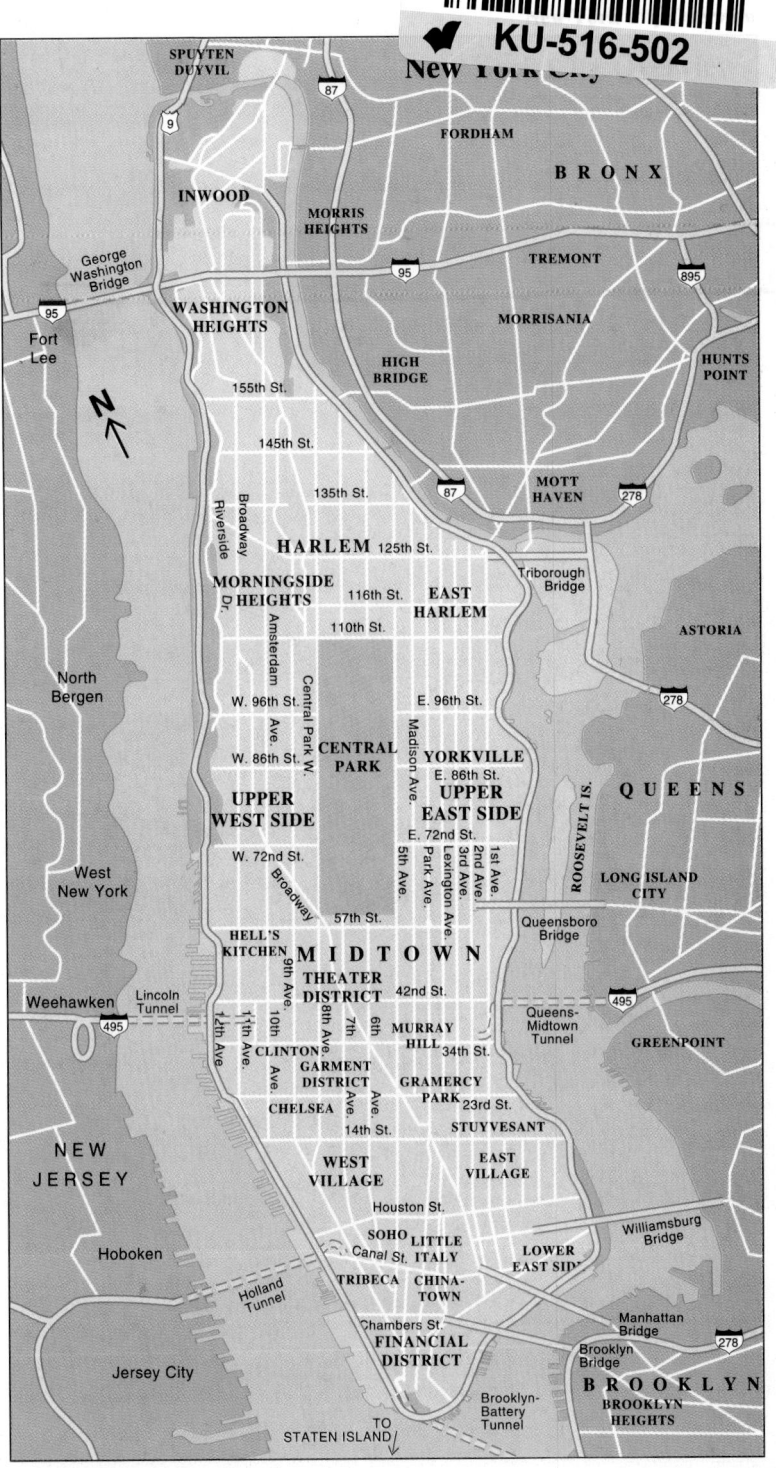

New York City

SPUYTEN
DUYVIL

87

9

INWOOD

BRONX

FORDHAM

MORRIS
HEIGHTS

George
Washington
Bridge

95

Fort
Lee

WASHINGTON
HEIGHTS

TREMONT

895

MORRISANIA

HIGH
BRIDGE

HUNTS
POINT

155th St.

Broadway
Riverside
Dr.

145th St.

135th St.

87

MOTT
HAVEN

278

HARLEM   125th St.

Triborough
Bridge

North
Bergen

MORNINGSIDE
HEIGHTS

116th St.

110th St.

EAST
HARLEM

ASTORIA

Amsterdam
Ave.

Central Park W.

W. 96th St.

E. 96th St.

278

West
New York

W. 86th St.

CENTRAL
PARK

Madison Ave.

E. 86th St.

YORKVILLE

QUEENS

UPPER
WEST SIDE

UPPER
EAST SIDE

ROOSEVELT IS.

LONG ISLAND
CITY

W. 72nd St.

E. 72nd St.

Lexington Ave.

Park Ave.

5th Ave.

3rd Ave.

2nd Ave.

1st Ave.

Broadway

57th St.

Queensboro
Bridge

HELL'S
KITCHEN

MIDTOWN

THEATER
DISTRICT

42nd St.

Queens-
Midtown
Tunnel

495

9th Ave.

8th Ave.

7th

6th

MURRAY
HILL

GREENPOINT

Weehawken

Lincoln
Tunnel

495

11th Ave.

10th

CLINTON

34th St.

GARMENT
DISTRICT

5th Ave.

12th Ave.

CHELSEA

GRAMERCY
PARK

23rd St.

14th St.

STUYVESANT

NEW
JERSEY

WEST
VILLAGE

EAST
VILLAGE

Houston St.

Hoboken

SOHO

Canal St.

LITTLE
ITALY

LOWER
EAST SIDE

Williamsburg
Bridge

Holland
Tunnel

TRIBECA

CHINA-
TOWN

Chambers St.

Manhattan
Bridge

278

Jersey City

FINANCIAL
DISTRICT

Brooklyn
Bridge

BROOKLYN

Brooklyn-
Battery
Tunnel

BROOKLYN
HEIGHTS

TO
STATEN ISLAND

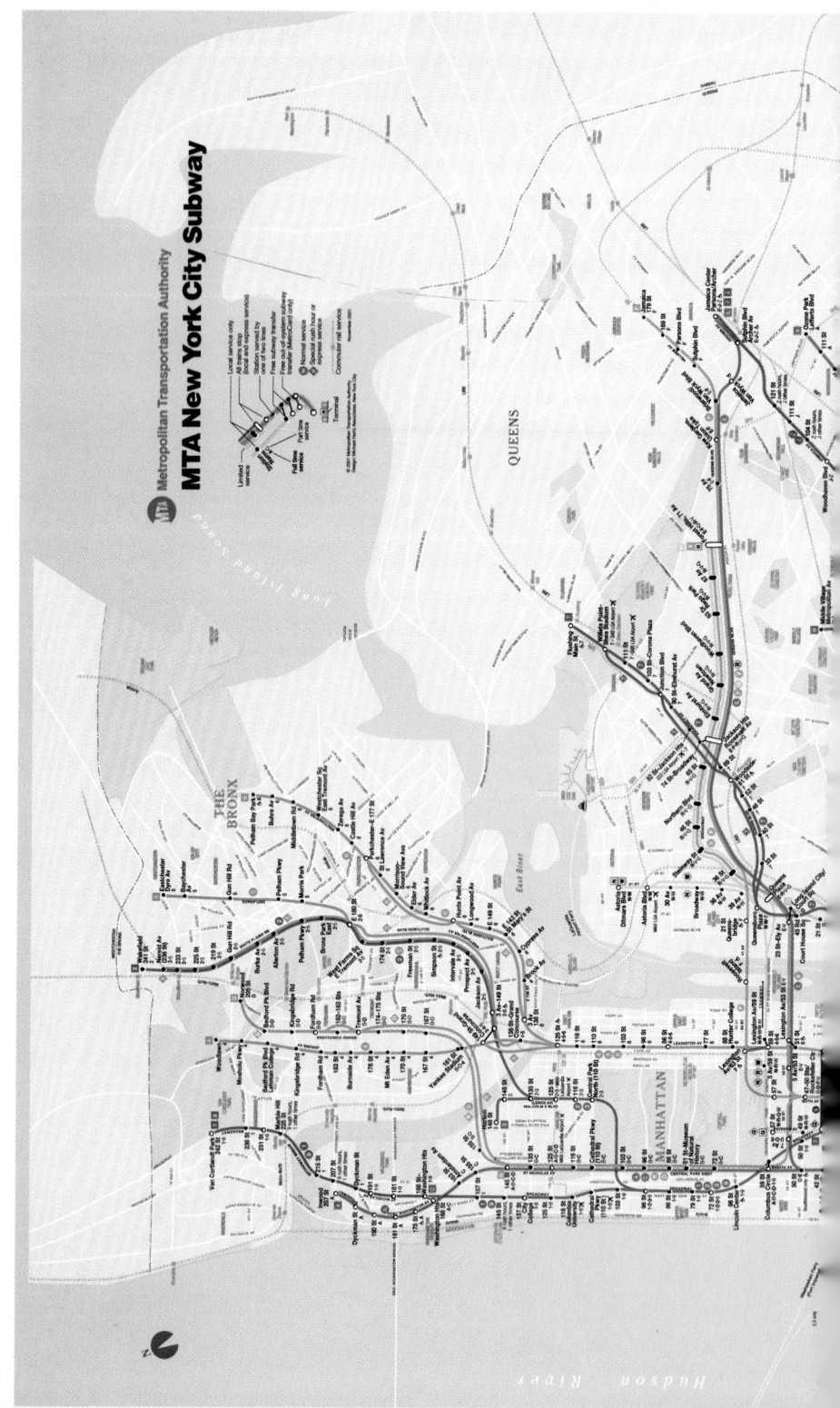

MTA New York City Subway

Metropolitan Transportation Authority

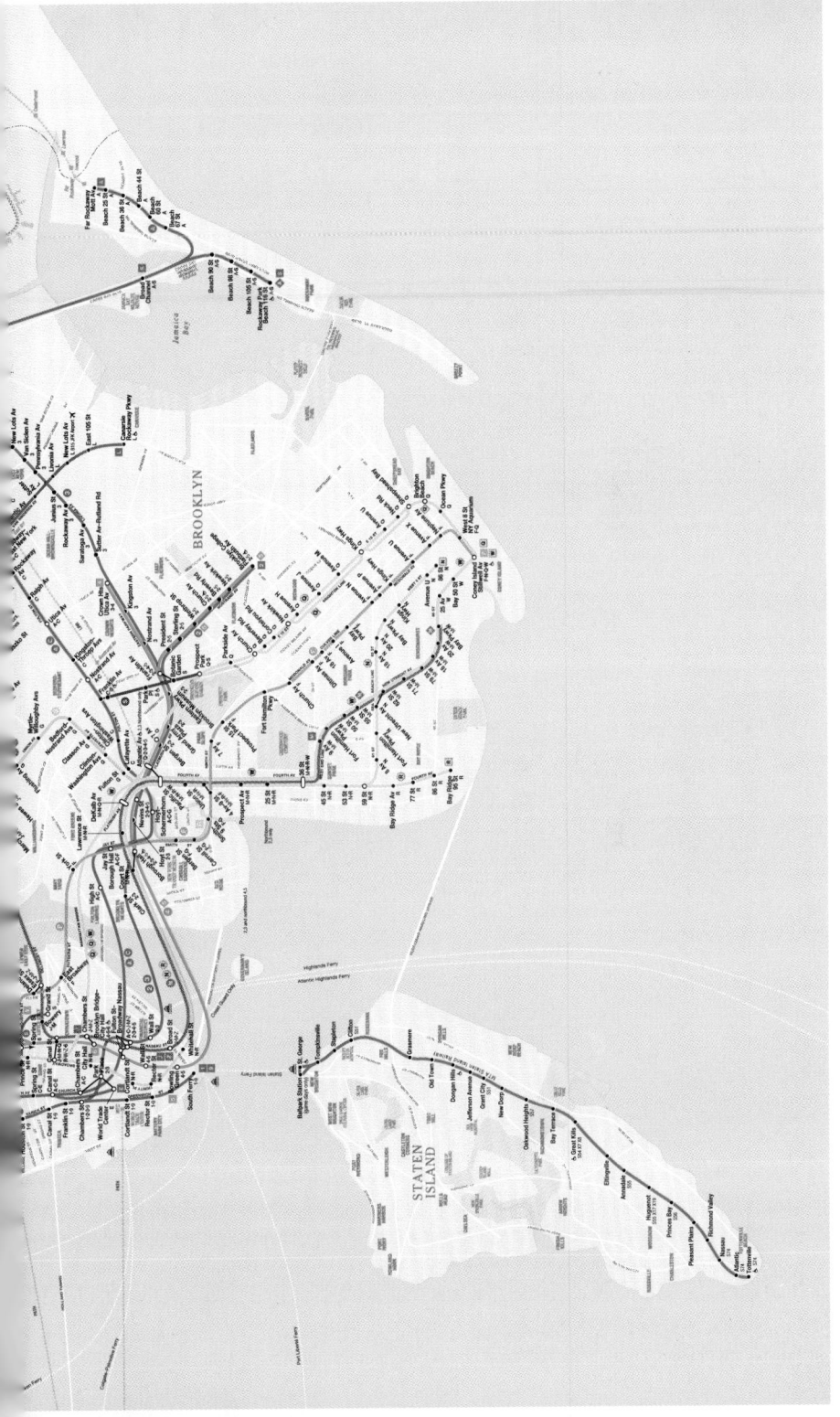

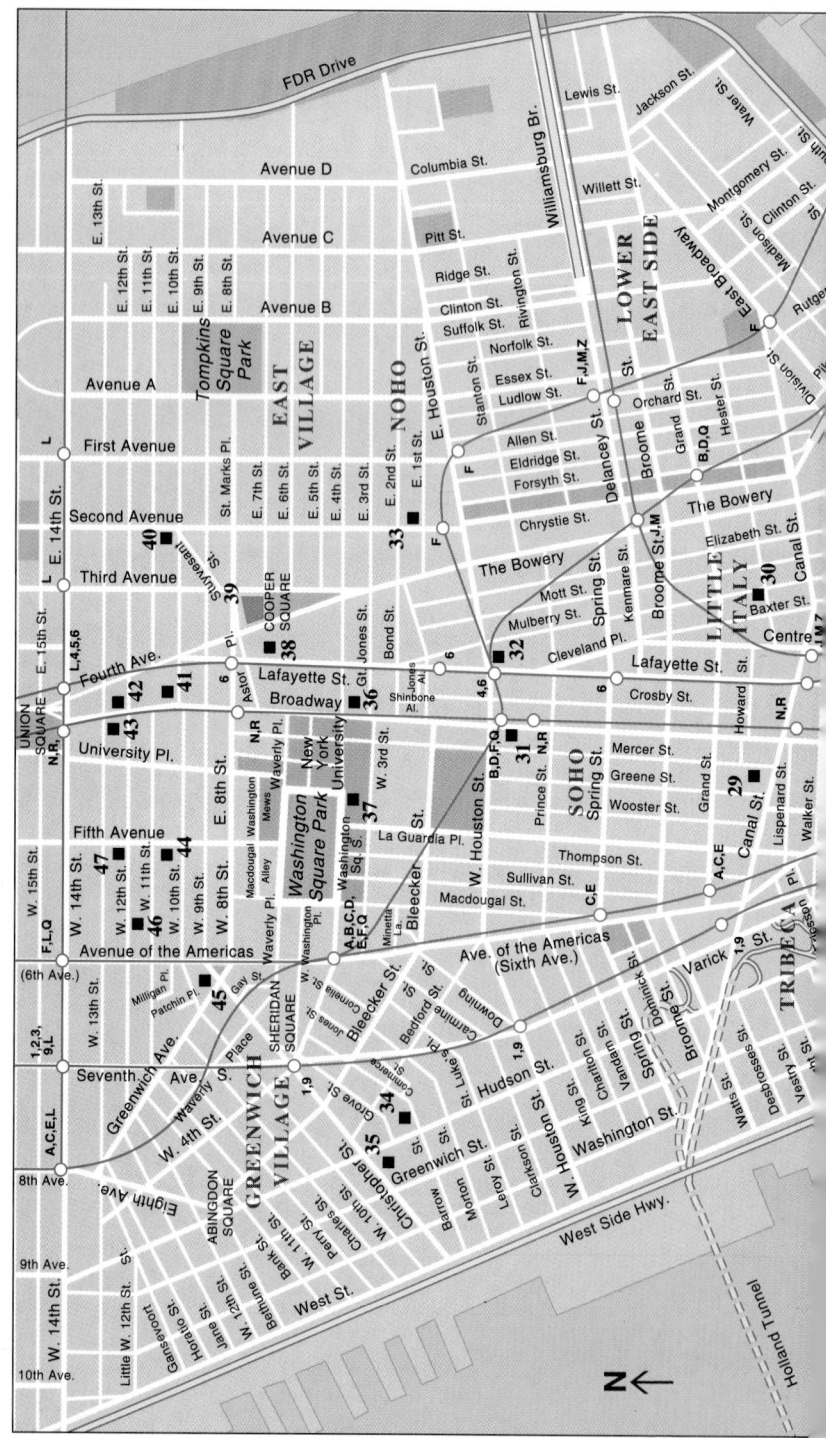

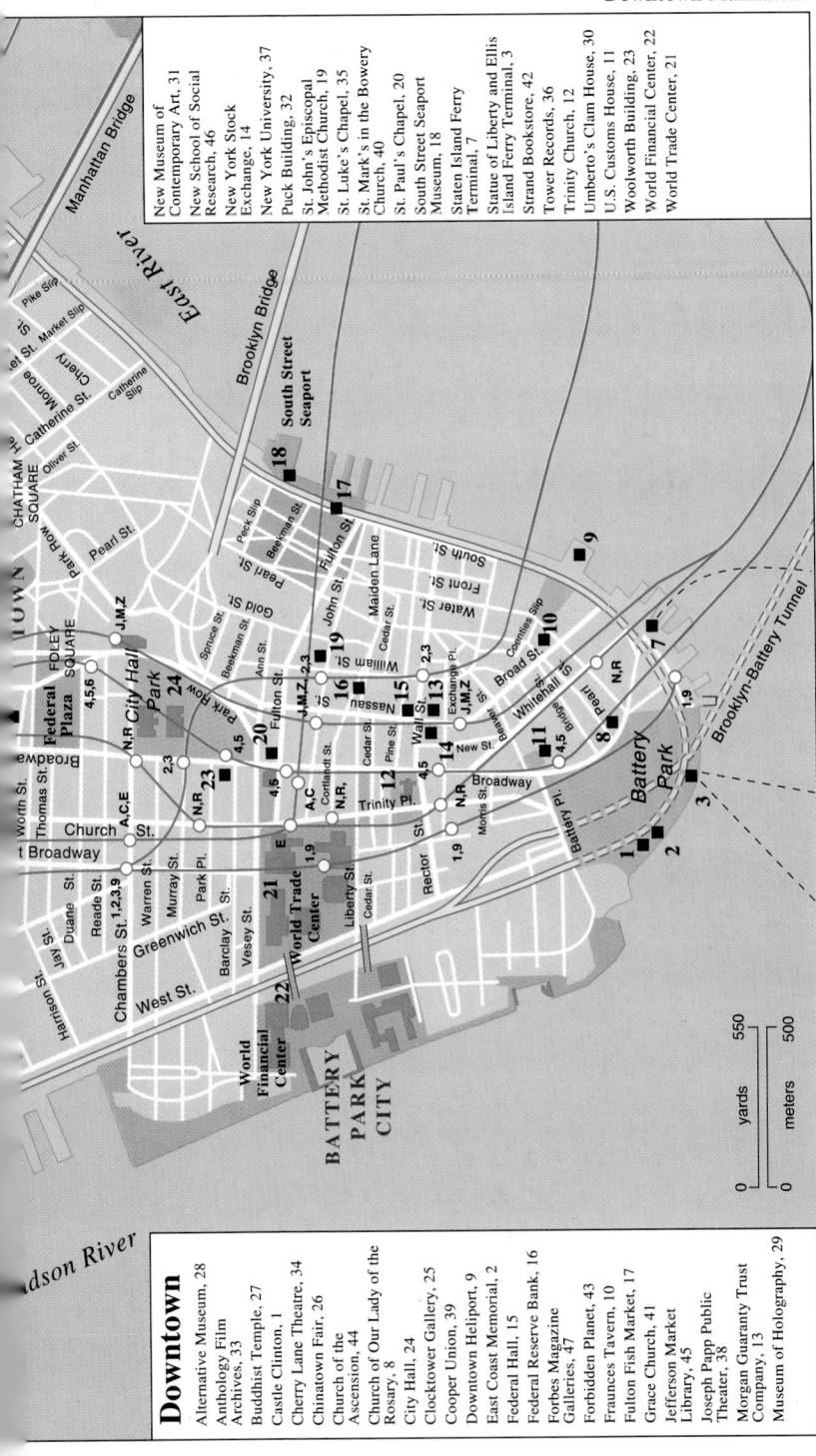

Downtown Manhattan

Downtown

Midtown Manhattan

East River

Queensboro Bridge

Queens-Midtown Tunnel

FDR Dr.

TURTLE BAY

United Nations

First Ave.

Second Ave.

Third Ave.

Lexington Ave.

Park Ave.

Park Ave.

Madison Ave.

Fifth Ave.

Sixth Ave.

Broadway

Seventh Ave.

Eighth Ave.

Ninth Ave.

Tenth Ave.

Eleventh Ave.

Twelfth Ave.

E. 56th St.
E. 55th St.
E. 54th St.
E. 53rd St.
E. 52nd St.
E. 51st St.
E. 50th St.
E. 49th St.
E. 48th St.
E. 47th St.
E. 46th St.
E. 45th St.
E. 44th St.
E. 43rd St.
E. 42nd St.
E. 41st St.
E. 40th St.
E. 39th St.
E. 38th St.
E. 37th St.
E. 36th St.
E. 35th St.
E. 34th St.
E. 33rd St.
E. 32nd St.
E. 60th St.
E. 59th St.
E. 58th St.
E. 57th St.

Second Ave.
Third Ave.

Citicorp Center

Grand Army Plaza

Park South

Central

Carnegie Hall

Museum of Modern Art

Rockefeller Center

Grand Central Terminal

New York Public Library

Bryant Park
W. 40th St.

MURRAY HILL

Empire State Building

HERALD SQUARE

GARMENT DISTRICT

Port Authority Bus Terminal

General Post Office

COLUMBUS CIRCLE

New York Convention & Visitors Bureau

TIMES SQUARE

Dyer Ave.

Tenth Ave.

HELL'S KITCHEN

Lincoln Tunnel

W. 60th St.
W. 59th St.
W. 58th St.
W. 57th St.
W. 56th St.
W. 55th St.
W. 54th St.
W. 53rd St.
W. 52nd St.
W. 51st St.
W. 50th St.
W. 49th St.
W. 48th St.
W. 47th St.
W. 46th St.
W. 45th St.
W. 44th St.
W. 43rd St.
W. 42nd St.
W. 41st St.
W. 39th St.
W. 38th St.
W. 37th St.
W. 36th St.
W. 35th St.
W. 34th St.

A,B,C,D,1,2,3,9
N,R
B,Q
4,5,6
4,5,6,S
7
6
E,F
B,D,F,Q
B,D,E
N,R
1,2,3,N,R,9
1,2,3,9
C,E
A,C,E
N,R

1 2 3 4 5 6 7 8 9 10 11 12 13 14 15 16 17 27 28 29 30 31 32 33 34 35 36 37 38 39 40 41 42 43 44 45 46 47 48 49 50 51 52 53 54 55 56 57 58 59 60 61 62 63 64 65 66 67 68

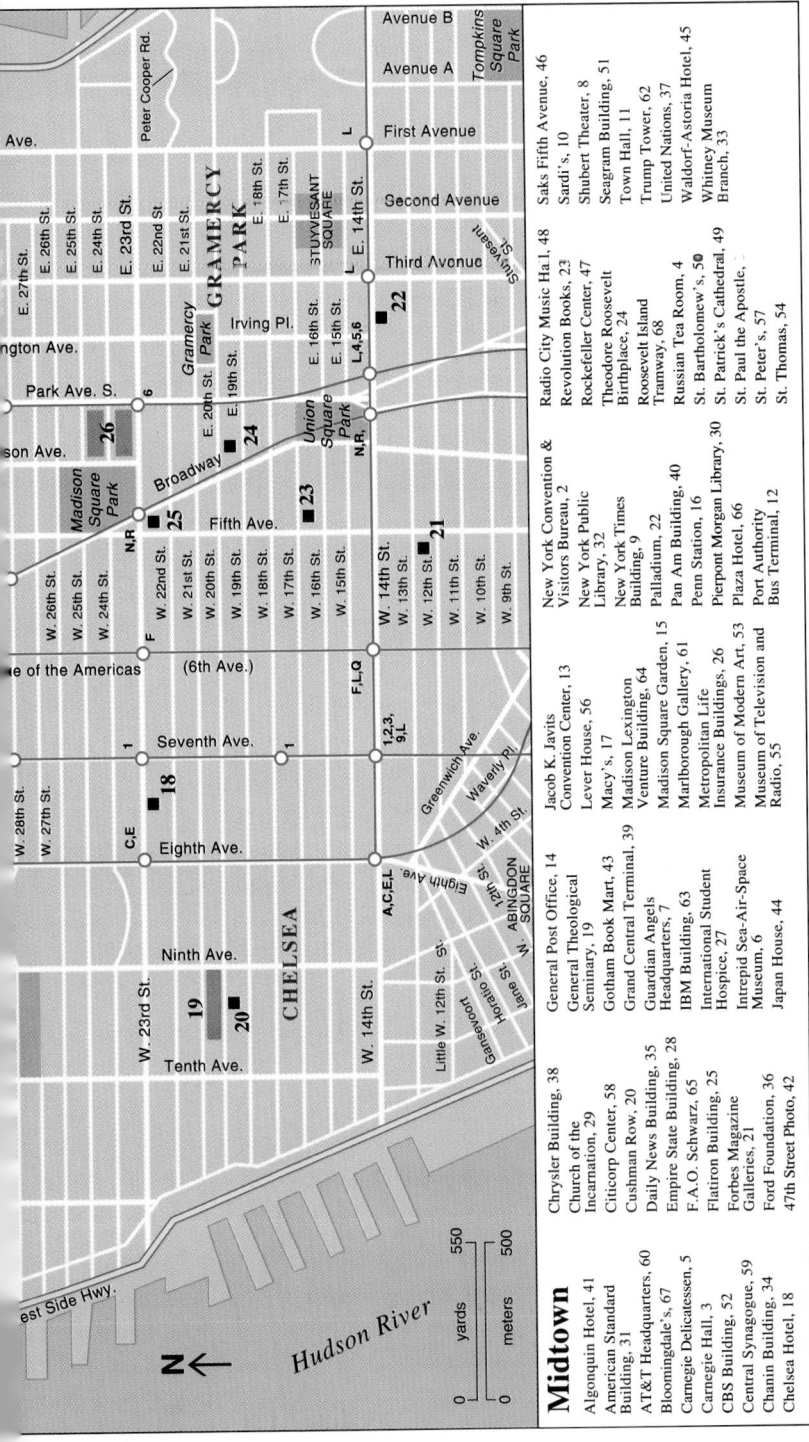

Uptown

American Museum of Natural History, 53
The Ansonia, 55
The Arsenal, 25
Asia Society, 14
Belvedere Castle, 36
Bethesda Fountain, 33
Blockhouse No. 1, 42
Bloomingdale's, 22
Bridle Path, 30
Cathedral of St. John the Divine, 47
Central Park Zoo, 24
Chess and Checkers House, 28
Children's Museum of Manhattan, 51
Children's Zoo, 26
China House, 19

Cleopatra's Needle, 38
Columbia University, 46
Conservatory Garden, 2
Cooper-Hewitt Museum, 7
The Dairy, 27
Dakota Apartments, 56
Delacorte Theater, 37
El Museo del Barrio, 1
Fordham University, 60
Frick Museum, 13
Gracie Mansion, 10
Grant's Tomb, 45
Great Lawn, 39
Guggenheim Museum, 9
Hayden Planetarium (at the American Museum of Natural History), 53
Hector Memorial, 50
Hotel des Artistes, 57

Hunter College, 16
International Center of Photography, 5
Jewish Museum, 6
The Juilliard School (at Lincoln Center), 59
Lincoln Center, 59
Loeb Boathouse, 34
Masjid Malcolm Shabazz , 43
Metropolitan Museum of Art, 11
Mt. Sinai Hospital, 4
Museum of American Folk Art, 58
Museum of American Illustration, 21
Museum of the City of New York, 3
National Academy of Design, 8
New York Convention & Visitors Bureau, 61

New York Historical Society, 54
New York Hospital, 15
Plaza Hotel, 23
Police Station (Central Park), 40
Rockefeller University, 20
7th Regiment Armory, 17
Shakespeare Garden, 35
Soldiers and Sailors Monument, 49
Strawberry Fields, 32
Studio Museum in Harlem, 44
Symphony Space, 48
Tavern on the Green, 31
Temple Emanu-El, 18
Tennis Courts, 41
Whitney Museum of American Art, 12
Wollman Rink, 29
Zabar's, 52

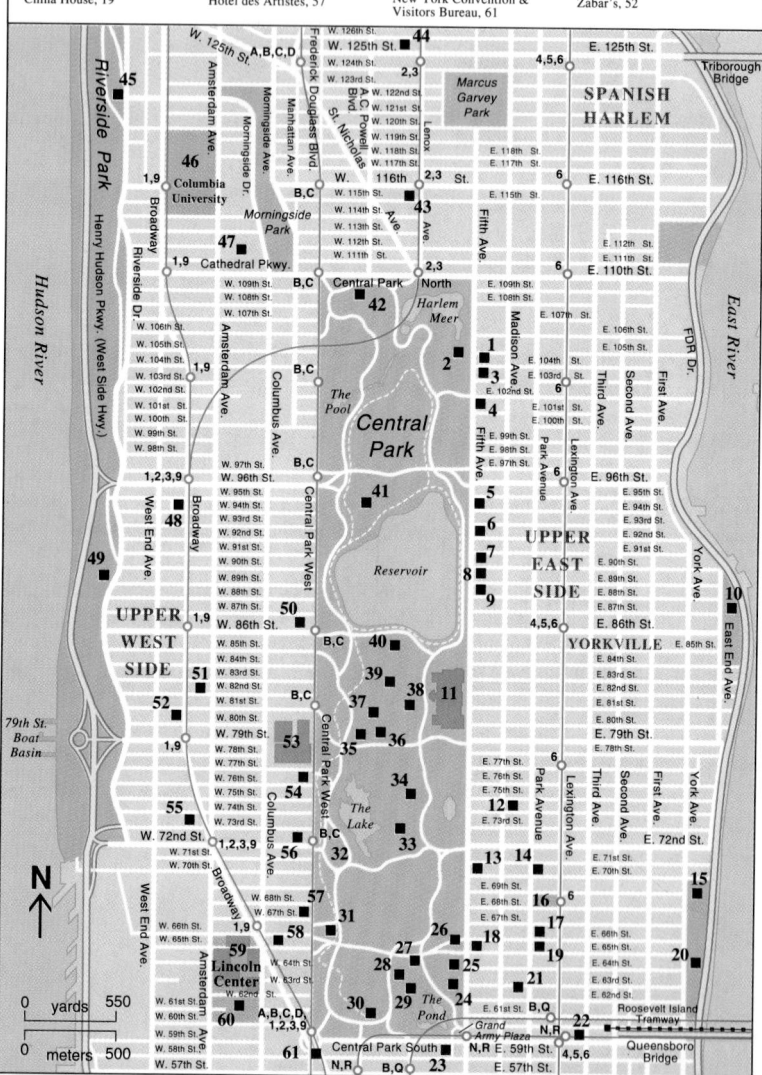

L.A. Westside

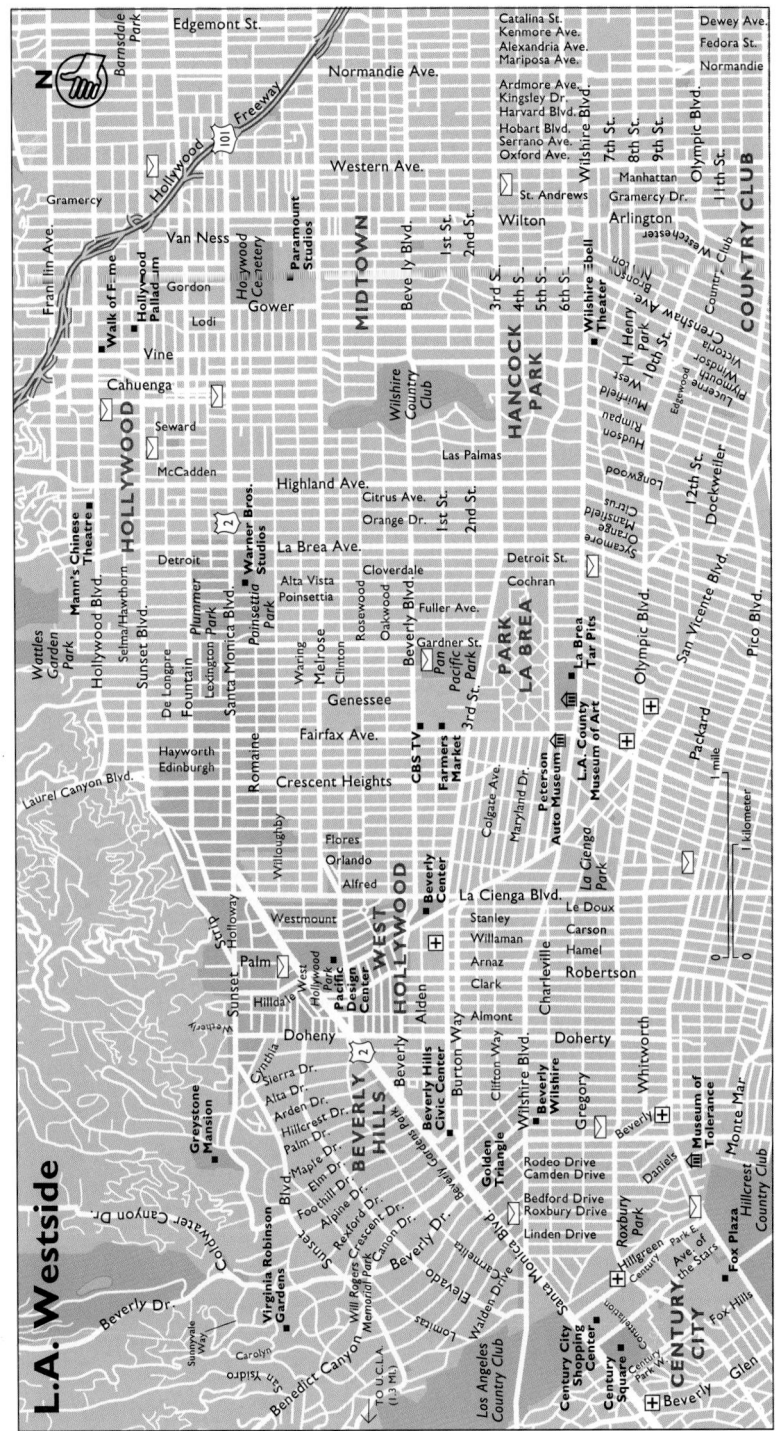

L.A. Westside

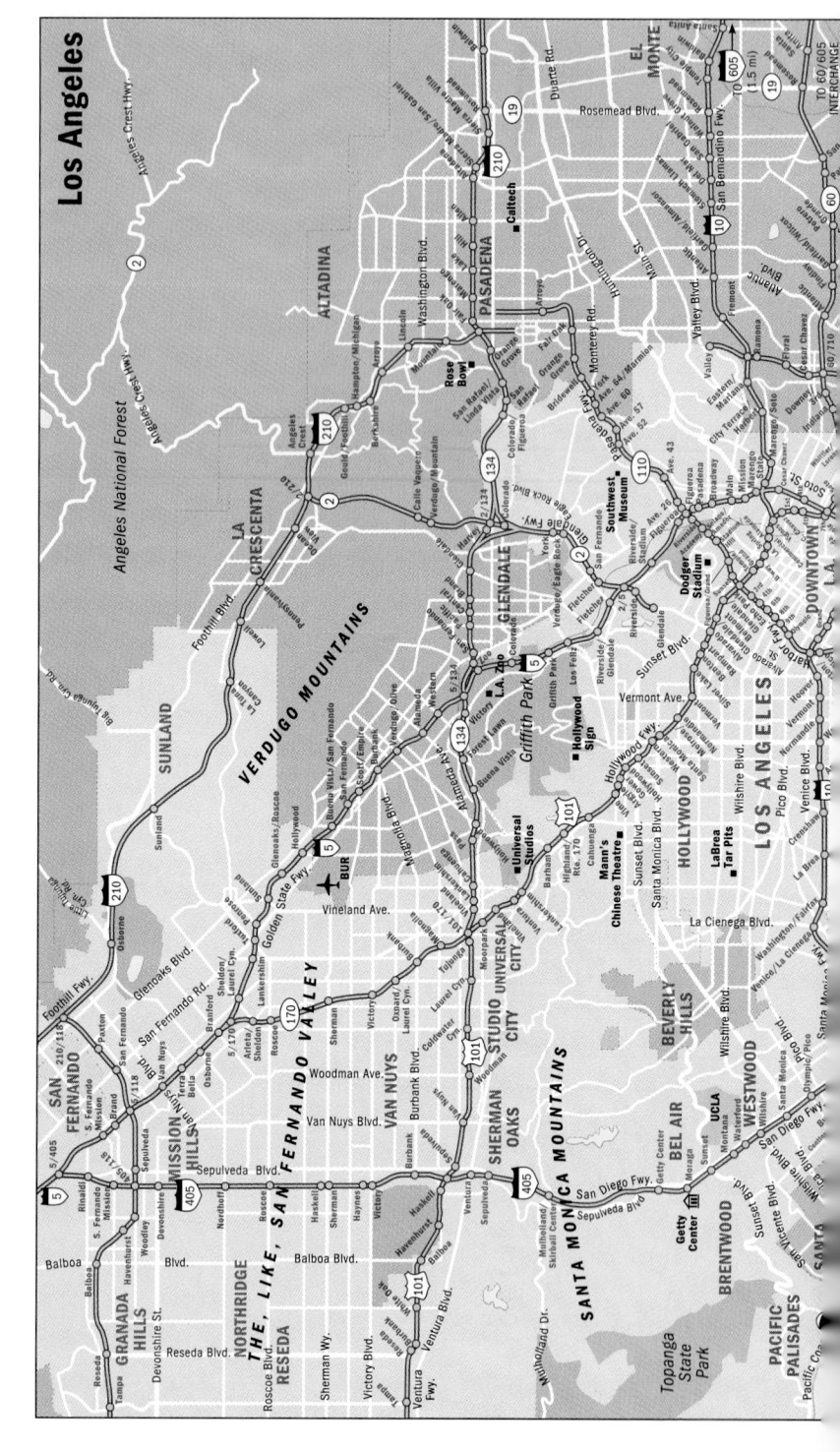

Los Angeles

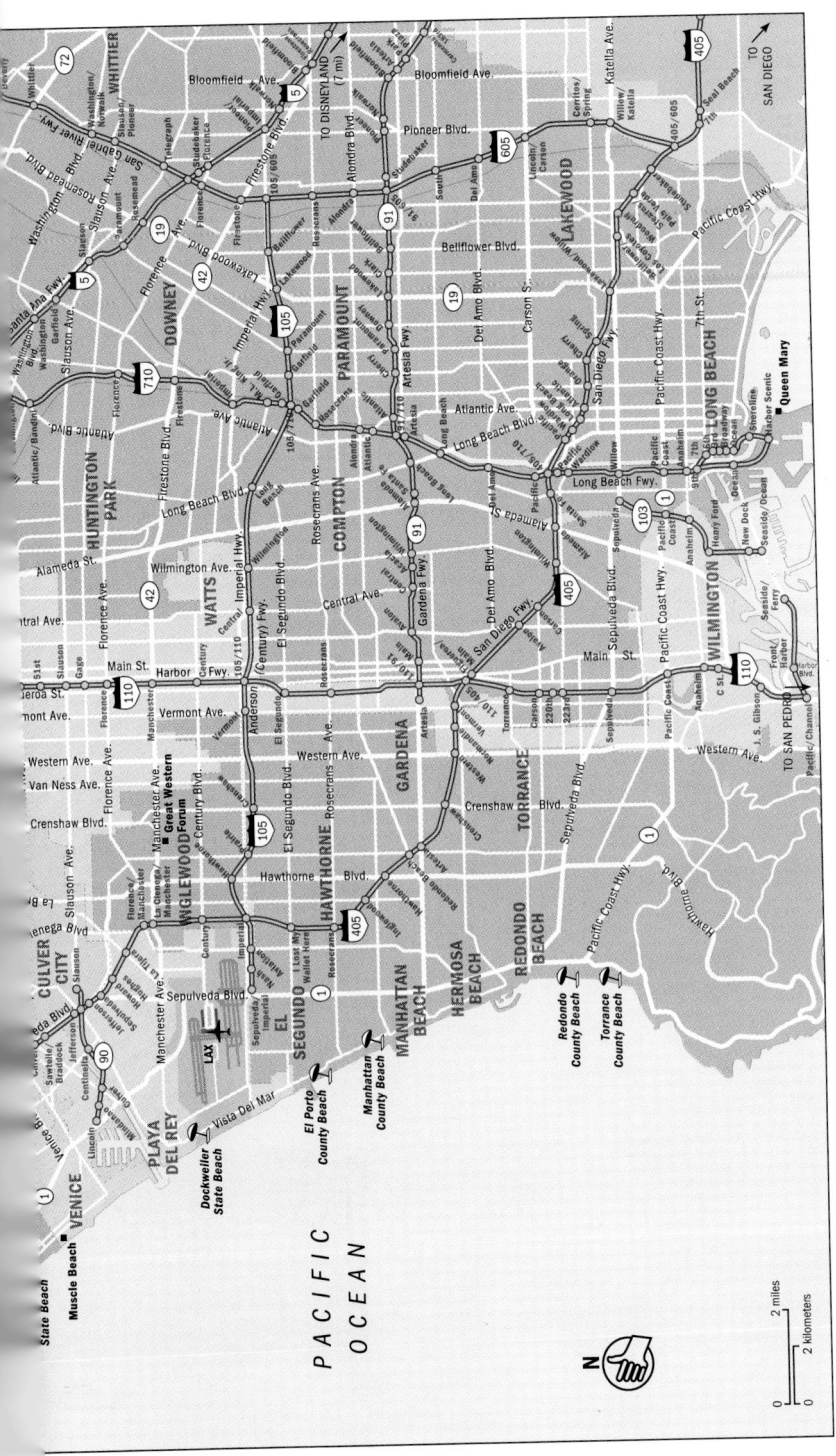

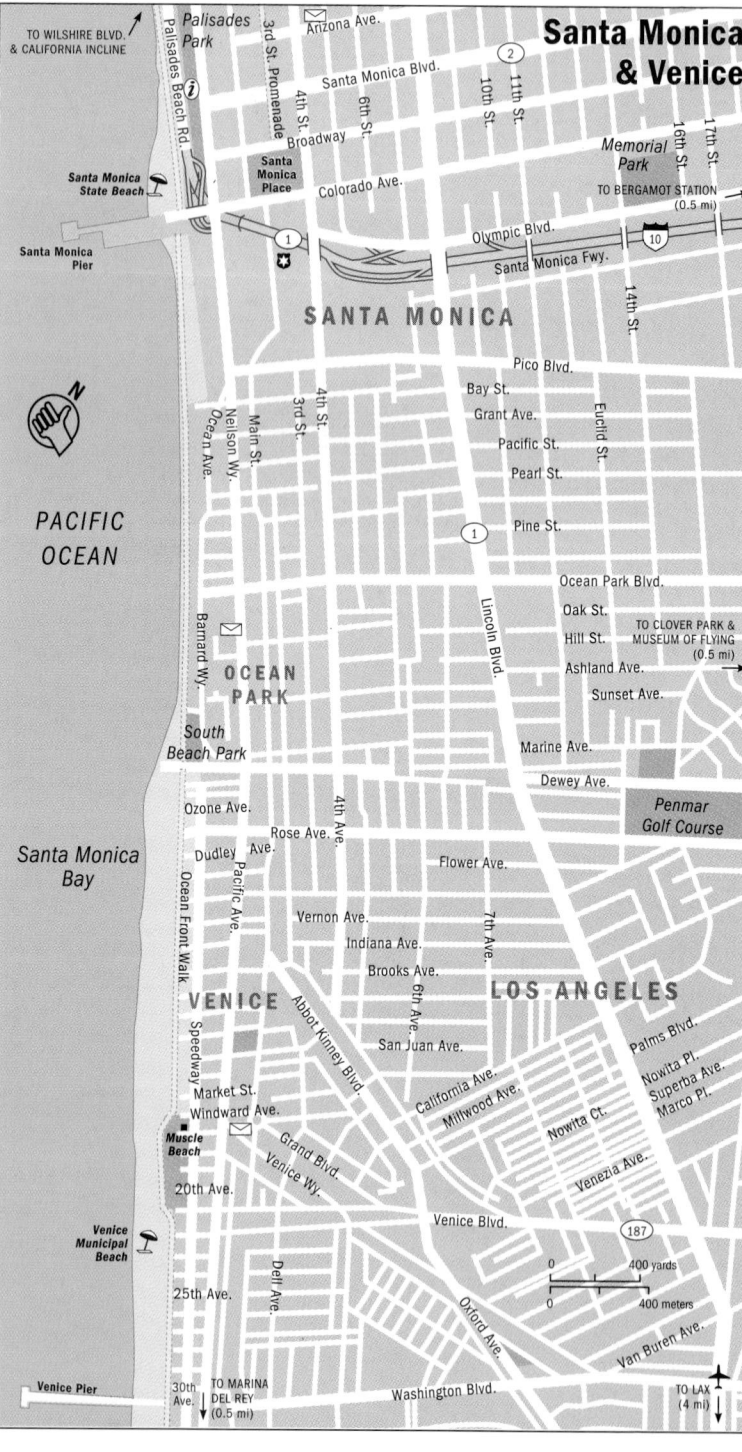

Santa Monica & Venice

TO WILSHIRE BLVD. & CALIFORNIA INCLINE
Palisades Park
Palisades Beach Rd.
3rd St. Promenade
Arizona Ave.
Santa Monica Blvd.
6th St.
Broadway
10th St.
11th St.
2
Memorial Park
16th St.
17th St.
4th St.
Santa Monica State Beach
Santa Monica Place
Colorado Ave.
TO BERGAMOT STATION (0.5 mi)
Santa Monica Pier
1
Olympic Blvd.
Santa Monica Fwy.
10
SANTA MONICA
14th St.
Pico Blvd.
Bay St.
Grant Ave.
Pacific St.
Euclid St.
Pearl St.
Neilson Wy.
Ocean Ave.
Main St.
3rd St.
4th St.
PACIFIC OCEAN
1
Pine St.
Ocean Park Blvd.
Oak St.
Hill St.
TO CLOVER PARK & MUSEUM OF FLYING (0.5 mi)
Lincoln Blvd.
Ashland Ave.
Barnard Wy.
OCEAN PARK
Sunset Ave.
South Beach Park
Marine Ave.
Dewey Ave.
Santa Monica Bay
Ozone Ave.
4th Ave.
Penmar Golf Course
Rose Ave.
Dudley Ave.
Flower Ave.
Ocean Front Walk
Pacific Ave.
Vernon Ave.
Indiana Ave.
7th Ave.
Brooks Ave.
6th Ave.
LOS ANGELES
VENICE
Abbot Kinney Blvd.
San Juan Ave.
Palms Blvd.
Speedway
California Ave.
Millwood Ave.
Nowita Ct.
Nowita Pl.
Superba Ave.
Marco Pl.
Market St.
Windward Ave.
Muscle Beach
Grand Blvd.
Venice Wy.
Venezia Ave.
20th Ave.
Venice Blvd.
187
Venice Municipal Beach
25th Ave.
Dell Ave.
0   400 yards
0   400 meters
Oxford Ave.
Venice Pier
30th Ave.
TO MARINA DEL REY (0.5 mi)
Washington Blvd.
Van Buren Ave.
TO LAX (4 mi)

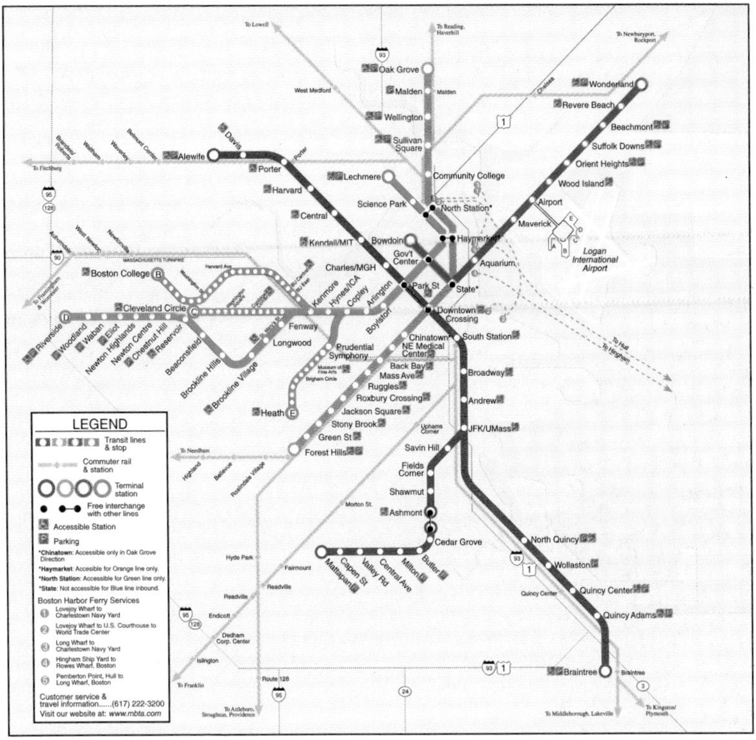
To Lowell
To Reading, Haverhill
To Newburyport, Rockport
Oak Grove
Malden
West Medford
Wellington
Sullivan Square
Wonderland
Revere Beach
Beachmont
Suffolk Downs
Orient Heights
Wood Island
Chelsea
Alewife
Davis
Porter
Harvard
Central
Kendall/MIT
Lechmere
Science Park
Community College
North Station*
Haymarket*
Bowdoin
Gov't Center
Airport
Maverick
Logan International Airport
Aquarium
State*
Park St
Charles/MGH
Downtown Crossing
Chinatown
South Station
NE Medical Center
Back Bay
Mass Ave
Ruggles
Roxbury Crossing
Jackson Square
Stony Brook
Green St
Forest Hills
Broadway
Andrew
JFK/UMass
Uphams Corner
Savin Hill
Fields Corner
Shawmut
Ashmont
Cedar Grove
Butler
Milton
Central Ave
Valley Rd
Capen St
Mattapan
North Quincy
Wollaston
Quincy Center
Quincy Adams
Braintree
To Hull
To Hingham
To Fitchburg
Brandeis/Roberts
Waltham
Waverley
Belmont Center
Auburndale
West Newton
Newtonville
MASSACHUSETTS TURNPIKE
To Framingham & Worcester
Boston College
Harvard Ave
Cleveland Circle
Riverside
Woodland
Waban
Eliot
Newton Highlands
Newton Centre
Chestnut Hill
Reservoir
Beaconsfield
Brookline Hills
Brookline Village
Longwood
Fenway
Kenmore
Hynes/ICA
Copley
Arlington
Boylston
Prudential
Symphony
Museum of Fine Arts
Brigham Circle
Heath
To Needham
Highland
Bellevue
Roslindale Village
Morton St.
Hyde Park
Fairmount
Readville
Endicott
Dedham Corp. Center
Islington
To Franklin
Route 128
To Attleboro, Stoughton, Providence
Quincy Center
Braintree
To Middleborough, Lakeville
To Kingston/Plymouth
LEGEND
Transit lines & stop
Commuter rail & station
Terminal station
Free interchange with other lines
Accessible Station
Parking
*Chinatown: Accessible only in Oak Grove Direction
*Haymarket: Accesible for Orange line only.
*North Station: Accessible for Green line only.
*State: Not accessible for Blue line inbound.
Boston Harbor Ferry Services
1 Lovejoy Wharf to Charlestown Navy Yard
2 Lovejoy Wharf to U.S. Courthouse to World Trade Center
3 Long Wharf to Charlestown Navy Yard
4 Hingham Ship Yard to Rowes Wharf, Boston
5 Pemberton Point, Hull to Long Wharf, Boston
Customer service & travel information......(617) 222-3200
Visit our website at: www.mbta.com

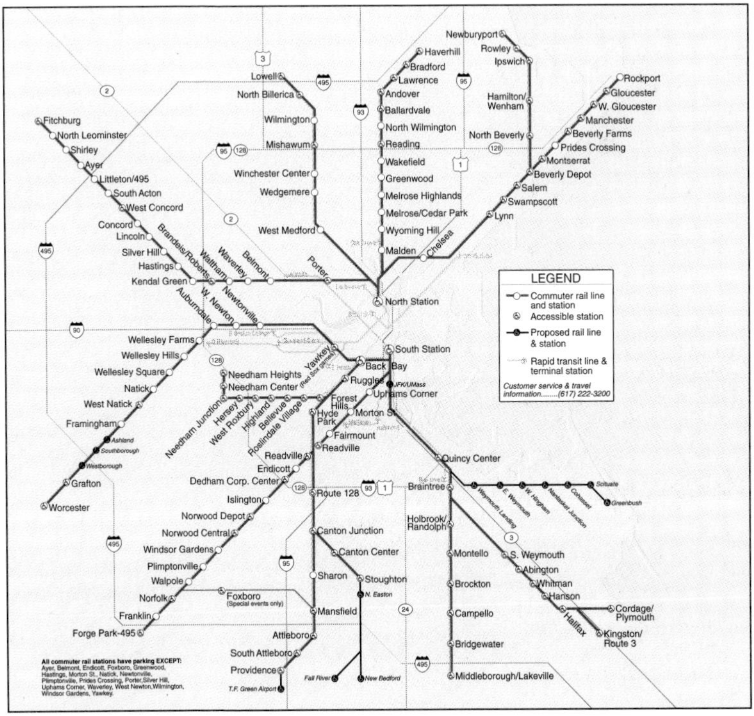
Newburyport
Rowley
Ipswich
Haverhill
Bradford
Lawrence
Andover
Ballardvale
North Wilmington
Reading
Wakefield
Greenwood
Melrose Highlands
Melrose/Cedar Park
Wyoming Hill
Malden
Chelsea
Lowell
North Billerica
Wilmington
Mishawum
Winchester Center
Wedgemere
West Medford
Porter
Belmont
Waverley
Waltham
Brandeis/Roberts
Rockport
Gloucester
W. Gloucester
Manchester
Beverly Farms
Prides Crossing
Montserrat
Hamilton/Wenham
North Beverly
Beverly Depot
Salem
Swampscott
Lynn
Fitchburg
North Leominster
Shirley
Ayer
Littleton/495
South Acton
West Concord
Concord
Lincoln
Silver Hill
Hastings
Kendal Green
North Station
Auburndale
W. Newton
Newtonville
Wellesley Farms
Wellesley Hills
Wellesley Square
Natick
West Natick
Framingham
Ashland
Southborough
Westborough
Grafton
Worcester
South Station
Back Bay
Yawkey
Ruggles
JFK/UMass
Uphams Corner
Needham Heights
Needham Center
Needham Junction
Hersey
West Roxbury
Highland
Bellevue
Roslindale Village
Forest Hills
Hyde Park
Morton St
Fairmount
Readville
Endicott
Dedham Corp. Center
Islington
Norwood Depot
Norwood Central
Windsor Gardens
Plimptonville
Walpole
Norfolk
Franklin
Forge Park-495
Foxboro (Special events only)
Route 128
Canton Junction
Canton Center
Sharon
Stoughton
N. Easton
Mansfield
Attleboro
South Attleboro
Providence
T.F. Green Airport
Fall River
New Bedford
Quincy Center
Braintree
Weymouth Landing
E. Weymouth
W. Hingham
Nantasket Junction
Cohasset
Scituate
Greenbush
Holbrook/Randolph
Montello
Brockton
Campello
Bridgewater
Middleborough/Lakeville
S. Weymouth
Abington
Whitman
Hanson
Halifax
Cordage/Plymouth
Kingston/Route 3
LEGEND
Commuter rail line and station
Accessible station
Proposed rail line & station
Rapid transit line & terminal station
Customer service & travel information........(617) 222-3200
All commuter rail stations have parking EXCEPT: Ayer, Belmont, Endicott, Foxboro, Greenwood, Hastings, Morton St., Natick, Newtonville, Plimptonville, Prides Crossing, Porter, Silver Hill, Uphams Corner, Waverley, West Newton, Wilmington, Windsor Gardens, Yawkey.

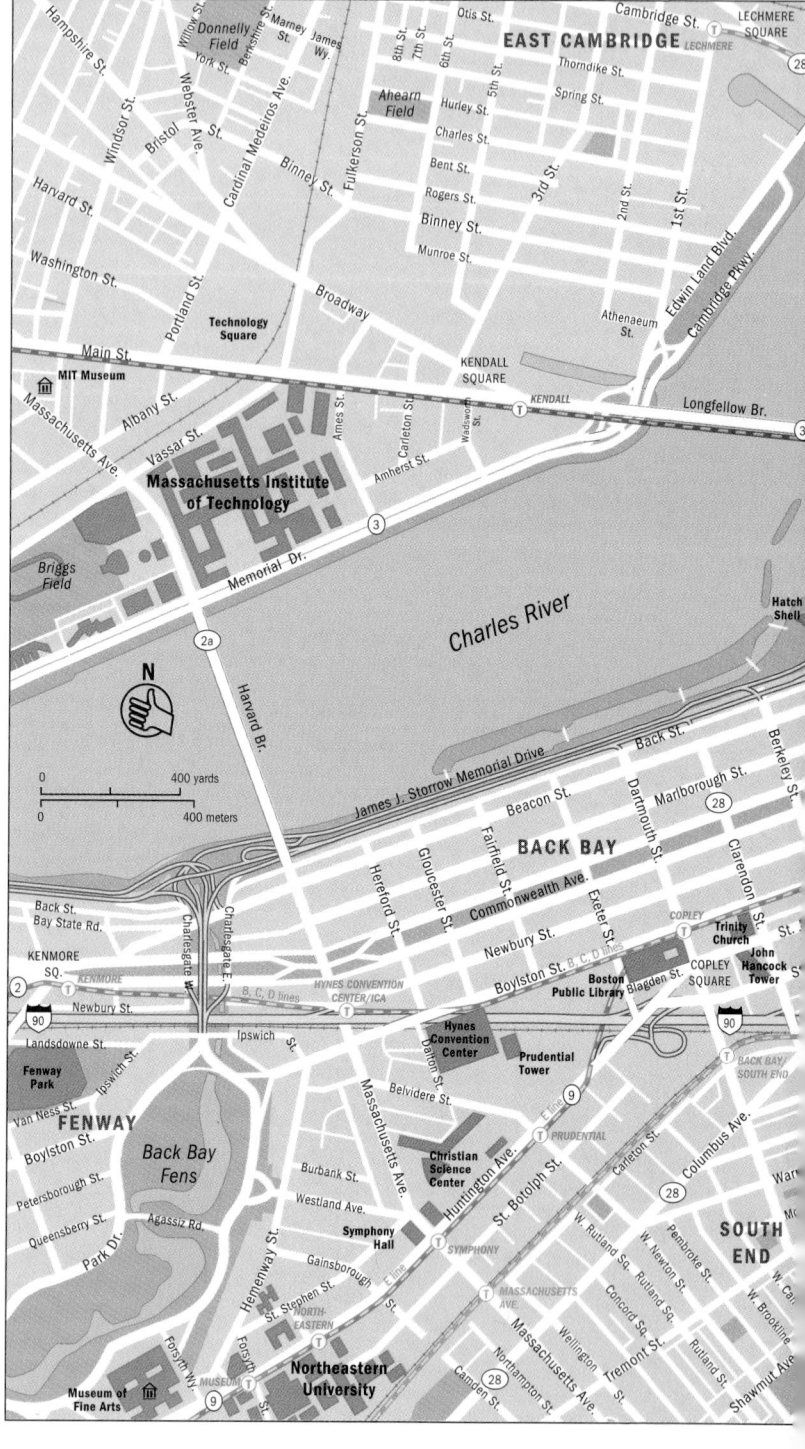

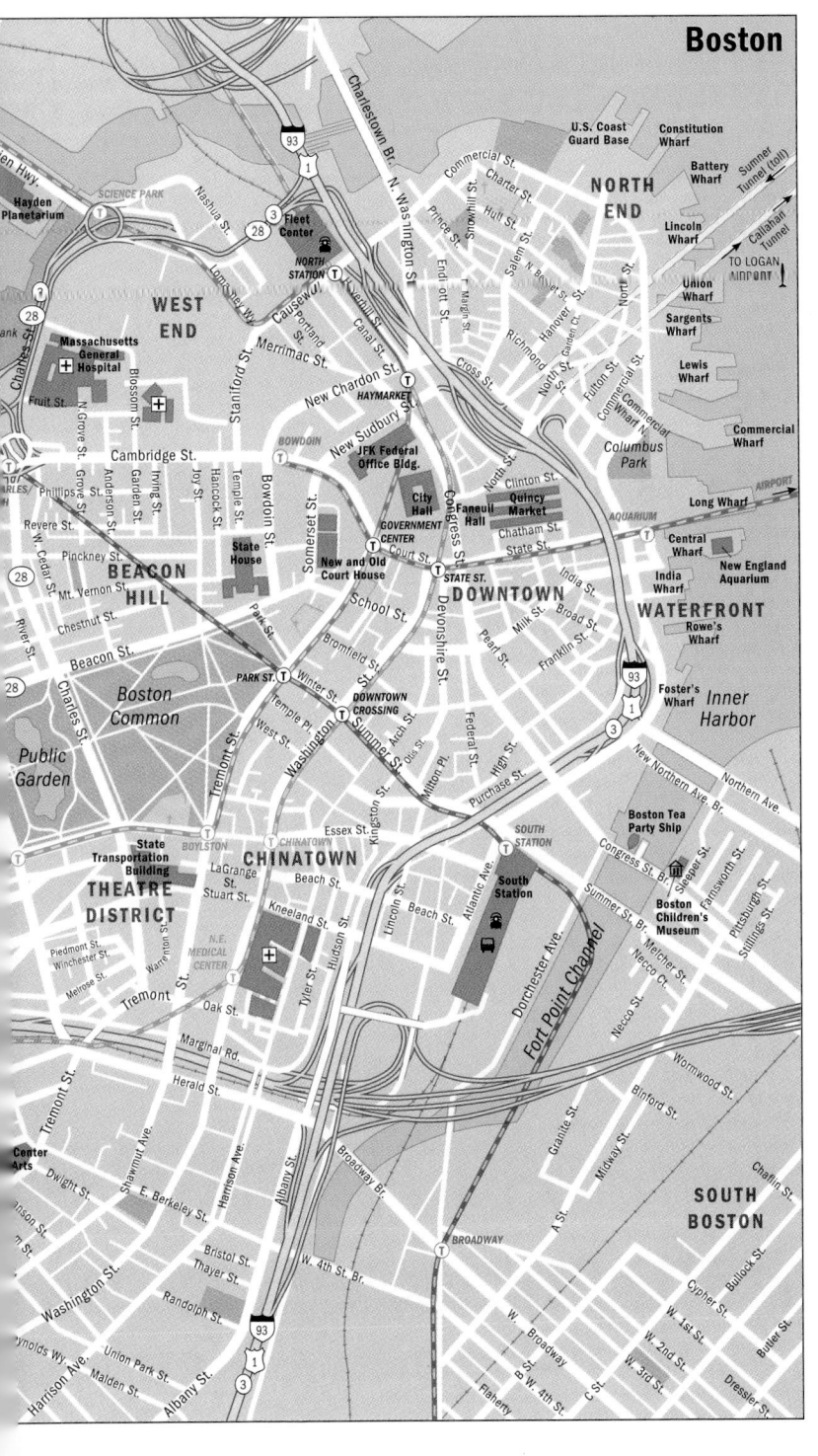

Boston

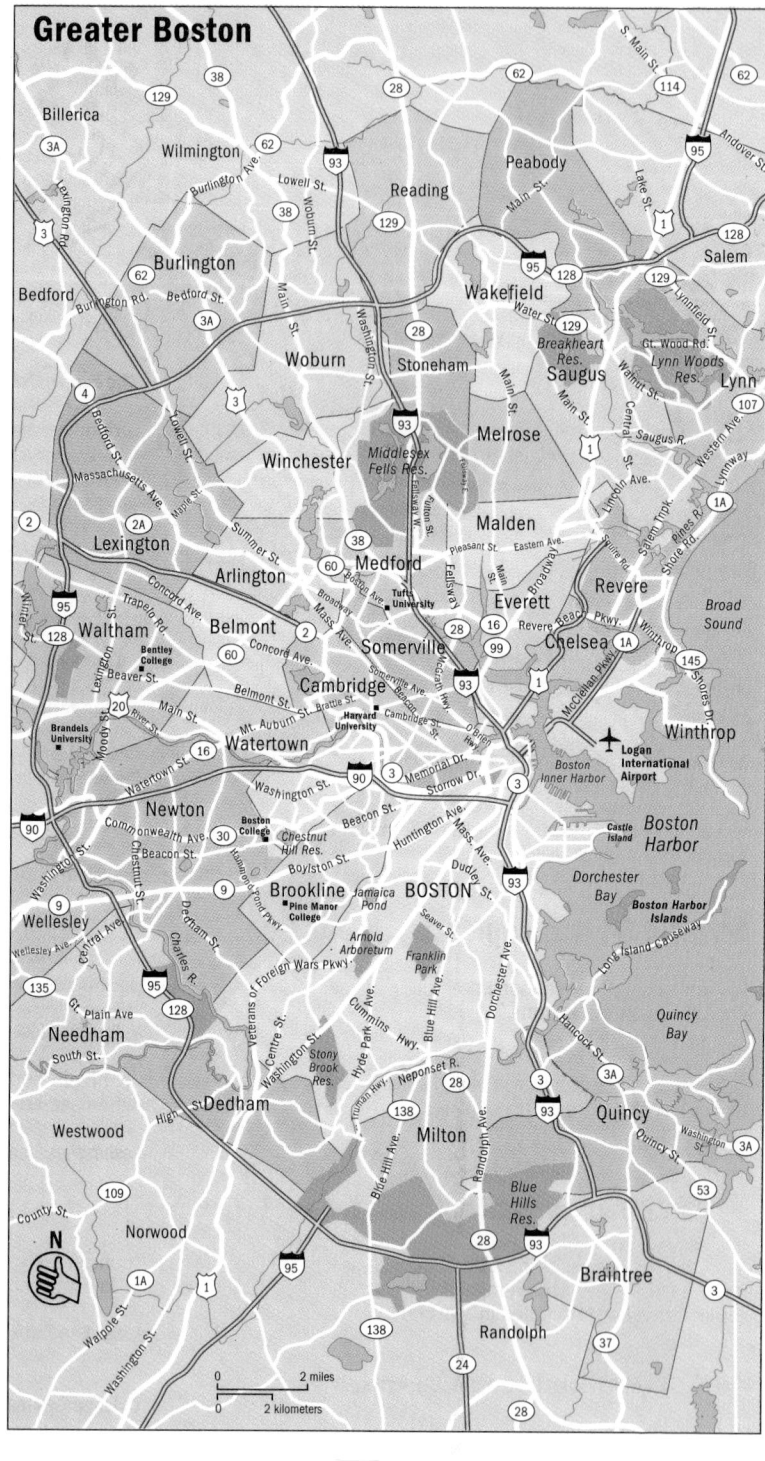

Greater Boston

✍ Let's Go writers travel on your budget.

"Guides that penetrate the veneer of the holiday brochures and mine the grit of real life."
—The Economist

"The writers seem to have experienced every rooster-packed bus and lunar-surfaced mattress about which they write."
—The New York Times

"All the dirt, dirt cheap."
—People

✍ Great for independent travelers.

"The guides are aimed not only at young budget travelers but at the independent traveler; a sort of streetwise cookbook for traveling alone."
—The New York Times

"A guide should tell you what to expect from a destination. Here *Let's Go* shines."
—The Chicago Tribune

"An indispensible resource, *Let's Go*'s practical information can be used by every traveler."
—The Chattanooga Free Press

✍ Let's Go is completely revised each year.

"A publishing phenomenon...the only major guidebook series updated annually. *Let's Go* is the big kahuna."
—The Boston Globe

"Unbeatable: good sight-seeing advice; up-to-date info on restaurants, hotels, and inns; a commitment to money-saving travel; and a wry style that brightens nearly every page."
—The Washington Post

✍ All the important information you need.

"*Let's Go* authors provide a comedic element while still providing concise information and thorough coverage of the country. Anything you need to know about budget traveling is detailed in this book."
—The Chicago Sun-Times

"*Let's Go* guidebooks take night life seriously."
—The Chicago Tribune

Let's Go Publications

Let's Go: Alaska & the Pacific Northwest 2002
Let's Go: Amsterdam 2002 **New Title!**
Let's Go: Australia 2002
Let's Go: Austria & Switzerland 2002
Let's Go: Barcelona 2002 **New Title!**
Let's Go: Boston 2002
Let's Go: Britain & Ireland 2002
Let's Go: California 2002
Let's Go: Central America 2002
Let's Go: China 2002
Let's Go: Eastern Europe 2002
Let's Go: Egypt 2002 **New Title!**
Let's Go: Europe 2002
Let's Go: France 2002
Let's Go: Germany 2002
Let's Go: Greece 2002
Let's Go: India & Nepal 2002
Let's Go: Ireland 2002
Let's Go: Israel 2002
Let's Go: Italy 2002
Let's Go: London 2002
Let's Go: Mexico 2002
Let's Go: Middle East 2002
Let's Go: New York City 2002
Let's Go: New Zealand 2002
Let's Go: Paris 2002
Let's Go: Peru, Ecuador & Bolivia 2002
Let's Go: Rome 2002
Let's Go: San Francisco 2002
Let's Go: South Africa with Southern Africa 2002
Let's Go: Southeast Asia 2002
Let's Go: Southwest USA 2002 **New Title!**
Let's Go: Spain & Portugal 2002
Let's Go: Turkey 2002
Let's Go: USA 2002
Let's Go: Washington, D.C. 2002
Let's Go: Western Europe 2002

Let's Go *Map Guides*

Amsterdam	New Orleans
Berlin	New York City
Boston	Paris
Chicago	Prague
Dublin	Rome
Florence	San Francisco
Hong Kong	Seattle
London	Sydney
Los Angeles	Venice
Madrid	Washington, D.C.

USA

INCLUDING COVERAGE OF CANADA

2002

D. Cody Dydek editor
Benjamin W. Fernandez associate editor
Nathaniel Mendelsohn associate editor

researcher-writers

Erik A. Beach

Brenna C. Farrell

Michael B. Marean

James Patrick McFadden

Todd Plants

Rahul Rohatgi

Kathryn A. Russo

Andrew Fayerweather Spofford

Arthur E. Koski-Karrell

Anne M. Tigani

Brian R. Walsh managing editor
Paul Guilianelli map editor

Macmillan

HELPING LET'S GO

If you want to share your discoveries, suggestions, or corrections, please drop us a line. We read every piece of correspondence, whether a postcard, a 10-page email, or a coconut. Please note that mail received after May 2002 may be too late for the 2003 book, but will be kept for future editions. **Address mail to:**

Let's Go: USA
67 Mount Auburn Street
Cambridge, MA 02138
USA

Visit Let's Go at **http://www.letsgo.com,** or send email to:

feedback@letsgo.com
Subject: "Let's Go: USA"

In addition to the invaluable travel advice our readers share with us, many are kind enough to offer their services as researchers or editors. Unfortunately, our charter enables us to employ only currently enrolled Harvard students.

Published in Great Britain 2002 by Macmillan, an imprint of Pan Macmillan Ltd.
20 New Wharf Road, London N1 9RR
Basingstoke and Oxford
Associated companies throughout the world
www.panmacmillan.com

Maps by David Lindroth copyright © 2002, 2001, 2000, 1999, 1998, 1997, 1996, 1995, 1994, 1993, 1992, 1991, 1990, 1989, 1988 by St. Martin's Press.

Published in the United States of America by St. Martin's Press.

ISBN: 0-333-90603-9
First edition
10 9 8 7 6 5 4 3 2 1

Let's Go: USA is written by Let's Go Publications, 67 Mount Auburn Street, Cambridge, MA 02138, USA.

Let's Go® and the thumb logo are trademarks of Let's Go, Inc.
Printed in the USA on recycled paper with biodegradable soy ink.

CONTENTS

MAPS

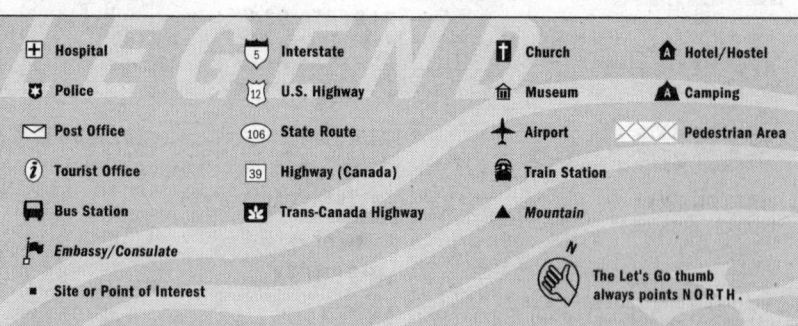

✚ Hospital	🛡 5 Interstate	✝ Church	⌂ Hotel/Hostel
🛡 Police	12 U.S. Highway	🏛 Museum	▲ Camping
✉ Post Office	106 State Route	✈ Airport	☓☓☓ Pedestrian Area
ⓘ Tourist Office	39 Highway (Canada)	🚂 Train Station	
🚌 Bus Station	Trans-Canada Highway	▲ Mountain	
⚑ Embassy/Consulate			
■ Site or Point of Interest		*N* The Let's Go thumb always points NORTH.	

RESEARCHER-WRITERS

Erik A. Beach   *Texas, Louisiana, Alabama, Oklahoma*

Steady as an old cowhand, assiduous as a seasoned rancher, and easygoing as a soulful jazzman, Erik deftly navigated the plains of the Lone Star State and the omnipresent hubbub of New Orleans. Venturing far from his native Wisconsin, Erik was always on the lookout for something new. By straying from the mainstream, he uncovered many a diamond in the rough, rewarding readers with a more diverse and authentic experience of the South.

Brenna C. Farrell   *Georgia, Carolinas, Tennessee, Kentucky*

Brenna the Intrepid had the most inauspicious beginning imaginable. But she persevered through rental car red tape, drunken rednecks, and American sketch to finish her trip in brilliant fashion. Frenetically sweeping through the majestic Appalachian trails, bustling Atlanta night spots, and kingly Memphis tourist traps, Brenna tackled the South with a Yankee's vengeance. Her fast wit and subtle charm endeared her to many a Southerner. Her diligent research and preternatural prose won over her editors.

Michael B. Marean   *The Rockies*

Mountain man Mike Marean traversed the Rockies, encountering Basque shepherds, Boulder-bred hippies, monstrously muscular Missoulians, and everyone in between. His uncanny lucky streak began the first day of his itinerary when he arrived at Going-to-the-Sun Road only hours after the first snowplow. Soon, he was charming natives left and right, scoring dates, and landing job offers. Neither bison jams nor editorial gaffes could derail Mike, whose easygoing spirit and talented writing made all of our lives a little easier.

James Patrick McFadden   *The Great Plains*

Over the course of seven weeks, Jim traveled farther than Sakakawea (and probably had more fun doing it). Notepad in hand, he took his trusty truck from the Dakotas to Texas and back again. Never missing a beat (or an opportunity to add new coverage), Jim delighted us with discursive sidebars. His steadfastness, dependability, and love of wheat made him an absolute joy to work with. From Omaha to OKC and Deadwood to Des Moines, Jim was a beacon shedding marvelous light on a misunderstood region.

Todd Plants   *The Great Lakes*

Footloose and fancy free, Todd enthusiastically worked his way around the magnificent Great Lakes. Early on in Chicago, he suffered some late-night willies outside a deserted Crate and Barrel and felt the general R-W blues, but by Ann Arbor, he was crafting copy like a wily veteran. Known for his love of all things American, from baseball to alt-country, this bespectacled and laid-back Michigander succinctly summarized the Great Lakes in two words: "Dontcha know?"

Rahul Rohatgi   *Florida, Deep South*

Blazing through Florida and the Deep South in his Lincoln chariot, Rahul somehow found time to churn out oodles of new coverage between bacchanalian forays. From lapdances to lightning strikes, baseball to BBQ, and Disneyworld to dead birds, Rahul's outlandish tales from the road kept us eager for his weekly phone calls. He finished his itinerary without the slightest hitch, bringing a big taste of the South up to New England—Rahuligan-style.

Kathryn A. Russo   *New England and Eastern Canada*

A native of Cape Canaveral, Katie rocketed her way through New England and Eastern Canada, leaving in her wake finely massaged prose and well-wrought write-ups. This freckly Floridian, possessing more grit than a French fur trapper, braved sleepless nights in cars, run-ins with toothless locals, and heavily greased scuzz in Montréal's clubs. In the end, she regaled us with philosophic insights on *québécois* culture, and served up New England like a delicious seven-course meal.

Andrew Fayerweather Spofford   *Southern New England, New York, Ontario,*
Western PA, Ohio, Indiana, Illinois, and St. Louis

Like the "giant" he is, Andrew journeyed all the way from Upstate New York to St. Louis in superhuman leaps and bounds. After snafus with rental car loopholes and testy tourist booth clerks, a frolicsome encounter with a synchronized swimming team brought him some much-needed rejuvenation. Already so famous around these parts that a popular sandwich bears his name, Andrew achieved further acclaim with his painstakingly researched and polished copy.

Arthur E. Koski-Karrell   *Pennsylvania, Delaware, and Maryland*

After three summers working for Let's Go, twice as a researcher and once as an editor, Art knew exactly what an editor would want. A pro at uncovering bars with no cover *and* a natural-born road-tripper, Art hit historic sights and splendid beaches while managing to eat his fill of Philly cheesesteak.

Anne M. Tigani   *Virginia and West Virginia*

A Richmond native, Annie gave Virginia coverage a local's flourish. She also attracted the attention of many male followers, undoubtedly impressed by her charm, humor, and press pass. Annie found fun in everything from plantations to model airplanes—and made sure her readers could do the same.

REGIONAL RESEARCHER-WRITERS

James Colbert, Mark Kirby, Bryden Sweeney-Taylor, Jakub Wrzesniewski	*Southwest USA*
Lily Fink, Bryn Lovejoy-Grinnell, Jeremy Kurzyniec, Beatrice Shu	*California*
Ashley Dayer, Brice Conklin, Emily Russin,	
Jessica Yin, Mike Weller, Nathaniel Towery	*Alaska & The Pacific Northwest*
Tiffany Lai, Emily van Dyke, Rani Yadav	*Boston and environs*
Seth Kleinerman, Daryl Sng, Avra van der Zee	*New York City and environs*
Keith Hahn, Brina Milikowsky, Alejandro Kauffmann	*San Francisco and environs*
Sarah E. Cohen	*Washington, D.C.*

REGIONAL EDITORS

Stephen M. Davis	*Editor, Alaska & The Pacific Northwest*
Natalie M. Carnes	*Associate Editor, Alaska & The Pacific Northwest*
Thomas M. Mercer	*Editor, Southwest USA*
Sarah Kennedy	*Associate Editor, Southwest USA*
Christopher R. Blazejewski	*Editor, California*
Angela Mi Young Hur	*Associate Editor, California*
Joseph Hearn	*Editor, Boston*
Eric Todrys	*Editor, New York City*
Nicole B. Usher	*Editor, Washington, D.C.*
Jean E. Huang	*Editor, San Francisco*

ACKNOWLEDGMENTS

The Let's Go 2002 series is dedicated to the memory of Haley Surti

TEAM USA THANKS: All who gave us sorely needed assistance: our phenomenal R-Ws; Steve, Nat, Tom, Sarah, Angela, Blaz, Joseph, Jean, Todrys, and Nikki; Harris, our fearless ME; and Guilianelli. Thanks also to Marly, Colin "The Beastie" Wambsgans, and the family Kiang. *Merci beaucoup* to Anne Jump. A special shout-out to those who helped with proofing: "Box o' Joe" Hearn, Keneddey, Bowman, Hur, and Mercer. Nice of you to show up.

CODY THANKS: Ben, for The Vision and the stupids. Than, for mail call and Karma Police. Joseph, thanks for the bo-nuts. Basement—how do you love it? GdB, EG, SV, SJ, SE, and SR, for hellos. Avi, Gavri, and Joey, for keeping some things in Somerville. The Crew. Pappas, my best friend; Pierce, the VIP; Kristian; and Carlie. Moshe and Tovah, you can always keep your stuff in my minivan. Last but not least: my parents, Bradley, Zac, Sam, and Teddy. Thank you for your love and support.

BEN THANKS: Cody, for the lovely tan and awesome leadership. Nat, for the tennis games and being da man. The Dirty South researchers. The Basement Crew. My summer roommates. Christine, my cutie. Shouts out to Alex, Brandon, Vlad, Phil, Roberto, Siegel, Sean, and Daves. To Michelle for getting me into this. Most of all, thanks to my family for being the light of my life. Mom, Dad, Samantha, Yia Yia, Grandpa, Grandma, aunts, uncles, cousins—you're the best. I love you Papu.

NATHANIEL (THAN)KS: Cody, for his witty and irreverent guidance. Ben, for his camaraderie and rap lyrics. The basement folks, how I knew thee and hopefully still will. My awesome researchers. All my friends, high school and college. Lauren, for making my summer so fun. My Mom and Dad and the rest of my family, I love you all so much. And the rest—watching baseball on TV, the Trauma Lounge and Iota, tennis breaks, my trusty steed, and for showing up.

Editor
D. Cody Dydek
Associate Editors
Benjamin W. Fernandez, Nathaniel Mendelsohn
Managing Editor
Brian R. Walsh
Map Editor
Paul Guilianelli

Publishing Director
Sarah P. Rotman
Editor-in-Chief
Ankur N. Ghosh
Production Manager
Jen Taylor
Cartography Manager
Dan Barnes
Design & Photo Manager
Vanessa Bertozzi
Editorial Managers
Amélie Cherlin, Naz F. Firoz, Matthew Gibson, Sharmi Surianarain, Brian R. Walsh
Financial Manager
Rebecca L. Schoff
Marketing & Publicity Managers
Brady R. Dewar, Katharine Douglas, Marly Ohlsson
New Media Manager
Kevin H. Yip
Online Manager
Alex Lloyd
Personnel Manager
Nathaniel Popper
Production Associates
Steven Aponte, Chris Clayton, Caleb S. Epps, Eduardo Montoya, Melissa Rudolph
Some Design
Melissa Rudolph
Office Coordinators
Efrat Kussell, Peter Richards

Director of Advertising Sales
Adam M. Grant
Senior Advertising Associates
Ariel Shwayder, Kennedy Thorwarth
Advertising Associate
Jennie Timoney
Advertising Artwork Editor
Peter Henderson

President
Cindy L. Rodriguez
General Manager
Robert B. Rombauer
Assistant General Manager
Anne E. Chisholm

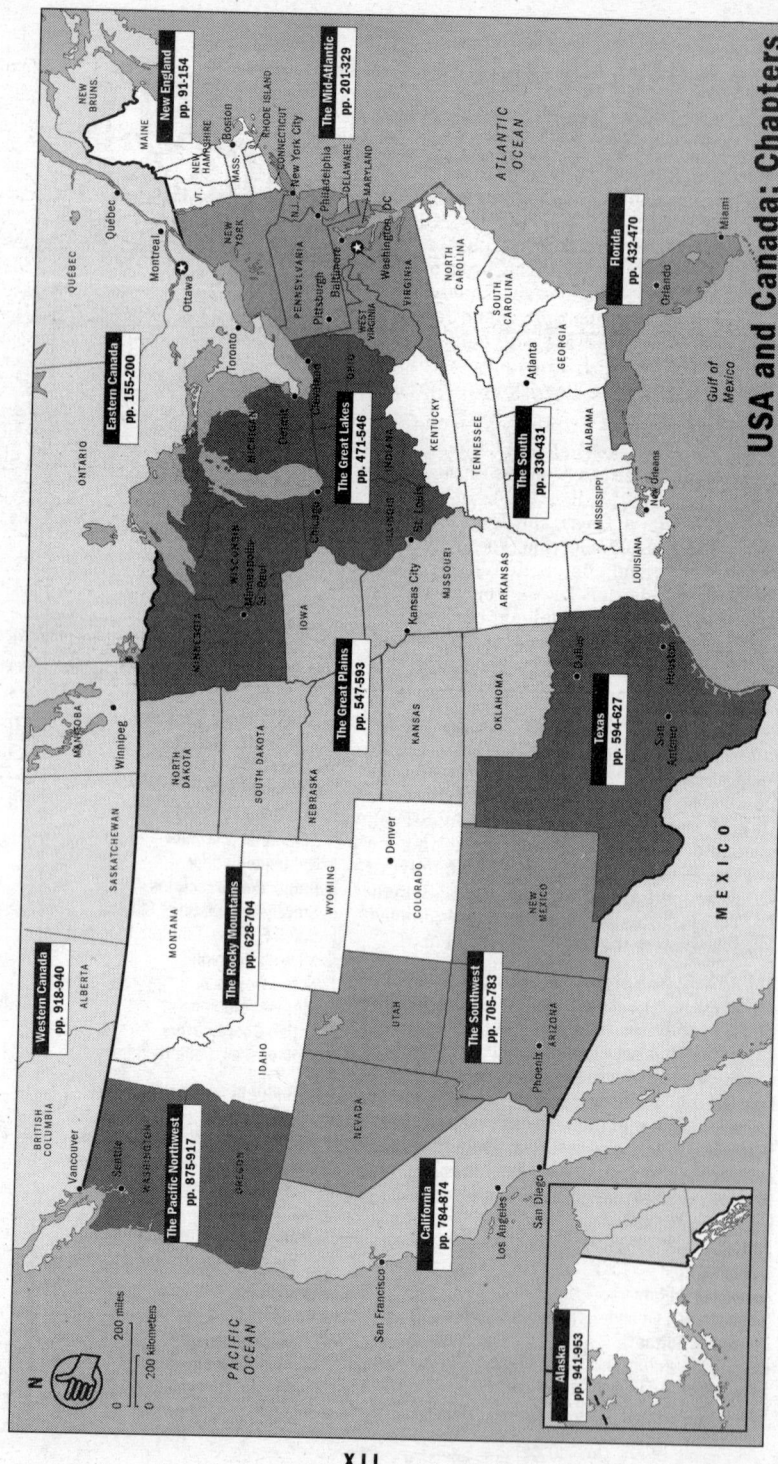

USA and Canada: Chapters

New England
pp. 91-154

The Mid-Atlantic
pp. 201-329

Eastern Canada
pp. 155-200

The Great Lakes
pp. 471-546

Florida
pp. 432-470

The South
pp. 330-431

The Great Plains
pp. 547-593

Texas
pp. 594-627

Western Canada
pp. 918-940

The Rocky Mountains
pp. 628-704

The Southwest
pp. 705-783

The Pacific Northwest
pp. 875-917

California
pp. 784-874

Alaska
pp. 941-953

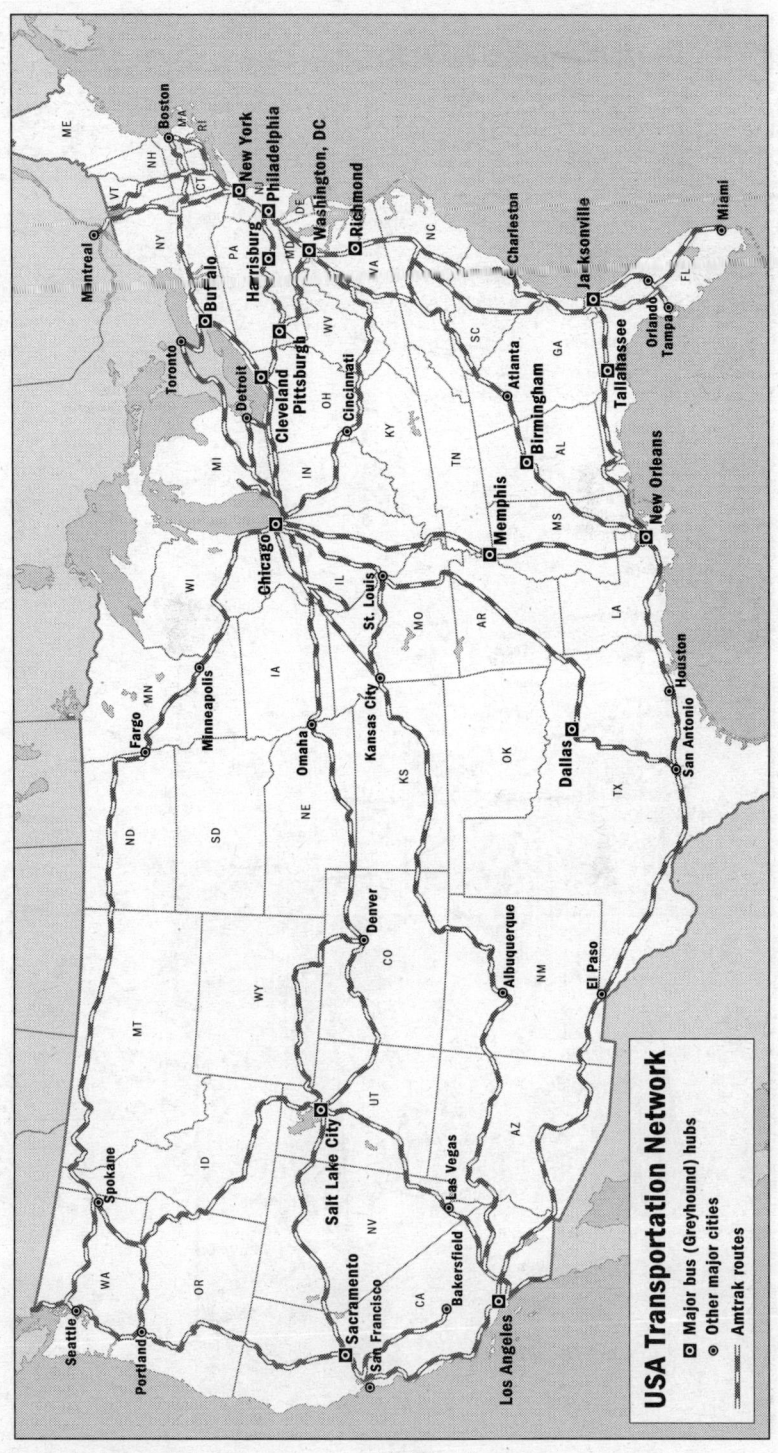

USA Transportation Network

- ⊡ Major bus (Greyhound) hubs
- ⊙ Other major cities
- ——— Amtrak routes

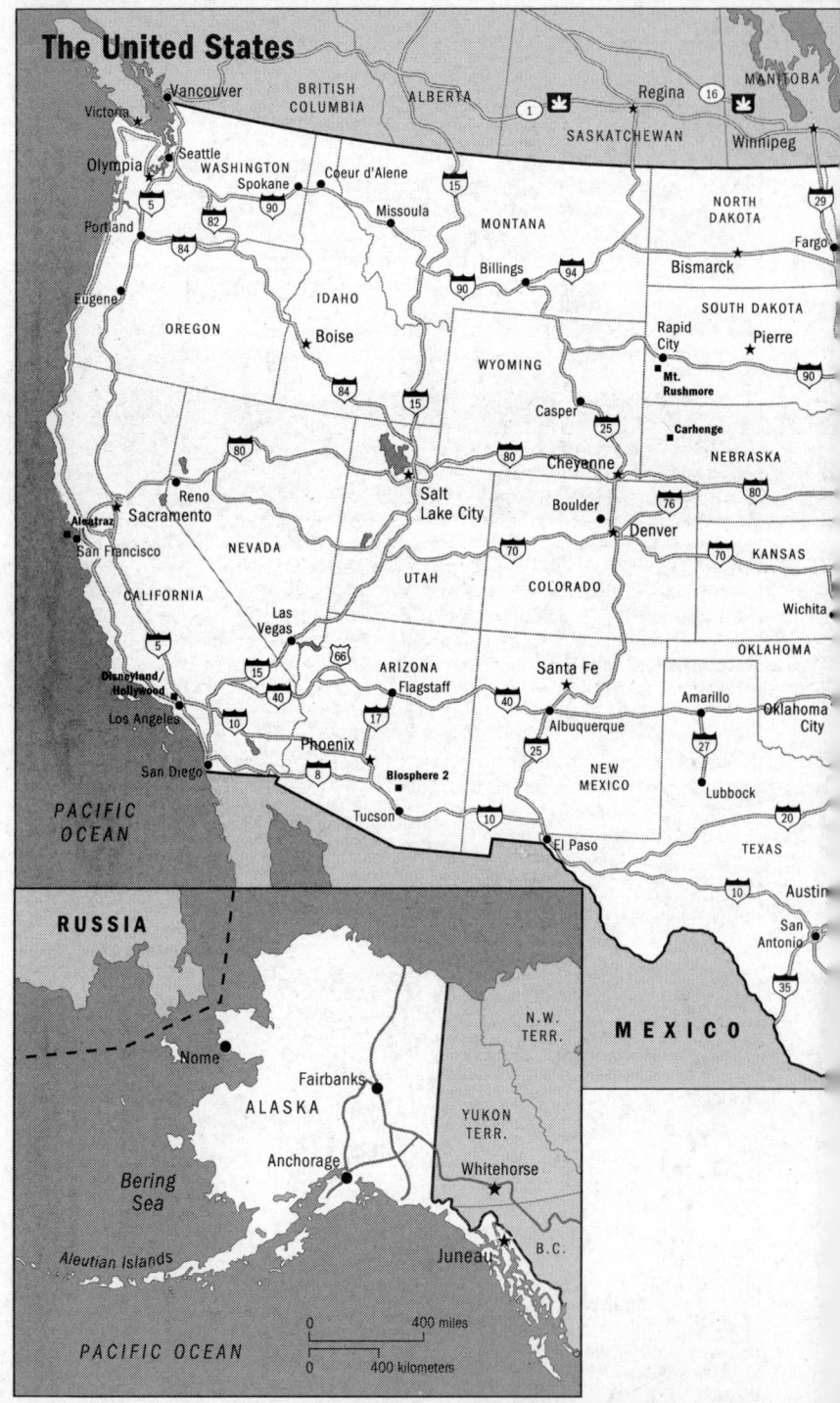

The United States

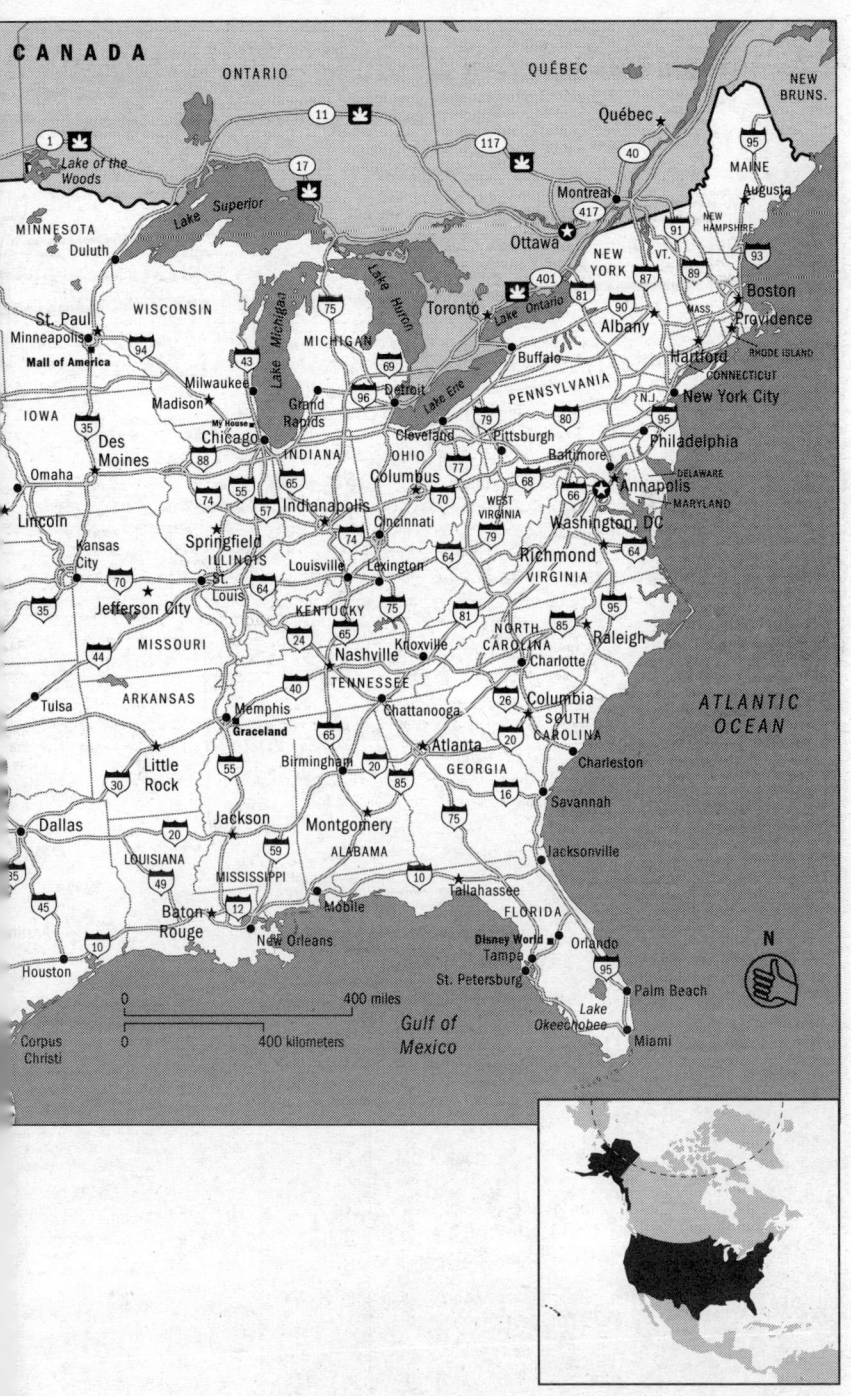

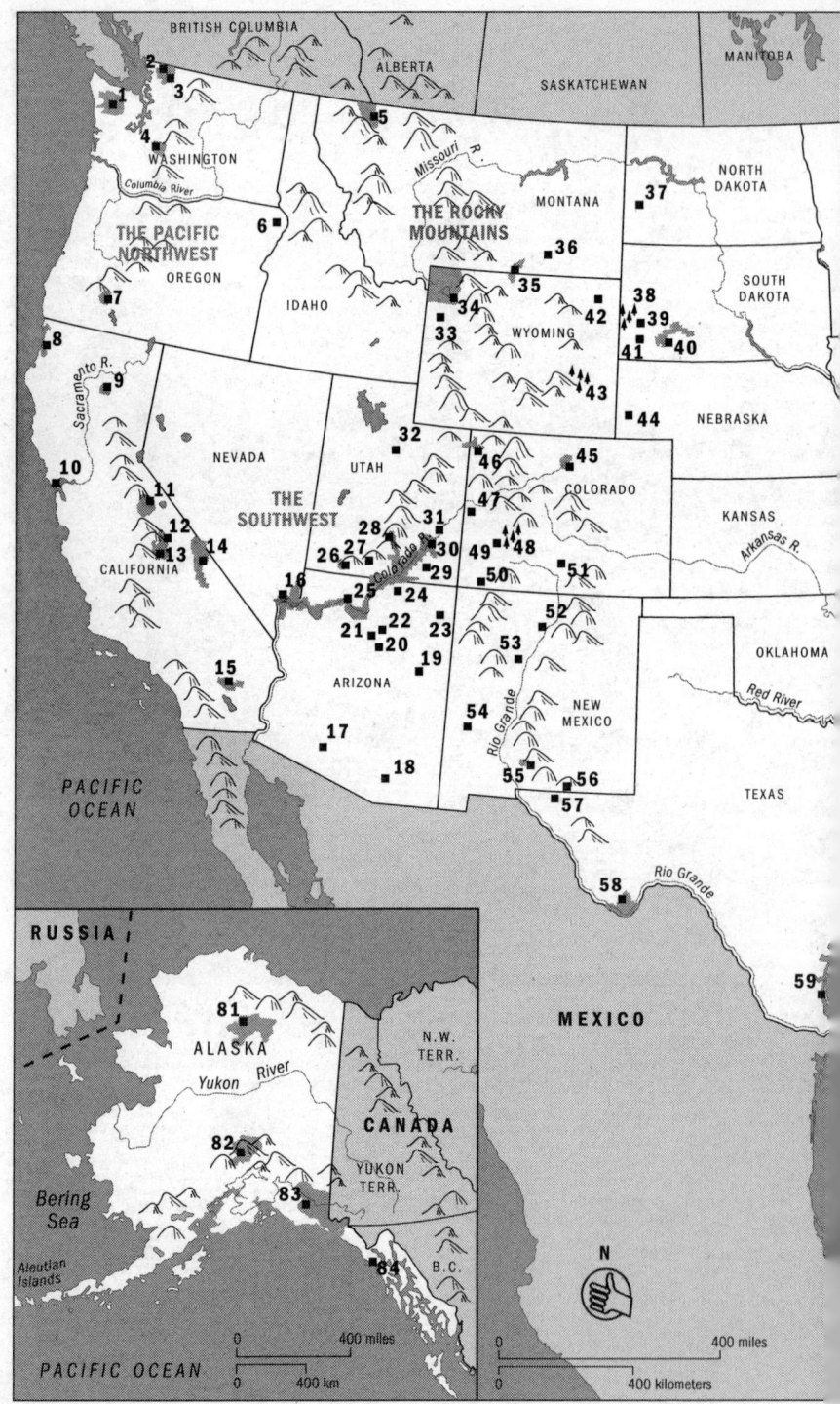

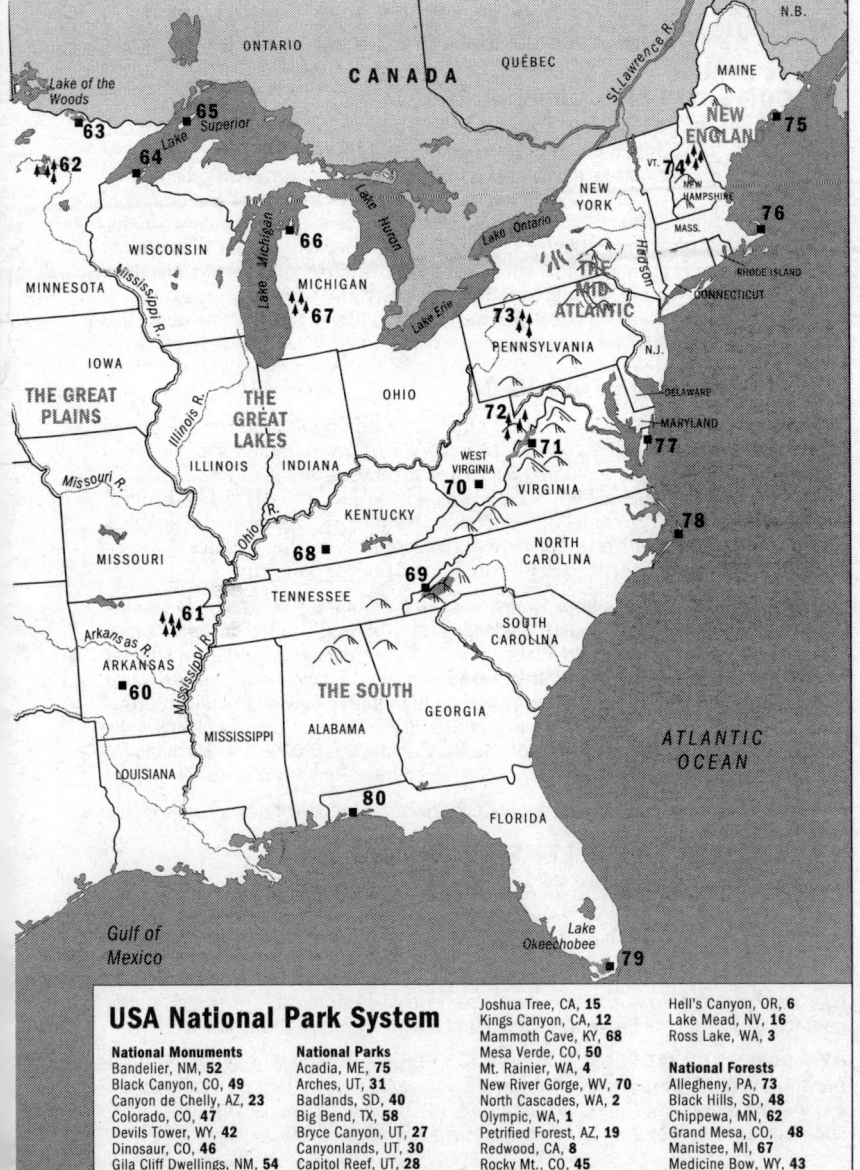

USA National Park System

National Monuments
Bandelier, NM, 52
Black Canyon, CO, 49
Canyon de Chelly, AZ, 23
Colorado, CO, 47
Devils Tower, WY, 42
Dinosaur, CO, 46
Gila Cliff Dwellings, NM, 54
Great Sand Dunes, CO, 51
Lassen Volcanic, CA, 9
Little Bighorn, MT, 36
Mt. Rushmore, SD, 39
Natural Bridges, UT, 29
Navajo, AZ, 24
Organ Pipe, AZ, 17
Petroglyph, NM, 53
Scotts Bluff, NE, 44
Sunset Crater, AZ, 21
Timpanogos Cave, UT, 32
Walnut Canyon, AZ, 20
White Sands, NM, 55
Wupatki, AZ, 22

National Parks
Acadia, ME, 75
Arches, UT, 31
Badlands, SD, 40
Big Bend, TX, 58
Bryce Canyon, UT, 27
Canyonlands, UT, 30
Capitol Reef, UT, 28
Carlsbad Caverns, NM, 56
Crater Lake, OR, 7
Death Valley, CA, 14
Denali, AK, 82
Everglades, FL, 79
Gates of the Arctic, AK, 81
Glacier, MT, 5
Glacier Bay, AK, 84
Grand Canyon, AZ, 25
Grand Teton, WY, 33
Great Smoky Mts., TN, 69
Guadalupe Mts., TX, 57
Hot Springs, AR, 60
Isle Royale, MI, 65

Joshua Tree, CA, 15
Kings Canyon, CA, 12
Mammoth Cave, KY, 68
Mesa Verde, CO, 50
Mt. Rainier, WA, 4
New River Gorge, WV, 70
North Cascades, WA, 2
Olympic, WA, 1
Petrified Forest, AZ, 19
Redwood, CA, 8
Rocky Mt., CO, 45
Saguaro, AZ, 18
Sequoia, CA, 13
Shenandoah, VA, 71
Theodore Roosevelt, ND, 37
Voyageurs, MN, 63
Wind Cave, SD, 41
Wrangell-St. Elias, AK, 83
Yellowstone, WY, 34
Yosemite, CA, 11
Zion, UT, 26

National Recreation Areas
Bighorn Canyon, MT, 35
Golden Gate, CA, 10

Hell's Canyon, OR, 6
Lake Mead, NV, 16
Ross Lake, WA, 3

National Forests
Allegheny, PA, 73
Black Hills, SD, 48
Chippewa, MN, 62
Grand Mesa, CO, 48
Manistee, MI, 67
Medicine Bow, WY, 43
Monongahela, WV, 72
Ozark, AR, 61
White Mts., NH, 74

National Lakeshores
Apostle Islands, WI, 64
Sleeping Bear Dunes, MI, 66

National Seashores
Assateague, MD, 77
Cape Cod, MA, 76
Cape Hatteras, NC, 78
Padre Island, TX, 59
Gulf Islands, FL, 80

HOW TO USE THIS BOOK

WELCOME TO LET'S GO: USA 2002!

The book you are now holding is the product of a lot of diligent labor, a lot of caffeine, and a lot of love. Three editors, ten researcher-writers, and dozens of regional editors and writers have spent half a year on a seemingly Sisyphean task: to meticulously research and document every budget-friendly nook and cranny of this great country. From cocktails in Key West to flightseeing in Fairbanks, yodeling from snowcapped mountaintops to braving Maine's frigid waters, our intrepid researchers saw everything. Meanwhile, the team of editors slaved away in a dank New England basement, lovingly crafting the witty and irreverent prose that is *Let's Go: USA*. These 1000 pages can never do justice to all the USA—and Canada—have to offer...but we think they come damn close. We hope you agree.

ORGANIZATION OF THIS BOOK

INTRODUCTORY MATERIAL. The first chapter of this book, **Discover the United States and Canada,** provides you with an overview of travel in the various regions of the USA and Canada, including **Suggested Itineraries** that give you an idea of what you shouldn't miss and how long it will take to see it. The **Life and Times** chapter provides you with a general introduction to the history, culture, and sometimes perplexing practices of North Americans. The **Essentials** section outlines the practical information you will need to prepare for and execute your trip.

COVERAGE. Our coverage hops, skips, and leaps around the continent, beginning (not in a dank basement) in **New England.** From there, it's on to **Eastern Canada** (*bien sûr!*), the sprawling **Mid-Atlantic** region, the sunny **South,** and even sunnier **Florida.** After that, it's off to the **Great Lakes**—dontcha know?—and the vast **Great Plains.** After a quick *yee-haw* in **Texas,** we get high in the **Rockies** and adventurous in the **Southwest.** We finish with a quick cruise up the Pacific Coast—**California,** the **Pacific Northwest, Western Canada,** and **Alaska.** Craving assistance? The **black tabs** in the margins will help you to navigate between chapters quickly and easily.

APPENDIX. How do we love the appendix? Check it out for a handy mileage chart.

A FEW NOTES ABOUT LET'S GO FORMAT

RANKING ESTABLISHMENTS. In each section (accommodations, food, etc.), we list establishments in order from best to worst. Our absolute favorites are so denoted by the highest honor given out by Let's Go, the Let's Go thumbs-up (🖐).

PHONE CODES AND TELEPHONE NUMBERS. The **phone code** for each region, city, or town appears opposite the name of that region, city, or town, and is denoted by the ☎ icon. **Phone numbers** in text are also preceded by the ☎ icon.

GRAYBOXES AND IKONBOXES. Grayboxes at times provide wonderful cultural insight, at times simply crude humor. In any case, they're usually amusing, so enjoy. **Whiteboxes,** on the other hand, provide important practical information, such as warnings (**M**), helpful hints, and further resources (**◨**).

A NOTE TO OUR READERS The information for this book was gathered by *Let's Go* researchers from May through August of 2001. Each listing is based on one researcher's opinion, formed during his or her visit at a particular time. Those traveling at other times may have different experiences since prices, dates, hours, and conditions are always subject to change. You are urged to check the facts presented in this book beforehand to avoid inconvenience and surprises.

DISCOVER THE UNITED STATES AND CANADA

Stretching from below the Tropic of Cancer to above the Arctic Circle and spanning the North American continent, the United States is big. It is a country defined by open spaces and an amazing breadth of terrain. From sparse deserts to lush forests to snow-capped peaks to rolling fields of grain, the American landscape sprouts new views from state to state—even from neighborhood to neighborhood.

America's accumulation of wealth and prestige since WWII has heightened both its patriotism and its interior divisions. Americans have reason to be proud: in this fair country, world-class creature comforts exist minutes away from acres of country quiet—and most of it is accessible, at least in theory, to everyone. However, the contrast between the overall abundance of wealth and the many who struggle to make ends meet is a constant confrontation. Though class lines aren't openly acknowledged, they drive people's daily lives, aspirations, and politics. Wealthy people may run the big show, but the middle-class masses inspire America's ideological orientation toward unpretentious family values. Through centuries of immigration, the US has absorbed and integrated millions of immigrants to create the cultural amalgamation that now defines the population, contributing to the proud spirit of diversity that pervades the country, and also clashing in situations of discrimination and misunderstanding.

America does indeed live up to its reputation as the land of plenty, but plentifulness leads often to too-muchness, as evidenced by the chain motels, cafes, and bookstores that all too frequently dot the landscape. Nonetheless, there remains a quality to the nation's cityscapes, byways, and wildernesses that is uniquely and unmistakably American.

While thousands of airplanes stream in and out of America's massive airports, the most rewarding way to see the country is still by car. The road trip is an authentic American institution that has captured the imagination of statesmen, writers, and lowly college students alike.

USA FACTS AND FIGURES

POPULATION: 284,736,000.

LARGEST CITIES: New York City, Los Angeles, Chicago, Houston, Philadelphia.

RELIGIOUS AFFILIATION: Protestant 58%, Roman Catholic 21%, other Christian 6%; Jewish 2%; Muslim 2%; other 2%; non-religious 9%.

MILES DRIVEN EACH YEAR: 1½ trillion (to the sun and back 7500 times).

URBAN/RURAL POPULATION: City mice 77%; country mice 23%.

ETHNICITY: White 73%; Black 12%; Hispanic 11%; Asian and Pacific Islander 3.5%; Native American 1%.

WHEN TO GO

In general, the US tourist season runs during the summer months between Memorial Day and Labor Day (May 27-Sept. 2, 2002); in Canada, the tourist season starts around mid-July. National parks become inundated with visitors during the high season, though cities are less affected. For regions where winter sports are big or where winters are mild, the tourist season is generally inverted (Dec.-Mar.).

NATIONAL HOLIDAYS

USA	
DATE IN 2002	**HOLIDAY**
January 1	New Year's Day
January 21	Martin Luther King, Jr. Day
February 18	Presidents Day
May 27	Memorial Day
July 4	Independence Day
September 2	Labor Day
October 14	Columbus Day
November 11	Veterans Day
November 28	Thanksgiving
December 25	Christmas Day

CANADA	
DATE IN 2002	**HOLIDAY**
January 1	New Year's Day
March 31	Easter Sunday
April 1	Easter Monday
May 20	Victoria Day
July 1	Canada Day
September 2	Labour Day
October 14	Thanksgiving
November 11	Remembrance Day
December 25	Christmas Day
December 26	Boxing Day

FESTIVALS

From music to magic, culture to kitsch, the USA and Canada are home to a remarkably varied selection of festivals. Some of the most popular American and Canadian festivals are listed below, along with the page numbers of their respective descriptions in the guide. This list is far from exhaustive; refer to the Sights and Entertainment sections of specific cities for more festivals.

USA	
MONTH	**FESTIVAL**
January	**Elvis Presley's Birthday Tribute,** Memphis, TN (p. 353)
	Western Stock Show, Rodeo, and Horse Show, Denver, CO (p. 674)
	Winter Carnival, St. Paul, MN (p. 540)
February	**Mardi Gras,** New Orleans, LA (p. 409)
	Ashland Shakespeare Festival, Ashland, OR (p. 914)
	Gasparilla Pirate Festival, Tampa, FL (p. 462)
March	**South by Southwest,** Austin, TX (p. 602)
April	**New Orleans Jazz and Heritage Festival,** New Orleans, LA (p. 409)
	Fiesta San Antonio, San Antonio, TX (p. 620)
May	**Memphis in May International Festival,** Memphis, TN (p. 353)
	Spoleto Festival USA, Charleston, SC (p. 371)
June	**Portland Rose Festival,** Portland, OR (p. 902)
	Chicago Blues Festival, Chicago, IL (p. 503)
	Summerfest, Milwaukee, WI (p. 529)
	Aspen Music Festival, Aspen, CO (p. 690)
July	**Tanglewood,** Lenox, MA (p. 146)
	Frontier Days, Cheyenne, WY (p. 670)
	Aquatennial, Minneapolis, MN (p. 540)
August	**Newport Folk Festival and JVC Jazz Festival,** Newport, RI (p. 148)
September	**Bumbershoot,** Seattle, WA (p. 876)
	La Fiesta de Santa Fe, Santa Fe, NM (p. 764)
November	**Hot Air Balloon Rally,** Albuquerque, NM (p. 771)
	Macy's Thanksgiving Day Parade, New York, NY (p. 201)

CANADA	
MONTH	**FESTIVAL**
January	**Annual Polar Bear Swim,** Vancouver, BC (p. 918)
February	**Winterlude,** Ottawa, ON (p. 194)
	Winter Carnival, Québec City, QC (p. 178)
May	**Stratford Shakespeare Festival** (through Nov.), Stratford, ON (p. 194)
	Canadian Tulip Festival, Ottawa, ON (p. 194)
June	**International Jazz Festival,** Montréal, QC (p. 168)
July	**Nova Scotia International Tattoo Festival,** Halifax, NS (p. 155)
August	**Canadian National Exhibition,** Toronto, ON (p. 193)

THINGS TO DO

Neither these two pages nor this book's one thousand pages can do justice to the vibrant, unparalleled, and, above all, diverse offerings of the North American continent. No two trips to the New World are ever the same, and visitors to two different regions may feel like they've visited different countries. There are, however, a few common themes in the States and Canada that deserve mention and that should be a part of any thorough exploration.

SCENIC DRIVES

News commentator and stalwart American patriot Charles Kuralt once said, "Thanks to the interstate highway system, it is now possible to travel from coast to coast without seeing anything." The interstate system is the fastest, most efficient, most sensible way of driving through America—and also the least rewarding. The incredible network of backroads in the US afford a view of the real country, unobstructed by vision-blocking soundproofers and gas-spewing trailers and with rest stops posessing more character than the next Burger King. The **Blue Ridge Parkway,** VA (p. 323), connects two national parks—Shenandoah and Great Smoky Mountains—passing tremendous green mountains and rustic Appalachian wilderness. In the North, the **Lake Superior North Shore Drive,** MN (p. 545), traces the dramatic, cliff-lined shore of the greatest Great Lake, passing waterfalls, lighthouses, and looming forests. Connecting San Antonio with Austin, TX, the **Texas Hill Country Drive** (p. 600) goes deep into the heart of Texas—broad-rim hats and dusty jeans country—where the Western landscape is dotted with historical immigrant communities and pristine vineyards. Just outside Phoenix, AZ, the **Apache Trail** (p. 755) curves around stark cactus-laden desert mountains, looming over deep blue reservoirs. The **San Juan Skyway** (p. 700), in southern CO, ascends to breathtaking heights under snow-capped mountains and past bottomless gorges. **Going-to-the-Sun Road** (p. 647), in the Waterton-Glacier Peace Park, MT, skirts mountainous landscape too beautiful for words, passing bubbling waterfalls and steep escarpments before descending into the rainforest.

MUST-SEE CITIES

Sure, everyone knows the biggies. New York has...well, everything. And for vivacity, glamour, great weather, and unbeatable smog, nothing tops Los Angeles. The multicultural metropolis of Toronto also offers unparalleled opportunities. But the real reason to buckle up for the great American journey, besides the great American wilderness, is to enjoy the smaller, less obvious cities and towns on the way. Lost between the twin giants of New York and Boston, the smaller college town of **Providence, RI** (p. 146), beckons with a slower, more inviting pace. The magnificent fortifications and twisting alleyways of **Québec City, QC** (p. 178), testify to the city's unmatched old-world character. The "staid" American Midwest boasts **Minneapolis-St. Paul, MN** (p. 534), a sprawling and unsung urban center with the sights and diversity to rival even the most famous of American cities. Travelers to **Savannah, GA** (p. 394) are rewarded with lush gardens, antebellum homes, and quaint Southern streets. The legendary nightlife of **Austin, TX** (p. 602), thrives on the city's mix of Southwestern grit, collegiate energy, and dot-com optimism. Only the most liberal-minded and fun-loving traveler need stop in the eclectic town of **Boulder, CO** (p. 682), a place of many Rocky Mountain highs. Countless adventurers find a warm welcome in **Flagstaff, AZ** (p. 738), perhaps the greatest crossroads in the US. The spirited city of **Portland, OR** (p. 902), known as the microbrewery capital of North America, is quickly becoming one of the most sought-after destinations on the continent.

COLLEGE TOWNS

America's colleges, from sprawling state universities to tiny liberal-arts academies, have engendered unique communities characterized by their youthful vitality and alternative spirit. The mountain hamlet of **Middlebury, VT** (p. 110) combines rural charm with a touch of collegiate rowdiness. An increasingly diverse student community gives the Southern establishment a run for its money in **Charlottesville, VA** (p. 318), a gorgeous town characterized by its rolling hills and splendid architecture. The student population of **Laramie, WY** (p. 673), has put a new spin on the region's traditional cowboy chic, while **Missoula, MT** (p. 641), has become one of the most fascinatingly cosmopolitan cities in the West. Even though it has become much more than just a college town, the quintessential liberal haven of **Berkeley, CA** (p. 847), is always worth a visit.

AMERICANA

America enshrines the biggest, smallest, and zaniest of everything. Kitschy roadside attractions dot the country's dusty roads, putting on public display a vast and truly baffling material culture, most often for a modest fee. The **Museum of Early American Farm Machinery and Very Old Horse Saddles with a History** houses rusted relics of happier days in Chalk Hill, PA (p. 277). Out west in Polson, MT, the **Miracle of America Museum** makes it clear that reg'lar old American living is downright miraculous (p. 643). **Wall Drug's** notorious billboards lure tourists to the Badlands of South Dakota from as far away as Amsterdam—that's right, in Holland—and have turned a marketing ploy into a cultural phenomenon (p. 557). At the **Tinkertown Museum** in Albuquerque, NM, the pants of the world's tallest man, among other thingamabobs, are walled in by countless glass bottles (p. 776). That's no match for the **Beer Can House** in Houston, TX, however, which needs no explanation (p. 617). Further evidence of American architectural ingenuity can be found at the **Corn Palace** in Mitchell, SD (p. 554); this gargantuan structure is rebuilt every year with a fresh crop. America also claims the world's largest **kaleidoscope** (Kaleidoworld in Mt. Tremper, NY, p. 239) and **wooden cross** (Cross in the Woods in Petoskey, MI, p. 499), neither of which can quite compete with the magnitude of **Carhenge**, a scale model of Stonehenge built from 36 old cars just north of Alliance, NE (p. 574). Bigger and brighter still are the casinos of **the Strip** in Las Vegas, NV (p. 707) and **the Boardwalk** in Atlantic City, NJ (p. 256). No tribute to the American value of individual rights stands so proud as **"The Tree That Owns Itself"** (and its shade) in Athens, GA (p. 392). And no tour of American kitsch would be complete without a trip to the heart and soul of all Americana, Elvis's **Graceland** (p. 356).

NATIONAL PARKS

From ancient glaciers to an endless sea of blinding white gypsum to haunting red buttes to endless pitch-black caves, the national parks of the US and Canada protect some of the most phenomenal natural beauty in the world. While much of the land's beauty can be seen along the byways, the truly miraculous works of nature are cared for by the National Park Service. The easternmost park in the US, **Acadia National Park**, ME (p. 97), features unspoiled rocky beaches and dense pine forests. **Shenandoah National Park**, VA (p. 321), made its way into history as America's first land reclamation project, and today lures travelers with its mountain vistas. **Great Smoky Mountains National Park**, TN (p. 348), the largest national park east of the Mississippi, also holds the distinctions of International Biosphere Reserve and World Heritage Site. By far the most popular parks, however, lie out west. Arguably the most famous (and most crowded) park in the US, **Yellowstone National Park**, WY (p. 651), wows visitors with attractions such as the Old Faithful geyser. **Grand Canyon National Park**, AZ (p. 732), wows visitors with...well, the Grand Canyon, while **Yosemite National Park**, CA (p. 868), draw hordes of trekkers, trailers, and tourists with its steep mountains and stunning waterfalls. Every local will tell you that you have to see their park "at least once in your life"; they speak the truth at these parks, known as the "big three" of the national park system. Smaller—but no less breathtaking—wonders can be found in the otherworldly hoodoos (pillar-like rock formations) of **Bryce Canyon National Park**, UT (p. 726), the varied and dramatic terrain of **Waterton-Glacier International Peace Park**, MT (p. 644), and the awesome mountains of **Grand Teton National Park**, WY (p. 660).

Canada also possesses a highly developed and well-maintained national park system. The world's largest tides ebb and flow at **Fundy National Park**, NB (p. 163), while nearby **Kouchibouguac National Park** (p. 165) features sandy beaches and acres of marshland. The Canadian Rockies also play host to gorgeous parklands, including the expansive icefields of **Jasper National Park**, AB (p. 937). Further west, the isolated **Pacific Rim National Park**, BC (p. 927), offers some of the best hiking, surfing, and diving on the continent.

◨ LET'S GO PICKS

BEST OPPORTUNITIES FOR PUBLIC BATHING: Hot springs are a therapeutic diversion from the hard work of travel; some of the best are at Hot Springs, AR (p. 429); Lolo Springs, MT (p. 642); Saratoga, WY (p. 673); and Calistoga, CA (p. 855). For just plain skinny dippin', try Hippie Hollow in Austin, TX (p. 605).

BEST SUNSPOTS: To watch the sun rise first, head to Cadillac Mt. in Acadia National Park, ME (p. 97). To see the best sunset on earth, go to the pier in Clearwater, FL (p. 464).

BEST FOR SPELUNKERS: Don't forget to explore the underground. Highest marks go to Mammoth Cave, KY (p. 335), and Carlsbad Caverns, NM (p. 782).

BEST GATORS: America's most impressive creatures. Get up close and scarily personal in Nachitoches, LA (p. 423); the Everglades, FL (p. 455); and St. Augustine, FL (p. 432).

MOST APPETIZING BEER NAMES: Montana's Moose Drool (p. 656) and Florida's Dolphin's Breath (p. 435) definitely rank among the nation's finest.

BEST BIG ART: Everything's big in America. Twenty-seven factory buildings are needed to hold the exhibits at the Museum of Contemporary Art in North Adams, MA (p. 143). The world's largest painting, a 360° mural, is housed in Atlanta, GA (p. 385). The still unfinished sculpture of Crazy Horse (p. 559) will be 563 ft. when it is completed, making the 60 ft. presidential heads on nearby Mt. Rushmore (p. 558) seem like child's play.

MOST CANADIAN LOCALE: Yarmouth, NS (p. 157), takes the Canadian cake.

BEST WAY TO ESCAPE AMERICA (OTHER THAN CANADA): Tibetan cuisine, rare in the US, is served authentically at the Snow Lion restaurant in Bloomington, IN (p. 484), owned by the Dalai Lama's nephew. Made in Tajikstan and shipped to Boulder, CO (p. 682), the building of the Dushanbe teahouse is a gift between sister cities—a tasty tribute to international relations.

BEST EXTRATERRESTRIALS: Many claim Roswell, NM (p. 781) and Sedona, AZ (p. 742) have hosted a few *really* long-distance travelers.

SUGGESTED ITINERARIES

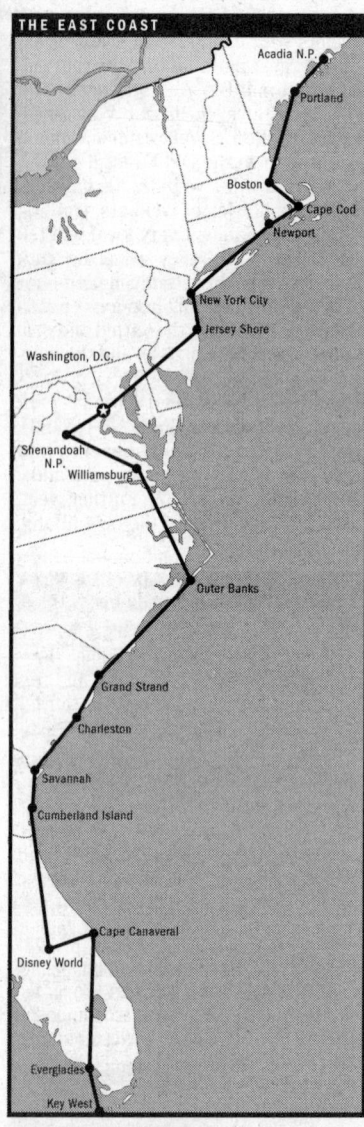

THE EAST COAST

Acadia N.P.
Portland
Boston
Cape Cod
Newport
New York City
Jersey Shore
Washington, D.C.
Shenandoah N.P.
Williamsburg
Outer Banks
Grand Strand
Charleston
Savannah
Cumberland Island
Cape Canaveral
Disney World
Everglades
Key West

Island, ME (p. 95) where mountain and ocean meet with spectacular results, and then head down the coast. The youthful Portland, ME (p. 92) will whet your appetite for city life, and the thriving culture of Boston, MA (p. 115) will satisfy it. Cape Cod (p. 134) awaits with pristine beaches, while Newport, RI (p. 148) preserves the must-see summer estates of America's wealthiest industrialists. Then on to New York City (p. 238), to which so many superlatives cannot do justice—give yourself some time to take it all in. The Jersey Shore (p. 256) offers R&R on what are arguably the best beaches in the Northeast. Washington, D.C. (p. 291) deserves a few days, as does the placid Shenandoah National Park (p. 321). They'll act out colonial history for you in Williamsburg, VA (p. 312), but you can find solitude on the long stretches of sand of the Outer Banks (p. 367). The more built-up Grand Strand (p. 377) and the city of Charleston, SC (p. 371) beckon partiers back to the mainland. Savannah (p. 394) and stunning Cumberland Island (p. 393) will leave Georgia on your mind, but Disney World (p. 441) will leave you blissfully mind-numb. Give the Space Coast of Florida (p. 445) a fly-by, and definitely explore the vast, mysterious Everglades (p. 455). Celebrate the end of your journey with umbrella drinks on sugar-white beaches in Key West (p. 459).

THE NORTH: TRACING THE US-CANA-DIAN BORDER (6 WEEKS) Crossing the continent at higher latitudes affords travelers time in the unique cities and less touristed parks of the North. Begin on the Canadian side of the border and take a whirlwind tour of the country's cosmopolitan eastern cities. Québec City (p. 178) and Montréal (p. 168) are predominantly French-speaking and overflow with culture. Titan Toronto (p. 186) boasts huge ethnic quarters and refreshing tidiness for such a big city. Cross the border at the spectacular Niagara Falls (p. 246) and head west for the oft-stigmatized and underestimated city of Detroit (p. 485). Move quickly on to the main course, though: Chicago (p. 503). Wind down in the friendly and scenic lakeside communities of Wisconsin at Door County (p. 529) and the Apostle Islands (p. 531). Next, head to the surprisingly hip twin cities of St. Paul and Minneapolis (p. 534). The charming city of Duluth, MN (p. 541) combines a thriving shipping industry with

EAST COAST: MAINE TO THE FLOR-IDA KEYS (6 WEEKS) I-95 and the sometimes commercial, sometimes scenic U.S. 1 parallel each other from the northern wilds of Maine down to the gorgeous Florida Keys. Despite the many state-levied tolls, this strip gives a true cross-section of American life and culture, and encourages on-a-whim diversions. Begin on Mt. Desert

DISCOVER

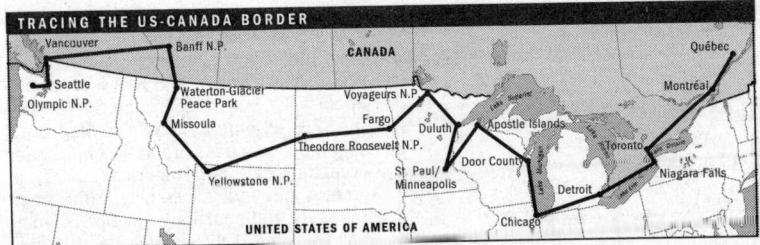

TRACING THE US-CANADA BORDER

endless waterfront recreation. Before leaving Minnesota, park the car and boat into the unspoiled expanse of Voyageurs National Park (p. 544). Stop in Fargo (p. 547), then speed out to the breathtaking Theodore Roosevelt (p. 551) and Yellowstone (p. 651) National Parks. Young and fresh, Missoula, MT (p. 641) provides a much-needed stop before heading north to Waterton-Glacier Peace Park (p. 644) and the popular Banff National Park (p. 934) in Canada. Out on the Pacific coast, choose among the lively city scenes of Vancouver (p. 918) and Seattle (p. 876) or one of the world's last remaining old-growth temperate rainforests at Olympic National Park (p. 893). Or take your time and do all three.

SOUTH BY SOUTHWEST (8 WEEKS)

Striking straight across the American South from sea to shining sea—and even dipping into Mexico—this route highlights old-fashioned Southern flavor, Mexican-infused Southwestern culture, and canyon country. It can be driven year-round. Warm up with big cities tempered by Southern hospitality in the triangle of Charleston, SC (p. 371), Savannah, GA (p. 394) and Atlanta (p. 380). Chug through Chattanooga, TN (p. 352), then follow virtually all American musical styles to their roots in Nashville (p. 342); Memphis (p. 353); Oxford, MS (p. 408); and New Orleans (p. 409). Experience the unadulterated Cajun culture of the Deep South in Acadiana, LA (p. 424) before heading out to the Texan trio of Houston (p. 613), San Antonio (p. 595), and Austin (p. 602). White Sands National

Monument, NM (p. 780) is truly otherworldly, while Truth or Consequences (p. 778) has phenomenal mineral baths. The cities of Santa Fe (p. 764) and Albuquerque (p. 771) are worth a couple of days each. After having your fill, head to the astonishing Petrified Forest and Painted Desert (p. 747). Flagstaff, AZ (p. 738) is an inviting Southwestern city in its own right, and makes a convenient base for exploring the region near the indescribable Grand Canyon (p. 732). Stop by the enormous Lake Powell (p. 749) for stunning scenery and great boating. To the north, the idyllic wilderness of Zion National Park (p. 727) and startling rock pillars of Bryce Canyon (p. 726) in Utah provide travelers with a last gasp of clean air and natural beauty before plunging into the glitz of Las Vegas (p. 707). In California, Joshua Tree National Park (p. 816) is a worthy stop in the desert on the way to the Pacific coast. Savor sunny San Diego (p. 808) before becoming starstruck in glamorous Los Angeles (p. 784).

THE AMERICAN WEST (3-6 WEEKS)

This is the West that has blown the minds of generations of westward wanderers. Acculturate yourself to the region with tours of Tucson (p. 756), Phoenix (p. 750), and Flagstaff, AZ (p. 738). Hit the must-see Grand Canyon (p. 732) from the South Rim, and then mosey through the more tranquil Bryce Canyon (p. 726) and Zion (p. 727) National Parks in Utah. On to Albuquerque (p. 771) and Santa Fe, NM (p. 764) as you approach more mountainous terrain. Spend some time in the authentic Western towns

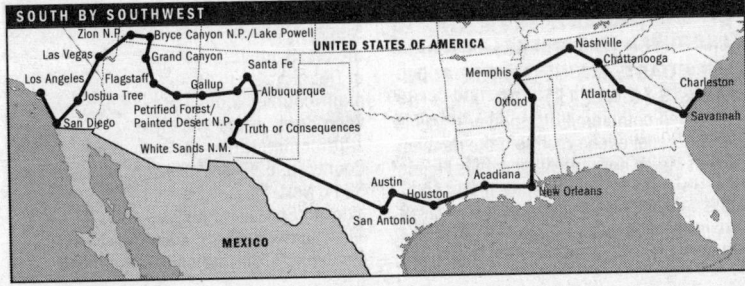

SOUTH BY SOUTHWEST

DISCOVER

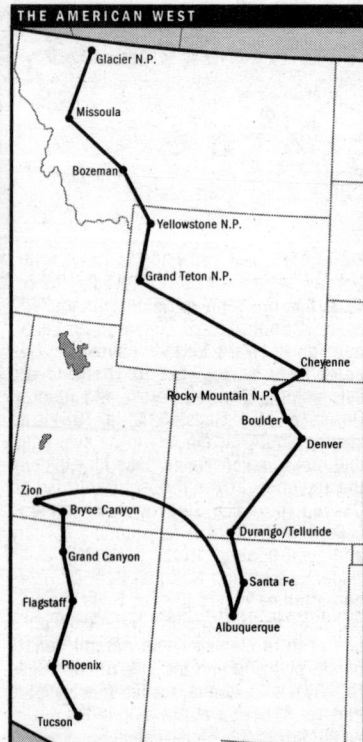

THE AMERICAN WEST

Glacier N.P.
Missoula
Bozeman
Yellowstone N.P.
Grand Teton N.P.
Cheyenne
Rocky Mountain N.P.
Boulder
Denver
Zion
Bryce Canyon
Durango/Telluride
Grand Canyon
Flagstaff
Santa Fe
Albuquerque
Phoenix
Tucson

ture. Las Vegas (p. 707), Tijuana (p. 814), and Joshua Tree (p. 816) are viable side trips. The 400 mi. stretch of shore-hugging Rte. 1 between L.A. and San Francisco—through Big Sur (p. 823) and Santa Cruz (p. 825)—is pure California: rolling surf, secluded beaches, dramatic cliffs, and eccentric locals. San Francisco (p. 827), a groovin' city in itself, is only 3-4hr. from Yosemite National Park (p. 868). From San Fran, the slightly inland Rte. 101 hits Napa Valley wine country (p. 853) before reuniting with Rte. 1 (and the coast) and passing through primordial Redwood National Park (p. 860). Once past the trees, rejoin I-5 for a trip through Oregon to Portland (p. 902). Side trips to Crater Lake (p. 913) and Mt. Hood (p. 907) are well worth it. Before resettling with a cappucino in Seattle (p. 876), commune with nature at Mt. St. Helens (p. 896) and Olympic National Park (p. 893). Vancouver, BC (p. 918) offers access to the outdoor havens of Vancouver Island (p. 926).

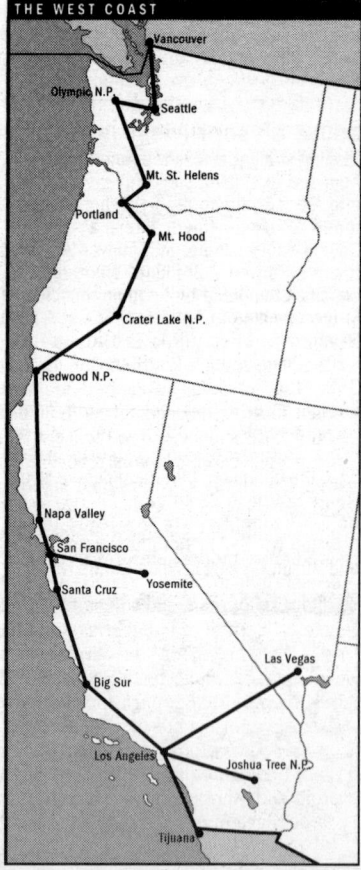

THE WEST COAST

Vancouver
Olympic N.P.
Seattle
Mt. St. Helens
Portland
Mt. Hood
Crater Lake N.P.
Redwood N.P.
Napa Valley
San Francisco
Santa Cruz
Yosemite
Las Vegas
Big Sur
Los Angeles
Joshua Tree N.P.
Tijuana

of Durango (p. 701) and Telluride, CO (p. 698), and take on the mile-high city of Denver (p. 674) and youthful Boulder (p. 682) before getting lost among the peaks of Rocky Mountain National Park (p. 685). Stop over in Cheyenne, WY (p. 670) for a boot-stompin' good time on your way to the magnificent Tetons (p. 660). The vastly popular Yellowstone National Park (p. 651) warrants an extra couple of days. Then, the towns of Bozeman (p. 638) and Missoula, MT (p. 641), culturally straddling East and West, make pleasant and unique stops for the weary. Cap off your trip with the purple mountains' majesty of rugged Glacier National Park (p. 644).

THE WEST COAST: FROM L.A. TO VANCOUVER (2-6 WEEKS). A tour of the West Coast offers the most cosmopolitan diversity, mountainscapes, and oceanfront property for your buck. Between sunny, boisterous Los Angeles and lush, mellow Vancouver, BC lies much natural (and artificial) diversion. L.A. (p. 784), America's western outpost of high culture, provides access to Hollywood (p. 788), famous art, and quintessential beach cul-

LIFE AND TIMES

THE UNITED STATES

HISTORY

BRIDGE OVER TROUBLED WATER

Archaeologists estimate that the first Americans crossed the Bering Sea from Siberia by **land bridge** during the last Ice Age, somewhere from 10,000 to 15,000 years ago. Scientists have raised different theories to explain this migration. Whether it was the pursuit of nomadic bison, a shift in living conditions in Asia, or simple wanderlust that drove them over the land bridge, the Asiatic peoples gradually inhabited all corners of their new continent. Fishing provided the main source of sustenance for societies of the Subarctic, Northwest Coast, and Plateau regions. The native peoples of California, in addition to fishing and small-game hunting, discovered a profitable method for extracting acorn flour. Nomadic families in the Great Basin region (modern-day Utah and Nevada) survived on wild seeds, insects, and small animals. The Native Americans of the nearby Plains Regions, hunters by trade, were greatly influenced by European colonization: the introduction of the horse by 16th-century Spanish explorers made bison hunting (and raiding) more profitable activities. Finally, the cultivation of staple crops such as corn (maize), beans, squash, and tubers enabled the creation of more sedentary societies in the Southwest and the Eastern Woodlands.

(UN)WELCOME EUROPEANS

The date of the first European exploration of North America is difficult to pinpoint. The earliest Europeans to stumble upon the "New World" were likely sea voyagers blown off-course by storms. History textbooks tell us that the "discovery" of the Americas was in 1492, when **Christopher Columbus** found his voyage to the East blocked by Hispaniola in the Caribbean Sea. Somehow believing that he had reached the spice islands of the East Indies, he dubbed the inhabitants "Indians." Columbus's arrival unleashed the unhappy tide of European conquest, which brought murder, disease, forced conversion, and other calamities to the natives.

Many Europeans came to the New World in search of gold and silver. While most were unsuccessful, colonial fever had taken hold, and European exploration persisted. The **Treaty of Tordesillas,** signed in 1494, divided the New World between Spain and Portugal, granting most of the Americas to Spain. While the Spanish expanded into the Southern regions of the modern-day US, the French and Dutch created more modest empires to the north. It was the English, however, who most successfully settled the vast New World. After a few unsuccessful attempts, the English finally managed to establish a colony at **Jamestown** in 1607. Their success hinged on a strain of indigenous weed called tobacco, which quickly became all the rage in England. While the Virginia settlements were founded for economic purposes, settlers came to the New World for a smattering of different reasons. A group of religious separatists known as **Puritans** fled persecution to settle in present-day Massachusetts. Similarly, a cadre of **Catholics** settled in the colony of Maryland. The colony of Georgia, founded in 1732, was conceived as a buffer state against Spanish-occupied Florida. Georgia also served as a dumping ground for debtors and other unsavory characters; some of these unsavory characters can still be found in Georgia (see **"Squeal Like a Pig,"** p. 382).

9

YOU SAY YOU WANT A REVOLUTION

In order to protect her holdings in the Americas, Great Britain entered into the French and Indian War against France (and her Indian allies) in 1754. Although ultimately successful, the struggle more than doubled Great Britain's government expenditures and raised awareness of the high price of colonialism. In order to offset the burden of this price on British taxpayers, the powers that be decided to shift more responsibility onto the American colonies, who had previously been taxed lightly. These new taxes angered colonists, who rallied against "taxation without representation." The leaders of the First Continental Congress were divided as to a course of action, but continued fighting between colonists and British troops convinced the Second Continental Congress to prepare the 13 colonies for war. In 1776, a **Declaration of Independence** was drafted. The date on which the declaration was adopted, July 4th, remains the most important national holiday for Americans. After eight years of fighting up and down the Eastern seaboard, British troops sailed off, and the colonists finally had a country of their own.

LIFE, LIBERTY, AND THE CONSTITUTION

After achieving its independence, the country experimented with a loose confederated government until 1787, when the state legislatures sent a distinguished group of 55 men to draft what was to become the world's first written **Constitution.** While **Federalists** supported a strong central government free from popular influence, **Jeffersonians** (Anti-Federalists) favored states' rights and were skeptical about the ability of centralized government to truly serve the people.

The **Bill of Rights,** a set of ten constitutional amendments passed shortly after the Constitution, has remained a cornerstone of the American political system. This document included the rights to free speech, freedom of the press, and freedom of religion—along with the controversial right to bear arms. Despite the supposed inalienability of these rights, the original words of the document's authors are still interpreted differently according to the political climate of each era. In the landmark court case *Plessy v. Ferguson* (1896), Justice Henry Billings Brown used the Constitution to support racial segregation, whereas Chief Justice Earl Warren cited the same document to destroy the practice in the 1950s. The power of the Constitution lies in its ability to be both timeless and timely, to represent the hopes of the nation's founders while accommodating the values of subsequent generations.

MANIFEST DESTINY

Looking beyond the Mississippi River, President Thomas Jefferson purchased the **Louisiana Territory** from Napoleon in 1803 for less than 3¢ an acre. The next year, Jefferson sent the Lewis and Clark expedition to explore the territory and to find an aqueous trade route to the Pacific Ocean. Lewis and Clark never found a trade route, but they did chart the vast extent of land that lay west of the Mississippi. The **Monroe Doctrine** (1823) struck a blow for American self-sufficiency and freedom from European influence. The philosophy of **Manifest Destiny,** first articulated in 1845, expressed the belief that the United States was destined by God to rule the continent. The acquisition of the Southwest, California, and Oregon territories gave the US access to the West Coast, and droves of people migrated west in covered wagons along the grueling Oregon Trail in search of land, fortune, and a new life.

The **Homestead Act** of 1862, which distributed government land to those who would farm it and live on it, prompted the cultivation of the Great Plains. This large-scale settlement led to bloody battles with the Sioux, Hunkpapas, and Cheyenne tribes who had long inhabited the Plains. From 1866 to 1891, the US fought a continuous war against the remaining 300,000 "Indians." At **Custer's Last Stand** in 1876, a group of Native Americans led by Crazy Horse and Sitting Bull massacred General Custer's army, prompting a furious reaction. The Native Americans were routed out, their land taken away, and their communities relegated to reservations. Much of the legend of the **Wild West** revolves around tall tales of brave white settlers and stoic cowboys rounding up cattle and fending off Indian attacks.

AMERICA'S PECULIAR INSTITUTION

The first **Africans** were brought to America in 1619, prisoners aboard a Dutch slave ship headed for Jamestown, Virginia. The infusion of African slave labor led to the decline of indentured servitude, a system by which poor Europeans would provide seven years of labor in exchange for their Atlantic crossing. From the late 16th century and into the 17th century, as the demand for cheap labor increased, white settlers systematically invaded and terrorized Native American communities in search of slaves. As white indentured servitude tapered off and Native Americans suffered fatally from European diseases, colonial America relied heavily on the African slave trade to fill the gap. Thousands of Africans were taken from their homes and forced across the Atlantic in the dark holds of slave ships, a harrowing journey known as the **Middle Passage.** Once in the US, they were auctioned. This practice would last until 1807, when the slave trade was abolished. Slave ownership, however, would continue until the late 19th century, forming one of the most brutal chapters in the country's short history.

Slavery exacerbated existing ideological differences between the North and the South. Because the federal government was designed to be relatively weak in order to prevent the "tyranny" of pre-Revolution days from reoccurring, each state could decide to allow or prohibit slavery independently. As the Northern states became more insistent that territories and new states should be kept free of slavery, the Southern states counteracted by citing the Revolutionary ideal of states' rights to self-determination. Northern abolitionists also joined with free African Americans to form the elusive **Underground Railroad,** an escape route in which "conductors" secretly transported slaves in covered wagons into the free northern states. Southerners who invaded the North to retrieve their "property" fueled existing tensions between these two separate halves of a nation, split by socioeconomic differences. It would take a fierce and bloody conflict to decide which identity would prevail.

"A HOUSE DIVIDED": THE CIVIL WAR

Tensions between the North and South came to a head when an anti-slavery Senator and future national hero, **Abraham Lincoln,** was elected President in 1860. South Carolina seceded from the Union, but Lincoln refused to officially recognize the secession. Twelve states followed in 1861, and 1862 witnessed the birth of a united **Southern Confederacy** under the lead of Jefferson Davis. Most federal forts in the South were converted to Confederate control, although Fort Sumter in Charleston, South Carolina, remained staffed by Union troops. On April 12, 1861, Southern troops fired at the fort, and the Civil War began. For four years the country endured a savage and bloody war, fought by the North to restore the Union and by the South to break it.

Lincoln led the North to victory, but the price was high. The war claimed more American lives than any other in history, and many families were divided against each other as brothers took up different uniforms and loyalties. Lincoln was assassinated on April 14, 1865, by a Southern sympathizer named John Wilkes Booth, but not before he left his mark on American history. Despite his untimely death, Lincoln would be forever memorialized in the public consciousness as the President who saved the Union and abolished slavery.

RECONSTRUCTION AND INDUSTRY

The period after the war brought Reconstruction to the South and Industrial Revolution to the North. The North's rapid industrialization rendered it a formidable contender in the world economy, while the South's agricultural economy began a slow decline. Injured and embittered by the war and dependent on an outdated agricultural tradition, Southerners struggled to readjust to the new economic and social situations forced upon them. The newly freed blacks faced a difficult transition from plantation to free life. **Jim Crow** laws continued to restrict blacks' freedom, while white politicians espousing the "separate but equal" doctrine prohibited blacks from frequenting the same establishments and schools as whites. Even drinking fountains were classified according to race. Though black colleges were founded and prominent blacks were able to gain some degree of political power, others were relegated to a life of share-cropping for white landowners.

During the North's **"Gilded Age"** of the 1870s, captains of industry such as George Vanderbilt, Andrew Carnegie, and John D. Rockefeller built commercial empires and enormous personal fortunes amid an atmosphere of widespread political and economic corruption. The burden of the concentration of massive wealth in a few hands landed most heavily on the powerless masses—on hapless farmers toiling in a dying agricultural economy and on workers facing low wages, violent strike break-ups, and unsafe working conditions. Yet the fruits of the industrial age, including railroads, telegraphs, and telephones, made transportation and communication across the vast nation easier.

GLOBAL IMPERIALISM AND WWI

The racism expressed in Jim Crow laws and Native American genocide didn't end at domestic borders. The United States' victory in the **Spanish-American War** in 1898 validated America's sense of white superiority, and the belief that its influence could be extended worldwide. The United States caught imperial fever, acquiring colonies in the Philippines, Puerto Rico, and Cuba. Meanwhile, large industrial monopolies came under attack from the Progressive Party. A new breed of journalists, the "muckrakers," began exposing the corruption rampant in big business.

In 1901, at age 42, **Teddy Roosevelt** became the youngest president in history. In response to the corrupt, monopolistic practices of big business, Roosevelt promoted anti-trust reforms to regulate large companies. In foreign affairs Roosevelt established the US as an international police power, recommending that the nation "speak softly and carry a big stick."

After vowing to keep the US out of "Europe's War," President **Woodrow Wilson** reluctantly entered **World War I** in its closing stages. US troops landed in Europe in 1917 and fought until Germany's defeat the next year. Though the metal-consuming war jump-started America's industrial economy and established the United States as a major international power, the frightful toll of the Great War—10 million people dead, including 130,174 Americans—disillusioned and shocked the nation.

ROARING 20S, GREAT DEPRESSION, AND WWII

Americans returned their attentions to their own continent, bursting with money but ruffled by the winds of change. Labor unrest and racial tension were blamed on communist influences, and the US would experience increased paranoia of communism (a **"Red Scare"**) over the course of 1919. The same year, the perceived moral decline of America was addressed with the immensely unpopular **Prohibition,** which outlawed all alcohol. Among the younger generations, however, restrictive conventions were exuberantly tossed aside. In celebration of the free-wheelin', booze-smugglin' **"Jazz Age,"** women shucked their undergarments aside and bared their shoulders to dance the Charleston. Women **suffragists** also mobilized for the right to vote, which the 19th Amendment to the Constitution granted in 1920.

The **"Roaring 20s"** were largely supported by overextended credit. The facade crumbled on "Black Thursday," October 24, 1929, when the New York Stock Exchange crashed, launching the **Great Depression.** In an urbanized, mechanized age, millions of workers (25-50% of the work force) were left unemployed and struggled to provide food and housing for their families. The United States was unable to rebound from the Great Depression as it had from previous depressions. The Depression imprinted a generation of Americans with a compulsion to hoard, an appreciation of money, and a skepticism of the economy. Under the guidance of President **Franklin D. Roosevelt,** the US began a decade-long recovery.

As the German Nazi regime plowed through Europe, anxious Americans largely stood aside and watched, unaware of the Holocaust. The Japanese attack on Pearl Harbor, Hawaii on December 7, 1941, brought America reluctantly into **World War II**. The war existed on two fronts, as the Allied powers fought both the Germans in Europe and the Japanese in the Pacific. The European front was resolved with the German surrender on May 8, 1945. The war in the Pacific continued until August, when the US dropped two newly developed **nuclear bombs** on Japan, at Hiroshima on August 6, 1945, and at Nagasaki three days later, killing 80,000 civilians.

THE COLD WAR: "WE WILL BURY YOU"

Empowered by nationalist pride and spared the wartime devastation of Europe and East Asia, the US economy boomed in the post-war era, securing the nation's status as the world's dominant economic and military power. The saccharine 50s are nostalgically recalled as a time of prosperity and social normalcy; TV sitcoms and suburban houses with glowing green lawns typified the American dream.

But while Elvis Presley shook his hound dog and Americans sported Buddy Holly glasses, the ideological gulf between the two nuclear powers—the democratic, capitalist America and the totalitarian, communist Soviet Union—initiated a half-century of **Cold War** between the two nations. Tension with the Soviet Union heightened as President Harry Truman exaggerated the Soviet threat in order to gain support for his foreign policy of **Communist containment**. Amid the anti-Communist hysteria, **McCarthyism** took root. A powerful congressional committee, labeled the House Un-American Activities Committee and led by Senator Joseph McCarthy, conducted witch-hunts in every facet of American public life. Reaching from politics to the film industry, McCarthyism was a move to expose all closet communists, though most accusations were groundless.

Fear of communism had grown in the US since the Russian Revolution in 1917, but the feverish intensity it gained during the McCarthy era ultimately led to American military involvement in Asia, where communism was beginning to take hold. From 1950 to 1953, the United States fought the **Korean War** on behalf of the South Koreans, who had been attacked by the Communist North Korean government. The precedents set in Korea were carried over to the Vietnam conflict. The Soviet launch of Sputnik, the first artificial satellite, in 1957, renewed fears that communism was getting ahead. The **Cuban Missile Crisis** in 1962, during which President John F. Kennedy narrowly negotiated the removal of Soviet missiles from a Cuban base, reinforced the notion that the United States must protect the world from Soviet invasion and nuclear assault.

In 1963, **President Kennedy** was assassinated during a campaign parade in Dallas, Texas, by Lee Harvey Oswald (see p. 610). The assassination of the young, charismatic President mirrored the loss of innocence that America was confronting. The cultural revolution that followed in the 60s tore the social fabric of the nation, ending in the long-fought civil rights movement and the turmoil of the Vietnam War.

MAKING LOVE AND PROTEST

High on its role as global policemen staying the tide of communism, the United States became embroiled in Vietnamese politics, culminating in a large-scale deployment of combat troops in 1965 to protect the South Vietnamese government from Ho Chi Minh's socialist government to the north. The **Vietnam War** became a symbol for America's credibility as a protector of nations struggling with communism, making retreat difficult even when it became apparent that the situation in Vietnam was not clear-cut and that victory was unlikely. Though many Americans supported the war at first, opposition grew as it dragged on and its moral premises were questioned. The use of TV and photographic media to cover the war contributed to the harsh and hopeless vision of the situation in Vietnam. The mounting human costs of Vietnam—and growing suspicion of America's motives—catalyzed wrenching generational clashes reflected vividly in the stacks of burning draft cards and anti-war demonstrations on college campuses. The mantra "Make Love, Not War," shouted among long-haired, scantily-clad bodies rolling in the mud at the 1969 **Woodstock** music festival, came to symbolize the hippie generation.

The Vietnam War was not the only cause that captured the hearts and lungs of idealistic young Americans. Rosa Parks's refusal to give up a bus seat in Montgomery, Alabama, in 1955 contributed to the **civil rights movement,** a time of intense protests by African Americans and other supporters, who organized countless demonstrations, marches, and sit-ins in the heart of a defiant and often violent South. Activists were drenched with fire hoses, arrested, and even killed by local mobs and policemen. The movement peaked with the March on Washington in 1963, where **Dr. Martin Luther King, Jr.** delivered his famous "I Have A Dream" speech, calling for non-violent racial integration. The tone of the civil rights movement changed as blacks became fed up with peaceful moderation, and turned to the more militant rhetoric of **Malcolm X,** a converted Black Muslim who espoused separatist "Black Power." The gun-toting Black Panthers resorted to terrorist tactics to assert the rights of African-Americans.

The second wave of the **women's movement** accompanied the civil rights movement. Sparked by Betty Friedan's landmark book *The Feminine Mystique*, American women sought to change the delineation between men's and women's roles in society, demanding access to male-dominated professions and equal pay. The sexual revolution, fueled by the introduction of the birth control pill, heightened debate over a woman's right to choose to have an abortion. The 1973 Supreme Court decision *Roe v. Wade* legalized abortion, but the battle between abortion opponents and pro-choice advocates still divides the nation today.

Despite a spate of civil rights legislation and anti-poverty measures passed under President Lyndon B. Johnson's **Great Society** agenda, the specter of the war overshadowed his presidency. By the end of these tumultuous years, the nation had dropped 7 million tons of bombs on Indochina—twice the amount used against America's World War II enemies—and victory was still unattainable. In 1972, as President Richard Nixon was attempting to "honorably" extricate the United States from Vietnam, five burglars were caught breaking into the Democratic National Convention Headquarters in the **Watergate** apartment complex. Their botched attempt to bug the Democratic offices eventually led to a broader scandal involving the President himself. Caught by his own audiotape, Nixon fought Congress but ultimately resigned from the Presidency.

By the mid-70s, America was firmly disillusioned with the idealistic counter-culture of the previous decade. More frivolous forms of fun, such as dancing in platform shoes and powder blue suits under flashing colored lights—a phenomenon known as **"disco"**—became the mark of a generation that just wanted to have fun. Unfortunately, the international situation continued to be tenuous. The oil-rich Arab nations boycotted the US, causing an **energy crisis** that drove up gas prices, frustrated autophile Americans, and precipitated an economic recession. The oil crisis also forced the US to develop more energy-efficient technology, lending economic credibility to the environmentalist movement.

THE BIG 80S

In 1980, **Ronald Reagan,** a politically conservative actor and former California governor, was elected to the White House. Reagan knew how to give the people what they wanted: money. He cut government spending on public programs and lowered taxes. Though the decade's conservatives did embrace certain right-wing social goals like school prayer and the campaign against abortion, the Reagan revolution was essentially economic. **Reaganomics** handed tax breaks to big business, spurred short-term consumption, and deregulated savings and loans. Although these measures were successful in the short-run by suppressing inflation and unemployment, long-term repercussions included a massive increase in the budget deficit. Whereas the US had been a creditor nation in 1980, the end of the decade saw the nation as the world's largest debtor.

On the foreign policy front, Reagan aggressively expanded the military budget and sent weapons and aid to right-wing "freedom fighters" in Guatemala, Nicaragua, and Afghanistan. The Iran-Contra affair at the end of his second term revealed that profit from arms sold to Iran had been used to fund the **Contras** of Nicaragua in their attempt to overthrow the leftist Sandinista regime. But even as the affair was received negatively by the American public, Reagan remained a popular president. For middle America, his administration represented a return to traditional values after the radicalism and revolution of the 60s and 70s, a legacy that helped his vice-president George Bush to victory in the 1988 presidential election.

THE 90S: "SLICK WILLY"

The US remained an active police force in the world through the early 90s, as President Bush instigated **"Operation Desert Storm"** in 1990 as a response to Iraq's invasion of neighboring Kuwait. The war freed Kuwait, but its popularity in the US was compromised by the recession that followed. The large deficit created by Reagan's administration prevented the typical cure of increased government spending, and the public replaced Bush in the 1992 Presidential election with the young, saxophone-tooting Democrat **Bill Clinton,** who promised a new era of government activism after years of laissez-faire rule.

Also in 1992, fire and riots swept Los Angeles in the wake of the **Rodney King** controversy. Although a videotape captured the scene of four white policemen brutally beating King, an African American, during a traffic stop, a jury acquitted the policemen of any wrongdoing. Angry mobs attributed the "not guilty" verdict to the color of King's skin. During the first 24 hours following the verdict, 25 murders took place, 1000 fires swept the city, and 2400 National Guardsmen moved in.

Clinton's young administration soon found itself plagued with its own problems, including a suspicious Arkansas real estate development called **Whitewater,** an alleged extramarital affair with Gennifer Flowers, and accusations of sexual harassment from Paula Jones. Clinton's public approval remained high, however, especially after the nation supported him in a struggle against the Congressional Republicans whose attempts to balance the budget led to two government shutdowns between 1995 and 1996. Clinton was elected to his second term in 1996.

A new scandal erupted in 1998, as reports of an inappropriate relationship between Clinton and 24-year-old White House intern **Monica Lewinsky** were plastered across American newspapers, magazines, and television. At first Clinton denied the allegations, although he would later admit that he lied. He was eventually **impeached** for perjury and obstruction of justice on the recommendation of Independent Counsel Kenneth Starr. The resulting trial in the Senate ended with a vote for informal censure over conviction, and Clinton remained in office.

2001'S NEWS

The beginning of the New Year saw the continued saga of one of the most controversial presidential elections in history. Normally decided in late November, the presidential race between **Al Gore** and **George W. Bush** extended all the way into December of 2000. While Gore won the popular vote by a margin of over 300,000, the fate of the election hinged on the state of **Florida** and its 25 electoral votes. In order to win a US presidential election, a candidate must gain 270 out of a possible 528 electoral votes. At the election's end, Gore was a mere three votes short of 270, though the outcome in Florida remained too close to call. Early tallies indicated that Bush barely won, but Florida state law necessitated an automatic recount. When the results of the automatic recount proved indecisive, a hand recount went into effect at the behest of the Florida Supreme Court. The US Supreme Court, however, struck the final blow to the Gore campaign by demanding a stop to the recount. Gore eventually conceded, and George W. Bush became only the third president in US history to lose the popular election.

The first months of the Bush administration witnessed a sharp decline in the stock market, ending six years of economic prosperity under Bill Clinton. Inflated technology stocks plummeted in value, causing the **NASDAQ** to fall over 60%. By the summer of 2001, markets had rebounded slightly, spurred by several interest rate increases by Alan Greenspan and the Federal Reserve. However, fears of a recession continue to worry investors.

Foreign policy also came under strain during the early Bush administration. An American **spy plane** collided with a Chinese fighter jet over China's Hainan Island. Initially refusing to release the 24-member crew that was aboard the spy plane, Chinese officials also denied UN inspectors access to the plane. Relations between the two countries soured for 11 days, as each nation blamed the incident on the other. The controversy ended on April 12 when a US apology convinced the Chinese to release the crew. Though the immediate conflict was over in a matter of days, policy makers remain apprehensive about the future of US-China relations.

The Republican-Democratic deadlock in the Senate swung to the side of the liberals as Vermont senator **Jim Jeffords** defected from the GOP, declaring himself an independent. Jeffords's switch gave the Democrats a one-seat edge in the Senate, allowing them the ability to block Republican-driven legislation. Tom Daschle, a Democratic senator from South Dakota, became the new Senate Majority Leader.

On June 11, **Timothy McVeigh** was executed by lethal injection for the worst act of domestic terrorism in US history. Over six years earlier, McVeigh's truck bomb annihilated the Alfred P. Murrah Federal building in Oklahoma City, killing 168 people and injuring hundreds more. McVeigh's execution did not go off without a hitch though, as federal investigators failed to disclose thousands of pages of documents to defense attorneys. Though the documents were not critical ones, the mishap embarrassed the FBI and generated some suspicion about the federal legal system.

A tragedy even greater than the Oklahoma City bombing struck the United States the morning of September 11. Four commercial jetliners were hijacked almost simultaneously, two eventually plowing into the Twin Towers of the World Trade Center in New York City, one slamming into the Pentagon in Washington, D.C., and another crash-landing into a field in rural Pennsylvania. Shortly after the attack on the World Trade Center, both towers collapsed, blanketing Lower Manhattan in smoke and debris. Thousands perished as a result of this terrorist attack, the worst ever committed on US soil. In the wake of this tragedy, Americans have been forced to confront their own vulnerability.

A CIVICS PRIMER

The US government functions on two separate levels. Certain laws are established on a national level by the **federal government,** while **states** and **localities** determine their own laws and regulations on matters that fall outside the federal government's scope. The federal government is further divided by focus into a system of three branches—the **executive, legislative,** and **judicial**—each of which can regulate the actions of the others. The **President** and **Vice President** head the executive branch and are elected every four years. Most federal agencies fall under the authority of the executive branch, which consists of thirteen departments. The heads of the departments, known as the Secretaries, comprise the Cabinet, and are used by the president as a source of advice and guidance for policy decisions. The legislative branch contains two representative bodies, the **House of Representatives** and the **Senate,** where laws and budgets are debated and passed before being submitted for presidential approval. The population of each state directly elects the members of these two bodies, jointly referred to as Congress. The **Supreme Court** of the United States, 13 circuit courts of appeal, and 90 district courts comprise the last branch of the federal government, the judicial branch. The Supreme Court's nine justices, appointed for life by the President and approved by the Senate, hold the power to strike down laws that violate constitutional principles.

Politics in the United States functions as a two-party system. Elected representatives in the US are usually members of the Republican or Democratic Parties, which span a narrow (and right-leaning) political spectrum. The Republican Party is more conservative and is divided into two warring camps: social traditionalists grudgingly share a tent with their libertarian, pro-business colleagues. The Democrats are also plagued by internal conflict, as the centrist "New Democrats" lock horns with the party's dwindling liberal contingent

THE ARTS

While the US's early artistic endeavors owed much to age-old European traditions, it did not take long for hearty American individualism to make its mark on the global canon. From the 19th century Transcendentalist literature of New England to the unique musical stylings of bluegrass and jazz, America has established itself time and again as an innovator in the theater of world arts.

LITERATURE

THE FIRST FEW PAGES

The first best-seller printed in America, the *Bay Psalm Book*, was published in Cambridge, MA, in 1640. Like much of the literature read and published in 17th- and 18th-century America, this chart-buster was religious in nature. Most of these early works gather dust on academic bookshelves; America did not create any enduring classics until the early 1800s, when her artists began to cultivate a substantial literary tradition expressing the unique American experience. James Fenimore Cooper's *Last of the Mohicans* (1826), Nathaniel Hawthorne's *Scarlet Letter* (1850), and Herman Melville's *Moby Dick* (1851)—among the first great American novels—all feature strong yet innocent individualists negotiating the raw American landscape. By the mid-nineteenth century, the **New England Transcendentalists** began writing sparse, less romantic works in a firm attempt to portray a down-to-earth culture distinct from that of their European forebears. The work of Henry David Thoreau (*Walden Pond*), Ralph Waldo Emerson, and Walt Whitman (*Leaves of Grass*) embodied a spirit of anti-materialism by focusing on self-reflection and a retreat into nature. Meanwhile, Mark Twain synthesized the intellectual refinement of a world traveler with the homespun tales of a Southern storyteller. His *Adventures of Huckleberry Finn* (1885) uses the motif of a young boy's journey to express social criticism and a unique treatment of the human spirit.

Literature provided 19th-century American women the opportunity both to express themselves and to comment critically on their society. In 1852, Harriet Beecher Stowe (see p. 152) published *Uncle Tom's Cabin*, an exposé of slavery that became internationally popular and is considered by some scholars to have contributed to the outbreak of the Civil War. Poet Emily Dickinson secretly scribbled away in her native Amherst, Massachusetts, home; her untitled, unpunctuated, and uncapitalized verses weren't discovered until after her death in 1886.

EARLY TWENTIETH CENTURY EXPLORATIONS

The 20s marked a time of increasing angst, and a reflective, self-centered movement fermented in American literature. F. Scott Fitzgerald's works (*The Great Gatsby*) portray restless individuals, financially secure but unfulfilled by their conspicuous consumption. Many writers moved abroad in search of refuge during this tumultuous time. This **Lost Generation** included Fitzgerald, Ernest Hemingway (*The Sun Also Rises*), T.S. Eliot (*The Waste Land*), Ezra Pound, and e.e. cummings, poets and writers whose sophisticated works conveyed the contemporary American experience. On the home front, poet and author Vladimir Nabokov (*Lolita*), a Russian émigré, redefined English prose style for a whole generation of writers. The Harlem Renaissance, a timely gathering of African-American artistic energy in New York City, fed off the excitement of the Jazz Age. Langston Hughes, Nella Larsen, and Zora Neale Hurston (*Their Eyes Were Watching God*) exposed the black American experience to a broad scope of readers.

As America struggled to recover from the Great Depression, the plight of decaying agricultural life and faltering industry of the **Deep South** and **West** began to infiltrate literature. William Faulkner (*The Sound and the Fury*) juxtaposed avant-garde stream-of-consciousness techniques with subjects rooted in the rural South. The plays of Tennessee Williams (*A Streetcar Named Desire*) portray the family dynamics within lower-class, uprooted Southern families. In his remarkable autobiography, *Black Boy* (1945), Richard Wright recounts the harsher side of the African-American experience in the South.

MODERN DESPAIR

In the conformist 50s, literature provided alternative commentary on America's underlying social problems. Ralph Ellison's *Invisible Man*, published in 1952, confronted a broad audience with the division between white and black identities in America. Gwendolyn Brooks, the first black writer to win a Pulitzer Prize, published intense poetry that highlighted social problems such as abortion, gangs, and drop-outs. The **Beats,** spearheaded by cult heroes Jack Kerouac (*On the Road*) and Allen Ginsberg ("Howl"), lived wildly and proposed a more free-wheeling attitude. Playwright, Arthur Miller, delved into the American psyche with *The Crucible* (1953), an allegory of McCarthyism (see p. 13).

As the rules of established society began to crumble in the **60s,** writers began to explore more outrageous material. Anne Sexton and Sylvia Plath led the movement toward "confessional poetry"; Sexton delves into the depths of her own mental breakdown, while Plath exposes her psychological deterioration and hints at her eventual suicide in *The Bell Jar* (1963). James Baldwin's essays and stories warn white America of the explosions to come and caution black America against the self-destructive excesses of racial hatred. John Cheever (*Bullet Park*) and John Updike (*Rabbit, Run*) explore the terrifying ennui of suburban America. The short stories of Flannery O'Connor ("Everything that Rises Must Converge") expose the eerie underbelly of the contemporary South.

Some 20th century authors reacted to the crisis of modernity by presenting contemporary problems in an absurdist light. The fiercely comic novels of Thomas Pynchon (*Gravity's Rainbow*) depict hapless heroes searching for answers in an ever-shifting universe. The farcical work of John Kennedy Toole (*A Confederacy of Dunces*) brims with endearingly disturbed characters. Carrying on the American absurdist tradition, Don DeLillo's *White Noise* (1985) heats up to the tune of a chemical holocaust.

In more recent fiction, the search for identity and the attempt to reconcile **artistic and social agendas** has continued. Toni Morrison (*Beloved*) won the Nobel Prize for her visceral interpretations of the tension between gender, ethnic, and cultural identities. Raymond Carver, in his numerous short stories, charts the hopelessly misdirected (yet strangely hopeful) lives of people stuck in the fog of modern society. The fast pace and commercialism of modern society has been the subject of many a novel. In *Bright Lights Big City* (1987), Jay McInerney exposes the fast-living Wall Street of the 80s. Most of Richard Ford's books, such as the best-selling *Independence Day* (not to be confused with the movie of the same title) are about guys in mid-life crises, a topic that reverberates strongly among Americans.

MUSIC

Weaned on the fertile—if not easy—intermingling of cultures, America has plenty of homegrown music. While American-born jazz, rock, and rap styles have imitators and innovators outside the States, American artists continue to dominate and define the musical genres that are rightfully their own.

ROOTS IN THE BLACK SOUTH

The unnerved climate of the South during and after slavery flooded the New World with renegade artists and musical styles. In the days of slave driving and

REGIONAL READS Many American writers have gained notoriety through their association with a particular region of the country. For those travelers seeking to add a literary component to their cross-country journey, *Let's Go* recommends the following regional picks:

New England: *The Scarlet Letter* (1850), by Nathaniel Hawthorne. The classic tale of sin and repression, set in colonial Massachusetts.

New York: *The Age of Innocence* (1920), by Edith Wharton. Set in the Golden Age of New York City, this novel explores the power of desire within the rigorously structured world of high society.

The South: *As I Lay Dying* (1930), by William Faulkner. Describes the odyssey of a Southern family across the landscape of rural Mississippi.

Texas: *Lonesome Dove* (1985), by Larry McMurtry. This epic novel present a fresh and innovative take on the mythical Texas.

The Plains: *O Pioneers!* (1913), by Willa Cather. The story of one woman's grit and determination, set against the backdrop of the Nebraska farmlands.

The Rockies: *The Virginian* (1925), by Owen Wister. The Western novel *par excellence*, this cowboy classic set the stage for an entire genre of writing.

The Southwest: *All the Pretty Horses* (1992), by Cormac McCarthy. This rich, elegantly written novel spins a tale of adventure and romance on both sides of the Mexican border.

California: *East of Eden* (1952), by John Steinbeck. A modern interpretation of the classic struggle between good and evil, this novel—set mainly in rural California—follows the story of two sets of brothers.

The Pacific Northwest: *Snow Falling on Cedars* (1994), by David Guterson. Set on an isolated island in Washington state, this novel explores the tragic legacy of the WWII Asian-American internment camps.

plantation farming, slaves sang work songs that fused African rhythm and call-and-response form with Christian hymns and a consciousness shaped by hardship and hope. After emancipation, music for still-oppressed blacks became a primary vehicle of African American religiosity, solidarity, and grievance. From ragtime, the upbeat, piano-banging dance music of the 19th century, to the Deep South's tradition of low-down, moanful blues, early African-American musics defined what would come to be called **soul**. Still a vital category of African-American music, soul encompasses a range of musical styles and expressions. The ecstatic joy of a rousing gospel chorus, the deep melancholy of timeless spirituals like "Swing Low, Sweet Chariot" and "Nobody Knows the Trouble I've Seen," and the reflective lyricism of current hip-hop all evince soul. Recent artists in rhythm and blues (R&B), jazz, pop, funk, and rap genres continue to be described as "soulful" in that they embody the legacy of a resilient and expressive African-American voice. In some ways, some say, even Michael Jackson is a soul artist.

BLUES

The blues epitomizes soul music. Thought to have originated from a blend of Northwest African calls and Native American song and verse forms, the blues allowed Southern black singers to vent the woes of hard love and a harder life. In the early 1900s, **W.C. Handy,** a diligent student of Southern music, introduced "blue" (flattened) notes into popular songs, giving birth to a distinctive, sorrowful sound. His most popular composition, "St. Louis Blues," remains one of the most recorded songs ever. Today, the blues attracts the "down and out" listener and artist, and has heavily influenced the development of other popular music styles, notably jazz and rock 'n' roll. To most Americans, nothing seems as appropriate as singin' the blues when your baby done left you or you're down in the dumps.

JAZZ

In the early 20th century, black musicians in New Orleans took Southern blues and ragtime, and the instruments of the brass band, into new territory with an intellectual music called jazz. Jazz's emphasis on **improvisation** and unique tonal and harmonic rules distinguished it from all other genres that feared performance spontaneity and occasional dissonance. Despite its roots in popular music, jazz certainly befits its label as "art music." It has long thrived on the tension between the popular and the elitist; it embraces both the catchy and the esoteric. As a medium of African-American artistic expression, jazz artists have used their music to convey social and political attitudes. The scintillating rhythms of jazz pioneer **Duke Ellington** and the deep, raspy voice of renowned horn-blower **Louis Armstrong** remain treasured remnants of the one true American art form.

Out of the black South still other musical styles were born: a bluesy, accordion-based music of the Creole-speaking population called **zydeco**, the uplifting **gospel** music of the church choir, and the foot-stomping, banjo-twanging Southern mainstay, **bluegrass.** But distinctively American musics also developed elsewhere.

COUNTRY

Country music began in the Appalachian Mountains among poor, rural whites putting a new spin on their ancestral European folk traditions. Simple melodies and sentimental lyrics served numerous ends: as work songs, as love songs and "cowboy ballads," and, when occasion called, as the rallying cry of an old-fashioned hoedown. The honky-tonk sounds of **Hank Williams** and **Ernest Tubb** dominated early country music. Commercially, country music didn't become popular until it was given a boost by radio, and Nashville's famous 30s program the *Grand Ole Opry* (see p. 345). Nowadays, the twangs of old-home superstars such as **Garth Brooks** and **Reba McIntyre** keep country in the limelight. Roadtrippers be warned: country music today monopolizes the radio waves over much of the continent.

FOLK

So-called American folk music is not a collective repository of ageless songs from nameless authors, but rather popular music by artists who maintain the spirit of such songs. From **Woody Guthrie**'s celebratory "This Land is Your Land," sung in the midst of the Great Depression, to the political and personal musical monologues of **Bob Dylan** or today's **Tracy Chapman,** American folk music keeps the tradition of simple melodies and direct lyrics alive. Folksters are still some of the most lucid social commentators, whether preaching love of country or satirizing American life.

ROCK 'N' ROLL

No one can say just who started rock 'n' roll, though **Elvis Presley** was the first to be crowned "King." His rock kingdom of **Graceland** is a popular attraction for Memphis tourists (see p. 356). What followed Elvis's success in the 50s and 60s was a contest of one-upmanship among rock 'n' roll musicians: when one band cranked up their amps, the next band cranked 'em up higher, and the next cranked 'em up with strategically-torn speakers, generating a wonderfully grating sound. **Chuck Berry**'s "Rock and Roll Music" (1957) inaugurated a new musical era not only in America, but in Europe (especially Britain) as well. In the decades after, rock 'n' roll's driving, danceable rhythms, rebellious attitude, and fascination with electric instruments would dominate the popular music charts. Today, rock music is familiar to all but the oldest generation of Americans. The general category of "rock" is divided chronologically into **oldies** (the Beach Boys, Jerry Lee Lewis), **classic rock** (Led Zeppelin, Bruce Springsteen), and **modern rock** (Pearl Jam, Dave Matthews); **pop, heavy metal,** and **alternative** also fall under the heading of "rock."

EAST COAST V. WEST COAST To be truly down with thug poetry, you must understand the conflict of the coasts. The grinding, bass-heavy west coast rap burst onto the musical forefront with the gangsta beats of **NWA** in the late 80s. The music of later west coast notables such as lyrically brilliant **Tupac Shakur** and ganja-loving **Snoop Dogg** brims with California love. Not to be outdone, east coast rappers tout the superiority of their Harlem 'hoods. The **Wu Tang Clan** and the late **Notorious B.I.G.** combine complex beats with abrasive lyrics to give New York "mad props" for being the home of the "real Gs." Though this lyrical battle raged mostly in the mid-90s, regional pride still infuses rap music.

RAP

Largely an urban phenomenon, rap music owes its beginnings to **reggae** DJs who improvised rhymes over pre-recorded music in a style called **dub.** The practice took off in New York City among dance DJs of all kinds in the late 70s. Soon, rap artists were keeping it real with syncopated rhymes over drum-heavy tape loops, record scratching, and digital samples. Lyrically, the subject-matter of rap music runs the gamut from hard-core sex and violence to class and race consciousness, from egoistic self-aggrandizement to lofty spiritual concerns.

FILM

Of all artistic media, American film has had, for better or worse, the greatest cultural impact, domestically and abroad in the 20th century. Popularly celebrated movie stars began setting fashions and influencing common perceptions of beauty and glamour well before World War II. Throughout the United States, movie catchphrases are part of the vernacular, movie stars are more recognizable (and occasionally have more political power) than politicians, and the archetypal Hollywood movie studio plot line is the foundation of the average American's grandest aspirations, or the American Dream.

SCENE ONE, TAKE ONE!

The most common aspects of American cinema can be traced back to their roots in the 1910s. Pioneering director D.W. Griffith (*The Birth of a Nation, Intolerance*) defined the medium, introducing both the stylistic plot conventions and the techniques like cuts, pans, and tracking that became the bread and butter of the Hollywood film studios.

Hollywood, California, owing to its sunny, film-friendly climate, proximity to a variety of photogenic terrain, and previous prominence as a theater center, quickly became the center of the movie business. As industry churned and began to give rise to a consumer market, America's thirst for quick, wrapped-and-packaged entertainment ballooned. By the period just after World War I, actors like Charlie Chaplin, Buster Keaton, and Mary Pickford were household names. Free from the control of domineering studios, these film artists brought a playful, exuberant, and innovative attitude to their work.

It was not long, however, before the wild success of the movies gave rise to expansion of the **studio system.** Giant production houses like Paramount, MGM, and Warner took up residence on the West Coast, and turned movies into big business. Despite their emphasis on the bottom line and their legacy of formulaic, happy-go-lucky, rather superficial films, American film's **golden age** nevertheless took place during the height of the studio era, fueled by those who transcended the studio system's confines. Victor Fleming's *Gone with the Wind* (1939), a Civil War epic, was the first large-scale movie extravaganza, redefining the bounds of cinematic scope. Frank Capra, in his surprisingly probing morality plays like *It's a Wonderful Life* (1946) and *Mr. Smith Goes to Washington* (1939), brought a conscience to entertainment. Michael Curtiz's *Casablanca* (1942), starring the moody Humphrey Bogart, fine-tuned the art of creating cinematic romance. In 1941, Orson Welles unveiled his intricate masterpiece, *Citizen Kane*, a landmark work whose innovations expanded contemporary ideas about the potential of film. Fantasy and mindless fun, however, still sold tickets: Walt Disney's animated *Snow White* (1937) and Fleming's *The Wizard of Oz* (1939) kept producers well-fed.

ALL GLITTER, SOME GOLD

The film industry met lean times following WWII. Heightened tensions with the Soviet Union and conflicts against communism abroad led to widespread communist witch-hunts at home. The film industry, under government pressure, took up the policy of **blacklisting** any artists with suspected ties to communism (or even leftism). The result of constant paranoia and dwindling box office returns—due to competition with television—resulted in a slew of films that were sensational enough to draw crowds away from their television sets and yet highly conservative and creatively stagnant. There were, of course, those who broke the mold, like master of suspense Alfred Hitchcock (*Strangers on a Train*) and the ever-free-thinking Orson Welles (*The Lady from Shanghai*).

The 50s also saw the emergence of a cult of **glamor** surrounding the most luminous stars. Cloaked in glitz and scandal, sex symbols Marilyn Monroe, James Dean, and Elizabeth Taylor drew audiences to movies by name recognition alone. Along with actors Marlon Brandon (*A Streetcar Named Desire*) and Audrey Hepburn (*Breakfast at Tiffany's*), these stars brought their own personal mystique to the screen, while adding much to the art of cinematic performance.

REBELS WITH A CAUSE

The 60s and early 70s saw widespread **social upheaval** and tension between generations. The studio system proved entirely incapable of responding to the demands of the young, more liberal-thinking audiences. *Cleopatra* (1963), starring Elizabeth Taylor, a last-ditch effort to attract crowds in the style of the 50s, proved to be a financial disaster. Rethinking their battle plans, many studios enlisted directors influenced by the French New Wave, and artists from other media to direct features, including Sidney Lumet, John Frankenheimer, and Robert Altman.

With the studios more willing to take a gamble, and the introduction of a movie ratings board (MPAA) to replace censorship, the work of a number of **innovative filmmakers** began to enter the mainstream. Stanley Kubrick, in *Dr. Strangelove* (1964), *2001: A Space Odyssey* (1968), and *A Clockwork Orange* (1971), brought a literary importance to filmmaking. Dennis Hopper's *Easy Rider* (1969), a film about countercultural youth rebellion, and the acclaimed documentary *Woodstock* (1970) opened the door to social critique. John Schlesinger's *Midnight Cowboy* (1969) demonstrated mature treatment of adult subjects.

By the 70s, experimentalism largely gave way to more polished treatment of equally serious issues. Film-schooled directors like Martin Scorsese (*Taxi Driver*), Francis Ford Coppola (*The Godfather*), and Michael Cimino (*The Deer Hunter*) brought technical skill to their exploration of the darker side of humanity. An influx of foreign filmmakers, like Milos Forman (*One Flew Over the Cuckoo's Nest*) and Roman Polanski (*Chinatown*), introduced a new perspective to American film.

BACK TO BUSINESS

Driven by the global mass distribution of American cinema and the development of high-tech special effects, the late 70s and 80s witnessed the revitalization of the **blockbuster**. Directors like George Lucas with his *Star Wars* trilogy, and Steven Spielberg with *E.T.* (1982) and *Raiders of the Lost Ark* (1981), created enormously successful movies whose success spanned the globe. Though such films were often criticized for their over-reliance on special effects and lack of story line, they almost single-handedly returned Hollywood to its former status as king.

Despite the profit-orientation of Hollywood, quite a bit of highly imaginative work came out of the period, including thoughtful critique of 80s materialism and self-absorption, *Rain Man* (1988), and disturbing exploration of the primal terror beneath the tranquil surface of suburbia, David Lynch's *Blue Velvet* (1986).

INDEPENDENTS, INDEPENDENCE DAY

The revival of the blockbuster continued strong into the 90s, with such high-budget money makers as the alien invasion flick *Independence Day* (1996) to the extravagant marine love-story *Titanic* (1997) still drawing the largest crowds. The recognition of independent, or **indie**, films—films that are either produced independently of any major studio or at least do not follow standard studio conventions—marks the most interesting turn for cinema in the last several years. Brothers Joel and Ethan Coen have created some of the most creative and original work of late, including the gruesome comedy *Fargo* (1996) and the hilarious, off-beat *The Big Lebowski* (1998). Quentin Tarantino's (*Reservoir Dogs*, *Pulp Fiction*) cool yet hyper-charged action, Mike Figgis's (*Leaving Las Vegas*) unpretentious drama, Steven Soderbergh's (*Traffic*) vibrant visual style, and Spike Lee's (*Malcolm X*) tackling of racial themes have all injected new life into American cinema. Hollywood has picked up on the indie trend and recently released a number of films with a distinctly un-Hollywood slant, like newcomer Sam Mendes's acclaimed exploration of suburban angst, *American Beauty* (1999).

VISUAL ART

Snobbish and Eurocentric art historians have often glossed over American art as a pale reflection of European trends. Notable modern art historians like Robert Rosenblum, however, reject that view, finding uniquely American themes in American art. Raw and uncontrolled nature, for one, is reflected not only in the grandiose 19th-century landscape paintings that sought to capture the beauty of the untamed West, but also in the unwieldy lines and shapes of a 20th-century American brand of abstract expressionism.

ART IN THE NEW WORLD

Colonial America produced art of a limited scope. Subject matter for New World artists was not an issue of prerogative: the only livelihood in art was in painting portraits for wealthy patrons. Some gifted (and willing) painters accompanied expeditions into unexplored territory in order to record the places and people they found. These two genres—portraiture and landscape painting—grew increasingly stylized into the mid-19th century. George Fuller made intimate portraits contrasting murky background with a glowing illumination of his subjects. Winslow Homer created memorable seaside scenes and sweeping Civil War era farmscapes. Combining loose watercolor technique and a shrewd observer's eye, Homer reproduced the many moods of nature on canvas. His style marked the growing creative freedom of American painters.

CHANGING ATTITUDES FOR THE NEW CENTURY

In the early 20th century, Alfred Stieglitz championed photography as a legitimate art form with meticulously composed stills. A zealous and influential advocate of art photography in the face of elitist skepticism, Stieglitz exhibited his work alongside that of a new crop of art photographers in his publications and venues. His wife Georgia O'Keefe preferred to paint surreal, pastel visions of desert bones and suggestive flowers. But other artists took a more socially engaged stance toward their vocation. In colorful, narrative paintings of distinctly American scenes, Edward Hopper and Thomas Hart Benton explored the innocence and mythic values of the country during its emergence as a superpower. While American painting captured the landscape aesthetic, **photography** became the medium of choice for artists with a social conscience. Lewis Hine photographed the urban poor, while Dorothea Lange and Walker Evans captured the plight of destitute farmers during the Great Depression. Ansel Adams's crisp landscapes, while not politically motivated *per se*, helped to establish the National Park system.

DRIVEN TO ABSTRACTION

By the 40s, the **abstract expressionist** movement in Europe had been reborn in the States, where country-wide anxiety over international unrest and the threat of war bore heavily on the American psyche. In this climate, many artists thought that realism's tight control over images was insincere. Willem de Kooning's masterful work documents the movement from realistic to abstracted images. Blending figurative images with vigorous strokes and splatters on a single canvas, de Kooning both juxtaposed old and new styles, and allowed them to comment on each other. The found-object compositions of Robert Rauchenburg, along with Jackson Pollock's energetic drip paintings, reflect the ironic mix of swaggering confidence and frenetic insecurity that characterized Cold War America.

The new art earned the appreciation of art purists through figures like Mark Rothko, who perfected the subtle aesthetics and emotional impact of abstract art in his color field paintings. Other artists strove for a more global impact. Jasper Johns incorporated iconic images like the American flag into his folksy paintings, ushering in the age of **pop** art. Practiced most memorably by Roy Lichtenstein and Andy Warhol, pop art used graphic, cartoonish images to satirize the icons of American life and popular culture, blurring the line between art and everything else. Warhol mass-produced loud, colorful images of American cultural icons like Marilyn Monroe and Elvis. Lichtenstein was the first to attempt to combine the "highbrow" art and "lowbrow" art of the mundane and popular.

NEW IN THE ART WORLD

In the 70s, photography finally came into its own as the back-to-basics 35mm photographs of Gary Winnogrand and Lee Friedlander, as well as the freakish work of Diane Arbus, stretched the bounds of art photography. The 80s art boom, stationed around private galleries in New York City and Los Angeles, began a retreat from the realism of photography, and ushered in a decade of slick, idyllic paintings. Julian Schnabel and David Hockney, in particular, garnered the accolades of art critics and investors with a taste for pretty things. But as part of an eventual backlash to 80s materialism, artists began to produce **ultra-realistic** depictions of the harshness in human life. The bare-all photographs of Nan Goldin opened up the seedy underbelly of urban life to photographic exploration. A master at exposing moments of pure, emotive expression, Goldin frames all her subjects—from prostitutes to couples smoking in bed—with thought and poignancy. The manipulated images of Cindy Sherman (a photographer who places herself in scenes taken out of anything from popular movie stills to gruesome pornography) and the odd body-part sculptures of Kiki Smith are typical of recent art that looks to deconstruct the meaning of identity and the human body. Abstract art, though, hasn't died on the gallery floor; Brice Marden's squiggly lines still sell big.

ARCHITECTURE AND PUBLIC ART

American architecture of earlier days may have scraped together the leftovers of passé European styles, but the 20th-century architect **Frank Lloyd Wright** gave America its own architectural mode. As a budding architectural genius, Wright left school at 18 for Chicago, where a boom in innovative construction was taking place. Wright signed on, embarking on a long and prolific career designing unique dwellings. His works, including the Fallingwater house in Pennsylvania (see p. 277) and the Robie House in Chicago (see p. 514), demonstrate an angular aesthetic and attention to environmental cohesiveness. More recently, Frank Gehry has moved the craft of architecture into the 21st century with his feats of impossible engineering and optical effects.

Public art has had an established role in most American cities; some devote a full 1% of their funds to it. Not only do sculptures and installations adorn city parks and the lobbies of public buildings, but experiential walk-through environments like Maya Ying Lin's Vietnam Veterans Memorial in Washington, D.C. (see p. 298) are often commissioned in larger cities.

THE MEDIA

America is wired. Images, sounds, and stories from the boob tube, radio, Internet, and advertisements infiltrate every aspect of the American lifestyle. Because of the media's power, constant debate centers on censorship and freedom. Censored or not, new media spread like (poison) ivy every second.

TELEVISION

Television sets are found in 98% of US homes. Competition between the six national **networks** (ABC, CBS, NBC, Fox, and two newcomers, UPN and WB), cable television, and satellite TV has triggered exponential growth in TV culture over the past few years. Some of the most popular shows airing during the pre-mium hours of prime time (8-11pm EST) include the trendy sitcoms *Friends* (NBC) and *Will and Grace* (NBC), the New York-set police drama *Law and Order* (NBC), and the irreverent cartoon *The Simpsons* (Fox). The newest fad of **reality television** is quickly occupying the most coveted time slots. Shows like *Survivor* (CBS) give countless coach potatoes hopes of winning huge cash prizes and gaining national fame (or ridicule). Wanna-be brainiacs hone their trivia skills in preparation for becoming contestants on the stress-filled game shows, *Who Wants to be a Millionaire* (ABC) and *The Weakest Link* (NBC). Late-night television is dominated by the comic stylings of talk-show hosts such as Conan O'Brien on *Late Night* (NBC) and David Letterman on *The Late Show* (CBS). **Teen shows** like *Dawson's Creek* (WB) overflow with high school stereo-types, from gushing girls to sensitive studs. Daytime programming concerns itself with similar lowbrow melodrama, offering a pastiche of trashy soap operas and trashier talk shows. Made-for-TV movies, national sporting events, and other special programming fill out the lineup on network television.

One need not be bound to the networks, however, as **cable** provides special-inter-est channels that cover every subject from cooking to sports to science fiction. Some hotel rooms come equipped with basic cable, while others will even offer pre-mium stations like HBO that air recently released movies along with stand-by favor-ites. Pay-per-view channels are also available in some hotel rooms, although (as the name suggests) the privilege comes at a cost.

Television is the point of entry to **world wide news** for most Americans. Twenty-four hour news coverage is available on CNN, a cable station. Each network pre-sents local and national nightly news, usually at 5 and/or 11pm EST, while prime-time "newsmagazines" like *60 Minutes* (CBS), *Dateline* (NBC), and *20/20* (ABC) specialize in investigative reports and exposés.

The **Public Broadcasting Station (PBS)** is commercial-free, funded by viewer contri-butions, the federal government, and corporate grants. Its repertoire includes edu-cational children's shows like *Sesame Street* and *Mister Roger's Neighborhood*, nature programs, mystery shows, and British comedy shows.

PRINT

Despite the onset of more sophisticated technologies like TV and the Internet, Americans still cherish the feel of glossy pages and the smell of newsprint. At first, strict censorship rules kept print confined to government-supported articles, ser-mons, and almanacs. By the 18th century, however, immigrant European printers with their brash, new ideas helped make "Hot off the presses!" part of the national idiom. Today, newsstands crowd city corners and transportation terminals throughout the country. Publications cover all areas of society, culture, and politics: whether it's for lounging away a Sunday afternoon at home or passing time in a doctor's waiting room, print media dominate the market.

Major daily newspapers include *The New York Times* and the *Washington Post*. Perfect for early-morning breakfast reading, they provide the local and international goings-on. Fashion magazines, *Cosmopolitan* and *Vogue*, dazzle readers with pictures of sculpted supermodels, while *The New Yorker* educates their subsrcibers with short stories and essays on current events. Entertainment magazines such as *People* chronicle American gossip, while *Rolling Stone* focuses on the music industry. Those interested in the ups and downs of the stock market swear by the *Wall Street Journal* and *Forbes;* those who prefer statistics about their favorite sports franchise flip through the pages of *Sports Illustrated*. Despite the range of publications, from glitzy **tabloids** like the *National Enquirer* to the most influential and respected news organs, almost all American media are criticized for being sensational and exploitative. But isn't that why we like it so much?

RADIO

Video might have killed the radio star, but before television transformed American culture, the radio was the country's primary source of entertainment and news. Classic comedy programs like *The Jack Benny Show* and the crackly sounding news coverage of Edward R. Murrow amused and informed Americans for decades. Even though the moving images and crisper sounds of television have reduced radio's earlier, widespread popularity, it remains a treasured medium. Radio is generally divided into AM and FM; talk radio comprises most of the low-frequency AM slots, and the high-powered FM stations feature most of the music. Each broadcaster owns a four-letter call-name, with "W" as the first letter for those east of the Mississippi River (as in WJMN), and "K" to the west (as in KPFA).

Radio is on everyone's wavelength. The more intellectually minded listen to **National Public Radio (NPR).** Full of classical music and social pundits debating important issues, the station gives even *Car Talk*, a show about car repair, an academic flair. For a less edifying but more outrageous time, many Americans obsess over the nationally broadcast talk shows of "shock jock" Howard Stern and politically contentious Rush Limbaugh. Supplying the country's regional needs, local area channels give up-to-the-minute news reports and air a wide range of music, from country western to the latest pop. College radio stations often play more alternative styles of music to appeal to younger listeners. While many people might surf the dial only to keep from dozing at the wheel, radio buzzes on as an integral part of the national media.

(NOT SO) CLOSE ENCOUNTERS Even more socially harmful than television violence and Internet pornography are space invaders on radio. On Halloween night, 1938, **Orson Welles** delivered over the airwaves the classic science-fiction novel *War of the Worlds*, a tale about ruthless aliens taking over Earth, as a news broadcast. Many listeners eager for some intergalactic warfare assumed the reports of invading aliens were real and prepared for the outer-space meanies. Some hid in cellars, others loaded their shotguns, and a few even covered their heads with wet towels to protect against poison gas. Once everyone dried the water from their ears, they realized that Welles's "invasion" was just a hoax. Duped citizens demanded that radio be more carefully regulated, but no steps were taken. The country must have learned its lesson, for no Americans similarly overreacted when *Independence Day* and *Mars Attacks!*, both featuring alien aggressors, invaded the theaters in 1996.

SPORTS

Nowhere do Americans express their team spirit so much as in and around the sports arena. For most die-hard fans, their favorite team or player serves as a modern-day tribe. Dressed in colorful uniforms and covered with face-paint, they fill stadiums or lounge at home, watching games on TV. In recent years, the all-around growing commercialism of sports and bloated player contracts have discouraged some fans, but the crack of a baseball bat and the swish of a basketball still resonate welcomingly throughout America.

AUTO RACING

Although baseball is officially America's favorite pastime, it is **NASCAR auto racing** that draws droves of fans to Daytona Beach, Florida in February with the Daytona 500 (see **Start Your Engines,** p. 437). Here, average family vehicles are transformed into over-185 mph powerhouses through the sponsorship of automobile manufacturers and brand-name companies like Spam, Cheerios, and Tide. The cars tear around a banked track hundreds of times, while wide-eyed and open-mouthed fans throw down countless beers and hot dogs. Now that's a sport!

THE NATIONAL PASTIME

For those who don't like fast-paced sports, pollution, or noisy fans, most large cities host **Major League Baseball (MLB)** teams. The slow, tension-building game of baseball—stopping play and changing sides so often that both the fans and the players need to partake of a seventh-inning stretch—captures the hearts of dreaming children and world-weary adults alike. Major-league games are often cheap and easy to get tickets to, and they are worth the price. Minor-league games are even cheaper, and are slowly gaining popularity among fans fed up with the multimillion-dollar contracts of the discontent big shots.

(AMERICAN) FOOTBALL

Like autoracing and beer-swilling, football and basketball rival baseball for the title of the country's favorite pastime. The **National Football League (NFL)** is full of beefy men made beefier by shoulder pads; this ain't no European "football." The American-rules game is especially dear to middle America, where the padded warriors of the gridiron are applauded for their heroic athleticism. Luckily, just as the grunts of the maniacal football season begin to fade, the squeaky sneakers of the equally maniacal basketball season take their place.

HOOP IT UP

Professional basketball teams hail from almost every major city, making up the **National Basketball Association (NBA).** NBA players have come a long way since the first teams were playing with peach baskets and Converse All-Star sneakers. Today, professional basketball players can jump so high and pass so fast that the Association had to move the three-point shooting line back in order to compensate. But football and basketball are not only for professionals: enthusiasm for college teams often surpasses that for the pros. Sticking with their school allegiances, many Americans are known to live and die by—and bet large amounts of money on—their college's football team in the bowl games or its basketball team in the NCAA tournament, fondly called March Madness.

OTHER SPORTS

Other sports claim smaller niches of the American spectatorship. The internationally publicized **US Open** (tennis) and **US Open** (golf) tend to appeal to those country club fans who prefer sipping lemonade over gulping beer. The **Kentucky Derby** (horse racing), a peculiarly American sporting event, hones the betting strategies of seasoned gamblers and tries the tolerance of seasoned boozers. Ice hockey is most

X-TREME FAILURE What happens when you relax the rules of football, pay players more for winning, and give teams names like the Orlando Rage? Naturally, you get a game full of so much bone-crunching action that it deserves the title of Extreme. Vince McMahon, the president of the **World Wrestling Federation (WWF)**, thinking that good old American football lacked the ferocious showiness of wrestling, created the **XFL (Xtreme Football League)** in 2001. To X-emplify the game's no-holds-barred nature, McMahon not only defied conventional spelling but eliminated such gentlemanly rules as the "fair catch." As the voice of the XFL, Jesse Ventura, the former-wrestler-turned-Governor of Minnesota, brought his trademark booming voice to the broadcast booth. Despite the hype, the league's shortage of skilled players and abundance of dumb team names fell a few yards short of a contract renewal. After only one season of abysmal ratings, the league was canceled, proving that regular football is already rough enough.

popular in the Northeast and the Great Lakes; the **National Hockey League (NHL),** comprised of both American and Canadian teams, endures the competition with its indoor cousin, basketball. **Major League Soccer (MLS)** and **women's basketball (WNBA)** are both up-and-coming, but not yet out-of-control sports.

PHYSICAL ALTERNATIVES

In the past decade, physical fitness has caught on among Americans. Workout enthusiasts have gone from Jane Fonda-type classic **aerobic workouts** to Billy Blanks's hard-core martial arts-inspired Tae Bo, from Cindy Crawford-style light exercise (helped along by a personal trainer) to "spinning" (group bike workouts set to pumping music) and kick-boxing. There is always a new way to burn fat, it seems. Along the beaches of California, you'll find hardbodies equipped with surf boards and in-line skates. In the Northeast, a new crop of suburban yuppies can be spotted powerwalking and cycling on expensive custom-made bikes. Of course, Americans like to do it all in as little time and as much style as possible; thus, the eight minute workout with matching Spandex gear. In the winter, skiing, snow-boarding, and ice skating are popular **recreational sports,** while during the rest of the year, families and bored teenagers nationwide turn to bowling and miniature golf for good, spherically shaped fun.

FOOD

There is more to American food than McDonald's and KFC, despite the common perception overseas. Due to the geographic and ethnic diversity of the States, however, it is not easy to nail down exactly what American food is. Ask the average American what he thinks is his native cuisine, and you'll probably hear about hamburgers, fried chicken, and hot dogs—basic **fast food** fare. Simply put, these offerings are what can be found anywhere in the country (and increasingly, the world), and are thus easily associated with "American food." The truth is that real American food is best found at the regional level, where agricultural production, immigration patterns, and local culture have resulted in food that goes beyond the hot dog (which is actually the German frankfurter, anyway).

Travelers through the States will probably come across some commonalities. Europeans, leave your light breakfasts on the continent; Americans cherish a big morning *repas*. The **lumberjack breakfast** is a favorite at many home-cookin' establishments and includes fried eggs, several strips of salty bacon, small links of breakfast sausage, hash browns (fried potatoes), buttered toast, pancakes (a.k.a. flapjacks) with maple syrup, coffee, and orange juice. Be sure to loosen your belt buckles. In the South, grits, a tasteless, mushy gruel is added to the mix, often topped with a gravy made from pork fat. For the non-lumberjack, a bowl of cereal and milk or oatmeal is an acceptable alternative.

Lunch and dinner (supper, in the middle of the country) are far less standardized than breakfast. Thick hamburgers, tender chicken breasts, and juicy ribeyes grace the lunch and dinner menus of nearly every chain restaurant, and are also popular **barbecue** items. Urbanites are often taken by the exotic allure of **international cuisine,** which is fairly abundant in most cities. However, Chinese takeout and pizza have become so Americanized that someone accustomed to the real thing may scarcely recognize the American versions. Many will still flock to the **staples** of their youth occasionally: a simple white bread sandwich for lunch and a dinner of neatly arranged meat, potatoes, and vegetables. Nevertheless, from Texas barbecued babybacks to New England clam chowder, "standard" American oats vary widely among regions.

NORTHEAST

America's English settlers first landed in the Northeast, bringing their cuisine with them. But the English staples of meats and vegetables quickly combined with uniquely American foodstuffs such as turkey, maple syrup, clams, lobster, cranberries, and corn. The results yielded such treasures as Boston brown bread, Indian pudding, New England clam chowder, and Maine boiled lobster. Seafood lovers rejoice: the shellfish in the Northeast are second to none.

SOUTHEAST

Be prepared for some good ol' home cookin'. Mamma's fried chicken, biscuits, mashed potatoes, grits, and collard greens are some of the highlights of Southeastern cuisine. Fried chicken is probably the most oft-eaten item inside the region (as evidenced by the popular national chain KFC), though pork products also prove popular among Southerners. Virginia ham is world-renowned, and ham biscuits provide a pleasant supplement to lunch and dinner dishes.

LOUISIANA

New Orleans chefs are among the best in the country, and creole or Cajun cooking will definitely tantalize your taste buds. Necessity compelled the earliest settlers of the region to make do with available food ingredients. Nowadays, however, locals and tourists alike regard smothered crawfish, fried catfish, jambalaya (rice cooked with ham, sausage, shrimp, and herbs), and gumbo (a soup with okra, meat, and vegetables) as delicacies. The faint of taste buds beware: Cajun and creole cooking can fry the mouth.

TEXAS

Lone Star State residents claim that Texas invented barbecue. From juicy tenderloins, to luscious baby back ribs, to whole pig roasts, Texans like to throw it on the grill. Eat at any of the many BBQ joints, though, and they'll tell you that the real secret's in the sauce. Be careful not to be too critical—disrespecting barbecue is fightin' words 'round these parts, as much of Texans' swelling pride lies under the grill. For those in the mood for something ethnic, enchiladas, burritos, and fajitas are scrumptious Tex-Mex options.

SOUTHWEST

Strongly influenced by Mexican cuisine, Southwestern food is America's oldest regional style. Much of the Southwest remained part of Mexico until 1848, when the territory was ceded to the United States. Consequently, the Mexican foodstuffs of corn, flour, and chilies are the basic components of Southwestern grub. Salsa made from tomatoes, chilies, and *tomatillos* adds a spicy notes to nearly all dishes, especially cheese- and chicken-filled quesadillas and ground beef tacos. Don't forget the Rolaids.

CALIFORNIA

Its images of pretentiousness and plasticity make California's health-conscious culinary revolution seem appropriate. Cooking California style means using fresh ingredients, and the result has been a wide array of fresh salads and blended smoothies. The wrapped sandwich, with its melange of ingredients, has recently become a trans-regional phenomenon. California's strong Asian contingent has had its share of influence on local cuisine, as the oriental chicken salad and Thai chicken wrap are among the most popular of their respective food categories.

CANADA

Geographically speaking, Canada is the second largest country in the world, sprawling over almost 10 million square kilometers (3.85 million sq. mi.). Still, just over 30 million people—roughly the population of California—inhabit Canada's ten provinces and three territories. Well over half the population crowds into the southern provinces of Ontario and Québec, while the newly declared territory, Nunavut, has under 30,000 people. Framed by the Atlantic to the east and the Pacific to the west, Canada extends from fertile southern farmlands to frozen northern tundra.

The name Canada is thought to derive from the Huron-Iroquois word *kanata* meaning "village" or "community." This etymology betrays the early settlers' dependence on indigenous peoples as well as the country's origins as a system of important trading posts. The early French and English colonists were both geographically and culturally distant from one another. To this day, **anglophones** and **francophones** fight to retain political dominance in the Canadian government. The concerns of the First Nation peoples and an increasing immigrant population have also become intertwined in the struggle.

O CANADA! A BRIEF HISTORY

Although archaeologists are uncertain about the exact timing, recent data indicates that the **first Canadians** arrived at least 10,000 years ago by crossing the Asian-Alaskan land bridge. Their descendents flooded the continent, fragmenting into disparate tribes. The first **Europeans** known to explore the area were the Norse, who settled in northern Newfoundland around the year 1000. England came next; John Cabot sighted Newfoundland in 1497. When Jacques Cartier, landing on the gulf of the St. Lawrence River, claimed the mainland for the French crown in 1534, he touched off a rivalry that persisted until Britain's 1759 capture of Québec in the Seven Years' War and France's total capitulation four years later.

The movement to unify the British North American colonies gathered speed after the American Civil War, when US military might and economic isolationism threatened the independent and continued existence of the British colonies. On March 29, 1867, Queen Victoria signed the **British North America Act** (BNA), uniting Nova Scotia, New Brunswick, Upper Canada, and Lower Canada (now Ontario and Québec). Though still a dominion of the British throne, Canada at last had its country—and its day: the BNA was proclaimed on July 1, now known as Canada Day.

Since that time, Canada has expanded both territorially and economically. The years following consolidation witnessed sustained economic growth and expansion. Westward travelers, often trekking toward the Pacific in search of gold, were greatly aided by the completion of a trans-continental railway in 1885. During this period, Canada grew to encompass most of the land it covers today. Participation in World War I earned the Dominion international respect and a charter membership in the League of Nations. It joined the United Nations in 1945 and was a founding member of the **North Atlantic Treaty Organization** in 1949. The Liberal government of the following decade created a national social security system and a national health insurance program. Pierre Trudeau's government repatriated Canada's constitution in 1981, freeing the nation from Britain in constitutional legality (though Elizabeth

II remains nominal head of state). Free to forge its own alliances, the country signed the controversial **North American Free Trade Agreement** (NAFTA) in 1992 under the leadership of Conservative Brian Mulroney.

In recent years, Canada has faced internal political tensions as well as an ever-increasing pressure to Americanize. Mulroney strove hard to mold a strong, unified Canada, but will probably go down in Canadian history as the leader who nearly tore the nation apart in an effort to bring it together. (Canadians today also revile Mulroney as the prime minister who introduced the universally bemoaned 7% Goods and Services Tax.) His numerous attempts to negotiate a constitution that all ten provinces would ratify (Canada's present constitution lacks Québec's support) consistently failed, fanning the flames of century-old regional tensions and leading ultimately to the end of his government.

The *québécois* **separatist movement** has a long and not entirely pleasant history. Though francophone nationalism has roots as far back as the colonial period, the separatist impulse truly took hold in 1960, when nationalist Liberals took power in Québec. In 1970, after a decade of bombings and robberies, the Front de Liberation du Québec kidnapped two Canadian officials, killing one. The crisis, which prompted Trudeau to declare a brief period of martial law, brought the issue to Québec's separation to a head. Support for the newly formed Parti Québécois was not universal, however, and a 1980 referendum saw 60% of *québécois* opposed of separation from the Dominion. In a more recent (1996) referendum, however, separation was rejected by a mere 1.2% margin. The struggle for an independent Québec thus continues in both the cultural and parliamentary arenas.

Canada has also locked horns with its **aboriginal peoples,** know as the First Nations. The Inuit and other peoples in the Northwest Territories have struggled for more political representation and have been largely successful: the 1999 creation of Nunavut represented a huge gain for First Nations in the north. The newly formed territory covers approximately 2 million sq. km (770,000 sq. mi.). About 85% of the region's 26,000 inhabitants are Inuit. While Nunavut's government mirrors that of the other provinces and territories, the new territory's political system is greatly influenced by Inuit customs and beliefs.

In addition to fretting over the independence wishes of their numerous constituents, Canadian policy-makers continue to struggle for Canada's **cultural independence** from the US. Media domination by their southern neighbor has put a bit of a strain on Canadian pride, so much so that Canada's radio stations are required by law to play 30% Canadian music. But increasing "brain drain," the southward emigration of Canada's intellectuals, has dashed many a hope for cultural renewal.

CANUCK CULTURE

Canada has two official languages, English and French. The *québécois* pronunciation of French can be perplexing to European speakers, and the protocol is less formal. There are also numerous native languages. Inuktitut, the Inuit language, is widely spoken in Nunavut and the Northwest Territories.

Most noted **Canadian literature** is post-1867. The opening of the Northwest and the Klondike Gold Rush (1898) provided fodder for the adventure tale—Jack London (*The Call of the Wild, White Fang*) and Robert Service (*Songs of a Sourdough, The Trail of '98*) both authored stories of prospectors and wolves based on their mining experience in the north. In the Maritimes, L.M. Montgomery penned one of the greatest coming-of-age novels of all times, *Anne of Green Gables* (1908). Prominent contemporary English-language authors include Margaret Atwood, best known for the futuristic best-seller *The Handmaid's Tale* (1986) and Sri Lankan-born novelist Michael Ondaatje, whose *The English Patient* (1992) received the prestigious Booker Prize. Canada also boasts three of the world's most authoritative cultural and literary critics: Northrop Frye, Hugh Kenner, and pop phenom Marshall McLuhan. The *québécois* literary tradition is becoming more recognized, and has been important in defining an emerging cultural and political identity.

ROASTED BEAVER TAIL? Despite the claims of some culinary cynics, Canadian cuisine does exist. Canadian cooking is a rich stew of different cultures and traditions, spiced with a hearty helping of Northern ingenuity. Foods such as tomato soup cake and Nanaimo bars (a hard, custard-like confection) reflect the nation's distinct cultural heritage. The *québécois* have also innovated in the culinary realm: staples include corn soup, *tourtière* (deep dish meat pie), and *poutine* (french fries with gravy and melted cheese).

Canada's contributions to the world of **popular music** encompass a range of artists and genres. Canadian rockers include Neil Young, Joni Mitchell, Bruce Cockburn, Rush, Cowboy Junkies, Barenaked Ladies, k.d. lang, Bryan Adams, Crash Test Dummies, Sarah McLachlan, and pop icons the Tragically Hip. Chart-toppers of the last few years include the inimitable (and who would want to?) Céline Dion, country cross-over Shania Twain, and Alanis Morissette. Canada is also home to *québécois* folk music and several world-class orchestras, including the Montréal, Toronto, and Vancouver Symphonies.

On the **silver screen,** Canada's National Film Board (NFB), which finances many documentaries, has gained worldwide acclaim. The first Oscar given to a documentary went to the NFB's 1941 *Churchill Island*. Recent figures of note include indy director Atom Egoyan, whose haunting film *The Sweet Hereafter* (1997) scored two Oscar nominations. *Québécois* filmmakers have also met with success. Director Denys Arcand caught the world's eye with the Oscar-nominated movie *Le déclin de l'empire américain* (1985). Arcand also directed the striking *Jésus de Montréal* (1989), which reflected the filmmaker's disillusionment with the Church.

Many famous **television** actors and comedians are from Canada, including Dan Aykroyd (*Blues Brothers, Ghostbusters*), Mike Myers (*Saturday Night Live, Wayne's World,* and *Austin Powers*), Michael J. Fox (*Back to the Future, Spin City*), newscaster Peter Jennings, *Jeopardy* host Alex Trebek, and Captain James T. Kirk himself, William Shatner (*Star Trek*). The comedy troupe SCTV spawned the careers of laughmasters Martin Short, Rick Moranis, and the late John Candy.

The *Toronto Globe and Mail* is Canada's national newspaper, distributed six days a week across the entire country. Every Canadian city has at least one daily paper; the weekly news magazine is *Maclean's.* The publicly owned **Canadian Broadcasting Corporation (CBC)** provides two national networks (one in English, one in French) for both radio and TV. Many Canadians, however, depend on cable and satellite networks beamed in from the US.

In the realm of sports, Canada possesses an athletic heritage befitting its northern latitudes. Popular sports include ice skating, skiing, and the perennial favorite, ice hockey. Canadians also enjoy a spirited game of **curling,** which involves pushing a 20kg stone across a sheet of ice. Some of Canada's other popular sports are derived from those of the First Nations. Lacrosse, the national game of Canada, was played long before the Europeans arrived. Finally, sports played in the US have crossed the border in full force; in addition to the **Canadian Football League (CFL),** Canada has two NBA teams and two Major League Baseball outfits.

ESSENTIALS

FACTS FOR THE TRAVELER

EMBASSIES & CONSULATES

Contact your nearest embassy or consulate for information regarding visas and passports to the United States and Canada. The **US State Department** provides contact info for US embassies and consulates abroad at http://usembassy.state.gov. A similar listing for the **Canadian Department of Foreign Affairs** can be found at www.dfait-maeci.gc.ca/dfait/missions/menu-e.asp. For more detailed info on embassies, consult www.embassyworld.com.

AMERICAN CONSULAR SERVICES ABROAD

US EMBASSIES
Australia, Moonah Pl., Yarralumla, ACT 2600 (☎02 6214 5600; fax 6214 5970; http://usembassy-australia.state.gov/embassy).

Canada, 490 Sussex Drive, Ottawa, ON K1N 1G8 (☎613-238-5335; fax 688-3091; www.usembassycanada.gov).

Ireland, 42 Elgin Rd., Ballsbridge, Dublin 4 (☎01 668 8777 or 668 7122; fax 668 9946; www.usembassy.ie).

New Zealand, 29 Fitzherbert Terr., Thorndon, Wellington (☎04 472 2068; fax 478 1701; http://usembassy.state.gov/wellington).

South Africa, 877 Pretorius St., Arcadia 0083 (☎012 342 1048; fax 342 2244; http://usembassy.state.gov/pretoria).

UK, 24 Grosvenor Sq., London W1A 1AE (☎ 0207 499 9000; fax 491 2485; www.usembassy.org.uk).

US CONSULATES
Australia, 553 St. Kilda Rd., Melbourne VIC 3004 (☎03 9526 5900; fax 9510 4646); 16 St. George's Terr., 13th fl., Perth WA 6000 (☎08 9202 1224; fax 9231 9444). MLC Centre, 19-29 Martin Pl., 59th fl., Sydney NSW 2000 (☎02 9373 9200; fax 9373 9125).

Canada, 615 Macleod Trail S.E., 10th fl., Calgary, AB T2G 4T8 (☎403-266-8962; fax 264-6630); Cogswell Tower, #910, Scotia Sq., 2000 Barrington St., Halifax, NS B3J 3K1 (☎902-429-2480; fax 423-6861); P.O. Box 65, Postal Station Desjardins, Montréal, QC H5B 1G1 (☎514-398-9695; fax 398-9748); 2 Place Terrasse Dufferin, Québec, QC G1R 4T9 (☎418-692-2096; fax 692-4640); 360 University Ave., Toronto, ON M5G 1S4 (☎416-595-1700; fax 595-0051); 1095 West Pender St., Vancouver, BC V6E 2M6 (☎604-685-4311; fax 685-5285).

New Zealand, Yorkshire General Bldg., 4th fl., 29 Shortland St., Auckland (☎9 303 2724; fax 366 0870).

South Africa, Monte Carlo Bldg., Heerengracht, Foreshore, Cape Town (☎021 421 4351; fax 425 3014); 2901 Durban Bay Building, 333 Smith St., Durban 4000 (☎031 304 4737; fax 301 0265); 1 River St., Killarney, Johannesburg (☎011 644 8000; fax 646 6916).

UK, Queen's House, 14 Queen St., Belfast, N. Ireland BT1 6EQ (☎028 9032 8239; fax 9024 8482); 3 Regent Terr., Edinburgh, Scotland EH7 5BW (☎0131 556 8315; fax 557 6023).

CANADIAN EMBASSIES
Australia, Commonwealth Ave., Canberra, ACT 2600 (☎02 6270 4000; fax 6273 3285; www.dfait-maeci.gc.ca/australia).

Ireland, 65 St. Stephen's Green, Dublin 2 (☎01 478 1988; fax 478 1285).

New Zealand, 61 Molesworth St., 3rd fl., Thorndon, Wellington (☎04 473 9577; fax 471 2082; www.dfait-maeci.gc.ca/newzealand).

South Africa, 1103 Arcadia St., Hatfield, Pretoria 0083 (☎012 422 3000; fax 422 3052).

UK, Canada House, Trafalgar Sq., London SW1Y 5BJ (☎0207 258 6600; fax 258 6333; www.dfait-maeci.gc.ca/london).

US, 501 Pennsylvania Ave. NW, Washington, D.C. 20001 (☎202-682-1740; fax 682-7726; http://canadianembassy.org).

CANADIAN CONSULATES

Australia, 123 Camberwell Rd., Hawthorn East, Melbourne, VIC 3123 (☎03 9811 9999; fax 9811 9969); 267 St. George's Terr., 3rd fl., Perth WA 6000 (☎08 9322 7930; fax 9261 7706); Quay West Bldg., 111 Harrington St., 5th fl., Sydney NSW 2000 (☎02 9364 3000; fax 9364 3098).

New Zealand, Jetset Centre, 9th fl., 48 Emily Pl., Auckland (☎09 309 3680; fax 307 3111).

South Africa, Reserve Bank Bldg., 60 St. George's Mall St., 19th fl., Cape Town 8001 (☎021 423 5240; fax 423 4893); 25/27 Marriott Rd., Durban 4000 (☎031 309 8434; fax 309 8432).

UK, 378 Stranmillis Rd., Belfast, N. Ireland BT9 5ED (☎028 660 212; fax 687 798); Port Rd., Rhoose, Vale of Glamorgan, Wales CF62 3BT (☎02920 719 172; fax 710 856); 30 Lothian Rd., Edinburgh, Scotland EH2 2XZ (☎0131 220 4333; fax 245 6010).

US, 3 Copley Pl., #400, Boston, MA 02116 (☎617-262-3760; fax 262-3415); 2 Prudential Plaza, 180 N. Stetson Ave., #2400, Chicago, IL 60601 (☎312-616-1860; fax 616-1877); 750 N. St. Paul Street, #1700, Dallas, TX 75201 (☎214-922-9806; fax 969-6935); 550 S. Hope St., 9th fl., Los Angeles, CA 90071 (☎213-346-2700; fax 620-8827); 200 S. Biscayne Blvd., Miami, FL (☎305-579-1600; fax 374-6774); 1251 Ave. of the Americas, New York, NY 10020 (☎212-596-1600; fax 596-1666); 555 Montgomery St., #1288, San Francisco, CA 94111 (☎415-834-3180, fax 834-3189).

CONSULAR SERVICES IN THE US AND CANADA

IN WASHINGTON, D.C. (USA)

Australia, 1601 Massachusetts Ave., 20036 (☎202-797-3000; fax 797-3168; www.austemb.org). **Ireland,** 2234 Mass. Ave., 20008 (☎202-462-3939; fax 232-5993; www.irelandemb.org). **New Zealand,** 37 Observatory Cir., 20008 (☎202-328-4800; fax 667-5227; www.nzemb.org). **UK,** 3100 Mass. Ave., 20008 (☎202-588-6500; fax 588-7870; www.britainusa.com/consular/embassy). **South Africa,** 3051 Mass. Ave., 20008 (☎202-232-4400; fax 265-1607; http://usaembassy.southafrica.net).

IN OTTAWA, ONTARIO (CANADA)

Australia, 50 O'Connor St., #710, K1P 6L2 (☎613-236-0841; fax 236-4376; www.ahc-ottawa.org). **Ireland,** 130 Albert St., #1105, K1P 5G4 (☎613-233-6281; fax 233-5835). **New Zealand,** 99 Bank St., #727, K1P 6G3 (☎613-238-6097; fax 238-5707; www.nzhcottawa.org). **UK,** 310 Summerset St. W., K2P 0J9 (☎613-230-2961; fax 230-2400; www.britain-in-canada.org). **South Africa,** 15 Sussex Drive, K1M 1M8 (☎613-744-0330; fax 741-1639).

> ### ⮢ ENTRANCE REQUIREMENTS.
> **Passport** (p. 35). Required for all visitors to the US and Canada.
> **Visa** (p. 45). A visa is usually required to visit the US and Canada, but can be waived.
> **Work Permit** (p. 87). Required for all foreigners planning to work in Canada or the US.
> **Driving Permit** (p. 78). Required for all those planning to drive.

DOCUMENTS AND FORMALITIES

PASSPORTS

REQUIREMENTS. All foreign visitors except Canadians need valid passports to enter the United States and to re-enter their own country. Returning home with an expired passport is illegal and may result in a fine. Canadians need to demonstrate proof of Canadian citizenship, such as a citizenship card with photo ID. The US does not allow entrance if the holder's passport expires in under six months.

PHOTOCOPIES. Be sure to photocopy the page of your passport with your photo, passport number, and other identifying info, as well as any visas, travel insurance policies, plane tickets, or traveler's check serial numbers. Carry one set of copies in a safe place, apart from the originals, and leave another set at home. Consulates also recommend that you carry an expired passport or an official copy of your birth certificate in a part of your baggage separate from other documents.

LOST PASSPORTS. If you lose your passport, immediately notify the local police and the nearest embassy or consulate of your home government. To expedite the replacement process, you will need to know all info from the previous passport; you must also show ID and proof of citizenship. In some cases, a replacement may take weeks to process, and it may be valid only for a limited time. Any visas stamped in your old passport will be irretrievably lost. In an emergency, ask for immediate temporary traveling papers that will permit you to re-enter your home country. Your passport is a public document belonging to your nation's government. You may have to surrender it to a US government official, but if you don't get it back in a reasonable amount of time, inform your country's nearest mission.

NEW PASSPORTS. File any new passport or renewal applications well in advance of your departure date. Most passport offices offer rush services for a steep fee. Citizens living abroad who need a passport or renewal should contact the nearest consular service of their home country.

Australia: Citizens must apply for a passport in person at a post office, a passport office, or an Australian diplomatic mission overseas. Passport offices are located in Adelaide, Brisbane, Canberra, Darwin, Hobart, Melbourne, Newcastle, Perth, and Sydney. New adult passports cost AUS$132 (for a 32-page passport) or AUS$198 (64-page), and a child's is AUS$66/AUS$99. Adult passports are valid for 10 years and child passports for 5 years. For more info, call toll-free (in Australia) 13 12 32, or visit www.passports.gov.au.

Canada: Citizens may cross the US-Canada border with any proof of citizenship.

Ireland: Citizens can apply for a passport by mail to either the Department of Foreign Affairs, Passport Office, Setanta Centre, Molesworth St., Dublin 2 (☎01 671 1633; fax 671 1092; www.irlgov.ie/iveagh), or the Passport Office, Irish Life Building, 1A South Mall, Cork (☎021 27 2525). Obtain an application at a local *Garda* station or post office, or request one from a passport office. 32-page passports cost IR£45/€57.14 and are valid for 10 years. 48-page passports cost IR£55/€69.84. Citizens under 16 or over 65 can request a 3-year passport (IR£10/€12.70).

New Zealand: Application forms for passports are available from any travel agency or Link Centre. Applications may be forwarded to the Passport Office, P.O. Box 10-526, Wellington, New Zealand (☎0800 225 050 or 04 474 8100; fax 474 8010; www.passports.govt.nz). Standard processing time is 10 working days. Adult passports (NZ$80) are valid 10 years; passports for children under 16 (NZ$40) are valid 5 years.

South Africa: Passports are issued only in Pretoria, but all applications must still be submitted or forwarded to the nearest South African consulate. Processing time is 4 months or more. Adult passports, which cost around ZAR192, are valid for 10 years. Passports for children under 16 (around ZAR136) are valid for 5 years.

United Kingdom: Application forms are available at passport offices, main post offices, travel agencies, and online (www.ukpa.gov.uk/forms/f_app_pack.htm). Apply by mail or in person to one of the passport offices, located in London, Liverpool, Newport, Peter-borough, Glasgow, or Belfast. Adult passports (UK£28) are valid for 10 years; under 16 (UK£14.80) are valid for 5. The process takes about 4 weeks, but the London office offers a 5-day, walk-in rush service for an additional UK£12. The UK Passport Agency can be reached by phone at 0870 521 0410. More info is available at www.open.gov.uk/ukpass/ukpass.htm.

United States: Citizens may cross the US-Canada border with any proof of citizenship.

VISAS

Citizens of most European countries, Australia, New Zealand, and Ireland can waive US visas through the **Visa Waiver Pilot Program.** Visitors qualify if they are trav-eling only for business or pleasure (*not* work or study) and are staying for fewer than 90 days. In addition, travelers must provide proof of intent to leave (such as a return plane ticket) and an I-94 form. Citizens of South Africa and some other coun-tries need a visa in addition to a valid passport for entrance to the US. To obtain a visa, contact a US embassy or consulate (see p. 33).

All travelers planning a stay of more than 90 days (180 days for Canadians) need to obtain a visa; contact the closest US embassy or consulate. The **Center for Inter-national Business and Travel (CIBT),** 23201 New Mexico Ave. NW, #210, Washington, D.C. 20016 (☎202-244-9500 or 800-925-2428), secures **B-2** (pleasure travel) visas to and from all possible countries for a variable service charge (six month visa around $45). If you lose your I-94 form, you can replace it at the nearest **Immigration and Nat-uralization Service (INS)** office (☎800-375-5283; www.ins.usdoj.gov), although it's unlikely that the form will be replaced within the time of your stay. **Visa extensions** are sometimes attainable with a completed I-539 form; call the forms request line at 800-870-3676. Be sure to double-check on entrance requirements at the nearest US embassy or consulate, or consult the Bureau of Consular Affair's web site (www.travel.state.gov/visa;visitors.html).

Citizens of Australia, Ireland, New Zealand, the UK, and the US may enter Canada without visas for stays of 90 days or less if they carry proof of intent to leave. South Africans need a visa to enter Canada (CDN$75 for a single person, CDN$400 for a family). Citizens of other countries should contact their Canadian consulate for more info. Write to Citizenship and Immigration Canada for the booklet *Applying for a Visitor Visa* at Information Centre, Public Affairs Branch, Jean Edmonds Tower S., 365 Laurier Ave. W., Ottawa, ON K1A 1L1 (☎613-954-9019 or 800-242-2100), or consult it online at http://cicnet.ci.gc.ca. Visa extensions are sometimes granted; phone the nearest Canada Immigration Centre.

IDENTIFICATION

When you travel, always carry two or more forms of identification on your person, including at least one photo ID; a passport combined with a driver's license or birth certificate is usually adequate. Many establishments, especially banks, may require several IDs in order to cash traveler's checks. Never carry all your forms of ID together; keep them in separate places in case of theft or loss.

STUDENT AND TEACHER IDENTIFICATION. The **International Student Identity Card (ISIC),** the most widely accepted form of student ID, provides discounts on sights, accommodations, food, and transportation. The ISIC is preferable to an institution-specific card (such as a university ID) because it is more likely to be recognized (and honored) abroad. All cardholders have access to a 24-hour emergency hel-pline for medical, legal, and financial emergencies (in North America call 877-370-ISIC). Holders of US-issued cards are also eligible for insurance benefits (see **Insur-ance,** p. 47). Many student travel agencies issue ISICs, including STA Travel in Aus-tralia and New Zealand; Travel CUTS in Canada; **usit** in the Republic of Ireland and Northern Ireland; SASTS in South Africa; Campus Travel and STA Travel in the UK; Council Travel and STA Travel in the US (see p. 71). The card is valid from Septem-ber of one year to December of the following year and costs AUS$13, UK£5, or

US$22. Applicants must be degree-seeking students of a secondary or post-secondary school and be of at least 12 years of age. Because of the proliferation of fake ISICs, some services (particularly airlines) require additional proof of student identity, such as a school ID. The **International Teacher Identity Card (ITIC)** offers the same insurance coverage but with limited discounts. The fee is AUS$13, UK£5, or US$22. Find more info at www.istc.org.

YOUTH IDENTIFICATION. The International Student Travel Confederation also issues a discount card to travelers who are 25 years old or under, but are not students. This one-year **International Youth Travel Card** (**IYTC;** formerly the **GO 25** Card) offers many of the same benefits as the ISIC. Most organizations that sell the ISIC also sell the IYTC ($22). If you are an ISIC card carrier and want to avoid buying individual calling cards or wish to consolidate all your means of communication during your trip, you can activate your ISIC's ISIConnect service, a powerful new integrated communications service (powered by eKit.com). With ISIConnect, one toll-free access number (☎800-706-1333 in the US, 877-635-3575 in Canada) gives you access to several different methods of keeping in touch via the phone and Internet, including: a reduced-rate international calling plan that treats your ISIC card as a universal calling card; a personalized voicemail box accessible from pa y phones anywhere in the world or for free over the Internet; faxmail service for sending and receiving faxes via email, fax machines, or pay phones; various email capabilities, including a service that reads your email to you over the phone; an online "travel safe" for storing (and faxing) important documents and numbers; and a 24hr. emergency help line (via phone or email at ISIConnect@ekit.com) offering assistance and medical and legal referrals. To activate your ISIConnect account, visit the service's comprehensive web site (www.isiconnect.ekit.com) or call the customer service number of your home country: in Australia 800 114 478; in Canada 877-635-3575; in Ireland 800 555 180 or 800 577 980; in New Zealand 0800 114 478; in the UK 0800 376 2366 or 0800 169 8646; in the US 800-706-1333; and in South Africa 0800 992 921 or 0800 997 285.

CUSTOMS

Upon entering the United States or Canada, you must declare certain items from abroad and pay a duty on the value of those articles that exceed the allowance established by the US or Canada's customs service. Keeping receipts for larger purchases made abroad will help establish values when you return. Upon returning home, you must declare all articles acquired abroad and pay a **duty** on the value of articles that exceed the allowance established by your country's customs service. Goods and gifts purchased at **duty-free** shops abroad are not exempt from duty or sales tax at your point of return; you must declare these items as well. "Duty-free" merely means that you need not pay a tax in the country of purchase. For more specific information on customs requirements, contact the following info centers.

 AMERICAN AND CANADIAN CUSTOMS DECLARATIONS. Entering the **US** as a *non-resident,* you are allowed to claim $100 of gifts and merchandise if you will be in the country for 72hr. *Residents* may claim $400 worth of goods. If 21, you may bring in 1L of wine, beer, or liquor. 200 cigarettes, 50 cigars (steer clear of Cubans), or 2kg of smoking tobacco are also permitted. Entering **Canada,** *visitors* may bring in gifts, each of which may not exceed CDN$60 in value. *Residents* who have been out of the country for 24hr. may claim an exemption of CDN$50. After 48hr. they may claim CDN$200, and after 7 days CDN$750. If you are of the legal drinking age in the province, and have been out of the country for 48hr. or more, you may bring in 1.5L of wine, 1.14L of liquor, or 24x355mL cans or bottles of beer or ale. You may also bring in 200 cigarettes, 50 cigars, or 200g of manufactured tobacco.

Australia: Australian Customs National Information Line (in Australia call 01 30 03 63, from elsewhere call +61 (2) 6275 6666; www.customs.gov.au).

Canada: Canadian Customs, 333 Dunsmuir St., Vancouver, BC V6B 5R4 (☎506-636-5064 or 800-461-9999; www.revcan.ca).

Ireland: Customs Information Office, Irish Life Centre, Lower Abbey St., Dublin 1 (☎01 878 8811; fax 878 0836; taxes@revenue.iol.ie; www.revenue.ie/customs.htm).

New Zealand: New Zealand Customhouse, 17-21 Whitmore St., Box 2218, Wellington (☎04 473 6099; fax 473 7370; www.customs.govt.nz).

South Africa: Commissioner for Customs and Excise, Private Bag X47, Pretoria 0001 (☎ 012 314 9911; fax 328 6478; www.gov.za).

UK: Her Majesty's Customs and Excise, Passenger Enquiry Team, Wayfarer House, Great South West Rd., Feltham, Middlesex TW14 8NP (☎020 8910 3744; fax 8910 3933; www.hmce.gov.uk).

US: US Customs Service, 1330 Pennsylvania Ave. NW, Washington, D.C. 20229 (☎ 202-354-1000; fax 354-1010; www.customs.gov).

MONEY

No matter how low your budget, if you plan to travel for more than a couple of days, you will need to keep handy a larger amount of cash than usual. Carrying it around with you, even in a money belt, is risky, and personal checks from another country, or even another state, will probably not be accepted no matter how many forms of identification you have (some banks don't even accept checks).

Many Canadian shops, as well as vending machines and parking meters, accept US coins at face value. Stores often convert the price of your purchase for you, but they are not legally obligated to offer a fair exchange. In almost all circumstances, you will receive Canadian change in return. (During the past several years, the Canadian dollar has been worth roughly 30% less than the US dollar.)

CURRENCY & EXCHANGE

The main unit of currency in the US and Canada is the **dollar ($)**, which is divided into 100 **cents (¢)**. Paper money is green in the US; bills come in denominations of $1, $5, $10, $20, $50, and $100. Coins are 1¢ (penny), 5¢ (nickel), 10¢ (dime), 25¢ (quarter), and $1. Paper money in Canada comes in denominations of $5, $10, $20, $50, and $100, which are all the same size but color-coded by denomination. Coins are 1¢, 5¢, 10¢, 25¢, $1, and $2. The $1 coin is known as the **Loonie** and the $2 coin is affectionately dubbed the **Toonie**. The chart below is based on rates published in late August, 2001.

THE GREENBACK (US DOLLAR)		THE LOONIE (CANADIAN DOLLAR)	
CDN$1 = US$0.65	US$1 = CDN$1.54	US$1 = CDN$1.54	CDN$1 = US$0.65
UK£1 = US$1.43	US$1 = UK£0.70	UK£1 = CDN$2.20	CDN$1 = UK£0.46
IR£1 = US$1.15	US$1= IR£0.87	IR£1 = CDN$1.76	CDN$1= IR£0.57
AUS$1 = US$0.52	US$1= AUS$1.91	AUS$1 = CDN$0.80	CDN$1= AUS$1.25
NZ$1 = US$0.43	US$1 = NZ$2.32	NZ$1 = CDN$0.66	CDN$1 = NZ$1.51
ZAR1 = US$0.12	US$1 = ZAR8.29	ZAR1 = CDN$0.19	CDN$1 = ZAR5.39

Banks generally have the best rates. Elsewhere, you can expect steep commission rates. A good rule of thumb is to use banks or money-exchanging centers that have at most a 5% margin between buy and sell prices. Convert in large sums to avoid numerous penalties, but don't exchange more than you'll need. ATM and credit cards (see p. 39) often get very good rates.

If using traveler's checks or bills, carry some in small denominations ($50 or less), especially for times when you are forced to exchange at poor rates. Also carry a range of denominations since charges may be levied per check cashed.

TRAVELER'S CHECKS

Traveler's checks (**American Express** and **Visa** are the most recognized) are one of the safest and least troublesome means of carrying funds. Several agencies and banks sell them for a small commission. Each agency provides refunds if your checks are lost or stolen, and many provide additional services, such as toll-free refund hotlines abroad, emergency message services, and stolen credit card assistance.

While traveling, keep check receipts and a record of which checks you've cashed separate from the checks themselves. It also helps to leave a list of check numbers with someone at home. Never countersign checks until you're ready to cash them, and always bring your passport with you to cash them. For lost or stolen checks, immediately contact a refund center (of the company that issued your checks) to be reimbursed; they may require a police report verifying the loss or theft. Ask about toll-free refund hotlines and the location of refund centers when purchasing checks, and always carry emergency cash.

American Express: Call 800 25 19 02 in Australia; in New Zealand 0800 441 068; in the UK 0800 521 313; in the US and Canada 800-221-7282. Elsewhere call the US collect +1 801-964-6665; www.aexp.com. Traveler's checks are available at a 1-4% commission at AmEx offices and banks, or commission-free at AAA offices (see p. 80). *Cheques for Two* can be signed by either of 2 people traveling together.

Citicorp: In the US and Canada call 800-645-6556; elsewhere call US collect +1 813-623-1709. Traveler's checks (available only in US dollars, British pounds, and German marks) at 1-2% commission. Call 24hr.

Thomas Cook MasterCard: In the US and Canada call 800-223-7373; in the UK call 0800 62 21 01; elsewhere call UK collect +44 1733 31 89 50. Checks available in 13 currencies at 2% commission. Thomas Cook offices cash checks commission-free.

Visa: In the US call 800-227-6811; in the UK call 0800 89 50 78; elsewhere call UK collect +44 20 7937 8091. Call for the location of their nearest office.

CREDIT CARDS

Credit cards are generally accepted in all but the smallest businesses in both the US and Canada. Major credit cards—**MasterCard** (along with its European counterparts **Euro Card** and **Access**) and **Visa** (with its European counterparts **Carte Bleue** or **Barclaycard**) are welcomed most often—can be used to extract cash advances in dollars (both US and Canadian) from associated banks and teller machines throughout both countries. Credit card companies get the wholesale exchange rate, which is generally 5% better than the retail rate used by banks and other currency exchange establishments. **American Express** cards also work in some ATMs, as well as at AmEx offices and major airports. All such machines require a **Personal Identification Number (PIN)**. You must ask your credit card company for a PIN before you leave; without it, you will be unable to withdraw cash with your credit card outside your home country. If you already have a PIN, check with the company to make sure it will work in Canada and the US.

CREDIT CARD COMPANIES. Visa (☎800-336-8472) and MasterCard (☎800-307-7309) are issued in cooperation with banks and other organizations. American Express (☎800-843-2273) has an annual fee of up to $55. AmEx cardholders may cash personal checks at AmEx offices abroad, access a 24hr. emergency medical and legal assistance hotline (in North America call 800-554-2639, elsewhere call US collect +1 715-343-7977), and enjoy American Express Travel Service benefits (including plane, hotel, and car rental reservation changes; baggage loss and flight insurance; mailgram and international cable services; and held mail). The Discover Card (in US call 800-347-2683, elsewhere call US +1 801-902-3100) offers cashback bonuses on most purchases.

CASH CARDS (ATM CARDS)

Cash cards—popularly called **ATM** (Automated Teller Machine) cards—are widespread in the US and Canada. Depending on the system that your home bank uses, you can most likely access your personal bank account from abroad. ATMs get the same wholesale exchange rate as credit cards, but there is often a limit on the amount of money you can withdraw per day (around $300). There is typically also a surcharge of $1-2 per withdrawal. Also, if your PIN is longer than four digits, ask your bank whether you need a new number.

The two major international money networks are **Cirrus** (☎800-424-7787) and **PLUS** (☎800-843-7587). To locate ATMs around the world, call the above numbers, or consult www.visa.com/pd/atm or www.mastercard.com/atm. Most ATMs charge a transaction fee that is paid to the bank that owns the ATM.

Visa TravelMoney (☎800-847-2399) is a system allowing you to access money with your Visa card from any Visa ATM. You deposit an amount before you travel (plus a small service fee), and you can withdraw up to that sum. These cards give you the same favorable exchange rate for withdrawals as a regular Visa. Obtain a card by visiting a nearby Thomas Cook or Citicorp office, or by checking with your local bank to see if it issues TravelMoney cards. **Road Cash** (☎877-762-3227; www.road-cash.com) issues cards in the US with a minimum $300 deposit.

DEBIT CARDS

Debit cards are a hybrid between credit and cash cards. They bear the logo of a major credit card, but purchases and withdrawals made with them are paid directly out of your bank account. Using a debit card like a credit card often incurs no fee (contact the issuing bank for details), gives you a favorable exchange rate, and frees you from having to carry large sums of money. Be careful, though: debit cards lack the theft protection that credit cards usually have.

GETTING MONEY FROM HOME

AMERICAN EXPRESS. Cardholders can withdraw cash from their checking accounts at any of AmEx's major offices and many representative offices (up to $1000 every 21 days; no service charge, no interest). AmEx "Express Cash" withdrawals from any AmEx ATM in the US and Canada are automatically debited from the cardholder's checking account or line of credit. Green card holders may withdraw up to $1000 in any seven-day period (2% transaction fee; minimum $2.50, maximum $20). To enroll in Express Cash, cardmembers may call 800-227-4669 in the US; elsewhere call the US collect +1 336-668-5041.

WESTERN UNION. Travelers from the US, Canada, and the UK can wire money abroad through Western Union's international money transfer services. In the US, call 800-325-6000; in Canada, 800-235-0000; in the UK, 0800 83 38 33. To wire money within the US using a credit card (Visa, MasterCard, Discover), call 800-CALL-CASH (225-5227). The rates for sending cash are generally $10-11 cheaper than with a credit card, and the money is usually available at the place you're sending it to within an hour. To locate the nearest Western Union location, consult www.westernunion.com.

FEDERAL EXPRESS. Some people choose to send money abroad in cash via FedEx to avoid transmission fees and taxes. While FedEx is reasonably reliable, note that this method is illegal. In the US and Canada, FedEx can be reached by calling 800-463-3339; in the UK, 0800 12 38 00; in Ireland, 800 535 800; in Australia, 13 26 10; in New Zealand, 0800 733 339; and in South Africa, 011 923 8000.

COSTS

The cost of your trip will vary considerably, depending on where you go, how you travel, and where you stay. For foreign travelers, the single biggest cost of the trip will probably be the round-trip **airfare** to North America (see **Getting There: By Plane**, p. 68). A car is necessary for traveling in many parts of the US and Canada, and travelers who plan on renting must also figure this expense into account (for information on car rental, see p. 81). It is a good idea to plan a daily **budget** for your trip before leaving.

STAYING ON A BUDGET. On land, **accommodations** start at about $12 per night in a hostel bed, while a basic sit-down meal costs about $10 depending on the region. If you stay in hostels and prepare your own food, you'll probably spend from $30-40 per person per day. A slightly more comfortable day (sleeping in hostels/guest houses and the occasional budget hotel, eating one meal a day at a restaurant, going out at night) would run $50-65; for a luxurious day, the sky's the limit. Transportation costs will increase these figures. **Gas** prices have risen significantly in the US over the past year. A gallon of gas now costs about $1.60 per gallon (40¢ per L), but prices vary widely according to state gasoline taxes. In Canada, gas costs CDN60-70¢ per L (CDN$2-2.65 per gallon). Finally, don't forget to factor in emergency reserve funds (at least $200) when planning how much money you'll need.

TIPS FOR SAVING MONEY. Considering that saving just a few dollars a day over the course of your trip might pay for days or weeks of additional travel, the art of penny-pinching is well worth learning. Learn to take advantage of freebies: for example, museums will typically be free once a week or once a month, and cities often host free open-air concerts and/or cultural events (especially in the summer). Bring a sleepsack (see p. 48) to save on sheet charges in hostels, and do your **laundry** in the sink (unless you're explicitly prohibited from doing so). You can split **accommodation** costs (in hotels and some hostels) with trustworthy fellow travelers; multi-bed rooms almost always work out cheaper per person than singles. The same principle will also work for cutting down on the cost of **restaurant** meals. You can also buy food in supermarkets instead of eating out. These simple tactics make the occasional splurge feel all the more rewarding.

TIPPING AND BARGAINING

In the US, it is customary to tip waitstaff and cab drivers 15-20% (at your discretion). Tips are usually not included in restaurant bills, unless you are in a party of 6 or more. At the airport and in hotels, porters expect at least a $1 per bag tip to carry your bags. Tipping is less compulsory in Canada; a good tip signifies remarkable service. Bargaining is generally frowned upon and fruitless in both countries.

TAXES

In the US, sales tax is similar to the European Value-Added Tax and ranges from 4-10% depending on the item and the place; in many states, groceries are not taxed. *Let's Go* lists sales tax rates in the introduction to each state; usually these taxes are not included in the prices of items.

In Canada, you'll quickly notice the 7% goods and services tax (GST) and an additional sales tax in some provinces. See the introductory sections for info on provincial taxes. Visitors can claim a rebate of the GST they pay on accommodations of less than one month and on most goods they buy and take home, so be sure to save your receipts and pick up a GST rebate form while in Canada. The total claim must be at least CDN$7 of GST (equal to CDN$100 in purchases) and made within one year of the date of the purchase; further goods must be exported from Canada within 60 days of purchase. A brochure detailing restrictions is available from local tourist offices or through Revenue Canada, Visitor's Rebate Program, 275 Pope Rd., Summerside, PEI C1N 6C6 (☎ 902-432-5608 or 800-668-4748).

SAFETY AND SECURITY

Crime is mostly concentrated in the cities, but being safe is a good idea no matter where you are. Newark, NJ; Atlanta, GA; St. Louis, MO; New Orleans, LA; Detroit, MI; Baltimore, MD; Miami, FL; and Washington, D.C., are the most dangerous cities in the United States, but that does not mean you should not visit them. Common sense and a little bit of thought will go a long way in helping you to avoid dangerous situations.

> **EMERGENCY = 911.** For emergencies in the US and Canada, dial **911.** This number is toll-free from all phones, including coin phones. In a very few remote communities, 911 may not work. If it does not, dial O for the operator and request to be connected with the appropriate emergency service. In national parks, it is usually best to call the **park warden** in case of emergency. *Let's Go* always lists emergency contact numbers.

PERSONAL SAFETY

EXPLORING. To avoid unwanted attention, try to blend in as much as possible and familiarize yourself with the area before you set out. The gawking camera-toter is a more obvious target for thieves and con artists than the low-profile traveler. Carry yourself with confidence; if you must check a map on the street, duck into a shop. If you are traveling alone, be sure someone at home knows your itinerary, and *never admit that you're traveling alone.*

Whenever possible, *Let's Go* warns of unsafe neighborhoods and areas, but there are some good general tips to follow. When walking at night, stick to busy, well-lit streets and avoid dark alleyways. Do not attempt to cross through parks, parking lots, or other large, deserted areas. Buildings in disrepair, vacant lots, and unpopulated areas are all bad signs. Keep in mind that a district can change character drastically between blocks and from day to night. Look for children playing, women walking in the open, and other signs of an active community. If you feel uncomfortable, leave as quickly and directly as you can, but don't allow fear of the unknown to turn you into a hermit. Careful, persistent exploration will build confidence and make your stay even more rewarding.

SELF DEFENSE. There is no sure-fire way to avoid all the threatening situations you might encounter when you travel, but a good self-defense course will give you concrete ways to react to different types of aggression. **Impact, Prepare,** and **Model Mugging** can refer you to local self-defense courses in the US (☎800-345-5425) and in Vancouver, BC, Canada (☎604-878-3838). Two- to three-hour workshops start at $50; full courses run $350-500. Both men and women are welcome.

GETTING AROUND. If you are using a **car,** learn local driving signals and wear a seatbelt. Children under 40 lbs. should ride only in a specially-designed carseat, available for a small fee from most car rental agencies. Study route maps before you hit the road. If your car breaks down, wait for the police to assist you. For long drives in desolate areas, invest in a cellular phone and a roadside assistance program (see p. 80). Be sure to park your vehicle in a garage or well-traveled area, and use a steering wheel locking device in larger cities. **Sleeping in your car** is one of the most dangerous (and often illegal) ways to get your rest.

Interstate **public transportation** is generally safe. Occasionally, bus or train stations can be unsafe; *Let's Go* warns of these stations where applicable. Within major US cities, the quality and safety of public transportation vary considerably. It is usually a good idea to avoid subways and intra-city buses late at night; if you must use these forms of transportation, try to travel in a large groups. **Taxis** are usually safe, although drivers do not always speak reliable English.

Let's Go does not recommend **hitchhiking** under any circumstances, particularly for women—see **Getting Around,** p. 82 for more info.

FINANCIAL SECURITY

PROTECTING YOUR VALUABLES. Theft in the US is more rampant in big cities and at night. To prevent easy theft, don't keep all your valuables (money, important documents) in one place. **Photocopies** of important documents allow you to recover them in case they are lost or lifted. Carry one copy separate from the documents and leave another copy at home. Label every piece of luggage both inside and out. *Don't put a wallet with money in your back pocket.* Never count your money in public and carry as little as possible—keep some aside in case of an emergency. If you carry a purse, buy a sturdy one with a secure clasp, and carry it crosswise on the side, away from the street with the clasp against you. Secure packs with small combination padlocks which slip through the two zippers. A **money belt** is the best way to carry cash; you can buy one at most camping supply stores. A nylon, zippered pouch with a belt that sits inside the waist of your pants or skirt combines convenience and security. A **neck pouch** is equally safe, although far less accessible and discreet. Valuables in a fanny pack will most likely be stolen.

CON ARTISTS & PICKPOCKETS. Among the more colorful fixtures of large cities are **con artists.** Con artists and hustlers often work in groups, and children are among the most effective. Con artists possess an innumerable range of ruses. Be aware of certain classics: sob stories that require money, rolls of bills "found" on the street, mustard spilled (or saliva spit) onto your shoulder, directions asked—all distracting you for enough time to snatch your bag. Try to rent a car with a phone so you can call the police; be careful when driving, and if you get bumped, be wary. In general, if you are harassed, do not respond or make eye contact, walk away quickly, and keep a solid grip on your belongings. Contact the police if a hustler is particularly insistent or aggressive.

In city crowds and especially on public transportation, **pickpockets** are amazingly deft at their craft. Rush hour is no excuse for strangers to press up against you on the subway. If someone stands uncomfortably close, move to another car and hold your bags tightly. Also, be alert in public telephone booths. If you must say your calling card number, do so very quietly; if you punch it in, make sure no one can look over your shoulder. The same applies to ATMs—make sure no one is looking over your shoulder when you enter your PIN. If at all possible, try to avoid using ATMs at night.

ACCOMMODATIONS & TRANSPORTATION. Never leave your belongings unattended; crime occurs in even the most demure-looking hostel or hotel. If you feel unsafe, look for places with either a curfew or a night attendant. *Let's Go* lists locker availability in hostels and train stations, but you'll need your own **padlock.** Lockers are useful if you plan on sleeping outdoors or don't want to lug everything with you, but don't store valuables in them. Most hotels also provide lock boxes free or for a minimal fee.

Be particularly careful on **buses;** carry your backpack in front of you, avoid checking baggage, and don't trust anyone to "watch your bag for a second." Thieves thrive on **trains;** professionals wait for tourists to fall asleep and then carry off everything they can. When traveling in pairs, sleep in alternating shifts; when alone, use good judgment in selecting a train compartment: never stay in an empty one, and use a lock to secure your pack to the luggage rack. Keep important documents and other valuables on your person.

If you travel by **car,** try not to leave valuable possessions—such as radios or luggage—in it while you are away. If your tape deck or radio is removable, hide it in the trunk or take it with you. If it isn't, at least conceal it under something else. Similarly, hide baggage in the trunk—although savvy thieves can tell if a car is heavily loaded by the way it sits on its tires.

Drivers should take necessary precautions against **carjacking,** which has become one of the most frequent crimes committed in the US. Carjackers, who are usually armed, approach their victims in their vehicles and force them to turn over the automobile. Carjackers prey on cars parked on the side of the road and cars stopped at red lights. If you are going to pull over on the side of the road, keep your doors locked and windows up at all times. Don't pull over to help a car in the breakdown lane; call the police instead. For info on the perils of **hitchhiking,** see p. 82.

DRUGS & ALCOHOL

In the US, the drinking age is 21; in Canada it is 19, except in Alberta, Manitoba, and Québec, where it is 18. Drinking restrictions are particularly strict in the

US; the youthful should expect to be asked to show government-issued identification when purchasing any alcoholic beverage. Drinking and driving is prohibited everywhere, not to mention dangerous and idiotic. Open beverage containers in your car will incur heavy fines; a failed breathalyzer test will mean fines, a suspended license, imprisonment, or all three. Most localities restrict where and when alcohol can be sold. Sales usually stop at a certain time at night and are often prohibited entirely on Sundays.

Narcotics like marijuana, heroin, and cocaine are highly illegal in the US and Canada. If you carry prescription drugs while you travel, it is important that you keep a copy of the prescription with you, especially at border crossings.

HEALTH

Common sense is the simplest prescription for good health. Travelers complain most often about their feet and their gut, so take precautionary measures: drink lots of fluids to prevent dehydration and constipation, wear sturdy, broken-in shoes and clean socks, and use talcum powder to keep your feet dry. To minimize the effects of jet lag, "reset" your body's clock by adopting the time of your destination as soon as you board the plane. It also helps to avoid caffeine and alcohol on the flight; stick to water instead.

BEFORE YOU GO

Preparation can help minimize the likelihood of contracting a disease and maximize the chances of receiving effective health care in the event of an emergency. For minor health problems, bring a compact **first-aid kit** (see p. 48). In your **passport,** write the names of any people you wish to be contacted in case of a medical emergency and list any **allergies** or medical conditions you would want doctors to be aware of. Allergy sufferers might want to obtain a full supply of any necessary medication before the trip. Matching a prescription to a foreign equivalent is not always easy, safe, or possible. Carry up-to-date, legible prescriptions or a statement from your doctor stating the medication's trade name, manufacturer, chemical name, and dosage. While traveling, be sure to keep all medication with you in your carry-on luggage.

IMMUNIZATIONS AND PRECAUTIONS

Travelers over two years old should be sure that the following vaccines are up to date: MMR (for measles, mumps, and rubella); DTaP or Td (for diptheria, tetanus, and pertussis), OPV (for polio), HbCV (for haemophilus influenza B), and HBV (for hepatitis B).

USEFUL ORGANIZATIONS & PUBLICATIONS

The **US Centers for Disease Control and Prevention,** or **CDC** (☎877-394-8747; www.cdc.gov/travel), is an excellent source of info for travelers, and maintains an international fax info service. The CDC's comprehensive booklet *Health Information for International Travelers*, an annual rundown of disease, immunization, and general health advice, is free on the web site or $22 via the Government Printing Office (☎202-512-1800). The **US State Department** (http://travel.state.gov) compiles Consular Information Sheets on health, entry requirements, and other issues for various countries. The **British Foreign and Commonwealth Office** also gives health warnings for individual countries (www.fco.gov.uk).

MEDICAL ASSISTANCE ON THE ROAD

The quality of health care in the US and Canada is very good. Before you leave, make sure you have some sort of travel insurance. Medicare (for US citizens in Canada) and most health insurance plans cover members' medical emergencies during trips abroad, but you should check with your insurance carrier to be sure. Occasionally insurance companies will require you to purchase additional coverage (see **Insurance,** p. 47).

ONCE IN THE US AND CANADA

ENVIRONMENTAL HAZARDS

Heat exhaustion and dehydration: Heat exhaustion, characterized by dehydration and salt deficiency, can lead to fatigue, headaches, and wooziness. Avoid it by drinking plenty of fluids (enough to keep your urine clear) and eating salty foods. Wear a hat, sunglasses, and a lightweight longsleeve shirt in hot sun, and take time to acclimate to a hot destination before seriously exerting yourself. Continuous heat stress can eventually lead to **heatstroke,** characterized by rising body temperature, severe headache, and cessation of sweating. Heatstroke victims must be cooled off with wet towels and taken to a doctor as soon as possible. The risks of heat exhaustion and dehydration are very high in the Southwest and in the desert.

Sunburn: If you're prone to sunburn, bring sunscreen with you. Apply it liberally and often to avoid burns and risk of skin cancer. If you are planning on spending time near water, in the desert, or in the snow, you are at risk of getting burned, even through clouds. If you get sunburned, drink more fluids than usual and apply Calamine or an aloe-based lotion.

Hypothermia and frostbite: A rapid drop in body temperature is the clearest warning sign of overexposure to cold. Victims may shiver, feel exhausted, have poor coordination or slurred speech, hallucinate, or suffer amnesia. Seek medical help, and *do not let hypothermia victims fall asleep*—their body temperature will continue to drop and they may die. To avoid hypothermia, keep dry, wear layers, and stay out of the wind. In wet weather, wool and synthetics such as pile retain heat. Most other fabric, especially cotton, will make you colder. When the temperature is below freezing, watch for **frostbite.** If a region of skin turns white, waxy, and cold, do not rub the area. Drink warm beverages, get dry, and slowly warm the area with dry fabric or steady body contact, until a doctor can be found.

High altitude: Travelers to high altitudes (e.g. the Rocky Mountains) must allow their bodies a couple of days to adjust to lower oxygen levels in the air before exerting themselves. Note that alcohol is more potent at high elevations.

INSECT-BORNE DISEASES

Many diseases are transmitted by insects—mainly mosquitoes, fleas, ticks, and lice. Be aware of insects in wet or forested areas, especially while hiking and camping. Mosquitoes are most active from dusk to dawn. Wear long pants and long sleeves, tuck your pants into your socks, and buy a mosquito net. Use insect repellents, such as DEET, and soak or spray your gear with permethrin (licensed in the US for use on clothing). Consider natural repellents like vitamin B-12 or garlic pills. To stop the itch after being bitten, try Calamine lotion or topical cortisones (like Cortaid), or take a bath with a half-cup of baking soda or oatmeal. Ticks—responsible for Lyme and other diseases—can be particularly dangerous in rural and forested regions. They are most common in the Northeast, the Great Lakes region, and the Pacific Northwest. Pause periodically while walking to brush off ticks using a fine-toothed comb on your neck and scalp. Do not try to remove ticks by burning them or coating them with nail polish remover or petroleum jelly.

Lyme disease: A bacterial infection carried by ticks and marked by a circular bull's-eye rash of 2 in. or more. Later symptoms include fever, headache, fatigue, and aches and pains. Antibiotics are effective if administered early. Left untreated, Lyme can cause problems in joints, the heart, and the nervous system. If you find a tick attached to your skin, grasp the head with tweezers as close to your skin as possible and apply slow, steady traction. Removing a tick within 24 hours greatly reduces the risk of infection.

FOOD- AND WATERBORNE DISEASES

Travelers in the US and Canada experience food- and water-related illness much less often than in most parts of the world, thanks to good water-treatment facilities and fairly well-maintained restaurant standards. The tap water in the US and Canada is treated to be safe for drinking.

Traveler's diarrhea: Results from drinking untreated water or eating uncooked foods; a temporary (and fairly common) reaction to the bacteria in new food ingredients. Symptoms include nausea, bloating, urgency, and malaise. Try quick-energy, non-sugary foods with protein and carbohydrates to keep your strength up. Over-the-counter anti-diarrheals (e.g. Imodium) may counteract the problems, but can complicate serious infections. The most dangerous side effect is dehydration; drink 8 oz. of water with ½ tsp. of sugar or honey and a pinch of salt, try uncaffeinated soft drinks, or munch on salted crackers. If you develop a fever or your symptoms don't go away after 4-5 days, consult a doctor. Consult a doctor for treatment of diarrhea in children.

Hepatitis A: A viral infection of the liver acquired primarily through contaminated water. Symptoms include fatigue, fever, loss of appetite, nausea, dark urine, jaundice, vomiting, aches and pains, and light stools. The risk is highest in rural areas and the countryside, but it is also present in urban areas. Ask your doctor about the vaccine (Havrix or Vaqta) or an injection of immune globulin (IG; formerly called gamma globulin).

Parasites: Giardiasis is present in the untreated water from streams or lakes and causes a very uncomfortable and difficult to treat intestinal disease. Drink only tap water, including public water fountains and campground pumps. If you are backpacking, carry water with you or use a water filter.

OTHER INFECTIOUS DISEASES

Rabies: Transmitted through the saliva of infected animals; fatal if untreated. By the time symptoms appear (thirst and muscle spasms), the disease is in its terminal stage. If you are bitten, wash the wound thoroughly, seek immediate medical care, and try to have the animal located. A rabies vaccine, which consists of 3 shots given over a 21-day period, is available but is only semi-effective.

Hepatitis B: A viral infection of the liver transmitted via bodily fluids or needle-sharing. Symptoms may not surface until years after infection. Vaccinations are recommended for health-care workers, sexually active travelers, and anyone planning to seek medical treatment abroad. The 3-shot vaccination series must begin 6 months before traveling.

Hepatitis C: Like hep B, but the mode of transmission differs. IV drug users, those with occupational exposure to blood, hemodialysis patients, and recipients of blood transfusions are at the highest risk, but the disease can also be spread through sexual contact or sharing items like razors and toothbrushes that may have traces of blood on them.

AIDS, HIV, & STDS

Acquired Immune Deficiency Syndrome (AIDS) is a growing problem around the world. The World Health Organization estimates that there are 30 million people infected with HIV, and women now comprise 40% of all new infections. In recent years, however, the spread of the disease has been markedly curbed in the US, though more than 900,000 Americans may be infected with HIV. The easiest mode of HIV transmission is through direct blood-to-blood contact with an HIV positive person; *never* share intravenous drug, tattooing, or other needles. A more common mode of transmission is sexual intercourse; wear a condom.

For more info on AIDS, call the **US Centers for Disease Control's** 24hr. hotline at 800-342-2437, or contact the **Joint United Nations Programme on HIV/AIDS (UNAIDS),** 20 av. Appia 20, CH-1211 Geneva 27, Switzerland (☎41 22 791 36 66, fax 22 791 41 87). The Council on International Educational Exchange's pamphlet, Travel Safe: AIDS and International Travel, is posted on their web site (www.ciee.org/Isp/safety/travelsafe.htm), along with links to other online and phone resources. If you are **HIV positive,** contact the Bureau of Consular Affairs, #4811, Department of State, Washington, D.C. 20520 (☎202-647-1488; fax 647-6074; http://travel.state.gov). According to US law, HIV positive persons are not permitted to enter the US. However, HIV testing is conducted only for those who are planning to immigrate permanently. Travelers from areas with particularly high concentrations of HIV positive persons or persons with AIDS may be required to provide more info when applying. Travelers to Canada who are suspected of being HIV positive will be required to submit to HIV testing.

Sexually transmitted diseases (STDs) such as gonorrhea, chlamydia, genital warts, syphilis, and herpes are easier to catch than HIV, and some can be just as deadly. **Hepatitis B** and **C** are also serious sexually transmitted diseases (see above). Warning signs for STDs include: swelling, sores, bumps, or blisters on sex organs, rectum, or mouth; burning and pain during urination and bowel movements; itching around sex organs; swelling or redness in the throat; fever, chills, and aches. If these symptoms develop, see a doctor immediately. Condoms may protect you from certain STDs, but oral or even tactile contact can lead to transmission.

INSURANCE

Travel insurance generally covers four basic areas: medical/health problems, property loss, trip cancellation/interruption, and emergency evacuation. Although your regular insurance policies may well extend to travel-related accidents, you may consider purchasing travel insurance if the cost of potential trip cancellation/interruption is greater than you can absorb.

Medical insurance (especially university policies) often covers costs incurred abroad; check with your provider. Medicare covers travel to Canada. Canadians are protected by their home province's health insurance plan for up to 90 days after leaving the country; check with the provincial Ministry of Health or Health Plan Headquarters for details. **Homeowners' insurance** (or your family's coverage) often covers theft during travel and loss of travel documents (passport, plane ticket, railpass, etc.) up to $500.

ISIC and **ITIC** provide basic insurance benefits, including $100 per day of in-hospital sickness for a maximum of 60 days, $3000 of accident-related medical reimbursement, and $25,000 for emergency medical transport (see **Identification,** p. 36). Cardholders have access to a toll-free 24hr. helpline whose multilingual staff can provide assistance in medical, legal, and financial emergencies overseas (US and Canada ☎877-370-4742, elsewhere call US collect +1 715-345-0505). **American Express** (☎800-528-4800) grants most cardholders automatic car rental insurance (collision and theft, but not liability) and ground travel accident coverage of $100,000 on flight purchases made with the card.

Prices for travel insurance purchased separately generally run about $50 per week for full coverage, while trip cancellation/interruption may be purchased separately at a rate of about $5.50 per $100 of coverage.

INSURANCE PROVIDERS. Council and **STA** (see p. 71) offer a range of plans to supplement insurance coverage. Other private insurance providers in the **US** and **Canada** include: **Access America** (☎800-284-8300; fax 804-673-1491); **Berkely/Carefree Travel Insurance** (☎800-323-3149 or 516-294-0220; fax 516-294-1821; info@berkely.com; www.berkely.com); **Globalcare Travel Insurance** (☎800-821-2488; fax 781-592-7720; www.globalcare-cocco.com); and **Travel Assistance International** (☎800-821-2828 or 317-818-2099; fax 317-575-2659; www.travelassistance.com). Providers in the **UK** include **Campus Travel** (☎01865 258 000) and **Columbus Travel Insurance** (☎020 7375 0011). In **Australia**, try **CIC Insurance** (☎9202 8000). In **Australia**, try **CIC Insurance** (☎02 9202 8000; fax 9202 8220).

PACKING

Pack according to the extremes of climate you may experience and the type of travel you'll be doing. Pack light: a good rule is to lay out only what you absolutely need, then take half the clothes and twice the money. The less you have, the less you have to lose (or store, or carry on your back). Any extra space left will be useful for any souvenirs or items you might pick up along the way. Don't forget the obvious things: no matter when you're traveling, it's always a good idea to bring a **warm jacket** or wool sweater, a **rain jacket** (Gore-Tex® is both waterproof and breathable), sturdy shoes or **hiking boots,** and **thick socks. Flip-flops** or waterproof sandals are must-haves for grubby hostel showers. You may also want to add one outfit beyond the jeans and t-shirt uniform, and maybe a nicer pair of shoes if you have the room. Remember that wool will keep you warm even when soaked through, whereas wet cotton is colder than wearing nothing at all.

SLEEPSACKS. Some youth hostels require that you have your own sleepsack or rent one of theirs. If you plan to stay in hostels you can avoid linen charges by making the requisite sleepsack yourself: fold a full size sheet in half the long way, then sew it closed along the open long side and one of the short sides. Sleepsacks can also be bought at any Hostelling International store.

WASHING CLOTHES. Laundromats are common in North America, but it may be cheaper and easier to use a sink. Bring a small bar or tube of detergent soap, a small rubber ball to stop up the sink, and a travel clothesline.

CONVERTERS AND ADAPTERS. In the US and Canada, electricity is 110V. 220V electrical appliances don't like 110V current. Visit a hardware store for an adapter (which changes the shape of the plug) and a converter (which changes the voltage). Don't make the mistake of using only an adapter (unless appliance instructions explicitly state otherwise).

TOILETRIES. Toothbrushes, towels, cold-water soap, talcum powder (to keep feet dry), deodorant, razors, tampons, and condoms are readily available. **Contact lenses,** on the other hand, can be expensive, so bring enough extra pairs and solution for your entire trip. Machines that heat-disinfect contact lenses will require a small converter (about $20) to 110V; consider switching temporarily to a chemical disinfection system. Also bring your glasses and a copy of your prescription in case you need emergency replacements.

FILM. If you're not a serious photographer, you might want to consider bringing a **disposable camera** or two rather than an expensive permanent one. Despite disclaimers, airport security X-rays *can* fog film, so either buy a lead-lined pouch, sold at camera stores, or ask the security to hand inspect it. Always pack it in your carry-on luggage, since higher-intensity X-rays are used on checked luggage.

FIRST-AID KIT. No matter how you're traveling, it's always a good idea to carry a first-aid kit including bandages, aspirin or another pain killer, antibiotic cream, a thermometer, a Swiss army knife with tweezers, moleskin, decongestant for colds, motion sickness remedy, medicine for diarrhea or stomach problems (Pepto Bismol and Imodium), sunscreen, insect repellent (you might want to get an extra-strength repellent if you plan on camping), burn ointment, and a syringe for emergency medical purposes (get an explanatory letter from your doctor).

OTHER USEFUL ITEMS. For safety purposes, you should bring a **money belt** and small **padlock.** Basic **outdoors equipment** (plastic water bottle, compass, waterproof matches, pocketknife, sunglasses, sunscreen, hat) may also prove useful. **Quick repairs** of torn garments can be done on the road with a needle and thread; also consider bringing electrical tape for patching tears. Other useful items include: an umbrella; sealable plastic bags (for damp clothes, soap, food, shampoo, and other spillables); alarm clock; safety pins; rope (makeshift clothesline and lashing material); towel; rubber bands; flashlight; cold-water soap; earplugs; tweezers; garbage bags; a small calculator for currency conversion; a pair of flip-flops for the shower.

IMPORTANT DOCUMENTS. Don't forget your passport, traveler's checks, ATM and/or credit cards, and adequate ID (see p. 45). Also check that you have a hostelling membership card (see p. 51) and a driver's license (see p. 78), if you need them.

ACCOMMODATIONS

HOTELS

Hotel rooms in the US vary widely in cost depending on the region in which the hotel is located. The cheapest hotel single in the Northeast would run about $60 per night, while it is possible to stay for $30 a night in a comparable hotel in the South, West, or Midwest regions. The most reliable national budget chains include Motel 6, Super 8, and Econolodge.

ESSENTIALS

HOTEL CHAIN	TELEPHONE	HOTEL CHAIN	TELEPHONE
Best Western	☎800-780-7234	La Quinta Inn	☎800-531-5900
Comfort Inn	☎800-228-5150	Motel 6	☎800-466-8356
Days Inn	☎800-325-2525	Ramada Inn	☎800-272-6232
Econolodge	☎800-446-6900	Red Carpet Inn	☎800-251-1962
Embassy Suites Hotel	☎800-362-2779	Select Inn	☎800-641-1000
Hampton Inn	☎800-426-7866	Sleep Inn	☎800-221-2222
Hilton Hotel	☎800-445-8667	Super 8 Motel	☎800-800-8000
Holiday Inn	☎800-465-4329	Travelodge	☎800 255 3050
Howard Johnson	☎800-654-2000	YMCA	☎800-922-9622

ESSENTIALS

Hotels tend to be more expensive with proximity to tourist attractions or cities. The best bargains are usually located on the outskirts of a city, typically on a busy road such as an interstate. Almost all hotels in the US take reservations, and for busy seasons they are highly recommended. Note that busy seasons can also mean an increase in the average price for any available hotel room.

HOSTELS

Hostels are generally dorm-style accommodations, often in single-sex large rooms with bunk beds, although some hostels do offer private rooms for families and couples. They sometimes have kitchens and utensils for your use, bike or moped rentals, storage areas, and laundry facilities. There can be drawbacks: some hostels close during certain daytime "lock-out" hours, have a curfew, don't accept reservations, impose a maximum stay, or, less frequently, require that you do chores. In the US and Canada, a bed in a hostel will average around $15.

For their various services and lower rates at member hostels, hostelling associations, especially **Hostelling International (HI),** can definitely be worth joining. HI hostels are scattered throughout both countries, and many accept reservations via the International Booking Network (Australia ☎02 9261 1111, Canada ☎800-663-5777, England and Wales ☎1629 58 14 18, N. Ireland ☎1232 32 47 33, Ireland ☎01 830 1766, New Zealand ☎09 379 4224, Scotland ☎8701 55 32 55, US ☎800-909-4776; www.hiayh.org/ushostel/reserva/ibn3.htm) for a nominal fee. HI's umbrella organization's web page (www.iyhf.org) lists the web addresses and phone numbers of all national associations and can be a great place to research hostelling in a specific region. Other comprehensive hostelling web sites include www.hostels.com and www.hostelbooking.com. To join HI, contact one of the following organizations:

Australian Youth Hostels Association (AYHA), 10 Mallett St., 3rd fl., Camperdown NSW 2050 (☎02 9565 1699; fax 9565 1325; www.yha.org.au). AUS$52, under 18 AUS$16.

Hostelling International-Canada (HI-C), 400-205 Catherine St., Ottawa, ON K2P 1C3 (☎800-663-5777 or 613-237-7884; fax 237-7868; info@hostellingintl.ca; www.hostellingintl.ca). CDN$35, under 18 free.

An Óige (Irish Youth Hostel Association), 61 Mountjoy St., Dublin 7 (☎01 830 4555; fax 830 5808; anoige@iol.ie; www.irelandyha.org). IR£10/€12.70, under 18 IR£4/€5.08.

Youth Hostels Association of New Zealand (YHANZ), P.O. Box 436, 193 Cashel St., 3rd Floor Union House, Christchurch 1 (☎03 379 9970; fax 365 4476; info@yha.org.nz; www.yha.org.nz). NZ$40, under 17 free.

Hostels Association of South Africa, 3rd fl. 73 St. George's St. Mall, P.O. Box 4402, Cape Town 8000 (☎021 424 2511; fax 424 4119; info@hisa.org.za; www.hisa.org.za). ZAR45.

Scottish Youth Hostels Association (SYHA), 7 Glebe Crescent, Stirling FK8 2JA (☎01786 89 14 00; fax 89 13 33; www.syha.org.uk). UK£6.

Youth Hostels Association (England and Wales) Ltd., Trevelyan House, 8 St. Stephen's Hill, St. Albans, Hertfordshire AL1 2DY, UK (☎0870 870 8808; fax 01727 84 41 26; www.yha.org.uk). UK£12.50, under 18 UK£6.25, families UK£25.

Hostelling International Northern Ireland (HINI), 22-32 Donegall Rd., Belfast BT12 5JN, Northern Ireland (☎02890 31 54 35; fax 43 96 99; info@hini.org.uk; www.hini.org.uk). UK£10, under 18 UK£6.

Hostelling International-American Youth Hostels (HI-AYH), 733 15th St. NW, #840, Washington, D.C. 20005 (☎202-783-6161; fax 783-6171; hiayhserv@hiayh.org; www.hiayh.org). $25, under 18 free.

BED AND BREAKFASTS

For a cozy alternative to hotel rooms, B&Bs (private homes with rooms available to travelers) range from the acceptable to the sublime. Hosts will sometimes go out of their way to be accommodating by accepting travelers with pets, giving personalized tours, or offering home-cooked meals. On the other hand, many B&Bs do not provide phones, TVs, or private bathrooms. Rooms in B&Bs generally cost $50-70 for a single and $70-90 for a double. For more info see Nerd World's Bed and Breakfasts by Region (www.nerdworld.com/users/dstein/nw854) or try **Bed & Breakfast Central Information (BBCI)**, P.O. Box 38279, Colorado Springs, CO 80937 (fax 719-471-4740; bbci@bbonline.com; www.bbonline.com/bbci). The National Network of Bed and Breakfast Reservations Services (TNN) provides links to booking agencies for each US state and certain regions of Canada (www.go-lodging.com).

YMCA AND YWCAS

Not all **Young Men's Christian Association (YMCA)** locations offer lodging; those that do are often located in urban downtowns, which can be convenient but a little gritty. YMCA rates are usually lower than a hotel's but higher than a hostel's and may include TV, air conditioning, pools, gyms, access to public transportation, tourist info, safe deposit boxes, luggage storage, daily housekeeping, multilingual staff, and 24hr. security. Many YMCAs accept women and families (group rates often available), and some will not lodge people under 18 without parental permission. There are several ways to make a reservation, all of which must be made at least two weeks in advance and paid for in advance with a traveler's check, US money order, certified check, Visa, or Mastercard in US dollars.

YMCA of the USA, 101 North Wacker Dr., Chicago, IL 60606 (☎888-333-9622; fax 312-977-0031; www.ymca.net). A listing of the nearly 2400 Ys across the US and info on prices, services available, phone numbers and addresses; no reservation service.

YMCA Canada, 42 Charles St., 6th fl., Toronto ON M4Y 1T4 (☎416-967-9622; fax 967-9618; services@ymca.ca; www.ymca.ca), offers info on Ys throughout Canada.

YWCA of the USA, Empire State Building, 350 Fifth Avenue, #301, New York, NY 10118 (☎212-273-7800; fax 465-2281; www.ywca.org). Publishes a directory ($8) on YWCAs across the US.

DORMS

Many **colleges and universities** open their residence halls to travelers when school is not in session (May-Sept.)—some do so even during term-time. These dorms are often close to student areas—good sources for info on things to do—and are usually very clean. Getting a room may take a couple of phone calls and require advanced planning, but rates tend to be low, and many offer free local calls. *Let's Go* lists colleges which rent dorm rooms among accommodations listings.

HOME EXCHANGES AND HOME RENTALS

Home exchange offers the traveler various types of homes (houses, apartments, condominiums), plus the opportunity to live like a native and to cut down on accommodation fees. For more info, contact **HomeExchange.Com** (☎805-898-9660; www.homeexchange.com), **Intervac International Home Exchange** (☎800-756-4663; www.intervac.com), or **The Invented City: International Home Exchange** (US ☎800-788-2489, elsewhere call 415-252-1141; www.aitec.edu.au/~bwechner/Documents/Travel/Lists/HomeExchangeClubs.html). Home rentals are more expensive than

ESSENTIALS

NEW CENTRAL HOSTEL

250-bed hostel open all year
bunks and large doubles with regular mattresses • 4 beds per room, private
rooms smoking and nonsmoking rooms

$20*

*per night (depending on bed and season)
travelers' check, VISA, MasterCard accepted
passport and travel documents requested • no membership required

pillows with cases, sheets and blankets provided
laundry • full kitchen
fax service • locker and safety deposit boxes

Check in: 24 hours a day • Check out: by 11 a.m.
No curfew • Parties / social activities

NEW CENTRAL HOSTEL
1412 Market Street
San Francisco, CA 94102
(415) 703-9988
Fax: (415) 703-9986

☐ **Shared Accommodations**
☐ **Double Rooms**
☐ **Private Rooms**
☐ **Free linen, kitchen**
☐ **Weekly Rates**

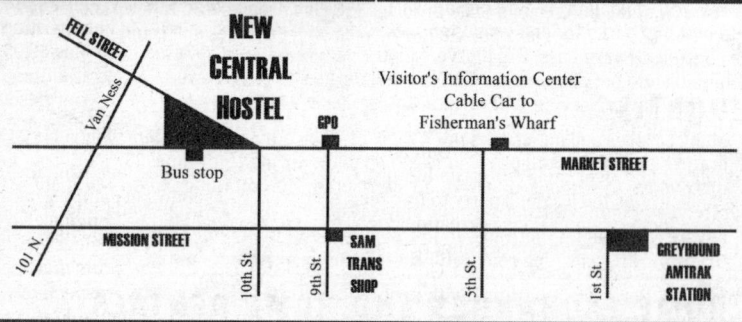

Transportation: city bus stops at front door
Attractions: Fisherman's Wharf, Haight-Ashbury, Union Square, Civic Center,
Golden Gate Bridge and Park, Alcatraz, Cable Cars, restaurants, shopping,
major museums and art galleries, bars, pubs and clubs

Visitor's Information Center, Post Office, hospital and downtown areas are all
within walking distance

exchanges, but they can be cheaper than comparable hotels. Both home exchanges and rentals are ideal for families with children, or travelers with special dietary needs; you often get your own kitchen, maid service, TV, and telephones.

FURTHER READING: ACCOMMODATIONS

Campus Lodging Guide (18th Ed.). B&J Publications ($15).

The Complete Guide to Bed and Breakfasts, Inns and Guesthouses in the US, Canada, and Worldwide, Pamela Lanier. Ten Speed Press ($17).

CAMPING AND THE OUTDOORS

Camping is probably the most rewarding way to slash travel costs. Considering the sheer number of public lands available for camping in both the United States and Canada, it may also be the most convenient option. Well-equipped campsites (usually including prepared tent sites, toilets, and water) go for $5-25 per night in the US and CDN$10-30 in Canada. **Backcountry camping,** which lacks all of the above amenities, is often free, but can cost up to $20 at some national parks. In general, the more popular the wilderness region, the better-equipped and the more expensive the campsites. Most campsites are first come first served, though a few accept reservations, usually for a small fee. Outside of national parks, the ubiquitous **Kampgrounds of America (KOA)** offer a ritzy kamping experience at a premium. All of the comforts of home go for about $20-30 a night for a tent site. It is not legal or safe to camp on the side of the road, even on public lands; *Let's Go* lists areas where dispersed roadside camping is permitted.

NATIONAL PARKS

National Parks protect some of the most spectacular scenery in North America (see p. 4). Though their primary purpose is preservation, the parks also host recreational activities such as ranger talks, guided hikes, marked trails, skiing, and snowshoe expeditions. For info, contact the **National Park Service,** Office of Public Inquiries, 1849 C St. NW, #1013, Washington, D.C. 20240 (☎202-208-4747). The slick and informative web page (www.nps.gov) lists info on all the parks, detailed maps, and fee and reservation data. The **National Park Foundation,** 1101 17th St. NW, #1102, Washington, D.C. 20066 (☎202-785-4500) distributes *The Complete Guide to America's National Parks* by mail-order ($16, plus $3 shipping); a guide to national parks is available online at www.nationalparks.org.

Entrance fees vary. The larger and more popular parks charge a $4-20 entry fee for cars and sometimes a $2-7 fee for pedestrians and cyclists. The **National Parks Pass** ($50), available at park entrances, allows the passport-holder's party entry into all national parks for one year. National Parks Passes can also be bought by writing to National Parks Pass, 27540 Ave. Mentry Valencia, CA 91355 (send $50 plus $3.95 shipping and handling) or on the National Parks Service web site. For an additional $15, the Parks Service will affix a **Golden Eagle Passport** hologram to your card, which will allow you access to sites managed by the US Fish and Wildlife Service, the US Forest Service, and the Bureau of Land Management. US citizens or residents 62 and over qualify for the lifetime **Golden Age Passport** ($10 one-time fee), which entitles the holder's party to free park entry, a 50% discount on camping, and 50% reductions on various recreational fees for the passport holder. Persons eligible for federal benefits on account of disabilities can enjoy the same privileges with the **Golden Access Passport** (free). Golden Age and Golden Access Passports must be purchased at a park entrance with proof of age or federal eligibility, respectively. All passports (not the Parks Pass) are also valid at National Monuments, Forests, Wildlife Preserves, and other national recreation sites.

Most national parks have both backcountry and developed **camping;** some welcome RVs, and a few offer grand lodges. At the more popular parks in the US and Canada, reservations are essential, available through MISTIX (☎619-452-8787 or 800-365-2267; http://reservations.nps.gov) no more than five months in advance. Indoor accommodations should be reserved months in advance. Campgrounds often observe first come, first served policies, and many fill up by late morning. Some limit your stay and/or the number of people in a group.

NATIONAL FORESTS

Often less accessible and less crowded, **US National Forests** (www.fs.fed.us) are a purist's alternative to parks. While some have recreation facilities, most are equipped only for primitive camping—pit toilets and no water are the norm. Entrance fees, when charged, are $10-20, but camping is generally free or $3-4. Some specially designated wilderness areas have regulations barring all vehicles. Necessary wilderness permits for backpackers can be obtained at the US Forest Service field office in the area. If you are interested in exploring a National Forest, *The Guide to Your National Forests* is available at all Forest Service branches, or call or write the main office (USDA, Forest Service, Office of Communications, Sydney R. Yates Bldg., 201 14th St. SW, Washington, D.C. 20050; ☎202-720-5881; fax 205-0885). This booklet includes a list of all national forest addresses; request maps and other info directly from the forest(s) you plan to visit. Reservations, with a one-time $16.50 service fee, are available for most forests, but are usually only needed during high season at the more popular sites. Write or call up to one year in advance to National Recreation Reservation Center, P.O. Box 900, Cumberland, MD 21501 (☎518-885-3639 or 800-280-2267; fax 301-722-9802; www.reserveusa.com).

CANADA'S NATIONAL PARKS

Less trammeled than their southern counterparts, these parks boast at least as much natural splendor. Park entrance fees range from CDN$3-7 per person, with family and multi-day passes available. Reservations are offered for a limited number of campgrounds with a CDN$7 fee. For these reservations, or for info on the over 40 parks and countless historical sites in the network, call Parks Canada, 25 Edy St., Hull, QC KIA OM5 (☎888-773-8888), or consult the useful web page (http://parkscanada.pch.gc.ca). A patchwork of regional passes are available at relevant parks; the best is the Western Canada Pass, which covers admission to all the parks in the Western provinces for a year (CDN$35 per adult, CDN$70 per group—up to seven people).

USEFUL PUBLICATIONS & RESOURCES

A variety of publishing companies offer hiking guidebooks to meet the educational needs of novice or expert. For information about camping, hiking, and biking, write or call the publishers listed below to receive a free catalog.

Automobile Association, A.A. Publishing. Orders and enquiries to TBS Frating Distribution Centre, Colchester, Essex CO7 7DW, UK (☎01206 25 56 78; www.theaa.co.uk).

Family Campers and RVers/National Campers and Hikers Association, Inc., 4804 Transit Rd., Bldg. #2, Depew, NY 14043 (☎/fax 716-668-6242). Membership fee ($25) includes their publication *Camping Today*.

Sierra Club Books, 85 Second St., 2nd fl., San Francisco, CA 94105 (☎415-977-5500; www.sierraclub.org/books). Publishes general resource books on hiking, camping, and women traveling in the outdoors, as well as books on hiking in Arizona, Florida, Arkansas, the Rockies, the California Desert, and hikes of northern California. All run $10-16.

The Mountaineers Books, 1001 SW Klickitat Way, #201, Seattle, WA 98134 (☎800-553-4453 or 206-223-6303; www.mountaineersbooks.org). Over 400 titles on hiking, biking, mountaineering, natural history, and conservation.

Wilderness Press, 1200 Fifth St., Berkeley, CA 94710 (☎800-443-7227 or 510-558-1666; www.wildernesspress.com). Over 100 hiking guides/maps, mostly for the western US.

Woodall Publications Corporation, 2575 Vista Del Mar Dr., Ventura, CA 93001, USA (☎800-323-9076 or 805-667-4100; www.woodalls.com). Woodall publishes the annually updated *Woodall's Campground Directory* ($22) as well as *Woodall's Campground Directory: Western Edition* ($15) and the *Camping Guide to the Far West* ($6).

For topographical maps of Canada, write the **Center for Topographic Information,** Canada Map Office, 130 Bentley Ave., Nepean, ON K1A 0E9 (☎613-952-7000 or 800-465-6277; http://maps.NRCan.gc.ca). In the US, contact the **US Geological Survey Information Services,** Box 25286, Denver CO 80225 (☎800-435-7627; http://mapping.usgs.gov/mac/findmaps.html).

WILDERNESS SAFETY

THE GREAT OUTDOORS. Stay warm, stay dry, and stay hydrated. The vast majority of life-threatening wilderness situations result from a breach of this simple dictum. On any hike, however brief, you should pack enough equipment to keep you alive should disaster befall. This includes raingear, hat and mittens, a first-aid kit, a reflector, a whistle, high-energy food, and extra water. Dress in warm layers of synthetic materials designed for the outdoors, or wool. Fleece jackets and Gore-Tex raingear are excellent choices. Never rely on cotton for warmth; in the wild, this "death cloth" will be absolutely useless should it get wet. Weather can change suddenly anywhere. Check **weather forecasts** and pay attention to the sky when hiking.

Whenever possible, let someone know when and where you are hiking, either a friend, your hostel, a park ranger, or a local hiking organization. If you are hiking in an area which might be frequented by bears, ask local rangers for info on bear behavior before entering any park or wilderness area, and obey posted warnings.

 ENVIRONMENTALLY RESPONSIBLE TOURISM. The idea behind responsible tourism is to leave no trace of human presence behind. A campstove is the safer (and more efficient) way to cook than using vegetation, but if you must make a fire, keep it small and use only dead branches or brush rather than cutting vegetation. Make sure your campsite is at least 150 ft. (50m) from water supplies or bodies of water. If there are no toilet facilities, bury human waste (but not paper) at least four inches (10cm) deep and above the high-water line, and 150 ft. or more from any water supplies and campsites. Always pack your trash in a plastic bag and carry it with you until you reach the next trash receptacle. For more information on these issues, contact one of the organizations listed below.

Earthwatch, 3 Clock Tower Pl., #100, Box 75, Maynard, MA 01754 (☎800-776-0188 or 978-461-0081; info@earthwatch.org; www.earthwatch.org).

Ecotourism Society, P.O. Box 668, Burlington, VT 05402 (☎802-651-9818; eco-mail@ecotourism.org; www.ecotourism.org).

National Audobon Society, Nature Odysseys, 700 Broadway, New York, NY 10003 (☎212-979-3066; travel@audobon.org; www.audobon.org).

Tourism Concern, Stapleton House, 277-281 Holloway Rd., London N7 8HN, UK (☎020 7753 3330; www.tourismconcern.org.uk).

WILDLIFE. The US contains varied climates and wildernesses, and within these are different kinds of dangerous wildlife. If you plan on doing any sort of hiking or camping, ask local rangers for information about wildlife in the area and obey all posted warnings. For more information, check out *How to Stay Alive in the Woods*, by Bradford Angier (Macmillan Press, $8).

If you are hiking in an area that might be frequented by **bears,** keep your distance. No matter how cute bears appear, don't be fooled—they're powerful and dangerous animals. If you see a bear at a distance, calmly walk (don't run) in the other direction. If the bear pursues you, back away slowly while speaking in low, firm tones. If you are attacked by a bear, get in a fetal position to protect yourself, put your arms over your neck, and play dead. In all situations, remain calm and don't make any loud noises or sudden movements.

Poisonous **snakes** are hazards in many wilderness areas in the US and Canada and should be carefully avoided. The two most dangerous are coral and rattlesnakes. Coral snakes reside in the Southwestern US and can be identified by black, yellow, and red bands. Rattlesnakes live in desert and marsh areas and will vigorously shake the rattle at the end of their tail when threatened. Don't attempt to handle or kill a snake; if you see one, back away slowly. If you are bitten, apply a pressure bandage and ice to the wound and immobilize the limb. Seek immediate medical attention for any snakebite that breaks the skin.

Mountain regions provide the stomping grounds for **moose**. These big, antlered animals have been known to charge humans, so never feed, walk toward, or throw anything at a moose. If a moose charges, get behind a tree immediately. If it attacks you, get on the ground in a fetal position and stay very still.

CAMPERS AND RVS

Much to the chagrin of more purist outdoorspeople, the US and Canada are havens for the corpulent, home-and-stove on wheels known as **recreational vehicles (RVs).** Most national parks and small towns cater to RV travelers, providing campgrounds with large parking areas and electric outlets ("full hook-up"). Especially for older travelers or families, RVs can be a convenient way to view the continent without sacrificing independence, mobility, and creature comforts.

Renting an RV will always be more expensive than tenting or hostelling, but the costs compare favorably with the price of staying in hotels and renting a car (see **Rental Cars,** p. 83), and the convenience of bringing along your own bedroom, bathroom, and kitchen makes it an attractive option.

ORGANIZED ADVENTURE TRIPS

Organized adventure tours offer another way of exploring the wild. Activities include hiking, biking, skiing, canoeing, kayaking, rafting, and climbing. Consult tourism bureaus, which can suggest parks, trails, and outfitters. Other good sources for organized adventure options are the stores and organizations specializing in camping and outdoor equipment listed above. Sales reps at REI, EMS, or Sierra often know of a range of cheap, convenient trips. They may give training programs for people who want to have an independent trip.

Specialty Travel Index, 305 San Anselmo Ave., #313, San Anselmo, CA 94960 (☎800-442-4922; www.specialtytravel.com), is a directory listing hundreds of tour operators worldwide.

AmeriCan Adventures & Roadrunner, P.O. Box 1155, Gardena, CA 90249 (☎800-TREK-USA or 310-324-3447; www.americanadventures.com). Organizes group adventure camping and hostelling trips (with transportation and camping costs included) in the US and Canada.

The Sierra Club, 85 Second St., 2nd fl., San Francisco, CA 94105 (national.outings@sierraclub.org; www.sierraclub.org/outings), plans many adventure outings at all of its branches throughout Canada and the US.

TrekAmerica, P.O. Box 189, Rockaway, NJ 07866 (☎973-983-1144 or 800-221-0596; www.trekamerica.com), operates small group adventure tours throughout the US, including Alaska, Hawaii, and Canada. Tours are for 18- to 38-year olds and run 1-9 weeks.

Roadrunner Hostelling Treks, 9741 Canoga Ave., Chatsworth, CA 91311 (☎800-873-5872 or +44 1892 51 27 00 in Europe and the UK; www.americanadventures.com), offers inexpensive guided trips (maximum 13 travelers) in the US and Canada which include hostel stays.

KEEPING IN TOUCH

BY MAIL

SENDING MAIL TO THE US AND CANADA

Envelopes should be marked "air mail" or "par avion" to avoid having letters sent by sea.

Australia: Allow 4-6 business days for regular **airmail** to the US; 5-7 work days to Canada. Postcards cost AUS\$1; letters up to 50g cost AUS\$1.50; packages up to ½kg AUS\$11.50, up to 2kg AUS\$40. **EMS** can get a letter to the US or Canada in 2-5 work days for AUS\$30. www.auspost.com.au/pac.

Ireland: Allow 4-6 business days for regular airmail to the US and Canada. Postcards and letters up to 25g cost IR£0.45/€0.57. Add IR£2.30/€2.92 for Swiftpost International. www.anpost.ie.

New Zealand: Allow 4-10 business days for regular airmail to the US and Canada. Postcards NZ$1.50. Letters up to 200g cost NZ$2.50-5; small parcels up to 0.5kg NZ$12.80, up to 2kg NZ$40.20. www.nzpost.co.nz/nzpost/inrates.

UK: Allow 4-6 business days for airmail to the US and Canada. Letters up to 20g cost UK£0.65; packages up to 0.5kg UK£4.55, up to 2kg UK£17.30. UK Swiftair delivers letters a day faster for UK£2.85 more. www.royalmail.co.uk.

Additionally, **Federal Express** (Australia ☎ 13 20 10, US and Canada ☎ 800-247-4747, New Zealand ☎ 0800 73 33 39; UK ☎ 0800 12 38 00; www.fedex.com) handles express mail services from most of the above countries to the US and Canada.

RECEIVING MAIL

General Delivery: Mail can be sent to the US through **General Delivery** to almost any city or town with a post office. Address letters to:

> Elvis PRESLEY
> General Delivery
> Post Office Street Address
> Memphis, TN 38101 or Victoria, BC V8W 1L0
> USA or CANADA.

The mail will go to a special desk in the central post office, unless you specify a post office by street address or postal code. As a rule, it is best to use the largest post office in the area, and mail may be sent there regardless of what is written on the envelope. It is usually safer and quicker to send mail express or registered. When picking up your mail, bring a form of photo ID, preferably a passport. There is generally no surcharge; if there is a charge, it generally does not exceed the cost of domestic postage. If the clerks insist that there is nothing for you, have them check under your first name as well. *Let's Go* lists post offices in the **Practical Information** section for each city and most towns.

ESSENTIALS

American Express: AmEx's travel offices throughout the world will act as a mail service for cardholders if you contact them in advance. Under this free **Client Letter Service,** they will hold mail for up to 30 days and forward upon request. Address the letter in the same way shown above. Some offices will offer these services to non-cardholders (especially those who have purchased AmEx Travelers Cheques), but you must call ahead to make sure. A complete list is available free from AmEx (☎800-528-4800).

SENDING MAIL HOME FROM THE USA AND CANADA

Aerogrammes, printed sheets that fold into envelopes and travel via airmail, are available at post offices. It helps to mark "airmail," though "par avion" is universally understood. Most post offices will charge exorbitant fees or simply refuse to send aerogrammes with enclosures. Airmail from the USA averages 4 to 7 business days, although times are more unpredictable from smaller towns. The cost is 70¢; a simple postcard is also 70¢. A **standard letter** can be sent abroad in about 4-7 business days for $1.50. For packages up to 4 lbs., use **Global Priority Mail,** for delivery to major locations in 3-5 business days for a flat rate ($5).

If regular airmail is too slow, **Federal Express** (US ☎800-247-4747) can get a letter from New York to Sydney in 2 business days for a whopping $30. By **US Express Mail,** a letter would arrive within 4 business days and would cost $15.

Surface mail is by far the cheapest and slowest way to send mail. It takes one to three months to cross the Atlantic and two to four to cross the Pacific—appropriate for sending large quantities of items you won't need to see for a while. When ordering books and materials from abroad, always include one or two **International Reply Coupons (IRCs)**—a way of providing the postage to cover delivery. IRCs should be available from your local post office and those abroad ($1.05).

BY TELEPHONE

CALLING HOME FROM CANADA AND THE USA

A **calling card** is probably your best and cheapest bet. Calls are billed either collect or to your account. **MCI WorldPhone** also provides access to MCI's Traveler's Assist,

PLACING INTERNATIONAL CALLS. To call the US or Canada from home or to call home from the US or Canada dial:

1. The **international dialing prefix**. To dial out of **Australia,** dial 0011; the **Republic of Ireland, New Zealand,** or the **UK,** 00; **South Africa,** 09; out of **Canada** or the **US,** 011.
2. The **country code** of the country you want to call. To call **Australia,** dial 61; the **Republic of Ireland,** 353; **New Zealand,** 64; **South Africa,** 27; the **UK,** 44; **Canada** or the **US,** 1.
3. The **city/area code.** *Let's Go* lists the city/area codes for cities and towns opposite the city or town name, next to a ☎.
4. The **local number.**

which gives legal and medical advice, exchange rate info, and translation services. Other phone companies provide similar services to travelers. **To obtain a calling card** from your national telecommunications service before you leave home, contact the appropriate company below.

US: AT&T (☎888-288-4685); **Sprint** (☎800-877-4646); or **MCI** (☎800-444-3333; from abroad dial the country's MCI access number).

Canada: Bell Canada **Canada Direct** (☎800-668-6878).

UK: British Telecom **BT Direct** (☎800 34 51 44).

Ireland: Telecom Éireann **Ireland Direct** (☎800 40 00 00).

Australia: Telstra **Australia Direct** (☎13 22 00).

New Zealand: Telecom New Zealand (☎0800 000 000).

South Africa: Telkom South Africa (☎10 219).

To call home with a calling card, contact the North American operator for your service provider. Wherever possible, use a calling card for international phone calls; long-distance rates for national phone services are often exorbitant. You can usually make direct international calls from pay phones, but if you aren't using a calling card you may need to drop your coins as quickly as your words. Prepaid phone cards and occasionally credit cards can be used for direct international calls, but they are still less cost-efficient. In-room hotel calls invariably include a surcharge.

The expensive alternative to dialing direct or using a calling card is using an international operator to place a **collect call.** An English-speaking operator from your home nation can be reached by dialing the appropriate service provider listed above, and they will typically place a collect call even if you don't possess one of their phone cards.

CALLING WITHIN THE USA AND CANADA

The simplest way to call within the country is to use a coin-operated phone. You can also buy **prepaid phone cards,** which carry a certain amount of phone time depending on the card's denomination. The time is measured in minutes or talk units (e.g. one unit/one min.), and the card usually has a toll-free access telephone number and a personal identification number (PIN). To make a phone call, you dial the access number, enter your PIN, and, at the voice prompt, enter the phone number of the party you're trying to reach. Phone rates tend to be highest in the morning, lower in the evening, and lowest on Sunday and late at night.

BY EMAIL AND INTERNET

Finding Internet access in the US and Canada should be no problem. Internet cafes abound, and most public libraries are Internet capable. Fees range from $2-5 per hr. Though in some places it's possible to forge a remote link with your home server, in most cases this is a much slower (and thus more expensive) option than taking advantage of free **web-based email accounts** (e.g., www.hotmail.com and www.yahoo.com). Travelers with laptops can call an Internet service provider via a **modem.** Long-distance phone cards specifically intended for such calls can defray

normally high phone charges; check with your long-distance phone provider to see if it offers this option. **Internet cafes** and the occasional free Internet terminal at a public library or university are listed in the **Practical Information** sections of major cities. For lists of additional cybercafes the US and Canada, check out www.net.cafeguide.com and www.cyberiacafe.net.

GETTING THERE

BY PLANE

When it comes to airfare, a little effort can save you a bundle. If your plans are flexible enough to deal with the restrictions, courier fares are the cheapest. Tickets bought from consolidators and standby seating are also good deals, but last-minute specials, airfare wars, and charter flights often beat these fares. The key is to hunt around, to be flexible, and to persistently ask about discounts. Students, seniors, and those under 26 should never pay full price for a ticket.

DETAILS AND TIPS

Timing: Airfares to the US and Canada peak in the summer, and holidays are also expensive periods in which to travel. Midweek (M-Th morning) round-trip flights run $40-50 cheaper than weekend flights, but the latter are generally less crowded and more likely to permit frequent-flier upgrades. Return-date flexibility is usually not an option for the budget traveler; traveling with an "open return" ticket can be pricier than fixing a return date when buying the ticket and paying later to change it.

Route: Round-trip flights are by far the cheapest; "open-jaw" (arriving in and departing from different cities) and round-the-world, or RTW, flights are pricier but reasonable alternatives. Patching one-way flights together is the least economical way to travel. Flights between capital cities or regional hubs will offer the most competitive fares.

Gateway Cities: Flights between capitals or regional hubs will offer the cheapest fares. The cheapest gateway cities in North America are typically New York, Chicago, Atlanta, Houston, and Los Angeles.

ESSENTIALS

Boarding: Whenever flying internationally, pick up tickets for international flights well in advance of the departure date, and confirm by phone within 72hr. of departure. Most airlines require that passengers arrive at the airport at least two hours before departure. One carry-on item and two pieces of checked baggage are the norm for non-courier flights. Consult the airline for weight allowances.

Fares: Round-trip fares from Western Europe to the US range from $100-400 (during the off season) to $200-550 (during the summer). Fares from Australia tend to the $900-1200 range.

BUDGET AND STUDENT TRAVEL AGENCIES

A knowledgeable agent specializing in flights to the US and Canada can make your life easy and help you save, too, but agents may not spend the time to find you the lowest possible fare—they get paid on commission. Those holding **ISIC and IYTC cards** (see **Identification,** p. 36) qualify for big discounts from student travel agencies. Most flights from budget agencies are on major airlines, but in peak season some may sell seats on less reliable chartered aircraft.

usit world (www.usitworld.com). Over 50 **usit campus** branches in the UK (www.usitcampus.co.uk), including 52 Grosvenor Gardens, London SW1W 0AG (☎0870 240 1010); Manchester (☎0161 273 1721); and Edinburgh (☎0131 668 3303). Nearly 20 **usit now** offices in Ireland, including 19-21 Aston Quay, O'Connell Bridge, Dublin 2 (☎01 602 1600; www.usitnow.ie), and Belfast (☎02890 327 111; www.usitnow.com). Offices also in Athens, Auckland, Brussels, Frankfurt, Johannesburg, Lisbon, Luxembourg, Madrid, Paris, Sofia, and Warsaw.

Council Travel (www.counciltravel.com). US offices include: Emory Village, 1561 N. Decatur Rd., Atlanta, GA 30307 (☎404-377-9997); 273 Newbury St., Boston, MA 02116 (☎617-266-1926); 1160 N. State St., Chicago, IL 60610 (☎312-951-0585); 931 Westwood Blvd., Westwood, Los Angeles, CA 90024 (☎310-208-3551); 254 Greene St., New York, NY 10003 (☎212-254-2525); 530 Bush St., San Francisco, CA 94108 (☎415-421-3473); 424 Broadway Ave E., Seattle, WA 98102 (☎206-329-4567); 3301 M St. NW, Washington, D.C. 20007 (☎202-337-6464). For US cities not listed, call 800-226-8624.

STA Travel, 6560 Scottsdale Rd., #F100, Scottsdale, AZ 85253 (☎800-781-4040; fax ☎602-922-0793; www.statravel.com). A student travel organization with countless offices worldwide. Ticket booking, travel insurance, railpasses, and more. US offices include: 297 Newbury St., Boston, MA 02115 (☎617-266-6014); 429 S. Dearborn St., Chicago, IL 60605 (☎312-786-9050); 7202 Melrose Ave., Los Angeles, CA 90046 (☎323-934-8722); 10 Downing St., New York, NY 10014 (☎212-627-3111); 4341 University Way NE, Seattle, WA 98105 (☎206-633-5000); 2401 Pennsylvania Ave., Ste. G, Washington, D.C. 20037 (☎202-887-0912); 39 Geary St., San Francisco, CA 94108 (☎415-391-8407). In the UK, 11 Goodge St., London W1P 1FE (☎151 7436 7779 for North American travel). In New Zealand, 10 High St., Auckland (☎64 309 0458). In Australia, 366 Lygon St., Melbourne 3053 (☎03 9349 4344).

StudentUniverse, 545 Fifth Ave., Suite 640, New York, NY 10017 (toll-free customer service ☎800-272-9676, outside the US 212-986-8420; help@studentuniverse.com; www.studentuniverse.com), is an online student travel service offering discount ticket booking, travel insurance, railpasses, destination guides, and much more. Customer service line open M-F 9am-8pm and Sa noon-5pm EST.

Travel CUTS (Canadian Universities Travel Services Limited), 187 College St., Toronto, ON M5T 1P7 (☎416-979-2406; fax 979-8167; www.travelcuts.com). 40 offices across Canada. Also in the UK, 295-A Regent St., London W1R 7YA (☎020 7255 1944).

Other organizations that specialize in finding cheap fares include:

Cheap Tickets (☎888-922-1849; www.cheaptickets.com) offers cheap domestic flights.

Travel Avenue (☎800-333-3335; www.travelavenue.com) searches for best available published fares and then uses several different consolidators to attempt to beat that fare. They also offer package deals, which include car rental and hotel reservations, to many destinations.

FLIGHT PLANNING ON THE INTERNET. The web is a great place to look for travel bargains—it's fast, it's convenient, and you can spend as long as you like exploring options without driving your travel agent insane.

Many airline sites offer special last-minute deals on the web. Other sites do the legwork and compile the deals for you—try www.bestfares.com, www.one-travel.com, www.lowestfare.com, and www.travelzoo.com.

STA (www.sta-travel.com) and **Council** (www.counciltravel.com) provide quotes on student tickets, while **Expedia** (msn.expedia.com) and **Travelocity** (www.travelocity.com) offer full travel services. **Priceline** (www.priceline.com) allows you to specify a price, and obligates you to buy any ticket that meets or beats it; be prepared for antisocial hours and odd routes. **Skyauction** (www.skyauction.com) allows you to bid on both last-minute and advance-purchase tickets.

Just one last note—to protect yourself, make sure that the site uses a secure server before handing over any credit card details. Happy hunting!

COMMERCIAL AIRLINES

The commercial airlines' lowest regular offer is the **APEX** (Advance Purchase Excursion) fare, which provides confirmed reservations and allows "open-jaw" tickets. Generally, reservations must be made seven to 21 days ahead of departure, with seven- to 14-day minimum-stay and up to 90-day maximum-stay restrictions. These fares carry hefty cancellation and change penalties (fees rise in summer). Book peak-season APEX fares early; by May you will have a hard time getting your desired departure date.

Although APEX fares are probably not the cheapest possible fares, they provide a sense of the average commercial price, from which to measure other bargains. Many airlines offer **"e-fares,"** special, last-minutes fares available over the internet; check airline web pages for details. **Microsoft Expedia** (http://msn.expedia.com) or **Travelocity** (www.travelocity.com) are pretty reliable web sites offering deals for student travelers. Specials in newspapers may be cheaper but have more restrictions and fewer available seats. Low-season fares should be appreciably cheaper than the peak-season (mid-June to Aug.) ones listed here.

NORTH AMERICAN CARRIERS

Air Tran (☎800-247-8726; www.airtran.com). Consumer Relations, Dept. INT, 9955 Air-Tran Blvd., Orlando, FL 32827. A budget carrier which also offers the "X-Fares Standby Program" for 18- to 22-year-olds (☎888-493-2737).

Air Canada (Canada ☎888-247-2262; www.aircanada.ca). P.O. Box 64239, Thorncliffe Outlet, 5512 4th St., NW Calgary, T2K 6J0. Ask about "Websaver" fares (US ☎800-776-3030, Canada 888-776-3030, W-F).

America West (☎800-235-9292; www.americawest.com). 4000 Sky Harbor Blvd., Phoenix, AZ 85034. Services primarily the Western US.

American (☎800-433-7300; www.americanair.com). P.O. Box 619612, Dallas-Ft. Worth International Airport, TX 75261. Offers "College SAAvers" fares for full-time students.

Continental (☎800-525-0280; www.flycontinental.com). Great deals for senior citizens in the "Freedom Club;" call 800-441-1135.

Northwest (☎800-225-2525; www.nwa.com). 5101 Northwest Dr., St. Paul, MN 55111-3034.

Southwest (☎800-435-9792; www.iflyswa.com). P.O. Box 36647-1CR, Dallas, TX 75235. A budget carrier with an ultra-friendly, laissez-faire attitude.

TWA (☎800-221-2000; www.twa.com). Customer Relations, 1415 Olive St., St. Louis, MO 63103. Offers last minute "TransWorld specials" via email.

United (☎800-241-6522; www.ual.com). P.O. Box 66100, Chicago, IL 60666.

TRAVELING FROM WITHIN NORTH AMERICA

Basic round-trip fares across the US (New York to Los Angeles) range from roughly $300-600. Flights that cover just a portion of the United States may actually be more expensive, depending on how frequented the route is (the more cheaper). Standard commercial carriers like American and United will probably offer the most convenient flights, but they can be expensive unless you manage to grab a special promotion or fare war ticket. You will probably find flying one of the following "discount" airlines a better deal, if any of their limited departure points is convenient for you.

TRAVELING FROM THE UK AND IRELAND

Airfares from Britain and Ireland peak between June and September and near holidays. Expect round-trip fares from either London or Dublin to New York or Boston to range from about $300 to $1100, to Los Angeles $500-1500.

European travelers will experience the least competition for inexpensive seats during the off season, but "off season" need not mean the dead of winter. Peak-season rates generally take effect from mid-May until mid-September. If you can, take advantage of cheap off-season flights within Europe to reach an advantageous point of departure for North America. (London is a major connecting point for budget flights to the US; New York City is often the destination.)

TRAVELING FROM AUSTRALIA AND NEW ZEALAND

Flights from Sydney to Los Angeles will cost between $900-1200. Traveling from Auckland to Los Angeles is a tad cheaper at around $700-1100. **Qantas** (☎ 13 13 13 or US ☎ 800-227-4500; www.qantas.com.au), **United** (see above), and **Air New Zealand** (New Zealand ☎ 0800 737 000; Australia ☎ 13 24 76; www.airnewzealand.co.nz) fly between Australia or New Zealand and the US. Advance purchase fares from Australia have extremely tough restrictions. If you are uncertain about your plans, pay extra for an advance purchase ticket that has only a 50% penalty for cancellation. Many travelers from Australia and New Zealand take **Singapore Air** (Australia ☎ 02 93 500 100; New Zealand ☎ 0800 808 909; www.singaporeair.com) or other East Asian carriers for the initial leg of their trip.

TRAVELING FROM SOUTH AFRICA

Traveling from either Cape Town or Johannesburg to New York will cost from $1000 to $1700. Most flights into the US will go through either Boston, New York, or Washington, D.C. Standard commercial carriers like Virgin Atlantic will probably offer the most convenient flights. **South African Airways** (www.saa.co.za), **American**, and **Northwest** (see above) connect South Africa with North America.

COURIER FLIGHTS

Those who travel light should consider courier flights. Couriers help transport cargo on international flights by using their checked luggage space for freight. Generally, couriers must travel with carry-ons only and must deal with complex flight restrictions. Most flights are round-trip only, with short fixed-length stays (usually one week) and a limit of one ticket per issue. Schedules and itineraries may also change or be canceled at the last moment (as late as 48hr. before the trip, and without a full refund), and check-in, boarding, and baggage claim are often much slower. As always, pay with a credit card if you can, and consider traveler's insurance against trip interruption. Generally, you must be over 21 (in some cases 18). In summer, the most popular destinations usually require an advance reservation of about two weeks (you can usually book up to two months ahead). Super-discounted fares are common for "last-minute" flights (three to 14 days ahead). Info on courier flights is available at www.courier.org.

STANDBY FLIGHTS

Traveling standby requires considerable flexibility in arrival and departure dates and cities. Companies dealing in standby flights sell vouchers rather than tickets, along with the promise to get to your destination (or near your destination) within a certain window of time (typically 1-5 days). You call in before your specific window of time to hear your flight options and the probability that you will be able to board each flight. You can then decide which flights you want to try to make, show up at the appropriate airport at the appropriate time, present your voucher, and board if space is available. Vouchers can usually be bought for both one-way and round-trip travel. You may receive a monetary refund only if every available flight within your date range is full; if you opt not to take an available (but perhaps less convenient) flight, you can only get credit toward future travel. Carefully read agreements with any company offering standby flights as tricky fine print can leave you in a lurch. To check on a company's service record in the US, call the Better Business Bureau (☎212-533-6200). It is difficult to receive refunds, and clients' vouchers will not be honored when an airline fails to receive payment in time. One established standby company in the US is Whole Earth Travel, 325 W. 38th St., New York, NY 10018 (☎800-326-2009; fax 212-864-5489; www.4standby.com) and Los Angeles, CA (☎888-247-4482), which offers one-way flights to Europe from the Northeast ($169), West Coast ($249), Midwest ($219), and Southeast ($199). Intracontinental connecting flights within the US or Europe cost $79-139.

TICKET CONSOLIDATORS

Ticket consolidators, or **"bucket shops,"** buy unsold tickets in bulk from commercial airlines and sell them at discounted rates. The best place to look is in the Sunday travel section of any major newspaper, where many bucket shops place tiny ads. Call quickly, as availability is typically extremely limited. Not all bucket shops are reliable establishments, so insist on a receipt that gives full details of restrictions, refunds, and tickets, and pay by credit card. For more info, check the web site **Consolidators FAQ** (www.travel-library.com/air-travel/consolidators.html).

TRAVELING WITHIN THE US AND CANADA

Travel Avenue (☎800-333-3335; www.travelavenue.com) searches for best available published fares and then uses several different consolidators to attempt to beat that fare. **NOW Voyager,** 74 Varick St., #307, New York, NY 10013 (☎212-431-1616; fax 219-1793; www.nowvoyagertravel.com) arranges discounted flights, within the US and to the world. Other consolidators worth trying are **Interworld** (☎305-443-4929; fax 443-0351); **Pennsylvania Travel** (☎800-331-0947); **Rebel** (☎800-227-3235; travel@rebeltours.com; www.rebeltours.com); **Cheap Tickets** (☎800-377-1000; www.cheaptickets.com); and **Travac** (☎800-872-8800; fax 212-714-9063; www.travac.com). Yet more consolidators on the web include the **Internet Travel Network** (www.itn.com); **Surplus-Travel.com** (www.surplustravel.com); **Travel Information Services** (www.tiss.com); **TravelHUB** (www.travelhub.com); and **The Travel Site** (www.thetravelsite.com). Keep in mind that these are just suggestions to get you started in your research; *Let's Go* does not endorse any of these agencies. As always, be cautious, and research companies before you hand over your credit card number.

TRAVELING FROM THE UK, AUSTRALIA, AND NEW ZEALAND

In London, the **Air Travel Advisory Bureau** (☎020 7636 5000; www.atab.co.uk) can provide names of reliable consolidators and discount flight specialists. From Australia and New Zealand, look for consolidator ads in the travel section of the *Sydney Morning Herald* and other papers.

GETTING AROUND

BY TRAIN

Locomotion is still one of the least expensive (and most pleasant) ways to tour the US and Canada, but keep in mind that discounted air travel may be cheaper, and much faster, than train travel. As with airlines, you can save money by purchasing your tickets as far in advance as possible, so plan ahead and make reservations early. It is essential to travel light on trains; not all stations will check your baggage.

AMTRAK

Amtrak is the only provider of intercity passenger train service in the US. (☎800-872-7245; www.amtrak.com. New York to Boston $60; New York to Chicago $150.) Most cities have Amtrak offices which directly sell tickets, but tickets must be bought through an agent in some small towns. The informative web page lists up-to-date schedules, fares, arrival and departure info, and makes reservations. **Discounts** on full rail fares are given to: senior citizens (15% off), Student Advantage cardholders (15% off; call 800-96-AMTRAK to purchase the $20 card), travelers with disabilities (15% off), ages 2-15 accompanied by an adult (50% off), children under 2 (free), and current members of the US armed forces, active-duty veterans, and their dependents (25% off; www.veteransadvantage.com). "Rail SALE" offers online discounts of up to 70%; visit the Amtrak web site for details and reservations. Amtrak also offers some **special packages:**

All-aboard America: This fare divides the Continental US into 3 regions: Eastern, Central, and Western.

Air-Rail Vacations: Amtrak and United Airlines allow you to travel in 1 direction by train and return by plane, or to fly to a distant point and return home by train. The train portion of the journey can last up to 30 days and include up to 3 stopovers. A multitude of variations are available; call 800-437-3441.

North America Rail Pass: A 30-day pass offered in conjunction with Canada's VIA Rail which allows unlimited travel and unlimited stops throughout the US and Canada for 30 consecutive days; $674 during peak season (June 1-Oct. 15) and $471 during off-season. A 15-day Northeastern North America Pass is available to international residents only; $400 during peak season, $300 off-season.

VIA RAIL

Via Rail, P.O. Box 8116, Station A, Montréal, QC H3C 3N3 (☎888-842-7245; www.via-ail.ca), is Amtrak's Canadian analog. **Discounts** on full fares are given to: students with ISIC card and youths under 24 (35% off full fare), seniors 60 and over (10% off), ages 2-15 accompanied by an adult (50% off), children under 2 (free on the lap of an

adult). Reservations are required for first-class seats and sleep car accommodations. "Supersaver" fares offer discounts of 35% and more. Call for details. The **Canrailpass** allows unlimited travel on 12 days within a 30-day period. Between early June and early October, a 12-day pass costs CDN$658 (seniors and youths and students with an ISIC, CDN$592). Off-season passes cost CDN$411 (seniors, youths, and students, CDN$370). Add CDN$33-56 for each additional day of travel. Call for info on seasonal promotions such as discounts on Grayline Sightseeing Tours.

BY BUS

Buses generally offer the most frequent and complete service between the cities and towns of the US and Canada. Often a bus is the only way to reach smaller locales without a car. In rural areas and across open spaces, however, bus lines tend to be sparse. *Russell's Official National Motor Coach Guide* ($15.70 including postage) is an invaluable tool for constructing an itinerary. Updated each month, *Russell's Guide* has schedules of every bus route (including Greyhound) between any two towns in the United States and Canada. Russell's also publishes two semiannual *Supplements* which are free when ordered with the main issue; a Directory of Bus Lines and Bus Stations, and a series of Route Maps (both $8.40 if ordered separately). To order any of the above, write **Russell's Guides, Inc.,** P.O. Box 278, Cedar Rapids, IA 52406 (☎319-364-6138; fax 365-8728).

GREYHOUND

Greyhound (☎800-231-2222; www.greyhound.com) operates the most routes in the US, and provides service to parts of Canada. Schedule information is available at any Greyhound terminal or agency, on their web page, or by calling them toll-free.

Advance purchase fares: Reserving space far ahead of time ensures a lower fare, although expect a smaller discount during the busy summer months. For tickets purchased more than 14 days in advance, fares anywhere in the US will be no more than $109 one-way. Fares are often reduced even more for 21-day advance purchases on many popular routes; call for up-to-date pricing or consult their web page.

Discounts on full fares: Senior citizens (10% off); children ages 2-11 (50% off); students with a Student Advantage card (up to 15% off); travelers with disabilities and special needs and their companions ride together for the price of one. Active and retired US military personnel and National Guard Reserves (10% off with valid ID) and their spouses and dependents may take a round-trip between any 2 points in the US for $179. With a ticket purchased 3 or more days in advance during the spring and summer months, a friend can travel along for free (some exceptions).

Ameripass: Call 888-454-7277. Allows adults unlimited travel through the US. 7-day pass $209, $188.10 seniors and students with valid ID; 10-day pass $259/$233.10; 15-day pass $319/$287.10; 21-day pass $369/$232.10; 30-day pass $429/$368.10; 45-day pass $469/$422.10; 60-day pass $599/$539.10. Passes for travel in the US and Canada: 15-day $399/$359.10, 21-day $439/$395.10, 30-day $499/$449.10, 45-day $569/$512.10, 60-day $639.10/$575.10. For travel exclusively through the western US and Canada, there is a 15-day option ($299/$269.10) and a 30-day option ($399/$359.10). Children's passes are half the price of adults. The pass takes effect the first day used. Before purchasing an Ameripass, total up the separate bus fares between towns to make sure that the pass is more economical, or at least worth the unlimited flexibility it provides.

International Ameripass: For travelers from outside the US. Those traveling inside the US can obtain a 4-day pass for $135, $135 seniors and students with valid ID; 7-day pass $185/$166.10; 10-day pass $239/$215.10; 15-day pass $285/$256.50; 30-day pass $385/$346.50; 45-day pass $419/$377.10; 60-day pass $509/$458.10. Passes for travel in the US and Canada: 15-day $339/$305.10, 21-day $389/$350.10, 30-day $449/$404.10, 45-day $499/$449.10, 60-day $559/$503.10. The western US and Canada pass is available for 15 days ($299/$269.10) or 30 days

($399/$359.10). Call 888-454-7277 for info. International Ameripasses are not available at the terminal; they can be purchased in foreign countries at affiliated agencies. Telephone numbers vary by country and are listed on the web page. Passes can also be ordered online at www.greyhound.com or purchased in Greyhound's International Office, in Port Authority Bus Station, 625 Eighth Ave., New York, NY 10018 (☎800-246-8572 or 212-971-0492; fax 402-330-0919; intlameripass@greyhound.com).

GREYHOUND CANADA TRANSPORTATION

Greyhound Canada Transportation, 877 Greyhound Way, Calgary, AB T3C 3V8 (☎800-661-TRIP; www.greyhound.ca), is Canada's main intercity bus company. The web page has full schedule info.

Discounts: Seniors 10% off; students 25% off with an ISIC; 10% off with other student cards; a companion of a disabled person free; ages 5-11 50% off; under 4 free. If reservations are made at least 7 days in advance, a friend travels half off. Children under 15 ride free with an adult if reserved 7 days in advance.

Canada Pass: Offers unlimited travel from the western border of Canada to Montréal on all routes for North American residents, including limited links to northern US cities. 7 day advance purchase required. 7-day pass CDN$249/CDN$224.10, 10-day pass CDN$319/CDN$287.10, 15-day pass CDN$379/CDN$341.10, 21-day pass CDN$419/CDN$377.10, 30-day pass CDN$449/CDN$404.10, 45-day pass CDN$535/$481.50, 60-day pass CDN$599/CDN$539.10. The Canada Plus Pass includes coast-to-coast travel and is slightly more expensive.

International Canada Pass: For foreign visitors. Same prices as the Canada Pass. The "Plus" pass adds travel to Québec and the Maritime provinces for a few dollars more; this pass can be purchased only overseas at select travel agencies, including those listed above for Greyhound Lines. Goods and services tax (GST) at 7% is added to fares.

BY CAR

"I" (as in "I-90") refers to Interstate highways, "U.S." (as in "U.S. 1") to US highways, and "Rte." (as in "Rte. 7") to state and local highways. For Canadian highways, "TCH" refers to the Trans-Canada Hwy., while "Hwy." or "autoroute" refers to standard automobile routes.

INTERNATIONAL DRIVING PERMIT

If you do not have a license issued by a US state or Canadian province or territory, you might want an **International Driving Permit (IDP)**. While the USA allows you to drive with a foreign license for up to a year, and in Canada for six months, it may help with police if your license is written in English. You must carry your home license with your IDP at all times. You must be 18 to obtain an IDP, it is valid for a year, and must be issued in the country in which your license originates. Contact these offices to apply:

Australia: Contact your local Royal Automobile Club (RAC) or the National Royal Motorist Association (NRMA) if in NSW or the ACT (☎08 9421 4444; www.rac.com.au/travel). Permits AUS$15.

Canada: Contact any Canadian Automobile Association (CAA) branch office or write to CAA, 1145 Hunt Club Rd., #200, Ottawa, ON K1V 0Y3. (☎613-247-0117; www.caa.ca/CAAInternet/travelservices/internationaldocumentation/idptravel.htm). Permits CDN$10.

Ireland: Contact the nearest Automobile Association (AA) office or write to the UK address below. Permits IR£4/€5.08. The Irish Automobile Association, 23 Suffolk St., Rockhill, Blackrock, Dublin (☎01 677 9481), honors most foreign automobile membership (24hr. breakdown and road service ☎800 667 788; toll-free in Ireland).

New Zealand: Contact your local Automobile Association (AA) or their main office at Auckland Central, 99 Albert St. Auckland City (☎9 377 4660; www.nzaa.co.nz). Permits NZ$10.

South Africa: Contact the Travel Services Department of the Automobile Association of South Africa at P.O. Box 596, 2000 Johannesburg (☎ 11 799 1400; fax 799 1410; http://aasa.co.za). Permits ZAR28.50.

UK: To visit your local AA Shop, contact the **AA Headquarters** (☎ 0870 600 0371), or write to: The Automobile Association, International Documents, Fanum House, Erskine, Renfrewshire PA8 6BW. For more info, see www.theaa.co.uk. Permits UK£4.

US: Visit any American Automobile Association (AAA) office or write to AAA Florida, Travel Related Services, 1000 AAA Dr., Heathrow, FL 32746 (☎ 407-444-7000; fax 444-7380). You don't have to be a member to buy an IDP/IADP. Permits $10. AAA Travel Related Services (☎ 800-222-4357) provides road maps, travel guides, emergency road services, travel services, and auto insurance.

AUTOMOBILE CLUBS

Most automobile clubs offer free towing, emergency roadside assistance, travel-related discounts, and random goodies in exchange for a modest membership fee. Travelers should strongly consider membership if planning an extended roadtrip.

■ **American Automobile Association (AAA),** (emergency road service ☎ 800-AAA-HELP/800-222-4357; www.aaa.com). Offers free trip-planning services, roadmaps and guidebooks, 24hr. emergency road service anywhere in the US, free towing, and commission-free traveler's checks from American Express with over 1,000 offices scattered across the country. Discounts on Hertz car rental (5-20%), Amtrak tickets (10%), and various motel chains and theme parks. AAA has reciprocal agreements with auto associations in other countries which often provide you full benefits while in the US. Memberships vary depending on which AAA branch you join, but hover between $50-60 for the first year; less for renewals and additional family members. Call 800-564-6222 to sign up.

■ **Canadian Automobile Association (CAA),** 1145 Hunt Club Rd., #200, Ottawa, ON K1V 0Y3 (☎ 800-CAA-HELP/800-222-4357; www.caa.ca). Affiliated with AAA (see above), the CAA provides the same membership benefits, including 24hr. emergency roadside assistance, free maps and tourbooks, route planning, and various discounts. Basic membership is CDN$62 and CDN$32 for associates; call 800-564-6222 to sign up.

Mobil Auto Club, 200 N. Martingale Rd., Schaumbourg, IL 60174 (info ☎ 800-621-558; emergency service 800-323-5880 for emergency service). Benefits include locksmith reimbursement, towing (free up to 10 mi.), roadside service, and car-rental discounts. $8 per month covers you and another driver.

ON THE ROAD

Tune up the car before you leave, make sure the tires are in good repair and have enough air, and get good maps. *Rand McNally's Road Atlas*, covering all of the US and Canada, is one of the best (available at bookstores and gas stations, $11). A **compass** and a **car manual** can also be very useful. You should always carry a spare tire and jack, jumper cables, extra oil, flares, a flashlight, and blankets (in case you break down at night or in the winter). Those traveling long undeveloped stretches of road may want to consider renting a **car phone** or purchasing a **cell phone** in case of a breakdown. When traveling in the summer or in the desert bring five gallons of **water** for drinking and for the radiator. In extremely hot weather, use the air conditioner with restraint; if you see the car's temperature gauge climbing, turn it off. Turning the heater on full blast will help cool the engine. If radiator fluid is steaming, turn off the car for half an hour. *Never pour water over the engine to cool it.* Never lift a searing hot hood. In remote areas, remember to bring food and water.

Sleeping in a car or van parked in the city is extremely dangerous—even the most dedicated budget traveler should not consider it an option. While driving, be sure to buckle up—seat belts are **required by law** in many regions of the US and Canada. The **speed limit** in the US varies considerably from region to region. Most urban highways have a limit of 55mph (89km per hr.), while rural routes range from 65mph (105kph) to 80mph (129kph). Heed the limit; not only does it save gas, but most local police forces and state troopers make frequent use of radar to catch speed demons. The **speed limit in Canada** is 50kph (31mph) in cities and 80kph (49mph) on highways. On rural highways the speed limit may be 100kph (61mph).

HOW TO NAVIGATE THE INTERSTATES

In the 50s, President Dwight D. "Ike" Eisenhower envisioned a well-organized **interstate highway system.** His dream has been realized: there is now a comprehensive, well-maintained, efficient means of traveling between major cities and between states. Luckily for the traveler, the highways are named with an intuitive numbering system. Even-numbered interstates run east-west and odd ones run north-south, decreasing in number toward the south and the west. North-south routes begin on the West Coast with I-5 and end with I-95 on the East Coast. The southernmost east-west route is I-4 in Florida. The northernmost east-west route is I-94, stretching from Montana to Wisconsin. Three-digit numbers signify branches of other interstates (e.g., I-285 is a branch of I-85) that often skirt around large cities.

RENTING

Car rental agencies fall into two categories: national companies with hundreds of branches, and local agencies that serve only one city or region. National chains usually allow you to pick up a car in one city and drop it off in another (for a hefty charge, sometimes in excess of $1000), and by calling their toll-free numbers, you can reserve a reliable car anywhere in the country. Generally, airport branches have more expensive rates. Most branches rent to ages 21-24 with an additional fee, but policies and prices vary from agency to agency and from branch to branch. If you're 21 or older and have a major credit card in your name, you may be able to rent where the minimum age would otherwise rule you out. **Alamo**(☎800-462-52663; www.alamo.com) rents to ages 21-24 with a major credit card for an additional $25 per day, **Enterprise** (☎800-736-8222; www.enterprise.com) rents to customers age 21-24 with a variable surcharge, and many **Dollar** (☎800-800-4000; www.dollar.com) and **Thrifty** (☎800-367-2277; www.thrifty.com) locations do likewise for varying surcharges. Some branches of **Budget** (☎800-527-0700; www.budget.com) rent to drivers under 25 with a surcharge that varies by location. **Hertz** (☎800-654-3131; www.hertz.com) policy varies with city. **Rent-A-Wreck** (☎800-944-7501; www.rent-a-wreck) specializes in supplying vehicles that are past their prime for lower-than-average prices; a bare-bones compact less than 8 years old rents for around $20-25; cars 3-5 years old average under $30.

Most rental packages offer unlimited mileage, although some allow you a certain number of miles free before the charge of 25-40¢ per mile takes effect. Quoted rates do not include gas or tax, so ask for the total cost before handing over the credit card; many large firms have added airport surcharges not covered by the designated fare. Return the car with a full tank unless you sign up for a fuel option plan that stipulates otherwise. And when dealing with any car rental company, be sure to ask whether the price includes insurance against theft and collision. There may be an additional charge for a collision and damage waiver (CDW), which usually comes to about $12-15 per day. Major credit cards (including MasterCard and American Express) will sometimes cover the CDW if you use their card to rent a car; call your credit card company for specifics.

CAR INSURANCE

Some credit cards cover standard insurance. If you rent, lease, or borrow a car, and you are not from the US or Canada, you will need a **green card,** or **International Insurance Certificate,** to certify that you have liability insurance and that it applies abroad. Green cards can be obtained at car rental agencies, car dealerships (for those leasing cars), some travel agents, and some border crossings.

BUYING

Adventures on Wheels, 42 Rte. 36, Middletown, NJ 07748 (☎732-495-0959 or 800-943-3579; info@wheels9.com; www.wheels9.com), sells travelers a motorhome, camper, minivan, station wagon, or compact car, organizes its registration and provides insurance, and guarantees they will buy it back after you have finished your travels. Cars with a buy-back guarantee start at $2500. Buy a camper for $6500, use it for six months, and sell it back for $3000-4000. The main office is in New York/New Jersey; there are other offices in Los Angeles, San Francisco, and Miami. Vehicles can be picked up at one office and dropped off at another.

ESSENTIALS

AUTO TRANSPORT COMPANIES

These services match drivers with car owners who need cars moved from one city to another. Would-be travelers give the company their desired destination and the company finds a car which needs to go there. The only expenses are gas, tolls, and your own living expenses. Some companies insure their cars; with others, your security deposit covers any breakdowns or damage. You must be at least 21, have a valid license, and agree to drive about 400 mi. per day on a fairly direct route. Companies regularly inspect current and past job references, take your fingerprints, and require a cash bond. Cars are available between most points, although it's easiest to find cars for traveling from coast to coast; New York and Los Angeles are popular transfer points. If offered a car, look it over first. Think twice about accepting a gas guzzler, since you'll be paying for the gas. With the company's approval, you may be able to share the cost with several companions.

Auto Driveaway Co., 310 S. Michigan Ave., Chicago, IL 60604 (☎312-939-3600 or 800-346-2277; nationalhq@autodriveaway.com; www.autodriveaway.com).

Across America Driveaway, 9905 Express Dr., Highland, IN 46322 (☎219-934-2000 or 800-619-7707; Schultz!@gte.net; www.schultz-international.com). Offices in L.A. (☎800-964-7874 or 310-798-3377) and Dallas (☎214-745-8893).

BY BICYCLE

Before you pedal furiously onto the byways of America astride your banana-seat Huffy, remember that safe and secure cycling requires a quality helmet and lock. A good helmet costs about $40—much cheaper than critical head surgery. U-shaped **Kryptonite** or **Citadel** locks ($30-60) carry insurance against theft for 1 or 2 years if your bike is registered with the police. **Bike Nashbar,** 4111 Simon Rd., Youngstown, OH 44512 (☎800-627-4227; fax 330-778-9456), will beat any nationally advertised in-stock price by 5¢, and ships anywhere in the US and Canada. They also field questions about repairs and maintenance (☎330-788-6464; open M-F 8am-6pm).

Adventure Cycling Association, P.O. Box 8308, Missoula, MT 59807 (☎406-721-1776 or 800-755-2453; fax 721-8754; acabike@aol.com; www.adv-cycling.org). A national, non-profit organization that researches and maps long-distance routes and organizes bike tours long and short for members (9-day trip $800; 75-day Great Divide Expedition, $3000). Annual membership $30; includes access to maps and routes and a subscription to *Adventure Cyclist* magazine.

The Canadian Cycling Association, 702-2197 Riverside Dr., Ottawa, ON K1H 7X3 (☎613-248-1353; fax 248-9311; general@canadian-cycling.com; www.canadian-cycling.com). Provides info for cyclists of all abilities, from recreational to racing. Distributes *The Canadian Cycling Association's Complete Guide to Bicycle Touring in Canada* (CDN$24), plus guides to regions of Canada, Alaska, and the Pacific Coast.

BY MOTORCYCLE

Those considering a long journey on a bike should contact the **American Motorcyclist Association,** 13515 Yarmouth Dr., Pickering, OH 43147 (☎614-856-1900 or 800-262-5646; fax 856-1920; ama@ama-cycle.org; ama-cycle.org), the linchpin of US biker culture. A full membership ($39 per year) includes a subscription to the extremely informative *American Motorcyclist* magazine, discounts on insurance, rentals, and hotels, and a kick-ass patch for your riding jacket. For an additional $25, members benefit from emergency roadside assistance, including pick-up and delivery to a service shop. And of course, take a copy of Robert Pirsig's *Zen and the Art of Motorcycle Maintenance* (1974) with you.

BY THUMB

Let's Go urges you to consider the great risks and disadvantages of **hitchhiking** before thumbing it. Hitching means entrusting your life to a randomly selected person who happens to stop beside you on the road. While this may be comparatively safe in some areas of Europe and Australia, it is generally *not* so in the US or Canada. We do not recommend it. We strongly urge you to find other means of transportation and to avoid situations where hitching is the only option.

SPECIFIC CONCERNS

FEMALE TRAVELERS

In the US, a woman should expect to be treated just as a man would be; though sexism still exists, it is considered unacceptable behavior. If you are treated unfairly because you are a woman, this is grounds for complaint.

Women exploring on their own inevitably face some additional safety concerns, but it's easy to be adventurous without taking undue risks. Generally, it is safe for women to travel in the US, but common sense still applies; women are targeted for muggings and swindlings, as well as general harassment. Watch out for vendors who may try to take advantage of you. Avoid downtrodden neighborhoods, especially at night, and avoid solitary, late-night treks or subway rides. If you are camping in isolated areas or traveling in big cities you are unfamiliar with, try to travel with partners. In more rural areas, rowdy bars can also be risky. Wherever you go, walk purposefully and self-confidently; women who look like they know what they are doing and where they are going are less likely to be harassed. When traveling, always carry extra money for a phone call, bus, or taxi. **Hitching** is never safe for lone women, or even for two women traveling together. Consider approaching older women or couples if you're lost or feel uncomfortable.

Your best answer to verbal harassment is no answer at all; feigning deafness, sitting motionless, and staring straight ahead at nothing in particular will do a world of good that reactions usually don't achieve. The extremely persistent can sometimes be dissuaded by a firm, loud, and very public "Go away!" Don't hesitate to seek out a police officer or a passerby if you are being harassed. *Let's Go: USA* lists emergency numbers (including rape crisis lines) in the **Practical Information** listings of most cities, and you can always dial **911**. An **IMPACT Model Mugging** self-defense course will not only prepare you for a potential attack, but will also raise your level of awareness of your surroundings and your confidence (see **Self Defense**, p. 42).

The **National Organization for Women**, or **NOW** (now@now.org; www.now.org) can refer women travelers to rape crisis centers and counseling services. Main offices include 150 W. 28th St., # 304, New York, NY 10001 (☎212-627-9895) and 733 15th St. NW, 2nd fl., Washington, D.C. 20005 (☎202-628-8669).

FURTHER READING

A Journey of One's Own: Uncommon Advice for the Independent Woman Traveler, Thalia Zepatos. Eighth Mountain Press ($14).

Adventures in Good Company: The Complete Guide to Women's Tours and Outdoor Trips, Thalia Zepatos. Eighth Mountain Press ($8).

Active Women Vacation Guide, Evelyn Kaye. Blue Panda Publications ($14).

Travelers' Tales: Gutsy Women, Travel Tips and Wisdom for the Road, Marybeth Bond. Traveler's Tales ($10).

TRAVELING ALONE

There are many benefits to traveling alone, among them greater independence and challenge. As a lone traveler, you have greater opportunity to interact with the region you're visiting. Without distraction, you can write a great travelogue in the grand tradition of Mark Twain, John Steinbeck, and Charles Kuralt.

Connecting: Solo Traveler Network, 689 Park Rd., Unit 6, Gibsons, BC V0N 1V7 (☎604-886-9099; info@cstn.org; www.cstn.org). Bimonthly newsletter features going solo tips, single-friendly tips, and travel companion ads. Annual directory lists holiday suppliers

ESSENTIALS

that avoid single supplement charges. Advice and lodging exchanges facilitated between members. Membership $40.

Travel Companion Exchange, P.O. Box 833, Amityville, NY 11701 (☎800-392-1256 or 631-454-0880; www.whytravelalone.com). Publishes the pamphlet *Foiling Pickpockets & Bag Snatchers* ($4) and *Travel Companions,* a bimonthly newsletter for single travelers seeking a travel partner (subscription $48).

FURTHER READING: TRAVELING ALONE

Traveling Solo, Eleanor Berman. Globe Pequot ($17).
The Single Traveler Newsletter, P.O. Box 682, Ross, CA 94957 (☎415-389-0227). 6 issues $29.

OLDER TRAVELERS

Senior citizens are eligible for a wide range of discounts on transportation, museums, movies, theaters, concerts, restaurants, and accommodations. If you don't see a senior citizen price listed, ask, and you may be delightfully surprised. The books *No Problem! Worldwise Tips for Mature Adventurers,* by Janice Kenyon (Orca Book Publishers; $16) and *Unbelievably Good Deals and Great Adventures That You Absolutely Can't Get Unless You're Over 50,* by Joan Rattner Heilman (NTC/ Contemporary Publishing; $13) are both excellent resources. For more information, contact one of the following organizations:

ElderTreks, 597 Markham St., Toronto, ON M6G 2L7 (☎800-741-7956; www.elder-treks.com). Adventure travel programs for the 50+ traveler in the USA or Canada.
Elderhostel, 11 Ave. de Lafayette, Boston, MA 02111 (☎877-426-8056; www.elderho-stel.org). Organizes 1- to 4-week "educational adventures" in the USA on varied subjects for those 55+.
The Mature Traveler, P.O. Box 15791, Sacramento, CA 95852 (☎800-460-6676). Deals, discounts, and travel packages for the 50+ traveler. Subscription $30.
Walking the World, P.O. Box 1186, Fort Collins, CO 80522 (☎800-340-9255; www.walkingtheworld.com), organizes trips for 50+ travelers to the USA.

BISEXUAL, GAY, & LESBIAN TRAVELERS

American cities are generally accepting of all sexualities, and thriving gay and lesbian communities can be found in most cosmopolitan areas. Most college towns are gay-friendly as well. In rural areas, however, homophobia can be rampant. In light of the anti-gay legislative measures narrowly defeated in various states, and not-so-isolated gay-bashing incidents, homophobia is still all too common.

BOOKSTORES AND INFORMATION SERVICES

Gay's the Word, 66 Marchmont St., London WC1N 1AB (☎+44 20 7278 7654; www.gaystheword.co.uk). The largest gay and lesbian bookshop in the UK, with both fiction and non-fiction titles. Mail-order service available.
Giovanni's Room, 1145 Pine St., Philadelphia, PA 19107 (☎215-923-2960; www.queerbooks.com). An international lesbian/feminist and gay bookstore with mail-order service (carries many of the publications listed below).
International Lesbian and Gay Association (ILGA), 81 rue Marché-au-Charbon, B-1000 Brussels, Belgium (☎+32 2 502 2471; www.ilga.org). Provides political information, such as homosexuality laws of individual countries.

FURTHER READING: BISEXUAL, GAY, AND LESBIAN TRAVELERS

Spartacus International Gay Guide 2001-2002. Bruno Gmunder Verlag ($33).
Damron Men's Guide, Damron Road Atlas, Damron's Accommodations, and *The Women's Traveller.* Damron Travel Guides ($14-19). For more info, call 800-462-6654 or check their web site (www.damron.com).

Ferrari Guides' Gay Travel A to Z, Ferrari Guides' Men's Travel in Your Pocket, Ferrari Guides' Women's Travel in Your Pocket, and *Ferrari Guides' Inn Places.* Ferrari Guides ($16-20). For more info, call 602-863-2408 or 800-962-2912. Purchase their guides online at www.ferrariguides.com.

Gayellow Pages USA/Canada, Frances Green. Gayellow pages ($16). Order by phone (212-674-0120), by email (gayellow@banet.net), or online at www.gayellowpages.com.

TRAVELERS WITH DISABILITIES

Federal law dictates that all public buildings should be wheelchair accessible, and recent laws governing building codes have made disabled access more the norm than the exception. Businesses, transportation companies, national parks, and public services are compelled to assist the disabled in using their facilities.

Those with disabilities should inform airlines, buses, trains, and hotels of their disabilities when making arrangements for travel; some time may be needed to prepare special accommodations. Call ahead to restaurants, hotels, parks, and other facilities to find out about the existence of ramps, the widths of doors, the dimensions of elevators, etc. Major airlines and **Amtrak** (☎800-872-7245; see p. 75) will accommodate disabled passengers if notified at least 72hr. in advance. Amtrak offers 15% discounts to disabled passengers, and hearing impaired travelers may contact Amtrak using teletype printers. **Greyhound** (see p. 77) will provide free travel for a companion; if you are without a fellow traveler, call Greyhound (☎800-752-4841) at least 48 hours, but no more than one week, before you leave and they'll arrange assistance where needed. Hertz, National, and Avis **car rental** agencies have hand-controlled vehicles at some locations (see **Renting,** p. 81). To visit a national park or any other sight managed by the US National Park Service, you can obtain a free **Golden Access Passport** (see **National Parks,** p. 55). The Green Book (http://members.nbci.com/thegreenbook/home.html) has a partial listing of disabled-access accommodations and sights in the USA and Canada.

USEFUL ORGANIZATIONS

Mobility International USA (MIUSA), P.O. Box 10767, Eugene, OR 97440 (voice and TDD ☎541-343-1284; www.miusa.org). Sells *A World of Options: A Guide to International Educational Exchange, Community Service, and Travel for Persons with Disabilities* ($35).

Society for the Advancement of Travel for the Handicapped (SATH), 347 Fifth Ave., #610, New York, NY 10016 (☎212-447-7284; www.sath.org). An advocacy group that publishes free online travel information and the travel magazine *OPEN WORLD* ($18, free for members). Annual membership $45, students and seniors $30.

TOUR AGENCIES

Directions Unlimited, 123 Green Ln., Bedford Hills, NY 10507 (☎800-533-5343). Books individual and group vacations for the physically disabled; not an info service.

The Guided Tour Inc., 7900 Old York Rd., #114B, Elkins Park, PA 19027 (☎800-783-5841; www.guidedtour.com). Organizes travel programs for persons with developmental and physical challenges in the USA and Canada.

MINORITY TRAVELERS

Racial and ethnic minorities sometimes face blatant and, more often, subtle discrimination and/or harassment, though regions in the US and Canada differ drastically in their general attitudes towards race relations. Verbal harassment is now less common than unfair pricing, false info on accommodations, or inexcusably slow or unfriendly service at restaurants. The best way to deal with such encounters is to remain calm and report individuals to a supervisor and establishments to the Better Business Bureau for the region (the operator will provide local listings);

contact the police in extreme situations. *Let's Go* always welcomes reader input regarding discriminating establishments.

In larger cities, African-Americans can usually consult chapters of the Urban League and the **National Association for the Advancement of Colored People,** or **NAACP** (www.naacp.org) for info on events of interest to African-Americans.

FURTHER READING: MINORITY TRAVELERS

Go Girl! The Black Woman's Book of Travel and Adventure, Elaine Lee. Eighth Mountain Press ($14).

The African-American Travel Guide, Wayne Robinson. Hunter Publishing ($13).

Traveling Jewish in America, Jane Moskowitz. Wandering You Press ($14.50).

TRAVELERS WITH CHILDREN

Family vacations often require that you slow your pace, and always require that you plan ahead. When deciding where to stay, remember the special needs of young children; if you pick a B&B or a small hotel, call ahead and make sure it's child-friendly. If you rent a car, make sure the rental company provides a car seat for younger children. Be sure that your child carries some sort of ID in case of an emergency or he or she gets lost, and arrange a reunion spot in case of separation when sight-seeing.

Restaurants often have children's menus and discounts. Virtually all museums and tourist attractions also have a children's rate. Children under two generally fly for free or 10% of the adult airfare on domestic flights (this does not necessarily include a seat). Fares are usually discounted 25% for children from 2 to 11.

FURTHER READING: TRAVELERS WITH CHILDREN

Kidding Around Boston; San Francisco; Washington D.C.; Indianapolis; Austin; Chicago; Cleveland; Kansas City; Miami; Milwaukee; Minneapolis/St. Paul; Nashville; Portland; Seattle. John Muir ($8).

Backpacking with Babies and Small Children, Goldie Silverman. Wilderness Press ($10).

How to take Great Trips with Your Kids, Sanford and Jane Portnoy. Harvard Common Press (US $10).

Have Kid, Will Travel: 101 Survival Strategies for Vacationing With Babies and Young Children, Claire and Lucille Tristram. Andrews McMeel Publishing ($9).

DIETARY CONCERNS

Vegetarians should have no problem finding suitable cuisine on either coast (the West Coast, especially, is extremely vegetarian friendly) and in most major cities, although small-town America may meet veggie requests with a long, blank stare and a pile of mashed potatoes. For more info, contact:

North American Vegetarian Society, P.O. Box 72, Dolgeville, NY 13329 (☎518-568-7970; navs@telenet.com; www.cyberveg.org/navs). Publishes *Transformative Adventures,* a guide to vacations and retreats ($15), and the *Vegetarian Journal's Guide to Natural Food Restaurants in the US and Canada* ($12).

Travelers who keep **kosher** should contact synagogues in larger cities for info on kosher restaurants; your own synagogue or college Hillel should have access to lists of Jewish institutions across the nation. You may also consult the kosher restaurant database at www.shamash.org/kosher.

The Jewish Travel Guide lists synagogues, kosher restaurants, and Jewish institutions in the US and Canada. Available from Vallentine-Mitchell Publishers, Newbury House 890-900, Eastern Ave., Newbury Park, Ilford, Essex, UK IG2 7HH (☎0181 599 8866; fax 599 0984). It is available in the US ($16) from ISBS, 5804 NE Hassallo St., Portland, OR 97213 (☎800-944-6190).

ALTERNATIVES TO TOURISM

For an extensive listing of "off-the-beaten-track" and specialty travel opportunities, try the **Specialty Travel Index**, 305 San Anselmo Ave., #313, San Anselmo, CA 94960 (☎415-455-1643 or 888-624-4030; www.specialitytravel.com; $6). **Transitions Abroad** (www.transabroad.com) publishes a bimonthly online newsletter for work, study, and specialized travel abroad.

STUDYING ABROAD

US. Foreign students can take advantage of most educational opportunities in the US, including secondary schools, colleges, English language programs for all levels, and even vocational training. Although revised immigration laws from 1996 prohibit foreign students from attending public elementary or middle school, public high schools (with a maximum stay of one year) and secondary institutions remain accessible with the **F-1 student visa**. Vocational students would need to secure an **M-1 visa**, which is more difficult to obtain than the F-1.

Those interested in studying in the US should first consider which program or institution they would like to join. The Web offers an exhaustive index of **study abroad** opportunities for foreign students, including www.petersons.com and www.studyabroad.com for academic programs and www.aipt.org for vocational and professional exchanges. Study abroad can also be arranged through particular institutions, such as universities and English language schools. Participation in a program needs to be secured before arranging for a visa, which should be done at the US Embassy or Consulate located in the country of permanent residence.

Most study abroad programs in the US require a base level of proficiency in English before admission can be granted. Applicants usually prove their skills by taking the **TOEFL**, a standardized test offered in most countries. Test times and locations can be obtained at www.toefl.org (toefl@ets.org) or by calling or writing TOEFL services: P.O Box 6151, Princeton, NJ 08541 (☎609-771-7100).

CANADA. Just as in the US, prospective students should choose and be accepted to a program of study before applying to live in Canada as a foreign student. Authorization for study in Canada occurs on a provincial level and requires proof of admission to an institution, financial solvency to pay all expenses incurred, and ability to meet other visitation requirements, such as visas. Here are some universities that offer study abroad programs in Canada:

Association of Commonwealth Universities (ACU), John Foster House, 36 Gordon Sq., London WC1H OPF (☎+44 020 7380 6700; www.acu.ac.uk). Publishes information about Commonwealth universities including those in Canada.

Plattsburgh State University of New York, Center for International Programs and Exchange, 133 Court St., Plattsburgh, NY 12901 (☎518-564-2086; www.plattsburgh.edu). Offers programs for American students in Montreal, Toronto, and Ottawa. Specialize in a range of subjects from literature to business administration.

WORKING ABROAD

US. Foreign students living in the US are prohibited from taking an off-campus job during the first year of their study and can only accept such a job after the first year upon permission from the INS. Technical students are allowed to work only as a function of their training. Visitors to the US under the regular visitation visa (the B-2 visa) are prohibited from taking any type of employment.

To work in the US without immigrating, one must obtain a work visa or participate in a cultural exchange program. **Work visas** are extremely difficult to procure and require the presence of extraordinary circumstances, such as extensive education or prominence in a particular academic or professional field. Cultural exchanges are easier to arrange and are intended to facilitate multi-culturalism in education, arts, and sciences. The US Information Agency organizes a variety of cultural exchanges (www.usinfo.state.gov).

CANADA. Foreign students living in Canada are allowed to work only under exceptional circumstances, such as unforeseen loss of expected funding. In order to work in Canada without immigrating, one must be sponsored by a Canadian employer who can prove that foreign assistance is needed to fill a Canadian employee market shortage. An Employment Authorization (EA) can be issued to a foreign worker only if he or she is sponsored by a Canadian employer and if a Human Resources Development Canada officer agrees that the foreign worker will produce a net benefit for Canada and Canadians.

OTHER RESOURCES

USEFUL PUBLICATIONS

MISCELLANEOUS

Specialty Travel Index, 305 San Anselmo Ave., #313, San Anselmo, CA 94960 (☎888-624-4030 or 415-455-1643; fax 459-4974; spectrav@ix.netcom.com; www.specialtytravel.com). Published twice yearly, this is an extensive listing of "off-the-beaten-track" travel opportunities. One copy $6, one-year subscription (2 issues) $10.

TRAVEL BOOK PUBLISHERS

Hippocrene Books, Inc., 171 Madison Ave., New York, NY 10016 (☎718-454-2366; fax 454-1391; contact@hippocrenebooks.com; www.netcom.com/~hippocre). Free catalogue. Publishes travel reference books and guides.

Hunter Publishing, 130 Campus Drive, Edison, NJ 08818 (☎800-255-0343; fax 417-0482; kimba@mediasoft.net; www.hunterpublishing.com). Has an extensive catalogue of travel books, guides, language learning tapes, and quality maps, and the *Charming Small Hotel Guide to New England* or *Florida* ($15).

Rand McNally, 150 S. Wacker Dr., Chicago, IL 60606 (☎312-332-2009 or 800-234-0679; fax 443-9540; storekeeper@randmcnally.com; www.randmcnally.com). Publishes a number of comprehensive road atlases (each $10).

Adventurous Traveler Bookstore, 245 S. Champlain St., Burlington, VT 05401 (☎800-282-3963 or 802-860-6776; www.adventuroustraveler.com).

Travel Books & Language Center, Inc., 4437 Wisconsin Ave. NW, Washington, D.C. 20016 (☎800-220-2665 or 202-237-1322; www.travelbks.com). Over 60,000 titles from around the world.

THE WORLD WIDE WEB

Listed here are some budget travel sites to start off your surfing; other relevant web sites are listed throughout the book. Because web site turnover is high, use search engines (such as www.google.com) to strike out on your own.

OUR PERSONAL FAVORITE...

▨ **Let's Go:** www.letsgo.com. Our constantly expanding web site features photos and streaming video, online ordering of all our titles, info about our books, a travel forum buzzing with stories and tips, and links that will help you find everything you ever wanted to know about the US and Canada

THE ART OF BUDGET TRAVEL

How to See the World: www.artoftravel.com. A compendium of great travel tips, from cheap flights to self defense to interacting with local culture.

Rec. Travel Library: www.travel-library.com. A fantastic set of links for general information and personal travelogues.

Lycos: cityguide.lycos.com. General introductions to cities and regions throughout the US and Canada, accompanied by links to history, news, and local tourism sites.

Microsoft Expedia: expedia.msn.com. Has everything you'd ever need to make travel plans on the web. Compare flight fares, look at maps, make reservations. FareTracker, a free service, sends you monthly mailings about the cheapest fares to any destination.
Shoestring Travel: www.stratpub.com. An alternative to Microsoft's huge site. A budget travel e-zine that features listings of home exchanges, links, and accommodations info.

INFORMATION ON THE USA AND CANADA

The CIA World Factbook (www.odci.gov/cia/publications/factbook/index.html) has tons of vital statistics on the United States and Canada. Check it out for an overview of either country's economy, and an explanation of its system of government.
Tourism Offices Worldwide Directory: http://mbnet.mb.ca/lucas/travel/tourism-offices.html. Lists tourism offices for all 50 states and Canada, as well as consulate and embassy addresses.
City Net: www.city.net. Dispenses info on renting a car, restaurants, hotel rates, and weather for a wide array of cities and regions across the US and Canada.

FURTHER READING: THE WORLD WIDE WEB

How to Plan Your Dream Vacation Using the Web, Elizabeth Dempsey. Coriolis ($25).
Nettravel: How Travelers Use the Internet, Michael Shapiro. O'Reilly & Associates ($25).
Travel Planning Online for Dummies, Noah Vadnai. IDG Books ($25).

ESSENTIALS

NEW ENGLAND

New England fancied itself an intellectual and political center long before the States were United. Students and scholars funnel into New England's colleges each fall, and town meetings still evoke the spirit of popular government that once inspired American colonists to create a nation. Numerous historic landmarks recount every step of the young country's break from "Old" England.

The region's unpredictable climate can be particularly dismal during the harsh, wet winter from November to March, when rivers, campgrounds, and tourist attractions freeze up. Nevertheless, today's visitors find adventure in the rough edges that troubled early settlers, flocking to New England's dramatic, salty coastline to sun on the sand, or heading to the slopes and valleys of the Green and White Mountains to ski, hike, bike, and canoe. In the fall, the nation's most brilliant foliage bleeds and burns, transforming the entire region into an earth-sized kaleidoscope.

HIGHLIGHTS OF NEW ENGLAND

SEAFOOD. Head to Maine (see below) for the best lobster around, and don't forget to try New England clam "chowda" before you leave.

SKIING. Enthusiasts flock to the mountains of New Hampshire and Vermont; the most famous resorts include Stowe (p. 111) and Killington (p. 107).

BEACHES. Cape Cod (p. 134) and Nantucket, MA (p. 141) have the region's best.

COLONIAL LANDMARKS. They're everywhere, but a walk along the Freedom Trail in Boston, MA (p. 115) is a great place to start.

SCENIC NEW ENGLAND. Take a drive along Rte. 100 in the fall, when the foliage is at its most striking, or hike the Appalachian Trail (p. 99) for a view on foot.

MAINE

Nearly a thousand years ago, Leif Eriksson and his band of Viking explorers set foot on the coasts of Maine. Moose roamed the sprawling evergreen wilderness, the cry of the Maine coon cat echoed through towering mountains, and countless lobsters crawled in the ocean deep. A millennium has not changed much. Forests still cover nearly 90% of Maine's land, an area larger than the entire stack of New England states to the south, and the inner reaches of the state stretch on for mile after uninhabited mile, while some more populated locales dot a harsh and jagged coastline.

ⓘ PRACTICAL INFORMATION

Capital: Augusta.

Visitor info: Maine Tourism Information, 325B Water St., Hallowell (☎207-623-0363 or 888-624-6345; www.visitmaine.com). Send mail to P.O. Box 2300, Hallowell 04347. **Bureau of Parks and Lands,** State House Station #22 (AMHI, Harlow Bldg.), Augusta 04333 (☎207-287-3821). **Maine Forest Service,** Bureau of Forestry, State House Station #22, Harlow Bldg., 2nd fl., Augusta 04333 (☎207-287-2791).

Postal Abbreviation: ME. **Sales Tax:** 6%.

MAINE COAST

As the puffin flies, the Maine coast from Kittery to Lubec measures 228 mi., but if untangled, all of the inlets and rocky promontories would stretch out for 3478 mi. The meandering, two-lane **U.S. 1** hugs the coastline, stringing the port towns

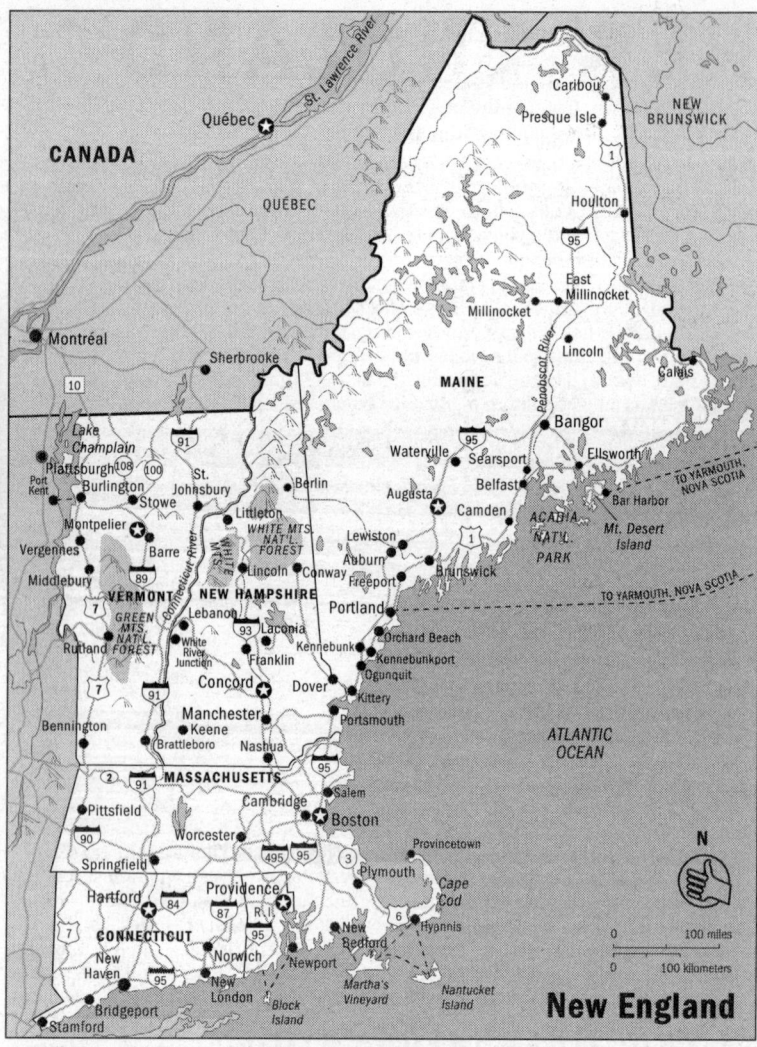

New England

together, and is the only option for most points north of Portland. In summer, the traffic pace is often slow; be prepared to take your time and stop at one of the innumerable makeshift red wooden lobster signs that bespeckle the roadsides for a freshly boiled one. Lesser roads and small ferry lines connect the remote villages and offshore islands. **Visitor info: Maine Information Center,** in Kittery, Visitor info 3 mi. north of the Maine-New Hampshire bridge. (☎207-439-1319. Open daily 8am-6pm; mid-Oct. to June 9am-5pm.) **Greyhound** serves points between Portland and Bangor along I-95, as well as the town of Brunswick, but to truly explore the coast you need a car.

PORTLAND   ☎207

During the 4th of July fireworks of 1866, a young boy playing on a Portland wharf inadvertently started a fire which destroyed over three-fourths of the city. The reconstruction efforts gave rise to the Victorian architecture in the Old Port

Exchange, which today forms a rather ironic backdrop to Portland's spirited youth culture. Here, teenagers and twenty-somethings gather in bars, restaurants, and cafes near the wharf and flood the streets in talkative groups or couples, even after stores close down. Outside the city, ferries run to the Casco Bay Islands while Sebago Lake provides sunning and water skiing.

■⚡ **ORIENTATION AND PRACTICAL INFORMATION.** Downtown sits near the bay, along **Congress St.** between State and Pearl St. A few blocks south lies the **Old Port,** on Commercial and Fore St. These two districts contain most of the city's sights and attractions. **I-295** (off I-95) forms the western boundary of downtown. **Concord Trailways,** 100 Sewall St. (☎828-1151; office open daily 5:30am-8:30pm), runs to Boston (2hr., 11 per day, $17) and Bangor (2hr., 4 per day, $21). Metro buses #3 and 5 run to and from the station. The **Greyhound/Vermont Transit** station (☎772-6587) is located at 950 Congress St., on the western outskirts of town. *Be cautious here at night.* Buses run to Boston (2hr., 9 per day, $15) and Bangor (2½-3½hr., 6 per day, $19). **Prince of Fundy Cruises,** P.O. Box 4216, 468 Commercial St., sends ferries to Yarmouth, NS, from the Portland International Ferry Terminal, on Commercial St. near the Million Dollar Bridge. Boats run May to mid-June and mid-September to late October. Ferries depart Portland at 9pm; the 11hr. trip takes the whole night. (☎775-5616, 800-341-7540 or 800-482-0955. Cabins available. $60, ages 5-14 $30; car $80, bike $7; late June to mid-Sept. $80/$40/$98/$10. Reservations strongly recommended.) **Metro Bus** services downtown Portland. Routes run 6am-7pm. (☎774-0351. $1, seniors with Medicaid card 50¢, under 5 free; transfers free.) **Visitors Information Bureau:** 305 Commercial St., at Center St. (☎772-5800. Open M-F 8am-6pm, Sa-Su 10am-6pm; mid-Oct. to mid-May M-F 9am-5pm, Sa-Su 10am-5pm.) **Internet access: JavaNet Cafe,** 37 Exchange St. (☎773-2469; open M-Th 7:30am-11pm, F 7:30am-11, Sa 8am-11, Su 8am-9pm; $8 per hr). **Post Office:** 400 Congress St. (☎871-8426; open M-F 8am-7pm, Sa 9am-1pm). **ZIP code:** 04112. **Area code:** 207.

▌ **ACCOMMODATIONS.** Portland has some inexpensive accommodations, but prices jump during the summer. At Exit 8 off I-95, **Super 8** and budget rates congregate. (☎854-1881. A few singles at $35; most start around $60.) The casual, elegant **Oak Leaf Inn,** 51A Oak St., has converted several of its guest suites into welcoming 4-6 bed dorms for stranded hostelers seeking the now nonexistent Portland Youth Hostel. (☎773-7882. Kitchen, towels and linen included, laundry. 20 beds total. Reservations strongly recommended. Dorms $22, nonmembers $27.) **The Inn at St. John,** 939 Congress St., is not located in an especially appealing neighborhood, but its upscale decor makes for a more elegant alternative. (☎773-6481 or 800-636-9127. Continental breakfast included. Kitchen, laundry facilities, and bike storage available. Free local calls and parking. Rooms with private bath are available. Singles and doubles start at M-Th $55, F-Su $65; in winter $50.) **Wassamki Springs,** 56 Saco St., in Scarborough, is the closest campground to Portland. Drive 6 mi. west on Congress St. (which becomes Rte. 22, then County Rd.), then turn right on Saco St. Flocks of migrant Winnebagos nest among cozy, fairly private sites bordering a lake encircled by sandy beaches. (☎839-4276. Free showers and flush toilets. Open May to mid-Oct. Reserve 2 weeks in advance, especially July-Aug. Sites for 2 people $21, with hookup $23-25; each additional person $4; lakefront sites $2 extra.)

▐ **FOOD.** Portland's harbor overflows with the ocean's fruits, but non-aquatic and vegetarian fare isn't too hard to find, either. A favorite among Portland's youth, **Federal Spice,** 225 Federal St., just off Congress St., spices all its entrees (all under $6) with fiery Caribbean, South American, and Asian ingredients. (☎774-6404. Open M-Sa 11am-9pm.) **Gilbert's Chowder House,** 92 Commercial St., is the local choice for seafood. For only $6, a large bowl of chowder in a bread bowl is a meal in itself. (☎871-5636. Open Su-Th 11am-9pm, F-Sa 11am-10pm; Oct.-May call for hours.) The homemade, organic pizza pies at the **Flatbread Company,** 72 Commercial St., are tasty and healthy treats ($7.75-13.50). Sit and enjoy the ocean view as your meal is fired in a huge clay oven. (☎772-8777. Open M-Th 11:30am-10pm, F-Sa 11:30am-10:30pm; in winter M-Th 11:30am-9:30pm, F-Sa 11:30am-10pm.)

NEW ENGLAND

◙ **SIGHTS.** Primordial offshore islands with secluded beaches and relatively undeveloped interiors lie just a ferry ride from the city proper. America's oldest ferry service, **Casco Bay Lines,** on State Pier near the corner of Commercial and Franklin, runs year-round to these nearby islands. Daily **ferries** depart approximately every hour for **Peaks Island.** (☎774-7871. Operates M-Sa 5:45am-10:30pm. Round-trip $5.25.) On the island, **Brad's Recycled Bike Shop,** 115 Island Ave., rents out bikes. (☎766-5631. $5 per hr., $8.50 for up to 3hr., $12 per day.) Waves crash on **Long Island's** quiet, unpopulated beach; Casco Bay Lines runs ten ferries there daily. Starting at Long Island, you can island-hop by catching later ferries to other islands (same price as Peaks ferry). Getting to more than two islands will take all day. **Two Lights State Park,** across the Million Dollar Bridge on State St. and south along Rte. 77 to Cape Elizabeth, is a great, uncrowded place to picnic. (☎799-5871. $2.)

The sea calls, but Portland does have landlubber activities. The **Portland Museum of Art,** 7 Congress Sq., at the intersection of Congress, High, and Free Streets, collects American art by John Singer Sargent and Winslow Homer. (☎775-6148 or 800-639-4067. Open June to mid-Oct. M-W and Sa-Su 10am-5pm, Th-F 10am-9pm. $6, students and seniors $5, ages 6-12 $1; free F 5-9pm.) The **Wadsworth-Longfellow House,** 489 Congress St., was the home of 19th-century poet Henry Wadsworth Longfellow and is now a museum of social history and US literature focusing on late 18th- and 19th-century antiques as well as on the life of the poet. (☎879-0427. House open June-Oct. daily 10am-5:30pm. Gallery and museum store also open Nov.-May W-Sa noon-4pm. $6, students and seniors $5, ages 6-18 $2. Price includes admission to a neighboring history museum with rotating exhibits. Tours every 30-40min.)

◙◙ **ENTERTAINMENT AND NIGHTLIFE.** Portland's vibrant, youthful culture shows in its many summer theater and orchestra performances; signs for these productions decorate the city, and schedules are available at the Visitors Center (see **Practical Information,** above). The **Portland Symphony** presents concerts renowned throughout the Northeast. (☎842-0800; 50% student discount.) Info on Portland's jazz, blues, and club scene packs the *Casco Bay Weekly* and *FACE*, both of which are free in many restaurants and stores.

Traditionally on the first Sunday in June, the **Old Port Festival** (☎772-6828) fills many blocks from Federal to Commercial St. with as many as 50,000 people. On summer afternoons during the **Noontime Performance Series,** a variety of bands perform in Portland's Monument Sq. and Congress Sq. (☎772-6828; late June to Aug.). For a taste of the hometown spirit, the **Portland Sea Dogs,** an AA minor-league baseball team, take the field from April to mid-September at **Hadlock Field** on Park Ave. Kids can run the bases after Sunday games. (☎879-9500. $4-6, under 17 $2-5.)

After dark, the Old Port area, known as "the strip," especially **Fore St.** between Union and Exchange St., livens up with pleasant (if touristy) shops and a few good pubs. **Brian Boru,** 57 Center St., provides a mellow pub scene. The nachos ($5) are good, as are $2 pints all day Sunday. (☎780-1506. Open daily 11:30am-1am.) **Gritty MacDuff's,** 396 Fore St., brews its own beer ($3 pints) for adoring locals and entertains with live bluegrass and jazz two to three times a week. (☎772-2739. No cover. Open daily 11:30am-1am.) The English pub around the corner, **Three Dollar Dewey's,** 241 Commercial St., serves over 100 different beers (36 on tap at $3-3.50), along with great chili (cup $3.50) and free popcorn. (☎772-3310. Open M-Sa 11:30am-midnight, Su noon-1am.) The **Dry Dock Restaurant & Tavern,** 84 Commercial St., is a great place to relax with a few drinks and friends. The bar is outside with a great waterfront view. (☎774-3550. Open daily 11am-1am.)

SOUTH OF PORTLAND ☎207

OLD ORCHARD BEACH
A kingdom of delightful tackiness, Old Orchard Beach reigns 10 mi. south of Portland on U.S. 1 (or take Exit 5 off I-95 south and follow signs). The plastic jewel in the beach's crown is the **Wonderland Arcade.** The rides aren't spectacular for those with high hopes, but the simple, happy carnival atmosphere is blissfully anachronistic. Parking costs $3, and East Grand Ave. is packed with seaside hotels and motels, the cheapest of which cost around $40 for a double.

KENNEBUNK

Kennebunk and its coastal counterpart 8 mi. east, **Kennebunkport,** are more tasteful (and expensive) than Old Orchard. Both of these towns are popular hideaways for wealthy authors and artists—Kennebunkport reluctantly grew famous as the summer home of former President Bush. Rare and used bookstores line U.S. 1 just south of Kennebunk, while art galleries fill the town itself. You could spend a day (and a fortune) exploring all the little shops in town. Even more scary than its monied homogeneity, though, is the **Maritime Productions' Chilling and Unusual Theater Cruise,** a 2hr. cruise and performance narrating true tales of haunted lighthouses, ghost ships, and cannibalism in New England's maritime past and present. (☎967-4938 or 967-5595. Departs twice daily from Kennebunkport Marina on Ocean Ave. 3:30pm matinee cruise $26, seniors $24, children $22; 6:30pm sunset cruise $30 all ages.) The 55 ft. gaff rigged **Schooner Eleanor** provides a more relaxed 2hr. yachting experience. (☎967-8809. Leaves from Arundel Wharf, Ocean Ave. $38. Call for reservations and times.) The **Kennebunk-Kennebunkport Chamber of Commerce,** 17 U.S. 100/Western Ave., in Kennebunkport, has a free guide. (☎967-0857. Open M-F 9am-5pm, Sa 10am-3pm, Su 11am-3pm; off-season M-F 9am-5pm.)

OGUNQUIT

South of Kennebunk on U.S. 1 lies Ogunquit, which means "beautiful place by the sea." The long, sandy shoreline is probably the best beach north of Cape Cod. Ogunquit also has one of New England's largest (although seasonal) gay communities. The **Ogunquit Welcome Center and Chamber of Commerce,** on U.S. 1, has info. (☎646-2939. Open M-Th noon-5pm, F 9am-8pm, Sa 10am-6pm; early Sept. to late May daily 9am-5pm.) The **Rachel Carson National Wildlife Refuge,** ½ mi. off U.S. 1 on Rte. 9, provides a secluded escape from the tourist throngs. A trail winds through the salt marsh, home to over 200 species of shorebirds and waterfowl. (☎646-9226. Office open M-F 8am-4:30pm, Sa-Su 10am-2pm; off-season M-F 8am-4:30pm. Trail open daily sunrise-sunset. Free.) In nearby Wells, the **Wells Reserve at Landholm Farm,** at the junction of U.S. 1 and Rte. 9, sprawls over meadows and beaches and offers tours of the estuary, bird life, and wildflowers. (☎646-1555. Visitors Center open mid-Jan. to Apr. M-F 10am-4pm, May-Oct M-Sa 10am-4pm, Su noon-4pm; Nov. to mid-Dec. M-F 10am-4pm.). Nearby **Perkins Cove,** which is accessible only by a very windy and narrow road, charms the argyle socks off the polo-shirt crowd with boutiques hawking seashell sculptures. The two **Barnacle Billy's** restaurants, about 60 ft. apart on Oar Weed Rd., practice an interesting division of labor. The original (a lobster pound) broils, bakes, and sautés lobsters, while their newer full-service location has a bigger menu. (☎646-5575. Both open daily noon-9:30pm.) Weather permitting, biking is the best way to travel Maine's rocky shores and spare yourself the thick summer traffic. **Wheels and Wares,** U.S. 1 on the Wells/Ogunquit border, rents mountain bikes. (☎646-5774. Open M-Tu 10am-9pm, W-Su 9am-7pm. $20 per day, $25 per 24hr.) **Moody,** just south of Ogunquit, has budget motels.

MT. DESERT ISLAND ☎207

Mt. Desert Island is anything but deserted. During the summer, the island swarms with tourists lured by the thick forests and mountainous landscape. Roughly half of the island is covered by Acadia National Park, which harbors some of the last protected marine, mountain, and forest environments on the New England coast. Bar Harbor, on the eastern side, is by far the most crowded and glitzy part of the island. Once a summer hamlet for the very wealthy, the town now welcomes a motley melange of R&R-seekers; though the monied have fled to the more secluded Northeast and Seal Harbor, the town still maintains its overpriced traditions.

■▪◪ **ORIENTATION AND PRACTICAL INFORMATION.** Mt. Desert Island is shaped roughly like a really big lobster claw, 14 mi. long and 12 mi. wide. To the east on Rte. 3 lie **Bar Harbor** and **Seal Harbor.** South on Rte. 198 near the cleft is **Northeast Harbor.** Across Somes Sound on Rte. 102 is **Southwest Harbor,** where fishing and shipbuilding thrive without the taint of tacky tourism. **Rte. 3** runs through Bar Harbor, becoming **Mt. Desert St.;** it and **Cottage St.** are the major east-west arteries.

Rte. 102 circuits the western half of the island. **Concord Trailways** (☎942-8686 or 888-741-8686; operates mid-June to early Sept.) leaves Bar Harbor daily from the Village Green at 195 Main St. and Bay Ferry Terminal for Bangor (1½hr., 4 per day, $25) and Boston (4¼hr., 2 per day, $57). **Beal & Bunker** (☎244-3575; open late June to Sept. daily 8am-4:30pm; call for winter hours) runs ferries from the Northeast Harbor town dock to Great Cranberry Island (20min.; 6 per day; $10, under 12 $5). **Bay Ferries** (☎888-249-7245), in Bar Harbor, runs to Yarmouth, NS (2¾hr.; 1-2 per day; $55, ages 5-12 $25, seniors $50, car $95, bike $25. Reservations recommended, $5 fee; car price does not include humans.) **Bar Harbor Bicycle Shop,** 141 Cottage St., rents bikes. (☎288-3886. Mountain bikes $10 for 4hr., $15 per day. Helmet, lock, and map included. 20% discount for rentals of 5 days or longer. Driver's license or credit card required. Open daily 8am-8pm; Sept.-June daily 9am-6pm.) **National Park Canoe Rentals,** at the north end of Long Pond off Rte. 102, in Pond's End (☎244-5854), or on the pier at the end of West St., Bar Harbor (☎288-0007), rents canoes and kayaks. (Kayaks only available at Long Pond location, which is open mid-May to mid-Oct. daily 8am-5pm. West St. location open daily 9am-8pm. Canoes $22 for 4hr., $32 per day; tandem kayaks $25 per half-day, $45 per day.)

Acadia National Park Visitors Center, 3 mi. north of Bar Harbor on Rte. 3., has info. (☎288-4932 or 288-5262. Open daily mid-June to mid-Sept. 8am-6pm; mid-Apr. to mid-June and mid-Sept. to Oct. 8am-4:30pm.) The **Park Headquarters,** 3 mi. west of Bar Harbor on Rte. 233, provides visitor info during the off season. (☎288-3338. Open year-round M-F 8am-4:30pm.) **Bar Harbor Chamber of Commerce:** 93 Cottage St. (☎288-5103. Open M-F 8am-5pm, Sa-Su noon-5pm; in winter M-F 8am-4pm.) **Mt. Desert Island Regional Chamber of Commerce,** on Rte. 3 at the entrance to Thompson Island (☎288-3411). In the same building is a state-owned **Acadia National Park Information Center** (☎288-9702). Both are open daily July-Aug. 9am-8pm; mid-May to June 10am-6pm and Sept. to mid-Oct. 9am-6pm. **Hotlines: Downeast Sexual Assault Helpline,** ☎800-228-2470; **Mental Health Crisis Line,** ☎800-245-8889; both 24hr. **Emergency: Acadia National Park Law Enforcement,** ☎288-3369. **Post Office:** 55 Cottage St. (☎288-3122; open M-F 8am-4:45pm, Sa 9am-noon). **ZIP code:** 04609. **Area code:** 207.

🛏 ACCOMMODATIONS. Grand hotels and prices linger from the island's exclusive resort days. Still, a few reasonable establishments do exist, particularly on **Rte. 3** north of Bar Harbor. Camping spots cover the island, especially on **Rte. 102** and **Rte. 198,** well west of town. Located in the parish house of St. Saviour's Episcopal Church, **Bar Harbor Youth Hostel (HI-AYH),** 27 Kennebec St., accommodates 20 guests in two large, cheery dorm rooms. A perfect location, common room with TV and piano, full kitchen, weekly movies, and free baked goods compensate for only two showers and an 11pm curfew. (☎288-5587. Linen $2. Lockout 9am-5pm. No reservations. Open mid-June to Sept. Dorms $12, nonmembers $15.) **Mt. Desert Island YWCA,** 36 Mt. Desert St., near downtown Bar Harbor, caters to women with its common room, kitchen, laundry, and Internet access. (☎288-5008. Open daily 9am-9pm; off-season M-F 9am-4pm. Reserve early. Singles with shared bath $30; doubles $50; solarium with 7 beds $20 per bed; weekly rates $90/$150/$65. $25 deposit.) **White Birches Campground,** in Southwest Harbor, on Seal Cove Rd. 1 mi. west of Rte. 102., has 60 widely spaced, wooded sites in a remote location. (☎244-3797. Free hot showers, bathrooms, laundry, pool. Reservations recommended, especially in summer. Open daily mid-May to mid-Oct. 8am-8pm for check-in. $20 for up to 4 people, with hookup $24; weekly $120/$144; each additional person $4.)

Acadia National Park campgrounds include **Blackwoods,** 5 mi. south of Bar Harbor on Rte. 3. The more than 300 wooded sites seem tightly packed when campgrounds reach full occupancy in summer. When the throngs depart, however, the charm of the campground's thick, deep, dark woods returns, as does the larger wildlife. (☎288-3274, reservations 800-365-2267. Reserve in summer. Mid-Mar. through Oct. $18; mid-Dec. to mid-Mar. free. Group sites also available.) **Seawall,** located off Rte. 102A on the western side of the island, 4 mi. south of Southwest Harbor and a 10min. walk from the ocean, is slightly more rustic, with toilets but no hookups.

(☎244-3600. Showers $1 per 6min. Open daily late May to Sept. 7:15am-9pm. First come, first served walk-in sites $12; drive-in and RV sites $18.)

◖ **FOOD.** To watch some flicks and chow down on a few slices, head over to ▨**Reel Pizza,** 33 Kennebec Place at the end of Rodick off Main. This movie theater-*cum*-pizzeria shows four films each evening for $5 and serves up creative pizza pies ($8.50-18), such as the "fantastic voyage," heaped with smoked salmon, roasted red peppers, and artichoke spread. (☎288-3828. Open daily 5pm to end of last screening.) The walls and ceilings at **Freddie's Route 66 Restaurant,** 21 Cottage St. in Bar Harbor, are absolutely crammed with campy license plates, wind-up metal cars, and boob tubes showing Casper the Friendly Ghost in black and white. The Cadillac burger is a well-spent $9; the seafood pie runs $15. (☎288-3708. Open mid-May to mid-Oct. daily 11am-3:30pm and 4:30-10pm.) **Beal's,** off Main St. at the end of Clark Point Rd. in Southwest Harbor, goes easy on the frills, offering lobster at superb prices on an outdoor, picnic-tabled patio overlooking the pier. Pick a live crustacean from a tank ($10-13), and (s)he'll be buttered and steaming red in minutes. (☎244-7178 or 800-245-7178. Open mid-May to early Sept. daily 9am-8pm; seafood is sold year-round daily 9am-5pm. Hours vary with weather.) **The Colonel's Deli Bakery and Restaurant,** on Main St. in Northeast Harbor, fixes sandwiches so big that it's hard to get one into your mouth ($6-10). Take one with you for a cheap dinner in the National Park. (☎276-5147. Open mid-Apr. to Oct. daily 6:30am-9pm.)

◐ **SIGHTS.** The staff at the **Mt. Desert Oceanarium,** at the end of Clark Pt. Rd. near Beal's in Southwest Harbor, knows its sea stuff. The main museum, reminiscent of a grammar school science fair, thrills children and some adults. (☎244-7330. Open mid-May to late Oct. M-Sa 9am-5pm. Ticket for all 3 facilities $13, ages 4-12 $10.) Cruises head out to sea from a number of points. **Bar Harbor Whale Watch Co.,** 1 West St. at the waterfront, offers various tours. (☎288-2386. Open May-Oct; call for exact schedule. Reservations recommended. Puffin- and whale-watching tours $35-45, ages 5-15 $20, under 5 $8; fishing and seal-watching trips $18/$15/$5.) **Wildwood Stables,** along Park Loop Rd. in Seal Harbor, takes tourists on explorations of the island via horse and carriage. (☎276-3622. 1hr. tour $13.50, seniors $12.50, ages 6-12 $7, ages 2-5 $4. 2hr. tour $17.50/$16.50/$8/$5. Reservations recommended.)

▣▨ **ENTERTAINMENT AND NIGHTLIFE.** Most after-dinner pleasures on the island are simple and cluster in Bar Harbor. **Ben and Bill's Chocolate Emporium,** 66 Main St., near Cottage St., boasts 50 flavors of homemade ice cream, including—no kidding—lobster. The fudge (¼lb. $2.75) is killer. (☎288-3281. Open mid-Feb. to Jan. daily 9am-midnight. Cones $3-4.) **Geddy's Pub,** 19 Main St., gives a backwoods backdrop of weathered wooden signs, beat-up license plates, and moose head trophies to the dancing frenzy that breaks out nightly. Live music until 10:30pm, when tables are moved aside for a DJ and dance floor. Pub-style dinner served until 9:30pm, pizzas ($10) until 10pm. (☎288-5077. No cover. Open Apr.-Oct. daily 11:30-12:30am; winter hours vary.) Locals prefer the **Lompoc Cafe & Brew Pub,** 36 Rodick St., off Cottage St., which features Bar Harbor Real Ale and live jazz, blues, Celtic, rock, and folk. (☎288-9392. Th open mic. No cover. Open May-Oct. daily 11:30am-1am. Shows F-Sa nights.) The Art Deco **Criterion Theater,** on Cottage St., shows mainstream movies in the summer. (☎288-3441. 2 evening movies daily. Box office opens 30min. before show. $7, seniors $6, under 12 $4.50; balcony seats $7.75.)

ACADIA NATIONAL PARK   ☎207

The jagged, rocky oceanside perimeter of Acadia National Park's 38,500 acres is gradually obscured, then enveloped by thick pine forests as you move inland. Fern-shrouded streams and 120 miles of hiking trails and carriage roads criss-cross the rugged, coastal terrain. Fearing the island would one day be overrun by cars, millionaire and expert horseman John D. Rockefeller funded the creation of these carriage roads, now accessible to mountain bikes.

NEW ENGLAND

With views of Long Pond, Echo Lake, and a watchtower that crowns the summit, **Beech Mountain** (0.5 mi.) is a pleasant trail for amateur hikers. **Precipice Trail** (1.5 mi.), one of the most popular and strenuous hikes, is closed June to late August to accommodate nesting peregrine falcons; be ready to use the iron ladders that are needed to finish the meandering cliff and ledge trail. Hike either the **Cadillac Mountain North** (4.5 mi.) or **South Ridge** (7.5 mi.) trails, or cruise up the paved **auto road** to the top. At 1530 ft., Cadillac Mountain is the highest point on the Atlantic seaboard north of Brazil; from its peak, be the first person in the US to witness ■**sunrise** on any summer morning (4-4:30am in summer).

About 4 mi. south of Bar Harbor on Rte. 3, **Park Loop Rd.** runs along the shore of the island, where great waves crash against steep granite cliffs. The sea comes into **Thunder Hole** with a bang at half-tide. Practice your backfloat in the relatively warm **Echo Lake** or at **Sand Beach,** both of which have lifeguards in the summer.

Touring the park by auto costs $10 for seven days, $5 per pedestrian or cyclist. Seniors can purchase a lifetime pass for $10. The *Biking and Hiking Guide to the Carriage Roads* ($6), available at the Visitors Center and in bookstores, offers invaluable directions for the more labyrinthine trails. To spend the night in or near the park (and you should!) see Mt. Desert Island's **Accommodations,** p. 96.

NORTHERN MAINE COAST   ☎207

Much like the coastal region south of Portland, the north offers the traveler unforgettable beaches, windswept ocean vistas, and verdant forests—for a price. Lodging in L.L. Bean country isn't cheap, but just passing through can give all the flavor without the guilt. U.S. 1 is northern Maine's only thoroughfare; public transportation is non-existent, and traffic barely creeps along on rainy weekends in Freeport.

FREEPORT

About 20 mi. north of Portland on I-95, Freeport once garnered glory as the "birthplace of Maine." The 1820 signing of documents declaring the state's independence from Massachusetts took place at the historic **Jameson Tavern,** 115 Main St., right next to L. L. Bean. Freeport is now known as the factory outlet capital of the world, with over 100 downtown stores attracting urbanites sick of the woods. The granddaddy of them all, **L.L. Bean,** began making Maine Hunting Shoes here in 1912. The megamogul now sells everything in outdoor gear and outfits America's youth with backpacks guaranteed for life. The factory outlet, 11 Depot St., behind Nine West Shoes, is the place for bargains. (☎552-7772. Open daily 9am-10pm; Jan. to late May 9am-9pm.) The multi-storied retail store, 95 Main St. (☎865-4761), is open 24 hours day, 365 days a year, and generates a madness that could transform even the biggest city slicker into a backwoods renegade.

CAMDEN

In the summer, khaki-clad crowds flock to Camden, 100 mi. north of Portland, to dock their yachts alongside the tall-masted schooners in Penobscot Bay. Cruises are generally out of the budgeteer's price range, but the **Camden-Rockport Lincolnville Chamber of Commerce,** on the public landing in Camden behind Cappy's Chowder House, can tell you which are most affordable. They also have info on the sparse budget accommodations. (☎236-4404 or 800-223-5459. Open M-F 9am-5pm, Sa 10am-5pm, Su 10am-4pm; mid-Oct. to mid-May closed Su.) The Camden Hills State Park, 1¼ mi. north of town on U.S. 1, is almost always full in July and August, but you are fairly certain to get a site if you arrive before 2pm. This beautiful coastal retreat offers more than 25 mi. of trails, including one which leads up to Mt. Battie and has a harbor view. (☎236-3109; reservations 287-3824 or 800-332-1501. Sites $17, ME residents $13, day use $2. Free showers. Open mid-May to mid-Oct.) The folks at Maine Sports, on U.S. 1, in Rockport just south of Camden, teach/lead/rent/ sell a wide array of sea-worthy vehicles. Kayaks will only be rented to those with paddling experience, but anyone can join a tour. (☎236-8797. Open daily 8am-9pm; Sept.-May daily 9am-6pm. 2hr. harbor tour $35. Full-day singles $30-45, doubles $40-

THE APPALACHIAN TRAIL Stretching 2160 mi. from Mt. Katahdin, ME, to Springer Mountain, GA, the Appalachian Trail, or "AT," follows the path of the Appalachian Mountains along the eastern United States. Use of the AT is free, although only foot travelers may access it. The Trail cuts through 14 states, 8 national forests, and 6 national parks. Generally, the AT is very accessible, crossed by roads along its entire length except for the northernmost 100 mi. Although many sections make excellent day hikes or overnights, about 2500 "through-hikers" attempt a continuous hike of the AT annually. Three-sided first come, first served shelters dot the trail, spaced about a day's journey apart. Hikers take advantage of streams and nearby towns to stock up on water and supplies. White blazes on rocks and trees mark the length of the main trail, while blue blazes mark side trails. For more info, contact the Center for AT Studies, P.O. Box 525, Hot Springs, NC 28743 (☎704-622-7601, M-Sa 10am-10pm; fax 704-622-7601; atcenter@trailplace.com; www.trailplace.com).

NEW ENGLAND

60, depending on whether it's a sea or lake kayak. Ask about overnights to nearby islands.) The **Maine State Ferry Service** (☎800-491-4883), 5 mi. north of Camden in Lincolnville, floats over to Islesboro Island. (20min., 7-9 per day; last return trip 4:30pm. Round-trip $4.50, with bike $8.50, car and driver $13. Parking $4.) The ferry also has an agency on U.S. 1 in Rockland, 517A Main St., that runs to North Haven, Vinalhaven, and Matinicus. (☎596-2202. Rates and schedules change with weather.)

SEARSPORT

Forty-five miles south of Bar Harbor on U.S. 1 lies Searsport, a respite from the commercialization of Camden and Freeport, but well-known as the antiques capital of Maine. Here, first-time buyers and lifelong collectors scour multitudinous shops for ancient and colonial treasures. A stay at the **Searsport Penobscot Bay Hostel (HI)**, 132 W. Main St./U.S. 1, merits a trip to this oceanside town. Once a sea captain's getaway, and later a bed and breakfast, the colonial homestead is now a spacious, relaxing, home-decorated hostel. (☎548-2506 or 877-334-6783. Open mid-Apr. through Oct. Office hours 8-10am, 5-10pm. Lockout 10pm. 10 beds. $15, nonmembers $18. Doubles $40/$50 per person.) Each of the 19th-century village buildings comprising the **Penobscot Marine Museum** features a different aspect of colonial New England maritime livelihood. The buildings, including Old Town Hall, the Congregational Church, and the historic home of Jeremiah Merithew, concentrate along **Church St.**, off U.S. 1. (☎548-2529. Open late May to mid-Oct. M-Sa 10am-5pm, Su noon-5pm. $6, seniors $5, ages 6-15 $2, families $14.)

NEW HAMPSHIRE

There are two sides to New Hampshire: the rugged landscape and natural beauty of the White Mountains, and the tax-free outlets, tourist traps, and state liquor stores that line most of the highways. The first colony to declare its independence from Great Britain, New Hampshire has retained its backwoods libertarian charm and its motto, "Live Free or Die!"

☑ PRACTICAL INFORMATION

Capital: Concord.
Visitor info: Office of Travel and Tourism, P.O. Box 856, Concord 03302 (☎603-271-2666 or 800-386-4664; www.visitnh.gov). **NH Parks and Recreation:** (☎271-3556). **Fish and Game Dept.,** 2 Hazen Dr., Concord 03301 (☎603-271-3421), furnishes info on hunting and fishing regulations and license fees. **U.S. Forest Service,** 719 North Main St., Laconia 03246 (☎603-528-8721). Open M-F 8am-4:30pm.
Postal Abbreviation: NH. **Sales Tax:** 8% on meals and lodgings. **Area Code:** 603.

PORTSMOUTH
☎ 603

Although New Hampshire's seacoast is the smallest in the nation, with only 13 miles fronting the Atlantic Ocean, the state makes the most of its toehold on the water. Portsmouth, once the colonial capital, is one of the nicest seaside towns north of Boston. Most buildings date to the 18th century, while a handful were built in the mid-17th century. Although not large by any standards, Portsmouth is exceptionally cultured—and expensive. History is the main attraction, seafood reigns supreme, and a pint of local ale is the mainstay after dinner.

⑦ PRACTICAL INFORMATION. Just 57 mi. north of Boston, Portsmouth is situated at the junction of U.S. 1, 1A, and I-95. The town is best navigated by foot; leave your car in one of the inexpensive lots (50¢ per hr.) downtown. State St. runs north-south through downtown and is bisected by Pleasant and Fleet St. **Buses: Vermont Transit/Greyhound,** 1 Market Sq. (☎436-0163), heads to Portsmouth from Boston (4 per day, 1¼hr., $13). **Public Transit: Seacoast Trolley** (☎431-6975) runs every hr. in summer 10am-5pm, with 17 stops in and around Portsmouth ($2). **Blue Star Taxi:** ☎436-2774. **Visitor info: Greater Portsmouth Chamber of Commerce,** 500 Market St., outside downtown. (☎436-1118. Open M-W 8:30am-5pm, Th-F 8:30am-7pm, Sa-Su 10am-5pm; in winter open M-F 8:30am-5pm.) **Hospital: Portsmouth Regional** (☎433-4006), a few miles from town at 333 Borthwick Ave. **Violence and Rape Hotline,** ☎800-336-3795. **Post Office:** 80 Daniel St. (☎431-1300; open M-F 7:30am-5:30pm, Sa 8am-noon). **Zip code:** 03801. **Area code:** 603.

⑥⬚ ACCOMMODATIONS AND FOOD. Portsmouth is not the best place to spend the night unless you can afford to part with your Ben Franklins. Accommodations in town are pricey; try U.S. 1A south of Portsmouth for typically drab motels. A nice alternative is **Camp Eaton** in York Harbor, ME, about 15 mi. north of Portsmouth off Rte. 1. Although the wooded sites are still pricey, oceanside vistas and immaculate bathrooms ease the pain. (☎207-363-3424. Sites $20-32 for 2.) The best bet may be to splurge and stay right in Portsmouth to take advantage of the great nightlife without having to drive out of town late at night.

Portsmouth offers plenty of other dining options, with many fine establishments dotting Market St. Unfortunately, great deals may be in short supply. ◪**The Friendly Toast,** 121 Congress St., a block and a half from Market Sq., is a local landmark, cluttered with the most ghastly artifacts the 50s could produce: mannequin limbs, pulp novels, formica furniture, and stroke-inducingly bad art. Most menu items ($6-7), such as the "mission burrito" ($6.25), are nearly "impossible" to finish. Breakfast is served all day. (☎430-2154. Open M-Th 7am-11pm, F 7am through Su 9pm.) At **Gilly's Lunchcart,** 175 Fleet St., semi-inebriated folk trail out the door of a nearby pub and into the street where heavenly hot dogs, burgers, and sandwiches await into the wee hours of any given night. Top it off with fries for $1.25 or chili cheese fries for $3. (Open M-Sa 11:30am-2:30am, Su 4pm-2:30am.)

⑥⬚ SIGHTS AND ENTERTAINMENT. Modern Portsmouth sells itself with its colonial past. The most prestigious and well-known example is **Strawbery Banke,** on the corner of Marcy and Hancock Streets. The community was first settled as Strawbery Banke in 1630 and did not assume the name of Portsmouth until 1653. The **museum** is a collection of these same original buildings from the period. To find the museum, just follow the signs that lead you toward the harbor and through a charming maze of shops. (☎433-1100. Open daily mid-Apr. to late Oct. 10am-5pm. $12, seniors $11, ages 7-17 $8. Tickets are good for 2 days.) Right across the street, snuggling the Piscataqua River, is **Prescott Park.** A great place to picnic or lounge, these well-tended gardens offer shade, fountains, and a pleasant respite from a day of budget travel. For something more technological, try the **USS Albacore,** a research submarine built locally at the Portsmouth Naval Shipyard. (☎436-3680. Open May-Oct. daily 9:30am-5pm; hours vary in winter. $5, seniors over 62 $3.50, ages 7-17 $2.) Deprive yourself of sleep and peace of mind with **Gravestones by Dusk,** a 1hr. tour of

North Cemetery. One of the Portsmouth's oldest graveyards, the cemetery holds the burial sites of some of the city's most important skeletons. (☎436-5096. Open Apr.-Oct. Tours run M-Su cost $10 per person. Times vary; call for reservations.)

NEW HAMPSHIRE SKI RESORTS   ☎603

The various ranges within the White Mountains offer numerous opportunities for skiing. **Ski New Hampshire** is a service which provides information and reservations for five resorts in the White Mountains. (☎745-8101 or 800-937-5493; www.skinh.com. P.O. Box 517, Lincoln 03251.) Winters in New England are long, so skiing is usually available from November through April, depending on the weather.

In North Conway close to the outlets, **Cranmore** offers 39 trails and ski vacations complemented by great shopping. The 350 ft. half-pipe, as well as the Children's Summer Camp, are huge summer draws. The slopes open in late Nov.; new this year is the Wild Cherry Grand Prix Tubing Center. (☎800-786-6754. Lift tickets $29, ages 6-12 $15; lift operates M-F 9am-4pm, Sa-Su 8:30am-4pm.) Located along U.S. 302 near North Conway, **Attitash** is expensive, but offers two mountains, 68 trails (20% beginner, 47% intermediate, 33% expert), and 25 acres of glades. Mountain biking, horseback riding, waterslides, rock climbing, trampolines, and an alpine slide keep visitors busy in summer. (☎374-2368. Lift tickets for weekends/weekdays/holidays $48/$42/$50, children $30/$27/$30. Alpine slide open 10am-6pm. Single ride $10, double $16. During the summer, all-day value pack $24, ages 2-7 $10.)

Just outside Pinkham Notch on Rte. 16, **Wildcat Mountain** offers a superb view of the Whites from its 4062 ft. peak, as well as 44 trails (25%, 40%, 35%). Gondola rides are $9 in the summer. (☎888-754-9453. Lift tickets for weekends/weekdays $49/$39, ages 13-17 and 65+ $39/$34, ages 6-12 $29/$27.) Three mi. east of Lincoln on Rte. 112, **Loon Mountain** guarantees less crowded conditions on their 43 trails by limiting ticket sales. They have biking and horseback riding when the weather warms and the annual Highland Games during the third week in September. (☎745-8111. Lift tickets for weekends/weekdays $47/$40, teens $41/$33, children $29/$25.) Just off I-93 in Franconia Notch State Park, **Cannon Mountain** has 42 trails (30%, 30%, 40%) at slightly lower prices than other local resorts. Summer hiking, biking, and swimming keep athletes in shape, while the Aerial Tramway (see p. 105) schleps the rest of us up the mountain. (☎823-5563. Lift tickets for weekends/weekdays $42/$30, teens $35/$30, children and seniors $27/$20.)

WHITE MOUNTAINS   ☎603

Consisting of 780,000 acres of mountainous national forest maintained by the US Forest Service, the White Mountains provide a playground for outdoor enthusiasts. Year-round hiking and camping, as well as warm weather alternatives like canoeing, kayaking, and fishing, supplement the White Mountains' intense winter skiing options. Campsites can be found throughout the mountains, near lakes and rivers, and deep within the wilderness. The White Mountain National Forest also holds dozens of geological wonders and offers a mostly undisturbed refuge for some awe-inspiring animals, like the moose and black bears that occasionally surprise hikers.

▌ TRANSPORTATION

The scenery on the ride to the White Mountains gives only a taste of the breathtaking views you'll soak in once you arrive. **Concord Trailways** (☎228-3300 or 800-639-3317) runs from Boston to Concord (14 per day, $12); Conway (1 per day, $26); and Franconia (1 per day, $27). **Vermont Transit** (☎800-451-3292) stops its Boston-to-Vermont buses in Concord (4 per day, $12.50) at the Trailways terminal, 30 Stickney Ave. The **Appalachian Mountain Club (AMC)** runs a **shuttle** between locations on the Appalacian Trail in the White Mountains. Consult AMC's *The Guide* for a complete map of routes and times; reservations are recommended for all stops and required for some. (☎466-2727. Service operates early June to early Oct. daily 8am-4pm. $8, nonmembers $9.)

🛈 ORIENTATION AND PRACTICAL INFORMATION

The White Mountains can be daunting to an unfamiliar traveler. The immense forest is bordered by a dozen or so distinctive towns and contains several commercial ski resorts. Many of this region's highlights can be found within three areas: **Pinkham Notch,** the popular center of the region; **Franconia Notch Area,** northwest of the National Forest; and **North Conway,** a buzzing gateway town. **Visitor info:** A map of the White Mountains area is super helpful; pick one up for free at local town info booths and the **White Mountain Attraction Center,** P.O. Box 10, N. Woodstock 03262, at Exit 32 from I-93. (☎745-8720. Open daily 8:30am-5:30pm.) **US Forest Service Ranger Stations** dot the main highways throughout the forest, also providing maps and info on trail locations and conditions as well as a handy free guide to the local **backcountry facilities.** Stations include: **Androscoggin** (☎466-2713), on Rte. 16, 5 mi. south of the U.S. 2 junction in Gorham; **Ammonoosuc** (☎869-2626), on Trudeau Rd. in Bethlehem, west of U.S. 3 on U.S. 302; and **Saco** (☎447-5448), on the Kancamangus Hwy. in Conway, 100 yd. off Rte. 16. (Ranger stations open daily 8am-4:30pm; Ammonoosuc only open M-F.) **Pinkham Notch Visitors Center** (☎466-2721 or 466-2727 for reservations), 10 mi. north of Jackson on Rte. 16 in Gorham, is the area's best source of info on weather and trail conditions. The center, run by the AMC, also handles reservations at any of the AMC lodgings and sells the complete line of AMC books, trail maps, and outdoor accessories. (Open daily 6:30am-10pm.)

🏕 CAMPING

The US Forest Service maintains over 20 **designated campgrounds:** six are directly accessible by car off the Kancamagus Hwy., the others are sprinkled along hiking trails. (☎877-444-6777 for reservations. Sites $12-16. Cars parked at campsite do not require a parking pass. Bathrooms and firewood usually available. Fee to change or cancel reservation $10. Reserve 2 weeks in advance, especially July-Aug.) Camping is less expensive or free of charge at the many backcountry **campsites,** which are only accessible via hiking trails. The **US Forest Service** (☎528-8721) and the AMC's free two-page handout, *Backpacker Shelters, Tentsites, Campsites, and Cabins in the White Mountains* offer helpful info. Regulations prohibit camping and fires above the tree line (approximately 4000 ft.), within 200 ft. of a trail, or within ¼ mi. of roads, huts, shelters, tent platforms, lakes, or streams. Rules vary depending on forest conditions; backpackers should call the Forest Service before settling into a campsite. Campers should note that a $5 **parking pass,** valid for one week, is required for any car parked at a trailhead in the forest.

🏠 ACCOMMODATIONS

The White Mountain Forest also rents land to the **AMC,** which has its main base at the Pinkham Notch Visitors Center and maintains eight backcountry huts, spaced about a day's hike apart, along the Appalachian Trail. Guests must provide their own sleeping bags or sheets; dinner and breakfast are included with each night's stay. (Bunk with 2 meals $66, children $44; AMC discounts available.) All huts open for full service June to mid-October; self-service rates with no meals are available at other times ($18, nonmembers $20; call the AMC for reservations). The club runs two car-accessible **lodgings** in the White Mountains: **Joe Dodge Lodge** (see **Pinkham Notch,** p. 103) and the **Crawford Hostel**—actually an isolated set of several spartan cabins situated against a mountainous backdrop east of Bretton Woods on U.S. 302. The hostel's main lodge includes a modest kitchen and library, while the front desk sells limited supplies, including trailguides, candy, and first-aid kit material. The cabins' 24 bunks fill up quickly, so make reservations. (☎278-5170, reservations through AMC 466-2727. Clean toilets, showers. Bring a sleeping bag/ linens and food. Curfew 9:30pm. $18, nonmembers $20.)

▓ OUTDOOR ACTIVITIES

If you intend to spend a lot of time in the area and are planning to do a significant amount of hiking, the *AMC White Mountain Guide* ($22; available in most bookstores and huts) is invaluable. The guide includes full maps and descriptions of all the mountain trails. Hikers should bring three layers of clothing in all seasons: one for wind, one for rain, and at least one for warmth, as weather conditions change at a moment's notice. Black flies and swarms of mosquitoes can ruin a trip, particularly in June, so carry insect repellent. After hiking, cycling is the next most popular way to tour the White Mountains. Many areas are accessible by bike, and paths are specifically provided for bikers in some locations. *The White Mountain Ride Guide* ($13) or the US Forest Service's bike trail guides, available at info centers, or *30 Bicycle Tours in New Hampshire* ($13), available at local bookstores and outdoor equipment stores, can help with planning. **Great Glen Trails Outdoor Center,** just north of Mt. Washington Auto Rd. on Rte. 16, rents some two-wheelers. (☎466-2333. Open daily 9am-5pm. Adult bike half-day $20, full-day $30.)

To see the National Forest without much exertion, drive the ▓**Kancamagus Scenic Highway,** which connects the towns of Lincoln and Conway. The 35 mi. drive requires at least an hour, though the vistas typically lure drivers to the side of the road for a picnic. Remember to purchase a **National Forest parking pass** ($5; valid for one week) if you plan to leave your car at a trailhead or picnic ground parking lot. Check your gas at Lincoln or North Woodstock (no gas is available for 35 mi.), then head east on the Kanc (officially Rte. 112; clearly marked) to enjoy the scenic splendor stretching all the way to Conway.

PINKHAM NOTCH ☎ 603

New Hampshire's easternmost Notch lies in the shadow of the tallest mountain in the Northeast, the 6288 ft. Mt. Washington. Pinkham's proximity to the peak makes it more crowded and less peaceful than some neighboring areas. The **Pinkham Notch Visitors Center,** the AMC's main info center in the White Mountains and the starting point for most trips up Mt. Washington, lies between Gorham and Jackson on Rte. 16. To get to Pinkham Notch from I-93 S, take Exit 35 and travel north on U.S. 3 until it meets U.S. 302; take U.S. 302 until it meets Rte. 16, then take Rte. 16 north.

From just behind the Pinkham Notch Visitors Center all the way up to the summit of Mt. Washington, **Tuckerman's Ravine Trail** takes 4-5hr. of steep hiking each way. Authorities urge caution when climbing—Mt. Washington claims at least one life every year. A gorgeous day here can suddenly turn into a chilling storm, with whipping winds and rumbling thunderclouds. It has never been warmer than 72°F atop Mt. Washington, and the average temperature on the peak is a bone-chilling 26.7°F. With an *average* wind speed of 35 mph and gusts that have been measured up to an astounding 231 mph, Mt. Washington is the windiest place in the world. If you take proper measures, however, the climb is stellar and the view on the way up well worth it. The **Lion's Head Trail** is a slightly less daunting hiking option, with more stable treadway in rough conditions. Motorists can take the **Mt. Washington Auto Rd.,** a paved and dirt road that winds 8 mi. to the summit. Motorists scaling the mountain by car receive bragging rights in the form of a free "This Car Climbed Mt. Washington" bumper sticker; delay affixing it to said bumper until your car has proven its engine and brakes can handle the challenge. The road begins at **Glen House,** 3 mi. north of the Visitors Center on Rte. 16. (☎466-3988. Road open daily June to Sept. 7:30am-6pm; May to June and Sept. to Oct. 8:30am-5pm. $17 per car and driver, $6 per passenger, ages 5-12 $4, seniors $2.) **Guided van tours** to the summit include a 30min. presentation on the mountain's natural history ($22, ages 5-12 $10). On even the most beautiful summer days, the summit is likely to be covered with clouds, giving you a slim chance of getting a good view. So enjoy the **snack bar,** offering sandwiches ($2-4) and drinks ($1-2) at reasonable rates. (☎466-3347. Open late May to mid-Oct. daily 8am-6pm.) A **museum** is run by the **Mt. Washington Observatory.** (☎466-3388. Open late May to mid-Oct. daily 9am-7pm.)

NEW ENGLAND

AMC's huts offer the best lodging near the mountain. At **Joe Dodge Lodge**, immediately behind the Pinkham Notch Visitors Center, a stay includes a comfortable bunk with two delicious and sizeable meals. The lodge offers over 100 bunks, but has no self-service kitchen—all meals are prepared and served by staff. Relax after each meal in the spacious library. (No reservations. $47, children $32; nonmembers $51/$35. Off-season $44, children $30; nonmembers $48/$32.) **Hermit Lake Shelter**, situated about 2hr. up the Tuckerman Ravine Trail, has bathrooms but no shower, and sleeps 72 people in eight lean-tos and three tent platforms ($8 per night; buy nightly passes at the Visitors Center). **Carter Notch Hut** is 4 mi. hike up the **19 Mile Brook Trail;** it has 40 bunks and a kitchen with a gas stove. Just 1½ mi. from Mt. Washington's summit sits **Lakes of the Clouds,** the largest, highest, and most popular of the AMC's huts with room for 90 people; additional sleeping space for six backpackers in its basement refuge room can be reserved from any other hut. (☎466-2727. $18, nonmembers $20. Reservations recommended for stays at all AMC huts.)

FRANCONIA NOTCH AREA ☎603

Located in the northwestern expanse of the forest, Franconia Notch is not actually part of the White Mountain National Forest but a state park owned and maintained by the state of New Hampshire. Formed by glacial movements that began during an ice age 400 million years ago, the Notch comprises imposing granite cliffs, waterfalls, endless woodlands, and the famous rocky profile known as the "Old Man of the Mountain," which has come to adorn New Hampshire state highway signs.

⚐ PRACTICAL INFORMATION. All but one of the area highlights are directly accessible from I-93. Beginning from Lincoln, traveling north on I-93, ⊠**The Flume,** a two-mile walk through a spectacular granite gorge, is the first essential stop within Franconia Notch (Pkwy. Exit 1). The moss-covered canyon walls are 90 ft. high, and the walk takes visitors over centuries-old covered bridges and past the 45 ft. Avalanche Falls. Tickets can be purchased from the **The Flume Visitors Center,** which also shows an excellent 15min. film that acquaints visitors with the landscape and geological history of the area. (☎745-8391; www.flumegorge.com. Open May-Oct. daily 9am-5pm; July-Aug. daily 9am-5:30pm. $8, ages 6-12 $5.) A 9 mi. **bike path** also begins at the Visitors Center and parallels I-93 north through the park.

⚐⚑ ACCOMMODATIONS AND FOOD. The beauty of Franconia Notch makes it an ideal place for camping. **Lafayette Place Campground,** with nearly 100 sites, is nestled smack in the middle of the Franconia Notch State Park. From the campground, the scenic **Pemi Trail** winds 2 mi. through the Notch forest and drops hikers at the Old Man of the Mountain Viewing Area. (☎823-9513. Open mid-May to mid-Oct., weather permitting. Lafayette's location makes it extremely popular; reservations are recommended at least two weeks in advance. Coin-operated showers. Sites for 2 adults $16, $8 each additional adult, children no extra charge.) For a bit more privacy set up tent at the **Fransted Campground,** 3 mi. north of the Notch on Rte. 18. Its relatively low elevation also makes it a warmer alternative. (☎823-5675. Open May to mid-Oct. Showers and bathroom. Family sites $18-22.) **Woodstock Inn & Station** offers a comfortable but not cheap—from $87—option to camping. (☎745-3951. Breakfast included. Jacuzzi and health club privileges.) Even if the Inn's prices are too rich for your blood, the endless menu next door at the **Woodstock Inn Brewery** is sure to please, with everything from not-so-standard sandwiches and salads ($6-$8) to Mexican fare and seafood. **Polly's Pancake Parlor,** on Rte. 117 in Sugar Hill, just 2 mi. from Exit 38 off I-93, is a homey cabin restaurant with a maple-leaf theme and a dining room overlooking Mt. Washington. The parlor offers a stack of six superb pancakes for $6 and unlimited pancakes for $11. (☎823-5575. Open May-Oct. daily 7am-3pm, Apr. and Nov. Sa-Su 7am-2pm.)

◙ SIGHTS. Franconia is best known for the **Old Man of the Mountain,** a 40 ft. human profile formed by five ledges of stone atop a 1200 ft. cliff on Cannon Mountain. Nathaniel Hawthorne addressed this geological visage in his 1850 story "The Great Stone Face," and the landmark has since graced state license plates as the symbol of the Granite State. The exit for "Old Man" parking is clearly marked, and a 10min. walk down the designated path brings viewers to the bank of **Profile Lake,** which affords the best available view. The 80-passenger **Cannon Mountain Aerial Tramway** climbs over 2,000 ft. in 7min. and carries visitors to the summit of the Great Cannon Cliff, a 1000 ft. sheer drop into the cleft between Mt. Lafayette and Cannon Mountain. The tram offers unparalleled vistas of Franconia Notch along its ascent. A "Play All Day Pass" ($22, children $18) includes the tram, access to the beach, and 1hr. bike or boat rentals. (☎823-8800. Open May-Oct. daily 9am-4:30pm; July-Aug. 9am-5pm. One-way $8, round-trip $10, ages 6-12 $6.) Right next to the tramway station sits the **New England Ski Museum.** Perfect for those summer travelers longing for the freshly groomed slopes of the northeast, the museum houses an impressive collection of skiing memorabilia. (☎823-7177. Open late May-early Oct. daily 9am-5pm; Dec.-Mar. M-Tu and F-Su 9am-5pm. Free.) Rather than riding the tramway, skilled mountaineers will enjoy climbing via the aptly named "Sticky Fingers" or "Meat Grinder" routes. Between Exits 1 and 2 on I-93, visitors can find a well-marked turn-off for **The Basin,** a whirlpool along the Pemigewasset River that has been carved out as a 15 ft. waterfall erodes a massive base of granite. It's fully wheelchair-accessible with a paved path to viewing areas. On summer days, the lifeguard-protected beach at **Echo Lake,** just off parkway Exit 3, offers cool but crowded waters. The lake is accessible even when the lifeguard is not on duty. (☎823-5563. Lifeguard on duty mid-June to Sept. daily 10am-5:30pm. $3, under 12 and over 65 free.)

🏔 **HIKING.** Myriad trails lead up into the mountains on both sides of Franconia Notch, providing excellent day hikes and views. Be prepared for severe weather, especially above 4000 ft. The **Lonesome Lake Trail,** a relatively easy hike, winds its way 1½ mi. from Lafayette Place Campground to **Lonesome Lake,** where the AMC operates its westernmost summer hut (see **Practical Information,** p. 104). The **Greenleaf Trail** (2½ mi.), which starts at the Aerial Tramway parking lot, and the **Old Bridle Path** (3 mi.), from Lafayette Place, are much more ambitious. Both lead up to the AMC's Greenleaf Hut near the summit of Mt. Lafayette and overlooking Echo Lake. This is a favorite destination for sunset photographers. From Greenleaf, a 7½ mi. trek east along **Garfield Ridge** leads to the AMC's most remote hut, the **Galehead.** This area can keep you occupied for days; adequate supplies and equipment are needed before starting out. A campsite on Garfield ridge costs $5.

NEAR FRANCONIA: LOST RIVER

Outside of Franconia Notch State Park, 🔲**Lost River,** located 6 mi. west of North Woodstock on Rte. 112, is a glacial gorge with numerous caves and rock formations. The reservation also maintains an elaborate nature garden and a forestry museum. The walk through the gorge is less than 1 mi., but can take a while; each creatively-named cavern (such as the Lemon Squeeze) is open for exploration to those agile (and willing) enough to wrench through. (☎745-8031. Open May-Oct. daily 9am-5pm. Last ticket sold 1hr. before close. $8.50, children 6-12 $5.)

NORTH CONWAY AND CONWAY ☎603

The town of North Conway serves as one of New Hampshire's most popular vacation destinations because of its proximity to ski resorts in winter, foliage in the fall, and hiking and shopping year-round. Rte. 16, the traffic-infested main road, houses **outlet stores** from big-buck labels like Banana Republic, J. Crew, Liz Claiborne, and Brooks Brothers. The town of Conway, several miles south, has fewer touristy shops but several excellent mealtime and lodging options.

🛈 **PRACTICAL INFORMATION.** A number of stores in the North Conway area rent outdoor equipment. For ski goods in winter or biking gear during other seasons, **Joe Jones,** in North Conway on Main St. at Mechanic St., is suitable. A second branch lies a few miles north of town on Rte. 302. (☎356-9411. Open July-Aug. daily 9am-9pm; Sept.-Nov. and Apr.-June Su-Th 10am-6pm, F-Sa 9am-6pm. Alpine skis, boots, and poles $18 for 1 day, $35 for 2 days; cross-country equipment $15/$26; snowboards $20/$38.) **Eastern Mountain Sports (EMS),** just north on Main St. in the lobby of the Eastern Slope Inn, distributes free info on the area, sells camping equipment, and rents tents (2-person $15 for 1 day, $20 for 3 days; 4-person $20 for 1 day, $25 for 3 days), sleeping bags ($10 for 1 day, $15 for 3 days), and other equipment. The knowledgeable staff can provide first-hand info on climbing and hiking in North Conway and offer their own summer school climbing school. (☎356-5433. Open June-Sept. M-Sa 8:30am-9pm, Su 8:30am-6pm; Oct.-May daily 8:30am-6pm.)

⌂ ACCOMMODATIONS. The ▣**White Mountains Hostel (HI-AYH)**, 36 Washington St. off Rte. 16 at the intersection of Rte. 153 in the heart of Conway, is maintained by incredibly friendly folk, kept meticulously clean, and proud to be environmentally friendly. The hostel has 43 comfy bunks on several floors, and each bed comes with clean linen and a pillow. (☎447-1001 or 800-909-4776, ext. 51. Kitchen and Internet access. Laundry $3. Reception 7-10am and 5-10pm. Check-out 10am. Reservations recommended during the summer and peak foliage season. Open Dec.-Oct. $19, nonmembers $22, includes light breakfast; private rooms $45/$48.) The hostel at the beautiful **Cranmore Mt. Lodge,** 859 Kearsarge Rd., North Conway, has 40 bunks. The lodge is a few miles from downtown, but its recreation room, pool, jacuzzi, trails, cable TV, refrigerator, microwave, and duck pond are all at the disposal of guests. A delicious full breakfast, included with each overnight stay, makes up for the tight bunkrooms and thin mattresses. Be sure to bring a warm blanket to ward off the nightly temperature drop. (☎356-2044 or 800-356-3596. Linen and towel available for a small fee. Check-in 3-9pm, check-out 11am. $17.)

▢ FOOD. As for eateries, **Horsefeathers** on Main St. in North Conway offers burgers for around $7 and an array of other entrees for a few bucks more, including several meatless options. (☎356-2687. Kitchen open daily 11:30am-11:45pm; bar open until 1am.) Across the way, adjacent to Olympia Sports, **Morning Dew,** 2686 Main St., caffeinates a great percentage of the local populus. This hole-in-the-wall coffee shack offers bagels, juice, and the daily paper in addition to every variety of coffee ($1-$2.50) or tea. (☎356-9366. Open daily 7am-9pm.) Stay wired with a bagful of penny candy from **Zeb's General Store,** which also sells everything New England, from pure maple syrup to wooden signs and moose memorabilia. (☎356-9294. Open mid-June to Dec. 9am-10pm; Jan.-May hours vary.) Several miles south in **Conway,** pink, green, and purple pastels shout **Cafe Noche,** 147 Main St., which offers authentic Mexican food with many vegetarian choices. Mexican tunes filter through the restaurant and onto the outdoor patio, shaded by a giant maple and colorful umbrellas. Local patrons recommend the Montezuma Pie, a sort of Mexican lasagna ($7.25), or the garden burger ($4.25), but warn against filling up on the unlimited chips and salsa. (☎447-5050. Open Su-Th 11:30am-9pm, F-Sa 11:30am-9:30pm.)

VERMONT

No other state is as aptly named as Vermont. The lineage of the name extends back to Samuel de Champlain, who in 1609 dubbed the area "green mountain" in his native French. The Green Mountain range defines Vermont, spanning the length of the state from north to south and filling most of its width as well. Over the past few decades, ex-urbanite yuppies have invaded, creating some tension between the original, pristine Vermont and the packaged Vermont of trendy businesses. Happily, the former still seems to prevail; visitors can frolic in any of the 30 state forests, 80 state parks, or the mammoth 186,000-acre Green Mountain National Forest.

▨ PRACTICAL INFORMATION

Capital: Montpelier.
Visitor info: Vermont Information Center, 134 State St., Montpelier 05602 (☎802-828-3237; www.travel-vermont.com). Open M-F 8am-8pm. **Dept. of Forests, Parks and Recreation,** 103 S. Main St., Waterbury 05676 (☎802-241-3670). Open M-F

7:45am-4:30pm. **Vermont Snowline** (☎802-229-0531) gives snow conditions. Nov.-May 24hr.

Postal Abbreviation: VT. **Sales Tax:** 5%; 9% on meals and lodgings. **Area code:** 802.

VERMONT SKI RESORTS   ☎802

Come winter, skiers pour into Vermont and onto the Northeast's finest slopes, which become havens for hikers and cyclists in the summer and fall. Towns surrounding each of the mountains make their livelihood on this annual avalanche, thus offering a range of accommodations options. For more info, contact **Ski Vermont**, 26 State St., P.O. Box 368, Montpelier 05601 (☎223-2439; www.skivermont.com; open M-F 7:45am-4:45pm). The Vermont Information Center (see **Practical Information,** above) also provides helpful info. Cheaper lift tickets can be found off-season before mid-December and after mid-March.

Just north of Stowe on Rte. 108 W. lies **Smuggler's Notch,** recently voted the #1 ski resort in the US by SKI Magazine. Smuggler's three mountains, 67 trails, and the only triple-black-diamond run in the East make it a hot spot in winter, while the resort's package deals and warm-weather canoeing and hiking options attract visitors throughout the year. (☎644-8851 or 800-451-8752. Lift tickets $44 weekday/$48 weekend, youth $32/$34; 5 night/5 day lodging lift packages start at $95 per adult per day in winter.) The family-friendly **Stowe Mountain Resort** offers one-day lift tickets for $54. Fifty-nine percent of the runs are ranked at the intermediate level (16% beginner, 25% expert). Stowe's summer facilities may be more impressive: a golf course and country club, mountain biking and alpine slides (single ride $8, ages 6-12 and seniors $7), and a skate park with a half-pipe. (☎253-3000 or 800-253-4754. All-day pass $15, junior/senior $12; half-day $8/$6.50.) West of Brattleboro on Rte. 100 in the town of West Dover, **Mt. Snow** boasts 134 trails (20% beginner, 60% intermediate, 20% expert), 26 lifts, excellent snowmaking capabilities, as well as the first snowboard park in the Northeast. In the summer, mountain bikers can take advantage of 45 mi. of trails. (☎800-245-7669. Open mid-Nov. to late Apr. M-F 9am-4pm, Sa-Su 8am-4pm. Lift tickets $52 weekends/$49 weekdays, ages 13-19 $46/$44, seniors and 12 and under $33/$31.)

At the junction of U.S. 4 and Rte. 100 N in Sherburne, **Killington's** seven mountains and 205 trails cover the most terrain and entertain the East's longest ski season (mid-Oct. to early June). Snowboarding and ice-skating are also popular here in winter, hiking and biking in the summer. (☎422-3333 or 800-621-6867. Lift tickets $56, ages 13-18 $49, 6-12 $26.) For some of the most reasonable lift ticket prices in Vermont, head to **Burke,** off I-91 in northern Vermont. Thirty percent of the trails are beginner, 40% intermediate, and 30% expert. In summer, visitors can find almost any activity, from rock climbing to fishing, as well as hike and bike 200 mi. of trails. (☎626-3305. Lift tickets Sa-Su $42, ages 13-18 $37, 12 and under $28; M-F $25; off-season $20.) In Jay on Rte. 242, **Jay Peak** sits just inside the US-Canadian border in Vermont's Northeast Kingdom, catching more snowfall each year than any other New England resort. With some of the East's best Glades and ample opportunities for woods-skiing, Jay Peak is an appealing option for thrill-seekers—63 trails, 40% of which are expert. Excellent fishing and mountain biking abound in summer. (☎988-2611 or 800-451-4449. Lift tickets $49, ages under 15 $37; after 2:45pm $12.)

Other resorts include **Stratton** (☎297-2200 or 800-787-2886; 90 trails, 12 lifts), on Rte. 30 N in Bondville, and **Sugarbush** (☎583-2381 or 800-537-8427; 112 trails, 18 lifts, 4 mountains). Cross-country resorts include the **Trapp Family Lodge,** Stowe (see p. 111); **Mountain Meadows,** Killington (☎775-7077; 90 mi. of trails); and **Woodstock** (☎457-1100; 40 mi. of trails).

BURLINGTON   ☎802

Tucked between Lake Champlain and the Green Mountains, the largest city in Vermont successfully bridges the gap between the urban and the rustic. Five colleges, including the University of Vermont (UVM), give the area a youthful, progressive flair; bead shops pop up next door to mainstream clothing stores without disrupting local harmony. Along Church St.—downtown's bustling marketplace—numerous sidewalk cafes offer both a taste of the middle-class hippie atmosphere and a great venue for people-watching.

⚡ PRACTICAL INFORMATION. Amtrak, 29 Railroad Ave., Essex Jct. (☎879-7298; open daily 8:30am-noon and 8-9pm), 5 mi. east of Burlington on Rte. 15, chugs to New York (9¾hr., 1 per day, $59) and White River Junction (2hr., 1 per day, $16). CCTA (see below) runs to downtown every 30min. M-F 5:55am-6:05pm, Sa 6:45am-7:40pm. **Vermont Transit,** 345 Pine St. (☎864-6811 or 800-451-3292; open daily 5:30am-7:30pm), at Main St., buses to Boston (4¾hr., 5 per day, $46.50); Montréal (2½hr., 4 per day, $19); White River Junction (2hr., 5 per day, $15); Middlebury (1hr., 3 per day, $7.50); Albany (4¾hr., 3 per day, $35). **Chittenden County Transit Authority (CCTA)** provides unbeatable access and frequent, reliable service. Pick up connections with Shelburne and other outlying areas downtown at the intersection of Cherry and Church St. (☎864-2282. Buses operate every 30min. M-Sa roughly 6:15am-9:20pm, depending on routes. $1; seniors, disabled, and under 18 50¢; 5 and under free.) **Ski Rack,** 85 Main St., rents bikes. (☎658-3313 or 800-882-4530. Mountain bikes $10 for 1hr.; $16 for 4hr.; $22 for 24hr. Helmet and lock included. In-line skates $10 for 4hr.; $14 per day. Credit card required. Open M-Th 10am-7pm, F 10am-8pm, Sa 9am-6pm, Su 11am-5pm.) **Visitor info: Lake Champlain Regional Chamber of Commerce,** 60 Main St., Rte. 100. (☎863-3489. Open M-F 8:30am-5pm, Sa-Su 9am-5pm; Oct.-May M-F 8:30am-5pm.) **Post Office:** 11 Elmwood Ave, at Pearl St. (☎863-6033. Open M-F 8am-5pm, Sa 8am-1pm.) **ZIP code:** 05401. **Area code:** 802.

☗ ACCOMMODATIONS. The Chamber of Commerce has the complete rundown on area accommodations. B&Bs are generally found in the outlying suburbs. Reasonably priced hotels and guest houses line **Shelburne Rd.** south of downtown. **Mrs. Farrell's Home Hostel (HI-AYH)** is a welcoming abode for the homesick traveler. In keeping with the local hippie slant, posters about everything from nuclear waste to vegan lifestyle make it a haven for peace, justice, and harmony. Six beds are split between a clean, comfortable basement and a lovely garden porch. Even if Mrs. Farrell has no available beds, she can refer you to an overflow location. The hostel is 3 mi. north of downtown via North Ave. and is accessible by public transportation; get directions when you call for reservations. (☎865-3730. Light breakfast included. Linen $1. Partial wheelchair access. Dorms $17.50, nonmembers $20.50.) The **North Beach Campsites,** on Institute Rd. 1½ mi. north of town by North Ave., have a spectacular view and access to a pristine beach on Lake Champlain. Take Rte. 127 to North Ave., or the "North Ave." bus from the main terminal on Pine St. (☎862-0942 or 800-571-1198. 137 sites. Showers 25¢ per 5min. Open Apr. to mid-Oct. Sites $20, with electricity $24, full hookup $27. Beach closes at 9pm; free to registered campers, $5 non-campers.) The **Shelburne Campground,** on Shelburne Rd., lies 1 mi. north of Shelburne and 5 mi. south of Burlington by Rte. 7; buses to Shelburne South stop right next to the campground. (☎985-2540. Pool, showers, and laundry. Open May-Oct. Sites for 2 $19, with water and electricity $21, full hookup $27; $5 each additional person.) See **Champlain Valley,** p. 109, for more camping.

☐ FOOD. Church Street Marketplace and its adjacent sidestreets have approximately 85 restaurants, making Burlington a food lover's paradise. Visitors could eat downtown for weeks without hitting the same place twice; not bad for a city of only 40,000. You don't have to be stoned to enjoy the food at **⬛Zabby and Elf's Stone Soup,** 211 College St. A taste of local flavor, this mostly vegetarian cafe specializes in the homey, hearty, and healthy. Sandwiches on freshly baked breads and hefty veggie meals from the hot and cold bars are perfect to go ($5). The never vitamin-packed but always tasty sweets ($1.25) go well with the greens. (☎862-7616. Open M-F 7am-7pm, Sa 8am-5pm. Credit cards not accepted.) The **Liquid Energy Cafe,** 57 Church St., fills California's shoes in the East with its attitude and bright, airy interior. Nonchalant staff and patrons define "chill" while concocting delicious smoothies ($3-$5) with unconventional ingredients and natural remedies; custom-build yours to cure anything from acne to asthma. (☎860-7666. Free Internet access. Open M-Th 7am-8pm, F 7am-9pm, Sa 9am-9pm, Su 9am-6pm.) **Ben & Jerry's,** 36 Church St., has been considered the company's birthplace (see p. 113) ever since its original shop, a converted gas station at 169 Cherry St., was burned down and abandoned. (☎862-9620. Open Apr.-Nov. Su-Th 11am-11pm, F-Sa 11am-midnight; Dec.-Mar. Su-Th 11am-

10pm, F-Sa 11am-11pm. Cones $2-3.) **Sweetwater's,** 120 Church St., incredibly high ceilings and vast wall paintings dwarf those who come for delicious $3-3.50 soups and $6-7 sandwiches. In the summer, ask to be seated outdoors to observe the goings-on of Church St. Marketplace. (☎864-9800. Open M-Sa 11:30am-2am, Su 10:30am-midnight; food served M-Sa until 1am, Su until 11pm.)

◘ **SIGHTS.** The **Shelburne Museum,** 7 mi. south of Burlington in Shelburne, houses one of the best collections of Americana in the country. A 19th-century General Store and adjacent apothecary are among the 37 buildings composing the splendid 45-acre museum. A covered bridge, lighthouse, and 1950s house are displayed beside Degas, Cassat, Manet, Monet, Rembrandt, and Whistler paintings. (☎985-3346. Open mid-May to Oct. daily 10am-5pm. Oct.-May hours vary; several buildings only open in summer. Tickets valid for 2 days; $17.50, ages 6-14 $7.) Five mi. farther south on U.S. 7, the **Vermont Wildflower Farm** has a seed shop and 6 acres of wildflowers. (☎425-3641. Open Apr.-Oct. daily 10am-5pm. $3; off-season $1.50.)

Amateur historians delight in Victorian **South Willard St.,** where you'll find **Champlain College** and the **University of Vermont,** founded in 1797. **City Hall Park,** in the heart of downtown, and **Battery St. Park,** on Lake Champlain near the edge of downtown, are bucolic. For insomniac boaters, the **Burlington Community Boathouse,** at the base of College St. at Lake Champlain, is open late to rent light craft for a cruise on the lake. (☎865-3377. Open mid-May to mid-Oct. daily 24hr.; rentals from 6am-midnight. Sailboats $25-35 per hr.) The **Spirit of Ethan Allen** scenic cruise departs from the boathouse at the bottom of College St. Live commentary complements the close-up view of the famous **Thrust Fault,** a geological wonder not visible from land. (☎862-8300. Cruises late May to mid-Oct. daily 10am, noon, 2, and 4pm. $9.90, ages 3-11 $4.65. Sunset cruise lasts 1hr. longer and sails at 6:30pm Su-Th. $11, ages 3-11 $5.70.) The **Ethan Allen Homestead** rests northeast of Burlington on Rte. 127. In the 1780s, Allen forced the surrender of Fort Ticonderoga and helped establish the state of Vermont. He built his cabin in what is now the Winooski Valley Park. (☎865-4556. Open mid-May to mid-June daily 1-5pm; June to mid-Oct. M-Sa 10am-5pm, Su 1-5pm. Last tour 4:15pm. $4, seniors $3.50, ages 5-17 $2, families $12.)

▨▥ **ENTERTAINMENT AND NIGHTLIFE.** UVM and several other nearby colleges fuel Burlington's youthful, kickin' atmosphere. The town's locus is Church St. Marketplace, a pedestrian haven for tie-dye seekers and ice cream lovers, where all are entertained by off-beat puppeteers and musicians. Pick up a free *Seven Days* newspaper to find out the skinny on what's happening in town. In the summer, the **Vermont Mozart Festival** (☎862-7352 or 800-639-9097) brings Bach, Beethoven, and Mozart to local barns, farms, and meadows. The **Discover Jazz Festival** (☎863-7992) features over 1000 musicians in both free and ticketed performances. The **Flynn Theater Box Office,** 153 Main St., handles sales for the Mozart and jazz performances. (☎863-5966. Open M-F 10am-5pm, Sa 11am-4pm.) The **Champlain Valley Folk Festival** (☎800-769-9176) croons in early August. Immortalized by ex-regulars Phish on their album *A Picture of Nectar,* **Nectar's,** 188 Main St., rocks with inexpensive food, such as the locally acclaimed gravy fries ($3-5), and nightly live tunes. (☎658-4771. Open M-F 5:45am-2am, Sa 7:30am-1am, Su 7:30am-2am. No cover.) The **Red Square,** 136 Church St., is one of Burlington's most popular night spots with live music nightly. Bands play in the alley if the crowd gets large. (☎859-8909. No cover.)

DAYTRIP FROM BURLINGTON: CHAMPLAIN VALLEY

Lake Champlain, a 100 mi. long lake between Vermont's Green Mountains and New York's Adirondacks, is often referred to as "Vermont's West Coast." You can take a bridge or a ferry across the lake; the ferry offers fantastic views. The **Lake Champlain Ferry,** located on the dock at the bottom of King St., sails daily from Burlington to Port Kent, NY, and back. (☎864-9804. 1hr. Late June to Aug. 12-14 per day, 8am-7:30pm; mid-May to late June and Sept. to mid-Oct. 9 per day, 8am-6:35pm. $3.50, ages 6-12 $1.25, car $13.25.) The same company also travels from Grand Isle to Plattsburg, NY, and 14 mi. south of Burlington from Charlotte, VT, to Essex, NY (either fare $2.50, ages 6-12 50¢, with car $7).

Mt. Philo State Park, 15 mi. south of Burlington off Rte. 7, offers pleasant camping and gorgeous views of the Champlain Valley; take the Vermont Transit bus from Burlington south along U.S. 7 toward Vergennes. (☎425-2390 or 800-658-1622. Open mid-May to mid-Oct. daily 10am-sunset. 7 tent sites without hookups $12, 3 lean-tos $15. Entrance fee $2, ages 4-14 $1.50.) The marsh of the **Missisquoi National Wildlife Refuge** sits at the northern end of the lake west of Swanton, VT along Rte. 78. Also north of the lake, **Burton Island State Park** is accessible only by ferry from Kill Kare State Park, 35 mi. north of Burlington and 3½ mi. southwest off U.S. 7 near St. Albans Bay. (☎524-6353 or 800-252-2363. Open late May to early Sept. daily 8am-8pm; call for schedule. $4.) The campground has 19 tent sites ($13) and 26 lean-tos ($19, $4 per each additional person). The state park on **Grand Isle,** just off U.S. 2 north of Keeler Bay, also offers camping. (☎372-4300. Open mid-May to mid-Oct. 123 sites for 4 $13, $3 each additional person; 34 lean-tos $17/$4; 1 cabin $34. Reservations are highly recommended, especially for summer weekends.)

MIDDLEBURY ☎802

Although most of Vermont's towns don't seem to play up their association with local colleges, Middlebury, "Vermont's Landmark College Town," basks in the energy and culture stimulated by Middlebury College. The result is a traditional Vermont atmosphere tinged with both vitality and history.

◪ PRACTICAL INFORMATION. Middlebury stretches along U.S. 7, 42 mi. south of Burlington. **Vermont Transit** stops at the Exxon station, 16 Court St., west of Main St. (☎388-4373; station open M-Sa 6am-9pm, Su 7am-9pm). Buses run to Burlington (1hr., 3 per day, $7.50); Rutland (1½hr., 3 per day, $7.50); Albany (3hr., 3 per day, $28); and Boston (6hr., 3 per day, $43). The **Addison County Transit Resources** provide free shuttle service from the station to the immediate Middlebury vicinity (☎388-1946). The downtown area may best be explored by foot, but for those who prefer wheels, the **Bike Center,** 74 Main St., rents bikes starting at $15 per day. (☎388-6666. Open M-Sa 9:30am-5:30pm.) The staff at the **Addison County Chamber of Commerce,** 2 Court St., in the historic Gamaliel Painter House, has area info. (☎388-7951. Open M-F 9am-5pm; limited weekend hours in summer.) **Internet access: Ilsley Public Library,** 75 Main St. (☎388-4095; open M, W, F 10am-6pm; Tu and Th 10am-8pm; Sa 10am-4pm). **Post Office:** 10 Main St. (☎388-2681; open M-F 8am-5pm, Sa 8am-12:30pm). **ZIP code:** 05753. **Area code:** 802.

⌂ ACCOMMODATIONS. Lodging with four walls and no mosquitoes does not come cheaply in Middlebury; be prepared to trade an arm and a leg for an extended stay. The **Sugar House Motor Inn,** just north of Middlebury on Rte. 7, offers basic motel rooms with free local calls, refrigerators, microwaves, and cable TV. (☎388-2770. Make reservations far in advance. Rooms start at $60 but the owner may be willing to make a deal off-season.) On the southern edge of Middlebury, the **Greystone Motel,** 2 mi. south of the town center on Rte. 7, has ten recently decorated, basic rooms with cable TV and refrigerator. (☎388-4935. Breakfast included. Reservations recommended. Singles $55; doubles Nov.-Apr. $75, May-Oct. $95.) The best budget accommodations are to be found in the great outdoors. **Branbury State Park,** 7 mi. south on U.S. 7, then 4 mi. south on Rte. 53, stretches along Lake Dunmore, offering idyllic frisbee fields and camping grounds. (☎247-5925. Open late May to mid-Oct. 40 sites $13; lean-tos $19. Canoe rentals $5 per hr., $30 per day; paddle boats $5 per 30min. Showers 25¢ per 5min.) **River's Bend Campground,** 3 mi. north of Middlebury off Rte. 7 on the Dog Team Rd. in New Haven, is clean and appropriately named, but is difficult to find. (☎388-9092 or 888-505-5159. 65 sites for 2 with water and electricity $22, river sites $26; $10 each additional adult. Fishing, swimming, picnicking facilities $4. Canoe rental $6 per hr. Showers 25¢ per 5min.)

◪▨ FOOD AND NIGHTLIFE. Middlebury's many fine restaurants cater chiefly to plump wallets, but the year-round presence of students ensures the survival of cheaper places. **Noonie's Deli,** in the Marbleworks building just behind Main St., is a student favorite and makes terrific $4-5 sandwiches on homemade bread. (☎388-0014. Open M-Sa 8am-8pm.) Students also flock to **Mister Up's,** a popular nighttime hangout on Bakery Ln. just off Main St., for a sizeable menu including sandwiches ($6-7) and an extensive salad bar. (☎388-6724. Open M-Sa 11:30am-midnight, Su 11am-midnight.) Decked with cacti, **Amigos,** 4 Merchants Row, offers fajitas, burritos, and other Mexican favorites. (☎388-3624. Live music F-Sa. Open M-Th 11:30am-9pm, F-Sa 11:30am-10pm, Su 11:30-9pm; bar open daily until midnight, depending on the crowd.) Night owls should check out **Angela's Pub,** 86 Main St. Whether it's live music, the juke box, or karaoke singers supplying the musical accompaniment, this hot spot is jumpin' at night. (☎388-0002. Open Tu-F 4pm-2am, Sa 6:30pm-1am.)

◪ **SIGHTS.** The **Vermont State Craft Center** at Frog Hollow exhibits and sells the artistic productions of Vermonters. (☎388-3177. Open M-Th 9:30am-5:30pm, F-Sa 9am-6pm, Su 11am-5pm.) Just behind the Center rests the **Marbleworks Memorial Bridge,** which provides a terrific view of the crumbling mills that once generated the town's power. **Middlebury College** hosts cultural events; the concert hall in the college **Arts Center,** just outside of town, has a terrific concert series. The campus **box office** has details on events sponsored by the college. (☎443-6433. Open Sept.-May Tu-Sa noon-4pm and 1hr. before start of show.) Tours from the **Admissions Office,** in Emma Willard Hall on S. Main St., showcase the campus. (☎443-3000. Tours Sept. to late May daily 9am and 1pm. In July and Aug. Self-guided tour brochures available.) Too poor for a pint? Trek ¾ mi. north of town to the **Otter Creek Brewery,** 793 Exchange St., for free samples. (☎800-473-0727. Tours daily at 1, 3, and 5pm.) Fifteen miles east of the Middlebury College campus, the **Middlebury College Snow Bowl** (☎802-388-4356) entertains skiers in winter with 15 trails and lifts.

STOWE   ☎802

Stowe winds gracefully up the side of Mt. Mansfield (Vermont's highest peak, at 4393 ft.). The village self-consciously fancies itself an American skiing hot spot on par with its ritzier European counterparts. In fact, Stowe has something of an obsession with all things Austrian, which may account for the proliferation of Austrian-type chalets and restaurants dotting the mountain's ascending road.

⧎ **PRACTICAL INFORMATION.** Stowe is 12 mi. north of I-89's Exit 10, which is 27 mi. southwest of Burlington. The ski slopes lie along **Rte. 108** (Mountain Rd.), northwest of Stowe. **Vermont Transit** (☎244-7689 or 800-872-7245; open daily 5am-9pm) comes only as close as **Depot Beverage,** 1 River Rd., in Waterbury, 10 mi. from Stowe. **Peg's Pick-up DBA Stowe Taxi** (☎253-9490) will take you into Stowe for less than $20, but you should call ahead. In winter, the **Stowe Trolley** runs irregularly between the important locations in the village. (☎253-7585. In summer, 1¼hr. tours M, W, F 11am, $5. In winter, every 20min. 8-10am and 2-4:20pm; every hr. 11am-1pm and 5-10pm. $1; weekly pass $10.) **Visitors Info: Stowe Area Association** on Main St. (☎253-7321 or 800-247-8693; open M-F 9am-8pm, Sa-Su 10am-5pm; late Apr. to early May closed Sa-Su). **Post Office:** 105 Depot St., off Main St. (☎253-7521; open M-F 7:15am-5pm, Sa 9am-noon). **ZIP code:** 05672. **Area code:** 802.

⧔ **ACCOMMODATIONS.** Easy access is one of many reasons to stay at the **Snow Bound Lodge,** 645 S. Main St., located about half a mile south of the intersection of Rte. 100 and 108. The owners, a friendly, older couple, make even the most weary travelers feel at ease with their engaging conversation and homemade breakfast. (☎253-4515. 10 beds. $20.) **Foster's Place,** on Mountain Rd., offers dorm rooms with a lounge, game room, and hot tub/sauna in a recently renovated school building. (☎253-9404. Singles July-Aug. $39; private bath $49; quad $75. Reservations recommended.) **Smuggler's Notch State Park,** 7248 Mountain Rd./Rte. 108, 8 mi. west of Stowe, just past the hostel, keeps it simple with hot showers, tent sites, and lean-tos. (☎253-4014. Open late May to mid-Oct. Sites for 4 $12, each additional person up to 8 \$4; lean-tos \$18/\$4. 2 night min. stay. Reservations recommended.) **Gold Brook Campground,** 1½ mi. south of the town center on Rte. 100, is the only camping area open year-round in Stowe. (☎253-7683. Showers, laundry, horseshoes. Sites for 2 \$18, with hookup \$20-29, \$5 each additional person.)

🍴 **FOOD.** The 🔲**Depot Street Malt Shoppe,** 57 Depot St., is reminiscent of decades past: felt sports pennants and plastic 45s deck the walls, while rock 'n' roll favorites liven up the outdoor patio seating. The cost of a 50s-style cherry or vanilla Coke has been adjusted for inflation, but prices remain reasonable, with meals ranging from \$3-6. (☎253-4269. Open daily 11:30am-9pm.) **Mac's Deli** is a convenient stop for a sandwich (\$3) or sub (\$4) to go. Located in Mac's Stowe Market, on S. Main St. by the intersection of Rte. 100 and Rte. 108, the deli has awful good sandwiches but no seating. They also serve piping hot soups at \$2.40 per lb. (☎253-4576. Open M-Sa 7am-9pm, Su 7am-8pm.) The **Sunset Grille and Tap Room,** 140 Cottage Club Rd. off Mountain Rd., is a favorite among sports fans with its 20 TVs (including 3 big screens) and pool and air hockey tables. The restaurant adjacent to the bar offers barbecue fare. (☎253-9281. Open daily for dining 11:30am-midnight; bar open until 2am.) The pub-like atmosphere of **The Shed,** 1859 Mountain Rd., along with six potent homemade microbrews and unbeatable Monday through Friday specials, including Tuesday \$2.50 pint night, make it another nighttime hot spot (☎253-4364).

🏔 **OUTDOOR ACTIVITIES.** Stowe's ski offerings include the **Stowe Mountain Resort** (☎253-3000 or 800-253-4754) and **Smuggler's Notch** (☎644-8851 or 800-451-8752; see **Vermont Ski Resorts,** p. 107). The hills are alive with the area's best cross-country skiing at the **Von Trapp Family Lodge,** on Luce Hill Rd., 2 mi. off Mountain Rd. Yes, it *is* the family from *The Sound of Music,* and it is divine. Don't stay here unless you have a rich uncle in Stowe—prices for lodging climb to \$845 in the high season. There's no charge to visit, though, and the lodge offers fairly cheap rentals and lessons for their cross-country ski trails. (☎253-8511 or 800-826-7000. Trail fee \$14; ski rentals \$16; lessons \$14-40 per hr.; ski school package includes all 3 for \$35; discounts for kids.) **A.J.'s Ski and Sports,** at the base of Mountain Rd., rents ski equipment in winter, bikes and in-line skates during other seasons. (☎253-4593. Skis, boots, and poles: downhill \$24 per day, \$46 2 days; cross-country \$12/\$22. Snowboard and boots \$24 per day. 20% discount with advance reservations. Mountain bike or in-line skates \$7 per hr., \$16 per half-day, \$24 full-day; helmet included. Open in summer daily 9am-6pm; in winter Su-Th 8am-8pm, F-Sa 8am-9pm.)

In summer, Stowe's frenetic pace drops off—as do its prices. **Action Outfitters,** 2160 Mountain Rd., serves your recreation needs. (☎253-7975. Mountain bikes \$6 per hr., \$14 per half-day, \$20 full day; in-line skates \$6/\$12/\$18; canoes \$20 per half-day, \$30 full day, including life jackets, paddles, and car rack. Open M-F 9am-5pm, Sa-Su 9am-5:30pm.) Stowe's 5½ mi. asphalt **recreation path,** perfect for cross-country skiing in the winter and biking, skating, or strolling in the summer, runs parallel to the Mountain Rd.'s ascent and begins behind the church on Main St. in Stowe. Before you set out on the path check out **Shaw's General Store,** 54 Main St., for pretty much anything, including Vermont-made shoes. (☎253-4040. Open daily 9am-5pm.)

Fly fishermen should head to the **Fly Rod Shop,** 3 mi. south of Stowe on Rte. 100, to pick up the necessary fishing licenses (\$38 per year, \$25 per week, \$11 per day; \$20 per year for VT residents) and rent fly rods and reels for \$10 per day. The owner can show you how to tie a fly, or you can stick around for free fly-fishing classes in the shop's own pond. (☎253-7346 or 800-535-9763. Open Apr.-Oct. M-F 9am-6pm, Sa 9am-5pm, Su 10am-4pm; after fishing season, M-F 9am-5pm, Sa 9am-4pm, Su 10am-4pm.) For a canoeing experience, try **Umiak,** Rte. 100, 1 mi. south of Stowe Center. The store (named after a unique type of kayak used by the Inuit) rents regular ol' kayaks and canoes in the summer and offers a full-day river trip for \$35 per person. (☎253-2317. Rental and transportation to the river included. Open Apr.-Oct. daily 9am-6pm; winter hours vary. Sport kayaks \$10 per hr., \$20 per 4hr.; canoes \$15/\$30.) Located in a rustic red barn, **The Nordic Barn at Topnotch,** 4000 Mountain Rd., offers 1hr. horseback-riding tours through woods and streams. No experience is necessary. (☎253-8585. Tours late May through Nov. daily 11am, 1, and 3pm. \$30. Reservations required.)

BEN & JERRY: TWO MEN, ONE DREAM, AND LOTS OF CHUNKS In 1978, Ben Cohen and Jerry Greenfield enrolled in a Penn State correspondence course in ice cream making, converted a gas station into their first shop, and launched themselves on the road to a double-scoop success story. Today, **Ben and Jerry's Ice Cream Factory,** north of Waterbury on Rte. 100, is a mecca for ice cream lovers. On a 30min. tour of the facilities, you can taste the sweet success of the men who brought "Lemongrad" to Moscow and "Cherry Garcia" to San Francisco. The tour tells Ben & Jerry's history, showcases the company's social consciousness, and awards a free sample at the end. (☎882-2586. *Tours Nov.- May daily every 30min. 10am-5pm; June every 20min. 9am-5pm; July-Aug. every 10min. 9am-8pm; Sept.-Oct. every 15min. 9am-6pm. $2, seniors $1.75, under 12 free.)*

NEAR STOWE: ROUTE 100 GLUTTONY

If you haven't already made yourself sick on **Ben & Jerry's** ice cream, Rte. 100 features a bona fide food fiesta south of Stowe. Begin at Ben & Jerry's and drive north on Rte. 100 towards Stowe. The first stop is the **Cabot Annex Store,** home to rich chocolate truffles and Vermont's best cheddar. (☎244-6334. Open daily 9am-6pm.) Cheddar samples are free, but be prepared fork over some cash for the chocolate. Leave room in your stomach for the **Cold Hollow Cider Mill.** In addition to the potent beverage, cider spin-offs include the 44¢ jelly and doughnuts. Light-of-money travelers should especially keep an eye out for free cider tastings and fudge samples in the adjacent building. (☎244-8771. Call for a cider-making schedule. Open daily 8am-6pm.) Finally, maple is everywhere at the **Stowe Maple Products** maple museum and candy kitchen. March and April is syrup season, but they sell the goods all year. (☎253-2508. Open daily 8am-6pm.)

WHITE RIVER JUNCTION ☎802

The intersection of I-89 and I-91 marks White River Junction, which serves as the bus center for most of Vermont. **Vermont Transit** (☎295-3011 or 800-552-8737; office open daily 7am-9pm), on U.S. 5, behind the Mobil station 1 mi. south of downtown White River Junction, makes connections to New York (7½hr., 3 per day, $56); Burlington (2hr., 4 per day, $17); Montréal (5hr., 4 per day, $42); and smaller centers on a less regular basis. **Amtrak** (☎295-7160; office open daily 9am-noon and 5-7pm), on Railroad Rd. off N. Main St., rockets once per day during weekdays and weekends to New York (7½hr.; $65); Essex Jct. (near Burlington, 2hr.; $25); Montréal (4½hr.; $39); and Philadelphia (9hr.; $76).

There's not much in White River Junction to attract tourists, but if you must stay in town, virtually the only choice for lodging is the old-style **Hotel Coolidge (HI-AYH),** 17 S. Main St., across the road from the retired Boston and Maine steam engine. From the bus station, walk to the right on U.S. 5 and down the hill past two stop lights (1 mi.) into town. The 26-bed dorm-style hostel-ette is tidy and relatively private. (☎295-3118 or 800-622-1124. Dorm beds $19, nonmembers $29.) The **Polkadot Restaurant,** 1 N. Main St., doles out cheap sandwiches ($2-5) and sit-down meals. (☎295-9722. Open M 5am-2pm, Tu-Su 5am-7pm.) Just east of the Junction on Rte. 4, across from the Texaco Station, the red clapboard **Four Aces Diner** serves up burgers for a good price ($4-6) and features 50's style jukeboxes. (☎603-298-6827. Open M 5am-3pm, Tu-Sa 5am-8pm, Su 7am-3pm.)

The **Vermont Welcome Center,** 100 Railroad Rd., in the Amtrak station building, next to the retired steam engine, can spill the not-so-juicy secrets of the area (☎295-6200; generally open Tu and Th mornings). **Post Office:** 195 Sykes Mt. Ave. (☎296-3246; open M-F 7:30-7pm, Sa 7:30am-noon). **ZIP code:** 05001.

NEAR WHITE RIVER JUNCTION: LEBANON, NH

For those seeking a pleasant way to the pass the time while waiting for their bus in White River Junction, the historic district of Lebanon lies across the border in New Hampshire at exit 18 off I-89. In contrast to the fast-paced shopping centers of its commercial counterpart, West Lebanon, located off Exit 19, Lebanon is the ideal place for a much-needed meal, sleep, or stretch. Heading into town, the spacious green of **Coburn Park** immediately welcomes visitors. Perfect for a stroll, the park puts them in the mood for a leisurely saunter around the neighborhood. Those who might be weary of walking can hop a ride on the **Advance Transit** bus line (☎802-295-1824) which carries passengers around the immediate area for free. For a bite to eat near the park, the popular Italian trattoria **Sweet Tomatoes**, 1 Court St., dishes up wood-fired pizzas, hardwood charcoal grill specialities, and pasta meals for around $10. (☎603-448-1711. Open for lunch M-F 11:30am-2pm; dinner Su-Th 5-9pm, F-Sa 5-9:30pm.) As for accommodations, pickings are slim in Lebanon, so your best may be one of the chain motels by Exit 18. The **Chamber of Commerce**, 1 School St. Village House, at the head of the park, provides information on the sites and goings-on around town. **Post Office:** 11 East Park (☎603-448-2348; open M-F 6am-6pm, Sa 6am-2:30pm). **Zip Code:** 03766.

BRATTLEBORO   ☎802

The colonial brick facade of Brattleboro's Main St. contains more than its fair share of sporting goods stores. Their presence is warranted by the town's popularity as a starting point for adventures in the southern Green Mountains and along the Connecticut River. Foliage season in October is the most beautiful, and thus the most expensive, time for a visit to this region of Vermont. Brattleboro's natural beauty, especially along its rivers, is its main attraction. The region can be explored by canoe from the **Vermont Canoe Touring Center**, 1 mi. north of town on Putney Rd. (☎257-5008. Open late May to early Sept. daily 9am-8pm; otherwise call for reservations. Rentals $10 for 1hr., 2hr. $15, half-day $20, and full-day $30.) The **Brattleboro Museum and Art Center** resides in the old Union Railroad Station at the lower end of Main St. and houses a changing and eclectic collection of very modern art. (☎257-0124. Open mid-May to Nov. Tu-Su noon-6pm. $3, seniors and students $2, under 12 free.) The **Gallery Walk** is a free walking tour of Brattleboro's plentiful art galleries on the first Friday of every month.

Economy lodgings such as **Super 8** and **Motel 6** proliferate on Rte. 9 (singles generally $49-69), although privately owned establishments can offer slightly better deals. The simple **Molly Stark Motel** sits 4 mi. west on Rte. 9. (☎254-2440. Singles start at $40 in winter, $55 in summer.) **Fort Dummer State Park** is 2 mi. south of town on U.S. 5; turn left on Fairground Ave. just before the I-91 interchange, then right on S. Main St., which becomes Old Guilford Rd., until you hit the park. Named for the first European settlement in Vermont, the park offers campsites with fireplaces, picnic tables, bathroom facilities, hiking trails, a playground, and a lean-to with wheelchair access. (☎254-2610. Day use of park $2, children $1.50. Hot showers 25¢ per 5min. Firewood $2.50 per armload. Reservations accepted. 51 sites. $12, $4 each additional person; ten lean-tos $18/$4.) **Molly Stark State Park**, 15 mi. west of town on Rte. 9 in a secluded location, provides basically the same facilities as Fort Dummer. (☎464-5460. RV sites without hookups for $11. Open May to mid-Oct.)

One mile north of town on Rte. 5, across Putney Rd. from the Vermont Canoe Touring Center, the casual **Marina Restaurant** is perched atop the bank of the West River, offering an unsurpassed view from the porch or outdoor terrace. Favorites include the $5.75 shrimp and chip basket and the $6 "rajun" Cajun chicken. (☎257-7563. Live music Su 3-6pm and W 7-10pm. Open in summer M-Sa 11:30am-10pm, Su 11am-9pm; winter hours vary.) With locally grown fruits, vegetables, and cider to boot, the **Farmers Markets** have what you need. (☎254-9567. W 11am-2pm on Main St.; Sa 9am-2pm on Rte. 9 2 mi. west of town.) At night, rock, blues, R&B, and reggae tunnel through the **Mole's Eye Cafe**, located downstairs at 4 High St., off Main St. Offering pub fare for under $7, the Mole's Eye is more a bar than a cafe. (☎257-0771. Live music F-Sa 9pm; cover $4. Open M-Th 4pm-1am, F-Sa 11:30am-1am.)

The **Amtrak** (☎254-2301) Montréaler train from New York and Springfield, MA, stops in Brattleboro behind the museum on Vernon St. Trains depart once per day for New York (6hr., $50) and Washington, D.C. (9¾hr., $79). **Greyhound** and **Vermont Transit** roll into town at the parking lot behind the Citgo station off Exit 3 on I-91, on Putney Rd. (☎254-6066. Open M-F 8am-4pm, Sa-Su 8am-3:20pm.) Buses run to New York (5hr., 4 per day, $41); Burlington (3½hr., 5 per day, $31); Montréal (6½hr., 4 per day, $59); and Boston (3hr., 2 per day, $25-31.50). The **Chamber of Commerce,** 180 Main St., provides the *Brattleboro Main Street Walking Tour,* detailed town maps, and brochures galore for outdoor activities. (☎254-4565. Open M-F 8:30am-5pm.) In the summer and fall seasons, an **info booth** (☎257-1112), on the Town Common off Putney Rd., operates from 9am-5pm. **Post Office:** 204 Main St. (☎254-4110; open M-F 7:30am-5:30pm, Sa 8am-1pm). **ZIP code:** 05301. **Area code:** 802.

MASSACHUSETTS

Massachusetts regards itself, with some justification, as the intellectual center of the nation. From the 1636 establishment of Harvard, the oldest college in America, Massachusetts has been a breeding ground for intellectuals and literati. The state also offers a variety of cultural and scenic attractions. Boston, the revolutionary "cradle of liberty" and later self-proclaimed "Hub of the Universe," has become an ethnically diverse city whose high cost of living does afford its residents general cleanliness and comparatively little crime. Resplendent during the fall, the Berkshire Mountains fill western Massachusetts with a charm that attracts thousands of visitors. The seaside areas, from Nantucket to Northern Bristol, feature the stark oceanic beauty that first attracted settlers to the North American shore.

▇ PRACTICAL INFORMATION

Capital: Boston, baby.

Visitor info: Office of Travel and Tourism, 10 Park Plaza (Transportation Bldg.), Boston 02202 (☎617-727-3201 or 800-447-6277 for guides; www.mass-vacation.com). Offers a complimentary, comprehensive *Getaway Guide.* Open M-F 8:45am-5pm.

Postal Abbreviation: MA. **Sales Tax:** 5%; no tax on clothing and pre-packaged food.

BOSTON   ☎617

Like many American cities, Boston reveals the limits of the "melting pot" metaphor. The city remains a sometimes uneasy mix of different racial, ethnic, religious, economic, and political groups. Its small geographical size and dramatically differentiated neighborhoods make the contrasts between these groups easy to see. The towering corporate sanctuaries of the Financial District are visible from the winding streets of the North End. Predominantly upper-class Beacon Hill is just across the Boston Common from the nation's first Chinatown. The South End, trendy and increasingly gay, abuts the less gentrified neighborhoods of Roxbury and Dorchester. Ironically, though, if Bostonians share one thing in common, it may be precisely this consciousness of the neighborhood boundaries that sometimes threaten to divide them. Walking the Freedom Trail will expose you to some of the earliest history of the United States, but wandering the streets of Boston's neighborhoods will give you a less glamorous glimpse of a still-evolving metropolis where ancient history is often less important—and less fascinating—than the lives and loves of the almost 800,000 residents who populate the metro area.

⊠ INTERCITY TRANSPORTATION

Airport: Logan International (☎561-1800), in East Boston. T: Blue Line-Airport. A free **Massport Shuttle** connects all terminals with the T stop. **US Shuttle** (☎877-748-8853) departs every 30min. to many areas in downtown Boston (24hr. service; 24hr. advanced reservation required). The **Airport Water Shuttle** runs between Rowes Wharf and Logan Airport (every 15min. M-F 6am-8pm; every 30min. F 8am-11pm, Sa 10am-11pm, Su 10am-8pm; $10). The **City Water Taxis** connect the airport with other landings (every 10min. Apr.-Oct. 15 daily 7am-7pm). A **taxi** to downtown costs $15-20.

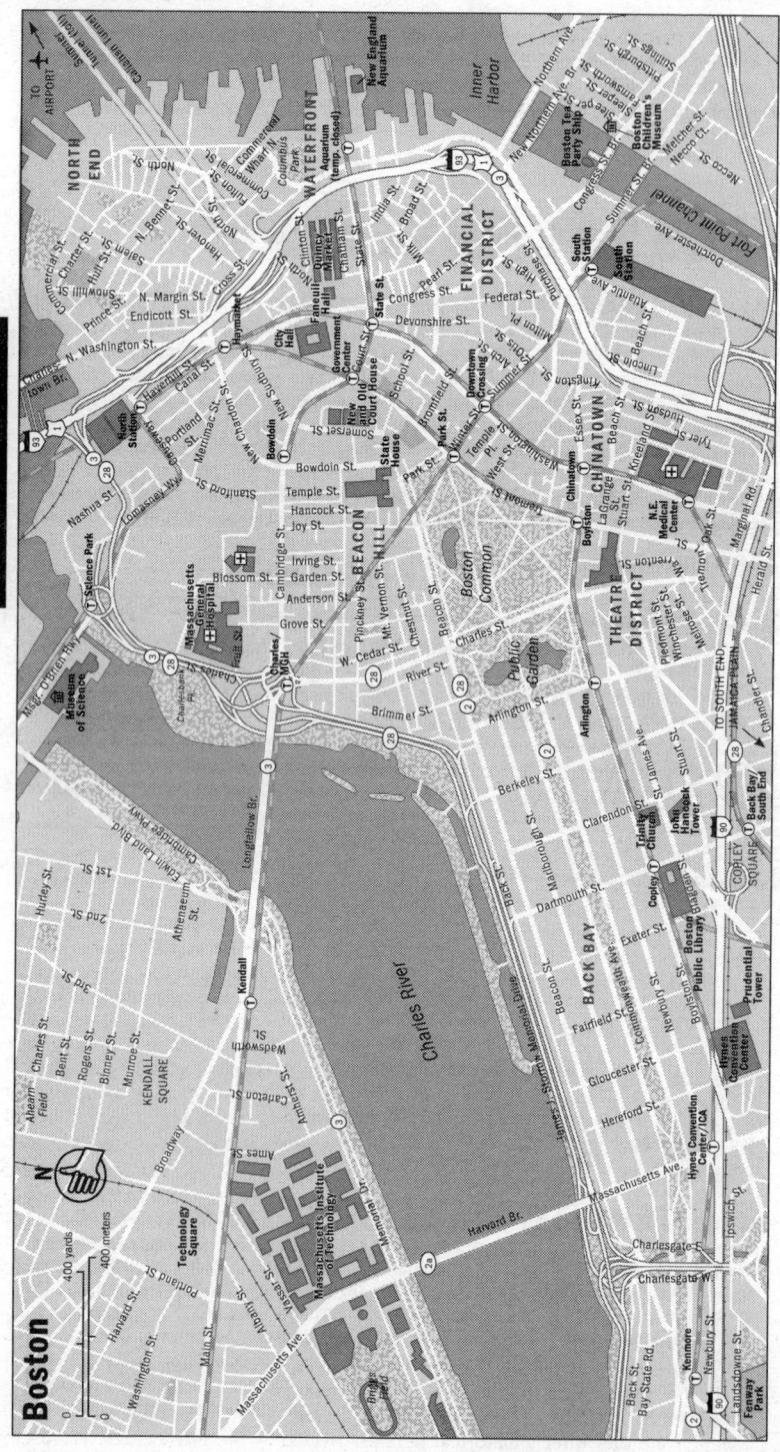

Boston

NEW ENGLAND

Trains: Amtrak. T: Red Line-South Station. Frequent daily service to New York City (5hr., $44-65); Washington, D.C. (9hr., $62-87); Philadelphia (7hr., $53-80); and Baltimore (8½hr., $62-87).

Buses: T: Red Line-South Station and T: Orange Line-Back Bay are the two main bus terminals. **Greyhound** provides daily service to New York City (4½hr., every 30min., $34); Washington, D.C. (10hr., every hr., $52); Philadelphia (7hr., every hr., $46); and Baltimore (10hr., every hr., $52). **Vermont Transit** (☎800-862-9671) goes north to Burlington (5hr., 6 per day, $45); Portland (2½hr., 8 per day, $24); and Montréal (8hr., 6 per day, $52). **Bonanza** (☎720-4110) has frequent daily service to Providence (16 per day, $8.75); Newport (5 per day, $15); and Woods Hole (1¾hr., 11-15 per day 8am-10pm, $15). **Plymouth & Brockton St. Railway** (☎508-746-0378) travels between South Station and Cape Cod; ride to Provincetown (3¼hr., 5 per day, $21). **Peter Pan Trailways** (☎800-343-9999) runs to Springfield (13 per day, $18); Albany (3 per day, $25); and New York City (21 per day, $34).

▣ LOCAL TRANSPORTATION

Public Transit: Massachusetts Bay Transportation Authority (MBTA) (☎722-3200 or 222-5000). The **subway** system, known as the **T**, consists of the Red, Green (which splits into B, C, D, and E lines), Blue, and Orange Lines. Maps available at info centers and T stops. Lines run daily 5:30am-12:30am. Fare $1, seniors 25¢, under 12 40¢. **MBTA Bus** service covers the city and suburbs more extensively than the subway. Fare 75¢, seniors 15¢. Bus and T schedules available at various subway stations, including Park St. and Harvard Sq. The **MBTA Commuter Rail** reaches suburbs and the North Shore, leaving from North Station, Porter Sq., Back Bay, and South Station T stops. Fares are determined by zone ($1-5.75). **Visitors passes** for the subway and buses 1-day $6, 3-day $11, 7-day $22.

Taxis: Checker Taxi, ☎536-7008. **Boston Cab,** ☎536-5010.

Car Rental: Dollar Rent-a-Car (☎634-0006 or 800-800-4000), at various locations including **Logan Airport.** Open 24hr. Under 25 $20 surcharge per day. 10% AAA discount. Must be 21 and have major credit card.

✦ ORIENTATION

Downtown Boston sits on a peninsula that juts into the protective waters of Boston Harbor. **Downtown** is still the same compact 3 sq. mi. settled in 1630, but important urban and residential neighborhoods, farther from the peninsula itself, have been incorporated into the city of Boston. Other neighborhoods actually on the Shawmut Peninsula include the **North End,** which lies—you guessed it—north (and east) of downtown, between downtown and the ocean. The **Fitzgerald Expressway (I-93)** divides downtown from the North End; the north-south interstate runs along the coast through Boston. Although I-93 is useful for getting in and out of Boston, tourists are more likely to experience the urban confusion that its renovation—a project nicknamed the "Big Dig" that has gone on forever and cost billions of dollars—has strewn throughout downtown. The North End, in turn, lies across the Charles River from up-and-coming **Charlestown. Chinatown** and the **Theater District** lie to the southwest of downtown. The Theater District's main artery, **Tremont St.,** continues into the South End (see below), where it's also more or less the main strip. West of the green **Boston Common,** the brownstones of **Back Bay** stand upon what was once a landfill. **Beacon St., Commonwealth Ave.,** and **Boylston St.** are parallel thoroughfares that run east-west throughout Back Bay. The **Mass. Pike (I-90),** which continues west across the state, separates Back Bay from the **South End.** Southwest of the South End lies **Jamaica Plain.** The **Fenway** spreads out along the Charles River to the west of Back Bay.

NEIGHBORHOODS

Downtown is the historical and financial center of the city, although other neighborhoods give it a run for its money as far as culture is concerned. Dining and shopping are generally expensive here, but downtown's sights and museums can be seen cheaply, and they offer a historical richness rivaled by few other cities. The predominately Italian **North End,** is small and easy to traverse on foot, though twisting roads make it easy to get lost. Stop here for incredible pastries and baked goods. **Charlestown,** across the river from Boston and adjacent to Cambridge, showcases the USS *Constitution* and a number of good restaurants; the neighborhood has profited from a healthy dose of new capital in recent years.

Chinatown is a densely packed enclave where, yes, you can get authentic Chinese food—even as late as 3 or 4am at many restaurants, which is true hardly anywhere else in Boston. The **Theater District** also scores well in the not-so-subtle-neighbor-hood-names contest. Boston used to boast many more theaters along Tremont St. than it does today, but plenty of standouts remain. This is also a good place to find chic, expensive bars. (Better ditch the dirty white hat.) Posh **Back Bay** is sort of like Boston's second downtown. Shopping is at its trendiest and most expensive on **Newbury St.; Copley Place** is a solid indoor alternative. You can also hit up the **John Hancock Observatory** and tons of hip bars and restaurants.

The **South End** is home to many galleries; it also boasts its fair share of eateries and nightlife, much of it gay- and lesbian-oriented and virtually all of it extremely gay-friendly. **Jamaica Plain** is worth the trip south for its stunning greenery—especially the Arnold Arboretum—and a quality of Mexican food unrivaled elsewhere in the city. It's also the home of the Sam Adams Brewery. The **Fenway** is the lively home of one of the world's foremost collections of art, the Museum of Fine Arts, as well as dance clubs that inhabit **Lansdowne St.**

🛈 PRACTICAL INFORMATION

Visitor info: Greater Boston Convention & Visitors Bureau, 2 Copley Pl., #105 (☎536-4100), in Back Bay. T: Green Line-Copley. Open M-F 8:30am-5pm. **Boston National Historic Park Visitors Center,** 15 State St. (☎242-5642), near the Old State House Downtown. T: Orange Line/Blue Line-State. Open daily 9am-5pm.

Hotlines: Rape Hotline, ☎492-7273. **Gay and Lesbian Helpline,** ☎267-9001.

Post Office: 25 Dorchester Ave. (☎267-8162), behind South Station. Open 24hr. **ZIP code:** 02205. **Area code:** 617. 10-digit dialing required.

🛏 ACCOMMODATIONS

Finding truly cheap lodging in Boston is almost always difficult, if not impossible. Planning ahead is essential in order to get a room during universities' move-in and graduation weeks in September, May, and June. Reservation services such as the free **Central Reservation Service** (☎800-332-3026 or 617-569-3800), **Boston Reservations** (☎332-4199; $5 fee), and the free **Hotel Reservations Network** (☎800-964-6835) promise to find discounted rooms even during sold-out periods like Boston's leaf-peeping craze, which peaks in early October. **Room tax** in Boston is 12.45%.

Hostelling International—Boston (HI-AYH), 12 Hemenway St. (☎536-9455). From T: Green Line-Hynes/ICA, turn left on Massachusetts Ave. (Mass. Ave.), then right on Boylston St.; Hemenway St. will be 1 block up, on your left. Laundry, kitchen, storage, in-room lockers, email kiosks. Shared bathrooms. $10 deposit for linen refunded at checkout. $5 refundable deposit for padlock. Reception 24hr. Check-in noon-10pm. Check-out 11am. Government-issued photo ID required for check-in. Reservations recommended. Wheelchair accessible. 6-bed dorms (co-ed or single-sex) $24 each person, nonmembers $27; doubles $72/$78.

Back Bay Summer Hostel (HI-AYH), 512 Beacon St. (☎353-3294), in Boston University's Danielsen Hall. From T: Green Line-Hynes/ICA, turn right on Mass. Ave., then left on Beacon St. Full kitchen, TV, laundry facilities. No sleeping bags; bedding included. $10 key deposit. Check-in noon. Check-out by 11am. Open roughly June 10-Aug. 15 (when school's out). Singles and doubles $29-54.

Beantown Hostel, 222 Friend St., 3rd fl. (☎723-0800), next to Hooters, and **Irish Embassy Hostel,** 232 Friend St., above the Irish Embassy Pub. From T: Orange Line/ Green Line-North Station, with the Fleet Center to your right, head down Causeway and turn left on Friend St. Check-in for both hostels at Beantown. 6-12 beds per room, both single-sex and co-ed. Free buffet Su and Tu 8pm in the **Irish Embassy Pub.** Lockers 50¢. Linen deposit $10 (no sleeping bags or sleep-sheets). Kitchen in Irish Embassy; laundry in Beantown. Check-out 10am. Curfew 1:45am. Reservations recommended. Dorms $22. Wheelchair access on Portland St.

YMCA of Greater Boston, 316 Huntington Ave. (☎536-7800). From T: Orange Line-Mass. Ave., take the back exit and go down the stairs to Huntington Ave. Nautilus equipment, swimming pool, laundry facilities. Basic, dormitory-style rooms (only some have A/C). Hallway bathrooms. $5 key deposit. Reception open 24hr. during the summer. Check-out 11am. 8 men-only rooms available Sept.-May. Singles $45; doubles $65; triples $81. With HI card, singles $42; doubles $58. Max. stay 10 nights. Must be 18 to rent a room. Wheelchair accessible.

YWCA Berkeley Residence, 40 Berkeley St. (☎375-2524), a 3min. walk from T: Orange Line-Back Bay. Hostel-style accommodations for women only. Rooms furnished with bed, bureau, desk, and closet; each floor has 2 spacious communal bathrooms. Breakfast included. On-site laundry. Reception 24hr. Singles $65; doubles and triples $100. Discounts available on longer stays (more than 14 nights).

The Buckminster, 645 Beacon St. (☎236-7050 or 800-727-2825), adjacent to Fenway Park. T: Green B, C, or D Line-Kenmore. Built in 1903, the Buckminster offers old-fashioned, fancy lodging for the tourist willing to put up a little cash. Private bath, TV, phone. Parking next door ($20 per night). Check-in 3pm. Check-out 11am. Singles $109-129; doubles $139-169; multi-bedroom suites $189-239. Wheelchair accessible.

The Farrington Inn, 23 Farrington Ave. (☎787-1860). From T: Green B Line-Harvard Ave., turn right onto Harvard Ave. from Commonwealth Ave. and pass the Brighton Ave. intersection; Farrington Ave. is a small side street on the right. The Farrington rents tidy singles, doubles, and apartments by the week. Whole apartments come complete with kitchen, living room, and bathroom. Showers, kitchens, TV, and A/C available in most rooms. Free parking and local calls. Reception daily 8am-6pm. Book ahead in summer. Sept.-Dec. about $450 per week; Jan.-Aug. about $350.

◨ FOOD

Boston is no longer just beans and cod: trendy bistros, pan-Asian diners, and ethnic restaurants of all stripes have hit the Hub in a major way. Then there are all the places that have been here forever, from greasy-spoon diners and barbecue joints to welcoming pubs. You can find anything here you want, from "chowda" and cheeseburgers to dim sum and *pad thai*.

DOWNTOWN

▨ **Blossoms Cafe,** 99 High St. (☎423-1911), at Federal St. From T: Red Line-South Station, cross I-93 on Summer St., turn right on High St., and walk past Federal St. This cafe serves salads with homemade dressings, soups, sandwiches, pizza, and hot entrees. Prices are surprisingly low for the Financial District: sandwiches are less than $5, and nothing is above $7. Open M-F 7am-3:30pm; lunch is served 11:30am-3pm. Cash only, but ATMs are on every corner. Wheelchair accessible.

▨ **Sultan's Kitchen,** 72 Broad St. (☎728-2828). From T: Orange Line/Blue Line-State, head toward the water on State St. for two blocks, then turn right on Broad St. and continue until you reach the corner of Custom House and Broad St. Behind its demure blue facade, you'll find some of the best Turkish food this side of the Atlantic. Try Sultan's famous *taramasalata* sandwich ($6.50), and of course, Turkey's legendary eggplant-based dish, "Swooning Imam" ($6.75). Open M-F 11am-5pm, Sa 11am-3pm.

Durgin Park, 340 North Market St. (☎227-2038), in Faneuil Hall. From T: Green Line/ Blue Line-Government Center, walk past City Hall to North Market to the left of Quincy

Market. Serving New England classics since 1827, its menu hasn't changed a bit: prime rib (2 cuts, $16 and $18), Yankee Pot Roast, cornbread, baked beans, and its famous Strawberry Shortcake, to name a few. Entrees $8-18. Open M-Sa 11:30am-10pm, Su 11:30am-9pm; lunch 11:30am-2:30pm. Wheelchair accessible.

Country Life Vegetarian, 200 High St. (☎951-2685), although the main entrance is on Broad St. From T: Blue Line/Orange Line-State, exit onto State St., take a left onto Atlantic Ave., turn right on High St. (under the I-93 overpass), and follow the blue and yellow signs to this self-serve, all-you-can-eat buffet restaurant that serves tasty veggies. Specialties include BBQ chickettes and Thai stir-fry. Lunch buffet $7, dinner $8, Su brunch $9. Open daily 11:30am-3pm; also Su and Tu-Th 5-8pm. Su brunch 10am-3pm.

THE NORTH END

Boston's "Little Italy" is the place to come for authentic Italian fare. If you just want to sip espresso and watch the passersby, head to **Caffè Paradiso,** 255 Hanover St. (☎742-1768; open daily 6:30am-2am) or **Caffè Vittoria,** 296 Hanover St. (☎227-7606; open M-F 8am-midnight, Sa-Su 1pm-12:30am). For cannoli to go, try **Mike's Pastry,** 300 Hanover St. (☎742-3050; open daily 9am-9pm) or **Modern Pastry,** 257 Hanover St. (☎523-3783; open in summer Su-Th 8am-10pm, F-Sa 8am-11pm; in winter Su-Th 8am-9pm, F-Sa 8am-10pm).

Monica's, 143 Richmond St. (☎227-0311). From T: Green Line/Orange Line-Haymarket, cross Fitzgerald Expwy. in the direction of Cross and Hanover St., turn right on Cross St., turn left on Hanover St., and take the first right off Hanover St. The four Iturralde brothers put their Italian, Argentinian, and Basque heritage to good use, creating Italian dishes with a twist. The figs and prosciutto over mixed greens shows the zest of Monica's fare. Pasta dishes $15-18. Open M-Sa 5:30-10:30pm, Su 4-10pm.

Artú, 6 Prince St. (☎742-4336), just off Hanover St. From T: Green Line/Orange Line-Haymarket, cross Fitzgerald Expwy. in the direction of Cross and Hanover St., turn right on Cross St., turn left on Hanover St., walk 2 blocks, and turn right on Prince St. This simple but tastefully appointed *rosticceria-trattoria* serves up a variety of traditional, hearty Italian *antipasti* ($3-12), *insalate, secondi,* and *dolci.* Locals rave about the grilled vegetable *antipasti* ($5.25) and the roast lamb *panini* (lunch only; $5). Dinner entrees start at $9.50. Open daily 11:30am-10:30pm; lunch served until 4pm.

CHINATOWN

Chinatown is the place to go for great Asian food, but it also happens to be the one place in Boston where you can get a full meal until 3 or 4am. Weekend morning dim sum is popular at **Chau Chow City,** 83 Essex St. (☎338-8158) and **China Pearl,** 9 Tyler St. (☎426-4338).

■ **Penang,** 685-691 Washington St. (☎451-6373). T: Orange Line-Chinatown or Orange Line/Red Line-Downtown Crossing. Though self-billed as Malaysian, the poly-ethnic menu is an amalgam of Indian, Cantonese, and Thai cuisines. The *roti canai* bread with curry dipping sauce ($3) is divine, and the hearty noodle-in-soup dishes ($4-6) are perfect for those with large appetites and small wallets. The service is impeccable, and the waiters are more than happy to help confused patrons pick an entree. Most entrees $6-14. Open Su-Th 11:30am-11:30pm, F-Sa 11:30am-midnight.

East Ocean City, 25-29 Beach St. (☎542-2504). From T: Orange Line-Chinatown, head south down Washington St., turn left on Beach St., and turn right on Harrison Ave.; it's on the right. Tuxedo-clad waiters hurry diners into an interior peopled with Hong Kong émigrés, who down rice dishes with beef, chicken, seafood, or vegetable toppings ($7-9) or marvel at the pan-fried shrimp ($12). Open Su-Th 11am-3am, F-Sa 11am-4am.

Dong Khanh, 83 Harrison Ave. (☎426-9410). From T: Orange Line-Chinatown, head south down Washington St., turn left on Beach St., and turn right on Harrison Ave.; it's on the right. This restaurant focuses on fantastic traditional Vietnamese cuisine such as *pho dac biet* (beef noodle soup; $4.50) and rice plates with meats and vegetables ($4-5). Open daily 9am-10pm. Cash only.

BACK BAY

■ **The Pour House Bar and Grill,** 907 Boylston St. (☎236-1767), at Hereford St. From T: Green B, C, or D Line-Hynes/ICA, turn left onto Mass. Ave., then immediately left onto Boylston St., and walk 1 block; it's on the left. Eating here won't put you in the poor house: the highest priced entree is $7, and a dirt-cheap breakfast is also served. A "Stately" burger menu features the Massachusetts (plain and proper) and the Hawaiian (teriyaki sauce with pineapple), all $3.25-4.50. "Burger Mania" every Sa 6-10pm, when all burgers are half-price. 21+ after 8pm. Open daily 8am-2am. Breakfast 8-11am, brunch Sa-Su 8am-3pm. Dinner served until 10pm. Wheelchair accessible.

Tridont Booksellers and Cafe, 338 Newbury St. (☎267-8688). From T: Green B, C, or D Line-Hynes/ICA, exit onto Mass. ave. and turn right on Newbury; it's a few blocks down on the right. A haven for the health food-seeking, liberal literati; customers lunch on veggie burgers and salads ($7-8) or sip fresh juice smoothies ($3-5) before or after perusing the wide selection of special interest books and periodicals. Come at night for luscious desserts ($4). Open daily 9am-midnight.

Emack and Bolio's, 290 Newbury St. (☎739-7995). From T: Green Line B, C, or D Line-Hynes/ICA, turn right on Newbury St. and walk 1½ blocks; it's on the right. *Boston Magazine's* pick for "Best Smoothie" is *the* place to be on a hot and muggy day in Boston. Sip a cool pink lemonade ($2.50) or get rejuvenated by the amazingly rich "energizer smoothie" ($4.50). Open daily 11am-11:30pm.

THE SOUTH END

The South End is quickly becoming the hottest neighborhood in the Boston culinary scene, especially in the area around Tremont St. Unfortunately, it's not right on the T, so you'll have to sashay from Back Bay Green and Orange Line stops.

■ **Bob the Chef's,** 604 Columbus Ave. (☎536-6204), at Northampton St. From T: Orange Line-Mass. Ave., turn right on Mass. Ave., walk 1 block, turn right on Columbus Ave., then walk another block. Across the street from the old NAACP building, Once a hangout for civil rights activists, Bob's now has a sleek new interior but the same spirit. Collard greens ($2.50) and "glori-fried" baked or barbecued chicken ($9-10) melt in your mouth. Entrees ($9-14) include two side dishes. Live jazz Th-Sa 7:30pm-midnight (cover $3-5). Su 11am-3pm all-you-can-eat brunch ($16, under 12 $11). Open Tu-W 11:30am-10pm, Th-Sa 11:30am-midnight, Su 11am-9pm.

Addis Red Sea, 544 Tremont St. (☎426-8727). From T: Orange Line-Back Bay, take the Columbus St. exit, turn left on Dartmouth St., walk 4 blocks, turn left on Tremont St., and walk 3 blocks along Tremont. The best Ethiopian restaurant in the city will introduce you to the joys of eating without utensils. Start off with the delightful *Ye-Miser Selatta* (lentils laced with tomatoes, onions, and peppers; $7). For entrees, choose from fish, chicken, beef, lamb, and vegetarian dishes ($8-12). Make sure not to lean on the *mesob* (Amharic for table), for it is very fragile. Open M-F 5-11pm, Sa-Su noon-11pm.

Le Gamin Cafe, 550 Tremont St. (☎654-8969), at Waltham St. From T: Orange Line-Back Bay/South End, exit onto Columbus Ave., turn right on Columbus, then make an immediate left on Dartmouth St., follow Dartmouth St. for 4 short blocks, turn left on Tremont, and walk for 3 blocks. Tucked into a romantic underground grotto on trendy Tremont St., Le Gamin attracts locals and visitors every night to try the expertly prepared crepes. All orders come with organic mesclun salad. Open daily 8am-midnight.

THE FENWAY

Near Boston University and Kenmore Sq., you'll find cheap student dives and a few late-night spots. Near the Symphony, there are a few good restaurants and bars.

■ **Betty's Wok & Noodle Diner,** 250 Huntington Ave. (☎424-1950), opposite Symphony Hall. T: Green E Line-Symphony. This new diner looks like a (stylish) throwback to the 50s, but there's nothing old about the incredibly fresh Asian-Latino cuisine. Entrees start at $8. For lunch, be adventurous and try a Cuban sandwich with fried yucca chips ($7). The lines are longest just before concerts at Symphony Hall, so join the crowd after 8pm to avoid a wait. Open Tu-Th noon-10pm, F-Sa noon-11pm.

Delihaus, 476 Commonwealth Ave. (☎247-9712). T: Green B, C, or D Line-Kenmore. The combination of greasy and delicious diner food, punk music, and late hours packs students into Delihaus when the clubs close. Pancakes $4, beer $3.50 (more for specialty Belgian brews), and perfect sweet potato fries with horseradish sauce $5. Open M-F 11am-2am, Sa-Su 9am-2am.

JAMAICA PLAIN

The restaurants in Jamaica Plain are some of the best bargains in the city, with a variety of ethnic cuisines to choose from. Because of the concentration of vegetarians that live here, most places cater to the herbivore demographic.

▨ **Bella Luna,** 405 Centre St. (☎524-6060). From T: Orange Line-Jackson Sq., turn right and walk 12 blocks down Centre St.; it's on your right. Come to Bella Luna and admire the artwork—both on the walls and on your plate—while you munch one of their many creations. The "Full Moon" pizza (pesto, basil, artichokes and tomatoes; $8-16) or the "Stavros Special" (feta, black olives, and mushrooms; $6-12) are flavorful enough to please carnivores and vegetarians alike. Open M-W 11am-3pm and 5-10pm, Th-F 11am-3pm and 5-11pm, Sa 11am-11pm, Su noon-10pm. Wheelchair accessible.

Centre St. Cafe, 669 Centre St. (☎524-9217), at Seaverns St. From T: Orange Line-Green St., take a left onto Green St. and a left at Centre St.; it's on your right. A paradise for vegetarians: organic and locally grown produce are the building blocks of the creative menu. Non-vegetarians can add shrimp ($4) and chicken ($2.50) to their entrees. Lunch entrees $6-10. Dinner $7-16. Open M-F 11:30am-3pm and 5-10pm, Sa-Su 9am-3pm and 5-10pm. Wheelchair accessible.

Acapulco Mexican Restaurant, 424 Centre St. (☎524-4328). From T: Orange Line-Stony Brook, turn left, walk down Boylston St., and turn left at Centre St.; it's on your left. This restaurant makes no secret of including authentic dishes such as *sopapilla* (fried dough with sugar and cinnamon; $3.50) and *tamal* (corn dough filled with potato and chicken; $3.25) alongside more typical fare (burritos and taco dishes will set you back about $8). Open M-W 4-10pm, Th noon-10pm, F noon-11pm, Sa-Su 1-11pm.

◉ SIGHTS

THE FREEDOM TRAIL

A great introduction to Boston's history lies along the red-painted line of the Freedom Trail, a 2½ mi. path through the historic landmarks of downtown Boston. Even on a trail dedicated to freedom, however, some sights charge admission. Starting at their **Visitors Center,** the National Park Service offers free tours of the trail's free attractions. (*Visitors Center* ☎536-4100. *T: Red/Green Line-Park Street. Open M-Sa 8:30am-5pm, Su 9am-5pm. Tours depart from the National Park Service office at 15 State St., opposite the entrance to the Old State House. In spring and fall M-F 2pm; Sa-Su 10, 11am, 2, and 3pm. In summer daily 10, 11am, 1, 2, and 3pm. Arrive 30min. early to sign up.*)

The Trail itself begins at another **Visitors Center,** in **Boston Common,** where you can pick up decent free maps or buy more detailed ones. (*T: Red/Green Line-Park St. Open M-Sa 8:30am-5pm, Su 9am-5pm.*) The Trail runs uphill to the **Robert Gould Shaw and 54th Regiment Memorial,** on Beacon St. The memorial honors the first black regiment of the Union Army in the American Civil War and their Bostonian leader, all made famous by the movie *Glory.* The Trail then crosses the street to the magnificent and ornate **State House.** (☎727-3676. *Open M-F 9am-5pm, Sa and holidays 10am-4pm. Free guided tours M-F 10am-3:30pm. Tours begin in Doric Hall on the 2nd floor.*) Passing the **Park St. Church,** the Trail reaches the **Old Granary Burial Ground** in which John Hancock, Samuel Adams, and Paul Revere rest. **King's Chapel and Burial Ground,** New England's oldest Anglican church, stands on Tremont St.; the latest inhabitants are Unitarian. Colonists founded the Chapel in 1686; more recently, the cemetery has become home of the earthly remains of John Winthrop. (*Chapel:* ☎227-2155. *Open in summer daily 9:30am-4pm; in spring and fall M and F-Sa 10am-4pm; in winter Sa 10am-2pm or by appointment. Unitarian services held W 12:15pm, Su 11am. Burial Grounds: open daily 8am-5:30pm; in winter 8am-3pm.*)

The **Old South Meeting House** was the site of the preliminary meeting that set the mood for the **Boston Tea Party.** *(☎ 482-6439. Open in summer daily 9:30am-5pm, in winter 10am-4pm. $3, students and seniors $2.50, under 6 free.)* Formerly the seat of British government in Boston, the **Old State House** now serves as a museum and the next stop on the trail. *(20 Washington St. ☎ 720-1713. Open daily 9am-5pm. $3, seniors and students $2, ages 6-18 $1.)* The Trail continues past the site of the **Boston Massacre** and through **Faneuil Hall,** a former meeting hall and current food court. Lectures are given every 30min. in the upstairs Great Hall when the city is not holding a function. *(Hall open daily 9am-5pm; enter through rear center doors.)* Heading into the North End, the path passes the **Paul Revere House.** *(19 North Sq. ☎ 523-2338. Open mid-Apr.-Oct. daily 9:30am-5:15pm; Nov. to mid-Apr. 9:30am-4:15pm. $2.50, seniors and students $2, ages 5-17 $1.)* Next, the **Old North Church** is where Revere's friend Robert Newman hung lanterns to warn the Charlestown rebels of the British approach. *(193 Salem St. ☎ 523-6676. Open in summer daily 9am-6pm; in winter 9am-5pm. Services on Su 9, 11am, and 4pm.)* **Copp's Hill Burying Ground** provides a resting place for numerous colonial Bostonians, including Prince Hall, a freed slave, soldier, and founder of Boston's first school for black children, as well as a nice view of the Old North Church.

Nearing its end, the Freedom Trail heads over the Charlestown Bridge to the newly renovated **USS *Constitution*** and its companion museum. *(☎ 426-1812. Open daily 9:30am until 10min. prior to sunset. Free tours every 30min. until 3:50pm.)* The final stop on the Trail is the **Bunker Hill Monument.** The obelisk is actually on Breed's Hill, the site of fortification during the battle; Bunker Hill is about a ½ mi. away. A grand view awaits those who climb the 294 steps to the top. *(Open daily 9am-4:30pm.)* To return to Boston, follow the Trail back over the bridge, take the T from the Orange Line-Community College stop near Bunker Hill, or hop on a **Harbor Ferry** from one of the piers near the *Constitution. (Ferries run between Lovejoy Wharf, adjacent to the Fleet Center, Boston Long Wharf, near the New England Aquarium, and the Charlestown Navy Yard/USS Constitution M-F every 20min. 6:30-11:10am and 3:10-6:30pm, every hr. 11:10am-3:10pm; Sa-Su every 30min. 10am-6pm. Fares collected aboard vessels. $1, ages 5-11 50¢.)*

DOWNTOWN

Downtown Boston is the historical and financial heart of the city, and it is usually the first and often the only place that many visitors to Boston see. Old and new rub shoulders in this mini-metropolis, where skyscrapers overshadow stately colonial buildings and subways rumble beneath the cobblestones. In the center of downtown Boston's three main districts—**Government Center, Downtown Crossing,** and the **Financial District**—is the sprawling **Boston Common,** where yuppies, hippies, and everyone in between come to sit in the sunshine.

GOVERNMENT CENTER. At the mouth of the Green/Blue Line-Government Center T stop lies a large brick plaza, home to the **JFK Building** and **City Hall.** City Hall's architecture was designed to express symbolically the structure of government: rising up from the plaza, the bricks of the lower level enclose the offices that the public use, while the highest reaches of the building hold offices reserved for the government. The plaza was originally intended to be a gathering place, but aside from the occasional concert, it serves mainly as a walkway from the T station to the bustling **Quincy Market** area, a commercialized outdoor market. It's worth the short walk to the **Holocaust Memorial,** six luminous 54 ft. high glass towers that pay tribute to all victims of the Holocaust, both Jews and Gentiles. Resembling smokestacks, the towers recall the six main concentration camps. The 6 million numbers etched into the towers, quotations from survivors, and facts about the Holocaust create a powerful, beautiful, and extremely educational memorial—it's especially sobering at night. To get there, walk past City Hall and turn left on Congress St.

DOWNTOWN CROSSING. Centered around **Washington St.,** Downtown Crossing is a great place to buy something quickly or cheaply (probably not both). At the heart of the Washington St. shopping district lies an emblem of bargain hunting, **Filene's Basement,** where there are generous discounts on many top-of-the-line labels. Independent shops and fancy department stores, which in pre-mall years drew suburban folks to Boston's best shopping, have long since given way to chains, but Downtown Crossing is still a convenient place to shop in the open air.

FORNICATING FALCONS Since 1987, the **Custom House Tower** has been the site of the nest of a pair of Peregrine falcons as part of an effort to restore the bird to Massachusetts. The Peregrine falcon is considered the fastest bird on earth, capable of diving from great heights at speeds of up to 200 mph to capture prey. Once prominent in the New England area, they suffered almost total extinction in the 50s because of the pesticide DDT. These falcons, one of the most productive pairs of falcons in New England, have laid 64 eggs and raised 36 chicks. The falcons are the two oldest Peregrines known to exist in the area and can often be seen hovering above downtown. Thanks to such recovery efforts, the Peregrine falcon was removed from the federal list of endangered species in 1999.

FINANCIAL DISTRICT. Boston's first skyscraper, the stylish 495 ft. **Custom House Tower,** and its signature clock stand out against their drab Financial District neighbors. The small **observation balcony** at the top of the tower is worth a visit: you can take in stunning views of the harbor and downtown area, as well as meet the **Peregrine falcons** who nest there. *(3 McKinley Sq. ☎310-6300. From T: Orange/Blue Line-State, walk down State St. towards the harbor to India St. Free tours to observation balcony daily 10am and 4pm.)* The **Batterymarch Building** was the first Art Deco building in the city of Boston. (It's now a Wyndham hotel.) One of the characteristics of the Art Deco style is the shifting of the exterior color from dark at the base to light at the top, giving the impression of greater height. *(60 Batterymarch St., at Broad St.)*

BOSTON COMMON. Bordered by Beacon, Boylston, and Tremont St., the **Boston Common** has been used over the centuries for public rallies and celebrations, recreation, military training, public punishment and burial, and pastureland for cows and sheep. In 1728, the first tree-lined pedestrian mall was laid out in the Common, and in the 19th century, enthusiasm for the American parks movement led to new walkways, statues, plaques, fountains, and gates. Today, you can picnic with squirrels and pigeons, wade in the **Frog Pond** in summer (the frogs have been evicted) or ice skate on it in the winter, watch old movies on a big screen for free during the **Classic Film Festival,** or take in some culture during the free **Shakespeare** performances in the Bandstand in late June. Upcoming events are posted at the **Visitor Information Center.** *(☎635-2147 for ice-skating info. T: Green/Red Line-Park Street. Classic films shown on the Parade Grounds June-Aug. Tu at dusk.)*

THE WATERFRONT. The waterfront area, bounded by Atlantic and Commercial St., runs along Boston Harbor from South Station to the North End. Stroll down Commercial, Lewis, or Museum Wharf for a view of the harbor and a breath of sea air. Catering to all ages, the **New England Aquarium,** on Central Wharf, presents cavorting penguins, giant sea turtles, and a bevy of briny beasts in a 200,000 gallon tank and over 70 galleries. Aboard *Discovery,* a floating platform moored next to the Aquarium, you can watch sea lions perform or visit the harbor seals and sea otters. A new IMAX theater is scheduled to open in fall 2001. *(☎973-5200 or 973-0223. From T: Orange/Blue Line-State, follow the signs as you walk toward the Harbor. Open Sept.-June M-F 9am-5pm, Sa-Su 9am-6pm; July-Aug. M-Tu and F 9am-6pm, W-Th 9am-8pm, Sa-Su 9am-7pm. $12.50, ages 3-11 $6.50, seniors $10.50. W 4-8pm $1 off.)* If you're having trouble getting your blood boiling about Revolutionary Boston, the **Boston Tea Party Ship and Museum,** on the Congress St. Bridge, is the place to come. Closed temporarily, the museum is scheduled to re-open in winter 2002. *(☎338-1773. From T: Red Line-South Station, walk down Atlantic Ave. to Congress St. and turn onto the bridge. Open spring and fall daily 9am-5pm, in summer 9am-6pm. $8, students $7, children $4.)*

THE NORTH END. The east tip of Boston contains the historic **North End.** *(T: Green/Orange Line-Haymarket.)* Now an Italian neighborhood, the city's oldest residential district overflows with window boxes, Italian flags, fragrant pastry shops, *crèches,* Sicilian restaurants, and Catholic churches. The most famous of the last, **Old St. Stephen's Church,** is the classic Colonial brainchild of Charles Bulfinch. *(24 Clark St.*

NEW ENGLAND

at Hanover St. ☎523-1230. Open daily 7am-dusk and during services.) Down the street, the sweet-smelling **Peace Gardens** provide a respite from the clamor of the North End.

CHINATOWN. Two blocks from South Station and southwest of the Common, Boston's **Chinatown** demarcates itself with an arch (and huge Fu dogs) at its Beach St. entrance, bilingual signs, and pagoda-topped telephone booths. This is *the* place for Asian food, and many restaurants stay open late. *Do not walk alone here at night.* Chinatown holds two big festivals each year. The first, **New Year**, usually celebrated on a Sunday in February, includes lion dances, fireworks, and kung fu exhibitions. The **August Moon Festival** honors a mythological pair of lovers at the time of the full moon, usually on the second or third Sunday in August. *(T: Orange Line-Chinatown.)*

BACK BAY. The elegant Back Bay district did not exist until 1857, when developers filled in the foul-smelling tidal flats between Beacon Hill and Brookline. The **Public Gardens** mark the eastern boundary of Back Bay, where the landfill project began. The heart of Back Bay is **Copley Square**, framed by H. H. Richardson's **Trinity Church** and the majestic **Boston Public Library**. Nearby, the **John Hancock Tower** soars above the neo-Gothic **New Old South Church**. The **Prudential Tower** on Huntington Ave. is alternately beloved and despised by locals, but it's a landmark either way. Radiating out from Copley Sq. are **Huntington Ave.**, the sculpture-studded **Commonwealth Ave.**, and **Boylston St.**, which runs parallel to upscale **Newbury St.**

PUBLIC GARDENS. Across from the Common on Charles St., the title characters from the children's book *Make Way for Ducklings* (hallowed in bronze) point the way to the **Public Gardens**, where pedal-powered **Swan Boats** glide around a quiet pond lined with shady willows. *(T: Green Line-Arlington. Swan rides $3 for 15min.)*

COPLEY SQUARE. The lush lawns and elegant fountains of Copley Sq. are hemmed in by Boston landmarks on all sides. *(T: Green Line-Copley.)* The John Hancock Observatory, on the 60th floor of the 790 ft., 62-story **John Hancock Tower**, is the tallest building in New England; the view of Boston and its environs is stunning. *(☎572-6429. Open M-Sa 9am-10pm, Apr.-Oct. Su 9am-10pm, Nov.-Mar. Su 9am-5pm. $6, seniors and ages 5-17 $4, military and children under 5 free.)* Dominating Copley Sq. is the Romanesque Revival **Trinity Church**, erected between 1872 and 1877 and widely regarded as the pinnacle of architect H. H. Richardson's career. The church's cloister and hidden garden are enchanting, perhaps because they are rather difficult to find—go around to Clarendon St. Founded on April 3, 1848, the **Boston Public Library** was the first major free municipal library in the US. When you first see it, however, it may feel more like an art museum than a large public research library. The greatest artistic treasures are hidden on the 3rd floor in the Sargent gallery, named for John Singer Sargent, who created the grand mural that adorns the walls. *(☎536-5400. Open M-Th 9am-9pm, F-Sa 9am-5pm. Free guided Art and Architecture Tours of the Library year-round M 2:30pm, Tu and Th 6pm, F-Sa 11am; Oct.-May Su 2pm.)*

NEWBURY AND BOYLSTON STREETS. The ritziest promenade in all of Boston is **Newbury St.**, where the city's rich and trendy go to see and be seen (and spend). In the eight-block stretch between Arlington St. and Mass. Ave., there are over 40 restaurants, more than 100 stores, 40 art galleries, and nearly 100 hair salons. The most upscale stores are clustered on the side of Newbury closest to the Public Gardens. **Boylston St.** runs parallel to Newbury St. and is considered the more modest of the two commercial strips. Fairly inexpensive bars can be found here, as well as common retail stores. *(T: Green Line-Arlington, Copley, or Hynes/ICA.)*

COMMONWEALTH AVENUE MALL. This 220 ft. wide Parisian boulevard is home to some of Back Bay's most impressive townhouses, with a tree-lined 100 ft. wide pathway cutting through the center. Frederick Law Olmsted designated the area part of his **Emerald Necklace** park system that encircles Boston and gives the Green line its color. The park is perhaps best known for its public sculptures—every block or so there is a sculpture or monument, ranging from former presidents to social activists to Viking **Leif Eriksson**, who, some 19th-century historians theorized, may have explored as far south as Boston and Cambridge. *(T: Green Line-Arlington.)*

JAMAICA PLAIN. Jamaica Plain offers the quintessentially un-Bostonian: ample parking, good Mexican food, and Mother Nature. Although it's one of the largest green spaces in the city of Boston, covering over 265 acres, many residents never make it to the lush fields of the **Arnold Arboretum,** 125 the Arborway, which now holds one of North America's largest collections of trees, vines, shrubs, and flowers. The variety of flowering species ensures that there will be blooms at any time of the year. On the second or third Sunday in May, **Lilac Sunday,** the Arboretum's collection of over 500 lilac plants are in full bloom. *(T: Orange Line-Forest Hills.* ☎*524-1718. Open daily dawn-dusk. $1 donation requested.)* When Frederick Law Olmsted designed the loop of green space around Boston that has become known as the Emerald Necklace, **Jamaica Pond,** between Perkins St. and Park Dr. on the Jamaicaway, was one of its key links. At 120 acres, this glacier-made pond is Boston's largest. Trails weave around the perimeter, making it a favorite place for jogging and walking. The 100-year-old boathouse rents small boats for leisurely sails around the pond. *(T: Orange Line-Green St.* ☎*635-7383.)* For an "educational" end to your south-of-Boston junket, swing by the ◙**Sam Adams Brewery,** 30 Germania St., and learn all you ever wanted to know about how beer is made on the 40min. tour, which includes tasting barley, smelling fresh Bavarian hops, and walking through the original Sam Adams Brewery. The highlight of the tour is the end, when those with 21+ ID learn how to "taste" beer. *(T: Orange Line-Stony Brook.* ☎*368-5000. Tours Th 2pm; F 2, 5:30pm; Sa noon, 1, and 2pm. $1 donation requested.)*

▥ MUSEUMS

◙ **Museum of Fine Arts (MFA),** 465 Huntington Ave. (☎267-9300), in the Fenway. T: Green E Line-Museum. Boston's most famous museum contains one of the world's finest collections of Asian ceramics, outstanding Egyptian Nubian art, a showing of Impressionists, and superb American art. Two unfinished portraits of George and Martha Washington, begun by Gilbert Stuart in 1796, merit a gander. Open M-Tu 10am-4:45pm, W-F 10am-9:45pm, Sa-Su 10am-5:45pm. $12; seniors and students $10; ages 7-17 M-F until 3pm $5, otherwise free; $2 off Th-F after 5pm; free W after 4pm. Special entrance fees apply for exhibits in the Gund Gallery.

◙ **Isabella Stewart Gardner Museum,** 280 the Fenway (☎566-1401), a few hundred yds. from the MFA. T: Green E Line-Museum. This astounding private collection remains exactly as Mrs. Gardner arranged it a century ago. The Venetian-style *palazzo* garners as much attention as the Old Masters, and the smell of the courtyard garden alone is worth the price of admission. Open Tu-Su 11am-5pm. $10, Sa-Su $11; students Tu and Th $5, W $3; seniors $7; under 18 free.

◙ **John F. Kennedy Presidential Library** (☎929-4500), Columbia Point, just off I-93 in Dorchester. T: Red Line-JFK/UMass, then take the free shuttle bus marked JFK to the library (every 20min. 8am-5pm). Dedicated "to all those who through the art of politics seek a new and better world." The looming white structure, designed by I.M. Pei, overlooks Dorchester Bay. No conspiracy theories here; the museum contains exhibits tracing Kennedy's career from the campaign trail to his tragic death. Open daily 9am-5pm. $8, seniors and students $6, children 13-17 $4, children under 12 free.

Museum of Science, Science Park (☎723-2500), on the Charles River. T: Green Line-Science Park. Contains the largest "lightning machine" in the world, a hands-on activity center, and live-animal demonstrations. Within the museum, the **Hayden Planetarium** features models, lectures, films, and laser and star shows. Travel the world in the **Mugar Omni Theater;** films on scientific subjects show on a 4-story, domed OmniMax screen. Exhibit hall open daily 9am-5pm; July 5 to early Sept. Sa-Th 9am-7pm, F 9am-9pm. Exhibit Hall $10, children and seniors $7. Omni Theater, Planetarium, and Laser Show $7.50/$5.50. Omni shows $2.50 off Tu-W after 7pm.

Children's Museum, 300 Congress St. (☎426-8850), on the waterfront. T: Red Line-South Station. Kids of all ages wind through hundreds of hands-on exhibits and learn a little something to boot. Open M-Th and Sa-Su 10am-5pm, F 10am-9pm. $7, ages 2-15 and seniors $6, under 2 $2. F 5-9pm $1.

Institute of Contemporary Art (ICA), 955 Boylston St. (☎266-5152), in Back Bay. T: Green Line B, C, or D-Hynes/ICA. Boston's lone outpost of the avant-garde attracts major modern artists while aggressively promoting lesser-known work. Innovative, thought-provoking exhibits change every 8 weeks. The museum also presents experimental theater and film. Open W and Sa-Su noon-5pm, Th noon-9pm, F noon-7pm. $6, seniors and students $4, children under 12 free. Free Th 5-9pm. 2 for 1 with AAA card.

🔲 ENTERTAINMENT

Publications such as *The Boston Phoenix*, *Stuff@Night*, and the *Boston Globe* Calendar section, and websites such as http://ae.boston.com and http://boston.city-search.com offer complete lists of what's happening in the Hub. For tickets to most events throughout the area, contact **Bostix** (☎723-5181), **Ticketmaster** (www.ticketmaster.com), or **NEXT** (☎423-6000). Although ticket prices can be steep, there are ways to cut costs. **Student rush** tickets go on sale for many shows 1hr. before the performance. Bostix sells **half-price remainder tickets** on the day of the show. Some venues accept **volunteer ushers,** which allows you to see the show at a reduced price or even free in exchange for less than 1hr. of stuffing programs or seating patrons. Contact individual venues for information on special pricing events.

THEATER

Boston is known as a try-out town; many shows test the waters here before heading for Broadway. The major theaters are clustered around the **Theater District** (T: Green Line-Boylston), including the **Wang Center,** a tour stop for blockbuster musicals *Phantom of the Opera* and *Miss Saigon*, as well as the home of the annual holiday production of *The Nutcracker*. Two of Boston's longest-running shows are thoroughly entertaining and worth the splurge to see them at the **Charles Playhouse. Blue Man Group** dazzles audiences of all ages with drums, music, paint, lights, twinkies, marshmallows, and rolls of toilet paper. (☎800-258-3626. $39-49, student rush $25.) **Shear Madness** is a wacky murder-mystery. (☎426-5225. $34, student rush $29.) The **Huntington Theater Company,** 264 Huntington Ave. (☎266-0800), in the Fenway, is a well-respected theater that produces quality contemporary and classic plays. For more avant-garde productions, check out what's playing at the **Boston Center for the Arts,** 539 Tremont St. (☎426-2748), in the South End.

CLASSICAL MUSIC AND DANCE

Symphony Hall, 301 Mass. Ave., is home to both the world-renowned **Boston Symphony Orchestra (BSO)** and her lighter-hearted little sister, the **Boston Pops.** (☎266-1492. Orchestra season Oct.-Apr., with concerts on Tu, Th, Sa night, F afternoon, and some F nights. $22-67; $10 rush tickets available Tu and Th 5pm, F 9am; $12 rehearsal tickets W night and Th morning. Pops season May-July Tu-Su nights. Balcony tickets $14-34, table tickets $36-53. Free concerts at the Hatch Shell on the Esplanade in early July.) The **Boston Ballet** (☎695-6950) performs at the Wang Center and is best known for its holiday performance of *The Nutcracker*, a six-week run that draws over 140,000 people.

SPORTS, ETC.

Catch a **Red Sox** game at **Fenway Park,** the oldest and the smallest baseball park in the major leagues. (☎482-4769 for tickets. Bleachers $14, grandstands $28, field boxes $45.) If you are a basketball or hockey fan, head to the **Fleet Center,** 50 Causeway St. Replacing the Boston Garden in 1995, this huge entertainment complex seats up to 20,000 for concerts, pro-wrestling, and figure skating. It is also the home of the **Celtics** and the **Bruins.** (☎624-1750. Box office summer hours M-F 10am-5pm; in season daily 10am-7pm. Celtics tickets $10-140, Bruins $20-140.)

The 106th **Boston Marathon** will occur in April 2002. The whopping 26 mi. run snakes from Hopkinton to Copley and over "Heartbreak Hill." Part of local tradition on Patriot's Day for over 100 years, the Boston Marathon attracts thousands of runners from all over the world who are cheered on by thousands of spectators lining the route. You don't need any tickets—just come. Since 1965, the **Head of the Charles Regatta**, the world's largest single-day crew race, has been a mecca for thousands of rowers and revelers who descend on the Charles River to participate in the pageantry. The Head of the Charles occurs the third weekend of October.

If ever a public pool parlor could be described as swank, it's **Boston Billiard Club**, 126 Brookline Ave. (☎ 536-7665), in the Fenway. **Jillian's**, 145 Ipswich St., at the end of Lansdowne St., has 55 billiard tables as well as arcade games on the second floor. (☎ 437-0300. 2 people $10 per hr., 4 people $14 per hr.)

◪ NIGHTLIFE

Before you set out to paint the town red, there are a few things to know about nightlife in Boston. First, nearly every place requires **21+ photo ID** to get in. Boston bars and clubs are notoriously strict about the minimum age. Second, **closing time is 2am**—"after hours" does not exist in Puritan Boston (though some restaurants in Chinatown do stay open until 3 or 4am). Do the math and you'll realize that the T stops running 2hr. before last call, so bring some extra cash for the taxi ride home. If **clubbing** is your thing, head to Lansdowne St. in Kenmore Sq. or Boylston St. in the Theater District. The **live music** scene in Boston is also fabulous, from Irish folk to jazz to rhythm and blues.

DANCE CLUBS

Avalon, 15 Lansdowne St. (☎ 262-2424). T: Green B, C, or D Line-Kenmore. Across the street from Fenway Park in a line of other clubs, the Avalon stands out with its trippy interior. The roomy dance floor, surrounded by 3 bars, offers house and techno dance music. Su is gay night. 19+ except on Sa 21+. Cover $10-15. Open daily 10pm-2am.

Axis, 13 Lansdowne St. (☎ 262-2437). T: Green B, C, or D Line-Kenmore. Th nights have international guest DJs downstairs and local DJs upstairs. F night Spin Cycle is mainly techno and house. Sa "X-nights" (cover $10; 21+). Cover ages 19-21 $15, 21+ $12. Open daily 10pm-2am.

Karma, 11 Lansdowne St. (☎ 617-421-9595). T: Green B, C, or D Line-Kenmore. The combined dance floor and stage area provide an intimate alternative to the super-sized clubs, and past performers Dido and Eddie Vedder prove that Karma puts its cozy venue to good use. Lose yourself among the hip college crowd. F nights drum and bass, Sa and Th nights house music. 19+. Cover $8-15. Open Th-Sa 10pm-2am.

Envy, 25 Boylston Pl. (☎ 542-3689). From T: Green Line-Boylston, cross the street and turn right, then make the first left. A huge club decked out in murals by a Hollywood film artist. DJ plays techno-ized 70s and 80s standards. Proper dress required. Beer $3.50-4, cocktails $5-6. Cover W $15; F-Sa $5. Open F-Sa and every other W 9pm-2am.

BARS AND PUBS

The Bell in Hand, 45 Union St. (☎ 617-227-2098), downtown. T: Orange/Blue Line-State. Take a left on Congress St., a right on North St., and a left on Union St.–it's on your right. Boasting the city's oldest liquor license, this labyrinthine space has 3 bars, live bands that play songs you know and like (W-Su), its own local brew courtesy of Sam Adams ($3.75), and a generally attractive crowd. Open daily until 2am.

Cactus Club, 939 Boylston St. (☎ 236-0200), in Back Bay. From T: Green Line-Hynes/ ICA, walk across the overpass towards the Convention Center; it's in the 2nd block on the left side of the street. A slightly timid crowd scopes but doesn't scam their yuppie neighbors; perhaps the margaritas ($5) are to blame for the slightly frosty pickup scene. The truly bold purchase their drinks in a "Big Bowl" ($11) with extra straws in the hopes of finding a friend or three with whom to share. Open daily 11:30am-2am.

Delux Cafe, 100 Chandler St. (☎ 338-5258), in the South End. From T: Orange Line-Back Bay, turn left on Dartmouth St., walk 1 block, turn left on Chandler St. and walk another block; it's on the right after Clarendon St. Bizarre is the keyword at Delux Cafe, where a shrine to Elvis sits beside a fake Christmas tree and golden oldies music competes for distraction with screenings of Scooby Doo episodes. Drinks $2.50-3.75. Open M-Sa 5pm-1am; dinner served until 11:30pm. Cash only.

Wonder Bar, 186 Harvard Ave. (☎351-2665), at Commonwealth Ave. in Allston. The Wonder Bar is *swank:* live jazz nightly, a downstairs lounge (velvet included), and a dress code to boot (no sneakers, no hats, no ripped jeans). The scene is at its most happening late into the night. Beer $3.75-4; wine $5-7. Live jazz nightly at 9:30pm. Bar open daily 5pm-2am; lounge Th-Sa 10:30pm-2am.

Sunset Grill & Tap, 130 Brighton Ave. (☎254-1331), in Allston. From T: Green B Line-Harvard Ave., walk right down Brighton Ave.; it's across the street from Pho Pasteur. Come to Sunset for the beer: with 112 varieties on tap, over 400 in bottles, and a selection that changes every 2 weeks, Sunset is a malt-lover's heaven. Beer starts at $3.50 a pint. "Midnight Madness" Su-Tu 11:30pm-1am: free appetizer buffet with a 2-drink min. purchase. Open daily 11:30am-1am.

LIVE MUSIC

▩ **Harper's Ferry,** 158 Brighton Ave. (☎254-9743), in Allston. From T: Green B Line-Harvard Ave., walk left down Brighton Ave. A must-stop for blues aficionados, this is Bo Diddley's favorite joint in town. In addition to live nightly rhythm and blues acts, Harper's promises a relaxed atmosphere, plenty of pool tables, and a casual down-home scene. Beer $3-4. Live music nightly at 9:30pm. Cover $2-10. Open daily 1pm-2am.

Wally's Cafe, 427 Mass. Ave. (☎424-1408), at Columbus Ave. in the South End, accessible via the #1 bus or T: Orange Line-Mass. Ave. Established in 1947, Wally's is Boston's longest-running jazz joint, and the place has only improved with age. The beer ($2.75, $3.75 during music) flows freely. Blues M 9pm-2am, jazz Tu-W and F-Sa 9pm-2am, Latin jazz Th 9pm-2am. 21+. Open M-Sa 9am-2am, Su noon-2am.

GAY AND LESBIAN NIGHTLIFE

For updated listings for gay and lesbian nightlife, pick up a copy of *Bay Windows*, available at many businesses in the South End. All bars and restaurants in the **South End** are gay-friendly, but some cater exclusively to a gay crowd (sorry, ladies, these are mostly boys' night out places). **The Eagle,** 520 Tremont St. (☎542-4494), draws an older male crowd. **The Fritz,** 26 Chandler St. (☎482-4428), is a popular gay sports bar. **Moonshine** and **Satellite Lounge** at Club Cafe, 209 Columbus Ave. (☎536-0966), are video bars that attract a mixed crowd of young gay professionals. **Jacque's,** 71 Broadway (☎426-8902), is the oldest gay bar in Boston, catering mostly to a transgendered crowd, with drag shows and live music. In the Fenway, strictly leather-and-Levis **Ramrod** has recently spawned another floor of non-leather earthly delights—**The Machine** (☎266-2986). If you wanna boogie, check out **Avalon Sundays** (see p. 128) for cruisy, crazy fun. On Friday and Saturday nights, the low-key gay bar **Chaps** transforms into **Vapor,** 100 Warrenton St. (☎695-9500), when a gay and lesbian crowd grooves to house and dance mixes under the lights. The most popular scene, however, is ▩**Axis Mondays** (p. 128), when a mixed straight and gay crowd pack the dance floor as one of area's best DJs spins the latest dance hits; at 12:30am, the real fun begins with a raunchy drag show—be prepared for foul language, fabulous costumes, and real attitude.

CAMBRIDGE   ☎617

Cambridge has thrived on intellectual life since the colonial era. Harvard, which boasts the nation's first college and many of the oldest graduate schools, was founded here in 1636. The Massachusetts Institute of Technology (MIT), founded in Boston in 1861, moved to Cambridge in 1916, giving the small city a second academic heavyweight. Town and gown mingle and contrast—not always amicably—creating diverse characters that change as you move from square to (not-square) square. Bio-tech labs and computer science buildings radiate out from MIT through Kendall Sq., and their gentrifying influence is slowly overtaking Central Sq. Harvard Sq., on the other side of the city, offers Georgian buildings, stellar bookstores and coffeehouses, and street musicians.

◪ PRACTICAL INFORMATION. Cambridge is best reached by a 10min. T ride from downtown Boston. The city's main artery, **Massachusetts Ave.** ("Mass. Ave."), runs parallel to the Red Line, which makes stops along the street. The **Kendall Sq./ MIT** stop is just across the Longfellow Bridge from Boston. The subway continues outbound through **Central Sq., Harvard Sq.,** and **Porter Sq.** The *Old Cambridge Walking Guide* makes for an excellent self-guided tour ($2). **Post Office:** 125 Mt. Auburn St., but it's always moving around due to construction. Follow the signs on Mt. Auburn west of Harvard Sq. (☎ 876-9280. Open M-F 7:30am-6pm, Sa 7:30am-3pm; self-service available M-F 7am-6:30pm, Sa 7am-3:30pm.) **ZIP code:** 02138. **Area code:** 617. For budget **accommodations,** head back to Boston (see p. 115).

◻ FOOD. Cambridge cuisine is a microcosm of the United Nations, from Portugal to Pamplona, Afghanistan to Algiers. At ◪**Charlie's Kitchen Bar and Grill,** 10 Eliot St., fickle tastes and changing trends don't bother anyone. Although it's occasionally frequented by ironic hipsters in search of kitsch, this joint offers a $5 double cheeseburger special that could become a staple of your diet—ask for the beer-battered french fries. (☎ 492-9646. Open Su-W noon-12:30am, Th-Sa noon-1:30am.) For a quick lunch, **Campo de' Fiori,** 1350 Mass. Ave., in the Holyoke Center, hits the spot with a scrumptious signature *pane romano*. The counter service is usually quick despite the crowds, making this an unusual but satisfying option on the fast food roster. (☎ 354-3805. Open M-F 8am-8pm, Sa 11am-6pm. *Pane romano* $3-4.50, sandwiches $4-6.) If you've had enough of pretentious Europhile eateries, head to **Pho Pasteur,** 35 Dunster St., in the Garage, for traditional Vietnamese cuisine that includes plenty of *pho* (soup), chicken, and noodle dishes. (☎ 864-4100. Open Su-W 11am-10pm, Th-Sa 11am-11pm.) Or hit **Spice,** 24 Holyoke St., for addictive *pad thai* ($8) and other Thai delicacies. (☎ 868-9560. Open M-Th 11:30am-3pm and 5-10pm, F 11:30am-3pm and 5-11pm, Sa-Su noon-10:30pm.) For an after-dinner treat, ◪**Herrell's Ice Cream,** 15 Dunster St., delivers ice cream lovers more than 2500 different possibilities, including frozen yogurt and "no-moo" vegan options. All flavors, fudges, and whipped creams are prepared on site. Lick your heart out in the a converted bank vault in the back decorated with aquatic murals. (Open daily noon-midnight.) When the munchies strike late at night, **Pinocchio's,** 74 Winthrop St., or "Noch's," as patrons lovingly dub it, serves Sicilian-style deep dish pizza with a variety of toppings, including tomato and basil, spinach, and good ol' pepperoni. (☎ 876-4897. Open M-Sa 11am-1am, Su 2pm-midnight. Slices around $2.)

◪ SIGHTS. The **Massachusetts Institute of Technology (MIT)** supports cutting-edge work in the sciences. Free campus tours highlight the Chapel, designed by Eero Saarinen, and an impressive collection of modern outdoor sculpture. Contact **MIT Information,** 77 Mass. Ave., for more details. (☎ 253-1875. T: Red Line-Kendall/MIT. Open M-F 9am-5pm. Tours M-F 10am and 2pm, meet in the lobby.) The **MIT Museum,** 265 Mass. Ave., contains a slide rule collection and wonderful photography exhibits, including famous stop-action photos of Harold Edgerton. (☎ 253-4444. Open Tu-F 10am-5pm, Sa-Su noon-5pm. $3, seniors and students $1, under 5 free.)

In all its red-brick-and-ivy dignity, **Harvard University,** farther down Mass. Ave. from Boston, finds space for Nobel laureates, students from around the world, and the occasional party. The **Harvard Events and Information Center,** 1350 Mass. Ave., at the Holyoke Center in Harvard Sq., distributes free guides to the university, its museums, and all upcoming events, as well as offering one-hour tours of Harvard Yard. Pick up a comprehensive map of Harvard for $1. (☎ 495-1573. Tours in summer M-Sa 10, 11:15am, 2, and 3:15pm, Su 1:30 and 3pm; Sept.-May M-F 10am and 2pm, Sa 2pm.) The university revolves around **Harvard Yard,** a grassy oasis amid the Cantabrigian bustle. The **Harry Elkins Widener Memorial Library** stands out as one of the largest academic libraries in the world, containing 4.5 million of the university's 13.5 million books. (Visitors are not allowed inside.) Ornate **Memorial Hall,** just outside the Yard's northern gate, is a secular cathedral dedicated to the Harvard-affiliated soldiers who died in the Civil War.

The most notable of Harvard's museums, the **Fogg Art Museum,** 32 Quincy St., gathers a considerable collection of works ranging from ancient Chinese jades to contemporary photography, as well as the largest Ingres collection outside of France. Across the street, the modern exterior of the **Arthur M. Sackler Museum,** 485 Broadway, holds a rich collection of ancient Asian and Islamic art. Another of Harvard's art museums, the **Busch-Reisinger Museum,** on the 2nd fl. of the Fogg, displays Northern and Central European sculpture, painting, and decorative arts, especially German Expressionism. (☎495-9400 for all 3. All open M-Sa 10am-5pm, Su 1-5pm. $5, seniors $4, students $3; free on W, Sa before noon, and for under 18. Wheelchair access on Prescott St.) Peering down at the Fogg, Le Corbusier's piano-shaped **Carpenter Center,** 24 Quincy St., displays student and professional work with especially strong photo exhibits and a great film series at the **Harvard Film Archive,** located inside the Center. Schedules are outside the door. (☎495-3251. Open M-Sa 9am-11pm, Su noon-11pm; during term-time, daily 9am-11pm. Most shows $6, students and seniors $5, under 8 free.) The **Botanical Museum,** one of Harvard's several **Museums of Natural and Cultural History,** 24 Oxford St., draws huge crowds to view the glass flowers. (☎495-3045. Open M-Sa 9am-5pm, Su 1-5pm. $5, seniors and students $4, ages 3-13 $3. Admission includes all the museums.)

The **Longfellow House,** 105 Brattle St. (☎876-4491), now a National Historic Site, headquartered the Continental Army during the early stages of the Revolution. The poet Henry Wadsworth Longfellow, for whom the house is named, lived here later. The ◪**Mt. Auburn Cemetery,** 580 Mt. Auburn St., lies about 1 mi. up the road at the end of Brattle St. The nation's first botanical garden/cemetery has 174 acres of beautifully landscaped grounds worked by Louis Agassiz, Charles Bullfinch, Dorothea Dix, Mary Baker Eddy, and Longfellow. Locals say it's the best birdwatching site in Cambridge. The central tower offers a stellar view of Boston and Cambridge. (☎547-7105. Open Su-Sa 8am-7pm; tower closes 1hr. earlier. Greenhouse: M-Sa 8am-4pm. Free. Wheelchair accessible.)

◪◪ **ENTERTAINMENT AND NIGHTLIFE.** In warm weather, street performers ranging from Andean folk singers to magicians crowd every brick sidewalk of Harvard Sq. and nearby **Brattle Sq.** The **American Repertory Theater (ART),** 64 Brattle St., in the Loeb Drama Center, produces shows from late November to early June. (☎547-8300. Box office open M 11am-5pm, Tu-Su 10am-5pm, or until showtime. Tickets $25-55. Student rush tickets available 30min. before shows, $12 cash only; seniors $5 off ticket price.)

Harvard Sq. is a lively scene weekend nights in the summertime, while other times of the year Harvard grads and undergrads crowd the bars, blowing off steam and throwing back shots. **Central Sq.** is a bar-hopper's heaven—a neighborhood not yet overrun by tourism. Here you'll also find some of the best live music anywhere.

The homespun acts of the ◪**The Cantab Lounge,** 738 Mass. Ave., are its primary claim to fame: Little Joe Cook and the Thrillers, who blend blues and 50s rock, take the stage Thursday through Saturday. (☎354-2685. Tu live bluegrass. Su and W folk or blues. W poetry slams. Cover W-Su $3-8. Open Su-W 8pm-1am, Th-Sa 8pm-2am. Beers $3-4. Bar food and sandwiches $4.50-7.) The **Cellar,** 991 Mass. Ave., in Central Sq., is frequented by Hemingway aspirants and students who think they're cool just because they've taken a five-minute walk out of Harvard Sq. But, hey, with pint-sized whiskey sours and gin and tonics (Su-Th $3, F-Sa $4), such delusion comes cheap. (☎876-2580. Open daily until 1am. Pilsner $3.)

The **Middle East,** 472 Mass. Ave., in Central Sq., features live bands every night. The Middle East is a well-known hot spot with a young crowd. (☎864-3278 or 492-5162. Cover for upstairs and downstairs average $5-8. Most shows 18+. Open Su-W 9pm-1am, Th-Sa 9pm-2am. Advance tickets for all shows are available at the Middle East Box Office and Ticketmaster locations. Bottled beers $3.50.) For live music, head to **Club Passim,** 47 Palmer St. This brick-floored, subterranean locale is a premier national venue that presents new and established folk and acoustic acts. Sitting in the intimate 125-seat audience, you can relive the days when Joan Baez graced the stage—and Bob Dylan played in between her sets. (☎492-5300. Open mic night Tu. Shows nightly 8pm. Cover $5-12. Open daily 11am-11pm. No alcohol.)

NEW ENGLAND

SALEM ☎978

Salem isn't trying that hard to free itself from certain stereotypes. The **Salem Witch Museum,** 19½ Washington Sq. N., gives a melodramatic but informative multimedia presentation that details the history of the infamous 17th-century witch trials. The museum also presents an interesting exhibit on the role of scapegoating throughout history. (☎745-1692. Open daily 10am-7pm; Sept.-June 10am-5pm. $6, seniors $5.50, ages 6-14 $4.) Escape the witch kitsch at the **Witch Trials Memorial,** off Charter St., where engraved stones commemorate the trials' victims.

Salem's ■**Peabody Essex Museum,** on the corner of Essex and Liberty St., recalls the port's former leading role in Atlantic whaling and merchant shipping. Admission includes tours of four historic Salem houses. (☎800-745-4054, recorded info 745-9500. Open M-Sa 10am-5pm, Su noon-5pm; Nov.-May closed M. $10, students and seniors $8, ages under 17 free.) Built in 1668 and officially named the Turner-Ingersoll Mansion, Salem's **House of Seven Gables,** 54 Turner St., became the "second most famous house in America" after the release of Nathaniel Hawthorne's Gothic romance of the same name. (☎744-0991. Open M-Sa 10am-5pm, Su noon-5pm. $8, ages 6-17 $5. Guided tour only.)

The **Salem Visitors Center,** 2 New Liberty St., has free maps, public restrooms, historical displays, and a gift shop. (☎740-1650. Open in summer daily 9am-6pm; in winter 9am-5pm.) Salem, 20 mi. northeast of Boston, is accessible by the Rockport/Ipswich commuter train from Boston's North Station (☎617-722-3200; $3.50), by bus #450 or 455 from Haymarket ($2.25), or by car from I-95 or U.S. 1 N. to Rte. 128 and Rte. 114. **Area code:** 978.

LEXINGTON ☎781

"Stand your ground. Don't fire unless fired upon, but if they mean to have a war, let it begin here," said Captain John Parker to the colonial Minutemen on April 19, 1775. Although no one is certain who fired the first shot, the American Revolution did indeed erupt in downtown Lexington. The site of the fracas lies in the center of town (Mass. Ave.) at the Battle Green, where a Minuteman Statue still stands guard. The fateful command itself was issued from across the street at the **Buckman Tavern,** 1 Bedford St. (☎862-5598), which housed the Minutemen on the eve of their decisive battle. The nearby **Hancock-Clarke House,** 36 Hancock St (☎861-0928), and the **Munroe Tavern,** 1332 Mass. Ave. (☎674-9238), also played significant roles in the birth of the Revolution. (All open Apr.-Oct. M-Sa 10am-5pm, Su 1-5pm. $4 per site, ages 6-16 $2. Combination ticket for all 3 houses $10.) All three can be seen on a 30min. tour that runs continuously. You can also survey exhibits on the Revolution at the **Museum of Our National Heritage,** 33 Marrett Rd./Rte. 2A, which emphasizes a historical approach to understanding popular American life. (☎861-6559. Open M-Sa 10am-5pm, Su noon-5pm. Free. Wheelchair accessible.) The hungry flock to the 33-acre **Wilson Farm,** 10 Pleasant St., for freshly picked fruits and veggies and over 30 varieties of freshly baked bread and pastry. (☎862-3900. Open M and W-F 9am-8pm, Sa 9am-7pm, Su 9am-6:30pm; call for winter hours.)

The road from Boston to Lexington is easy. Drive straight up Mass. Ave. from Boston or Cambridge, or bike the **Minuteman Commuter Bike Trail** to downtown Lexington (access off Mass. Ave. in Arlington, or Alewife in Cambridge). MBTA bus #62 from Alewife in Cambridge runs to Lexington (75¢). An excellent model and description of the Battle of Lexington decorates the **Visitors Center,** 1875 Mass. Ave., behind the Buckman Tavern. Learn also about what's happening in town. (☎862-2480. Open Apr.-Oct daily 9am-5pm, off-season 10am-4pm.) **Area code:** 781.

CONCORD ☎978

Concord, site of the second conflict of the American Revolution, is famous both for its military history and for its status as a 19th-century intellectual center. The **Concord Museum,** 200 Lexington St., on the Cambridge Turnpike, lies across the street from Ralph Waldo Emerson's 19th-century home. This recently refurbished museum houses a reconstruction of Emerson's study alongside Paul Revere's lantern. Period rooms, with an exhaustive collection of decorative arts, walk you through three centuries of Concord's history. (☎369-9763. Open M-Sa 9am-5pm, Su noon-5pm; Jan.-Mar. M-Sa 11am-4pm, Su 1-4pm. $7, seniors and students $6, ages 6-18 $3, families $16.) Down the road from the museum, you'll find the **Orchard House**, 399 Lexington Rd., home of the illustrious and multi-talented Alcotts, where Louisa May wrote *Little Women*. (☎369-4118. Open M-Sa 10am-4:30pm, Su 1-4:30pm; Nov.-Mar. M-F 11am-3pm, Sa 10am-4:30pm, Su 1-4:30pm. $7, students and seniors $6, ages 6-17 $4, families $16. Guided tour only.) Farther down the road lies **Wayside**, 455 Lexington Rd., the former residence of the Alcotts and Hawthornes. (☎360-6075. Open May to Oct. M-Th 10am-5pm. $4, under 17 free. Guided tour only.) Today, Emerson, Hawthorne, Alcott, and Thoreau reside on "Author's Ridge" in the **Sleepy Hollow Cemetery** on Rte. 62, three blocks from the center of town.

Over the **Old North Bridge**, you'll find the spot from which "the shot heard 'round the world" was fired. From the parking lot, a five-minute walk brings you to the **North Bridge Visitors Center**, 174 Liberty St., where you can learn about the town's history, especially its involvement in the Revolutionary War. (☎369-6993. Open Apr.-Oct daily 9am-5pm; in winter 9am-4pm.) The **Minuteman National Historical Park**, best explored along the adjacent 5½ mi. **Battle Rd. Trail**, includes an impressive **Visitors Center** that hosts battle re-enactments and a multimedia presentation on the "Road to Revolution." (☎781-862-7753. Off Rte. 2A between Concord and Lexington. Open Apr.-Nov. daily 9am-5pm; in winter 9am-4pm.)

A night's stay in Concord will suck your wallet dry; consider making the trek 13 mi. northwest to the secluded, family-run **Friendly Crossways Hostel and Conference Center**, 247 Littleton County Rd. in Littleton. Set in rural Massachusetts on 40 acres of gardens, forests, and cornfields, this big, beautiful hostel offers an escape from a busier (and costlier) New England. Buffet-style meals (breakfast $5, lunch $10, dinner $15) are served in the dining hall, or guests may use the kitchen. (☎456-9386 or 456-3649. Linen $5. Check-in 8-10am and 5-11pm; after 10pm ring the owner's private residence. Check-out before 10am. 50 beds, $12-17, nonmembers add $3.) Both Littleton and Concord, north of Boston, are served by commuter rail trains from **North Station**. (☎722-3200. Fare $2.50, seniors and ages 5-11 $1.25.) **Area Code:** 978.

NEAR CONCORD: WALDEN POND

In 1845, Thoreau retreated 1½ mi. south of Concord "to live deliberately, to front only the essential facts of life" (though the harsh essence of *his* life was eased from time to time by his mother's home cooking; she lived within walking distance of his cabin). He wrote his famous book *Walden* here. The **Walden Pond State Reservation**, on Rte. 126, draws picnickers, swimmers, and boaters and is mobbed in summer (though still mighty pleasant). No camping, pets, or "novelty flotation devices" are allowed. (☎369-3254. Open daily 7am-8pm. Parking $2.) When Walden Pond swarms with crowds, head east from Concord center on Rte. 62 to another of Thoreau's haunts, **Great Meadows National Wildlife Refuge**, on Monsen Rd. (☎443-4661. Open daily dawn-dusk. Free.)

PLYMOUTH   ☎508

Despite what American high school textbooks say, the Pilgrims' first step onto the New World was *not* at Plymouth. They stopped first at Provincetown—but promptly left because the soil was so inadequate. **Plymouth Rock** itself is a rather small stone that has (dubiously) been identified as the actual rock on which the Pilgrims disembarked. It served as a symbol of liberty during the American Revolution, then was moved three times and chipped away by tourists before ending up at its current home, beneath an extravagant portico on Water St., at the foot of North St. After several vandalization episodes, it's under tight security.

Three miles south of town off Rte. 3A, the historical theme-park ▓**Plimoth Plantation** recreates the Pilgrims' early settlement. In the **Pilgrim Village**, costumed actors play the roles of actual villagers carrying out their daily tasks, based upon William Bradford's record of the year 1627, while the **Wampanoag Summer Encampment** represents a Native American village of the same period. The plantation sends a historian to England each summer to gather more information about each villager. (☎746-1622. Open Apr.-Nov. daily 9am-5pm. $20, ages 6-12 $12.) The **Mayflower II,** built in the 50s to recapture the atmosphere of the original ship, is docked off Water St. (Open Apr.-Nov. daily 9am-5pm. $8, ages 6-12 $6. Admission to both sights $22, seniors and students $20, ages 6-12 $14.) The nation's oldest museum in continuous existence, the **Pilgrim Hall Museum,** 75 Court St., houses Puritan crafts, furniture, books, paintings, and weapons. (☎746-1620. Open Feb.-Dec. daily 9:30am-4:30pm. $5, seniors $4.50, ages 5-17 $3, families $14.) The natives chow down at **Wood's Seafood Restaurant,** Town Pier. A fish sandwich with fries is about $4; prices vary with fresh market prices. (☎746-0261. Open June-Aug. daily 11am-9pm; Sept.-May 11am-8:30pm.) Zip back to modern times at **Sean O'Toole's Public House,** 22 Main St., with live music and a traditional Irish pub atmosphere. (☎746-3388. Open daily 4:30pm-12:30am.) **Plymouth Visitors Information Center** is located at 130 Water St. (☎747-7525 or 800-872-1620. Open Apr.-May daily 9am-5pm; June 9am-6pm; July-Aug. 9am-9pm; Sept.-Nov. 9am-5pm.) **Area code:** 508.

CAPE COD ☎508

Henry David Thoreau once said: "At present [this coast] is wholly unknown to the fashionable world, and probably it will never be agreeable to them." Often so perceptive, Thoreau, in this case, was sadly mistaken. In 1602, when English navigator and Jamestown colonist Bartholomew Gosnold landed on this peninsula in southeastern Massachusetts, he named it in honor of all the cod he caught in the surrounding waters. In recent decades, tourists have replaced the plentiful cod, and the area has as many taffy shops as fishermen. This small strip of land supports a diverse set of landscapes—long, unbroken stretches of beach, salt marshes, hardwood forests, deep freshwater ponds carved by glaciers, and desert-like dunes sculpted by the wind. Thankfully, the Cape's natural landscape has been protected from the tide of commercialism by the **Cape Cod National Seashore.** Blessed with an excellent hostel system, Cape Cod is an option for budget travelers, though in general it attracts more affluent tourists. The Cape also serves as the gateway to **Martha's Vineyard** and **Nantucket,** two islands with unsurpassed natural beauty. Ferries run from Falmouth, Woods Hole, and Hyannis to Martha's Vineyard, and from Hyannis to Nantucket; see **Martha's Vineyard** (p. 139) and **Nantucket** (p. 141) for info.

✦⁊ ORIENTATION AND PRACTICAL INFORMATION

Terminology for locations on the Cape can be confusing. **"Upper Cape"** refers to the more suburbanized and developed part of Cape Cod closer to the mainland. Proceeding eastward away from the mainland, you travel "down Cape" until hitting the **"Lower Cape."** The National Seashore encompasses much of this area. Cape Cod resembles a bent arm, with **Woods Hole** at its armpit, **Chatham** at the elbow, and **Provincetown** at its clenched fist. Travel times on the peninsula are often inconsistent; a drive from the Sagamore bridge to Provincetown can take anywhere from 2 to 4hr. Leaving the Cape can be equally annoying; the area's weekend warriors can turn a Sunday departure into a hellacious six-hour odyssey.

If you're up for some exercise, cycling is the best way to travel the Cape's gentle slopes. The park service can give you a free map of trails or sell you the detailed *Cape Cod Bike Book* ($3; available at most Cape bookstores). The 135 mi. **Boston-Cape Cod Bikeway** connects Boston to Provincetown. If you want to bike this route, pick up a bicycle trail map of the area. These are available at some bookstores and most bike shops. The trails that line either side of the **Cape Cod Canal** in the National Seashore rank among the country's most scenic, as does the 25 mi. **Cape Cod Rail Trail** from Dennis to Wellfleet. For discount coupons good for bargains at restaurants, sights, and entertainment venues throughout the Cape, pick up a free copy of *The Official 2002 Guide to Cape Cod* or the *Cape Cod Best Read Guide,* available at most Cape info centers. **Area code:** 508.

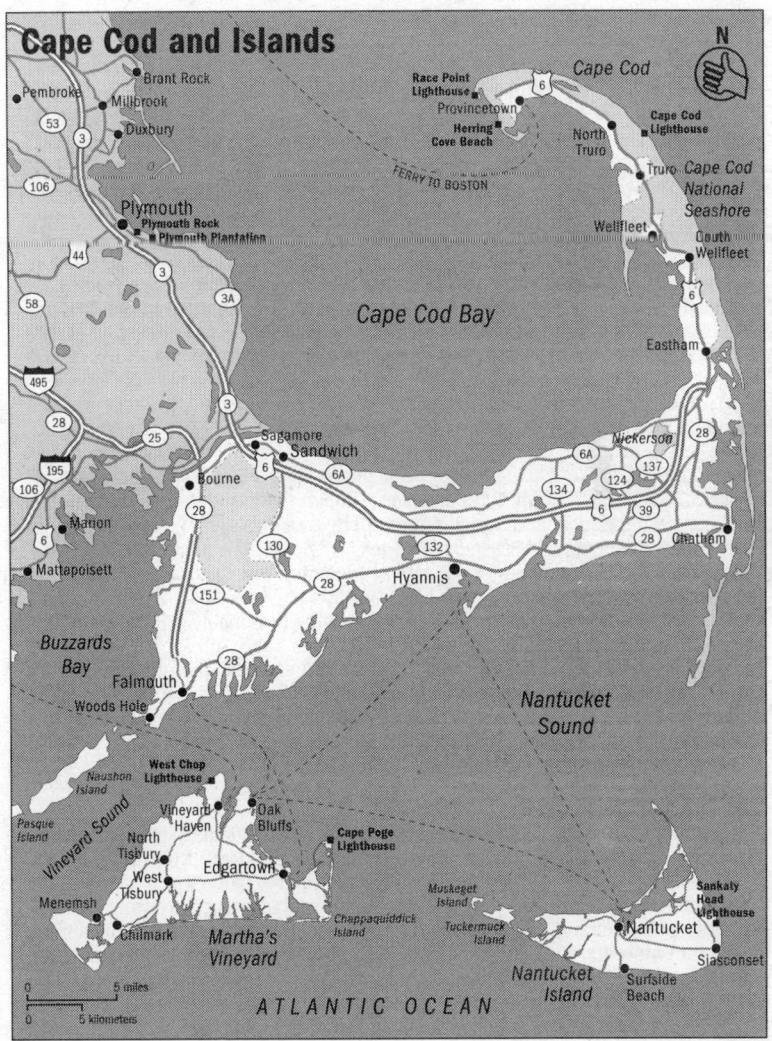

Cape Cod and Islands

HYANNIS

☎508

Tattooed midway across the Cape's upper arm, Hyannis is not the Cape Cod most people expect. JFK did indeed spend his summers on the beach in nearby Hyannisport, but the town itself sees more action as a transportation hub and tourist site than a home to rich. Ferries to the islands and buses to destinations along the Cape leave from Hyannis; "duckmobile" tours show you around land and water, and Cape Cod Central Railway gives scenic tours of the area out of Hyannis. Check out the **JFK Museum**, 397 Main St. (☎790-3077; open M-Sa 10am-4pm, Su 1-4pm) and the **Edna Hibel Museum of Art**, 337 Main St. (☎778-7877), on a free afternoon.

A great place to stay in Hyannis is the **Heritage House**, 259 Main St., which is centrally located and has both indoor and outdoor pools. (☎775-7000. Rooms run $45-169.) Hyannis also has restaurants in every price range, including **Mainstreet Seafood & Grill**, 462 Main St. (☎771-8585), which boasts the "Best Chowder on Cape Cod." The town also sports a few good beaches. **Kalmus Park**, on Ocean St. in Hyannisport, is popular with windsurfers. **Orrin Keyes,** on Sea St., attracts more of a local crowd. **Veteran's Park Beach,** off Ocean St., is great for families. All three beaches have parking (M-F $8, Sa-Su $10), lifeguards, bathhouses, snack bars, picnic areas, and wheelchair accessibility. **Plymouth & Brockton** (☎ 771-6191) runs five Boston-to-Provincetown buses per day with 30min. layovers at the **Hyannis Bus Station,** 17 Elm St. Other stops besides Boston (1¾hr., $14) and Provincetown (1½hr., $10) include Plymouth, Barnstable, Yarmouth, Eastham, Wellfleet, and Truro. **Bonanza Bus Lines** (☎ 800-556-3815) operates a line to New York City (6hr., 7 per day, $29).

SANDWICH   ☎ 508

The oldest town on the Cape, Sandwich cultivates an old-fashioned charm, more old New England-y than touristy. The beauty and workmanship of Sandwich glass was made famous by the Boston & Sandwich Glass Co., founded in Sandwich in 1825. Master glass blowers shape works of art from blobs of molten sand at **Pairpoint Crystal,** 851 Sandwich Rd., just across the town border in Sagamore. (☎ 888-2344. Open M-F 9am-6pm, Sa 10am-6pm, Su 11am-6pm. No glass blowing after 4pm M-Su. Free.) To enjoy the town's collection of older pieces, tiptoe through the light-bending exhibits at the **Sandwich Glass Museum,** 129 Main St., in Sandwich Ctr. (☎ 888-0251. Open Apr.-Dec. daily 9:30am-5pm; Feb.-Mar. W-Su 9:30am-4pm. $3.50, ages 6-12 $1.) The landscaped gardens at the **Heritage Plantation of Sandwich,** 67 Grove St., are worth a visit by themselves, though the plantation also features a working 1912 carousel and antique automobiles. (☎ 888-3300. Open mid-May to mid-Oct. daily 10am-5pm. $9, seniors $8, ages 6-18 $4.50. Wheelchair accessible.)

Sandwich has a number of great B&Bs, including the **Captain Ezra Nye House** (☎ 888-6142; $90-125) and the **Isaiah Jones Homestead** (☎ 888-9648; $99-160), which are the cheapest accommodations in town. Eat at the reasonably priced **Tavern** (dinner $7-15), which is popular with locals. If you have a free afternoon, stop by the **Sandwich Art Gallery,** 153 Main St., which houses impressive Impressionist paintings of the Cape (☎ 833-2098), and munch on the scones while you sip gourmet tea at the **Dunbar Tea Shop,** 1 Water St. (☎ 833-2485). Sandwich lies at the intersection of Rte. 6A and Rte. 130, about 13 mi. from Hyannis. The **Plymouth & Brockton** bus makes its closest stop in Sagamore, 3 mi. northwest along Rte. 130.

CAPE COD NATIONAL SEASHORE

As early as 1825, the Cape had suffered so much manmade damage that the town of Truro required local residents to plant beach grass and keep their cows off the dunes. Further conservation efforts culminated in 1961 with the creation of the **Cape Cod National Seashore,** which includes much of the Lower Cape from Provincetown to Chatham and has largely escaped the commercialism that afflicts most American seacoasts. Over 30 mi. of wide, soft, uninterrupted beaches lie under the tall clay cliffs and towering 19th-century lighthouses of this protected area. Just a short walk away from the lifeguards, the sea of umbrellas fades into the distance.

Beachgoers at the Cape face a difficult question: ocean or bay? While the ocean beaches entice with whistling winds and surging waves, the water on the bay side rests calmer and gets a bit warmer. The National Seashore oversees six beaches: **Coast Guard** and **Nauset Light** in Eastham; **Marconi** in Wellfleet; **Head of the Meadow** in Truro, and **Race Point** and **Herring Cove** in Provincetown. Herring Cove has special facilities which allow disabled travelers access to the water. (Parking at all beaches $7 per day, $20 per season; mid-Sept. to late June free.)

To park at any other beach, a town permit is required. While each town has a different beach-parking policy, all require proof of lodging in their town. Permits generally cost $5-10 per day, $20-25 per week, or $50-100 per season and can be bought at town halls. Call the appropriate town hall before trying to get around the parking permit; beaches are sometimes miles from any other legal parking and police with tow trucks hover like vultures. Parking lots fill up by 11am or earlier; it is often easier to rent a bike and ride in. Most town beaches do not require bikers and walkers to pay an entrance fee. Wellfleet and Truro stand out among the ocean beaches as great examples of the Cape's famous endangered sand dunes. **Cahoon Hollow Beach,** with spectacular, cliff-like dunes, and **Duck Harbor Beach,** overlooking the bay in Wellfleet, provide two particularly beautiful vistas.

Among the best of the seashore's 11 self-guided **nature trails,** the **Great Island Trail,** in Wellfleet, traces an eight-mile loop through pine forests and grassy marshes and along a ridge with a view of the bay and Provincetown. The **Atlantic White Cedar Swamp Trail,** a 1.25 mi. walk, beginning at Marconi Station site in south Wellfleet, leads to dark, swampy waters under towering trees. The **Buttonbush Trail,** a 0.3 mi. walk with Braille guides and a guide rope for the blind, leaves the Salt Pond Visitors Center (see below). There are also three park **bike trails:** Nauset Trail (1.5 mi.), Head of the Meadow Trail (2 mi.), and Province Lands Trail (5 mi.). The accessible **National Seashore's Salt Pond Visitors Center,** at Salt Pond, off Rte. 6 in Eastham, offers a free ten-minute film every 30min. and a museum with exhibits on the Cape's natural and contemporary history. (☎255-3421. Open daily 9am-5pm; Sept.-June 9am-4:30pm.) **Camping** on the national seashore is illegal. Permits for fishing and campfires can be purchased at the Visitors Center.

PROVINCETOWN ☎508

At Provincetown, Cape Cod ends and the wide Atlantic begins. The National Seashore protects two-thirds of "P-Town" as conservation land; the inhabited third touches the harbor on the south side of town. This former whaling village has diversified and now includes a prominent gay and lesbian contingent. P-Town is far from inexpensive, but there are some options for the budget travelers. Commercial St., the town's main drag, is home to countless art galleries, novelty shops, and trendy eateries, as well as parades and, yes, drag shows.

☑ PRACTICAL INFORMATION. The **Plymouth & Brockton Street Railway** (☎771-6191) has buses connecting to a local in Hyannis, which will take you all the way to Provincetown (3¼hr.; $23 one-way, $45 round-trip). **Bay State Cruises** sends regular and high-speed ferries between Boston and P-town. (☎487-9284 or 617-748-1428. 3hr.; $18 one-way, seniors $15, ages 5-14 $14. High-speed ferries run late May to early Oct. 2hr.; $28.) **Boston Harbor Cruises** uses high-speed catamarans to make the trip in 1½hr. (☎617-227-4321. $25 one-way, $45 round-trip; seniors $21/$38; ages 4-12 $19/$34.) To get around in Provincetown, Herring Cove Beach, and North Truro, take **The Shuttle.** Tickets are available on the bus or at the Chamber of Commerce. (☎385-8326 or 800-352-7155; TDD 385-4163. Runs daily late June to mid-Sept. every 20min. 7:15am-12:15am; mid-Sept. to mid-Oct. in Provincetown only. $1; seniors, disabled, and under 17 50¢; under 6 free. 1-day pass $3, bulk tokens 25% discount.) **Ptown Bikes,** 42 Bradford St., hands out free locks and maps with their beach cruisers and mountain bikes. (☎487-8735. Open daily 9am-7pm. $3.50 per hr., min. 2hr. $10-17 per day, $69 per week. Helmet $1 per day, $5 per week.) You'll find the helpful **Provincetown Chamber of Commerce** at 307 Commercial St. (☎487-3424. Open June-Sept. daily 9am-4pm; reduced off-season hours.) National Seashore information can be found at the **Province Lands Visitors Center,** Race Point Rd. off Rte. 6. (☎487-1256. Open May 15-Sept. daily 3 per day 9am-5pm.) **Area Code:** 508.

⌂ ACCOMMODATIONS. Provincetown teems with expensive places to lay your head—the most comfortable budget options are the hostels 10 mi. away in Truro or a bit farther in Eastham. But if the temptation of P-town nightlife is too much, a few decent quasi-cheap accommodations exist. Prices here plummet in the off season. **Outermost Hostel,** 28 Winslow St., is a short walk from the center of town at a quiet location 300 ft. past the Pilgrim Monument. Thirty less-than-firm beds in five cramped cottages go for $15 each, including kitchen access and parking. (☎487-4378. Linen rental $3. Key deposit $10. Reception daily 8-9:30am and 5:30-9:30pm. Check-out 9:30am. No curfew. Reservations recommended for weekends and July-Aug.) **The Cape Codder,** 570 Commercial St., in the quiet East End, welcomes you in crisp, classic Cape Cod style—right down to the wicker furniture and private beach access. Room 16 has a view of the beach. Shared bathrooms are clean, and antique tubs are a quaint plus. (☎487-0131. Parking and continental breakfast. Singles and doubles $45-70 in-season, $30-60 off-season; each additional person $5.) **Dunham House Bunk and Brew,** 3 Dyer St., has five rooms, named and decorated according to squares on a Monopoly board, available in the homestead of proprietor Jack's great-grandfather. The "Brew" in the name refers to available coffee and beer, but youngsters should know that the friendly Jack still cards. (☎487-3330. Rooms with shared bath $39-74.) When the great American Realist Edward Hopper wanted to paint a guest house, he chose the **Sunset Inn,** 142 Bradford St.; it inspired his famous "Rooms for Tourists." The house has changed little, and the warmth and light that Hopper depicted still welcome weary travelers. (☎487-9810 or 800-965-1801. Parking and continental breakfast. Rooms with shared bath $69-79, with private bath $112-149.) **Dune's Edge Campground,** 386 Rte. 6, on the right side at the East End, offers 100 shaded sites packed together in an idyllic setting. (☎487-9815. Office open July-Aug. 8am-10pm, May-June and Sept. 9am-8pm. Sites $28, with partial hookup $34.)

⌂ FOOD. Sit-down meals in Provincetown are expensive. The Commercial St. extension next to MacMillian Wharf and the Aquarium Mall farther west on Commercial St. offer a selection of fast food with nearby benches and picnic tables. For a gourmet picnic, head to the East End's **Angel Foods,** 467 Commercial St. (☎487-6666. Open in season 8am-10pm; reduced off-season hours.) **Mayflower Family Dining,** 300 Commercial St., has given visitors cheap food since 1921. Mayflower is cheaper than it is good, and portions can be small, but it's still worth seeking out in this haven for overpriced cuisine. Try the fish and chips ($8.50) or crab cakes ($10), or splurge on the cheapest lobster in town, about $12 for 1¼lb. (☎487-0121. Open Apr.-Nov. daily 11:30am-10pm. Cash only.) **Spiritus,** 190 Commercial St., dishes out spirit-lifting whole-wheat pizza. It doubles as an art gallery and hoppin' coffee and ice cream shop. (☎487-2808. Open Apr.-Oct. daily noon-2am. Cheese slices $2.) **Cafe Crudite,** 338 Commercial St., is a casual restaurant with deliciously fresh vegetarian, vegan, and macrobiotic options including tasty Greek salad ($7.25), eggless salad sandwich ($6), lots of tofu options, and daily specials at lunch and dinner. (☎487-6237. Lunch served F-M 11:30am-4pm, dinner from 5:30pm.) **Cafe Edwidge,** 333 Commercial St. serves up to-die-for $7.50 French toast with fresh fruit. (☎487-4020. Breakfast daily 8am-1pm, dinner 6-10pm. Open May-Oct.)

◙♫ SIGHTS AND ENTERTAINMENT. Provincetown's natural waterfront provides spectacular walks. Directly across from Snail Rd. on Rte. 6, an unlikely path will lead you to a world of rolling **sand dunes;** look for shacks where writers such as Tennessee Williams, Norman Mailer, and John Dos Passos penned their days away. From Race Point Rd., you can reach the **National Seashore beaches** as well as **walking and biking trails.** The **Visitors Center** offers free daily guided tours and activities during the summer. The 1¼ mi. **Breakwater Jetty,** at the west end of Commercial St., takes you away from the crowds and down to a secluded peninsula of endless beach that bears two working lighthouses and the remains of a Civil War fort.

Provincetown is acknowledged as the site of the Pilgrims' 1620 arrival in Massachusetts, which is marked by **Pilgrim Monument** and the **Provincetown Museum,** on High Pole Hill just north of the center of town. (☎487-1310. Open Apr.-Nov. daily 9am-5pm, July-Aug. 9am-7pm. $6, ages 4-12 $3.) The **Provincetown Art Association and Museum,** 460 Commercial St., lies near the artsy East End and was founded in 1914 during Provincetown's heyday as a seasonal artists' colony. The museum houses an enchanting sculpture garden. (☎487-1750. Open July-Aug. daily noon-5pm and 8-10pm; Apr.-Sept. reduced hours. $3, seniors and children $1.)

Today, Provincetown seafarers carry photo lenses, not harpoons, when they go whale hunting. **Whale-watching cruises** rank among P-town's most popular attractions. Cruise companies claim that whales are sighted on 99% of the journeys, and most promise free trips to that unlucky 1%. Tickets are about $19 for a three-hour tour, but don't bring as many clothes as Ginger. Coupons can be found in most local publications and at the Chamber of Commerce. **Cape Cod Whale Watch** (☎487-4079 or 800-559-4193), **Dolphin Fleet** (☎349-1900 or 800-826-9300), and **Portuguese Princess** (☎487-2651 or 800-422-3188) all leave from MacMillian Wharf.

◪ **NIGHTLIFE.** Provincetown's nightlife is almost totally gay- and lesbian-oriented. Most of the clubs and bars on Commercial St. charge a cover of about $5 and shut down at 1am. The venues are generally 21+ but may not always be too strict about carding. (*Let's Go* does not recommend falsifying your identity—let alone using a fake ID.) Live music drives **Antro**, 258 Commercial St. (behind the Ben & Jerry's), with nightly shows and techno music after 10:30pm. (☎487-8800; $15 shows at 8:30pm and 10pm; $5 after the shows. Open May-Oct. daily) **Governor Bradford**, 312 Commercial St., has drag karaoke nightly, never charges cover, and offers $3 beer. (☎487-2781. Open daily 11:30am-1am; kitchen closes at 11pm.) **Vixen**, 336 Commercial St., caters mostly to women, with big-name shows and a steamy dance floor. (☎487-6424. Open nightly 5pm-1am.) **Steve's Alibi**, 291 Commercial St., is a local hangout with a laid-back atmosphere and tiny tables crunched together to promote socializing. (☎487-2890. $5-10 cover for shows nightly at varying times. Open daily 11am-1am.) The **Crown and Anchor**, 247 Commercial St., has two cabarets, a lobby bar, the "Wave Video" bar with pool table, games, and a dance floor that sometimes hosts circuit parties in the summer. (☎487-1430. $15 shows in the cabarets daily 7, 8:30, and 9pm. Open daily noon-1am.)

MARTHA'S VINEYARD ☎508

Native American Wampanoags have long called the island home—even before its "discovery" in 1602 by Bartholemew Gosnold—and they still retain part of their original lands in the rural southwestern part of the island. In the 1800s, the island profited from the prosperity of successful whalers and fishermen. By the 1960s, the Vineyard was a liberal hippie haven; aging hipsters still appreciate the "clothing-optional" beaches. In the past decade, the Vineyard has seen an unbelievable boom in wealth and population—during the summers, that is. Even though the Vineyard economy depends on summer tourism, locals have mixed feelings about the new construction, inflated real estate values, and damage to the fragile ecosystem. Still, there's a reason why honeymooners, celebrities, even presidents and royalty flock here: the island's unparalleled natural beauty. To experience the best of the Vineyard, you really need more than a day, and it's best to have a car, though public transportation is somewhat more extensive than on neighboring Nantucket.

◪ **PRACTICAL INFORMATION. Bonanza Bus Lines** (☎800-751-8800) stops at the Ferry Terminal in Woods Hole and departs, via Bourne, for Boston (1¾hr.; 11-15 per day 8am-10pm; $21) and New York City (6hr.; 6 per day, early Sept. to late June 5 per day; $49). The **Steamship Authority** sends 24 **ferries** per day on the 45min. ride from Woods Hole to Vineyard Haven and Oak Bluffs. (☎477-8600 or 693-9130. Oak Bluffs: May-Oct. daily 10:45am-6:15pm; Vineyard Haven: year-round 7am-9:30pm. Reserve cars months in advance in summer. $5.50; ages 5-12 $2.75; cars $52, Oct.-May $31; bikes $3.) **Martha's Vineyard Regional Transit Authority** runs summer shuttles between and within the various towns on the island. Maps and schedules (available at the ferry terminals) detail all 11 routes, including the popular route between South Beach and Edgartown. (Recorded info ☎627-7448, additional info 693-4633. 75¢ per town. Most buses have bike racks.) **Island Transport** supplements the coverage with trips in and out of Oak Bluffs to Vineyard Haven and Edgartown (☎693-1589. Late May to late June and early Sept. to early Oct. every 30min. Su-Th 8am-6:30pm, F-Sa 8am-11:30pm; late June to early Sept. every 15-30min. 6am-12:30am. Oak Bluffs to Vineyard Haven or Edgartown $2.25.) **Martha's Bike Rental,** at the corner of Beach St. and Beach Rd., Vineyard Haven, rents the wheeled creatures. (☎693-6593. 3-speed $12 per day, mountain or hybrid $18 per day. Open June-Aug. daily 8am-6pm; mid-Mar. to Nov. 9am-5pm. **Taxis: AdamCab,** ☎693-3332 or 281-4462. **Visitor info: Martha's Vineyard Chamber of Commerce,** Beach Rd., Vineyard Haven. (☎693-0085. Open M-F 9am-5pm.) **Post Office:** Beach Rd., Vineyard Haven. (☎693-2815. Open M-F 8:30am-5pm, Sa 9:30am-1pm.) **ZIP code:** 02568. **Area code:** 508.

◪ **ACCOMMODATIONS.** Truly budget accommodations in Martha's Vineyard are almost nonexistent. The Chamber of Commerce provides a list of inns and guest houses; all recommend reservations for July and August, especially for weekend stays. **Martha's Vineyard Hostel (HI-AYH),** Edgartown-West Tisbury Rd. in West Tisbury, provides 78 of the cheapest beds on the island. The hostel's facilities include a kitchen, a grill, a ping-pong table, and a volleyball court. Linens are provided, but bring your own towel. (☎693-2665. Internet access. Bikes $15 per day. Lockers 75¢. Light chores required. Open Apr. to early Nov. daily 7:30am-10pm; dorms and kitchen open 7:30-10am and 5-10pm. Reservations essential. $22, nonmembers $19.) **Attleboro House,** 42 Lake Ave. in Oak Bluffs, has 11 tiny rooms with character: colorful wallpaper and bedspreads, mirrors, and chairs add to the good vibes. All rooms have porches. (☎693-4346. Check-in 1pm. Check-out 11am. Doubles with shared bath $89-95, suites $115-200; each additional person $15-25.) The Victorian **Nashua House,** 30 Kennebec Ave., in Oak Bluffs, is a stellar deal for those who desire more privacy than a hostel can provide. (☎693-0043. Check-in 2pm. Check-out 11am. Singles and doubles with shared bath $59-109; each additional person $20.) **Martha's Vineyard Family Campground,** 1½ mi. from Vineyard Haven on Edgartown Rd., offers 185 shaded sites in an oak forest. (☎693-3772. Laundry, store, playground, and game room. Office open daily 8am-9pm; in spring and fall 8:30-10:30am and 5-8pm. Check-in 2pm. Check-out noon. No pets or motorcycles. 2-person sites $34; each additional person $10, ages 2-18 $3. Cabins with 4-6 beds $90-100.)

⬭ FOOD. Reasonably cheap sandwich and lunch places do exist on the Vineyard, especially in Vineyard Haven and Oak Bluffs. Fried-food shacks across the island sell clams, shrimp, and potatoes, which generally cost at least $15. Several **farm stands** sell inexpensive produce; the Chamber of Commerce map shows their locations. **◼The Newes From America,** 23 Kelley St., in Edgartown, serves traditional pub fare in an old-time Colonial tavern replete with wooden cupboards and lanterns. (☎627-4397. Open daily 11:30am-midnight; kitchen open Su-W 11:30am-10pm, Th-Sa 11:30am-11pm. Sandwiches $6-8; fish and chips $9.50. Beer $3.50.) **Louis',** 350 State Rd., in Vineyard Haven, serves up classy Italian take-out that won't break the bank. Try the $6 fresh pasta with meat sauce or the $5.50 vegetable calzone. (☎693-3255. Open M-Sa 11am-8:30pm, Su 4-8:30pm. Cheese pizzas $8.75-16.75.) **Black Dog Bakery,** on Water St. in Vineyard Haven, tempts patrons with a range of creative and delicious pastries and breads (40¢-$3.25), but *please* don't buy another sweatshirt. (☎693-4786. Open in summer daily 5:30am-7pm.) An island institution, **Mad Martha's,** 117 Circuit Ave. in Oak Bluffs, scoops out outstanding homemade ice cream and frozen yogurt, offering over 26 tasty if uninventive flavors. (☎693-9151. Open in-season daily 11am-11pm. 2 scoops $3.) Other locations are at 7 N. Water St. in Edgartown (☎617-627-8761), and at 8 Union St. in Vineyard Haven (☎617-693-5883).

◐ SIGHTS. Exploring the Vineyard can involve much more than zipping around on a moped. Head out to the countryside, hit the beach, or trek down one of the great trails. **Felix Neck Wildlife Sanctuary,** on the Edgartown-Vineyard Haven Rd., offers five trails that meander through 350 acres, all leading to water. There is also a small exhibit room. (☎627-4850. Office open June-Sept. M-Sa 8am-4pm, Su 10am-3pm; Oct.-May Tu-Sa 8am-4pm, Su 10am-3pm. $3, seniors and ages 3-12 $2.) **Menemsha Hills Reservation,** off North Rd. in Menemsha, has 4 mi. of trails along the rocky Vineyard Sound beach, leading to the island's second-highest point. **Cedar Creek Tree Neck,** on the western shore, harbors 250 acres of headland off Indian Hill Rd. (with trails throughout), while the **Long Point** park in West Tisbury preserves 633 acres and a shore on the Tisbury Great Pond.

Two of the best beaches on the island, **South Beach,** at the end of Katama Rd., 3 mi. south of Edgartown, and **State Beach,** on Beach Rd. between Edgartown and Oak Bluffs, are free and open to the public. South Beach boasts sizeable surf and an occasionally nasty undertow. State Beach's warmer waters once set the stage for parts of *Jaws,* the granddaddy of classic beach-horror films. For the best sunsets on the island, stake out a spot at **Aquinnah** or the **Menemsha Town Beach.**

Chicama Vineyards, off State Rd. in West Tisbury, offers free tours and wine tasting. (☎693-0309. Open late May to early Oct. M-Sa 11am-5pm, Su 1-5pm; mid-Oct. to mid-May M-Sa 1-4pm. 25min. tours late May to early Oct. M-Sa noon, 2, and 4pm; Su 2 and 4pm.) **Oak Bluffs,** 3 mi. west of Vineyard Haven on Beach Rd., is the most youth-oriented of the Vineyard villages. Highlights of a tour of **Trinity Park,** near the harbor, include the famous "Gingerbread Houses" (minutely detailed, elaborate pastel Victorian cottages) and Oak Bluffs' **Flying Horses Carousel,** at the end of Circuit Ave. It's the oldest carousel in the nation, built in 1876, and composed of 20 handcrafted horses. Snatch the brass ring and win a free ride. (☎693-9481. Open mid-June to Aug. daily 10am-10pm; Easter to mid-June and Sept.-Oct. hours vary. $1.) Also check out the **Dreamland Game Room,** across from Flying Horses. (☎693-5163. Open in summer daily 10am-11pm.) **Aquinnah,** 22 mi. southwest of Oak Bluffs on State Rd., offers just about the best view of the sea in all of New England. The native Wampanoag frequently saved sailors shipwrecked on the breathtaking **Gay Head Cliffs.** The 100,000-year-old precipice shines brilliantly and supports one of the island's five lighthouses. **Menemsha** and **Chilmark,** northeast of Aquinnah, share a scenic coastline; Chilmark claims to be the only "working" fishing town on the island. Tourists can fish off the pier. **Vineyard Haven** has more artsy boutiques and fewer tacky t-shirt shops than other towns on the island.

NANTUCKET ☎508

Nantucket has entered modern lore as Martha's Vineyard's conservative little sister. Rampant affluence has given the islands' residents an influential stance in fighting for the preservation of its charms: dune-covered beaches, beautiful wild flowers, cobblestone streets, and spectacular bike paths. Over 36% of Nantucket is protected from development. The island shows the visitor few hints of the neon-signed, Wal-Mart world just 14 mi. over the water on the Cape. Even with all this privilege, it is possible to enjoy a stay on the island without holding up a convenience store, thanks to the hostel a few miles south of the island's only town.

⁊ PRACTICAL INFORMATION. In Hyannis there are two ferry companies, each two blocks from the bus station, that run ferries to Nantucket. Both companies have slow boats (about 2hr. one-way) and fast boats (1hr.). **Hyline** runs slightly faster boats to Straight Wharf on Nantucket. (☎778-2600. Slow boat: 5 per day in summer, 3 per day in winter; $13.50 one-way, ages 5-12 $6.75. Fast boat: 6 per day year-round; $33/$25.) The **Steamship Authority** floats into Steamboat Wharf on Nantucket. (☎477-8600. Slow boat: 4-6 per day 7am-8:30pm; $13 one-way, ages 5-12 $6.50. Fast boat: 6 per day; $23/$17.25.) Both ferries charge $5 for bicycles. **Nantucket Regional Transit Authority** (☎228-7025) runs five shuttle bus routes throughout the island. Buses to **Sconset** and **Surfside** (where the hostel is) leave from Washington and Main St. (near the lamp post), buses to **Miacomet** leave from Washington and Salem St. (a block up from Straight Wharf), and buses to **Madaket** and **Jetties Beach** leave from Broad St. in front of the Peter Foulger Museum. (Buses depart every 30min. 7am-11:30pm; the Surfside bus runs every 40min. 10am-5:20pm. Fare is 50¢-$1, seniors 25-50¢, under 6 free.) **Young's Bicycle Shop** rents bikes from Steamboat Wharf. All-terrain or hybrid bikes (with baskets for picnic supplies) are $25 per day and $90 per week, though if you bring the bike back by 5pm the same day, you save $5. Children's bikes are $15 per day and $65 per week. (☎228-1151. Open daily 8am-6pm; in winter 9am-5pm.) Bus map, schedules, and multi-day passes are available at the **Visitors Center,** 25 Federal St. (☎228-0925; open daily 9am-5:30pm). Renting bikes is a great option: there are three beautiful **bike paths** that wind from town through wildflower paths and along dune-covered beaches (to Madaket Beach 5 mi., Surfside Beach 2½ mi., and Siasconset 6 mi). **Area code:** 508.

⌐ ACCOMMODATIONS. There once was a hostel from Nantucket...and there still is. Besides this one hostel and the occasional affordable inn, sleeping here is generally expensive. If you're interested in private baths and more extravagance than the hostel offers, call the **Nantucket Accommodations Bureau**, Fort Dennis Dr. (☎228-9559), which has listings for the cheapest inns—still more elegant than many hotels on the mainland—and "granny rooms," singles or suites that a house owner rents out. **Nantucket Hostel (HI-AYH)**, 31 Western Ave., is best reached by bike; it's 3½ mi. from town, at the end of the Surfside Bike Path. (☎228-0433. 3 large rooms with 49 bunk beds. Full kitchen. Linen and towels provided. Check-in 5-10pm. Lockout 10am-5pm. Curfew 11pm. Reservations essential. $19, nonmembers $22.) The beautiful Victorian **Nesbitt Inn**, 21 Broad St., up from the Steamboat Wharf, is one of the least expensive inns on Nantucket. (☎228-2446. Shared bath. Breakfast included. Reception 7am-10pm. Reservations required. Check-in noon. Check-out 11am. Singles $75; rooms with double beds $85; with king-sized bed $95; Oct.-Apr. $10 less.)

◘ FOOD. There are no cheap full-service restaurants on Nantucket—standard entrees run $15-20. For meals, the best-tasting budget options are the two sandwich shops in town. Make your own with ingredients from the **A&P Supermarket**, just to the right of Straight Wharf. (☎938-3468. Open M-Sa 7am-9pm, Su 7am-7pm.) **Henry's** is the first establishment you'll see after getting off the ferry on Steamboat Wharf. No surprises with traditional cold-cut or hot sandwiches ($4-5), but they're pretty well executed. Garden salads run $4-8. (☎228-0123. Open May to mid-Oct. daily 9am-10pm. Cash only.) **Mac's Place,** 6 Harborview Way, at the Children's Beach, serves full breakfasts ($8 and under) on a patio overlooking Children's Beach. Fresh doughnuts are 60¢; eat a few outside with your feet dangling in the sand. (☎228-3127. Open June-Sept. daily 7am-5pm; kitchen open until 2pm. Cash only.)

◙ SIGHTS. For a great bike trip, head east from Nantucket Town on Milestone Rd. and turn left onto any path that looks promising. For a day on the sand, **Dionis** and **Jetties** both have rolling dunes and calm water (Jetties is also the closest beach to town, and predictably more busy). For isolated expanses made for walking, head east to the beaches of **Siasconset** and **Wauwinet**. **Nobadeer** and **Cisco** are good areas for surfing. **Nantucket Island Community Sailing** rents kayaks (1-person kayaks $15 per hr.; 2-person kayaks $25). You can only kayak in the protected waters of Nantucket Sound, but if you head across the harbor to an isolated beach on the Coatue peninsula, you'll be able to enjoy a peaceful picnic. **Barry Thurston's**, at Candle St. and Washington St., rents out rods and reels and is helpful to beginners. To get there, turn left on the third street up from Straight Wharf and walk a block. (☎228-9595. Necessary equipment $20 per day. Open Apr.-Dec. daily 8am-6pm.)

The popular **Nantucket Whaling Museum**, on Broad St. (☎228-1736), in Nantucket Town, explains the glories and hardships of the old whaling community through exhibits and talks on whales and whaling. The **Peter Foulger Museum**, next door (☎228-1894), features a special exhibit on the whaleship *Essex*, which was rammed by a whale, leaving the crew floating around the South Pacific for months. The story of the *Essex* supposedly inspired *Moby Dick*. Both museums are located in front of Steamboat Wharf. (Whaling Museum open late May to early Oct. M-Sa 10am-5pm, Su noon-5pm; end of April to May and Oct. Foulger Museum open daily 11am-4pm. Both museums $12, ages 7-17 $8, 6 and under free, family pass $35. Ticket good for 7 historical sites as well as the 90min. walking tour, offered June-Oct. M-Sa 10:30am and 2:30pm; May M-Sa 10:30am.)

WESTERN MASSACHUSETTS

THE BERKSHIRES ☎413

Cultural events in the summer and rich foliage in the fall make the Berkshires an attractive destination for a weekend getaway. Sprinkled with small New England towns, the Berkshires offer fudge shops, country stores, and scenic rural drives, as well as pristine colleges and their associated college towns and art museums.

⚔🖋 ORIENTATION AND PRACTICAL INFORMATION

Comprising the western third of Massachusetts, the Berkshire region is bordered to the north by Rte. 2 (the Mohawk Trail) and Vermont and to the south by the Mass. Pike and Connecticut. **Peter Pan Bus Lines** runs buses from South Station to Springfield, where you can catch a **Bonanza** connection to Williamstown. (☎800-343-9999. 4hr.; daily 10am. $33.) **Visitor info: Berkshire Visitors Bureau,** 2 Berkshire Common, Plaza Level, in Pittsfield (☎443-9186 or 800-237-5747. open M-F 8:30am-5pm) and an **information booth** (open M-F 9am-5pm) on the east side of Pittsfield's rotary circle. Berkshire County's 12 state parks and forests cover 100,000 acres and offer numerous camping and hiking options. For info, stop by the **Region 5 Headquarters,** 740 South St., in Pittsfield. (☎442-8928. Open M-F 8am-5pm.) **Area code:** 413.

NORTH ADAMS

Once a large industrial center—100 trains per day passed through its state-of-the-art Hoosac Tunnel—North Adams went into decline for many years. Bolstered by a new art museum, however, the city is on the upswing again, as it finds new uses for its many factory buildings. The two-year-old ⬛**Mass. MoCA,** 87 Marshall St., comprises 27 old factory buildings and is the largest center for contemporary visual and performing arts in the country. The museum exhibits art that, because of its complexity, can't be exhibited anywhere else in the US. (☎662-2111. Open June-Oct. daily 10am-6pm; Nov.-May W-M 11am-5pm. $8, ages 6-16 $3; Nov.-May $6, seniors $4, ages 6-16 $2.) The **Contemporary Artists Center,** 189 Beaver St. (Rte. 8N), also displays stunning modern art. (☎663-9555. Open W-Sa 11am-5pm, Su noon-5pm. Free.)

North Adams is also home to the **Western Gateway,** on the Furnace St. bypass off Rte. 8, a railroad museum, a gallery, and one of Massachusetts's five Heritage State Parks. (☎663-6312. Open daily 10am-5pm. Free; donations accepted. Live music in summer Th 7pm.) On Rte. 8, ½ mi. north of downtown North Adams, lies **Natural Bridge State Park,** home to a white marble bridge formed during the last Ice Age. (May-Oct. ☎663-6392 and Nov.-Apr. 663-6312. Open late May to mid-Oct. daily 9am-5pm. Parking $2.) There is also a **Visitors Center** on Union St. (Rte. 2 and 8), on the east side of town. (Open 10am-4pm.)

WILLIAMSTOWN

Williamstown's surrounding wooded hills beckon from the moment you arrive. The **Hopkins Memorial Forest** offers over 2250 acres that are free for hiking and cross-country skiing. Take Rte. 7 N (North St.), turn left on Bulkley St., follow Bulkley to the end, and turn right onto Northwest Hill Rd. (☎597-2346). For bike, snowshoe, or cross-country ski rentals, check out **The Mountain Goat,** 130 Water St. (☎458-8445).

At **Williams College,** the second-oldest college in Massachusetts after Harvard, homework-laden students have to make time to enjoy their stunning surroundings—and to dis rival **Amherst College** (see p. 144). Nicknamed "Ephs" (after college founder Ephraim Williams), Williams students seem to have a strange obsession with their mascot, a purple cow, but maybe that's just what the long winters here do to you. Maps of the beautiful campus are available from the admissions office, 988 Main St., in Mather House. (☎597-2211. Open M-F 8:30am-4:30pm. 2-6 tours M-F year-round. 1-2 tours Sa June-Nov.) An especially exquisite jewel in Williams' crown is the **Williams College Museum of Art,** 15 Lawrence Hall Dr., #2, which houses medieval to contemporary works of art, including sculpture, paintings, and photos. (☎597-2429. Open Tu-Sa 10am-5pm, Su 1-5pm. Free. Wheelchair accessible.)

Located ½ mi. down South St. from the info booth, the **Clark Art Institute,** 225 South St., displays a collection of 14th- to 16th-century European and American works. (☎458-2303. Open July-Aug. daily 10am-5pm; Sept.-June Tu-Su 10am-5pm. Free Nov.-June and on Tu, $5 for permanent exhibit July-Oct. Ages 18 and under and students free. Tours July-Aug. daily 3pm. Wheelchair accessible.) In summer, check out the star-studded ⬛**Williamstown Theater Festival.** (☎597-3400. Box office open June-Aug. Tu-Sa 11am-intermission of 1st evening performance, Su 11am-4pm.) Performances are given Tuesday through Sunday on the Main Stage ($33-43), on the Nikos Stage (about $20 except for $3 F afternoons), and in the Free Theater.

Williamstown has many affordable motels east of town on Rte. 2. The welcoming **Maple Terrace Motel,** 555 Main St./Rte. 2, has bright rooms with cable TV and refrigerators, a heated outdoor pool, and continental breakfast. (☎458-9677. Reception open daily 8am-10:30pm. Check-in 1pm. Check-out 11am. Doubles Nov.-May $51-81; June-Oct. $73-118.) Comfortable **Chimney Mirror Motel,** 295 Main St., is a cheaper but less lavish choice. (☎458-5202. A/C, breakfast. Singles $65-75, winter $45; doubles $95-105, winter $60.) For affordable meals that happen to bear the names of famous actors and actresses, stop by **Papa Charlie's,** 28 Spring St., for a "Dick Cavett" or an "Olympia Dukakis"—feta, avocado, tomatoes, and dressing in a pita. (☎458-5969. Open M-Th 8am-9pm, F-Sa 8am-10pm, Su 9am-8pm. Cash only.) Serving up Herrell's ice cream and delightful lunchtime specials (quiche $3, sandwiches $5), **Lickety Split,** on Spring St., is hopping in the early afternoon. (Open May-Oct. daily 11:30am-10pm, Nov.-Apr. 11:30am-4pm; lunch until 3pm. Cash only.)

LENOX

Tanglewood, one of the Berkshires' greatest treasures, is the famed summer home of the **Boston Symphony Orchestra.** South on Rte. 7, a short distance west of Lenox Center on Rte. 183 (West St.), Tanglewood concerts include a variety of musical genres, but its bread and butter, as it were, is top-notch classical music. Lawn tickets and picnics make for a great evening or Sunday afternoon. Chamber concerts entertain on Thursday evenings, the Boston Pops give three summer concerts, and the young musicians of the Tanglewood Music Center, a premier training institute, perform throughout the summer. The summer ends with a **jazz festival** over Labor Day weekend. (☎637-5165. Orchestral concerts held late June to early Sept. F 8:30pm with 6pm prelude, Sa 8:30pm, Su 2:30pm. Auditorium/"Music Shed" $17-88, lawn seats $14-17. Students with valid ID should inquire about discounts. Free lawn tickets for children under 12. Open rehearsals held Sa 10:30am. Call for schedule.)

Dubbed "a delicate French chateau mirrored in a Massachusetts pond" by Henry James, **The Mount,** 2 Plunkett St. at the southern junction of Rte. 7 and 7A, is the newly restored home of **Edith Wharton.** The Mount offers tours, special events, and lecture series. (☎637-1899. Open late May-late Oct. daily 9am-5pm. $7.50, seniors $7, ages 13-18 $5, ages 6-12 $3, ages 5 and under free.) Visit **Shakespeare & Company,** 70 Kemble St. (Rte. 7A), at the new Founders Theater and enjoy enchanting productions of plays written both by Shakespeare and by Berkshires authors such as Edith Wharton and Henry James. (☎637-3353. Late May-late Oct. $10-100.) At **Pleasant Valley Wildlife Sanctuary,** enjoy an amble through the 1500 acres and 7 mi. of trails in this Massachusetts Audobon Society Sanctuary. (☎637-0320. Open July-Sept.)

THE FIVE COLLEGE AREA   ☎413

Aside from rampant tourism, another way to keep cool shops and museums afloat is to pack an area full of college students—in the case of the **Five College Area,** nearly 30,000. Named for the five prestigious liberal arts colleges located in Amherst, Northampton, and South Hadley, the Five College Area is possessed of all the best attributes of a college town: terrific restaurants that cater to student budgets, impressive art museums, bike trails, and a host of great state parks.

AMHERST

Founded by Noah Webster in 1821, **Amherst College,** near the intersection of Rte. 9 and 116, was originally intended to be a ministry for young men with great intelligence and few funds. It is now a top co-educational liberal arts institution ornamented with beautiful classical architecture, including an eye-catching Greek Revival chapel. However, Amherst College's charms extend beyond the beautiful architecture of its buildings and the elegance of its landscaping. The **Wildlife Sanctuary,** located to the east of the tennis courts on campus, includes plenty of hiking and jogging trails. The Norwottuck Rail Trail runs through the Bird Sanctuary here. It's a seven-mile jog or bike ride to the Connecticut River.

Located next to Stearns Steeple on the east side of the main quadrangle, the **Mead Art Museum** has an impressive 12,000-piece permanent collection strong in early American and European Renaissance art. (☎542-2335. Open Sept. to mid-May Tu-W and F-Su 10am-4:30pm, Th 10am-9pm; mid-May through Aug. Tu-Su 1-4pm. Free.) A visit to Amherst would hardly be complete without a brief tribute to **Emily Dickinson** at her family's homestead at 280 Main St. Born here on December 10, 1830, Dickinson lived here nearly all her life and composed nearly 1800 poems. (☎542-8161. Grounds open daily 10am-5pm; homestead open for guided tours only. Tours $5, seniors and students $4, ages 6-18 $3, under 6 free.)

Bay Rd., right next to Atkins Farms, leads to **Hampshire Shakespeare**, a festival of "Shakespeare Under the Stars" performed between late June and early August. The performance venue is at the Hartsbrook School. From Rte. 9 E, turn south on Rte. 47, then turn left onto Bay Rd., drive 1 mi.; the school is on the right. (☎548-8118. Plays $12, seniors and students $9, children $6.) **Amherst Brewing Co.**, 24-36 N. Pleasant St., offers booze and grub in a stylish setting. Menu choices such as fish and chips ($9.50) and jambalaya ($13) delight diners. (☎253-4400. Pints $4, mixed drinks $5-6. Live music Th-Su. The Amherst Jazz Orchestra plays every 1st and 3rd M. Open daily 11am-1am; kitchen open until midnight.) **Antonio's**, 31 N. Pleasant St., is lauded as the pizza capital of the Northeast by locals. Slices run $1.50-3. (☎253-0808. Open daily 10am-1am.)

The **Country Belle Motel**, 329 Russell St., is a convenient and economical accommodation on Rte. 9 in Hadley, which lies between Northampton and Amherst. This homey motel has an outdoor pool, easy access to the Norwottuck Bike Trail, cable TV, and A/C. Breakfast is included. (☎586-0715. Nov.-Apr. $50, May-Dec. $60-80.)

NORTHAMPTON

Built in the late 19th century, **Smith College,** on College Ln., off Main St. in downtown Northampton, has become one of the largest and most esteemed women's colleges in the country. The money to buy the land, construct the first buildings, and begin the endowment came from Sophia Smith's bequest of the fortune that she herself had inherited at age 65. Smith sought to "furnish for [her] own sex means and facilities for education equal to those which are afforded now in our colleges to young men." Smith's campus is full of elegant wood and brick buildings attractively set on a hillside that overlooks downtown Northampton. Attractions include the beautiful **Lyman Plant House,** a beautiful botanical garden that makes a stop by the campus well worth your time. (☎585-2740. Open daily 8:30am-4pm. Free.) The campus is easily navigable by bike or foot. For Northampton info, visit **Historic Northampton,** 46 Bridge St. The collection features more than 10,000 photographs, manuscripts from the 17th to the 20th centuries, and fine art. (☎584-6011. Open Tu-F 10am-4pm, Sa-Su noon-4pm. Historic house tours Sa-Su noon-4pm.)

Tickets to the **Calvin Theater & Performing Arts Center,** 19 King St. (☎586-0851), usually run $28-45 for the big-name performances, which have recently included Emmylou Harris, the Alvin Ailey Dance Theater, Arlo Guthrie, and Wynton Marsalis. For fine foreign and domestic film and stage entertainment, stop by the **Academy of Music,** 274 Main St. (☎584-8435), down the hill from Smith College. This attractive building features great performances on and off the screen. For small-scale films, sit back and relax at the **Pleasant St. Theater,** 27 Pleasant St. (☎586-5828).

The **Best Western of Northampton,** 117 Conz St., on Rte. 5 off Exit 18 of I-91, has free breakfast, cable TV, in-room fridges and jacuzzis, and an outdoor pool. (☎586-1500. In summer, rooms $89-139; in winter, rooms $69-99. Under 15 free. Wheelchair accessible rooms available.) **Paul & Elizabeth's Natural Foods Restaurant,** 150 Main St., in Thornes Market, serves delectable wheat rolls alongside the daily specials, which are reason enough to dine here. But there's also a full selection of lunch and dinner dishes. If the grilled tofu kebabs ($11) sound too intimidating, plenty of seafood and pasta dishes ($8.50-14) await. (☎584-4832. Open Su-Th 11:30am-9pm, F-Sa 11:30am-9:45pm.) **Pizzeria Paradiso,** 12 Crafts Ave., uses a traditional wood-fired brick oven to yield divine thin-crust pizza. (☎586-1468. Open daily 5-10:30pm.)

SPRINGFIELD

For the budget traveler, Springfield is no more than a transportation hub, so pull out quickly. **Visitor info: Greater Springfield Convention and Visitors Bureau,** in the Tower Sq. Bldg. at 1500 Main St. (☎787-1548; open M-F 9am-5pm). Budget motels are in West Springfield, at Exits 13A and 13B off I-91. **Peter Pan Bus Line,** 1776 Main St. (☎781-3320; open 5:30am-9:45pm), runs to Boston (2hr., 16 per day, $20) and New York (3½hr., 16 per day, $32). **Amtrak,** at 66 Lyman St. (open 5am-12:45am), runs to New York (3½hr., 7 per day, $36) and Boston (2½hr., 2 per day, $21).

RHODE ISLAND

Despite its smallest-state status, Rhode Island has never felt pressure to conform. Founded by religious outcast Roger Williams during colonial days, it was the first state to pass laws against slavery. Though you can drive through the whole of Rhode Island in 45 minutes, the Ocean State's 400-mile coastline deserves a longer look. Small, elegant hamlets bespeckle the shores winding to Connecticut, exuding pure New England charm.

▨ PRACTICAL INFORMATION

Capital: Providence.
Visitor info: Dept. of Tourism, 1 West Exchange St., Providence 02903 (☎401-222-2601 or 800-556-2484; www.visitrhodeisland.com). Open M-F 8:30am-4pm. **Division of Parks and Recreation,** 2321 Hartford Ave., Johnston 02919 (☎401-222-2632). Open M-F 8:30am-4pm.
Postal Abbreviation: RI. **Sales Tax:** 7%.

PROVIDENCE   ☎401

Seven colleges inhabit the seven hills of Providence, luring a community of students, artists, and academics to join the native working class and state representatives. Providence has cobbled sidewalks and colonial buildings, a college town atmosphere, and more than its share of bookstores and cafes. In the area around the colleges, students on tight budgets support a plethora of inexpensive restaurants and shops. Affordable accommodations are hard to find, but Providence's compact size makes it a pleasurably walkable city. Its local color stems in part from constant allegations of crooked city government: longtime mayor Buddy Cianci, who served a jail term and a term of office on probation for attacking his estranged wife's suspected lover, is recently under indictment for new corruption charges.

▨▨ **ORIENTATION AND PRACTICAL INFORMATION.** The downtown business district clusters in the area bounded by **I-95** on the west, **I-195** to the south, the Providence River to the east, and the state capitol to the north. **Brown University** and the **Rhode Island School of Design (RISD),** pronounced *RIZ-dee,* sit atop a steep hill, a 10min. walk east of downtown. **Amtrak,** 100 Gaspee St. (☎727-7379 or 800-872-7245; station open daily 5am-11pm; ticket booth open 5am-9:45pm), operates from a gleaming white structure near the state capitol, a 10min. walk from Brown University or downtown. Trains set out for Boston (1hr., 11 per day, $17-19; 4 high-speed Acela trains per day take only 30min.) and New York (4hr., 12 per day, $44-63; 4 Acela trains, 3¼hr.). **Greyhound,** 102 Fountain St. in downtown Providence (☎454-0790; station open daily 6:30am-8:30pm), runs buses to Boston (1hr.; 12 per day; M-F $7.50, Sa-Su $8.50) and New York (5hr.; 13 per day; M-F $22, Sa-Su $24). **Bonanza,** 1 Bonanza Way at Exit 25 off I-95 (☎751-8800; station open daily 4:30am-11pm), also has frequent service to Boston (1hr., 18 per day, $9) and New York (4hr., 6 per day, $37). **Rhode Island Public Transit Authority (RIPTA)**, 265 Melrose St. (☎781-9400; M-F 7am-7pm, Sa 8am-6pm), runs an **info booth** at Kennedy Plaza, which provides route and schedule assistance and free bus maps. RIPTA's service includes Newport ($1.25) and other points. (Buses run daily 5am-midnight; hours vary. Fare 25¢-$5; base fare $1.25; within Providence, 50¢.) **Yellow Cab** (☎941-1122) provides taxi service in the Providence metro area.

Visitor info: Providence/Warwick Convention and Visitors Bureau, 1 Sabin St. in downtown (☎274-1636 or 800-233-1636; open M-Sa 9am-5pm). The **Providence Preservation Society**, 21 Meeting St. at the foot of College Hill, provides detailed info on historic Providence. (☎831-7440. Open M-F 9am-5pm.) On street parking is scarce and meter-maids are many; **Metropark** (☎274-9290) has several lots in town, including 28 Pine St. **Post Office:** 2 Exchange Terr. (☎421-4361; open M-F 7:30am-5:30pm, Sa 8am-2pm). **ZIP code:** 02903. **Area code:** 401.

ACCOMMODATIONS. Downtown motel rates make Providence an expensive overnight stay. Rooms fill up well in advance for the graduation season in May and early June. Head 10 mi. south on I-95 to Warwick/Cranston for cheaper motels.

Catering largely to the international visitors of the universities, the stained-glass-windowed **International House of Rhode Island**, 8 Stimson Ave., off Hope St. near the Brown campus, has three comfortable, welcoming rooms that fill up quickly. Reservations are required and should be made far in advance. Amenities include kitchen, private bath, TV, and a fridge. (☎421-7181. Reception M-F 9:30am-5pm. Singles $50, students $35; doubles $60/$45; $5 per night discount for stays of 5 nights or more. Many international visitors stay for weeks at a time.) Three mi. outside of Providence on Rte. 6 in Seekonk, MA, the **Town 'n' Country Motel** has clean, comfortable rooms. (☎336-8300. Singles $44; doubles $50.) The nearest **campgrounds** lie 30min. from downtown. One of the closest, **Colwell's Campground**, in Coventry, RI, provides showers and hookups for 75 sites along the Flat River Reservoir. From Providence, take I-95 S. to Exit 10, then head west 9½ mi. on Rte. 117 to Peckham Ln. (☎397-4614. Check-in 9am-7pm. Sites $14, with electricity $16.)

FOOD. Three areas in Providence boast impressive food: **Atwells Ave.** in the Italian district, on Federal Hill just west of downtown; **Thayer St.**, on College Hill to the east, home to off-beat student hangouts and ethnic restaurants; and **Wickenden St.**, in the southeast corner of town, with many inexpensive international eateries. **Geoff's Superlative Sandwiches**, 163 Benefit St., attracts a diverse clientele with 102 creatively-named sandwiches, such as the "Buddy Cianci," the "Marlene Dietrich," and the "Embryonic Journey." Grab a green dessert from the huge pickle barrel on your way out. (☎751-2248. Sandwiches $4-6. Open M-F 8am-9pm, Sa-Su 10am-9pm.) Shoot the breeze with Providence locals at the **Seaplane Diner**, 307 Allen's Ave., 5min. from downtown, near I-195. A classic diner, Seaplane has quick service and cheap homestyle breakfasts and lunches. (☎941-9547. Open M-F 5am-3pm, Sa 5am-1pm, F-Sa midnight-4am.) **Loui's Family Restaurant**, 286 Brook St., is the home-away-from-home for many college students. Recently, students have rallied to save the diner from Brown's expansion. Try the "Henry Hample" ($3), a vegan eggplant Florentine sub, or any number of specials drawn on placards above the counter. (☎861-5225. Open daily 6am-3pm.) For Italian food head to **The Original Riccotti's**, 133 Atwells Ave. on Federal Hill. As "home of the 29 in. sub" ($13.50), Ricotti's is a bargain for two or more. (☎621-8100. Open M-F 8am-8pm, Sa 10am-8pm.)

SIGHTS. Exhibiting just a smattering of this world-renowned art school's collection, the **RISD Museum of Art**, 224 Benefit St., gathers Egyptian, Indian, Impressionist, medieval, and Roman art, as well as a gigantic 12th-century Japanese Buddha, into a small but pleasant space. (☎454-6500. Open Tu-Su 10am-5pm. $5, students $2, seniors $4, ages 5-18 $1. Free every 3rd Th 5-9pm and last Sa of month.) The 350-year-old neighborhood of **College Hill** is home to many of Providence's notable historic sights. **Brown University**, established in 1764, includes several

18th-century buildings and provides a fitting starting point for a historic walking tour of Providence. The Office of Admissions, housed in the historic **Carliss-Brackett House,** 45 Prospect St., former home of the inventor of the elevator, gives free 1hr. walking tours of the campus. (☎863-2378. Open M-F 8am-4pm. Tours M-F 10, 11am, 1, 3, and 4pm.) In addition to founding Rhode Island, in 1638 Roger Williams founded the *first* **First Baptist Church of America.** Rarely crowded, its 1775 incarnation stands today at 75 N. Main St. (☎454-3418. Open M-F 10am-noon and 1-3pm, Sa 10am-noon. Free.) From atop the hill, gaze at the impressive **Rhode Island State Capitol,** which boasts the 4th-largest free-standing marble dome in the world. (☎222-2357. Open M-F 8:30am-4:30pm. Free tours M-F 10 and 11am; reservations appreciated for individual groups. Free self-guide booklets available in room 220.)

John Quincy Adams called the **John Brown House Museum,** 52 Power St., "the most magnificent and elegant private mansion" on the continent. Today, the 18th-century home of the Rhode Island entrepreneur and revolutionary is not so "private"; tour buses galore crowd outside. (☎331-8575. Open Tu-Sa 10am-5pm, Su noon-4pm. $6, seniors and students $4.50, ages 7-17 $3.) The New England textile industry was born in 1793 when Samuel Slater used plans smuggled out of Britain to build the first water-powered factory in America. In Pawtucket, the **Slater Mill Historic Site,** 67 Roosevelt Ave., preserves fabric heritage with working machinery in three historic buildings. (☎725-8638. Open June-Nov. M-Sa 10am-5pm, Su 1-5pm; Dec.-May Sa-Su 1-5pm. Tours leave roughly every 2hr. $7, seniors $6, 6-12 $5.50.) If you're ready for some hardball, the **Pawtucket Red Sox** take the field April through early September in the splendid **McCoy Stadium,** 1 Columbus Ave. in Pawtucket. (☎724-7300. Box seats $8; general admission $5, seniors and under 13 $4.)

🎭🎬 **ENTERTAINMENT AND NIGHTLIFE.** For film, theater, and nightlife listings, read the "Weekend" section of the Friday *Providence Journal* or the *Providence Phoenix.* The nationally acclaimed **Trinity Repertory Company,** 201 Washington St., offers $12 student rush tickets 2hr. before performances when available. (☎351-4242. Tickets $32-42.) For splashier productions, contact the **Providence Performing Arts Center,** 220 Weybosset St., which hosts a variety of concerts and Broadway musicals. (☎421-2787. Box office open M-F 10am-6pm, Sa noon-5pm.) The **Cable Car Cinema and Cafe,** 204 S. Main St., shows artsy and foreign films in a kinder, gentler setting—on couches instead of chairs. Occasional weekend film festivals featuring Brown and RISD students' work are a cinematic treat. Call ahead for a schedule. (☎272-3970. Tickets $7.50.)

Brownies, townies, and RISDs rock the night away at several hot spots throughout town. Mingle with the local artist community at **AS220,** 115 Empire St. between Washington and Westminster St., a cafe/bar/gallery/music and improv performance space. (☎831-9327. Open M-F 10am-1am, Sa 1-5pm and 7pm-1am, Su 7pm-1am. Cover $3-5.) Gay and straight alike favor **Gerardo's,** 1 Franklin Sq. on Allen's Ave., where DJ beats and karaoke fill a neon pink and blue disco dance hall. (☎274-5560. Th-Su cover varies; open Su-Th 4pm-1am, F-Sa 4pm-2am.)

NEWPORT ☎401

Money has always found its way into Newport. Once supported by slave trade profits, the coastal town later became the summer home of America's elite and thus the site of some of the nation's most opulent mansions. Today, Newport is a high-priced tourist town, but its numerous arts festivals—and the awe-inspiring extravagance of its mansions—are reason enough for those on a tight budget to visit.

🔏 **PRACTICAL INFORMATION.** The place to start any visit to Newport is the **Newport County Convention and Visitors Bureau,** 23 America's Cup Ave. in the Newport Gateway Center (☎845-9123 or 800-976-5122; www.gonewport.com; open Su-Th 9am-5pm, F-Sa 9am-6pm). **Bonanza Buses** (☎846-1820) depart from the Center, as do the buses of **Rhode Island Public Transit Authority (RIPTA)** (see p. 146). **Ten**

Speed Spokes, 18 Elm St., rents bikes. (☎ 847-5609. Open M-Th 10am-6pm, F-Sa 9am-6pm, Su 11am-5pm. Mountain bikes $5 per hr., $25 per day. Must have credit card and photo ID.) **Post Office:** 320 Thames St. (☎ 847-2329; open M-F 8:30am-5pm, Sa 9am-1pm). **ZIP code:** 02840. **Area code:** 401.

▌ ACCOMMODATIONS. Guest houses account for the bulk of Newport's accommodations. Most offer a bed and continental breakfast with colonial intimacy but not for colonial prices. Those willing to share a bathroom or forego a sea view might find a double for $75; singles are almost nonexistent. Many hotels and guest houses book solid two months in advance for summer weekends. The best weekday deal in the area is the **Newport Gateway Hotel,** 31 W. Main Rd., just across the town line in Middletown. The Gateway has clean, comfortable doubles with A/C and cable TV, a few minutes from Newport's harborfront. (☎ 847-2735. Su-Th $45-95; F-Sa $125-195 with 2-night minimum. $15 each additional person.) Just up the road, **Motel 6,** 249 J.T. Connel Hwy, provides a second affordable option for budget travelers. Follow Broadway out of Newport into Middletown, turn left on W. Main St., and follow Connelton Hwy. for 1½ mi. (☎ 848-0600 or 800-466-8356. Singles $50-56; doubles $56-62, $3 each additional person.) **Fort Getty Recreation Area,** on Fort Getty Rd. on Conanicut Island, provides a peaceful respite. (☎ 423-7264, reservations ☎ 423-7211. RV sites $25; tent sites $20. Showers and beach access. Reservations recommended 1-2 months in advance. Tent sites available late May-Oct.)

█ FOOD. While many Newport restaurants are pricey, cheap food does exist. Most of Newport's restaurants line up on **Thames St.,** where ice cream parlors abound. Good, hearty breakfasts like the "Portuguese Sailor" (chorizo sausage and eggs; $5) are prepared before your eyes at the **Franklin Spa,** 229 Spring St. (☎ 847-3540; open M-W 6am-2pm, Th-Sa 6am-3pm, Su 7am-1:30pm.) Shack up with some choice mollusks alongside a severely incapacitated lobster boat at **Flo's Clam Shack,** Rte. 138A/Aquidneck Ave., across from Easton Beach. (☎ 847-8141. Fried clams $11. Open Su-Th 11am-9pm, F-Sa 11am-10pm, call for off-season hours.) **Dry Dock Seafood,** 448 Thames St., serves fresh fish. (☎ 847-3974. Entrees $7-15, baked fish of the day $9. Open daily 11am-9pm; off-season Tu-Su 11am-9pm.) **Mel's Cafenio,** 25 Broadway St., is the place to find locals on lunch break, skimming newspapers and enjoying cheap non-seafood fare. (☎ 849-6420. Open daily 6am-3pm.)

◨ SIGHTS. George Noble Jones built the first "summer cottage" in Newport in 1839, thereby kicking off an extravagant string of palatial summer estates. Five of the mansions lie south of downtown on Bellevue Ave. A self-guided walking tour or a guided tour by the **Preservation Society of Newport,** 424 Bellevue Ave., will allow you to ogle at the extravagance; purchase tickets at any mansion. (☎ 847-1000. Open M-F 9am-5pm; mansions open M-F 10am-5pm. $10-15, ages 6-17 $4. Combination tickets available.) **The Marble House** is the must-see of the mansions. Built for $11 million in 1892 as a 39th birthday present for William K. Vanderbilt's wife Alva, it contains over 500,000 cubic ft. of marble, silk walls, and rooms covered entirely in gold. (☎ 847-1000. Open Apr.-Oct. M-F 10am-5pm; Jan.-Mar. Sa-Su 10am-4pm. $9, ages 6-17 $4.) The father of William Mayes, a notorious Red Sea pirate, opened the **White Horse Tavern** at Marlborough St. and Farewell St. in 1687, making it the oldest continuously operated drinking establishment in the country. The tavern makes off like a bandit with its entrees ($30) but serves up beer for $3-4. (☎ 849-3600. Open W-M 11:30am-2:30pm for lunch and 6-10pm each day for dinner.) The oldest synagogue in the US, the restored Georgian **Touro Synagogue,** 85 Touro St., dates back to 1763. (☎ 847-4794. Visits by free tour only. Tours every 30min. late May to late June M-F 1-2:30pm, Su 11am-2:30pm; early July to early Sept. Su-F 10am-4:30pm. Call for off-season tour schedule.) Die-hard tennis fans will feel right at home in Newport, where the **Tennis Hall of Fame,** 194 Bellevue Ave., has the largest tennis museum in the world. (☎ 849-3990. Open daily 9:30am-5pm. $8, students and seniors $6, under 17 $4, families $20.) Eight miles north of Newport in Portsmouth, the **Green Animals**

Topiary Gardens, Cory's Lane, holds 21 shrubs amazingly sculpted as giraffes and lions. (☎683-1267. May-Oct. open daily 10am-5pm. $10, ages 6-17 $4.)

Newport's gorgeous beaches are frequently as crowded as the streets. The most popular is **Easton's Beach,** or First Beach, on Memorial Blvd. (☎848-6491. Open late May to early Sept. M-F 9am-9pm, Sa-Su 8am-9pm. Parking M-F $8, Sa-Su $10; before 10am in the summer $6.) For a nice walk by the sea, traverse the **Cliff Walk,** a 3½ mi. dirt trail on Newport's eastern shore. Start at Easton Beach or halfway through the trail at Narragansett Ave. **Fort Adams State Park,** south of town on Ocean Dr. 2½ mi. from the Visitors Center, offers showers, picnic areas, and two fishing piers. (☎847-2400. Park open sunrise to sunset.) Good beaches also line Little Compton, Narragansett, and the shore between Watch Hill and Point Judith; for more details pick up a free *Ocean State Beach Guide*, available at the **Visitors Center.**

🎵 **ENTERTAINMENT.** From June through August, Newport gives lovers of classical, folk, blues, jazz, and film each a festival to call their own. The oldest and best-known jazz festival in the world, the **Newport Jazz Festival** has seen the likes of Duke Ellington and Count Basie; bring your beach chairs and coolers to Fort Adams State Park to join the fun. Also at Fort Adams State Park, folk singers (former acts include Bob Dylan, Joan Baez, and the Indigo Girls) entertain at the **Newport Folk Festival.** (Info for both festivals ☎847-3709. Jazz Festival Aug. 9-11, 2002; Folk Festival Aug. 2-4, 2002. Tickets $40 per day, under 12 $15.) The **Newport Music Festival** will bring classical musicians from around the world for two weeks of concerts in the ballrooms and lawns of the mansions. (☎846-1133; box office ☎849-0700. July 12-28, 2002. Box office open daily 10am-5pm. Tickets $33-38.)

A number of pubs and clubs line Thames St., making it a happening area at night. **One Pelham East,** 274 Thames St., packs 'em in for alternative cover bands. (☎847-9460. Live music nightly; cover varies. Open M-F 3pm-1am, Sa-Su 1pm-1am.) The **Newport Blues Cafe,** 286 Thames St., has rocking blues music seven nights per week. (☎841-5510. Open 6pm-1am. Dinner 6-10pm; live music after 9:30pm. Cover varies; non-passport foreign IDs not accepted.) For art films, go to the **Jane Pickens Theater,** 49 Touro St. (☎846-5252. $7, senior $4.) For more mainstream flicks, head across the street to the **Opera House Cinema,** 19 Touro St. (☎847-3456. $7, children $4.)

NEAR NEWPORT: BLOCK ISLAND

A popular daytrip 10 mi. southeast of Newport in the Atlantic, sand-blown **Block Island** possesses an untamed natural beauty. Block Island was originally called by its Mohegan name *Manisses,* or "Isle of Little God." One-quarter of the island is protected open space; local conservationists hope to increase this figure to 50%. The 11 sq. mi. island is not as well known as its larger Massachusetts counterparts, Martha's Vineyard and Nantucket, but countless visitors still swell its population during the summer months. The **Interstate Navigation Co.** (☎783-4613) provides **ferry service** to Block Island from Galilee Pier in Point Judith, RI. (1¼hr. 8-9 per day, Sept.-June schedule varies. $8.40, ages 5-11 $4.60. Cars by reservation $26.30, driver and passengers extra; bikes $2.30.) Additional summer service runs from New London, CT. (2hr. Mid-June to mid-Sept. Sa-Th 1 per day, F 2 per day. $15, ages 5-11 $9.) **Viking Lines** (☎631-668-5709) also runs a daily ferry from Montauk, Long Island, to Block Island during the summer. (1¾hr. 1 per day, 9am. $25, ages 5-12 $10.)

The island does not permit camping; it's best to take a daytrip unless you're willing to shell out $60 or more for a room in a guest house. Moderately priced restaurants hover near the ferry dock in Old Harbor; several dot New Harbor 1 mi. inland. Cycling is the ideal way to explore the tiny (7 mi. by 3 mi.) island; the **Old Harbor Bike Shop,** directly to the left of the ferry exit, rents all manner of wheeled conveyances from mountain bikes to Geo Trackers. (☎466-2029. Mountain bikes $5-8 per hr., $20-30 per day; mopeds $32/$80. Tracker SUVs $80 half-day, $140 full-day. Must be 21+ with credit card. Open mid-May to mid-Oct. daily 8:30am-7pm.) The **Block Island Chamber of Commerce** (☎466-2982) is located at the ferry dock in Old Harbor Drawer D and in an office behind Finn's Fish Market. (Open in summer daily 9am-5pm; off-season hours vary.) **Area code:** 401.

CONNECTICUT

Connecticut, the third-smallest state in the Union, contrasts a patchwork quilt of industrialized centers (like Hartford and New Haven) with serene New England villages and lush woodland beauty. Perhaps it is this diversity that attracted such famous residents as Mark Twain, Harriet Beecher Stowe, Noah Webster, and Eugene O'Neill, and inspired the birth of the American Impressionist movement and the American musical—both Connecticut originals. Home to Yale University and the nation's first law school, Connecticut has an equally rich intellectual history. This doesn't mean that the people of Connecticut don't know how to let their hair down—this is the state that also brought us the lollipop, the three-ring circus, and the largest casino in the United States.

◪ PRACTICAL INFORMATION

Capital: Hartford.
Visitor info: Connecticut Vacation Center, 865 Brook St., Rocky Hill 06067 (☎800-282-6863; www.ctbound.org). Open M-F 9am-4:30pm.
Postal Abbreviation: CT. **Sales Tax:** 6%.

HARTFORD
☎860

Hartford may be the world's insurance capital, but it has more to offer travelers than financial protection: several high-quality museums, a lively theater scene, and the only hostel in all of Connecticut and Rhode Island. As Mark Twain, one of the the town's most prized former residents, boasted, "of all the beautiful towns it has been my fortune to see, this is the chief."

◪ **PRACTICAL INFORMATION.** Hartford marks the intersection of I-91 and I-84. Union Place, in the northeast part of the city between Church and Asylum St., houses **Amtrak,** which runs trains north and south (☎727-1778; office open M-F 6am-7:30pm, Sa-Su 6:30am-7:30pm), and **Greyhound** (station open daily 5:45am-10pm), which runs buses to New York (2½hr., 34 per day, $20) and Boston (2½hr., 14 per day, $21). **Visitor info: Greater Hartford Convention and Visitors Bureau,** 1 Civic Center Plaza, 3rd fl. (☎728-6789 or 800-446-7811; open M-F 9am-4:30pm); the **Old State House,** 800 Main St., which provides free Internet access and tourist info (☎522-6766; open M-F 10am-4pm, Sa 11am-4pm); and **Connecticut Transit's Information Center,** at State and Market St., which doles out more helpful info (☎525-9181; open M-F 7am-11pm). **Parking: Hilton Lot,** corner of Ford and Pearl St. (☎244-2077), is centrally located. **Taxi: Yellow Cab** (☎666-6666). **Post Office:** 141 Weston St. (☎524-6074; open M-F 7am-6pm, Sa 7am-3pm). **ZIP code:** 06101. **Area code:** 860.

◪◪ **ACCOMMODATIONS AND FOOD.** The excellent **Mark Twain Hostel (HI-AYH),** 131 Tremont St., offers welcoming accommodations not far from the center of town. Tremont St. is past the Mark Twain House on Farmington Ave. and is accessible by the "Farmington Ave." bus west. (☎523-7255. Check-in 9am-10pm. Dorms $18, nonmembers $20.) In the heart of downtown, the **YMCA,** 160 Jewell St., by Bushnell Park, offers dorm-like rooms at reasonable rates and use of a gym, pool, and racquetball courts. (☎246-9622. $5 key deposit. Must be 18+ with ID. Check-in 7:30am-10pm. Check-out noon. No reservations. Singles $19, with private bath $24.) Many restaurants lie within a few blocks of downtown. Hartford's oldest eatery, the **Municipal Cafe,** 485 Main St., is a friendly lunch or dinner place. If you make it past the wooden alligator at the door, you'll reap the benefits of delicious $4-6 entrees. (☎278-4844. Open daily 10am-2:30pm.) **Black-Eyed Sally's BBQ & Blues,** 350 Asylum St., serves cheap, down-home cooking. Sally's image warns patrons that the only thing worse than a barbecue sandwich without sauce is "skinny dippin' with yer mother." (☎278-7427. Open M-W 11:30am-10pm, Th 11:30am-11pm, F 11:30am-midnight, Sa 5pm-midnight, Su 5-9pm. Live blues Th-Sa nights.)

NEW ENGLAND

⑤ SIGHTS. The ▨**Wadsworth Athenaeum,** 600 Main St., has absorbing collections of contemporary and Baroque art, including one of three Caravaggios in the US. (☎278-2670. Open Tu-Su 11am-5pm. $7, seniors and students $5, ages 6-17 $3. Free all day Th and Sa before noon. Call ahead for tour and lecture info.) Designed by Charles Bulfinch in 1796, the gold-domed **Old State House,** 800 Main St., housed the state government until 1878. Now, historic actors welcome tourists to the chambers and a museum of oddities. (☎522-6766. Open M-F 10am-4pm, Sa 11am-4pm. Free.) The **Mark Twain House,** 351 Farmington Ave. (☎247-0998), and **Harriet Beecher Stowe House,** 71 Forest St., both just west of the city center on Farmington Ave., colorfully reflect their authors' life and times. From the Old State House, take any "Farmington Ave." bus west. An entertaining tour of the intricately textured Twain homestead, where the author penned *The Adventures of Huckleberry Finn,* poignantly recalls Twain's energetic life and family tragedies. After the publication of *Uncle Tom's Cabin,* Stowe, whom Abraham Lincoln called "the little lady that started the big war," lived in her homey cottage next door. (Open M-Sa 9:30am-5pm, Su noon-5pm; Jan.-Apr. and Nov. closed Tu. $9, seniors $8, ages 13-18 $7, ages 6-12 $5. Stowe House: ☎522-9258. Open June to early Oct. M-Sa 9:30am-4:30pm, Su noon-4:30pm; off-season closed M. $6.50, seniors $6, ages 6-16 $2.75.)

⌧ ENTERTAINMENT. Hartford is home to a burgeoning 20-block **Arts & Entertainment District** downtown. The **Hartford Stage Company,** 50 Church St., a Tony Award-winning regional troupe, mounts productions of classics and contemporary works. (☎527-5151. Tickets $25-55; call for showtimes.) **TheaterWorks,** 233 Pearl St., is an off-Broadway-type theater that shows recent American plays. (☎527-7838. Tickets $18-25; performances Tu-Sa 8pm, Su 2:30pm.) For more show options, head to **The Bushnell,** 166 Capitol Ave., home of Hartford's symphony, ballet, and opera companies. (☎987-5900. Box office open M-Sa 10am-5pm, Su 12-4pm.)

NEW HAVEN   ☎203

Simultaneously university town and depressed city, New Haven has gained a reputation as something of a battleground—academic types and a working-class population live uneasily side by side. While most of New Haven continues to decay, Yale has begun to renovate its neo-Gothic buildings, convert its concrete sidewalks to brick, and generate a thriving collegiate coffeehouse, bar, and bookstore scene.

⚅ PRACTICAL INFORMATION. New Haven lies at the intersection of I-95 and I-91, 40 mi. south of Hartford, and is laid out in nine squares. Between Yale University and City Hall, the central square, called **the Green,** provides a pleasant escape from the hassles of city life. *At night, don't wander too far from the immediate downtown and campus areas; surrounding sections are notably less safe.* **Amtrak,** Union Station on Union Ave. Exit 1 off I-91 (☎773-6178; ticket office open daily 6:30am-10pm), runs out of a newly renovated station to New York (1½hr., 13 per day, $41); Boston (2½hr., 8 per day, $33); Washington, D.C. (6hr., 13 per day, $69); and Mystic (1¼hr., 6 per day, $23). Also at Union Station, **Greyhound** (☎772-2470; ticket office open daily 6:15am-8pm) runs frequently to: New York (2½hr., 11 per day, $20); Boston (4hr., 13 per day, $29); and Providence (2½hr., 13 per day, $19.50). **Taxi: MetroTaxi,** ☎777-7777. **Visitor info: Greater New Haven Convention and Visitors Bureau,** 59 Elm St. (☎777-8550; open M-F 8:30am-5pm) and another location at 350 Long Wharf Dr. **Internet access: New Haven Public Library,** 133 Elm St. ½hr. access per day with photo ID. (☎946-8130. Open M-Th 9am-9pm, F-Sa 9am-5pm, Su 1-5pm. Closed Sa-Su in July and Aug.) **Post Office:** 50 Brewery St. (☎782-7000; open M-F 8am-6pm, Sa 8am-1pm). **ZIP code:** 06511. **Area code:** 203.

⚑ ACCOMMODATIONS. Inexpensive lodgings are sparse in New Haven; the hunt quickens around Yale Parents Weekend (mid-October) and Commencement (early June). Head 10 mi. south on I-95 to **Milford** for affordable motels. **Hotel Duncan,** 1151 Chapel St., located in downtown New Haven, has old-fashioned charm, inexpensive rooms with cable TV, and the oldest manually operated elevator in the state. John

Hinckley enjoyed a comfortable stay here while he was stalking Jodie Foster in the fall of 1980, a few months before he shot President Reagan. (☎787-1273. Singles $44; doubles $60; suite with fridge $70. Reservations recommended for F-Su.) **Motel 6,** 270 Foxon Blvd., Exit 8 off I-91, keeps 58 rooms at good prices. (☎469-0343 or 800-466-8356. $56 per person, $6 each additional person.) **Hammonasset Beach State Park,** 20min. east on I-95 N from New Haven, Exit 62 in Madison, offers 558 sites in a beautiful setting. (☎245-1817. Office open mid-May to Oct. 8am-11pm. Sites $12.)

◖ FOOD. For great authentic Italian cuisine, work your way along Wooster St., in Little Italy 10min. east of downtown. The finest brick oven pizza can be found at **◪Pepe's,** 157 Wooster St. Try a small red or white sauce clam pie for $9. (☎865-5762. Open M and W-Th 4-10pm, F-Sa 11:30am-11pm, Su 2:30-10pm.) No condiments are allowed at **Louis' Lunch,** 263 Crown St. Cooked vertically in original cast iron grills, these $3.50 burgers are too fine for ketchup or mustard. (☎562-5507. Open Tu-W 11am-4pm, Th-Sa 11am-2am.) Indian restaurants dominate the neighborhood southwest of downtown, by Howe St. The $6 all-you-can-eat lunch buffet at **India Palace,** 65 Howe St., is one of the best deals in town. (☎776-9010. Open until 10:30pm; lunch served M-F 11:30am-3pm.) **Claire's Corner Copia,** 1000 Chapel St., recently voted best vegetarian restaurant by *Connecticut Magazine*, serves hearty portions of kosher vegetarian cuisine. Claire's offerings include Italian, Mexican, and Middle Eastern dishes. (☎562-3888. Open M-F 8am-9pm, Sa-Su 8am-10pm.)

◉ SIGHTS. The Yale University Campus provides the bulk of the city's sights and museums. Each campus building was designed in the English Gothic and Georgian Colonial styles, many of them with intricate moldings and a few with gargoyles. The **Yale Visitors Center** faces the Green at 149 Elm St. (☎432-2300. Open M-F 9am-4:45pm, Sa-Su 10am-4pm. Free tours M-F 10:30am and 2pm, Sa-Su 1:30pm. Tours last 1¼hr.) Wander into the charming Old Campus, bordered by Chapel, College, Elm, and High St., and view Connecticut Hall, the university's oldest building. One block north, on the other side of Elm St., **Sterling Memorial Library,** 120 High St., is designed to resemble a monastery—even the telephone booths are shaped like confessionals. Apparently the creator of the massive **Beinecke Rare Book and Manuscript Library** wasn't fond of windows: this massive modern white structure has none. Instead, it's paneled with Vermont marble cut thin enough to be translucent. The building protects one of five Gutenberg Bibles in the US and an extensive collection of William Carlos Williams's writings. (121 Wall St. ☎432-2977. Open M-F 8:30am-5pm, Sa 10am-5pm. Closed Sa in Aug.)

Open since 1832, the **Yale University Art Gallery,** 1111 Chapel St., on the corner of York, claims to be the oldest university art museum in the Western Hemisphere. The museum holds over 100,000 pieces from around the world, including works by Monet and Picasso. (☎432-0600. Open Sept.-July Tu-Sa 10am-5pm, Su 1-6pm. Free.) The **Peabody Museum of Natural History,** 170 Whitney Ave., Exit 3 off I-91, houses Rudolph F. Zallinger's Pulitzer Prize-winning mural depicting the North American continent before European settlement. Check out the 100-million-year-old, three-ton turtle and a mummy residing in the "house of eternity." (☎432-5050. Open M-Sa 10am-5pm, Su noon-5pm. $5, seniors and ages 3-15 $3.)

◪◪ ENTERTAINMENT AND NIGHTLIFE. Pick up a free copy of *The Advocate* to find out what's up. The **Shubert Theater,** 247 College St., brings in such top Broadway productions as *Kiss Me Kate*. (☎562-5666 or 800-228-6622. Box office open M-Sa 10am-5pm, Su 11am-3pm.) The **Yale Repertory Theater,** 1120 Chapel St., boasts illustrious alums like Meryl Streep, Glenn Close, and James Earl Jones. (☎432-1234. Open M-F 10am-5pm. Tickets $20-39. Half-price student rush tickets on the day of a show.) In summer, the city hosts **concerts** on the Green (☎946-7821), including the **New Haven Symphony** (☎865-0831, box office ☎776-1444; open M-F 10am-5pm). During the last two weeks of June, New Haven hosts the **International Festival of Arts & Ideas,** an extravaganza of theater, music, visual arts, dance, and "ideas." (Many events are free. Call 888-278-4332 for more info.)

Toad's Place, a club at 300 York St., has hosted gigs by Bob Dylan, the Stones, and George Clinton. (☎562-5694, recorded info ☎624-8623. Box office open daily 11am-6pm; buy tickets at the bar after 8pm. Bar open Su-Th 8pm-1am, F-Sa 8pm-2am; closed when there is not a show.) **Bar,** 254 Crown St., is a hip hangout, replete with pool table, lounge room, dance floor/theater, homemade beer and brick-oven pizza. The party every Tuesday night attracts a large gay crowd. (☎495-8924. Open Su-Tu 4pm-1am, W-Th 11:30am-2:30am and 4pm-1am, F 11:30am-2am, Sa 5am-2am.)

MYSTIC AND THE CONNECTICUT COAST   ☎860

Connecticut's coastal towns were busy seaports in the days of Herman Melville and Richard Henry Dana, but the dark, musty inns filled with tattooed sailors swapping sea stories are history. Today, sea lovers of a different ilk fill its lodgings: both sailing enthusiasts and vacationers just looking for a stroll by the shore seek the coast. **Mystic Seaport,** 1 mi. south on Rte. 27 from I-95 at Exit 90, offers a look back at Melville's Connecticut, with 17 acres of recreated village and a working wood-only shipyard where a reproduction of the notorious slave ship *Amistad* was completed in 1999. (☎572-5315. Open Apr.-Oct. daily 9am-5pm; Nov.-Mar. 10am-4pm. $16, seniors $15, ages 6-12 $8. Audio tours $3.50.) Seaport admission entitles visitors to **Sabino Charters'** steamboat cruise on the **Mystic River** for a few dollars more. (☎572-5351. 30min. trips mid-May to early Oct. daily on the hr. 11am-4pm. $5, ages 6-12 $4 after Seaport admission.) For some indoor aquatic life, don't miss the seals, penguins, sharks, and dolphins that await at one of the Northeast's finest aquariums, the **Mystic Marinelife Aquarium,** 55 Coogan Blvd., at Exit 90 off I-95. (☎572-5955. Open daily 9am-5pm, July to early Sept. 9am-6pm; $15, seniors $14, ages 3-12 $10.) The **Denison Pequotsepos Nature Center,** 1½ mi. east of downtown at 109 Pequotsepos Rd., offers a relaxing refuge from the droves of tourists with great bird watching and 10 mi. of scenic trails. (☎536-1216. Park center open M-Sa 9am-5pm, Su 10am-4pm; park open dawn-dusk. $6, seniors $5, ages 6-12 $4.)

The **Sea Breeze Motel,** 5 mi. north of Mystic at 812 Stonington Rd./Rte. 1, rents big rooms with A/C and cable TV. (☎535-2843. Singles $49, F-Sa $99; doubles $99, F-Sa $129. Rates lower in winter.) Close to Mystic are the **Seaport Campgrounds,** on Rte. 184, 3 mi. north on Rte. 27 from Mystic. (☎536-4044. Open mid-Apr. to Mid-Nov. daily. Sites $28, with water and electricity $32; $5 each additional person; seniors 10% discount.) **Mystic Pizza,** 56 W. Main St., the town's most renowned eatery, has been serving its tasty "secret recipe" pizzas since 1973. The 1988 Julia Roberts film by the same name further contributed to the popularity of this lively, but sometimes touristy restaurant/take-out joint. (☎536-3737 or 536-3700. Open 10am-11pm. Slices $2; small pizza $5.25; large $9.75.) For consistently good seafood, head to **Cove Fish Market,** a classic New England take-out stand 1 mi. east of downtown on Old Stonington Rd. (☎536-0061. Open mid-May through early Sept. M-Th 11am-7pm, F-Su 11am-8pm. Fish market open year-round 9am-6pm.) **Trader Jack's,** 14 Holmes St., near downtown, a popular nightspot, pours $2.75 domestics. (☎572-8550. No cover. Food 5pm-midnight; last call Su-Th 1am, F-Sa 2am. Happy hour M-F 4:30-6:30pm.)

To find out info on attractions and accommodations visitors should check out the **Mystic Tourist and Information Center,** Bldg. 1d in Old Mystick Village, off Rte. 27. (☎536-1641. Open M-Sa 9am-6pm, Su 10am-5pm.) It is almost impossible to find budget-friendly lodgings in Mystic, and pricier offerings need to be reserved well in advance. **Post Office:** 23 E. Main St. (☎536-8143; open M-F 8am-5pm, Sa 8:30am-12:30pm). **ZIP code:** 06355. **Area code:** 860.

EASTERN CANADA

> ## HIGHLIGHTS OF EASTERN CANADA
>
> **FOOD.** Fresh seafood abounds, particularly on Prince Edward Island (p. 165). Delicious *québécois* cuisine fills the restaurants of Québec City, QC (p. 181).
>
> **COASTAL TOWNS.** Buy "cheese" in the photo-opportune towns of Yarmouth, NS (p. 157) and Fundy, NB (p. 163).
>
> **NIGHTLIFE.** Québec offers up terrific nightlife opportunities in Montréal (p. 168). What's more, the drinking age is a mere 18.
>
> **TORONTO.** Ethnic neighborhoods and fabulous museums provide fodder for long days of exploration (p. 186).

NOVA SCOTIA

Around 1605, French colonists joined the indigenous Micmac Indians in the Annapolis Valley and on the shores of Cape Breton Island. During the American Revolution, Nova Scotia declined the opportunity to become the 14th American state, establishing itself as a refuge for fleeing British loyalists. Subsequent immigration waves infused Pictou and Antigonish Counties with a Scottish flavor. As a result of these multinational immigrants, Nova Scotia's population is a cultural "mixed salad." This diversity is complemented by the province's four breathtaking geographies: the rugged Atlantic coast, the lush Annapolis Valley, the calm Northumberland Strait, and the magnificent highlands of Cape Breton Island.

⚡ PRACTICAL INFORMATION

Capital: Halifax.
Visitor Info: Tourism Nova Scotia, P.O. Box 519, Halifax B3J 2R7 (☎902-425-5781 or 800-565-0000; www.explore.gov.ns.ca).
Drinking Age: 19.
Postal Abbreviation: NS. **Harmonized Sales Tax:** 15% GST.

 All prices in this chapter are listed in Canadian dollars unless otherwise noted.

ATLANTIC COAST
☎902

LIGHTHOUSE ROUTE
Nova Scotia's **Lighthouse Route** (Hwy. 3) extends south of Halifax and continues along the Atlantic Coast the whole way to Yarmouth, linking coastal villages. Here, dilapidated fishing boats and lobster traps are tools of a trade, not just props for tourists. Blue signs with lighthouse symbols clearly mark the route's twists and turns. The main draw at **Peggy's Cove,** located off Hwy. 333, 43km southwest of Halifax, is the lighthouse-turned-post office that sits atop an enormous peninsula of rocks; tourists crawl like ants on its smooth surface. Picturesque houses bespeckle a rocky highland landscape as mammoth gulls flap about. The town recently stepped into the limelight when local fishermen bravely weathered the sea and fog in their own vessels to search for survivors of the 1998 Swissair flight 111 plane crash. Early arrivals miss the crowds, and early birds wake up with $2 espresso and $1 fresh cookies at **Beales Bailiwick.** (☎823-2099. Open Apr.-Nov. daily 9am-8pm.)

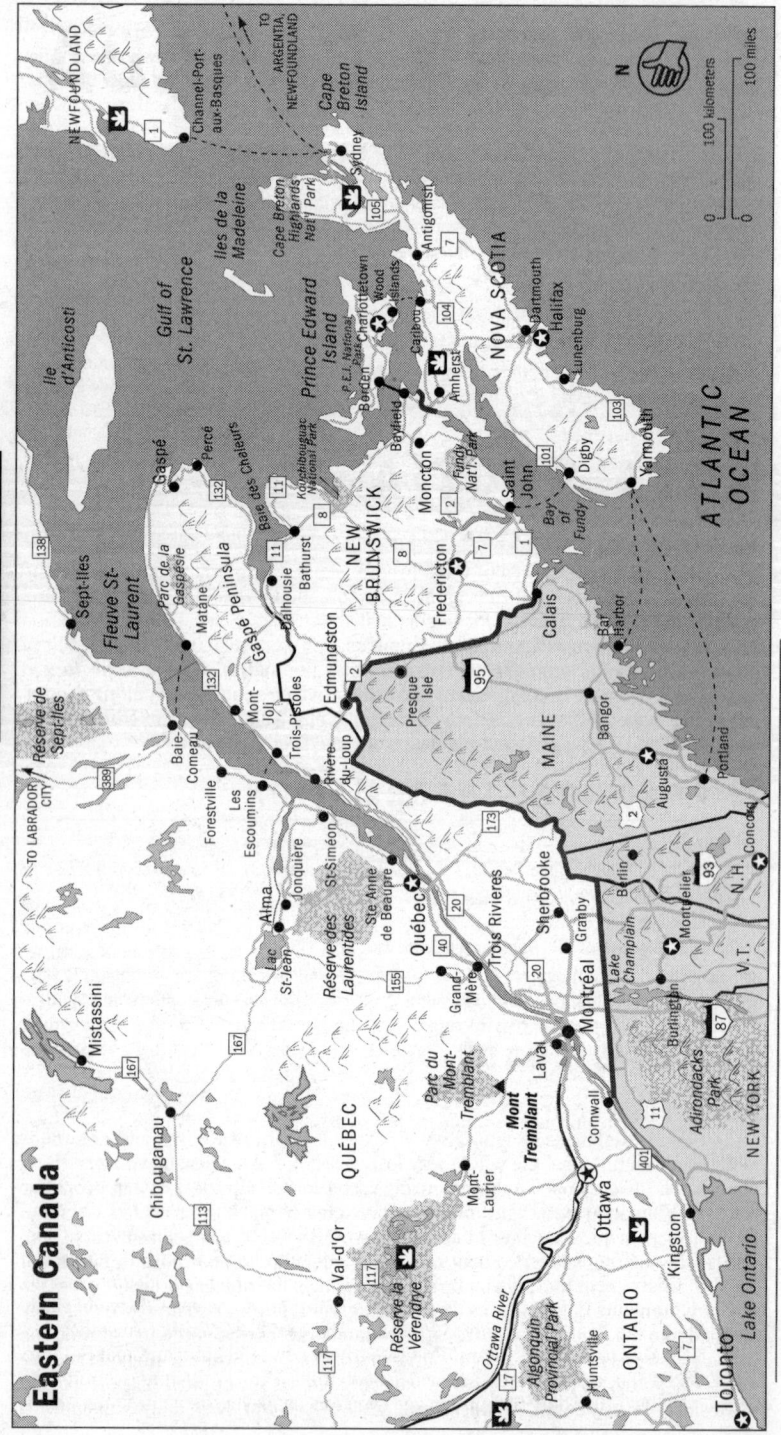

Eastern Canada

N

100 kilometers
100 miles

NEWFOUNDLAND

TO ARGENTIA, NEWFOUNDLAND

1

Channel-Port-aux-Basques

Cape Breton Island

Sydney

106

Cape Breton Highlands Nat'l Park

Iles de la Madeleine

Antigonish

7

Dartmouth

Halifax

Lunenburg

NOVA SCOTIA

Gulf of St. Lawrence

Ile d'Anticosti

Prince Edward Island

Charlottetown

P.E.I. National Park

Wood Islands

104

Caribou

Amherst

103

Digby

Yarmouth

ATLANTIC OCEAN

Gaspé

Percé

132

Borden

Springhill

101

Bay of Fundy

Fundy Nat'l Park

Saint John

Parc de la Gaspésie

Matane

Gaspé Peninsula

11

Bathurst

8

Moncton

2

Fredericton

7

St. Andrews

Digby

Baie des Chaleurs

Dalhousie

11

Kouchibouguac National Park

NEW BRUNSWICK

8

1

Bar Harbor

138

Sept-Iles

Fleuve St-Laurent

132

Mont-Joli

Trois-Pistoles

Rivière-du-Loup

Edmundston

2

Presque Isle

95

Calais

Bangor

Portland

Réserve de Sept-Iles

Baie-Comeau

Forestville

Les Escoumins

173

MAINE

Augusta

2

TO LABRADOR CITY

389

Alma

Jonquière

St-Siméon

Ste-Anne de Beaupré

Sherbrooke

Granby

Berlin

93

N.H.

Concord

Mistassini

167

Lac St-Jean

Réserve des Laurentides

Québec

20

Trois-Rivières

20

Montpelier

V.T.

167

155

Grand-Mère

Laval

Montréal

Lake Champlain

Burlington

87

Chibougamau

QUÉBEC

Parc du Mont-Tremblant

Mont Tremblant

Cornwall

Adirondacks Park

NEW YORK

113

Val-d'Or

Mont-Laurier

11

117

Réserve la Vérendrye

117

Ottawa River

Ottawa

401

Kingston

Lake Ontario

117

17

Algonquin Provincial Park

Huntsville

ONTARIO

7

Toronto

MAHONE BAY

Offering a few more tourist amenities is the slightly larger coastal town of Mahone Bay; take Hwy. 333 W to Hwy. 3 and head west for about 90km. The **Tourist Office** is at 165 Edgewater St. (☎ 624-6151. Open July-Aug. daily 9am-7pm; May and Oct. 10am-5pm; June and Sept. 10am-6pm.) The **Wooden Boat Festival** (☎ 624-0347), a celebration of the region's heritage, happens in early August. It includes a boat-building contest and race, and a parade of old-style schooners. Avast, ye scurvy dog! **Mug & Anchor Pub,** 634 Main St., in the Mader's Wharf complex, tames a mate's appetite for seafood (fish and chips $8) and draft beer. (☎ 624-6378. Open daily 11am-9:30pm; bar open Su-Th 11am-midnight, F-Sa 11am-1am. Beer pints $4.70.)

LUNENBURG

Dark-trimmed Victorian houses and occasional German flags hint at Lunenburg's status as Canada's oldest German settlement and a UNESCO World Heritage Site. The town may be better known for producing the undefeated racing schooner **Bluenose,** which now adorns the Canadian dime and Nova Scotia's license plate. Explore ocean-going history at the **Fisheries Museum of the Atlantic,** on Bluenose Dr. by the harbor front. (☎ 634-4794. Open mid-May to mid-Oct. daily 9:30am-5:30pm; call for winter hours. $7, seniors $5.50, ages 6-17 $2.) Several B&Bs dot the roadsides in this area, but prices hover around $55 for singles and $65 for doubles. Call the **Tourist Office,** in the blockhouse on Blockhouse Hill Rd., for info on lodgings. (☎ 634-8100 or 634-3656. Open July-Sept. daily 9am-8pm; May-June and Oct. 8am-6pm.) For cheap sleeping, stay at the **Lunenburg Board of Trade** campgrounds by the Tourist Office. (☎ 634-8100. 55 sites. $18.50, with hookup $23-24.)

OVENS NATURAL PARK

Steeped in lore that extends from Native Canadian legends to tales of the Nova Scotia Gold Rush, ⚑**Ovens Natural Park** has an almost spiritual quality, marred only by efforts to package it for tourists. The park features a trail along a cliff to a set of natural sea caves (the "ovens" from which the area takes its name) and the region's best **campground.** Overlooking the ocean, amenities include access to free hot showers, a heated swimming pool, flush toilets, a restaurant, and a store. The camp also offers boat tours ($18, ages 6-12 $14) of the nearby caves. (☎ 766-4621. Open May-Oct. Check-in before dusk. 65 sites. $20, with water and electricity $23, full hookup $28-35. Private cottages from $50. Park admission $5; seniors and ages 5-12 $3.)

LAHAVE

Hwy. 332 continues along the shore and into the town of **East LaHave,** where a **cable ferry** runs across the LaHave River to LaHave. (Every 30min. 7am-11pm, by demand 11pm-7am. $3 per car or person.) There is no actual ferry terminal, just a small turnoff from the road with a sign, so be on the lookout. The **LaHave Marine Hostel (HI-C),** above the **LaHave Bakery,** is run by the bakery proprietor. A homey apartment with a wood-burning stove, the hostel overlooks the river, has eight beds, and offers kitchen and laundry facilities ($1). Forego cooking for yourself and try some delicious cheese and herb bread ($2.75) downstairs. Call ahead or arrive during bakery hours. (☎ 688-2908. Bakery open daily 9am-7pm; mid-Sept. to June 10am-5pm. Hostel open June-Oct. Dorms $12, nonmembers $14.)

YARMOUTH

The port of Yarmouth, 339km from Halifax on the southwestern tip of Nova Scotia, has a major **ferry terminal,** 58 Water St., where boats set out across the Bay of Fundy to Maine (open daily 8am-5pm). Life here seems to revolve around the ferries. **Bay Ferries** (☎ 742-6800 or 888-249-7245) provides service to Bar Harbor, ME. (2½hr.; 2 per day; US$58, seniors US$53, ages 5-12 US$29; car US$95, bike US$25. Reservations recommended. Car prices do not include driver/passenger.) **Prince of Fundy Cruises** sail 11hr. from Yarmouth to Portland, ME. (☎ 800-341-7540. Cruise departs daily May to mid-Oct. 10am. Prices: early May to mid-June and mid-Sept. to mid-Oct. US$60, ages 5-14 US$30; car US$80, bike US$7; mid-June to mid-Oct. US$80/$40/$98/$10. Add US$3 passenger tax.) **Avis** can rent you a car at 42 Starr's

EASTERN CANADA

Rd., and at a desk in the ferry terminal. (☎742-3323. $30-60 per day with 200 free km, 15¢ each additional km. Reserve ahead; must be 21+.) The **Visitors Center,** 228 Main St., uphill and visible from the ferry terminal, houses both **Nova Scotia Information** (☎742-5033) and **Yarmouth Town and County Information.** (☎742-6639. Both open May to mid-Oct.; hours vary.) The **Ice House Hostel** and adjacent **Churchill Mansion Inn** overlook Darling Lake, 15km from Yarmouth on Hwy. 1 E. Take Old Post Rd. on the left; the hostel and inn are on your right. Seven beds are split between the hostel and a cabin outside the inn. Guests have access to all inn facilities. (☎649-2818. Open May-Nov. Shared bath. Pickup from ferry upon special request. Laundry, Internet access. Dorms $10 or US$7. Reservations recommended.) **Area code:** 902.

HALIFAX   ☎902

Once upon a time there was a little peninsula in Nova Scotia. And on that peninsula there stood a hill, and upon that hill was built a star-shaped fortress that became a strategic stronghold for the British in their ongoing skirmishes with the French. This Halifax Citadel, finished in 1749, took 28 years to complete. Today, this buzzing seaport city attracts droves of linen-clad wayfarers in search of maritime souvenirs. Despite being Eastern Canada's largest city and having first-rate nightlife, Halifax is manageable, tree-filled, and laid-back.

◩️ ORIENTATION AND PRACTICAL INFORMATION. The major north-south thoroughfare, **Barrington St.,** runs straight through downtown. Approaching the Citadel and the Public Garden, Sackville St. cuts east-west parallel to Spring Garden Rd., Halifax's shopping thoroughfare. Downtown is flanked by the less affluent North End and the mostly quiet and arboreal South End, on the ocean. Traffic is light, and parking is available by the waterfront for $3-7. **VIA Rail,** 1161 Hollis St. (☎494-7920 or 800-561-3952; open daily 9am-5:30pm), at South St. in the South End near the harbor, runs trains to Montréal ($146, students $127) and Québec City ($173/$116). **DRL Bus Lines** and **Acadian Lines** share a terminal at 6040 Almon St. (☎454-9321; open daily 6:30am-7pm), near Robie St.; take bus #7 or 80 on Robie St. DRL travels down the coast to Yarmouth (6hr., 1-2 per day, $51). Acadian covers most of the remainder of Nova Scotia and Canada: Annapolis Royal (3-5hr., 1 per day, $31); Charlottetown, P.E.I. (8½hr., 1-2 per day, $60); and North Sydney (6-8hr., 2 per day, $56). Students receive a 10% discount, seniors 25%, ages 5-11 50%. For public transportation, **Metro Transit** is efficient and thorough; maps and schedules are available at any Visitors Center. (☎490-6600. Fare $1.65, seniors and ages 5-15 $1.15, under 5 free. Buses run daily roughly 6am-11pm. Bus info M-F 7:30am-10pm.) **FRED (Free Rides Everywhere Downtown)** operates during the summer daily 11am-6pm (☎423-3848; www.downtownhalifax.ns.ca). **Dartmouth/Woodside-Halifax Ferry,** on the harbor front, departs every 15-30min. (☎490-6600. June-Sept. M-F 6:30am-11:30pm, Sa 6:30am-11:30pm, Su noon-6pm; Oct.-May no Su service. Same fares as Metro Transit.) **Halifax International Visitors Center:** 1595 Barrington St. (☎490-5946. Open daily 8:30am-8pm; off-season M-F 8:30am-4:30pm. Free Internet access.) **Hotlines: Sexual Assault,** ☎425-0122. **Crisis Centre,** ☎421-1188. Both 24hr. **Royal Canadian Mounted Police:** ☎426-1323. **Post Office:** 1680 Bedford Row (☎494-4000; open M-F 7:30am-5:15pm). **Postal code:** B3K 5M9. **Area code:** 902.

▝ ACCOMMODATIONS. Affordable summer accommodations come easy, but popular ones, like the universities and the hostel, are usually booked. Expect snafus during major events, such as the Tattoo Festival (see **Entertainment,** below). The **Halifax Heritage House Hostel (HI-C),** 1253 Barrington St., is a three-minute walk from the heart of downtown. Behind the brick facade is a newly renovated hostel with a high-ceilinged TV room, kitchen, laundry facilities, and four- to eight-bed dorms. (☎422-3863. Office open 7am-1am. Parking $5. Check-in after 2pm. Dorms $18, nonmembers $23.) Just a short distance from pubs and clubs, **St. Mary's University,** 923 Robie St., has hundreds of rooms in the summer. (☎420-5049 or 420-5485. Free linen, towels, and local calls. Open May-Aug.; call for reservations. Singles $28;

doubles $43.) **Dalhousie University,** 6136 University Ave., also has a large selection of summer housing options with linen, towels, Internet access, and use of gym facilities. (☎494-8840. Open May-Aug.; call ahead for reservations and directions. Singles $37, students $25; doubles $56/$43. Prices include tax.) **Laurie Provincial Park,** 25km north of Halifax on Hwy. 2, offers rustic campsites on Grand Lake. (☎861-1623. Open June-Sept. No showers. Check-in before dusk. Sites $10.)

🍴 **FOOD.** Dozens of downtown restaurants double as nightspots come dusk. Grab a bite before 9 or 10pm, as most places close their doors or kitchens when the sun goes down; then, let the drinking begin. **Granite Brewery,** at 1222 Barrington St., produces three of their own microbrewed beer labels and tasty pub food. The "Peculiar" brew (pints $5.50) is a sweet, smooth complement to the hearty $5.25 beef-and-beer stew. (☎423-5660. Open M-Sa 11:30am-1am, Su noon-11:30pm.) At **Mediterraneo Restaurant,** 1571 Barrington St., students and civilians gather over Middle Eastern dishes. (☎423-4403. Open M-Sa 7am-10pm, Su 7am-9pm. Falafel sandwich $4-5, full breakfast served until closing for $2.50-5.) For great food in a casual, fun atmosphere, try **The Atrium,** 1740 Argyle St., which is also a popular nightspot. (☎422-5453. Open M-Tu 11am-2am, W-Su 11am-3:30am. Kitchen closes at 9pm. Seafood dishes around $6-8, daily specials $6-7. Famous 15¢ wings daily 4-9pm.)

📷 **SIGHTS.** Stroll up to the star-shaped **Halifax Citadel National Historical Park,** in the heart of Halifax on Sackville St., and the old **Town Clock,** at the foot of **Citadel Hill,** for a fine view of the city and harbor. A one-hour film tells the history of the British fortress. Come any day at noon to see the preparation for the **noonday cannon firing.** Guided tours lasting 45min. are the best way to take in the little known stories about the fort's history; call for schedule. (☎426-5080. Open mid-June to early Sept. daily 9am-6pm; early Sept. to mid-Oct. and mid-May to mid-June 9am-5pm. In summer $6, seniors $4.50, ages 6-16 $3, family $14.75. Parking $2.75. Nov.-Apr. free.)

The **Halifax Public Gardens,** across from the Citadel near the intersection of South Park and Sackville St., are ideal for strolling, snoozing, or picnicking. The Roman statues, Victorian bandstand, gas lamps, exquisite horticulture, and overfed loons on the pond are all properly British. From July through September, watch for concerts on Sunday afternoons at 2pm. (☎424-4248. Open daily 8am-sunset.)

The 186 car-free wooded acres that comprise **Point Pleasant Park** at the southern tip of Halifax (take bus #9 from Barrington St. downtown) remain one of England's last imperial holdings, leased to the city of Halifax for 999 years at the bargain rate of one shilling per year. Inside the park, the **Prince of Wales Martello Tower,** an odd fort built by the British in 1797, honors Prince Edward's obsession with round buildings—with no corners, there's no place for ghosts to hide. (☎426-5080. Tower open July-Sept. daily 10am-6pm.) A little farther from downtown, **The Dingle** or **Sir Sandford Fleming Park** on Dingle Rd. provides ocean access for escaping the occasionally scorching summer heat. But if you're really *hot* (wink wink), go to **Crystal Crescent Beach,** off Hwy. 349, Halifax's clothing-optional locale.

> **BOOM.** What do you get when you cross 200 tons of TNT, a few barrels of butane, a hell of a lot of picric acid, and a lone spark? On Dec. 6, 1917, the citizens of Halifax discovered the answer—the biggest boom before the Atomic Age. Tragically, over 2000 people lost their lives when *Mont Blanc,* a French ship heavy with acid and TNT, collided with *Imo,* a Belgian relief ship. Both vessels began to burn, luring hapless spectators to the docks. An hour later, the explosion leveled 132 hectares (325 acres) of the city. The **Maritime Museum of the Atlantic** has an exhibit and short film on the explosion. (*1675 Lower Water St.* ☎424-7490. *Open M-Sa 9:30am-5:30pm, Su 1-5:30pm. In winter, open Tu-Sa 8:30am-5pm, Su 1-5pm. June to late Oct. $6, seniors $5, ages 6-17 $2; family $15. Late Oct. to May 31 free.*)

EASTERN CANADA

⚞⚟ ENTERTAINMENT AND NIGHTLIFE. The **Neptune Theater,** 1593 Argyle St., presents the area's most noteworthy professional stage productions. (☎429-7070. Box office open Tu-Sa 9am-9pm, Su 11am-9pm. Tickets $18-33, student and senior discounts.) **The Nova Scotia International Tattoo Festival** is Halifax's biggest summer event. The festival runs from June 28 to July 7, and features military groups and international performers; at noon, the Metro area fills with free entertainment. At 7:30pm, a two-hour show begins in the Metro Centre. (☎420-1114, ticket info 451-1221. Tickets $18-29, seniors and under 13 $10-22.) The **Atlantic Jazz Festival** (☎492-2225 or 800-567-5277) jams for a week in mid-July with ticketed and free concerts. From Sept. 13-23, street performers display random talents from magic tricks to chalk art at **Buskerfest** (☎429-3910). At the end of September, the **Atlantic Film Festival** (☎422-3456) shows Canadian and international films. The **Halifax Event Line** (☎451-1202) and **Civic Events and Festivals Line** (☎490-6776, ext. 2) offer info.

Halifax boasts an intoxicating nighttime scene—the pub per capita ratio is "the highest in Canada," which makes bar-hopping common and easy. The free *Coast* lists special goings-on. **The Dome** (that's "the Liquordome" to locals), 1740 Argyle St., is a four-club establishment that offers dining by day, and attracts a twenty- and thirty-something crowd to party at nightfall. (☎422-6907. Cover $3-6. Open nightly 11pm-4am.) The **Seahorse Tavern,** 1665 Argyle St., is the oldest tavern in Nova Scotia. Purple-haired students chat with paralegals in a dark basement room with carved woodwork and benches aplenty. (☎423-7200. Open M-W noon-1am, Th-Sa noon-2am.) Amid nautical decor, the **Lower Deck** in the Historic Properties region on Upper Water St., offers excellent Irish folk music. (☎425-1501. Cover $2-5. Open daily 11am-12:30am.) Huge and always packed, **Peddler's Pub,** in Barrington Place Mall on Granville St., is a favorite for good pub food. (☎423-5033. Open M-Sa 11am-10:30pm, Su 11am-8pm. Wings $5; steamed mussels $4.50.) The city's hottest gay spot and best sound system are both inside **Reflections Cabaret,** 5184 Sackville St. (☎422-2957), where pounding bass overtakes dancers' heartbeats nightly until 4am.

CAPE BRETON ISLAND ☎902

Located north of Halifax and set against the awesome canvas of the Atlantic Ocean, Cape Breton Island offers wonderful vistas and overflows with Acadian and Gaelic heritage. To top it all off, the impressive mountains and valleys of Cape Breton Highlands National Park accentuate the Island's natural grandeur.

⚟ PRACTICAL INFORMATION. The **Port Hastings Visitor Information Centre,** just up the hill from the Canso Causeway in Port Hastings, hands out info on the area. Be sure to pick up a copy of *Dreamers and Doers* to find out the latest happenings. (☎625-4201. Open mid-May to June and Sept. to mid-Oct. daily 9am-5pm, July and Aug. 8:30am-8:30pm.) **Acadia Bus Lines,** 99 Terminal Rd. in Sydney (☎564-5533), runs buses to Halifax (6hr., 2 per day, $40-60). Even though Cape Breton lacks any public transportation, there are a number of privately-owned (read: expensive) **shuttle services** from which to choose; check the *Cape Breton Post* and the Visitors Centre for listings. **Taxi:** Guy's Taxi, ☎625-1434. **Post Office:** 11 Lover's Ln. (☎625-1677; open M-F 8:30am-5pm, Sa 9am-2pm). **Postal code:** B9A 1N2. **Area code:** 902.

⚞⚟ ACCOMMODATIONS AND FOOD. To avoid the pricey bed and breakfasts on the island, head straight to the town of Mabou. The **■Mabou River Hostel and Guesthouse (HI-C),** 19 Mabou Ridge Rd., is a little bit hostel and a lotta home; the gracious owners keep the accommodations immaculate and welcoming. With its restaurant, hair salon, and bike and kayak rental, the Mabou exceeds the expectations of even the most demanding hostelers. Also included are the usual hostel facilities: kitchen, parking, laundry, full continental breakfast ($3), and Internet access. (☎945-2356 or 888-627-9744. Check-in 2-10pm. $18, nonmembers $22; private rooms $42; doubles with shared bath $48.) For a taste of standard pub food and rich music, head to the **Red Shoe Pub,** just down the street from the hostel. Locals and visitors alike cram in to see live performances nightly. (☎945-2626. Occasional cover charge depending on the entertainment. Open W-Su noon-1am, M-Tu noon-11pm;

kitchen open daily noon-9pm.) A trip to Cape Breton would be incomplete without sampling the area's seafood. At **Baddeck Lobster Suppers,** 17 Ross St., the famished can fill themselves to the gills with fresh Atlantic lobster and seafood chowder. (☎295-3307. Open June-Oct. daily 4-9pm.)

◖▢ SIGHTS AND ENTERTAINMENT. Cape Breton's greatest strength and most appealing quality is its natural splendor. By car, the best way to take in the surrounding scenery is on the ▣**Cabot Trail.** With its fair share of awe-inspiring moments, the drive winds along steep rocky cliffs by the coast and takes as much as two days to complete. A worthy stop along the Trail is the area of Baddeck on Hwy. 105 North of Port Hastings. Here, at the **Alexander Graham Bell Museum,** 559 Chebacto St., visitors can learn about the creative genius of the "queerest man fooling around the live-long day," as his neighbors here once referred to him. The museum delves into Bell's personal life and work with the deaf. (☎ 295-2069. Open June daily 9am-6pm, July and Aug. 8:30am-7:30pm, Sept. to mid-Oct. 8:30am-6pm, mid-Oct. through May 9am-5pm. $4.25, seniors $3.25, students and youth $2.25.) Another valuable diversion off the Trail is **Meat Cove,** a fishing village which serves as a prime spot for whale watching and picnicking. In the Acadian village of **Chéticamp,** on the western coast of the island, amateur art collectors can procure pieces of the traditional folk art For those more interested in critiquing art rather than buying it, **Les Trois Pignons,** 15584 Main St., displays some of the finest local works. (☎ 222-2642. Open July and Aug. daily 8am-6pm, off-season 9am-5pm. $3.)

CAPE BRETON HIGHLANDS NATIONAL PARK

While driving in the area is breathtaking, exploring the national park area on foot or bike will reveal mountain passes, steep descents, and rocky coastal vistas that will dwarf visitors in their grand majesty. There are 27 hiking and walking trails ranging from 20min. family strolls to challenging overnight adventures. The **Skyline Loop** is an especially popular trail of intermediate difficulty, and known for moose sightings. **Black Brook Beach** is a gorgeous spot to stop for lunch or relax in the sun. ($3.50, $2.50 seniors, $1.50 students and children, under 7 free, families $8.) The park also has six serviced **campgrounds** and two wilderness grounds, each with 10-20 sites ($15-21). There are two **Visitors Centers,** one located at the entrance to the park in the east at Ingonish, and the other at the entrance just beyond Chéticamp on the west coast. (Ingonish: ☎285-2866; Chéticamp: ☎224-3403. Both open June-Aug. daily 8am-8pm, Sept.-Oct. and mid-May to June 9am-5pm.)

NEW BRUNSWICK

Powerful South Indian Ocean currents sweep around the tip of Africa and ripple thousands of kilometers through the Atlantic before coming to a spectacular finish at New Brunswick. The Bay of Fundy witnesses the world's highest tides, which can ebb and flow through a staggering 48-foot cycle. Away from the ocean's violent influence, vast unpopulated stretches of forest swathe the land in timeless wilderness. In the 17th century, French pioneers established the farming and fishing nation of *l'Acadie* on the northern and eastern coasts. Later, British Loyalists, fleeing in the wake of the American Revolution, settled on the shores of the bay. After complaining about the distant government in Halifax, the colonists were granted self-government by the Crown, and New Brunswick was born. Over a third of the province's population is French-speaking, but English is more widely used.

⑦ PRACTICAL INFORMATION

Capital: Fredericton.

Visitor Info: Dept. of Economic Development and Tourism, P.O. Box 6000, Fredericton E3B 5C3 (☎658-6622). Call **Tourism New Brunswick** (☎800-561-0123) from anywhere in Canada.

Postal Abbreviation: NB. **Drinking Age:** 19. **Harmonized Sales Tax:** 15%. **Area Code:** 506.

SAINT JOHN ☎ 506

The city of Saint John (never abbreviated to distinguish it from St. John's, Newfoundland) was founded literally overnight on May 18, 1783, by the United Empire Loyalists, a band of about 10,000 American colonists holding allegiance to the British crown. But the town's remarkable history is a mere detail to the thousands who flock here just to witness the Bay of Fundy's tides and the "Reversing Falls."

■ ▣ **ORIENTATION AND PRACTICAL INFORMATION.** Saint John's downtown is bounded by **Union St.** to the north, **Princess St.** to the south, **King Sq.** to the east, and **Market Sq.** and the harbor to the west. Fort Latour Harbor Bridge (toll 25¢) on Hwy. 1 links Saint John to West Saint John, as does a free bridge on Hwy. 100. **Via Rail** (☎ 857-9830) has a station in Moncton; take an SMT bus from Saint John. **SMT,** 300 Union St. (☎ 648-3500), buses to Moncton (2hr., 2-4 per day, $23); Montréal (14hr., 2 per day, $94); and Halifax (6-6½hr., 5 per week, $65). Station open daily 7:30am-9pm. **Saint John Transit** runs until roughly 12:30am. (☎ 658-4700. Fare $1.75, under 15 $1.45.) Late June to early October, 2hr. tour of historic Saint John leaves from Barbours General Store at Loyalist Plaza, Reversing Falls, and Rockwood Park Campsite ($15, ages 6-14 $5). **NFL Bay Ferries** (☎ 888-249-7245) on Lancaster St. (follow ferry signs after Exit 109 from Hwy. 1), crosses to Digby, NS (3hr.; 2-3 per day; $30, seniors $25, ages 5-12 $15, cars $60). The **City Center Information Center,** at Market Sq., has info. (☎ 658-2855. Open daily 9am-8pm, Sept.-May 9am-6pm.) **Parking:** Reasonably priced lots are located at Water St. and Chipman Hill; free streetside parking can be found outside of downtown. **Taxis: Century Taxi,** ☎ 696-6969. **Post Office:** Station B, 41 Church Ave. W., in West Saint John. (☎ 672-6704. Open M-F 8am-5pm.) **Postal code:** E2L 3W9. **Area Code:** 506.

▐ **ACCOMMODATIONS.** There are number of nearly identical motels on the 1100 to 1300 blocks and then farther along on the 1700 block of **Manawagonish Rd.** in the western part of town. (Singles $35-50.) Saint John Transit has bus directions (see **Practical Information,** above); by car, avoid the 25¢ bridge toll by taking Hwy. 100 into West Saint John, turn right on Main St., and head west until it turns into Manawagonish Rd. The rooms at the **Saint John YMCA/YWCA (HI-C),** 19-25 Hazen Ave., are clean and unremarkable. Access to recreational facilities, pool, and workout room is included. From Market Sq., head two blocks up Union St.; the hostel is on the left. (☎ 634-7720. Laundry. Key Deposit $10. Open daily 5am-11pm; guests arriving on evening ferry can check in later. Reservations recommended in summer. Singles $20, nonmembers $30.) The **University of New Brunswick at Saint John** on Tucker Park Rd. offers neat, furnished rooms a ten-minute drive from downtown. Take Somerset St. onto Churchill Blvd. and turn left onto Tucker Park Rd. (☎ 648-5768. Open May-Aug. Reception M-F 8am-4pm. Singles $29, students $18; doubles $42/$30.) Partially wooded tent sites at the **Rockwood Park Campground** are off Lake Drive S. in Rockwood Park. Take the "University" bus to Mt. Pleasant; follow the signs. (☎ 652-4050. Showers. Open May-Sept. Sites $15, with hookup $18; weekly $65/$95.)

▐ **FOOD.** The butcher, baker, fishmonger, produce dealer, and cheese merchant sell fresh goodies at **City Market,** 47 Charlotte St., between King and Brunswick Sq. The market may be the best place to get your daily **dulse,** sun-dried seaweed from the Bay of Fundy; it is best described as "ocean jerky." (☎ 658-2820. Open M-Th 7:30am-6pm, F 7:30am-7pm, Sa 7:30am-5pm.) **Billy's Seafood Company,** 49-51 Charlotte St., is scrumptious, though pricey. Fresh oysters (6 for $10) and fish and chips ($11) are superb; splurge for the lobster. (☎ 672-3474. Open M-Th 11am-10pm, F-Sa 11am-11pm, Su 4-10pm.) **Reggie's Restaurant,** 26 Germain St., is the local hub, providing homestyle North American fare. The plentiful breakfast special ($4.25) is served all day. (☎ 657-6270. Open M-Tu 6am-7pm, W-F 6am-8pm, Sa-Su 6am-6pm.)

◪ **SIGHTS.** Saint John's main attraction is the **Reversing Falls,** a natural phenomenon caused by the powerful Bay of Fundy tides (for more on the tides see **Fundy,** below). Though the name may suggest 100 ft. walls of gravity-defying water, the "falls" are actually beneath the surface of the water. Two hours before high tide, and again 2hr. after, patient spectators see the flow of water at the nexus of the Saint John River and Saint John Harbor slowly halt and change direction. More amazing than the event itself is the number of people captivated by it. The **Reversing Falls Tourist Center,** at the west end of the Hwy. 100 bridge (take the westbound "East-West" bus), distributes tide schedules and shows a 12min. film on the phenomenon. Thrill-seekers with a few extra dollars should ride the Reversing Falls in a jet boat tour for $25. (☎658-2937, tours 634-8987. Center open May-Oct. daily 8am-8pm. Screenings every 15min.; $1.75.) **Moosehead Breweries,** 89 Main St., in West Saint John, is the oldest independent brewery in Canada. (☎635-7000. 1hr. tours with samples mid-June to Aug. M-Th 1pm and 3pm. Tours limited to 20 people; make reservations 2-3 days in advance. Free.)

FUNDY NATIONAL PARK   ☎506

Twice each day, the world's largest tides withdraw over one kilometer into the Bay of Fundy, leaving a variety of aquatic lifeforms high and dry on a vast stretch of seashore. The dramatic contrast between the two tidescapes, and the rapidity with which the waters rise and fall (1m per 3min.), is enough to draw thousands of tourists each year to Fundy National Park. Located an hour's drive southeast of Moncton on Hwy. 114, the park occupies 260 square kilometers of New Brunswick's coast and offers exquisite campgrounds and recreation facilities, as well as a variety (wooded, oceanside, swampy, etc.) of hiking trails. Visits to the park in chillier September and October catch the fall foliage and avoid the crush of vacationers.

▸ PRACTICAL INFORMATION. Park Headquarters, P.O. Box 1001, Alma E4H 1B4, in the southeastern corner of the Park facing the Bay, includes the administration building and the **Visitors Center.** (☎887-6000. Open mid-Jun. to early Sept. daily 8am-10pm; mid-May to mid-June and early Sept. to early Oct. daily 8am-4:30pm, weekends until 5pm; in winter 8am-4:30pm, weekends 9am-4pm.) The other Visitors Center, **Wolfe Lake Information,** is at the northwest entrance off Hwy. 114. (☎432-6026. Open late June to early Sept. daily 10am-6pm.) No public transportation serves Fundy; the nearest bus depots are in Moncton and Sussex. (Entrance fee $3.50 per day, seniors $2.75, ages 6-16 $1.75; family $7.) The free and invaluable park newspaper *Salt and Fir*, available at the entrance stations and Visitors Centers, includes a map of hiking trails and campgrounds. **Weather info:** ☎887-6000.

▸ CAMPING AND ACCOMMODATIONS. The park operates four **campgrounds** totaling over 600 sites. Getting a site is seldom a problem, but landing one at your campground of choice may be a little more difficult; reservations are highly recommended. **Headquarters Campground,** closest to civilization with its washer and dryer, kitchen, shower, and playground, is usually in highest demand. (Open year-round. Sites $12, with hookup $19. Wheelchair accessible) **Chignecto North Campground,** off Hwy. 114, 5km inland from the headquarters, provides more private wooded sites. (Open mid-May to mid-Oct. Sites $13, with hookup $17-19. Partial wheelchair access.) **Point Wolfe Campground,** scenically located along the coast 7km west of headquarters, stays cooler and more insect-free than the inland campgrounds and has direct access to several beautiful oceanside hikes. (Open late June to early Sept. Sites $12). Year-round wilderness camping is also available in some of the most scenic areas of the park, especially **Goose River** along the coast. The campsites, all with fireplaces, wood, and an outhouse, take a $3 per person per night permit fee. Or opt for a degree of domestication while remaining burrowed within the park's splendor at the **Fundy National Park Hostel (HI-C),** near Devil's Half Acre about 1km south of the park headquarters. The 24-bed hostel has a full kitchen, showers, laundry facilities and a common room. (☎887-2216. Open June-Sept. Check-in 8-10am and 5-10pm. Dorms $12, nonmembers $17. Wheelchair accessible.)

▸ FOOD. Refuel with basic groceries or a home-cooked meal at **Harbor View Market and Coffee Shop,** 8598 Main St. in Alma. The breakfast special of two eggs, toast, bacon, and coffee runs $4.50. (☎887-2450. Open July-Aug. daily 7am-10pm.) A trip into Alma is more than worthwhile if only for a sticky bun ($1) from ▨**Kelly's Bake**

Shop, 8587 Main St. Replenish lost hiking calories (plus some!) with fresh baked bread, cookies, pies, and peanut butter balls. (☎887-2460. Open July-Aug. 7am-8pm, off-season 10am-5:30pm.) For seafood caught locally and hauled in daily, **Collins Lobster,** just behind Kelly's Bake Shop, is a well-known favorite. Its takeout lobster ($8 per lb. live, $8.75 cooked) is a fine catch. (☎887-2054. Open 10am-6pm daily.)

⚠ OUTDOOR ACTIVITIES. The park maintains 104km of trails year-round, about 35km of which are open to mountain bikes. Be sure to bring your own though—no rental outfits serve the island. *Salt and Fir* contains detailed descriptions of all trails, including where to find waterfalls and ocean views. Moose are most common along Hwy. 114 between Wolfe Lake and Caribou Plain. Hike the ◪**Caribou Plain Trail** (3½km loop) at dusk and you'll likely spot several dining in the swamps. Deer live throughout the park; thieving raccoons run thick. Peregrine falcons are harder to spot. Most recreational facilities operate only during the summer season (mid-May to early Oct.), and include free daily interpretive programs designed to help visitors get to know the park. The park staff leads beach walks and evening theatre and campfire gatherings, usually involving storytelling, forest education, and singing. For a fee, visitors can take a spooky nocturnal three-hour tour through the woods. (Tours held twice per week $12, children $8, family $33.)

MONCTON   ☎506

A small and unremarkable town on the surface, Moncton boasts a recently revived downtown and a couple of the most peculiar natural attractions found in all of Eastern Canada. The Petitcodiac River that flows through the center of Moncton is usually nothing more than red mud flats, but twice a day the tidal bore rushes in as two dramatic waves and raises the river by the rate of three meters per hour. This strange phenomenon can best be viewed near the end of Main St. at the suitably named, **Tidal Bore Park,** where tide schedules are available. Moncton, site of a huge Acadian settlement before many were expelled in 1758, traces its cultural heritage from 1604 to present at **The Acadian Museum,** located on the campus at Université de Moncton, the only Francophone university outside of Québec. (☎858-4088. Open M-F 10am-5pm, Sa-Su 1-5pm. $2, seniors and students $1.)

The Pump House, 5 Orange Ln., is a firehouse-themed brewery that churns out eight original beers on-site. Plenty of vegetarian options and the wood-fired brick oven pizza ($3-8) will quench any hunger. (☎855-2337. Open M-W 11am-midnight, Th 11am-1am, F-Sa 11am-2am, Su noon-midnight.) **Graffiti,** 897 Main St., designs good-sized portions of Greek and Mediterranean fare in a funky atmosphere. Popular souvlaki dishes and filet mignon shish kebabs are a bargain at $5-9. (☎382-4299. Open Su-Th 11am-11pm, F and Sa 11am-midnight.) For a hangout that has both a lively nightlife and a rejuvenating breakfast, head to **Doc Dylan's,** 841 Main St. (☎382-3627. Open daily 11am-2am, Sa-Su 10:30am-4pm.) Saturday morning early birds flock to the **Farmers Market** off Robinson St., where locals peddle everything from apples to hand-knit mittens. (☎383-1749. Open daily 7am-1pm.)

Although there are no registered hostels in Moncton, try the **Université de Moncton,** which rents rooms in the summer at two of its residences. (☎858-4008. Singles with shared bath $25-35, seniors and students $18-30.) By far the most common creature in the area is the bed and breakfast. The reasonably priced ◪**Downtown Bed & Breakfast,** 101 Alma St., with its sunroom and French toast breakfast, is clean, cozy, and charming. (☎855-7108. Towels, Internet. Singles $58; doubles $69. Off-season prices negotiable.) More intrepid travelers can try the sites at **Magnetic Hill Campground,** near the intersection of the Trans-Canada Hwy. and Mountain Rd. (☎384-0191. Open May through Oct. Showers and laundry. Sites $16.)

The **Tourist Information Center,** located in the City Hall Building at 655 Main St., gives the scoop on the area. (☎853-3590. Open late May to early Sept. daily 8:30am-8pm, off-season M-F 8:30am-4:30pm.) **SMT,** 961 Main St. (☎859-5060), on the corner of Bonnacord, runs buses to Saint John (2hr., 3 per day, $23); Halifax (4hr., 3 per day $45); and Montréal (9hr., 2 per day, $105). **Codiac Transit,** the local bus line,

MAGIC, MAGNETS, OR MIND GAME? Still a mystery after all these years, **Magnetic Hill,** at the corner of Mountain Rd. and Trans-Canada Hwy., wows visitors with its seemingly outright defiance of physics. Local folklore about Magnetic Hill began in 1933, when newspaper reporters watched their Ford Roadster roll uphill without them. Since then, the hill was recorded as having magnetic properties, and it was only recently that people began to acknowledge the optical illusion in effect. Though a bit hokey, the thrill of rolling "uphill" still puzzles the mind and is well worth the cost of $3 per car. (☎ 853-3540. Open late June to early Oct. daily 8pm-8pm.)

operates Monday through Saturday from 7am-6pm. (☎ 857-2008 for schedules and fares. Open M-F 6am-4:30pm. Call for additional hours on Th and F evenings.) **Bike Rental: Gary's,** 239 Weldon St. (☎ 855-2394), provides two-wheeled transportation for $25 per day. **Taxi: Air Cab** (☎ 857-2000), rides from the airport to town for $15. **Post Office:** 281 St. George St. (☎ 857-7240; open M-F 8am-5:30pm).

NEAR MONCTON: KOUCHIBOUGUAC NATIONAL PARK

Unlike Fundy's rugged forests and high tides, **Kouchibouguac National Park** (the name means "river of the long tides") features warm lagoon waters, salt marshes, peat bogs, and white sandy beaches. Bask in the sun along the 25km stretch of barrier islands and sand dunes, or float down canoe waterways. Rent canoes ($6 per hr., $30 per day), kayaks ($6 per hr., $30 per day), and bikes ($4 per hr., $26 per day) at **Ryans Rental Center** in the park between the South Kouchibouguac Campground and Kelly's Beach. (☎ 876-8918. Open June-Aug. daily 8am-9pm; May Sa-Su 8am-5pm.) The park runs two campgrounds in the summer. **South Kouchibouguac** has 311 sites with showers. (Late June to early Sept. $16.25; with hookup $22. Mid-May to late June and early Sept. to mid-Oct. $13/$18. Reservations recommended.) **Côte-à-Fabien** has 32 sites ($14), but no showers. Off-season campers stay at primitive sites within the park and campgrounds just outside the park. (Entrance fee $3.50, ages 6-16 $1.75.) The **Visitors Center** is at the park entrance on Hwy. 117 just off Hwy. 11, 90km north of Moncton. (☎ 876-2443. Open daily 8am-8pm; mid-Sept. to mid-June 9am-5pm. Park administration open year-round M-F 8am-4:30pm.)

PRINCE EDWARD ISLAND

Prince Edward Island, now more commonly called "P.E.I." or "the Island," began as St. John's Island. The name switch came in 1799, when residents renamed their home to honor Prince Edward, son of King George III, in response to his interest in the territory's welfare. The smallest province in Canada attracts most of its visitors thanks to the beauty made famous by Lucy Maud Montgomery's novel *Anne of Green Gables*. The fictional work did not exaggerate the wonders of natural life on the island; the soil, made red by its high iron-oxide content, contrasts with the green crops and shrubbery, turquoise waters, and purple roadside lupin. On the north and south shores are some of Canada's finest beaches. Relentlessly quaint island towns all over P.E.I. seem to exist more for visitors than for residents.

🛈 PRACTICAL INFORMATION

Charlottetown is the capital of P.E.I.; **Queen St.** and **University Ave.** are its main thoroughfares, straddling **Confederation Centre** on the west and east, respectively. The most popular beaches—**Cavendish, Brackley,** and **Rustico Island**—lie on the north shore in the middle of the province, opposite Charlottetown. The longest continuous marine span bridge in the world, **Confederation Bridge** meets P.E.I. at Borden-Carleton, 56km west of Charlottetown on Hwy. 1.

Ferries: Northumberland Ferry (☎888-249-7245 from P.E.I. and Nova Scotia), in Wood Islands 61km east of Charlottetown on Trans-Canada Hwy. To Caribou, NS (1¼hr.; 6-10 per day; pedestrians $11, seniors $9, vehicles $49).

Taxis: City Cab, ☎892-6567. Runs 24hr.

Bike Rental: MacQueens, 430 Queen St. (☎368-2453). Road and mountain bikes $25 per day, $100 per week; children half-price. Must have credit card or $75 deposit. Open M-Sa 8:30am-5:30pm, 10am-2pm.

Beach Shuttles: ☎566-3243. Picks up at the **P.E.I. Visitor Information Centre** at 178 Water St. and the hostel (call for additional points), and drops off in Cavendish (45min.; June and Sept. 2 per day, July-Aug. 4 per day; $10, same-day round-trip $18).

Visitor Info: P.E.I. Visitor Information Centre, P.O. Box 940, Charlottetown C1A 7M5 (☎368-4444 or 888-734-7529). Open June daily 8am-8pm; July-Aug. 8am-10pm; Sept. to mid-Oct. 9am-6pm; mid-Oct. to May M-F 9am-4:30pm.

Internet access: CyberDeck Cafe, 115 Queen St. (☎569-2787; open M-Sa 10am-midnight, Su noon-5pm).

Crisis Line: Crisis Centre, ☎566-8999. 24hr.

Drinking Age: 19.

Post Office: 135 Kent St. (☎628-4400), Charlottetown C1A 7N7. Open M-F 8am-5:15pm. **Postal abbreviation:** PEI. **Area code:** 902.

ACCOMMODATIONS

B&Bs and **country inns** crowd every nook and cranny of the province; some are open year-round, but the most inexpensive are closed off-season. Rates hover around $35-40 for singles and $50 for doubles, but you won't land those prices unless you call in advance. Many of the island's Visitors Centers, including Charlottetown's, display daily vacancy listings for the island's inns, B&Bs, campgrounds, and other accommodations. Fifteen farms participate in a provincial **Farm Vacation** program, in which tourists spend time with a farming family. (☎651-2620. Doubles from $35.)

The **Charlottetown International Hostel (HI-C),** 153 Mt. Edward Rd., across the yard from the University of P.E.I. (UPEI), is housed in a large green barn. Take Belvedere one long block east of University Ave., then turn left onto Mt. Edward Rd. (☎894-9696. Kitchen facilities, showers, TV lounge. Linen $1. Bike rental $15. Open June to early Sept. Check-in 7-10am and 4pm-midnight. Curfew midnight. Lockout 10am-4pm. Dorms $15.50, nonmembers $19.50.) Located off of Belvedere Rd., the **UPEI** runs a dorm-style B&B in Marian and Bernardine Halls, but lacks the Victorian frills. (Sept.-May ☎566-0486; June-Aug. ☎566-0442. Marian: July-Aug. singles $37, doubles $46.50; May-June $32/$39. Bernardine: $47/$53/$46/$48. Check-in for all locations at Bernardine Hall.) The **Midgell Centre,** right off of Rt. 2 in Morell, houses 60 people in its spacious barns. (☎961-2963. Open mid-June to mid-Sept. Kitchen, showers, lockers, linens, laundry. $15.)

Prince Edward Island National Park operates three campgrounds during the summer and one off-season. Reservations are strongly recommended, and must be made at least three days in advance. (☎800-414-6765 for reservations; info 672-6350 or 963-2391. In summer, 462 primitive sites with showers, toilets, kitchen access, laundry facilities $15-19; 110 sites with hookup $21. In winter, primitive sites $8.) **Cavendish Campground** has a beachside location—reservations are particularly handy. (Seasons vary, but expect to find a campground open mid-June to mid-Sept.) Privately-owned campgrounds fill the island and provide an alternative when campsites are unavailable at the national park (info available at Visitors Centers).

FOOD

The quest for food often boils down to the search for **lobster.** The coveted crustaceans start around $9 per lb. Fresh seafood, including world-famous **Malpeque oysters,** is sold along the shores of the island, especially in North Rustico on the north shore. The back of the *P.E.I. Visitor's Guide* lists fresh seafood outlets. The **Charlottetown Farmers Market**, on Belvedere Ave. opposite UPEI, sells the freshest fruits and veggies around in summer. (☎368-4444. Open July-Aug. W and Sa 9am-2pm; in winter Sa 9am-2pm.) The young clientele at **Beanz**, 52 University Ave., basks on a sunny terrace and washes down homemade sandwiches ($3-4) with great espresso. (☎892-8797. Open M-F 6:30am-6pm, Sa 8am-6pm, Su 9am-5pm.) **Shaddy's**, 44 University Ave., has lobsters (seasonal $20-24) and non-aquatic Lebanese and Canadian fare. (☎368-8886. Open daily 10am-9:30pm. Sandwiches $4-7.)

◐ SIGHTS

Green Gables House, off Hwy. 6 in Cavendish just west of Hwy. 13, is a shrine for adoring Lucy Maud Montgomery readers, a surprising number of whom are from Japan. The traditionally furnished house and its surroundings served as inspiration for this P.E.I. native's first novel; add a few sappy L.M. Montgomery films and memorabilia, and most visitors can't escape without purchasing a special edition copy of *Anne*, if not a commemorative thimble. Arrive in early morning or the evening to escape crowds. (☎963-3370. Open July-Aug. daily 9am-8pm; May-June and Sept.-Oct. 9am-5pm. $5, seniors $4, ages 6-16 $2.50, families $12. Off-season discounts.)

Prince Edward Island National Park consists of a 32km coastal strip embracing some of Canada's finest beaches. Wind-sculpted sand dunes and salt marshes undulate along the park's terrain. The park is home to many of the Island's 300-odd species of birds. (☎963-7830 or 963-7831. Campgrounds, programs, and services from early July to mid-Aug.) The stretches of beach on the **eastern coast** of P.E.I. are less touristed than those in the west, perhaps due to the rougher surf. **Lakeside,** a beach 35km east of Charlottetown on Hwy. 2, is unsupervised and often nearly deserted on summer weekdays. Trot along the surf atop a sturdy steed from **Gun Trail Ride,** located beside the golf course. (☎961-2076. Open June to early Sept. daily 9am-9pm. $10.) **Basin Head Beach,** 95km east of Charlottetown, makes a relaxing daytrip, with over 11km of unsupervised white sand. Celtic concerts are held throughout the summer at the ▧**College of Piping,** 619 Water St. E., in Summerside. Scottish *ceilidhs*, with bagpipes and traditional dance, happen Monday and Friday at 7pm. Call for a full schedule. (☎877-224-7473. $12, seniors $11, students and children $7.)

QUÉBEC

Home to 90% of Canada's French-speaking population, Québec continues to fight for political and legal recognition of its separate cultural identity. Originally populated by French fur trading settlements along the St. Lawrence River, Québec was ceded to the British in 1759. Ever since, anti-federalist elements within *québécois* society have rankled under control of the largely Anglicized national government. Visitors may be tipped off to the underlying struggles by the occasional cry for "Liberté!" scrawled across a building or sidewalk, but the tensions are mostly a focus behind closed doors in Ottawa. Instead, Montreal's renowned nightlife and Québec City's centuries-old European flair distinguish Québec among Canada's provinces.

◪ PRACTICAL INFORMATION

Capital: Québec City.

Visitor Info: Tourisme Québec, C.P. 979, Montréal H3C 2W3 (☎800-363-7777, in Montréal 514-873-2015; www.tourisme.gouv.qc.ca). Open daily 9am-5pm. **Canadian Parks Service,** Québec Region, 3 Passage du D'or, C.P. Box 6060, Haute-Ville GIR 4V7 (☎800-463-6769, in Québec City 418-648-4177).

Postal Abbreviation: QC. **Drinking Age:** 18.

Provincial Sales Tax: 7.5%, plus 7% GST.

EASTERN CANADA

MONTRÉAL ☎ 514

This island city, named for the royal mountain in its midst, has been coveted territory for over 300 years. Wars and sieges have brought governments in and out like the tide, including a brief takeover by American revolutionaries in late 1775. Despite, or perhaps as a result of, these conflicts, Montréal has grown into a diverse city with a cosmopolitan air. Although less than an hour from the US border, Montréal has grown to be the second largest French-speaking city in the world, and its European legacy is immediately evident. Fashion that rivals Paris, a nightlife comparable to London, and cuisine from around the globe all attest to this international influence. Whether you credit Montréal's global flavor or its large student population, it is hard not to be swept up by the vibrancy coursing through the *centre-ville*.

■ INTERCITY TRANSPORTATION

Airports: Dorval (info ☎394-7377; www.admtl.com), 25min. from downtown by car. From the Lionel Groulx Métro stop, take bus #211 to Dorval Train Station, then transfer to bus #204. **L'Aérobus** (☎931-9002) runs a minivan to Dorval from 777 rue de la Gauchetière, at University St., stopping at any downtown hotel if you call in advance. Vans run M-F every 20min. 5:20am-11pm, Sa-Su every 30min. $12, under 5 free. Taxi to downtown $30-35. A 2nd airport, **Mirabel International** (☎450-476-3010, info 800-465-1213), is 45min. from downtown by car. Taxi to downtown $60.

Trains: Central Station, 895 rue de la Gauchetière Ouest, under Queen Elizabeth Hotel. Métro: Bonaventure. Served by **VIA Rail** (☎989-2626 or 800-561-9181, in the US 800-842-7245; www.viarail.com). To: Québec City (3hr.; 3-4 per day; $51, seniors $46, students $33, ages 2-11 $26); Ottawa (2hr., 4 per day, $40/$36/$26/$20); and Toronto (4-5½hr., 6 per day, $97/$87/$63/$49). Discount tickets must be bought 5 or more days prior. Open daily 6am-9pm. **Amtrak** (☎800-842-7245) goes to New York (10hr., 1 per day, US$65) and Boston (13hr., 1 per day, US$115). Open daily 8am-5pm.

Buses: Voyageur, 505 bd. de Maisonneuve Est (☎842-2281). Métro: Berri-UQAM. To: Toronto (6¾hr.; 5 per day; $78, students $54); Ottawa (2½hr., 17-18 per day, $29); and Québec City (3hr., 15 per day, $40/$30). **Greyhound** (☎287-1580). To New York City (7½-8¾hr., 7 per day, $103.50) and Boston (7hr., 7 per day, $84).

Driver/Rider Service: Allo Stop, 4317 rue St-Denis (☎985-3032). Matches passengers with member drivers; part of the rider fee goes to the driver. To: Québec City ($15), Toronto ($26), Sherbrooke ($9), New York City ($50), and Boston ($42). Riders and drivers fix their own fees for rides over 1000 mi. Annual membership fee required ($6, drivers $7). Open daily 9am-6pm.

▐ LOCAL TRANSPORTATION

Public Transit: STCUM Métro and Bus (☎288-6287). Safe and extremely efficient. The 4 Métro lines and most buses operate daily 5:30am-12:30am; some have early morning schedules as well. Get maps at the tourist office or any Métro station booth. Buses are well-integrated; transfer tickets from bus drivers are valid as subway tickets, and vice versa. Fare for train or bus $2, 6 tickets $8.50. 1-day unlimited tourist pass $5, 3-day $14; weekly $13.50. Passes sold at any downtown Métro station.

Taxis: Taxi Pontiac, ☎761-5522. **Champlain Taxi Inc.,** ☎273-2435.

Car Rental: Via Route, 1255 rue MacKay (☎871-1166), at Ste-Catherine. Rates from $40 per day; special 4hr. rental $25. Must be 21+ with credit card. Open M-F 7am-7pm, Sa 7:30am-5pm, Su 9am-9pm.

Bike Rental: Cycle Pop, 1000 rue Rachel Est (☎526-2525). Métro: Mont-Royal. 21-speeds $20 per day, $40 per weekend. Open M-W 10am-6pm, Th-F 10am-9pm, Sa-Su 9am-5pm. Credit card or $250 deposit required.

✦ ORIENTATION

Two major streets divide the city, making orientation convenient. The one-way **bd. St-Laurent** (also called **"The Main"**) runs north through the city, splitting Montréal and its streets east-west. The Main also serves as the unofficial French/English divider; English **McGill University** lies to the west, while slightly east is **St-Denis**, a parallel two-way thoroughfare which defines the French student quarter (also called the *quartier latin* or the "student ghetto"). **Rue Sherbrooke**, which is paralleled by **de Maisonneuve** and **Ste-Catherine** downtown, runs east-west almost the entire length of Montréal. The **Underground City** runs north-south, stretching from **rue Sherbrooke** to **rue de la Gauchetière** and **rue St. Antoine.** A free map from the tourist office helps navigation. **Parking** is expensive and often difficult to find along the streets (meters are 25¢ for 10min.; $30 tickets are common); try the lots—especially those on the outskirts—for more reasonable parking prices.

NEIGHBORHOODS

Montréal has matured from a riverside settlement of French colonists into a hip, cosmopolitan metropolis. A stroll along **rue Ste-Catherine,** the flashy commercial avenue, is a must; it is here where European fashion tussles Canada, fragments of overheard conversation morph between English and French, and upscale retail intermingles with tacky souvenir stores and debaucherous nightclubs.

A small **Chinatown** orients itself along rue de la Gauchetière, near Vieux Montréal's Place d'Armes. **Little Greece**, a bit farther than you might care to walk from downtown, is just southeast of the Outremont Métro; stroll by rue Hutchison between av. Van Horne and av. Edouard-Charles. At the northern edge of the town's center, **Little Italy** occupies the area north of rue Beaubien between rue St-Hubert and Louis-Hémon. Walk east from Métro: Beaubien. Rue St-Denis, home to the city elite at the turn of the century, still serves as the **Latin Quarter's** main street, although restaurants of all flavors are also clustered along rue Prince Arthur (Métro: Berri-UQAM or Sherbrooke). **Bd. St-Laurent,** north of Sherbrooke, is perfect for walking or biking. Originally settled by Jewish immigrants, this area now functions as a sort of multicultural welcome wagon, home to Greek, Slavic, Latin American, and Portuguese immigrants. Many attractions between **Mont-Royal** and the **Fleuve St-Laurent** are free, from parks (Mont-Royal and Lafontaine) and universities (McGill, Montréal, Concordia, UQAM) to architectural spectacles. **Carré St-Louis** (Métro: Sherbrooke) hosts a beautiful fountain and sculptures. **Le Village,** the gay village, is located along rue Ste-Catherine Est between rue St-Hubert and Papineau. Both the Latin Quarter (above) and the area along rue St-Denis foster a very liberal, gay-friendly atmosphere (Métro: Sherbrooke or Mont-Royal).

⏹ PRACTICAL INFORMATION

Visitor Info: Infotouriste, 1001 rue de Square-Dorchester (☎873-2015 or 800-363-7777; www.tourisme.montreal.org), at Peel and Ste-Catherine between rue Peel and rue Metcalfe. Métro: Peel. Open daily 7am-8pm; Sept.-June 9am-6pm. In **Old Montréal,** 174 rue Notre-Dame Est at Place Jacques Cartier. Open daily 9am-7pm; daily Sept.-Oct. 9am-5pm; Nov. to early Mar. Th-Su 9am-5pm; daily late Mar. to early June 9am-5pm.

Youth Travel Office: Tourisme Jeunesse, 4800 rue St-Denis (☎252-3117 or 844-0287). Métro: Sherbrooke. A non-profit organization that inspects and ranks all officially recognized youth hostels in Québec. Open M-W and Sa 10am-6pm, Th-F 10am-9pm, Su 10am-5pm. **Travel CUTS,** McGill Student Union, 3480 rue McTavish (☎398-0647). Métro: McGill. Specializes in budget travel for college students. Open M-F 9am-5pm.

Currency Exchange: Currencies International, 1250 rue Peel (☎392-9100). Métro: Peel. Open in summer M-W 8:30am-8pm, Th-F 8:30am-9pm, Sa 8:30am-7pm, Su 9am-6pm; call for winter hours. **Thomas Cook,** 777 rue de la Gauchetière Ouest (☎397-4029). Métro: Bonaventure. Open M-F 8:30am-7pm, Sa 9am-4pm, Su 10am-3pm. Rue Ste-Catherine is lined with other small *bureaux de change*—watch out for high commissions.

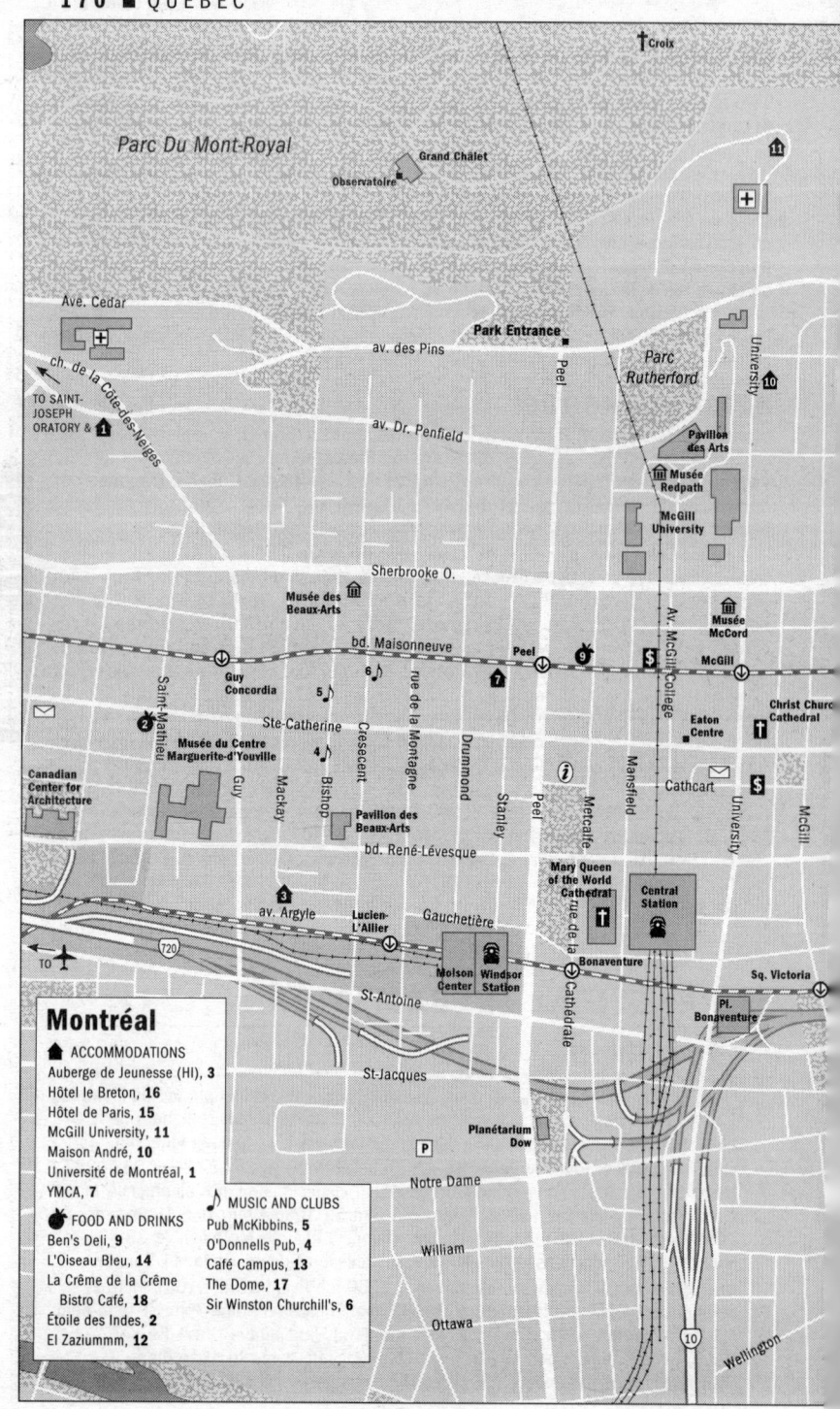

Montréal

ACCOMMODATIONS
Auberge de Jeunesse (HI), **3**
Hôtel le Breton, **16**
Hôtel de Paris, **15**
McGill University, **11**
Maison André, **10**
Université de Montréal, **1**
YMCA, **7**

FOOD AND DRINKS
Ben's Deli, **9**
L'Oiseau Bleu, **14**
La Crème de la Crème
  Bistro Café, **18**
Étoile des Indes, **2**
El Zaziummm, **12**

MUSIC AND CLUBS
Pub McKibbins, **5**
O'Donnells Pub, **4**
Café Campus, **13**
The Dome, **17**
Sir Winston Churchill's, **6**

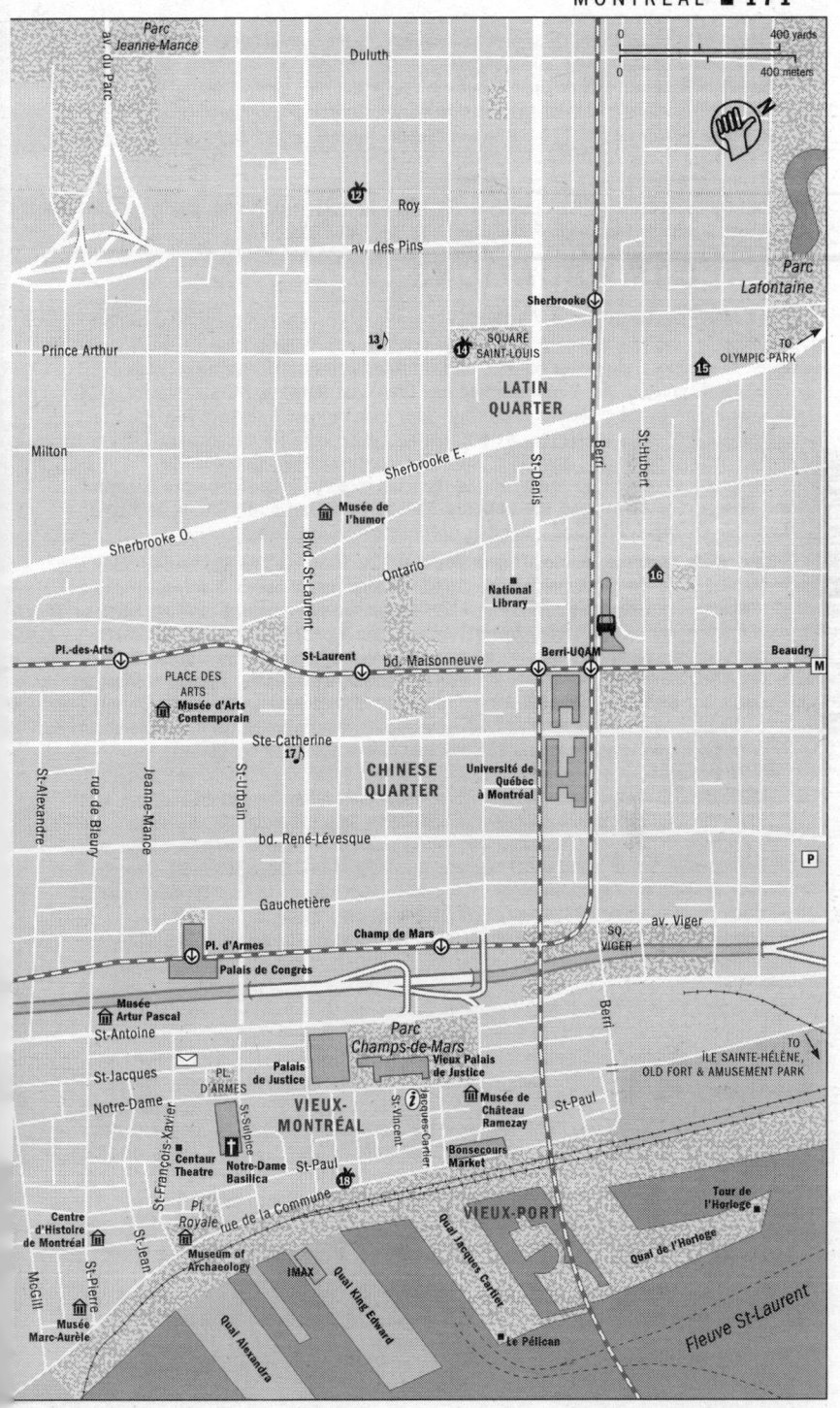

Parc
av. Jeanne-Mance

Duluth

12

Roy

av. des Pins

Sherbrooke

Parc
Lafontaine

Prince Arthur

13

SQUARE
SAINT-LOUIS

14

TO
OLYMPIC PARK

15

Milton

LATIN
QUARTER

Sherbrooke E.

St-Denis

Berri

St-Hubert

Sherbrooke O.

Musée de
l'humor

Blvd. St-Laurent

Ontario

National
Library

16

Pl.-des-Arts

St-Laurent

bd. Maisonneuve

Berri-UQAM

Beaudry

M

PLACE DES
ARTS
Musée d'Arts
Contemporain

Ste-Catherine

17

CHINESE
QUARTER

Université de
Québec
à Montréal

St-Alexandre

rue de Bleury

Jeanne-Mance

St-Urbain

bd. René-Lévesque

P

Gauchetière

Pl. d'Armes

Champ de Mars

av. Viger

SQ.
VIGER

Palais de Congrès

Musée
Artur Pascal

St-Antoine

Parc
Champs-de-Mars

Berri

TO
ÎLE SAINTE-HÉLÈNE,
OLD FORT & AMUSEMENT PARK

St-Jacques

Notre-Dame

PL.
D'ARMES

Palais
de Justice

VIEUX-
MONTRÉAL

Vieux Palais
de Justice

i

Musée de
Château
Ramezay

St-Paul

St-François Xavier

St-Sulpice

Centaur
Theatre

Notre-Dame
Basilica

St-Vincent

Jacques-Cartier

St-Paul

Bonsecours
Market

18

Centre
d'Histoire
de Montréal

Pl.
Royale

rue de la Commune

VIEUX-PORT

Tour de
l'Horloge

St-Jean

Museum of
Archaeology

IMAX

Quai King Edward

Quai Jacques Cartier

Quai de l'Horloge

McGill

St-Pierre

Musée
Marc-Aurèle

Quai Alexandra

Le Pélican

Fleuve St-Laurent

0   400 yards
0   400 meters

Most ATMs are on the PLUS system and charge only the normal transaction fee for withdrawals abroad; ask your bank about fees.

American Express, 1141 bd. de Maisonneuve (☎284-3300), at Peel. Métro: Peel. Travel agency; traveler's checks and currency exchange. Open M-F 9am-5pm.

Hotlines: Tél-Aide, ☎935-1101. **Gay and Lesbian Hotline,** ☎252-4429; **Sexual Assault,** ☎934-4504. **Suicide-Action,** ☎723-4000. All operate 24hr. **Rape Crisis,** ☎278-9383. Operates M-F 9:30am-4:30pm; call Tél-Aide after hours.

Post Office: Succursale (Postal Station) "B," 1250 rue Université (☎395-4539), at Cathcourt. Open M-F 8am-5pm. **Postal code:** H3B 3B0. **Area code:** 514.

⚓ ACCOMMODATIONS

The **Québec Tourist Office** (☎800-363-7777) is the best resource for info about hostels, hotels, and *chambres touristiques* (rooms in private homes or small guest houses). B&B singles cost $25-40, and doubles run $35-75. Or, take your B&B inquiries directly to the **Downtown Bed and Breakfast Network,** 3458 av. Laval, H2X 3C8, near Sherbrooke; the managers run their own modest hideaway and maintain a list of 80 other homes downtown. (☎289-9749 or 800-267-5180; www.bbmontreal.qc.ca. Open daily 9am-9pm. Singles $40-65; doubles $45-75.)

Ranging from quaint to seedy, any of the least expensive *maisons touristiques* and hotels cluster around **rue St-Denis.** The area, which abuts Vieux Montréal, flaunts lively nightclubs and a number of funky cafes and bistros.

▨ Auberge de Jeunesse, Montréal Youth Hostel (HI-C), 1030 rue MacKay (☎843-3317). Métro: Lucien-L'Allier. Airport shuttle drivers will stop here if asked. If only the life of a hosteler were always this cushy; with a full bathroom in every room, a complete kitchen, laundry facilities, pool tables, Internet access, and a *petit café* whipping up gourmet creations, the Montréal Youth Hostel is synonymous with heaven. The 250 beds (4-10 per room) fill quickly in summer, attesting to Montréal's popularity. If you're hesitant to check out nightlife alone, join staff and guests for a biweekly pub crawl (Tu and F 8:30pm). Some parking. Linen $2.10. 1-week max. stay; in winter 10 days. Reception 24hr. Dorms $21, nonmembers $25. Private doubles $26/$32 per person.

McGill University, Bishop Mountain Hall, 3935 rue de l'Université, H3A 2B4 (☎398-6367). Métro: McGill. Follow Université through campus, then catch your breath and bear right when the road seems to terminate in a parking lot atop the steep hill. Kitchenettes on each floor. 1000 beds. Fast, free Internet access. Common room with TV, towels and linen provided, and laundry facilities. Full breakfast M-Th 7:30-9:30am $6. Reception daily 7am-10pm; a guard will check you in late. Open May 15 to Aug. 15. Singles $40, students and seniors $33; weekly $230/$200; prices include tax.

Hôtel Le Breton, 1609 rue St-Hubert (☎524-7273), around the corner from the bus station and 2 blocks east of St-Denis. Métro: Berri-UQAM. Although the neighborhood is neither particularly wholesome nor safe-feeling, the 13 rooms are clean and comfortable with a TV, some with A/C. Reception 8am-midnight. Make reservations 2 weeks in advance. Non-smoking rooms available. Front door remains locked. Rooms $40-55.

Université de Montréal, Residences, 2350 rue Edouard-Montpetit, H2X 2B9 (☎343-6531), off Côte-des-Neiges. Métro: Edouard-Montpetit. Located on the edge of a beautiful campus; try the East Tower for great views. Laundry facilities. Free local calls, sink in each room. Reception 24hr. The noon check-out is strictly enforced. Cafe with basic foods open M-F 7:30am-2:30pm. Open early May to mid-Aug. Singles $26. Parking $7.

Hôtel de Paris, 901 rue Sherbrooke E. (☎522-6861). Métro: Sherbrooke. Misleading in appearance, the facade of this seemingly modest-sized 19th-century flat conceals a brand new 100-bed hostel with kitchen and a score of hotel rooms. The dorms lack the comfort of the hotel rooms, but come much cheaper. Single-sex dorm rooms $19. Linen $2. Hotel rooms start at $55.

Maison André Tourist Rooms, 3511 rue Université (☎849-4092). Métro: McGill. Mme. Zanko spins great yarns in her antique, well located house. Guests have been returning to this bastion of European cleanliness and decor for over 30 years. No smoking. Singles $26-35; doubles $38-45; $10 each additional person. Reservations recommended.

SMOKED MEAT ON RYE Any true Montréalian (not those artsy downtown types) will agree that Smoked Meat—a spicy, salty, greasy cured beef brisket—is a delicacy not to be compared with anything else in the world. The great landmark ▨ **Ben's Delicatessen**, at Metcalfe, in the heart of downtown, is often said to be the originator of this artery-clogging delicacy, which can resemble pastrami or even corned beef. *(990 bd. de Maisonneuve. ☎ 844-1000.)* The story has it that Ben Kravitz, a native Lithuanian, longed for the briskets of his native land and, in an effort to recreate them, invented Smoked Meat. Famous in Montréal, cafes as far away as Halifax fly in meat from Ben's to serve to their adoring customers. A proper Smoked Meat sandwich is served hot with mustard on seedless rye, with fries, vinegar, a half-sour pickle, and black cherry soda. *(At Ben's, that'll be about $6.)*

YMCA, 1450 rue Stanley at Ste-Catherine's (☎ 849-8393), downtown. Métro: Peel (right across the street from the station). A far cry from luxury, the Y compensates with impeccable, ideally located rooms (they're tiny, but equipped with TV and phone) and newly renovated facilities. Singles $40 for men, $46 for women; doubles $56; triples $66; quads $76. Reserve 2 weeks in advance.

Camping Alouette, 3449 rue de l'Industrie (☎ 450-464-1661), 30km from the city. Follow Autoroute 20, take Exit 105, and follow the signs to the campground. Find the privacy that is lacking in Montréal's bustling hostels. Pool, laundry facilities, a small store, and a daily shuttle to and from Montréal. Showers 25¢. Sites for 2 $19, with hookup $27; each additional person $2. Shuttle $10 per person round-trip.

◪ BON APPÉTIT

Affordably to astonomically priced restaurants pack in along **bd. St-Laurent** and on the western half of **Ste-Catherine.** In the Latin Quarter, energetic **rue Prince Arthur** jams Greek, Polish, and Italian restaurants into a tiny area, and maître d's stand in front of their restaurants to court you. The accent changes slightly at **av. Duluth,** where Portuguese and Vietnamese establishments prevail. Extending north of Maisonneuve on **Rue St-Denis,** you'll find the French Student Quarter, which has many small cafes and eateries, most catering to student budgets. If you'd like wine at an unlicensed restaurant, buy your own at a *dépanneur* or at the **SAQ (Sociéte des alcohols du Québec);** the eateries are concentrated on **bd. St-Laurent,** north of Sherbrooke, and in the pedestrian precincts of rue Prince Arthur and rue Duluth.

All restaurants are required by law to post their menus outside (although many white out the prices), so shop around. Consult the free *Restaurant Guide,* published by the **Greater Montréal Convention and Tourism Bureau** (☎ 844-5400), which lists over 130 restaurants by type of cuisine. For preparing your own meals, head to the markets: the **Atwater Market** (Métro: Lionel-Groulx); the **Marché Maisonneuve,** 4375 rue Ontario Est (Métro: Pie-IX); the **Marché St-Jacques** (Métro: Berri-UQAM, at Ontario and Amherst); or the **Marché Jean-Talon** (Métro: Jean Talon). Call 937-7754 9am-4pm daily. All markets open M-W 8am-6pm, Th 8am-8pm, F 8am-9pm, Sa-Su 8am-5pm. Closest to the Montréal hostel is Provigo **SuperMarché,** on the corner of Maisonneuve and rue du Fort. (☎ 932-3756. Open daily 8am-9pm.)

▨ **La Crème de la Crème Bistro Café,** 21 rue de la Commune Est (☎ 874-0723), down by the water in Old Montreal. Provincial French decor and refreshingly reasonable prices distinguish this brick basement cafe from the other eateries lining Old Montréal's streets. Baguette sandwiches served with salad are $7-9, but even more impressive are their scandalously large wedges of chocolate cake ($3-4). Open June-Sept. daily 11am-midnight. Hours vary during other seasons.

Au Pain Doré, 5214 Côte des Neiges (☎ 342-8995), near rue Jean Brillant. As if Montréal's nightlife didn't offer enough opportunity for indulgence, the pastries of pleasure here are another reason to splurge. Chocolatines are excellent, as are the croissants, breads, muffins, and everything else. Also offers a selection of cheeses. Baguettes $1.50-4. Open M-W 8:30am-7pm, Th-F 8:30am-7:30pm, Sa-Su 8:30am-5:30pm.

EASTERN CANADA

Étoile des Indes, 1806 Ste-Catherine Ouest (☎932-8330), near St-Mathieu. Métro: Guy-Concordia. The best Indian fare in town, according to locals. The brave should try their bang-up Bangalore *phal* dishes. Dinner entrees $5-15; lunch specials $5-8 are your best bet for value. Open M-Sa noon-2:30pm and 5-11pm; Su 5-11pm.

El Zaziummm, 51 Roy Est (☎844-0893), a St-Laurent side street. Festive-colored patio floorboards suggest the good times that seem to flow like sangria at this Mexican eatery. Entrees $8-15. Open M-Tu 4-11pm, W-Su noon-11:30pm; in winter daily 4-11pm.

L'Oiseau Bleu, 3603 av. Laval (☎286-6654), in Sq. Saint-Louis. This ice cream parlor vends great licks to the kids, lovers, punks, and others who meander through the park. Cones $1.50-2.50, wraps and sandwiches $4-6. Open May-Nov. daily noon-11pm.

◉ SIGHTS

MONT-ROYAL, LE PLATEAU, AND THE EAST

Package tickets for the Funiculaire, Biodôme, Gardens, and Insectarium are a decent deal. *($22.50, students and seniors $15.75, ages 6-17 $12.)*

BIODÔME. The fascinating ▨Biodôme is the most recent addition to Olympic park. Housed in the former Olympic Vélodrome, the Biodôme is a "living museum" in which four complete ecosystems have been reconstructed: the Tropical Forest, the Laurentian Forest, the St-Laurent marine ecosystem, and the Polar World. Stay alert and you might spot the more elusive of the 6200 vertebrates subsisting here. *(4777 av. Pierre-de-Coubertin. Métro: Viau. ☎868-3000. Open in summer daily 9am-7pm; off-season 9am-5pm. $9.50, seniors and students $7, ages 6-17 $4.75.)*

ST. JOSEPH'S. The dome of ▨St. Joseph's Oratory, second in height among the world's domes to only that of St. Peter's Basilica in Rome, stands in testimony to the chapel's grandeur. An acclaimed religious site that attracts pilgrims from all over the globe, St. Joseph's is credited with a long list of miracles and unexplained healings. The **Votive Chapel,** where the crutches and canes of thousands of healed devotees hang for all to see, keeps warm with the heat of 10,000 candles. *(3800 ch. Queen Mary. Métro: Côte-des-Neiges. ☎733-8211. Open daily 6am-9:30pm.)*

FUNICULAIRE. Home to the 1976 summer Olympic games, **Olympic Park** still provides entertainment enough for a day away from the city's center. The park's daring architecture is poignantly represented by the inclined tower (the world's tallest) adjoined to what now serves as the Expos's stadium—together, the two form a structure uncannily similar to the starship *Enterprise* from TV's *Star Trek.* Riding the Funiculaire to the top grants a panoramic view of Montréal. *(3200 rue Viau. Métro: Viau, Pie IX. ☎252-8687. Tours offered daily in both French and English. Call for times. $5.25, ages 5-17 $4.25. Funiculaire open June-Sept. M noon-9pm, Tu-Th 10am-9pm, F-Su 10am-11pm; early Sept. to mid-June M noon-6pm, Tu-Su 10am-6pm. $9, seniors and ages 5-17 $5.50.)*

THE GARDENS. In the summer, a free shuttle will take you across the park to the **Jardin Botanique (Botanical Gardens).** The Japanese and Chinese landscapes showcase the largest *bonsai* and *penjing* collections outside of Asia. Beware: the gardens also harbor an **insectarium** with astounding collections of mounted and live exotic bugs, including at least a dozen live fist-sized spiders. *(4101 rue Sherbrooke Est. Métro: Pie-IX. ☎872-1400. Gardens open daily 9am-7pm; Sept.-June 9am-5pm. $9.50, seniors and students $7, ages 6-17 $4.75; Sept.-June $6.75/$5.25/$3.50.)*

PARC DU MONT-ROYAL. The Parc du Mont-Royal, which climbs up to the mountain that is the city's namesake, was inaugurated in 1876. From rue Peel, hardy hikers can take a foot path and stairs to the top or to the lookouts on Camillien-Houde Pkwy. and the Mountain Chalet. Like New York's Central Park, this one is also a Frederick Law Olmsted original. The **30m cross** at the top of the mountain commemorates the 1643 climb by de Maisonneuve, the founder of Montréal. In winter, his proverbial progeny gather here to ice-skate, toboggan, and cross-country ski. In summer, Mont-Royal welcomes joggers, cyclists, picnickers, and amblers. *(Camilien-Houde Pkwy. Métro: Mont-Royal or Bus #11. ☎844-4928. Officially open 6am-midnight.)*

MCGILL. The **McGill University** campus extends up Mont-Royal. Composed predominantly of Victorian-style buildings set on pleasant greens, the university symbolizes the city's British heritage. For a look around campus, stop by the **McGill Welcome Center** for a tour. *(Burnside Hall Building, Room 115.* ☎ *398-6555. Open M-Sa 9am-5pm.)* The campus also contains the site of the 16th-century Native American village of **Hochelaga** and the **Redpath Museum of Natural History,** with rare fossils and two genuine Egyptian mummies. *(Main gate at rue McGill and Sherbrooke. Métro: McGill.* ☎ *398-4086. Open M-Th 9am-5pm, Su 1-5pm; Sept. to late June M-F 9am-5pm, Su 1-5pm. Free.)*

THE UNDERGROUND CITY

For those who are attracted to the chic, cosmopolitan Montréal but could do without its sub-zero winters, hibernation is always an option. Twenty-nine kilometers of tunnels link Métro stops and form the ever-expanding "prototype city of the future," connecting railway stations, two bus terminals, restaurants, banks, cinemas, theatress, hotels, two universities, two department stores, 1700 businesses, 1615 housing units, and 1600 boutiques. And there aren't any streets to speak of; rather, residents bustle through the hallways of this sprawling mall-like, "sub-urban" city.

PLACE BONAVENTURE. The underground city can be entered from most downtown Métro stops, though a good start to an adventure is the **Place Bonaventure.** Canada's largest commercial building sports a melange of shops, each selling products imported from a different country. The tourist office supplies treasure maps of the tunnels and underground attractions. *(900 rue de la Gauchetière Ouest. Métro: Bonaventure.* ☎ *397-2325. Shops open daily 9am-9pm.)*

MCGILL. At the McGill stop lies some of the Underground City's finest offerings. Here, beneath the **Christ Church Cathedral** wait the **Promenades de la Cathédrale,** one of the Underground's primary shopping complexes. *(635 rue Ste-Catherine Ouest. Church* ☎ *843-6577. Open daily 8am-6pm. Promenades* ☎ *849-9925.)* Three blocks east, passing through Centre Eaton, of grand department store fame, the **Place Montréal Trust** is famous for its modern architecture and decadent shopping area.

VIEUX MONTRÉAL (OLD MONTRÉAL)

In the 17th century, the city of Montréal struggled with Iroquois tribes for control of the area's lucrative fur trade and erected walls encircling the settlement for defense. Today the remnants of those ramparts delineate the boundaries of Vieux Montréal, the city's first settlement, on the stretch of river bank between **rue McGill, Notre-Dame,** and **Berri.** The fortified walls that once protected the quarter have crumbled, but the beautiful 17th- and 18th-century mansions of politicos and merchants retain their splendor. Take the Métro to **Place d'Armes** or **Champ-de-Mars.**

BASILIQUE NOTRE-DAME-DE-MONTRÉAL. A couple blocks south of the Place d'Armes, Notre-Dame-de-Montréal towers above the memorial to de Maisonneuve in the bordering square. One of North America's largest churches and an historic center for the city's Catholic population, the neo-Gothic basilica once hosted Québec separatist rallies. Most impressive are the extremely ornate and detailed hand-painted designs covering the pillars and ceiling. *(116 rue Notre-Dame Ouest.* ☎ *842-2925. Open daily 7am-8pm; early Sept. to late June M-Sa 7am-6pm, Su 1:30-6pm. Free.)*

CATHÉDRALE MARIE REINE DU MONDE. On the block bordered by René-Lévesque, Cathédrale, and Metcalfe, Cathédrale Marie Reine du Monde is a scaled-down replica of St. Peter's in Rome and rivals Notre-Dame-de-Montréal for grandeur. A Roman Catholic basilica, it stirred tensions when it was built in the heart of Montréal's Anglo-Protestant area. *(*☎ *866-1661. Open M-F 7:30am-7:30pm, Sa 7:30am-8:30pm, Su 8:30am-7:30pm. At least 3-4 masses offered daily. Free.)*

CHÂTEAU RAMEZAY. The grand Château Ramezay, built in 1705 for the French viceroy, houses a museum of *québécois*, British, and American artifacts. Take a step back in time and a stroll along the 18th-century Governor's garden and sidewalk cafe. *(280 rue Notre-Dame Est. Métro: Champ-de-Mars.* ☎ *861-3708. Open daily 10am-*

6pm; Oct.-May Tu-Su 10am-4:30pm. $6, students $4, seniors $3, under 18 $3. Tours available by reservation. Partially wheelchair accessible; assistance may be required.)

OTHER ATTRACTIONS. The **St-Sulpice Seminary,** built in 1685, is the oldest building in Montréal and a still-functioning seminary. The clock over the facade, built in 1701, is also the oldest public timepiece in North America and chimes today as a symbol of continuity. *(130 rue Notre-Dame Ouest. Métro: Place D'Armes.)* At rue Bonsecours and rue St-Paul stands the 18th-century **Notre-Dame-de-Bonsecours,** founded as a sailors' refuge by Marguerite Bourgeoys, leader of the first order of non-cloistered nuns. The church displays archaeological finds from beneath its floors. *(400 rue St-Paul Est. Métro: Champ-de-Mars. ☎282-8670.)* **Place Jacques Cartier** is the site of Montréal's oldest market. Here the modern European character of Montréal is most evident; cafes line the square, and street artists strut their stuff during the summer. *(Rue St. Paul. Métro: Champ-de-Mars.)* The **Vieux Palais de Justice,** built in 1856 in Place Vauquelin, is the place where Charles de Gaulle declared, "Vive le Québec libre!" **Rue St-Jacques** in the Old City, established in 1687, is Montréal's Wall St.

ÎLE STE-HÉLÈNE AND ST-LAURENT

By car, you can take either of two bridges to Île Ste-Hélène: the Pont Jacques Cartier or the Pont de la Concorde. To avoid traffic and the hassle of finding parking, the Métro stop at Île Ste-Hélène provides a convenient starting-off point; buses depart from the stop to the island's attractions.

LA RONDE. The best among many good reasons to visit Île Ste-Hélène, **La Ronde** amusement park boasts a free-fall drop and one of the largest wooden roller coasters in North America. *(Métro: Jean-Drapeau. ☎872-4537 or 800-797-4537. Rides open in summer daily 11am-11pm, grounds open until midnight; hours vary off-season. Unlimited passes $29.)* The **International Fireworks Competition** takes place every June and July at La Ronde, but you can avoid the park's steep prices by watching from Mont-Royal or the crowded Pont Jacques-Cartier *(☎872-4537).*

LE VIEUX FORT. Originally built in 1820 to defend Canada's inland waterways from the imperialistic Americans to the south, Le Vieux Fort now protects the **Stewart Museum,** which houses a large collection of weapons, war instruments, and strategic maps. Sit tight for musket firing by costumed colonials daily in summer at 3pm. *(Métro: Île-Sainte-Hélène. ☎861-6701. Open June-Aug. daily 10am-6pm; Sept.-May W-M 10am-5pm. $6, students and seniors $4, families $12.)*

EAU DE FUN. Saute-Moutons Jet-Boating tours are a unique but expensive way for even the most devoted landlubbers to experience the rapids of the St. Lawrence without getting soaked. *(Clock Tower Pier. Métro: Champ-de-Mars. ☎284-9607. Open in summer 10am-6pm. Prices start at $60. Call ahead.)* **Les Descentes sur le Saint-Laurent** in LaSalle provides **rafting adventures.** *(Free shuttle from the Visitors Center at 1001 rue du Square-Dorchester. Métro: Peel. ☎767-2230 or 800-324-7238. 1½hr. tours. Prices and departure times vary, but begin around $30.)*

🏛 MUSEUMS

Musée des Beaux-Arts, 1380 rue Sherbrooke Ouest (☎285-2000). Métro: Guy-Concordia. Located only about 5 blocks west of the McGill entrance, this museum's small permanent collection touches upon all major artistic periods and includes Canadian and Inuit work. Open Tu-Su 11am-6pm. Permanent collection free. Temporary exhibits $12, seniors and students $6, under 12 $3; half-price W 5:30-9pm.

McCord Museum, 690 rue Sherbrooke Ouest (☎398-7100). Métro: McGill. Textiles, paintings, and an immense photographic archive trace Canada's history from Confederation onward. Open June-Sept. daily 10am-5pm; Sept.-June Tu-F 10am-6pm, Sa-Su 10am-5pm. $9.50, seniors $7, students $5, ages 7-12 $3, families $19. Free Sa 10am-noon.

Montréal Museum of Archaeology and History (Pointe-à-Callière), 350 Place Royale (☎872-9150), near Vieux-Port. This museum and national historic site opened in 1992, filled with the products of more than 10 years of archaeological digs. This innovative journey through the city's history is the next best thing to time travel. Open Tu-F 10am-5pm, Sa-Su 11am-6pm. $9.50, seniors $7, students $5.50, ages 6-12 $3, under 5 free.

Canadian Centre for Architecture, 1920 av. Baile (☎939-7026). Métro: Guy-Concordia or Atwater. Houses one of the world's most important collections of architectural prints, drawings, photographs, and books. Open in summer Tu-W and F-Su 11am-6pm, Th 11am-9pm; hours vary in other seasons. $6, seniors $4, students $3, under 12 free.

Musée d'Art Contemporain, 185 rue Ste-Catherine Ouest (☎847-6226), at Jeanne-Mance. Métro: Place-des-Arts. Here you can view works by *québécois* artists, as well as textile, photography, and avant-garde exhibits. Open Tu and Th-Su 11am-6pm, W 11am-9pm. $6, seniors $4, students $3, under 12 free; W 6-9pm free.

Montréal Museum of Decorative Arts, 2200 rue Crescent (☎284-1252). Métro: Guy-Concordia, then transfer to bus #24 "Pie-IX." Stop by for a slew of innovative and absurd decorative pieces. Open Tu-Su 11am-6pm, W 11am-9pm. $4, students $3, under 12 free.

◪ NIGHTLIFE

Combine a loosely enforced drinking age of 18 with thousands of taps flowing unchecked till 3am and what results is the unofficially titled "nightlife capital of North America." Most pubs and bars offer the ever-popular weekday "happy hour," usually from 5-8pm, where bottled drinks may be two-for-one, and mixed drinks may be double their usual potency. Although it has its share of skanky peep shows and *châteaux de sexe*, Montréal is less a depot of debauchery and more a youthful city surging with energy at twilight and after. In summer, restaurants spill onto outdoor patios and streets clog with strollers, thespians, and couples holding hands. **Rue Prince Arthur** at St-Laurent is devoted solely to pedestrians who mix and mingle at cafes by day and clubs by night (Métro: Sherbrooke). **Rue St-Denis,** north of Ste-Catherine, is rising as a nighttime hot spot.

◪ Pub McKibbins, 1426 Bishop (☎288-1580). Fine fermented drinks within the dark mahogany confines of an enchanting Irish pub. Trophies and brass tokens ornament the walls, and dart boards entertain the crowds; a fieldstone fireplace warms the quarters in winter. Ground yourself with the Shepard's Pie ($9) before your next Guinness. Open daily 11am-3am; kitchen closes at 10pm.

O'Donnells Pub, just down the street at 1224 Bishop (☎877-3128), south of Ste-Catherine. Enticing weekday dinner specials (fish and chips on F $7). The tartan stools and cozy booths are quickly claimed W-Sa, when live traditional Irish music filters into the street, luring in all passers-by. Open daily noon-3am, kitchen closes at 10pm.

Sir Winston Churchill's, 1459 Crescent (☎288-0616). Perhaps the most impressive ratio of counter length to total area of any bar in all of Montréal. As if covering every inch of wall with bar counter weren't enough, 2 island watering holes take up the remaining floorspace. Every M is "dare to bare all"—we're talking drinking too heavy for even Sir Winston, himself. Open daily 10:30am-3am.

Café Campus, 57 Prince Arthur (☎844-1010). Unlike the more touristy meat-market discothèques, this hip club gathers a friendly student and twenty-something crowd. Tu night is retro night, when sloshing pitchers of beer go for a measly $6. Cover: dancing $3, live music $5-15. Open M-Sa 7pm-3am, Su 8:30pm-3am.

The Dome, 32 rue Ste-Catherine Est (☎875-5757), at the corner of St-Laurent. Attracts a more international crowd to bump and grind. Cover $5. Open F-Sa, 10pm-3am.

GAY AND LESBIAN NIGHTLIFE

Most of Montréal's gay and lesbian hot spots can be found in the **gay village** along rue St-Catherine between St-Hubert and Papineau. While most of the village's establishments cater to *hommes*, a few *femme*-friendly locales are interspersed throughout the neighborhood.

Le Drugstore, 1366 rue Ste-Catherine Est (☎868-9278). Métro: Beaudry. A 3-story gay megaplex featuring several distinctively themed bars. Crowd is mostly male, though women are welcome. Ground floor is wheelchair accessible. Open M-F 7pm-6am.

La Track, 1584 rue Ste-Catherine Est (☎521-1419). Métro: Papineau. This all-male dance club fills to the brim, especially on weekends. Wheelchair accessible. W theme nights. No cover. Bar open daily 10am-3am; club open W-Sa 9pm-3am, Su 3pm-3am.

Sisters, 1333 rue Ste-Catherine Est (☎522-4717). Métro: Beaudry. Since the closing of several popular girl bars in 2000, Sisters has picked up the slack, offering intimate tables, disco dancing, and a well-equipped bar. Tu "Boyz in the House" night. Cover F-Sa $5. Open Th-Sa 10pm-3am.

🎵 ENTERTAINMENT

THEATRE

Productions in both French and English sustain another genre of nighttime entertainment in Montréal: theatre. The **Théâtre du Nouveau Monde,** 84 rue Ste-Catherine Ouest, hosts French productions. (☎866-8667. Métro: Place-des-Arts.) The **Théâtre du Rideau Vert,** 4664 rue St-Denis (☎844-1793), stages *québécois* works. **Centaur Theatre,** 453 rue St-François-Xavier, has English-language plays, performed mainly September through May. (☎288-1229, ticket info 288-3161. Métro: Place-d'Armes.) The city's exciting **Place des Arts,** 260 bd. de Maisonneuve Ouest, at rue Ste. Catherine Ouest and rue Jeanne Mance (☎842-2112 for tickets), houses the **Opéra de Montréal** (☎985-2258), the **Montréal Symphony Orchestra** (☎842-9951), and **Les Grands Ballets Canadiens** (☎849-8681). The **National Theatre School of Canada,** 5030 rue St-Denis (☎842-7954), stages excellent student productions during the academic year. **Théâtre Saint-Denis,** 1594 rue St-Denis (☎849-4211), hosts traveling productions like *Cats.* Theatergoers should peruse the **Calendar of Events** (available at tourist offices and newspaper stands), or call **Telspec** for ticket info (☎790-2222; open M-Sa 9am-9pm, Su noon-6pm). **Admission Ticket Network** also has tickets for various events. (☎790-1245 or 800-361-4595. Open daily 8am-midnight. Credit card required.)

SEASONAL AND OTHER ENTERTAINMENT

Like much of the city, Vieux Montréal is best seen at night. Street performers, artists, and *chansonniers* in various *brasseries* set the tone for lively summer evenings of clapping, stomping, and singing along. Real fun goes down on **St-Paul,** near the corner of St-Vincent. For a sweet Sunday afternoon, **Parc Jeanne-Mance** reels with bongos, dancing, and handicrafts (May-Sept. noon-7pm).

Québec is no different from the rest of Canada in its obsession with hockey. Between October and April, be sure to attend a **Montréal Canadiens** hockey game at the new **Molson Centre,** 1250 rue de la Gauchetière Ouest, where Les Habitants (a nickname for the Canadiens) play. Dress and behavior at games can be quite formal; jackets and ties are not uncommon. (☎932-2582. Métro: Bonaventure. Call well in advance to reserve tickets.) Baseball is also popular here, and the local MLB team, the **Montréal Expos,** plays at Olympic Park. (☎790-1245. Métro: Pie-IX.)

But *Montréalais* don't just like to watch; in early June, the one-day **Tour de l'ile,** a 64km circuit of the island, is the largest cycling event in the world, with 45,000 mostly amateur cyclists pedaling their wares. (Call 521-8356 by Apr. to participate. Separate days for adults and children.)

Jazz fiends will command the street the first week of July in 2002, during the annual **Montréal International Jazz Festival** (☎871-1881), with over 300 free outdoor shows scattered over a dozen stages near Métro Place-des-Arts. During the third week in June, Montreal swoons during the **Mondial de la Bière,** when over 75 beers are available for tasting and visitors discover the happy marriage of spirits, music, and cuisine. (☎722-9640; www.festivalmondialbiere.qc.ca. Day pass $10.)

QUÉBEC CITY   ☎418

Dubbed the "Gibraltar of America" because of the stone escarpments and military fortifications protecting the port, Québec City (generally shortened to just "Québec") sits high on the rocky heights of Cap Diamant where the Fleuve St-Laurent narrows and is joined by the St-Charles river. The name Québec is derived

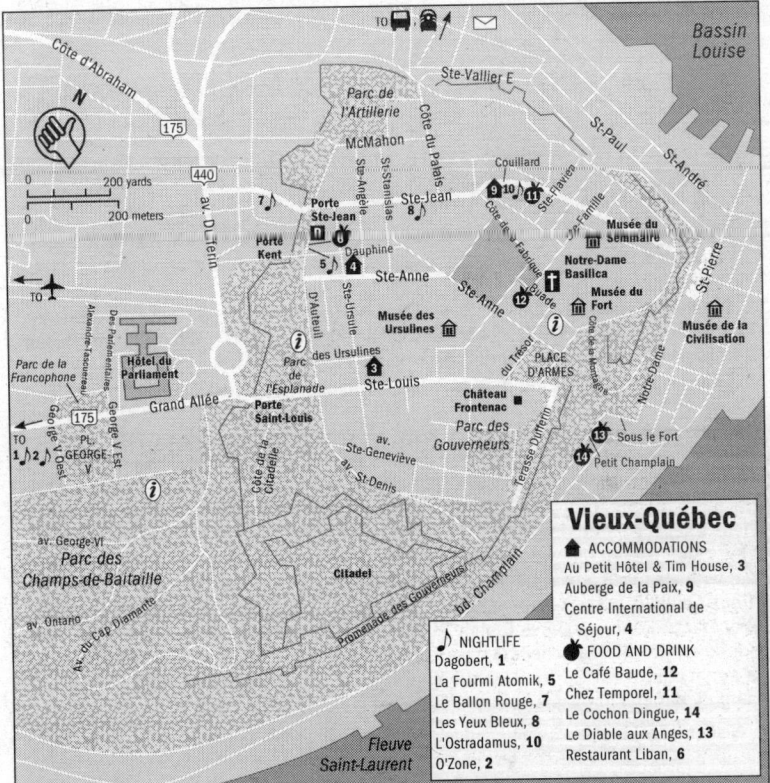

Vieux-Québec

🏠 ACCOMMODATIONS
Au Petit Hôtel & Tim House, 3
Auberge de la Paix, 9
Centre International de
Séjour, 4

🍎 FOOD AND DRINK
Le Café Baude, 12
Chez Temporel, 11
Le Cochon Dingue, 14
Le Diable aux Anges, 13
Restaurant Liban, 6

♪ NIGHTLIFE
Dagobert, 1
La Fourmi Atomik, 5
Le Ballon Rouge, 7
Les Yeux Bleux, 8
L'Ostradamus, 10
O'Zone, 2

EASTERN CANADA

from the Algonquin word *kebek*, which means "place where the river narrows."
Passing through the portals of North America's only walled city is like stepping into
a European past; horse-drawn carriages greet visitors to the winding maze of
streets in the Old City (Vieux Québec), and there are enough sights and museums to
satisfy even the most voracious history buff for weeks. Along with the historical
attachment, Canada's oldest city boasts a thriving French culture, standing apart
from Montréal as the center of true *québécois* culture. Never assume that the locals
speak English—it has yet to make solid inroads here.

🚃 TRANSPORTATION

Airport: Québec's airport (☎ 692-0770) is far out of town and inaccessible by public transit. Taxi to downtown $30. By car, turn right onto Rt. de l'aéroport and then take either
bd. Wilfred-Hamel or, beyond it, Autoroute 440 to get into the city. **Autobus La Québecois** runs a shuttle service between the airport and the major hotels of the city. (☎872-
5525. M-F 6 per day 8:45am-9:45pm, Sa 7 per day 9am-8:45pm, Su 7 per day 9am-
11:35pm. $9, under 12 free.)

Trains: VIA Rail, 450 rue de la Gare du Palais (☎ 692-3940), in Québec City. To: Montréal
(3hr.; M-F 4 per day, Sa-Su 3 per day; $53, seniors $48, students $34, ages 2-11
$26); Toronto (8hr., 4 per day, $133/$120/$86/$67); and Ottawa (3hr., 3 per day,
$77/$69/$50/$39). Open daily 6am-8:30pm. Nearby stations at 3255 ch. de la
Gare, in Ste-Foy (open M-F 6am-9pm, Sa-Su 7:30am-9pm) and 5995 St-Laurent, Autoroute 20, in Lévis (open Th-M 4-5am and 8-10:30pm, Tu 4-5am, W 8-10:30pm).

Buses: Orléans Express, 320 Abraham Martin (☎ 525-3000). Open daily 5:30am-1am.
Outlying stations at 3001 ch. des Quatre-Bourgeois, in Ste-Foy (☎ 650-0087; open M-
Sa 6am-1am, Su 7am-1am), and 63 Hwy. Trans-Canada Ouest (Hwy. 132), in Lévis

(☎837-5805; open daily 6am-2am). To: Montréal (3hr.; every hr. 6am-8pm and 9:30-11pm; $35, seniors $26, ages 5-11 $17); Ste-Anne-de-Beaupré (25min., 3 per day, $5); and the US via Montréal or Sherbrooke.

Public Transit: Société de Transport de la Communauté Urbaine de Québec (STCUQ), 270 rue des Rocailles (☎627-2511 for route and schedule info). Open M-F 6:30am-10pm, Sa-Su 8am-10pm. Buses operate daily 6am-1am, although individual routes and hours of operation vary significantly. $2.25, students $1.50, seniors and children $1.30; advance-purchase tickets $1.60/$1/$1; under 5 free.

Taxis: Coop Taxis Québec, ☎525-5191.

Driver/Rider Service: Allo-Stop, 665 rue St-Jean (☎522-0056), will match you with a driver heading for Montréal ($15). Must be a member ($6 per year, drivers $7). Open daily 9am-6pm, Tu and F until 7pm.

Car Rental: Pelletier, 900 bd. Pierre Bertrand (☎681-0678). $35 per day, $50 with insurance; 250km free, 11¢ each additional km. Must be 25+ with credit card deposit of 20%. Open M-F 7am-8pm, Sa-Su 8am-4pm.

Internet access: Café Internet du Palais Montcalm, 995 Rue D'Youville (☎692-4909).

◼✸🛈 ORIENTATION AND PRACTICAL INFORMATION

Québec's main thoroughfares run through both the Old City *(Vieux Québec)* and the more modern city outside it, generally parallel in an east-west direction. Within **Vieux Québec,** the main streets are **St-Louis, Ste-Anne,** and **St-Jean.** Most streets in Vieux Québec are one-way, the major exception being rue d'Auteuil, which borders the walls inside Vieux Québec—it's the best bet for parking. Outside the walls of Vieux Québec, both St-Jean and St-Louis continue (St-Jean eventually joins ch. Ste-Foy and St-Louis becomes **Grande Allée**). **Bd. René-Lévesque,** the other major street outside the walls, runs between St-Jean and St-Louis. The Basse-ville (lower town) is separated from the Haute-ville (upper town, Old Québec) by an abrupt cliff roughly paralleled by rue St-Vallier Est.

Visitor info: Bureau d'information touristique du Vieux-Québec, 835 rue Wilfred Laurier (☎649-2608), in the Old City just outside the walls. Open daily 8:30am-7pm; Thanksgiving (mid-Oct.) to May 9am-5:30pm. Dealing primarily with provincial tourism, Maison du tourisme de Québec, 12 rue Ste-Anne (☎800-363-7777). Open daily 8:30am-7:30pm; early Sept. to mid-June 9am-5pm.

Hotlines: Tél-Aide distress center, ☎686-2433. Operates daily noon-midnight. **Viol-Secours (sexual assault line),** ☎522-2120. Counselors on duty M-F 9am-4pm and on-call 24hr. **Center for Suicide Prevention,** ☎529-0015. Operates daily 8am-midnight. **Info-Santé,** ☎648-2626, handles bi-gay-lesbian concerns. **Poison Control,** ☎656-8090.

Emergency: Police, ☎911 (city); 800-461-2131 (province). **Info-Santé (medical info),** ☎648-2626. Both 24hr.

Post Office: 300 rue St-Paul (☎694-6176). Open M-F 8am-5:45pm. **Postal code:** G1K 3W0. **Area code:** 418.

🛏 ACCOMMODATIONS

Le Transit, 1050 av. Turnbull, G1R 2X8 (☎647-6802; call 8am-noon or 4-9pm), will help with bed and breakfast referrals. Rooms start at $50 for one or two people, and hosts are usually bilingual. If parking is a problem (usually the case in Vieux Québec) and you must make use of the underground parking areas, ask your host about discount parking passes.

▧ **Centre International de Séjour (HI-C),** 19 rue Ste-Ursule (☎694-0755), 1 block north of rue St-Jean at Dauphine. Follow Côte d'Abraham uphill from the bus station until it joins av. Dufferin. Turn left on St-Jean, pass through the walls, and walk uphill, to your right, on Ste-Ursule. If driving, follow St-Louis into the Old City and take the 2nd left past the walls onto Ste-Ursule. Diverse, young clientele, fabulous location, and an array of extras (laundry, microwave, TV, pool table, ping-pong tables, living room, kitchen, cafeteria,

Internet access) make this place prime pickin's. Reduced-rate parking at a city garage. Breakfast 8-10am (continental $3.75, full $4.50). Check-out 10am. Lockout 11pm, but the front desk will let you in if you flash your key. 250 beds $17, nonmembers $21; private rooms $46/$50. Usually full July-Aug.; make reservations or arrive early.

Auberge de la Paix, 31 rue Couillard (☎ 694-0735). Take St-Jean into Vieux Québec, and take Couillard when it branches left. If you can manage without TV or Internet access for a few days, check yourself into this friendly, conveniently located "peace hostel" (look for the peace sign suspended above the door). The atmosphere is laid-back (there are no locks on the doors, but this doesn't seem to be a problem). Continental breakfast from 8-10am. Curfew 2am with all-day access. Kitchen open all day. 60 beds in 14 co-ed rooms, $19. Linen $2.50. Reservations necessary July-Aug.

Au Petit Hôtel, 3 ruelle des Ursulines (☎ 694-0965), just off of rue Ste-Ursule. This tidy little hotel is a great deal for 2 people. 14 rooms with TV, free local phone, private bath, and refrigerator in each; A/C in some. May-Oct. rooms from $60 for 1 or 2 occupants; Nov.-May rooms from $45. Free parking in winter ($5 May-Oct.).

Tim House, 84 rue Ste-Louis (☎ 694-0776). Adjacent to Au Petit Hôtel and run by the same folks (check-in at Au Petit). A lovely B&B. 3rd fl. rooms have shared baths; a delectable breakfast is included. Rooms $40-70, depending on the season. Reservations necessary. Parking $5.

Montmartre Canadien, 1675 ch. St-Louis (☎ 686-0867). Located on the outskirts of the city near Sillery, this small white house behind the main building at 1669 is ideal for those willing to trade proximity for privacy. Located in a religious sanctuary run by Assumptionist monks, the grounds have a relaxed, almost ascetic setting. Take bus #25 or 11. Dirt-cheap, immaculate singles $17; doubles $30; triples $42. Common showers. Reserve 2-3 weeks in advance.

You can obtain a list of nearby **campgrounds** from the **Maison du Tourisme de Québec** (see **Practical Information,** p. 180), or write to **Tourisme Québec,** C.P. 979, Montréal H3C 2W3 (☎ 800-363-7777; open daily 9am-5pm). A good camping option is **Municipal de Beauport,** 95 rue de la Serenité, Beauport. Take Autoroute 40E, get off at Exit 321 at rue Labelle onto Hwy. 369, turn left, and follow the signs marked "camping." Bus #55 to 800 will also take you to this 135-site campground on a hill over the Montmorency River. A swimming pool, canoes ($8 per hr.), showers (50¢ per 5min.), and laundry facilities ($1 per load) are available. (☎ 666-2228. Open June to early Sept. Sites $20, with hookup $25; $120/$150 per week.)

☕ L'HAUTE CUISINE

In general, rue Buade, St-Jean, and Cartier, as well as the **Place Royale** and **Petit Champlain** areas offer the widest selection of food and drink. The **Grande Allée** may seem like heaven to the hungry, but its prices may encourage you to keep strolling.

The best bet for a simple and affordable meal doesn't have to be a fast-food joint. Traditional *québecois* food is not only appetizing, but often economical. One of the most filling yet inexpensive meals is a *croque monsieur*, a large, open-faced sandwich with ham and melted cheese (about $6), usually served with salad. *Québecois* French onion soup, slathered with melted cheese, can be found in virtually every restaurant and cafe. It is usually served with either bats of French bread or *tourtière,* a thick meat pie. Other specialties include the ever-versatile *crêpe,* stuffed accordingly to serve as either an entree or a dessert. The ■**Casse-Crêpe Breton,** 1136 St-Jean, offers many choices of fillings in their "make your own combination" crêpes for dinner ($3.75-6), as well as scrumptious dessert options. (Open daily 7:30am-midnight.) **Pâtisserie au Palet d'Or,** 60 rue Garneau, bursts with culinary excellence—$6 will score you the *menu du jour:* an entree, salad, beverage, and a choice of many sweet, doughy desserts. (☎ 692-2488. Open daily 7am-9pm.)

■ **Le Diable aux Anges,** 28 bd. Champlain and 39 Petit Champlain (☎ 692-4674). Absorbs the European aura of rue Petit Champlain with its dimly lit, colonial interior. A number of traditional *québecois* dishes and sinfully named desserts offer seldom-found variety to the usual cafe/bistro. Breakfast is the best value, with many items offered a la carte.

Try the *oeuf gaspésien* ($10), an English muffin topped with smoked salmon, poached egg, and hollandaise sauce, with herbed potatoes and beans. Open daily 10am-11pm.

Le Café Buade, 31 rue Buade (☎ 692-3909), is renowned for its succulent prime rib, but it'll cost you $15-20. For those short on money, breakfast ($4) and lunch specials ($11) are large and delicious. Open daily 7am-midnight.

Le Cochon Dingue, 46 bd. Champlain (☎ 692-2013), meaning "crazy pig," is quickly becoming a culinary landmark in Québec. Consider spending your money on a few extra chocolate pear pies ($4) instead of the hog-themed t-shirt. Open June-Aug. M-Th 7am-midnight, F 7am-1am, Sa-Su 8am-1am; Sept.-May M-F 7am-11pm, Sa-Su 8am-11pm.

Chez Temporel, 25 rue Couillard (☎ 694-1813). Stay off the tourist path but remain within your budget at this genuine *café québécois*, discreetly tucked in a side alley off rue St-Jean, near the Auberge de la Paix. Besides the usual cafe staples (salads and soups $4-7), it offers some unique drinks ($4.50). Open daily 7am-2am.

Restaurant Liban, 23 rue d'Auteuil (☎ 694-1888), off rue St-Jean. Grab a great lunch or a late-night bite to go, or enjoy it on their outdoor patio. Tabouleh and hummus plates $3.50, both with pita bread. Excellent falafel ($4.50). Open daily 9am-4:30am.

👁 SIGHTS

The **Fortifications of Québec** compose a 6.5km stretch of wall surrounding Vieux Québec, inside of which are most of the city's historic attractions. Monuments are clearly marked and explained; still, you'll get more out of the town if you consult the *Greater Québec Area Tourist Guide*, which contains a walking tour of the Old City and is available at any Visitors Center. Don't be tempted by bus tours; although it takes one to two days to explore all of Vieux Québec's narrow, hilly streets and historic sites on foot, this is by far the best way to absorb its charm. The **Funiculaire** will carry passengers between Upper-Town and Place Royal and the Quartier Petit-Champlain for $1.25. (☎ 692-1132. Open 7:30am-midnight.)

CAP DIAMANT. Climbing to the top of Cap Diamant for a view of the city is a good way to orient oneself. Take Terrasse Dufferin to the Promenade des Gouverneurs. Just north is the **Citadel,** the largest North American fortification still guarded by troops—who knows why? Visitors can catch a tour of the **changing of the guard** daily at 10am and the **beating of the retreat** Wednesday-Saturday at 6pm. (☎ 694-2815. Open Apr. to mid-May daily 10am-4pm; mid-May to mid-June daily 10am-5pm; mid-June to Aug. 9am-6pm; Sept. 9am-4pm; Oct. 10am-3pm. $60, seniors $5, under 18 $3, families $14.)

PLACE-ROYALE AND QUARTIER PETIT-CHAMPLAIN. One of Old Québec's highlights is the crowded thoroughfare of **Rue du Petit-Champlain.** Along either side of this narrow passageway, modern visitors will find a host of cafes, craft shops, trendy boutiques, and restaurants. Each evening, the **Café-Théâtre le Petit Champlain** presents *québécois* music, singing, and dancing. (*68 rue du Petit-Champlain.* ☎ 692-2631. Call for schedules. Tickets for most shows $25-30.) **Place-Royale,** home to the oldest permanent European settlement in Canada (dating from 1608), can be reached quickly by taking rue Sous-le-Fort from the bottom of the Funiculaire. The **Centre d'interprétation Place-Royale** provides free 45min. tours of this historic district. (☎ 643-6631. Open daily 10am-5pm.) Dating back to 1688, **L'Eglise Notre-Dame-des-Victoires** is the oldest church in Canada. (*32 rue Sous-le-Fort.* ☎ 692-1650. Open May to mid-Oct. M-F 9:30am-5pm, Sa-Su 9:30am-4:30pm; mid-Oct. to Apr. 10am-4:30pm. Admission and tours free.) The **Musée de la Civilisation** celebrates Québec's past, present, and future, with tours in English and French. Follow the series of signs at the bottom of the Funiculaire. (*85 rue Dalhousie.* ☎ 643-2158. Open late June to early Sept. 10am-7pm; off-season Tu-Su 10am-5pm. $7, seniors $6, students $4.)

PARLIAMENT HILL. The **Assemblée Nationale,** at Grande Allée and av. Honore-Mercier, is located just outside the wall of the city. Finished in 1886, the building was designed in the style of Louis XIV. Lively debates can be observed from the visitors' gallery, and both English and French speakers have recourse to simultaneous translation earphones. (☎ 643-7239. Open late June to early Sept. M-F 9am-4:30pm, Sa-Su 10am-4:30pm; mid-Sept. to mid-June hours vary. 30min. tours are free, but advance reservations are recommended.) The **Capital Observatory,** just off Grande Allée, offers breathtaking views of the city from 230m above sea level, the highest observing place in town. (1037 rue de la Chevrotière. ☎ 644-9841. Open daily 10am-5pm. $4, seniors and students $3.)

BATTLEFIELDS. The **Parc des Champs-de-Bataille** or **Plains of Abraham,** located adjacent to the Citadel along av. George-VI, can be reached from Grande Allée. The interpretation center has exhibits on the history of the battlefields, where French forces under Montcalm fell to the British under General Wolfe in 1759. (☎ 648-4071. Open mid-May to early Sept. daily 10am-5:30pm; call for times during the rest of the year.) Located on the premises of the Battlefields Park, the **Musée du Québec** houses eclectic modern and québécois art while playing host to visiting exhibitions. (☎ 646-3330. Open June through early Sept. 3 daily 10am-6pm, W 10am-9pm; mid-Sept.-May 31 Tu-Su 10am-5pm, W 10am-9pm. $7, students $2.75, seniors $6.)

CHÂTEAU FRONTENAC. The Château Frontenac, with its grand architecture and green copper roofs, is perhaps the most recognizable structure in the city and is thought to be the most photographed hotel in the world. Should you be windswept by the hype, the hotel provides tours of its opulence, highlighting its place in history with photographs of famous visitors, including the Allied leaders that conferenced here during World War II. (1 rue des Carrières. ☎ 692-3861 or 691-2166. Tours mid-May to mid-Oct. daily on the hr. 10am-6pm, mid-Oct. to mid-May Sa-Su on the hr. 1-5pm; reservations highly recommended. $6.50, seniors $5.50, under 16 $3.75.)

OTHER ATTRACTIONS. With its shimmering golden altar and ornate stained-glass windows, the **Basilique Notre-Dame de Québec** is one of the oldest cathedrals in North America. Located at rue de Buade and rue Ste-Famille, the Basilique shows a fantastic 45min. light show, the **"Act of Faith,"** which relays the history of the church. (☎ 694-4000. Open daily 9:30am-4:30pm. Free. Shows daily May-Oct.; times vary. $7.50.) The **Musée de l'Amérique-française,** located on the grounds of the **Québec Seminary** just down the street from the Basilica, is an excellent museum whose informative exhibits recount the details of Francophone settlement in North America. (9 rue de l'Université. ☎ 692-2843. Open Tu-Su 10am-5pm. $4, students and seniors $3.)

🎵🎬 ENTERTAINMENT AND NIGHTLIFE

Images of "Le Bonhomme de Neige" will plaster the snow-covered city in anticipation of the raucous annual **Winter Carnival,** which breaks the tedium of northern winters from February 1 to 17, 2002 (☎ 626-3716). The annual **Summer Festival,** with free outdoor concerts, will mean packed hostels from July 4 to July 14, 2002 (☎ 529-5200). Throughout the summer, the **Plein Art** exhibition floods the Pigeonnier on Grande-Allée with arts and crafts (☎ 694-0260). **Les nuits Black,** Québec's main jazz festival, bebops the city for two weeks in late June. But Québec's most festive day of the year—eclipsing even Canada Day—is June 24, **la Fête nationale du Québec** (St-Jean-Baptiste Day). This celebration of québécois culture features free concerts, a bonfire, and 5 million roaring drunk acolytes of John the Baptist. (☎ 640-0799.)

OUTSIDE THE WALLS

The Grande Allée's many restaurants are interspersed with bar discothèques, where twenty-something crowds dance till dawn. **Dagobert,** 600 Grande Allée Est, saturates the air with pop and dance sounds. Two dance floors and an adjoining bar give plenty of room to mingle. (☎ 522-0393. No cover. Outside bar open daily 2pm-2am, inside club 10pm-3am.) A bit less hectic is **O'Zone,** 570 Grande Allée, where the folks linger at the bar before going to the 2nd-story dance floor for rock, dance, and hip-hop. (☎ 529-7932. No cover. Open M-Sa 11am-3am, Su 1pm-3am.) The gay scene in Québec City is limited, but alive. **Le Ballon Rouge,** 811 rue St-Jean, several blocks beyond the walls of the Old City, is a favorite dance club where dimly lit pool tables coexist with neon rainbows. (☎ 647-9227. No cover. Open daily 5pm-3am.)

INSIDE THE WALLS

Québec City's young, visible punk contingent clusters around rue St-Jean and several nearby sidestreets, but more laid-back nightclubs find a niche here too. A traditional Québec evening awaits at **Les Yeux Bleux**, 1117½ rue St-Jean, a local spot where *chansonniers* perform nightly. (☎694-9118. No cover. Open daily 8pm-3am.) **La Fourmi Atomik,** 33 rue d'Auteuil, has underground rock and themed music nights. (☎694-1473. 18+. No cover. Open daily 1pm-3am; Oct.-May 4pm-3am.) **L'Ostradamus**, 29 rue Couillard, throws live jazz and techno over its smoke-drenched, "spiritual" ambience. (☎694-9560 Cover $4. Open daily 8pm-3am.)

▶ DAYTRIP FROM QUÉBEC CITY: ÎLE-D'ORLÉANS

Named in honor of the god of wine (and sex), the **Île-d'Orléans** was originally called *Île de Bacchus* because of the multitudinous wild grapes fermenting there. The Île-d'Orléans remains a sparsely populated retreat of small villages and endless strawberry fields. The island is located about 10km downstream from Québec on the St-Laurent, making it an ideal excursion by car (public transportation doesn't access the island, and the highway stretch to the island makes biking impossible). Take Hwy. 75 to Autoroute 440 Est, on to Hwy. 368, and cross over the only bridge leading to the island (Pont de l'Île). A tour of the island covers 64km. **The Manoir Mauvide-Genest,** in St-Jean, once home to the king's surgeon, is now a private museum flaunting crafts and traditional colonial furniture. (*1451 ch. Royal.* ☎829-2630. *Open June to mid-Oct. daily 9am-5pm. Free, but donations are appreciated.*)

Exiting Île-d'Orléans, turn right (east) onto Hwy. 138 (bd. Ste-Anne) to view the splendid **Chute Montmorency** (Montmorency Falls). In winter, vapors from the falls form a frozen mist that screens the running water. About 20km along Hwy. 138 lies **Ste-Anne-de-Beaupré** (Orléans Express buses link it to Québec City for $5, see **Practical Information**). This small town's *raison d'être* is the famous double-spired **Basilique Ste-Anne-de-Beaupré,** which houses the alleged forearm bone of St. Anne, mother to the Virgin Mary. How did it get to Canada? The pilgrims who visit by the hundreds of thousands each year don't question the logistics, and the church's miraculous healing power is evidenced by the racks of discarded crutches inside. (*10018 av. Royale.* ☎827-3781. *Open early May to mid-Sept. daily 6am-9:30pm.*)

ONTARIO

Now an Anglo political counterbalance to French Québec, this populous central province raises the ire of peripheral regions of Canada due to its high concentration of power and wealth. In the south, world-class Toronto shines—multicultural, enormous, vibrant, clean, and generally safe. Yuppified suburbs, an occasional college town, and farms surround this sprawling metropolis. In the east, the national capital Ottawa sits on Ontario's border with Québec. To the north, layers of cottage country and ski resorts give way to a pristine wilderness that is as much French and Native Canadian as it is British.

▶ PRACTICAL INFORMATION

Capital: Toronto.

Visitor Info: Customer Service Branch of the **Ontario Ministry of Culture, Tourism, and Recreation** (☎800-668-2746, 24hr. automated info). Send written requests to **Tourism Ontario**, 1243 Islington Ave., Suite 200, Toronto, ON M8X 2Y3.

Drinking Age: 19. **Postal Abbreviation:** ON. **Sales Tax:** 8%; 5% on rooms; 7% GST.

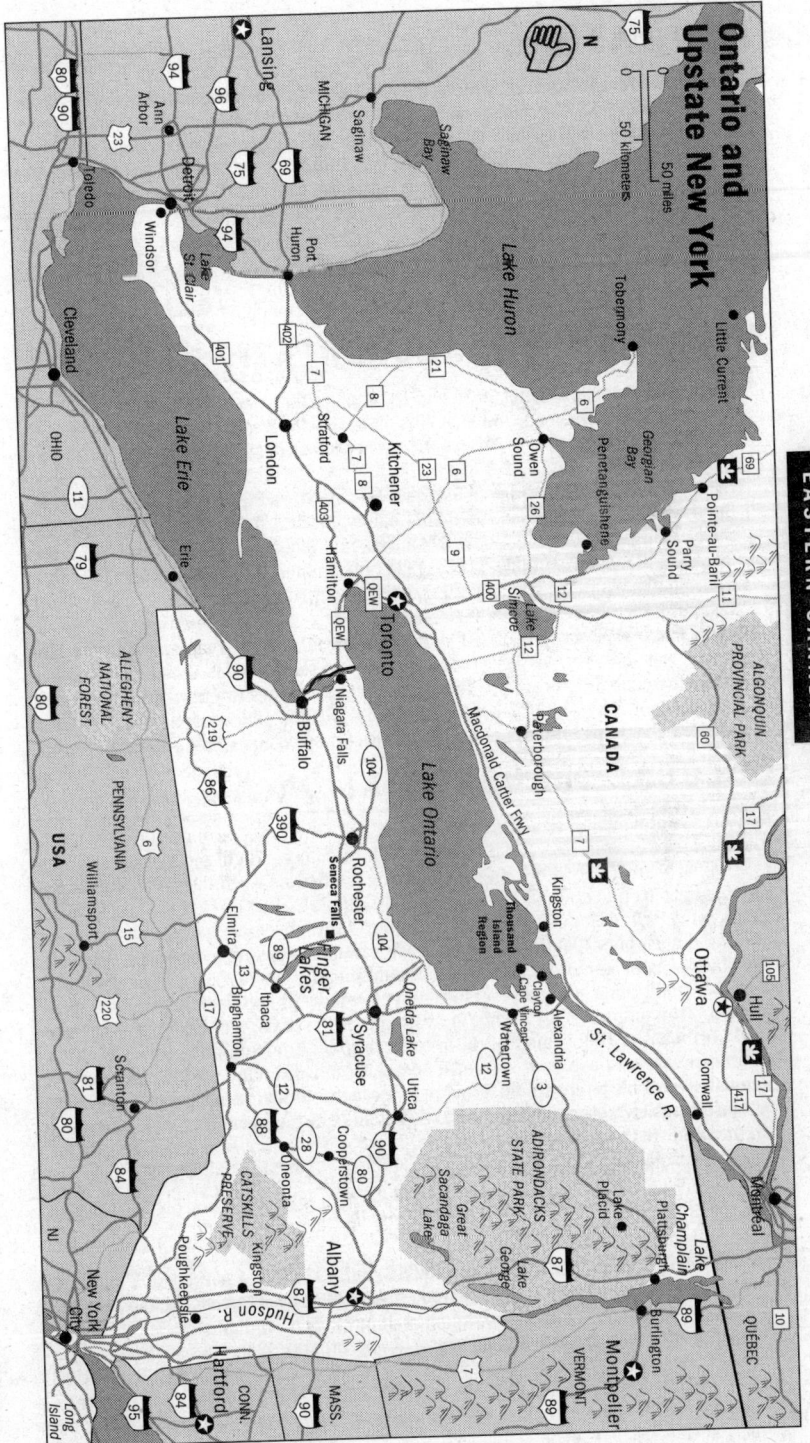

Ontario and Upstate New York

N

50 kilometres
50 miles

TORONTO

☎ **416**

Once a prim and proper Victorian city where even window-shopping was prohibited on the Sabbath, Toronto is now dubbed the world's most multicultural city by the United Nations. The city has spent millions in recent years on spectacular public works projects: the world's tallest free-standing structure (the CN tower), the biggest retractable roof (the Sky Dome), and outstanding lakefront development. Cosmetically, Toronto aspires to the urban grandeur of New York, drawing Hollywood producers seeking to make a New York movie at Toronto prices. But New York it is not; one film crew, after dirtying a street to make it look more like a gritty "American" avenue, went on coffee break and returned to find their set spotless again, swept by the vigilant city maintenance department.

✈ INTERCITY TRANSPORTATION

Airport: Pearson International (☎247-7678), about 20km west of Toronto via Hwy. 401. Take bus #58A west from Lawrence W. subway. **Pacific Western Transportation** (☎905-564-6333) runs buses every 20min. to downtown hotels ($14.25, round-trip $24.50). Buses run 5:30am-12:15am.

Trains: All trains leave from **Union Station,** 65 Front St. (☎366-8411), at Bay and York. Subway: Union. **VIA Rail** (☎366-8411) cannonballs to Montréal (5½hr., 7 per day, $99); Windsor (4hr., 4-5 per day, $74); New York City (12hr., 1-2 per day, $95); and Chicago (11hr., 1-2 per day, $160). Ticket office open M-F 6am-11:30pm, Sa 6am-6:30pm, Su 7am-11:30pm; station open M-Sa 5:30am-12:45am, Su 6:30am-12:45am.

Buses: Trentway-Wagar (☎393-7911) and **Greyhound** (☎367-8747) operate from 610 Bay St., just north of Dundas St. Subway: St. Patrick or Dundas. Trentway-Wagar has service to Montréal (7hr., 7 per day, $82). Greyhound goes to Ottawa (5½-7hr., 9 per day, $59); Calgary (49hr., 3 per day, $161); Vancouver (2½ days, 3 per day, $182), and New York City (11hr., 6 per day, $108). Ticket office open daily 5am-1am.

▣ LOCAL TRANSPORTATION

The TTC's subway and streetcars are the easiest way to get around the city, but if you must drive, avoid rush hour (4-7pm). A flashing green light means that you can go straight or turn left freely, as the opposing traffic has a red light. **Parking** on the street is hard to find and usually carries a 1hr. limit, except on Sunday and at night (until 7am), when spaces are free and abundant. Day parking generally costs inbound daytrippers $3-4 at outlying subway stations; parking overnight at the subway stations is prohibited. Parking lots within the city run at least $12 for 24 hours (7am-7am), although some all-day lots downtown on King St. sell unguarded spots for $4-6. Free, unmetered parking is available in **Rosedale,** a residential neighborhood northeast of Bloor and Sherbourne St., about 3km from downtown. To combat transportation problems, city officials enforce traffic and parking regulations zealously, so don't tempt them. Towing is a common occurrence, even for locals; the **non-emergency police number** (☎416-808-2222) has an answering system to help you find your car's temporary new home.

Ferries: Toronto Island Ferry Service (☎392-8194, recording 392-8193). Ferries to Centre Island, Wards Island, and Hanlans Point leave from the foot of Bay St. Service daily about every 30min. 8am-11:45pm; less often in winter. Round-trip $5; seniors, students, and ages 15-19 $3; ages 2-14 $2.

Public Transit: Toronto Transit Commission (TTC) (☎393-4000). A network of 2 long subway lines and many bus and streetcar routes. After dark, buses are required to stop anywhere along a route at a female passenger's request. Subway service begins M-Sa 6am and Su 9am, with the last trains leaving downtown at 1:30am; buses cover subway routes after that. Fare $2 (5 tokens $10), seniors and students with ID $1.50, under 13 50¢ (10 for $4). M-Sa 1-day travel pass $7.50. Su and holidays, families receive unlimited travel for $7.50. Free transfers among subway, buses, and streetcars, but only at stations.

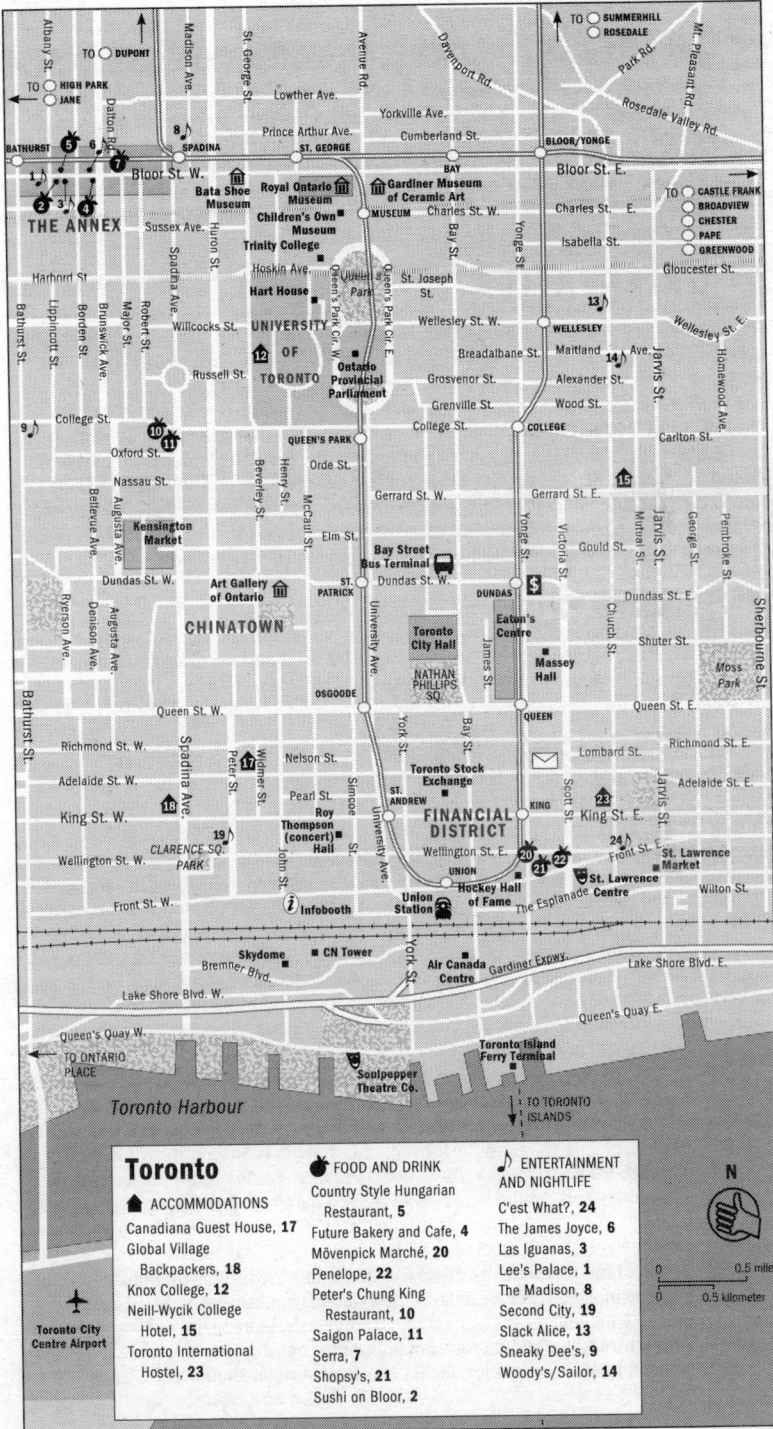

Toronto

ACCOMMODATIONS

Canadiana Guest House, **17**
Global Village
   Backpackers, **18**
Knox College, **12**
Neill-Wycik College
   Hotel, **15**
Toronto International
   Hostel, **23**

FOOD AND DRINK

Country Style Hungarian
   Restaurant, **5**
Future Bakery and Cafe, **4**
Mövenpick Marché, **20**
Penelope, **22**
Peter's Chung King
   Restaurant, **10**
Saigon Palace, **11**
Serra, **7**
Shopsy's, **21**
Sushi on Bloor, **2**

**ENTERTAINMENT
AND NIGHTLIFE**

C'est What?, **24**
The James Joyce, **6**
Las Iguanas, **3**
Lee's Palace, **1**
The Madison, **8**
Second City, **19**
Slack Alice, **13**
Sneaky Dee's, **9**
Woody's/Sailor, **14**

Taxis: Co-op Cabs, ☎504-2667.

Jump-On/Jump-Off Service: Moose Travel Co. Ltd. (☎905-853-4762 or 888-816-6673). A series of expeditions founded by former backpackers, in which you can hop on and off a bus full of hostelers at dozens of destinations throughout Eastern Canada at your own convenience. 4-9 days of travel time can spread over 5 months. Offers 3 routes through Ontario and Québec ($239-399) and discounted rail connections to western routes.

Bike Rental: Brown's Sports and Bike Rental, 2447 Bloor St. W. (763-4176). $22 per day, $45 per weekend, $55 per week. $300 deposit or credit card required. Open M-W 9:30am-6pm, Th-F 9:30am-8pm, Sa 9:30am-5:30pm.

✦ ORIENTATION

Toronto's streets form a grid pattern. Addresses on north-south streets increase toward the north, away from Lake Ontario. **Yonge St.** is the main north-south route, dividing the city and the streets perpendicular to it into east and west. Numbering for both sides starts at Yonge St. and increases as you move away in either direction. West of Yonge St., the main arteries are **Bay St., University Ave., Spadina Ave.,** and **Bathurst St.** The major east-west routes include, from the water north, **Front St., Queen St., Dundas St., College St., Bloor St.,** and **Eglington St.** For an extended stay or travel outside the city center, it is best to buy the *Downtown and Metro Toronto Visitor's Map Guide* from a drug store or tourist shop ($2.95). The *Ride Guide*, free at all TTC stations and info booths, explains metro area transit.

NEIGHBORHOODS

Downtown Toronto splits into many distinctive neighborhoods. Thanks to zoning regulations that require developers to include housing and retail space in commercial construction, many people live downtown. **Chinatown** centers on Dundas St. W. between Bay St. and Spadina Ave. Formerly the Jewish market of the 1920s, **Kensington Market,** on Kensington Ave., Augusta Ave., and the western half of Baldwin St., is now a largely Portuguese neighborhood with many good restaurants, vintage clothing shops, and an outdoor bazaar. The strip of old factories, stores, and warehouses on **Queen St. W.,** from University Ave. to Bathurst St., is a good place to shop during the day and go club-hopping at night. The ivy-covered Gothic buildings and magnificent quadrangles of the **University of Toronto** occupy about 200 acres in the center of the city. **The Annex,** Bloor St. W. at the Spadina subway, has an artistic ambience and an excellent range of budget restaurants (see **Food,** below). Afterwards, hit the numerous bars and nightclubs along Bloor St. heading west. **Yorkville,** just north of Bloor between Yonge St. and Avenue Rd., was once the communal home of flower children and folk guitarists. **Cabbagetown,** just east of Yonge St., bounded by Gerrard St. E., Wellesley, and Sumach St., takes its name from the Irish immigrants who used to plant the vegetable in their yards. The **Gay and Lesbian Village,** around Church and Wellesley St., offers fine outdoor cafes.

On Front St. between Sherbourne and Yonge St., the **Theater District** supports enough venues to whet any cultural appetite. Music, food, ferry rides, dance companies, and art all dock at the **Harbourfront** (☎973-3000), on Queen's Quay W. from York to Bathurst St., on the lake. The three main **Toronto Islands,** accessible by ferry (see **Local Transportation,** above), offer beaches, bike rentals, and an amusement park. East from the harbor, the beaches along and south of Queen's St. E., between Woodbine and Victoria, boast a popular boardwalk. Five km east of the city center, the rugged 16m stretch of **Scarborough Bluffs** rises over the lakeshore.

Three more ethnic enclaves lie 15 to 30min. from downtown by public transit. **Corso Italia** surrounds St. Clair W. at Dufferin St.; take the subway to St. Clair W. and bus #512 west. **Little India** is at Gerrard St. E. and Coxwell; ride the subway to Coxwell, then take bus #22 south to the second Gerard St. stop. Better known as **"the Danforth,"** Greektown (subway: Pape) is on Danforth Ave. at Pape Ave.

◪ PRACTICAL INFORMATION

Visitor Info: The **Metropolitan Toronto Convention and Visitors Association (MTCVA),** 207 Queens Quay W. (☎203-2500 or 800-363-1990), mails out info and answers questions by phone. For in-person assistance, head to the **Info T.O.,** 255 Front St. W., at the Metro Toronto Convention Centre. Open daily 8am-5pm.

Student Travel Office: Travel CUTS, 187 College St. (☎979-2406), just west of University Ave. Subway: Queen's Park. Open M and Th-F 9am-5pm, Tu 9:30am-5pm, W 9am-7pm, Sa 10am-3pm.

Currency Exchange: Toronto Currency Exchange, 363 Yonge St. (☎598-5096), at Dundas St., offers the best rates around. Open daily 10am-8pm. Also at 2 Walton St. (☎599-5821). Open daily 10am-7pm. **Royal Bank of Canada,** 200 Bay St. Plaza (☎800-769-2511), exchanges around the city. Branches generally open M-F 10am-4pm; call for each branch's specific hours.

Hotlines: Rape Crisis, ☎597-8808. **Services for the Disabled, Info Ability,** ☎800-665-9092. **Toronto Gay and Lesbian Phone Line,** ☎964-6600. Open M-F 7-10pm. **Events Hotline,** ☎392-0458.

Post Office: Adelaide Station, 31 Adelaide St. E. (☎214-2353 or 214-2352). Subway: King. Open M-F 8am-5:45pm. **Postal code:** M5C 1J0. **Area code:** 416 (city), 905 (outskirts). In text, 416 unless noted otherwise.

◪ ACCOMMODATIONS

Cut-rate hotels concentrate around Jarvis and Gerrard St. The University of Toronto provides cheap sleep for budget travelers; contact the **U of T Housing Service,** 214 College St., at St. George St., for $20-45 rooms. (☎978-8045. Open M-F 8:45am-5pm.) The **Downtown Association of Bed and Breakfast Guest Houses** places guests in renovated Victorian homes. (☎483-8032; singles $50-85, doubles $75-130.) Because it is difficult to regulate these registries, visit a B&B before you commit.

Global Village Backpackers, 460 King St. W. (☎703-8540 or 888-844-7875). Subway: St. Andrew. An efficient, highly social backpacker support system. 195 beds in the centrally located, brightly colored former Spadina Hotel. Travelers convene at the outdoor patio, where BBQs are held nightly 7-9:30pm. Lockers ($1) and Internet access. Kitchen, laundry ($1.50), in-house Travel CUTS branch. Reception 24hr. Dorms $25; doubles $60 during summer, slightly less off-season. $2-4 off for ISIC or HI members.

Canadiana Guest House & Backpackers, 42 Widmer St., off Adelaide St. W. (☎598-9090 or 877-215-1225). Subway: Osgoode. 70 extra-long, wood-stained beds in attractive, newly renovated Victorian townhouses. A slightly older and quieter hostel crowd. A/C, laundry ($3), and Internet. Kitchen and locker facilities available. Check-in 8am-midnight during summer; in winter 8am-11pm. Dorms $25; private doubles $60.

Neill-Wycik College Hotel, 96 Gerrard St. E. (☎977-2320 or 800-268-4358). Subway: Dundas. Small, clean rooms, some with beautiful views of the city and a roof deck perfect for recuperating from a tiring day of travel. Continental breakfast included. Kitchen on every fl. Laundry ($2), sauna, family rooms, and lockers available. Open early May to late Aug. Check-in after 4pm. Check-out 10am. Dorms $20; singles $35; doubles $60. Students, seniors, and HI members get a 20% discount. No discount on dorms.

Toronto International Hostel (HI-C), 76 Church St. (☎971-4440 or 877-848-8737), at King. Subway: King. Recently relocated hostel in a great downtown location. Kitchen, laundry facilities ($3), and a lounge. Linen $2. Reception 24hr. Check-in after noon. Check-out 11am. Dorms $20, nonmembers $24. Reservations recommended in the summer. Additional location June-Aug. at 160 Mutual St. (☎971-7073; $22.50/27).

Knox College, 59 St. George St. (☎978-0168; call M-F 10am-5pm). Subway: Queen's Park or St. George. In the heart of campus, Canada's picturesque Presbyterian Seminary offers huge rooms with wooden floors. Open mid-May to late Aug. Singles $45, students $35; doubles $60. Reserve rooms at least 3 weeks ahead of time.

YWCA-Woodlawn Residence, 80 Woodlawn Ave. E. (☎923-8454), off Yonge St. Subway: Summerhill. 144 rooms for women only, in a nice neighborhood uptown. Breakfast, kitchen, TV lounges, linen ($5 deposit), and laundry facilities. Reception M-F 7:30am-11:30pm, Sa-Su 7:30am-7:30pm. Small, neat singles $48-54; doubles $62; private bath available. Beds in basement dormitory $22. 10% senior discount.

◘ FOOD

An immigration surge has made Toronto a haven for international food, with over 5000 restaurants squeezed into the metropolitan area. **Village by the Grange,** at McCaul and Dundas near the Art Gallery of Ontario, is a vast collection of super-cheap restaurants and vendors—Chinese, Thai, Middle Eastern, you name it (generally open 11am-7pm). "L.L.B.O." posted on the window of a restaurant means that it has a liquor license. Some of the standouts can be found on **Bloor St. W.** and in **Chinatown.** For fresh produce, go to **Kensington Market** or the **St. Lawrence Market** at King St. E. and Sherbourne, six blocks east of the King subway stop.

THE ANNEX

Serra, 378 Bloor St. W. (☎922-6999). Subway: Spadina. A quiet, tastefully decorated oasis amid the bustle of the Annex. Delicately prepared angel hair and grilled chicken ($12.45). Open M-F noon-10pm, Sa-Su 5-11pm.

Sushi on Bloor, 515 Bloor St. W. (☎516-3456). Subway: Bathurst. This friendly, well-lit joint is filled with hipsters scarfing down fresh sushi (6 pieces $4-5), including lunch ($6) and dinner (starting from $5.50) specials. Open daily noon-midnight.

Future Bakery & Cafe, 483 Bloor St. W. (☎922-5875). Subway: Bathurst. Fresh cakes ($4.25) and huge breakfasts pastries charge up the young student crowd by day, and beer ($4-5) on the patio winds them down after dark. Open daily 7:30am-2am.

Country Style Hungarian Restaurant, 450 Bloor St. W. (☎537-1745). Subway: Bathurst. Hearty stews, soups, and casseroles, just like in Hungary. Meals come in small (plenty) and large (huge) portions. Schnitzel $9.75. Entrees $4-11. Open daily 11am-10pm.

CHINATOWN

Saigon Palace, 454 Spadina Ave. (☎968-1623), at College St. Subway: Spadina. An unassuming Vietnamese restaurant with great spring rolls and natural juice drinks ($3). Bee or vegetable dishes over rice $4-8. Open M-Th 9am-10pm, F-Sa 9am-11pm.

Peter's Chung King Restaurant, 281 College St. W. (☎928-2936). Subway: Spadina. A picture of Chris de Burgh (of "Lady in Red" fame) adorns the window, with Chris's note proclaiming "Wonderful Food!" He's not the only one who thinks so: Peter's is consistently named one of Toronto's best Chinese restaurants. Garlic shrimp $9; soy-sauteed green beans $7. Open M-Th noon-10pm, F noon-11pm, Sa 1-11pm, Su 1-10pm.

THEATER/ST. LAWRENCE DISTRICT

◙ **Mövenpick Marché** (☎366-8986), in BCE Place at Yonge and Front St. Probably the only restaurant that requires a map. Browse through and select a meal from the 14 culinary stations, including bakery, bar, pasta, seafood, salad, and grill. Entrees run $8-10. Open Su-Th 7:30am-2am, F-Sa 7:30am-4am.

Shopsy's, 33 Yonge St. (☎365-3333), at Front St. 1 block from Union Station. Other locations at 284A King St. W. (☎599-5464) and 1535 Yonge St. (☎967-5252). The definitive Toronto deli. 300 seats. Snappy service. Hot dog $3.79. Open M 6:30am-10pm, Tu-W 6:30am-11pm, Th-F 6:30am-midnight, Sa 8am-midnight, Su 8am-9pm.

Penelope, 6 Front St. E. (☎351-9393). Subway: Union. Generous portions of Greek fare in the middle of the financial district. Pre-theatre dinner special $11; mouth-watering roast lamb $13. Open daily 10:30am-11pm.

THE DANFORTH

Mr. Greek, 568 Danforth Ave. (☎947-1159), at Carlaw. Subway: Pape. A friendly, bustling cafe serving shish kebabs, salads, and wine amidst Greek music. Classic gyros or souvlaki dinner $10.50. Open Su-Th 10:30am-1am, F-Sa 10:30am-4am.

◉ SIGHTS

A walk through the city's neighborhoods can be one of the most rewarding activities in Toronto. Streetside conversations change languages frequently, and the main thoroughfares are usually full of frenetic activity. For an organized expedition, the **Royal Ontario Museum** leads ten free **walking tours.** (☎586-5513. Tours June-Sept. W 6pm and Su 2pm. Destinations and meeting places vary; call for specific info.) The green and tidy **University of Toronto** conducts free 1hr. walking tours of Canada's largest university. Tours meet at the Nona MacDonald Visitors Center at King's College Circle. (☎978-5000. Tours June-Aug. M-F 11am and 2pm, Sa 11am.)

ARCHITECTURE. Toronto's **CN Tower** stands as the world's tallest free-standing structure, a mammoth concrete symbol of human ingenuity that is visible from nearly every corner of the city. Its other claims to fame include the world's longest metal stairway and the world's highest wine cellar. The tower offers a heavenly view (especially on a cloudy day), and despite the frightening void below, trusting souls lie down on the observation deck's sturdy glass floor. *(Subway: Union. ☎360-8500. Open daily 9am-11pm. $16, seniors $14, ages 4-12 $11. $5.50 more for the Sky Pod.)*

The curving twin towers and two-story rotunda of the innovative **City Hall** are at Queen and Bay St.; brochures for self-guided tours of this 60s creation are available. *(Subway: Osgoode. ☎338-0338. Open M-F 8:30am-4:30pm.)* In front of City Hall, **Nathan Phillips Sq.** is home to a reflecting pool (which becomes a skating rink in winter) and numerous events, including live music every Wednesday (June to early Oct. noon-2pm). The Ontario government meets in the stately Provincial Parliament Buildings, at Queen's Park in the heart of the city. *(Subway: Queen's Park. ☎325-7500. 30min. tours daily 9am-4pm late May-early Sept. Call ahead for Parliamentary schedule. Free gallery passes available at south basement door when the house is in session.)* Straight from a fairy tale, the 98-room **Casa Loma**, atop a hill near Spadina a few blocks north of the Dupont subway stop, is a classic tourist attraction. An eerie underground tunnel and two imposing towers add to the grandeur of this display of late Victorian opulence. *(☎923-1171 or 923-1172. Open daily 9:30am-4pm. $10, seniors and ages 14-17 $6.50, ages 4-13 $6.)* Visitors are treated to a tour of 19th-century Toronto next door at the **Spadina House**, a six-acre estate relic from 1866. *(285 Spadina Rd. ☎392-6910. Open Apr.-Sept. Tu-Su noon-5pm. $5, seniors and ages 12-17 $3.25, ages 6-11 $3.)*

FAUNA. The **Metro Toronto Zoo** keeps over 6600 animals in a 710-acre park that features sections re-creating the world's seven geographic regions and rare wildlife including a Tasmanian devil. *(Meadowvale Rd. off Exit 389 on Hwy. 401. Take bus #86A from Kennedy Station. ☎392-5900. Open mid-Oct. to mid-Mar. daily 9:30am-4:30pm; mid-Mar. to mid-May and early Sept. to mid-Oct. 9am-6pm; late May to early Sept. 9am-7:30pm. Last entry 1hr. before closing. $15, seniors $11, ages 4-14 $9. Parking $6.)*

SCIENCE. The **Ontario Science Center** presents more than 650 interactive exhibits showcasing humanity's greatest innovations. *(770 Don Mills Rd., at Eglington Ave. E. ☎696-3127. Museum open daily 10am-5pm. $12, ages 13-17 and seniors $7, ages 5-12 $6; with Omnimax film $17/$11.)*

HOCKEY. No trip to Toronto is complete without a visit to the **Hockey Hall of Fame,** the glorified home of Canada's national pastime. Get in on the action in several interactive exhibits, or call your own bilingual play-by-play of some of hockey's greatest goals. Check out the 100-year-old Great Hall, which houses the coveted Stanley Cup beneath a beautiful stained glass dome. *(In BCE Place, 30 Yonge St. Subway: BCE Place. ☎360-7765. Open mid-June to early Sept. M-Sa 9:30am-6pm, Su 10am-6pm; off-season M-F 10am-5pm, Sa 9:30am-6pm, Su 10:30am-5pm. $12, seniors and under 18 $7.)*

🏛 MUSEUMS

Art Gallery of Ontario (AGO), 317 Dundas St. (☎979-6648), on three blocks of University Ave. downtown. Subway: St. Patrick. Showcases an enormous collection of Western art from the Renaissance to the 90s, concentrating on Canadian artists. Exhibits in the past year have featured the treasures of Russia's Hermitage. Open Tu and Th-F 11am-6pm, W 11am-8:30pm, Sa-Su 10am-5:30pm. $6 suggested donation.

YOUR CHARIOT AWAITS... If you find the subway crowded but don't want to hail a cab, rickshaws will sweep you off your feet. Originally from Hong Kong, these human-drawn carriages have caught on all over Canada. In Toronto, companies like **Rickshaw Services of Toronto** (☎410-4593) will cart you through the city streets courtesy of other people's backs. Rates are about $3 per block per person.

Bata Shoe Museum, 327 Bloor St. (☎979-7799). Subway: St. George. Housed in a shoe-box-shaped edifice, the diverse collection focuses on the often stepped-over role of footwear in human culture. Open Tu-W and F-Sa 10am-5pm, Th 10am-8pm, Su noon-5pm. $6, seniors and students $4, ages 5-14 $2, families $12. Free first Tu of every month.

George R. Gardiner Museum of Ceramic Art, 111 Queen's Park (☎586-8080). Subway: Museum. Traces the history of ceramics. Open M, W, F 10am-6pm; Tu, Th 10am-8pm; Sa-Su 10am-5pm. $5, students and seniors $3. Free first Tu of every month.)

Royal Ontario Museum (ROM), 100 Queen's Park (☎586-5549), across the street from the Gardiner Museum. Subway: Museum. Houses artifacts from ancient civilizations, a bat cave, and a giant *T. rex.* Open M-Th and Sa 10am-6pm, F 10am-9:30pm, Su 11am-6pm. $15, seniors and students $10, ages 5-14 $8. F after 4:30pm free.

◪ OUTDOOR ACTIVITIES

Toronto crawls with **biking** and **hiking** trails. For a map of the trails, call **MetroParks** (☎392-8186), which has info on local facilities and activities. It might not be the Caribbean, but the **beaches** on the southeast now support a permanent community. A popular "vacationland," the **Toronto Islands Park,** on Centre Island, has a boardwalk, bathing beaches, canoe and bike rentals, and an amusement park. The park is on a 9km strip of connected islands opposite downtown. (Open mid-May to early Sept.)

♫ ENTERTAINMENT

The monthly *Where Toronto*, available free at tourism booths, gives the lowdown on arts and entertainment. **T.O. Tix** sells half-price tickets on performance day at 208 Yonge St., north of Queen St. at Eaton's Centre. (☎536-6468. Subway: Queen. Open Tu-Sa noon-7:30pm; arrive before 11:45am for first dibs.) **Ticketmaster** (☎870-8000) supplies tickets for many Toronto venues, but with a hefty service charge.

Ontario Place, 955 Lakeshore Blvd. W., features cheap summer entertainment, including music and light shows. (☎314-9811, recording 314-9900. Park open mid-May to early Sept. daily 10:30am-midnight.) Top pop artists perform in the **Molson Amphitheater.** (☎260-5600. Ticketmaster handles tickets; $20-125.) **Roy Thompson Hall,** 60 Simcoe St., at King St. W., is both Toronto's premier concert hall and the home of the **Toronto Symphony Orchestra,** from September to June. (☎593-4828, box office 872-4255. Subway: St. Andrews. Open M-F 10am-6pm, Sa noon-5pm, Su 2hr. before performances. Tickets $25-85, $25-50 for matinees. $15 rush tickets available on concert days M-F 11am and Sa 1pm.)

The **St. Lawrence Centre,** 27 Front St. E., stages excellent drama and chamber music recitals. (☎366-7723. Box office open M-Sa 10am-6pm; in winter performance days 10am-8pm, non-performance days 10am-6pm. Possible student and senior discounts.) **Canadian Stage** performs free summer Shakespeare ($12 donation suggested) at **High Park,** on Bloor St. W. at Parkside Dr. Year-round shows at the St. Lawrence Centre include new Canadian works and classics. (Box office 368-3110. Subway: High Park. Open M-Sa 10am-6pm. Call for schedule.) Several blocks west in the Harbourfront Centre, the **Soulpepper Theatre Company,** 231 Queen's Quay W., presents famous masterpieces. (☎973-4000. $21-45, students $25, rush tickets $18.)

Canada's answer to Disney is **Canada's Wonderland,** 9580 Jane St., 1hr. from downtown but accessible by public transit; take **Vaughn Transit** (☎905-832-8527) from the Richmond Hill area or the **Go Bus** (☎869-3200) from the Yorkdale or York Mills subway stations ($3.75 each way). Splash down water rides or ride on coasters. (☎905-

832-7000. Open late June to early Sept. daily 10am-10pm; open in fall Sa-Su, times vary. Waterpark open in summer daily 11am-7pm. $45, seniors and ages 3-6 $24.)

From April to early October, the **Toronto Blue Jays** play hardball at the enormous modern monstrosity, **Sky Dome**, Front and Peter St. (☎341-1111, tickets 341-1234. Subway: Union, follow the signs. Tickets $7-42.) To get an inside look at the Sky Dome, take the **tour.** (☎341-2770. Times vary. $12.50, seniors and under 16 $8.50.) The Sky Dome is also the home of the **Toronto Argonauts** of the Canadian Football League, as well as concerts and other events throughout the year. (Argonauts: ☎489-2746; concerts: ☎341-3663.) Hockey fans head for **The Air Canada Centre**, 40 Bay St., to see the **Maple Leafs.** (☎815-5700. Subway: Union. Tickets $30-160.)

Toronto's rich cultural offerings include several world-class **festivals**. Film fans choose the **Bloor Cinema**, 506 Bloor St. W. (☎532-6677), at Bathurst, or the **Cinematheque Ontario**, 317 Dundas St. W. (☎923-3456), at McCaul St. The ten-day **Toronto International Film Festival** (☎967-7371), being held Sept. 5-14, 2002, with its showings of classic, Canadian, and foreign films is one of the most prestigious festivals on the art-house circuit. In June, the **Toronto International Dragon Boat Race Festival** (☎598-8945) continues a 2000-year-old Chinese tradition, including performances and foods. From August 16 through September 2, the **Canadian National Exhibition (CNE)**, the world's largest annual fair, brings an international carnival to Exhibition Place. (☎393-6000. Open daily 10am-midnight. $9, seniors and children $5, under 6 free.) The city also rocks with the second-largest **gay pride celebration** in the world, also in late June, and a growing **street festival** and **fringe theatre festival** in mid-July.

☒ NIGHTLIFE

Toronto offers a seemingly limitless selection of bars, pubs, dance clubs, and late-night cafes, including the **Second Cup Coffee Co.**, a T.O. institution which has branches all over town. The city stops alcohol distribution daily at 2am, and most clubs close down then. The most interesting new clubs are on trendy **Queen St. W.** in the **Entertainment District**, and on **College St. W.** and **Bloor St. W.** The free entertainment magazine, *Now* and *Eye*, comes out every Thursday. The gay scene centers on **Wellesley and Church St.** For info on the gay scene, pick up the free, biweekly *fab*.

THE ANNEX

The James Joyce, 386 Bloor St. (☎324-9400). Subway: Spadina. The connection to Joyce is in this bar's Irish heritage, not its literary pretensions. Live Celtic music every night is the highlight of this traditional Irish pub. No cover. Open daily 11:30am-2am.

Lee's Palace, 529 Bloor St. W. (☎532-1598), just east of the Bathurst subway stop. Live alternative music nightly downstairs; batcave-like DJ dance club, the **Dance Cave**, swings upstairs. Box office opens 8pm, shows begin 10pm. Cover $3-20 downstairs; open M-Sa noon-2am. Cover after 10pm $4 upstairs F-Sa; open daily 2pm-2:45am.

The Madison, 14 Madison Ave. (☎927-1722), at Bloor St. Subway: Spadina. 1 pool room, 4 patios, and a laid-back but crowded atmosphere attract students and yuppies. 16 beers on tap. Pints $5. Wings $9. Open daily 11am-2am.

Las Iguanas, 513 Bloor St. W. (☎532-3360). Subway: Spadina. For a less yuppie atmosphere, soon-to-be-intoxicated Canucks are drawn to this bar's faux-calfskin booths and kitschy margaritas ($5). Su is wing night. Open M-F noon-2am, Sa-Su 11am-2am.

DOWNTOWN

The Second City, 56 Blue Jays Way (☎343-0011 or 888-263-4485), at Wellington St., just north of the Sky Dome. Subway: Union. One of North America's wackiest, most creative comedy clubs. Spawned comics Dan Akroyd, John Candy, Martin Short, Mike Myers, and a hit TV show (SCTV). Free improv sessions M-Th 9:30pm and Sa midnight. Free F midnight howl with guest improv troupe. M-Th show 8pm $21, F-Sa 8pm and 10:30pm $25-27, Su touring company's production $14. Reservations required.

C'est What?, 67 Front St. E. (☎867-9499). Subway: Union. A mellow manifestation of Canada's multiculturalism. A great bar, with lots of live music and homemade micro-brews and wines. Open M-F noon-2am, Sa 11am-2am, Su 11am-1am.

COLLEGE ST.

Sneaky Dee's, 431 College St. W. (☎603-3090), at Bathurst. A popular (if generic) bar replete with cheap beer ($2.50-4) and pool tables in back. DJ and dancing upstairs W-Sa 9:30pm. Open M-Th 11am-4am, F 11am-5am, Sa 9am-5am, Su 9am-4am.

THE DANFORTH

Iliada Cafe, 550 Danforth Ave. (☎462-0334). Subway: Pape. Sip frappes and nibble at fresh baklava ($2.75) in this softly lit hangout spot, which serves a young, dyed, and pierced clientele. Open Su-Th 9am-2am, F-Sa 9am-3am.

THE GAY AND LESBIAN VILLAGE

Woody's/Sailor, 465-467 Church St. (☎972-0887), by Maitland. Subway: Wellesley. *The* gay bar in the Church and Wellesley area. Don't miss "Bad Boys Night Out" Tu and "Best Chest" Th at midnight. Bottled beer $4.50. Open daily noon-2am.

Slack Alice, 562 Church St. (☎969-8742). Subway: Wellesley. This cafe and bar offers international food (entrees $7-14), a patio, and a happy hour from 4-7pm. Mostly a gay and lesbian crowd. A DJ and dancing on weekends. Open daily 11am-2am.

▣ DAYTRIPS FROM TORONTO

ONATION'S NIAGARA ESCARPMENT

As beautiful as its name is strange, Onation's Niagara Escarpment passes west of Toronto as it winds its way from Niagara Falls to Tobermory at the tip of the Bruce Peninsula. Along this rocky 724km ridge, the **Bruce Trail** snakes through parks and private land. Hikers are treated to spectacular waterfalls, the breathtaking cliffs along **Georgian Bay,** and unique flora and fauna. Because the Escarpment is registered as a UN world biosphere reserve, future land development is limited to that which can exist symbiotically with the natural environment. For maps and Escarpment info, write or call the **Niagara Escarpment Commission,** 232 Guelph St., George-town L7G 4B1 (☎905-877-5191). Specifics on the Bruce Trail can be obtained from the **Bruce Trail Association,** P.O. Box 857, Hamilton ON L8N 3N9 (☎905-529-6821).

STRATFORD

The **Stratford Shakespeare Festival,** held in nearby Stratford since 1953, has proven to be the lifeblood of this picturesque town named for the Bard's own village. The renowned festival runs from early May to early November, with about 15 Shakes-pearean and non-Shakespearean plays performed in three theatres. During mid-summer (July-Aug.), up to six different shows play per day (none on M), with mati-nees beginning at 2pm and evening performances at 8pm. For complete info, call 800-567-1600. Tickets are expensive ($49-79), but a few good deals lower the stakes, including **rush tickets,** sold at 9am on the morning of the show at the box office, the-atre, or at 9:30am by phone ($38-50); matinees for seniors and students from Sep-tember to November (from $22); general student discounts ($27); and half-price for some performances in the fall. (Box office open M-Sa 9am-8pm, Su 9am-2pm.)

OTTAWA   ☎613

Legend has it that in the mid-19th century, Queen Victoria chose Ottawa as Can-ada's capital by closing her eyes and pointing a finger at a map, but perhaps politi-cal savvy rather than blind chance guided her to this once remote logging town. As a stronghold for neither the French nor English, Ottawa became a perfect compro-mise. Now, faced with the tough task of forging national unity while preserving local identities, Ottawa continues to play cultural diplomat to larger Canada.

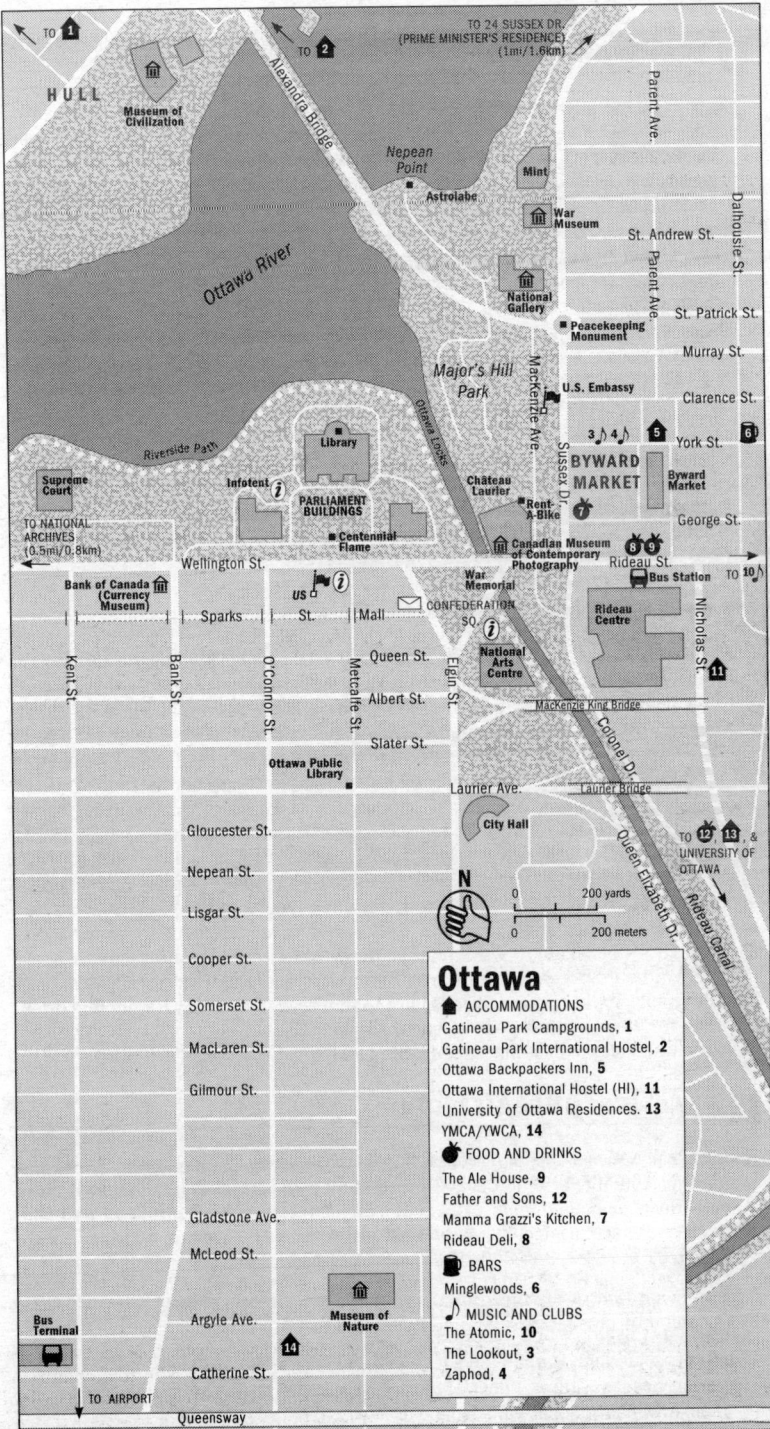

Ottawa

🏠 ACCOMMODATIONS

Gatineau Park Campgrounds, **1**
Gatineau Park International Hostel, **2**
Ottawa Backpackers Inn, **5**
Ottawa International Hostel (HI), **11**
University of Ottawa Residences, **13**
YMCA/YWCA, **14**

🍎 FOOD AND DRINKS

The Ale House, **9**
Father and Sons, **12**
Mamma Grazzi's Kitchen, **7**
Rideau Deli, **8**

🍺 BARS

Minglewoods, **6**

♪ MUSIC AND CLUBS

The Atomic, **10**
The Lookout, **3**
Zaphod, **4**

▐ TRANSPORTATION

Airport: Ottawa International (☎248-2125), 20min. south of the city off Bronson Ave. Take bus #97 from MacKenzie King Bridge. Info desk in arrival area open 9am-9pm. **Kasbary Transport, Inc.** (☎736-9993), runs shuttles between the airport and all downtown hotels (every 30min. 4:40am-2am; call for later pickup. $9, seniors and ages 11-18 $6). Call for pickup from smaller hotels.

Trains: VIA Rail, 200 Tremblay Rd. (☎244-8289), east of downtown, off the Queensway at Alta Vista Rd. To: Montréal (2hr., 4 per day, $40); Toronto (4hr., 5 per day, $85); and Québec City via Montréal (7hr., 2 per day, $75). Ticket office open M-F 5am-9pm, Sa 6:30am-7pm, Su 8:20am-9pm.

Buses: Voyageur, 265 Catherine St. (☎238-5900), between Kent and Lyon. Serves primarily Eastern Canada. To Montréal (2½hr., every hr. 7am-11pm, $29). **Greyhound** (☎237-7038) leaves from the same station, bound for Western Canada and southern Ontario. To Toronto (5hr., 7 per day, $56.50). For service to the US you must first go to Montréal or Toronto; the Québec City-bound passes through Montréal (6hr., every hr., $64.20). Station open daily 6:30am-12:30am. The blue **Hull City** buses (☎819-770-3242) connect Ottawa to Hull, across the river.

Public Transit: OC Transpo, 1500 St. Laurent (☎741-4390). Buses congregate on Rideau Centre. Fare $2.25, express (green buses) $3.50, ages 6-11 $1.25.

Taxis: Blue Line Taxi, ☎238-1111. **Capital,** ☎744-3333.

✷ ORIENTATION

The **Rideau Canal** divides Ottawa into the eastern lower town and the western upper town. West of the canal, Parliament buildings and government offices line **Wellington St.,** one of the city's main east-west arteries, which runs directly into the heart of downtown and crosses the canal. **Laurier** is the only other east-west street which permits traffic from one side of the canal to the other. East of the canal, Wellington St. becomes **Rideau St.,** surrounded by a fashionable shopping district. North of Rideau St. lies the **Byward Market,** a shopping area which hosts a summertime open-air market and much of Ottawa's nightlife. **Elgin St.,** a primary north-south artery stretching from the Queensway (Hwy. 417) to the War Memorial just south of Wellington in front of Parliament Hill, is also home to a number of pubs and nightlife spots. **Bank St.,** which runs parallel to Elgin three blocks to the west, services the town's older shopping area. The canal itself is a major access route. In winter, thousands of Ottawans skate to work on this, the world's longest skating rink; in summer, power boats breeze by regularly. Bike paths and pedestrian walkways also line the canals. Parking downtown is hard to find as well as to pay for; meters often cost 25¢ for 10min. Stash your car near the hostels and hop on the OC Transpo buses or walk; all the best places are within walking distance of each other.

▐ PRACTICAL INFORMATION

Visitor Info: National Capital Commission Information Center, 90 Wellington St. (☎239-5000 or 800-465-1867 in Canada), opposite the Parliament Bldg. Open early May-early Sept. daily 9am-9pm; early Sept.-early May 9am-5pm. For info on Hull and Québec province, contact the **Association Touristique de l'Outaouais,** 103 rue Laurier, Hull (☎819-778-2222 or 800-265-7822). Open mid-June to Sept. M-F 8:30am-8pm, Sa-Su 9am-6pm; off-season M-F 8:30am-5pm, Sa-Su 9am-4pm.

Hotlines: Ottawa Distress Centre, ☎238-3311 (English). **Tél-Aide,** ☎741-6433 (French). **Rape Crisis Centre,** ☎562-2333. All 24hr.

Bi-Gay-Lesbian Info: Gayline-Telegai (☎238-1717) has info. Open daily 7-10pm.

Internet access: Ottawa Public Library, 120 Metcalf St. (☎236-0301). Open M-Th 10am-8pm, F noon-6pm, Sa 10am-5pm.

Post Office: Postal Station B, 59 Sparks St. (☎844-1545), at Elgin St. Open M-F 8am-6pm. **Postal code:** K1P 5A0. **Area code:** 613 in Ottawa; 819 in Hull.

ACCOMMODATIONS

In downtown Ottawa, fantastic budget options exist only if you avoid hotels. Advance reservations are strongly recommended, especially if you stay through Canada Day (July 1). A complete list of B&Bs can be found in the *Ottawa Visitors Guide;* **Ottawa Bed and Breakfast** represents ten B&Bs in the Ottawa area. (☎563-0161. Singles $49-54; doubles $59-64.)

- **Ottawa International Hostel (HI-C),** 75 Nicholas St., K1N 7B9 (☎235-2595), in downtown Ottawa. The site of Canada's last public hanging, the former Carleton County Jail now incarcerates travelers. Cells contain 4-8 bunks and minimal personal space. Communal showers, kitchen, laundry facilities, lounges, and a cast of friendly regulars. Internet (25¢ per 8min.) Linen $2. In winter, doors locked 2-7am. Dorms $16, nonmembers $21; private rooms from $46/$50. Parking $4.28 per day.

- **Gatineau Park International Hostel (HI-C),** 66 Carman Rd. (☎819-459-3180), 20min. from downtown Ottawa. Take Hwy. 5 north to its end, turn left at the intersection, and the hostel is 5km down the road, on the left. Take bus #1 "Maniwaki" and ask the driver to stop at the intersection of Hwy. 105 and Chemin Carman. Call the hostel in advance for shuttle service from here. Dorms $17, nonmembers $20.

- **University of Ottawa Residences,** 90 University St. (☎564-5400), in the center of campus, an easy walk from downtown. From the bus and train stations, take bus #95. Clean dorms in a concrete landscape. Free linen, towels. Open early May to late Aug. Check-in 4:30pm. Parking $9 per day; $7.50 per half-day. Singles $38; doubles $50. Students with ID $27.50/$40.

- **YMCA/YWCA,** 180 Argyle Ave. (☎237-1320), at O'Connor St., close to the bus station and only a 10min. walk from Ottawa's main sights; walk left on Bank St. and right on Argyle. Good-sized rooms in a high-rise. Free local calls from most rooms. Gym facilities. Reception Su-Th 7am-11pm, F-Sa 24hr. Singles with shared bath $41, with private bath $49; doubles $49; suites $67. Parking $9.25. Weekly and group rates available.

- **Ottawa Backpackers Inn,** 203 York St. (☎241-3402 or 888-394-0334). This 32-bed heritage abode has both a prime downtown location and hands out free coffee and linens. Facilities include two full kitchens, television, and Internet access. Reception 7am-midnight. No curfew. 4- and 6-bed dorms $18.

- **Gatineau Park** (☎819-827-2020; reservations 456-3016), northwest of Hull. Three rustic campgrounds within 45min. of Ottawa: **Lac Philippe Campground,** 248 sites with facilities for family camping, trailers, and campers; **Lac Taylor Campground,** with 33 semi-rustic sites; and **Lac la Pêche,** with 36 campsites accessible only by canoe. Lac Philippe and Lac Taylor are open year-round; daily 9am-6pm, in winter 9:30am-6pm. La Pêche is available mid-May to mid-Oct. Camping permits required for Taylor and Philippe ($16; mid-June to mid-Oct. $19) available at the campground entrance. Pay for a site at La Pêche ($15; off-season $12) on Eardley Rd.

FOOD

Ottawa's **Byward Market,** on Byward St. between York and Rideau St., is full of tables with fresh produce, plants, flowers, and the sweet-smelling maple syrup. (☎562-3325. Open daily in warmer weather 8am-5pm. Boutiques open later.)

- **Father and Sons,** 112 Osgoode St. (☎239-1173), at the eastern edge of the U of O campus, is a student favorite. The menu presents quality, tavern-style food with some Lebanese and/or vegetarian dishes thrown in. The Lebanese dip ($6) and the triple-decker sandwich ($8) are delicious. Open daily 7am-2am; in winter 7am-midnight.

- **Mamma Grazzi's Kitchen,** 25 George St. (☎241-8656). This little Italian hideaway is located in a stone building in one of the oldest parts of Ottawa. The thin-crust pizza ($8-13) is well worth the wait. Open Su-Th noon-10pm, F-Sa noon-11pm.

The Ale House, 115 Rideau St. (☎562-5678). Brick walls and exposed ceiling pipes give a dark ambience to this former coffee joint restyled as a pub. Lunch and dinner options include burgers ($6-7), pasta ($8-9), and wraps ($6-9). Or, if you prefer, skip straight to the bar. Open daily 8am-1am or 2am, depending on the crowd.

Rideau Deli, 113 Rideau St. (☎562-8147). Quick-stop sandwiches are rarely so tasty ($2). Open M-W 9:30am-6pm, Th-F 9:30am-7pm, Sa 9:30am-5pm, Su 11:30am-5pm.

◉ SIGHTS

THE HUB. Parliament Hill, on Wellington at Metcalfe St., distinguished by Gothic architecture, towers over downtown. Warm your hands or raise a skeptical *québécois* eyebrow over the **Centennial Flame** at the south gate, lit in 1967 to mark the 100th anniversary of the Dominion of Canada's inaugural session of Parliament. The Prime Minister can occasionally be spotted at the central parliament structure, **Centre Block,** which contains the House of Commons, Senate, and Library of Parliament. Free tours of Centre Block (in English or French) depart every 30min. from the white **Infotent** by the Visitors Center. *(☎992-4793. Tours mid-May to Sept. M-F 9am-8pm, Sa-Su 9am-5pm; Sept. to mid-May daily 9am-3:30pm. Info-tent open mid-May to mid-June daily 9am-5pm; mid-June to Aug. 9am-8pm.)* On display behind the library, the bell from Centre Block is the only part of the original 1859-66 structure to survive a 1916 fire; according to legend, the bell crashed to the ground after chiming at midnight on the night of the flames. A carillon of 53 bells now hangs in the Peace Tower. When Parliament is in session, you can watch Canada's government officials debate during the official **Question Period** in the House of Commons chamber. *(Mid-Sept. to Dec. and Feb. to mid-June M-Th 2:15-3pm, F 11:15am-noon. Passes required; for info call 992-4793.)*

Those interested in trying to make a statuesque soldier smile should attend the 30min. **Changing of the Guard** ceremony, on the broad lawns in front of Centre Block. *(☎993-1811. Late June to late Aug. daily 10am, weather permitting.)* At dusk, Centre Block and its lawns transform into the set for **Sound and Light: Wind Odyssey,** which relates the history of the Parliament Buildings and the nation. *(Shows mid-May to early Sept. Performances alternate between French and English; for specifics, call ☎239-5100)* A five-minute walk west along Wellington St., the **Supreme Court of Canada** *(☎995-5361)* cohabits with the **Federal Court.** *(Open daily 9am-5pm; Sept.-May hours vary. Alternating French and English 30min. tours every 30min.; no tours Sa-Su noon-1pm. Free.)*

PARKS AND OTHER ATTRACTIONS. East of the Parliament Buildings at the junction of Sparks, Wellington, and Elgin St. stands **Confederation Sq.** with its enormous **National War Memorial,** dedicated by King George VI in 1939. The structure symbolizes the triumph of peace over war, an ironic message on the eve of World War II. **Nepean Point,** several blocks northwest of Rideau Centre and the Byward Market, behind the National Gallery of Canada, grants a panoramic view of the capital. The **Governor-General,** the Queen's representative in Canada, resides at **Rideau Hall** *(☎991-4422)*. During the open houses on New Year's Day or Canada Day the public sneaks an otherwise elusive peak of the interior. Otherwise, gawk from 24 Sussex Drive, the **Prime Minister's residence.** Free tours leave from the main gate at 1 Sussex Dr. *(☎800-465-6890 for tour info)*. See the production of "Loonies" ($2 coins) at the **Royal Canadian Mint.** *(320 Sussex Drive. ☎993-8990 or 800-276-7714. Tour schedule varies.)*

Ottawa has managed to skirt the traditional urban vices of pollution and violent crime; the multitude of parks and recreation areas may make you forget you're in a city at all. A favorite destination for Ottawans who want to cycle, hike, or fish, **Gatineau Park** (see **Accommodations,** above) occupies 356 sq. km in the northwest. Artificial **Dow's Lake,** accessible by the Queen Elizabeth Dwy., extends off the Rideau Canal 15min. south of Ottawa. **Dow's Lake Pavilion,** near Preston St., rents pedal boats, canoes, and bikes in the summer and ice skates and sleighs during the winter. *(101 Queen Elizabeth Driveway. ☎232-1001. Open mid-May to Sept. daily 8am-8pm. Rentals by the hr. and half-hour. Prices vary.)*

🏛 MUSEUMS

Geographically concentrated and manageable, many of Ottawa's notable museums (most of which are wheelchair accessible) double as architectural marvels.

🖼 National Gallery, 380 Sussex Dr. (☎990-1985 or 800-319-2787). A spectacular glass-towered building adjacent to Nepean Pt. holds the world's most comprehensive collection of Canadian art, complemented by outstanding European, American, and Asian works. The facade, a work of art in itself, is a modern interpretation of the nearby neo-Gothic Library of Parliament. Open May-Oct. daily 10am-6pm, Th 10am-8pm; hours vary off-season. Free; special events $10-12, students and seniors $6-8, under 18 free.

Canadian Museum of Civilization, 100 Laurier St. (☎776-7000). Housed in a striking, sand-dune-like structure across the river in Hull. Offers life-sized dioramas that attempt to put 1000 years of Canadian history into perspective. Open Apr.-Oct. daily 9am-6pm, Th. 9am-9pm; hours vary off-season. $8, seniors $7, students $6, ages 2-12 $4.

Canadian War Museum, 330 Sussex Dr. (☎776-8600), located next to the National Gallery. Outside stands a poignant exhibit of Canadian citizens at war from colonial times to UN Peacekeeping Missions. Open daily 9:30am-5pm, Th 9:30am-8pm. Closed M mid-Oct. through May. $4, students and seniors $3, children $2.

Canadian Museum of Contemporary Photography, 1 Rideau Canal (☎990-8257). Check out the impressive collection at this museum, on the steps between the Château Laurier and the Ottawa Locks. Time stands still here as modern Canadian life is freeze-framed. Open M-W and F-Su 10am-6pm, Th 10am-8pm. Free.

Canadian Museum of Nature, 240 McLeod St. (☎566-4700). A multimedia exploration of the natural world. For something creepy-crawly, check out the bug petting zoo, where nothing bites...hard. Open May to early Sept. daily 9:30am-5pm, Th 9:30am-8pm; off-season hours vary. $6, seniors and students $4, ages 3-12 $2.50, families $13; free after 5pm.

National Library Archives, 395 Wellington St. (☎995-5138). History buffs can get lost among the oodles of Canadian publications, old maps, photographs, letters, and historical exhibits. Reading room open M-F 8:30am-10pm, Sa-Su 8am-6pm. Call ahead for a tour.

Laurier House, 335 Laurier Ave. E. (☎992-8142). Liberal Prime Minister William Lyon Mackenzie King governed from the elegant house for most of his lengthy tenure. Admire all that he accumulated, including the crystal ball he used to consult his long-dead mother on matters of national importance. Open Apr. to mid-Oct. Tu-Sa 9am-5pm, Su 12-5pm. $2.25, seniors $2, students $1.25, under 5 free.

National Museum of Science and Technology, 1867 St. Laurent Blvd. (☎991-3044). Explore the world of modern technology with hands-on exhibits. The entrance is on Lancaster Rd., 200m east of St. Laurent. Open May-Sept. daily 9am-5pm; hours vary off-season. $6, seniors and students $5, ages 6-14 $2, family rate $12.

🎵🎬 ENTERTAINMENT AND NIGHTLIFE

Those pubcrawlers who recall nightlife being centered across the Ottawa River may want to reconsider before heading over to **Hull, Québec.** At one time grinding until 3am, many nightclubs have since been bought out due to increasing crime. As a result of Ottawa's decision to allow nightspots to serve alcohol until 2am, the capital city is once again where it's at. For a taste of it all, wander about **Byward Market** and the nearby area, where streets overflow with pedestrians in the evening.

The Atomic, 137 Besserer Street, lures clubbers through its silver doors with the most up-to-date music scene in Canada, spinning techno and rave still virgin to the airwaves. (☎241-2411. Open Th 10pm-3am, cover $5; F 10pm-5am, cover $7 before 1am, $10 after; Sa 10pm-8am, cover $10 before 1am, $12 after.) While not in the classiest area, experience life, the universe, and a bit of everything else at **Zaphod,** 27 York St., in Byward Market, a popular alternative club famous for their $6.50 Pangalactic Gargle Blasters. (☎562-1010. Live bands on weekends, music on weekdays. Cover $2-10 depending on the band playing. Open daily 3pm-2am.) **The Look-**

out, 41 York St. next to Zaphod's, is a hoppin' gay club with intense dancing. (☎789-1624. Open daily 3pm-2am.) **Minglewoods,** 101 York St. on the corner of Dalhousie, has slew of domestic beers on tap. The three levels include a bar, pool room, and dance floor. (☎562-2611. Open daily from 11:30am-2am.)

Ottawans seem to celebrate everything, even the bitter Canadian cold. All-important is **Canada Day,** July 1, which involves fireworks, partying in Major's Hill Park and Centre Block, concerts, and all-around merrymaking. During the first three weekends of Feb., **Winterlude** (☎239-5000) lines the Rideau Canal with ice sculptures illustrating how it feels to be an Ottawan in the winter (frozen). For a week in mid-May, the **Tulip Festival** (☎567-5757) explodes with a kaleidoscope of more than a million buds around Dow's Lake. Music fills the air during the **Dance Festival** (☎996-5051), in mid-June, and the **Jazz Festival** (☎241-2633), in mid-July; both hold free and pricey recitals and concerts. During Labor Day weekend, hundreds of balloons from around the globe soar at the **Hot Air Balloon Festival** (☎819-243-2330).

MID-ATLANTIC

From the Eastern seaboard of New York south through Virginia, the mid-Atlantic states claim not only a large slice of the nation's population, but several of its major historical, political, and economic centers. This region has witnessed the rotation of US capitals; first Philadelphia, PA; then Princeton, NJ; Annapolis, MD; Trenton, NJ; New York City, and finally Washington, D.C. During the Civil War, the mid-Atlantic even housed the Confederacy's capital, Richmond, VA. Urban centers (and suburban sprawl) cover much of the land, but the great outdoors have survived. The Appalachian Trail meanders through the region and New York's Adirondacks compose the largest US park outside of Alaska.

HIGHLIGHTS OF THE MID-ATLANTIC

NEW YORK, NY. The Big Apple combines world-class museums (p. 225) with top-notch arts and entertainment venues (p. 229).

WASHINGTON, D.C. The impressive Smithsonian Museum (p. 301), the White House (p. 300), the Capitol (p. 298), and a slew of monuments (p. 298) comprise some of the coveted attractions of the nation's capitol.

SCENIC DRIVES. The Blue Ridge Pkwy. (p. 323) is justifiably famous. A more hidden drive is the gorgeous backcountry road from Carter's Grove Plantation to Colonial Williamsburg, VA (p. 312).

HISTORIC SITES. Four-time battlefield Fredericksburg, VA (p. 310); Harper's Ferry, WV (p. 325); and Gettysburg, PA (p. 271) are the best places to relive the Civil War. Philadelphia, PA (p. 258) abounds with colonial landmarks.

NEW YORK

This state offers a little bit of everything: the excitement of New York City, the grandeur of Niagara Falls, and the fresh natural beauty of the Catskills and the Adirondacks. While "The City" attracts cosmopolitan types looking for adventure year-round, those seeking a more mellow New York experience head upstate. Here, surrounded by the beauty of some of the state's landscape, you may find it difficult to remember that smog and traffic exist. The cities that dot upstate New York have a sweet natural flavor that hold its own against the tang of the Big Apple.

🔲 PRACTICAL INFORMATION

Capital: Albany.
Visitor info: Division of Tourism, 1 Commerce Plaza, Albany 12245 (☎518-474-4116 or 800-225-5697; www.iloveny.state.ny.us). Operators available M-F 8:30am-5pm.
New York State Office of Parks and Recreation and Historic Preservation, Empire State Plaza, Agency Bldg. 1, Albany 12238 (☎518-474-0456). Open M-F 9am-5pm.
Bureau of Public Lands of the **Division of Lands and Forests,** DEC, 50 Wolf Rd., #438, Albany 12233 (☎518-457-7433, campground info 457-2500).
Postal Abbreviation: NY. **Sales Tax:** 7-9%, depending on county.

NEW YORK CITY   ☎212

Immensity, diversity, and a tradition of defying tradition characterize the city known as the "Crossroads of the World." Since its earliest days, New York has scoffed at the timid offerings of other American cities. It boasts the most immi-

Mid-Atlantic

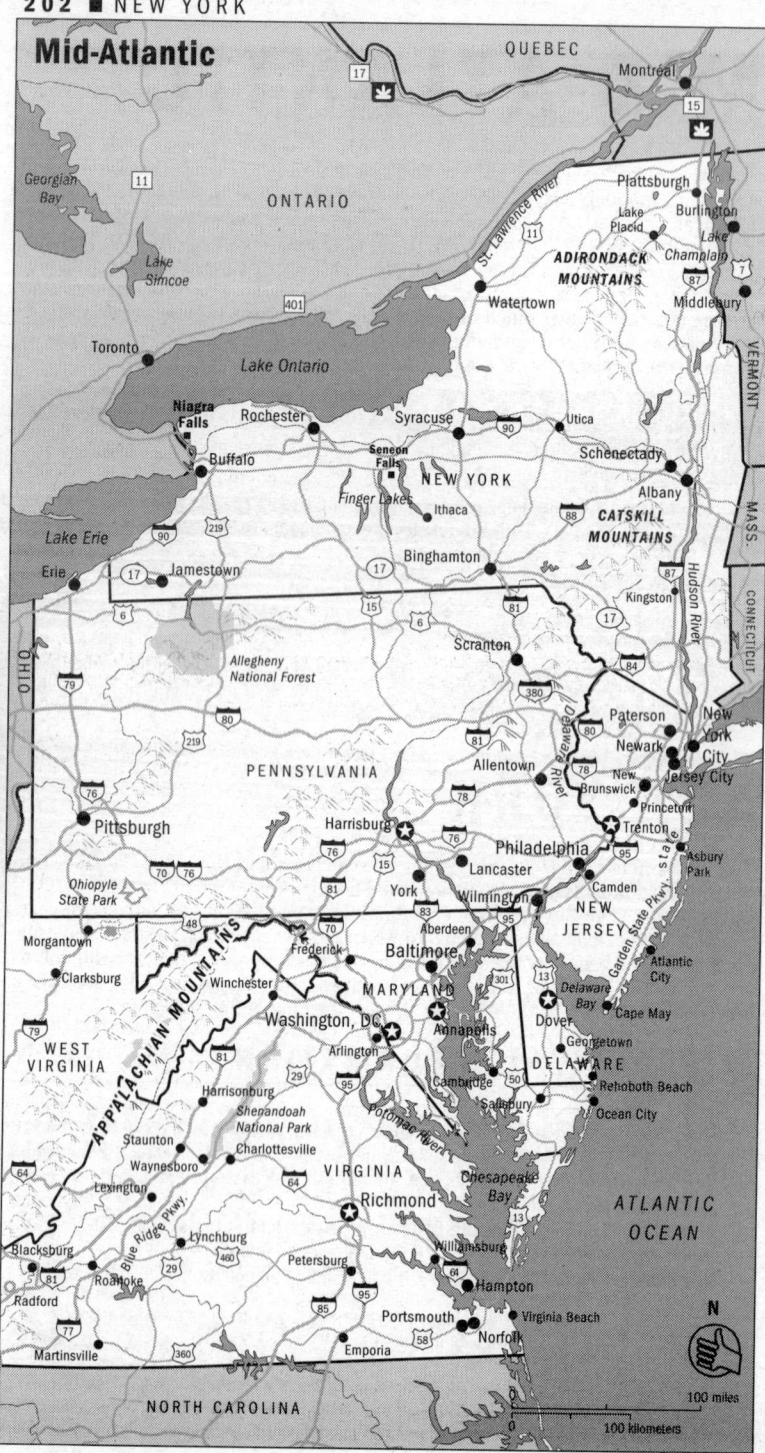

grants and the biggest museum in the Western Hemisphere. Even the vast blocks of concrete have their own gritty charm. Returning from a dull vacation in Westchester, author O. Henry noted, "there was too much fresh scenery and fresh air. What I need is a steam-heated flat and no vacation or exercise."

New York City is full of folks. The stars are invisible behind the array of lights. The buildings soar; the subways scream; the people scramble. All is rushed. There may be grime, but for every inch of it, there's a yard of silver lining. Countless people mean countless pockets of culture—you can find every kind of ethnicity, food, art, language, attitude. It's possible to be alone, but that's not the point—plunge into the fray and you'll find eight million stories, curmudgeonly humor, innovative ideas, and a fair share of madness. Meanwhile, there's flamenco at an outdoor cafe, jazz in an historic speakeasy, house and techno in a flashy club—whatever the question, New York has the answer.

For the coverage this city deserves, see our city guide, *Let's Go: New York City 2002*, and the *Let's Go Map Guide: New York City*.

✈ INTERCITY TRANSPORTATION

Airports: Three airports serve the New York metropolitan area.

John F. Kennedy Airport (JFK) (☎718-244-4444), at the end of the Van Wyck Expressway, in southern Queens. JFK handles most international and many domestic flights. The airport is located 12 mi. from midtown Manhattan, but the drive can take up to 45min. A bus runs every 15min. from any airport terminal to the Howard Beach-JFK subway station. From there, take the A train to Manhattan (1hr.). A taxi from JFK to Manhattan costs $30 (plus tolls and tip).

LaGuardia Airport (☎718-533-3400), off Exit 7 on the Grand Central Parkway, in northern Queens. LaGuardia is 6 mi. from midtown; the drive is approximately 25min. Domestic flights leave from here. The M60 bus (daily 4:50am-1am; $1.50) goes into Manhattan. Alternatively, the MTA Q33 and Q47 buses transfer at the 74th St./Broadway-Roosevelt Ave./Jackson Hts. subway stop in Queens to the 7, E, F, G, or R trains into Manhattan. Travel time: at least 1½hr. Taxis to Manhattan are $16-26 (plus tolls and tip).

Newark International Airport (☎973-961-6000), 12 mi. west of midtown in Newark, NJ, on I-95 at Exit 14. Domestic and international flights. Olympia Airport Express (☎964-6233) travels between Newark and Grand Central, Penn Station, and Port Authority every 20-30min. 6am-midnight (25min.-1hr., $10; tickets may be purchased on the bus). New Jersey Transit Authority (NJTA) (☎973-762-5100) runs an Air Link bus #302 ($4) between the airport and Newark's Penn Station (not Manhattan's). From there bus #108 ($3.25, exact change) goes to Port Authority. PATH trains (☎800-234-7284; $1) run from Newark Penn Station into Manhattan.

Trains: Grand Central Terminal, 42nd St. and Park Ave. (Subway: 4, 5, 6, 7, S to 42nd St.-Grand Central), handles **Metro-North** (☎800-638-7646) commuter lines to Connecticut and NY suburbs. **Amtrak** (☎800-872-7245) runs out of **Penn Station,** 33rd St. and 8th Ave. (Subway: 1, 2, 3, 9, A, C, E to 34th St./Penn Station). To: Washington, D.C. (3-4hr., $67-118); Boston, MA (4-6hr., $50-71); and Philadelphia (1½hr., $43 77). The **Long Island Railroad (LIRR)** (☎718-217-5477) and **NJ Transit** (☎973-762-5100) commuter rails also chug from Penn Station. Nearby at 33rd St. and 6th Ave., you can catch a **PATH** train to New Jersey (☎800-234-7284).

Buses: Greyhound and **Peter Pan** buses leave the **Port Authority Terminal,** 42nd St. and 8th Ave. (☎435-7000; subway: A, C, E to 42nd St.-Port Authority). Watch for con artists and pickpockets, especially at night. To: Boston (4½hr., $42); Philadelphia (2hr., $21); and Washington, D.C. (4½hr., $42).

▣ LOCAL TRANSPORTATION

Public Transit: The **Metropolitan Transit Authority (MTA)** runs the city's subways, buses, and trains. The subway system is quite extensive and operates 24hr. a day, 365 days a year. Groups of 4 may find a cab to be cheaper and more expedient for short distances. Long distances are best traveled by subway; once inside, a passenger may transfer onto any other train without restrictions. Subway maps are available in any subway station. You'll see glass globes outside of most subway entrances. If the globe is green, the entrance is open 24hr. A red globe indicates that the entrance is somehow restricted. **Buses** are often slower than subways, but are relatively safer and cleaner. Buses stop roughly every 2 blocks and run crosstown (east-west), as well as uptown and downtown (north-south). Ring to get off. Look for blue signposts announcing bus numbers or glass-walled shelters displaying a map of the route and a schedule of arrival times. In the outer boroughs, some of the buses are run by independent contractors. Be sure to grab a borough bus map. **MetroCards** are the main form of currency for the subway and buses. Buy a card with a pre-set value. With the purchase of a $15 card, you get 1 free ride. MetroCards can make free subway-bus, bus-subway, and bus-bus transfers. When the card is swiped on the initial ride, a free transfer (good for 2hr., good from subway to bus, bus to subway, and bus to bus) is stored on your MetroCard. The 1-day ($4), 7-day ($17), and 30-day ($63) "Unlimited Rides" MetroCards (as opposed to "Pay-Per-Ride" cards) allow unlimited use, and are good for tourists visiting many sights.

> **! SUBWAY SAFETY.** In crowded stations (most notably those around 42nd St.), pickpockets find work; violent crimes occasionally occur in stations that are deserted. Stay alert and stick to well-lit areas; most stations have clearly marked "off-hours" waiting areas that are under observation and significantly safer. When boarding, pick a car with a number of other passengers in it, or sit near the middle of the train, in the conductor's car. *For safety reasons, try to avoid riding the subways between midnight and 7am, especially above E. 96th St. and W. 120th St. and outside Manhattan.*

Taxis: Most people in Manhattan hail yellow (licensed) cabs on the street.
Car Rental: AAMCAR Rent-a-Car, 315 W. 96th St. (☎222-8500), between West End Ave. and Riverside Dr. **Avis,** ☎800-831-2847. **Dollar,** at JFK (☎718-656-2400); at LaGuardia (☎718-779-5600, 800-800-4000). **Enterprise,** ☎800-736-8222. **Hertz,** ☎800-831-2847.

✈ ORIENTATION

NYC comprises **five boroughs:** the Bronx, Brooklyn, Manhattan, Queens, and Staten Island. Flanked on the east by the "East River" (actually a strait) and on the west by the Hudson River, **Manhattan** is a sliver of an island, measuring only 13 mi. long and 2½ mi. wide. **Queens** and **Brooklyn** are on the other side of the East River. Residential **Staten Island,** southwest of Manhattan, has repeatedly sought secession from the city. North of Manhattan sits the **Bronx,** the only borough connected by land to the rest of the US. The five boroughs united to form one city in 1898.

BOROUGHS

MANHATTAN

Above 14th St., Manhattan is an organized grid of avenues running north-south and streets east-west. Streets run consecutively, and their numbers grow as one travels north. Avenues are slightly less predictable: some are numbered while others are named. The numbers of the avenues increase as one goes west. **Broadway,** which follows an old Algonquin trail, defies the rectangular pattern and cuts diagonally across the island, veering east of Fifth Ave. at 23rd St. Central Park and Fifth Ave. (south of 59th St., north of 110th St.) separate the city into the East Side and West Side. **Below 14th St.,** the city dissolves into a confusing tangle of old, narrow streets, which becomes complicated south of Houston St., where streets are not numbered. The **Financial District/Wall St. area,** set over the original Dutch layout, is full of narrow, winding, one-way streets. **Greenwich Village,** only slightly less confusing, is especially complicated west of Sixth Ave. The **East Village and Alphabet City** are gridlike, with alphabetized avenues from Ave. A to Ave. D east of First Ave.

BROOKLYN

The **Brooklyn-Queens Expressway (BQE)** pours into the **Belt Parkway** and circumscribes Brooklyn. Ocean Parkway, Ocean Ave., Coney Island Ave., and diagonal Flatbush Ave. run from the beaches of southern Brooklyn to Prospect Park in the heart of the borough. The streets of western Brooklyn (including those in Sunset

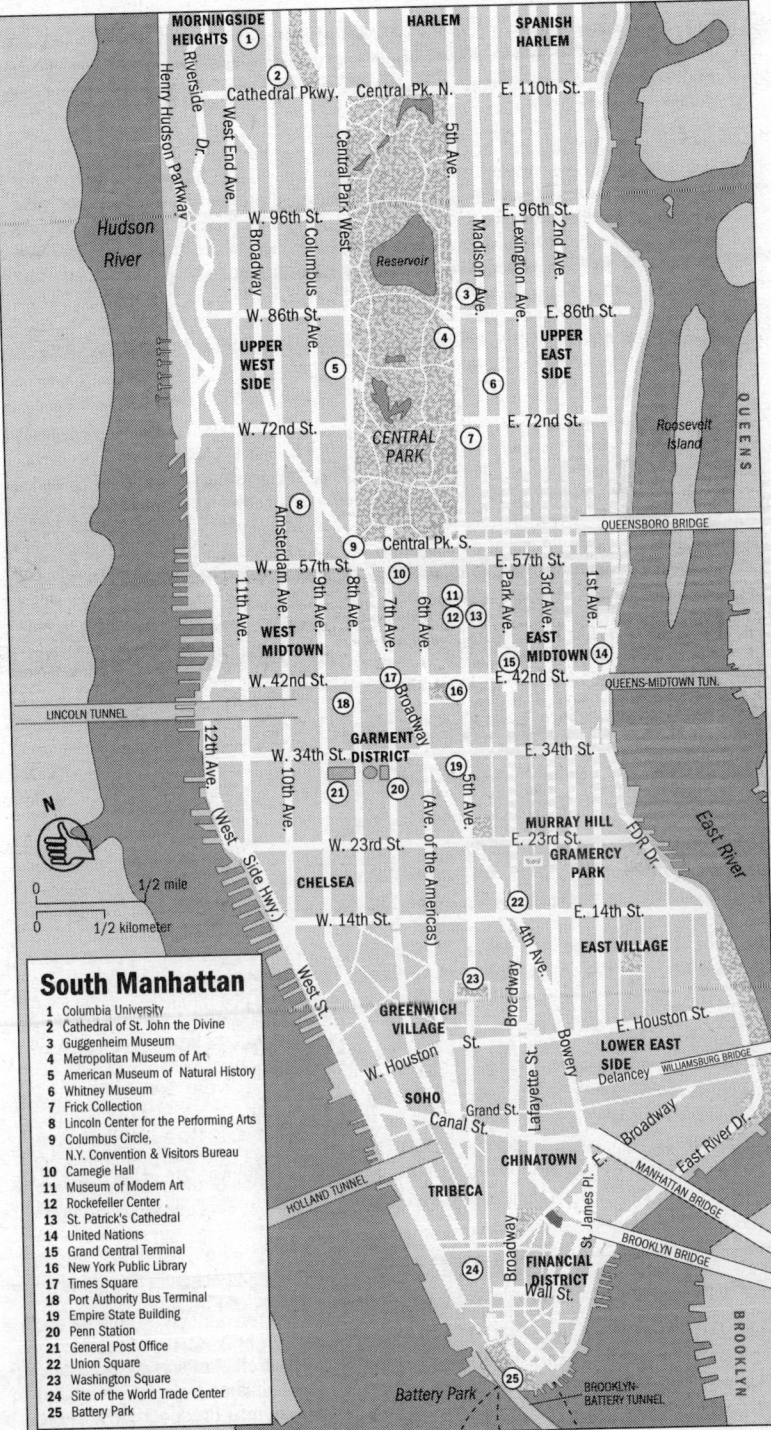

South Manhattan

1 Columbia University
2 Cathedral of St. John the Divine
3 Guggenheim Museum
4 Metropolitan Museum of Art
5 American Museum of Natural History
6 Whitney Museum
7 Frick Collection
8 Lincoln Center for the Performing Arts
9 Columbus Circle,
   N.Y. Convention & Visitors Bureau
10 Carnegie Hall
11 Museum of Modern Art
12 Rockefeller Center
13 St. Patrick's Cathedral
14 United Nations
15 Grand Central Terminal
16 New York Public Library
17 Times Square
18 Port Authority Bus Terminal
19 Empire State Building
20 Penn Station
21 General Post Office
22 Union Square
23 Washington Square
24 Site of the World Trade Center
25 Battery Park

Park, Bensonhurst, Borough Park, and Park Slope) are aligned with the western shore and thus collide at a 45-degree angle with central Brooklyn's main arteries. In northern Brooklyn, several avenues—Atlantic Ave., Eastern Parkway, and Flushing Ave.—travel from downtown east into Queens.

QUEENS

The streets of Queens resemble neither the orderly grid of Upper Manhattan nor the haphazard angles of Greenwich Village; instead, a mixed bag of urban planning techniques has resulted in a logical—but extremely complicated—system. Streets generally run north-south and are numbered from west to east, from 1st St. in Astoria to 271st St. in Glen Oaks. Avenues run perpendicular to streets and are numbered from north to south, from Second Ave. to 165th Ave. The address of an establishment or residence often tells you the closest cross-street (for example, 45-07 32nd Ave. is near the intersection with 45th St.). Pick up the very useful *Queens Bus Map* (free) available on most Queens buses.

THE BRONX

Major highways cut the Bronx up into many pieces. The **Major Deegan Expwy. (I-87)** runs up the western border of the borough, next to the Harlem River. The **Cross-Bronx Expressway (I-95)** runs across the borough before turning north on its easternmost edge. Up the center of the borough runs the **Bronx River Pkwy.** Several avenues run north-south, including **Jerome Ave.** on the western side of the borough and **White Plains Rd.** and **Boston Rd.** on the eastern side of the borough. Streets running east-west include **Tremont Ave.** and **Fordham Rd.** and the **Bronx** and **Pelham Pkwy.**

STATEN ISLAND

Unlike the rest of the city, Staten Island is quite spread out. Pick up much-needed maps of Staten Island's bus routes as well as other pamphlets at the **Chamber of Commerce**, 130 Bay St. Bear left from the ferry station onto Bay St.

🛈 PRACTICAL INFORMATION

Visitor info: The Official New York City Visitor Information Center, 810 Seventh Ave. (☎484-1222), between 52nd and 53rd St. Open M-F 8:30am-6pm, Sa-Su 9am-5pm. Other locations in Grand Central and Penn Station.

Hotlines: AIDS Hotline, ☎447-8200. Open daily 9am-9pm; 24hr. recording. **Crime Victims' Hotline**, ☎577-7777. **Sex Crimes Report Line**, ☎267-7273. Both 24hr.

Bi-Gay-Lesbian Concerns: Callen-Lorde Community Health Center, 356 W. 18th St. between Eighth and Ninth Ave. (☎271-7200; www.callen-lorde.org). Open M 12:30-8pm, W 8:30am-1pm and 3-8pm, Tu and Th-F 9am-4:30pm. **Gay Men's Health Crisis (GMHC)**, 119 W. 24th St. between Sixth and Seventh Ave. (☎367-1000). Walk-in counseling M-F 11am-8pm. GMHC's **Geffen Center** (☎367-1100) provides confidential (not anonymous) HIV testing. **Hotline:** ☎ 807-6655 or 800-243-7692. Open M-F 10am-9pm, Sa noon-3pm. **Gay and Lesbian Switchboard** (☎989-0999; glnh@glnh.org). Open M-F 6-10pm, Sa noon-5pm. 24hr. recording.

Medical Services: Walk-in Clinic, 55 E. 34th St. (☎252-6001, ext. 2), between Park and Madison Ave. Open M-Th 8am-8pm, Sa 9am-3pm, Su 9am-2pm.

Post Office: 421 8th Ave. (☎330-2902), across from Madison Sq. Garden. Open 24hr. For General Delivery, mail to and use the entrance at 390 9th Ave. **ZIP code:** 10001.

Area code: 212 or 646 (Manhattan); 718 (other 4 boroughs); 917 (cell phones). In text 212, unless noted.

🏠 ACCOMMODATIONS

The cost of living in New York is *very high*. A night at a full-service establishment runs $125 (plus 13.4% hotel tax), but you can get a bed for under $60 a night.

HOTELS AND B&BS

🏨 **Gershwin Hotel**, 7 E. 27th St. (☎545-8000; fax 684-5546), between Madison and Fifth Ave. Subway: 6, N, R to 28th St. This chic hotel full of pop art, modern furniture, and artsy twenty-somethings seems like a set from Alice in Wonderland—MTV-style. Private rooms come with bathrooms, cable TV, A/C, and phones. Economy rooms (single or double occupancy only) $99, standard rooms (single or double occupancy only) $169. $15 extra for Th to Sa. 8-12 bed dorms $30.

▨ **Carlton Arms Hotel,** 160 E. 25th St. (☎679-0680), between Third and Lexington Ave. Subway: 6 to 23rd St. Each room is decorated by a different artist in this boutique hotel. The rooms (54 in total) are spacious, although summer travelers should note that there is no A/C. Singles $70, with bath $85; doubles $90/$100; triples $110/$120; quads $105/$117. $5-11 discounts for students and foreign travelers. Pay for 7 or more nights up front and get a 10% discount.

▨ **Hotel Stanford,** 43 W. 32nd St. (☎563-1500 or 800-365-1114; fax 629-0043), between Fifth Ave. and Broadway. Subway: B, D, F, N, Q, R to 34th St. This Korean District hotel's lobby glitters with sparkling ceiling lights and a polished marble floor. Rooms are impeccably clean, with firm mattresses, plush carpeting, private bathrooms, cable TV, phones, A/C, refrigerators. Continental breakfast included. Singles $120-150; doubles and twins $150-180; suites $200-250.

▨ **Akwaaba Mansion,** 347 MacDonough St. (☎718-455-5958; fax 718-774-1744), in Brooklyn's Bedford-Stuyvesant. Subway: A, C to Utica Ave.; turn to Stuyvesant Ave., make a left, and walk 4 blocks to MacDonough St. This B&B won an award from the New York Landmarks Preservation Society, and photographers come here to do fashion and advertising shoots. Each of the 18 rooms has its own theme; all are decorated in African cultural decor. Rooms comfortably accommodate two. Call at least a month in advance to reserve a room. Rooms $120-135; weekends $135-150.

▨ **Colonial House Inn,** 318 W. 22nd St. (☎243-9669 or 800-689-3779; fax 633-1612), between Eighth and Ninth Ave. Subway: C, E to 23rd St. A gay-friendly comfortable B&B in a classy Chelsea brownstone. All rooms have cable TV, A/C, and phone; some have bath and fireplace. Sun deck with a "clothing optional" area. 24hr. desk and concierge. Continental breakfast included. Reservations are encouraged and require 2 nights' deposit within 10 days of reservation. Double bed "economy" room $80-99; queen-size bedroom $99-125, with private bath and fridge $125-140.

Larchmont Hotel, 27 W. 11th St. (☎989-9333; fax 989-9496), between Fifth and Sixth Ave. Subway: N, R, L, 4, 5, 6 to 14th St./Union Sq. Spacious, clean rooms in a white-washed brownstone on a quiet block. A/C, TV, desks, closets, and wash basins in all rooms. Shared bath. Continental breakfast included. Reserve 5-6 weeks in advance. Singles $70-95; doubles $90-115; queen-size bed $109-125.

Hudson Hotel, 356 W. 58th St. (☎554-6000), between Eighth and Ninth Ave. Subway: A, C, B, D, 1, 9 to 59th St. The luxuries don't stop at this new hotel: customized greenhouses, utopian garden courtyard, an Olympic size pool, etc. The decadent rooms with oak walls and art exhibits, as well as an ultra-modern bathroom. Standard rooms run $155-255, with suites as high as $500, but there are occasional $95 specials.

Bed & Breakfast on the Park, 113 Prospect Park W. (☎718-499-6115; fax 718-499-1385), between 6th and 7th St., on Brooklyn's Prospect Park. Subway: F to Seventh Ave./Park Slope; then 2 blocks east and 2 blocks north. A magnificently restored brownstone jam-packed with Victoriana. Classy furnishings (Rococo armoires, oriental carpets, damask) are museum-quality. Gourmet breakfast in sumptuous (not-so) common room. 8 doubles (2 with shared bath), each in a different style, $125-300.

ThirtyThirty, 30 E. 30th St. (☎689-1900 or 800-804-4480; fax 689-0023), between Park Ave. South and Madison Ave. A sleek, modern hotel in a prime location at relatively budget prices. All rooms have cable TV, A/C, iron, hair dryer, and phones with voicemail. Singles $125; doubles $165; suites $245.

St. Mark's Hotel, 2 St. Mark's Pl. (☎674-2192; fax 420-0854), at Third Ave. Subway: 6 to Astor Pl. Functional, clean rooms in an exciting location. Call ahead for reservations. All rooms have private bath and cable TV. Singles $99-109; doubles $113-131. Cash and travelers checks only.

Chelsea Pines Inn, 317 W. 14th St. (☎929-1023; fax 620-5646), between Eighth and Ninth Ave. Subway: A, C, E to 14th St.; L to Eighth Ave. This gay-owned and operated inn is an amenity-laden haven of rooms decorated with vintage film posters. A/C, cable TV, phone with answering machine, refrigerator, and showers in all rooms. 3-day min.

stay on weekends. Rooms with private showers and shared toilet $99-169; with queen-size bed and private bath $129-189; suites $139-199.

Murray Hill Inn, 143 E. 30th St. (☎683-6900 or 888-996-6376), between Third and Lexington Ave. Subway: 6 to 28th St. Simple, floral-print rooms at reasonable prices. 5 floors—no elevator. All rooms have A/C, cable TV, and phone. 21-day max. stay. Check-in 2pm. Check-out noon. Singles $75, with private bath $115; doubles $95/$125.

Hotel 17, 225 E. 17th St. (☎475-2845; fax 677-8178), between Second and Third Ave. Subway: L to Third Ave. This historic 120-room hotel served as the setting for Woody Allen's *Manhattan Murder Mystery*. All rooms have A/C and cable TV. Some rooms have fireplaces (good); many have frankly disastrous wallpaper (not as good). Check-in 2pm. Check-out noon. Must be over 18. Singles $70-75; doubles $80-95; triples $140-150. Weekly rates: singles $425; doubles $600. No credit cards.

HOSTELS

▨ **Jazz on the Park,** 36 Duke Ellington Blvd./W. 106th St. (☎932-1600; fax 932-1700), at Central Park West. Subway: B, C to 103rd St. The Jazz riffs to the tune of clean, brightly-colored hostel-dom. Lockers and A/C make you a real cool cat. Enough activities that you might not actually leave the hostel—live jazz in the downstairs lounge; all-you-can-eat barbecues on the terrace W and Su in summer ($5); and Sunday gospel brunches. Linen and towels included. 12- to 14-bed dorms $30; 6- to 8-bed dorms $32; 4-bed dorms $34; private rooms (full or bunk beds) $88; prices include tax.

▨ **New York International HI-AYH Hostel,** 891 Amsterdam Ave. (☎932-2300; fax 932-2574), at 103rd St. Subway: 1, 9, B, C to 103rd St. In a block-long building resides the mother of all youth hostels—the largest in the US, with 90 dorm-style rooms and 624 beds. Soft carpets and spotless bathrooms. Linen and towels included. Credit card reservations a must. Check-in 24hr. Nov.-Apr. 10- to 12-bed dorms $27; 6- to 8-bed dorms $30; 4-bed dorms $33. May-Oct. $29/$32/$35. Nonmembers $3 more. Groups of 4-9 may get private rooms with bathroom ($120); groups of 10 or more definitely will.

Sugar Hill International House, 722 St. Nicholas Ave. (☎926-7030), at 146th St. Subway: A, B, C, D to 145th St. A brownstone with large and spacious rooms (25-30 beds total), a quiet family feel, garden out back, and an adorable but spoiled dog. Friendly staff is a living library of Harlem history and entertainment. Rooms for 2-10 people. All-female room available. Internet access $1 per 10min. Facilities include kitchens, stereo, and library. Key deposit $10. 2-week max. stay. Check-in 9am-10pm. Check-out 11am. Call 1 month in advance during off-season. No reservations accepted July-Sept.; call the morning of your intended stay. Passport ID required. No smoking. Rooms $25-30.

Chelsea Center Hostel, 313 W. 29th St. (☎643-0214; fax 473-3945), between Eighth and Ninth Ave. Subway: 1, 2, 3, 9, A, C, E to 34th St. To enter, ring the labeled buzzer at the door. Knowledgeable, multilingual staff dispenses New York tips. Room for 20 guests in this quiet residential-home-turned-hostel. 15 stay in a spacious basement room with a summer-camp feel; the rest in a bedroom on the main floor. A lovely garden adds to the charm. 2 showers. Linen and light breakfast included. Check-in 8:30am-10:45pm. Flexible lockout 11am-5pm. Cash and traveler's checks only. Dorms $30.

Chelsea International Hostel, 251 W. 20th St. (☎647-0010; fax 727-7289), between Seventh and Eighth Ave. Subway: 1, 9, C, E to 23rd St. Scandinavians and other Europeans make up the bulk of the clientele of this enclosed hostel with funky youth travelers. The congenial staff offers pizza W night. There's a backyard garden, but the smallish rooms themselves are merely utilitarian. Kitchens, laundry room, TV rooms. Internet access 20¢ per min. Key deposit $10. Check-in 8am-6pm. Reservations recommended. 4- and 6-person dorms $27; private rooms $65.

Uptown Hostel, 239 Lenox Ave. (☎666-0559; fax 663-5000), at 122nd St. Subway: 2, 3 to 125th St. Bunk beds in clean, comfy rooms. Spacious hall bathrooms. Brand new common room and kitchen add to the atmosphere. Key deposit $10. Check-in 11am-8pm. Lockout June-Aug. 11am-4pm. Call well in advance in summer, 2 days in advance the rest of the year. Sept.-May singles $20, doubles $25; June-Aug. singles $22/$30.

Central Park Hostel, 19 W. 103rd St. (☎678-0491; fax 678-0453), between Manhattan Ave. and Central Park West. Subway: B, C to 103rd St. Clean, air-conditioned rooms. Shared bathrooms. Linen/towels provided. Lockers available. Key deposit $2. 13-day max. stay. No curfew. Dorm $25; private double $75.

International Student Hospice, 154 E. 33rd St. (☎228-7470; fax 228-4689), between Lexington and Third Ave. Subway: 6 to 33rd St. Up a flight of stairs in a brownstone with a brass plaque saying "I.S.H." This non-profit establishment better resembles a house full of bric-a-brac than a hostel. Rooms for 1-4 people; tiny hall bathroom. Call ahead. $28 per night including tax; $20 per night if you pay for a week up front.

◘ FOOD

New York will dazzle you with its culinary bounty. City dining, like the population, spans the globe, ranging from sushi bars to wild combinations like Afghani/Italian and Mexican/Lebanese.

LOWER MANHATTAN: SOUTH OF HOUSTON ST.

Chinatown features Thai and Vietnamese cuisine, in addition to inexpensive, delicious Chinese. The Lower East Side is known for its delicatessens, while Little Italy has, well, Italian food.

⬛ Hop Kee, 21 Mott St. (☎964-8365), down the stairs at the corner of Mosco St. Subway: 4, 5, 6, J, M, N, R, Z to Canal St. Bare bones in the ambience department, but this is *real* Chinese food. Their specialties include salted pork chop with hot peppers ($8.25) and seafood in a basket ($17). Open daily 11am-4am. Cash only.

⬛ Thailand Restaurant, 106 Bayard St. (☎349-3132), between Baxter and Mulberry St. Subway: 4, 5, 6, J, M, N, R, Z to Canal St. Simple and quiet, but head and shoulders above the other joints. Known for homemade Thai desserts like sweet rice with egg custard and coconut milk ($1.50). Open daily 11:30am-11pm.

⬛ Vietnam, 11-13 Doyers St. (☎693-0725), between Bowery and Pell St. Subway: 4, 5, 6, J, M, N, R, Z to Canal St. All of the standards—brittle spring rolls, noodle soups—and then some. Try the tasty, filling Vietnamese crepes ($6). Ask about the more innovative items like the stir-fried salmon with black bean sauce ($7). Open daily 11am-9:30pm.

⬛ El Sombrero, 108 Stanton St. (☎254-4188), at Ludlow St. Subway: F, J, M, Z to Delancey St.-Essex St. If the gods ate at a Mexican restaurant, lived on a budget, and didn't mind a little kitsch, they'd dine here. Fajitas Mexicana $10. Hours vary; open Su-Th approximately 10am-midnight, F-Sa approximately 10am-3am. Cash only.

New Silver Palace, 52 Bowery (☎964-1204), at Canal St. Subway: 4, 5, 6, J, M, N, R, Z to Canal St. An enormous mecca for dim sum lovers ($3-5; served until 4pm) and a popular spot for Chinatown wedding banquets. Open daily 9am-10:30pm.

H.S.F. Restaurant, 46 Bowery (☎374-1319), between Bayard and Canal St. Subway: 4, 5, 6, J, M, N, R, Z to Canal St. Wonderful dim sum ($3-5; served 11am-5pm), or order the buffet special and cook up veggies, dumplings, etc. in a pot of boiling broth at your table ($20 per person; served after 5pm). Open Su-Th 8am-midnight, F-Sa 8am-2am.

Rice, 227 Mott St. (☎226-5775), between Prince and Spring St. Subway: 6 to Spring St. Fantastic food on rice. The basics—basmati, brown, sticky, Japanese—are options, in addition to the more exotic Thai black or Bhutanese red ($1-4). The sauces range from mango chutney to Aleppo yogurt ($1). Open daily noon-midnight. Cash only.

Joe's Shanghai, 9 Pell St. (☎233-8888), between Bowery and Mott St. Subway: 4, 5, 6, J, M, N, R, Z to Canal St. The true source of Joe's acclaim is his *xiao long bao* ($7), crab meat and pork dumplings in a savory soup. Be prepared for communal tables and long lines of *bao* addicts on weekends. Open daily 11am-11:15pm. Cash only.

Bouley Bakery, 120 W. Broadway (☎964-8362), between Duane and Reade St. Subway: 1, 2, 3, 9, A, C to Chambers St. This world-class restaurant also has an adjoining cafe, which serves light meals and desserts. Peckish travelers can take away sandwiches such as the satisfying roast beef on mountain bread ($7.25), or the "torpedo," a baguette roll with prosciutto and mozzarella ($2.50). Cafe open daily 8am-6pm.

Penang, 109 Spring St. (☎274-8883), between Mercer and Greene St. Subway: N, R to Prince St. Excellent Malaysian cuisine served in a beautiful and exotic setting. Savor the *roti canai* ($4.25) or the hearty *poh-piah* (steamed spring rolls; $6). Vegetarians should try the tasty *kari sayur campur* ($12.50). Open M-Th noon-midnight, F-Sa noon-1am.

Le Gamin Cafe, 50 MacDougal St. (☎254-4678), between Prince and Houston St. Subway: C, E to Spring St. This *établissement* offers simple but elegant French fare. The *salade de chèvre chaud aux noix* (goat cheese croutons, tomato, mesclun, and walnuts; $9) is a favorite. Cafe au lait $3. Crepes $3.25-9.50. Open daily 8am-midnight.

Space Untitled, 133 Greene St. (☎260-8962), between Prince and Houston St. Subway: N, R to Prince St. Huge, warehouse-like cafe with plenty of barstools and chairs to make yourself comfortable. Sandwiches $3-6; sumptuous desserts $1.75-4.50. Coffee $1.50-4. Open M-Th 7am-10pm, F 7am-11pm, Sa 8am-11pm, Su 8am-9pm.

Katz's Delicatessen, 205 E. Houston St. (☎254-2246), between Orchard and Ludlow St. Subway: F to Second Ave. A Lower East Side institution since 1888. The food is orgasmic (as Meg Ryan confirmed in *When Harry Met Sally*), but you pay extra for the atmosphere. Gyros $5.10, knishes $2.25, franks $2.15, sandwiches around $9. Open Su-Tu 8am-10pm, W-Th 8am-11pm, F-Sa 8am-3am.

Lombardi's Coal Oven Pizza, 32 Spring St. (☎941-7994), between Mott and Mulberry St. Perhaps the oldest pizzeria in the United States (opened 1905), credited with creating the New York-style thin-crust pizza. A large pie feeds 2 ($13.50). Open M-Th 11:30am-11pm, F-Sa 11:30am-midnight, Su 11:30am-10pm. Cash only.

Alfanoose, 150 Fulton St. (☎349-3622), at Broadway. Subway: 2, 3, 4, 5, A, C, J, M, Z to Fulton St. If you can skirt the rush, their falafel is well worth the price ($3.25). Open M-F 10am-9:30pm, Sa-Su 11am-9:30pm.

Hong Kong Egg Cake Co., on the corner of Mott and Mosco St. Located in a small red shack—just follow the line wrapped around the corner. Cecilia Tam will make you a dozen bite-size, sweet egg cakes ($1) fresh from the skillet that she's been working for 20 years. Open W-Th and Sa-Su 10:30am-5pm.

Chinatown Ice Cream Factory, 65 Bayard St. (☎608-4170), at Elizabeth St. Satisfy your sweet tooth with homemade lychee, taro, ginger, red bean, or green tea ice cream. 1 scoop $2.20, 2 scoops $4, 3 scoops $4.80. Open in summer M-Th 11:30am-11:30pm, F-Su 11:30am-midnight; rest of the year daily noon-11pm.

Ciao Bella, 285 Mott St. (☎431-3591), between Prince and E. Houston St. Possibly the best ice cream in the city: dense, smooth and rich. Their downtown location is little more than a storefront, but benches outside invite devotees to linger. Small $3.50, large $4.50. Open M-Sa 11am-11pm, Su 11am-10pm.

Economy Candy, 108 Rivington St. (☎254-1531), between Ludlow and Essex St. Subway: F, J, M, Z to Delancey St.-Essex St. This candy warehouse sells imported chocolates, jams, and countless confections, all at rock-bottom prices. 10 lb. bag of assorted candy $12. Open Su-F 8:30am-6pm, Sa 10am-5pm.

THE VILLAGES: FROM HOUSTON ST. TO 14TH ST.

Both Greenwich Village and the East Village present a wide array of budget dining options, spanning every imaginable cuisine.

▓ **Corner Bistro,** 331 W. 4th St. (☎242-9502), on the corner of Jane St. at Eighth Ave. Subway: A, C, E, L to 14th St.-Eighth Ave. Known for transcendent hamburgers ($4.50-5.50) and cold beer ($2-3). Arrive early—or late—if you want to get a seat. Open M-Sa 11:30am-4am, Su noon-4am. Cash only.

▓ **Max,** 51 Ave. B (☎539-0111), between E. 3rd and 4th St. Subway: F to Second Ave. Eating in the Max's garden is like having dinner in an old Italian neighborhood. The food fits the ambience (pasta $9-11, entrees $11-15). Open daily noon-midnight. Cash only.

▓ **National Cafe,** 210 First Ave. (☎473-9354), at E. 13th St. Subway: L to First Ave. The decor may not be much to talk about, but this is great home cooking, Cuban style. It's hard to find a better lunch special in the city; from 10:30am-3pm the National serves an entree of the day, rice and beans or salad, plantain, and a cup of soup for $4.60. Everything on the garlic-heavy menu is well under $10. Open M-Sa 10:30am-10pm.

John's Pizzeria, 278 Bleecker St. (☎243-1680), between Seventh Ave. S. and Morton St. Subway: 1, 9 to Christopher St. Widely regarded as Manhattan's best pizzeria and a great place to enjoy a pie. Two sizes, small and large, $10-20. No slices. Open M-Th 11:30am-11:30pm, F-Sa 11:30am-12:30am, Su noon-11:30pm. Cash only.

Yakitori Taisho, 5 St. Mark's Pl. (☎228-5086), between Second and Third Ave. Subway: 6 to Astor Pl. This tiny eating space serves good Japanese fare at wonderful prices. 10 *yakitori* (skewers of exquisitely tender pieces of chicken and vegetables) $12, cold ramen $4, chicken teriyaki $7. Open daily 11am-11pm.

Frank, 88 Second Ave. (☎420-0202), between E. 5th and E. 6th St. Subway: 6 to Astor Pl. An adorable sliver of a place with a friendly bistro feel. Pasta $9-13; entrees $12-14. M-F 5:30-7pm is *aperitivo* hour—free *antipasti* until 6:30pm. Expect to wait on the sidewalk for seats. Open M-Th 10:30am-4pm and 5pm-1am, F-Sa 10:30am-4pm and 5pm-2am, Su 10:30am-4pm and 5pm-midnight.

2nd Ave. Delicatessen, 156 Second Ave. (☎677-0606), at 10th St. Subway: 6 to Astor Pl. *The* definitive New York deli. The Lebewohl family has proudly maintained this strictly kosher joint since 1954. Try the *babka* ($3.25), *kasha varnishkes* ($4), or mushroom barley ($4), all reputed to be among the best in the city, or go for the classic pastrami or corned beef sandwiches ($8-11). Open M-Sa 10am-8:30pm, Su 11am-7pm.

Dojo Restaurant, 26 St. Mark's Pl. (☎674-9821), between Second and Third Ave. Subway: 6 to Astor Pl. One of the most popular restaurants and hangouts in the East Village serving an incredible variety of (largely) vegetarian and Japanese foods with St. Mark's Pl. ambience. Soyburgers with brown rice and salad $3.50. Dojo salad with carrot dressing $5. *Yakisoba* $5-7. Open Su-Th 11am-1am, F-Sa 11am-2am. Cash only.

Elvie's Turo-Turo, 214 First Ave. (☎473-7785), between E. 12th and 13th St. Subway: L to First Ave. Filipino food served cafeteria-style—just point to what you want. Dishes include *pancit* (a stir-fried rice noodle dish), chicken adobo, and barbecued pork and chicken. One dish (plus rice) $4, 2 for $5.75. Open M-Sa 11am-9pm, Su 11am-8pm.

MIDTOWN: FROM 14TH TO 59TH ST.

Fashionable gay men dine in pairs at Chelsea's trendy restaurants. The area just south of Murray Hill is home to a collection of Indian restaurants, earning the area the name Curry Hill. Restaurant Row in the Theater District is a favorite spot for pre-theater dining.

▨ Kitchen, 218 Eighth Ave. (☎243-4433), at 21st St. Subway: C, E to 23rd St. Bear with the narrow confines of Kitchen—the Mexican dishes (take-out only) are well worth the squeeze. Burrito stuffed with a filling of your choice, pinto beans, rice, and green salsa $6.75. Open M-Sa 9am-10:30pm, Su 11am-10:30pm.

Curry in a Hurry, 119 Lexington Ave. (☎683-0900), at 28th St. Subway: 6 to 28th St. Lots of tasty food at good prices make this a favorite Curry Hill locale. Chicken or lamb curries $4.50; vegetarian dishes $3.50-3.75; platters (main dishes, basmati rice, *naan*, and salad) $6.50-8.50. Open daily noon-midnight.

Sapporo, 152 W. 49th St. (☎869-8972), between Sixth and Seventh Ave. Subway: B, D, F, Q to 47th-50th St.-Rockefeller Center. A simple Japanese diner, with big portions and astounding flavors. Ramen $7.30. Open M-Sa 11am-11:30pm, Su 11am-10:30pm.

Hourglass Tavern, 373 W. 46th St. (☎265-2060), between Eighth and Ninth Ave. Servers flip an hourglass at your table when you sit down, and the time limit is strictly enforced. Delicious *prix-fixe* entrees $12-14. Open M-W 5-11:15pm, Th-F 5-11:30pm.

Little Pie Co., 407 W. 14th St. (☎414-2324), between Ninth and Tenth Ave. Subway: A, C, E, L to 14th St.-Eighth Ave. Small but perfect. Grab a 5 in. old-fashioned apple pie ($5) to go, or snack at the diner-style counter. Open M-F 10am-8pm, Sa-Su noon-7pm.

FROM 59TH ST. TO 96TH ST.

An overwhelming quantity of restaurants line Second and Third Ave. on the Upper East Side. On both sides of the park, you'll find food from all over the world.

▨ Saigon Grill, 1700 Second Ave. (☎996-4600), at 88th St. Subway: 4, 5, 6 to 86th St. Also at 2381 Broadway (☎875-9072). Some of the best Vietnamese in the city and a rare bargain on the Upper East Side. Dishes come chock-full of vegetables. Open daily 11:30am-11:30pm.

Big Nick's Burger Joint and Pizza Joint, 2175 Broadway (☎362-9238), at 77th St. Subway: 1, 9 to 79th St. Also at 70 W. 71st St. at Columbus Ave. (☎799-4444). Two times a joint, Big Nick's will satisfy your munchies and then some. Nick's dishes tried-and-true pizza, plate-sized burgers ($5-6.75; or go for the 1 lb. sumo burger, $7.50), and breakfast dishes from their vast menu. Free delivery. Open 24hr., "sometimes 25."

Barking Dog Luncheonette, 1678 Third Ave. (☎831-1800), at 94th St. Subway: 6 to 96th St. Enjoy big, tasty portions like "'Mom's Lovin' Meatloaf" ($11) in this restaurant full of dog paraphernalia, from the doghouse-shaped entrance to the pictures of celebrities and their hounds. Salads $5-9; sandwiches $6-8. Specials (M-F 5-7pm) come with soup or salad and dessert. Open daily 8am-11pm.

El Pollo, 1746 First Ave. (☎996-7810), between 90th and 91st St. Subway: 4, 5, 6 to 86th St. Excellent Peruvian fare. While known for its roasted, marinated, 7-flavored chicken, this restaurant also serves up delicacies like fried sweet plantains ($3) and *papas con ají* ($5). Half-chicken $6. Open M-F 11am-11pm, Sa-Su 12:30pm-10:45pm.

Le Pain Quotidien, 1131 Madison Ave. (☎327-4900), between 84th and 85th St. Subway: 4, 5, 6 to 86th St. Purveyors of some of the freshest breads in the city. Pick up a *baguette à l'ancienne* ($2.50). Open M-F 7:30am-7pm, Sa-Su 8am-7pm.

Zabar's, 2245 Broadway (☎787-2000), between 80th and 81st St. Subway: 1, 9 to 79th St. This Upper West Side institution sells everything you need for a 4-star meal at home. Cheeses, smoked salmon, and beautiful bread lure droves of shoppers into the gourmet grocery store. Open M-F 8am-7:30pm, Sa 8am-8pm, Su 9am-6pm.

HARLEM AND MORNINGSIDE HEIGHTS

Copeland's, 547 W. 145th St. between Broadway and Amsterdam Ave. (☎234-2357). Subway: 1, 9, A, B, C, D to 145th St. Excellent soul food accompanied by live music in an elegant dining room. Entrees pricey ($11-26); check out Copeland's cafeteria next door—no atmosphere but same food, entrees $4-11. Only open for dinner, except for Su (noon-9pm); cafeteria M-F 8am-11:30pm, Sa 8am-12:30am, Su 8am-1am.

Sylvia's, 328 Lenox Ave. (☎996-0660), at 126th St. Subway: 2, 3, to 125th St. The sumptuous soul food has enticed New Yorkers for close to 40 years; now European tour groups arrive in buses. Sylvia accents her "World-Famous Talked-About BBQ Ribs Special" with sweet spicy sauce and a side of collard greens and macaroni and cheese ($11). Open M-Sa 7:30am-10:30pm, Su 11am-8pm.

Sugar Shack, 2611 Frederick Douglass Blvd./Eighth Ave. (☎491-4422), at 139th St. An artsy crowd frequents this sexy lounge and soul food restaurant (entrees $10-12). Try the phenomenal daiquiris ($6-12) or the chocolate martini. Open M 7pm-midnight, Tu-W 5:30-11pm, Th 5:30pm-1am, F-Sa 5:30pm-2am, Su 11am-5pm.

Manna's Too!!, 486 Lenox Ave. (☎234-4488), between 134th and 135th St. Subway: 2, 3, to 135th St. Boasts the best salad bar in Harlem, along with a variety of soul food options and fresh veggies. Homemade cakes $2.50; an enormous and sinful piece of double chocolate cake $2. Open M-Sa 7am-8pm, Su 10am-7pm. Cash only.

Amir's Falafel, 2911A Broadway (☎749-7500), between 113th and 114th St. Subway: 1, 9 to 110th St., 116th St. Small and simple with low-priced Middle Eastern staples for vegetarians and meat lovers alike. Sandwiches ($3-5) and vegetarian platters ($5) made with care. Open daily 11am-11pm. Cash only.

Koronet Pizza, 2848 Broadway (☎222-1566), at 110th St. Subway: 1, 9 to 110th St. Slices larger than life for $2.25. Open Su-W 10am-2am, Th-Sa 10am-4am. Cash only.

BROOKLYN

For the trendiest in Brooklyn restaurants, head to Smith St. in Williamsburg. Flatbush, especially on Church Ave., is the spot for West Indian eateries. Brooklyn's Chinatown is located in Sunset Park. Ethnic enclave Brighton Beach is full of Russian and Ukrainian food, while Coney Island is known for its pizza and hot dogs.

■ **Grimaldi's,** 19 Old Fulton St. (☎718-858-4300), between Front and Water St., in Fulton Ferry. Subway: A, C to High St. Delicious thin crust brick-oven pizza with wonderfully fresh mozzarella, sold only by the pie. Come admire the all-Sinatra decor (it was one of his favorite joints). Small pies $12, large $14; toppings $2 each. Open M-Th 11:30am-11pm, F-Sa noon-midnight, Su noon-11pm. Cash only.

Bliss, 191 Bedford Ave. (☎718-599-2547), between 6th and 7th St., in Williamsburg. Subway: L to Bedford Ave. Don't be surprised when your *chili con pan* comes meat-free in this vegetarian hot spot. Specialties include the marinated tofu sandwich ($7) or the Bliss Bowl ($8). BYOB. Open M-F 8am-11pm, Sa-Su 10am-11pm. Cash only.

Oznot's Dish, 79 Berry St. (☎718-599-6596), at N. 9th St., in Williamsburg. Subway: L to Bedford Ave. Oznot's exterior resembles a modern painting, and the interior is exquisite. The Mediterranean food is good, especially the lunch *meze* platter of pita, hummus and olives ($7). Open daily 11am-4:30pm and 6pm-midnight.

Planet Thailand, 115 Berry St. (☎718-599-5758), between N. 7th and 8th St., in Williamsburg. Subway: L to Bedford Ave. The menu is expansive, with reasonably priced Thai ($8) and a new Japanese menu which is a bit pricier (sushi dinner $11). DJ every night at 9pm. Open Su-W 11:30am-1am, Th-Sa 11:30am-2am. Cash only.

Caravan, 193 Atlantic Ave. (☎718-488-7111), between Court and Clinton St., in Brooklyn Heights. Subway: 2, 3, 4, 5, M, N, R to Court St./Borough Hall. Caravan prides itself on its couscous and tandoori oven-baked bread. *Prix-fixe* lunch ($8) includes an entree, hummus and *baba ghanoush*, soup or salad, dessert, and Moroccan coffee. Belly dancing and live band Sa at 8pm. Open M-F 11am-10pm, Sa-Su noon-midnight.

Brooklyn Moon, 745 Fulton St. (☎718-243-0424), at S. Elliott Pl., in Fort Greene. Subway: G to Fulton St.; C to Lafayette Ave. Salmon burger $6.50; apple salad $4.25. The Moon holds open mic night on F at 10:30pm, when aspiring bards from all over NYC come forth. Open M-Th noon-10pm, F-Sa 11:30am-midnight, Su 11:30am-10pm.

Totonno Pizzeria Napolitano, 1524 Neptune Ave. (☎718-372-8606), between 15th and 16th St., in Coney Island. Subway: B, D, F, N to Coney Island. A Coney Island legend, this joint serves pizza by the pie that vies for the coveted title of finest pizza in New York. Pies $13-14.50. No slices. Open W-Su noon-8:30pm. Cash only.

Primorski Restaurant, 282 Brighton Beach Ave. (☎718-891-3111), between Brighton Beach 2nd and 3rd St. Subway: D to Brighton Beach. Serves Ukrainian specialties in a festive atmosphere. Russian music and disco M-Th 8pm-midnight, F-Sa 9pm-2am, Su 8pm-1am. Open daily 11am-2am.

Sahadi Importing Company, 187-189 Atlantic Ave. (☎718-624-4550), between Court and Clinton St., in Brooklyn Heights. Subway: 2, 3, 4, 5, M, N, R to Court St./Borough Hall. A popular Middle Eastern emporium that stocks spices, seasonings, dried fruits, and an array of spreads and dips. Open M-F 9am-7pm, Sa 8:30am-7pm.

QUEENS AND THE BRONX

Queens offers visitors some of the best and most reasonably priced ethnic cuisine: Greek in Astoria, Indian in Jackson Heights, Chinese and Korean in Flushing, and West Indian in Jamaica. The Bronx's culinary heart beats in Belmont, where you'll find some of the city's best Italian food.

■ **Elias Corner,** 24-02 31st St. (☎718-932-1510), at 24th Ave., in Astoria, Queens. Subway: N, W to Astoria Blvd. With no menus, outdoor dining, and fresh everything, this fantastic seafood restaurant has a distinctly Greek character. Try the delicious *tsatziki*, calamari, or grilled octopus as appetizers ($3-6 depending on plate size). Whole grilled fish $7-14. Often crowded. No reservations. Open daily 4-11pm or midnight. Cash only.

■ **Dominick's,** 2335 Arthur Ave. (☎718-733-2807), near E. 186th St., in the Bronx. No menu here and no set prices—regulars are happy to give advice. Linguine with mussels and marinara ($7), marinated artichoke ($7), and veal *francese* ($12) are all house specials. Arrive before 6pm or after 9pm, or expect a 20min. wait. Open M, W-Th, and Sa noon-10pm; F noon-11pm; Su 1-9pm.

Flushing Noodle, 135-42 Roosevelt Ave. (☎ 718-353-1166), in Flushing, Queens. Subway: 7 to Main St.-Flushing. Duck from the bustle of Flushing's big streets into this Chinese noodle shop, among the finest in Queens. Noodles $3.75-5. Lunch specials $5.

Jackson Diner, 37-47 74th St. (☎ 718-672-1232), at 37th Ave., in Jackson Heights, Queens. Subway: E, F, G, R to Jackson Heights/Roosevelt Ave.; 7 to 74th St./Broadway. Possibly the best Indian food in the city. The colorful setting is a departure from other, more ornate Indian restaurants. Lunch specials $6-7.50. Weekend lunch buffet (11:30am-4pm) $8. Open M-F 11:30am-10pm, Sa-Su 11:30am-10:30pm. Cash only.

Emilia's, 2331 Arthur Ave. (☎ 718-367-5915), near E. 186th St., in the Bronx. Delicious food in large portions. The *calamari fra diavolo* ($15) is especially good. Entrees $13-18. Lunch special $10. Open M-F and Su noon-10pm, Sa noon-11pm.

Nick's Pizza, 108-26 Ascan Ave. (☎ 718-263-1126), between Austin and Burns St., in Forest Hills, Queens. Subway: E, F, G, R to Forest Hills/71st Ave. Some of the best pizza in Queens, served in a classy setting. Flaky crust and delectable sauce and toppings (small pizzas $11, large $13, toppings $2 extra; no slices). Open M-Th 11:30am-9:30pm, F 11:30am-11:30pm, Sa 12:30-11:30pm, Su 12:30-9:30pm.

Jai-Ya, 81-11 Broadway (☎ 718-651-1330), in Elmhurst, Queens. Subway: R to Elmhurst Ave. Great Thai food, with 3 degrees of spiciness, from mild to "help-me-I'm-on-fire." Most dishes $7-11.25. Vegetarian options available. Lunch specials ($5.25-8.50) M-F 11:30am-3pm. Open M-F 11am-midnight, Sa 11:30am-midnight, Su 5pm-midnight.

The Lemon Ice King of Corona, 52-02 108th St. (☎ 718-699-5133), at Corona Ave., in Corona, Queens. Subway: 7 to 111th St.; a healthy walk back 1 block to 108th and south 10 blocks. The Emperor of Cool scrapes up juicy frozen treats outdoors. Every flavor you could want, including bubble gum, blueberry, cantaloupe, cherry, and, of course, lemon (80¢-$2). Open daily 10am-12:30am.

Galaxy Pastry Shop, 37-11 30th Ave. (☎ 718-545-3181), in Astoria, Queens. Subway: N to 30th Ave.; make a right on 30th Ave. and walk east to 37th St. A hangout for young locals, the Galaxy offers great pastries to ruin your diet. The baklava ($1.20) tastes like the answer to a Dionysian prayer. Open daily 6:30am-3am.

◎ SIGHTS

THE STATUE OF LIBERTY AND ELLIS ISLAND

The Statue of Liberty stands at the entrance to New York Harbor, long a symbol of hope for millions of immigrants who had just completed the arduous voyage across the Atlantic. In 1886, the French government presented Frederic-Auguste Bartholdi's sculpture to the US as a sign of goodwill. Instead of taking the long, slow climb to the top, take the elevator to the top of Richard Morris Hunt's pedestal, which offers enchanting views of New York and the towering statue above you. While the Statue embodies the American Dream, Ellis Island chronicles the harsh realities of life in the New World, housing a museum describing immigrant experience. *(Ferries run in a Battery Park-Liberty Island-Ellis Island loop, daily every 30min. 9:30am-3pm. Subway: 1, 9 to South Ferry; 4, 5 to Bowling Green; N, R to Whitehall St. ☎ 363-3200. Tickets for ferry, the Statue of Liberty, and Ellis Island: $8, seniors $6, ages 3-17 $3, under 3 free.)*

LOWER MANHATTAN

The southern tip of Manhattan is a motley assortment of cobblestones and financial powerhouses. The Wall St. area, less than ½ mi. long, is the most densely built in all New York, creating one of the highest concentrations of skyscrapers in the world. Crooked streets retain NY's original Dutch layout; lower Manhattan was the first part of the island to be settled.

WALL STREET AND THE FINANCIAL DISTRICT. Once the northern border of the New Amsterdam settlement, Wall St. takes its name from the wall built in 1653 to shield the Dutch colony from a British invasion from the north. By the early 19th century, the area was the financial capital of the US. On the southwest corner of

Wall and Broad St. stands the **New York Stock Exchange,** where over 3000 companies exchange 228 billion shares of stock valued at $13 trillion. The observation gallery overlooks the exchange's zoo-like main trading floor. *(☎ 656-5165 or 656-5168. Open M-F 9am-4:30pm. Tickets handed out on a first come, first served basis beginning at 8:45am.)* Around the corner, at the end of Wall St., rises the seemingly ancient **Trinity Church.** Its steeple and cemetery—which houses the grave of Alexander Hamilton—are delicately crafted, an anomaly amid the canyons of the Financial District. At the intersection of Battery Pl., Broadway, and Whitehall St., is **Bowling Green,** the site of the city's first mugging: here, Peter Minuit purchased Manhattan for the equivalent of $24 in trade goods. This spot eventually became the city's first park. The Beaux Arts **U.S. Custom House,** 1 Bowling Green, overlooks the park. A few blocks northwest lies the former site of the **World Trade Center.** On September 11, 2001, two hijacked commercial jets crashed into the WTC's Twin Towers. Approximately an hour after the crash, both 110-story buildings collapsed in a cloud of rubble. Thousands were killed in the worst terrorist attack ever to have hit the United States. *(At the time that this book went to press, rescue efforts were just underway.)*

CIVIC CENTER. Fittingly, the city's center of government is located immediately north of its financial district, as the city tries to keep unscrupulous dealings to a minimum. **City Hall** is the neighborhood's center, and around it revolve myriad courthouses, civic buildings, and federal buildings. Completed in 1811, City Hall may be the finest piece of architecture in the city. New York's mayor keeps his offices in this elegant Neoclassical structure. The building's interior is not presently open to the public. *(Broadway at Murray St., off Park Row.)* The neo-Gothic **Woolworth Building** towers south of City Hall. F.W. Woolworth reportedly paid $15.5 million to house the headquarters of his five-and-dime store empire in this sumptuous 1913 skyscraper, once known as the "Cathedral of Commerce." Arches and mosaics adorn the resplendent lobby. *(233 Broadway, between Barclay St. and Park Pl.)* A block and a half south on Broadway, **St. Paul's Chapel** is Manhattan's oldest public building in continuous use; it hasn't missed a day since George Washington prayed here on his inauguration day. *(Between Vesey and Fulton St. Open M-F 9am-3pm, Su 7am-3pm.)*

SOUTH STREET SEAPORT. The shipping industry thrived here for most of the 19th century, when New York was the most important port city in the US. During the 20th century, bars, brothels, and crime flourished. But in the mid-1980s, the Seaport Museum teamed up with the Rouse Corporation, which built Boston's Quincy Market, the St. Louis Union Station, and Baltimore's Harborplace, to design the 12-block "museum without walls," which features old schooners, sailboats, and houses. *(Visit the Seaport Museum Visitors Center, 209 Water St., for info on the myriad sights of the area. ☎ 748-8600.)* The pervading fishy stench comes from the **Fulton Fish Market,** the largest fresh-fish mart in the country (and a notorious former mafia stronghold), on South St., on the other side of the overpass. *(☎ 748-8786. Market opens at 4am. Crack-of-dawn tours available June-Oct.)* The seaport also reeks of Malldom USA. **Pier 17** houses your typical shopping center offerings.

CHINATOWN AND LITTLE ITALY

Mott and **Pell St.,** the unofficial centers of Chinatown, boil over with Chinese restaurants and commercial activity. Every inch of the old red and green awnings lining the storefronts are decorated with Chinese-style baby jackets, bamboo hats, and miniature Buddhas. If it's labels you're into, Canal is the street for you. Don't let the low-priced merchandise snooker you, though—creative labeling abounds in several stores and those are *not* Rolexes. During the Chinese New Year, the area's frenetic pace accelerates to a fever pitch.

Immigration has propelled Chinatown into what was once Italian territory. Since the 1960s, Little Italy's borders have receded in the face of an aggressively expanding Chinatown, and much of the neighborhood's authenticity has disappeared due to the temptation of tourism. **Mulberry St.** remains the heart of the neighborhood.

LOWER EAST SIDE

The Lower East Side was once the most densely settled area in New York; 240,000 immigrants lived within one square mile. Initially populated by Irish immigrants in the mid-1800s, the area saw a large influx of Eastern Europeans in the 50 years preceding WWI. Post-WWII migrants to the area were mostly African-Americans and Puerto Ricans, and in the 1980s and 90s Latin Americans and Asians began to move into the area. Main thoroughfares such as East Broadway continue to reflect the multicultural aspect of the neighborhood. Traces of the Jewish ghetto also persist on Orchard St., an historic shopping area that fills up on Sundays. If you need guidance, visit the **Lower East Side Visitors Center.** *(261 Broome St., between Orchard and Allen St. ☎888-825-8374. Open Su-F 10am-4pm.)*

For a taste of the neighborhood as it was, try the **Lower East Side Tenement Museum,** 90 Orchard St. Tours lead through three meticulously restored apartments of immigrant families: the Gumpertzes in 1870, the Rogarshevskys in 1918, and the Baldizzis in 1939. *(☎431-0233. Call for info on tours of tenement and neighborhood. $9, seniors and students $7.)* The **Eldridge Street Synagogue** *(12 Eldridge St.)* and **Congregation Anshe Chesed** *(172-176 Norfolk St., at Stanton St.)* are two splendid old synagogues.

SOHO AND TRIBECA

The architecture in **SoHo**—the area bounded by Houston St. on the north, Canal St. on the south, Broadway on the west, and Crosby St. on the east—is American Industrial, notable for its cast-iron facades. Its inhabitants are New York's prospering *artistes*. Here, **galleries** reign supreme (see **Galleries,** p. 227) and chic boutiques fill in the cracks. While the shopping in SoHo is probably well beyond a budget traveler's means, those seeking that hidden gem should check out the **Antiques Fair and Collectibles Market** on the corner of Broadway and Grand St. *(Open Sa-Su 9am-5pm.)*

TriBeCa, or triangle below Canal St., has been anointed (by resident Robert DeNiro and others) as one of the hottest neighborhoods in the city. Hidden inside the industrial warehouses are lofts, restaurants, bars, and galleries, maintaining SoHo's trendiness without the upscale airs. Admire the cast-iron edifices lining White St., Thomas St., and Broadway, the 19th-century Federal-style buildings on Harrison St., and the shops, galleries, and bars on Church and Reade St.

GREENWICH VILLAGE

The area west of Broadway, between Houston and 14th St., or the Village, has undergone a relentless process of cultural ferment that layered grime, activism, and artistry atop a tangle of quaint, meandering streets. The area, once covered in farms and hills, developed in the mid-19th century into a staid high-society playground. Real-estate values plummeted at the turn of the century as German, Irish, and Italian immigrants found work in the industries along the Hudson River. Some fifty years later, the Beat movement crystallized in the Village, and the 60s saw the growth of a homosexual community around Christopher St. The Village's nonconformist ethos conflicted with the aims of the city government in the late 60s. Violent clashes between police and homosexuals resulted in the Stonewall Riots of 1969, a powerful moment of awakening in the gay rights movement. In the 70s the punk scene exploded and added mohawked rockers to the Village's diverse cast of characters. The 80s and 90s saw a gentrification process that has made the Village a fashionable and comfortable settlement for wealthier New Yorkers with a bit more spunk than their uptown counterparts.

WASHINGTON SQUARE AND SURROUNDINGS. Washington Square Park has a rich history. The latter half of the 18th century saw the area converted into a potter's field for the burial of the poor and unknown (around 15,000 bodies lie buried here) and then as a hanging-grounds during the Revolutionary War. In the 1820s the area metamorphosed into a park and parade ground. Soon, high-toned residences made the area the center of New York's social scene. On the north side of the park is **The Row.** Built largely in the 1830s, this stretch of stately brick residences soon became an urban center populated by writers, dandies, and professionals.

At the north end of the Park stands the **Washington Memorial Arch,** built in 1889 to commemorate the centennial of George Washington's inauguration. Until 1964, Fifth Ave. actually ran through the arch; residents, however, complained of the noisy traffic and the city truncated the most esteemed of avenues. The country's largest private university, **New York University** is notable for some of the least appealing contemporary architecture in the Village. On the southeast side of the park, where Washington Sq. South meets LaGuardia Pl., you'll find NYU's **Loeb Student Center,** garnished with pieces of scrap metal purported to represent birds in flight.

WEST VILLAGE. The area of Greenwich Village west of 6th Ave. boasts eclectic summer street life and excellent nightlife. A visible gay community thrives around **Sheridan Sq.,** at the intersection of Seventh Ave., W. 4th St., and Christopher St. These are the home waters of the 1969 Stonewall Riot that helped galvanize the gay community. The neighborhood is also a destination for those making literary pilgrimages. **Chumley's,** between Grove and Barrow St., is a former speakeasy and hangout for such authors as Ernest Hemingway and John Dos Passos. *(86 Bedford St.)* Off 10th St. and Sixth Ave. you'll see an iron gate and street sign that reads **"Patchin Place."** e.e. cummings, Theodore Dreiser, and Djuna Barnes lived in the 145-year-old buildings that line this path. **75½ Bedford St.** is the narrowest building in the Village, only 9½ ft. in width. Writer Edna St. Vincent Millay lived here in the 20s, when she founded the nearby **Cherry Lane Theater.** *(38 Commerce St.)* Actors Lionel Barrymore and Cary Grant also appreciated the cramped quarters.

EAST VILLAGE

The East Village—north of Houston St., east of Broadway, and south of 14th St.— was carved out of the Bowery and the Lower East Side in the early 1960s, when artists and writers moved here to escape high rents in Greenwich Village. Today East Village residents span a wide spectrum, with punks, hippies, ravers, rastas, guppies, goths, and beatniks all coexisting. Diversity, however, does not always breed harmony; many poorer residents of the East Village feel that wealthier newcomers have pushed them out by raising rents. These tensions have forged the East Village into one of the most overtly politicized neighborhoods of the city.

ST. MARK'S PLACE. Full of pot-smoking flower children and musicians in the 1960s, this street gave Haight-Ashbury a run for its hashish. In the late 1970s, it taught London's Kings Road how to do punk, as mohawked youths hassled passersby from the brownstone steps off Astor Place. Nowadays, those 60s and 70s youths still line the street—in their old-tattooed-geezer incarnations. The present-day St. Mark's Pl. is a drag full of tiny ethnic eateries, street level shops, sidewalk vendors selling trinkets of all kinds—from plastic bug-eye sunglasses to PVC fetish wear—music shops, and, of course, tattoo shops.

ASTOR PLACE. The **Joseph Papp Public Theater** resides at Lafayette St., housed in what was once a library donated by John Jacob Astor. *(☎598-7150.)* The intersection of **Astor Place,** at Lafayette, E. 8th St., and Fourth Ave., is distinguished by a large black cube balanced on its corner. (If you push it, it will turn.)

ALPHABET CITY. East of First Ave. and south of 14th St., the avenues run out of numbers and adopt letters. During the area's heyday in the 60s, Jimi Hendrix played open-air shows here to bright-eyed love children. There has been a great deal of drug-related crime in the recent past, although locals have done an admirable job of making the area livable and have started a number of community gardens. Alphabet City's extremist Boho activism has made the neighborhood chronically ungovernable; police officers in 1988 set off a riot when they attempted to evict a band of the homeless and their supporters in **Tompkins Sq. Park.** *(E. Seventh St. and Ave. A.)*

LOWER MIDTOWN

UNION SQUARE. So named because it was the union of the Bowery and Bloomingdale Rd. (now Fourth Ave. and Broadway), Union Square and the surrounding area sizzled with high-society aristocrats before the Civil War. Today, the scent of herbs and fresh bread wafts through the air, courtesy of the ◪**Union Square Green-market.** *(Between Broadway and Park Ave., and 14th and 17th St.)*

GRAMERCY. In 1831 Samuel Ruggles, a developer fond of greenery, drained a marsh to create the **Gramercy Park,** at the south end of Lexington Ave., between 20th and 21st St., and laid out 66 building lots around its perimeter. Today, the neighborhood surrounding the private park is a thriving residential area. Two blocks west and two blocks north of Gramercy Park is the eminently photogenic **Flatiron Building.** Considered the world's first skyscraper, it was originally named the Fuller Building, but its dramatic wedge shape, imposed by the intersection of Broadway, Fifth Ave., 22nd St., and 23rd St., quickly earned it its current name.

MURRAY HILL. So named because Robert Murray, a rich man in revolutionary times, made his country home close to the present-day intersection of 37th St. and Park Avenue. The highlight of Murray Hill is the **Pierpont Morgan Library.** The original library building was completed in 1906 and designed by Charles McKim in the style of a Renaissance *palazzo. (29 E. 36th St., at Madison Ave.)*

CHELSEA. Home to some of the most fashionable clubs, bars, and restaurants in the city, Chelsea has lately undergone something of a rebirth. A large gay and lesbian community and an increasing artsy-yuppie population have given the area, west of Fifth Ave. between 14th and 30th St., the flavor of a lower-rent West Village. Chelsea has become home to innovative **art galleries** that escape SoHo's exorbitant rent (see **Museums and Galleries,** p. 225). The historic **Hotel Chelsea,** between Seventh and Eighth Ave., has sheltered many an artist, most famously Sid Vicious of the Sex Pistols. Edie Sedgwick torched the place with a cigarette between Warhol films. Countless writers spent their days searching for inspiration here, including Arthur Miller, Vladimir Nabokov, and Dylan Thomas. *(222 W. 23rd St. ☎ 243-3700.)*

EMPIRE STATE BUILDING AND HERALD SQUARE. The Empire State Building remains New York's classic landmark, continuing to dominate postcards, movies, and the city's skyline. The limestone and granite structure, with glistening ribbons of stainless steel, stretches 1454 ft. into the sky, and its 73 elevators run through 2 mi. of shafts. The nighttime view from the top is spectacular. *(Fifth Ave. between 33rd and 34th St. ☎ 736-3100. Observatory open daily 9:30am-midnight; tickets sold until 11:30pm. $11.50, seniors and ages 4-12 $8.50.)*

East on 34th St., between Seventh Ave. and Broadway, in Herald Sq., stands **Macy's,** the Goliath of department stores. It sponsors the **Macy's Thanksgiving Day Parade,** a NYC tradition buoyed by ten-story Snoopys, marching bands, and floats. For cheaper clothing, the area surrounding Macy's, between Broadway and Eighth Ave. in the 30s, is the **Garment District,** once a red light district, which, in the 1930s, purportedly contained the largest concentration of apparel workers in the world.

HELL'S KITCHEN

Located from 34th to 59th St. west of Eighth Avenue, Hell's Kitchen purportedly got its name from a policemen fed up with his beat. Once a badland for ruffians and a breeding-ground for violence, this is the neighborhood that bore the "Westies"—the gangs that inspired Leonard Bernstein's 1957 *West Side Story.* Slowly swept by a wave of gentrification, this neighborhood paints urban renewal over a gritty core. The neighborhood is home to the **Jacob Javits Center,** host to some of the grandest-scale events in the world, like its famous motorcycle and car shows. *(Along Twelfth Ave. between 34th and 38th St.)*

MIDTOWN

FIFTH AVENUE. A monumental research library in the style of a classical temple, the main branch of the **New York Public Library,** between 40th and 42nd St., is a breath of fresh air from the skyscrapers lining Fifth Ave. On sunny afternoons, throngs of people perch on the marble steps. This is the world's seventh largest research library; see the immense 3rd fl. reading room. *(☎ 869-8089. Open M-Sa 10am-6pm, Tu-W 11am-7:30pm. Free tours Tu-Sa 11am and 2pm.)* **Bryant Park** spreads out behind the library. The stage at the head of the park hosts free cultural events throughout the summer, including screenings of classic films, jazz concerts, and live comedy. (☎ 484-1222 for a schedule of events. Open 7am-9pm.) **St. Patrick's Cathedral,** New York's most famous church and the largest Catholic cathedral in America, stands at 51st St. Designed by James Renwick, its twin spires stretch 330 ft. into the air. On 59th St., at the southeast corner of Central Park, sits the legendary **Plaza Hotel,** built in 1907 at astronomical cost. Its 18-story, 800-room French Renaissance interior flaunts five marble staircases, countless ludicrously named suites, and a two-story Grand Ballroom. The stores on Fifth Ave. from Rockefeller Center to Central Park are the ritziest in the city. At **Tiffany & Co.,** on 57th St., everything from jewelry to housewares shines; the window displays are works of art in themselves, especially around Christmas. **F.A.O. Schwarz,** at 58th St., is one of the world's largest toy stores.

ROCKEFELLER CENTER. The main entrance to Rockefeller Center is on Fifth Ave. between 49th and 50th St. **The Channel Gardens,** so named because they sit between the **Maison Française** on the left and the **British Empire Building** on the right, usher the pedestrian toward **Tower Plaza.** This sunken space, topped by the gold-leafed statue of **Prometheus,** is surrounded by the flags of over 100 countries. During spring and summer an **ice-skating rink** lies dormant beneath an overpriced cafe. The rink, which is better for people-watching than for skating, reopens in winter in time for the **annual Christmas tree lighting,** one of New York's greatest traditions.

Behind Tower Plaza is the **General Electric Building,** a 70-story skyscraper. NBC, which makes its home here, offers an hour-long tour that traces the history of the network, from their first radio broadcast in 1926 through the heyday of TV programming in the 1950s and 60s to today's sitcoms. The tour visits six studios including the infamous 8H studio, home of Saturday Night Live. (30 Rockefeller Plaza.) A block north is **Radio City Music Hall.** Narrowly escaping demolition in 1979, this Art Deco landmark received a complete interior restoration shortly thereafter. Radio City's main attraction is the Rockettes, a high-stepping long-legged troupe of dancers. Tours of the Music Hall take the visitor through The Great Stage and various rehearsal halls. (On the corner of Sixth Ave. and 51st St. ☎ 664-3700. NBC Tour: from the GE Building. $17.50, seniors and children $15. Radio City Music Hall tours given M-Sa 10am-5pm, Su 9am-5pm. $16, under 12 $10.)

PARK AVENUE. A luxurious boulevard with greenery running down its center, **Park Avenue** from 45th St. to 59th St. is lined with office buildings and hotels. Completed in 1913, **Grand Central Terminal** is a train station of monumental proportions. The richly classical main facade is on 42nd St.; on top stands a beautiful sculpture of Mercury, Roman god of transportation. Inside, the Main Concourse is abuzz with commuters. In the middle of the Concourse sits an information booth, which may be the most popular meeting place in New York. (Between 42nd and 45th St.) Several blocks uptown the **Waldorf-Astoria** is the *crème de la crème* of Park Avenue hotels. (Between 49th and 50th St.) Completed in 1919, **St. Bartholomew's Church,** at 50th St., draws heavily upon Byzantine architecture. A monument of modern architecture, Ludwig Mies Van der Rohe's dark and gracious **Seagram Building** stands a few blocks uptown. (375 Park Ave., between 52nd and 53rd St.)

UNITED NATIONS. Founded in 1945 in the aftermath of World War II to serve as "a center for harmonizing the actions of nations" (and meeting with limited success since then), the **United Nations** is located along what would be First Ave. But the UN is international territory and not under the jurisdiction of the US—as evidenced by the member nations' 189 flags flying outside at equal height, in flagrant violation of American custom. The complex consists of the Secretariat Building (the skyscraper), the General Assembly Building, the Hammarskjöld Library, and the Conference Building. The only way into the General Assembly Building is by guided tour. (Between 42nd and 48th St. ☎ 963-4475; General Assembly 963-7713. Tours, in 20 languages, depart from the UN visitor's entrance at First Ave. and 46th St. Children under 5 not admitted on tour. 1hr.; every 15min. daily 9:15am-4:45pm. $7.50, seniors $6, students $5, ages 4-14 $4; disabled 20% discount.) To return to the spirit of go-get-'em American capitalism, head to the nearby **Chrysler Building.** A spire influenced by radiator grille design tops this Art Deco palace of industry. (On 42nd St. and Lexington Ave.)

TIMES SQUARE AND THEATER DISTRICT. At 42nd St., Seventh Ave., and Broadway, the city offers up one of the largest electronic extravaganzas in the world. Times Square may have given New York its reputation as a dark metropolis covered with strip clubs, neon, and filth, but today the smut is at least partially cleaned up. Madame Tussaud's and AMC united to rebuild the Liberty, Empire, and Harris theaters into a wax museum and 29-screen movie megaplex. The historic Victory Theater, where Abbot met Costello and Houdini made an elephant disappear, is now the eerily Orwellian "New Victory" Theater. While some theaters have been converted into movie houses or simply left to rot as the cost of live productions has skyrocketed, approximately 37 theaters remain active (most of them grouped around 45th St.). One highlight of the Theater District is **Shubert Alley,** a half-block west of Broadway between 44th and 45th St. Originally built as a fire exit between the Booth and Shubert Theaters, the alley now serves as a private street for pedestrians. After shows, fans often hover at stage doors to get their playbills signed.

57TH ST. AND CENTRAL PARK SOUTH. Luxury hotels, such as the **Essex House,** the **St. Moritz,** and the **Plaza,** overlook Central Park from their perch on Central Park South, between Fifth and Eighth Ave., where 59th St. should be. Two blocks south, 57th St. is filled with galleries, stores, and New York's musical mecca, **Carnegie Hall** (see p. 233). In the late 1950s, the threat of Carnegie's replacement by an enormous red skyscraper generated a city-wide campaign, led by violinist Isaac Stern, to save the building. In 1960, the campaign convinced the city government to purchase the building. Decades of patchwork maintenance and periodic facelifts left the hall in various stages of disrepair until 1985 when a $60 million restoration and repair program returned the building to its earlier splendor. (☎ 903-9791 for tours. 1hr. tours M-Tu and Th-F at 11:30am, 2, and 3pm. Open M-Tu and Th-F 11am-4:30pm. Free. Museum and tours closed July-Aug. $6, seniors and students $5, under 12 $3.)

CENTRAL PARK

Until the mid-1800s the 843 acres that are now Central Park were considered a social and geographical wasteland. The area was home to over 1600 of the city's poorest residents, including Irish pig farmers, German gardeners, and the black Seneca Village population, all squatters, who occupied shantytowns, huts, and caves on the site. Around 1850 some of New York's wealthiest citizens began to advocate for the creation of a park, claiming that the public space would ameliorate social ills. In truth, the upper class had long envied the public grounds of London and Paris and now sought a playground of their own. Their voices were heard, and in 1857 Frederick Law Olmstead collaborated with Calvert Vaux to win the rights to design the park. Their Greensward plan took 15 years to implement, employing over 20,000 workers. The result is a beautiful park very well-used by New Yorkers.

 Central Park is fairly safe during the day, but less so at night. Don't be afraid to go to events in the Park at night, but take large paths and go with someone. Do not wander the darker paths at night, especially if you are a woman. In an **emergency,** use one of the call-boxes located throughout the park. **24hr. Park Line,** ☎570-4820.

Expansive fields such as the **Sheep Meadow,** from 66th to 69th St., and the **Great Lawn,** from 80th to 85th St., complement developed spaces such as the **Mall,** between 66th and 71st St.; the **Shakespeare Garden,** at 80th St.; and the **Imagine Mosaic,** on the western side of the park at 72nd St., commemorating the music and dreams of John Lennon. Don't miss the park's free performances—at Central Park Summerstage and Shakespeare in the Park—come June, July, and August. (☎ 360-3444; parks and recreation info 360-8111, M-F 9am-5pm. Free park maps at Belvedere Castle, located mid-park at 79th St.; the Charles A. Dana Discovery Center, at 110th St. near 5th Ave.; the North Meadow Recreation Center, mid-park at 97th St.; and the Dairy, mid-park near 65th St.)

UPPER EAST SIDE

Since the late 19th and early 20th centuries, when some of New York's wealthiest citizens built elaborate mansions along **Fifth Avenue,** the Upper East Side has been home to the city's richest residents. Today, some of these parkside mansions have been turned into museums, such as the Frick Collection and the Cooper-Hewitt Museum. They are just two of the world-famous museums that line **Museum Mile,** from 82nd to 104th St. on Fifth Ave. (see p. 225). **Park Avenue** from 59th to 96th St. is lined with dignified apartment buildings. Lexington and Third Ave. are commercial, but as you go east, the neighborhood becomes more and more residential.

HOUSES OF WORSHIP. The imposing Romanesque synagogue **Temple Emanu-El** is home to some fine stained-glass windows. *(1 E. 65th St. at Fifth Ave.)* While the temple fits its surroundings, the multi-domed **Church of St. Jean Baptiste** seems positively out of place on busy Lexington Ave. *(On the corner of Lexington Ave. and 76th St.)* To get a good look at its splendid paired towers and Corinthian porticoes, cross over to the other side of the avenue. Equally anomalous is **St. Nicholas Russian Orthodox Church** which is exuberantly topped by five onion domes. *(15 E. 97th St.)*

OLD BOYS' CLUBS. Designed by Stanford White to resemble a 16th-century Italian palazzo, **The Metropolitan Club** *(1 E. 60th St.)* was founded in 1891 by a group of distinguished gentlemen who were disgruntled with the rejection of some of their friends from the very exclusive **Union Club.** *(101 E. 69th St.)* Inversely, **The Knickerbocker Club** was founded in 1871 by Union men who believed that the club's admissions policies had become *too* lax and liberal. *(2 E. 62nd St.)*

UPPER WEST SIDE

While Central Park West and Riverside Drive flank the Upper West Side with residential quietude, Columbus Ave., Amsterdam Ave., and Broadway are abuzz with action. The gods of organic fruit and progressive politics will reward you for wandering their domain (between 59th and 110th St., west of Central Park).

LINCOLN CENTER. Broadway intersects Columbus Ave. at Lincoln Center, the cultural hub of the city, between 62nd and 66th St. Power broker Robert Moses masterminded Lincoln Center when Carnegie Hall seemed fated for destruction in 1955. The ensuing construction forced the eviction of thousands and erased a major part of Hell's Kitchen. The complex was designed as a modern version of the public plazas of Rome and Venice, and despite the opinions of critics (*The Times* called it "a hulking disgrace"), the airy architecture, along with the performances that take place here, has made it one of New York's most admired locales. Performance spaces for opera, ballet, and classical music take center stage (see p. 232).

APARTMENTS OF THE RICH AND FAMOUS. The Dakota may be the city's most famous apartment building. When constructed in 1884, the complex was surrounded by open land and shanties, and so far removed from the city that someone remarked, "It might as well be in the Dakota Territory." The name stuck, and architect Henry Hardenbergh even gave the elegant building a frontier flare. *(1 W. 72nd St.)* A couple blocks uptown is the **Ansonia Hotel,** which bristles with ornaments, curved Veronese balconies, and towers. Constructed in the Beaux-Arts style in 1904, the Ansonia has 2,500 apartments as well as various cafes, tea rooms, writing rooms, and a dining room seating 550. *(2109 Broadway.)* **The El Dorado** showcases flashy Art Deco detailing in a full array of gold. The lobby is a national landmark and well worth a stop if you can convince the security guards that you won't sneak a visit to the stars who reside there. *(300 Central Park West, between 90th and 91st St.)*

HARLEM

Over the years Harlem has entered the popular psyche as the archetype of America's frayed edges, but you won't believe the hype once you've actually visited the place. The largest neighborhood in all of Manhattan, Harlem extends from 110th

Street to the 150s, between the Hudson and East Rivers. Between 1910 and 1920, during a collapse in the real-estate market, Harlem began its transformation into a black neighborhood. The 1920s brought prosperity to Harlem and welcomed the artistic and literary movement known as the Harlem Renaissance.

In the 1960s, riding the tidal wave of the Civil Rights movement, the radical Black Power movement thrived here. In spite of the activism, though, Harlem's economic welfare was declining rapidly. In the 1970s and 80s, members of the community recognized the need for economic revitalization as a route to empowerment. Today, thanks to the economic boom of the 1990s, pockets of Harlem are thriving again.

MORNINGSIDE HEIGHTS. The center of the neighborhood is **Columbia University.** The campus, designed by prominent New York architects McKim, Mead and White, is urban (don't come looking for grass), yet removed from surrounding Morningside Heights. Its centerpiece, the majestic Roman Classical Low Library, looms over College Walk, the school's central promenade that bustles with academics, students, and quacks. *(Morningside Dr. and Broadway, from 114th to 120th St.)*

A cathedral where creation is not only for the divine, the unfinished **St. John the Divine,** has been under construction since 1892. St. John's is the largest cathedral in the world and one of the most worldly, featuring altars and bays dedicated not only to the sufferings of Christ, but also to the experiences of immigrants and victims of genocide and AIDS. *(Amsterdam Ave. between 110th and 113th St. Open M-Sa 7am-6pm, Su 7am-8pm. Suggested donation $2, seniors and students $1. Vertical tours—you go up—given on the first and 3rd Sa of the month at noon and 2pm. $10. Reservations necessary. Regular horizontal tours Tu-Sa 11am, Su 1pm. $3.)* Near Columbia is **Riverside Church.** The observation deck in the tower commands an amazing view. Concerts make use of the world's largest carillon (74 bells), a gift of John D. Rockefeller, Jr. *(120th St. and Riverside Dr. Bell tower open Tu-Sa 10:30am-5pm, Su 9:45-10:45am. Admission to observation deck Tu-Sa $2, seniors and students $1. Free tours Su 12:30pm.)* Diagonally across Riverside Dr. lies **Grant's Tomb,** the resting place of you-know-who.

SUGAR HILL. In the 1920s and 30s, African-Americans with "sugar" (i.e., money) moved here. In addition to leaders W.E.B. DuBois and Thurgood Marshall and musical legends Duke Ellington and W.C. Handy, some of the city's most notable gangsters operated here. (Wesley Snipes starred as one in the film *Sugar Hill.*) The area is also the birthplace of Sugarhill Records, the rap label that created the Sugarhill Gang, whose 1979 "Rapper's Delight" became the first hip hop song to reach the Top 40. *(143rd to 155th St. between St. Nicholas and Edgecombe Ave.)*

STRIVER'S ROW. A group of impressive 1891 brownstones presents a combination of architectures, from neo-Colonial to Italian Renaissance. Originally envisioned as a "model housing project" for middle-class whites, legend says Striver's Row acquired its nickname from lower class Harlemites who felt their neighbors were striving to attain uppity middle-class status. *(138th and 139th St. between Powell and Frederick Douglass Blvd.)*

WASHINGTON HEIGHTS

North of 155th St., Washington Heights affords a taste of urban life with an ethnic flavor. You can eat a Greek dinner, buy Armenian pastries and vegetables from a South African, and discuss the Talmud with a **Yeshiva University** student. Fort Tryon Park is home to **The Cloisters,** a museum specializing in medieval art (see p. 225).

BROOKLYN

The Dutch named this area Breuckelen, or "Broken Land." Displaying typical resilience, the city of Brooklyn refused when asked to join New York City in 1833, claiming that the two cities shared no interests except common waterways. Not until 1898 did the citizenry decide in a close vote to join New York City's boroughs. Today, Brooklyn is New York City's most populous borough. In the coverage below, neighborhoods are arranged from north to south.

WILLIAMSBURG AND GREENPOINT. Having become home to a growing number of artists in the last decade, **Williamsburg** has the galleries to match its artsy population (see **Galleries,** p. 227). **Greenpoint,** bounded by Java St. to the north, Meserole St. to the south, and Franklin St. to the west, is Brooklyn's northernmost border with Queens and home to a large Polish population. The birthplace of Mae West, Brooklynese, and the Union's Civil War ironclad Monitor, Greenpoint is also home to charming Italianate and Grecian houses built during the shipbuilding boom of the 1850s. The **Russian Orthodox Cathedral of the Transfiguration** is marked by five striking, copper-covered, onion-shaped domes. *(228 N. 12th St.)* **Brooklyn Brewery** is a busy factory during the week and a lively spot on the weekend for the curious and for those who just want to knock one back. *(79 N. 11th St.)*

FULTON LANDING. Fulton Landing hearkens back to days when the ferry—not the subway or the car—was the primary means of transportation between Brooklyn and Manhattan. Completed in 1883, the nearby **Brooklyn Bridge**—spanning the gap between lower Manhattan and Brooklyn—is the product of elegant calculation, careful design, and human exertion. A walk across the bridge at sunrise or sunset is one of the most exhilarating strolls New York City has to offer. *(From Brooklyn: entrance from the end of Adams St. Subway: A, C to High St.-Brooklyn Bridge. From Manhattan: entrance from Park Row. Subway: 4, 5, 6 to Brooklyn Bridge-City Hall.)*

BROOKLYN HEIGHTS AND DOWNTOWN. Brooklyn Heights, a well-preserved 19th-century residential area, sprang up with the development of steamboat transportation between Brooklyn and Manhattan in 1814. Rows of posh Greek Revival and Italianate houses in this area essentially created New York's first suburb. **Montague Street,** the main drag, has the stores, cafes, and mid-priced restaurants of a cute college town. The view of the Manhattan skyline from the **Promenade,** by the East River between Remsen and Orange St., is jaw-dropping. *(Subway: 2, 3 to Clark St.)* **Downtown** is the location of Brooklyn's Civic Center, and strolling through you'll find several grand municipal buildings. *(Subway: 2, 3, 4, 5, to Borough Hall; M, N, R to Court St.)*

PARK SLOPE AND PROSPECT PARK. Park Slope is a residential neighborhood with charming brownstones. Seventh Ave. has long been the neighborhood's main drag, but Fifth Ave.'s budding thrift stores, gay bars, and even an art gallery or two, give it a hipper edge. The neighboring **Propect Park** is the borough's answer to Manhattan's Central Park. Frederick Law Olmsted and Calvert Vaux designed the park in the mid-1800s and supposedly liked it better than their Manhattan project. You'll find a zoo, an ice skating rink, a children's museum, and plenty of wide open spaces within its confines. *(Bounded by Prospect Park West, Flatbush Ave., Ocean Ave., Parkside Ave., and Prospect Park Southwest. Subway: 2, 3 to Grand Army Plaza; F to 15 St./Prospect Park; D, Q, S to Prospect Park.)* In the middle of Grand Army Plaza, the 80-foot-high **Memorial Arch,** built in the 1890s to commemorate the North's Civil War victory, marks one of the park's entrances. **The Brooklyn Botanic Garden,** adjacent to the park, is a 52-acre fairyland. The **Fragrance Garden for the Blind** is an olfactory carnival—with mint, lemon, violet, and other appetizing aromas. The more formal **Cranford Rose Garden** crams in over 100 blooming varieties of roses. *(1000 Washington Ave.; other entrances on Eastern Pkwy. and on Flatbush Ave. ☎ 718-623-7000. Open Apr.-Sept. Tu-F 8am-6pm, Sa-Su 10am-6pm; Oct.-Mar. Tu-F 8am-4:30pm, Sa-Su 10am-4:30pm. $3, seniors and students $1.50, under 16 free. Free Tu all day and Sa 10am-noon; seniors free F.)*

CONEY ISLAND. At one time a resort for the City's elite, until the subway made it accessible to the masses, legendary Coney Island is now fading. The **Boardwalk** squeaks nostalgically as tourists are jostled by roughnecks. Enjoy a hot dog at the original **Nathan's,** at Surf and Sitwell Ave. The **Cyclone,** built in 1927, was once the most terrifying roller coaster ride in the world. *(834 Surf Ave.)* Meet walruses, sharks, or other marine beasties at the **New York Aquarium.** *(Surf Ave. and W. 8th St. At Surf and W. 8th St. ☎ 718-265-3474. Summer tickets sold M-F 10am-5:15pm, Sa-Su 10am-6:15pm. $9.75; seniors and ages 2-12 $6.)*

MID-ATLANTIC

QUEENS

Queens is notable primarily for its ethnic communities rather than its sights or museums. Unlike Brooklyn, which contains many distinctive neighborhoods but remains united as a whole, Queens is a more of a collection of independent towns.

ASTORIA AND LONG ISLAND CITY. In the northwest corner of Queens lies Astoria, where Greek-, Italian-, and Spanish-speaking communities mingle amid lively shopping districts and cultural attractions. Long Island City is just south, across the river from the Upper East Side. Two sculpture gardens make for a worthwhile daytrip from Manhattan. The **Isamu Noguchi Garden Museum** contains a wide variety of the Noguchi's oeuvre: from the sculptures that stand around the shimmering water of *The Well* to his *akari* lamps. *(32-37 Vernon Blvd., at 10th St. and 33rd Rd. ☎ 718-204-7088. Subway: N to Broadway. Open Apr.-Oct. W-F 10am-5pm, Sa-Su 11am-6pm. Suggested donation $4, seniors and students $2.)* Sculptor Mark di Suvero created the curiosity that is the **Socrates Sculpture Park**. Thirty-five stunning day-glo and rusted metal abstractions cluster on the site of what was once an illegal dump. *(At the end of Broadway, across the Vernon Blvd. intersection. ☎ 718-956-1819. Park open daily 10am-dusk. Free.)*

FLUSHING AND FLUSHING MEADOWS PARK. Flushing boasts colonial neighborhood landmarks, a bustling downtown, and a huge Asian immigrant population. *(Subway: 7 to Main St.-Flushing.)* Nearby **Flushing Meadows-Corona Park** was the site of the 1939 and 1964 World's Fair, and now holds **Shea Stadium** (home of the Mets), the **USTA National Tennis Center** (where the U.S. Open is played), and the simple yet interesting **New York Hall of Science**. *(On the corner of 111th St. and 48th Ave. ☎ 718-699-0005, ext. 365.)* The **Unisphere**, a 380-ton steel globe in front of the nearby New York City Building, hovers over a fountain in retro-futuristic glory. This is the structure that nasty alien crashed into in the 1997 *Men In Black*.

THE BRONX

The borough takes its name from Jonas Bronck, the European who settled in the area with his family in 1639. Until the turn of the 19th century, the area consisted largely of cottages, farmlands, and wild marshes. In the 1840s, the tide of immigration swelled and brought scores of Italian and Irish settlers to the borough. Since then, the flow of immigrants (now mostly Hispanic and Russian) has never stopped. This relentless stream has created vibrant ethnic neighborhoods (including a Little Italy to shame its Manhattan counterpart).

THE BRONX ZOO. The most popular reason to come to the Bronx is the **Bronx Zoo/Wildlife Conservation Park**. The largest urban zoo in the US, it houses over 4000 animals. Soar into the air on the **Skyfari** aerial tramway ($2) that runs between Wild Asia and the **Children's Zoo**. *(Entrances on Bronx Park S., Southern Blvd., E. Fordham Rd., and the Bronx River Pkwy. Subway: 2, 5 to West Farms Sq./E. Tremont Ave. Follow Boston Rd. for 3 blocks until the Bronx Park S. gate. ☎ 718-330-1234. Open Apr.-Oct. M-F 10am-5pm, Sa-Su 10am-5:30pm; parts of the zoo close Nov.-Apr. $9, seniors and ages 2-12 $5; W free.)*

NEW YORK BOTANICAL GARDEN. Located adjacent to the Zoo, the 250-acre garden is the city's most extensive botanical garden. One can scope out the 40-acre **hemlock forest,** kept in its natural state. Although it costs an extra few dollars to enter, the **Conservatory** deserves a visit; the gorgeous domed greenhouse contains a few different ecosystems of exquisite plant life. *(Kazimiroff Blvd. ☎ 718-817-8700. Subway: 4 to Bedford Park Blvd./Lehman College; B, D to Bedford Park Blvd. Walk 8 blocks east or take the Bx26 bus. Train: Metro-North Harlem line goes from Grand Central Terminal to Botanical Garden station, which is right outside the main gate. Open Apr.-Oct. Tu-Su 10am-6pm; July-Aug. Th and Sa grounds open until 8pm; Nov.-Mar. Tu-Su 10am-4pm. $3, seniors and students $2, ages 2-12 $1; W all day and Sa 10am-noon free.)*

BELMONT. Arthur Ave. is the center of this uptown Little Italy, which is home to wonderful homestyle southern Italian cooking. To get a concentrated sense of the area, stop into **Arthur Avenue Retail Market.** *(2334 Arthur Ave. between 186th and Crescent St.)* The **Church of Our Lady of Mt. Carmel** holds high mass in Italian daily at 10:15am, 12:45, and 7:30pm. Signs of a recent Kosovar influx permeate the area; the

Kosovar flag with its red background and spidery bird is hung in the window fronts of many stores and eateries. *(627 187th St., at Belmont Ave. Subway: 4, B, D to Fordham Rd.; then walk 10 blocks east–or take Bx12–to Arthur Ave. and head south.)*

YANKEE STADIUM. In 1923, Babe Ruth's success as a hitter inspired the construction of the Yankees' own ballpark. The aging stadium's frequent facelifts have kept it on par with younger structures. The Yankees played the first night game here in 1946, and the first message scoreboard tallied runs here in 1954. Inside the 11.6-acre park (the field measures only 3½ acres), monuments honor Yankee greats like Lou Gehrig, Joe DiMaggio, and Babe Ruth. The Yankees offer tours of the Stadium, but do yourself a favor and go to a ballgame. *(E. 161st St., at River Ave. ☎ 718-293-6000. Subway: 4, B, D to 161st St. Tours daily at noon. $10; seniors and under 15 $5.)*

STATEN ISLAND

Unless you have a vested interest in Fresh Kills, the world's largest landfill, it is more trouble to get to Staten Island than it is worth. However, the 30min. ferry ride from Manhattan's Battery Park to Staten Island is a perfect opportunity to cruise by the Statue of Liberty for free. The island is also connected to Brooklyn by the **Verrazano-Narrows Bridge,** the world's 2nd-longest (4260 ft.) suspension span. Because of the distances (and some dangerous neighborhoods in between), it's a bad idea to walk from one site to the next. Plan excursions with the bus schedule in mind.

Sights on the island cluster around the beautiful 19th-century **Snug Harbor Cultural Center,** housing the **Newhouse Center for Contemporary Art,** a small art gallery with a sculpture show in summer, and the **Staten Island Botanical Gardens.** *(1000 Richmond Terr. ☎ 718-448-2500. Call for hours. Suggested donation $2. Gardens 718-273-8200.)*

🏛 MUSEUMS

For listings of upcoming exhibits consult *Time Out: New York*, *The New Yorker*, *New York* magazine and Friday's *The New York Times* (Weekend section). Most museums are closed on Monday and are jam-packed on weekends. Many museums request a "donation" in place of an admission fee—don't be embarrassed to give as little as a dollar. Most are free one weeknight.

UPPER WEST SIDE

▣ **American Museum of Natural History** (☎ 769-5100), Central Park West, between 77th and 81st St. Subway: B, C to 81st St. You're never too old for the Natural History Museum, one of the world's largest museums devoted to science. The main draw is the 4th fl. dinosaur halls, which display real fossils in 85 percent of the exhibits (most museums use fossil casts). Perhaps the most impressive part of the museum is the sparkling Hayden Planetarium within the Rose Center for Earth and Space. The giant screen is sure to impress. Open Su-Th 10am-5:45pm, F-Sa 10am-8:45pm. Suggested donation $10, seniors and students $7.50, under 12 $6. IMAX ☎ 769-5034.

New York Historical Society, 2 W. 77th St. (☎ 873-3400), at Central Park West. Subway: B, C to 72nd St., 81st St. Founded in 1804, this is New York's oldest continuously operated museum. The block-long Neoclassical building houses both a library and museum for history buffs. Children shouldn't miss the Kid City exhibit. Open Tu-Su 11am-5pm. Suggested donation $5, seniors and students $3, children free.

WASHINGTON HEIGHTS

▣ **The Cloisters** (☎ 923-3700), at Fort Tryon Park. Subway: A to 190th St.; then follow Margaret Corbin Dr. 5 blocks north. Crowning a hilltop at the northern tip of Manhattan, this tranquil branch of the Metropolitan Museum of Art incorporates pieces of 12th- and 13th-century French monasteries into its own medieval design. The tremendous collection includes the Unicorn Tapestries; the Treasury, where the museum's most fragile offerings are found; and the Robert Campin's altarpiece, one of the first known oil paintings. Open Mar.-Oct. Tu-Su 9:30am-5:15pm, Nov.-Feb. Tu-Su 9:30am-4:45pm.

UPPER EAST SIDE

■ **Metropolitan Museum of Art,** 1000 Fifth Ave. (☎535-7710, concerts and lectures 570-3949), at 82nd St. Subway: 4, 5, 6 to 86th St. The largest in the Western Hemisphere, the Met's art collection includes 3.3 million works from around the world. Highlights include the Egyptian Art collection (including the completely reconstructed Temple of Dendur), the awesome European paintings collection, and an extensive collection of American art. Also of note is the Costume Institute, which houses over 75,000 costumes and accessories from five continents from the 17th century to the present, and the collection of Greek and Roman Art, recently overhauled. Don't miss the Gubbio Studiolo, a Renaissance study completely decorated in wood inlay. Open Su and Tu-Th 9:30am-5:15pm, F-Sa 9:30am-8:45pm. Suggested donation $10, seniors and students $5.

■ **Frick Collection,** 1 E. 70th St. (☎288-0700), at Fifth Ave. Subway: 6 to 68th St. Henry Clay Frick left his house and art collection to the city, and the museum retains the elegance of his chateau. The Living Hall displays 17th-century furniture, Persian rugs, Holbein portraits, and paintings by El Greco, Rembrandt, Velázquez, and Titian. The courtyard is inhabited by elegant statues surrounding the garden pool and fountain. Open Tu-Sa 10am-6pm, Su 1-6pm. $7, seniors and students $5. Under 10 not allowed, under 16 must be accompanied by an adult.

Museum of the City of New York, 1220 Fifth Ave. (☎534-1672), at 103rd St. Subway: 6 to 103rd St. This fascinating museum details the history of the Big Apple, from the construction of the Empire State Building to the history of Broadway theater. Cultural history of all varieties is on parade: from model ships and NYC paintings to hot pants and Yankees World Series trophies. Open W-Sa 10am-5pm, Su noon-5pm. Suggested donation $7; seniors, students, and children $4.

The Jewish Museum, 1109 5th Ave. (☎423-3200), at 92nd St. Subway: 6 to 96th St. The gallery's permanent collection details the Jewish experience throughout history, ranging from ancient Biblical artifacts and ceremonial objects to contemporary masterpieces by Marc Chagall, Frank Stella, and George Segal. Open Su-M and W-Th 11am-5:45pm, Tu 11am-8pm. $8, seniors and students $5.50; Tu 5-8pm pay-what-you-wish.

Whitney Museum of American Art, 945 Madison Ave. (☎570-3676), at 75th St. Subway: 6 to 77th St. The only museum with a historical mandate to champion the works of living American artists has assembled the largest collection of 20th- and 21st-century American art in the world. Even the modern-art skeptic will be impressed by Jasper John's *Three Flags* and Frank Stella's *Brooklyn Bridge*. Open Tu-Th 11am-6pm, F 1-9pm, Sa-Su 11am-6pm. $10, seniors and students $8, under 12 free; F 6-9pm pay-what-you-wish.

Museum of American Illustration, 128 E. 63rd St. (☎838-2560), between Lexington and Park Ave. Established in 1981 by the Society of Illustrators, this treasure of a museum owns over 1500 works by such legendary artists as Rockwell, Pyle, and Wyeth. Open Tu 10am-8pm, W-F 10am-5pm, Sa noon-4pm. Free.

Cooper-Hewitt Museum, 2 E. 91st St. (☎849-8400), at Fifth Ave. Subway: 4, 5, 6 to 86th St. Occupying the splendid Carnegie Mansion since 1967, the Cooper-Hewitt holds a collection of over 250,000 objects—one of the largest collections of design in the world. Unfortunately, the vast majority of this permanent collection is never on display to the public. Make an appointment if you want to see more. Open Tu 10am-9pm, W-Sa 10am-5pm, Su noon-5pm. $8, seniors and students $5, under 12 free; Tu 5-9pm free.

Guggenheim Museum, 1071 Fifth Ave. (☎423-3500), at 89th St. Subway: 4, 5, 6 to 86th St. The building, an inverted white quasi-ziggurat designed by Frank Lloyd Wright, is a modern architectural masterpiece. The Guggenheim contains a large collection of significant works in the fields of cubism, surrealism, American minimalism, and abstract expressionism, including works by Picasso, Matisse, Van Goh, Gaugin, Manet, and Cézanne. Open Su-W 9am-6pm, F-Sa 9am-8pm. $12, students and seniors $8, under 12 free; F 6-8pm "pay-what-you-wish."

MIDTOWN

▨ Museum of Modern Art (MoMA), 11 W. 53rd St. (☎708-9400), between Fifth and Sixth Ave. Subway: E, F to Fifth Ave.-53rd St. or B, D, Q to 50th St. One of the most extensive post-Impressionist collections in the world. Founded in 1929 in response to the Met's reluctance to embrace modern art. Monet's sublime *Water Lily* room, numerous Picassos, and a great design collection are among the highlights. In summer 2002, in order to expand, the MoMA will be temporarily moved to Long Island City, Queens. **MoMA Queens** will be located at 45-20 33rd St. Open Sa-Tu and Th 10:30am-5:45pm, F 10:30am-8:15pm. $10, seniors and students $6.50, under 16 free.

Museum of Television and Radio, 25 W. 52nd St. (☎621-6600), between Fifth and Sixth Ave. Subway: E, F to 53rd St. More archive than museum, this shrine to modern media contains over 100,000 easily accessible TV and radio programs. The museum also hosts a number of film screenings that focus on topics of social, historical, or artistic interest. Open Tu-W and F-Su noon-6pm, Th noon-8pm; F until 9pm for theaters only. Suggested donation $6, seniors and students $4, under 13 $3.

Pierpont Morgan Library, 29 E. 36th St. (☎985-0610), at Madison Ave. J.P. Morgan and son left a stunning collection of rare books, sculptures, and paintings, including hand-written sheet music by Beethoven and Mozart, Thoreau's journal, a Guttenberg Bible, and a 12th-century, jewel-encrusted triptych believed to contain fragments of the Holy Cross. Open Tu-F 10:30am-5pm, Sa 10:30am-6pm, Su noon-6pm. $8, seniors and students $6, under 12 free.

DOWNTOWN

The Museum for African Art, 593 Broadway (☎966-1313), between Houston and Prince St. Subway: N, R to Prince St.; B, D, F, Q to Broadway-Lafayette. Features two exhibitions of stunning African and African-American art on such themes as storytelling, magic, religion, and mask-making. Hands-on sculpture workshops available. Open Tu-F 10:30am-5:30pm, Sa-Su noon-6pm. $5, seniors and students $2.50.

New Museum of Contemporary Art, 583 Broadway (☎219-1222), between Prince and Houston St. Subway: N, R to Prince St.; B, D, F, Q to Broadway-Lafayette. Supports the newest and, usually, the most controversial in contemporary art, making it one of the premier museums of modern art in the world. Open W and Su noon-6pm, Th-Sa noon-8pm. $6; seniors, students, and artists $3; under 18 free; Th 6-8pm free.

BROOKLYN

Brooklyn Museum of Art, 200 Eastern Pkwy. (☎718-638-5000), at Washington Ave. Subway: 2, 3 to Eastern Parkway/Brooklyn Museum. The museum's enormous Oceanic and New World art collection takes up the central 2-story space on the first floor. You'll find outstanding Ancient Greek, Roman, Middle Eastern, and Egyptian galleries on the 3rd fl. Open W-F 10am-5pm, Sa-Su 11am-6pm. Open first Sa of the month 11am-11pm. Suggested donation $6, seniors and students $3, under 12 free.

GALLERIES

New York's galleries provide a riveting—and free—introduction to the contemporary art world. To get started, pick up a free copy of *The Gallery Guide* at any major museum or gallery. Published every two to three months, it lists the addresses, phone numbers, and hours of nearly every showplace in the city. Most galleries are open Tuesday to Saturday, from 10 or 11am to 5 or 6pm. Galleries are usually only open on weekdays in the summer, and many are closed in August.

SOHO. The area between Broadway and West Broadway south of Houston St. is a wonderland of galleries. **Drawing Center** specializes exclusively in original works on paper. *(35 Wooster St. between Grand and Broome St. ☎219-2166. Open Tu-F 10am-6pm, Sa 11am-6pm; closed Aug.)* **Artists Space** gives lesser-known artists a chance to shine. *(38 Greene St., 3rd fl., at Grand St. ☎226-3970. Open Tu-Sa 11am-6pm.)* One of the more commercial spaces is **Pop International,** which sells works by pop art icons such as Warhol, Lichtenstein, and Haring. *(473 W. Broadway, between Prince and W. Houston St. Open M-Sa 10am-7pm, Su 11am-6pm.)* For something out of ordinary, head to **Shakespeare's Fvlcrum.** The gallery's owner wears transparent vixen clothing and displays Actual Art, works that require the forces of nature for completion. *(500 Canal St. ☎ 966-6848. Open Tu-Sa 11am-6pm, Su-M 1-6pm.)* Other spaces in SoHo include **Exit Art/ The First World** *(548 Broadway, between Prince and Spring St., 2nd fl.)* and **Thread Waxing Space.** *(476 Broadway, between Broome and Grand St., 2nd fl.)*

CHELSEA. Many of the galleries originally in SoHo have been lured by cheaper rents to Chelsea's warehouses; the area west of Ninth Ave., between 17th and 26th St., is rife with display spaces. At the heart of the Chelsea arts scene is **Dia Center for the Arts,** a massive four-floor gallery with a definite sensibility for catching the pulse of current art. *(548 W. 22nd St., between Tenth and Eleventh Ave. ☎ 989-5566. Open W-Su noon-6pm; closed mid-June to mid-Sept. $6, seniors and students $3.)* A couple doors down from Dia is **Sonnabend.** *(536 W. 22nd St., between Tenth and Eleventh Ave. ☎ 627-1018. Open Tu-Sa 10am-6pm; closed Aug.)* Aspiring fashionistas should head to **The Museum at Fashion Institute of Technology.** The museum displays several exhibits related to everything fashionable—from photography to mannequin displays. *(Seventh Ave. and 27th St. ☎ 217-5800. Open Tu-F noon-8pm, Sa 10am-5pm.)*

UPPER EAST SIDE. A ritzy neighborhood with chi-chi showplaces to match. The **Fuller Building** harbors 12 floors of galleries. *(41 E. 57th St. between Park and Madison Ave. Most open M-Sa 10am-5:30pm; Oct.-May most closed M.)* Across the street, you'll find **Pace Gallery:** four floors dedicated to the promotion of widely disparate forms of art from primitive to ultra-modern. *(32 E. 57th St. between Park and Madison Ave. Open June-Sept. M-Th 9:30am-6pm, F 9:30am-4pm; Oct.-May Tu-Sa 9:30am-6pm.)* **Sotheby's** is one of the most respected auction houses in the city, selling everything from Degas to Disney. Auctions open to anyone, but a few of the more popular require a first come, first served ticket. *(1334 York Ave., at 72nd St. ☎ 606-7000, ticket office 606-7171. Open M-Sa 10am-5pm, Su 1-5pm; closed Sa-Su in summer.)*

Other galleries include **Leo Castelli** *(59 E. 79th St., between Park and Madison Ave.)*; **Gagosian** *(980 Madison Ave., at 77th St.)*; **M. Knoedler & Co., Inc.** *(19 E. 70th St., between Madison and Fifth Ave.)*; and **Acquavella** *(18 E. 79th St., between Madison and Fifth Ave.).*

WILLIAMSBURG. The few Bohemian pilgrims who moved into Brooklyn's Williamsburg in the 80s have witnessed the neighborhood transform into one of the city's artistic centers. The epicenter of the Williamsburg arts scene is **The Williamsburg Art and Historical Center.** The works of local and international artists is on display in the beautiful second floor gallery. *(135 Broadway, between Bedford and Driggs Ave. ☎ 718-486-7372. Open Sa-Su noon-6pm.)* **Pierogi** hosts two big-name solo shows a month, but still displays hundreds of affordable works by emerging artists. *(177 N. 9th St., between Bedford and Driggs Ave. ☎ 718-599-2144. Open F-M noon-6pm.)* **Lunar Base** stands out amidst a gaggle of other galleries on Grand St., boasting bold abstract works. *(197 Grand St. ☎ 718-599-2905. Open Th-Su 1-7pm.)*

LONG ISLAND CITY. Long Island City is the center of the Queens arts scene. **P.S. 1 Contemporary Art Center,** presents cutting-edge exhibitions within a converted public school. *(22-25 Jackson Ave. ☎ 718-784-2084. Open W-Su noon-6pm. Suggested donation $5, seniors and students $2. Wheelchair accessible.)* A spacious converted warehouse, **New York Center for Media Arts** features rotating installations of multimedia art work. *(45-12 Davis St., off Jackson Ave. ☎ 718-472-9414. Open Th-Su noon-6pm.)*

⬚ SHOPPING

There is no easier place to blow your dough than NYC—stores run the gamut from the world's (2nd) largest department store to sidewalk stands peddling bootleg Top 40 selections. Here's a quick walking tour of the city, style-wise.

The best place to start is downtown on the **Lower East Side,** where hip, new designers sell their uneven hemlines and poly-nylon-rubber-day-glo shirts. (Orchard, Stanton, and Ludlow St.) Next stop is **Chinatown,** where you can pick up a (fake) Kate Spade from any of the million vendors along Canal St. Not to worry: they'll stick the label on for you. Pick up other imitation items right off the sidewalk, from CDs to Polo shirts. Walk up to **SoHo** to spend some major cash, this time on hip but established designers. Wooster, Prince, and West Broadway are home to the likes of Rowley and Sui, but Broadway is cheaper, with the NYC staple Canal Jeans Co. (between Spring and Prince St.). **Greenwich Village** has a mishmash of offerings, from the city's largest comic book store (Forbidden Planet) to Cheap Jack's Vintage Clothing and the city's best used bookstore, the Strand, 828 Broadway, at 12th St. Just east of Broadway is the more risqué **East Village,** a den of tattoo parlors, silver trinkets, sex shops, and cheap CD stores (centered on St. Mark's Pl.). Find some fashionable enclaves on 9th St. farther east and a number of good vintage stores all over. In **Herald Square** you'll find department stores, such as Macy's. Designer flagships line **Fifth Ave.** between 42nd and 59th St. Peruse these for a look at the really unattainable—Chanel, Armani, Prada, Louis Vuitton, Tiffany's & Co., etc. plus elite department stores like Bergdorf, Saks, and Bloomingdale's. To keep the kids quiet while you shop at Versace, stop at F.A.O. Schwarz on 5th Ave. and 58th St. **Uptown** has everything, from cute boutiques along **Columbus Ave.** on the West Side to the cheapest kicks and FuBu gear on 125th St. in **Harlem.** The outer boroughs are a mixed bag, too far for most short-term visitors, although **Brooklyn** has the hippest vintage warehouse: Domsey's in Williamsburg.

◗ ENTERTAINMENT

Publications with noteworthy entertainment and nightlife sections are the *Village Voice, Time Out: New York, New York* magazine, and the Sunday edition of *The New York Times. The New Yorker* has the most comprehensive theater survey.

THEATER

Broadway is currently undergoing a revival and ticket sales are booming. Mainstream musicals receive more than their fair share of attention. Tickets cost about $50 each when purchased through regular channels. **TKTS** sells 25-50% discounted tickets to many shows on the day of the performance from a booth in the middle of Duffy Sq.—in the northern part of Times Sq., at 47th and Broadway. (☎768-1818 for recorded info. Tickets sold M-Sa 3-8pm for evening performances, W and Sa 10am-2pm for matinees, Su 11am-7pm for matinees and evening performances. $2.50 service charge per ticket.) For info on shows and tickets, call the **NYC/ON STAGE hotline** at 768-1818. **Ticketmaster** (☎307-4100 or 800-755-4000) takes credit cards, but charges at least $2 more than other outlets.

Off-Broadway theaters have between 100 and 499 seats; only Broadway houses have over 500. Off-Broadway houses frequently offer more off-beat, quirky shows, with shorter runs. Occasionally these shows have long runs or make the jump to Broadway houses. Tickets cost $15-45. Many of the best Off-Broadway houses huddle in the Sheridan Sq. area of the West Village. TKTS also sells tickets for the larger Off-Broadway houses. **Off-Off-Broadway** means cheaper, younger theaters.

Shakespeare in the Park (☎539-8750) is a New York summer tradition. From June through August, two plays are presented at the **Delacorte Theater** in Central Park, near the 81st St. entrance on the Upper West Side, just north of the main road. Tickets are free, but lines form early.

GENERAL ENTERTAINMENT VENUES

▣ **Knitting Factory,** 74 Leonard St. (☎219-3055), between Broadway and Church St. Features several shows nightly ranging from indie rock to jazz and hip hop. The multilevel performance space also hosts a summertime jazz festival. Cover $5-20. Box office open M-F 10am-11pm, Sa-Su 2-11pm. Bar open M-F 4:30pm-2am, Sa-Su 6pm-2am.

Beacon Theater, 2130 Broadway (☎307-7171), at 74th St. Subway: 1, 2, 3, 9 to 72nd St. Attached to the Beacon Hotel, this mid-sized venue hosts a wide variety of music acts, as well as other performances and plays. Call for schedule. Tickets usually $25-50. Box office open M-F 11am-6pm, Su noon-5pm.

CHEAP SEATS To the budget traveler, the Great White Way's major theatrical draws may seem locked away in gilded Broadway cages. Never fear, however, *Let's Go* is here! Er, that is to say, you can find cheap tickets, compadre. Should **Ticketmaster** and **TKTS** (see above) fail, other avenues remain open to you.

Rush Tickets: Some theaters distribute them on the morning of the performance; others make student rush tickets available 30min. before showtime. Lines can be extremely long, so get there *early*. Call the theater before to find out their policy.

Cancellation Line: No rush luck? Some theaters redistribute returned or unclaimed tickets several hours before showtime. You might have to sacrifice your afternoon—but, come on, Dame Edna is worth it! Once again, call before.

Hit Show Club: 630 9th Ave. (☎581-4211), between 44th and 45th St. This free service distributes coupons redeemable at the box office for 30% or more off regular ticket prices. Call for coupons via mail or pick them up them up at the club office.

Standing-room Only: Sold on the day of show, tend to be around $15 or $20. Call first, as some theaters can't accommodate standing room.

Brooklyn Academy of Music, 30 Lafayette Ave. (☎718-636-4100), between St. Felix St. and Ashland Pl. Subway: 2, 3, 4, 5, D, Q to Atlantic Ave.; B, M, N, R to Pacific St. The oldest performing arts center in the country, the Brooklyn Academy of Music (BAM) focuses on new, non-traditional, multicultural programs—with the occasional early classical music performance. Jazz, blues, performance art, opera, and dance also take the stage. The **Brooklyn Philharmonic Orchestra** performs here Oct.-Mar. Manhattan Express Bus ("BAM bus") departs round-trip from 120 Park Ave. at 42nd St. for each performance ($5, round-trip $10).

Brooklyn Center for Performing Arts, 2900 Campus Road (☎718-951-4500 or 951-4522), at Hillel Place, one block west of the junction of Flatbush and Nostrand Ave. on the campus of Brooklyn College. Season Oct.-May. Tickets $20-40.

Cathedral of St. John the Divine, 1047 Amsterdam Ave. (☎662-2133), at 112th St. This beautiful church offers an impressive array of classical concerts, art exhibitions, lectures, plays, movies, and dance events. The NY Philharmonic performs on occasion, and soprano saxophonist Paul Winter gives annual Winter Solstice concert. Prices vary.

Colden Center for the Performing Arts, 65-30 Kissena Blvd. (☎718-793-8080), at Queens College. Subway: 7 to Flushing-Main St.; then buses Q17, Q25, or Q34 to the corner of Kissena Blvd. and the Long Island Expwy. 2143-seat theater hosts jazz, classical, and dance concerts Sept.-May. Summer box office hours M-W noon-4pm.

Collective Unconscious, 145 Ludlow St. (☎254-5277), between Rivington and Stanton St. Subway: F to Delancey St. A popular performance space run by 21 local artists, this venue and studio space debuts performances from the downtown artistic community. Rev. Jen's Anti-Slam Comedy Act (W) brings in a big crowd. BYOB. Cover $3-5.

The Kitchen, 512 W. 19th St. (☎255-5793), between Tenth and Eleventh Ave. Subway: C, E to 23rd St. World-renowned showcase for arts events in an unassuming location. Features experimental and avant-garde film and video, as well as concerts, dance performances, and poetry readings. Ticket prices vary by event.

Merkin Concert Hall, 129 W. 67th St. (☎501-3330), between Broadway and Amsterdam Ave. Subway: 1, 9 to 66th St. An intimate theater, sometimes known as "the little hall with the big sound." Season Sept.-June. Tickets $8-50, with occasional free concerts. Box office open M-F noon-4pm.

92nd Street Y, 1395 Lexington Ave. (☎996-1100), at 92nd St. The Upper East Side's cultural mecca. The Y's Kaufmann Concert Hall seats only 916 people and offers an intimate setting unmatched by New York's larger halls, with flawless acoustics and the ambience of a Viennese salon. Notable series include Jazz in July, Chamber Music at the Y, Lyrics and Lyricists, and Young Concert Artists. Tickets $15-35. Closed June-Aug.

Radio City Music Hall, 1260 Sixth Ave. (☎247-4777), at 50th St., boasts a bill of great performers that reads like an invitation list to the Music Hall of Fame; Ella Fitzgerald, Frank Sinatra, Ringo Starr, and Sting have all performed at the legendary venue. Tickets for events generally start at $30. Box office 50th St. and Sixth Ave. Open regularly M-Sa 10am-8pm, Su 11am-8pm. In summer, M-F 10am-8pm, Sa-Su noon-5pm.

Symphony Space, 2537 Broadway (☎864-5400), at 95th St. Subway: 1, 2, 3, 9 to 96th St. Under renovation until March 2002. Open Tu-Sa 1-7pm. Tickets by phone Th-Sa noon-6pm. Most movies $8, other events up to $45.

JAZZ JOINTS

The **JVC Jazz Festival** blows into the city with all-star performances from June to July. Tickets go on sale in early May, but many events are outdoors and free. Check the newspaper or call 501-1390. Annual festivals sponsored by major corporations bring in local talent and industry giants. The concerts take place throughout the city (some free) but center at TriBeCa's **Knitting Factory** (☎ 219-3055 in spring).

▨ **Small's,** 183 W. 10th St. (☎929-7565), at Seventh Ave. Subway: 1, 9 to Christopher St. Small's serves no alcohol, and thus is allowed to stay open all night. It's a splendid after-hours spot and a late, late night showcase for musicians who still have chops left over from performances at other clubs. Cover $10. Free show Sa 6:30-9pm. Call ahead for early bird specials (no cover). Open Su-Th 10pm-8am, F-Sa 6:30pm-8am.

Smoke, 2751 Broadway (☎864-6662), between 105th and 106th St. This sultry cocktail lounge jumps with excellent jazz seven nights a week. Although slightly congested, the intimate space swells with music and an animated atmosphere. Jam sessions M at 10pm and Th at midnight. W funk, Su Latin jazz. Happy hour daily 5-8pm. Cover Th-Sa $10-20. $10 drink min. Open daily 5pm-4am.

Detour, 349 E. 13th St. (☎533-6212), between First and Second Ave. Subway: L to First Ave. Great nightly jazz and no cover—a perfect mix. One-drink minimum. Happy hour (2-for-1 drinks) M-F 4-7pm. Open M-Th 3pm-2am, F-Su 3pm-4am. Wheelchair accessible. Mixed drinks $6, bottled beer $4.

Apollo Theatre, 253 W. 125th St. (☎749-5838; box office 531-5305) between Frederick Douglass and Adam Clayton Powell Blvd. Subway: A, B, C, D to 125th St. This Harlem landmark has heard Duke Ellington, Count Basie, Ella Fitzgerald, and Billie Holliday. A young Malcolm X shined shoes here. A big draw is W's legendary Amateur Night ($13-30). Order tickets through Ticketmaster (☎307-7171) or at the box office. Open M-Tu and Th-F 10am-6pm, W 10am-8:30pm, Sa noon-6pm.

Fez, 380 Lafayette St. (☎533-2680), between 3rd and 4th St., under Time Cafe. Subway: 6 to Bleecker St. This lushly appointed, Moroccan-decorated performance club draws a photogenic crowd, especially on Th when the Mingus Big Band holds court. Sets at 9:30pm and 11:30pm. $18, students pay $10 for second set. Reservations suggested. Cover $5-30; 2-drink min. Open Su-Th 6pm-2am, F-Sa 6pm-4am.

Birdland, 315 W. 44th St. (☎581-3080), between Eighth and Ninth Ave. Subway: 1, 2, 3, 7, 9, C, E, N, Q, R, W to 42nd St. Said by Charlie Parker to be the "jazz corner of the world," this dinner club serves up Cajun food and splendid jazz in a classy, neon-accented setting. Music charge, including a complimentary drink, $20-35. Open daily 5pm-2am; first set nightly at 9pm, 2nd at 11pm. Reservations recommended.

Lenox Lounge, 288 Lenox Ave. (☎427-0253), between 124th and 125th St. Subway: 2, 3 to 125th St. The lounge is quintessential Harlem; intimate, offbeat, and bursting with great jazz. The original 1939 decor—smooth red booths and tiled floors—make this one of Harlem's hidden gems. Jazz Th-M $10-15; M night jam session $5. 2-drink min. First set 10pm; last set 1am. Open daily noon-4am.

ROCK, POP, PUNK, FUNK

New York City has a long history of producing bands on the vanguard of popular music and performance, from the Velvet Underground to Sonic Youth. **Music festivals** provide the opportunity to see tons of bands at a (relatively) low price. The **CMJ Music Marathon** (☎877-633-7848) runs for four nights in the fall, including over 400 bands and workshops on the alternative music scene. **The Digital Club Festival** (☎ 677-3530), a newly reconfigured indie-fest, visits New York in late July. The **Macintosh New York Music Festival** presents over 350 bands over a week-long period.

▨ **Mercury Lounge,** 217 E. Houston St. (☎260-4700), between Essex and Ludlow St. Once a gravestone parlor, the Mercury has attracted an amazing number of big-name acts, running the gamut from folk to pop to noise. A spectacular sound system attracts hipsters to the nightly shows. Cover varies (cash only). Box office open M-Sa noon-7pm.

Arlene Grocery and Butcher Bar, 95 Stanton St. (☎358-1633), between Ludlow and Orchard St. Every night this venue hosts at least three bands back-to-back-to-back. Mostly local indie acts, but big names like Sheryl Crow have also played in this intimate space. Bob Dylan once stopped by, but only to use the bathroom. Stop by next door at the Butcher Bar—a leg of the "grocery"—where drafts cost $5. Cover F-Sa $5.

Bowery Ballroom, 6 Delancey St. (☎533-2111; tickets 866-468-7619), between Chrystie St. and The Bowery. Subway: J, M, Z to Bowery. This medium-sized club retains some of the details from its original 1929 Beaux Arts construction. The venue attracts popular bands, and its stage has recently been graced by REM, the Black Crowes, and the Red Hot Chili Peppers. Tickets $10-20.

CBGB/OMFUG (CBGB's), 315 Bowery (☎982-4052), at Bleecker St. The initials have stood for "country, bluegrass, blues, and other music for uplifting gourmandizers," since CBGB's 1973 opening, but the New York Dolls, Television, the Ramones, Patti Smith, and Talking Heads rendered this venue synonymous with punk. The music remains loud, raw, and hungry. Shows nightly around 8pm. Cover $3-10. Next door, **CB's Gallery,** 313 Bowery (☎677-0455) presents softer live music.

Continental, 25 Third Ave. (☎529-6924), at Stuyvesant St. A dark club that hosts the loud set nightly. Come for noise, rock, and local punk. Iggy Pop, Debbie Harry, and Patti Smith have all played here—recently. Check lamp posts and fliers for shows and times. Shot of anything $2 with a beer. Cover up to $7.

Tonic, 107 Norfolk St. (☎358-7501), between Delancey and Rivington St. This converted wine brewery is home to a downstairs lounge (DJ; no cover) and a small-sized performance space for avant-garde musicians (cover $6-12). Lounge open daily 9pm-3am. Evening performance times vary. Sunday brunch with $10 cover and a band.

FILMS

Many films open in New York weeks before they're distributed elsewhere, and the response of Manhattan audiences and critics can shape a film's success or failure. Big-screen fanatics should check out the cavernous **Ziegfeld,** 141 W. 54th St., one of the largest screens left in America. (☎765-7600. Subway: 1, 9 to 51st St.) Eight screens project art-house cinema at the **Angelika Film Center,** 18 W. Houston St., at Mercer St. (☎995-2000. Subway: 6 to Bleecker St.; B, D, F, Q to Broadway-Lafayette.) **Anthology Film Archives,** 32 2nd Ave., at E. 2nd St., is a forum for independent filmmaking. (☎505-5181. Subway: F to 2nd Ave.) The **New York International Film Festival** is here every October; check the *Village Voice* or *Time Out.*

OPERA AND DANCE

You can do it all at **Lincoln Center;** there's usually opera or dance at one of its many venues. (☎546-2656. Subway: 1, 9 to 66th St.) Check *The New York Times* listings. The **Metropolitan Opera Company's** premier outfit plays on a Lincoln Center stage as big as a football field. You can stand in the orchestra, $16; or all the way back in the Family Circle, $12. (☎362-6000. Season runs Sept.-Apr. M-Sa. Box office open M-Sa 10am-8pm, Su noon-6pm. Regular tickets run over $250; upper balcony around $50. The cheapest seats have an obstructed view.)

Next to the Met, the **New York City Opera** has come into its own. "City" has a split season (Sept.-Nov. and Mar.-Apr.) and keeps its ticket prices low. (☎870-5570. Tickets $25-92; $10 rush tickets, call the night before and wait in line morning of.) **Dicapo Opera Theatre,** 184 E. 76th St., between 3rd and Lexington Ave., is a small company that garners standing ovations after *every* performance. (☎288-9438. Subway: 6 to 77th St. Tickets around $40.)

The **New York State Theater** in Lincoln Center is home to the late George Balanchine's **New York City Ballet.** Tickets for the *Nutcracker* in December sell out almost immediately. (☎870-5570. Season Nov.-Feb. and May-June. Tickets $12-65.) The **American Ballet Theater** dances at the Metropolitan Opera House. (☎477-3030, box office 362-6000. Tickets $17-75.) **City Center,** 131 W. 55th St., has some of the city's best dance, from modern to ballet, including the **Alvin Ailey American Dance Theater** (☎581-7907) in December. The dance company **De La Guarda** (think disco in a rainforest with an air show overhead) performs at 20 Union Sq. East. (☎239-6200. Standing-room only $40-45, some $20 tickets sold 2hr. before.) Other venues for dance include **Dance Theater Workshop,** 219 W. 19th St. (☎924-0077), between Seventh and Eighth Ave.; **Joyce Theater,** 175 Eighth Ave. (☎242-0800), between 18th and 19th St.; and **Thalia Spanish Theater,** 41-17 Greenpoint Ave. (☎718-729-3880), between 41st and 42nd St., in Sunnyside, Queens.

CLASSICAL MUSIC

Lincoln Center has the most selection in its halls. The **Great Performers Series,** featuring famous and foreign musicians, packs the Avery Fisher and Alice Tully Halls and the Walter Reade Theater from October until May (see above for contact info; tickets from $10). **Avery Fisher Hall** presents the annual **Mostly Mozart Festival.** Show up early; there are usually recitals 1hr. before the main concert that are free to ticketholders. (☎875-5766. July-Aug. Tickets $15-50.) The **New York Philharmonic** begins its regular season in mid-September. Seniors and students can sometimes get $10 tickets day-of; call ahead. Check about seeing morning rehearsals. (☎875-5709. Tickets $10-60.) For a few weeks in late June, Kurt Masur and friends lead the posse at **free concerts** on the Great Lawn in Central Park, at Prospect Park in Brooklyn, at Van Cortlandt Park in the Bronx, and elsewhere (☎875-5709). Free outdoor events at Lincoln Center occur all summer (☎875-4000).

If you're wondering how to get to **Carnegie Hall,** head to 7th Ave. at 57th St. (☎247-7800. Box office M-Sa 11am-6pm, Su noon-6pm. Tickets $10-60.) A good, cheap way to absorb New York musical culture is to visit a **music school.** Except for opera and ballet productions ($5-12), concerts at these schools are free and frequent: the **Juilliard School of Music,** Lincoln Center (☎769-7406), the **Mannes School of Music** (☎580-0210), and the **Manhattan School of Music** (☎749-2802).

SPORTS

Most cities are content to field a major-league team in each big-time sport. New York opts for the Noah's Ark approach: two baseball teams, two hockey teams, NBA and WNBA basketball teams, two football teams, and a lonely MLS soccer squad. New York hosts a number of world-class events. Get tickets three months in advance for the prestigious **U.S. Open,** held in late August and early September at the USTA Tennis Center in Flushing Meadows, Queens. (☎888-673-6849. $33-69.) On the 3rd Sunday in October, 2 million spectators witness the 22,000 runners of the **New York City Marathon.** The race begins on the Verrazano Bridge and ends at Central Park's Tavern on the Green. The **New York Mets** bat at **Shea Stadium** in Queens. (☎718-507-6387. $13-30.) The legendary **New York Yankees** play ball at Yankee Stadium in the Bronx. (☎718-293-4300. $8-30.) Both the **New York Giants** and the **Jets** play football across the river at **Giants Stadium** in East Rutherford, NJ. (☎516-560-8200. From $25.) The **New York/New Jersey Metrostars** play soccer in the same venue. The **New York Knickerbockers** (that's the Knicks to you), as well as the WNBA's **Liberty,** play basketball at **Madison Sq. Garden** (☎465-5867; from $22 and $8, respectively) and the **New York Rangers** play hockey there (from $25). The **New York Islanders** hit the ice at the Nassau Veterans Memorial Coliseum in Uniondale. (☎882-4753. Tickets from $14.)

◪ NIGHTLIFE

When the sun sets over the Hudson, the insomniac empress Gotham loosens her corset and takes down her hair. The city is awash with nightlife options: see performance art; hear live hip hop; sip a highball; work it at a drag show; learn to salsa. Whether you prefer Times Square's blinding lights or a Harlem jazz club, a smoky Brooklyn bar or a Lower East Side be-seen-ery, allow yourself to succumb to the city's dark side. At the end of it all, a 4:30am cab ride home through empty streets with the windows down will inevitably make your spirits soar.

MID-ATLANTIC

BARS

No one bar scene defines NYC in the way that pubs define Ireland or cruisy Hollywood bars define Los Angeles. NYC doesn't merely have every type of bar, but does them all well. Bars are loosely ranked, but personal preference depends on your own social or alcoholic slant.

▨ **The Whitehorse Tavern,** 567 Hudson St. (☎243-9260), at W. 11th St. Subway: 1, 9 to Christopher St. Dylan Thomas drank himself to death here, pouring 18 whiskies through an already tattered liver. Boisterous locals squeeze into one of NYC's oldest bars to pay homage to the poet. Beer $3.50-5. Open Su-Th 11am-2am, F-Sa 11am-4am.

▨ **bOb Bar,** 235 Eldridge St. (☎777-0588), between Houston and Stanton St. Subway: F to Second Ave. Small and laid-back, with a hip hop-inclined crowd and graffiti-esque paintings covering the walls. While Tu alternates between Latin, reggae, and hip hop (free), Th is strictly hip hop (cover $5 after 10pm; women $3). Open daily 7pm-4am.

▨ **Izzy Bar,** 166 First Ave. (☎228-0444), at E. 10th St. Subway: L to First Ave. Izzy Bar is a wooden-decor-laden, votive-glowing hangout; it's also one of the East Village's best music spots, whether it be for the DJs spinning house or hip hop, or for the live jazz (Su). Coronas $5. Cover up to $10. Open daily 7pm-4am.

▨ **Beauty Bar,** 231 E. 14th St. (☎539-1389), between Second and Third Ave. Subway: L to Third Ave. Unless you knew this was a bar, it would be easy enough to walk by "Thomas Hair Salon." Crowded all week, with slightly punk patrons drawn by the cheap cocktails (amaretto sour $4). Beer $3-4.50. Open Su-Th 5pm-4am, F-Sa 7pm-4am.

Idlewild, 145 E. Houston St. (☎477-5005), between First and Second Ave. Subway: F to Second Ave. This eclectic bar appropriated JFK's former name to lift the theme bar to new heights. Idlewild is shaped like an airplane, replete with a fuselage-shaped interior and reclining seats with tray tables. Beer $4-5. Open Tu-W 8pm-3am, Th-Sa 8pm-4am.

Orchard Bar, 200 Orchard St. (☎673-5350), between Houston and Stanton St. Subway: F to Second Ave. A long, narrow haunt frequented by hip Lower East Side scenesters. The bar is too cool for a sign—keep your eyes wide. F is house with one of NY's best DJs, Rob Salmon (free). Beer $4-5. Other drinks $5-6. Open W-Su 6pm-4am.

Fun, 130 Madison St. (☎964-0303), at Pike St. Subway: F to East Broadway. In-the-know hipsters chill at this "never a cover, never a guest list" hangout. Whimsical decor, complete with hydraulic lifts for the bartenders and wall video projections. VJs and DJs rotate nightly. Drinks start at $9 but are worth the fun. Open M-Sa 8pm-4am.

Naked Lunch Bar and Lounge, 17 Thompson St. (☎343-0828), at Grand St. Subway: 1, 9, A, C, E to Canal St. Adorned with the roach-and-typewriter theme found in the William Boroughs book of the same name. Unbeatable martinis like the Tanqueray tea ($8). Sometimes a $7 cover F-Sa after 10pm. Open Tu-F 5pm-4am, Sa 9pm-4am.

Milady's, 160 Prince St. (☎226-9069), at Thompson St. Subway: C, E to Spring St. A rough in the overbearing diamond mine that is SoHo. Down-to-earth neighborhood haunt that claims the only pool table in SoHo (a bit of a stretch) and a cast of affable regulars. Everything (even martinis) under $6. Open daily 11am-4am.

Cafe Noir, 32 Grand St. (☎431-7910), at Thompson St. Subway: 1, 9, A, C, E to Canal St. Cool in so many ways. The patrons, the bartenders, and the street-front windows all provide this bar/lounge/restaurant with a classy but unaffected feel. Draft beers $5-6. Entrees $12-22. Open daily noon-4am.

The Village Idiot, 355 W. 14th St. (☎989-7334), between Eighth and Ninth Ave. Subway: A, C, E, L to 14th St.-Eighth Ave. Honky-tonk, New York style. The beer is still cheap ($1.25 mugs of MGD), the music still loud (and still country), and the ambience still as close to a roadhouse as this city gets. Open daily noon-4am.

Tribe, 132 First Ave. (☎979-8965), at St. Mark's Pl. Subway: 6 to Astor Pl. Behind the frosted glass windows lies a chic, friendly bar with colorful but subtle back lighting, complete with comfortable lounging areas. DJ nightly: M live music and DJ, Tu salsa/Latin. Beer $5; cocktails $5-10. Open daily 5pm-4am.

d.b.a., 41 First Ave. (☎475-5097), between E. 2nd and 3rd St. Subway: F to Second Ave. A bar for the serious beer drinker. With 19 premium beers on tap (around $5), well over 100 bottled imports and microbrews, and 45 different tequilas, d.b.a. lives up to its motto—"drink good stuff." Mellow jazz and a sassy crowd. Open daily 1pm-4am.

Bbar (Bowery Bar), 40 E. 4th St. (☎475-2220), at the Bowery. Subway: F to Second Ave. Bbar has long held court on Bowery as a flagship of cooler-than-thou-ness. While newer spots may challenge its cachet, the crowd still has attitude to burn. Beer $5. Tu night is "Beige," Erich Conrad's wonderfully flamboyant gay party. Open Su-Th 11:30am-3am, F-Sa 11:30am-4am.

Coyote Ugly, 153 First Ave. (☎477-4431), between E. 9th and 10th St. Subway: L to First Ave. If you've seen the movie, you know what Coyote Ugly is like: a honky-tonk bar with good-looking bartenders and people whoopin' it up atop the bar. For those who like country music on the jukebox and a cheap beer in the hand. Open noon-4am.

McSorley's Old Ale House, 15 E. 7th St. (☎473-9148), at Third Ave. Subway: 6 to Astor Pl. Their motto is, "We were here before you were born," and unless you're 148 years old, they're right. It can get frat-boyish at times, but then that might just be your thing. Only 2 beers: light and dark. Two-fisters take note: mugs come 2 at a time ($3 for 2). Open M-Sa 11am-1am, Su 1pm-1am.

Sake Bar Decibel, 240 E. 9th St. (☎979-2733), between Stuyvesant St. and Second Ave. Subway: 6 to Astor Pl. All things Japanese are seriously fashionable in the East Village, and sake is no exception. This hidden bar, located down a flight of stairs, draws in a random mix of multi-ethnic hipsters. Over 60 kinds of *sake* $4-6 per glass. Minimum order $8 per person during busy weekend hours. Open M-Sa 8pm-3am, Su 8pm-1am.

The Evelyn Lounge, 380 Columbus Ave. (☎724-2363), at 78th St. Subway: B, C to 81st St. A somewhat upscale bar for the after-work set, with fireplaces and settees creating a homey setting. Great live music downstairs Tu-Th 9:30pm-1:30am. Drinks ($9 martinis) are a bit pricey but cover the cost of comfy couches colonized by cultured cliques. Enticing bar menu $7-14. Open daily 6pm-4am.

Montero's Bar & Grill, 73 Atlantic Ave. (☎718-624-9799), at Hicks St. Subway: 2, 3, 4, 5, M, N, R to Court St./Borough Hall. Heavily bedecked with nautical paraphernalia, this friendly dive still looks like the longshoremen's bar it once was. Beer $3. Open M-Sa 10am-4am, Su noon-4pm.

Teddy's, 96 Berry St. (☎718-384-9787), at N. 8th St., in Greenpoint. Subway: L to Bedford Ave. An eclectic mix of artists and wizened Brooklynites visits Teddy's for its great jukebox and friendly atmosphere. A wide variety of specialty martinis and low-priced Brooklyn beers ($2-4). Open Su-Th 10am-2:30am, F-Sa 11am-4am.

Pete's Candy Store, 709 Lorimer St. (☎718-302-3770), between Frost and Richardson St. Subway: L to Lorimer St. A lively local crowd flocks to the soda-shop-turned-bar for the free live music every night, but it's the Bucket of Joy (Stoli, Red Bull, 7-Up and straws) that makes this place worth the walk. Open Su-Tu 5pm-2am, W-Sa 5pm-4am.

DANCE CLUBS

Carefree crowds, unlimited fun, massive pocketbook damage—these foundations of the New York club scene make it an unparalleled institution of boogie. Many parties move from space to space each week. It can pay to call ahead to put your name on the guest list. Come after 11pm unless you crave solitude, but the real party starts around 1 or 2am. A few after-hours clubs keep at it until 5-6am, or even later.

▩ Centrofly, 45 W. 21st St. (☎627-7770), between Fifth and Sixth Ave. Where the beautiful people and music aficionados come to dance to the latest house and techno. Although patrons rave about the martinis ($11), it's the psychedelic lights and retro-chic decor that put the "fly" in Centrofly. Manhattan's clubbing elite tend to show up here on Th. Cover $20. Open M-Sa 10pm-5am.

Hush, 17 W. 19th St. (☎989-4874), between Fifth and Sixth Ave. Subway: F, N, R to 23rd St. This mid-sized club, run in part by the ex-head of security at Studio 54, spreads house, trance, and hip hop over two rooms. Dress nicely. Open F-Sa 11pm-4am.

Cheetah, 12 W. 21st St. (☎206-7770), between Fifth and Sixth Ave. Subway: F, N, R to 23rd St. A self-consciously trendy crowd struts it at this cheetah-print decorated club. Th is Clique (female DJ rotation with open bar 10-11pm). F is British house (open bar 10-

11pm). Sa is Cherchez La Femme (hip hop and R&B with open bar 10-11pm). Cover usually $20-25. Open 10pm-4am.

Nell's, 246 W. 14th St. (☎675-1567), between Seventh and Eighth Ave. Subway: 1, 2, 3, 9, A, C, E to 14th St.; L to Eighth Ave. Upstairs is a mellow space for mingling; downstairs is for dancing. No sneakers, jeans, or work boots. Cover M-W $10, Th-Su $15. Open M 8pm-2am, Tu and Th-Su 10pm-4am, W 9pm-3am.

NV/289 Lounge, 289 Spring St. (☎929-6868), near Varick St. Subway: C, E to Spring St. Gothic playground meets post-industrialism and results in a web of ceiling pipes over curtain-laden, sconce-enhanced chambers. Two bars and dance floors. W and Su nights feature great R&B, hip hop, and reggae vibes. Cover $10-20. Happy hour W-Th 6-10pm. Open W-Su 10pm-4am.

Ohm, 16 W. 22nd St. (☎229-2000, guest list 774-7749), between Fifth and Sixth Ave. Subway: F, N, R to 23rd St. A flashy, stylish club, with a towering ceiling, three bars, and a quality restaurant. House (of the high-BPM Euro variety) dominates the playlist on Sa, and gets mixed up with Latin (salsa, merengue, freestyle) on F. Downstairs, hip hop beats reign. Cover $20. Open Th-Sa 10pm-4am.

Shine, 285 West Broadway (☎941-0900), at Canal St. Subway: A, C, E to Canal St. It's "The Show" on Sa that lives up to its name, with not just great hip hop and house but also dancers and the occasional Elvis impersonator. Cover Th $10, F-Sa $20, Su $5. Open daily 10pm-4am.

Spa, 76 E. 13th St. (☎388-1062), between Broadway and Fourth Ave. Subway: 4, 5, 6, L, N, Q, R, W to Union Sq. Don't be intimidated by the elegance of the crowd or the Herculean-sized bouncers. Just wear black and walk in with attitude. "Rock and Roll W"; other nights have hip hop, house, and R&B to get you in the dancing groove. Th is a very popular gay night. Cover F-Sa $20-25. Open Tu-Sa 10pm-4am.

GAY AND LESBIAN NIGHTLIFE

Gay nightlife in New York is centered in Chelsea, especially along Eighth Ave. in the 20s, and the West Village, on Christopher St. Park Slope in Brooklyn is home to a growing lesbian community.

■ **Bar d'O,** 29 Bedford St. (☎627-1580). Subway: 1, 9 to Christopher St. A cozy, sultry-lit lounge. Superb performances by drag divas (Tu and Sa-Su nights 10:30pm, $5). Even without the fine chanteuses, this is a damn fine place for a drink. M night is "Pleasure" for women. Go early for the atmosphere, around midnight for the performances, and 2am to people-watch/gender-guess. Cover $3. Opens at 10pm.

■ **Splash,** 50 W. 17th St. (☎691-0073), between Fifth and Sixth Ave. Subway: 1, 9 to 18th St.; F to 23rd St. One of the most popular gay mega-bars. Enormous complex on two floors. Cool, almost sci-fi decor provides a sleek backdrop for a very crowded scene, with a dance floor that completes the evening. Cover varies, peaking at $7. Drinks $4-7. Open Su-Th 4pm-4am, F-Sa 4pm-5am.

Stonewall, 53 Christopher St. (☎463-0950). Subway: 1, 9 to Christopher St. Legendary bar of the Stonewall Riots. Join the lively and diversified crowd in this recently renovated bar to toast the brave drag queens who fought back. Upstairs, the Club at Stonewall has a dance floor. $2 frozen margaritas Sa-Su 2:30-9pm. Open daily 2:30pm-4am.

Henrietta Hudson, 438 Hudson St. (☎243-9079), between Morton and Barrow St. Subway: 1, 9 to Christopher St. A young, clean-cut lesbian crowd presides at this neighborhood bar. Mellow in the afternoon, jam-packed at night and on the weekends. Also gay male and straight friendly. DJs Th-Sa. Su is Girl Parts, a cover band highlighting lesbian-friendly music. Cover Th-Sa $3-5. Open M-F 4pm-4am, Sa-Su 1pm-4am.

g, 223 W. 19th St. (☎929-1085), between Seventh and Eighth Ave. Subway: 1, 9 to 18th St. Glitzy, popular bar shaped like an oval racetrack—somehow an appropriate architectural metaphor, given the pumped-up Chelsea clientele that speeds around this circuit trying to win glances. Fortunately, the famous frozen Cosmos satisfy the thirst of those logging their miles. No cover. Open daily 4pm-4am.

La Nueva Escuelita, 301 W. 39th St. (☎631-0588), at Eighth Ave. Subway: A, C, E to 42nd St. Drag Latin dance club that throbs with merengue, salsa, and arguably the best drag shows in New York. Largely, but not entirely, gay Latin crowd. F, starting at 10pm, is Her/She Bar, with go-go gals, performances, and special events. Cover Th $5; F $10; Sa $15; Su 7-10pm $5, after 10pm $8. Open Th-Sa 10pm-5am, Su 7pm-5am.

Boiler Room, 86 E. 4th St. (☎254-7536), between First and Second Ave. Subway: F to Second Ave. A popular locale catering to alluring alternative types, NYU college students, and eager refugees from the sometimes stifling Chelsea clone scene. Terrific jukebox gives the evening a democratic spin. Open daily 4pm-4am.

Wonder Bar, 505 E. 6th St. (☎777-9105), between Ave. A and B. Done up in zebra chic and laid back neutrals, the Wonder Bar is frequented by a chill gay bohemian crowd and the occasional curious breeder. Open daily 6pm-4am.

MISCELLANEOUS HIPSTER HANGOUTS

There are some New York institutions that defy characterization. Here's a short list.

ABC No Rio, 156 Rivington St. (☎254-3694), between Clinton and Suffolk St. A nonprofit, community-run art space. The center is open to the public and hosts a myriad of community events from art exhibitions of local teenagers to hard-core and punk shows. No alcohol or beverages served. All ages. Cover $2-5.

Halcyon, 227 Smith St. (☎718-260-9299), between Butler and Douglass St. Subway: F, G to Bergen St. The hippest Brooklyn hangout south of Flatbush Ave., Halcyon combines record store, cafe, and lounge. The laid back atmosphere allows you to soak in the sounds of the DJ while playing one of their old, forgotten board games like Twixt. BYOB. No cover. Open Su and Tu-Th 8pm-midnight, F-Sa 9pm-2am.

Galapagos, 70 N. 6th St. (☎718-782-5188), between Kent and Wythe St. Subway: L to Bedford Ave. A bit deserted at night; go with a friend. Once a mayonnaise factory, this space is now a futuro-sleek bar that puts up parties, vaudeville performances on M, and a weekly film series (Su 7 and 9:30pm, M 8:30pm; $5 cover). DJs Tu-Sa. Open Su-Th 6pm-2am, F-Sa 6pm-4am.

The Anyway Cafe, 34 E. 2nd St. (☎533-3412), at Second Ave. Subway: F to Second Ave. Sample Russian-American culture at this dark, leopard-spotted hangout. Numerous literary readings during the week, as well as jazz F and Sa nights, and Russian folk on Su. Music every night at 9pm. Open M-Th 5pm-2am, F-Sa 5pm-4am, Su noon-1am.

Nuyorican Poets Cafe, 236 E. 3rd St. (☎505-8183), between Ave. B and C. Subway: F to Second Ave. NYC's leading joint for poetry slams (check out the F night slam at 10pm) and spoken-word performances; several regulars have been featured on MTV. A mixed bag of doggerel and occasional gems. If you don't like the poets, don't worry—there's likely to be a heckler in the house. Cover $5-12.

LONG ISLAND ☎631

Long Island, a sprawling suburbia stretching 120 miles the east of Manhattan, is both a home to over 2.7 million New Yorkers (excluding those who live in the Queens and Brooklyn) and a sleepy summertime resort for wealthy Manhattanites. It is both expensive and difficult to navigate without a car.

🛈 PRACTICAL INFORMATION. Long Island Convention and Visitors Bureau: ☎631-951-2423. **Long Island Railroad (LIRR)** services the island from Penn Station in Manhattan and stops in Jamaica, Queens (subway: E, J, Z) before proceeding to "points east." (☎718-217-5477. 34th St. at 7th Ave. Subway: 1, 2, 3, 9, A, C, E. $4.75-15.25; lower in off-peak hours.) To reach **Fire Island,** take the LIRR to Sayville, Bayshore, or Patchogue. The **Sayville ferry** serves Cherry Grove, the Pines, and Sailor's Haven. (☎589-8980. Round-trip $9-11, under 12 $5.) The **Bay Shore ferry** sails to Fair Harbor, Ocean Beach, Ocean Bay Park, Saltaire, and Kismet. (☎516-665-3600. Round-trip $11.50, under 12 $5.50.) The **Patchogue ferry** (☎516-475-1665) shuttles to Davis Park and Watch Hill (round-trip $10, under 12 $5.50). The Hamptons are accessible by LIRR or by car. Take the Long Island Expressway to Exit 70. Make a right onto Rte. 111 (Manorville Rd.). When the road ends, make a left onto the Montauk Hwy. Towns are located near the highway. **Area code:** 631 and 516; 631 unless noted.

FIRE ISLAND

A gay hot spot and extraordinarily well-preserved site off Long Island's shores, Fire Island is a 32 mi. long barrier island buffering the South Shore from the roaring waters of the Atlantic. Cars are allowed only on the easternmost and westernmost tips of the island; there are no streets, only "walks." A hip countercultural enclave during the 60s and home to the disco scene of the 70s, the island's communities, both gay and straight, still party loud.

Cherry Grove and the Pines are the main gay communities on the island. Both towns host establishments that advertise themselves as "guest houses." Be aware that some of these may not be legally accredited (due to such things as fire code violations), and that some may not be lesbian-friendly. When planning lodging, be advised that many places require a two-night minimum on the weekends, so call ahead. **The Cherry Grove Beach Hotel** is a good bet, centrally located on the Main Walk of Cherry Grove and close to the beach. The economy room starts at $90 mid-week during July, but costs $450 for a two-night stay during the weekend. (☎597-6600. Open May-Oct. Reservations required.)

There is a very established schedule to gay nightlife in Fire Island. A night in Cherry Grove usually begins at the **Ice Palace** (☎597-6600), attached to the Cherry Grove Beach Hotel, where you can disco till dawn. Most go to the Pines for late-night partying; you can catch a water taxi from the docks at Cherry Grove. A ten-minute walk up the beach from Cherry Grove, the Pines has traditionally looked down at its uninhibited neighbor. You may want to bring along a flashlight to navigate the often poorly lit boardwalks here. The Pines' active, upscale nighttime scene, unfortunately, has a bit of a secret club feel to it—you need to be in the know or somehow be able to look like you know the schedule. **Low Tea,** from 5-8pm, is at the bar/club next to the Botel (big hotel). Move on to disco **High Tea** at 8pm at the Pavilion, but make sure you have somewhere to disappear to during "disco nap" time (after 10pm). Around 1:30am you can emerge unabashedly to dance until dawn at the **Island Club and Bistro,** better known as the Sip and Twirl. The Pavilion becomes hot again late-night on weekends, including Sundays during the summer.

THE HAMPTONS AND MONTAUK

West Hampton, Southampton, Bridgehampton, and East Hampton make up the entity known as the Hamptons, where the upper crust of society roam the sidewalks before heading to the beach for the afternoon. As a result of the clientele, the prices are high here. Try going to Montauk, at the eastern tip of Long Island, for (slightly) budget accommodations. The **Blue Haven Motel,** 533 W. Lake Ln. (☎631-668-5943), offers good clean rooms for comparatively cheap prices: $170 on the weekends but almost $100 less during the week.

Many beaches in the Hamptons require a permit to park, but anyone can walk on for free. Sights include the **Montauk Point Lighthouse and Museum,** off Rte. 27 at the far eastern tip of the island, which was built in 1796 by special order of President George Washington. (☎631-668-2544. Open June-Sept. M-F and Su 10:30am-6pm, Sa 10:30am-7:30pm; other times call for info. $4, seniors $3.50, under 12 $2.50.) Whaling buffs shouldn't miss the **Sag Harbor Whaling Museum,** at the corner of Main and Garden St. in Sag Harbor. (☎631-725-0770. Open May-Sept. M-Sa 10am-5pm, Su 1-5pm. $3, seniors $2, ages 6-13 $1. Tours by appointment; $2.)

THE CATSKILLS   ☎845

The Catskills, home of Rip Van Winkle's century-long repose, remained in a happy state of somnambulant obscurity for centuries. In the early 1960s, holiday camps of the kind portrayed in the hit 80s film *Dirty Dancing* began to wake the area from its slumber. After the purple haze of Woodstock fully jolted the region to life in 1969, the Catskills had to undergo an extensive detox period. Barring the occasional flashback, such as the 1994 and 1999 repetitions of the rock festival, the state-managed Catskill Forest Preserve is today the region's best attraction, offering travelers pristine miles of hiking and skiing trails, diminutive villages, and crystal-clear fishing streams.

🔀 PRACTICAL INFORMATION. Traveling from I-87, the region is most easily explored by following Rte. 28 W. **Adirondack/Pine Hill Trailways** provides excellent service through the Catskills. The main stop is in **Kingston,** 400 Washington Ave., on the corner of Front St. (☎331-0744 or 800-858-8555; ticket office open M-F 5:45am-11pm, Sa-Su 6:45am-11pm). Buses run to New York City (2hr., 9-15 per day, $19; Tu-Th same-day round-trip $26). Other stops in the area include Woodstock, Pine Hill, Saugerties, and Hunter; each connects with New York City, Albany, and Utica. Four stationary **tourist cabooses** dispense info, including the extremely useful *Ulster County: Catskills Region Travel Guide.* Located at the traffic circle in Kingston, on Rte. 28 in Shandaken, on Rte. 209 in Ellenville, and on Rte. 9 W in Milton. (Open May-Oct. 9am-5pm; hours vary depending on volunteer availability.) Rest stop **Visitors Centers** along I-87 can advise you about area sights and distribute excellent, free maps of New York State. **Area code:** 845, unless otherwise noted.

CATSKILL FOREST PRESERVE

The 250,000-acre **Catskill Forest Preserve** contains many small towns and outdoor adventure opportunities. Ranger stations distribute free permits for backcountry camping, which are necessary for stays over three days. Still, most of the **campgrounds** listed below sit at gorgeous trailheads that mark great day-long jaunts. Reservations are vital in summer, especially weekends. (☎800-456-2267. Sites $9-16; phone reservation fee $8.50; $2-3 more for partial hookup at some sites. Open May-Sept.) The **Office of Parks** (☎518-474-0456) distributes brochures on the campgrounds. Required permits for **fishing** (non-NY residents $20 for five days) are available in sporting goods stores and at many campgrounds. **Ski season** runs from November to mid-March, with popular slopes down numerous mountainsides along Rte. 28 and Rte. 23A. Although hiking trails are maintained, some lean-tos are dilapidated and crowded. For more info, call the **Dept. of Environmental Conservation** (☎256-3000). **Adirondack Trailways** buses from Kingston pass most trailheads.

WOODSTOCK

Signs advertising "Tie-Dyed T-shirts" and "Last incense for 20 mi. sold here" might suggest to you that Woodstock, between Phoenicia and Kingston, is *the* place to be for aging hippies. Although the famed 1969 concert was actually held in nearby Saugerties, Woodstock has been a haven for artists since the turn of the century. The tie-dyed legacy has gradually faded, however, and Woodstock has become expensive and touristy. Still, neo-hippies operate out of the **Woodstock School of Art** on Rte. 212, accessible from Rte. 28 via Rte. 375. In addition to housing art classes, a small gallery pays homage to Woodstock's artistic tradition. (☎914-679-2388. Open M-Sa 9am-3pm.)

MT. TREMPER

🖾Kaleidoworld, on Rte. 28, fiercely competes with nature for the title of most spectacular attraction in the Catskills. The two largest kaleidoscopes in the world are displayed here, with the largest (56 ft.) leaving Woodstock-era veterans muttering, "I can see the music!" The adjacent Crystal Palace (included in admission) features hands-on kaleidoscopes. (☎688-5800. Open daily 10am-7pm; mid-Oct. to July closed Tu. $10, seniors $8, kids under 4 ft. 6 in. $8.) **Kenneth L. Wilson,** on Wittenburg Rd. 3¾ mi. from Rte. 212 (make a hard right onto Wittenburg Rd., then turn right at the next intersection), has wooded **campsites,** showers, and a quiet, wholesome atmosphere. The beach features a gorgeous panorama of mountains surrounding the looking-glass-shaped lake. Canoe rentals, fishing, and hiking round out the options. (☎679-7020. Sites $14, plus a $2.50 service charge. Registration 8am-9pm. Day use $3, seniors free M-F. Canoes half-day $10, full-day $15.)

PHOENICIA

Phoenicia is another beautiful spot in the Catskills. The **Esopus Creek,** to the west, has great trout **fishing,** and **The Town Tinker,** 10 Bridge St., rents inner-tubes for river-riding. (☎688-5553; www.towntinker.com. Inner-tubes $7 per day, with seat $10. Driver's license or $50 deposit required. Tube taxi transportation $3. Life jackets $2. Open mid-May to Sept. daily 9am-6pm; last rental 4:30pm.) If tubes don't float your boat, the wheezing, 100-year-old **Catskill Mountain Railroad** can shuttle you for six scenic miles from Bridge St. to Mt. Pleasant. (40min. Runs late May to late Oct. Sa-Su, 1 per hr. 11am-5pm. $4, round-trip $6, under 12 $2.) At the 65 ft. high **Sundance Rappel Tower,** off Rte. 214, visitors return to earth the hard way. (☎688-5640. 4 levels of lessons; beginner 3-4hr., $22. Lessons only held when a group of 8 is present. Reservations 1 week in advance required.) For a trip to the peak, head to Woodland Valley campground (below), where a 9¾ mi. hike to the 4204 ft. summit of **Slide Mt.** lends a view of New Jersey, Pennsylvania, and the Hudson Highlands.

The somewhat primitive **Woodland Valley** campground, off High St., 7 mi. southeast of Phoenicia, has flush toilets and showers, and provides access to many hiking trails. (☎688-7647. Sites $12, plus a $2.50 service charge. Register between 8am-9pm. Open late May to early Oct.) The **Cobblestone Motel,** surrounded by mountains on Rte. 214, has friendly managers, an outdoor pool, and clean, newly renovated rooms, most with a kitchen and fridge. (☎688-7871. Doubles $49, large doubles $60, with kitchenette $69; 1-bedroom cottages $80, 3-room cottages with kitchen $99.)

PINE HILL

Pine Hill is nestled near **Belleayre Mt.,** which offers hiking trails and ski slopes. (☎254-5600 or 800-942-6904. Ski lift, lesson, and rental package M-F $62, Sa-Su $71; children $59/$63.) **Belleayre Hostel** is a lodging bargain; follow Rte. 28 past Big Indian, making a left on Main St. at the big white "Pine Hill" sign, then another left into the second parking lot. Bunks and private rooms in a rustic setting near Phoenicia. Amenities include a recreational room, kitchen access, laundry ($2), a picnic area, Internet access, and sporting equipment. (☎254-4200. Bunks $15; private rooms $30/$40; cabins for up to 6 $60.)

HUNTER MT. AND HAINES FALLS

From Rte. 28, moving north on Rte. 42 and then east onto Rte. 23A leads through a gorgeous stretch along **Hunter Mt.,** one of the most popular ski areas on the east coast (ski info ☎518-263-4223, accommodations 800-775-4641). During festivals held throughout the summer and fall, Hunter Mt. offers **Skyride,** the longest, highest chairlift in the Catskills. ($6, ages 3-12 $4, under 6 free.) Motels and outdoor stores dot the highway. Past Hunter Mt., **North Lake/South Lake campground** in Haines Falls has 219 campsites near two lakes, a waterfall, and hiking. (☎518-589-5058. $16, plus a $2.50 service charge; reserve 2 days in advance. Day use $5. Canoe rental $15.)

ALBANY   ☎518

Although Albany proclaims itself "the most livable city in America," it suffers from an unhappy reversal of clichés. The city once known as Fort Orange comes up short in comparison with its southern sibling, the Big Apple. Established six years before the Pilgrims landed on the New England shore, it is the oldest continuous European settlement in the original 13 colonies and the capital of New York State.

🛈 **PRACTICAL INFORMATION. Amtrak,** at the intersection of East St. and Rensselaer, across the Hudson from downtown Albany (☎462-5710; station open daily 3:30am-midnight), has service to: New York City (2½hr., 11-13 per day, $41) and Buffalo (5hr., 4 per day, $47). **Greyhound,** 34 Hamilton St. (☎434-8095, schedule information 800-231-2222; station open 24hr.), runs buses to: Utica (1½-2hr., $22); Syracuse (3hr., $31); Rochester (4½hr., $37); and Buffalo (5-6hr., $49). *Be careful here at night.* From the same station, **Adirondack Trailways** (☎436-9651) connects to other upstate locales: Lake George (1¾hr., 3 per day, $12); Lake Placid (4½hr., 1 per day, $27); and Kingston (1hr., 6 per day, $10). For local travel, the **Capital District Transportation Authority (CDTA),** 110 Watervliet Ave. (☎482-8822), serves Albany ($1), Troy ($1.25), and Schenectady ($1.35). Schedules are available at the Amtrak and Trailways stations. The **Albany Visitors Center,** 25 Quackenbush Sq. at Clinton Ave. and Broadway, runs trolley tours of downtown (☎434-0405; late June to late Sept. F 1pm and Sa 10:30am; $10, seniors $9, under 15 $5) and Albany's historic homes (open M-F 11am-4pm, Sa-Su 10am-4pm; trolley tour W 10am). **Post Office:** 45 Hudson Ave. (☎462-1359; open M-F 8am-5:30pm). **ZIP code:** 12207. **Area code:** 518.

⌐▐◖ **ACCOMMODATIONS AND FOOD.** **Pine Haven Bed & Breakfast,** 531 Western Ave., offers gorgeous rooms with phone, TV, and A/C in an inviting setting. The big Victorian house stands at the convergence of Madison and Western Ave.; parking is in the rear. (☎482-1574. Breakfast included. Reservations needed. Single with shared bath $59; double $74; private bath $74/$89.) **Thompson's Lake State Park,** on Rte. 157 north of East Berne, 18 mi. southwest of Albany, offers the closest camping, with 140 primitive sites, fishing, hiking, and a swimming beach. Follow Rte. 443 out of Albany and look for the signs for Thompson's Lake. (☎872-1674. Sites $13. One-time service fee $2.75.)

In "downtown" Albany, the best eating option entails getting "locked away" at the **Big House Brewing Company,** 90 N. Pearl St., at Sheridan St. The Big House serves pizzas, sandwiches, and burgers at prices that don't cry larceny ($6-7), alongside Al Capone Amber Ale. (☎445-2739. Open Tu-Sa 4pm-late. Happy hour 4-7pm. Live bands Th-F. Dancing F-Sa.) At **Stone Soup Deli,** 484 Central Ave., wash down a sandwich and salad ($4.75) with one of a variety of organic shakes ($2-3). Remember to bring your favorite tunes; there's a tape deck for your listening pleasure. (☎482-2667. Open M-F 9am-8pm, Sa 9am-6pm, Su 10am-6pm.)

◙ **SIGHTS.** Albany's sights are centered around the **Rockefeller Empire State Plaza,** between State and Madison St., a $1.9 billion, towering, modernist Stonehenge. The plaza houses state offices, stores, a bus terminal, a post office, and a food court. (Free parking M-F after 2pm.) The huge flying saucer at one end of the Plaza is the **Empire Center for the Performing Arts,** also known as "The Egg," a venue for theater, dance, and concerts. (☎473-1845. Box office open M-F 10am-5pm, Sa noon-3pm; in summer M-F 10am-4pm; tickets $15-30.) Across the street, the **New York State Museum** has in-depth exhibits on the state's history, people, and wildlife. (☎474-5877. Open daily 9:30am-5pm. Free.) The magnificent **New York State Capitol,** adjacent to the Plaza, has provided New York politicians with luxury quarters since 1899. (☎474-2418. Call ahead for daily tour times. Tours begin M-F at 10am, noon, 2, and 3pm, at the senate staircase on the 1st fl. Free.)

Bounded by State St. and Madison Ave. north of downtown, **Washington Park** has tennis courts, paddle boats, and plenty of room for celebrations and performances. The **Park Playhouse** stages free musical theater from July to mid-Aug. (☎434-2035. Open Tu-Su 8pm.) On Thursday during June, July, and August folks come **Alive at Five** to free concerts at the **Tricentennial Plaza,** across from Fleet Bank on Broadway. (☎434-2032.) For events, call the **Albany Alive Line** at 434-1217, ext. 409.

Biking aficionados traverse the **Mohawk-Hudson Bikeway,** which passes along old railroad grades and canal towpaths as it weaves through the capital area. (☎386-2225. Maps available at the Visitors Center.) Rentals can be had at the **Down Tube Cycle Shop,** 466 Madison Ave. (☎434-1711. Open M-F 11am-7pm, Sa 10am-5pm. Full-day $25, 2-days $35.)

COOPERSTOWN   ☎607

To earlier generations, Cooperstown evoked images of novelist James Fenimore Cooper's frontiersman hero, Leatherstocking, who roamed the woods around Lake Otsego. Tiny Cooperstown now recalls a different source of American legend and myth—baseball. Tourists file through the Baseball Hall of Fame, eat in baseball-themed restaurants, and sleep in baseball-themed motels. Fortunately for the tepid fan, baseball's hometown is surrounded by some non-baseball rural attractions like the Fenimore Art Museum and Glimmerglass State park.

◪ **PRACTICAL INFORMATION.** Cooperstown is accessible from I-90 and I-88 via Rte. 28. Street parking is rare in Cooperstown; park in the free lots just outside of town on Rte. 28, on Glen Ave. at Maple St., or near the Fenimore House. From these lots, it's an easy 5-15min. walk to Main St. (Rte. 31). **Trolleys** also leave from the lots, dropping off riders at the Hall of Fame, the Farmer and Fenimore museums, Doubleday Field, the Chamber of Commerce, and downtown. (Trolleys run late June to mid-Sept. daily 8:30am-9pm; early June and late Sept. to Oct. Sa-Su 8:30am-6pm; all-day pass $2, children $1.) **Pine Hall Trailways** (☎800-858-8555) picks up visitors at Clancy's Deli on Rte. 28 and Elm St. for New York City (5½hr., 2-3 per day, $41) and Kingston (3¼hr., 1-2 per day, $21). **Cooperstown Area Chamber of Commerce and Visitor Information Center:** 31 Chestnut St., on Rte. 28 near Main St. (☎547-9983; generally open daily 9am-5pm, but hours vary; call ahead). **Post Office:** 40 Main St. (☎547-2311; open M-F 8:30am-5pm, Sa 8:30am-noon). **ZIP code:** 13326. **Area code:** 607.

▐▌▐▌ ACCOMMODATIONS AND FOOD. Summertime lodging in Cooperstown seems to require a Major League baseball player's salary, and during peak tourist season (late June to mid-Sept.), many accommodation-seekers strike out. Fortunately, there are alternatives waiting on deck. The **Mohican Motel,** 90 Chestnut St., offers large beds, cable TV, and A/C at relatively affordable Cooperstown-area prices. (☎547-5101. Late June to early Sept. 2- to 6-people rooms range from $76-160; rates are about 50% lower in off-season.) **Glimmerglass State Park,** 8 mi. north of Cooperstown on Rte. 31 on the east side of Lake Otsego, has 37 pristine campsites in a gorgeous lakeside park. Daytime visitors can swim, fish, and boat ($6 per vehicle) from 8am-6pm. (☎547-8662, 800-456-2267 for reservations and a heinous $8 service charge. Sites $13; $2.75 registration fee; showers, dumping station; no hookups. Register daily 11am-9pm.) Closest to the Hall of Fame, **Cooperstown Beaver Valley Campground,** off Rte. 28 10min. south of Cooperstown, has spacious wooded sites, pool, recreation area, and boat rentals. (☎293-8131 or 800-726-7314. Sites $28, with hookup $31.)

The **Doubleday Cafe,** 93 Main St., hits a two-run dinger with a tasty bowl of chili ($4) and eye-catching memorabilia of the Babe and other baseball greats on the walls. (☎547-5468. Open daily 7am-10 or 11pm, depending on crowd; bar closes after kitchen.) For elegant but affordable dining, the uncapitalized **hoffman lane bistro,** off Hoffman Ln., off Main St. across from the Hall of Fame, has light, airy rooms with checkered black-and-white tablecloths. Their crabcakes ($8) leave customers rooting for more. (☎547-7055. Open M-Sa 11:30am-3:30pm and 5-9:30pm. Late-night menu served until midnight. Clams over linguine $6.) A Cooperstown institution, **Schneider's Bakery,** 157 Main St., has been feeding the locals delicious 50¢ "old-fashioneds" (doughnuts less sweet and greasy than their commercial cousins) since 1887. (☎547-9631. Open M-Sa 6:30am-5:30pm, Su 7am-1pm.)

◙ SIGHTS. The ▨**National Baseball Hall of Fame and Museum** on Main St. is an enormous, glowing monument to America's national pastime. The building is home to priceless memorabilia—everything from the bat with which Babe Ruth hit his famous "called shot" home run in the 1932 World Series to the infamous jersey worn by 65 lb. White Sox midget Eddie Gaedel. The museum also features a multimedia tribute to the sport, a candid display on African-American ballplayers' experiences in the Negro Leagues, art and movies about baseball, and history tracing the myth-making game to ancient Egyptian rituals. One exhibit reads, "In the beginning, shortly after God created Heaven and Earth, there were stones to throw and sticks to swing." You'll have to fight the crowds: the daily turnstile count at the museum in the summer exceeds the town population. (☎547-7200. Open daily 9am-9pm; Oct.-Apr. 9am-5pm. $9.50, seniors $8, ages 7-12 $4.)

The free **annual ceremonies** for new inductees takes place on either the last weekend of July or the first weekend of August, on the field adjacent to the **Clark Sports Center** on Susquehanna Ave., a 10min. walk from the Hall. During the festivities, fans scramble for contact with the many Hall of Famers who sign autographs (at steep prices) along Main St. The annual **Hall of Fame Game** between two rotating Major League teams concludes the festival on Monday at 2pm in the delightfully intimate Doubleday Field. Plan accordingly—over 40,000 visitors are expected. Rooms must be reserved months in advance.

THEY MIGHT BE GIANTS Before the 1919 Black Sox scandal deceived Americans nationwide, the **Cardiff Giant** was the centerpiece of an earlier and equally controversial fraud. Its creator, local entrepreneur George Hull, commissioned the statue in 1868 for $2600 following an argument with a Methodist Minister, who remembering Genesis 6:4, "There were giants in the earth in those days," firmly believed that giants had once roamed the Earth. Thinking he could exploit this readiness to believe the Bible, Hull planned to bury and then "discover" the stone Giant. The next year, the Giant was unearthed by workmen digging a well on Hull's brother-in-law's farm. Soon, with crowds coming from miles around to see Hull's "fossilized giant," he sold his interest in the statue for a whopping $40,000. Over the ensuing months, Hull's creation was shown to increasingly skeptical crowds, and when P.T. Barnum displayed his own copy of the Giant two blocks away from the "real" one, it was widely recognized as a hoax. Today, the original lives at the **Farmer's Museum** (see **Sights,** above).

Nearby, the **Fenimore Art Museum,** Lake Rd./Rte. 80, features American folk art, Hudson River School paintings, James Fenimore Cooper memorabilia, and an impressive collection of Native American art. (☎547-1400 or 888-547-1450. Open daily 10am-5pm; Oct.-Dec. and Apr.-May Tu-Su 10am-4pm. $9, ages 7-12 $4.) Across the street, the **Farmer's Museum** offers exhibits on 19th-century rural life, with an operating farmstead and a recreated village. (☎547-1450. Open Apr.-May Tu-Su 10am-4pm, June-Sept. daily 10am-5pm, Oct.-Nov. 10am-4pm. $9, ages 7-12 $4. Combination tickets with Hall of Fame and Fenimore Art Museum $22.)

ITHACA AND THE FINGER LAKES ☎607

According to Iroquois legend, the Great Spirit laid his hand upon the earth, and the impression of his fingers made the Finger Lakes: Canandaigua, Cayuga, Seneca, and others. Whether it was the Great Spirit or mere Ice Age glaciers, the results are spectacular. Vladimir Nabokov, Kurt Vonnegut, and Thomas Pynchon have all brooded on the cliff at Cornell University. Thirsty trekkers refresh themselves in the waterfalls of Ithaca's ruggedly carved gorges or sip another divine nectar that flows here—the rich wine of the Finger Lakes area's acclaimed vineyards.

🛈 PRACTICAL INFORMATION. Ithaca Bus Terminal (☎272-7930; open M-Sa 6:30am-6pm, Su noon-5pm), 710 W. State St. at Rte. 13 houses **Short Line** (☎277-8800) and **Greyhound** (☎272-7930), with service to New York City (5hr., 12 per day, $37); Philadelphia (7hr., 2per day, $52); and Buffalo (4hr., 5 per day, $27). **Tompkins Consolidated Area Transit (T-CAT)** (☎277-7433) is your only choice for getting out to Cayuga Lake without a car. Buses stop at Ithaca Commons, westbound on Seneca St. and eastbound on Green. (Fare 75¢-$2, seniors and students 50¢. Buses run daily.) The **Ithaca/Tompkins County Convention and Visitors Bureau,** 904 E. Shore Dr., Ithaca 14850, has the best map of the area ($2.50), hotel and B&B listings, and brochures. (☎272-1313 or 800-284-8422. Open late May to early Sept. M-F 8am-5pm, Sa 10am-5pm, Su 10am-4pm; mid-Sept. to late May M-F 8am-5pm.) **Post Office:** 213 N. Tioga St., at E. Buffalo (☎272-5455; open M-F 7am-6pm, Sa 7am-1pm). **ZIP code:** 14850. **Area code:** 607.

🛈 ACCOMMODATIONS. As befits the town where Vladimir Nabokov penned *Lolita*, Ithaca is filled with cheap roadside motels, no questions asked. In summer, however, rooms are scarce and rates rise from about $40 to $100 per night. **Elmshade Guest House,** 402 S. Albany St., at Center St. three blocks from the Ithaca Commons, offers large, impeccably clean, well-decorated rooms with shared bath, cable TV, and a generous continental breakfast. This B&B is by far the best budget option in Ithaca. From the bus station, walk up State St. and turn right onto Albany St. (☎273-1707. Singles $40; doubles $60. Reservations recommended.) **The Economy Inn,** 658 Elmira Rd./Rte. 13, has just the basics, but is close to Buttermilk Falls and 2 mi. from downtown Ithaca. Rooms have A/C, cable TV, refrigerator, and free local calls. (☎277-0370. Singles from $30, Sa-Su $48; doubles $38/$65.) **The Wonderland Motel,** 654 Elmira Rd., has a pool, A/C, and free local calls. (☎272-5252. Continental breakfast included. Singles from $45; doubles from $55; Nov.-Mar. $35/$45. Rates significantly higher on weekends.) Three of the nearby state parks with camping are **Robert H. Treman** (☎273-3440), on Rte. 327 off Rte. 13; **Buttermilk Falls** (☎273-5761), Rte. 13 south of Ithaca; and **Taughannock Falls** (☎387-6739), north on Rte. 89. (Sites $15; $2 walk-on fee or $7.50 reservation fee by calling 800-456-2267. Cabins $122-239 per week plus $11 reservation fee.) The *Finger Lakes State Parks* has info on all area state parks and is available at any tourist office or park.

◘ **FOOD.** Restaurants in Ithaca center on **Ithaca Commons** and **Collegetown.** For a night on the town, the free *Ithaca Times*, available at most stores and restaurants, has complete listings of entertainment options. The ◪**Rongovian Embassy to the USA ("The Rongo"),** Rte. 96 on the main strip in Trumansburg about 10 mi. from Ithaca, is worth the drive. Seek asylum in amazing Mexican entrees at this offbeat and inexpensive restaurant/bar. Travelers unsatisfied with reality can plot a trip to "Nearvarna" on the huge wall map that features the nation of Rongovia and other fictitious destinations. (☎387-3334. Restaurant open Tu-Su 5-10pm; bar Tu-Su 4pm-1am. Bands Tu-Su; cover $5. Enchiladas $6; beer $2.) **Moosewood Restaurant,** 215 N. Cayuga, at Seneca St. in the Dewitt Mall, features an amazing selection of wonderfully fresh and creative vegetarian options. (☎273-9610. Open daily 11:30am-4pm and 6-9pm. Lunch $6.50; dinner $10-13. No reservations.) **Just a Taste,** 116 N. Aurora, near Ithaca Commons, has an extensive selection of fine wines ($2-5 glass), 25 beers, and tempting *tapas.* (☎277-9463. Open Su-Th 11:30am-3:30pm and 5:30-10pm, F-Sa 11am-3:30pm and 5:30-11pm.) **Joe's Restaurant,** 602 W. Buffalo St., at Rte. 13 (Meadow St.), serves Italian and American entrees ($8-20) with Joe's bottomless salad. (☎273-2693. Open Su 2-10pm, M-Th 4-10pm, F-Sa 4-11pm.)

◙ **SIGHTS. Cornell University,** youngest of the Ivy League schools, sits on a *steep* hill in Ithaca between two tremendous gorges. The **Suspension Bridge** above Fall Creek provides a heart-pounding walk above one gorge, while the **Central Avenue Stone Arch Bridge** above Cascadilla Creek has a brilliant sunset view. The **Information and Referral Center** in the Day Hall Lobby has info on campus sights and activities. (☎254-4636. Open M-F 8am-5pm; telephone staffed Sa 8am-5pm and Su noon-1pm. Tours Apr.-Nov. M-F 9, 11am, 1, and 3pm, Sa 9am and 1pm, Su 1pm; Dec.-Mar. daily 1pm.) The boxy but strangely pleasing cement edifice rising from the top of the hill—designed by I.M. Pei—houses Cornell's **Herbert F. Johnson Museum of Art,** at the corner of University and Central. The small collection of European and American painting and sculpture includes works by Giacometti, Matisse, O'Keeffe, de Kooning, and Hopper; the rooftop sculpture garden yields an amazing view. (☎255-6464. Open Tu-Su 10am-5pm. Free.) At **Cornell Plantations,** a series of botanical gardens surround Cornell's great geological wonders. (☎255-3020. Open daily sunrise to sunset. Free.) Adventurous hikes into the Cornell gorge include the 1½ mi. **Founder's Loop,** which is well worth the time. The free *Passport to the Trails of Tompkins County*, available from the Visitor's Bureau, is a comprehensive guide.

The fertile soil of the Finger Lakes area has made it the heart of New York's wine industry. Three designated **wine trails** provide opportunities for wine tasting and vineyard touring; locals say that the fall harvest is the best time to visit. The ten vineyards closest to Ithaca lie on the **Cayuga Trail,** with most located along Rte. 89 between Seneca Falls and Ithaca; call 800-684-5217 for info. The Finger Lakes Association (see **Practical Information,** above) has info on the **Seneca Lake Trail,** 21 wineries on the east side (Rte. 414) and west side (Rte. 14) of the lake, and the **Keuka Trail,** seven wineries along Rte. 54 and Rte. 76. Some wineries offer free picnic facilities and tours. All give free tastings; some require purchase of a glass ($2).

⊠ **NIGHTLIFE.** The area near Cornell called Collegetown, centering on College Ave., harbors student hangouts and access to a romantic path along the gorge. A smoky, red-walled cafe, **Stella's**, 403 College Ave., wears its pretension well. The dazzling $2.55 Italian soda with heavy cream and a few martinis might encourage you to strut your stuff at Stella's adjoining blue-walled jazz bar. (☎277-8731. Restaurant open daily 7am-1:30am; in summer M-F 8am-1am, Sa-Su 10am-1am. Jazz bar open daily 11am-1am.) Downtown, live bands and hip hop acts perform at **The Haunt**, 702 Willow Ave. (☎275-3447; 18+; small cover charge). High-minded moviegoers head to the **Cornell Cinema**, 104 Willard Straight Hall on the Cornell campus, a traditional art-house theater with thrilling programming and prices, (☎255-3522. Tickets $4.50; seniors, students, and under 12 $4.) A favorite among Cornell students, **Ruloff's**, 411 College St., exudes that classic college bar type of atmosphere. At half past midnight, the bartender spins the "wheel of fortune" to pick the late-night drink special. (☎272-6067. Open M-Sa 11:30am-1am, Su 10am-1am.)

BUFFALO   ☎716

Girded by steel and concrete highways, Buffalo is a big, furry, overgrown town in a high-rise disguise. Fiery chicken wings and electric blues bands burn off the lingering pain of the Bills' four recent Super Bowl defeats and the minor-league status of Bison baseball. From the downtown skyline to the small-scale pastel charm of historic Allentown, Buffalo trades the cosmopolitan for honest, modern Americana.

⚀ **PRACTICAL INFORMATION.** Greyhound (☎855-7533 and 800-231-2222; station open 24hr.) buses from 181 Ellicott St. at N. Division St. To: New York (8½hr., 15 per day, $65); Boston (11½hr., 10 per day, $57); Niagara Falls, ON (1hr., 11 per day, $4); and Toronto (2½hr., 12 per day, $16). **Amtrak** (☎856-2075; office open M-F 7am-3:30pm) leaves from 75 Exchange St. at Washington St. for New York (8hr., 3 per day, $59) and Toronto (4hr., 1 per day, $16). The **Niagara Frontier Transit Authority (NFTA)** (☎855-7211 or 283-9319) offers bus and rail service throughout the city (fare $1.25), as well as free rides on the Main St. Metrorail and service to Niagara Falls (bus #40 "Grand Island" leaves from 181 Ellicott St.; 13 per day; fare $1.85, seniors and ages 5-11 85¢). **Taxi:** Cheektowaga Taxi (☎822-1738). **Visitors Center:** 617 Main St., in the Theater District. (☎852-2356 or 800-283-3256. Open M-F 9am-5pm, Sa-Su 10am-2pm. Tour $5.) **Post Office:** 701 Washington St. (☎856-4604; open M-F 8:30am-5:30pm, Sa 8:30am-1pm). **ZIP code:** 14203. **Area code:** 716.

⚐ **ACCOMMODATIONS.** The **Buffalo Hostel (HI-AYH)**, 667 Main St., houses 48 beds and spotless floors in a safe neighborhood downtown. Friendly staff lead frequent group outings and make travelers feel at home. (☎852-5222. Free linen, access to microwave, pool table, laundry facilities. Reception daily 8-11am and 4pm-midnight. Dorms $19, nonmembers $22.) Otherwise, budget lodgings are a rarity in Buffalo; **chain motels** congregate around the airport and I-90 8 to 10 mi. northeast of downtown. See **Niagara Falls** (p. 246) for campsites in the area.

⊡⊠ **FOOD AND NIGHTLIFE.** Frank and Teressa's Anchor Bar, 1047 Main St., serves up the original Buffalo Wing, invented here in 1964. (☎886-8920. 10 wings $6, 20 wings $10. Open Su noon-11pm, M-Th 11am-11pm, F-Sa 11am-1am.) Among the cute, boxy buildings of Allentown, the gothic facade of **Gabriel's Gate**, 145 Allen St., doesn't frighten its lunch crowd, which feasts on taco salads ($5.45) or garden souvlaki ($6) under stuffed mooseheads or on the shaded patio. (☎886-0602. Open Su-Th 11:30am-1am, F-Sa 11:30am-2am.) The city's surprisingly lively nightlife centers on **Chippewa St.** and **Franklin St.**, and on **Elmwood Ave.** The *Buffalo Beat* has event listings. **The Calumet Arts Cafe**, 56 W. Chippewa St., plays live jazz and blues on the weekends. (☎855-2220. Open M-W 5:30-10pm, Th-Sa 5:30pm-4am.) **City SPoT**, on the corner of Delaware and Chippewa St., is the hip place to go for a wide array of cheap coffee and tea concoctions. (☎856-2739. Open 24hr.)

SIGHTS AND ENTERTAINMENT. The **Albright Knox Art Gallery,** 1285 Elmwood Ave., bus #32 "Niagara," houses over 6000 modern pieces, including a wonderful collection of Abstract Expressionist works. (☎882-8700. Open Tu-Sa 11am-5pm, Su noon-5pm. $5, seniors and students $4, families $10; free Sa 11am-1pm.) At the **Naval and Military Park,** on Lake Erie at the foot of Pearl and Main St., visitors can climb aboard a guided missile cruiser, a destroyer, and a WWII submarine. (☎847-1773. Open Apr.-Oct. daily 10am-5pm; Nov. Sa-Su 10am-4pm. $6, seniors and ages 6-16 $3.50.) An 1881 floating marine bicycle swims among the 300-piece collection at the **Pedaling History Bicycle Museum,** 3943 N. Buffalo Rd., Rte. 240/277 in Orchard Park, 12 mi. southeast of Buffalo. (☎662-3853. Open M-Sa 11am-5pm, Su 1:30-5pm; mid-Jan. to early Apr. M and F-Sa 11am-5pm, Su 1:30-5pm. $4.50, seniors $4, ages 7-15 $2.50, families $12.50.)

In winter, **Rich Stadium** (☎649-0015), in Orchard Park, hosts the four-time Super Bowl loser **Buffalo Bills.** The **HSBC Arena,** 1 Seymour H. Knox III Plaza (☎855-4000), is where hockey's **Buffalo Sabres,** who lost in the Stanley Cup Finals in 1999, slap the puck. The summer brings family fun with **Buffalo Bison** baseball (☎846-2000) at **Dunn Tire Park,** on Swan St. From I-90, take the Elm St. exit.

NIAGARA FALLS ☎716

One of the seven natural wonders of the world, Niagara Falls also claims the title of one of the world's largest sources of hydroelectric power and daredevil risk-takers. Since 1901, when a 63-year-old schoolteacher, Annie Taylor, was the first to survive the beer-barrel plunge, the Falls have attracted many thrill-seekers. Modern day Taylors beware—heavy fines and possible death await the daring. For those of a sounder mind, outlet shopping, cheap motels, and neon lights cram the streets.

TRANSPORTATION

Trains: Amtrak (☎285-4224), at 27th and Lockport St. 1 block east of Hyde Park Blvd. Take bus #52 to Falls/Downtown. To New York City ($60) and Toronto ($16). Open Th-M 7am-11pm, Tu-W 7am-3pm.

Buses: Niagara Falls Bus Terminal (☎282-1331), 4th and Niagara St., sells **Greyhound** tickets for use in Buffalo. Open M-F 9am-4pm, Sa-Su 9am-noon. To get a bus in Buffalo, take a 1hr. trip on bus #40 from the Niagara Falls bus terminal to the **Buffalo Transportation Center,** 181 Ellicott St. (see Buffalo **Practical Information,** p. 245).

Public Transit: Niagara Frontier Metro Transit System, 343 4th St. (☎285-9319), provides local city transit. Fare $1.25. **ITA Buffalo Shuttle** (☎800-551-9369) has service from Niagara Falls info center and major hotels to Buffalo Airport ($22).

Taxis: Blue United Cab, ☎285-9331. **Niagara Falls Taxi** in Canada, ☎905-357-4000.

ORIENTATION AND PRACTICAL INFORMATION

Niagara Falls spans the US-Canadian border; addresses given here are in NY, unless noted. Take **U.S. 190** to the Robert Moses Pkwy., or else skirt the tolls (but suffer traffic) by taking Exit 3 to Rte. 62. In town, Niagara St. is the main east-west artery, ending in the west at **Rainbow Bridge,** which crosses to Canada (pedestrian crossings 25¢, cars $2.50). Numbered north-south streets increase toward the east. Outside of town, stores, restaurants, and motels line **Rte. 62 (Niagara Falls Blvd.)** Customs procedures, though relaxed, are inevitable when crossing the border. Many places in the Niagara area accept both American and Canadian currency.

Visitor info: Orin Lehman Visitors Center (☎278-1796), in front of the Falls' observation deck; the entrance is marked by a garden. Open daily May-Sept. 8am-6:15pm; Oct. to mid-Nov. 8am-8pm; mid-Nov. to Dec. 8am-10pm; Jan.-Apr. 8am-6:15pm. An **info center** (☎284-2000) adjoins the bus station on 4th and Niagara St., a 10min. walk from the Falls. Open daily 8:30am-7:30pm; mid-Sept. to mid-May 9am-5pm. **Niagara**

Falls Tourism, 5515 Stanley Ave., ON L2G 3X4 (☎905-356-6061; www.discoverniagara.com), has info on the Canadian side. Open daily 8am-8pm; off-season 8am-6pm. On the Canadian side, tune in to 105.1FM CFL2 for tourist info.

Post Office: 615 Main St. (☎285-7561). Open M-F 7:30am-5pm, Sa 8:30am-2pm. **ZIP code:** 14302. **Area code:** 716 (NY), 905 (ON). In text, 716 unless otherwise noted.

▌ ACCOMMODATIONS

Many newlyweds spend part of their honeymoon by the awesome beauty of the Falls, which are especially romantic at night. Cheap motels (from $25) advertising free wedding certificates line **Lundy's Lane** on the Canadian side and **Rte. 62** on the American side, while many moderately priced B&Bs overlook the gorge on **River Rd.** between the Rainbow Bridge and the Whirlpool Bridge on the Canadian side. Reservations are always recommended.

Niagara Falls International Hostel (HI-C), 4549 Cataract Ave. (☎905-357-0770 or 888-749-0058), Niagara Falls, ON, just off Bridge St. An excellent hostel in a former brothel near the Falls, about 2 blocks from the bus station and VIA Rail. 88 beds; can be cramped when full, but the staff is friendly, funky, and casual. Family rooms, laundry facilities, Internet access, pub crawls, nature hikes, barbecues, and parking. Check-out 10am. Reception 24hr. CDN$18, nonmembers CDN$22. Linen CDN$1.

Niagara Falls International Hostel (HI-AYH), 1101 Ferry Ave. (☎282-3700). From bus station, walk east on Niagara St., turn left onto Memorial Pkwy.; the hostel is at the corner of Ferry Ave. *From the Falls, avoid walking alone on Ferry Ave. at night.* 44 beds in a friendly old house. Kitchen, TV lounge, limited parking. Family rooms available. Open Feb. to mid-Dec. Linen $1.50. Check-in 7:30-9:30am and 4-11pm. Lockout 9:30am-4pm. Curfew 11:30pm; lights out midnight. Dorms $14, nonmembers $17.

Olde Niagara House, 610 4th St. (☎285-9408). A country B&B just 4 blocks from the falls. Dorms $18-20 per person. Rooms with breakfast $45-55; in winter $35-45; student singles $25-45/$25-35.

All Tucked Inn, 574 3rd St. (☎282-0919 or 800-797-0919). Clean, nicely colored rooms with shared baths. Common TV room. Singles from $39; doubles from $59. Off-season $27/49. Continental breakfast included; discounts for *Let's Go* toters.

YMCA, 1317 Portage Rd. (☎285-8491), a 20min. walk from the Falls; at night take bus #54 from Main St. 58 beds. Fee includes full use of YMCA facilities; no laundry. Key deposit $10. Check-in 24hr. Dorm rooms for men only; singles $25, $96 weekly. Men and women can sleep on mats in the gym for $15.

Niagara Glen-View Tent & Trailer Park, 3950 Victoria Ave. (☎800-263-2570), Niagara Falls, ON. Close to the Falls, hiking trail across the street. Ice, showers, laundry facilities, pool. Shuttle from driveway to the foot of Clifton Hill in summer every 30min. 8:45am-2am. Sites CDN$35, with hookup CDN$42 from June-Sept.; $28/$35 May and Oct. Office open daily 8am-11pm. Park open May to mid-Oct.

▐ FOOD

A favorite among backpackers, **The Press Box Restaurant,** 324 Niagara St., stuffs their sacks with filling meals at astoundingly low prices. On Mondays, feast on buffalo wings for a mere 15¢ apiece. (☎284-5447. Open daily 9am-11pm.) **Sardar Sahib,** 626 Niagara St., serves authentic and filling Indian food, emphasizing vegetarian specialities. (☎282-0444. Open daily 11:30am-midnight. Entrees $10 or less.) On the Canadian side, the restaurants on **Victoria Ave.** by Clifton Hill are touristy but inexpensive. **Simon's Restaurant,** 4116 Bridge St., ON, serves big breakfasts with giant homemade muffins (CDN69¢) and hearty, homestyle dinners. (☎905-356-5310. Open M-Sa 5:30am-8pm, Su 5:30am-2pm.) **The Peninsula Bakery and Restaurant,** 4568 Erie Ave., ON, off Bridge St., has authentic Pan-Asian food. (☎905-374-8176. Open M 10:30am-7pm, Tu-Su 10:30am-10pm. Malaysian stir-fried noodles CDN$7.50.)

⊙ SIGHTS

Although tourist snares abound on both sides, they're less rampant on the American shore. Official sights give more bang for your buck. From late November to mid-January, Niagara Falls holds the **Festival of Lights** (☎905-374-1616), combining snow, ice, and spray from the Falls with concerts, fireworks, and night parades for a wondrous wintertime spectacle.

AMERICAN SIDE. The **Maid of the Mist Tour** is an exhilarating, drenching 30min. boat ride to the foot of both falls that has been thrilling tourists for over 150 years. *(☎284-4233. Tours in summer every 30min. M-Th. Open daily 10am-6pm. $8.50 plus 50¢ elevator fee, ages 6-12 $4.80.)* The **Caves of the Wind Tour** lends out yellow raincoats for an exciting body-soaking hike to the base of the Bridal Veil Falls, including an optional walk to Hurricane Deck, where gale-force waves slam down on you from above. *(☎278-1730. Open May to mid-Oct.; hours vary depending on season and weather conditions. Trips leave every 15min. $6, ages 6-12 $5.50. Must be at least 42 in.)* For the less adventurous, **Niagara Wonders,** a 20min. movie on the Falls, plays in the info center. *(☎278-1783. Shows daily every 45min. 9am-9pm; in fall M-Su 10am-6pm. $2, ages 6-12 $1.)*

The **Master Pass,** available at the park's Visitors Center, covers admission to the theater, Maid of the Mist, **Schoellkopf's Geological Museum** in Prospect Park (home of the "greatest rock and flow story ever told"), a modest **Aquarium,** and the **Viewmobile,** a tram-guided tour of the park. *(Master Pass $24, ages 6-12 $17. Museum: ☎278-1780. Open daily May-Sept. 9am-7pm, Apr.-May and Sept.-Oct. 9am-5pm. $1. Dramatic film every 30min. Aquarium: 701 Whirlpool St. ☎285-3575. Open daily 9am-7pm. $6.75, ages 4-12 $4.75. Viewmobile: ☎278-1730. Runs daily every 15min. Su-Th 10am-8pm, F-Sa 10am-10pm. $4.50, children $3.50.)*

Continuing north, the **Niagara Power Project** features interactive demonstrations, videos, and displays on energy, hydropower, and local history. While there, you can cast off the fishing platform to reel in salmon, trout, or bass. *(5777 Lewiston Rd. ☎286-6661. Open daily 9am-5pm. Free.)* Further north in Lewiston, NY, the 200-acre state **Artpark**, at the foot of 4th St., focuses on visual and performing arts, with a variety of demonstrations. The theater presents opera, pops concerts, and rock shows. *(☎800-659-7275. Shows May-Dec.; call for schedule. Box office open M-F 9am-5pm, later on event days. Tickets $15-33.)* **Old Fort Niagara,** a French castle built in 1726, guards the entrance to the Niagara River and is now a prime picnic spot. A series of special re-enactments throughout the summer brings the fort back to 18th-century life. *(☎745-7611. Follow Robert Moses Pkwy. north from Niagara Falls. Open daily June-Aug. 9am-5:30pm; hours vary off-season. $6.75, seniors $5.50, ages 6-12 $4.50.)*

CANADIAN SIDE. On the Canadian side of Niagara Falls (across Rainbow Bridge), **Queen Victoria Park** provides the best view of Horseshoe Falls. The Falls are illuminated for 3hr. every night, starting 1hr. after sunset. Parking in Queen Victoria is expensive (CDN$9.75). **Park 'N' Ride** is a better deal, offering parking at Rapids View, across from Marineland at the south end of Niagara Pkwy. **People Movers** buses efficiently and comfortably take you through the 30km area on the Canadian side of the Falls, stopping at attractions along the way. *(☎357-9340. Mid-June to early Sept. daily 9am-11pm; hours vary off season. CDN$5.50, children CDN$3.)* Bikers, in-line skaters, and walkers enjoy the 32km **Niagara River Recreation Trail,** which runs from Fort Erie to Fort George and passes many interesting historical sights.

High above the crowds and excitement, **Skylon Tower** has the highest view of the falls at 236m; on a clear day, you can see as far as Toronto. Its 159m **Observation Deck** offers a calming, unhindered view of the falls above the swarms of tourists. *(5200 Robinson St. ☎356-2651. Open daily 8am-11:30pm; in winter hours change monthly. CDN$9, seniors CDN$8, children CDN$4.50.)* The **Discovery Pass** includes passage to **Journey Behind the Falls,** a tour behind Horseshoe Falls; **Great Gorge Adventure,** a long boardwalk next to the famous Niagara River Rapids, home to many lucky and not-so-lucky daredevils over the years; the **Spanish Aero Car,** an aerial cable ride over the whirlpool waters; and several other prime attractions. *(Pass: CDN$32, children*

CDN$17. Journey: ☎354-1551. CDN$7, children CDN$3.50. Adventure: ☎374-1221. Open daily mid-June to early Sept. 9am-8:30pm; hours fluctuate off-season. CDN$6, children CDN$3. Aero Car: ☎354-5711. Open year-round but hours vary; in winter, operation often closed due to inclement weather. CDN$6, children CDN$3.)

Commercialism can be as much of a wonder as any natural one. The Canadian side of the falls offers the delightfully tasteless **Clifton Hill,** a collection of wax museums, funhouses, and overpriced shows. **Ripley's Believe It or Not Museum** displays wonders like wax models of unicorn men and a scary selection of medieval torture devices. Unfortunately, the authentic New Guinea Penis Guard, used for protection from hungry mosquitoes, is not for sale. *(4960 Clifton Hill. ☎356-2238. Open during summer daily 9am-2am; hours change off season. CDN$8.50, seniors CDN$6.50, ages 6-12 CDN$4.)*

NORTHERN NEW YORK

THE ADIRONDACKS   ☎518

In 1892, the New York State legislature demonstrated uncommon foresight, establishing the **Adirondacks State Park,** the largest US park outside Alaska and one of the few places left in the Northeast where hikers can spend days without seeing another soul. Unfortunately, increased pollution and development in recent years have damaged fish and tree populations, alerting locals and naturalists to the fragility of a seemingly immortal ecosystem. Despite this human intrusion, much of the area retains the splendor that has awed visitors for over a century.

🛈 PRACTICAL INFORMATION. The **Adirondack Mountain Club (ADK)** is the best source of info on outdoor activities in the region. Its offices are located at 814 Goggins Rd., Lake George 12845 (☎668-4447; open M-Sa 8:30am-5pm; Jan.-Apr. M-F 8:30am-4:30pm), and at Adirondack Loj Rd., P.O. Box 867, Lake Placid 12946 (☎523-3441; open Sa-Th 8am-8pm, F 8am-10pm), adjoining the Adirondack Loj. Call the Lake Placid number for the scoop on outdoor skills classes such as canoeing, rock climbing, whitewater kayaking, and wilderness medicine. For the latest backcountry info, visit ADK's **High Peaks Information Center,** 3 mi. east of Lake Placid on Rte. 73, then 5 mi. down Adirondack Loj Rd. The center also has washrooms and sells basic outdoor equipment, trail snacks, and a variety of extremely helpful guides to the mountains for $11-25. (Open M-Th 8am-5pm, F 8am-10pm, Sa-Su 8am-8pm.) Rock climbers should consult the experienced staff at the **Mountaineer** in Keene Valley, between I-87 and Lake Placid on Rte. 73. Snowshoes rent for $16 per day; ice-climbing boots and crampons $20 per day; rock shoes $12 per day. (☎576-2281. Open Su-Th 9am-5:30pm, F 9am-7pm, Sa 8am-7pm; off-season M-F 9am-5:30pm, Sa 8am-5:30pm, Su 10am-5:30pm.) The ADK and the Mountaineer can provide basic info on the conditions and concerns of backwoods travel.

Adirondacks Trailways (☎800-858-8555) services the region. From Albany, buses set out for Lake Placid and Lake George. From the Lake George bus stop at Lake George Hardware, 35 Montcalm St., buses go to Lake Placid (2 per day, $14.40); Albany (4 per day, $11); and New York City (5 per day, $42). **Area code:** 518.

🛏 ACCOMMODATIONS. The ADK also runs two lodges near Lake Placid. The ▧**Adirondack Loj** lures hikers off the trails with its cozy atmosphere. Situated on Heart Lake, the log cabin has 38 bunks and a den decorated with deer and moose trophies and warmed by an imposing fieldstone fireplace. In summer, guests swim, fish, and canoe on the premises (canoe or kayak rental $5 per hr., guests $3); in winter, they explore the wilderness trails by renting snowshoes for $10 per day or cross-country skis for $20. (☎523-3441. Breakfast included, lunch $4.50, dinner $14. Reservations highly recommended. Bunks $32; private room $52. Lean-tos, campsites, and cabins also available.) For a more rustic experience, hike 3½ mi. from the closest trailhead to the **John's Brook Lodge** in Keene Valley (call the Adirondack Loj for reservations); from Lake Placid, follow Rte. 73 15 mi. through Keene to Keene

Valley and turn right at the Ausable Inn. The hike runs slightly uphill, but the meal that awaits you will reward the effort. A great place to meet friendly New Yorkers, John's Brook is no secret; beds fill completely on weekends. Make reservations one day in advance for dinner, earlier for a weekend. Bring sheets or a sleeping bag. (Rates start at $30 for a bunk July to early Sept.; dinner $14.)

Free camping is easy to come by. Inquire about the location of free trailside shelters before you plan a hike in the forest, or camp for free anywhere on public land in the **backcountry** as long as you are at least 150 ft. away from a trail, road, water source, or campground and below 4000 ft. in altitude. The State Office of Parks and Recreation (see New York **Practical Information,** p. 201) has more details.

◪ **SIGHTS AND ACTIVITIES.** Of the six million acres in the Adirondacks Park, 40% are open to the public, offering a slew of outdoor activities. The 2000 mi. of winding trails that pass through the forest provide spectacular mountain scenery for hikers, snowshoers, and cross-country skiers; the rivers and streams that cross the mountains offer canoers and whitewater rafters the same, as well as the adventure of seasonal rapids. The hard-core outdoor enthusiast might consider conquering Mt. Marcy, the state's highest peak (5344 ft.), or taking advantage of a dozen well known alpine centers. For those who prefer spectator sports, the town of Lake Placid, venue of the 1932 and 1980 winter Olympic Games, frequently hosts national and international competitions. Tupper Lake and Lake George have carnivals every January and February; Tupper also hosts the **Tin Man Triathlon** in mid-July. In September, the hot air balloons of the **Adirondack Balloon Festival** paint the sky over Glens Falls.

LAKE PLACID ☎518

Tucked away beneath the High Peaks Mountains, Lake Placid lives and breathes winter sports. Host to the Olympic Winter Games in both 1932 and 1980, this modest town has seen thousands of pilgrims and, aside from the manifold motels, has remained charmingly untainted by its popularity. World-class athletes train year-round in the town's extensive facilities, lending an international flavor which distinguishes Lake Placid from its Adirondack neighbors. The setting of the Adirondack High Peaks Region attracts droves of hikers and backpackers each year, although many would-be campers end up pitching their tents in a motel room—in the winter, temperatures can dip down to -40° F.

◪ **PRACTICAL INFORMATION.** Lake Placid sits at the intersection of Rte. 86 and Rte. 73. The town's Olympic past defines the Lake Placid of today; the **Olympic Regional Development Authority,** 216 Main St., Olympic Center, operates the sporting facilities. (☎523-1655 or 800-462-6236. Open M-F 8:30am-4pm.) Find info on food, lodging, and area attractions at the **Lake Placid-Essex County Visitors Bureau,** also in the Olympic Center. (☎523-2445; www.lakeplacid.com. Open daily 9am-5pm; winter closed Su.) **Adirondack Trailways** (☎800-225-6815 for bus info) stops at Lake Placid Video, 324 Main St., and has extensive service in the area. Destinations include New York City ($62) and Lake George ($15). **Weather info:** ☎523-1363. **Internet access:** Lake Placid Public Library, 67 Main St. (☎523-3200; open M-F 11am-5pm, Sa 11am-4pm). **Post Office:** 201 Main St. (☎523-3071; open M-F 8:30am-5pm, Sa 8:30am-2pm). **ZIP code:** 12946. **Area code:** 518.

◪ **ACCOMMODATIONS.** If you avoid the resorts on the west end of town, both lodgings and food can be had cheaply in Lake Placid. The **White Sled,** 3½ mi. east of town on Rte. 73, has a standard bunkhouse with 38 beds, three bathrooms, kitchen and barbecue facilities, and cable TV. For a little more, sleep in one of 15 motel rooms or rent the ten-bed cottage. The owner can provide visitors with information on Lake Placid and the Adirondacks, and if you're lucky, she will prepare her specialty, blueberry buckle. (☎523-9314. Bunks $18; motel rooms from $55.) If you prefer to stay right in town, the **High Peaks Hostel** offers slightly more crowded living quarters with Olympic proximity and a higher price. Located at 337½ Main St., across from the bowling alley and just a few blocks from Olympic Center, the hostel has kitchen facilities, a TV, a common room, and 14 bunks in two rooms. (☎ 523-3764. $20.) **Meadowbrook State Park,** 5 mi. west of town on Rte. 86 in Ray Brook, and **Wilmington Notch State Campground,** about 8 mi. east of Lake Placid on Rte. 86, are the region's best camping areas, although they may disappoint those who anticipate pristine Adirondack splendor. Both offer shady, wooded sites which accommodate two tents without hookups. (Meadowbrook ☎ 891-4351. Sites $10. Wilmington Notch ☎ 946-7172. Sites $12, $2.75 surcharge for a first time registration.) Unquestionably one of the state's most beautiful campgrounds, **Ausable Point** is located an hour from Lake Placid, 12 mi. south of Plattsburgh on Rte. 9, situated right on Lake Champlain. (☎ 561-7080. $16, $19 with electricity; $2.50 surcharge for first time registration.) For reservations at any New York State campground, call 800-456-2267.

🄲 **FOOD.** Lake Placid Village, concentrated primarily along Main St., has a number of reasonably priced dining establishments. Glut at the **Hilton Hotel's** lunch buffet, 1 Mirror Lake Drive, which includes sandwiches, soups, salads, and a hot entree for only $7.50. (☎ 523-4411. Buffet from noon-2pm.) The **Black Bear Restaurant,** 157 Main St., across from the municipal parking lot, caters to the diets of athletes in training, dishing out organic foods, vegetarian and vegan sandwiches, and smoothies. Daily specials ($6-8) and a hearty breakfast ($3-6) or lunch ($6) will leave both your stomach and your wallet full. (☎ 523-9886. Open 6am-10pm, depending on the crowd.) **The Cottage,** 5 Mirror Lake Dr., offers a spectacular view of Mirror Lake, where you can sometimes catch the US national canoeing or kayaking teams at practice. The awesome sandwiches and salads are all under $8. (☎ 523-9845. Food served 11:30am-10pm; bar open 11:30am-midnight or 1am, depending on crowd.) **Mud Puddles,** 3 School St., is one of Lake Placid's few late-night hot spots. (☎ 523-4446. No cover M-F; Sa-Su $3. Open 8am-3am.)

🄶 **SIGHTS.** If you're planning to visit most of Lake Placid's Olympic attractions, the **Olympic Sites Passport** is your best bargain. For $17 per person, the pass includes entrance to the **Olympic Jumping Complex** (including chairlift and elevator ride), the **Mt. Van Hoevenberg Sports Complex,** the **Winter Olympic Museum,** and choice of either the **Scenic Gondola Ride** to the top of Little Whiteface or access to the **Veterans Memorial Highway** that climbs Whiteface Mt. Purchase at any Olympic venue or at the Olympic Center Box Office (☎ 523-1655 or 800-462-6236).

The **Olympic Center** in downtown Lake Placid houses the 1932 and 1980 hockey arenas, as well as the petite, memorabilia-stuffed **Winter Sports Museum.** The museum features an eight-minute intro video to Lake Placid and its Olympic history. (☎ 523-1655, ext. 226. Open daily 10am-5pm. $4, seniors $3, children under 6 $2.) Purchase tickets for a guided tour of the **Olympic Ski Jumps,** which, along with the **Kodak Sports Park,** make up the **Olympic Jumping Complex,** just east of town on Rte. 73. Admission gets you a chairlift and elevator ride to the top, where you can watch summertime jumpers soaring off the AstroTurf-covered Olympic ramp into a swimming pool. (Open 9am-4pm. $8, seniors and children $5.) About 5 mi. east of town on Rte. 73, the **Olympic Sports Complex** (☎ 523-4436) at Mt. Van Hoevenberg offers bobsled rides down the actual Olympic track, no matter the season. In colder weather, the bobsleds run on ice and will set you back a chilly $30 per ride; in warmer weather, the sleds grow wheels and, oddly enough, cost only $25 per ride. While at the complex, consider whipping yourself into shape Olympian-style by taking a **mountain bike** run down one of the several cross-country ski paths. Bike rentals are available inside the complex. (☎ 523-2811. Open daily mid-June to early Sept.; on weekends early Sept. to early Oct. Bikes $10-40 per day; required helmet $3 per day.) Popular **Tour Boat Cruises** travel 16 narrated miles across Lake Placid on turn-of-the-century crafts. Glimpse at impressive estates accessible by vehicles only in the winter when the lake partially recedes and locals drive across. (☎ 523-9704. Cruises depart daily at 10:30am and 2:30pm; Sa-Su 10:30am, 2:30, and 4pm. $7.25, seniors $6.25, children $5.25.) For a bird's eye view, drive up Whiteface

Mountain on the **Veterans Memorial Highway** just 11 mi. east of Lake Placid on Rte. 86. The alpine-style tollbooth at the bottom of the hill has info about the highway and is the starting point for a self-guided nature walk. Stop at one or two of the many parking areas on your way up for spectacular mountain vistas before reaching the observatory at the summit. (☎946-7175. Open daily mid-May through early Oct. 8:30am-5pm, longer if weather permits. $8 car and driver; $5 motorcycle and driver; $4 each passenger.) Best saved until after you have safely traversed the mountains, the tasting room of **Swedish Hill Winery,** 1 mi. east of downtown on Rte. 73, pours up 16 selections of locally produced award-winning wine. (☎523-2498. Open M-Sa 10am-6pm, Su noon-6pm. $3.)

THOUSAND ISLAND SEAWAY ☎315

The Thousand Island region of the St. Lawrence Seaway spans 100 mi. from the mouth of Lake Ontario to the first of the many locks on the St. Lawrence River, forming a natural US-Canadian border. Although lucky Canada scored two-thirds of the islands when the two nations first parcelled them out, the US took the larger islands, thus laying claim to 50% of the total area. Surveys conducted by the US and Canadian governments determined that there are over 1700 islands in the seaway. The requirements for being an island stipulated that at least one square foot of land should sit above water year-round and at least one tree should grow on it. These islands and countless rocky shoals make navigation tricky in the area. Locals divide people into two groups: those who *have* hit a shoal and those who *will* hit a shoal. But don't let this dire prediction deter you; not only is the Thousand Island region a fisherman's paradise with some of the world's best bass and muskie catch, it's the only area in the nation with a salad dressing named after it.

⁊ PRACTICAL INFORMATION. The Thousand Island region hugs the St. Lawrence just 2hr. from Syracuse by way of I-81 N. From south to north, **Cape Vincent, Clayton,** and **Alexandria Bay** ("Alex Bay" to locals) are the main towns in the area, although Alex Bay is by far the most cosmopolitan of the three. For Wellesley Island, Alexandria Bay, and the eastern 500 islands, stay on I-81 until you reach Rte. 12 E. For Clayton and points west, take Exit 47 and follow Rte. 12 until you reach Rte. 12 E. The **Clayton Chamber of Commerce,** 510 Riverside Dr., Clayton 13624, has the free *Clayton Vacation Guide* and *Thousand Islands Seaway Region Travel Guide.* (☎686-3771. Open daily mid-June to mid-Sept. 9am-4pm, mid-Sept. to mid-June M-F 9am-4pm). The **Alexandria Bay Chamber of Commerce,** 11 Market St., Alexandria Bay 13607, is just off James St. (☎482-9531. Open May to Sept. daily 8am-6pm.) The **Cape Vincent Chamber of Commerce** welcomes visitors at 175 James St., by the ferry landing. (☎654-2481. Open May-Oct. Tu-Sa 9am-5pm; also late May to early Sept. Su-M 10am-4pm.) **Greyhound,** 540 State St. in Watertown (open M-F 8:30am-1pm and 3-5pm; Sa-Su only at departure times), runs to New York City (7½hr., 2 per day, $47.50); Syracuse (1¾hr., 2 per day, $8.50); and Albany (5hr., 2 per day, $36). **Thousand Islands Bus Lines** leaves for Alexandria Bay and Clayton from the same station, M-F at 1pm (☎287-2782; $5.60 to Alexandria, $3.55 to Clayton); return trips leave Clayton from the **Nutshell Florist,** 234 James St. (☎686-5791), at 8:45am, and Alexandria from the **Dockside Cafe,** 17 Market St. (☎482-9849), at 8:30am. **Internet access: Cape Vincent,** at the corner of Broadway and Real St. (☎654-2132. Open Tu and Th 9am-8pm, Sa-Su 9am-1pm.) Clayton's **Post Office:** 236 John St. (☎686-3311; open M-F 9am-5pm, Sa 9am-noon). **ZIP code:** 13624. Alexandria Bay's **Post Office:** 13 Bethune St. (☎482-9521; open M-F 8:30am-5:30pm, Sa 8:30am-1pm). **ZIP code:** 13607. Cape Vincent's **Post Office:** 362 Broadway St., across from the village green. (☎654-2424. Open M-F 8:30am-1pm and 2-5:30pm, Sa 8:30-11:30am.) **ZIP code:** 13618. **Area code:** 315.

⁊ ACCOMMODATIONS AND CAMPING. The peaceful **Tibbetts Point Lighthouse Hostel (HI-AYH),** 33439 County Rte. 6, along the western edge of the seaway on Cape Vincent, is situated where Lake Ontario meets the St. Lawrence River. Take Rte. 12 E into town, drive straight onto Broadway, and follow the river until the road ends.

The lighthouse is still active, and the hypnotic rhythm of the waves lulls you to sleep at night. (☎654-3450. Open mid-May to Oct. Check-in 5-10pm. 2 houses with 26 beds. Linen $1. Full kitchen with microwave. Dorms $12, nonmembers $15.) **Burnham Point State Park,** on Rte. 12 E, 4 mi. east of Cape Vincent and 11 mi. west of Clayton, sports 52 campsites and three picnic areas. (☎654-2324. Open late May to early Sept. daily 8am-10pm. Showers. Tent sites $13, prime sites on the water $15. Boat dockage $6 for the day, $13 overnight. $2.50 surcharge for each registration. Wheelchair accessible.) **Keewaydin State Park,** just south of Alex Bay, maintains 41 sites along the St. Lawrence River. Campers can take a dip in an Olympic-size swimming pool for free, which may explain why the park teems with tents in the thick of summer. (☎482-3331. Open late May to early Sept. daily 8am-11pm. Pool open 10am-7pm. Showers. Sites $13; $2.50 surcharge.) For reservations at any New York State campground, call 800-456-2267.

◙ EXPLORING THE SEAWAY. Any of the small towns that dot Rte. 12 will serve as a fine base for exploring the region, although Clayton and Cape Vincent tend to be less expensive than Alexandria Bay. **Uncle Sam Boat Tours,** 604 Riverside Dr. (☎686-3511), in Clayton, and on James St. in Alexandria Bay (☎482-2611), delivers the best view of the islands and the plush estates situated atop them, along with a fact-packed live narration and some sage wisdom on shoal-avoidance. Tours highlight **Heart Island** and its famous **Boldt Castle;** they do not cover the price of admission to the castle. (Tourism council: ☎800-847-5263. Uncle Sam: 2¼hr. tours leave daily from Alexandria Bay late Apr. to Oct. $13.50, children 12 and under $6.75. Daily lunch and dinner cruises $20.50-27.50 must be reserved in advance.) Endorsed by maniacal boaters, the **Antique Boat Museum,** 750 Mary St. in Clayton, houses practically every make and model of hardwood, freshwater boat ever conceived. (☎686-4104. Open daily mid-May to mid-Oct. 9am-5pm. $6, seniors $5, students $2, children under 5 free.) **French Creek Marina,** 250 Wahl St. (☎686-3621), off Strawberry Lane, just south of the 12/12E junction, rents 14 ft. fishing boats ($50 per day), launches boats ($5), and provides overnight docking ($20). **Fishing licenses** are available at sporting goods stores or at the **Town Clerk's Office,** 405 Riverside Dr. in Clayton. (☎686-3512. Open M-F 9am-noon and 1-4pm. $11 per day, $20 per 5 days, $35 per season.) No local store rents equipment; bring rods or plan to buy.

CASTLE FOR SALE When the island and the deteriorating Boldt castle were finally purchased, it was not by some famous personality or royal wannabe, but rather by the Thousand Islands Council for the staggering figure of...$1. The stipulations involved in the purchase decreed that the property could never be used for commercial enterprises, so the admission cost visitors pay today contributes to the castle's continual improvement rather than filling its coffers. Ironically, the council has since invested over $15 million in revamping the place. Despite this investment, another clause in the contract prevents the council from ever completing the project. Since George Boldt's architectural dream never materialized during his wife's lifetime, the castle is to remain permanently under construction. (☎482-9724. Open daily mid-May to mid-Oct. 10am-6:30pm. $4.25, ages 6-12 $2.50.)

NEW JERSEY

Travelers who refuse to get off the interstates envision New Jersey as a conglomeration of belching chemical plants and ocean beaches strewn with garbage and gamblers. This false impression belies the quieter delights of the state with the highest ratio of parkland to total land area in the Union. A closer look reveals that there is more to New Jersey than commuters, chemicals, and craps; the interior blooms with fields of corn, tomatoes, and peaches, and placid sandy beaches outline the southern tip of the state. The state shelters quiet hamlets, the Pine Barrens forest, and two world-class universities that clashed in the first ever intercollegiate football game: Rutgers and Princeton. Certainly, Atlantic City is gaudy and glitzy, and the Turnpike remains the zone of the road warrior, but those straying from the path will be pleasantly surprised. Hey, Bruce Springsteen calls it home.

◪ PRACTICAL INFORMATION

Capital: Trenton.

Visitor info: State Division of Tourism, 20 W. State St., P.O. Box 826, Trenton 08625 (☎609-292-2470; www.state.nj.us/travel). **New Jersey Dept. of Environmental Protection and Energy,** 401 E. State St., Trenton 08625 (☎609-292-2797).

Postal Abbreviation: NJ. **Sales Tax:** 6%; no tax on clothing.

ATLANTIC CITY   ☎609

More than any other American city, the geography of Atlantic City is subconsciously implanted into the minds of generations of Americans. For over 50 years, board-gaming strategists have been passing "Go" to collect their $200 and buying properties in efforts to control this coastal city as reincarnated on the *Monopoly* board. The opulence of Boardwalk and Park Place gradually faded into neglect, still visible in decrepit streets and alleys, and then into a megadollar tackiness. Casinos rose from the rubble of the boardwalk in the 1970s, and these days, Atlantic City's beachside hot spot status is assured by the waves of urban professionals looking for a fast buck, quick tan, and maybe even a loose romance. Velvet-lined temples of glitter (each with a dozen restaurants and big-name entertainment) overlook the beach and draw all kinds, from international princes to local paupers.

▛ TRANSPORTATION

Atlantic City lies halfway down New Jersey's eastern seashore, accessible via the **Garden State Pkwy.** and the **Atlantic City Expwy.** and easily reached by train from Philadelphia or New York.

Airport: Atlantic City International (☎645-7895 or 800-892-0354). Located just west of Atlantic City in Pamona. Served by Spirit, USAirways, and Continental.

Trains: Amtrak, at Kirkman Blvd., near Michigan Ave. Follow Kirkman to its end, bear right, and follow the signs. To New York (5½hr., 5 per day, $54). Open daily 6am-10:15pm.

Buses: Greyhound (☎609-340-2000). Buses travel every 30min. between Port Authority (NYC) and most major casinos (2½hr., casino drop-off rates $30 round-trip). Many casinos, in addition to the round-trip discounts, will give gamblers between $15 and $20 in coins upon arrival. (Trump Plaza offers $20 for starting your gambling spree at their casino.) **New Jersey Transit** (☎215-569-3752 or 800-582-5946) offers hourly service between NYC and the transit station on Atlantic Ave. between Michigan and Ohio St. ($25, seniors $11 each way). **Gray Line Tours** (☎800-669-0051) offers daytrips to Atlantic City (3hr.; $22 on weekdays, $24 on weekends). Your receipt is redeemable for cash, chips, or food from casinos when you arrive. The bus drops riders at the casino and picks you up later the same day. Call for nearest NYC bus pickup locations. Call 800-995-8898 for info about economical overnight packages. Terminal open 24hr.

✴◪ ORIENTATION AND PRACTICAL INFORMATION

Attractions cluster on and around the Boardwalk, which runs east-west along the Atlantic Ocean. Running parallel to the Boardwalk, Pacific and Atlantic Ave. offer cheap restaurants, hotels, and convenience stores. *Atlantic Ave. can be dangerous after dark, and any street farther out can be dangerous even by day.* Getting around is easy on foot and more pleasant on the boardwalk than in the neighborhoods. **Parking** at the Sands Hotel is free, but "for patrons only," so spend a dollar at the slots. Lots near the boards run $3-7.

Visitor info: Atlantic City Convention Center and Visitors Bureau, 2314 Pacific Ave. (☎888-228-4748). Open daily 11am-7pm. Another Visitors Center is on the Atlantic Expwy. approx. 1 mi. after the Pleasantville Toll Plaza. Open daily 9am-5pm.

Hospital: Atlantic City Medical Center (☎344-4081), at Michigan and Pacific Ave.

Hotlines: Rape and Abuse Hotline, ☎646-6767. 24hr. **Gambling Abuse,** ☎800-426-2537. 24hr. **AIDS Hotline,** ☎800-281-2437.

Post Office: Illinois and Pacific Ave. (☎345-4212). **ZIP code:** 08401. **Area code:** 609.

ACCOMMODATIONS

Large, red-carpeted, and overpriced beachfront hotels have bumped smaller operators a few streets back. Smaller, privately owned hotels along **Pacific Ave.,** one block from the Boardwalk, charge about $60-95 in the summer, when the local population surges to 250,000. Reserve ahead, especially on weekends, or face the plight of forking over all your blackjack earnings for mediocre lodging. Many hotels lower their rates mid-week and in winter, when water temperature and gambling fervor drop significantly. If you have a car, it pays to stay in **Absecon,** about 8 mi. from Atlantic City; Exit 40 from the Garden State Pkwy. leads to Rte. 30 and cheap rooms.

Inn of the Irish Pub, 164 St. James Pl. (☎344-9963), near the Ramada Tower just off the Boardwalk, has spacious, clean rooms with floral wall designs: the best budget accommodations in town. Porch is equipped with relaxing rocking chairs and refreshing Atlantic breeze. There's never a dull night in the house as the downstairs bar offers lively entertainment. Coin-op laundry in hotel next door. Key deposit $5. Doubles with shared bath $53-65, with private bath $75-85; quad with shared bath $85-99.

Comfort Inn, 154 South Kentucky Ave. (☎348-4000 or 888-247-5337), near the Sands. Basic rooms with king size or 2 queen size beds and, true to Atlantic City swank, a jacuzzi. Breakfast, free parking, and a heated pool. Sept.-May $59, June $69-79, July $89, Aug. $99, early Sept. $69. Rooms with ocean views $20 extra, but come with fridge, microwave, and a bigger jacuzzi. Call well in advance for Sa-Su and holidays.

Seacomber Motel, 1630 Albany Ave. (☎348-3171). A bit out of the way—right off the Atlantic Expwy. on the way into town—the Seacomber has standard, uninspiring rooms but provides free shuttle to boardwalk and casinos. Daily room service, cable/HBO, restaurant in lobby. Doubles $39-59; quads $55-79; all with private bath. *Be careful in the surrounding neighborhood after dark.*

Shady Pines Campground, 443 S. 6th Ave., in Absecon (☎652-1516), 6 mi. from Atlantic City; take Exit 12 from the Expwy. This leafy, 140-site campground also sports a pool, playground, laundry and firewood service, and new showers and restrooms. Open Mar.-Nov. Sites $26, with water and electricity $29.

FOOD

The food in Atlantic City is, for the most part, reasonable. Although not recommended by nutritionists, 75¢ hot dogs and $1.50 pizza slices crowd the Boardwalk. Some of the best deals in town await at the casinos, where all-you-can-eat lunch ($7) and dinner ($11) buffets lie in wait. Less tacky and more tasty food can be found a little further from the seashore. For the scoop on local dining, pick up a copy of *Shorecast Insider's Guide at the Shore* or *Whoot* (both free). For real deal-seekers, loiter in casinos and score the free snacks provided to high rollers.

Atlantic City's most affordable eats are a mere flight of stairs away from the otherwise pricey town's cheapest beds. At one of the few AC spots where locals rule, the **Inn of the Irish Pub,** 164 St. James Pl., no item on the menu exceeds $6. The lunch special (M-F 11:30am-2pm) includes a pre-selected sandwich and a cup of soup for $2. Domestic drafts are $1. (☎345-9613. Open 24hr.) **Pacific Ave.** is cramped with steak, sub, and pizza shops. There's never a dull moment at the vibrant **White House Sub Shop,** 2301 Arctic Ave. Sinatra was rumored to have had these immense subs ($4-9) flown to him while he was on tour. (☎345-1564 or 345-8599. Open M-Th 10am-midnight, F-Sa 10am-1am, Su 11am-11pm.) For the best pizza in town, hit **Tony's Baltimore Grille,** 2800 Atlantic Ave., at Iowa Ave. Tourists can't resist the personal jukeboxes, but budget travelers will appreciate the $3-6 pasta and pizza. (☎345-5766. Open daily 11am-3am. Bar open 24hr.) One of the more palatable boardwalk options, **Custard and Snack House,** between South Carolina and Ocean Ave., makes 37 flavors of ice cream and yogurt, ranging from peach to tutti-frutti (one scoop $2.25). If it's too chilly for dessert, try the coffee, tea, or hot cocoa, all $1. (☎345-5151. Open Su-Th 10am-midnight, F-Sa 10am-3am.)

🌀 CAINO, THE BOARDWALK, AND BEACHES

All casinos on the Boardwalk fall within a dice toss of one another. The farthest south is **The Hilton** (☎347-7111), between Providence and Voston Ave., and the farthest north is **Showboat** (☎343-4000), at Delaware Ave. and Boardwalk. If you liked *Aladdin*, you'll love the **Taj Mahal**, 1000 Boardwalk (☎449-1000). Donald Trump's glittering castle is too ostentatious to be missed; neglected payments on this tasteless tallboy cast the financier into his billion dollar tailspin. You, too, can board a magic carpet ride to bankruptcy! Speaking of *Monopoly*, Trump owns three other hotel casinos in the city: **Trump Plaza** (☎441-6000) and **Trump World's Fair** (☎344-6000) on the Boardwalk and **Trump Castle** (☎441-2000) at the Marina. Many a die is cast at **Caesar's Boardwalk Resort and Casino** (☎348-4411), at Arkansas Ave. The **Sands** (☎441-4000), at Indiana Ave., stands tall and flashy with its seashell motif. And, as if you couldn't guess, all are open 24hr.

There's something for everyone in Atlantic City, thanks to the Boardwalk. Those under 21 (or those tired of the endless cycle of winning and losing) **gamble for prizes** at one of the many arcades that line the Boardwalk. It feels like real gambling, but the teddy bear in the window is easier to win than the convertible on display at Caesar's. The **Steel Pier,** an extension in front of the Taj Mahal, juts into the coastal waters with a ferris wheel that spins riders over the Atlantic. It also offers the rest of the usual amusement park suspects: roller coaster, tilt-a-whirl, carousel, kiddie rides, and many a game of "skill." Rides cost $2-5 each. (Open daily noon-midnight; call the Taj Mahal for winter hours.) When you tire of spending money, check out the **beach. Ventnor City,** just west of Atlantic City, offers more tranquil shores.

CAPE MAY ☎ 609

Lying at the southern extreme of New Jersey's coastline, Cape May is the oldest seashore resort in the US, and the money here is no younger. Once the summer playground of Upper Eastside New Yorkers, the town still carries the signs of affluent infiltration in the elegant restaurants of Beach Ave. but is no longer characterized by it. The resort's main attraction, however, continues to be the sparkling white beaches—perfect for play or a nap under the rays—which shun the commercialism of more modern beach towns. At night, candles flicker in the windows of 19th-century B&Bs by the shore, infusing the streets with Victorian romance.

🚃🚌 ORIENTATION AND PRACTICAL INFORMATION. Despite its geographic isolation, Cape May is easily accessible by car or bus. Start digging for loose change as you follow the tollbooth-laden Garden State Pkwy. as far south as it goes, watch for signs to Center City, and you'll end up on Lafayette St. Alternately, take the slower, scenic Ocean Dr. 40 mi. south along the shore from Atlantic City. Rte. 55 brings beachgoers from Philadelphia. **NJ Transit** (☎215-569-3752 or 800-582-5946) makes a local stop at the bus depot on the corner of Lafayette and Ocean St. To: Atlantic City (2hr., 18 per day, $3.45); Philadelphia (3hr., 18 per day, $13.60); and New York City (4½hr., 3 per day, $27). **Cape Area Transit (CAT)** run buses on Pittsburgh Ave., Beach Dr., Lafayette St., and Ocean Ave. (☎889-0925 or 800-966-3758. Operates late June to Sept. daily 6 10am-10pm; late May to late June and Sept. 6 to mid-Oct. F 4-10pm, Sa 10am-10pm, Su 10am-4pm. $1 exact change.) **Cape May Seashore Lines** runs old-fashioned trains to further attractions along the 26 mi. to Tuckahoe four times per day. (☎884-2675. $8, children $5.) Bike the beach with the help of **Shields' Bike Rentals,** 11 Gurney St. (☎884-2453. Open 7am-7pm. $4 per hr., $9 per day; tandems $12 per hr.; surreys $24 per hr.) **Faria's,** 311 Beach Ave., rents beach necessities. (☎898-0988. Surfboard $16-20; umbrella or chair $6; bodyboard $8-16; wetsuit $15. Open Apr.-Sept. daily 9am-4pm.) **Welcome Center:** 405 Lafayette St. (☎884-9562; open daily 8:30am-5pm). **Chamber of Commerce:** 513 Washington St. Mall (☎465-7181; open M-F 9am-5pm, Sa-Su 10am-6pm) and in the **historic kiosk** at the south end of the mall. **Post Office:** 700 Washington St. (☎884-3578; open M-F 9am-5pm, Sa 8:30am-12:30pm). **ZIP code:** 08204. **Area code:** 609.

ⓘ ACCOMMODATIONS. Sleeping does not come cheaply in Cape May. Luxurious hotels and Victorian B&Bs along the beach run $85-250 per night. Further from the shore, prices drop. Although the **Hotel Clinton,** 202 Perry St., may lack presidential suites and A/C, the Italian family-owned establishment offers 16 breezy rooms, the most affordable rates in town, and priceless warmth and welcome from the charismatic proprietors. (☎884-3993. Open mid-June to Sept. Singles $36-40; doubles $46-50. Reservations recommended.) Next door, the **Parris Inn,** 204 Perry St., rents a variety of spacious, comfortable rooms, most with private baths, A/C, and TV. (☎884-8015. Open mid-Apr. to Dec. Singles $65-75; doubles $85-115. Lower rates off-season.) Campgrounds line U.S. 9 just north of Cape May. In a prime seashore location, **Camp Island,** 709 Rte. 9, is connected to Cape May by the Seashore Line, a restored railroad that makes four trips per day ($3.50). The fully equipped campground features two pools, a playground, a store, and laundry facilities. (☎800-437-7443. Sites $24-36, full hookup $26-39.) More primitive, but only ten blocks from Cape May, **Depot Travel Park,** 800 Broadway, 2 mi. north on Rte. 626 (Seashore Rd.) off Rte. 9, is convenient for beach seekers. (☎884-2533. Open May-late Sept. Sites with water and electricity $23, full hookup $28.)

ⒸⓂ FOOD AND NIGHTLIFE. Cape May's cheapest food is the generic pizza and burger fare along **Beach Ave.** You'll have to shell out a few more clams for a more substantial meal at one of the pricey and plush beachside restaurants. Crawling with pedestrians hunting for the most heavenly fudge and saltwater taffy, the **Washington St. Mall** supports several popular food stores and eateries. A meal at the pub-like **Ugly Mug,** 426 Washington St. Mall, is worth battling through the initially suffocating smokescreen. Fresh air can be had on the patio as you inhale a New England cup o' chowder for $2.25 or the ever-popular "oceanburger" for $5.75. (☎884-3459. Open M-Sa 11am-2am, Su noon-2am. Hot food served until 11pm. Free pizza M 10pm-2am.) At the newly launched **Gecko's,** in the Carpenter St. Mall, Mexican chefs help hungry patrons triple their southwestern delight for $5.50 with the three-sister quesadilla. (☎898-7750. Open daily 10am-10pm.)

The rock scene collects around **Carney's,** on Beach Ave., with nightly entertainment in the summer beginning at 10pm. Unwind on the weekend with Sunday jams 3-7pm. (☎884-442. Drafts $3.50-5. Open daily 11:30am-2am.) A chic crowd congregates at **Cabana's,** across from the beach at the corner of Decatur St. and Beach Ave. You'll have to find a lot of sand dollars if you want a pricey entree, but there is no cover for the nightly blues or jazz. (☎884-8400. Open daily noon-2am.)

ⓐ HITTING THE BEACH. Cape May's sands actually sparkle, dotted with the famous Cape May "diamonds" (quartz pebbles to the geology buffs). You can get horizontal and soak up some sun on a city-protected beach (off Beach Ave.), but you must pick up a **beach tag,** required for beachgoers over 11. Tags are available from roaming vendors or from the **Beach Tag Office,** located at Grant and Beach Dr. (☎884-9522. Open daily 9:30am-5:30pm. Tags required June-Sept. daily 10am-5:30pm. Daily $4, 3-day $8, weekly $11, seasonal $17.) Those in search of exercise and a spectacular view of the seashore can ascend the 199 steps to the beacon of the 1859 **Cape May Lighthouse** in **Cape May Point State Park,** west of town at the end of the point. (☎884-8626. Park open 8am-dusk. Lighthouse open Apr.-Nov. daily 8am-dusk; Dec.-Mar. Sa-Su 8am-dusk. $4, ages 3-12 $1.) The behemoth of a bunker next to the lighthouse is a WWII gun emplacement, used to scan the shore for German U-boats. In summer, several shuttles ($5, ages 3-12 $4) run the 5 mi. from the bus depot on Lafayette St. to the lighthouse. Even migratory birds flock to Cape May for a break from the long, southbound flight. Sneak a peak at these feathered vacationers from the **Cape May Bird Observatory**, 701 E. Lake Dr., on Cape May Point, a birdwatcher's paradise. Bird maps, field trips, and workshops are all available here. (☎884-2736. Open Tu-Su 10am-5pm.)

PENNSYLVANIA

In 1681, Englishman William Penn, Jr. established the colony of Pennsylvania (Latin scholars can trace the etymology to "Penn's woods") in order to protect his fellow Quakers from persecution. Since then, Pennsylvania has clung to the ideals of freedom from the drafting of the Declaration of Independence in Philadelphia to the present. In 1976, Philadelphia groomed its historic shrines for the nation's bicentennial, and today the colonial monuments serve as the centerpiece of the city's ambitious renewal. Pittsburgh, the steel city with a raw image, was once dirty enough to fool streetlights into burning during the day but has recently began a cultural renaissance. Removed from the noise of its urban areas, Pennsylvania's landscape has retained much of the rustic beauty first discovered by colonists centuries ago, from the farms of Lancaster County to the gorges of the Allegheny Plateau.

◪ PRACTICAL INFORMATION

Capital: Harrisburg.

Visitor info: Pennsylvania Travel and Tourism, 453 Forum Bldg., Harrisburg 17120 (☎800-847-4872; www.state.pa.us). **Bureau of State Parks,** Rachel Carson State Office Bldg., 400 Market St., Harrisburg 17108 (☎888-727-2757). Open M-F 8am-4:30pm.

Postal Abbreviation: PA. **Sales Tax:** 6%.

PHILADELPHIA   ☎215

With his band of Quakers, William Penn founded the City of Brotherly Love in 1682, after it had served as a colonial hub for 100 years. But it was Ben, not Penn, that transformed the town into the urban metropolis it is today. Benjamin Franklin, ingenious American ambassador, inventor, womanizer, and wit, almost singlehandedly built Philadelphia into an American colonial capital. Sightseers will eat up Philly's historic attractions, world-class museums, and architectural accomplishments. Be sure to save room, though—the city's ethnic neighborhoods deliver endless culinary choices, while the native cheesesteak is a staple.

◪ INTERCITY TRANSPORTATION

Airport: Philadelphia International (☎937-6800 for info, 24hr.), 8 mi. southwest of Center City on I-76. The 20min. **SEPTA Airport Rail Line** runs from Center City to the airport. Trains leave 30th St., Suburban, and Market East Stations daily every 30min. 5:25am-11:25pm; $5 at window, $7 on train. Last train from airport 12:10am. **Airport Limelight Limousine** (☎782-8818) will deliver you to a hotel or a specific address downtown; $8 per person. Taxi to downtown $25.

Trains: Amtrak, 30th St. Station (☎824-1600), at Market St., in University City. To: New York (2hr.; 30-40 per day; $45, express trains $71); Boston (7hr., 10 per day, $59-69); Washington, D.C. (2hr., 33 per day, $42); Baltimore (2hr., 10 per day, $40); and Pittsburgh (8hr., 2 per day, $54-82). Office open M-F 5:10am-10:45pm, Sa-Su 6:10am-10:45pm. Station open 24hr.

Buses: Greyhound, 1001 Filbert St. (☎931-4075 or 800-231-2222), at 10th and Filbert, in downtown Philadelphia 1 block north of Market near the 10th and Market St.

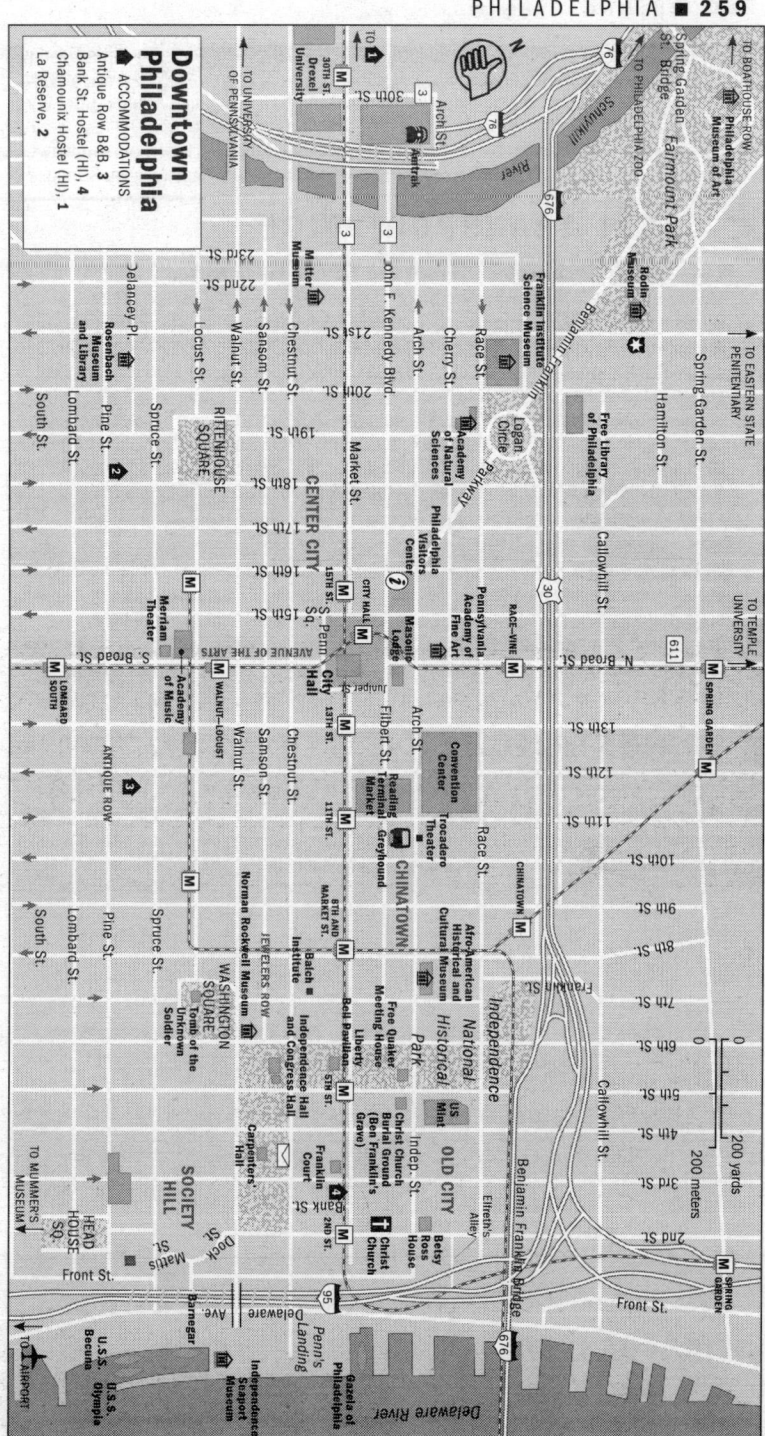

MID-ATLANTIC

subway/commuter rail stop. A populated, safe area. To: New York (2hr., 32 per day, $21); Boston (7hr., 24 per day, $55); Baltimore (2hr., 12 per day, $18); Washington, D.C. (3hr., 12 per day, $21); Pittsburgh (7hr., 8 per day, $38); and Atlantic City (2hr., 12 per day, $8.50). Station open daily 24hr. **New Jersey Transit** (☎569-3752), in the same station. To: Atlantic City (1hr., $10); Ocean City (2hr., $11); and other points on the New Jersey shore. Operates daily with buses to Atlantic City nearly every 30min.

▣ LOCAL TRANSPORTATION

Public Transit: Southeastern Pennsylvania Transportation Authority (SEPTA), 1234 Market St. (☎580-7800; www.septa.org). Extensive bus and rail service to the suburbs. Buses serve the 5-county area; most operate 5am-2am, some 24hr. 2 major subway routes: the blue east-west **Market St. line** (including 30th St. Station and the historic area) and the orange north-south **Broad St. line** (including the stadium complex in south Philadelphia). *The subway is unsafe after dark;* buses are usually safer. Subway connects with commuter rails—the **R5** main line local runs through the western suburb of Paoli ($3.75-4.25). The SEPTA **R7** runs north to Trenton, NJ ($5). Pick up a free SEPTA system map, Philly's best street map, at any subway stop. Fare $1.60, 2 tokens $2.30, transfers 40¢. Unlimited all-day pass for both $5. In the tourist area, purple **Phlash** buses come by every 10min. and hit all major sights. Fare $1.50, day-pass $3.

Taxis: Yellow Cab, ☎922-8400. **Liberty Cab,** ☎389-2000.

Car Rental: Budget (☎492-9400), downtown at 21st and Market St., or in the 30th St. Station. Reliable and easy to find but relatively expensive. Rates start $28 per day with unlimited mi.; $25 per day surcharge for under 25. Major credit card required.

Bike Rental: Frankenstein Bike Work, 1529 Spruce St. (☎893-4467). Open May-Sept. only Tu-Sa 10am-6pm, Su noon-4pm. Call ahead for M service. Cruisers $12 for 4hr., $15 per day.

✵ ORIENTATION

Penn planned his city as a logical and easily accessible grid, though the prevalence of one-way streets can cause many a migraine behind the wheel. The north-south streets ascend numerically from the **Delaware River,** flowing from **Penn's Landing** and **Independence Hall** on the east side to the **Schuylkill River** (SKOO-kill) on the west. The first street is **Front;** the others follow consecutively from 2 to 69 across the Schuylkill River. This **Center City** area is distinguished from poor South Philly, poor Northeast Philly, and rich Northwest Philly. The intersection of **Broad (14th) St.** and **Market** is the focal point of Center City, marked by the ornate City Hall. This framework sounds simple, but Penn omitted the alleys in his system. Some can accommodate cars while others are too narrow, but street addresses often refer to alleys not pictured on standard AAA-type maps of the city. The **SEPTA transportation map,** available free from the tourist office, is probably the most complete map of the city.

Due to the proliferation of one-way streets, horrendous traffic, and outrageous parking fees, **driving** is not a good way to get around town. Parking near the historic sights will break the bank ($10 per day), but lower priced options scatter at a farther but walkable distance. Meterless two-hour parking spaces can sometimes be found in the Washington Sq. district or on the cobblestones of Dock St. Day-long deals require vehicles to be in by 10am and out by 6pm. A well-secured lot on the corner of Race and 8th adheres to this policy ($5 all day). At 10th between Race and Vine St., a larger lot discounts on weekends and evenings ($4 Sa-Su and after 3pm.) Park outside the city and ride Philly's system of **buses** and its **subway** to most major downtown destinations. *Public transportation can be unsafe after dark.*

NEIGHBORHOODS

The **Historic District** stretches from Front to 6th St. and from Race to South St. The hip **Washington Square District** runs from 6th to Broad St. and Market to South St., and the affluent **Rittenhouse Square District** lies directly to the west. **Chinatown** comprises the blocks around 10th and Arch St., while the **Museums District** takes up the northwest quadrant made by Market and Broad St. Across the Schuylkill River, **University City** includes the sprawling campuses of the **University of Pennsylvania (UPenn)** and **Drexel University.**

🗊 PRACTICAL INFORMATION

Visitor info: 1525 John F. Kennedy Blvd. (☎636-1666), the UFO-like building by the fountain at 16th St. Free city guide with great map. Open daily 9am-6pm; in winter 9am-5pm. The **National Park Service Visitors Center** (☎597-8974, 627-1776 for a recording), at 3rd and Chestnut St., has info on **Independence Park,** including maps, schedules, and a branch of the tourist office. Open daily 9am-6pm; in winter 9am-5pm.

Hotlines: Suicide and Crisis Intervention, ☎686-4420. **Youth Crisis Line,** ☎787-0633. **Women Against Abuse,** ☎386-7777. All 24hr.

Gay, Lesbian, and Bisexual Info: Gay and Lesbian Counseling Services, ☎732-8255. Operates M-F 6-9pm, Su 5-8pm. **William Way Lesbian, Gay, and Bisexual Community Center** (☎732-2220). Info about gay events and activities. Open M-F noon-10pm, Sa 10am-5pm, Su 10:30am-8:30pm.

Post Office: 2970 Market St. (☎895-8000), at 30th St. across from the Amtrak station. Open 24hr. **ZIP code:** 19104. **Area code:** 215.

🗊 ACCOMMODATIONS

Aside from its two hostels, inexpensive lodging in Philadelphia is uncommon, but if you make arrangements a few days in advance, comfortable rooms close to Center City can be had for around $60. The motels near the airport at Exit 9A on I-95 sacrifice location to be the most affordable motels in the area. The personable proprietors at **Antique Row Bed and Breakfast** and **La Reserve** (see below) will recommend rooms if they lack vacancy. **Bed and Breakfast Connections/Bed and Breakfast of Philadelphia,** in Devon, PA, books in Philadelphia and southeastern Pennsylvania but requires 20% payment. (☎610-687-3565. Call 9am-7pm. Singles $60-90; doubles $75-250. Reserve at least a week in advance.) The closest camping is across the Delaware River in New Jersey at **Timberline Campground,** 117 Timber Ln., 15 mi. from Center City. Take U.S. 295 S to Exit 18B (Clarksboro), follow straight through the traffic light ½ mi. and turn right on Friendship Rd. Timber Ln. is one block on the right. (☎609-423-6677. Sites $18, full hookup $24.)

▩ Chamounix Mansion International Youth Hostel (HI-AYH) (☎878-3676 or 800-379-0017), in West Fairmount Park. Take bus #38 from lower Market St. to Ford and Cranston Rd.; take Ford Rd., turn left on Chamounix Dr., and follow to hostel. A young, energetic staff maintains uncommonly lavish hosteling in a converted mansion. Showers, kitchen, laundry, TV/VCR, piano, bikes, and Internet access ($1 per 5 min.). Free parking, discounted bus tokens, and free summer orchestra passes. 80 beds. A few private rooms are available for families and couples. Linen $2. Check-in 8-11am and 4:30pm-midnight. Lockout 11am-4:30pm. Curfew midnight. Dorms $13, nonmembers $17.

▩ Bank Street Hostel (HI-AYH), 32 S. Bank St. (☎922-0222 or 800-392-4678). From the bus station, walk down Market St.; it's between 2nd and 3rd St. Subway: 2nd St. Very social hostel rests in a prime location in the historic district and near the waterfront and South St. Travelers convene nightly to watch movies on the lounge's big screen TV. A/C, free coffee and tea, laundry facilities, kitchen, pool table, Internet access ($5 per 30min.). Linen $2. Lockout 10am-4:30pm, but they'll hold baggage. Curfew M-F 12:30am, Sa-Su 1am. 70 beds. Dorms $18, nonmembers $21. Cannot reserve rooms via phone; must mail payment in advance—call for details.

Antique Row Bed and Breakfast, 341 S. 12th St. (☎592-7802). Enchanting traditional B&B at the heart of colonial rowhouses. The engaging owner offers her guests expert restaurant referrals and serves her own hearty morning meal. Four apartments cater toward longer visits with TV, utilities, and laundry. Free local calls. $60-100, depending on size of suite; reduced rate for longer stays.

La Reserve (a.k.a. **Bed and Breakfast Center City**), 1804 Pine St. (☎ 735-1137 or 735-0582). Entertains guests with an extravagant dining room that is often the site of lively dinner parties and visits from local musicians. Personable owner is a reliable source of Philadelphia advice and sidesplitting humor. Full breakfast. Plush doubles $80-130.

Motel 6, 43 Industrial Hwy. (☎610-521-6650 or 800-466-8356), in Essington, Exit 9A off I-95. A generic option: large standard rooms with A/C and cable. Doubles $56-65.

⬛ FOOD

Street vendors are at the forefront of Philly specialties, hawking **cheesesteaks, hoagies, soft pretzels,** and **fruit salad.** Ethnic eateries gather in several specific areas: hip **South St.,** between Front and 7th St.; **18th St.** around Sansom St.; and **2nd St.,** between Chestnut and Market St. **Chinatown,** bounded by 11th, 8th, Arch, and Vine St., offers well-priced vegetarian restaurants. The quintessential Philly cheesesteak rivalry squares off at 9th and Passyunk Ave., in South Philadelphia; **Pat's King of Steaks** (☎468-1546), the legendary founder of the cheesesteak, faces larger, more neon **Geno's Steaks** (☎389-0659). Both offer cheesesteaks for $5-6 and stay open 24hr. Whichever establishment you choose to visit, ordering a cheesesteak and the subsequent consumption of one will be an adventure. Prepare to order quickly and convincingly or risk being ejected to the back of the line. Be sure to grab a fistful of napkins to stay the flood of grease that will pour from the sandwich. You may need a shower afterwards, but no Philly visit is complete without a cheesesteak.

Fresh fruit and other foodstuffs pack the mobbed streets of the immense **Italian Market,** which spans the area around 9th St. below Christian St. The **Reading Terminal Market,** 12th and Arch St., stocks globally diverse food under one roof—fabulous for lunch. Since 1893, food stands have clustered in the indoor market selling fresh produce and meats. Check the pamphlet available at vendors for events. (☎922-2317. Open M-Sa 8am-6pm.)

HISTORIC DISTRICT

Famous 4th St. Delicatessen, (☎922-3274), 4th and Bainbridge St. A Philadelphia landmark since 1923, the Delicatessen has earned its stellar reputation by faithfully serving Jewish deli favorites like corned beef sandwiches ($7.50) in its antique dining room. Open M-Sa 7:30am-6pm, Su 7:30am-4pm.

Jim's Steaks, 400 South St. (☎928-1911). South St. bustles with activity, and at the heart of it rests this time warp back to 50s Philadelphia. People come in droves for the authentic Philly hoagie ($3.50-5) and fries ($1.25); pass the time in line by inspecting the impressive wall of fame. Open M-Th 10am-1am, F-Sa 10am-3am, Su noon-10pm.

Pink Rose Pastry Shop, (☎592-0565), at 4th and Bainbridge St., across from the Delicatessen. Friendly students serve up the widest selection of homemade delicacies at intimate tables graced with freshly-cut flowers. Simply unforgettable sour cream apple pie ($4.50) and chocolate midnight cake ($5) with a latte ($2.75) will leave you crooning for more. Open M-Th 9am-10:30pm, F-Sa 9am-11:30pm, Su 9am-8:30pm.

CHINATOWN

⬛ **Singapore,** 1006 Race St. (☎923-0303). Health-conscious Chinese food cravers flock to this therapeutic restaurant for options like the vegetarian roast duck ($8) or celery with bean curd ($7). Open M-Th 11:30am-10pm, F 11:30am-11pm, Sa-Su noon-11pm.

⬛ **Rangoon,** 112 9th St. (☎829-8939). Simple, pink, and plastic decor belies the complex, spicy scents of Burmese cuisine wafting onto the sidewalk. The crisp lentil fritters ($9) will whet your appetite for the tasty mint kebab ($9). Open daily 11:30am-10pm.

Sang Kee Duck House, 238 9th St. (☎925-7532). Locals of all types pack the large, new dining room for a taste of the extensive menu (shrimp seaweed soup $5). Open M-Th 10am-11pm, F-Sa 10am-midnight, Su 10am-10pm.

CENTER CITY

▩**Jamaican Jerk Hut,** 1436 South St. (☎545-8644). This tropical paradise brightens an otherwise bleak block. While chefs jerk your Negril garlic shrimp ($10) to perfection, Bob Marley tunes jam in the backyard veranda. Open M-Th 10am-1am, F-Sa 10am-3am, Su 5-10pm. Live music F-Sa 7pm.

Sabbaba Restaurant, 1240 Pine St. (☎735-8111). Fresh Middle Eastern cuisine is attentively served in this friendly Antique Row refuge. Feta and salad in grape leaves ($5) and lemon-marinated shwarma ($8) go down deliciously, while walnut baklava desserts ($1.50) are made before your eyes. Open M-Sa 11am-12am, Su noon-10pm.

Samson St. Oyster House, 1516 Sansom St. (☎567-7683). Businesspeople and professionals seek seafood delight in the nautically bedecked dining room. Oysters top the menu ($7.25 for a half-dozen), but broiled bluefish ($7.50) and the popcorn shrimp po' boy ($6.25) are also great catches. Open daily 11am-11pm.

Alaska, 123 S. 18th St. (☎563-4424). Quiet cafe serves up creamy creations amid the bustle of downtown. Features 3 diverse ice cream brands including Philly's famed Bassett's (regular $3). Open M-Th 11:30am-10pm, F-Su 11:30am-11pm.

UNIVERSITY CITY

▩**Tandoor India Restaurant,** 106 S. 40th St. (☎222-7122). Northern Indian cuisine with bread fresh from the clay oven (ask to see it). Slightly cafeteria-like atmosphere, but $6 lunch and $9 dinner buffets are delicious values. 20% student discount with valid ID. Open M-F 11:30am-3pm and 4:30-10pm, Sa-Su 11:30am-3:30pm and 4:30-10pm.

Smokey Joe's, 210 S. 40th St. (☎222-0770), between Locust and Walnut St. The most popular UPenn bar and restaurant features hearty meals at student-friendly prices. All-you-can-eat pasta, broiled salmon, or BBQ baby ribs ($8). Lighter eaters can opt for the Palestra deal (salad, healthy sub, and drink for $7). Open daily 11am-2am; July-Aug. closed Su. In summer, no lunch Sa-Su. Local groups occasionally perform Su-Tu 10pm.

Abner's Cheesesteaks, 3813 Chestnut St. (☎662-0100), at 38th and Chestnut St. Local fast food attracts tipsy UPenn students deep into the night and a more professional set for lunch. Onion-laden cheesesteak, large soda, and fries for $6. Open Su-Th 11am-midnight, F-Sa 11am-3am.

◉ SIGHTS

INDEPENDENCE MALL

REVOLUTIONARY SIGHTS. The **Independence National Historical Park,** a small green bounded by Market, Walnut, 2nd, and 6th St., is comprised of a hash of historical buildings. (☎597-8974. Open June-Aug. daily 9am-6pm; Sept.-May 9am-5pm. Free.) Begin your trip down American history memory lane at the **Visitors Center,** at 3rd and Chestnut St., which dispenses detailed maps and brochures pertinent to the area (see **Practical Information,** above). One of the most popular of Philadelphia's historic landmarks, **Independence Hall** abounds with revolutionism and tourism. After Jefferson elegantly drafted the Declaration of Independence, the delegates signed the document here in 1776 and reconvened in 1787 to ink their names onto the US Constitution. (Between 5th and 6th St. on Chestnut St. Open daily 9am-8pm; arrive early in summer to avoid a long line. Free guided tours daily every 15-20min. In summer, tours usually conclude around 6pm in favor of an open house format.) The US Congress first assembled in nearby **Congress Hall,** at Chestnut and 6th St. While soaking up the history, guests can take a reclining rest in one of the plush Senate chairs. (Self-guided tour with rangers available to answer questions.) Its predecessor, the First Continental Congress, united against the British in **Carpenters' Hall,** in the middle of the block bounded by 3rd, 4th, Walnut, and Chestnut St., now a mini-museum heralding the carpenters responsible for such architectural achievements as Old City Hall and the Pennsylvania State House. (Open Tu-Su 10am-4pm.) North of Independence Hall, in its own pavilion, rests the country's most revered bell. Nowadays at the **Liberty Bell Pavilion,** freedom may ring but the (cracked) Liberty Bell does not. *(Open 9am-8pm. Free.)*

OTHER SIGHTS. The rest of the park preserves residential and commercial buildings of the Revolutionary era. On the northern edge of the Mall, a replica of Ben Franklin's home presides over **Franklin Court,** between 3rd and 4th St. The original abode was unsentimentally razed by the statesman's heirs in 1812 in order to erect an apartment complex. That project didn't endure, and today's re-created home reflects Franklin's pragmatic eclecticism. The home contains an underground museum, a 20min. movie, a replica of his printing office, and phones that allow guests to lend an ear to the quips of long-dead political and literary luminaries. *(318 Market St. Open daily 10am-6pm. Free.)* On a more somber note, in Washington Sq., a statue of the army general and first American president namesake nobly presides over the **Tomb of the Unknown Soldier,** where an eternal flame commemorates the fallen heroes of the Revolutionary War.

Adjacent to the house where Jefferson drafted the Declaration of Independence, the **Balch Institute for Ethnic Studies** is a more academic glimpse into events in America's social history, such as the plight of Japanese Americans during World War II. *(18 S. 7th St. ☎ 925-8090. Open M-Sa 10am-4pm. $3; students, seniors, and under 12 $1.50; Sa 10am-noon free.)* Across the street, the **Atwater-Kent Museum** offers still more Franklin exhibits; by the end, you will probably be convinced that the guy is your close friend. *(15 S. 17th. ☎ 922-3031. Open M-Th 10am-5pm, F 10am-3pm, Su noon-5pm.)*

OUTSIDE INDEPENDENCE MALL

COLONIAL MADNESS. A penniless Ben Franklin arrived in Philadelphia in 1723 and strolled by the colorful and clustered rowhouses that line the narrow **Elfreth's Alley,** near 2nd and Arch St. The vigorous neighborhood—the oldest continuously inhabited street in America—provides a shaded retreat from 21st century blaring horns and a window into the daily lives of Philadelphia patriots. A museum gives a peak inside and some alley history. *(126 Elfreth's Alley. Open Tu-Sa 10am-4pm, Su noon-4pm; Jan.-Feb. Sa 10am-4pm, Su noon-4pm.)* At the **Betsy Ross House,** arguably the most celebrated female patriot speaks through child-oriented placards to convey the seamstress' skills that led her to sew the first Stars and Stripes in 1777. *(239 Arch St. ☎ 627-5343. Open daily 10am-5pm. Suggested donation $2, children $1.)*

OTHER SIGHTS. For those who like to get off on the good foot, the Temple University School of Podiatric Medicine houses the **Shoe Museum,** on the corner of 8th and Race St. This 6th fl. collection features footwear from the famous feet of Reggie Jackson, Lady Bird Johnson, Dr. J, Nancy Reagan, and others. *(☎ 625-5243. Tours W and F 9am-noon; tours are limited, call for appointment.)* The powder-blue "marvel near the mint," **Benjamin Franklin Bridge,** off Race and 5th St., in addition to connecting Philadelphia to New Jersey, provides an expansive view of the city for un-vertigoed folks. The bridge adds a touch of urban art after dark, with its deep, sweeping blue highlighted by hundreds of hue-shifting lights.

SOCIETY HILL AND THE WATERFRONT

Society Hill proper begins to the east of where Independence Mall ends, on Walnut St. between Front and 7th St. Independence Mall may halt at Walnut St., but the history continues to preside in 200-year-old townhouses over cobblestone walks illuminated by electric "gaslights."

HISTORICAL SIGHTS. Flames don't have a chance in **Head House Sq.,** at 2nd and Pine St., which holds the distinction of being America's oldest firehouse and marketplace and now houses restaurants and boutiques. Bargain hunters can test their haggling skills at an outdoor **flea market** on summer weekends. *(☎ 790-0782. Open June-Aug. Sa noon-11pm, Su noon-6pm.)* South of Head House Sq., the **Mummer's Museum** at Washington Ave. swells with the glamour of old costumes. Each January, looking somewhat like a Village People reunion, Philadelphia construction workers, policemen, and other sequin- and feather-clad participants join in a rowdy New Year's Day parade. *(1100 S. 2nd St. ☎ 336-3050. Open Tu-Sa 9:30am-5pm, Su noon-5pm; closed Su July-Aug. Free string band concerts Tu evenings. $2.50, seniors and children $2.)*

ON THE WATERFRONT. A looming, neon sign at the easternmost end of Market St. welcomes visitors to **Penn's Landing,** the largest freshwater port in the world. The lavishly appointed USS *Olympia*, the oldest steel warship still afloat, served as Admiral Dewey's flagship during the Spanish-American War. The USS Becuna, a WWII submarine, also bobs at the dock. *(☎923-8181. Open daily 10am-5pm. $4, seniors $3, children $2.)* Philadelphian shipbuilding, cargo, and immigration unfold at the **Independence Seaport Museum.** Kids can get their sea legs under them at the "Boats Float" exhibit, which welcomes junior sailors aboard ships. *(☎925-5439. Open 10am-5pm. Museum $5, seniors $4, children $2.50; museum and ships $7.50/$6/$3.50.)* Finish the waterfront day in relaxing fashion at a free **waterfront concert** April to October. *(☎629-3257. Big bands Th nights, children's theater Su.)*

CENTER CITY

As the financial and commercial hub of Philly, there's barely enough room to accommodate the professionals who cram into **Center City,** the area bounded by 12th, 23rd, Vine, and Pine St. Although rife with business activity during the daytime, the region retires early at night.

ART AND ARCHITECTURE. The country's first art museum and school, the **Pennsylvania Academy of Fine Art** dwells at Broad and Cherry St. Permanent displays include artwork by Winslow Homer and Mary Cassatt, while current students and accomplished alumni get their own exhibit each May. *(118 N. Broad St. ☎972-2060. Open M-Tu and Th-Sa 10am-5pm, W 10am-8pm, Su 11am-5pm. Tours M-F 11:30am and 1:30pm, Sa-Su noon and 2pm. $5, seniors and students with ID $4, ages 5-11 $3; additional charge for special exhibits.)* Presiding over Center City, the granite and marble **City Hall,** at Broad and Market St., remains the nation's largest working municipal building. Until 1908, it reigned as the tallest building in the US, aided by the 37 ft. statue of William Penn stretching toward the heavens. A sentimentally historic municipal statute prohibited building higher than the apex of Penn's hat until Reagan-era entrepreneurs overturned the law in the mid-80s, launching independent and historical Philadelphia into the modernism of the skyscraper era. Unless you're afraid of heights, a commanding view of the city awaits in the building's tower. *(☎686-2840. Open M-F 10am-4pm; last elevator 4pm. Suggested donation $1. Tour daily 12:30pm.)* Across from City Hall, behind an alluring gate, lurks the mysterious **Masonic Temple.** The heavy wooden doors vault collections of books and other artifacts dating back to 1873 that can be viewed on a 45min. tour. *(1 N. Broad St., at JFK Blvd. ☎988-1917. Tours M-F every hr. 10am-3pm except noon; Sept.-June Sa 10 and 11am. Free.)*

RITTENHOUSE SQUARE

Masons of a different ilk left their mark in the brick-laden **Rittenhouse Sq. District,** a ritzy neighborhood southeast of Center City. This shaded region of town cradles the musical and dramatic pulse of the city, housing multiple performing arts centers. Not short on other means of tourist entertainment, Rittenhouse Sq. offers visitors two distinctly dissimilar museum options. For best results, digest your lunch before digesting the bizarre and often gory medical abnormalities displayed at the highly intriguing **Mütter Museum.** Among the potentially unsettling fascinations are a wall of skulls and human horns. *(19 S. 22nd St. ☎563-3737. Open Tu-Sa 10am-4pm. $8, seniors, students with ID, and ages 6-18 $5.)* Just south of the square, the more benign **Rosenbach Museum and Library** permanently displays the original manuscript of James Joyce's *Ulysses* and the collected illustrations of Maurice Sendak, among rotating exhibits. *(2010 Delancey St. ☎732-1600. Open Sept.-July Tu-Su 11am-4pm. Guided 1¼hr. tours $5; seniors, students, and children $3. Last tour 2:45pm.)*

PARKWAY/MUSEUM DISTRICT

Once nicknamed "America's Champs-Elysées," the **Benjamin Franklin Pkwy.** has seen better days. While it sports a United Nations-esque international flag row cutting through Philadelphia's streets, the surrounding areas suffer from a lack of upkeep. Nevertheless, the Parkway supports some of Philly's finest cultural attractions.

MID-ATLANTIC

SCIENCE. A modern assemblage of everything scientific, the **Franklin Institute** at 20th and Ben Franklin Pkwy., would make the old inventor proud and is even more interactive than standard science museums. The newly installed skybike allows guests to explore scientific theories while pedaling through the air. (☎ 448-1200. *Open daily 9:30am-5pm. $9.75, over 62 and ages 4-11 $8.50.*) Within the scientific depths of the Institute, the **Imax Theater** thrills audiences with 180° and 4½ stories of optical oohs and aahs. (☎ 448-1111. *Shows every hr. Su-Th 10am-4pm, F-Sa 10am-9pm except for 6pm. $7.50. Advance tickets recommended.*) Not to be outdone, **Fels Planetarium** boasts an advanced computer-driven system that projects a simulation of life billions of years beyond ours. Lively laser shows flash and blind on Friday and Saturday nights. (☎ 448-1388. *Shows M-F 12:15 and 2:15pm; Sa 10:15am, 12:15, and 2:15pm. $6, seniors and children $5. Exhibits and a show $12.75/$10.50. Exhibits and both shows $14.75/$12.50.*) Opposite Fels, at the **Academy of Natural Sciences**, 19th and Ben Franklin Pkwy., budding archaeologists can try their hand at dinosaur fossil digging. Through May 2002, guests will be able to trace the origins of life by playing sleuth in a microbial world. (☎ 299-1000. *Open M-F 10am-4:30pm, Sa-Su and holidays 10am-5pm. $8.50, seniors and military $7.75, ages 3-12 $7. Wheelchair accessible.*)

ART. Sylvester Stallone may have etched the sight of the **Philadelphia Museum of Art** into the minds of movie buffs everywhere when he bolted up the stately front stairs in *Rocky*, but it is the artwork that has solidified the museum's fine reputation. A world-class collection includes Cezanne's *Large Bathers* and Toulouse-Lautrec's *At the Moulin Rouge*, as well as extensive Asian, Egyptian, and decorative art collections. Lighten up from 5:30-8:30pm on Wednesday evenings with free films, talks, music, and food. (*Benjamin Franklin Pkwy. and 26th St.* ☎ 763-8100. *Open Tu and Th-Su 10am-5pm, W 10am-8:45pm. Tours daily 10am-3pm. $8; seniors, students, and ages 5-18 $5; free Su before 1pm.*) A casting of the Gates of Hell outside the **Rodin Museum**, guards the portal of human passion, anguish, and anger in the most extensive collection of the prolific sculptor's works this side of the Seine. (*22nd St.* ☎ 563-1948. *Open Tu-Su 10am-5pm. $3 suggested donation.*)

BOOKS AND INMATES. The Free Library of Philadelphia, scores with a library of orchestral music and one of the nation's largest rare book collections. Philadelphia art students frequently seek sketching subjects and inspiration amid the classical architecture of the building. (*20th and Vine St.* ☎ 686-5322. *Open M-W 9am-9pm, Th-F 9am-6pm, Sa 9am-5pm; Oct.-May also Su 1-5pm.*) In a reversal of convention, guests pay to get into prison, not out of it, at the castle-like **Eastern State Penitentiary**, on Fairmount Ave. at 22nd St. Once a ground-breaking institution of criminal rehabilitation, self- and other-guided tours twist through the moldering dimness Al Capone once called home. (☎ 236-3300. *Open May to early Nov. Th-Su 10am-5pm. Tours every hr. 10am-4pm. $7, seniors and students $5, children $3, under 5 not permitted.*)

UNIVERSITY CITY

The **University of Pennsylvania (UPenn)** and **Drexel University,** located across the Schuylkill from Center City, are in west Philly within easy walking distance of the 30th St. subway station. The Penn campus, a thriving assemblage of luscious green lawns, red brick quadrangles, and young Ivy League minds, contrasts sharply with the dilapidated buildings and lower-middle-class community surrounding it. Ritzy shops and hip cafes spice up 36th St. A statue of the omnipresent Benjamin Franklin, who founded the university in 1740, greets visitors at the entrance to the Penn campus on 34th and Walnut St. *Much of the area surrounding University City is unsafe at night—try not to travel alone.*

U-CITY SIGHTS. The **University Museum of Archeology and Anthropology** journeys through three floors of the world's major cultures under a beautiful stone-and-glass rotunda. (*33rd and Spruce St.* ☎ 898-4001. *Open June-Aug. Tu-Sa 10am-4:30pm; Sept.-May Tu-Sa 10am-4:30pm, Su 1-5pm. Suggested donation $5, students and over 62 $2.50.*) In 1965, Andy Warhol had his first one-man show at the **Institute of Contemporary Art,** which has always stayed on the cutting edge of art and technology. (*36th and Sansom St.*

☎898-7108. Open during academic terms W-F noon-8pm, Sa-Su 11am-5pm. $3; seniors, students, and artists $2; Su 11am-1pm free.) North of the University area, the **Philadelphia Zoo,** the oldest zoo in the country, houses more than 1700 animals, wild exhibits, and kid-friendly programs. (34th and Girard St. ☎243-1100. Open M-F 9:30am-4:45pm, Sa-Su 9:30am-5:45pm. $10, seniors and ages 2-11 $8. Parking $5.)

⚠ OUTDOOR ACTIVITIES

Philly's finest outdoor opportunities can be found in the resplendent **Fairmount Park.** Larger than any other city park and covered with bike trails and picnic areas, the park offers city-weary vacationers the adventure of the great outdoors, not to mention stirring vistas of the Schuylkill River, within a stone's throw of urban museums. The Grecian ruins by the waterfall immediately behind the museum comprise the abandoned **Waterworks.** Free tours featuring Waterworks' architecture, technology, and social history meet on Aquarium Dr. behind the Art Museum. (☎685-4935. Open Sa-Su 1-3:30pm.) Further down the river, Philly's traditional dominance in the rowing world is apparent in the line of crew clubs forming the historic **Boathouse Row.** (Admission to most mansions $2.50.) The Museum of Art hosts $3 guided tours of Boathouse Row on Wednesday and Sunday and trolley tours to some of the mansions in Fairmount Park. The area is also Philly's most popular **in-line skating** spot. Rental blades are available from **Wilburger's** kiosk, on Kelly Dr. south of Boathouse Row, but you'll have to share the paths with the many joggers seeking recreation and a refreshing river breeze. (☎765-7470. Open May to early Sept. W-F 4-8pm, Sa-Su 9am-6pm. $5 per hr., $25 per day.) In the northern arm of Fairmount Park, trails follow the secluded Wissahickon Creek for 5 mi., as the concrete city fades to a distant memory. The **Japanese House and Garden,** off Montgomery Dr. near Belmont Ave., is designed in the style of a 17th-century *shoin;* the authentic garden offers the utmost in tranquility. (☎878-5097. Open May to early Sept. Tu-Su 10am-4pm; mid-Sept. to Oct. Sa-Su 10am-4pm. $2.50, seniors and students $2.) *Some neighborhoods surrounding the park are not safe. The park is not safe at night.*

🎭 ENTERTAINMENT

The **Academy of Music,** Broad and Locust St., modeled after Milan's La Scala, houses the **Philadelphia Orchestra.** Under Wolfgang Sawallisch's expert baton-waving direction, the orchestra performs from September to May. (☎893-1930. Tickets $15-90. $5 general admission tickets go on sale at the Locust St. entrance 45min. before F-Sa concerts. Tu and Th student rush tickets 30min. before show $8.) The theater also hosts the six yearly runs of the **Pennsylvania Ballet.** (☎551-7000. Tickets $20-85.)

The **Mann Music Center,** on George's Hill near 52nd and Parkside Ave. in Fairmount Park, hosts the Philadelphia Orchestra, jazz, and rock concerts with 5000 seats under cover and 10,000 on outdoor benches and lawns. Tickets are also available from the Academy of Music box office on Broad and Locust St. From June through Aug., free lawn tickets for the orchestra are available from the Visitors Center at 16th and JFK Blvd. on the day of a performance. (☎567-0707. Real seats $10-32.) The **Robin Hood Dell East** (☎685-9560), Strawberry Mansion Dr. in Fairmount Park, brings in top names in pop, jazz, gospel, and ethnic dance in July and August The Philadelphia Orchestra holds several free performances here in summer, and as many as 30,000 people gather on the lawn.

Many of Philadelphia's most appealing cultural events take a leave of absence with the city's students come summertime. During the school year, however, theatrical entertainment bustles like a library during final exams. The students of the world-renowned **Curtis Institute of Music,** 1726 Locust St., give free concerts (mid-Oct. to Apr. M, W, and F at 8pm). **Merriam Theater,** 250 S. Broad St., Center City, stages performances ranging from student works to Broadway hits. (☎732-5446. Box office open M-Sa 10am-5:30pm.) The **Old City,** from Chestnut to Vine and Front to 4th St., comes alive the for the **First Friday** celebration on the first Friday of every month (Oct.-June). The streets fill with live music, and many art galleries open their doors, enticing visitors with free food and sparkling wine.

Philly gets physical with plenty of sports venues. Philly's four professional teams play a short ride away on the Broad St. subway line. Philadelphia's boys of summer, the baseball **Phillies** (☎ 463-1000), and football's **Eagles** (☎ 463-5500) play games at **Veterans Stadium**, at Broad St. and Pattison Ave.; the **First Union Center**, across the street, fills to capacity on winter nights to support the NBA's **76ers** (☎ 339-7676) and the NHL's **Flyers** (☎ 755-9700). Call 336-3600 for general First Union Center information. General admission tickets for baseball and hockey start at $10; football and basketball tickets go for $15-50.

◪ NIGHTLIFE

Check the Friday *Philadelphia Inquirer* for entertainment listings. *City Paper*, distributed Thursday, and the *Philadelphia Weekly*, distributed on Wednesday, have weekly listings of city events (free at newsstands and markets). Along **South St.** toward the river, a diverse club crowd jams to the sounds of live music on weekends. Many pubs line **2nd St.** near Chestnut St., close to the Bank St. hostel. Continuing south to Society Hill, especially near **Head House Sq.**, a slightly older crowd fills dozens of streetside bars and cafes. **Delaware Ave.** (a.k.a. **Columbus Blvd.**), running along Penn's Landing, has recently become a trendy local hot spot, full of nightclubs and restaurants attracting droves of young urban professionals and students. Gay and lesbian weeklies *Au Courant* (free) and *PGN* (75¢) list events taking place throughout the Delaware Valley region. Most bars and clubs that cater to a gay clientele congregate along **Camac St., S. 12th St.,** and **S. 13th St.**

◪ **Kat Man Du,** Pier 25 (☎ 629-1724), at N. Columbus Blvd. Hawaiian-shirt-clad partiers take refuge in the shadows of the Ben Franklin Bridge. Rock and hip hop boom over the palm trees and open-air deck at Philly's hottest summer venue. Happy hour M-F 5-7pm, $2 calls and domestic beers. 50¢ drafts Tu and Th 10pm-midnight. Cover M-Th after 8:30pm $5; F-Sa $8; Su $2, after 5pm $5. Open daily noon-2am.

The Khyber, 56 S. 2nd St. (☎ 238-5888). A speakeasy during the days of Prohibition. A young crowd now gathers legally to listen to a range of punk, metal, and hip hop music. The ornate wooden bar was shipped over from England in 1876. Belly-pleasing vegetarian sandwiches are $3. Happy Hour M-F 5-7pm. Live music daily from 10pm. Cover $5-15. Open daily 11am-2am.

The Trocadero (☎ 922-5483), at 10th and Arch St. Aged 120 years, "the Troc," the oldest operative Victorian theater in the US, hosts local as well as big-name bands. The upstairs balcony bar is sometimes open on non-show nights. Cover $6-16. Advance tickets through Ticketmaster. Box office open M-F noon-6pm, Sat. noon-5pm.

Warmdaddy's (☎ 627-8400), at Front and Market St. Though entrees tend toward the pricey, Bayou dreamers will eat up this Cajun club renowned for its blues, diversity, and W night seafood bashes ($22 per person for lobster, shrimp, and crab). Sets start at 7pm in summer, 8:30pm in winter. Tu free jam night. Cover W-Th and Su $5, F-Sa $10. Open Tu-Sa 5pm-2am, Su noon-2am.

Dirty Franks, (☎ 574-0070), at 13th and Pine St. Always busy, this Washington Sq. fixture delivers on the rock, reggae, and blues W-Sa and is a favorite local hangout all week. Friendly bartenders and $3 drafts. Happy hour M-F 5-7pm, $1 off bottled beers and cocktails. Cover for shows $3-7. Open M-Sa 5pm-2am, Su 5pm-1am.

Moriarty's, 1116 Walnut St. (☎ 627-7676). Though tucked near the office buildings of downtown, this Irish pub still draws a healthy crowd late into the night. Extensive menu is served until 1am. Over 20 beers on tap, ESPN on the TV, and private booths galore. Open Su-Th 11am-1am, F-Sa 11am-2am.

Woody's, 202 S. 13th St. (☎ 545-1893). An outgoing gay crowd frequents this lively club. Lunch daily noon-3:30pm. Happy hour 5-7pm daily with 25¢ off all drinks. M karaoke, Tu trivia night. Dance to country tunes Tu and Su, or grind to house music F-Sa. W is all ages night. Bar open M-Sa 11am-2am, Su noon-2am.

🏷 DAYTRIP FROM PHILADELPHIA

VALLEY FORGE

It was the winter of 1777-78, not the British, that almost crushed the Continental Army. When George Washington selected Valley Forge as the winter camp for his 12,000 troops following defeat at Germantown in October, the General could not have predicted the wretched fate that would befall his troops. Three arduous months of starvation, bitter cold, and disease nearly halved his forces. Subsisting on crude meals of flour-and-water "firecake," and at times without blankets or even shoes, the soldiers were nourished by hope alone. But it was not until Baron Friedrich von Steuben arrived with fresh troops and supplies that recovery seemed possible. Renewed, the Continental Army left Valley Forge and its harrowing memory on June 19, 1778, to win the Battle of Monmouth and help forge a nation.

The hills that once tried the frost-bitten soldiers roll through **Valley Forge National Historical Park.** Slightly more comfortable than frostbite is the 10 mi. self-guided auto tour which begins at the **Visitors Center.** The center also features a small museum and 18min. film. The tour passes **Washington's headquarters,** reconstructed soldier huts and fortifications, and the Grand Parade Ground where the Continental Army drilled. Visitors can also hop aboard a **bus tour.** The park has three picnic areas but no camping; those seeking to pitch a tent can obtain information at the Visitors Center. Joggers can take a revolutionary trip down memory lane on a paved 6 mi. trail through deer-populated forests. (☎ 610-783-1077. Park open daily sunrise-sunset. Grounds free. Center open daily 9am-5pm. Film shown every 30min. 9am-4:30pm. Washington's headquarters $2, under 17 free. Audio tapes $9; tape player $15; no players rented after 2pm. Tours every hr. 9:30am-4pm. $5.50, children $4.50.)

Valley Forge lies 30min. from Philadelphia by car. To get there, take I-76 west from Philly for about 12 mi. Get off at the Valley Forge exit (Exit 24), then take Rte. 202 S for 1 mi. and Rte. 422 W for 1½ mi. to another Valley Forge exit. **SEPTA** runs buses to the Visitors Center M-F only; catch #125 at 16th and JFK (fare $3.10).

LANCASTER COUNTY ☎ 717

The Amish, the Mennonites, and the Brethren, three groups of German Anabaptists who fled persecution in Deutschland (thus the misnomer "Pennsylvania Dutch"), sought freedom to pursue their own religion in the rolling countryside of Lancaster County in the 18th century. They successfully escaped censorship, but they have not escaped attention. The simplicity of the undeveloped, unassuming Amish lifestyle continues to fascinate a technologically dependent society. As a result, the chief industry in Lancaster County is now tourism. Thousands of visitors flock to this pastoral area every year to glimpse a modest way of life that eschews modern conveniences like motorized vehicles, television, and cellular phones. Point but don't shoot; many Amish have religious objections to being photographed.

🏷🏷 **ORIENTATION AND PRACTICAL INFORMATION.** Lancaster County covers an area almost the size of Rhode Island. County seat Lancaster City, in the heart of Dutch country, has red brick row houses huddled around historic **Penn Sq.** The rural areas are mostly accessible by car (unless you've got a horse and buggy), but it is easy to see the tourist sites with a bike or the willingness to walk the mile or two between public transportation drop-offs. You won't need to be married to travel the country roads of Lancaster where **Intercourse** suspiciously leads to **Paradise.** From Paradise, **U.S. 30 W** plots a straight course into **Fertility.** And you thought these were wholesome people. In all seriousness, visitors should be aware that the area is heavily Mennonite, so most businesses and all major attractions close on Sunday. **Amtrak,** 53 McGovern Ave. (☎ 291-5080), in Lancaster City, runs to Philadelphia (1hr., 8-10 per day, $14) and Pittsburgh (6½hr., 2 per day, $48). **Capital Trailways** (☎ 397-4861; open daily 8am-10pm), in the same location, buses to Philadelphia (3hr., 1 per day, $14) and Pittsburgh (6hr., 3 per day, $44). **Red Rose Transit,** 45 Erick

Rd., serves Lancaster and the surrounding countryside. (☎397-4246. Buses run M-F 9am-3:30pm and after 6:30pm, Sa-Su all day. Base fare $1, over 65 free.) The **Pennsylvania Dutch Visitors Bureau,** 501 Greenfield Rd., on the east side of Lancaster City off Rte. 30, dispenses info on the region, including excellent maps and walking tours. (☎299-8901 or 800-735-2629. Open M-Sa 8am-6pm, Su 8am-5pm; Sept.-May daily 8:30am-5pm.) **Post Office:** 1400 Harrisburg Pike (☎396-6900; open M-F 7:30am-4:30pm, Sa 9am-2pm). **ZIP code:** 17604. **Area code:** 717.

⌂ ACCOMMODATIONS. Hundreds of hotels and B&Bs cluster in this area, as do several working farms with guest houses. Visitors Centers can provide room information or, as part of a religious outreach mission, the amicable staff at the **Mennonite Information Center** (see **Sights,** below) will try to find you a Mennonite-run guest house for about the same price. About the only things that outnumber cows here are the campgrounds. The spotless rooms at the **Kendig Tourist Home,** 105 N. Ronks Rd., left off Rte. 30 E just past Flory's Campgrounds, offer maximum comfort at minimal cost. Hear the horses hooves and neighs of the Amish neighbors from dawn until the wee hours. (☎393-5358 or 687-6294. All rooms come with TV, some with A/C and private bath. Singles $26; doubles $36.) The **Pennsylvania Dutch Motel,** 2275 N. Reading Rd., at Exit 21 off the Pennsylvania Turnpike, has spacious, clean rooms with cable TV and A/C. The helpful hostess eagerly distributes written directions to major sights. (☎336-5559. Singles $50; doubles $60; prices lower Nov.-Mar.) The wilderness setting at the **Sickman's Mill Campground,** 671 Sand Hill Rd., off State Rd. 272, 6mi. south of Lancaster, keeps things quiet. Amenities include fishing, playground, and firewood, in addition to tours of the 19th-century mill ($4). Inner tube rental is available. (☎872-5951. Office open daily 10:30am-9pm. Sites $15.)

◨ FOOD. Amish food, wholesome and generous in portion, is characterized by a heavy potato and vegetable emphasis. A palatable alternative to high-priced "family-style" restaurants endures at the **Farmers Markets** and produce stands which dot the roadway. At the ◨**Central Market,** in downtown Lancaster City at the northwest corner of Penn Sq., simply dressed Pennsylvania Dutch invade the city to sell affordable fresh fruit, meats, cheeses, vegetables, sandwiches, and desserts alongside more conventionally dressed vendors (open Tu and F 6am-4pm, Sa 6am-2pm). The Lancaster restaurant scene surrounds the market. One of the most convenient culinary options can be found in Central Mall: **Isaac's Deli,** 44 N. Queen St., with the $5.25 Phoenix sandwich (ham, sliced pineapple, provolone) and classic $3 ice cream float. (☎394-5544. Open M-Th 10am-9pm, F-Sa 10am-10pm, Su 11am-9pm.) Nearby, **My Place,** 12 N. Queen St., can provide a slice of Italy or scrumptious pizza ($1.30) in Amish country. The filling cheesesteak hoagie ($4) will satisfy the ravenous, while light eaters can pick at generous salads for $2-3. (☎393-6405. Open M-Th 10:30am-10pm, F-Sa 10:30am-11pm.) The huge **Bird-in-Hand Market** complex on Rte. 340 at the corner of Maple Ave. is more pricey than the Amish road stands but offers an array of non-perishable goods as well as traditional ready-to-eat options. (☎393-9674. Open M-Sa 6am-8pm. Entrees $6-10.) At the **Amish Barn,** 3029 Old Philadelphia Pike, quilts surround the tables where patrons feed on Amish specialties such as $2 chicken corn soup and $3.50 Amish apple dumpling. (☎768-8886. Open late May to early Sept. daily 7:30am-9pm; early Sept. through Oct. and Apr.-May 8am-8pm; Nov. 8am-7pm.) Except for the chains, most restaurants close on Sunday.

PIE IN YOUR EYE The most distinctive culinary specialty of Lancaster County is the traditional Amish dessert, **shoofly pie,** popularized in the days before the refrigerator (or in contemporary Amish houses without refrigerators) because of its resistance to spoiling. Once removed from the oven, its treacly sweetness attracted droves of flies and thus gained its name from the constant "shoo fly" calls of its baker. Of equal authenticity if less publicity is the **whoopie pie,** a cookie-sized object with buttercream frosting sandwiched between two rounds of chocolate, pumpkin, or red velvet cake. These can be found at most bake shops for about 50¢ per pie.

HERSHEY'S CANDYLAND Around the turn of the century, Milton S. Hershey, a Mennonite resident of eastern Pennsylvania, discovered how to mass market a rare and expensive luxury—chocolate. Today, the company that bears his name operates the world's largest chocolate factory, in Hershey, about 45min. from Lancaster. East of town at **Hersheypark,** the **Chocolate World Visitors Center** presents a free, automated tour through a simulated chocolate factory. After the tour, visitors emerge into a pavilion full of chocolate cookies, discounted chocolate candy, and fashionable Hershey sportswear. Near the Visitors Center, the **Hershey Museum** probes more deeply into Milton Hershey's life and showcases his 19th-century Apostolic Clock with an hourly procession of clockwork apostles past a clockwork Jesus, while Satan periodically appears and a rooster crows to announce Judas's betrayal. (Park: ☎534-3900. Open June M-F 10am-10pm; July-Aug. M-F 10am-10pm, Sa-Su 10am-11pm; call for hours May to early June and Sept. $30, over 54 and ages 3-8 $17; after 5pm $16. Visitors Center: ☎800-437-7439. Opens with park and closes 2hr. earlier. Free; parking $5. Museum: ☎534-3439. Open June-Aug. daily 10am-6pm; Sept.-May 10am-5pm. $5, seniors $4.50, ages 3-15 $2.50. Theme park: ☎534-3860. Open mid-June to Aug. daily 10am-8pm; Sept. to mid-June 10am-5pm. $5.25, seniors $4.75, ages 3-12 $4.)

◪ **SIGHTS.** To develop an understanding and appreciation of Amish culture, visit the informative **People's Place,** 3513 Old Philadelphia Pike, on Main St./Rte. 340, in Intercourse, 11 mi. east of Lancaster City. The complex covers most of a block with bookstores craft shops, and a quilt museum. An exhibit called **20Q,** referring to the 20 most-asked questions about the Amish, details the nuances of their unique lifestyle. The film, *Who Are the Amish?*, takes care of any lingering curiosity. (☎768-7171. Open M-Sa 9:30am-8pm; early Sept. to late May M-Sa 9:30am-5pm. Film shown every 30min. 9:30am-5pm. $5, seniors $4, under 12 $2.50. Film and 20Q $8/$7/$4.) To get the story from the people who live it, stop in the **Mennonite Information Center** (☎299-0964), on Millstream Rd. off Rte. 30 east of Lancaster. The Mennonites, unlike the Amish, believe in outreach and established this center to help tourists distinguish between the two faiths. Exceptionally cordial hostesses also offer to guide guests through a Mennonite Tabernacle reproduction.

For the most authentic exploration of Amish country by car, wind through the verdant fields off U.S. 340 near Bird-in-the-Hand. Cyclists can capture the anti-electricity spirit on the tourism office's **Lancaster County Heritage Bike Tour,** a 46 mi., reasonably flat route past covered bridges and historic sites. A visit to Lancaster is not complete without using the locals' preferred mode of transportation; **Ed's three-mile buggy ride,** on Rte. 896, 1½ mi. south of U.S. 30 W in Strasburg, bumps along an hour of scenic backwoods and countryside. (M-Sa 9am-dusk. $7, under 10 $3.50.) **Amish Country Tours** offers 2½hr. trips that include visits to one-room schools, Amish cottage industries, authentic farms, and a vineyard. (☎786-3600. Tours given Apr.-Oct. M-Sa 10:30am and 2pm, Su 11:30am. $18, ages 4-11 $11.) Tourist offices have info on the pseudo-Amish experiences available, from staying in an Amish-style house to watching a blacksmith. Old country crafts and food can be found at the **Pennsylvania Dutch Folk Festival,** at Exit 31 off I-81 S. (☎610-683-8707. Late June to early July. $10, ages 5-12 $5.)

GETTYSBURG ☎717

July 1-3, 1863, remain as perhaps the most memorable dates of the US Civil War. On those three sweltering summer days, Union and Confederate forces clashed at Gettysburg in a climactic battle in the otherwise peaceful southern Pennsylvania countryside. The Union forces would ultimately prevail, derailing Southern hopes of advancement, but at a high price: over 50,000 casualties between North and South. Four months later, President Lincoln arrived in Gettysburg to dedicate the Gettysburg National Cemetery, where 979 unidentified Union soldiers rest. Today, the National Soldier's Monument towers where Lincoln delivered his legendary Gettysburg Address. Each year, thousands of visitors visit these fields and are reminded of the President's call to "resolve that these dead shall not have died in vain."

⊉ PRACTICAL INFORMATION. Inaccessible by Greyhound or Amtrak, Gettysburg is in south-central Pennsylvania, off U.S. 15, about 30 mi. south of Harrisburg. **Towne Trolley** makes in-town trips, but doesn't serve the battlefield. (Runs Apr.-Oct. $1.) The **Gettysburg Travel Council**, 35 Carlisle St., is in the old train depot where Lincoln disembarked. (☎334-6274. Open daily 9am-5pm.) **Post Office:** 115 Buford Ave. (☎337-3781; open M-F 8am-4:30pm, Sa 9am-noon). **ZIP code:** 17325. **Area code:** 717.

⌂⍾ ACCOMMODATIONS AND FOOD. Follow Rte. 34 N to Rte. 233 to reach the closest hostel, **Ironmasters Mansion Hostel (HI-AYH)**, 20 mi. away from Gettysburg, within the entrance of Pine Grove Furnace State Park and left at the Twirly Tap ice cream sign. Unusually large and luxurious, the 1820s building holds 46 beds in a tranquil and gorgeous area. Spacious porches, an ornate dining room, and the decadent jacuzzi make this hostel seem more like a Club Med resort. (☎486-7575. Reception 7:30-9:30am and 5-10pm. Laundry. Linen $2. Internet access $3 per 15min. Dorms $14, nonmembers $15. By reservation only Dec.-Feb.) **Artillery Ridge**, 610 Taneytown Rd., 1 mi. south of the Military Park Visitors Center, maintains over 200 sites with access to showers, stables, laundry, a pool, nightly movies, a pond, and bike rentals. Don't rely on catching a meal out of the pond; local regulations mandate catch-and-release. (☎334-1288. Open Apr.-Nov. Sites $16.50, with hookup $24; each additional person $4.) Multiple motels line Steinwehr Rd. near the battlefield, but finding summer rates below $100 is difficult. Slightly cheaper options, such as the $79 per night **Red Carpet Inn,** 2450 Emmitsburg Rd. (☎334-5026 or 800-336-1345), are 4 mi. west of town on Steinwehr Rd., which becomes Emmitsburg.

Hefty rations persist in the town's square and just beyond the entrance to the battlefield. At the **Dobbin House,** 89 Steinwehr Rd., Gettysburg's first building (ca. 1776), guests can create their own grilled burger ($6) under the candlelight and view an Underground Railroad shelter used for the protection of runaway slaves during the Civil War. (☎334-2100. Open Su-Th 9am-10pm, F-Sa 10am-11:30pm. Jazz on the 1st W of each month from 7:30pm.) Near the battlefield, **General Pickett's Restaurant,** 571 Steinwehr Rd., charges $6-10 for a Southern-style all-you-can-eat buffet. (☎334-7580. Open M-Sa 11am-3:15pm and 4:30-8pm, Su 11am-8pm.)

◉ SIGHTS. Visitors can explore Gettysburg in many ways. A sensible start is the **National Military Park Visitors Information Center,** 97 Taneytown Rd., which distributes free maps for an 18 mi. self-guided driving tour. (☎334-1124, ext. 431. Visitors Center open daily 8am-6pm; early Sept. to late May 8am-5pm. $3, seniors and under 15 $2. Park open daily 6am-10pm.) General admission to the battlefield is free, but prepare to spare a penny or two for a more in-depth look at the historic grounds. Enlightening **park rangers** squeeze into the family wagon to personally guide you through the monuments and landmarks. (2hr. tour $30 for up to 5 people. Personal tours are popular so arrive by 9am to ensure a time slot.) If you're not comfortable with inviting a stranger ranger into your car, just follow the free walking tour.

Surround yourself with chilling sights and sounds of battle at the **Cyclorama Center,** next to the Visitors Center. The center shows a 20min. film on the battle every hour, and a 30min. light show revolves around a 9500 sq. ft. mural of the battle. (☎334-1124, ext. 499. Open daily 9am-5pm. $3, seniors $2.50, ages 6-16 $2.) Artillery Ridge Campgrounds (see above) rents **bikes** and conducts **horseback tours** by reservation. (Bikes $25 per day, $15 per half-day. 1hr. horseback tour $23, 2hr. tour $45.) Adjacent to the campground's office is a meticulously detailed diorama of the Gettysburg battle, along with other exhibits. ($4.50, seniors and children $3.50.) **Historic Tours** trundles visitors around the battlefield in buses that are nearly as old as the Battle of Gettysburg itself. (☎334-8000. $12, children $9.) Straight out of a Stephen King novel, candlelit **ghost walks,** leaving from 55 Steinwehr Ave., reawaken the dead. (☎337-0445 or 334-8838. Walks at 8:15, 8:45, and 9pm. $6.50 under 8 free.)

The grim **Jennie Wade House,** 528 Baltimore St., preserves the kitchen where Miss Wade, the only civilian killed in the battle of Gettysburg, was mortally wounded by a stray bullet. The hole in the wall, through which the fatal bullet traveled, is still visible today. Legend has it that unmarried women who pass their finger through the fatal bullet hole will be engaged within a year. (☎334-4100. Open May-Aug. daily 9am-9pm; Sept.-Apr. 9am-5pm. $5.75, ages 6-11 $3.50.)

PITTSBURGH   ☎412

Those who come to the City of Steel expecting sprawling industry and hordes of soot-encrusted American Joes are bound to be disappointed. The decline of the steel industry has meant cleaner air and rivers, and a recent economical renaissance has produced a brighter urban landscape. City officials are desperate to provide Pittsburgh with a new image, going so far as to propose a theme park filled with robotic dinosaurs. Throughout renewals, Pittsburgh's neighborhoods have maintained strong and diverse identities. Admittedly, some of the old, sooty Pittsburgh survives in the suburbs, but one need only ride up the Duquesne Incline and view downtown from atop Mt. Washington to see how thoroughly Pittsburgh has entered a new age—and to understand why locals are so proud of "The 'Burgh."

▐▀ TRANSPORTATION

Airport: Pittsburgh International (☎472-5526), 18 mi. west of downtown by I-279 and Rte. 60 N in Findlay Township. The Port Authority's **28x Airport Flyer** bus serves downtown and Oakland from the airport (daily every 30min. 6am-midnight; $2). **Airline Transportation Company** (☎321-4990 or 471-8900) runs to downtown (M-F every hr. 7am-11:30pm, reduced service Sa; $14). Cab to downtown $30.

Trains: Amtrak, 1100 Liberty Ave. (☎471-6170), at Grant on the northern edge of downtown next to Greyhound and the post office. Generally safe inside, *but be careful walking from here to the city center at night.* To: Philadelphia (8½-11½hr., 2 per day, $48-89); New York (10-13hr., 2 per day, $65-121); and Chicago (9½-10hr., 3 per day, $57-106). Station open daily 6am-midnight.

Buses: Greyhound (☎392-6526), on 11th St. at Liberty Ave. near Amtrak. To Philadelphia (7hr., 9 per day, $40) and Chicago (8-12hr., 9 per day, $56). Open 24hr.

Public Transit: Port Authority of Allegheny County (PAT) (☎442-2000). Downtown: bus fare free until 7pm; subway (between the 3 downtown stops) free. Beyond downtown: bus fare $1.60, transfers 25¢, all-day weekend pass $4; subway $1.60, ages 6-11 half-price for bus and subway. Schedules, maps at most subway stations.

Taxi: Yellow Cab, ☎665-8100.

✳️🔢 ORIENTATION AND PRACTICAL INFORMATION

Pittsburgh's downtown, the **Golden Triangle,** is shaped by two rivers—the **Allegheny** to the north and the **Monongahela** to the south—which flow together to form a third, the **Ohio.** Streets in the Triangle that run parallel to the Monongahela are numbered one through seven. The **University of Pittsburgh** and **Carnegie-Mellon University** lie east of the Triangle in Oakland. Don't venture to one of Pittsburgh's many tight-knit neighborhoods without getting directions first—the city's streets and 40-odd bridges are notoriously difficult to navigate. To keep yourself oriented, pick up the detailed *Pittsburgh StreetMap* ($4) in any convenience store.

Visitor info: Pittsburgh Convention and Visitors Bureau, 425 Sixth Ave., 30th fl. (☎281-7711 or 800-359-0758; www.pittsburgh-cvb.org). Open M-F 9am-5pm, Sa-Su 9am-3pm. There are 4 **Visitors Centers:** downtown, Station Sq. at the foot of Mt. Washington, and 2 at the airport.

Parking: Gateway Center Garage, 400 Liberty Ave. (☎765-1938), located next to the info booth just outside Point State park.

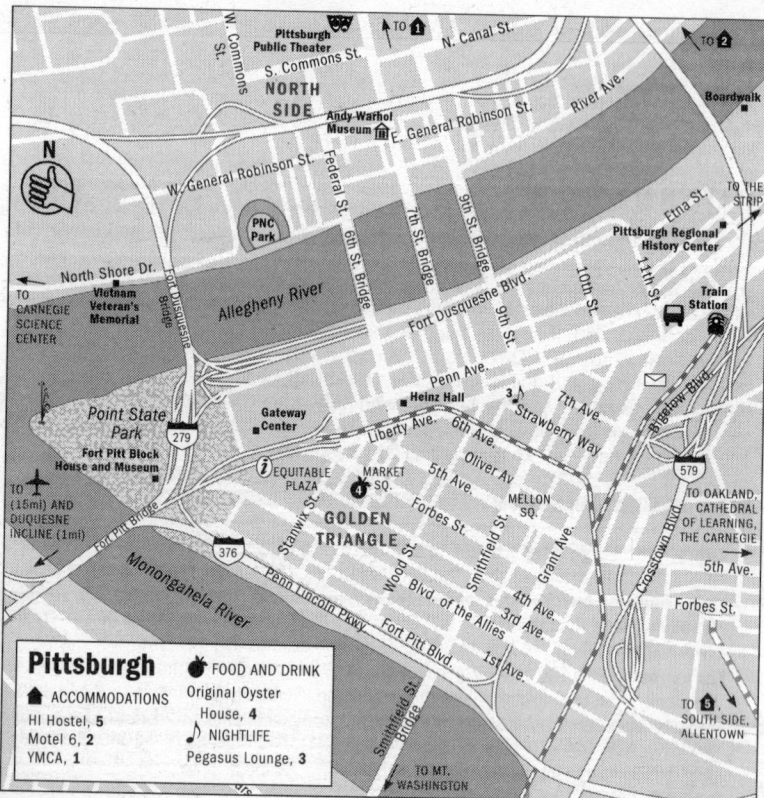

Pittsburgh

🏠 **ACCOMMODATIONS**
HI Hostel, **5**
Motel 6, **2**
YMCA, **1**

🍎 **FOOD AND DRINK**
Original Oyster
House, **4**
♪ **NIGHTLIFE**
Pegasus Lounge, **3**

Hotlines: Rape Action Hotline, ☎765-2731. Operates 24hr. **Gay, Lesbian, Bisexual Center,** ☎422-0114. Operates M-F 6:30-9:30pm, Sa 3-6pm.
Post Office: 700 Grant St. (☎642-4472). Open M-F 7am-6pm, Sa 7am-2:30pm. **ZIP code:** 15219. **Area code:** 412.

🏠 ACCOMMODATIONS

Once a bank, the sparkling ■**Pittsburgh Hostel (HI-AYH),** 830 E. Warrington Ave., across the river and up a steep hill in Allentown 1 mi. south of downtown, delivers clean, grade-A hostel living. Amenities include spacious rooms, kitchen, A/C, free parking, a great 4th-floor common room view, and an elevator in a vault. Take bus #52, "Allentown." *Be careful walking around the nearby area at night.* (☎431-1267. Linen $1, towels 50¢. Check-in 8-10am and 5pm-midnight. Lockout 10am-5pm. Laundry. Dorms $19, nonmembers $22. Semi-private singles $23/$26; doubles $41/$47; quads or family rooms $45-52. Wheelchair accessible.) The **Allegheny YMCA,** 600 W. North Ave., has men's singles in the North Side. (☎321-8594. Laundry, gym, pool. Dorms $28, $83 per week; $5 key deposit.)

Several inexpensive motels can be found on the city's outskirts near the airport. **Motel 6,** 211 Beecham Dr., off I-79 at Exit 60A, 10 mi. from downtown, supplies standard lodging with TV and A/C. (☎922-9400. Reservations suggested for summer weekends. Singles $39; doubles $45; $3 per extra person.) **Pittsburgh North Campground,** 6610 Mars Rd., in Cranberry Township, has the area's closest camping, 20min. north of downtown; take I-79 to the Cranberry/Mars exit. (☎724-776-1150. Office open daily 8am-9pm. 110 campsites, showers, swimming. Tent sites for 2 $20, with hookup $27.50; each additional adult $3, each additional child $2.)

🖸 FOOD

Aside from the pizza joints and bars downtown, **Oakland** is the best place to look for a good inexpensive meal. Collegiate watering holes and cafes pack **Forbes Ave.** around the University of Pittsburgh; colorful eateries and shops line **Walnut St.** in Shadyside and **E. Carson St.** in South Side. The **Strip District** on Penn Ave. between 16th and 22nd St. (north of downtown along the Allegheny) bustles with Italian, Greek, and Asian cuisine; the Saturday morning **Farmers Market** sells an abundance of fresh produce and fish.

🖾 Cafe Zinho, 238 Spahr St. (☎363-1500), in Shadyside, just east of Oakland. An intimate, tastefully decorated cafe serving light, scrumptious selections. Try the ornately presented chicken salad sandwich ($8). Open Tu-Th 11:30am-3pm and 5:30pm-10pm, F-Sa until 11pm.

The Original Oyster House, 20 Market Sq. (☎566-7925). Pittsburgh's oldest and perhaps cheapest restaurant and bar. Serves seafood platters ($4-6) and fresh fish sandwiches ($3-5) in a smoky marble and wrought-iron bar decorated with panoramic shots of Miss America pageants from ages past. Open M-Sa 9am-11pm.

Zenith Tea Room, at 26th and Sarah St. in the South Side (☎481-4833). Attached to a gallery cluttered with antiques and artwork for sale, the tea room treats patrons to a creative selection of vegetarian entrees ($9), sandwiches ($5), and home-brewed iced teas. If you see something you like, be sure to try it while you have the chance—the menu changes every week. Open Th-Sa 11:30am-9pm, Su 11:30am-3pm.

Union Grille, 413 S. Craig St. (☎681-8620), off Forbes Ave., in Oakland. Gains notoriety for its "honest American food" and cheap draughts ($1.75-3). Veggie sandwiches ($7), crabcakes ($6-14), and house wine ($3.25) please yuppies and students alike. Open M-Th 11:30am-10pm, F-Sa 11:30am-11pm, Su 11:30am-9pm.

🖸 SIGHTS

The **Golden Triangle** is home to **Point State Park** and its famous 200 ft. fountain. A ride up the **Duquesne Incline,** 1220 Grandview Ave., in the South Side, grants a spectacular view of the city. (☎381-1665. Open M-Sa 5:30am-12:45am, Su 7am-12:45am; round-trip $3.60.) Founded in 1787, the **University of Pittsburgh** stands in the shadow of the 42-story **Cathedral of Learning,** at Bigelow Blvd. between Forbes and 5th Ave. in Oakland. The Cathedral, built in part thanks to the dimes of Depression-era Pittsburgh schoolchildren, features 25 "nationality classrooms" decorated by artisans from the city's many ethnic traditions. (☎624-6000. Cassette-guided tours M-F 9am-2:30pm, Sa 9:30am-2:30pm, Su 11am-3pm. $2.30, seniors $2, ages 8-18 50¢.) **Carnegie-Mellon University** (☎268-2000) puts up scholars nearby on Forbes Ave.

The **Andy Warhol Museum,** 117 Sandusky St., on the North Side, is the world's largest museum dedicated to a single artist, supporting seven floors of the Pittsburgh native's material, from pop portraits of Marilyn to screenings of films like *Eat* (39min. of a man eating) and a series of pieces entitled *Oxidation,* made from synthetic polymer paint and urine on canvas. (☎237-8300. Open W-Th and Sa-Su 10am-5pm, F 10am-10pm. $8, seniors $7, students and children $4.) A 20min. walk into the North Side, **The Mattress Factory,** 505 Jacksonia Way, off East Commons, is actually a museum recognized as the best facility of site-specific installation art in the US. Known for its cutting-edge style, the Factory makes even its exterior, a crumbly warehouse, seem like a work of art. (☎231-3169. Open Tu-Sa 10am-5pm, Su 1-5pm. $6, seniors and students $4.)

Back when Pittsburgh was a bustling steel metropolis, Andrew Carnegie was its biggest robber baron—and its biggest benefactor. Carnegie's most spectacular gift, **The Carnegie,** 4400 Forbes Ave., across the street from the Cathedral of Learning, holds both an art museum and a natural history collection. (☎622-3131 or 622-3289 for tours. Open Tu-Sa 10am-5pm, Su 1-5pm; July-Aug. M 10am-5pm. $6, seniors $5, students and ages 3-18 $4.) Feel an earthquake, climb aboard a WWII submarine, or gaze at a cool miniature railroad and village at the **Carnegie Science Center,** 1 Allegheny Ave. (☎237-3400; open Su-F 10am-6pm, Sa 10am-9pm; $10, seniors and ages 3-18 $8; with OmniMax or planetarium $14/$10).

Off I-376, east of town in Penn Hills, an eastern suburb of Pittsburgh, lies the first Hindu temple in the US. The **Sri Venkateswara (S.V.) Temple** (☎373-3380) is modeled after a temple in Andhra Pradesh, India, and has become a major pilgrimage site for American Hindus since its completion. Non-Hindus can walk through the Great Hall and observe prayer.

🎭🎵 ENTERTAINMENT AND NIGHTLIFE

Most restaurants and shops carry the weekly *In Pittsburgh* or *City Paper*, great sources for free, up-to-date entertainment listings, nightclubs, and racy personals. The acclaimed **Pittsburgh Symphony Orchestra** performs September through May at **Heinz Hall,** 600 Penn Ave. (☎392-4900), downtown. The **Pittsburgh Public Theater,** in Allegheny Sq. on the North Side, is world-renowned, but charges a pretty penny. (☎316-1600. Box office open Oct.-July M 10am-5:30pm, Tu-Sa 10am-showtime, Su noon-7pm. Tickets $20-42; students and children under 27 $10 for shows Su-Th.) At brand new **PNC Park** on the North Side, the **Pirates** (☎321-2827) hit the hardball from April through September, while the **Steelers** (☎323-1200) storm the gridiron down the road at Heinz Stadium from September through December.

For nightlife, the Strip downtown is still relatively dense with revelers (relatively, that is, in a town that closes down at 5pm). The hip crowd fills **E. Carson St.** on the South Side, which overflows with regular guys and gals on weekend nights. **Metropol** and the more intimate **Rosebud,** 1600 Smallman St., in the Strip District, fill a spacious warehouse with two dance floors of steely partygoers. (☎261-4512. Cover $5. Doors open 8pm.) **Nick's Fat City,** 1601-1605 E. Carson St., South Side, features popular local rock 'n' roll bands and $2.75 draughts of Yuengling, a favorite PA brew. (☎481-6880. Cover varies. Open Tu-Sa 11am-2am.) **Jack's,** on E. Carson at S. 12th, South Side, repeatedly earns the moniker "Best Bar in the 'Burgh" by offering lifesaving specials like 25¢ hot dogs (M), 10¢ wings (W), and $1 beers (M-W) to a rowdy but friendly local crowd. (☎431-3644. 21+. Open M-Sa 7am-2am, Su 11am-2am.) The gay and lesbian community flocks to the **Pegasus Lounge,** 818 Liberty Ave., downtown, for house and drag shows. (☎281-2131. Open Tu-Sa 9pm-2am.)

OHIOPYLE STATE PARK ☎724

Lifted by steep hills and cut by cascading rivers, southwest Pennsylvania encompasses some lovely forests. Native Americans dubbed this region *Ohiopehhle* ("white frothy water") for the grand Youghiogheny River Gorge (*YOCK-a-GAY-nee*—or "The Yock" to locals), now the focal point of Pennsylvania's Ohiopyle State Park. The park's 19,000 acres offer hiking, fishing, hunting, rafting, and a variety of winter activities. The latest addition to the park, a bike trail that winds 28 mi. north from the town of Confluence to Connellsville, was converted from a riverside railroad bed. Recently named one of the 19 best walks in the world, the trail is just one section of the "rails to trails" project connecting Pittsburgh and Washington, D.C.

Throngs come each year to raft Ohiopyle's 8 mi. long class III rapids. Some of the best whitewater rafting in the East, the rapids take about 5hr. to conquer. Four outfitters front Rte. 381 in "downtown" Ohiopyle: **White Water Adventurers** (☎800-992-7238), **Wilderness Voyageurs** (☎800-272-4141), **Laurel Highlands River Tours** (☎800-472-3846), and **Mountain Streams** (☎800-723-8669). Trip prices on the Yock vary dramatically ($30-60 per person per day), depending on the season, day of the week, and difficulty. If you're an experienced river rat (or if you enjoy flipping boats), any of the above companies will rent you equipment. (Rafts about $12-15 per person; canoes $20; inflatable kayaks about $20-26.) In order to float anything, you need a **launch permit** from the park office. (M-F free, Sa-Su $2.50. Call at least 30 days in advance for Sa permits. Rental companies provide free permits.) To begin your trip, park at **Old Mitchell Parking Lot,** 7 mi. northwest of downtown, and purchase a $2.50

token. At the end of your trip, a shuttle will take you and your equipment back to your car. The Falls Market and Overnight Inn (see below) sells **fishing licenses** required in the park ($15 for 3 days; $30 per week; $35 per season, residents $17). If rafting isn't for you, outfitters in Ohiopyle rent mountain bikes for use on the park's excellent trails, including the local section of the Pittsburgh-Cumberland railbed. Bike rental prices vary (generally $3-4 per hr.).

Inexpensive motels around Ohiopyle are scarce. The excellent **Ohiopyle State Park Hostel (HI-AYH)**, on Ferncliffe Rd., sits next to a freight railroad line in the center of town off Rte. 381. (☎329-4476. Check-in 6-10pm. Check-out 7-9am. Curfew 10pm. 24 bunks, kitchen, laundry facilities. Dorms $15, nonmembers $18. Private rooms $30/$36, each additional person $5.) Down the street on Rte. 381, **Falls Market and Overnight Inn** rents quality rooms with shared baths. The downstairs store has groceries and a restaurant/snack bar. (☎329-4973. A/C, cable TV, VCR, laundry facilities. Store open daily 7am-9pm; in winter 7am-6:30pm. Triples $60; each additional person $10.) There are 226 **campsites** in Ohiopyle. (☎888-727-2757. Su-Th $15, F-Sa $17; PA residents $12/$14. Call at least 30 days in advance for summer weekends.)

Ohiopyle borders on Rte. 381, 64 mi. southeast of Pittsburgh via Rte. 51 and U.S. 40. **Greyhound** serves Uniontown, 20 mi. to the west on U.S. 40, and travels to Pittsburgh (1¼hr., 1-2 per day, $14). The **Park Information Center**, P.O. Box 105, lies just off Rte. 381 on Dinnerbell Rd. (☎329-8591; open daily 8am-4pm; Nov.-Apr. M-F 8am-4pm). **Post Office:** Green St. (☎329-8605; open M-F 7:30am-4:30pm, Sa 7:30-11:30am). **ZIP code:** 15470. **Area code:** 724.

NEAR OHIOPYLE: FALLINGWATER

Fallingwater, 8 mi. north of Ohiopyle on Rte. 381, is a masterpiece by the king of modern architecture, Frank Lloyd Wright. Designed in 1935 for Pittsburgh's wealthy Kaufmann family, "the most famous private residence ever built" blends into the surrounding terrain; huge original boulders are part of its architecture. The family wanted the house to be near the Bear Run Waterfall, but Wright daringly built it over the waterfall. As a result, the water's gentle roar can be heard in every room. A $12 million reinforcement project will be undertaken in the coming years before the house's steel girding bends beyond repair. (☎329-8501. Open Tu-Su 10am-4pm; Nov.-Dec. and Mar. Sa-Su only. Reservations required. Tours Tu-F $10, ages 6-18 $7; Sa-Su $15/$8. Children under 6 must be left in child care; $2 per hr.) The singular **Museum of Early American Farm Machines and Very Old Horse Saddles with a History** (☎438-5180), on U.S. 40 in Chalk Hill, exhibits rusted and zany Americana, as wascaly wabbits run amok amid a 12-ton cast-iron steam engine from 1905, a "cowboy's going courting saddle," and saddles from the Civil War.

DELAWARE

Tiny Delaware serves as a sanctuary from the sprawling cities of the Boston-New York-Washington megalopolis. Small in size but charming in its own particular way, Delaware is well represented by the state insect, the ladybug, adopted in 1974 after an ardent campaign by elementary school children. Delaware was first to ratify the US Constitution on Dec. 7, 1787—and proudly totes its tag as the "First State." The history of Delaware has since been dominated by the wealthy DuPont clan, whose gunpowder mills marked the start of what would become one of the world's biggest chemical companies. Tax-free shopping, scenic beach towns—and yes, convenient location—lure visitors from all along the country's eastern shores.

> **NICE TO MEET YOU** Delaware, although rightfully esteemed by Americans as the first state to ratify the Constitution, is small—so small that when two Delawareans meet for the first time, they ask each other, "What exit are you from?"

MID-ATLANTIC

▶ PRACTICAL INFORMATION

Capital: Dover.

Visitor info: Duke of York and Federal St., Dover 19903 (☎302-739-4266 or 800-292-9507; www.state.de.us). Open M-F 8am-4:30pm. **Delaware State Chamber of Commerce,** 1201 N. Orange St., Wilmington 19899 (☎800-422-1181).

Postal Abbreviation: DE. **Sales Tax:** 0%; 8% on accommodations.

LEWES   ☎302

Explored by Henry Hudson and founded in 1613 by the Dutch, Lewes was Delaware's first town and has attracted colonists, pirates, hardy fishermen, and now summer renters. Nevertheless, Lewes (pronounced Lewis) hasn't changed much with the times. Featuring Victorian gingerbread houses, quiet streets, and a genuine lack of tourist culture, this ferry town has remained old-fashioned for ages. The town has plotted out a walking tour of its colonial attractions, but the main draw remains Lewes's beautiful beach, which draws an older and wealthier vacationing set away from the bustling boardwalk of nearby Rehoboth Beach.

■▶ ORIENTATION AND PRACTICAL INFORMATION. Unless you own a private chopper, automobile is the only sensible way to reach Lewes. From points north, Rte. 1 S brings you directly to Lewes before simply accessing Savannah Rd., which dissects Lewes. From the west, begin traveling east on Rte. 404, then take Rte. 9 E at Georgetown. This will land you at Rte. 1, where you continue south until Savannah Rd. The best public transportation option is the **Delaware Resort Transit** (☎800-553-3278) shuttle bus, which runs from the ferry terminal through Lewes to Rehoboth and Dewey Beach (every 30min.; operates late May to early Sept. daily 7am-3am; $1, seniors and disabled 40¢, day pass $2). **Seaport Taxis** (☎645-6800) will take you door to door anywhere in Lewes for a small fee. Note that the beach is not in town—a bridge separates the two, and it's a long walk to the beach without a car. Thankfully, the beach does offer abundant parking. **Post Office:** 116 Front St. (☎645-6548; open M-F 8:30am-4pm). **ZIP code:** 19958. **Area code:** 302.

▶◻ ACCOMMODATIONS AND FOOD. A charming, kid-friendly seven-room B&B with a lavish vegetarian breakfast, the **Savannah Inn,** 330 Savannah Rd., tops other Lewes accommodations in price and earth-friendly philosophy. Don't be fooled by the hints of peeling paint; this building is well-maintained and clean. (☎645-5592. No A/C. Oct.-May no breakfast and $10 off room rates. Double rooms with shared bath $70, largest rooms sleep 3-4 and run $75-80.) **Captain's Quarters,** 406 Savannah Rd., offers clean, quiet, and comfy doubles. (☎645-7924. Check-in 3pm, check-out 11am. $70, on summer weekends $85; each additional person $5.) Over 150 sandy campsites are available in **Cape Henlopen State Park,** off Rte. 1. From the north, bypass Savannah Rd. and continue on Rte. 1 for ½ mi. before signs direct you to take a left. These sites, a short hike from the beach, feature new restroom and visitors' facilities. (☎645-2103. Campground open Apr.-Oct. Park open year-round 7am-11pm. Sites for 4 $25, with water $27; each additional person $2.)

The few restaurants in Lewes cluster primarily on 2nd St. **Rosa Negra,** 128 2nd St., offers huge plates of Italian fare in a subtly decorated dining room. Be an anxious early bird, though, because the post-6pm menu is 25% pricier. (☎645-1980. Early bird special daily 5-6pm; choice of 8 pastas and 9 sauces for $7 combo; seniors $6. Open daily 5-9pm.) Sniff the rich aroma of brews like "linzer torte" and "coconut kiss" at **Oby Lee Coffee Roasters,** 124 2nd St. Tiptoe around the several bags of coffee bean imports piled on the floor to order sandwiches ($2-4) and the "opposite of Hot Cocoa" Vanilla Dream. (☎645-0733. Open daily 7am-10pm.) Locals jam to live music (Tu-Sa) at the wood-paneled **Rose and Crown Restaurant and Pub,** 108 2nd St. (☎645-2373. Happy hour daily 4-6pm; $1 off drafts. Open daily 11am-1am.)

MID-ATLANTIC

⊙ SIGHTS. While the towns on the Eastern Shore pride themselves on their independence from the tourism industry, Lewes is struggling to turn itself into a vacationer's historical playground. The waterfront in town sports several fishing piers, as well as the **ferry** to Cape May. (☎644-6030. 8 per day; $18 per vehicle, $4 per passenger. Office open daily 8:30am-4:30pm.) The **Lewes Chamber of Commerce,** 20 King's Hwy., operates out of the Fisher-Martin House and offers useful Lewes info and a free walking tour of founders' houses, old meeting places, and buildings that saw action during the War of 1812. (☎645-8078. Open in summer M-F 10am-4pm, Sa 9am-3pm, Su 10am-2pm; off-season closed Sa-Su.) Secluded among sand dunes and scrub pines 1 mi. east of Lewes on the Atlantic Ocean is the 4000-acre **Cape Henlopen State Park** (see **Accommodations,** above). The family-oriented beach caters to youngsters frolicking in the waves under the watchful eyes of lifeguards, while parents and young couples can soak up the rays from their lawn chairs. The **Seaside Nature Center,** the park's museum on beach and ocean life, is home to a seabird nesting colony, sparkling white "walking dunes," and a two-mile paved trail ideal for biking or skating. (☎645-6852. Open M-Sa 9am-4pm, Su noon-4pm. Trail open daily 8am-sunset. $5 per car; bikes and walkers free.)

REHOBOTH BEACH ☎302

Rehoboth Beach is between Lewes and Ocean City, both geographically and culturally. While Lewes tends to be quiet and family-oriented and Ocean City attracts rowdy underage high-schoolers, Rehoboth is home to its share of cotton candy, mini-golf, fast-food, beach volleyball, and discount t-shirt shops clustered along the boardwalk but has also preserved its antique beach cottage appeal. Well-heeled Washington-area families and a growing gay population constitute the summer crowd, supplemented by daytrippers seeking relaxation as much as sand and sun.

◪▨ ORIENTATION AND PRACTICAL INFORMATION. Rehoboth is located about 6 mi. south of Lewes. To reach the town from Rte. 1, take Rte. 1B to Rehoboth Ave. and follow it to the water. The vibrant section of town is very concentrated within the beachside boardwalk, so walking is the preferred mode of transportation. **Greyhound/Trailways,** 251 Rehoboth Ave. (☎227-7223 or 800-231-2222), stops next to the Chamber of Commerce. **Buses** go to and from Baltimore (3½hr., 1 per day, $28.75), Philadelphia (4hr., 2 per day, $30.75), and Washington, **D.C.** (3½hr., 3 per day, $32.75). The **Rehoboth Beach Chamber of Commerce,** 501 Rehoboth Ave., a recycled railroad depot next to an imitation lighthouse, doles out Delaware info and coupons. (☎227-2233 or 800-441-1329. Open M-F 9am-5pm, Sa-Su 9am-noon.) Surf the web at **Avenue Video and Internet,** 71 Rehoboth Ave. (☎227-5999. $4 per 15min. Open Su-Th 10am-10pm, F-Sa 10am-11pm.) **Post Office:** Rehoboth Ave. and 2nd St. (☎227-8406; open M-F 9am-6pm, Sa 10am-3pm). **ZIP code:** 19971.

▟◻ ACCOMMODATIONS AND FOOD. Inexpensive lodgings, mostly charming bed and breakfasts, abound in Rehoboth. **Mr. and Mrs. Downs of the Lord Baltimore,** 16 Baltimore Ave., half a block from the boardwalk, have rented out clean, antiquated rooms with TVs, refrigerators, and A/C for over 25 years. (☎227-2855. Check-in 2pm, check-out 11am. Singles and doubles with shared bath $40-55, with private bath $56-65; in winter $25-50; each additional person $5.) **The Abbey Inn,** 31 Maryland Ave., is just a street away from the noise of Rehoboth Ave. (☎227-7023. 2-day min. stay. Open late May to early Sept. Singles and doubles with shared bath from $48, rooms for 3-4 people with shared bath $61, suite with private bath $105; 15% surcharge on weekends.) The wooded **Big Oaks Family Campground,** 1 mi. off Rte. 1 on Rd. 270, offers a rugged alternative to town lodging. Shaded sites, a bathhouse, and a pool are all available. (☎645-6838. Sites $28.50, with hookup $33.)

Rehoboth is known for its bargain, high-quality beach cuisine and its many bars. **Cafe Papillon,** 42 Rehoboth Ave., in the Penny Lane Mall offers an authentic European twist to a very American town. French cooks speaking the international language of good food serve up fresh crepes ($2.75-7), croissants ($2-3.50), and $5-7 baguette sandwiches. (☎227-7568. Open May-Oct. daily 8am-11pm.) Refuel after some late-night skinny dipping at **Nicola's Pizza**, 8 1st St. Customers of all kinds are drawn by the enticing aroma of an Italian kitchen and indulge themselves with satisfying and economical pasta dishes for $4-7. (☎227-6211. Open daily 11am-3am.) For filling breakfasts like Mom used to make, saunter over to the **Royal Treat**, 4 Wilmington Ave., where a stack of pancakes and bacon is $5.50. The restaurant doubles as an ice-cream parlor in the afternoon and evening, catering to traditionalists with an old-fashioned ice cream soda and genuine Hershey's syrup on hot fudge sundaes, both for $3.50. (☎227-6277. Breakfast 8-11:30am; ice cream 1-11:30pm.)

🎭🏠 **ENTERTAINMENT AND NIGHTLIFE.** Partygoers head out early as well, given the 1am last calls. **The Summer House Saloon**, 228 Rehoboth Ave., across from City Hall, is one of Rehoboth's favorite spots to flirt. Young twenty-something crowds take advantage of nightly drink specials and island and hip hop music to get their game on. (☎227-3895. M half-price half-pound burger, reduced-price bucket o' beer night, F half-price hurricanes. Open June-Aug. daily 5-11pm, bar open until 2am; Sept.-May Tu, F, Sa only.) Beer lovers bow down to **Dogfish Head Brewings & Eats**, 320 Rehoboth Ave. With inventive house brews like the luscious Buxom Blond Barleywine, who can blame them? Live music Friday and Saturday whips up the partying crowds. (☎226-2739. Happy hour M-F 4-7pm; pints $2. Open M-F 4pm-1am, Sa-Su noon-1am.) A new addition to the Rehoboth bar scene, the **Full Moon Saloon** uses the universal appeal of live classic rock 'n' roll to attract young and old. (Happy hour M-Th 5-8pm; $1 drafts. Open M-Sa 10am-1am, Su 11am-1am.) At **The Blue Moon**, 35 Baltimore Ave., a predominantly gay crowd grooves to techno beats. (☎227-6515. Happy hour M-F 4-6pm. Open daily 4pm-1am.)

MARYLAND

Once upon a time, folks on Maryland's rural eastern shore captured crabs, raised tobacco, and ruled the state. Across the bay in Baltimore, workers loaded ships and ran factories. Then the federal government expanded, industry shrank, and Maryland had a new focal point: the Baltimore-Washington Pkwy. Suburbs grew, Baltimore revitalized, and the Old Line State acquired a new, liberal urbanity. As D.C.'s homogenized commuter suburbs continue to swell beyond the limits of Maryland's Montgomery and Prince George counties, Baltimore revels in its immensity, whereas Annapolis, the capital, remains a small town of sailors. The mountains of the state's western panhandle are largely pristine to this day.

🛈 PRACTICAL INFORMATION

Capital: Annapolis.
Visitor info: Office of Tourism, 217 E. Redwood St., Baltimore 21202 (☎800-543-1036; www.mdisfun.org). **Dept. of Natural Resources**, 580 Taylor Ave., Annapolis 21401 (☎410-260-8186). Open M-F 8am-4:30pm.
Postal Abbreviation: MD. **Sales Tax:** 5%.

BALTIMORE ☎410

Nicknamed "Charm City" for its mix of small-town hospitality and big-city flair, Baltimore still manages to capture the hearts of visitors with its lively restaurant and bar scene, first-class museums, and loving attention to historical sights. Birthplace of the *Star-Spangled Banner*, Baltimore lies just north of the nation's capital and is now home to two major sports teams which provide year-round spectacle—win or lose—for its proud residents.

Central Baltimore

TO EDGAR ALLAN
POE HOUSE

UNIVERSITY OF
MARYLAND
AT BALTIMORE

Penn St.
Emory St.
Washington Blvd.
Greene St.
Paca St.
Eutaw St.
Lombard St.
Redwood St.
Baltimore St.

Edgar Allan
Poe Grave

LEXINGTON MARKET

Fayette
Lexington
Marion
St.
Eutaw
St.
Saratoga St.
Josephine St.
Howard St.

TO B&O
RAILROAD
MUSEUM

Babe Ruth Birthplace/
Baltimore Orioles Museum

Orioles Park at
Camden Yards

200 meters
200 yards

Camden
Station

Pratt Street

Camden St.
Conway St.
Barre St.
Howard St.
Sharp St.
Welcome St.

Convention
Center

Baltimore
Arena

CHARLES CENTER

Liberty Street

N. Charles St.
Saint Paul St.
Lexington St.
Davis St.

Light St.

Convention
Center

S. Charles St.
Lee St.
SCIENCE CENTER (136k)
TO MARYLAND
SCIENCE CENTER (136k)

Clipper City

Calvert St.

Harborplace

Inner Harbor

Patapsco R.

World Trade
Center, Top of
the World

National
Aquarium

Maritime
Museum

Columbus
Center for
Marine
Biology

Pier Six
Concert
Pavilion

Museum of
Public Works

Jewish
Historical
Society

South St.
Water St.
Commerce St.
Gay Street
Frederick St.
Market Pl.

City Hall

Holocaust
Memorial

City Life
Museums

Star Spangled Banner,
Flag House and Museum

President St.
Albemarle St.
High St.
Exeter St.
Fleet St.
Aliceanna St.
Eastern Ave.

Civil War
Museum

LITTLE
ITALY

Front St.
Lombard St.
Pratt St.
Granby St.
Central Ave.

Jones Falls Expwy.

Falls way

Low St.

Colvin St.

Fayette
St.

Baltimore St.

Asquith St.

Museum of
Mankind

Baltimore's southern heritage is visible in its many neighborhoods. In Roland Park, for instance, every house has a front porch and everyone greets you in a friendly "Bawlmer" accent. Certain natives have gained notoriety for digging beneath this genial southern complacency: John Waters's films capture the city's twisted side, while Edgar Allan Poe's writing evokes its gloominess.

▐ TRANSPORTATION

Baltimore lies 35 mi. north of D.C. and about 150 mi. from the Atlantic Ocean. To get to Baltimore from D.C., take the **Baltimore-Washington Pkwy. (I-295). Exit 53 for Rte. 395** leads right into **Inner Harbor.** Without traffic, the trip takes under 1hr.

Airport: Baltimore-Washington International (BWI) (☎859-7111), on I-195 off the Baltimore-Washington Pkwy., about 10 mi. south of the city center. Take MTA bus #17 to the Nursery Rd. light rail station. Airport shuttles to hotels (☎859-0800) run daily every 30min. 5:45am-11:30pm ($11 to downtown). For D.C., shuttles leave every hr. 5:45am-11:30pm ($26-34). Amtrak trains run to Baltimore ($5) and D.C. ($12). MARC commuter trains are cheaper but slower, and only run M-F (Baltimore $3.25, D.C. $5).

Trains: Penn Station, 1500 N. Charles St. (☎800-872-7245), at Mt. Royal Ave. Easily accessible by bus #3 or 11 from Charles Station downtown. Amtrak trains run every 30min.-1hr. to New York ($62-71); Washington, D.C. (from $19); and Philadelphia (from $35). On weekdays, 2 **MARC commuter lines** (☎800-325-7245) connect Baltimore to D.C.'s Union Station (☎859-7400 or 291-4268) via Penn Station (with stops at BWI Airport) or **Camden Station** (☎613-5342), at the corner of Howard and Camden St. near Oriole Park. Both are $5.75. Ticket window open daily 5:30am-9:30pm.

Buses: Greyhound (☎800-231-2222) has 2 locations: downtown at 210 W. Fayette St. (☎752-7682), near N. Howard St., and 5625 O'Donnell St. (☎752-0908), 3 mi. east of downtown near I-95. Connections to New York ($24), Washington, D.C. ($6), and Philadelphia ($15).

Public Transit: Mass Transit Administration (MTA), 300 W. Lexington St. (☎539-5000 or 800-543-9809), near N. Howard St. Operator available M-F 6am-9pm. Bus, Metro, and light rail service to most major sights in the city and outlying areas. Some buses run 24hr. Metro operates M-F 5am-midnight, Sa 6am-midnight. Light rail operates M-F 6am-11pm, Sa 8am-11pm, Su 11am-7pm. Base fare $1.35; may be higher depending on distance traveled. Bus #17 runs from the Nursery Rd. light rail to BWI Airport.

Water Taxi: Harbor Boating, Inc., 1615 Thames St. Main stop at Inner Harbor (563-3901 or ☎800-658-8947). Stops every 8-18min. (Nov.-Mar. every 40min.) at the harbor museums, Harborplace, Fells Point, Little Italy, and more. Service May-Aug. daily 9am-midnight, Apr. and Sept.-Oct. 9am-9pm, Nov.-Mar. 9am-6pm. 1-day unlimited rides $4.50, under 11 $2. Ticket includes coupons for Baltimore attractions.

Taxis: Checker Cab, ☎685-1212. **Royal Cab,** ☎327-0330.

✦ ▐ ORIENTATION AND PRACTICAL INFORMATION

The southern end of the **Jones Falls Expressway (I-83)** halves Baltimore near the Inner Harbor, and the **Baltimore Beltway (I-695)** circles the city. **I-95** cuts across the southwest corner of the city as a shortcut to the wide arc of the Beltway. During rush hour, these roads slow to a crawl. The city is divided into quarters by **Baltimore St.** (east-west) and **Charles St.** (north-south). Directional prefixes indicate every other street's relation to these main streets.

The **Inner Harbor,** near the corner of Pratt and Charles St., is a scenic tourist trap and home to historic ships, a shopping mall, and an aquarium. The museum-laden **Mount Vernon** neighborhood—served by city buses #3, 9, and 11—occupies **N. Charles St.,** north of **Baltimore St.,** around **Monument St.** and **Centre Ave.** Ethnic **Little Italy** sits a few blocks east of the Inner Harbor, past the **Jones Falls Expressway.** Continuing past Little Italy, a short walk to the southeast brings you past Broadway to bar-happy **Fells Point.** Old-fashioned **Federal Hill** preserves Baltimore history, while the area east of **Camden Yards** has recently been re-urbanized.

Baltimore, like any other major US city, lacks free parking. Either come fisting shiny quarters or expect to pay garages about $9 per day. Meters and garages away from the harbor are less expensive.

Visitor info: Baltimore Area Visitors Center, 451 Light St. (☎837-7024). Located in a red-trimmed, white trailer, the user-friendly center provides dozens of maps, brochures offering discounts to sights and restaurants, and the city's helpful *Quickguide*. Open in summer M-Sa 9am-7pm, Su 10am-5pm; in winter daily 9am-5pm.

Traveler's Aid: ☎685-3569 (M-F 8:30am-3:30pm) or 685-5874, voice-mail only. Two desks at **BWI Airport** (☎859-7209). Open M-F 9am-9pm, Su 1-9pm.

Help Lines: Suicide: ☎531-6677. **Sexual Assault and Domestic Violence:** ☎828-6390. Both operate 24hr. **Gay and Lesbian:** ☎837-8888. Operates daily 7pm-midnight.

Post Office: 900 E. Fayette St. (☎347-4425). Open M-F 7:30am-9pm, Sa 7:30am-5pm. **ZIP code:** 21233. **Area code:** 410 or 443; in text 410 unless otherwise noted.

▚ ACCOMMODATIONS AND CAMPING

Expensive chain hotels dominate the Inner Harbor, and reputable inexpensive hotels are hard to find. For a convenient way to reserve B&Bs, call **Amanda's Bed and Breakfast Reservation Service**, 1428 Park Ave. (☎225-0001 or 800-899-7533. Open M-F 8:30am-5:30pm, Sa 8:30am-noon. Rates from $50.)

Duke's Motel, 7905 Pulaski Hwy. (☎686-0400), in Rosedale off the Beltway. The bullet-proof glass in the front office is nothing to worry about—all the neighborhood motels have it. The area is actually safer than most parts of downtown Baltimore. Clean and efficiently run. Simple rooms have A/C and cable TV. $5 key deposit and ID required. King-sized beds optional. Singles from $45; doubles from $50.

Quality Inn Inner Harbor, 1701 Russell St. (☎727-3400 or 800-221-2222), near the Beltway in South Baltimore, about 1 mi. from Inner Harbor. Cable TV, data ports, pool, and continental breakfast. Some rooms have fridge and microwave. *Be careful at night.* Singles M-Th $72, F-Su $85; doubles $77/$90. AARP/AAA and military 10% discount.

Capitol KOA, 768 Cecil Ave. (☎923-2771, 987-7477 or 800-562-0248), in Millersville, between D.C. and Baltimore. From D.C., take Rte. 50 E (John Hanson Hwy.) to Rte. 3 N (Robert Crain Hwy.). Bear right after 8 mi. onto Veterans Hwy.; after a short distance, turn left under the highway onto Hog Farm Rd.; follow blue signs. Pool, volleyball courts, and bathroom/shower facilities centrally located. Free shuttles to MARC commuter train, New Carollton Metro, and Union Station. Standard max. stay 2 week; varies based upon availability. Open late Mar. through Oct. Sites for 2 $30; water and electricity $34; full hookup $39; 1-room kabins $49, 2 rooms $59. Each additional adult $5, child $3.

◖ FOOD

▨ Mugavero's Confectionery, 300 S. Exeter St. (☎539-9798). This menu-less deli has been a fixture for 54 years thanks to the unwavering service of the friendly proprietor. Patrons can invent their own sandwiches or entrust their sandwich to the owner-operator's creative imagination ($4). Open daily 10am-9pm, sometimes later. Cash only.

▨ Amicci's, 231 S. High St. (☎528-1096). Mediterranean zest is apparent on the menu as well as the Italian movie decor; *ziti la rosa* (ziti in tomato pesto served with shrimp in marsala sauce; $13) is a standout. Live large with the renowned *pane rotundo*, jumbo shrimp stuffed into a round loaf of soft Italian bread ($6). 11 immense pasta dishes under $10. Open M-Th noon-10pm, F-Sa noon-11pm, Su noon-9pm.

▨ The Fudgery, 301 Light St. (☎539-5260), on the first fl. in the Light St. Pavilion. Nirvana for chocolate cravers. Musically inclined staff sings while preparing heavenly fudge. Products are pricey ($6 per half-pound slice) but worth the sacrifice for a delectable (and entertaining) treat. Open M-Th 9am-10pm, F-Sa 9am-11:30pm, Su 9am-9pm.

Phillip's Restaurant, 301 Light St. (☎800-782-2722), on the first fl. in the Light St. Pavilion. Loyal fans and families flock to the Inner Harbor's seafood hot spot for magnificent marine dishes. Sandwiches ($6-13) are just as delicious as the expensive entrees

($12 and up). Tykes under 5 eat for free. Try **Phillip's Seafood Market** right next door for inexpensive takeout. Open M-F 9am-10pm, Sa 9am-11pm, Su 9am-8pm.

👁 SIGHTS

Baltimore's gray harbor ends with a colorful bang in the **Harborplace,** a five-square-block body of water bounded on three sides by an aquarium, shopping malls, a science museum, and a bevy of boardable ships. The nation's first pier-pavilion, the Harborplace mall is Baltimore's most imitated building. Crowds flock to Harborplace's Pratt St. and Light St. Pavilions and to the Gallery across the street for shopping and air-conditioned bliss. (☎332-4191. Open M-Sa 10am-9pm, Su 10am-6pm.) The **National Aquarium,** at Pier 3, 501 E. Pratt St., makes the Inner Harbor worthwhile. Multilevel exhibits and tanks show off rare fish, big fish, red fish, and blue fish along with the biology and ecology of oceans, rivers, and rainforests. The Children's Cove (level 4) lets visitors handle inter-tidal marine animals. (☎576-3800. Open July-Aug. daily 9am-8pm; Mar.-June and Sept.-Oct. Sa-Th 9am-5pm, F 9am-8pm; Nov.-Feb. Sa-Th 10am-5pm, F 10am-8pm. Aquarium remains open 2hr. after last entrance time. $14, seniors $10.50, children $7.50, under 3 free.)

Several ships bob by the aquarium; most belong to the **Baltimore Maritime Museum** (☎396-3453), at Piers 3 and 4. Visitors may board the USS *Torsk* submarine (which sank the last WWII Japanese combatant ships), the lightship *Chesapeake*, and the Coast Guard cutter *Roger B. Taney.* At the Inner Harbor's far edge, the kid-oriented **Maryland Science Center,** 601 Light St., stuns audiences with its five-story IMAX screen, 38-speaker sound system, and 50 ft. planetarium. (☎685-5225. Open June-Aug. M-Th 9:30am-6pm, F-Su 10am-8pm; Sept.-May M-F 10am-5pm, Sa-Su 10am-6pm. $11; seniors, military, and ages 13-17 $10; 4-12 $8.50; under 4 free.) **Fort McHenry National Monument,** at the foot of E. Fort Ave. and Lawrence Ave., commemorates the fort's victory against British forces in the War of 1812; the battle inspired Francis Scott Key's *The Star-Spangled Banner.* (☎962-4290. Open June-Aug. daily 8am-8pm, Sept.-May 8am-5pm. $5, seniors and under 16 free.)

The **Walters Art Gallery,** 600 N. Charles St., at Centre St., keeps one of the world's largest private art collections, spanning five millennia. The museum's most esteemed possession is the Ancient Art collection, with sculptures and metalwork from Egypt, Greece, and Rome. (☎547-9000. Open Tu-F 10am-4pm, Sa-Su 11am-5pm. Tours W noon and Su 1:30pm. $5, seniors and students with ID $3, ages 6-17 $1, under 18 free Sa before noon.) The **Baltimore Museum of Art,** 10 Art Museum Dr., at N. Charles and 31st St., exhibits a fine collection of Americana and modern art. The museum's **sculpture gardens** make great picnic grounds. (☎396-7100. Open W-F 11am-5pm, Sa-Su 11am-6pm. $6, seniors and students $4, under 18 free; Th free.) The **Baltimore Zoo,** Exit 7 off I-83, offers a new chimpanzee exhibit, the spectacular Palm Tree Conservatory, a lake surrounded by lush greenery, and a simulated savanna with elephants and Siberian tigers. (☎396-7175. Open M-F 10am-4pm, Sa 10am-8pm, Su 10am-5:30pm; in winter until 4pm. $9, seniors and ages 2-16 $5.50.)

🎵 ENTERTAINMENT

Vacationing in Baltimore can be expensive, but fortunately for the budget traveler, much of the city's finest entertainment can be enjoyed free of charge. At **Harborplace,** performers are constantly entertaining tourists with magic acts, juggling, and clowning around during the day. At night, dance, dip, and dream to the sounds of anything from country to calypso to oldies at the Harborplace (occasional Th-Sa nights). The **Baltimore Museum of Art** offers free summer jazz concerts in its sculpture garden. **Jazzline** (☎466-0600) lists jazz shows from September to May; call for schedules and info. When the music isn't free in Baltimore, it's still just as good. Big-name musicians perform several times a week from May to October at **Pier 6 Concert Pavilion** (☎625-3100). Tickets ($15-30) are available at the pavilion or through Ticketmaster (☎625-1400 or 481-7328). The **Baltimore Symphony Orchestra** plays at Meyerhoff Symphony Hall, 1212 Cathedral St., from September to May and during their month-long Summerfest. (☎783-8000. Box office open M-F 10am-6pm, Sa-Su noon-5pm, and 1hr. before performances. Call for Summerfest dates. Tickets $15-52.) The **Lyric Opera House,** down the street at 110 W. Mt. Royal Ave., near Maryland Ave., hosts the **Baltimore Opera Company** from late October to April. (☎727-6000. Box office open M-F 10am-5pm. Tickets $24-109.)

The **Arena Players,** an African-American theater group, performs comedies, drama, and dance at 801 McCullough St., at Martin Luther King, Jr. Blvd. (☎728-6500. Box office open M-F 9am-5pm. Tickets start at $15.) The **Showcase of Nations Ethnic Festivals** celebrate Baltimore's ethnic neighborhoods with a different culture featured each week (June-Sept.). The festivals take place all over the city; call the Baltimore Visitors Bureau (☎800-282-6632) for info.

The beloved **Baltimore Orioles** play ball at **Camden Yards,** just a few blocks from the Inner Harbor at the corner of Russell and Camden St. Tickets for Orioles games range from $7 (standing room) to $35 (reserved boxes). Call 547-6234 to order tickets. The 2001 NFL Champion **Ravens** represent Baltimore's second chance at professional football. The Ravens, formerly the Cleveland Browns, play in **Raven Stadium,** adjacent to Camden Yards. To order individual game tickets, call 481-7328. Just outside of Baltimore, head off to the races at **Laurel** (☎792-7775; on Rte. 216 off I-95) and **Pimlico Race Tracks** (☎542-9400) on Rte. 129. The two tracks hold thoroughbred horse races for much of the spring, summer, and fall. **The Preakness Stakes** (☎542-9400, ext. 4484 for tickets), leg two of the Triple Crown, is run annually at Pimlico on the third Saturday in May.

NIGHTLIFE

Last call in Baltimore happens at 2am; hearty partiers should plan to start their evenings early. After 2am, check out Fells Point to meet throngs of fellow revellers.

Cat's Eye Pub, 1730 Thames St. (☎276-9866), in Fells Point. An older crowd of regulars packs it in every weeknight for live blues, jazz, folk, or traditional Irish music (M-Th 9pm, F-Sa 4pm). Over 25 different drafts and 60 bottled beers. Happy hour M-F 4-7pm. Live blues Su 4-8pm. Occasional cover for national musical acts. Open daily noon-2am.

Bohager's, 701 S. Eden St. (☎563-7220), in Fells Point. Bohager's is an enclosed tropical paradise for college students and locals. Under a 29,000 sq. ft. retractable dome, patrons rage to live island music until the wee hours of the morning. Tickets available at the club or through Ticketmaster (☎481-7328). Happy hour Th-F 5-8pm. Open M-F 11:30am-2am, Sa-Su 3pm-2am.

Greene Turtle, 720 Broadway (☎342-4222). With foosball, pool (50¢), and an extensive CD jukebox, this relaxed bar is popular with the Baltimore college crowd, the Ravens, and anyone else interested in tanking up for next to nothing. $1.50 drafts and half-price appetizers during happy hour (M-F 4-7pm). Open daily 11:30am-2am. Sandwiches $5-7.50. Sa-Su special yields ½lb. spicy steamed shrimp for $4.50.

Hippo, 1 W. Eager St. (☎547-0069), across the street from Central Station. Baltimore's largest gay bar provides pool tables, videos, and a packed dance floor in an industrial setting. Happy hour 4-8pm daily. First Su of every month is Ladies' Tea, one of the largest lesbian events this side of the Mississippi (6-10pm). Men's Night Th. Cover Th-F $3, Sa $6. Saloon open daily 4pm-2am; dance bar open Th-Sa 10pm-2am.

ANNAPOLIS ☎410

Settled in 1649, Annapolis became the capital of Maryland in 1694. The fine Georgian houses once packed in colonial aristocrats and their slaves. Annapolis made history when the Continental Congress ratified the Treaty of Paris here in 1784, marking the official end of the American Revolution. After its 1783 stint as temporary capital of the US (hot on the heels of Philadelphia, New York, and Trenton, NJ), Annapolis relinquished the national limelight in favor of a more tranquil existence. Now, guests are treated to a taste of what coastal America once was: pastel row houses with gorgeous gardens, friendly strollers, and an endless array of boats.

■⑦ ORIENTATION AND PRACTICAL INFORMATION. Annapolis lies southeast of U.S. 50 (also known as U.S. 301), 30 mi. east of D.C. and 30 mi. south of Baltimore. From D.C. take U.S. 50 E, which begins at New York Ave. and can also be accessed from the Beltway (I-495). From Baltimore, follow Rte. 2 S to US 50 W, cross the Severn River Bridge, and then take Rowe Blvd. into the city.

The city extends south and east from two landmarks: **Church Circle** and **State Circle. School St.,** in a blatantly unconstitutional move, connects Church and State. **East St.** runs from the State House to the Naval Academy. **Main St.** (where food and entertainment congregate) starts at Church Circle and ends at the docks. The downtown area of Annapolis, besides being a vibrant town center, is also very safe. Downtown Annapolis is compact and easily walkable, but finding a parking space—unless in an expensive lot or in the public garage ($7-11 per day)—can be tricky. Parking at the **Visitors Center** ($1 per hr., $8 max. weekdays, $4 max. for the weekend) is the best bet. There is also free weekend parking in State Lots A and B at the corner of Rowe Blvd. and Calvert St.

Greyhound stops at the local bus stop in the football field parking lot at Rowe Blvd. and Taylor St. and sends buses to Washington, D.C. (1hr., 4 per day, $10.50); Philadelphia (5-6hr., 2 per day, $42); and Baltimore (3hr., 5 per day, $10). **Mass Transit Administration** (☎539-5000 or 800-543-9809) has an express (#210) that runs to Baltimore Monday through Friday (1hr., $2.85) and a local (#14) that runs daily (1½hr., $1.35). Buses leave from St. John's and College Ave. and St. John's and Calvert St. **Annapolis Dept. of Public Transportation** operates a web of city buses connecting the historic district with the rest of town. (☎263-7964. Buses run M-Sa 5:30am-10pm, Su 8am-7pm. Base fare 75¢, over 60 or disabled 35¢.) **Annapolis Cab Co.,** ☎268-0022. **Checker Cab,** ☎268-3737. **Visitor info: Annapolis and Anne Arundel County Conference and Visitors Bureau,** 26 West St., has free maps and brochures. (☎280-0445; www.visit-annapolis.org. Open daily 9am-5pm.) **Post Office:** 1 Church Circle (☎263-9292; open M-F 8:30am-5pm). **ZIP code:** 21401. **Area code:** 410.

⋔ ACCOMMODATIONS. The heart of Annapolis lacks cheap motels but has plenty of elegant and pricey bed and breakfasts. In general, these B&Bs prove a better choice than the hotels scattered about western Annapolis. Rooms should be reserved in advance, especially for weekends and the busy summer months. **Bed and Breakfasts of Maryland** aids in arranging accommodations in Annapolis. (☎800-736-4667, ext. 15. Open M-F 9am-5pm, Sa 10am-3pm.) **Amanda's** offers a similar service. (☎225-0001. Open M-F 8:30am-5:30pm, Sa 8:30am-noon.) All lodgings listed are near the dock and within walking distance of major attractions.

Scotlaur Inn, 165 Main St., atop Chick and Ruth's Delly, has ten tiny guest rooms. This homey "bed and bagel," which is less fancy than the other B&Bs, is far more affordable. Huge complimentary breakfasts are available from **Chick & Ruth's** (see **Food,** below) and more than compensate for the rooms' lack of luxury. (☎268-5665. A/C, TV, and private baths. Rooms range from $80-95.) **Gibson's Lodgings,** 110 Prince George St., 1 block from City Dock on Randall St., offers a patio and spacious common parlors among its three ivy covered buildings and 18 rooms. (☎268-5555. Continental breakfast and courtyard parking included. Single rooms start at $79; doubles at $109. Rollaway $20 extra. $10 discount in off season. One wheelchair accessible room available.) **Flag House Inn,** 26 Randall St., has a prime location next to the visitors entrance to the Naval Academy and, true to its name, six flags waving from the porch. (☎280-2721 or 800-437-4825. TV, A/C, and free off-street parking. King-sized beds and private baths in each of the 5 rooms. Breakfast included. Try to reserve 2-4 weeks in advance. Rooms begin at $95; 2-person suites $145; 4-person suites $230.)

◖ FOOD. Most restaurants in the area cluster around **City Dock,** an area packed with people in summertime (especially Tu at 7:30pm, when the spinnaker races finish at City Dock). The best place to find cheap eats is the Market House food court at the center of City Dock, where a hearty meal costs under $5. Numerous newspaper clippings adorn the walls at **Chick & Ruth's Delly,** 165 Main St., paying homage to an Annapolis institution of over 30 years. Dishes named for local and national politicians include the "Al Gore" chicken salad ($5). Omelettes ($3-7), corned beef sandwiches ($5), and malted milkshakes ($2.75) highlight an inexpensive menu. (☎269-6737. Open M-Tu 6:30am-4pm, W-Th and Su 6:30am-10pm, F-Sa 6:30am-11pm. Delivery available.) The Middle Eastern **Full Moon Cafe,** 137 Prince George St., a block up East St. from the Naval Academy, attracts vegetarians, who flock here to sample creamy hummus ($4) and other light options. (☎280-1956. Poetry slams Tu 9:30pm; cover $3. Live music Th-Sa. Weekend brunch until 2pm.)

🅂 **SIGHTS.** The **US Naval Academy,** 52 King George St., is the institution that most typifies Annapolis. At the academy, harried, short-haired "plebes" (first-year students) in official sailor dress try desperately to remember and flawlessly recite the words of Navy fight songs while the rest of the undergraduates, "middies" (midshipmen), scream orders. The first stop should be the **Armel-Leftwich Visitors Center,** in the Halsey Field House. Tours include historic Bancroft Hall, the crypt, a dorm room, and the athletic facilities where the middies test their seafaring prowess on land. Visitors also view the original Tecumseh, a shiphead carving on the third ship in the US Navy named after an Indian chief by joking midshipmen. The name stuck, and the icon is now one of the academy's mascots. (☎263-6933. Tours every 30min. M-Sa 9:30am-3:30pm, Su 12:15-3:30pm. $5.50, seniors $4.50, students $3.50.)

Built from 1772 to 1779, the Corinthian-columned **State House,** 90 State Circle, is the oldest working capitol building in the nation. It was the US Capitol Building from 1783 to 1784, and the Treaty of Paris was signed inside on January 14, 1784. Visitors can explore the historical exhibits and silver collection, or watch the state legislature bicker in two exquisitely adorned marble halls from mid-January until mid-April. (☎974-3400. Open daily 9am-5pm. Tours 11am and 3pm. Free.) **Historic Hammond-Harwood House,** 19 Maryland Ave., at King George St., an elegant 1774 building designed by Colonial architect William Buckland, retains period decor right down to the candlesticks. The house is most renowned for its impeccably preserved colonial doorway. (☎263-4683. Open M-Sa 10am-4pm, Su noon-4pm. Tours every hr.; last tour 1hr. before closing. $5, ages 6-18 $3, military in uniform free.) The **William Paca House,** 186 Prince George St., is the first Georgian-style home built in Annapolis. The elegant house overlooks two acres of lush vegetation, and the garden hides shaded benches that gaze upon trellises, water lilies, and gazebos. (☎263-5553. Open M-Sa 10am-4pm, Su noon-4pm; Jan.-Feb. F-Sa 10am-4pm, Su noon-4pm. Tours given every hr. on the half-hour; arrive at least 1hr. before closing. House $5, garden $4, both $7. $10 joint tickets for Hammond-Harwood and William Paca houses.)

It's difficult to escape the eats and greets at Annapolis' spirited **City Dock** which is easily accessed by following Main St. to its aquatic dead end. The city's main hub of activity, restaurants, and touristy shops line the waterfront, and Naval Academy ships (skippered by fresh-faced "plebes" in the summertime) ply the waters. The civilian yachtsmen congregate at bars to simultaneously flex their alcohol tolerance and biceps, earning the street its nickname, **"Ego Alley."** Smaller cruise boats leave on tours from April through October. (☎268-7600. Boats depart M-F every hr. 11am-4pm, Sa-Su every hr. 11am-7pm. $6, under 12 $3.)

🎭🎬 **ENTERTAINMENT AND NIGHTLIFE.** Locals and tourists generally engage in one of two activities: wandering along City Dock or schmoozing 'n' boozing at upscale pubs. Bars and taverns line downtown Annapolis, drawing crowds every night. If you want more culture than drink can provide, Annapolis also has performance options. Theatergoers can check out **The Colonial Players, Inc.,** 108 East St., for innovative and often unknown works. (☎268-7373. Performances Th 8pm, Su 2:30 and 8pm. Tickets Th and Su $7, seniors and students $5; F-Sa $10.) During the summer, the **Annapolis Summer Garden Theater,** 143 Compromise St., offers musical "theater under the stars" in an open courtyard theater near the **City Dock.** (Tickets $10, seniors and students $8.)

McGarvey's, 8 Market Space, hosts mainly locals, who pack in among naval pilot-donated helmets on the candle-lit mezzanine level. (☎263-5700. Happy hour M and W 10pm-2am. Th 6pm-2am the house beer is only $1.50. Open M-Sa 11:30am-2am, Su 10am-2am.) **Armadillo's,** a sports bar at 132 Dock St., sports a homey brick interior and a cordial, talkative staff. (☎280-0028. Happy hour M-F 4-7pm. Live music W-M 9:30pm. 21+ upstairs. Open daily 9am-1:30am.) At the **Ram's Head Tavern,** 33 West St., beer connoisseurs, midshipmen, and tourists enjoy 135 different beers, including international microbrews. (☎268-4545. Happy hour M-F 4-7pm and midnight daily. Open M-Sa 11am-2am, Su 10am-2am.)

ASSATEAGUE & CHINCOTEAGUE, VA ☎757

Crashing waves, windswept dunes, wild ponies galloping free—if it sounds like the stuff of a childhood fantasy, that's because it is. Local legend has it that ponies first came to Assateague Island by swimming ashore from a sinking Spanish galleon—a story so captivating that it became the premise of Marguerite Henry's classic children's story, *Misty of Chincoteague.* A less romantic and more likely theory is that miserly colonial farmers put their horses out to graze on Assateague to avoid mainland taxes. Whatever their origins, the famous wild ponies now roam free across the unspoiled beaches and forests of the picturesque island.

■∄ ORIENTATION AND PRACTICAL INFORMATION. Telling the two islands apart, especially since their names are sometimes used interchangeably, can often leave visitors bewildered. Assateague Island is the longer barrier island facing the ocean, while Chincoteague Island is nestled between Assateague and mainland Eastern Shore. The best way to get to Assateague Island is by car. From Rte. 50, take Rte. 611 south. If traveling from points south, use Rte. 113 north to Rte. 376 east in Berlin, Md. Follow Rte. 376 to access Rte. 611 and continue to the island. To reach Chincoteague and the Chincoteague Wildlife Refuge (which is actually on Assateague Island) from Rte. 50, take U.S. 13 south at Salisbury and turn east onto State Rd. 175. **Buses:** to reach the island by bus, take a **Greyhound** (☎800-752-4841) to Ocean City, via daily routes from Greyhound stations in Baltimore (3½hr., 3 per day, $30) or Washington, D.C. ($5hr., 4 per day, $40). **Trailways** runs buses from **Salisbury, MD** ($8) and **Norfolk, VA** ($42), stopping at T's Corner store on U.S. 13 (☎824-5935), 11 mi. from Chincoteague. From Ocean City, take a **taxi** to the island (☎289-1313; about $30). **Visitor info: Chincoteague Chamber of Commerce,** P.O. Box 258, Chincoteague, VA 23336. The Chamber is located at 6733 Maddox Blvd. (☎336-6161; www.chincoteaguechamber.com. Open in summer M-Sa 9am-4:30pm, Su 12:30-4:30pm; off-season M-Sa 9am-4:30pm.) **ZIP code:** 23336. **Area code:** 757.

⌐☐ ACCOMMODATIONS AND FOOD. Due to Assateague's lack of civilization, visitors eat and sleep on **Chincoteague Island,** across an inlet from southern Assateague. Motels line the sides of **Maddox Boulevard** near the Chincoteague-Assateague causeway. Midway down this motel mile, the **Mariner,** 6273 Maddox Blvd., offers spotless rooms with wide, comfortable beds and features an outdoor pool and continental breakfast. (☎336-6565 or 800-221-7490. Four efficiency apartments are available for $125; doubles start at $79, in winter $65; smaller economy rooms $61/$50. Reserve in advance; the 10 economy rooms go fast.) Across from the Mariner, the clean and quiet **Sea Hawk Motel,** 6250 Maddox Blvd., offers slightly smaller rooms with cable and pool access. (☎336-6527. Rooms $70-80, in winter $49-59; 1 double bed $59.) **Maddox Family Campground,** off to the right immediately before the causeway, has 550 sites, many with shade. (☎336-3111. Pool and playground. Open Mar.-Dec. Sites $21.70; all have hookups.)

For fresh, absurdly cheap seafood takeout (no seats), head to **Melvin's Seafood,** situated in the family backyard of 3117 Ridge Rd., on the south side of the island (follow signs from Main St.). Don't be bashful, just drive right into their driveway where the owner family sells crab cakes for $8, a dozen steamed crabs for $12, and oyster sandwiches for $3.50. (☎336-3003. Open daily 7am-7pm.) Locals swear by the all-you-can-eat steamed crabs ($18) and patriotic decor at **Wright's Seafood Res-**

taurant, Wright Rd. From southbound Rte. 175, turn left on Atlantic Rd., go straight for 1½ mi., and turn left on Wright Rd. (☎824-4012. Open Tu-Sa 4-9pm, Su noon-9pm. Entrees $10-23.) Chincoteague's most beloved dessert, nighttime snack, or breakfast treat is a Belgian waffle topped with ice cream and fruit ($5) from **Muller's Old Fashioned Ice Cream Parlor,** 4034 Main St. Single scoops are $1.50, extra scoops are $1. (☎336-5894. Open daily 11am-11pm when the family is in residence.)

⚡ OUTDOOR ACTIVITIES. Maryland and Virginia share Assateague Island, which is divided into three distinct parts. The **Assateague State Park,** Rte. 611 in southeast Maryland, is a 2 mi. stretch of picnic areas, beaches, bathhouses, and campsites. Fishing without a license is permitted, but you must supply your own equipment. (☎410-641-2120 or 888-432-2267. Open daily 8am-sunset. $2 per person, seniors free. Campsite registration open 8am-10pm. 2-night min. stay on weekends. Sites $20, with hookup $30.)

The **Assateague Island National Seashore** claims most of the long sandbar north and south of the park and has its own campground and beaches, most of which are inaccessible by car. The ranger station distributes $5 back-country camping permits from noon until 5pm; they go quickly, so arrive early. The **Barrier Island Visitors Center,** on Rte. 611, provides maps and info, an introduction to the park, and films on the park's natural treasures. (☎641-1441. Open daily 9am-5pm.) Secluded beach-combing to the north of the state park provides unguided, but adventurous, opportunities to unlock the park's natural treasures. Three meandering, ½ mi. nature trails give visitors a closer look at the island's flora and fauna: the **Forest Trail** offers the best viewing tower, but the **Marsh Trail** has fewer mosquitoes. If you feel safer within the confines of your own car, rental driving tours ($2) are available. Notorious gnats pester visitors all over the island, so bring plenty of repellent. (Campsites May-Oct. $14; Nov. to Apr. $10. Water, cold showers, grill; no hookups.)

The **Chincoteague National Wildlife Refuge** stretches across the Virginia side of the island. Avid bird-watchers flock here to see rare species such as peregrine falcons, snowy egrets, and black-crowned night herons. The wild pony roundup, held the last consecutive Wednesday and Thursday in July, brings hordes of tourists to Assateague. During slack tide, local firemen herd the ponies together and swim them from Assateague to Chincoteague Island, where the fire department auctions off the foals the following day. The adults swim back to Assateague and reproduce, providing next year's crop. Can't make the round-up? Ponies can be seen almost every day along the refuge's trails, especially the Wildlife Loop Rd. (open 5am-10pm; for cars 3pm-sunset), which begins at the Visitors Center. If you are lucky enough to spot one of these awesome creatures, be careful to gawk from a safe distance—the ponies may appear harmless but can strike at random. For more info, visit the **Chincoteague Refuge Visitor Contact Station.** (☎804-336-6122. Open daily 9am-4pm. $5 per car.)

OCEAN CITY ☎410

Ocean City is a lot like a kiddie pool—it's shallow and plastic, but can be a lot of fun if you're the right age. This ten-mile strip of prime Atlantic beach packs endless bars, all-you-can-eat buffets, hotels, mini-golf courses, boardwalks, flashing lights, and sun-seeking tourists into a thin region between the ocean and the Assawoman Bay. Tourism is unabashedly the town's only industry, and Ocean City is not afraid to shake its money-maker. The siren call of senior week beckons droves of recent high school and college graduates to alcohol- and hormone-driven fun, turning O.C. into a city-wide block party in June. Proceed with caution if you're driving, but otherwise, full steam ahead; the scantily clad grads tend to prance the Ocean City streets recklessly. July and August cater more to families and professional singles looking for inexpensive fun in the sun.

◼◼ ORIENTATION AND PRACTICAL INFORMATION. Driving is the most sensible mode of transportation to reach the ocean resort. From the north, follow Rte. 1, which becomes Coastal Highway (Philadelphia Ave.). From the west, Rte. 50

leads directly to Ocean City. From points south, take Rte. 113 to Rte. 50 and follow
it to town. Ocean City runs north-south, with numbered streets linking the ocean to
the bay. Most hotels are in the lower numbered streets toward the ocean; most
clubs and bars are uptown toward the bay. **Trailways** (☎289-9307; open daily June-
Aug. 7-8am and 10am-5pm; Sept.-May 10am-3pm), at 2nd St. and Philadelphia Ave.,
buses to Baltimore (3½hr., 3 per day, $30) and Washington, D.C. (5hr., 4 per day,
$40). **Public buses** run up and down the strip and are the best way to get around
town. (☎723-1607. 24hr. $1 per day for unlimited rides.) **The Ocean City Visitors Cen-
ter,** 4001 Coastal Hwy., at 40th St. in the Convention Center, gives out discount coupons. (☎800-626-2326. Open June-Aug. M-W 8:30am-5pm, Th-Sa 8:30am-8pm; Sept.-
May daily 8:30am-5pm.) **Post Office:** 11805 Coastal Hwy. (☎524-7611). **ZIP code:**
21842. **Area code:** 410.

⌂⌂ ACCOMMODATIONS AND FOOD. The **Whispering Sands,** 15 45th St., rents
out 11 spacious rooms with kitchen access. Lodging, available on a daily or a full-
summer basis, draws a mostly European crowd in a location convenient to nightlife. The personable owner gladly provides visiting advice and conversation. (☎723-
1874; Nov.-Apr. 202-362-3453 or 954-761-9008. A/C in all rooms but one. Open May-
Oct. $70-75.) **Ocean City International Student Services,** 9 Somerset St., in the south
end of town, is a cheap summer boarding house for predominantly international
college students. Private rooms and dorm rooms have access to kitchen, TV, living
room, deck, hammock, and grill. (☎289-4542. Open Apr.-Oct. Cost averages $87 per
week. Reservations necessary.) The **Cabana Motel,** 1900 Coastal Hwy./Philadelphia
Ave., caters to families, with small, comfortable rooms outfitted with A/C and TV.
(☎289-9131. Open May-Oct. Singles and doubles $80-95; prices decrease in May and
fall seasons.) The serene **Atlantic House Bed and Breakfast,** 501 N. Baltimore Ave.,
only a few bucks more, offers free breakfast and a wholesome change of pace from
the Ocean City motel trend. (☎289-2333. A/C, cable TV, parking. Rooms with shared
bath from $62; with private bath from $132.) **Ocean City Travel Park,** 105 70th St., runs
the only in-town campground. (☎524-7601. Tents and RVs $25-38.)

Besides the beach, food is Ocean City's prime attraction. With freshly caught fish
and a friendly atmosphere, **The Embers,** 24th St. and Coastal Hwy., flaunts the biggest seafood buffet and most potent fish stench in town. (☎289-3322 or 888-436-
2377. Open July-Aug. daily 2-10pm; Sept.-June 3-9pm.) When filling your belly matters more than aesthetics, **Fat Daddy's Sub Shop,** 216 S. Baltimore Ave., a grimy but
economical dive around the corner from the hostel, offers satisfying deli sandwiches ($2-4.50) and subs ($4-6) on the beach until the early morning. (☎289-4040.
Open daily 11am-4am. Free delivery.) Breakfast is the best meal of the day at the
seaside **Brass Balls Saloon,** between 11th and 12th St. on the boardwalk. Enjoy Oreo
waffles ($4.75) or light, fluffy omelettes ($4.25-5.25) under a mural of smiling celebrities. (☎289-0069. Open May-Oct. daily 8:30am-2am.)

⊡⊡ ENTERTAINMENT AND NIGHTLIFE. Ocean City's star attraction is its
beautiful **beach.** The wide stretch of surf and sand runs the entire ten-mile length of
town and can be accessed by taking a left onto any of the numerous side streets off
of Philadelphia and Baltimore Ave. The breaking waves know no time constraints,
but beachgoers are technically limited to 6am-10pm. When the sun goes down,
hard-earned tans glow under the glaring lights of Ocean City's bars and nightclubs.
An amusement park for adults, the island oasis **Seacrets,** on 49th St., features 11
bars, including two floating bars on the bay. Barefoot barflies wander from bar to
bar, sipping the signature frozen rum runner mixed with piña colada ($5.25) to the
strains of three live bands nightly. A magnificent sunset view ushers in the early
revelers. (☎524-4900. Cover $3-5. Open M-Sa 11am-2am, Su noon-2am.) The elder
statesman of the bayside clubs, **Fager's Island,** 60th St. in the bay, attracts hordes
across a plank walkway to its island location. No one seems to know the source of
the classical music tradition, but the 1812 Overture rings aloud daily with the sunset. Start the week with a festive bang at the Monday night deck party. (☎524-5500.
Happy hour Su-Th 4-7pm. Live music nightly. Cover M $7. Open daily 11am-2am.)

WASHINGTON, D.C. ☎ 202

Like many a young adult fresh out of college, the fledgling United States government quickly realized that independence meant little without a place to stay. Both Northern and Southern states wanted the capital on their turf. The final location—100 square miles pinched from Virginia and Maryland—was a compromise, an undeveloped swamp wedged between north and south. Congress commissioned French engineer Pierre L'Enfant to design the city.

Washington's wide avenues remained mostly empty, with a smattering of slave markets and boarding houses the only companions for the elegant government buildings. The city had hardly begun to expand when the British torched it in 1814; a post-war vote to give up and move the capital failed in Congress by just eight votes. Washington continued to disgust foreign diplomats—the district was a first stop for slave traders, whose shackled cargo awaited sales on the Mall and near the White House. The cessation of the slave trade after the Civil War transformed Washington from the Union's embarrassing appendage to its jugular vein.

The discrete cities of Federal Washington and local Washington coexist in the District. Federal Washington, the town of press conferences, power lunches, and presidential intrigue, is what most visitors come to see. The other part of Washington, the "second city," consists of a variety of communities, some prosperous, others overcome by poverty, drugs, and crime. These areas, sometimes within a few blocks of the seats of government, surprise many tourists with the troubling paradoxes of American democracy.

For everything about Washington, D.C. you always wanted to know but were afraid to ask, check out the wildly revamped *Let's Go: Washington, D.C. 2002*, available at fine bookstores.

◼ INTERCITY TRANSPORTATION

Airports: Ronald Reagan National Airport (☎ 703-417-8000). Metro: National Airport. It's best to fly here from within the US; National is on the Metro and closer to the city. Taxi $10-15 from downtown. The **Super Shuttle** (☎ 800-258-3826) runs between National and downtown M-F every 30min. **Dulles International Airport** (☎ 703-369-1600) is much farther from the city. Taxis cost $40+ from downtown. The **Washington Flyer Dulles Express Bus** (☎ 888-927-4359) hits the West Falls Church Metro every 30min. 6-10am and 6-10:30pm, every 20min. from 10am-2pm, every 15min. from 2-6pm ($8). **Buses** to downtown (15th and K St. NW) take about 45min. and leave M-F every 30min. 5:20am-10:20pm; Sa-Su every hr. 5:20am-12:20pm, every 30min. 12:50-10:20pm ($16; family rate for groups of 3 or more $13 each).

Trains: Union Station, 50 Massachusetts Ave. NE (☎ 484-7540). **Amtrak** to: New York (3½hr.; $67 reserved, $118 metroliner); Baltimore (40min., $21); Philadelphia (2hr., $50); and Boston (8½hr., $68). Maryland's commuter train, **MARC** (☎ 410-859-7400, 24hr.), departs from Union to Baltimore ($5.75) and the suburbs.

▣ LOCAL TRANSPORTATION

Public Transit: Metrorail and Metrobus (METRO), 600 5th St. NW (☎ 637-7000; M-F 6am-10:30pm, Sa-Su 8am-10:30pm), is relatively safe. Fare $1.10-3.25, depending on time and distance traveled. 1-day Metro pass $5. **Flash Pass** ($20) allows unlimited bus (and sometimes Metro) rides for 2 weeks. Trains run M-F 5:30am-midnight, Sa-Su 8am-2am. For bus transfers, get a pass on the platform *before* boarding the train. The **Metrobus** system serves Georgetown, downtown, and the suburbs. Fare $1.10.

Taxis: Yellow Cab, ☎ 544-1212.

Car Rental: Bargain Buggies Rent-a-Car, 3140 N. Washington Blvd. (☎ 703-841-0000), in Arlington, rents for $23 per day, $150 per week; 100 free mi. per day, 20¢ each additional mi. Must be 18 with major credit card or $250 cash deposit. Open M-F 8am-7pm, Sa 9am-3pm, Su 9am-noon.

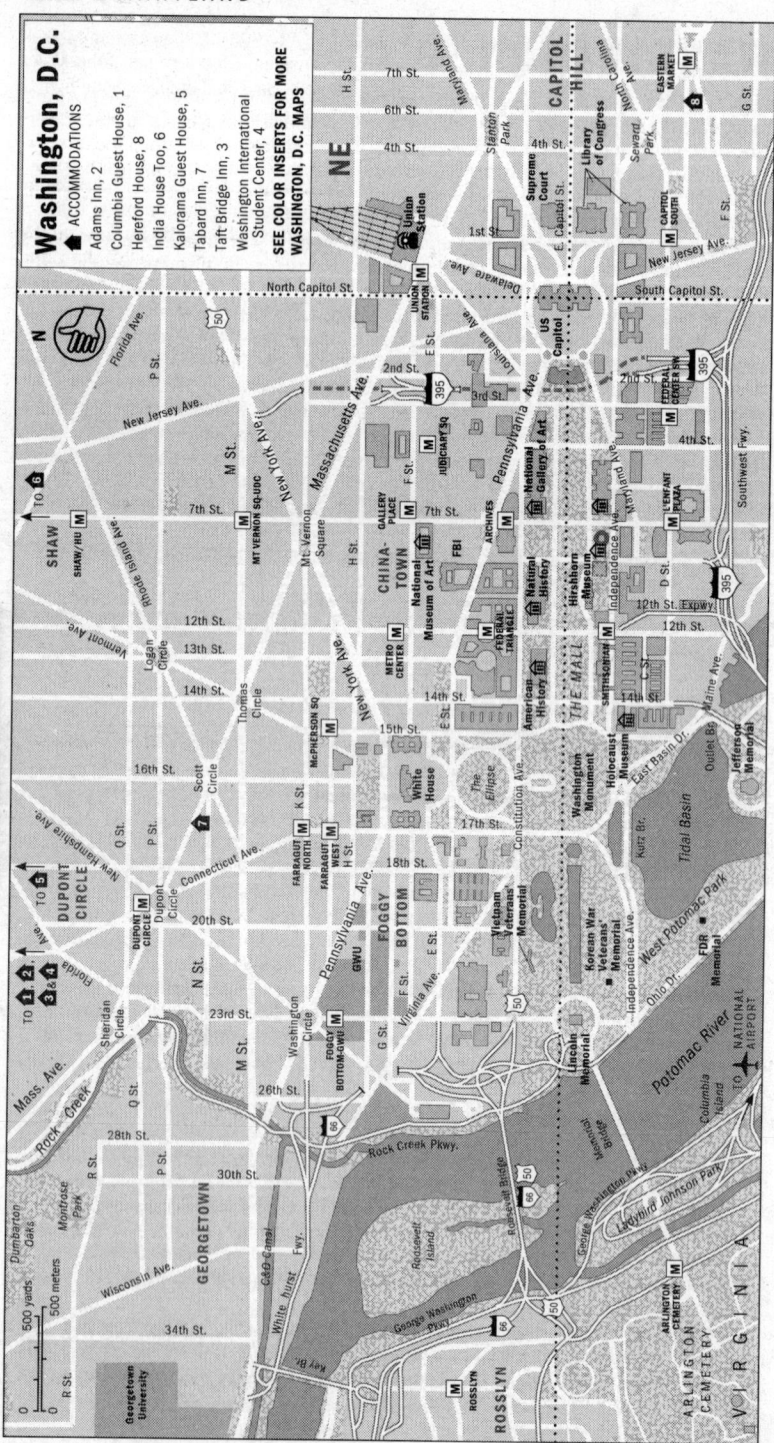

Washington, D.C.

▲ ACCOMMODATIONS

Adams Inn, 2
Columbia Guest House, 1
Hereford House, 8
India House Too, 6
Kalorama Guest House, 5
Tabard Inn, 7
Taft Bridge Inn, 3
Washington International
Student Center, 4

SEE COLOR INSERTS FOR MORE
WASHINGTON, D.C. MAPS

Bike Rental: Big Wheel Bikes, 315 7th St. SE (☎543-1600). Metro: Eastern Market. Mountain bikes $5 per hr. (min. 3hr.), $25 per business day. $32 per 24hr. Major credit card required for deposit. Open Tu-F 11am-7pm, Sa 10am-6pm, Su noon-5pm.

✈ ORIENTATION

Diamond-shaped D.C. stretches its tips in the four cardinal directions. The **Potomac River** forms the jagged southwest border, its waters flowing between the district and Arlington, VA. **North Capitol St., East Capitol St.,** and **South Capitol St.** slice up the city into four quadrants: NW, NE, SE, and SW. The **Mall** stretches west of the Capitol. The suffixes of the quadrants distinguish otherwise identical addresses. For instance, you might find both an 800 G St. NW *and* an 800 G St. NE.

Washington's streets lie in a simple grid. Streets that run east-to-west are labeled alphabetically in relation to the north-south division, which runs through the Capitol. Since the street plan follows the Roman alphabet, in which "I" and "J" are the same letter, there is no J St. After W St., east-west streets take on two-syllable names, then three-syllable names, then the names of trees and flowers. The names run in alphabetical order, but sometimes repeat or skip a letter. Streets running north-south are numbered (1st St., 2nd St., etc.) all the way out to 52nd St. NW and 63rd St. NE. Addresses on lettered streets indicate the number of the cross street. For instance, 1100 D St. SE is on the corner of D and 11th.

Major roads include **Pennsylvania Ave., Connecticut Ave., Wisconsin Ave., 16th St. NW, K St. NW, Massachusetts Ave., New York Ave.,** and **North Capitol St.** Washington, D.C. is ringed by the **Capital Beltway/I-495** (except where it's part of I-95); the Beltway is bisected by **U.S. 1,** and meets **I-395** from Virginia. The high-speed **Baltimore-Washington Pkwy.** connects Washington, D.C. to Baltimore. **I-595** trickles off the Capital Beltway east to Annapolis. **I-66** heads west into Virginia.

NEIGHBORHOODS

Postcard-perfect and pristine white, **Capitol Hill** symbolizes the democratic dream with the Capitol building, Supreme Court, and the Library of Congress. The **Mall** is flanked by the Smithsonian Museums and the National Gallery of Art. Monuments and memorials fill the Mall's west end, as cherry trees bud and blossom along the brink of the Tidal Basin. **Foggy Bottom** has evolved from underdeveloped swampland to the stomping grounds of the State Dept. The Bottom's blockbuster, though, is the White House at 1600 Pennsylvania Ave. The **Federal Triangle** area is home to a growing commercial and banking district. The International Trade Center and the Ronald Reagan Building share the wide avenues with federal agencies like the FBI. It's a wonderful (corporate) life in glass-walled **Farragut,** where government agencies, lobbying firms, and lawyers make their home.

There's more to D.C. than politics, though, and the neighborhoods comprising up the **Second City** bustle with sights, shops, and eateries. **Adams-Morgan** is a hub of nightlife and good food. **Chinatown,** more of a block than a neighborhood, offers the most authentic Chinese cuisine in the District. Fashionable and picturesque **Georgetown** has the feel of a college town with Georgetown University nearby and enough nightlife to keep college students dazed and happy. Ever-trendy **Dupont Circle** hosts foodies, art sophisticates, and diplomats. The **Upper Northwest,** an upper-class residential neighborhood, is home to American University and the National Zoo. The **U District,** a historically African-American area, now rocks out nightly—and deafens passersby—as its clubs blast punk and techno until the sun rises.

🛈 PRACTICAL INFORMATION

Visitor info: Washington, D.C. Convention and Visitors Association (WCVA), 1212 New York Ave., #600 NW (☎789-7000; www.washington.org). Open M-F 9am-5pm. **D.C. Committee to Promote Washington,** 1212 New York Ave. NW, #200 (☎347-2873 or 800-422-8644). **Meridian International Center,** 1630 Crescent Pl. NW (☎667-6800). Metro: Dupont Circle. Office open M-F 9am-5pm.

MID-ATLANTIC

Hotlines: Rape Crisis Center, ☎333-7273. 24hr. **Gay and Lesbian Hotline,** ☎833-3234. Operates 7-11pm. **Traveler's Aid Society,** ☎546-3120. Offices at Union Station, National and Dulles Airports, and downtown at 512 C St. NE. Hours vary.

Hospitals and Clinics: Children's National Medical Center, 111 Michigan Ave. NW (☎884-5000). **Georgetown University Medical Center,** 3800 Reservoir Rd. NW (☎687-2000). **Whitman-Walker Clinic** (☎797-3500) provides AIDS and STD counseling. **Planned Parenthood,** 1108 16th St. NW (☎347-8500).

Internet access: Atomic Grounds, 1555 Wilson Blvd., #105 (☎703-524-2157), in Arlington. Open M-F 6:30am-6:30pm, Sa-Su 8am-6:30pm.

Post Office: 900 Brentwood Rd. NE (☎636-1532). Indescribably inconvenient location. Open M-F 8am-8pm, Sa 8am-6pm, Su noon-6pm. **ZIP code:** 20066. **Area code:** 202.

ᚠ ACCOMMODATIONS

Come nightfall, you're seeking sanctuary from the tourist dregs. But wherever should one squat in the District? Don't trip unwittingly into some chandeliered lobby. Trick these gold-digging taverns by shacking up with them on weekends or in summer months when discount rates crop up. Hostels also offer unbeatable rates and the chance to mingle with an international crowd. Don't forget that D.C. adds a 14.5% occupancy tax to your bill. Damn feds.

HOSTELS AND STUDENT CENTERS

India House Too, 300 Carroll St. (☎291-1195), on the border of D.C. and Takoma Park. Metro: Takoma. Walk straight from Metro stop on Carroll St. toward the hill on the right. Colorful mural-painted walls decorate the interior of this young, make-yourself-at-home hostel. The suburban neighborhood doesn't offer much in the way of nightlife, but the hostel is only steps away from the Metro. Free linens and use of kitchen. No A/C. Laundry facilities and free Internet access. Pool and foosball tables in basement. Reservations preferred. 4-6 bed dorm rooms $15; private rooms $36 (no private bath).

Washington International Student Center, 2451 18th St. NW (☎667-7681 or 800-567-4150), in the fun-packed Adams-Morgan area. Metro: Woodley Park-Zoo. A friendly and experienced staff manage the clean and cozy establishment, consisting of 5 A/C-equipped bedrooms, each with 3-4 sets of bunk beds (38 beds total). 2 kitchens and 3 shared bathrooms. Internet access $1 per 8min. No lockout. Key deposit $5. Breakfast included. Lockers available. Free parking first 2 nights. Check-in 8:30am-10:30pm. Reserve at least a week in advance, especially in summer. Beds $17 per night.

HOTELS

Taft Bridge Inn, 2007 Wyoming Ave. (☎387-2007), at the intersection of 20th and Wyoming. Quiet hotel with beautifully decorated antique-filled rooms in a stately 19th-century Georgian building. All rooms have modem, phone, voicemail, and A/C; cable TV in all rooms with private bath. Laundry. Full breakfast included. Parking $9 per day. Wheelchair accessible. Singles $59-79, with private bath $119-124; high-season singles $99-119; additional person $15.

Hereford House, 604 S. Carolina Ave. SE (☎543-0102), at 6th St., 1 block from the Eastern Market Metro. No sign marks this 4-room, 6-bed, British-style B&B in a townhouse run by a friendly English hostess. Shared baths, laundry facilities, A/C, refrigerator, living room, homecooked breakfast, and garden patio. No smoking. No credit cards. 50% due for reservation, balance due on arrival. Singles $58-72; doubles $74-82. Discounted weekly or monthly leases available.

GUEST HOUSES

Kalorama Guest House at Kalorama Park, 1854 Mintwood Pl. NW (☎667-6369), off Columbia Rd., a block south of 18th St. This quiet, Victorian guest house offers 19th-century appeal with 20th-century convenience. Some suites with TV and phone. Internet hookup available in certain rooms. Continental breakfast included. Limited parking behind guest house by reservation only, $7 per night. Reception M-Tu 8am-8pm, W-Su 8am-10pm. Reservations with credit card required, payment due upon arrival. Singles with shared bath $55-70, with private bath $70-95; doubles $60-75/$75-100.

The Columbia Guest House, 2005 Columbia Rd. NW (☎265-4006), just off Connecticut Ave. Eccentric, patrician townhouse with dark wood paneling, polished hardwood floors, ornate fireplaces, and neatly furnished rooms (some with A/C and private bath). Most of the clientele are students or other budget travelers. Singles $25-30; doubles $35-45; triples $50-65; each additional occupant $10. Students 10-15% discount.

Adams Inn, 1744 Lanier Pl. NW (☎745-3600 or 800-578-6807), 2 blocks north of the center of Adams Morgan. 3 elegant Victorian townhouses and a carriage house with garden. Cable TV, pay phones, and laundry. Rooms vary in size, but all have A/C, private sinks, and period furnishings. Friendly, helpful staff. Continental breakfast included. Limited parking $7 per night. Internet access in office. Reception M-Sa 8am-9pm, Su 1-9pm. Reservations require first night deposit. Singles $65, with private bath $75; additional person $10. ISIC 10% discount. Limited special weekly rates.

Tabard Inn, 1739 N St. NW (☎785-1277), between 17th and 18th St., just south of the Circle. 3 townhouses connected by a maze of passages, stairways, and lounges. Features beautiful rooms decorated with ornate furniture. Offers a patio, bar, and lounges. Rooms have A/C and phone. Breakfast included. Reception 24hr. Singles $65-95, with private bath $99-155; doubles $90-110/$114-170; each additional person $15.

◖ FOOD

How does one feast like a senator on an intern's slim budget? Savvy natives go grubbing at happy hours. Bars often leave out free appetizer platters to bait early evening clients (see **Nightlife**). As for budget eateries, **Adams-Morgan** and **Dupont Circle** are home to the *crème de la crème* of succulent ethnic delights. Suburban **Bethesda, MD** features over 100 different restaurants within a four-block radius.

ADAMS-MORGAN

▨**Meskerem,** 2434 18th St. NW (☎462-4100), near Columbia Rd. An ecstatic, sun-themed decor lights up this 3-floor restaurant named after the Ethiopian month marking spring. Appetizers include *sambussas* (vegetable, shrimp, or meat-filled dough shells; $3.25-5.25). Live music F-Sa. Lunch entrees $5-10.50, dinner entrees $8.50-13. Free delivery. Open daily noon-midnight.

Mixtec, 1792 Columbia Rd. NW (☎332-1011), near 18th St. Voted the Very Best Bargain Restaurant by the *Washingtonian* from 1997 to 2000. Mexican specialties and favorites include *tacos al carbón* (two small tortillas filled with beef; $7), nachos ($6.50), and refreshing fruit drinks ($1.75). Appetizers $3-6.50; entrees $6.50-13. Open M-Th 8am-10:30pm, F 8am-11pm, Sa 9am-11pm, Su 9am-10:30pm.

So's Your Mom, 1831 Columbia Rd. NW (☎462-3666). This busy sandwich shop offers first-rate sandwich ingredients (such as imported meats and cheeses), portions as big as your mom, and unexpected sandwich choices (sliced beef tongue $6). Sandwiches $3.50-6.50. Freshly baked goods include cinnamon rolls and muffins ($1.25-2). Takeout only. Open M-F 7am-8pm, Sa 8am-7pm, Su 8am-3pm. Cash only.

BETHESDA

▨**Thyme Square Cafe,** 4735 Bethesda Ave. (☎301-657-9077). The friendly service, colorful decorations, and healthy vegetarian and vegan dishes radiate wholesomeness. Start off your meal with multigrain bread served with sweet potato spread; then savor steamed Beijing vegetable pot stickers ($8), or the avocado "PLT" (grilled portabella, lettuce, tomato, avocado, and eggless mayo on toasted multigrain bread; $7.50). Open M-Th 11:30am-9:30pm, F-Sa 11:30am-10pm, Su 11am-9:30pm.

Philadelphia Mike's, 7732 Wisconsin Ave. (☎301-656-0103), near Middleton Ave. Mike's successfully replicates the gooey taste of an authentic Philly cheesesteak ($4-8) served over the counter in a modest, pizza-shop atmosphere. Also serves burgers and deli sandwiches ($4-8), breakfast subs (under $3), and daily lunch specials ($3). Open M-F 8am-9pm, Sa 9am-9pm, Su 9am-4pm.

Grapeseed, 4865 Cordell Ave. (☎301-986-9592). Aimed at making connoisseurs of us all, Grapeseed provides an unpretentious environment for experimentation in the intimidating field of wine tasting. Serves dishes in both *tapas*-sized ($4-12) and full entree-sized portions ($17-23) with accompanying wine recommendations. Wine can be ordered by the bottle, by the glass, or by the taste (a 2½ oz. pour). Open for lunch M-F 11:30am-2pm; dinner M-Th 5-10pm, F-Sa 5-11pm.

Tastee Diner, 7731 Woodmont Ave. (☎301-652-3970), at Cheltenham Dr. The aged wooden booths, long counter, and table jukeboxes look like they've been here since the place opened in 1935. The prices haven't changed much either; breakfast is still served around the clock for a few bucks. Deliciously greasy hamburgers $2.25-6.25, side of fries $1.25. Daily dinner specials (M-F 11am-9pm, Sa-Su noon-9pm) take up home-cooking with a vengeance. Open 24hr.

CHINATOWN (FEDERAL TRIANGLE)

Go-Lo's, 604 H St. NW (☎347-4656). Lavishly decorated and divided into smaller rooms, the restaurant provides greater intimacy than its H St. counterparts. Bring a group of 6 or more for the family-style luncheon, featuring 5 entrees, soup, egg rolls, and shrimp cakes ($8 per person). Lunch specials ($5-6) vary daily. Entrees $6-22. Open Su-Th 10:30am-10:30pm, F-Sa 10:30am-midnight.

Szechuan Gallery, 617 H St. NW (☎898-1180). A scene from the movie *True Lies* was filmed here, and they've got autographed pictures to prove it. Locally renowned for its unusual dishes such as *congee*, a delicious rice soup ($5). Lunch specials $5-8, dinner entrees $9-14. Open Su-Th 11am-10pm, F-Sa 11am-11pm.

Hunan Chinatown, 624 H St. NW (☎783-5858). Upscale restaurant serving standard Chinese food; locals maintain that the cuisine is well worth the added expense. Lunch items include Kung Pao chicken ($6.75); dinners include tea smoked duck ($15) and local favorite Hunan lamb ($14). Open Su-Th 11am-10pm, F-Sa 11am-11pm.

DUPONT CIRCLE

▧ Lauriol Plaza, 1865 18th St. NW (☎387-0035), Dupont's hottest spot serves Latino food in copious quantities to large, well-dressed after-work crowds. The complimentary chips and salsa are unusually addictive. Appetizers like fried plantains and guacamole $2.50-7; entrees $7-16. Su brunch entrees $6-9 (11am-3pm). Free parking. No reservations. Open Su-Th 11:30am-11pm, F-Sa and holidays 11:30am-midnight.

Pizzeria Paradiso, 2029 P St. NW (☎223-1245), near 21st St. A modest awning hides the surprisingly airy, light-filled restaurant. Their brick oven bakes up some of the most genuinely Italian thin-crust pizza in town (8 in. $7-10; 12 in. $12-16). Toppings 75¢-$1.75. Also offering an array of panini sandwiches ($5-7) and salads ($3-5). Open daily M-Th 11:30am-11pm, F 11:30am-midnight, Sa 11am-midnight, Su noon-10pm.

City Lights of China, 1731 Connecticut Ave. NW (☎265-6688), between R and S St. This award-winning restaurant serves delicious Chinese food in a spacious dining room. Special steamed dishes for the calorie-conscious. Entrees $8-14. Open M-Th 11:30am-10:30pm, F 11:30am-11pm, Sa noon-11pm, Su noon-10:30pm.

Luna Grill & Diner, 1301 Connecticut Ave. NW (☎835-2280), south of Dupont Circle. Friendly and slightly eccentric waitstaff serves high-quality diner fare in a moon-themed dining room. Salads, pastas, sandwiches ($6-10), and entrees ($10-16), all taste better, come larger, and cost more than in your typical diner. Reservations accepted for weekday lunch only. Open M-F 8am-11pm, Sa 10am-midnight, Su 10am-10pm.

GEORGETOWN

▧ Cafe La Ruche, 1039 31st St. NW (☎965-2684, takeout 965-2591), 2 blocks south of M St. The name means "the beehive," and this place certainly gets buzzing when late-night romantics move in for dessert and coffee. Serves up French fare, including soups ($4), salads ($4-9), quiche ($8), and sandwiches ($7-9). Desserts around $5. Open M-Th 11:30am-11:30pm, F 11:30am-1am, Sa 10am-1am, Su 10am-10:30pm.

Thomas Sweet, 3214 P St. NW (☎337-0616), at the intersection with Wisconsin Ave. A local ice cream parlor that serves cheap bagel sandwich breakfasts ($1-3), sandwiches ($4-6), and over 30 flavors of homemade ice cream and frozen yogurt (single scoop cone $2). Open M-Th 8am-midnight, F-Sa 8am-1am, Su 9am-midnight. Cash only.

Marvelous Market, 3217 P St. NW (☎333-2591), on the corner of P St. and Wisconsin Ave. Reminiscent of a neighborhood market, it sells the basics—produce, fresh bread, cheese, and flowers. Almost everything is made on the premises. Grab a homemade sandwich ($5.25-5.50), freshly baked pizza ($5-11), or coffee ($1-3) and relax in the adjacent window-enclosed dining area. Open M-Sa 8am-8pm, Su 8am-7pm.

Moby Dick House of Kabob, 1070 31st St. NW (☎333-4400), near the corner of M and 31st St. Featuring traditional Iranian dishes with mouth-watering, lean, marinated meats. Try the *kubideh* and *chenjeh* combo served with rice and clay-oven pita bread ($9.25) or enjoy one of Moby's famous sandwiches ($4-5). Open Su-Th 11am-10pm, F-Sa 11am-4am. Cash only.

Amma Vegetarian Kitchen, 3291 M St. NW (☎625-6025), at the corner of M and 33rd St. Traditional south Indian cuisine in a spare, spotless dining room. Enjoy regional specialities like *idli sambar* (steamed rice-flour cakes with a dazzling vegetable sauce; $4). Open for lunch M-F 11:30am-2:30pm, Sa 11:30am-3:45pm; Su noon-3:45pm; dinner M-Th 5:30-10pm, F-Su 5:30-10:30pm.

Patisserie Poupon, 1645 Wisconsin Ave. NW (☎342-3248), near the corner of Wisconsin and Q St. A bakery known for its decadent French pastries ($1-2). Sandwiches, quiches, and salads $4-7. Open Tu-Sa 8am-6:30pm, Su 8am-4pm.

Georgetown Cafe, 1623 Wisconsin Ave. NW (☎333-0215), at the corner of Q St. This all-hours cafe is the perfect place to grab a late-night snack and is often packed come 3am. Offers 'round-the-clock breakfast as well as your typical sandwiches ($4-7) and pizzas ($7-10), along with some more exotic fare. Happy hour daily 4-8pm. Open 24hr.

Bistro Med, 3288 M St. NW (☎333-0955), at the corner of M and 33rd St., offers Turkish-style pizzas such as the *lahmacun*, a favorite with ground beef ($7) as well as entrees ($10-17) including the *merguez de marocaine* (lamb sausage with eggplant and couscous; $11). Special late-night brunch served Th-Sa 11:30pm-5am. Open M-Th 11:30am-1am, F 11:30am-5am, Sa 10:30am-5am, Su 10:30am-1am.

UPPER NORTHWEST

Chipotle Mexican Grill, 2600 Connecticut Ave. NW (☎299-9111). Chipotle chefs prepare fresh burritos and tacos ($4.75-5.50) in assembly-line fashion using the ingredients you select. Perfect for hungry customers on the go. Chicken entrees recommended, vegetarian options available. Open daily 11am-10pm.

Jandara, 2606 Connecticut Ave. NW (☎387-8876). Celestial decorations and heavenly blues and purples create an out-of-this-world atmosphere. The food is equally stunning with specialty dishes like *gaeng ped yang* (slices of roasted duck simmered in a red curry sauce with pineapple; $9). Lunch menu features reduced price entrees ($5-10). Open Su-Th 11:30am-10:30pm, F-Sa 11:30am-11pm.

Yanni's, 3500 Connecticut Ave. NW (☎362-8871). Bright, airy neighborhood restaurant with extra-friendly service and homestyle Greek cooking (e.g. fresh herbs and a whole lot of olive oil). Try charbroiled octopus, crunchy on the outside and delicately tender within, served with rice and vegetables ($12). Appetizers $4-7, entrees $7-16. Outdoor seating available. Open daily 11:30am-11pm.

Faccia Luna, 2400 Wisconsin Ave. NW (☎337-3132). A wood-fired oven bakes up thin, crisp-yet-tender crusts. The dining room is welcoming with intimate brick alcoves and booths. Basic pie $6.50-12; toppings $1.25-2 each. Appealing lunch specials ($5-6; M-F 11:30am-2pm) include an entree and drink. Open M-Th 11:30am-11pm, F-Sa 11:30am-midnight, Su noon-11pm.

Mama Maria and Enzio's, 2313 Wisconsin Ave. NW (☎965-1337), near Calvert St. Amazing southern Italian cuisine served in a 9-table dining room, with a casual, family atmosphere. Appetizers $6-12, pastas $9-13. Lunch entrees $7-11. Open for lunch M-F 11:30am-3pm; dinner M-Sa 5-10:30pm.

Firehook Bakery & Coffeehouse, 3411 Connecticut Ave. NW (☎362-2253). A local branch serving the main Alexandria bakery's fresh breads ($3-4), sinfully rich cookies ($1.40), and sandwiches ($5.50) as well as a variety of coffee drinks ($1.10-2.50). Open M 7am-8pm, Tu-Th 7am-10pm, F-Sa 7am-11pm, Su 8am-9pm.

👁 SIGHTS

CAPITOL HILL

Capitol Hill is the heart of American government, Washington's principal tourist attraction, and one of democracy's most potent icons.

THE CAPITOL. The US Capitol may be an endless font of cynicism, but it still evokes the glory of the republican ideal. The **East Front** faces the Supreme Court. From the times of frontiersman Andrew Jackson (1829) to peanut-farmin' Jimmy Carter (1977), most presidents were inaugurated here. Recent presidential inaugurations have taken place on the mall-facing West Front. The East Front entrance brings you into the 180 ft. high **rotunda**, where soldiers slept during the Civil War. From the lower-level crypt, visitors can climb to the second floor for a view of the House or Senate visitors chambers. Americans may obtain a free gallery pass from the office of their representative or senator in the House or Senate office buildings near the Capitol. Foreigners may get one-day passes by presenting identification at the "appointments desks" in the crypt. *(Metro: Capitol South. ☎ 225-6827. Open daily Mar.-Aug. 9am-8pm; Sept.-Feb. 9am-4:30pm. Tours Mar.-Aug. M-F 9am-7pm, Sa 9am-4pm; Sept.-Feb. M-Sa 9am-4pm. Free.)* The real business of Congress, however, is conducted in **committee hearings.** Most are open to the public; check the *Washington Post's* "Today in Congress" box for times and locations. The free **Capitol subway** (the **"Capitol Choo-Choo"**) shuttles between the basement of the Capitol and the House and Senate office buildings; a buzzer and flashing light signals an imminent vote.

SUPREME COURT. In 1935, the justices of the Supreme Court decided it was time to take the nation's separation of powers literally and moved from their makeshift offices in the Capitol into a new Greek Revival courthouse across the street. Oral arguments are open to the public; show up before 8:30am to be seated, or walk through the standing gallery to hear 5min. of the argument. *(1 1st St. ☎479-3000. In session Oct.-June M-W 10am-noon and 1-3pm for 2 weeks every month. The courtroom itself is open when Justices are on vacation. Court open M-F 9am-4:30pm. Free.)*

LIBRARY OF CONGRESS. The Library of Congress, between East Capitol and Independence Ave., is the world's largest library, with 113,026,742 objects stored on 532 mi. of shelves, including a copy of *Old King Cole* written on a grain of rice. The collection was torched by the British in 1814, and was restarted from Thomas Jefferson's personal collection. The collection is open to anyone of college age or older with a legitimate research purpose—a tour of the facilities and exhibits is available for tourists. *(1st St. SE. ☎707-5000.)* The **Jefferson Building's** green copper dome and gold-leafed flame seals a spectacular octagonal reading room. *(Great Hall pen M-Sa 8:30am-5:30pm. Visitors Center and galleries open 10am-5:30am. Free.)*

UNION STATION. Trains converge at Union Station, two blocks north of the Capitol. Colonnades, archways, and domed ceilings hark back to imperial Rome—if Rome was filled with stores and a food court. *(50 Massachusetts Ave. NE. Metro: Union Station. ☎371-9441. Retail shops open M-Sa 10am-9pm, Su 10am-6pm.)*

MONUMENTS

WASHINGTON MONUMENT. With a $9.4 million restoration project completed just a year ago, this shrine to America's first president is even more impressive. The Washington Monument was once nicknamed the "the Beef Depot monument" after the cattle that grazed here during the Civil War. Construction was temporarily halted during the war and later resumed; the rock that was then used came from a different quarry, which explains the different colors of the monument's stones. The

Reflecting Pool mirrors Washington's obelisk. *(Metro: Smithsonian. Admission to the monument by timed ticket. Apr.-Aug. monument open daily 8am-midnight, ticket kiosk open from 7:30am until all tickets distributed; Sept.-Mar. monument open 9am-5pm, ticket kiosk from 8:30am. Free. No tickets needed after 8pm Apr.-Aug.)*

VIETNAM VETERANS MEMORIAL. Maya Ying Lin, who designed the Vietnam Veterans Memorial, received a "B" when she submitted her memorial concept for a grade as a Yale senior—but beat her professor in the public memorial design competition. In her words, the monument is "a rift in the earth—a long, polished black stone wall, emerging from and receding into the earth." The wall contains the names of the 58,132 Americans who died in Vietnam, indexed in books at both ends of the structure. *(Constitution Ave. at 22nd St. NW. Metro: Foggy Bottom/GWU. ☎634-1568.)*

LINCOLN MEMORIAL. The Lincoln Memorial, at the west end of the Mall, recalls the rectangular grandeur of Athens' Parthenon. From these steps, Martin Luther King, Jr. gave his "I Have a Dream" speech during the 1963 March on Washington. A seated Lincoln presides over the memorial and everything that takes place below it. Climbing the 19 ft. president is a federal offense; a camera will catch you if the rangers don't. *(Metro: Smithsonian or Foggy Bottom/GWU. ☎426-6895. 24hr.)*

KOREAN WAR MEMORIAL. The 19 colossal polished steel statues of the Korean War Memorial trudge up a hill, rifles in hand, an eternal expression of weariness mixed with fear frozen upon their faces. The statue is accompanied by a black granite wall with over 2000 sandblasted photographic images from this war, in which 54,000 Americans lost their lives. The memorial is at the west end of the Mall, near Lincoln. *(Metro: Smithsonian or Foggy Bottom/GWU. ☎632-1002.)*

FRANKLIN DELANO ROOSEVELT MEMORIAL. Occupying a long stretch of West Potomac Park (the peninsula between the Tidal Basin and the Potomac River) just a short walk from the Jefferson or Lincoln Memorials, the Franklin Delano Roosevelt Memorial is more of a stone garden than a monument. Whether to display the disabled Roosevelt in his wheelchair was hotly debated when the memorial was being planned; in compromise, Roosevelt is seated, a position based on a famous picture taken at Yalta. The memorial is laid out in four "rooms" of red granite, each representing a phase of FDR's presidency. *(Metro: Smithsonian. ☎376-6704.)*

JEFFERSON MEMORIAL AND TIDAL BASIN. A 19 ft. bronze Thomas Jefferson stands in the domed rotunda of the Jefferson Memorial, designed to resemble Jefferson's own Monticello. The memorial overlooks the Tidal Basin, where pedalboats ply a polluted pond in and out of the shrine's strange shadow. Quotes from the Declaration of Independence, the Virginia Statute of Religious Freedom, *Notes on Virginia*, and an 1815 letter adorn the walls. *(Metro: L'Enfant Plaza. ☎426-6821.)*

SOUTH OF THE MALL

US HOLOCAUST MEMORIAL MUSEUM. A block off the mall lies the US Holocaust Memorial Museum, where excellent displays chronicle the rise of Nazism, the events leading up to the war in Europe, and the history of anti-Semitism. Films show troops entering concentration camps, shocked by the mass graves and emaciated prisoners they encountered. An eternal flame burns in "The Hall of Remembrance." *(100 Raoul Wallenberg Pl. SW. Metro: Smithsonian. ☎488-0400. Open in summer daily 10am-8pm; in winter 10am-5:30pm. Free. Get in line early for tickets.)*

BUREAU OF ENGRAVING AND PRINTING. Also known as "the Mint," the Bureau offers tours of the presses that annually print over $20 billion worth of money. The love of money has made this the area's longest line; expect to grow old while you wait. *(At 14th and C St. SW. Metro: Smithsonian. ☎847-2808. Open M-F 9am-2pm. Free.)*

FEDERAL TRIANGLE

An architectural marvel houses the Smithsonian's **National Building Museum.** Montgomery Meigs's Italian-inspired edifice remains one of Washington's most beautiful. *(F St. NW, between 4th and 5th St. Metro: Judiciary Sq. ☎272-2448. Open M-Sa*

10am-4pm, Su noon-4pm; until 5pm in summer. Suggested donation $3, seniors and students $2.) At the **National Archives,** visitors line up to view the original Declaration of Independence, US Constitution, and Bill of Rights. *(8th St. and Constitution Ave. NW. Metro: Archives-Navy Memorial. ☎ 501-5000. Open daily Apr.-Aug. 10am-9pm; Sept.-Mar. 10am-5:30pm. Free.)* Interstate felons may wish to avoid the **Federal Bureau of Investigation;** for everyone else, tour lines form on the **J. Edgar Hoover Building**'s outdoor plaza. *(☎ 324-3447. Open M-F 8:45am-4:15pm. Free.)*

John Wilkes Booth shot President Abraham Lincoln during a performance at **Ford's Theater.** National Park Rangers describe the events with animated gusto during a 20min. talk. *(511 10th St. NW. Metro: Metro Center. ☎ 426-6924. Open daily 9am-5pm. Free.)* The **Old Post Office** rebukes its contemporary neighbors with arched windows, conical turrets, and a clock tower, all sheathing a shopping mall. *(Pennsylvania Ave. and 12th St. NW. Metro: Federal Triangle. ☎ 289-4224. Tower open mid-Apr. to mid-Sept. 8am-10:45pm; off-season 10am-6pm. Shops open M-Sa 10am-8pm, Su noon-6pm.)* The **National Museum of Women in the Arts** houses works by the likes of Mary Cassatt, Georgia O'Keeffe, and Frida Kahlo in a former Masonic Temple. *(1250 New York Ave. NW. Metro: Metro Center. ☎ 783-5000. Open M-Sa 10am-5pm, Su noon-5pm. Free.)*

WHITE HOUSE AND FOGGY BOTTOM

WHITE HOUSE. With its simple columns and expansive lawns, the White House seems a compromise between patrician lavishness and democratic simplicity. Thomas Jefferson proposed a contest for the design of the building, but his entry lost to that of amateur architect James Hoban. The President's staff works in the West Wing, while the First Lady's cohorts occupy the East Wing. Staff who cannot fit in the White House work in the nearby **Old Executive Office Building.** The President's official office is the **Oval Office,** site of many televised speeches, but the public tour is limited to public reception areas. *(1600 Pennsylvania Ave. NW. ☎ 456-7041. Open by tour only Tu-Sa 10am-noon. Free. Get tickets at the White House Visitors Center, 1450 Pennsylvania Ave. NW, at the corner of 15th and E St.)*

AROUND LAFAYETTE PARK. Historic homes surround Lafayette Park north of the White House. These homes include the Smithsonian-owned **Renwick Gallery** craft museum, which has some remarkable works, such as the 80s sculptures *Ghost Clock* and *Game Fish.* *(17th St. and Pennsylvania Ave. NW. Metro: Farragut West. ☎ 357-2700. Open daily 10am-5:30pm. Free.)* Once housed in the Renwick's mansion, the **Corcoran Gallery** now boasts larger quarters, displaying American artists such as John Singer Sargent, Mary Cassatt, and Winslow Homer. *(17th St. between E St. and New York Ave. NW. ☎ 639-1700. Open M, W, and F-Su 10am-5pm, Th 10am-9pm. Suggested donation $3, seniors and students $1, families $5.)* Nearby, the **Octagon,** a curious building designed by Capitol architect William Thornton, is reputedly filled with ghosts. Tour guides explain the history of the house. *(Open Tu-Su 10am-4pm. $5, seniors and students $3.)*

THE KENNEDY CENTER FOR THE PERFORMING ARTS. A few blocks above Rock Creek Pkwy., the John F. Kennedy Center for the Performing Arts rises like a marble sarcophagus. One could fit the Washington Monument in the gargantuan **Grand Foyer,** were it not for the 18 Swedish chandeliers, shaped like cubical grape clusters. *(25th St. and New Hampshire Ave. NW. Metro: Foggy Bottom-GWU. ☎ 467-4600. Open daily 10am-midnight. Free tours every hr. M-F 10am-5pm, Sa-Su 10am-1pm.)* Across the street is Tricky Dick's beloved **Watergate Complex.**

GEORGETOWN

Georgetown's quiet, narrow, tree-lined streets are sprinkled with trendy boutiques and points of historic interest that make for an enjoyable walking tour. Retired from commercial use since the 1800s, the **Chesapeake & Ohio Canal** extends 185 mi. from Georgetown to Cumberland, MD. Today, the towpath where trusty mules pulled barges on the canal belongs to the National Park Service.

The **Dumbarton Oaks Mansion,** former home of John Calhoun, holds a beautiful collection of Byzantine and pre-Columbian art. The 1944 Dumbarton Oaks Conference helped write the United Nations charter. The spectacular pre-Columbian art gallery was designed by Phillip Johnson. The beautiful gardens are the best cheap date place in town. *(1703 32nd St. NW. ☎339-6401. Art gallery open Tu-Su 2-5pm. Suggested donation $1. Gardens open Apr.-Oct. daily 2-6pm; Nov.-Mar. 2-5pm. $5, seniors and children $3.)* In 1789, when Archbishop John Carroll learned where the new capital would be built, he quickly founded **Georgetown University,** the first Catholic institution of higher learning in the US. *(37th and O St.)*

UPPER NORTHWEST

Washington National Zoological Park saw two new arrivals in January 2001, Mei Xiang and Tian Tian, two giant pandas, arrived from China to live in the zoo's newly refurbished panda habitat. The zoo's orangutans are allowed to swing through the park via a series of 40 ft. high towers. The Valley Trail (marked with blue bird tracks) connects the bird and sealife exhibits, while the red Olmsted Walk (marked with elephant feet) links land-animal houses. *(3001 Connecticut Ave. Metro: Woodley Park-Zoo. ☎673-4800. Grounds open May to mid-Sept. daily 6am-8pm; mid-Sept. to Apr. 6am-6pm. Buildings open daily 10am-6pm, off-season 10am-4:30pm. Free.)*

The **Washington National Cathedral** was built from 1907 to 1990. Rev. Martin Luther King, Jr. preached his last Sunday sermon from the pulpit. The elevator rises to the Pilgrim Observation Gallery, revealing D.C. from the highest vantage in the city. At the **Medieval Workshop,** children can carve stone, learn how a stained-glass window is created, or, for $2, mold a gargoyle out of clay. *(Massachusetts and Wisconsin Ave. NW. Metro: Tenleytown, then take the #30, 32, 34, or 36 bus toward Georgetown; or walk up Cathedral Ave. from the equidistant Woodley Park-Zoo Metro. ☎537-6200 or 364-6616. Cathedral open May-Aug. M-F 10am-9pm, Sa 10am-4:30pm, Su 12:30-4:30pm; Sept.-Apr. M-Sa 10am-5pm, Su 12:30-4pm. Suggested donation $3 for tour, under 12 $1.)*

DUPONT CIRCLE

Once one of Washington's swankier neighborhoods, Dupont Circle attracted embassies because of its stately townhouses and large tracts of land. Today, it is a haven for the international, artsy, and gay crowds; this mix of business, politics, and pleasure make it one of the most exciting parts of the city.

The **Art Gallery District,** bounded by Connecticut Ave., Florida Ave., and Q St., contains over two dozen galleries displaying everything from contemporary photographs to tribal crafts. *(General information ☎232-3610.)* Nearby, the **Phillips Collection,** was the first museum of modern art in the US. Everyone gapes at Auguste Renoir's masterpiece, *Luncheon of the Boating Party,* in the Renoir room. Works by Delacroix, Miró, and Turner line the Annex. *(Q St. NW at 1600 21st St. ☎387-2151. Open Tu-Sa 10am-5pm, Su noon-7pm. $7.50, seniors and students $4, under 12 free.)*

The stretch of Massachusetts Ave. between Dupont Circle and Observatory Circle is also called Embassy Row. Before the 30s, Washington socialites lined the avenue with extravagant edifices; status-conscious diplomats found the mansions perfect for their purposes. Flags line the entrance to the **Islamic Center,** a brilliant white building within which stunning designs stretch to the tips of spired ceilings. *(2551 Massachusetts Ave. NW. ☎332-8343. No shorts allowed; women must cover their heads, arms, and legs. Open daily 10am-5pm; prayers held 5 times daily.)*

🏛 MUSEUMS ON THE MALL

The **Smithsonian** is the catalogued attic of the United States, containing over 140 million objects. The Institute began as the brainchild of **James Smithson,** a British chemist who, though he never himself visited the US, left 105 bags of gold sovereigns—the bulk of his estate—to "found at Washington, under the name of the Smithsonian Institution, an establishment for the increase and diffusion of knowledge among men." The Smithsonian Museums on the Mall constitute the world's largest museum complex. The **Smithsonian Castle,** on the south side of the mall, has an introduction to and info on the Smithsonian buildings. *(Metro: Smithsonian or Federal Triangle. ☎357-2700. All Smithsonian museums are free, wheelchair accessible, and open daily 10am-5:30pm, with extended summer hours determined annually.)*

MID-ATLANTIC

National Air and Space Museum, on the south side of the Mall across from the National Gallery, is the world's most popular museum, with 7.5 million visitors per year. Airplanes and space vehicles dangle from the ceilings; the Wright brothers' original biplane hangs in the entrance gallery. The space-age atrium holds a moon rock, worn smooth by tourists' fingertips. Walk through the Skylab space station, the Apollo XI command module, and a DC-7.

National Museum of American History, on the north side of the Mall, closest to the Washington Monument, houses several centuries' worth of machines, photographs, vehicles, harmonicas, and uncategorizable US detritus. When the Smithsonian inherits quirky artifacts of popular history, like Dorothy's slippers from *The Wizard of Oz,* they end up here. Hands-on exhibits are geared toward children.

Museum of Natural History, east toward the Capitol from American History, ruminates on the earth and its life in 3 big, crowded floors of exhibits. Objects on display in the spectacular golden-domed, Neoclassical buildings include dinosaur skeletons, the largest African elephant ever captured, and an insect zoo with live creepy-crawlies. Visitors still line up to see the cursed Hope Diamond.

National Gallery of Art (☎737-4215), east of Natural History, is not technically a part of the Smithsonian, but a close cousin of the Institute due to its location on the mall. The **West Wing** houses its pre-1900 art in a domed marble temple in the Western Tradition, including works by El Greco, Raphael, Rembrandt, Vermeer, and Monet. Leonardo da Vinci's earliest surviving portrait, *Ginevra de' Benci,* the only one of his works in the US, hangs among a fine collection of Italian Renaissance Art. The **East Building** houses the museum's 20th-century collection, including works by Picasso, Matisse, Mondrian, Miró, Magritte, Pollock, Warhol, Lichtenstein, and Rothko. The building also holds the museum's temporary exhibits. The National Gallery recently unveiled an outdoor **Sculpture Garden.** Open M-Sa 10am-5pm, Su 11am-6pm.

Hirshhorn Museum and Sculpture Garden, on the south side of the mall west of Air and Space. The 4-story, slide-carousel-shaped brown building has outraged traditionalists since 1966. Each floor consists of 2 concentric circles: an outer ring of rooms with modern, postmodern, and post-postmodern paintings, and an inner corridor of sculptures. The museum claims a comprehensive set of 19th- and 20th-century Western sculpture.

National Museum of African Art and the **Arthur M. Sackler Gallery** hide together underground in the newest museum facility on the Mall, to the west of the Hirshhorn. The Museum of African Art displays artifacts from sub-Saharan Africa such as masks, textiles, ceremonial figures, and musical instruments. The Sackler Gallery showcases an extensive collection of art from China, South and Southeast Asia, and Persia. Exhibits include illuminated manuscripts, Chinese and Japanese painting, jade miniatures, and friezes from Egypt, Phoenicia, and Sumeria.

Freer Gallery of Art (☎357-4880) just west of the Hirshhorn, displays American and Asian art. The static American collection consists of the holdings of Charles L. Freer, the museum's benefactor, and focuses on works by James McNeill Whistler. The strong Asian collections include bronzes, manuscripts, and jade.

🔊 ENTERTAINMENT

MUSIC

The D.C. punk scene is one of the nation's most lively. The biggest rock events take place at the sports arenas: **RFK Stadium** in the summer and the **USAir Arena** year-round. Tickets for many shows are available from **Protix** (☎410-481-6500, 703-218-6500, or 800-955-5566) or **Ticketmaster** (☎432-7328). The **U District,** D.C.'s ear-blasting epicenter, has sent the D.C. punk and rock scene off the Richter scale for decades. *Be careful in the area at night.* On weekends in summer, shows from jazz and R&B to the **National Symphony Orchestra** occupy the outdoor, 4200-seat **Carter Barron Amphitheater,** set into Rock Creek Park at 16th St. and Colorado Ave. (☎426-6837. Tickets vary from free to around $20.)

THEATER AND DANCE

Arena Stage, 6th St. and Maine Ave. SW, is often called the best regional theater company in America. (☎488-4377. Metro: Waterfront. Box office open M-Sa 10am-8pm, Su noon-8pm. Tickets $25-45, lower for smaller stages, students 35% off, seniors 20% off; half-price rush usually available 1½hr. before show.) The **Kennedy Center** (☎416-8000), at 25th St. and New Hampshire Ave., offers scores of ballet, opera and dramatic productions, most of them expensive ($10-75); however, most productions offer half-price tickets the day of performance to students, seniors, military, and the disabled; call 467-4600 for details. The **Millennium Stage** presents free performances in the Grand Foyer of the Kennedy Center. The prestigious **Shakespeare Theater**, at the Lansburgh, 450 7th St. NW at Pennsylvania Ave., offers a Bard-heavy repertoire. Standing-room tickets are available 2hr. before curtain. (☎547-1122, TTY 638-3863. Metro: Archives-Navy Memorial. $10.) In the **14th St. theater district**, tiny repertory companies explore and experiment with enjoyable results (check *CityPaper* for listings). **Woolly Mammoth**, 1401 Church St. NW (☎393-3939; Metro: Dupont Circle); **Studio Theater**, 1333 P St. NW, at 14th St. (☎332-3300; Metro: Dupont Circle); and **The Source Theater**, 1835 14th St. NW (☎462-1073; Metro: U St.-Cardozo), between S and T St., are all fine theaters in the neighborhood near Dupont Circle. Tickets for all three run $25. *Use caution in this area at night.*

SPORTS

The 20,000-seat **MCI Center**, 601 F St. NW, in Chinatown, is D.C.'s premier sports arena. (☎628-3200. Metro: Gallery Pl.-Chinatown.) The NBA's **Washington Wizards** continue their struggle against dismal play and a lame mascot. (Tickets $19-85.) The **Washington Capitals** skate from October through April. (Tickets $20-75.) Three-time Superbowl champions the **Washington Redskins** draw crowds to **Fed-Ex Stadium**, Raljon Dr., in Raljon, MD, from September through December. (☎301-276-6050. Tickets $40-60.) At **Robert F. Kennedy Stadium**, the **D.C. United** play soccer mid-April through October. (☎608-1119. Tickets $12-40.)

◪ NIGHTLIFE

BARS AND CLUBS

Talk about leading a double life. When darkness falls, Washington swaps the flesh-toned nylons for the fishnet stockings. D.C. denizens who crawl through red tape by day paint the town red by night. If you find yourself taking Jell-O bodyshots off a beautiful stranger at an all-you-can-drink-fest, just don't say we didn't warn you. Here's our advice on tripping the light fantastic: if you ache for a pint of amber ale, swing by the Irish pub-laden **Capitol Hill**. If you like girls (or boys) who wear Abercrombie & Fitch, hit up **Georgetown**, where youthful prepsters go to get happy. Gay and lesbian travelers traipse nightly through the glam **Dupont Circle**, while **Adams-Morgan** plays host to an international crowd. To party with rock stars, head to none other than U District for the best live rock 'n' roll in all of Dixieland.

- ▨ **Dragonfly**, 1215 Connecticut Ave. NW (☎331-1775). Beauty may be fleeting, but there is no better place to revel it than amidst the chic clientele of Dragonfly. Ice-white interior, pod-like chairs, techno music, and video projections. Drinks are expensive, but good sushi is served all night at reasonable prices. DJs every night. No cover. Open M-Th 5:30pm-1am, F 5:30pm-2am, Sa 6pm-2am, Su 6pm-1am.

- ▨ **Club Zei**, 1415 Zei Alley (☎842-2445), between 14th and 15th and H and I St. NW. Metro: McPherson Square. The streets of D.C. are abuzz about Club Zei's mix of hot hip hop and high-energy house music. The crowd tends to be a mix of D.C. college students. No sneakers or athletic gear; jeans okay. 18+. Cover $10. Open Th-Sa 10pm-3am.

- ▨ **State of the Union**, 1357 U St. NW (☎588-8810), near 14th St. Throbbing hip hop, techno, and other jazzy genres keep the crowd bouncing on a small dance floor under murals and busts of famous commies. Happy hour (daily until 8:30pm) means half-price drinks, with specialty twists on Russian faves—Starburst vodka, comrade? The back room has a moveable wall for summer patio action. 21+. Occasional $7 drink min. Open M-Th 5pm-2am, F-Sa 5pm-3am, Su 7pm-3am.

Club Heaven and Club Hell, 2327 18th St. NW (☎332-8899), near Columbia Rd. **Hell** is a hip, smoky bar greasily ornamented with pimpish gold tables and loud alterna-music. Happy hour Tu-Th until 10pm. No cover. **Heaven** looks more like an old townhouse with scuffed wood, comfy couches, a small bar, and 3 TVs, but the dance floor throbs to pounding beats of techno that spill out onto the back patio. Domestic beer $3, imports $4-5. Mixed techno and progressive F-Sa. Cover W $2-3, Th-Sa $5. Both open Su-Th 7pm-2am, F-Sa 7pm-3am.

The Common Share, 2003 18th St. NW (☎588-7180). With rock-bottom drink prices (beers and mixed drinks $2), this is the first stop on many a pub crawl. Upstairs looks like an unfurnished frat house, with college students and plenty of alcohol. Open M-Th 5:30pm-2am, F 5:30pm-3am, Sa 6pm-3am.

Blue Room, 2123 18th St. (☎332-0800). Chic *tapas* restaurant by day, alluring lounge and dance club by night. Trendy mid-twenties to early-thirties clientele gravitates to this stylish, blue world with polished chrome. Beers $4-9, cocktails $5-8. Tu live music on, Th-Sa down tempo deep house. Like Destiny's Child, the club starts jumping at 11:30pm; closing time is around 3am. Proper dress required.

GAY BARS AND CLUBS

The *Washington Blade* is the best source of gay news and club listings; published every Friday, it's available in virtually every storefront in Dupont Circle.

■ **J.R.'s,** 1519 17th St. NW (☎328-0090). D.C.'s busiest bar for good reasons: beautiful bartenders, beautiful barhoppers, beautiful interior. Packed every night with "guppies" (gay urban professionals). M Show-tune Sing-a-Long; W South Park. Happy hour (M-F 5-8pm) specials include $7 all-you-can-drink (Th 5:30-8pm). Open M-Th 11:30am-2am, F-Sa 11:30am-3am, Su noon-2am.

Badlands, 1415 22nd St. NW (☎296-0505), near P St. Stark exterior and limited hours proves that Badlands was built with a singular purpose: to host packed wild gay dance parties. The Annex upstairs is home to a mellower video bar with pool table, but most come for drag karaoke F-Sa. Tu and Th are under 21 nights. Th no cover with a college ID. Cover $4 F-Sa 9-10pm, $8 after 10pm. Open Th-Sa 9pm-very late, Su 9pm-2am.

The Fireplace, 2161 P St. NW (☎293-1293). 2-floor video bar catering to mostly older professional males and the men who love them. Look for the "outdoor" fireplace, complementing the gentlemen's club brick exterior. Happy hour M-F 1-8pm. Weekends and evenings can get pretty packed. No cover. Open Su-Th 1pm-2am, F-Sa til 3am.

Club Chaos, 1603 17th St. NW (☎232-4141), at Q St. Metro: Dupont Circle. Different nights cater to different crowds, though all nights are usually boisterously fun, crowded, and gender- and orientation-mixed. Happy hour Tu-F 5-8pm. Tu gay bingo, W lesbian night, Th Latin night. The best drag show in town happens Sa at 10pm. Open Tu-Th 4pm-1am, F-Sa 4pm-2am, Su 11am-1am.

◪ DAYTRIPS FROM D.C.

ARLINGTON, VA

The silence of the 612-acre **Arlington National Cemetery** honors those who sacrificed their lives in war. The Kennedy Gravesites hold the remains of President John F. Kennedy, his brother Robert F. Kennedy, and his wife Jacqueline Kennedy Onassis. The Eternal Flame flickers above JFK's simple memorial stone. The **Tomb of the Unknowns** honors all who died fighting for the US and is guarded by soldiers from the Army's Third Infantry (changing of the guard every 30min.; Oct.-Mar. every hr.) Robert E. Lee's home, **Arlington House**, overlooks the cemetery; tours are self-guided. (☎703-697-2131. Metro: Arlington Cemetery. Cemetery open Apr.-Sept. daily 8am-7pm; Oct.-May 8am-5pm. Free.) Head down Custis Walk in front of Arlington House, exit the cemetery through Weitzel Gate, and walk for 20min. to get to the **Iwo Jima Memorial,** based on Joe Rosenthal's Pulitzer Prize-winning photo of Marines straining to raise the US flag on Mt. Suribachi. The **Pentagon,** the world's largest office building, shows just how huge military bureaucracy can get. It also stands as a reminder of the events of September 11, 2001, when a hijacked plane crashed into a corner of the building, killing close to 200 individuals. (☎695-1776. Metro: Pentagon. Tours every hr. M-F 9am-4pm. Free.)

ALEXANDRIA, VA

Alexandria, VA traces its colonial origins over a century further back than Washington, D.C. Courtesy of a massive 80s restoration effort, **Old Town Alexandria** (Metro: King St.) has cobblestone streets, brick sidewalks, tall ships, and quaint shops. Sights cluster along **Washington** and **King St.** George Washington and Robert E. Lee used to pray at **Christ Church,** 118 N. Washington St. (☎703-549-1450), at Cameron St., a red brick Colonial building with a domed steeple. Both slept in **Robert E. Lee's Boyhood Home,** 607 Oronoco St. (☎703-548-8454), near Asaph St. Thirty-seven different Lees inhabited the **Lee-Fendall House,** 614 Oronoco St. (☎703-549-1789).

MT. VERNON

George Washington had a fabulous estate called Mt. Vernon, easily accessible to Washingtonians in Fairfax County, VA. Visitors can see Washington's bedroom and tomb and the estate's fields, where slaves once grew corn, wheat, and tobacco. To get there, take the Fairfax Connector 101 bus from the Huntington Metro stop, or take I-395 S to George Washington Pkwy. S, which becomes Mt. Vernon Hwy. in Alexandria; use the Mt. Vernon exit. (☎703-780-2000. Open Apr.-Aug. daily 8am-5pm; Sept.-Oct. and Mar. 9am-5pm; Nov.-Feb. 9am-4pm. Grounds close 30min. later. $9, seniors $8, ages 5-11 $4, under 5 free.)

VIRGINIA

If Virginia is obsessed with its past, it has good reason: many of America's formative experiences—the English settlement of North America, the shameful legacy of the slave trade, the final establishment of American independence, and much of the Civil War—took place in Virginia. More recently, the state has begun to abandon its Old South lifestyle in search of a more cosmopolitan image. The western portion of the state, with montane forests and fascinating underground caverns, provides a welcome respite from nostalgia and relentless Southern heat.

🛈 PRACTICAL INFORMATION

Capital: Richmond.
Visitor info: Virginia Division of Tourism, 901 E. Byrd St., 19th fl., Richmond 23219 (☎804-786-4484 or 800-847-4882; www.virginia.org). Open M-F 8am-5pm. **Dept. of Conservation and Recreation,** 203 Governor St., Richmond 23219 (☎804-786-1712). Open daily 8am-5pm.
Postal Abbreviation: VA. **Sales Tax:** 4.5%.

RICHMOND ☎804

The Civil War is still being waged in this capital city, once known as the "Cradle of the Confederacy." As recently as four years ago, residents vehemently lobbied against the inclusion of Confederate General Robert E. Lee's mosaic portrait along the scenic Canalwalk, and the inclusion of tennis great Arthur Ashe's statue alongside secessionist heroes such as Jefferson Davis and Stonewall Jackson. At the same time, the city honors the rich African-American heritage of Jackson Ward, an area that once rivaled Harlem as a center of Black thought and culture. Aside from its history, Richmond offers a diverse range of festivals, sports, and a hip nightlife.

MID-ATLANTIC

☞ TRANSPORTATION

Trains: Amtrak, 7519 Staple Mills Rd. (☎264-9194 or 800-872-7245). To: Washington, D.C. (2¼hr., 8 per day, $24); Williamsburg (1¼hr., 2 per day, $19); Virginia Beach (3¼hr., 2 per day, $27); New York City (6hr., 8 per day, $111); Baltimore (3½hr., 8 per day, $48); and Philadelphia (4¾hr., 8 per day, $71). Open 24hr. **Taxi** to town $17-18.

Buses: Greyhound, 2910 N. Blvd. (☎254-5910 or 800-231-2222). 2 blocks from downtown. Take GRTC bus #24 north. To: Washington, D.C. (2hr., 17 per day, $19); Charlottesville (1½hr., 4 per day, $17.50); Williamsburg (8 per day, 1hr., $8.50); Norfolk (2½hr., 9 per day, $19.50); New York City (6½hr., 25 per day, $56); Baltimore (3hr., 25 per day, $22); and Philadelphia (6hr., 15 per day, $35).

Public Transit: Greater Richmond Transit Co., 101 S. Davis Ave. (☎358-4782). Maps available in the basement of City Hall (900 E. Broad St.), the 6th St. Marketplace Commuter Station, and in the Yellow Pages. Most buses leave from various locations along Broad St. downtown. Bus #24 goes to the Greyhound station. Fare $1.25, seniors 50¢; transfers 15¢.

Taxi: Veterans Cab, ☎276-8990; **Yellow Cab**, ☎222-7300; **Star Cab**, ☎754-8556.

✴ ⁊ ORIENTATION AND PRACTICAL INFORMATION

Broad Street is the city's central artery, and the streets that cross it are numbered from west to east. Most parallel streets to Broad St., including **Main St.** and **Cary St.**, run one-way. Both I-95, leading north to Washington, D.C., and I-295 encircle the urban section of the city. The **Court End** and **Church Hill** districts, on Richmond's eastern edges, comprise the city's historic center. Farther southeast, **Shockoe Slip** and **Shockoe Bottom** overflow with after-dark partiers. **Jackson Ward**, in the heart of downtown (bounded by Belvedere, Leigh, Broad, and 5th St.) is currently undergoing renovations for an expanded City Center, which will revitalize the relatively rundown community. **The Fan**, named such because the neighborhood shape resembles the cooling device, is bounded by the Boulevard, I-95, the walk of statues along **Monument Ave.**, and **Virginia Commonwealth University.** The pleasant bistros and boutiques of **Carytown**, past the Fan on Cary St., and the tightly knit working community of **Oregon Hill** add texture to the cityscape.

Visitor info: Metro Richmond Convention and Visitors Bureau, 1710 Robin Hood Rd. (☎358-5511 or 358-5512), Exit 78 off I-95/64, in a converted train depot. Helpful 9 min. video introduces the city's attractions. Bus/van tours available, as well as maps of downtown and the metro region. Offers same-day discounted accommodations. Open June-Aug. daily 9am-7pm; off-season 9am-5pm.

Help Lines: Traveler's Aid, ☎225-7470. M-F 8:30am-4:30pm. **Rape Crisis**, ☎643-0888. **AIDS/HIV**, ☎800-533-4148. M-F 8am-5pm. **Crisis Pregnancy Center**, ☎353-2320. **Women's Health Clinic**, ☎800-254-4479.M-F 8am-5pm, Sa 7am-noon. **Richmond Organization for Sexual Minority Youth (ROSMY)**, ☎353-2077.

Post Office: 1801 Brook Rd. (☎775-6133). Open M-F 7am-5pm, Sa 10am-1pm. **ZIP code:** 23219. **Area code:** 804.

☞ ACCOMMODATIONS

Budget motels in Richmond cluster on **Williamsburg Rd.**, at the edge of town, and along **Midlothian Turnpike**, south of the James River; however, public transport to these areas is unreliable. As usual, the farther you stay from downtown, the less you pay. The Visitors Center can reserve accommodations, often at $20-35 discounts (see above).

Massad House Hotel, 11 N. 4th St. (☎648-2893). Surround yourself with antique furnishings, oil paintings, and a European atmosphere 5 blocks from downtown and the capitol. A/C and cable TV. Singles $53; doubles $58. Student and seniors 10% off.

MID-ATLANTIC

Downtown Richmond

ACCOMMODATIONS
Cadillac Motel, 1
The Inns of Virginia, 2
Massad House Hotel, 5
Pocahontas State Park, 8

FOOD
3rd St. Diner, 4
Bottom's Up, 7
Coppola's Deli, 6
Ma-Masu's, 3

TO SCIENCE MUSEUM
OF VIRGINIA (1 mi)
& (600 yd)

TO MONUMENT AVE. &
VIRGINIA MUSEUM
OF FINE ARTS (1.5 mi)

TO (i) WASHINGTON,
HWY. & (10 mi)

Cary St.

Cumberland St.

THE FAN

Monroe
Park

Virginia
Commonwealth
University

Iglewood St.

Hollywood
Cemetery

Cherry St.

Albemarle St.

Laurel St.

Pine St.

Spring St.

Belvidere St.

Gilmer St.

Belvidere St.

Henry St.

Monroe St.

Madison St.

Jefferson St.

Adams St.

Foushee St.

1st St.

2nd St.

3rd St.

Main St.

Cary St.

Canal St.

Byrd St.

Byrd St.

Public Library

CARYTOWN

Black History Museum
and Cultural Center

Maggie Walker
House

Jackson St.

JACKSON
WARD

Clay St.

Marshall St.

4th St.

5th St.

Broad St.

6th St.

Grace St.

Franklin St.

Leigh St.

7th St.

8th St.

9th St.

10th St.

11th St.

12th St.

John Marshall
House

Richmond
City Hall

Valentine
Museum

White House
& Museum
of the
Confederacy

State
Capitol

Bell
Tower

Governor's
Mansion

COURT
END

Governor St.

National Park
Service Civil
War Visitor
(i) Center

Canalwalk

James River

Manchester Bridge

SHOCKOE
SLIP

13th St.

12th St.

Shockoe Slip

15th St.

14th St.

Mayos
Island

Mayos Bridge

307

Richmond Trerbfront Trail

TO RTE. 288 (9 mi)
&

Dock St.

17th St.

18th St.

19th St.

20th St.

21st St.

22nd St.

23rd St.

24th St.

25th St.

Main St.

Grace St.

Franklin St.

Farmer's
Market

Edgar Allan
Poe Museum

SHOCKOE
BOTTOM

CHURCH
HILL

St. John's

Jefferson Ave.

TO RICHMOND NATL.
BATTLEFIELD PARK

N

0   200 yards

0   200 meters

Chamberlayne

Mosby St.

17th St.

The Inns of Virginia, 5215 W. Broad St. (☎ 288-2800), 3 mi. from town; use bus #6. After being renamed two years ago, this motel with modest, but clean rooms and a lavish lobby seeks stability under new ownership. Provides A/C, cable TV, and an outdoor pool. Rooms $39-79; weekly rate $196.

Cadillac Motel, 11418 Washington Hwy. (☎ 798-4049), 10 mi. from town; no public transportation. Take I-95 to Exit 89. Not the Cadillac of motel rooms, but decent sleeping quarters with A/C and cable TV. Singles $32-45; doubles $36-55.

Pocahontas State Park, 10301 State Park Rd. (☎ 796-4255; reservations 225-3867 or 800-933-7275). From Richmond, take I-95 south to Rte. 288 and connect to Rte. 10. The park is 10 mi. south on Rte. 10 and Rte. 655 in Chesterfield. Showers, biking, boating, picnic areas, and the 2nd largest pool in Virginia. Rent a canoe or paddleboat ($5 per hr.). Open year-round. Sites $18. No hookups.

🔲 FOOD

College students strapped for cash dominate the downtown Richmond cuisine scene—which ranges from greasy spoons to inexpensive Southern and ethnic foods. The outdoor **Farmers Market,** N. 17th and E. Main St., brings the freshest country crops into the city, brimming with farm fruits, veggies, and homemade delicacies. Surrounding the market in **Shockoe Bottom,** pizza and deli food top the menu. The self-proclaimed "artsy" crowd of Virginia Commonwealth University convene in hip coffeehouses and restaurants.

▨ Bottom's Up, 1700 Dock St. (☎ 644-4400), at 17th and Cary St. Named "Richmond's Best Pizza" 5 years in a row. Choose-your-own-pizza adventure, or go with signatures such as the Jo-Jo (tomatoes, feta, and shrimp) or the Chesapeake (spicy crab meat). Pizza $3-5.25 per slice. Drafts $3.25-4.25, bottles $2.75-4.50. Open M-W 11:30am-11pm, Th 11:30am-midnight, F 11:30am-2am, Sa noon-2am, Su noon-11pm.

Coppola's Deli, 1116 E. Main St. (☎ 255-0454). One of the best-kept secrets of downtown Richmond; has a sandwich to suit every personality and culinary persuasion. Local favorites include the Acropolis (feta, black olives, and tomato; $5.25) and the cheese tortellini ($2). Open M-W 10am-8pm, Th-Sa 10am-9pm, Su 11am-4pm.

Ma-Masu's, 2043 W. Broad St. (☎ 355-8063). Not to be confused with "Mamma Zu's." Ma-Masu, "Spiritual Mother" extraordinaire, inducts her guests to Liberian culture with a colorful mural. *Keli-willy* (fried plantains with spices and onions) and toywah beans $6, collard greens $2.50, coconut juice $2. Delivery available. Open M-F 11am-9pm.

3rd St. Diner (☎ 788-4750), at the corner of 3rd and Main St. Locals are served cheap eats by tattooed, pierced waitresses in combat boots. All-day breakfast special (2 eggs biscuit or toast, and homefries, grits, or Virginia fried apples; $3.75) and dinner sandwiches ($4-7) curb a late-night greasy-spoon craving. Open 24hr.

👁 SIGHTS

AROUND ST. JOHN'S CHURCH. St. John's Church is the site of Patrick Henry's famed 1775 "Give me liberty or give me death" speech. Actors recreate the speech during the summer Sundays at 2pm. *(2401 E. Broad St. ☎ 648-5015. 25 min. tours M-Sa 10am-3:30pm, Su 1-3:30pm. Summer Su tours after 3:30pm. $3, seniors 62+ $2, ages 7-18 $1.)* Nearby is the **Edgar Allen Poe Museum,** where visitors try to unravel the mysterious death (theories range from rabies to murder) of the enigmatic author in Richmond's oldest house. Inspect a coffin fragment and a lock of hair to draw your own conclusions, then bristle with fear as Poe's bust glares at you from a spooky archway in the garden. *(1914 E. Main St. ☎ 888-648-5523. Open Tu-Sa 10am-5pm, Su 11am-5pm. Tours every hour, last one at 4pm. $6; seniors, students, and AAA $5; under 9 free.)*

COURT END DISTRICT. Richmond's most important sites can be found in the **Court End** district. The **State Capitol,** at 9th and Grace St., is a Neoclassical masterpiece designed by Thomas Jefferson. The building was the seat of the Confederate government during the Civil War. Meet the real George Washington at the imposing Houdon statue, the only statue for which George actually posed. *(☎ 698-1788. Open daily 9am-5pm.)*

CONFEDERATE SOUTH. The Civil War South is celebrated at the Museum of the Confederacy. To feel most welcome, wear hometown gray while wandering through the first floor's memorial to the "Great War of Northern Agression." Of interest are the poignant painting "Last Meeting of Lee and Jackson" and the collection of artifacts and documents detailing gruesome Confederate medical treatments. The museum also runs 45min. tours through the White House of the Confederacy next door, where a South-shall-rise-again feeling is almost palpable. *(1201 E. Clay St. ☎ 649-1861; www.moc.org. Open M-Sa 10am-5pm, Su noon-5pm. $6, seniors $5, ages 7-18 $3, under 7 free. Tours every 30min. M, W, F-Sa 10:30am-4pm; Tu and Th 11:30am-4pm; Su 12:30-4:30pm. $7, seniors $6, students $4. Combination tickets: adults $9.50, seniors $9, ages 7-18 $5.)* There are no cupids of candied hearts in The Valentine Museum—just the South's largest collection of costumes and textiles. Fantastic additions to the cultural elitism of the 18th century, ruffles and layers abound—and that's just the men's clothing. Admission price includes a Wickham House tour. *(1015 E. Clay St. ☎ 649-0711. Open Tu-Sa 10am-5pm, Su noon-5pm. House tours on the hour 11am-4pm. $5, seniors and students $4, ages 7-12 $3.)*

SHOCKOE SLIP. South of Court End, the Shockoe Slip district, running from Main, Canal, and Cary St. between 10th and 14th St., features fancy shops in restored and warehouses, but few bargains. The **Shockoe Bottoms Arts Center** crams in 120 artist's cutting edge creations. *(2001 E. Grace St. ☎ 643-7959. Open Tu-Sa 10am-5pm, Su 1-5pm. Free)* Also in the Slip, the **Canalwalk,** linking the **Kanawha Canal** next to the James River, has gorgeous vistas, swaying trees, and stylish eateries.

JACKSON WARD. Jackson Ward, the heart of African-American Richmond, was recently listed by National Trust for Historic Preservation as one of the 11 most endangered sites in the country. The tiny Black History Museum and Cultural Center of Virginia showcases rotating exhibits on African-American history, including regional African wall hangings and a Woolworth's counter. *Be careful in this area at night. (00 Clay St. ☎ 780-9093. Open Tu-Sa 10am-5pm, Su 11am-5pm. $4, seniors and students $3, under 12 $2. Wheelchair accessible.)*

THE FAN. In the Fan, **Monument Ave.,** a boulevard lined with trees, gracious old houses, and towering statues of Virginia heroes, is a Richmond memory lane. The statue of Robert E. Lee faces south toward his beloved Dixie; Stonewall Jackson faces north so that the general can perpetually scowl at the Yankees. The statue of African-American tennis hero Arthur Ashe, who died of AIDS, created a storm of controversy when built at the end of the avenue. *Be very careful at night.*

CARYTOWN. Located past the Fan near the VCU campus, this tiny stretch of Cary St. is full of little boutiques, cheap restaurants, and culture galore. Find great deals on used CD's in the basement dungeon of **Plan 9 Records,** 3012 W. Cary St. (☎ 353-9996). Then put together the perfect outfit at **Bygones** thrift store, 2916 W. Cary St. (☎ 353-1919), or the trendier upscale **Pink,** 3158 W. Cary St. (☎ 353-08843), before grabbing a yummy sandwich from **Coppola's Deli,** 2900 W. Cary St. (☎ 353-6969). *Be—you guessed it—careful in this area at night.*

VIRGINIA MUSEUM OF FINE ARTS. On Thursdays in summer from 6:30-9pm, the Virginia Museum of Fine Arts—the South's largest art museum—draws sell-out crowds to its sculpture garden for **Jumpin',** one of Virginia's most dynamic musical performance cycles. *(2800 Grove Ave. ☎ 340-1400. Open Tu-W and F-Su 11am-5pm, Th 11am-8pm. Suggested donation $5. Jumpin': ☎ 367-8148. Tickets $10.)*

🎵🎭 ENTERTAINMENT AND NIGHTLIFE

One of Richmond's most entertaining and delightful diversions is the marvelous old **Byrd Theatre,** 2908 W. Cary St. (☎ 353-9911). Movie buffs buy tickets from a tuxedoed agent and are treated on weekends to a pre-movie Wurlitzer organ concert. All shows are 99¢; on Saturday the balcony opens for $1 extra. Free concerts abound downtown and at the **Nina Abody Festival Park,** near the bottom of 17th St. *Style Weekly,* a free magazine available at the Visitors Center, and its younger counterpart, *Punchline,* found in most hangouts, both list concert lineups. Cheer on the

Richmond Braves, Richmond's AAA minor-league baseball team, on Boulevard St. for a fraction of major-league prices. (☎359-4444. Boxes $7, reserved seats $5, general $4.) Student-driven nightlife enlivens **Shockoe Slip** and sprinkles itself throughout the **Fan.** After dark, **Shockoe Bottom** turns into a college-party central, with transient bars pumping bass-heavy music early into the morning.

■ **Havana '59,** 16 N. 17th St. (☎649-2822). Tipsy patrons sway with the palm trees while puffing on stogies at this salsa cabana. Though you won't sunburn in this Havana, you might scorch your wallet eating dinner (entrees $15-26). Try a Cuban *flan* ($6) or cigar (from $5.25) instead. Open M-Sa 4:30pm-2am; Su 11am-3:30pm and 5:30-11pm.

Matt's Pub and Comedy Club, 109 S. 12th St. (☎643-5653), pours out a bit of Brit wit in wooden walls reminiscent of the old country. Stand-up comedy F 8 and 10:30pm, Sa 8 and 11pm; reservations recommended. Open F-Sa 11:30am-2am. Tex-Mex and pub fare $3-7; microbrews and drafts $2.75-$3.60; cocktails $3.25. Cover around $8.50.

Medley's, 1701 E. Main (☎648-2313). An older crowd drowns their sorrows with live blues and French-Cajun food. Po' boy sandwiches $5.50-9; gumbo $8. Cover F-Sa $3-5. Open W-Sa 6pm-2am.

FREDERICKSBURG   ☎540

Sometimes popularity really hurts. Fredericksburg is smack dab between the Union Capital at Washington, D.C., and the Confederate capital at Richmond. A foothold in Fredericksburg during the Civil War meant control of the road between the capitals and, thus, a distinct military advantage. As a result, Fredericksburg experienced a river of bloodshed as men battled for control of the city. Years before the battle of Fredericksburg shattered the silent landscape with gunshots, the colonial post was already established as an important tobacco port on the banks of the Rappahanock River. After the Civil War dust cleared in 1865, Fredericksburg lay stained with carnage. The town has recovered, mixing gorgeous city plantations and somber battlefields with cafes and elegant boutiques. This town offers some of the finest in antique shopping and historical reenactments, without the notorious crowds of Williamsburg.

■■ **ORIENTATION AND PRACTICAL INFORMATION.** Fredericksburg's position on I-95 directly between Washington and Richmond makes it an easily accessible and pleasant destination en route to either capital. Exit 130A off I-95 and onto Rte. 3 accesses the city, which is divided into two parts by **Lafayette Boulevard.** South of Lafayette lie personal residences, while the **Historic Downtown** crams museums, historical sites, and chic cafes into a network of one-ways that is easily traversed by foot. **William St. (Rte. 3)** runs northeast over the Rappahanock River into Falmouth. One-way **Caroline St.** is the main historic and commercial route.

Amtrak, 200 Lafayette Blvd. (☎872-7245 or 800-872-7245), near Caroline St., runs trains through twice daily as a stop on the long line from Maine to Florida. (No ticket office. Call for reservations.) **Virginia Railway Express (VRE),** in the same building, makes several trips daily to Union Station in D.C. (☎703-684-1001 or 800-743-3873. Station open M-F 7am-7pm. Fare $7.) **Greyhound/Trailways,** 1400 Jefferson Davis Hwy. (☎373-2103), buses to Washington, D.C. (1¼hr., $10), Baltimore (1hr., $22), and Richmond (1hr., $13). **Fredericksburg Regional Transit,** 1400 Jefferson Davis Hwy., offers extended bus service around the city with Caroline St. and Princess Anne St. as main thoroughfares. (☎372-1222. 25¢ per ride.) **Yellow Cab** (☎371-7075) and **Virginia Cab Service** (☎373-5111) provide taxis. **Fredericksburg Visitors Center,** 706 Caroline St. at the corner of Charlotte St., offers extensive free info on Historic Fredericksburg, including a walking tour, bike tours, maps, admission passes to sights, and a 14min. orientation video about the town. (☎373-1776 or 800-678-4748. Open daily 9am-7pm; in winter 9am-5pm.) **Post Office:** Princess Anne St., between Charlotte St. and Lafayette Blvd. (☎373-6543. Open M-F 8:30am-5pm, Sa 9am-2:30pm.) **ZIP code:** 22401. **Area code:** 540.

ᚾ ACCOMMODATIONS. Chain motels rule the areas around Fredericksburg's Exits 118, 126, 130, and 133 off I-95, while historic B&Bs scattered near the Rappahanock River cost more than a few pence. Snag a copy of the *Traveler Discount Guide* at area restaurants for discount coupons.

Econolodge, 7802 Plank Rd., Exit 130B off I-95, then left at the first light, is where you'll forfeit colonial romance for the cheapest rates in Williamsburg. Desks, A/C, cable TV, and rosy interiors make for a comfortable stay. (☎786-8374. Singles $39; doubles $54.) Ascend the grand staircase at the **Fredericksburg Colonial Inn,** 1707 Princess Anne St., to encounter walls decorated with Civil War memorabilia. (☎371-5666. TV, fridges, A/C, breakfast, and morning paper. Singles and doubles $70; suites $95.) **Selby House,** 226 Princess Anne St., four blocks from the historic district, is a fragrant Victorian bed and breakfast operated by a certified Civil War battlefield tour guide. (☎373-7037. Private bathrooms, A/C, and lounge with cable TV. Breakfast included. Singles $62; double with canopy bed $75.)

ᚾ FOOD. Nearly every fast food and restaurant chain known to man accompanies the motel mania off Exits 130A and 130B. Supermarkets thrive along the same strip, including **Ukrops,** 4250 Plank Rd. (☎785-2626). The locals head to **Caroline St.** for a barrage of healthy options and less congested dining.

Sammy T's, 801 Caroline St., a block from the Visitors Center, was formerly the Fredericksburg Post Office but now delivers a comprehensive menu capable of pleasing poultry cravers (chicken parmesan $8.50) and animal lovers (vegan sandwich $7). Those of age can wash down their meal with a bottle from an impressive selection of imports. (☎371-2008. Open M-Sa 11am-10pm, Su 11am-9pm.) **Lee's Ice Cream,** 821 Caroline St., peddles the most decadent dessert in Fredericksburg. Choose Kahlua fudge or Arbuckle's, a finely ground chocolate chip. (☎370-4390. Open M-Th 11am-10pm, F-Sa 11am-midnight, Su 10am-10pm. Single scoop $2, double $3, triple $3.25.) At **La Familia Castiglia's,** 324 William St., an effervescent family staff greets customers with grins as wide as the broad menu. Indulge in the sumptuous veal marsala ($10) but not before a seafood start with $6.50 fresh mussels in wine sauce. (☎373-6650. Open daily 10:30am-10:30pm.) While prescriptions are being filled in the back of **Goolrick's Pharmacy,** 901 Caroline St., patrons climb baby blue barstools to chow on cheap chicken salad ($2.50) in this time warp to the 50s. Thick milkshakes ($3) and freshly squeezed lemonade ($1) refresh on steamy summer days. (☎373-3411. Open M-F 8:30am-7pm, Sa 8:30am-6pm.)

ᚾ SIGHTS. Mansions, medicine, and Monroe (James, not Marilyn) take center stage in Fredericksburg's **Historic District. Kenmore Plantation,** 1201 Washington Ave., was built in 1775 for Fielding Lewis and his wife, George Washington's sister, Betty. After being dazzled by the elegant dining room gawk at the garden so pristine it looks artificial. (☎373-4255. Open Mar.-Dec. M-Sa 10am-5pm, Su noon-4pm. $6, ages 6-17 $3. Grounds free.) Since George was a bit busy founding a nation, he wanted his aging mother to be near his sister Betty. The result is the **Mary Washington House,** 1200 Charles St., with tours packed with 18th-century trinkets. (☎373-1569. Open Mar.-Nov. daily 9am-5pm; Dec.-Feb. 10am-4pm. $4, children $1.50.) Learn why leeches purify the blood at the **Hugh Mercer Apothecary Shop,** 1020 Caroline St., which offers fascinating insights into old-fashioned medical practices. (☎373-3362. Open Mar.-Nov. daily 9am-5pm; Dec.-Feb. 10am-4pm. $4, ages 6-18 $1.50.) **The James Monroe Museum,** 908 Charles St., originally Monroe's law office, is a repository of memorabilia. Parisian-purchased, Louis XVI-influenced furniture includes the desk where James drafted his famous doctrine. (☎654-1043. Open Mar.-Oct. daily 9am-5pm; Nov.-Feb. 10am-4pm. $4, seniors $3.20, children $1.)

ᚾᚾ ENTERTAINMENT AND NIGHTLIFE. In the olden times, sundown meant bedtime. Well, not much has changed in Fredericksburg. Though flanked by **Mary Washington College** on the north, the town and its students usually quiet down when the tourists retire to their lodgings. The town does have a few postprandial pleasures. The **Colonial Theatre,** 907 Caroline St. (contact the Visitors Center at 800-678-4748), showcases symphonic performances and the occasional play. At the **Klein Theater,** College Ave. and Thornton Ave. (☎654-1124), the **Fredericksburg Theatre Co.** performs in the summer. ($18-20. Performances W-Sa 8pm, Su 2pm.)

Predominantly folk music attracts a local crowd to the trendy, purple walls of **Orbits,** 406 Lafayette Blvd. Roaming Rastafarians jam to a monthly reggae performance. You can open your mouth for an open mic night Monday or for a $5.50 intercontinental alliance of pesto nachos. (☎371-2003. Cover F-Sa $5.Open M-Th 11:30am-10pm, F-Sa 11:30am-2am, Su 11:30am-4pm. Drafts $3.) **The Underground,** 106 George St., in the basement of George St. Grill, takes its name literally with its dark basement location and alternative rock players. While aged waitresses serve a relatively refined crowd upstairs, head-banging persists down below F-Sa and makes holding a brew ($2.75) difficult. (☎371-9500. Open F-Sa. Opening vary with shows; call ahead.)

NEAR FREDERICKSBURG: NATIONAL BATTLEFIELD PARKS

What today is a vast and serene green expanse witnessed bloody decimation between December 1862 and May 1864. Under the leadership of Confederate generals Robert E. Lee and "Stonewall" Jackson and Union Generals Ambrose E. Burnside, Joseph Hooker, and Ulysses S. Grant, four devastating Civil War battles were contested in the 20 mi. that surround the town. Today, a 76 mi. driving tour winds through the battlefields of **Fredericksburg, Chancellorsville,** the **Wilderness,** and **Spotsylvania,** paying homage to the many soldiers who risked their lives for the Confederate stripes.

Three walking tours—the **Sunken Road Walking Tour** following the entrenchment line at Fredericksburg, the **Chancellorsville History Trail,** and the **Spotsylvania History Trail**—encircle the battlefields and provide strategic viewpoints of all major sights of battle, including the Bloody Angle at Spotsylvania. A captivating and comprehensive journey into the Civil War, the battlefields inspire everyone to be a history buff for at least a day. Six rotating tours offered by rangers highlight different features of the battlefield. Stop by the **Visitors Center,** 1013 Lafayette Blvd., for info. (☎373-6122. Open daily 8:30am-6:30pm; in winter 9am-5pm. $4, under 17 free.)

WILLIAMSBURG   ☎757

After its colonial prosperity, Williamsburg fell upon hard economic times until philanthropist John D. Rockefeller, Jr. restored a large chunk of the historic district, now known as **Colonial Williamsburg,** in the 1920s. Nowadays a fife-and-drum corps marches down the streets, and costumed wheelwrights, bookbinders, and blacksmiths go about their tasks using 200-year-old methods. Travelers who visit in late fall or early spring will avoid the crowds, heat, and humidity of summer. However, they will also miss the extensive array of special summer programs, such as the July 4 artillery demonstration and outdoor colonial dancing. December visitors will find an array of charming Colonial Christmas activities.

▐ TRANSPORTATION

Airport: Newport News/Williamsburg International Airport, 20min. away in Newport News, with frequent connections to Dulles by United Express and USAir. Take Rte. 199 W. to I-64 S.

Trains: Amtrak, 408 N. Boundary St. (☎229-8750 or 800-872-7245), behind the fire station. To: New York (7½-8hr., 2 per day, $78-111); Washington, D.C. (3½hr., 2 per day, $38-45); Philadelphia (6hr., 2 per day, $61-76); Baltimore (5hr., 2 per day, $45-54); and Richmond (1hr., 2 per day, $19-20). Station open Tu-Th 7:30am-5pm, Su-M and F-Sa 7:30am-10:30pm.

Buses: Greyhound (☎229-1460 or 800-231-2222), in the same location. To: Richmond (1hr., 8 per day, $10); Norfolk (1-2hr., 9 per day, $10); Washington, D.C. (3-4hr., 8 per day, $29); Baltimore (6-7hr., 8 per day, $45); and Virginia Beach (2½hr., 4 per day, $14). Ticket office open M-F 8am-5pm, Sa 8am-2pm, Su 8am-noon.

Public Transit: James City County Transit (JCCT) (☎220-1621). Bus service along Rte. 60, from Merchants Sq. in the historic district west to Williamsburg Pottery or east past Busch Gardens. Operates M-Sa 6:30am-5:15pm. Fare $1 plus 25¢ per zone-change. **Williamsburg Shuttle** (☎220-1621), provides service between Colonial Williamsburg and Busch Gardens every 30min. Operates June-Aug. daily 9am-9pm. All-day pass $1.

Taxi: Yellow Cab, ☎245-7777. **Williamsburg Limousine Service,** ☎877-0279. To Busch Gardens or Carter's Grove $6-10 one-way. To Jamestown and Yorktown $20 round-trip. Call between 8:30am-midnight.

Bike Rental: Bikes Unlimited, 759 Scotland St. (☎229-4620), rents bikes for $15 per day. $5 deposit required. Open M-F 9am-7pm, Sa 9am-5pm, Su noon-4pm.

⚡🔋 ORIENTATION AND PRACTICAL INFORMATION

Williamsburg lies some 50 mi. southeast of Richmond between Jamestown (10 mi. away) and Yorktown (14 mi. away). **The Colonial Parkway,** which connects the three towns, has no commercial buildings and is a beautiful route between historic destinations. The general Colonial Williamsburg area is accessed by I-64 and the Colonial Pkwy. exit.

Visitor info: Williamsburg Area Convention and Visitors Bureau, 201 Penniman Rd. (☎253-0192), ½ mi. northwest of the train station. Provides a free Visitor's Guide to Virginia's Historic Triangle. Open M-F 8:30am-5pm. **Colonial Williamsburg Visitors Center,** 102 Information Dr. (☎800-447-8679), 1 mi. northeast of the transport center. Tickets and transportation to Colonial Williamsburg. Maps and guides to historic district, including a guide for the disabled. Info on prices and discounts for Virginia sights. Open in summer daily 8:30am-8pm; winter hours vary.

Post Office: 425 N. Boundary St. (☎229-4668). Open M-F 8am-5pm, Sa 9am-2pm. **ZIP code:** 23185. **Area code:** 757.

🎯 ACCOMMODATIONS

The hotels operated by the **Colonial Williamsburg Foundation** are generally more expensive than other lodgings in the area. **Rte. 60 W** and **Rte. 31 S** are packed with budget motels, which grow cheaper the farther they are from the historic district. At the various B&Bs around William and Mary, guests pay more for gorgeous colonial decor. Guest houses don't serve breakfast, but still offer the bed, a reasonable price, abounding warmth, and "like-home" feelings.

🖼 Lewis Guest House, 809 Lafayette St. (☎229-6116), a 10min. walk from the historic district, rents three comfortable rooms, including an upstairs unit with private entrance, kitchen, partial A/C and shared bath. Rooms $25-35.

Carter Guest House, 903 Lafayette St. (☎229-1117). Two doors down from Lewis Guest House are 2 lovely, spacious rooms with 2 beds and a shared bath. Be forewarned: no bed till you're wed! Mrs. Carter—a woman of traditional Southern values—will not let unmarried men and women sleep in the same room. Singles $25; doubles $35.

Bryant Guest House, 702 College Terr. (☎229-3320). Offers rooms with private baths, TV and limited kitchen facilities in a stately, exquisitely landscaped brick home. Singles $35; doubles $45; 5-person suite $55.

Jamestown Beach Campsites, 2217 Jamestown Rd. (☎229-7609), immediately adjacent to the Jamestown Settlement. One of the largest campgrounds in the area. Frolic by the pool and waterslide or splash around in the more natural James River. Don't disturb the peace; quiet hours (11pm-8am) are strictly enforced. Sites $20; with water and electricity $25; full hookup $28. Six-person maximum at each campsite.

🍴 FOOD

Instead of rowdy farmers and proper colonists, most of the authentic-looking "taverns" in Colonial Williamsburg are packed with sweaty tourists and are overpriced (lunch $5-10, dinner from $18). Jumping back into the 21st century for food proves the most price-savvy option.

▒ **Chowning's Tavern** (☎220-7012), on Duke of Gloucester St. Odd dishes like "Bubble and Squeak" (cabbage and potatoes $5) and "Welsh Rarebit" (bread in beer sauce with ham, $7) will have you chowing down like George Washington. After 9pm, the merriment continues as costumed waiters sing 18th-century ballads and challenge guests to card games ($3-7). Cover $3. Open daily 11am-midnight.

Green Leafe Cafe, 765 Scotland St. (☎220-3405). This classy restaurant draws William and Mary students with its hearty sandwiches ($5-6) like the pan-fried pumpernickel. 30 brews on tap ($2.75-4), including savory Virginia micros. Su "Mug Night" means half-price beer. Open daily 11am-2am.

The Cheese Shop, 424 Prince George St. (☎220-0298 or 800-468-4049). On weekdays, tourists overflow out the doors at this gourmet shop and deli. The local Virginia ham sandwich ($4) vies with the international Braunschweiger ($3.75). Outdoor seating only. Open M-Sa 10am-6pm, Su 11am-5pm.

👁 SIGHTS

Colonial Williamsburg will have you spending 1774 treasury notes and singing "my hat, it has three corners" while you dodge horse droppings all the way to the milliner's. The historic district itself doesn't require a ticket—walk around, march behind the fife-and-drum corps, and lock yourself in the stocks for free. Also open to the public is a colonial flea market where you can test your haggling skills or just peaceably buy a tri-cornered hat for $9. Most of the "colonial" shops and two of the historic buildings—the **Wren Building** and the **Bruton Parish Church**—are also open to the public. Monday's *Visitor's Companion* newsletter lists free events and evening programs. (☎800-447-8679. Most sights open 9:30am-5pm; see the *Visitor's Companion newsletter*. $32, ages 6-12 $16. 2-day pass $38/$19.)

The real fun of Colonial Williamsburg comes from interacting with its history. Trade shops afford wonderful opportunities to learn from skilled artisans such as the carpenter, and slightly less-skilled workmen like the brickmaster, who may invite you to take off your shoes and join him in stomping on wet clay. Colonial denizens are quick to play up their antiquated world view (admitted Floridians are likely to be greeted with startled cries of "Spanish territory!").

Spreading west from the corner of Richmond and Jamestown Rd., the **College of William and Mary** is the second oldest college in the US. The **Sir Christopher Wren Building** was built two years after the college received its charter and restored with Rockefeller money. (Tours M-F 10am and 2:30pm.)

🏃 DAYTRIPS FROM WILLIAMSBURG

JAMESTOWN AND YORKTOWN
The **"Historic Triangle"** brims with United States history. More authentic and less crowded than Colonial Williamsburg empire, Jamestown and Yorktown show visitors where it all *really* began. At the **Colonial National Park**, southwest of Williamsburg on Rte. 31, you'll see the remains of the first permanent English settlement in America (1607), as well as exhibits explaining colonial life. The **Visitors Center** offers a hokey film, a free 30min. "living history" walking tour, and a 45min. audio tape tour ($2) for the five-mile **Island Loop Route**. The **Old Church Tower**, built in 1639, is the only 17th-century structure still standing. Also featured is a statue of **Pocahon-**

BRIDGE O' LOVE A jaunt across the **Crim Dell Bridge** at William and Mary College means risky business. According to student lore, the fate of many a love life has been sealed in a single crossing (or shall we say in crossing singly?). Superstition dictates that those who tread the bridge's path alone will never marry. And if passion leads a couple to smooch with the bridge underfoot, destiny has eternally bound them together. Maybe this chance to say "I Do" has something to do with Playboy naming the bridge the "second most romantic spot on a college campus."

tas. In the remains of the settlement itself, archeologists have uncovered the original site of **Jamestown Fort.** (☎ 229-1733. Open daily 9am-5pm; off-season 9am-4:30pm. Visitors Center closes 30min. after park. $5.)

The nearby **Jamestown Settlement** is a commemorative museum with changing exhibits, a reconstruction of James Fort, a Native American village, and full-scale replicas of the three ships that brought the original settlers to Jamestown in 1607. The 20min. dramatic film details the settlement's history, including a discussion of settler relations with the indigenous Powhatan tribe. (☎ 229-1607. Open daily 9am-5pm. $10.75, ages 6-12 $5.25.)

The British defeat at **Yorktown** in 1781 signaled the end of the Revolutionary War. The Yorktown branch of **Colonial National Park** vividly re-creates the significant last battle with an engaging film and an electric map. The Visitors Center rents cassettes and players ($2) for driving the battlefield's seven-mile automobile route. (☎ 757-898-3400. Visitors Center open daily 8:30am-5pm; last tape rented at 3:30pm. $4, under 17 free.) Brush up on your high school history as you listen to the rallying cries of revolutionary figures like Benjamin Franklin and Patrick Henry foretelling independence won at Yorktown. The **Yorktown Victory Center,** one block from Rte. 17 on Rte. 238, boasts an intriguing "living history" exhibit: in an encampment in front, soldiers from the 1781 Continental Army take a break from combat. (☎ 757-887-1776. Open daily 9am-5pm. $8, seniors $6.75, ages 6-12 $4.)

JAMES RIVER PLANTATIONS

Built near the water to ease the planters' commercial and social lives, these country houses buttressed the slave-holding Virginia aristocracy. Reconstructed **Carter's Grove Plantation,** 6 mi. east of Williamsburg on Rte. 60, maintains the colonial feel. Also redone were the slave quarters. The **Winthrop Rockefeller Archaeological Museum,** built unobtrusively into a hillside, provides a case study in archaeology. (☎ 757-229-1000, ext. 2973. Plantation open Tu-Su 9am-5pm; Nov.-Dec. 9am-4pm. Museum and slave quarters open Mar.-Dec. Tu-Su 9am-5pm. $20, ages 6-12 $12.)

Berkeley Plantation, halfway between Richmond and Williamsburg on Rte. 5, claims to be the site of the invention of bourbon by British settlers. Beautiful, terraced box-wood gardens stretch from the original 1726 building to the James River. (☎ 804-829-6018. Open daily 8am-5pm. $9.50, seniors and ages 13-16 $6.50, ages 6-12 $2.50. Grounds alone $5/$3.60/$2.50.) To reach **Shirley Plantation,** follow Rte. 5 west from Williamsburg, or east from Richmond. Surviving war after war, this 1613 plantation has an exquisite mansion featuring a seemingly unsupported three-story staircase. (☎ 800-232-1613. Open daily 9am-5pm. $9, ages 13-21 $6, ages 6-12 $5.)

BEER AND ROLLER COASTERS

At **Busch Gardens,** proceed with caution; an arduous journey fraught with dangerous dragons, monsters, and angry gods awaits the innocent tourist in "17th-Century Europe." Visitors over 21 can indulge in a home-brewed Anheuser-Busch beer, but consume in moderation lest your stomach churn after a pulsating 70 mph scream on the **Apollo's Chariot** roller coaster. (☎ 253-3350. Open late June through Aug. Su-F 10am-10pm, Sa 10am-11pm; Sept.-Oct. M and F 10am-6pm, Sa-Su 10am-7pm; call for winter hours. $41, seniors $36, ages 3-6 $26, after 5pm $19 for all.)

A three-day ticket ($50) is good for both Busch Gardens and **Water Country: USA,** 2 mi. away. Thirty-five water rides, slides, and attractions laced with a 1950s surfing theme keep barefooted waterbabies splashing with delight. (Open late May to mid-June Sa-Su 10am-6pm; mid-June to mid-Aug. daily 10am-8pm; Sept. Sa-Su 10am-7pm. Hours vary; call ahead. $30, ages 3-6 $23; after 3pm $19 for all.)

VIRGINIA BEACH ☎ 757

Virginia's largest city, once the capital of the cruising collegiate crowd, is now gradually shedding its playground image and maturing into a family-oriented vacation spot. As with its nearby neighbors Norfolk, Newport News, and Hampton, the streets of this former Spring Break spot now welcome parents and their baby carriages alongside tipsy twenty-somethings. Fast-food joints, motels, and cheap discount stores (hallmarks of every beach town) still abound. Virginia Beach is distinguished from its East Coast counterparts by beautiful ocean sunrises, a substantial dolphin population, and frequent military jet flyovers.

▐ TRANSPORTATION

Trains: Amtrak (☎245-3589 or 800-872-7245). The nearest train station, in Newport News, runs 45min. bus service to and from the corner of 19th and Pacific St. When leaving, you must call to reserve your train ticket. To Newport News from: Baltimore (5½hr., $63); New York City (8hr., $111); Philadelphia (7hr., $80); Richmond (2hr., $24); Washington, D.C. (4½hr., $52); and Williamsburg (45min., $17).

Buses: Greyhound, 1017 Laskin Rd. (☎422-2998 or 800-231-2222). Connects with Maryland via the Bridge-Tunnel. Station located ½ mi. from the ocean. From: Richmond (3½hr., $17.50); Washington, D.C. (6½hr., $32); and Williamsburg (2½hr., $15).

Public Transit: Virginia Beach Transit/Trolley Information Center (☎437-4768), Atlantic Ave. and 24th St. Info on area transportation and tours, including trolleys, buses, and ferries. Trolleys transport riders to most major points in Virginia Beach. The Atlantic Avenue Trolley runs from Rudee Inlet to 42nd St. (May-Sept. daily noon-midnight; 50¢, seniors and disabled 25¢, 3-day passes $3.50). Other trolleys run along the boardwalk, the North Seashore, and to Lynn-haven Mall. **Hampton Roads Regional Transit (HRT)** (☎222-6100), in the Silverleaf Commuter Center at Holland Rd. and Independence St., connects Virginia Beach with Norfolk, Portsmouth, and Newport News. ($1.50, seniors and disabled 75¢, children under 38 in. free.)

Bike Rental: RK's Surf Shop, 305 16th St. (☎428-7363), in addition to aquatic equipment, rents bikes for $4 per hr. or $16 per day. Open June-Sept. daily 9am-10pm, Oct.-May 11am-6pm; bikes must be returned 2hr. before closing.

Taxi: Yellow Cab, ☎460-0605. **Beach Taxi,** ☎486-4304.

✦ ▐ ORIENTATION AND PRACTICAL INFORMATION

In Virginia Beach, east-west streets are numbered and the north-south avenues, running parallel to the beach, have ocean names. Prepare to feel like a thimble on a Monopoly board: **Atlantic** and **Pacific Avenue** comprise the main drag. **Arctic, Baltic,** and **Mediterranean Avenues** are farther inland.

Tourist Office: Virginia Beach Visitors Center, 2100 Parks Ave. (☎437-4888 or 800-446-8038), at 22nd St. Info on budget accommodations and area sights. Helpful, knowledgeable docents. Open Sept.-May daily 9am-8pm; June-Aug. 9am-5pm.

Internet access: WebCity Cybercafe, 1307 Atlantic Avenue, #112, on the boardwalk. $5 per 30min.

Post Office: 2400 Atlantic Ave. (☎428-2821), at 24th St. and Atlantic Ave. Open M-F 8am-4:30pm. **ZIP code:** 23458. **Area code:** 757; 10-digit dialing required.

▐ ACCOMMODATIONS AND CAMPING

As could be expected with an ocean resort, a string of endless motels lines the waterfront in Virginia Beach. Oceanside, Atlantic and Pacific Ave. buzz with activity during the summer and boast the most desirable hotels. If you reserve in advance, rates are as low as $45 in winter and $65 on weekdays in summer.

▣ **Angie's Guest Cottage, Bed and Breakfast, and HI-AYH Hostel,** 302 24th St. (☎428-4690). Filled with friendly staff, sparklingly clean rooms, and plenty of boogie boards in a prime area of town, only 1 block from the oceanfront. Kitchen, lockers available. Linen $2. No lockout. No A/C. Open Apr.-Sept. Check-in 10am-9pm. 2-day min. stay for private rooms. Dorms $14.50, nonmembers $17; off-season $11.50/$13. Private singles with A/C $31; doubles $48 per person; substantially less off-season.

Ocean Palms Motel, 2907 Arctic Ave. (☎428-8362), at 30th St. Not likely to be mistaken for a 5-star hotel, the brick building skimps on aesthetics, but offers the second cheapest rates (after Angie's) in the immediate resort area. TV, A/C, kitchen. $30-60 per night, holidays excluded. Cash or traveler's checks only.

First Landings, 2500 Shore Dr. (☎800-933-7275 or 412-2300 for reservations), about 8 mi. north of town on Rte. 60; take the North Seashore Trolley. Beachfront sites thrive on the natural beauty of Virginia's shore. Desirable location makes the park very popular; call at least 11 months ahead for reservations. The park features picnic areas, a private swimming area on a sprawling beach, a bathhouse and boat launching areas. Cabins Apr.-May and Sept.-Nov. $65-75, June-Aug. $85-95.

🍴 FOOD

Prepare for more $6 all-you-can-eat breakfast specials than you have ever previously encountered. Alternatively, fish for a restaurant on **Atlantic Avenue,** where each block is a virtual buffet of fried, fatty, sweet, or creamy dining options.

▨ The Jewish Mother, 3108 Pacific Ave. (☎422-5430). Let Mama fill your belly with deli in this popular Virginia chain restaurant. Unfold a newspaper format menu to find humongous sandwiches with a scoop of potato salad ($4.50-6.75), followed up by overwhelming desserts ($3.50-4.50). Transforms into a local barfly's delight after 11pm with live music nightly; W blues jam, Su karaoke. Cover $3. Open M-F 8am-1am, Sa 8am-3am, Su 7am-2am.

▨ Giovanni's Pasta Pizza Palace, 2006 Atlantic Ave. (☎425-1575). Speedy service, scrumptious rolls, and savory fare make Giovanni's a must-eat on the boardwalk. Tasty, inexpensive Italian pastas, pizzas, hot strombolis ($6-11), and a fabulous veggiboli ($6) await. Open daily noon-11pm.

Cuisine and Co., 3004 Pacific Ave. (☎428-6700). This sophisticated escape serves up Martha Stewart-approved over-the-counter gourmet lunches. Typical treats include creamy tuna melts ($5), a chunky chicken salad ($5.25), and decadent cookies ($7.50 per lb.). Open M-Sa 9am-8pm, Su 9am-6pm.

Ellington's Restaurant, 2901 Atlantic Ave. (☎428-4585), inside the Oceanfront Inn, on the boardwalk. Patrons gaze over the ocean while enjoying some of the most overlooked food in the city, like huge lunch salads ($7) and affordable dinner entrees ($8-17). Try the Mexi Burger with guacamole and cheddar-jack cheese ($8). Open daily 7am-10pm.

👁 SIGHTS

The **beach and boardwalk,** jam-packed with college revelers, bikini-clad sunbathers, and families, is the *raison d'être* at Virginia Beach. The **Old Coast Guard Station,** 24th St. and oceanfront, offers historic exhibits and a **Tower Cam** for voyeuristic peeks of sunbunnies. (☎422-1587. Open daily M-Sa 10am-5pm, Su noon-5pm. $3, seniors and military with ID $2.50, ages 6-18 $1, under 6 free.) The frequent roar of F-14 and Tomcat jet engines will also remind you of the naval base nearby. (Visitor info ☎433-3131.) The **Virginia Marine Science Museum,** 717 General Booth Blvd., is home to over 50 species of fish, sharks and stingrays. (☎425-3474, excursion trips 437-2628. Open daily 9am-9pm; off-season 9am-5pm. $9, seniors $8, ages 4-11 $6.)

🎵🎭 ENTERTAINMENT AND NIGHTLIFE

On summer nights, the Virginia beach boardwalk becomes a haunt for lovers and teenagers, and **Atlantic Ave.,** a.k.a. "Beach Street, USA," hums with minstrel shows and street performers. Rousing jazz and classic rock performances can be heard every other block. Larger outdoor venues at 7th, 17th, and 24th St. draw bigger names and bigger crowds. (☎440-6628 for more info. Schedules for the main events are posted along the street. Free.) Gay and lesbian bars can be found away from Virginia Beach in the chi-chi Ghent neighborhood of nearby Norfolk.

▨ Chicho's, 2112 Atlantic Ave. (☎422-6011), on "The Block" of closet-sized college bars clustered between 21st and 22nd St. One of the hottest spots on the hot-spot strip fea-

MID-ATLANTIC

tures gooey pizza dished out from the front window (slices $2.25-3.25), tropical mixed drinks ($5-7), and live rock 'n' roll music M. Open M-F 3pm-2am, Sa-Su 11am-2am.

Harpoon Larry's, 216 24th St. (☎422-6000), at Pacific Ave., 1 block from the HI-AYH hostel, serves tasty fish in an everyone-knows-your-name atmosphere. Affable staff welcomes twenty- and thirty-somethings to escape the sweat and raging hormones of "The Block." Specials include crabcakes ($7) and rum runners (Tu, Th; $2). Shout "¡Arriba!" W with 25¢ jalapeno poppers. Happy hour M-F 7-9 pm. Open daily noon-2am.

Peabody's, 209 21st St. (☎422-6212). Boogie your body, not your board, at the biggest dance floor on the beach. A young, scantily clad crowd bops to Top 40 hits, especially during Peabody's "Hammertime" when drinks are only $1.50 (daily 7-9pm). All-you-can-eat fresh crab legs and shrimp $15. Peabody's scores big with the fresh-faced crowd on its theme nights: F College Night (free admission with college ID) and Sa Summer Saturdaze (discount with tropical attire). Cover $5. Open Th-Sa 7pm-2am.

Mahi Mah's, 615 Atlantic Ave. (☎437-8030), at 7th St., inside the Ramada Hotel. Sushi, live music, and ocean views. Wine "flights" offered W 5-9pm: choose 4 tastes ($2 each) from a selection of whites and reds. Mouth-watering sushi ($6 rolls 11am-5pm, extended menu after 5pm), including the Dragon Roll (crab, cucumber, and avocado wrapped in eel; $10.50). Outdoor band entertains nightly. Open daily 7am-1am.

CHARLOTTESVILLE ☎804

Thomas Jefferson, composer of the Declaration of Independence and colonial Renaissance man, built his dream house, Monticello, high atop his "little mountain" just southeast of Charlottesville. Around his personal paradise, Jefferson endeavored to create the ideal community. In an effort to breed further intellect (not to mention keep him busy in his old age), Jefferson humbly created the University of Virginia (UVA). Jefferson would be proud to know his time was not wasted—today the college sustains Charlottesville economically, geographically, and culturally.

▐ TRANSPORTATION

To reach Charlottesville by car, I-64 runs east-west and is the city's main feeder. From points north and south, Rte. 29 leads directly into Charlottesville where it becomes Emmet St.

Airport: Charlottesville-Albemarle Airport, ☎973-8341, 1 mi. west of Charlottesville on Rte. 29 on Airport Rd. Served by USAir, United, and Delta. Fares and destinations vary, call for information. Hertz, Avis, and National rental cars available.

Trains: Amtrak, 801 W. Main St. (☎434-296-4559 or 800-872-7245), 7 blocks from downtown. To: Washington, D.C. (3hr., 2 per day, $29); New York City (8hr., 1 per day, $141); Baltimore (4hr., 1 per day, $71); and Philadelphia (5½hr., 1 per day, $108). Open daily 5:45am-9:45pm.

Buses: Greyhound/Trailways, 310 W. Main St. (☎295-5131), within 3 blocks of downtown. To: Richmond (1hr., 3 per day, $17.50); Washington, D.C. (3hr., 5 per day, $18); Norfolk (4½hr., 3 per day, $35); Baltimore (5½hr., 5 per day, $42); and Philadelphia (7hr., 4 per day, $53). Open daily 6:15am-10pm.

Public Transit: Charlottesville Transit Service (☎296-7433). Bus service within city limits. Maps available at both info centers, on the buses, the Chamber of Commerce, City Hall, Charlottesville Transit Office (4th St.), and the UVA Student Center in Newcomb Hall. Buses operate M-Sa 6:30am-midnight. Fare 75¢, seniors and disabled 35¢, under 6 free. The more frequent UVA buses technically require UVA student ID, but others report that a studious look usually suffices.

Taxi: Yellow Cab, ☎295-4131. **AAA Cab Co.,** ☎975-5555.

✦ ▐ ORIENTATION AND PRACTICAL INFORMATION

Charlottesville streets are numbered from east to west, using compass directions; 5th St. NW is 10 blocks from (and parallel to) 5th St. NE. There are two downtowns: **The Corner,** on the west side across from the university, home to student-run delis and coffeeshops, and **Historic Downtown,** about a mile east and a tad higher on the price scale. The two are connected by east-west **University Avenue,** which starts as Ivy Rd. and becomes Main St. after a bridge terminates in The Corner district.

Visitor info: Chamber of Commerce, 415 E. Market St. (☎295-3141), at 5th St. Within walking distance of Amtrak, Greyhound, and downtown. Maps, guides, and info about special events available. Open M-F 9am-5pm. **Thomas Jefferson Visitors Center** (☎977-1783, ext. 121), off I-64 on Rte. 20. Arranges discount lodgings and travel packages to Jeffersonian sights. "The Pursuit of Liberty," a free 30min. film about Jefferson's life, is shown every hr. 10am-4pm). Also features a free exhibit with 400 original Jeffersonian objects. Open Mar.-Oct. daily 9am-5:30pm; Nov.-Feb. 9am-5pm. **University of Virginia Information Center** (☎924-7969), at the Rotunda in the center of campus. Offers brochures, a university map, and tour information. Open daily 8:45am-4:45pm. The larger **University Center** (☎924-7166), Exit 120A off U.S. 250 W, is home to the campus police and hands out transport schedules, campus maps, entertainment guides, and hints on budget accommodations. Open 24hr.

Campus Police: ☎4-7166 on a UVA campus phone.

Hotlines: Region 10 Community Services: ☎972-1800. Open 24hr. **Mental Health:** ☎977-4673. Open 24hr. **Sexual Assault Crisis Center:** ☎977-7273. Open 24hr. **Lesbian and Gay:** ☎982-2773. Operates Sept.-May M-W 7-10pm, Su 6-10pm. **Women's Health Clinic** (in Richmond): ☎800-254-4479. Open 24hr.

Post Office: 513 E. Main St. (☎963-2525). Open M-F 8:30am-5pm, Sa 10am-1pm. **ZIP code:** 22902. **Area code:** 804.

⌂ ACCOMMODATIONS

Emmet Street (U.S. 29) is home to generic hotels and motels ($40-60) that tend to fill up during summer weekends and big UVA events. The Budget Inn, 140 Emmet St., is the closest motel to the university, and offers big rooms with lots of sunlight and cable TV. (☎293-5141. Reception 24hr. 36 rooms, $42-58, each additional person $5.) Equally attractive to the budget traveler is the Econo Lodge, located at 400 Emmet St., with an outdoor pool, cable TV, and continental breakfast. (☎296-2104. Reception 24hr. 60 rooms, $42-62.) Charlottesville KOA Campground, Rte. 708, 10 mi. outside Charlottesville (take U.S. 20 S to Rte. 708 W), has shaded campsites to keep guests cool, and a recreation hall, pool, and volleyball court to entertain. (☎296-9881 or 800-KOA-1743. Laundry facilities. Fishing and pets allowed. 73 sites. Open Mar.-Oct. $20, with water and electricity $24, full hookup $27.)

⌂ FOOD

Students and tourists dictate the menus in Charlottesville. Intellectual crowds dine at **The Corner** on University Ave. across from the university where good, cheap food overflows each plate. The chain motels on Emmet St. are complemented by fast food chains. For a glitzier culinary experience, a stroll down the cobblestone streets by the **Downtown Mall** unveils romantic, unique eateries, most of which offer outdoor dining in summer.

▨ **The Hardware Store,** 316 E. Main St. (☎977-1518 or 800-426-6001), in the Downtown Mall. It requires a handyman's dexterity to go bottoms-up on the half-meter and full meter beer tubes ($5-10). The Store sends patrons to the head of the class with the *summa cum laude* sandwich (smoked salmon and swiss on pumpernickel; $8.75). Try the specialty pierogies ($5). Open M-Th 11am-9pm, F-Su 11am-10pm.

▨ **Southern Culture,** 633 W. Main St. (☎979-1990). Delve deep into Cajun culture with the *pasta jambalaya* ($14) or the more affordable Cajun burger ($6) served up by an amicable staff. Every Tu is Mardi Gras night. Open M-Th 5-10pm, F-Sa 5-10:30pm, Su 11am-2:30pm and 5-10pm.

Littlejohn's, 1427 University Ave. (☎977-0588). During lunch hours, this deli becomes as overstuffed with students and workers as its sandwiches. In the wee, wee hours of the morning, barflies trickle into Littlejohn's to kick back and relax with the Easy Rider (baked ham, mozzarella, and coleslaw $3.50). Many, many beers ($2-3). Open 24hr.

◉ SIGHTS

Jefferson oversaw every stage of development of his beloved **Monticello,** 1184 Monticello Loop, a home that truly reflects the personality of its brilliant creator. The house is a quasi-Palladian jewel filled with fascinating innovations, such as a fireplace dumbwaiter to the wine cellar and a mechanical copier, all compiled or conceived by Jefferson. The grounds include orchards and flower gardens and afford magnificent views. (☎984-9822. Open Mar.-Oct. daily 8am-5pm; Nov.-Feb. 9am-4:30pm. $11, ages 6-11 $6.) Just west of Monticello on the Thomas Jefferson Pkwy. (Rte. 53) is the partially reconstructed **Michie Tavern,** which includes an operating grist mill and a general store. (☎977-1234. Open daily 9am-5pm. $8, seniors and AAA $7, under 6 $3. Last tour 4:20pm.) To reach **Ash Lawn-Highland,** 1000 James Monroe Pkwy., the 535-acre plantation home of President James Monroe, continue east to the intersection with Rte. 795, 2½ mi. east of Monticello, and make a right. Although less distinctive than Monticello, Ash Lawn reveals more about family life in the early 19th century and hosts living history exhibitions including banjo music. Kids are mesmerized by the colorful peacocks in the backyard. (☎293-9539. Open daily 9am-6pm; Nov.-Feb. 10am-5pm. Tour $7, seniors $6.50, ages 6-11 $4. AAA discount 10%. Wheelchair accessible.)

Most activity on the grounds of the **University of Virginia** clusters around the **Lawn** and fraternity-lined **Rugby Road.** Jefferson's Monticello is visible from the lawn, a terraced green carpet that is one of the prettiest spots in American academia. Professors live in the Lawn's pavilions; Jefferson designed each one in a different architectural style. Privileged Fourth Years (never called seniors) are chosen each year for the small Lawn singles. Room 13 is dedicated to ne'er-do-well **Edgar Allen Poe,** who was kicked out for gambling. The early-morning clanging of the bell that used to hang in the **Rotunda** provoked one incensed student to shoot at the building. (☎924-7969. Open daily 8:45am-4:45pm. Tours mid-Mar. through Apr. M-F 10am and 1pm; May to mid-June M-F 10am; mid-June through Oct. M-F 10am and 1pm, Sa 10am; Nov. to mid-Mar. M-F 10am.) The **Bayley Art Museum,** on Rugby Rd., features changing exhibits and a small permanent collection that includes a cast of Rodin's *The Kiss.* (☎924-3592. Open Tu-Su 1-5pm. Free.)

♫▓ ENTERTAINMENT AND NIGHTLIFE

This preppy college town is full of jazz, rock, and pubs. A kiosk near the fountain in the center of the Downtown Mall has posters with club schedules; the free *Weekly C-ville* can tell you who's playing when. English-language opera and musical theater highlight the **Summer Festival of the Arts** in the Box Gardens behind Ash Lawn. (☎293-4500. Open June-Aug. M-F 9am-5pm.) Ash Lawn also hosts a "Music at Twilight" series on Wednesday evenings at 8pm ($10, seniors $9, students $8). There's daily skating at the **Charlottesville Ice Park,** 230 W. Main St., at the end of the Downtown Mall (☎817-1423; call ahead for times and prices).

▓ **Buddhist Biker Bar and Grille,** 20 Elliewood Ave. (☎971-9181). UVA students and local twenty-somethings flock to this bar, known for its huge lawn and its drink specials (beers $2.50-3.50). The food ain't bad either—try the spinach dip ($5) or stuffed mushrooms ($3.75). $1 beers M, $2 cocktails W. Live bluegrass Th. Open M-Sa 5pm-2am.

▓ **Orbit,** 102 14th St. NW (☎984-5707). The hottest new bar and restaurant among C-ville locals. The recently opened downstairs features a *2001: A Space Odyssey* theme, and the garage-door windows open on hot summer evenings. Upstairs has 8 pool tables and another bar with extensive taps, including many imports ($2.50-4). Tu ladies shoot pool for free, W live DJ, Th $2 drafts, Su live acoustic music. Open daily 5pm-2am.

Baja Bean, 1327 W. Main St. (☎293-4507). Cheap burritos, tamales, and chimichangas go down smooth for under $8 at this Mexican bar and restaurant. Every 5th day of the month is the Cinco Celebration, a fiesta highlighted by $3 Coronas. Happy hour M-F 4-6pm; $1.50 pints of Bud Light and $2 cocktails. W night dance parties (9pm-midnight) with lasers and DJ-fueled music. Open daily 11am-2am.

The Max, 120 11th St. SW (☎295-6299 or 295-8729). Tu features Top 40 DJ and dancing, while Charlottesville turns to its southern roots with line dancing W. F-Sa brings live
country rock. Cover usually $5. Drafts around $2. Open Th-Su 8pm-1:30am.

TRAX, 122 11th St. SW (☎295-8729, 800-594-8499 for tickets and shows), next door
to its rhyming neighbor Max, opens its doors as a concert venue Th-Sa for everything
from heavy metal and rap to Christian rock. Tickets $5-20, depending on band.

SHENANDOAH NATIONAL PARK ☎540

Shenandoah National Park was America's first great nature reclamation project. In
1926, Congress authorized Virginia to purchase a 280-acre tract of over-logged,
over-hunted land. A 1936 decree from Franklin Roosevelt sought to improve the
land, experimenting with trappers to foster new life upon the slowly rejuvenating
soil. Today an enthralling national park spans 196,000 acres and contains 500 miles
of trails and more plant species than all of Europe. On clear days, visitors can see
miles of ridges and treetops. Such unspoiled views, however, are a rare commodity,
as pollution has mixed with the natural dew in the area to create a murky mist
cloaking the peaks. Shenandoah's amazing multicolored mountains—covered with
foliage in the summer, streaked with brilliant reds, oranges, and yellows in the
fall—offer relaxation and recreation throughout the year.

ORIENTATION AND PRACTICAL INFORMATION

The park runs nearly 75 mi. along the famous 105 mi. **Skyline Drive,** which extends
from Front Royal in the north to Rockfish Gap in the south before evolving into the
Blue Ridge Parkway. Miles are measured north to south and denote the location of
trails and stops. Three major highways divide the park into sections. The **North Section** runs from Rte. 340 to Rte. 211, the **Central Section** from Rte. 211 to Rte. 33, and
the **South Section** from Rte. 33 to I-64. Entrance fee is $10 per vehicle, or $5 per
hiker, biker, or bus passenger. Admission for disabled persons is free. Pass is valid
for seven days and is necessary for re-admittance. Most facilities hibernate in the
winter; call ahead. Skyline Dr. closes during and following bad weather.

The **Dickey Ridge Visitors Center,** at Mi. 4.6, and the **Byrd Visitors Center,** at Mi. 51,
answer questions and maintain small exhibits about the park, including a 12min.
introductory slide show. (Dickey Ridge: ☎635-3566. Byrd: ☎999-3688. Both open
Apr.-Oct. daily 8:30am-5pm; July-Aug. 8:30am-6pm. Dickey is open through Nov., F-
Sa only.) The stations and their knowledgeable rangers conduct informative presentations on local wildlife, guide short walks among the flora, and then wax
romantic, outdoors-style, with lantern-lit evening discussions. Pick up a free
Shenandoah Overlook visitor newsletter for a complete listing of programs. Com-
prehensive and newly updated, the *Guide to Shenandoah National Park and
Skyline Drive* ($7.50 and worth every penny) is available at both Visitors Centers.
For general park info call 999-3397 (daily 8am-4:30pm) or 999-3500 for a recorded
message. Send mail to: **Superintendent,** Park Headquarters, Shenandoah National
Park, Rte. 4, P.O. Box 348, Luray, VA 22835. In an emergency call 800-732-0911.

Greyhound sends two buses a day from Washington, D.C. ($40), Richmond ($25),
and Charlottesville ($8), to Waynesboro, near the park's southern entrance; no bus
or train serves Front Royal, near the park's northern entrance. **Area code:** 540.

ACCOMMODATIONS

The Bear's Den (HI-AYH), 18393 Blue Ridge Mountain Rd., 35 mi. north of Shenandoah
on Rte. 601, in a miniature stone castle, can hold 20 mountain-weary travelers
within its two standard dorm rooms; another room has one double bed and two
bunk beds. Take Rte. 340 N to Rte. 7 E and follow it for 10 mi. to 601 N; travel ½ mi.
on 601 and turn right at the gate. Aside from the more standard amenities, the hostel also offers simple, straightforward hiking trails geared towards inexperienced
woodsfolk. A convenience store spares budget-travelers a 9 mi. trek to the nearest
supermarket. (☎554-8708. 5 day max. stay. Reception 7:30-9:30am and 5-10pm.

Check-out 9:30am. Front gate locked and quiet hours begin at 10pm; 24hr. access to hikers' basement room. Beds $12, nonmembers $15; private room for 2 $30/$36, each additional person $12/$15. Camping $6/$7 per person with use of hostel facilities, $3 without.) The park also maintains three affordable "lodges," essentially motels with nature-friendly exteriors. **Skyland,** Mi. 42 on Skyline Dr., offers wood-furnished cabins and more upscale motel rooms. (☎999-2211. Cabins: Open Apr.-Oct. $52-102. Motel rooms: Open Mar.-Nov. $113-170. Up to $10 more in Oct.) **Big Meadows,** Mi. 51, has similar services, with a historic lodge and cabins. (☎999-2221. Cabins: Open late Apr. to Nov. $75-85. Lodge: $68-115. Up to $10 more in Oct.) **Lewis Mountain,** Mi. 57, operates regular cabins and tent cabins. (☎999-2255. Cabins: $62-67; $2 more in Oct. Tent cabins: $17-22.) Reservations are necessary at all three lodges, which can be accessed at 800-999-4714; call up to six months in advance.

▨ CAMPING

The park service (☎800-365-2267) maintains four major campgrounds: **Mathews Arm** (Mi. 22), **Big Meadows** (Mi. 51), **Lewis Mountain** (Mi. 58), and **Loft Mountain** (Mi. 80). The latter three have stores, laundry, and showers, but no hookups. Heavily wooded and uncluttered by RVs, Mathews Arm and Lewis Mountain make for the happiest campers. Sites at Mathews Arm, Lewis Mountain, and Loft Mountain are $14, at Big Meadows $14-17. Reservations are possible only at Big Meadows.

Backcountry camping is free, but you must obtain a permit at park entrances, Visitors Centers, ranger stations, or the park headquarters. Camping without a permit or above 2800 ft. is illegal and unsafe. Trail maps and the PATC guide can be obtained at the Visitors Center. The PATC puts out 3 topographical maps ($5 each). The Appalachian Trail (AT) runs the length of the park. The **Potomac Appalachian Trail Club** (PATC), a volunteer organization, maintains six cabins in backcountry areas of the park. Campers who feel that they are sufficiently ready for a backpacking trip but not totally comfortable with staying in the woods on their own might consider staying at one of these rustic accommodations. You must reserve space in the cabins in advance by writing to the club at 118 Park St. SE, Vienna, VA 22180 or calling 703-242-0693 or 242-0315 (M-Th 7-9pm, Th-F noon-2pm). You may be under a roof but you'll still be in the wilderness, so bring lanterns and food; the primitive cabins contain only bunk beds, blankets, and stoves. (One group member must be 21+. Su-Th $15 per group, F-Sa $25.) Also available are 12 three-sided shelters strewn at eight- to ten-mile intervals along the AT. Unwritten trail etiquette usually reserves the cabins for those hiking large stretches of the trail.

▧ OUTDOOR ACTIVITIES

DRIVING
Many visitors choose to experience the park by taking a ride along Skyline Dr. and stopping occasionally to take short hikes, enjoy the views at scenic overlooks, or picnic. The drive is lined with seven picnic areas (located at Mi. 5, 24, 37, 51, 58, 63, and 80) with bathrooms, potable water, and scenic eating spots. The trusty *Guide to Shenandoah and Skyline Drive* includes an extensive hikes section with descriptions of every trail in the park.

HIKING
The trails off Skyline Dr. are heavily used and safe for cautious day-hikers with maps, appropriate footwear, and water. If you do not feel comfortable hiking on your own or want to try a longer hike, you might consider one of the free ranger-led tours arranged by the Visitors Center. The middle section of the park, from **Thorton Gap** (Mi. 32) to **South River** (Mi. 63), bursts with photo opportunities and moving views, although it tends to be crowded. Rangers recommend purchasing *Hiking Shenandoah Park* ($13), a guide detailing the distance, difficulty, elevation, and history of 59 hikes.

Whiteoak Canyon Trail (Mi. 42.6; 4.5 mi., 4hr.). A strenuous hike that opens upon an impressive 86 ft. waterfall and rewards those who ascend the 1040 ft. of trail with tremendous views of the ancient Limberlost hemlocks.

Limberlost Trail (5 mi. round-trip from Whiteoak Canyon, 2-3hr.; 1 mi. wheelchair-accessible loop from trailhead; 1hr.) slithers into a hemlock forest. Weaving through orchards and remaining relatively level, Limberlost is recommended for beginners.

Old Rag Mountain Trail (Mi. 45; 8.8 mi., 6-8hr.). Main trail starts outside the park; from U.S. 211, turn right on Rte. 522, then right on Rte. 231. Trail scrambles up 3291 ft. to triumphant views of the valley below. Be careful in damp weather, as rocks can get slippery. $3 fee for Old Rag hikers 10 and older who have not paid Shenandoah admission.

Stony Man Nature Trail (Mi. 41.7; 1.5 mi., 1½hr.). Independent hikers can gain altitude on this self-guided trail, which gradually climbs to the park's second-highest peak.

OTHER ACTIVITIES

There are two other ways to explore Shenandoah: by boat or beast. **Downriver Canoe Co.** in Bentonville offers canoe, kayak, raft, and tube trips. From Skyline Dr. Mi. 20 follow U.S. 211 W for 8 mi., then take U.S. 340 N 14 mi. to Bentonville; turn right onto Rte. 613 and go 1 mi. (☎635-5526 or 800-338-1963.) Pick up a guided **horseback ride** at the Skyland Lodge at Mi. 42. (Riders must be 4 ft. 10 in. 1hr. rides $20. Open Mar.-Oct.; call for times and reservations.)

NEAR SHENANDOAH   ☎540

LURAY CAVERNS

Mother Nature worked millions of years to sculpt the limestone bowels of the earth into delicate marvels of color and form. Chances are, it will seem like a million years as you wait in line to explore **Luray Caverns'** moist, 57° tunnels filled with mineral formations. A Mexican band entertains the droves of tourists as they wait in line to play some underground music of their own on the "Stalacpipe Organ." Exit 264 off I-81 to U.S. 211. (☎743-6551. Open mid-June through Aug. daily 9am-7pm; mid-Mar. to mid-June and Sept.-Oct. 9am-6pm; Nov. to mid-Mar. M-F 9am-4pm, Sa-Su 9am-5pm. $14, seniors $12, ages 7-13 $6; $2 AAA discount.)

ENDLESS CAVERNS

Escape the tourist congestion of Luray Caverns to discover the beauty of creation at **Endless Caverns,** 1800 Endless Caverns Rd. The wildest of the caves was discovered in 1800 by two boys hunting a rabbit. Where the rabbit scurried remains a mystery, but chances are he had plenty of space to hop with 5½ mi. of passages documented and an unknown number still unexplored. Cave temperature is cool and the tour is relatively physical, so wear a jacket and sturdy shoes. Follow signs from the intersection of U.S. 11 and U.S. 211 in New Market. (☎896-2283. Open June-Aug. daily 9am-7pm; Sept.-Nov. and Mar.-June 9am-5pm; Nov.-Mar. 9am-4pm. $12, ages 3-12 $6; $1 AAA discount.)

SKYLINE CAVERNS

The smallest and the closest to D.C., **Skyline Caverns,** located on U.S. 340, 1 mi. from the junction of Rte. 340 and Skyline Dr., tends an orchid-like garden of white rock spikes. Don't hold your breath in anticipation of the next formation: one grows every 7000 years. Most notable are the anthodites (crystals), which cannot be found anywhere else in the world. (☎540-635-4545 or 800-296-4545. Open June-Aug. daily 9am-6:30pm; Mar.-May and Sept.-Nov. 9am-5pm; Nov.-Mar. 9am-4pm. $12; seniors, AAA, and military $10; ages 7-13 $6.)

SCENIC DRIVE: BLUE RIDGE PARKWAY   ☎540

The beauty of unrestrained wilderness does not end at the southern gates of Shenandoah. Your jaw will continue to drop as you weave through the world's longest scenic drive, the 469 mi. Blue Ridge Parkway. Continuous with Skyline Dr., the parkway winds through Virginia and North Carolina, connecting the Shenandoah (Virginia) and Great Smoky Mountains (Tennessee) National Parks and offering an endless array of stunning vistas along the way. Administered by the National Park

Service, the parkway sprouts hiking trails, campsites, and picnic grounds with humbling mountain views. While still accessible in the winter, it lacks maintenance or park service between November and April. The steep, bending roads can be treacherous, so exercise caution, especially during inclement weather. Also be on the alert for darting deer, not an uncommon sight among the wild woods.

From Shenandoah National Park, the road extends south through Virginia's **George Washington National Forest** from Waynesboro to Roanoke. The forest's **Visitors Center** (☎291-1806), 12 mi. off the parkway at Mi. 70 at the intersection of Rte. 130 and Rte. 11 in Natural Bridge, distributes info on hiking, camping, canoeing, and swimming at Sherando Lake (4½ mi. off the parkway at Mi. 16; user fee $8).

Across from the forest's Visitors Center, a water-carved *Arc de Triomphe*, the **Natural Bridge,** towers 219 ft. above green-lined falls and an underground river. One of the seven natural wonders of the world, the Bridge still bears the initials carved into the side by vandalous George Washington. The nightly "Drama of Creation" light and sound show chronicles the biblical seven days of creation. (☎291-2121 or 800-533-1410. Bridge open daily 8am-9pm. Drama show Su-F 9pm, Sa 9 and 10pm. $8; seniors, AAA, military, and students $7; ages 6-15 $4. Wheelchair accessible.)

Hiking trails vary in difficulty and duration, offering naturalists of all ages and abilities a chance to explore the peaks and valleys of Blue Ridge. **Humpback Rocks,** a formation of green volcanic rock (Mi. 5.8), is an easy hike to the namesake emerald mounds. The **Mountain Farm Trail** (Mi. 5.9) is another easy hike, about 20min., and leads to a reconstructed homestead. Three- to five-mile trails start from **Peaks of Otter** (Mi. 84), where you can camp at the lowest point on the parkway among peaks as high as 4500 ft. For wheelchair accessibility, try the ¼ mi. **Linn Cove Viaduct Access Trail** (Mi. 304.4 in North Carolina). If you're hard-core and have the time to spare, venture onto the **Appalachian Trail,** which leads all the way to Georgia or Maine.

The opulent manor at **Moses H. Cone Memorial Park** (Mi. 294) rents canoes on Price Lake, Mi. 291. (☎295-3782. Open June-Aug. daily 8:30am-6pm; May and Sept.-Oct. Sa-Su 10am-6pm. $4 for 1hr., $3 per additional hr.) The Park Service hosts a variety of ranger-led activities, including history talks, campfire circles, guided nature walks, slide shows, and musical demonstrations; info is available at the **Visitors Centers** (see below). At the intersections of I-81 and I-64, where Skyline Dr. melts into Blue Ridge Parkway, the college town of **Lexington** drips with Confederate pride. Check out the **Lee Chapel and Museum,** at the center of the Washington and Lee campus, which holds Confederate General (and college namesake) Robert E. Lee's crypt and his trusty horse Traveler's remains. (☎463-8768. Open M-Sa 9am-5pm, Su 1-5pm. Free.) For accommodations and further attractions, contact the **Lexington Visitors Center,** 106 E. Washington St. (☎463-3777). Other cities and towns along the Parkway also offer accommodations, mostly motels (rates $35-55).

For general info on the parkway, call the park service in Roanoke, VA (☎857-2490) or write to **Blue Ridge Parkway Superintendent,** 199 Hemphill Knob Rd., Asheville, NC 28801 (☎828-298-0398). Twelve **Visitors Centers** line the Parkway at Mi. 6, 64, 86, 169, 218, 294, 305, 316, 365, and 382, located at entry points where highways intersect the Blue Ridge (most open daily 9am-5pm). **Area code:** 540.

ROANOKE   ☎540

Long hailed as the cultural and economic capital of Southwest Virginia, Roanoke began in 1881 as a small pioneer settlement called "Big Lick," after a large salt marsh where deer fed. Soon after, the Norfolk and Western Railroads met in a junction within the city, launching it into industrial fame and fortune; one can still see the railyards that transformed the tiny town along Norfolk Ave. With its myriad museums, musical and theater performances, and thriving downtown, Roanoke has earned its title, the "Star of Southwest Virginia."

The **Center in the Square** complex is Roanoke's cultural mecca. Downstairs lies the **Mill Mountain Theatre,** now in its 38th season. The all-star 2002 season boasts *The Jungle Book, Annie Get Your Gun,* and *Death of A Salesman.* (☎342-5740. Box office open Tu-Sa 10am-5pm.) Take a trip through Roanoke's history, from Native American and frontier life to the present, at the **History Museum & Historical Society of Western Virginia.** The tiny Theatre History Gallery houses costumes, chandeliers, furniture, and a Miller pump organ from Roanoke's own theaters. (☎342-5770. Open daily 10am-5pm. $2, seniors and children $1.) The **Mill Mountain Zoo,** off Jefferson Rd., houses two magnificent bald eagles rescued from injury, a clouded leopard, a Himalayan crested porcupine, and Bernice, a python with amelanism (a condition similar to albinism). Make sure to visit the Sichuan Takin, the beast whose pelt may have been the golden fleece sought by Jason and the Argonauts. (☎343-3241. Open M-Th 10am-4:30pm, F-Su 10am-7:30pm. $6.30, seniors and AAA $5.70, under 12 $4.20, under 2 free. ZooChoo tickets $1.58 per person, under 2 free.)

Budget lodging in Roanoke is scarce. **Econolodge,** 308 Orange Ave., offers standard rooms at the cheapest rates in town. (☎343-2413. A/C, cable, continental breakfast. $35-59, seniors and AAA 10% off.) Don't be fooled by the lush lobby of the **Ramada Inn,** 1927 Franklin Rd.; the rooms provide only the bare essentials. (☎343-0121. A/C, cable, breakfast, outdoor pool. $46-99, AAA/AARP/military discount.)

Savvy budget diners should stick close to the **Historic Farmers Market District** and the surrounding blocks. ▓**Saltori's Cafe & Spirits,** 202 Market Square SE, offers overstuffed sandwiches ($6-7) and an overwhelming assortment of caffeinated beverages, including black velvet tea (ginseng, mint, and licorice) for $1.15. (☎343-6644. Open M-Th 8:30am-11pm, F-Sa 8:30am-1am, Su 9am-11pm.) For cheap Indian eats, try **Nawab Indian Cuisine,** 118A Campbell Ave. SE. Nawab's lunch buffet ($7) is the most food for your money. Vegans and vegetarians may choose from 15 entrees ($9-11); the daily luncheon special runs $6. (☎345-5150. Open daily for lunch 11:30am-2:30pm; for dinner Su-Th 5-10pm, F-Sa 5-11pm.) Although downtown Roanoke has countless culinary and cultural options, the city is sorely lacking for entertainment when the sun goes down. The younger crowd frequents **Awful Arthur's,** 108 Campbell Ave. SE, a no-frills, everybody-knows-your-name bar. Try the Awful Margarita ($6) and oyster shooters (beer and vodka with tabasco seasoning; $2-3). Standard domestic bottles and drafts are $1.75-2. (☎344-2997. Happy hour daily 11am-7pm. Live rock and blues Th. Open daily 11am-2am.)

Greyhound, 26 Salem Ave. SW (☎343-7885 or 800-231-2222; open daily 9am-5pm), runs to Washington, D.C. (5hr., 7 per day, $36) and Richmond (4hr., 4 per day, $28). **Valley Metro,** 1108 Campbell Ave. SE, handles local transportation. (☎982-2222. Maps available at the Visitors Center. M-Sa 5:45am-8:45pm. Fare $1.25, seniors and disabled 60¢, children under 6 free; free transfers.) **Taxi: Liberty Cab,** ☎344-1776. **Post Office:** 419 Rutherford Ave. NE (☎985-8765; open M-F 7:30am-5:30pm, Sa 9am-noon). **ZIP code:** 24022. **Area code:** 540.

WEST VIRGINIA

With 80% of the state cloaked in untamed forests, hope of commercial expansion and economic prosperity once seemed a distant dream for West Virginia. When the coal mines—formerly West Virginia's primary source of revenue—became exhausted, the state appeared doomed, until government officials decided to capitalize on the area's evergreen expanses, tranquil trails, and raging rivers. Today, thousands of tourists forge paths into West Virginia's breathtaking landscape.

◪ PRACTICAL INFORMATION

Capital: Charleston.

Visitor info: Dept. of Tourism, 2101 Washington St. E., Bldg. #17, Charleston 25305; P.O. Box 30312 (☎800-225-5982; www.callwva.com). **US Forest Service,** 200 Sycamore St., Elkins 26241 (☎304-636-1800). Open M-F 8am-4:45pm.

Postal Abbreviation: WV. **Sales Tax:** 6%.

HARPERS FERRY ☎304

A bucolic hillside town overlooking the Shenandoah and Potomac rivers, Harpers Ferry earned its fame when a band of abolitionists led by John Brown raided the US

Armory in 1859. Although Brown was captured and executed, the raid brought the divisions over slavery into the national spotlight. Brown's adamant belief in violence as the only means to overcome the problem of slavery soon gained credence. Soon, the town was in a major theater of conflict, changing hands eight times during the Civil War. Today, Harpers Ferry attracts more mild-mannered guests: outdoor enthusiasts who come to enjoy the town's surrounding wilderness.

ORIENTATION AND PRACTICAL INFORMATION. Located on West Virginia's border with Maryland, Harpers Ferry is close enough to Washington, D.C., for a convenient daytrip. **Amtrak,** on Potomac St., has one train per day to Washington, D.C. ($18); reservations are required, as no tickets are sold at the station. The same depot serves the **Maryland Rail Commuter (MARC)** (☎800-325-7245; open M-F 5:30am-8:15pm), a cheaper and more frequent service to D.C. (M-F 2 per day; $7.25). The **Appalachian Trail Conference (ATC),** which runs buses to Charles Town for $2. **Blue Ridge Outfitters** (☎304-535-6331), 2 mi. west of Harpers Ferry towards Charles Town, rents bikes for $20 per day. **Visitor info:** ☎535-6223. **Visitors Center:** just inside the park entrance off Rte. 340 (☎535-6298; open daily 8am-5pm). Admission is $5 per car, $3 per hiker or bicyclist, and lasts for three consecutive days. Shuttles leave the parking lot for town every 10min. **Post Office:** on the corner of Washington and Franklin St. (open M-F 8am-4pm, Sa 9am-noon). **ZIP code:** 25425. **Area code:** 304.

ACCOMMODATIONS. Ragged hikers find a warm welcome and a roof over their heads at the social and spacious **Harpers Ferry Hostel (HI-AYH),** 19123 Sandy Hook Rd., at Keep Tryst Rd. off Rte. 340 in Knoxville, MD. This renovated auction house, replete with a backyard trail to pulsating Potomac overlooks, spreads guests into four rooms with 37 well-cushioned beds. (☎301-834-7654. Closed Nov. 15 to Mar. 15. Check-in 7-9am and 6-11pm. Laundry, limited parking. 3-night maximum stay. Beds $15, nonmembers $17. Camping $6/$9, includes use of hostel kitchen and bathrooms. "Primitive" campsites $3/$4.50. Credit card number required for phone reservation.) For private quarters, the **Hillside Motel,** 19105 Keep Tryst Rd., in Knoxville, MD, has 19 clean, adequate rooms. Location next to a restaurant and a liquor store may be the wildest local alternative on a Saturday night. (☎301-834-8144. Singles $36; doubles $45; lower winter rates.) Camp along the **C&O Canal,** where free camping sites lie 5 mi. apart, or in one of the five Maryland state park campgrounds within 30 mi. of Harpers Ferry. (For more information, call the ranger station at 301-739-4200.) **Greenbrier State Park,** on Rte. 40 E off Rte. 66, has 165 campsites and outdoor recreation revolving around a lake. (☎301-791-4767 or 888-432-2267. Open May-Oct. Sites $20, with hookup $25.)

FOOD. Harpers Ferry has sparse offerings for hungry hikers on a budget; most restaurants in town are pricey dining rooms in hotels and B&Bs. **Rte. 340** welcomes the fast food fanatic with various chain restaurants indicated by highway signs. Across the street from the Hillside Motel lies the **Cindy Dee Restaurant,** 19112 Keep Tryst Rd. at Rte. 340. Enough chicken ($5) is fried here to singlehandedly clog all your arteries, but the homemade apple dumpling ($2.50) is delectable. (☎301-695-8181. Open daily 7am-9pm.) The historic area, especially High St. and Potomac St., caters to lunchtime noshers but vacates for dinner. For nightlife and varied cuisine, the tiny **Shepherdstown,** 11 mi. north of Harpers Ferry, is practically a bustling culinary metropolis in these quiet parts. From the Ferry, take Rte. 340 S for 2 mi. to Rte. 230 N or bike 13 mi. along the C&O towpath. Amid the colonial architecture of E. German St. lies the **Mecklinburg Inn,** 128 E. German St., where rock 'n' roll and $1.75 Rolling Rock provide alliterative entertainment on open mic night every Tuesday from 9pm to midnight. (☎876-2126. Happy hour M-F 4:30-6:30pm. 21+ after 5pm. Open M-Th 3pm-12:30am, F 3pm-1:30am, Sa 1pm-2am, Su 1pm-12:30am.)

SIGHTS. Parking in town is nonexistent, so it's necessary to park at the Visitors Center and board the free bus to town or foot the 20min. walk. The bus stops at **Shenandoah St.,** where a barrage of replicated 19th-century shops and replicated 19-century people will greet you. The **Harpers Ferry Industrial Museum,** on Shenandoah

St., describes the methods used to harness the powers of the Shenandoah and Potomac Rivers and details the town's status as the endpoint of the nation's first successful rail line. The unsung stories of the Ferry captivate visitors at **Black Voices from Harpers Ferry,** on the corner of High and Shenandoah St., where fettered slaves express their opinions of John Brown and his fiery raid. The plight of Harpers Ferry's slaves is also elaborated in the **Civil War Story,** next door on High St. Informative displays detail the importance of Harpers Ferry's strategic location to both the Union and Confederate armies. A ticket is required to enter some of the exhibits, but the park's *Lower Town Trail Guide* facilitates historical exploration. Park rangers provide free 45min. to 1hr. tours of the town (in summer daily 10:30am-4pm). In addition, the park offers occasional battlefield demonstrations, parades, and other re-enactments of Harpers Ferry's history (☎535-6298 for the schedule).

The **John Brown Museum,** on Shenandoah St. just beyond High St., is the town's most captivating historical site. A 30min. video chronicles Brown's raid of the armory with a special focus on the moral and political implications of his actions. A daunting, steep staircase hewn into the hillside off High St. follows the **Appalachian Trail** to **Upper Harpers Ferry,** which has fewer sights but is graced with interesting historical tales. Allow 45min. to ascend past **Harper's House,** the restored home of town founder Robert Harper, and **St. Peter's Church,** where a pastor flew the Union Jack during the Civil War to protect the church.

◪ OUTDOOR ACTIVITIES. After digesting the historical significance of Harpers Ferry, many choose to immerse themselves in the town's flourishing outdoors. Go to the park's Visitors Center for trail maps galore. The **Maryland Heights Trail,** the town's most popular trail located across the railroad bridge in the Lower Town of Harpers Ferry, wanders for 4 mi. through Blue Ridge Mountains, including precipitous cliffs and glimpses of crumbling Civil War-era forts. More wooded, the 4 mi. **Loudon Heights Trail** starts in Lower Town off the Appalachian Trail. Both trails take a little over 3hr. to hike. History dominates the **Bolivar Heights Trail,** which starts at the northern end of Whitman Ave. Along the trail, exhibits and a three-gun battery now frame the Civil War battle line where Stonewall Jackson and his Confederate troops prevailed in battle. His horse didn't fail him; neither should your feet on the easy 1.1 mi. loop. The **Chesapeake & Ohio Canal** towpath, off the end of Shenandoah St. and over the railroad bridge, serves as a lasting reminder of the town's industrial roots and the point of departure for a day's bike ride to Washington, D.C. The **Appalachian Trail Conference,** 799 Washington St. at Washington and Jackson St., offers catalogs that feature deals on hiking books, trail info, and a maildrop for hikers. (☎535-6331. Open late May-Oct. M-F 9am-5pm, Sa-Su 9am-4pm; Nov. to mid-May M-F 9am-5pm. Membership $30, seniors and students $25.)

River & Trail Outfitters, 604 Valley Rd., 2 mi. out of Harpers Ferry off Rte. 340, in Knoxville, MD, rents canoes, kayaks, inner tubes, and rafts and organizes everything from scenic daytrips to wild overnights. For a more placid ride, Shenandoah River calm water floats run $15. (☎301-695-5177. Canoes $55 per day; raft trips $55-60 per person, children $40; tubing $32 per day.) At **Butt's Tubes, Inc.,** on Rte. 671 off Rte. 340, you can buy a tube for the day and sell it back before you go. (☎800-836-9911. Open M-F 10:30am-3pm, last pickup at 5pm; Sa-Su 10am-4pm, last pickup at 6pm. $5-20.) Horse activities in the area include a variety of recreational trips offered through **Elk Mountain Trails** (☎301-834-8882).

NEW RIVER GORGE ☎304

The New River Gorge is an electrifying testament to the raw beauty and power of nature. One of the oldest rivers in the world, the New River carves a narrow gouge through the Appalachian Mountains, creating precipitous valley walls that tower an average of 1000 ft. above the white waters. These steep slopes remained virtually untouched until 1873 when industrialists drained the region to uncover coal and timber. With the coal mines now defunct, the Gorge has come full circle, reverting to a natural marvel burgeoning with wildlife.

MID-ATLANTIC

◪ PRACTICAL INFORMATION. Greyhound stops at 105 Third Ave. in Beckley. (☎253-8333. Open M-F 7am-noon and 1-8:30pm, Sa 7am-noon and 3-8:30pm, Su 7-9am and 4-8:30pm.) **Amtrak** runs through the heart of the gorge, stopping on Rte. 41 N in Prince and Hinton. (☎253-6651. Trains Su, W, and F. Open Su, W, and F 10:30am-7pm; Th and Sa 7am-2:30pm.) Rentals are available at **Ridge Rider Mountain Bikes,** 103 Keller Ave., off U.S. 19 in Fayetteville. (☎574-2453 or 800-890-2453. Open daily 9am-6pm. Half-day $25, full-day $35.) **Area code:** 304.

⌐ ACCOMMODATIONS. Budget motels can be found off I-77 in Beckley ($45-60), while smaller lodges and guest houses are scattered through Fayetteville. Call 800-225-5982 for accommodations info. The aptly named **Whitewater Inn,** on the corner of Appalachian Dr. off U.S. 19, features small but clean rooms at affordable rates. (☎574-2998. Rooms $30-45.) **Canyon Ranch** (☎574-3111 or 574-4111), off Gatewood Rd. next to Cunard Access, offers four rooms with A/C and shared bath. Many raft companies operate private campgrounds, while four public campgrounds dot the area. The most central public campground, **Babcock State Park,** on Rte. 41 south of U.S. 60, 15 mi. west of Rainelle, is the largest public campground in the gorge and has 26 shaded sites. (☎438-3004 or 800-225-5982. $13, with electricity $17.) On Ames Heights Rd., ½ mi. north of the New River Gorge Bridge, the **Mountain State Campground** offers tent sites with platforms (by request) and six-person primitive cabins. (☎574-0947. 2 night min. stay. Open Apr.-Oct. Sites $6-7; cabins $60.)

◙ SIGHTS. Where Rte. 19 crosses the river at the park's northern end, the man-made grandeur of the **New River Gorge Bridge,** the second highest bridge in the US, overlooks the Canyon Rim cut of the gorge. The Visitors Center at this site offers a decent vista, but if you're feeling adventurous, descending the stairs to the lower level lookout yields a spectacular view, not to mention a day's worth of exercise. Towering 876 ft. above New River, the bridge claims the world's largest single steel arch span. On **Bridge Day** (☎800-927-0263), the 3rd Saturday in October, thousands of extreme sports enthusiasts leap off the bridge by bungee or parachute. (☎707-793-2273 or www.newrivercvb.com to register. $60 fee. Limited to 300 jumpers.) For more stable flying, charter planes offer **scenic plane rides** ($10) at the Fayetteville airstrip, 2 mi. south of town. Retired coal miners lead tours down a mine shaft at the **Beckley Exhibition Coal Mine,** on Ewart Ave. in Beckley, 20 mi. south of Fayetteville at New River Park. Explore the mining industry as you ride behind a 30s engine through 150 ft. of underground passages. Bring a jacket for the 58°F tunnels. (☎256-1747. Open Apr.-Oct. daily 10am-5:30pm. $9, seniors $8, ages 4-12 $6, under 4 free.) **Horseback riding** trips are another way to explore the gorge; try **New River Trail Rides, Inc.,** which features 2½hr. rides, sunset trips, and overnight adventures year-round. (☎888-742-3982. Rides start at $39.)

◪ OUTDOOR ACTIVITIES. The **New River Gorge National River,** which runs north from Hinton to Fayetteville, falling over 750 ft. in 50 mi., is now protected, and the park service oversees the fishing, rock climbing, canoeing, mountain biking, and world-class rafting in the gorge. Whitewater rapids range from the family-friendly class I to the panic-inducing class V. A state info service (☎800-225-5982) connects you to some of the nearly 20 outfitters on the New River and the rowdier Gauley River, or pick up a brochure at the **Fayetteville County Chamber of Commerce,** 310 Oyler Ave. (☎465-5617), in Oak Hill. **USA Raft,** at the intersection of Rte. 16 and Rte. 19 in Fayetteville, runs some cheap express trips. (☎800-346-7238. New River: Su-F $48, Sa $58. Gauley River: upper portion $55/$65, lower portion $66/$76.)

Though the renowned rapids draw the most tourists, the park's numerous trails provide hikers with a sense of fulfillment and an appreciation for the river and the industry that once flourished here. The most rewarding trails are the 2 mi. **Kaymoor Trail** and the 3.4 mi. **Thurmond Minden Trail.** Kaymoor starts at the bridge on Fayette Station Rd. and runs past the abandoned coke ovens of Kaymoor, a coal mining community that shut down in 1962. Thurmond Minden, left off Rte. 25 before Thurmond, has vistas of the New River and Thurmond. For a vertical challenge, climb the **Endless Wall** which runs southeast along the New River and is accessible from a trail off the parking lot at Canyon Rim Visitors Center. The park operates four **Visitors Centers: Canyon Rim** (☎574-2115), off Rte. 19 near Fayetteville at the northern extreme of the park; **Grandview** (☎763-3145), on Rte. 9 near Beckley; **Hinton** (☎466-1597), on Rte. 20; and **Thurmond** (☎465-8550), on Rte. 25 off I-19. Grandview attracts visitors in May when the rhododendrons are in bloom; otherwise, most stop at Canyon Rim, which has info on all park activities. (Canyon Rim and Grandview open June-Aug. daily 9am-8pm; Sept.-May 9am-5pm. Hinton open June-Aug. daily 9am-5pm; Sept.-May Sa-Su 9am-5pm. Thurmond open daily 9am-5pm.)

MONONGAHELA NATIONAL FOREST   ☎304

Mammoth Monongahela National Forest sprawls across the Eastern portion of the state, sustaining wildlife, limestone caverns, weekend canoers, fly fisherman, spelunkers, and skiers. Over 500 campsites and 600 miles of winding wilderness hiking trails lure adventurers to this outdoor haven. Surrounded by luscious green thicket, Monongahela's roads are indisputably scenic, though the beauty of **Rte. 39** from Marlinton down to Goshen, VA, past Virginia's swimmable Maury River, is unsurpassed. The **Highland Scenic Hwy.** (Rte. 150) runs near the Nature Center and stretches 43 mi. from Richwood to U.S. 219, 7 mi. north of Marlinton. Tempted as you may be to feast your eye on the forest's natural splendor, driving through the often fog-filled sinuous roads can be treacherous, so keep your eyes on the road.

Aside from displaying an informative wildlife exhibit that includes hissing rattlesnakes, the Nature Center conducts free weekend tours of the **Cranberry Glades** (tours June-Aug. Sa-Su 2pm). Wrapping 6 mi. around the glades is the **Cow Pasture Trail,** which features glimpses of a WWII German prison camp and beaver dams. Two popular short hikes in the area are the panoramic **High Rocks Trail,** leading off of the Highland Scenic Hwy., and the awesome 2 mi. **Falls of Hills Creek,** off Rte. 39/55 south of Cranberry Mountain Nature Center. *Remove valuables from vehicles, as thieves are common in this area.*

Those with several days might choose to hike, bike, or cross-country ski a part of the **Greenbrier River Trail,** a 75 mi., 1% grade track from Cass to North Caldwell (trailhead on Rte. 38 off U.S. 60). Lined with numerous access points and campgrounds, the trail offers multiple vistas and arguably the highest concentration of butterflies in West Virginia. **Watoga State Park** (☎799-4087), in Marlinton, has maps. For downhill delights, head over to **Canaan Valley** and the 54 trails at **Snowshoe** resort, just outside the National Forest. (☎572-1000. Open Nov.-Apr. daily 8:30am-10pm. Lift tickets $38, seniors and students $30; Sa-Su $44. Ski rental $26, children $18.) In summer, mountain biking is preferred. For area **fishing,** anglers can cast their lines for the abundant trout that flow through the Williams and Cranberry Rivers. For all types of gear, try **Elk River** (☎572-3771 or 572-4173), off Rte. 219 in Slatyfork. Trails to the National Forest begin right out the door; the outfitter also gives year-round fly-fishing tours and runs a rustic B&B ($45-85 per night).

Each of Monongahela's six districts has a campground and a recreation area, with ranger stations off Rte. 39 east of Marlinton and in the towns of Bartow and Potomack (open M-F 8am-4:30pm). The forest **Supervisor's Office,** 200 Sycamore St., in Elkins, distributes a full list of sites and fees and provides info about fishing and hunting. (☎636-1800. Open M-F 8am-4:45pm.) Established sites are $5; sleeping in the backcountry is free. Indicate backcountry plans at the **Cranberry Mountain Nature Center,** near the Highland Scenic Hwy. at the junction of Rte. 150 and Rte. 39/55. (☎653-4826. Open Apr.-Nov. daily 9am-5pm.) **Cranberry Campground,** in the Gauley district, 13 mi. from Ridgewood on Forest Rd. 76, has hiking trails through cranberry bogs and $6 campsites. Most public transportation in the forest area comes into White Sulphur Springs at the forest's southern tip. **Greyhound** will drop passengers off along Rte. 60, but does not run outbound from the forest. (☎800-231-2222 for times and fares.) **Amtrak** stops Su, W, and F at 315 W. Main St., across from the Greenbrier resort. A flag stop in downtown Alderson can also be requested Su, W, or F. Trains run to Washington, D.C. (from White Sulphur Springs $61, from Alderson $72) and Charlottesville ($34/$38). **Area code:** 304.

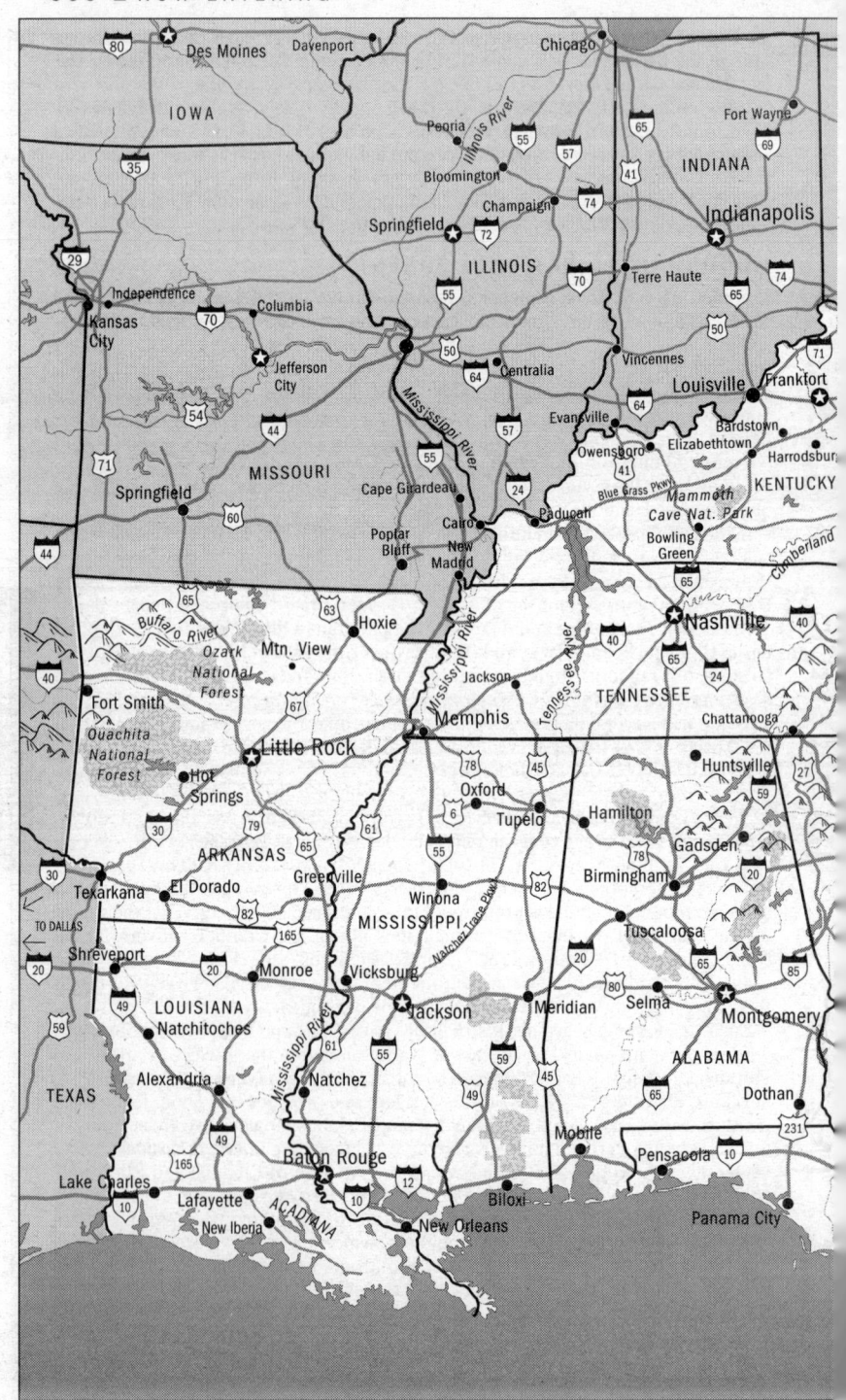

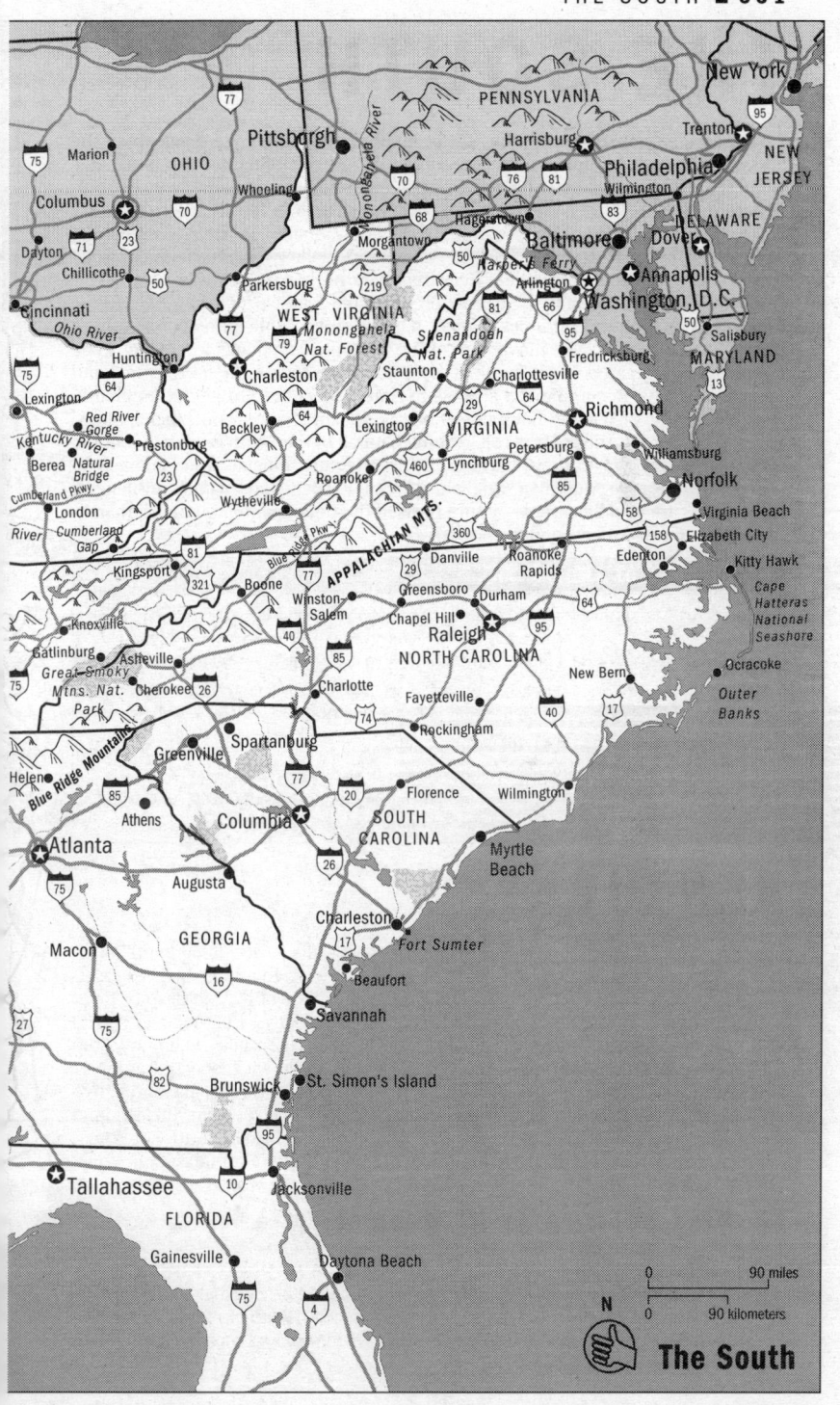

The South

THE SOUTH

The American consciousness has become much more homogeneous since the 1860s, when regional differences ignited the bloodiest conflict in the nation's history. Yet differences persist between North and South, as much in memory as in practice: what's known as "the Civil War" up North is here rather defiantly referred to as "The War Between the States." And outside the area's commercial capitals—Atlanta, Nashville, Charlotte, and New Orleans—Southerners continue to live slower-paced and friendlier lives than their northern cousins.

Perhaps the greatest unifying characteristic of the South is its legacy of extreme racial division: slavery continues to place a nearly unbearable burden on Southern history, and the civil rights movement of the 50s and 60s remains too recent to be comfortably relegated to textbook study. At the same time, racial tensions and interactions have inspired many strands of American culture rooted in the South, from the novels of William Faulkner to nearly *all* American music: gospel, blues, jazz, country, R&B, and rock 'n' roll. Although much of the South remains poor, the area maintains a rich cultural heritage; its architecture, cuisine, and language all borrow from Native American, English, African, French, and Spanish influences. Landscapes are equally varied—nature blessed the region with mountains, marshlands, sparkling beaches, and fertile soil.

HIGHLIGHTS OF THE SOUTH

FOOD. Some of the best Southern barbecue is at Dreamland in Mobile, AL (p. 402). New Orleans, LA (p. 409) has spicy and delicious Cajun cuisine. Southern "soul food" completes the spirit—Nita's Place, Savannah, GA (p. 394) will take you higher.

MUSIC. Make time for Tennessee—Nashville (p. 342) is the country music hot spot, but if you're a believer, you'll be heading to Graceland (p. 353).

CIVIL RIGHTS MEMORIALS. The Martin Luther King Center in Atlanta, GA (p. 380) and the Birmingham Civil Rights Institute, AL (p. 400) will move you to tears.

OLD SOUTH. Charm and Elegance. Nowhere is the antebellum way of life so well-kept as in stately Charleston, SC (p. 371) or Savannah, GA (p. 394).

KENTUCKY

Legendary for the duels, feuds, and stubborn spirit of its earlier inhabitants (such as the infamous Daniel Boone), but gentler than its past, Kentucky invites travelers to kick back, take a shot of local bourbon, grab a plate of burgoo (a spicy meat stew), and relax amid rolling hills and bluegrass. These days, Kentuckians' spirits erupt on the highways—they drive fast. Appropriately, Kentucky is home to the only American sports car, the Corvette. Of course, the most respected mode of transport is still the horse. Louisville ignores its vibrant cultural scene and active nightlife at Derby time, and Lexington devotes much of its most beautiful farmland to breeding champion racehorses. Farther east, the Daniel Boone National Forest preserves the virgin woods of the Kentucky Highlands, where trailblazers first discovered a route across the mountains to what was then the West.

🔼 PRACTICAL INFORMATION

Capital: Frankfort.
Visitor info: Kentucky Dept. of Travel 500 Mero St., 22nd fl., Frankfort 40601 (☎502-564-4930 or 800-225-8747; www.kentuckytourism.com). **Kentucky State Parks,** 500 Mero St., 10th fl., Frankfort 40601 (☎800-255-7275; www.kystateparks.com).
Postal Abbreviation: KY. **Sales Tax:** 6%.

LOUISVILLE ☎502

Louisville (pronounced "Lua-Vul" by locals) is caught between two pasts. One past left a legacy of smokestacks, stockyards, and the occasional crumbling structure; the other shines with beautiful Victorian neighborhoods, ornate buildings, and the elegant, twin-spired Churchill Downs. Louisville's premier attraction, however, remains the Kentucky Derby; this extravagant event, the nation's most prestigious horse race, will pack the city with visitors May 4, 2002.

■🚶 **ORIENTATION AND PRACTICAL INFORMATION.** Interstates through the city include **I-65** (north-south expressway), **I-71**, and **I-64.** The easily accessible **Watterson Expwy.**, also called **I-264**, rings the city, while the **Gene Snyder Frwy. (I-265)** circles farther out. In central downtown, **Main St.** and **Broadway** run east-west, and **Preston Hwy.** and **19th St.** run north-south. The **West End,** beyond 20th St., is a rough area. The **Louisville International Airport** (☎368-6524) is 15min. south of downtown on I-65. A taxi downtown is $13-15, or take bus #2 into the city. **Greyhound,** 720 W. Muhammad Ali Blvd. (☎561-2805), at 7th St., runs to Indianapolis (1¼hr., 9 per day, $17.50); Cincinnati (2hr., 10 per day, $19.50); and Chicago (5hr., 7 per day, $38). Station open 24hr. **Transit Authority River City's (TARC)** extensive bus system serves most of the metro area. (☎585-1234. Runs daily 5am-11:30pm. Fare 75¢, $1 M-F 6:30-8:30am and 3:30-5:30pm.) Two free trolley routes service Main St. and 4th St. downtown from 8am-5pm. **Taxis: Yellow Cab,** ☎636-5511. **Highland Cycle,** 1737 Bardstown Rd., rents bikes. (☎458-7832. Open M-F 9am-5:30pm, Sa 9am-4:30pm. Bikes from $3.25 per hr., $12 per day.) **Visitor info: Louisville Convention and Visitors Bureau,** 3rd and Market St. (☎584-2121; open M-Sa 8:30am-5pm, Su noon-4pm). **Hotlines: Rape Hotline** (☎581-7273) and **Crisis Center** (☎589-4313), both open 24hr.; **Gay/Lesbian Hotline** (☎454-7613; daily 6-10pm). **Post Office:** 1420 Gardner Ln. (☎454-1766; open M-F 7:30am-7pm, Sa 7:30am-3pm). **ZIP code:** 40213. **Area code:** 502.

🛏 **HITCHIN' POSTS.** Lodging in downtown Louisville is easy to find but pricey. Budget motels are on **I-65** near the airport or across the river in **Jeffersonville. Newburg Rd.,** 6 mi. south, is also a budget haven. To get Derby Week lodging, make reservations six to 12 months in advance and prepare to spend big; after Mar. 13, the Visitors Bureau will help you to secure a room for the event.

Motel 6, Exit 117 off I-65, is about a 30min. drive from downtown, but has clean, comfortable rooms and is easy to find. Only a short drive from the airport, it's not far from Bardstown and its surrounding attractions. (☎543-4400. Singles $37; doubles $42.) **Super 8,** 927 S. 2nd St., has basic rooms. An airport shuttle can be secured by appointment. (☎584-8888. Singles $53; doubles $58. Some wheelchair accessible rooms.) The local installation of the **KOA** regime, 900 Marriot Dr., has paved camping convenient to downtown. Follow I-65 N across the bridge and take Exit 1. (☎282-4474. Grocery, playground, free pool access, mini golf, and fishing lake. Sites for 2 $23, with hookup $28; $4 each additional person, under 18 $2.50. Kabins for 2 $35. Rates drop mid-Nov. to mid-Mar.)

🍽 **OATS AND HAY.** Louisville's food is varied, but good budget fare can be hard to find in the heart of downtown. **Bardstown Rd.** is lined with cafes, budget eateries, and local and global cuisine, while **Frankfort Rd.** is rapidly becoming Bardstownized with restaurants and chi-chi cafes of its own. Downtown, **Theater Sq.,** at Broadway and 4th St., provides plenty of good lunch options. ■**Twice Told,** 1604 Bardstown Rd., was the first coffeehouse in Louisville, and it's still hot after all these years. Poetry readings, comedy, punk, jazz, and blues entertain at the stage in the back, but get in earlier for a $5.75 portabella melt. (☎456-0507. Some shows free; cover can go as high as $10. Open M-Th noon-midnight, F noon-1am, Sa 9am-1am. Open stage every Tu. Shows M-Sa at 9pm.) The giant teapot in front of **Lynn's Paradise Cafe,** 984 Barret Ave., marks a Louisville landmark that combines delicious food with an atmosphere that celebrates childhood: from the plastic toy figures on the tables to the artwork of local elementary students that flavors the walls. Dinner prices rack up quickly; breakfast and lunch are more manageable for those on a budget. (☎583-3447. Open Tu-Su 7am-10pm.) **Mark's Feed Store,** 1514 Bardstown Rd., serves award-winning barbecue in a dining room decorated with large metal signs advertising animal feed. (☎459-6275. Open Su-Th 11am-10pm, F-Sa 11am-11pm. Sandwiches $4-5, BBQ dinners under $8. Free dessert M after 4pm.)

◙ **NOT JUST A ONE-HORSE TOWN.** The **Highlands** strip runs along Baxter/Bardstown and is bounded by Broadway and Trevilian Way on the south. This "anti-mall" of unfranchised cafes, pizza pubs, antique shops, and record stores is worth a gander (buses #17 and 23). Nearby, the **American Printing House for the Blind,** 1839 Frankfort Ave., runs a small but fascinating museum on the development of Braille and other lesser-known systems for aiding the blind. (☎895-2405. Open M-F 9am-4:30pm; guided tours 10am and 2pm. Free.) Farther south, near the University of Louisville, the impressive galleries of the **J.B. Speed Art Museum,** 2035 S. 3rd St., house a large collection ranging from Dutch tapestries to contemporary art, as well as a stylish sculpture court. Take bus #2 or 4. (☎634-2700. Open Tu-W and F 10:30am-4pm, Th 10:30am-8pm, Sa 10:30am-5pm, Su noon-5pm. Free; parking $1.50 per hr.)

The **Belle of Louisville,** an authentic paddle-wheel craft built in 1914, docks at 4th St. and River Rd. (☎574-2355. 2hr. cruises depart from Riverfront Plaza early June to early Sept., call for schedule and prices.) Nearby, the world's tallest baseball bat (120 ft.) leans against the **Hillerich and Bradsby Co. (Louisville Slugger Factory and Museum),** 800 W. Main. Inside awaits a nostalgic film and a tour showing how Sluggers are made. H&B will even give you a free miniature bat at the tour's end. (☎588-7228. Open M-Sa 9am-5pm; Apr.-Nov. also open Su noon-5pm. $6, seniors $5, children $3.50.)

Onward, chicken soldiers, to the **Harland Sanders Museum** and **Kentucky Fried Chicken International Headquarters,** 1441 Gardiner Ln., off the Watterson Expwy. at Newburg Rd. A room of artifacts and a short film honor the white-suited Colonel who brought us fried chicken with his secret recipe of 11 herbs and spices. (☎874-1000. Open M-F 8am-5pm. Free, as it should be.)

▨ **WIN, PLACE, OR SHOW.** Each year, on the first Saturday in May, Louisville stages the nation's most prestigious horse race, the **Kentucky Derby,** also referred to as the **Run for the Roses.** The rollicking, week-long extravaganza leading up to the big day corrals over 500,000 visitors, but when the horses leave the gate, the stands are still for "the most exciting two minutes in sports"; after all, $15 million ride on each Derby Day. Even if you miss the Derby, be sure to visit **Churchill Downs,** 700 Central Ave., 3 mi. south of downtown. Take bus #4 to Central Ave. You don't have to bet to admire the twin spires, the colonial columns, the gardens, and the sheer scale of the track. (☎636-4400. Races occur late Apr.-Nov.; schedules and prices vary. Tours available through the Kentucky Derby Museum. $2, seniors $1, under 13 free.)

The **Kentucky Derby Festival** kicks off with 64 tons of fireworks at **Thunder Over Louisville,** the largest fireworks show in North America, and continues for two weeks with balloon and steamboat races, concerts, and a parade. All of this is mere prelude to the climactic 80,000 mint juleps consumed at the **Run for the Roses,** the first Saturday in May. A one- to ten-year waiting list stands between you and a ticket for the Derby, but never fear—on Derby morning, tickets are sold for standing-room-only spots in the infield ($35). Get in line early for good seats, lest the other 125,000 spectators get there first. Amazingly, no one is turned away. The **Kentucky Derby Museum,** at Gate One at Churchill Downs, offers a short film on a 360° screen, footage of every Derby ever recorded (including Secretariat's record 1973 run), a simulated horse race for betting practice, tips on exactly what makes a horse a "sure thing," and tours of the Downs every day. (☎637-1111. Open M-Sa 9am-5pm, Su noon-5pm. Last tour at 4:15pm. $7, seniors $6, ages 5-12 $3, under 5 free.)

▣▨ **HORSIN' AROUND.** The free weekly arts and entertainment newspaper, *Leo,* is available at most downtown restaurants or the Visitors Center. All's well that ends well at the **Kentucky Shakespeare Festival** at the zoo and in Central Park, during June and July. (☎583-8738. Performances 8pm. Free.) **The Louisville Palace,**

BILLIONS IN BULLION Security is so tight at Fort Knox, the holding station for American gold bullion reserves, 30 mi. south of Louisville, that all visitors can do is drive by. The best bet for those planning a heist is to examine the model used in the movie *Goldfinger*, which can be found at the nearby **Patton Museum**. The museum, north of Fort Knox off U.S. 31 W, holds exhibits on the history of armored warfare and more tanks than you can shake a stick at. (☎ 624-3812. *Open May-Sept. M-F 9am-4:30pm, Sa-Su 10am-6pm; Oct.-June Sa-Su 10am-4:30pm. Free.*)

625 S. 4th Ave. (☎ 583-4555), is one of only 15 remaining "atmospheric theaters." Go to see both the lavish Spanish Baroque interior and the Broadway shows, comedy acts, and big-name music acts that play there.

Clubs cluster on Baxter Ave. near Broadway. **Phoenix Hill Tavern,** 644 Baxter Ave., features blues, rock, and reggae on four stages, including a deck and roof garden. (☎ 589-4957. Cover $2-5. Open W-Th and Sa 8pm-3:30am, F 5pm-3:30am.) For gay nightlife, make **The Connection,** 120 Floyd St. This black-and-white-and-mirrored-all-over club features four venues under one roof. The different bars have different theme nights and varying hours, but Monday through Saturday at least two are open after 10pm. (☎ 585-5752. Cover $2-5. Open M-W 5pm-2am and Th 5pm-4am; Dance Bar open Th-Sa 10pm-4am. Showroom open F-Sa 10:30pm-3:30am.)

NEAR LOUISVILLE

BARDSTOWN. Kentucky's second-oldest city, 17 mi. east on Rte. 245 from I-65 Exit 112, is proudly known as the "Bourbon Capital of the World." In 1791, Kentucky Baptist Reverend Elijah Craig left a fire unattended while heating oak boards to make a barrel for his aging whiskey. The boards were charred, but Rev. Craig carried on, and bourbon was born in that first charred wood barrel. Today, 90% of the nation's bourbon hails from Kentucky, and 60% of that is distilled in Nelson and Bullitt Counties. **Jim Beam's American Outpost,** 15 mi. west of Bardstown in Clermont off Rte. 245, features the "master distiller emeritus" himself, Jim Beam's grandson, Booker Noe, who narrates a film about bourbon. Jim Beam's has free sampling (M-Sa), as well as free lemonade, coffee, and bourbon candies. (☎ 543-9877. Open M-Sa 9am-4:30pm, Su 1-4pm. Free.) Tours are offered at **Maker's Mark Distillery,** 19 mi. southeast of Bardstown, follow signs from downtown, on Rte. 52 E in Loretto; come any day but Sunday to buy a bottle of bourbon in the gift shop, and you can hand-dip it yourself in the label's famous trademark red wax. (☎ 865-2099. Tours M-Sa every hr. 10:30am-3:30pm, Su every hr. 1:30-3:30pm. Free.) The **Oscar Getz Museum of Whiskey History,** in Spalding Hall at 114 N. 5th St., offers a fascinating look at Kentucky's favorite beverage, and also on the state's other contribution to alcohol history—rabid Prohibitionist Carry Nation. (☎ 348-2999. Open May-Oct. M-Sa 9am-5pm, Su 1-5pm; Nov.-Apr. Tu-Sa 10am-4pm, Su 1-4pm.) **Bardstown Visitors Center:** 107 E. Stephen Foster Ave. (☎ 348-4877 or 800-638-4877. Open M-F 8am-6pm, Sa 9am-6pm, Su 11am-3pm; Oct.-Mar. M-Sa 8am-5pm.)

MAMMOTH CAVE. Hundreds of enormous caves and narrow passageways cut through ▧**Mammoth Cave National Park,** 80 mi. south of Louisville off I-65, then west on Rte. 70. Mammoth Cave comprises the world's longest network of cavern corridors—over 365 mi. in length. The first tours ran here in 1816. The original tour guides were slaves who worked the cave's saltpeter mining operation, shut down by the New Madrid earthquake in 1811. Nowadays tours are guided by park rangers. Devout spelunkers try the 6hr. "Wild Cave Tour" during the summer (16+; $35); less ambitious types generally take the 2hr., 2 mi. historical walking tour ($8, seniors $4, ages 6-12 $5). Those in a rush can always opt for the unguided "Discovery Tour" ($3.50, seniors and ages 6-12 $2). Other tours accommodate disabled visitors (1½hr., $7). The caves are a chilly 54°F; the park also features numerous above-ground walking trails. (Visitors Center: ☎ 758-2328 or 800-967-2283. Open daily 7:30am-7pm; off-season 8am-6pm. Reservations recommended.) Camping with toilets is available at the Headquarters campground, near the Visitors Center. (☎800-967-2283. Sites $14, showers in summer $2; reservations recommended.) For RV sites, check out **Maple Springs Campground**, across the river from the Visitors Center by ferry, or by a 35 mi. detour. (☎800-967-2283. $25; reservations required.) **Backcountry camping** permits can be obtained at the Visitors Center. **Greyhound** travels to **Cave City**, just east of I-65 on Rte. 70. **Time zone:** Central (1hr. behind Eastern).

BOWLING GREEN. Home of the classic American sports car, the Corvette, auto enthusiasts inevitably pay their respects here. The extensive **National Corvette Museum**, 350 Corvette Dr. off I-65 Exit 28, displays 'Vettes from the original chrome-and-steel '53 to futuristic concept cars; the display rotates constantly. (☎800-538-3883. Open daily 8am-5pm. $8, ages 6-16 $4.50, seniors $5.) To see some action, visit the **General Motors Corvette Assembly Plant**, Exit 28 off I-65. With luck comes a chance to test-start one of the mint condition products. (☎270-745-8419. Tours M-F 9am and 1pm. Free.) **Time zone:** Central (1hr. behind Eastern).

LEXINGTON ☎859

In the early 1800s, Lexington was known as "the Athens of the West"; wealth from tobacco and hemp farms helped fund one of the most active cultural scenes west of the Appalachians and left a legacy of historic mansions near downtown. These days Lexington's most high-profile money comes from horse farming. Farms that have raised some of the most famous racehorses in the world ring the city in the scenic "bluegrass country" for which eastern Kentucky is famous. Within the Lexington city limits, the University of Kentucky (UK) keeps the banner of high culture flying.

▛ TRANSPORTATION

Airport: Blue Grass, 4000 Versailles Rd. (☎255-7218), southwest of downtown. Ritzy downtown hotels run shuttles, but there is no public transportation. Taxi to downtown about $20.

Buses: Greyhound, 477 New Circle Rd. NW (☎299-0428; open M-F 7:30am-11pm, Sa-Su 7:30-6pm). To: Louisville (2hr., 4 per day, $16-17); Cincinnati (1½hr., 7 per day, $18-19); and Knoxville (4hr., 4 per day, $41-44).

Public Transit: LexTran, 109 W. Louden Ave. (☎253-4636). Buses leave from the Transit Center, 220 E. Vine St., on a long block between Limestone and Rose St., generally 15min. before and after the hour. Serves the university and city outskirts. Most routes run 6am-midnight. Fare $1, ages 6-18 80¢, seniors and disabled 50¢. Transfers free. On racing days, LexTran runs a $1 shuttle to Keeneland.

Taxis: Lexington Yellow Cab, ☎231-8294.

✴❼ ORIENTATION AND PRACTICAL INFORMATION

New Circle Rd. (Rte. 4/U.S. 60 bypass) loops the city, intersecting with many roads that connect the downtown district to the surrounding towns. **High, Vine,** and **Main Sts.** running east-west and **Limestone St.** and **Broadway** running north-south provide the best routes through downtown. Beware of the many curving one-way streets downtown and near UK.

Visitor info: Lexington Convention and Visitors Bureau, 301 E. Vine St., at Rose St. (☎233-7299 or 800-845-3959; www.visitlex.com). Open in summer M-F 8:30am-5pm, Sa 10am-5pm, Su noon-5pm; off-season closed Su.

Hotlines: Crisis Intervention, ☎253-2737 or 800-928-8000. **Rape Crisis,** ☎253-2511 or 800-656-4673. Both 24hr.

Hospitals: St. Joseph East Hospital, 150 N. Eagle Creek Dr. (☎268-4800). **Lexington Women's Diagnostic Center,** 1701 Bobolink Dr. (☎277-8485).

Internet access: Lexington Public Library, 140 E. Main St. (☎231-5500), at Limestone St. Open M-Th 9am-9pm, Su 1-5pm.

Post Office: 210 E. High St. (☎254-6156). Open M-F 8am-5pm, Sa 9am-noon. **ZIP code:** 40507. **Area code:** 859.

ACCOMMODATIONS

A concentration of horse-related wealth pushes up accommodation prices. The cheapest places are outside the city on New Circle Rd. or near I-75. The Visitors Center can help you find a room. (☎233-1221 or 800-848-1224. Open M-F 8:30am-5pm, Sa 10am-5pm, Su noon-5pm.)

Catalina Motel, 208 W. New Circle Rd. (☎299-6281). Follow Broadway north of the city, and turn left onto New Circle Rd. Large, clean rooms with A/C, cable TV, pool, and free local calls. Singles $30; doubles $40.

Microtel, 2240 Buena Vista Dr. (☎299-9600), off I-75 at the Winchester Rd. (Rte. 60) Exit. Take bus #7. Pleasant motel rooms with window seats. A/C, cable; wheelchair-accessible rooms available. Singles Su-Th $45, F-Sa $52; doubles $52/$56.

Kentucky Horse Park Campground, 4089 Ironworks Pike (☎259-4257 or 800-370-6416), 10 mi. north of downtown off I-75 at Exit 120. Groomed camping plus laundry, showers, basketball courts, swimming pool, and modem hookup available. Wide open tent sites. RV sites nicely mix shade and lawn. 2-week maximum stay. Apr.-Oct. $13; with hookup $18; seniors $15.50; Nov.-Mar. $11/$14/$12.

FOOD AND NIGHTLIFE

With a menu of fantastic international and veggie/vegan meals that change nightly, ▨**Alfalfa Restaurant,** 557 S. Limestone St. near UK, serves up great, affordable food. Dinners range in price from $7-14, while filling soups and salads price out between $2.50 and $7.25. (☎253-0014. Live jazz, folk, and other music Tu-Sa 8-10pm. No cover. Open M 11am-2pm, Tu-Th 11am-2pm and 5:30-9pm, F-Sa 10am-2pm and 5:30-10pm, Su 10am-2pm.) ▨**Ramsey's** serves at five locations in the Lexington area, but the true experience can only be found at 496 E. High St. at Woodland. Real stick-to-your-ribs Southern food abounds; even the veggies are cooked with pork parts. Entrees go for $8-10, sandwiches $6-8. (☎259-2708. Open Su 10am-11pm, M-Tu 11am-11pm, W-F 11am-1am, Sa 10am-1am. Drinks specials 4-7pm.) At the **Parkette Drive-In,** 1230 E. New Circle Rd. between Liberty and Winchester Rd., bargain food comes to you in a classic 50s setting. Booths inside let carless folks join in the nostalgia. (☎254-8723. Open Su 11am-10pm, M-Th 11am-11pm, F-S a 11am-midnight.)

Lexington's nightlife surpasses expectations for a town its size, but lacks any real center. Generally, the area around Main St. west of Limestone St. and the eastern fringes of UK are most active. For current info, read the "Weekender" section of the Friday *Herald-Leader*, or pick up a free *Ace*. **The Bar,** 224 E. Main St., a popular disco cabaret/lounge complex, caters to gays and lesbians. (☎255-1551. Cover F $4, Sa $5. Lounge open M-Sa 4pm-1am; club open Tu-Th 11pm-1am, F 10pm-1am, Sa 10pm-3:30am.) **Lynagh's Pub and Club,** in University Plaza at Woodland and Euclid St., is a casual, well-populated neighborhood bar near UK. Music plays next door to the pub. (Pub: ☎255-1292. Cover from $3-$15. Open M-Sa 11am-1am, Su noon-11pm. Club: ☎255-6614. Open Tu-Sa 4-9pm for pool and darts; music 9pm-1am.)

SIGHTS

CITY ATTRACTIONS. To escape the stifling swamp conditions farther south, antebellum plantation owners built beautiful summer retreats in milder Lexington. The most attractive of these stately houses preen only a few blocks northeast of the town center, in the **Gratz Park** area near the old Public Library. Wrap-around porches, stone foundations, and rose-covered trellises distinguish these old estates from the neighborhood's newer homes. The **Hunt Morgan House** stands at the end of the park across from the Carnegie Literacy Center, at W. 2nd St. Built in 1814 by John Wesley Hunt, the first millionaire west of the Alleghenies, the house witnessed the birth of Thomas Hunt Morgan, who won a 1933 Nobel Prize for proving the existence of the gene. The house's most colorful inhabitant, however, was

Confederate General John Hunt Morgan, the "Thunderbolt of the Confederacy." As legend has it, Hunt Morgan, while being pursued by Union troops, rode his horse up the front steps and into the house, leaned down to kiss his mother, and rode out the back door. *(201 N. Mill St. ☎ 233-3290 or 253-0362. Tours Tu-Sa 10am-4pm, Su 2-5pm at 15min. past the hr. $5, students $3. In the week before Halloween, Gratz Park "ghost tours" begin here in the evenings—brief tours of the area that focus on the neighborhood's many other-worldly inhabitants.)* Hollywood jewelry designer George W. Headley's exotic creations are displayed at the **Headley-Whitney Museum.** Included on the museum grounds is the fanciful "Shell Grotto," a former carriage house that Headly studded with thousands of seashells. *(4435 Old Frankfort Pike. ☎ 255-6653. Open Tu-F 10am-5pm, Sa-Su noon-5pm Closed Jan. $6, students $4, seniors $5.)*

HORSE ATTRACTIONS. Lexington horse farms are pretty places to visit; the Visitors Bureau can help you arrange tours of open farms. **Three Chimneys Farm** raised the 1977 Triple Crown winner Seattle Slew. *(On Old Frankfort Pike 4 mi. from I-64 and 8½ mi. from New Circle Rd. ☎ 873-7053. Tours by reservation only. $5-10 tip customary.)* **Kentucky Horse Park** has extensive equine facilities, a museum tracing the history, science, and pageantry of these animals, and many live examples. The last weekend in April, the horse park hosts the annual Rolex tournament qualifier for the US equestrian team. *(4089 Ironworks Pkwy. off Ironworks Pike, Exit 120 off I-75. ☎ 233-4303. Open mid-Mar. to Oct. daily 9am-5pm; Nov. to mid-Mar. W-Su 9am-5pm. $12, ages 7-12 $6; Nov.-Mar. $9/ $5.50; live horse shows and horse-drawn vehicle tours included. 45min. horse ride and tour in addition to entrance fee $13; pony rides $4. Parking $2. Wheelchair accessible.)* Every April, the **Keeneland Race Track,** west on U.S. 60 across from the airport, holds the final prep race for the Kentucky Derby. The track kitchen may have the best breakfast deal in town: around $4 for a cafeteria-style full breakfast and the chance to chat with a jockey or horse owner. *(4201 Versailles Rd. ☎ 254-3412 or 800-456-3412. Races Oct. and Apr.; post time 1pm. $2.50. Workouts free and open to the public mid-Mar. to Nov. 6-10am. Breakfast daily 5:30-11am except the first 2 weeks in Feb.)*

⚑ DAYTRIPS FROM LEXINGTON

WHITE HALL

At Exit 95 off I-75, the elegant Georgian-Italianate mansion **White Hall** was home to abolitionist (not boxer) Cassius M. Clay, cousin of Senator Henry Clay. Cassius Clay was known not only for his views on abolition, but also for firing a cannon at tax collectors and for his book on the finer points of knife-fighting—a field in which he had good deal of personal expertise. *(☎ 623-9178. 45min. guided tours only. Open Apr.-Oct. daily 9am-5:30pm, last tour at 4:30pm; early Sept. to Oct. W-Su only. $5, under 13 $2.50, under 6 free.)*

BEREA

Further south, **Berea,** off Exit 76 or 77 from I-75, is a local crafts capital. High-priced and highly touristed crafts stores tend to dominate, but the town retains much of its charm nonetheless. At **Churchill Weavers,** 100 Churchill Dr., off U.S. 25, visitors can take a self-guided tour of the loomhouse and view one of the few remaining examples of the handloom industry. *(☎ 859-986-3127. Loomhouse open M-F 9am-noon, 12:30-4pm.)* **Berea College,** located in the center of town, is known far and wide for its progressive past and present. The college, founded in 1855, educated women and African-Americans before the Civil War; students of the college now are given work to do in lieu of paying tuition. Many students help operate the handsome **Boone Tavern,** 100 Main St. Stop by for lunch to enjoy the classy atmosphere without having to spend a fortune for a meal. Lunch prices start at $6, while dinners range from $13-25 *(☎ 859-985-3700 or 800-366-9358).* Information on these and other attractions is available at the **Tourist and Convention Commission,** 201 N. Broadway. *(☎ 859-986-2540 or 800-598-5263. Open M-Sa 9am-5pm, Su 1-5pm.)*

THE SOUTH

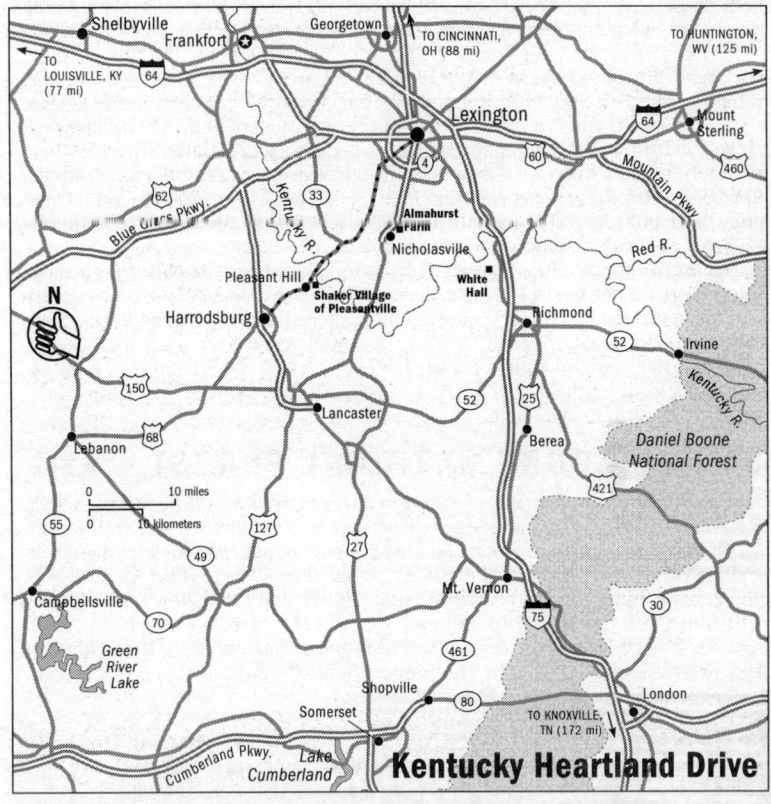

Kentucky Heartland Drive

SCENIC DRIVE: KENTUCKY HEARTLAND

A drive along the Kentucky Heartland Drive is a drive through Kentucky history, with a bit of beautiful scenery thrown in for good measure. The scenic route actually begins on S. Broadway in Lexington and ends in Harrodsburg. About five miles south of New Circle Rd., the hustle, bustle, and endless strip malls fade away, replaced by verdant pastures and the miles of horse fences that run along U.S. 68. The drive takes roughly 45min. to 1hr.

This is classic Kentucky horse country. Thoroughbreds, some of which are more valuable than the cars that pass them, graze alongside the road. The most famous horse farm in the area is **Almahurst Farm,** 9 mi. south of Lexington, marked by a signpost by the side of the road. The farm was given to a certain James Knight in honor of his service in the Revolutionary War and has since raised a number of minor horse racing legends. Five miles after Almahurst, U.S. 68 enters the **Kentucky**

WHISKEY BUSINESS All bourbon is whiskey, but not all whiskey is bourbon. So what makes bourbon so special? It's all in the making, codified by the US government. For alcohol to be bourbon, it must fulfill these 6 requirements: 1. It must be aged in a new white oak barrel, flame-charred on the inside. (Scotch, alternatively, must be aged in used barrels.) 2. It must age at least 2 years in that barrel. 3. It must be at least 51% corn. 4. It cannot be distilled over 160 proof (80% alcohol). 5. It cannot go into the barrel over 125 proof. 6. It can have no additives or preservatives.

River Gorge. Limestone shelves overgrown with ivy lead up to what is undoubtedly the scenic high point of the trip: the Kentucky River itself.

Two historical attractions mark the further edge of the drive. The first of these, the **Shaker Village of Pleasant Hill,** is about 30 mi. from Lexington. The Shakers, a religious sect that spread to Kentucky in the early 19th century, marked themselves for impermanence by making celibacy an article of faith. This village was closed in 1910, but the buildings are preserved here as part of a "living history" production that involves tours, guided or otherwise, and craft demonstrations. **Riverboat excursions** are also run from here. (☎ 859-734-5411 or 800-734-5611. Open daily 9:30am-5:30pm. $10, ages 12-17 $5.50, ages 6-11 $3.50; with river trip $14/ $7.50/$4.50. Oct.-Mar. reduced hours and prices. Wheelchair accessible.)

Eight miles south of the Shakers is historic **Harrodsburg,** the oldest permanent English settlement west of the Alleghenies. Visitors can watch faux 18th-century craftspeople demonstrate their skills in the center of town at **Old Fort Harrod State Park,** Lexington and College St. The Park is a replica of the stockade built here in 1774. The Harrodsburg **Visitors Center,** 103 Main St. at U.S. 68, hands out information and a local tourbook. (☎ 734-2364 or 800-355-9192. Open M-F 9am-5pm; mid-June to Oct. also Sa 10am-3pm.)

DANIEL BOONE NATIONAL FOREST ☎ 606

The Daniel Boone National Forest cuts a vast green swath through Kentucky's Eastern Highlands. Encompassing 670,000 acres of mountains and valleys, the forest is layered with a gorgeous tangle of chestnut, oak, hemlock, and pine, as well as pristine lakes, waterfalls, and extraordinary natural bridges. This is bluegrass country, where seasoned backpackers and Lexington's daytrippers still find the heart of old Appalachia deep in the forest—though, by some reports, you're less likely these days to stumble onto feuding Hatfields and McCoys than into some farmer's hidden field of marijuana, reputedly Kentucky's leading cash crop.

◪ PRACTICAL INFORMATION. Six US Forest Service Ranger Districts administer the National Forest. Ranger offices supply trail maps and specifics about the portions of the 269 mi. **Sheltowee Trace** that pass through their districts. Sheltowee was the name the Shawnee gave to Daniel Boone, meaning— enigmatically enough—"Big Turtle." **Stanton Ranger District,** 705 W. College Ave., includes the **Red River Gorge and Natural Bridge.** (☎ 663-2852. Open M-F 8am-4:30pm.) To the north, **Morehead Ranger District,** 2375 KY 801 S. (☎ 784-6428), 2 mi. south of Rte. 60, includes **Cave Run Lake.** The **Morehead Tourism Commission,** 150 E. First St., Morehead 40351 (☎ 784-6221), has more info. To the south, **London Ranger District** (☎ 864-4163), on U.S. 25 S, covers Laurel River Lake, close to Cumberland Falls; Laurel River Lake's **Visitors Center** is at Exit 41 off I-75. (☎ 878-6900 or 800-348-0095. Open M-Sa 9am-5pm, Su 10am-2pm.) For forest-wide info, contact the **Forest Supervisor,** 1700 Bypass Rd., Winchester (☎ 745-3100). **Greyhound** buses from Lexington to Morehead (1½hr., 1 per day, $14-15); London (1¾hr., 3 per day, $18-19); and Corbin (2hr., 4 per day, $20-21). **Area code:** 606.

STANTON RANGER DISTRICT

The Mountain Pkwy. runs through Stanton Ranger District, providing easy access to the District's two principle attractions: **Natural Bridge State Resort Park** and **Red River Gorge Geological Area.** South of the Parkway, **Natural Bridge,** off Rte. 11, is the area's absolute must-see site. A rather steep ¾ mi. trail leads to the top of the bridge itself, where an expansive view of the surrounding wilderness stretches unobstructed by any sort of railings; walk a little further for a spectacular view of the bridge itself. The **Red River Gorge Area,** on the other side of the Parkway, contains some of the most varied and ecologically rich terrain in this part of the country. A 32 mi. circuit (Rte. 77 E to Rte. 715) runs through the 900 ft. single-lane **Nada Tunnel,** an old railroad tunnel cut directly through the rock (scary as hell!), and past the restored **Gladie Historic Site Log House** (open 10am-6pm). Along the way, the drive curves around picturesque mountain roads and forests. Take a 1¼ mi. hike past the beautiful **Rock Bridge,** down Rock Bridge Rd. near the junction of Rte. 715 and Rte. 15. A few mi. north of Rock Bridge is **Sky Bridge** (off Rte. 715), which only requires a fairly-level ¼ mi. hike to reach the top. Standing high above the sheer drop-offs and green gorges on both sides is magical.

Both sites are best approached via the Slade Exit off Mountain Pkwy., where a **red tourist caboose,** run by the **Natural Bridge/Powell County Chamber of Commerce,** hands out info on the weekends. (☎663-9229. Open Sa-Su 10am-5pm.) Budgetary concerns are best met by staying at the campgrounds at Natural Bridge or the Red River Gorge Area. Near Natural Bridge, **Whittletown** has 40 well-shaded sites, and **Middle Fork** has 46 open sites. (☎663-2214. Sites $8.50, 10% discount for seniors; with hookup $16 for 2 adults; $1 per additional adult, under 16 free. No reservations.) Near Red River Gorge, **Koomer Ridge Campground,** Route 15, of the Mountain Parkway between Exits 33 and 40, has lush, shaded sites. (☎663-2852. Mid-Apr. to Oct. $10 per single unit, $15 per double; Nov. to mid-Apr. all units $5.) You can pitch a tent anywhere in the forest, as long as you stay more than 300 ft. from roads, marked trails, and water source. **Abner's Motel,** 87 E. College Ave., at Exit 22 in Stanton, offers large rooms with A/C and cable. (☎663-4379. Singles $36; doubles $45.)

LONDON RANGER DISTRICT

There's boating, fishing, hiking, and just hanging out at the **Laurel River Lake. Camping** is available at two densely wooded Forest Service campgrounds on the lake, both off Rte. 193 and adjacent to marinas: **Grove** with 56 sites and **Holly Bay** with 94 sites. (☎877-444-6777. Walk-in sites $7 for 1 person, $10 for 2; drive-in sites $10/$15; with electricity and water $15/$25. Reservations recommended.) Visitors to giant **Cumberland Falls**—"The Niagara of the South"—can camp at the state park that surrounds the falls. The campground, 18 mi. west of Corbin on Rte. 90, is signposted off Rte. 90. (☎528-4121. Open Apr.-Oct. 50 sites. Sites $8.50, seniors $7.20; RVs $14/$12.) Water mist during a full moon creates the fantastic moonbows for which the Cumberland Falls are famous. **Sheltowee Trace Outfitters,** on Rte. 90, 5 mi. east of the state park, arranges guided, 7hr. rafting trips down the Falls' class III rapids. (☎800-541-7238. Runs 9am-4:30pm with equipment, guide, and lunch. $51, ages 6-12 $40.25. Canoe trips on more placid sections of the river are $16 per person.)

CUMBERLAND GAP

Stretching from Maine to Georgia, the majestic Appalachian Mountain Range proved a formidable obstacle to the westward movement of early American settlers, but not to bison. By following these animals, Native Americans learned of the Cumberland Gap, a natural break in the mountains. Frontiersman Daniel Boone became famous when he blazed the Wilderness Trail through the Gap in 1775, thereby opening the West to colonization. The **Cumberland Gap National Historic Park,** best reached by U.S. 25 E from Kentucky or U.S. 58 from Virginia, sits on 20,000 acres shared by Kentucky, Virginia, and Tennessee. The Cumberland Gap **Visitors Center** (☎606-248-2817), on U.S. 25 E in Middleboro, KY, has a film and slide show on the Gap's history, as well as a small museum that narrates the story of the Gap and its significance to American history. (Park and Visitors Center open daily 8am-6pm; off-season 8am-5pm.) The park's 160-site **campground,** on U.S. 58 in Virginia, has hot showers (sites $10, with electricity $15). **Backcountry camping** requires a free permit from the Visitors Center. A panoramic view of Virginia, Kentucky, and Tennessee is a short trip away from **Pinnacle Rock** (4 mi. from the Visitors Center).

THE SOUTH

TENNESSEE

Sloping from the majestic Great Smoky Mountains to the verdant Mississippi lowlands, Tennessee makes and breaks stereotypes with the smooth ease of Jack Daniels. Those enchanted with the last state to secede from the Union (and the first to rejoin) often express their affection in the form of song—an ode to Davy Crockett deems this land the "greatest state in the land of the free," Dolly Parton finds her Heartsong in the mountains, and there ain't no place the Grateful Dead would rather be. Tennessee's economy is industry-based, with the world's largest Bible-producing business, but it is music that fuels the state's soul.

⚿ PRACTICAL INFORMATION

Capital: Nashville.

Visitor info: Tennessee Dept. of Tourist Development, 320 6th Ave., Nashville (☎741-2159; www.state.tn.us/tourdev). Open M-F 8am-4:30pm. **Tennessee State Parks Information,** 401 Church St., Nashville (☎800-421-6683).

Postal Abbreviation: TN. **Sales Tax:** 6-8%.

NASHVILLE   ☎615

Long-forgotten Francis Nash is one of only four Revolutionary War heroes honored with US city names (Washington, Wayne, and Knox are the others), but his tenuous foothold in history pales in comparison to Nashville's notoriety as the banjo-pickin', foot-stompin' capital of country music. Large, eclectic, and unapologetically heterogeneous, Tennessee's capital is not only the home of the Country Music Hall of Fame, but also "the Wall Street of the South." The city houses both the Southern Baptists and centers of higher learning such as Fisk University and Vanderbilt.

▐ TRANSPORTATION

Airport: Metropolitan (☎275-1675), 8 mi. south of downtown. An airport **shuttle** (☎275-1180) operates out of major downtown hotels ($11, round-trip $17). Bus fare downtown $1.55 with a transfer. Taxi to downtown $20.

Buses: Greyhound, 200 8th Ave. S. (☎255-3556), at Broadway downtown. Borders on a rough neighborhood, but the station is well lit. To: Memphis (4hr., 6 per day, $27-29); Chattanooga (2½hr., 5 per day, $18-19); Birmingham (3½hr., 7 per day, $26-28); and Knoxville (3½hr., 7 per day, $22-24). Station open 24hr.

Public Transit: Metropolitan Transit Authority (MTA) (☎862-5950). Buses operate on limited routes, usually once per hr. Times vary route to route, but none runs before 5:30am or after 11:15pm M-F; less frequent service Sa-Su. Fare $1.45, transfers 10¢.

Taxis: Nashville Cab, ☎242-7070. **Music City Taxi,** ☎262-0451.

Car Rental: Thrifty, 414 11th Ave. N. (☎248-8888), downtown. $33 per day. Must be over 25 with a major credit card.

✴⚿ ORIENTATION AND PRACTICAL INFORMATION

Nashville's streets are fickle, often interrupted by curving parkways and one-ways. Names change constantly and without warning; **Broadway,** the main east-west thoroughfare, melts into **West End Ave.** just outside downtown at Vanderbilt and I-40. In downtown, numbered avenues run north-south, parallel to the Cumberland River. The curve of **James Robertson Pkwy.** encloses the north end, becoming **Main St.** on the other side of the river (later **Gallatin Pike**) and **McGavock St.** at the south end.

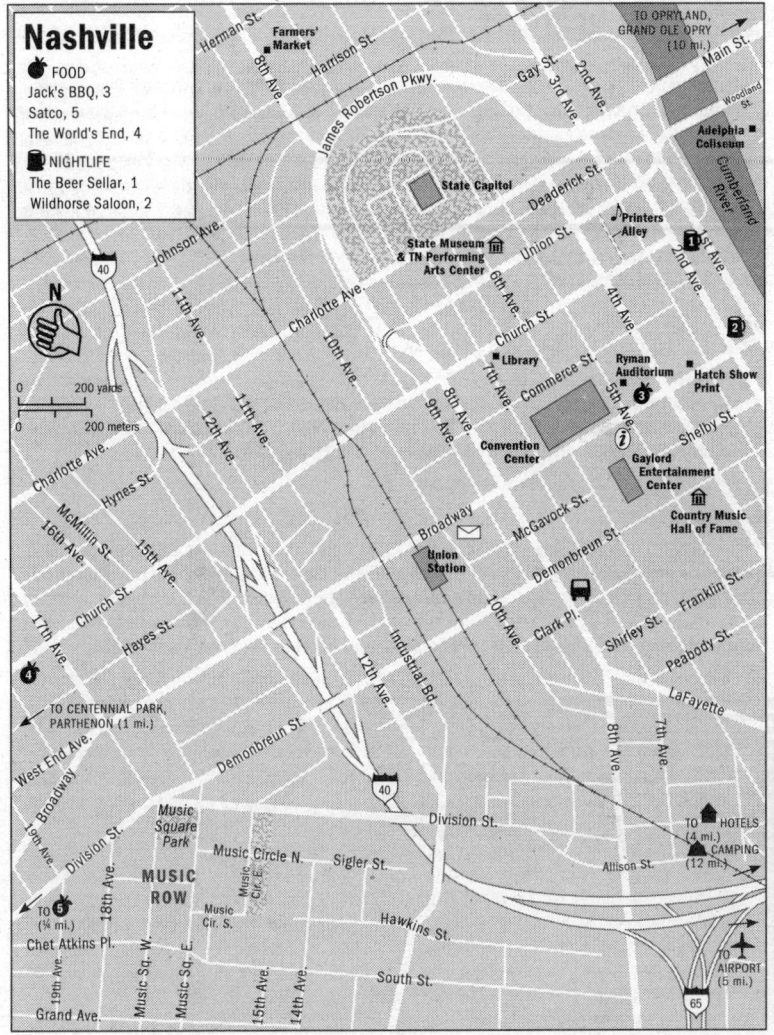

Nashville

🍎 **FOOD**
Jack's BBQ, 3
Satco, 5
The World's End, 4

🍺 **NIGHTLIFE**
The Beer Sellar, 1
Wildhorse Saloon, 2

THE SOUTH

The area south of Broadway between 2nd and 7th Ave. and the region north of James Robertson Pkwy. are both unsafe at night.

Visitor info: Nashville Visitors Bureau, 501 Broadway (☎259-4747), in the Gaylord Entertainment Center (previously the Nashville Arena), I-65 at Exit 84, James Robertson Pkwy. Open daily 8:30am-7pm; off-season 8:30am-5:30pm.

Hotlines: Crisis Line, ☎244-7444. **Rape Hotline,** ☎256-8526. Both 24hr. **Gay and Lesbian Switchboard,** ☎297-0008. Operates nightly 6-9pm.

Hospital: Metro General Hospital, 1818 Albion St. (☎341-4000).

Internet access: Nashville Public Library, 615 Church St. (☎862-5800), between 6th and 7th Ave. Open M-Th 9am-8pm, F 9am-6pm, Sa 9am-5pm, Su 2-5pm.

Post Office: 901 Broadway (☎255-3613), next to Union Station. Open M-F 7:30am-6pm, Sa 9am-2pm. **ZIP code:** 37202. **Area code:** 615.

▌ ACCOMMODATIONS

Finding a room in Nashville is expensive, especially in summer. Make reservations well in advance. Budget motels concentrate around **W. Trinity Ln.** and **Brick Church Pike,** off I-65. Dirt-cheap hotels inhabit the area around **Dickerson Rd.** and **Murfreesboro,** but the neighborhood is seedy at best. Closer to downtown (but still sketchy), several motels huddle on **Interstate Dr.** just over the Woodland St. Bridge. **The Cumberland Inn,** 150 W. Trinity Ln. at Exit 87A off I-65 N, has cheerful rooms with A/C and laundry. (☎226-1600 or 800-704-1028. Singles $30; doubles $35.) The spacious rooms of **Knights Inn,** 1360 Brick Church Pike, at Exit 87B on I-65, offer a great end to a day out with A/C, cable, and free coffee and donuts. (☎226-4500 or 800-843-5644. Singles $30; doubles $38; weekends $35/$41.) Rooms at **The Liberty Inn,** 2400 Brick Church Pike, Exit 87B off I-65, dispense justice with cable, A/C, and roomy showers. (☎228-2567. Singles and doubles $30-36. Wheelchair accessible.) Two campgrounds are stationed near Opryland USA. **Nashville Holiday Travel Park,** 2572 Music Valley Dr., has a wooded area for tenting and crowded RV sites. (☎889-4226 or 800-547-4480. Sites for 2 $21; water and electricity $33; full hookup $41; each additional person over 11 $4.) **Opryland KOA,** 2626 Music Valley Dr., has a pool and live summer music. (☎889-0286. Sites $23; with hookup $36. 1-room cabins with A/C and electricity $40, 2-room cabins $49.)

▐ FOOD

In Nashville, music influences even the local delicacies; **Goo-Goo Clusters** (peanuts, pecans, chocolate, caramel, and marshmallow), sold most places, bear the initials of the Grand Ole Opry. Nashville's other finger-lickin' traditions, barbecue or fried chicken followed by pecan pie, are no less sinful. Restaurants for collegiate tastes and budgets cram **21st Ave., West End Ave.,** and **Elliston Pl.,** near Vanderbilt.

- **Loveless Cafe,** 8400 Rte. 100 (☎646-9700 or 800-889-2432). A Nashville country cookin' tradition. Feast on nationally renowned biscuits made from scratch with home-made preserves, country ham ($10), fried chicken ($11), and good ol' Southern hospitality. Open M-F 8am-2pm and 5-9pm, Sa-Su 8am-9pm. Reservations recommended.
- **SATCO (San Antonio Taco Company),** 416 21st Ave. S. (☎327-4322). Tex-Mex and beer abound at this student hangout. Fajitas $1.50, tacos $1; large combo platters $5. Single beers $2, bucket of 6 $10. Open Su-W 11am-midnight, Th-Sa 11am-1am.
- **Jack's Bar-B-Que,** 416 Broadway (☎254-5715). If the flashing neon of winged pigs above the door isn't enough to draw you in, consider the pull of tender pork. Sandwiches $3-4, plates $7-11. Open M-Th 10:30am-10pm, F-Sa 10:30am-11pm, Su noon-8pm; off-season M-W 10:30am-3pm, Th 10:30am-10pm, F-Sa 10:30am-11pm.
- **The World's End,** 1713 Church St. (☎329-3480). It's the end of the world as we know it, and I feel like a burger or a salad ($5-8), or maybe a beer ($2.50). Open Su and Tu-Th 4pm-12:30am, F-Sa 4pm-1:30am; happy hour nightly until 8pm.

◉ SIGHTS

COUNTRY MUSIC HALL OF FAME. Music Row, home of Nashville's signature industry, centers around Division and Demonbreun St. from 16th to 19th Ave. S., bounded to the south by Grand Ave. *(Take bus #3 to 17th Ave. and walk south.)* The new **Country Music Hall of Fame,** sings the praises of country stars from Jimmie Rodgers to Dolly Parton and celebrates the stylish glitz and twang of their gun-studded cars, embroidered suits, and Technicolor cowboy boots. Elvis's 24-karat gold-plated Cadillac glitters on display while scores of videos and listening stations put you in touch with the music. *(222 5th Ave. S. ☎416-2001. Open daily 10am-6pm; June-Aug. Th 10am-10pm. $15, ages 6-15 $8, under 6 free.)*

PARTHENON. Nashville's pride and joy awaits in **Centennial Park,** a 15min. walk west along West End Ave. from Music Row. The "Athens of the South" boasts a full-scale replica of the **Parthenon.** Built as a temporary exhibit for the Tennessee

Centennial in 1897, the Parthenon met with such success that it was rebuilt to last, much like its Ancient namesake. In its first floor gallery, the building also houses the **Cowan Collection of American Paintings,** an erratic but refreshing selection of 19th- and early 20th-century American art. (☎862-8431. Open Tu-Sa 9am-4:30pm, Su 12:30-4:30pm; Apr.-Oct. closed Su. $3.50, seniors and ages 4-17 $2. Wheelchair accessible.)

TENNESSEE STATE CAPITOL. A comely Greek Revival structure atop the hill on Charlotte Ave. next to downtown, the Capitol offers, among other things, tours of the tomb of former President James Knox Polk. (☎741-1621. Open 9am-4pm. Tours every hr. M-F 9-11am and 1-3pm, Sa-Su self-guided tours only. Free. Wheelchair accessible.)

VAN VECHTEN GALLERY. Fisk University's Carl Van Vechten Gallery consists of a portion of the private collection of Alfred Steiglitz and Georgia O'Keeffe; outstanding Steiglitz photographs hang among works by Picasso, Renoir, and others. (At Jackson St. and D.B. Todd Blvd. off Jefferson St. ☎329-8543. Open Tu-F 10am-5pm, Sa 1-5pm and Su 1-5pm during the academic year. Free, though donations accepted. Wheelchair accessible.)

CHEEKWOOD MUSEUM. If you tire of the downtown area, you can rest at the **Cheekwood Botanical Garden and Museum of Art.** The well-kept gardens offer a respite from the flashiness of downtown and complement the museum's 19th-century art perfectly. The museum also hosts high-caliber temporary exhibits on contemporary art. (8 mi. southwest of town on Forrest Park Dr. between Rte. 100 and Belle Meade Blvd. Bus #3 "West End/Belle Meade" from downtown to Belle Meade Blvd. and Page Rd. ☎356-8000. Open Tu-Sa 9:30am-4:30pm, Su 11am-4:30pm. $10, seniors $8, college students and ages 6-17 $5.)

BELLE MEADE MANSION. Near Cheekwood Museum, the **Belle Meade Mansion,** dubbed "The Queen of Tennessee Plantations," is a pleasant change of pace from the excitement of neon lights and amplifiers that pervades Music City. This lavish 1853 plantation was the site of the nation's first thoroughbred breeding farm and host to seven US presidents, including the 380 lb. William Howard Taft, who spent some time lodged in the bathtub there. Prior to Taft's second visit, his hosts installed a rather amply proportioned shower. (5025 Harding Rd. ☎356-0501 or 800-270-3991. Open M-Sa 9am-5pm, Su 11am-5pm. 2 guided tours per hr.; last tour 4pm. $10, seniors $8.50, ages 6-12 $4. The bottom floor of the mansion is wheelchair accessible.)

HERMITAGE. The impressive array of original furnishings of Andrew Jackson's graceful manor, the **Hermitage,** encourages breaking away from the sociable squeeze of downtown for a couple of hours. Admission includes a 16min. film, access to the house and grounds, and a visit to nearby Tulip Grove Mansion and Church. (4580 Rachel's Ln., Exit 221A off I-40. ☎889-2941. Open daily 9am-5pm. $10, seniors and students $9, ages 6-12 $5, families $30. All of the grounds, except for the nature trail and the second floor of the mansion itself, are wheelchair accessible.)

♫ ENTERTAINMENT

The setting for America's longest-running radio show, the **Grand Ole Opry (GOO),** 2804 Opryland Dr., at Exit 11 off Briley Pkwy., features live music and a museum showcasing a host of treasures such as Marty Robbin's race car and a suit belonging to Randy Travis. (☎889-6611. Museum open M-Th 10am-5pm, F 10am-8pm, Sa 10am-10pm. Free. Live music F 7:30pm, Sa 6:30 and 9:30pm; $25. The F *Tennessean* lists performers. Tours F-Sa 10:30am-2:30pm. $8.65, ages 4-11 $4. Call for reservations.) Once the home of the Opry and the stomping grounds of such legendary performers as Hank Williams and Patsy Cline, the **Ryman Auditorium,** 116 Fifth Ave. N., now hosts live music most nights and offers tours during the day. (☎889-3060. Open for self-guided tours 9am-4pm; $8, ages 4-11 $4. Showtimes and prices vary.) The **Tennessee Performing Arts Center,** Deaderick and 6th Ave. N., hosts the Nashville Symphony, Opera, Ballet, and other highbrow entertainment. (☎782-4000, for tickets 255-2787.) Listings for the area's music and events fill the free publications *Nashville Scene* and *Rage*, available at most area establishments. The Visitors Center hands out a list of gay and lesbian establishments.

Two new major-league franchises dominate the Nashville sports scene. The National Football League's **Tennessee Titans** play at **Adelphia Coliseum,** across the river from downtown at 460 Great Circle Rd. (☎565-4000. Tickets $12-52.) The **Nashville Predators,** a National Hockey League team, play at the **Gaylord Entertainment Center,** 501 Broadway. (☎770-2000 for info or 770-2040 for tickets. $10-95.)

▶ NIGHTLIFE

Nightlife downtown centers Broadway and 2nd Ave., where large tourist attractions like the Hard Rock Cafe and Planet Hollywood draw large crowds. Parking down here on a summer evening—especially when something is going on at the Gaylord Entertainment Center—can be either a huge hassle or a huge expense. Near Vanderbilt, **Elliston Pl.** hops with an array of college-oriented music venues.

■ **Bluebird Cafe,** 4104 Hillsboro Rd. (☎383-1461), in strip mall in Green Hills. This famous bird sings country, blues, and folk. Garth Brooks got his start here. $7 per person food/drink minimum if you sit at a table. Open daily 5:30pm until the singing stops (usually between 11pm and 1am). Early show 7pm; cover begins around 9:30pm ($4-10). No cover Su. Reservations recommended Tu-Sa.

Wildhorse Saloon, 120 2nd Ave. N. (☎902-8211). Bring your cowboy boots, hat, and two-step through the night in this huge country dance hall and birthplace of the TNN dance show. Dance lessons M-F 6-9pm, Sa-Su 2-9pm. Live music Tu-Sa. Cover $4-6 after 7pm. Open Su-Th 11am-1am, F-Sa 11am-3am.

The Beer Sellar, 107 Church St. (☎254-9464). For a more relaxed setting head to the subterranean calm of the Beer Sellar. Choose from 50 different drafts ($2.50-4.50) and 135 bottled beers. Happy hour M-F 2pm-7pm. Open daily 2pm-3am.

KNOXVILLE ☎865

Knoxville was settled after the Revolutionary War and named for Washington's Secretary of War, Henry Knox. Once the capital of Tennessee, the city hosted the 1982 World's Fair (which attracted 10 million visitors) and continues to be home to the 26,000 students of the University of Tennessee (UT). Shaded by the stunning Great Smoky Mountains and hemmed by vast lakes created by the Tennessee Valley Authority, Knoxville offers friendly urbanity.

▶ **PRACTICAL INFORMATION.** Downtown stretches north from the **Tennessee River,** bordered by **Henley St.** and the **World's Fair Park** to the west. **Greyhound,** 100 E. Magnolia Ave. (☎522-5144; open 24hr.), at Central St., buses to Nashville (3hr., 6 per day, $22-24); Chattanooga (2hr., 3 per day, $14-15); and Lexington (4hr., 6 per day, $39-41). *Avoid this area at night.* **Public transit: KAT** buses run M-F from 6:15am-6:15pm or later, depending on the route; buses start running at 7:15am on Sa; a few lines also run Su. (☎637-3000. Fare $1, transfers 20¢.) Two **free trolley** lines run throughout the city: Blue goes downtown and eastward, while Orange heads downtown and westward to the park and UT (Orange line: 7am-6pm; Blue line: 6am-6:20pm). **Gateway Regional Visitors Center,** 900 Volunteer Landing, along the river on the southeast side of downtown, also hosts a small museum. (☎971-5550. Open M-Sa 9am-5pm, Su 1-5pm.) **Internet access:** Lawson McGhee Library, 500 W. Church Ave. (☎215-8750; open M-Th 9am-8:30pm, F 9am-5:30pm; Sept.-May Sa-Su 1-5pm as well). **Post Office:** 501 Main St. (☎525-4683; open M-F 7:30am-5:30pm). **ZIP code:** 37901. **Area code:** 865.

▶ **ACCOMMODATIONS.** Many not-quite-budget motels sit along **I-75** and **I-40,** just outside the city. The **Knoxville Hostel,** 404 E. 4th St. features not only clean rooms, a kitchen, and a comfortable common room, but also free Internet access and continental breakfast. *Be careful around this neighborhood at night. If you arrive at the Greyhound station, call the hostel and they will pick you up.* (☎546-8090. Free telephone use. Laundry. No lockout. Office open 8am-4pm. $15 per night.) If you're a woman, consider staying in the **YWCA's** transit room at

ANYONE FOR FUSION HANGMAN? Shrouded in secrecy and fenced in from outsides, the city of Oak Ridge was created in 1942 for the sole purpose of working on atomic bombs as part of the Manhattan Project. The city, 20 mi. from Knoxville on Rte. 62 or 162, was opened to the public in 1949 and hosts the **American Museum of Science and Energy.** The museum is "dedicated to personalizing science and technology," and succeeds to a great extent with excellent interactive exhibits on the evolution of energy technology (including, yes, computerized games of "fusion hangman"). Some viewers, however, may find the relative lack of information on how science and technology were "personalized" to the citizens of Hiroshima and Nagasaki rather eerie. The museum also operates a bus tour of the first nuclear reactor to operate at full capacity and the once top-secret Y-12 Plant, where the uranium used in the "Little Boy" bomb was produced. *(300 S. Tulane Ave. ☎576-3200. Open M-F 9am-5pm. The museum may begin charging admission in spring 2001. Tours M-F 12:30pm.)*

420 W. Clinch St., downtown at Walnut St. The clean, pleasing room is located right in the heart of downtown within walking distance of many of Knoxville's attractions. (☎523-6126. Call ahead M-F 9am-5pm. Single with shared bath down the hall $12.) Edinburgh split-level it is not, but the **Scottish Inns,** 301 Callahan Rd., at Exit 110 off I-75, keeps clean, inviting rooms equipped with A/C, free local calls, cable TV, and an outdoor pool. (☎689-7777; fax 688-7749. Singles $30; doubles $33; on weekends $31/$37.) **Yogi Bear's Jellystone Park Campground,** 9514 Diggs Gap Rd., at Exit 117 off I-75, is located closer to the city than most other campgrounds. It features a pool, clubhouse, restaurant, and laundry, as well as cartoon cheer. (☎938-6600 or 800-238-9644. Sites with water and electricity $18; full hookup $25.)

❑ FOOD. The Strip (part of Cumberland Ave. along campus proper) is lined with student hangouts, bars, and restaurants. **Market Sq.,** a popular plaza to the east of World's Fair Park, presents restaurants, fountains, and shade, but mostly shuts down at night. The other center of chowing, browsing, and carousing, **Old City,** spreads north up Central and Jackson St. and stays active later than Market Sq. **The Tomato Head,** 12 Market Sq., beckons with gourmet pizzas (9 in. $6-18.25) and sandwiches ($4.25-6). Veggie options galore. (☎637-4067. Open M 11am-3pm, Tu-Th 11am-10pm, F-Sa 11am-11pm.) The ever-popular **Calhoun's on the River,** 400 Neyland Dr., claims to serve the "best ribs in America." (☎673-3355. Open M-Th 11am-10:30pm, F-Sa 11am-11pm, Su 11am-10pm. Meat on ribs $10-16; meat in a sandwich $7.) The **Crescent Moon Cafe,** 705 Market St. in an alley between Church Ave. and Cumberland Ave. offers budget- and health-friendly gourmet experiences. Lunch specials and sandwiches go for $6.25 and include a side. (☎637-9700. Open M-F 8am-10am and 11am-2:15pm. Dinner by reservation on the first F of each month.)

◙ SIGHTS. The must-see ▨**Museum of Appalachia,** 16 mi. north of Knoxville at I-75 Exit 122, in Norris, is actually a village with houses, barns, a school, a spectacular Hall of Fame building complete with a dulcimer exhibit, livestock, and the cabin where Samuel Langhorne Clemens (Mark Twain) was conceived. Full of personal anecdotes and the tools and household items that make up the materials of the everyday, this museum does a splendid job of paying tribute to the uniqueness of Appalachian culture (from farm tools to evangelical road signs) without turning its subject into spectacle. (☎494-7680 or 494-0514. Open daily 8am-5pm, June-Aug. 8am-8pm; live music Apr.-Dec. 9:30am-5pm. $7, ages 6-15 $4, families $17; senior and AAA discounts.) For a taste of down-home Appalachia, visit the **Farmers Market,** 15 mi. from downtown on I-640, Exit 8. (☎524-3276. Open M-Sa 10am-6pm, Su noon-6pm.)

The self-guided **Cradle of Country Music Tour** runs through the eastern end of downtown; sights include the theater where Roy Acuff made his first public performance as well as the hotel where Hank Williams spent the last night of his life. Maps and information are available at the Visitors Center. Since the tour is self-guided, feel free to visit as few or as many of the sights as you please. Picnickers

THE SOUTH

will appreciate **Krutch Park,** across the street from Market Sq., a tiny, perfectly manicured oasis of green in the midst of downtown. Larger expanses of greenery can be found at **Ijams Nature Center,** 2915 Island Home Ave., 2 mi. east of downtown across Gay St. Bridge. (☎577-4717. Grounds open daily 8am-dusk. Museum open M-F 9am-4pm, Sa noon-4pm, Su 1-5pm. Free.)

World's Fair Park has been undergoing major reconstructive surgery but is slated to reopen sometime in 2002. The park will emerge with a vast new expanse of greenery extending down toward the river, and a giant addition to the Convention Center. The golden "sunsphere," instantly recognizable from nearly anywhere in the city, will continue to delight visitors. The **Knoxville Museum of Art,** 1050 World's Fair Park Dr., in the Park, houses high-caliber changing exhibits as well as an interesting permanent collection. (☎525-6101. Open Tu-Th and Sa 10am-5pm, F 10am-9pm, Su noon-5pm. Free, donations accepted; charge for special exhibits.) The **Women's Basketball Hall of Fame,** 700 Hall of Fame Dr., celebrates the history of women in basketball and generates excitement for the game today. (☎633-9000. Open June-Aug. M-Sa 9am-8pm; Sept.-May M-Th 10am-6pm, F-Sa 10am-8pm, Su noon-6pm. $8, seniors and ages 6-15 $6, under 6 free. Wheelchair accessible.) Nearby, the **James White Fort,** 205 E. Hill Ave., still preserves portions of the original stockade built in 1786 by Knoxville's first citizen and founder, while informative tours give you the inside scoop on life in Kentucky in the 18th century. (☎525-6514. Tours run continuously until 3:30pm. Open M-Sa 9:30am-4:30pm. $5, children 5-12 $2, seniors and AAA $4.25.)

🎭🎵 **ENTERTAINMENT AND NIGHTLIFE.** UT sports some fantastic teams, particularly **football** and **women's basketball;** call 974-2491 for tickets. From April through September the **Knoxville Smokies,** an AA baseball team, hit the field. (☎637-9494. Tickets $6-9.) Knoxville will be in full bloom April 5-28, 2002 for the **Dogwood Arts Festival** (☎637-4561), featuring food, folks, fun, and a lot of trees. Old City has the highest concentration of nightlife in the area. **Fiction,** 214 W. Jackson Ave., spins a web of lights and music into a dance club experience. (☎525-3675. Cover $3-8. Open M and F-Sa 10pm-3am.) The **Rainbow Club,** 133 S. Central St., an upscale gay bar in the area, features happy hour nightly from 5-7pm. (☎522-6610. Live music M-W and F. Cover on weekends. Open daily 5pm-3am.) The **Tennessee Theatre,** 604 S. Gay St., plays classic movies and hosts major bands (☎522-1174). For goings-on around town, pick up a free copy of *Metro Pulse.*

GREAT SMOKY MOUNTAINS ☎865

The largest wilderness area in the eastern US, Great Smoky Mountains National Park encompasses 500,000 acres of gray-green Appalachian peaks bounded by misty North Carolina and Tennessee valleys. Black bears, wild hogs, groundhogs, wild turkeys, and a handful of red wolves inhabit the area, as well as more than 1500 species of flowering plants. Whispering conifer forests line the mountain ridges at elevations of over 6000 feet. Spring sets the mountains ablaze with wildflowers and azaleas; in June and July, rhododendrons burst into their full glory, and by mid-October, the mountains become a vibrant quilt of autumnal color. Unfortunately, the area has not remained untouched by human presence. Fifty years ago, a visitor at Newfound Gap could see, on average, 93 miles. Today, poorer air quality has cut visibility to only 15 miles.

🛈 PRACTICAL INFORMATION

Great Smoky Mountains National Park has two **Visitors Centers. Sugarlands** (☎436-1291), on Newfound Gap Rd. 2 mi. south of Gatlinburg, TN, next to the park's headquarters, shows a 20min. film on the history and features of the park, and contains an exhibit on the plants and animals that inhabit the Great Smoky Mountains. On the North Carolina side of the park, **Oconaluftee** (☎828-497-1900 or 828-497-1904), 4 mi. north of Cherokee, shares its grounds with an outdoor Mountain Farm Museum made up of historic buildings relocated from throughout the park and preserved in the 1950s. (Both Visitors Centers open daily 8am-7pm; off-season hours vary.) Rte. 441, known as the Newfound Gap Rd., is the only road connecting the Tennessee and North Carolina sides of the park. The *Smokies Guide* (25¢) details the park's tours, lectures, activities, and changing natural graces.

Buses: East Tennessee Human Resource Agency (ETHRA), 298 Blair Bend Rd. in Loudon (☎800-232-1565), offers transportation from Knoxville and other towns in the vicinity. Operates M-F 8am-4:30pm. Call at least 48hr. in advance to schedule a trip. Fares $2 and up.

Info line: ☎436-1200 (operates daily 8:30am-4:30pm). **Area code:** 865.

⬛⬛ GRUB 'N' SLUMBER

Motels lining Rte. 441 and Rte. 321 decrease in price with distance from the park. Small motels cluster in both Cherokee and Gatlinburg. In general, Cherokee motels are cheaper (from $35) and Gatlinburg motels are nicer (from $45); prices soar on weekends. In Cherokee, the **Gateway Inn,** 2418 Rte. 441, south of town, supplies serviceable if somewhat shabby rooms for fantastic rates. (☎828-497-3777. TV, A/C, heat. Singles $25; doubles $29.) In Tennessee, **The Scenic Motel,** 8254 Rte. 73 in Townsend, offers charming rooms with A/C, TV, fridges, and microwaves just minutes from the park. (☎864-448-2300. Rooms $20-140.) **Bell's Wa-Floy Retreat,** 3610 East Pkwy., is 10 mi. east of Gatlinburg on Rte. 321. This Christian retreat community includes a pool, tennis courts, and meditation area. (☎436-5575. Check-in before 10pm. Reservations required. $15 first night HI-YHA members, $25 nonmembers; thereafter, HI-YHA $12, nonmembers $25.)

Ten **campgrounds** lie scattered throughout the park, each with tent sites, limited trailer space, water, and bathrooms (no showers or hookups). **Smokemont, Elkmont,** and **Cades Cove** accept reservations from mid-May to late October (sites $14-17, cancellation fee $10); the rest are first come, first served (sites $12-14). In summer, reserve spots near main roads at least eight weeks in advance. (☎800-365-2267, park code GRE; 10am-10pm.) **Backcountry camping** is by reservation only; **permits** are free at the Visitors Center. (☎436-1231. Office open daily 8am-6pm.)

Authentic Tennessee cookin' is the order of business at ⬛**Smokin' Joe's Bar-B-Que,** 8215 Rte. 73, near the intersection with 321 in Townsend. With succulent, slow-cooked meats and homemade side dishes like BBQ beans, Joe's smokes the competition. (☎448-3212. Usually open Su-Th 11am-9pm, F-Sa 11am-10pm; off-season hrs. vary. Dinners come with 2 sides, meat, bread, and choice of sauce; sandwiches $2.50-4.50.) **Jernigan's Country Restaurant,** on U.S. 19 near the intersection with Acquoni Rd., satisfies hungry customers with heaping portions of delicious homestyle cooking. (☎497-2307. Open daily 7am-3pm; closed W in winter.) **Hearth and Kettle,** Rte. 321 in Townsend, serves up $9-15 entrees, and a host of $4-8 sandwiches and sandwich platters. (☎448-6059. Open daily 7am-9:30pm.)

⬛ OUTDOOR ACTIVITIES

HIKING

Over 900 mi. of hiking trails and 170 mi. of road meander through the park. Rangers at the Visitors Centers will help you devise a trip appropriate for your ability. Great Smoky Mountains National Park is known for its phenomenal **waterfalls,** and many of the park's most popular hikes culminate in stunning waterfall views. Less crowded but equally scenic areas not accessible from Rte. 441 include **Cosby** and **Cataloochee,** both on the eastern edge of the park. A backcountry camping **permit,** free from the Visitors Centers, is also required to hike off marked trails. *Wherever you go, bring water and don't feed the bears.*

Rainbow Falls (5.5 mi., 4hr.). This moderate to strenuous hike reveals the Smokies' highest single-plunge waterfall, and is the park's most popular hike.

Laurel Falls (2.5 mi., 2hr.). One of the easiest hikes on the Tennessee side of the park, it follows a paved trail through a series of cascades before reaching the 60 ft. falls.

Ramsay Cascades (8 mi., 5hr.), is a fairly strenuous hike. The trailhead is located in the Greenbrier area. The cascades themselves fall 100 ft. down the mountainside.

Chimney Tops (4 mi., 2hr.), is a steep scramble leading up to two 4755 ft. rock spires. Breathtaking views away at the top.

Andrews Bald (3.6 mi., 2hr.). This fairly easy-going hike heads downslope to a bald hill-top with excellent views of the southern section of the park.

Charlies Bunion (8 mi., 4hr.). Tracing the Appalachian Trail and the state-line ridge, this difficult hike offers splendid views.

BIKING

Biking is permitted along most roads within in the park, with the exception of the Roaring Fork Motor Nature Trail. The best opportunities for cyclists can be found in the **Foothills Parkway** and in **Cades Cove** (see p. 351). While the Smokies boast no **mountain biking** trails, a few gravel trails in the park, including the **Gatlinburg Trail** and the **Oconaluftee River Trail,** allow bicycles. **Bike rental** is available in the Cades Cove area; for info call 448-9034.

FISHING

Forty species of fish swim in the park's rivers and streams. Fishing is permitted throughout the park, although the brook trout (native only to the Smokies) is off-limits due to extensive habitat restoration programs. All anglers over 12 (over 15 in North Carolina) must possess a valid Tennessee or North Carolina **fishing license.** The park itself does not sell licenses; check with local Chambers of Commerce for purchasing information. The Smokies permit fishing in open waters year-round from 30min. before sunrise to 30min. after sunset.

RIDING

Over 500 mi. of the park's trails are open to horses. Five **horse camps** are located within the park: **Anthony Creek, Big Creek, Cataloochee, Roundbottom,** and **Towstring.** Reservations are required (☎ 800-362-2267; http://reservations.nps.gov). **Cades Cove Riding Stables** provides 1hr. guided rides in addition to scenic hayrides and frequent carriage rides. (☎ 448-6286. Open daily 9am-5pm. 1hr. rides $15; 25-30min. carriage rides every 30min., $7; 2hr. hayrides F-M 7pm, $8.) **Smokemont Riding Stables,** on the North Carolina side of the park, offers rides as well. (☎ 828-497-2373. Open daily 9am-4:30pm. 1hr. ride $15, 2hr. ride $35.)

NEAR SMOKY MOUNTAINS: CHEROKEE RESERVATION

The **Cherokee Indian Reservation,** on the southeast border of the national park, features a number of museums, shops, attractions, and—most notably—a casino. Three historical attractions stand in marked contrast to miles and miles of rampant commercialism. From May to October, the reservation offers a tour of the **Oconaluftee Indian Village,** a re-created mid-18th-century Native American village. (☎ 828-497-2315. Open May 15-Oct. 25 daily 9am-5:30pm. $12, ages 6-13 $5.) Cherokee lifestyle, legends, and history are featured at the **Museum of the Cherokee Indian** on Drama Rd. off Rte. 441. (☎ 828-497-3481. Open M-Sa 9am-8pm, Su 9am-5pm. $8, ages 6-13 $5, AAA and AARP discount.) **"Unto these Hills,"** an outdoor drama, retells the story of the Cherokees and the Trail of Tears. (☎ 828-497-2111. Open mid-June-Aug. 8:30pm with a pre-show beginning at 7:45pm.) The **Cherokee Visitors Center,** 498 Tsali Blvd., provides information; follow signs from Rte. 441 or Rte. 19. (☎ 800-438-1601. Open M-F 7:45am-5pm, Sa-Su 8:45am-5:30pm.) Role the dice at **Harrah's Cherokee Casino,** 777 Casino Dr. (☎ 828-497-8866 or 877-811-0777; 21+; Open daily 24hr.). **Smoky Mountain Jamboree,** US 441 N. at Acquoni Rd., jams classic country, bluegrass, rock 'n' roll, and gospel, but no alcohol is allowed. (☎ 497-5521. Open June-Oct. Tu-Sa. Shows start at 8pm; ticket office opens at 6pm. $12.50, under 13 free with paying adult.)

The **Nantahala Outdoor Center (NOC),** 13077 U.S. 19 W, 13 mi. southwest of Bryson City, NC, and just south of the National Park, beckons with cheap beds, three restaurants, and the great outdoors. (☎888-662-1662; call ahead. Showers, kitchen, and laundry facilities. Bunks in simple cabins $14.) The NOC's **whitewater rafting expeditions** are pricey, but with some amount of rafting competency, you can rent your own raft for a trip down the Nantahala River. (Rafts Su-F $19, Sa $22. 1- or 2-person inflatable "ducks" Su-F $31/$24, Sa $34/$27. Rafters must be 60 lb. Group rates available. Higher prices weekends in July-Aug. Prices include transportation to site and all necessary equipment.) The **Appalachian Trail** runs through here. **Mountain bike** rentals start at $30, helmets and car racks are included. (☎888-662-1662). The NOC staff can assist if you need help planning a daytrip.

SCENIC DRIVE: CADES COVE LOOP DRIVE

The Cades Cove loop road begins 24 mi. (40min. driving time) from Newfound Gap Rd., near the Sugarlands Visitors Center. May through September, from 7-10am on Wednesday and Saturday, the loop is closed to car traffic in order to accommodate bicyclists. The main features of the one-way loop road are the stone and wooden buildings, some of which date as far back as the 1820s. Numerous private homes, three beautifully simple churches (one of which, the Methodist church, was built in 115 days for $115), a blacksmith shop, and a sawmill are accessible from the loop. Near the blacksmith shop and sawmill, at the far end of the loop, is the **Cades Cove Visitors Center** (open May-Aug. 9am-7pm; off-season hours vary). All of the historic buildings have been preserved to look more or less as they did when the federal government bought the land in 1927 and the 500 inhabitants of Cades Cove began to move elsewhere. Pamphlets providing information on each building and on the cove in general are available at the information station at the start of the loop ($1).

Most visitors, however, also spend a good deal of time gawking at the **wildlife**—deer are nearly ubiquitous, and many hikers also spot the occasional black bear. Wild European boars, turkeys, river otters, and that unfortunate animal known as both "groundhog" and "woodchuck" also inhabit the Cove, although they are more rarely seen by visitors. Drivers in a hurry beware: frequent animal sightings and the lines of cars they inevitably form as each family scurries for its cameras can make driving times astronomical. Unless you happen to be by one of the two roads that cut across the valley, there's no way of evading holdups. During summers, expect the 11 mi. of road to take anywhere between 1½ to 3hr.

Those wishing either to avoid traffic jams or to get closer to the historic experience can rent **horses** at the entrance to the loop across from the ranger station. (☎448-6286. Open Mar.-Nov. 9am-5pm. 1hr. guided horse rides $15. Hayrides $6-8, 1 per day except Tu and Th. Buggy rides $7.) **Bikes** are available at the same location. (☎448-9034. Open June-Aug. Tu and Th-Su 9am-7pm, M and W 7am-7pm, no rental after 4:30pm; May and Sept. daily 9am-5pm, no rental after 2:30pm. $3.25 per hr.)

MOUNTAINS OF FUN A mythical American village created by Dolly Parton in the Tennessee hills, **Dollywood** dominates Pigeon Forge. The park celebrates the cultural legacy of the east Tennessee mountains and the country songmistress herself, famous for some mountainous topography of her own. In Dolly's world, craftspeople demonstrate their skills and sell their wares, 30 rides offer thrills and chills, and country favorites perform. While Dolly asserts that she wants to preserve the culture of the Tennessee mountains, she also seems to want you to pay to come again—Dollywood's motto is "Create Memories Worth Repeating." (1020 Dollywood Ln. ☎865-428-9488. Open year-round; mid-June to mid-Aug. daily, most days 9am-9pm, but hrs. vary. $31, over 59 $26, ages 4-11 $22; enter after 3pm during the summer and get in free the next day. Discount coupons available at tourist centers, restaurants, and motels.)

CHATTANOOGA ☎ 423

Anyone approaching Chattanooga by road will soon be made well aware of the city's star attraction: insistent signs for Ruby Falls flank the city in a 60 mi. radius. Chattanooga itself is, indeed, well-advertised and clearly commercial. Its downtown teems with tourists in peak season. But while the prices and developments of its beautiful mountain attractions may leave some visitors longing for the National Park Service, the city once famous mainly for its "choo-choo" connection, cultivates a certain charm nonetheless.

⊅ PRACTICAL INFORMATION. Chattanooga straddles the Tennessee/Georgia border at the junction of I-24, I-59, and I-75. **Greyhound,** 960 Airport Rd. (☎892-1277; station open 6am-10pm), buses to Atlanta (2hr., 8 per day, $18-19); Nashville (3½hr., 5 per day, $18-19); and Knoxville (2hr., 4 per day, $14-15). **Chattanooga Area Transportation Authority (CARTA)** runs buses 5am-11pm (☎629-1473; fare $1, transfers 20¢, children 50¢/10¢). **Visitors Center:** 2 Broad St., next to the aquarium (☎756-8687 or 800-322-3344; open daily 8:30am-5:30pm). **Internet access: Public Library,** 1001 Broad St. at 10th St. (☎757-5310. Open M-Th 9am-9pm, F-Sa 9am-6pm; Sept.-May also Su 2-6pm.) **Post Office:** 900 Georgia Ave., between Martin Luther King Blvd. and 10th St. (☎267-1609. Open M-F 7:30am-5:30pm.) **ZIP code:** 37402. **Area code:** 423.

⌂⌂ ACCOMMODATIONS AND FOOD. Budget motels congregate on the highways coming into the city and on **Broad St.** at the base of Lookout Mountain. **Holiday Trav-l-Park,** 1709 Mack Smith Rd., in Rossville ½ mi. off I-75 at the East Ridge exit, enlivens tent and RV sites with a Civil War theme. (☎706-891-9766 or 800-693-2877. Laundry, pool. 2-person site $17, with water and electricity $21, full hookup $23; cabins $36, each additional person $2.) Two nearby lakes, **Chickamauga** and **Nickajack,** are surrounded by campgrounds. The **⊠Pickle Barrel,** 1012 Market St., downtown, moves beyond cucumbers to scrumptious sandwiches, such as the spicy black bean burger ($5.25). The open-air deck upstairs is a must in nice weather. (☎266-1103. 21+ after 9pm, except families. Open M-Sa 11am-3am, Su noon-3am.)

⊙⊅ SIGHTS AND ENTERTAINMENT. Downtown Chattanooga, a small area between 10th St. and the river, is full of attractions, shops, and restaurants. The biggest catch in town is the **Tennessee Aquarium,** 1 Broad St. on Ross's Landing, with the largest turtle collection in the world, as well as 7000 other animals and an IMAX screen. (☎800-322-3344. Open M-Th 9am-6pm, F-Su 9am-8pm; Oct.-Apr. daily 10am-6pm. $13, ages 3-12 $7; IMAX $7.25/$5; both $17/$10.) Somewhat lower-profile is the **International Towing and Recovery Hall of Fame and Museum,** 401 Broad St. A big room full of gleaming tow trucks celebrates the unsung inventor of these vehicles, a Chattanooga native. (☎267-3132. Open M-F 10am-4:30pm, Sa-Su 11am-5pm. $4, seniors and ages 5-18 $3, under 6 free.) The **Chattanooga Regional History Museum,** 400 Chestnut St., charts the city's involvement in the forced Cherokee removal in 1838 (the "Trail of Tears") and in the Civil War. (☎265-3247. Open M-F 10am-4:30pm, Sa-Su 11am-4:30pm. $4, seniors $3.50, children $3.) A **riverwalk pathway** runs between downtown, near the aquarium, and the **Bluff View Art District.** Bluff View is a small district of upscale shops and cafes, anchored by the **Hunter Museum of Art,** 10 Bluff View. The museum houses the South's most complete American art collection. (☎267-0968. Open Tu-Sa 10am-4:30pm, Su 1-4:30pm. $5, seniors $4, students $3, ages 3-11 $2.50. Wheelchair accessible.) The riverfront shuts down for nine nights in mid-June for the **Riverbend Festival,** featuring good live music. (☎265-4112. $23-30.)

The **Incline Railway** takes passengers up an insane 72.7° grade up **Lookout Mountain** to an observation deck (also accessible by car) for an expansive view which, on a clear day, encompasses six states. (Incline: $9, ages 3-12 $4.50. Lookout Mountain: Take S. Broad or bus #15 or 31 and follow signs. Open daily June-Aug. 8:30am-9:15pm, Sept.-May 9am-5:15pm. Wheelchair accessible.) The nature trail

Rock City Gardens combines the natural spectacle of scenic outlooks and narrow rock passages with decidedly less organic additives: the trail has been outfitted with strategically placed shops and finishes with a cave decked out with colorful elves and fairy tale dioramas. (☎706-820-2531. Open June-Aug. daily 8:30am-8pm; Sept.-May 8:30am-6pm. $12, ages 3-12 $6.50.) One thousand feet inside the mountain, the ▨**Ruby Falls** cavern formations and a 145 ft. waterfall—complete with colored lights and sound effects—add a little Disney-style pizzazz to a day of sightseeing. (☎821-2544. Open daily 8am-8pm. 1hr. tour. $11.50, ages 3-12 $5.50.)

For entertainment listings, check the free weekly *Outlook*, available at many restaurants and shops. The **Chattanooga Lookouts,** a minor league baseball farm team for the Reds, play at the new **BellSouth Park,** at 2nd and Chestnut St. (☎267-2208 or 800-852-7572. Tickets $4-8, $2 for seniors and children under $12.)

NEAR CHATTANOOGA: CHICKAMAUGA CREEK

The same railroads that immortalized Chattanooga in song gave the area great strategic importance in the Civil War. In the fall of 1863 some of the hardest fighting of the war took place here, near **Chickamauga Creek,** about 3 mi. over the Georgia border on U.S. 27. Chickamauga was the nation's first military park, initially intended as an opportunity for professional military study. As a result, the events of the battle are presented in mind-boggling detail on countless plaques across the park. The **Visitors Center** is on U.S. 27. (☎706-866-9241. Open daily 8am-5:45pm, off-season 8am-4:45pm. 26min. video shown every hr.; $3, seniors and children $1.50. Audio tour rentals until 3hr. before closing; $3 plus a $20 deposit. Park open until dusk.)

MEMPHIS   ☎901

Memphis is a music mecca, especially for Elvis fans. The city has seen the creation of practically every important American music trend in the past century, including rock 'n' roll and soul, but most visitors make the Memphis pilgrimage to see Graceland, the former home of the King and the tackiest mansion in the US. Beyond Graceland, Memphis offers a rich array of musical monuments, and popular blues clubs along Beale St. keep the city's greatest tradition alive. Genuine Southern accents like great barbecue, historic mansions, and manicured parks provide the perfect accompaniment to the more obvious musical treats.

▛ TRANSPORATION

Airport: Memphis International, 2491 Winchester Rd. (☎922-8000), south of the southern loop of I-240. Taxi fare to the city around $22—negotiate in advance. Public transport to and from the airport $1.10; service is sporadic and the trip can be confusing.

Trains: Amtrak, 545 S. Main St. (☎526-0052), at Calhoun on the southern edge of downtown. The surrounding area can be less than safe, but the Main St. Trolley line runs to the station. To: New Orleans (8½hr., 1 per day, $44-86); Chicago (10½hr., 1 per day, $84-150); and Jackson (4½hr., 1 per day, $30-59).

Buses: Greyhound, 203 Union Ave. (☎523-1184), at 4th St. downtown. *The area is unsafe at night.* To: Nashville (4hr., 13 per day, $27-29); Chattanooga (9hr., 4 per day, $37-39); and Jackson (4-5hr., 7 per day, $29-31). Open 24hr.

Public Transit: Memphis Area Transit Authority (MATA) (☎274-6282), corner of Auction Ave. and Main St. Bus routes cover most suburbs but run infrequently. The major downtown stops are at the intersections of Front and Jefferson St., and 2nd St. and Madison Ave.; the major routes run on Front, 2nd, and 3rd St. Buses run M-F from 5:30am, Sa-Su from 6am and stop between 6pm and midnight, depending on the route. $1.10, transfers 10¢. Refurbished 19th-century **trolley cars** cruise Main St. (M-Th 6am-midnight, F 6am-1am, Sa 9:30am-1am, Su 10am-6pm) and roll along the Riverfront (M-Th 6:30am-midnight, F 6:30am-1am, Sa 9:30am-1am, Su 10am-6pm). 50¢; seniors 25¢, M-F 11am-1:30pm 25¢; children under 5 free. 1-day pass $2, 3-day $5.

Taxis: In taxi-deprived Memphis, expect a long wait. **City Wide,** ☎324-4202.

✦⧫ ORIENTATION AND PRACTICAL INFORMATION

Downtown, named avenues run east-west and numbered ones run north-south. **Madison Ave.** divides north and south addresses. Two main thoroughfares, **Poplar** and **Union Ave.**, run east-west; **2nd** and **3rd St.** are the major north-south routes downtown. **I-240** and **I-55** encircle the city. **Bellevue** becomes **Elvis Presley Blvd.** and leads you south straight to Graceland. Marvelous **Midtown** lies east of downtown.

Help Lines: Crisis Line, ☎274-7477. 24hr. **Gay/Lesbian Switchboard,** ☎324-4297. Operates daily 7:30-11pm.

Hospital: Baptist Memorial Hospital, 899 Madison Ave. (☎227-2727).

Visitor info: Tennessee Welcome Center, 119 Riverside Dr. (☎543-6757), at Jefferson St. Open 24hr. The uniformed **blue suede brigade** roaming the city will happily give you directions or answer questions—just stay off of their blue suede shoes.

Internet access: Cossitt-Goodwin Public Library, 33 S. Front St. (☎526-1712), at Monroe. Open M-F 10am-5pm.

Post Office: 555 S. 3rd St. (☎521-2559). Open M-F 8:30am-5:30pm, Sa 10am-2pm. **ZIP code:** 38101. **Area code:** 901.

⌐ SINCE M'BABY LEFT ME, I GOT A NEW PLACE T'DWELL

A few downtown motels have prices in the budget range; otherwise, more distant lodgings are available near Graceland at **Elvis Presley Blvd.** and **Brooks Rd.** For the celebrations of Elvis's historic birth (Jan. 8) and death (Aug. 15), as well as for the Memphis in May festival, book six months to one year in advance.

Memphis Hostel, 340 W. Illinois St. (☎942-3111), Exit 12C off I-55. Located in the Days Inn Riverbluff, the hostel consists of hotel rooms furnished with bunk beds instead of regular hotel fare. While lacking the hominess (and kitchen) that marks most hostels, such affordable accommodations ($15 per night) so near to downtown and the Mississippi River are a steal.

Days Inn Riverbluff, 340 W. Illinois St. (☎948-9005), Exit 12C off I-55. Pleasant accommodation in a scenic (if somewhat rundown) location near downtown, next to the Mississippi. Cable, A/C, coffee, doughnuts, and newspaper. Rooms start at $45, but Visitors Center flyers can bring rates down to $33.

American Inn, 3265 Elvis Presley Blvd. (☎345-8444), Exit 5B off I-55. You can't help falling in love with the large rooms and even larger Elvis-themed mural in the lobby. Cable, A/C. Singles $30; doubles $40.

Memphis/Graceland KOA, 3691 Elvis Presley Blvd. (☎396-7125), right next door to Graceland with pool, laundry, and free shuttle to Beale St. No privacy, but the location is great. Sites for 1-2 people $21, with hookup $32. Kabins with A/C $37; each additional person $4.

Memphis South Campground, 460 Byhalia Rd. (☎662-429-1818), Coldwater, MS, 20 mi. south of Memphis, at Exit 280 off I-55. A relaxing, green spot with a pool and laundry. Office open daily 8-10am and 4pm-8pm. Sites $12, with water and electricity $15, full hookup $17; each additional person $2.

◖ MEALS FIT FOR THE KING

In Memphis, barbecue is as common as rhinestone-studded jumpsuits; the city even hosts the **World Championship Barbecue Cooking Contest** in May. But don't fret if gnawing on ribs isn't your thing—Memphis has plenty of other Southern restaurants with down-home favorites like fried chicken, catfish, chitterlings, and grits.

Rendezvous, 52 2nd St. (☎523-2746), around back on "Downtown Alley." A Memphis legend, serving large portions of ribs ($12-15) and cheaper sandwiches ($3-6), but be prepared to wait an hour. Open Tu-Th 4:30-10:30pm, F-Sa 11am-11:30pm.

Downtown Memphis

🏠 **ACCOMMODATIONS**
Days Inn Riverbluff, **11**
American Inn, **12**
Memphis/
  Graceland KOA, **14**
Memphis Hostel, **13**

🍺 **BARS**
Newby's, **6**

🍎 **FOOD**
Huey's, **4**
The Map Room, **2**
The North End, **1**
Rendezvous, **3**
Tops BBQ, **5**

🎵 **MUSIC AND CLUBS**
B.B. King's Blues Club, **9**
Elvis Presley's Memphis, **10**
This Is It!, **8**
Rum Boogie Cafe, **7**

The Pyramid

North Parkway

Overton Ave.

Jackson Ave.

Market Ave.

Cook
Convention
Center

Exchange Ave.

State Office
Building

Poplar Ave.

City
Hall

Civic Center

Washington Ave.

Adams Ave.

Memphis Belle

Wolf River

Mud Island
Park

Monorail and Walkway

River
Museum

Jefferson
Davis Park

Confederate
Park

Jefferson Ave.

TO VICTORIAN
VILLAGE (1/2mi)

Amphitheater

COURT
SQUARE

Court Ave.

Mississippi River

Main St. Mall

Madison Ave.

"Downtown Alley"

Front St. Dell

Union Ave.

AutoZone
Stadium

Monroe Ave.

Peabody
Hotel

Gayoso Ave.

Center for
Southern Folklore

Peabody Pl.

TO SUN STUDIO,
PINK PALACE MUSEUM,
BROOKS MUSEUM OF ART,

Beale St.

Orpheum

Handy
Park

W.C. Handy
Museum

Tom Lee
Park

Elvis Statue

A. Schwab

Beale St.

Hunt-
Phelan
Home

Linden Ave.

Rock 'n'
Soul Museum

Lt. George W. Lee Ave.

Robert
Church
Park

TO GRACELAND, MEMPHIS INT'L
AIRPORT ✈, NATIONAL
ORNAMENTAL METAL MUSEUM,

Vance Ave.

Linden Ave.

Huling Ave.

Pontotoc Ave.

Nettleton Ave.

National
Civil Rights
Museum

Butler Ave.

Butler Ave.

Vance Ave.

Butler Ave.

Calhoun Ave.

AMTRAK

St. Paul Ave.

St. Paul Ave.

0   100 yards
0   100 meters

N

THE SOUTH

Tops Bar-B-Q, 1286 Union Ave. (☎725-7527). If you want good BBQ, and you want it fast and without frills, make tracks to the smoking chimney of Tops. A sandwich and two sides goes for $4.25. Open daily 8:30am-11:45pm.

The North End, 346 N. Main St. (☎526-0319), at Jackson St. downtown, specializes in tamales, wild rice, stuffed potatoes, and Creole dishes ($3-12). The orgasmic hot fudge pie is known as "sex on a plate" ($3.75). Very extensive beer list—domestics from $2.75, imports from $3.50. Happy hr. daily 4-7pm. Open daily 11am-3am. Live music on the weekends starts around 10pm.

The Map Room, 2 S. Main St. (☎543-8686), where everything seems to move in delightfully slow motion. Business folk, travelers, and neo-hippies lounge on the sofas to read loaned books and sip "lateas." Sandwiches such as pimento-and-cheese ($3.50) are a respite from Memphis's otherwise meaty options. Live music daily. Open 24hr.

Huey's, 77 S. 2nd St. (☎527-2700), downtown. Voted best burgers ($4) in Memphis since 1984. Huey's patrons show their appreciation by launching toothpicks into the ceiling with straw-blowguns. Open M-Sa 11am-3am, Su noon-3am. Live music Su 4pm.

P and H Cafe, 1532 Madison Ave. (☎726-0906). The initials aptly stand for Poor and Hungry. The "beer joint of your dreams" serves grill food to students and locals. The friendly waitresses and the kitschy decor are the real draw. During Death Week in Aug., P and H hosts the infamous "Dead Elvis Ball." Open M-F 11am-3am, Sa 5pm-3am.

◉ MEMPHIS MUSIC AND MARVELS

GRACELAND. Bow down before **Graceland,** Elvis Presley's home and the paragon of Americana that every Memphis visitor must see. Surrender yourself to the crush of tourists, the mansion's crowd-control methods and audio-tape tour, and the tacky, abundant commercialism; it's all part of the delightful orgy of gaudiness. You'll never forget the faux-fur furnishings, mirrored ceilings, carpeted walls, and yellow-and-orange decor of Elvis's 1974 renovations. By tour's end, even those who aren't die-hard Elvis fans may be genuinely moved. Be sure to ooh and ahh at the blinding sheen of the **Trophy Building,** where hundreds of gold and platinum records line the wall. The King and his court are buried next door in the **Meditation Gardens.** *(3763 Elvis Presley Blvd. Take I-55 S to Exit 5B or bus #13 "Lauderdale." ☎332-3322 or 800-238-2000. Expect to wait 1-2hr. on summer weekends. Ticket office open M-Sa 9am-5pm, Su 10am-4pm; Nov.-Feb. mansion tour closed Tu. Attractions remain open 2hr. after ticket office closes. $16, students and seniors $14.40, ages 7-12 $6.)*

MORE ELVIS. If you love him tender, love him true—visit the peripheral Elvis attractions across the street from the mansion. The **Elvis Presley Automobile Museum** houses a fleet of **Elvis-mobiles** that includes pink and purple Cadillacs and a battalion of golf carts and motorized toys. Meanwhile, an indoor drive-in movie theater shows clips taken from 31 Elvis movies of the King on the move. *($7, students and seniors $6.30, children $3.) Walk a Mile in My Shoes,* a free 20min. film with performance footage, screened every 30min., contrasts the early (slim) years with the later (fat) ones. **Elvis Airplanes** features the two Elvis planes: the *Lisa Marie* (named for Elvis's daughter) complete with blue suede bed and gold-plated seatbelt and the tiny *Hound Dog II* Jetstar. *($6, seniors $5.40, children $3.)* The **Sincerely Elvis** exhibit glimpses into Elvis's private side; see the books he read, the pajamas he wore, the TVs he shot, and home movies with his wife Priscilla. *($5, seniors $4.50, children $2.50.)* The **Platinum Tour Package** discounts admission to the mansion and all attractions. *($25, students and seniors $22.50, ages 7-12 $12.)* All have wheelchair access except the airplanes and two rooms in the mansion tour.

Every year on the week of August 15 (the date of Elvis's death), millions of the King's cortege get all shook up for **Elvis Week,** an extended celebration that includes a pilgrimage to his junior high school and a candlelight vigil. The days surrounding his birthday, January 8, also see some Kingly activities.

ELVIS WHO? THE BLUES AND MORE. Long before Sam Phillips and Sun Studio produced Elvis, Jerry Lee Lewis, U2, and Bonnie Raitt, historic Beale St. saw the invention of the blues. Recently ousted from Beale St. by rampant commercialism, the ⬛**Center for Southern Folklore** celebrates local folk cultures with exhibitions, live music, and general exuberance. *(119 S. Main St.* ☎*525-3655. Open Su-Th 11am-7pm, F-Sa 11am-11pm. Lunch M-F 11am-2pm. Galleries free; shows around $5.)* The center can give you info on the **Music and Heritage Festival,** which fills Beale St. during Labor Day weekend. Gospel, country, blues, and jazz accompany dance troupes and craft booths. *(*☎*525-3655. Open 11am-11pm. Free.)* The city's musical legacy also includes the soul hits of the Stax label and rockers like Big Star. For an idea of how all these different elements influenced each other and American culture at large, head over to the must-see ⬛**Rock 'n' Soul Museum.** Numerous artifacts are on display; best of all, the audio tour contains a hundred complete songs, from early blues classics to Isaac Hayes' theme from *Shaft.* *(145 Lt. George W. Lee Ave., one block south of Beale St.* ☎*543-0800. Open daily 10am-6pm. $8.50, seniors $7.50, ages 5-17 $5. Wheelchair accessible.)* Pay your respects to **Sun Studio,** the legendary one-room recording studio where Elvis was discovered, Johnny Cash walked the line, Jerry Lee Lewis was consumed by great balls of fire, and Carl Perkins warned everyone to stay off of his blue suede shoes. *(706 Union Ave.* ☎*521-0664. 30min. tours every hr. on the ½hr. Open daily 10am-6pm. $8.50, under 12 free, AAA discount; some memorabilia is on display at the upstairs gift shop for free. Wheelchair accessible.)* Memphis is also home to soul music legend **Al Green's Full Gospel Tabernacle,** where Sunday services display powerful music, dancing, speaking in tongues, and even exorcisms. *(787 Hale Rd.* ☎*396-9192. Services Su 11am-2:30pm; arriving late and leaving early is bad form.)*

MUD ISLAND. A quick monorail ride over the Mississippi to **Mud Island** allows you to ogle the renowned World War II B-17 *Memphis Belle,* and stroll and splash along a 1½ mi. scale model of the Mississippi River. **Free tours** of the Riverwalk and Memphis Belle run several times daily. Also on the island, the **Mississippi River Museum** charts the history and culture of the river over the past 10,000 years with artifacts, videos, and life-sized replicas of steamboats, ironclads, and cafes for your perusal. *(Monorail leaves from 125 Front St.* ☎*576-7241 or 800-507-6507. Open daily 10am-7:15pm; early Sept. to late May Tu-Su 9am-4:15pm. Museum $8, seniors $6. Wheelchair accessible.)*

MORE MUSEUMS. The powerful ⬛**National Civil Rights Museum** is housed at the site of Martin Luther King, Jr.'s assassination in the **Lorraine Motel** at Calhoun St. Historical documents, graphic photographs of lynching victims, and films chronicle the struggles of the Civil Rights Movement. *(450 Mulberry St.* ☎*521-9699. Open M-Sa 9am-6pm, Su 1-6pm; Sept.-May 9am-5pm, Su 1-5pm; $8.50, students with ID and seniors $7.50, ages 4-17 $6.50.)* The four seamlessly connected buildings of the **Brooks Museum of Art,** in the southwest corner of Overton Park east of downtown, showcase artwork as diverse as its architecture. *(1934 Poplar Ave.* ☎*544-6200. Open Tu-F 10am-4pm, first W of each month 10am-8pm, Sa 10am-5pm, Su 11:30am-5pm. $5, seniors $4, students $2; W free. Wheelchair accessible.)* South of downtown, the **National Ornamental Metal Museum,** the only such institution in the US, displays fine metalwork from contemporary artists. In the back is a working blacksmith shop and a sculpture garden with a view of the river. *(374 Metal Museum Dr., Exit 12C from I-55.* ☎*774-6380. Open Tu-Sa 10am-5pm, Su noon-5pm. $4, seniors $3, students $2.)*

The **Pink Palace Museum and Planetarium** is a fascinatingly strange conglomeration of exhibits ranging from a shrunken head (with recipe) to local history to a room-sized clockwork circus in miniature, as well as the obligatory IMAX theater. The museum also includes a walk-through replica of the world's first self-service grocery store, a Memphis Piggly-Wiggly complete with shelves stocked with vintage 1916 dry and canned goods. The museum itself is a pink marble mansion originally built to house Piggly-Wiggly founder Clarence Saunders, who relinquished the house after losing his fortune on Wall Street. *(3050 Central Ave.* ☎*320-6362. Open M-Th 9am-4pm, F-Sa 9am-9pm, Su noon-6pm. $7, seniors $6.50, ages 3-12 $4.50; IMAX film $6.50/ $6/$5; planetarium show $3.50/$3/$3. Package deals available. Wheelchair accessible.)*

THE SOUTH

AQUAMMODATIONS William Faulkner once said of Memphis that "the Delta meets in the lobby of the **Peabody Hotel.**" Every day at 11am and 5pm, the hotel rolls out the red carpet, and the ducks that live in their own luxury suites on the top floor ride down the elevator, with the help of a personal attendant, and waddle about the premises to John Phillip Sousa's *Stars and Stripes Forever* or *King Cotton March. (149 Union Ave, in downtown.* ☎ *529-4000.)*

HISTORIC MEMPHIS. Memphis is home to a few tastefully ornate houses. **Victorian Village** is a cluster of 19th-century houses around the intersection of Orleans St. and Adams Ave., all in various stages of restoration. Two of these are open for visitation: **Mallory-Neeley House** and **Woodruff-Fontaine House.** *(Village open M-Sa 10am-4pm, Su 1-4pm, with the last tours leaving at 3:30pm. Mallory Neeley: 652 Adams Ave.* ☎ *523-1484. Closed M and Jan.-Feb. Woodruff-Fontaine: 680 Adams Ave.* ☎ *526-1469. Closed Tu. Each house $5, seniors $4, students $3.50. Joint admission to both houses: $9/$7.50/$5.50. Limited wheelchair access.)* **A. Schwab,** a small family-run department store (ca. 1876), still offers old-fashioned bargains. The mezzanine houses a "museum" of never-sold relics, including an array of voodoo potions. Elvis bought some of his ensembles here. *(163 Beale St.* ☎ *523-9782. Open M-Sa 9am-5pm. Free tours upon request.)*

PARKS AND GARDENS. Memphis has almost as many parks as museums, each offering a slightly different natural setting. Brilliant wildflowers and a marvelous Heinz of roses (57 varieties) bloom and grow forever at the **Memphis Botanical Garden.** *(750 Cherry Rd. in Audubon Park off Park Ave.* ☎ *685-1566. Open M-Sa 9am-6pm, Su 11am-6pm; Nov.-Feb. M-Sa 9am-4:30pm, Su 11am-4:30pm. $4, students and seniors $3, ages 6-17 $2. Free every Tu after noon.)* Across the street, the **Dixon Galleries and Garden** flaunts its manicured landscape and a collection of European art which includes works by Renoir, Degas, and Monet. *(4339 Park Ave.* ☎ *761-2409. Open Tu-Sa 10am-5pm, Su 1-5pm. $5, seniors $4, students free. On M, only the gardens are open; admission is half-price. Seniors free on Tu.)* **Lichterman Nature Center** in East Memphis is a 65-acre wildscape with forests, wildlife, 3 mi. of trails, and a picnic area. *(5992 Quince Rd.; entrance at 1680 Lynnfield Rd.* ☎ *767-7322. Open M-Th 9am-4pm, F-Sa 9am-5pm, Su noon-5pm; last tickets are sold 1 hr. before closing. $6, seniors $5.50, ages 3-12 $4.50; free Tu 1pm-4pm.)*

♫ ARE YOU LONESOME TONIGHT?

BEALE ST. BLUES
W.C. Handy's 1917 "Beale St. Blues" claims that "You'll find that business never closes 'til somebody gets killed." Beale has changed a lot since Handy's day; today's visitors are more likely to encounter the Hard Rock Cafe and all the mega-commercialism that comes with it. But despite all the change, the strip between 2nd and 4th St. is still the place most visitors come for live music, and few clubs have set closing times. On Friday nights, a $10 wristband lets you wander in and out of any club on the strip. You can save a few bucks by buying a drink at one of the many outdoor stands and soaking up the blues and acrobatics of street performers as you meander from show to show. Hot blues joints wax and wane with the moon; ask the folks at the **Center for Southern Folklore** (see p. 357), who are veritable archives of local info. The free *Memphis Flyer* and the "Playbook" section of the Friday morning *Memphis Commercial Appeal* can also tell you what's goin' down in town.

B.B. King's Blues Club, 143 Beale St. (☎ 524-5464 or 800-443-0972). The club's namesake still makes appearances. Happily mixes young and old, tourist and native, and the occasional celebrity. Wash down entrees ($7-18) with a $3.25 beer. Cover $3-$7; when B.B. himself plays, $35-100. Open M-F 4:30pm-1am, Sa-Su 11am-12:30am.

Elvis Presley's Memphis, 126 Beale St. (☎ 527-6900), Graceland-sponsored. Serves Elvis grub such as fried peanut butter and banana sandwiches ($5.75). Open Su-Th 11am-midnight, F-Sa 11am-1am. Shows begin 8:30-9:30pm. Su gospel brunch.

This is It!, 167 Beale St. (☎527-8200). A much smaller club than either of the big names, This is It! is about as close as it's going to get to the old Beale atmosphere. Cover Th-Sa $5. Open M-Tu 5pm-1am, W-Th 5pm-2am, F-Sa 5pm-4am, Su 7pm-1am. Shows generally at 8:30pm.

Rum Boogie Cafe, 182 Beale St. (☎528-0150). Friendly, relaxed atmosphere and honest homegrown blues with a touristy crowd. Check out the celebrity guitars hanging from the ceiling and the original Stax records sign. Music at 9:30pm. Open Su-Th 8:30am-12:20am, F-Sa 9:30am-1:30am.

NIGHTLIFE OFF BEALE ST

For a more off-the-beaten-track club, try **Wild Bill's,** 1580 Vollintine Rd., which capitalizes on the juke joint/hole-in-the-wall tradition. (☎726-5473. Live music F-Su; it's best to arrive after 11pm. Cover $5 F-Su. Open M-Th 7am-11pm, F-Su 7am 'til late.) The hot gay spot, **J-Wag's Lounge,** 1268 Madison, served as the bar in *The People vs. Larry Flynt.* (☎725-1909. DJ music F-Sa. Open 24hr.) For a collegiate atmosphere, try the **Highland St.** strip near **Memphis State University,** with hopping bars like **Newby's,** 539 S. Highland St. (☎452-8408. Happy hour 4-7pm. Live music W-Sa around 10:30pm. Cover $3-10. Open daily 3pm-3am.)

ENTERTAINMENT

The majestic **Orpheum Theater,** 203 S. Main St., shows classic movies in the summer at 7:15pm on Friday along with an organ prelude and a cartoon. The grand old theater, with 15 ft. high chandeliers, has occasional live music and Broadway shows. (☎525-3000. Box office open M-F 9am-5pm and sometimes before shows. Movies $6, students and seniors $5. Music and shows $15-45.) **Memphis in May** (☎525-4611) celebrates through the month with concerts, art exhibits, food contests, and sporting events. The **Memphis Redbirds,** swing their AAA bats in Autozone Park downtown. (☎721-6000. Tickets $5-15; discounts for seniors, military, and under 14.)

▶ DAYTRIPS FROM MEMPHIS

SHILOH NATIONAL MILITARY PARK

On the morning of Apr. 6, 1862, Confederate troops, under the command of General A.S. Johnston, surprised General Grant's army of Tennessee, which was camped in the woods and fields around Shiloh. The next two days witnessed the largest artillery concentration seen in North America to that date. The park's Visitors Center gives a pamphlet to the 9½ mi. automobile path and shows a 25min. video every 30min. From Memphis, take U.S. 64 E 100 mi. to U.S. 45 S and follow the signs. (☎901-689-5275. Park open during daylight hrs.; Visitors Center open daily 8am-5pm. $2, under 16 free, family $4.)

THE MISSISSIPPI DELTA

South of Memphis, U.S. 61 runs to Vicksburg through the swamps and flatlands of the Mississippi Delta region, where cotton was king and the blues were born. Times are still hard in **Clarksdale, MS,** 70 mi. south of Memphis, where some of the most famous musicians were born and are now glorified at festivals and in museums. The **Delta Blues Museum,** 1 Blues Alley, displays photographs and rare artifacts, including one of B.B. King's guitars and a guitar created by the artists of ZZ Top out of the late Muddy Waters' cabin wood. (☎662-627-6820. Open M-F 9am-5pm. $6.) Twenty miles north on U.S. 49, across the river in Arkansas, lies **Helena.** The legendary King Biscuit Time radio show was first broadcast here in 1941, featuring live music from Sonny Boy Williamson. The first weekend of October, the town hosts the **King Biscuit Blues Festival,** the largest free blues festival in the South. The **Delta Cultural Center,** 141 Cherry St., displays exhibits on the rich land and poor people that figure so prominently in regional culture. (☎870-338-4350 or 800-358-0972. Open M-Sa 10am-5pm, Su 1-5pm. Free.)

NORTH CAROLINA

North Carolina can be split neatly into three regions: down-to-earth mountain culture in the west, mellow sophistication in the Research Triangle of the central piedmont, and beach culture in the east. Largely untouched by development, the natural beauty of the "Old North State" continues to be one of its greatest assets. Visitors in a hurry—definitely out of pace with most of the state—should stick to the scenery at the extremes of the state, in the Appalachian Mountains and the Outer Banks.

▰ PRACTICAL INFORMATION

Capital: Raleigh.
Visitor info: Dept. of Commerce, Travel and Tourism, 301 N. Wilmington St., Raleigh 27601-2825 (☎919-733-4171 or 800-847-4862; www.visitnc.com). **Dept. of Natural Resources and Community Development,** Division of Parks and Recreation, 1615 Mail Service Ctr., Raleigh 27699 (☎919-733-4181).
Postal Abbreviation: NC. **Sales Tax:** 6%.

THE RESEARCH TRIANGLE   ☎919

Large universities and their students dominate "the Triangle," a regional identity born in the 50s with the creation of a spectacularly successful Research Triangle Park, where Nobel Prize-winning scientists toil for dozens of high-tech and biotech firms. **Raleigh,** the state capital and home to North Carolina State University (NC State), is a historic town that has recently renovated its tourist attractions. **Durham,** formerly a major tobacco producer, now supports multiple hospitals and medical research projects devoted to finding cancer cures. It's also purported to be one of the country's more gay-friendly cities. The University of North Carolina (UNC), chartered in 1789 as the nation's first state university, is located just 20 miles down the road in **Chapel Hill.** College culture predominates here—nearly every other store specializes in UNC t-shirts—and the music scene thrives.

▐ TRANSPORTATION

Airport: Raleigh-Durham International (☎840-2123; www.rdu.com), 10 mi. from both downtown Raleigh and Durham, located on U.S. 70. A taxi to downtown Raleigh or Durham costs about $27.
Trains: Amtrak, 320 W. Cabarrus St., Raleigh, 4 blocks west of the Civic Ctr. (☎833-7594). To Washington, D.C. (6hr., 2 per day, $43-78) and Richmond (3½hr., 2 per day, $28-50). Open 24hr.
Buses: Greyhound has a station in both Raleigh and Durham. **Raleigh:** 314 W. Jones St. (☎834-8275). To: Durham (40min., 9 per day, $6.50); Chapel Hill (80min., 4 per day, $10); and Charleston, SC (7½hr., 2 per day, $59). Open 24hr. **Durham:** 820 W. Morgan St., 1 block off Chapel Hill St. downtown, 2½ mi. northeast of Duke (☎687-4800). To Chapel Hill (25min., 4 per day, $8) and Washington, D.C. (6hr., 6 per day, $50). Open daily 7:30am-9:30pm. The **Chapel Hill** bus station is no longer open, but Triangle-area buses still pick up and drop off passengers in front of the old building at the corner of Franklin St. and Columbia St. Tickets must be bought at the next station on the route.
Public Transit: Capital Area Transit, Raleigh (☎828-7228). Buses run M-Sa. Fare 75¢; transfers free. **Durham Area Transit Authority (DATA),** Durham (☎683-3282). Most routes start downtown at Main and Morgan St. on the loop. Operates daily; hours vary by route; fewer on Su. Fare 75¢; seniors, under 18, and disabled 35¢; transfers free; children under 43 in. free. **Chapel Hill Transit,** Chapel Hill (☎968-2769). Buses run 5:40pm-8pm. Office open M-F 4:45am-10pm. Fare 75¢. There is also a free shuttle on the UNC campus.
Taxis: Cardinal Cab, ☎828-3228.

PRACTICAL INFORMATION

Visitor info: Raleigh Visitors Center, 301 N. Blount St. (☎733-3456). Open M-F 8am-5pm, Sa 10am-5pm, Su 1-5pm. **Durham Convention Center and Visitors Bureau,** 101 E. Morgan St. (☎800-446-8604). Open M-F 8:30am-5pm, Sa 10am-2pm. **Visitor info Center and Chapel Hill Chamber of Commerce,** 104 S. Estes Dr. (☎967-7075). Open M-F 9am-5pm.

Hotline: Rape Crisis, ☎919-403-6562. 24hr.

Post Office: Raleigh: 311 New Bern Ave. (☎828-5902). Open M-F 8am-5:30pm, Sa 8am-noon. **ZIP code:** 27611. **Durham:** 323 E. Chapel Hill St. (☎683-1976). Open M-F 8:30am-5pm. **ZIP code:** 27701. **Chapel Hill:** 125 S. Estes St. (☎967-6297). Open M-F 8:30am-5:30pm, Sa 8:30am-noon. **ZIP code:** 27514.

Area code: 919.

ACCOMMODATIONS

Raleigh's budget lodging can be found on Capital Blvd., about 2½ mi. northeast of town, a mile or so inside the 440 beltline. Perhaps the best bargain in the Triangle, the **Carolina-Duke Motor Inn,** Guess Rd. exit off I-85, provides travelers with a clean, budget-priced rooms, laundry facilities, and a shuttle to both the Duke and V.A. hospitals. (☎286-0771 or 800-438-1158 for reservations. Pool, A/C, cable TV, free local calls, and continental breakfast included. DATA access across the street. Singles $40; doubles $48; each additional person $3. 10% AARP/AAA discount. Wheelchair accessible.) In Raleigh, a pleasing option is the **Regency Inn,** 300 N. Dawson St., at Lane St. (☎828-9081; fax 821-0654. A/C, cable TV, and coffee. Singles $44; doubles $48.) Reasonably priced accommodations are slightly harder to come by in Chapel Hill; the **Red Roof Inn,** 5623 Chapel Hill Blvd. at the intersection of U.S. 15-501 and I-40, offers standard rooms. (☎489-9421; fax 489-8001. A/C, disabled access, free local calls, and cable TV. Singles $47-53; doubles $54-59; $4 each additional person.) Area camping is best at **Falls Lake State Recreation Area,** about 12 mi. north of Raleigh, off Rte. 98. (☎676-1027. Reservations taken with 7-14 days notice if you are staying more than 7 days. Open year-round. $12, with hookup $17.)

FOOD

Each of the area's major universities has spawned a region of affordable and interesting eateries nearby; Raleigh's **Hillsborough St.,** Durham's **9th St.,** and Chapel Hill's **Franklin St.** all cater to a college (and thus budget-oriented) crowd, with the Franklin St. area offering the most variety. ■**Skylight Exchange,** 405½ W. Rosemary St. (the entrance is in an alley off of Rosemary), a block over from Franklin, doubles as a cafe and used book/music store. The Exchange is home to a vast array of sandwiches ($3-8) and, most importantly, the legendary 50¢ cup of coffee. (☎933-5550. Live music M-Sa 9pm. Open daily 11am-11pm.) The ■**Ramshead Rathskellar,** 157½ E. Franklin St., has been a local legend since 1948. The uniquely decorated interior of "the Rat" has seen more than 50 years of Tarheels come and go. (☎942-5158. Open M-W 11am-2:30pm and 5-9pm, Th 11am-2:30pm and 5-9:30pm, F 11am-2:30pm and 5-10pm, Sa 11:30am-10:30pm, Su 11:30am-9pm. Sandwiches under $8, meals $6-17.) In Raleigh, **Big Ed's,** 220 Wolfe St. in City Market, entices costumers with award-winning homestyle fare such as biscuits and country-cooked meats and vegetables. (☎836-9909. Open M-F 7am-2pm, Sa 7am-noon. Filling platters around $6.) In Durham, **Elmo's Diner,** 776 and 9th St., serves breakfast all day for about $5. (☎416-3823. Open Su-Th 6:30am-10pm, F-Sa 6:30am-11pm.)

THE SOUTH

⊙ SIGHTS

RALEIGH. Raleigh has grown rapidly in recent years—to the extent that it now needs a bypass to bypass its old bypass—but its downtown area still retains much of the character of an old North Carolina town, with added gleaming tourist attractions. Across from the capitol building are the **North Carolina Museum of History** and the **Museum of Natural Sciences** which features "Willo, the dinosaur with a heart," a rare dinosaur fossil with an iron concretion within the ribcage. *(Museum of History: 5 E. Edenton St. ☎ 715-0200. Open Tu-Sa 9am-5pm, Su noon-5pm. Free. Museum of Natural Sciences: 11 W. Jones St. ☎ 733-7450. Open M-Sa 9am-5pm, Su noon-5pm. Free.)* The area around **Moore Square,** a few blocks southeast of the capitol, is a small district of youthful artsiness. Adjacent to the Square is **City Market,** a collection of shops, cafes, and bars.

CHAPEL HILL. Chapel Hill and neighboring Carrboro are virtually inseparable from the **University of North Carolina at Chapel Hill.** The university's **Smith Center** hosts sporting events and concerts. Until 1975, NASA astronauts trained at UNC's **Morehead Planetarium,** which now projects several different shows per year and houses a small museum. *(250 E. Franklin St. ☎ 549-6863. Open M-Sa 10am-5pm and 7-9:45pm, Su 12:30-5pm and 7-9:45pm. $4.50, students, seniors, and children $3.50. Exhibits free.)*

DURHAM. Durham's main attractions center around the Duke family and their principle legacy, **Duke University,** which is split up into East and West Campuses. The neo-gothic **Duke Chapel,** completed in the early 30s, looms grandly at the center of West Campus. Over a million pieces of stained glass and a host of statues depicting both Christian and Southern figures grace the chapel. *(☎ 684-2572. Open daily Sept.-May 8am-10pm; June-Aug. 8am-8pm. Free; self-guided tour available.)* Nearby on Anderson St. the 55-acre **Sarah P. Duke Gardens** showcase both native and non-native plants in a lush, shaded setting complete with ponds and a vine-draped gazebo. *(☎ 684-3698. Open daily 8am-dusk. Free.)* At the other end of Durham, the **Duke Homestead and Tobacco Museum,** details, you guessed it, the history of both the Duke family and the tobacco industry. This funky-smelling museum provides a rare opportunity to watch old TV ads for cigarettes as well as to learn everything you ever wanted to know about tobacco farming. *(2828 Duke Homestead Rd., off Guess Rd. ☎ 477-5498. Open Apr.-Oct. M-Sa 9am-5pm, Su 1-5pm; Nov.-Mar. Tu-Sa 10am-4pm, Su 1-4pm. Free. Call to schedule Homestead tours.)* The 1988 movie *Bull Durham* was filmed in the **Durham Bulls'** ballpark. The AAA farm team for the Tampa Bay Devil Rays still plays here, minus Kevin Costner. *(☎ 687-6500. Check www.durhambulls.com for more info.)*

♫ 📺 ENTERTAINMENT AND NIGHTLIFE

Pick up a free copy of the *Spectator* and *Independent* weekly magazines, available at most restaurants, bookstores, and hotels, for listings of Triangle news and events. Chapel Hill offers the best nightlife, especially in terms of music. A number of live music clubs congregate near the western end of Franklin St., where it becomes Main St. in the neighboring town of Carrboro. **Cat's Cradle,** 300 E. Main St. in Carrboro, is the area's main venue, hosting a wide variety of local and national acts. Recent performers range from Kool Keith to L7. *(☎ 967-9053. Show times vary widely. Cover usually around $10.)* Another nearby club focusing on indie and rock 'n' roll is **Local 506,** 506 W. Franklin St. *(☎ 942-5506. 21+. Cover around $5.)* **Gotham,** 306 W. Franklin St., #H facing Rosemary St., offers more of a dance club environment. Ads boast that Gotham offers "the hottest gay and lesbian Friday night in the triangle." *(☎ 967-2852. Call for hours.)* Nightlife in Raleigh and Durham is harder to come by. **ComedySportz,** 204 Wolfe St. in Raleigh's City Market, turns stand-up into a sporting event: the home team, the Hillsborough Malamutes, takes on all comers. *(☎ 829-0822. F 8:30pm, Sa 7:30 and 9:45pm. Sa matinee 4:45pm. $10.)*

CHARLOTTE ☎704

The third-largest banking center in the nation and the largest city of the Carolinas, Charlotte seems unhaunted by any legacy of its past. The gleaming "uptown" region bustles with well-funded charm and vigor, attracting visitors with its top-notch science museum, ritzy clubs and bars, and successful sports teams. But beneath the veneer, patches of the past can still be found. Off Stonewall St., near the edges of Charlotte's city center, a set of concrete steps can be seen under the I-277 overpass. They don't lead anywhere; before the predominantly black neighborhood of Brooklyn was bulldozed in the 60s, they would have been the front steps of a small house. Now they stand, in comparison to the polish of uptown Charlotte, as a somewhat eerie reminder of that which can be forgotten in the process of "urban renewal."

⚐ PRACTICAL INFORMATION. Amtrak, 1914 N. Tryon St. (☎376-4416) and **Greyhound,** 601 W. Trade St. (☎372-0456) stop in Charlotte. Both stations are open 24hr. **Charlotte Transit,** 901 N. Davidson St., operates local buses. (☎336-3366. Fare $1, $1.40 for outlying areas; free transfers.) Within the uptown area, **Center City Circuit** runs free shuttles; call 332-2227 for info. **Info Charlotte,** 330 S. Tryon St., offers free parking off 2nd St. (☎331-2720 or 800-722-1994; open M-F 8:30am-5pm, Sa 10am-4pm, Su 1-4pm). **Hotlines: Rape Crisis,** ☎375-9900. **Suicide,** ☎358-2800. **Gay/Lesbian Switchboard,** ☎535-6277. Operates Su-Th 6:30-10pm. **Post Office:** 201 N. McDowell (☎333-5135; open M-F 7:30am-6pm, Sa 9am-1pm). **ZIP code:** 28204. **Area code:** 704.

⚏⚐ ACCOMMODATIONS AND FOOD. There are several clusters of budget motels in the Charlotte area: off I-85 at Sugar Creek Rd., Exit 41; off I-85 at Exit 33 near the airport; and off I-77 at Clanton St., Exit 7. The **Continental Inn,** 1100 W. Sugar Creek Rd., has immaculate, inviting rooms. (☎597-8100. A/C, cable. Singles $36, doubles $40; weekends $40/$45.) **Motel 6,** 3430 St Vardell Ln., Exit 7 on I-77, has clean, standard rooms and a convenient location. (☎527-0144 or 800-466-8356. Cable, A/C, laundry, pool, and free local calls. Singles $35, $40 on the weekend. $6 each additional person.)

Two areas outside of uptown offer attractive dining options. North Davidson ("NoDa"), around 36th St., is home to a small artistic community inhabiting a set of historic buildings. South from city center, the **Dilworth** neighborhood, along East and South Blvds., is lined with restaurants serving everything from ethnic cuisine to pizza and pub fare. Tally ho veggie lovers! Organic health food is the name of the game at **Talley's Green Grocery and Cafe,** 1408-C East Blvd., an upscale grocery with a deli counter offering sandwiches for under $6. (☎334-9200. Open M-Sa 7:30am-9pm, Su 10am-7pm.) East of downtown, the colorful **Antony's Caribbean Cafe,** 2001 E. 7th St., spices up life with cheerful decor and delicious food. (☎342-0749. Call for hrs.) The sign outside of **Bill Spoon's Barbecue,** 5524 South Blvd., reads "We cook the whole pig. It makes the difference." It does. Serving east Carolina-style BBQ, this place supplies the hungry traveler with a pork sandwich for only $3.20. (☎525-8865. Open M-F 10:30am-3pm.) The **Charlotte Regional Farmers Market,** 1801 Yorkmont Rd., behind the Coliseum, hawks local produce, baked goods, and crafts year-round. (☎357-1269. Open Tu-Sa 8am-6pm, May- Aug. additional Su hrs. 12:30-6pm.)

◻ SIGHTS. Most of Charlotte's museums are clustered around the intersection of Tryon St. and Trade St. at the very center of the city. The largest and most publicized of these is **The Discovery Place,** 301 N. Tryon St., a hands-on science museum that draws crowds with its OmniMax theater, flight simulator, and planetarium. (☎372-6261 or 800-935-0553. Open M-Sa 9am-6pm, Su 1-6pm; during the off season the museum closes at 5pm. One attraction $7.50, seniors $6.50, ages 6-12 $6, ages 3-5 $5. Theater and museum $12/$11/$10/$8.) The excellently curated **Mint Museum of Craft and Design,** 220 N. Tryon St., features an eclectic array of exhibits, from furniture to pottery to technology. Admission also pays for the **Mint Museum of Art,** 2730

THE SOUTH

Randolph Rd., across town, which displays American decorative and visual arts. (Both museums: ☎337-2000. Open Tu-Sa 10am-5pm, Su noon-5pm; art museum also open 10am-10pm on Tu. $6, students and seniors $5, ages 6-17 $3.) Look for the **Museum of the New South,** exploring post-Reconstruction Charlotte and the Carolina Piedmont area, scheduled to reopen fall 2001 at College St. and 7th St. (☎333-1887).

🎭🎵 **ENTERTAINMENT AND NIGHTLIFE.** Charlotte is a big sports town. Basketball's **Hornets** (men) and **Sting** (women) play in the **Coliseum** (☎357-4700), and the National Football League's **Panthers** play in Ericsson Stadium (☎358-7538). The Charlotte **Knights** play AAA minor league baseball at Knights Castle, off I-77 S at Exit 88 in South Carolina. (☎364-6637. Tickets $5, seniors and children $3.50.)

For nightlife, arts, and entertainment listings, grab a free *Creative Loafing* in one of Charlotte's shops or restaurants or check the E&T section in the F *Charlotte Observer*. **Amos' Southend,** 1423 S. Tryon St., beckons with live music every night and pool and foosball tables. (☎377-6874. Cover $5-12. Open daily 9pm-2am.)

CAROLINA MOUNTAINS

The sharp ridges and rolling slopes of the southern Appalachian range create some of the most spectacular scenery in the Southeast. Amid this beauty flourishes a melange of diverse personalities, from scholars to ski bums to farmers to artists. The aptly named High Country includes the territory between Boone and Asheville, 100 mi. to the southwest, and fills the upper regions of the Blue Ridge Mountains. The central attraction of the mountains is the Blue Ridge Parkway (see p. 323), a national parkway that snakes through the mountains from northern Virginia to southern North Carolina. Views from many of the Parkway's scenic stops are simply staggering, particularly on rainy days when the peaks are wreathed in mist. Southwards is the Great Smoky Mountains National Park (see p. 348).

BOONE ☎828

Named for frontiersman Daniel Boone, Boone is nestled among the breathtaking mountains of the High Country. The small town lives on year-round, populated by summer tourists, winter skiers, locals, and the students of Appalachian State University (ASU). **Horn in the West,** in an open-air amphitheater located near Boone off Rte. 105, dramatizes the part of the American Revolution fought in the southern Appalachians. (☎264-2120. Shows June-Aug. Tu-Su 8pm. $12, under 12 $6; group rates upon request; AAA and senior discount $1. Reservations recommended.) In July, the festival **An Appalachian Summer** brings to town high-caliber music, art, theater, and dance sponsored by ASU. (☎800-841-2787. $12-24 for individual shows.)

Downhill skiers enjoy the Southeast's largest concentration of alpine resorts: **Appalachian Ski Mountain,** off Rte. 221/321 (☎800-322-2373; lift tickets $23, Sa-Su $35); **Ski Beech,** 1007 Beech Mt. Pkwy., off Rte. 184 in Banner Elk (☎800-438-2093; lift tickets $28/$45); **Ski Hawksnest,** 2058 Skyland Dr., in the town of Seven Devils (☎888-429-5763; lift tickets $22/$39); and **Sugar Mountain,** in Banner Elk off Rte. 184 (☎898-4521; lift tickets $30/$47). Lift prices are approximate, it's best to call ahead to the resort for latest specific ski package prices. **Boone AppalCart** (see below) runs a free winter shuttle to Sugar Mountain. Call 800-962-2322 for **daily ski reports.**

The 5 mi. road to **Grandfather Mountain,** off Rte. 221, near the intersection of Rte. 221 and the Parkway, provides an unparalleled view of the entire High Country area. (☎800-468-7325. Mountain open daily 8am-7pm, no entrance after 6pm; Nov.-Mar. 8am-5pm with no entry after 4pm, weather permitting.) At the top, a private park features a 1 mi. high suspension bridge, a museum, and a small zoo ($12, seniors $11, ages 4-12 $6, under 4 free). Hiking or camping on Grandfather Mt. requires a **permit** ($5), available at the park entrance or at several area stores including **Mast General Store,** 630 W. King St. in downtown Boone. (☎262-0000. Open M-Sa 10am-6pm, Su 1pm-6pm.) Nearby **Blowing Rock,** 7 mi. south of Boone on Rte. 321, delights travelers with its unusual air currents. (☎828-295-7111. Open Apr.-Dec. daily 8:30am-7pm; Jan.-Feb. Sa-Su as weather permits. $4, ages 6-11 $1.)

Catering primarily to vacationing families, Boone fronts more than its share of expensive motels and B&Bs. Scratch the surface, though, and you'll find inexpensive rooms and campsites. The **Boone Trail Motel,** 275 E. King St./U.S. 421, just south of downtown, is close to all the action and features clean, if not particularly luxurious rooms. (☎264-8839. Singles Apr.-July $30-40; doubles $30-60. In winter, rooms as low as $21/$25.) Along the Pkwy. near Boone, spectacular tent and RV sites without hookups ($12) are available at the **Julian Price Campground,** Mi. 297 (☎963-5911. Open May-Oct.; sites around Loop A are on a lake.) Hungry travelers should visit **Our Daily Bread,** 627 West King St., for delightful sandwiches, salads, and $3-7 vegetarian specials. (☎264-0173. Open M-F 8am-6pm, Sa 11am-5pm, Su noon-5pm.)

The **Boone AppalCart,** 274 Winklers Creek Rd., provides local bus service. (☎264-2278. Red: M-F 7:30am-11pm, Sa 8:30am-5pm. Green: M-F 7am-11pm, Sa 9am-5pm. Blue: M-F 7:30am-6pm. Fare 50¢; those wanting to make a transfer should notify the driver when they board.) The **North Carolina High Country Host Visitors Center,** 1700 Blowing Rock Rd., has info. (☎264-1299 or 800-438-7500. Open M-Sa 9am-5pm, Su 9am-3pm.) Hikers should invest in the invaluable, large-scale map *100 Favorite Trails* ($3.50), available at book stores. **Post Office:** 1544 Blowing Rock Rd. (☎264-3813.; open M-F 8:30am-5pm, Sa 8:30am-noon). **ZIP code:** 28607. **Area code:** 828.

ASHEVILLE ☎828

Hazy blue mountains, deep valleys, and spectacular waterfalls all supply a splendid backdrop to this tiny town. Once a coveted layover for the nation's well-to-do, Asheville housed enough Carnegies, Vanderbilts, and Mellons to fill a 1920s edition of *Who's Who on the Atlantic Seaboard.* Monuments such as the Biltmore Estate reflect the rich history of the town's gilded citizenry. The population these days tends more toward dreadlocks, batik, and vegetarianism, providing funky nightlife and festivals all year. In contrast to the laid-back locals, Asheville's sights are fanatically maintained and its downtown meticulously preserved, making for a pleasant respite from the Carolina wilderness.

▌ PRACTICAL INFORMATION. Greyhound, 2 Tunnel Rd. (☎253-8451; open daily 8am-9pm), 2 mi. east of downtown, near the Beaucatcher Tunnel, sends buses to Charlotte (2½-5hr.; 5 per day; M-Th $26, F-Su $28); Knoxville (2hr., 5 per day, $25-27); Atlanta (6¾hr., 1 per day, $32-34); and Raleigh (8-12hr., 5 per day, $49-52). The **Asheville Transit System,** 360 W. Haywood St. (☎253-5691), handles bus service within city limits. Pick up a copy of bus schedules and routes from the Visitors Center or visit the **Asheville Transit Center,** 49 Coxe Ave. across from the Post Office, to wait for transfers or ask questions. (Fare 75¢, transfers 10¢, short trips in downtown free. Discounts for seniors, disabled, and multi-fare tickets.) For Visitor info, check the **Chamber of Commerce,** 151 Haywood St., Exit 4C off I-240, on the northwest end of downtown. (☎800-257-1300; www.ashevillechamber.org. Open M-F 8:30am-5:30pm, Sa-Su 9am-5pm.) **Post Office:** 33 Coxe Ave., off Patton Ave. (☎271-6420; open M-F 7:30am-5:30pm, Sa 9am-1pm). **ZIP code:** 28802. **Area code:** 828.

▐ ACCOMMODATIONS. The cheapest lodgings are on **Tunnel Rd.,** east of downtown, while slightly more expensive (and fewer) options can be found on **Merrimon Ave.,** just north of downtown. The ritziest of the budget circle hover around the Biltmore Estate on **Hendersonville Ave.,** south of downtown. The **Log Cabin Motor Court,** 330 Weaverville Hwy., 10min. north of downtown, this motel provides immaculate, inviting cabins with cable TV, and laundry; some have fireplaces and kitchenettes, though none have A/C. (☎645-6546. Singles from $32; doubles from $53; each additional person $5.) The **In Town Motor Lodge,** 100 Tunnel Rd., offers spacious rooms just minutes from downtown for great prices. All rooms have A/C, cable TV, and pool; ask for one with a balcony. (☎252-1811. Singles Su-Th $32, F-Sa $44; doubles $36/$48.) **Powhatan,** on Wesley Branch Rd. 12 mi. southwest of Asheville off Rte. 191, is the closest campsite in the Pisgah National Forest. Wooded sites on a 10-acre trout lake provide opportunities for fishing, swimming, and hiking. (☎670-5627. Open Apr.-Oct. 31. Gates close 11pm. $14, no hookups.) **Bear Creek RV Park and Campground,** 81 S. Bear Creek Rd., features "luxury" camping with a pool, laundry facilities, groceries, and a game room. Follow signs from I-40 Exit 47. (☎800-833-0798. Sites $20, with water and electricity $22; RV sites with hookup $26-31.)

🍴🎭 **FOOD AND ENTERTAINMENT.** You'll find the greasy links of most fast-food chains on **Tunnel Rd.** and **Biltmore Ave.** The **Western North Carolina Farmers Market,** at the intersection of I-40 and Rte. 191, sells fresh produce and crafts. (☎253-1691. Open Apr.-Oct. daily 8am-6pm; Nov.-Mar. 8am-5pm.) The **Laughing Seed Cafe,** 40 Wall St., behind Patton Ave., caters to your vegetarian and vegan fantasies with sumptuous dishes and reasonable prices. Sunday brunch draws a bustling crowd—and never disappoints. (☎252-3445. Open M and W-Th 11:30am-9pm, F-Sa 11:30am-10pm, Su 10am-9pm. Salads $2.50-8 and sandwiches $4-7.) For an atmosphere with a bit more attitude hit **Beanstreets,** 3 Broadway St., for a cup of coffee or sandwiches and omelettes for under $5.50. (☎255-8180. Open M-W 7:30am-6pm, Th-F 7:30am-midnight, Sa 7am-midnight, and Su 9am-4pm.)

For a small town, Asheville really grooves. The downtown area, especially the southeast end around the intersection of Broadway and College St., offers music, munchies, and movies. Those in search of something a little more, well, European can find it at 🏛**Old Europe,** 18 Battery Park Ave., near Wall St., which doubles as a dessert shop and bar. Pastries are handmade by the Hungarian owners. (☎252-0001. Cookies under $1, pastries under $4; beer $3.) Every Sunday night from June to September **The New Ebony Bar & Grill,** 19 Eagle St., takes the party to the streets, closing Eagle St. to traffic in order to accommodate rollicking live music, dancing, and rows of folding chairs. (☎645-0305. Open nightly 5pm-late.) Indie and artsy flicks play at the **Fine Arts Theater,** 36 Biltmore Ave. (☎252-1537. $6.50, matinees and seniors $5.) A popular bar, **Barley's Taproom,** 42 Biltmore Ave., hops with locals, $3 beers from 42 taps, and pool tables upstairs. (☎255-0504. Live music Tu, Th, and Su. Open M-Sa 11:30am-2am, Su noon-midnight.)

Summer shouldn't be anyone's season of discontent, not with free **Shakespeare in Montford Park.** (☎254-4540. Performances June-Aug. F and Su 7:30pm at Hazel Robinson Amphitheater.) During the last weekend in July, put your feet on the street along with thousands of others at North Carolina's largest free street fair, **Bele Chere Festival** (☎259-5800). The free weekly paper, *Mountain Express,* and *Community Connections,* a free gay publication, feature entertainment listings.

🔲 **SIGHTS.** George Vanderbilt's palatial **Biltmore Estate,** 1 North Pack Sq., 3 blocks north of I-40 Exit 50, was built in the 1890s. Modeled on the chateaux of the Loire valley, the Biltmore is the largest private home in America. A tour can take all day; try to arrive early. Tours of the surrounding gardens and the Biltmore winery (with wine tasting for those 21 and over) are included in the admission price. (☎274-6333 or 800-543-2961. Open daily 9am-5pm. $33, ages 10-15 $25, disabled $24; Nov.-Dec. $2-3 more. Winery open M-Sa 11am-7pm, Su noon-7pm.) Meanwhile, free scenery blooms at the **Botanical Gardens,** 151 Weaver Blvd., (☎252-5190) as well as the North Carolina Arboretum, Exit 2 on I-26 or Exit 47 on I-40, (☎665-2492). Both attractions are open dawn to dusk.

Four museums pack into **Pack Place** downtown: the Asheville Art Museum, the YMI Culture Center, Health Adventure, and the Colburn Gem and Mineral Museum. Tickets for all four can be purchased inside Pack Place. The **Asheville Art Museum** (☎253-3227) displays 20th-century American artwork, while the **YMI Culture Center** focuses solely on African-American art (☎252-4614). The kid-oriented **Health Adventure** lets you become one with your body (☎254-6373), and the **Colburn Gem and Mineral Museum** showcases all that glitters. (☎254-7162. $4, $3 students, seniors, and children 4-15. All 4 museums open Tu-Sa 10am-5pm; Art Museum and Health Adventure also Su 1-5pm; Gem and Mineral Museum June-Oct. Su 1-5pm. 1 museum $4; students, seniors, and ages 4-15 $3; all 4 museums $12/$9.)

The **Thomas Wolfe Memorial,** between Woodfin and Walnut St., celebrates one of the early 20th century's most influential American authors. The Visitors Center houses an exhibit on Wolfe's life and his impact other authors, and shows a compelling biographical film. The inside of the novelist's boyhood home is closed due to fire, but tours of the exterior of are available. (☎253-8304. Open Apr.-Oct. M-Sa 9am-5pm, Su 1-5pm; Nov.-Mar. Tu-Sa 10am-4pm, Su 1-4pm. Tours every hr. on the half hour. $1, students 50¢.) The scenic setting for *Last of the Mohicans* rises up almost ½ mi. in **Chimney Rock Park,** 25 mi. southeast of Asheville on Rte. 74A. After driving to the base of the Chimney, take the 26-story elevator to the top, or walk up for a 75 mi. view. (☎625-9281 or 800-277-9611. Ticket office open daily 8:30am-5:30pm; in winter 8:30am-4:30pm. Park open 1½hr. after office closes. $11, ages 6-12 $5; in winter $7/$4.)

NORTH CAROLINA COAST

Lined with barrier islands that shield inlanders from Atlantic squalls, the Carolina Coast has a history as stormy as the hurricanes that pummel its beaches. England's first attempt to colonize North America ended in 1590 with the peculiar disappearance of the Roanoke Island settlement. Later in its history, the coast earned a name as "The Graveyard of the Atlantic"—over 600 ships have foundered on the Outer Banks' southern shores. The same wind that sank ships lifted the world's first powered flight in 1903, thanks to some assistance from the Wright brothers, and now forms the basis of much of the area's recreational activity: hang-gliding, paragliding, windsurfing, and good ol' kite-flying.

OUTER BANKS   ☎252

The Outer Banks explode in the north with a burst of insistent glitz that tapers into an endearing tranquility in the south. The three contiguous towns of Kitty Hawk, Kill Devil Hills, and Nags Head are located on the northern half of Bodie Island, which, like many other well-touristed beach areas on the East Coast, is heavily trafficked and dense with stores. Crowds become less overpowering farther south on Rte. 12. Ocracoke Island, despite its growing popularity with visitors, retains the feel of a small community.

◖ ORIENTATION

The Outer Banks consist of four narrow islands strung along half the length of the North Carolina coast. **Bodie Island,** the northernmost island, is joined to the mainland by U.S. 158 and serves as most travelers' point of entry. For much of Bodie Island, Rte. 12 (known as the Beach Road) and U.S. 158 (called the Bypass) run parallel until the north edge of the **Cape Hatteras National Seashore.** After that, Rte. 12 continues south through the park to the great sandy elbow that is **Hatteras Island,** connected by a bridge to Bodie. **Ocracoke Island,** the southernmost island, is linked by ferry to Hatteras Island and towns on the mainland. Both Hatteras and Ocracoke are almost entirely park land. **Roanoke Island,** the only one of the four not on the Atlantic coast, lies between Bodie and the mainland on U.S. 64 and includes the town of **Manteo.** Directions to locations on Bodie Island are usually given in terms of distances in mi. (marked as MP for Mile Post) from the Wright Memorial Bridge. There is **no public transit** on the Outer Banks. The flat terrain makes hiking and biking pleasant, but ferocious traffic calls for extra caution and travel time.

▐ PRACTICAL INFORMATION

Ferries: Free ferries run between Hatteras and Ocracoke (40 min., daily 5am-midnight). **Toll ferries** run to Ocracoke (☎800-345-1665) from Cedar Island (☎800-856-0343; 2¼hr.), east of New Bern on Rte. 12, off U.S. 70, and from Swan Quarter (☎800-773-1094; 2½hr.), on U.S. 264. Call ahead for schedules and reservations. $1 per pedestrian, $2 per cyclist, $10 per car.

Taxis: **Beach Cab** (☎441-2500), for Bodie Island and Manteo.

Bike Rental: Pony Island Motel (☎928-4411) on Ocracoke Island. $2 per hr., $10 per day. Open daily 8am-10pm.

Visitor info: Outer Banks Visitors Bureau, 704 S. Rte. 64 (☎473-2138 or 800-446-6262), in Manteo; info for all the islands except Ocracoke. Open M-F 8:30am-6pm, Sa-Su noon-4pm by phone only. **Cape Hatteras National Seashore Information Centers: Whalebone Junction** (☎441-6644), Rte. 12 at the northern entrance to the park. Open Apr.-Nov. daily 9am-5pm. **Bodie Island** (☎441-5711), Rte. 12 at Bodie Island Lighthouse. Open June-Aug. daily 9am-6pm; Sept.-May 9am-5pm. **Ocracoke Island** (☎928-4531), next to the ferry terminal at the south end of the island. Open Apr.-Nov. daily 9am-6pm; Sept.-May 9am-5pm. **Hatteras Island** (☎995-4474), Rte. 12 at the Cape Hatteras Lighthouse. Open daily 9am-6pm, off-season 9am-5pm.

Internet access: Dare County Library (☎441-4331), 400 Mustian St., Kill Devil Hills, on the 158 Bypass. Open M and Th-F 9am-5:30pm, Tu-W 10am-7pm, Sa 10am-4pm.

Post Office: 3841 N. Croatan Hwy., Kitty Hawk (☎261-2211), MP 4 on the 158 Bypass. Open M-F 9am-4:30pm, Sa 10am-noon. **ZIP code:** 27949. **Area code:** 252.

■ ACCOMMODATIONS AND FOOD

Most motels line **Rte. 12** on crowded Bodie Island. For more privacy, go farther south; **Ocracoke** is the most secluded. On all three islands, rooming rates are highest from late May to early September. Reservations are needed seven to ten days ahead for weeknights and up to a month in advance for weekends. Long tent spikes (for the loose dirt), tents with fine screens (to keep out biting "no-see-ums"), and strong insect repellent are all recommended. Sleeping on the beach may result in fines.

BODIE ISLAND

Outer Banks International Hostel (HI-AYH), 1004 W. Kitty Hawk Rd., is the best deal in the northern islands. From Rte. 158, turn south onto The Woods Rd. (2nd traffic light after the Wright Memorial Bridge), continue until the end of the road, then turn right onto Kitty Hawk Rd. This clean and friendly hostel has 40 beds, two kitchens, A/C, heat, volleyball, and shuffleboard. (☎261-2294. Members $15, non-members $18; private rooms for one person $30/$35; for 2 $40/$50. Camping spot on the grounds $12, $6 each additional person; tent rental $6.) The **Nettlewood Motel,** MP 7, Beach Rd., offers clean, cheery rooms and private access to a sandy, uncluttered strip of beach. (☎441-5039. TV, A/C, heat, refrigerators, pool. Doubles are equipped with a kitchenette. June 15-Aug. 25 singles $50, doubles $72; May 25-June 14 and Aug. 26-Sept. 29 $41/$52; Jan. 1-May 24 and Sept. 30-Dec. 31 $33/$38.)

Tortuga's Lie, MP 11 Beach Rd., serves Caribbean-influenced seafood and grill items in a straight-up casual setting. Grab a Carib Burger for $7 or try an order of Jamaican Jerk Chicken with beans and rice for $9. Desserts baked fresh by "a little local lady." (☎441-7299. W sushi night. Open Su-Th 11:30am-midnight, F-Sa 11:30am-1am. No reservations—expect to wait.) For a more stylized take on casual cuisine, stop by the **Flying Fish Cafe,** MP 10 Bypass 158, and experience American and Mediterranean cuisine in a dining area breezy with unassuming class. Early bird specials before 6pm are all priced under $10. (☎441-6894. Open daily 5-10pm.)

MANTEO

Snuggled in between the 7-11 and BP gas station on U.S. 64, the **Scarborough Inn** exists in romantic defiance to the standardized service that flanks it. Antique furnishings and wraparound porches lead the resistance. (☎473-3979. A/C, fridges, microwaves, and free bicycle use for guests over 18. May 15-Sept. 15 singles or doubles $60-65; Mar. 16-May 14 and Sept. 16-Nov. 30 $45-50; Dec. 1-Mar. 15 $35-40.)

Try bratwurst on the beach at **The Weeping Radish,** across the street from the Inn. The Radish, America's oldest restaurant/brewery, offers authentic German food and beer brewed according to the 1516 *Reinheitsgebot,* or Purity Law, which

decreed that only four ingredients—malt, hops, yeast, and water—may be used
to make beer. Check out the adjacent mini-theme park. (☎473-1157. Microbrewery tours daily 4pm with added times during peak season. Open daily 11:30am-
9pm; bar open until 10pm. 0.5L beer $3.50.) The **Manteo Waterfront** encourages
one's inner pedestrian with tree-lined, restaurant-dotted streets conducive to
strolling. The **Full Moon Cafe** overlooks the waterfront with a view of the *Elizabeth II* and features an impressive array of sandwiches ($6-9) and wraps ($6-8)
with several vegetarian options. (☎473-6666. Open daily 4:30pm-9pm.) Farther
down Queen Elizabeth Ave. **Poor Richard's Sandwich Shop** offers more standard
fare, including $3-5 sandwiches, in a bright, relaxed setting (☎473-3333. Open
M-F 8am-8pm, Sa 11am-3pm.)

HATTERAS AND OCRACOKE

⛺**Ocracoke Island Wayfarer Hostel** combines the graceful charm of a bed and breakfast with hostel practices and prices. The thoroughly inviting, immaculate hostel
beckons from the tree-lined quiet of 125 Lighthouse Rd. Going south on Rte. 12,
take a left at the Island Inn; the hostel will be on your left. (☎928-3411. Office
hours 9-11am and 4-9pm. Free bike use, A/C, kitchen, 2 porches. Dorms $19; pri-
vate room $39.) The bright, clean, wood-paneled rooms at the **Sand Dollar Motel,** off
Rte. 12 in Ocracoke, exude a beach-cabin allure. Turn right at the Pirate's Chest
gift shop, right again at the Back Porch restaurant, and left at the Edwards Motel.
(☎928-5571. Open Apr.-late Nov. Refrigerators, A/C, heat, pool, and breakfast.
Queen bed $70, 2 double beds $75; off-season rates vary.)

Occupying a counter along the back wall of Styron's General Store (est. 1920) at
the corner of Lighthouse and Creek Rd. in Ocracoke, the **Cat Ridge Deli** specializes
in Thai-influenced cuisine, with wraps for around $6. (☎928-3354. Open M-Sa 11am-
7pm, Su 11am-5pm.) Sea lovers can sail on over to **Jolly Roger** on Silver Lake Harbor
off of Rte. 12 for the only waterfront dining in Ocracoke. Inhale the sea breeze
along with locally caught fresh fish specials (market price) and sandwiches ($4-8).

CAPE HATTERAS NATIONAL SEASHORE

Three oceanside campgrounds off Rte. 12 along the Cape Hatteras National Seashore are open mid-April to early October: **Oregon Inlet,** on the southern tip of
Bodie Island; **Frisco,** near the elbow of Hatteras Island; and **Ocracoke,** in the middle of Ocracoke Island. **Cape Point** in Buxton is open late May to early September. All four have water, restrooms, cold-water showers, and grills. Ocracoke is
closest to the ocean, with its campsites clustered near the water. Frisco, with its
winding roads and scalloped hills, takes the prize for most interesting terrain.
Ocracoke sites ($17) can be reserved from mid-May to early September. (☎800-
365-2267; http://reservations.nps.gov). All other sites ($17) are rented on a first
come, first served basis. Listings of open sites at all four campgrounds are
posted at Whalebone Junction. Contact **Cape Hatteras National Seashore** (☎473-
2111) for park concerns.

◎🎫 SIGHTS AND OUTDOORS

The **Wright Brothers National Memorial,** MP 8 on U.S. 158, marks the spot where
Orville and Wilbur Wright took to the skies in history's first powered flight. (☎441-
7430. Open June through August daily 9am-6pm; winter 9am-5pm. Exhibits and
reproductions of the Wright gliders are on display in the Visitors Center. $2 per
person, $4 per car.) Kitty Hawk Aero Tours offers 30min. airplane tours of the
area. (☎441-4460. $29-39 per person.)

Flying of a different sort goes on at the nearby **Jockey's Ridge State Park,** MP 12 on
U.S. 158, where **Kitty Hawk Kites** takes aspiring hang gliding pilots under its wing.
Beginner lessons including flights start at $65. (☎441-4124 or 877-359-8447.) Those
preferring to explore things at ground level can shuffle through the 6 million truck-
loads of sand that make up the tallest dunes on the east coast. (Park ☎441-7132.
Open daily 8am-8:45pm; off-season hrs. vary. Free.)

A ROCK OF AGES IT ISN'T Lighthouses, built to ward ships from dangerous stretches of coasts, are generally taken as cultural symbols of safety and stability against the changing currents around them—as fixed points in a sea of change. They are also extremely large and very heavy. Given these two generalizations, it may come as a surprise that all 203 feet of the Cape Hatteras lighthouse were moved more than half a mile in the summer of 1999. The long-planned move, necessary to save the lighthouse from the ravages of erosion, was accomplished in only 23 days. Having already weathered two hurricanes in its new position, the lighthouse seems stable as ever; of course, by current estimates they'll have to do it all over again in another 100 years.

Roanoke Island is a locus of historical and cultural draws. Facing the Manteo Waterfront, **Roanoke Festival Park** (follow signs from the highway), staffed largely by persons in 16th-century garb, is centered around its interactive, kid-friendly museum and the sailing ship *Elizabeth II*, a replica of a 16th-century English merchant ship. (☎475-1500. Park open daily 9am-7pm; ship 10am-6pm; hrs. vary off-season. $8, students $5). In summer, students from the North Carolina School for the Arts perform at the Park's outside pavilion (suggested donation adults $5, students/ seniors $3). The **Fort Raleigh National Historic Site,** off U.S. 64, offers several attractions. The **Lost Colony,** the longest-running outdoor drama in the US, has been performed here since 1937 and commemorates the first English colony in America, which mysteriously disappeared in 1590. (☎473-3414 or 800-488-5012. Shows June-Aug. M-Sa 8:30pm. $16, seniors $15, under 11 $8.) Verdant paths unfold into sculpted array of flowers, antique statues, and fountains in the **Elizabethan Gardens** (☎473-3234. Open daily 9am-8pm; off-season hrs. vary. $5, seniors $4.50, ages 6-18 $1, under 5 free with adult.) Located 1 mi. west of U.S. 64 on Airport Rd., 3 mi. north of Manteo, The **North Carolina Aquarium** showcases the underwater scene from the coastal plain to the Gulf Stream. (☎473-3493. Open June-Aug. daily 9am-7pm; off-season 9am-5pm. $4, seniors and military $3, ages 6-17 $2.) A pass for the aquarium, gardens, and Festival Park can be purchased at any of the locations for $14 (adult) or $6 (6-18 yrs); with Lost Colony ticket $28/$14.

SCENIC DRIVE: CAPE HATTERAS NAT'L SEASHORE

Get two shores for the price of one along the entire 70 mi. expanse of the **Cape Hatteras National Seashore:** one that faces out to the Atlantic Ocean and another that looks across the Pamlico Sound to North Carolina's mainland. The park's main appeal is this unique landscape, dotted with dunes, stunted trees, and occasional stretches of marshland. Driving south from Hatteras to Ocracoke, the water stretches out to the horizon on either side; the park offers magnificent, largely empty beaches on both coasts.

Rte. 12 is the main artery of the park, running all the way from the northern entrance of the park at the Whalebone Junction information center to the town of Ocracoke, except for a 40min. stretch from Hatteras to Ocracoke that is covered by a free ferry. For its entire length, Rte. 12 is a paved two-lane road. Total transport time from Whalebone to Ocracoke is about 2½hr.

All of the major attractions of the park are accessible and clearly marked from Rte. 12. The chief of these are the Outer Banks' three **lighthouses** on Bodie, Hatteras, and Ocracoke islands. The tallest of these—and the tallest lighthouse in North America—is the 257-step Cape Hatteras lighthouse, built in 1870. The lighthouse is open for climbing 10am-6pm during the summer. Another set of attractions along Rte. 12 serves to remind visitors that lighthouses have a value apart from the picturesque: various **shipwrecks** are visible from spots on the shore. The schooner *A. Barnes* can be seen from Coquina Beach on Bodie Island, across from the lighthouse. For a schedule of the various daily programs run at the Visitors Centers located at each lighthouse, pick up a copy of the free paper *In The Park.*

Another part of the seashore's appeal is its rich wildlife, on display at the **Pea Island National Wildlife Refuge** on the northern tip of Hatteras Island. Adjoining the **Visitors Center** (☎473-1131) is the marsh-country **Charles Kuralt Nature Trail,** which affords trekkers a chance to glimpse grackles, pelicans, and the Carolina salt marsh snake. (Visitors Center usually open daily 9am-4pm in summer; off-season open weekends only. Beaches in the Refuge are open only during daylight.) Farther south, the **Pony Pasture** on Rte. 12 in Ocracoke acts as the stomping ground for a herd of horses peculiar to the island.

SOUTH CAROLINA

South Carolina's pride in the Palmetto State may seem extreme. Inspired by the state flag, the palmetto tree logo decorates hats, bottles and bumper stickers across the landscape. To some, pride lies in the unrivaled beaches of the Grand Strand; others revel in the stately elegance of Charleston. Columbia offers an impressive art and cultural experience without the smog and traffic that plague the New South metropoloi of neighboring states. Tamed for tourists and merchandising, the Confederate legacy of the first state to secede from the Union is groomed as a cash cow. In recent years, South Carolina has been in the national news for its refusal to remove the controversial Confederate flag from the statehouse. In July 2000, state legislators approved moving the flag from the Statehouse dome to the lawn. However, the NAACP plans to boycott the state until it is removed entirely.

⚑ PRACTICAL INFORMATION

Capital: Columbia.
Visitor info: Dept. of Parks, Recreation, and Tourism, Edgar A. Brown Bldg., 1205 Pendleton St., #106, Columbia 29021 (☎803-734-1700; www.travelsc.com). **US Forest Service,** 4931 Broad River Rd., Columbia 29210 (☎803-561-4000).
Postal Abbreviation: SC. **Sales Tax:** 5%, 6% in Charleston.

CHARLESTON ☎843

Built on rice and cotton, Charleston's antebellum plantation system yielded vast riches now seen in its numerous museums, historic homes, and ornate architecture. An accumulated cultural capital of 300 years flows like the long, distinctive drawl of the natives. Several of the south's most renowned plantations dot the city, while two venerable institutions, the College of Charleston and the Citadel, add a youthful eccentricity. Horse-drawn carriages, cobblestone streets, pre-Civil War homes, beautiful beaches, and some of the best restaurants in the Southeast explain why Charleston often heads the list of the nation's top destinations.

▟ TRANSPORTATION

Trains: Amtrak, 4565 Gaynor Ave. (☎744-8264), 8 mi. west of downtown. To: Richmond (6¾hr., 2 per day, $82-124); Savannah (1¾hr., 2 per day, $23-35); and Washington, D.C. (9½hr., 2 per day, $110-166.) Open daily 6am-10pm.
Buses: Greyhound, 3610 Dorchester Rd. (☎747-5341 or call 800-231-222 for schedules and fares), in N. Charleston. *Avoid this area at night.* To: Myrtle Beach (2½hr., 1 per day, $22-24), Savannah (2¾hr., 2 per day, $22-24) and Charlotte (4½hr., 2 per day, $39-41). **CARTA's** "Dorchester/Waylyn" bus goes to town from station area. Return on "Navy Yard: 5 Mile Dorchester Rd." bus.
Public Transit: CARTA, 36 John St. (☎724-7420). Fare 75¢, seniors and disabled 25¢, 1-day pass $2, 3-day $5. CARTA's **Downtown Area Shuttle (DASH)** is made up of 5 trolley routes that circle downtown daily 8am-11pm. Visitors Center has free schedules.

Bike Rental: The Bicycle Shoppe, 280 Meeting St. (☎ 722-8168), between George and Society St. $4 per hr., $15 per day. Open M-Sa 9am-7pm, Su 1pm-5pm.
Taxis: Yellow Cab, ☎ 577-6565.

◢✦ 🛈 ORIENTATION AND PRACTICAL INFORMATION

Old Charleston lies at the southernmost point of the mile-wide peninsula below **Calhoun St.** The major north-south routes through the city are **Meeting, King,** and **East Bay St.** The area north of the Visitors Center is mostly rundown and uninviting. **Savannah Hwy./U.S. 17** cuts across the peninsula going south to Savannah and north across two towering bridges to Mt. Pleasant and Myrtle Beach. There are plenty of metered parking spaces; there are also plenty of police officers giving tickets.

Hotlines: Crisis Line, (☎ 744-4357 or 800-922-2283). 24hr. general counseling and referral. Teen concerns 747-8336; operates M-F 4pm-8pm. **People Against Rape,** ☎ 745-0144 or 800-241-7273. Operates 24hr.

Visitor info: Charleston Visitors Center, 375 Meeting St. (☎ 853-8000 or 800-868-8118; www.charlestoncvb.com), across from Charleston Museum. Open 8:30am-5:30pm Apr.1-Oct. 39, 8:30am-5pm Nov. 1-Mar. 31.

Post Office: 83 Broad St. (☎ 577-0690). Open M-F 9am-5pm, Sa 10am-noon. Also houses a cute little postal museum. **ZIP code:** 29402. **Area code:** 843.

⌂ ACCOMMODATIONS

Motel rooms in historic downtown Charleston are expensive. Cheap motels are a few miles out of the city, around Exits 209-11 on I-26 W in N. Charleston, or across the Ashley River on U.S. 17 S in Mt. Pleasant—not practical for those without cars.

Bed, No Breakfast, 16 Halsey St. (☎ 723-4450). The only budget option within walking distance of downtown. Two guest rooms available in this historical house. $65-95.

Masters Inn Economy, 6100 Rivers Ave. (☎ 744-3530 or 800-633-3434), at I-26 Exit 211B, 11 mi. from downtown. Spacious rooms with A/C and cable. Pool, free local calls, and laundry. Singles $37; doubles $43; Sa-Su $43/$50.

Seagrass Inn, 2355 Aviation Ave. (☎ 744-4900), behind Waffle House. Clean, comfortable rooms with cable, pool, A/C. Singles from $40.

Motel 6, 2058 Savannah Hwy. (☎ 556-5144), 5 mi. south of town. Clean and pleasant, but far from downtown and often full. Rooms $40, $6 each additional person.

Campground at James Island County Park (☎ 795-9884 or 800-743-7275). Take U.S. 17 S to Rte. 171 and follow the signs. Spacious but unwooded sites. The spectacular park is made up of 16 acres of lakes, bicycle and walking trails, and a small water park. Bike and boat rental. Tent sites $19; primitive sites $13; full hookup $25. Seniors and Good Sam members 10% off.

🍴 FOOD

Charleston has some of the best food in the country. While most restaurants cater to big-spending tourists, there are plenty of budget-friendly opportunities to sample the Southern cooking, barbecue, and fresh seafood that has made the low country famous. Alluring options wait on nearly every street; don't hesitate to wander around and discover a restaurant that appeals to you.

Hyman's Seafood Company, 215 Meeting St. (☎ 723-6000). Since 1890, this casual restaurant has offered 15-25 different kinds of fresh fish daily ($7-15), served in any one of 7 styles. No reservations; expect long waits. Open daily 11am-11pm.

Southend Brewery, 161 E. Bay St. (☎ 853-4677). Outstanding ribs, eclectic pizzas, and home brewed beers entice many to frequent this 3-story brewhouse. Open Su-W 11:30am-10:30pm, Th-Sa 11:30am-11:30pm. Bar open until 1am.

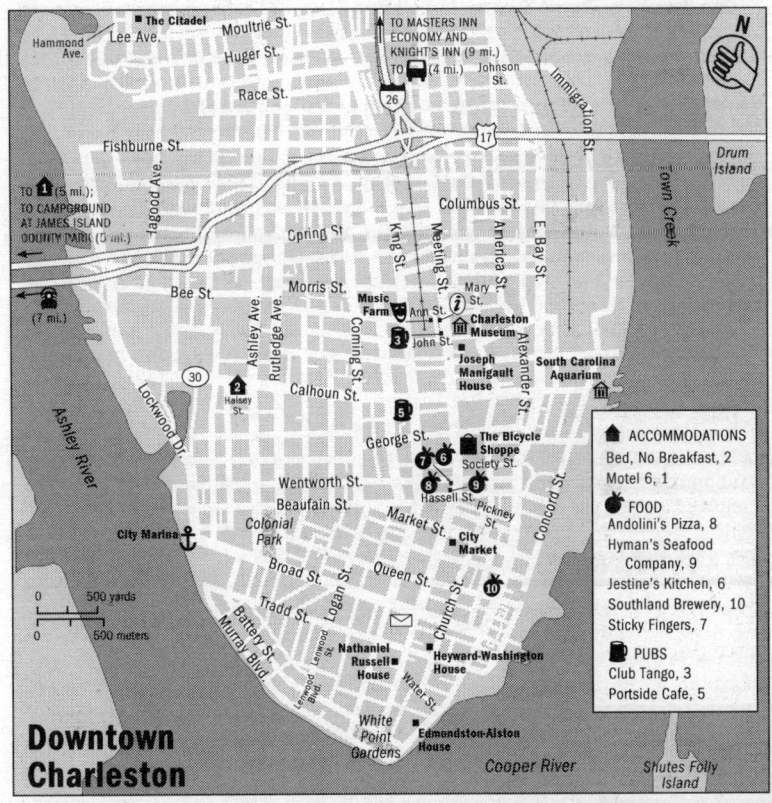

Downtown Charleston

Map labels:
The Citadel · Hammond Ave. · Lee Ave. · Moultrie St. · Huger St. · Race St. · Fishburne St. · TO MASTERS INN ECONOMY AND KNIGHT'S INN (9 mi.) · TO (4 mi.) Johnson St. · 26 · 17 · Immigration St. · Tagood Ave. · Columbus St. · Drum Island · E. Bay St. · America St. · Town Creek · TO (5 mi.); TO CAMPGROUND AT JAMES ISLAND COUNTY PARK (5 mi.) · Spring St. · King St. · Meeting St. · (7 mi.) · Bee St. · Morris St. · Ashley Ave. · Rutledge Ave. · Coming St. · Music Farm · Ann St. · Mary St. · Alexander St. · Charleston Museum · 30 · Halsey St. · Calhoun St. · Joseph Manigault House · South Carolina Aquarium · George St. · The Bicycle Shoppe · Society St. · Ashley River · Lockwood Dr. · Wentworth St. · Beaufain St. · Hassell St. · Pinckney St. · Concord St. · City Marina · Colonial Park · Market St. · City Market · Broad St. · Logan St. · Queen St. · Church St. · Tradd St. · Battery St. · Murray Blvd. · Linwood St. · Nathaniel Russell House · Heyward-Washington House · Water St. · White Point Gardens · Edmondston-Alston House · Cooper River · Shutes Folly Island

0 500 yards
0 500 meters

◆ ACCOMMODATIONS
Bed, No Breakfast, 2
Motel 6, 1

🍎 FOOD
Andolini's Pizza, 8
Hyman's Seafood Company, 9
Jestine's Kitchen, 6
Southland Brewery, 10
Sticky Fingers, 7

🍺 PUBS
Club Tango, 3
Portside Cafe, 5

Jestine's Kitchen, 251 Meeting St. (☎722-7224). If you had a Southern country grandma, and this grandma had a restaurant, it would probably be something like Jestine's. Excellent crispy fried chicken with 2 fresh veggies $8. Open Tu-Th 11am-9:30pm, F-Sa 11am-10pm, Su 11am-9pm.

Andolini's Pizza, 82 Wentworth St. (☎722-7437), at King St. Reputedly the best pizza place in the south, Andolini's makes all items from scratch. Large thin crust cheese pie $11. Calzones from $5. Open M-Th 11am-11pm, F-Sa 11am-midnight, Su noon-10pm.

Sticky Fingers, 235 Meeting St. (☎853-7427). Voted the best barbecue in town on numerous occasions. Pulled pork sandwich $6. Ribs $12-26. Open daily 11am-10pm.

🍥 SIGHTS

Charleston's ancient homes, historical monuments, churches, galleries, and gardens can be seen by foot, car, bus, boat, trolley, or horse-drawn carriage. **City Market,** downtown at Meeting St., keeps the market place way of doing business abuzz in its newly restored 19th-century building. (Open daily from about 9am-5pm.)

PLANTATIONS AND GARDENS. The 300-year-old **Magnolia Plantation and Magnolia Gardens** is by far the most majestic of Charleston's plantations. Visitors enjoy the Drayton family's staggering wealth by exploring their 50 acres of gorgeous gardens with 900 varieties of camelia and 250 varieties of azalea. Other attractions include a hedge maze, bike or canoe rental, swamp, and bird sanctuary. (On Rte. 61, 10 mi. out of town off U.S. 17. ☎571-1266 or 800-367-3517. Open daily 8am-5:30pm. $10, teens $8, ages 6-12 $5. House $16/$14/$11; nature trail $15/$12/$8; swamp garden $5, ages 6-12

$3; canoes or bikes $3 per 3hr.) A bit farther down the road is **Middleton Place,** a more manicured plantation with working stables, gardens, and house. *(On Rte. 61, 14 mi. northwest of downtown. ☎ 556-6020. Open daily 9am-5pm. $15, seniors $14, ages 6-12 $7; gardens and stables $23; AAA discount.)* Even farther out, but well worth the trip, **Cypress Gardens** lets you paddle your own boat out onto the eerie swamps filled with gators. *(3030 Cypress Gardens Rd. ☎ 553-0515. Open daily Feb.-Dec. 9am-5pm.)*

CHARLESTON MUSEUM AND HISTORIC HOMES. Across the street from the Visitors Center stands the **Charleston Museum,** the country's oldest museum. *(360 Meeting St. ☎ 722-2996. Open M-Sa 9am-5pm, Su 1pm-5pm. $8, children $4.)* Although a combo ticket is available for the museum and two historic homes located nearby (the 18th-century **Heyward-Washington House** and **Joseph Manigault House**), just pick one house and save your money. *(Heyward-Washington House: 87 Church St. ☎ 722-0354. Joseph Manigault House: 350 Meeting St. ☎ 723-2926. Both homes open M-Sa 10am-5pm, Su 1-5pm. Museum and 1 home $12; museum and 2 homes $18. One house $8, ages 3-12 $4.)* The **Nathaniel Russell House** and **Edmondston-Alston House** are similar, more unrefined 19th-century homes. *(Nathaniel Russell: 51 Meeting St. ☎ 723-1623. Open M-Sa 10am-5pm, Su 2-5pm. $7, under 6 free. Edmondston-Alston: 21 E. Battery. ☎ 722-7171. Open Su-M 1:30-4:30pm, Tu-Sa 10am-4:30pm. $8, under 6 free.)*

PATRIOT'S POINT AND FORT SUMTER. Climb aboard four Naval ships, including a submarine and the giant aircraft carrier *Yorktown,* in **Patriot's Point Naval and Maritime Museum,** the world's largest Naval museum. *(Across the Cooper River in Mt. Pleasant. ☎ 884-2727. Open daily Apr.-Sept. 9am-6pm, ships close at 7:30pm; Oct.-Mar. 9am-5pm, ships close at 5:30pm. $12.50, seniors/military $11, ages 6-11 $6, under 7 free.)* **Fort Sumter Tours** offers boat excursions to the National Historic Site from the City Marina (limited handicap access available only at City Marina) off Lockwood Blvd. or Patriots Point. *(☎ 881-7337. 2¼hr. total, 1hr. on Fort; 1-3 per day from each location. $11, seniors $10, ages 6-11 $6, under 6 free.)*

BEACHES. Over the James Island Bridge and U.S. 171, about 20 mi. southeast of Charleston, **Folly Beach** is popular with local students from the Citadel, College of Charleston, and USC. **Isle of Palms** is more wide open and extends for miles down toward the less-crowded **Sullivan's Island.** To get there, cross the Cooper River Bridge, drive 10 mi. down Hwy 17 N, and turn right onto the Isle of Palms Connector. *(Folly Beach: ☎ 588-2426. Isle of Palms: ☎ 886-3863.)*

SOUTH CAROLINA AQUARIUM. This brand new aquarium has quickly become Charleston's biggest attraction. Although a bit overpriced, exhibits showcasing aquatic life from the region's swamps, marshes, and oceans are well-executed and extremely interesting. *(At the end of Calhoun St. on the Cooper River, overlooking the harbor. ☎ 720-1990; www.scaquarium.org. Open daily July-Aug. 9am-7pm; Nov.-Feb. 10am-5pm; Mar.-June and Sept.-Oct. 9am-5pm. $14, ages 13-17 and seniors $12, ages 4-12 $7.)*

BULL ISLAND. To get away from human civilization, take a ferry to Bull Island, a 5000-acre island off the coast of Charleston. The boat is often greeted by dolphins swimming in some of the cleanest water on the planet, while the island is home to 278 different species of bird and 16 mi. of hiking trails. *(☎ 881-4582. ½hr. ferries depart from Moore's Landing 5 mi. east of US 17 between Mt. Pleasant and Awendaw. Departs Mar.-Nov. Tu and Th-Sa 9am and 12:30pm; returns Tu and Th-Sa noon and 4pm; Dec.-Feb. Sa 10am; returns 3pm. Round-trip $30, under 12 $15.)*

🎵🎭 ENTERTAINMENT AND NIGHTLIFE

With nearby colleges and a constant tourist presence, Charleston's nightlife beats strong. Free copies of *City Paper,* in stores and restaurants, list concerts and other events. Big name bands take center stage nightly at the **Music Farm,** 32 Ann St. (☎ 853-3276). Nearby, on 39 John St., **Club Tango** (☎ 577-2822), lures hot-steppers to the alley between John and Hutson St. as night falls. The more relaxed scene at **Portside Cafe,** 462 King St., combines an outdoor patio, an excellent blend of nouveau American and Southern food (with sandwiches under $7 and barbecue starting at $8), and nightly live music. (☎722-0409. Open M-Sa 11am-4pm and 5-10pm.) In late May and early June the city explodes with music, theater, dance, and opera as Charleston hosts **Spoleto Festival USA,** the nation's most comprehensive arts festival. (☎722-2764. Tickets $10-75.)

▓ DAYTRIP FROM CHARLESTON: BEAUFORT

Listen closely, and you will hear a musical language spoken in the coastal islands of southeastern South Carolina. During the slave trade, numerous African cultures merged with the European cultures of slave traders to produce **Gullah,** a unique blend of language, food, arts, and religion. After the Civil War, Gullah largely faded across the South, except in the geographically isolated South Carolina lowcountry. Bridges allow easy access to the area and exploration of this unique culture. St. Helena is considered the center of Gullah, largely due to the preservation efforts of the **Penn Center** (☎838-8545), about 1 mi. down Martin Luther King Jr. Dr. off U.S. 21, the first school for freed slaves in the south. King wrote his "I Have a Dream" speech on retreat at the center. The center preserves the area's unique heritage in the **York W. Bailey Museum.** (☎838-2474. Open M-Sa 11am-4pm. $4, children $2.)

The best way to truly experience Gullah is on the **Gullah 'n' Geechie Tours,** led by community activist, historian, scholar, and all around expert Kitty Greene. More than a leisurely drive, Greene carefully conveys the Gullah culture by examining its language, religion, art, family, and food. Included is a trip to a "praise house," the 300-year-old religious center for local plantation slaves. (☎838-7516 or 838-3758. 2hr. tours leave from 847 Sea Island Parkway in St. Helena. M-F 9:45am, 1:45, and 4:30pm; Sa by arrangement. $17, children $12; reservations required.)

One of the Palmetto State's strangest sites is the **Kingdom of Oyotunji,** a Yoruba African village in Sheldon, 10 mi. north of Beaufort on Rte. 17. The 30-year-old sanctuary for African priests is led by a self-proclaimed African king and his several wives. The heartfelt yet bizarre tour is worth every cent of its $5 charge; make an appointment beforehand to speak with the king. (☎846-8900. Open 10am-dusk.)

Stately Beaufort hosts the lively **Gullah Festival** every May and chows at the packed **Shrimp Festival** every October Beaufort is 60 mi. from both Savannah and Charleston, on Rte. 21, 15 mi. south of I-95 Exit 33. From the **Greater Beaufort Visitors Center,** 1106 Carteret St., travel 5 mi. south on Rte. 210 to St. Helena. (☎986-5400. Open daily 9am-5:30pm.) **Greyhound,** 1307 Boundary Rd. (☎524-4646), runs to Savannah (1hr., 4 per day, $11.50-12.50). **Area code:** 843

COLUMBIA ☎803

Soon after the Revolutionary War, upstate resentment forced Charleston aristocrats to relocate the capital to the middle of the state, on Colonel Thomas Taylor's plantation along the Congaree River. As planned, Columbia quickly rose to prominence, only to be leveled by Sherman's marching torch. Yet Columbia has moved beyond its Civil War shadow with a thriving art community, historic neighborhoods, and an upscale entertainment district near the Congaree River. Town and gown prosper together, as the University of South Carolina (USC) adds its substantial cultural resources to the city.

▓▓ ORIENTATION AND PRACTICAL INFORMATION. The city is laid out in a square, bordered by Huger St. (running north-south), Harden St. (north-south), Blossom St. (east-west), and Calhoun St. (east-west). **Assembly St.** is the main drag, running north-south through the heart of the city. **Gervais St.** is its east-west equivalent. The Congaree River marks the city's western edge.

Columbia Metropolitan Airport, 3000 Aviation Way (☎822-5000), is in West Columbia; a taxi to downtown costs about $13-15. **Amtrak,** 850 Pulaski St. (☎252-8246), sends one train per day to Miami (15hr.; $68-168); Washington, D.C. (10hr., $70-138); and Savannah (2½hr., $24-47). The station is open daily 10am-5:30pm and 11pm-6:45am. **Greyhound,** 2015 Gervais St. (☎256-6465), at Harden, sends buses to Charlotte (1½hr., 5 per

> **A PIG PRIMER** Southerners have always found unique ways to prepare all parts of the pig. Chitlins, a tasty (but smelly) fall treat, are pig intestines cleaned, boiled, fried, and then seasoned. Hogmau is boiled and seasoned pig stomach. Throughout the South, pickled pig's feet soak in pool hall countertop jars. And those in a hurry can always grab a pig's ear sandwich.

day, M-Th $15, F-Su $16); Atlanta (5 hr., 9 per day, $43-46); and Charleston (2½ hr., 3 per day, $22-24). **Atlantic Express** runs public buses through Columbia from 5:30am to midnight. Most main routes depart from pickup/transfer depots at Sumter St. and Laurel St. and at Assembly St. and Taylor St. (☎217-9019. Call for schedules. Fare 75¢, seniors and disabled 25¢, under 6 free. Free transfers.) **Columbia Metropolitan Convention and Visitors Bureau,** 801 Lady St., has maps and info. (☎254-0479. Open M-F 8:30am-5pm, Sa 10am-4pm; winter hrs. vary.) For info on USC, try the **University of South Carolina Visitors Center,** 937 Assembly St. (☎777-0169 or 800-922-9755. Open M-F 8:30am-5pm, Sa 9:30am-2pm. Free visitor parking pass.) **Post office:** 1601 Assembly St. (☎733-4643; open M-F 7:30am-6pm). **ZIP code:** 29202. **Area code:** 803.

ⅰ ACCOMMODATIONS. Generally, the cheapest digs lie furthest from the city center. One convenient option located only a short drive from downtown is the **Masters Inn,** 613 Knox Abbott Dr. Take Blossom St. across the Congaree River, where it becomes Knox Abbott Dr. The inn offers free local calls and morning coffee, a pool, and cable TV. (☎796-4300. Singles $33-35; doubles $35-37.) Inexpensive motels also line the three interstates (I-26, I-77, and I-20) that circle the city. **Knights Inn,** 1987 Airport Blvd., may not be a castle, but it has a great deal of amenities for a low price. All rooms have refrigerators, microwaves, cable TV, A/C, free local calls, and pool access. (☎794-0222. Singles and doubles Su-Th $35, F-Sa $39; 10% senior discount.) The **Sesquicentennial State Park** offers 1400 acres, swimming and fishing, a nature center, hiking and biking trails, and 87 wooded sites with electricity and water. Public transportation does not serve the park; take I-20 to the Two Notch Rd./U.S. 1, Exit 17, and head northeast for 3 mi. (☎788-2706. Gate open Apr.-Oct. daily 7am-9pm; Nov.-Mar. 7am-6pm. Campsites $16. Entrance $1.50 per person.)

❐ FOOD. It's little wonder that **Maurice's Piggie Park,** 800 Elmwood Ave. and 1600 Charleston Hwy., owns the world record for "Most BBQ sold in one day." Maurice's cash "pig" is his exquisite, mustard-based sauce that covers the $4.50 Big Joe pork BBQ sandwich. (☎256-4377. Open M-Sa 10am-10pm.) **Groucho's,** 611 Harden St., has received high marx from the collegiate crowd for 60 years, proving the allure of "dipper" sandwiches ($6) served with one of Groucho's special sauces. (☎799-5708. Open M-Sa 11am-4pm, Su noon-4pm; June-Aug. M-Sa 11am-4pm.) For healthy, organic temptations try **Rosewood Market,** 2803 Rosewood Dr., which features a grocery store as well as a deli-style counter. A small order of BBQ tofu goes for $2.50, or choose from a selection of desserts sweetened with fruit juice. (☎765-1083 or 888-203-5950. Deli open M-Sa 9am-9pm, Su 10am-6pm.) Or head to the **Columbia State Farmers Market,** 1001 Bluff Rd., across from the football stadium, for a chance to experience the Palmetto State's produce in all its raw, unadulterated glory. (☎737-4664. Open M-Sa 6am-9pm, Su 1-9pm.)

◪ SIGHTS. Over 2000 animals roam in re-created natural habitats at **Riverbanks Zoo and Garden,** on I-126 at Greystone Blvd., northwest of downtown, which has been ranked as one of the top ten zoos in the country. In addition to an undersea fish and reptile kingdom, desert, interactive Southern farm, and bird pavilion, look for the new gorillas and koala bears joining the zoo's ranks. (☎779-8717. Open M-F 9am-4pm, Sa-Su 9am-5pm. $7.25, students $6, seniors $5.75, ages 3-12 $4.75.)

Bronze stars mark the impact of Sherman's cannonballs on the **Statehouse,** located between Sumter St., Assembly St., and Gervais St. Lawmakers spent $70 million to restore Columbia's dominant structure to its turn-of-the-century glory. (☎734-2430. Open M-F 9am-5pm, Sa 10am-5pm, 1st Su each month 1-5pm. Free tours

THE SECRET OF LIFE Unknown to the rest of the world, mankind's secrets to wisdom and prosperity reside in **Elberton, GA** ("the granite capital of the world"), 150 mi. from Columbia. In 1980 a "group of Americans who seek the age of reason" sent a large check to a local mining firm with engraving instructions. On a hilltop 8 mi. out of town, several giant slabs of granite answer humanity's most burning questions. In English, Russian, Chinese, Hebrew, Swahili and Greek, the guidestones advise humanity to reproduce wisely, unite under a new living language, keep the population under 500 million, and resolve disputes in a world court. To prevent confusion, "Let these be guidestones" is announced in Babylonian Cuniform, Classical Greek, Sanskrit and Egyptian Hieroglyphics at the top of the tablets.

available.) Across Sumter St. from the Statehouse the **Horseshoe,** the heart and original campus of USC, exudes verdant grace. At the head of the green, sitting at the intersection of Bull and Pendleton St., **McKissick Museum** explores the folklife of South Carolina and the southeast through music, science, art, and history. (☎777-7251. Open M-F 9am-4pm, Sa-Su 1-5pm. June-Aug. Free.) The **South Carolina Confederate Relic Room and Museum,** 301 Gervais St., scheduled to reopen in its new location in the State Museum by Jan. 2002, houses an impressive and well-maintained collection of Civil War artifacts. (☎898-4921. Call for hrs. Free.) Two 19th-century mansions, the **Robert Mills Historic House and Park** and the **Hampton-Preston Mansion,** 1616 Blanding St., 3 blocks east of Sumter St., compete in elegance as twin survivors of Sherman's Civil War rampage. Both have been lovingly restored with period fineries. (☎252-1770. Tours every hr. Tu-Sa 10:15am-3:15pm, Su 1:15-4:15pm. Tours $4, students $2.50, under 5 free. Buy tickets at Mills House Museum Shop.)

🖪 **NIGHTLIFE.** Columbia's nightlife centers around the collegiate **Five Points District** (junction of Harden St. and Devine St.) and the blossoming, slightly more mature **Vista area** (Gervais St. before the Congaree River). The decor of the **Knock Knock Club,** 634 Harden St., speaks easy to the days of Prohibition while gamecocks (USC students) live it up and are blissfully oblivious to the days when alcohol was illegal. (☎799-1015; open M-F 5pm-5am, Sa-Su 7pm-2am). Students also drink the night away at **Jungle Jim's,** 724 Harden St. (☎256-1390; open M-F 5pm-3am, Sa-Su 7pm-2am). In the Vista, the **Art Bar,** 1211 Park St., attracts a diverse crowd with its troop of life-size plastic robots lined up against one wall. (☎929-0198; open M-F 8pm-late, Sa-Su 8pm-2am). The **Alley Cafe,** 911 Lady St., serves dinner as well as drinks while supporting a thriving lesbian scene in a "straight-friendly" atmosphere. (☎771-277; open Tu-F 5pm-11pm, Sa 5pm-2am). The weekly publication *Free Times* gives details on Columbia's club and nightlife scene. *In Unison* is a weekly paper listing gay-friendly nightspots.

MYRTLE BEACH AND THE GRAND STRAND   ☎ 843

Each summer, millions of Harley-riding, RV-driving Southerners make Myrtle Beach the second-most-popular summer tourist destination in the country. During spring break and in early June, Myrtle Beach is thronged with rambunctious students on the lookout for a good time. The rest of the year, families, golfers, shoppers, and everyone else partakes in the unapologetic tackiness of the town's theme restaurants, amusement parks, and shops. The pace slows significantly on the rest of the 60 mi. Grand Strand. South of Myrtle Beach, Murrell's Inlet, a quaint port stocked with good seafood, and Pawley's Island are both dominated by private homes. Georgetown, once a critical Southern port city, showcases its history with white-pillared homes on 18th-century-style rice and indigo plantations.

🖪🖪 **ORIENTATION AND PRACTICAL INFORMATION.** Most attractions are on **Rte. 17/Kings Hwy.,** which splits into a Business Route and Bypass 4 mi. south of Myrtle Beach. **Ocean Blvd.** runs along the ocean, flanked on either side by endless ranks of cheap motels. Avenue numbers repeat themselves after reaching 1st Ave. in the middle of town; be sure to note whether the Ave. is "north" or "south." Also, take care not to confuse north **Myrtle Beach** with the town **North Myrtle Beach,** which has an almost identical street layout. **Rte. 501** runs west toward Conway, I-95, and, most importantly, the factory outlet stores. Unless otherwise stated, addresses on the Grand Strand are for Myrtle Beach. **Greyhound,** 511 7th Ave. N (☎448-2471; open M-F 7am-6:45pm, Sa-Su 10am-6:45pm), runs to Charleston (2½hr.; 1 per day; $22-24). **Coastal Rapid Public Transit (CRPTA),** 1418 Third Ave., provides minimal busing; pick up a copy of schedules and routes from the Chamber of Commerce or from area businesses. (☎488-0865. Runs daily 6am-2:30am. Local fares $1.10-2.10.) Rent bikes at **The Bike Shoppe,** 711 Broadway, at Main St. (☎448-5335. Open M-F 8am-6pm, Sa 8am-5pm. Cruisers $5 per half-day, $10 per day; mountain bikes $10/$20.) **Myrtle Beach Chamber of Commerce:** 1200 N. Oak St., parallel to Kings Hwy., at 12th N. (☎626-7444 or 800-356-3016. Open daily 8:30am-5pm. **Mini Golf:** everywhere. **Post Office:** 505 N. Kings Hwy. (☎626-9533), at 5th Ave. N. Open M-F 8:30am-5pm, Sa 9am-1pm. **ZIP code:** 29577. **Area code:** 843.

⌨ ACCOMMODATIONS AND CAMPING. There are hundreds of motels lining Ocean Blvd., with those on the ocean side fetching higher prices than those across the street. Cheap motels also dot Rte. 17. Prices plummet Oct. through Mar.—as low as $20-30 a night for one of the luxurious hotels right on the beach. Call the free **Myrtle Beach Lodging Reservation Service,** 1551 21st Ave. N., #20. (☎626-9970 or 800-626-7477. Open May-Aug. M-F 8:30am-7pm; Sept.-Apr. 8:30am-5pm.) **Sea Banks Motor Inn,** 2200 S. Ocean Blvd., across the street from the ocean, offers rooms with large windows, cable, laundry, and pool and beach access. (☎448-2434 or 800-523-0603. Singles $45; doubles $68; mid-Sept. to mid-Mar. $20-26/$26-31.) The **Hurl Rock Motel,** 2010 S. Ocean Blvd., has big, clean (and rock-free) rooms with access to a pool and hot tub. (☎626-3531 or 888-487-5762. Must be 25+ to rent a single. Singles $45; doubles $54-75; as low as $22/$25 during the off season.) **David's Landing,** 2708 S. Ocean Blvd., features large, modern one- and two-room apartments. (☎626-8845 or 800-561-3504. Must be 25+ to rent. June-Aug. $45-75; Sept.-May $25-40.) **Huntington Beach State Park Campground,** 3 mi. south of Murrell's Inlet on U.S. 17, is located in a diverse environment including lagoons, salt marshes, and a beach. Gators come within yards of the sites. (☎237-4440. Open daily 6am-10pm, off-season 6am-6pm. Tent sites Apr.-Oct. $12; Nov.-Mar. $9.50. Full hookup $26/$21. Day use $4.) **Myrtle Beach State Park Campground,** 3 mi. south of town off U.S. 17, is more crowded and less attractive than Huntington, but its 350 sites come with access to a beach, fishing pier, pool, and nature trail, as well as showers and laundry. (☎238-5325. Office open daily 8am-5pm. Sites $22. Cabins for 4-8 $440 per week. Day use $2.)

⌨ ALL YOU CAN EAT. The Grand Strand tempts hungry motorists to leave the highway with over 1800 restaurants serving every type of food in every type of setting imaginable. Massive, family-style all-you-can-eat joints beckon from beneath the glow of every traffic light. **Rte. 17** offers countless steakhouses and fast food restaurants. Meanwhile, seafood is best on **Murrell's Inlet.** With license plates on the walls and peanut shells on the floor, the **River City Cafe,** 404 21st Ave. N., celebrates a brand of American informality bordering on delinquency: peruse the enthusiastic signatures of patrons as you polish off a burger or knock back a beer. (☎448-1990. Open daily 11am-10pm.) While most of the restaurants in Broadway at the Beach sacrifice food quality for elaborate decor, **Benito's,** in the northeast part of the complex, puts together fancy brick oven pizzas ($5-15) and calzones ($6-7), as well as $9-12 pasta dishes. (☎444-0006. Open daily 11am-10:30pm.) Split your belly with one of the monstrous sandwiches at **Dagwood's Deli,** 400 11th. Ave. N. All sandwiches ($4-8) are made with fresh bread and served with pickles and chips. (☎448-0100. Open M-Sa 11am-9pm.)

⌨ SIGHTS AND NIGHTLIFE. The boulevard and the length of the beach are both called "the strand," and while you're on it the rule of the land is watch or be watched. Strutting is preferable to mere walking, while signs curb cruising aspirations with the command "You may not cross this point more than twice in two hours." Meanwhile, families, newlyweds, foreigners, and students flock to Myrtle Beach to lie out, eat out, and live out American beach culture. Coupons are everywhere; you should never pay full price for any attraction in Myrtle Beach. Pick up a copy of the *Sunny Day Guide*, *Myrtle Beach Guide*, or *Strand Magazine*.

The colossal **Broadway at the Beach,** Rte. 17 Bypass and 21st Ave. N., is a sprawling complex determined to stimulate and entertain. In addition to theaters, a water park, mini golf, rides, theme restaurants, nightclubs, and 100 shops, **Butterfly Pavilion** (☎839-4444) showcases over 40 species of butterflies in free flight while **Ripley's Aquarium** (☎916-0888 or 800-734-8888) features sharks and sting rays swimming overhead. (Open daily 9am-11pm. $15, ages 5-11 $9, ages 2-4 $3.) Meanwhile, **Alligator Adventure,** Barefoot Landing, Rte. 17 in North Myrtle Beach, provides another opportunity for animal-directed voyeurism with over 800 gators. (☎361-0789. Open daily 9am-10pm. $12, seniors $10, ages 4-12 $8.)

Escaping from the real world can be as simple as reducing its size. Sports of highly specialized skill become the realm of the common enthusiast in parks that scale down the stakes. **Mini golf** holes outnumber permanent residents, with the most elaborate courses clustering on Kings Hwy., while faster-paced adventures go down at **NASCAR Speedpark** as seven different tracks, all with varying speed and difficulty, cater to the need for speed. (☎918-8725. $25 unlimited rides, under 13 $11.) The 9100-acre **Brookgreen Gardens,** Rte. 17 opposite Huntington Beach State Park south of Murrell's Inlet, offer a respite from downtown's more frenzied antics. A large collection of American sculpture rests on over 9000 oak-shaded, relaxing acres. (☎235-6001. Open daily 9:30am-5pm. $8.50, ages 6-12 $4.)

For a night on the town, **Celebrity Square** facilitates stepping out in any style with *ten* nightclubs, each offering a different take on the immortal drinking and dancing combo. Elsewhere, **Club Millennium 2000,** 1012 S. Kings Hwy. (☎445-9630), and **2001,** 920 Lake Arrowhead Rd. (☎449-9434), offer more opportunity for adventure during a hot-steppin' odyssey.

GEORGIA

Georgia presents two faces: the rural southern region contrasts starkly with the sprawling commercialism of the north. But the state somehow manages to balance its many different identities. The cosmopolitan capital city of Atlanta boasts of Coca-Cola and Ted Turner's CNN, both of which have networked the globe. Savannah fosters a different sort of life from the Atlanta metropolis by stubbornly preserving its distinctive antebellum atmosphere. And while collegiate Athens breeds "big" bands, Georgia's Gold Coast mellows in slow-paced seaside existence. This state of countless contradictions was called home by two former presidents as well: Jimmy Carter's hometown of Plains and Franklin D. Roosevelt's summer home in Warm Springs both stand on red Georgia clay. No matter where you go in Georgia, however, one thing remains constant—the peachy Southern hospitality.

THE SOUTH

▨ PRACTICAL INFORMATION

Capital: Atlanta.

Visitor info: Dept. of Industry and Trade, Tourist Division, 285 Peachtree Center Ave., Atlanta 30303 (☎404-656-3590 or 800-847-4842; www.georgia.org), in the Marriot Marquis 2 Tower, 10th fl. Open M-F 8am-5pm. **Dept. of Natural Resources,** 205 Butler St. SE, #1352, Atlanta 30334 (☎404-656-3530 or 800-864-7275). **U.S. Forest Service,** 1800 NE Expwy., Atlanta 30329 (☎404-248-9142). Open W-Su 11am-7:30pm.

Postal Abbreviation: GA. **Sales Tax:** 4-7%, depending on county.

ATLANTA ☎ 404

An increasingly popular destination for twenty- and thirty-somethings craving big city life but weary of more manic metropoloi, Atlanta strives to be cosmopolitan with a smile. Although it has not yet caught up to the likes of Los Angeles or New York City, Atlanta continues to expand with corporate bigwigs, international sports events, and a wave of newcomers encouraging its growth. Northerners, Californians, the third-largest gay population in the US, and a host of ethnicities have diversified this unofficial capital of the South. A nationwide economic powerhouse, Atlanta holds offices for 400 of the Fortune 500 companies, including the headquarters of Coca-Cola, Delta Airlines, the United Parcel Service, and CNN. Nineteen colleges, including Georgia Tech, Morehouse College, Spelman College, and Emory University, call "Hotlanta" home. The city is just as blessed with subtle gems; getting lost on Atlanta's streets reveals a seemingly endless number of trendy restaurants and beautiful old houses.

■ INTERCITY TRANSPORTATION

Atlanta sprawls across ten counties in the northwest quadrant of the state at the junctures of I-75, I-85, and I-20. **I-285** (the "Perimeter") circumscribes the city.

Flights: Hartsfield International Airport (general info, international services, and flight info ☎ 530-2081; www.atlanta-airport.com), south of the city. MARTA (see **Public Transit**) is the easiest way to get downtown, with 15min. rides departing every 8min. from the Airport Station daily 5am-1am ($1.75). **Atlanta Airport Shuttle** (☎ 524-3400) runs vans from the airport to over 100 locations in the metropolis and outlying area (every 15min. daily 7am-11pm; shuttle downtown $14). Taxi to downtown $20.

Train: Amtrak, 1688 Peachtree St. NW (☎ 881-3062), 3 mi. north of downtown at I-85, or 1 mi. north of Ponce de Leon on Peachtree St. Take bus #23 from "Arts Center" MARTA station. To: New York (19hr., 1 per day, $107-191) and New Orleans (10½hr., 1 per day, $50-89). Open daily 7am-9:30pm.

Buses: Greyhound, 232 Forsyth St. SW (☎ 584-1728), across from "Garnett" MARTA station. To: New York (18-23hr., 14 per day, $93-98); Washington, D.C. (15hr., 12 per day, $75-79); and Savannah (5hr., 6 per day, $45). Open 24hr.

▐ LOCAL TRANSPORTATION

Public Transit: Metropolitan Atlanta Rapid Transit Authority (MARTA) (☎ 848-4711; schedule info M-F 6am-11pm, Sa-Su 8am-10pm). Clean, uncrowded trains and buses provide hassle-free transportation to Atlanta's major attractions. Rail operates M-F 5am-1am, Sa-Su and holidays 6am-12:30am in most areas. Bus hours vary. Fare $1.75, exact change needed, or buy a token at station machines; transfers free. Unlimited weekly pass $13. Pick up a system map at the **MARTA Ride Store,** Five Points Station downtown, or at the airport, Lindbergh, or Lenox stations. The majority of trains, rail stations, and buses are wheelchair accessible.

Taxis: Atlanta Yellow Cab, ☎ 521-0200. **Checker Cab,** ☎ 351-1111.

Car Rental: Atlanta Rent-a-Car, 3185 Camp Creek Pkwy. (☎ 763-1110), just inside I-285 2½ mi. east of the airport. 10 other locations in the area including 2800 Campelton Rd. (☎ 344-1060) and 3129 Piedmont Rd. (☎ 231-4898). $25 per day, 100 free mi. per day, 24¢ per additional mi. Must be 21 with major credit card.

◀ ORIENTATION

Maneuvering around Atlanta's main thoroughfares, arranged much like the spokes of a wheel, challenges even the most experienced native. **Peachtree St.** (one of over 100 streets bearing the name in Atlanta), is a major north-south road, while two other significant roads, **Spring St.** and **Piedmont Ave.,** run parallel to Peachtree. On the eastern edge of the city, **Moreland Ave.** runs the length of the city, through Vir-

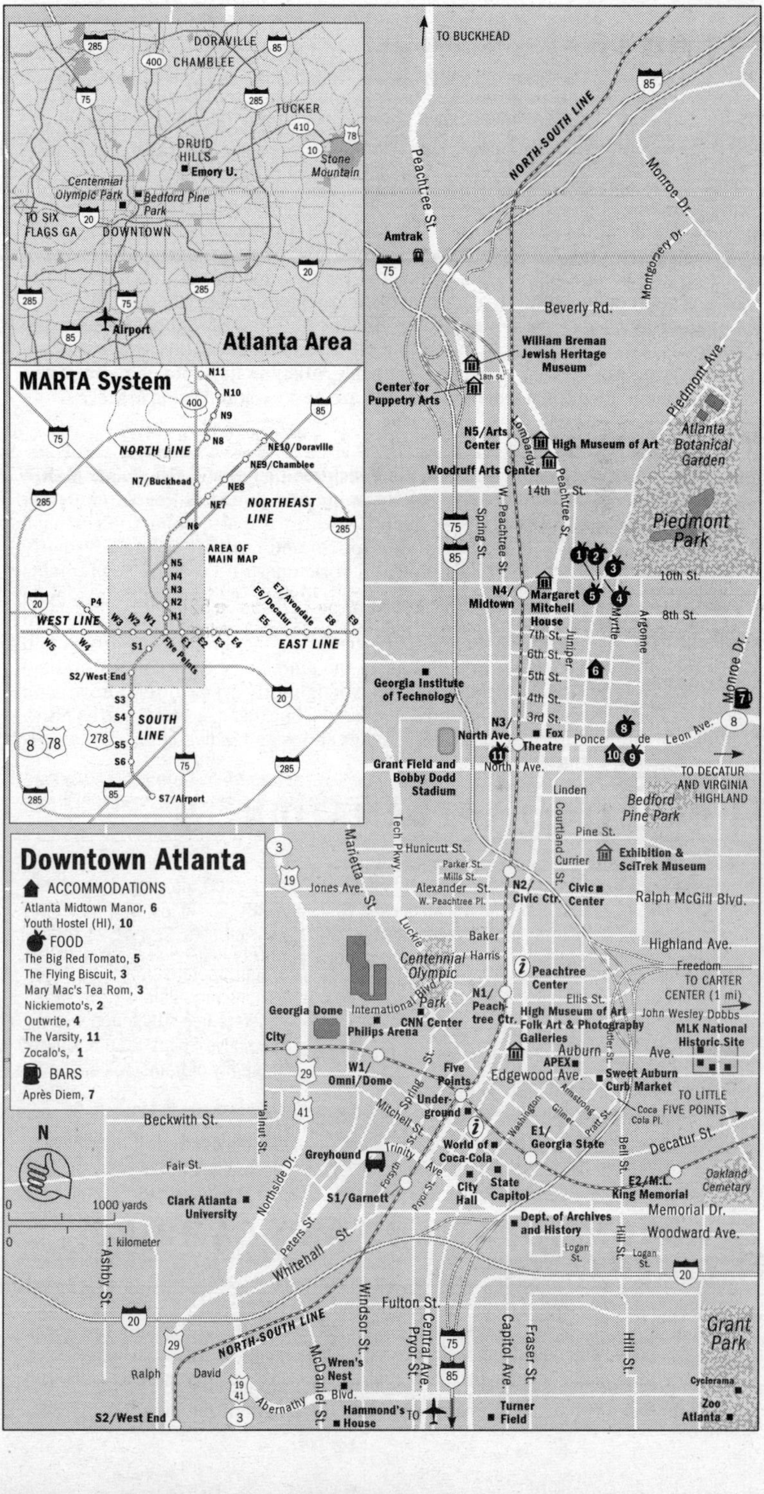

Atlanta Area

TO BUCKHEAD

DORAVILLE
CHAMBLEE
285 400 85
75 TUCKER
295 410 78
DRUID 10
HILLS Stone
Emory U. Mountain
Centennial
Olympic Park Bedford Pine
Park
TO SIX 20
FLAGS GA DOWNTOWN
285 75 85
75
Airport

MARTA System

N11
N10
N9
400
NORTH LINE
N8
75 NE10/Doraville
NE9/Chamblee
N7/Buckhead NE8
NE7 NORTHEAST
285 N6 LINE
AREA OF
MAIN MAP 285
N5
N4 E7/Avondale
N3 E6/Decatur E8
P4 N2 E5 E9
WEST LINE W3 N1 E4
W2 W1 Five E1 E2 E3 EAST LINE
W5 W4 S1 Points
S2/West End
S3
8 78 278 S4 SOUTH
S5 LINE
S6
285 75 285
85
S7/Airport

Downtown Atlanta

⌂ **ACCOMMODATIONS**
Atlanta Midtown Manor, **6**
Youth Hostel (HI), **10**
🍴 **FOOD**
The Big Red Tomato, **5**
The Flying Biscuit, **3**
Mary Mac's Tea Rom, **3**
Nickiemoto's, **2**
Outwrite, **1**
The Varsity, **11**
Zocalo's, **1**
🍸 **BARS**
Après Diem, **7**

N
1000 yards
1 kilometer
Ashby St.

Peachtree St.
North-South Line
Monroe Dr.
85

Amtrak
75
Beverly Rd.
Montgomery Dr.

William Breman
Jewish Heritage
Museum
8th St.
Center for
Puppetry Arts Piedmont Ave.
N5/Arts Piedmont
Center High Museum of Art Atlanta
Woodruff Arts Center Botanical
Peachtree St. Garden
W. Peachtree St.
14th St. Piedmont
Park
Spring St. 1 2 10th St.
3
75 N4/ 5
85 Midtown 4 8th St.
Margaret Myrtle
Mitchell Argonne
House 7th St. Juniper
6th St.
5th St. 6
Georgia Institute 4th St.
of Technology 3rd St. Monroe Dr.
N3/ Fox 8 7
North Ave. Theatre
Ponce de Leon Ave. 8
Grant Field and 10 9
Bobby Dodd North Ave.
Stadium Linden Bedford
Pine Park TO DECATUR
Courtland St. AND VIRGINIA
Pine St. HIGHLAND
Marietta St. 3 Hunicutt St.
19 Parker St. Currier Exhibition &
Jones Ave. Mills St. SciTrek Museum
Alexander St. Ralph McGill Blvd.
W. Peachtree Pl.
Tech Pkwy. N2/ Civic
Baker Civic Ctr. Center Highland Ave.
Centennial Harris Freedom
Olympic TO CARTER
Park i Peachtree CENTER (1 mi)
Center John Wesley Dobbs
Georgia Dome Ellis St. MLK National
International Blvd. N1/ High Museum of Art Ave. Historic Site
CNN Center Peach- Folk Art & Photography
Philips Arena tree Ctr. Galleries TO LITTLE
City Auburn APEX Sweet Auburn FIVE POINTS
Ave. Curb Market Coca
W1/ Five Edgewood Ave. Cola Pl.
Omni/Dome Points Armstead St. Gilmer St.
Under- Washington St. Decatur St.
ground E1/ Oakland
Beckwith St. World of Georgia State Cemetery
41 Coca-Cola E2/M.L.
Greyhound i King Memorial
Fair St. City State King Memorial Memorial Dr.
Clark Atlanta Hall Capitol Woodward Ave.
University S1/Garnett Dept. of Archives
Peters St. and History 20
Pryor St. Logan St.
Whitehall St. Hill St.
Fulton St. Logan St. Grant
Central Ave. Park
North-South Line Capitol Ave. Fraser Ave.
20 75 Cyclorama
29 85
Ralph David Wren's Zoo
McDaniel St. Nest Turner Atlanta
3 Blvd. Field
S2/West End Abernathy St. Hammond's TO
House

TO DECATUR AND VIRGINIA HIGHLAND · TO LITTLE FIVE POINTS · TO CARTER CENTER (1 mi)

THE SOUTH

"SQUEAL LIKE A PIG" One of Georgia's more dubious claims to fame is the film *Deliverance*, shot in the woodlands of the state's northeastern corner. In the 1972 film, directed by John Boorman, four Atlanta businessmen get more than they bargain for on a fishing trip to the Georgia backcountry. Their disturbing encounter with the depraved locals has been the stuff of nightmares—not to mention more than a few horrendous pig jokes. See the movie.

ginia Highland, Little Five Points (L5P), and East Atlanta. Major east-west roads include **Ponce de Leon Ave.** and **North Ave.** Navigating Atlanta requires a full arsenal of transportation strategies, from walking to public transportation to driving. The city is more a conglomeration of several distinct regions and neighborhoods than a single metropolis. The outlying areas of Buckhead, Virginia Highlands and Little Five Points are easiest to get to by car, but once you've arrived, the restaurant- and bar-lined streets encourage walking. Meanwhile, Atlanta's most popular attractions are centered in downtown and midtown and are best explored using MARTA.

NEIGHBORHOODS

Sprouting out of downtown Atlanta, the **Peachtree Center** and **Five Points MARTA** stations deliver hoards of tourists to shopping and dining at **Peachtree Center Mall** and **Underground Atlanta,** respectively. Downtown is also home to **Centennial Olympic Park** as well as Atlanta's major sports and concert venues. Directly southwest of downtown the city's oldest historic quarter, the **West End** remains an African-American neighborhood with a rich history. From Five Points, head northeast to **Midtown** (from Ponce de Leon Ave. to 17th St.) for museums and **Piedmont Park.** The **Little Five Points (L5P)** district, a local haven for artists and youth subculture, lies east of Five Points, at the junction of Euclid and Moreland Ave. North of L5P, **Virginia Highland,** a trendy neighborhood east of Midtown and Piedmont Park, attracts yuppies and college kids. **Buckhead,** a swanky area north of Midtown on Peachtree St., houses designer shops and dance clubs, and accessible on MARTA ("Buckhead").

🔢 PRACTICAL INFORMATION

Visitor info: Atlanta Convention and Visitors Bureau, 233 Peachtree St. NE, (☎521-6600 or ☎800-285-2682; www.atlanta.com), Peachtree Center, #100, downtown. Open M-F 8:30am-5pm. Automated **information service** (☎222-6688). For maps, and brochures while in town stop in at the **Visitors Center,** 65 Upper Alabama St. (☎521-6688). Located on the upper level of Underground Atlanta, at MARTA "Five Points." Open M-Sa 10am-6pm, Su noon-6pm. Gray Line Tours depart from the Visitors Center Tu-Sa 9am and 1:30pm, M 1:30pm. $35, children 6-12 $30.

Bi-Gay-Lesbian Organizations: The Atlanta Gay and Lesbian Center, 159 Ralph McGill Blvd., #600 (☎523-7500; www.aglc.org). Also see *Gay Yellow Pages* (☎892-6454).

Hotline: Rape Crisis Counseling, ☎616-4861. Operates 24hr.

Post Office: Phoenix Station (☎521-2963). At the corner of Forsyth and Marietta St., one block from MARTA "Five Points." Open M-F 9am-5pm. **ZIP code:** 30301. **Area code:** 404 roughly inside the I-285 perimeter, 770 outside. Listings 404 unless noted. 10-digit dialing required.

🏠 ACCOMMODATIONS AND CAMPING

Atlanta Hostel, 223 Ponce de Leon Ave., attached to the Woodruff B&B (☎875-9449), in Midtown. From MARTA: North Ave. station, exit onto Ponce de Leon, about 3½ blocks east at Myrtle St., or take bus #2 and ask the driver to stop. Clean, dorm-style rooms with free coffee and doughnuts in the morning. No sleeping bags allowed, but free blankets are distributed. Laundry facilities, pool table, kitchen, and Internet terminal. Luggage storage $1. Linen $1. Free lockers. Dorms $18; private rooms $39-$49.

Masters Inn Economy, 3092 Presidential Pkwy. in Doraville (☎770-454-8373 or 800-633-3434), off Chamblee Tucker Rd., Exit 94 off I-85. Clean, large rooms with king-size beds, local calls, cable TV, and pool. Singles $40, F-Sa $44; doubles $44/$49.

Motel 6, 2820 Chamblee Tucker Rd. in Doraville (☎770-458-6626), Exit 94 off I-85. Spacious and immaculate rooms. Offers free local calls, morning coffee, and A/C. Under 18 stay free with parents. Singles $46; $6 each additional person.

Atlanta Midtown Manor, 811 Piedmont Ave. NE (☎872-5846 or 800-724-4387). Nestled on a shaded lane in the center of Atlanta, Midtown Manor's 3 Victorian houses offer charming rooms with antique furnishings, A/C, and TV. Free coffee, doughnuts, and street parking. Shared bath, private costs extra. Fills up in summer; reservations recommended. Laundry. Singles $79; doubles $99.

Stone Mountain Family Campground (☎770-498-5710), on U.S. 78 (see p. 388). Gorgeous sites; one-third are on the lake. Bike rentals, free laser show, and Internet access. Max. 2-week stay. Sites $20-26; full hookup $30-35. Entrance fee $6 per car.

◖ FOOD

From Vietnamese to Italian, baked to fried to fricasseed, Atlanta dining cooks up ample options, no matter what you're craving. "Soul food," designed to nurture the spiritual as well as the physical, is the heart of this town's palate. Some favorite dishes include fried chicken, ribs, okra, sweet potato pie, and peach cobbler. Have a taste of the South and dip cornbread into "pot likker," water used to cook greens. For a sweet treat (60¢), you can't beat the Atlanta-based **Krispy Kreme Doughnuts,** whose glazed delights are a Southern institution. The factory store, 295 Ponce de Leon Ave. NE (☎876-7307), continuously bakes their wares, visible through the back window. (Open Su-Th 5:30am-midnight, F-Sa 24hr.; drive-through open daily 24hr.) More substantial fare, from cow's feet to ox tails, is available at the **Sweet Auburn Curb Market** in the Sweet Auburn District, 209 Edgewood Ave., a depot for soul food's raw materials since 1923. (☎659-1665. Open M-Sa 8am-6pm.)

BUCKHEAD

For cheap eats in diamond-studded Buckhead, head over to the **Kroger** supermarket, 3330 Piedmont Rd. NE, in the Piedmont Peachtree Crossing Shopping Center. The deli serves sandwiches ($3-5) and chicken dinners ($6), among other dishes.

▨ **Fellini's Pizza,** 2809 Peachtree Rd. NE (☎266-0082), welcomes hungry customers with its bright yellow awnings and spacious deck, complete with fountain. Four other Atlanta locations, including 909 Ponce de Leon (☎873-3088). Slices $1.45, toppings 40¢ extra; pies $8.50-12.50. Open M-Sa 11:30am-2am, Su 12:30pm-midnight.

East Village Grille, 248 Buckhead Ave. NE (☎233-3345). Located smack-dab in the middle of the Buckhead nightlife scene, this trusty diner serves up late-night munchies (including $3 breakfast specials) to inebriated locals. Kitchen open M-F 11am-midnight, Sa-Su 11am-2am; bar open daily 11am-4am.

BUFORD HIGHWAY

Little Szechuan, 5091-C Buford Hwy. (☎770-451-0192), at I-285, Exit 25. In the heart of the ethnically diverse Buford Hwy. area, lunch specials for $6 are served in not-so-little doses. Open M and W-Sa 11:30am-9:30pm, Su noon-9:30pm.

Pho Hoa, 5150 Buford Hwy., #C-120 (☎770-455-8729), at I-285, Exit 25. Vietnamese noodle soup, *pho,* provides a healthy one-dish alternative for any meal of the day. Open daily 10am-10pm.

MIDTOWN

Tortillas, 774 Ponce de Leon Ave. (☎892-0193). The student crowd munches dirt-cheap and tasty Mexican food, with soft chicken tacos ($1.75) and a large variety of burritos (from $3). Try the patio for open-air eating. Open Su-Th 11am-10pm, F-Sa 11am-11pm.

The Varsity, 61 North Ave. NW at Spring St. (☎881-1707), at I-85. MARTA: North Ave. The world's largest drive-in and originator of the assembly-line school of food preparation. Best known for the greatest onion rings in the South and the 2 mi. of hot dogs sold daily. Most menu items around $2. Open Su-Th 9am-11:30pm, F-Sa 9am-12:30am.

Mary Mac's Tea Room, 224 Ponce De Leon Ave. (☎876-1800), at Myrtle; take the "Georgia Tech" bus north. A "revival of Southern hospitality" with a 40s atmosphere and amazing cinnamon rolls ($3.75 per dozen after 5pm). An entree and side from the Southern-style menu goes for $9. Cash only. Open M-Sa 11am-8:30pm, Su 11am-3pm.

10TH ST.

Zocalo's, 187 10th St. (☎249-7576). Gourmet Mexican for the frugal-minded. Gorgeously fresh, authentic dinners start at $8.75. Open M-Th 11:30am-2:30am and 5:30pm-11pm, F-Sa 11:30am-midnight, Su 8:30am-10pm.

Nickiemoto's, 990 Piedmont Ave. (☎ 253-2010). If sushi's your pleasure, head to Nickiemoto's to soothe your palate. Combo plates start at $10.50. Open M-Th 11:30am-11pm, F 11:30am-midnight, Sa noon-midnight, Su 2-11pm.

Outwrite Bookstore & Coffeehouse, 991 Piedmont Ave. (☎ 607-0082). With rainbow-wigged mannequin heads gracing the windows, specialty coffees and sandwiches in the back corner, and inviting tables and chairs up front, this gay and lesbian bookstore and coffeehouse has a relaxed, stylish air. Open Su-Th 9am-11pm, F-Sa 9am-midnight.

Big Red Tomato Bistro, 980 Piedmont Rd. (☎870-9881). For Italian fare and a warm, romantic ambience, cozy up to the Big Red Tomato. Entrees $8-20. Open Su-Tu 5:30-10pm, W-Th 5:30-11pm, F-Sa 5:30-midnight.

The Flying Biscuit, 1001 Piedmont Ave. (☎874-8887). As expected, biscuits are the forte here. Breakfast lovers will gobble up the orange-scented French toast ($6). Breakfast served all day. Open daily 7am-11pm.

VIRGINIA HIGHLAND

Fontaine's Oyster House, 1026½ N. Highland Ave. (☎872-0869). Dive into Fontaine's for all things oyster: have them on the half-shell (half-dozen for $5) or eat them roasted in one of 8 ways ($8-15). Don't be afraid to sink your teeth into some juicy alligator too. Open M and W-F 10:30am-4am, Tu 4pm-4am, Su 10:30am-midnight. Restaurant closes at midnight, 11:30pm on Su.

Panita Thai Kitchen, 1043 Greenwood Ave. (☎888-9228) off N. Highland. Lose yourself in vine-covered trellises and authentic Thai food in this graceful restaurant in Virginia Highland. Vegetarian meals from $11; chicken and duck dishes from $12; and gourmet meals from $16. Open daily noon-midnight.

Everybody's, 1040 N. Highland Ave. (☎873-4545), has received high accolades for selling Atlanta's best pizza. Their inventive pizza salad, a colossal mound of greens and chicken on a pizza bed ($10.75), is more than enough for two. Open M-Th 11:30am-11pm, F-Sa 11:30am-1am, Su noon-10:30pm.

Majestic Food Shop, 1031 Ponce de Leon Ave. (☎875-0276), at Cleburne. For the ravenous insomniac people-watcher, there is no place better. The late, late night scene for Highland and L5P with doormen to prevent weekend nocturnal crowding. The Majestic offers "food that pleases" such as burgers ($2), grits ($1.15), and the like. Open 24hr.

Manuel's Tavern, 602 N. Highland Ave. (☎525-3447). A prime spot between L5P and the Highland, this casual bar and grill is a hangout for local media and the longtime stomping grounds of Atlanta's Democrats; Jimmy Carter is known to swing by for a burger ($5.50) and a beer. Open M-Sa 11am-2am, Su 11am-midnight.

LITTLE FIVE POINTS

La Fonda Latina, 1150 Euclid Ave. (☎577-8317). Lounge under the glow of palm leaves fashioned from neon lights and enjoy the vibrantly decorated walls while savoring a Cuban sandwich ($6.25-7) or 10 in. quesadillas ($5-7). Open M-Th 11:30am-11pm, F-Sa 11:30am-midnight, Su 12:30-11pm.

Bridgetown Grill, 1156 Euclid Ave. (☎653-0110). Try the mango pork with black beans, rice, and plantains ($13) in this colorful atmosphere. Open M-Th 11:45am-10pm, F-Sa 11:45am-11pm.

◉ SIGHTS

SWEET AUBURN DISTRICT

Atlanta's sights are scattered, but the effort it takes to find them pays off. The most powerful are the MLK sites along Auburn Ave. in Sweet Auburn. Reverend Martin Luther King, Jr.'s birthplace, church, and grave are all part of the 23-acre ◪**Martin Luther King, Jr. National Historic Site.** The **Visitors Center** houses poignant displays of photographs, videos, and quotations oriented around King's life and the civil rights struggle. *(450 Auburn Ave. NE. MARTA: King Memorial. ☎331 5190. Open daily 9am 6pm.)* The Visitors Center administers tours of the **birthplace of MLK,** 501 Auburn Ave. Arrive early to sign up: advance reservations are not accepted *(☎331-5190).* Across the street from the Visitors Center stands **Ebenezer Baptist Church,** where King gave his first sermon at age 17 and co-pastored with his father from 1960 to 1968. *(407 Auburn Ave. ☎688-7263. Open June-Aug. daily 9am-6pm, Sept.-May 9am-5pm.)* King's **grave** and reflecting pool are located next door at the **Martin Luther King, Jr. Center for Non-violent Social Exchange.** The center holds a collection of King's personal effects, an overview of his role model, Gandhi, and an exhibit on Rosa Parks. *(449 Auburn Ave. NE. ☎331-5190. Open June-Aug. daily 9am-6pm; winter 9am-5pm.)* Plaques lining Sweet Auburn point out the architecture and prominent past residents of this historically African-American neighborhood. All sites are free.

DOWNTOWN AND AROUND

From March through November, the **Atlanta Preservation Center** offers walking tours of six popular areas, including Druid Hills, the setting of *Driving Miss Daisy.* *(537 Peachtree St. NE. ☎876-2041. $5, students and seniors $4.)*

GRANT PARK. In Grant Park, directly south of Oakland Cemetery and Cherokee Ave., the 116-year-old **Cyclorama,** the world's largest painting (48 ft. tall and 348 ft. in circumference) continues to twirl viewers on a revolving platform through the 1864 Battle of Atlanta, just as it did in 1893 when it first opened. *(800 Cherokee Ave. SE. ☎624-1071. Take bus #31 or 97 from Five Points. Open June-Sept. daily 9:30am-5:30pm; Oct.-May 9:30am-4:30pm. $5, seniors $4, ages 6-12 $3.)*

ZOO ATLANTA. Next door to the park, the zoo boasts komodo dragons, an artist-elephant, Allen the orangutan, a petting zoo, two giant pandas of Chengdu, and most recently, a silverback gorilla and Sumatran tiger. *(800 Cherokee Ave. SE. ☎624-5600 or 624-5856. Take bus #31 or 97 from Five Points. Open Apr.-Oct. M-F 9:30am-4:30pm, Sa-Su 9:30am-5:30pm; Nov.-Mar. daily 9:30am-4:30pm. $15, seniors $11, ages 3-11 $10.)*

WORLD OF COCA-COLA. Two blocks from the capitol, the World of Coca-Cola details "the real thing's" rise from its humble beginnings in Atlanta to a position of world domination. The ode to Coca-Cola culture includes exhibits bursting with ads, slogans, and press accounts of the soft drink. A replica soda fountain, complete with a "jerk" demonstrating cola concocting, informs and entertains. The whole experience ends with a bang rather than a fizzle in the sampling room, where guests enthusiastically partake of 46 different soft drinks from around the world. *(55 Martin Luther King, Jr. Dr. ☎676-5151. Open June-Aug. M-Sa 9am-6pm, Su 11am-6pm; Sept.-May M-Sa 9am-5pm, Su noon-6pm. $6, seniors $4, ages 6-12 $3.)*

UNDERGROUND ATLANTA. Adjacent to the WOC, this redeveloped part Atlanta gets down with six subterranean blocks of urban marketplace and over 120 chain restaurants, shops, and night spots. Descend at the entrance beside the Five Points subway station. *(☎523-2311. Shops open June-Sept. M-Sa 10am-9:30pm, Su 11am-7pm; Oct.-May M-Sa 10am-9pm, Su noon-6pm. Bars and restaurants close later.)*

CNN. High-tech Atlanta reigns with multinational business powerhouses situated in the **Five Points District. Turner Broadcasting System** offers a behind-the-scenes peek with its **Cable News Network (CNN) Studio Tour,** at Techwood Dr. and Marietta St. Witness anchors broadcasting live, and get the inside scoop on production techniques and special effects. *(☎827-2300. 45min. tours given every 10-15 min. Open*

> # THE REAL STORY ON THE REAL THING In the
> year 1886, chemist Dr. John Smyth Pemberton created a headache powder advertised
> to relieve even the greatest pangs. As old Southern lore will tell it, a customer walked
> into Jacob's pharmacy shortly thereafter and asked the pharmacist to mix the powder
> with tonic water right there in the store, as his headache prevented him from waiting
> any longer to swallow the cure. This concoction, with its still secret formula, marked the
> birth of Coca-Cola and has not changed in over a century.

daily 9am-6pm. $8, seniors $6, ages 5-12 $5.) You're invited to join the punditocracy in
the studio audience of *CNN Talk Back Live*, but they'll warn you not to pick your
nose on camera. *(M-F 3pm. Take MARTA west to the Omni/Dome/GWCC Station at W1. Free.)*

OLYMPICS. Despite the tragic bombing that occurred here during the Olympics,
Centennial Olympic Park, next to CNN and the Georgia World Congress Center,
delights children of all ages with the youthful **Fountain of Rings**—splashing and giggling encouraged. *(Four 20min shows daily: 12:30, 3:30, 6:30, and 9pm.)*

CARTER PRESIDENTIAL CENTER. This charming museum, north of Little Five
Points, traces Georgia peanut farmer Jimmy Carter's political career through interesting, and at times humorous, exhibits and films. Attached to the museum, the
Jimmy Carter Library, one of only ten Presidential libraries in the country, serves as an
archival depository for historical materials from the Carter Administration. *(441 Freedom Pkwy. ☎331-0296. Take bus #16 to Cleburne Ave. Museum open M-Sa 9am-4:45pm, Su
noon-4:45pm; grounds open to the public daily 6am-9pm. $5, seniors $4, under 16 free.)*

WEST END

AFRICAN-AMERICAN HISTORY. Dating from 1835, the West End is Atlanta's oldest neighborhood. Experience several eccentric twists on the historic home tradition at the **Wren's Nest.** Home to author Joel Chandler Harris, who popularized the
African folktale trickster Br'er Rabbit, the Wren's Nest offers a glimpse into middle class life as it was at the beginning of the century. The house sparks further
interest with a look into Harris's bedroom which has been left untouched since
his death. Energetic professional storytellers continue the house's legacy, entertaining young and old alike. *(1050 R.D. Abernathy Blvd. Take bus #71 from West End Sta-
tion/S2. ☎753-7735. Open Tu-Sa 10am-2pm. $7, seniors and teens $5, ages 4-12 $4.)* The
Hammonds House displays unique contemporary and historic works in Georgia's
only collection dedicated entirely to African-American and Haitian art. *(503 Pee-
ples St. SW. ☎752-8730. Open Tu-F 10am-6pm, Sa-Su 1-5pm. $2; seniors, students, and chil-
dren $1.)* Slave-born Alonzo F. Herndon built the 1910 Beaux-Arts Classical
mansion, the **Herndon Home.** A prominent barber and founder of Atlanta Life
Insurance Co., Herndon became Atlanta's wealthiest African-American in the
early 1900s. *(587 University Pl. NW. Take bus #3 from Five Points station to the corner of Martin
Luther King, Jr. Dr. and Maple and walk 1 block west, turn right on Walnut and walk 1 block.
☎581-9813. Open Tu-Sa 10am-4pm. Tours every hr., last tour 4pm. $5, students $3, W Community Day: donations accepted.)*

MIDTOWN

SCITREK. Near Piedmont Park (see **Outdoors,** below), **SciTrek (Science and Technology Museum of Atlanta),** with over 150 interactive exhibits for all ages, is one of the
nation's top science centers. *(395 Piedmont Ave. NE. ☎522-5500. Take MARTA to Civic Center, walk three blocks east on Ralph McGill Blvd., and turn left on Piedmont. Open M-Sa 10am-
5pm, Su noon-5pm. $7.50; seniors, students, military, and ages 3-17 $6.)*

MARGARET MITCHELL. Reopened in 1997 after two arson-related fires, the **Margaret Mitchell House** and *Gone With the Wind* **Movie Museum** sit at 10th and Peachtree
St., adjacent to the Midtown MARTA station. See the apartment where Mitchell
wrote *Gone With the Wind,* as well as her typewriter and autographed copies of
the novel. The Movie Museum includes the door to "Tara," the portrait of Scarlet at

which Clark Gable hurled a cocktail onscreen (complete with stain), and other original props from the movie set. *(990 Peachtree St. ☎249-7015. Open daily 9:30am-5pm. $12, seniors and students $9, ages 6-17 $5. 1hr. tours every 10min.; last tour at 4:30pm.)*

WOODRUFF ARTS CENTER. Culture vultures, here's your place. To the west of Piedmont Park, the Woodruff Arts Center and the **High Museum of Art,** Richard Meier's award-winning building of glass, steel, and white porcelain, offer a bit of refinement. The museum's permanent collection contains one of Andy Warhol's Marilyn Monroe paintings, while recent visiting exhibits have brought renowned works of Picasso, Rockwell, and Michelangelo. *(WAC: 1280 Peachtree St. NE. ☎733-4200. Take MARTA to Arts Center and exit Lombardy Way. High Museum of Art: ☎733-4400. Open Tu-Sa 10am-5pm, Su noon-5pm. $8, seniors and students with ID $6, ages 6-17 $4.)* The **Folk Art & Photography Galleries,** a satellite facility of the High Museum, houses additional exhibits one block south of Peachtree Center Station. *(30 John Wesley Dobbs Ave. NE. ☎577-6940. Open M-Sa 10am-5pm, and the first Th of every month 10am-8pm. Free.)*

WILLIAM BREMAN JEWISH HERITAGE MUSEUM. The William Breman Jewish Heritage Museum, the largest Jewish museum in the southeast, features a powerful, gripping Holocaust exhibit and a gallery tracing the history of the Atlanta Jewish community from 1845 to the present. *(1440 Spring St. NW. ☎873-1661. From Peachtree Center Station, walk three blocks north to 18th St. and Spring St. Open M-Th 10am-5pm, F 10am-3pm, Su 1-5pm. $5, seniors and students $3, under 7 free.)*

CENTER FOR PUPPETRY ARTS. Across the street from the Jewish Heritage Museum, the Center for Puppetry Arts stages live shows and offers puppet-making workshops. The center's museum showcases puppet history and culture throughout the world and invites you to try your hand at manipulating different types of puppets. Also on display are traditional Punch and Judy figures and some of Jim Henson's original Muppets. *(1404 Spring St. NW, at 18th St. ☎873-3391. Open Tu-Sa 9am-5pm, Su 11am-5pm, M closed, though box office is open. $8; seniors, students, and children $7. Puppet workshop ages 5 and over, $5.)*

FERNBANK MUSEUM OF NATURAL HISTORY. The Fernbank Museum of Natural History, off Ponce de Leon Ave., sports dinosaurs, an IMAX theater, discovery centers, and fossils embedded in the limestone floor tiles. *(767 Clifton Rd. NE. ☎929-6300. Take bus #2 from North Ave. or Avondale Station. Open M-Sa 10am-5pm, Su noon-5pm. Museum $12, seniors and students $11, ages 3-12 $10; IMAX film $10/$9/$8; both $17/$15/$13.)* The adjacent **R.L. Staton Rose Garden,** on the corner of Ponce de Leon and Clifton Rd., blossoms with gorgeous blooms from spring into December.

BUCKHEAD

A drive through **Buckhead** (north of midtown and Piedmont Park, off Peachtree near W. Paces Ferry Rd.) uncovers Atlanta's Beverly Hills—the sprawling mansions of Coca-Cola bigwigs and other specimens of high culture. This area is also very conducive to wining and dining experiences, with the area around the intersection of W. Paces Ferry and Peachtree St. offering a string of dance clubs, bars, and restaurants frequented by Atlanta's twenty-somethings. One of the most exquisite residences in the Southeast, the Greek Revival **Governor's Mansion,** has elaborate gardens and one of the finest collections of furniture from the Federal Period. *(391 W. Paces Ferry Rd. ☎261-1776. Tours Tu-Th 10-11:30am. Free.)* In the same neighborhood, discover the **Atlanta History Center/Buckhead.** The **Atlanta History Museum,** 130 W. Paces Ferry Rd. NW, traces Atlanta's development from a rural area to an international cityscape. Its Civil War Gallery spotlights the stories of both Confederate and Union soldiers, while the Folklife Gallery expounds on Southern culture from grits to banjos. Also on the grounds are the **Swan House,** a lavish Anglo-Palladian Revival home built in 1928, and the **Tullie Smith Farm,** an 1845 Yeoman farmhouse. (☎814-4000. Open M-Sa 10am-5:30pm, Su noon-5:30pm. Ticket sales end at 4:30pm. $10, seniors and students $8, ages 6-17 $5; tours of the houses are each an additional $1.)

⚄ OUTDOOR ACTIVITIES

Located in the heart of Midtown, **Piedmont Park** is a hotbed of fun, free activities. Look for the Dogwood Festival, an art festival, in the spring and the Jazz Festival in May. In June the park celebrates with the **Gay Pride Festival**, and on July 4th it draws 55,000 people to the world's largest 10K race. Every summer Turner Broadcasting and HBO present "Screen on the Green," a series of free films projected once a week in the meadow (behind the Visitors Center). To the north, the vast park sprawls around the 60-acre **Atlanta Botanical Garden**, 1345 Piedmont Ave. NE. Stroll through 15 acres of landscaped gardens, a 15-acre hardwood forest with trails, and an interactive children's garden focusing on health and wellness. (☎876-5859. MARTA: Lindburgh Center, bus #31. Open Mar.-Sept. Tu-Su 9am-7pm; Oct.-Feb. Tu-Su 9am-6pm. $7, seniors $5, students and ages 6-12 $4.) The Garden's **Dorothy Chapman Fuqua Conservatory** houses hundreds of species of endangered plants. (Take bus #36 from Arts Center Station or bus #31 from Five Points on Su. Opens at \10am.)

Sixteen miles east of the city on U.S. 78, **Stone Mountain Park** provides a respite from the city with a dose of nature and a fabulous Confederate Memorial carved into the world's largest mass of granite. The "Mt. Rushmore of the South" features Jefferson Davis, Robert E. Lee, and Stonewall Jackson and rises 825 ft. The hike up the **Confederate Hall Trail** (1½ mi.) is rewarded with a spectacular view of Atlanta. The mount is surrounded by a 3200-acre recreation area and historic park; check out the dazzling (and free) laser show on the side of the mountain summer nights at 9:30pm. (☎770-498-5690. Take bus #120 "Stone Mountain" from the Avondale subway stop. Park gates open daily 6am-midnight; attractions open 10am-8pm; off-season 10am-5pm. $7 per car; other attractions $5.50-7.)

🎭 ENTERTAINMENT

For hassle-free fun, buy a MARTA pass (see **Practical Information,** p. 382) and pick up one of the city's free publications on music and events. *Creative Loafing*, *Music Atlanta*, the *Hudspeth Report*, or "Leisure" in the Friday edition of the *Atlanta Journal and Constitution* will give you the scuttlebutt. Look for free summer concerts in Atlanta's parks.

The **Woodruff Arts Center** (see **Midtown,** p. 386) houses the Atlanta Symphony, the Alliance Theater Company, Atlanta College of Art, and the High Museum of Art. **Atlantix,** 65 Upper Alabama St., sets you up with half-price rush tickets to dance, theater, music, and other attractions throughout the city. (☎770-772-5572. MARTA: Five Points. Walk-up service only, Tu 11am-3pm, W-Sa 11am-6pm, Su noon-3pm.) The **Philips Arena**, 100 Techwood Dr., hosts concerts, the **Atlanta Hawks** basketball team, and the **Atlanta Thrashers** hockey team (☎878-3000 or 800-326-4000). In 2002 Atlanta will host the NCAA Men's Final Four Basketball Tournament, and in 2003 the NCAA Women's Final Four. The National League **Atlanta Braves** play at **Turner Field,** 755 Hank Aaron Dr., which features a Coke bottle over left field that erupts with fireworks after home runs. (☎522-7630. MARTA: West End; bus #105. Call Ticketmaster at 800-326-4000. Tickets $5-15, $1 skyline seats available game day.) One-hour tours of Turner Field, including a glimpse from the $200,000 skyboxes, are offered. (☎614-2311. Open non-game days M-Sa 9:30am-4pm, Su 1-4pm; game days M-Sa 9:30am-noon; off-season M-Sa 10am-2pm. $7, children $4, under 3 free.) See the **Atlanta Falcons** play football at the **Georgia Dome,** site of the 2000 Super Bowl, and the world's largest cable-supported dome. Public tours are available by appointment. (☎223-8600. MARTA: Omni/Dome/World Congress Center. Open M-F 8:30am-5pm. $2, seniors and ages 3-12 $1.)

Six Flags Over Georgia, 7561 Six Flags Rd. SW at I-20 W, is one of the largest theme/amusement parks in the nation. Take bus #201 "Six Flags" from Hamilton Homes. Check out the 54 mph roller coaster "Georgia Scorcher," along with the two new roller coasters: "Acrophobia," which features a 200 ft. drop, and "Dejavu," which takes you both forward and backward along the tracks. (☎770-948-9290. Open mid-May to Aug. M-F 10am-9pm, Sa 10am-10pm; hours vary rest of year. $41, children and seniors $20.50; 2-day pass $51.50/$31.)

☑ NIGHTLIFE

Atlanta's rich nightlife lacks a true focal point. Fortunately, it also lacks any limits, and young people can be found partying 'til the wee hours and beyond. Scores of bars and clubs along Peachtree Rd. and Buckhead Ave. in **Buckhead** cater to a very young crowd; pricier **Midtown** greets the glitzy and the glamorous. Alternative **Little Five Points** plays hosts to bikers and goths, while **Virginia Highland** and up-and-coming **East Atlanta** feature an eclectic mix of all of types imaginable.

BARS AND PUBS

Lu Lu's Bait Shack, 3057 Peachtree Rd. NE (☎262-5220). Cool off with a 96 oz. fishbowl in the heart of Buckhead's popular and young nightlife scene. Open Tu-F 5pm-4am, Sa 5pm-3am.

Rock Bottom Brewery, 3242 Peachtree Rd. NE (☎264-0253). Stainless steel brewing tanks encased in glass greet visitors as they enter this spacious brewpub, tastefully removed from the Buckhead bedlam. Enjoy a pint of Hooch Pilsner or Iron Horse Stout with your pizza ($8-10) or entree ($8-15). Open M-Th 11:30am-midnight, F-Sa 11:30am-1am, Su 11:30am-11pm.

Apres Diem, 931 Monroe Dr. (☎872-3333), in Midtown, features delicious, stylishly presented food, 12 kinds of coffee drinks, and a hip night scene with an international, gay-friendly crowd. Open Su-Th 11:30am-midnight, F-Sa 11:30am-2am.

Masquerade, 695 North Ave. NE (☎577-8178; concert info 577-2007), occupies an original turn-of-the-century mill. The bar has three different levels: "heaven," with live music from touring bands; "purgatory," a more laid-back pub and pool house; and "hell," a dance club offering everything from techno to 1940s big band jazz. An outside space provides dancing with lights and celestial views. The 4000-seat amphitheater caters to metal and punk tastes. Cover $3-8 and up. 18+. Open W-Su 8pm-4am.

Blind Willie's, 828 N. Highland Ave. NE (☎873-2583), in Virginia Highland. Feel your way over here for a dazzling line-up of live blues, zydeco, and folk acts. Live music starts around 10pm. Cover $5-10. Open Su-Th 8pm-2am, F 8pm-3am, Sa 8pm-2:30am.

The Vortex, 438 Moreland Ave. (☎688-1828), in the Little Five Points district. Many bikers park their choppers here, the home of Atlanta's best burger, for a drink at their favorite watering hole. Open M-Sa 11am-2am, Su 11am-midnight.

9 Lives Saloon, 1174 Euclid Ave. (☎659-2760). If you're not too intimidated by the often rambunctious crowd that gathers outside at the main intersection of L5P, or by the pierced bouncers flanking the entrance, venture into "Atlanta's only rock 'n' roll club" for live music W-Sa and a bar that encourages you to "name your poison." Open Tu-Th 4pm-4am, Sa midnight-3am, Su midnight-12am.

Flatiron, 520 Flat Shoals Ave. (☎688-8864), anchoring the expanding East Atlanta scene. Bears the catchphrase, "If you love this country, you'll love this bar." Open Su-Th 11am-2am, F-Sa 11am-3pm.

Fountainhead Lounge, 485 Flat Shoals Ave. SE (☎522-7841). If the streets of East Atlanta seem uncrowded, it's because everyone is packed into this hip hideout. Couches near the bar and tables in the small upstairs offer rest for the weary, but be prepared to stand with the rest of the trendsetters. DJ spins F-Sa. Open M-Sa 7pm-3am.

DANCE CLUBS

On hot Atlanta nights, everyone who's anyone ends up at **Backstreet** (see below).

Chaos, 3067 Peachtree Rd. NE (☎995-0064). One of the largest—and newest—clubs in Buckhead, Chaos manages to avoid the cheesy commercialism of some of its neighbors. M hip hop; other nights Top 40 and techno. Cover $10 for men ($5 with ubiquitous coupon), women free. Open M-F 9pm-4am, Sa 9pm-3am.

Tongue & Groove, 3055 Peachtree Rd. NE (☎261-2325). An international crowd frequents this hangout, Buckhead's answer to some of Atlanta's swanker establishments. W Latin night, Th house, F hip hop with no cover for ladies, Sa Euro night. Cover W and F $5; Sa $10, women free until midnight. Open W-Sa 9pm-4am, Su 11:30am-2am.

THE SOUTH

The Riviera, 1055 Peachtree St. NE (☎607-8050). Like the Midtown crowd it serves, the Riv is fun, flashy, and full of itself. Still, nothing beats the opportunity to get down with Atlanta's hottest. Shoot pool and/or kamikazes while cooling off from the dance floor. Frequent live music shows. Cover $15. Open daily 10pm-6am.

GAY AND LESBIAN NIGHTLIFE

Most of Atlanta's gay culture centers around **Midtown** and several blocks north in **Ansley Sq.** (near Piedmont and Monroe). For information on gay happenings and special events in Hotlanta, check out the free *Southern Voice* newspaper, available everywhere.

Blake's, 227 10th St. (☎892-5786). Midtown males flock to this friendly bar, where see-and-be-seen is a way of life. Also a popular destination for the young lesbian crowd. Open daily 3pm-2am.

Burkhart's, 1492 Piedmont Ave. NE (☎872-4403), in Ansley Sq. Both slightly less pretentious and slightly more cruisy than Blake's, this bar is Atlanta's other gay mainstay. Popular events include Su tea dances with free food. Open M-F 4pm-4am, Sa 2pm-3am, Su 2pm-midnight.

Backstreet, 845 Peachtree St. NE (☎873-1986), is Atlanta's most popular gay club and *the* hangout for all the city's late-night partiers. With a vast dance floor, several balconies, three full bars, and an upstairs patio, the behemoth Backstreet is a devilishly delightful emporium of sights and sounds. Required quarterly "membership" $10; cover F-Sa $5. Open daily 24hr.

HELEN   ☎706

When your town's major industry dries up and tourism is stagnant, there is but one thing to do—redevelop and bill yourself as a Bavarian village. In the 1960s, four Helen businesswomen transformed this once sleepy lumber town into Georgia's own Little Germany. Biergartens and cobblestone streets line the overwhelmingly convincing downtown district; strict building codes ensure that even fast-food cabins fit the image. Burn off your wiener schnitzel exploring the nearby Chattahoochee River, Appalachian Trail, and Unicoi State Park. Willkommen, y'all!

Stroll down Helen's Main St. and check out **Charlemagne's Kingdom,** 8808 N. Main St., a scale replica of Germany (what else?) It includes over 6000 handpainted models. (☎878-2200. Open daily 11am-6pm. $5, ages 6-12 $2.50.) Helen's greatest virtue lies in its proximity to some of Georgia's finest natural landmarks. The magnificent twin waterfalls at **Anna Ruby Falls,** 5 mi. down Rte. 356 in the Chattahoochee National Forest, thunder over 100 ft. into tributaries of the Chattahoochee. (☎878-3574. Open daily 9am-8pm; off-season 9am-6pm. $2 per car.) Deep inside the National Forest rises **Brasstown Bald,** Georgia's highest peak and only several miles from the Appalachian Trail. A steep half-mile hike leads to an observation deck, where on a clear day you can see peaks in four states. Take Rte. 75, then make a left on Rte. 180. (☎896-2556. Open Apr.-May Sa-Su 10am-5:30pm, June-Nov. daily 10am-6pm. $3 parking fee.) Various rafting packages at **Wildewood Outfitters,** 7272 S. Main St., let you float way down yonder on the Chattahoochee. (☎865-4451 or 800-553-2715. Trip information 9am-2pm summer only. Store open M-Sa 10am-6pm, Su noon-6pm. Last trip leaves 2pm. From $16 per person, including transportation.) Become one of the thousands of tourists to "Tube the Hooch" with **Cool River Tubing,** located behind the Welcome Center. (☎878-3665 or 800-896-4595. Open June-Aug. daily 10am-6pm, weather permitting. Under 6 free.) Like any good German town, Helen packs tens of thousands in for **"The World's Longest Oktoberfest,"** held from mid-September through November (☎878-1619).

Most tourists rent mountain cabins and chalets, but try the major motel chains lining Main St. for a cheaper option. The **Alpine Village Inn,** 1005 Edelweiss St., is a fun alternative, sporting four garden-side "haus" with cable TV, free cookies, and continental breakfast. (☎800-844-8466. Singles and doubles $49-69.) **Unicoi State Park,** 2 mi. up Rte. 356, offers 84 campsites in either a mountain or lakeside setting. (☎800-573-9659. Primitive sites $14; water and electricity $18; full hookup $20.

Park open 24hr.) ▊**Fred's Famous Peanuts,** 17 Clayton Rd., off Rte. 356, offers roasted peanuts, peanut brittle and Fred's specialty, Cajun Fried Peanuts ($2.50 for a large bag) served daily from spring to fall. (☎878-3124. Open seasonally, hrs. vary). The owner's German mother supervises the schnitzel construction at **Alt Heidelburg,** in White Horse Sq. (☎878-2986. Open daily 11:30am-9pm.)

Helen lies 85 mi. northeast of Atlanta, nestled in the mountains of the Chatta-hoochee National Forest. From I-85, follow I-985N, exit on U.S. 129N and then take Rte. 75 into town. Bavarian sights are accessible by foot from the **Alpine Helen/ White County Welcome Center,** 726 Brucken Strasse. (☎800-858-8027. Open M-Sa 0am 5pm, Su noon 1pm.) **Poct Office:** at S. Main St. and Brucken Strasse (☎878-2422; open M-F 8:30am-5pm, Sa 8:30am-noon). **ZIP code:** 30545. **Area code:** 706.

ATHENS ☎706

There's a lot to live up to when a city's namesake contains the famed Parthenon, but the state of Georgia has done its best to help create a bohemian feel to this hamlet in the hills. In 1795 a group of Georgia lawmakers chose Athens to host the first publicly chartered college in the country, the University of Georgia (UGA). UGA breathes life into the normally sleepy town: when school is in session, 30,000 students crowd the small downtown area looking for fun. Even in summer, over 10,000 students roam the city. Its enormous size, resources, and influence have forged an artsy downtown, a prolific music scene, Georgia football fever, and a hot nightlife.

▊ **PRACTICAL INFORMATION.** Situated 70 mi. northeast of Atlanta, Athens can be reached from I-85 via U.S. 316, which runs into U.S. 29. The **Athens-Ben Epps Airport,** 1010 Ben Epps Dr., 3½ mi. from downtown (☎549-5783), is a small commuter airport; it's easier to fly into Atlanta and take a **commuter shuttle** (☎800-354-7874) to various points in and around Athens ($30). **Greyhound,** 220 W. Broad St. (☎549-2255; station open M-F 7:30am-9:15pm, Sa-Su 7:30am-2:30pm and 7-9:15pm), buses to Atlanta (2hr., 3 per day, $17). The **Athens Transit System** runs buses on 30min. and 1hr. loops around downtown, UGA, and surrounding residential areas. Look for "The Bus" signs to catch a ride. Schedules and info are available at the Welcome Center and Information Center on Washington St. (☎613-3430. Buses run M-F 6:15am-7:15pm, Sa 7:30am-7pm. $1, seniors 50¢, ages 6-18 75¢.) Two blocks north of the UGA campus is the **Athens Welcome Center,** 280 E. Dougherty St., in the Church-Waddel-Brumby House. (☎353-1820. Open M-Sa 10am-6pm, Su noon-6pm.) The **UGA Visitors Center,** at the intersection of College Station Rd. and River Rd. on campus, provides info on UGA attractions. (☎542-0842. Open M-F 8am-5pm, Sa 9am-5pm, Su 1pm-5pm.) Help is available from **Helpline Georgia** (☎800-338-6745) and **Community Connection** (☎353-1313). **Post Office:** 575 Olympic Dr. (☎800-275-8777; open M-F 8:30am-6pm). **ZIP code:** 30601. **Area code:** 706.

▊ **ACCOMMODATIONS.** Many of the city's affordable motels line **W. Broad St.,** also known as the Atlanta Hwy. (U.S. 78), a few mi. from downtown. Hotels jack up their prices during Georgia football weekends in the fall. For those seeking quality budget accommodations, the **Hawk's Nest Hostel,** about 15min. south of downtown, provides a private sanctuary in the form of a cabin next to the main house. The owner can point all the ins and outs of town. (☎769-0563. Call ahead for reservations and directions. $10, $18 per cabin group.) In the Five Points District, the **Downtowner Motor Inn,** 1198 S. Milledge Ave., has rooms drenched in pastel colors near campus with A/C, continental breakfast, free local calls, and cable. Some rooms have fridge and microwave. (☎549-2626. Singles $42-45; doubles $50; each additional person $2. Senior, UGA student, and AAA member discounts.) A full-service campground with secluded sites, **Pine Lake RV Campground,** Rte. 186, 12 mi. outside of Athens off Rte. 441 in Bishop, has full hookups and fishing lakes. (☎769-5486. Open daily 8am-dark. Sites $16.50, full hookup $19.50. Wheelchair accessible.)

THE SOUTH

❏ FOOD. A university town always has its share of quirky, inexpensive, and delicious food, and downtown Athens is no exception. Low key and without frills, **Weaver D.'s,** 1016 E. Broad, boasts the best-known grub in town. Good BBQ and fried chicken (around $6) pack in natives and visitors alike. The sign outside reads "Automatic For the People," owner Dexter Weaver's favorite expression; it inspired the title of REM's 1992 album. (☎353-7797. Open M-F 11am-6pm.) For home cookin' in a help-yourself atmosphere, head down to **Wilson's Soul Food,** 351 N. Hull St. Buffet is the name of the game: try the ribs, collard greens, and corn muffins. A full meal will run about $6-7. (☎353-7289. Open M-Th 8am-4pm, F 8am-5:30pm, Sa 8am-3pm.) **The Grit,** 199 Prince Ave., is Athens at its crunchiest and coolest, serving up scrumptious, healthy meals, including a great weekend brunch. International dishes from Mexico, the Middle East, and Italy give the menu a foreign flair. The vegetable samosas ($5.50) are a popular choice on the all-vegetarian menu. (☎543-6592. Open M-F 11am-10pm, Sa-Su brunch 10am-3pm and dinner 5-10pm. Entrees $3-6.) No Athenian culinary experience is complete without an immense 50¢ scoop from **Hodgson's Pharmacy,** 1220 S. Milledge Ave., maybe the last place on earth where ice cream comes so cheap. (☎543-7386. Open M-Sa 9am-7pm, Su 2-7pm.)

◆⅃ SIGHTS AND ENTERTAINMENT. UGA takes up most of the space in town and its free attractions are the prime reason to visit. Walk around the inviting **North Campus** (free maps available at UGA Visitors Center) or tour one of the state's grandest cultural institutions, the **Georgia Museum of Art,** 90 Carlton St., in the university's Performing and Visual Arts Complex. The museum houses a collection of over 8000 works and shows famous exhibits year-round. (☎542-4662. Open Tu and Th-Sa 10am-5pm, W 10am-9pm, Su 1-5pm. Free.) Folk cures for diabetes, epilepsy, and the flu grow at the **State Botanical Garden of Georgia,** 2450 S. Milledge Ave. Five mi. of trails through grandiose gardens and forest provide good exercise. (☎542-1244. Open Oct.-March daily 8am-6pm, Apr.-Sept. 8am-8pm; Visitors Center open Tu-Sa 9am-4:30pm, Su 11:30am-4:30pm. Free.) For an in-depth look at Athens's old and new, take the 1½hr. **Classic City Tour.** This fascinating $10 driving tour tells the stories of the antebellum homes, the Civil War, and the university. Alternatively, the **Historic Interiors Tour** takes visitors inside Athens's beautiful houses. (☎353-1820 or 208-8687 for reservations. Tours leave from the Welcome Center daily. Free driving tour 2pm, $20 interiors tour 4pm.)

Georgia's sporting past may elicit mixed emotions, but a visit to the popular **Butts-Mehre Heritage Hall,** 1 Selig Circle, will turn you into a Bulldog fan in a hurry. (☎404-542-9094. Open M-F 8am-5pm, Su 2pm-5pm. Free.) Don't miss a tour of the ⬛**Collegiate Tennis Hall of Fame,** near Butts-Mehre at the Dan Magill tennis complex. Legendary UGA men's tennis coach and "Godfather of College Tennis" Dan Magill leads the personalized tours. (☎542-8064 or call the UGA Visitors Center to schedule tours. Free.) Ancient Greece meets Civil War America at Athens's grandest Greek Revival mansion, the **Taylor-Grady House,** 634 Prince Ave., which once housed the newspaperman who coined the term "New South." The 13 Doric columns supposedly represent the original 13 colonies. (☎549-8688. Open M-F 10am-1pm and 2:30-5pm. $3.) Athenian legend recalls that Prof. W.H. Jackson deeded that the white oak standing at Dearing and S. Finley St. own itself and its shade. The original **"Tree that Owns Itself"** died in 1942 but was reborn from one of its own acorns. The **Morton Theater,** 195 W. Washington St., was the first theater in the US to be owned and run by African Americans. Ticket prices aren't what they were in 1910, but they're still low. (☎613-3770. $5-15.)

◪ NIGHTLIFE. Nightlife in Athens centers on the three blocks north of campus. Read the free weekly *Flagpole Magazine,* available at local restaurants, to find out the specifics on shows and entertainment. If on an R.E.M. pilgrimage, check out the **40 Watt Club,** 285 W. Washington St., where the group started out and where many bands today attempt to follow their lead. (☎549-7871. Cover $5-12. Open daily 10pm-3am.) Appealing to a slightly more mature crowd, **The Globe,** 199 N. Lumpkin St., draws grad students in droves. The big brass bar offers over 100 types of beer.

(☎353-4721. Open M-Tu 4pm-1am, W-Sa 4pm-2am.) Once an old Shell gas station, **Jittery Joe's,** 1210 S. Milledge Rd., is now a posh, 90s coffee sophisticate. Cozy and remote, Joe's provides a relaxed atmosphere for late night conversations. (☎208-1979. Open M-Th 6:30am-midnight, F 6:30am-1am, Sa 8:30am-1am, Su 8:30am-midnight.) In the Five Points District, **Sons of Italy,** 1573 S. Lumpkin St., packs 'em in with a roadside ping-pong table and an outdoor bar with patio. (☎543-2516. Open M-Sa 11am-2am, Su 11am-midnight.) In late June, **Athfest** features hundreds of local bands playing in the downtown area. (☎548-1973. $10 per day, $15 for both days.)

OKEFENOKEE SWAMP   ☎912

Nearly 400,000 acres in southeastern Georgia make up the ecologically diverse **Okefenokee National Wildlife Refuge,** established in 1937 to preserve the nearby swamp. "The Land of the Trembling Earth" contains a wide range of habitats: alligators, catfish and bass populate the creeks, rivers, and lakes; black bears and white-tailed deer roam the "prairies." Only a few of the refuge's trails can be traversed by foot—rent a canoe or take a guided boat tour to explore the water. Fishing is allowed. A popular nine-mile scenic drive through the refuge shows off much of the wildlife through a series of trails and overlooks. Lucky visitors can catch a glimpse of the red-cockaded woodpecker, one of the refuge's endangered species. (Refuge open daily 30min. before sunrise until 7:30pm. $5 per vehicle.)

Three entrances guide visitors into the refuge, each offering their own unique opportunities for sighting wildlife. At the **East Entrance,** the main access located 11 mi. southwest of Folkston off Rte. 121/23, a brief stop at the **Richard S. Bolt Visitors Center** provides a wealth of trail maps and info on the indigenous species (☎496-7836; open daily 9am-5pm). Knowledgeable and friendly guides lead one-hour boat tours of the Suwanee Canal, accessible through the East Entrance. (☎496-7156 for tours. $10.50, ages 5-11 $6.75. Canoe rentals $22.) The **West Entrance** is found at Stephen C. Foster State Park, 17 mi. east of Fargo off Hwy. Spur 177. An entrance fee of $5 is good for 7 days and works at both entrances.

The **Okefenokee Swamp Park** flanks the **North Entrance,** 8 mi. south of Waycross off U.S. 1. This private establishment makes the swamp available to landlubbers. Admission includes a one-hour guided railroad tour through the wetlands and a chance to see gators, otters, and other swamp creatures from a safe distance. The Nature Center located inside the park offers lectures and a small museum on Walt Kelly, the creator of the Okefenokee-based comic strip "Pogo." (☎283-0583. Open daily 9am-5:30pm. $10, seniors and ages 5-11 $9. 1hr. boat tour $18, canoe tour $16. Boat tours depend on guide availability and water level.)

Conveniently located across from the East Entrance on Rte. 121, the **Okefenokee Pastimes Campground** sports nature trails and a gallery featuring regional artists. (☎496-4472. Primitive sites $12; each additional person $5. Full hookup $18; each additional person $3. Cabins $45, with private bath $60.) **Stephen C. Foster State Park,** at the West Entrance, is the only campground located within the refuge. (☎637-5274. Feb.-June sites $13, full hookup $15; June-Feb. $16/$18.) Waycross, near the North entrance to the refuge, has a number of cheap motels along U.S. 1. Just off U.S. 1/23, opposite the Okefenokee Swamp Park, lies **Laura S. Walker State Park** (from U.S. 1/23, make a left onto Rt. 177 and drive 4 mi.) An 18-hole golf course complements various overnight facilities. A large lake in the middle of the park provides a fresh, cool opportunities for campers—if they are willing to pay the $2 swimming fee. (☎287-4900 or 800-864-7275 for reservations. Closed to non-overnighters by 10pm. Tent sites $13. Full hookup $15, sites by the water $16.)

NEAR OKEFENOKEE SWAMP: CUMBERLAND ISLAND

About 50 miles east of Okefenokee Swamp, the 17½ miles of salt marsh, live oak forest, and sand dunes laced with trails and a few decaying mansions make **Cumberland Island National Seashore** the gem of the Georgia Coast Isles. The National Park Service allows only 300 visitors per day to the island, so a jaunt to the enchanted playground of the Carnegies is rewarded with seclusion; you can walk all day on the hard-packed beaches without seeing a soul. Phone reservations are necessary for entry into the parks. (☎912-882-4335. Open M-F 10am-4pm.) The **ferry,** the only way to access the island, leaves from St. Mary's at the end of Rte. 40. (45min. Mar.-Nov. Su-Tu 2 per day, W-Sa 3 per day; Dec.-Feb. Th-M 2 per day. $16, under 12 $11.)

Nearby **St. Mary's,** voted the best small town in America by *Money* magazine, offers overnight stays near Cumberland. About 3 mi. outside downtown, **Cumberland Kings Bay Lodges,** 603 Sand Bar Dr., provides comfortable mini-suites for 1-4 people. Each room comes with fridge, stove, and microwave. (☎800-831-6664 or 912-882-8900. Breakfast included. Laundry on first floor. Singles $30, doubles $40-50. Discounts for seniors and military.)

SAVANNAH   ☎912

In February 1733, General James Oglethorpe and a ragtag band of 120 vagabonds founded the city of Savannah and the state of Georgia at Tamacraw Bluff on the Savannah River. General Sherman later spared the city during his famous rampage through the South. Some say he found it too pretty to burn, even presenting Savannah to President Lincoln as a Christmas gift. Today, the general's reaction is still believable to anyone who sees Savannah's antique stores and stately old trees, its Federalist and English Regency houses amid spring blossoms. More recently, the movie *Forrest Gump* has popularized a certain bench in Chippewa Sq., while John Berendt's best-seller *Midnight in the Garden of Good and Evil* continues to attract readers to this lovable town and its welcoming inhabitants.

▓▐ ORIENTATION AND PRACTICAL INFORMATION. Savannah rests on the coast of Georgia at the mouth of the **Savannah River,** which runs north of the city along the border with South Carolina. The city stretches south from bluffs overlooking the river. The restored 2½ sq. mi. **downtown historic district,** bordered by East Broad, Martin Luther King, Jr. Blvd., Gwinnett St., and the river, is best explored on foot. *Do not stray south of Gwinnett St.; the historic district quickly deteriorates into an unsafe area.* **Tybee Island,** Savannah's beach, 18 mi. east on U.S. 80 and Rte. 26, makes a fine daytrip. Try to visit the city at the beginning of spring, when Savannah's streets are lined with flowers. **Amtrak,** 2611 Seaboard Coastline Dr. (☎234-2611; open Sa-Th 4:30am-12:15pm and 5pm-12:45am, F 4:30am-12:45am), chugs to Charleston (1½hr., 2 per day, $18-35). **Greyhound,** 610 W. Oglethorpe Ave. (☎232-2135; open 24hr.), at Fahm St., sends buses to Jacksonville (2½hr., 12 per day, $22); Charleston (3hr., 2 per day, $24); and Atlanta (6hr., 5 per day, $67). **Chatham Area Transit (CAT),** 124 Bull St. (☎233-5767), in the Chatham County Court House, runs buses daily 7am-11pm. (Fare 75¢; seniors 37¢; no transfers. Weekly pass $12. Free CAT shuttle runs through the historic area daily M-Sa 7am-9pm, Su 9:40am-5pm.) The **Savannah Visitors Center,** 301 Martin Luther King, Jr. Blvd., at Liberty St., in a lavish former train station, offers a reservation service for local inns and hostels (☎877-728-2662). $5 parking pass allows unlimited use of all metered parking and city lots and garages for 2 days. (☎944-0460. Open M-F 8:30am-5pm, Sa-Su 9am-5pm.) **Post Office:** 2 N. Fahm St., at Bay St. (☎235-4619. Open M-F 7:30am-6pm, Sa 9am-3pm.) **ZIP code:** 31402. **Area code:** 912.

▐ ACCOMMODATIONS. Downtown motels cluster near the historic area, Visitors Center, and Greyhound station. For those with cars, **Ogeechee Rd. (U.S. 17)** has several budget options. **Savannah International Youth Hostel (HI-AYH),** 304 E. Hall St., is located in a restored Victorian mansion in the historic district. (☎236-7744. Closed Dec.-Feb. Internet access. Linen $1. Bikes $10. Check-in 7-10am and 5-11pm; call for late night check-in. Lockout 10am-5pm. 3 night max. stay. Dorms $18; private rooms $35.) **Thunderbird Inn,** 611 W. Oglethorpe Ave., has the least expensive rooms downtown. The modest exterior belies the pleasant furnishings within. (☎232-2661. Su-Th singles $40; F-Sa $50. 5% off with mention of *Let's Go*.) The rooms at **Motel 6,** 4071 Rte. 17 in Richmond Hill, 20 mi. south of downtown, have cable, A/C, free local calls, and laundry. (☎756-3543 or 800-466-8356. Singles Su-Th $34, F-Sa $35. Additional adult $6.) **Skidaway Island State Park,** 13 mi. southeast of downtown off Diamond Causeway, is inaccessible by public transportation; follow Liberty St. east from downtown until it becomes Wheaton St.; turn right on Waters Ave. and follow it to the Diamond Causeway. Sites feature bathrooms, heated showers, electricity, and water. (☎598-2300 or 800-864-7275. Open daily 7am-10pm. Check-in before 10pm. Sites $16, with hookup $18.) **Fort McAllister State Park,** Exit 90 off I-95, has wooded sites with water and electricity, some with a water view, all located on an island surrounded by marsh. (☎727-2339. Office open daily 8am-5pm; campground open 7am-10pm. Check-in before 10pm. Parking $2. Sites $13, with hookup $15.)

🄲 **FOOD. Nita's Place,** 129 E. Broughton St., gives reason enough to come to Savannah. You can read enthusiastic letters from satisfied customers pressed beneath the glass tabletops while you experience the uplifting power of soul food. The dessert-like squash casserole, a delight beyond description, will make you a believer. (☎238-8233. Open M-Th 11:30am-3pm, F-Sa 11:30am-3pm and 5-8pm.) **Wall's BBQ,** 515 E. York Ln., in an alley between York and Oglethorpe, is a tiny, no-nonsense restaurant consisting of a counter, a few tables, and amazing ribs ($4.50-$12) and BBQ sandwiches ($4.50). The baked deviled crabs ($3) are not to be missed. (☎232-9754. Open Th-Sa 11am-9pm.) **Mrs. Wilkes Boarding House,** 107 W. Jones St., is a Southern institution. Friendly strangers gather around large tables for homestyle atmosphere and food. Luscious fried chicken, butter beans, and superb biscuits are favorites, but don't leave before dessert! (☎232-5997. Open M-F 8-9am and 11am-3pm.) **Clary's Cafe,** 404 Abercorn St., has been family owned since 1903. The famous weekend brunch features $4 malted waffles. (☎233-0402. Open M-Tu and Th-F 7am-4pm, W 7am-5pm, Sa-Su 8am-4:30pm.) The **Voo-Doo Cafe,** 321 Habersham St., is open for breakfast and lunch with entrees (including wraps, salads, and pasta) under $10 dollars and tables outside that look onto Troup Sq. (☎447-1999. Open M-F 10:30am-3:30pm; Sa-Su brunch 8:30am-3:30pm.)

🄶 **SIGHTS.** Most of Savannah's 21 squares contain some distinctive centerpiece. Elegant antebellum houses and drooping vine-wound trees often cluster around the squares, adding to the classic Southern aura. Bus, van, and horse carriage **tours** leave every 10-15min. from the Visitors Center ($13-15), but walking it can be more rewarding. Two of Savannah's best-known historic homes are the **Davenport House,** 324 E. State St., on Columbia Sq., and the **Owens-Thomas House,** 124 Abercom St., a block away on Oglethorpe Sq. The Davenport House, earmarked to be razed for a parking lot, was saved in 1955. Tours explore the 1st fl. every 30min.; the 3rd fl. is open to explore at your leisure. (Davenport: ☎236-8097. Open M-Sa 10am-4pm, Su 1-4pm. Last tour 4pm. $7, under 18 $3.50, under 7 free. Owens-Thomas: ☎233-9743. Open M noon-5pm, Tu-Sa 10am-5pm, Su 2-5pm. Last tour 4:30pm. $8, students $4, seniors $7, ages 6-12 $2.) The **Green Meldrim House,** 14 W. Macon St., on Madison Sq., is a Gothic Revival mansion that served as one of General Sherman's headquarters during the Civil War. (☎233-3845. Open Tu and Th-F 10am-4pm, Sa 10am-1pm. Tours every 30min., last tour 30min. before closing. $5, $2 students.)

Girl Scouts past and present explore their heritage with a pilgrimage to the **Juliette Gordon Low Birthplace,** 142 Bull St., near Wright Sq. The Girl Scouts' founder was born here on Halloween 1860, which might explain the Girl Scouts' door-to-door treat technique. The house contains an interesting collection of Girl Scout memorabilia, but sorry, no cookies. (☎233-4501. Open M-Tu and Th-Sa 10am-4pm, Su 12:30-4:30pm. $8, students $5.) The **Negro Heritage Trail Tour,** 502 E. Harris St., visits sights such as the First African Baptist Church, which served as a hideout for runaway slaves. (☎234-8000. 2hr. tours leave daily from Visitors Center, 1 and 3pm. $15, students and under 13 $9.)

Savannah's four forts once protected the city's port from Spanish, British, and other invaders. The most interesting, **Fort Pulaski National Monument,** 15 mi. east of Savannah on U.S. 80 E. and Rte. 26, marks the Civil War battle where rifled cannons first pummeled walls. (☎786-5787. Open daily 9am-5pm; extended hrs. in summer; Visitors Center closes 5pm. $2, under 16 free.)

THE SOUTH

BETTER HOMES AND GARDENS A notorious and sophisticated antique dealer, a scandalous and flamboyant drag queen, and the prim and proper members of the Married Women's Card: these are a few of the characters that have recently seized the attention of readers in 11 different countries. The colorful plot of *Midnight in the Garden of Good and Evil*, a *New York Times* best-seller, revolves around a highly publicized fatal shooting at Mercer House, a venerable and elegant old home on Monterey Sq. Was it murder or self-defense? Although the social elite about town have denounced "The Book's" exposure of their secrets in indignant whispers, tourism has skyrocketed by 46%, and it's hard to find a local who doesn't claim to be actually referred to in the book, however vaguely. **"The Book" Gift Shop,** 127 E. Gordon St. (☎233-3867), at Calhoun Sq., a fan club, midnight tours, and a Hollywood adaptation all attest to the interest that "The Book" has generated.

Special events in Savannah include the **Annual NOGS Tour of the Hidden Gardens of Historic Savannah** in late April, when private walled gardens are opened to the public. Green is the theme of the **St. Patrick's Day Celebration on the River,** a five-day, beer- and fun-filled party which packs the streets and warms celebrants up for the **Annual St. Patrick's Day Parade,** the second-largest in the US. (Celebration: ☎234-0295. Parade: ☎233-4804, begins at 10:15am.) A free paper, *Creative Loafing,* found in restaurants and stores, has the latest in news and entertainment.

◪ **NIGHTLIFE.** The waterfront area (River St.) offers endless oceanfront dining opportunities, street performers, and a friendly pub ambience. **Kevin Barry's Irish Pub,** 117 W. River St., features live Irish folk music. (☎233-9626. Music W-Sa after 8:30pm. Cover $2. Open M-F 2pm-3am, Sa 11:30am-3am, Su 12:30pm-2am.) **The Warehouse Bar and Grill,** 18 E. River St., boasts the "coldest, cheapest beer in town" with draft beers starting at $1.50. (☎234-6003. Open M-Sa 11am-3am, Su 12pm-2am.) If frozen drinks are your pleasure, head to **Wet Willies,** 101 E. River St., with its casual dining and irresistible frozen daiquiris for $4-6. (☎233-5650. Open Su-Th 11am-1am, F-Sa 11am-2pm.) Local college students eat, drink, and shop at **City Market.** Delivering better than the rest, **Malone's Bar and Grill,** 27 W. Barnard St., serves up dancing, drinks, and live music Wednesday through Sunday. The lower floor opens up to a game room, while techno and rap beat upstairs Friday and Saturday night when the top level is 18+. (☎234-3059. Happy hour 4-8pm. Open M-Sa 11am-3am, Su noon-2am. Restaurant open until 1am.) Hustlers will enjoy the ten pool tables and over 80 beers at **B&B Billiards,** 411 W. Congress St. (☎233-7116. Open M-Sa 4pm-3am. Free pool Tu and Th.) For the best alternative scene and a gay- and lesbian-friendly atmosphere check out **Club One,** 1 Jefferson St. near Bay St., where the Lady Chablis, a character featured in *Midnight in the Garden of Good and Evil* (see above), performs regularly. (☎234-1124. Cover $3-10. Open M-Sa 5pm-3am, Su 5pm-2am.) Live music rocks Wednesday through Saturday nights at **The Velvet Elvis,** 127 W. Congress St., behind the giant crown in the front window and the smattering of Elvis paraphernalia decking the walls. (☎236-0665. Cover $3-5. Open M-Sa 6:30pm-3am.)

ALABAMA

The "Heart of Dixie" and the "cradle of the Confederacy" is often remembered for its controversial role in the civil rights movement of the 1960s, when Governor George Wallace fought a vicious campaign opposing integration. Today, this once stalwart defender of segregation strives to broaden its image and reconcile its past. The legacy of that past comprises Alabama's most poignant attractions, as museums, statues, and sites pay homage to those who were vilified 30 years ago. There is much more to this state than its history, however; Southern cuisine, local festivities, and nationally acclaimed gardens combine to create the 'Bama of today.

◪ PRACTICAL INFORMATION

Capital: Montgomery.

Visitor info: Alabama Bureau of Tourism and Travel, 401 Adams Ave., Montgomery 36104 (☎334-242-4169 or 800-252-2262; www.touralabama.org). Open M-F 8am-5pm. **Division of Parks,** 64 N. Union St., Montgomery 36104 (☎800-252-7275). Open daily 8am-5pm.

Postal Abbreviation: AL. **Sales Tax:** 4%, plus county tax.

MONTGOMERY ☎334

Today Montgomery stands still and quiet, in sharp contrast to its tumultuous past as the first capital of the Confederacy and the birthplace of America's civil rights movement. Montgomery's role in the movement took off in 1955, when local authorities arrested Rosa Parks, a black seamstress, because she refused to give up her seat to a white man on a city bus. The success of an ensuing bus boycott, organized by local minister Dr. Martin Luther King, Jr., encouraged nationwide reform. Montgomery relies on its prominent past to overcome a nondescript today; civil rights movement battlegrounds are the main attractions.

■◪ ORIENTATION AND PRACTICAL INFORMATION. Downtown follows a grid pattern: Madison Ave. and Washington Ave. are the major east-west routes; Union St. and Decatur St. run north-south. West of downtown, **I-65** runs north-south and intersects **I-85**, which forms downtown's southern border. **Greyhound,** 950 W. South Blvd. (☎286-0658; open 24hr.), at Exit 168 on I-65, runs to Mobile (3hr., 8 per day, $31); Atlanta (4hr., 6 per day, $29-31); and Tuskegee (45min., 6 per day, $9.50). **Downtown Area Runabout Transit (DART)** runs local buses 6am-6pm (fare $1.50, no transfers). **Taxis: Yellow Cab,** ☎262-5225. **Visitors Center:** 300 Water St., in Union Station (☎262-0013; open M-Sa 8:30am-5pm, Su noon-4pm). **Hotlines: Council Against Rape,** ☎286-5987. Operates 24hr. **Post Office:** 135 Catoma St. (open M-F 7:30am-5:30pm, Sa 8am-noon). **ZIP code:** 36104. **Area code:** 334.

▐▐ ACCOMMODATIONS AND FOOD. For those with a car, South Blvd., Exit 168 off I-65, overflows with inexpensive beds—beware the cheapest of the cheap, which are fairly seedy. Downtown is the comfortable and newly renovated ◪**Town Plaza,** 743 Madison Ave., at N. Ripley St. near the Visitors Center. Rooms come with all the perks: A/C, TV, free local calls, and fridges. (☎269-1561. Singles $26; doubles $32.) Right next to I-65 on W. South Blvd., **The Inn South,** 4243 Inn South Ave., greets travelers with an unusually dramatic lobby for a budget motel. (☎288-7999 or 800-642-0890. Continental breakfast, free local calls, cable. Singles $29, Sa-Su $34; doubles $36; each additional person $2. Wheelchair accessible.) The site of a 1763 French stronghold, **Fort Toulouse Jackson Park,** 12 mi. north of Montgomery on Ft. Toulouse Rd. off U.S. 231, has 39 rustic sites with water and electricity in beautiful woods. Other sites grace the Coosa River. (☎567-3002. Registration daily 8am-5pm. Make reservations at least 2 weeks in advance in spring and fall. Sites $11, with hookup $14; seniors $8/$11.)

◪**Martin's,** 1796 Carter Hill at Mulberry, is a popular and friendly local place, offering their fried chicken dinner with three vegetables for $7. (☎265-0757. Open M-F 11am-3pm and 4-7:45pm, Su 10:45am-1:45pm.) **El Reys,** 1031 East Fairview, provides 20 vegetarian burrito options ($5.50-8.50) in a collegiate setting. (☎832-9688. Open M-Sa 11am-10pm, Su 4-10pm.) The oldest restaurant (and combination magazine stand) in town, **Chris',** 138 Dexter Ave. makes hot dogs like nobody else. The special ($2) comes with mustard, onions, sauerkraut, and chili sauce. (☎265-6850. Open M-Th and Sa 10am-7pm, F 10am-8pm.) Snag a bag of peaches for $2.50 at the **Montgomery State Farmers Market,** 1655 Federal Dr. at Coliseum Blvd., north of town near Gunter Air Force Base. (☎242-5350. Open daily 7am-5pm.)

THE SELMA TO MONTGOMERY MARCH In the Selma of 1964, only 1% of eligible blacks had the right to vote due to state-imposed restrictions. In 1965, to protest these conditions, civil rights activists organized an ill-fated march on the state capitol that was quashed by billy club-swinging troops. Their spirits battered but not destroyed, the marchers tried again, this time encouraged by the likes of Dr. Martin Luther King, Jr., Joan Baez, Sammy Davis, Jr., Harry Belafonte, Lena Horne, and Mahalia Jackson. A second march was also turned back, but the third time proved the charm. The 54 mi. trek from Selma to Montgomery prompted a weary Dr. King to declare the movement the "greatest march ever made on a state capitol in the South." Six months later, Congress passed the Voting Rights Act, which prohibited states from using prerequisites to disqualify voters on the basis of color.

◙ **SIGHTS.** The brand new **Rosa Parks Library and Museum,** 251 Montgomery St., features an innovative multimedia recreation of December 1, 1955, when Rosa Parks refused to give up her seat. (☎241-9615. Open M-F 9am-5pm, Sa 9am-3pm. $5, under 12 $3.) Maya Lin, the architect who designed the Vietnam Veterans Memorial in Washington, D.C. (p. 299), also designed Montgomery's newest sight, the **Civil Rights Memorial,** 400 Washington Ave., in front of the Southern Poverty Law Center. The outdoor monument, over which water continuously flows, pays tribute to 40 activists who died fighting for civil rights. (☎264-0286. Open 24hr. Free. Wheelchair accessible.) The legacy of African-American activism and faith survives one block away, at the 112-year-old **King Memorial Baptist Church,** 454 Dexter Ave. This is where the 1955 bus boycott was organized. The basement mural chronicles Dr. King's role in the nation's struggle for civil rights. (☎263-3970).

The **Hank Williams Museum,** 118 Commerce St., features the star's outfits, memorabilia, and the '52 Cadillac in which he died. (☎262-3600. Open M-Sa 9am-6pm, Su 1-4pm. $5.25, under 12 $1.50.) The tormented soul and grinning prankster finally burned out his brilliant flame at age 29 from heavy drug and alcohol abuse. **Old Alabama Town,** 301 Columbus at Hull St., reconstructs 19th-century Alabama with over 40 period buildings, including a pioneer homestead, an 1892 grocery, and an early African-American church. Knowledgeable guides provide excellent background to the sights. (☎240-4500. $7, seniors $6.10, students and ages 6-18 $3. Tickets sold M-Sa 9am-3pm; grounds open until 4:30pm.) A modest exterior hides the exquisitely decorated **State Capitol,** Bainbridge St. and Dexter Ave. On the front steps, a bronze star commemorates the spot where Jefferson Davis took the oath of office as president of the Confederacy. (☎242-3935. Open M-F 9am-5pm, Sa 9am-4pm. Guided tours available. Free.) The **First White House of the Confederacy,** 644 Washington Ave., contains period furnishings and many of President Jefferson Davis's personal belongings. (☎242-1861. Open M-F 8am-4:30pm. Free.)

The **F. Scott and Zelda Fitzgerald Museum,** 919 Felder Ave., off Carter Hill Rd. at Dunbar, contains a few of her bad paintings as well as some of his original manuscripts. (☎264-4222. Open W-F 10am-2pm, Sa-Su 1-5pm. Free.) The **Montgomery Museum of Fine Arts,** 1 Museum Dr. (for directions see Shakespeare Festival below), houses a collection of 19th- and 20th-century American paintings along with "Artworks," a hands-on gallery and art studio for kids. (☎244-5700. Open Tu-W and F-Sa 10am-5pm, Th 10am-9pm, Su noon-5pm. Free, but donations appreciated.)

🎭 **ENTERTAINMENT.** The **Alabama Shakespeare Festival,** the fifth largest in the world, is staged at the **State Theater** on the grounds of the 250-acre private estate, **Wynton M. Blount Cultural Park;** take East Blvd. 15min. southeast of downtown, or Exit 6 off I-85, onto Woodmere Blvd. The theater also hosts contemporary plays. (☎271-5353 or 800-841-4273. Box office open M-Sa 10am-6pm, Su noon-4pm, until 9pm on performance nights. Tickets $25-30; previews the week before opening $21.) For some blues and beer, try **1048,** 1048 E. Fairview Ave., near Woodley Ave. (☎834-1048. Usually no cover. Open daily 4pm-2am, music daily at 10:30pm.) The Thursday *Montgomery Advertiser* lists other entertainment options.

NEAR MONTGOMERY

TUSKEGEE. After Reconstruction, "emancipated" blacks in the South remained segregated and disenfranchised. **Booker T. Washington,** a former slave, believed that blacks could best improve their situation through hard work and learning a trade. The curriculum at the college Washington founded, the Tuskegee Institute, revolved around such practical endeavors as agriculture and carpentry, with students constructing almost all of the campus buildings. Today, a more academically oriented **Tuskegee University** fills 160 buildings on 5000 acres; the buildings of Washington's original institute comprise a national historical site. (☎ 727-8347 for tours.) On campus is the **George Washington Carver Museum,** which has exhibits and informative films. Artist, teacher, scientist, and head of the Agricultural Dept., Carver discovered many practical uses for the peanut, including axle grease and peanut butter. (☎ 727-3200. Open daily 9am-5pm. Free.) Across the street from the campus on Montgomery Rd. lies **The Oaks,** a restoration of Washington's home. The home, down to the bricks themselves, was built by students in just one year from 1899-1900, and was the first with electricity in Macon County. Call the museum to schedule a tour (available daily 10am-4pm). To get to Tuskegee, take I-85 toward Atlanta and exit at Rte. 81 S. Turn right at the intersection of Rte. 81 and Old Montgomery Rd. onto Rte. 126., or simply take Exit 32 and follow the signs. **Greyhound** (☎ 727-1290) runs from Montgomery (45min., 6 per day, $8-9). **Area code:** 334.

SELMA. Selma is more infamous than famous—the small, historic Southern town was shaped by two momentous events that took place 100 years apart. As a stronghold for the Confederate armies (Selma's arsenal produced two-thirds of the South's ammunition during the last years of the war), its fall in 1865 marked a decisive victory for the North. A century later, Selma gained notoriety from its involvement in the voting rights movement, specifically the brutal beatings inflicted on marchers by state troopers at Pettus Bridge that injured 65 people and sent 17 to the hospital (see **The Selma to Montgomery March,** on p. 398). The **National Voting Rights Museum & Institute,** 1012 Water Ave., houses memorabilia concerning the Voting Rights Act of 1965. The Institute will sponsor a Bridge Crossing Jubilee to commemorate the march with music, storytelling, and art on March 1-3 2002. (☎ 418-0800. Open Tu-F 9am-5pm, Sa 10am-3pm. $4, $2 students.) The **Brown Chapel AME Church and King Monument,** 410 Martin Luther King St., served as the headquarters for many civil rights meetings. (☎ 874-7897. Tours available by appointment M-Sa 10am-4pm, Su 1-4pm.) A map available from the Visitors Center will lead you to other Civil Rights points of interest in Selma. **The Old Depot Museum,** 4 Martin Luther King St., explores the history of Selma with artifacts of past and present, some dating back thousands of years to the area's original inhabitants. (☎ 874-2197. Open M-Sa 10am-4pm. $4, seniors $3, students $2.)

Downtown Selma is bordered by **Jeff Davis Ave.** to the north and the **Alabama River** to the south. **U.S. 80,** which becomes **Broad St.,** runs straight through town. **Greyhound,** 434 Broad St. (☎ 874-4503; open daily 6:45am-10:45pm), runs to Montgomery (1hr., 6 per day, $12). **Visitors Center:** 2207 Broad St. (☎ 875-7485; open daily 8am-8pm). **Post Office:** 1301 Alabama Ave. (☎ 874-4678; open M-F 8am-4:40pm, Sa 8am-noon). **Zip code:** 36703. **Area code:** 334.

BIRMINGHAM ☎ 205

Birmingham, like its English namesake, sits atop soil rich in coal and iron ore—minerals responsible for its lightning-quick growth following the Civil War. "The Magic City" became the first industrial center of the South and the largest city of Alabama, a distinction it still carries. But for most people, Birmingham recalls the struggle for black civil rights in the 1960s. Leaders like the Revs. Martin Luther King and Fred Shuttlesworth faced some of their toughest fights in what was labeled "Bombingham" after dozens of bombs rocked the city in the early 60s. Despite adversity, black culture thrived. Today's Birmingham has turned the corner and focused its efforts on building a substantial medical research community. The city does not shy from its turbulent past, however. Some of the most powerful and moving civil rights monuments in the South are located downtown.

⚡🔢 ORIENTATION AND PRACTICAL INFORMATION. Downtown Birmingham is a regular grid, with numbered avenues running east-west and numbered streets running north-south. Richard Arrington, Jr. Blvd. is the one exception, running along what would have been called 21st St. The only complication is that downtown is in fact two grids, northside and southside, divided by railroad tracks—thus both avenues and streets are designated "N." or "S." **I-65, I-20/59,** and **Rte. 31** form a U around downtown, leaving the southern side exposed. Five Points and the University of Alabama-Birmingham lie south of 6th Ave. S. Birmingham is accessible by several major interstates. **I-20** approaches from Atlanta to the east; **I-65** runs north to Nashville and south to Mobile; and from New Orleans **I-59** runs northeast into the heart of the city. **Amtrak,** 1819 Morris Ave. (☎324-3033; open daily 8:30am-5pm), sends one train per day to Atlanta (5hr., $39) and New Orleans (7hr., $47). **Greyhound,** 618 19th St. N. (☎251-3210; open daily 24hr.), buses to Montgomery (2hr., 5 per day, $20); Mobile (6-8hr., 6 per day, $41); Atlanta (3hr., 12 per day, $22-24); and Nashville (3-4½hr., 7 per day, $26). Birmingham's **Metropolitan Area Express (MAX)** and **Downtown Area Runabout Transit (DART)** handle local transportation. (☎521-0101. MAX: M-F 6am-6pm; $1, transfers 25¢. DART: M-F 9am-4pm, 50¢.) **Taxi: Yellow Cab** (☎252-1131). The **Greater Birmingham Convention and Visitors Center,** 2200 9th Ave. N., 1st fl., will answer your questions. (☎458-8000 or 800-458-8085. Open M-F 8:30am-5pm.) **Hotlines: Crisis Center,** ☎323-7777. **Rape Response,** ☎323-7273. Both operate 24hr. **Gay info line:** ☎326-8600. **Post Office:** 351 24th St. N. (☎521-0302; open M-F 6am-11pm). **ZIP code:** 35203. **Area code:** 205.

🔢🔢 ACCOMMODATIONS AND FOOD. Relatively cheap hotels and motels dot the Greater Birmingham area along the various interstates. The closer to downtown, the more expensive the room. A pleasant non-chain option in the city is **The Ranchouse Inn,** 2127 7th Ave. S., just north of Five Points. (☎322-0691. Singles $40; doubles $45. Wheelchair accessible.) Along I-20 in the eastern section of town lies the **Motel Birmingham,** 7905 Crestwood Blvd. Comfortable rooms surround landscaped garden courtyards. A/C, cable and a pool complete the package. (☎956-4440 or 800-338-9275. Exit 132 off I-20, then left on Crestwood. Rooms for 1-4 $45-55.) Visitors may camp in Alabama's largest (10,000 acres) state park, **Oak Mountain State Park,** 15 mi. south of Birmingham off I-65 in Pelham at Exit 246. Horseback rides, golf, hiking, and an 85-acre lake with beach and fishing are all available in the area. (☎620-2527 or 800-252-7275. Basic sites $10.50; water and electricity $14; full hookup $16.50. Parking $1.)

With over 60 joints to choose from, barbecue reigns as the local specialty. **Five Points South,** an old streetcar suburb near the University of Alabama-Birmingham, at the intersection of 6th Ave. S. and 20th St. S., is the best place to eat cheap and meet young people. **Jim 'N Nick's Barbecue,** 744 29th St. S., roasts chicken, pork, and beef BBQ sandwiches ($3) on a hickory wood fire in a brick pit out back. Finish off dinner with a tasty piece of homemade pie. (☎323-7082. Open M-Th 10:30am-9pm, F 10:30am-10pm.) Birmingham's oldest seafood wholesaler doubles as the **Fish Market Restaurant,** 611 Richard Arrington, Jr. Blvd. S., a no-frills joint with cheap catch of the sea; fish entrees run $5-8. (☎322-3330. Open M-Th 10am-9pm, F-Sa 10am-10pm.) In 20 short years, ⬛**Hosie's Barbecue and Fish,** 321 17th St. N. in downtown, has become *the* place for tasty and cheap wings, catfish and other Southern delights. (☎326-3495. Open M 11am-8pm, Tu-Th 11am-10pm, F-Sa 11am "till the customers stop walking.")

◼ SIGHTS. Birmingham's efforts to reconcile its ugly past have culminated in the **Birmingham Civil Rights District,** centered on the intersection of 16th St. and 6th Ave. N., a six-block tribute to the fight for freedom and equality. The powerful ⬛**Birmingham Civil Rights Institute,** 520 16th St. N., traces the nation's civil rights struggle through the lens of Alabama's own segregation battle. Traditional displays and documentary footage balance the imaginative exhibits on living through the Jim Crow era. The institute also highlights contemporary human rights issues across the globe and serves as a public research facility. (☎328-9696. Open Tu-Sa 10am-5pm, Su 1-5pm. $6, seniors $3, college students $2, under 18 free. Su free.) Across the street from the Institute is the **Sixteenth St. Baptist Church,** 1530 6th Ave.

N., which served as the center of Birmingham's civil rights movement. Four young black girls died in the church in a September 1963 bombing by white segregationists. (☎251-9402. Open Tu-F 10am-4pm, Sa by appointment. $2 suggested donation.) Protests spurred on by the deaths occurred in nearby **Kelly-Ingram Park,** at the corner of 6th Ave. and 16th St., where statues and sculptures commemorating the civil rights demonstrations now grace the green lawns.

In the same area as Kelly-Ingram Park is the **Alabama Jazz Hall of Fame,** 1631 4th Ave. N., in the Carver Theatre. Jazz greats from Erskine Hawkins to Sun Ra and his Intergalactic Arkestra each get a small display on their life work. (☎254-2731. Open Tu-Sa 10am-5pm, Su 1-5pm. Free.) Bama's sports greats, from Willie "The Say Hey Kid" Mays to runner Carl Lewis, are immortalized in the **Alabama Sports Hall of Fame,** at the corner of Civic Center Blvd. and 22nd St. N. (☎323-6665. Open M-Sa 9am-5pm, Su 1-5pm. $5, seniors $4, students $3.) Birmingham remembers its days as the "Pittsburgh of the South" at the gigantic **Sloss Furnaces National Historic Landmark,** adjacent to the 1st Ave. N. viaduct off 32nd St. downtown. Though the blast furnaces closed 20 years ago, they stand as the only preserved example of 20th-century iron-smelting in the world. Ballet, drama, and music concerts are held in a renovated furnace shed next to the stacks. (☎324-1911. Open Tu-Sa 10am-4pm, Su noon-4pm. Free tours Sa-Su 1, 2, and 3pm.) Two blocks away is the **Birmingham Museum of Art,** 2000 8th Ave. N., the largest municipal art museum in the South, including over 18,000 works and a sculpture garden. (☎254-2565. Open Tu-Sa 10am-5pm, Su noon-5pm. $3.50 suggested donation.)

For a breather from an educational vacation, revel in the marvelously sculpted grounds of the **Birmingham Botanical Gardens,** 2612 Lane Park Rd, off U.S. 31. Spectacular floral displays, an elegant Japanese Garden, and an enormous greenhouse vegetate on 67 acres. (☎879-1227. Garden Center open daily 8am-5pm. Gardens open daily dawn-dusk. Free.) Alternatively, visit the 70-acre **Visionland** amusement complex, 16 mi. southwest of Birmingham at I-20 and I-459. (☎481-4750. Open late May to mid-August M-F 10am-8pm, Sa 10am-10pm, Su noon-8pm; mid-Aug. to late Oct. Sa 10am-10pm, Su noon-8pm. $23, seniors $15, under 48 in. $18.)

■■ **ENTERTAINMENT AND NIGHTLIFE. Historic Alabama Theater,** 1817 3rd Ave. N., renovated in 1927, is booked 300 nights of the year with films, concerts, and live performances. Their organ, the "Mighty Wurlitzer," entertains the audience pre-show. (☎252-2262. Order tickets through Ticketmaster 715-6000, or at the box office 1hr. prior to show. Showtimes generally 7pm; Su 2pm. Films $6, seniors and children under 12 $5.) In addition to the theater's **Infoline** (☎251-0418), the free *Birmingham Weekly* and the biweekly *black & white* list local entertainment events. Those lucky enough to visit Birmingham during Father's Day weekend in mid-June can hear everything from country to gospel to big name rock groups at **City Stages.** The three-day festival, held in Linn Park, is the biggest thing to hit town all year and includes food, crafts, and children's activities. (☎251-1272. $18; weekend pass $25.)

Nightlife centers around **Five Points South** (Southside). On spring and summer nights, many grab outdoor tables or loiter by the fountain until late. The hippest people jam year-round at **The Nick,** 2514 10th Ave. S., which locals call "*the* place." The poster-covered exterior says it clear and proud: "The Nick...rocks." (☎252-3831. Happy hr. M-F 3-9pm. Live music M-W. Cover $4-7; usually free M. Open M-F 3pm-late, Sa 8pm-6am.) Live bands from reggae to alternative entertain a collegiate crowd at **The Hippodrum,** 2007 Highland Ave. (☎933-6565. Hrs. vary, live music Tu-Sa. No horses allowed. Cost depends on program.)

DAYTRIPS FROM BIRMINGHAM

MOUNDVILLE. When white settlers first came across **Moundville,** 60 mi. southwest of Birmingham on I-59/20, they believed they had come across the city of some lost classical race. Archaeology would eventually place the two dozen flat-topped earthen mounds, the highest at 58 ft., as the work of the same Mississippian civilization that built **Effigy Mounds** in Iowa (see p. 569). From 1000-1500 AD, the site was the ceremonial capital of a city of 10,000 people; the exact purposes of the mounds, and the causes of their builders' disappearance, are unknown. To reach the park from I-59/20, take Exit 71A to Rte. 69 south 13 mi. (☎371-2572. Park open daily 8am-8pm; Visitors Center open 9am-5pm. $4, students and ages under 16 $2.)

HUNTSVILLE. Eighty miles north of Birmingham, Huntsville was the first English-speaking settlement in Alabama and the location of Alabama's constitutional convention in 1819. Far more momentous, however, was the 1950 decision to locate the nation's rocket program here, initially proposed by Wernher von Braun. The 363 ft. replica of a Saturn V rocket at the **US Space and Rocket Center** is easily recognizable for miles. This self-proclaimed "fun center of the universe" features various space-flight simulators, an IMAX theater, and tours to the nearby Marshall Space Flight Center. (☎837-3400. Open daily 9am-6pm; off-season 9am-5pm. $15, ages 3-12 $11.)

Budget motels and chain restaurants cluster on **University Drive,** northwest of downtown. The **Knights Inn,** 4404 University Dr., chivalrously offers one reasonable lodging option. (☎864-0388. Singles $33, doubles $40-$50; prices increase during the weekend.) **Monte Sano State Park,** east of town off U.S. 431, has pleasant campsites in the midst of extensive recreational facilities. (☎534-6589. Primitive sites $10, water and electricity $15, full hookup $16.) **RV sites** are also available adjacent to the Space and Rocket Center (☎830-4987; full hookup $14). For food downtown, try the friendly **Wild Rose Cafe,** 121 N. Side Square, a traditional lunch counter serving up quality meat-and-three (vegetables, that is) platters on Styrofoam plates for $6. (☎539-3658. Open M-F 7am-2:30pm.)

Greyhound, 601 Monroe St. (☎534-1681; terminal hours 7:30am-11:45pm), runs buses to Nashville (2hr., 4 per day, $15-16); Birmingham (2¼hr., 4 per day, $16-17); and Memphis (7hr., 4 per day, $46-49). A **tourist shuttle,** mostly aimed at shoppers, runs every hr. between downtown, points on University Dr., and the Space and Rocket Center. (M-F 6am-6pm, Sa 8:40am-7:10pm. $1, all-day pass $2.) Meanwhile, **Huntsville Shuttle** also runs 11 other routes daily 6am-6pm. ($1, seniors and children under 7 50¢, transfers free.) For more info on both shuttles call 532-7433. **Taxis: Huntsville Cab Co.,** ☎539-8288. **Visitors Center:** 700 Monroe St., in the Von Braun Center. (☎533-5723. Open M-Sa 9am-5pm, Su noon-5pm.) **Area code:** 256.

MOBILE   ☎251

Though Bob Dylan lamented being stuck here, Mobile (*mo-BEEL*) has had plenty of fans in its time—French, Spanish, English, Sovereign Alabama, Confederate, and American flags have each flown over the city since its founding in 1702. This historical diversity is revealed in local architecture: antebellum mansions, Italianate dwellings, Spanish and French forts, and Victorian homes line azalea-edged streets. Today, Mobile offers an untouristed version of New Orleans. The site of the first Mardi Gras, the city still holds a two-week long Fat Tuesday celebration—without the hordes that plague its Cajun counterpart.

■■◪ **ORIENTATION AND PRACTICAL INFORMATION.** The downtown district borders the Mobile River. **Dauphin St.** and **Government Blvd. (U.S. 90),** which becomes **Government St.** downtown, are the major east-west routes. **Royal St.** and **Broad St.** are major north-south byways. **Water St.** runs along the river downtown, becoming the **I-10 causeway. Frontage Rd.,** also known as the **Beltline,** lies west of downtown.

Amtrak, 11 Government St. (☎432-4052), runs the "Gulf Breeze" from Mobile to New York City via bus service to Birmingham or Atlanta. Three trains per week roll to New Orleans (2½hr.; $32). **Greyhound,** 2545 Government Blvd., at Pinehill St. west of downtown (☎478-6089; open 24hr.), runs buses to Montgomery (3hr., 7 per day, $28); New Orleans (2½hr., 8 per day, $23); and Birmingham (6hr., 5 per day, $37). **Mobile Transit Authority (MTA)** has major depots at Bienville Sq., the Royal St. parking garage, and the Adams Mark Hotel. (☎344-5656. Runs M-F 6am-6pm; reduced service on Sa. Fare $1.25, seniors and disabled 60¢, transfers 10¢.) **Yellow Cab,** ☎476-7711. **Visitor info: Fort Condé Info Center,** 150 S. Royal St., in a reconstructed French fort near Government St. (☎208-7304. Open daily 8am-5pm.) **Hotlines: Rape Crisis,** ☎473-7273. **Helpline,** ☎431-5111. Both 24hr. **Post Office:** 250 St. Joseph St. (☎800-275-8777; open M-F 7am-5pm, Sa 9am-noon.) **ZIP code:** 36601. **Area code:** 251.

↑ ACCOMMODATIONS. A slew of affordable hotels lines I-65 on Beltline, from Exit 5 (Spring Hill Rd.) to Exit 1 (Government Blvd.), and Rte. 90 west of downtown. **Family Inn,** 980 S. Beltline Rd., I-65 at Airport Blvd., sports firm beds, free local calls, continental breakfast, cable, and an outdoor pool. (☎344-5500. Singles $28; doubles $40.) Downtown, the **Budget Inn,** 555 Government St., offers basic, clean rooms with cable TV and A/C. (☎433-0590. Singles $35; doubles $40.) **I-10 Kampground,** 6430 Theodore Dawes Rd. E., lies 7½ mi. west on I-10, south off Exit 13. This is a great place...if you like RVs. (☎653-9816 or 800-272-1263. Pool, playground, and laundry facilities. RV hookup $20; each additional person $1.)

▣▦ FOOD AND NIGHTLIFE. Mobile's Gulf location means fresh seafood (surf) and Southern cookin' (turf). **◪Wintzell's Oyster House,** 605 Dauphin St., is a long-time local favorite that offers oysters "fried, stewed, or nude." Beat the one-hour oyster-eating record of 21½ dozen and the meal is on them. Happy hour specials run M-F 4pm-7pm; 25¢ appetizers and $4.25 pitchers of beer. (☎432-4605. Open M-Sa 11am-10pm, Su noon-8pm.) For turf, **◪Dreamland,** 3314 Old Shell Rd., has ribs that will put you in a blissful food coma, not to mention stain your shirt. (☎479-9898. Open M-Sa 10am-10pm, Su 11am-9pm. Half-slab $9, half-chicken $6.50.) To mix with the locals of Mobile, head to the well-worn and well-populated bar at **Hayley's,** 278 Dauphin St. (☎433-4970. Open daily 3pm-3am. Beer $2.50.) Eighteen pool tables, darts, and half-pound hamburgers ($4.50) make **Solomon's,** 5753 Old Shell Rd. at University Rd., the quintessential brew and cue college hangout. (☎344-0380. Happy hour daily 11am-7pm. Open 24hr., though not all of 'em are so happening.)

◪ SIGHTS. Mobile's attractions lie scattered inland, around downtown, and near the bay. Three historic districts—Detonti Sq., Dauphin St., and Church St.—encompass the downtown area. The city's varied influences have led to an architecture unique to Mobile. In particular, the 27 buildings of the **Church St. East Historic District** showcase Federal, Greek Revival, Queen Anne, and Victorian architecture. **Bay City Tours** leads a 1hr. tour of downtown departing from the Visitors Center at Fort Condé—call for reservations. (☎479-9970. Tours $12.50 per person.)

Antebellum homes dominate the attractions of Old Mobile. In the **DeTonti Historical District,** north of downtown, brick townhouses with wrought-iron balconies surround the restored **Richards-DAR House Museum,** 256 North Joachim St. The house's stained glass and Rococo chandeliers blend beautifully with its antebellum Italianate architecture and ornate iron lace. (☎208-7320. Open M-F 11am-3:30pm, Sa 10am-4pm, Su 1-4pm. Tours $5, children $2. Free tea and cookies.) **Oakleigh Historical Complex,** 350 Oakleigh Pl., 2½ blocks south of Government St. at George St., features a cantilevered staircase. (☎432-1281. Open M-Sa 10am-4pm. Tours every 30min.; last tour 3:30. $5, seniors and AAA $4.50, ages 12-18 and students $3, ages 6-11 $2.)

For its lush rose and oriental gardens, bayou boardwalk, and 900-acre setting, *Southern Living* magazine has ranked **Bellingrath Gardens,** 12401 Bellingrath Gardens Rd., Exit 15A off I-10, one of the top three public gardens in the country. You can also tour the Bellingrath Museum Home. (☎973-2217. Open daily 8am-dusk. Gardens $8, ages 5-11 $5.) The **USS Alabama,** moored 2½ mi. east of town at Battleship Park (accessible from I-10), fought in every major Pacific battle during WWII. Open passageways let landlubbers explore the ship's depths. (☎433-2703. Open daily 8am-6pm. $8, ages 6-11 $4. Parking $2. 25% off coupon available at Fort Condé Visitors Center.) Downtown, **Spanish Plaza,** Hamilton and Government St., honors Mobile's sister city (Málaga, Spain) and recalls Spain's early presence in Mobile.

February is a big month for Mobile. Locals await the blooming of the 27 mi. **Azalea Trail** and enjoy the parades, costumes, and "throws" of the oldest Fat Tuesday around at Mobile's **Mardi Gras.** (Azalea Festival and Run: ☎334-473-7223. Mardi Gras: Jan. 30-Feb. 12, 2002.) Mobile's tricentennial falls in 2002; call 342-4386 for a listing of events throughout the year. The *Mobile Traveler,* available at Fort Condé Visitors Center, has an updated list of all Mobile attractions.

THE SOUTH

MISSISSIPPI

The "Deep South" bottoms out in Mississippi. The legacy of extravagant cotton plantations, dependence upon slavery, and subsequent racial strife and economic ruin are more visible here than in any other state. In the 1850s, Natchez and Vicksburg were two of the most prosperous cities in the nation, but during the Civil War, the state was devastated by the siege of Vicksburg and the burning of Jackson. Hatred and injustice drowned Mississippi into the 1960s as blacks protested against continuing segregation and whites reacted with campaigns of terror. However, despite its tribulations, Mississippi has been home to a number of remarkable triumphs. Ironically, one of the least literate states in the nation has produced literary giants the likes of William Faulkner, Eudora Welty, and Tennessee Williams. Also hailing from Mississippi, musicians Bessie Smith, W.C. Handy, and B.B. King brought their riffs up the "Blues Highway" to Memphis, Chicago, and the world.

▇ PRACTICAL INFORMATION

Capital: Jackson.
Visitor info: Division of Tourism, P.O. Box 1705, Ocean Springs 39566 (☎800-927-6378; www.visitmississippi.org). **Department of Parks**, P.O. Box 451, Jackson 39205 (☎800-467-2757).
Postal Abbreviation: MS. **Sales Tax:** 7%.

JACKSON   ☎601

Jackson makes a concerted effort to overcome Mississippi's spotty past and lingering backwater image. One billboard even claims that Jackson is as "Rome was to Renaissance Europe." Impress your friends with the word "hyperbole"—Jackson simply ain't all that. Nonetheless, as the state's political and cultural capital, Jackson strives to bring the world to its people. North Jackson's lush homes and plush country clubs epitomize wealthy Southern living, while shaded campsites, cool reservoirs, and national forests invite exploration only minutes away.

◼▇ **ORIENTATION AND PRACTICAL INFORMATION.** West of I-55 and north of I-20, downtown is bordered on the north by **Fortification St.**, on the south by **South St.**, and on the west by **Gallatin St.** North-south **State St.** bisects the city. **Jackson International Airport** (☎932-2859) lies east of downtown off I-20. **Amtrak**, 300 W. Capitol St. (☎355-6350; open daily 9:30am-7pm), runs to Memphis (4hr., 7 per week, $31) and New Orleans (4½hr., 7 per week, $17). **Greyhound**, 201 S. Jefferson (☎353-6342), sends buses to Montgomery (5hr., 7 per day, $48-51); Memphis (4hr., 8 per day, $26); and New Orleans (4½hr., 4 per day, $28). Station is open 24hr.; *avoid this area at night.* **Jackson Transit System (JATRAN)** provides limited public transportation service. Maps are posted at most bus stops downtown and available at JATRAN headquarters, 1025 Terry Rd. (☎948-3840. Open M-F 8am-4:30pm. Transit runs M-F 5am-7pm, Sa 5:30am-7pm. Fare $1, transfers free.) **Taxi: City Cab,** ☎355-8319. **Visitor info: The Convention and Visitors Bureau**, 921 N. President St., downtown (☎960-1891; open M-F 8am-5pm). 24hr. **Rape Hotline:** ☎982-7273. **Post Office:** 401 E. South St. (open M-F 7am-6pm, Sa 8am-noon). **ZIP code:** 39205. **Area code:** 601.

◼ **ACCOMMODATIONS.** If you have a car, head for the motels along **I-20** and **I-55. Sun 'n' Sand Motel**, 401 N. Lamar St., downtown, is a 60s time warp—there's even a Polynesian suite. (☎354-2501. Pool, cable TV. Singles $35-40; each additional person $5.) **Parkside Inn**, 3720 I-55 N, at Exit 98B, is neither the cleanest nor the newest motel around, but is a good bargain. (☎982-1122. Pool, cable TV, free local calls, microwave and fridge. Singles $29; doubles $39.) For camping, head to **Timberlake Campgrounds;** take I-55 N to Lakeland East (Exit 98B), turn left after 6 mi.

onto Old Fannin Rd. and go 4 mi. (☎992-9100. Office open daily 8am-5pm. Pool, video games, tennis and basketball courts, playground. 16 tent sites $12, full hookup $17; Oct.-Apr. $10/$13; seniors $1 discount.)

▣▨ FOOD AND NIGHTLIFE. Franchised grease palaces can be found north between I-55 and I-220, on County Line Rd., dubbed "restaurant alley" by natives. For the real Jackson scene, the **▨George St. Grocery,** 416 George St., is the place to be. Packed with state politicians by day and students by night, it offers an all-you-can-eat Southern lunch buffet for $7.50. (☎969-3573. Restaurant open M-Th 11am-9pm, F 11am-10pm, Sa 5-10pm. Live music Th-Sa 9pm-2am.) **Keifer's,** 705 Poplar St., off State St., 1½ mi. north of downtown, serves gyros and other tasty pita wraps ($4.50-5.50) amid hanging greenery. (☎355-6825. Open Su-Th 11am-10pm, F-Sa 11am-11pm.) **Hal & Mal's Restaurant and Brew Bar,** 200 S. Commerce St., stages live music in an old warehouse. (☎948-0888. Cover up to $5 F-Sa. Restaurant open M 11am-3pm, Tu-Th 11am-10pm, F 11am-10:30pm. Bar open M-Th until 11pm, F-Sa until 1am.) On Thursday, pick up the *Clarion-Ledger* for a list of weekend events.

▣ SIGHTS. The **Mississippi Museum of Art,** 201 E. Pascagoula, at Lamar St., displays a small assortment of both local and international art on a rotating basis. (☎960-1515. Open M and W-Sa 10am-5pm, Tu 10am-8pm, Su noon-5pm. $5, seniors $4, students $3, ages 6-17 $2.) Adjacent to the MMA, the out-of-this-world **Russell C. Davis Planetarium** has both an IMAX film and an astronomical sky show. (☎960-1550. Show times vary, so call ahead. $4.50, seniors and under 12 $2.50, 2-show ticket $3.60/$2.)

The **Old State Capitol Museum,** at the intersection of Capitol and State St., houses an excellent collection documenting Mississippi's turbulent history. (☎359-6920. Open M-F 8am-5pm, Sa 9:30am-4:30pm, Su 12:30-4:30pm. Free.) The **New State Capitol,** 400 High St., between West and President St., was completed in 1903. A recent restoration project preserved the *beaux arts* grandeur of the building. (☎359-3114. Open M-F 8am-5pm, self-guided tours. Free.) Tour the grandiose **Governor's Mansion,** 300 E. Capitol St., one of only two inhabited governor's mansions in the country with public tours. (☎359-3175. Tours Tu-F every 30min. 9:30-11am. Free.)

The **Mississippi's Agriculture and Forestry Museum,** 1150 Lakeland Dr., ½ mi. east of I-55 Exit 98B, is a fascinating historical account of the changing practices of agriculture and land use in the state, from King Cotton to logging to crop dusting. The actual crop dusting aircraft is presented on site in the **National Agricultural Aviation Museum.** The complex also contains many restored buildings and farm implements. (☎800-844-8687. Open M-Sa 9am-5pm, Su 1-5pm; closed Su early Sept. to late May. $4, seniors $3, ages 6-18 $2, under 6 50¢.)

VICKSBURG ☎601

Vicksburg's verdant hills and prime Mississippi River location were host to one of the major battles of the Civil War. President Lincoln called the town the "key," and maintained that the war "can never be brought to a close until that key is in our pocket." After a 47 day siege, the Confederate General Pemberton surrendered to Ulysses S. Grant's army on July 4, 1863, claiming he chose the date in order to gain better surrender terms from the Union. The city held quite a grudge—it refused to celebrate the Fourth of July until the late 1940s. Today Vicksburg is a sleepy river town with the battlefield as its main attraction. Lush parks lend the city a relaxed, pastoral feel, while brick roads and casino riverwalks recreate the old way of life.

▨ PRACTICAL INFORMATION. A car is necessary in Vicksburg. The bus station, the Visitors Center, downtown, and the far end of the sprawling military park mark the city's extremes. **Greyhound** (☎638-8389; open daily 7am-8:30pm) pulls out at 1295 S. Frontage Rd. for Jackson (1hr., 6 per day, $11.50). The **Tourist Information Center,** on Clay St. across from the military park (I-20 Exit 4, turn west), has a helpful map of sights. (☎636-9421 or 800-221-3536. Open daily 8am-5pm; in winter Sa-Su 8am-4pm.) **Post Office:** 3415 Pemberton Blvd., just off U.S. 61 S. (636-1071. Open M-F 8am-5pm, Sa 8am-noon.) **ZIP code:** 39180. **Area code:** 601.

⌐ ACCOMMODATIONS. Inexpensive lodging comes easy in Vicksburg. The **Hillcrest Motel,** 40 Rte. 80 E, ¼ mi. east from I-20 Exit 4, offers well-worn but spacious rooms and a pool. (☎638-1491. Singles $26; doubles $32.) The **Beechwood Motel,** 4449 E. Clay St., a block west of the Hillcrest, offers cable, microwave and fridge. (☎636-2271. Singles $27; doubles $35.) Most hotels cluster near the park; don't expect to stay downtown, unless you choose the **Relax Inn Downtown,** 1313 Walnut St. (☎631-0097. Microwave and fridge. Singles $35; doubles $40.) **Magnolia RV Park,** 211 Miller St., has 68 full RV hookups, a pool, game room, and playground. Head south on Washington (I-20 Exit 1A), and take a left on Rifle Range Rd. to Miller St. (☎631-0388. Office open daily 8:30am-8pm. Sites $18.) Closer to the military park and the highway is **Battlefield Kampground,** 4407 I-20 Frontage Rd., off Exit 4B. (☎636-2025. Sites $12; with water and electricity $15; full hookup $18.)

◫◪ FOOD AND NIGHTLIFE. Chow down at ◪**Walnut Hills,** 1214 Adams St., where all-you-can-eat round table dinners (Su-F 11am-2pm) of catfish, ribs, and sides cost $10. (☎638-4910. Open M-F 11am-9pm, Su 11am-2pm.) While downtown, indulge in home-cooked meals at **Burger Village,** 1220 Washington St., for $4.25-5.25. Old fashioned burgers are nothing but 100% all-American beef. (☎638-0202. Open M-Sa 9am-6pm.) Only in America do you find a place like the **Red Carpet Washateria and Lanes,** 2904 Clay St., a bowling alley, pool room, and laundromat all in one. (☎631-0890. Laundry open daily 7am-9pm. Lanes open M-Th noon-11pm, F-Sa noon-1am, Su noon-10pm. $2.50 per game.) Despite the Red Carpet's many thrills, high-rollers might prefer spending their time at one of the four **casinos** that line the river.

◙ SIGHTS. Vicksburg is a mecca for thousands of touring schoolchildren, Civil War buffs, and Confederate and Union army descendents. Memorials and markers of combat sites riddle the grassy 1700-acre ◪**Vicksburg National Military Park,** lending the grounds a sacred air. The park blockades the eastern and northern edges of the city, with its Visitors Center on Clay St., about ½ mi. west of I-20 Exit 4B. Driving along the 16 mi. path, you have three options: guide yourself with a free map available at the entrance, buy an informative audio tour, or hire a person to help navigate the sights. (☎636-0583. Park center open daily 8am-5pm. Grounds open daily 7am-8pm; in winter 7am-5pm. $4 per car. Tape $5, CD $8. Live guide $25.) Within the park, the sunk and saved Union **USS Cairo Museum** contains countless artifacts salvaged in the early 1960s from the old ironclad. (☎636-2199. Usually open daily 9:30am-6pm; off-season 8am-5pm. Free with park fee.) The **Old Courthouse Museum,** 1008 Cherry St., is an excellent Civil War museum. During the siege of Vicksburg in 1863, Confederate troops used the cupola as a signal station and held Union prisoners in the courtroom. (☎636-0741. Open M-Sa 8:30am-5pm, Su 1:30-5pm; early Oct. to early Apr. until 4:30pm. $3, seniors $2.50, under 18 $2.)

For an escape from Vicksburg's war-related attractions, the **Attic Gallery,** 1101 Washington St., has a collection of Southern contemporary art and an eclectic display of glassware, pottery, books, and jewelry. (☎638-9221. Open M-Sa 10am-5pm. Free.) Vicksburg's finest contribution to the historical home circuit, the **Martha Vick House,** 1300 Grove St., was home to the daughter of the city's founder, Reverend Newitt Vick. (☎638-7036. Open M-Sa 9am-5pm, Su 2-5pm. $5, under 12 free.)

NATCHEZ   ☎601

In the late 18th century, Natchez distinguished itself as one of the wealthiest towns on the Mississippi. Of the 13 millionaires in Mississippi at the time, 11 had their cotton plantations here. After the Civil War, the cotton-based economy crumbled, and the days of the mansion owners passed. Many of the homes remain, though, affording visitors the opportunity to gaze at elegant dwellings from a vanquished era.

⚑ PRACTICAL INFORMATION. Greyhound makes connections to Vicksburg (1½hr., 1 per day, $16) and New Orleans (4½hr., 2 per day, $36) at the **Natchez Bus Station,** 103 Lower Woodville Rd. at Rte. 61. (☎445-5291. Open M-F 8am-5:30pm, Sa 8am-noon and 1-5pm, Su 2-5pm.) The **Natchez Bicycle Center,** 334 Main St., rents bikes with basket, helmet, lock, and repair kit. (☎446-7794. Open Tu-F 10am-5:30pm, Sa 10am-3pm; other times by appointment. $15 per 4hr., $20 per day.) **Visitors Center:** 640 S. Canal St., near the U.S. 84 Mississippi Bridge. (☎442-5849. Open daily 8:30am-6pm; early Nov. to Feb. 8:30am-5pm.) **Post Office:** 214 N. Canal St. (☎442-4361; open M-F 8:30am-5pm, Sa 10am-noon). **ZIP code:** 39120. **Area code:** 601.

⌂❒ ACCOMMODATIONS AND FOOD. The intersection of **U.S. 61** and **Highland Blvd.** has lots of high-quality rooms. **Scottish Inns,** 40 Sgt. Prentiss Dr./U.S. 61, a coral-colored complex, has clean rooms equipped with fridges and microwaves. (☎442-9141 or 800-251-1962. Singles $28; doubles $40.) Close to the Mississippi Bridge and Visitors Center is the **Natchez Inn,** 218 John Junkin Dr./U.S. 84, with tidy rooms, a pool, and cable TV. (☎442-0221 or 800-647-624. A/C, cable TV, and free local calls. Singles $35; doubles $40.) The secluded campground in **Natchez State Park** is less than 10 mi. north of Natchez on U.S. 61 in Stanton. (☎442-2658. 10 primitive sites $9; 50 sites with water and electricity $13; full hookup $14; seniors $10.)

Lots of cafes and diners dish up budget eats in Natchez. **Cock of the Walk,** 200 N. Broadway, earns its title and stature with spicy catfish and complimentary jalapeno cornbread served in a bare wood dining room evocative of tough frontiersmen. (☎446-8920. Open daily 5pm until around 8:30. Catfish fillet $11.) The **Pig Out Inn,** 116 S. Canal St., serves down-home, home-smoked, faster-than-fast-food BBQ with a spicy sauce on the side. (☎442-8050. Open M-Sa 11am-9pm. Sandwiches $4, with 2 sides and drink $6.50.) **Mammy's Cupboard,** 555 Rte. 61, 4 mi. south of town, serves home cookin' ($6-7.50), like chicken pot pie and desserts (about $2.50) in a country cottage beneath a huge statue of Mammy, the stereotypical Southern black mother. (☎445-8957. Open Tu-Sa 11am-2pm.)

◩ SIGHTS. Natchez Pilgrimage Tours, 200 State St. at Canal St., supervises tours of the restored manors left from Natchez's cotton days. A helpful staff has free tour schedules, maps, and pamphlets, plus a guidebook that details the histories of the 32 homes that Pilgrimage oversees. The central office sells tickets for individual house tours or tickets for a 35min. horse-drawn carriage tour and a 55min. air-conditioned bus tour. (☎800-647-6742 or 446-6631. Open M-Sa 9am-5pm, Su 12:30-5pm. Guide book $5. House tours $6, children $3. Horse tour $10/$5. Bus tour $15/$7.50. Call ahead for seasonal schedules and prices.) The largest octagonal house in America, **Longwood,** 140 Lower Woodville Rd., astounds visitors with its imaginative floorplan; however, the six-story edifice remains unfinished. The builders, hired from the North, abandoned work at the beginning of the Civil War to fight for the Union, leaving only the basement completed and furnished. (☎442-5193. Open daily 9am-5pm. Tours every 30min., last tour 4:30pm.) **Stanton Hall,** 401 High St., on the other hand, arose under the direction of local Natchez architects and artisans. Completed in 1857, the mansion features French mirrors, Italian marble, and exquisite chandeliers. (☎442-6282. Open daily 9am-5pm. Tours every 30min., last tour 4:30pm.)

For centuries, the Natchez Indians flourished on this fertile land. The arrival of the French incited fighting in 1730, and French military successes brought an end to the thriving Natchez community. The **Grand Village of the Natchez Indians,** 400 Jefferson Davis Blvd., off U.S. 61 S., pays homage to the tribe with a small museum that documents their history and culture, as well as mounds. (☎446-6502. Open M-Sa 9am-5pm, Su 1:30-5pm. Free.) The **Natchez Museum of Afro-American History and Culture,** 301 Main St., features exhibits of cotton harvesting and Afro-American religion, education, and home life in Natchez. (☎445-0728. Open Tu-Sa 1-4:30pm. Requested donation $5, children $1.) The 500 mi. **Natchez Trace Pkwy.** leads north from Natchez to Nashville, TN. Rambling through forests, swamps, and countryside, the road passes through historic landmarks and a beautiful national park.

THE VINE THAT ATE THE SOUTH So some refer to the leafy kudzu plant, which seems to cover everything in the Deep South that stands still: trees, telephone poles, abandoned buildings, occasionally entire hillsides. Local legend has it that nervous Southern mothers often keep watch over their children on summer nights, for fear that the vine—capable of growing a foot daily—will choke their sleeping infants. Defined as a "weed" and a "pest plant" for its tendency to obliterate native vegetation, kudzu is nonetheless admired for its ability to enshroud ordinary landscape in surreal, biomorphic abstraction. Aesthetics aside, however: it's still best to close the window before turning out the light...

OXFORD ☎ 662

When westward explorers first decided to incorporate this quaint town in northern Mississippi, they decided to name it "Oxford" in hopes of getting the state government to open a university here. The plan worked brilliantly, eventually landing Oxford the University of Mississippi (Ole Miss). The school gained notoriety in the early 60s, when James Meredith attempted to be the first black student to enroll. Mississippi Governor Ross Burnett openly defied federal law, banning Meredith until the National Guard arrived. Above all, however, Oxford is the "little postage stamp of native soil" that William Faulkner determined "was worth writing about." The resulting work is widely regarded as the greatest American literature to date.

◪ PRACTICAL INFORMATION. Oxford is 30 mi. east of I-55 on Rte. 6 (take Exit 243), 55 mi. south of Memphis and 140 mi. north of Jackson. **Oxford Tourism Info Center,** 111 Courthouse Sq., offers free audio walking tours and loads of info on Faulkner. (☎800-758-9177. Open M-F 9am-5pm, Sa 10am-4pm, Su 1-4pm.) **Greyhound,** 2625 W. Oxford Loop (☎234-0094), runs to Memphis (1½hr., 1 per day, $19); Nashville (9hr., 1 per day, $59); and New Orleans (14½ hr., 2 per day, $79). **Internet access:** Public Library, 401 Bramlett Blvd. at Jackson Ave. (☎234-5751; open M-Th 9:30am-8pm, F-Sa 9:30am-5:30pm, Su 2-5pm). **Post Office,** 401 McElroy Dr. (☎513-4685; open M-F 9am-5pm, Sa 9:30am-12:30pm). **ZIP code:** 38655. **Area code:** 662.

◪ ACCOMMODATIONS. Spend a night in Southern comfort at the **Oliver-Britt House Inn,** 512 Van Buren Ave., an unpretentious B&B. Five comfortable but small rooms fit in this turn-of-the-century house. (☎234-8043. Breakfast on weekends. Rooms $79-105, $10 surcharge F-Sa, $20 on football weekends.) **Ole Miss Motel,** 1517 E. University Ave., has well-worn but quaint rooms. (☎234-2424. Singles from $32; doubles from $42.) As a last resort, try the motels on the commercial strip of Jackson Ave., near Rte. 6 southwest of downtown. **Wall Doxy State Park,** 23 mi. north of town on Rte. 7, is a scenic spot with an expansive lake. (☎252-4231. Campsites with water and electricity $6, RV sites with dump stations $11. Cabins $43-49 per night, 3-night minimum stay. Entrance fee $2 per car, 50¢ per pedestrian or bicyclist.)

◪◪ FOOD AND ENTERTAINMENT. Food and such is best found at **Courthouse Sq.,** at Jackson Ave. and Lamar Blvd. It's hip to be at **Square Books,** 160 Courthouse Sq., a true Southern bookstore. Read tall tales while sampling coffee drinks ($2) and pastries ($3) on a balcony overlooking the downtown area. (☎236-2262. Both open M-Th 9am-9pm, F-Sa 9am-10pm, Su 10am-6pm.) The **Bottletree Bakery,** 923 Van Buren Ave., serves large deli sandwiches ($6-7) and fresh pastries. (☎236-5000. Open Tu-F 7am-4pm, Sa 9am-4pm, Su 9am-2pm.) **Ajax Diner,** 118 Courthouse Sq., serves more substantial food: meat-and-two platters are $6, and traditional po' boy sandwiches are $5. (☎232-8880. Open M-Sa 11:30am-10:30pm.) At night, live music rolls from **Proud Larry's,** 211 S. Lamar, which keeps on burnin' all year. (☎236-0050. Music M-W and Su 10pm-midnight, F-Sa 10pm-1am. Cover $5-7.) For local listings, check the free weekly *Oxford Town.*

◙ **SIGHTS.** Faulkner remains the South's favorite son, and his home, **Rowan Oak,** is Oxford's biggest attraction. It lies just south of downtown on Old Taylor Rd. Faulkner, entranced by the home's history (it had belonged to a Confederate general), bought the place in 1930 and named the property after the rowan tree, a symbol of peace and security. True to form, the pastoral and tree-covered location meant little sound and less fury, which gave Faulkner peace of mind to work. The plot outline of his 1954 novel *A Fable* is scribbled in pencil on the walls of the study. (☎234-3284. Open Tu-F 10am-noon and 2-4pm, Sa 10am-4pm, Su noon-4pm. Grounds open sunrise to sunset. Free self-guided tours.)

Outside of Faulkner, Oxford's sights are all affiliated with another symbol of Southern intellectualism, Ole Miss. The town's covered sidewalks and tall cedar trees help to make it a fitting home for the **Center for the Study of Southern Culture** in the old Barnard Observatory at Ole Miss, where visitors can pick up pamphlets or attend conferences, including the ever-popular **Faulkner Conference** in late July or early August. (☎915-5993. Center open M-F 8am-5pm. Free.) Blues buffs will revel in the memorabilia, sheet music, and over 40,000 records at the **Ole Miss Blues Archive,** Farley Hall room #340, one of the largest such collections in the world. (☎915-7753. Open M-F 9am-5pm. Free.) The **University Museums,** on University Ave., contain four main collections ranging from classical Greek pottery to 19th-century scientific instruments, as well as a small but impressive collection of Southern folk and "outsider" art. (☎915-7073. Open Tu-Sa 10am-4:30pm, Su 1-4pm. Free.)

LOUISIANA

After exploring the Mississippi River valley in 1682, Frenchman René-Robert Cavalier proclaimed the land "Louisiane," in honor of Louis XIV. The name has endured three centuries, though French ownership of the vast region clearly has not. The territory was tossed between France, England, and Spain before Thomas Jefferson and the US snagged it in the Louisiana Purchase of 1803. Nine years later, a smaller, redefined Louisiana was admitted to the Union. Each successive government lured a new mix of settlers to the bayous: Spaniards from the Canary Islands, French Acadians from Nova Scotia, Americans from the East, and free blacks from the West Indies. Louisiana's multinational history, Creole culture, and Napoleonic legal system are unlike anything found in the 49 other states.

▧ PRACTICAL INFORMATION

Capital: Baton Rouge.
Visitor info: Office of Tourism, P.O. Box 94291, Baton Rouge 70804 (☎225-342-7317 or 800-261-9144; www.louisianatravel.com). Open M-F 8am-4:30pm. **Office of State Parks,** P.O. Box 44426, Baton Rouge 70804 (☎225-342-8111 or 888-677-1400; www.crt.st.la.us). Open M-F 9am-5pm.
Postal Abbreviation: LA. **Sales Tax:** 8%.

NEW ORLEANS ☎504

First explored by the French, *La Nouvelle Orléans* was secretly ceded to the Spanish in 1762, though the citizens didn't find out until 1766. Spain returned the city to France just in time for the United States to grab it in the Louisiana Purchase of 1803. Centuries of cultural cross-pollination have resulted in a vast melange of Spanish courtyards, Victorian verandas, Cajun jambalaya, Creole gumbo, and French *beignets*. New Orleans has its own style of cooking, its own distinct accent, and its own way of making music. At the start of the 20th century, its musicians even invented the musical style that came to be known as jazz.

The city's nickname, "the Big Easy," reflects the carefree attitude characteristic of this fun-loving place. While New York may claim to be "the city that never sleeps," N'awlins holds the title for "the city that won't stop partying." Day or night, there's always something going on. The only thing that stifles this vivacity is the heavy, humid air that slows folks to a near standstill during the summer. But when the day's heat finally retreats into the night, the city jumps with drinking and dancing into the early morning. Come late February, there's no escaping the month-long celebration of Mardi Gras, the climax of the city's already festive mood.

✈ INTERCITY TRANSPORTATION

Airport: Moisant International (☎464-0831), 15 mi. west of the city. Cab fare to the Quarter is set at $24 for 1-2 people; $10 each additional person. The **Louisiana Transit Authority,** 118 David Dr. (☎818-1077; open M-F 8am-4pm) runs buses from the airport to Elk St. downtown, M-Sa every 15-30min. 5:30am-5:40pm. After 5:40pm, buses go to Tulane Ave. and Carollton Ave. (mid-city) until 11:30pm. Fare $1.50; exact change needed. Pickup on the upper level, near the exit ramp.

Trains: Amtrak, 1001 Loyola Ave. (☎800-872-7245), in the Union Passenger Terminal, a 10min. walk to Canal St. via Elk. To: Houston (8hr., 3 per week, $50-89); Jackson (4hr., 7 per week, $18-36); and Atlanta (12hr., 7 per week, $50-89). Station open 24hr. Ticket office open Tu, Th, and Su 6:15am-11pm; M, W, and F-Sa 6:15am-8:30pm.

Buses: Greyhound, 1001 Loyola Ave. (☎524-7571 or 800-231-2222), in the Union Passenger Terminal. To: Austin (11hr., 5 per day, $84) and Baton Rouge (2hr., 9 per day, $11). Open 24hr.

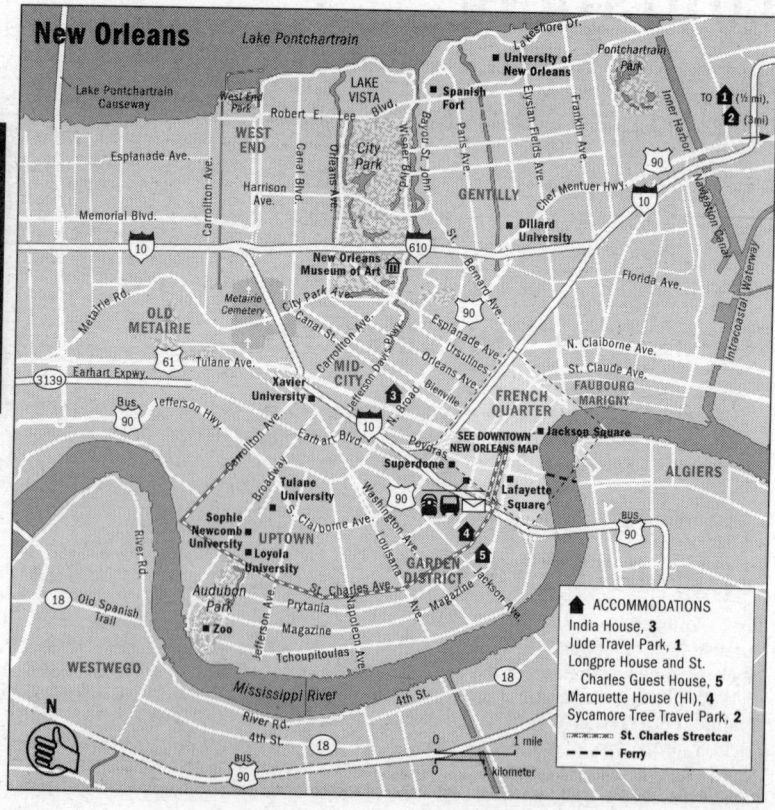

New Orleans

ACCOMMODATIONS
India House, **3**
Jude Travel Park, **1**
Longpre House and St.
    Charles Guest House, **5**
Marquette House (HI), **4**
Sycamore Tree Travel Park, **2**
▬▬▬ St. Charles Streetcar
– – – – Ferry

Downtown New Orleans

➤ ACCOMMODATIONS
Depot House at Mme. Julia's, 1
Hotel LaSalle, 4

🍴 FOOD AND DRINKS
Acme Oyster House, 3
Café du Monde, 21
Central Grocery, 22
Clover Grill, 19
Croissant d'Or, 23
Gumbo Shop, 12
Johnny's Po' boys, 8
Laura's Candies, 6
Mama Rosa's, 5
Mother's Restaurant, 2
The Praline Connection, 28
Royal Blend, 13

♪ MUSIC AND CLUBS
735 Nightclub, 16
Bourbon Pub and Parade Disco, 17
Café Brasil, 31
Café Lafitte, 18
Checkpoint Charlie's, 27
Crescent City Brewhouse, 9
d.b.a, 29
Dragon's Den, 26
El Matador, 25
House of Blues, 7
Lafitte's Blacksmith Shop, 20
Molly's at the Market, 24
O'Flaherty's Irish Pub, 10
Pat O'Briens, 15
Preservation Hall, 14
Shim Sham Club, 11
Snug Harbor, 30

Downtown New Orleans

THE SOUTH

▣ LOCAL TRANSPORTATION

Public Transit: Regional Transit Authority (RTA), 2817 Canal St. (☎248-3900; open M-F 8am-5pm). Most buses pass Canal St., at the edge of the French Quarter. Major buses and streetcars run 24hr. $1.25, seniors and disabled passengers 40¢; transfers 25¢. 1-day pass $5, 3-day pass $12; passes sold at major hotels in the Canal St. area. Office has bus schedules and maps.

Taxis: Checker Yellow Cabs, ☎943-2411. **United Cabs,** ☎522-9771.

Bikes: French Quarter Bicycles, 522 Dumaine St. (☎529-3136), between Decatur and Chartres. Open M-F 11am-7pm, Sa 10am-6pm. $5 per hr., $25 per 24hr., $87.50 per week (includes lock, helmet, and map). Also rents wheelchairs and baby joggers. Credit card or $200 cash deposit required.

◪ ORIENTATION

Most sights in New Orleans are located within a central area. The city's main streets follow the curve of the **Mississippi River,** hence its nickname "the Crescent City." Directions from locals reflect watery influences—lakeside means north, referring to **Lake Ponchartrain,** and "riverside" means south. Uptown lies west, up river; downtown lies down river. The city is concentrated on the east bank of the Mississippi. However, **"The East"** refers only to the easternmost part of the city. **Parking** in New Orleans is relatively easy. To park near the French Quarter, head for the residential area starting at Esplanade St. just east of the Quarter, where many streets have no meters and no restrictions. Avoid parking on deserted streets at night. After sunset, it's often best to take a cab or the St. Charles Streetcar.

NEIGHBORHOODS

Less populated regions of the city, like Algiers, are on **the West Bank,** across the river. Tourists flock to the small **French Quarter (Vieux Carré),** bounded by the Mississippi River, **Canal St., Rampart St.,** and **Esplanade Ave.** Streets in the Quarter follow a grid pattern, making foot travel easy. The residential **Garden District** (uptown, bordered by **St. Charles Ave.** to the north and **Magazine St.** to the south) is distinguished by its elegant homes. The scenic **St. Charles Streetcar** route (fare $1.25), easily picked up at Canal St. and Carondelet St., passes through parts of the **Central Business District** ("CBD" or "downtown"), the Garden District via St. Charles Ave., and **S. Carollton Ave** (near Tulane and Loyola universities).

SAFETY IN NEW ORLEANS. New Orleans is not as dangerous as it used to be, as the city has increased its police force and made an effort to keep tourists safe. But New Orleans still has high crime rates, and many areas that you want to avoid. Many neighborhoods change character very quickly, and danger may lurk one block from a tourist attraction. The tenement areas directly north of the French Quarter and directly northwest of Lee Circle pose particular threats to personal safety. At night, stick to busy, well-lit roads and never walk alone after dark. Make some attempt to downplay the tourist image (e.g., don't wear a t-shirt that has the words "New Orleans" anywhere on it), and have a good idea of where you want to go. Avoid all parks, cemeteries, and housing projects at night.

▣ PRACTICAL INFORMATION

Visitor info: The **New Orleans Welcome Center,** 529 St. Ann St. (☎566-5031; www.neworleanscvb.com), by Jackson Sq. in the French Quarter. Open daily 9am-5pm.

Hotlines: Cope Line, ☎523-2673, for crises. **Rape Hotline,** ☎483-8888. Both 24hr.

Hospital: Charity Hospital, 1532 Tulane Ave. (☎568-2311).

Internet access: New Orleans Public Library, 219 Loyola Ave., 1½ blocks west of Canal St. (☎529-7323). Open M-Th 10am-6pm, Sa 10am-5pm.

Post Office: 701 Loyola Ave. (☎800-275-8777), near the bus station. Open M-F 7am-9pm, Sa 8am-8pm, Su noon-5pm. **ZIP code:** 70113. **Area code:** 504.

ACCOMMODATIONS

Finding inexpensive yet decent rooms in the **French Quarter** can be as difficult as staying sober during Mardi Gras. Luckily, other parts of the city compensate for the absence of cheap lodging downtown. Several **hostels** pepper the area and cater to the young and almost penniless, as do guest houses near the **Garden District**. Accommodations for Mardi Gras and the Jazz Festival get booked up to a year in advance. During peak times, proprietors will rent out any extra space—be sure you know what you're paying for. Rates tend to sink in the off season (most of the summer months) when business is slow; negotiation can pay off.

■ **India House,** 124 S. Lopez St. (☎821-1904), at Canal St. What this bohemian haunt lacks in tidiness it compensates for in character. Young backpackers come here to celebrate freedom and camaraderie. Kitchen, pool, and separate alligator pond out back. 1pm check-out designed for those with "morning grogginess." No lockout or curfew. Free linen. Key deposit $5. Dorms $14, up to $17 in peak times.

■ **Marquette House New Orleans International Hostel (HI-AYH),** 2249 Carondelet St. (☎523-3014), in the Garden District. The cleanest and classiest hostelling experience in New Orleans. Courtyards link several separate buildings with 176 beds, A/C, kitchens, and study rooms; wheelchair accessible. Exceptionally quiet. Linen $2.50. No lockout or curfew, no alcohol permitted. Key deposit $5. Dorms $16.50, nonmembers $19.50. Private rooms with queen-sized bed and pull-out sofa $50, each additional person over 2 people $10. Weekly rates available.

St. Charles Guest House, 1748 Prytania St. (☎523-6556). In a serene neighborhood near the Garden District. A big 3-building complex with 38 rooms, 8 with shared baths. Lovely pool and sunbathing deck. Continental breakfast included. No-frills backpacker's singles $25-45. Rooms with 1 queen-sized bed or 2 twins $45-85.

Depot House at Mme. Julia's, 748 O'Keefe Ave. (☎529-2952) located ½ mi. from the Quarter and in the CBD. This B&B has plain, but comfortable rooms for 1 or 2 people ($65-75). Shared bathrooms. Continental breakfast included. Reservations required.

Longpre House, 1726 Prytania St. (☎581-4540), in a 145-year-old house 1 block south of St. Charles, shows its age a bit. A 25min. walk from the Quarter. Dorm check-in 8am-10pm, 11am for private rooms. Free coffee and linen. No curfew. Dorms $12, in peak times $16. Singles and doubles with shared bath $35, with private bath $40.

Hotel LaSalle, 1113 Canal St. (☎523-5831 or 800-521-9450), 3 blocks from Bourbon St., downtown. Convenient location, spartan accommodations. Rooms are well maintained with TVs and phones. Lobby staffed 24hr. Continental breakfast included. Singles $33, with bath $65; doubles $45/$78.

St. Bernard State Park (☎682-2101), 18 mi. southeast of New Orleans; take I-10 Exit 246A, turn left onto Rte. 46 for 7 mi., then right on Rte. 39 S. for 1 mi. 51 sites with water and electricity. Office open daily 7am-9pm. Sites $12.

Jude Travel Park and Guest House, 7400 Chef Menteur Hwy./U.S. 90 (☎241-0632 or 800-523-2196), just east of the eastern junction of I-10 and U.S. 90, Exit 240B. Bus #98 "Broad" drives past the front gate to #55 "Elysian Fields," which heads downtown. Pool and hot tub, showers, laundry, 24hr. security, shuttle bus to French Quarter. 46 tent/RV sites $20; 5 room guest house available, rates rise at peak times.

Sycamore Tree Travel Park, 10910 Chef Menteur Hwy./U.S. 90 (☎244-6611), 3 mi. east of the eastern junction of I-10 and U.S. 90. Same RTA service as Jude Travel Park. Pool, showers, and laundry facilities. Sites $14, full hookup $20.

FOOD

If the eats in the Quarter prove too trendy, touristy, or tough on the budget, there are plenty of other options, most notably on **Magazine St.** and in the Tulane area. The French Market, between Decatur and N. Peters St., on the east side of the French Quarter, sells pricey fresh vegetables.

SHO' NUFF, GOOD STUFF New Orleans offers a long list of regional specialties that have evolved from the mixing of Acadian, Spanish, Italian, African, French, and Native American cuisines. **Jambalaya** (a Cajun jumble of rice, shrimp, oysters, sausage, and ham or chicken mixed with spices) and **gumbo** (chicken or seafood stew over rice) grace practically every menu in New Orleans. A Southern breakfast of grits, eggs, bacon, and buttermilk biscuits satisfies even the most ardent eaters. **Creole** cuisine (a mixture of Spanish, French, and Caribbean) is famous for red beans and rice, **po' boys** (French bread sandwiches filled with sliced meat or seafood and vegetables; "dressed" means with mayo, lettuce, tomatoes, pickles, etc.), and shrimp or crawfish *étouffée*. Get some of the best Creole pralines ($1.25) at **Laura's Candies,** 600 Conti St. (☎525-3880; open daily 9am-7pm).

FRENCH QUARTER

Cafe du Monde, 800 Decatur St. (☎525-4544), near the French Market. The consummate people-watching paradise since 1862 really only does 2 things: hot *café au lait* and scrumptious *beignets* (each $1.25). Open 24hr. To take home some of that chicory coffee (15 oz. of the grind $4.60), cross the street to the Cafe du Monde Gift Shop, 813 Decatur St. (☎581-2914 or 800-772-2927; open daily 9:30am-6pm).

Johnny's Po' boys, 511 St. Louis St. (☎524-8129). This French Quarter institution offers 40 varieties of the famous sandwich ($4-7.50). Decent Creole fare (jambalaya $4.25, gumbo $6.25) is also on the menu. Open M-F 8am-4:30pm, Sa-Su 9am-4pm.

Gumbo Shop, 630 St. Peter St. (☎525-1486). Sit under a broad-leafed palm and savor a bowl of seafood okra or chicken *andouille* gumbo ($7); po' boys $5-8, entrees from $10. Expect a line. Open daily 11am-11pm.

Sabrina and Gabrielle's Secret Garden, 538 St. Philip St. (☎524-2041). A romantic rendezvous for the dinnertime crowd. A pleasant courtyard and gracious service add to the mood. Cajun and Creole specials come with soup and salad ($7-15). Open Su-Th 5:30-10pm, F-Sa 5:30-11pm.

Central Grocery, 923 Decatur St. (☎523-1620), between Dumaine and St. Philip St. Try an authentic *muffuletta* (deli meats, cheeses, and olive salad on Italian bread) at the place that invented them. A half ($5) serves 1; a whole ($9) is best split between 2. Open M-Sa 8am-5:30pm, Su 9am-5:30pm.

Acme Oyster House, 724 Iberville St. (☎522-5973). At the bar, patrons slurp fresh oysters shucked before their eyes (6 for $4, 12 for $6.50), or sit at the red checkered tables for a po' boy ($5-9). Open Su-Th 11am-10pm, F-Sa 11am-11pm.

Croissant d'Or, 617 Ursulines St. (☎524-4663). Fair-priced French pastries, sandwiches, and quiches. *Carré Mocca* $1.30, chocolate mousse $1.50. Open daily 7am-5pm.

Mama Rosa's, 616 N. Rampart (☎523-5546). Locals adore this Italian *ristorante*. Rosa's pizza was once rated among the 9 best in the country by *People* magazine. 14 in. cheese pie $9. Open Su-Th 11am-10pm, F-Sa 11am-11pm.

Royal Blend, 621 Royal St. (☎523-2716). Quiet garden setting offers escape from hustle of Royal St. Over 20 hot and iced coffees available, as well as a mighty fine selection of teas—you can even brew your own. Light meals (croissant sandwiches, quiches, and salads) $5-6; pastries $1-2. Open M-Th 6:30am-8pm, F-Sa 7am-midnight, Su 6:30am-6pm. Internet cafe upstairs.

Clover Grill, 900 Bourbon St. (☎598-1010). The Clover has been open 24hr. since 1950, serving greasy and delicious burgers ($4 and up) grilled under an American-made hubcap. The waiters behind the counter love to entertain and compliment patrons—for extra tips, of course.

OUTSIDE THE QUARTER

Camellia Grill, 626 S. Carrollton Ave. (☎866-9573). Take the St. Charles Streetcar to the Tulane area. Classic, counter-service diner where cooks don't mind telling the whole restaurant about their marital problems. Big drippin' plates, crowds (especially weekend mornings), and excellent service. Chef's special omelette ($7), "whole meal" sandwiches $6-7. Open M-Th 9am-1am, F 9am-3am, Sa 8am-3am, Su 8am-1am.

▨ **Franky and Johnny's,** 321 Arabella (☎899-9146), southwest of downtown toward Tulane off Tchoupitoulas St. A noisy local hangout where you can sample alligator soup ($3 a cup), crawfish pie ($4), or boiled crawfish ($6-11 for 2 lb., seasonal, Feb.-June). Open Su-Th 11am-10pm, F-Sa 11am-midnight.

Taqueria Corona, 5932 Magazine St. (☎897-3974), between State and Nashville St. Some of the best Mexican food around. Loud but cozy atmosphere. Deliciously hot burritos $3-7.25. Open daily 11:30am-2pm and 5-9:30pm.

Tee Eva's, 4430 Magazine St. (☎899-8350). Eva sells bayou cooking to go from her kitchen window. Creole pralines $2, and 9 oz. snow balls for $1.50. Crawfish pie $3; sweet potato and pecan pie $2. Large 9 in. pies $10-17, by order only. Soul food lunches change daily ($4-6). Open daily 11am-7pm.

Joey K's Restaurant, 3001 Magazine St. (☎891-0997), at 7th St. Friendly neighborhood eatery, especially for the midday meal—lunch specials start at $6 and feature "Creole pot" cooking, fried seafood, and daily specials including stuffed eggplant. Sandwiches $4.50-6 and 18 oz. beer $2.50. Open M-F 11am-10pm, Sa 8am-10pm.

Cafe Atchafalaya, 901 Louisiana Ave. (☎891-5271), at Laurel St. Take the #11 bus "Magazine St." This cozy cottage serves mouth-watering traditional Southern cuisine. Simple dishes like red beans and rice with salad ($6.50) and an appetizer of fried green tomatoes ($3.50) are expensive but exquisite. Laid-back service. Lunch Tu-F 11:30am-2pm, Sa-Su 8:30am-2pm; dinner Th-Tu 5:30-9pm, F-Sa 5:30-9:30pm.

The Praline Connection, 542 Frenchman St. (☎943-3943). Finger-lickin' good soul food: fried chicken and seafood, stuffed crab, and *étouffées* along with daily lunch specials. Entrees from $9. Open Su-Th 11am-10:30pm, F-Sa 11am-midnight.

Mother's Restaurant, 401 Poydras St. (☎523-9656), downtown at Tchoupitoulas St., 4 blocks southwest of Bourbon St. Serving up po' boys ($7-10) and some of the best jambalaya in town ($7.25). Open M-Sa 5am-10pm, Su 7am-10pm.

The Trolley Stop Cafe, 1923 St. Charles Ave. (☎523-0090). Breakfast served 24hr. and it's busy all the time, partly thanks to the police officers who convene here. Most lunch and dinner specials under $5.50; breakfast specials $3.75-4.50.

☯ SIGHTS

FRENCH QUARTER

Allow *at least* a full day in the Quarter. The oldest section of the city is famous for its ornate wrought-iron balconies; French, Spanish, and uniquely New Orleans architecture; and a raucous atmosphere. Known as the **Vieux Carré** (*view-ca-RAY*), or Old Square, the historic district of New Orleans offers dusty used book and record stores, museums, and tourist traps. **Bourbon St.** is packed with touristy bars, strip clubs, and clowns. **Decatur St.** has more mellow coffeeshops and bars.

ROYAL STREET. A streetcar named "Desire" once rolled down Royal St., now one of the French Quarter's most aesthetically pleasing avenues. With balconies of wrought-iron oak leaves and acorns spanning three tiers, **LaBranche House,** at Royal and St. Peter St., may be the most photographed building in the French Quarter.

JACKSON SQUARE. During the day, most of the activity in the French Quarter centers on Jackson Sq., a park dedicated to Gen. Andrew Jackson, victor of the Battle of New Orleans. The square swarms with artists, mimes, musicians, psychics, magicians, and con artists. **St. Louis Cathedral** is the oldest operational Catholic cathedral in the US. (*Tours every 15-20min. 9am-5pm daily; cathedral open 6:30am-6:30pm daily. Free.*) Behind the cathedral lies **St. Anthony's Garden,** bordered by **Pirate's Alley** and **Père Antoine's Alley.** Legend has it that the former was the site of covert meetings between pirate Jean Lafitte and President Andrew Jackson, as they conspired to plan the Battle of New Orleans. Pirate's Alley is also home to **Faulkner House Books,** where the late American author wrote his first novel. Upholding the literary tradition, the bookshop is a treasure-trove of Faulkner first editions and quality hardcovers. (*624 Pirate's Alley. ☎524-2940. Open daily 10am-6pm.*)

FRENCH MARKET. The historic French Market takes up several city blocks just east of Jackson Sq., toward the water, along N. Peters St. (☎ 522-2621. *Shops open daily 9am-8pm.*) The market begins at the famous **Cafe du Monde** (see p. 414). Vendors sell everything from watermelons to earrings. For a map of the whole strip, stop at the **Visitors Center.** (*700 Decatur, under Washington Artillery Park.* ☎ 596-3424. *Open daily 8:30am-5pm.*) Since 1791, visitors have been able to purchase fresh fruits, vegetables, herbs, and spices at the **Farmers Market,** which never closes.

TOURS OF THE QUARTER. The **Jean Lafitte National Historical Park and Preserve** conducts free 1½hr. walking tours through the Quarter. Daily presentations on regional topics occur at 3pm. (*419 Decatur St.* ☎ 589-2636. *Tours daily 9:30am. Office open daily 9am-5pm.*) It's always a great night to stroll the **Moon Walk,** a promenade stretching alongside the "Mighty" Mississippi. The walk offers a fantastic riverside view and a chance for Michael Jackson jokes. *Don't go alone at night.*

OTHER ATTRACTIONS. At the southwest corner of the Quarter, the **Aquarium of the Americas** houses an amazing collection of sea life and birds. Among the 500 species are black-footed penguins, endangered sea turtles, and extremely rare white alligators. (*1 Canal St.* ☎ 565-3033. *Open daily 9:30am-7pm May-Aug., 9:30am-6pm Sept.-Apr. $13.50, seniors $10, ages 2-12 $6.50.*) The steamboat **Natchez** breezes down the Mississippi on 2hr. cruises, featuring live jazz and narration on riverside sights. Pick up two-for-one coupons at the Visitors Center or fork over $16.75 per person at the regular fee. (☎ 586-8777 *or* 800-233-2628. *Departs 11:30am and 2:30pm, near the aquarium and across from Jackson Brewery.*)

OUTSIDE THE QUARTER

WATERFRONT. The **Riverwalk,** a multimillion dollar conglomeration of overpriced shops overlooking the port, stretches along the Mississippi. (*Open M-Sa 10am-9pm, Su 11am-7pm.*) Take a chance on the newly opened **Harrah's New Orleans Casino,** at Canal and the river. Experience an endless Mardi Gras as quarters plink into endless rows of slot machines. (☎ 800-427-7247. *21+. Open 24hr.*) For an up-close view of the Mississippi River and a bit of African-American history, take the free **Canal St. Ferry** to Algiers Point. The Algiers of old was home to many of New Orleans's African Americans and is a beautiful neighborhood to explore by foot. At night, the ferry's outdoor observation deck affords a panoramic view of the city's sights. (*Departs daily 5:45am-midnight, every 30min. from the end of Canal St. Cars $1 round-trip.*)

WAREHOUSE ARTS DISTRICT. Relatively new to the downtown area, the Warehouse Arts District, near the intersection of St. Charles and Julia St., contains several revitalized warehouse buildings that house contemporary art galleries. The galleries feature widely attended exhibition openings the first Saturday of every month, the biggest of which is **White Linen Night,** the first Saturday in August, when thousands take to the streets donned in their fanciest white finery. In an old brick building with a modern glass-and-chrome facade, the **Contemporary Arts Center** mounts exhibits ranging from puzzling to positively cryptic. (*900 Camp St.* ☎ 528-3805. *Open Tu-Su 11am-5pm. Exhibits $5, seniors and students $3, under 12 free; Th free.*) In the rear studio of the **New Orleans School of Glassworks and Printmaking Studio,** observe as students and instructors transform blobs of molten glass into vases and sculptures. (*727 Magazine St.* ☎ 529-7277. *Open M-F 11am-5pm; winter M-Sa 11am-5pm. Free.*) **The Jonathan Ferrara Gallery** hosts an annual "No Dead Artists: A Juried Exhibition of New Orleans Art Today" every April. Ferrara was nationally recognized for his involvement in "Guns in the Hands of Artists," a 1996 program in which people turned in guns that were then made into works of art. (*841 Carondelet St.* ☎ 522-5471. *Open Tu-Sa noon-6pm. Free.*) Just west of the warehouse district the **Zeitgeist Multi-Disciplinary Arts Center** offers films, musical performances, and art exhibitions. Their mission is "something for and against everyone!" A huge exhibition of communist art is slated for May through June, 2002. (*1724 Oretha Castle Haley Blvd. 4 blocks north of St. Charles St.* ☎ 525-2767. *Call for times and schedule.*) A few blocks farther west on St. Charles St., in **Lee Circle,** stands a bronze Confederate Gen. Robert E. Lee. The general continues to stare down the Yankees: he faces due North.

BEFORE YOU DIE, READ THIS: Being dead in New Orleans has always been a problem. Because the city lies 4-6 ft. below sea level, a 6 ft. hole in the earth fills up with 5 ft. of water. At one time coffins literally floated in the graves, while cemetery workers pushed them down with long wooden poles. One early solution was to bore holes in the coffins, allowing them to sink. Unfortunately, the sight of a drowning coffin coupled with the awful gargling sound of its immersion proved too much for the squeamish families of the departed. Burial soon became passé, and stiffs were laid to rest in beautiful raised stone tombs. Miles and miles of creepy, cool marble tombs now fill the city's graveyards and ghost stories.

ST. CHARLES STREETCAR. Much of the Crescent City's fame derives from the **Vieux Carré,** but areas uptown have their fair share of beauty and action. The **St. Charles Streetcar** still runs west of the French Quarter, passing some of the city's finest buildings, including the 19th-century homes along **St. Charles Ave.** *Gone With the Wind*-o-philes will recognize the whitewashed bricks and elegant doorway of the house on the far right corner of Arabella St.—it's a replica of Tara. Frankly, my dear, it's not open to the public. For more views of fancy living, get off the streetcar in the **Garden District,** an opulent neighborhood around Jackson and Louisiana Ave. French, Italian, Spanish, and American architectural legacies create an extraordinary combination of colors, ironwork, and gardens. Some houses are raised above the ground for protection from the swamp on which New Orleans rests.

HISTORIC HOMES AND PLANTATIONS

Called the "Great Showplace of New Orleans," **Longue Vue House and Gardens** epitomizes the grand Southern estate with lavish furnishings, opulent decor, and sculpted gardens dating back to the 1930s. On the way, pause for a peek at the 85 ft. tall monument among the raised tombs in the **Metairie Cemetery,** where country/rock legend Gram Parsons is buried in the Garden of Memories. *(Longue Vue House: 7 Bamboo Rd., off Metairie Rd.* ☎*488-5488. Open M-Sa 10am-4:30pm, Su 1-5pm. Tours every hr. $10, seniors $9, students $5, under 5 free. Tours available in English, French, German, Spanish, Italian, and Japanese.)* **River Rd.** curves along the Mississippi River across from downtown New Orleans, accessing several plantations preserved from the 19th century; copies of *Great River Road Plantation Parade: A River of Riches*, available at the New Orleans or Baton Rouge Visitors Centers, contain a good map and descriptions of the houses. Pick carefully, since a tour of all the privately owned plantations is quite expensive. Those below are listed in order from New Orleans to Baton Rouge.

HERMANN-GRIMM HISTORIC HOUSE. Built in 1831, the house exemplifies French style, replete with a large central hall, guillotine windows, a fan-lit entrance, and the original parterre beds. On Thursdays from October to May trained volunteers demonstrate period cooking in an 1830s Creole kitchen. *(820 St. Louis St.* ☎*525-5661. Open M-F 10am-4pm. Tours every hr.; last tour 3:30pm. $6, ages 8-18 $5.)*

GALLIER HOUSE MUSEUM. The elegantly restored residence of James Gallier, Jr., the city's most famous architect, displays the taste and lifestyle of the wealthy in the 1860s. *(1118-1132 Royal St.* ☎*525-5661. Open M-F 10am-4pm. Last tour 3:30pm. $6, students, seniors and ages 8-18 $5, under 8 free.)*

SAN FRANCISCO PLANTATION HOUSE. Beautifully maintained since 1856, the San Francisco is an example of the Creole style, with a bright blue, peach, and green exterior. *(Rte. 44, 2 mi. northwest of Reserve, 42 mi. from New Orleans on the east bank of the Mississippi. Exit 206 off I-10.* ☎*535-2341 or 888-322-1756. Tours Mar.-Oct. daily 10am-4:30pm; Nov.-Feb. 10am-4pm. $8, ages 12-17 $4, ages 6-11 $3.)*

OAK ALLEY. The name Oak Alley refers to the magnificent driveway bordered by 28 evenly spaced oaks. The oaks correspond to 28 columns surrounding the Greek Revival house. The Greeks wouldn't have approved, though: the mansion is bright pink. *(3645 Rte. 18, between St. James and Vacherie St.* ☎*800-463-7350. Tours Mar.-Oct. daily every 30min. 9am-5:30pm; Nov.-Feb. 9am-5pm. $10, ages 13-18 $6, ages 6-12 $4.)*

HOUMAS HOUSE. This plantation served as the setting for the movie *Hush,*
Hush, Sweet Charlotte, starring Bette Davis and Olivia de Havilland. Huge, moss-
draped oaks shade the spacious grounds and beautiful gardens. "Southern Belle"
guides lead tours in authentic antebellum attire. *(40136 Rte. 942, in Burnside just over*
halfway to Baton Rouge. ☎888-323-8314. Open daily 10am-5pm; Nov.-Jan. 10am-4pm. $8,
ages 13-17 $6, ages 6-12 $3.)

NOTTOWAY. The largest plantation home in the South, Nottoway is often called
the "White Castle of Louisiana." A 64-room mansion with 22 columns, a large ballroom, and a 3-story stairway, it was David O. Selznick's first choice for filming
Gone with the Wind, but the owners wouldn't allow it. *(Rte. 405, between Bayou*
Goula and White Castle, 18 mi. south of Baton Rouge on the southern bank of the Mississippi.
☎225-545-2730. Open daily 9am-5pm. Admission and 1hr. tour $10, under 12 $4.)

🏛 MUSEUMS

National D-Day Museum, 945 Magazine St. (☎527-6012). Founded by renowned historian Stephen Ambrose, the museum features vivid personal accounts of the WWII experience, as well as an award-winning documentary film on the economic and political
nature of the War. Open daily 9am-5pm. $10, seniors and students $6, ages 5-17 $5.

Louisiana State Museum, P.O. Box 2448 (☎800-568-6968), oversees 5 separate museums. The **Old US Mint,** 400 Esplanade, focuses not on currency or fresh breath, but on
the history of jazz. **Cabildo,** 701 Chartres St., features a wonderful history of Mardi
Gras. **Presbytère,** 751 Chartres St., delves into Louisiana history and has a death mask
of Napoleon. **1850 House,** 523 St. Ann St., is, not surprisingly, a recreated house from
the time period. **Mme. John's Legacy,** 632 Dumaine St., showcases French Colonial
architecture and an exhibit on contemporary self-taught Louisiana artists. All open Tu-
Su 9am-5pm. Old US Mint, Cabildo, Presbytère: $5, seniors and students $4. 1850
House, Mme. John's Legacy: $3/$2. Under 12 free for all museums.

New Orleans Museum of Art (NOMA) (☎488-2631), in City Park. Take the Esplanade bus
from Canal and Rampart St. This magnificent museum houses art from North and South
America, a small collection of local decorative arts, opulent works by the jeweler Fab-
ergé, and a strong collection of French paintings. Free tours available at 11am and
2pm. Open Tu-Su 10am-5pm. $6, seniors and ages 3-17 $5.

Historic New Orleans Collection, 533 Royal St. (☎523-4662). Located in the aristocratic
18th-century Merieult House, this impressive cultural research center oozes with Louisiana's history. The History Tour explores New Orleans past, while the Williams Residence
Tour showcases the eclectic home furnishings of the collection's founders. Gallery open
Tu-Sa 10am-4:30pm; free. Tours 4 times daily; $4.

Musée Conti Wax Museum, 917 Conti St. (☎525-2605). A great mix of the historically
important, sensationally infamous, and just plain kitschy. Perennial favorites include a
voodoo scene, and a mock-up of Madame Lalaurie's torture attic. Open M-Sa 10am-
5:30pm, Su noon-5:30pm. $6.75, seniors $6.25, under 17 $5.75.

Confederate Museum, 929 Camp St. (☎523-4522), in a brownstone building just south
of Lee Circle. The state's oldest museum, with a wide collection of Civil War records and
artifacts. Open M-Sa 10am-4pm. $5, students and seniors $4, under 12 $2.

New Orleans Pharmacy Museum, 514 Chartres St. (☎565-8027), in the Quarter. This
apothecary shop was built by America's first licensed pharmacist in 1823. On display
are 19th-century "miracle drugs," voodoo powders, and the still-fertile botanical garden.

Louisiana Children's Museum, 420 Julia St. (☎523-1357). This place invites kids to play
and learn as they star in their own news shows, run their own cafe, or shop in a re-created mini-mart. Kids under 16 must be accompanied by an adult. Open M-Sa 9:30am-
4:30pm, Su noon-4:30pm; Sept.-May closed M. $6.

Louisiana Nature and Science Center (☎246-5672), Joe Brown Memorial Park. Go east
on I-10 and take Exit 244; the park is off Read Blvd. Trail walks, exhibits, planetarium,
laser shows, and 86 acres of natural wildlife preserve. From Basin St., take bus #64
"Lake Forest Express" ($1.25) to reach this wonderful escape. Open Tu-F 9am-5pm, Sa
10am-5pm, Su noon-5pm. $4.75, seniors $3.75, ages 3-12 $2.50.

⚠ OUTDOOR ACTIVITIES

The St. Charles Streetcar eventually makes its way to **Audubon Park,** near **Tulane University.** Audubon contains lagoons, statues, stables, and the award-winning **Audubon Zoo,** where white alligators swim in a re-created Louisiana swamp. (☎581-4629. Free museum shuttle between park entrance and zoo every 15min. Zoo open daily 9:30am-5pm; in summer Sa-Su until 6pm. $9, seniors $5.75, ages 2-12 $4.75.)

One of the most unique sights in the New Orleans area, the coastal wetlands along Lake Salvador make up a segment of the **Jean Lafitte National Historical Park** called the **Barataria Preserve,** 7400 Barataria Blvd.; south of New Orleans, take Business 90 to Rte. 45. There's a daily park-sponsored foot tour through the swamp at 11am. (☎589-2330. Open daily 7am-5pm; extended summer hours; Visitors Center open daily 9am-5pm. Free.) Many commercial boat tours operate around the park; **Cypress Swamp Tours** will pick you up from your hotel for free, but the tour itself is damn expensive. (☎581-4501 or 800-633-0503; call for reservations. 2hr. tours at 9:30, 11:30am, 1:30, and 3:30pm. $22, ages 6-12 $12.)

🎭 ENTERTAINMENT

THEATER
Le Petit Théâtre du Vieux Carré, 616 St. Peters St., is one of the city's most beloved and historical theaters. The oldest continuously operating community theater in the US, the 1789 building replicates the early 18th-century abode of Joseph de Pontalba, Louisiana's last Spanish governor. About five musicals and plays go up each year, as well as three fun productions in the "Children's Corner." (☎522-9958. Box office open M-Sa 10:30am-5:30pm, Su noon-5pm. Most tickets around $25.)

MUSIC
Uptown tends to house authentic Cajun dance halls and popular university hangouts, while the Marigny is home to New Orleans's alternative/local music scene. Check out *Off Beat,* free in many local restaurants, or the Friday *Times-Picayune* to find out who's playing where.

Born at the turn of the century in **Armstrong Park,** traditional New Orleans jazz still wails nightly at the tiny, dim, historic **Preservation Hall,** 726 St. Peters St.; jazz is in its most fundamental element here. With only two small ceiling fans trying to move the air around, most people can only stay for one set, so you can usually expect to find a place. (Daytime ☎522-2841, otherwise 523-8939. No food or drink allowed. Cover $5. Doors open at 8pm; music begins at 8:30pm and ends at midnight.)

Keep your ears open for **Cajun** and **zydeco** bands, which use accordions, washboards, triangles, and drums to perform hot dance tunes (true locals two-step expertly) and saccharine waltzes. Anyone who thinks couple-dancing went out in the 50s should try a *fais-do-do,* a lengthy, wonderfully energetic traditional dance. The locally based **Radiators** do it up real spicy-like in a rock-Cajun-zydeco style.

FESTIVALS
New Orleans's **Mardi Gras** celebration is the biggest party of the year, a world-renowned, epic bout of lascivious debauchery that fills the three weeks leading up to Ash Wednesday. Parades, gala, balls, and general revelry take to the streets, as tourists pour in by the plane-full (flights into the city and hotel rooms fill up months in advance). In 2002, "Fat Tuesday" falls on Feb. 12; the biggest parades and the bulk of the partying will take place the two weeks prior to that. The ever-expanding **New Orleans Jazz and Heritage Festival** attracts 7000 musicians from around the country to the city's fairgrounds. The likes of Aretha Franklin, Bob Dylan, Patti LaBelle, and Wynton Marsalis have graced this slightly "classier" fest, where music plays simultaneously on 12 stages in the midst of a huge food and crafts festival. The biggest names perform evening riverboat concerts. The festival grows bigger and, unfortunately, more commercialized each year. (☎522-4786; Apr. 26-May 5, 2002.)

GIMME SOME SKIN French quarter shops sell beads for $1-5, but why buy them when you can *earn* them for free? Down on the 700th block of Bourbon St., and especially near the balconies above the Cat's Meow and Tricou House, lie the best bead bartering locations. Women (and even men) who flash body parts on the street earn beads. Only in New Orleans is exposing oneself so colorfully rewarded.

☑ NIGHTLIFE

Life in New Orleans is and always will be a party. On any night of the week, at any time of the year, the masses converge on **Bourbon St.** to drift in and out of bars and shop for romantic interludes. Though the street has become increasingly touristy of late, much of Bourbon's original charm remains. Several sleazy strip clubs and cross-dressing joints maintain the sense of sinful excitement that is the essence of the Quarter. To escape the debauchery of Bourbon St., go uptown to the Tulane area or east of the Quarter on Frenchman St. Some flee to Decatur St., between St. Ann and Barracks St.

While the Quarter offers countless bars and jazz, blues, and brass venues, be assured that there's more to New Orleans entertainment. When locals burn out on Bourbon, they head uptown toward **Tulane University,** or to the **Marigny,** an up-and-coming district northeast of the Quarter. New Orleans has a vibrant gay scene. *Ambush* and *Eclipse* will tell you what's happening; both are available at **Faubourg Marigny Books,** 600 Frenchmen St. (☎943-9875. Open M-F 10am-8pm, Sa-Su 10am-6pm.) Gay establishments cluster toward the northeast end of Bourbon St., and St. Ann St. is known to some as the **"Lavender Line."**

Bars in New Orleans stay open late, and few keep a strict schedule; in general, they open around 11am and close around 3am. Most blocks feature at least one establishment with cheap draft beer and Hurricanes (sweet juice-and-rum drinks). *All establishments are 21+ unless otherwise noted.*

BARS

FRENCH QUARTER

Pat O'Brien's, 718 St. Peters St. (☎525-4823). Housed in the first Spanish theater in the US, this busy bar, one of the best in the French Quarter, bursts with happy (read: drunk) patrons. Home of the original Hurricane; purchase your first in a souvenir glass ($8, $6 without glass). Open Su-Th 10am-4am, F-Sa 10am-5am.

Lafitte's Blacksmith Shop, 941 Bourbon St. (☎523-0066), at Phillip St. Appropriately, one of New Orleans's oldest standing structures is a bar. Built in the 1730s, the building is still lit by candlelight after sunset. Named for the scheming hero of the Battle of New Orleans, it offers shaded relief from the elements of the city. Live piano 8pm until late. Beers $4. Open weekdays 11:30am-2am, weekends 11:30am-6am.

Molly's at the Market, 1107 Decatur St. (☎525-5169). Molly's offers tasty and widely acclaimed frozen Irish coffee ($4.50), as well as a hang-out space for eclectic locals. Vibrant late night retreat from the touristy frenzy of the Quarter. Open daily 10am-6am.

Crescent City Brewhouse, 527 Decatur St. (☎522-0571). The only microbrewery in New Orleans, this classy brewpub sells its own 5 blends (12 oz. $4, 20 oz. $5). Glass walls and balcony make for good people-watching, a wonderful activity when set to live jazz (nightly 6-9pm). Open Su-Th 11am-10pm, F-Sa 11am-midnight.

O'Flaherty's Irish Channel Pub, 514 Toulouse St. (☎529-1317). O'Flaherty's bills itself as the meeting point of the disparate Celtic nations. Eavesdrop on Gaelic conversation while listening to Scottish bagpipes, watching Irish dances, and/or singing along to Irish tunes. Irish music weekdays at 8pm, weekends at 9pm. Special Irish breakfast Su starting at 8am, $8. Cover $2-10. Open daily M-F noon-2am, Sa-Su noon-3am.

Jimmy Buffett's Margaritaville Cafe, 1104 Decatur (☎592-2565), at Ursulines. Jimmy got his start singing on Bourbon St. Today, you can relax at this "island in the city," which draws a mixed crowd of families and twenty-somethings. Live music daily 3pm-midnight. Bar open daily 11am-midnight; restaurant open daily 11am-10:30pm.

OUTSIDE THE QUARTER

Snug Harbor, 626 Frenchmen St. (☎949-0696), near Decatur St. Regulars include big names in modern jazz like Charmaine Neville and Ellis Marsalis. The cover is steep ($12-18), but the music and its fans are authentic. All ages. Shows nightly 9 and 11pm. Bar open daily 5pm-1am; restaurant open Su-Th 5-11pm, F-Sa 5pm-midnight.

F&M Patio Bar, 4841 Tchoupitoulas St. (☎895-6784), near Napoleon. Mellow twenty-somethings, students, lawyers, and ne'er-do-wells dance together on pool tables all through the night. Food served after 6pm, mostly fajitas ($4) and burgers ($5.25) from the patio grill. Open M-Th 6pm-4am, F 1pm-6am, Sa 3pm-6am, Su 8pm-4am.

Cafe Bracil, 2100 Chartres (☎949-0851), at Frenchmen St. Unassuming by day, Brasil is full on weekend nights with locals who come to see a wide variety of New Orleans talent. All ages. Cover F-Sa $6-10 after 11pm. Open daily 7pm until late.

Checkpoint Charlie's, 501 Esplanade (☎947-0979), grunges it up like the best of Seattle, but with a wide variety of live music 7 nights a week starting at 10:30pm. You can do your laundry here as well. Julia Roberts sat on these machines in *The Pelican Brief.* Beer $2.25. No cover. Open and serving food 24hr.

Carrollton Station, 8140 Willow St. (☎865-9190), at Dublin St. A cozy neighborhood club with live R&B and friendly folks. As one of the regulars says, "a place with character full of characters." 12 beers on tap ($2-4) and nearly 40 varieties of rum. Music Th-Su at 10pm. Cover varies. Open daily 3:30pm-2am.

d.b.a., 618 Frenchmen St. (☎942-3731), next to Snug Harbor. A taste of Manhattan in the Big Easy, this classy, beautifully wood-paneled bar has live music 2-3 nights a week as well as monthly beer and tequila tastings. Open M-F 5pm-4am, Sa-Su 3pm-5am.

Jimmy's, 8200 Willow (☎861-8200). When school is in session, this is where the college crowd chills. Occasional live music, daily drink specials. Open daily 9pm until late.

Dragon's Den, 435 Esplanade (☎949-1750), upstairs from Siam Cafe. This opium den-like establishment bills itself as a "social aid and pleasure club." Live music daily 10:30pm, Th poetry slam and open mic 8pm. Monday 2 for 1 hot sake is always a big draw. No cover M-Th; F-Sa $6. Open daily 6pm til dawn; food served til 1am.

DANCE CLUBS

FRENCH QUARTER

House of Blues, 225 Decatur St. (☎529-2624). A sprawling complex with a large (over 1000 capacity) music/dance hall, and a balcony and bar overlooking the action. 18+. Cover usually $5-10, but big names cost up to $30. Restaurant open Su-Th 11am-11pm, F-Sa 11am-midnight. Concerts nightly 9:15pm.

735 Nightclub and Bar, 735 Bourbon St. (☎581-6740). Great music and a hip mixed crowd keep this dance club energized well into the night. Techno, progressive house, and trance plays downstairs, with 80s music on the 2nd floor. 18+. Cover $5, under 21 $10. Open W-Su 10pm-3am.

Shim Sham Club, 615 Toulouse St. (☎299-0666). The last 3 digits of their phone number should give you an accurate idea of this place—an incredible variety of live music, burlesque shows, and "glitter glam rock 'n' roll" shows every Sa. No cover before 11pm; varies after 11. Open daily 2pm-6am.

OUTSIDE THE QUARTER

Tipitina's, 501 Napoleon Ave. (☎891-8477, concert info 897-3943). The best local bands and some big national names, such as the Neville Brothers, John Goodman, and Harry Connick, Jr., playing so close you can almost touch them. Su evenings 5-9pm feature Cajun *fais-do-dos.* Cover $4-25. 18+. Usually music W-Su starting at 10:30pm, but call ahead for times and prices.

The Red Room, 2040 St. Charles (☎528-9759). Latin beats and rhythm and blues mark this swanky throwback to the opulent, jazzy side of the 30s. One of the mellowest, classiest clubs. Be sure to dress up, or you'll look drab against the posh red decor. 18+. Cover $5-10. Open 7pm-2am, Sa until late. Music starts at 9pm.

Maple Leaf Bar, 8316 Oak St. (☎866-9359). The best local dance bar, offering zydeco, brass band, and Cajun music; everyone does the two-step. Large, pleasant, covered patio. Cover $7. Open daily 3pm. Poetry readings Su 3pm, free. Music and dancing start Su 9pm, M-Sa 10:30pm.

Mid City Lanes, 4133 S. Carrollton Ave. (☎482-3133), at Tulane Ave. Uncut N'awlins. The "home of Rock 'n' Bowl" is bowling alley by day, dance club by night (you can bowl at night, too). Featuring good food and local zydeco, blues, and rock 'n' roll, this is where the locals party. Lanes $12 per hr. Music Tu-W 8:30pm, Th 9:30pm, F-Sa 10pm. 18+. Cover $5-7. Open Tu-Th noon-1am, F-Sa noon-2am.

El Matador, 504 Esplanade (☎569-8361). A good mix of patrons and a wide range of musical styles make this nightclub a good escape from the predictable drunken mayhem of more touristy locations. Usually no cover, but it varies. Live flamenco show 7:30pm Sa. Open M-Th 9pm until late, F-Su 4pm until late.

GAY AND LESBIAN NIGHTLIFE

Cafe Lafitte in Exile, 901 Bourbon St. (522-8397). This gay bar and one-time haunt of playwright Tennessee Williams was formerly located in the current Lafitte's Blacksmith Shop—it moved in 1953, hence the name. All 24 hours of the day are happy here, but 4-9pm is when you'll find drink specials.

Bourbon Pub & Parade Disco, 801 Bourbon St. (☎529-2107). This gay dance bar has a "tea dance" on Su with $5 all-you-can-drink beer. Dance upstairs at the Parade Disco nightly from 10pm; it lasts 'til you fall off. Open 24hr.

BATON ROUGE   ☎225

Once the site of a tall cypress tree marking the boundary between rival Native American tribes, Baton Rouge ("red stick") has blossomed into Louisiana's capital and second largest city. State politics have shaped this town—it was once the home of notorious governor, senator, and populist demagogue "Kingfish" Huey P. Long. The presence of Louisiana State University (LSU) adds an element of youth, but Baton Rouge has a simple meat-and-potatoes flavor in contrast to the flamboyant sauciness of New Orleans.

In a move reminiscent of Ramses II, Huey Long ordered the construction of the unique **Louisiana State Capitol,** a magnificent, modern skyscraper, completed over a mere 14 months in 1931 and 1932. Toward the back of the first floor of the capitol stands a display marking the spot where Long was assassinated in 1935. The **observation deck,** on the 27th fl., provides a fantastic view of the surrounding area. (☎342-7317. Open daily 8am-4pm. Free.) The **Old State Capitol,** 100 North Blvd., resembles a cathedral, with a fantastic spiral staircase and domed stained glass. Inside are interactive political displays. (☎342-0500 or 800-488-2968. Open Tu-Sa 10am-4pm, Su noon-4pm. $4, seniors $3, students $2; $1 off with brochure from the new capitol.) **Magnolia Mound Plantation,** 2161 Nicholson Dr., built in 1791, is a colonial plantation spanning 16 acres with its out buildings (slave and work houses) still standing. (☎343-4955. Open Tu-Sa 10am-4pm, Su 1-4pm. $8, seniors and students $6, ages 5-17 $3. Last tour 3:15pm.) The **LSU Rural Life Museum,** 4560 Essen Ln., just off I-10, depicts the life of 18th- and-19th century Creoles through their furnished shops, cabins, and storage houses—in all, 24 buildings are spread over 10 acres. Adjacent to the museum are the lakes, winding paths, and flowers of the **Windrush Gardens.** (☎765-2437. Both open daily 8:30am-5pm. $5, seniors $4, ages 5-11 $3.)

Baton Rouge's cheapest accommodations are located on the outskirts of town. One of the best deals for can be found at **Motel 6,** 2800 I-10 Frontage Rd., off I-10 just west of Baton Rouge across the Mississippi River, in Port Allen. (☎343-5945. Singles $40; doubles $46.) The **KOA Campground,** 7628 Vincent Rd., 1 mi. off I-12 at the Denham Springs exit, keeps 110 well-maintained sites, clean facilities and a big pool. (☎664-7281 or 800-562-5673. Sites $20; full RV hookup $27.) Downtown, sandwich shops and cafes line 3rd St. Head to LSU at the intersection of Highland Rd. and Chimes St. for cheaper chow and an abundance of bars. **Louie's Cafe,** 209 W. State St., grills up fabulous omelettes for $5.25-11. (☎346-8221. Open 24hr.)

When you want a good sit-down meal, check out **The Chimes**, 3357 Highland Rd., a big restaurant and bar with more than 120 different beers. Start the meal with an appetizer of Louisiana alligator—farm-raised, marinated, and fried, served with Dijon mustard sauce— for $7, then dig into some $7 crawfish *étoufée*. (☎383-1754. Open M-Sa 11am-2am, Su 11am-midnight.) Close to downtown, **Greyhound**, 1253 Florida Blvd. (☎383-3811 or 800-231-2222; open 24hr.), at 13th St., sends buses to New Orleans (2hr., 8 per day, $10) and Lafayette (4hr., 12 per day, $10). *The area is unsafe at night.* **Visitor info: State Capitol Visitors Center,** on the 1st fl. of the State Capitol. (☎342-7317. Open daily 8am-4:30pm.) **Baton Rouge Convention and Visitors Bureau,** 730 North Blvd. (☎383-1825 or 800-527-6843; open M-F 8am-5pm). **Post Office:** 750 Florida Blvd., off River Rd. (☎800-275-8777; open M-F 7:30am-5pm, Sa 8am-12:30pm). **ZIP code:** 70821. **Area code:** 225.

NATCHITOCHES   ☎318

The oldest city in Louisiana, Natchitcoches (pronounced *NAK-ah-tish*), was founded in 1714 by the French to facilitate trade with the Spanish in Mexico. The town was named after the original Native American inhabitants of the region. Its strategic location along the banks of the Red River meant Natchitoches should have become a major port city, much like New Orleans. However, fate (or, in reality, a big logjam) changed the course of Natchitoches's history, redirecting the Red River and leaving the town high and dry. Now called the Cane River National Heritage Area, only a 35-mile stretch of what used to be the Red River remains.

🛂 **PRACTICAL INFORMATION.** Downtown Natchitoches is organized in a grid-like fashion, with **Front St.** following the **Cane River** and numbered streets running parallel behind it. Most of the historic homes and plantations lie about 18 mi. south of town, off **Rte. 1 S.** The **Greyhound** bus station at 331 Cane River Shop Center (☎352-8341; open M-F 8am-11am and noon-4pm), sends buses to New Orleans (6½hr., 11 per day, $48-51) and Houston (8-10hr., 3 per day, $57-60). **Visitor info: Natchitoches Convention and Visitors Bureau,** 781 Front St. (☎352-8072 or 800-259-1714; open M-F 8am-6pm, Sa 9am-5pm, Su 10am-4pm). **Post Office:** 240 Saint Denis St. (☎352-2161; open M-F 8am-4:30pm, Sa 9am-11pm). **ZIP code:** 71457. **Area code:** 318.

🛏 **ACCOMMODATIONS.** Don't say we didn't tell you: Natchitoches isn't a cheap town. As the "B&B Capital" of Louisiana, Natchitoches abounds with cozy rooms in historic homes. Unfortunately, most are far from budget-friendly. If the wallet's not a primary concern, ask at the **Natchitoches Convention and Visitors Bureau** for a listing of the area's top-notch B&Bs. During the Christmas Festival, room rates (even for motels!) can be as much as triple, and reservations are booked months in advance.

A good bet for a cheaper motel is west of town, where I-49 meets **Rte. 6.** One of the best deals is the **Microtel Inn**, 5335 Rte. 6 W. Brand new rooms come well-furnished with A/C, cable, and free local calls. Access to pool and continental breakfast included. (☎214-0700 or 888-771-7171. Singles $46; doubles $55. 10% off for AAA.) Campers have the advantage here. The 600,000-acre **Kisatchie National Forest** offers plenty of rustic, outdoor living in one of nature's untouched gems, but be forewarned—most of the roads are gravel and poorly marked, campsites are difficult to find, and all sites are primitive ($2-3 per night). You must check-in first with the **Kisatchie Ranger District,** Rte. 6 W, ¼ mi. past the Microtel Inn, for maps, camping information, and park conditions. (☎352-2568. Open M-F 8am-4:30pm.)

🍴 **FOOD AND NIGHTLIFE.** **Lasyone's,** 622 2nd St., is the place to go for down-home cooking. Their specialty is the meat pie—have it by itself ($2.50) or get the full meal that comes with salad bar and two veggies ($7). Lunch specials are $5.25. (☎352-3353. Open M-Sa 7am-7pm.) **Almost Home,** 5820 Rte. 1 N Bypass, lets you take what (and how much) you want from their buffet-line of traditional Southern fare. The price is set at one meat and three veggies for $6, except on Friday night when they have an all-you-can-eat seafood dinner for $10. (☎352-2431. Open M-Sa 6am-2:30pm, F night seafood dinner 5-9pm.) Drink with a friendly, local crowd at **Pioneer Pub,** 812 Washington St., opposite the Visitors Center. (☎352-4884. Live music Th-Sa at 9pm. Open daily 11:30am-2am.) Being home to **Northwestern State University,** located along Rte. 6 on the western side of town, Natchitoches has its share of rowdy college bars.

◘ ♫ SIGHTS AND ENTERTAINMENT. Much of Natchitoches's charm can be found near the Cane River, along **Front St.,** where coffeeshops and antique parlors are the primary residents of historic buildings dating back to the mid-19th century. To see everything of significance that lies within city limits from the comfort of a large, green trolley, take a ride with the **Natchitoches Transit Company,** 100 Rue Beau Port. (☎356-8687. Call for departure times. 1hr. tour $8, seniors $7, ages 3-12 $5.)

Many of the popular tourist destinations are outside the city limits. For the next generation of handbags and belts, drive out to **▨Bayou Pierre Gator Park & Show,** 8 mi. north of Natchitoches off Rte. 1 N. (look for the big school bus in the shape of a gator off Rte. 1). Originally a conservation project for the scaly beasts, the park now entertains visitors with regular feeding shows and swamp-suspended walkways. According to the owner, the alligators respond well to the Country and Cajun tunes blaring from the speakers. Check out the "world's largest folding pocketknife" in the gift shop. (☎354-0001 or 877-354-7001. Open mid-Apr. through Oct. daily 10am-6pm; call for hrs. during the winter months when the alligators are hibernating. $6, ages 3-12 $4.50.) A string of plantation homes follow the Cane River, south of downtown along Rte. 1. The **Melrose** plantation, 14 mi. south on Rte. 1 then left on Rte. 493, is unique in origin; its female founder was an ex-slave herself. Writers William Faulkner, John Steinbeck, and Sherwood Anderson all stayed on the plantation, and it was the home of the painter Clementine Hunter, Louisiana's most celebrated primitive artist. (☎379-0055. Open daily noon-4pm. $6, ages 13-17 $4, ages 6-12 $3.) The **Kate Chopin House,** 20 mi. south off Rte. 1, houses the Bayou Folk Museum and is especially interesting for those curious about the roots of the feminist movement. Author of the controversial novel *The Awakening,* Kate Chopin broke with convention by doing such things as cigar-smoking and beer-drinking in a quiet Southern town. (☎379-2233. Open M-Sa 10am-5pm, Su 1-5pm. $5, under 18 $3.)

While Natchitoches may not see a *white* Christmas, she'll most definitely see a *light* Christmas. The town's residents spend months putting up some 300,000 Christmas bulbs, only to be greeted in-turn by 150,000 camera-toting tourists flocking like moths to the **City of Lights.** The peak of the month-long exhibition (Dec. 2, 2002 to Jan. 3, 2003) is the first weekend in December (Dec. 7-8, 2002), when a carnival-like atmosphere fills the air during the **Festival of Lights.**

ACADIANA

Throughout the early 18th century, the English government in Nova Scotia became increasingly jealous of the prosperity of French settlers *(Acadians)* and deeply offended by their refusal to kneel before the British Crown. During the war with France in 1755, the British rounded up the Acadians and deported them by the shipload in what came to be called *le grand dérangement,* "the Great Upheaval." Of the 7000 Acadians who went to sea, one-third died of smallpox and hunger. Those who survived sought refuge along the Atlantic Coast, but were met suspicion and forced into indentured servitude. The Acadians soon realized that freedom waited in French Louisiana. The "Cajuns" (as they are known today) of St. Martin, Lafayette, New Iberia, and St. Mary parishes are descendants of these settlers.

Several factors have threatened Acadian culture since the relocation. In the 1920s, Louisiana passed laws forcing Acadian schools to teach in English. Later, during the oil boom of the 70s and 80s, oil executives and developers envisioned the Acadian center of Lafayette (see below) as the Houston of Louisiana and threatened to flood the area with mass culture. The proud people of southern Louisiana have resisted homogenization—the state is officially bilingual.

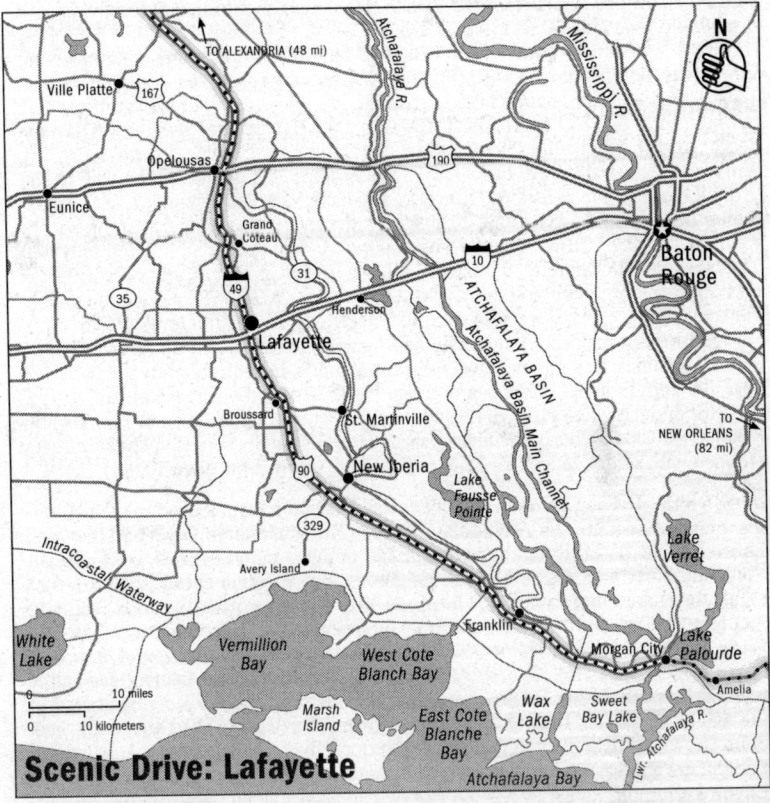

Scenic Drive: Lafayette

THE SOUTH

LAFAYETTE

☎337

The center of Acadiana, Lafayette is the perfect place to try boiled crawfish or dance the two-step to a fiddle and accordion. Though the city's French roots are often obscured by the chain motels that have accompanied its growth, there is no question that the Cajuns still own the surrounding countryside, where Cajun music and Creole zydeco heat up dance floors every night of the week, and locals continue to answer their phones with a proud *bonjour*.

■🛈 ORIENTATION AND PRACTICAL INFORMATION. Lafayette stands at a crossroads. **I-10** leads east to New Orleans and west to Lake Charles; **U.S. 90** heads south to New Iberia and the Atchafalaya Basin; **U.S. 167** runs north into central Louisiana. Most of the city is west of the **Evangeline Thwy. (U.S. 49)** which runs north-south. Establishments are concentrated along Johnson St. (U.S. 167) and Ambassador Caffery Pkwy. **Amtrak**, 133 E. Grant St., sends three trains per week to New Orleans (4hr., $21); Houston (5½hr., $35); and San Antonio (10hr., $55). **Greyhound**, 315 Lee Ave. (☎235-1541), buses to New Orleans (3½hr., 10 per day, $17.50); Baton Rouge (1hr., 12 per day, $11); and New Iberia (30min., 2 per day, $7.50). Station open 24hr. The **Lafayette Bus System**, 1515 E. University, is centered at Lee and Garfield St. (☎291-8570). Infrequent service M-Sa 6:30am-6:30pm. 75¢, ages 5-12 50¢, seniors and disabled 35¢.) **Taxi: Yellow/Checker Cab Inc.,** ☎237-6196. **Hospital: University Medical Center,** 2390 W. Congress (☎261-6000; 24hr.). **Visitor info: Lafayette Parish Convention and Visitors Commission,** 1400 N. Evangeline Thwy. (☎232-3808; open M-F 8:30am-5pm, Sa-Su 9am-5pm). **Post Office:** 1105 Moss St. (☎800-275-8777; open M-F 8am-5:30pm, Sa 8am-12:30pm). **ZIP code:** 70501. **Area code:** 337.

ⲅⲓ⍁ ACCOMMODATIONS AND FOOD. Hostelers should head straight for the downtown **Blue Moon Guest House,** 215 E. Convent St. Take Exit 103A from I-10, turn right on Johnston and left on Convent. The Blue Moon offers spacious common areas, deck, and backyard. Kitchen, Internet access, bikes available. (☎654-1444. Check-in 5pm-10pm; check-out 10am. Lockout 10am-5pm. Dormitory $15; private rooms $40-70.) Inexpensive hotels line the Evangeline Thwy. **Travel Host Inn South,** 1314 N. Evangeline Thwy., offers clean rooms with cable TV, outdoor pool, and breakfast. (☎233-2090 or 800-677-1466. Singles $35; doubles $41.) One campground close to the center of Lafayette, **Acadiana Park Campground,** 1201 E. Alexander, off Louisiana Ave., has 75 sites with access to tennis courts and a soccer field. (☎291-8388. Office open Sa-Th 8am-5pm, F 8am-8pm. Full hookup only $9.) The lakeside **KOA Lafayette,** 5 mi. west of town on I-10 at Exit 97, has over 200 sites and offers a store, mini-golf course, and two pools. (☎235-2739. Office open daily 7:30am-8:30pm. Sites $19; with water and electricity $24.50; full hookup $26.)

Cajun restaurants with live music and dancing have popped up all over Lafayette. Unfortunately, some demand substantial funds. In central Lafayette, **Chris' Po' boys,** 631 Jefferson St., offers seafood platters ($7-10) and—whadda ya know—po' boys for under $6. (☎234-1696. Live blues and Cajun F nights. Open M-Th 10:30am-8:30pm, F 10:30am-9pm.) The **Judice Inn,** 3134 Johnston St., serves up great burgers (topped with secret sauce) for $2-3. (☎984-5614. Open M-Sa 10am-10pm.)

◻ SIGHTS. Driving through south-central Louisiana means driving over America's largest swamp, the Atchafalaya Basin. The **Atchafalaya Fwy.** (I-10 between Lafayette and Baton Rouge) crosses 32 mi. of swamp and cypress trees. To get down and dirty and possibly see some gators, exit at Henderson (Exit 115), turn right, then immediately left for 5 mi. on Rte. 352. From there, follow signs to **McGee's Landing,** 1337 Henderson Rd., which sends four 1½hr. **boat tours** into the Basin each day. (☎228-2384 or 800-445-6681. Tours daily 8, 10am, 1, and 3pm. $12, seniors and under 12 $10, under 2 free.) The **Acadian Cultural Center/Jean Lafitte National Park,** 501 Fisher Rd., has an overly melodramatic 40min. documentary, but the exhibits on Cajun history and culture are terrific. (☎232-0789. Open daily 8am-5pm. Shows every hr. 9am-4pm. Free.) Next door, the re-creation of an Acadian settlement at **Vermilionville,** 1600 Surrey St., has music, crafts, food, and dancing on the Bayou Vermilion banks. (☎233-4077 or 800-992-2968. Open daily 10am-4pm. Live bands Sa-Su 1-4pm. Cajun cooking lessons daily 10:30am, 12:30, and 1:30pm. $8, seniors $6.50, ages 6-18 $5.) **Acadian Village,** 200 Greenleaf Rd., features 19th-century Cajun homes with a fascinating array of artifacts and displays. Take Johnston (U.S. 167 S) to Ridge Rd., then left on Broussard, and follow the signs. While at the village, view Native American artifacts at the **Mississippi Valley Missionary Museum.** (☎981-2364 or 800-962-9133. Both open daily 10am-5pm. $7, seniors $6, children $4.) The 450-year-old **St. John's Cathedral Oak,** 914 St. John St., shades the entire lawn with spidery branches spreading 145 ft.; each branch weighs around 72 tons.

◪ ENTERTAINMENT. While in Lafayette, be sure to take advantage of the many local music performances. Lafayette kicks off spring and fall weekends with **Downtown Alive!,** a series of free concerts featuring everything from New Wave to Cajun and zydeco. (☎291-5566. Apr.-June and Sept.-Nov. F 5:30pm; music 6-8:30pm.) The **Festival International de Louisiane,** is a francophone tribute to southwestern Louisiana. (☎232-8086. Call for dates.) The **Breaux Bridge Crawfish Festival** in nearby Breaux Bridge (10 mi. east on I-10) features crawfish races, live music, and a crawfish-eating contest. (☎332-6655. May 3-5, 2002.) To find the best zydeco in town, pick up a copy of *The Times,* free at restaurants and gas stations. **Randol's,** 2320 Kaliste Saloom Rd., romps with live Cajun and zydeco music nightly and doubles as a restaurant. (☎981-7080. Open Su-Th 5-10pm, F-Sa 5-11pm.) **Grant St. Dance Hall,** 113 Grant St., features bands playing everything from zydeco to metal. (☎237-8513. 18+. Cover usually $5-10. Only open days of shows, which start at 10pm.) At **El Sid O's Blues and Zydeco,** 1523 Martin Luther King Dr., you might get a glimpse of the legendary Buckwheat Zydeco. (☎318-235-0647. Open F-Su 7pm-2am.)

NEW IBERIA AND ENVIRONS ☎337

While Lafayette was being invaded by oil magnates eager to build a Louisiana oil-business center, New Iberia continued to maintain links to its bayou past. Most plantations in southern Louisiana are still private property, but **Shadows on the Teche,** 317 E. Main St. at the Rte. 14/Rte. 182 junction, welcomes the public with over 17,000 family documents and a first-hand look at antebellum life in the South. (☎369-6446. Open daily 9am-4:30pm. $7, ages 6-11 $4; AAA discount.) **Avery Island,** 7 mi. away on Rte. 329 off Rte. 90 (50¢ toll to enter the island), sizzles with the world-famous **Tabasco Pepper Sauce Factory,** where the McIlhenny family has produced the famous condiment for nearly a century. Tours every 15min. include free recipes and samples. (Tours and gift shop open daily 9am-4pm. Free.) Bring sunglasses for the 1hr. **Airboat Tour** of the shallow swamps and bayous of Lake Fausse Pointe. At Marshfield Landing; take Hwy 86, turn right on Black Line Rd., then right on Marshfield Rd. (☎229-4457. Open Feb.-Oct. Tu-Su 8am-5pm. $15. Reservations required.)

Picturesque campsites on the banks of the Bayou Teche are available at **Belmont Campgrounds,** 1000 Belmont Rd., at the junction of Rte. 31 and 86. Within the well-kept grounds are nature trails and fishing areas in the stocked pond. (☎369-3252. Sites with showers and laundry $11; full hookup $17.)

New Iberia lies 21 mi. southeast of Lafayette on U.S. 90. **Amtrak** stops at an unstaffed station, 402 W. Washington St., at Railroad St. Three trains per week set out for Lafayette (30min., $4) and New Orleans (3hr., $20). **Greyhound,** 1103 E. Main St. (☎364-8571), buses to New Orleans (4hr., 4 per day, $28) and Lafayette (40min., 2 per day, $7). Station open M-F 8am-5pm, Sa 8am-noon. The **Iberia Parish Convention and Visitors Bureau,** 2704 Rte. 14 (☎888-942-3742; open daily 9am-5pm), and the **Greater Iberia Chamber of Commerce,** 111 W. Main St. (☎364-1836; open M-F 8:30am-5pm) have maps. **Area code:** 337.

ARKANSAS

"The Natural State" lives up to its nickname, encompassing the Ozark and Ouachita mountains, the clear waters of Hot Springs, and miles of lush pine forests. The state's subcultures are as varied as its geography. The bluesy Mississippi Delta region seeps into southeast Arkansas, while the northern mountains support a close-knit, no-pretenses community. All across Arkansas, however, one thing remains constant—travelers are easily accepted into the friendly family (which happens to include "friendly" former President Bill Clinton).

THE SOUTH

PRACTICAL INFORMATION

Capital: Little Rock.

Visitor info: Arkansas Dept. of Parks and Tourism, One Capitol Mall, Little Rock 72201 (☎501-682-1191 or 800-628-8725; www.arkansas.com). Open M-F 8am-5pm.

Postal Abbreviation: AR. **Sales Tax:** 6%.

LITTLE ROCK ☎501

Located squarely in the middle of the state along the Arkansas River, Little Rock became the ideal spot for a major trading city in the 19th century. A small rock just a few feet high served as an important landmark for boats pushing their way upstream, and, lo and behold, Little Rock was born. The capital was the focus of a nationwide civil rights controversy in 1957, when Governor Orval Faubus and local white segregationists violently resisted nine black students who entered Central High School under the shields of the National Guard. Fortunately, Little Rock has since become a more integrated community and cosmopolitan center for the state.

⚑ PRACTICAL INFORMATION. Little Rock is at the intersection of I-40 and I-30, 140 mi. west of Memphis. Downtown, numbered streets run east-west. Near the river, Markham St. is 1st St. and Capitol is 5th St. The east side of Markham St. is now President Clinton Avenue. **Greyhound,** 118 E. Washington St. (☎372-3007), is in North Little Rock; take bus #7 or 18. Runs to St. Louis (8½hr., 1 per day, $48); New Orleans (13½hr., 5 per day, $74); and Memphis (2½hr., 9 per day, $22). **Amtrak,** 1400 W. Markham St. (☎372-6841), runs from Union Station at Victory St.; take bus #1 or 8. Trains go every day to St. Louis (7hr., $62-72); Dallas (6½hr., $69-80); and Malvern ($9), near Hot Springs. (Station open Su and W-Th 6pm-1:30am, M 9:30am-7:30pm, Tu 3:30pm-1:30am, F-Sa 6am-4pm.) **Central Arkansas Transit (CAT)** operates an extensive bus system through downtown and surrounding towns. (☎375-1163. Runs M-F 6am-11pm, with reduced service on weekends. Fare $1, seniors 50¢, transfers 10¢.) CAT also runs trolleys from the business district to River Market (M-F 11am-2pm; 25¢). **Little Rock Convention and Visitors Bureau,** 400 W. Markham St. in the Robinson Center at Broadway. (☎376-4781. Open M-F 9am-5pm.) **Internet access: Main Library,** 100 Rock St., near River Market. (☎918-3000. Open M-Tu, and Th 9am-8pm, W and F-Sa 9am-6pm, Su 1-5pm.) **Post Office:** 600 E. Capitol (☎375-5155; open M-F 7am-5:30pm). **ZIP code:** 72701. **Area code:** 501.

⚑ ACCOMMODATIONS. Budget motels are particularly dense on I-30 southwest of town and at the intersection of I-30 and I-40 in North Little Rock. **Master's Inn Economy,** 707 I-30, at 7th St. (Exit 140), is one of the few acceptable downtown motels, with spacious rooms, a pool, and complimentary breakfast. (☎372-4392 or 800-633-3434. Singles $35-42; doubles $47; each additional adult $4. Under 18 free with parent.) The **Cimarron Motel,** 10200 I-30 (Exit 130), has 33 basic rooms and a pool. (☎565-1171. Key deposit $5. Singles $30; doubles $35.) If saving money is your only objective, **King's Motel,** 10420 I-30, has relatively comfortable cheap rooms, but no frills. (☎565-1501. Key deposit $5. Singles $25; doubles $30.) **Maumell Park,** 9009 Pinnacle Valley Rd., on the Arkansas River, has 129 sites and is situated near the beautiful Pinnacle Mountain State Park. From I-430, take Rte. 10 (Exit 9) west 3 mi., then turn right on the Pinnacle Valley Rd. for 3 mi. (☎868-9477. Sites with water and electricity $15. Boat launch $2; free for campers.)

◨◪ FOOD AND NIGHTLIFE. The downtown lunch crowd heads to the **River Market,** 400 E. Markham St., for a wide selection of food shops, coffee stands, and delis. (☎375-2552. Market open M-Sa 7am-6pm, but many shops are only open lunch hrs. Outdoor vegetable market Tu and Sa 7am-3pm.) **Vino's,** 923 W. 7th St. at Chester St., is Little Rock's original microbrewery with cheap Italian fare; slices are under $1, and calzones start at $5. (☎375-8466. Cover $3-15. Open M-W 11am-10pm, Th 11am-midnight, F 11am-1am, Sa 11:30am-midnight, Su 1-9pm. Live music Th-Sa.) **Juanita's,** 1300 S. Main St., is a local favorite, serving $6 Mexican lunches. Dinner runs $11-12. (☎372-1228. Cover up to $10. Open for lunch M-F 11am-2:30pm, Sa 11am-3pm; dinner M 5:30-9pm, Tu-Th 5:30-10pm, F 5:30-10:30pm, Sa 3-10:30pm. Bar open M-F 11am-close. Live music most nights.)

◫ SIGHTS. Tourists can visit the **"little rock"** at Riverfront Park, a pleasant place for a walk along the Arkansas River. From underneath the railroad bridge at the north end of Louisiana St., look straight down; the rock is part of the embankment. The **State Capitol,** at the west end of Capitol St., may look familiar—it's a small-scale replica of the US Capitol in Washington, D.C. When the Legislature is not in session, which is most of the year after springtime, visitors can freely explore the building and its chambers. (☎682-5080. Open M-F 8am-6pm, Sa-Su 10am-5pm.) In the middle of downtown, the **Arkansas Territorial Restoration,** 200 E. Third St., displays life in 19th-century Little Rock. Period actors show off old-time tricks of living in frontier Arkansas. (☎324-9351. Open M-Sa 9am-5pm, Su 1-5pm; tours every hr. until 4pm, except noon. $2, seniors $1, children 50¢.) Little Rock's most important attraction lies at the corner of 14th St. and Park. **Central High School** remains a fully functional (and fully integrated) school, so it's closed to visitors. But in a restored Mobil station across the street, a **Visitors Center,** 2125 W. 14th St., contains an exhibit on the "Little Rock Nine." (☎374-1957. Open M-Sa 10am-4pm, Su 1-4pm. Free.) Construction of the **Clinton Presidential Library** began last year and should be finished sometime in late 2003 or 2004. Right next to the River Market district, the Library will update the old Little Rock skyline. (☎370-8000 for information or to donate to the fund.)

HOT SPRINGS ☎501

Hot Springs has long had problems with tourism. In 1820, the citizens of the Arkansas Territory asked the government to protect the area in order to prevent it from becoming as overly commercial as other spa resorts. Despite all efforts of the National Park Service, Hot Springs is currently home to such varied tourist traps as alligator farms, wax museums, and horse tracks. Nevertheless, the town delivers the soothing relaxation it has advertised for nearly two centuries. Once you've bathed in these 143°F springs, you'll realize why everybody from Al Capone to the feds jumped into the bathhouse craze of the 20s.

⚄ PRACTICAL INFORMATION. Hot Springs is about 1½hr. from Little Rock via I-30. **Greyhound,** 229 W. Grand Ave. (☎623-5574), downtown, operates buses twice a day to Little Rock (1½hr., $13) and Dallas (6hr., $51). Station open M-F 8am-12:30pm and 3:30-7:30pm, Sa 8am-noon and 6-7:15pm. **Visitors Center,** 629 Central Ave., downtown off Spring St. (☎321-2277 or 800-543-2284; open daily 9am-5pm). **Post Office:** 100 Reserve St., at Central Ave. in the Federal Building (☎623-8217; open M-F 8am-4:30pm, Sa 9am-1pm). **ZIP code:** 71901. **Area code:** 501.

⌂⌂ ACCOMMODATIONS AND FOOD. In the days when the bathhouses were active, the local government gave a free bath to anyone who could prove financial need. You won't get quite the same treatment these days, but Hot Springs remains almost as budget-friendly in terms of lodging. Good deals can be found in the old-time motor inns north and south of town along **Rte. 7.** Check for cleanliness and safety before taking cheap rooms—many of the motels are pretty run down. The **Tower Motel,** 755 Park Ave., offers immaculately clean rooms with wonderfully soft bedding. Call ahead; if no one's staying, the motel shuts down. (☎624-9555. Rooms for 1-2 people $45-50. Cash only.) Walk from Bathhouse Row and the entertainment area to the **Margarete Motel,** 217 Fountain St., just a stone's throw away from the national park. It offers great deals on large rooms, many of which have kitchens. (☎623-1192. Singles $30; doubles $45; slightly higher late Jan. to mid-Apr.) The closest campgrounds are at **Gulpha Gorge,** part of **Hot Springs National Park.** Follow Rte. 70 (Grand Ave.) 1 mi. east to Exit 70B, turn left, and drive ½ mi. north; it's on the left. (☎624-3383, ext. 640 for info and emergencies. Primitive sites $8.) **Hot Springs KOA,** 838 McClendon Rd., Exit 4 off Rte. 70, offers free shuttles to town. (☎624-5912 or 800-562-5903. Water and electric sites $23.50, full hookup $25.50.)

A number of restaurants line the strip near the bathhouses. **Granny's Kitchen,** 362 Central Ave., cooks up hearty country food. Lunch can get crowded, so arrive early. (☎624-6183. Open daily 7am-7pm. Plate lunches $5, dinners $6-10.) Right across from Bathhouse Row, **Maggie's Pickle Cafe,** 414 Central Ave., serves a tasty lunch. Save room for their famous fried dill pickles (8 for $3). Cold sandwiches go for $4-5. (☎623-4091. Open W-Su 11am 'til "lunchtime is over.") The truly hungry can join the locals south of town at **King's,** 3310 Central Ave., which serves authentically Americanized (i.e. greasy) Chinese food at low, low prices: all-you-can-eat lunch buffet $5, dinner buffet $6. (☎318-1888. Buffet daily 11am-2:30pm and 5-9pm.)

◎ SIGHTS. Still percolating through the earth after 4000 years, water gushes to the planet's crust in Hot Springs at a rate of 850,000 gallons per day. Visitors can fill bottles in the parking lot of the Visitors Center or bathe in one of the many bathhouses; lots of people cart the stuff away by the carload. Hot Springs' heyday came when all the fancy bathhouses on "Bathhouse Row," operated at full capacity; today, only the **Buckstaff,** 509 Central Ave., retains masseuses and spas. (☎623-2308.

Open M-Sa 7-11:45am and 1:30-3pm; Nov.-Mar. Sa 7-11:45am. Bath $15, whirlpool $1.50 extra; massage $18.) Around the corner, the **Hot Springs Health Spa,** N. 500 Reserve, at Spring St., offers large co-ed hot tubs and whirlpools. Bathing suits are required. (☎321-9664. Open daily 9am-9pm. Bath $13; 30min. massage $17.50.) The price for a hands-on, full treatment bath is lowest in the hot springs at the **Downtowner,** 135 Central Ave., but the quality is still comparable to the more expensive options elsewhere. (☎624-5521 or 800-251-1962. Open M-Tu and Th-F 7-11am and 1:30-3:15pm, W 7-11am, Sa 7-11am and 2-4:15pm. Bath $12.50, whirlpool $1.50 extra; massage $16.)

Bathe yourself in information about the 20th-century leisure class at **Hot Springs National Park.** It's the only park which is essentially built in a city. Interestingly, the **Fordyce Bathhouse Visitors Center** used to be a well-respected establishment on Bathhouse Row, now it shows a 17min. film on the history of the area and of the park, set aside as a national reserve by Andrew Jackson in 1832, long before the park system existed. The partially-restored bathhouse (those pesky stains from the "mercury rub" treatment for syphilis just don't come off), complete with obscure medical equipment, is also open for 2hr. self-guided tours. Ask at the front desk about guided tours. A number of trails run behind the bathhouses through the park, including the paved **Grand Promenade,** a 15min. walk, where visitors in the 20s paraded their highfalutin St. Louis fashions. The **Visitors Center** is located at 369 Central Ave. (☎624-3383, ext. 640. Open daily 9am-6pm. The front desk has a helpful chart for disabled and hearing-impaired visitors.)

Hot Springs's natural beauty, like its schlocky tourist-oriented economy, is unmistakable. Folks can gaze at the green-peaked mountains while cruising Lake Hamilton on the **Belle of Hot Springs,** 5200 Central Ave., a 1½hr. narrated tour alongside Lake Ouachita and Lake Hamilton mansions. (☎525-4438. June-Aug. 3 trips per day, 5 on Sa; Sept.-May 2 per day; call for times. $10, seniors $8.50, ages 2-12 $5. Lunch and dinner cruises extra.) A free shuttle runs from the Visitors Center to **Hot Springs Mountain Tower,** in the National Park, with a beautiful view of the surrounding mountains and lakes. Turn off Central Ave. onto Fountain St. and follow the signs. (☎623-6035. Open daily mid-May to Aug. 9am-9pm; Sept.-Oct. and Mar. to mid-May 9am-6pm; Nov.-Feb. 9am-5pm. $5, seniors $4, ages 5-11 $3.)

SCENIC DRIVE: ARKANSAS ROUTE 7

Arkansas isn't known as the "Natural State" for nothing: most of the northern and eastern parts of the state are rural, marked by the Ouachita and Ozark National Forests. Arkansas Rte. 7, a scenic byway that travels through both ranges in its 160 mi. journey from Hot Springs north to Harrison, is perhaps the best way to see this part of the state, where the sky is deep blue and there's a whole lot of banjo music on the radio. Considered one of the prettiest drives in the country, it's especially beautiful during the multicolored fall season.

The road begins as Central Ave. in Hot Springs. Immediately after the small town of Jessieville, the road enters into the **Ouachita National Forest.** The helpful **ranger station** in Jessieville, on the west side of the road, can provide info; a short, wheelchair-accessible trail runs behind the station. (☎501-948-5313. Open Oct.-Apr. M-F 8am-4:30pm; May-Sept. daily.) The main trail of the park, the 192 mi. **Ouachita National Recreation Trail,** running from eastern Oklahoma to central Arkansas, intersects Rte. 7 just north of Jessieville. Fifteen miles of densely wooded forest follow, much of it developed in the 30s by the Civilian Conservation Corps. This part of the drive is particularly popular in fall, when viewing the diverse foliage here has become a bit of a local ritual. Numerous trailheads are well-marked, and Ouachita also boasts eleven practice shooting ranges. About 40 mi. north of Hot Springs, Rte. 7 crosses the Fourche LaFave River, dammed in 1942 to form **Nimrod Lake.** After passing through the town of Ola, Rte. 7 intersects with Rte. 154 in the tiny crossroads town of Centerville. A right turn on Rte. 154 will take you on a fantastic detour 16 mi. east to **Petit Jean State Park.** (☎501-727-5441. Open daily 8am-10pm.) Petit Jean offers a healthy portion of geological goodies—including the secluded Cedar Falls and a natural bridge—as well as pleasant facilities and an extensive trail network climbing all the way to the summit of Petit Jean Mountain.

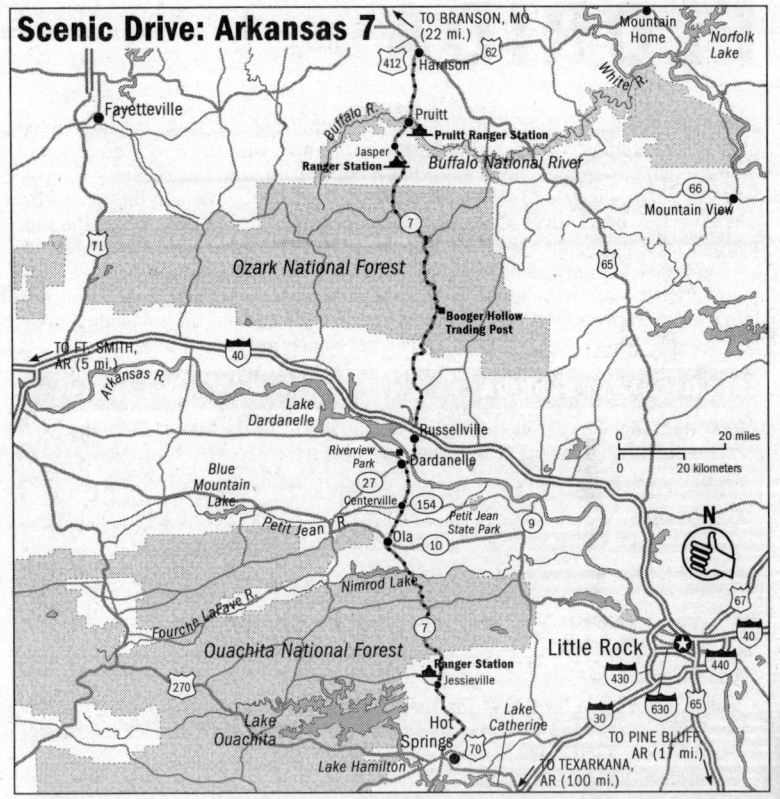

Scenic Drive: Arkansas 7

Back on Rte. 7, the road crosses the dammed Arkansas River, 8 mi. north of Centerville. For a view of the dam and accompanying Lake Dardanelle, take a left just before the river at the sign for **Riverview Park** and drive about 1½ mi. Continue north through Russelville, where the highway intersects I-40. Eighteen miles north of Russelville, enter the deep backwoods of America in the **Ozark National Forest,** a land of forested mountains and one-room country churches. The only ranger station on Rte. 7 is north of much of the forest just outside of Jasper. (☎501-968-2354. Open M-F 8am-4:30pm.) Further north, the road comes out of the forest and runs through what's known as Arkansas's **"Grand Canyon."** The road descends from here, running 6 mi. to the town of Jasper and then entering the **Buffalo National River,** a national park that follows the sandstone and limestone bluffs of the river for almost all of its 150 mi. length. The **Pruitt Ranger Station,** at the entrance to the park, can give info on the numerous boating options. (☎870-741-5443. Open generally Mar.-Sept. M-F 9am-5pm.) Twelve miles north, the road ends with a bit of a whimper at the town of Harrison; from here, head 35 mi. north to Branson, MO (p. 589).

THE SOUTH

FLORIDA

Ponce de León landed in St. Augustine on the Florida coast in 1513, in search of the elusive Fountain of Youth. Although the multitudes who flock to Florida today aren't seeking fountains, many find their youth restored in the Sunshine State— whether they're dazzled by Disney World or bronzed by the sun on the state's seductive beaches. Droves of senior citizens also migrate to Florida, where the sun-warmed air is just as therapeutic as Ponce de León's fabled magical elixir.

Florida's recent population boom has strained the state's natural resources; commercial strips and tremendous development have turned many pristine beaches into tourist traps. Still, it is possible to find a deserted spot on the peninsula on which to plop down with a paperback and get some sand in your toes.

HIGHLIGHTS OF FLORIDA

BEACHES. White sand, lots of sun, clear blue water. Pensacola (p. 469) and St. Petersburg (p. 464) win our thumbs-up for the best of the best.

DISNEY WORLD. Orlando's cash cow...er, mouse (p. 441). What else is there to say?

EVERGLADES. The prime Florida haunt for fishermen, hikers, canoers, bikers, and wild-life watchers (p. 455). Check out the unique mangrove swamps.

KEY LIME PIE. This famous dessert hails from the Florida Keys (p. 458).

🛈 PRACTICAL INFORMATION

Capital: Tallahassee.

Visitor info: Florida Division of Tourism, 126 W. Van Buren St., Tallahassee 32399 (☎888-735-2872; www.flausa.com). **Division of Recreation and Parks,** 3900 Commonwealth Blvd., #506, Tallahassee 32399 (☎850-488-6131).

Postal Abbreviation: FL. **Sales Tax:** 6%.

ST. AUGUSTINE   ☎904

Spanish adventurer Pedro Menéndez de Aviles founded St. Augustine in 1565, making it the first European colony in North America and the oldest continuous settlement in the United States. Thanks to preservation efforts, much of St. Augustine's Spanish flavor remains intact. This city's pride lies in its provincial cobblestone streets and *coquina* rock walls rather than in its token beaches. A one-time robber baron's playground, St. Augustine now emphasizes beaches, golf, sun and historical fun. And forget L.A.'s high-priced plastic surgeons—eternal youth costs just $5.75 around here, in the form of admission to the famed Fountain of Youth.

▶🛈 ORIENTATION AND PRACTICAL INFORMATION

St. Augustine started minimal public transportation in 2001. For $1, **Public Street Corner** bus service will drop or pick up passengers at most street corners. (☎823-4816 for updated schedules and information.) Fortunately, most of the town lies within a 10-15min. walk from the hostel, motels, and bus station. Narrow streets, one-ways, and abundant parking meters can make driving unpleasant. The major east-west routes, **King St.** and **Cathedral Place,** run through the downtown and become the Bridge of Lions that leads to the beaches. **San Marco Ave.,** also known as **Avenida Menéndez,** runs north-south. **Castillo Dr.** grows out of San Marco Ave. near the center of town. **Saint George St.,** a north-south pedestrian route, contains most of the shops and many sights in St. Augustine. **Greyhound,** 100 Malaga St. (☎829-6401; station open daily 7:30am-8pm), has service to Jacksonville (1hr., 5 per day, $9.50) and Daytona Beach

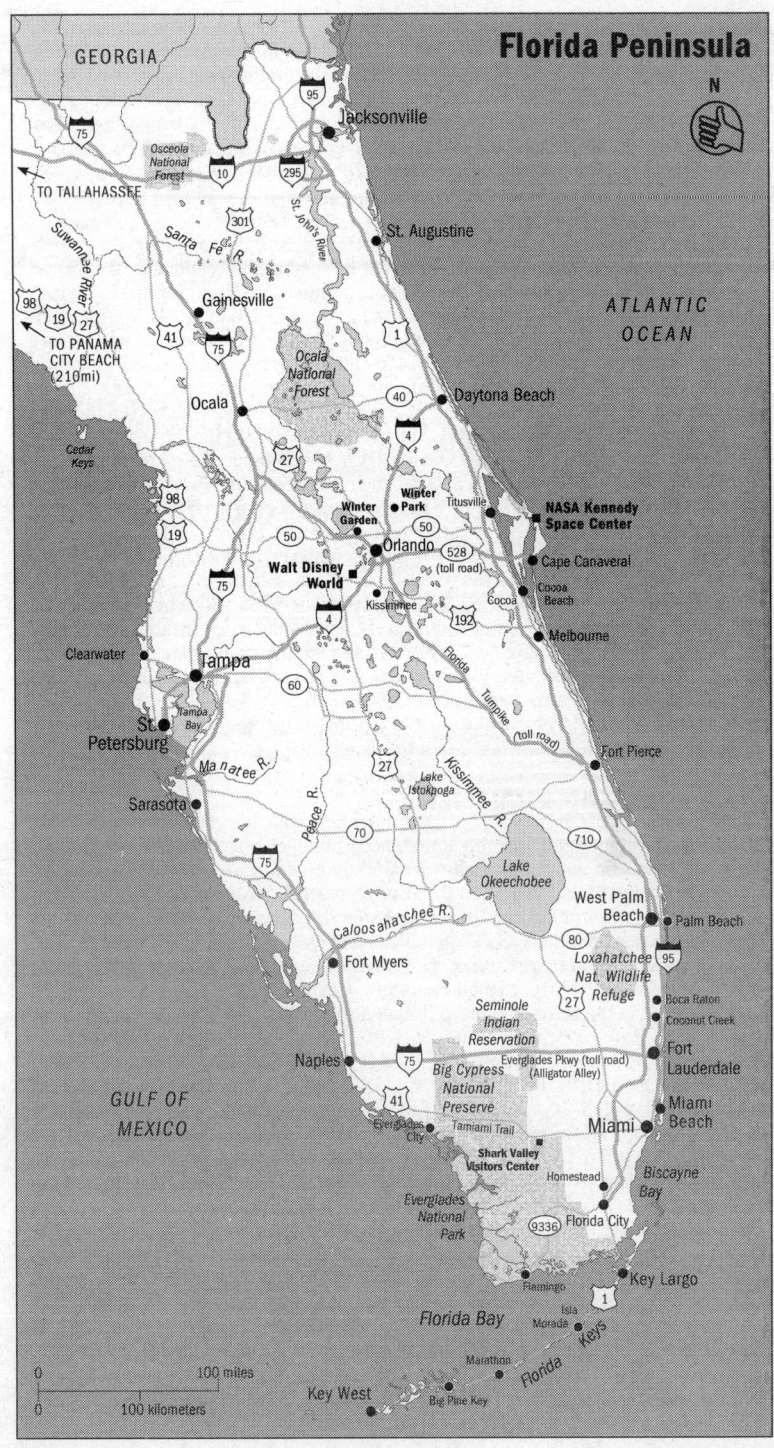

Florida Peninsula

N

GEORGIA

95 Jacksonville

75

Osceola
National
Forest

10

295

TO TALLAHASSEE

301

St. John's River

St. Augustine

Santa Fe R.

98

19

27

41

75

Gainesville

ATLANTIC
OCEAN

Suwannee River

TO PANAMA
CITY BEACH
(210mi)

Ocala
National
Forest

1

40 Daytona Beach

Ocala

4

Cedar
Keys

27

98

19

50

Winter
Garden

Winter
Park

Titusville

NASA Kennedy
Space Center

50

Orlando

528
(toll road)

Cape Canaveral

75

Walt Disney
World

4

Kissimmee

Cocoa

Cocoa
Beach

192

Melbourne

Clearwater

60

Tampa

Florida Turnpike (toll road)

St.
Petersburg

Tampa
Bay

Manatee R.

Fort Pierce

Peace R.

Sarasota

27

Lake
Istokpoga

Kissimmee R.

70

710

75

Lake
Okeechobee

Caloosahatchee R.

West Palm
Beach

Palm Beach

80

95

Fort Myers

Loxahatchee
Nat. Wildlife
Refuge

Boca Raton

27

Coconut Creek

Seminole
Indian
Reservation

Fort
Lauderdale

Naples

75

Big Cypress
National
Preserve

Everglades Pkwy (toll road)
(Alligator Alley)

41

Miami
Beach

GULF OF
MEXICO

Everglades
City

Tamiami Trail

Miami

Shark Valley
Visitors Center

Homestead

Biscayne
Bay

Everglades
National
Park

9336

Florida City

Flamingo

Key Largo

Florida Bay

Isla
Morada

1

Florida Keys

Marathon

0   100 miles

0   100 kilometers

Key West

Big Pine Key

FLORIDA

(1¼hr., 5 per day, $12.50); if the station is closed, the driver accepts cash. **Ancient City Taxi:** ☎824-8161. **Visitors Center:** 10 Castillo Dr., at San Marco Ave. From the Greyhound station, walk 3 blocks north on Riberia St., then right and 4 blocks on Orange St. Center provides walking tour maps and sightseeing package discounts. (☎825-1000. Open daily late May to early Sept. 8am-7:30pm; Oct.-Apr. 8:30am-5:30pm.) **Post Office:** 99 King St., at Martin Luther King, Jr. Ave. (☎829-8716; open M-Tu and Th-F 8:30am-5pm, W 8:30am-5:30pm, Sa 9am-1pm). **ZIP code:** 32084. **Area code:** 904.

⛢ ACCOMMODATIONS

Spacious dorms, beautiful private rooms, helpful management and a great location make the ⛢**Pirate Haus** hostel, 32 Treasury St., a must-visit. From Rte. 16 E, make a left on King St. and then left on Charlotte St.; parking is available. Weary travelers are pampered by a lively common room, big lockers, Internet access, and a tasty pancake breakfast. (☎808-1999 or 877-466-3864. A/C, free lockers, $5 key/linen deposit. Office hours 8-10am and 5-10pm, no lockout for registered guests. Dorms $12-15 for HI members; nonmembers $2 extra. Private rooms $34; under 14 free.) The **Sunrise Inn,** 512 Anastasia Blvd., is the best option among the motels along A1A. (☎829-3888. A/C, cable TV, phones and pool. Check-in/check-out 10am. Singles Su-Th $26, F-Sa $32; 2-4 people $32.) Right down the road, the **Seabreeze Motel,** 208 Anastasia Blvd., has clean rooms with refrigerators and pool access. (☎829-8122. A/C, cable TV, and free local calls. Kitchenette available. Singles M-F $35-40, Sa-Su $42; doubles $40/$45.) The **American Inn,** 42 San Marco Ave., near the Visitors Center, rents small rooms close to the restaurants and historic sights. (☎829-2292. TV, A/C, and pool. Singles M-F $45, Sa-Su $55; doubles $55/$65.) Nearby Salt Run and the Atlantic Ocean provide opportunities for great windsurfing, fishing, swimming, and hiking near the 139 campsites of the **Anastasia State Recreation Area,** on Rte. A1A, 4 mi. south of the historic district. From town, cross the Bridge of Lions and turn left past the Alligator Farm. (☎461-2033. Office open daily 8am-sunset. Sites $17.50; with electricity $19.60. Vehicle entrance fee $3.75, pedestrians $1. Reservations recommended for weekends at least 2 months in advance.)

⛢⛢ FOOD AND NIGHTLIFE

The bustle of daytime tourists and abundance of budget eateries make lunch in St. Augustine's historic district a delight. With a mix of sidewalk cafes and restaurant bars, **Saint George St.** is where you find the good stuff. Stroll down the pedestrian mall and the let the whiff of a cruller or croissant drag you inside for a quick bite. At the **Bunnery Bakery and Cafe,** 35 Hypolita St., delectable sandwiches, *panini*, and salads draw locals and tourists alike. The inventive and filling chicken walnut sandwich is just $5. (☎829-6166. Open 8am-4pm. Cash or check only.) An excellent healthy option is the **Manatee Cafe,** 179 San Marco Ave., just past the Fountain of Youth. They prepare cuisine with pure filtered water and certified organically grown produce. Tasty grilled hummus pita reuben ($5.25) gets originality points. (☎826-0210. Open Th-Tu 8am-4pm.) If, my dear, you do give a damn, go to **Scarlett O'Hara's,** 70 Hypolita St., at Cordova St., where monster burgers run $6 and live music entertains nightly. (☎824-6535. Happy hour M-F 4-7pm. Occasional $2 cover. Open daily 11:30am-12:30am.) **Peterson Bakery,** 113½ King St., has a carefully arranged and tasty array of fresh donuts, pastries, and other delights in the morning. (☎829-2964. Open M-F 6:30am-4:30pm, Sa 7am-4:30pm.)

St. Augustine supports a variety of bars, many on A1A, the historic district or on Anastasia Blvd. *Folio Weekly,* available at most grocery and convenience stores, contains event listings. Saint George St. provides tourists with free music and relatively cheap drinks. Local string musicians play on the two stages in the **Milltop,** 19½ Saint George St., a tiny bar situated above an old mill in the restored district. (☎829-2329. Music daily from 1pm until closing. Cover varies. Open M-Sa 11am-1am, Su 11am-10pm.) Throw back a Dolphin's Breath Lager at the **Oasis Deck and Restaurant,** 4000 Rte. A1A S./Beach Blvd., featuring nightly musical entertainment. (☎471-3424 or 471-2451. Happy hour 4-7pm. Open daily 6:30am-1am.) Cheap flicks and bargain eats await the weary traveler at **Pot Belly's,** 36 Granada St., across from the Lightner Museum (see **Sights,** below). This combination pub, deli, and cinema serves a range of junk food to tables in the theater. Remarkably cheap movie tickets run $3.75, and the ice cream drinks are divine. (☎829-3101. Shows start around 6:30 and 8:45pm.)

⊙ SIGHTS

GATORS. Across the Bridge of Lions, the ▨St. Augustine Alligator Farm allows visitors to get up close and personal with some of nature's finest reptilians. This century-old park is the only place in the world where all 23 known crocodilian species live. Stay for the hourly presentations or the daily 1:30pm feedings—for the gators, that is. *(On Rte. A1A S. ☎824-3337. Open daily 9am-6pm; in winter 9am-5pm. $14.25, ages 5-11 $8.50. Discounts for AAA/CAA, military and seniors available.)*

FOUNTAIN OF YOUTH. No trip to St. Augustine would be complete without a trek down beautiful Magnolia Drive to the **Fountain of Youth,** the infamous legend that sparked Ponce de Leon's voyage to the New World. A guided tour will take you through hundreds of years of Spanish conquistador history in minutes. To fully capture the historical significance of the place, take a swig of the sulfury libation and try to ignore the fact that the water now runs through a pipe. *(11 Magnolia Ave. ☎829-3168 or 800-356-8222. Go right on Williams St. from San Marco Ave. and continue until it dead ends into Magnolia Ave. Open daily 9am-5pm. $5.75, seniors $4.75, ages 6-12 $2.75.)*

SPANISH HERITAGE. Actors in period costumes describe the customs and crafts of the Spanish New World at the **Spanish Quarter,** a living museum that walks you through the daily activities of a military garrison community. *(29 Saint George St. ☎825-6830. Open Su-Th 9am-6pm, F-Sa 9am-7pm. $6.50; students and ages 6-18 $4; seniors, military, and AAA members 10% discount.)* Other 18th-century homes and shops fill the Restored Area. The oldest masonry fortress in the continental US, **Castillo de San Marcos National Monument** has 14 ft. thick walls built of *coquina*, the local shell-rock. The fort (a four-pointed star complete with drawbridge and moat) contains a museum, a large courtyard surrounded by livery quarters for the garrison, a jail, a chapel, and the original cannon brought overseas by the Spanish. *(1 Castillo Dr., off San Marco Ave. ☎829-6506. Open daily 8:45am-4:45pm. $4, under 16 and seniors with Golden Age Passport free. Occasional tours; call ahead.)* Tucked away from the hustle and bustle of the historic district off San Marco Ave., **La Leche Shrine and Mission of Nombre de Dios** is the birthplace of American Catholicism. The first Mass in the US was held here over 400 years ago. A 208 ft. cross commemorates the city's founding by Pedro Menéndez de Aviles. *(27 Ocean St., off San Marco Ave. ☎824-2809. Open M-F 8am-5:30pm, Sa-Su 9am-5pm. Mass M-F 8:30am, Sa 6pm, Su 8am. Free, donation suggested.)*

HISTORICAL SIGHTS. The historic district centers on Saint George St., beginning at the Gates of the City near the Visitors Center and running south past Cadiz St. and the Oldest Store. **Sightseeing Trains** help the tired traveler off his feet and onto a red trolley that hits all the major attractions. Board and exit at your convenience; expect a train every 15-20 minutes. *(170 San Marco Ave. ☎829-6545 or 800-226-6545. Operates 8:30am-5pm. 20 stops. $12, ages 6-12 $5.)* The original **Ghostly Experience** walking tour will send chills up your spine as you saunter through the historical regions of St. Augustine and learn about the city's most celebrated spirits. *(☎461-1009 or 888-461-1009. Meets at Milltop water wheel nightly at 7:45pm. $6, under 6 free. $1 discount at Visitors Center.)* Not surprisingly, the oldest continuous settlement in the US holds some of the nation's oldest stuff. The **Gonzalez-Alvarez House** on 14 St. Francis is the oldest house on the National Registry of Historic Places. Many passed through its doors from its construction in the 1600s until 1918, when it became a museum. *(14 Saint Francis St. ☎824-2872. Open daily 9am-5pm. Last admission 4:30pm. $5, students $3, seniors $4.50, families $12.)* The **Oldest Store Museum** holds over 100,000 items from the 18th- and 19th-centuries, some of the store's original inventory. *(4 Artillery Ln. ☎829-9729. Open daily 10am-4pm. $5, ages 6-12 $1.50.)*

FLORIDA

RESTORED HOTELS. A student-guided tour through **Flagler College** shows what college living ought to be like. Housed in the restored **Ponce de Leon Hotel,** the school was constructed by railroad and Standard Oil tycoon Henry Flagler. Edison himself outfitted the hotel with electricity. The stained glass windows in the large banquet room were designed by Tiffany before he became famous, and the room now serves as a dining hall for undergraduates. *(☎829-6481, ext. 383. Tours mid-May to mid-Aug. daily on the half-hour 11am-4pm. $4, under 12 free.)* In 1947, Chicago publisher and art lover Otto Lightner converted the Alcazar Hotel across the street into the **Lightner Museum** to hold an impressive collection of cut, blown, and burnished glass, as well as old clothing and oddities like nun and monk beer steins. 18th-century musical instruments play daily at 11am and 2pm. *(☎824-2874. Open daily 9am-5pm. Last admission 4:30pm. $6, students and ages 12-18 $2.)*

DAYTONA BEACH ☎386

When locals first started autoracing on the hard-packed sands along the ocean in Daytona Beach, they were combining the two aspects of life that would come to define the entire town mentality: speed and sand. Daytona played an essential role in the founding of the **National Association of Stock Car Auto Racing (NASCAR)** in 1947, and the mammoth Daytona International Speedway still hosts several big races each year. While the hard-packed sands no longer host races, 23 miles of Atlantic beaches pump the lifeblood of the community. Every spring break season brings flocks of college students to roost in the 500-foot-wide sands and ample nightlife.

⬛ ORIENTATION. Daytona Beach lies 53 mi. northeast of Orlando and 90 mi. south of Jacksonville. **I-95** parallels the coast and the barrier island. **Atlantic Ave. (Rte. A1A)** is the main drag along the shore, a scenic drive up A1A goes to St. Augustine and Jacksonville. **International Speedway Blvd. (U.S. 92)** runs east-west, from the ocean, through the downtown area and to the racetrack and airport. Daytona Beach is a collection of smaller towns that have expanded and converged but preserved their individual street-numbering systems. Many street numbers are not consecutive and navigation can be difficult. To avoid the gridlock on the beach, arrive early (8am) and leave early (around 3pm). You'll pay $5 to drive onto the beach (permitted 8am-7pm, $3 after 3pm), and police strictly enforce the 10 mph speed limit. Free parking is plentiful during most of the year but sparse during peak seasons, especially Speedweeks, Bike Week, Biketoberfest, and the Pepsi 400 (see **Start Your Engines,** below), not to mention spring break (usually mid-Feb. to Apr.).

🏮 PRACTICAL INFORMATION. Amtrak, 2491 Old New York Ave. in DeLand (☎734-2322; open daily 8:30am-7pm), 24 mi. west on Rte. 92, tracks to Miami (7hr., 2 per day, $84). **Greyhound,** 138 S. Ridgewood Ave. (☎255-7076; station open daily 7am-10:30pm), behind the antique mall, 4 mi. west of the beach, goes to Orlando (80min.; 7 per day; $9, F-Su $10) and Jacksonville (2hr.; 10 per day; $17, F-Su $18). **Votran County Transit Co.,** 950 Big Tree Rd., operates local buses as well as a trolley that covers Rte. A1A between Granada Blvd. and Dunlawton Ave. All buses have bike racks. On certain parts of the beach where driving is prohibited, free beach trams transport beachgoers. (☎761-7700. Service M-Sa 6am-7:30pm, Su 7am-6:30pm; trolley runs Sa until midnight. $1, seniors and 6-17 50¢, transfers free. Free maps available at hotels.) **Taxi: Yellow Cab,** ☎255-5555. **Daytona Beach Area Convention and Visitors Bureau:** 126 E. Orange Ave., on City Island inside the Chamber of Commerce. (☎255-0415 or 800-854-1234. Open M-F 9am-5pm.) **Rape Crisis and Sexual Abuse Line:** ☎254-4106. Operates 24hr. **Post Office:** 220 N. Beach St. (open M-F 8am-5pm, Sa 9am-noon). **ZIP code:** 32115. **Area code:** 386.

🬑 ACCOMMODATIONS. Almost all of Daytona's accommodations front **Atlantic Ave./Rte. A1A,** either on the beach or across the street; those off the beach offer the best deals. Daytona operates on seasonal/off-season rates. Spring break and race events drive prices to absurd levels. Off-season rates are more motel-like. Almost all the motels facing the beach cost $35 for an off-season single; on the other side of the street it's $25. The **Camellia Motel,** 1055 N. Atlantic Ave. (Rte. A1A), across the street from the beach, is an especially welcoming retreat, with cozy, bright rooms, free local calls, cable TV, and A/C. Most travelers should feel at home: the owner speaks English, French, German, Czech, Slovak, and Polish. (☎252-9963. Singles $35; doubles $42; each additional person $10. During spring break, singles $60; each additional person $10. Rooms with kitchens cost $10 more. Reserve early.) The **Streamline Hotel,** 140 S. Atlantic Ave. (A1A), one block north of E. International Speedway Blvd., stands out amid low level motels. Location is excellent—right near the boardwalk—but rooms are not luxurious. (☎258-6937. Key deposit $5. Singles $21, doubles $24; during special events $150-200. No reservations.) For a truly unique sleeping experience, try the **Travelers Inn,** 735 N. Atlantic Ave., "where the automobiles are king and guests are royalty." Each of 22 rooms has a different theme, from Jimi Hendrix to NASCAR. (☎253-3501 or 800-417-6466. Rooms for 1-2 people, some bigger units. All rooms $49; prices triple during events.)

Tomoka State Park, 2099 N. Beach St., 8 mi. north of Daytona and 70min. from Disney World, has 100 sites under a tropical canopy. Enjoy salt-water fishing, nature trails, and a sculpture museum. Take bus #3 to Domicilio and walk 2 mi. north. (☎676-4050. Open daily 8am-sunset. Sites $11, with electricity $13; Nov.-Apr. $17/ $19; seniors and disabled FL residents 50% discount. $3.25 entrance fee.) **Nova Family Campground,** 1190 Herbert St., in Port Orange, is south of Daytona Beach and 3 mi. from the shore. From I-95, take Exit 85 to Dunlawton Ave. E. Make a left onto Clyde Morris Blvd. and a right on Herbert St., or take bus #7 or 15 from downtown or the beach. (☎767-0095. Reception daily 8am-7pm. Pool and laundry facilities. Sites $16, with electricity and water $20, full hookup $22; higher during events.)

◖ **FOOD.** One of the most famous (and popular) seafood restaurants in the area is ▨**Aunt Catfish's,** 4009 Halifax Dr., on the corner of Dunlawton Ave. just next to the Port Orange Bridge on the mainland. Lunch and earlybird specials include a hot bar and salads all for under $8. Finish every meal at Catfish's with the Boatsinker Pie ($4.50), a chocolate-encrusted fudge dessert that has been lauded by *Bon Appetit.* (☎767-4768. Open M-Sa 11:30am-10pm, Su 9am-2pm.) "If it swims…we have it," boasts **B&B Fisheries,** 715 E. International Speedway Blvd. Take out your choice of fresh fish for lunch from $3.25. (☎252-6542. Open M-F 11am-8:30pm, Sa 4-8:30pm; takeout M-Sa 11:30am-8:30pm.)

▧ **START YOUR ENGINES.** The center of the racing world is the **Daytona International Speedway,** host of NASCAR's Super Bowl: the Daytona 500 (Feb. 17, 2002). **Daytona USA,** 1801 W. International Speedway Blvd., allows fans and non-fans alike the opportunity to experience the Great American Race. Exhibits include a new simulation ride, an IMAX film on the history of Daytona, and a fun teaching program on NASCAR commentating. The breathtaking **Speedway Tour** is a unique chance to see the garages, grandstands and famous 31° banked turns up close. For the true motorhead, the $99 **Richard Petty Driving Experience** puts a fan in a stock car for a ride-along at 145 mph. (☎947-6800; call 253-7223 for NASCAR tickets. Open daily 9am-7pm. $12, seniors $10, ages 6-12 $6. Tours daily 9am-5pm on the hour and half-hour $6.) **Bike Week** draws biker mamas for various motorcycle duels, and **Biketoberfest** brings them back for more. (Bikeweek: Mar. 1-10, 2002. Biketoberfest: Oct. 17-20, 2002.) **Speedweek** (Feb. 2-17, 2002) precedes the Daytona 500.

▨ **NIGHTLIFE.** When spring break hits, concerts, hotel-sponsored parties, and other events cater to students seeking fun. News about these travels fastest by word of mouth, but the *Calendar of Events* and *SEE Daytona Beach,* available at the Chamber of Commerce, make good starting points. Closing time in Dayton is around 2:30am and all clubs stick to it. On more mellow nights, head to the boardwalk to play volleyball or shake your groove thing at the **Oceanfront Bandshell,** an open-air amphitheater constructed entirely of *coquina* rock. Dance clubs thump along Seabreeze Blvd. near the corner of N. Atlantic Ave. Witness live jazz at the **St. Regis Bar and Restaurant,** 509 Seabreeze Blvd. (☎252-8743. Happy hour with 2-for-1 drinks F 5-7pm. Live music F-Sa 8-11pm. Open Tu-Sa 6-11pm.) **Ocean Deck,** 127 S. Ocean Ave., where "every day is like a weekend," stands out among the clubs with its beachfront location and live music. A house band plays reggae, jazz, and calypso every night except Sunday, when a rock band takes over. (☎253-5224. Music nightly 9:30pm-2:30am. 21+ after 9pm. Open daily 11am-3am; full menu until 2am.)

ORLANDO ☎407

When Walt Disney was flying over the small towns of Central Florida in search of a place to put his Florida operation, he marveled at the endless number of lakes and streams that still dominate the Orlando area. But amidst this beautiful setting, he also foresaw a world full of thrill-packed amusement rides and life-sized, cartoonish figures. While Orlando is older than Disney World, most of the city's resources are dedicated to servicing the tourism industry that is the life-blood of the economy. Theme parks, hotels, diners and other kitschy treats line every major street; even downtown Orlando, 20 miles from Disney, overflows with tourists. Plan your time wisely—there are many ways to spend your money in this land of illusions.

▐ TRANSPORTATION

Airport: Orlando International, 1 Airport Blvd. (☎825-2001); from the airport take Rte. 436 N, exit to Rte. 528 W. (the Bee Line Expwy.), then head east on I-4 to the exits for downtown. City bus #42 or 51 make the trip for $1. **Mears Motor Shuttle,** 324 W. Gore St. (☎423-5566), has a booth at the airport for transportation to most hotels. No shuttle reservations are necessary from the airport (for return, call 1 day in advance).

Trains: Amtrak, 1400 Sligh Blvd. (☎843-7611), 3 blocks east of I-4. Take S. Orange Ave., head west on Columbia, then take a right on Sligh. To Jacksonville (3-4hr., 2 per day, $20-39). Station open daily 7:15am-7:45pm.

Buses: Greyhound, 555 N. John Young Pkwy. (☎292-3424). To Kissimmee (40min., 7 per day, $7) and Jacksonville (2½-4hr., 10 per day, $25-27). Open 24hr.

Public Transit: LYNX, 78 W. Central Blvd. (☎841-8240; open M-F 6:30am-8pm, Sa 7:30am-6pm, Su 8am-6pm). Buses operate daily 6am-9pm (hrs. vary with route). Fare $1, transfers 10¢ and are good for the entire day. Downtown terminal between Central and Pine St., 1 block west of Orange Ave. and 1 block east of I-4. Schedules available at most shopping malls, banks, and at the downtown terminal. Look for signposts with a colored claw. Serves the airport, downtown, and all major parks.

Taxis: Yellow Cab, ☎422-4455.

✴▐ ORIENTATION AND PRACTICAL INFORMATION

Orlando lies at the center of hundreds of small lakes, toll highways, and amusement parks. Streets are divided north-south by **Rte. 17/92 (Orange Blossom Trail)** and east-west by **Colonial Dr.** The **Bee Line Expwy. (Rte. 528)** and the **East-West Expwy. (Rte. 408)** exact several tolls for their convenience. The major artery is **I-4,** which actually runs north-south through the center of town despite being labeled an east-west highway. The parks—**Disney World, Universal Studios** and **Sea World**—await 15-20 mi. southwest of downtown on I-4 W; Winter Park is 3-4 mi. northeast.

Visitor info: Orlando Official Visitor Center, 8723 International Dr., #101 (☎363-5872), several mi. southwest of downtown; take bus #8. Ask for the free "Magic Card" and get discounts at sites, restaurants, and hotels. Open daily 8am-7pm, tickets sold 8am-6pm.

Hotlines: Rape Hotline, ☎740-5408. **Crisis Hotline,** ☎843-4357. **Crisis Info,** ☎425-2624.

Post Office: 46 E. Robinson St. (☎425-6464). Open M-F 7am-5pm, Sa 9am-noon. **ZIP code:** 32801. **Area code:** 407.

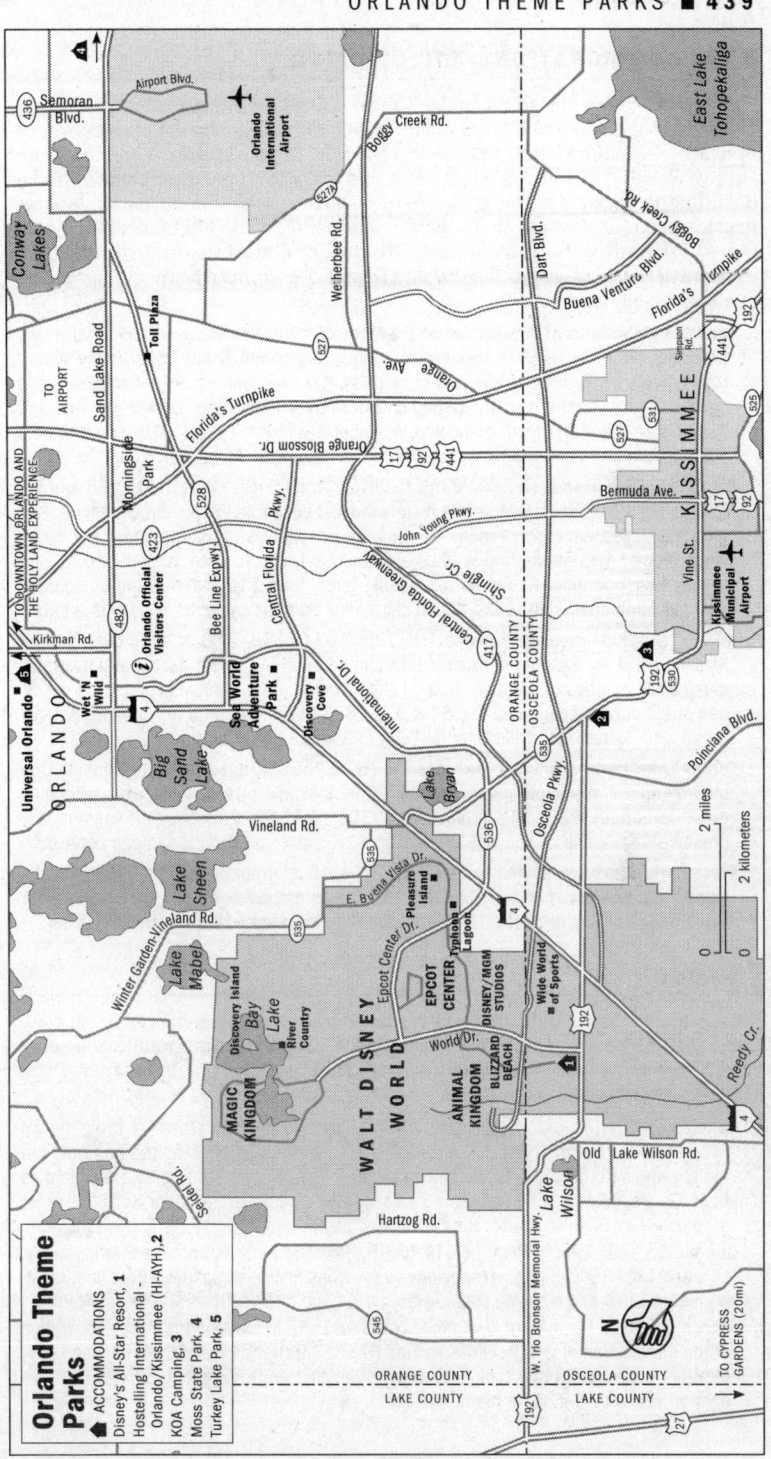

Orlando Theme Parks

🛏 ACCOMMODATIONS
Disney's All-Star Resort, **1**
Hostelling International -
Orlando/Kissimmee (HI-AYH), **2**
KOA Camping, **3**
Moss State Park, **4**
Turkey Lake Park, **5**

FLORIDA

⬛ ACCOMMODATIONS AND CAMPING

Orlando does not cater to the budget traveler. Prices for hotel rooms rise exponentially as you approach Disney World; plan to stay in a hostel, downtown, or in nearby Kissimmee. **U.S. 192,** or Irlo Bronson Memorial Highway, runs from Disney World to downtown Kissimmee, and is probably the best place to find a deal. Public transportation goes from Kissimmee to the major parks. **International Drive,** a north-south thoroughfare that parallels the interstate, is the center of Orlando's lodging world. Most accommodations provide free transportation to nearby Universal and Disney. Reservations are recommended at all accommodations.

Hostelling International-Orlando Resort (HI-AYH), 4840 W. Irlo Bronson Memorial Hwy./ Rte. 192 (☎396-8282), in Kissimmee. Lakeside location 5 mi. from Disney World. Super-clean, motel-style rooms with bunk beds, A/C, swimming pool, lake access, and shuttle transportation to theme parks, downtown and the airport. Lockers, linens, and towels free. Laundry facilities available. Reception 24hr. Dorms $16, nonmembers $19; private rooms from $35. Ages 6-17 half-price, under 6 free.

Disney's All-Star Resorts (☎934-7639), in Disney World. From I-4, take Exit 25B and follow the signs to Blizzard Beach—the resorts are just behind it. Pricey, but a great deal for groups. Large theme decorations from surfboards to cowboy boots adorn the courtyards. Pools, A/C, phone, fridge ($10 extra per day), and food court. Free parking and Disney transportation. All rooms two double beds, from $100, depending on season; $10 per additional adult (up to 4). No charge for children under 18 when with adults.

KOA, 4771 W. Irlo Bronson Memorial Hwy./Rte. 192 (☎396-2400 or 800-562-7791), in Kissimmee, 5 mi. east of I-4. Closest KOA campground to Disney, it's big and has facilities for all varieties of camper. Shaded sites available. Pool, tennis courts and volleyball on grounds. Reception 24hr. Sites $22-28. RV $38, $40 with full hookup. Kabins: 1-bed $40, 2-bed $50. Discounts for KOA, AAA and AARP available.

Turkey Lake Park, 3401 S. Hiawassee Rd. (☎299-5581), near Universal Studios. One of Orlando's 2 municipal campgrounds. Offers lakeside beach, trails, and swimming pool. Open daily 7:30am-7pm; in winter 7:30am-5:30pm. 200-400 tent sites, mostly primitive $7. RV sites $15, with full hookup $17. Cabins $28; $25 damage deposit.

Moss Park, 12901 Moss Park Rd. (☎273-2327), 10 mi. from the airport. 2nd municipal campgrounds. Garnished with Spanish moss, sites are lovely but off the beaten path. Open daily 8am-7pm. Sites $15, with water and electricity $18; park entrance $1.

⬛ FOOD

Most eating in the Orlando area is either fine dining or done on-the-run in between park rides. Prices are exorbitant inside theme parks; visitors should pack some food if they have space. Cheap buffets and ethnic eateries line International Dr., U.S. 192, and Orange Blossom Trail.

⬛ Bakely's, 345 W. Fairbanks Ave. (☎645-5767), in Winter Park. Take I-4 to Fairbanks Ave., Exit 45. The variety at this restaurant/bake shop is as large as the portions; the menu ranges from waffles to quesadillas (under $6). The $5.50 burgers are Orlando's best. On weekdays from 11am-3pm, "salary saver" meals go for under $6. Save room for the 6-layer Boston cream cake ($3). Open Su-Th 7am-11pm, F-Sa 7am-midnight.

Champ's, 132 E. Central Blvd. (☎649-1230), downtown across from the Public Library. Lilia and Chef George cook up specialty sandwiches and tasty pastries. Breakfast sandwiches ($1.50) and a hearty soup/salad lunch combo ($4). Open M-Sa 6am-6pm.

Azteca's, 809 N. Main St. in Kissimmee (☎933-8155). In historic downtown Kissimmee at the intersection of Orange Blossom Trail (U.S. 17-92) and U.S. 192. At this authentic Mexican restaurant, *pollo* (chicken) is the specialty, and the lunch specials ($4) are light on your wallet. Call for hours.

🎵🍺 ENTERTAINMENT AND NIGHTLIFE

Relatively inexpensive bars line **N. Orange Ave.**, the city's main drag. **Tabu**, 46 N. Orange Ave., provides a safe haven for twenty-somethings in search of the South Beach scene. (☎648-8363. Tu college night; Th women drink free until midnight. 21+. Open T-Su 9pm-3am.) Improv comedy shows will keep you in stitches at the ⬛SAK Comedy Lab, 380 W. Amelia St., at Hughey Ave. Audience participation and clean humor are the trademarks of this intimate club. SAK launched Wayne Brady of ABC-TV's "Whose Line is it Anyway?" (☎648-0001. Shows Tu 9pm; Th-F 8 and 10pm; Sa 8, 10pm, and midnight. $3-12.) **Church Street Station**, 129 W. Church St., on the corner of Church and Garland St., is a slick, block-long entertainment, shopping, and restaurant complex built inside an old train depot. The main attractions are **Rosie O'Grady's Good Time Emporium**, which features Dixieland jazz and **Cheyenne**, one of the few places in downtown to get your two-step on. (☎422-2434. $19, children $12. Open daily 11am-11pm; clubs and bars close later.)

DISNEY WORLD ☎407

Disney World is the Rome of central Florida: all roads lead to it. The name is more apt than one might imagine; Disney indeed creates a "world" of its own among the lakes, forests, hills, and streams. Within the Magic Kingdom, theme parks, resorts, golf courses, theater, restaurants, and nightclubs all work together to make fun the buzzword. The four major theme parks—Magic Kingdom, EPCOT, Disney/MGM Studios and Animal Kingdom—are the primary suppliers. Of course, the only setback is that magical amusement comes with a price—everything in Walt Disney's World costs almost thrice as much as in the real world. But in the end the corporate empire that is Disney leaves no one unhappy or bored, and despite the lighter load on the wallet, wins the prize of best park in the US.

🛈 PRACTICAL INFORMATION

Disney dominates **Lake Buena Vista**, 20 mi. west of Orlando via I-4. (☎824-4321. Call daily 8am-10pm.) The $48 one-day entrance fee (ages 3-9 $37) admits you to one of the four parks, allowing you to leave and return to the same park later in the day. A much better option is the **Park-Hopper Pass**, which buys admission to all four parks for several days (4-day $204, ages 3-9 $162; 5-day $230/$183). The **Park Hopper Plus**, includes a set number of days of admission plus free access to other Disney attractions (5-day, with 2 extras $262/$209; 6-day with 3 extras $294/$236; 7-day with four extras $326/$262). The Hopper passes allow for unlimited transportation between attractions on the Disney monorail, boats, buses, and trains. Multi-day passes need not be used on consecutive days and never expire. Attractions that charge separate admissions include **River Country** ($16/$12.50); **Typhoon Lagoon** ($30/$24); **Pleasure Island** ($20, 18+ unless with adult); **Blizzard Beach** ($30/$24), and **Disney's Wide World of Sports Complex** ($9/$7). For descriptions, see **Other Disney Attractions** (p. 443). *Never pay full gate fare for a Disney park.* Official Tourist Info Centers and the like all sell Park Hopper passes for an average $10-15 less.

Disney World opens its gates 365 days a year, but hours fluctuate with the season. Expect the parks to open at 9am and close between 7pm and 11pm, but call beforehand—the schedule is set a month in advance. The parks get busy during the summer when school is out, but the enormously crowded peak times are Christmas, Thanksgiving, and the month around Easter. More people visit between Christmas and New Year's than at any other time of year, but the parks are least crowded in January, when most kids are trapped in school. To experience the animated fun, arrive early. Disney has expanded the **FASTPASS** option from the Animal Kingdom into other parks and most of the major rides. Show up for your assigned time to ride and bypass the line. Otherwise, expect a 45min. to 2hr. wait.

FLORIDA

 THE PARKS

MAGIC KINGDOM

Seven lands comprise the Magic Kingdom: **Main St., USA; Tomorrowland; Fantasyland; Liberty Sq.; Frontierland; Adventureland;** and **Mickey's Toontown Fair.** More than any of the other Disney parks, this is geared toward children.

MAIN ST., USA AND TOMORROWLAND. As the entrance to the "Most Magical Place on Earth," Main St. captures the spirit and bustle of early 20th-century America. The architects employed "forced perspective" here, building the ground floor of the shops nine-tenths of the normal size and making the 2nd and 3rd floors progressively smaller. Every afternoon the "Magical Moments Parade" traverses this mystical street. Tomorrowland received a neon- and stainless-steel facelift that skyrocketed it out of the space-race days of the 60s and into a futuristic intergalactic nation. The indoor roller coaster **Space Mountain** rules this land, providing chills and thrills no child (or adult) can ever forget.

MICKEY'S TOONTOWN AND FANTASYLAND. Meet your favorite characters at the **Hall of Fame** and **Mickey's Country House.** Children can swarm Mickey who, during the day, walks about the grounds. **Fantasyland** brings some of Disney's all-time favorite animated films to life. **Peter Pan's Flight, Snow White's Scary Adventures** and the recently-added **Many Adventures of Winnie the Pooh** let riders experience live animation. For some saccharine but heartwarming enjoyment, meet the mechanical children of **"It's a Small World."** Their classic song inspires kids and adults alike.

LIBERTY SQUARE AND FRONTIERLAND. Welcome to Americana, Disney style. Liberty Sq. introduces visitors to the educational and political aspects of American history; Frontierland showcases America as penned by Mark Twain. **The Hall of Presidents** in Liberty Sq. is an exhibit on U.S. heads of state from the original George W. (Washington) to the current (Bush). In Frontierland, take a lazy raft ride over to **Tom Sawyer Island** and do some exploring like Tom himself, or stay in the main park and take on the two big rides, **Splash Mountain** and **Big Thunder Mountain Railroad.**

ADVENTURELAND. This is the least serious, and therefore most fun, land in the park. Sail on the classic **Pirates of the Caribbean** and uncover hidden treasures. As one of the original rides from the park's opening, **The Jungle Cruise** proves its popularity through its endurance. A tongue-in-cheek take on exploration, the boat ride down the world's most amazing rivers supplies good, wet fun.

EPCOT CENTER

In 1966, Walt dreamed up an "Experimental Prototype Community Of Tomorrow" (EPCOT), which would evolve constantly to incorporate new ideas from US technology—eventually becoming a self-sufficient, futuristic utopia. At present, Epcot splits into **Future World** and **World Showcase.**

The trademark 180 ft. high geosphere that forms the entrance to **Future World** houses the Spaceship Earth attraction, where visitors board a "time machine" for a tour through the evolution of communications and AT&T's latest ad campaign. At the Wonders of Life, **Body Wars** takes visitors on a tour of the human body (with the help of a simulator). The immensely popular Journey Into Imagination pavilion screens **Honey, I Shrunk the Audience,** which boasts stellar 3D effects.

At the **World Showcase,** an architectural style or monument, as well as typical food and crafts, represent 11 countries from around the world. People in indigenous costumes perform various forms of cultural entertainment. Every night at 9pm, Epcot presents a magnificent mega-show called IllumiNations, with music from the represented nations accompanied by dancing fountains, laser lights, and fireworks. The World Showcase Pavilions specialize in regional cuisine. The all-you-can-eat meat, seafood, and salad buffet ($19) at **Restaurant Akershus,** in the Norway Pavilion, is the closest one gets to a Disney dining bargain. It is wise to make reservations early in the morning at Guest Relations. The regional cafes (no reservations required) present cheaper options, but no real bargains.

DISNEY-MGM STUDIOS

Disney-MGM Studios (DMS) set out to create a "living movie set." Restaurants resemble their Hollywood counterparts and movie characters stroll the grounds signing autographs and posing for photo ops. DMS is built around several core shows; plan your day according to the ones you want to see. Stunt shows and mini-theatricals take place continually, although DMS also features some of the best thrill rides of all of the parks. The newest addition to DMS is **Who Wants to Be a Millionaire? Play It!**, based on the hit TV game show. The set, sounds, and performance replicate the real show, save affable host Regis Philbin. The **Indiana Jones Epic Stunt Spectacular** shows off some of the greatest scenes from the trilogy in live action, and the popular **Star Tours** takes your virtual ship into enemy fire Star Wars style. The real reason to cough up the money for this particular park, however, is the **Magic of Disney Animation,** a tour that introduces you to actual Disney animators, teaches you how they create Disney animated films, and offers a sneak peak at the sketches of upcoming Disney classics.

DISNEY'S ANIMAL KINGDOM

If fake plastic characters and make-believe are getting to be too much, Disney's newest theme park, the Animal Kingdom, is a heavy dose of reality. **Kilimanjaro Safaris** depart for the exotic Harambe preserve, where elephants, hippos, giraffes and other creatures of the African savannah roam. A **Maharajah Jungle Trek** drops riders among tigers, tapirs and bats. Animal Kingdom is not all about immersion in foreign lands—like any Disney park shows and rides make up a large part of the attraction. **DINOSAUR** puts the traveler in the middle of the early Cretaceous, but the lengthy wait and short ride make it uninviting. **It's Tough to be a Bug!**, another 3D Disney spectacular put on by the cast of the animated flick *A Bug's Life.*

OTHER DISNEY ATTRACTIONS

Besides the three main parks, Disney offers several other draws with different themes and separate admissions. **Blizzard Beach,** the most intense but least thematic of three water parks, was built on the harrowing premise of a melting mountain. Ride a ski lift to the peak of Mt. Gushmore and take the fastest water-slide in the world (Summit Plummet) down the 120 ft. descent. **Typhoon Lagoon,** a 50-acre water park, centers on one of the world's largest wave-making pools and the seven-foot waves it creates. Besides eight water slides, the lagoon has a creek for inner-tube rides and a saltwater coral reef stocked with tropical fish and harmless sharks. Built to resemble a swimming hole, **River Country** offers water slides, rope swings, and plenty of room to swim. Water parks fill up early on hot days, so you might get turned away. For $9.25 visit **Disney's Wide World of Sports Complex** (☎939-1500) and test your skills in the **NFL Experience.** The larger than life **Downtown Disney** is a neon conglomeration of theme restaurants, nightlife, and shopping. **Pleasure Island** is the hedonistic Disney with an attitude. Choose among the nightclubs—country, R&B, jazz, 70s and techno. (18+ unless accompanied by parent; admission fee $20.)

LIFE BEYOND DISNEY   ☎407

The big non-Disney theme parks band together in competition with Mickey. "Flex Tickets," their version of a mouse trap, combine admission prices at a discount. A four-park ticket covers Sea World, both Universal Studios parks, and Wet 'n' Wild, and allows seven days of visiting with unlimited admissions and free transportation ($160, ages 3-9 $128). The five-park ticket (call Universal City Travel at ☎800-224-3838) adds Busch Gardens in Tampa (see p. 463) and lasts ten days ($197/$158).

FLORIDA

A HORSE OF A DIFFERENT COLOR Back in 1933, when Prohibition was repealed, the last thing August A. Busch, Sr. expected to receive in celebration of his resumed brewery business was a bunch of European war horses. His son, August Jr., introduced the first Budweiser Clydesdale hitch as a surprise gift to his father, and these magnificent steeds have now become a renowned symbol of Anheuser-Busch, the most popular beer company in America. As the most widely traveled horses in the world, the Bud Clydesdales must have white stockings on all four legs, a blaze of white on the face, and a black mane and tail to make the team. You can get a firsthand look at these brawny beasts at the stables in Orlando's Sea World (p. 444) or Tampa's Busch Gardens (p. 463).

👁 THE PARKS

SEA WORLD

One of the US's largest marine parks, **Sea World Adventure Park** makes a splash with marine-themed shows, rides and exhibits. In recent years, it has re-invented itself from simply a repository of cutting-edge marine technology to a full-fledged park emphasizing the mystery and dark side of sea creatures. Eels, barracudas, sharks, and other beasties lick their chops in **Terrors of the Deep,** the world's largest collection of dangerous sea creatures. In Shamu Stadium, the talented killer whale family remains Sea World's big draw. **The Shamu Adventure** thrills with plenty of amazing aquatic acrobatics executed smartly by a whole family of Orcas and their trainers. Whale belly flops send waves of 52°F salt water into the cheering "soak zone"; try to wear a swimsuit. **Journey to Atlantis** gets rave reviews as the park's first roller coaster, and spring 2000 brought the much anticipated **Kraken,** a floorless ride billed as the highest, fastest, and longest coaster in Orlando. *(12 mi. southwest of Orlando off I-4 at Rte. 528. ☎351-3600. Take bus #8. Open daily 9am-7pm; extended hours in summer. $48, ages 3-9 $39. Parking $6. Sky Tower ride $3 extra. Most hotel brochure displays and hostels have coupons for $2-3 off regular admission. Discovery Cove admission by reservation only.)*

CYPRESS GARDENS

Cypress Gardens lies southwest of Orlando in Winter Haven. The botanical gardens feature over 8000 varieties of plants and flowers with winding walkways and electric boat rides for touring. Hoop-skirted Southern Belles patrol the grounds. Despite all the pretty flowers, the **water-ski shows** attract the biggest crowds and the loudest applause. *(Take I-4 southwest to Rte. 27 S, then Rte. 540 W. ☎863-324-2111. Open daily 9:30am-5pm; call ahead for exact hrs. Water-ski shows daily 11am and 4:30pm; times and frequency vary with crowd size. Park admission $33, ages 6-12 $17.)*

UNIVERSAL STUDIOS ESCAPE

A less cartoonish alternative to Disney World is Universal: nothing magical, just movie rides that thrill, spin, and make you squeal. With its three parks, **Universal Studios Florida, Islands of Adventure,** and **CityWalk,** Universal is no longer an afterthought to the "other park" down I-4; its attractions are also must-sees in Orlando. *(I-4 Exit 29B or 30B. ☎363-8000. Open daily 9am, closing times vary. CityWalk open until 2am. Each park is $46, ages 3-9 $37; look for discount "upgrade" tickets to other park. CityWalk is ungated and free. Parking $7.)*

UNIVERSAL STUDIOS FLORIDA. The original park to "ride the movies" showcases a mix of rides and behind-the-scenes extravaganzas. Rid the world of invading aliens on **Men In Black: Alien Attack,** the park's newest attraction. **Back to the Future...The Ride,** one of the staples of any Universal visit, utilizes seven-story Omni-iMax surround screens and spectacular special effects. A studio tour of **Nickelodeon,** the children's network, offers an interactive look at the sets, stages and slime. Just don't say "I don't know!"

ISLANDS OF ADVENTURE. This park encompasses 110 acres of the most technologically sophisticated rides in the world. Five islands portray different themes, ranging from cartoons to Jurassic Park to Marvel Superheroes. **The Amazing Adventures of Spider Man** is the crown jewel of Orlando theme parks; new technology and several patents sprung from its conception. A fast-moving car whizzes around a 3D video system as you and Pete Parker find the stolen Statue of Liberty. The most entertaining island is the pastel-overload **Seuss Landing,** home of the **Green Eggs & Ham Cafe** (green eggs and ham-wich $5.60) and the **Moose Juice Goose Juice** stand. **The Cat in the Hat** turns the Theodore Geisel classic into a ride on a wild couch that loops its way through the story. If that's too tame, the **Dueling Dragons** is the world's first inverted, dueling, near-miss roller coaster.

CITYWALK. The free CityWalk greets the eager tourist upon entering Universal Studios. A mix of unique restaurants, a few clubs, and free evening parking make it an appealing alternative to Pleasure Island. **The NASCAR Cafe, NBA City,** and **Emeril's** are a few of the pricey theme restaurants that line the main street. Two 21+ clubs, **Bob Marley's** and **The Groove,** charge $4-5 cover.

COCOA BEACH AND CAPE CANAVERAL ☎ 321

Cape Canaveral and the surrounding "Space Coast" were ground zero during the Cold War. Once the great Space Race began heating up, the area took off—it became the base of operations for every major space exploration feat from the Apollo moon landings to the current International Space Station effort. Today, the enormous Kennedy Space Center occupies most of the coastal regions and surrounding wildlife refuge, but the towns of Cocoa Beach and nearby Melbourne provide the typical Atlantic beach atmosphere. Beware summer launch dates, when tourists pack the area and hotel prices follow NASA into the stratosphere.

◼◪ ORIENTATION AND PRACTICAL INFORMATION. The Cocoa Beach area, 50 mi. east of Orlando, consists of mainland towns Cocoa and Rockledge, ocean-front towns Cocoa Beach and Cape Canaveral, and Merritt Island in between. Both **I-95** and **U.S. 1** run north-south on the mainland, while **Rte. A1A** (North Atlantic Ave.) is the beach's main drag, running through Cocoa Beach and Cape Canaveral. **Greyhound,** 302 Main St. (☎636-6531; station open daily 7am-5:30pm), in Cocoa, 8 mi. inland, runs to Orlando (1hr., 2 per day, $8.50-9.50) and Daytona (1¾hr., 4 per day, $13.50-14.50). **Space Coast Area Transit** (☎633-1878) runs North Beach and South Beach routes and makes stops at every town in Brevard County from 8am to 5pm. (Fare $1; students, seniors, and disabled 50¢; transfers free.) **Taxi: Royal Cab** (☎267-7061), **Yellow Cab** (☎636-1234). **Blue Dolphin Shuttle** (☎433-0011) connects Cocoa Beach with Orlando International Airport ($25) and the Kennedy Space Center ($8 round-trip). Call in advance. **Visitor info: Cocoa Beach Chamber of Commerce,** 400 Fortenberry Rd. on Merritt Island (☎459-2200; open M-F 8:30am-5pm). **Space Coast Office of Tourism,** 8810 Astronaut Blvd. (A1A), #102 (☎800-936-2326; open M-F 8am-5pm). **Post Office:** 333 Crockett Blvd., Merritt Island (☎453-1366; open M-F 8:30am-5pm, Sa 9am-1pm). **ZIP code:** 32952. **Area code:** 321. 10-digit dialing required.

◪◲ ACCOMMODATIONS AND FOOD. Across from the beach, **Motel 6,** 3701 N. Atlantic Ave. (A1A) beats the rates of most accommodations in Cocoa Beach. (☎783-3103. A/C, TV, pool, laundry, shuffleboard. Singles Su-Th $42-47, F-Sa $46-50.) Behind the Greyhound station and the water tower is the **Dixie Motel,** 301 Forrest Ave., recently renovated with clean rooms, floor-to-ceiling windows, A/C, cable TV, and a swimming pool. (☎632-1600. Laundry available. Singles $40; doubles $50; off-season $45/$55.) Pitch your tent at scenic **Jetty Park Campgrounds,** 400 E. Jetty Rd., at the northern tip of Cape Canaveral. (☎455-1380. 6 people per site. Jan.-Apr. primitive sites $18, with water and electricity $22, full hookup $25; May-Dec. $16/$20/$23. Reserve 3 months in advance, especially before shuttle launches.)

Lines awaiting "famous" New York style pizza stream out the door of **Bizzarro,** #4 1st Ave. off AIA in Indialantic. Grab a round or Sicilian slice for $1.50. (☎724-4799. Open M-Th 11am-9pm, F-Sa 11am-11pm, Su noon-9pm.) There's nothing like soy milk, tofu, and spelt on the beach; buy it at **Sunseed Food Co-op,** 6615 N. Atlantic Ave. (A1A), an impressive depot of all things organic, natural, and healthy. (☎784-0930. Open M-W 10am-7pm, Th-F 10am-8pm, Sa 10am-7pm, Su 11am-6pm.) The **Tea Room,** 6211 N. Atlantic Ave. (A1A), combines home cookin' and a little TLC to rev up your engine. Daily breakfast specials run around $3; pastries range 50¢-$1.25. (☎783-5527. Open M-F 6:30am-2pm, Sa-Su 8am-2pm.)

◐ **THE FINAL FRONTIER.** All of **NASA's** shuttle flights take off from the **Kennedy Space Center,** 18 mi. north of Cocoa Beach on Rte 3. Accessible by car via Rte. 405E off I-95 or Rte. 528E from the Beeline Expwy.; from Cocoa Beach, take Rte. A1A until it turns west onto Rte. 528, then follow Rte. 3 N to the Spaceport. Public transport: Blue Dolphin Shuttle (see **Practical Information,** above). The recently renovated **Kennedy Space Center Visitors Complex** provides a huge welcoming center for visitors, complete with two 3-D IMAX theaters, a Rocket Garden, and continuously updated exhibits on the latest in space exploration. KSC offers three tours of their 220 sq. mi. grounds. The **Kennedy Space Center Tour** departs continuously from 9:30am to 5pm, hitting the three main attractions: the LC 39 Observation Gantry, Apollo/Saturn V Center, and the International Space Station Center. The **Then & Now Tour** highlights historic launch sites. See where the initial Apollo missions blasted off, and where the brave Mercury astronauts lived and trained. A new addition in 2001, the **NASA Up Close Tour** provides access to facilities that are restricted on the standard tour. Check out the shuttle launch pad, the humongous VAB building (where the shuttle is put together), and the Crawler Transporter. With NASA's ambitious launch schedule, you may have a chance to watch the space shuttles *Endeavor,* *Columbia, Atlantis,* or *Discovery* thunder off into the blue yonder above the Cape. For $15, KSC will transport you to a viewing area to watch the fiery ascension. (☎452-2121; 449-4444 for launch info and schedules. Open daily in summer 9am-8:30pm; in winter 9am-5:30pm. Standard Kennedy Space Center grounds tours $25, ages 3-11 $15; Up Close and Then & Now tours an additional $20 per person.)

Surrounding the NASA complex, the **Merritt Island National Wildlife Refuge** stirs with sea turtles, manatees, wild hogs, otters, and over 300 species of birds, including several endangered ones. Take Exit 80 off I-95, east on Garden St. to SR 402. (☎861-0667. Open daily sunrise-sunset. Visitors Center open M-F 8am-4:30pm, Sa-Su 9am-5pm.) Just north of Merritt Island, **Canaveral National Seashore,** the northeastern shore of the wildlife refuge, covers 67,000 acres of undeveloped beach and dunes. Take Rte. 406 E off US 1 in Titusville. (☎407-867-0677. Open daily 6am-8pm. $5 per car. Closed 3 days before and 1 day after NASA launches.)

FORT LAUDERDALE   ☎954

City streets and highways may be fine for most city's transportation needs, but Fort Lauderdale adds a third way: canals. Intricate waterways connect ritzy homes with the intercoastal river—owning a yacht (over 40,000 in town) is both practical and stylish. "The Venice of America" also boasts 23 miles of beach which makes Fort Lauderdale fun even for those who can't afford a yacht. And for the aquaphobic, trendy Las Olas Blvd. offers some of the best shopping in South Florida.

▐ **TRANSPORTATION**

Airport: Fort Lauderdale/Hollywood International, 1400 Lee Wagoner Blvd. (call 359-1200 for recorded ramblings; 359-6100 for a human), 3½ mi. south of downtown on U.S. 1, or take I-595 E from I-95 to Exit 12B. Take bus #1 from downtown.

Trains: Amtrak, 200 SW 21st Terr. (☎587-6692), just west of I-95, ¼ mi. south of Broward Blvd. Take bus #22 from downtown. To Orlando (4¾hr., 2 per day, $29-56). Open daily 7:15am-9:15pm.

Buses: Greyhound, 515 NE 3rd St. (☎764-6551), 3 blocks north of Broward Blvd. down-town. *Be careful in the surrounding area, especially at night.* To: Orlando (5hr., 7 per day, $36-38); Daytona Beach (6½-7hr., 6 per day, $30-32); and Miami (1hr., 17 per day, $5). Open 24hr.

Public Transit: Broward County Transit (BCT) (☎357-8400; M-F 7am-10pm, Sa 7am-8pm, Su 8am-7pm). Most routes go to the terminal at the corner of 1st St. NW and 1st Ave. NW, downtown. Routes 11 and 36 run north-south on A1A through the beaches. Get a system map at any terminal. Operates daily 6am-11pm, every 30min. on most routes. $1, transfer 15¢; seniors, under 18, and disabled 50¢ (with ID). 7-day passes ($9), all-day passes ($2.50), and 10-ride passes ($8) available at beachfront hotels, libraries, and the central terminal. **IMAX** (☎761-3543) runs loops through downtown and on the beach strip between Sunrise Blvd. and Las Olas Blvd. F-Sa every 30min. 6pm-1am. Free. **Tri-Rail** (☎728-8445 or 800-874-7245) connects West Palm Beach, Fort Lauderdale, and Miami. Trains run M-F 4am-10pm, Sa-Su 6:30am-10pm. Sched-ules available at airport, motels, or Tri-Rail stops. $2-5.50, 50% discount for children, disabled, students and seniors with Tri-Rail ID.

Taxis: Yellow Cab, ☎777-7777. **Public Service Taxi,** ☎587-9090.

Car Rental: Alamo, 2601 S. Federal Hwy. (☎525-4713). Open 24hr. $39 per day, $225 per week with unlimited mi. Must be 21+ with a major credit card. $20 per day sur-charge for those under 25.

Bike Rental: Mike's Cyclery, 5429 N. Federal Hwy. (☎493-5277). Open daily 10am-7pm. A variety of bicycles $20 per day, $50 per week. Some racing bikes cost slightly more. Credit card deposit required.

■✷ ORIENTATION AND PRACTICAL INFORMATION

North-south **I-95** connects West Palm Beach, Fort Lauderdale, and Miami. **Rte. 84/I-75 (Alligator Alley)** slithers 100 mi. west from Fort Lauderdale across the Everglades to Naples and other small cities on Florida's Gulf Coast. **Florida's Turnpike** originates in Orlando and runs parallel to I-95. Fort Lauderdale is bigger than it looks. The city extends westward from its 23 mi. of beach to encompass nearly 450 sq. mi. Streets and boulevards are east-west and avenues are north-south. All are labeled NW, NE, SW, or SE according to quadrant. **Broward Blvd.** divides the city north-south, while **Andrews Ave.** cuts east-west. The brick-and-mortar downtown centers around **Federal Hwy. (U.S. 1)** and **Las Olas Blvd.**, about 2 mi. west of the oceanfront. Between downtown and the waterfront, yachts fill the ritzy inlets of the **Intracoastal Waterway. The strip** (a.k.a. Rte. A1A, Fort Lauderdale Beach Blvd., 17th St. Causeway, Ocean Blvd., and Seabreeze Blvd.) runs 4 mi. along the beach between **Oakland Park Blvd.** to the north and Las Olas Blvd. to the south.

Visitor info: Greater Fort Lauderdale Convention and Visitors Bureau, 1850 Eller Dr., Ste. #303 (☎765-4466), in the Port Everglades. Particularly useful *Superior Small Lodg-ings,* a comprehensive and detailed list of low-priced accommodations. For published info, call ☎800-227-8669. Open M-F 8:30am-5pm. **Chamber of Commerce,** 512 NE 3rd Ave. (☎462-6000), 3 blocks off Federal Hwy. at 5th St. Open M-F 8am-5pm.

Hotlines: First Call for Help, ☎467-6333. **Sexual Assault and Treatment Center,** ☎761-7273. Both operate 24hr.

Post Office: 1900 W. Oakland Park Blvd. (☎527-2028). Open M-F 7:30am-7pm, Sa 8:30am-2pm. **ZIP code:** 33310. **Area code:** 954.

▛ ACCOMMODATIONS

Hotel prices increase exponentially as you approach prime beachfront and spring break. High season runs from mid-February through early April. Motels just north of the strip are the cheapest, and many hotels offer off-season deals for under $35. The **Greater Fort Lauderdale Lodging and Hospitality Association,** 1412 E. Broward Blvd., provides a free directory of area hotels (☎567-0766; open M-F 9am-5pm). The *Fort Lauderdale News* and the *Miami Herald* occasionally sport listings by local

FLORIDA

residents who rent rooms to tourists in spring. Sleeping on the well-patrolled beaches is illegal and virtually impossible between 9pm and sunrise. Instead, several new hostels in the area provide cheap and plentiful housing options.

Fort Lauderdale Beach Hostel, 2115 N. Ocean Blvd. (A1A) (☎567-7275). On A1A north between Sunrise and Oakland Park Blvds., or take bus #11 from the central terminal. The newest entrant to the hostelling business, FLBH is conveniently located several blocks from the beach. Both Owners and guests share the laid-back and friendly attitude that characterizes the area. Free local phone calls and Internet access. Free daytime pickup from anywhere in Ft. Lauderdale. Breakfast included. Free lockers. $10 linen deposit. Bed $16-18.

Floyd's Hostel/Crew House, 445 SE 16th St. (☎462-0631; call ahead, bus #1 or #40 from downtown, get off at 17th St.). A recent expansion makes Floyd's a homey hostel catering to international travelers and boat crews. Over 50 beds, 8 kitchens, 8 living rooms with cable TV, and 8 bathrooms. Dorm rooms have 4 beds. Free daytime pickup from anywhere in the Ft. Lauderdale area. The owners got engaged thanks to *Let's Go: USA 1995* (ask them for details). Free food, including pasta, beans, and cereal; local calls; linen; lockers; and laundry. Check-in by midnight or call for special arrangement. Passport or American driver's license required. Internet access. Beds $16, $115 for a week; foreign workers get 5th day free in the summer; private rooms $40, $55 in winter.

Quiet Waters County Park, 401 S. Powerline Rd. (☎360-1315), off I-95's Exit 37B; take Hillsboro Blvd. west to Powerline Rd. From downtown, take bus #11 to Pompano Sq. Mall, then switch to bus #95. Fully equipped lake-side campsites (tent, grill, and free admission to beach) for up to 5-30 people ("don't feed the gators!"). Normal water sports and see-it-to-believe-it 8-person "boatless water skiing" at the end of a cable. No electricity or RVs. Office hours 8:30am-6pm. Check-in 2-6pm. Sites $25. Entry fee $2, children $1. $25 refundable deposit. Wheelchair accessible.

▣▨ FOOD AND NIGHTLIFE

The clubs along the strip offer massive quantities of free grub during Happy Hour; wieners, chips, and hors d'oeuvres come on surfboard-sized platters or you can opt for the all-you-can-eat pizza and buffets. However, these bars have hefty cover charges (from $5) and drink minimums (from $3). The **Ocean Drive Cafe,** 401 Ft. Lauderdale Beach Blvd. (A1A), is one affordable option along the strip that provides both savory dishes and a great vantage point—people-watching breaks up a long day of sun and surf. Try the $7 homemade calzones or munch on a veggie burger for $6.50. (☎779-3351. Open daily 8:30am-midnight.) **La Spada's,** 4346 Seagrape Dr., off Commerical Blvd., boasts "the best damn hoagies in town," and judging by the size of the local crowd it seems that everyone agrees. Subs run $5-7; the foot-long Italian sub is an absolute must. (☎776-7893. Open M-Sa 10am-8pm, Su 11am-8pm.) The traditional diner **Lester's,** 250 Rte. 84, furnishes each table with its own jukebox, mixing golden oldies with mouth-watering shakes and burgers. Breakfast is served all day, but come in between 3 and 7pm for the "twilight" menu, when $7 can get you a full entree, drink, salad and desert. (☎525-5641. Open daily 24hr.)

Several popular nightspots line Ft. Lauderdale Beach Blvd. next to the beach. The **Elbo Room** sits on prime real estate at the corner of A1A and Las Olas Blvd; a camera on the second floor patio transmits the beach/strip scene to www.theelboroom.com. The booming sidewalk bar, chock full of scantily-clad beach beauties, is among the most visible and packed scenes on the strip. (☎463-4615. Live music nightly. Open M-Th 11am-2am, F-Sa 11am-3am, Su noon-2am.) **Club Atlantis,** 219 S. Ft. Lauderdale Beach Blvd., is a popular hangout for the crazy youth. Mud wrestling and freakin' grace the dance floors. If you're hungry, grab a $5 buffet during the day. (☎779-2544. Cover varies. Open daily 9pm-4am.) In the popular Las Olas district, **O'Hara's Jazz Cafe,** 722 E. Las Olas Blvd., combines stacked sandwiches with nightly jazz and blues acts for a laid-back night out. (☎524-1764. Live music nightly. Open M-F 11:30am-2am, Sa 11:30am-3am, Su noon-2am.)

LIVING THE JAI LIFE President Harry Truman and Eleanor Roosevelt were fans. Babe Ruth tried it, but failed. Anointed by Guinness as the **"fastest game in the world,"** Jai Alai generally still remains unknown to Americans outside the state of Florida. Players from the Basque region of France and Spain brought the game to the Sunshine State in the 20s, where it blossomed as a betting sport. Brave players whip the *pelota*, a rubber ball encased in layers of goat skin, from their *cesta*, a curved throwing/catching basket. Wild spins and speeds exceeding 180 mph aim to keep the opponent from cleanly catching and releasing the pelota. **Dania Jai-Alai,** off U.S. 1 10min. south of Fort Lauderdale sports one of the largest *frontons* (courts) in the state. *(301 E. Dania Beach Blvd.* ☎ *927-2841. Games Tu and Sa noon and 7:15pm, W-F 7:15pm, Su 1pm. General admission $1.50; reserved seats from $2.50.)*

👁 SIGHTS

Fort Lauderdale is a pleasant medium between the pretension of Miami Beach and the Redneck Riviera of panhandle beaches. Parts of "AIA: Beachfront Ave." demonstrate the class and sophistication of Vanilla Ice—signs for Jello might mean nude women. Yet Fort Lauderdale's well maintained palm-lined shore, emerald waters, and pink brick sidewalks make Miami Beach look shabby.

ON THE WATER. Fort Lauderdale Beach doesn't have a dull spot on it, but most of the action is between Las Olas Blvd. and Sunrise Blvd. **Los Olas Waterfront,** 2 W. 2nd St., the latest on-the-beach mall, boasts clubs, restaurants, and bars to entertain you until the ocean lures you back. Tour the city's waterways aboard the **Jungle Queen,** 801 Seabreeze Blvd., located at the Bahia Mar Yacht Center, on Rte. A1A three blocks south of Las Olas Blvd. The captain's commentary keeps you acquainted with the changing scenery as the 550-passenger riverboat cruises up the New River. (☎462-5596. 3hr. tours daily 10am, 2, and 7pm. $12.50, ages 2-10 $8.25; 7pm tour $26/$13.75, dinner included.) The **Water Taxi,** 651 Seabreeze Blvd/Rte. A1A, offers a different way to get around town. The nautical mode of transit makes 20 stops along the Intracoastal Waterway and the New River. (☎467-6677. Call 30min. before pickup. Open daily 10am until they get tired. $14; under 12 $7, free on Su when accompanied by an adult. All-day service $16.) **Water Sports Unlimited,** 301 Seabreeze Blvd/Rte. A1A, on the beach, rents equipment for a variety of water sports, including wave runners. Parasailing trips are $65 (600 ft., 8min. duration), plus a little more if you want to get dipped. (☎467-1316. Open daily 9am-6:30pm.)

ON DRY LAND. Landlubbers can walk among three acres of tropical gardens, exotic birds, and thousands of live butterflies at **Butterfly World,** west of Florida's Turnpike, Exit #69, in Coconut Creek. (3600 W. Sample Rd. ☎977-4400. Open M-Sa 9am-5pm, Su 1-5pm, gate closes 5pm. $13, ages 4-12 $8.) Learn to fly-fish and reel in the virtual "big one" at the **International Game Fishing Association's Fishing Hall of Fame & Museum,** 300 Gulf Stream Way, off I-95 at Griffin Rd., Exit 26. Upon entering the museum look directly up at the ceiling—large replicas of world-record catches adorn the hall. Adventures begin with the inspirational film, *Journeys,* in a big screen theater. (☎922-4212. Open daily 10am-6pm. $5, seniors $4.50, children $4. Wheelchair accessible. IGFA members free.) Amidst the commercial world of the beachfront area sits the secluded **Bonnet House,** 900 N. Birch Rd., a historic plantation, South Florida style. Forty-five spider monkeys roam the 35 subtropical acres. (☎563-5393. Open W-F 10am-1:30pm, Sa-Su noon-2:30pm. Closed mid-Aug. thru mid-Sept. $9, students $7, seniors $8, children under 6 free.)

MIAMI AND MIAMI BEACH ☎305

Miami's Latin heart pulses to the beat of the largest Cuban population this side of Havana—speaking Spanish is very useful. Beautiful buildings and beautiful people have established the city as a tourist haven. When it's cold in New York or smoggy in Los Angeles, Miami Beach seems to be the preferred hangout for an inordinate amount of celebrities, and the hopping nightclub scene lets the lay person enjoy the lifestyle along with them. But it's not all bikinis and sand—Miami is the starting point to one of America's greatest natural habitats, the Everglades, and also the gateway to the Florida Keys and Caribbean America.

▆ TRANSPORTATION

Airport: Miami International (☎876-7000), at Le Jeune Rd. and NW 36th Ave., 7 mi. northwest of downtown. Bus #7 runs downtown; many other buses make downtown stops. From downtown, take bus "C" or "K" to South Miami Beach.

Trains: Amtrak, 8303 NW 37th Ave. (☎835-1223), near Northside station of Metrorail. Bus "L" goes directly to Lincoln Rd. Mall in South Miami Beach. To: Orlando (5hr., 2 per day, $33-64); New Orleans (24hr., 3 per week, $206-387); and Charleston (13-14hr., 2 per day, $64-149). Open daily 6:30am-10pm.

Buses: Greyhound, Miami Station, 4111 NW 27th St. (☎871-1810). To: Atlanta (17-19hr., 13 per day, $85.50); Orlando (5-9hr., 10 per day, $36); and Fort Lauderdale (1hr., every hr., $5). Open 24hr.

Public Transit: Metro Dade Transportation (☎770-3131; info M-F 6am-10pm, Sa-Su 9am-5pm). The extensive Metrobus network converges downtown, where most long trips transfer. Over 70 routes, but the major, lettered bus routes A, C, D, G, H, J, K, L, R, S, and T serve Miami Beach. After dark, some stops are patrolled (indicated with a sign). Buses run M-F 4am-2:30am. $1.25; transfers 25¢, to Metrorail 25¢. Call for weekend schedule. Exact change only. The **Metrorail** services downtown's major business and cultural areas. Rail runs daily 5am-midnight. $1.25, rail-to-bus transfers 50¢. The **Metromover** loop downtown is linked to the Metrorail stations. Runs daily 5am-midnight. Fare 25¢, seniors 10¢, free transfers from Metrorail. **Tri-Rail** (☎800-874-7245) connects Miami, Fort Lauderdale, and West Palm Beach. Trains run M-Sa 4am-8pm, Su 7am-8pm. M-F $6.75, Sa-Su $4; students, ages 5-12, and seniors 50% off. The **Electrowave** (☎843-9283) offers shuttles along Washington Ave. from S. Pointe to Dade Blvd. Runs M-W 8am-2am, Th-Sa 8am-4am, Su and holidays 10am-2am. 25¢; pick up a brochure or just hop on in South Beach.

Taxis: Metro, ☎888-8888. **Central Cab,** ☎532-5555. Flat fare from airport to Miami Beach $24; otherwise $3 for first mile, $2 per mile.

Bike Rental: Miami Beach Bicycle Center, 601 5th St. (☎531-4161), at the corner of Washington Ave., Miami Beach. Open M-Sa 10am-7pm, Su 10am-5pm. $5 per hr., $20 per day, $70 per week. Must be 18+ with credit card or $200 cash deposit.

✴ ORIENTATION

Three highways criss-cross the Miami area. **I-95,** the most direct route north-south, merges into **U.S. 1 (Dixie Hwy.)** just south of downtown. U.S. 1 runs to the Everglades entrance at Florida City and then continues as the Overseas Hwy. to Key West. **Rte. 836 (Dolphin Expwy),** a major east-west artery through town, connects I-95 to **Florida's Turnpike,** passing the airport in between. If you're headed to Florida City, taking Rte. 836 and the Turnpike will allow you to avoid the traffic on U.S. 1.

When looking for street addresses, pay careful attention to the systematic street layout; it's easy to confuse North Miami Beach, West Miami, Miami Beach, and Miami addresses. Streets in Miami run east-west, avenues north-south; both are numbered. Miami divides into NE, NW, SE, and SW quadrants; the dividing lines (downtown) are **Flagler St.** (east-west) and **Miami Ave.** (north-south). Some numbered streets and avenues also have names—e.g., Le Jeune Rd. is SW 42nd Ave., and SW 40th St. is Bird Rd. Get a map that lists both numbers and names.

Several causeways connect Miami to **Miami Beach.** The most useful is **MacArthur Causeway,** which becomes 5th St. in Miami Beach. Numbered streets run east-west across the island, increasing as you go north. In South Miami Beach, **Collins Ave. (A1A)** is the main north-south drag. Parallel to Collins are the club-filled **Washington Ave.** and the beachfront **Ocean Ave.** The commercial and entertainment district sits between 6th and 23rd St.

The heart of **Little Havana** lies between SW 12th Ave. and SW 27th Ave.; take bus #8, 11, 17, or 37. **Calle Ocho** (SW 8th St.) is central; one block north, the corresponding section of **W. Flagler St.** is a hub of Cuban business. **Coconut Grove,** south of Little Havana, centers on the shopping and entertainment district on **Grand Ave.** and **Virginia St. Coral Gables,** an upscale residential area, rests around the intersection of **Coral Way (SW 24th St.)** and **Le Jeune Rd.** A **car** can be useful to get around the city and its rather extensive suburbs, but watch where you park. Posted signs indicate different parking zones; should you leave your car in a residential zone for even a few moments, you may return to find it towed. Never leave valuables visible in your car; automobile theft and break-ins are common.

▓ PRACTICAL INFORMATION

Visitor info: Miami Beach Visitors Center, 420 Lincoln Rd. (☎672-1270). Open M-F 9am-6pm, Sa-Su 10am-4pm. **Info booth,** 401 Biscayne Blvd. (☎539-2980), downtown outside of Bayside Marketplace. Open daily 10am-6:30pm. In South Beach, **The Art Deco Welcome Center,** 1001 Ocean Dr. (☎531-3484) has tour info. Open M-F 11am-6pm, Sa 10am-10pm, Su 11am-10pm, extended hours in winter. **Coconut Grove Chamber of Commerce,** 2820 McFarlane Ave. (☎444-7270). Open M-F 9am-5pm. **Greater Miami Convention and Visitors Bureau,** 701 Brickell Ave. (☎539-3000 or 800-283-2707), 27th fl. of Barnett Bank Bldg. downtown. Open M-F 9am-5pm.

Internet Access: Space Taco, 1659 Washington Ave. (☎695-8786) in Miami Beach. $4 per 30min. Open daily 7:30am-midnight. **Kafka's Cafe,** 1464 Washington Ave. (☎673-9669) in Miami Beach. 13 computers, $9 per hr. Open daily 9am-11pm.

Hotlines: Crisis Line, ☎358-4357. **Rape Treatment Center and Hotline** (☎585-7273), at Jackson Memorial Hospital, 1611 NW 12th Ave. Both 24hr. **Gay Hotline,** ☎759-5210. **Abuse Hotline,** ☎800-342-9152.

Post Office: 500 NW 2nd Ave. (☎639-4284), downtown. Open M-F 8am-5pm, Sa 9am-1:30pm. **ZIP code:** 33101. **Area code:** 305.

▛ ACCOMMODATIONS

Cheap rooms abound in South Miami Beach's Art Deco hotels. Finding a "pull-manette" (in 40s lingo), a room with a refrigerator, stove, and sink, will save you money. In South Florida, many inexpensive hotels are likely to have 2-3 inch cockroaches ("palmetto bugs"). Hostels, all located in Miami Beach, are the cheapest option. In general, high season for Miami Beach runs late December through mid-March; during the off season, when rooms are empty, hotel clerks are quick to bargain. The **Greater Miami and the Beaches Hotel Association,** 407 Lincoln Rd. #10G, can help you find a place to crash (☎531-3553; open M-F 9am-5pm), and the Miami Beach Visitors Center (see **Practical Information,** above) can finagle you the cheapest rates. **Camping** is not allowed in Miami Beach.

▨ **Banana Bungalow,** 2360 Collins Ave. (☎538-1951), at 23rd St. along the northern edge of the Art Deco district. Banana Bungalow is known as "party central"–the festive atmosphere around its pool/bar area hops all year long. All rooms have A/C and cable TV, though not all the fixtures work. Check out the room before you take it. 180 bunk beds. Free coffee, tea, and toast. Full bar with grill poolside. Kayak/canoe rentals $10 per 2hr. Free lockers in dorms. $20 key/linen deposit. Internet access 20¢ per min. Limited, free, guarded parking. Dorms $17, private rooms $75 depending on season.

The Tropics Hotel/Hostel, 1550 Collins Ave. (☎531-0361), across the street from the beach. From the airport, take bus "J" to 41st St., transfer to bus "C" to Lincoln Rd., and walk

1 block south on Collins Ave. Next to parking garage. Clean, large rooms with 4-8 beds, A/C, private baths, phone, pool access, and an outdoor, common kitchen. Lockers at front desk, none in rooms. Free linen. $10 key deposit. Internet access 20¢ per min. Dorms $18; private singles or doubles $50. Discounts available for ISIC holders.

Miami Beach International Travelers Hostel (9th St. Hostel) (AAIH/Rucksackers), 236 9th St. (☎534-0268 or 800-978-6787; www.sobehostel.com), at Washington Ave. From the airport, take bus "J" to 41st and Indian Creek, then transfer to bus "C" or "K." Central location, but difficult parking. Lively international atmosphere near the beach. Laundry, common room with TV and movie library. Internet access, $8 per hr. All rooms (maximum 4 people) with A/C and bath. Dorms $15, $13 with any hostelling membership or student ID; private singles or doubles $55, off-season $36.

Sea Deck Hotel and Apartments, 1530 Collins Ave. (☎538-4361). Basic, cozy, and clean pullmanettes with floral bedspreads open onto a tropical courtyard. Limited parking available. Pullmanettes $49, other rooms $67, suites $78. *Let's Go* toters get 10% off.

The Clay Hotel and International Hostel (HI-AYH), 1438 Washington Ave. (☎534-2988 or 800-379-2529), in the heart of the Art Deco

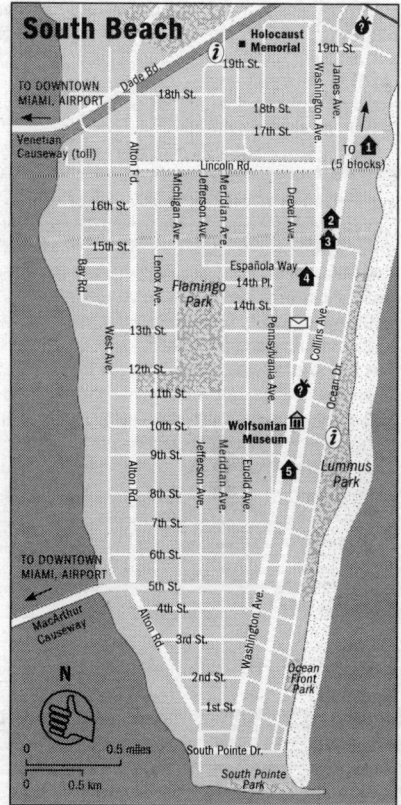

South Beach

🍴 FOOD
Famous 11th Street Diner, 6
Wolfie's, 1

🔺 ACCOMMODATIONS
Banana Bungalow, 2
The Clay Hotel and Int'l. Hostel, 5
Sea Deck Hotel and Apartments, 4
Miami Beach Int'l. Travelers Hostel, 7
The Tropics Hotel/Hostel, 3

district; take bus "C" from downtown. This historic building and center of Al Capone's Miami gambling syndicate was often featured on the TV series *Miami Vice*. Great archways in a Mediterranean-style building. International crowd. Kitchen, laundry facilities, A/C. Open 24hr. Dorm rooms of 4-8 beds come with phone and fridges; some also have TV. Lockers $1 per day. Linen/key deposit $10. Dorms $15, nonmembers $17; private rooms $45-81.

🔲 FOOD

Miami's rich ethnic diversity has made it a haven for top-notch Latin cuisine. Cuban specialties include *medianoche* sandwiches (a sort of club sandwich on a soft roll, heated and compressed); bright red *mamey*-flavored ice cream and shakes; hearty *frijoles negros* (black beans); and *picadillo* (shredded beef and peas in tomato sauce, served with white rice). For sweets, seek out a *dulcería* (sweetshop), or sample thimble-sized shots of strong, sweet *café cubano* (around 35¢). For other treats, try *plátanos*, large starchy bananas served fried or caramelized, and *mojitos*,—rum, lime and mint spritzers. Florida stone crabs are in season from October to May; seafood lovers will be easily caught by their sweet, meaty claws. Cheap restaurants are not common in Miami, but an array of bakeries can sustain you.

FLORIDA

▨ **Macarena,** 1334 Washington Ave. (☎531-3440), in Miami Beach. Dance your way to wonderful food in an atmosphere that's intimate and festive. This place is a favorite of the Julio Iglesias family. *Paella* ($14, lunch $7) and the best rice pudding you'll encounter ($5.50) make for the perfect Spanish treat. Wine comes from their own vineyards. Flamenco dancing W and F; ladies night Th; live salsa on Sa. Open daily for lunch 12:30-3:30pm; dinner Su-Tu 7pm-1am, W-Th 7pm-1:30am, F-Sa 7pm-5am.

▨ **Wolfie's,** 2038 Collins Ave. (☎538-6626), at 21st St. in South Beach. "Famous the world over," this mega-deli is a throwback to old Miami Beach. Dessert selection is unreal, especially the 6 in. thick cheesecake ($3.95). Look for luminaries in the "celebrity room." Open 24hr.

11th St. Diner, 1065 Washington Ave. (☎534-6373), at 11th St., in Miami Beach. Classic diner with the requisite soda fountain and ancient Coca-Cola clock. Originally built and operated in Wilkes-Barre, PA, the diner (the actual train car) was moved down to the Art Deco district and reopened in 1992. Breakfast all day ($3-7), sandwiches ($4-7), and grill items. Best shakes in Miami ($3.95). Open 24hr., making it a popular spot for beating the munchies after a long night of revelry.

King's Ice Cream, 1831 SW 8th St./Calle Ocho (☎643-1842), in Miami. Tropical fruit *helado* (ice cream) flavors include a regal coconut (served in its own shell), *mamey,* and mango (just $1 for a small cup). Open M-Sa 10am-11pm, Su 1-11pm.

Flamingo Cafe, 1454 Washington Ave. (☎673-4302), near the Clay Hostel, in Miami Beach. Small counter with friendly service, all of which is in Spanish. Beef tacos and salad $2.75, *frijoles con queso* $2.75. Lunch specials $5-7. Open M-Sa 7am-10pm.

◉ SIGHTS

South Beach, or "SoBe" for short, between 6th and 23rd St., is the reason to come to Miami. The liberal atmosphere, hot bodies, Art Deco design and excellent sand make these 17 blocks seem like their own little world. Going **topless** is forbidden, but an oft-ignored offense. **Ocean Dr.** is America's ultimate see-and-be-seen strip, lined with many a bar or cafe for dodging the sun. **Walking tours** start at the **Oceanfront Auditorium,** 1001 Ocean Dr. at 10th St. (☎672-2014. 1½hr. tours Th 6:30pm and Sa 10:30am; $10. 1¼hr. self-guided tours run daily 11am-4pm; $5.) The **Holocaust Memorial,** 1933-45 Meridian Ave., across from the Miami Beach Visitors Center, commemorates the 6 million Jews who fell victim to Nazi terrorism in WWII. Marvel at the 42-foot bronze arm that protrudes from the ground with sculptured people attempting to climb it to freedom. (☎538-1663. Open daily 9am-9pm. Free.) **The Wolfsonian,** 1001 Washington Ave., examines the art of design from 1885-1945 through over 70,000 objects. The exhibits include Russian propaganda, London subway signs, and a rather funny "plastics" room. (☎531-1001. Open M-Tu and F-Sa 11am-6pm, Th 11am-9pm, Su noon-5pm. $5, students and seniors $3.50. Free Th 6-9pm.)

A stroll through the lazy streets of **Coconut Grove** uncovers an unlikely combination of haute boutiques and tacky tourist traps. People-watching abounds at the open-air mall, CocoWalk, along Grand Ave. On the bayfront between the Grove and downtown stands the **Vizcaya Museum and Gardens,** 3251 S. Miami Ave. European antiques, tapestries, and art fill this 70-room Italianate mansion, surrounded by ten acres of lush gardens. (☎250-9133. Open daily 9:30am-5pm; last entry 4:30pm. $10, $5 ages 6-12, ISIC holders discount.)

On the waterfront downtown, Miami's sleek **Bayside** shopping center hops nightly with talented street performers. (Open M-Th 10am-10pm, F-Sa 10am-11pm, Su 11am-9pm.) The **American Police Hall of Fame and Museum,** 3801 Biscayne Blvd., celebrates America's "men in blue" with a memorial engraved with names of officers who have died in the line of duty. On the upper level, exhibits feature grisly execution equipment, including a gas chamber and "Old Sparky," Florida's infamous electric chair. (☎573-0070. Open daily 10am-5:30pm. $6, $4 seniors, $3 ages 6-12, free for police officers; discounts at Visitors Center.)

Scenic **Coral Gables** boasts one of the most beautiful planned communities in the region houses the **University of Miami.** Nearby, the family-friendly **Venetian Pool,** 2701 DeSoto Blvd., founded in 1923, once drew Hollywood stars like Esther Williams and Johnny Weissmuller. Waterfalls and Spanish architecture dress up this swimming hole. (☎460-5356. Open summer M-F 11am-7:30pm, Sa-Su 10am-4:30pm; hours vary in winter and spring. $8.50, under 12 $4.50; Nov.-Mar. $5/$2. Children under 36 mos. or 38 in. not admitted.)

🎵🎬 ENTERTAINMENT AND NIGHTLIFE

For the latest on Miami entertainment, the "Living Today," "Lively Arts," and Friday "Weekend" sections of the *Miami Herald* are logical places to start. Weekly *Oceandrive,* the *New Times, Street,* and the *Sun Post* list local happenings. *TWN* and *Miamigo* are the major gay papers. **Performing Arts and Community Education (PACE)** manages more than 400 concerts each year (jazz, rock, soul, dixieland, reggae, salsa, and bluegrass); most are free. **Carnaval Miami,** the nation's largest Hispanic festival, fills 23 blocks of Calle Ocho in early Mar. with salsa, music, and the world's longest conga line. Some call it the world's largest block party.

Nightlife in the Art Deco district of South Miami Beach starts late (usually after midnight) and continues until well after sunrise. Gawk at models and stars while eating dinner at one of Ocean Blvd.'s open cafes or bars, then head down to Washington Ave., between 6th and 7th St., for some serious fun. Miami Beach's club scene is transient; what's there one week may not be there the next. Many clubs charge covers only after midnight. Most clubs have dress codes, and everyone dresses to the nines, even on so-called "casual" nights. **Bash,** 655 Washington Ave., stands out among its neighbors; the large indoor dance floor grooves to house and progressive while the courtyard in back jams to worldbeat. (☎538-2274. Fashion shows on Th; Brazilian parties on F. 21+. Cover $10 Th, $20 Sa-Su. Open Th-Su 10pm-5am.) The beautiful and famous go to **Liquid,** 1439 Washington Ave., owned by Madonna chum Ingrid Casares and Madonna brother Michael Ciccone. (☎532-9154. 21+. Cover $20. Open 10pm-5am.) Arrive before midnight to dodge the cover and long lines at the **Groove Jet,** 323 23rd St. The front room of this massive hall plays trance, dance, and house; the back room churns out alternative rock. (☎532-2002. 21+. Cover $10 after midnight. Open Th-Su 11pm-5am.)

A few gay and mixed clubs call Miami Beach home as well, including **Score,** 727 Lincoln Rd. Mall. Clientele is mixed and features frequent theme nights. (☎535-1111. 21+. No cover. Open M-Sa 3pm-5am, Su 3pm-2am.) The recently expanded **Twist,** 1057 Washington Ave., is a two-story gay club with an outdoor lounge and rockin' dance floor. (☎538-9478. Cover varies. Open daily 1pm-5am.)

EVERGLADES ☎305

Encompassing the entire tip of Florida and spearing into Florida Bay, **Everglades National Park** spans 1.6 million acres of one of the world's most unique and fragile ecosystems. Vast prairies of sawgrass spike through broad expanses of shallow water, creating the famed "river of grass," while tangled mazes of mangrove swamps wind up the western coast. To the south, delicate coral reefs lie below the shimmering blue waters of the bay. A host of species found nowhere else in the world inhabits these lands and waters: American alligators, dolphins, sea turtles, and various birds and fishes, as well as the endangered Florida panther, Florida manatee, and American crocodile.

🛈 PRACTICAL INFORMATION

The main entrance to the park, the **Ernest Coe Visitors Center,** 40001 Rte. 9366, sits just inside the eastern edge of the Everglades. (☎242-7700. Open daily 8am-5pm.) Rte. 9366 also cuts 40 mi. through the park past campgrounds, trailheads, and canoe waterways to the **Flamingo Visitors Center** (☎695-2945; open daily 8am-5pm, in

FLORIDA

winter 7:30am-5pm) and the heavily developed Flamingo Outpost Resort. At the northern end of the park off U.S. 41 (Tamiami Trail), the **Shark Valley Visitors Center** provides access to a 15 mi. loop through a sawgrass swamp that can be accessed by foot, bike, or a 2hr. tram. **Shark Valley** is an ideal site for those who want a taste of the freshwater ecosystem but can't venture too deep into the park. (☎221-8776. Open daily 8:30am-6pm. Tram tours May-Nov. daily 9:30, 11am, 1, and 3pm; Dec.-Apr. daily every hr. 9am-4pm; $10, seniors $9, under 12 $5.50. Reservations recommended. Wheelchair access available with reservations. Bike rental daily 8:30am-3pm; $4.25 per hr., including helmets.) The **Gulf Coast Visitors Center,** 800 Copeland Ave. S., in Everglades City in the northwestern end of the park, provides access to the western coastline and the vast river network throughout the park. (☎695-3311. Open 8:30am-5pm in summer; extended hours in winter.) For other area information on lodgings and discounts on nearby attractions, check out the **Tropical Everglades Visitors Center,** on U.S. 1 in Florida City. (☎245-9180 or 800-388-9669. Open daily 9am-5pm.) **Emergency: Park headquarters** (☎247-7272). **Entrance fee:** Ernest Coe $10 per car, $5 bike- or walk-in; Shark Valley $8/$4; Gulf Coast free. **Area code:** 305.

Summer visitors can expect to get eaten alive by swarming mosquitoes. The best time to visit is winter or spring, when heat, humidity, storms, and bugs are at a minimum and wildlife congregate in shrinking pools of evaporating water. *Wear long-sleeve clothing and bring insect repellent at all times.*

■ ACCOMMODATIONS

Outside the eastern entrance to the park, **Florida City** offers some cheap motels along U.S. 1. But the ▨**Everglades International Hostel,** 20 S.W. 2nd Ave., located off Rte. 9336, presents a far better option. The owner, Owhnn (yeah, that's how it's spelled), has created a home away from home. Hang out with fellow travelers in the gazebo, the gardens, or the kitchen house—which also has a large-screen TV with a free video collection. (☎305-248-1122 or 800-372-3874. Internet access available. Bike rental $5. Canoe rental $20. Linen $2. Dorms $13, $14 with A/C; private rooms $33/35. $3 nonmember surcharge. Cash only.) The only option for lodging inside the park, **Flamingo Lodge,** 1 Flamingo Lodge Hwy., has large rooms with A/C, TV, private baths, pool, and a great view of the Florida Bay. (☎695-3101 or 800-600-3813. Continental breakfast included in summer. Singles and doubles $65; Nov.-Dec. and Apr. $79; Jan.-Mar. $95. Reservations recommended.) A few **campgrounds** line Rte. 9336; all have drinking water, grills, dump sites, and restrooms, but none have hookups. (☎800-365-2267. Reservations required Nov.-Apr. Sites free in summer; in winter $14.) **Backcountry camping** inside the park is accessible primarily by boat (see **Sights,** below). Required **permits** are available on a first come, first served basis at the Flamingo and Gulf Coast Visitors Centers (Dec.-Apr. $10 for 1-6 people; May-Nov. free). Applications must be made in person at least 24hr. beforehand.

Near the northwest entrance, motels, RV parks, and campgrounds scatter around Everglades City. The **Barron River Villa, Marina, and RV Park** offers 67 RV sites, 29 on the river, and precious motel rooms with TV and A/C. (☎695-3331 or 800-535-4961. RV sites: full hookup $18, on the river $20; Oct.-Apr. $28/$34. Motel rooms: May-Aug. $41; Sept.-Dec. $49; Jan.-Apr. $57.)

▢ FOOD

Right across the street from the hostel, **Rosita's,** 199 Palm Dr., offers the best Mexican food in the area. Breakfast eggs ($4) can get you ready for a long day of exploring the park, or come back at night for some great *chiles rellenos* or $8 *mole.* (☎246-3114. Open daily 8:30am-9pm.) Up Rte. 997 in Homestead, the **Main St. Cafe,** 128 N. Krome Ave., guarantees a good time when the community comes together for open mic nights. Try one of their gourmet smoothies for $2-4 or the all-you-can-eat soup and salad bar for $8. (☎245-7575. Th teen open mic 8-11pm; F open mic 7pm-midnight; Sa folk country and acoustic rock 7pm-midnight. Open M-W 10am-5pm, Th-Sa 10am-midnight.)

MAIL CALL After a fire destroyed the local post office in 1953, Ochopee, FL, town leaders searched for a new location. Postmaster Sidney Brown quickly chose a small shack, originally an irrigation pipe shed for a tomato farm; ever since, the country's smallest post office has serviced a three-county area in a room barely big enough for two. Cram into the Ochopee mail room on U.S. 41 (Tamiami Trail) between the Gulf Coast and Shark Valley entrances to Everglades National Park.

◪ OUTDOOR ACTIVITIES

The park is literally swamped with fishing, hiking, canoeing, biking, and wilderness observation opportunities. *Forget swimming; alligators, sharks, and barracuda patrol the waters.* From November through April, the park sponsors amphitheater programs, canoe trips, and ranger-guided Slough Slogs (swamp tours).

HIKING

Visitors to the Everglades can walk the well-developed short trails to explore the wildlife without exerting too much energy. Two of the best start at the **Royal Palm Visitors Center,** 4 mi. inside the park from the main entrance. The famous **Anhinga Trail** offers the best opportunities to see alligators, anhinga birds, turtles, and giant crickets. For a spectacular view from horizon to horizon, the **Pa-hay-okee overlook,** on the main road, is worth the half-mile trip it takes to get there.

BOATING

If you really want to experience the Everglades, start paddling. The 99 mi. **Wilderness Waterway** winds its way from the northwest entrance to the Flamingo station in the far south. Adventurous camping spots along the journey include chickees (wooden platforms elevated above mangrove swamps), beaches, and groundsites. (Free in summer; $10 in winter.) **Everglades National Park Boat Tours,** at the Gulf Coast Visitors Center, rents canoes. (☎695-2591 or 800-445-7724. $20 per day.) The same company offers two boat tours into the park. Naturalists on the **Ten Thousand Island Cruise** lead the relaxing 1½hr. jaunt through the heart of the coastal "Ten Thousand Islands," and into the Gulf of Mexico, with the occasional manatee, bottle-nosed dolphin, and bald eagle sighting. Shorter canoe trails wind from Rte. 9336; the **Hell's Bay Canoe Trail** threads through mangrove swamps past primitive campsites like Pearl Bay. Canoes are also available at the **Flamingo Marina.** (☎695-3101 or 800-600-3813. $22 for 4hr., $32 per day; $40 deposit.)

GARDENS AND GATORS

For a truly bizarre time, head up U.S. 1 to Homestead and the **Coral Castle,** 28655 South Dixie Hwy., in Homestead. In the 1920s, little Latvian immigrant Ed Leedskalnin turned hundreds of tons of dense coral rock into a magnificent garden of beautiful sculptures. (☎305-248-6344. Open M-Th 9am-6pm, F-Su 9am-7pm. Guided tours daily. $7.75, seniors $6.50, ages 7-12 $5. Discounts at Visitors Center.) View gators, crocs, and snakes at the **Everglades Alligator Farm,** 40351 SW 192 Ave., 4 mi. south of Palm Dr. There are thousands of gators, from little hatchlings clambering for the sun to 18-footers clambering for...um...you. (☎305-247-2628 or 800-644-9711. Open daily 9am-6pm. $9, ages 4-10 $5. Wildlife shows $8. Discounts at Visitors Center.)

FLORIDA KEYS

Intense popularity has transformed this long-time haven for pirates, smugglers, and treasure hunters into supreme beach vacationland. Whether smothered in tourists or outcasts, the Keys retain an "anything goes" mentality. When former Key West mayor Tony Tarracino arrived here decades ago, he did a quick inventory of bars and strip clubs, and concluded that he'd reached heaven (see p. 461). If this sounds more like hell, take a dive. Gardens of coral 6 mi. off the coast grant relative solitude to scuba divers and snorkelers, as long as they don't mind millions of colorful fish, and form a 100-yard wide barrier reef between Key Largo and Key West. Don't believe the hype; sharks are scarce here.

⚡ PRACTICAL INFORMATION

The **Overseas Hwy. (U.S. 1)** bridges the divide between the Keys and the southern tip of Florida, stitching the islands together. **Mile markers** section the highway and replace street addresses. The first marker, Mi. 126 in Florida City, begins the long countdown to zero in Key West. **Greyhound** runs to the Keys from Miami ($32), stopping in Homestead, Key Largo, Marathon, Big Pine Key, and Key West. Most bus drivers can be convinced to stop at mile markers along the side of the road. Tiny Greyhound signs along the highway indicate bus stops (usually hotels), where you can buy tickets or call the Greyhound **info line** on the red phones provided. **Biking** along U.S. 1 is treacherous due to fast cars and narrow shoulders; instead of riding, bring your bike on the bus.

KEY LARGO   ☎ 305

Over half a century ago, Hollywood stars Humphrey Bogart and Lauren Bacall immortalized the name "Key Largo" in their hit movie. Quick-thinking locals of Rock Harbor, where some of the scenes were shot, soon changed the name of their town to Key Largo to attract tourists. It sure worked. Key Largo works as the gateway to the rest of the enchanting, laid-back islands. While some (older) visitors still come to see the relics of the moviemaking past, more are drawn to Key Largo's greatest natural asset: the coral reefs. Pennekamp State Park was the country's first completely *underwater* park, and divers of all abilities flock to the isle for the chance to glimpse at the reef ecosystem and the numerous shipwrecks.

⚡ **PRACTICAL INFORMATION.** Greyhound (☎871-1810), Mi. 102 at the Howard Johnson, goes to Miami (3 per day, 1¾hr., $12.50-14.50) and Key West (4 per day, 3 hr., $26-29). Station open daily 8am-6pm. **Mom's Taxi:** ☎852-6000. **Key Largo Chamber of Commerce/Florida Keys Visitors Center:** 106000 U.S. 1, Mi. 106 (☎451-1414 or 800-822-1088; open daily 9am-6pm). **The Key Largo Tourist and Reservation Center:** 103360 U.S. 1, Mi. 103 (☎453-0066; open M-Sa 9am-8pm, Su 10am-6pm). **Post Office:** 100100 U.S. 1, Mi. 100 (☎451-3155; open M-F 8am-4:30pm). **ZIP code:** 33037. **Area code:** 305.

⚐ **ACCOMMODATIONS. Ed and Ellen's Lodgings,** 103365 U.S. 1, Mi. 103.4, offers clean, large rooms with cable TV, A/C, and kitchenettes as well as help with diving or snorkeling reservations. (☎451-9949 or 888-333-5536. Doubles $49-79; off-season $39-49; each additional person $10. Rates may vary on weekends, holidays, special events, and lobster season.) A few lodgings near downtown Key Largo boast reasonable rates. The **Bay Cove Motel,** 99446 Overseas Hwy., Mi. 99.5, borders a small beach on the bay side of the island. Rooms have cable TV, A/C and mini-fridges. (☎451-1686. Doubles $50-80 depending on season and availability.) The waterside **Hungry Pelican,** Mi. 99.5, boasts beautiful bougainvillea vines, tropical birds in the trees, and tidy, cozy rooms with double beds, fridges, and cable. Free use of paddle boats, canoes, and hammocks afford amazing sunset views. Complimentary continental breakfast is available every morning. (☎451-3576. Rooms $50-115; each additional person $10.) Reservations are necessary for the popular **John Pennekamp State Park Campground** (see **Sights,** below); the 47 sites are clean, convenient, and well worth the effort required to obtain them. Pets not allowed, and a maximum stay of 14 days is enforced. (☎451-1202. $24; with electricity $26.)

◻ **FOOD.** Seafood restaurants litter the Overseas Hwy., offering varying degrees of price, quality, specialty and view. Follow your meal from the boat to the plate at **Calypso's,** 1 Seagate Dr., on the marina across from Key Largo Fisheries, near Mi. 99. The coconut shrimp ($6) is a sweet, fried delight. (☎451-0600. Open M and W-Th noon-10pm; F-Sa noon-11pm.) **Alabama Jack's,** 58000 Card Sound Rd., between Homestead and Key Largo, east of Overseas Highway, rocks the southern Florida wetlands with live country music Saturday 2-5pm and Sunday 2-7pm. It is probably the southernmost place to enjoy "hoppin' john," a Southern dish of black-eyed peas, rice and ham. (☎248-8741. Open M-F 11am-7pm, Sa-Su 11am-7:30pm.)

◨ **SIGHTS.** Key Largo is the self-proclaimed "Dive Capital of the World" and many diving instructors offer their services via highway billboards. The best place to go is the nation's first underwater sanctuary, **John Pennekamp State Park,** Mi. 102.5, 60 mi. from Miami. The park extends 3 mi. into the Atlantic Ocean, safeguarding a part of the coral reef that runs the length of the Keys. (☎451-1202. $2.50 per vehicle with 1 occupant, $1.50 walk- or bike-in; $5 per vehicle with 2 occupants, each additional person 50¢.) The park's **Visitors Center** hands out maps of the reefs, info on boat and snorkeling tours, and films on the park. To see the reefs, visitors must take a boat or rent their own. (☎451-9570. Open daily 8am-5pm. 19 ft. motor boat $28 per hr. Deposit required. Call 451-6325 for reservations.) **Scuba trips** from the Visitors Center run at 9:30am and 1:30pm. (☎451-6322. $37 per person for a two-tank dive. Deposit required.) A **snorkeling tour** also allows you to partake of the underwater quiet. (☎451-1621. 2½hr. total, 1½hr. water time. Tours 9am, noon, and 3pm. $25, under 18 $20. Equipment $5. Deposit required.) A relatively new addition, **Glass Bottom Boat Tours,** provides a crystal clear view of the reefs without wetting your feet. (☎451-1621. 2½hr. Tours 9:15am, 12:15, and 3pm. $18, under 12 $10.)

KEY WEST ☎305

The small "last island" of the Florida Keys, Key West has always drawn its fair share of colorful characters. Henry Flagler, Ernest Hemingway, and Jimmy Buffett have all called the quasi-independent "Conch Republic" home. Nowadays thousands of tourists hop on the Overseas Highway to glimpse the past, frequent the over 300 bars, and kick back under the sun. The crowd is as diverse as Key West's past: families spend a week enjoying the water; 20-somethings come to party and work; and a swinging gay population finds a haven of clubs and resorts oriented exclusively to them. Key West is as far south as you can get in the U.S. without going to Hawaii. This is the end of the road—enjoy it.

█▊ **ORIENTATION AND PRACTICAL INFORMATION.** Key West lies at the end of U.S. 1, 155 mi. southwest of Miami (3-3½hr.). Divided into two sectors, the eastern part of the island, known as **New Town,** harbors tract houses, chain motels, shopping malls, and the airport. Beautiful old conch houses fill **Old Town,** west of White St. **Duval St.** is the main north-south thoroughfare in Old Town; Truman Ave. (U.S. 1) is a major east-west route. A car is the easiest way to get to Key West, though driving in town is neither easy nor necessary. **Greyhound,** 3535 S. Roosevelt Blvd. (☎296-9072; open daily 8am-6pm), at the airport, runs to Miami (4½hr., 3 per day, $32-36). **Key West Port and Transit Authority,** at City Hall, has Clockwise ("Old Town") and counterclockwise ("Mallory Sq. Rte.") routes. (☎292-8161. Service daily 7am-10:30pm, about every 1½hr. Fare 75¢, seniors and students 35¢.) **Keys Moped & Scooter,** 523 Truman Ave., rents wheeled adventures. (☎294-4724. Open daily 9am-6pm. Bikes $4 per half-day, $30 per week. Mopeds $18 per 9am-5pm, $23 per 24hr. Electric cars $29 per hr.) **Keys Taxi:** ☎296-6666. **Visitor info: Key West Welcome Center,** 3840 N. Roosevelt Blvd., a private reservation service just north of the intersection of U.S. 1 and Roosevelt Blvd. (☎296-4444 or 800-284-4482. Open M-Sa 9am-7:30pm, Su 9am-6pm.) **Key West Chamber of Commerce,** 402 Wall St. (☎294-2587 or 800-527-8539), in old Mallory Sq. Open M-F 8:30am-6:30pm, Sa-Su 8:30am-6pm. **The Key West Business Guild Gay and Lesbian Information Center,** 728 Duval St. (☎294-4603). Open M-F 9am-5pm. **Hotlines: Help Line,** ☎296-4357. Operates 24hr. **Internet access: Internet Isle Cafe,** 118 Duval St. (☎293-1199). $8 per hr. Open daily 8am-11pm. **Post Office:** 400 Whitehead St. (☎294-2557), 1 block west of Duval at Eaton. Open M-F 8:30am-5pm, Sa 9:30am-noon. **ZIP code:** 33040. **Area code:** 305.

FLORIDA

 ACCOMMODATIONS. Key West is packed virtually year-round, particularly from January through March, so reserve rooms far in advance. In Old Town the multi-colored 19th-century clapboard houses capture the charming flavor of the Keys. B&Bs are the most common types of establishments, and even "reasonably priced" means over $50. Some of the guest houses in the Old Town are for gay men exclusively. *Do not park overnight on the bridges*—this is illegal and dangerous. **Key West Hostel (HI-AYH),** 718 South St., offers rooms with 6-12 beds and shared bath, as well as a common room with TV. (☎296-5719. Internet access $8 per hr. Lockers $1. Free parking and linens. Reception 24hr. Bike rentals $8 per 24hr. Reservations essential Dec.-Mar. Call to check availability or for late arrival. Dorms $18.50, nonmembers $21.50. Key deposit $5.) **Caribbean House,** 226 Petronia St., has festive Caribbean-style rooms with A/C, cable TV, free local calls, and fridge. Rooms have comfy double beds, and continental breakfast is included. (☎296-1600 or 800-543-4518. Reservations not accepted for cottages. Rooms from $49, in winter $69; cottages $69/$89.) The rooms at the **Wicker Guesthouse,** 913 Duval St., on the main drag, have pastel decor, private baths, A/C and cable TV; most have kitchenettes, but none have phones. Kitchen, pool access, free parking, and breakfast included. (☎296-4275 or 800-880-4275. Reservations recommended; ask for summer specials. Rooms $89-105; late Dec. to May $130-150.) **Eden House,** 1015 Fleming St., just 5 short blocks from downtown, is a brightly painted, Art Deco-style hotel. Clean rooms with private or shared bath. (☎296-6868 or 800-533-5397. Pool, jacuzzi, hammock area, and kitchens. Bike rentals $10 per day. Join other guests for free happy hour daily 4-5pm. Rooms with shared bath $105; off-season $80.) **Boyd's Campground,** 6401 Maloney Ave, sprawls over 12 oceanside acres and offers full facilities, including showers. Take a left off U.S. 1 onto Macdonald Ave., which becomes Maloney. (☎294-1465. $35-57; in winter $39-68 for 2 people; each additional person $8. Waterfront sites $6-14 extra. Water and electricity $10 extra, full hookup $15 extra.)

 FOOD AND NIGHTLIFE. Expensive and trendy restaurants line festive **Duval St.** Sidestreets offer lower prices and fewer crowds. **Blue Heaven,** 729 Thomas St., one block from the Caribbean House offers the best grub in town. Blue Heaven serves healthy breakfasts with fresh banana bread ($2-9), Caribbean or Mexican lunches ($2.50-10), and heavenly dinners ($9-19) that include plantains, corn bread, and fresh veggies. (☎296-8666. Open M-Sa 8am-3pm, 6-10:30pm; Su 8am-1pm, 6-10:30pm.) **Garden Cafe,** 310 Duval St., markets half-pound burgers in an outdoor paradise for $5.75. Monster portabella and veggie burgers are $6.25. (☎294-2991. Open M-F 10am-1am, Sa-Su 10am-2am. Clothing-optional.) The best Cuban fare can be found at **El Siboney,** 900 Catherine St., where $7 buys a ton of food. (☎296-4184. Open M-Sa 11am-9:30pm.)

The free *Island News,* found in local restaurants and bars, list dining spots, music, and clubs; *Celebrate!* covers the gay and lesbian community. Nightlife in Key West revs up at 11pm and winds down very late. The action centers around upper Duval St. **Capt. Tony's Saloon,** 428 Greene St., the oldest bar in Key West and reputedly one of Tennessee Williams's preferred watering holes, has been serving away since the early 30s. Bras and business cards festoon the ceiling. Tony Tarracino, the 83-year-old owner and former mayor of Key West, enters through a secret door on weekends. (☎294-1838. Live entertainment daily and nightly. Open M-Sa 10am-2am, Su noon-2am.) An unabashed meat market under the stars, **Rick's,** 202 Duval St., boasts well-placed body shots and a hot clientele. (☎296-4890. Happy hr. daily 3-6pm features $2 longneck Bud. W and Th $7 all-you-can-drink nights. Open M-Sa 11am-4am, Su noon-4am.) For a real party, with both tourists and locals, stop by **Sloppy Joe's,** 201 Duval St., undoubtedly Hemingway's favorite hangout. Grab a table and the *Sloppy Joe's News* to learn the latest on "Papa" look-alike contests and upcoming entertainment. (☎294-5717. Open M-Sa 9am-4am, Su noon-4am.) Search for your lost shaker of salt in **Margaritaville,** on Duval St., the Jimmy Buffet-inspired bar that specializes in, that's

"BRAINS DON'T MEAN SHIT" This brief profundity sums up the philosophy of Captain Tony Tarracino, gun runner, mercenary, casino owner, and one-time mayor of Key West. "All you need in this life is a tremendous sex drive and a great ego," proclaimed the Captain, who escaped to Key West over 40 years ago while evading the New Jersey bookies he cheated, having used a battered TV set to get racing results before they came over the wire. Tarracino arrived to find an island populated by bar-hoppers, petty criminals, and other deviants. In this setting, he thrived. Tony attempted to organize his local popularity into a political campaign, and after four unsuccessful bids, he was finally voted mayor in 1989, on the slogan, "Fighting for your future: what's left of it." Although he wasn't re-elected, Tarracino is certain that history will exonerate him. "I'll be remembered," he vows. With his own bar, countless t-shirts that bear his image, and even a feature film about his life, this is no idle assertion. But for now, Tony T. isn't going anywhere—he even mocks his own mortality. "I know every stripper in this town," he boasts. "When I'm dead, I've asked them all to come to my casket and stand over it. If I don't wake up then, put me in the ground."

right, margaritas. True Parrotheads may not appreciate the infestation of hundreds of tourists. (☎296-3070. Open daily 11am-2am.) Most gay clubs line Duval St. south of Fleming Ave; **801 Bourbon**, 801 Duval St., is very popular. (☎294-4737. Open daily 11am-4am.) Key West nightlife reaches its annual exultant high during **Fantasy Fest** (☎296-1817; the third week in Oct.).

🄶 **SIGHTS.** Traversing Key West by bike or moped is more convenient and comfortable than driving. For those inclined towards riding, the **Conch Tour Train**, a fascinating 1½hr. narrated ride through Old Town, leaves from Mallory Sq. at 3840 N. or from Roosevelt Blvd., next to the Quality Inn. (☎294-5161. Runs daily 9am-4:30pm. $18, ages 4-12 $9.) **Old Town Trolley** runs a similar narrated tour 9am-5:30pm, but you can get on and off throughout the day at 9 stops. (☎296-6688. Full tour 1½hr. $18, ages 4-12 $9.) The **glass-bottomed boat** *Fireball* cruises to the reefs and back at noon, 2, and 6pm. (☎296-6293. 2-2½hr. Tickets $20, at sunset $25, ages 5-12 $10/$12.50.)

No one can leave Key West without a visit to the **Ernest Hemingway Home**, 907 Whitehead St., where "Papa" wrote *For Whom the Bell Tolls* and *The Snows of Kilimanjaro*. Take a tour, or traipse through on your own among 50 descendants of Hemingway's cat, half of which have extra toes. (☎294-1136. Open daily 9am-5pm. $9, ages 6-12 $5.) A tour of the **Harry S. Truman Little White House Museum**, 111 Front St., provides a fascinating view of one of America's greatest leaders. (☎294-9911. Open daily 9am-5pm. $10, children $5. Includes tour.) The **Audubon House**, 205 Whitehead St., shelters fine antiques and a collection of original engravings by naturalist John James Audubon. (☎294-2116. Open daily 9:30am-5pm. $8, seniors $7.50, students $5, ages 6-12 $3.50.)

Down Whitehead St., past the Hemingway House, you'll come to the southernmost point in the continental US at the fittingly named **Southernmost Beach**. A small, conical monument marks the spot, along with some hustlers who might offer to take your picture; they may not give your camera back until you pay them. The **Mel Fisher Maritime Heritage Society Museum**, 200 Greene St., showcases the amazing discovery of the Spanish galleon *Atocha*, which sank off the Keys in the 17th century with hundreds of millions in gold and silver. An illuminating film is included in the entrance fee. (☎294-2633. Open daily 9:30am-5pm; last film 4:30pm. $6.75, students $5.50, ages 6-12 $3.50.)

Before the nightlife begins in Key West the sun has to go down. At the **Mallory Sq. Dock,** street entertainers (including Tomas the incredible living statue) and hawkers of tacky wares work the crowd, while boats parade in revue during the daily **Sunset Celebration.** After the sun finally slips into the Gulf, it's time to drink.

GULF COAST

TAMPA   ☎ 813

Even with year-round warm weather and perfect beaches, Tampa has managed to avoid the plastic pink flamingos that plague its Atlantic Coast counterparts. While most tourists wait on line at Busch Gardens, Tampa's main theme park, the rest of the bay city provides a less commercial vacation spot. Ybor City, Tampa's Cuban district, is a rejuvenated hotbed of culture, where the sun-bleached tourist can find most of the good restaurants, bars, and clubs. Downtown is not very inviting, but a few gems proudly display Tampa's charm.

⊞◪ ORIENTATION AND PRACTICAL INFORMATION. Tampa wraps around Hillsborough Bay and sprawls northward. **Nebraska Ave.** and **Dale Mabry Rd.** parallel **I-275** as the main north-south routes; **Kennedy Blvd., Columbus St.** and **Busch Blvd.** are main east-west arteries. With some exceptions, numbered streets run north-south and numbered avenues run east-west. **Ybor City**, Tampa's Latin Quarter and nocturnal playland, is bounded roughly by Nuccio Pkwy. on the north, 22nd St. on the south, Palm St. on the east, and 5th St. on the west. *Be careful not to stray outside these boundaries, since the area can be dangerous.* **Tampa International Airport** (☎870-8700), is located 5 mi. west of downtown. HART-line bus #30 runs between the airport and downtown Tampa. **Amtrak,** 601 Nebraska Ave. (☎221-7600; ticket office open daily 5:30am-10:45pm), at the end of Zack St., 2 blocks north of Kennedy St., runs to Miami (5hr., 1 per day, $32) and New Orleans (20hr., 3 per week, $78). **Greyhound,** 610 E. Polk St. (☎229-2174; open daily 5am-midnight), buses to Atlanta (11-14hr., 8 per day, $62.50); Orlando (1-3hr., 7 per day, $17.50); and Miami (7-10hr., 7 per day, $37). **Hillsborough Area Regional Transit (HARTline)** provides public transportation. (☎254-4278. $1.50, seniors and ages 5-17 55¢; exact change required.) The **Tampa Town Ferry** (☎223-1522) runs between the Florida Aquarium and Lowry Park Zoo. **Visitor info: Tampa/Hillsborough Convention and Visitors Association,** 111 Madison St. at Ashley Dr. (☎223-1111 or 800-826-8358; open M-Sa 9am-5pm). **Hotlines: Crisis Hotline,** ☎234-1234. **Helpline,** ☎251-4000. **Post Office:** 401. S Florida Ave. (☎800-725-2161; open 8am-5pm). **ZIP code:** 33601. **Area code:** 813.

▌ ACCOMMODATIONS. Dedicated to the art of staying young at heart, owner Mark Holland started the Gram Parsons Foundation as a way to memorialize the late 70s singer-songwriter. That dedication has turned into a bed and breakfast of the best type. **Gram's Place Bed & Breakfast/Hostel,** 3109 N. Ola Ave., occupies a refurbished train car. There's always music playing, and the outdoor jacuzzi, patio and BYOB bar add to the bohemian, eclectic attitude. If you don't bring the good times with you, they'll provide them. (☎221-0596. From I-275, take Martin Luther King Blvd. west to Ola Ave., then left on Ola. Dorms: $15 June-Nov., $25 Dec.-May. B&B theme rooms $65 June-Nov., $80 in Dec.-May; with private bath $95.) **Villager Lodge,** 3110 W. Hillsborough Ave., 5 mi. from the airport at Exit 30 off I-275, has 33 small rooms with A/C, cable, and pool access. (☎876-8673. Singles $39-45; doubles $43-48; each additional person $5.) **Super 8 Motel,** 321 E. Fletcher Ave., 3 mi. from Busch Gardens in northwest Tampa, offers clean rooms with cable TV, pool access, and breakfast; some rooms have a fridge and stove. Pool and cable. Coffee and doughnuts each morning. (☎933-4545. Singles Sa-Su $39, M-F $37; doubles $46; king size suites $55; slightly more Jan.-Mar. Students with ID 10% discount.) The rooms at the **Garden View Motel,** 2500 E. Busch Blvd., have cable, A/C, and pool access. Discount tickets to Busch Gardens are available at the front desk. (☎933-3958. Singles $30-35; doubles $40-50. Students with ID 10% discount.)

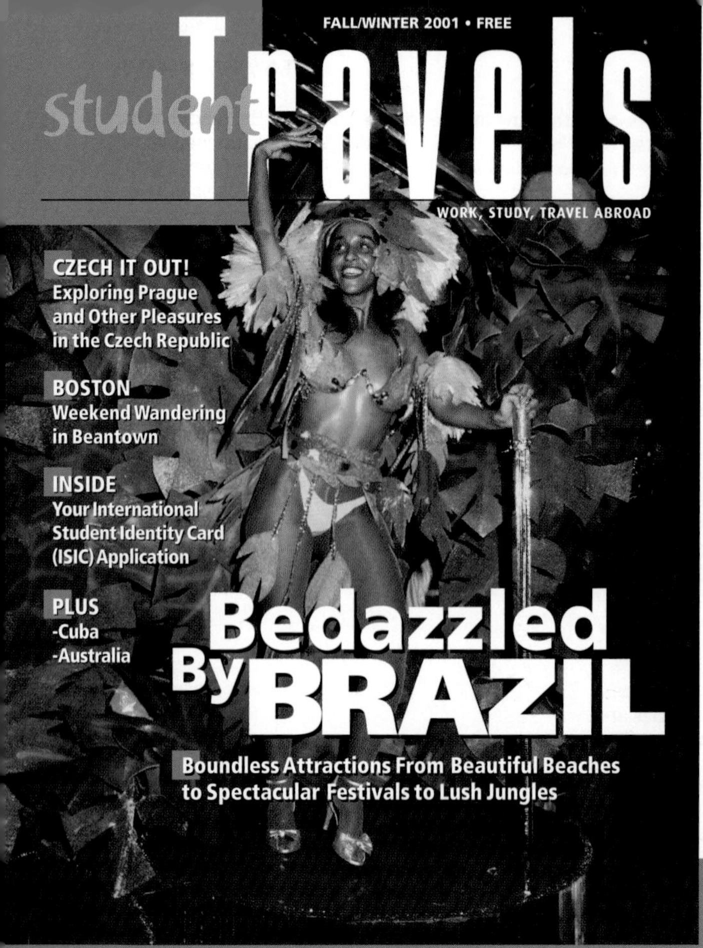

◘ **FOOD.** Tampa is blessed with many inexpensive restaurants. Heading that list is ⊠**Skipper's Smokehouse,** 910 Skipper Rd., off Nebraska Ave., a giant complex of thatched huts, wreckage, and wood planks in the northern outskirts of town. Scarf down a yummy tender fried alligator tail sandwich ($5.50). Skipper's also has a separate oyster bar and "Skipper Dome," where guests groove to blues, zydeco, reggae and worldbeat tunes—a Tampa must-see. (☎971-0666. Cover varies. Happy hr. Th-F 4-8pm. Restaurant and bar open Tu 11am-10pm, W F 11am-11pm, Sa noon-11pm, Su 1-10pm.) The original hand-rubbed marinade behind **Kojak's House of Ribs,** 2808 Gandy Blvd., reminds you that you're still in the South. (☎837-3774. Open Tu-Th 11am-9:30pm, F-Sa 11am 10pm, Su 4pm-9pm. Ribs with 2 sides $8.50.) Tampa's gulf shore heritage is evident at **Cafe Creole,** 1330 E. 9th Ave., an Ybor City joint known for oysters and jambalaya. (☎247-6283. Live jazz Th-Sa night. Happy hr. M-F 4-7pm. Open M-Th 11:30am-10pm, F 11:30am-11:30pm, Sa 5-11:30pm. Entrees $6-18.)

◙ **SIGHTS.** Tampa blossomed only after the success of Ybor City, a planned community once known as the cigar capital of the world. Early 20th-century stogie manufacturer Vincent Martínez Ybor employed a wide array of immigrants, marking the area with a rich and varied ethnic heritage. The **Ybor City State Museum,** 1818 9th Ave., details the rise and fall of the neighborhood's tobacco empire and the workers behind it. Photographs examine the art and culture of the hand-rolled cigar. (☎247-6323. Open daily 9am-5pm. Neighborhood walking tours Sa 10:30. $2, under 7 free.) A 1½hr. **Ybor City Ghostwalk** spins haunting tales about the city's history. The tour leaves from **Joffrey's Coffee Co.,** 1616 E. 7th Ave. (☎242-9255. Tours Th-Sa 7pm, Su 4pm. $11 in advance, $12.50 on site; children $7.50.) Buses #8, 3, and 46 run to Ybor City from downtown. The free Tampa-Ybor Trolley runs during lunchtime between the two areas; schedules are available at the Visitors Center.

The **Florida Aquarium,** 701 Channelside Dr., invites you to mash your face to the glass for a *tête-à-tête* with fish from Florida's various lagoons. Snakes, tarantulas, and scorpions star in the wildly creepy "Frights of the Forest" exhibit. (☎273-4000. Open daily 9:30am-5pm. $13, seniors $12, ages 3-12 $8.) A former resort hotel, Spanish-American war headquarters, and now a college administration building, the **Henry B. Plant Museum,** 401 W. Kennedy Blvd., in a wing of the University of Tampa's Plant Hall, showcases 19th-century railroad tycoon Henry Plant's lavish collection of European sculptures, paintings, and other knick-knacks. (☎254-1891. Open Tu-Sa 10am-4pm, Su noon-4pm. Free; suggested donation $5. Tours at 1:30pm.) Downtown, the **Tampa Museum of Art,** 600 N. Ashley Dr., houses a noted collection of ancient Greek and Roman works as well as a series of changing, family-oriented exhibits. (☎274-8130. Open Tu-W and F-Sa 10am-5pm, Th 10am-8pm, Su 1-5pm. Tours Th 5-8pm, Sa 10am-noon. $5, seniors $4, ages 6-18 $3. Free Su and W 5-9pm.)

It's never Miller time at **Busch Gardens,** 3000 E. Busch Blvd., Anheuser Busch's addition to the world of Floridian theme parks. The underwhelming roller coasters—Kumba, Montu, and Gwazi—mistakenly get top billing. The true highlights of this park are the wildlife exhibits. Over 2500 animals roam, fly, slither, and swim through the African-themed zoo areas; the Edge of Africa safari experience remains among the park's most popular attractions. (☎987-5082. Open daily 9:30am-7pm. $48, ages 3-9 $39. Parking $6.) The nearby **Adventure Island,** 10001 Malcolm McKinley Dr., serves as Busch Garden's water park. (☎987-5660. Open June 1 to Aug. 5 M-Th 9am-7pm, F-Su 9am-8pm. $25, ages 3-19 $23. Parking $4. Busch Gardens/Adventure Island combo ticket $60, ages 3-9 $50.)

▥▧ **ENTERTAINMENT AND NIGHTLIFE.** Brief yourself on city entertainment with the free *Tampa Weekend* or *Weekly Planet*, found in local restaurants, bars, and streetcorners; gay travelers should check out the free *Stonewall*. Every year in the first week of February, the **Jose Gasparilla** (☎358-8070), a fully-rigged pirate ship loaded with hundreds of exuberant "pirates," invades Tampa, kicking off a month of parades and festivals. The **Gasparilla Sidewalk Art Festival** (☎876-1747), awaits the gathering of worldwide talent. Thousands pack Ybor City every October for **"Guavaween"** (☎621-7121), a Latin-style Halloween celebration.

FLORIDA

With over 35 clubs and bars in a condensed area, **Ybor City** really does offer it all. Most nighttime hangouts are located on the well-lit 7th Ave. and 9th Ave.; use caution when walking down side streets. National blues, jazz, and reggae acts jam every weekend at the **Blues Ship Cafe**, 1910 E. 7th Ave. (☎248-6097. Tu open mic, W open jam. 18+. $5 cover for bands. Restaurant and bar open M-F 5pm-3am, Sa-Su 1pm-3am.) Ybor offers a diverse range of clubs. **The Castle**, 2004 N. 16th St. at 9th St., caters to the goth in you, but is open to all who enter the friendly sanctum. (☎247-7547. F-Sa goth nights, Su gay night, M 80s night. 18+. Cover $4. Open F-M 9:30pm-3am.) Spanning the pop spectrum, country line-dancing swings to everything from Alan Jackson to Puff Daddy at **Spurs**, 1915 7th Ave. (☎247-7787. Open Th-Sa 6pm-3am; free dance instructions 7-9pm.) During the week, many restaurants close at 8pm, and clubs don't open until 10pm.

ST. PETERSBURG AND CLEARWATER ☎727

Twenty-two miles southwest of Tampa, across the bay, St. Petersburg caters to a relaxed community of retirees and young singles. The town enjoys 28 miles of soft white beaches, emerald-colored and bathtub-warm water, and about 361 days of sunshine per year. The St. Petersburg-to-Clearwater stretch caters to beach bums and city strollers alike. While the outdoor scenery draws the crowds, indoor activities will captivate as well—museum exhibits on Salvador Dali and JFK rival even the most superlative of sunsets.

■ **ORIENTATION AND PRACTICAL INFORMATION.** In St. Petersburg, **Central Ave.** parallels numbered avenues running east-west in the downtown area. **34th St. (U.S. 19), I-275,** and **4th St.** are major north-south thoroughfares. The beaches line a strip of barrier islands on the far west side of town facing the Gulf. Several causeways, including the **Clearwater Memorial Causeway (Rte. 60),** access the beaches from St. Pete. Clearwater sits at the far north of the strip; **Gulf Blvd.** runs down the coastline, through Belleair Shores, Indian Rocks Beach, Indian Shores, Redington Shores, Madeira Beach, Treasure Island, and St. Pete Beach. The stretch of beach past the huge pink Don Cesar Hotel, in St. Pete Beach, and Pass-a-Grille Beach have the best sand with less pedestrian and motor traffic. **St. Petersburg Clearwater International** (☎535-7600) sits right across the bay from Tampa, off Roosevelt St. **Airport Connection Limo** (☎572-1111) runs $19 shuttles. **Greyhound,** 180 9th St. N. (☎898-1496; open daily 4:30am-11pm), in St. Pete, buses to Panama City (9-10hr., 3 per day, $62-68) and Clearwater (30min., 7 per day, $8). The Clearwater station is located at 2811 Gulf-to-Bay Blvd. (☎796-7315; open daily 6am-9pm). **Pinellas Suncoast Transit Authority (PSTA)** (☎530-9911), handles public transit. Most routes depart from Williams Park at 1st Ave. N. and 3rd St. N. (fare $1). To reach Tampa, take express bus #100X from the Gateway mall (fare $1.50). The **downtown looper** hits all the attractions, shopping centers, and hotels in downtown St. Pete for 50¢. A green trolley runs up and down the Pier (free). A 1-day unlimited bus pass is $2.50.
   Visitor info: St. Petersburg Area Chamber of Commerce, 100 2nd Ave. N. (☎821-4715). Open M-F 8am-5pm, Sa 9am-4pm, Su noon-3pm. **The Pier Information Center,** 800 2nd Ave. NE (☎821-6164), is open M-Sa 10am-8pm, Su 11am-6pm. Several downtown kiosks also provide maps and discount books. **Crisis Lines: Rape Crisis,** ☎530-7233. **Helpline,** ☎344-5555. **Florida AIDS Hotline,** ☎800-352-2437. All operate 24hr. **Post Office:** 3135 1st Ave. N., at 31st St. (☎323-6516. Open M-F 8am-6pm, Sa 8am-noon.) **ZIP code:** 37370. **Area code:** 727.

■ **ACCOMMODATIONS.** St. Petersburg and Clearwater offer two hostels, as well as many cheap motels lining **4th St. N.** and **U.S. 19** in St. Pete. Some establishments advertise singles for as little as $25, but these tend to be very worn down. To avoid the worst neighborhoods, stay on the north end of 4th St. and the south end of U.S. 19. Several inexpensive motels cluster along Gulf Blvd. on the beaches. The **Clearwater Beach International Hostel (HI-AYH),** 606 Bay Esplanade Ave., is located off Mandalay Ave. at the Sands Motel in Clearwater Beach. Rooms fit 8, but are not always very clean. The hostel features a common room with TV and a pool. (☎443-1211. Internet access $1 per 8min. Office hours 9am-noon and 5pm-9pm. Linen and key deposit $5. Dorms $13, nonmembers $14, surcharge for credit card payments. Private rooms $30-40.) Located in downtown St. Pete at the Bay Park Arms Hotel, the **St. Petersburg Youth Hostel**, 326 1st Ave. N., consists of one four-person room with private bath in a large historic hotel. (☎822-4141. Common room, TV, A/C. Youth hostel card or student ID required. Bunks $15. Also rents historic hotel rooms, with A/C and private bath, some with TV and fridge, for $39.) The **Treasure Island Motel**, 10315 Gulf Blvd., across the street from the beach, has big rooms with A/C, fridge, color TV, pull-out couch, and use of a beautiful pool. Catch dinner off a pier in back. (☎367-3055. Singles and doubles $45.) The **Grant Motel**, 9046 4th St. N., located 4 mi. north of St. Pete on U.S. 92. All rooms have A/C, fridge, and pronounced country decor, including straw hats and lacy curtains. The beautifully landscaped grounds include an outdoor pool. (☎576-1369. Reservations strongly recommended. Singles and doubles $43. Weekly apartments $37-49 per day.)

Fort De Soto County Park, 3500 Pinellas Bayway S., composed of 5 islands, has the best camping around and ranks among the best state parks in Florida. The small island centers around the old Spanish fort De Soto. (☎582-2267. 2-night min. stay, 14-day max. stay. Max. 2 sites per individual per day. Front gate locked at 9pm. Curfew 10pm. Check-out 1pm. No alcohol. $23 Aug.-Dec.; $33 Jan.-July. Reservations must be made in person either at the park office, 501 1st Ave. N., #A116, or at the Parks Dept., 631 Chestnut St. in Clearwater. Park office: ☎582-7738; open 8am-4:30pm. Parks Dept.: ☎464-3347; open 8am-5pm.)

◘ FOOD. Dockside Dave's, 13203 Gulf Blvd. S. in Madeira Beach, is one of the best-kept secrets on the islands. The half-pound grouper sandwich (market price, around $8) is simply sublime. (☎392-9399. Open M-Sa 11am-10pm, Su noon-10pm.) St. Petersburg's cheap, health-conscious restaurants cater to its retired population, and generally close by 8 or 9pm. City polls have repeatedly ranked **Tangelo's Bar and Grille**, 226 1st Ave. NE, as a top Cuban restaurant, and the polls never lie. Their imported sauce accents the $5.50 Oaxacan *mole negro* chicken breast sandwich. (☎894-1695. Open M-Sa 11am-7pm, Su seasonally.) Also in St. Pete is the **Fourth Street Shrimp Store**, 1006 4th St. N., purveyor of all things shrimp. Filling shrimp-taco salads cost $7. (☎822-0325. Open Su-Th 11am-9pm, F-Sa 11am-9:30pm.) A traditional local favorite in Clearwater Beach is **Frenchy's Cafe**, 41 Baymont St. The house specialty, boiled shrimp, comes dusted in their secret seasonings for $13. Or go for the original grouper burger ($6-7) with a variety of toppings. (☎446-3607. Open M-Th 11:30am-11pm, F-Sa 11:30am-midnight, Su noon-11pm.)

◙ SIGHTS. Grab a copy of *See St. Pete* or the *St. Petersburg Official Visitor's Guide* for the lowdown on area events, discounts, and useful maps. Downtown St. Pete is cluttered with museums and galleries that make it worth the effort to leave the beach. Relive the 60s at the ◙**Florida International Museum**, 100 2nd St. North. The brand new exhibit, **Cuban Missile Crisis: When the Cold War Got Hot**, takes visitors through a day in the life in the atomic age. **John F. Kennedy: The Exhibition**, provides a comprehensive look at JFK's personal and political life through hundreds of personal artifacts. (☎822-3693 or 800-777-9882. Open M-Sa 9am-6pm, Su noon-6pm; last tours leave by 4:30pm. $14, seniors $13, students $8, ages 6-18 $6). Melting clocks and phallic symbols mark the exhaustive ◙**Salvador Dali Museum**, 1000 3rd St. S., the largest private collection of the surrealist's work in the world. Guided tours provide some intriguing explanations of the great master's puzzling works. (☎823-3767 or 800-442-3254. Open M-W and F-Sa 9:30am-5:30pm, Th 9:30am-8pm, Su noon-5:30pm. $9, seniors $7, students $5, under 11 free.) The **Tampa Bay Holocaust Memorial Museum**, 55 5th St. S., covers pre-war Europe to the birth of Israel in the fourth-largest museum of its kind in the country. A Nazi boxcar sitting in the center atrium once transported Jews to the camps. (☎820-0110. Open M-F 10am-5pm, Sa-Su noon-5pm. $6, students and seniors $5, under 19 $2.)

FLORIDA

Beaches are the most worthwhile—but not the only—attraction for the coastline. The nicest beach may be **Pass-a-Grille Beach,** but its parking meters eat quarters for breakfast. Check out **Clearwater Beach,** at the northern end of the Gulf Blvd. strand, where mainstream beach culture is the norm in a decidedly fantastic white sand beach setting. The **Sunsets at Pier 60 Festival** (☎449-1036) brings arts and entertainment to the Clearwater Beach daily from 2hr. before sundown until 2hr. after. The **sunsets** that happen every night are perhaps the most beautiful in all of the East Coast; the blazing sun gently dips below the horizon.

◪ **NIGHTLIFE.** St. Pete caters to those who want to end the night by 9 or 10pm; most visitors and locals looking for nightlife either head to Tampa or to the beach. Clearwater hotels, restaurants, and parks often host free concerts. Free copies of *Weekly Planet* or *Tampa Tonight/Pinellas Tonight* grace local restaurants and bars. A smattering of establishments hit the bull's-eye for those looking for a night on the town. **Beach Nutts,** 9600 W. Gulf Blvd., Treasure Island, has fresh grouper ($7.25) and decent burgers ($5), but go for the ambience; the restaurant/bar's newly expanded porch has a spectacular view of the beach, and bands play nightly. (☎367-7427. Open M-Sa 11am-2am, Su 1pm-2am.) Locals wind down with a beer and a game of pool at the **Beach Bar,** 454 Mandalay Ave. If you're not in the mood for darts on the weekend, then walk around the corner to groove on their dance floor. (☎446-8866. Dancing F-Sa 9pm-2am. 21+. Bar open daily 10am-2am.) The younger crowd likes to make a dash for the mainland and party at **Liquid Blue,** 22 North Ft. Harrison St., Clearwater's premier nightspot for techno and weekly drink specials. (☎446-4000. 18+. Cover varies. Open Tu-Sa 9pm-2am.)

GAINESVILLE ☎352

Break from the beach-and-theme-park monotony at Gainesville, Florida's version of a university town. The University of Florida (UF) lends the town a notably attractive population and an air of high culture mixed with equal parts bohemian, frat house, and even Old South. From the dizzying clubs to drag racing to professional theater, Gainesville has a little of something for everyone. Located in lush North Central Florida, Gainesville and surrounding Alachua County also provide ample opportunities for the nature lover.

▣▮ **ORIENTATION AND PRACTICAL INFORMATION.** Gainesville is accessible primarily by **I-75. Main St.** divides the town into east and west, **University Avenue** (referred to locally as "The Avenue") divides it into north-south. The city follows a grid system: streets run north-south and avenues east-west. The University of Florida is located on the west side of town at the intersection of University Ave. and SW 13th St. (or **U.S. 441**). **Amtrak** stops in Waldo, 14 mi. northeast of Gainesville at an unstaffed station at U.S. 301 and State Rd. 24 (☎468-1403). One train per day runs to Miami (9hr., $29-80) and Tampa (3½hr., $19-38); pay on board. Some hotels will provide transportation from the station for a fee. **Greyhound,** 516 S.W. 4th Ave. (☎376-5252; station open M-Sa 7am-11pm, Su and holidays 10am-10pm) heads to Miami (9hr., 8 per day, $47-54); Tampa (3-5hr., 7 per day, $23-27); and Orlando (2½hr., 8 per day, $24). **Regional Transit System** runs trains and buses around the city. (☎334-2602. $1; seniors, students, and disabled 50¢; $2 buys a 1-day unlimited pass. M-F 6am-7pm, Sa-Su 7am-7pm.) Taxi: Gator Cab Co., ☎375-0313. **Visitors Center: The Alachua County Visitors and Convention Bureau:** 30 E. University Ave., downtown (☎374-5231; open M-F 8:30am-5pm); **Alachua County Official Welcome Center,** 3833 N.W. 97th Blvd., located right off I-75 at Exit 77. (☎374-5231; open daily 10am-5:30pm). **Post Office:** 401 SE 1st Ave. (☎371-7009; open M-Sa 8am-5:30pm, Sa 8am-noon). **ZIP code:** 32601. **Area code:** 352 or 904. Listings 352 unless noted.

▮ **ACCOMMODATIONS.** Plenty of motels are located right off the interstate or on 13th St., increasing in price as you approach the University of Florida. On football or Gatornationals race weekend, rates are at least double at any place you can squeeze into. The **Gainesville Lodge,** 413 W. University Rd., is a downtown steal, only a short stumble from the nightclubs. (☎376-1224. TV, A/C, and pool. Singles $36;

doubles $40.) The **Cape Cod Inn**, 3820 SW 13th St., features decor that will make New Englanders nostalgic. All rooms come with cable, pool, and continental break-fast. (☎371-2500. Singles $44; doubles $47.) An expensive and luxurious treat, the **Magnolia Plantation**, 309 SE 7th St. in downtown, is one of Florida's best B&Bs. (☎375-6653 or 800-201-2379. Rooms $90-105, cottages $150-250.) Sleep amid bona-fide Floridian flora and fauna at **Paynes Prairie State Reserve** (see **Sights,** below), 10 mi. south on U.S. 441. (15 tent and 35 RV sites with water $11, with electricity $13.)

[] FOOD. Gainesville's diverse university population seems to have one taste they agree on: cheap food. University Ave. and 13th St. hold the standard college eater-ies: cheap pizza, burger, and taco joints. **Farah's,** 1120 W. University Ave., doles out delectable Mediterranean cuisine. The *dolmathes* (rolled grape leaves stuffed with rice and meat) are unique specialties and come in either a $3.50 appetizer (6 leaves) or a $9 meal platter. (☎378-5179. Live jazz Sa 8pm. Open M-Tu 11am-10pm, W-Sa 11am-11pm.) **Leonardo's By the Slice,** 1245 W. University Ave., offers basic pastas ($4-6) and beautiful pizzas (slices $2-4), with a cafe that sells breakfasts and treats throughout the day. (☎375-2007. Open M-Th 9am-10pm, F 9am-11pm, Sa 10am-11pm, Su 11am-10pm.) To see where frantic UF students get their caffeine fix when final exams roll around, check out **Maude's Classic Cafe,** 101 S.E. 2nd Place. Imagine the "John Lennon," a large piece of lemon poppyseed cake with whipped cream for only $2.75. (☎336-9646. Open Su-W 10am-midnight, Th-Sa 10am-2am.)

⬕ SIGHTS. The town's lifeblood, The **University of Florida** provides most of the area's culture and happenings. The UF Cultural Complex, at Hull Rd. and S.W. 34th St., holds two free museums. The **Samuel P. Harn Museum of Art** displays 19th and 20th century painting and sculpture, mostly American or Caribbean. (☎392-9826. Open Tu-F 11am-5pm, Sa 10am-5pm, Su 1pm-5pm. Free.) Next door, the **Florida Museum of Natural History** has one of the largest collections of natural history arti-facts in the Southeast. (☎846-2000. Open M-Sa 10am-5pm, Su 1pm-5pm. Free.) Down Museum Rd. lies the **Bathouse.** Locals traditionally gather at sunset, turning their backs to the alligators in Lake Alice to watch the bats fly from their abode. **Ben Hill Griffin Memorial Stadium,** more commonly known as "The Swamp," hosts home football games for the school's highly successful "Fightin' Gators." The school's football program is so popular that when UF helped develop a new sports drink, it was dubbed Gatorade (☎384-3261 or 877-428-6742).

North Central Florida's natural beauty also surrounds Gainesville. Teeming with gators, wild horses, and herds of buffalo, the 21,000 acres of **Paynes Prairie State Reserve** lie 10 mi. south on U.S. 441. The natural landscape was the site of many bat-tles during the 18th-century Seminole Wars. A tower overlooks the many miles of verdant, wet prairie landscape. Hike the trail either on your own or with an expert; in the winter, park rangers lead overnight expeditions through the basin. (☎466-3397 or 466-4100 for reservations. Open daily 8am-sunset. $3.25 per car.) A big hole in the ground may not sound like interesting sightseeing but the **Devil's Millhopper State Geological Site,** 4732 NW 53rd Ave., is an anomaly worth checking out. The 120 ft. deep, 500 ft. wide natural sinkhole was named for its funnel-like shape and the discovery of fossilized bones and teeth at its bottom—legend claims bodies were once fed to the devil here. (☎955-2008. Open M-F 9am-5pm, Sa-Su 9am-sunset. $2 parking.) **Poe Springs Park,** 28800 NW 182nd Ave., just over 3 mi. west of High Springs on County Rd., is a prime picnic spot and boasts sparkling natural springs and nature trails along the Santa Fe river. (☎904-454-1992. Open 9am-dusk. $4.)

Gainesville has its share of the esoteric. **The Fred Bear Museum,** at I-75 and Archer Road, glorifies archery and bowhunting. The walls display an endless parade of stuffed animals that met the famed archer's deadly aim. (☎376-2411. Open daily 10am-6pm except holidays. $5, seniors $4, ages 6-12 $3, families $12.) The **Retire-ment Home for Horses,** Mill Creek Farm, County Rd. 235-A, in Alachua, houses over 80 equine retirees, many of which were abused or neglected by previous owners. Admission is two carrots, but the horses request as many as you can smuggle in. (☎904-462-1001. Open Sa only, 11am-3pm.)

FLORIDA

🔳🎵 ENTERTAINMENT AND NIGHTLIFE. The annual **Downtown Music Festival & Art Show** showcases the local music scene; the likes of Tom Petty and Sister Hazel hail from Gainesville. The 3-day festival features 50 bands. (☎336-8360. Early Nov.) For live tunes year-round, head to the **Gainesville Community Plaza,** E. University Ave. and S.E. 1st St., where bands play every Friday night. (☎334-5064. Shows start at 8pm. Free.) The biweekly *Moon, Gator Times,* and UF's daily *Alligator* list local events and nightlife info. Look for them at Gainesville restaurants and street corners. In March, drag racing fans flock to Gainesville for the annual **Mac Tools Gatornationals,** a series of NHRA-sponsored competitions. See all the action at the **Gainesville Raceway,** 11211 N. County Rd. 225 (☎377-0046). The pulse and mood of UF—and the town in general—rise and fall with the school's football team. Home games fill up **The Swamp** (see **Sights**), and tickets go quickly for big matchups. (☎375-4683 or 800-344-2867 for tickets and information.)

Clubs dot the intersection of W. University Ave. and 2nd St. downtown. **Orbit Lounge,** 238 W. University Ave., is the place in town for hip hop and techno, with three floors of dancing, a cigar lounge, and nightly drink specials. (☎335-9800. 18+. Cover $5. Open Th-Sa 10pm-2am.) Follow your ears to the wickedly hip **Soulhouse,** 15 S.W. 2nd Pl. and 1st St., off S. Main St. The house is a local secret known for its notorious beanbag room. (☎377-7685. Cover $5. Open M-Th 10pm-2am, F-Sa 10am-3am.) **Lush,** 6 E. University Ave., covers everything from reggae to R&B to hip hop. Thursday through Saturday guarantee drink specials and killer DJs. Make sure to wash behind the ears—a dress code is enforced. (☎381-9044. Cover varies. Open M-Sa 10pm-2am.) A supposed oyster bar turns into the place for live local bands at **Purple Porpoise,** 1728 W. University Ave., every Thursday. (☎376-1667. Open daily 11am-2am.) Another popular college club, **:08,** 201 W. University Ave., has a stuffed alligator gracing its University Ave. entrance. (☎384-0888. Open Th-Sa 9pm-2am.)

PANAMA CITY BEACH ☎850

The people in PCB are quick to say that their home isn't just a hot spring break destination for the college crowd. But don't bother coming unless you're ready to have fun, Panama City Beach-style. Suntan lotion is the perfume of choice along these miles of snow-white beach and turquoise waters of the Gulf of Mexico, billed as the "world's finest beaches." Heart of the "Redneck Riviera," PCB puts on no airs; leave those black suits and cell phones in Miami. Water parks, roller coasters, and surf shops complement the 27 miles of sandy shore.

🔳🄵 ORIENTATION AND PRACTICAL INFORMATION. After crossing Hathaway Bridge, **Front Beach Rd.** forks off from U.S. 98, (as does Thomas Dr.,) and runs along the gulf. Also known as the "Miracle Strip," Front Beach Rd. is the place to see and be seen. **Greyhound,** 917 Harrison Ave. (☎785-7861; open daily 7am-8:45pm), stops at the junction of U.S. 98 and U.S. 79 and continues on to Orlando (8-11hr., 3 per day, $62) and Atlanta (9hr., 3 per day, $51). **Bay Town Trolley,** 1021 Massalina Dr., shuttles along the beach, running M-F 6am-6pm. (☎769-0557. Fare 50¢, students and seniors 25¢; $1 to cross bridge.) **AAA Taxi:** ☎785-0533. **Yellow Cab:** ☎763-4691. **Panama City Beach Convention and Visitors Bureau:** 17001 Panama City Beach Pkwy., at corner of U.S. 98 and U.S. 79. (☎800-722-3224; www.pcbeach.com. Open daily 8am-5pm.) **Domestic Violence and Rape Crisis Hotline:** ☎763-0706. **Crisis and Mental Health Emergency Hotline:** ☎769-9481, ext. 405. Both 24hr. **Post Office:** 420 Churchwell Dr. (☎800-275-8777; open M-F 8:30am-5pm, Sa 9am-12:30pm). **ZIP code:** 32401. **Area code:** 850.

🄵 ACCOMMODATIONS. Depending on the Strip location and the time of year, rates range from can-do to outrageous. High season runs from the end of April until early September; rates drop in fall and winter. Call well in advance for summer reservations. Rates generally correspond to distance from the beach. One exception is the **Sugar Beach Motel,** 16819 Front Beach Rd., with beach access, TV and in-room movies, A/C, pools, and hot tub; kitchenettes are available. (☎800-528-1273. Singles $59-75; doubles $80-115.) **La Brisa Inn,** 9424 Front Beach Rd., ½ mi. from the beach, has clean, spacious rooms with two double beds, a pool, free cable, and coffee.

(☎235-1122 or 800-523-4369. Singles or doubles $45-79.) **Panama City Beach KOA,** 8800 Thomas Dr., two blocks south of U.S. 98 and directly across the street from the clubs, maintains 114 sites with showers, laundry, pool, cable TV, and storage. (☎234-5731 or 800-562-2483. Sites with water $20; full hookup $30; kabins $40; in winter $16/$23/$30. Reservations recommended 3 months in advance.) Or camp on the beach at **St. Andrews State Recreation Area,** 4607 State Park Ln., 3 mi. east of PCB at the east end of Thomas Dr. Call ahead (up to 60 days) for reservations at this popular campground. All 176 sites are beneath the pines and on or close to the water. (☎233-5140. Sites $17, with electricity or waterside $19; in winter $10/$12.)

◨◪ **FOOD AND NIGHTLIFE.** Buffets stuff the Strip and Thomas Dr. along the Grand Lagoon. "Early bird" specials, offered around 5pm, get you the same food at about half the price. **Scampy's,** 4933 Thomas Dr., offers seafare in a smaller, less harried atmosphere than the mega-troughs. (☎235-4209. Open M-F 11am-10pm, Sa-Su 11am-11pm. 17 different lunch specials $4-7.50, seafood salad $8, dinner entrees $11-20.) Cool off at **Sharky's,** 15201 Front Beach Rd., with a hard lemonade ($3.25). More adventurous spirits will savor their signature appetizer, "shark bites" (fried shark cubes; $7). Raw oysters go for $2 per dozen daily 4-6pm. (☎235-2420. Live performers on the beach deck most nights. Cover $8. Open daily 11:30am-11pm.)

Bars are a stumble away along the strip and Thomas Dr.; most have occasional live bands. The largest club in the US (capacity 8000) and MTV's former Spring Break headquarters, **Club LaVela,** 8813 Thomas Dr., offers eight clubs and 48 bar stations under one jammin' roof. Live bands work the Rock pavilion every night. Wet t-shirt, bikini, and male hard body contests fill the weekends and every night during Spring Break. (☎234-3866. 18+. No cover during the day; cover varies at night. Open daily 10am-4am.) Next door, **Spinnaker,** 8795 Thomas Dr., contains a family restaurant (fresh seafood $8-20), a pool deck, and a playground for kids. This enormous beach clubhouse hosts live bands throughout the week. (☎234-7882. Live music Th-F starting at 6:30pm, Sa-Su 1pm. Happy hour 9-11pm. 18+. Cover $5-10. Restaurant open daily 11am-10pm; club open daily 10pm-4am.) The back patio bar at **Harpoon Harry's,** 12627 Front Beach Rd., overlooks the beach. Build a midnight sandcastle with their famous $7.50 margarita buckets. (☎234-6060. Open daily 11am-2am.)

◨◪ **SIGHTS AND ENTERTAINMENT.** Over 1000 acres of gators, nature trails, and beaches make up the **St. Andrews State Recreation Area** (see **Accommodations,** above; open daily 8am-sunset; $4 per car). **Glass-bottom boat trips** take you on a dolphin-watching excursion and sail to Shell Island from Treasure Island Marina, 3605 Thomas Dr. (☎234-8944. 3hr. trips at 9am, 1, and 4:30pm. $15, seniors $14, under 12 $8.) Also in the Marina, the world's largest speed boat, the **Sea Screamer,** 3601 Thomas Dr., cruises the Grand Lagoon. (☎233-9107. In summer 4 cruises per day; spring and fall 2 per day; call for times. $14, ages 4-12 $8.) Sister to the Screamer is the **Sea Dragon,** an authentic pirate ship that fashions swashbucklers out of both young and old. (☎234-7400. 2hr. cruises in daytime, evening, and sunset; call ahead for times. $16, seniors $13, ages 2-14 $11.) **Miracle Strip Amusement Park** is adjacent to **Shipwreck Island Water Park,** 2000 Front Beach Rd. The largest amusement complex in northeast Florida, these parks both have a number of thrill rides and shows for those who've had enough of the beach. (Amusement park: ☎234-5810. Open summer Su-F 6-11pm, Sa 1-11:30pm; spring and fall hours vary. $16, seniors $10.75. Water park: ☎234-0368. Open summer daily 10:30am-5:30pm; spring and fall hours vary. $22.50, seniors $12.75. Admission to both parks $31.25.) An assortment of dolphin shows, parasailing outfits, and amusement parks lines **Front Beach Rd.**

PENSACOLA   ☎850

Pensacola's military-infused population and reputation for conservatism have been a part of the city's make-up since before the Civil War, when three forts on the shores of Pensacola formed a triangular defense to guard the deep-water ports. Most visitors, however, will be drawn to the area for its sugar-white beaches and the secluded, emerald waters along the Gulf Island National Seashore. For those seeking solace from sunburn, the naval aviation museum provides ample diversion.

FLORIDA

At the **Naval Aviation Museum,** inside the Naval Air Station, at Exit 2 off I-10, the excitement of more than 130 planes of past and present, dangling from the ceiling or parked within arm's reach, will have pilot wanna-bes soaring on natural highs. (☎452-3604. Open daily 9am-5pm. 1½hr. tours daily at 9:30, 11am, 1, and 2:30pm. Museum free.) For fun that doesn't involve winged killing machines, head across the Pensacola Bridge. From the Visitors Center at the **Naval Live Oaks Area,** 1801 Gulf Breeze Pkwy., relaxing paths meander through a forest originally harvested for shipbuilding. (☎934-2600. Open 8am-5:50pm.) Pay $1 to cross the bridge to Santa Rosa Island for some of the best beaches around. ◪**Fort Pickens,** where Apache leader Geronimo was once imprisoned, commands the west part of the island. A $6 fee lets you explore the ruins and sunbathe on the seashore. (Park open 7am-10pm.)

Hotels along the beach cost at least $65. Better options lie inland, north of downtown on Pensacola Blvd., near I-10 (a 15min. drive to the beach). The **Civic Inn,** 200 N. Palafox St., is near downtown and budget friendly. The rooms are clean and well-furnished. (☎432-3441. A/C, TV. Singles Su-Th $40, F-Sa $48; doubles $48/$58.) At the western edge of Santa Rosa Island, the **Fort Pickens Campground** on the Gulf Islands National Seashore offers electric ($20) and non-electric ($15) sites within walking distance of gorgeous beaches. (☎934-2622 for camping info, 800-365-2267 for reservations.) ◪**Hopkins House,** 900 Spring St., has incredibly popular, all-you-can-eat delicious family-style dinners on Tuesday and Friday evenings ($8), as well as regular lunch and breakfast specials such as biscuits, grits, and any omelette for only $3.50. (☎438-3979. Open Tu-Su 7-9:30am and 11am-2pm, Tu and F 5-7:30pm.) The owner of **King's BBQ,** 2120 N. Palafox St., built the drive-through stand (with picnic tables for those who want to sit down) with his own hands. Dinners with coleslaw, potato salad, baked beans, and bread go for $8.25, while sandwiches cost $5.25. (☎433-4479. Open M-F 10:30am-6:30pm.)

The city buttresses Pensacola Bay. **Palafox St.** and **I-110** are the main north-south byways; **Government St.** and **Main St.** run east-west. Main St. becomes **Bayfront Pkwy.** along the edge of the bay and runs over the **Pensacola Bay Bridge.** On the other side, **Pensacola Beach Rd.** leads to Santa Rosa Island and Pensacola Beach. **Amtrak,** 980 E. Heinburg St. (☎433-4966 or 800-872-7245; open M, W, F midnight-1pm; Tu and Th 5:30am-1pm; Sa 5:30am-8:30am) stops by on its east-west route between New Orleans (7hr., 3 per week, $30-65) and Orlando (13hr., 3 per week, $50-108). **Greyhound,** 505 W. Burgess Rd. (☎476-4800; open 24hr.) heads to Orlando (9hr., 7 per day, $62); Atlanta (9-14hr., 5 per day, $51); and New Orleans (4-7hr., 2 per day, $31). A **trolley** runs two lines through downtown, complete with tours; stops line Palafox St. (M-F 9am-3pm; 25¢). During the summer, two free Tiki Trolley shuttles run along the beach (F-Sa 10am-3am, Su 10am-10pm). **Taxi: Yellow Cab,** ☎433-3333. **Pensacola Convention and Visitors Bureau:** 1401 E. Gregory St., near the Pensacola Bay Bridge (☎800-874-1234; open daily 8am-5pm). **Post office:** 101 S. Palafox St. (open M-F 8am-5pm). **ZIP code:** 32501. **Area code:** 850.

GREAT LAKES

During the Ice Age, massive sheets of ice flowed from the north, carving out huge basins. These glaciers eventually receded and melted, leaving expanses of rich topsoil, numerous basin pools, and five inland seas. Together, the Great Lakes comprise 15% of the earth's drinkable freshwater supply and an invaluable network of transport arteries for the surrounding region. Lake Superior is the world's largest freshwater lake, and its unpopulated, scenic coast hosts a significant wolf population. The sports lover's paradise of Lake Michigan boasts swimming, sailing, deep-water fishing, and sand dunes. Lake Erie has suffered from industrial pollution, but due to strict regulations, this shallow lake is gradually reclaiming its former beauty. The first Great Lake to be seen by Europeans, Lake Huron is still the least developed, though not in size or recreational potential. The runt of the bunch, Lake Ontario, still covers an area larger than New Jersey.

The Great Lakes region is not all uncharted beauty—Minneapolis and St. Paul have the panache of any coastal metropolis, while Chicago dazzles visitors with world-class music, architecture, and cuisine.

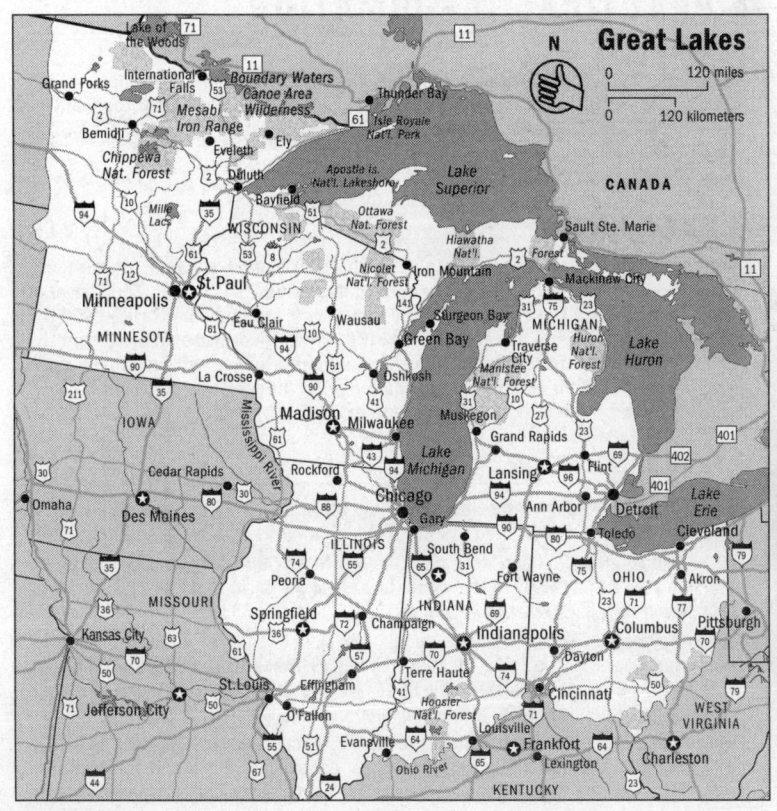

HIGHLIGHTS OF THE GREAT LAKES

FOOD. Wisconsin cheese, Chicago pizza (p. 508), "pasties" in Michigan's Upper Peninsula (p. 499), and Door County's fishboils (p. 530) are some regional specialties.

RECREATIONAL ACTIVITIES. Canoeing and kayaking are popular in the northern reaches of the Great Lakes; Grand Traverse Bay (p. 496) is an recreation hot spot.

SCENIC VISTAS. Reach the top of the Log Slide in MN (p. 501) or the Dune Climb in MI (p. 496), and you'll never want to come down.

SCENIC DRIVES. In MI, see the Lake Michigan shore on U.S. 31 and Rte. 119 (p. 498); Brockway Mountain Dr. (p. 502); or the dirt roads of Pictured Rocks State Park (p. 501). In MN, drive Rte. 61 N from Duluth along the Lake Superior shore (p. 545).

OHIO

The glaciers that carved out the Great Lakes flattened the northern half of Ohio, creating the state's perfect farmland now patched with cornfields and soybean plants. The southern half, spared the bulldozing, rolls with endless wooded hills. The strikingly similar cities of Cincinnati, Cleveland, and Columbus, combined with unending farms and friendly small towns such as Oberlin, give Ohio its cheerfully acknowledged "Middle American" status.

⚡ PRACTICAL INFORMATION

Capital: Columbus.

Visitor Info: State Office of Travel and Tourism, 77 S. High St., 29th fl., Columbus 43215 (☎614-466-8844; www.ohiotourism.com). Open M-F 8am-5pm. **Ohio Tourism Line** (☎800-282-5393). **Division of Parks and Recreation,** Fountain Sq., Columbus 43224 (☎614-265-7000).

Postal Abbreviation: OH. **Sales Tax:** 5.75%.

CLEVELAND   ☎216

The city formerly known as the "Mistake on the Lake" has undertaken an extensive facelift in recent years in an attempt to correct its beleaguered image. The arrival of the Rock and Roll Hall of Fame and three new sports stadiums has brightened the previously bleak visage of abandoned urbanity. Now, the downtown area is on the verge of flourishing, but Cleveland's outlying neighborhoods still face many challenges. Cleveland itself will remain a challenge for budget travelers until a new downtown hostel, scheduled for completion in 2003, opens up.

🚌 TRANSPORTATION

Airport: Cleveland Hopkins International (☎265-6030), 10 mi. southwest of downtown in Brook Park. RTA line #66X "Red Line" to Terminal Tower $1.50. Taxi to downtown $20.

Trains: Amtrak, 200 Cleveland Memorial Shoreway NE (☎696-5115), across from Brown Stadium east of City Hall. To: New York City (12hr., 1 per day, $104-128); Chicago (7hr., 3 per day, $75-92); and Pittsburgh (3hr., 2 per day, $33-40). Open 24hr.

Buses: Greyhound, 1465 Chester Ave. (☎781-1841), at E. 14th St., 7 blocks from Terminal Tower. Near RTA bus lines. To: New York City (9-14hr., 12 per day, $83); Chicago (5¼-7½hr., 16 per day, $44); Pittsburgh (2½-4½hr., 12 per day, $24); and Cincinnati (4½-6½hr., 12 per day, $40). Most eastbound buses stop over in Pittsburgh.

Public Transit: Regional Transit Authority (RTA), 315 Euclid Ave. (☎621-9500, TDD 781-4271; open M-F 6:30am-6:30pm). Bus lines, connecting with Rapid Transit trains, travel from downtown to most of the metropolitan area. Service daily 5am-midnight; call for info on "owl" after-midnight service. Train fare $1.50. Bus fare $1.25, express $1.50, downtown loop 50¢, 1-day pass $4; ask the driver for free transfer tickets. The **Waterfront Line** serves the Science Center, Rock and Roll Hall of Fame, and the Flats.

Taxis: Americab, ☎429-1111.

✦🔁 ORIENTATION AND PRACTICAL INFORMATION

Terminal Tower in **Public Sq.** cleaves the city into east and west. Many street numbers correspond to the distance of the street from Terminal Tower; e.g., E. 18th St. is 18 blocks east of the Tower. To reach Public Sq. from **I-90** or **I-71,** follow the Ontario Ave./Broadway exit. From **I-77,** take the 9th St. exit to Euclid Ave., which runs into Public Sq. **The Flats,** along both banks of the Cuyahoga River, and **Coventry Rd.** in Cleveland Heights are the happenin' spots for food and nightlife.

Visitor Info: Cleveland Convention and Visitors Bureau, Tower City Center (☎621-4110 or 800-321-1001), 1st fl. of Terminal Tower at Public Sq. Open M-F 10am-4pm.

Internet access: Cleveland Public Library, 525 Superior Ave (☎623-2904). 15min. limit. Open M-Sa 9am-6pm, Su 1-5pm; closed Su in summer.

Hotline: Rape Crisis Line, ☎619-6192 or 619-6194. Operates 24hr.

Post Office: 2400 Orange Ave. (☎443-4494; after 5pm 443-4096). Open M-F 7am-8:30pm, Sa 8:30am-3:30pm. **ZIP code:** 44101. **Area code:** 216; 440 or 330 in suburbs. In text, 216 unless otherwise noted.

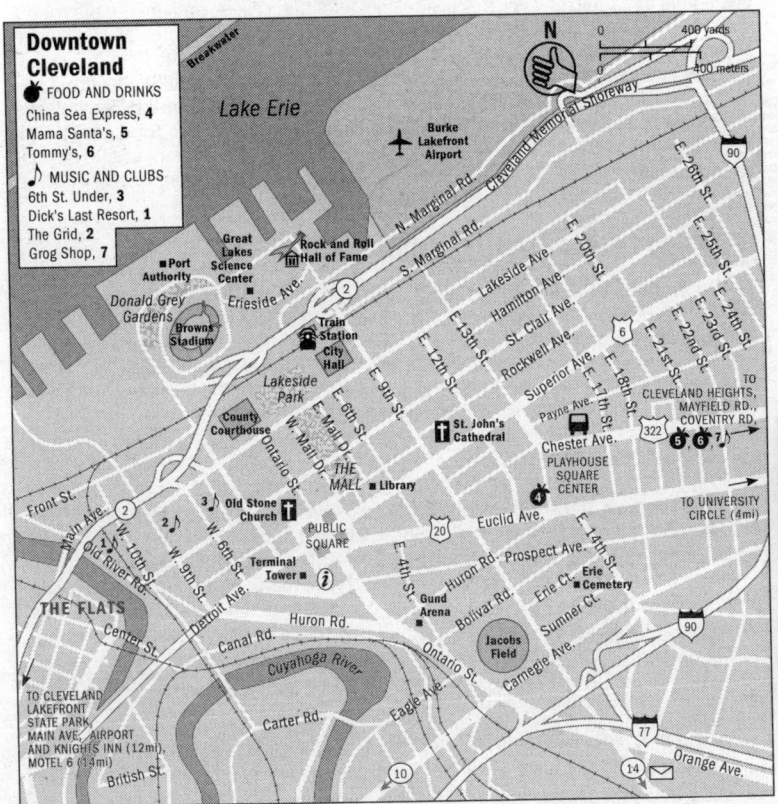

ACCOMMODATIONS

With hotel taxes (not included in the prices listed below) as high as 14.5%, budget lodging pickings are slim in Cleveland. So-called "budget" motels tend to run at least $60. **Cleveland Private Lodgings,** P.O. Box 18557, Cleveland 44118, will place you in a home around the city for as little as $45. (☎321-3213. Call M-F 9am-noon or 3-5pm. Allow 2-3 weeks for a letter of confirmation or earlier by email.) Travelers with cars might consider staying in the suburbs or near the airport, where prices tend to be lower, or heading south to the **Cuyahoga Valley National Park** (see p. 476), where hosteling and camping are options. Off Exit 235 on I-71, 15 mi. southwest of the city, **Motel 6,** 7219 Engle Rd., has comfy rooms with cable TV and A/C. (☎440-234-0990. Singles $46, F-Sa $56; doubles $52/$62.) Close to the airport, **Knights Inn,** 22115 Brookpark Rd., Exit 9 off I-480, has standard motel rooms. Take the first two rights after the freeway. (☎440-734-4500. Singles $45; doubles $55. Must be 21+.)

FOOD

The delis downtown satiate most hot corned beef cravings, but Cleveland has more to offer elsewhere. A healthy dose of hipness infuses the shops near **Coventry Rd.** in Cleveland Heights. Italian cafes and restaurants cluster in Little Italy, around **Mayfield Rd.** Seafood and standard pub fare are abundant in **the Flats.** Over 100 vendors hawk produce, meat, and cheese at the old-world style **West Side Market,** 1979 W. 25th St., at Lorain Ave. (☎771-8885. Open M and W 7am-4pm, F-Sa 7am-6pm.)

Tommy's, 1824 Coventry Rd. in Cleveland Heights, up the hill from University Circle, whips up tantalizing veggie cuisine, like a falafel, veggie, and cheese pie for $5. Take bus #9X east to Mayfield and Coventry Rd. (☎321-7757. Open M-Th 7:30am-10pm, F-Sa 7:30am-11pm, Su 9am-10pm.) **Mama Santa's,** 12305 Mayfield Rd., in Little Italy just east of University Circle, serves generous portions of Sicilian food in a no-frills setting. (☎231-9567. Open M-Th 11am-10:45pm, F-Sa 11am-11:45pm; closed most of Aug. Lasagna and *cavatelli* with meatballs both $7.) For good, cheap Chinese food downtown, the **China Sea Express,** 1507 Euclid Ave., offers an all-you-can-eat lunch buffet for $5.75, including soup, salad, and an assortment of other dishes. (☎861-0188. Open Su-Th 11am-9pm, F-Sa 11am-10pm.)

SIGHTS AND OUTDOORS

The aspirations of a new Cleveland are revealed in the made-over downtown—a self-declared "Remake on the Lake." The **Rock and Roll Hall of Fame,** 1 Key Plaza, is a dizzying exploration of the rock music world where one can listen to hundreds of history-making tunes while reveling in the fashion sense of rock stars, from Jim Morrison's scout uniform to Elvis's sequined capes. (☎781-7625. Open daily 10am-5:30pm, W until 9pm. $15, seniors and ages 9-11 $11.50. $5 W after 6pm.) Next door, the **Great Lakes Science Center,** 601 Erieside Ave., holds doodads and gizmos galore. (☎694-2000. Open Su-Th 9:30am-5:30pm, Sa 9:30am-6:45pm. $8, seniors $7, ages 3-17 $6; with IMAX $11/$10/$8. Parking for Hall of Fame and Science Center $7.) **Cleveland Lakefront State Park,** accessible via Lake Ave., Cleveland Memorial Shoreway, or Lakeshore Blvd., is a 14 mi. park near downtown with beaches and great picnic areas. (☎881-8141. Open daily 6am-11pm. Everett Beach closes at dusk.)

Seventy-five cultural institutions cluster in **University Circle,** a micro-Smithsonian 4 mi. east of the city. The world-class **Cleveland Museum of Art,** 11150 East Blvd., exhibits a survey of art from the Renaissance to the present, with exceptional collections of Impressionist and modern art. (☎421-7340. Open Su 10am-5pm; Tu, Th, and Sa 10am-6pm; W and F 10am-9pm. Free.) Nearby, the **Cleveland Museum of Natural History,** 1 Wade Oval Dr., displays the only existing skull of the fearsome dinosaur Pygmy Tyrant *(Nanatyrannus)* and one freaky-looking Ohio mastodon. (☎231-4600. Open M-Sa 10am-5pm, Su noon-5pm. $6.50; students, seniors, and ages 7-18 $4.50; ages 3-6 $3.50.) The lovely, stream-laden **Cleveland Botanical Garden,** 11030 East Blvd., provides a peaceful respite from the urban decay that haunts much of the city. (☎721-1600. Open Apr.-Oct. until dusk.) The **Cleveland Orchestra**, 11001 Euclid Ave., one of the nation's best, performs at Severance Hall. (☎231-7300. Box office open Sept.-May M-F 9am-6pm, Sa 10am-6pm. Tickets from $25.)

🎵🎭 ENTERTAINMENT AND NIGHTLIFE

Baseball's **Cleveland Indians** (☎420-4200) hammer the hardball at **Jacobs Field**, 2401 Ontario St. Tickets are difficult to get; the best bet is a 1hr. **stadium tour**. (☎241-8888 for tickets. May-Sept. every 30min. M-Sa 10am-2pm, June-Aug. Su noon-2:30pm when the team is away. $6, seniors and under 15 $4.) The **Cleveland Cavaliers** (☎420-2000) run the ball around **Gund Arena**, 1 Center Ct. (Nov.-Apr.), as do their female colleagues, the WNBA **Cleveland Rockers** (June-Aug.).

Playhouse Square Center, 1519 Euclid Ave. (☎771-4444), a 10min. walk east of Terminal Tower, is the second-largest performing arts center in the US. Inside, the **State Theater** hosts the **Cleveland Opera** (☎575-0900) and the renowned **Cleveland Ballet** (☎426-2500) from October to June. The **Cleveland Cinematheque** (☎421-7450), at the Institute of Art, screens offbeat and foreign films for $6.

Most of Cleveland's nightlife is focused in **the Flats**. **Dick's Last Resort**, 1096 Old River Rd., hosts cover bands that rock the crowds with hits from the 50s, 60s, 70s, and 80s Thursday through Saturday nights, while a swing band plays Sundays. (☎241-1234. Open M-Th 11am-1am, F-Sa 11am-2am, Su 10am-11pm.) **6th St. Under**, 126 W. 6th St., hosts jazz and R&B jam sessions in one of the most chill downtown venues. (☎589-9313. Live music Th-Sa. Open Tu-Th 5pm-12:30am, F 5pm-2:30am, Sa 9pm-2:30am, Su 8:30pm-2:30am.) Punk rock and grunge fans head for the **Grog Shop**, 1765 Coventry Rd. in Cleveland Heights, for local and national acts. (☎321-5588. Open M-Sa 7pm-2am, Su 2pm-2am.) Gays and lesbians frequent **The Grid**, 1281 W. 9th St., with a comfortable bar and a high-tech dance floor. (☎623-0113. Male strippers W, F-Su. Open M-Sa 5pm-2:30am, Su 4pm-2:30am.) For info on clubs and bands, pick up a copy of *Scene* or the *Free Times*. The *Gay People's Chronicle* and the biweekly *Out lines* are available at gay clubs, cafes, and bookstores.

🔷 DAYTRIPS FROM CLEVELAND

CEDAR POINT AMUSEMENT PARK

Recently declared "best amusement park in the world" by *Amusement Today*, Cedar Point Amusement Park off U.S. 6, 65 mi. west of Cleveland in Sandusky, earns its superlatives. The world's highest and fastest inverted roller coasters (riders are suspended from above), a "training coaster", and the brand new **Millennium Force** (310 ft., 90 mph) offer a grand old adrenaline rush for all. Patriotic laser light shows take to the sky in summer at 10pm. (☎419-627-2350 or 800-237-8386. Open June-Aug. daily 10am-11pm; Sept. to early Oct. hours vary. $39, seniors $23, children under 4 or shorter than 4 ft. $15. Parking $7.)

SEA AND INVENTURE

The **Marine Park** at **Six Flags**, 1100 Sea World Dr., 30 mi. south of Cleveland off Rte. 43 in Aurora, presents Shark Encounter, penguins, and wet, crowd-pleasing shows. (☎330-995-2121. Open mid-June to late Aug. daily 10am-10pm; mid-May to mid-June 10am-7pm; late Aug. to late Oct. 10am-8pm. Adults and those over 4 ft. $40, under 4 ft. $20. Parking $8.) Innovative juices flow at **Inventure Place** and the **National Inventor's Hall of Fame**, 221 S. Broadway in Akron, 35 mi. south of Cleveland. Adults will find several levels of exhibits celebrating famous inventors, while children and the young at heart will delight in the hands-on inventing workshops on the ground floor. (☎762-6565 or 800-968-4332. Open Tu-Sa 9am-5pm, Su noon-5pm; Sept.-Mar. W-Sa 9am-5pm, Su noon-5pm. $7.50, seniors, students, and children $6.)

FOOTBALL HALL OF FAME

The **Pro Football Hall of Fame**, 2121 George Halas Dr. NW in Canton, 60 mi. south of Cleveland, honors the pigskin greats. O.J. Simpson's jersey and helmet are displayed, but not his glove. (☎330-456-8207. Take Exit 107A from I-77. Open daily 9am-8pm; early Sept. to late May 9am-5pm. $12, seniors $8, ages 6-14 $6.)

GREAT LAKES

CUYAHOGA VALLEY NATIONAL PARK ☎ 330

Just 10 mi. south of Cleveland lies the northern edge of the surprisingly scenic **Cuyahoga Valley National Park,** established by Congress first as a National Recreation Area in the face of looming development in 1974 and then adopted as a National Park in 2000. The **Cuyahoga River,** which once caught fire during the height of Cleveland's pollution woes a few decades ago, winds 22 mi. through the dense forests and open farmland of the park, passing stables, aqueducts, and mills along the way. The best way to see the soothing natural beauty of the park is by hiking or biking its long trails. The **Ohio & Erie Canal Towpath Trail** runs through shaded forests and past the numerous locks used in the canal during its heyday. For some wheels, go to **Century Cycles,** 1621 Main St. in Peninsula, which rents bikes for $5 per hr. (☎657-2209. Open M-Th 10am-8pm, F-Sa 10am-6pm, Su 10am-5pm.) At **Hale Farm & Village,** 2686 Oak Hill Rd., 2 mi. south of Peninsula, role-playing artisans and farmers help recreate the rustic frontier life of 1848. (☎666-3711. Open June-Oct. M-Sa 10am-5pm, Su 12-5pm. $12, seniors $10, ages 3-12 $7.) **Beaver Marsh** was once an auto salvage yard until beavers built a dam and changed the environment into a flourishing swamp. To see the park by rail, hop on the **Cuyahoga Valley Scenic Railroad,** which runs several excursions along the river's banks, from Peninsula, Independence, and Akron. (☎657-2000. Closed Jan. $11-20, seniors $10-18, children $7-12. Call ahead for reservations.) The park also has a few seasonal attractions. In the summer, the **Cleveland Orchestra** performs evening concerts at the **Blossom Music Center,** 1145 W. Steels Corners Rd. in Cuyahoga Falls, a few mi. south of the park. (☎920-8040. Lawn seating $20-50.) In winter, **Boston Mills/Brandywine Ski Resorts** (☎467-2242) offers 16 lifts, snow tubing, and night skiing on both sides of the Cuyahoga.

The genteel ▓**Stanford House Hostel (HI-AYH),** 6093 Stanford Rd. in Boston, is the best accommodations option both in the park and in Cleveland. The spacious hostel was built as a farmhouse in 1843 by George Stanford. Explore the hiking and biking trails nearby. From Exit 12, turn right onto Boston Mills Rd., drive about 5 mi., then turn right on Stanford Rd. (☎467-8711. Call ahead. 7-night max. stay. Linen $2. Laundry $1.75. Check-in 5-10pm. Check-out 9am. Curfew 11pm. 4-bed dorms and a smattering of family and private rooms. Dorms $14, under 18 $7.) **Tamsin Park,** 5000 Akron-Cleveland Rd., 3 mi. south of Boston in Peninsula, offers the only **camping** around. (☎656-2859. Open May to Oct. 1. Sites $24, with hookup $30.)

The village of Peninsula serves as the center of the park, and is home to most of its restaurants. **Fisher's Cafe and Pub,** 1607 Main St., serves delicious pancakes and $3-6 breakfast specials. (☎657-2651. Open M-Th 8am-10pm, F-Sa 8am-midnight, Su 8am-9pm.) **Tommy's Drive-In & Dairy Whip,** 1208 Aurora Rd., a few mi. east of the park in Macedonia, delivers the pleasing Tommyburger (with Tommy's own special sauce) and creamy $1.50 milkshakes. (☎467-1004. Open in summer M-Sa 11am-10pm, Su noon-10pm; in spring and fall closes at 9pm.) The Park Service operates three Visitors Centers, including the Depression-era **Happy Days Visitor Center,** on Rte. 303, off Rte. 8 in Peninsula. (☎650-4636. Open daily 8am-5pm; closed M-Tu in winter.) **Post Office:** 1921 Bronson Ave., off Rte. 303 in Peninsula. (☎657-2500. Open M-F 8am-5pm, Sa 8am-noon.) **ZIP code:** 44264. **Area code:** 330.

COLUMBUS ☎ 614

Rapid growth, a huge suburban sprawl, and some gerrymandering have nudged Columbus's population beyond that of Cincinnati or Cleveland. The main drag, High St., heads north from the towering office complexes of downtown to the lively galleries in the Short North. It ends in the collegiate cool of Ohio State University (OSU), America's largest university with over 60,000 students. Columbus is America without glitz, fame, pretentiousness, smog—the clean, wholesome land of *Family Ties.* Bexley, a city suburb, was the model for the hit sitcom's setting.

▓▐ ORIENTATION AND PRACTICAL INFORMATION. Columbus, a planned capital city, is laid out in an easy grid. High St., running north-south, and Broad St., running east-west, are the main thoroughfares, dividing the city into quadrants.

Greyhound, 111 E. Town St. (☎221-2389 or 800-231-2222), offers service from downtown to Cincinnati (2hr., 13 per day, $17); Cleveland (3hr., 12 per day, $18); and Chicago (7-10hr., 7 per day, $47.50). The **Central Ohio Transit Authority (COTA),** 177 S. High St., runs in-town transportation until 11pm or midnight, depending on the route. (☎228-1776. Open M-F 8:30am-5:30pm. $1.10, express $1.50.) **Taxi: Yellow Cab,** ☎444-4444. **Greater Columbus Visitors Center,** 111 S. 3rd St., on the 2nd fl. of City Center Mall. (☎221-6623 or 800-345-4386. Open M-F 8am-5pm.) **Post Office:** 850 Twin Rivers Dr. (☎469-4521. Open M-F 7am-8pm, Sa 8am-2pm.) **ZIP code:** 43216. **Area code:** 614.

▛▞ ACCOMMODATIONS AND FOOD. The **Heart of Ohio Hostel (HI-AYH),** 95 E. 13th Ave., 1 block from OSU, offers quality facilities (including a piano) and loans out bikes to guests. Stay free if you put on a 1hr. concert. (☎294-7157. Check-in 7:30-9:30am and 5-10pm. Lockout 9:30am-5pm. Dorms $14, nonmembers $17; 4 nights for $50.) **Motel 6,** 5910 Scarborough Dr., 20min. from downtown off I-70 at Exit 110A, has what you'd expect. (☎755-2250. Singles $37-45; $6 per each additional adult.) More standard motels are located around the same area.

High St. features a variety of tasty budget restaurants. The **J&G Diner,** 733 N. High St., serves filling Belgian waffles ($4) and "hippie" or "rabbi" omelettes ($7) amid evocative paintings of a green-clad Cinderella figure. (☎294-1850. Open M-F 10am-10pm, Sa-Su 9am-10pm.) **Bernie's Bagels and Deli,** 1896 N. High St., has healthy $3-5 sandwiches. (☎291-3448. Open M-Sa 10am-2am, Su 5pm-2am.) **La Bamba,** 1980 N. High St., is the colorful home of the $5.65 burrito "Bigger Than Your Head." The proof is on the wall—a picture of the OSU football team in which each player sports a burrito for a head. (☎294-5004. Open Tu-Sa 11am-3am, Su-M 11am-midnight.)

◙ SIGHTS. Ohio State University (OSU) rests 2 mi. north of downtown. **The Wexner Center for the Arts,** N. High St. by 15th Ave., was controversial modernist architect Peter Eisenman's first public building. The four galleries display avant-garde art in all media, and the performance spaces host dance, music, and theater productions. (☎292-3535. Exhibits open Tu-W and F-Sa 10am-6pm, Th 10am-9pm, Su noon-6pm. $3, students and seniors $2; Free Th 5-9pm. Wheelchair accessible.) The **Columbus Museum of Art,** 480 E. Broad St., hosts Impressionist and European Modernist works. (☎221-6801. Open Tu-W and F-Su 10am-5:30pm, Th 10am-8:30pm. $6, seniors and students $4, under 5 free; Free Th 5-8:30pm.) Fire, water, explosions, nylon mittens, uranium, and kids add up to some good ol' fun at the **Center of Science and Industry (COSI),** 333 W. Broad St. (☎288-2674; open daily 10am-5pm; $12, seniors $10, ages 2-12 $7; wheelchair accessible.) Several blocks east is the very first link in the **Wendy's** restaurant chain (see graybox, p. 478). Nearby, James Thurber's childhood home, the **Thurber House,** 77 Jefferson Ave., off E. Broad 1 block west of I-71, is decorated with drawings by the famous author. (☎464-1032. Open daily noon-4pm. Free. Tours Su $2, students and seniors $1.50.)

For some good Germanica, march down to the **German Village,** south of Capitol Sq. This area, first settled in 1843, is now the largest privately funded historical restoration in the US, full of stately homes and beer halls. At **Schmidt's Sausage Haus,** 240 E. Kossuth St., traditional German oompah bands Schnickel-Fritz, Schnapps, and Squeezin' 'n' Wheezin' lead polkas at 7pm. Between dances, *lederhosen*-clad servers will bring you an $8.50 plate of homemade sausage. (☎444-6808. Polkas W-Th at 7pm and F-Sa at 8pm in summer; no W show in winter. Open Su-M 11am-9pm, Tu-Th 11am-10pm, F-Sa 11am-11pm.) You can grab free samples at **Schmidt's Fudge Haus,** one block west of the Sausage Haus (☎444-9217; call for hours). The **German Village Society Meeting Haus,** 588 S. 3rd St., knows all. (☎221-8888. Open M-F 9am-4pm, Sa 10am-2pm. Open M-Sa noon-9pm, Su noon-6pm; shorter hours in winter.) Ask about **Oktoberfest,** for some reason held in early September.

▟▞ ENTERTAINMENT AND NIGHTLIFE. Four free weekly papers available in shops and restaurants—*The Other Paper, Columbus Alive, The Guardian,* and *Moo*—list arts and entertainment options. The **Clippers,** a minor league affiliate of the NY Yankees, swing away from April to early September. (☎462-5250. Tickets $5-

AMERICAN BEEFCAKE When R. David Thomas was a boy, he held the cartoon character Wimpy close to his heart. A character on *Popeye*, Wimpy spent every episode incessantly gobbling hamburgers. In doing so, he cut an inspiring figure for the future fast-food entrepreneur. Born in 1932, Dave Thomas spent his early childhood in Atlantic City, dropping out of high school in 10th grade to pursue his culinary dreams. In 1969, he opened the **first Wendy's restaurant** in Columbus. From there, the freckled face and red pigtails of his daughter spread across the US like a midwest prairie fire. Today, Wendy's is an international fast-food chain, and Dave Thomas is a multimillionaire who hasn't forgotten his humble beginnings; he still loves to play the part of Wimpy, slipping out of meetings to devour a quick burger...or three.

8.) The eccentric **Gallery V,** 694 N. High St., exhibits contemporary paintings, sculptures, and works in less common media. (☎228-8955. Open Tu-W and F-Sa noon-6pm, Th noon-9pm; in winter Tu-Sa 11am-5pm.)

When you overdose on art, Columbus has a sure cure: rock 'n' roll. Bar bands are a Columbus mainstay; it's hard to find a bar that doesn't have live music on the weekend. Bigger national acts stop at the **Newport,** 1722 N. High St. (☎228-3580. Tickets $5-40.) A famed chocolate martini and a lively, crowded atmosphere highlight the **Union Station Video Cafe,** 630 N. High St., which entertains a primarily gay crowd. (☎228-3740 or 228-3546. Show tunes Su 6pm. Beers $2.50-3.50. Open daily 11am-2:30am.) A few blocks south from that hip joint is the **Brewery District,** where barley and hops have replaced the coal and iron of the once industrial area.

NEAR COLUMBUS

A 1hr. drive south of Columbus, the area around **Chillicothe** (pronounce *CHILL-i-cozy* with a lisp) features several interesting attractions. The **Hopewell Culture National Historical Park,** 16062 Rte. 104, swells with 23 enigmatic Hopewell burial mounds spread over 13 acres, with a museum that theorizes about the mounds' configuration. (☎740-774-1126. Museum open daily 8:30am-6pm; Sept.-May 8:30am-5pm. Grounds open dawn to dusk. $4 per car, $2 per pedestrian.) From mid-June to early September, the Sugarloaf Mountain Amphitheater, on the north end of Chillicothe off Rte. 23, presents **Tecumseh,** a drama re-enacting the life and death of the Shawnee leader. A behind-the-scenes tour will answer questions about how the stunt men dive headfirst off the 21 ft. cliff. (Shows M-Sa 8pm. $14, F-Sa $16; under 10 $6 everyday. Tour every hr. 2-5pm $3.50, children $2.) **Scioto Trail State Park,** 10 mi. south of Chillicothe off U.S. 23, has walk-in **camping** across from Stuart Lake. (☎740-663-2125. Sites $9, with electricity $13.)

CINCINNATI   ☎513

Longfellow called it the "Queen City of the West." Founded by German pig salesmen, Cincinnati has also earned the less regal nickname of "Porkopolis." Located just across the Ohio River from Kentucky, Cincinnati has the feel—and sometimes the accent—of a Southern city. Its stellar ballet, world-class zoo, and one-of-a-kind chili make it a highlight of the region, drawing travelers from all over.

▐ TRANSPORTATION

Airport: Greater Cincinnati International (☎859-767-3151), in Kentucky, 12 mi. south of Cincinnati and accessible by I-75, I-71, and I-74. **Jetport Express** shuttles to downtown (☎859-767-3702; $12, $16 round-trip), or call the **Transit Authority of Northern Kentucky (TANK)** (☎859-331-8265) for alternate shuttling info.

Trains: Amtrak, 1301 Western Ave. (☎651-3337), in Union Terminal. To Indianapolis (4hr., 1 per day, $19-35) and Chicago (8-9hr., 1 per day, $19-36). Open M-F 9:30am-5pm and Tu-Su 11pm-6:30am. *Avoid the area to the north, especially Liberty St.*

GREAT LAKES

Buses: Greyhound, 1005 Gilbert Ave. (☎352-6012), past the intersection of E. Court and Broadway. To: Louisville, KY (2hr., 10 per day, $21); Cleveland (4-6hr., 10 per day, $40); and Columbus (2hr., 11 per day, $17). Open 24hr.

Public Transit: Cincinnati Metro and **TANK,** both in the bus stop in the Mercantile Center, 115 E. 5th St. (☎621-9450; open M-F 8am-5pm). Most buses run out of Government Sq., at 5th and Main St., to outlying communities. In summer 50¢, in winter 65¢, winter rush-hour 80¢; extra to suburbs. Office has schedules and info.

Taxi: Yellow Cab, ☎241-2100.

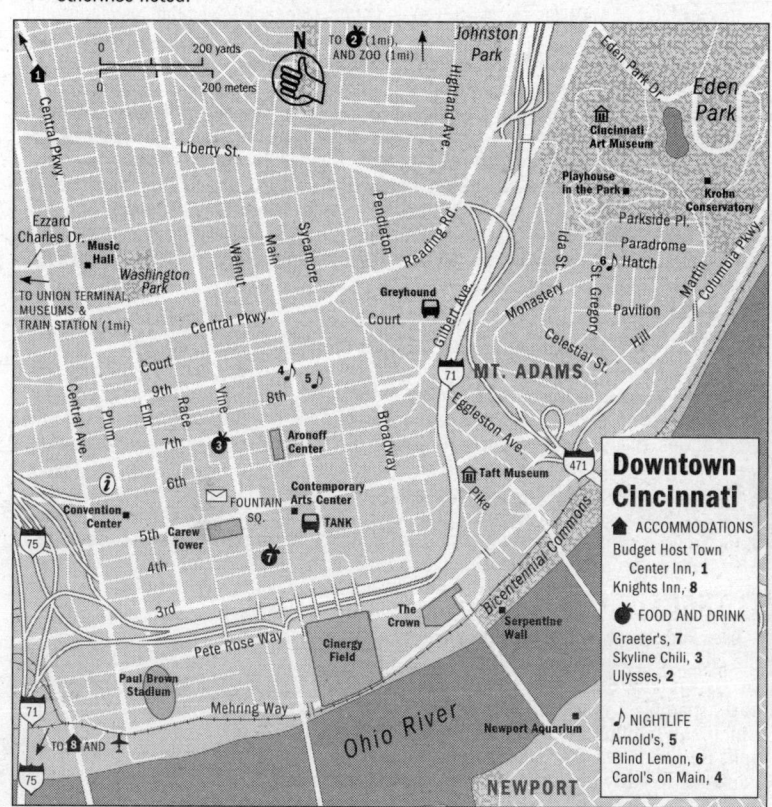 ORIENTATION AND PRACTICAL INFORMATION

The downtown business district is a simple grid centered around **Fountain Sq.,** at **5th** and **Vine St.** Cross streets are numbered and designated E. or W. by their relation to Vine St. The **University of Cincinnati** spreads out from Clifton, the area north of the city. **Cinergy Field,** the **Serpentine Wall,** and the **Riverwalk,** all to the south, border the river that marks the Ohio and Kentucky divide.

Visitor Info: Cincinnati Convention and Visitors Bureau, 300 W. 6th St. (☎621-2142 or 800-246-2987). Open M-F 9am-5pm. **Info Booth** in Fountain Sq. has limited offerings. Open M-Sa 9am-5pm.

Hotlines: Rape Crisis Center, 216 E. 9th St. (☎872-9259), downtown. 24hr. **Gay/Lesbian Community Switchboard,** ☎591-0222.

Post Office: 525 Vine St. (☎684-5667), on the Skywalk. Open M-F 8am-5pm, Sa 8am-1pm. **ZIP code:** 45202. **Area codes:** 513; Kentucky suburbs 859. In text, 513 unless otherwise noted.

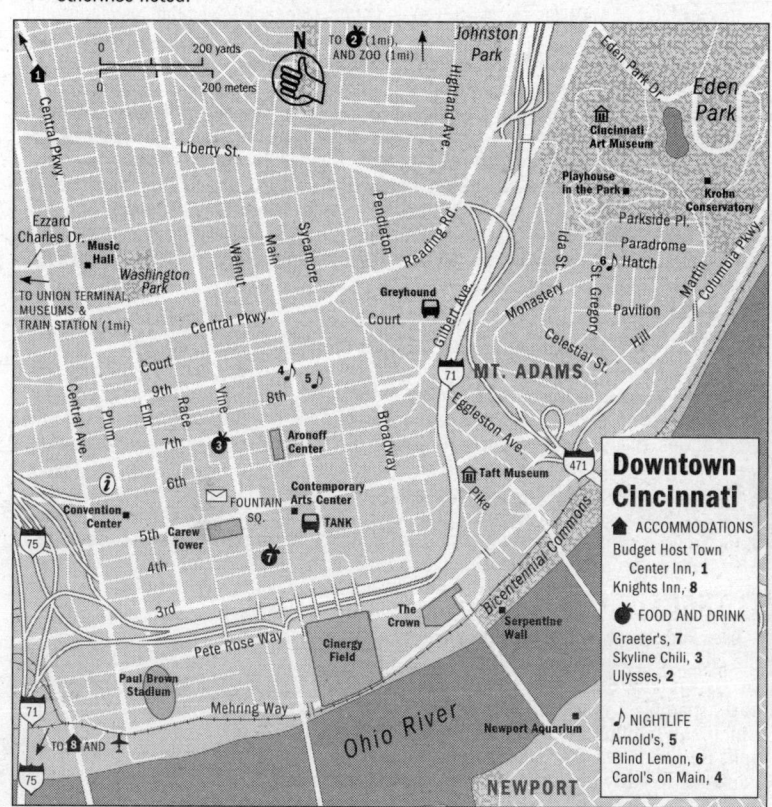

Downtown Cincinnati

🏠 ACCOMMODATIONS
Budget Host Town Center Inn, 1
Knights Inn, 8

🍴 FOOD AND DRINK
Graeter's, 7
Skyline Chili, 3
Ulysses, 2

♪ NIGHTLIFE
Arnold's, 5
Blind Lemon, 6
Carol's on Main, 4

GREAT LAKES

🏠 ACCOMMODATIONS

Few cheap hotels can be found in downtown Cincinnati. About 30 mi. north of Cincinnati in Sharonville, budget motels cluster along Chester Rd.; 12 mi. south of the city, inexpensive accommodations line I-75 at Exit 184. Closer by, the motels at Central Pkwy. and Hopple St. offer solid, semi-cheap lodging. **Knights Inn-Cincinnati/ South**, 8048 Dream St., Florence, KY, just off I-75 at Exit 180, has renovated rooms with an Arthurian flair and friendly service. (☎859-371-9711. Cable TV, A/ C, outdoor pool. Singles $36-40; doubles $40-45. 21+.) Ten minutes from downtown and the University of Cincinnati, **Budget Host Town Center Inn**, 3356 Central Pkwy., Exit 3 off I-75, is a smallish motel with a pool, and A/C and satellite TV in faded but comfortable rooms. (☎283-4678 or 800-283-4678. Singles $45-60; doubles $50-65.) Twenty-five miles east of the city, outside the I-275 loop, **Stonelick State Park** has 115 campsites at the edge of Stonelick Lake and provides welcome relief from Cincinnati's pricey lodgings. (☎625-6593. Sites $11, with electricity $15.)

🍴 FOODSTUFFS

Cincinnati's greatest culinary innovation is its chili; it consists of noodles topped with meat, cheese, onions, and kidney beans…and a distinctive secret ingredient.

Skyline Chili, everywhere. Locations all over Cincinnati, including 643 Vine St. (☎241-2020), at 7th St., dish up the best beans in town. The secret ingredient has been debated for years; some say chocolate, but curry is more likely. 5-way large chili $5.55, cheese coney (hot dog) $1.25. Open M-F 10:30am-8pm, Sa 11am-4pm.

Ulysses, 209 W. McMillan (☎241-3663), in Clifton. One-table vegetarian restaurant with a distinctive hippie aura; draws ravenous herbivores from all over town. Try the zesty and refreshing fruit smoothies ($1.75) or the veggie chili ($2.75). Open in summer M-Sa 11am-8pm; in winter 11am-9pm.

House of Sun, 35 E. 7th St. (☎721-3600), between Vine and Walnut St. Plentiful, cheap Chinese cuisine makes this a favorite among locals. Try the lunch special, which includes soup, entree, and fried rice for $5.25. Open M-Sa 11am-9:30pm.

Graeter's, 41 E. 4th St. (☎381-0653), between Walnut and Vine St. downtown. One of 15 locations. Since 1870, Graeter's has been sending sweet-toothed locals into sensory bliss with delectable ice cream blended with giant chocolate chips (single cone $1.75). Sandwiches and baked goods also served. Open M-F 7am-6pm, Sa 7am-5pm.

👁 SIGHTS

Downtown Cincinnati orbits around the **Tyler Davidson Fountain**, 5th and Vine St., a florid 19th-century masterpiece and an ideal people-watching spot. To the east, the expansive garden at **Procter and Gamble Plaza** is just one mark that the giant company has left on its hometown. Around **Fountain Sq.** are business complexes and great shops, connected by a series of 2nd fl. skywalks; the observation deck at the top of **Carew Tower** provides the best view in the city.

Close to Fountain Sq., the **Contemporary Arts Center**, 2nd fl. of the Mercantile Center at 115 E. 5th St., has a strong national reputation. (☎721-0390. Open M-Sa 10am-6pm, Su noon-5pm. $3.50, seniors and students $2; M free. Wheelchair accessible.) Also downtown is the **Taft Museum**, 316 Pike St. at the east end of 4th St., which houses a prodigious collection of Rembrandts and Whistlers. (☎241-0343. Open M-Sa 10am-5pm, Su 1-5pm. $4, students and seniors $2, under 18 free; W and Su free.) **Eden Park**, northeast of downtown and Mt. Adams, provides a nearby respite from the city with rolling hills, a pond, and cultural centers. Take bus #49 to Eden Park Dr. (Open daily 6am-10pm.) The collections at the **Cincinnati Art Museum**, inside the park, span 5000 years, from Near Eastern artifacts to Andy Warhol's rendition of Cincinnati's infamous baseball great Pete Rose. (☎721-5204. Open Tu-Sa 10am-5pm, Su noon-6pm. $5, seniors and students $4, under 18 free, Sa by donation. Free mid-June to early Sept.) The nearby **Krohn Conservatory** is one of the largest public greenhouses in the world, boasting a lush rainforest and a butterfly garden. (☎421-5707. Open daily 10am-5pm. Free; donations accepted. Wheelchair accessible.)

🎵 ENTERTAINMENT

The free newspapers *City Beat, Everybody's News*, and *Downtowner* list the happenings around town. The cliff-hanging community of **Mt. Adams** supports a thriving arts and entertainment district. Perched on its own wooded hill in Eden Park, the **Playhouse in the Park,** 962 Mt. Adams Circle, performs theater-in-the-round. (☎421-3888. Performances mid-Sept. to June Tu-Su. Tickets $26-40; senior rush 2hr. before show, student rush 15min. before show, both $13.50.)

The **Music Hall,** 1243 Elm St. (☎721-8222), hosts the **Cincinnati Symphony Orchestra** and the **Cincinnati Pops Orchestra** (☎381-3300) from September through May (tickets $16.50-63). The orchestra's summer seasons (June-July) take place at **Riverbend,** near Coney Island (tickets $17-37). The **Cincinnati Opera** performs in the Music Hall as well (☎888-533-7149; tickets $12-90). For updates, call **Dial the Arts** (☎621-4744). The **Cincinnati Ballet Company** (☎621-5219) is at the **Aronoff Center for the Arts,** 650 Walnut, which also hosts a Broadway series. (☎241-7469. Ballet performances Oct.-May. Tickets $12-47, matinee $9-40; musical tickets $15-65. Wheelchair accessible.)

Escape the highbrow lot and beat the summer heat in the world's largest recirculating pool at the **Coney Island Amusement Center,** 6201 Kellogg Ave., off I-275 at the Kellogg Ave. exit. (☎232-8230. Pool open daily 10am-8pm; rides M-F noon-9pm, Sa-Su 11am-9pm. Pool $12, ages 4-11 $10, seniors $8; rides $7, ages 4-11 $5; both $17/$15/$13.) In Mason, 24 mi. north of Cincinnati, off I-71 at Exit 24, stop by at **Paramount's King Island.** This fun center cages **The Beast,** the world's longest wooden roller coaster, which spreads its tentacles over 35 acres and 2 ZIP codes. (☎573-5800 or 800-288-0808. Open late May to late Aug. Su-F 9am-10pm, Sa 9am-11pm. $40, seniors and ages 3-6 $20. Parking $6. Wheelchair accessible.) Sports fans watch baseball's **Reds** (☎421-7337; tickets $5-28) and football's **Bengals** (☎621-3550; tickets $35-50) at **Cinergy Field,** 201 E. Pete Rose Way.

🎭 NIGHTLIFE

Overlooking downtown from the east, **Mt. Adams** has spawned some off-beat bars and late-night coffeeshops. Antiques adorn the walls of **Blind Lemon,** 936 Hatch St., at St. Gregory St., while live blues and acoustic rock fill its courtyard. (☎241-3885. No cover. Domestic draft $2. Music M-Sa 9:30pm, Su 7pm. Open M-Th 5pm-2:30am, F 4pm-2:30am, Sa-Su 3pm-2:30am.) For a drink straight out of the 19th century, try Cincinnati's oldest tavern, **Arnold's,** 210 E. 8th St., between Main and Sycamore. This wood-paneled mainstay provides good, uncomplicated beer ($3) as well as pasta and sandwiches ($4-13). After 9pm, Arnold's does ragtime, bluegrass, and swing. (☎421-6234. Open M-F 11am-1am, Sa 4pm-1am.) **Carol's On Main,** 825 Main St., inserts funk and style into downtown Cincinnati. Drawing theater groups and thirty-something yuppies galore, this restaurant/bar is known for great food (Cock-a-Noodle-Do salad $8.50) and late hours. (☎651-2667. Bar open Su 4pm-1:30am, M-Tu 11:30am-1:30am, W-F 11:30am-2:30am, Sa 4pm-2:30am.)

INDIANA

The cornfields of southern Indiana's Appalachian foothills give way to expansive plains in the industrialized north, where Gary's smokestacks spew black clouds over the waters of Lake Michigan and urban travel hubs string along the interstates. Despite its lofty official motto—"The Crossroads of America"—Indiana is a modest, slow-paced state, where farms roll on and on, big cities are a rarity, and countless Hoosier school boys grow up dreaming of becoming the next Larry Bird.

🔃 PRACTICAL INFORMATION

Capital: Indianapolis.
Visitor Info: Indiana Division of Tourism, 1 N. Capitol, #700, Indianapolis 46204 (☎ 800-289-6646; www.state.in.us/tourism). **Division of State Parks,** 402 W. Washington, #W-298, Indianapolis 46204 (☎ 317-232-4125).
Postal Abbreviation: IN. **Sales Tax:** 5%.

INDIANAPOLIS   ☎ 317

Surrounded by flat farmland, Indianapolis feels like a model Midwestern city. Folks shop and work all day among downtown's skyscrapers and then drive home to sprawling suburbs in the evening. Life ambles here—until May, when 350,000 spectators and crew members overrun the city, and the road warriors of the Indianapolis 500 speed into the spotlight.

🔃🔃 ORIENTATION AND PRACTICAL INFORMATION. The city is laid out in concentric circles, with a dense central cluster of skyscrapers and low-lying outskirts. The very center of Indianapolis is just south of **Monument Circle,** at the intersection of **Washington St. (U.S. 40)** and **Meridian St.** Washington St. divides the city north-south; Meridian St. divides it east-west. **I-465** circles the city and provides access to downtown. **I-70** cuts through the city east-west. Plentiful metered parking can be found along the edges of the downtown area. **Indianapolis International Aiport** (☎ 487-7243) is located 7 mi. southwest of downtown off I-465, Exit 11B; take bus #8 "West Washington." A taxi ride to downtown runs $17. **Amtrak,** 350 S. Illinois St. (☎ 263-0550; open daily 7am-2:30pm, 11pm-6:30am), behind Union Station, rolls to Chicago (5hr., 1 per day, $18-34) and Cincinnati (3hr., 1 per day, $19-34); trains travel east-west only. **Greyhound,** 350 S. Illinois St. (☎ 267-3071; open 24hr.), buses to Chicago (4hr., 12 per day, $33); Cincinnati (3-7hr., 4 per day, $21); and Bloomington (1hr., 2 per day, $16). **Indy Go,** 209 N. Delaware St., handles public transportation. (☎ 635-3344. Office open M-F 8am-6pm, Sa 9am-4pm. $1, children under 6 free.) **Taxis: Yellow Cab,** ☎ 487-7777. **Visitor Info: Indianapolis City Center,** 201 S. Capitol Ave., in the Pan Am Plaza, has a helpful model of the city. (☎ 237-5200 or 800-323-4639. Internet access $1 per 5min. Open M-F 10am-5:30pm, Sa 10am-5pm, Su noon-5pm.) **Hotlines: Rape Crisis Line,** ☎ 800-221-6311. **Gay/Lesbian Switchboard,** ☎ 251-7955. **Post Office:** 125 W. South St. (☎ 464-6376), across from Amtrak. Open M-W and F 7am-5:30pm, Th 7am-6pm. **ZIP code:** 46206. **Area code:** 317. **Time zone:** Central.

🛏 PIT STOP. Budget motels line the I-465 beltway, 5 mi. from downtown. Make reservations a year in advance for the Indy 500, which drives up rates throughout May. The **Fall Creek YMCA,** 860 W. 10th St., just north of downtown, has small, dorm-style rooms with access to a pool, a gym, and laundry facilities. (☎ 634-2478. Free parking. 87 rooms for men only. Key deposit $5. Singles $25, with bath $30; $77/$87 per week.) Head to **Motel 6,** 6330 Debonair Lane, at Exit 16A off I-465, for clean, pleasant rooms with A/C and cable TV. (☎ 293-3220. Singles $35-40; doubles $41-46.) **Dollar Inn,** 6331 Crawfordsville Rd., off I-465 at Exit 16A, is not the lap of luxury, but a good deal nonetheless. The decent rooms have cable TV, including HBO. (☎ 248-8500. Check-out 11am. 21+. Key deposit $2. Singles $26-31; doubles $31.) The **Indiana State Fairgrounds Campgrounds,** 1202 E. 38th St., has 170 sod-and-gravel sites, mostly packed by RVs. To get close to nature, go elsewhere. (☎ 927-7520. Take bus #4 or 39 from downtown. Busy during the state fair. Sites $16, full hookup $19.)

🔃 HIGH-OCTANE FUEL. Ethnic food stands, produce markets, and knick-knack vendors fill the spacious **City Market,** 222 E. Market St., a renovated 19th-century building. As if America didn't have enough malls, Indianapolis's newly constructed **Circle Centre,** 49 West Maryland St. (☎ 681-8000), contains a slew of restaurants and a food court. **Bazbeaux Pizza,** 334 Massachusetts Ave. (☎ 636-7662), and 832 E. Westfields Blvd. (☎ 255-5711), is Indianapolis's favorite pizza. The Tchoupitoulas pizza is a Cajun masterpiece (serves 2 $12). Construct your own culinary wonder ($5.75) from a choice of 53 toppings. (Both locations open M-Th 11am-10pm, F-Sa 11am-

11pm, Su 4:30-10pm.) **The Abbey,** 771 Massachusetts Ave., is a popular coffee and sandwich shop with another location at 923 Indiana Ave. The decaffeinated can sit in overstuffed velvet chairs while sipping cappucino for $2.25. (☎269-8426. Open Su 11am-midnight, M-Th 8am-midnight, F 8am-1am, Sa 11am-1am.)

◙ **SUNDAY DRIVE.** The newly restored canal at **White River State Park,** near downtown, entices locals to stroll, bike, or nap on the banks. Pedal boats are available for rent at **Central Canal Rental** (☎634-1824). The **Visitors Center,** 801 Washington Ave., is located inside the park's old pumphouse. (☎233-2434 or 800-665-9056. Open M-F 8:30am-7pm, Sa 10am-7pm, Su noon-7pm.) Near the park entrance, the **Eiteljorg Museum of American Indians' and Western Art,** 500 W. Washington St., features an impressive collection of art from the Old West—both white and Native American. (☎636-9378. Open Tu-Sa 10am-5pm, Su noon-5pm; in summer also M 10am-5pm. Tours daily at 1pm. $6, seniors $5, students with ID and children $3.) It may be far from downtown, but the **Indianapolis Museum of Art,** 1200 W. 38th St., is well worth a visit. The museum's beautiful 152 acres offer nature trails, art pavilions, the Eli Lilly Botanical Garden, a greenhouse, and a theater. (☎923-1331. Open Tu-W and F-Sa 10am-5pm, Th 10am-8:30pm, Su noon-5pm. Free; special exhibits $5.)

A majestic stained-glass dome graces the marbled interior of the **State House,** between Capitol and Senate St. near W. Washington St. (☎233-5293. Open daily 8am-4:30pm, main floor only Sa-Su. 2-4 guided 1hr. tours per day M-F. Self-guided tour brochures are available inside. Free.) Animal lovers should check out the seemingly cageless **Indianapolis Zoo,** 1200 W. Washington St., which holds one of the world's largest enclosed whale and dolphin pavilions. (☎630-2001. Open daily 9am-5pm; Sept.-May 9am-4pm. $9.75, seniors $7, ages 3-12 $6. Parking $3.) Wolves and bison roam under researchers' supervision at **Wolf Park,** on Jefferson St. in Battle Ground, 1hr. north of Indianapolis off I-65. The howling wolves are let out into the moonlight some nights. (☎765-567-2265. Open May-Nov. Tu-Su 1-5pm; open later for wolf howls, F-Sa 7:30pm. Tu-Sa $4, ages 6-13 $3; Su $5/$3.)

🏎 **DAYS OF THUNDER.** When the **Indianapolis Motor Speedway,** 4790 W. 16th St., off I-465 at the Speedway Exit, lies dormant, buses full of tourists rather than racecars steered by speedsters drive around the 2½ mi. track. Take bus #25. (☎481-8500. Track tours daily 8am-4pm. $3, ages 6-15 $1.) The adjacent **Speedway Museum** houses Indy's Hall of Fame. (☎484-6747. Open daily 9am-5pm. $3, ages 6-15 $1.) The country's passion for fast cars reaches fever pitch during the **500 Festival**—a month of parades and hoopla leading up to race day. (Call 636-4556 for info on the festival.) The festivities begin with time trials in mid-May and culminate with the bang of the **Indianapolis 500** starter's gun the Sunday before Memorial Day. Tickets for the race go on sale the day after the previous year's race and usually sell out within a week. NASCAR's **Brickyard 400** sends stock cars zooming down the speedway in early August. (☎800-822-4639 for ticket order forms for any event.)

🎭🎵 **IN THE FAST LANE.** The **Walker Theatre,** 617 Indiana Ave., named in honor of African-American beautician Madame Walker, America's first female self-made millionaire, is now the home of the biweekly **Jazz on the Avenue.** Take a 15min. walk northwest of downtown. (☎236-2087. F 6-10pm. $5.)

By day a somewhat bland area, the **Broad Ripple** area, 6 mi. north of downtown at College Ave. and 62nd St., transforms after dark into a center for nightlife. The party fills the clubs and bars and spills out onto the sidewalks off Broad Ripple Ave. until about 1am on weekdays and 3am on weekends. The **Monkey's Tale,** 925 E. Westfield Blvd. (☎253-2883), is a good place to meet other happening folks and play a tune on the jukebox. The attached **Jazz Cooker** heats up when the Dick Liswell Trio begins jamming (F-Sa at 10pm). **Average Joe's Sports Pub,** 814 Broad Ripple Ave., is a standard bar offering five pool tables and $2.75 beers. (☎253-5844. Open M-F 5pm-3am, Sa 6pm-3am, Su 6pm-midnight.) If you need some laughs, head to the **Crackers Comedy Club,** 6281 N. College Ave., at Broad Ripple Ave. (☎255-4211; shows Tu-Sa, M amateur night). After the clubs close, make a run for tacos ($2.50) and burritos ($4.50) at **Paco's Cantina,** 723 Broad Ripple Ave. (☎251-6200; open 24hr.)

BLOOMINGTON

☎812

The region's rolling hills create an exquisite backdrop for Bloomington's most prominent institution, Indiana University. Its college town atmosphere, nightlife hot spots, and die-hard fans of Hoosier basketball help Bloomington keep pace with its northern neighbor Indianapolis.

▲▐ ORIENTATION AND PRACTICAL INFORMATION. Bloomington lies south of Indianapolis on Rte. 37; **N. Walnut** and **College St.** are the main north-south thoroughfares. **Greyhound,** 219 W. 6th St. (☎332-1522; station open M-F 9am-5pm, Sa-Su noon-4pm), connects Bloomington to Chicago (5hr., 2 per day, $52) and Indianapolis (1hr., 2 per day, $16). **Bloomington Transit** sends buses on seven routes. Service is infrequent; call 332-5688 for info. (75¢, seniors and ages 5-17 35¢.) **Yellow Cab** (☎336-4100) charges by zone. The **Visitors Center,** 2855 N. Walnut St., offers free local calls. (☎334-8900 or 800-800-0037. Open May-Oct. M-F 8:30am-5pm, Sa 9am-4pm, Su 10am-3pm; Nov.-Apr. M-F 8:30am-5pm, Sa 10am-3pm; 24hr. brochure area.) **Internet access: Monroe County Public Library,** 303 E. Kirkwood Ave. (☎349-3050; open M-Th 9am-9pm, F 9am-6pm, Sa 9am-5pm, Su 1-5pm). **Post Office:** 206 E. 4th St., two blocks east of Walnut St. (☎334-4030. Open M and F 8am-6pm, Tu-Th 8am-5:30pm, Sa 8am-1pm.) **ZIP code:** 47404. **Area code:** 812. **Time zone:** Central.

▐ ACCOMMODATIONS. Budget hotels are located around the intersection of N. Walnut St. and Rte. 46. **College Motor Inn,** 509 N. College Ave., is close to the university and offers plush rooms with basic cable and comfortable furniture. (☎336-6881. Singles from $45; doubles from $50.) **Motel 6,** 1800 N. Walnut St., provides big, clean rooms, free HBO, and an outdoor pool. (☎332-0820. Singles $36 Su-Th, $40 F-Sa; doubles $42/$46.) **Paynetown State Recreation Area,** 10 mi. southeast of downtown on Rte. 446, has open field campsites in a well-endowed park on Lake Monroe with access to hiking trails. Boat rentals are available. (☎837-9490. Primitive sites $7, with shower $12, with electricity $15. Vehicle registration $5, in-state $3.)

▐ FOOD. Downtown Sq. boxes a wealth of veggie-heavy restaurants, bookstores, and cute clothing shops into a two-block radius, on Kirkwood Ave. near College Ave. and Walnut St. **◪Snow Lion,** 113 S. Grant St., just off Kirkwood Ave., is owned by the Dalai Lama's nephew and is one of only a few Tibetan restaurants in the country. *Momo* Dinner ($7) and Tibetan Butter Tea ($1.50) make for a splendid meal. (☎336-0835. Open daily 11am-10pm.) **The Laughing Planet Cafe,** 322 E. Kirkwood Ave., serves up organic delights made from local produce, such as superb $4 burritos. (☎323-2233. Open daily 11am-9pm.) Join hordes of Hoosiers at **Jimmy John's,** 430 E. Kirkwood Ave., home of the "World's Greatest Sandwiches." (☎332-9265. Open M-W 10:30am-midnight, Th-Sa 10:30am-4am, Su 10:30am-midnight.)

▨ NIGHTLIFE. Bloomington's nightlife scene is about what you would expect from a college town in Middle America: beer and rock. **The Crazy Horse,** 214 W. Kirkwood Ave., drafts an alcohol army of 80 beers. (☎336-8877. Open M-W 11am-1am, Th-Sa 11am-2am, Su noon-midnight.) Everyone who's anyone (at IU, that is) shimmies over to **Nick's,** 423 E. Kirkwood Ave., to play drinking games. (☎332-4040. Beers $2-3. Open M-Sa 11am-2am, Su noon-midnight.) **Bluebird,** 216 N. Walnut St., showcases local musical talent. (☎336-2473. Open M-Sa 9pm-3am.) The doors at **Rhino's,** 325½ S. Walnut St (☎333-3430.), are open to those under 21 for dancing and performances. **Bullwinkle's,** 201 S. College Ave., caters to a gay crowd with drag shows (M and W) and dance music. (☎334-3232. Open M-Sa 7pm-3am.)

◪ SIGHTS. The **Tibetan Cultural Center,** 3655 Snoddy Rd., offers meditation and info on Tibetan culture. (☎334-7046. Grounds open Sa-Su noon-4pm. Center open Su noon-3pm.) IU's architecturally striking **Art Museum,** E. 7th street on campus, maintains an excellent collection of Oriental and African artworks. (☎855-5445. Open Tu-Sa 10am-5pm, Su noon-5pm. Free.) Nearby, the **Mathers Museum of World**

Cultures, 416 N. Indiana St., near E. 8th St., features somewhat interesting archaeology displays, idiophones, and chordophones. Check out the lively exhibit on the South American Carnival. (☎855-6873. Open Tu-F 9am-4:30pm, Sa-Su 1-4:30pm.) **Oliver Winery,** 8024 N. State Rd. 37, not only has beautiful grounds, but also offers free (and generous) tastings of all of its 15 wines, including the local favorite, blackberry wine. (☎876-5800 or 800-258-2783. Open M-Sa 10am-6pm, Su noon-6pm.)

MICHIGAN

Orbiting the earth in a space shuttle, Michiganders would have no trouble identifying their state; with its 3000 miles of coastline along four of the Great Lakes, Michigan easily lays claim to the title of "Most Readily Apparent State When Viewed from Space." Michigan's industrially developed Lower Peninsula paws the Great Lakes like a huge mitten, while its pristine and oft-ignored Upper Peninsula hangs above, quietly nursing moose, wolves, and vacation homes. The state once famous for its booming automotive industry is now starting to make waves as a natural getaway, blending coastal character with thousands of freshwater lakes.

⁊ PRACTICAL INFORMATION

Capital: Lansing.
Visitor Info: Michigan Travel Bureau, 333 S. Capitol, Ste. F, Lansing 48909 (☎888-784-7328 or 800-543-2937; www.michigan.org). **Dept. of Parks and Recreation,** Information Services Center, P.O. Box 30257, Lansing 48909 (☎517-373-9900). Entry to all state parks requires a motor vehicle permit; $4 per day, $20 annually. Call ☎800-447-2757 for reservations at any state park campground.
Postal Abbreviation: MI. **Sales Tax:** 6%.

DETROIT   ☎313

Long the ugly step-sister of America's big cities, Detroit has no where to go but up. Violent race riots in the 60s caused a massive flight to the suburbs; the population has more than halved since 1967, turning neighborhoods into ghost towns. The decline of the auto industry in the late 70s added unemployment to the city's ills, beleaguering an already depressed area. Today, the five gleaming towers of the riverside Renaissance Center symbolize the hope of a city-wide renewal; even a huge swath of downtown Detroit is slowly being reborn as a commercial center and city park. The aggressive tourism industry focuses attention on Detroit's attractions: Michigan's largest and most comprehensive museums, a fascinating ethnic history, a vibrant music festival scene, and the still-visible (though soot-blackened and slightly crumbling) evidence of the city's former architectural grandeur.

⌐ TRANSPORTATION

Airport: Detroit Metropolitan (☎942-3550 or 800-351-5466), 2 mi. west of downtown off I-94 at Merriman Rd. in Romulus. **Checkered Sedan** (☎800-351-5466) offers taxi service to downtown for $36.
Trains: Amtrak, 11 W. Baltimore (☎873-3442), at Woodward. To Chicago (6hr., 3 per day, $19-50) and New York (16hr., 1 per day, $72-135). Open daily 5:45am-11:30pm. For Canadian destinations, go through **VIA Rail,** 298 Walker Rd., Windsor, ON (☎519-256-5511 or 800-561-3949). To Toronto (4hr., 5 per day, CDN$7; 40% discount with ISIC card.)
Buses: Greyhound, 1001 Howard St. (☎961-8011). *At night, the area is unsafe.* To: Chicago (5½hr., 8 per day, $24); Cleveland (4hr., 9 per day, $20); and Ann Arbor (1hr., 5 per day, $7). Station open 24hr.; ticket office open daily 6am-12:30am.

GREAT LAKES

Public Transit: Detroit Dept. of Transportation (DOT), 1301 E. Warren St. (☎933-1300). Policed public transport system serves downtown, with limited service to the suburbs. Many buses stop service at midnight. Fare $1.25, transfers 25¢. **DOT Attractions Shuttle** (☎259-8726) delivers camera-toting tourists to the metro area's most popular sights 10am-5:45pm. All-day ticket $5. **People Mover,** 150 Michigan Ave. (☎962-7245 or 800-541-7245). Ultramodern elevated tramway circles the Central Business District on a 2.7 mi. loop; worth a ride just for the view. Runs M-Th 7am-11pm, F 7am-midnight, Sa 9am-midnight, Su noon-8pm. Fare 50¢. **Southeastern Michigan Area Regional Transit (SMART)** (☎962-5515 or 223-2100). Bus service to the suburbs. Fare $1.50, transfers 25¢. Get free maps of the system at the office on the first fl. of First National Bank at 600 Woodward Ave. Buses run 4am-midnight, depending on route.

Taxis: Checker Cab, ☎963-7000.

✴📞 ORIENTATION AND PRACTICAL INFORMATION

Detroit lies on the Detroit River, which connects Lakes Erie and St. Clair. Across the river to the south, the town of **Windsor, ON,** can be reached by tunnel just west of the Renaissance Center (toll $2.50), or by the Ambassador Bridge. Detroit is a tough town, but you probably won't encounter trouble during the day, especially within the People Mover loop. Driving is the best way to negotiate this sprawling city where good and bad neighborhoods alternate at whim; public transportation is often inefficient and less safe.

Detroit's streets form a grid. **The Mile Roads** run east-west as major arteries. **Eight Mile Rd.** is the city's northern boundary and the beginning of the suburbs. **Woodward Ave.** heads northwest from downtown, dividing city and suburbs into "east side" and "west side." **Gratiot Ave.** flares out northeast from downtown, while **Grand River Ave.** shoots west. **I-94** and **I-75** pass through downtown. For a particularly helpful map, check the pull-out in the invaluable *Detroit Metro Visitor's Guide.*

Visitor Info: Convention and Visitors Bureau, 211 W. Fort St. (☎202-1813 or 800-338-7648). Open M-F 8:30am-5pm. **Hotlines: Crisis Hotline,** ☎224-7000. **Sexual Abuse Helpline,** ☎876-4180. Both operate 24hr.

Bi-Gay-Lesbian Organizations: Triangle Foundation of Detroit, ☎537-3323. **Between the Lines,** ☎248-615-7003. **Affirmations,** 195 W. 9 Mile Rd. 48220 (☎248-398-7105), in Ferndale, has a large library and info on gay nightlife.

Post Office: 1401 W. Fort St. (☎226-8304; open 24hr.). **ZIP code:** 48233. **Area codes:** 313, 810, and 248 (north); or 734 (southwest). In text, 313 unless otherwise noted.

⌂ ACCOMMODATIONS

Detroit's suburbs harbor loads of chain motels. Ones near the airport in **Romulus** tend to be overpriced, and others along **E. Jefferson,** near downtown, can be skanky. For a mix of convenience and affordability, look along **Telegraph Rd.** off I-94, west of the city. If the exchange rate is favorable, good deals can be found in **Windsor** just across the border. The *Detroit Metro Visitor's Guide* lists accommodations by area and includes price ranges.

▨ Country Grandma's Home Hostel (HI-AYH), 22330 Bell Rd. (☎734-753-4901), in New Boston, 6 mi. south of I-94 off I-275, between Detroit and Ann Arbor. Take Exit 11B, turn right, and then make an immediate right onto Bell Rd. Though it's inaccessible by public transportation, the comfort and hospitality make it worth the trip. 6 beds, kitchen, and free parking. Dorms $11, nonmembers $14. Call for required reservations and directions. Wheelchair accessible.

Shorecrest Motor Inn, 1316 E. Jefferson Ave. (☎568-3000 or 800-992-9616), as close to downtown as the budget traveler can get. Clean, comfortable singles $69; doubles $89. Key deposit $5. Reservations recommended. Wheelchair accessible.

University of Windsor, 401 Sunset Ave. (☎519-973-7074), in Windsor, just over the Ambassador Bridge, rents rooms from early May to late Aug. Free use of university facil-

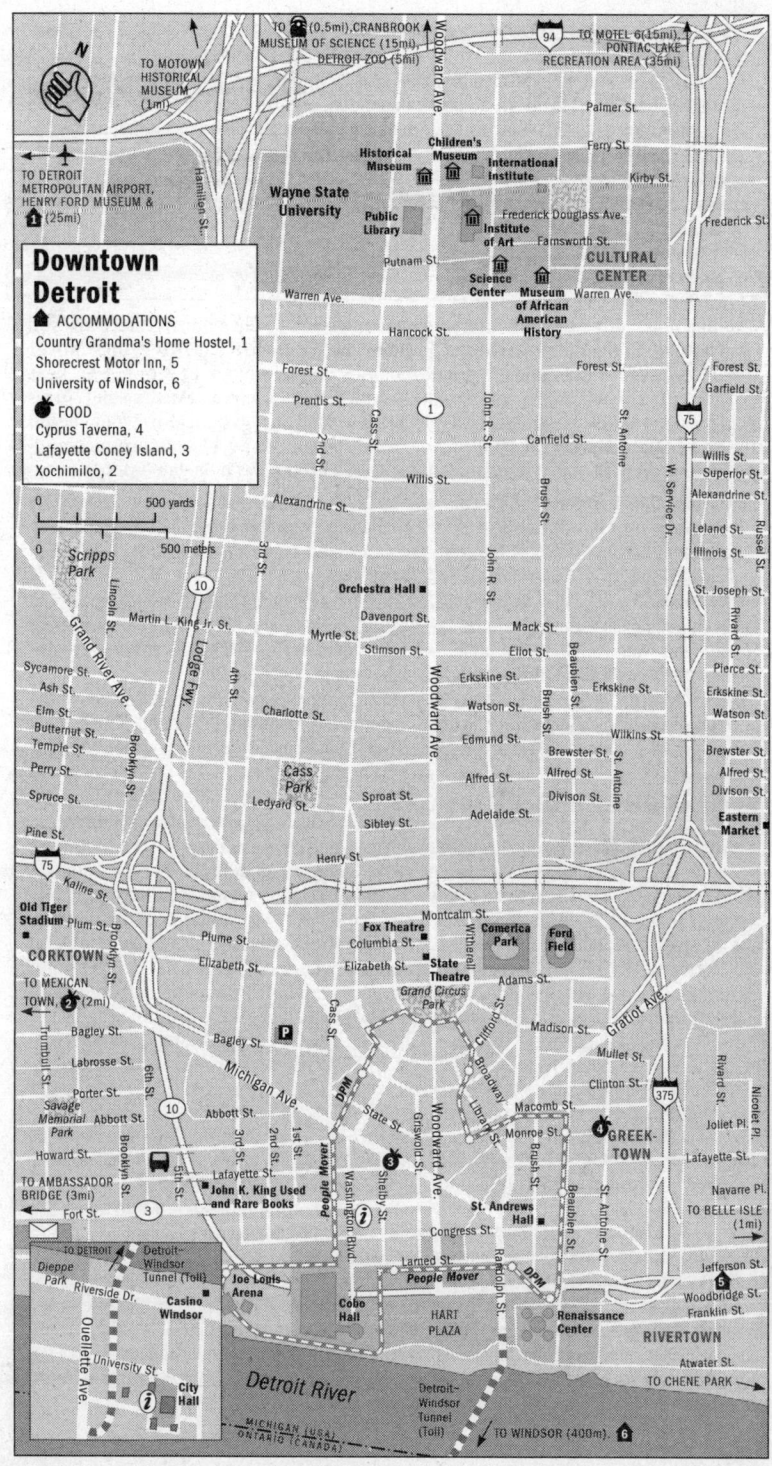

N

TO MOTOWN
HISTORICAL
MUSEUM
(1mi)

TO 🎭 (0.5mi),CRANBROOK
MUSEUM OF SCIENCE (15mi),
DETROIT ZOO (5mi)

Woodward Ave.

94 TO MOTEL 6(15mi),
PONTIAC LAKE
RECREATION AREA (35mi)

Palmer St.

Ferry St.

TO DETROIT
METROPOLITAN AIRPORT,
HENRY FORD MUSEUM &
(25mi)

Hamilton St.

Wayne State
University

Historical
Museum

Children's
Museum

International
Institute

Kirby St.

Frederick St.

Public
Library

Frederick Douglass Ave.

Institute
of Art

Famsworth St.

CULTURAL
CENTER

Putnam St.

Science
Center

Museum
of African
American
History

Warren Ave.

**Downtown
Detroit**

🏠 ACCOMMODATIONS

Country Grandma's Home Hostel, 1
Shorecrest Motor Inn, 5
University of Windsor, 6

🍎 FOOD

Cyprus Taverna, 4
Lafayette Coney Island, 3
Xochimilco, 2

Warren Ave.

Hancock St.

Forest St.

Forest St.

Forest St.

Garfield St.

Prentis St.

Cass St.

John R St.

Canfield St.

St. Antoine

75

Willis St.
Superior St.
Alexandrine St.

W. Service Dr.

Russel St.

0   500 yards
0   500 meters

Willis St.

2nd St.

Brush St.

Leland St.
Illinois St.

Scripps
Park

Alexandrine St.

3rd St.

St. Joseph St.

10

Orchestra Hall ■

Davenport St.

Mack St.

Rivard St.

Pierce St.

Lincoln St.

Martin L. King Jr. St.

Myrtle St.

Stimson St.

Eliot St.

Beaubien St.

Erkskine St.

Erkskine St.

Watson St.

Grand River Ave.

Brooklyn St.

Lodge Fwy.

4th St.

Woodward Ave.

Erkskine St.

Watson St.

Edmund St.

Brush St.

Wilkins St.

Sycamore St.
Ash St.

Elm St.
Butternut St.
Temple St.

Perry St.

Spruce St.

Charlotte St.

Cass
Park

Ledyard St.

Sproat St.

Alfred St.

Alfred St.

St. Antoine

Brewster St.
St. Antoine

Brewster St.

Alfred St.
Divison St.

Sibley St.

Adelaide St.

Divison St.

Eastern
Market

Pine St.

75

Kaline St.

Henry St.

Old Tiger
Stadium

Plum St.

Montcalm St.

CORKTOWN

Brooklyn St.

Plume St.

Fox Theatre

Columbia St.

Comerica
Park

Ford
Field

TO MEXICAN
TOWN, 🍎 (2mi)

Elizabeth St.

Elizabeth St.

State
Theatre

Witherell

Adams St.

Bagley St.

Grand Circus
Park

Clinton St.

Madison St.

Gratiot Ave.

Labrosse St.

6th St.

Michigan Ave.

Bagley St.

P

Cass St.

Broadway

Mullet St.

Porter St.

Savage
Memorial
Park

Abbott St.

10

Abbott St.

3rd St.

2nd St.

1st St.

State St.

Griswold St.

Library St.

Macomb St.

Clinton St.

375

Joliet Pl.

Nicolet Ave.

Howard St.

Monroe St.

GREEK-
TOWN

Lafayette St.

TO AMBASSADOR
BRIDGE (3mi)

3

John K. King Used
and Rare Books

Lafayette St.

Washington Blvd.

People Mover

3

Shelby St.

St. Andrews
Hall ■

Beaubien St.

St. Antoine St.

TO BELLE ISLE
(1mi)

Fort St.

Congress St.

Navarre Pl.

TO DETROIT

Dieppe
Park

Riverside Dr.

Detroit-
Windsor
Tunnel
(Toll)

Casino
Windsor

Joe Louis
Arena

Larned St.

People Mover

Renaissance
Center

Randolph St.

DPM

Jefferson St.

Woodbridge St.

5

Franklin St.

Ouellette Ave.

University St.

City
Hall

Cobo
Hall

HART
PLAZA

RIVERTOWN

Atwater St.

TO CHENE PARK

Detroit River

MICHIGAN (USA)
ONTARIO (CANADA)

Detroit-
Windsor
Tunnel
(Toll)

TO WINDSOR (400m) 6

ities. Singles CDN$32, CDN$19 for students with college ID; doubles CDN$40. Wheelchair accessible.

Motel 6, 32700 Barrington St. (☎248-583-0500), 15 mi. north of downtown off I-75 in Madison Heights, just off 12 Mile Rd. Enormous, well-kept, cookie-cutter rooms with free local calls and HBO. Singles $43; doubles $49. Reservations recommended.

Pontiac Lake Recreation Area, 7800 Gale Rd. (☎248-666-1020), in Waterford 45min. northwest of downtown; take I-75 to Rte. 59 W, a right on Will Lake northbound and left onto Gale Rd. Huge wooded sites in rolling hills, just 4 mi. from the lake. 176 sites with electricity $11. Vehicle permit $4.

◖ FOOD

Although many downtown restaurants have migrated to the suburbs, there are still some in-town budget dining options. In **Greektown,** at the Greektown People Mover stop, Greek restaurants and excellent bakeries line one block of Monroe St. near Beaubien St. To snag a *pierogi*, cruise Joseph Campau Ave. in **Hamtramck** (*Ham-TRAM-eck*), a Polish neighborhood northeast of Detroit. No budget traveler should miss the **Eastern Market,** at Gratiot Ave. and Russell St., an 11-acre produce-and-goodie festival with everything imaginable. (☎833-1560. Open Sa 4am-5pm.)

Lafayette Coney Island, 118 W. Lafayette (☎964-8198). Detroit's most famous culinary establishment, Lafayette doles out its $2.10 coney dogs and $2.85 chili cheese fries to Detroiters from all walks of life. Join the crowd and bring some antacids. Open M-Th 7:30am-4am, F-Sa 7:30am-5am, Su 9:30am-4am.

Xochimilco, 3409 Bagley St. (☎843-0129). The highlight of Detroit's Mexicantown. The curious should try poking around the buzzing markets and shops that line the street while they wait (briefly) for a table. The house specialities—enchilada and burrito platters—are cheap ($5-8), huge, and delicious. Open daily 11am-2am.

Cyprus Taverna, 579 Monroe St. (☎961-1550). A local favorite for Greek cuisine. In the heart of Greektown, it features tasteful decor and a charmingly subdued atmosphere. Entrees $9-13. Open Su-Th 11am-2am, F-Sa 11am-4am.

◉ ⚑ SIGHTS AND OUTDOORS

Detroit's art isn't confined to museums. Artist and activist Tyree Guyton created the block-long **Heidelburg Project,** an ever-changing amalgamation of polka dots and found objects. (To get there, turn west on Heidelburg St. from Mt. Elliott, which is between I-94 and E. Jefferson, and follow the dots.) For wandering bibliophiles, **John K. King Used and Rare Books,** 901 W. Lafayette, holds over a million books on four floors. (☎961-0622. Open M-Sa 9:30am-5:30pm.)

Those roars you hear rumbling in the suburbs come from the animatronic dinosaur exhibit at the well-funded **Detroit Zoological Park,** just off the Woodward exit off Rte. 696 in Royal Oak. North America's first National Amphibian Conservation Center is the newest attraction, and joining it in 2002 will be the world's largest polar bear exhibit. For a simple pleasure, stick your head into the observatory globes in the middle of the prairie dog exhibit. (☎248-398-0900. Open Apr.-Oct. daily 10am-5pm, Nov.-Mar 10am-4pm. Open mid-May through Aug. Su until 6pm, late June to late Aug. W until 8pm. $7.50, ages 2-18 and seniors $5.50, under 2 free. Parking $3.)

Fifteen mi. north of Detroit in posh Bloomfield Hills, **Cranbrook's** scholarly campus holds public gardens, several museums, and an art academy. Far and away the best of the lot is the **Cranbrook Institute of Science,** 39221 N. Woodward Ave., with rotating exhibits emphasizing educational fun. (☎248-645-3209 or 877-462-7262. Open Sa-Th 10am-5pm, F 10am-10pm. $7; seniors, students, and children $4.) The largest urban island park in the US and one of the best escapes from Detroit's hectic pace, **Belle Isle,** located 3 mi. from downtown via the MacArthur Bridge. maintains a conservatory, nature center, aquarium, maritime museum, and a small zoo for animal lovers with short attention spans. (☎852-4078. Accessible daily 6am-10pm; all attractions open 10am-5pm. $2 each, ages 2-12 $1; zoo $3/$1.)

🏛 MUSEUMS

Detroit Institute of Arts, 5200 Woodward Ave. (☎833-7900). One of the nation's finest museums, with Van Gogh's "Self-Portrait" and Diego Rivera's mural "Detroit Industry"— one masterpiece that will never go on loan. Open W-F 11am-4pm, Sa-Su 11am-5pm, first F of each month 11am-9pm. Suggested donation $4, children and students $1.

Henry Ford Museum, 20900 Oakwood Blvd., off I-94 in Dearborn. (☎982-6100, 271-1620 for 24hr. info). Take SMART bus #200 or 250. More than just a tribute to planes, trams, and automobiles, its exhibits deliver a comprehensive commentary on 20th century America. The premices boast the limousine in which President Kennedy was assassinated and the chair in which Lincoln was shot. Next to the museum lies **Greenfield Village,** where over 80 historic edifices from around the country have been placed; visit the workshop of the Wright Brothers or the factory where Thomas Edison researched. Museum and village open daily 9am-5pm. Museum or village $12.50, seniors $11.50, ages 5-12 $7.50. Combination ticket, $24/$23/$15, valid 2 consecutive days.

Automotive Hall of Fame, 21400 Oakwood Blvd. (☎240-4000). Glorifies the innovators of the car industry with an interactive tour through the industry's history. Open June-Oct. daily 10am-5pm; Nov.-May Tu-Su 10am-5pm. $6, seniors $5.50, ages 5-12 $3.

Museum of African-American History, 315 E. Warren Rd. (☎494-5800). Exhibits include harrowing accounts of the history of slavery and displays of present-day African-American culture. Open Tu-Su 9:30am-5pm. Suggested donation $5, under 13 $3.

Motown Historical Museum, 2648 W. Grand Blvd. (☎875-2264), east of Rosa Parks Blvd., about 1 mi. west of the Lodge Freeway/Rte. 10. Take the "Dexter Avenue" bus. Downstairs, the Jackson 5, Marvin Gaye, Smokey Robinson, and Diana Ross recorded in the primitive Studio A. Open Su-M noon-5pm, Tu-Sa 10am-5pm. $6, under 12 $3.

🎵🎭 ENTERTAINMENT AND NIGHTLIFE

Newly renovated and restored, Detroit's theater district, around Woodward and Columbia, is witnessing a cultural revival. The **Fox Theatre,** 2211 Woodward Ave., near Grand Circus Park, features high-profile drama, comedy, and musicals, as well as the nation's largest movie theater hall (seats 5000) for occasional epic films. (☎983-3200. Box office open M-F 10am-6pm. Tickets $25-100; movies under $10.) The **State Theater,** 2115 Woodward Ave. (☎961-5450; 810-932-3643 for event info), brings in a variety of popular concerts and is also home to **Ignition,** a giant party that enlists DJs from a local radio station to play alternative dance music. (Cover starts at $5. Sa 10pm-2am.) **Orchestra Hall,** 3711 Woodward Ave., at Parsons St., houses the Detroit Symphony Orchestra. (☎962-1000, box office 576-5111. Open M-F 9am-5pm. Half-price rush tickets 1½hr. prior to show for seniors and students with ID.) For some of Detroit's best jazz, check out the **Harmony Park** area near Orchestra Hall. The weekly *Metro Times* contains complete entertainment listings.

For info on the trendiest nightspots, pick up a free copy of *Orbit* in record stores and restaurants. *Between the Lines,* also free, has entertainment info for gays, lesbians, and bisexuals. Alternative fans looking for a little live music should check out **St. Andrews Hall,** 431 E. Congress, which hosts local and national alternative acts. (☎961-6358. Shows F-Su. Advance tickets sold through Ticketmaster; $7-10.) **Shelter,** the dance club downstairs, draws young, hip crowds on non-concert nights. Young party animals take advantage of Ontario's lower drinking age (19) at bars and clubs along **Ouellette Ave.** in Windsor (see below).

Detroit's numerous **festivals** draw millions of visitors. A new and rousingly successful downtown tradition, the ■**Detroit Electronic Music Festival** (☎393-9200; www.demf.org) has lured over one million ravers to Hart Plaza each of its first two Memorial Day weekends. Hip jazz fans jet to the riverbank during Labor Day weekend for the four-day **Ford Detroit International Jazz Festival** (☎963-7622). With more than 70 acts on three stages and mountains of international food at the World Food Court, it's the largest free jazz festival on the continent. The nation's oldest state fair, the **Michigan State Fair** (☎369-8250), at Eight Mile Rd. and Woodward Ave., gathers together bake-offs, art, and livestock birth exhibits during the two weeks before Labor Day. A two-week extravaganza in late June, the international **Freedom Festival** (☎923-7400), celebrates the friendship between the US and Canada by igniting North America's largest fireworks display over the Detroit River. **Detroit's African World Festival** (☎494-5853) brings over a million people to Hart Plaza on the 3rd weekend in August for free reggae, jazz, and gospel concerts.

Sports fans won't be disappointed in Detroit. During the dog days of summer, baseball's **Tigers** round the bases in the newly built **Comerica Park,** 2100 Woodward Ave. (☎471-2255; tickets $8-35). Football's **Lions** continue to hit the gridiron at the **Pontiac Silverdome,** 1200 Featherstone Rd., until their new stadium, **Ford Field,** is ready for action in August, 2002. (☎800-616-7627, tickets $15-35). Inside the **Joe Louis Arena,** 600 Civic Center Dr., the Red Wings play their hockey (☎645-6666; tickets $20--40), and 30min. oustide Detroit in Auburn Hills, basketball's Pistons hoop it up at **The Palace of Auburn Hills,** Two Championship Dr. (☎377-0100s; tickets $10-60).

NEAR DETROIT: WINDSOR, ON   ☎519

Playing second fiddle to Detroit is hardly a glamorous job, but Windsor rises to the task. Combining cultural highlights, natural attractions, and a vibrant nightlife, Windsor offers tourists much more than just the abandoned buildings so common across the river. Because the town weathered the decline of the auto industry better than its American counterparts, Michiganders are often spotted shopping in Windsor's malls and partying at one of its many bars. Of course, that may have more to do with the favorable exchange rates and the low drinking age (19), but it makes the Windsor crowd a cosmopolitan and exciting mix.

For a small industrial city, Windsor scores big with its collection of contemporary art. Stroll through the "museum without walls" at the **Windsor Sculpture Garden,** part of a 6 mi. long riverfront green area in Assumption and Centennial Parks between the Ambassador Bridge and Curry Ave. Visitors are enchanted by Inuit artist Pauta Saila's *Dancing (Polar) Bear.* (☎253-2300. Open daily dawn to dusk. Free.) The city's other major exhibit space, **The Art Gallery of Windsor,** 401 Riverside Dr. West, provides a showcase for a rotating cast of Canada's best modern artists. (☎977-0013. Open Tu-Th 11am-7pm, F 11am-9pm, Sa-Su 11am-5pm. Free.) Beauty of the natural type is on display at **Point Pelee National Park of Canada,** 407 Robson Street, Leamington, ON, 45 mi. southeast of downtown. The park is famous for its bird- and butterfly- watching. (☎322-2365. Open April and Sept. through mid-Oct. daily 6am-9:30pm, mid-Oct. to Mar. 7am-6:30pm, May 5am-9:30pm. CDN$3.25, seniors CDN$2.40, students CDN$1.60, family CDN$8.55; guided butterfly tours in Sept. $20 including T-shirt.) Locals come from miles around to dine at the ▨**Tunnel Bar-B-Q,** 58 Park St. East, across from the tunnel exit. Hailed as having North America's best ribs a few years back, the restaurant serves up a great half-strip rib dinner for CDN$14. (☎258-3663. Open Su-Th 8am-2am, F and Sa 8am-4am.)

The rest of Windsor's culinary and nightlife activity is centered along Ouelette (OH-let) Ave. downtown. Family run for two generations, the **Aar-D-Vark Blue Cafe,** 89 University Ave. W., is an even better take on the traditional Chicago blues joint. (☎977-6422. Live music Tu-Su. Open M-F noon-2am, Sa 4pm-2am, Su 7pm-2am.) Hipsters too edgy for the blues can bust it to the latest house or drum and bass at **Amsterdam,** 26 Pelissier St. On Fridays a DJ is flown in from as far away as Europe. (☎977-7232. Cover F-Sa after 12:30am CDN$5. Open daily 6pm-2am.) Those with too much cash can rid themselves of the burden at the shiny **Windsor Casino,** 377 Riverside Dr. With three floors of gambling, the casino sucks cash from across the border 24hr. a day. (☎800-991-8888 for reservations, 800-991-7777 for info. 19+.)

Canada's national rail service **VIA Rail,** 298 Walker Rd. (☎256-5511 or 800-561-3949. Ticket window open M-Sa 5:15am-9pm, Su 6am-9pm.), provides service to Toronto (4hr.; 5 per day; CDN$79, 40% discount with ISIC card). **Transit Windsor,** 3700 North Service Rd. E., sends buses throughout the city. (☎944-4111. Fare CDN$2.15, students CDN$1.50.) **Taxi: Veteran's Cab,** ☎256-2621. **The Convention and**

Visitors Bureau of Windsor, Essex County, & Pelee Island, 333 Riverside Dr. W., #103 (☎255-6530 or 800-265-3633; www.city.windsor.on.ca/cvb. Open M-F 8:30am-4:30pm.) **Post Office:** City Centre, corner of Park St. and Ouellette Ave. (☎253-1252; open M-F 8am-5pm). **Postal code:** N9A 4K0. **Area code:** 519.

ANN ARBOR ☎734

For a small town tucked between some major industrial hubs, Ann Arbor hasn't fared too badly. Named after Ann Rumsey and Ann Allen, wives of two of the area's early pioneers (who supposedly enjoyed sitting under grape arbors), the city has managed to prosper without losing its relaxed charm. In 1837, the gargantuan and well-respected University of Michigan moved to town, giving rise to a hip collage of leftists, granolas, yuppies, and Middle Americans.

ORIENTATION AND PRACTICAL INFORMATION. Ann Arbor's streets lie in a grid, but watch out for the *slant* of Packard St. and Detroit St. **Main St.** divides the town east-west, and **Huron St.** cuts it north-south. The central campus of the **University of Michigan (U of M),** where restaurants and bars live, lies four blocks east of Main St. and south of E. Huron (a 5min. walk from downtown). Although street meter parking is plentiful, authorities ticket ruthlessly. One-way streets and frequent dead ends also make driving near campus stressful. **Amtrak,** 325 Depot St. (☎994-4906; ticket window open daily 7am-11pm), sends three trains per day to Chicago (5hr., $37-43) and Detroit (1hr., $13-15). **Greyhound,** 116 W. Huron St. (☎662-5511; open M-Sa 8am-6:30pm, Su 8am-9am and noon-6:30pm), buses to Detroit (1-1½hr., 4 per day, $9-10); Chicago (6hr., 5 per day, $29-31); and Grand Rapids (2-4hr., 3 per day, $19). **Ann Arbor Transportation Authority (AATA),** 331 S. 4th Ave., provides public transit service in Ann Arbor and a few neighboring towns. (☎996-0400 or 973-6500. Buses run M-F 6:45am-10:45pm, Sa-Su 8am-6:15pm. Fare 75¢, students and seniors 35¢. Station open M-F 7:30am-9pm, Sa noon-5:30pm.) AATA's **Nightride** provides safe door-to-door transportation. (Call 663-3888 to book a trip; the wait is 5-45min. Runs M-F 11pm-6am, Sa-Su 7pm-6am. Fare $2.) **Commuter Transportation Company** offers frequent shuttle service between Ann Arbor and the Detroit Metro Airport. Vans depart Ann Arbor 5am-7pm and return 7am-midnight. (☎941-9391 or 800-488-7433. $24, round-trip $48. Door-to-door service for up to 4 people $65-75. Reserve up to 48hr. in advance.) **Visitor Info: Ann Arbor Convention and Visitors Bureau,** 120 W. Huron St., at Ashley. (☎995-7281 or 800-888-9487. Open M-F 8:30am-5pm.) **Hotlines: Sexual Assault Crisis Line,** ☎483-7273. **U. Michigan Sexual Assault Line,** ☎936-3333. **S.O.S. Crisis Line,** ☎485-3222. All 24hr. **U. Michigan Gay/Lesbian Referrals,** ☎763-4186. Operates M-F 9am-5pm. **Post Office:** 2075 W. Stadium Blvd. (☎665-1100; open M-F 7:30am-5pm). **ZIP code:** 48103. **Area code:** 734.

ACCOMMODATIONS. Due to the many business travelers and college sports fans who flock to the town, expensive hotels, motels, and B&Bs dominate the lodging scene in Ann Arbor. Reservations are always advisable, especially during the school year. Reasonable rates exist at discount chains farther out of town or in **Ypsilanti,** 5 mi. southeast along I-94. Just south of I-94 on the outskirts of Ann Arbor, good ol' **Motel 6,** 3764 S. State St., rents well-kept, reliable rooms. (☎665-9900. Singles $46-56; doubles $52-62.) The **Hotel Embassy,** 200 E. Huron, at 4th Ave., a short walk from campus, offers tidy rooms in the middle of the action. (☎662-7100. Key deposit $3. Singles $59.) Seven campgrounds lie within a 20 mi. radius of Ann Arbor. Both the **Pinckney Recreation Area,** 8555 Silver Hill (☎426-4913), in Pinckney, and the **Waterloo Recreation Area,** 16345 McClure Rd. (☎475-8307), in Chelsea, have primitive ($6) and modern ($14) sites; both require a $4 vehicle permit.

FOOD. Where there are students, there are cheap eats. Here the cheapest cram the sidewalks of **State St.** and **S. University St.,** while the more upscale line **Main St.** Next to the Kerrytown shops, growers haul their crops to the popular **Farmers Market,** 315 Detroit St. (☎994-3276. Open May-Dec. W and Sa 7am-3pm; Jan.-Apr. Sa

8am-3pm.) At ✉**Zingerman's Deli,** 422 Detroit St., even *goyim* line up for huge, excellent deli sandwiches for $6-12. (☎663-3354. Open daily 7am-10pm.) For an even more complete meal, try the gigantic portions at **Casey's Tavern,** 304 Depot St., across from the train station. The Caesar Steak Sandwich ($8) makes both locals and passers-through rave. (☎665-6775. Open M-Th 11am-11pm, F-Sa 11am-midnight.) In the birthplace of Domino's, **Pizza House,** 618 Church St., reigns supreme as the best in town. (☎995-5095. Open daily 10:30am-4:30am. Pizzas $7-22.) Plants tremble at the mention of **Seva,** 314 E. Liberty, Ann Arbor's long-established veggie haven. Its earthy decor complements a meatless menu that covers Mexican, stir-fry, and all points in between. (☎662-1111. Open M-Th 10am-9pm, F 10:30am-10pm, Sa 9am-10pm, Su 10am-9pm. Entrees $7-10.) **Krazy Jim's Blimpy Burger,** 551 S. Division, near campus, is a favorite of kollege kids for their great, self-proclaimed $1.70 "cheaper than food" burgers. (☎663-4590. Open daily 11am-10pm.)

🖼🎵 SIGHTS AND ENTERTAINMENT. Most of Ann Arbor's attractions stem from its identity as home to a major university. At the **University of Michigan Museum of Art (UMMA),** 525 S. State St., at the corner of S. University St., a limited but impressive collection of artwork from around the world decorates the galleries. Two pieces by Picasso highlight the museum's cache. (☎764-0395. Open Tu-W and F-Sa 10am-5pm, Th 10am-9pm, Su noon-5pm. Free.) The **University of Michigan Exhibit Museum of Natural History,** 1109 Geddes Ave., at Washtenaw, displays an assortment of dinosaur skeletons and other exhibits on zoology, astronomy, and geology. The planetarium offers indoor star-gazing on weekends. (☎764-0478. Open M-Sa 9am-5pm, Su noon-5pm. Museum free; planetarium $3, seniors and kids $2.) Outside the university, the **Ann Arbor Hands-On Museum,** 219 E. Huron St., presents a tactile wonderland of exhibits designed to be felt, turned, touched, pushed, and plucked by children of all ages. (☎995-5437. Open Tu-Sa 10am-5pm, Su noon-5pm. $6; seniors, students, and children $4.) Numerous local artists display their creations at the **Artisans' Market,** 315 Detroit St., which shares the Farmers Market grounds. (Open May-Dec. Su 11am-4pm.) It's nigh-impossible to get tickets for a **Wolverine football** game at U of M's 115,000 capacity stadium, but fans can give it a shot by calling the athletics office at 764-0247.

As tens of thousands of students depart for the summer, locals indulge in a little celebration. In late July, thousands pack the city to view the work of nearly 600 artists at the **Ann Arbor Summer Art Fair** (☎995-7281; July 17-20, 2002). The **Ann Arbor Summer Festival** (☎647-2278) draws crowds from mid-June through early July for a collection of comedy, dance, and theater productions, as well as musical performances including jazz, country, and classical. The festival includes nightly outdoor movies at **Top of the Park,** on top of the Fletcher St. parking structure, next to the Health Services Building. The **County Events Hotline** (☎930-6300) has more info. Classical music lovers should contact the **University Musical Society,** in the Burton Memorial Clock Tower at N. University and Thouper, for info on area performances. (☎764-2538 or 800-221-1229. Open M-F 10am-5pm, Sa 10am-1pm. Tickets $10-55.)

🌙 NIGHTLIFE. The monthlies *Current, Agenda, Weekender Entertainment,* and the weekly *Metrotimes,* all free and available in restaurants, music stores, and elsewhere, print up-to-date nightlife and entertainment listings. For gay and lesbian info pick up a copy of *OutPost* or *Between the Lines.* The **Blind Pig,** 208 S. First St., is the hottest spot in town for live music, with rock 'n' roll, reggae, blues, and swing. (☎996-8555. 19+. Cover $5-15. Open nightly until 2am.) Showcasing big names Friday and Saturday, the **Bird of Paradise,** 207 S. Ashley, sings with live jazz every night. (☎662-8310. Cover $3-5.) **The Nectarine,** 516 E. Liberty, is the place for young hipsters to shake their groove thing to DJ-controlled dance music. (☎994-5436. Open Tu-Sa until 2am; Tu and F are gay nights.) The laid back **Ashley's,** 338 S. State St., keeps over 60 beers on tap. (☎996-9191. Open nightly until 2am.) **Conor O'Neill's,** 318 S. Main St., is a hearty Celtic-flavored hangout for locals and students. (☎665-2968. Open daily 11am-2am.) On weekends, locals hang out at **Del Rio,** 122 W. Washington St., at Ashley, for cheap burgers and Mexican food, good vegetarian options, and free jazz Sunday evenings. (☎761-2530. Open nightly until 1:45am with jazz until 9:30pm. Cash only.) Sports fans should join the ESPN camera crew at **Touchdown Cafe Grill & Bar,** 1220 S. University on campus, to guzzle beer and indulge their inner quarterback with enormous TVs. (☎665-7777. Open nightly until 2am.)

GRAND RAPIDS   ☎616

From its humble beginning as one among many fur trading posts, Grand Rapids worked hard to distinguish itself from its neighbors. While many towns opted for tourist chic with quaint, old-fashioned looks, Grand Rapids plowed ahead to become a city of concrete and tall buildings. While attractive to businesses, Grand Rapids offers precious little in the way of entertainment for the traveler. Most use it as a transportation hub to reach the rest of western Michigan.

⚆ PRACTICAL INFORMATION. Most of Grand Rapids' streets are neatly gridded. The town is quartered by the north-south Division St. and the east-west Fulton St. **Greyhound,** 190 Wealthy St. (☎456-1709; station open daily 6:45am-10pm), connects to: Detroit (3½hr., 4 per day, $19-23); Chicago (4½hr., 3 per day, $27-29); and Ann Arbor (3hr., 1 per day, $18-21). **Amtrak,** 507 Wealthy St., at Market, has service to the south and west, including Chicago (4hr.; 1 per day; $32-46, round-trip $58). The station, which does not sell tickets, only opens when trains pass through. **Grand Rapids Transit Authority (GRATA),** 333 Wealthy St. SW, sends buses throughout the city and suburbs. (☎776-1100. Runs M-F 5:45am-11:15pm, Sa 6:30am-9:30pm, Su 8am-7:45am. Fare $1.25, seniors 60¢; 10-ride pass $9.) **Veterans Taxi:** ☎459-4646. The **Grand Rapids-Kent County Convention and Visitors Bureau,** 134 Monroe Center (☎459-8287 or 800-678-9859; open M-F 9am-7pm) and the **West Michigan Tourist Association,** 1253 Front Ave. NW (☎456-8557 or 800-442-2084; open M-Th 8:30am-5pm, F 8:30am-6pm, Sa 9am-1pm), furnish general area info. **Suicide, Drug, Alcohol, and Crisis Line,** ☎336-3535. Operates 24hr. **Internet access:** Free at the **Grand Rapids Public Library,** 1100 Hynes SW, Suite B (☎988-5400; open M-Th 9am-9pm, F, Sa 9am-5:30pm, in summer Su 1-5pm). **Post Office:** 225 Michigan St. NW (☎532-2109; open M-F 8am-5:30pm, Sa 9am-12:30pm). **ZIP code:** 49503. **Area code:** 616.

⚐ ACCOMMODATIONS. Most of the cheaper motels and restaurants cluster south of the city along Division and 28th St. **The Grand Rapids Inn,** 250 28th St. SW, offers serviceable rooms at rock-bottom prices. (☎452-2131. Singles from $33, doubles from $40.) Men are in luck at the **YMCA,** 33 Library St. NE, downtown. (☎222-9626. $26, $15 each additional night; no reservations.) Just 12 mi. northeast of downtown, **Grand Rogue Campgrounds,** 6400 W. River Dr., sports wooded, riverside sites. Take Rte. 131 north to Comstock Park Exit 91, then head left on W. River Dr. for 4 mi. (☎361-1053. $20, with hookup $26.)

⚐⚏ FOOD AND NIGHTLIFE. Throngs of locals pack the **Beltline Bar and Café,** 16 28th St. SE, for Grand Rapids' most popular Mexican food. Wet burritos, the house specialty, start at $5. (☎245-0494. Open M-Tu 7am-midnight, W-Sa 7am-1am, Su noon-10:30pm.) The **⚏Four Friends Coffeehouse,** 136 Monroe Center, has excellent coffee concoctions (from $1), fresh muffins ($1.25), and delicious sandwiches ($3) in a trendy atmosphere. (☎456-5356. Live music on F and Sa during the school year. Open M-Th 7am-10pm, F 7am-midnight, Sa 8am-midnight; Sept.-May open until 11pm.) The **Grand Rapids Brewing Company,** 3689 28th St. SE, makes tasty $6 burgers, steaks, and $3.50 handcrafted beers. (☎285-5970. Open M-Th and Su 11am-10pm, F-Sa 11am-11pm, Su noon-10pm; bar open M-Th 11am-midnight, F-Sa 11am-1am.)

Detailed listings on events and nightlife in Grand Rapids can be found in *On the Town* or *In the City*, both available in most shops, restaurants, and kiosks. The artsy Eastown District houses the bulk of the local music scene; dance clubs overshadow other forms of city nightlife. The wild **Diversions,** 10 Fountain NW, is *the* place to show off your stylin' moves. (☎451-3800. Karaoke W and Sa at 10pm. Cover usually $5, free for 21+. Open daily 8pm-2am, dance floor opens at 10pm.)

◙ **SIGHTS.** The attractive **Public Museum of Grand Rapids,** 272 Pearl St. NW, show-cases marvels such as one of the world's largest whale skeletons (76 ft.), an antique, 50-animal carousel, and a planetarium. (☎456-3977. Open M-Sa 9am-5pm, Su noon-5pm. $6, seniors $5, ages 3-17 $2.50. Planetarium $2.) The largest year-round conservatory in Michigan, the **Frederik Meijer Gardens,** 3411 Bradford St. at Beltline, keeps over 100 sculptures among numerous tropical plants on 70 acres. A $12.8 million addition and a three-story replica of a Da Vinci horse sculpture were purchased in celebration of the millennium. (☎957-1580. Open M-W and F-Sa 9am-5pm, Th 9am-9pm, Su noon-5pm; Sept.-May M-Sa 9am-5pm, Su noon-5pm. $6, seniors $5, students $4, children $2.50.) Architecture enthusiasts shouldn't miss the **Meyer May House,** 450 Madison Ave. SE, designed by Frank Lloyd Wright in his famous multi-tiered style. (☎246-4821. Open Tu and Th 10am-2pm and most Su 1pm-5pm. Free.)

LAKE MICHIGAN SHORE

The freighters that once powered the rise of Chicago still steam along the coast of Lake Michigan, but have long since been supplanted by pleasure boats. With dunes of sugary sand, superb fishing, abundant fruit harvests, and deep winter snows, the eastern shore of Lake Michigan is any vacationer's dreamland. The coastline stretches 350 miles north from the Indiana border to the Mackinac Bridge; its southern end is a scant two hours from downtown Chicago.

⁊ PRACTICAL INFORMATION

Many of the region's attractions lie in the small coastal towns that cluster around Grand Traverse Bay in the north. **Traverse City,** at the southern tip of the bay, is famous as the "cherry capital of the world." Fishing is best in the Au Sable and Manistee Rivers. However, the rich Mackinac Island Fudge, sold in numerous specialty shops on and around the Island, seems to have the biggest hold on tourists ("fudgies" to locals; see **Mackinac Island,** p. 497). The main north-south route along the coast is U.S. 31. Numerous detours, marked by green "Lake Michigan Circle Tour" signs, twist closer to the shoreline, providing an excellent way to explore the coast. Coastal accommodations can be quite expensive; for cheaper lodging, head inland. Based in Grand Rapids, the **West Michigan Tourist Association,** 1253 Front Ave. NW, hands out info on the area. (☎456-8557 or 800-442-2084. Open M-Th 8:30am-5pm, F 8:30am-6pm, Sa 9am-1pm.) The Lake Michigan Shore's **area codes** are 616 and 231.

SOUTHERN MICHIGAN SHORE

HOLLAND   ☎616

Thirty mi. southwest of Grand Rapids off I-196, Holland was founded in 1847 by Dutch religious dissenters and remained mostly Dutch well into the 20th century. The town cashes in on its heritage with a bevy of tacky, Dutch-inspired attractions; still, it's worth visiting around May when the tulips bloom. The small but high-quality **Holland Museum,** 31 W. 10th St., displays ceramics, furniture from the home country, and exhibits on town history. (☎392-9084. Open M, W, F-Sa 10am-5pm; Th 10am-8pm; Su 2-5pm. $3, seniors and students $2.) The harvest at the jubilantly arrayed **Veldheer Tulip Gardens,** 12755 Quincy St., at U.S. 31, would be the envy of the Amsterdam market. (☎399-1900. Open daily 8am-6pm. $5, ages 3-13.) Next door, the **DeKlomp Wooden Shoe and Delftware Factory** caters to tourists who want to walk home in a wooden or porcelain souvenir. (☎399-1900. Open M-F 8am-6pm, Sa-Su 9am-5pm. Free.) A nearby "authentic" **Dutch Village,** 12350 James St., at U.S. 31, is worth a look, although its oversized wooden shoe and windmill attractions can resemble a mini-golf course *sans* holes. (☎396-1475. Open late Apr. to mid-Oct. daily 9am-5pm, July to mid-Oct. 9am-7pm. $6.50, ages 3-11 $5.) DeZwaan, the nation's only operating Dutch windmill, turns on **Windmill Island,** at the corner of Lincoln and 7th St. downtown. (☎355-1030. Open May-Oct. daily with variable hours; call for info. $5.50, ages 5-12 $2.50, under 5 free.)

The **Blue Mill Inn,** 409 U.S. 31, at 16th St., rents decent singles from $52 and doubles from $64. (☎392-7073 or 888-258-3140. Off-season rates lower.) **Holland State Park,** 2215 Ottawa Beach Rd., 8 mi. west of Holland, has 306 sparsely wooded sites nestled between Lake Macatawa and Lake Michigan. (☎399-9390 or 800-447-2757. Sites $15; vehicle permit $4.) **Greyhound,** 171 Lincoln Ave. (☎396-8664), runs through Holland to Detroit (4hr., 2 per day, $26-28); Chicago (4hr., 3 per day, $27-29); and Grand Rapids (35min., 3 per day, $9-10). **Amtrak,** in the same building, runs a daily train to Chicago (3hr., $31). Reserve train tickets in advance; there are no Amtrak representatives at the station. (Station open M-F 7-11am and 12:30-4:30pm.) **Holland Convention and Visitors Bureau:** 76 E. 8th St. downtown (☎394 0000 or 800-506-1299; open M-F 8am-5pm, May-Oct. also Sa 10:30am-3pm).

GRAND HAVEN   ☎616

Thirty-five miles west of Grand Rapids off I-96, Grand Haven is one of the best beach communities in the area. The town offers a relaxed, resort-like atmosphere and lots of sand—so pure that auto manufacturers use it to make cores and molds for engine parts. The small downtown area attracts visitors to its pleasant "boardwalk" along the lake. In the heart of downtown, **Washington St.** is lined with shops, restaurants, and laid-back people. The groovy **Musical Fountain,** at the end of Washington St., pulses with water and light to the beat of different music each night. (☎842-4910 or 842-2550. Operates June-Aug. around 9:30pm.)

An upscale northwoods hostel, the ▓**Khardomah Lodge,** 1365 Lake Ave., has charmingly decorated rooms and enormous common areas. Its Americana character, warm service, and convenient location to the beach, make it one of the best budget lodgings on all of Michigan's lakeshore. (☎842-2990. Kitchen, shared bath. Reservations strongly recommended. Doubles $58, $10 each additional person.) Campers will love picturesque **Grand Haven State Park,** 1001 Harbor Dr. (☎847-1309 or 800-447-2757; open early Apr.-Oct.; $15 plus $4 permit for site and hookup). **Grand Haven Area Visitors Bureau:** 1 S. Harbor Dr., at Washington St. (☎842-4499 or 800-303-4096; open in summer M 9:30am-5pm, Tu-F 8:30am-5pm, Sa 10am-2pm).

CENTRAL MICHIGAN SHORE

MANISTEE   ☎231

Manistee's claim to be a "Victorian Port City" is overshadowed by the impressive trio of natural beauties that surround it. Lake Michigan tempts boaters, swimmers, and beachgoers, while fishing buffs are drawn to Manistee Lake. Manistee National Forest blankets the outskirts of the city, catering to hikers, bikers, and campers.

There are several relatively inexpensive motel options in and near Manistee. The friendly **Riverside Motel,** 520 Water St., has dock space for boats and large waterfront rooms. (☎723-3554. Summer singles $69-99, doubles $69-109; winter $29-69/ $35-79. Reservations recommended.) Fourteen mi. north in Onekama, the **Traveller's Motel,** 5606 Eight Mile Rd., half a block from Rte. 22, rents large rooms with kitchenettes. (☎889-4342. Singles $45; doubles $60; with kitchenettes for up to 6 people $80; in winter $32/$42/$55.) **Manistee National Forest** supplies copious camping at 11 campgrounds in the area ($5 per person; no reservations). Those who enjoy roughing it are free to camp anywhere in the forest.

More info on hiking and canoeing is available from the **Manistee Ranger Station,** 412 Red Apple Rd., just south of downtown of U.S. 31. (☎723-2211. Open M-F 8am-5pm, Sa-Su 8:30am-5pm.) Those interested in fishing the area's lakes and rivers with a guide should contact the Manistee Area Charterboat organization (☎889-5815). Thirty mi. to the south, the **Lake Michigan Car Ferry** shuttles people and cars between Ludington and Manitowoc, WI, granting easy access to Wisconsin's major cities and attractions. (☎800-841-4243. 4hr., late June to Aug. 2 per day, in spring and fall 1 per day; $38, seniors $35, ages 5-15 $17, cars an additional $46. Reservations recommended.) The **Manistee Economic Council and Chamber Alliance (MECCA),** 50 Filer St. in Briny Bldg., #224, is a pilgrimage site for those seeking brochures on local attractions. (☎723-4325. Open M-F 8am-5:30pm.)

SLEEPING BEAR DUNES   ☎ 231

The Sleeping Bear Dunes lie along the western shores of the Leelanau Peninsula, 20 mi. west of Traverse City on Rte. 72. According to Chippewa legend, the mammoth sand dune represents a sleeping mother bear, waiting for her drowned cubs—the Manitou Islands—to finish a swim across the lake after fleeing a forest fire. Each cub has a distinctive personality—South Manitou is small and more civilized, while rugged North Manitou is vast and untamed. The sleepy town of **Empire** serves as the gateway to the **Sleeping Bear Dunes National Lakeshore,** which includes both the Manitou Islands and 25 mi. of lakeshore on the mainland. Near the historic Fishtown shops, **Manitou Island Transit,** in Leland, makes daily trips to South Manitou and ventures five times per week in July and August to North Manitou. (☎256-9061. Check-in 9:15am. Call ahead for schedule in May-June and Sept.-Nov. Round-trip $22, under 12 $13.) **Camping** is available on both islands with the purchase of a **permit** ($5; plus required park entrance fee $7 for 7 days; buy at the Visitors Center); the Manitou Islands do not allow cars.

Willing climbers can be king of the sandhill at **Dune Climb,** 5 mi. north of Empire on Rte. 109. From there, a strenuous 2½ mi. hike over sandy hills leads to Lake Michigan in all its refreshing glory. If you'd rather let your car do the climbing, drive to an overlook along the 7 mi. **Pierce Stocking Scenic Drive,** off Rte. 109 just north of Empire, where a 450 ft. sand cliff descends to the cool water below. (Open mid-May to mid-Oct. daily 9am-10pm.) For maps and info on the numerous cross-country skiing, hiking, and mountain biking trails in the lakeshore area, stop by the helpful **National Parks Service Visitors Center,** 9922 Front St., in Empire (☎326-5134; open in summer daily 9am-6pm; mid-Sept. to mid-June 9am-4pm).

The Sleeping Bear Dunes have four **campgrounds: DH Day** (☎334-4634), in Glen Arbor, with 83 primitive sites ($10); **Platte River** (☎325-5881 or 800-365-2267), off the southern shore, with 179 sites and showers ($14, with electricity $19); and two cheaper **backcountry campsites** accessible by 1½ mi. trails (no reservations; $5 permit required, available at Visitors Center or at either developed campground). The Platte River (at the southern end of the lakeshore) and the Crystal River (at the northern end) are ideal for canoeing or for lazy floating. **Crystal River Outfitters,** 6249 Western Ave. (Rte. 22), near Glen Arbor, offers 1-4hr. kayak excursions. (☎334-7490. $12.50-20 per person.) **Riverside Canoes,** 5042 Scenic Hwy. (Rte. 22), at Platte River Bridge, lets less adventurous types play with water toys. (☎325-5622. Inner tubes $4-6 for 1hr., $11-13 for 2hr.; canoes $25-29; kayaks $16.)

TRAVERSE CITY   ☎ 231

Named after the "Grand Traverse" that French fur traders once made between the Leelanau and Old Mission Peninsulas, Traverse City offers the summer vacationer a slew of sandy beaches and more than a bowl full of cherries (half of the nation's cherries are produced in the surrounding area). In the summer, swimming, boating, and scuba diving interests focus on Grand Traverse Bay; free beaches and activities bespeckle the shore. The scenic waterfront also makes for excellent biking. The **TART** bike trail runs 8 mi. along E. and W. Grand Traverse Bay, while the 30 mi. loop around Old Mission Peninsula, north of the city, provides great views of the Bay. **McLain Cycle and Fitness,** 750 E. 8th St., rents bikes and dispenses biking info. (☎941-7161. Open M-Sa 9am-6pm, Su 11am-4pm. $15 per day, $30 all weekend.)

Most other attractions in the Traverse City area focus on its fruit. The annual **National Cherry Festival** (☎947-4230), held the first full week in July, is a rousing tribute to the fruit's annual harvest with concerts, parties and lots of cherry pie. In early to mid-July, five orchards near Traverse City let visitors pick their own cherries, including **Amon Orchards,** 10 mi. north on U.S. 31. (☎938-9160. Open daily 9am-6pm. $1.25 per lb.; eat while you pick for free.) More sophisticated fruit connoisseurs can indulge their taste buds at one of the area's many well-respected wineries. The scenic **Château Grand Traverse,** 12239 Center Rd., 8 mi. north of Traverse City on Rte. 37, offers free tours and tastings. (☎223-7355 or 800-283-0247. Open June-Aug. M-Sa 10am-7pm, Su noon-6pm; May and Sep.-Oct. M-Sa 10am-6pm, Su noon-6pm; Nov.-Apr. M-Sa 10am-5pm, Su noon-5pm. In summer, tours on the hr. noon-4pm.)

East Front St. (U.S. 31) is lined with motels, but it is nearly impossible to find a room for under $50 in the popular summer months. **Northwestern Michigan College,** 1701 E. Front St., West and East Halls, has some of the cheapest beds in the city. (☎995-1409. Linen $9. Reserve several weeks in advance. Open early June to Aug. Singles $31; doubles $40; suite with bathroom $55.) For those who prefer to commune with nature, or at least with 300 other campers, **Traverse City State Park,** 1132 U.S. 31 N, 2 mi. east of town, has 344 wooded sites across the street from the beach. (☎922-5270 or 800-447-2757. Sites with hookup $15; $4 vehicle permit fee.) Front St. downtown offers a range of appealing food options. **Poppycock's,** 128 E. Front St., doles out $5-7 gourmet sandwiches (vegetarian and otherwise). (☎941-7632. Open in summer M-Th 11am-10pm, F-Sa 11am-10:30pm, Su noon-9pm; in winter M-Th 11am-9pm, F-Sa 11am-10pm.) The **U & I Lounge,** Front St. downtown, is the hottest bar in town, thanks in part to the tasty local beer. (☎946-8932. Open M-Sa 11am-2am, kitchen until 1:35am; Su noon-2am, kitchen until 1:15am.) For more entertainment info, pick up the weekly *Northern Express* at corner kiosks around the city.

Indian Trails and **Greyhound,** 3233 Cass Rd. (☎946-5180), tie Traverse City to Detroit (9hr., 3 per day, $37-41) and to the Upper Peninsula via St. Ignace (3hr., 1 per day, $18). Call the **Bay Area Transportation Authority** and they'll pick you up; a 24hr. notice is preferred. (☎941-2324. Available M-Sa 6am-1:30am, Su 8am-1:30am. Fare $2, seniors $1.) **Traverse City Convention and Visitors Bureau:** 101 West Grandview Pkwy./U.S. 31 N (☎947-1120 or 800-872-8377; open daily 9am-6pm). **Post Office:** 202 S. Union St. (☎946-9616; open M-F 8am-5pm). **ZIP code:** 49684.

NORTHERN MICHIGAN SHORE

STRAITS OF MACKINAC   ☎231

Only fur'ners say *"mack-i-NACK"*—in the Land of the Great Turtle (as early Native Americans called it), Mackinac is pronounced *mack-i-NAW.* Even though tourists, not troops, flock to **Mackinaw City,** Colonial **Fort Michilimackinac** still guards the straits between Lake Michigan and Lake Huron. Along with Fort Michilimackinac, **Fort Mackinac** (on Mackinac Island, see below) and **Historic Mill Creek** (3½ mi. south of Mackinaw City on Rte. 23) form a trio of State Historic Parks in the area. (☎436-4100. All open mid-June to early Sept. daily 9am-6pm; early Sept. to Oct. and May to mid-Oct. 10am-5pm. Each park $8, ages 6-17 $5, families $20.) The five-mile **Mackinac Bridge** ("Mighty Mac"), connecting Mackinaw City to St. Ignace in the Upper Peninsula, is the world's longest suspension bridge. A local tradition not to be missed is the annual **Labor Day Bridge Walk,** where Michigan's governor leads thousands of pilgrims across the bridge from Mackinaw City to St. Ignace.

The best lodging deals in the area lie across the Mackinac Bridge and away from the lakeshore on the I-75 Business Loop in St. Ignace. Five min. from the docks, the lakeside **Harbor Light Motel,** 1449 State St. (on business I-75), rents newly refurbished rooms with cable TV. Join other travelers for a late-night bonfire on the beach. (☎906-643-9439. Singles $45, doubles $47.) Back near Mackinaw City, campers can crash at the enormous **Mackinac Mill Creek Campground,** 3 mi. south of town on Rte. 23. Most of its 600 sites lie near the lake. (☎436-5584. Sites $15, full hookup $17.50; cabins $40.) Sites at the **Wilderness State Park,** 11 mi. west of the city on Wilderness Park Dr., have showers and electricity. (☎436-5381. $15; 4- to 8-person cabins $40; 20-person bunkhouse $55. $4 permit required.)

For transportation outside the city, **Indian Trails** (☎517-725-5105 or 800-292-3831) has a flag stop at the Big Boy restaurant on Nicolet Ave. One bus runs north and one south per day; buy tickets at the next station. The **Michigan Dept. of Transportation Welcome and Travel Information Center,** on Nicolet St. off I-75 at Exit 338, has loads of helpful info on lodging, food and area attractions. (☎436-5566. Open daily 8am-6pm; Sept. through mid-June 9am-5pm. Free reservation service.)

GREAT LAKES

MACKINAC ISLAND   ☎ 231

Posh Mackinac Island, a 16-minute ferry ride from the mainland, has long been considered Mackinaw City's classier cousin. The prohibition of cars on the heavily touristed island, and the resulting proliferation of horse-drawn carriages, have given it a snobbish air and a decidedly equine aroma. Nevertheless, travelers flock to the island for its coastal, old-world charm.

The main draws include **Fort Mackinac,** magnificent Victorian homes, and countless beaches. (Fort ☎436-4100. Open mid-June to mid-Aug. daily 9:30am-6:30pm; mid- to late Aug. 9:30am-5pm. $8, ages 6-17 $5, under 6 free.) Connoisseurs will immediately recognize the island as the birthplace of Mackinac Fudge, sold in shops all over the island and along the entire Michigan coastline (1 lb. box $7). **Horse-drawn carriages** cart guests on tours all over the island, showcasing architectural wonders such as the ritzy Grand Hotel. (Carriage tours ☎906-847-3325. Open daily 9am-5pm. $15, ages 4-11 $7.50.) Saddle horses ($25 per hr.) are also available at various stables around the isle. Perhaps the best way to see the island and escape the tourist mayhem is by bicycle. Rentals line Main St. by the ferry docks ($4 per hr.). Encompassing 80% of the island, **Mackinac Island State Park** features a circular 8.2 mi. shoreline road for biking and hiking.

Transportation to the island via ferry is quick and pleasant, providing terrific views of the Mackinac Bridge. Three ferry lines leave Mackinaw City and St. Ignace with overlapping schedules, though service from St. Ignace is less frequent. **Shepler's** (☎800-828-6157) offers the fastest service. The catamarans operated by **Arnold Transit Co.** (☎847-3351 or 800-542-8528) are a fun way to jet to the island. During the summer, a ferry leaves Mackinaw City every 30min. from 8am-11pm (round-trip $15.50, under 16 $7.50, bike passage $6.50). Prices on the island are exorbitantly high; the mainland is the place to stay. For food, **Mighty Mac** cooks it good and cheap, with huge ¼ lb. burgers for under $4. (☎847-8039. Open daily 8am-8pm.) The invaluable *Mackinac Island Locator Map* ($1) and the *Discover Mackinac Island* book ($2) can be found at the **Mackinac Island Chamber of Commerce,** on Main St. (☎906-847-3783 or 800-454-5257. Open daily 8am-7pm; Oct.-May 9am-5pm.)

SCENIC DRIVE: NORTHERN MICHIGAN SHORE DRIVE

Cherry trees, tranquil lake shores, and intimate resort villages dot the Northern Michigan Shore. Once a trade route used by Native Americans and French fur traders, the path along the coast now shows of the diversity of Michigan's lands.

U.S. 31 winds its way 65 mi. north from Traverse City to Petoskey, where tortuous Rte. 119 takes over and completes the 31 mi. journey to Cross Village. It takes about 3hr. to do justice to the drive, stopping along the way to admire both the natural and man-made wonders that line the route. Although the roads are generally well maintained, drivers should exercise special caution on the spectacular 27 mi. stretch of Rte. 119 between Cross Village and Harbor Springs, known as the **Tunnel of Trees.** This patch of road is extremely narrow and twists through many sharp curves, necessitating slow speeds and care in passing. Luckily, the slow pace is rewarded with more time to absorb the natural beauty of the area.

Just 12 mi. outside of bustling Traverse City, lush cherry orchards line the road around the sleepy town of **Acme.** Twenty mi. north of Acme, then west on Barnes Park Road, the village of **Torch Lake** harbors pristine, isolated beaches on **Grand Traverse Bay** at **Barnes County Park.** More cherry trees line the route north of **Atwood,** one of the most prolific areas of the cherry harvest.

Rolling hills and increasingly elaborate homes mark the entrance into **Charlevoix** (*SHAR-le-voy*), a resort village that inhabits the narrow strip of land between Lake Michigan and Lake Charlevoix. The yacht-filled, highbrow town now attracts more tourists than it did earlier in the century, when one-time resident Ernest Hemingway used the area as the setting for many of his Nick Adams stories. The **Charlevoix Area Chamber of Commerce,** 408 Bridge St., dishes the dirt on area attractions such as golfing, boating, and shopping. (☎547-2101. Open in summer M-Sa 9am-6pm; in winter M-F 9am-5pm.) Lodging rarely comes cheap in this coastal resort town, but the

DEER SEASON Lasting only two weeks in late November, "Deer Season" might seem relatively innocuous to the unwary traveler, yet in this part of the country, Deer Season is fraught with cultural significance. Many schools in the Upper Peninsula and the northern Lower Peninsula close on Opening Day (the first day of Deer Season) because of the sheer number of student absences. The song "The Second Week of Deer Camp" is played incessantly on the radio. Hunter's orange, an eye-catching fabric hue designed to prevent accidental shootings, becomes *de rigueur* in every bar and tavern. The same old jokes are bandied around with equal enthusiasm each year: "What's the difference between beer nuts and deer nuts? Beer nuts are $2.50; deer nuts are under a buck." Groan if you want, but he has a gun....

Colonial Motel, 6822 U.S. 31 S, is better than the rest with free coffee, A/C, and cable TV. (☎547-6637. Open May-Oct. Singles $38-60; doubles $48-70; off-season rates lower.) Campers who don't mind doing without showers and electricity can bask in 90 sites on the shores of Lake Michigan at **Fisherman's Island State Park**, on Bells Bay Rd., 5 mi. south of Charlevoix on U.S. 31. (☎547-6641 or 800-447-2757; rustic sites $6; vehicle permit $4). Charlevoix also serves as the gateway to **Beaver Island,** the Great Lakes' most remote inhabited island. Hiking, boating, biking, and swimming abound on the island's 53 sq. mi., just a 2¼hr. ferry trip from shore. **Ferries** depart from 102 Bridge St. 1-3 times per day. (☎547-2311 or 888-446-4095. Round-trip $31, ages 5-12 $15.50; bikes $12.) **Beaver Island Chamber of Commerce: ☎**448-2505.

PETOSKEY   ☎231

Eighteen miles north of Charlevoix on the mainland, the slightly larger resort town of Petoskey is best known for its Petoskey Stones, fossilized coral from an ancient sea that remains strewn about the area's beaches. Another vacation haunt of Hemingway, the town honors him with a dedication at the **Little Traverse History Museum,** on the waterfront downtown at 100 Depot Ct. (☎347-2620; open summers M-F 10am-4pm, Sa-Su 1-4pm; $1). Nearby, off northbound U.S. 31, the **Sunset Park Scenic Overlook** is an unbeatable place to watch the sun sink below the horizon.

The cheapest rooms in town are at homely **North Central Michigan College,** 1515 Howard St., which rents single dorm rooms within a suite. (☎348-6611 or 348-6612 for reservations. Linen provided. Singles $30; doubles $40; 4-person suite $70. Reservations recommended; cash or check only.) If dorm life isn't your thing, the major chains clump around the junction of U.S. 31 and U.S. 131. Petoskey's **Gaslight District,** just off U.S. 31 downtown, features local crafts and foods in period shops. In the heart of the district, the nautical-themed **Roast and Toast Cafe,** 309 E. Lake St., serves pasta and chicken dishes for $7-10. (☎347-7767. Open daily in summer 7am-9:30pm; in winter 7am-8pm.) The **City Park Grill** sells sandwiches ($6-8) in an elegant 1910 setting dear to Hemingway. (☎347-0101. Live entertainment W-Sa 10pm. $2-3 cover. Open Su-Th 11:30am-10pm, F-Sa 11:30am-11pm, bar open later.)

Although it lies 20 mi. east of Petoskey in a remote woodland just outside Indian River, the **Cross in the Woods,** 7078 Rte. 68 (☎238-8973), is worth seeing. Here, a 31 ft. bronze Jesus cleaved onto a 55 ft. tall wooden cross—the world's tallest—forms an anguished yet oddly imposing monument to the national obsession with size.

UPPER PENINSULA

A multi-million-acre forestland bordered by three of the world's largest lakes, Michigan's Upper Peninsula (U.P.) is among the most scenic, unspoiled stretches of land in the world. In 1837, though, Michigan only grudgingly accepted this "wasteland to the north" in the unpopular deal that gave the territory statehood. From the start, Michigan exploited most of the land, laying waste to huge tracts of forest destined for the fireplaces of Chicago. In the past century, however, the now-protected forests have once again won the hearts of nature lovers.

GREAT LAKES

Only 24,000 people live in the U.P.'s largest town, **Marquette.** The region is a paradise for fishing, camping, hiking, snowmobiling, and escaping hectic urban life. Hikers here enjoy numerous treks, including Michigan's section of **North Country Trail,** a national scenic trail extending from New York to North Dakota. The **North Country Trail Association,** 49 Monroe Center NW, Suite 200B, Grand Rapids 49503 (☎616-454-5506), provides details on the path. A vibrant spectrum of foliage makes autumn a beautiful time to hike; in the winter, skiers and snowmobilers replace hikers as layers of snow blanket the trails. After the ice thaws, dozens of pristine rivers beckon canoers. Those who heed the call of the water should contact the **Michigan Association of Paddlesport Providers,** P.O. Box 270, Wellston, MI 49689 (☎616-862-3227).

Outside the major tourist towns, motel rooms in the U.P. generally start at around $24. The peninsula has 200 **campgrounds,** including those at both national forests (call 800-447-2757 for reservations). Sleep with your dogs or bring extra blankets—temperatures in these parts drop to 50°F, even in July. For regional cuisine, indulge in the Friday night **fish-fry:** all-you-can-eat whitefish, perch, or walleye buffets served in almost every restaurant in every town. The local ethnic specialty is a **pasty** (*PASS-tee*), a meat pie imported by Cornish miners in the 19th century.

⦿ PRACTICAL INFORMATION

Helpful **Welcome Centers** guard the U.P. at its six main entry points: **Ironwood,** 801 W. Cloverland Dr. (☎932-3330; open June-Aug. daily 8am-6pm, in winter daily 8am-4pm); **Iron Mountain,** 618 S. Stephenson Ave. (☎774-4201; open June-Aug. daily 7am-5pm, in winter 8am-4pm); **Menominee,** 1343 10th Ave. (☎863-6496; open June-Aug. daily 8am-5pm, in winter 8am-4pm); **Marquette,** 2201 U.S. 41 S (☎249-9066; open daily 9am-6pm); **Sault Ste. Marie,** 943 Portage Ave. W. (☎632-8242; open June-Sept. daily 8am-6pm, Oct.-May daily 9am-5pm); and **St. Ignace,** on I-75 N just north of the Mackinac Bridge (☎643-6979; open June-Aug. daily 8am-6pm, Sept.-May daily 9am-5pm). The invaluable *Upper Peninsula Travel Planner* is published by the **Upper Peninsula Travel and Recreation Association** (☎800-562-7134; info line staffed M-F 8am-4:30pm). For additional help planning a trip into the wilderness, write to or call the **U.S. Forestry Service** at the **Hiawatha National Forest,** 2727 N. Lincoln Rd., Escanaba 49829 (☎786-4062). **Area code:** 906.

SAULT STE. MARIE AND THE EASTERN U.P.   ☎906

The shipping industry rules in gritty Sault ("Soo") Ste. Marie, where "the locks" are the primary attraction for both tourists and prospective residents. Back in the day, St. Mary's River dropped 21 vertical feet over one mile in this area, rendering the river impassable by boat. In 1855, entrepreneurs built the first lock here, opening up industrial opportunities that led the region to relative economic prosperity. Now the busiest in the world, the city's four locks float over 12,000 ships annually, gradually lowering them through successive, emptying chambers. A 2hr. **Soo Locks Boat Tour,** which leaves from both 1157 and 515 E. Portage Ave., grants a close-up look at the locks' operation. (☎632-6301 or 800-432-6301 for departure times. Open mid-May to mid-Oct. $17, ages 13-18 $14.50, ages 4-12 $7.50, under 4 free.) For landlubbers, the **Locks Park Historic Walkway** runs parallel to the water for 1 mi., allowing visitors a close-up view of the 1000 ft. long supertankers that use the locks.

On the waterfront, at the end of Johnston St., lies the **Museum Ship Valley Camp,** a 1917 steam-powered freighter housing the **Marine Hall of Fame.** (☎632-3658. Open July-Aug. daily 9am-9pm; mid-May to June and Sept. to mid-Oct. 10am-6pm. $7.25, children $3.75.) A different, wilder side of the Soo rewards intrepid travelers who cross the 2 mi. long **International Bridge** into Ontario (toll $1.50). Although the Canadian Sault Ste. Marie is more urban and larger than its American cousin, it has more immediate access to wilderness. The **Agawa Canyon Train Tour** is an all-day excursion into a picturesque North that gives new meaning to the words "sparsely populated." (☎800-242-9287. Departs from the Station Mall, 129 Bay St. Operates early June to late Oct. In summer, CDN$56, seniors CDN$48, ages 5-18 CDN$18, under 5 CDN$13. In fall when the trees are in full color, CDN$75/CDN$75/CDN$45/CDN$20.)

The Ontario side of the city is also home to the area's best lodging deal. **The Algonquin Hotel (HI-C),** 864 Queen St. E., features intimate private rooms in a welcoming atmosphere just 1 mi. from the bridge. (☎705-253-2311. Singles CDN$21.25, nonmembers $28; doubles CDN$33/CDN$39.60.) Otherwise, affordable lodgings line the I-75 Business Spur on the American side. The **Mid City Motel,** 304 E. Portage, is a relaxed establishment in the shadow of the campy Tower of History, a glorified observation tower. (☎632-6832. Singles $36-48; doubles $45-58.) Just down the road, get stuffed with a Paul Bunyan burger ($7) at **The Antlers,** 804 E. Portage St. (☎632-3571. Open daily 11am-10:30pm.) Animal lovers beware—the walls of the wildly popular restaurant have eyes (and heads and bodies).

West of the city, the uncrowded eastern branch of the **Hiawatha National Forest** and the appealing town of **Paradise** are other attractions in the eastern U.P. At **Tahquamenon Falls State Park** (☎492-3415), 15min. east of Paradise, amateur voyageurs can rent a **canoe** ($10 per half-day) or **rowboat** ($12 per person) at the Lower Falls, or gawk at the spectacular 50 ft. Upper Falls (no barrel riders here). North of Tahquamenon, over **300 shipwrecks** protected in an Underwater Preserve lie off Whitefish Point, affording divers an unbeatable opportunity to search for sunken treasure.

MIDDLE OF THE PENINSULA ☎906

The western branch of the **Hiawatha National Forest** dominates the middle of the Peninsula, offering limitless wilderness activities and many rustic **campsites** ($7-11; pit toilets, no showers; first come, first served). **Rapid River** is home to the southern office of the west branch on Rte. 2. In the north, **Munising,** on Rte. 28, accesses the forest and the not-to-be-missed **Pictured Rocks National Lakeshore,** where water saturated with copper, manganese, and iron oxide paints the cliffs with multicolored bands. **Pictured Rocks Boat Cruise** (☎387-2379), at the city dock in Munising, gives the best view. Tours last approximately 3hr. ($24, ages 6-12 $10, under 6 free; rates subject to change), but various car- or foot-accessible overlooks within the park offer spectacular glimpses of their own. The Forest and Lakeshore share a **Visitors Center** at the intersection of Rte. 28 and Rte. 58 in Munising (☎387-3700; open mid-May to mid-Oct. daily 8am-6pm; mid-Oct. to mid-May M-Sa 9am-4:30pm). From Munising, Rte. 58—a bumpy, partially unpaved gem of a road—weaves along the lakeshore past numerous trailheads and campsites; spare tires are often necessary for extensive travel in the Hiawatha Forest. For a paved (but less scenic) alternative from Munising to Grand Marais, go east on Rte. 28, then north on Rte. 77.

Within the park, **Miner's Falls,** 10 mi. east of Munising off Rte. 58, rewards visitors with a rocky and staggeringly beautiful waterfall. Two mi. father up the road, ▨**Miner's Castle Overlook** allows trekkers to walk up to the edge of the cliffs, providing an unbeatable image of multicolored rocks and deep blue water as far as the eye can see. Twenty mi. east of Miner's Castle off Rte. 58, visitors can stroll, birdwatch, or collect smooth stones along the shore at **Twelve Mile Beach** (self-registered campsites $10; running water only). For some comic relief, travelers should make a pilgrimage to the center of all things "Yooper," **Da Yooper's Tourist Trap,** 490 N. Steel St., 12 mi. west of Marquette on U.S. 41. This little roadside themepark is the ultimate attraction for oversized sports equipment—their rifle and chainsaw are worthy of the *Guinness Book of World Records.* Come on down to da tourist trap, dontcha know? (☎800-628-9978. Open M-Th, Sa 9am-8pm, F 9am-9pm, Su 9am-7pm.) From atop the sandy **Log Slide,** 5 mi. west of Grand Marais on Rte. 58, the adventurous can survey the magnitude of Lake Superior; in the winter months, "polar bears" (read: fat guys with balls of steel) take the plunge in the ice water.

As an alternative to the developed campsites at Twelve Mile Beach, **backcountry camping permits** for 1-6 people ($15) are available from the Munising or **Grand Sable Visitors Center,** 2 mi. west of Grand Marais on Rte. 58. (☎494-2660. Open mid-May to early Oct. daily 9am-7pm.) For non-campers, the **Poplar Bluff Cabins,** Star Rte. Box 3118, have lakeview rooms with kitchens. Head 12 mi. east of Munising on Rte. 28, then 6 mi. south from Shingleton on Rte. 94 to get there. (☎452-6271. Cottages $40-50 per night, from $200 per week. Free use of boats on lake.)

GREAT LAKES

KEWEENAW PENINSULA   ☎906

In 1840, Dr. Douglas Houghton's mineralogical survey of the Keweenaw (*KEE-wa-naw*) Peninsula, a curved finger of land on the U.P.'s northwest corner, incited a copper mining rush which sent the area booming. When mining petered out around 1969, the land was left barren and exploited. Today, reforestation and government support have helped Copper Country find new life as a tourist destination. Every year, 250 inches of snow fall on the towering pines, smooth-stone beaches, and low mountains of the Keweenaw. Visitors ski, snowshoe, and snowmobile in winter and enjoy the gorgeous green coasts during the summer.

The rugged **Porcupine Mountain Wilderness State Park** (☎885-5275 or 800-447-2757), affectionately known as "The Porkies," hugs Lake Superior at the base of the peninsula. Eight miles inside the park on Rte. 107, **Lake of the Clouds** etches out a path between rugged cliffs and mountains, giving way to a spectacular overlook view of the Big Carp River valley below. The park also sports campsites ($9-14 sites with toilets and showers, electricity at Union; rustic sites $6), rustic cabins for 2-8 ($32; reservations required), and paths into the **Old Growth Forest,** the largest tract of uncut forest between the Rockies and the Adirondacks. The **Visitors Center,** near the junction of Rte. 107 and South Boundary Rd. inside the park, provides required **permits** good for all Michigan state parks. (Open in summer daily 10am-6pm.)

The twin towns of **Houghton** and **Hancock** link the Porkies to the rest of the Keweenaw. Eight miles north of Hancock on Rte. 203, **McLain State Park** is home to some of the best camping in Copper Country. The campground rests along a 2 mi. agate beach and harbors an impressive lighthouse. (☎482-0278. Sites with electricity $14; required vehicle permit $4.) From the state park, U.S. 41 winds north through the Keweenaw. By far the most scenic path to the tip of the peninsula, the breathtaking ⊠**Brockway Mountain Dr.** (6 mi.), between Eagle Harbor and Copper Harbor, is a must for those who want to reach the summit. Rising 1337 ft. above sea level, its peak provides some of the best panoramic views on the entire U.P. The drive is accessible from Rte. 26 off U.S. 41. In **Copper Harbor,** the northernmost town in Michigan, the **Keweenaw Adventure Company,** 145 Gratiot St. (☎289-4303), can make anyone's wilderness dreams come true with kayaking outings (2½hr. intro paddle $26); bike rentals (half-day $25, full-day $35); and more.

ILLINOIS

The "Land of Lincoln" is one of compromise between sharply contrasting lifestyles, from the bustling urban center of Chicago to the vast farm country of most of the rest of the state. First known for its arable soil, the growth of big industry diversified Illinois and made its extremes more disparate. Always a gateway between east and west, present-day Illinois encompasses patches of coastal sophistication amid acres and acres of Midwestern prairie. Visitors benefit from this diversity, finding a little bit of everything American in the mix of terrains and attitudes.

⚡ PRACTICAL INFORMATION

Capital: Springfield.

Visitor Info: Illinois Office of Tourism (☎800-226-6632; www.enjoyillinois.com). **Springfield Office of Tourism,** 109 N. Seventh St., Springfield 62701 (☎800-545-7300).

Postal Abbreviation: IL. Sales Tax: 6.25-8.75%, depending on the city.

CHICAGO ☎312

Situated snugly along the banks of Lake Michigan—the only topological boundary to its development—Chicago is the Midwestern version of urban sprawl. A burgeoning commercial center by the mid-1800s, the town drew millions of immigrants and freed slaves who encountered more tribulation than economic triumph. Machine politics soon flourished, blurring any line between organized government and organized crime. Thus, the "Windy City" was named for its politicians' hot air, not for its cold, fierce gusts. Today, Chicago proudly weaves this checkered past into its brighter present. From renowned museums to a varied and vibrant music and entertainment scene, Chicago's offerings please any visitor. Even a simple stroll along Lake Michigan during a sunny day shows off the city's splendor.

✈ INTERCITY TRANSPORTATION

Airports: O'Hare International (☎773-686-2200), off I-90. One million planes take off and land here every minute. Well, maybe not that many, but it's a really big number. Depending on traffic, a trip between downtown and O'Hare can take up to 2hr. The blue line **Rapid Train** runs between the Airport El station and downtown (40min.-1hr., $1.50). **Midway Airport** (☎773-767-0500), on the western edge of the South Side, often offers less expensive (though less frequent) flights. To get downtown, take the El orange line from the Midway stop. **Airport Express** (☎888-284-3826) connects to downtown hotels from O'Hare (45min.-1hr.; every 5-10min. 6am-11:30pm; $20) and Midway (30-45min.; every 10-15min. 6am-10:30pm; $15).

Trains: Amtrak, Union Station, 225 S. Canal (☎558-1075), at Adams St. just west of the Loop, is Amtrak's nationwide hub. The bus is the easiest way to get there; buses #1, 60, 125, 151, and 156 all stop at the station. Otherwise, take the El to State and Adams, then walk 7 blocks west on Adams. To: Milwaukee (1½hr., 5 per day, $20); Detroit (8hr., 3 per day, $37-42); and New York (19hr., 2 per day, $106-131). Station open 6:15am-10pm; tickets sold daily 6am-9pm. Lockers $1 per day.

Buses: Greyhound, 630 W. Harrison St. (☎408-5980), at Jefferson and Desplaines Ave. Take the El to Linton or buses #60, 125, 156, or 157 to the terminal. The hub of the central US and home-base for several smaller companies covering the Midwest. To: Detroit (6-7hr., 6 per day, $27-29); Milwaukee (2hr., 13 per day, $14); St. Louis (5-7hr., 9 per day, $33); and Indianapolis (3½-4½hr., 9 per day, $29-31). Station and ticket office open 24hr.

⊏ LOCAL TRANSPORTATION

Public Transportation: The **Chicago Transit Authority (CTA),** 350 N. Wells (☎836-7000 or 888-968-7282), 7th fl., runs efficient trains, subways, and buses. The **elevated rapid transit train system,** called the **El,** encircles the Loop. Some downtown routes run underground but are still referred to as the El. The El operates 24hr., but late-night service is infrequent and unsafe in many areas. Some buses do not run all night; call the CTA for schedules and routes. Extremely helpful CTA maps are available at many stations and the Water Tower Information Center. Don't step blindly onto a train; many are "express" and different routes may run along the same track. Train and bus fare is $1.50; add 25¢ for express routes. Get a transfer (30¢), which allows for up to 2 more rides on different routes during the following 2hr., from bus drivers or when you enter the El stop. Buy or add value to **transit cards** (from $3 for 2 rides; $13.50 for 10 rides or $16.50 for 10 rides and transfers) at all CTA stations and some supermarkets and museums. CTA also offers a variety of consecutive-day passes for tourists, available at airports and Amtrak stations: 1-day $5, 2-day $9, 3-day $12, and 5-day $18. On Sa from mid-June through mid-Oct., a **Loop Tour Train** departs on a free 40min. elevated tour of the downtown area at 12:15, 12:55, 1:35, and 2:15pm (tickets must be picked up at the Chicago Office of Tourism; see **Practical Information,** below).

Taxis: Yellow Cab, ☎829-4222. **Flash Cab,** ☎773-561-1444.

GREAT LAKES

Car Rental: Dollar Rent-a-Car (☎800-800-4000), at O'Hare and Midway. $26 per day, $170 per week; under 25 surcharge $15 per day.

METRA, 547 W. Jackson (☎836-7000), distributes free maps and schedules for its extensive commuter rail network, with 11 rail lines and 4 downtown stations. (Open M-F 8am-5pm; fare $2-6.60, depending on distance.)

PACE (☎836-7000) operates the suburban bus system. Numerous free or cheap shuttle services run throughout the loop, with schedules available just about everywhere.

✦ ORIENTATION

Chicago has overtaken the entire northeastern corner of Illinois, running north-south along 29 mi. of the southwest Lake Michigan shorefront. The city sits at the center of a web of interstates, rail lines, and airplane routes; most cross-country traffic swings through the city. A good map is essential for navigating Chicago; pick up a free one at the tourist office or any CTA station.

Although flat and sprawling, the grids mostly make sense, and navigation is pretty straightforward, either by car or ubiquitous public transportation. At the city's center is the **Loop,** Chicago's downtown business district and hub of the public transportation system. The block numbering system begins from the intersection of State and Madison, increasing by about 800 per mi. The Loop is bounded by the Chicago River to the north and west, Lake Michigan to the east, and Roosevelt Rd. to the south. Directions in *Let's Go* are usually from downtown. South of the Loop, numbered east-west streets increase towards the south. Many ethnic neighborhoods lie in this area (see **Neighborhoods,** below), but farther out, avoid the struggling South Side. Most of the city's best spots for food and nightlife jam the first few mi. north of the Loop. **Lake Shore Dr.,** a scenic freeway hugging Lake Michigan (beware the 45 mph speed limit), offers express north-south connections.

To avoid driving (and parking) in the city, daytrippers can leave their cars in one of the suburban park-and-ride lots ($1.75); call CTA (see below) for info. Parking downtown costs around $8-15 per day. Check out the lots west of the South Loop, across the canal from the Sears Tower, for the best deals.

Chicago is a big city with big city problems. It is a good idea to stay within the boundaries made apparent by tourist maps. Aside from small pockets such as Hyde Park and the U. of Chicago, areas south of the loop and west of the "little ethnic" enclaves are mostly industrial or residential and pose a safety threat to the unwary tourist. **Cabrini Green** (bounded by W. Armitage Ave. on the north, W. Chicago Ave. on the south., Sedgwick on the east, and Halsted on the west), an infamously dangerous public housing development, sits within tourist map borders—other unsafe neighborhoods are usually outside them.

NEIGHBORHOODS

The diverse array of enclaves that compose the Windy City justifies its title as a "city of neighborhoods." North of the Loop, LaSalle Dr. loosely defines the west edge of the posh **Near North** area, whose activity is largely centered along the **Magnificent Mile** of Michigan Ave. between the Chicago River and Oak St. The trendy restaurant- and nightlife-packed **River North** district lines N. Clark St., just north of the Loop and west of Michigan Ave. The primarily residential **Gold Coast** shimmers on N. Lakeshore Dr. between Oak St. and North Ave. Northwest of the Gold Coast, the **Bucktown/Wicker Park** area, at the intersection of North, Damen and Milwaukee Ave., is the place to be for artsy, cutting-edge cafes and nightlife. **Lincoln Park,** a hotbed of hip activity, revolves around the junction of N. Clark St., Lincoln Ave., and Halsted St. To the north near the 3000s of N. Clark St. and N. Halsted St., Lincoln park melts into **Lakeview,** (a gay-friendly area teeming with food and nightlife), and then becomes **Wrigleyville** in the 4000s. **Andersonville,** 5 mi. farther down N. Clark St. north of Foster Ave., is the historic center of the Swedish community, though immigrants from Asia and the Middle East have recently settled here.

MORTON GROVE

SKOKIE

NILES

Harlem Ave.

Skokie Blvd.

Crawford Ave.

N. Shore Channel

Northwestern University

EVANSTON

Sheridan Rd.

LINCOLNWOOD

Rogers Park

TO O'HARE INT'L AIRPORT (4mi.)

Forest Preserve

Milwaukee Ave.

Lincoln Ave.

Western Ave.

Ashland Ave.

Broadway

Loyola University of Chicago

HARWOOD HEIGHTS

Lawrence Ave.

Andersonville

Uptown

Lake Michigan

Irving Park

Wrigleyville

Wrigley Field

Belmont Ave.

Lakeview

Lincoln Park

Fullerton St.

N. Br. Chicago R.

North Ave.

Bucktown

Lincoln Park

Lincoln Park Zoo

Frank Lloyd Wright Home & Studio

Grand Ave.

Humboldt Park

Wicker Park

Near North

OAK PARK

Austin

Garfield Park

Chicago R.

Madison St.

United Center

Greektown

Loop

CICERO

Cook County Hospital

Douglas Park

U. of Illinois at Chicago

Grant Park

Near South Side

Cermak Rd.

BERWYN

Pilsen

Chinatown

Des Plaines R.

Chicago Sanitary and Ship Canal

Bridgeport

Comiskey Park

Back of the Yards

Burnham Park

Damen Ave.

55th St.

Garfield Blvd.

Museum of Science and Industry

Chicago Midway Airport

Marquette Park

55th St.

University of Chicago

Hyde Park

Jackson Park

Englewood

BEDFORD PARK

79th St.

BURBANK

Pulaski Rd.

Kedzie Ave.

Western Ave.

Dan Ryan Woods

Ashland Ave.

Halsted St.

95th St.

EVERGREEN PARK

OAK LAWN

S. Chicago Ave.

Mackinaw Ave.

Ewing Ave.

Calumet R.

111th St.

WORTH

Morgan Park

Pullman

ALSIP

Calumet Sag Channel

BLUE ISLAND

Lake Calumet

William W. Powers State Conservation Area

Little Calumet R.

Chicago
♠ ACCOMMODATIONS
Arlington House, 2
Chicago International Hostel, 1

0   2 miles
0   2 kilometers

N

The near south and west sides are filled with other vibrant ethnic districts. The center of the Chinese community lies 2 mi. south of the Loop, at Cermak Rd. and Wentworth Ave. The German community has scattered, but the beer halls, restaurants, and shops in the 3000s and 4000s of N. Lincoln Ave. remain. The former residents of **Greektown** have also moved, but S. Halsted St., just west of the Loop, houses authentic Greek restaurants. The area is bustling and safe until the restaurants close, at which point tourists clear out. Nearby **Little Italy** has fallen prey to the **University of Illinois at Chicago (UIC),** and little of the once-bustling district remains. Jewish and Indian enclaves center on Devon Ave., from Western Ave. to the Chicago River. The **Pilsen** neighborhood, southwest of the loop, around 18th St., offers a slice of Mexico. The search for Polish cuisine leads hungry travelers near Bucktown to N. Milwaukee Ave. between blocks 2800 and 3100. Chicago's Polish population is the largest of any city outside Warsaw.

⑦ PRACTICAL INFORMATION

Visitor Info: Chicago Office of Tourism, 78 E. Washington St. (☎ 744-2400 or 800-226-6632). Open M-F 10am-6pm, Sa 10am-5pm, Su noon-5pm. In the same building is the **Chicago Cultural Center Welcome Center,** 77 E. Randolph St., at Michigan Ave. Open M-F 10am-6pm, Sa 10am-5pm, Su noon-5pm. **Chicago Visitor Information Center,** 163 E. Pearson St. (☎ 744-2400), at Michigan Ave., is located in the Water Tower Pumping Station. Open M-F 9:30am-7pm, Sa 10am-7pm, Su 11am-6pm. On the lake sits the **Navy Pier Info Center,** 600 E. Grand (☎ 595-7437). Open Su-Th 10am-10pm, F-Sa 10am-noon. The **International Visitors Center,** 520 N. Michigan Ave. (☎ 645-1836), aids foreign visitors with their itineraries. Call for assistance.

Hotlines: Crisis Line, ☎ 800-866-9600. **Rape Crisis Line,** ☎ 847-872-7799. Both 24hr.

Bi-Gay-Lesbian Concerns: Gay and Lesbian Hotline/Anti-Violence Project, ☎ 871-2273. **Gay and Lesbian Hotline,** ☎ 773-929-4357. Both 24hr. For current info on events and nightlife, pick up a copy of the *Windy City Times* or *Gay Chicago* at Lakeview's **Unabridged Books,** 3251 N. Broadway (☎ 773-883-9119).

Medical Services: Northwestern Memorial Hospital, 251 E. Huron St. near Michigan Ave. (☎ 908-2000); emergency division at 250 E. Erie St. nearby (☎ 926-5188). Open 24hr. Farther out, **Cook County Hospital,** 1835 W. Harrison (☎ 633-6000). Take the Congress A train to the Medical Center Stop. Open 24hr.

Internet access: Free at the **Chicago Public Library.** Main branch at 400 S. State St., at Congress. Open M 9am-7pm; Tu and Th 11am-7pm; W, F, and Sa 9am-5pm; Su 1-5pm.

Post Office: 433 W. Harrison St. (☎ 654-3895), at the Chicago River. Free parking. Open 24hr. **ZIP code:** 60607. **Area code:** 312 (downtown) or 773 (elsewhere in Chicago); 708, 630, or 847 (outside the city limits). In text, 312 unless otherwise noted.

⌂ ACCOMMODATIONS

A cheap, convenient bed can be found at one of Chicago's many hostels. The motels on **Lincoln Ave.** in Lincoln Park are accessible by car and moderately priced. Motel chains off the interstates, about 1hr. from downtown, are out of the way and expensive (from $35), but are an option for late-night arrivals. **Chicago Bed and Breakfast,** P.O. Box 14088, Chicago 60614 (☎ 773-248-0005 or 800-375-7084), runs a referral service. Few B&Bs have parking, but the majority are near public transit. (2-night minimum stay. Singles from $75; doubles from $85. Reservations required.) Chicago has a 15% tax on most accommodation rates.

HOSTELS

▨ **Hostelling International—Chicago (HI-AYH),** 24 E. Congress Pkwy. (☎ 360-0300), off Wabash St. in the Loop. Take the El Orange Line to State & Van Buren, walk 1 block east to Wabash St., turn right, walk 1 block to Congress. In the land of hostels, this brand new, immense, and amenity-packed hostel is king. Its location offers easy access to the major museums during the day, but *be careful on the deserted streets of the*

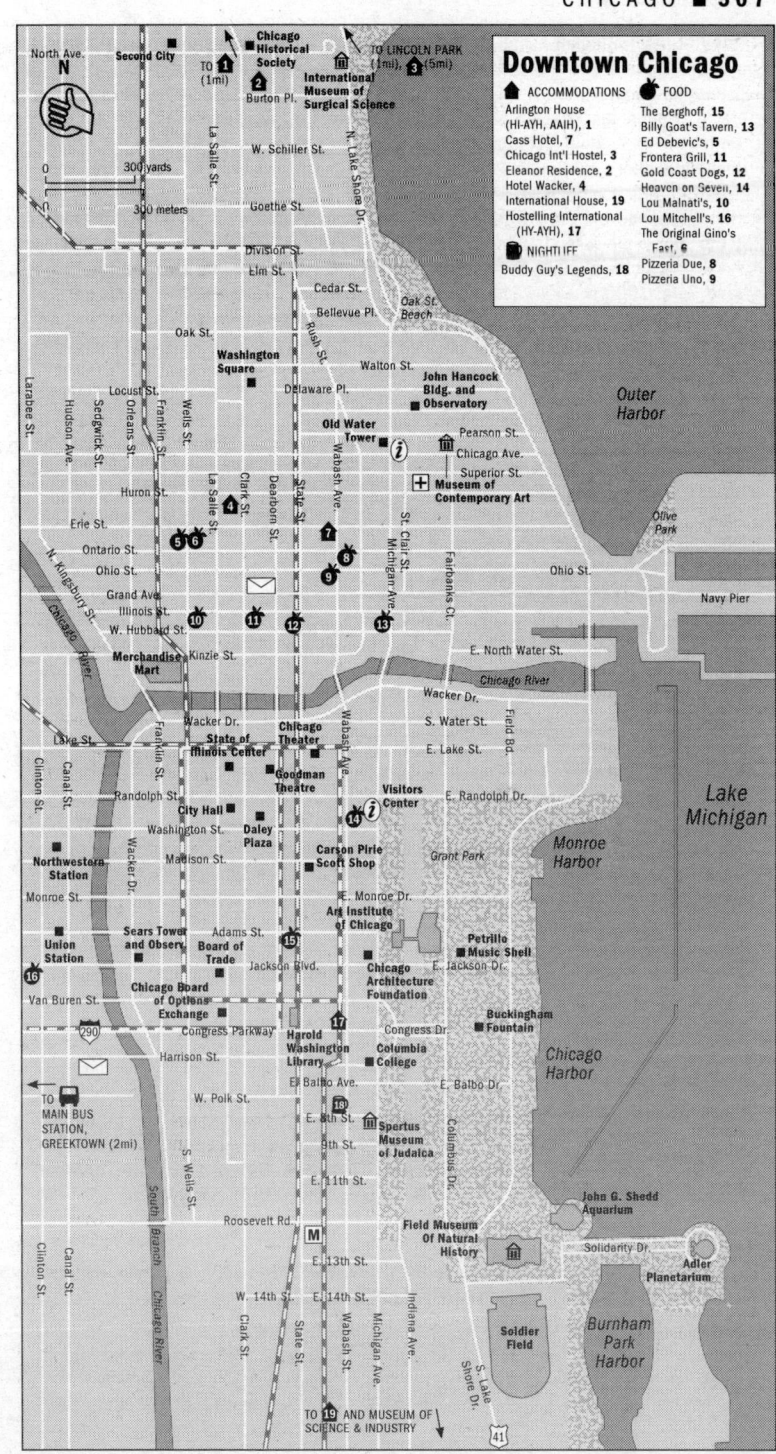

Loop at night. Student center, performance center, library, kitchen, laundry. All rooms with A/C. Dorms $19-20, nonmembers $22-23. Reservations recommended.

Eleanor Residence, 1550 N. Dearborn Pkwy. (☎664-8245). *Women only, must be over 18.* A location near Lake Michigan, Lincoln Park, and the Gold Coast is the ideal setting for a majestic common room and lobby, as well as spotless rooms. Singles $65, breakfast and dinner included. Reserve at least 1 day in advance; 1-night deposit required.

Chicago International Hostel, 6318 N. Winthrop St. (☎773-262-1011). Take the Howard St. northbound train to Loyola Station; walk 3 blocks south on Sheridan Rd. to Winthrop, and ½ block south. Simple, sunny rooms with 4-6 beds, near Loyola University. A fairly safe location during the day close to the lake, beaches, and the fantastic Heartland Cafe, 7000 N. Glenwood Ave. (☎773-465-8005). *Don't wander around the surrounding area alone at night.* Lockers $1. Linens provided. Free parking. Kitchen and laundry access. Key deposit $5. Check-in 7-10am and 4pm-midnight. Lockout 10am-4pm. Curfew 2am. Dorms $25; doubles $35, with bath $40.

Arlington House, 616 W. Arlington Pl. (☎773-929-5380 or 800-467-8355), off Clark St. just north of Fullerton in the Lincoln Park area. The social atmosphere and brilliant location ensure a lively stay in this enormous Lincoln Park hostel. The dorm rooms are tidy, breezy, and social. The private rooms, however, are sometimes poorly kept and not worth the price. Safe, central neighborhood near food and nightlife. Kitchen, TV room, laundry facilities. Dorms $19.50; private singles with shared bath $41, with private bath $51. Reservations recommended.

HOTELS AND GUEST HOUSES

Cass Hotel, 640 N. Wabash Ave. (☎787-4030 or 800-227-7850), just north of the Loop. Take El to State St. Reasonable rates and convenient location near the Magnificent Mile make this newly renovated hotel a favorite find of the budget-conscious. The in-house bar promotes bonding, and the $2 breakfast downstairs at the coffeeshop is a great deal. Parking available ($26 per day). Key deposit $5. Laundry room. Singles from $79; doubles from $84. Reservations recommended. Wheelchair accessible.

International House, 1414 E. 59th St. (☎773-753-2270), Hyde Park, off Lake Shore Dr. Take the Illinois Central Railroad from the Michigan Ave. station (20min.) or METRA South Shore Line to 59th St. and walk a half-block west. On the grounds of the University of Chicago; *don't wander off campus at night. Students only.* Expansive common areas filled with student activity augment neat, spacious singles with shared bath. Kitchen and laundry; tennis courts, game room, weight room, cafeteria. Linen provided. Rooms $38. Reservations with credit card required.

Hotel Wacker, 111 W. Huron St. (☎787-1386), at N. Clark St. Insert your own joke. A green formerly neon sign on the corner makes this place easy to find. Small, well-appointed rooms have reasonable prices. TV, A/C, phone. Key and linen deposit $5. Check-in 24hr. Singles $50; doubles $65. Wheelchair accessible.

◘ FOOD

Chicago's many culinary delights, from pizza to po' boy sandwiches, are among its main attractions. One of the best guides to city dining is the monthly *Chicago* magazine, which includes an extensive restaurant section, indexed by price, cuisine, and quality. It can be found at tourist offices and newsstands everywhere.

PIZZA

Chicago's deep-dish pizza is known 'round the world, either standard-style, with the cheese on top, or stuffed, with "toppings" in the middle.

■ **Lou Malnati's,** 439 N. Wells St. (☎828-9800), at Hubbard downtown. The name may not be as famous as Uno's, but the pizza is just as fantastic. A Chicago mainstay for 30 years, Lou's is a local sports memorabilia-themed chain with bubbling deep-dish masterpieces. Thoughtful travelers can even FedEx one of their creations to Aunt Maude in

Boise. There are seven other branches throughout the city and suburbs. Pizzas $5-20. Open M-Th 11am-11pm, F-Sa 11am-midnight, Su noon-10pm.

Pizzeria Uno, 29 E. Ohio St. (☎321-1000), and younger sister **Due,** 619 N. Wabash Ave. (☎943-2400). It may look like any other Uno's, but this is where the delicious legacy of deep-dish began. Lines are long, and pizza takes 45min. to prepare. Individual-sized pies ($5) take less time (25min.). Same short menu at Due (right up the street), with a terrace and more room than Uno's. Uno open M-F 11:30am-1am, Sa 11:30am-2am, Su 11:30am-11:30pm. Due open Su-Th 11am-1:30am, F-Sa 11am-2am.

The Original Gino's East, 633 N. Wells St. (☎988-4200), at Ontario downtown. Bring a marker to claim history on the heavily decorated walls of this legendary deep-dish joint. Pizza $9-23. Mini-pizza weekday lunch special $4. Open daily 11am-11pm.

'ROUND THE LOOP

Many of Chicago's best restaurants, from ragin' Cajun to tried-and-true German, inhabit the streets of the Loop.

▨ Lou Mitchell's, 565 W. Jackson Blvd. (☎939-3111), 2 blocks west of the Sears Tower. Undoubtedly the city's best breakfast place, this retro diner has been stuffing faithful customers for 75 years. Visitors should plan to leave the diet elsewhere and indulge in a sinfully good omelette ($6-8) and the "world's finest cup of coffee" ($1.50). Lines are long but move fast, and female customers get a free box of Milk Duds while they wait. Cash only. Open M-Sa 5:30am-3pm, Su 7am-3pm.

Heaven on Seven, 111 N. Wabash Ave. (☎263-6443), 7th fl. of the Garland Bldg. This is heaven Cajun-style, from the Mardi Gras and voodoo decor to endless hot sauce and spicy cuisine. The line is long, but hell, the jambalaya is great ($6; entrees $9-11). Open M-F 8:30am-5pm, Sa 10am-3pm.

Billy Goat's Tavern, 430 N. Michigan (☎222-1525), underground on lower Michigan Ave. Descend through what looks like a subway entrance in front of the Tribune building. The gruff service in this bar/diner was the inspiration for the legendary *Saturday Night Live* "Cheezborger, cheezborger—no Coke, Pepsi" skit. Surprisingly good cheezborgers $2.50. "Butt in anytime" M-F 6am-2am, Sa 10am-3am, Su 11am-2am.

Gold Coast Dogs, 418 N. State St. (☎527-1222), at Hubbard St. Hot dogs are sacred in Chicago, but only when they're done Second City-style with a veritable salad of relish, onions, pickles, tomatoes, etc. on top. Locals rank Gold Coast's among the best. Hot dogs from $2. Open M-F 7am-10pm, Sa-Su 11am-8pm.

The Berghoff, 17 W. Adams St. (☎427-3170). Take the El to Adams. This dim, cavernous German restaurant filled with lunching traders has been a Chicago institution for over 100 years. Bypass the pricey dining room and head for the "cafe" section, which is really more of a bar. Bratwurst $4.50, stein of Berghoff's own beer $3. Open M-Th 11am-9pm, F 11am-9:30pm, Sa 11am-10pm.

RIVER NORTH

River North houses some of the trendiest eateries in town, as well as Chicago's pizza institutions (see **Pizza,** above).

▨ Frontera Grill, 455 N. Clark St. (☎661-1434), between Illinois and Hubbard. Take El Red Line to Grand/State. A delightful departure from chain tacos and burritos, Frontera delivers what many claim is the best authentic Mexican cuisine in the region. Entrees ($7-22) change often but are always superb. The usual 2hr. wait is bearable if you snag a bar seat and order appetizers (from $3). Lunch: open Tu-Th 11:30am-2:30pm, Sa 10:30am-2:30pm. Dinner: open Tu 5:20-10pm, W-Th 5-10pm, F-Sa 5-11pm. Reservations accepted for parties of 5 or more.

Ed Debevic's, 640 N. Wells St. (☎664-1707), at Ontario across from Gino's East Pizza. This faux 50s diner trades heavily in kitsch. With a bright aqua interior and a DJ spinning classic tunes, Ed Debevic's is not the spot for a quiet dinner for two. Still, they serve up great burgers ($7) and shakes ($4) with a side of attitude—their slogan warns, "The better you tip, the nicer we are." Open Su-Th 11am-10pm, F-Sa 11am-midnight.

SOUL FOOD SOUTH OF THE LOOP

The area of the Loop between Jackson and Roosevelt St. is the South Loop, home to good, cheap American-style soul food like ribs, fried chicken, and greens. More of the same peppers the South Side, but travelers should be very careful south of the Loop, especially after dark.

■ **Army & Lou's,** 422 E. 75th (☎ 773-483-6550), on the South Side. Locals from all over the city come here for a surprisingly upscale setting and some of the best southern fare north of the Mason-Dixon line. Fried chicken with 2 sides $9, mixed greens with ham $8. Open M and W-Su 9am-10pm.

Dixie Kitchen & Bait Shop, 5225 S. Harper St. (☎ 773-363-4943), tucked back in a parking lot at 52nd in Hyde Park, this new place is fast becoming a local hot spot. Fried green tomatoes ($4.25) and oyster po' boy sandwiches ($8) are among Dixie's southern highlights. Fried catfish $10. Blackened Voodoo beer $2. Open M-Th and Su 11am-10pm, F-Sa 11am-11pm.

The Smokedaddy, 1804 W. Division St. (☎ 773-772-6656), west of the Loop in Wicker Park. Fantastic ribs ($8), vegetarian BBQ sandwiches ($5.50), and pulled pork sandwiches ($5.50) merit the "WOW" proclamation of the neon sign out front. Open M, F, and Sa 11:30am-1am; Tu-Th 5pm-1am; Su 11:30am-1am. Live blues nightly.

CHINATOWN

Chinatown is lined with restaurants. Take the Red Line to Cermak/Chinatown to get here, *but don't go too far south of Cermak St. after dark.*

Hong Min, 221 W. Cermak Rd. (☎ 842-5026). Spartan decor, Epicurean dining. Daily dim sum and fresh oysters are local favorites. Sweet-and-sour fish $8. Open Su-Th 10am-2am, F-Sa 10am-3am. Dim sum M-F 10am-3pm, Sa-Su 10am-4pm.

Three Happiness, 209 W. Cermak Rd. (☎ 842-1964). The smaller of 2 locations, this site receives constant local acclaim. Chicken entrees around $7. Open daily 9am-2am.

GREEKTOWN

■ **The Parthenon,** 314 S. Halsted St. (☎ 726-2407). The golden ratio ain't in the architecture, but the staff converses in Greek, the murals transport you to the Mediterranean, and the food wins top awards. The tasty Greek Feast family-style dinner ($15) includes everything from *saganaki* (flaming goat cheese) to *baklava*. Open daily 11am-1am.

Rodity's, 222 S. Halsted St. (☎ 454-0800), between Adams St. and Jackson Blvd. With slightly cheaper fare than the other Greektown options (daily specials under $9), Rodity's prepares more than generous portions of *spanakopita* ($7.75) and other delectable Greek treats. Open Su-Th 11am-midnight, F-Sa 11am-1am.

LINCOLN PARK

■ **Cafe Ba-Ba-Reeba!,** 2024 N. Halsted St. (☎ 935-5000), just north of Armitage. Well-marked by the colorful, glowing facade, the sprawling Ba-Ba-Reeba pleases with unbeatable *tapas* ($3-8) and hearty Spanish *paellas* ($10-15 per person; there will be plenty to take home). The outdoor terrace provides some of the best people-watching in town. Glass of *sangria* $3.50. Reservations recommended. Open for lunch Sa and Su noon-5pm; dinner Su-Th 5-10pm, F-Sa 5pm-midnight.

■ **Potbelly Sandwich Works,** 2264 N. Lincoln Ave. (☎ 773-528-1405), between Belden and Webster. Potbellied locals might have had one too many Italian sandwiches from this laid-back deli, appropriately decorated with a potbelly stove and a player piano. Huge, delicious subs $4. Be sure to try the yogurt smoothies ($2.45). Open daily 11am-11pm. Call for additional locations.

Penny's Noodle Shop, 950 W. Diversey Ave. (☎ 773-281-8448), at Sheffield. One of the best budget options in town, the unassuming Penny's delivers outstanding, generous Asian noodle dishes (all under $6) to scores of locals who pack the place at all hours. No reservations; sit at the counter or prepare to wait. Open Su and Tu-Th 11am-10pm, F-Sa 11am-10:30pm.

Crêpe de Paris, 2433 N. Clark St. (☎ 773-404-1300), great for a late breakfast, this little cafe duplicates a Parisian *crêperie* with sugary success. Travelers with a sweet tooth can bite into scrumptious crepes oozing with Nutella ($5-7). Vegetarian options are plentiful; lunch and dinner crepes $4-7. Open Su-Th 10am-10pm, F-Sa 10am-11pm.

ANDERSONVILLE

Kopi, A Traveller's Cafe, 5317 N. Clark St. (☎ 773-989-5674), near Foster St. in Andersonville. A 10min. walk from the Berwyn El, 4 blocks west on Berwyn. As visitors quickly learn, *kopi* is Indonesian for (really good) "coffee." For perfect reading material while sipping the coffee, the cafe includes much of the *Let's Go* series in its extensive travel library. Espresso $1.50. Music M and Th nights. Open M-Th 8am-11pm, F 8am-midnight, Sa 9am-midnight, Su 10am-11pm.

Ann Sather, 929 W. Belmont Ave. (☎ 773-348-2378). Take El Red Line to Belmont. This authentic Swedish diner draws a huge breakfast crowd with their wildly popular, gooey cinnamon rolls ($4). Although there hasn't yet been a formal study, locals report that they're addictive. Open Su-Th 7am-10pm, F-Sa 7am-11pm. Call for other locations.

BUCKTOWN/WICKER PARK

Kitsch'n on Roscoe, 2005 W. Roscoe St. (☎ 773-248-7372), at Damen Ave. in nearby Roscoe Village. Kitsch abounds at this breakfast and lunch spot, which serves a surprisingly good "Kitsch-n Sink Omelette" and "Jonny's Lunch Box" (soup, sandwich, fruit, and a snack cake served in a lunch box) on campy theme tables. Star Trek, anyone? Meals $3-12. Open for breakfast and lunch: Tu-F 7:30am-2pm, Sa-Su 9am-3pm. Dinner: Su and Tu-F 5-9pm, Sa 5-10pm.

Zoom Kitchen, 1646 N. Damen Ave. (☎ 773-278-7000). Visit this space-age diner for fresh sandwiches ($4-6) prepared just as you like them. The friendly staff will top your meal with handfuls of veggies picked from the giant piles behind the counters. Open M-Sa 11am-10pm, Su 10am-8pm.

◎ SIGHTS

Chicago's sights range from well-publicized museums to undiscovered back streets, from beaches and parks to towering skyscrapers. The tourist brochures, bus tours, and downtown area reveal only a fraction of Chicago. As a famous art historian once said, "no one will learn the city of Chicago without using their feet."

THE LOOP

When Mrs. O'Leary's cow kicked over a lantern and started the **Great Fire of 1871,** Chicago's downtown flamed into a pile of ashes. The city rebuilt with a vengeance, turning the functional into the fabulous and creating one of the most concentrated clusters of architectural treasures in the world. The downtown area, hemmed in by the Chicago River and Lake Michigan, grew upward rather than outward.

TOURS. Visitors can explore this street museum via **walking tours,** organized by the **Chicago Architectural Foundation.** The 2hr. tours, one of early skyscrapers and one of modern architecture, start at the foundation's gift shop. Highlights include Louis Sullivan's arch, the Chicago window, and Mies van der Rohe's revolutionary skyscrapers. *(224 S. Michigan Ave. ☎ 922-8687. $12 for 1 tour, $18 for both.)*

CHICAGO BOARD OF TRADE. Those who prefer to explore the Loop on their own can observe the frantic trade of Midwestern farm goods at the world's oldest and largest commodity exchange, the Chicago Board of Trade. For tours, contact the **Visitors Office.** *(141 W. Jackson Blvd., on the 5th fl. ☎ 435-3590. Open M-F 8am-2pm. Tours M-F 9:15am, every 30min. 10am-12:30pm. Free.)*

SEARS TOWER. A few blocks west on Jackson, the **Sears Tower** is undoubtedly Chicago's most immediately recognizable architectural landmark. Built in 1973 and named for American retail giant Sears-Roebuck, its former tenant, the Tower is the second-tallest building in the world (first, in the minds of staunch Chicagoans). Its

1454ft. tall stature impresses all, but few know about the 25,000 *miles* of plumbing wrought throughout the building. On a clear day, visitors to the 103rd fl. Skydeck can see three bordering states, as well as the city's second-tallest structure, the Amoco Building. *(233 S. Wacker Dr., enter on Jackson. ☎875-9696. Open daily 10am-10pm; Oct.-Apr. 10am-8pm. $9.50, seniors $7.75, youth $6.75. Lines are long, usually at least 1hr.)*

THE PLAZA. The **Bank One Building and Plaza** sits about two blocks northeast at the corner of Clark and Monroe St. One of the world's largest bank buildings, it leads gazes skyward with its diamond-shaped, diagonal slope. Back on the ground, Marc Chagall's vivid mosaic, *The Four Seasons*, lines the block and sets off a public space often used for concerts and lunchtime entertainment. The mural is a fabulous sight at night, when it is lit by various colored bulbs. Two blocks north at the corner of Clark and Washington St., the Methodist **Chicago Temple,** the world's tallest church, sends its Babel-esque steeples heavenward. *(77 W. Washington St. ☎236-4548. Tours M-F 2pm, Sa-Su 9:30am and noon.)*

STATE STREET. State and Madison St., the most famous intersection of "State St., that great street," forms the focal point of the Chicago street grid as well as another architectural haven. Here, Louis Sullivan's beloved **Carson Pirie Scott** store is adorned with exquisite ironwork and the famous extra-large Chicago window. Sullivan's other masterpiece, the **Auditorium Building,** sits several blocks south at the corner of Congress St. and Michigan Ave. Intricate design and flawless acoustics highlight this Chicago landmark.

OTHER ARCHITECTURAL WONDERS. Burnham and Root's **Monadnock Building,** 53 W. Jackson, deserves a glance for its serene, alternating bays of purple and brown rock. Just to the southeast, the **Sony Fine Arts Theatre** screens current artistic and foreign films in the grandeur of the **Fine Arts Building.** *(418 S. Michigan Ave. ☎939-2119. Open M-Th. $8.25; students $6; seniors, children, or matinee $5.)* In 1988, the city held a contest to design a building in honor of the late mayor. The result is the $144 million **Harold Washington Library Center,** a researcher's dream and a postmodern architectural delight. *(400 S. State St. ☎747-4300. Open M-Th 9am-7pm, F-Sa 9am-5pm, Su 1-5pm. Tours M-Sa noon and 2pm, Su 2pm.)* On the north side of the Loop, at Clark and Randolph, the **State of Illinois Building** is a postmodern town square designed by Helmut Jahn in 1985; the elevator to the top gives a thrilling (and free) view of its sloping atrium, circular floors, and hundreds of employees.

SCULPTURE. In addition to its architectural masterpieces, Chicago is decorated with one of the country's premier collections of outdoor sculpture. Large, abstract designs punctuate many downtown corners, making a walking tour of Loop outdoor sculpture a terrific way to spend an afternoon. The Chicago Cultural Center sells the *Loop Sculpture Guide* for $4 (see **Practical Information,** above). The piece known simply as "The Picasso" at the foot of the **Daley Center Plaza,** at Washington and Dearborn St., is an unofficial symbol of Chicago, although no one is quite sure if it represents a bird, dog, or woman. *(☎443-3054 for more info.)* Directly across Washington St. rests surrealist Joan Miró's *Chicago*, the artist's voluptuous gift to the city. *(69 W. Washington. St.)* Three blocks south on Dearborn at Adams, Alexander Calder's *Flamingo*, a stark red structure that is half-statue, half-mobile, stands in front of the Federal Center Plaza. Calder's other Chicago masterpiece, *The Universe*, swirls in the lobby of the Sears Tower.

NEAR NORTH

TRIBUNE TOWER. The city's ritziest district lies north of the Loop along the lake, just past the Michigan Ave. Bridge. An international design competition in the 1920s resulted in the Tribune Tower, a Gothic skyscraper just north of the bridge which overlooks this stretch. The tower is also home to Chicago's largest newspaper, *The Chicago Tribune. (435 N. Michigan Ave.)*

THE MART. Over 8 mi. of corridors fill the nearby Merchandise Mart; the entrance is on N. Wells or Kinzie, north of the river. One of the largest commercial buildings in the world (25 stories high and 2 blocks long), it even has its own ZIP code. The first two floors house a mediocre public mall; the remainder contains private show-rooms where design professionals converge to choose home and office furnishings. **Tours at the Mart** guides visitors through the building. (☎ 312-644-4664. Bus #114. 2hr. tours Th and F 1:30pm. $12, seniors $10, students $9.)

NAVY PIER. Big, bright, and always festive, Navy Pier, east of Grant Park on Lake Michigan, captures the carnival spirit 365 days a year. No small jetty, the mile-long pier has it all: a concert pavilion, dining options, nightspots, sightseeing boats, a spectacular ferris wheel, a crystal garden with palm trees, and an Omnimax theater. Now *that's* America. From here, explorers can rent **bicycles** to navigate the Windy City's streets. (600 E. Grand Ave. Take El Red Line to Grand/State and transfer to a free pier trolley bus. Bike rental open June-Sept. daily 8am-11pm, May 8am-8pm, Apr. and Oct. 10am-7pm. $9 per hr., $36 per day.)

MAGMILE. Chicago's showy Magnificent Mile, a row of glitzy shops along N. Michigan Ave. between the Chicago River and Oak St., can magnificently drain the wallet. Several of these retail stores, including **Banana Republic** and **Crate & Barrel,** were designed by some of the country's foremost architects and merit a look. The area is also home to one of the country's few **Virgin Megastores,** a music store palace full of popular American albums and British albums. The relatively plain **Chicago Water Tower** and **Pumping Station** stick out among the ritzy stores at the corner of Michigan and Pearson Ave. Built in 1867, these structures were the only ones in the area to survive the Great Chicago Fire. The pumping station houses the multimedia show *Here's Chicago* and a comprehensive tourist center (see **Practical Information,** above). Across Pearson St., expensive, trendy stores pack **Water Tower Place,** the first urban shopping mall in the US. One block north, the **John Hancock Building** (Chicago's third-tallest) rockets toward the sky in black steel and glass.

OLD TOWN. The bells of the pre-fire **St. Michael's Church** ring 1 mi. north of the MagMile in **Old Town,** a neighborhood where eclectic shops and nightspots fill gentrified streets. Architecture buffs will enjoy a stroll through the W. Menomonee and W. Eugenie St. area. In early June, the **Old Town Art Fair** attracts artists and craftsmen nationwide. (Take bus #151 to Lincoln Park and walk south down Clark or Wells St.)

NORTH SIDE

LINCOLN PARK. Urban renewal has made **Lincoln Park,** a neighborhood just west of the park bearing the same name, a popular choice for wealthy residents. Bounded by Armitage to the south and Diversey Ave. to the north, lakeside Lincoln Park offers splendid harbors and parks. Cafes, bookstores, and nightspots pack its tree-lined streets. Some of Chicago's liveliest clubs and restaurants lie in the area around N. Clark St., Lincoln Ave., and N. Halsted St.

LAKEVIEW. North of Diversey Ave. on N. Clark St., the streets of Lincoln Park become increasingly diverse as they melt into the community of Lakeview around the 3000s block. In this self-proclaimed "gay capital of Chicago," supermarket shopping plazas alternate with tiny markets and vintage clothing stores, while apartment towers and hotels spring up between aging two-story houses. Polish diners share blocks with Korean restaurants, and Mongolian eateries face Mexican bars in this ethnic potpourri.

WRIGLEYVILLE. Around the 4000s block of N. Clark, Lakeview shifts into **Wrigleyville.** Even though the **Chicago Cubs** haven't won a World Series since 1908, Wrigleyville residents remain fiercely loyal to their hometown team. Tiny, ivy-covered **Wrigley Field,** 1060 W. Addison, just east of the junction of Graceland and N. Clark, is the North Side's most famous institution. A pilgrimage here is a must for the serious or curious baseball fan, and for *Blues Brothers* nuts who want to visit the famous pair's falsified address. Tours of the historic park are available when the Cubs are away. Call 773-404-2827 for details. Along Clark St. in both Lakeview and Wrigleyville, restaurants, sports bars, and music clubs abound. Window shopping here beckons in the funk, junk, and 70s revival stores. For an alternative form of nightlife, go bowling, one of the most cherished midwest pastimes, at **Southport Lanes &**

Billiards. The 75 year-old Southport is one of the only remaining alleys anywhere to use pin-boys to set the lanes. *(3325 N. Southport Ave. near N. Clark St. ☎ 773-472-1601. Open 24hr. Game prices vary; tips appreciated.)* An even more raucous bowling experience awaits at the **Diversey Rock-n-Bowl**, in Lakeview, where "athletes" guzzle beers and bowl to deafening rock music. *(2211 W. Diversey. ☎ 773-227-5800. Open 24hr.)*

NEAR WEST SIDE

The Near West Side, bounded by the Chicago River to the east and Ogden Ave. to the west, assembles a veritable cornucopia of vibrant ethnic enclaves. **Greektown** and **Little Italy** draw culinary acclaim from all over the city (see **Food**, above).

HULL HOUSE. The primary inedible attraction on the Near West Side lies a few blocks north on Halsted, where activist Jane Addams devoted her life to historic Hull House. This settlement house bears witness to Chicago's role in turn-of-the-century reform. Although the house no longer offers social services, it has been painstakingly restored as a small museum. *(800 S. Halsted St. Take El Blue Line to Halsted/U of I or bus #8 "Halsted." ☎ 413-5353. Open M-F 10am-4pm, Su noon-5pm. Free.)*

SOUTH OF THE LOOP

HYDE PARK AND THE UNIVERSITY OF CHICAGO. Seven mi. south of the Loop along the lake, the scenic campus of the **University of Chicago** dominates the **Hyde Park** neighborhood. A former retreat for the city's artists and musicians, the park's community underwent urban renewal in the 50s and is now an island of intellectualism in a sea of degenerating neighborhoods. University police patrol the area bounded by 51st St. to the north, Lakeshore Dr. to the east, 61st St. to the south, and Cottage Grove to the west, but don't test these boundaries, even during the day. Lakeside Burnham Park, east of campus, is fairly safe during the day but not at night. The impressive **Oriental Institute, Museum of Science and Industry** (see **Museums**, p. 515), and **DuSable Museum of African-American History** are all in, or border on, Hyde Park. *(From the Loop, take bus #6 "Jefferson Express" or the METRA Electric Line from the Randolph St. Station south to 59th St.)*

ROBIE HOUSE. On campus, Frank Lloyd Wright's famous ▨**Robie House** blends into the surrounding trees. A seminal example of Wright's Prairie Style, which sought to integrate house with environment, its low horizontal lines now hold University offices. *(5757 S. Woodlawn, at the corner of 58th St. ☎ 708-848-1976. Tours M-F 11am-3pm, Sa-Su 11am-3:30pm. $8, over 64 and ages 7-18 $7.)*

PULLMAN. In 1885, George Pullman, inventor of the sleeping car, attempted to create a model working environment so that his Palace Car Company employees would be "healthier, happier, and more productive." The result of this quest was the town of **Pullman**, 14 mi. southeast of downtown. It was considered the nation's ideal community until 1894, when a stubborn Pullman evicted fired workers from their homes. The community soon after held a monumental strike and Pullman's vision was shattered. In the center of town, **Hotel Florence** houses a museum and gift shop. *(11111 S. Forrestville Ave. I-94 W to 111th St. Illinois Central Gulf Railroad to 111th St. and Pullman or METRA Rock Island Line to 111th St. ☎ 773-785-8181.)* The **Historic Pullman Foundation Visitors Center** leads guided tours. *(11141 S. Cottage Grove Ave. ☎ 773-785-3111. Tours leave the first Su of each month May-Oct. at 12:30 and 1pm. $5, students and seniors $4.)*

WEST OF THE LOOP

OAK PARK. Gunning for the title of the most fantastic suburb in the US, the magnificent town of Oak Park sprouts off of Harlem St., 10 mi. west of downtown on I-290. *(I-290 W to Harlem St.)* Frank Lloyd Wright endowed the downtown area with 25 of his spectacular homes and buildings, all of which dot the Oak Park Historic District. Here, his one-time home and workplace, the ▨**Frank Lloyd Wright House and Studio,** offers an unbeatable look at his interior and exterior stylings. *(951 Chicago Ave. ☎ 708-848-1976. Open daily 10am-5pm. 45min. tours of the house M-F 11am, 1, and 3pm, Sa-Su every 20min. 11am-3:30pm. 1hr. self-guided tours of Wright's other Oak Park homes can be* *taken with a map and audio cassette available daily 10am-3:30pm. Guided tours Mar.-Nov. Sa-Su every hr. 11am-4pm; Dec.-Feb. Sa-Su every hr. noon-2pm. $9, seniors and under 18 $7; combination interior/exterior tour tickets $14/$10.)* Visitors should also stop by the fomer home of another American giant, Ernest Hemingway. Throughout the year, fans flock to the **Ernest Hemingway Birthplace and Museum** to take part in the many events honoring this legendary master of the novel. *(Birthplace: 339 N. Oak Ave., Museum: 200 N. Oak Park Ave. ☎ 708-848-2222. Th, F, and Su 1-5pm, Sa 10am-5pm. $6 combined ticket, seniors and under 18 $4.50.)* Swing by the **Visitors Center** for maps, guidebooks, tours, and local history. *(158 Forest Ave. ☎ 708-848-1500 or 888-625-7275. El Green Line to Harlem.)*

🏛 MUSEUMS

Chicago's major museums admit visitors free at least one day per week. The first five listings, known as the Big Five, provide a diverse array of exhibits, while a handful of smaller collections target specific interests. Lake Shore Drive has been diverted around Grant Park, linking the Field Museum, Adler, and Shedd; the compound, known as Museum Campus, offers a free shuttle between museums. Visitors who plan on seeing all five, plus the Sears Tower Observation Deck, can also save money by purchasing a half-price CityPass, which grants admission to the sights as well as discount coupons for food and shopping ($33.75, seniors $25, ages 3-11 $22.25; available at each included attraction).

Art Institute of Chicago, 111 S. Michigan Ave. (☎443-3600), at Adams St. in Grant Park; take the El Green, Brown, Purple, or Orange Lines to Adams. The city's premier art museum, with four millennia of art from Asia, Africa, Europe, and beyond. Highlight tour daily 2pm, includes Wood's *American Gothic.* Pull a Ferris Bueller and stand real close to Seurat's *A Sunday Afternoon on the Island of La Grande Jatte,* among others. Open M and W-F 10:30am-4:30pm, Tu 10:30am-8pm, Sa-Su 10am-5pm. $10, students and children $6, under 6 free. Free on Tu.

Field Museum of Natural History, 1400 S. Lake Shore Dr. (☎922-9410), at Roosevelt Rd. in Grant Park; take bus #146 from State St. Sue, the largest *T. rex* skeleton ever unearthed, presides over excellent geology, anthropology, botany, and zoology exhibits. Other highlights include Egyptian mummies, Native American halls, and a dirt exhibit. Open daily 8am-5pm, Sept.-May 9am-5pm. $8; seniors, students, and ages 3-11 $4; under 3 free. Free on W. Parking $7 per day.

Shedd Aquarium, 1200 S. Lake Shore Dr. (☎939-2438), in Grant Park. The world's largest indoor aquarium has over 6600 species of fish in 206 tanks. The Oceanarium features beluga whales, dolphins, seals, and other marine mammals in a giant pool that appears to flow into Lake Michigan. On the ground floor, penguins defend their nests against their handlers. Open daily 9am-6pm, Th until 10pm, Oceanarium until 8pm; Sept.-May M-F 9am-5pm, Sa-Su 9am-6pm. Feedings M-F 11am, 2, and 3pm. Combined admission to Oceanarium and Aquarium $15, seniors and ages 3-11 $11; Aquarium free on M. Oceanarium $6, seniors and ages 5-17 $5. Tour of Oceanarium $3.

Museum of Science and Industry, 5700 S. Lake Shore Dr. (☎773-684-1414), at 57th St. in Hyde Park; take bus #6 "Jeffrey Express" or METRA South Shore line to 57th St. The expansive Museum features the *Apollo 8* command module, a full-sized replica of a coal mine, a cantilevered 727 airplane, and Omnimax shows. Call for schedule. Open daily 9:30am-5:30pm. $9, seniors $7.50, ages 3-11 $5; with Omnimax $15/$12.50/ $10. Free on Th, except Omnimax. Parking $7 per day.

Adler Planetarium, 1300 S. Lake Shore Dr. (☎922-7827), on Museum Campus in Grant Park. Aspiring astronauts can discover their weight on Mars, read the news from space, and examine astronomy tools. Open June-Aug. Sa-W 9am-6pm, Th-F 9am-9pm; Sept.-May M-F 9am-5pm, Sa-Su 9am-6pm. $5, seniors and ages 4-17 $4. Free on Tu and Th evenings. Some exhibits $5 extra. Skyshow daily on the hr. $5.

Museum of Contemporary Art, 220 E. Chicago Ave. (☎280-2660), 1 block east of Michigan Ave.; take #66 "Chicago Ave." bus. The MCA showcases outstanding permanent and temporary collections of modern art in its ultra-modern exhibition space. Call to see whether their extensive collection of Calder mobiles are on display. If not, Warhol, Javer, and Nauman still highlight a vibrant list of artists. Open Tu 10am-8pm, W-Su 10am-5pm. $8, students and seniors $5, under 12 free; free on Tu.

Museum of Holography, 1134 W. Washington Blvd. (☎226-1007), just west of the loop. This unconventional museum explores the wild world of holograms. The hologram pictures of famous people are fantastic. Open W-Su 12:30-5pm. $2.50.

Spertus Institute of Jewish Studies, 618 S. Michigan Ave. (☎322-1747), near Harrison downtown; take El Red Line to Harrison. An impressive collection of synagogue relics rests on the first fl., as does the diminutive but moving Holocaust Memorial. Open Su-W 10am-5pm, Th 10am-8pm, F 10am-3pm. Artifact center open Su-Th 1-4:30pm. $5; students, seniors, and children $3; free on F.

Terra Museum of American Art, 664 N. Michigan Ave. (☎664-3939), at Erie St. One of few galleries to exclusively showcase American art from colonial times to the present, focusing on 19th-century Impressionism. Open Tu 10am-8pm, W-Sa 10am-6pm, Su noon-5pm. $7, seniors $3.50, students and teachers with ID and under 12 free; free on Tu and first Su of month. Free tours Tu-F noon and 6pm, Sa-Su noon and 2pm.

International Museum of Surgical Science, 1524 N. Lake Shore Dr. (☎642-6502), at North Ave. A sculpture of a surgeon holding his wounded patient marks the entrance to this unique museum, a harrowing journey through the history of surgery. Highlights, if they can be so called, include a fascinating collection of gallstones and bladderstones. Open Tu-Sa 10am-4pm. $5, seniors and students $3.

🏞 OUTDOOR ACTIVITIES

A string of lakefront parks fringe the area between Chicago proper and Lake Michigan. On sunny afternoons, a cavalcade of sunbathers, dog walkers, in-line skaters, and skateboarders storms the shore. Close to downtown, the two major parks are **Lincoln** and **Grant**. Lincoln extends across 5 mi. of lakefront on the north side, and rolls in the style of a 19th-century English park: winding paths, natural groves of trees, and asymmetrical open spaces. The **Lincoln Park Zoo**, the nation's oldest, is an excellent spot for a stroll among the gorillas and lions. (Open daily 10am-5pm, summer Sa-Su until 7pm. Free.) Next door, the **Lincoln Park Conservatory** encloses fauna from varied ecosystems in its glass palace. (☎742-7736. Open daily 9am-5pm. Free.)

Grant Park, covering 14 lakefront blocks east of Michigan Ave., follows the 19th-century French park style: symmetrical and ordered, with corners, a fountain in the center, and wide promenades. The Grant Park Concert Society hosts free summer concerts here in the **Petrillo Music Shell,** 520 S. Michigan Ave. (☎742-4763). Colored lights illuminate **Buckingham Fountain** from 9-11pm. On the north side, Lake Michigan lures swimmers and sun-bathers to **Lincoln Park Beach** and **Oak St. Beach.** Be aware that the rock ledges are restricted areas, and swimming from them is illegal. Although the beaches are patrolled 9am to 9:30pm, they can be unsafe after dark. The **Chicago Parks District** (☎747-2200) has further info.

Starting from the Hyde Park area in the south, the **Lake Shore Drive** offers sparkling views of Lake Michigan all the way past the city and one of the best views of the downtown skyline. At its end, Lake Shore becomes Sheridan Rd., which twists and turns its way through the picturesque northern suburbs. Just north of Chicago is **Evanston,** a lively, affluent college town (home to Northwestern University) with an array of parks and nightclubs. Ten minutes farther north is upscale **Wilmette,** home to the ornate and striking 🏛**Baha'i House of Worship,** 100 Linden Ave. at Sheridan Rd. This out-of-the-way and not very touristy architectual wonder is topped by a stunning nine-sided dome. (☎847-853-2300. Open daily 10am-10pm; Oct.-May 10am-5pm. Services M-Sa 12:15pm, Su 1:15pm.)

The 🏛**Indiana Dunes State Park** and **National Lakeshore** lie 45min. east of Chicago on I-90. The State Park's gorgeous dune beaches on Lake Michigan are packed on summer weekends, when Chicagoans flee the frantic pace of the city for swimming and sunning. Options for the more adventuresome include hikes through dunes, woods, and marshes. Info about the State Park is available at the **Visitors Center,** 1600 N. 25 East in Chesterton (☎219-926-1952). Obtain Lakeshore details at their Visitors Center, 1100 N. Mineral Springs Rd. in Porter (☎219-926-7561).

♫ ENTERTAINMENT

The free weeklies *Chicago Reader* and *New City,* available in many bars, record stores, and restaurants, list the latest events. The *Reader* reviews all major shows, with times and ticket prices. *Chicago* magazine has exhaustive club, music, dance, and opera listings, along with theater reviews. *The Chicago Tribune* includes an entertainment section every Friday. *Gay Chicago* provides info on social activities and other news for the area's gay community.

THEATER

One of the foremost theater centers of North America, Chicago's more than 150 theaters show everything from blockbuster musicals to off-color parodies. Downtown theaters cluster just north of the Loop and around Michigan Ave. and Madison Ave. Smaller, community-based theaters are scattered throughout the city. Most tickets are expensive. Half-price tickets are sold on the day of performance at **Hot Tix Booths,** 108 N. State St., or on the 6th fl. of 700 N. Michigan Ave. Purchases must be made in person. (☎977-1755. Open M-F 10am-7pm, Sa 10am-6pm, Su noon-5pm.) **Ticketmaster** (☎559-1212) supplies tickets for many theaters; ask about senior, student, and child discounts at all Chicago shows. The "Off-Loop" theaters on the North Side specialize in original productions, with tickets usually under $18.

▓ **Steppenwolf Theater,** 1650 N. Halsted St. (☎335-1888), where Gary Sinise and the eerie John Malkovich got their start and still stop by. Tickets Su-Th $40, F-Sa $45; half-price Tu-F after 5pm, Sa-Su after noon. Office open Su-M 11am-5pm, Tu-F 11am-8pm, Sa 11am-9pm.

Goodman Theatre, 200 S. Columbus Dr. (☎443-3800), presents consistently solid original works. Tickets around $18-40; half-price after 6pm, or after noon for matinee. Box office open M-F 10am-5pm; 10am-8pm show nights, usually Sa-Su.

Shubert Theater, 22 W. Monroe St. (☎977-1700), presents big-name Broadway touring productions. Tickets $15-70. Box office open M-Sa 10am-6pm.

Annoyance Theatre, 3747 N. Clark St. (☎773-929-6200), in Wrigleyville. Original works that play off pop culture, such as *Co-ed Prison Sluts.* Often participatory comedy. Tickets ($5-10) sold just before showtime, usually 8 or 9pm.

Bailiwick Repertory, 1225 W. Belmont Ave. (☎773-327-5252), in the Theatre Bldg. A mainstage and experimental studio space. Tickets from $10. Box office open W noon-6pm, Th-Su noon until showtime.

COMEDY

Chicago boasts a plethora of comedy clubs. The most famous, ▓**Second City,** 1616 N. Wells St. (☎642-8189), at North Ave. in Old Town, spoofs Chicago life and politics. Second City graduated Bill Murray and late greats John Candy, John Belushi, and Gilda Radner, among others. Most nights a free improv session follows the show. **Second City Etc.** offers more comedy next door at 1608 N. Wells. (☎642-6514. Shows for both M-Th 8:30pm, F-Sa 8 and 11pm, Su 8pm. Box office hours daily 10:30am-10pm. Tickets $15. Reservations recommended; during the week you can often get in if you show up 1hr. early.) Watch improv actors compete to bust your gut at **Comedy Sportz,** 2851 N. Halsted (☎773-549-8080; shows F-Sa 8 and 10:30pm).

DANCE, CLASSICAL MUSIC, AND OPERA

Ballet, comedy, live theater, and musicals are performed at **Auditorium Theatre,** 50 E. Congress Pkwy. (☎922-2110; box office open M-F 8:30am-5pm). From October through May, the **Chicago Symphony Orchestra,** conducted by Daniel Barenboim, resonates at **Symphony Center,** 220 S. Michigan Ave. (☎294-3333). **Ballet Chicago** pirouettes in theaters throughout Chicago. (☎251-8838. Tickets $12-45.) The acclaimed **Lyric Opera of Chicago** performs from September through March at the **Civic Opera House,** 20 N. Wacker Dr. (☎332-2244). While other places may suck your wallet dry, the **Grant Park Music Festival** affords a taste of the classical for free. From mid-June through late August, the acclaimed Grant Park Symphony Orchestra plays a few free evening concerts per week at the Grant Park Petrillo Music Shell. (Usually W-Su; schedule varies. Call 552-8500 for details.)

SEASONAL EVENTS

The city celebrates summer on a grand scale. The **Taste of Chicago** festival cooks for eight days through July 4th. Seventy restaurants set up booths with endless samples in Grant Park, while crowds chomp to the blast of big name bands. (Free entry; food tickets 50¢ each.) The Taste's fireworks are the city's biggest and most popular. The first week in June, the **Blues Festival** celebrates the city's soulful music; the **Chicago Gospel Festival** hums and hollers in mid-June; and Nashville moves north for the **Country Music Festival** at the end of June. The ¡Viva Chicago! Latin music festival steams up in late August, while the **Chicago Jazz Festival** scats Labor Day weekend. All festivals center at the Grant Park Petrillo Music Shell. The Mayor's Office's **Special Events Hotline** (☎744-3370) has more info on all six free events.

The regionally famous **Ravinia Festival** (☎847-266-5100), in the northern suburb of Highland Park, runs from late June to early September. The Chicago Symphony Orchestra, ballet troupes, folk and jazz musicians, and comedians perform throughout the festival's 14-week season. (Shows M-Sa 8pm, Su 7pm. Lawn seats $8; other tickets $15-35. On certain nights, the Orchestra allows students free lawn admission with student ID. Call ahead. Round-trip on the METRA costs about $7; the festival runs charter buses for $12. The bus ride takes 1½hr.)

SPORTS

The National League's **Cubs** step up to bat at **Wrigley Field,** 1060 W. Addison St., at N. Clark St. in Wrigleyville, one of the few ballparks in America to retain the early grace and intimate feel of the game. (☎773-404-CUBS; www.cubs.com. Tickets $10-22.) The **White Sox,** Chicago's American League team, swing on the South Side at the new **Comiskey Park,** 333 W. 35th St. (☎674-1000; tickets $12-24). The **Bears** of the NFL kick off at **Soldier Field Stadium,** at McFetridge Dr. and S. Lakeshore Dr. (☎708-615-2327). The **Bulls** have won many an NBA championship at the **United Center,** 1901 W. Madison just west of the Loop, known fondly as "the house that Michael Jordan built." (☎943-5800. Tickets $30-450.) Hockey's **Blackhawks** skate in his shadow there. (☎455-4500. Tickets $25-100.) **Sports Information** (☎976-4242) has up-to-the-minute info on local sports events. For tickets to all games, call **Ticketmaster** (Bulls and Blackhawks ☎559-1212; White Sox ☎831-1769; Cubs ☎773-404-CUBS).

◪ NIGHTLIFE

"Sweet home Chicago" takes pride in the innumerable blues performers who have played here. Jazz, folk, reggae, and punk clubs throb all over the **North Side.** The **Bucktown/Wicker Park** area, west of Halsted St. in Northwest Chicago, stays open late with bucking bars and dance clubs. Aspiring pickup artists swing over to **Rush** and **Division St.,** an intersection that has replaced the stockyards as one of the biggest meat markets in the world. Full of bars, cafes, and bistros, **Lincoln Park** is frequented by singles and young couples, both gay and straight. The vibrant center of gay culture is between 3000 and 4500 **N. Halsted St.;** many of the more festive and colorful clubs and bars line this area. For more upscale raging, raving, and discoing, there are plenty of clubs near **River North,** in Riverwest, and on Fulton St.

BARS AND BLUES JOINTS

◪**The Green Mill,** 4802 N. Broadway Ave. (☎773-878-5552). El Red Line: Lawrence. Founded as a Prohibition-era speakeasy. Mafiosi-in-training can park themselves in Al Capone's old seat. An authentic jazz club, this hot spot draws late-night crowds after other clubs shut down. The cover-free jam sessions on weekends after the main acts finish are reason enough to chill until the wee hours. Cover $5-8. Open daily until 4am.

The Hideout, 1354 W. Wabansia Ave. (☎773-227-4433). El Brown Line: Clybourn and North, West Town. Nestled in a municipal truck parking lot, this creative joint is the insider's indie rock club. Some weekends, the lot fills with special "kid's shows" geared toward families who still like to rock. Arrangements with a top record company has established the club as one on the nation's best places to catch rising alt-country acts. Cover $5-10 Tu-F. Open M 8pm-2am, Tu-F 4pm-2am, Sa 7pm-3am.

B.L.U.E.S., 2519 N. Halsted St. (☎773-528-1012). El to Fullerton, then take the east-bound "Fullerton" bus. Crowded and intimate, with unbeatable music. Success here led to the larger **B.L.U.E.S. etc.,** 1124 W. Belmont Ave. (☎773-525-8989). El to Belmont, then 3 blocks west on Belmont. The place for huge names: Albert King, Bo Diddley, Dr. John, and Wolfman Washington have played here. Live music every night 9pm-1:30am. 21+. Cover for both places M-Th $6-8, F-Sa $8-10.

Buddy Guy's Legends, 754 S. Wabash Ave. (☎427-1190). Buddy officially plays in Jan., but he is known to stop by when not on tour. The rest of the time, major and rising blues stars take over and enchant crowds in the soul-filled space. Blues M-Th 5pm-2am, F 4pm-2am, Sa 5pm-3am, Su 6pm-2am. 21+. Cover Su-W $8, Th $7, F-Sa $12.

Metro, 3730 N. Clark St. (☎773-549-0203), in Wrigleyville. At this outstanding live alter-native and pop music venue, local bands are showcased every Su. 18+; occasionally all ages are welcome. Cover $5-12; much more for big bands.

Wild Hare & Singing Armadillo Frog Sanctuary, 3530 N. Clark St. (☎773-327-4273), between Addison and Roscoe St., in Wrigleyville. El: Addison. Live Roots Reggae acts sing Jah's praises in front of both dreadlocked hipsters and yuppies. No cover before 9:30pm. Cover $5-8 W-Su; W ladies free. Open Su-F until 2am, Sa until 3am.

Checkerboard Lounge, 423 E. 43rd St. (☎773-624-3240), at King Dr. Drive or take a cab. The true Blues bar experience, the Checkerboard is the most authentic, intimate joint in town. The down-and-out neighborhood infuses the music with its spirit; be care-ful. Cover $5-7. Open M-F 1pm-2am.

DANCE CLUBS

▣**Funky Buddha Lounge,** 728 W. Grand Ave. (☎666-1695. El Blue Line: Chicago), West Town just west of River North. Extremely trendy, eclectic dance club and lounge where hip-hop and funk blend with crazy leopard, velvet, and Buddha decor. Su gay night. Cover $10-20. Open M-W 10pm-2am, Th-F 9pm-2am, Sa 9pm-3am, Su 6pm-2am.

▣**Berlin,** 954 W. Belmont Ave. (☎773-327-7711). El Red or Brown line: Belmont, in Lake-view. Anything and everything goes at Berlin, a mainstay of Chicago's gay nightlife scene. Crowds pulsate to house/dance music amid drag contests, disco nights, The Art-ist Formerly Known As Prince night, and other theme parties. W ladies night. 21+. Cover F-Sa after midnight $5. Open M-F until 4am, Sa until 5am.

Smart Bar, 3730 N. Clark St. (☎773-549-4140), downstairs from the Metro. Resident DJ spins punk, techno, hip-hop and house. 21+. Cover $5-9; Metro concertgoers free. Opening times vary (around 10pm); closes around 4am on weekends.

Crobar Night Club, 1543 N. Kingsbury St. (☎413-7000). El Red Line: North & Clybourn. Cavernous, candle-strewn dance club where a young, leather-clad crowd slithers to house beats in cages and on the floor. GLEE gay night Su. Cover $5-20. Open W, F, and Su 10pm-4am; Sa 10pm-5am.

SPRINGFIELD ☎217

Springfield, "the town that Lincoln loved," owes much to its most distinguished former resident. A hotbed of political activity during the increasingly fractured antebellum years, the small town hosted the heated Lincoln-Douglass debates of 1858, attracting the attention of the entire nation. Although Springfield has since declined from national prominence into near obscurity, the town welcomes tour-ists to learn everything about Honest Abe.

◪ **PRACTICAL INFORMATION. Amtrak,** 3rd and Washington St. (☎753-2013; sta-tion open daily 6am-9:30pm), near downtown, runs trains to Chicago (3½hr., 3 per day, $21-44) and St. Louis (2hr., 3 per day, $19-31). **Greyhound,** 2351 S. Dirksen Pkwy. (☎800-231-2222; depot open 8am-noon and 2-8pm, Sa-Su 8am-noon and 2-4pm), on the eastern edge of town, rolls to Chicago (5hr., 6 per day, $40); Indianapolis (7hr., 2 per day, $49); St. Louis (2hr., 4 per day, $26); and Bloomington (1hr., 1 per day, $57). **Springfield Mass Transit District:** 928 S. 9th St. Pick up maps at transit headquar-ters, most banks, or the Illinois State Museum. (☎522-5531. Buses operate M-Sa

6am-6pm. Fare 75¢, seniors 35¢, transfers free.) The **downtown trolley** system is designed to take tourists to eight designated places of historic interest. (☎528-4100. Trolleys run W-Su 9am-4pm. Hop-on/off fare $10, seniors $9, kids 5-12 $5; circuit fare $5.) Taxi: **Lincoln Yellow Cab,** ☎523-4545. **Springfield Convention and Visitors Bureau:** 109 N. 7th St. (☎789-2360 or 800-545-7300; open M-F 8am-5pm). **Internet access: Lincoln Library,** 326 S. 7th St. (☎753-4900; open M-Th 9am-9pm, F 9am-6pm, Sa 9am-5pm; Sept.-May also Su noon-5pm). **Post Office:** 411 E. Monroe, at Wheeler St. (☎788-7470; open M-F 8am-4:30pm). **ZIP code:** 62701. **Area code:** 217.

▐▌ ACCOMMODATIONS AND FOOD. Bus service to the cheap lodgings off I-55 and U.S. 36 on Dirksen Pkwy. is limited. Downtown hotels may be booked solid on weekdays when the legislature is in session, but ask the Visitors Bureau about weekend packages. Rooms should be reserved early for holiday weekends and the **State Fair** (Aug. 9-18, 2002). Take bus #3 "Bergen Park" to Milton and Elm St. and walk a few blocks east to the **Dirksen Inn Motel/Shamrock Motel,** 900 N. Dirksen Pkwy., for clean, pleasant rooms with refrigerators. (☎523-5302. Reception daily 8am-10pm. Rooms $30.) **Mister Lincoln's Campground,** 3045 Stanton Ave., off Stevenson Dr., has free showers. Take bus #10. (☎529-8206. Reception daily 8am-8pm; in winter 8am-6pm. Sites $16, with hookup $21; cabins with A/C $25.) Interesting cuisine is sparse in Springfield. Still, you can get some kicks on historic Rte. 66 at the **Cozy Drive-In,** 2935 S. 6th St., a family-owned diner devoted to roadside memorabilia and great greasy food. (☎525-1992. Open M-Sa 8am-8pm. Cozy Dog $1.50.)

▣ SIGHTS. Springfield makes money by zealously re-creating Lincoln's life. Walking from sight to sight allows you to retrace the steps of the monumental man himself. Happily, many Lincoln sights are free. (Info line ☎800-545-7300.) The **Lincoln Home Visitors Center** screens a 19min. film on "Mr. Lincoln's Springfield" and doles out free tickets to see the **Lincoln Home,** 426 S. 7th St. The only house Abe ever owned and the main Springfield draw, it sits at 8th and Jackson St. in a restored 19th-century neighborhood replete with hoops-playing girls and rickety board-walks. (☎492-4241. Open Apr.-Sept. daily 8am-6pm. 10min. tours every 5-10min. from the front of the house. Arrive early to avoid the crowds.) The magnificent limestone **Old State Capitol,** where Lincoln delivered his stirring and prophetic "House Divided" speech in 1858, also witnessed the epic Lincoln-Douglass debates. (☎785-7961. Open Mar.-Oct. daily 9am-5pm, Nov.-Feb. 9am-4pm. Last tour 1hr. before closing. Donation suggested.) Lincoln, his wife Mary Todd, and three of their sons rest at the massive **Lincoln Tomb,** 1500 Monument Ave., at Oak Ridge Cemetery. (☎782-2717. Open Mar.-Oct. 9am-5pm daily, Nov.-Feb. 9am-4pm.)

Those unwilling to endure all of Lincolnland should walk to the **Dana-Thomas House,** 301 E. Lawrence Ave., six blocks south of the Old State Capitol. Built in 1902, the stunning and well-preserved home was one of Frank Lloyd Wright's early experiments in Prairie Style and still features Frank's original fixtures. (☎782-6776. Open W-Su 9am-4pm. 1hr. tours every 15-20min. Suggested donation $3.) Rte. 66, that fabled American highway of yesteryear, is remembered in Springfield by **Shea's,** 2075 Peoria Rd., a truck shop with masses of memorabilia, including gas pumps, signs, and license plates. (☎522-0475. Open Tu-F 7am-4pm, Sa 7am-noon.)

WISCONSIN

Oceans of milk and beer flood the Great Lakes' most wholesome party state. French fur trappers first explored this area in search of lucrative furry creatures. Later, miners burrowed homes in the hills during the 1820s lead rush (earning them the nickname "badgers"), and hearty Norsemen set to clearing vast woodlands. By the time the forests fell and the mines were exhausted, German immigrant farmers had set dairy cows to graze and planted rolling fields of barley for beer amid the state's 15,000 lakes. Visitors to "America's Dairyland" pass cheese-filled country stores to delight in the ocean-like vistas of Door County and the ethnic *fêtes* (and less refined beer bashes) of Madison and Milwaukee.

☑ PRACTICAL INFORMATION

Capital: Madison.

Visitor Info: Division of Tourism, 123 W. Washington St., P.O. Box 7976, Madison 53707 (☎608-266-2161 or 800-432-8747; www.tourism.state.wi.us).

Postal Abbreviation: WI. **Sales Tax:** 5-5.5%, depending on county.

MILWAUKEE   ☎414

Home to beer and countless festivals, Milwaukee is a city given to celebration. Ethnic communities take turns throwing rollicking city-wide parties each summer weekend, giving the city its reputation for *gemütlichkeit* (hospitality). Milwaukee's famous beer industry fuels the revelry, supplying more than 1500 bars and taverns with as much of the good stuff as anyone could ever need—or take. Aside from merrymaking, the city boasts top-notch museums, German-inspired architecture, and a long expanse of scenic lakeshore.

▛ TRANSPORTATION

Airport: General Mitchell International Airport, 5300 S. Howell Ave. (☎747-5300). Take bus #80 from 6th St. downtown (30min.). **Limousine Service,** ☎769-9100 or 800-236-5450. 24hr. pickup and dropoff from most downtown hotels. $10, round-trip $18. Reservations required.

Trains: Amtrak, 433 W. St. Paul Ave. (☎271-0840), at 5th St. downtown. In a fairly safe area, but less so at night. To Chicago (1½hr., 6 per day, $20) and St. Paul (6½hr., 1 per day, $45-98). Open M-Sa 5:30am-10pm, Su 7am-10pm.

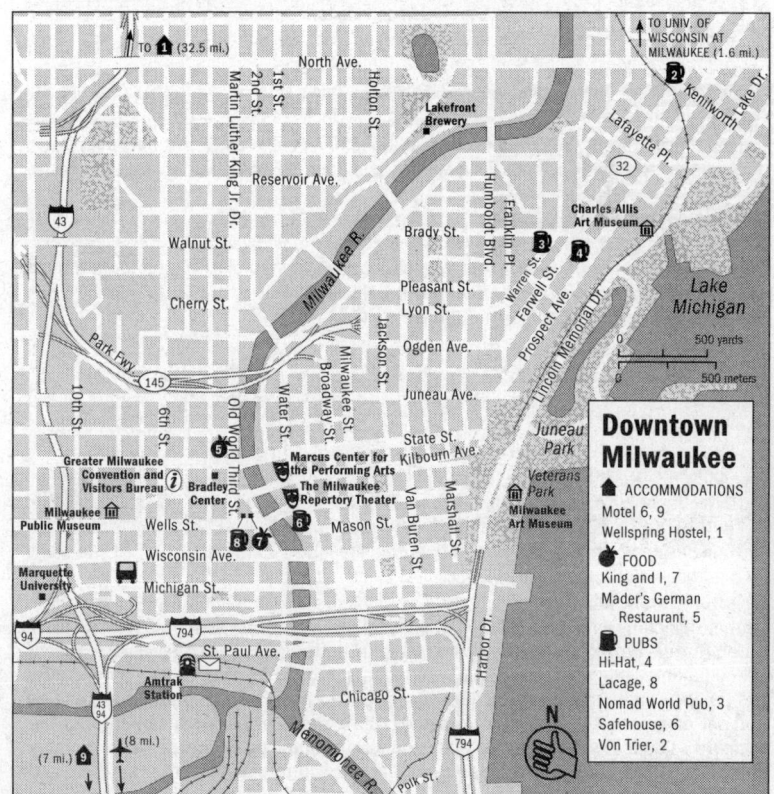

Downtown Milwaukee

🏠 ACCOMMODATIONS
Motel 6, 9
Wellspring Hostel, 1

🍎 FOOD
King and I, 7
Mader's German Restaurant, 5

🍺 PUBS
Hi-Hat, 4
Lacage, 8
Nomad World Pub, 3
Safehouse, 6
Von Trier, 2

GREAT LAKES

Buses: Greyhound, 606 N. 7th St. (☎272-2156), off W. Michigan St., 3 blocks from the train station. To Chicago (2-3hr., 16 per day, $14) and Minneapolis (7-9hr., 6 per day, $49). Station open 24hr.; office open daily 6:30am-11:30pm. **Coach USA Milwaukee** (☎262-544-6503 or 262-542-8861), in the same terminal, covers southeastern Wisconsin. **Badger Bus,** 635 N. James Lovell St. (☎276-7490 or 608-255-1511), across the street, burrows to Madison (1½hr., 6 per day, $10). Open daily 6:30am-10pm. *Be cautious at night.*

Public Transit: Milwaukee County Transit System, 1942 N. 17th St. (☎344-6711). Efficient metro area service. Most lines run 5am-12:30am. Fare $1.50, seniors and children 75¢; weekly pass $11. Free maps at the library or at Grand Ave. Mall info center. Call for schedules. The **Trolley** (☎344-6711) runs downtown, with service to festivals and Brewers games. Fare 50¢, seniors 25¢. Operates June-Aug. M-Th 6:30am-10pm, F 6:30am-midnight, Sa 10am-midnight, Su 10am-6pm. Call for winter schedules.

Taxis: Veteran, ☎291-8080. **Yellow Taxi,** ☎271-6630.

✦❷ ORIENTATION AND PRACTICAL INFORMATION

Most of Milwaukee's action is centered on the east side of downtown, which lies between **Lake Michigan** and 10th St. Address numbers increase north and south from **Wisconsin Ave.,** the center of east-west travel. Most north-south streets are numbered, increasing from Lake Michigan toward the west. The **interstate system** forms a loop around Milwaukee: **I-43 S** runs to Beloit, **I-43 N** runs to Green Bay, **I-94 E** is a straight shot to Chicago, **I-94 W** goes to Madison and then Minneapolis/St. Paul, **I-794** cuts through the heart of downtown Milwaukee, and **I-894** (the downtown bypass) connects with the airport.

Visitor Info: Greater Milwaukee Convention and Visitors Bureau, 400 W. Wisconsin, located in the Midwest Express Center lobby (☎273-7222 or 800-554-1448). Open M-F 9am-5pm; in summer also Sa 9am-2pm, Su 11am-3pm.

Hotlines: Crisis Intervention, ☎257-7222. **Rape Crisis Line,** ☎542-3828. Both operate 24hr. **Gay People's Union Hotline,** ☎562-7010. Operates daily 7-10pm.

Post Office: 345 W. St. Paul Ave. (☎800-272-8777), south along 4th Ave. from downtown, by the Amtrak station. Open M-F 7:30am-8pm. **ZIP code:** 53201. **Area code:** 414.

⌂ ACCOMMODATIONS

Downtown lodging options tend to be expensive; travelers with cars should head out to the city's two hostels. **Bed and Breakfast of Milwaukee** (☎277-8066) finds rooms in picturesque B&Bs around the area (from $55).

Milwaukee Summer Hostel (HI), McCormick Hall on Marquette University's campus, 1530 W. Wisconsin (☎288-3232 or 961-2525). Take bus #10 or 30 down Wisconsin to 16th St. Recently opened as a hostel and centrally located, this place has all the comforts of, well, college. Laundry facilities, free Internet access, no curfew, and parking nearby ($3.50). Open June to mid-Aug. Check-in 8-11am, 5-10pm. Dorm beds $17, nonmembers $20. Private rooms with bath $55/$60.

University of Wisconsin at Milwaukee (UWM), Sandburg Hall, 3400 N. Maryland Ave. (☎229-4065 or 299-6123). Take bus #30 north to Hartford St. Close to East Side restaurants and bars, the UWM sports spotless, unadorned dorm suites, divided into single and double bedrooms. Laundry facilities, cafeteria, free local calls. 2-day advance reservations required. Open June to mid-Aug. Singles with shared bath $33; doubles $60.

Wellspring Hostel (HI-AYH), 4382 Hickory Rd. (☎675-6755), in Newburg. Take I-43 N to Rte. 33 W to Newburg and exit on Main St.; Hickory Rd. intersects Newburg's Main St. just northwest of the Milwaukee River. The idyllic setting, far from downtown on a riverside farm, is worth the 45min. drive for those looking to get back to nature. Well-kept with 25 beds, kitchen, and nature trails. Linen $3. Office open daily 8am-8pm. Dorms $15, nonmembers $18. Private room with bath $40. Reservations required.

Motel 6, 5037 S. Howell Ave. (☎482-4414), near the airport off I-894, in a remodeled building 15min. from downtown. Any airport shuttle will take you within walking distance of this dependable chain motel, which houses airy rooms with A/C, cable, and a pool. Singles $44; doubles $50; Sa-Su $50/$56.

FOOD

Milwaukee is best known for its food and beer. German influences run especially strong, as *bier*-guzzling locals take pride in the best *wurst* this side of the Atlantic. On a distinctly less exotic note, Milwaukeeans take advantage of nearby Lake Michigan with a local favorite called the **Friday night fish fry.** For those who prefer to skip straight to the sweet stuff, extra-creamy ice cream, known as **frozen custard,** is the Dairy State's special treat.

German restaurants are scattered along nearly every street in the city—particularly downtown, where most have highbrow prices and continental attitude to match their 100 or so years of experience. Polish and Serbian influences dominate the **South Side,** and good Mexican food prevails in **Walker's Point,** at National and 5th St. **East Side** eateries are cosmopolitan and quirky, with a mix of ethnic flavors. Downtown, the Riverwalk project has revitalized the **Water St. entertainment district,** which boasts hot new restaurants for a range of palates. On the north end of the Riverwalk, **Old World Third St.** is home to the city's best brew-pubs.

Leon's, 3131 S. 27th St. (☎383-1784). A cross between *Grease* and *Starlight Express,* Leon's scoops some of the best frozen custard in town (2 scoops $1.25). Hot dogs $1.10. Open Su-Th 11am-midnight, F 11am-12:30am, Sa 11am-1am.

Casablanca, 730 W. Mitchell St. (☎383-2363), on the South Side. Herbivores feast on falafel and tabouli at the unbeatable all-you-can-eat lunch buffet ($5) in this serene Middle Eastern storefront. Carnivores get their fix with delectable shish kebabs ($5-7). Entrees $5-10. Lunch buffet Tu-F 11am-2pm. Open Tu-Sa 11am-9pm, Su noon-6pm.

Mader's German Restaurant, 1037 N. Old World Third St. (☎271-3377), downtown. In a town known for its German cuisine, Mader's is a local favorite; the *schnitzels* and *schaumtorte* are worth the steep prices. The stern decor of suits of armor along the halls conjure images of old Bavaria. Entrees from $12. Open M 11:30am-9pm, Tu-Th 11:30am-10pm, F-Sa 11:30am-11pm, Su 10:30am-9pm. Reservations recommended.

King and I, 823 N. 2nd St. (☎276-4181). The lunch buffet ($6.50) is a favorite at this elegant Thai place. Entrees $9. Open M-F 11:30am-10pm, Sa 5-11pm, Su 4-9pm.

SIGHTS

BREWERIES. Although many of Milwaukee's breweries have left, the city's name still evokes images of a cold one. No visit to the city would be complete without a look at the yeast in action. The **Miller Brewery,** a corporate giant that produces 43 million barrels of beer annually, leads a free 1hr. tour followed by a trip to the biergarten for three generous samples. (*4251 W. State St. ☎931-2337. 2 tours per hr. M-Sa 11am-3:30pm; 3 per hr. during busy days; call for winter schedule. Under 18 must be accompanied by adult. ID required.*) The **Lakefront Brewery,** off Pleasant St., produces five popular year-round beers and several seasonal specials, including pumpkin beer and cherry lager. (*1872 N. Commerce St. ☎372-8800. Tours F 3:30pm; Sa 1:30, 2:30, and 3:30pm, Su 12:30pm. $3 for plastic cup, $5 for tour with souvenir mug.*) One of the state's most renowned microbreweries, **Sprecher Brewing,** 5 mi. north of the city on I-43 then east on Port Washington St., doles out four beer samples following a one-hour tour. (*701 W. Glendale. ☎964-2739. Tours M-F 1-4pm every hr., Sa every 30min. 1-3pm. $2, under 21 free. Reservations required.*) Most breweries offer discounts for non-drinkers.

MUSEUMS. Several excellent museums dot the shores of Milwaukee. The newly expanded, spectacular **Milwaukee Art Museum,** on the lakefront downtown, is worth a visit just for its innovative architecture: moveable, sail-like wings jut out from the building and control its light and temperature, sheltering Haitian folk art,

19th-century German art, and American works from folk to Warhol. *(700 N. Art Museum Dr. ☎224-3200. Open Tu, W, Sa 10am-5pm; Th noon-9pm; F 10am-9pm. $6, seniors and students $4, under 12 free.)* One of the nation's first and finest natural history spots, the **Milwaukee Public Museum,** at N. 8th St., attracts visitors with dinosaur bones, a replicated Costa Rican rainforest, and a re-created European village. *(800 W. Wells St. ☎278-2700 or 278-2702 for recorded info. Open daily 9am-5pm. $6.50, seniors $5, ages 4-17 $4. IMAX Theater $4. Parking available.)* The **Charles Allis Art Museum** houses a fine collection of East Asian and Classical artifacts in a surprisingly intimate mansion. *(1801 N. Prospect Ave. at E. Royal Pl., 1 block north of Brady. ☎278-8295. Take bus #30 or 31. Open W-Su 1-5pm. $3, students and seniors $2, children free.)*

PARKS. Better known as "The Domes," the **Mitchell Park Horticultural Conservatory,** at 27th St., recreates a desert and a rainforest and mounts seasonal floral displays in a series of seven-story conical glass domes. *(524 S. Layton Ave. Take bus #10 west to 27th St., then #27 south to Layton. ☎649-9830. Open daily 9am-5pm. $4, seniors and students 6-17 $2.50, under 6 free.)* The **Boerner Botanical Gardens,** in Whitnall Park between Grange and Rawsen St. in suburban Hales Corners, cultivate billions of beautiful blossoms as well as host open-air concerts on Thursday nights. *(5879 S. 92nd St. ☎425-1130. Open mid-Apr. to Oct. daily 8am-7pm. Parking $3.50.)* County parks line much of Milwaukee's waterfront, providing free recreational areas and trails.

OTHER SIGHTS. A road warrior's nirvana, locally headquartered **Harley-Davidson** gives 1hr. tours of its engine plant that will enthrall the aficionado. *(11700 W. Capitol Dr. ☎342-4680. Tours Apr.-Aug. M-F 9:30, 11am, and 1pm; Dec.-May M, W, and F 9:30, 11am, and 1pm. Call ahead; the plant sometimes shuts down in summer. Reservations required for groups larger than 6. Closed shoes must be worn.)* For a brush with Olympic glory, amateur ice skaters should head to daily open skates at the **Pettit National Ice Center,** next to the state fairgrounds. Home to the US Speed-skating team, the Pettit encloses several hockey and figure-skating rinks. *(500 S. 84th St. at I-94. ☎266-0100. Call for open skating schedules. $5, seniors and children $4. Skate rental $2.50.)*

♫ ENTERTAINMENT

The modern **Marcus Center for the Performing Arts,** 929 N. Water St., across the river from Père Marquette Park, is the area's major arts venue and plays host to the **Milwaukee Symphony Orchestra,** the **Milwaukee Ballet,** and the **Florentine Opera Company.** *(☎273-7121. Symphony tickets $17-52, ballet $13-62, opera $15-80. Ballet and symphony offer half-price senior and student rush tickets.)* During the summer months, the center's Peck Pavilion hosts **Rainbow Summer,** a series of free lunchtime concerts—jazz, bluegrass, you name it. *(☎273-7121. Concerts M-F noon-1:15pm.)* **The Milwaukee Repertory Theater,** 108 East Wells St., stages innovative shows alongside the classics from September through May. *(☎224-1761. Tickets $8-30; half-price student and senior rush tickets available 30min. before shows.)*

The **Milwaukee Brewers** baseball team steps up to bat at the brand new, convertible **Miller Park,** at the interchange of I-94 and Rte. 41 *(☎902-4000 or 800-933-7890; tours available, call for schedule)*, while the **Milwaukee Bucks** hoop it up at the **Bradley Center,** 1001 N. 4th St., downtown *(☎227-0500)*.

Summertime livens up Milwaukee's cultural scene with countless free festivals and live music events. On any given night, a free concert is happening somewhere; call the **Visitors Bureau** *(☎273-7222)* to find out where. On Thursdays in summer, **Cathedral Park Jazz** *(☎272-0993)* jams for free in **Cathedral Square Park,** at N. Jackson St. between Wells and Kilbourn St. In Père Marquette Park, between State and Kilbourn St., **River Flicks** *(☎270-3560)* screens free movies at dusk Thursdays in August.

Locals line the streets far in advance for ■**The Great Circus Parade** *(☎356-8341)*, held in mid-July, a re-creation of turn-of-the-century processions with trained animals, daredevils, costumed performers, and 65 original wagons. **Summerfest,** the largest and most lavish of Milwaukee's festivals, spans 11 days in late June and early July. Daily life halts as a potpourri of big-name musical acts, culinary specialties, and an arts and crafts bazaar take over. *(☎273-3378 or 800-273-3378.)*

Tickets M-Th $9, F-Su $10.) In early August, the **Wisconsin State Fair** rolls into the fairgrounds toting 12 stages, exhibits, contests, rides, fireworks, and a pie-baking contest. (☎266-7000 or 800-884-3247. $7, seniors $5, ages 7-11 $3.) Ethnic festivals also abound during festival season. The most popular are: **Polish Fest** (☎529-2140) and **Asian Moon** (☎481-9829), both in mid-June; **Festa Italiana** (☎223-2193), in mid-July; **Bastille Days** (☎271-7400), around Bastille Day (July 14); **German Fest** (☎464-9444), in late July; **Irish Fest** (☎476-3378), in mid-August; **Mexican Fiesta** (☎383-7066), in late August; **Indian Summer Fest** (☎774-7119), in early September; and **Arabian Fest** (☎342-1120), in mid-September. (Most festivals $7, under 12 free; some free plus price of food.) Pick up a copy of the free weekly *Downtown Edition* for more info.

NIGHTLIFE

Milwaukee never lacks something to do after sundown. The downtown business district gets a bit seedy at night, but the area along **Water St.** between Juneau and Highland Ave. offers hip, lively bars and clubs. Nightspots that draw a college crowd cluster around the intersection of **North Ave.** and **North Farwell St.**, near the UW Campus. One of the hottest places to be in Milwaukee after hours is bar- and coffeehouse-lined **Brady St.**, which runs east-west between Farwell and the river. **South 2nd St.** is a hothouse for eclectic, ultra-trendy nightclubs, including dance clubs, sports bars, lounges, and the town's best gay bars.

■ **Safehouse,** 779 N. Front St. (☎271-2007), across from the Pabst Theater downtown. A brass plate labeled "International Exports, Ltd." welcomes guests to this bizarre world of spy hideouts, James Bond music, and drinks with names like Rahab the Harlot. A briefing with "Moneypenny" in the foyer is just the beginning of the intrigue. Draft beer $2.75; 24 oz. specialty drinks from $5. Cover $1-3. Open M-Th 11:30am-1:30am, F-Sa 11:30am-2am, Su 4pm-midnight.

Hi-Hat, 1701 Brady St. (☎225-9330), 3 blocks west of Farwell Ave. Assorted live acts play in this trendy jazz joint, while Milwaukee's hep night-hawks roost in the cavernous depths below. The Su brunch is a local favorite. Beer $2-6. M-W swing and jazz. No attitude, no dress code, no cover. Open daily 4pm-2am, Su 10am-3pm for brunch.

Nomad World Pub, 1401 E. Brady St. (☎224-811), down the street from Hi-Hat. The TV here plays two shows: Packers games and cricket. State law in Wisconsin requires the football, but the crowd of foreign expats demands the cricket. Like the barflies, all the beer is imported. Open Su-Th 4pm-2am, F-Sa 4pm-2:30am.

Von Trier, 2235 N. Farwell Ave. (☎272-1775), near Brady St. *Deutsch* down to the last detail, Von Trier is a packed biergarten with fantastic outdoor seating. The intricate wood carvings, big oak bar, and walls lined with steins create a laid-back atmosphere for enjoying some serious beer. A house special is German beer topped with German gin ($5). Beer from $2. Open Su-Th 4pm-2am, F-Sa 4pm-2:30am.

Lacage, 801 S. 2nd Ave. (☎383-8330). The largest pub in town attracts a mostly twenty- and thirty-something gay clientele, but they consider themselves "straight-friendly" and crowds are often mixed due to the welcoming atmosphere. DJs spin to keep 2 large floors grooving. F and Sa the bar splits: dancing on one side and drag shows on the other. Cover W $2, Th $3, F-Sa $5. Open Su-Th 9pm-2am, F-Sa until 2:30am.

MADISON   ☎608

Locals in Madison refer to their city as "The Isthmus." For those who have forgotten their seventh-grade geography, that's a narrow strip of land that connects two larger landmasses. In other words, it's a rather awkward place to build a city. Madison's development owes much to Judge James Doty, who in 1836 cajoled lawmakers into moving the capital to the thin sliver of land sandwiched between lakes Menona and Mendota. The resulting proximity of the Capitol to the University now gives Madison its peculiar flavor, blending the youth culture of activity and activism with the solemn, austere atmosphere of Midwestern government.

ORIENTATION

Madison's main attractions are centered around the Capitol and the University of Wisconsin-Madison. Pedestrian-only **State St.**, which connects the two, is the city's hub for eclectic food, shops, and nightlife. The northeast and southwest ends of the isthmus house malls, chain restaurants, and chain motels and are joined by **Washington Ave./US 151**, the city's main thoroughfare. **I-90** and **I-94** are joined through the city, but separate on either side of it. I-94 E goes to Milwaukee, then Chicago; I-94 W goes to Minneapolis/St. Paul; I-90 E goes directly to Chicago through Rockford, IL; I-90 W goes to Albert Lea, MN.

PRACTICAL INFORMATION

Greyhound, 2 S. Bedford St. (☎257-3050), has buses to Chicago (3-5hr., 8 per day, $21-33) and Minneapolis (6hr., 3 per day, $39-41). **Badger Bus** (☎255-6771) departs from the same address at 10pm. **Madison Metro Transit System,** 1101 E. Washington Ave. (☎266-4466), serves downtown, campus, and environs ($1.50). **Greater Madison Convention and Visitors Bureau:** 615 E. Washington Ave. (☎255-2537 or 800-373-6376; open M-F 8am-5pm). **Internet access: Madison Public Library,** 201 W. Mifflin St. (☎266-6300; open M-W 8:30am-9pm, Th-F 8:30am-6pm, Sa 9am-5pm). **Taxi: Union Cab,** ☎242-2000. **Post Office:** 3902 Milwaukee St., at Rte. 51 (☎246-1249; open M 7:30am-7pm, Tu-F 7:30am-6pm, Sa 8:30am-2pm). **ZIP code:** 53714. **Area code:** 608.

ACCOMMODATIONS

Among the motels stretching along Washington Ave. (U.S. 151), near the intersection with I-90, rates start at $40 per weeknight and rise dramatically on weekends. From the Capitol, Bus A shuttles the 5 mi. between the Washington Ave. motels and downtown. Prices steepen downtown, starting around $60.

Hostelling International—Madison (HI-AYH), 141 S. Butler St.(☎441-0144), near State St. This brand new, ideally located hostel is a good bet for social, nightlife-loving travelers. Cheerful, homey setting and spotless rooms. Open year-round. Office hours 8-11am and 5-9pm. 24 beds; 34 beds June-Aug. Kitchen, laundry, Internet access. Dorms $16, nonmembers $19; private rooms $35/$38; discounts for bikers, families, and groups of 5 or more.

Memorial Union, 800 Langdon St. (☎265-3000), on the UW campus. Large, elegant rooms with excellent lake and city views, cable TV, A/C, and free parking. The 8 rooms fill up to a year in advance, so call ahead. Rooms from $60. The no-frills **college cafeterias** here dole out the quickest, cheapest food in town. Meals from $5-8.

Select Inn, 4845 Hayes Rd. (☎249-1815), near the junction of I-94 and U.S. 151. Large rooms with cable TV, A/C, and whirlpool. Continental breakfast included. Singles from $42; doubles from $47; Sa-Su $52/$57.

Motel 6, 1754 Thierer Rd. (☎241-8101), behind Denny's. A solid choice with A/C and cable TV. Singles from $42; doubles from $48.

Lake Kegonsa State Park, 2405 Door Creek Rd. (☎873-9695), 20min. south on I-90 in Stoughton. Pleasant sites in a wooded area near the beach. Showers, flush toilets. Sites $9, WI residents $7; more on weekends. Parking permits $7/$5 per day.

FOOD

Good, unique restaurants pepper Madison; clusters of them spice up the university and Capitol areas. **State St.** hosts a variety of cheap restaurants, including chains and Madison originals.

Himal Chuli, 318 State St. (☎251-9225). This State St. storefront stirs up excellent Nepalese favorites, such as *tarkari, dal,* and *bhat*. In English, that's great veggie meals and lentil soup ($3). Meat entrees $8-10. Open daily 11am-8pm.

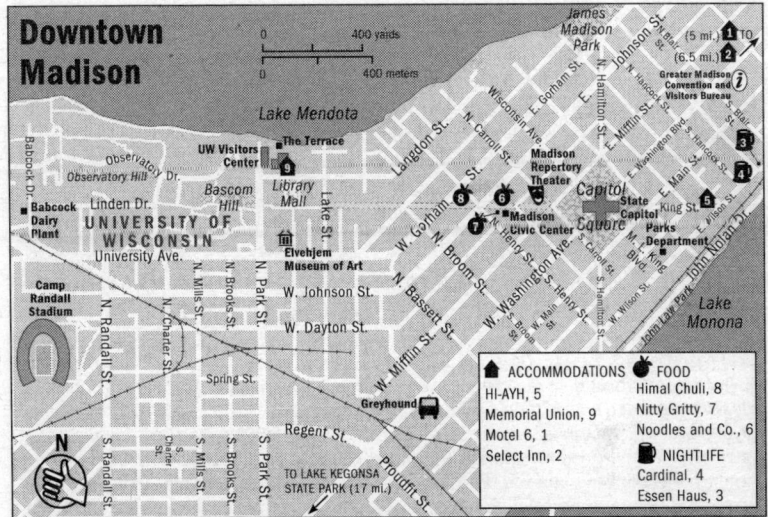

Downtown Madison

Lake Mendota

James Madison Park

(5 mi.) **1** TO
(6.5 mi.) **2**

Greater Madison Convention and Visitors Bureau **i**

3

4

The Terrace

UW Visitors Center

Observatory Dr.
Observatory Hill

Bascom Hill

Library Mall

Madison Repertory Theater

Capitol

State Capitol

King St.

State Parks Department

5

Babcock Dr.

Linden Dr.

Babcock Dairy Plant

UNIVERSITY OF WISCONSIN

University Ave.

Elvehjem Museum of Art

8 **6**

7 Madison Civic Center

Capitol Square

Camp Randall Stadium

W. Johnson St.

W. Dayton St.

Lake Monona

Spring St.

Greyhound

Regent St.

TO LAKE KEGONSA STATE PARK (17 mi.)

N

▲ ACCOMMODATIONS	🍎 FOOD
HI-AYH, 5	Himal Chuli, 8
Memorial Union, 9	Nitty Gritty, 7
Motel 6, 1	Noodles and Co., 6
Select Inn, 2	♪ NIGHTLIFE
	Cardinal, 4
	Essen Haus, 3

Nitty Gritty, 223 N. Frances St. (☎ 251-2521), near State St. A popular college hangout, this laid-back grill celebrates a gazillion birthdays each day with balloons and free beer (for the birthday person only). Just don't wear your birthday suit. Entrees $3-7. Open M-Th 11am-2am, F-Sa 11am-2:30am, Su 5pm-midnight.

Noodles and Co., 232 State St. (☎ 257-6393), at Johnson St. A global array of tasty noodle dishes is just about all there is in this corner shop, where pan-fried noodles and *pad thai* share counter space with Stroganoff and Wisconsin-style macaroni and cheese. Entrees $3-6. Open M-Th 11am-9pm, F-Sa 11am-10pm, Su noon-8pm.

👁 ♪ SIGHTS AND ENTERTAINMENT

DOWNTOWN. With its double nature as a seat of government and home to a thriving college scene, there's lots to see on the isthmus. The imposing, Roman Renaissance-style **State Capitol,** in Capitol Sq. at the center of downtown, boasts beautiful ceiling frescoes. (☎ 266-0382. Open daily 6am-8pm. Free tours from the ground fl. info desk M-Sa on the hr. 9-11am and 1-3pm, Su 1-3pm.) Every Saturday morning from late April to early November, visitors swarm the Capitol grounds for the Farmers Market, an attraction full of farmers selling their crops and Madison radicals advocating animal rights. Leading out from the Capitol, Madison's pedestrian-only **State St.** exudes a lively college atmosphere, sporting many offbeat clothing stores and record shops. The **Madison Civic Center** frequently stages arts and entertainment performances in the Oscar Mayer Theatre, and hosts the **Madison Symphony Orchestra.** *(211 State St. ☎257-3734. Office open M-F 11am-5:30pm, Sa 11am-2pm. Season runs late Aug. to May. Tickets from $20.)* The building is also home to the rotating contemporary exhibits of the **Madison Art Center.** *(☎257-0158. Open Tu-Th 11am-5pm, F 11am-9pm, Sa 10am-9pm, Su 1-5pm. Free.)* The **Madison Repertory Theatre,** also located in the Civic Center, performs classic and contemporary works. *(☎ 266-9055. Showtimes vary; tickets $6.50-22.)* At the southwest end of State St. is the **University of Wisconsin–Madison (UW),** where students and locals pass their days and nights hanging out at Memorial Union's gorgeous, lakeside **Union Terrace.** In summer, the terrace is home to free weekend concerts on the lakeshore. The concerts move indoors in winter.

UNIVERSITY OF WISCONSIN. UW itself has a few noteworthy museums. One of the state's most acclaimed art museums, the **Elvehjem Museum of Art** *(EL-vee-hem)* boasts an astounding collection of Ancient Greek coins and vases, several galleries of American and European painting, and decorative arts dating from 2300 BC. *(800*

GREAT LAKES

BARABOO'S BIZARRE The Greatest Show on Earth is in Baraboo, Wisconsin—permanently. Twenty miles northwest of Madison along the Baraboo River, a swath of bank has been set aside by the State Historical Society to honor the one-time winter home of the world-famous **Ringling Brothers** circus. The **Circus World Museum,** in Baraboo, packs a full line-up of events from big-top performances to street parades. *(426 Water St.* ☎ *356-8341. Open in summer daily from 9am-6pm, mid-July through mid-Aug 9am-9pm. Big top shows at 11am, 3:30, and 7:30pm. $15, seniors $13, ages 5-11 $8.)* Baraboo, however, has more to offer than plumed horse parades. The **fantastical sculpture garden of Dr. Evermore** lies just south of Baraboo on Rte. 12. Here iron relics from an industrial age are given new life by the good doctor's welding torch. The centerpiece is a massive palace/rocketship structure which has been recognized by *Guinness* as the largest junk sculpture in the world.

University Ave. ☎ *263-2246. Open Tu-F 9am-5pm, Sa-Su 11am-5pm. Free.)* UW produces its own Babcock brand of ice cream at the **Babcock Dairy Plant.** An observation deck allows visitors to watch their favorite flavor being made. *(1605 Linden Dr., near Charter St. and Observatory Dr.* ☎ *262-3045. Store open M-F 9:30am-5:30pm, Sa 10am-1:30pm.)* Also part of UW, the outdoor **Olbrich Botanical Gardens** and indoor **Bolz Conservatory** house a plethora of plant life. The Gardens showcase floral settings, from butterfly-attracting plants to an English herb garden; free-flying birds, waterfalls, and tropical plants grace the inside of the conservatory dome. *(3330 Atwood Ave.* ☎ *246-4550. Gardens open daily 8am-8pm; Sept.-May M-Sa 10am-4pm, Su 1am-5pm. Free. Conservatory open M-Sa 10am-4pm, Su 10am-5pm. $1, under 5 free; free W and Sa 10am-noon.)* Aspiring botanists can trek along the 6 mi. walking loop which encircles the 1200 acres of trees at the **University Arboretum** off I-94. *(1207 Seminole Hwy.* ☎ *263-7888. Open M-Sa 7am-10pm, Su 10am-10pm.)* For more info visit the **UW Visitors Center,** at the corner of Observatory Dr. and N. Park St., on the west side of the Memorial Union.

OUTSIDE MADISON. Some of Madison's most unique sights are far from the isthmus. Forty-five minutes west of Madison off U.S. 14, **House on the Rock** is an unparalleled multilevel house built into a chimney of rock. The 40-acre complex of gardens and fantastic architecture features wall-to-wall-to-ceiling shag carpeting and the world's largest carousel—of its 269 animals, not one is a horse. *(5754 Rte. 23, in Spring Green.* ☎ *935-3639. Open daily 9am-7pm. $19.50, ages 7-12 $11.50, ages 4-6 $5.50.)* Nine miles north of the House on the Rock, Frank Lloyd Wright's famed **Taliesin** home and school, on Rte. 23 in Spring Green, sprawls across acres of prairie. ASk at **Visitors Center** about tours of the area. *(Rte. 23 at Rte. C.* ☎ *588-7900. Open May-Oct. daily 8:30am-5:30pm. Prices vary; call for rates and schedules.)*

🏞 OUTDOOR ACTIVITIES

For more personal contact with nature, Madison's many parks and lakeshores offer endless recreational activities. There are 13 gorgeous public **beaches** for swimming or strolling along the two lakes (call 266-4711 for info). Back on dry land, **bicycling** is possibly the best way to explore the isthmus and surrounding park lands. **Budget Bicycle Center,** 1230 Regent St. (☎ 251-8413), loans out all types of two-wheel transportation ($7-15 per day). Hikers and picnickers should head to **Picnic Point.** A bit of a hike off University Bay Dr., this spot provides great views of the college. For other city parks, the **Parks Department,** 215 Martin Luther King Jr. Blvd., in the Madison Municipal Building, can help with specific park info. (☎266-4711. Office open M-F 8am-4:15pm; park open daily 4am-dusk. Admission to Madison parks is free.)

🌙 NIGHTLIFE

Fueled by the 40,000-plus students who pack the reputed party school, Madison's nightlife scene is active and eclectic. Clubs and bars are scattered throughout the isthmus, particularly along **State St.** and **U.S. 151.**

GREAT LAKES

Essen Haus, 514 E. Wilson St. (☎255-4674), off U.S. 151. This lively German bar and grill plays host to live polka bands, semi-rowdy crowds, and ten-gallon hats. Incredible beer selection (from $1.50). Open Tu-Th 3pm-2am, F-Sa 3pm-2:30am, Su 3-11pm.

Cardinal, 418 E. Wilson St. (☎251-0080), near Essen Haus. Salsa Cubana and other themed dance nights bring some spice to the Madison nightlife scene. Renowned for its quirky, mixed crowds, Cardinal is the liveliest dance club in the city. Cover $4-5. Hours. vary; call first. Usually open Su-Th until 2am, F-Sa until 2:30am.

Rainbow Room, 131 W. Main St. (☎251-5838), near the Capitol. The decor feels like the Land of Oz but see the strippers on Th night and you'll know this ain't Kansas. Instead, the Rainbow is the center of Madison's gay nightlife. Live DJ or band weekends. No cover. Open Su-Th 10am-2am, F-Sa 10am-2:30am.

DOOR COUNTY   ☎920

Jutting out like a ▨thumb from the Wisconsin mainland between Green Bay and Lake Michigan, the Door Peninsula exudes a coastal spirit unlike any other in the nation's heartland. With 250 miles of rocky coastline, Lake Michigan's ocean-like tides, miles of bike paths, acres of apple and cherry orchards, and stunning scenery, Door County is the Midwest's vacationland. Despite its undeniable popularity as a tourist destination, the Door has managed to carefully avoid the fast-paced, neon-lit commercialism that plagues so many resort communities. Its 12 villages swing open on a summer-oriented schedule, so visitors are advised to make reservations for just about everything if they plan to be on the peninsula during a weekend in either July or August. Temperatures can dip to 40°F at night, even in July.

■ ✦ 7 ORIENTATION AND PRACTICAL INFORMATION

Door County begins north of **Sturgeon Bay,** where Rte. 42 and Rte. 57 converge and then split again. Rte. 57 runs up the eastern coast of the peninsula; Rte. 42 runs up the western. The peninsula's west coast, which borders the Green Bay, tends to be artsier and more expensive. The colder, calmer, and less expensive east coast, contains most of the peninsula's park area. From south to north along Rte. 42, **Egg Harbor, Fish Creek, Ephraim, Sister Bay,** and **Ellison Bay** are the largest towns. Public transportation comes only as close as **Green Bay,** 50 mi. southwest of Sturgeon Bay, where **Greyhound** has a station at 800 Cedar St. (☎432-4883; open M-F 6:30am-5pm, Sa-Su 6:30am-6:50am, 10am-noon and 3:30-5:10pm). To Milwaukee (3 per day, $20). Reserve tickets at least a day in advance. **Door County Chamber of Commerce:** 6443 Green Bay Rd., on Rte. 42/57 entering Sturgeon Bay (☎743-4456 or 800-527-3529; open Apr.-Oct. M-F 8:30am-5pm, Sa-Su 10am-4; Nov.-Mar. M-F 8:30am-4:30pm). **Post Office:** 359 Louisiana, at 4th St. in Sturgeon Bay (☎743-2681; open M-F 8:30am-5pm, Sa 9:30am-noon). **ZIP code:** 54235. **Area code:** 920.

▌ ACCOMMODATIONS AND CAMPING

Unique, country-style lodgings crowd Rte. 42 and Rte. 57 (from $60 in summer); reservations for July and August should be made far in advance. The **Century Farm Motel,** 10068 Rte. 57, 3 mi. south of Sister Bay on Rte. 57, rents intimate, carefully maintained two-room cottages hand-built by the owner's grandfather in the 20s and still sturdy. (☎854-4069. Open mid-May to mid-Oct. A/C, TV, private bath, fridge. $45-60.) A bevy of gnome statues, 1000 Barbies, 600 animated store-window mannequins, and 35 cars grace the premises of the **Chal-A Motel,** 3910 Rte. 42/57, 3 mi. north of the bridge in Sturgeon Bay, which also houses guests in large, homey rooms. (☎743-6788. July-Aug. singles $49, doubles $59; Nov. to mid-May $29/$34; mid-May to June $34/$39.) Relaxed but convenient, the **Lull-Abi Motel,** 7928 Egg Harbor Rd./Rte. 42 in Egg Harbor, soothes visitors with spacious rooms, a patio, an indoor whirlpool, and free coffee. (☎868-3135. Open May to mid-Oct. Doubles $50-84, depending on season. Suites with wet bar and refrigerator $62-95.)

Four out of the area's five **state parks** (all but **Whitefish Dunes**) offer outstanding camping ($10, WI residents $8; F-Sa $12/$10). All state parks require a motor vehicle permit ($7/$5 per day; $25/$18 per year; $3 per hr.). **Peninsula State Park,** just past Fish Creek village on Rte. 42, contains 20 mi. of shoreline and 17 mi. of trails alongside the largest of the state park campgrounds. (☎868-3258. 469 sites with showers and toilets. Make reservations *well* in advance or come in person to put your name on the waiting list for one of 70 walk-in sites.) The relatively uncrowded **Potawatomi State Park,** 3740 Park Dr., sits just outside Sturgeon Bay off Rte. 42/57, south of the bridge. (☎746-2890. 125 campsites, 19 open to walk-ins.) **Newport State Park** is a shaded wildlife preserve at the tip of the peninsula, 7 mi. from Ellison Bay off Rte. 42. Vehicles are permitted, but sites are accessible by hiking only. (☎854-2500. 16 sites, 3 open to walk-ins.) The untamed **Rock Island State Park** offers 40 remote sites on Washington Island. (☎847-2235. Open mid-Apr. to mid-Nov.)

▐ FOOD AND DRINK

Many people come to Door County just for **fishboils**, a Scandinavian tradition dating back to 19th-century lumberjacks in which cooks toss potatoes, spices, and whitefish into a large kettle over a wood fire. To remove the fish oil from the top of the water, the boilmaster judges the proper time to toss kerosene into the fire, producing a massive fireball; the cauldron boils over, signaling chow time—like other regional dishes, it's much better than it sounds. Most fishboils conclude with a slice of cherry pie, made from famous Door Peninsula cherries. Door County's best-known fishboils bubble up at **The Viking Grill**, in Ellison Bay. (☎854-2998. Mid-May to Oct. every 30min. 4:30-8pm. $13.25, under 12 $9.75; regular dining 6am-10pm.)

Door cooks up much more than just fishboils. **White Gull Inn,** 4225 Main St. in Fish Creek, is the peninsula's breakfast spot of choice, serving delicious cherry-stuffed french toast ($6) in an elegant country inn. (☎868-3517. Open daily 7:30am-9pm. Lunch from $6, dinner from $18. Reservations required for dinner.) **Al Johnson's Swedish Restaurant,** 700-710 Bayshore Dr. in the middle of Sister Bay on Rte. 42, has excellent entrees from $9 and goats on the thick sod roof, just as the Vikings liked it. (☎854-2626. Open daily 6am-9pm; in winter daily 7am-8pm.) At the ▨**Bayside Tavern,** on Rte. 42 in Fish Creek, Bob cooks up his world-famous chili ($4). At night, it's a lively bar with local music on Monday and Saturday (cover $6) and open-mic on Thursday. (☎868-3441. Open Su-Th 11am-2am, F-Sa 11am-2:30am.)

Catch the Packers game with cheeseheads at **Husby's Food & Spirits,** on Rte. 42 entering Sister Bay from the south. The well-chosen beer selection includes $2.50 imports, while the menu ranges from Mexican to fish fry. (☎854-2624. Open M-Th 11am-2am, F-Sa 11am-2:30am, Su 9am-2am.) Just across the street, local favorite **Sister Bay Bowl and Supper Club** rolls out generous portions of chicken, fish, and sandwiches along with a six-lane bowling alley. (☎854-2841. Open daily 11:30am-2pm, 5-10pm; in winter 11:30am-2pm, 5-9pm. Entrees from $5, bowling from $3.)

◉ SIGHTS

Most of Door County's sights are located on the more populated West Side. At the base of the peninsula, Sturgeon Bay houses the intriguing **Door County Maritime Museum,** 120 N. Madison St. downtown. The museum offers the best insight into the area's ship-building, water-charting history with antique boats and interactive, hands-on exhibits. (☎743-5958. Open May-Oct. daily 9am-6pm, Nov.-Apr. 10am-5pm. $3.) The nearby **Door County Historical Museum,** 4th Ave. and Michigan St., explains such important traditions as the fishboil, cherry orchards, and commercial fishing. (☎743-5809. Open May-Oct. daily 10am-4:30pm. Suggested donation $2.)

The award-winning **Door Peninsula Winery,** 5806 Rte. 42 in Sturgeon Bay, invites vine- (or orchard-) lovers to partake of 30 different fruit wines. (☎743-7431 or 800-551-5049. 15-20min. tours and tastings daily in summer 9am-6pm; off-season 9am-5pm.) The park also hosts the musical troupe **American Folklore Theatre,** home to the Door County hit *Lumberjacks in Love.* (☎869-2329. $11, ages 13-19 $6.50, ages 6-

12 $3.50.) Just north of the Peninsula State Park, on Rte. 42 between Fish Creek and Ephraim, is the fabulous ▓**Skyway Drive-In,** showing double features at great prices. (☎854-9938. Current release double-feature $6, ages 6-11 $3. Call for schedules.)

The shipping town of **Green Bay,** 50 mi. south of Sturgeon Bay at the foot of the Door peninsula, is best known as home to the Green Bay Packers. Unless you know a Packer, you won't find a ticket, but the appropriately green and yellow Lambeau Field is worth a look. (☎496-5719. Tickets $32-39.) The unique **Packer Hall of Fame,** 855 Lombardi Ave., across from the stadium, has a cathedral-like feel, for thousands come here to worship their gridiron heroes. (☎499-4281. Open daily 9am-5pm. Tours of Lambeau Field June-Aug. only; 1½hr, $8, under 15 $5.50.)

▓ OUTDOOR ACTIVITIES

EAST SIDE

Biking is the best way to take in the largely untouched lighthouses, rocks, and white-sand beaches of the Door's rugged eastern coastline; village tourist offices have free bike maps. **Whitefish Dunes State Park,** off Rte. 57 on the peninsula's east side, glimmers with Wisconsin's most extensive sand dunes, hiking/biking/skiing trails, and a well-kept wildlife preserve. (Open daily 8am-8pm. $7 vehicle permit required.) Just north of the Dunes on Cave Point Rd. off Rte. 57, **Cave Point County Park** has some of the best views on the peninsula. (Open daily 6am-9pm. Free.)

Five mi. north of Cave Point in the sleepy town of Jacksonport, **Lakeside Town Park** offers a wide, sandy expanse of beach backed by a shady, picnic-perfect park and playground. (Open daily 6am-9pm. Free.) Another natural highlight of the East Side lies 3 mi. to the north in laid-back **Baileys Harbor.** Here, waves and wind have carved miles of sand ridges that swirl along the coastline. Trails at the **Ridges Sanctuary,** north of Baileys Harbor off Rte. Q, enable exploration of over 30 of the ridges, great birdwatching, and a unique boreal forest at **Toft's Point.** (☎839-2802. Nature center open daily 9am-4pm. $2.) Adjoining the sanctuary on Ridges Rd. is **Baileys Harbor Ridges Beach,** a usually uncrowded stretch of sand ideal for secluded swimming. Just past the ridges off Rte. Q, **Cana Island Lighthouse** juts out from the Lake, beckoning visitors to cross the narrow sandpath (at low tide) or wade through the frigid waters (at high tide) to reach its oft-photographed shores. (Reached from Cana Island Rd. off Rte. Q. No phone. No facilities. Open daily 10am-5pm. Free.)

WEST SIDE

The West Side's recreational offerings are fewer, but no less exciting. **Peninsula State Park,** in Fish Creek, visitors rent boats and ride bicycles along 20 mi. of shoreline road. Sunbathing at Nicolet Beach is a more relaxed way to get close to nature. At the top of **Eagle Tower,** 1 mi. and 110 steps up from the beach, a clear day allows a glimpse of Michigan's shores across the waters of Green Bay. (Open daily 6am-11pm. Vehicle permit required. $3 per hr.) Directly across from the Fish Creek entrance, **Nor Door Sport and Cyclery,** 4007 Rte. 42, rents out bikes and winter equipment. (☎868-2275. From $3 per hr., $10 per day. Cross-country skis $9 per day.)

APOSTLE ISLANDS ☎ 715

The National Lakeshore protects 21 of the breathtaking islands off the coast of Wisconsin, as well as a 12 mi. stretch of mainland shore. Glaciers created these land masses that once supported loads of shipping activity during the Voyageur fur trade. Lighthouses still dot six of the islands and recall their industrially prosperous past. Today, summer tourists with all levels of outdoor experience enjoy kayaking, hiking, spelunking, and camping among the unspoiled sandstone bluffs.

▓ **PRACTICAL INFORMATION.** All Apostle Islands excursions begin in the sleepy mainland town of **Bayfield** (pop. 686), in northwest Wisconsin on the Lake Superior coast. The **Bay Area Rural Transit (BART),** 300 Industrial Park Rd., 21 mi. south on Rte. 13 in Ashland, offers a shuttle to Bayfield (☎682-9664; 4 per day, M-F

POWWOW. Throughout the Midwest, and scattered around the rest of the country, are hundreds of small nations, commonly known as Indian Reservations. Countless stereotypes exist regarding reservation conditions—many Americans think of them now as hotbeds for casinos and gambling. But instead of pouring money into a tribal casino, tourists can go to a party, Native American-style. Most reservations have two powwows annually, making for a wonderful mix of celebration and reverence. In the words of one young dancer, "A powwow is a family." The festival, often a 4-day weekend affair for $5-10, normally comes with free camping. Food from vendors' trucks is ridiculously cheap and satisfying, and crafts are also sold for fair prices. To learn more on the **Menominee** reservation, in Keshena, call 715-799-3341. For info on other locations, stop by the tribal offices, call the above number, or pick up a local reservation newspaper or the international publication, *Indian Country Today*.

7am-5pm; $1.80, students $1.50, seniors $1.10). **Bayfield Chamber of Commerce,** 42 S. Broad St. (☎779-3335 or 800-447-4094; open M-Sa 8am-5pm, Su 10am-2pm). **National Lakeshore Headquarters Visitors Center,** 410 Washington Ave., distributes hiking info and **camping permits** (☎779-3398; open daily 8am-6pm, mid-Sept. to mid-May W-Su 8am-4:30pm; $15 permit for 2 weeks, must be 14 consecutive days). **Weather:** ☎682-8822. Bayfield's **Post Office:** 22 S. Broad St. (☎779-5636; open M-F 9am-4:30pm, Sa 9am-11am). **ZIP code:** 54814. **Area code:** 715.

✦ ACCOMMODATIONS. In summer months, the budget pickings are slim in Bayfield. Would-be lodgers without reservations may be out of luck on July and August weekends; it's wise to call far in advance to reserve a room. The best deal in town is **The Seagull Bay Motel,** off Rte. 13 at S. 7th St., offering spacious, smoke-free rooms with cable TV and a lake view. (☎779-5558. From $65; mid-Oct. to mid-May $35.) Just south on Rte. 13, **Lakeside Lodging** has rooms with a private entrance and bath, patio, and continental breakfast. (☎779-5545. Open mid-May to mid-Oct. In summer, reservations recommended 1 month in advance. Rooms $65.) **Dalrymple Park,** ¼ mi. north of town on Rte. 13, has 30 campsites in a grand setting under tall pines on the lake. (No showers; self-regulated; no reservations. Sites $12.) **Apostle Islands Area Campground,** ½ mi. south of Bayfield on County Rd. J off Rte. 13, has a few sites overlooking the islands. (☎779-5524. Sites $13, with hookup $17, with full sewer and cable $22, with view $24; Reservations recommended 1 month in advance in July-Aug.) The Chamber of Commerce has info on **guest houses** (from $35).

◖ FOOD. With a look that is more Key West than Midwest, **Maggie's,** 257 Manypenny Ave., serves satisfying burgers ($6) in a flamingo-filled decor. (☎779-5641. Open Su-Th 11am-10pm, F-Sa 11am-11pm.) The **Gourmet Garage,** just south of Bayfield on Rte. 13, has lots of pies. (☎779-5365. Open daily 9am-6pm.) **Greunke's Restaurant,** 17 Rittenhouse Ave. at 1st St., specializes in huge breakfasts by day ($4-6) and famous fishboils by night. (☎779-5480. Open M-Sa 6am-10pm, F-Su 7am-9:30pm. Fishboils W-Su 6:30-8pm; $11, children $6.) **Egg Toss Cafe,** 41 Manypenny Ave., serves a variety of breakfasts and sandwiches in a patio setting. (☎779-5181. Open daily 6am-2pm.) Outfit your stomach at the **Wild By Nature Market,** 100 Rittenhouse Ave., with bulk trail food or $4-5 wraps. (☎779-5075. Open daily 9am-6pm.)

◷▲ SIGHTS AND OUTDOORS. Though often overshadowed by Bayfield and Madeline Island (see below), the other 21 islands have their own subtle charms. The sandstone quarries of Basswood and Hermit Islands and the abandoned logging and fishing camps on some of the other islands serve as silent reminders of a more vigorous era. The restored **lighthouses** on Sand, Raspberry, Long, Michigan, Outer, and Devil's Islands offer spectacular views of the surrounding country. **Sea caves,** carved out by thousands of years of winds and water, pocket the shores of several islands. The **Apostle Islands Cruise Service** runs narrated three-hour tours for a less exorbitant fee than most companies. From late June to early September, the cruise service runs an inter-island shuttle that delivers campers and lighthouse lovers to their destinations. (☎779-3925 or 800-323-7619. Tours of the entire archipelago depart the Bayfield City Dock mid-May to mid-Oct. daily 10am. $25, children $14. Call for additional tours and departure times.) The best beach on the mainland is **Bay View Beach,** just south of Bayfield along Rte. 13, near Sioux Flats, reached by a poorly marked path to the left about 8 mi. out of town. **Swimming** in chilly Lake Superior can be quite uncomfortable. **Trek and Trail,** at Rittenhouse and Broad St., rents bikes and kayaks. (☎800-354-8735. Bikes $5 per hr., $20 per day; 4hr. kayak rental $20, all equipment included. Renters must complete $50 safety course.)

Bayfield is the proud home of some awfully good apples. The first full weekend of October, up to 40,000 gather for the street fairs at the **Apple Festival.** The **Bayfield Apple Company,** on County J near the intersection of Betzold Rd., has fresh-picked fruit and tasty jam. (☎779-5700 or 800-363-4526. Open May-Jan. daily 9am-6pm.)

MADELINE ISLAND   ☎715

Several hundred years ago, the Ojibwe tribe came to Madeline Island from the Atlantic in search of the megis shell, a light in the sky purported to bring prosperity and health. The island maintains its allure, as thousands of summer visitors seek the clean, sandy beaches of this relaxing retreat.

The **Madeline Island Motel,** on Col. Woods Ave. across from the ferry landing, has private patios, as well as clean rooms named for local personalities. (☎747-3000. Mid-June through Sept. doubles $95; Oct.-May $60.) Rooms in the area fill during the summer; call ahead for reservations. Madeline Island has two campgrounds. **Big Bay Town Park,** 6½ mi. from La Pointe off Big Bay Rd., sits next to tranquil Big Bay Lagoon. (☎747-6913. Sites $10, with electricity $13. No reservations accepted.) Across the lagoon, **Big Bay State Park** rents 55 primitive sites. (☎747-6425; Bayfield office 779-4020; for reservations 888-475-3386. Reservations $4. Sites $10-12. Daily vehicle permit $7, WI residents $5.) **Tom's Burned Down Cafe,** 1 Middle Rd., fills your belly with good, healthy food despite being little more than an outdoor bar with an awning. The obvious questions are answered by the numbered responses on the wall: "1. Yes there was a fire—10 years ago" and "2. The tent goes up in spring and comes down in fall." (☎747-6100. Open daily 10-2am. Sandwiches $7, pizzas $9.)

With roughly five streets, Madeline Island is easy to navigate. **Visitor Info: Madeline Island Chamber of Commerce,** on Middle Rd. (☎747-2801 or 888-475-3386; open M-Sa 8am-4pm). **Madeline Island Ferry Line** shuttles between Bayfield and La Pointe on Madeline Island. (☎747-2051 or 747-6801. 20min. ride; in summer daily every 30min. 9:30am-6pm, every hr. 6:30-9:30am and 6-11pm. $4, ages 6-11 $2; bikes $1.75; cars $9.25—driver not included. Mar.-June and Sept.-Dec. ferries run less frequently and prices drop.) In winter, the state highway department builds a road across the ice. During transition periods, the ferry service runs **windsleds** between the island and the mainland. "Moped Dave" rents scooters at **Motion to Go,** 102 Lake View Pl., about one block from the ferry. (☎747-6585. $7.50 per hr., $65 per day. Mountain bikes $7/$26. Open July-Aug. daily 8am-8pm, May-June 8:30am-7pm, Sept. to mid-Oct. 9am-7pm.) La Pointe's **Post Office** is just off the dock on Madeline Island. (☎747-3712. Open M-F 9am-4:20pm, Sa 9:30am-12:50pm.) **ZIP code:** 54850.

MINNESOTA

In the 19th century, floods of German and Scandinavian settlers forced the native tribes from the rich lands now known as Minnesota. Minnesota's white pioneers transformed the southern half of the state into a stronghold of commercial activity; however, the north remains largely untouched, an expanse of wilderness quilted with over 14,000 lakes. Attempts at preserving this rugged wilderness have helped raise awareness about Minnesota's natural resources and the culture of the Ojibwe, the state's Native American antecedents.

GREAT LAKES

🛈 PRACTICAL INFORMATION

Capital: St. Paul.
Visitor Info: Minnesota Office of Tourism, 100 Metro Sq., 121 7th Pl. E., St. Paul 55101
(☎800-657-3700; www.exploreminnesota.com). Open M-F 8am-5pm.
Postal Abbreviation: MN. **Sales Tax:** 6.5%.

MINNEAPOLIS AND ST. PAUL ☎612

Native son Garrison Keillor wrote that the "difference between St. Paul and Minne-apolis is the difference between pumpernickel and Wonder bread." Keillor's quote plays on St. Paul's characterization as an old Irish Catholic, conservative town and Minneapolis's reputation as a young, fast-paced metropolis of the future. Minneap-olis's theaters and clubs rival those of New York, while both the traditional capitol and the cathedral rest atop St. Paul. In both cities, consumer culture, the bohemian youth world, corporate America, and an international community thrive together.

▐ TRANSPORTATION

Downtown Minneapolis lies about 10 mi. west of downtown St. Paul via **I-94. I-35** splits in the Twin Cities, with **I-35 W** serving Minneapolis and **I-35 E** serving St. Paul. **I-494** runs to the airport and the Mall of America, while **I-394** heads to downtown Minneapolis from the western suburbs.

Airport: Twin Cities International, 15min. south of the cities on Rte. 5 (☎726-5555), off I-494 in Bloomington. Take bus #7 to Washington Ave. in Minneapolis or bus #54 to St. Paul. **Airport Express** (☎827-7777) shuttles to either downtown and to some hotels roughly every 30min. 6am-midnight. To: Minneapolis ($13) and St. Paul ($10).

Trains: Amtrak, 730 Transfer Rd. (☎651-644-1127 or 800-872-7245), on the east bank off University Ave. SE, between the Twin Cities. City bus #7 runs from the station to St. Paul, and #16 connects to both downtowns. To: Chicago (8hr., 1 per day, $58-101) and Milwaukee (6hr., 1 per day, $51-93). Open daily 6:30am-11:30pm.

Buses: Greyhound, in Minneapolis, 590 Hawthorne Ave. (☎371-3325), at 9th St. N. downtown. In St. Paul, 166 W. University Ave. (☎651-222-0507), 2 blocks west of the capitol. To: Chicago (9-12hr., 11 per day, $49-52) and Milwaukee (6-9hr., 8 per day, $44-47); both routes depart from Minneapolis and St. Paul stations. Minneapolis station open daily 5:30am-1am. St. Paul station open daily 6:15am-9pm.

Public Transit: Metropolitan Transit Commission, 560 6th Ave. N. (☎373-3333), serves both cities. Most major lines end service by 12:45am; some buses operate 24hr. $1.25, seniors and ages 6-12 50¢ discount; disabled 75¢. Peak fare (M-F 6-9am and 3:30-6:30pm) $1.75. Express 50¢ more. Bus #16 connects the 2 downtowns 24hr. (50min.); bus #94 (b, c, or d) takes 30min.

Taxis: Yellow Taxi, ☎824-4444 in Minneapolis; ☎651-222-4433 in St. Paul.

✳🛈 ORIENTATION AND PRACTICAL INFORMATION

Curves and one-way streets tangle both of the downtown areas; even the numbered grids in the cities are skewed, making north-south and east-west designations tricky without a map.

Visitor Info: Minneapolis Convention and Visitors Association, 40 S. 7th St. (☎661-4700), near Hennepin Ave. in the City Center skyway. Open M-F 10am-7pm, Sa 10am-6pm, Su noon-6pm. **St. Paul Convention and Visitors Bureau,** 175 W. Kellogg, #502 (☎800-627-6101), in the RiverCentre. Open M-F 8:30am-5pm.

Hotlines: Crisis Line, ☎340-5400. **Rape/Sexual Assault Line,** ☎825-4357. Both 24hr. **Gay-Lesbian Helpline,** ☎822-8661 or 800-800-0907. M-F noon-midnight, Sa 4pm-midnight. **Gay-Lesbian Information Line,** ☎822-0127. M-F 2-10pm, Sa 4-10pm.

Internet access: Minneapolis Public Library, 300 Nicollet Mall, downtown (☎630-6000). Open M-Th 9am-9pm, F 9am-6pm, Sa 10am-6pm.

Downtown St. Paul
FOOD
Mickey's Diner, 1
TO AMTRAK
TO MINNEAPOLIS

Downtown Minneapolis
ACCOMMODATIONS
Evelo's Bed and Breakfast, 7
City of Lakes International House, 9
Hotel Amsterdam, 5
FOOD
Taco Morelos, 8
NIGHTLIFE
Fine Line Music Cafe, 1
First Avenue and 7th St. Entry, 4
Gay 90s, 3
Loring Bar and Cafe, 6
The Quest, 2
TO ST. PAUL
TO AIRPORT

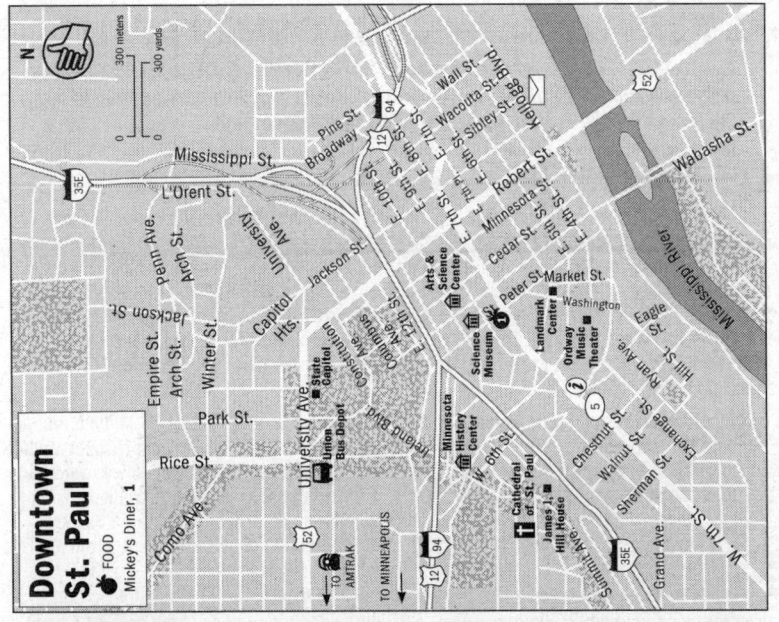

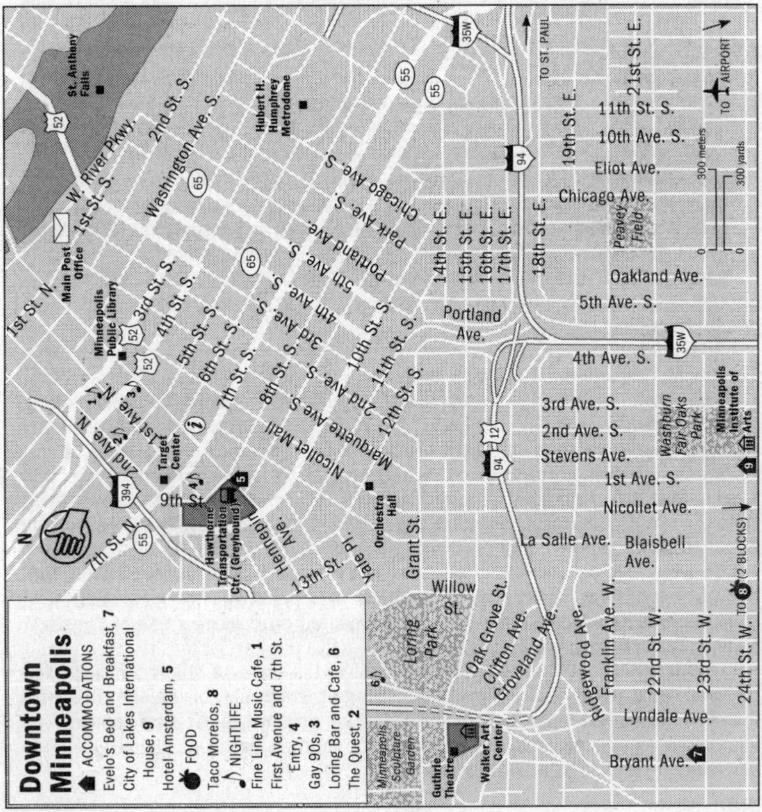

Post Office: In Minneapolis, 100 S. 1st St. (☎349-6388), at Marquette Ave. on the river. Open M-F 7am-11pm, Sa 9am-1pm. **ZIP code:** 55401. In St. Paul, 180 E. Kellogg Blvd. (☎651-293-3268). Open M-F 8am-6pm, Sa 8:30am-1pm. **ZIP code:** 55101. **Area codes:** Minneapolis 612, St. Paul and eastern suburbs 651, southwestern suburbs 952, northwestern suburbs 763. In text, 612 unless otherwise noted.

ACCOMMODATIONS

The Twin Cities are filled with unpretentious, inexpensive accommodations. The Visitors Centers have lists of **B&Bs** (but no price info), while the **University of Minnesota Housing Office** (☎624-2994) keeps a list of local rooms ($15-60) which rent on a daily or weekly basis. The section of I-494 at Rte. 77, near the Mall of America, is lined with budget chain motels from $40. The nearest private campgrounds are about 15 mi. outside the city; the closest state park camping is in the **Hennepin Park** system, 25 mi. out. Call **The Connection** (see **Practical Information,** above) for info.

City of Lakes International House, 2400 Stevens Ave. S. (☎871-3210), Minneapolis, south of downtown by the Institute of Arts. Take bus #10, 17, or 18 from Nicollet Mall to 24th St. and walk 2 blocks east to Stevens. From airport, take bus #7 downtown and then buses above. This clean hostel has a strong community atmosphere. Kitchen, TV, lockers, on-site parking, Internet access. Bike rentals ($4-6 per night). Linen $2, towel $1. Key deposit $20. Check-in daily 9am-noon, 6:30pm-midnight. Checkout 11am. Call for reservation. Beds $18, students and foreigners $16; 2 singles $38.

Evelo's Bed and Breakfast, 2301 Bryant Ave. (☎374-9656), South Minneapolis. Convenient location just off Hennepin Ave., a 15min. walk from uptown; take bus #17 from downtown to Bryant Ave. Kind owners rent out 3 lovingly cared for rooms in a house with fine Victorian artifacts. Reservations and deposit required. Singles $55; doubles $75.

Kaz's Home Hostel (☎822-8286), in South Minneapolis. Bright shag carpet, a ton of family photos, a dog, and friendly hosts make this house better than home. Kitchen, laundry facilities. Towels $1. No children allowed. Call for reservations and directions. Checkout 9am. Lockout 9am-5pm. Curfew 11pm. 2 beds in a large 2nd fl. room $10.

Hotel Amsterdam, 828 Hennepin Ave. (☎288-0459), between 8th and 9th St. in downtown Minneapolis. Quiet considering its location above the wildly popular **Saloon** nightclub, this warm hotel offers visitors comfortable rooms and easy access to downtown action and attractions. "The inn that's out" is geared toward the BGLT community, but all are welcome. Reservations recommended. Singles from $33; doubles from $38.

FOOD

The Twin Cities' cosmopolitan, cultured vibe is reflected in their culinary choices. Posh, big city restaurants share the streets with intimate cafes. **Uptown** Minneapolis, around the intersection of Lake St. and Hennepin Ave., packs plenty of funky restaurants and bars with reasonable prices. In downtown Minneapolis, the **Warehouse District,** on 1st Ave. N between 8th St. and Washington Ave., and **Nicollet Mall,** a pedestrian stretch of Nicollet Ave., attract locals and tourists with trendy shops and cafes. In St. Paul, **Grand Ave.,** between Lexington and Dale, is lined with laid-back restaurants and bars. South of downtown, Nicollet turns into **Eat Street,** a 17-block stretch of international cuisine. In downtown St. Paul, **Lowertown,** along Sibley St. near 6th St., is the newest nighttime hot spot. Near the U of M campus between the downtowns, **Dinkytown,** on the east bank of the river, and the **Seven Corners** area of the **West Bank,** on Cedar Ave. across the river, cater to student appetites. To get to either one, follow the signs off of I-94 for East Bank or West Bank. In the Twin Cities, many forego restaurants for the plentiful **cafes** (see p. 537). For do-it-yourselfers, pick up fresh produce the **St. Paul Farmers Market,** on Wall St., between E. 4th and 5th St. downtown. (☎651-227-6856. Open late Apr. to mid-Nov. Sa 6am-1pm.)

MINNEAPOLIS

■ **Chino Latino,** 2916 Hennepin Ave. at Lake St. (☎824-7878), Uptown. An amazing array of gold sequins dangles above the outside entrance, but beware: "no iron gut, no service" at this Latin-Asian fusion. The trendiest restaurant in town packs in the (young, hipper-than-thou) crowds with its satay bar ($7-9) and pu pu platter ($28; serves an army). Open M-F 4:30pm-1am, Sa-Su 11am-1am. Reservations strongly recommended.

Bryant Lake Bowl, 810 W. Lake St. (☎825-3737), at Bryant St. near Uptown. Built in the 30s, this funky bowling alley-*cum*-bar-*cum*-cabaret is also—surprise—a really good, inexpensive restaurant. The "BLB Scramble" (a breakfast dish of eggs and vegetables), ravioli, soups, and sandwiches ensure that the stylish patrons throw strikes with pleasantly full stomachs. Bowling $3. Entrees from $4. Open daily 8am-1am.

Taco Morelos, 14 26th St. W. at Nicollet Ave. (870-0053). Hispanophiles can practice their Spanish at this authentic Mexican establishment. Try the three amigos enchiladas (one enchilada with each of three sauces, $10) or gorge on their famous tacos ($2 each). Entrees from $6. Open Su-Th 9am-10pm; F-Sa 9am-2am.

Mud Pie, 2549 Lyndale Ave. S. (☎872-9435; www.mudpiefoods.com), at 26th St., Uptown. Try the delicious veggie burger $7. Open M-Th 11am-11pm, F 11am-midnight, Sa 10am-midnight, Su 10am-11pm; brunch weekends 10am-2pm.

ST. PAUL

■ **Cafe Latte,** 850 Grand Ave. (☎651-224-5687), at Victoria St. More gourmet than its prices and cafeteria-style setup would suggest. Meals are consistently wonderful; desserts are to die for. Chicken-salsa chili ($5) and turtle cake ($4) fill the 2 floors with chic, hungry locals. Open M-Th 9am-11pm, F-Sa 9am-midnight, Su 9am-10pm.

Mickey's Diner, 36 W. 7th St. (☎651-698-0259), at St. Peter St. A real 30s diner on the National Register of Historic Places, Mickey's offers food that outshines its bright history and chrome-and-vinyl decor. Steak and eggs from $6; pancakes $2.50. Open 24hr.

◧ CAFES

More so than anywhere else outside of Seattle, cafes are an integral part of the Twin Cities' nightlife. Particularly in Uptown Minneapolis, quirky, one-of-a-kind coffeehouses caffeinate the masses and draw crowds as large as any bar. Come hungry, since most complement their java with some of the cheapest food in town.

■ **Uncommon Grounds,** 2809 Hennepin Ave. S. (☎872-4811), at 28th St., Uptown. The self-described "BMW of coffeeshops" uses only the most secret ingredients to make the tastiest coffees and teas around. With its velour booths and relaxing music in its smoke-free interior, this coffeeship lives up to its name. Espresso $1.30, Iced Chai $4.50, Turtle Mocha $3.20, Zoom $1.65. Open M-F 5pm-1am, Sa-Su 10am-1am.

Pandora's Cup and Gallery, 2516 Hennepin Ave., at 25th St., Uptown. One of the newest coffee spots in town, Pandora's is also the most lively, with hordes of twenty-somethings packing the shop's 2 stories inside and out. The tragically hip sip their espresso ($1.35-2) and munch on PB&J "sammiches" ($2) and free ginger snaps. Coffee drinks $1.35-4.50. Sandwiches $2-5. $1 minimum. Open daily 7am-1am.

Plan B Coffeehouse, 2727 Hennepin Ave. (☎872-1419), between 27th and 28th St. Plan B is first-rate. The desk toward the back may be littered with boring dictionaries, but the animated conversation, artwork, and mismatched furniture tell a different story. Try the "tripper's revenge" ($3.75). Open Su-Th 8am-midnight, F-Sa 8am-1am.

Muddy Waters, 2401 Lyndale Ave. S. (☎872-2232), at 24th St., Uptown. The linoleum tables and vinyl chairs of this self-proclaimed "caffeine canteen" recall a smoky 50s diner, but the music, stylish mosaic, outstanding coffee, and pierced staff keep it on the cutting edge. Mochas, cereal and milk, and spaghetti-o's (with half a bagel $4) are just the beginning of the eclectic menu. Open Su-Th 7am-1am, F-Sa 8am-1am.

GREAT LAKES

 SIGHTS

MINNEAPOLIS

LAKES AND RIVERS. In the land of 10,000 lakes, Minneapolis boasts many of its own. **Lake Calhoun,** on the west end of Lake St. Uptown, is the largest of the bunch and a recreational paradise. Scores of in-line skaters and runners loop the lake on all but the coldest days. Ringed by stately mansions, serene **Lake of the Isles** is an excellent place to commune with Canadian geese. Just southeast of Lake Calhoun on Sheridan St., **Lake Harriet** brings out the locals with tiny paddleboats and a band-shell with nightly free concerts in summer. The city maintains 28 mi. of lakeside trails around the three lakes for strolling and biking. **Calhoun Cycle Center,** three blocks east of Lake Calhoun, rents out bikes for exploring the paths. *(1622 W. Lake St. ☎827-8231. Open M-Th 10am-8pm, F-Sa 9am-9pm, Su 9am-8pm. $15-20 per half day, $24-32 per day. Must have credit card and driver's license.)* At the northeast corner of Lake Cal-houn, the **Minneapolis Park and Recreation Board** handles canoe and rowboat rentals. *(☎370-4964. Open daily 10am-8pm. Canoes $6 per hr., rowboats $11 for 4hr. $10 deposit.)*

You can get a good look at the Mighty Mississippi from several points in town. Off Portland Ave. downtown, **Stone Arch Bridge** offers pedestrians and bikers a scenic view of **St. Anthony Falls.** The **Visitors Center** at the **Upper St. Anthony Lock and Dam,** at Portland Ave. and West River Pkwy., provides a sweeping view of the falls and a helpful explanation of the locks that allow big boats access to the city. *(☎651-332-5336. Observation tower open mid-Mar. to mid-Dec. daily 9am-10pm.)* Several mi. down-stream, **Minnehaha Park** *(near the airport; take bus #7 from Hennepin Ave. downtown)* allows a gander at the much more impressive **Minnehaha Falls,** immortalized in Longfel-low's *Song of Hiawatha.* *(Off Minnehaha Ave., south of Godfrey Pkwy.)*

MUSEUMS. The lakes are only the beginning of Minneapolis's appeal—locals and visitors have plenty to do during the (at least) six months of frigid winter. The **Min-neapolis Institute of Arts,** south of downtown, has an exceptionally varied and well-chosen collection, including Rembrandt's *Lucretia* and the world-famous *Dory-phoros,* Polykleitos's perfectly proportioned man. *(2400 3rd Ave. S. ☎870-3131. Take bus #9. Open Tu-W and Sa 10am-5pm, Th-F 10am-9pm, Su noon-5pm. Free.)* A few blocks southwest of downtown, the world-renowned ▨**Walker Art Center** counts daring exhibits by Lichtenstein, Rothko, and Warhol among its amazing galleries of con-temporary art. *(725 Vineland Pl. at Lyndale Ave. ☎375-7622. Open Tu-W and F-Sa 10am-5pm, Th 10am-9pm, Su 11am-5pm. $6; seniors, students, and ages 12-18 $4; free Th and 1st Sa of the month.)* Next to the Walker lies the **Minneapolis Sculpture Garden,** the largest urban sculpture garden in the US. The tongue-in-cheek, postcard-friendly **Spoon-bridge and Cherry** is the highlight of the worthwhile gardens; the adjacent **Cowles Con-servatory** houses an array of plants and a Gehry fish sculpture. *(Gardens open daily 6am-midnight; conservatory open Tu-Sa 8am-8pm, Su 10am-5pm. Free.)* Frank Gehry also holds the honor of having designed the Cities' most unique and controversial struc-ture: the **Weisman Art Museum,** on the East Bank of the U of M campus. The inde-scribable metallic pseudo-building was the rough draft for his famous Guggenheim Bilbao. Check out the inspired collection of modern art, including works by O'Keeffe and Hartley. *(333 E. River Rd. ☎625-9494. Open Tu, W, F 10am-5pm, Th 10am-8pm, Sa-Su 11am-5pm. Free.)* The **Museum of Questionable Medical Devices,** north of the river near St. Anthony Falls, has a sure cure for everything. The fully operational phrenological device is one of the highlights of the collection. *(201 Main St. SE. ☎379-4046. Open Tu-Th 5-9pm, F-Sa noon-9pm, Su noon-5pm. Donation requested, toenails preferred.)*

ST. PAUL

ARCHITECTURE. St. Paul's history and architecture are among its greatest assets. Nowhere is this more evident than along **Summit Ave.,** the nation's longest continu-ous stretch of Victorian houses. The avenue includes a former home of novelist **F. Scott Fitzgerald** *(599 Summit Ave.; currently a private residence)* and the Minnesota **Gover-nor's Mansion,** now home of the state's most famous ex-wrestler, Governor Jesse

SHOP 'TIL YOU DROP About 10min. south of downtown, the **Mall of America,** Bloomington, corrals an indoor roller coaster, ferris wheel, mini-golf course, and 2 mi. of stores. Welcome to the largest mall in America, the consummation of an American love affair with all that is obscenely gargantuan. With hundreds of specialty stores, a movie megaplex, amusement park, and aquarium, plus all your old favorites and a large and better-than-average food court, the Mall is a good idea for a day of mind-numbing entertainment or a good old-fashioned shopping spree. *(60 E. Broadway. ☎883-8800. From St. Paul, take I-35 E south to I-494 W to the 24th Ave exit. Open M-F 10am-9:30pm, Sa 9:30am-9:30pm, Su 11am-7pm.)*

"The Body" Ventura. *(1006 Summit Ave. ☎651-297-2581. Tours May-Oct. F 1-3pm. Reservations required. Free.)* Also on Summit, the magnificent home of railroad magnate **James J. Hill** offers 1¼hr. tours every 30min. *(240 Summit Ave. ☎651-297-2555. Open W-Sa 10am-3:30pm. $5, seniors $4, ages 6-15 $3. Reservations preferred.)* Golden horses top the ornate **state capitol,** on Aurora Ave. at Cedar St., the world's largest unsupported marble dome. *(☎651-296-3962. Open M-F 9am-5pm, Sa 10am-4pm, Su 1-4pm. Tours on the hr. M-F 9am-4pm, Sa 10am-3pm, Su 1-3pm. Free.)* Overlooking the capitol at the end of Summit Ave. stands the **Cathedral of St. Paul,** a scaled-down version of St. Peter's in Rome. *(239 Selby Ave. ☎651-228-1766. Mass M-F 7:30am and 5:15pm, no evening mass F; Sa mass 8am and 7pm; Su 8am, 10, noon, and 5pm. Tours M, W, F 1pm. Free.)*

HISTORICAL SIGHTS. Along the river, the innovative, exciting ▨**Minnesota History Center** houses ten interactive, hands-on exhibit galleries on Minnesota history. *(345 Kellogg Blvd. W. ☎800-657-3773; www.mnhs.org. Open W-Sa 10am-5pm, Th 10am-8pm, Su noopn-5pm; July-Aug. also open M 10am-5pm. Free.)* Downtown's **Landmark Center** is a grandly restored 1894 Federal Court building replete with towers and turrets, along with a collection of pianos, a concert hall, and four courtrooms. *(75 W. 5th St. ☎651-292-3228. Open M-W and F 8am-5pm; Th 8am-8pm; Sa 10am-5pm; Su 1-5pm. Free tours Th 11am, Su 1pm.)* Out front, **Rice Park** is an ideal place for a stroll or a picnic.

AMUSEMENTS. Out in suburban Apple Valley, the **Minnesota Zoo** harbors local and exotic animals in their natural habitats. The snow monkeys and the Northern Trails are must-sees. *(13000 Zoo Blvd. Take Rte. 77 S to zoo exit and follow signs. ☎952-431-9200 or 952-432-9000. Open June-Aug. M-Sa 9am-6pm, Su 9am-8pm; Sept. daily 9am-6pm; Oct.-May 9am-4pm. $8, seniors $5, ages 3-12 $4, under 3 free.)* In Shakopee, even the most daring thrill-seekers can get their jollies at **Valleyfair,** a quality amusement park with five coasters and the brand new Power Tower, which drops over ten stories. *(1 Valleyfair Dr. Take Rte. 169 south to Rte 101 W. ☎952-445-7600 or 800-386-7433. Open June-Aug. daily; hours vary so call first. Usually 10am-10pm. $29; seniors and kids under 48 in. $9.)*

♫ ENTERTAINMENT

Second only to New York in number of theaters per capita, the Twin Cities are always full of drama and music. Most parks feature free evening concerts in the summer. The thriving alternative, pop, and classical music scenes fill out the wide range of cultural options. For more info, read the free *City Pages.*

THEATER

The renowned repertory ▨**Guthrie Theater,** 725 Vineland Pl., Minneapolis, adjacent to the Walker Art Center just off Hennepin Ave., draws lots of praise for its mix of daring and classical productions. (☎377-2224. Season Apr.-Nov., also shows in Dec. Box office open M-F 9am-8pm, Sa 9am-8pm, Su 10am-7pm. Tickets $16-44, seniors and students $5 discount. Rush tickets 15min. before show $12.50, line starts 1-1½hr. before show.) Touring Broadway shows take the stage at either the **Historic State Theatre,** 805 Hennepin Ave. downtown, or the **Orpheum Theatre,** across the street at 910 Hennepin Ave. N. (Call 673-0404 for tickets to Broadway shows and Ticketmaster at 989-5151 for all others.) For family-oriented productions, the **Children's Theater Company,** at 3rd Ave. and 24th St., next to the Minneapolis Institute of

Arts, comes through with first-rate plays. (☎874-0400. Season Sept.-June. Box office open M-Sa 9am-5pm; summer hours vary slightly. Tickets $18-27; students, seniors, and children $12-21. Rush tickets 15min. before show $8.) The ingenious **Théâtre de la Jeune Lune,** 105 1st St. N., stages critically acclaimed, off-the-beaten-path productions in an old warehouse. (☎332-3968, box office 333-6200. Open M-F 10am-6pm. Tickets $10-28.) **Brave New Workshop,** 3001 Hennepin Ave. in Uptown, stages satirical sketch comedy shows and improv in an intimate club. (☎332-6620. Box office open M-F 9:30am-5pm, Sa 10am-11pm, Su noon-5pm. Tickets $14-20.)

MUSIC

The Twin Cities' vibrant music scene offers everything from opera and polka to hip-hop and alternative. **Sommerfest,** a month-long celebration of Viennese music put on by the **Minnesota Orchestra,** is the best of the cities' classical options during July and August; **Orchestra Hall,** 1111 Nicollet Mall, downtown Minneapolis, hosts the event. (☎800-292-4141. Box office open M-Sa 10am-6pm. Tickets $15-50; rush tickets for students 30min. before show $10.) Nearby **Peavey Plaza,** on Nicollet Mall, holds free nightly concerts and occasional film screenings. The **St. Paul Chamber Orchestra,** the **Schubert Club,** and the **Minnesota Opera Company** all perform at St. Paul's glass-and-brick **Ordway Music Theater,** 345 Washington St., which also hosts touring Broadway productions. (☎651-224-4222. Box office open M-F 9am-5pm, Sa 10am-5pm, Su 11am-5pm. Tickets $20-55.) Outside the city in Chanhassen, **Paisley Park,** the studio complex of the artist **Prince,** draws bands from all over.

SPORTS

The puffy **Hubert H. Humphrey Metrodome,** 900 S. 5th St., in downtown Minneapolis, houses baseball's **Minnesota Twins** (☎375-7450) and football's **Minnesota Vikings** (☎333-3865). Basketball's **Timberwolves** howl at the **Target Center,** 600 1st Ave. (☎337-0900), between 6th and 7th St. in downtown Minneapolis. The expansion NHL team, the **Wild,** takes to the ice at St. Paul's **RiverCentre** this winter (☎651-222-9453). The soccer craze hits the Midwest with the minor-league **Thunder,** at the **National Sports Center** in suburban Blaine (☎785-3668).

FESTIVALS

Countless festivals celebrate the coming of summer and liven up the dreary cold days. In late January to early February, the fun ten-day **St. Paul Winter Carnival,** near the state capitol, cures cabin fever with ice sculptures, ice-fishing, and skating contests. In July, the 12-day **Fringe Festival** for the performing arts (tickets $4-5) stages edgy plays around town. On the 4th of July, St. Paul celebrates **Taste of Minnesota** with fireworks, concerts, and regional and ethnic cuisine from hordes of local vendors. On its coattails rides the nine-day **Minneapolis Aquatennial,** with concerts and art exhibits glorifying the much talked about lakes. The first weekend in August, the excellent **Uptown Art Fair** takes over the junction of Hennepin and Lake, drawing thousands of people. In the two weeks prior to Labor Day, just about everyone in town heads to the **Minnesota State Fair,** at Snelling and Como St. in St. Paul (☎651-642-2200), the nation's largest. With cheese curds and walleye-on-a-stick, the fair provides a sampling of the area's flavor. ($5, seniors and ages 5-12 $4, under 5 free.)

◪ NIGHTLIFE

Minneapolis's vibrant youth culture feeds the Twin Cities' nightlife. The post-punk scene thrives in the Land of 10,000 Aches: **Soul Asylum** and **Hüsker Dü,** as well as the best bar band in the world, **The Replacements,** rocked here before they went big (or bad). A cross-section of the diverse nightlife options can be found in the downtown **Warehouse District** on Hennepin Ave., in **Dinkytown** by the U of M, and across the river on the **West Bank** (bounded on the west by I-35 W. and to the south by I-94), especially on **Cedar Ave.** The Twin Cities card hard, even for cigarettes, so carry your ID with you. The top floor of the **Mall of America** (see **Shop 'til You Drop,** p. 539) invites bar-hopping after the screaming kids have gone to bed.

Loring Bar and Cafe, 1624 Harmon Pl. (☎332-1617), off Hennepin Ave. near I-94. Velvet-draped and bohemia-soaked, the Loring oozes character and attitude from its indoor, light-strung trees to its artsy waitstaff. Live music, a theatrical feel, and a see-and-be-seen outdoor patio keep the stylish patrons satisfied. Beer starts at $4; wine $4.50; entrees $9. Cover (for live music) $3-5. Open daily 9am-1am.

The Quest, 110 5th St. N. (☎359-0915), between 1st Ave. N. and 2nd Ave. N. in the Warehouse District. Once owned by Prince, this poppin' dance club pays homage to his purple highness with purple windows and lots of funk. Live salsa on M and house music draw in a young, cosmopolitan crowd. Cover $5-10. hours vary; call ahead.

Ground Zero, 15 4th St. NE (☎378-5115), off Hennepin Ave. just north of the river, has cages for dancing and wild theme nights for adventurous clubgoers. Bondage A Go-Go on Th and Sa. Open M, W, and Su until 1am; Tu and Th until 2am; F-Sa until 3am.

First Avenue and 7th St. Entry, 701 1st Ave. N. (☎332-1775), downtown Minneapolis, rocks with the area's best live music several nights a week. First Ave. is where cutting-edge twenty-somethings go to dance and be seen. Music from grunge to hip hop. Cover $6-10, for concerts $10-30. Open M-F 8pm-2am, Sa-Su 7pm-3am.

Fine Line Music Cafe, 318 1st Ave. N. (☎338-8100), in the Warehouse District. Even musicians love to sit in the audience at the Fine Line, where a range of local and national folk, blues, rock, and jazz acts induce toe-tapping from the accessible stage. Cover $6-8. Open daily 8pm-1am. Nightly shows at 9pm.

The Gay 90s (☎333-7755), on Hennepin Ave. at 4th St., claims the seventh highest liquor consumption rate of all clubs in the nation. This superplex hosts thousands of mostly gay and lesbian partiers in its many bars and showrooms, though the straight crowd is sizeable. Drag shows upstairs W-Su. Open M-Sa 8am-1am, Su 10am-1am.

DULUTH ☎218

If cities were sold at auctions, Duluth would fetch a high price: the people are nice, the parks are clean, the streets are safe, and the location is amazing. Bidders on a vacation to Duluth can expect to eat well, find relatively inexpensive lodging, and watch some serious shipping action. As the largest freshwater port in the world, Duluth harbors huge ships from over 60 different countries. The recently restored area of Canal Park, along Lake St., has tempted microbreweries, restaurants, theaters, and museums to occupy the old factories and depots down on the wharf, turning a once-overlooked tourist destination into a hot spot of northern activity.

◪ PRACTICAL INFORMATION. Greyhound, 4926 Grand Ave. (☎722-5591), stops 3 mi. west of downtown; take bus #1 "Grand Ave. Zoo" from downtown. Buses run only to Minneapolis (3½hr., 3 per day, $19-20). Buy tickets daily 6:30am-5:45pm. The **Duluth Transit Authority,** 2402 W. Michigan St. (☎722-7283), buses within the city (peak fare M-F 7-9am and 2:30-6pm $1, off-peak 50¢). The **Port Town Trolley** (☎722-7283) moves tourists around. (Runs late May to early Sept. daily 11am-7pm; fare 50¢.) The **Convention and Visitors Bureau,** 100 Lake Place Dr. at Endion Station in Canal Park (☎722-4011; open M-F 8:30am-5pm), and the **Summer Visitors Center** at Vista dock on Harbor Dr. (☎800-438-5884; open mid-May to mid-Oct. daily 8:30am-7pm; hours vary). **Crisis Line:** ☎726-1931. **Post Office:** 2800 W. Michigan St. (☎723-2555; open M-F 8am-5pm, Sa 9am-1pm). **ZIP code:** 55806. **Area code:** 218.

◪ ACCOMMODATIONS. Motel rates rise and rooms fill during the warm months. The postcard-worthy **College of St. Scholastica,** 1200 Kenwood Ave., Exit 258 off I-35 N, rents out quiet dorm rooms with free local calls, kitchen access, and laundry facilities. (☎723-6000 or 800-447-5444; ask for the housing director. Singles $21; doubles $40. Reservations recommended. Open early June to mid-Aug.) Motels line London Rd.; the **Chalet Motel,** 2 mi. west of downtown at 1801 London Rd., offers decent rooms decorated with fantastical medieval characters. (☎728-4238 or 800-235-2957. Apr.-Sept. Sa-Su singles $55, doubles $68; M-F $45/$58. Lower in winter.) A few mi. south of town, the warm **Duluth Motel,** 4415 Grand Ave., houses visitors in affordable, well-kept rooms. (☎628-1008. In summer from $35; in winter $25.)

With a decidedly less urban feel, the rocky **Jay Cooke State Park,** southwest of Duluth on I-35 Exit 242, draws in families and travelers with hiking, snowmobiling, cross-country skiing, and 83 campsites among the tall trees of the St. Louis River valley. (☎384-4610 or 800-246-2267 for reservations. Open daily 9am-9pm, park gates open until 10pm. Backpack sites $7, sites with showers $12, plus electricity $15. Vehicle permit $4. Reservations recommended; $7.25 reservation fee.)

◨◪ FOOD AND NIGHTLIFE. Upscale **Fitger's Brewery Complex,** 600 E. Superior St., and the **Canal Park** region, south from downtown along Lake Ave., feature plenty of pleasant eateries. The **Brewhouse,** in Fitger's Brewery Complex, has beer and pub food. (☎726-1392. Live entertainment F and Sa; cover $1-2. Open daily 11am-1am. Grill closes 10pm. Big Boat Oatmeal Stout from $2.75.) The **DeWitt-Seitz Marketplace,** in the middle of Canal Park Dr., has slightly pricier restaurants. The friendly staff at the **Blue Note Cafe,** 357 Canal Park Dr., serves delicious sandwiches ($5-7) and desserts ($3.25) in a coffeehouse setting. (☎727-6549. Open M-Th 9am-10pm, F-Sa 9am-11pm, Su 9am-8pm.) Located in an old pipe-fitting factory in Canal Park, **Grandma's Sports Garden** has dining, a bar, and a huge dance floor. (☎722-4724. Restaurant open June-Aug. daily 11am-10pm; Sept.-May daily 11:30am-10pm. Club open daily 11:30am-1am; dancing W-Sa nights.) Get your freak on at any of the trendy clubs on Tower Ave. across the river in Superior, WI. **Hall of Fame,** 1028 Tower Ave., spins all kinds of music. (☎715-394-4225. Open daily til 2am. Beer $2.50.)

◪◩ SIGHTS AND ENTERTAINMENT. Duluth's proximity to majestic Lake Superior is its biggest draw; many visitors head right down to **Canal Park** and watch the big ships go by at the ◧**Aerial Lift Bridge.** Accompanied by deafening horn blasts, the unique Aerial Lift Bridge climbs 138 ft. in 1min. to allow vessels to pass; late afternoon is prime viewing time. Ships load at the **Ore Docks Observation Platform,** at 35th Ave. W. and Superior St. downtown. The **Boatwatcher's Hotline** (☎722-6489) has up-to-the-minute info on ship movements. Within Canal Park, the **Lake Superior Maritime Visitors Center** prepares extensive displays on commercial shipping in Lake Superior. (☎727-2497. Open daily 10am-9pm.) Canal Park also serves as the beginning and end of the **Duluth Lakewalk,** a beautiful three-mile promenade.

A 39-room neo-Jacobean mansion built on iron-shipping wealth, **Glensheen,** 3300 London Rd., lies on the eastern outskirts of town and provides visitors with a glimpse of Duluth's most prosperous period. (☎726-8863 or 888-454-4536. Open May to Oct. 9:30am-4pm; off-season hours vary. $8.75, seniors and ages 12-15 $7, ages 6-11 $4; reservations recommended.) Waterfront tours aboard the giant steamer **William A. Irvin** reveal more of Duluth's shipping past. (☎722-7876 May-Oct.; 722-5573 year-round. Open May daily 10am-4pm; June-Aug. Su-Th 9am-6pm, F-Sa 9am-8pm; Sept. to mid-Oct. Su-Th 10am-4pm, F-Sa 10am-6pm. $6.50, students and seniors $5.50, ages 3-12 $4.) Across the Aerial Lift Bridge, **Park Point** has excellent but cold swimming areas, parks, and sandy beaches. The scenic **Willard Munger State Trail** links West Duluth to Jay Cooke State Park, providing 14 mi. of paved path perfect for bikes—**Willard Munger Inn,** 7408 Grand Ave., rents both. (☎624-4814 or 800-982-2453. Bikes $10 per half-day, $13 per day; in-line skates $10/$14.)

Featuring fascinating exhibitions on animal life in Lake Superior and loads of hands-on displays, the brand new ◧**Great Lakes Aquarium,** 353 Harbor Dr., is the world's only all-freshwater aquarium. (☎740-3474. Open late May to Sept. M-Th 9am-9pm, F-Su 9am-6pm; call for off-season hours. $11, seniors $9, children 4-7 $6, under 4 free.) History buffs should seek out the outstanding **Karpeles Manuscript Library Museum,** which houses original drafts of the Bill of Rights, Handel's Messiah, and the Emancipation Proclamation. (☎728-0630. Open June-Aug. daily noon-4pm; Sept.-May Tu-Su noon-4pm. Free.) **The Depot,** 506 W. Michigan St., a former railroad station, features four performing arts groups and several museums. (☎727-8025. Open June-Aug. daily 9:30am-6pm; Sept.-May M-Sa 10am-5pm, Su 1-5pm. $8.50 includes all museums and a trolley ride; ages 3-11 $5.25, families $23.50.)

CHIPPEWA NATIONAL FOREST ☎218

Gleaming white stands of birch lace the Norway pine forests of the **Chippewa National Forest,** home to the highest density of breeding bald eagles—America's national symbol—in the continental US. The national forest shares territory with the **Leech Lake Indian Reservation,** home to 4560 Ojibwe tribespeople. The Ojibwe, mistakenly called Chippewa, migrated from the Atlantic coast in the 1700s. In the mid-1800s, the US government forced them onto reservations such as Leech Lake.

Cheap, plentiful, and available in varying degrees of modernity, **camping** is the way to stay in the forest. The Forest Office (see above) has info on campsites; over 400 of them are free. Billboards for private campgrounds string the edges of Rte. 71 along the western border of the forest. For those who prefer more permanent forms of shelter, modern lakeside cabins at **Stony Point Resort,** 8724 Stoney Point Camp Trail NW, 7 mi. east of town off Rte. 200 then 4 mi. north on Onigum Rd., sleep up to 12 people. (☎547-1665 or 800-338-9303. Open May-Sept.; from $156 for 4-person cabin with A/C.) The **National Forest Campground** next door provides a budget-friendly alternative. (☎877-444-6777. Self-regulated sites $18.)

For the northbound traveler, **Walker,** a small town in the southwest corner of the park and reservation, is an ideal gateway. **Leech Lake Area Chamber of Commerce** is on Rte. 371 downtown (☎547-1313 or 800-833-1118; open May-Sept. M-F 9am-5pm, Sa 10am-3pm; winter open Sa 10am-1pm). The **Forest Office** (☎547-1044), just east of town on Rte. 371, has the dirt on outdoor activities (open M-F 7:30am-4:30pm). **Greyhound** runs from Minneapolis to Walker (5½hr., 1 per day, $35), stopping at Hardee's (☎214-849-8966). Buy tickets from the driver. Leaves daily for the Twin Cities at 12:20pm. **Post Office:** 602 Michigan Ave. (☎547-1123; open M-F 9am-4pm, Sa 9am-11:30pm). **ZIP code:** 56484. **Area code:** 218.

IRON RANGE ☎218

It was the cry of *"Goald!"* that brought a flood of miners to join loggers and trappers already in the area, but it was the staying power of iron that kept them here. The Iron Range—120 mi. of wilderness and small towns along Minnesota Rte. 169—produces over 50% of the country's steel. Although taconite mining techniques have usurped the profitability of their underground mines, Iron Rangers continue to celebrate their heritage proudly with exhibitions of past industrial glory.

CHISOLM

Off Exit 38 on Rte. 169, the town of **Chisolm** cultivates its iron-laden history at the **Ironworld Discovery Center,** W. Rte. 169 at Rte. 73. Half amusement park and half museum, Ironworld leads interested teams of pseudo-miners on a trolley ride through historical equipment and above an obsolete open-pit mine. (☎254-3321 or 800-372-6437. Open mid-June to mid-Sept. daily 9:30am-5pm; genealogy research center open year-round M-F 8am-4:30pm. $9, senior citizens $7, students under 18 $7, under 6 free.) On the way out, the 85 ft. tall **Iron Ore Miner Statue** is a conspicuous tribute to the workers of the Iron Range's glory days.

EVELETH

The Iron Range could also be named the Hockey Player Range after its other major export. As the home of the **U.S. Hockey Hall of Fame,** 801 Hat Trick Ave., Eveleth, 10 mi. east of Chisolm on Rte. 53, attracts ice fans nationwide. Focusing on collegiate and Olympic success, the Hall honors American-born players of the world's hardest hitting sport. (☎744-5167 or 800-443-7825. Open M-Sa 9am-5pm, Su 10am-3pm. $6, seniors and ages 13-17 $5, ages 6-12 $4, under 6 free.) Further proof that they take their hockey seriously in Eveleth can be found at the 107 ft. long **World's Largest Hockey Stick,** at Grant and Monroe St. Follow the signs marked "Big Stick."

SOUDAN

For those who feel the need to dig deeper, the town of Soudan, 50 mi. northeast of Chisolm on Rte. 169, features an unforgettable journey ½ mi. underground in a high-speed elevator, or "cage," at the ◪**Soudan Underground Mine State Park,** off Rte. 1. This, the "Cadillac of underground mines," offers fascinating tours given by retired miners and their families. Visitors go by train almost a mile into the underground maze to glimpse the dark, difficult lives of ore workers in the Iron Range. Bring sturdy shoes and a jacket—it's always a chilly 50°F underground. (☎753-2245. Park open June-Aug. daily 9am-6pm; tours given every 30min. 10am-4pm. $6, ages 5-12 $4, under 5 free; $4 state park vehicle permit required.) Next door, the **McKinley Park Campground** rents semi-private campsites overlooking a lake. (☎753-5921. Sites $12, with hookup $16. Canoe and paddleboat rentals $4 per hr.)

ELY

The charming town of **Ely** serves as a launching pad into both the **Boundary Waters Canoe Area Wilderness** (see **Boundary Waters,** p. 546) and the Iron Range, and so supports its share of wilderness outfitters and attractions. The **International Wolf Center,** just north of downtown at 1396 Rte. 169, houses three timber wolves, packs BWCAW permits, and has informative displays on *Canis lupus.* (☎365-4695. Open May-June and Sept.-Oct. daily 9am-5pm, July-Aug. 9am-7pm, Nov.-Apr. F-Su 10am-5pm. $5.50, seniors $5, ages 6-12 $2.75. Call for wolf presentation times.) **Stony Ridge Resort,** 60 W. Lakeview Pl. off Shagawa Rd., has some RV or tent campsites and cabins. (☎365-6757. RV and tent sites $15 with water, electricity, and showers. 1 bedroom cabins from $65 for weeknights. Canoe rental $15 per day.)

VOYAGEURS NATIONAL PARK   ☎218

Voyageurs National Park sits on Minnesota's boundary with Ontario, accessible almost solely by boat. Named for the French Canadian fur traders who once traversed this area, the park invites today's voyagers to leave the auto-dominated world and push off into the longest inland lake waterway on the continent. Preservation efforts have kept the area much as it was in the late 18th century, and wolves, bear, deer, and moose roam freely. As the traders did, today's visitors can also travel by canoe to camp in these northern woods. Sadly, undeveloped can mean unregulated; water should be boiled for at least 2min. before consumption, and some fish in these waters contain mercury. Ticks bearing Lyme disease have been found as well; visitors should take precautions (see **Preventing Disease,** p. 45).

Many of the numerous campsites in the park are accessible only by water. Several car-accessible sites lie outside Voyageurs in the state forest, including **Wooden Frog,** about 4 mi. from Kabetogama Lake Visitors Center on Rte. 122 (☎757-3274; 62 primitive sites $9, showers available at lodge $3), and **Ash River,** 3 mi. from the Visitors Center on Rte. 129 (☎757-3489; primitive sites $9). The **Ash Trail Lodge,** 10 mi. east of Rte. 53 on Rte. 129, is a good option for the wilderness-challenged, offering roomy cabins, a restaurant/bar, and lots of socializing in a wooded environment. (☎374-3131 or 800-777-4513. 3 bedrooms $50.) **International Falls,** the inspiration for Rocky and Bullwinkle's hometown of Frostbite Falls, offers other lodging options and a few attractions outside Voyageurs. Rte. 53 is loaded with motels. **The Tee Pee Motel,** 1501 2nd Ave. at Rte. 53, features homey rooms with cable, fridge, and A/C. (☎283-8494. Singles $39; doubles $60.) **International Voyageurs RV Campground,** 5min. south of town on Rte. 53, offers decent camping with showers and laundry. (☎283-4679. Sites for 2 $9, full hookup $18; each additional person $2; under 12 free.)

The park can be accessed through **Crane Lake, Ash River, Kabetogama Lake,** or **Rainy Lake** (all east of Rte. 53), or through **International Falls,** at the northern tip of Rte. 53 just below Ft. Frances, ON. The **State of Minnesota Travel Information Center,** Rte. 53 and Rte. 11, in downtown International Falls, hands out info on travel. (☎285-7623; open M-Sa 8am-6pm, Su 9am-3pm). For more help, stop by the three Visitors Centers in the park: **Rainy Lake,** at the end of Rte. 11, 12 mi. east of International Falls (☎286-5258; open mid-May-Sept. daily 9am-5pm; Oct. to mid-May W-Su 9am-4:30pm); **Ash River,** 8 mi. east of Rte. 53 on Rte. 129, then 3 mi. north (☎374-3221; open mid-May to Sept. daily 9am-5pm); and **Kabetogama Lake,** 1 mi. north of Rte. 122; follow the signs (☎875-2111; open mid-May to Sept. daily 9am-5pm).

WHERE IT ALL BEGINS Near Chippewa, step across the Mighty Mississippi at its source at the **Beginning of the Mississippi,** in **Lake Itasca State Park,** 30 mi. west of Chippewa National Forest on Rte. 200. More like a vacation home than a cheap place to spend the night, the ▨**Mississippi Headwaters Hostel (HI-AYH)** within the park attracts locals and travelers alike. The hostel stays open in the winter to facilitate access to the park's excellent cross-country skiing. (☎266-3415. Laundry, kitchen, multiple bathrooms. Linen $2-4. $4 per day vehicle permit required for entrance to park. Private rooms available. 2-night min. stay some weekends. Check-in Su-Th 5-10pm, F-Sa 5-11pm. Check-out M-F 10am, Sa-Su noon. Dorms $15-17, nonmembers $18-20.) The **park office,** through the north entrance and down County Rd. 122, has camping info. (☎266-2100. Office open M-F 8am-4:30pm, Sa-Su 8am-4pm; mid-Oct. to Apr. M-F 8am-4:30pm. Ranger on call after hours.)

SCENIC DRIVE: NORTH SHORE DRIVE

Vast and mysterious, Lake Superior shapes the landscape of Northeastern Minnesota with its jagged, glacier-carved edges and seemingly limitless surface. Scenic overlooks on the lake's North Shore allow harrowing views down steep cliffs toward the fickle waters below. Inland, the **Sawtooth Mountains** hover over the lake with stunning rock formations and tall, sweeping birch trees.

The true Lake Superior North Shore extends 646 mi. from Duluth, MN to Sault Ste. Marie, ON; but **Rte. 61,** winding 150 mi. along the coast from Duluth to Grand Portage, gives travelers an abbreviated version of the spectacular journey. Most of the small, touristy fishing towns along the shore maintain Visitors Centers. The **R.J. Houle Visitor Information Center** (☎834-4005 or 800-554-2116), 21 mi. from Duluth up Rte. 61 in scenic **Two Harbors,** has lodging guides and info for each town along the MN stretch of the North Shore. (Open Su-Th 10am-4pm, F-Sa 9am-7pm; mid-Oct. to May W-Sa 9am-1pm.) Rte. 61 is often glutted with boat-towing pickup trucks and family-filled campers on summer weekends. Accommodations flanking the roadside fill up fast in summer; make reservations early. Remember to bring warm clothes; temperatures can drop into the low 40s (°F) on summer nights.

Striking views of the jagged cliffs that descend to the massive lake are Rte. 61's greatest appeal. State parks scattered along the route not only afford more in-depth looks at the shore but, in many cases, stunning attractions of their own. Twenty miles northeast of the Visitors Center, **Gooseberry Falls** crashes down to the lake with five rugged waterfalls and scenic overlooks. The adventuresome can climb on the middle or lower falls for a head-on view. (☎834-3855. Visitors Center open daily 9am-7pm; park open daily 8am-10pm.) **Camping** near the cataract is an appealing lodging option. (Primitive sites with shower $12; vehicle permit $4.)

Eight miles down the road, the **Split Rock Lighthouse** takes visitors back to the lake's industrial heyday and elevates them to a birds-eye view atop a 130 ft. cliff. (☎226-6372. Open mid-May to mid-Oct. daily 9am-7pm; call for winter hours. $6, seniors $5, ages 6-12 $4.) Rte. 61 becomes more convoluted as it enters the **Lake Superior National Forest** and passes over countless winding rivers toward **Tofte,** where the 1526 ft. **Carlton Peak** dominates the landscape. The pine-paneled **Cobblestone Cabins,** off Rte. 61 2 mi. north of Tofte, offer the road-weary a place to stay and access to a cobblestone beach, canoes, a woodburning sauna, and kitchenettes. (☎663-7957. Open May-Oct. Cabins from $40.)

GRAND MARAIS

Near the north end of the 150 mi. scenic drive, this fishing resort town and former artists' colony is both a popular tourist spot and a good place to sleep and eat. **Nelson's Traveler's Rest,** on Rte. 61, ½ mi. west of town, provides fully equipped cabins with a lake view. (☎387-1464 or 800-249-1285. Single cabins from $35; doubles from $49. Open mid-May to mid-Oct.; call in advance.) **Grand Marais Recreation Area RV Park–Campground,** off Rte. 61 in Grand Marais, has wooded and mostly private primitive sites by the lake. (☎387-1712 or 800-998-0959. Office open 6am-10pm. Primitive sites $15, with water and electricity $18; discounted use of municipal pool.)

Cheap and popular with locals and fishermen, **South of the Border Cafe,** 4 W. Rte. 61, in Grand Marais, specializes in huge breakfasts (served all day) and satisfying diner food. The bluefin herring sandwich (fried, of course) will run you $2.75; breakfast less than $4. (☎387-1505. Open daily 5am-2pm.) No sweet tooth can accuse **World's Best Doughnuts,** at the intersection of Wisconsin and Broadway, of false advertising. (☎387-1345. Open late May to mid-Oct. daily 7:30am until sold out, usually around 4pm. Doughnuts 50¢.) The **Grand Marais Chamber of Commerce:** N. Broadway off Rte. 61. (☎387-2524 or 888-922-5000. Open M-Sa 9am-5pm.)

BOUNDARY WATERS. Grand Marais also serves as a gateway to the **Boundary Waters Canoe Area Wilderness (BWCAW),** a designated wilderness comprising 1.2 million acres of lakes, streams, and forests. The BWCAW is understandably finicky about when, where, and how many people it will allow to enter; phoning ahead is essential (day permits free, camping permits $10 per person per trip). One mile south of Grand Marais, the **Gunflint Ranger Station** distributes permits. (☎877-550-6777. Open June-Sept. daily 6am-8pm, Oct.-Apr. 8am-4:30pm, May 6am-6pm.) Running northwest from town, the 60 mi. paved **Gunflint Trail** (County Rd. 12) is the only developed road offering access to the wilderness from Rte. 61; resorts and outfitters gather on this lone strip of civilization. **Bear Track Outfitting Co.,** 2011 W. Rte. 61, across from the Gunflint Ranger Station, rents boats and sells camping necessities. (☎387-1162. 1-day canoe rental $240, including accessories. 1-day kayak rental $32.)

A good option for those who would rather not camp in the Wilderness, the well-kept, seldom-full cabins of **"Spirit of the Land" Island Hostel (HI-AYH)** are located on an island in Seagull Lake, near the end of the Gunflint Trail. The Christian-oriented **Wilderness Canoe Base** leads canoe trips and summer camps for various groups. Call from Grand Marais to arrange a boat pickup. (☎388-2241 or 800-454-2922. Full kitchen, outhouses. Beds $16, nonmembers $18, F-Sa $18/$20. Sleeping bag $5, sleepsack $3. Meals $4-6. Hot showers free. Saunas $3. Canoe rental $10 per half day, $18 per day. Snowshoe rentals in winter. Closed Nov.-Dec.)

GREAT PLAINS

In 1803, the Louisiana Purchase doubled America's size, adding French territory west of the Mississippi at the bargain price of 4¢ per acre. Over time, the plains spawned legends of pioneers and cowboys and of Native Americans struggling to defend their homelands. The arrival of railroad transportation and liberal land policies spurred an economic boom, until a drought during the Great Depression transformed the region into a dust bowl. Since the 1930s, the region has been struggling to settle on an effective course of development. Modern agriculture has reclaimed the soil, and the heartland of the United States now thrives on the trade of farm commodities. The Plains are also a vast land of prairies, where open sky stretches from horizon to horizon, broken only by long, thin lines of trees. Grasses and grains paint the land green and gold. The land rules here, as its inhabitants know. While signs of humanity are unmistakable—checkerboard farms, Army posts, and railroad corridors—the region's most staggering sights are the work of nature, from the Badlands and the Black Hills to the mighty Missouri and Mississippi Rivers.

HIGHLIGHTS OF THE GREAT PLAINS

NATIONAL PARKS AND MONUMENTS. Discover the uncrowded gems of Theodore Roosevelt National Park, ND (p. 551), and the Badlands, SD (p. 554), or join the crowds in the Black Hills around Mt. Rushmore (p. 558).

HISTORICAL SITES. Scotts Bluff National Monument, NE (p. 574), and Chimney Rock, NE (p. 574) will fascinate anyone interested in the pioneers.

NORTH DAKOTA

An early visitor to the site of present-day Fargo declared, "It's a beautiful land, but I doubt that human beings will ever live here." Posterity begs to differ. The stark, haunting lands that so intimidated early settlers eventually found willing tenants, and the territory became a state along with South Dakota on Nov. 2, 1889. The inaugural event was not without confusion—Benjamin Harrison concealed the names when he signed the two bills, so both Dakotas claim to be the 39th state. North Dakota lies just a bit too far north to attract throngs of summer tourists, but those who do visit are greeted by awe-inspiring natural beauty minus the crowds.

🖊 PRACTICAL INFORMATION

Capital: Bismarck.
Visitor info: Tourism Dept., 400 E. Broadway, #50, Bismarck 58501 (☎ 701-328-2525 or 800-435-5663; www.ndtourism.com). **Parks and Recreation Dept.,** 1835 Bismarck Expwy., Bismarck 58504 (☎ 328-5357). **Game and Fish Dept.,** 100 N. Bismarck Expwy., Bismarck 58501 (☎ 328-6300). All state offices open M-F 8am-5pm.
Postal Abbreviation: ND. **Sales Tax:** 7%.

FARGO   ☎ 701

Although it is North Dakota's largest city, Fargo existed in anonymity until the Oscar-winning 1996 film *Fargo* brought it name recognition. However, very little of the movie was filmed in the town, and its parodied accents are more northern Minnesota than North Dakota. Fargo and its sister city, Moorhead, MN, are home to 20,000 students who pack lectures at North Dakota State University, Moorhead State, and Concordia College. The region's northern European cultural heritage continues to flourish. The **Heritage Hjemkomst Center**, 202 1st Ave. N. in Moorhead,

GREAT PLAINS

Great Plains

pays a moving tribute to the two cities' Norwegian heritage. Inside looms the Hjemkomst (*YEM-komst*), a 76 ft. Viking ship replica built by Moorhead native Robert Asp that sailed the 6100 mi. from Duluth, MN to Bergen, Norway in 1982. Outside, a 72 ft. stave church replica, built by Moorhead native Guy Paulson, looms over visitors. (☎ 218-299-5511. Open M-W and F-Sa 9am-5pm, Th 9am-9pm, Su noon-5pm. $3.50, seniors and students $3, ages 4-17 $1.50.) The **Scandinavian Hjemkomst Festival** is a big draw, complete with cultural exhibits, music and dance shows, and food. (☎ 800-235-7654. June 19-23, 2002.) From June to August, **Trollwood Park Weekends** (☎ 241-8160) feature similar events.

Cheap chain motels abound at I-29 and 13th Ave.; take Exit 64 off I 20. **The Sunset Motel,** 731 W. Main, in West Fargo, about 3 mi. west off I-29 Exit 65, offers clean rooms, free local calls, continental breakfast, and an indoor pool with a snazzy two-story waterslide. (☎ 282-3266 or 800-252-2207. Call early on weekends. Singles $26-29; doubles $44-49; kitchenettes $5 extra.) Follow signs from I-94 Exit 351 to **Lindenwood Park,** at 17th Ave. and S. 5th St. The campground offers sites close to the peaceful Red River of the North. The park also has extensive trails ideal for mountain biking. (☎ 232-3987. Sites $8, with hookup $15.)

Erbert & Gerbert's, 68 Broadway, puts together great club sandwiches and subs on freshly baked bread. Vegetarians will be delighted with the "Jacob Bluefinger" ($3.40). There are plenty of meat options as well. (☎ 235-3445. Open F-Sa 10:30am-2am, Su-Th 10:30am-11pm.) **Cafe Aladdin,** 530 N. 6th Ave., is popular for its scrumptious Greek and Middle Eastern food ($4-7.50) and sweet, flaky baklava for $1.75. (☎ 298-0880. Open M 10:30am-8pm, Tu-Sa 10am-8pm.) NDSU students tend to go to the bars along Broadway near Northern Pacific Ave. The newest and most frequented dance club in the city is **Old Broadway,** 22 Broadway, with two levels of dance floors and plenty of people-watching spots. (☎ 237-6161. Cover F-Sa $2. Open M-Sa 4pm-1am.) If it's culture you're craving, head to the **Fargo Theater,** 314 Broadway. The recently restored theater now shows art films. (☎ 239-8385. Tickets $6.50.)

Fargo and Moorhead flank the Red River of the North on the west and east, respectively. The cities are connected by numbered streets running north-south and numbered avenues running east-west. Main Ave. is the central east-west thoroughfare and intersects I-29. **Hector International Airport** is at 2801 32nd Ave. NW (☎ 241-8168), off N. 19th Ave. in northern Fargo. **Amtrak** can be found at 420 N. 4th St. (☎ 232-2197). **Greyhound** is at 402 Northern Pacific (N.P.) Ave. (☎ 293-1222. Open daily 6:30am-6:20pm and 9:30pm-1:20am.) **Metro Area Transit,** 502 North Pacific Ave., runs buses across the city (☎ 232-7500; operates M-Sa). Sort out your visit at the **Fargo-Moorhead Convention and Visitors Bureau,** 2001 44th St. SW, off 45th St. Follow the blue signs from I-29 Exit 63B. (☎ 282-3653 or 800-235-7654. Open May-Aug. M-Sa 8am-7pm, Su 9am-6pm; Sept.-Apr. M-F 8am-5pm, Sa 10am-4pm.) **Crisis Line:** ☎ 235-7335; 24hr. **Post Office:** 657 N. 2nd Ave. (open M-F 7:30am-5:30pm, Sa 8am-2pm). **ZIP code:** 58103. **Area code:** 701.

BISMARCK   ☎ 701

Bismarck is hardly a rough, urban capital. The city is impeccably clean, the people are open and friendly, and the scenery is spectacular. Even with only about 55,000 residents, it still has the look and feel of a large town. The city was founded on land that defies the notion that all prairies are flat. The terrain displays an array of colors, textures, and shapes. Seas of yellow wildflowers, grids of green farmland, and fields of golden wheat blend with surprising harmony. The city of Bismarck itself offers a number of upscale restaurants and lively nightspots. As far as North Dakotan cities go, Bismarck is the most interesting and comfortable place to spend a few days relaxing, enjoying the scenery, and learning about pioneer culture.

◼◪ ORIENTATION AND PRACTICAL INFORMATION. Bismarck is on I-94, about halfway between Fargo and Theodore Roosevelt National Park. The Missouri River separates Bismarck from Mandan, its neighbor to the west. Washington and 9th St. are the main north-south thoroughfares and are intersected by Main Ave.,

I-94, ROAD OF CONCRETE WONDERS Two gargantuan concrete monuments separated by 131 mi. of interstate symbolize the past and present of North Dakota. Looming on the horizon in Jamestown, ND, at Exit 258, is the world's largest buffalo—a towering 24 ft., monument to the animals that once roamed the Plains. Near the statue, a herd of real buffalo regards their concrete brother apathetically from behind a protective fence. With luck, you'll see White Cloud, a rare (one in six billion) albino buffalo sacred to many Native American tribes. In Salem, 131 mi. west of Jamestown, at Exit 127, Salem Sue, the world's largest Holstein Cow (38 ft. tall and 50 ft. long), keeps an eye on the interstate and the seas of cows that munch on the grasses of the Plains. ($1 suggested donation.)

Divide Ave., and Interstate Ave., all of which run east-west. The **Bismarck Municipal Airport** (☎222-6502) is located on University Dr., 2 mi. southeast of the city. **Greyhound**, 3750 E. Rosser Ave. (☎223-6576; open daily 9am-1pm and 3:30-8pm), runs buses to Fargo (4hr., 4 per day, $32-35) and Billings (7½hr., 4 per day, $65-69). For a taxi, try **Taxi 9000** (☎223-9000). **Internet access** is free at the **Bismarck Public Library**, 515 N. 5th St. (Open M-Th 9am-9pm, F 9am-6pm, Sa 9am-5pm, Su 1-5pm. 1hr. time slots.) **Bismarck-Mandan Visitors Center:** 1600 Burnt Boat Rd., Exit 157 off I-94. (☎222-4308. Open daily 7am-7pm.) **Post Office:** 220 E. Rosser Ave. (☎221-6550; open M-F 7:45am-5:30pm, Sa 10am-noon). **ZIP code:** 58501. **Area code:** 701.

⌂ ACCOMMODATIONS AND FOOD. Budget motels abound at I-94 Exit 159. The **Bismarck Motor Hotel**, 2301 E. Main Ave., offers clean rooms with a microwave and a fridge. (☎223-2474. Singles $34.50; doubles $44.50.) The best value around is the **Select Inn**, 1505 Interchange Ave., Exit 59 off I-94. The rooms are clean and spacious, with laundry access and continental breakfast. (☎223-8060 or 800-641-1000. Singles $43; doubles $50. AAA discount.) Camping is relaxing in the beautiful **Fort Abraham Lincoln State Park** (see **Sights**, below), 7 mi. south on Rte. 1806 in Mandan. Tent sites line the banks of the Missouri River and feature an amazing view of the surrounding prairie. (☎663-9571. $7, with electricity $12; vehicle fee $4.)

With an enormous menu of pasta, chicken, seafood, and sandwiches ($5.50-10), the **⊠Walrus**, 1136 N. 3rd. St. in Arrowhead Plaza, is a popular local favorite. The $9.50 Italian sausage pizziola is a house specialty. (☎250-0020. Open M-Sa 10:30am-1am.) Bismarck offers a surprising array of posh restaurants, each with a unique ambience. What **Happy Joe's**, 2921 North 11th St., lacks in atmosphere, it makes up for with fantastic pizza. Lunch specials including a beverage go for $3.15, whole pizzas $7-11. (☎355-1146. Open Su-Th 7am-10pm, F-Sa 7am-11pm.) Housed in the old train depot, **Fiesta Villa** (☎222-8075), 411 E. Main Ave., serves quesadillas, tacos, and other Mexican fare, complemented by homemade sauces ($6-9). Enjoy your selection inside the historic building or soak up the atmosphere on the open-air patio.

◙ SIGHTS. The **North Dakota State Capitol**, 600 E. Boulevard Ave, was built between 1932-34 with a budget of only $2 million. To stretch the money to the max, the usual dome-style capitol design was replaced by a more efficient 19-story office-style building. Inside, visitors view examples of Art Deco architecture in beautiful Memorial Hall. The observation deck on the 19th floor is a great place to see the prairie and the Capitol's 130 acres of well-manicured grounds. (☎328-2471. Open M-F 7am-6pm. 30-45min. tours leave every hr. M-F 8am-4pm; June-Aug. additional tours Sa 9am-4pm, Su 1-4pm. Free.) Right next door to the Capitol is the **North Dakota Heritage Center**, 612 E. Boulevard Ave., an excellent historical museum with exhibits ranging from anthropology to Dust Bowl photography. (☎328-2666. Open M-F 8am-5pm, Sa 9am-5pm, Su 11am-5pm. Free.) On Rte. 1806 in Mandan, **Fort Abraham Lincoln State Park** houses "On-a-Slant" Mandan Indian village and replicas of the cavalry post and Victorian-style home of Lt. Col. George Armstrong Custer. Those wishing to "visit the General" can follow a host dressed in period garb through the Custer home. (☎663-3069 or 663-9571. Open June-Aug. Buildings open daily 9am-7pm; park 9am-9:30pm. $4, high school students $2; vehicle fee $4.)

🎭🎬 **ENTERTAINMENT AND NIGHTLIFE.** The **Bismarck Symphony** (☎258-8345) plays in the magnificent **Belle Mehus Auditorium,** 201 N. 6th St. The symphony celebrates holidays in style—8000 people turn up for their 4th of July concert on the Capitol steps. A variety of musical programs run throughout the year, and chamber music can be heard every Sunday afternoon. Locals agree that the coolest place to be in Bismarck these days is **Borrowed Buck's Roadhouse,** 118 S. 3rd St. Decorated like an old service station, Buck's has a full dance floor and a live DJ every night. Rock music is the focus, but Wednesdays are "Dance Ranch," featuring good country music. Live bands take the stage at Bucks once or twice a month; the performances are well-advertised around the city. (☎224-1545. 21+. Open M-F 4pm-1am, Sa noon-1am.) If only one night a week of country isn't enough for you, there's always **Lonesome Dove,** 3929 Memorial Hwy. on the border of Mandan, the *real* country joint in Bismarck. Lonesome Dove has a large dance floor and live, toe-tappin' country music six nights a week. (☎663-2793. Open daily noon-1am.)

SCENIC DRIVE: SAKAKAWEA TRAIL

Drivers along Rte. 200 in North Dakota witness an extraordinary transformation, as smooth prairie hills and azure kettle ponds abruptly give way to jutting buttes and canyons. The change in terrain occurs without warning and can be startling. Aside from the scenery, the Sakakawea Trail offers travelers interested in Lewis and Clark or Native American history ample opportunity to learn and explore the countryside. The Sakakawea Trail begins in **Washburn,** north of Bismarck on Rte. 83. At the junction of Rte. 83 and Rte. 200A lies the **Lewis and Clark Interpretive Center.** The museum presents an overview of the wilderness journey, and visitors can don buffalo robes and schlep around with a cradle board just like the one Sakakawea once wore. (☎701-462-8535. Open June-Aug. daily 9am-7pm; Sept.-May 9am-5pm.) Two miles away at **Fort Mandan,** modern-day trailblazers can enter a replica of the expedition's rugged riverside lodgings. (☎701-462-8535. Open daily 8:30am-sunset.)

About 10 mi. west of Washburn, a scenic overlook is marked with a small sign. On the left-hand side lie the Arroda Lakes, blue and sparkling against the green land. On the right, vibrantly colored fields greet the Missouri River. Down the road, plaques and sign posts mark the former site of **Historic Fort Clark;** over time, forceful prairie winds eradicated any evidence of its existence on the plains. About 8 mi. west of Fort Clark, you can follow signs to the **Knife River Indian Villages National Historic Site.** There is a 15min. video detailing the life of Plains Indians and a ½ mi. wheelchair accessible trail to the Knife River. (☎701-745-3309. Open June-Aug. daily 7:30am-6pm; Sept.-May 8am-4:30pm. Earth lodge tours 9am-4pm. Free.)

After the Knife River Indian Villages, there's not much standing in the way of **Theodore Roosevelt National Park** other than 65 mi. of farms and tiny Plains towns. Just before the junction with Rte. 85, however, the landscape begins to change dramatically. At first, only a few solitary buttes break the tranquility of the hills. Then—before you know it—they are everywhere; the earth becomes a stark red and white and dotted with jagged formations. The southern entrance to Theodore Roosevelt National Park lies in the tiny frontier town of **Medora,** about 35 mi. south on Rte. 85 and another 15 mi. west on I-94. Signs on Rte. 85 N also point the way to the northern entrance to the park, 16 mi. north on U.S. 85.

THEODORE ROOSEVELT NAT'L PARK ☎701

After his mother and his wife died on the same day, pre-White House Theodore Roosevelt moved to his ranch in the Badlands for a dose of spiritual renewal. He was so influenced by the red- and brown-hued lunar formations, horseback riding, big-game hunting, and cattle ranching in this unforgiving land that he later claimed, "I never would have been President if it weren't for my experiences in North Dakota." Inspired by his wilderness days, Roosevelt created numerous national parks, monuments, and bird refuges. Theodore Roosevelt National Park was created in 1947 as a monument to his conservationist policies. Visitors can garner the inspiration he did among the quiet canyons, secluded glens, and dramatic rocky spires that adorn the park. Roosevelt National Park teems with wildlife; prairie dogs, bighorn sheep, and bison have greeted many visitors.

GREAT PLAINS

⚑ PRACTICAL INFORMATION. The park is split into southern and northern units and bisected by the border separating Mountain and Central Time Zones. The entrance to the more-developed southern unit is just north of I-94 in **Medora**, a revamped tourist haven. **Greyhound** serves Medora from the Sully Inn (see below), with buses to Bismarck (3½hr., 3 per day, $25-27) and Billings (6hr., 2 per day, $52-55). There is no ticket office in Medora; buy your ticket during the Dickinson layover. The park entrance fee ($5 per person or $10 maximum per vehicle, under 17 free) covers admission to both units of the park for seven days. The **South Unit's Visitors Center,** in Medora, maintains a mini-museum displaying T.R.'s guns, spurs, and old letters, as well as a beautiful 14min. film treating T.R.'s relationship with the land. (☎623-4466. Open daily 8am-8pm; Sept. to mid-June 8am-4:30pm.) The **North Unit's Visitors Center** has an interesting exhibit on the nature and wildlife in the park. (☎842-2333. Open daily 9am-5:30pm Central Time.) For more info, write to **Theodore Roosevelt National Park,** P.O. Box 7, Medora 58645, or call the Visitors Center.

Medora lacks a real pharmacy and grocery store. However, both the **Ferris Store,** 251 Main St. (☎623-4447; open daily 8am-8pm) and **Medora Convenience and Liquor,** Pacific Ave. (☎623-4479; open daily 7am-10pm), sell basic pharmaceutical goods, food and cooking items. There is a 24hr. **Walmart** in Dickinson (30 mi. east on I-94). **Dakota Cyclery,** 275 3rd Ave., rents bikes. (☎623-4808. Open daily 9am-6pm. $20-30 for 4hr.; full-day $30-45.) The Cyclery also leads bike tours of the plains and badlands at 10am and 2pm daily. Off-road biking is not allowed in either unit of Theodore Roosevelt National Park. **South unit time zone:** Mountain (2hr. behind Eastern). **North unit time zone:** Central (1hr. behind Eastern). Medora's **Post Office:** 355 3rd Ave. (☎623-4385; open M-Sa 8am-7pm; window service M-F 8am-4:30pm, Sa 8:15am-9:45am). **ZIP code:** 58645. **Area code:** 701.

⬧⬧ ACCOMMODATIONS AND FOOD. Free backcountry camping permits are available at the Visitors Centers. **Cottonwood Campgrounds** lies just inside the south entrance. In the north, **Juniper Campground,** 5 mi. west of the north unit entrance, is in a beautiful valley. The campground is a popular buffalo night spot all year, so be aware. (Both campgrounds have toilets and running water; sites $10). It's not easy to find inexpensive, non-camping lodging in Medora. Despite its name, the **Sully Inn,** 428 Broadway, offers clean rooms at the lowest rates in town, free local calls, cable TV, and 10% off in its bookstore. (☎623-4455. Singles $60, in winter $40; doubles $65/$45; under 13 free.) Teddy Roosevelt was known to bunk down at the **Rough Riders Hotel,** 301 3rd Ave. The hotel's room rates are far from budget, but the restaurant serves reasonable breakfasts and lunches in an upscale atmosphere for $4-7. (☎623-4444, ext. 497. Open daily 7am-8:30pm. In winter, B&B only.) The **Iron Horse Saloon,** 160 Pacific Ave., offers great American standards year-round; prices range from $4-7. (☎623-9894. Open June-Sept. daily 6am-1am; Oct.-May 10am-1am.)

⬧ OUTDOOR ACTIVITIES. Painted Canyon Overlook, 7 mi. east of Medora off I-94, has its own **Visitors Center** with picnic tables and a breathtaking view of the Badlands. The occasional buffalo roams through the parking lot. The **Painted Canyon Trail** is a worthwhile 1 mi. loop that undulates gently through shady wooded areas and scorching buttes. (☎575-4020. Open daily 8am-6pm; mid-Apr. to late May and early Sept. to mid-Nov. 8:30am-4:30pm. Free.) The **south unit** is busier and more crowded than the north unit, consisting of a 36 mi. **scenic automobile loop** from which all sights and trails are accessible. **Peaceful Valley Ranch,** 7 mi. into the park, offers a variety of horseback riding excursions, 1½hr. or longer. (☎623-4568. Rides leave daily 8:30am-2pm, evening ride 6pm. $20.) The **Ridgeline Trail** is a short, self-guided hiking trail about 0.5 mi. long. Signs along the way instruct about the ecology and geology of the terrain. The 0.8 mi. **Coal Vein Trail** traces a seam of lignite coal that ignited and burned from 1951 to 1977. The searing heat of the blaze served as a natural kiln, baking the adjacent clay and sand. **Buck Hill** is accessible by car, but a short climb up a steep paved path earns you a full view of the Badlands landscape. Constant winds continue to morph the soft sands of **Wind Canyon.** A short dirt path leads you along the bluffs for a close look at the canyon walls and the river below.

The third largest **petrified forest** in the US lies a day's hike into the park; if you prefer to drive, ask the ranger for directions and expect to walk about ¾ mi. For more info on hiking, pick up a copy of the *Backcountry Guide* at one of the Visitors Centers. Learn more about Teddy Roosevelt through a tour of his **Maltese Cabin,** circa 1883. Tours leave periodically from the **Southern Unit Visitors Center** in the summer.

The less-visited **north unit** of the park is 70 mi. from the south unit on U.S. 85. Equally as scenic as the south unit, it is infinitely more conducive to hiking and exploring. Most of the land is wilderness, resulting in virtually unlimited **backcountry hiking** possibilities. The seclusion provides ample opportunity for wildlife contact, but be careful not to surprise the buffalo; one ranger advises singing while hiking so they can hear you coming. For those eager to escape the crowds but reluctant to leave the car, the north unit boasts a **14 mi. scenic drive;** the drive connects the entrance and Visitors Center to **Oxbow Overlook,** and is as unsullied as possible. Everyone can enjoy the **Little Mo Trail.** Weaving through woodlands and badlands, ¾ of the 1 mi. trail is wheelchair accessible. The **Buckhorn Trail** is a long but relatively easy 11 mi. walk that includes a visit to a prairie dog town. The **Caprock Coulee Trail** (1½ mi. round-trip) connects with the Buckhorn Trail and journeys on fairly level ground through prairie and dry-water gulches. Seasoned hikers and adventurers will thrive on the challenging **Achenbach Trail.** The 16 mi. sojourn features numerous vertical drops and uphill climbs as it winds around the Little Missouri River, visible from the **River Bend Outlook.**

🎭 **ENTERTAINMENT.** The popular **Medora Musical** is a comical singing, dancing, and theatrical experience that attracts hordes of people nightly. The show, held in the open-air **Burning Hills Amphitheater** west of town, incorporates the magnificent natural landscape into the performance. The Medora Musical also stages various outside talent acts, ranging from magicians to comedians to Argentinian Gauchos. (Shows early June to early Sept. nightly 8:30pm. $19-21, ages 6-18 $11-12.) Before the show, clog your arteries at the **Pitchfork Fondue.** The "chef" puts ten steaks on a pitchfork and dips them into a vat of boiling oil for 5min. ($19.50, under 18 $11, includes buffet. Reservations required.) Tickets for both are available at 335 4th St. at the **Harold Schafer Heritage Center** (☎623-4444), or by calling 800-623-6721.

SOUTH DAKOTA

With fewer than ten people per square mile, South Dakota has the highest ratio of sights-to-people in all of the Great Plains. Colossal manmade attractions such as Mt. Rushmore and the Crazy Horse Memorial and stunning natural spectacles such as the Black Hills and the Badlands make tourism the state's largest industry. The buffalo once again roam parts of the state, as do adventure-seeking tourists. Small and patient, down-to-earth and friendly, South Dakota is the highlight of the Plains.

🛈 PRACTICAL INFORMATION

Capital: Pierre.

Visitor info: Department of Tourism, 711 E. Wells Ave., Pierre 57501 (☎605-773-3301 or 800-732-5682; www.travelsd.com). Open M-F 7am-7pm. **US Forest Service,** 330 Mt. Rushmore Rd., Custer 57730 (☎605-673-4853). Open M-F 7:30am-4:30pm. **Game, Fish, and Parks Dept.,** 523 E. Capitol Ave., Foss Bldg., Pierre 57501 (☎605-773-3391), has info on state parks and campgrounds. Open M-F 8am–5pm. Call 800-710-2267 for campground reservations.

Postal Abbreviation: SD. **Sales Tax:** 4%.

SIOUX FALLS   ☎ 605

South Dakota's eastern gateway, Sioux Falls is the typical "nice guy": quiet, friendly, clean-cut, and a little boring—a better stopping point than a destination in itself. The city's namesake rapids are at Falls Park, north of downtown on Falls Park Dr. The Sioux River Greenway Recreation Trail circles the city from Falls Park in the northeast to the Elmwood golf course in the northwest. At **Buffalo Ridge,** 5 mi. west of Sioux Falls on I-90, Exit 390, you can visit a ghost town with over 50 exhibits portraying life in the Old West. A herd of over 50 buffalo also makes appearances near the town from time to time. (☎528-3931. Open early Apr.-Oct. sunrise to sunset. $4, children 5-12 $3.) The **Corn Palace,** 604 N. Main St., in Mitchell, 70 mi. west of Sioux Falls on I-90, poses as a regal testament to the "a-maize-ing" power of corn. Dating back to 1892, the structure is refurbished with a new crop every year. (☎800-257-2676. Open June-Aug. daily 8am-9pm, May and Sept. daily 8am-5pm, Oct.-Apr. M-F 8am-5pm. Free.) During summer, head to the Visitors Center (see below) for the **Wells Fargo Falls Park Light and Sound Show.** The spectacle enhances the natural beauty of Sioux Falls, the city's namesake, with a little help from technology. (Nightly June-Aug., starting at 9pm. Free.) **Great Bear Ski Valley,** 5901 E. Rice St., has skiing, snowboarding, and snowshoeing. (Call 367-4309 after Dec. 1 for lift ticket and rental prices.)

Budget motels flank 41st St. at Exit 77 off I-29. The **Select Inn,** 3500 Gateway Blvd., is a particularly good value. (☎361-1864. Continental breakfast included. Singles $38; doubles $47, with two double beds $52; AAA discounts.) There are a number of state parks nearby; **Split Rock City Park,** 20 mi. northeast in Garretson has the cheapest camping. From I-90 E, take Rte. 11 N. (Corson) and drive 10 mi. to Garretson; turn right at the sign for Devil's Gulch, and it will be on your left before the tracks. (Pit toilets and drinking water. Sites $4-6.) The ◪**Zandbroz Variety Store,** 209 S. Phillips St., offers everything from fantastic sandwiches ($2-3) and sundaes ($3-4) to free gift-wrapping of purchases. The 1920s lunch counter is built of some of the first marble to be used in the Dakotas. (☎331-5137. Open M-Sa 9am-9pm, Su noon-5pm.)

A tucked-away spot with big-name comedy acts, **The Funny Bone,** 431 N. Phillips St., showcases local talent along with Hollywood imports. (☎339-4816. Box office open M-F 9am-6pm, Sa noon-6pm. Cover $7-10.) Dance the night away at South Dakota's best dance club, the **ACME,** 305 N. Main St., where clubbers overflow from the spacious dance floor onto the back patio. (☎339-1131. 21+, W 18+. No cover. Open W 9pm-1am, Th-Sa 7pm-2am.) **Jack Rabbit Buses,** 301 N. Dakota Ave. (☎336-0885; open daily 7:30am-5pm), hop to Minneapolis (6hr., 2 per day, $47); Omaha (4hr., 2 per day, $35); and Rapid City (9hr., 1 per day, $102). **Sioux Falls Transit** buses run during the day for $1 with free transfers. (☎367-7183. Buses operate M-Sa.) **Taxi: Yellow Cab,** ☎336-1616. **Visitors Center:** in Falls Park, near the corner of Phillips and 6th. (☎367-7430. Open mid-Apr. through Sept. daily 9am-9pm, Oct. to mid-Apr. Sa-Su 9am-5pm.) Be sure to take the free climb up the Visitors Center's observation tower for a glimpse at the surrounding countryside. **Post Office:** 320 S. 2nd Ave. (☎357-5000; open M-F 7:30am-5:30pm, Sa 8am-1pm). **ZIP code:** 57104. **Area code:** 605.

THE BADLANDS   ☎ 605

When architect Frank Lloyd Wright first saw the Badlands it appeared to him as "an endless supernatural world more spiritual than earth but created out of it." Earlier explorers, when faced with the mountainous rock formations that suddenly appear out of the prarie, were less enthusiastic; "Hell with the fires out," General Alfred Sully called these arid and treacherous formations. The French (perhaps erroneously) translated the Sioux name for the area, *mako sica,* as *les mauvaises terres:* "bad lands." Some 60 million years ago, when much of the Great Plains was under water, tectonic shifts thrust up the Rockies and the Black Hills. Mountain streams deposited silt from these nascent highlands into the area now known as the Badlands, capturing and fossilizing the remains of wildlife that once wandered these flood plains in layer after multicolored layer. Erosion has carved spires and steep sills into the earth, and it is still at work today. According to geologists, the Badlands lose about 2 inches every year; at that rate they will disappear in 500,000 years—so hurry up before it's too late. Late spring and fall in the Badlands offer pleasant weather that can be a relief from the extreme temperatures of mid-summer and winter; no matter how bad it gets, though, it is always well worth a visit.

⁊ PRACTICAL INFORMATION

Badlands National Park lies about 50 mi. east of Rapid City on I-90. **Driving tours** of the park can start at either end of Rte. 240, which winds through wilderness in a 32 mi. detour off I-90 (Exit 110 or 131). The **Ben Reifel Visitors Center,** 5 mi. inside the park's northeastern entrance, serves as the Park Headquarters. (☎433-5361. Open June to mid-Aug. daily 7am-8pm; mid-Aug. to May 8am-5pm.) Another ranger station, the **White River Visitors Center,** is located 55 mi. to the southwest off Rte. 27 in the park's less-visited southern section. (☎455-2878. Open June-Aug. 10am-4pm, hrs. may vary.) Both Visitors Centers have potable water. The **entrance fee** is $10 per car, $5 per person (a free copy of *The Prairie Preamble* with trail map included). The **National Grasslands Visitors Center (Buffalo Gap),** 708 Main St., in Wall, has several films and an exhibit on the complex ecosystem of the surrounding area. (☎279-2125. Open June-Aug. daily 8am-6pm, Sept.-May 8am-4:30pm.) **Area code:** 605.

⌂◱ ACCOMMODATIONS AND FOOD

The **Badlands Inn** sits just outside the park, south of the Ben Reifel Visitors Center in Interior. The Inn offers comfortable rooms with free local calls and great sunrise views. (☎433-5401 or 800-341-8000. Singles $32-40, with 2 people $37-50; doubles $40-57.) In Wall, 35 mi. away, **The Homestead,** 113 6th Ave., offers equally comfortable rooms with cable TV and A/C along the main tourist drag. Next to the Ben Reifel Visitors Center inside the park, **Cedar Pass Lodge** rents cabins with A/C and showers. (☎433-5460. Open mid-Apr. to mid-Oct. 1 person $46, each additional person $4. Fills up early; call ahead.)

Two campgrounds lie within the park. **Cedar Pass Campground,** just south of the Ben Reifel Visitors Center, has sites with water and restrooms ($10). It's best to get there early, since it sometimes fills up by late afternoon in summer. At **Sage Creek Campground,** 13 mi. from the Pinnacles entrance south of Wall (take Sage Creek Rim Rd. off Rte. 240), you can sleep in an open field; there are restrooms, but no water and no fires allowed—but hey, it's free. **Backcountry camping** (½ mi. from the road and out of sight) allows a more intimate introduction to this austere landscape, but water must be brought along. For more info, contact one of the rangers. Wherever you sleep, don't cozy up to the bison; nervous mothers can become very protective.

At the lodge's mid-priced **restaurant** (the only one in the park), brave diners try the $3.45 buffalo burger (open May 15 to late Oct. daily 7am-8:30pm; hrs. may vary). When your stomach demands more loving fare, head to the **Cuny Table Cafe** (☎455-2957), 8 mi. west of the White River Visitor Center on Rte. 2, only a short detour to or from Wounded Knee. It's worth the drive to get the area's best Indian Tacos ($5)—home-cooked fry bread piled with veggies, beans, and beef raised in the backyard. For generous breakfasts near the Ben Reifel Visitors Center, try the **A&M Cafe,** on Rte. 44 in Interior. (☎433-5340. Open daily 6:30am-9:30pm.)

🔼 OUTDOOR ACTIVITIES

The 244,000-acre park protects large tracts of prairie and stark rock formations. The Ben Reifel Visitors Center has a video on the Badlands, as well as a wealth of info on nearby camping and activities. Park rangers offer free talks and excursions into the park daily in summer; check the handy *Prairie Preamble* for the schedule.

HIKING

Hiking is permitted throughout the entire park, although climbing on the formations is discouraged. Rangers do encourage hikers to explore the backcountry, and offer guidance in planning routes. For backcountry hikers, it's a good idea to bring a compass, a map, and lots of water. Despite the burning heat in summer, long pants are advisable to protect from poison ivy, stinging and biting insects, and the park's one venomous snake—the prairie rattlesnake. Five hiking trails begin off Loop Rd. near the Ben Reifel Visitor Center.

Door Trail (0.8 mi., 30min.) is wheelchair accessible for the first 100m. The rest of the trail winds through buttes and crevices for spectacular views of the surrounding country-side. Self-guiding brochure (50¢) available at the start of the trail.

Window Trail, more of a scenic overlook than an actual hike, consists of a wheelchair accessible ramp with a splendid view.

Cliff Shelf Nature Trail (0.5 mi., 40min.) also sells self-guiding brochures (50¢). Half of the trail is wooded and unpaved. Wooden steps connect this less-traveled, tranquil half to the trodden wooden plank path.

Notch Trail (1.5 mi., 1½-2hr.) demands sure footing and a willingness to climb a shaky ladder at a 45° angle. Not for the faint of heart. The trail blazes around narrow ledges before making its way to the grand finale: an unbelievable view of the Cliff Shelf and White River Valley.

Saddle Pass Trail (0.2 mi., 30min.), for more experienced hikers, involves a quick scramble up the Badlands Wall before connecting with the longer and more level **Castle** and **Medicine Root Trails.**

DRIVING

A scenic drive along Rte. 240/Loop Rd. is an excellent way to see the park. The road makes its way through rainbow-colored bluffs and around hairpin turns, all the while affording views of many distinct types of Badlands terrain. The Loop Rd. serves as an excellent introduction to the entire northern portion of the park. The gravel Sage Creek Rim Rd., west of Rte. 240, has fewer people and more animals; highlights are Roberts Prairie Dog Town and the park's herds of bison and antelope. Across the river from the Sage Creek campground lies another prairie dog town and some popular bison territory. Fresh buffalo chips reveal recent activity.

RIDING

Travelers interested in exploring the area on horseback can check out **Badlands Trail Rides,** 1.5 mi. south of the Ben Reifel Visitors Center on Rte. 377. While the trails do not lead into Badlands National Park itself, they cover territory on the park's immediate outskirts. (☎433-5453 or 386-4470. Open in summer daily 8am-7pm. $20 for 1hr. ride; $15 for 30min. ride.)

RAPID CITY   ☎605

Rapid City's location makes it a convenient base from which to explore the Black Hills and the Badlands. In summer, the area welcomes three million tourists, over 60 times the city's permanent population. Pick up a map of the Rapid City Circle Tour at the Civic Center or at any motel; the route leads you to numerous free attractions and includes a jaunt up Skyline Drive for a bird's-eye view of the city and the seven concrete dinosaurs of Dinosaur Park. Runners, walkers, and bikers should traverse the eight-mile **Rapid City Riverwalk** along Rapid Creek.

HAVE YOU DUG WALL DRUG? There is almost no way to visit the Badlands without being importuned by advertisements from **Wall Drug,** 510 Main St., a towering monument to the success of saturation advertising. (☎279-2175. Open daily 6am-10pm; mid-Sept. to Apr. 6:30am-6pm.) After seeing billboards for Wall Drug from as far as Greenland and Amsterdam, Holland, travelers feel obligated to make a stop in Wall to see what all the ruckus is about—much as they must have done 60 years ago, when Wall first enticed parched travelers with free water.

Rapid City accommodations are more expensive during the summer. Make reservations; motels often fill weeks in advance, especially during the first two weeks in August, when nearby Sturgis hosts its annual motorcycle rally. Winter travelers are in luck because of an abundance of off-season bargains (Sept.-May). **Big Sky Motel,** 48 Tower Rd., is located just south of town on a service road off Mt. Rushmore St. (large billboards guide the way). Many rooms have great views, but can be chilly. (☎348-3200 or 800-318-3208. Singles $40; doubles $56; lower off-season.) **Camping** is available at **Badlands National Park, Black Hills National Forest,** and **Custer State Park.**

The Millstone Family Restaurant, 2010 W. Main St., cooks up large, hot portions of turkey, pot roast, chicken, and ham. The excellent salad bar features bread pudding, fresh cheeses, and soups. (☎343-5824. Open daily 6am-11pm.) The cosmopolitan **Once Upon a Vine,** 513 6th St., offers the city's best wine selection. The chef puts together delectable sandwiches ($4.50-5.75) for gourmet taste buds. The curried chicken salad on hazelnut bread ($4.75) is superb. (☎343-7802. Open M-Sa 11am-2pm, 5-9pm; F-Sa until 10pm.) Nightlife lines **Main St.** between 6th and Mt. Rushmore St. For a beer as black as the Hills, toss back a Smokejumper Stout ($3) at the **Firehouse Brewing Co.,** 610 Main St., *the* bar in Rapid City. Located in a restored 1915 firehouse, the company brews five beers in-house and serves sandwiches, burgers, and salads for $6-10. (☎348-1915. Open M-Th 11am-midnight, F-Sa 11am-2am, Su 4-10pm.) After dinner at the firehouse, head upstairs to **Fat Boys Saloon** for pool, foosball, music, and more beer. (☎348-1915. Open M-Sa 7pm-2am.)

Driving in Rapid City is easy; roads are laid out in a sensible grid pattern. **St. Joseph St.** and **Main St.** are the main east-west thoroughfares, and Mt. Rushmore/ Rte. 16 is the main north-south route. Many north-south roads are numbered, and numbers go up as you move from east to west, beginning at **East Blvd.** East streets are denoted as such (St. Joseph St. becomes East St. Joseph, etc.). **Jack Rabbit Lines** scurries east from the Milo Barber Transportation Center, 333 6th St. (☎348-3300), downtown, with one bus daily to Pierre (4hr., $36), Sioux Falls (10hr., $86), and Omaha (12hr., $105). **Powder River Lines,** also in the center, runs to Billings (8hr., 1 per day, $60) and Cheyenne (8hr., 1 per day, $65). Station open M-F 8am-5pm, Sa-Su 10am-noon and 2-5pm. **Grayline Tours** leads regional tours based out of Rapid City. Take a flight from **Rapid City Regional Airport** (☎393-9924), off Rte. 44 8½ mi. east of the city. **Rapid Ride** runs **buses** M-F 6:35am-6:05pm. (☎394-6631. $1, seniors 50¢. Pick up schedule at terminal in the Milo Barber Transportation center.) **Rapid City Chamber of Commerce and Visitors Information Center:** 444 Mt. Rushmore Rd. N., in the Civic Center. (☎343-1744. Open M-F 8am-5pm.) **Post Office:** 500 East Blvd., several blocks east of downtown. (☎394-8600. Window service M-F 8am-5:30pm, Sa 8:30am-12:30pm.) **ZIP code:** 57701. **Area code:** 605.

BLACK HILLS REGION

The Black Hills, named for the dark hue that distance lends the green pines covering the hills, have long been considered sacred by the Sioux. The Treaty of 1868 gave the Black Hills and the rest of South Dakota west of the Missouri River to the tribe. But when gold was discovered in the 1870s, the US government snatched back the land. The dueling monuments of Mt. Rushmore (a national memorial, see p. 558) and Crazy Horse (an independent project, see p. 559) strikingly illustrate the clash of the two cultures that reside among these hills. Today, the area, which contains a trove of natural treasures, including Custer State Park, Wind Cave National Park, and Jewel Cave National Monument, attracts millions of visitors annually.

BLACK HILLS NATIONAL FOREST ☎ 605

Most of the land in the Black Hills is part of the Black Hills National Forest and exercises the "multiple use" principle—mining, logging, ranching, and recreation all take place in close proximity. Must-see attractions like reptile farms and Flintstone campgrounds lurk around every bend of the sinuous roads. The forest itself provides opportunities for backcountry hiking and camping, as do park-run campgrounds and private tent sites. In the hills, the **Visitors Center,** on I-385 at Pactola Lake, has details on backcountry camping and $7 waterproof maps. (☎343-8755. Open June-Sept. daily 8:30am-6pm.) **Backcountry camping** in the national forest is free. Camp 1 mi. away from any campground or Visitors Center and at least 200 ft. off the side of the road (leave your car in a parking lot or pull off); open fires are prohibited, but controlled fires in provided grates are allowed. Good campgrounds include **Pactola,** on the Pactola Reservoir just south of the junction of Rte. 44 and U.S. 385; **Sheridan Lake,** 5 mi. northeast of Hill City on U.S. 385 (north entrance for group sites, south entrance for individuals); and **Roubaix Lake,** 14 mi. south of Lead on U.S. 385 (sites for all three $16-18). All National Forest campgrounds are quiet and wooded, offering fishing, swimming, and pit toilets, but no hookups. (Call 877-444-6777 for reservations.) The national forest extends into Wyoming with a **ranger station** in Sundance. (☎307-283-1361. Open M-F 7:30am-5pm.) The Wyoming side of the forest permits campfires, allows horses, and draws fewer visitors. The hostel in Deadwood (see p. 561) is the cheapest indoor accommodation in these parts.

I-90 skirts the northern border of the Black Hills from Spearfish in the west to Rapid City in the east; **U.S. 385** twists from Hot Springs in the south to Deadwood in the north. The road system that winds through the hills covers beautiful territory. Don't expect to get anywhere fast, though—these tortuous routes will hold you to half the speed of the interstate. Pick up a $7 map at ranger station or Visitors Centers. The off season in the Black Hills offers stellar skiing and snowmobiling (see **Lead,** p. 561), but many attractions close or have limited hours, and most resorts and campgrounds close for the winter. Unless you are astride a flashy piece of chrome and steel, steer clear of the Hills in early August, when over 12,000 motorcyclists converge on the area for the **Sturgis Rally** (☎605-347-9190; Aug. 5-11, 2001).

Of the **Grayline tours,** P.O. Box 1106, Rapid City, 57709, tour #1 is the most complete. Make reservations or call 1hr. before departure for pickup from motels in Rapid City. (☎342-4461. Runs daily mid-May to mid-Oct., 9hr., $36 includes admission prices.) The **Black Hills Visitor Information Center,** Exit 61 off I-90, in Rapid City, has info. (☎355-3700. Open daily 8am-8pm; off-season 8am-5pm; hours subject to change.) **Area code:** 605.

MOUNT RUSHMORE ☎ 605

Mt. Rushmore National Memorial stands alone among all the tourist sites in the regions. Historian Doane Robinson originally conceived of this "shrine of democracy" in 1923 as a memorial for local Western heroes; sculptor Gutzon Borglum chose four presidents instead. Borglum initially encountered opposition from those who felt the work of God could not be improved, but the tenacious sculptor defended the project's size, insisting that "there is not a monument in this country as big as a snuff box." Throughout the Depression work progressed slowly; a great setback occurred when the nearly completed face of Thomas Jefferson had to be blasted off Washington's right side and moved to his left due to insufficient granite. In 1941, the 60 ft. heads of George Washington, Thomas Jefferson, Theodore Roosevelt, and Abraham Lincoln were finished. The 465 ft. tall bodies were never completed, as work ceased when US funds were diverted to WWII, but the millions of visitors who come here every year don't seem to mind the disembodiment.

From Rapid City, take U.S. 16 and 16A to Keystone and Rte. 244 up to the mountain. Remote parking is free, but the lot fills early. There is an $8 per car "annual parking permit" for the lot adjacent to the entrance. The **info center** (☎574-3198) details the monument's history and has ranger tours. A state-of-the-art **Visitors Center** (☎574-3165) chronicles the history of the monument, the lives of the featured presidents, and shows a film explaining how the carving was accomplished. About 90% of the sculpting was done with dynamite. (Both info center and Visitors Center open June-Aug. daily 8am-10pm; off-season hours generally 8am-5pm.)

From the Visitors Center, along the **Presidential Trail**, it is 0.6 mi. and over 300 steps down on a planked wooden path to **Borglum's Studio.** Here visitors can stare at Borglum's full-bodied plaster model of the carving as well as tools and designs for Mt. Rushmore (open May-Sept. daily 9am-6pm). During the summer, the **Mt. Rushmore Memorial Amphitheater** hosts a monument-lighting program. A patriotic speech and film commence at 9pm, and light floods the monument 9:30-10:30pm. Trail lights are extinguished at 11pm.

Horsethief Campground lies 4 mi. west of Mt. Rushmore on Rte. 244. Former President George Bush fished here in 1993; rumor has it that the lake was overstocked with fish to guarantee his success. (☎877-444-6777. Water and flush toilets in the woods. Lakeside sites $20. Sites set back from the lake $16. Reservations recommended on weekends and during peak times.) The rather commercialized **Mt. Rushmore KOA/Palmer Gulch Lodge** lies 7 mi. west of Mt. Rushmore on Rte. 244. With campsites for two ($25, with water and electricity $32) or kabins ($45-52) come showers, stoves, pool, laundry, and free shuttle service to Mt. Rushmore. (☎574-2525 or 800-562-8503. Open May-Oct. Make reservations early, up to 2 months in advance for cabins and special requests.)

CRAZY HORSE MEMORIAL   ☎605

According to sculptor Korczak Ziolkowski, "When the legends die, the dreams end. When the dreams end, there is no more greatness." The Crazy Horse Memorial, which at its completion will be the world's largest sculpture, concretizes these words as a living tribute to the revered Native American leader. A famed warrior, Crazy Horse garnered respect by refusing to sign treaties or live on a government reservation. In 1877, Crazy Horse was treacherously stabbed by a white soldier.

As a reminder to whites that native peoples have their own heroes, Lakota Chief Henry Standing Bear commissioned Ziolkowski to sculpt the memorial in 1947. To no one's surprise, the project didn't receive any initial government funding. The sculptor went solo for years, later refusing $10 million in federal funding. Today, seven of his ten children carry on the work. Crazy Horse's completed face was unveiled in June 1998 (all four of the Rushmore heads could fit inside it), and part of his arm is now visible; eventually, his entire torso and head will be carved into the mountain. The memorial, 17 mi. southwest of Mt. Rushmore on U.S. 16/385, includes the Indian Museum of North America, the Sculptor's Studio-Home, and the Native American Educational and Cultural Center where native crafts are displayed and sold. The orientation center shows a moving 17min. video. (☎673-4681; www.crazyhorse.org. Open daily 7am-dark; Oct.-Apr. 8am until dark. Monument lit nightly, about 10min. after sunset, for 1hr. $8, $19 per carload; with a senior $7/$14; under 6 free. $2 AAA discount per car. Free coffee at the restaurant.)

WIND CAVE AND JEWEL CAVE   ☎605

In the cavern-riddled Black Hills, the subterranean scenery often rivals the above-ground sites. Local entrepreneurs will attempt to lure you into the holes in their backyards, but the government owns the area's prime underground real estate: **Wind Cave National Park** (☎745-4600), adjacent to Custer State Park on U.S. 385, and **Jewel Cave National Monument** (☎673-2288, 800-967-2283 for tour reservations), 11 mi. west of the U.S. 385/U.S. 16 junction in Custer. There is no public transportation to the caves. Bring a sweater on all tours—Wind Cave remains a constant 53°F, Jewel Cave 49°F. **Area code:** 605.

WIND CAVE

Wind Cave was discovered in 1881 by Tom Bingham, who heard the sound of air rushing out of the cave's only natural entrance. In fact, the wind was so strong it knocked his hat off. Air forcefully gusts in and out of the cave due to outside pressure changes. When Tom returned to show his friends the cave, his hat got sucked in. Today, scientists estimate that only 5% of a potential 2000 mi. of passageways has been discovered. Currently, 100 mi. have been explored, and geologists have even found a lake over 200 ft. long in the cave's deepest depths. Wind Cave is known for its "boxwork," a honeycomb-like lattice of calcite covering its walls. There are five tours; all have more than 150 stairs. The **Garden of Eden Tour** is the least strenuous. (1hr., 7 per day June-Aug. 8:40am-5:30pm. Call for off-season times. $6, seniors and ages 6-15 $3.) The **Natural Entrance Tour** and the **Fairgrounds Tour** are both moderately strenuous and one or the other leaves about every 30min. (1¼hr. and 1½hr. respectively, June-Aug. 9am-6:30pm. Call for off-season times. $8, seniors and ages 6-16 $4.) Light your own way on the more rigorous **Candlelight Tour.** (Limited to 10 people. 2 hr. June-Aug. 10:30am and 1:30pm. $9, seniors and kids $4.50. Under 8 not admitted. "Non-slip" soles on shoes required.) The rather difficult **Caving Tour,** an intro to basic caving, is limited to ten people ages 16 and over who can fit through a 10 in. high passageway. (Parental consent required for under 18. 4hr. tour at 1pm. $20, seniors $10. Reservations required.) In the afternoon, all tours fill about 1hr. ahead of time, so buy tickets early (☎800-967-2283). **Wind Cave National Park Visitors Center,** RR1, P.O. Box 190, Hot Springs 57747, can provide more info. (☎745-4600. Open June to mid-Aug. daily 8am-7:30pm; winter hours vary. Parts of some tours are wheelchair accessible.) The **Elk Mountain Campground,** part of Wind Cave National Park, rarely fills up during the summer, though it is an excellent site in the woods with potable water and restrooms. (Sites $10.)

JEWEL CAVE

In contrast to nearby Wind Cave's boxwork, the walls of this labyrinth (the 2nd longest cave in the US) are covered with a layer of calcite crystal. The ½ mi. **Scenic Tour** includes 723 stairs and a peek at a 27 ft. cave formation that bears a striking resemblance to a strip of bacon. (Leaves roughly every 20min. 8:30am-6pm; in winter call ahead. $8, ages 6-16 $4.) The **Historic Tour** is more interesting. (Every hr. 9am-5pm; in winter call ahead. $8, ages 6-16 $4.) Reservations, pants, a long-sleeve shirt, knee-pads, sturdy boots, and a willingness to get down and dirty are required for the 4hr. **Spelunking Tour,** limited to five people ages 16 and up. (Runs June-Aug. daily 12:30pm. $20; you must be able to fit through an opening only 8½ in. by 2 ft.) The **Visitors Center** has more info. (☎673-2288. Open daily 8am-7:30pm; mid-Oct. to mid-May 8am-4:30pm.) Behind the Visitors Center, Jewel Cave offers visitors two alluring hiking tails. The **Roof Trail** is short, but provides a memorable introduction to the Black Hills' beauty. The bucolic 3½ mi. **Canyons Trail** winds through small canyons, through fields, and up forested hills before returning to the Visitors Center.

CUSTER STATE PARK   ☎605

Peter Norbeck, governor of South Dakota in the late 1910s, loved to hike among the thin, towering rock formations that haunt the area south of Sylvan Lake and Mt. Rushmore. In order to preserve the land, he created Custer State Park. The spectacular **Needles Hwy. (Rte. 87)** within the park follows his favorite hiking route (see below). Norbeck designed this road to be especially narrow and winding so that newcomers could experience the pleasures of discovery. **Iron Mountain Road (U.S. 16A)** from Mount Rushmore to near the Norbeck Visitors Center (see below) takes you through a series of tunnels, "pigtail" curves, and switchbacks. The park's **Wildlife Loop Road** brings you past prairie dog towns, popular bison wallows, and wilderness areas that are near prime hiking and camping territory. If you are "lucky," one of Custer's **1500 bison** will come up to your car. Don't get out; they are dangerous.

The **entrance fee** is $5 per person, $10 per carload for a seven-day pass from May to October. (Nov.-Apr. $2 per person, $5 per car). The **Peter Norbeck Visitors Center,** on U.S. 16A, ½ mi. west of the State Game Lodge, serves as the park's info center. (☎255-4464. Open June-Aug. daily 8am-8pm; early Sept. to Oct. and May 9am-5pm.) Eight **campgrounds** in the park charge $12-16 and have showers and restrooms, but no hookups. Primitive camping ($2 per night) is available in the **French Creek Natural Area;** the Visitors Center can give you more info. Over 200 of the park's 400+ sites are reserveable. The entire park fills by 3pm in the summer. (Call 800-710-2267 daily

June-Sept. 7am-7pm, early Sept. to late May 7am-5pm. $5 non-resident users fee.) The **Elk Mountain Campground** in Wind Cave National Park is an excellent alternative and rarely fills up. Motels in the surrounding area include the convenient **Chalet Motel**, on 16A just west of the Stockade Lake entrance to the park. (☎673-2393 or 800-649-9088. Call ahead. Rooms start at $42.) Food is available at all park lodges, but the general stores in Custer, Hermosa, and Keystone generally charge less. **The Bank Coffee House**, 548 Mt. Rushmore Rd., serves $3-5 sandwiches and $3 pie. (☎605-673-5698. Open June-Aug. daily 6am-8pm, Sept.-May M-Sa 6am-9pm.)

At 7242 ft., **Harney Peak** is the highest point east of the Rockies and west of the Pyrenees. At the top are a few mountain goats and a great view of the Black Hills. Bring water and food, wear good shoes, and leave as early in the morning as possible. For less extreme hikers, the park provides 30 lower-altitude trails. You can also hike, fish, paddle boats, or canoe at popular **Sylvan Lake**, on Needles Hwy. (☎574-2561. Kayaks $4 per person per 30min.) Horse rides are available at **Blue Bell Lodge**, on Rte. 87 about 8 mi. from the south entrance. (☎255-4531, stable 255-4571. 1hr. for $18, under 12 $15.) Mountain bikes can be rented at the **Legion Lake Resort**, on U.S. 16A 6 mi. west of the Visitors Center. (☎255-4521. $8.50 per hour, $22 per half-day, $36 per day.) All lakes and streams permit fishing with a daily license ($7; non-residents $12; 3-day non-resident license $30). Licenses and equipment are available at the area lodges. Trout fishing is best in summer. The strong granite of the Needles makes for great rock climbing. For more info contact **Granite Sports/Sylvan Rocks** at the corner of Elm and Main St. in Hill City. (☎574-2121 or 574-2425. Open daily 8:30am-8:30pm; off-season hours vary.) **Area code:** 605.

LEAD ☎605

Lead (rhymes with *bead*, not *bed*) is actually named for the ore veins that marked the path to gold in the mines of this town. The **Black Hills Mining Museum**, 323 West Main St., offers a 50min. guided tour of Black Hills mining history as well as a 20min. video about area mines. Those who want the feeling of panning for gold (with uncharacteristic 100% success) can pay an extra $4 per person for **gold panning** as part of their tour. The small museum also houses exhibits on cultural history and technological advances. (☎584-1605. Open in summer daily 9am-5pm; in winter Tu-Sa 9am-4:30pm. $4.75, seniors $4.25, students $3.75, families $15.) The **Ponderosa Motor Lodge**, on U.S. 14A just outside of Lead heading toward Deadwood, offers a variety of cabins nestled among the pines and stocked with TVs and fridges but no phones. (☎584-3321. $50-65 depending on season and size.) **Hanna Campground** lies about 9 mi. from town off U.S. 85; turn onto the dirt road just south of the junction with 14A at Cheyenne Crossing (pit toilets and water; sites $11; open mid-May to mid-Sept.). Interesting sandwich combos ($4.75-9) are the main fare at the **Stampmill Saloon**, 305 W. Main St. (☎584-1984; open Su-Th 11am-9pm, F-Sa 11am-10pm).

Wintertime in the Black Hills provides fine skiing and snowboarding opportunities. **Terry Peak Ski Area** and **Deer Mountain** are both west of Lead off U.S. 85. (Terry: ☎584-2165 or 342-7609. Lift ticket $32, under 13 $25, over 69 and under 5 free. Ski rental $18, junior ski rental $12, snowboard rental $25. Deer: ☎584-3230 or 800-410-3337. Lift ticket weekends and holidays $24, children $19. Weekdays $20/$16. Ski rental $15, snowboard rental $22.50.) **Lead Chamber of Commerce:** 640 W. Main St. (☎584-1100; open M-F 9am-3pm). **Post Office:** 329 W. Main St. (☎584-2110. Open M-F 8:15am-4:15pm, Sa 10am-noon.) **ZIP code:** 57754. **Area code:** 605.

DEADWOOD ☎605

Continue along Main St. from Lead for 3 mi., and you'll find yourself in Deadwood. Gunslingers **Wild Bill Hickock** and **Calamity Jane** sauntered into this town during the height of the Gold Rush. Bill stayed just long enough—two months—to spend eternity here. They lie side-by-side in the **Mt. Moriah Cemetery**, just south of downtown. ($1, ages 5-12 50¢—is nothing sacred?) If you have a car, take Cemetery St. off of Rte. 85 and follow the signs. Hiking up the hill on foot is quite a challenge, but **Alkali Ike Tours** will drive you on their 1hr. narrated bus tour. Tickets are sold at the booth on Main St., just outside Saloon #10. (☎578-3147. July-Aug. 5 tours per day. $6, ages

7-13 $3, under 7 free.) The forever immortalized **Saloon #10**, 657 Main St., is where Hickock was shot holding black aces and eights, the infamous "dead man's hand." Every summer the shooting is re-enacted on location. (☎578-3346. 1, 3, 5, and 7pm.) At 7:45pm Tuesday through Sunday outside of Saloon #10, assassin Jack McCall is apprehended by authorities, and those willing to pay $8 can follow the angry mob to a comical re-enactment of **McCall's trial** in the **Old Town Hall**, 12 Lee St. (☎578-3583 for ticket reservations. Pick up reserved tickets at the Old Town Hall.) If you still can't get enough, there are **random shootouts** along Main St. at 2, 4, and 6pm. Listen for gunshots and the sound of Calamity Jane's whip.

If Lead is where the gold is found, then Deadwood is where the gold is lost. It's a challenge to avoid **gambling** entertainment in Deadwood—casinos line **Main St.**, and even the most innocent-looking establishments may hide slot machines within. At the **Buffalo Saloon**, 658 Main St. (☎578-1300), you can gamble 24hr. a day, seven days a week, and there's live music outside the Stockade. For the fun of gambling without the high stakes, many casinos offer nickel slot machines. **Free parking** is available in the Sherman St. parking lot on Rte. 85 heading towards Lead. If you lose most of your money at the gambling tables, you can probably still afford to stay at ▧**Hostelling International Black Hills at the Penny Motel (HI-AYH)**, 818 Upper Main St. Look for the Penny Motel sign. A great kitchen, comfortable beds, and super clean rooms await. (☎578-1842 or 877-565-8140. Dorms $12, nonmembers $15. One private room $36. Motel singles $49; doubles $56.) The **Whistler Gulch Campground**, off U.S. 85, has a pool, laundry facilities, and showers. (☎578-2042 or 800-704-7139. Sites $20, full hookup $30.) Casinos monopolize the food and dining market; you might have to shop around to find a decent meal. The **Deadwood History and Information Center**, 3 Siever St. (☎800-999-1876), is open in summer daily 8am-7pm and in winter 8am-5pm. **Area code:** 605.

SPEARFISH   ☎ 605

Located on the northern edge of the Black Hills, Spearfish makes a pleasant, short stop on the way to or from the Black Hills. Nearby, the spectacular **Spearfish Canyon Scenic Byway** (U.S. 14A) winds through 20 miles of forest along Spearfish Creek. Amazing views of the Black Hills, waterfalls, and picnic spots await around every corner of the Byway. The site where *Dances with Wolves* was filmed is marked by a small sign and lies 2¾ miles west of U.S. 14A on Rte. 222.

There are no trout native to the Black Hills, but you can feed tens of thousands of hatchery-raised fish at the unique **D.C. Booth National Fish Hatchery**, 423 Hatchery St. View the Booth home, stroll through the manicured gardens, or check out the old railroad "fish car." (☎642-7730. Grounds open daily dawn to dusk. Buildings open May-Sept. M-F 9am-6pm.) Dick Termes paints rotating spheres and calls his work, cleverly enough, Termespheres; more than 30 examples are on display at the **Termesphere Gallery.** Go south on Main St. and follow it as it becomes Colorado Blvd.; turn right on Christensen Dr. and go about 1½ mi. (☎642-4805. Open M-Sa 9am-5pm or just show up; if they're home, you can look.) The **Passion Play Amphitheater** attracts large audiences with the **Passion Play,** which recounts the last week of Jesus's life. The outdoor show features 23 professional actors, Spearfish townspeople as extras, and live camels and donkeys. (☎800-457-0160. Performances every Su, Tu, and Th from the beginning of June to late Aug. Reserved tickets $12-18, unreserved seats $10, under 12 half-price. Tickets are sold only at the amphitheater.)

The weary traveler can ring in at **Bell's Motor Lodge**, on Main St. at the east edge of town. (☎642-3812. Open May-Sept. Free local calls, TV, pool. Singles $36; doubles $48.) The **Canyon Gateway Hotel,** south of town on U.S. 14A, offers cozy rooms in a pleasant setting. (☎642-3402 or 800-281-3402. No phones. Singles $41; doubles $45.) Three and four miles west of U.S. 14A on Rte. 222 are two spectacular campgrounds: **Rod and Gun Campground** and **Timon Campground** (pit toilets and potable water; sites $11). Right in town, at the southern end of Canyon St. two blocks west of Main St., the **Spearfish City Campground**, 404 S. Canyon, has 57 sites with full hookups. (☎642-1340. Showers 25¢. Reservations needed Sa-Su. Sites for 1 person $12, each additional person $1; full hookup $21.) For authentic English pub fare like fish and chips, trot on over to the **Knight's Cellar,** 404 Main St. Live music by local artists on Wednesday, Friday, and Saturday. (☎642-4292. Open daily 3-11pm.) The **Spearfish Ranger Station,** 2014 N. Main St., has free maps and hiking advice. (☎642-4622. Open M-F 8am-5pm, Sa 8am-4:30pm; in winter M-F 8am-4:30pm; foyer with maps and info open 24hr.) The **Chamber of Commerce:** 106 W. Kansas St., at Main St. (☎642-2626 or 800-626-8013. Open June-Aug. M-F 8am-6pm, Sept.-May M-F 8am-5pm.) **Post Office:** 120 Yankee St., north of downtown off North Ave. (☎642-2521. Open M-F 8:30am-4:30pm, Sa 9:30am-noon.) **ZIP code:** 57783. **Area code:** 605.

IOWA

Named for the Ioway Native Americans who farmed along the state's many river banks, Iowa contains one fourth of all US Grade A farmland. Farming *is* the way of life in Iowa, a land where men are measured by the size of their John Deere tractor, not the by the kind of car they drive. Fertile and beautiful, the state ripples with gentle hills. Created by wind-blown quartz silt, the striking Loess Hills in the west are a geological rarity found only in Iowa and China. The Mississippi River Valley in Eastern Iowa offers amazing views of the Mighty Miss from limestone bluffs. Despite its distinctly American landscape, Iowa preserves its European heritage in small towns that maintain their German, Dutch, and Scandinavian traditions.

⑫ PRACTICAL INFORMATION

Capital: Des Moines.
Visitor info: Iowa Dept. of Economic Development, 200 E. Grand Ave., Des Moines 50309 (☎800-345-4692 or 888-472-6035; www.traveliowa.com).
Postal Abbreviation: IA. **Sales Tax:** 5%; some towns add an additional 1-2%.

DES MOINES   ☎515

Des Moines suffers from an image problem. Around the city, residents are silently glum about the condition of the capital, apparently oblivious to the renewal their city has experienced in the last decade. Like many American cities, Des Moines has experienced a rebound of late: the Skywalk, a third-floor maze of passageways connecting buildings downtown, is without equal in the Midwest. A beautiful system of interconnecting parks traces the area's rivers and presents a welcome contrast to the now-bustling downtown area. From the World Pork Expo (June 6-8, 2002) to world-class art, Des Moines's offerings run the gamut from kitsch to class.

⌐ TRANSPORTATION

I-80 and U.S. 65 encircle Des Moines; I-235 bisects the circle.

Airport: Des Moines International, 5800 Fleur Dr. at Army Post Rd. (☎256-5195), 5 mi. southwest of downtown; take bus #8 "Havens" M-F. Taxi to downtown around $10.

Buses: Greyhound, 1107 Keo Way (☎243-1773 or 800-231-222) at 12th St., just northwest of downtown; take bus #4 "Urbandale." To: Iowa City (2hr.; 7 per day; $22, Sa-Su $24); Omaha (2hr.; 9 per day; $24, Sa-Su $32); Chicago (8hr.; 12 per day; $41, Sa-Su $44); and St. Louis (10hr.; 5 per day; $66, Sa-Su $70). Station open 24hr.

Public Transit: Metropolitan Transit Authority (MTA), 1100 MTA Lane (☎283-8100), south of the 9th St. viaduct. Open M-F 8am-5pm. Buses run M-F approximately 6am-10pm, Sa 6:45am-5:50pm. Fare $1, seniors (except M-F 3-6pm) and disabled persons 50¢ with MTA ID card; transfers 10¢. Routes converge at 6th and Walnut St. Maps at the MTA office, Convention and Visitors Bureau, or any Dahl's or Hy-Vee.

Taxis: Yellow Cab, ☎243-1111.

Car Rental: Enterprise, 5601 Fleur Dr. just outside the airport (☎285-2525), with speedy airport pickup. $42 with 150 mi. per day, 30¢ each additional mi. Weekend special: F-M $10 per day with 150 in-state mi. per day. Must be 21+ with major credit card. No surcharge for under 25. Open M-F 7:30am-6pm, Sa 9am-1pm.

■🔢 ORIENTATION AND PRACTICAL INFORMATION

Numbered streets run north-south, named streets east-west. Addresses begin with zero downtown at the **Des Moines River** and increase as you move east or west; **Grand Ave.** divides addresses north-south. Other east-west thoroughfares are **Locust St.,** and moving north, **University Ave.** (home to Drake University), and **Hickman Rd.** Note that Des Moines and West Des Moines are different places, and the numbered streets within each are not the same.

Visitor info: Greater Des Moines Convention and Visitors Bureau, 405 6th Ave. (☎286-4960 or 800-451-2625), along Locust in the Skywalk. Open M-F 8:30am-5pm. Up a few blocks is the **Chamber of Commerce,** 700 Locust (☎286-4950; open M 9:30am-5pm, Tu-Th 8am-5pm, F 8am-4pm).

Internet access: Des Moines Public Library, 100 Locust (☎283-4152), and all other branches. Free 1hr. per day. It's best to sign up one day in advance, particularly on M. Open M-W 10am-9pm, Th-F 10am-6pm, Sa 10am-5pm.

Post Office: 1165 2nd Ave., downtown just north of I-235 (☎283-7585). Open M-F 7:30am-5:30pm. **ZIP code:** 50318. **Area code:** 515.

🛏 ACCOMMODATIONS

Finding cheap accommodations in Des Moines is usually no problem, though you should make reservations at least one month in advance for visits during the State Fair in August and during the high school sports tournament season in March Beware of the 7% hotel tax. Several campgrounds can be found west of the city off I-80 and cheap motels are sprinkled along I-80 and Merle Hay Rd., 5 mi. northwest of downtown. Take bus #4 "Urbandale" or #6 "West 9th" from downtown.

🏚 **The Carter House Inn,** 640 20th St. (☎288-7850), at Woodland St. in historic Sherman Hill. The Nelson family has converted this old Victorian home into a beautifully furnished and immaculately clean B&B. A large home-cooked breakfast is served on fine china, by candlelight, to classical music. Rooms $65-75. Student discounts around 15% can be arranged if extra rooms are available. Only 4 rooms available; call ahead.

Motel 6, 4817 Fleur Dr. (☎287-6364), at the airport, 10min. south of downtown. Newly renovated rooms with free local calls and HBO. Singles Su-Th $40, F-Sa $45; doubles $46/$52. AARP discount available. Two wheelchair-accessible rooms.

Iowa State Fairgrounds Campgrounds, E. 30th St. (☎262-3111 or 800-545-3247; fax 262-6906), at Grand Ave. Take bus #1 "Fairgrounds" to the Grand Ave. gate and follow East Grand Ave. straight east through the park. No fires. Check-in until 10pm. Make reservations well in advance, especially in summer. Open mid-Apr. to Oct. Sites with water and electricity $12; full hookup $15. Fee collected in the morning.

🍴 FOOD

Good eating places tend to congregate on **Court Ave.** downtown. West Des Moines also boasts an assortment of budget eateries along Grand Ave. and in the antique-filled **Historic Valley Jct.** The supermarkets **Dahl's** and **Hy-Vee** are sprinkled throughout the city and have cafeterias that serve hot food for cheap. At Dahl's, breakfast is under $3 and lunch and dinner under $5. Hy-Vee is a little more expensive, but offers an all-you-can-eat Chinese lunch and dinner buffet ($5). The popular **Farmers Market** (☎243-6625) sells loads of fresh fruit and vegetables, baked goods, and ethnic food on Saturday mornings (mid-May to Oct. 7am-noon), and Court Ave. between 1st and 4th St. is blocked off for the extravaganza.

■ **Big Daddy's Bar-B-Q,** 1000 E. 14th St. (☎262-0352), sends 5 or 6 people to the hospital every year with its killer sauces, which, according to locals, are "just that damn hot." The especially adventurous—or insane—are encouraged to try the "Last Supper," "ER," or "Code Blue" sauces; the "Final Answer" is reserved for only the highest pain thresholds. Rib platters for two $9; beef, pork, or chicken sandwiches $4; cornbread 75¢ per slice. Open Tu-Sa 11am-5pm; takeout Tu-Th 11am-6pm, F-Sa 11am-7pm.

Bauder's Pharmacy and Fountain, 3802 Ingersoll (☎255-1124), at 38th St. With an authentic lunch counter, soda fountain, and old-fashioned ice cream, Bauder's makes a convincing stab at nostalgia. Ice cream $1.25 per scoop; shakes, floats, and malts $2.50. Bauder's also sells simple sandwiches for $2-3. Open M-F 8:30am-7pm, Sa 9am-5pm, Su 10am-3pm.

Stella's Blue Sky Diner, 400 Locust St. (☎246-1953), at the Skywalk level in the Capital Sq. Mall. At this old-school diner, you can slide into a vinyl booth and enjoy classic food while enveloped in pure 50s tack. Breakfast $3-5; 10 different hamburgers all under $5. Open M-Th 6:30am-6pm, Sa 8am-6pm.

◉ SIGHTS

Renovations on the inspiring gold-domed **State Capitol** began in 1999 and are slated to be completed in 2003. The view of the Des Moines skyline from the Capitol is a must-see. (☎281-5591. Open M-F 8am-5pm, Sa-Su 8am-4pm. Free tours M-Sa 9:30am-2:30pm; call for exact times.) Built on urban renewal land east of the Des Moines River, the geodesic greenhouse and outdoor gardens of the **Botanical Center,** 909 E. River Dr., house exotic flora and fauna. (☎323-8900. Open M-Th 10am-6pm, F 10am-9pm, Sa-Su 10am-5pm. $1.50, students 50¢, seniors 75¢.) Located at the base of the Capitol complex parking lot, the **Iowa Historical Building,** 600 E. Locust St., features exhibits on topics as diverse as soil profiles, coal mining, Native American culture, and the history of the miniskirt. Check out the Wall of Iowa Pride, full of self-esteem-boosting affirmations from Iowans great and small. (☎281-5111. Open Tu-Sa 9am-4:30pm, Su noon-4:30pm. Free.)

Most cultural sights cluster west of downtown on Grand Ave. The intimate **Des Moines Art Center,** 4700 Grand Ave., is composed of three buildings. The museum exhibits an interesting collection of African art, gigantic sculptures, and a smattering of paintings by favorites like Picasso, Monet, and Andy Warhol. (☎277-4405. Open T-W and F-Sa 11am-4pm, Th 11am-9pm, Su noon-4pm. Free.) Behind the Art Center lie the immaculately groomed **Rose Garden** and **Greenwood Pond,** a small, still-water lagoon where you can relax in the sun (or ice skate in the winter). Across from Greenwood Pond, the **Science Center of Iowa,** 4500 Grand Ave., has exhibits for kids, dazzling laser shows set to popular music, and planetarium spectacles. (☎274-6868. Open M-Sa 10am-5pm, Su noon-5pm. $5.50, seniors and ages 3-12 $3.50.)

♫▥ ENTERTAINMENT AND NIGHTLIFE

The **Civic Center,** 221 Walnut St. (☎243-1120), sponsors theater and concerts; call for info. On Thursday the Des Moines *Register* publishes "The Datebook," a helpful listing of concerts, sporting events, and movies. *Cityview,* a free local weekly, lists free events and is available at the Civic Center box office and most supermarkets. The **Iowa State Fair,** one of the nation's largest, captivates Des Moines for ten days in mid-August with prize cows, crafts, cakes, and corn. (Runs Aug. 8-18, 2002. $7 per day, children over 5 $4; $2 less if purchased in advance.) Tickets for **Iowa Cubs** baseball games are a steal. Chicago's farm team plays at **Sec. Taylor Stadium,** 350 SW 1st St. Call for game dates and times. (☎243-6111. General admission $5.50, children $3.50; reserved grandstand $7.50, children $5.50.) **Jazz in July** (☎280-3222) presents free concerts throughout the city every day of the month; pick up a schedule at restaurants, Wells Fargo banks, or the Visitors Bureau. **Music Under the Stars** presents free concerts on the steps of the State Capitol (☎237-1386; June-July Su 7-9pm.)

Court Ave., in the southeast corner of downtown, serves as the focal point for much of Des Moines's nightlife scene. At **Papa's Planet,** 208 3rd St., twenty- and thirty-somethings move to 80s and 90s dance music on two dance floors. Classic rock cover bands play on the patio outside. (☎284-0901. Live music F-Sa. 25¢ beers on Th with $5 cover; F-Sa cover $3-5 includes drink specials. 21+. Open Th-Sa 7pm-2am.) **Java Joe's,** 214 4th St., a mellow coffeehouse with Internet access ($1 per 10min.), sells exotic coffee blends and beer ($2.50-3). Vegetarians will delight in the creative array of sandwiches, all for $3-5. (☎288-5282. Open M-Th 7:30am-11pm, F-Sa 7:30am-1am, Su 9am-11pm.)

▶ DAYTRIPS FROM DES MOINES

PELLA

Forty-one miles east of Des Moines on Rte. 163, Pella blooms in May with its annual **Tulip Time** festival, featuring Dutch dancing, a parade, concerts, and glockenspiel performances (☎888-746-3882; May 2-4, 2002). For a dose of Dutch culture available year-round, visit the **Jaarsma Bakery,** 727 Franklin St. (☎641-628-2940). Also open year-round is the **Pella Historical Village,** 507 Franklin St. (☎641-628-2409; open M-F 9am-5pm; $2, seniors and students $1).

PRAIRIE CITY

Twenty miles east of Des Moines on Rte. 166, you will see signs for the **Neal Smith National Wildlife Refuge,** a veritable time machine transporting visitors to Iowa's prairie days. Project officials hope eventually to restore 8600 acres of original prairie. For now, the refuge is home to 18 bison as well as a beautiful and informative learning center. In August, the big bluestem grass grows to 6ft. (☎994-3400. Open Tu-Sa 9am-4pm, Su noon-5pm. Free.)

MADISON COUNTY

Twenty miles south of Des Moines lies Madison County, immortalized in the novel and movie *The Bridges of Madison County.* **Winterset,** the county seat, is where American tough guy John Wayne was christened Marrion Robert Morrison in 1907. The **John Wayne Birthplace,** 216 S. 2nd St., has been converted to a museum featuring two rooms of memorabilia and two rooms authentically furnished in the turn-of-the-century style. (☎462-1044. Open daily 10am-4:30pm. $2.50, seniors $2.25, children $1.) For information on the county's famous **covered bridges,** visit the **Madison County Chamber of Commerce,** 73 Jefferson St. (☎462-1185 or 800-298-6119; open M-F 9am-5pm, Sa 9am-4pm, Su 11am-4pm).

IOWA CITY ☎319

Iowa City served a stint as the state capital in the mid-19th century. But while it is no longer the seat of the state government, Iowa City is still the cultural center of Iowa. Home to the University of Iowa, this town exudes youthful exuberance and energy. Don't come expecting pitchfork-toting farmers: Iowa City is better known for college football, shopping, inexpensive restaurants, and an active nightlife.

◢ PRACTICAL INFORMATION. Iowa City is off I-80, 112 mi. east of Des Moines. North-south **Madison** and **Gilbert St.** and east-west **Market** and **Burlington St.** mark off downtown. **Greyhound** and **Burlington Trailways** are both located at 404 E. College St. (☎337-2127. Station open M-F 6:30am-8pm, Sa-Su 10am-8pm.) Buses travel to Des Moines (2-4hr.; 8 per day; $22, Sa-Su $24); Chicago (4¼-6½hr.; 8 per day; $40, Sa-Su $38); St. Louis (12hr.; 1 per day; $64, Sa-Su $68); and Minneapolis (8-12hr.; 5 per day; $57, Sa-Su $60). The free **Cambus** runs daily all over campus and downtown. (☎335-8633. M-F 5am-midnight, Sa-Su noon-midnight; summer M-F 6:30am-6pm, Sa-Su noon-6pm.) **Iowa City Transit** runs a free downtown shuttle daily from 6:30am-6:30pm, as well as other routes. (☎356-5151. M-F 6:30am-10:30pm, Sa 6:30am-7pm. Fare 75¢, seniors with pass 35¢.) The **Convention and Visitors Bureau,** 408 1st Ave., sits across the river in Coralville off U.S. 6. (☎337-6592 or 800-283-6592. Open M-F

8am-5pm, Sa-Su 10am-4pm.) More area info is available at the University of Iowa's **Campus Information Center,** in the **Iowa Memorial Union** at Madison and Jefferson St. (☎335-3055. Open M-F 8am-8pm, Sa 10am-8pm, Su noon-4pm; reduced hrs. in summer and breaks.) **Internet access: Iowa City Public Library,** 123 S. Linn St. (☎356-5200; open M-Th 10am-9pm, F-Sa 10am-6pm, Su 1-5pm). **Post Office:** 400 S. Clinton St. (☎354-1560; open M-F 8:30am-5pm, Sa 9:30am-1pm). **ZIP code:** 52240. **Area code:** 319.

ⅢⅢ ACCOMMODATIONS AND FOOD. Six blocks from downtown is **Haverkamp's Linn Street Homestay,** 619 N. Linn St., an unbeatable value. This 1907 bed and breakfast contains three reasonably priced rooms; call ahead for reservations. (☎337-4636. Rooms $35-50.) Cheap motels line U.S. 6 in **Coralville,** 2 mi. west of downtown, and **1st Ave.** at Exit 242 off I-80. The cheapest of the bunch is the **Big Ten Inn,** 707 1st Ave. off U.S. 6. (☎351-6131. Singles $33; doubles $46.) Nearby is the **Capri Motor Lodge,** 705 2nd St. Clean, efficient, and a short drive to downtown, the motor lodge offers cable TV and a morning coffee. (☎354-5100. Singles $35; doubles $40.) **Kent Park Campgrounds,** 15 mi. west on U.S. 6, has 86 secluded first come, first served sites near a lake. (☎645-2315. Check-in by 10:30pm. $6, with electricity $10.)

Downtown boasts cheerful, moderately-priced restaurants and bars. At the open-air **Pedestrian Mall,** on College and Dubuque St., the melodies of street musicians drift through the eateries and shops, and vendors sell food until 3am if demand is strong. For an unforgettable dining experience in an Iowa institution, dine at **Hamburg Inn #2 Inc.,** 214 N. Linn St. "The Burg," as it is known to locals, serves huge portions of breakfast staples, burgers, and desserts. Nearly everything on the menu is under $7. (☎337-5512. Open daily 6am-11pm.) North one block, **Pagliai's Pizza,** 302 Bloomington St., tosses up crusty, crumbly thin-crust pizzas for $6-11. (☎351-5073. Open M-Sa 4pm-midnight, Su 4pm-11pm.) **Masala,** 9 S. Dubuque St., Iowa City's award-winning vegetarian Indian restaurant, has a $6.25 lunch buffet. Student discounts are given. (☎338-6199. Open daily 11:15am-2:30pm and 5-10pm.)

◙ SIGHTS. The **Old Capitol** building between Clinton and Madison St. is the focus of the **Pentacrest,** a formation of five university buildings. The gorgeous Capitol was restored with much attention to detail: brass spittoons on the floor, wood in the stove bins, and upholstered curtains on the windows. (☎335-0548. Open M-Sa 10am-3pm, Su noon-4pm.) Another Pentacrest building, the **Museum of Natural History** at Jefferson and Clinton St., details Iowa's history, focusing on Native American culture and local fauna. (☎335-0482. Open M-Sa 9:30am-4:30pm, Su 12:30-4:30pm. Free.) A short drive from downtown lies the **Plum Grove Historic Home,** 1030 Carroll St. Explore the 1840s home and garden of the first governor of the Iowa Territory. (☎351-5738. Open June-Oct. W-Su 1-5pm.) In West Branch, 15min. northeast of the city (Exit 254 on I-80; follow signs) lies the **Herbert Hoover National Historic Site.** The over 100-acre site beautifully recreates the feel of an 1870s American town, complete with a ½ mi. trail through "restored" prairie. (☎643-2541. Open daily 9am-5pm. $2, seniors $1, under 16 free. Wheelchair accessible.)

◪ NIGHTLIFE. Ever the college town, Iowa City is loaded with places to...well, get loaded. Many bars double as dance clubs, and loud music seems to be the common denominator downtown. **The Union Bar,** 121 E. College St., brags that it's the "biggest damn bar in college football's 'Big Ten.'" (☎339-7713. 18+ with college ID. Cover usually $5.) A new addition to the Iowa City scene, the nicely groomed **Et Cetera,** 114 S. Dubuque St., attracts a young, impeccably dressed crowd. (☎341-5872. Cover F-Su $5. Open daily 8pm-2am.) The more traditional **Deadwood,** 6 S. Dubuque St., is often lauded as the city's best bar, touting live bluegrass, classic rock, and folk acts. (☎351-9417. Open daily 10am-2pm.) Local musicians play Thursday to Saturday at 9:30pm in **The Sanctuary,** 405 S. Gilbert St., a restaurant and bar with 120 beers, comfortable sofas, and a decent menu. (☎351-5692. Cover $3. Open daily 4pm-2am; closes earlier in summer.) In summer, the **Friday Night Concert Series** (☎354-0863; 5-9pm) offers everything from jazz to salsa to blues, while **Just Jazz Saturdays** (6:30-9pm), features exactly what it advertises.

SCENIC DRIVE: GREAT RIVER ROAD

With its winding roads, sheer limestone cliffs, and breathtaking views of the Mississippi River, the **Great River Road** allows travelers to appreciate the diversity of Iowa's natural and built environments. The drive begins in **Sabula,** an island community of 750 held in place by the extensive lock and dam system on the Mighty Mississippi. From Sabula its a 45 mi. drive to **Dubuque,** Iowa's oldest city. Dubuque is a rather unattractive industrial city, but provides travelers with an opportunity to fill their tanks and their tummies before continuing on the road.

After Dubuque, travelers have the choice of continuing on the official Great River Road, a series of county, state, and US roads marked with distinctive road signs, or staying on Rte. 52 N. and driving the **Balltown Rd.,** a stretch of road tracing the high bluffs overlooking the Mississippi. Both routes reconvene in the town of **Guttenberg.** This historical river town is the home to **Lock and Dam No. 10,** and the path to the river from Rte. 52 is marked by signs. Hungry travelers can find gourmet sandwiches ($3.75-5) at the sassy **Guttenberg Bakery and Cafe,** 422 S. River Park Dr., but "if you are grouchy, irritable, or just plain mean, there will be a $10 charge just for putting up with you." (☎319-252-2225. Open Tu-Sa 6am-2pm, Su 7am-1pm.)

To finish the drive, pick up Rte. 340 north and pass through **McGregor.** The quiet town features a small-town commercial strip, reminiscent of the time before malls destroyed the quintessential American downtown. Three miles north lies **Marquette,** the official terminus of the journey. From Marquette, however, travelers may opt to visit the **Effigy Mounds National Monument.**

Scenic Drive: Great River Road

IS THIS HEAVEN, RAY? Movie buffs and baseball fanatics alike may want to go the distance to the **Field of Dreams** in Dyersville, where the movie *Field of Dreams* was shot. (☎888-875-8404. Open Apr.-Nov. daily 9am-6pm. Free.) In the film, mysterious voices direct a farmer (played by Kevin Costner) to build a baseball field amidst Iowa's acres of corn. The folks there will provide you with free bats, balls, and gloves so you can try to hit one into the stands, er, stalks. Pick up a souvenir at one of many shops. Dyersville is about 25 mi. west of Dubuque in northeast Iowa. Take Rte. 20 west from Dubuque to Rte. 136 N.; go right after the tracks for 3 mi.

EFFIGY MOUNDS

Mysterious and striking, the Effigy Mounds are earthy windows into North American prehistory. Built by Native Americans as early as 1000 BC, the enigmatic effigies are low-lying mounds of piled earth formed into distinguishable geometric and animal shapes. Though they once covered much of the Midwest, farmers' plows have ensured that only a scattering of them remain, mostly in western Wisconsin and eastern Iowa. One of the largest concentrations of intact mounds composes the **Effigy Mounds National Monument,** 151 Rte. 76, 100 mi. west of Madison in Marquette, Iowa. Offering striking views of the Mississippi from high, rocky bluffs, the trails winding through the park explore the lives of these indigenous people and the meaning the mounds had for them. Guided tours are available and recommended. Take Rte. 18 W from Madison. (☎319-873-3491. Visitors Center open daily 8am-5pm.) **Wyalusing State Park,** just across the Mississippi in Wisconsin, offers more than 110 campsites overlooking the stunning confluence of the Wisconsin River and the Mighty Mississippi, as well as its own assortment of mounds and trails. (☎608-996-2261. Campsites Su-Th $10, F-Sa $12.)

SPIRIT LAKE AND OKOBOJI   ☎712

Not to be outdone by its neighbors, Iowa boasts its own Great Lakes: Spirit Lake, West Okoboji Lake, and East Okoboji Lake, all popular vacation destinations. West Okoboji Lake ranks with Switzerland's Lake Geneva and Canada's Lake Louise as one of the world's three blue-water lakes, carved out by a glacier 10,000 years ago and continuously replenished with spring water since then.

It's hard to miss the **amusement park** in **Arnold's Park,** off Rte. 71, with its roller coaster, kiddie rides, and ice cream shops. (☎332-2183 or 800-599-6995. Hours vary. $14 with rides, children 3-4 ft. tall $10, under 3 ft. free; $5 without rides.) The park's **Roof Garden** plays open air concerts, including an annual **Blues and Zydeco Festival** (call for info). One block west of the amusement park is **Abbie Gardner Historic Log Cabin.** (☎332-7248. Open June-Sept. M-F noon-4pm, Sa-Su 9am-4pm. Free, but donation suggested.) The museum presents a 13min. video explaining the unfurling of the dispute between encroaching settlers and members of the Sioux that led to the Spirit Lake Massacre of March 1857. Theater buffs can catch a production of the **Stephens College Okoboji Summer Theater** (☎332-7773; box office open M 10am-6pm, Tu-Sa 10am-9pm, Su 1-7pm; $10-13). For a dose of the outdoors, you can hike, skate, or bike **The Spine,** a 14½ mi. trail that runs through the area; bike rental ($10 per day) is available at **Allan's Hardware Hank,** on Rte. 71 (☎332-7131).

Budget accommodations in the immediate lake area are scarce, especially in summer. Cheap motels line U.S. 71 in Spencer, about 15 mi. south of Okoboji. **The Northland Inn,** at the junction of Rte. 9 and Rte. 86 just north of West Okoboji Lake, offers wood-paneled rooms and a continental breakfast. (☎336-1450. May-Sept., 1 bed for 1-2 people $55, 2 beds for up to 4 people $65; Oct.-Apr. 1 bed $30, 2 beds $40.) Pitch your tent year-round at tranquil **Marble Beach Campground** in the state park on the shores of Spirit Lake. (☎336-4437, in winter 337-3211.) Other camping options include **Emerson Bay** and **Gull's Point,** both off Rte. 86 on West Okoboji Lake. Sites at all three campgrounds cost $11, $16 with electricity. The **Koffee Kup Kafe,** off U.S. 71 in Arnold's Park, serves up an all-day power breakfast (eggs, bacon, pancakes, hash browns, and juice) for $5.25. Those craving more simplicity can try a variety of tasty pancakes ($1-3), also served all day. (☎332-7657. Open daily 6am-2pm.) **Tweeter's,** off U.S. 71 in Okoboji, is a local lunch spot that grills burgers ($6-7), tosses salads ($5-6), and melts sandwiches. (☎332-9421. Open daily 11am-midnight, in winter 11am-11pm.) The **Iowa Great Lakes Chamber of Commerce,** at the **Iowa Welcome Center** just through the gate to the amusement park, overflows with info about the area. (☎322-2107 or 800-839-9987. Open M-F 9am-5pm.) **Area code:** 712.

NEBRASKA

Nebraska often has it rough—imagine having to deal with persistent accusations of being "boring," "endless," or "the Great American Desert." Nebraska's landscape is in actuality its greatest attraction. Central Nebraska features the Sandhills, a breathtakingly huge windblown dune region with cattle, ranches, windmills, and tiny towns. The Panhandle offers Western-style mountains and canyons, historical trails, and National Monuments. For the more urbane traveler, Omaha and Lincoln feature quality sports, fine music, and some of the best Grade A meat in America. While the urge might be to speed through the Cornhusker State, patient travelers will be rewarded with a true Great Plains experience.

🏛 PRACTICAL INFORMATION

Capital: Lincoln.
Visitor info: Nebraska Tourism Office, P.O. Box 94666, Lincoln 68509 (☎402-471-3796 or 800-228-4307; www.visitnebraska.org). Open M-F 8am-5pm. **Nebraska Game and Parks Commission,** 2200 N. 33rd St., Lincoln 68503 (☎402-471-0641). Open M-F 8am-5pm.
State Beverage: Kool-Aid. **Postal Abbreviation:** NE. **Sales Tax:** 5-6.5%, depending on city.

OMAHA   ☎402

Omaha is a city of seemingly endless sprawl, spreading over miles and miles of the Nebraska prairie. The heart of the city, however, exudes a healthy compactness. Omaha's museums, world-renowned zoo, and sports complex are the envy of other medium-sized cities. The Old Market in downtown Omaha lures visitors with a surprisingly large concentration of quiet cafes, breweries, and nightclubs. Overall, the town seems to settle comfortably into its role as Gateway to the West.

◢◪ ORIENTATION AND PRACTICAL INFORMATION. Omaha rests on the west bank of the Missouri River, brushing up against Iowa's border. While it wears a facade of geometric order, Omaha is actually an imprecise grid of numbered streets (north-south) and named streets (east-west). **Dodge St.** (Rte. 6) divides the city east-west. **I-80** runs across the southern half of town and intersects with **I-480/Rte. 75** (the Kennedy Expwy.). *At night, avoid N. 24th St., Ames Ave., and the area north of I-480.* **Amtrak,** 1003 S. 9th St. (☎342-1501; open 10:30pm-11:30am, 12:30-4pm), at Pacific St., chugs to Chicago (9½hr., 1 per day, $100) and Denver (8hr., 1 per day, $87-128). **Greyhound,** 1601 Jackson (☎341-1906; open 24hr.), runs to Des Moines (2-2½hr., 3 per day, $24); Cheyenne (8½hr., 5 per day, $74-78); and Lincoln (1hr., 4 per day, $11-12). **Metro Area Transit (MAT),** 2222 Cumming St., handles local transportation. Schedules are available at Park Fair Mall, at 16th and Douglas St. near the Greyhound station, and at the library, 14th and Farnam St. (☎341-0800. Open M-F 8am-4:30pm. Fare $1.25, transfers 5¢.) The **Greater Omaha Convention and Visitors Bureau,** 6800 Mercy Rd., #202, at the Ak-Sar-Ben complex off S. 72 St. north of I-80, dispenses tourist info. (☎800-332-1819. Open M-F 8am-4:30pm.) **Hotlines: Rape Crisis,** ☎345-7273. 24hr. **First Call for Help,** ☎444-6666. M-F 8am-5pm. **Internet access: Omaha Public Library,** 215 S. 15th St., between Douglas and Farnham. (☎444-4800. Open M-Th 9am-9pm, F-Sa 9am-5:30pm, Su 1-5pm.) **Post Office:** 1124 Pacific St. (☎348-2696; open M-F 7:30am-6pm, Sa 7:30am-noon). **ZIP code:** 68108. **Area code:** 402.

⌂ ACCOMMODATIONS. Motels in Omaha are not particularly budget-friendly. For better deals, head for the outskirts; start around 60th and L St. and head west from there. It's fun to stay at the **YMCA,** 430 S. 20th St. The Y offers clean, cheap singles. (☎341-1600. $5 per day for use of facilities; free parking. Men-only rooms with shared bath $11; either-sex rooms with private bath $12.) The **Satellite Motel,** 6006 L St., south of I-80 Exit 450 (60th St.), is a round two-story building with lots of personality. Clean, wedge-shaped rooms come equipped with fridge, microwave, coffee-maker, and cable TV. (☎733-7373. Summer singles $40-42, doubles $50-52; winter $38-40/$48-50.) Outdoorsfolk should head to the **Haworth Park Campground,** in Bellevue on Payne St. at the end of Mission Ave. Take the Exit for Rte. 370 E. off Rte. 75, turn right onto Galvin Rd., left onto Mission Ave., and right onto Payne St. before the toll bridge. Tent sites are separate from the RV area but not entirely out of view. (☎291-3379 or 293-3098. Showers, toilets, and shelters. Open daily 6am-10pm; stragglers can enter after hrs. Check-out 3pm. Sites $5, with hookup $10.)

◘ FOOD FOR THOUGHT. It's no fun being a chicken, cow, or vegetarian in Omaha, with a fried chicken joint on every block and a steakhouse in every district. Once a warehouse area, the brick streets of the **Old Market,** on Jackson, Howard, and Harney St. between 10th and 13th, now feature popular shops, restaurants, and bars. The **Farmers Market,** 11th and Jackson St. (☎345-5401), is held on Saturday 8am-12:30pm from mid-May to mid-October and on Wednesday 4-8pm from mid-July to mid-August. **The Diner,** 409 S. 12 St., is as straightforward as its name suggests, serving up hot, heaping portions (including "breakfast by the number") in next to no time. Everything on the menu is under $6; pancakes run $3-4. (☎341-9870. Open M-Sa 6am-4pm.) **Délice European Cafe,** 1206 Howard St., in the Old Market, sells scrumptious pastries and deli fare ($2-6) in a light, spacious setting. They also serve wine and beer to help make your meal appropriately European. The patio affords shaded views of the Court St. area. (☎342-2276. Open M-Th 7:30am-9pm, F-Sa 7:30am-11pm, Su 7:30am-6pm.) **McFoster's Natural Kind Cafe,** 302 S. 38th St., at Farnam St., sells healthy dishes ($4-13), including free-range chicken, vegan eggplant parmesan, and artichoke specialties. (☎345-7477. Live blues Th. Open M-Th 11am-10pm, F-Sa 11am-11pm, Su 10am-3pm. Wheelchair accessible.) **Upstream Brewing,** 514 S. 11th St., at Jackson St., dishes out creative entrees ($9-18) that can be wolfed down inside, out on the patio, or up on the rooftop deck. Pizza and burgers run $6-8; a selection of eight home-brewed beers is also available. (☎344-0200. Open M-Sa 11am-1am, Su 11am-midnight.)

◙ SIGHTS. The **Durham Western Heritage Museum,** 801 S. 10th St., occupies the former Union Train Station, an impressive Art Deco structure. The restored station houses exhibits on the railroad as well as the men and women who first settled the West. (☎444-5071. Open Tu-Sa 10am-5pm, Su 1-5pm. $5, seniors $4, ages 3-12 $3.50.) Within a monumental Art Deco edifice, Omaha's **Joslyn Art Museum,** 2200 Dodge St., displays a decent collection of 19th- and 20th-century American and European art. From mid-July to mid-August, the museum hosts free "Jazz on the Green" concerts each Thursday 7:30-9pm. (☎342-3300. Open Tu-Sa 10am-4pm, Su noon-4pm. $6, seniors and college students $4, ages 5-17 $3.50, free Sa 10am-noon.) See the gargantuan remnants of US airpower of the last half-century in an equally enormous **Strategic Air and Space Museum,** Exit 426 off I-80. The museum displays various military aircraft, including a B-52 bomber, as well as exhibits on military history. (☎800-358-5029. Open daily 9am-5pm. $6, seniors and military $5, ages 5-12 $3.)

One of the largest indoor jungles in the nation, complete with monkeys, low-flying bats, and exotic birds, has made the **Henry Doorly Zoo,** 3701 S. 10th St., the number one tourist attraction between Chicago and Denver. (☎733-8401. Exit at 13th St. off I-80, at Bert Murphy Blvd. Open M-Sa 9:30am-5pm, Su 9:30am-6pm; early Sept.-late May daily 9:30am-5pm. $8, seniors over 62 $6.50, ages 5-11 $4.25.) Just down the road is the **Simmons Wildlife Safari Park.** Drive your all-terrain vehicle (or beat-up Chevette) 4½ mi. through a nature preserve with bison, pronghorns, moose, wolves, and other beasts roaming inside. (☎944-9453. Open Apr.-Oct. 9:30am-5pm. $10 per car. Sa-Su guided tram tours an additional $1.)

GREAT PLAINS

🎵📺 **ENTERTAINMENT AND NIGHTLIFE.** At I-80 and 13th St. (across the street from the zoo) is **Johnny Rosenblatt Stadium,** where you can watch the minor league **Omaha Golden Spikes** round the bases from April to early September (☎734-2550. General admission $4. Box seat $6-8. $1 off all tickets for high school students and seniors. Wheelchair accessible.) The stadium has also hosted the NCAA College Baseball World Series every June since 1950. In late June and early July, **Shakespeare on the Green** stages free performances in Elmwood Park, on 60th and Dodge St. (☎280-2391. Th-Su 8:30pm.)

Punk and progressive folk have found a niche at the several area universities; check the window of the **Antiquarian Bookstore,** 1215 Harney, in the Old Market, for the scoop on shows. Several good bars await nearby. **The Dubliner,** 1205 Harney, below street level, stages live traditional Irish music on Friday and Saturday evenings (☎342-5887; cover $2-3). The **13th Street Coffee Company,** 519 13th St., keeps 20 types of beans on hand and brews three different varieties every day. The Mexican latte—chocolate, orange, cinnamon, steamed milk, a double shot, and whipped cream—is particularly rich and tasty. (☎345-2883. Live music F-Sa 9pm. Internet access $5 per hr. Open Su-Th 6:30am-11pm, F-Sa 6:30-midnight.) **The Max,** 1417 Jackson, is one of the most popular gay bars in the state. With five bars, a disco dance floor, DJ, fountains, patio, the Max is Omaha's gay haven. (☎346-4110. 21+. Cover F-Sa $3. Open daily 4pm-1am. Happy hour 4-7pm.) For country tunes and line dancing, head to **Guitars and Cadillacs,** 10865 W. Dodge Rd. On Friday and Saturday the club hosts after-hours dancing (1-3am) for those 18 and over. (☎333-5500. Open Tu-W 7pm-1am, Th 8pm-1am, F 6pm-3am, Sa 7pm-3am, and Su 6pm-1am.)

LINCOLN   ☎402

The spirit of Lincoln rises and falls with the success of its world-famous college football team, the Nebraska Cornhuskers. Many youngsters spend their childhoods running wind sprints, weightlifting, and practicing—all for the dream of stepping onto the field at Nebraska. Life does go on off the field, however. Lincoln houses the Nebraska state legislature, the only one-house legislature in the Union, as well as quality restaurants and scenic parks.

🛈 **PRACTICAL INFORMATION.** Lincoln's grid makes sense. Numbered streets increase as you go east; lettered streets progress through the alphabet as you go north. **O St.** is the main east-west drag. It becomes Cornhusker Hwy. (U.S. 6) if you head west of the city and Rte. 34 if you head east. **R St.** runs along the south side of the **University of Nebraska-Lincoln (UNL).** Most downtown sights lie between 7th and 16th St. and M and R St. **Lincoln Airport** (☎458-2480) is located 5 mi. northwest of downtown on Cornhusker Hwy., or take Exit 399 off I-80. **Amtrak,** 201 N. 7th St. (☎476-1295; open M-W 7:30am-4pm and daily 11:30pm-7am), runs once daily to Omaha (1hr., $9-16); Denver (7½hr., $70-125); and Chicago (11hr., $74-132). Prices vary with availability. **Greyhound,** 940 P St. (☎474-1071; ticket window open M-F 6:30am-5:30pm, Sa 9:30am-5:30pm), sends buses to Omaha (1 hr., 4 per day, $11.50); Chicago (12hr., 6 per day, $50); Kansas City (6-10hr., 3 per day, $49); and Denver (9-18hr., 4 per day, $68). **Star Trans,** 710 J St., handles public transportation. Schedules are available on the bus, at the office, and at many locations downtown. (☎476-1234. Buses run M-Sa 6am-6pm. Fare 85¢, seniors 40¢, ages 5-11 50¢.) **Visitors Center:** 201 N. 7th St., in the Haymarket district. (☎434-5348 or 800-423-8212. Open M-F 9am-8pm, Sa 8am-5pm, Su noon-5pm; in winter M-F 9am-6pm, Sa 10am-4pm, Su noon-4pm.) **Internet access: Lincoln Public Library,** 136 S. 14th St., at N St. (☎444-8500. Open M-Th 9am-9pm, F-Sa 9am-6pm, Su 1:30pm-5:30pm.) **Post Office:** 700 R St. (☎458-1844; open M-F 7:30am-6pm, Sa 9am-1pm). **ZIP code:** 68501. **Area code:** 402.

🏠 **ACCOMMODATIONS.** There are few inexpensive motels downtown. Many cheaper places to flop lie east of the city center around the 5600 block of Cornhusker Hwy. (U.S. 6). The **Cornerstone Hostel (HI-AYH),** 640 N. 16th St., at U St. just south of Vine St., is conveniently located in a church basement in the university's downtown campus and rarely fills up. While the basement can get stuffy in summer, the sound of the organ drifting from upstairs will take your mind off the heat. (☎476-0355 or 476-0926. Two single-sex rooms; 5 beds for women, 3 for men. Full kitchen and laundry facilities. Free parking and linen. Curfew 11pm. Dorms $10, nonmembers $13.) **The Great Plains Budget Host Inn,** 2732 O St., has large rooms with fridges. Take bus #9 "O St. Shuttle." (☎476-3253 or 800-288-8499. Free parking and kitchenettes available. Singles $42; doubles $48; 10% AAA discount.) The 199 sites at the **Nebraska State Fair Park Campground,** 2400 N. 14th St. at Cornhusker, are conveniently located but next to a highway and train tracks; take bus #7 "Belmont." (☎473-4287. Open Apr.-Oct. Sites for 2 $14, with electricity $16, full hookup $18; each additional person $1. Fills up early in Aug., but no reservations accepted.) To get to the more pleasant **Camp-A-Way,** 1st and Superior St., take Exit 401 or 401a from I-80, then Exit 1 on I-180/Rte. 34. While located next to a highway, the 81 sites are peaceful and shaded. (☎476-2282. Showers, laundry, pool, and convenience store. Reservations recommended during fair time in Aug. Sites $14, water and electricity $18.50, full hookup $22.)

🍴🌙 **FOOD AND NIGHTLIFE. Historic Haymarket,** 7th to 9th and O to R St., is a renovated warehouse district near the train tracks, with cafes, bars, several restaurants, and a **farmers market.** (☎435-7496. Open mid-May to mid-Oct. Sa 8am-noon.) All downtown buses connect at 11th and O St., two blocks east of Historic Haymarket. Breakfast is served all day at **Kuhl's,** 1038 O St. The Lincoln special—two eggs, toast, hash browns, and ham, bacon, or sausage—sets the local standard ($5.75); other breakfasts run $3-6. (☎476-1311. Open M-F 6am-7pm, Sa 6am-4pm, Su 7am-3pm.) **Maggie's Bakery and Vegetarian Vittles,** 311 N. 8th St., sustains Lincoln's vegetarians and vegans with delicious $1.50-2 pastries and $6 lunch specials. (☎477-3959. Open M-F 8am-3pm.) **Valentino's,** 232 N. 13th St., a regional chain with roots in Lincoln, offers pasta dishes for $5-7 and a $3-5 all-you-can-eat pizza buffet Friday and Saturday from 8-11pm. (☎475-1501. Open Su-Th 11am-10pm, F-Sa 11am-11pm.) **Ja Brisco,** 700 P St., serves pizzas, pasta, and deli sandwiches ($6-10) that are sure to please. (☎434-5644. Open daily 11am-10:30pm. Wheelchair accessible.)

Nightspots abound in Lincoln, particularly those of the sports-bar variety. For the biggest names in Lincoln's live music scene, try the suitably dark and smoky **Zoo Bar,** 136 N. 14th St., where blues is king. (☎435-8754. 21+. Cover $3-10. Open M-Sa 3pm-1am, occasionally on Su.) **Q,** 226 S. 9th St. between M and N, is a great gay and lesbian bar with a large dance floor. (☎475-2269. Tu college night; 19+. Open Tu-Su 8pm-1am.) For the best of the college sports bar genre, head to **Iguana's** at 1426 O St. (☎476-8850. Happy hour F 3-7pm; free appetizers. Open M-Sa 7pm-1am.)

☉ **SIGHTS.** The "Tower on the Plains," the 400 ft. **Nebraska State Capitol Building,** at 14th and K St., wows with its streamlined exterior and detailed interior, highlighted by a beautiful mosaic floor. Although exterior renovations continue, the inside is untouched and remarkably beautiful. (☎471-0448. Open M-F 8am-5pm, Sa 10am-5pm, Su 1-5pm. Free 30min. tours are given every 30min. M-F in summer, every hr. Sa-Su.) The **Museum of Nebraska History** on Centennial Mall, a renamed portion of 15th St., has a phenomenal collection of headdresses, moccasins, jewelry, and other beautiful artifacts in its exhibit on the Plains Indians. (☎471-4754. Open M-F 9am-4:30pm, Sa 9am-5pm, Su 1:30-5pm. Free.) The **University of Nebraska State Museum,** 14th and U St., in Morrill Hall, boasts an amazing fossil collection that includes the largest mounted mammoth of any American museum. (☎472-6302. Open M-Sa 9:30am-4:30pm, Su 1:30-4:30pm. Requested donation $2.) In the same building, the **Mueller Planetarium** lights up the ceiling with several shows daily and laser shows several days a week. (☎472-2641. Planetarium $5; seniors, students, and under 13 $4. Laser shows $5, with college ID $4, under 12 $3.)

In addition to livestock, crafts, and fitter family contests, the **Nebraska State Fair** offers car races, tractor pulls, and plenty of rides to please all comers. (☎473-4109. Aug. 23 to Sept. 2, 2002. $5.) **Pioneers Park,** 3201 S. Coddington Ave., ¼ mi. south off W. Van Dorn, is a sylvan paradise perfect for a prairie picnic. The Pioneer Park Nature Center harbors bison and elk within its sanctuary and is also the starting point for 5 mi. of trails. (☎441-7895. Open M-Sa 8:30am-8:30pm, Su noon-8:30pm; Sept.-May M-Sa 8:30am-5pm, Su noon-5pm. Free. Wheelchair accessible.)

> **CARHENGE OR BUST** Everything looks the same as you drive through the plains and bluffs of western Nebraska, until, suddenly, a preternatural power sweeps the horizon and the ultimate shrine to bizarre Americana springs into view—Carhenge. Consisting of 36 old whitewashed cars, this oddly engaging sculpture has the same orientation and dimensions as Stonehenge in England. When asked why he built it, the artisan Reinders replied, *"plane, loqui deprehendi,"* or, "clearly, I spoke to be understood." This wonder can be found right off Rte. 385, 2 mi. north of Alliance, NE, which is 60 mi. northeast of Scotts Bluff. (☎800-738-0648. Open daily 24hr.)

SCOTTS BLUFF   ☎308

Known to the Plains Indians as *Ma-a-pa-te* ("hill that is hard to go around"), the imposing clay and sandstone highlands of **Scotts Bluff National Monument** were landmarks for people traveling the Mormon and Oregon Trails in the 1840s. For some time the bluff was too dangerous to cross, but in the 1850s a single-file wagon trail was opened just south of the bluff through narrow **Mitchell's Pass,** where traffic wore deep marks in the sandstone. Today, a half-mile stretch of the original **Oregon Trail** is preserved at the pass; tourists can gaze out at the distant horizons to the east and west as pioneers once did. The **Visitors Center,** at the entrance on Rte. 92, will tell you of the mysterious death of Hiram Scott, the fur trader who gave the Bluffs their name. Don't miss the 12min. slide show. (☎436-4340. Open daily 8am-7pm; in winter 8am-5pm. $5 per carload, $2 per motorcycle.) To get to the top of the bluffs, hike the challenging **Saddle Rock Trail** (1½ mi. each way) or motor up **Summit Dr.** At the top, you'll find two short **nature trails.** Guides are available at the trailheads for 50¢. The **North Overlook** is a 0.5 mi. paved walk for a view of the North Platte River Valley. The **South Overlook** is 0.2 mi. and provides a spectacular view of Scotts Bluff. Take U.S. 26 to Rte. 71 to Rte. 92; the monument is on Rte. 92 about 2 mi. west of **Gering** (*not* in the town of Scottsbluff). A 1.2 mi. bike trail links Gering with the base of the bluffs. From July 11-14, 2002, the 81st annual **Oregon Trail Days Festival** packs the towns near Scotts Bluff with festive folk. Twenty miles east on Rte. 92, just south of Bayard, the 500 ft. spire of **Chimney Rock,** visible from more than 30 mi. away, marks another landmark which once inspired travelers of the Oregon Trail. A gravel road leads from Rte. 92 to within ½ mi. of the rock. There you can find the first graveyard of settlers on the Oregon Trail. Unfortunately, there is no path up to the base of the rock due to the rough terrain and rattlesnakes. The Nebraska State Historical Society operates a **Visitors Center.** (☎586-2581. Open daily 9am-6pm; in winter 9am-5pm. $2, under 18 free.) **Area code:** 308. **Time Zone:** Mountain.

KANSAS

In 1935, a University of Chicago professor conducted a study and determined that respondents would cut off their little toe for $100, but would only move to Kansas if given $10,000. Needless to say, enthusiasm for Kansas has picked up since then. The state continues to serve as an important stopover for cross-country travelers, and its inhabitants are quick to sing the praises of the Sunflower State. Grueling feuds over Kansas's slavery status before the Civil War gave rise to the term "Bleeding Kansas." The wound has since healed, and Kansas now presents a serene blend of small-town charm and miles of farmland. Highway signs subtly remind that "every Kansas farmer feeds 75 people—and *you.*"

⁊ PRACTICAL INFORMATION

Capital: Topeka.
Visitor info: Division of Travel and Tourism: 700 S.W. Harrison, #1300, Topeka 66603 (☎785-296-2009 or 800-252-6727; www.travelks.com). Open M-F 7am-10pm, Sa-Su

GEOGRAPHIC CENTER OF THE US. Have you ever wanted to be the center of the action? Go 2 mi. northwest of Lebanon, KS. Sit by the stone monument and feel special—you are the center of the United States.

7:30am-10pm. **Kansas Wildlife and Parks,** 512 S.E. 25th Ave., Pratt 67121 (☎316-672-5911; www.kdwp.state.ks.us). Open M-F 8am-5pm.

State Reptile: Ornate box turtle. **State Amphibian:** Barred tiger salamander.

Postal Abbreviation: KS. **Sales Tax:** 4.9%, plus 1.6% in most cities.

WICHITA   ☎316

In 1541, Coronado came to the site of present-day Wichita in search of the mythical, gold-laden city of Quivira. Upon arriving, he was so disappointed that he had his guide strangled for misleading him. Wichita continued this inauspicious pattern of existence through most of the 19th century, fending off cattle thieves and struggling to stay alive. Beginning with the 20th century, however, Wichita's economy took off as a center of aviation manufacturing and an agricultural commodities hub for the southern and central Plains. Downtown gives off a suburban vibe, but as the Old Town area gets revamped, yuppies party further and further into the Kansas night.

🔢 PRACTICAL INFORMATION. Wichita lies on I-35, 170 mi. north of Oklahoma City and about 200 mi. southwest of Kansas City. A small and quiet downtown makes for easy walking or parking. **Broadway** is the major north-south artery. **Douglas Ave.** divides the numbered east-west streets to the north from the named east-west streets to the south. **Kellogg Ave. (U.S. 54)** is the main commercial strip east and west of town; through downtown it serves as an expressway. The closest **Amtrak** station, 414 N. Main St. (☎283-7533; station open Su-Tu and Sa midnight-8am, W-F midnight-4pm), 25 mi. north of Wichita in the town of Newton, sends one very early train northeast to Kansas City (5hr., $49-72) and another west to Dodge City (2½hr., $39-57). **Greyhound,** 312 S. Broadway, 2 blocks east of Main St. and 1½ blocks southwest of the transit station (☎265-7221; open daily 3-6pm), services Kansas City (3-5hr., 3 per day, $29-33); Oklahoma City (4hr., 3 per day, $29-33); and Denver (12-23hr., 3 per day, $72-82). **Wichita Transit,** 214 S. Topeka Blvd., runs 18 bus routes in town. (☎265-7221. Station open M-F 8am-5pm. Buses run M-F 6am-7pm, Sa 7am-6pm. Fare $1, seniors 50¢, ages 6-17 75¢; transfers 25¢.) **Convention and Visitors Bureau:** 100 S. Main St., at Douglas Ave. (☎265-2800 or 800-288-9424. Open M-F 8am-5pm.) **Internet access: Public Library,** 223 S. Main St. (☎261-8500; open M-Th 10am-9pm, F-Sa 10am-5:30pm, Su 1-5pm). **Post Office:** 330 W. 2nd St., at Waco. (☎262-6245. Open M-F 8am-5:30pm, Sa 9am-noon.) **ZIP code:** 67202. **Area code:** 316.

🏠 ACCOMMODATIONS. Wichita offers a bounty of cheap hotels. South Broadway has plenty of mom-and-pop places, *but be wary of the neighborhood.* The chains line **E. and W. Kellogg Ave.** 5 to 8 mi. from downtown. Only 10 blocks from downtown, the **Mark 8 Inn,** 1130 N. Broadway, has small, comfortable rooms with free local calls, cable TV, A/C, fridge, and laundry facilities. (☎265-4679 or 888-830-7268. Singles $30; doubles $33; no checks.) The **English Village Inn,** 6727 E. Kellogg, though American, urban, and a motel, keeps large rooms with aging furnishings in tidy repair for very reasonable rates. (☎683-5613 or 800-365-8455. Cable and HBO in the rooms, popcorn in the lobby. Singles from $32; doubles from $36.) **USI Campgrounds,** 2920 E. 33rd St., right off Hillside Rd., is the most convenient of Wichita's hitchin' posts, with laundry, showers, playground, and storm shelter, in case there's a twister a-comin'. (☎838-0435. RV sites $22.50; no tents.)

🍴 FOOD. Beef is what's for dinner in Wichita. The newly renovated **Old Town** area is a good choice for lunch, with several restaurants offering $5 buffets and other specials. The **River City Brewing Company,** 150 N. Mosley, is one of the newest dining spots in the neighborhood, with hearty entrees ranging from $6-10. (☎263-2739.)

> **BOOZE, BOOTS, AND BOVINES** In its heyday in the
> 1870s, Dodge City, KS ("the wickedest little city in America"), was a haven for gun-
> fighters, prostitutes, and other lawless types. At one time, the main drag had a saloon
> for every 50 citizens. Disputes were settled man to man, with a duel; the slower draw
> ended up in Boot Hill Cemetery, so named for the boot-clad corpses buried there. Leg-
> endary lawmen Wyatt Earp and Bat Masterson earned their fame cleaning up the
> streets of Dodge. Today, the town's most conspicuous residents, about 50,000 cows,
> reside on the feedlots on the east part of town. Hold your nose and whoop it up during
> the **Dodge City Days,** complete with rodeo, carnival, and lots of steak. You'll know
> when you're getting close. (☎620-225-2244. July 26-Aug. 4, 2002.)

Open daily 11am-10pm.) Neon lights are on **N. Broadway** around 10th St., with all
kinds of fairly authentic Asian food, mostly Vietnamese. If you eat only one slab
here, make it one from **Doc's Steakhouse,** 1515 N. Broadway, where the most expensive entree—a 17 oz. T-bone with salad, potato, and bread—is only $10. Take bus
#13 "N. Broadway." (☎264-4735. Open M-Th 11:30am-9:30pm, F 11:30am-10pm, Sa
4-10pm.) The large paper umbrellas hanging from the ceiling at **Pho 99,** 1015 N.
Broadway, may be questionable, but the food certainly isn't. Thirty-two kinds of hot
pho and vermicelli dishes are $4-6; only in Kansas would Vietnamese noodles be
accompanied by strips of ribeye steak. (☎267-8188. Open daily 10am-8:30pm.)

🖸 **SIGHTS.** The **Four Museums-on-the-River** are located within a few blocks of each
other; take the trolley or bus #12 "Riverside." Walk through the rough and tumble
cattle days of the 1870s in the **Old Cowtown,** 1871 Sim Park Dr., lined with many original buildings. (☎264-6398 or 264-0671. Open M-Sa 10am-5pm, Su noon-5pm; Nov.-
Mar. Sa-Su only. $7, seniors $6.50, ages 5-11 $3.50, under 5 free; seniors 2-for-1 Tu
and W. Call for special events info.) The **Mid-America All-Indian Center and Museum,**
650 N. Seneca, displays Native American artifacts. The late Blackbear Bosin's awe-
inspiring sculpture, *Keeper of the Plains,* stands guard over the confluence of the
Arkansas and Little Arkansas Rivers. The center holds the **Mid-America All-Indian
Intertribal Powwow** in late July with traditional dancing, foods, arts, and crafts.
(☎262-5221. Open M-Sa 10am-5pm, Su 1-5pm; Jan.-Mar. closed M. $2, ages 6-12 $1.)

Wichita's newest and most impressive piece of riverfront architecture houses the
city's most fun and interactive museum, **Exploration Place,** 300 N. McLean Blvd.
Come here to learn how to shoot air out of a cannon or to see how tornadoes and
steam currents propagate. (☎263-3373 or 877-904-1444. Open M noon-6pm, Tu-Th
9am-6pm, F-Sa 9am-9pm, Su 9am-6pm. $7, seniors $6.50, ages 5-15 $5, ages 2-4 $2.)
Botanica, 701 N. Amindon, the Wichita botanical gardens, displays a wide collection
of flora from the Americas as well as Asian floral species. Large indoor exhibits
afford a chance to beat the heat, and the outdoor exhibits are spellbinding. (☎264-
0448. Open M-Sa 9am-5pm, Su 1-5pm. $4.50, seniors $4, students $2.)

LAWRENCE   ☎785

Home to the flagship University of Kansas (KU), Lawrence offers numerous first-
rate artistic, historical, cultural, and social activities. The University
of Kansas's **Watkins Community Museum of History,** 1047 Massachusetts St., whets the
appetites of Kansas history buffs. (☎841-4109. Open Tu-Sa 10am-4pm, Su 1:30-4pm.
Free.) The main attractions, however, are two tours through downtown Lawrence.
The first self-guided tour, **Quantrill's Raid: The Lawrence Massacre,** traces the events
leading up to the murder of over 200 men by pro-slavery vigilantes on August 21,
1863. (1½hr. driving tour begins at 1111 E. 19th St.) A second tour, **House Styles of
Old West Lawrence,** provides a look at gorgeous 19-century homes. (45min. walking,
25min. driving. Maps at the Visitors Center, Chamber of Commerce, and library.)

Lawrence's inexpensive hotels are located around Iowa and 6th St., just west of
campus. The town also offers several bed and breakfast options. Three blocks from
downtown, the **Halcyon House Bed and Breakfast,** 1000 Ohio St., is extremely close to

local attractions and good parking. (☎841-0314. Breakfast included. 2 ground-floor rooms $49.) The traditional **Westminster Inn and Suites**, 2525 W. 6th St., offers several amenities to make stays more comfortable, including a pool and free day passes to the nearby health club. (☎841-8410. Breakfast included. Singles M-Th $54, F-Su $64; doubles $64/$74; $5 AAA discount. 2 wheelchair accessible rooms.)

Downtown Lawrence features both traditional barbecue joints and more health-conscious offerings. The **Wheatfields Bakery and Cafe**, 904 Vermont St., serves up large sandwiches ($5-6.50) on French bread, freshly baked rye, or focaccia. Plenty of vegetarian options are available. (☎841-5553. Open M-Sa 6:30am-8pm, Su 7:30am-4pm.) **Cafe Nova**, 745 New Hampshire St., brews several varieties of coffee each day, offering multiple sweeteners from maple syrup to sweet cream. Seasonal offerings include pastas, salads, and $3-4 sandwiches. (☎841-3282. Internet access $6 per hr. Open M-W 7am-12am, Th-Sa 7am-2am, Su 7am-1am.) The **Free State Brewing Company**, 636 Massachusetts St., brews over 50 beers yearly and always has at least five on tap. Beers are $2.50, while sandwiches are $6 and pasta dishes run $8-10. (☎843-4555. M $1.25 beers. Open M-Sa 11am-12am, Su noon-11pm.) For live music and a neighborhood-bar atmosphere, head down to the well-equipped **Jazzhaus**, 926½ Massachusetts St. Performers range from local groups to the occasional regional act. (☎749-3320. Cover $3-4. Open daily 4pm-2am.)

Lawrence lies just south of I-70 in northeastern Kansas. **Amtrak**, 413 E. 7th St. (☎800-872-7245; call for hours), chugs once daily to Chicago (1hr., $12-17). **Greyhound**, 2447 W. 6th St. (☎843-5622; ticket window open M-F 7:30am-4pm, Sa 7:30am-noon), runs buses to Denver (10-12hr., 3 per day, $62-66); Dallas (12-14hr., 6 per day, $70-74); and Kansas City, MO (1hr., 4 per day, $12-13). The **Lawrence Transit System (the "T")**, 930 E. 30th St., handles local transportation. Pick up schedules on any bus, at the office, or at the library. (☎312-7054. Open M-F 6am-8pm, Sa 7am-8pm. 50¢, seniors and disabled 25¢.) **Visitors Center:** 2nd and Locust St. (☎865-4499 or 888-529-5267; open M-Sa 8:30am-5:30pm, Su 1-5pm). **Lawrence Chamber of Commerce:** 734 Vermont St., #101 (☎865-4411; open M-F 8am-5pm). **Post Office:** 645 Vermont St. (☎843-1681; open M-F 8am-5:30pm, Sa 9am-noon). **ZIP code:** 66045. **Area code:** 785.

MISSOURI

Pro-slavery Missouri applied for statehood in 1818, but due to Congress's fear of upsetting the balance of free and slave states, it was forced to wait until Maine entered the Union as a free state in 1821. Missouri's Civil War status as a border state was a harbinger of its future ambiguity; close to the center of the country, Missouri still defies regional stereotyping. Its large cities are defined by wide avenues, long and lazy rivers, numerous parks, humid summers, and blues and jazz wailing into the night. In the countryside, Bible factory outlets stand amid firework stands and barbecue pits. Missouri's patchwork geography further complicates characterization. In the north, near Iowa, amber waves of grain undulate. Along the Mississippi, towering bluffs inscribed with Native American pictographs evoke western canyonlands, while Hannibal's spelunkers enjoy some of the world's largest limestone caves, made famous by Mark Twain's Tom Sawyer.

∎ PRACTICAL INFORMATION

Capital: Jefferson City.
Visitor info: Missouri Division of Tourism, P.O. Box 1055, Jefferson City 65102 (☎573-751-4133 or 800-877-1234; www.visitmo.org). Open M-F 8am-5pm; toll-free number operates 24hr. **Dept. of Natural Resources,** Division of State Parks, P.O. Box 176, Jefferson City 65102 (☎573-751-2479 or 800-334-6946). Open M-F 8am-5pm.
Postal Abbreviation: MO. **Sales Tax:** Varies, averaging 6.75%.

ST. LOUIS ☎314

Located directly south of the junction of the Mississippi, Missouri, and Illinois rivers, St. Louis gained prominence in the 18th and 19th centuries as the US expanded west. St. Louis has also played an important role in American music history: the city contributed both to the development of the blues and witnessed Scott Joplin's invention of ragtime in the early 20th century. Generally considered the best baseball town in America, St. Louis is also home to innovative musicians, infamous ghettoes, and the magnificent Gateway Arch, a silvery landmark of expansion.

▐ TRANSPORTATION

Airport: Lambert-St. Louis International (☎426-8000), 12 mi. northwest of the city on I-70. Hub for **TWA**. MetroLink and Bi-state bus #66 "Maplewood-Airport" provide easy access to downtown ($1.25). Taxis to downtown are less economical ($20). A few westbound Greyhound buses stop at the airport.

Trains: Amtrak, 550 S. 16th St. (☎331-3000). To: Chicago (6hr., 3 per day, $27-58) and Kansas City (5½hr., 2 per day, $26-52). Office open daily 6am-1am.

Buses: Greyhound, 1450 N. 13th St. (☎231-4485), at Cass Ave. Bi-State bus #30 "Cass" takes less than 10min. from downtown. *Be cautious at night.* To Chicago (6½hr., 11 per day, $31) and Kansas City (5hr., 5 per day, $28).

Public Transit: Bi-State (☎231-2345). Info and schedules available at the **Metroride Service Center** in the St. Louis Center (☎982-1485; open M-F 6am-8pm, Sa-Su 8am-5pm). **MetroLink,** the light-rail system, runs from 5th St. and Missouri Ave. in East St. Louis to Lambert Airport M-Sa 5am-midnight and Su 6am-11pm. Travel for free in the "Ride Free Zone" (from Laclede's Landing to Union Station) M-F 11:30am-1pm. Fare for Bi-State or MetroLink $1.25, transfers 10¢; seniors and ages 5-12 50¢/5¢. Day pass $4, available at MetroLink stations. **Shuttle Bug,** a small bus painted like a ladybug, cruises around Forest Park and the Central West End. (M-F 6:45am-6pm, Sa-Su 10am-6pm. $1.25.) The **Shuttle Bee** buzzes around Forest Park, Clayton, Brentwood, and the Galleria. (M-F 6am-11:30pm, Sa 7:30am-10:30pm, Su 9:30am-6:30pm. $1.25.)

Taxis: Yellow Cab, ☎361-2345.

▐ ORIENTATION AND PRACTICAL INFORMATION

U.S. 40/I-64 runs east-west through the entire metropolitan area. Downtown, **Market St.** divides the city running north-south. Numbered streets parallel the Mississippi river, increasing to the west. The historic **Soulard** district borders the river south of downtown. **Forest Park** and **University City,** home to **Washington University** and old, stately homes, lie west of downtown; the Italian neighborhood called **The Hill** rests south of these. St. Louis is a driving town: parking comes easy, wide streets allow for lots of meters, and private lots are cheap ($2-8 per day).

Visitor info: St. Louis Visitors Center, 308 Washington Ave. (☎241-1764). Open daily 9:30am-4:30pm. The *Official St. Louis Visitors Guide* and the monthly magazine *Where: St. Louis,* both free, contain helpful info and decent maps.

Hotlines: Rape Hotline, ☎531-2003. **Suicide Hotline,** ☎647-4357. **Kids Under 21 Crisis,** ☎644-5886. All 24hr. **Gay and Lesbian Hotline,** ☎367-0084. Operates M-Sa 6-10pm.

Hospitals: Barnes-Jewish Hospital, 216 S. Kingshighway Blvd. (☎747-3000). **Metro South Women's Health Center,** 2415 N. Kingshighway Blvd. (☎772-1749).

Post Office: 1720 Market St. (☎436-4114). Open M-F 8am-8pm, Sa 8am-1pm. **ZIP code:** 63103. **Area code:** 314 (in St. Louis), 636 (in St. Charles), 618 (in IL); in text, 314 unless noted.

ACCOMMODATIONS

Most budget lodging is far from downtown. For chain motels, try **Lindbergh Blvd. (Rte. 67)** near the airport, or the area north of the I-70/I-270 junction in **Bridgeton**, 5 mi. beyond the airport. **Watson Rd.** near Chippewa is littered with cheap motels; take bus #11 "Chippewa-Sunset Hills" or #20 "Cherokee."

Huckleberry Finn Youth Hostel (HI-AYH), 1908 S. 12th St. at Tucker Blvd. (☎241-0076), 2 blocks north of Russell Blvd. in the Soulard District. Take bus #73 "Carondelet." A very accommodating hostel with TV, lockers, full kitchen, free parking, and friendly staff. Linen $3. Key deposit $5. Reception daily 8-10am and 6-10pm. Check-out 9:30am. Dorm-style rooms with 10-12 beds $15, nonmembers $18. Ask about work opportunities, such as whitewashing the fence.

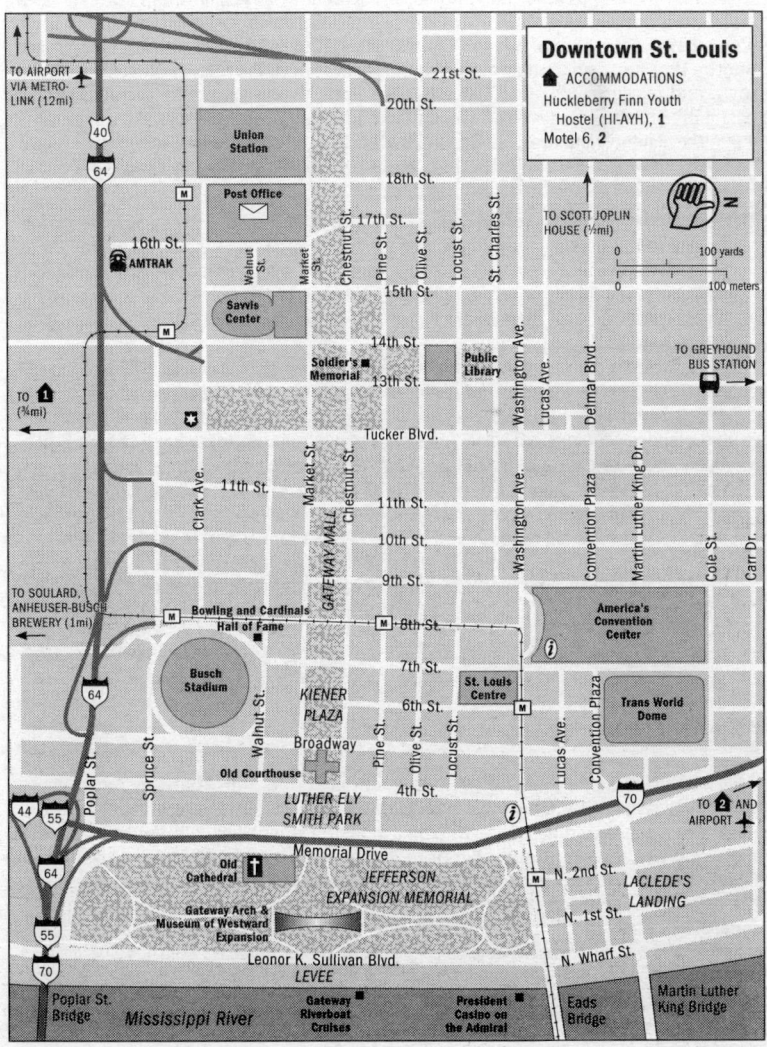

Downtown St. Louis

🏠 ACCOMMODATIONS
Huckleberry Finn Youth
Hostel (HI-AYH), **1**
Motel 6, **2**

Motel 6, 4576 Woodson Rd. (☎427-1313), Exit 236 off I-70, near the airport. From downtown, Metrolink to the airport or take bus #4 "Natural Bridge." Most motels match the price but not the cleanliness. A/C, pool. Singles $46-52; doubles $52-58.

Royal Budget Inn, 6061 Collinsville Rd. (☎618-874-4451), 20min. east of the city off Exit 6 of I-55/I-70 in Fairmont City, IL. Clean, one-bed purple-lit rooms with an aqua-green Taj Mahal flavor. Rooms Su-Th $35, F-Sa $38.

Horseshoe Lake State Park, 3321 Rte. 111 (☎618-931-0270), north off I-70 in Granite City, IL. Sites are on an island (connected by a causeway) in a very secluded area. No electricity or showers. Sites $7.

☀ FOOD

In St. Louis, the difference of a few blocks can mean vastly different cuisine. The area surrounding **Union Station,** at 18th and Market St. downtown, is being revamped with hip restaurants and bars. The **Central West End** offers coffeehouses and outdoor cafes; a slew of impressive restaurants await just north of Lindell Blvd. along **Euclid Ave.** (MetroLink to "Central West End" and walk north, or catch the Shuttle Bug.) St. Louis's historic Italian neighborhood, **The Hill,** southwest of downtown and just northwest of Tower Grove Park, produces plenty of inexpensive pasta; take bus #99 "Lafayette." Cheap Thai, Philippine, and Vietnamese restaurants spice the **South Grand** area, at Grand Blvd. just south of Tower Grove Park; board bus #70 "Grand." The intellectual set hangs out on **University City Loop,** on Delmar Blvd. between Skinker Blvd. and Big Bend Blvd.

Blueberry Hill, 6504 Delmar Blvd. (☎727-0880), on the Loop. Eclectic rock 'n' roll restaurant with 9 different rooms including the "Duck Room" and the "Elvis Room." Walls decked with record covers, Howdy Doody toys, a *Simpsons* collection, and giant baseball cards. The jukebox plays 2000 songs, and live bands play F-Sa and some weeknights (cover $4-15). Burgers are big and juicy ($4.75). 21+ after 8pm. Open M-Sa 11am-1am, Su 11am-midnight.

Ted Drewe's Frozen Custard, 4224 S. Grand Blvd. (☎352-7376); or 6726 Chippewa (☎481-2652), on Rte. 66. *The* place for the summertime St. Louis experience since 1929. Standing in line for the "chocolate-chip banana concrete shake" is rewarding; the blended toppings are thick enough to hang in an overturned cup ($1.60-3.60). Open June-Aug. daily 11am-midnight; Sept.-Dec. and Feb.-May 11am-11pm.

Pho Grand, 3195 S. Grand Blvd. (☎664-7435), in the South Grand area. Good Vietnamese food, with vegetarian and thinly cut beef options. Their specialty is *pho* (noodle soup; $4); entrees are $4-6. Open Su-M and W-Th 11am-10pm, F-Sa 11am-11pm.

Mangia Italiano, 3145 S. Grand Blvd. (☎664-8585). Offers fresh pasta made on site ($5-9), jazz on weekend nights, a handpainted mural wall, and mismatched tables. Food served M-F noon-10pm and Sa-Su 12:30-10:30pm; bar open until 1:30am.

Kaldi's Coffeehouse and Roasting Company, 700 De Mun Ave. (☎727-9955), in Clayton. Home-roasted java and the food is fresh. Intellectuals dig into panini ($5) and whole-wheat pizza ($3) in this intimate, veggie-friendly establishment. Open daily 7am-11pm.

👁 SIGHTS

DOWNTOWN. The nation's tallest monument at 630 ft., the **Gateway Arch** towers gracefully over all of St. Louis and southern Illinois. The ground-level view is impressive, but the 4min. ride to the top in quasi-futuristic elevator modules is more fun. Waits are shorter after dinner or in the morning but are uniformly long on Saturday. Beneath the arch, the underground **Museum of Westward Expansion** adds to the appeal of the grassy park complex known comprehensively as the **Jefferson Expansion Memorial.** The museum celebrates the Louisiana Purchase and its exploration. *(☎982-1410. Museum and arch open daily 8am-10pm; in winter 9am-6pm. Tickets for 1 attraction $6, ages 13-16 $4, ages 3-12 $2.50; 2 attractions $10/$8/$5; 3 attractions $14/ $12/$7.50. Limited wheelchair access.)* Scope out the city from the water with **Gateway Riverboat Cruises;** tours leave from the docks in front of the arch. *(☎621-4040 or 800-878-7411. 1hr. tours 11am-3:30pm. $9, ages 3-12 $4.)*

Beneath the arch, St. Louis's oldest church, **Old Cathedral,** holds masses daily. *(209 Walnut St. ☎231-3250.)* Within walking distance is the magnificently ornate **Old Courthouse,** across the highway from the arch. In 1847, Dred Scott sued for freedom from slavery here. *(11 N. 4th St. ☎655-1600. Open daily 8am-4:30pm. Tours usually every hr. in summer, less frequently in winter. Free. Limited wheelchair access.)*

It's a strike either way at the **International Bowling Museum and Hall of Fame** and the **St. Louis Cardinals Hall of Fame Museum,** across from Busch Stadium. The amusing bowling museum features little-known facts about bowling (only here can you learn how monopolistic German dwarfs played Sunday night games with gold and silver pins), while the baseball museum exhibits memorabilia from the glory days of St. Louis hardball. *(111 Stadium Plaza. ☎231-6340. Open in summer M-Sa 9am-5pm, Su noon-5pm; Oct.-Mar. daily 11am-4pm; game days until 6:30pm. $6, ages 5-12 $4. Includes 4 frames in the lanes downstairs. Wheelchair accessible.)* Historic **Union Station,** 1 mi. west of downtown, houses a shopping mall, food court, and entertainment center in a magnificent structure that was once the nation's largest and busiest railroad terminal. *(18th and Market St. ☎421-6655. MetroLink to Union Station.)* "The Entertainer" lives on at the **Scott Joplin House,** just west of downtown at Geyer Rd., where the ragtime legend lived and composed from 1901 to 1903. The detailed one-hour tour delves into Joplin's long-lasting influence on American music and his tortured love life and includes a few live performances of ragtime classics. *(2658 Delmar Blvd. ☎340-5790. Open in summer M-Sa 10am-5pm, Su noon-6pm. $2, ages 6-12 $1.25. Wheelchair accessible.)*

SOUTH AND SOUTHWEST OF DOWNTOWN. Soulard is bounded by I-55 and Seventh St.; walk south on Broadway or 7th St. from downtown, or take bus #73 "Carondelet." In the early 70s, the city proclaimed this area a historic district, because it once housed German and East European immigrants, many of whom worked in the breweries. At Lafayette and 7th St., the district surrounds the bustling **Soulard Farmers Market,** where fresh produce abounds. *(730 Carroll St. ☎622-4180. Open W-F 8am-5:30pm, Sa 6am-5:30pm; hours vary among merchants.)* The end of 12th St. features the largest brewery in the world, the **Anheuser-Busch Brewery,** 12th and Lynch St. The 1½hr. tour is markedly less thrilling than sampling the beer at the end. *(1127 Pestalozzi St. Take bus #40 "Broadway" south from downtown. ☎577-2626. Tours June-Aug. M-Sa 9am-5pm; Sept.-May 9am-4pm. Get free tickets at the office. Wheelchair accessible.)*

The internationally acclaimed 79-acre **Missouri Botanical Garden** thrives north of Tower Grove Park on grounds left by entrepreneur Henry Shaw. The Japanese Garden is guaranteed to soothe the weary budget traveler. *(4344 Shaw Blvd. From downtown, take I-44 west by car or ride MetroLink to "Central West End" and hop on bus #13 "Union-Missouri Botanical Gardens" to the main entrance. ☎800-642-8842. Open M 9am-8pm, Tu-Su 9am-5pm. $7, seniors $5, under 12 free. Guided tours daily at 1pm. Wheelchair accessible.)* **Grant's Farm,** the former home of President Ulysses S. Grant, is now a bustling wildlife preserve. The tram-ride tour crosses a terrain where over 1000 animals roam and interact freely, as evidenced by the zebrass (donkey-zebra). Do you know what's preserved in Grant's Farm? *(10501 Gravois Rd. Take I-55 west to Reavis Barracks Rd. and turn left onto Gravois. ☎843-1700. Open May-Aug. Tu-Sa 9:30am-4pm, Su 10am-5pm.; call for Apr. and Sept. hours. Free. Parking $4.)*

WEST OF DOWNTOWN. Forest Park, the country's largest urban park, contains three museums, a zoo, a planetarium, a 12,000-seat amphitheater, and a grand canal, as well as countless picnic areas, pathways, and flying golf balls. Take MetroLink to Forest Park and catch the Shuttle Bug. All Forest Park sites are wheelchair accessible. Marlin Perkins, the late host of TV's *Wild Kingdom*, turned the **St. Louis Zoo** into a world-class institution, replete with frisbee-playing sea lions. *(☎781-0900. Open late May-early Sept. W-M 9am-5pm, Tu 9am-dusk; Sept.-May daily 9am-5pm. Free.)* Atop **Art Hill,** a statue of France's Louis IX, the city's namesake, raises his sword in front of the **St. Louis Art Museum,** which contains masterpieces of Asian, Renaissance, and Impressionist art. *(☎721-0072. Open Tu 1:30-8:30pm, W-Su 10am-5pm. Main museum free; special exhibits usually $8, seniors and students $6, ages 6-12 $4; free Tu.)*

From Forest Park, head east a few blocks to gawk at the Tudor homes of the **Central West End.** The vast **Cathedral Basilica of St. Louis** is a unique amalgam of architectural styles, with mosaics depicting church history in Missouri. *(4431 Lindell Blvd. MetroLink stop "Central West End" or bus #93 "Lindell" from downtown. Tours ☎533-0544. Open daily 6am-7pm, off-season 6am-5pm. Tours M-F 10am-3pm, Su after noon Mass. Wheelchair accessible.)* At a shrine of a different sort, monster truck enthusiasts pay homage to **Bigfoot,** the "Original Monster Truck," who lives with his descendants near the airport. *(6311 N. Lindbergh. ☎731-2822. Open M-F 9am-6pm, Sa 9am-3pm. Free.)*

The Loop, just northwest of the Central West End, has more than just shops full of ethnic items and cafes full of intellectuals—the sidewalk, for instance. All along the loop runs the **St. Louis Walk of Fame,** with stars and biographies celebrating famous St. Louisians like Kathleen Turner, Kevin Kline, Tennessee Williams, Bob Costas, and John Goodman. *(6504 Delmar Blvd. ☎727-7827.)*

♫ ENTERTAINMENT

Founded in 1880, the **St. Louis Symphony Orchestra** is one of the country's finest. **Powell Hall,** 718 N. Grand Blvd., holds the 101-member orchestra in acoustic and visual splendor. The symphony has a "summer series" in June at the Music School and in July at Queenie Park. (☎534-1700. Performances Sept.-May Th-Sa 8pm, Su matinee 3pm. Box office open M-Sa 9am-5pm and before performances. Tickets from $10; rush tickets often available for half-price on day of show.)

St. Louis offers theatergoers many choices. The outdoor **Municipal Opera,** the "Muny," performs tour productions of hit musicals on summer nights in Forest Park. Back rows provide 1456 free seats on a first come, first served basis. (☎361-1900. Box office open June to mid-Aug. daily 9am-9pm. Tickets $7-41.) Productions are also regularly staged by the **St. Louis Black Repertory,** 634 N. Grand Blvd. (☎534-3807), and the **Repertory Theatre of St. Louis,** 130 Edgar Rd. (☎968-4925). The **Fox Theatre,** 537 N. Grand, was originally a 1930s movie palace, but now hosts Broadway shows, classic films, and Las Vegas, country, and rock stars. (☎534-1111. Open M-Sa 10am-6pm, Su noon-4pm. Tours Tu, Th, Sa at 10:30am. Th and Sa $8, Tu $5; under 12 $3. Call for reservations.) **Metrotix** (☎534-1111) has tickets to most events.

A recent St. Louis ordinance permits gambling on the river for those over 21. The **President Casino on the Admiral** floats below the Arch on the Missouri side. (☎622-3000 or 800-772-3647. Open Su-Th 8am-4am, F-Sa 24hr. $2.) On the Illinois side, the **Casino Queen** claims "the loosest slots in town." (☎618-874-5000 or 800-777-0777. Open daily 9am-6:30am.) Parking for both is free; both are wheelchair accessible.

Six Flags St. Louis, 30min. southwest of St. Louis on I-44 at Exit 261, reigns supreme in the kingdom of amusement parks. Last year brought the addition of the vaunted "Boss" wooden roller coaster, which features a 570° helix. (☎636-938-4800. Hours vary by season. $39, seniors and under 48 in. $19.50.) The **St. Louis Cardinals** play ball at **Busch Stadium** April through early October. (☎421-3060; tickets $10-35). The 2000 Super Bowl champion **Rams,** formerly of L.A., have brought the ol' pigskin back to St. Louis in shining fashion at the **Trans World Dome** (☎425-8830; tickets $32). The **Blues** hockey team slices ice at the **Savvis Center** at 14th St. and Clark Ave. (☎843-1700 or 622-5400; tickets from $15).

♥ NIGHTLIFE

Music rules the night in St. Louis. The *Riverfront Times* (free at many bars and clubs) and the *Get Out* section of the *Post-Dispatch* list weekly entertainment. The *St. Louis Magazine,* published annually, lists seasonal events. For beer and live music, often without a cover charge, St. Louis offers **Laclede's Landing,** a collection of restaurants, bars, and dance clubs housed in 19th-century industrial buildings north of the Arch on the riverfront. In the summer, bars take turns sponsoring "block parties," with food, drink, music, and dancing in the streets. (☎241-5875. 21+. Generally open 9pm-3am, with some places open for lunch and dinner.) Other nightlife hot spots include the bohemian **Loop,** along Delmar Blvd.; **Union Station** and its environs; and the less touristy and quite gay-friendly **Soulard** district.

Brandt's Market & Cafe, 6525 Delmar Blvd. (☎727-3663), a Loop mainstay, offers live jazz, along with beer, wine, espresso, and a varied menu. Open daily 11am-midnight.

Mississippi Nights, 914 N. 1st St. (☎421-3852), hosts big local and national bands. Box office open M-F 11am-6pm.

Train Wreck, 720 N. 1st St. (☎436-1006), features alternative cover bands in its night-club F and Sa nights. Cover $3. Open Su-Th 11am-10pm, F-Sa 11am-3am.

Z, 2005 Locust St. (☎241-5700). A hip, young crowd grooves to DJ beats Tu through Sa, and enjoys a varied selection of live Latin, jazz, and funk acts. Open for dinner Th-Sa 8:30-11pm; live music Tu Sa 0pm 3am.

1860 Hard Shell Cafe & Bar, 1860 S. 9th St. (☎231-1860), in the Soulard district. Hosts some gritty blues and rock performances. Live music nightly and Sa-Su after-noons. Cover $3 after 9pm F-Sa. Open M-F 9am-1:30am, Sa-Su 10am-12:30am.

Clementine's, 2001 Menard (☎664-7869), also in the Soulard area. Contains a crowded restaurant and St. Louis's oldest gay bar (established in 1978). Open M-F 10am-1:30am, Sa 8am-1:30am, Su 11am-midnight.

◪ DAYTRIP FROM ST. LOUIS: HANNIBAL

Hannibal hugs the Mississippi River 100 mi. west of Springfield, IL, and 100 mi. northwest of St. Louis. Founded in 1819, the town remained a sleepy village until Samuel Clemens (a.k.a. Mark Twain) distinguished his boyhood home by making it the setting of *The Adventures of Tom Sawyer*. Tourists flock to Hannibal to imag-ine Tom, Huck, and Becky romping around the quaint streets and nearby caves. Despite all its tourist traps, Hannibal retains its small-town hospitality and charm.

The **Mark Twain Boyhood Home and Museum,** 208 Hill St. (☎221-9010), marks the downtown historic district with restored rooms and an assortment of memora-bilia from the witty wordsmith's life. Across the street sit the **Pilaster House** and **Clemens Law Office,** where a young Twain awoke one night to find a murdered man lying on the floor next to him. Further down Main St., the new **Mark Twain Museum** includes a collection of Norman Rockwell's *Tom and Hucks.* (☎221-9010. Open June-Aug. daily 8am-6pm; off-season hours vary dramatically. All sites included $6.) The **Mark Twain Riverboat,** at Center St. Landing, steams down the Mississippi for a one-hour sightseeing cruise that is part history, part folklore, and part advertisement for the land attractions. (☎221-3222. Late May to early Sept. 3 per day; May and Sept.-Oct. 1 per day. $9, ages 5-12 $6; dinner cruises 6:30pm $26/ $18.) Both Injun Joe's ghost and rare bats haunt the **Mark Twain Cave,** 1 mi. south of Hannibal on Rte. 79, the complex series of caverns Twain explored as a boy. Graffiti from as early as the 1830s still mark the walls. (☎221-1656. Open June-Aug. daily 8am-8pm; Apr.-May and Sept.-Oct. 9am-6pm; Nov.-Mar. 9am-4pm. 1hr. tour $12, ages 5-12 $6.) From June to August, nearby **Cameron Cave** provides a slightly longer and far spookier lantern tour ($14, ages 5-12 $7). Every 4th of July weekend, 100,000 fans converge on Hannibal for the fence-painting, frog-jump-ing fun of the **Tom Sawyer Days** festival (☎221-2477).

As befits a state bordering the Deep South, Hannibal is home to some tasty barbe-cue establishments. At ◪**Bubba's,** 101 Church St., the specialty is catfish, but don't miss the pit-smoked BBQ pork and beef sandwiches ($5.50) that come with home-style vegetable sides such as cole slaw and jambalaya. (☎221-5552. Open daily 11am-9pm.) Cool down with an ice cream ($1.50) at the **Main St. Soda Fountain,** 207 S. Main St., home to a hundred-year-old soda fountain. (☎248-1295. Open Tu-Su from 11:30am until late evening.)

From **Trailways Bus Lines,** at the junction of MM and 61 (☎800-992-4618), in front of Abel's Quik Shop, buses blaze to Cedar Rapids (1 per day, $60) and St. Louis (1 per day, $23). The **Hannibal Convention and Visitors Bureau,** 505 N. 3rd St., offers free local calls (☎221-2477; open M-F 8am-6pm, Sa 9am-6pm, Su 9:30am-4:30pm). **Post Office:** 801 Broadway (☎221-0957; open M-F 8:30am-5pm, Sa 8:30am-noon). **ZIP code:** 63401. **Area code:** 573.

GREAT PLAINS

KANSAS CITY ☎ 816

With over 200 public fountains and more miles of boulevard than Paris, Kansas City looks and acts more European than one might expect from the "Barbecue Capital of the World." KC has a strong tradition of booze and good music. When Prohibition stifled most of the country's fun in the 20s, Mayor Pendergast let the good times continue to roll. The Kansas City of today maintains its big bad blues-and-jazz rep in a metropolis spanning two states: the highly suburbanized and mostly bland half in Kansas (KCKS) and the quicker-paced commercial half in Missouri (KCMO).

⌐ TRANSPORTATION

Airport: Kansas City International (☎243-5237), 18 mi. northwest of KC off I-29 (take bus #29). **KCI Shuttle** (☎243-5000 or 800-243-6383) departs over 100 times daily, servicing downtown, Westport, Crown Center, and Plaza of KCMO and Overland Park, Mission, and Lenexa of KCKS (one-way $13, round-trip $21). Taxi to downtown $25-30.

Trains: Amtrak, 2200 Main St. (☎421-3622), at Pershing Rd., next to the renovated old Union Station (take bus #27). To St. Louis (5-6½hr., 2 per day, $26-52) and Chicago (10hr., 2 per day, $49-98). Open 24hr.

Buses: Greyhound, 1101 N. Troost (☎221-2835). Take bus #25. *Stay alert—the terminal is in an unsafe area.* To St. Louis (5hr., 5 per day, $30) and Chicago (10-15hr., 6 per day, $45). Open daily 5:30am-midnight.

Public Transit: Kansas City Area Transportation Authority (Metro), 1200 E. 18th St. (☎221-0660), near Troost. Excellent downtown coverage. $1, $1.20 for Independence, MO; seniors and disabled 50¢. Free transfers. Buses run 5am-1am. **Downtowner Shuttles** run north-south on Main St. and east-west on 11th St. M-F 6:30am-6pm. Fare 25¢.

Taxis: Yellow Cab, ☎471-5000.

✴ 🛈 ORIENTATION AND PRACTICAL INFORMATION

The KC metropolitan area sprawls almost interminably, making travel difficult without a car. Most sights worth visiting lie south of downtown on the Missouri side or in the 18th and Vine Historic District. All listings are for KCMO, unless otherwise indicated. Although parking around town is not easy during the daytime, there are many lots that charge $5 or less per day. **I-70** cuts east-west through the city, and **I-435** circles the two-state metro area. KCMO is laid out on an extensive grid with numbered streets running east-west from the Missouri River well out into suburbs, and named streets running north-south. **Main St.** divides the city east-west.

Visitor info: Convention and Visitors Bureau of Greater Kansas City, 1100 Main St., #2550 (☎221-5242 or 800-767-7700), 25th fl. of the City Center Sq. Bldg. Open M-F 8:30am-5pm. Locations in the Plaza and Union Station open M-F 10am-6pm, Sa-Su noon-6pm. **Missouri Tourist Information Center,** 4010 Blue Ridge Cut-Off (☎889-3330 or 800-877-1234); follow signs from Exit 9 off I-70. Open Mar.-Nov. daily 8am-5pm, Dec.-Feb. M-Sa 8am-5pm.

Hotlines: Crisis Line, ☎531-0233. **Gay and Lesbian Hotline,** ☎931-4470. **Suicide Prevention,** ☎888-233-1639. **Troubled Youth Line,** ☎741-1477. **Women and Children's Center,** ☎452-8535. All operate 24hr.

Hospitals: Truman Medical Center, 2301 Holmes St. (☎556-3000). **Women's Clinic of Johnson County,** 5701 W. 119th St. (☎491-4020).

Internet access: Kansas City Public Library, 311 E. 12th St. (☎221-2685). Open M-Th 9am-9pm, F-Sa 9am-5pm, Su 1-5pm.

Post Office: 315 W. Pershing Rd. (☎374-9361), at Broadway (take bus #40 or 51). Open M-F 8am-6:30pm, Sa 8am-2:30pm. **ZIP code:** 64108. **Area code:** 816 in Missouri, 913 in Kansas; in text 816 unless noted.

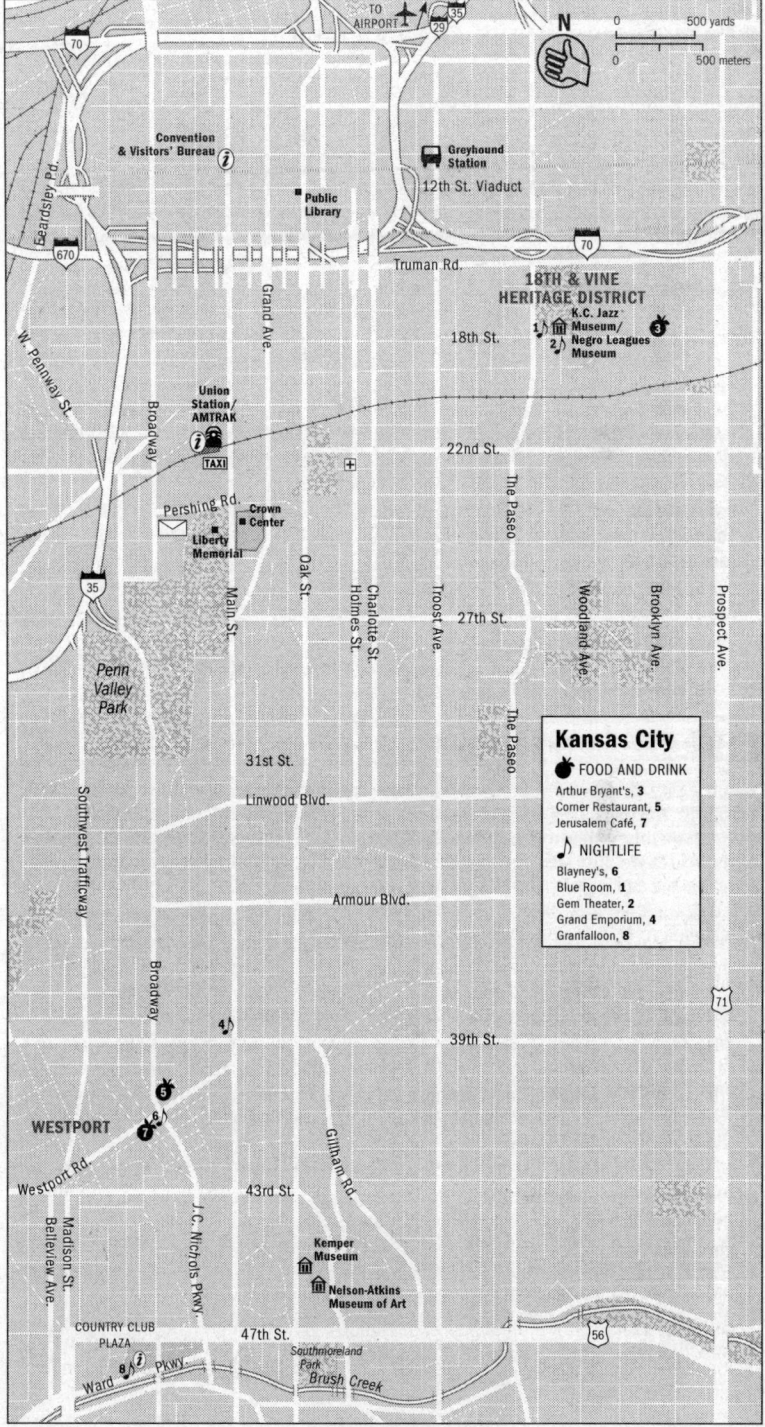

Kansas City

🍎 FOOD AND DRINK

Arthur Bryant's, **3**
Corner Restaurant, **5**
Jerusalem Café, **7**

🎵 NIGHTLIFE

Blayney's, **6**
Blue Room, **1**
Gem Theater, **2**
Grand Emporium, **4**
Granfalloon, **8**

ACCOMMODATIONS AND CAMPING

The least expensive lodgings are near the interstates, especially I-70, and towards Independence. Downtown, most hotels are either expensive, uninhabitable, or unsafe—sometimes all three. For help finding a bed in an inn or a home closer to downtown (from $50), call **Bed and Breakfast Kansas City** (☎913-888-3636).

Serendipity Bed and Breakfast, 116 S. Pleasant St. (☎833-4719 or 800-203-4299), 20min. from downtown KC in Independence. A Victorian mansion with all the trimmings and an ample breakfast. Historic tours and train pickups are available in a 1926 Studebaker, weather and time permitting. Singles $30-80; doubles $45-100.

American Inn (☎800-905-6343), a chain that dominates the KC budget motel market, has locations at 4141 S. Noland (☎373-8300); Woods Chapel Rd. (☎228-1080) off I-70 at Exit 18; 1211 Armour Rd. (☎471-3451) in North Kansas City off I-35 at Exit 6B; and 7949 Splitlog Rd. (☎913-299-2999) in KCKS off I-70 at Exit 414. Despite the gaudy neon facades, the rooms inside are large, cheap, and good-looking, with A/C, free local calls, cable, and outdoor pools. Rates are subject to a rather annoying game: the motels have a cheap set of rooms (singles from $30; doubles from $45) that sell immediately, leaving more expensive rooms remaining (singles $46-56, doubles $50-60). American does offer a 10% AAA discount.

Interstate Inn (☎229-6311), off I-70 at Exit 18. A great deal if you get one of a small set of walk-in, non-reserveable singles and doubles ($30); other singles $44-79.

YMCA, 900 N. 8th St. (☎913-371-4400) in KCKS. Varying rooms for men. Take bus #1 or 4. $84 per week plus $10 key deposit.

Lake Jacomo (☎229-8980), 22 mi. southeast of KCMO. Take I-470 south to Colbern, then head east on Colbern for 2 mi. 10-12 forested campsites, lots of water activities, and a nifty dam across the street. Reservations are accepted. Sites $10, with electricity $14, plus water $16, full hookup $20.

BBQ AND OTHER GRUB

Kansas City rustles up a herd of barbecue restaurants that serve unusually tangy ribs. The **Westport** area, at Westport Rd. and Broadway just south of 40th St., has eclectic menus, cafes, and coffeehouses. Ethnic fare clusters along **39th St.** just east of the state line. For fresh produce, visit **City Market,** at 5th and Walnut St. along the river. (☎842-1271. Open Su-F 9am-4pm, Sa 6am-4pm.)

Arthur Bryant's, 1727 Brooklyn St. (☎231-1123). Take the Brooklyn exit off I-70 (bus #110 from downtown). A KC tradition, this restaurant is invariably on the short list for best barbecue in the country. "Sandwiches"—little wimpy triangles of bread drowning in a mass of perfectly-cooked meat—are $7. Vegetarians should probably head elsewhere. Open M-Th 10am-9:30pm, F-Sa 10am-10pm, Su 11am-8:30pm.

Strouds, 1015 E. 85th St. (☎333-2132), at Troost, 2 mi. north of the Holmes exit off I-435. All-you-can-eat portions of vegetables and potatoes are served along with entrees. The $11 chicken-fried steak is deadly good in size and taste; save room for homemade cinnamon rolls (usually included in the price). Open M-Th 4-9:30pm, F 11am-10:30pm, Sa 2-10:30pm, Su 11am-9:30pm.

d-Bronx, 3904 Bell St. (☎531-0550), on the 39th St. restaurant row. A New York deli transplanted to middle America. 35 kinds of subs (half-sub $3-6, whole $6-10) and huge brownies ($1.50). Open M-Th 10:30am-10:30pm, F-Sa 10:30am-midnight.

Jerusalem Cafe, 431 Westport Rd. (☎756-2770). Vegetarians can breathe a sigh of relief at this healthy (and tasty) sanctuary. Sandwiches with rice and salad $4-5, entrees $8-10. Open M-Sa 11am-10pm, Su noon-8pm.

Corner Restaurant, 4059 Broadway (☎931-6630), in the heart of Westport. Large breakfast specials, including plate-sized pancakes ($3) and biscuits and gravy ($5). Lunch and dinner specials $5-8. Open M-F 7am-3pm and 5-9pm, Sa-Su 7am-2pm.

⑥ SIGHTS

Jazz once flourished in what has been recently designated as the **18th and Vine Historic District** (☎474-8463). The **Kansas City Jazz Museum,** 1616 E. 18th St., brings back the era with classy displays, music listening stations, neon dance hall signs, and everything from Ella Fitzgerald's eyeglasses to Louis Armstrong's lip salve. In the same building swings the **Negro Leagues Baseball Museum,** where the era of segregation of the American pastime is recalled with photographs, interactive exhibits, and bittersweet nostalgia. Take bus #108 "Indiana." (Jazz museum: ☎474-8463. Baseball museum: ☎221-1920. Both open Tu-Sa 9am-6pm, Su noon-6pm. One museum $6, under 12 $2.50; both museums $8/$4.) The nearby **Black Archives of Mid-America,** 2033 Vine St., holds a large collection of paintings and sculpture by African-American artists, focusing on local black history. Take bus #108 "Indiana." (☎483-1300. Open M-F 9am-4:30pm, tours start 10am. $2, under 17 50¢.)

A taste of KC's masterpieces is available at the **Nelson-Atkins Museum of Art,** 4525 Oak St., three blocks northeast of Country Club Plaza. The museum contains one of the best East Asian art collections in the world and a sculpture park with 13 Henry Moores. Renovations scheduled to be completed in 2003 may lead to exhibit closings; call ahead. Take bus #147, 155, 156, or 157. (☎561-4000. Open Tu-Th 10am-4pm, F 10am-9pm, Sa 10am-5pm, Su noon-5pm. Jazz F 5:30-8:30pm. $5, students $2, ages 6-18 $1; free Sa. Free tours Tu-Sa until 2pm, Su until 3pm.) Two hundred tons of treasure and local history were unearthed from a nearby field in 1988 after lying for nearly 150 years at the bottom of the Missouri River. Now, these findings rest at the **Steamboat Arabia Museum,** 400 Grand Ave. Displayed items include bottles of bourbon, plates, stationery, clothing, and most of the original logs from the ship. (☎471-4030. Open M-Sa 10am-5pm, Su noon-4pm. $8.50, seniors $8, ages 4-12 $4.75.)

A few blocks to the west at 47th and Southwest Trafficway, **Country Club Plaza,** known as "the Plaza," is the oldest and perhaps most picturesque shopping center in the US. Modeled after buildings in Seville, Spain, the Plaza boasts fountains, sculptures, hand-painted tiles, and reliefs of grinning gargoyles. During summer, the Plaza hosts free concerts on the weekends. Take buses #139, 140, 147, 151, 155, 156, or 157 (☎753-0100). **Crown Center** sits 2 mi. north of the Plaza, near Pershing Rd. The center, headquarters of Hallmark Cards, houses a maze of restaurants and shops, plus the children's **Coterie Theatre** and the **Ice Terrace,** KC's only public outdoor ice-skating rink. On the 3rd level of the center, say "I care!" and see how cards and accessories are made at the **Hallmark Visitors Center.** Take bus #140, 156, 157, or any trolley. (Crown Center: 2450 Grand Ave. ☎274-8444. Coterie: ☎474-6785. $8, children $6. Ice Terrace: ☎274-8412. Rink open Nov.-Dec. Su-Th 10am-9pm, F-Sa 10am-11pm; Jan.-Mar. daily 10am-9pm. $5, under 13 $4. Rentals $1.50. Visitors Center: ☎274-3613 or 274-5672 for a recording. Open M-F 9am-5pm, Sa 9:30am-4:30pm.)

🎵 ENTERTAINMENT

The **Missouri Repertory Theatre,** 50th and Oak St., stages American classics. (☎235-2700. Season Sept.-May. Tickets $25 and up, students and seniors $3 off. Box office open M-F 10am-5pm; call for weekend hours.) **Quality Hill Playhouse,** 303 W. 10th St., produces off-Broadway plays and revues year-round. (☎235-2700. Tickets around $20, seniors and students $2 off.) Late June to mid-July, the **Heart of America Shakespeare Festival** (☎531-7728) in Southmoreland Park, 47th and Oak St., puts on free shows nearly every night at 8pm. In Shawnee Mission, KS, the **New Theatre Restaurant,** 9229 Foster St., stages dinner theater productions of classic comedies and romances, attracting nationally recognized actors. Take Metcalf Ave. and turn into the Regency Park Center between 91st and 95th St. (☎913-649-7469. Box office open M-Sa 9am-6pm and Su 11am-3pm. Tickets $22-44; buffet meal included.)

Sports fans will be pierced to the heart by **Arrowhead Stadium,** at I-70 and Blue Ridge Cutoff, home to football's **Chiefs** (☎920-9400 or 800-676-5488; tickets from $30) and soccer's **Wizards** (☎472-4625; tickets $10-15). Next door, a water-fountained wonder, **Kauffman Stadium** (☎921-8000 or 800-676-9257), houses the **Royals** baseball team (tickets $7-17, M and Th most seats half-price). A stadium express bus runs from downtown and Country Club Plaza on game days.

 NIGHTLIFE

In the 20s, jazz musician Count Basie and his "Kansas City Sound" reigned at the River City bars; 20 years later, saxophonist Charlie "Bird" Parker spread his wings and soared. The Crown Center rocks annually with the **Kansas City International Jazz Festival,** on the last weekend in June. (☎888-337-8111. Tickets from $12.) The restored **Gem Theater,** 1615 E. 18th St., stages old-time blues and jazz. (☎842-1414. Box office open M-F 10am-4pm.) Across the street, the **Blue Room,** 1600 E. 18th St., cooks four nights a week with some of the smoothest acts in town. (☎474-2929. Cover F-Sa $5. Bar open M and Th 5-11pm, F-Sa 7pm-1am.) The **Grand Emporium,** 3832 Main St., twice voted the best blues club in the US, has live music five nights a week. (☎531-1504. Live music M and W-Sa. Cover $5-15. Open daily noon-3am.)

The young and the beautiful strut their stuff in the up-and-coming **Granfalloon,** 608 Ward Pkwy., in the Plaza area. During the daytime, this noisy hot spot serves up sandwiches ($5-6.50) and salads ($4-6); at night, patron's attentions are drawn to $1.50 domestic beer specials. (☎753-7850. Open daily 9am-2:30am.) Bars also cluster in the Westport area. Intense rhythm and blues pours onto the newly built deck at **Blayney's,** 415 Westport Rd. (☎561-3747; cover $2-7; open Tu-Th 8pm-3am, F-Sa 6pm-3am). The music at **Kiki's Bon-Ton Maison,** 1515 Westport Rd., ranges from reggae to hard rock, while the Cajun cookin' clears your sinuses. (☎931-9417. Cover $3. Open M-Th 11am-10pm, F 11am-11pm, Sa 11am-1:30am, Su 11:30am-8pm.)

The Westport area is also ground zero for dance clubs. "Retro" and "disco" are the key words at **America's Pub,** 520 Westport Rd. (☎531-1313. Cover $5. Open Tu-Sa 8pm-2:30am.) Elevated barstools provide excellent people-watching opportunities, while an oh-so-young crowd gyrates on the packed dance floor. Across the street at the **Have a Nice Day Cafe,** 415 Mill St., hipsters groove to dance, disco, pop, and rock beats on a raised dance floor. A slightly more middle-aged crowd congregates at the bar to watch the several TVs. (☎931-9110. Cover $5. Open M-Sa 5pm-1:30am.) **The Hurricane,** 4040 Broadway, caters to both young and old with different local acts each night. (☎752-0884. Beers $3. Cover $5. Open daily 8pm-3am.)

▓ DAYTRIP FROM KANSAS CITY: INDEPENDENCE

The buck stops at Independence, the hometown of former President Harry Truman and a 15min. drive east of KC on I-70 or U.S. 24. The **Harry S. Truman Library and Museum,** at U.S. 24 and Delaware St., has a replica of the Oval Office and exhibits about the man, the times, and the presidency. Ongoing renovations mean some exhibits will be closed; call ahead for info. (☎833-1225 or 800-833-1225. Open M-W and F-Sa 9am-5pm, Th 9am-9pm, Su noon-5pm. $5, seniors $4.50, ages 6-18 $3.) Just down the street, the **Harry S. Truman Home,** 219 N. Delaware St., known as the "Summer White House," provides a glimpse into the president's home life. Get tickets to tour the Victorian mansion at the **Truman Home Ticket and Info Center,** 223 Main St. (☎254-2720. Open daily 8:30am-5pm. $3, under 18 free.)

Independence's history goes back farther than just Truman. The Santa Fe, Oregon, and Mormon Trails all began here. Walk a part of these historic trails with the info provided by the **National Frontier Trails Center,** 318 W. Pacific. (☎325-7575. Open M-Sa 9am-4:30pm, Su 12:30-4:30pm; $3.50, seniors $3, ages 5-18 $2.) The gothic **Vaile Mansion,** 1500 N. Liberty St., built in 1881, has 112 windows of various sizes and two-foot thick walls. (☎325-7430. Open Apr.-Oct. and Dec. M-Sa 10am-4pm, Su 1-4pm. $4, seniors $3.50, ages 6-16 $1.) On the bluffs overlooking downtown Kansas City hovers the computer-designed world headquarters of the **Community of Christ,** formerly the **Reorganized Church of Jesus Christ of Latter-Day Saints,** 1001 W. Walnut

St. Modeled after the chambered nautilus, the structure is a bizarre and beautiful seashell that spirals up nearly 200 ft. to a pinnacled point. (☎521-3030. Tours M-Sa 9-11:30am and 1-5pm, Su 1-5pm. Organ recitals Su 3pm; daily in summer. Free.)

BRANSON   ☎417

The Presley family had no idea what the impact would be when they opened a tiny music theater on **West Rte. 76.** Over 7 million tourists, mostly retirees, clog Branson's strip each year to visit the "live country music capital of the Universe." If Branson keeps growing at this pace, it may eclipse Nashville as *the* place to go for country music. Billboards, motels, and giant showplaces beckon the masses that visit Branson each year to embrace this collage of all things plastic or franchised. Branson boasts over 30 indoor theaters, and a few outdoor ones as well. Most of them have two shows a day, one in the afternoon and one around 8pm. Box office prices for most shows run between $18-40, but it all depends on who's playing. *Never* pay full price for a show or attraction in Branson. Coupon books, including the *Best Read Guide*, offer dozens of discounts. Big-name country acts, such as Loretta Lynn and Billy Ray Cyrus, play the **Grand Palace,** 2700 W. Rte. 76. (☎336-1220 or 800-884-4536. Shows Apr.-Dec. $35-50, children $12-50.) Take a break from country with the **Platters,** who hit it big with doo-wop tunes in the 50s and still pack in crowds at the Hughes Bros. Celebrity Theater. (☎336-3688. $22, under 13 free.)

Competition is fierce among accommodations, and the consumers win out most of the time. Motels along Rte. 76 generally start around $25, but prices often increase during the busy season from July to September. Some less tacky, inexpensive motels line Rte. 265, 4 mi. west of the strip or Gretna Rd. at the west end of the strip. **Budget Inn,** 315 N. Gretna Rd., has slightly dim but spacious rooms with A/C, free local calls, cable, and pool access very close to the action. (☎334-0292. Rooms from $24.50.) Branson's location along Lake Taneycomo and Table Rock Lake makes it a popular camping area as well; over 20 campgrounds and RV parks lie within a 10 mi. radius. **Indian Point,** at the end of Indian Point Rd., south of Rte. 76, has lakeside sites with swimming and a boat launch. (☎338-2121 or 888-444-6777. Reception Su-Th 9am-7pm, F-Sa 8am-8pm. Sites $12, with electricity $16.)

The off season runs from January to March; many attractions close. **Branson Chamber of Commerce:** on Rte. 248 just west of the Rte. 248/65 junction. (☎334-4136. Open M-F 8am-6pm, Sa 8am-5pm, Su 10am-4pm.) **Greyhound's** nearest location is 20 mi. south in Harrison, AR, but there is a flag stop in town at Bob Evans, on the corner of Rte. 76 and Rte. 65. **Jefferson Shuttle** (☎339-2550) also leaves from Bob Evans and runs once daily to Kansas City ($35) and Springfield, Mo. ($48). **Area code:** 417.

OKLAHOMA

In 1838 and 1839, President Andrew Jackson forced the relocation of "The Five Civilized Tribes" from the southeastern states to the designated Oklahoma Indian Territory in a tragic march which came to be known as "The Trail of Tears." After rebuilding their tribes in Oklahoma, the Indians were again dislocated in 1889 by "Boomer Sooners" who settled practically half the territory in a one-day land rush. The "Dirty Thirties" turned Oklahoma into the wasteland depicted in *The Grapes of Wrath.* Oklahoma has since overcome this history; the state instead promotes its Native American character and emphasizes its rich immigrant heritage.

◨ PRACTICAL INFORMATION

Capital: Oklahoma City.

Visitor info: Oklahoma Tourism and Recreation Dept., 15 N. Robinson, #801, Oklahoma City 73152 (☎521-2406 or 800-652-6552; www.travelok.com), in the Concord Bldg. at Sheridan St. Open M-F 8am-5pm.

Postal Abbreviation: OK. Sales Tax: 8%. **Tolls:** Damn annoying. Oklahoma is fond of tollbooths, so keep a wad of bills (and a roll of coins for unattended booths) handy.

TULSA
☎ **918**

Though Tulsa is not Oklahoma's political capital, it is in many ways the center of the state. First settled by Creek Native Americans arriving on the Trail of Tears, Tulsa's location on the banks of the Arkansas River made it a logical trading outpost. The town's Art Deco skyscrapers, French villas, Georgian mansions, and distinctively large Native American population reflect its varied heritage. Rough-riding motorcyclists and slick oilmen have recently joined the city's cultural melange, seeking the good life on the Great Plains.

■☐ ORIENTATION AND PRACTICAL INFORMATION. Tulsa is divided neatly into one sq. mi. quadrants. Downtown surrounds the intersection of **Main St.** (north-south) and **Admiral Blvd.** (east-west). Numbered streets lie in ascending order north or south from Admiral. Named streets run north-south in alphabetical order; those named after western cities are west of Main St., while eastern cities lie to the east. **Tulsa International Airport** (☎838-5000; call M-F 8am-5pm) is just northeast of downtown and accessible by I-244 or U.S. 169. **Greyhound,** 317 S. Detroit Ave. (☎584-4428), departs for Oklahoma City (2hr., 8 per day, $18); St. Louis (7-10hr., 6 per day, $76); Kansas City (7hr., 3 per day, $39); and Dallas (7hr., 4 per day, $47). Station open 24hr. **Metropolitan Tulsa Transit Authority,** 319 S. Denver, runs local buses. (☎582-2100. Open M-F 7am-5:30pm, Sa 8am-noon. Buses operate M-F 5am-8:30pm, Sa 6am-8pm. Fare $1, transfers 5¢, seniors and disabled 50¢, ages 5-18 75¢, under 5 free.) **Taxis: Yellow Cab,** ☎582-6161. **Hospitals: Hillcrest Medical Center,** 1120 S. Utica Ave. (☎579-1000), and **Center for Women's Health,** 1822 E. 15th St. (☎749-4444). **Tulsa Metro Chamber:** 616 S. Boston Ave. (☎585-1201 or 800-558-3311; open M-F 8am-5pm). **Internet access: Tulsa Public Library,** 400 Civic Center (☎596-7977; open Sept.-Apr. M-Th 9am-9pm, F-Sa 9am-5pm, Su 1-5pm). **Post Office:** 333 W. 4th St. (☎232-2176; open M-F 7:30am-5pm). **ZIP code:** 74103. **Area code:** 918.

☐ ACCOMMODATIONS. Decent budget accommodations are scarce downtown. The best deal can be found at the **YMCA,** 515 S. Denver. (☎583-6201. 6 rooms for women. Pool, track, weight rooms, and racquetball courts. $20 per day plus $20 deposit.) Also close to downtown, the **Village Inn,** 31st St. and Riverside Dr., offers uncommon amenities. Take the Riverside Dr. exit of I-44. (☎743-2009. Rooms have free local calls, cable TV, fridge, and whirlpool. Check-out 11am. Singles Su-Th $38, F-Sa $33; doubles $48/$43.) You can also try the budget motels around the junction of **I-44** and **I-244** (Exit 222 from I-44); take bus #17 "Southwest Blvd." **Georgetown Plaza Motel,** 8502 E. 27th St., off I-44 at 31st and Memorial St., offers clean, if frayed, rooms with free local calls and cable TV. (☎622-6616. Singles $28, with microfridge $31; doubles $34.) The **Gateway Motor Hotel,** 5600 W. Skelley, at Exit 222 C, has functional rooms decorated in pea-green and timber fashion. (☎446-6611. Check-out 11am. Singles $29-35; doubles $35.) The 250-site **Mingo RV Park,** 801 N. Mingo Rd., at the northeast corner of the I-244 and Mingo Rd. intersection, provides laundry and showers in a semi-urban setting. (☎832-8824 or 800-932-8824. Reception daily 8:30am-8pm. Sites with full hookup $25.)

☐☑ FOOD AND NIGHTLIFE. Most downtown restaurants cater to lunching businesspeople, closing on weekends and at 2pm on weekdays. **Nelson's Buffeteria,** 514 S. Boston Ave., is an old-fashioned diner that has served their blue plate special (two scrambled eggs, hash browns, biscuit and gravy $2.50) and famous chicken-fried steak ($6) since 1929. (☎584-9969. Open M-F 6am-2pm.) For extended hours, S. Peoria Ave. has more to offer. **The Brook Restaurant,** 3401 S. Peoria, in a converted movie theater, has classic Art Deco appeal. A traditional menu of chicken, burgers, and salads ($6-8) is complemented by an extensive list of $4.50-5.25 signature martinis. (☎748-9977. Open M-Sa 11am-2am, Su 11am-11pm.) For really extended hours, try **Mama Lou's Restaurant,** I-44 and W. Skelly Dr., where breakfast—including two eggs, three pancakes, hash browns, and bacon for $4.35—is served all day long. (☎445-1700. Open 24hr.)

Read the free *Urban Tulsa*, at local restaurants, and *The Spot* in the Friday *Tulsa World* for up-to-date specs on arts and entertainment. Good bars line the 3000s along S. Peoria Ave., an area known as **Brookside,** and 15th St. east of Peoria. Let the party-animal inside reveal itself at **ID Bar**, 3340 S. Peoria Ave. With a posh interior and quality DJs, this newly-opened dance club has a clearly un-Oklahoman feel. (☎743-0600. Live music W. 21+. Cover F-Sa $5-7. Open W-Su 9pm-2am.) 18th and Boston Ave. raises a ruckus at night, catering to the young adult crowd. College kids flock to the blues-happy **Steamroller**, 1738 Boston Ave., commonly billed as the "snob-free, dork-free, band-and-brewski place to be." (☎583-9520. Local bands Th-Sa 10pm. Cover $5. Open M-W 11am-10pm, Th-F 11am-2am, Sa 5pm-2am.)

SIGHTS AND ENTERTAINMENT. Perched atop an Osage foothill 2 mi. northwest of downtown, the **Thomas Gilcrease Museum**, 1400 Gilcrease Museum Rd., houses the world's largest collection of Western American art, as well as 250,000 Native American artifacts. Take the Gilcrease exit off Rte. 412 or bus #47. (☎596-2700. Open M-Sa 9am-5pm, Su 11am-5pm; Mid-Sept. to mid-May closed M. $3 donation requested.) The **Philbrook Museum of Art**, 2727 S. Rockford Rd., presents tastefully selected works of Native American and international art in a renovated Italian Renaissance villa, complete with a grassy sculpture garden. Take bus #5 "Peoria." (☎749-7941 or 800-324-7941. Open Tu-W and F-Sa 10am-5pm, Th 10am-8pm, Su 11am-5pm. $5, seniors and students $3, under 13 free.) The ultra-modern, gold-mirrored architecture of **Oral Roberts University**, 7777 S. Lewis Ave., rises out of an Oklahoma plain about 6 mi. south of downtown between Lewis and Harvard Ave.; take bus #12. In 1964, Oral had a dream in which God commanded him to "Build Me A University," and Tulsa's biggest tourist attraction was born. The **Visitors Center,** located in the Prayer Tower, offers free tours. (☎495-6807. Open June-Aug. M-Sa 9am-5pm, Su 1-5pm; Sept.-May 10am-5pm, Su 1-5pm. Tours begin every 15min.)

Tulsa thrives during events like the **International Mayfest** (☎582-6435; May 16-19, 2002). The city also hosts the **Oklahoma Jazz Hall of Fame** ceremonies and concerts at Greenwood Park (300 N. Greenwood Dr.; June 13-16, 2002). The **Intertribal Powwow**, at the Tulsa Fairgrounds Pavilion (Expo Sq.), attracts Native Americans and thousands of onlookers for a three-day festival of food, crafts, and nightly dance contests. (☎744-1113. August 9-11, 2002. $5 per person, $16 per "family" of four.)

NEAR TULSA: TAHLEQUAH

Oklahoma's strong Native American heritage started in Tahlequah, 66 miles southeast of Tulsa on Rte. 51. Cherokees removed from their Appalachian homelands in the 1830s by the federal government were plopped down in eastern Oklahoma. The Indians, suffering from the loss of nearly ¼ of their population along the Trail of Tears, started anew by placing the capital in this sleepy hamlet. In the center of town, on Cherokee Sq., still stands the capitol building of the **Cherokee Nation,** 101 S. Muskogee Ave. (Rte. 51/62/82). Built in 1870, the building, together with other tribal government buildings such as the Supreme Court building and the Cherokee National Prison (one and two blocks south of Cherokee Sq. respectively), formed the highest authority in Oklahoma until statehood in 1907. Across from the northeast corner of Cherokee Sq., the **Visitors Center**, 123 E. Delaware St., offers free maps of the major sites downtown. (☎456-3742. Open M-F 9am-5pm.)

The **Cherokee Heritage Center**, 4 mi. south of town on Rte. 82, reminds visitors of the injustice perpetrated against Native Americans. In the **Ancient Village**, local Cherokee recreate a 16th-century Cherokee settlement with ongoing demonstrations of skills such as bow making and basket weaving. Right next door, the well-executed **Cherokee National Museum** presents an amazing wealth of information on the Trail of Tears removal, replete with artifacts and personal histories. (☎456-6007 or 888-999-6007. Village and Museum open Feb.-Apr. M-Sa 10am-5pm; May-Oct. daily 10am-5pm; Nov.-Dec. M-Sa 10am-5pm, Su 1-5pm. Last tour 4:15pm. $8.50, under 13 $4.25, 10% AAA discount.) **Area code:** 918.

OKLAHOMA CITY ☎405

At noon on Apr. 22, 1889, a gunshot sent settlers scrambling into the Oklahoma Territory—the land rush was afoot. By sundown, Oklahoma City, set strategically along the Santa Fe Railroad, was home to over 10,000 homesteaders. These settlers have since multiplied, maintaining the thriving stockyards and horse shows that often vanished with the civilizing of the Old West. In recent years, Oklahoma City has had more than its share of tragedy; the city remains an unobstrusive and tranquil place, in spite of the traumatic 1995 bombing of the Alfred R. Murrah federal office building and the devastating 1999 tornado which left whole sections of the city in ruin. Despite the trauma, Oklahoma City continues to develop and grow.

■🛈 **ORIENTATION AND PRACTICAL INFORMATION.** Oklahoma City is constructed on a nearly perfect grid; **Santa Fe Ave.** divides the city east-west, and **Reno Ave.** divides it north-south. Cheap and plentiful parking makes driving the best way to go. **Will Rogers World Airport** (☎680-3200), is on I-44 southwest of downtown, Exit 116 B. To get to the **Greyhound** station, 427 W. Sheridan Ave. (☎235-6425), at Walker St., take city bus #4, 5, 6, 8, or 10. *Be careful at night.* Buses run to Tulsa (2hr., 7 per day, $15); Fort Worth (5hr., 5 per day, $43); and Kansas City (10hr., 6 per day, $78). Station open 24hr. **Amtrak,** 100 S. E.K. Gaylord Blvd., rumbles to Ft. Worth (4½ hr., 1 per day, $30-58). The station is open 24hr., but unattended. **Oklahoma Metro Transit** has bus service M-Sa 6am-6pm; all routes radiate from the station at 200 N. Shartel St. The office at 300 S.W. 7th distributes free schedules. (☎235-7433. Open M-F 8am-5pm. Fare $1, seniors and ages 6-17 50¢.) Look for the **Oklahoma Spirit** trolley downtown and in Bricktown. (Runs M-Sa every 15min. 9am-11pm, Su 10am-6pm. Fare 50¢.) **Yellow Cab,** ☎232-6161. The **Oklahoma City Convention and Visitors Bureau,** 189 W. Sheridan at Robinson St., has info. (☎297-8910. Open M-F 8:30am-5pm.) **Internet access: Oklahoma City Public Library,** 131 Dean McGee (☎231-8650; open M and W-F 9am-6pm, Tu 9am-9pm, Sa 9am-5pm). **Post Office:** 305 N.W. 5th St. (☎232-2176; open M-F 6am-10pm, Sa 8am-5pm). **ZIP code:** 73102. **Area code:** 405.

🛏 **ACCOMMODATIONS.** Ten minutes from downtown and 5min. from the big mall and lots of food, **Flora's Bed and Breakfast,** 2312 N.W. 46th St., has two traditional rooms available. (☎840-3157. Singles $55; doubles $60.) Other cheap lodging in OKC lies along the interstate highways, particularly on I-35 north of the I-44 junction. **The Royal Inn,** 2800 S. I-35, south of the junction with I-40, treats you to free local calls, HBO, and adequate rooms. (☎672-0899. Singles $28.50; doubles $34.) Behind a strip mall are the 172 sites of **RCA,** 12115 Northeast Expwy./I-35 N. Take southbound Frontage Rd. off Exit 137; it's ¼ mi. to the red-and-white "RV" sign. (☎478-0278. Pool, laundry, and showers. Open daily 8am-8pm; in winter 8am-6pm. Sites $12.) In contrast, **Lake Thunderbird State Park** offers campsites near a beautiful lake fit for swimming or fishing. Take I-40 east to Choctaw Rd. (Exit 166), then south 10 mi. until the road ends and make a left for another mi. (☎360-3572. Office open M-F 8am-5pm, with a host for late or weekend arrivals. Showers available. Sites $7-8, with water and electricity $15-18, full hookup $20-22; huts $45.)

◧🖾 **FOOD AND NIGHTLIFE.** Oklahoma City contains the largest feeder cattle market in the US, and beef tops most menus. Most places downtown close early in the afternoon after they've served business lunchers. A notable exception is the **Peacock Restaurant,** 517 W. Reno Ave., where gyros, Greek spaghetti, and goulash are the house favorites. (☎232-1759. Open M-F 5:30am-8pm, Sa 6am-8pm, Su 6am-2pm. Most entrees under $6.) A number of after-hours restaurants lie immediately east of town on Sheridan Ave. (in the Bricktown district) and north of downtown, along Classen Blvd. and Western Ave. Everyone's fighting for the rights to the late Leo's recipes at **Leo's Original BBQ,** 3631 N. Kelley St., a classic, hickory smoking outfit in the northwest reaches of town. (☎424-5367. Open M 11am-2pm, Tu-Sa 11am-7pm.) Unfortunately, nightlife here is almost as rare as the elusive jackalope. The Bricktown district has restaurants with live music. The **Bricktown Brewery,** 1 N.

Oklahoma St., at Sheridan Ave., brews 5 beers daily. (☎232-2739. Live music Tu and F-Sa 9pm. Upstairs 21+. Cover $5 for bands. Open Su-M 11am-10pm, Tu-Th 11am-midnight, F-Sa 11am-1:30am.) **Studio 54 at Bricktown,** 15 E. California, a crowded, brand new dance club, provides great views of Oklahoma City—and of the dressed-to-impress clientele. (☎235-3533. Tu ladies night. Open Tu-Su 8pm-2am.)

SIGHTS AND ENTERTAINMENT. Monday morning is the time to visit the **Oklahoma City Stockyards,** 2500 Exchange Ave. (☎235-8675), the busiest in the world. Take bus #12 from the terminal to Agnew and Exchange Ave. Cattle auctions (M-Tu) begin at 8am and may last into the night. Visitors enter free of charge via a cat-walk soaring over cow pens and cattle herds, leading from the parking lot northeast of the auction house. The auction is as Old West as it gets; only those with a wide-brim cowboy hat, blue jeans, boots, and faded dress shirt fit in.

Plant lovers should make a bee-line for **Myriad Gardens,** 301 W. Reno Ave., where a 70 ft. diameter glass cylinder, called the Crystal Bridge, perches above a large pond. The gardens include both a desert and a rainforest. (☎297-3995. Open M-Sa 9am-6pm, Su noon-6pm. $4, seniors and students $3, ages 4-12 $2. Gardens open daily 7am-11pm. Free.) The **National Cowboy and Western Heritage Museum,** 1700 N.E. 63rd St., features an extensive collection of Western art. (☎478-2250. Open daily 9am-5pm. $8.50, seniors $7, ages 6-12 $4, under 6 free.) The **Oklahoma City National Memorial,** at 5th and Harvey downtown, is a powerful tribute to the victims of the 1995 bombing of the Murrah Federal Bldg. The **Red Earth Festival** is the country's largest celebration of Native America; the Myriad Convention Center hosts art fairs and dance competitions. (☎427-5228. June 7-9, 2002. $7.) Fall visitors should check out the **Deep Deuce Jazz Festival** at N.E. 2nd and Walnut St. (☎424-2552; Oct. 5-6, 2002) and the **World Championship Quarter Horse Show** (☎948-6800; Nov. 3-16, 2002.)

TEXAS

Covering an area as long as the stretch from North Carolina to Key West, Texas has more the brawn of a country than a state. The fervently proud, independent citizens of the "Lone Star State" seem to prefer it that way: where else do you see "Don't Mess With Texas" on official road signs and "No firearms allowed" at restaurants and museums? After revolting against the Spanish in 1821 and splitting from Mexico in 1836, the Republic of Texas stood alone until 1845, when it entered the Union as the 28th state. The state's unofficial motto proclaims that "everything is bigger in Texas;" this truth is evident in prolific wide-brimmed hats, styled and sculpted ladies' coifs, boat-sized American autos, giant ranch spreads, countless steel skyscrapers, and oil refineries the size of small towns.

HIGHLIGHTS OF TEXAS

FOOD. Drippin' barbecue and colossal steaks reign supreme in the state where beef is king and vegetables are for the cows. Some of the best beef awaits in Austin (p. 602) and Amarillo (p. 622).

SAN ANTONIO. Remember the Alamo! A city rich with Spanish heritage (p. 620).

RODEOS/COWBOYS. The ol' West lives on in Fort Worth (p. 612) and at the Mesquite Rodeo in Dallas (p. 611), with the finest rope-riders in the land.

7 PRACTICAL INFORMATION

Capital: Austin.

Visitor info: Texas Travel Information Centers (☎800-452-9292; www.tourtexas.com), near state lines on all major highways into Texas. Call 8am-6pm (centers open daily 8am-5pm) for a free guidebook. **Texas Division of Tourism,** P.O. Box 12728, Austin 78711 (☎800-888-8839). **Texas Parks and Wildlife Dept.,** Austin Headquarters Complex, 4200 Smith School Rd., Austin 78744 (☎512-389-8950 or 800-792-1112).

Postal Abbreviation: TX. **Sales Tax:** 6-8.25%.

SAN ANTONIO   ☎210

The skyline may be dominated by aging office buildings, but no Texan city preserves its rich heritage better than the romantic San Antonio. Founded in 1691 by Spanish missionaries, the city is home to the famed Alamo, historic Missions, and La Villita, once a village for San Antonio's original settlers and now a workshop for local artisans. Many attractions, including the magnificent (albeit slightly artificial) Riverwalk, make San Antonio a popular vacation destination. Though both Native Americans and Germans have at one time claimed San Antonio as their own, Spanish speakers (55% of the population) outnumber any other group; the city's food, architecture, and language reflect this influence.

⌐ TRANSPORTATION

Flights: San Antonio International Airport, 9800 Airport Blvd. (☎207-3411), north of town. Accessible by I-410 and U.S. 281. Bus #2 ("Airport") connects the airport to downtown at Market and Alamo. Taxi to downtown $14-15.

Trains: Amtrak, 350 Hoefgen St. (☎223-3226), facing the northern side of the Alamodome. To: Houston (5hr., 3 per week, $30); Dallas (9hr., 1 per day, $28); and Los Angeles (27hr., 4 per week, $135). Open daily 10am-4pm.

Buses: Greyhound, 500 N. Saint Mary's St. (☎270-5824). To: Houston (4hr., 9 per day, $21) and Dallas (5-6hr., 15 per day, $34). Open 24hr.

Public Transit: VIA Metropolitan Transit, 800 W. Myrtle (☎362-2020). Buses operate daily 5am-midnight; many routes stop at 6pm. Infrequent service to outlying areas. Fare 75¢, transfers 5¢. One-day "day tripper" passes $2, available at 260 E. Houston St.

Taxis: Yellow Cab, ☎226-4242.

Car Rental: American Auto Rental, 3249 SW Military Dr. (☎922-9464). $20.80 per day with 100 free mi. Must be 21 with credit card or cash deposit. Customer pickup service available for $12. Open M-Sa 9am-6pm.

7 PRACTICAL INFORMATION

Visitor info: 317 Alamo Plaza (☎207-6748), downtown across from the Alamo. Open daily 8:30am-6pm. Free maps and brochures.

Hotlines: Rape Crisis, ☎349-7273. 24hr. **Supportive Services for the Elderly and Disabled,** ☎226-9212. Referrals and transport.

Hospital: Metropolitan Methodist Hospital, 1310 McCullough Ave. (☎208-2200).

Internet access: San Antonio Public Library, 600 Soledad St. (207-2534). Open M-Th 9am-9pm, F-Sa 9am-5pm, Su 11am-5pm.

Post Office: 615 E. Houston (☎800-275-8777), 1 block from the Alamo. Open M-F 8:30am-5:30pm. **ZIP code:** 78205. **Area code:** 210.

TEXAS

■ ACCOMMODATIONS AND CAMPING

For cheap motels, try **Roosevelt Ave.**, a southern extension of Saint Mary's St., and **Fredericksburg Rd.** Inexpensive motels also line **Broadway** between downtown and Brackenridge Park. Drivers should follow **I-35 N** to find cheaper and often safer lodging within a 15 mi. radius of town.

Bullis House Inn San Antonio International Hostel (HI-AYH), 621 Pierce St. (☎223-9426), 2 mi. north of downtown on Broadway, right on Grayson. From the bus station, walk to Navarro St. and take bus #11 or 15 to Grayson and New Braunfels; walk 2 blocks west. A spacious, ranch-style hostel in a quiet neighborhood. Pool, kitchen, and Internet access. Fills quickly in summer. Breakfast $4.50. Linen $2. Key deposit $10. Reception daily 8am-10pm. No curfew. $16.75, nonmembers $19.75.

Villager Lodge, 1126 E. Elmira (☎222-9463 or 800-584-0800), about 3 blocks east of St. Mary's, 1 mi. north of downtown. Take bus #8. The caring management provides the cleanest rooms at this price. Cable TV, 5 free local calls, and A/C; some rooms fridge and microwave. Outdoor pool. Small singles for $27, large singles or doubles $34.

Capri Motel, 1718 Roosevelt Ave. (☎533-2583), about 2 mi. south of downtown near the missions. Fairly clean rooms at reasonable prices. Singles $35; doubles $40.

Alamo KOA, 602 Gembler Rd. (☎224-9296 or 800-833-7785), 6 mi. from downtown; take bus #24 ("Industrial Park") from the corner of Houston and Alamo downtown. From I-10 E, take Exit 580/W.W. White Rd., drive 2 blocks north, then take a left onto Gembler Rd. Beautiful, well-kept grounds with lots of shade. Each site has a grill and patio. Showers, laundry facilities, pool, and free movies. Reception daily 7:30am-9:30pm. Sites $20, full hookup $23-25; additional person $3.

◖ FOOD

Expensive cafes and restaurants surround the **Riverwalk**—breakfast alone can clean you out if you don't settle for a muffin and coffee. North of town, Asian restaurants open onto **Broadway** across from Brackenridge. On weekends, hundreds of carnival food booths crowd the walkways of **Market Sq.** Come late in the day when prices drop and vendors are willing to haggle. (☎207-8600. Open daily 10am-8pm; Sept.-May 10am-6pm.) **Pig Stand** diners offer cheap but decent grub all over this part of Texas; the branches at 801 S. Presa, off S. Alamo, and 1508 Broadway (both near downtown) stay open 24hr. The omnipresent **Bill Miller's BBQ,** one location at 501 N. Saint Mary's St., at Pecan St., grills serious BBQ. (☎212-4343. Open M-F 8am-6pm.)

☒ Mi Tierra, 218 Produce Row (☎225-1262), in Market Sq. Perpetually smiling *mariachi* musicians serenade patrons. Delicious chicken enchiladas with chocolate *mole* sauce $8.50. Lunch specials $7. Grab dessert on the run from their bakery. Open 24hr.

Rosario's, 910 S. Alamo St. (☎223-1806), at S. Saint Mary's St., is widely acknowledged by locals to be the best eatery in town. Scrumptious chicken quesadillas for $6 uphold the reputation. Live music F-Sa nights. Open M 10:45am-3pm, Tu-Th 10:45am-10pm, F-Sa 11am-12:30am.

Liberty Bar, 328 E. Josephine St (☎227-1187). A friendly local hangout with daily specials and sandwich plates $6-8. Try the Karkade (iced hibiscus and mint tea with fresh ginger and white grape juice). Open M-Th 11am-10:30pm, F-Sa 11am-midnight, Su 10:30am-10:30pm.

Josephine St. Steaks/Whiskey, 400 Josephine St. (☎224-6169), at McAllister. Specializes in thick Texan steaks, but offers an array of tasty dishes in a relaxed atmosphere. Entrees $5-12, lunch specials $5-7. Open M-Th 11am-10pm, F-Sa 11am-11pm.

Twin Sisters, 124 Broadway and 6322 N. New Braunfels (☎354-1559). Some of the best vegetarian eats around. Try the Caesar with eggless tofu salad ($8) or the tofu quesadillas ($6). Open M-F 9am-3pm.

Madhatters, 36036 Avenue B at Brackenridge Park (☎821-6555), just off Broadway at Mulberry. Features over 50 teas and a famous Sunday brunch in a casual, fun space. Breakfast specials ($4) M-F. Open M-F 7:30am-10pm, Sa 9am-10pm, Su 9am-3pm.

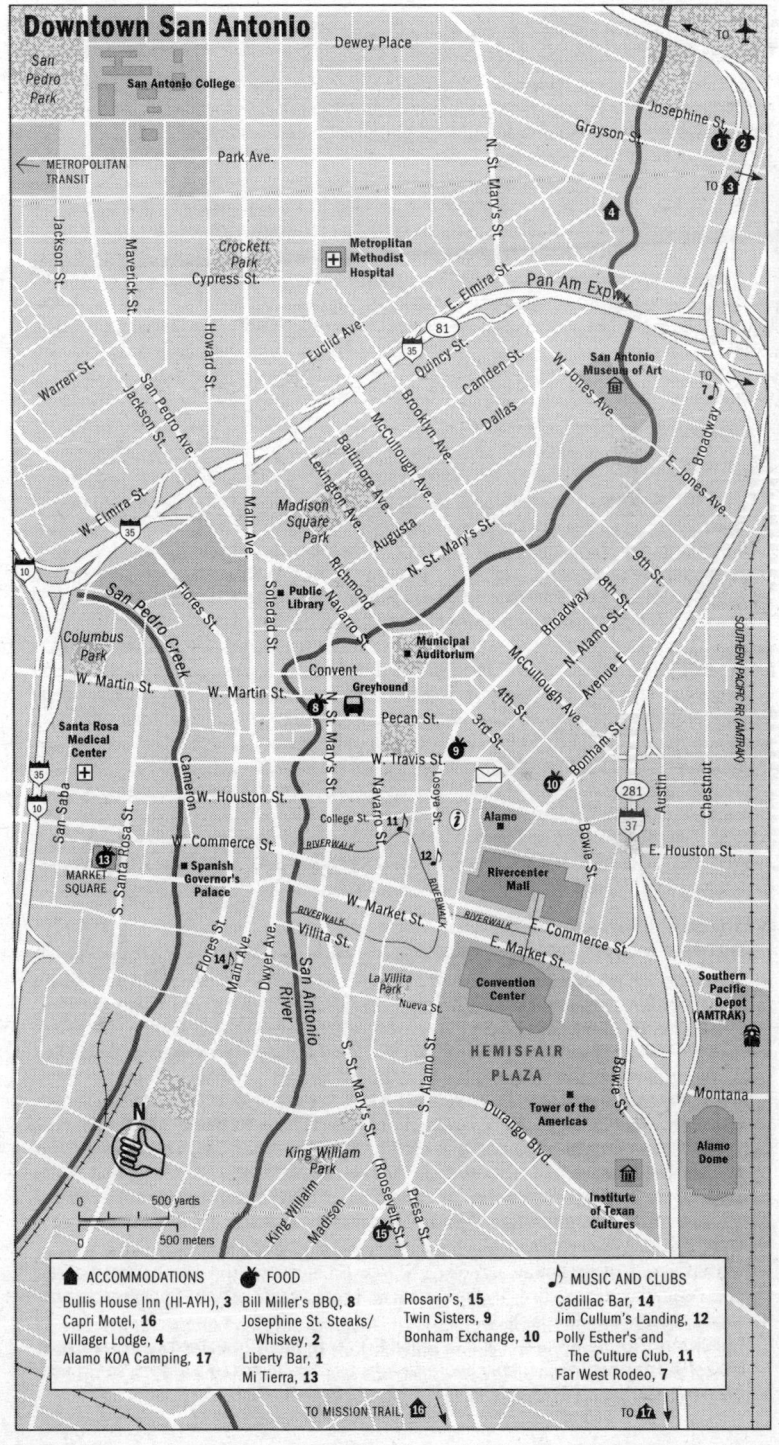

Downtown San Antonio

🏠 ACCOMMODATIONS

Bullis House Inn (HI-AYH), **3**
Capri Motel, **16**
Villager Lodge, **4**
Alamo KOA Camping, **17**

🍴 FOOD

Bill Miller's BBQ, **8**
Josephine St. Steaks/
    Whiskey, **2**
Liberty Bar, **1**
Mi Tierra, **13**

Rosario's, **15**
Twin Sisters, **9**
Bonham Exchange, **10**

♪ MUSIC AND CLUBS

Cadillac Bar, **14**
Jim Cullum's Landing, **12**
Polly Esther's and
    The Culture Club, **11**
Far West Rodeo, **7**

TO MISSION TRAIL, **16** ↓   TO 🚐 ↓

👁 SIGHTS

Much of historic San Antonio lies in the present-day downtown and surrounding areas. The city may seem diffuse, but almost every major site or park is within a few miles of downtown and is accessible by public transportation.

DOWNTOWN

THE ALAMO. "Be silent, friend, here heroes died to blaze a trail for other men." **The Alamo,** which has always been set apart from the other missions, is not maintained by the National Historical Park but by the Daughters of the Republic of Texas. The site was deeded to the state in 1905 by Clara Driscoll, in order that "the sacred shrine be saved from the encroachments of commercialism." If the core of Texas pride were stored in a strongbox, it would be deposited here. Disobeying orders to retreat with their cannons, the 189 defenders of the Alamo, outnumbered 20 to one, held off the Mexican army for 12 days. Then, on the morning of the 13th day, the Mexicans commenced the infamous *deguello* (throat-cutting). Forty-six days later, General Sam Houston's small army defeated the Mexicans at San Jacinto amid cries of "Remember the Alamo!" (☎ 225-1391. *At the center of Alamo Plaza near Houston and Alamo St. Open M-Sa 9am-5:30pm, Su 10am-6:30pm. Free.*)

OTHER MISSIONS. The five missions along the river once formed the soul of San Antonio; the city preserves their remains in the San Antonio Missions National Historical Park. To reach the missions, follow the brown and white "Mission Trail" signs beginning on S. Saint Mary's St. downtown. **Mission San José,** a.k.a. the "Queen of the Missions," has remnants of its own irrigation system, a gorgeous sculpted rose window, and numerous restored buildings. As the largest of San Antonio's missions, it best conveys the self-sufficiency of these institutions. **Mission Concepción** is the oldest unrestored stone church in North America. Traces of the once-colorful frescoes are still visible. **Mission San Juan Capistrano** and **Mission San Francisco de la Espada,** smaller and simpler than the others, evoke the isolation of such outposts. Between them lies the Espada Aqueduct, the only remaining waterway built by the Spanish. (☎ 534-8833 *for info on all missions. Bus #42 stops within walking distance of Mission Concepción and right in front of Mission San José. The main Visitors Center is located at Mission San José. San José: 6701 San José Dr. off Roosevelt Ave.* ☎ 922-0543. *4 Catholic masses held each Su 7:45, 9, 10:30am, and a noon "Mariachi Mass." Concepción: 807 Mission Rd., 4 mi. south of the Alamo off E. Mitchell St.* ☎ 534-1540. *San Juan: 9101 Graf St.* ☎ 534-0749. *San Francisco: 10040 Espada Rd.* ☎ 627-2021. *All missions open daily 9am-5pm. Free.*)

SECULAR SAN ANTONE

DISTRICTS. Southwest of the Alamo, black signs indicate access points to the 2½ mi. **Paseo del Río (Riverwalk),** a series of well-patrolled shaded stone pathways which follow a winding canal built by the WPA in the 30s. Lined with picturesque gardens, shops, and cafes, and connecting most of the major downtown sights, the Riverwalk is the hub of San Antonio's nightlife. To ride the river, try **Yanaguana Cruise Services.** Buy tickets at the Rivercenter Mall; board almost anywhere along the river. (*315 E. Commerce St.* ☎ 244-5700 *or* 800-417-4139. *Open daily 9am-10pm. $5.25, Seniors $3.65.*) A few blocks south, the recreated artisans' village, **La Villita,** 418 Villita, contains restaurants, craft shops, and art studios. (☎ 207-8610. *Shops open daily 10am-6pm, restaurant hours vary.*) On weekends, **Market Sq.,** between San Saba and Santa Rosa St., features the upbeat tunes of Tejano bands and the omnipresent buzzing of frozen margarita machines. (☎ 207-8600. *Open daily 10am-8pm; Sept.-May 10am-6pm.*)

HEMISFAIR PLAZA. The site of the 1968 World's Fair, **HemisFair Plaza,** on S. Alamo, draws tourists with nearby restaurants, museums, and historic houses. The observation deck of the **Tower of the Americas** rises 750 ft. above the Texas Hill Country; the view is best at night. Inside the park, the **Institute of Texan Cultures** showcases 27 ethnic and cultural groups and their contributions to the history of Texas. (*600 HemisFair Park.* ☎ 207-8617. *Open Su-Th 9am-10pm, F-Sa 9am-11pm. $3, seniors $2, ages 4-11 $1. Institute of Texan Cultures:* ☎ 458-2300, *open Tu-Su 9am-5pm.*)

OTHER ATTRACTIONS. Clown around at the **Hertzberg Circus Museum.** In addition to over 20,000 items of circus memorabilia, Hertzberg features special events such as mimes, jugglers, and magicians on weekends. *(210 W. Market St. ☎207-7810. Open M-Sa 10am-5pm, Su 1pm-5pm. $2.50, seniors $2, children 3-12 $1.)* Home to the **San Antonio Spurs,** the **Alamodome,** at Hoefgen St., resembles a Mississippi riverboat. *(100 Montana. ☎207-3600. Take bus #24 or 26. Tours Tu and F 11am and 1pm, except during scheduled events. $4, seniors and ages 4-12 $3.)* The **San Antonio Museum of Art,** housed in the former Lone star Brewery just north of the city center, showcases an extensive collection of Latin American folk art, as well as Texan furniture and an impressive variety of pre-Columbian, Egyptian, Oceanic, Asian, and Islamic art. *(200 W. Jones Ave. ☎978-8100. Open Tu 10am-9pm, W-Sa 10am-5pm, and Su noon-5pm. $5, seniors and students with ID $4, ages 4-11 $1.75; free Tu 3-9pm. Free parking.)*

OUTSIDE CITY CENTER

BRACKENRIDGE PARK. To escape San Antonio's urban congestion, amble down to **Brackenridge Park,** 5 mi. north of the Alamo. The 343-acre show ground includes playgrounds, a miniature train, and a driving range. The main attraction of the park is a lush, perfumed Japanese tea garden with pathways weaving in and out of a pagoda and around a goldfish pond. Directly across the street, the **San Antonio Zoo,** one of the country's largest, keeps over 3500 animals from 800 species in reproductions of their natural settings, including an extensive African mammal exhibit. *(Park: 3910 N. Saint Mary's St. ☎223-9534. Take bus #8. Open daily 5am-11pm. Train: 9am-6:30pm daily, $2.25, $1.75 children. Zoo: 3903 N. Saint Mary's St. ☎734-7184. Open June-Aug. daily 9am-6pm; Sept.-May 9am-5pm. $7, seniors and ages 3-11 $5.)*

A LITTLE SOMETHING DIFFERENT. The phallic, 140-million-year-old stalactites and stalagmites of **Natural Bridge Caverns** change continuously; some grow as much as an inch every hundred years. *(26495 Natural Bridge Caverns Rd. ☎651-6101. Take I-35 N to Exit 175 and follow the signs. Open June-Aug. daily 9am-6pm; off-season 9am-4pm. $12, ages 4-12 $7. 1¼hr. tours every 30min.)* If you have an itchy trigger finger, **A Place to Shoot** is—well, just that. *(13250 Pleasanton Rd. ☎628-1888. Exit 46 off I-410 S. Open M-F 10am-7pm, Sa-Su 9am-7pm; $7 per person; $5 per 25 clays. 50¢ earplug rental.)* If you're in the mood to see some cowboy paraphernalia, visit the **Texas Pioneer, Trail Driver and Texas Ranger's Museum.** It contains a splendid collection of artifacts, old guns, documents, and portraits. *(3805 Broadway. ☎822-9011. Open May-Aug. M-Sa 10am-5pm, Su noon-5pm; $3, seniors $2, ages 6-12 $1.)*

🎵🎭 ENTERTAINMENT AND NIGHTLIFE

In late April, **Fiesta San Antonio** (☎227-5191) ushers in spring with concerts, parades, and plenty of Tex-Mex celebrations to commemorate the victory at San Jacinto and to pay homage to the heroes of the Alamo. Every first Friday of the month is a fiesta in San Antonio: the art galleries along S. Alamo put on a huge event called Artswalk, featuring free food and drink. (☎207-6748 for info.) For excitement after dark any time, any season, stroll down the Riverwalk. *The Friday Express* or weekly *Current* (available at the tourist office) will guide you to concerts and entertainment.

The **Sam's Burger Joint,** 330 E. Grayson (☎223-2830), for the **Puro Poetry Slam** every Tuesday night at 10pm ($2). Sam's also features live music and the "Big Monster Burger," 1 lb. of beef for $7. For authentic **Tejano music,** a Mexican and country amalgam, head to the **Cadillac Bar,** 212 S. Flores, where every weeknight a different band whips the huge crowd (anywhere from 500-1000 people) into a cheering and dancing frenzy. (☎223-5533. 21+. Open M-Sa 11am-2am.) Right around the corner from the Alamo, the **Bonham Exchange,** 411 Bonham, San Antonio's biggest gay dance club, plays high-energy music with some house and techno on the side. A younger, more mixed crowd files in on Wednesdays for college night. (☎271-3811. Cover for 21+ $3-5, for 18-20 up to $10. Open M-Th 4pm-2am, F 4pm-3am, Sa 8pm-3am.) Some of the best traditional jazz anywhere happens at **Jim Cullum's Landing,** 123 Losoya, in the Hyatt downtown. The legendary Cullum plays with his jazz band M-Sa 8:30pm-1am.

HOW MANY WORDS CAN YOU MAKE FROM "SCHLITTERBAHN?" The entire economy of New Braunfels, TX, depends on the inner tube. Almost 2 million visitors per year come to this town, hoping to spend a day floating along the waters of the spring-fed **Comal River**. **Rockin' "R" River Rides** will send you off with a life jacket an a trusty tube and pick you up downstream 2½hr. later. *(193 S. Liberty. ☎830-620-6262. Open May-Sept. daily 9am-7pm. Tube rentals $9, bottomless floats $7. Car keys, proper ID, or $25 deposit required for rental.)* If the Comal doesn't float your boat, head for the chlorinated waters of **Schlitterbahn**, a 65-acre extravaganza of a waterpark with 17 waterslides, nine tube chutes, and five gigantic hot tubs. The park has recently added the planet's only uphill watercoaster, the Master Blaster. To find both attractions, take I-35 to Exit 189, turn left, and follow the signs for Schlitterbahn. *(400 N. Liberty. ☎830-625-2351. Open May-Sept. Call for hrs.; generally around 10am-8pm. Full-day passes $27.50, ages 3-11 $22.75.)*

Tidy dress is recommended at this sophisticated venue. The improv jazz quintet Small World performs on Sunday nights. (☎223-7266. All ages. Cover M-Th $3.50, F-Sa $6.50, Su no cover. Open M-Sa 4:30pm-1am, Su noon-1am.) Also along the Riverwalk, **Polly Esthers** and **The Culture Club,** 212 College St., pump up the crowd with 70s disco on the 2nd floor and 80s retro on the 3rd floor. (☎220-1972. 21+. Cover $3-7. Open Su-W 8pm-2am, Th 8pm-3am, F-Sa 8pm-4am.) **Far West Rodeo**, 3030 Rte. 410 NE, plays two types of music—country *and* Western. With an indoor rodeo on Friday and Saturday nights, a mechanical bull and two dance floors; bring your ten-gallon hat to enjoy the fun. (☎646-9378. Cover $3-6. 18+. Open W-Th 7pm-2am, F-Sa 8pm-2am.)

SCENIC DRIVE: TEXAS HILL COUNTRY DRIVE

Parts of the **Texas Hill Country** are as country as they come. Rolling expanses of scraggly brush interrupted by jagged hills dominate the landscape, while rusty pickup trucks driven by big men in big hats dominate the roads. Longhorns graze roadside as vehicles hurtle past at 70 mph. Yet the Texas Hill Country is more than ranches and cattle: the limestone-rich soil is well suited for wine-making and peach-growing. There is a noticeable German influence in the area, dating back to 1846 with the founding of **Fredericksburg**—stop off at a *biergarten* to sample some German cuisine. Finally, a series of well-maintained parks offers campers and day visitors alike the chance to experience the natural beauty of Texas firsthand.

Driving through the Hill Country at a leisurely pace takes about two days, and links San Antonio and Austin. Although not the most direct route between these two cities, unique diversions and beautiful scenery make up for a few extra miles. From San Antonio, take I-35 to New Braunfels. After high-priced visits to the **Schlitterbahn** and/or **Natural Bridge Caverns** (see p. 599), you might be eager for less touristy attractions. From New Braunfels, take Rte. 46 west for 6½ mi., then turn left on Herbelin Rd. Here you'll find **Dry Comal Creek Vineyards,** 1741 Herbelin Rd., which offers free tastings and tours of the small vineyard. (☎830-885-4121. Open W-Su noon-5pm.) Yes, Texas makes wine—in fact, the state is currently fifth in the nation in wine production. Twenty-five miles past Dry Comal Creek along Rte. 46 west is **Guadalupe River State Park,** where you can swim in the cliff-lined river or camp in nearby sites. (☎830-438-2656, 512-389-8900 for reservations. Open M-F 8am-8pm, Sa 8am-10pm. Day entrance $4 per person, children under 12 free; $15 for water and electricity, $12 for water only. Additional charge of $3 per person, under 12 free.)

Further down Rte. 46 is **Boerne** (pronounced BUR-nee), an antique lover's paradise. A string of converted barns and old farmhouses sell a wide array of odds and ends. After 12 mi. of twists through a series of low hills along the way to **Bandera,** Rte. 46 intersects with Rte. 16; take Rte. 16 north. Bandera's central street passes through a row of ramshackle buildings that could serve as backdrops for old cowboy movies. Consistent with the image, Bandera is home to the ⚑**Frontier Times Museum,** 510 13th St., which has cowboy memorabilia and odd knick-knacks like

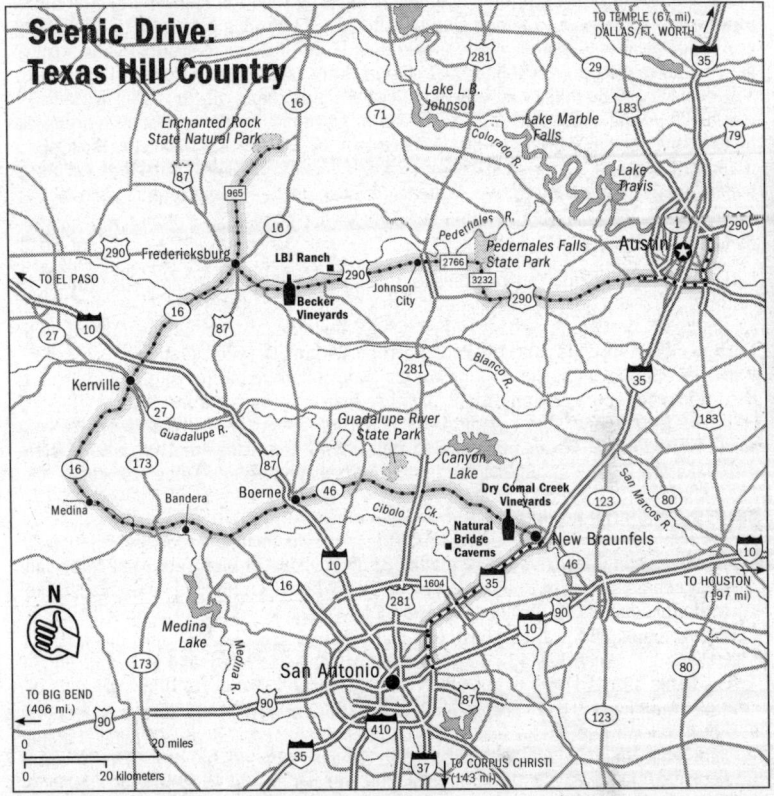

Scenic Drive:
Texas Hill Country

Peruvian shrunken heads. (☎830-796-3864. Open M-Sa 10am-4:30pm, Su 1pm-4:30pm. $2, ages 6-18 25¢.) Continuing down 15 mi. of zig-zag roads through dramatic countryside, Rte. 16 north then brings you to the town of **Medina**, the "apple capital of Texas." Stop off at **Love Creek Orchards** (☎800-449-0882), on Rte. 16 on the north side of town, to buy some fresh cider for the trip ($5 per ½ gallon).

Leaving Medina on Rte. 16 north, the next 35 mi. winds through some of the most breathtaking country around. Be especially cautious driving this leg of the trip; hairpin turns and steep inclines can be treacherous. Safety aside, the real reason to proceed slowly is to enjoy the surrounding scenery. On the way through **Kerrville**, stop by the **Cowboy Artists of America Museum**, 1550 Bandera Hwy. (from Rte. 16 north, take Rte. 173 south). Action-packed scenes of the Wild West demonstrate the creative side of America's gun-toting heroes. (☎830-896-2553. Open June-Aug. M-Sa 9am-5pm, Su 1-5pm; Sept.-May Tu-Sa 9am-5pm, Su 1-5pm. $5, ages 6-18 $1, seniors $3.50.) Twenty-two miles along Rte. 16 from Kerrville sits historic **Fredericksburg,** a German-rooted town of beer and sausage. For history buffs, Fredericksburg's **Admiral Nimitz Museum,** 340 E. Main St., contains an excellent exhibit on the Pacific theater of World War II. (☎830-997-4379. Open daily 10am-5pm. $5, students $3.)

Eighteen miles north of Fredericksburg on Rte. 965 lies **Enchanted Rock State Natural Park,** has the double allure of being a natural wonder (a tree-less, 440 ft. dome of pink granite) as well as a place to pitch one's tent. It also offers hiking—a relatively easy scramble to the top—and rock-climbing for the experienced. (☎800-792-1112. Open daily 8am-5pm. Entrance fee $5, under 12 free. 46 Regular tent sites available with shower, water, and grill $9. 60 primitive sites $7. No RVs or trailers permitted. Reservations strongly recommended.)

Back in Fredericksburg, take U.S. 290 E heading towards **Johnson City,** the birthplace of 36th President Lyndon Baines Johnson. Ten miles east of Fredericksburg you'll find **Becker Vineyards,** on Jenschke Ln., which offers free tours of the winery as well as tastings. (☎830-644-2681. Open daily 10am-5pm.) Follow U.S. 290 to Johnson City. Nine miles east is **Pedernales Falls State Park,** off Rte. 2766. Waterfalls, extensive hiking trails, tent sites, and swimming/tubing areas make it a favorite getaway from Austin, which lies 60 mi. east on U.S. 290. (☎800-792-1112. Park open daily 8am-10pm, office open M-Th 8am-7pm, F 8am-10pm, Sa-Su 8am-8pm; entrance fee $4 per person, under 12 free. Water and electric sites $16, primitive sites $7.)

AUSTIN ☎512

If the "Lone Star State" still inspires images of rough-and-tumble cattle ranchers riding horses across the plains, Austin does its best to put the stereotype to rest. In recent years, big money and big industry have become increasingly prominent, with Fortune 500 companies and Internet startups seeking to redefine the city's essence. With booming growth, the population has skyrocketed, and driving in and around Austin has become quite an ordeal. Austin's history of musical innovation (the city is known as the "Live Music Capital of the World"), plus the 50,000 college students at the University of Texas, make it a vibrant city. A liberal, alternative oasis in a traditional state, Austin should be the first stop on any traveler's Texas itinerary.

⌐ TRANSPORTATION

Airport: Austin Bergstrom International, 3600 Presidential Blvd. (☎530-2242). Heading south from the city on I-35, go east on Ben White Blvd. (Rte. 71) 8 mi. from downtown. Take bus #100. Taxi to downtown $12-14.

Trains: Amtrak, 250 N. Lamar Blvd. (☎476-5684 or 800-872-7245); take bus #38. To: Dallas (6hr., daily, $29-42); San Antonio (3hr., daily, $12-19); and El Paso (19hr., 4 per week, $98-121). Office open daily 7am-9:30pm.

Buses: Greyhound, 916 E. Koenig, (☎800-231-2222 or 458-4463), several mi. north of downtown off I-35. Easily accessible by public transportation. Bus #7 and 15 stop across the street and run downtown. To: San Antonio (2hr., 13 per day, $13.50); Houston (3½hr., 7 per day, $17); and Dallas (3hr., 11 per day, $25). Schedules and prices vary. Station open 24hr.

Public Transit: Capitol Metro, 106 E. 8th St. (☎474-1200 or 800-474-1201; call M-F 6am-10pm, Sa 6am-8pm, Su 7am-6pm). Fare 50¢; students 25¢; seniors, children, and disabled free. Buses run 4am-midnight; most start later and end earlier. Office has maps and schedules (open M-F 7:30am-5:30pm). The **'Dillo Bus Service** (☎474-1200) runs downtown (on Congress, Lavaca, San Jacinto, and 6th St.) M-F every 10-15min. during rush hrs.; varies during off-peak times. The 'Dillos, which look like trollies on wheels, are always free. Park for free in the lot at Bouldin and Barton Springs.

Taxis: American Yellow Checker Cab, ☎472-1111.

Bike Rental: If you come upon a **completely yellow bicycle,** hop on it for free—compliments of the city. Just make sure to leave it in a conspicuous spot for the next person to use. Most buses have bicycle racks. **Waterloo Cycles,** 2815 Fruth St. (☎472-9253), offers rentals $15 per day, $20 on weekends. Fee includes helmet. Lock rental $5. Delivery available. Open M-W and F-Sa 10am-7pm, Th 10am-8pm, Su noon-5pm.

▄▞ ORIENTATION AND PRACTICAL INFORMATION

The majority of Austin lies between **Mopac Expwy./Rte. 1** and **I-35,** both running north-south and parallel to one another. UT students inhabit central **Guadalupe St. ("The Drag"),** where plentiful music stores and cheap restaurants thrive on their business. The state capitol governs the area a few blocks to the southeast. South of the capitol dome, **Congress Ave.** features upscale eateries and classy shops. The many bars and clubs of **6th St.** hop and clop at night. Much nightlife has moved to the growing **Warehouse District,** around 4th St., west of Congress. Away from the urban gridiron, **Town Lake** offers a haven for the town's joggers, rowers, and cyclists.

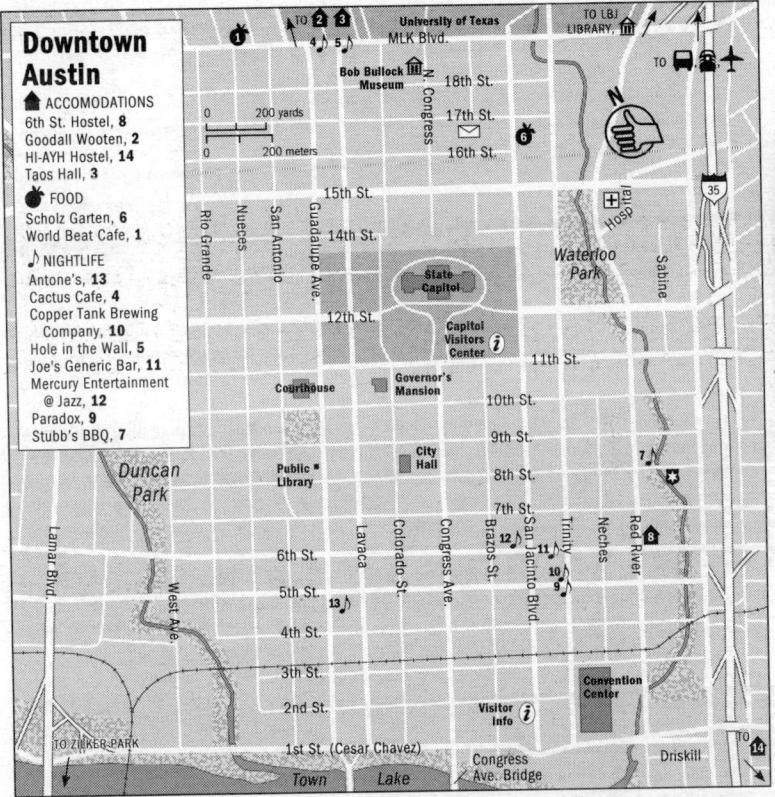

Downtown Austin

🏠 ACCOMMODATIONS
6th St. Hostel, **8**
Goodall Wooten, **2**
HI-AYH Hostel, **14**
Taos Hall, **3**

🍴 FOOD
Scholz Garten, **6**
World Beat Cafe, **1**

♪ NIGHTLIFE
Antone's, **13**
Cactus Cafe, **4**
Copper Tank Brewing Company, **10**
Hole in the Wall, **5**
Joe's Generic Bar, **11**
Mercury Entertainment @ Jazz, **12**
Paradox, **9**
Stubb's BBQ, **7**

Visitor info: Austin Convention and Visitors Bureau/Visitors Information Center, 201 E. 2nd St. (☎478-0098 or 800-926-2282). Open M-F 8:30am-5pm, Sa-Su 9am-5pm.

Hospital: St. David's Medical Center, 919 E. 32nd St. (☎476-7111). Off I-35, close to downtown. Open 24hr.

Hotlines: Crisis Intervention Hotline, ☎472-4357. **Austin Rape Crisis Center Hotline,** ☎440-7273. Both operate 24hr. **Outyouth Gay/Lesbian Helpline,** (☎800-969-6884; www.outyouth.org). Lines Open W, F, Su 5:30-9:30pm.

Internet access: Austin Public Library, 800 Guadalupe St. (☎974-7599). Open M-Th 10am-9pm, F-Sa 10am-6pm, Su noon-6pm.

Post Office: 510 Guadalupe (☎800-275-8777 or 494-2210) at 6th St. Open M-F 7am-6:30pm, Sa 8am-3pm. **ZIP code:** 78701. **Area code:** 512.

🏠 ACCOMMODATIONS

If you insist on your Motel 6, cheap accommodations lie along **I-35,** running north and south of Austin. However, this funkified city is a great place to find cheap options with character. In town, **co-ops,** run by college houses at UT, peddle rooms and meals to hostelers. Patrons have access to all their facilities, including fully stocked kitchens. Unfortunately, most UT co-ops only have space available from May through August. Call 476-5678 for information about several co-ops. If you plan to stay in a co-op, it's strongly advised to make the arrangements before you arrive in Austin. Since the co-ops are more residential than commercial, it's often difficult even to reach someone over the phone. If you're interested in camping, however, a 10-20min. drive separates Austin and the nearest campgrounds.

■ **Hostelling International-Austin (HI-AYH),** 2200 S. Lakeshore Blvd. (☎800-725-2331 or 444-2294), about 3 mi. from downtown. From the Greyhound station, take bus #7 "Duval" to Burton and walk 3 blocks north. From I-35, exit at Riverside, head east, and turn left at Lakeshore Blvd. Beautifully situated, quiet hostel with a 24hr. common room overlooking Town Lake. Features live music by local acts M-Sa. 40 dorm-style beds, single-sex rooms. No curfew. No alcohol. Linen provided; no sleeping bags allowed. Rents bikes, kayaks, and canoes ($10 each). Reception open daily 8-11am and 5-10pm; you must arrive by 10pm or call ahead to check in. $15.50, nonmembers $18.50.

■ **6th St. Hostel,** 604 6th St. (☎495-9772 or 866-467-8356). If you want to be where the action is and leave peace and quiet behind, stay here. The hostel advertises "free earplugs (for those who sleep)." 24hr. reception, free coffee and tea, free pickup/drop-off from airport/train/bus station (just call them). Game room with pool table, small kitchen. Linen provided; no sleeping bags allowed. Purchase a hostel wrist band for $5 and get discounts, free cover at over 20 6th St. hot spots. $18, private rooms $40-60.

Taos Hall, 2612 Guadalupe (☎476-5678), at 27th St. The UT co-op where you're most likely to get a private room. For stays of a week or more, they'll draft you into the chore corps. Open June-Aug. Three meals and a bed $20.

21st St. Co-op, 707 W. 21st St. (☎476-5678). Take bus #39 on Airport Blvd. to Koenig and Burnet, transfer to the #3 S, and ride to Nueces St.; walk 2 blocks west. Treehouse-style building arrangement and hanging plants recall Robinson Crusoe's island home; its residents call it the "Ewok Village." A bit grungy, but only from all the good fun. Suites with A/C, and common room on each floor. $15 per person for 3 meals and kitchen access. Fills up rapidly in summer.

The Goodall Wooten, 2112 Guadalupe (☎472-1343). The "Woo's" comfortable, clean, institutional-style rooms are essentially UT dorms, but come with private baths, small fridges, balcony, and access to a big-screen TV lounge, laundry, basketball courts, and a free computer lab. Linen $10. Reception M-Sa 9am-5pm and 8pm-midnight, Su 1-5pm and 8pm-midnight. Call ahead. Singles $30; doubles $35.

McKinney Falls State Park, 5808 McKinney Falls Pkwy. (☎243-1643, reservations 389-8900), southeast of the city. Turn right on Burleson off Rte. 71 E, then right on McKinney Falls Pkwy. Caters to RV and tent campers. Swimming permitted in the stream; 7 mi. of hiking trails. Primitive sites (accessible only by foot) $9; with water and electricity $12. Daily park usage fee $2, under 13 free. Open daily 8am-10pm.

Austin Lonestar RV Resort (☎444-6322 or 800-284-0206), 6 mi. south of the city along I-35 off Exit 227 on the northbound service road. Offers a pool, clean bathrooms, a game room, laundry facilities, a grocery store, and a playground. RV and tent sites with water and electricity $34-36; 3rd night free if on a weekday. Cabins for 4 $39; for 6 $49. 10% off with AAA.

◖ FOOD

Scores of fast-food joints line the west side of the UT campus on **Guadalupe St.** Around **6th St.**, south of the capitol, the battle for happy hour business rages with unique intensity; patrons can often enjoy drink specials and free hors d'oeuvres. Although a bit removed from downtown, **Barton Springs Rd.** offers a diverse selection of inexpensive restaurants, including Mexican and Texas-style barbecue joints. The **Warehouse District** has more expensive seafood and Italian eateries. **The Kerbey Lane Cafe,** 3704 Kerbey Lane, is an Austin institution; try them for breakfast. (☎451-1436. Open daily 24hr. Locations throughout town.) Prepare your own meals from groceries purchased at the **Wheatsville Food Co-op,** 3101 Guadalupe. The only food co-op in Texas features organic foods and is a community gathering place to boot (☎478-2667; open daily 9am-11pm).

■ **Ruby's BBQ,** 512 W. 29th St. (☎477-1651). Ruby's barbecue is good enough to be served on silver platters, but that just wouldn't seem right in this cow-skulls-and-butcher-paper establishment. The owners only order meat from farm-raised, grass-fed cows. A scrumptious brisket sandwich goes for $4.25. Open daily 11am-midnight.

WHERE HAVE ALL THE HIPPIES GONE?

About 15 mi. northeast of downtown Austin lies Hippie Hollow, Texas's only public nude swimming and sunbathing haven. Here, free spirits go au naturel in the waters of the lovely Lake Travis. Take Mopac (Rte. 1) north to the Exit for F.M. 2222. Follow 2222 west and turn left at the I-620 intersection; Comanche Rd. will be on your right. (7000 Comanche Trail. ☎473-9437. 18+ only. Open daily 8am-9pm, no entry after 8:30pm. $5 per car, pedestrians $2.)

World Beat Cafc, 600 MLK, (☎236-0197). This eclectic cafe has African specialties such as yam *fu fu* with *egusi* or okra vegetable soup ($5) as well as damn good burger/fries specials on Tu, Th, and Su ($2.75). Open M-Sa 11am-9pm, Su noon-7pm.

Magnolia Cafe, 1920 S. Congress (☎455-0000); another location at 2304 Lake Austin Blvd. (☎478-8645). A colorful, lively place with a variety of healthy, tasty dishes. Try 2 "Tropical Turkey" tacos for $6.50. Open daily 24hr.

Guero's, 1412 S. Congress (☎447-7688), across the river from downtown. This wholesome Mexican restaurant is very popular with locals, as well it should be. Lunch specials $6-8, combo plates $8.50-12.50. Open M-F 11am-11pm, Sa-Su 8am-11pm.

Trudy's Texas Star, 409 W. 30th St. (☎477-2935); another location at 8800 Burnet Rd. (☎454-1474). Fine Tex-Mex dinner entrees ($5.25-8) and a fantastic array of margaritas. Famous for *migas,* a corn tortilla soufflé ($5.25). M happy hour all day. Open Su-Th 10am-midnight, F-Sa 11am-2am; bar always open until 2am.

Threadgill's, 301 W. Riverside Dr. (☎472-9304); another location at 6416 N. Lamar Blvd. (☎451-5440). A legend in Austin since 1933, serving up terrific Southern soul food and $8 fried chicken among creaky wooden floors, slow-moving ceiling fans, and antique beer signs. Surprisingly large variety of vegetarian and non-dairy options. Live music Th starting at 7pm. Open M-Sa 11am-10pm, Su 10am-9:30pm.

Scholz Garten, 1607 San Jacinto Blvd. (☎474-1958), near the capitol. UT students and state politicians alike gather at this Austin landmark, recognized by the legislature for "epitomizing the finest traditions of the German heritage of our state." Popular chicken-fried steak dinners ($7.30) and sausage and bratwurst po' boys ($5.30). Open M-W 11am-10pm and Th-Sa 11am-11pm.

Casa De Luz, 1701 Toomey Rd. (☎476-2535). Those familiar with macrobiotic cooking (essentially vegetarian) will enjoy the lovingly prepared meals served in a tranquil, communal setting. Lovers of furry, fishy, or feathered fare might find themselves asking "Where's the beef?" All meals are $9, except brunch, $11. Open M-F 11:30am-2pm and 6-8pm, Sa-Su 11:30am-2pm for brunch.

👁 SIGHTS

Not to be outdone, Texans built their **state capitol,** at Congress Ave. and 11th St., 7 ft. higher than the national one. (☎463-0063. Open M-F 7am-10pm, Sa-Su 9am-8pm. 45min. tours every 15min. Free.) The **Capitol Visitors Center,** 112 E. 11th St., is located in the southeast corner of the capitol grounds. (☎305-8400. Open daily 9am-5pm.) There is a free two-hour garage at 12th and San Jacinto St. Near the capitol, you can tour the **Governor's Mansion,** 1010 Colorado St. (☎463-5516. Free tours M-F every 20min. 10-11:40am.) From March to November, the **Austin Convention and Visitors Bureau** sponsors free walking tours of the area. (☎454-1545. Tours Th-F 9am, Sa-Su 9, 11am, 2pm. Tour starts at the capitol steps.)

The **University of Texas at Austin (UT)** is both the wealthiest public university in the country, with an annual budget of almost a billion dollars, and America's largest, with over 50,000 students. UT forms the backbone of city cultural life. Bus #20 heads to the **Lyndon B. Johnson Library and Museum,** 2313 Red River St. The first floor focuses on Texas-native LBJ and the history of the American presidency; the 8th floor features a model of the Oval Office. (☎916-5137. Open daily 9am-5pm. Free.)

If you've ever wondered about "The Story of Texas," the brand-spanking new **Bob Bullock Texas State History Museum,** 1800 N. Congress, is waiting to tell it to you in three stories of exhibits and two IMAX theaters. (☎936-8746. Open M-Sa 9am-6pm, Su 1-6pm. Exhibits $5, seniors $4.25, under 19 free; IMAX $6.50, seniors $5.50, under 19 $4.50; cheaper combination tickets available.)

The downtown **Austin Museum of Art,** 3809 W. 35th St., has rotating exhibitions every few months (☎495-9224). The museum was formerly housed in a Mediterranean-style villa, and the grounds are still open to the public. (☎458-8191. Grounds open Tu-Sa 10am-5pm, Su noon-5pm. Free.) The **Mexic-Arte Museum,** 419 S. Congress, features a permanent collection of Mexican masks and photos, as well as revolving exhibits. (☎480-9373. Open M-Sa 10am-6pm.) The Austin Arts Guild sponsors an arts and crafts festival the first week of April (☎494-9224, ext. 300 for info). Just before dusk, head underneath the south side of the **Congress Ave. Bridge,** near the Austin American-Statesman parking lot, and watch for the massive swarm of ■**Mexican free-tail bats** that emerge from their roosts to feed on the night's mosquitoes. When the bridge was reconstructed in 1980, the engineers unintentionally created crevices which formed ideal homes for the migrating bat colony. The city began exterminating the night-flying creatures until **Bat Conservation International** moved to Austin to educate people about the bats' harmless behavior and the benefits of their presence—the bats eat up to 3000 lbs. of insects each night. Today, the bats are among the biggest tourist attractions in Austin. The colony, seen from mid-March to November, peaks in July, when a fresh crop of pups increases the population to around 1½ million. For **flight times,** call the bat hotline (☎416-5700, ext. 3636).

Mt. Bonnell Park, 3800 Mt. Bonnell Rd., off W. 35th St., offers a sweeping view of Lake Austin and Westlake Hills from the highest point in the city. On hot afternoons, Austinites come in droves to riverside **Zilker Park,** 2201 Barton Springs Rd., just south of the Colorado River; take bus #30. (☎477-7273. Open daily 5am-10pm. Free.) Flanked by walnut and pecan trees, **Barton Springs Pool,** a spring-fed swimming hole in the park, stretches 1000 ft. long and 200 ft. wide. The pool's temperature hovers around 68°F. (☎499-6710. Pool open F-W 5am-10pm, Th 5-9am and 7-10pm. M-F $2.50, Sa-Su $2.75; ages 12-17 $1, under 12 50¢. Free 5-8am and 9-10pm daily.) The **Barton Springs Greenbelt** offers challenging hiking and biking trails.

♫ ▣ ENTERTAINMENT AND NIGHTLIFE

Beverly Sheffield Zilker Hillside Theater, across from the Barton Springs pool, hosts free outdoor bands, ballets, plays, musicals, and symphony concerts every weekend from May to October (☎397-1463 for events schedule). In mid-March, the **South by Southwest Music, Media, and Film Festival** draws entertainment industry's giants and thousands of eager fans (☎467-7979). Austin's smaller events calendar is a mixed bag, like the **Spamarama** in early April. Spam fans from all walks of life pay homage to...this, er, product...with food, sports, and live music at the **Spam Jam.** Bibliophiles won't want to miss **Half Price Books,** 3110 Guadalupe St. (☎451-6383. Open M-Sa 10am-10pm, Su noon-9pm.)

Austin has replaced Seattle as the nation's underground music hot spot, so keep an eye out for rising indie stars, as well as old blues, folk, country, and rock favorites. On weekends, nighttime swingers seek out dancing on **6th St.,** an area bespeckled with warehouse nightclubs and fancy bars. More mellow cigar-smoking night owls gather at the **4th St. Warehouse District.** Still another area for nightlife in Austin is along **Red River St.,** with a series of bars and clubs that have all of the grit of 6th St., but less of the glam. The weekly *Austin Chronicle* and *XL-ent* provide details on current music performances, shows, and movies. The *Gay Yellow Pages* is free at stands along Guadalupe St. An alternative to the bars and clubs is the Austin coffeehouse scene. ■**Mojo's Daily Grind,** 2714 Guadalupe St., is simply "the hub of subculture in Austin." (☎477-6656. DJs spinning music Th-Sa nights. Open 24hr.) Also check out **Spider House,** 2908 Froth St. just off Guadalupe, with its large booths in a dark interior along with patio seating. (☎480-9562. Open daily 8am-2am.)

▓ **Antone's,** 213 W. 5th St. (☎474-5314). Antone's has attracted the likes of B.B. King and Muddy Waters. This blues paradise was also the starting point for Stevie Ray Vaughn. All ages. Shows at 10pm. Cover $5-25. Open daily 9pm-2am.

▓ **Mercury Entertainment @ Jazz,** 214 E. 6th St. (☎478-6372). Representing the new side of Austin that has moved away from the usual country music and classic rock, the Mercury caters to hip twenty-somethings looking for the latest in jazz, funk, and hip-hop. Cover $9 and up for ages 18-20, $6 and up for 21+. Open daily 9:30pm-2am.

Stubb's BBQ, 801 Red River (☎480-8341). Don't miss Stubb's fabulous (but pricey) Sunday gospel brunch—all-you-can-eat buffet plus live gospel for $15 (reservations required, sittings at 11am and 1pm). Otherwise, the 21+ club downstairs hosts nightly acts. Swing by earlier for some scrumptious, inexpensive grub like beef brisket and 2 side dishes for $7.25. All ages welcome for amphitheater shows. Cover $5-25. Shows at 10:30pm. Open Tu-W 11am-10pm, Th-Sa 11am-1am, Su 11am-9pm.

Oilcan Harry's, 211 W. 4th (☎320-8823). One of the biggest and best gay bars in Austin. Strip shows 10:30pm-1:30am on Tu and Su. 21+. No cover except W (18+ $12 cover, 21+ $7 cover). Open Su-Th 2pm-2am, F-Sa 8pm-4am.

Copper Tank Brewing Company, 504 Trinity St. (☎478-8444). Probably the city's best microbrewery, with its namesake copper tanks dispensing brewskis right behind the bar. W $1 beers, Th $1 any drink, F $2 any drink. 21+. Open Tu-F 5pm-2am, Sa 8pm-2am.

Hole in the Wall, 2538 Guadalupe St. (☎472-5599), at 26th St. Its self-effacing name belies the popularity of this renowned music spot, which features a mix of punk/alternative and country-western bands. Music nightly. 21+. Cover $3-5; no cover Su-M. Open M-F 11am-2am, Sa-Su noon-2am.

Cactus Cafe, at 24th and Guadalupe St. (☎475-6515), in the Texas Union. Features adventurous acoustic music every night. Specializing in folk-rock and Austin's own "New Country" sound, the Cactus gave Lyle Lovett his start. No smoking permitted. Music starts 9pm. All ages welcome. Cover $2-15. Open M-F 8pm-1am, Sa 8pm-2am.

Joe's Generic Bar, 315 E. 6th St. (☎480-0171). Find your way here for some raunchy Texas-style blues that are anything but generic. 21+. No cover. Open M-Sa 7:30pm-2am, Su 8pm-midnight.

Broken Spoke, 3201 S. Lamar St. (☎442-6189). For some honky-tonk, good old-fashioned country twang, put on your spiffiest Western dress and make tracks for the Broken Spoke. The restaurant serves the world's best chicken fried steak dinner for $8.25, is open Tu-Th 10:30am-10:30pm, F-Sa 10:30am-11:30pm. Music/dancing W-Sa, 8pm-midnight. All ages. Cover $4-10.

Paradox, 311 E. 5th St. (☎469-7615), at Trinity. In a city hurting for dance clubs, this 12,000 square ft. warehouse-style dance club plays alternative, hip-hop, and high energy dance music. Raid your parents' closet for retro night on Su. Cover $5-10. Open Th-Su 9pm-4am.

DALLAS
☎214

Dallas began as a trading outpost at a fort across the Trinity River in 1841. Rapidly boosted by the oil industry, Dallas is now the nation's largest inland city. Nevertheless, it has yet to be recognized as the cosmopolitan center it aspires to be—visitors are more fascinated by the image of oil and cowboys fostered by the television show *Dallas*. In truth, golf courses and swimming pools far outnumber genuine ropers or oilers here; one gets the feeling that Dallas never quite abandoned the yuppiedom of the 80s. The city's overwhelming prosperity means slim-pickings for slim wallets. There are some interesting attractions, but lack of affordable accommodations downtown can make Dallas a tough city for budget travelers to navigate.

▐ TRANSPORTATION

Airport: Dallas-Ft. Worth International (☎972-574-8888), 17 mi. northwest of downtown; take bus #202 ($2). For door-to-gate service, take the **Super Shuttle,** 729 E. Dallas Rd. (☎800-258-3826). 1st passenger $16; additional passengers $6. 24hr. service. Taxi to downtown $38.

Trains: Amtrak, 400 S. Houston St. (☎653-1101), in Union Station. To: Los Angeles (42hr., 4 per week, $138); Austin (6½hr., 1 per day, $22); and Little Rock (7½hr., 1 per day, $53). Open daily 9am-6:30pm.

Buses: Greyhound, 205 S. Lamar St. (☎655-7727), 3 blocks east of Union Station. To: New Orleans (13hr., 11 per day, $78); Houston (4hr., 11 per day, $34); and Austin (4hr., 15 per day, $28). Open 24hr.

Public Transit: Dallas Area Rapid Transit (DART), 1401 Pacific Ave. (☎979-1111; open M-F 5am-10pm, Sa-Su 8am-6pm). Buses radiate from 2 downtown transfer centers, East and West, and serve most suburbs. Darts daily 5:30am-9:30pm, to suburbs 5:30am-8pm. Fare $1, $2 to suburban park-and-ride stops; transfers free. Maps at Elm and Ervay St. office (open M-F 7am-6pm). DART Light Rail runs north-south through downtown (5:30am-12:30am; fare $1).

Taxis: Yellow Cab Co., ☎426-6262 or 800-749-9422.

⚡❷ ORIENTATION AND PRACTICAL INFORMATION

Most of Dallas lies within the I-635 loop, which is bisected east-west by I-30 and north-south by I-35 E (Stemmons Fwy.) and U.S. 75 (Central Expwy.). Nicer suburbs stretch along the northern reaches of Central Expwy. and the Dallas North Toll Rd. northwest of downtown. Many of downtown Dallas's shops and restaurants lie underground in a maze of tunnels accessible from any major office building. Navigating the freeways can be confusing, and parking in downtown Dallas is a pain—many parking meters are in effect until 10pm every day of the week.

Visitor info: Dallas Convention and Visitors Bureau, in the Old Red Courthouse, 100 S. Houston St. at the intersection with Main St. Open M-F 8am-5pm, Sa-Su 9am-5pm. Administrative office at 1201 Elm S., Renaissance Tower, 20th fl. (☎571-1000; 24hr. hotline 571-1301).

Hotlines: Suicide and Crisis Center, ☎828-1000. Contact Counseling, ☎972-233-2233, for general counseling. Both 24hr.

Internet access: Dallas Public Library, 1515 Young at Ervay (☎670-1400). Open M-Th 9am-9pm, F-Sa 9am-5pm, Su 1-5pm. Be careful around this area.

Dallas Gay and Lesbian Community Center: 2701 Reagan St. (☎528-9254).

Post Office: 401 Dallas-Ft. Worth Turnpike (☎800-275-8777), take Sylvan exit. Open daily 24hr. Downtown branch: 1201 Main St. ZIP code: 75201; for General Delivery, 75221. Area codes: 214, 817, and 972. In text, 214 unless otherwise noted.

▐ ACCOMMODATIONS

Cheap lodging in Dallas is nearly impossible to come by; big events such as the Cotton Bowl (Jan. 1) and the State Fair in October exacerbate the problem. Look 15-20min. along three major roads for inexpensive motels: north of downtown on U.S. 75, north along I-35, and east on I-30. Bed and Breakfast Texas Style, 4224 W. Red Bird Ln., will place you in a home, usually near town, with friendly residents anxious to make y'all as comfortable as possible. It's an especially good deal for two people. Call a few days ahead. (☎972-298-8586. Open M-F 8:30am-4:30pm. Singles from $55; doubles from $65.) The Super 7 Motel Mesquite, 3629 U.S. 80 E, lies 15min. from downtown; after bearing right onto U.S. 80 from I-30, exit at Town East Blvd. Rooms come with TV and free local calls. (☎972-613-9989. Singles $30.50; doubles $35.) Downtown, the Paramount Hotel, 302 S. Houston St., near Dealey Plaza and the West End, stands 2½ blocks from the Light Rail and CBD West transfer center. (☎761-9090. Singles $69; doubles $79.)

Near Lake Joe Pool, 20-30min. southwest of the city, Cedar Hill State Park provides 355 tent and RV sites. Take I-35 E to Rte. 67 and turn right onto FM 1382; the park is on the left. A swimming area, marina, jet-ski rental, and three walking trails are all located in the park. Reserve at least two weeks in advance. (☎972-291-3900, call 512-389-8900 for reservations. Office open M-F 10am-5pm, Sa-Su 10am-10pm; 24hr. gate access with reservations. Sites $15, primitive $7. Additional $5 daily fee for

TEXAS

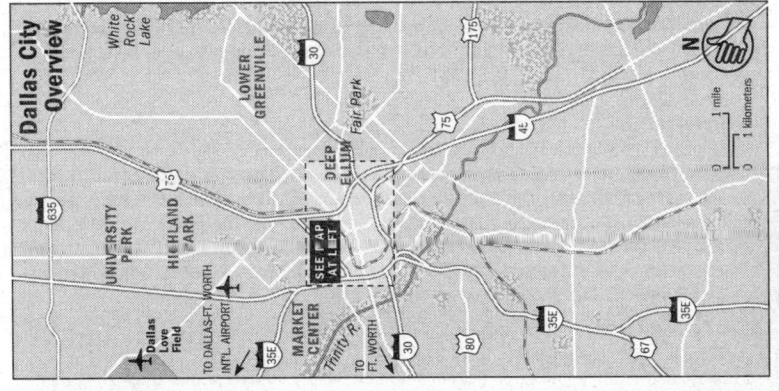

Dallas City Overview

White Rock Lake

LOWER GREENVILLE

Fair Park

DEEP ELLUM

SEE MAP AT LEFT

UNIVERSITY PARK

HIGHLAND PARK

MARKET CENTER

Dallas Love Field

TO DALLAS-FT. WORTH INTL. AIRPORT

TO FT. WORTH

Trinity R.

N

1 mile

1 kilometers

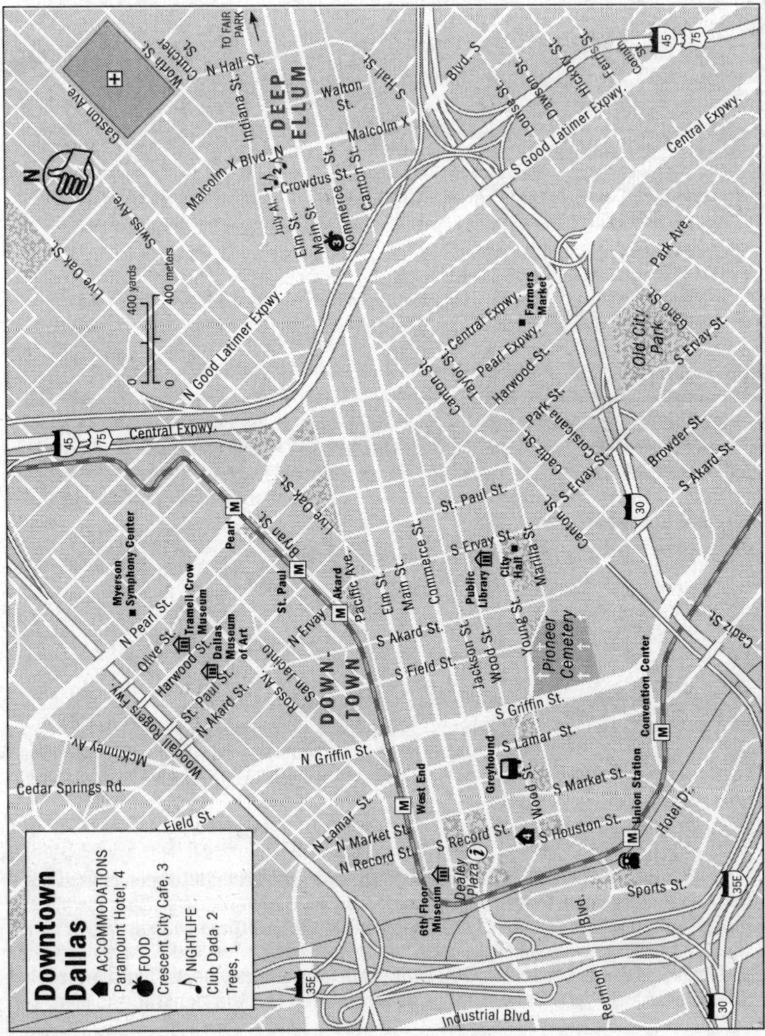

Downtown Dallas

♦ ACCOMMODATIONS
Paramount Hotel, 4

⚑ FOOD
Crescent City Cafe, 3

♪ NIGHTLIFE
Club Dada, 2
Trees, 1

World St.
Crutcher St.
N Hall St.
Indiana St.
Walton St.
DEEP ELLUM
Malcolm X Blvd.
Malcolm X
Crowdus St.
Commerce St.
Canton St.
S Hall St.
Blvd. S.
Louise St.
Dawson St.
Harry St.
Carson St.
Central Expwy.
N Good Latimer Expwy.
Gaston Ave.

TO FAIR PARK

N

400 yards
400 meters

Live Oak St.
Swiss Ave.
Elm St.
Main St.
July Al.

Central Expwy.

Canton St.
Taylor St.
Central Expwy.
Pearl Expwy.
Harwood St.
Cadiz St.
Corsicana St.

Farmers Market

Old City Park

S Ervay St.
Good St.
Browder St.
S Akard St.
Park Ave.

Myerson Symphony Center
Pearl M
Bryan St.
St. Paul M
Akard M
Trammell Crow Museum
Dallas Museum of Art
Olive St.
N Pearl St.
Harwood St.
St. Paul St.
N Akard St.
Ross Av.
San Jacinto
Pacific Ave.
N Ervay
Elm St.
Main St.
Commerce St.
S Akard St.
S Field St.
St. Paul St.
S Ervay St.
City Hall
Public Library
S Ervay St.
Marilla St.
Young St.
Wood St.
Cadiz St.
Canton St.
Pioneer Cemetery

DOWN-TOWN

Woodall Rogers Fwy.
McKinney Av.
Cedar Springs Rd.
Field St.

N Griffin St.
S Griffin St.
N Lamar St.
S Lamar St.
N Market St.
S Market St.
N Record St.
S Record St.
S Houston St.
Wood St.
West End
Greyhound
Convention Center M
Union Station M
Hotel Dr.
6th Floor Museum
Dealey Plaza
Sports St.
Reunion Blvd.

Industrial Blvd.

each adult.) Another option for RV campers is **Sandy Lake RV Park,** 1915 Sandy Lake Rd.; take I-35 E north of the city to Exit 444, then go left under the highway about a mile. (☎972-242-6808. Office open M-F 8am-8pm, Sa 8am-7pm, Su 1-6pm. Sites $25.)

▷ FOOD

Dallas supports more restaurants per capita than any other in the US (four times more than New York City). While many restaurants tend to be rather pricey, there are a few that offer great food at reasonable prices. For the lowdown on dining options, pick up the "Friday Guide" of the *Dallas Morning News.* Stock up on the freshest produce at the **Farmer's Market,** 1010 S. Pearl, next to International Marketplace. (☎939-2808. Open daily 7am-6pm.)

◪ EatZi's, 3403 Oaklawn Ave. (☎526-1515), at Lemmon Ave., 1 mi. east of Oaklawn exit from 35E, north of downtown. Take the #2 or 51 bus from downtown. A paradise for the frugal gourmet, this grocery, cafe, kitchen, and bakery forms a venue of glorious food. Sounds of Vivaldi and surround heapings of focaccia ($3), sandwiches ($4-7), and a multitude of delights. Enjoy numerous free sample platters. Open daily 7am-10pm.

Crescent City Cafe, 2615 Commerce (☎745-1900). One of the city's most popular lunch spots, the Crescent City Cafe serves up New Orleans cooking in the heart of Deep Ellum. 3 *beignets* (rumored to be better than those of the Cafe du Monde in New Orleans) $1.50, half a *muffaletta* (an Italian sandwich) $6.25. Open M-Sa 8am-3pm.

Sonny Bryan's Smokehouse, 302 N. Market St. (☎744-1610), in the West End. A landmark of Dallas BBQ, although a little more commercialized than your average BBQ joint. Try a beef sandwich ($4.25) or combine 3 smokehouse delicacies ($13). Vegetarian options available. Open M-Th 11am-10pm, F-Sa 11am-11pm, Su noon-9pm.

Baker's Ribs, 2724 Commerce (☎748-5433), east of downtown in Deep Ellum. If good BBQ is what you're craving, Baker's is the answer. A hearty meal between walls covered in banjos, washpans, cowboy pictures, and other pieces of Texan glory. Sandwiches ($3.75), combination plates ($7.25-9.50). Open M-Th 11am-7pm, F-Su 11am-9pm.

◉ SIGHTS

Oil-flushed Dallas is packed with showy displays of 20th-century architecture and sculpture. Located in the heart of downtown, historic Dallas can easily be seen on a walking tour. Dallas is more notorious for its recent history, however; JFK's assassination during a campaign parade in 1963 is permanently preserved in various museums and landmarks.

JFK SIGHTS. The **6th Floor Museum** is located at 411 Elm St. at Houston St. in the former Texas School Book Depository building. Stand on the sixth floor and look out the window through which Lee Harvey Oswald allegedly fired the shot that killed President John F. Kennedy on Nov. 22, 1963. Nowadays this fascinating museum is devoted to the Kennedy legacy, tracing the dramatic and macabre moments of the assassination through various media. (☎747-6660. *Open daily 9am-6pm. $7, seniors, students, and children 6-18 $6. Audio cassette rental $3.*) To the south of the depository, Elm St. runs through **Dealy Plaza,** a national landmark beside the infamous grassy knoll where Kennedy's convertible passed as the shots were fired. Philip Johnson's **Memorial** to Kennedy looms nearby at Market and Main. The cenotaph (open tomb), is a symbol of the freedom of JFK's spirit and is most striking when viewed at night. For more intrigue, check out the **Conspiracy Museum.** *(110 Market St. ☎741-3040. Open daily 10am-6pm. $7, students and seniors $6, children $3.)*

ART AND ARCHITECTURE. The **Dallas Museum of Art's** architecture is as graceful and beautiful as its collections of Egyptian, African, Early American, Impressionist, modern, and decorative art. *(1717 N. Harwood St. ☎922-1200. Open Tu-W and F 11am-5pm, Th 11am-9pm, Sa-Su 11am-5pm. Free. Special exhibits $5-8. Parking $2 first hr., $1 each additional hr.)* Directly across Harwood St., the ◪**Trammel Crow Center** has a must see collection of Asian art. A beautiful sculpture garden has works by Rodin, Maillol, and Bourdelle. *(2010 Flora St. at Hardwood and Olive. ☎979-6430. Open Tu-Su 11am-6pm except Th 11am-9pm. Free.)* The ubiquitous **I.M. Pei** designed many downtown Dallas buildings. One of his creations, the spectacular **Fountain Place** at the Wells Fargo Bldg., is on Ross St. just past Field St. The **Morton H. Meyerson Symphony Center,** 2301 Flora St., a few blocks east, and the imposing **Dallas City Hall,** 100 Marilla St. off of Young St., were also designed by Pei. Free tours of the Symphony Center are sometimes available. *(☎670-3600. Tours on selected M, W, F-Sa 1pm.)*

ATTRACTIONS. At the **Dallas World Aquarium,** admission is steep, but the multilevel rainforest exhibit with caged bats, swimming penguins, sleepy crocodiles, and birds zooming by your head make this aquarium worth the plunge. The museum anchors northeast of the West End, a block north of Ross Ave. *(1801 N. Griffin St. ☎720-2224. Open daily 10am-5pm. $11.85, seniors and children $6.50.)* On the east shore of White Rock Lake, resplendent flowers and trees fill the 66-acre **Dallas Arboretum.** The lake also provides a haven for walkers, bikers, and in-line skaters. *(8617 Garland Rd. ☎327-8263. Take bus #19 from downtown. Open M-F 10am-6pm, Sa-Su 8am-6pm; Nov.-Feb. daily 10am-5pm. $6, seniors $5, ages 6-12 $3. Parking $3.)*

FAIR PARK. Home to the state fair since 1886, **Fair Park** earned national landmark status for its Art Deco architecture. During the fair, **Big Tex**—a 52 ft. smiling cowboy float—towers over the land; only a huge ferris wheel, the **Texas Star,** looms taller. The 277-acre park also hosts the **Cotton Bowl** on January 1. In association with the Smithsonian Institute, **The Woman's Museum: An Institute for the Future** features a timeline of US women's history from 1500 to the present, as well as exhibits on famous American women. *(3800 Parry Ave. ☎915-0860. Open Tu-Sa 10am-5pm, Su noon-5pm. $5, seniors and children 5-12 $3.)*

HISTORIC DALLAS. Thirty-five late 19th-century buildings from around Dallas (including a dentist's office, a bank, and a farmstead which still raises animals) have been restored and moved to **Old City Park,** the city's oldest and most popular recreation and lunch spot. *(1717 Gano. ☎421-5141. Located 9 blocks south of City Hall at Ervay St. Open daily 9am-6pm. Exhibit buildings open Tu-Sa 10am-4pm, Su noon-4pm. $7, seniors $5, children $3.)* The **West End Historic District and Marketplace,** full of broad sidewalks, shops, and restaurants, lies north of Union Station. *(Most stores open M-Sa 11am-10pm, Su noon-6pm.)* Dallas's **mansions** are in the **Swiss Avenue Historic District** and along the streets of the **Highland Park** area, between Preston Rd. and Hillcrest Ave. south of Mockingbird Ln.

🎵 ENTERTAINMENT

The Observer, a free weekly found in stands across the city, has unrivaled entertainment coverage. For the scoop on Dallas's **gay scene,** pick up copies of the *Dallas Voice* and *Texas Triangle* in **Oak Lawn** shops and restaurants.

Prospero works his magic at the **Shakespeare in the Park** festival, at Samuel-Grand Park just northeast of Fair Park. During June and July (no performances the last week of June), two free plays run six nights per week. *(☎559-2778. Performances Tu-Su 8:15pm. Gates open 7:30; arrive early. $4 optional donation.)* At Fair Park, the **Music Hall** showcases **Dallas Summer Musicals.** *(☎421-0662 or 373-8000 for tickets; 696-4253 for half-price tickets on show days. Shows run June-Oct. $9-70.)* The **Dallas Symphony Orchestra** plays in the Symphony Center, at Pearl and Flora St. in the arts district. *(☎692-0203. Sept.-May. Box office open M-F 10am-6pm. Tickets $12-87.)*

If you come to Dallas looking for cowboys, the **Mesquite Rodeo,** 1818 Rodeo Dr., is the place to find them. Take I-30 east to I-635 S to Exit 4 and stay on the service road. Nationally televised, the rodeo is one of the most competitive in the country. *(☎972-285-8777 or 800-833-9339. Shows Apr. to early Oct. F-Sa 8pm. Gates open at 6:30pm. $10, seniors $7, children 3-12 $4. Dinner $9.50, children $6.50.)*

Six Flags Over Texas, 20 mi. from downtown off I-30 at Rte. 360 in Arlington, between Dallas and Fort Worth, boasts 38 rides, including the speedy, looping roller coasters "Batman: The Ride" and "Mr. Freeze." *(☎817-640-8900. Open June to early Aug. daily from 10am; late Aug.-Dec. and Mar.-May Sa-Su from 10am. Closing times vary. $41, over 55 or under 4 ft. $20.50. Parking $8.) Across the highway lies the mammoth 47-acre waterpark, **Hurricane Harbor.** Shoot down superspeed water flumes or experience simulated seasickness in the one million gallon wave pool. (☎817-265-3356. Open late May to early Aug. daily 10:30am-8pm. $27, seniors and under 4 ft. $13.50, parking $7.) Find coupons for both parks on soda cans and at Dallas or Ft. Worth tourist information offices.

In Dallas, the moral order is God, country, and the **Cowboys.** Football fanatics flock to **Cowboys Stadium** at the junction of Rte. 12 and Rte. 183, west of Dallas in Irving. (☎972-785-5000. Sept.-Jan. Ticket office open M-F 9am-5pm. Tickets from $36.) **The Ballpark in Arlington,** 1000 Ballpark Way, plays host to the **Texas Rangers.** (☎817-273-5100. Apr.-Sept. Ticket office open M-F 9am-6pm, Sa 10am-4pm, Su noon-4pm. Tickets $4-30.) Experience the mystique of the game with a tour of the locker room, dugout, and the press box on the **ballpark tour.** (☎817-273-5098. Non-game days, tours M-Sa 9am-4pm, Su noon-4pm every hr.; hours vary for game days. $5, seniors and students $4, ages 4-18 $3.)

NIGHTLIFE

For nightlife, head to **Deep Ellum,** east of downtown. In the 20s, the area was a blues haven for legends Blind Lemon Jefferson, Lightnin' Hopkins, and Robert Johnson; in the 80s, Bohemians revitalized the area. The first Friday of every month is **Deep Friday,** when a $7 wrist band gets you in to 9 Deep Ellum clubs featuring mostly local rock acts. Other nightlife epicenters include **Dallas Alley,** an amalgam of seven differently themed clubs located in the touristy **West End** (☎880-7420; $3-6); **Lower Greenville Ave.;** and **Yale Blvd.,** near Southern Methodist University's fraternity row. Many gay clubs rock north of downtown in **Oak Lawn.**

Trees, 2709 Elm St. (☎748-5009), rated the best live music venue in the city by the *Dallas Morning News,* occupies a converted warehouse with a loft full of pool tables and tree trunks in the middle of the club. Bands tend to play alternative rock music. 17+. Cover $2-10. Open W-Sa 9pm-2am.

Club Dada, 2720 Elm St. (☎744-3232). A former haunt of Edie Brickell and the New Bohemians, this hoppin' club boasts an eclectic clientele. Live local acts and a recently added outdoor patio and add to the fun. 21+. Cover W-Sa $3-5. Open W-Th 7pm-2am, F-Sa 5pm-2am, Su 8pm-2am.

Poor David's Pub, 1924 Greenville Ave. (☎821-9891), stages live music ranging from Irish folk tunes to reggae. Tickets available after 6pm at the door; cash only. Cover $1-20. Open M-Sa 8pm-2am; closed nights when no performance is scheduled.

Green Elephant, 5612 Yale Blvd. (☎750-6625). Full of pseudo-60s psychedelica, the Elephant is the bar of choice near SMU. Open M-Sa 11am-2am, Su 6pm-2am.

Roundup, 3912 Cedar Springs Rd. (☎522-9611), at Throckmorton. A huge, cover-free country-western bar that packs a large, mixed crowd on weekends. Free dance lessons Th 8:30pm. Bar open M-F 3pm-2am, Sa-Su noon-2am; club open Th-Su 8pm-2am.)

FORT WORTH   ☎817

If Dallas is the last Eastern city, Fort Worth is undoubtedly the first Western one. Dallas's slightly less refined neighbor lies less than 40min. west on I-30, providing a worthwhile daytrip and some raw Texan entertainment. Fort Worth is divided into three cultural districts, each marked by red brick streets: the **Stockyards Historic District, Sundance Square,** and the **Cultural District.**

The **Stockyards Historic District,** located along East Exchange Ave., 10min. north of downtown on Main St., attracts a throng of felt hat and leather boot hipsters. A walk along Exchange Ave., the main drag, provides a window into the Wild West, offering a slew of saloons, restaurants, shows, and gambling parlors. The **White Elephant Saloon,** 106 Exchange Ave., with its live country music (7 nights a week), brass footrails, and prodigious collection of cowboy hats, is a local favorite. (☎624-1887. Su-Th no cover; F-Sa $8 cover. Open Su-Th noon-midnight, F-Sa noon-2am.)

Just down the road at 121 Exchange Ave., the **Cowtown Coliseum** (☎625-1025 or 888-269-8696) hosts two weekly events: **rodeos** happen Friday and Saturday at 8pm ($8.50, seniors $7, children $5), and **Pawnee Bill's Wild West Show** features sharp-shooting, trick-roping, and a bullwhip act every Saturday and Sunday at 2:30 and 4:30pm. ($7.50, seniors $6, ages 3-12 $4.) To uncover the mystery of cattle raising, visit the **Cattle Raisers Museum,** 1301 7th St. between the Stockyards and Cultural Districts. (☎332-8551. Open M-Sa 10am-5pm, Su 1pm-5pm. $3, seniors and children 13-18 $2, children 4-12 $1.) The **Chisholm Trail Round-Up,** a three-day jamboree in the Stockyards during either the second or third week of June, preserves the heritage of the cowhands who led cattle drives to Kansas 150 years ago. (☎624-4741. Calls taken M-F 9am-6pm, Sa 9am-7pm, Su 11am-5pm.) The **Armadillo Races** are a Round-Up must-see; children and visitors are allowed to try their hand at making the crit-ters move. For more on the stockyards, pick up a copy of the *Stockyards Gazette* at the **Visitors Center,** 130 E. Exchange Ave. **Billy Bob's Texas,** 2520 Rodeo Plaza, ropes in the crowds for some honky-tonk night clubbing with big names in country music. With 100,000 sq. ft. of floor space, including a restaurant, pool tables, and 42 bar stations, the place bills itself as the world's largest honky-tonk. (☎624-7117. Free dance lessons Th 7pm. Professional bull-riding F-Sa 9 and 10pm. Under 18 must be accompanied by parent. Afternoon cover $1; Su-M after 6pm $3; Tu-Th $4; F-Sa $6.50-11, depending on performers. Open M-Sa 11am-2am, Su noon-2am.)

Downtown, **Sundance Sq.,** a pedestrian-friendly area, offers quality shops, muse-ums, and restaurants. In the square, the **Sid Richardson Collection,** 309 Main St., dis-plays an impressive stash of 55 paintings by the Western artists Remington and Russell. (☎332-6554. Open Tu-W 10am-5pm, Th-F 10am-8pm, Sa 11am-8pm, Su 1-5pm. Free.) Be sure to visit the little boys/girls room before going to the **Water Gar-dens** at Commerce and 5th St., where the wet stuff cascades down a series of man-made terraces as onlookers picnic in the shade. (Open daily 7am-11:30pm. Free.)

A few minutes west of downtown along 7th St., the **Cultural District** offers an array of intimate collections and exhibitions. The **Kimbell Museum,** 3333 Camp Bowie Blvd., touted as "America's best small museum," displays masterpieces from Car-avaggio to Cézanne. (☎332-8451. Open Tu-Th and Sa 10am-5pm, F noon-8pm, Su noon-5pm. Free, special exhibits $10, seniors and students $8, children 3-18 $6.) To see the newest art in the oldest art museum in Texas, visit the **Modern Art Museum,** 1309 Montgomery St. near the Kimbell. (☎738-9215. Open Tu-F 10am-5pm, Sa 11am-5pm, Su noon-5pm. Free.) **Ft. Worth Visitor's Bureau:** ☎336-8791. **Area code:** 817.

HOUSTON   ☎713

Born in 1836 when New York brothers Augustus and John Allen came slicing through the weeds of the Buffalo Bayou, Houston now spreads its borders as a huge mega-metropolis. Houston's expansive superhighways, awe-inspiring glass-and-steel skyscrapers, enormous oil plants, and massive strip malls provide a play-ground for the city's 1.8 million people. As if all this was not enough, the Houston-based NASA space center reaches toward the stars. Tangled interstates and heavy construction downtown (much of it directed toward a light rail system set to be completed in 2004) can make driving in Houston difficult. Even though Houston's suburbs sprawl as far as the eye can see, the downtown area itself is quite manage-able. But while the city grapples with its burgeoning borders, it continues to offer the cultural benefits of a large city in distinctive Texan style.

▬ TRANSPORTATION

Flights: Houston Intercontinental Airport (☎281-230-3100), 25 mi. north of downtown. Get to city center via **Express Shuttle** (☎523-8888); buses daily every 30min. to 1hr., depending on the destination hotel in the downtown area. Runs 7am-11:30pm; $19-20, ages 12-18 $6, under 12 free. **Hobby Airport,** 7800 Airport Blvd. (☎640-3000), lies about 10 mi. south of downtown and specializes in regional travel.

Trains: Amtrak, 902 Washington Ave. (☎224-1577), *in a rough neighborhood.* During the day, catch a bus west on Washington Ave. (away from downtown) to Houston Ave.; at night, call a cab. To San Antonio (5hr., 3 per week, $31-56) and New Orleans (9hr., 3 per week, $50-89). Open M-Tu, Th, and Sa 7am-9pm; Su, W, and F 7am-midnight.

Buses: Greyhound, 2121 Main St. (☎759-6565). *At night call a cab—this is an unsafe area.* To: Dallas (4-5hr., 10 per day, $32); San Antonio (3½hr., 11 per day, $20); and Santa Fe (24hr., 5 per day, $119). Open 24hr.

Public Transit: Metropolitan Transit Authority (☎635-4000). Offers reliable service anywhere between NASA (15mi. southeast of town) and Katy (25 mi. west of town). Operates M-F 6am-9pm, Sa-Su 8am-8pm; less frequently on weekends. The METRO operates a free trolley throughout downtown. Free maps available at the **Houston Public Library,** 500 McKinney (☎236-1313), at Bagby St. or at a Metro Rides store. Fare $1, seniors 40¢, ages 5-11 25¢; day pass $2. Open M-F 9am-9pm, Sa 9am-6pm, Su 2-6pm.

Taxis: United Cab, ☎699-0000.

✦🛈 ORIENTATION AND PRACTICAL INFORMATION

Though the flat Texan terrain supports several mini-downtowns, the true downtown Houston, a squarish grid of interlocking one-way streets, borders the **Buffalo Bayou** at the intersection of I-10 and I-45. **The Loop (I-610)** encircles the city center with a radius of 6 mi. Anything inside the Loop is easily accessible by car or bus. The shopping district of **Westheimer Blvd.** (uptown Houston) grows ritzier to the west. Nearby, restaurants and shops line **Kirby Dr.** and **Richmond Ave.;** the upper portion of Kirby Dr. winds past spectacular mansions. *Be careful in some areas of south and east Houston, as they may be unsafe.* The downside to Houston's booming economy is the ongoing roadwork—be on the look-out for detours.

Visitors Info: Greater Houston Convention and Visitors Bureau, in City Hall, at the corner of McKinney and Bagby St. (☎437-5200 or 800-446-8786). Open daily 9am-4pm.

Hotlines: Crisis Center, ☎228-1505. **Rape Crisis,** ☎528-7273. **Women's Center,** ☎528-2121. All 24hr. **Gay and Lesbian Switchboard of Houston** (☎529-3211; www.gayswitchboardhouston.org) has entertainment info. Operates daily 8am-11pm.

Hospital: Columbia Bellaire Medical Center, 5314 Dashwood (☎512-1200), has a 24hr. emergency room. **Columbia Woman's Hospital of Texas,** 7600 Fannin (☎790-1234).

Internet access: Houston Public Library (see Public Transit, above).

Post Office: 701 San Jacinto St. (☎800-275-8777). Open M-F 8am-5pm. **ZIP code:** 77052. **Area codes:** 713, 281, and 832 (in text 713, unless indicated).

🛏 ACCOMMODATIONS

A few cheap motels dot the **Katy Freeway (I-10W)** and **S. 59th St.** Budget accommodations along **S. Main St.** are more convenient, but not all are safe. Prices start at $30 for a single room. (Bus #8 goes down S. Main.)

Perry House, Houston International Hostel, 5302 Crawford St. (☎523-1009), at Oakdale St., in the museum district near Hermann Park. From the Greyhound station, take bus #8 or #15 south to Southmore St.; walk 6 blocks east to Crawford St. and 1 block south to Oakdale St. 30 beds in 6 spacious rooms. Well-equipped kitchen. Internet ($3 per hr.). Lockout 10am-5pm, common area open all day. Free use of bicycles with a $20 deposit (check out the bicycle store next door). Dorms $15.

YMCA, 1600 Louisiana Ave. (☎659-8501), between Pease and Leeland St. Downtown location features cubicle-like rooms, all singles, with daily maid service. Some have private baths. Key deposit $10; towel deposit $2.50. Newly renovated. Singles $25-35. **Another branch,** 7903 South Loop East (☎643-2804), is farther out (off the Broadway exit from I-610 near I-45) but less expensive. Take bus #50 to Broadway. Key deposit $10. Singles $22.

White House Motel, 9300 S. Main (☎666-2261). Close to I-610. Large, decently maintained rooms at solid prices. There's also an "Olympic Pool," (outdoor) but don't get your gold-medal hopes up too high. Singles $33; doubles $38.

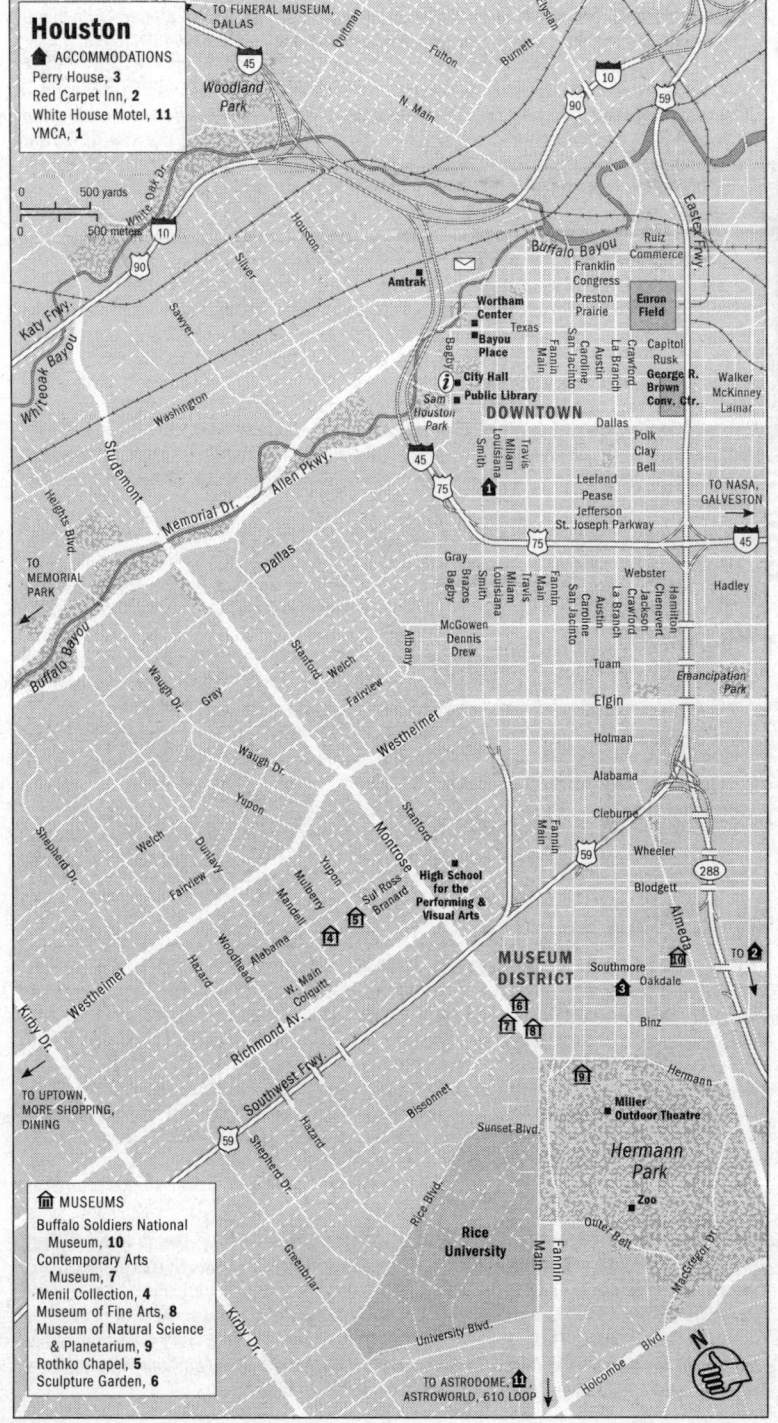

Houston

ACCOMMODATIONS
Perry House, **3**
Red Carpet Inn, **2**
White House Motel, **11**
YMCA, **1**

0   500 yards
0   500 meters

TO FUNERAL MUSEUM, DALLAS

Woodland Park

Quitman
Fulton
Burnett
Dysan

N. Main

Buffalo Bayou

Ruiz
Commerce

Amtrak

Franklin
Congress
Preston
Prairie

Wortham Center

Bayou Place

Texas

City Hall

Public Library

Sam Houston Park

DOWNTOWN

Enron Field

Capitol
Rusk

George R. Brown Conv. Ctr.

Walker
McKinney
Lamar

Crawford
La Branch
Caroline
Austin
San Jacinto
Fannin
Main

Dallas

Polk
Clay
Bell

Leeland
Pease
Jefferson
St. Joseph Parkway

TO NASA, GALVESTON

Smith
Louisiana
Milam
Travis

Gray
Brazos
Bagby

Louisiana
Milam
Travis
Main
Fannin
San Jacinto
Austin
Caroline
Crawford
La Branch

McGowen
Dennis
Drew

Webster
Hamilton
Chenevert
Jackson
Crawford

Hadley

Tuam

Emancipation Park

Elgin

Holman

Alabama

Cleburne

Wheeler

Blodgett

High School for the Performing & Visual Arts

MUSEUM DISTRICT

Southmore

Oakdale

Binz

Almeda

TO

Memorial Dr.
Allen Pkwy.
Dallas

Buffalo Bayou

TO MEMORIAL PARK

Heights Blvd.
Studemont

Washington

Katy Frwy.
Whiteoak Bayou

Silver
Sawyer
Houston
White Oak Dr.

Shepherd Dr.
Waugh Dr.
Gray
Stanford
Welch
Fairview
Albany
Westheimer

Waugh Dr.
Yupon

Welch
Dunlavy
Fairview

Montrose
Stanford

Mulberry
Mandell
Sul Ross
Branard

Woodhead
Alabama
Hazard

W. Main
Colquitt

Richmond Av.

Southwest Frwy.

TO UPTOWN, MORE SHOPPING, DINING

Kirby Dr.
Westheimer

Bissonnet

Sunset Blvd.

Hermann Park

Miller Outdoor Theatre

Zoo

Outer Belt

Hermann

MacGregor Dr.

Shepherd Dr.
Hazard

Rice Blvd.

Greenbriar

Kirby Dr.

Rice University

Fannin
Main

University Blvd.

Holcombe Blvd.

N

TO ASTRODOME, ASTROWORLD, 610 LOOP

MUSEUMS
Buffalo Soldiers National Museum, **10**
Contemporary Arts Museum, **7**
Menil Collection, **4**
Museum of Fine Arts, **8**
Museum of Natural Science & Planetarium, **9**
Rothko Chapel, **5**
Sculpture Garden, **6**

Red Carpet Inn, 6868 Hornwood Dr. (☎981-8686 or 800-251-1962). Near the Bellaire exit off U.S. 59 S/SW Fwy. Plain but well-kept rooms. Free coffee and continental breakfast. Singles $29; doubles $35.

Most campgrounds in the Houston area lie a considerable distance from the city center. **KOA Houston Central,** 1620 Peachleaf, has sites with pool and shower access. From I-45 N, go east on Aldine-Bender Rd., then turn right on Aldine-Westfield Rd., and then right again on Peachleaf. (☎281-442-3700 or 800-562-2132. Sites for 2 $18, with hookup $24; each additional adult $5. 1-room cabins $30, 2-room $40.)

▯ FOOD

Houston's port has witnessed the arrival of many immigrants (today the city's Indochinese population is the second largest in the nation), and its restaurants reflect this diversity. The city's cuisine features Mexican, Greek, Cajun, Asian, and Southern soul food. Look for reasonably priced restaurants along the chain-laden streets of **Westheimer** and **Richmond Ave.,** especially where they intersect with **Fountainview.** Houston has two **Chinatowns:** a district south of the George R. Brown Convention Center along Main St. and a newer area on **Bellaire Blvd.** called **DiHo.** Many small Mexican restaurants line the strip malls outside of the downtown region and are usually a good value for an empty stomach. For authentic Mexican fare, try Houston's East End.

Goode Company BBQ, 5109 Kirby Dr. (☎522-2530), near Bissonnet St. The mesquite-smoked brisket, ribs, and sausage links (all smothered in homemade sauce) will make your mouth water. Sandwiches from $3.50; one meat and two veggie dishes, $7-10. Also features gift shop with that utensil you've always wanted. Open daily 11am-10pm.

One's A Meal, 607 W. Gray St. (☎523-0425), at Stanford St. This family-owned institution serves everything from chili 'n' eggs ($6) to a gyro with fries ($6). Try the Greek pizza (6 in., $6) and colossal breakfast special (egg, bacon, sausage or ham, grits or hash browns, toast or biscuits, and juice for—you guessed it—$6). Open 24hr.

Ragin' Cajun, 4302 Richmond Ave. (☎623-6321). A local favorite that specializes in fish, Cajun-style. Indoor picnic tables and a casual atmosphere. Po' boys $6-9, cup of gumbo $4. Open M-Th 11am-10pm, F-Sa 11am-11pm.

Alfreda's Cafeteria, 5101 Almeda Rd. (☎523-6462). Close to Perry House. Alfreda's proudly advertises as "Black Family Owned" and serves great, cheap soul food. The special of the day includes meat and two vegetables for just $3.90. Open daily 6am-8pm.

◉ SIGHTS

JOHNSON SPACE CENTER. The city's most popular attraction, **Space Center Houston** is technically not even in Houston, but 20 mi. from downtown in Clear Lake, TX. The active Mission Control Center still serves as HQ for modern-day Major Toms. When astronauts ask, "Do you read me, Houston?" these folks answer. Admission includes tours of the mission control center and other astronaut training facilities. Among the attractions are out-of-this-world harnesses that will have you bouncing around like a real spaceman. The complex also houses models of Gemini, Apollo, and Mercury craft. *(1601 NASA Rd. 1. ☎281-244-2100 or 800-972-0369. Take I-45 south to NASA Rd. exit, then head east 3 mi. or take bus #246. Open June-Aug. daily 9am-7pm; Sept.-May M-F 10am-5pm, Sa-Su 10am-7pm. $15, seniors $14, ages 4-11 $11. Parking $3.)*

BAYOU BEND. The American decorative art from 1620-1870 at **Bayou Bend Collection and Gardens** in **Memorial Park** is an antique-lover's dream. The collection, housed in the mansion of millionaire Ima Hogg (we're not just hamming it up), daughter of former Gov. Jim "Boss" Hogg, includes John Singleton Copley portraits. *(1 Westcott St. ☎639-7750, ext 7750. Collection open Tu-Sa 10am-5pm, Su 1-5pm. $10, seniors and students $8.50, ages 10-18 $5, under 10 not admitted. Gardens open Tu-Sa 10am-5pm, Su 1-5pm. $3, under 10 free. 1½hr. garden tours by reservation.)*

HERMANN PARK. Museums, gardens, paddle boats, and golfing are all part of **Hermann Park,** 388 acres of beautifully landscaped grounds by Rice University and the Texas Medical Center. Near the northern entrance of the park, the **Houston Museum of Natural Science** offers a six-story glass butterfly center, some formidable looking dinosaurs (all dead), a splendid display of gems and minerals, a planetarium, an IMAX theatre, and a hands-on gallery geared towards grabby little children. At the southern end of the park, crowds flock to see more animated attractions—such as gorillas, hippos, and reptiles—in the **Houston Zoological Gardens.** The park grounds also encompass the Miller Outdoor Theater (see **Entertainment,** below), a children's zoo, golf course, sports facilities, a kiddie train, and a Japanese garden. *(Museum of Natural Science: 1 Hermann Circle Dr.* ☎ *639-4629. Exhibits open M-Sa 9am-6pm, Su 11am-6pm. Museum $4, seniors and under 12 $3, ages 3-11 $2; IMAX $6.50/$4.50/$4.50; planetarium $4/$3/$3; butterfly center $4/$3/$3. Zoo: 1513 N. MacGregor.* ☎ *523-5888. Open daily 10am-6pm. $2.50, seniors $2, ages 3-12 50¢.)*

ART ATTRACTIONS. The Museum of Fine Arts hosts Impressionist and post-Impressionist Art, as well as works from Asia, Africa, and the American West. The museum's **Sculpture Garden** includes pieces by artists such as Matisse and Rodin. Across the street, the **Contemporary Arts Museum** features changing exhibits. *(Museum of Fine Arts: 1001 Bissonet.* ☎ *639-7300. Open Tu-W and Sa 10am-7pm, Th-F 10am-9pm, Su 12:15-7pm. $5, students and seniors $2.50; free Th. Garden: 5101 Montrose St. Open daily 9am-10pm. Free. Contemporary Arts Museum: 5216 Montrose St.* ☎ *284-8250. Open Tu-W and F-Sa 10am-5pm, Th 10am-9pm, Su noon-5pm. Suggested donation $3.)*

The Menil Foundation exhibits an array of artwork in four buildings grouped within a block of each other. The **Menil Collection** includes an eclectic assortment of Surrealist paintings and sculptures; Byzantine and medieval artifacts; and European, American, and African art. *(1515 Sul Ross.* ☎ *525-9400. Open W-Su 11am-7pm; chapel closes at 6pm. Free.)* A block away, the **Rothko Chapel** houses 14 of the artist's paintings in a sanctuary. Worshipping fans of modern art will delight in Rothko's ultra-simplicity; others will wonder where the paintings are. *(3900 Yupon.* ☎ *524-9839. Open daily 10am-6pm. Free.)*

JUST FOR FUN. In downtown, earthly pleasures can be found underground. Hundreds of shops and restaurants line the 18 mi. **Houston Tunnel System,** which connects all the major buildings in downtown Houston, extending from the Civic Center to the Tenneco Building and the Hyatt Regency. Duck into the air-conditioned passageways via any major building or hotel. *(Most entries closed Sa-Su.)* Many a Bacchanalian feast must have preceded the construction of the **Beer Can House,** 222 Malone, off Washington Ave. Adorned with 50,000 beer cans, strings of beer-can tops, and a beer-can fence, the house was built by the late John Mikovisch, an upholsterer from the Southern Pacific Railroad. At 5¢ a can, the tin abode has a market price of $2500 for the decorations alone.

SAN JACINTO. The **San Jacinto Battleground State Historical Park** is the most important monument to Lone Star independence. The 18min. battle brought Texas its freedom from Mexico and gave the city its namesake in the person of Sam Houston. A ride to the top of the 50-story **San Jacinto Monument** yields a stunning view of the area. The **museum** inside the monument celebrates Texas history. While you're there, check out the *Battleship Texas,* the only surviving naval vessel to have served in both World Wars. *(Monument:* ☎ *281-479-2421. 21 mi. east on Rte. 225 and 3 mi. north on Rte. 134. Open daily 9am-6pm. $3, seniors $2.50, under 12 $2. Museum:* ☎ *281-479-2431. Open daily 9am-6pm. Free. 40min. projector, multimedia slide show daily every hr., 10am-5pm. $3.50/$3/$2.50. Combo tickets with elevator ride $6/$5/$4. Battleship:* ☎ *281-479-2431. Right next to monument. Open daily 10am-5pm. $5, seniors $4, ages 6-18 $3, under 6 free.)*

OTHER MUSEUMS. If you've always wondered what the Bob Marley song "Buffalo Soldier" is about, check out **Buffalo Soldiers National Museum.** The small museum highlights the role of the Buffalo soldiers in taming the Wild West and also features exhibits on African American military history from the Revolutionary War to the present. The **Holocaust Museum** in the museum district features a chilling architectural style that recalls the concentration camps. The museum also has a rotating art gallery and two films about the Holocaust. *(Buffalo Museum: 1834 Southmore. ☎942-8920. Open M-F 10am-5:30pm, Sa 10am-3pm, closed Su. Free. Holocaust Museum: 5401 Caroline St. ☎942-8000. Open M-F 9am-5pm, Sa-Su 12-5pm. Free.)*

♫ ENTERTAINMENT

From April to October, symphony, opera, and ballet companies and various professional theaters stage free performances at the **Miller Outdoor Theatre** in Hermann Park (☎284-8352). The annual **Shakespeare Festival** struts and frets upon the stage from late July to early August. The downtown **Alley Theatre**, 615 Texas Ave., puts on Broadway-caliber productions at moderate prices. (☎228-8421. Tickets $32-44; Su-Th $12 student rush tickets 1hr. before the show.) For downtown entertainment, **Bayou Place,** 500 Texas Ave., holds a multiscreen movie complex, a pool hall, a live music venue, and a Hard Rock Cafe. **Jones Hall,** 615 Louisiana Blvd. (☎227-3974), stages more of Houston's highbrow entertainment. The **Houston Symphony Orchestra** performs here September through May. (☎227-2787. Tickets $20-70.) Between October and May, the **Houston Grand Opera** produces six operas in the nearby **Wortham Center,** 500 Texas Ave. (☎546-0200. Tickets $35-200; 50% student discount available at noon on the day of some shows, $20-70 off tickets bought 1hr. before start time.) The **Houston Ballet** also performs in the Wortham Center from September to June (tickets $41-101).

The **Astros** play ball at **Enron Field,** a new stadium located at the intersections of Texas, Crawford, and Congress St. near Union Station downtown (☎295-8000). With the Astros leaving the Astrodome behind, there's plenty of space to house the **Houston Livestock Show and Rodeo** (☎713-629-3700; Feb. to mid-March). Houston's basketball team, the **Rockets,** hoop it up at the **Compaq Center,** 10 Greenwald Plaza (☎843-3995). August 2002 will mark the first NFL game for the new **Houston Texans,** who will play at the spanking-new **Reliant Stadium**, 8400 Kirby Dr. (☎336-7700).

◼ NIGHTLIFE

A growing number of upscale bars, restaurants, and clubs surround **Market Square. Main St.** also boasts a growing club scene. Most of Houston's nightlife, however, happens west of downtown around Richmond and Westheimer Ave. Several gay clubs cluster on lower Westheimer, while enormous, warehouse-style dancehalls line the upper reaches of Richmond. A variety of bars and music clubs fill the streets in between.

   City Streets, 5078 Richmond Ave. (☎840-8555), is a multivenue complex with 6 different clubs offering everything from country and live R&B to disco and a pool hall. Cover $2-5, good for all 6 clubs. Open W-F 5pm-2am, Sa 7:30pm-2am.

   Sam's Boat/Sam's Place, 5720 Richmond Ave. (☎781-2628). Good-natured drinkers gather on the patio to drink, chat, and hear live music. Live music Tu 5pm-2am, F 8pm-2am, Sa 6pm-2am. Cover up to $3. Open daily 11am-2am; food served until 2am.)

   Valhalla (☎348-3258), in the center of the Rice campus across from the library. Stop by for "gods, heroes, mythical beings, and cheap [75¢] beer." Open M-F 4pm-2am, Su 7pm-2am.)

   Rich's, 2401 San Jacinto (☎759-9606). The 2-story gay dance club boasts an awesome sound system. Cover $5. Open Su-Th 9pm-2am, F-Sa 9pm-4am.

GALVESTON ISLAND   ☎409

In the 19th century, Galveston was the "Queen of the Gulf," Texas's most prominent port and wealthiest city. The glamour came to an abrupt end on Sept. 8, 1900, when a devastating hurricane ripped through the city, claiming 6000 lives. The Galveston hurricane still ranks as one of the worst natural disasters in US history. Today, the narrow, sandy island of Galveston (pop. 60,000), 50 mi. southeast of Houston on I-45, will never be mistaken for a posh, hopping beach area, but it's a worthwhile stop for a little fun in the sun or a chance to view the exquisite architecture downtown.

◢ PRACTICAL INFORMATION. Galveston's streets follow a grid: lettered avenues run east-west, while numbered streets run north-south. **Seawall Blvd.** follows the southern coastline. Most routes have two names; Ave. J and Broadway, for example, are the same street. Greyhound-affiliated **Kerrville Bus Co.,** 714 25th St. (☎765-7731; station open M-F 8am-7pm, Sa 8am-3:15pm), travels to Houston (1½hr., 4 per day, $13-14). **Galveston Island Convention and Visitors Bureau,** 2428 Seawall Blvd. (☎763-4311 or 888-425-4753; open daily 8:30am-5pm), is conveniently located on the beach. **Heritage Visitors Center,** 2328 Broadway in the Ashton Villa (☎762-3933; open M-Sa 10am-5pm, Su 12pm-5pm) dispenses info. **Post Office:** 601 25th St. (☎763-1527; open M-F 8am-5pm, Sa 8am-5pm). **ZIP code:** 77550. **Area code:** 409.

◪◖ ACCOMMODATIONS AND FOOD. The price of lodging in Galveston fluctuates by season, rising to exorbitant heights ($50 and way up) during the summer, holidays, and weekends. However, travelers should also beware of dilapidated, extremely cheap motels along the beach. Far and away the best option is the ◪**Sandpiper Motel,** 201 Seawall Blvd. (☎765-9431), right on the beach. All digs are former hotel rooms, so $18.50 nets you a TV, fridge, room phone, balcony, big commons area, and an outdoor pool. Those looking to spend a night outdoors can head to **Bayou Shores RV Resort,** 6310 Heards Ln., off 61st St., located on a peaceful waterfront with laundry facilities and bug-free restrooms and showers. (☎744-2837. Sites for 2 with full hookup $22, waterfront sites $25; $3 each additional person.) **Galveston Island State Park,** on 13½ Mile Rd., 6 mi. southwest of Galveston on FM3005 (a continuation of Ashton Blvd.), rents tent sites. (☎737-1222. Restrooms, showers, and barbecue pits available. $12, plus $3 entrance fee per person.)

The oldest restaurant on the island, **The Original Mexican Cafe,** 1401 Market, cooks up great Tex-Mex meals with homemade flour tortillas. Lunch specials run $6-8. (☎762-6001. Open M-Th 11am-9:30pm, F 11am-10pm, Sa-Su 8am-10pm.) **Benno's,** 1200 Seawall Rd., serves tasty Cajun seafood. (☎762-4621. Open Su-Th 11am-10pm, F-Sa 11am-11pm. Po' boys $5.25.) Indulge your sweet tooth at **LaKing's Confectionery,** 2323 Strand St., a large, old-fashioned ice cream parlor. (☎762-6100. Open Su-Th 10am-8:30pm, F 10am-9pm, Sa 9:30am-10pm; closes earlier in the winter.)

◪◪ SIGHTS AND OUTDOORS. Galveston recently spent more than $6 million to clean up and restore its shoreline, which still has only shallow water on the beaches: don't expecting a white sand, postcard shot. Nevertheless, the money was well spent—finding a pleasant beach is easy. The only beach in Galveston which permits alcoholic beverages is **Apffel Park,** on the far eastern edge of the island (known as East Beach). **#3 Beach Pocket Park** (numbers 1 and 2 were destroyed by the ocean) lies on the west end of the island, east of Pirates Beach, with bathrooms, showers, playgrounds, and a concession stand. (Car entry for beaches generally $5. Open daily 9am-9pm; some open later.) Catch a ferry to **Bolivar Island,** where bathing suit restrictions are rumored to be less stringent, at Ferry Rd. (off the far eastern end of Seawall, across from the Sandpiper Motel).

Strand St., near the northern coastline, between 20th and 25th St., is a national landmark, with many Victorian buildings. The district, restored with authentic gas lights and brick-paved walkways, holds a hodgepodge of cafes, restaurants, and shops. The elegant **Moody Mansion,** 2618 Broadway, features handcarved wood and stunning stained glass. (☎762-7688. Open M-Sa 10am-4pm, Su 12-4pm. $6, seniors $5, ages 6-18 $3.) The **Galveston Island Trolley** runs between the seawall beach area and Strand St. Pick up the trolley at either Visitors Center. (☎762-2903. Runs M-Th and Su 10am-6pm, F-Sa 10am-8pm. 60¢, 30¢ seniors and children under 12.)

You'll find fabulous and pricey attractions at **Moody Gardens;** turn onto 81st from Seawall. The shop and restaurant-packed area makes room for three glass pyramids. One houses over 30 interactive space exhibits and three IMAX ride-film theaters (rides every 15min.), a second contains a tropical rainforest and 2000 exotic species of flora and fauna, and the third features an aquarium. The newest attraction is Palm Beach, an artificial white sand beach. (☎683-4200 or 800-582-4673. Open summer daily 10am-9pm; winter Su-Th 10am-6pm, F-Sa 10am-9pm. Attrac-

TEXAS

tions $8 each, ride/films $8, aquarium $11, seniors and children $1 off; $29 day pass, everything half price after 6pm.) The antique locomotives at the **Galveston Railroad Museum,** 123 Rosenberg Ave., will honk the horn of train enthusiasts. (☎765-5700. Open daily 10am-4pm. $5, seniors $4.50, children 4-12 $2.50.)

CORPUS CHRISTI   ☎361

Corpus Christi's economy depends almost entirely on its shore side location; while local refineries are fed by the crude oil found offshore in the Gulf, year-round warm beaches bring the tourists in droves. Vacationers crowd the beaches in the summer, only to be replaced in the cooler months by "winter Texans," many of them elderly mobile home owners fleeing the chill of the northern states. Corpus Christi is defined equally by its pricey knick-knacks, cheap gas, natural stretches of sand, and the encroaching waste that floats in from the Gulf.

▐ **TRANSPORTATION. Greyhound,** 702 N. Chaparral (☎882-9206; open daily 8am-2:30am). To: Dallas (9-10hr., 7 per day, $42); Houston (5hr., 9 per day, $21-22); and Austin (5-7½hr., 4 per day, $25). **Regional Transit Authority (The "B")** (☎289-2600) buses within Corpus Christi; pick up maps and schedules at the Visitors Center or at **The B headquarters,** 1806 S. Alameda (☎883-2287; open M-F 8am-5pm). City Hall, Port Ayers, Six Points, and the Staples St. stations serve as central transfer points. (Runs M-Sa 5:30am-9:30pm, Su 11am-6:30pm. Fare 50¢; students, seniors, and children 25¢; disabled 10¢; Sa 25¢; transfers free.) The **Harbor Ferry** follows the shoreline and stops at the aquarium (daily 10:30am-6:30pm, $1 each way). On the north side of Harbor Bridge, the free **Beach Shuttle** also travels to the beach, the Aquarium, and other attractions (runs May-Sept. 10:30am-6:30pm). **Taxi: Yellow Cab,** ☎884-3211.

▐ **PRACTICAL INFORMATION.** Corpus Christi's tourist district follows **Shoreline Dr.,** which borders the Gulf Coast, 1 mi. east of the downtown business district. **Convention and Visitors Bureau,** 1823 Chaparral, 6 blocks north of I-37 and 1 block from the water. (☎561-2000 or 800-766-2322. Open daily 9am-5pm.) **Medical Care: Spohn Hospital Shoreline,** 600 Elizabeth St. (☎881-3000). **Hotlines: Hope Line** (☎855-4673) and **Battered Women and Rape Victims Shelter** (☎881-8888); both operate 24hr. **Internet access:** Corpus Christi Public Library, 805 Comanche. (☎880-7000. Open M-Th 9am-9pm, F-Sa 9am-6pm, Su 2pm-6pm.) **Post Office:** 809 Nueces Bay Blvd. (☎800-275-8777. Open M-F 7:30am-5:30pm, Sa 8am-1pm.) **ZIP code:** 78469. **Area code:** 361.

▐ **ACCOMMODATIONS AND CAMPING.** Cheap accommodations are scarce downtown, and posh hotels and motels take up much of the shoreline. The best motel bargains lie several mi. south on Leopard St. (take bus #27) or I-37 (take #27 Express). The **Super 8,** 910 Corn Products Rd., provides a reasonable budget option. (☎289-1216. Singles $33, doubles $37.) Campers should head for the **Mustang State Park** or the **Padre Island National Seashore** (see below). Nueces River **City Park** (☎241-1464), off I-37 N from Exit 16 and approximately 18 mi. from downtown Corpus, has free tent sites, but only pit toilets and no showers. Pick up a camping permit from the ranger station on your way into the park.

▐ ▌ **FOOD AND NIGHTLIFE.** The mixed population and seaside locale of Corpus Christi have resulted in a wide range of cuisines. Non-chain restaurants can be found on the south side of the city, around Staples St. and S. Padre Island Dr. For delectable Mexican, try **Martha's Mexican Restaurant,** 1001 3rd St., near the library and City Hall. The $5 daily lunch specials and evening entertainment Tuesday through Saturday make Martha's a magnificent option. (☎904-0016. Open M-Sa 11am-10pm.) **BJ's,** 6335 S. Padre Island Dr., serves four topping, crispy-crusted pizzas (8 in.; $5) while patrons shoot pool and drink 300 varieties of beer. (☎992-6671. Open M-Sa 11am-10:30pm, Su noon-9:30pm.) **The Purple Parrot,** 2900 N. Shoreline Dr. (☎883-7100 or 800-883-8507), next to the USS Lexington, boasts bay-view decks, a courtyard with constant music, and beach volleyball courts. Right next door is **Pier 99,** 2822 N. Shoreline Dr., which specializes in fried fresh fish, such as $7 shrimp or oyster baskets. (☎887-0764. Open daily 11am-10pm.)

Get your groove on at **Stinger's** and **Dead Eye Dick's,** both at 301 N. Chaparral. Stomp to country and rock music at Stinger's, then shake it to traditional dance tunes at Dick's. (☎887-0029. Open W-Sa 11am-2am. Cover $5 W-Th, $8 F-Sa.)

⬛ **SIGHTS.** Corpus Christi's most significant sight is the shoreline, bordered by miles of rocky seawall and wide sidewalks with graduated steps down to the water. Overpriced seaside restaurants, sail and shrimp boats, and aggressive, hungry seagulls overrun the piers. The best beach is Port Aransas, reachable by ferry (on Rte. 361). To find beaches that allow swimming (some lie along Ocean Dr. and north of Harbor Bridge), just follow the signs. On the north side of Harbor Bridge, the **Texas State Aquarium,** 2710 N. Shoreline Blvd., showcases underwater creatures from the Gulf of Mexico. (☎881-1200 or 800-477-4853. Open M-Sa 9am-6pm, Su 10am-6pm; early Sept. to late May closes at 5pm. $9, seniors $7.50, ages 4-12 $5.25.)

Just offshore floats the aircraft carrier **USS Lexington,** a World War II relic now open to the public. In her day, the "Blue Ghost" set more records than any carrier in the history of naval aviation. Be sure to check out the crews' quarters—you won't complain about small hostel rooms ever again. (☎888-4873 or 800-523-9539. Open daily 9am-6pm; early Sept. to late May 9am-5pm. $10, seniors $8, ages 4-12 $5.) Lay down a few clams on your favorite pooch at the **Corpus Christi Greyhound Race Track,** I-37 at Navation exit. (☎289-9333 or 800-580-7223. Grandstand admission $1.)

PADRE ISLAND ☎361

With over 80 mi. of painstakingly preserved beaches, dunes, and wildlife refuge land, the **Padre Island National Seashore (PINS)** is a priceless (though debris-flawed) gem, sandwiched between the condos of North Padre Island and the spring-break hordes of South Padre Island. The seashore provides excellent opportunities for windsurfing, swimming, or surf fishing. Driving is permitted at most places on the beach, though four-wheel-drive is recommended. Padre Island is divided into several areas; gain entrance to each area through the access roads. Access 1a is at the far northern tip of the island near Port Aransas, while Access 6 is closest to PINS. For up-to-date info on prices and activities within PINS, call 800-766-2322. Garbage from nearby ships frequently litters the sands, but a lucky few may spot one of the endangered Kemp's Ridley sea turtles nurtured by PINS. A yearly pass into PINS costs $10 for cars, $5 for hikers and bikers. Day pass $5. Windsurfing or launching a boat from the Bird Basin will dock you an extra $5. Many beachcombers avoid these fees by going to the free **North Beach.** Cast your own line or just take a look at what others are catchin' at **Bob Hall Pier,** Access Rd. 4, the main fishing pier on the island. (☎949-0999. Open daily 24hr. $1.)

Five miles south of the entrance station, **Malaquite Beach** makes your day on the sand as easy as possible with restrooms and rental picnic tables. In summer, the rental station is set up on the beachfront. (Inner tubes $2 per hr., chairs $1 per hr., body boards $2.50 per hr.) The **Malaquite Visitors Center** has free maps and exhibits about the island. (☎949-8068. Open daily summer 8:30am-6pm; winter 8:30am-4:30pm.) Motorists enter the PINS via the JFK Causeway, from the Flour Bluff area of Corpus Christi. PINS can only be reached by car.

Visitors with four-wheel-drive and a taste for solitude should make the 60 mi. trek to the **Mansfield Cut,** the most remote and untraveled area of the seashore; loose sands prevent most vehicles from venturing far onto the beach. Call the **Malaquite Ranger Station** (☎949-8173), 3½ mi. south of the park entrance, for emergency assistance. No wheels? Hike the **Grasslands Nature Trail,** a ¾ mi. loop through sand dunes and grasslands. Guide pamphlets are available at the trailhead.

The **PINS Campground,** less than 1 mi. north of the Visitors Center, consists of an asphalt area for RVs, restrooms, and cold-rinse showers—no soap is permitted on PINS (sites $8). Outside of this area—excluding the 5 mi. pedestrian-only beach—wherever vehicles can go, camping is free. For camping with amenities, the **Padre Balli County Park,** Access 5 on Park Rd. 22, 3½ mi. from the JFK Causeway, near the National Seashore, provides running water, electricity, laundry, and hot showers for campers. (☎949-8121. Sites with water and hookup $15 plus $5 water key deposit; beach tent sites $6. 3-day max. stay.) **Area code: 361.**

TEXAS

WESTERN TEXAS

On the far side of the Río Pecos lies a region whose stereotypical Texan character verges on self-parody. This is the stomping ground of Pecos Bill—the mythical cowpoke who was raised by coyotes and who lassoed a tornado. The land was colonized in the days of the Republic of Texas, during an era when the "law west of the Pecos" meant a rough mix of vigilante violence and frontier gunslinger machismo. The border city of El Paso and its Chihuahuan neighbor, Ciudad Juárez, beckon way, *wayyyy* out west—700 mi. from the Louisiana border—while Big Bend National Park dips down into the desert, cradled by a curve in the Río Grande.

AMARILLO   ☎ 806

Named for the yellow clay of a nearby lake (*amarillo* is "yellow" in Spanish), Amarillo opened for business as a railroad construction camp in 1887 and, within a decade, became one of the nation's largest cattle-shipping markets. For years, the economy depended largely on the meat industry, but the discovery of oil gave Amarillo a kick in the 20s. Amarillo is now the prime overnight stop for motorists en route from Dallas, Houston, or Oklahoma City to Denver and other Western destinations. It's little more than a one-day city—but what a grand, shiny truck stop it is.

The outstanding **Panhandle-Plains Historical Museum,** 2401 4th Ave., in nearby Canyon (I-27 S to Rte. 87), has fossils, local history and geology exhibits, and a collection of Southwestern art. (☎651-2244. Open M-Sa 9am-5pm, Su 1-6pm; in summer daily until 6pm. $4, seniors $3, ages 4-12 $1.) The **American Quarter Horse Heritage Center and Museum,** 2601 I-40 E, at Exit 72B, presents the heroic story of "America's horse." (☎376-5181 or 888-209-8322. Open M-Sa 9am-5pm, Su noon-5pm. $4, seniors $3.50, ages 6-18 $2.50.) At **Cadillac Ranch,** Stanley Marsh III has planted ten Cadillacs at the same angle as the Great Pyramids of Cheops. Get off I-40 at the Hope Rd. exit, 9 mi. west of Amarillo, cross to the south side of I-40, turning right immediately at the end of the bridge. Drive ½ mi. down the highway access road to the west.

Amarillo is a popular place for travelers to hang up their Stetson for the evening. Budget motels proliferate along the entire stretch of I-40, I-27, and U.S. 287/87 near town. Prices rise near the downtown area. **Camelot Inn,** 2508 I-40 E, at Exit 72A, a pink, castle-like motel with palatial rooms, a princely staff, cable, and breakfast, ranks among the best of the I-40 offerings. (☎373-3600. Singles $26-36; doubles $33-36; varies seasonally. 21+.) Kampers flock to the **KOA Kampground,** 1100 Folsom Rd., 6 mi. east of downtown; take I-40 to Exit 75, head north to Rte. 60, then east 1 mi. (☎335-1792. Reception daily 8am-10pm; early Sept. to late May 8am-8pm. Pool, laundry, and free coffee. Sites $20, with water and electricity $24, full hookup $25.) Dine amid fountains and Mexican murals at **Abuelo's,** 3501 45th St. The *cena mexicana* ($10) is scrumptious. (☎354-8294. Open Su-Th 11am-10pm, F-Sa 11am-11pm.)

Amarillo sprawls at the intersection of I-27, I-40, and U.S. 287/87; you'll need a car to explore. Rte. 335 (the Loop) encircles the city. Amarillo Blvd. (historic Rte. 66) runs east-west, parallel to I-40. **Greyhound,** 700 S. Tyler (☎374-5371; station open 24hr.), buses to Dallas (8hr., 4 per day, $56-59) and Santa Fe (6-10hr., 4 per day, $57-60). **Amarillo City Transit,** 801 S.E. 23rd, operates eight bus routes departing from 5th and Pierce St. (☎378-3094. Buses run every 30min. M-Sa 6am-6pm. Maps at office. Fare 75¢.) The **Texas Travel Info Center,** 9400 I-40E, at Exit 76, has state info. (☎335-1441. Open daily 8am-5pm.) **Amarillo Convention and Visitors Bureau:** 1000 S. Polk, at 10th St. (☎374-1497 or 800-692-1338. Open M-F 8am-5pm.) **Post Office:** 505 E. 9th Ave., at Buchanan St. (Open M-F 7:30am-5pm.) **ZIP code:** 79105. **Area code:** 806.

PALO DURO CANYON STATE PARK   ☎ 806

Known as the "Grand Canyon of Texas," Palo Duro covers 16,000 acres of jaw-dropping beauty. The beautiful 16 mi. **scenic drive** through the park begins at the HQ. Rangers allow backcountry **hiking,** but the majority of visitors stick to the marked trails. Most hikers can manage the 2 mi. **Sunflower Trail,** or the 2 mi. **Paseo del Río Trail,** but only experienced hikers should consider the rugged 9 mi. **Running Trail.**

BIG TEXAN WOMEN The 72 oz. steak at the **Inn of the Big Texan,** at Lakeside Exit 75 from I-40, seems impossible to eat. Anyone who scarfs the steak in 1hr. gets it free; the defeated pay $54. Over 32,000 have tried to consume the beast; the names, weights (before), and home cities of some of the 5100 success stories are listed under the glass-top bar. A third of the women have been victorious, compared to only a fifth of the men. (☎372-6000 or 800-657-7177. Open daily 10:30am-10:30pm.)

Avid bikers enjoy the 4 mi. **Capitol Peak Mountain Bike Trail.** The official play of the State of Texas, the musical ◼**Texas,** performed in Pioneer Amphitheater, is a must-see. The performance covers the state's early days against the backdrop of the canyon's scenery. (☎655-2181. In summer M-Sa 8:30pm. $8-23, under 13 $5-23.)

Backcountry camping is allowed in designated areas. (☎512-389-8900 for reservations. Primitive sites $9; with water $10; hookup $12; cabins $65.) The **Chuckwagon Restaurant,** 1½ mi. along the drive, sells sandwiches ($3) and a small selection of groceries. (☎488-2152. Open Th-Tu 8:30am-8pm, W 8:30am-7pm, Th-Sa.) **Old West Stables,** ¼ mi. farther, rents horses with a saddle and riding hat. (☎488-2180. Open 10am-6pm. $20 per hr., wagon rides $8. Reservations recommended.)

The park is 23 mi. south of Amarillo. Take I-27 to Exit 106 and head east on Rte. 217; from the south, get off I-27 at Exit 103. (Park open daily 7am-10pm; in winter 8am-10pm. $3, under 12 free.) *Temperatures in the canyon frequently climb to 100°F; bring at least 2 quarts of water.* The park headquarters, just inside the park, has maps of hiking trails and info on park activities. (☎488-2227. Open daily 7am-10pm; in winter 8am-5pm.) A ½ mi. past the HQ, the **Visitors Center** displays exhibits on the canyon's history (open M-Sa 9am-5pm, Su 1-5pm). **Area code:** 806.

GUADALUPE MOUNTAINS NATIONAL PARK ☎915

Rising austerely above the parched west Texas desert, these peaks form the highest and most remote of the west Texas ranges. Mescalero Apaches hunted and camped on these lands, until they were driven out by the US army. Before being forced out, Apache chief Geronimo claimed that the greatest gold mines in the world were hidden in the peaks. Despite the country's craze for gold, few settlers bought the prophecy; by the late 1800s, only a handful of miners inhabited the rugged region. Today, Guadalupe Mountains National Park encompasses 86,000 acres of desert, caves, canyons, and highlands. Drivers can glimpse the park's most dramatic sights from U.S. 62/180: **El Capitán,** a 2000 ft. limestone cliff, and **Guadalupe Peak,** the highest point in Texas (8749 ft.). The mountains promise over 80 mi. of challenging desert trails to those willing to explore the area. Entrance to the park is currently free, though a fee is planned for 2002. **Carlsbad, NM** (see p. 782), 55 mi. northeast, makes a good base town, with many cheap motels, campgrounds, and restaurants.

The major park trailhead is at Pine Springs Campground, near the headquarters (see below). From this starting point, imposing **Guadalupe Peak** can be scaled in a difficult but rewarding full-day hike (5-6hr., 8.4 mi.). A shorter trek (2-3hr., 4.2 mi.) traces the sheltered streambed of **Devil's Hall.** A full-day hike (9 mi., 6-7hr.) leads from the campground to the **Bowl,** a high-country forest of Douglas Fir and Ponderosa Pines. The **Spring Trail** (1-2hr., 2.3 mi.) leads from the **Frijole Ranch,** about 1 mi. north of the Visitors Center, to a mountain spring frequented by park wildlife. Beginning at the **McKittrick Visitors Center,** several mi. northeast of the main Visitors Center, a trail leads up scenic McKittrick Canyon to the historic **Pratt Cabin.**

The park's lack of development is attractive to backpackers, but it creates some inconveniences. The nearest gas and food spot is the **Nickel Creek Cafe,** 5 mi. north of Pine Springs. (☎828-3295. Open M-Sa 7am-2pm and 6-9pm. Burgers $4. Cash only.) The park's two simple campgrounds, **Pine Springs,** just past park headquarters, and **Dog Canyon,** south of the New Mexico border at the north end of the park, have water and restrooms but no hookups or showers. (☎828-3251. Reservations for groups only. Sites $8.) Dog Canyon is accessible only via Rte. 137 from Carlsbad, NM (72 mi.), or by a full-day hike from the **Main Visitors Center** at Pine Springs, off U.S. 62/180. (☎828-3251. Open daily June-Aug. 8am-6pm; Sept.-May 8am-4:30pm. After hours, info is posted on the outside bulletin board.) Free **backcountry camping** permits are available at the Visitors Center.

Guadalupe Park lies 110 mi. east of El Paso. For additional info, contact the Visitors Center or write to **Guadalupe Mountains National Park,** HC 60, Box 400, Salt Flat 79847. **TNM&O Coaches** (☎505-887-1108) runs along U.S. 62/180 between Carlsbad, NM, and El Paso and will make a flag stop at the Pine Springs Visitors Center if you call ahead (from Carlsbad 2½hr., $26). **Area code:** 915.

EL PASO   ☎915

The largest of the US border towns, El Paso boomed in the 17th century as a stopover on an important east-west wagon route that followed the Río Grande through "the pass" (*el paso*) between the Rocky Mountains and the Sierra Madre. Today, the El Paso-Ciudad Juárez metropolitan area has nearly three million inhabitants, a number that keeps growing due to an increase in the cross-border enterprises fueled by NAFTA. Nearly everyone in El Paso speaks Spanish, and the majority of denizens are of Mexican ancestry. After dark, activity leaves the center of town, migrating toward the suburbs and south of the border to raucous Ciudad Juárez.

◼◪ ORIENTATION AND PRACTICAL INFORMATION. San Jacinto Plaza, at the corner of Main and Oregon, is the heart of El Paso. **I-10** runs east-west and **U.S. 54** north-south from the city. El Paso is divided into east and west by **Santa Fe Ave.** and into north and south by **San Antonio Ave.** *Tourists should be wary of the streets between San Antonio and the border late at night.* **Amtrak** trains depart from Union Train Depot, 700 San Francisco St. (☎545-2247), two blocks west of the Civic Center, for San Antonio (12½hr., 3 per week, $146) and Tucson (6hr., 3 per week, $96). **Greyhound,** 200 W. San Antonio (☎532-2365; open 24hr.), across from the Civic Center, has daily service to Dallas (12hr., 7 per day, $60) and Los Angeles (16hr., 6 per day, $45). **Sun Metro** runs buses all through the city, departing from San Jacinto Plaza. Bus #33 runs 50min. to downtown from the airport. (☎533-3333. $1, students 50¢.) **Visitors Center:** 1 Civic Center Plaza, at Santa Fe and San Francisco. (☎544-0062. Open daily 8am-5pm.) **Post Office:** 219 E. Mills, between Mesa and Stanton. (☎532-2652. Open M-F 9am-5pm, Sa 8am-noon.) **ZIP code:** 79901. **Area code:** 915.

◪◪ ACCOMMODATIONS AND FOOD. El Paso offers safer, more appealing places to stay than Ciudad Juárez. Several good budget hotels can be found in the town center near Main St. and San Jacinto Square. The best place in town is the ◼**El Paso International Hostel,** 311 E. Franklin, between Stanton and Kansas in the Gardner Hotel. From the airport, take bus #33 to San Jacinto Park, walk two blocks north to Franklin, turn right, and head east 1½ blocks. The hostel takes great pride in meeting the needs of backpackers. (☎532-3661. Dorms $15.) **Budget Lodge Motel,** 1301 N. Mesa, at California, is six blocks from the University of Texas at El Paso (UTEP) and a short walk from the bus and train stations. (☎533-6821. A/C, cable TV. Singles $30; doubles $35.) Camping can be found at **Hueco Tanks State Historical Park** (see below), 32 mi. east of town (sites $10).

El Paso's cheap restaurants cluster around Stanton and Texas. **La Malinche,** 301 Texas, near San Jacinto Square, dishes large portions of Mexican food. *Menudo* (a local specialty) is served Saturday and Sunday. (☎544-8785. Open M-Sa 7:30am-4pm.) **Manolo's Cafe,** 122 S. Mesa, between Overland and San Antonio, serves $2 *menudo* and $1 burritos. (☎532-7661. Open M-Sa 7am-6pm, Su 7:30-4pm.)

◼◪ SIGHTS AND OUTDOORS. Most visitors are either stopping on the long drive through the desert or heading south to Ciudad Juárez. For a whirlwind tour, hop aboard the **Border Jumper Trolleys,** departing from the Visitors Center. Historic **San Jacinto Plaza** swarms with daily activity and affords an opportunity to rest on a shaded bench. For a commanding view of the city, its Mexican counterpart, and the Sierra Madre, head northwest of downtown along Stanton and make a right turn on Rim Road (which becomes Scenic Dr.) to reach **Murchison Park,** at the base of the

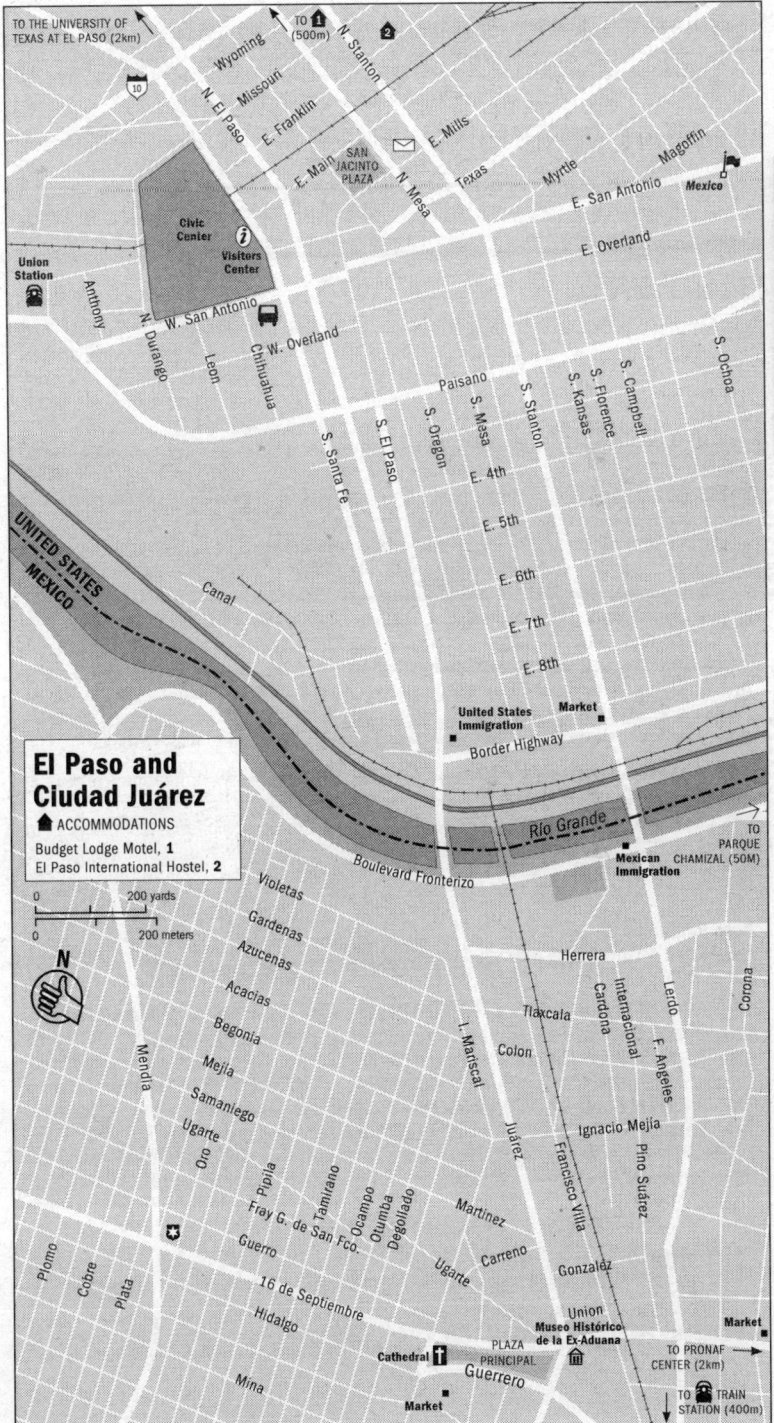

TEXAS

TO THE UNIVERSITY OF
TEXAS AT EL PASO (2km)

TO 1
(500m)

2

Wyoming

Missouri

N. Stanton

N. El Paso

E. Franklin

E. Main

E. Mills

SAN
JACINTO
PLAZA

N. Mesa

Texas

E. San Antonio

Myrtle

Magoffin

Mexico

E. Overland

Union
Station

Civic
Center

Visitors
Center

Anthony

N. Durango

Leon

Chihuahua

W. San Antonio

W. Overland

Paisano

S. Santa Fe

S. El Paso

S. Oregon

S. Mesa

S. Stanton

S. Kansas

S. Florence

S. Campbell

S. Ochoa

E. 4th

E. 5th

Canal

E. 6th

E. 7th

E. 8th

United States
Immigration

Market

Border Highway

UNITED STATES

MEXICO

Río Grande

TO
PARQUE
CHAMIZAL (50M)

Boulevard Fronterizo

Mexican
Immigration

El Paso and
Ciudad Juárez

🏠 ACCOMMODATIONS

Budget Lodge Motel, 1
El Paso International Hostel, 2

0   200 yards
0   200 meters

N

Violetas

Gardenas

Azucenas

Acacias

Begonia

Mejia

Samaniego

Ugarte

Oro

Mendia

Pipila

Tamirano

Fray G. de San Fco.

Ocampo

Otumba

Degollado

Guerro

Plomo

Cobre

Plata

16 de Septiembre

Hidalgo

Mina

I. Mariscal

Colon

Juárez

Martinez

Ugarte

Carreno

Herrera

Tlaxcala

Cardona

Internacional

Ignacio Mejia

Francisco Villa

Gonzalez

Lerdo

F. Angeles

Pino Suárez

Corona

Market

Union
Museo Histórico
de la Ex-Aduana

TO PRONAF
CENTER (2km)

PLAZA
PRINCIPAL

Cathedral

Guerrero

Market

TO TRAIN
STATION (400m)

ridge. **Hueco Tanks State Historical Park,** 32 mi. east of town off U.S. 62, has the best rock climbing and bouldering in Texas. Call ahead because only 70 people are allowed in the park at one time. (☎849-6684. Open Oct.-Apr. 8am-6pm; May-Sept. M-Th 8am-6pm, F-Su 7am-7pm. Park admission $4, children free.)

◪ **NIGHTLIFE.** Most nightlife seekers make a run for the border to Ciudad Juárez. If you decide to stick to the US side, **The Tap,** 408 E. San Antonio, remains El Paso's nightlife staple, serving authentic Mexican food (burritos $1.75-4) and drinks under its neon lights. (Open M-Sa 7am-2am, Sa noon-2am.) **OP,** 301 S. Ochoa, is El Paso's premier gay club. (☎533-6055. Open Th and Su 9pm-2am, F-Sa 9pm-4am.)

BIG BEND   ☎915

Roadrunners, coyotes, wild pigs, mountain lions, and a few black bears make their home in Big Bend National Park, an 800,000-acre tract (about the size of Rhode Island) cradled by the mighty meander of the Río Grande. Spectacular canyons, vast stretches of the Chihuahua Desert, and the airy Chisos Mountains occupy this literally and figuratively "far-out" spot. The high season for visitation is in the early spring—during the summer, the predominantly desert park is excruciatingly hot.

◧ **TRANSPORTATION.** There is no transportation service into or around the park. **Amtrak** offers trains from El Paso to Alpine (4½hr.; $39-48), 103 mi. north of the park. From there, rent a car from **Aerflite Auto Rental,** 414 E. Holland Ave., next to the Sonic. (☎837-3463 or 800-894-3463. From $36 per day, 10¢ per mi. Must be 21+. Deposit required. Call for reservations.) Three roads lead south from U.S. 90 to the park: from Marfa, U.S. 67 to Rte. 170; from Alpine, Rte. 118; from Marathon, U.S. 385. The fastest route to the park headquarters is via U.S. 385. There are two **gas stations** within the park, one at **Panther Junction** (☎477-2294; open Sept.-Mar. daily 7am-7pm, Apr.-Aug. 8am-6pm; 24 hr. credit card service), next to the park headquarters, and at **Río Grande Village** (☎477-2293; open daily Mar.-May 9am-8pm, June-Feb. 9am-6pm). The **Study Butte Store** also sells gas. (Open 24 hr. Credit cards only.)

◪◪ **ORIENTATION AND PRACTICAL INFORMATION. Park headquarters** is at **Panther Junction,** 26 mi. inside the park. (☎477-2251. Open daily 8am-6pm; vehicle pass $10 per week, pedestrians and bikers $5. National park passes accepted.) For info, write the Superintendent, Big Bend National Park, Box 129, 79834. **Ranger stations** are located at Río Grande Village, Persimmon Gap, Castolon, and Chisos Basin (Persimmon open daily 8am-5pm; Chisos open daily 9am-4:30pm; others closed June-Oct.). The Río Grande Village Store has **public showers** (75¢). **Emergency:** ☎477-2251 until 5pm; afterwards, call 911. **Post Office:** In Panther Junction, next to park headquarters (open M-F 8am-4pm). **ZIP code:** 79834. **Area code:** 915.

◪◪ **ACCOMMODATIONS AND FOOD.** The expensive **Chisos Mountains Lodge,** in the Chisos Basin, 10 mi. from park headquarters, offers the only motel-style shelter in the park. Reservations are a must for high season. In the lodge is the only restaurant in the park, serving three square meals a day. (☎477-2291. Restaurant open daily 7am-8pm. Singles $78, doubles $84, $10 per each additional person.) Just west of the park lie Terlingua, Lajitas, and Study Butte, three dusty hamlets with a few restaurants and motels. The closest budget motel to the park, the **Chisos Mining Co. Motel,** on Rte. 170, ¾ mi. west of Rte. 118, provides clean rooms with A/C. (☎371-2254. Singles $37, doubles $47, 5-6 person cabins with kitchenettes $60.) For a more rustic experience stay at the **Terlingua Ranch Resort,** 17 mi. north on Rte. 118 from Rte. 170 and then 16 mi. east. (☎371-2416. Singles and doubles $38.)

The developed campsites in the park are run on a first come, first served basis. During holidays and spring the campgrounds fill early; call park headquarters for availability. The **Chisos Basin Campground** (water and flush toilets; $8) stays cooler than other campgrounds in the summer. The **Río Grande Village Campground** (flush toilets and water; $8) is near the only showers in the park. Most areas of the park are open to **backcountry camping;** get a free permit from one of the Visitors Centers.

Restaurants are scarce in the Big Bend area, though there are some options near Terlingua and Lajitas. **Ms. Tracy's Cafe,** on Rte. 118 just south of Rte. 170, with a patio and decorative cacti, serves eggs, burritos, and a number of vegetarian entrees. (☎371-2181. Open Oct.-May 7am-9:30pm, June 7am-2pm, July-Sept. 7am-5pm.) **The Hungry Javelina,** on Rte. 170 about ¾ mi. from Rte. 118, is a pink, yellow, and green pastel trailer with picnic tables and an amazing view of the Chisos Mountains. (☎371-2181. Open June-Sept. M-F 8am-3pm, Oct.-May daily 8am-3pm.)

▲ OUTDOOR ACTIVITIES. Big Bend encompasses several hundred miles of hiking trails, ranging from 30min. nature walks to backpacking trips several days long. *When hiking in the desert, always carry at least a gallon of water per person per day.* The 43 mi. **scenic drive** to Santa Eleña Canyon is handy for those short on time. Many of the park's roads can **flood** during the "rainy" late summer months.

Park rangers at the Visitors Centers are happy to suggest hikes and sights. Pick up the *Hiker's Guide to Big Bend* pamphlet ($2), available at Panther Junction. The **Lost Mine Trail** (3hr., 4.8 mi.) leads to an amazing view of the desert and the Sierra de Carmen in Mexico. Also in the Chisos, the **Emory Peak** (6hr., 9 mi.) requires an intense hike. An easier walk (1½hr., 1.7 mi.) ambles through the **Santa Eleña Canyon** along the Río Grande. Canyon walls rise as high as 1000 ft. over the riverbank.

Though upstream damming has markedly decreased the river's flow, rafting is still big fun on the Río Grande. Free permits and info are available at the Visitors Center. Several companies offer **river trips** down the 118 mi. of designated Río Grande Wild and Scenic River within park boundaries. **Far-Flung Adventures,** next door to the Starlight Theater Bar and Grill in Terlingua, organizes one- to seven-day trips. (☎371-2489 or 800-359-4138. 1-day trip to Santa Eleña around $125 per person if water flows permit; 1-day trip to Colorado Canyon $110.). Rent your own equipment at **Big Bend River Tours,** with shuttle services for pickup downriver also available. (☎424-3219 or 800-545-4240. Canoes $45 per day; kayaks $35 per day.)

ROCKY MOUNTAINS

Created by immense tectonic forces some 65 million years ago, the Rockies mark a vast wrinkle in the North American continent. Sculpted by wind, water, and glaciers over eons, their weathered peaks extend 3000 miles from northern Alberta to New Mexico and soar to altitudes exceeding two vertical miles. Cars overheat and humans gulp thin alpine air as they ascend into grizzly bear country. Dominated by rock and ice, the highest peaks of the Rockies are accessible only to veteran mountain climbers and wildlife adapted for survival in scant air and deep snow.

Although the whole of the Rocky Mountain area supports less than 5% of the US population, every year millions flock to its spectacular national parks, forests, and ski resorts, while hikers follow the Continental Divide along the spine of the Rockies. Nestled in valleys or appearing out of nowhere on the surrounding plains, the region's mountain villages and cowboy towns welcome travelers year-round.

HIGHLIGHTS OF THE ROCKY MOUNTAINS

HIKING. Memorable trails include the Gunnison Rte. in the Black Canyon, CO (p. 696); the hike to Monument Canyon at the Colorado National Monument (p. 693); and just about anything in the Grand Tetons (p. 660).

SKIING. The Rockies are filled with hot spots, but try Sawtooth, ID (p. 633); Vail, CO (p. 688); or Jackson Hole, WY (p. 663).

SCENIC DRIVES. Going-to-the-Sun Rd. in Glacier National Park (p. 644) is unforgettable, as is phenomenally high San Juan Skyway in Colorado (p. 700). The Chief Joseph Scenic Hwy. (p. 660) explores the rugged Wyoming wilderness.

ALPINE TOWNS. Aspen, CO (p. 690), and Stanley, ID (p. 633): two of the loveliest.

IDAHO

Idaho is a land of tremendous geographic diversity. The Rocky Mountains divide the state into three distinct regions, each with its own natural aesthetic. Northern Idaho possesses the greatest concentration of lakes in the western US, interspersed by lush green valleys and rugged mountain peaks. In Central Idaho, plentiful ski slopes, hiking trails, and hot springs span against the semi-arid landscape. To the southeast, world-famous potatoes are cultivated in valleys rich with volcanic sediment. With miles of untouched National Forest and wilderness ripe for adventure, little has changed since Lewis and Clark first laid eyes on the state in 1805.

⚐ PRACTICAL INFORMATION

Capital: Boise.

Visitor info: Idaho Information Line, ☎800-837-4843; www.visitid.org. **State Parks and Recreation Dept.**, 5657 Warm Springs Ave., Boise 83712 (☎334-4199). **Skier Info,** ☎800-243-2754. **Idaho Outfitters and Guide Association,** 711 N. 5th St.; P.O. Box 95, Boise 83702 (☎342-1438; www.ioga.org; open in summer M-F 8:30am-4pm).

Hotlines: Mental Health Emergency, ☎334-0808 or 800-600-6474. **Women's Crisis Line,** ☎343-7025. **Rape Crisis Line,** ☎345-7273. **Gay Community Center,** ☎336-3870.

Postal Abbreviation: ID. **Sales Tax:** 5%. **Area code:** 208.

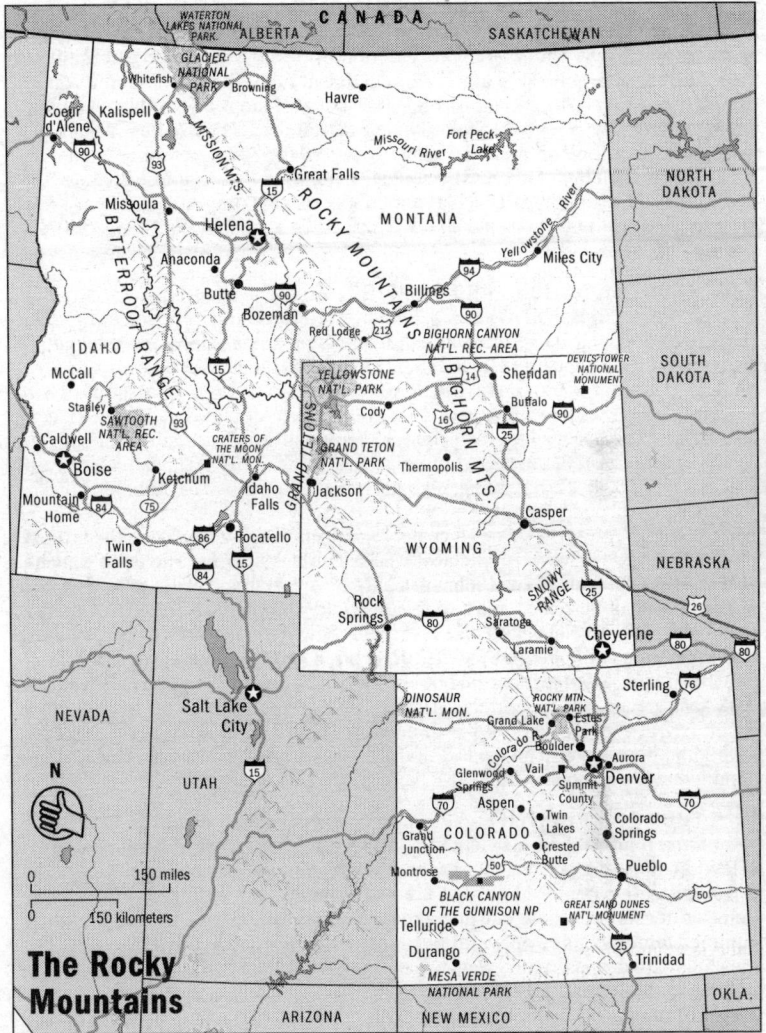

The Rocky
Mountains

BOISE ☎208

Built along the banks of the Boise River, Idaho's surprisingly cosmopolitan capital straddles the boundary between desert and mountains. A network of parks protects the natural landscape of the river banks, creating a greenbelt perfect for walking, biking, or skating. Most of the city's sights cluster in the ten-block area between the Capitol and the River, making Boise supremely navigable. A revitalized downtown offers a vast array of ethnic cuisine as well as a pulsing nightlife.

◪ **PRACTICAL INFORMATION.** The pedestrian-friendly Grove is a brick walkway between Main and Front St. **Greyhound,** 1212 W. Bannock (☎343-3681), a few blocks west of downtown, runs to Salt Lake City (7hr., 3-4 per day, $44-47); Portland (11hr., 3 per day, $38-43); and Seattle (14hr., 3 per day, $38-41). **Boise Urban Stages** run several routes throughout the city. (☎336-1010. Maps available at Visitors Center. Buses operate M-F 5:15am-7:40pm, Sa 7:45am-6:10pm. Fare 75¢, seniors 35¢, ages 6-18 50¢; all fares 35¢ on Sa.) **McU's Sports,** 822 W. Jefferson St. (☎342-7734), rents a good selection of outdoor gear and offers hiking tips. The **ski shop** is located at 2314 Bogus Basin Rd. (☎336-2300. In-line skates $5 for 1hr., $15 for 8hr. Mountain bikes $15 per half-day, $25 per day. Ski equipment $16 per day, kids $13. Night skiing $13, children $11.) **Visitors Center:** 850 W. Front St., at Boise Centre on the Grove. (☎344-5338. Open M-F 10am-4pm, Sa 10am-2pm.) **Internet access: Boise Public Library,** 715 S. Capitol Blvd. (☎384-4114; open M 10am-6pm, Tu-Th 10am-9pm, F 10am-6pm, Sa 10am-5pm). **Post Office:** 770 S. 13th St. (☎433-4308; open M-F 7:30am-5:30pm, Sa 10am-2pm). **ZIP code:** 83702. **Area code:** 208.

⌂⌂ ACCOMMODATIONS AND CAMPING. A recent addition to the town of Nampa, **Hostel Boise (HI-AYH),** 17322 Can-Ada Rd., is located 15-20min. from downtown Boise. This country-style home has mountain views, evening campfires, and Internet access ($1 per 15min.). To get to the hostel, take Exit 38 off I-84 W and turn right onto Garrity Blvd., which turns into Can-Ada Rd. (☎467-6858. Dorm-style beds $12-15.) Inexpensive motels bunch around Exit 53 of I-84, near the airport. The **Cabana Inn,** 1600 Main St., in downtown Boise, offers newly renovated rooms in a Spanish-style villa, featuring TV, A/C, fridges, and microwaves. (☎343-6000. Reservations recommended. Singles $42-52; doubles $45-52.) **University Inn,** 2360 University Dr., next to Boise State University, has free local calls, cable TV, and HBO, as well as pool and jacuzzi and a shuttle to the airport. (☎345-7170 or 800-345-7170. Singles $48.50; doubles $54.50.) The **Boise National Forest Office/Bureau of Land Management,** 1387 S. Vinnell Way, provides info about Boise campgrounds, most of which are RV-oriented. (☎373-4007. Open M-F 7:45am-4:30pm.) **Fiesta RV Park,** 11101 Fairview Ave., features a pool, running water, and a pay phone. (☎375-8207. Reception Oct.-May daily 8am-6pm; June-Sept. 8am-8pm. Sites $21; partial hookup $23, full hookup $24.) The **Americana RV Park Kampground,** 3600 Americana Terrace Blvd., has sites overlooking the Boise River. (☎344-5733. Showers $3. Full hookup $22 per night, $125 per week; each additional person $2.) The closest non-RV campground is at **Bogus Basin,** about 45min. outside of Boise. (Open M-F 9am-5pm.)

▢▣ FOOD AND NIGHTLIFE. You may be surprised to discover that Boise offers much more than just baked potatoes and french fries. Besides its fine selection of potato wedges, there are also 80 restaurants of varying cuisines. The downtown area, centered around **8th and Main St.,** is bustling with lunchtime delis, coffeeshops, ethnic cuisine, and several stylish bistros. During the warm summer months, sidewalks and outdoor patios are packed with people. For amazingly fresh and creative vegetarian food, try **Kulture Klatsch,** 409 S. 8th. This hip and multi-kultural eatery has an extensive veggie menu, including numerous vegan options, and hosts live music with no cover five nights a week. (☎345-0452. Open M 7am-3pm, Tu-Th 7am-10pm, F 7am-11pm, Sa 8am-11pm, Su 8am-3pm. Breakfasts $3-8, lunch specials $5, dinners $7-9.) **Moon's Kitchen,** 815 W. Bannock St., is a vintage 50s diner that has been serving classic American food and famous malts since 1955. (☎385-0472. Open M-Sa 8am-3pm, Su 9am-1pm. Breakfast $4.50-7, shakes $4.) Those wishing to stay in this century should try the casual yet trendy **Bittercreek Alehouse,** 246 N. 8th St., in the middle of downtown Boise. The burgers and pita sandwiches ($6-9) are a perennial favorite among regulars. (☎345-1813. 21+ after 10pm. Open daily 11am-late.)

Musicians perform on Main St. from 5-9pm, while vendors from nearby restaurants hawk food and beer. Cheap beer and live music draw the locals to **Blues Bouquet,** 1010 Main St., downtown Boise's only western saloon. (☎345-6605. 21+. Open M-F 1pm-2am, Sa-Su 8pm-2am.) Live music can also be found Monday nights at **The Balcony,** 150 N. 8th St., #226, one block from the Grove Center. People from all around gather at this gay-friendly bar to dance and play pool. (☎336-1313. Happy hour daily 2-7pm. 21+. Open 2pm-2am.)

BOISE'S BASQUE BACKGROUND In 1848, the California Gold Rush brought a flood of immigrants to the US. Among them were the Basques, who moved from a small corner of Spain to the goldfields of the Sierras. Unable to find jobs, the American Basques spread through the Western rangelands and mountains to become shepherds. Today, southern Idaho is home to the largest concentration of Basque population outside of Europe. Basque culture is preserved at the **Basque Museum and Cultural Center** at the corner of Grove St. and Capital Blvd. in downtown Boise. This fascinating museum includes a gallery featuring Basque art and a replica of a Basque herder's house. *(☎343-2671. Open Tu-F 10am-4pm, Sa 11am-3pm. Free; donations appreciated.)*

◉ **WHO IS JULIA DAVIS?** The logical starting point for exploring Boise is the beautiful **Julia Davis Park.** Free parking is available along Capitol Blvd. near the museums. The **Boise Tour Train** covers around 75 city sights in 1¼hr. Tours begin and end in the parking lot at Julia Davis Park. (☎342-4796. Tours June to early Sept. M-Sa 5 per day 10am-3pm, Su 4 per day noon-3:45pm; in fall, W-F 2 per day at noon and 1:30pm, Sa 4 per day 10:30am-3pm, Su 3 per day noon-3pm. $7, seniors $6, ages 4-12 $4.50.) To learn about Idaho and the Old West at your own pace, stroll through the **Historical Museum,** 610 Julia Davis Dr., which showcases a replica 19th-century bar complete with a display of a two-headed calf. Other notable exhibits include Native American artifacts and a timeline of Ernest Hemingway's life. (☎334-2120. Open M-Sa 9am-5pm, Su and holidays 1-5pm. Free; donations encouraged.) The **Boise Art Museum,** 670 Julia Davis Dr., displays an impressive selection of contemporary international and local works while offering educational programs, lectures, and tours. (☎345-8330. Open year-round Tu-F 10am-5pm, Sa-Su noon-5pm; June-Aug. M 10am-5pm. $4, seniors and students $2, ages 6-18 $1; free the 1st Th of every month.) Raptors perch and dive at the **World Center for Birds of Prey,** 566 W. Flying Hawk Ln. From I-84, take the Exit 50 and go south on S. Cole; turn right onto W. Flying Hawk Ln. (☎362-3716. Open daily 9am-5pm; Nov.-Feb. 10am-4pm. $4, seniors $3, children $2, under 4 free.) To enjoy the city's outdoor opportunities, try the 22 mi. **Boise River Greenbelt.** In the summer, visitors can go tubing in the river at Berber Park. The ever-growing **Boise Shakespeare Festival** (☎336-9221) hits town from June to September. Every year in late June, Boise hosts a **River Festival** (☎338-8887; June 27-30, 2002), featuring hot-air balloons, a carnival, live music, fireworks, and sporting events. Upcoming events are showcased in Thursday's *The Boise Weekly*.

KETCHUM AND SUN VALLEY ☎208

In 1935, Union Pacific heir Averill Harriman sent Austrian Count Felix Schaffgotsch to scour the western US for a site to develop a ski resort that would rival Europe's best. The Count finally settled on the small mining and sheep-herding town of Ketchum in Idaho's Wood River Valley. Sun Valley was quickly recognized as a world-class ski resort, fulfilling Harriman's dream. While Ketchum's permanent population is only 5300, traffic extends for miles in each direction during peak months. Ketchum has matured into a bustling western town, filled with pricey eateries and saloons. However, the real attraction remains in the hills outside of town.

🛈 **PRACTICAL INFORMATION.** The best time to visit is during the rare "slack" period (late Oct. to late Nov. and May to early June). **Sun Valley Express** runs one bus daily to the Boise airport. (☎877-622-8267. Leaves Ketchum 8:30am, return bus from the Boise airport leaves at 2:45pm. Summer $57-62; winter $59-64. Reservations recommended.) **KART,** Ketchum's **bus service,** tours the city and its surrounding areas. (☎726-7576. Runs daily 7:20am-midnight. Maps available at Chamber of Commerce. No fare.) **Sawtooth National Recreation Area (SNRA) Headquarters,** 6 mi. north of Ketchum off Rte. 75, stocks detailed info on the recreation area, hot springs, and area forests and trails, including National Recreation Area maps for $6-7 and local hiker Margaret Fuller's excellent trail guides for $14-18. (☎ 727-5013, 727-5000, or 800-280-2267. Open daily 8:30am-5pm.) **Chamber of Commerce/Visitors Center:** 4th and Main St. in Ketchum. (☎ 726-3423 or 800-634-3347; www.visitsunvalley.com. Open in peak season daily 9am-6pm, hours vary during spring and fall.) **Internet: Newslink Cafe,** 360 E. Sun Valley Rd. (☎726-8388. $3 per 15min., $4 per 30min., $5 per hr. Open M-F 7:30am-6pm, Sa 9am-6pm.) **Post Office:** 151 W. 4th St. (☎ 726-5161; open M-F 8am-5:30pm, Sa 11am-2pm). **ZIP code:** 83340. **Area code:** 208.

⚐ ACCOMMODATIONS. From early June to mid-October, camping is the best option for cheap sleep in the Sun Valley area. Check with the **Ketchum Ranger Station,** on Sun Valley Rd., just outside of Ketchum on the way to Sun Valley. (☎622-5371. Open M-F 8:30am-5pm, Sa-Su 8am-5:30pm.) **Boundary Campground,** 3 mi. northeast of town on Trail Creek Rd. past the Sun Valley resort, is closest to town and has nine wooded sites near a creek. (Restrooms, water, picnic area. Sites $11.) There are also free primitive "dispersed" campsites further along Trail Creek. Up Rte. 75 into the SNRA lie several scenic camping spots; the cheapest ($10) are **Murdock** (11 sites) and **Caribou** (7 sites). They are, respectively, 2 and 3 mi. up the unpaved North Fork Rd., which begins as a paved road to the right of the Visitors Center. The $11 **North Fork** (29 sites) and **Wood River** (30 sites) are 8 mi. north of Ketchum, along Rte. 75. For North Fork, take the first campground road north of SNRA headquarters; Wood River is 2 mi. north. The **High Country Motel and Cabins,** 765 S. Main in Bellevue, with spacious, wood-paneled rooms and cable TV, is the best deal around. (☎788-2050 or 800-692-2050. Rooms $55-80.)

◨▨ FOOD AND NIGHTLIFE. Ketchum's small confines bulge with over 80 restaurants, catering to the gourmet tastes of resort visitors. Ketchum's cheapest eats can be found at **The Hot Dog Adventure Company,** 210 N. Main St. A vast array of hot dogs ($2-4), including veggie dogs, corn dogs, bratwurst, and Polish sausage, are served with fries and shakes. (☎726-0117. Open M-Sa noon-6pm and 10:30pm-2:30am.) The soups and chowders ($4-6) at the **Burger Grill,** corner of 4th and Main, are filling and inexpensive. (Open M-Sa 11am-8pm. Burgers $5-7.) Chase back some stiff drinks for only $1 on Sunday and Tuesday at Hemingway's old haunt, **Whiskey Jacques,** 251 Main St. (☎726-5297, take-out 726-3200. Live music 9:30pm-2am most nights. Cover $3. Open daily 4pm-2am.) The **Pioneer Saloon,** on Main St., always packs a heavily local crowd. (☎726-3139. Bar opens 4pm.)

⚡ OUTDOOR ACTIVITIES. The **Wood River and Sun Valley trail system** consists of over 20 mi. of paved trails follow Rte. 75 south of town. The trail begins in Bellevue and continues through Ketchum and Sun Valley, passing by ski slopes and historic sites. The *Wood River Trails* pamphlet, available at the Visitors Center, has more info. Visible for miles around, **Bald Mountain,** or "Baldy," is a beacon for serious skiers. Two plazas serve Baldy River Run on the north side of town and Warm Springs on the south side. The gentle slopes of **Dollar Mountain** are perfect for beginners. (☎800-786-8259, ski conditions 800-635-4150. Full-day lift ticket $59, under 12 $32.)

The Sawtooth area is nationally renowned for its stunning mountain bike trails, which traverse the gorgeous canyons and mountain passes of the SNRA. Beware: trails might be snowbound or flooded well into July. Take a high-speed quad to the top of Bald Mountain and ride down on a mountain bike during summer months. (☎622-2231. Open in summer daily 9am-3:45pm. $15 per ride, $20 per day.) Inquire about trail conditions at **Formula Sports,** 460 N. Main St. (☎726-3194. Bikes from $12 per 4hr., $18 per day; tandems $20/$30.) **The Elephant's Perch,** 280 East Ave., at East Ave. and Sun Valley Rd., has a complete stock of outdoor gear. (☎726-3497. Open daily 9am-6pm. Bikes $12 per 4hr., $20 per day. Backpack $15 per day, sleeping bag $25 per day, tents $20 per day, ski packages $12-30 per day.) Inquire about biking trails at the Chamber of Commerce or the SNRA Headquarters.

After a hard day of biking or hiking, Ketchum locals soak their weary legs in one of several hot springs. Hidden in the hills and canyons of Ketchum, the hot springs are no longer a well-kept secret. Melting snow and rain can bury the springs under-

THE SUN VALLEY ALSO RISES Ernest Hemingway's love affair with both rugged outdoor sports and wealthy celebrities fits Ketchum's dualistic spirit. After spending many of his vacations hunting and fishing in the Sawtooth Range, the author built a cabin in Sun Valley where he died from a self-inflicted gunshot wound on July 2, 1961. While Hemingway's house is off-limits, there are a number of sites in town that commemorate the author. His grave is located in the Ketchum Cemetery, just north of town on Rte. 75. The **Ketchum-Sun Valley Heritage and Ski Museum,** at the corner of 1st St. and Washington Ave., displays exhibits on Hemingway's life. (☎726-8118. Open daily 1-4pm.) A bust of Hemingway is tucked away in a shady spot along the river at the **Hemingway Memorial,** about 1 mi. outside of Sun Valley on the way to Boundary Campground (see above). Each year on Hemingway's birthday, July 21, the community library hosts a lecture. (☎726-3493.)

water, rendering them inaccessible in spring and early summer. The springs are safe for swimming once the current subsides in July. The Chamber of Commerce has suggestions on which pools are safe and accessible. Two of the more accessible, non-commercial springs are **Warfield Hot Springs,** on Warm Springs Rd., 11 mi. west of Ketchum, and **Russian John Hot Springs,** 8 mi. north of the SNRA headquarters on Rte. 75, just west of the highway. An alternative to these pools can be found at **Easley Hot Springs,** 12 mi. north of Ketchum on Rte. 75. (☎726-7522. Open Tu and Th-Sa 11am-7pm, W 11am-4pm, Su 11am-5pm. $4, seniors $2.50, children $3.) For the best info on **fishing,** including equipment rentals, stop by **Silver Creek Outfitters,** 500 N. Main St. (☎726-5282. Open M-Sa 9am-6pm, Su 9am-5pm; longer hours in peak season. Fly rods, waders, and boots $15 per day.)

SAWTOOTH   ☎208

Established by Congress in 1972, the Sawtooth National Recreation Area (SNRA) sprawls over 756,000 acres of National Forest, including 217,000 acres of untouched wilderness. The park is home to four mountain ranges, with more than 40 peaks topping 10,000 feet. The Sawtooth and White Cloud Mountains tower above the surrounding landscape in the north, while the Smokey and Boulder Mountains dominate the southern horizon. Over 300 mountain lakes, and the headwaters of four of Idaho's major rivers, are interspersed throughout the park's dense forest. The Sawtooth Scenic Byway (Rte. 75) spans 60 miles of National Forest land between Ketchum and Stanley, crossing the Galena Pass at 8701 feet. Pause at the Galena Overlook, 31 miles north of Ketchum, for a spectacular view of the park.

◪ PRACTICAL INFORMATION. The tiny (pop. 69), frontier-style town of **Stanley,** located 60 mi. north of Ketchum at the intersection of Rte. 21 and 75, serves as a northern base for exploring Sawtooth. The small business district is located one block south of Rte. 21, along Ace of Diamonds St. The **Stanley Ranger Station** offers maps, SNRA passes, and sage outdoor advice. The station is located 3 mi. south of Stanley on Rte. 75. (☎774-3000. Open M-Sa 8am-4:30pm; off-season M-F 8am-5pm.) At the entrance to Redfish Lake (5 mi. south of Stanley and 55 mi. north of Ketchum on Rte. 75), the **info booth** dispenses a wide range of info about hiking, camping, and outdoor sports. (☎774-3536. Sporadic hours; the booth is usually staffed during sunny, busy weekends.) The **Redfish Lake Visitors Center** can provide additional information about the park, including educational programs about wildlife and geology. (☎774-3376. Open late May to mid-June Sa-Su 9am-5pm; mid-June to early Sept. daily 9am-5pm.) Stanley's **post office:** Ace of Diamonds St. (☎774-2230. Open M-F 8-11am and noon-5pm.) **Chamber of Commerce:** Rte. 21, P.O. Box 8 (☎774-3411 or 800-878-7950). **ZIP code:** 83278. **Area code:** 208.

⌂ ACCOMMODATIONS. The SNRA boasts 33 campgrounds scattered throughout the park; consult a ranger for help in selecting (and locating) a campsite. **Alturas Lake,** 21 mi. south of Stanley on Rte. 75 (the turn-off is marked about 10 mi. north of

Galena Pass) has three campgrounds with fishing and swimming. (Vault toilets and water. 55 sites $11-13.) The area around **Redfish Lake,** 5 mi. south of Stanley off Rte. 75, is a scenic but sometimes overcrowded spot. The eight campgrounds in the area are conveniently close to Stanley and many trailheads. (Sites $11-13.)

East on Rte. 75, past the town of Stanley, numerous sites are available alongside the wild and scenic **Salmon River.** (Water available; no hookup. First come, first served sites $11, $5.50 with Golden Age and Golden Access, free with Golden Eagle.) One of the best campgrounds is **Mormon Bend,** 5 mi. east of Stanley on Rte. 75, with 15 sites close to whitewater rafting opportunities. Other scenic and inviting spots are **Casino Creek,** 8 mi. east of Stanley on Rte. 75, the **Salmon River Campground,** 9 mi. east of Stanley on Rte. 75, and **Upper and Lower O'Brien,** 2 mi. past Sunbeam Dam. In most areas, a trailhead pass is required for parking. Pick them up at the Stanley Ranger Station (see **Practical Information,** above).

For a real bed, Stanley provides more scenic and more reasonable lodging than Ketchum. At **Danner's Log Cabin Motel,** on Rte. 21, ex-mayor and Stanley history buff Bunny Danner rents historic cabins built by goldminers in 1939. The office, built in 1906, was the first building in town and originally served as the ranger station. (☎774-3539. Cabins $55-85; spring and fall $36-80.) The brand new **Sawtooth Adventure Hostel,** on Rte. 75 in Lower Stanley, is the best deal around. (☎866-774-4644. Linens $3. $15 per night, $80 per week.) The intrepid staff also operates **Sawtooth Adventure Rentals** next door, renting kayaks ($25) and rafts ($85 for 6 people).

🍴🛏 **FOOD AND NIGHTLIFE.** Dining options are rather limited in Stanley. Stock up on food and gas at **Jerry's Country Store and Motel,** on Rte. 75 in Lower Stanley, before exploring the SNRA. Fishing licenses and supplies are available. (☎774-3566 or 800-972-4627. Open M-Sa 8:30am-9pm, Su 9am-7pm.) Locals rave about the $5 deli sandwiches at **Papa Brunee's,** Ace of Diamonds St., downtown. Papa also serves various sizes of pizza for $4-11. (☎774-2536. Open daily 11am-10pm.) The local watering hole is the **Rod and Gun Club Bar,** at the end of Ace of Diamonds St. This authentic western bar has pool tables, Internet access ($5 per 30min.), a big dance floor, and live music on weekends. (☎774-9920. 21+. Open daily 4pm-2am.)

🏔 **OUTDOOR ACTIVITIES.** The rugged backcountry of the SNRA is perfect for hiking, boating, fishing, and mountain biking. Pick up a free map of the area and inquire about trail conditions at SNRA headquarters before heading into the park, particularly in early summer, when trails may be flooded. Much of the backcountry stays buried in snow well into the summer. Watch out for black bears; ranger stations have information about necessary precautions.

Redfish Lake is the source of many trails; some popular, leisurely hikes include those to **Fishhook Creek** (excellent for children), **Bench Lakes,** and the **Hell Roaring trail.** The long, gentle loop around **Yellow Belly, Toxaway,** and **Petit Lakes** is a moderate overnight suitable for novices. Two miles northwest of Stanley on Rte. 21, the 3 mi. Iron Creek Rd. leads to the trailhead of the 5.5 mi. **Sawtooth Lake Hike.** Bionic hikers can try the steep, 4 mi. hike to **Casino Lakes,** which begins at the Broadway Creek trailhead southeast of Stanley.

The Sawtooths have miles of mountain biking, but check a map first; riding is allowed in National Forest areas but prohibited in the Sawtooth Wilderness. **Riverwear,** on Rte. 21 in Stanley, rents bikes from $17 per day. (☎774-3592. Open daily 7am-10pm.) The 18 mi. **Fischer/Williams Creek Loop** is the most popular biking trail, ascending to an elevation of 8280 ft. Beginners will enjoy riding the dirt road that accesses the North Fork campgrounds from the Visitors Center. This gorgeous passage parallels the North Fork of the Wood River for 5 mi. before branching off into other narrower and steeper trails, suitable for more advanced riders. These trails can be combined into loops; consult the trail map or the ranger station. The steep **Boulder Creek Rd.,** 5 mi. from SNRA headquarters, leads to pristine Boulder Lake and an old mining camp.

Topographical maps ($4) and various trail books ($3-20), including Margaret Fuller's invaluable books ($14-18), are available at **McCoy's Tackle and Gift Shop,** on Ace of Diamonds St. McCoy's also sells sporting goods, fishing tackle, and licenses.

(☎774-3377. Open June-Sept. daily, hours vary.) **Sawtooth Rentals,** just north of the Rte. 21/75 junction, specializes in water vehicle rentals. (☎774-3409 or 800-243-3185. Kayaks $30 per day, doubles $40; rafts $15 per person per day; mountain bikes $25 per day.) For boat tours of the lake, head for **Redfish Lake Lodge Marina.** (☎774-3536. Open in summer daily 7am-8:30pm. 1½hr. tours $8, ages 6-12 $5; $32 minimum; hours vary. Paddleboats $5 per 30min. Canoes $7.50 per hr., $25 per half-day, $40 per day. Outboards $12.50 per hr., $42 for half-day, $80 per day.)

The most inexpensive way to enjoy the SNRA waters is to visit the **hot springs** just east of Stanley. **Sunbeam Hot Springs,** 10 mi. east of Lower Stanley on Rte. 75, triumphs over the rest. Be sure to bring a bucket or cooler to the stone bathhouse; you'll need to add about 20 gallons of cold Salmon River water before you can get into these hot pools (120-130°F). High water can wash out the hot springs temporarily. Check with locals for info about other hot springs.

CRATERS OF THE MOON ☎208

The unearthly landscape at Craters of the Moon National Monument first drew national attention in the early 1920s. An early visitor to the landscape claimed it was "the strangest 75 square miles on the North American continent." The park's twisted lava formations were formed by the same geological hot spot responsible for the thermal activity in Yellowstone National Park. Located 70 mi. southeast of Sun Valley at the junction of Rte. 20 and 26/93, the park's unusual craters and rock formations make for an interesting visit. ($4 per car, $2 per individual.)

There are 52 sites scattered throughout the monument's single campground, located just past the entrance station. (Water but no hookup; $10.) Wood fires are prohibited, but charcoal fires are permitted. Camping at unmarked sites in the dry lava wilderness of the park is permitted with a free backcountry permit, available at the **Visitors Center** (☎527-3257; open in summer daily 8am-6pm; off-season 8am-4:30pm). **Echo Crater,** a short four-mile hike from the Tree Molds parking lot, is one of the most popular backcountry campsites.

The Visitors Center has videos, displays, and printed guides that outline the area's geological past. A seven-mile drive winds through much of the monument, guiding tourists to the major sights. Several short trails lead to more unusual rock formations and a variety of caves; the Visitors Center has guides. Don't forget sturdy shoes, water, sunscreen, and hats; the rocks are black and there are no trees for miles. For more information, write the **Superintendent,** Craters of the Moon National Monument, Box 29, Arco, ID 83213.

The town of **Arco,** 18 mi. east of the Craters of the Moon on Rte. 20, claims to be the "first city in the world lighted by atomic energy." Arco is also the closest source of services and lodgings for travelers visiting the monument. Cheap rooms with telephones and cable TV are available at the **D-K Motel,** 316 S. Front St. (☎527-8282 or 800-231-0134. Singles $31; doubles $34-41.) The **Arco Deli Sandwich Shop,** on Rte. 20/26/93, at Grand Ave. and Idaho St., serves fresh deli sandwiches (go figure) to a local crowd. (☎527-3757. Open M-Sa 8am-8pm. Foot-long sandwiches $7.) The **Chamber of Commerce,** on Grand Ave., has info on local attractions. If you're traveling from Arco to Sun Valley (see p. 631), you can also pick up a free cassette tour of the Central Idaho Rockies. (☎527-8977. P.O. Box 46, Arco, ID 83213.)

MONTANA

If there is one part of the scenery that dominates the Montana landscape more than the pristine mountain peaks and shimmering glacier lakes, it's the sky. Welcome to Big Sky country. With 25 million acres of national forest and public lands, Montana's population of grizzly bears, mountain lions, and pronghorn antelope outnumber the people. Small towns, set against unadulterated mountain vistas, offer a true taste of the Old West. Copious fishing lakes, 500 species of wildlife (not including millions of insect species), and beautiful rivers combine with mountains, glaciers, hot springs, and thousands of ski trails to make Montana an American paradise.

🛂 PRACTICAL INFORMATION

Capital: Helena.

Visitor info: Travel Montana, P.O. Box 7549, Missoula 59807 (☎406-444-2654 or 800-847-4868; www.visitmt.com). **National Forest Information,** Northern Region, Federal Bldg., 200 E. Broadway, Box 7669, Missoula 59807 (☎406-329-3511).

Gay/Lesbian info: PRIDE!, P.O. Box 775, Helena 59624 (☎406-442-9322; www.gay-montana.com).

Postal Abbreviation: MT. **Sales Tax:** 0%.

BILLINGS   ☎406

Located at the junction of I-90 and I-94 and served by many major airlines, Billings is more of a stopover, or point of entry, than a destination. Billings's lodgings are dispersed throughout the city. The **Cherry Tree Inn,** 823 N. Broadway at 9th Ave., is a terrific bargain, with immaculate and spacious rooms at chopped-down prices. Take Exit 450 off I-90 and head north on 27th St.; turn left onto 9th Ave. (☎252-5603 or 800-237-5882. A/C, phones, cable TV. Singles $42; doubles $48.) Near the Interstate, **Motel 6,** 5400 Midland Rd., offers clean rooms at decent rates. (☎252-0093. A/C, phones, pool, cable TV. Singles $41; doubles $46.)

Downtown, **Jake's,** 2701 1st Ave. N., serves delicious burgers and sandwiches ($6-8), and has a large selection of microbrews on tap. (☎259-9375. Bar open M-Th 11:30am-1am, F 11:30am-2am, Sa 4:30pm-2am. Restaurant open M-F 11:30am-2pm and 5:30-10pm, Sa 5:30-10:30pm.) Also downtown, **Cafe Jones,** 2712 2nd Ave. N., is a coffeehouse/juice bar that also prepares salads ($4-5) and sandwiches for around $5. (☎259-7676. Open M-F 7am-4pm, Sa 8am-noon.) **Khanthaly's Eggrolls,** 1301 Grand Ave., serves tasty Laotian cuisine at Laotian prices. From downtown, head west on 6th Ave. N. and bear right at the fork onto Grand Ave. (☎259-7252. Open M-Sa 11am-9pm. Entrees $2-6, spring rolls $1.50.)

Plunge into a satisfying Black Jack Burger and sample some of Montana's finest beer at the **Montana Brewing Co.,** 113 N. Broadway. The large outdoor patio always draws a crowd during the summer. (☎252-9200. Open daily 11am-2am. Burgers $5-6, sandwiches $5-6, draft beers $3.) Strap on a cowboy hat and boots and hit the dance floor at **Desperados,** 145 Regal St., Billing's premier bar and dance hall. Catch some fresh air on the spacious front deck, complete with bar, pool table, and seating area. (☎248-3404. Open Tu-Sa 8pm-2am; M 6pm-2am deck only.)

The **Billings Logan International Airport,** 1901 Terminal Circle (☎238-3420) is located at the end of N. 27th St. Both **Greyhound** and **Rimrock Trailways** operate from 2502 1st Ave. N. (☎245-5116; open 24hr.); buses run to Bozeman (3hr., 5 per day, $23-25); Missoula (7-9hr., 5 per day, $46-49); and Bismarck (9hr., 4 per day, $56-59). For car rentals, head to **Thrifty,** 2600 6th Ave. N. In summer, rentals start around $48 per day with 150 free mi. and $245-260 per week with 1050 free mi. (☎259-1025 or 800-847-4389. Open daily 5:30am-11:30pm. 25¢ each additional mi. $20 per day surcharge for ages 21-24.) **Billings Metropolitan Transit** runs buses M-F approximately 6:45am-6:30pm, Sa 8:45am-5:45pm. Maps are available at stores, banks, and the library. (☎657-8218. 75¢, seniors 25¢.) **Visitors Center:** 815 S. 27th St. (☎252-4016 or 800-735-2635. Open May 31-Sept. 6 daily 8:30am-6pm; off-season M-F 8:30am-5pm.) **Post Office:** 841 S. 26th St. (☎657-5700; open M-F 8am-5pm, Sa 10am-2pm). **ZIP code:** 59101. **Area code:** 406.

LITTLE BIG HORN

Little Big Horn National Monument, 60 mi. southeast of Billings off I-90 on the Crow Reservation, marks the site of one of the most dramatic episodes in the conflict between Native Americans and the US government. Here, on June 25, 1876, Sioux and Cheyenne warriors, led by Sioux chiefs Sitting Bull and Crazy Horse, retaliated for years of genocide by annihilating five companies of the US Seventh Cavalry under the command of Lt. Colonel George Armstrong Custer. White stone graves mark where the US soldiers fell. The exact Native American casualties are not

ROCKY MOUNTAINS

known, since their families and fellow warriors removed the bodies from the battlefield almost immediately. The renaming of the monument, formerly known as the Custer Battlefield Monument, signifies the government's admission that Custer's brutal acts against Native Americans merit no glorification. Congress also prescribed that a memorial be built in honor of the Native Americans killed at the battle. This memorial, toward which the Cheyenne have been working since 1925, is still being built; the completion date is unknown.

Rangers give great explanatory talks in the summer every hour daily, from 9am-6pm. Visitors can ride through the monument guided by an audio tour that narrates the progression of the battle. ($13. Open daily 8am-8pm.) A one-hour **bus tour** leaves the Visitors Center at 9, 10:30am, noon, 2, and 3:30pm ($10; seniors $8, under 12 $5). The **Visitors Center** has a small movie theater and an electronic map of the battlefield. (☎638-2621, ext. 124. Monument open late May to early Sept. daily 8am-9pm; Visitors Center open 8am-7:30pm. In fall, monument and Visitors Center open 8am-6pm; in winter 8am-4:30pm. Entrance $10 per car, $5 per person.)

HELENA ☎406

As Montana's capital city, Helena has successfully modernized while still retaining the historical feel of the Old West. A product of the 1864 Gold Rush at Last Chance Gulch, Helena has transformed itself from a humble mining camp into a sophisticated city equipped with a symphony, several theaters, and an outdoor walking mall downtown. Since it is situated halfway between Glacier and Yellowstone National Parks, Helena provides a pleasant stopover for travelers tackling the two parks. The city is an outdoors destination in itself, offering numerous hiking, boating, and fishing opportunities.

🔼 **PRACTICAL INFORMATION.** I-15, U.S. 12, and U.S. 287 intersect Helena. **Rimrock Trailways,** at the High Country Travel Plaza Truck stop, 3122 U.S. 12 E. (☎442-5860), buses to Missoula ($20; departs 8:15am, 6:45pm), Bozeman ($17; departs 8:15am, 6:45pm), and Billings ($36; departs 8:15am, 6:45pm), with Greyhound connections in Missoula and Bozeman. **Helena Area Chamber of Commerce,** 225 Cruse Ave., has visitor information. (☎442-4120. Open M-F 8am-5pm.) **Post Office:** 2300 N. Harris (☎443-3304). **ZIP code:** 59601. **Area code:** 406.

🔳 **ACCOMMODATIONS AND FOOD.** Budget accommodations aren't that easy to find in Helena. **Budget Inn Express,** 524 N. Last Chance Gulch, has an attractive downtown location and large, tidy rooms. (☎442-0600 or 800-862-1334. Laundry, cable, kitchenettes. Singles $38; doubles $43.) The **Helena Campground and RV Park,** 5820 N. Montana Ave., north of Helena, just west of I-15, has grassy, shaded tent sites. (☎458-4714. Laundry, showers. Sites $22, full hookup $23, cabin $38.) Just to the southeast of Helena, a number of free to $10 public campgrounds line Canyon Ferry Reservoir. The free Fish Hawk campground, on West Shore Drive is reserved for tents and has toilets but no drinking water. Take either Canyon Ferry Rd. or Rte. 284 from U.S. 12. The **BLM/BOR Canyon Ferry Office** at 7661 Canyon Ferry Rd. (☎475-3319), has more info.

Rub elbows with state legislators and officials at the **Windbag Saloon and Grill,** 19 S. Last Chance Gulch (in the walking mall), and enjoy Montana-sized burgers for $6-7. (☎443-9669. Open M-Sa 11am-2pm and M-Th 5:30-9:30pm, F-Sa 5-10pm.) For a taste of regional flavor, head over to **Bert & Ernie's,** 361 N. Last Chance Gulch, and sink your teeth into a juicy half-pound burger ($6-7). The Santa Fe burger is a local favorite, while deli sandwiches ($6-7) and heart-healthy entrees—designated by a heart on the menu—satisfy burger-phobes. (☎443-5680. Open M-Sa 11am-9pm.)

🔲 **SIGHTS AND OUTDOORS.** A logical starting point for exploration of Helena, the **Montana Historical Society,** 225 N. Roberts St. (☎444-2694. Open June-Aug. M-F 8am-6pm, Sa-Su 9am-5pm. Open in winter M-F 8am-5pm, Sa 9am-5pm. Free.) The society runs several tours of Helena, including the popular hour-long

Last Chance Tour Train. (☎442-1023. May 11am, 1, 3pm; June 10, 11am, 1, 2, 3pm; July-Aug. every hr. 10am-6pm; Sept. 11am, 1, 3pm. $5.50, ages 4-12 $4.50, under 4 free.) The **State Capitol** building, 6th and Montana Ave., has several pieces of notable artwork, including C.M. Russell's *Lewis and Clark Meeting the Flathead Indians at Ross' Hole* and a statue of Jeannette Rankin, the first woman elected to the US Congress. (Self-guided tours M-F 6am-6pm, Sa-Su 8am-5pm; in summer guided tours every hr., M-Sa 9am-4pm, Su noon-4pm. Free.) The gold vanished from **Last Chance Gulch** long ago; today this walking mall offers restaurants, shops, and public artwork. Housed in the old jail, the **Myrna Loy Center,** 15 N. Ewing St. (☎443-0287), is a multipurpose theater, presenting foreign film, dance, music, and performance art.

Take in all of Helena and the surrounding area from the top of **Mt. Helena** (elevation 5460 ft.); the trail begins from the Adams St. Trailhead, just west of Reeders Alley. Observe the Missouri River just as Lewis and Clark did by taking a boat tour of the **Gates of the Mountains,** 18 mi. north of Helena, just off I-15. The boat stops near Mann Gulch, where a 1949 forest fire killed 13 smokejumpers. (☎458-5241. June: M-F 2 tours per day, Sa-Su 4 per day. July-Aug.: M-F 3 per day, Sa-Su 7 per day. Sept.: M-F 2 per day, Sa-Su 3 per day. Call for times. $9, seniors $8, ages 4-17 $6.)

BOZEMAN ☎ 406

Surrounded by world-class hiking, skiing, and fishing, Bozeman has lately become a magnet for outdoor enthusiasts. To Montanans, however, Bozeman remains "that boisterous college town." Cowboy hats and pickup trucks are still popular among many students at Montana State University, but a recently diversified student body reflects the growing cultural vibrancy of this thriving community.

🛈 PRACTICAL INFORMATION. Greyhound and **RimRock Stages,** 1205 E. Main St. (☎587-3110), both serve Bozeman. To: Butte (1½hr., 4 per day, $16-17); Billings (3-4hr., 4 per day, $23-25); Helena (2hr., 1 per day, $16-17); and Missoula (5hr., 4 per day, $25-33). Open M-F 7:30am-5pm, 7pm-midnight; Sa-Su 7:30am-noon, 3:30-5:30pm, 7pm-midnight. **Budget Rent-a-Car,** at the airport, rents for $80 per day. (☎388-4091. Open daily 7am-11pm, or until last flight. 100 free mi., 25¢ per additional mi. Ages 21-24 $15 per day surcharge; credit card required.) **Bozeman Area Chamber of Commerce:** 2000 Commerce Way, at the corner of 19th Ave. and Baxter Ln. (☎586-5421 or 800-228-4224; www.bozemanchamber.com. Open M 9am-5pm, Tu-F 8am-5pm.) **Internet access: Library,** 220 E. Lamme St. (☎582-2400; open M-Th 10am-8pm, F-Sa 10am-5pm, Su 1-5pm, closed Su in summer). **Post Office:** 32 E. Babcock St. (☎586-2373; open M-F 9am-5pm). **ZIP code:** 59715. **Area code:** 406.

🛈 ACCOMMODATIONS. A number of budget motels line Main St. and 7th Ave. north of Main. The **Bozeman International Backpackers Hostel,** 405 W. Olive St., situated on a quiet street near the university, has a relaxed and welcoming atmosphere. The first floor is a comfortable living and eating area, while the upstairs and basement have rooms with bunkbeds. There are only 18 beds; call ahead to reserve a place. Owners advise where to eat, drink, and hike; they also rent bikes. The hostel offers a large kitchen and laundry. (☎586-4659. $14; 1 double $32. Bikes half-day $6, full-day $10.) The **Alpine Lodge,** 1017 E. Main St., has reasonable prices and spacious rooms, with breakfast included. Call ahead to reserve a room. (☎586-0356 or 888-922-5746. Summer $35.) Across the street, the **Blue Sky Motel,** 1010 E. Main St., offers comfortable rooms off an enclosed front porch that runs the length of the motel. (☎587-5241. Singles $43; pets an additional $3.) The **Bear Canyon Campground** has great views of the surrounding countryside. The park is 4 mi. east of Bozeman, south of I-90 at Exit 313. (☎587-1575 or 800-438-1575. Laundry, showers, and pool. $15 for 2, with water and electricity $18-20; full hookup $22; each additional person $2.) **Spire Rock Campground,** 22 mi. south of Bozeman on U.S. 191, is one of several national forest campgrounds that line the highway. ($7 per night, second car $12.)

(sidebar, vertical text) ROCKY MOUNTAINS

📷🎵 FOOD AND NIGHTLIFE. Thrifty eateries aimed at the college crowd line W. College near the university. Now a popular chain throughout Montana, the original **Pickle Barrel** resides at 809 W. College. Enormous sandwiches with fresh ingredients and free pickles have drawn MSU students for years. A hefty half-sandwich is $4.60-5.40. (☎587-2411. Open daily 10:30am-10pm; in winter 11am-10:30pm.) Stop by **tombo's**, 27 S. Wilson, for giant bowls of hearty rice and noodles. Both vegetarian and meat dishes are available. (☎585-0234. Open M-Sa 11am-8pm, Su noon-6pm, closed Su in summer. Bowls $4.75-7.) **Charlie's Deli and Coffeehouse**, 104 W. Main St., at the corner of Wilson and Main, serves delicious sandwiches on thick slices of bread for a reasonable price. Try a specialty sandwich ($4-0) or build your own ($5). A pickle and chips are included. (☎587-5580. Open M-F 9am-4:30pm, Sa 10am-4:30pm, Su noon-4pm.) Locals and travelers thirsty for good beer and great live music should head over to the **◼Zebra Cocktail Lounge**, in the basement at the corner of Rouse Ave. and Main St. The large selection of beers and the supercool atmosphere always draw a young and hip crowd. (☎585-8851. Music every other night. Open daily 8pm-2am.) Sample some of Montana's best beer at the **Spanish Peaks Brewery**, 14 N. Church. (☎585-2296. Alehouse open daily 11am-2am.) Get the low-down on music and nightlife from the weekly *Tributary* and *The BoZone*

📷🏔 SIGHTS AND OUTDOORS. Get up close and personal with dinosaurs and other artifacts of Rocky Mountain history at the **Museum of the Rockies**, 600 West Kagy Blvd., near the university. Dr. Jack Horner (the basis for the main character in *Jurassic Park*) and other paleontologists make this their base for excavating prehistoric remains throughout the West. While you're there, check out the exhibit on Native American culture. (☎994-2251. Open daily 8am-8pm, in winter M-Sa 9am-5pm, Su 12:30-5pm. $7, ages 5-18 $4, under 5 free.)

Surrounded by three renowned trout-fishing rivers—Yellowstone, Madison, and Gardiner—the small town of **Livingston**, about 25 mi. east of Bozeman off I-90, is an angler's heaven. This is gorgeous country; *A River Runs Through It* was shot in Bozeman and Livingston. Livingston's Main St. features a strip of circa-1900 buildings, housing bars (with gambling), restaurants, fishing outfitters, and a few modern businesses. **Dan Bailey's**, 209 W. Park St., sells licenses (2-day $15, season $50), and rents gear. (☎222-1673 or 800-356-4052. Open M-Sa 7am-7pm, Su 8am-5pm; in winter M-Sa 8am-6pm. Float tubes $15, rod and reel $10, waders and boots $10.)

Bozeman provides its share of downhill thrills. The world-class ski area, **Big Sky**, 45 mi. south of town on U.S. 191, has over 120 trails and short lift lines. The Lone Peak trams reach an altitude of 11,166 ft. and offer extreme skiing options. (☎800-548-4486. Full-day ticket $54, ages 11-17 and college students with I.D. $42, under 10 free. Rentals: skis $26-40, kids' skis $19, snowboard $34. Season mid-Nov. to mid-Apr.) More intimate and less expensive than Big Sky, **Bridger Bowl Ski Area**, 15795 Bridger Canyon Rd., 16 mi. northeast of town, has trails for a variety of abilities. (☎586-2389 or 800-223-9609. Season early Dec. to early Apr. Full-day ticket $34, seniors $28, children 6-12 $13, under 6 free. Rentals: skis $20, junior skis $10, snowboard $30.) In summer, scenic **lift rides** soar up Big Sky. (Open June to early Oct. daily 9:45am-5pm; $13, under 10 free.) Equestrian types gallop at nearby **Dalton's Big Sky Stables**, on the spur road off U.S. 191 about 2 mi. before Big Sky's entrance. (☎995-2972. Open June-Sept. $30 per hr., $50 per 2hr.; 1 day's notice required). **Yellowstone Raft Co.** shoots the rapids of the Gallatin River 7 mi. north of the Big Sky area on U.S. 191. Trips meet at the Yellowstone Raft Co. office, between mileposts 55 and 56 on U.S. 191. (☎995-4613 or 800-348-4376. Half-day $39, children $30.)

RED LODGE ☎406

The small historic mining town of Red Lodge (pop. 2000) is nestled in the foothills of the Beartooth Mountains. The Absaroka (Crow) Indians are the region's original inhabitants, and legend has it that the name "Red Lodge" derives from the red clay adhering to Absaroka tepees. Today, Red Lodge offers a plethora of outdoor activities and entertainment, from world-class rodeos to skiing at Red Lodge Mountain.

> **SHAKESPEARE IN THE PARK** No, New York's famed production didn't make a wrong turn at W. 86th St. and Central Park West to end up in Montana. Rather, this is **Montana Shakespeare in the Park**, a roving band of thespians who make the rounds of the Big Sky state from early July to Labor Day. In the words of one young Montanan, "In the summer, if I'm not camping, I'm watching this." (☎ 406-994-3901; http://opal.msu.montana.edu/wwwmtsip.)

🗓 PRACTICAL INFORMATION. The closest bus stop is in Billings (60 mi. northeast), but the **Red Lodge Shuttle** offers affordable transportation between Billings and Red Lodge (☎ 446-2257 or 888-446-2191). The folks at the **Visitors Center**, 601 N. Broadway, on the north side of town, can help you occupy your time. (☎ 446-1718. Open in summer daily 8am-7pm; in winter M-F 9am-5pm.) **Hospital: Beartooth Hospital and Health Clinic**, 600 W. 21st St. (☎ 446-2345). **Internet access:** Free at the **Public Library,** 3 W. 8th St. (☎ 446-1905. Open M-F 9am-6pm.) **Post Office:** 119 S. Hauser (☎ 446-2629; open M-F 8am-4:30pm, Sa 9am-1pm). **ZIP code:** 59068. **Area code:** 406.

🏨🍴 ACCOMMODATIONS AND FOOD. Most accommodations in Red Lodge are expensive. **The Eagles Nest,** 702 S. Broadway, has affordable rates and a location both adjacent to Rock Creek and close to downtown. (☎ 446-2312. Phone, cable TV. Singles $36; doubles $46; ski-house for 8 with kitchen $125.) Four miles north of Red Lodge on Rte. 212, the **Red Lodge KOA** has 75 shaded sites on Rock Creek. (☎ 446-2364 or 800-562-7540. Open late May to mid-Sept. Sites $20, full hookup $26; kabins $40.) A number of free and inexpensive campsites can be found south of Red Lodge on U.S. 212, along Rock Creek.

Stop by the sophisticated **Bridge Creek Backcountry Kitchen & Bar,** 116 S. Broadway downtown, for lunch or dinner. The lunch combinations (soup plus salad or sandwich for $6) are a great value. (☎ 446-9900. Open daily 11am-9pm.) **Genesis Natural Foods Grocery and Deli,** 123½ S. Broadway, specializes in vegetarian salads and sandwiches. (☎ 446-3204. Open M-F 8am-6pm, Sa 9am-5pm. Sandwiches $4.50-5.50, salads $4-6.) Sample microbrews ($3.75) and creative wraps ($5-6) at the **Red Lodge Alehouse,** 9 N. Broadway (☎ 446-1426). Wallpapered with personalized license plates and irreverent bumper stickers, the raucous **▧Snow Creek Saloon** is one of the best bars around. (☎ 446-2542. Live music on weekends. Open daily 2pm-2am.)

🏔🎿 SIGHTS AND OUTDOORS. Red Lodge Mountain offers 69 runs and over 1600 newly expanded acres of skiable terrain. The mountain's 2400 ft. vertical drop provides some of the finest skiing and snowboarding in the region. A variety of cross-country skiing options are also available. (☎ 446-2610 or 800-444-8977. Open early Nov. to mid-Apr. $36, ages 13-18 $33, 12 and under $14. Rentals $17, snowboards $30.) The **Red Lodge Nordic Center** (☎ 446-9191), located 2 mi. west of Red Lodge on Rte. 78, has over 9 mi. of groomed trails ranging in difficulty. The roads along Rock Creek south of town are good for beginners. Mountain bikers converge at Red Lodge each year in late July for the **Fat Tire Frenzy,** an off-road and slalom competition. The **Meeteetse Trail,** off U.S. 212 south of Red Lodge, and the **Silver Run Trails** near the West Fork of Rock Creek are popular among mountain bikers.

A number of other festivals and special events attract visitors to Red Lodge in both winter and fall. Hosted jointly by the town and the ski area, the **Winter Carnival,** held the first weekend in March, makes good use of abundant snow with ice sculptures, sledding, and music. (Call 446-2610 for info.) The 4th of July **Home of Champions Rodeo** celebrates a local infatuation with the cowboy sport. Red Lodge's first settlers were miners who came from all over Europe, and today Red Lodge pays tribute to this multicultural heritage with the week-long **Festival of Nations** held each August. Every summer weekend Friday-Sunday, beginning at 7pm, **Bearcreek Downs,** 7 mi. east of Red Lodge on Rte. 308, features pig races that draw visitors from all over the world. The races are sponsored by the Bearcreek Saloon where you can get a healthy portion of beef, but no pork. (☎ 446-3481. Open Th-Su 2pm-2am. Burgers $5.) For a more refined style of entertainment, hit up the **Round Barn**

Restaurant and Theater, just north of Red Lodge on U.S. 212. (☎446-1197. Performances every weekend.) For the past six years, Harley-Davidson enthusiasts have gathered in Red Lodge in mid-July for the celebratory **Iron Horse Rodeo.** The festivities include a motorcycle trip down the Beartooth Hwy. and Chief Joseph Hwy. Riders stop at five locales along the way, picking up a playing card along the way; the rider with the best poker hand at the end picks up a pretty $1000. Other events include a street dance, live music, and the motorcycle decathlon. (Info ☎733-5634.)

MISSOULA ☎406

A liberal haven in a largely conservative state, Missoula attracts new residents every day with its revitalized downtown and bountiful outdoors opportunities. Home to the University of Montana, downtown Missoula is lined with bars and coffeehouses spawned by the large student population. Four different mountain ranges and five major rivers surround Missoula, supporting skiing during the winter as well as fly fishing, hiking, and biking during the summer months.

⚐ PRACTICAL INFORMATION. Flights stream into the **Missoula International Airport,** 5225 Rte. 10 W (☎728-4381); follow Broadway (which turns into Rte. 10/200) west out of town 6 mi. **Greyhound:** 1660 W. Broadway (☎549-2339); to Bozeman (6hr., 4 per day, $24-30) and Spokane (4hr., 5 per day, $31-33). From the same terminal, **RimRock Stages** serves Whitefish via St. Ignatius and Kalispell (3½hr.; 1 per day; M-Th $23, F-Su $25) and Helena (2½hr.; 1 per day; M-Th $19, F-Su $20). Catch a ride on the reliable **Mountain Line City Buses** from the Transfer Center, located behind the County Courthouse at the corner of Ryman and Pine St., or a curbside around town. (☎721-3333. Buses operate M-F 6:45am-6:15pm, Sa 9:45am-5:15pm. Fare 85¢.) **Taxis: Yellow Cab** (☎543-6644). **Rent-A-Wreck,** 1905 W. Broadway, provides free transportation to and from the airport and great prices on rentals. (☎721-3838. 25+. $27 per day. 150 free mi., 25¢ each additional mi.) **Missoula Chamber of Commerce:** 825 E. Front St. at Van Buren. (☎543-6623; www.missoulachamber.com. Open in summer M-F 8am-7pm, Sa 10am-6pm; early Sept. to late May M-F 8am-5pm.) **Internet access: Cyber Shock,** 821 S. Higgins (☎721-6251; open M-F 7am-2am, Sa 10am-2am, Su noon-2am; $4 per hr.). **Post Office:** 1100 W. Kent, between Brooks and South St. (☎329-2200; open M-F 8am-6pm, Sa 9am-1pm). **ZIP code:** 59801. **Area code:** 406.

⌂ ACCOMMODATIONS. There are no hostels in Missoula, but there are plenty of inexpensive alternatives along **Broadway.** Rooms at the **City Center Motel,** 338 E. Broadway, are adorned with large murals and have cable, fridges, and microwaves. (☎543-3193. May-Sept.: singles $42, doubles $48. Sept.-Dec.: singles $35, doubles $42.) To reach the **Aspen Motel,** 3720 Rte. 200 E in East Missoula, get off I-90 at Exit 107 and travel ½ mi. east. Enjoy the clean rooms, cable, and A/C. (☎721-9758. Singles $38; 1-bed doubles $44.50; 2-bed $55.) The **Sleepy Inn Motel,** 1427 W. Broadway, is conveniently located near the bus depot. Carpeted rooms are equipped with cable and A/C. (☎549-6484. Singles $38; doubles $48.) The **Missoula/El-Mar KOA Kampground,** 3450 Tina Ave., just south of Broadway off Reserve St., is one of the best KOAs around, offering shaded tent sites apart from RVs. Pool, hot tub, minigolf courses, arcade, and 24hr. laundry facilities are available. (☎549-0881 or 800-562-5366. 2 people $20, water and electricity $26, full hookups $26-31, kabins $38-43; each additional person $3.)

⚃⚄ FOOD AND NIGHTLIFE. Missoula, the culinary capital of Montana, boasts a number of innovative, delicious, and thrifty eating establishments. Head downtown, north of the Clark Fork River along Higgins Ave., and check out the array of restaurants and coffeehouses that line the road. Located at the corner of Higgins and Spruce, **⚐Worden's** is a popular local deli, serving a wide variety world-class sandwiches in three sizes: 4 in. ($4.25), 7 in. ($5.75), and 14 in. ($10.75). You can also pick up groceries while you munch. (☎549-1293. Open M-Th 8am-10pm, F-Sa 8am-11pm, Su 9am-9pm.) The **Farmers Market** and the **Peoples Market** showcase edible and inedible wares at N. Higgins (open in summer Sa 9am-noon and Tu 5:30-7pm). **Torrey's**, 1916 Brooks St., prides itself on serving healthy, low-fat meals reminiscent of Mom's homecooking. All meals are $3. (☎721-2510. Open M-F 11:30am-3pm.) **Tipu's Tiger International Deli**, 531 S. Higgins, serves scrumptious vegetarian options from around the world, including a large selection of vegan dishes. Meals range from $3-6. (☎549-6902. Open daily 8am-8pm.) Hungry UM students crowd **Food for Thought**, 540 Daly, for breakfast and lunch. The A+ sandwich makes the grade at $5.25. (☎721-6033. Open daily 7am-4pm, breakfast served until 11am weekdays, 2pm weekends. Omelettes $5-6, huge bowl of vegan chili with roll $3.)

College students swarm the downtown bar area around Front St. and Higgins Ave. during the school year; bars have a more relaxed atmosphere in summer. One of the most popular bars in town, **The Iron Horse Brew Pub**, 501 N. Higgins, always packs a crowd. The indoor seating area is spacious, and a large patio fills up during the summer months. (☎728-8866. Open daily 11am-2am.) Live music and an affable waitstaff make **Sean Kelly's**, 130 W. Pine St., the place to be on weekends. (☎542-1471. Open daily 11am-2am.) Follow the advice of **The Kettle House Brewing Co.**, 602 Myrtle, one block west of Higgins between 4th and 5th, and "support your local brewery." The Kettle House has its priorities straight: it doesn't serve food, only a delectable assortment of beers. (Open M-Th 3-9pm, F-Sa noon-9pm; no beer served after 8pm. 2 free samples, then $2.75 for pints.)

▣ **SIGHTS.** Missoula's hottest sight, the **Smokejumper Center**, 7 mi. west of town on Broadway (5765 Rte. 10, just past the airport), is the nation's largest training base for smokejumpers, aerial firefighters who parachute into flaming, remote forests. (☎329-4934. Open daily 8:30am-5pm. Tours May-Sept. every hr. 10-11am and 2-4pm. Free.) The handcrafted **Carousel**, in Caras Riverfront Park, is one of the oldest hand-carved carousels in America. (☎549-8382. Open June-Aug. daily 11am-7pm; Sept.-May 11am-5:30pm. $1, seniors and under 19 50¢.) **Out to Lunch**, also in Caras Riverfront Park, offers free performances in the summer, every Wednesday 11:30am-1:30pm; call the Missoula Downtown Association (☎543-4328) for more info. The **Western Montana Fair and Rodeo**, held the second week in August, has live music, a carnival, fireworks, and commercial concession booths. (☎721-3247. August 6-11, 2002. Open 10am-10pm.) The *Independent* and *Lively Times* offer the lowdown on the Missoula music scene (available at newsstands and cafes), while the *Entertainer*, in the Friday *Missoulian*, has movie and event schedules. You can soak your weary feet at the **Lolo Hot Springs**, 35 mi. southwest of Missoula on Hwy 12. The 103-105° springs served as an ancient meeting place for local Native Americans, and were frequented by explorers Lewis and Clark in 1806. (☎273-2290 or 800-273-2290. $6, 12 and under $4.)

▨ **OUTDOOR ACTIVITIES.** Nearby parks, recreation areas, and surrounding wilderness areas make Missoula an outdoor enthusiast's dream. Bicycle-friendly Missoula is located along both the Trans-America and the Great Parks bicycle routes; all major streets have designated bike lanes. **Open Road Bicycles and Nordic Equipment**, 517 S. Orange St., has bike rentals. (☎549-2453. Open M-F 9am-6pm, Sa 10am-5pm, Su 11am-3pm. $3.50 per hr., $17.50 per day.) The national **Adventure Cycling**, 150 E. Pine St., is the place to go for info about the Trans-America and Great Parks routes. (☎721-1776 or 800-755-2543. Open M-F 8am-5pm.) The **Rattlesnake Wilderness National Recreation Area**, 11 mi. northeast of town off the Van Buren St. exit on I-90, and the **Pattee Canyon Recreation Area**, 3½ mi. east of Higgins on Pattee Canyon Dr., are highly recommended for their biking trails. Call Adventure Cycling for more information. **Missoulians on Bicycle** is a local organization that hosts rides and events for cyclists; write to P.O. Box 8903, Missoula 59807 for more information, or check www.missoulabike.org.

Alpine and Nordic **skiing** keep Missoulians busy during winter; Pattee Canyon has groomed trails that are conveniently close to town, and **Marshall Mountain** is a great place to learn how to downhill ski. (☎258-6000. Full-day $19, seniors and under 13 $15; skis $12, snowboard $16; night skiing and free shuttles from downtown.) Experienced skiers should check out the extreme **Montana Snowbowl**, 12 mi. northwest of

Missoula, with a vertical drop of 2600 ft. and over 35 trails. (☎549-9777 or 800-728-2695. Open Nov.-Apr. daily 9:30am-4pm. Full-day $29, children $13, under 5 free.)

Floating on rafts and tubes is a favorite activity for locals on weekends. The Blackfoot River, along Rte. 200 east of Bonner, makes a good afternoon float. Call the **Montana State Regional Parks and Wildlife Office**, 3201 Spurgin Rd., for information about rafting locations. (☎542-5500. Open M-F 8am-5pm.) Rent tubes ($3 per day) or rafts ($40; credit card required) from the **Army and Navy Economy Store**, 322 N. Higgins. A $20 deposit is required. (☎721-1315. Open M-F 9am-7:30pm, Sa 9am-5:30pm, Su 10am-5:30pm.) **Pangaea Expeditions** runs rafting trips leaving from Bernice's Bakery at 190 S. 3rd St. W. (☎721-7719. 2hr. $25, half day $40-45, full-day $55.)

Hiking opportunities also abound in the Missoula area. The relatively easy half-mile round-trip hike to the "M" (for the U of M, not Missoula) on Mount Sentinel, offers a tremendous view of Missoula and the surrounding mountains. The Rattlesnake Wilderness National Recreation Area, named after the shape of the river (there are no rattlers for miles), is 11 mi. northeast of town off the Van Buren St. exit from I-90, and makes for a great day of hiking. Other popular areas include Pattee Canyon and **Blue Mountain,** located south of town. Maps ($6) and information on longer hikes in the Bitterroot and Bob Marshall areas, are available from the **US Forest Service Information Office,** 200 E. Broadway; the entrance is at 200 Pine St. (☎329-3511. Open M-F 7:30am-4pm.) For equipment rentals, stop by **Trailhead,** 110 E. Pine St., at Higgins St. (☎543-6966. Open M-F 9:30am-8pm, Sa 9am-6pm, Su 11am-6pm. Tents M-F $9, Sa-Su $18; backpacks $9-15; sleeping bags $5-9.)

Western Montana is **fly-fishing** country, and Missoula is at the heart of it all. Fishing licenses are required and can be purchased from the **Department of Fish, Wildlife, and Parks,** 3201 Spurgin Rd. (☎542-5500), or from local sporting goods stores. **Kingfisher,** 926 E. Broadway, offers licenses ($15-50) and pricey guided fishing trips. (☎721-6141. Open summer daily 7am-8pm, off-season daily 9am-5pm.) **Grizzly Hackle Outfitting,** 215 W. Front, sells licenses at $15 per 2 days, $10 for each additional 2-day period and leads even pricier guided trips. (☎721-8996 or 800-297-8996. Open summer daily 8am-6pm, off-season daily 10am-5pm.)

FROM MISSOULA TO GLACIER

The ▓**Miracle of America Museum,** 58176 U.S. 93 at the southern end of **Polson,** houses one of the country's greatest collections of Americana, with large displays of old posters, uniforms, furniture, and weapons. A general store, saddlery shop, barber shop, soda fountain, and gas station sit among the classic memorabilia. The museum celebrates Live History Day the third weekend in July. (☎883-6804. Open June-Sept. daily 8am-8pm; Oct.-May M-Sa 8am-5pm, Su 2-6pm. $3, ages 3-12 $1.)

The **National Bison Range** was established in 1908 in an effort to save the dwindling number of bison from extinction. At one time 30-70 million of these animals roamed the plains, but after years of over-hunting the population dropped to less than 1000. The Range is home to 350-500 buffalo in addition to deer, antelope, elk, bighorn sheep, and mountain goats. The two-hour Red Sleep Mountain self-guided tour offers a spectacular view of the Flathead Valley and the best chance for wildlife observation. To access the range, travel 40 mi. north of Missoula off U.S. 93, then 5 mi. west on Rte. 200, and 5 mi. north on Rte. 212. (☎644-2211. Visitors Center open M-F 8am-4:30pm; summer hours vary, call ahead. Red Sleep Mountain drive open mid-May to mid-Oct. daily 7am-dusk. $4 per vehicle; Federal Recreation Passes accepted.) Fresh fruit stands line **Flathead Lake,** the largest natural lake west of the Mississippi. Renowned for its fresh cherries and fresher fish, the lake is located along U.S. 93 between Polson and Kalispell.

St. Ignatius Campground and Hostel, off U.S. 93 in **St. Ignatius** (look for the camping sign), offers lodging in its recently renovated "earthship," an eco-friendly structure built into a hillside and made from recycled tires and aluminum cans. Faux cave paintings decorate the plaster walls. The hostel provides skiing equipment for $5 or less and is a convenient blasting-off point for exploring the backcountry. (☎745-3959. Showers, laundry, kitchen. $12; sites for 1 $10, for 2 $12.) **RimRock Stages** (☎745-3501) makes a stop ½ mi. away in St. Ignatius, at the Malt Shop on Blaine St.

WATERTON-GLACIER PEACE PARK

Waterton-Glacier transcends international boundaries to encompass one of the most strikingly beautiful portions of the Rockies. Both established in 1932, the two parks are connected by a natural unity of landscape and wildlife. The massive Rocky Mountain peaks span both parks, providing sanctuary for many endangered bears, bighorn sheep, moose, mountain goats, and gray wolves. Perched high in the Northern Rockies, Glacier is sometimes called the "Crown of the Continent," and the high alpine lakes and glaciers shine like the jewels.

🔼 PRACTICAL INFORMATION

Technically one park, Waterton-Glacier is actually two distinct areas: the small **Waterton Lakes National Park** in Alberta, and the enormous **Glacier National Park** in Montana. There are several **border crossings** nearby: **Piegan/Carway** at U.S. 89 (open daily 7am-11pm); **Roosville** on U.S. 93 (open 24hr.); and **Chief Mountain** at Rte. 17 (open mid- to late May daily 9am-6pm, June-Aug. 7am-10pm, Sept. 9am-6pm). The fastest way to Waterton is to head north along the east side of Glacier, entering Canada through Chief Mountain. Since snow melt can be unpredictable, the parks are usually in full operation only from late May to early September; it is worth your while to check conditions in advance. The *Waterton Glacier Guide*, provided at any park entrance, has dates and times of trail, campground, and border crossing openings. To find out which park areas, hotels, and campsites will be open when you visit, contact the **Park Headquarters,** Waterton Lakes National Park, Waterton Park, AB T0K 2M0 (☎ 403-859-2224), or Glacier National Park, West Glacier, MT 59936 (☎ 406-888-7800). Mace and firewood are not allowed into Canada.

GLACIER NATIONAL PARK ☎ 406

❋ ORIENTATION

There are few roads in Glacier, and the locals like it that way. Glacier's main thoroughfare is the **Going-to-the-Sun Rd.** which connects the two primary points of entry, West Glacier and St. Mary. **U.S. 2** skirts the southern border of the park and is the fastest route from Browning and East Glacier to West Glacier. At the "Goat Lick," about halfway between East and West Glacier, mountain goats traverse steep cliffs to convene and lap up the natural salt deposits. **Rte 89** heads north along the eastern edge of the park past St. Mary. Anyone interested in visiting the northwestern section of the park must braved the unpaved and pothole-ridden **Outside North Fork Rd.** While most of Glacier is primitive backcountry, a number of villages provide lodging, gas, and food: Many Glacier, St. Mary, and East Glacier in the east and West Glacier, Apgar, and Polebridge in the west.

▣ TRANSPORTATION

Amtrak (☎ 226-4452) traces a dramatic route along the southern edge of the park. The station in West Glacier is open mid-May to Sept.; the train stops at an unstaffed station in the winter. Trains chug daily to East Glacier (1½hr., $17), Whitefish (30 min., $5), Seattle (14hr., $120), and Spokane (6hr., $50-60); Amtrak also runs from East Glacier to Chicago (32hr., $250) and Minneapolis (23hr., $172-207). Fares subject to change; call 800-872-7245 for more info. **RimRock Stages** (☎ 800-255-7655), the only bus line that nears the park, stops in Kalispell at the Kalispell Bus Terminal, 3794 U.S. 2 E., and goes to Missoula (M-Th $19, F-Su $20) or Billings (M-Th $61, F-Su $65). As in most of the Rockies, a car is the most convenient mode of transport, particularly within the park. **Rent-A-Wreck**, 3582 U.S. 93 S., in Kalispell, rents cars. (☎ 755-4555. $37.50 per day. 100 free mi., 21¢ each additional mi. Must be 21; under 25 $5 per day surcharge.) **Glacier Park, Inc.'s** famous red jammer buses are currently out of service as they undergo repairs, but bus tours are still available departing from Lake McDonald and Many Glacier; check www.glacierparkinc.com for updates. **Sun Tours** offers additional tours of the park, leaving from East Glacier and St. Mary. (☎226-9220 or 800-786-9220. $45 for all day tour.) Shuttles for hikers ($8-17; under 12 50% off) roam the length of Going-to-the-Sun Rd. from early July to early September; schedules are available at Visitors Centers (☎888-9187).

🛈 PRACTICAL INFORMATION

Admission is $10 per week per car and $5 for pedestrians and cyclists. Yearly passes are available for $20. The accessible and knowledgeable rangers at each of the three Visitors Centers can give you the inside scoop on campsites, day hikes, weather, flora, and fauna. **St. Mary** guards the east entrance of the park. (☎ 732-7750. Open mid-May to mid-June daily 8am to 5pm; mid- to late June 8am to 6pm; late June to early Sept. 8am to 9pm; early Sept. to mid-Oct. 8am-5pm.) **Apgar** is located at the west entrance. (☎888-7939. Open late May to late June daily 8am-4:30pm; late June to early Sept. 8am-8pm; early Sept. to late Oct. 8am to 4:30 pm.) A third Visitors Center graces **Logan Pass** on the Going-to-the-Sun Rd. (Open early to late June daily 9am-4:30 pm; late June to early Sept. 9am-7pm; early to late Sept. 10am-4:30pm; early to mid-Oct. 10am-4pm.) The **Many Glacier** ranger station can also help answer important questions. (Open late May to late June daily 8am-4:30 pm; late June to early Sept. 8am-6pm; early to mid-Sept. 8am-4:30pm.)

Visitors planning overnight backpacking trips must obtain the necessary **backcountry permits.** With the exception of the Nyack/Coal Creek camping zone, all backcountry camping must be done at designated campsites that are equipped with pit toilets, tent sites, food preparation areas, and food hanging devices. During the summer season (June 1-Sept. 30), the fee for overnight camping is $4 per person per night for adults (17 and over); $2 for ages 9-16; there are no fees for winter permits. Advance reservations are available after April 16 each year for a $20 fee and must be made more than 24hr. in advance. Reservations can be made in person at the Apgar Permit Center and other park offices, over the web at www.nps.gov/glac/home.htm, or by writing to Backcountry Reservation Office, Glacier National Park, West Glacier, MT 59936. The free *Backcountry Camping Guide* is available at Visitors Centers and permit stations. The **Backcountry Permit Center,** located next to the Visitors Center in Apgar, is an invaluable resource for those seeking to explore Glacier's less-traveled areas. (Open early May early July daily 8am-4pm; early July to mid-Sept. 7am-4pm; mid-Sept. to late Oct. 8am-4pm.) Backcountry permits are also available at other Visitors Centers. **Kalispell Regional Medical Center:** 310 Sunny View Ln. (☎ 752-5111), north of Kalispell off Rte. 93. **Post Office:** In West Glacier. (☎888-5591. Open M-F 8:30am-12:30pm and 1:30-4:45pm.) **ZIP code:** 59936. **Area code:** 406.

🛏 ACCOMMODATIONS

Staying indoors within Glacier is expensive, but several affordable options lie just outside the park boundaries. On the west side of the park, the small town of **Polebridge** provides access to Glacier's remote and pristine northwest corner. From Apgar, take Camas Rd. north, and take a right onto the poorly-marked gravel Outside North Fork Rd., just past a bridge over the North Fork of the Flathead River. (Avoid Inner North Fork Rd.—your shocks will thank you.) From Columbia Falls, take Rte. 486 north. Follow the signs through town to the **North Fork Hostel,** 80 Beaver Dr., where the wooden walls and kerosene lamps are reminiscent of a deep woods hunting retreat. The price includes showers, but no flush toilets. During the winter, old-fashioned wood stoves warm frozen fingers and toes after skiing or snowshoeing. Call ahead for a $25 pickup from the West Glacier Amtrak station. (☎888-5241. Check-in 10pm, check-out noon. Lockout 9am-5pm. Light chores. Free use of canoes, mountain bikes, snowshoes, and nordic ski equipment. Showers $4 for non-lodgers. Linen $2. Reservations recommended, especially during winter. Dorms $15, $12 after 2 nights; cabins $30; log homes $65.)

To the east, inexpensive lodging is just across the park border in **East Glacier.** You can check in at the grocery counter of **Brownies Grocery (HI-AYH),** 1020 Rte. 49, and head upstairs to the spacious hostel on the second floor, feasting your eyes on a stunning view of the Rockies from the porch. (☎226-4426. Open May-Sept., weather permitting. Kitchen, showers, linens, and laundry provided. Check-in by 9pm, call ahead for late arrivals. Check out 9am. Light chores. Reservations recommended. Dorms $13, nonmembers $16; private singles $18/$21; doubles $26/$29; triples $26/$29; family room for 4-6 $36/$38. Tent sites $10. Extra bed $5. Key deposit $5. Credit card required.) The **Backpacker's Inn Hostel,** 29 Dawson Ave., just south of the East Glacier Amtrak station and behind Serrano's Mexican Restaurant, has 14 clean beds in co-ed rooms and hot showers for only $10 per night. A private room with a queen-sized bed and full linens (1 guest $20 per night, 2 guests $30) is also available. (☎226-9392. Open May-Sept. Sleeping bags $1.) The one budget motel, the **Swiftcurrent Motor Inn** in Many Glacier Valley, has one-bedroom cabins for $41 and two-bedroom cabins for $51. (☎732-5531. Open early June to early Sept. No toilets.) The distant offices of **Glacier Park, Inc.,** handle reservations for all in-park lodging. (☎406-756-2444. Write 106 Cooperative Way, #104, Kalispell, MT 59901.)

🍴 FOOD

To hungry backpackers, the homemade pastries ($1-3) at the **Polebridge Mercantile Store** (☎888-5105) are as splendid as the surrounding peaks. Gas, gifts, and public pay phones are also available. The **Northern Lights Saloon** next door serves fabulous $5.50 cheeseburgers and $3 cold pints in a one-room log cabin with slices of tree trunk for barstools. (Kitchen open June-Sept. daily 4-9pm; bar open until midnight.) At **Brownies Grocery** (see above), travelers can refuel with a thick huckleberry shake ($4) or a backpack-friendly sandwich ($5).

Sample homemade Montana delicacies at the **Whistle Stop Restaurant** in East Glacier next to Brownies Grocery, best known for its "world-famous" huckleberry french toast and $6-7 omelettes. (☎226-9292. Open daily 7am-9pm.) A few buildings farther down from the Whistle Stop on Rte. 89, the **Restaurant Thimbleberry** boasts delicious homemade berry pies ($2.25 per slice), as well as burgers ($4-6) and sandwiches ($4-6). Dinner is served with fresh fruit and succulent corn-on-the-cob. For those who have a hankering for huckleberries, fresh huckleberry jam and syrup is available for purchase. (☎226-5523. Open daily 7am-9:30pm.) In St. Mary on Rte. 89, just north of the park entrance, the **Park Cafe** provides sustenance to those who dare to traverse the Going-to-the-Sun Rd. The incredible homemade pies ($2.75 per slice), the "Hungry Hiker" special (2 eggs with hash browns and toast, $3.50) and the vegetarian Caribbean Burrito ($4.75) are all local favorites. (☎732-4482. Open May-Sept. M-F 7:30am-9pm; Sa-Su 7:30am-10pm.)

🥾 HIKING

There are bears and mountain lions out there. Familiarize yourself with the precautions necessary to avoid an encounter. Ask the rangers about wildlife activity in the area in which you plan to hike. Most of Glacier's spectacular scenery lies off the main roads and is accessible only by foot. An extensive trail system has something for everyone, from short, easy day hikes to rigorous backcountry expeditions. Stop by one of the Visitors Centers for maps with day hikes.

Avalanche Lake (4 mi., 3hr.). This breathtaking trail is easily the most popular day hike in the park.

Trail of the Cedars (0.3 mi., 20min.) begins at the same trailhead, north of Lake McDonald on the Going-to-the-Sun Rd. Also offers a shorter, wheelchair accessible hike.

Numa Ridge Lookout hike (12 mi., 9hr.) begins from the Bowman Lake campground, near Polebridge. After climbing 2930 ft., the hike ends with sweeping vistas of Glacier's rugged northeast corner.

Grinnell Glacier Trail (11 mi., 7hr.) passes within close proximity of several glaciers. Trailhead at the Many Glacier Picnic Area. On a clear day, from **Scenic Point,** you can see the Sweetgrass Hills, nearly 100 mi. away; the Scenic Point trailhead is ¼ mi. east of the Two Medicine Ranger Station (6.3 mi; 5hr).

Hidden Lake Nature Trail (3 mi., 460 ft. elevation gain, approx. 2hr.) begins at the Logan Pass Visitor Center and offers a chance to stretch your legs while winding along the Going-to-the-Sun Rd.

OUTDOOR ACTIVITIES

BIKING

Opportunities for bicycling are limited and confined to roadways and designated bike paths; cycling on trails is strictly prohibited. Although the Going-to-the-Sun Rd. is a popular **bike route,** only experienced cyclists with appropriate gear and legs of titanium should attempt this grueling ride. The sometimes nonexistent shoulder of the road can create hazardous situations. From mid-June through August, bike traffic is prohibited 11am-4pm from the Apgar campground to Sprague Creek, and eastbound (uphill) from Logan Creek to Logan Pass. The Inner Fork Rd. (which runs from Kintla Lake to Fish Creek on the west side of the park) and the old logging roads in the Flathead National Forest are good for **mountain biking.** Ask at a Visitors Center for more details. **Equestrian** explorers should check to make sure trails are open; there are steep fines for riding on closed trails. **Trail rides** from Mule Shoe Outfitters ($35 for 2hr.) are available at Many Glacier (☎732-4203), Apgar (☎888-5010), and Lake McDonald (☎888-5121).

BOATING

The **Glacier Park Boat Co.** (☎257-2426) provides **boat tours** that explore all of Glacier's large lakes. Tours leave from **Lake McDonald** (☎888-5727; 1hr., 4-5 per day, $9); **Two Medicine** (☎226-4467; 45min., 5 per day, $10); **Rising Sun** at St. Mary Lake (☎732-4430; 1½hr., 5 per day, $10); and **Many Glacier** (☎732-4480; 1¼hr., $10). The tours from Two Medicine, Rising Sun, and Many Glacier provide access to Glacier's backcountry, and there are sunset cruises from Rising Sun and Lake McDonald. **Glacier Raft Co.,** in West Glacier, leads trips down the middle fork of the Flathead River. (☎888-5454 or 800-235-6781; half-day $41, under 13 $29; full-day trip $75 with lunch, under 13 $49.) You can rent **rowboats** ($10 per hr.) at Lake McDonald, Many Glacier, Two Medicine, and Apgar; **canoes** ($10 per hr.) at Many Glacier, Two Medicine, and Apgar; **kayaks** ($10 per hr.) at Apgar and Many Glacier; and **outboards** ($17 per hr.) at Lake McDonald and Two Medicine. (Outboards at Apgar are $19 per hr.)

FISHING

No permit is needed to **fish** in the park, and limits are generally high, though some areas are restricted and certain species may be catch-and-release. It's all explained in *Fishing Regulations,* available at Visitors Centers. Lake Ellen Wilson, Gunsight Lake, and Lake Elizabeth are good places to sink a line. Outside the park, on Blackfeet Indian land, you *do* need a special permit, and everywhere else in Montana you need a state permit.

SCENIC DRIVE: GOING-TO-THE-SUN ROAD

The high country of Glacier National Park is a paradise of purple mountains, cascading waterfalls, alpine wildflowers, and permanent snowpack. The Going-to-the-Sun Rd. winds its way through the mountains from St. Mary to West Glacier, tantalizing visitors with its sweeping vistas, expansive valleys, and gushing waterfalls. This fifty-mile scenic drive is always a highlight of the park; however, drivers should keep their eyes on the road, as hairpin turns, narrow shoulders, and thousand-foot dropoffs present a constant threat. Sun Tours will do the driving for you if you would prefer to sit back and enjoy the scenery (see **Practical Information,** above). Going-to-the-Sun runs through the mountains from St. Mary to Apgar, and driving time runs between two and three hours, depending on weather and traffic

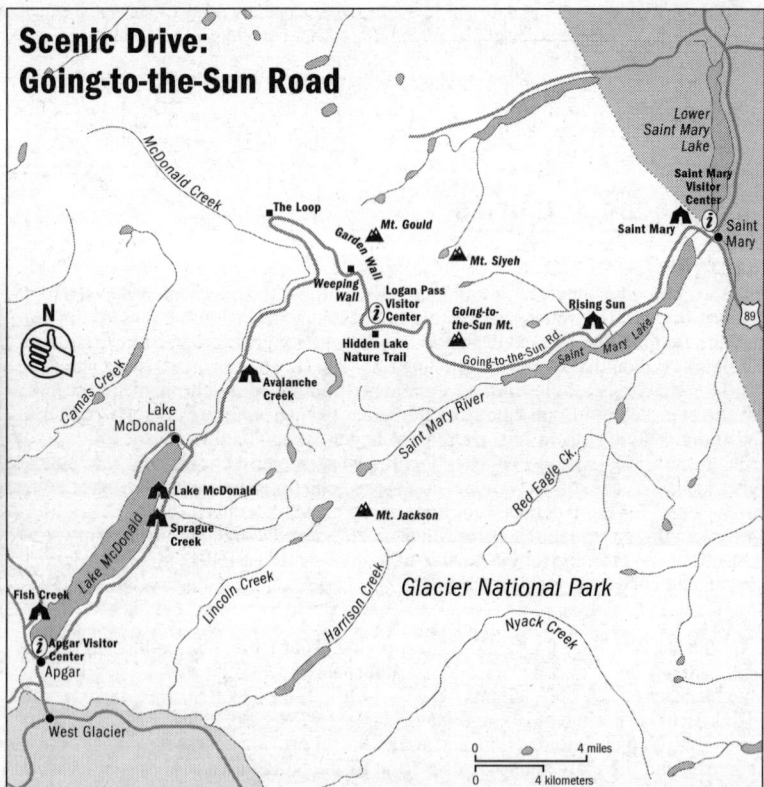

Scenic Drive: Going-to-the-Sun Road

conditions. Due to late-melting snow and early winters, high portions of the road (near Logan Pass) are usually only open from late May or early June to late October. Vehicles over 21 feet in length or 8 feet in width are prohibited.

Travelers can begin from either Apgar or St. Mary. Some prefer starting at St. Mary, as the road hugs the inside of the mountains for the majority of the drive. Beginning from St. Mary, the drive passes through **Two Dog Flats,** the windswept plains of the Rocky Mountain front as it follows the blue-green waters of **St. Mary Lake.** Campgrounds and a full-service boat dock are available at **Rising Sun,** just before the road turns to offer a stunning view of **Wild Goose Island** and the looming snowcapped peaks that have graced many a postcard. Going-to-the-Sun Mountain and Mount Siyeh appear to the right as the road ascends toward **Logan Pass,** where the road crosses the Continental Divide at an elevation of 6646 ft. Visit the **Logan Pass Visitor Center** for information on wildlife, and keep an eye out for mountain goats strolling through the parking lot. The road begins its descent below the treeline along the **Garden Wall.** From **Bird Women Falls Overlook,** cascading waterfalls on distant mountains are visible. Slow down as you pass the **Weeping Wall,** where water rushes down the cliffs onto the road below, spraying the windshields of unexpecting drivers. At **The Loop,** a giant hairpin turn, the road goes back into trees and follows McDonald Creek until it reaches **Lake McDonald.**

NEAR GLACIER   ☎ 406

WHITEFISH

Whitefish's proximity to skiing, Glacier National Park, Flathead Lake and other outdoor attractions has largely contributed to its recent boom. Fortunately, the sprawling shops and malls that are spreading throughout the Flathead Valley haven't detracted from Whitefish's vibrant downtown where bars crowd with ski bums in winter and cyclists in summer.

The Big Mountain, southwest of the park in Whitefish, has 78 superb ski trails in the winter. (☎800-858-5439. Full-day $47; seniors, students, and ages 7-18 $34; night skiing $14. Rentals $22, seniors and ages 7-12 $14, snowboards $28.) Mountain bikers take over the trails in the summer. (Bikes $25 per half day. Lift ticket $15 per day or $12 per ride.) Other activities include horseback riding, gondola rides, and frolf (frisbee golf).

The **Tally Lake District** of the Flathead National Forest has great (but hard-core) mountain bike trails. **Glacier Cyclery,** 326 2nd St., sells maps ($6) and rents bikes. (☎862-6446. Half-day $20, full-day $25-35; helmet included.) After a long day of skiing or biking, many crash at one of Whitefish's two hostels. **The Bunkhouse Traveler's Inn and Hostel,** 217 Railway St., has a summertime sundeck and offers winter ski pickup. (☎862-3377. Closes in spring and fall; call ahead to see if they're open. Kitchen and laundry facilities. Linens $3. Dorms $13; private rooms $30.) The **Non-Hostile Hostel,** 300 E. 2nd St., is one helluva friendly place. This apartment-like hostel has Internet access ($2 for email, $8 per hr.), a pool table, and the **Wrap and Roll Cafe** (wraps starting at $4) downstairs. (☎862-7383. Open Tu-Su. Rooms $13.)

After working up an appetite on the slopes, head over to **Truby's,** 115 Central Ave., for a wood-fired pizza. The lunch special is hard to beat: half a gourmet pizza, a salad, and a soda for $6. (☎862-4979. Lunch served M-Sa 11am-3pm.) Park visitors with a hankering for Mexican cuisine should check out **Serrano's,** 10 Central Ave., across the street from the Great Northern Saloon. Large appetizers ($3-7) and entrees ($7-14) and a friendly staff are bound to please even the toughest critic. (☎862-5600. Open daily 11:30am-10pm.) Whitefish is the area's nightlife hot spot; the **Dire Wolf Pub,** 845 Wisconsin Ave., on the way to Big Mountain, is a local favorite featuring live music during the ski season. Burgers and sandwiches ($5-6) satisfy mountain-sized appetites. (☎862-4500. Open daily 11am-2am.) The **Great Northern Saloon,** 27 Central St., rocks on the patio in summer and offers a variety of cures for the tired skier or snowboarder. (☎862-2816. Open daily 11am-2am.) Both bars serve burgers and sandwiches ($5-6). The Monday night special ($1 Miller Lite) starts the week off on a good note. The **Black Star Brewery,** 2 Central Ave., pours up samples of good beer. (☎863-1000. Open M-Sa noon-6pm; in winter M-Sa 3-7pm.)

RimRock buses (☎800-255-7655) stop at the Conoco station across E. 2nd St. and run to Missoula (1 per day; M-Th $23, F-Su $25). Whitefish can be reached by **Amtrak;** call 800-872-7245 for schedules and fares. **Post Office:** 424 Baker St. (☎862-2151. Open M-F 8:30am-5:30pm, Sa 10am-2pm.) **ZIP code:** 59937.

BROWNING

The center of the Blackfeet Indian Reservation, Browning, 12 mi. east of East Glacier, provides a glimpse into the past and present of Native American life. The **Museum of the Plains Indian,** at the junction of U.S. 2 and U.S. 89, displays traditional Native American clothing, artifacts, and crafts. (☎338-2230. Open June-Sept. daily 9am-4:45pm; Oct.-May M-F 10am-4:30pm. $4, ages 6-12 $1; groups of 10 or more $1 per person; Oct.-May free.) During **North American Indian Days** (Th-Su the 2nd weekend in July), Native Americans from the surrounding Blackfeet Reservation and elsewhere gather for a celebration that includes tribal dancing, rodeo, and a fantastic parade 11am on Saturday. Call **Blackfeet Planning** (☎338-7406) for more details.

WATERTON LAKES NAT'L PARK, AB   ☎403

Only a fraction of the size of its Montana neighbor, Waterton Lakes National Park offers spectacular scenery and activities without the crowds that plague Glacier during July and August. The town of Waterton is a genuine alpine town, complete with a Swiss-style chalet. Bighorn sheep and mule deer frequently wander down the the surrounding slopes into town, causing unexpected traffic delays. Admission is CDN$4 per day, CDN$8 per group of two to seven people (free in the winter).

ROCKY MOUNTAINS

ROCKY MOUNTAINS

◪ PRACTICAL INFORMATION. The only road from Waterton's park entrance leads 8½km south to **Waterton Park.** En route, stop at the **Waterton Visitors Center,** 8km inside the park on Rte. 5 for a schedule of events and hikes. (☎859-5133. Open mid-June to Aug. daily 8am-8pm; mid-May to mid-June 8am-6pm; Sept.-Oct. 9am-6pm, although hours may vary depending on weather.) In the off season, pick up info at **Park Administration,** 215 Mt. View Rd. (☎859-2224; open M-F 8am-4pm). Greenbacks (US dollars) can be exchanged for Loonies (Canadian dollars) at the **Tamarack Village Sq.** on Mt. View Rd. (☎859-2378; open July-Aug. daily at least 9am-6pm, May-June and Sept.-Oct. usually 9am-5pm). **Pat's Gas and Cycle Rental,** Mt. View Rd., Waterton, rents bikes. (☎859-2266. Mountain bikes CDN$6 per hr., CDN$30 per day.) **Ambulance:** ☎859-2636. **Post Office:** in Waterton on Fountain Ave. at Windflower Ave. (open M, W, and F 8:30am-4:30pm; Tu and Th 8:30am-4pm). **Postal code:** T0K 2M0. **Area code:** 403.

▌▐ ACCOMMODATIONS AND FOOD. At the entrance to the park, the enormous (and enormously pricey) **Prince of Wales Hotel** perches on a small hill overlooking both Middle and Upper Waterton Lakes. The kilted waitstaff serves traditional high tea from June 15 to Sept. (☎859-2231. Daily 2-4:30pm. CDN$25.) If high tea isn't in your budget, the view from the lobby is free—and just as satisfying.

The park's three campgrounds are much more affordable. **Belly River,** on Chief Mountain Hwy. outside the park entrance, has scenic and uncrowded primitive sites for CDN$10. **Crandell,** on Red Rock Canyon Rd., is situated in a forest area with sites for CDN$13. Camp with 200 of your best RV pals at **Townsite** in Waterton Park, which has showers and a lakeside vista, but no privacy. The walk-in sites are satisfactory and generally the last to fill (sites CDN$17, walk-in sites CDN$15, full hookup CDN$23). **Backcountry camping** is CDN$6 per person per night and requires a permit from the Visitors Center (call 859-5133 for a CDN$10 permit, up to 90 days in advance). The backcountry campsites are rarely full, and several, including beautiful **Crandell Lake,** are less than a 1hr. hike from the trailhead.

Travelers preferring to stay indoors should reserve one of the 21 comfy beds, with thick mattresses, at the **Waterton International Hostel (HI),** in the Waterton Lakes Lodge. One of the cushiest hostels around, amenities include a 15% discount at the health club and pool next door, laundry, and kitchen. (☎859-2151, ext. 2016. CDN$21, nonmember CDN$25, family room CDN$28/32 per person, ages 6-17 CDN$11/15.) The **Country Bakery and Lunch Counter,** 303 Windflower Ave., directly across the street from the Waterton Lakes Lodge, cooks up CDN$2.75 meat pies and CDN$3.50-5.50 waffles. (☎859-2181. Open M-Sa May-Sept. 7am-7pm.)

◪ OUTDOOR ACTIVITIES. Waterton Lakes includes 120 mi. of trails of varying difficulty. In addition to exploring the snowcapped peaks of Waterton Lakes, many of these trails link up with the network of trails in Glacier National Park. **Waterton-Glacier International Peace Park Hike,** a free guided hike, takes off every Saturday morning at 10am (July-Sept.) from the Bertha Trailhead, just south of the Waterton townsite, and crosses the border into the US. After 8.5 mi. of moderately easy hiking led by interpreters from both the US and Canada, participants can take a boat back from the Goat Haunt Ranger Station. The **Carthew-Alderson Trail** starts from Cameron Lake and leads through 18km of incredible views on its way back into town (11.8 mi. one-way, 1440 ft. elevation gain, 6-7hr.) A shorter day hike follows the shore of Cameron Lake. (2.3 mi., no elevation gain, approximately 1hr.) The **Hiker Shuttle** runs from Tamarack Village Sq. in town to Cameron Lake and other trailheads. (☎859-2378. Reservations strongly recommended. CDN$7.50) The popular **Crypt Lake Trail** leads past waterfalls in a narrow canyon, through a 20m natural tunnel, and after 6km arrives at icy, green Crypt Lake, which straddles the international border. (10½ mi. round-trip, 2100 ft. elevation gain, 5-6hr.) To get to the trailhead, you must take the **water taxi** run by **Waterton Shoreline Cruises** in Waterton Park (☎859-2362). The boat leaves four times a day (CDN$12, ages 4-12 CDN$6). The marina also runs a 2hr. boat tour of Upper Waterton Lake (open mid-May to mid-Sept.; CDN$22, ages 13-17 CDN$12, ages 4-12 CDN$8). Gear is available for purchase at **Waterton Outdoor Adventures** in the Tamarack Village Sq., which also sponsors guided hiking tours. (☎859-2378. Open 9am-6pm.) Horses are allowed on many trails. **Alpine Stables,** 1km north of the townsite, conducts trail rides. (☎859-2462. Open May-Sept. 1hr. ride CDN$17, 4hr. CDN$52.)

Fishing in Waterton requires a **license** (CDN$6 per week, CDN$13 per season), available from the park offices, campgrounds, warden stations, and service stations in the area. Lake trout cruise the depths of **Cameron** and **Waterton Lakes,** while northern pike prowl the weedy channels of **Maskinonge Lake.** Most of the backcountry lakes and creeks support rainbow and brook trout. Try the creek that spills from Cameron Lake, about 200m to the east of the parking lot, or hike 1½km to Crandell Lake for plentiful fish. Rent **rowboats, paddleboats,** or **canoes** at Cameron Lake (2 people $17 first hr., $14 per additional hr.; 4 people CDN$20/$17). On summer evenings at 8:30pm, take in a free **interpretive program** at the **Cameron Theater** in town or at the Crandell campsite. There are programs daily in summer at 8:30pm; the Visitors Center has a schedule.

WYOMING

The ninth-largest state in the Union, Wyoming is also the least populated. This is a place where livestock outnumber citizens, and men don cowboy hats and boots for real. Yet this rugged land was more than just a frontier during westward expansion. It was the first state to grant women the right to vote without later repealing it, and the first to have a national monument (Devils Tower, p. 669) and a national park (Yellowstone, p. 651) within its borders. Those expecting true Western flavor, however, will not be disappointed; Wyoming boasts the "Rodeo Capital of the World" (Cody, p. 666), where cowboys and cowgirls thrill audiences nearly every night throughout the summer with a genuine taste of the Old West.

◪ PRACTICAL INFORMATION

Capital: Cheyenne.

Visitor info: Wyoming Business Council Tourism Office, I-25 at College Dr., Cheyenne 82002 (☎307-777-7777 or 800-225-5996; www.wyomingtourism.org). Info center open daily 8am-5pm. **Dept. of Commerce, State Parks and Historic Sites Division,** 122 W. 25th St., Herschler Bldg., 1st fl. E., Cheyenne 82002 (☎307-777-6323; http://spacr.state.wy.us/sphs/index1.htm). Open M-F 8am-5pm. **Game and Fish Dept.,** 5400 Bishop Blvd., Cheyenne 82006 (☎307-777-4600; http://gf.state.wy.us). Open M-F 8am-5pm.

Hotlines: Mental Health Services, ☎800-252-1246. **Battered Women's Emergency Line,** ☎307-733-7466. **Gay & Lesbian of Wyoming United,** ☎307-778-7645.

Postal Abbreviation: WY. **Sales Tax:** 5%.

YELLOWSTONE NATIONAL PARK ☎307

Yellowstone National Park holds the distinction of being the world's first national park, as well as the largest park in the contiguous US. Yellowstone is also one of the largest active volcanoes in the world, with over 300 geysers and thousands of thermal fissures spewing steam and boiling water from beneath the earth's crust. The park's natural hot springs are popular among tourists and local wildlife alike: bison and elk gather around the thermal basins for warmth during the winter months.

Today, Yellowstone is still recovering from the devastating forest fires that burned over a third of the park in 1988. The destruction is especially evident in the western half of the park, where charred tree stumps line the roads. Despite the fires, however, Yellowstone has retained its rugged beauty, and the park's roads are clogged with RVs and tourists eagerly snapping photos of geysers and wildlife. With the reintroduction of wolves in 1995, all of the animals that lived in the Yellowstone area before the arrival of Europeans still roam the landscape, with the exception of the black-footed ferret.

✸ ORIENTATION

Yellowstone is huge; both Rhode Island and Delaware could fit within its boundaries. Yellowstone's roads are designed in a figure-eight configuration, with side roads leading to park entrances and some of the lesser-known attractions. The natural wonders that make the park famous (e.g. Old Faithful) are scattered along the Upper and Lower Loops. Construction and renovation of roads are planned for the next 80 years; call ahead or consult *Yellowstone Today*, available at the entrance, to find out which sections will be closed during your visit. Travel through the park can be arduously slow regardless of construction. The speed limit is 45 mph, and steep grades, tight curves, and frequent animal crossings increase driving delays.

Yellowstone can be a dangerous place. While roadside wildlife may look tame, these large beasts are unpredictable and easily startled, particularly mothers with babies. Stay at least 75 ft. from any animal and at least 300 ft. away from bears. Both black bears and grizzly bears inhabit Yellowstone; take all necessary precautions. Consult a ranger about proper precautions before entering the backcountry. If you should encounter a bear, inform a ranger for the safety of other visitors. Bison, regarded by many as mere overgrown cows, can actually travel at speeds of up to 30 mph; visitors are gored every year. Yellowstone's geothermal activity can also prove dangerous. The crust surrounding thermal basins, geysers, and hot springs is thin, and the water in these pools is boiling. Stay on the boardwalks at all times. Finally, watch for "widow makers," dead trees that can fall over at any time, especially during high winds.

▐ TRANSPORTATION

The bulk of Yellowstone National Park lies in the northwest corner of Wyoming, with slivers in Montana and Idaho. **West Yellowstone, MT,** and **Gardiner, MT,** are the most developed and expensive entrance points to the park. **Cooke City, MT,** the northeast entrance to the park, is a small rustic town nestled in the mountains. From Cooke City, you can pick up the **Beartooth Hwy.** (U.S. 212; open only in summer) and ascend the surrounding slopes for a breathtaking view of eastern Yellowstone. **Cody** (see p. 666) lies to the east of the park along Rte. 14/16/20. The southern entrance to the park is bordered by **Grand Teton National Park** (see p. 660). The **Entrance fee** is $20 for cars, $10 for pedestrians, and $15 for motorcycles; the pass is good for one week at Yellowstone and Grand Teton.

Buses: Greyhound: West Yellowstone Office Services, 132 Electric St., West Yellowstone (☎646-0001). To: Bozeman (2hr., 1 per day, $17); Salt Lake City (9hr., 1 per day, $51); and Boise (17hr., 1 per day, $99). **Powder River Transportation** departs from Cody (see p. 666).

Car Rental: Big Sky Car Rental, 415 Yellowstone Ave. (☎646-9564 or 800-426-7669), West Yellowstone, MT. $45 per day, 10% discount for 7 days or more, unlimited mi. Must be 21 with a credit card. Open May to mid-Oct. daily 8am-5pm.

Bike Rental: Yellowstone Bicycle and Video, 132 Madison Ave. (☎646-7815), West Yellowstone, MT. Mountain bikes with helmet and water $3.50 per hr., $12.50 per half-day, $19.50 per day. Open May-Oct. daily 8:30am-8:30pm; Nov.-Apr. 11am-7pm.

Horse Rides: AmFac (☎344-7311; call at least a day ahead), from Mammoth Hot Springs, Roosevelt Lodge, and Canyon Village. Late May to early Sept. $23.50 per hr., $35.50 per 2hr. From early June to early Sept., **stagecoach rides** ($6.75, ages 2-11 $5.50) are available at Roosevelt Lodge.

Tours: With time and transportation, you can do better on your own, but **AmFac Parks and Resorts** (☎344-7311) offers the cheapest tours. 8-9hr. bus tours of part of the park leave daily from Old Faithful Inn, Grant Village, Lake Yellowstone Hotel, Fishing Bridge RV Park, and Canyon Lodge and Bridge campground. ($26-34; ages 12-16 $14-16.)

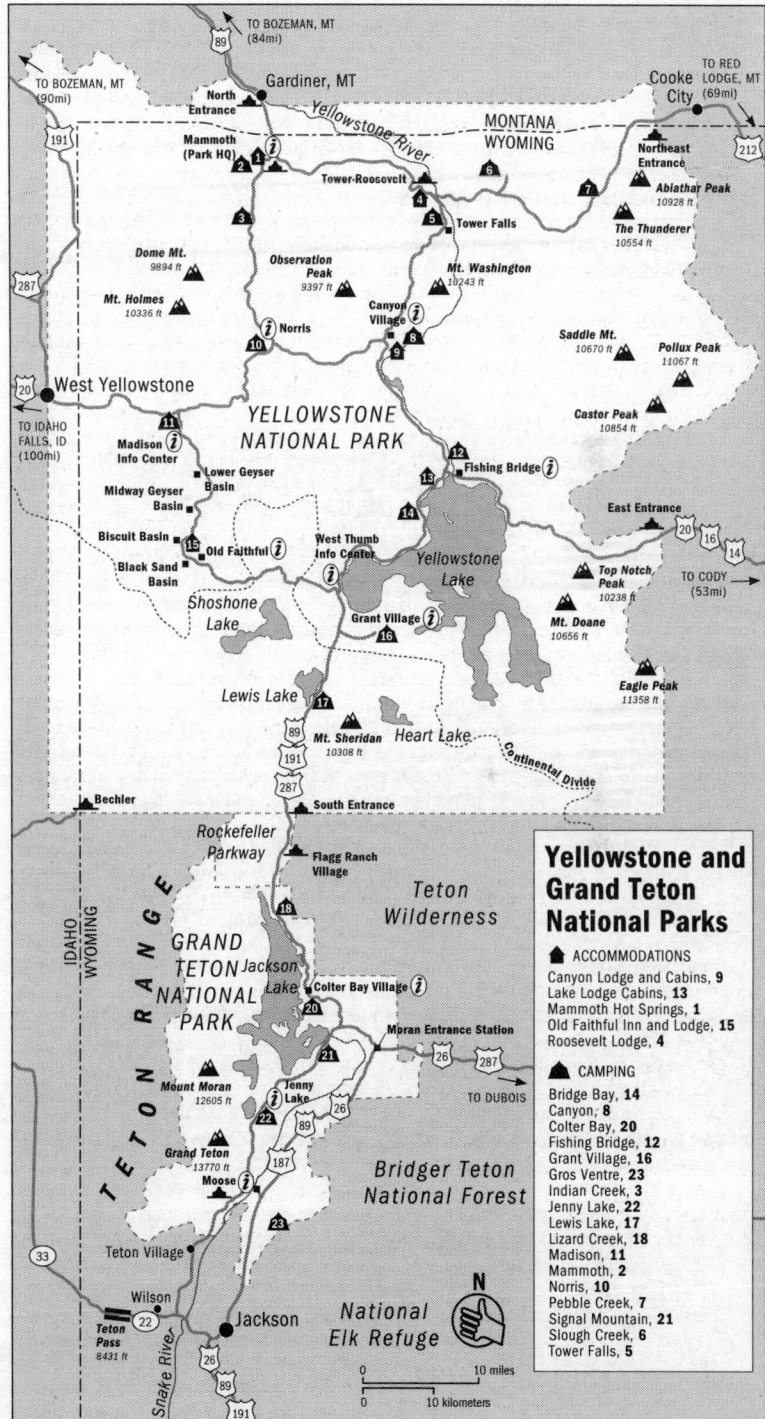

TO BOZEMAN, MT (84mi)
89

TO BOZEMAN, MT (90mi)

Gardiner, MT

Cooke City

TO RED LODGE, MT (69mi)

North Entrance

Yellowstone River

MONTANA
WYOMING

212

191

Mammoth (Park HQ) 1 2
i

Northeast Entrance

Tower-Roosevelt 4 6 7
5 Tower Falls

Abiathar Peak 10928 ft

The Thunderer 10554 ft

3

287

Dome Mt. 9894 ft

Observation Peak 9397 ft

Mt. Washington 10243 ft

Mt. Holmes 10336 ft

Norris i
10

Canyon Village i
8
9

Saddle Mt. 10670 ft

Pollux Peak 11067 ft

West Yellowstone

20

TO IDAHO FALLS, ID (100mi)

YELLOWSTONE NATIONAL PARK

Castor Peak 10854 ft

Madison Info Center i
11

Lower Geyser Basin

Midway Geyser Basin

Biscuit Basin

Old Faithful i
15

Black Sand Basin

Shoshone Lake

West Thumb Info Center i

Fishing Bridge i
12
13

14

East Entrance

20 16 14

TO CODY (53mi)

Yellowstone Lake

Top Notch Peak 10238 ft

Grant Village i
16

Mt. Doane 10656 ft

Lewis Lake

17

89
191

Mt. Sheridan 10308 ft

Heart Lake

Eagle Peak 11358 ft

Continental Divide

287

Bechler

South Entrance

Rockefeller Parkway

Flagg Ranch Village

Teton Wilderness

IDAHO
WYOMING

TETON RANGE

GRAND TETON NATIONAL PARK

18

Jackson Lake

Colter Bay Village i

20

Moran Entrance Station

21

Mount Moran 12605 ft

Jenny Lake i
22

26 287

TO DUBOIS

Grand Teton 13770 ft

Moose i

89
187

Bridger Teton National Forest

33

Teton Village

23

Wilson

Teton Pass 8431 ft

22

Jackson

National Elk Refuge

N

Snake River

26
89
191

Scale
0   10 miles
0   10 kilometers

Yellowstone and Grand Teton National Parks

▲ ACCOMMODATIONS

Canyon Lodge and Cabins, 9
Lake Lodge Cabins, 13
Mammoth Hot Springs, 1
Old Faithful Inn and Lodge, 15
Roosevelt Lodge, 4

▲ CAMPING

Bridge Bay, 14
Canyon, 8
Colter Bay, 20
Fishing Bridge, 12
Grant Village, 16
Gros Ventre, 23
Indian Creek, 3
Jenny Lake, 22
Lewis Lake, 17
Lizard Creek, 18
Madison, 11
Mammoth, 2
Norris, 10
Pebble Creek, 7
Signal Mountain, 21
Slough Creek, 6
Tower Falls, 5

ROCKY MOUNTAINS

Full-day tours around the park's figure-eight road system also available, leaving from Gardiner, MT, and Mammoth Hot Springs. ($36-38; ages 12-16 $18.) **Grayline Tours** runs from West Yellowstone through both loops. Free pickup from area motels and campgrounds. (☎406-646-9374 or 800-523-3102. $40.) Alternatively, **Buffalo Bus Lines,** 415 Yellowstone Ave. (☎406-646-9564 or 800-426-7669), in West Yellowstone, tours Lower Loop every day and Upper Loop M, W, and F ($38, under 17 $25).

⏻ PRACTICAL INFORMATION

The park's high season extends from about mid-June to mid-September. If you visit during this period, expect large crowds, clogged roads, and filled-to-capacity motels and campsites. Most of the park shuts down from November to mid-April, then gradually reopens as the snow melts.

Over 95% (almost 2 million acres) of Yellowstone is backcountry. To venture overnight into the wilds of Yellowstone, you need a free **backcountry permit** from a ranger station (near all major Visitors Centers). There is almost always space available in the backcountry, although the more popular areas fill up July and August. You can reserve a permit in person between 24 and 48hr. in advance. To reserve a permit ahead of time ($20), write to the **Backcountry Office** (P.O. Box 168, Yellowstone National Park 82190; ☎344-2160 or 344-2163; open daily 8am-5pm) to receive a **trip planning worksheet.** Before heading into the backcountry, visitors must watch a short film outlining safety regulations. No firearms, pets, or mountain bikes are permitted in the backcountry. In many backcountry areas campfires are not permitted, and in particularly dry years none may be permitted at all; plan on bringing a stove and related cooking gear. Consult a ranger before embarking on a trail; they can offer tips on how to avoid bears, ice, and other natural hindrances. The **Backcountry Trip Planner,** available at Visitors Centers and the Backcountry Office, contains information on trails, campsites, and necessary safety precautions.

Fishing and **boating** are both allowed within the park, provided you follow a number of regulations. Permits are required for fishing; areas may be closed due to feeding patterns of bears, and the park's three native species are catch-and-release only (permits age 16 and older $10 for 10-day pass, $20 for season; available at rangers stations and Visitors Centers). In addition to the lake, popular fishing spots include the Madison and Firehole rivers; the Firehole is available for fly fishing only. To go boating or even floating on the lake, you'll need a **boating permit** (motorized vessels $10 for 10-day pass, $20 for season; motor-free boats $5 for 10-day pass, $10 for season), available at backcountry offices (check *Yellowstone Today*), Bridge Bay marina, a few park entrances, and the Lewis Lake campground. **AmFac** (☎344-7311) rents row boats ($7 per hr.), outboards ($30 per hr.), and dockslips ($12-18 per night) at Bridge Bay Marina from mid-June to early September. Parts of Yellowstone Lake and some other lakes are limited to non-motorized boating; inquire at the Lake Village or Grant Village ranger stations for more advice.

Visitor info: Most regions of the park have their own central station. All centers offer general information and backcountry permits, but each has distinct hiking and camping regulations and regional exhibits. All stations are usually open late May to early Sept. daily 8am-7pm; Albright and Old Faithful are open through the winter.

Albright Visitors Center (☎344-2263) at Mammoth Hot Springs: history of Yellowstone Park and the beginnings of the National Park idea.

Grant Village (☎242-2650): wilderness and the 1988 fire.

Fishing Bridge (☎242-2450): wildlife and Yellowstone Lake.

Canyon (☎242-2550): bison; **Old Faithful** (☎545-2750): geysers; **Norris** (☎344-2812): geothermic features of the park.

Info centers: Madison (☎344-2821; open 8am-7pm), and at **West Thumb** (open 9am-5pm), on the southern edge of the Lake. **West Yellowstone Chamber of Commerce,** 30 Yellowstone Ave. (☎406-646-7701 or 646-9488 for lodging info), West Yellowstone, MT, 2 blocks west of the park entrance. Open late May to early Sept. daily 8am-8pm; early Sept. to late May M-F 8am-4pm.

General Park information: ☎344-7381, TDD 344-2386.

Radio information: Tune in to 1610AM for park info.

Medical services: Lake Clinic, Pharmacy, and **Hospital** (☎242-7241), across the road from the Lake Yellowstone Hotel. Clinic open late May to mid-Sept. daily 8:30am-8:30pm. Emergency room open May-Sept. 24hr. **Old Faithful Clinic** (☎545-7325), near the Old Faithful Inn. Open early May to mid-Oct. daily 8:30am-5pm; May and mid-Sept. to mid-Oct. open M-W and Sa-Su. **Mammoth Hot Springs Clinic** (☎344-7965), open year-round M-F 8:30am-1pm and 2-5pm. The **Clinic at West Yellowstone,** 236 Yellowstone Ave. (☎406-646-7668), in West Yellowstone. Open late May to early Sept. M-F 8:30am-5:30pm, Sa 8am-2pm; off-season hours vary.

Disabled Services: All entrances, Visitors Centers, and ranger stations offer the *Visitor Guide to Accessible Features.* Fishing Bridge RV Park, Madison, Bridge Bay, Canyon, and Grant campgrounds have accessible sites and restrooms; Lewis Lake and Slough Creek each have sites. Write the **Accessibility Coordinator,** P.O. Box 168, Yellowstone National Park, WY, 82190, for more info, or call 344-2018 or (TDD only) 344-2386.

Post Office: There are 5 post offices in the park at **Lake, Old Faithful, Canyon, Grant,** and **Mammoth Hot Springs** (☎344-7764). All open M-F 8:30am-5pm. Specify which station at Yellowstone National Park when addressing mail. **ZIP code:** 82190. In **West Yellowstone, MT:** 209 Grizzly Ave. (☎406-646-7704). Open M-F 8:30am-5pm, Sa 8-10am. **ZIP code:** 59758.

Area codes: 307 (in the park), 406 (in West Yellowstone, Cooke City, and Gardiner, MT). In text, 307 unless otherwise noted.

🛏🍴 ACCOMMODATIONS AND FOOD

Camping is much cheaper, but affordable indoor lodging can be found with advanced preparation. Lodging within the park can be hard to come by on short notice but is often a better deal than the motels along the outskirts of the park. During peak months, the cost of a motel room can skyrocket to $100, while in-park lodging remains relatively inexpensive. Without reservations, affordable lodgings within the park are scarce, and nearby motels fill early in the afternoon.

IN THE PARK

AmFac Parks and Resorts (☎344-7311; www.amfac.com) controls all accommodations within the park, employing a unique code to distinguish between cabins: "Roughrider" means no bath, no facilities; "Budget" offers a sink; "Economy" guarantees a toilet and sink; "Pioneer" offers a shower, toilet, and sink; "Frontier" is bigger, more plush; and "Western" is the biggest and most plush. Facilities are located close to cabins without private bath. Reserve cabins well in advance of the June to September tourist season. Buying food at the restaurants, snack bars, and cafeterias in the park can be expensive; stick to the **general stores** at each lodging location. The stores at Fishing Bridge, Lake, Grant Village, and Canyon sell lunch-counter style food. (Open daily 7:30am-10pm, though times may vary by around 30min.)

Roosevelt Lodge, in the north of the park, 19 mi. north of Canyon. A favorite of Teddy Roosevelt, who seems to have frequented every motel and saloon west of the Mississippi. Provides some of the cheapest and most scenic indoor accommodations around, and is located in a relatively isolated section of the park. Roughrider cabins with wood-burning stoves $46. Frontier cabins with full bath $84.

Mammoth Hot Springs, 18 mi. west of Roosevelt area, near the north entrance, makes a good base for early-morning wildlife sighting excursions. Lattice-sided Budget cabins $52. Frontier cabins (some with porches) from $84. Hotel room without bath $63.

Old Faithful Inn and Lodge, 30 mi. southwest of the west Yellowstone entrance, is a sea awash with ice cream-toting tourists and RVs, but is conveniently located. Pleasant Budget cabins $42. Frontier cabins $65. Well-appointed hotel rooms without bath from $68, with private bath $91.

Lake Lodge Cabins, 4 mi. south of Fishing Bridge, is a cluster of cabins from the 20s and 50s, all just a stone's throw from Yellowstone Lake. Pioneer cabins $50. Larger Western cabins $111. Next door, **Lake Yellowstone Hotel and Cabins** has yellow Frontier cabins with no lake view for $83.

Canyon Lodge and Cabins, 15 mi. north of Fishing Bridge, overlooking the Grand Canyon of Yellowstone (as the name implies). Less authentic and more expensive than Roosevelt Lodge's cabins, but centrally located and more popular among tourists. Pioneer cabins $54. Frontier cabins $78. Western cabins $111.

WEST YELLOWSTONE, MT

Guarding the west entrance of the park, West Yellowstone capitalizes on the hordes of tourists who pass through en route to the park. The closest of the border towns to popular park attractions, West Yellowstone has numerous budget motels, with more reasonable prices than Gardiner.

Grab an inexpensive breakfast or lunch at the **Running Bear Pancake House,** at the corner of Madison and Hayden (☎406-646-7703; open daily 7am-2pm) or stockpile provisions at the **Food Round-Up Grocery Store,** 107 Dunraven St. (☎406-646-7501. Open in summer daily 7am-10pm; in winter 7am-9pm.) Prepare yourself for a day at the park at the **Timberline Cafe,** 135 Yellowstone Ave., which specializes in homemade pies (and satisfying hungry customers). Burgers are $5-7.50, while sandwiches and omelettes run $6-7. (☎646-9349. Open daily 6:30am-10pm.)

West Yellowstone International Hostel (AAIH/Rucksackers), 139 Yellowstone Ave. (☎406-646-7745 or 800-838-7745), at the **Madison Hotel,** provides the best indoor budget accommodations around the park. The friendly staff and welcoming lobby make travelers feel at home. Internet access $5 per hr. Open late May to mid-Oct. Dorms $20; private singles and doubles $40.

Lazy G Motel, 123 Hayden St. (☎406-646-7586), has an affable staff and spacious 70s-style rooms featuring queen-sized beds, refrigerators, and TVs. Singles $43; doubles $53, with kitchenette $53-63.

Ho Hum Motel, 126 Canyon (☎406-646-7746), is a straightforward motel that offers clean, comfortable rooms with 1 queen bed for $40 and 2 queen beds for $50.

GARDINER, MT

Marking the original entrance to the park, Gardiner is smaller and less touristy than West Yellowstone; it is also significantly more pricey. The town clusters along U.S. 89 and has a great view of the park's northern fringe. Load up on cheap food at **Food Farm,** on U.S. 89 across from the Super 8. (☎406-848-7524. Open M-Sa 7am-9pm, Su 8am-8pm.) A few blocks west on U.S. 89, **Helen's Corral Drive-In** rounds up killer ½ lb. burgers. (Open in summer daily 11am-11pm. Burgers $3.75-6.75.)

The Town Cafe and Motel (☎406-848-7322), on Park St. across from the park's northern entrance. These wood-paneled, carpeted rooms are one of the best deals in town. TVs but no phones. Singles $45, Oct.-May $35; doubles $55/$45.

Jim Bridger Court Modern Cabins (☎406-848-7371), on U.S. 89, has clean, no-frills cabins with a sheltered front stoops and a terrific view. TVs but no phones. 1 queen bed $50, 2 queen beds $65.

Hillcrest Cottages (☎406-848-7353 or 800-970-7353), on U.S. 89 across from the Exxon, rents out deluxe cabins with kitchenettes. Open May to early Sept. Singles $60; doubles $70; $6 per additional adult, $2 per additional child under 18.

COOKE CITY, MT

Cooke City is located at the northeast corner of the park. The Nez Percé slipped right by the US cavalry here, Lewis and Clark deemed the area impassable, and even today few people visit this rugged little town. Nonetheless, Cooke City is a great location for exploring the remote backcountry of Yellowstone and is conveniently situated between the park and the junction of two scenic drives: the **Beartooth Hwy (Rte. 212)** and the **Chief Joseph Scenic Hwy (Rte. 296),** which traces the route traveled by the Nez Percé from Cooke City to Cody, WY.

The **Grizzly Pad Grill and Cabins,** on Rte. 212 on the eastern side of town offers the Grizzly Pad Special—an incredible milkshake, fries, and a large cheeseburger for only $7. (☎406-838-2161. Open in summer daily 7am-9pm; off-season hours vary. closed mid-Oct. to late Dec. and mid-Apr. to late May.) Popular among locals, **The**

Miner's Saloon, on Rte. 212 downtown, is the best place to go for a buffalo burger ($6.50) and a frosty Moose Drool beer. (☎406-838-2214. Open daily noon-2am.)

Yellowstone Yurt Hostel (☎406-838-2349), at the corner of W. Broadway and Montana St. (turn north onto Republic St. from U.S. 212). Rustic lodging in a round tent with a skylight, wood stove, and 6 bunks. $14 buys a bunk, a hot shower, and use of an outdoor kitchen. Bring a sleeping bag. Check-in before 10pm; call ahead for late arrivals.

Antler's Lodge (☎406-838-2432). Built in 1936, each cabin has its own personality and a great mountain view. Ernest Hemingway spent several nights editing *For Whom the Bell Tolls* here. Singles without kitchens $45; doubles $55.

◤ CAMPGROUNDS

Campsites fill quickly during the summer months, so be prepared to make alternate arrangements. Call **Park Headquarters** (☎344-7381) for info on campsite vacancies. **AmFac,** P.O. Box 165, Yellowstone National Park 82190 (☎344-7311), runs five of the 12 developed campgrounds within the park: **Canyon, Grant Village, Madison, Bridge Bay** (all $15), and **Fishing Bridge RV** ($28; RVs only). AmFac accepts advance reservations (☎344-7311) as well as same-day reservations (☎344-7901). Reservations are accepted up to two years in advance, and during peak summer months (especially on weekends and holidays) all available sites may be reserved beforehand. On quieter days it is possible to reserve a site before 9am. The two largest AmFac campgrounds, **Grant Village** (425 sites) and **Bridge Bay** (430 sites), are your best bet for last-minute reservations.

The 7 National Park campgrounds do not accept advance reservations. During the summer, these smaller campgrounds generally fill by 10am, and finding a site can be frustrating. Check-out time is 10am, and the best window for claiming a campsite is between 8 and 10am. Two of the most beautiful campgrounds are **Slough Creek Campground** (29 sites, 10 mi. northeast of Tower Jct.; open late May to Oct.; $10) and **Pebble Creek Campground** (32 sites; no RVs; open mid-June to early Sept.; $10). Both are located in the northeast corner of the park, between Tower Falls and the Northeast Entrance—generally the least congested area—and offer relatively isolated sites and good fishing. You can also try **Lewis Lake** (85 sites; $10), halfway between West Thumb and the South Entrance, or **Tower Falls** (32 sites; $10), between the Northeast entrance and Mammoth Hot Spring. **Norris** (116 sites; open late May-late Sept.; $12); **Indian Creek,** between the Norris Geyser Basin and Mammoth Hot Springs (75 sites; open mid-June to mid-Sept.; $10); and **Mammoth** (85 sites; open year-round; $12) are less scenic but still great places to camp. Campgrounds at Grant Village, Fishing Bridge, and Canyon have coin laundries ($1.25 wash, $1 dry) and pay showers ($3). The lodges at Mammoth and Old Faithful have showers for $3 (towels and shampoo included) but no laundry facilities.

◉ SIGHTS

AmFac (☎344-7311) offers tours, horseback rides, and chuckwagon dinners. However, these outdoor activities are expensive, and—given enough time—Yellowstone is best explored on foot. Visitors Centers give out informative self-guiding tour pamphlets with maps for each of the park's main attractions (25¢, except for Old Faithful, Mammoth Hot Springs, and Canyon 50¢). Trails to these sights are accessible from the road via walkways, usually extending ¼ to 1½ mi. into the various natural environments.

Yellowstone is set apart from other National Parks and Forests in the Rockies by its **geothermal features**—the park protects the largest geothermic area in the world. The bulk of these geothermal wonders can be found on the western side of the park between Mammoth Hot Springs in the north and Old Faithful in the south. The most dramatic thermal fissures are the **geysers.** Incredibly hot molten rock, close to the surface of the earth in the geothermic areas superheats water until it boils and bubbles and eventually builds up enough pressure to burst through the cracks with steamy force. The extremely volatile nature of this area means that attractions may change, appear, or disappear due to forces beyond human control.

ROCKY MOUNTAINS

Beware: the crust around many of Yellowstone's thermal features is thin, and boiling, acidic water lies just beneath the surface. Stay on the marked paths or, in the backcountry, keep a good distance from hot springs and fumaroles.

While bison-jams and bear-gridlock may make wildlife seem more of a nuisance than an attraction, wildlife viewing in Yellowstone affords a unique opportunity to see a number of native species co-existing in their natural environment. The best times for viewing are early morning and just before dark, as most animals nap in the shade during the hot midday. The road between Tower-Roosevelt and the northeast entrance, in the Lamar Valley, is one of the best places to see wolves and grizzlies (among other species). Consult a ranger for more specific advice.

OLD FAITHFUL AREA

Yellowstone's trademark attraction, Old Faithful is the most predictable of the large geysers and has consistently pleased audiences since its discovery in 1870. Eruptions typically occur every 45min. to 2hr. (average 80min.) and are usually 106 ft. to 184 ft. in height. Eruptions last anywhere from 1½ to 5min. Predictions for the next eruption, usually accurate to within 10min., are posted at the Old Faithful Visitors Center. Old Faithful lies in the **Upper Geyser Basin,** 16 mi. south of the Madison area and 20 mi. west of Grant Village. Numerous other geysers and hot springs flow in this area and trails connect them all. The spectacular **Morning Glory Pool** is an easy 1½ mi. from Old Faithful, and provides an interesting diversion between eruptions.

FIREHOLE RIVER

Between Old Faithful and Madison, along the Firehole River, lay the **Midway Geyser Basin** and the **Lower Geyser Basin.** Many of these geysers are visible from the side of the road, although stopping for a closer look is highly recommended. The **Excelsior Geyser Crater,** a large, steaming lake created by a powerful geyser blast, and the **Grand Prismatic Spring,** the largest hot spring in the park, sit about 5 mi. north of Old Faithful and are well worth the trip. Eight miles north of Old Faithful gurgles the **Fountain Paint Pot,** a bubbling pool of hot milky mud. All four types of geothermal activity present in Yellowstone (geysers, mudpots, hot springs, and fumaroles) are found along the trails of the Firehole River. There is a strong temptation to wash off the grime of camping in the hot water, but swimming in the hot springs is prohibited. You can **swim** in the Firehole River, three-fourths of the way up Firehole Canyon Dr. (just south of Madison Jct.), but prepare for a chill; the name of the river is quite deceiving. Call park info (☎344-7381) to make sure the river is open.

NORRIS GEYSER BASIN

Fourteen miles north of Madison and 21 mi. south of Mammoth, the colorful **Norris Geyser Basin** is both the oldest and the hottest active thermal zone in the park. The geyser has been erupting hot water at temperatures up to 459°F for over 115,000 years. **Echinus,** in the Black Basin, is the largest known acid-water geyser, erupting 40-60 ft. every 35-90min. Its neighbor, **Steamboat,** is the tallest active geyser in the world, erupting over 300 ft. for anywhere from 3-40min. However, Steamboat's eruptions are entirely unpredictable: after nine years of inactivity, Steamboat surprised a group of campers on May 2, 2000.

MAMMOTH HOT SPRINGS

Shifting water sources, malleable limestone deposits, and temperature-sensitive, multicolored bacterial growth create the most rapidly changing natural structure in the park: the hot spring terraces resembling huge wedding cakes at **Mammoth Hot Springs,** 21 mi. to the north of the Norris Basin and 19 mi. west of Tower. On the day of your visit, ask a local ranger where to find the most active springs. Also ask about area trails, which feature some of the park's best wildlife viewing. AmFac offers **horse rides** (see **Practical Information,** p. 652) just south of the Hot Springs, and **swimming** is permitted in the **Boiling River,** 2½ mi. north. Call the info line (☎344-7381) to make sure that this area is open.

GRAND CANYON

The east side's featured attraction, the **Grand Canyon of the Yellowstone,** wears rusty red and orange hues, created by hot water acting on the volcanic rock. The canyon is 800-1200 ft. deep and 1500-4000 ft. wide. For a close-up view of the mighty **Lower Falls** (308 ft.), hike down the short but steep **Uncle Tom's Trail** (over 300 steps). **Artist Point** on the southern rim and **Inspiration Point** on the northern rim offer broader canyon vistas and both are accessible from the road between Canyon and Fishing Bridge. Keep an eye out for bighorn sheep along the canyon's rim. At dawn or dusk, the bear-viewing area (at the intersection of Northern Rim and Tower roads) should have you dusting off your binoculars. **Horse rides** are available at Canyon, as well as in the Tower-Roosevelt area 19 mi. north (see **Practical Information,** p. 652).

YELLOWSTONE LAKE AREA

Situated in the southeast corner of the park, **Yellowstone Lake** is the largest high-altitude lake in North America and home to a recovery program for the cutthroat trout. While the surface of the lake may appear calm, geologists have found evidence of geothermal features at the bottom. **AmFac** offers lake cruises that leave from the marina at Bridge Bay. (☎344-7311. Open early June to mid-Sept. daily. 5-7 per day. $9, ages 2-11 $5.) Geysers and hot springs in **West Thumb** dump an average of 3100 gallons of water into the lake per day. Notwithstanding this thermal boost, the temperature of the lake remains quite chilly, averaging 45°F during the summer. Early visitors to the park cooked freshly-caught trout in the boiling water of the **Fishing Cone,** but this is no longer permitted. Due to efforts to help the endangered cutthroat population, fishing off the **Fishing Bridge** is now forbidden. The sulphurous odors of **Mud Volcano** can be distinguished from miles away, but these unique turbulent mudpots are worth the assault on your nose. Located 6 mi. north of Fishing Bridge and 10 mi. south of Canyon Jct., the unusual geothermal features have descriptive names such as **Dragon's Mouth, Sour Lake,** and **Black Dragon's Cauldron.**

OFF THE (EXTREMELY WELL) BEATEN PATH

Most visitors to Yellowstone never get out of their cars and miss out on over 1200 mi. of trails in the park. Options for exploring Yellowstone's more pristine areas range from short dayhikes to long backcountry trips. When planning a hike, pick up a topographical trail map ($8-9) at any Visitors Center and ask a ranger to describe the network of trails. Some trails are poorly marked, so allow extra time (at least 1hr.) in case you get lost. The 1988 fires scarred over a third of the park; hikers should consult rangers and maps on which areas are burned. Burned areas have less shade; hikers should equip themselves with hats, extra water, and sunscreen.

In addition to the self-guiding trails at major attractions, many worthwhile sights are only a few miles off the main road. The **Fairy Falls Trail,** near Old Faithful, offers a unique perspective on the Midway Geyser Basin. The trail begins in the parking lot marked Fairy Falls just south of Midway Geyser Basin and is 5¼ mi. round-trip. The trail to the top of **Mt. Washburn** is enhanced by an enclosed observation area and offers sweeping views of the park. This trail begins at Chittenden Rd. or Dunraven Pass parking areas and totals about 6 mi. round-trip. The free *Backcountry Trip Planner* and rangers can help plan more extended trips.

SCENIC DRIVE: NORTH FORK DRIVE

Linking Yellowstone National Park with Cody, WY, the **Buffalo Bill Cody** scenic byway, also known as U.S. 14/16/20, bridges the majestic peaks of the Absaroka Mountains (*ab-SOR-ka*) with the sagebrush lands of the Wyoming plains. This 52 mi. drive winds through the canyon created by the North Fork of the Shoshone River and is a spectacular departure from or entrance to Yellowstone. The high granite walls and sedimentary formations of the **Shoshone Canyon** are noticeable from the road, as is the smell of sulfur from the DeMaris springs located in the Shoshone River. Once the world's tallest dam, the **Buffalo Bill Dam Visitors Center and Reservoir** celebrates man's ability to control the flow of water to fit human needs. Built between 1904 and 1910, the Buffalo Bill Dam measures 350 ft. in height. (Visi-

tors Center ☎527-6076. Open May and Sept. daily 8am-6pm, June-Aug. 8am-8pm.)
West of the dam, **strange rock formations,** created millions of years ago by volcanic
eruptions in the Absarokas, dot the dusty hillsides. Sagebrush and small juniper
trees gradually lead into the thick pine cover of the **Shoshone National Forest,** the
nation's first national forest. This area, known as the **Wapiti Valley,** is home to over
18 dude ranches. Keep an eye out for a variety of wildlife, including grizzly bears,
while traveling through the valley. The **East Entrance** to Yellowstone National Park
guards the west end of the scenic byway and is closed in winter.

The **Chief Joseph Scenic Hwy (Rte. 296)** connects Cooke City, MT, to Cody, WY,
passing through rugged sagebrush-covered mountains across the summit of Dead
Indian Hill. This scenic byway traces the route traveled by the Nez Percé Indians in
skillfully evading the US army in the summer of 1877. From Cody, follow the Buffalo Bill Cody scenic byway back into eastern Yellowstone, completing a spectacular drive through the western half of Wyoming.

GRAND TETON NATIONAL PARK   ☎ 307

One of the most impressive skylines in the Rockies, twelve Teton peaks tower over
12,000 feet. The Grand Tetons are the youngest mountains in the entire Rocky
Mountain system, their jagged peaks sculpted by glaciers more than 3000 feet thick.
When French trappers from the Hudson Bay Company first observed the three
most prominent peaks—South Teton, Grand Teton, and Mt. Teewinot—they
dubbed the mountains *"Les trois tetons,"* meaning "the three breasts." Later discovering that the three nipples were surrounded by numerous smaller peaks, the
erstwhile Frenchmen renamed the range *"Les grands tetons."* Grand Teton
National Park was officially established in 1929, and delights hikers with miles of
strenuous trails and steep rock cliffs along the range's eastern face.

▓▓ ORIENTATION AND PRACTICAL INFORMATION

Scenic Teton vistas are accessible from Rte. 89, which runs the length of the park,
connecting Yellowstone to Jackson. Teton Park Rd. gives a closer look at the peaks
between Jackson Lake Jct. and Moose Jct. and provides access to Jackson Lake.
There are two entrance stations to the park, at Moose and at Moran Jct. The stretch
of Rte. 89 that runs between Moran Jct. and Jackson does not pass through either
entrance, offering excellent (and free) views of the Tetons. Those who elect to
enter the park pay an **entrance fee** of $20 per car, $10 per pedestrian or bicycle, and
$15 per motorcycle. The pass is good for seven days in the Tetons and Yellowstone.

To **backcountry camp** between January 1 and May 15 in a mountain canyon or on
the shores of a lake, advance reservations are required. To make a reservation, submit an itinerary and $15 to the **permit office.** (☎739-3309 or 739-3397; fax 739-3438.
Write to Grand Teton National Park, Moose HQ, Attn.: Permits, P.O. Drawer 170,
Moose 83012.) After May 15, three-fourths of all backcountry spots are available
first come, first served; get a free permit up to 24hr. in advance at the Moose, Colter
Bay (permit office open daily 8am-6pm), or Jenny Lake Visitors Centers. The staff
can also help plan routes and find campsites. Wood fires are only permitted within
existing fire grates; be sure to check with rangers before singing 'round the campfire. Snow often remains at high-elevation campsites into July, and the weather can
become severe (deadly to those who are unprepared) any time of the year. Severe
weather gear is strongly advised.

> **Public Transit: Grand Teton Lodge Co.** (☎543-2811 or 800-628-9988) runs in summer
> from Colter Bay to Jackson Lake Lodge ($3 each way). Shuttles also run to the Jackson
> Hole airport (5 per day, $20) and Jackson (3 per day, $15).

> **Visitor info:** Visitors Centers and campgrounds have free copies of the *Teewinot* newspa-
> per which has info on special programs, hiking, camping and news. For general info,
> info on ranger-led activities, and a visitor's packet, contact **Park Headquarters** (☎739-
> 3600) or write the **Superintendent,** Grand Teton National Park, P.O. Drawer 170, Moose
> WY 83012.

Moose Visitors Center (☎ 739-3399), Teton Park Rd., at the southern tip of the park, ½ mi. west of Moose Jct. Open early June to early Sept. 8am-7pm; early Sept. to mid-May 8am-5pm.

Jenny Lake Visitors Center (☎ 739-3392), next to the Jenny Lake Campground. Open early June to early Sept. daily 8am-7pm, early Sept. to early Oct. 8am-5pm.

Colter Bay Visitors Center (☎ 739-3594), on Jackson Lake in the northern part of the park. Open early June to early Sept. daily 8am-8pm; early May to mid-May and early Sept. to early Oct. 8am-5pm; late May to early June 8am-7pm.

Info lines: Weather, ☎ 739-3611. **Wyoming Hwy. Info Center,** ☎ 733-1731. **Wyoming Dept. of Transportation,** ☎ 888-996-7623. **Road Report,** ☎ 336-6600 or 888-996-7623. **Backcountry Permits and River Info,** ☎ 739-3309.

Emergency: Sheriff's office, ☎ 733-2331. **Park dispatch,** ☎ 739-3300.

Medical Services: Grand Teton Medical Clinic, Jackson Lake Lodge (☎ 543-2514, after hours 733-8002). Open late May to mid-Oct. daily 10am-6pm. **St. John's Hospital,** 625 E. Broadway (☎ 733-3636), in Jackson.

Post Office: In Moose (☎ 733-3336), across from the Park HQ. Open M-F 9am-1pm and 1:30-5pm, Sa 11am-12:30pm. **ZIP code:** 83102. **Area code:** 307.

▉ CAMPGROUNDS AND BACKCOUNTRY CAMPING

To stay in the Tetons without emptying your savings account, find a tent and pitch it; call 739-3603 for camping info. The park service maintains five campgrounds, all first come, first served. Campsites are generally open mid-May to late Sept. or early Oct. (vehicle sites $12, bicycle campsites $3). Maximum length of stay is 14 days at all sites except Jenny Lake (7 day maximum stay). All have restrooms, cold water, fire rings, dump stations, and picnic tables. RVs are welcome at all the campsites, with the exception of Jenny Lake, but only Colter Bay (sites $31) and Flagg Ranch sites have hookups. There is a maximum of six people and one vehicle per site, but Colter Bay and Gros Ventre accept larger groups. The 49 sites at **Jenny Lake** are among the most beautifully developed in the US. Mt. Teewinot towers 6000 ft. above tents pitched at the edge of the lake. These sites usually fill before 8am; get there early. **Lizard Creek,** closer to Yellowstone than the Tetons, has 60 spacious, secluded sites along the northern shore of Jackson Lake. The campsites fill up by about 2pm. While not exactly a wilderness experience, the 350 crowded sites at **Colter Bay** offer the most amenities, including $3 showers, a grocery store, a laundromat, and two restaurants. At **Signal Mountain,** along the southern shore of Jackson Lake, the 86 sites are roomier and more secluded than at Colter Bay. The campground is usually full by 10am. **Gros Ventre** is the biggest campground (360 sites, 5 group sites), located along the edge of the Gros Ventre River, close to Jackson. However, the Tetons are hidden from view by Blacktail Butte. The campsite rarely fills and is the best bet for late arrivals. (☎ 739-3516; Jan.-May 739-3473.)

▉▉ ACCOMMODATIONS AND FOOD

The Grand Teton Lodge Co. runs all indoor accommodations in the park. (Reservations ☎ 543-2811 or 800-628-9988; or write **Reservations Manager,** Grand Teton Lodge Co., P.O. Box 240, Moran 83013. Deposits often required.) Most lodges are pricey, but there are two options for affordable, rustic cabins at Colter Bay, open late May to early October. **Colter Bay Tent Cabins** are the cheapest, but provide the least shelter from the elements. The cabins are charming but primitive log and canvas shelters with dusty floors, wood-burning stoves, tables, and bunks. Sleeping bags, cots, and blankets are available for rent. (☎ 543-2828. Office open early June to early Sept. 24hr. Tent cabins $33 for 2; each additional person $4. Restrooms and $3 showers nearby.) **Colter Bay Log Cabins** maintains 208 quaint log cabins near Jackson Lake. The cabins with shared baths are probably the best deal in the entire Jackson Hole area; book early. Inquire with the staff about local hikes and excursions. (☎ 543-2828. Open late May to late Sept. 2-person cabins with semi-private bath from $33, with private bath $68-98; 2-room cabins with bath $102-125.)

ROCKY MOUNTAINS

The best way to eat in the Tetons is to bring your own food. Non-perishables are available at **Dornan's General Store** in Moose. (☎733-2415. Open daily 8am-8pm.) Jackson has an **Albertson's** supermarket, 105 Buffalo Way, at the intersection of W. Broadway and Rte. 22. (☎733-5950. Open daily 6am-midnight.) The **Chuck Wagon Restaurant,** in Colter Bay, serves breakfast (buffet $8.50) and dinner and will cook your catch of the day for $10, provided you deliver it to the restaurant by 4pm. (☎543-1077. Open daily 6:30-11am, 5:30-9pm.) The adjacent **Cafe Court** has affordable cafeteria-style food. (Open daily 11am-10pm. Sandwiches and salads $3-7.)

⚑ OUTDOOR ACTIVITIES

While Yellowstone wows visitors with geysers and mudpots, the Grand Tetons boast some of the most scenic mountains in the US, if not the world. Only 2-3 million years old, the Tetons range between 10,000-13,770 ft. in elevation. The absence of foothills creates spectacular mountain vistas that accentuate the range's steep rock faces. These dramatic rocks draw scores of climbers, but less seasoned hikers can still experience the beauty of the Teton's backcountry. A number of self-guiding trails allow even novices to get off the beaten path for a few hours.

HIKING

All Visitors Centers provide pamphlets about the day hikes and sell numerous guides and maps ($3-10). Rangers also lead informative hikes; check the *Teewinot* or at Visitors Centers for more info. Before hitting the trail or planning extended hikes, be sure to check in at the ranger station; trails at higher elevations may still be snow-covered. Prime hiking season does not begin until well into July during years with heavy snowfall.

The Cascade Canyon Trail (14 mi. with boat ride, 18 mi. without boat ride; 6-8hr.) begins on the far side of tranquil Jenny Lake and follows Cascade Creek through U-shaped valleys carved by glaciers. The **Hidden Falls Waterfall** is located ½ mi. up; views of Teewinot, Mt. Owen, and Grand Teton are visible to the south. Hikers with more stamina can continue upwards towards **Inspiration Point** (another ½ mi.), but only the lonely can trek 6¾ mi. further to **Lake Solitude** (9035 ft). Guides for Cascade Canyon available (for a small fee) at Visitors Centers. Hikers can reach the Cascade Canyon Trial by following part of the 6.6 mi trail around Jenny Lake or by taking one of the shuttles offered by Teton Boating. (☎733-2703. Boats leave from Jenny Lake Visitors Center every 20min. beginning at 8am; last boat returns from other side at 6pm. One-way $4, ages 7-12 $3; round-trip $6/$4.)

Taggert Lake (3.2 mi., 2hr.) is another self-guided hike. This moderate trail winds through a broad spectrum of plant life, including the remains of a 1985 forest fire, and emerges for spectacular views of the mountains at the lake. The trail begins in the Taggert Lake parking area, 3 mi. north of Moose.

Hermitage Point (8.8 mi., 4hr.). Beginning at Colter Bay, this hike offers a unique perspective on Jackson Lake and is a prime spot for observing wildlife.

The Amphitheater Lake Trail (9.8 mi., 8hr.), beginning just south of Jenny Lake at the Lupine Meadows parking lot, takes you to one of the park's glacial lakes. Lupines, the purple flowers visible all along the roads throughout the park, bloom from June to July.

Static Peak Divide (15.6 mi., 10hr.) is a loop trail up 4020 ft. from the Death Canyon trailhead (4.5 mi. south of Moose Visitors Center). Offers some of the best vistas in the park. The Death Canyon area is prime for longer two- to three-day hikes.

The Cunningham Cabin Trail (0.8 mi., 1hr.) relives the history of cattle ranching in the valley. The trail begins 6 mi. south of Moran.

CLIMBING

Two climbing guide companies offer more extreme backcountry adventures, including four-day packages that let beginners work their way up to the famed Grand Teton. **Jackson Hole Mountain Guides and Climbing School,** 165 N. Glenwood St. in Jackson, offers a one-day beginner course for $80; more advanced (and more expensive) programs are also available. (☎733-4979 or 800-239-7642. Reservations necessary.) **Exum Mountain Guides** has similar classes and rates. A one-day begin-ners' rock-climbing course runs $95, and guided 1-2 day climbs range between $120-200. (☎733-2297. Reservations necessary.)

BOATING, FISHING, AND BIKING

Boating is permitted on a number of lakes; Jackson, Jenny, and Phelps Lakes allow motorboats; hand-powered crafts are also allowed on most lakes. Permits for boat-ing can be obtained at the Moose or Colter Bay Visitors Centers. (Motorized boats $10 for 7 days, $20 annual; non-motorized $5/$10.) Grand Tetons Lodge Company rents boats at Colter Bay and Jenny Lake and offers scenic cruises of Jackson Lake, leaving from Colter Bay. (Colter Bay Marina ☎543-2811; Jenny Lake 733-2703. Cruises $15, ages 3-11 $7. Canoes $9 per hr.; motor boats $18 per hr.; 2hr. min.) **Fish-ing** is permitted within the park with a Wyoming license, available at Moose Village Store, Signal Mountain Lodge, Colter Bay Marina, and Flagg Ranch Village. ($10 Wyoming Conservation stamp required with all fishing licenses. Residents $3 per day; $15 per season, ages 14-18 $3. Non-residents $10 per day; $65/$15 per season.) The **Grand Teton Lodge Company** offers float trips on the Snake River. (☎543-2811 or 800-628-9988. $39.50, ages 6-11 $20.) **Mountain biking** is a popular activity on roads in the park, but is strictly forbidden on hiking trails.

Outdoor equipment rentals can be found both in Jackson and at Moose Village. **Adventure Sports,** a division of Dornan's in Moose, rents bikes and provides advice on where to trek. (☎733-3307. Open daily 9am-6pm; spring and fall hours vary. Mountain bikes from $8 per hr. Credit card or deposit required.) **Snake River Angler,** next to Dornan's, rents rods for $15 per day. (☎733-3699. Open daily 8am-8pm, off-season 9am-6pm.) Next door, **Moosely Seconds** rents equipment. (Open daily 8am-9pm. Climbing shoes $6-10, crampons $10, ice axes $6, trekking poles $4.)

WINTER ACTIVITIES

In the **winter,** all hiking trails and the unploughed sections of Teton Park Rd. are open to **cross-country skiers.** Pick up winter info at Moose or Colter Bay Visitors Centers. Naturalists lead free **snowshoe hikes** from the Moose Visitors Center. (☎739-3399. Jan.-Mar. Th-Tu at 1pm.) **Snow Creek Nordic & Snowshoe Center** in Jackson offers over 9 mi. of groomed skiing trails, as well as guided cross-country and snowshoe tours of the Tetons. (☎733-8833 or 800-443-6139. Trail fee $8 per day, seniors and children $5. Ski tours $45 per half-day, $70 per day. Snowshoe tours $30 per half-day.) **Snowmobiling** along the park's well-powdered trails and up into Yellowstone is a noisy but popular winter activity; pick up a free permit at Moose Visitors Center (Moose is *the* Visitors Center in the winter) and grab a map and guide at the Jackson Chamber of Com-merce. **Grand Teton Park Snowmobile Rental** (☎733-1980 or 800-563-6469), near Moran Jct., rents snowmobiles for only $79 per ½ day ($119 per day), including clothing, hel-met, and boots. A well-developed snowmobile trail runs from Moran to Flagg Ranch, and numerous other snowmobiling opportunities exist in the valley. The Colter Bay and Moose parking lots are available for parking in the winter. All **campgrounds** close in winter, but **backcountry snow camping** (only for those who know what they're doing) is allowed with a permit purchased from the Moose Visitors Center. Before making plans, consider that temperatures regularly drop below -20°F. Be sure to carry extreme weather clothing and check with a ranger station for current weather condi-tions and avalanche danger; many early trappers froze to death in the 10 ft. drifts.

JACKSON   ☎307

Jackson Hole, the valley that separates the Teton and Gros Ventre mountain ranges, is renowned for its world-class skiing. However, skiing is not the area's only attraction. Grand Teton National Park, only a few miles north of Jackson, is a pop-ular destination for hiking, biking, and rafting along the Snake River. In recent years, the small town of Jackson (pop. 5000) has exploded into a cosmopolitan epi-center. Downtown Jackson is lined with chic restaurants, faux-Western bars, and expensive lodgings. The area's true beauty, however, can only be appreciated by exploring the nearby Tetons or navigating the winding Snake River.

⊞⊞ ORIENTATION AND PRACTICAL INFORMATION. Downtown Jackson is centered around the intersection of Broadway St. and Cache St. and is marked by the **Town Sq. Park.** The majority of shops and restaurants are within a four-block radius of this intersection. South of town, W. Broadway becomes U.S. 191/89/26 at the intersection with Rte. 22. To get to **Teton Village;** take Rte. 22 to Rte. 390 (Teton Village Rd.), just before the town of Wilson. Winding backroads, unpaved at times, connect Teton Village to Moose and the southern entrance of the National Park. North of Jackson, Cache St. turns into Rte. 89, leading directly into the park.

Public Transportation: Jackson START runs buses late May to mid-September 6am-10:30pm, early December to early April 6am-11pm. (☎733-4521. Free in town, $1 on village road, $2 to Teton Village; under 9 free.) **Jackson Hole Express** (☎733-1719 or 800-652-9510) runs to the Salt Lake City airport (5½hr., 3 per day, $45) and the Idaho Falls airport (2hr., 4 per day, $20). Reservations are required. **Leisure Sports,** 1075 Rte. 89, has the best deals on camping and backpacking rentals, as well as boating equipment. (☎733-3040. Open summer/winter daily 8am-6pm, fall/spring daily 8:30am-5:30pm. Tents $7.50-25, sleeping bags $5-8, backpacks $3.50-7.50. Canoes and kayaks $35 per day, rafts $90-110 per day.) **Jackson Hole and Greater Yellowstone Information Center,** 532 N. Cache St., has info. (Open early June to early Sept. daily 8am-7pm; in winter M-F 8am-5pm, Sa-Su 10am-2pm.) **Grayline Tours** (☎733-4325 or 800-443-6133) offers guided tours of Grand Teton (8hr.; leaves Jackson M, W, and Sa 8:30am; returns 4pm) and Yellowstone's Lower Loop (11hr.; leaves Tu, Th, and Su 7:30am; returns 6:30pm). Both tours run $60; call for reservations. **Internet access: Jackson Library,** 125 Virginian Ln. (☎733-2164; open M-Th 10am-9pm, F 10am-5:30pm, Sa 10am-5pm, Su 1-5pm). **Post Office:** Powderhorn and Maple Way. (☎733-3650. Open M-F 8:30am-5pm, Sa 10am-1pm.) **ZIP code:** 83002. **Area code:** 307.

⊩ ACCOMMODATIONS. Jackson draws hordes of visitors year-round, making rooms expensive and hard to find without reservations. **☒The Hostel X (HI-AYH),** 12 mi. northwest of Jackson in Teton Village, lets skiers and others stay close to the slopes without mortgaging their home. Each room has a private bath and maid service. Other amenities include a lounge with TVs and games and a ski-waxing room. The hostel is a close stumble from the Mangy Moose (see **Nightlife,** below) next door. (☎733-3415. 4 beds in dorm rooms; 20 rooms with king-size beds. $48 for 1-2 people; $60 for 3-4.) Rooms are costly during peak months, but **The Pioneer,** 325 N. Cache St., is a bargain during the spring. It offers lovely rooms with microwaves, refrigerators, free local calls, and handcrafted quilts. (☎733-3673 or 888-320-3673. Open mid-May to early Oct. Singles peak at $90 in the summer.) For those on a serious budget, **The Bunkhouse,** 215 N. Cache St., in the basement of the Anvil Motel, is a viable option. (☎733-3668. Showers, coin laundry, and ski storage. Beds $22.)

For those willing to rough it, the primitive campgrounds in Grand Teton National Park and the **Bridger-Teton National Forest** are the cheapest accommodations in the area. **Gros Ventre** campground (see p. 661) is only a 10min. drive from Jackson. There are 45 developed campgrounds in the Bridger-Teton National Forest, including several along U.S. 26 west of Jackson. The publication *The Bridge,* available at the Visitors Center in Jackson, and the National Forest offices have additional info. (Some have water, no showers. $5-15.) Dispersed camping is free within the National Forest; campers must stay at least 200 ft. from water and 100 ft. from roads or trails. Consult with a ranger beforehand, as some areas may be restricted.

⊡ FOOD. Jackson has dozens of restaurants, but few are suited to the budget traveler. **The Bunnery,** 130 N. Cache St., attracts both locals and tourists with its special O.S.M. bread (made of oats, sunflower, and millet) and $7.50 classic club. (☎733-5474. Open daily 7am-10pm. Sandwiches $6-8; omelettes $5.50-7.50.) For a homeopathic remedy, or just a healthy bite to eat, try the **Harvest Bakery and Cafe,** 130 W. Broadway, a New Age jack-of-all-trades. Stop in for breakfasts priced under $5, soup and salad ($6), fresh pastries ($2), and $3-4.50 smoothies. (☎733-5418. Cafe open 7am-4pm. Bakery open M-Sa 7am-8pm, Su 8am-4pm; in winter 8am-6pm.) A popular family restaurant, **Bubba's,** 515 W. Broadway, serves generous portions of ribs and sides. (☎733-2288. Open in summer daily 7am-10pm; in winter 7am-9pm. Spare ribs $8.75.) **LeJay's 24 Hour Sportsmen Cafe,** at the corner of Glenwood and Pearl, draws an eclectic crowd hungry for authentic Western cooking after the bars close. (☎733-3110. Open 24hr. Ribs, steaks, burgers, sandwiches, and breakfast all start at $3.50.) At **Mountain High Pizza Pie,** 120 W. Broadway, you can build your own pizza or choose from a large selection of pies ($10-17) or subs for $6. (☎733-3646. Open in summer daily 11am-midnight; in winter 11am-10pm.)

🔼 OUTDOOR ACTIVITIES. Jackson puts on a good show, but the feature presentation here is the quality of outdoor adventure. World-class skiing, climbing, and whitewater rafting all lie within minutes of Jackson, and the plethora of guiding companies can make anyone feel extreme. **Whitewater rafting** on the legendary Snake River is a popular activity. **Barker-Ewing,** 45 W. Broadway, runs tours of varying lengths and difficulty levels. (☎733-1000 or 800-448-4202. 8 mi. tour $36-40, ages 6-12 $30-34; 16 mi. tour $65/$50; overnight 16 mi. adventure $115/$85.) **Mad River,** 1255 S. Rte. 89, 2 mi. south of Town Sq., offers similar trips with a promise of "small boats, big action." (☎733-6203 or 800-458-7238. 8 mi. trip $39, 12 and under $29; scenic/whitewater combo $69/$49.) During winter months, skiing enthusiasts flock to Jackson to experience pure Wyoming powder. **Jackson Hole Mountain Resort,** 12 mi. north of Jackson in Teton Village, has some of the best runs in the US, including the jaw-droppingly steep Corbet's Couloir. (☎733-2292. Open Dec. 4 to April 2. Lift tickets $56, seniors and under 14 $28.) Even after the snow melts, the **aerial tram** whisks tourists to the top of Rendezvous Mountain (elevation 10,450 ft.) for a panoramic view of the valley. (☎733-2292. Open late May to late June daily 9am-5pm; late June to early Sept. 9am-7pm; early to late Sept. 9am-5pm. $15, seniors $13; ages 6-17 $5.) Located in the town of Jackson, **Snow King** offers less expensive and more relaxed skiing. (☎733-5200. Lift tickets full-day $30, half-day $20, night $14; juniors and seniors $20/$12/$9. $8 per hr.) Snow King also has summer rides to the summit for views of the Tetons. ($8 round-trip; ride down $1.) Jackson Hole is a prime locale for **cross-country skiing. Skinny Skis,** 65 W. Delorney in downtown Jackson, can point you in the right direction. (☎733-6094. Rentals with skis, boots, and poles full-day $15, half-day $10.)

🌃🌃 ENTERTAINMENT AND NIGHTLIFE. When the sun goes down on a long day of skiing, hiking, or rafting, Jackson has bars, concerts, and festivals to suit all tastes. Catch cowboy fever at the **JH Rodeo,** held at the fairgrounds, two blocks west of the Snow King ski area. (☎733-2805. Late May to early Sept. W and Sa 8pm. $9, reserved tickets $11, families $28, ages 4-12 $7.) Over Memorial Day weekend, the town's population explodes as tourists, locals, and nearby Native American tribes pour in for the dances and parades of **Old West Days.** World-class musicians roll into Teton Village each summer for the **Grand Teton Music Festival,** early July to late August. (☎733-1128. Festival orchestra concerts F-Sa 8pm; $30, students $15. Spotlight concerts Th 8pm; $25/$12.50. Chamber music concerts Tu-W 8pm; $15/$7.50. Open rehearsal F 9:30am; $5/$2.50.) The **Jackson Hole Fall Arts Festival** (☎733-3316; mid-Sept.) showcases artists, musicians, and dancers in a week-long celebration.

Head straight from the slopes to **The Mangy Moose,** in Teton Village at the base of Jackson Hole Ski Resort, a quintessential après-ski bar. The atmosphere is more sedate during the summer, but in winter, the Mangy Moose is the place to be. The entertainment lineup has featured everything from Blues Traveler to Dr. Timothy Leary. (☎733-4913. Dinner daily 5:30-10pm; bar open 11:30am-2am. Cover $3-15.) Jackson is home to the award-winning **Snake River Brewery,** 265 S. Millward St. One particularly powerful beer is the "Zonkers Stout" (pints $3, pitchers $10), named the best stout at the 1999 Colorado Beer Festival. (☎739-2337. Open daily noon-1am; food served until 11pm.) Live music and good beer make the **Stagecoach Bar,** 7 mi. west of Jackson on Rte. 22 in Wilson, a popular nightspot, particularly on Thursday Disco Night. (☎733-4407. Live music Su, sometimes Sa. Open daily 11am-2am.)

SCENIC DRIVE: CENTENNIAL SCENIC DRIVE

Passing through some of the most beautiful country on earth, this all-day drive is like a vacation unto itself. For 162 mi., the Centennial Scenic Byway passes by the high peaks, roaring whitewater rivers, and broad windswept plains of western Wyoming. The drive is open all year but may occasionally close due to snow.

Begin your drive in the small frontier town of **Dubois,** home of the **National Bighorn Sheep Interpretive Center,** 907 W. Ramshorn (☎455-3429; open Th-M 9am-5pm). As you leave town on Rte. 26, the crumbly breccia of the volcanic Absaroka mountains will become visible to the north. The high towering mountain is **Ramshorn Peak** at 11,920 ft. The road follows the **Wind River,** a favorite swimming spot for moose, especially early in the morning. Aspen groves are found along the river and the road. A "grove" of these delicate trees is actually just one tree with many different branches rising up from a root system that can go for miles. The road gently rises through a conifer forest and reaches **Togwotee Pass,** elevation 9544 ft.

As the road begins to descend, the famed panorama of the Teton mountain range becomes visible. The highest peak is the Grand Teton (13,770 ft.); the exhibit at the Teton Range Overlook labels each visible peak in the skyline. After entering **Grand Teton National Park** (see p. 660), the road winds through the flat plain of the Buffalo Fork River, a strikingly beautiful contrast to the high peaks and mountain forests. This floodplain is the beginning of the wide, long valley known as Jackson Hole; early trappers referred to any high mountain valley as a Hole.

Once in the park, the road follows the legendary Snake River, renowned for its whitewater rafting and kayaking. As you near **Jackson** (see p. 663), the National Elk Refuge, the winter home of some 6000-7000 elk, is visible to the east. The town of Jackson, once home to mountain men, explorers, and trappers, now caters to tourists. To bypass Jackson, take U.S. 189/191 south. As the Tetons fade out of sight, the Wind River Range appears on the horizon. You will soon spot the highest peak in Wyoming, **Gannet Peak** (13,804 ft.). The drive ends in the tiny, authentically Western town of **Pinedale.** The **Museum of the Mountain Man,** located in Pinedale, chronicles the history of the Plains Indians, the fur trade, and the settlement of western Wyoming. (☎877-686-6266. Open early May to late Sept. daily 10am-6pm.)

CODY   ☎307

The self-proclaimed "Rodeo Capital of the World," Cody is home to the longest-running rodeo in the US. For 63 straight years, the Cody Nite Rodeo has thrilled audiences every night during the summer (June 1-Aug. 31). Meanwhile, the Cody Stampede annually attracts the country's most prestigious cowboys in celebration of July 4th. Praised for its breathtaking scenery and Western charm, Cody is only 54 miles from Yellowstone National Park along the Buffalo Bill Cody Scenic Byway.

🖪 PRACTICAL INFORMATION. Cody lies at the junction of Rte. 120, 14A, and 14/16/20. The town's main street is **Sheridan Ave.,** which turns into **Yellowstone Ave.** west of town. **Powder River Transportation** (☎800-442-3682) runs buses to Denver (14hr., 1 per day, $78); Cheyenne (9hr., 1 per day, $68); and Billings (3hr., 1 per day, $27) from the Cody Chamber of Commerce. **Powder River Tours** offers guided daytrips through Yellowstone National Park and departs from several locations in town (☎527-3677 or 800-442-3682, ext. 114. $60, 16 and under $30, seniors $54. Reservations recommended.) The **Chamber of Commerce Visitors Center** is at 836 Sheridan Ave. (☎587-2297. Open M-Sa 8am-6pm, Su 10am-3pm; off-season M-F 8am-5pm.) **Internet access:** Free at the **Library,** corner of 11th St. and Sheridan Ave. (☎527-8820. Open M-F 10am-5:30pm, Sa 10am-1pm; winter hours vary.) **Post Office:** 1301 Stampede Ave., 1 mi. south of downtown on 13th St. (☎527-7161. Open M-F 8am-5:30pm, Sa 9am-noon.) **ZIP code:** 82414. **Area code:** 307.

🖪🖪 ACCOMMODATIONS AND FOOD. Rates go up in the summertime, but a strip of reasonable motels lines **W. Yellowstone Ave.** Just a block from downtown, the **Pawnee Hotel,** 1032 12th St., has 18 unique rooms. (☎587-2239. Rooms $22-38.) The

A TRUE COWBOY Cody's namesake, Col. William F. "Buffalo Bill" Cody, was an authentic Western hero who rode for the Pony Express, fought with the Kansas Jayhawkers during the Civil War (a Union guerilla group), and later helped build the first transcontinental railroad. Hunting to supply meat for the men working on the railroad, Cody was affectionately named "Buffalo Bill." Cody catapulted the image of the cowboy across the world with his outdoor extravaganza, Buffalo Bill's Wild West Show. The Wild West Show toured both the United States and Europe, attracting the attention of royalty and statesmen. The **Buffalo Bill Historical Center,** 720 Sheridan Ave., keeps Cody's legacy alive with four museums under one roof: the **Buffalo Bill Museum,** the **Whitney Gallery of Western Art,** the **Plains Indians Museum,** and the **Cody Firearms Museum.** (☎587-4771. Open June to mid-Sept. daily 7am-8pm; mid-Sept. to Oct. 8am-5pm; Nov.-Mar. Tu-Su 10am-3pm; Apr. 10am-5pm; May 8am-8pm. $10, students $6, ages 6-17 $4. Tickets good for 2 consecutive days.)

Rainbow Park Motel, 1136 17th St., is a bargain in the winter, but prices jump during the more popular summer months. Carpeted, wood-paneled rooms have phone, HBO, and A/C. (☎587-6251. In winter singles $34, doubles $43; in summer $75/$82.) **Buffalo Bill State Park** offers two campgrounds on the Buffalo Bill Reservoir with incredible views. The **North Shore Bay Campground** (☎527-6274) is located 9 mi. west of town on U.S. 14/16/20. **Peter's Cafe and Bakery,** at 12th St. and Sheridan Ave., a popular local establishment, serves cheap breakfasts (3 buttermilk pancakes $3) and stacks thick subs (including vegetarian options) starting at $3. (☎527-5040. Open M-Sa 6:45am-8:45pm, Su 6:45am-2:30pm.) Celebrate the women of the Wild West at **Annie Oakley's Cowgirl Cafe,** on Sheridan Ave. downtown. The Buzz Tails appetizer (sauteed rattlesnake; $10) appeals to the adventurous traveler. (☎587-1011. Open daily 11am-10pm. Burgers $5-8, sandwiches $5-6, wraps $5-6.)

🄲🄽 **SIGHTS AND OUTDOORS.** To this day, as numerous billboards proclaim, Cody is Rodeo—a visit to this cowboy town is your best chance to catch the sport. The **Cody Nite Rodeo** performs every night from June through August at 8:30pm. (☎587-5155. Tickets $11-13, ages 7-12 $5-7.) Each year over the 4th of July weekend, the **Cody Stampede Professional Rodeo Cowboy Association Rodeo,** voted by the cowboys themselves as the best "large outdoor rodeo" in the world, rough-rides into town. (☎587-5155. Tickets $15; reserve ahead.) The **Cody Trolley Tour** offers a one-hour tour of the city, visiting frontier sites and portraying the historical Old West. (☎527-7043. $11, seniors over 62 $9, ages 6-12 $6.) **Rafting** trips on the Shoshone provide more energetic diversions. To make arrangements, call **Wyoming River Trips,** 1701 Sheridan Ave., at Rte. 120 and 14. (☎587-6661 or 800-586-6661. Open May-Sept. Easy 2hr. trip $20, half-day trip $50.) For equine adventures, try **Cedar Mountain Trail Rides.** (☎527-4966. $18 per hr., $30 per 2hr., $60 per 4hr., $100 per day.)

SHERIDAN ☎307

Sheridan, the hub of northeast Wyoming and southern Montana area, offers stunning views of the surrounding prairie, as well as an authentic Western atmosphere. **King's Saddlery and Cowboy Museum,** 184 N. Main St. in the building behind their main store, ropes 'em in with over 550 remarkably crafted, award-winning saddles on display. Watch as ropes and saddles are made in their warehouse. Each saddle takes four to six weeks to complete and can cost $1800-6000. (☎672-2702, 672-2755, or 800-443-8919. Open M-Sa 8am-5pm. Free.) The **Trail End State Historic Site,** 400 Clarendon Ave., showcases the impressive mansion and gardens of rags-to-riches cattle baron, former Wyoming governor, and US senator, John B. Kendrick. (☎674-4589. Open June-Aug. daily 9am-6pm; Sept. to mid-Dec. W-Su daily 1-4pm. $2 for non-residents, $1 for residents, under 18 free.)

Sheridan Inn, at 5th and Broadway, saw scores of colorful characters in its day; Buffalo Bill Cody used the porch to audition cowpokes aspiring to his *Wild West Show.* (☎674-5440. Guided tours M, W, and Sa 2pm. $3, seniors $2, under 12 free;

call ahead.) Locals flock to town several days a week for **polo** games (☎ 751-3802 for schedule and information; June to mid-Sept.). There are motels aplenty along Main St. and Coffeen Ave. The **Aspen Inn,** 1744 N. Main St., offers the best deal. (☎ 672-9064. Singles $36; doubles $48.) Kamping can be found at the **Sheridan KOA** with the typical KOA amenities: laundry, showers, water, pool, restaurant, video arcade, etc. Go south at Exit 20 off I-90, turn right at the Port of Entry, take an immediate right on Rte. 338 and go about ¾ mi. (☎ 674-8766. $17 for 2, water and electricity $24, full hookup $26; kabins $32. Each additional person $2.50.) Camping is more rustic at **Connor Battlefield Campground,** which offers pit toilets, water, fishing, and $9 sites. (In Ranchester, 14 mi. north of Sheridan; take Rte. 14 west at Exit 9 off I-90, turn left on to Gillette St. and follow the signs to the battlefield/campground.) Find good, hearty meals at the **Sheridan Palace Restaurant,** 138 North Main St., not far from King's Saddlery. The menu features delicious burgers and sandwiches ($5-6) with a good selection of freshly made pies ($2.50 per slice) for dessert. (☎ 672-2391. Open M-Th 6am-7:30pm, F-Sa 6am-9:30pm.) The **Mint Bar,** 151 Main St., has been pleasing customers since 1907. (☎ 674-9696. Open M-Sa 8am-2am.)

Powder River buses leave twice daily for Billings (2hr., $28) and Cheyenne (8hr., $59) from the **Evergreen Inn,** 580 E. 5th St. (☎ 674-6188. Terminal open daily 3am-11:30pm.) The **Sheridan Chamber of Commerce** sits just off I-90 at Exit 23. (☎ 672-2485 or 800-453-3650. Open M-F 8am-7pm, Sa-Su 8am-5pm; in winter M-F 8am-5pm.) The Sheridan **Ranger Station** is on the south end of town at 1969 S. Sheridan Ave, off Coffeen St. (☎ 672-0751. Open M-F 8am-4:30pm.) **Post Office:** 101 E. Laucks St. (☎ 672-0713. Open M-F 7:30am-5:30pm, Sa 8am-noon.) **ZIP code:** 82801. **Area code:** 307.

BUFFALO   ☎ 307

Situated at the crossroads of I-90 and I-25, Buffalo is also the eastern terminus of the **U.S. 16 Scenic Byway.** Before heading for the mountains, however, absorb some Old West character in the elegant rooms of the **Occidental Hotel,** 10 N. Main St., which opened its doors as the town hall in 1880 and, as the story goes, was won by the Smith Family in a 1917 poker game. The hotel was the setting for Owen Wister's western novel, *The Virginian.* (☎ 684-0451. Open in summer M-Sa 10am-5pm. $2.)

Budget motels line **Main St. (Rte. 87)** and **Fort St.,** as well as the area around I-25. The friendly management at the **Mountain View Motel and Campground,** 585 Fort St./ U.S. 16, keeps appealing pine cabins with TV, A/C, and heat. (☎ 684-2881. Showers and laundry. Cabins $59; in winter $35; up to 6 people in big cabin with kitchenette $85/$50. Sites $15; with hookup $18.) A few doors down, the **Z-Bar Motel,** 626 Fort St., has TVs, refrigerators, free local calls, and A/C. (☎ 684-5535 or 888-313-1227. Singles $45, Nov.-Apr. $34; doubles $54/37. Kitchen $6 extra.) **Tom's Main Street Diner,** 41 N. Main St., is a great little eatery downtown. Lunch specials ($4-5.75) and $2 pie are the best. (☎ 684-7444. Open M and W-Sa 5:30am-2pm, Su 8am-1pm.) **Dash Inn,** 620 E. Hart St., serves great chicken, ribs, and Mexican entrees for $4-5. (☎ 684-7930. Open Tu-Su 11am-9:30pm; in winter M-Sa 11am-8pm.)

There is no bus service to Buffalo; **Greyhound** (☎ 674-6188) goes to nearby Sheridan and Gillette. **Just Gone Fishing,** 777 Fort St., sells fishing licenses (non-residents $10), as well as tackle, US Forest Service maps, camping gear, and hiking supplies. (☎ 684-2755. Open in summer daily 7am-6pm, in winter 8:30am-5pm.) The **Buffalo Chamber of Commerce Visitors Center,** 55 N. Main St. has info. (☎ 684-5544 or 800-227-5122. Open June-Aug. M-F 8am-6pm, Sa-Su 10am-4pm; Sept.-May M-F 8am-5pm.) The **US Forest Service Offices,** 1425 Fort St., sells maps of the area for $4-7. (☎ 684-1100. Open M-F 8am-4:30pm.) **Post Office:** 193 S. Main St. (☎ 684-7063. Open M-F 8am-5pm, Sa 10am-noon.) **ZIP code:** 82834. **Area code:** 307.

BIGHORN MOUNTAINS   ☎ 307

The **Bighorn National Forest** may be one of the best kept secrets in the Rocky Mountains; it is relatively uncrowded and offers great hiking and wildlife viewing. The Bighorns erupt from the hilly pasture land of northern Wyoming, a dramatic backdrop to grazing cattle, sprawling ranch houses, and valleys full of wildflowers. Visitors can hike through the woods or follow **scenic highways U.S. 14/14A** in the north and **U.S. 16** in the south to waterfalls, layers of prehistoric rock, and views above the clouds. The **Medicine Wheel** on U.S. 14A is a mysterious 80 ft. wide stone formation at 10,000 ft. dating from around AD 1300; prepare for a 3 mi. round-trip hike from where the dirt road off the highway ends. This site is sacred to 89 Native American tribes, and several people pray there each day. **Cloud Peak Wilderness** offers sheer solitude. Registration at major trailheads is required to enter the Cloud Peak area. The most convenient access to the wilderness area is from the trailheads off U.S. 16, around 20 mi. west of Buffalo. From the **Hunter Corrals Trailhead**, move to beautiful **Seven Brothers Lake**, 3 mi. off U.S. 16 on Rd. 19 (13 mi. west of Buffalo on U.S. 16), an ideal base for day-hikes into the high peaks beyond. You can also enter the wilderness area on U.S. 14/14A to the north. To get to the top of 13,175 ft. Cloud Peak, most hikers enter at **West Tensleep Trailhead**, accessible from the town of **Tensleep** on the western slope, 55 mi. west of Buffalo on U.S. 16. Tensleep was so named because it took the Sioux ten sleeps to travel from there to their main winter camps. Check with a forest office to find out about more out-of-the-way treks, and always check on local conditions with a ranger before any hike. A listing of all the Bighorn's attractions along with other helpful information and a map of the area can be found in *Bighorn Bits and Pieces*, available at all of the Visitors Centers.

Campgrounds fill the forest. **Doyle Campground**, near a fish-rich creek, has 18 sites ($9) and toilets, but no water. (Drive 26 mi. west of Buffalo on U.S. 16 and south 6 mi. on Hazelton Rd./County Rd. 3—it's a rough ride.) There is no fee to camp at the uncrowded **Elgin Park Trailhead**, 16 mi. west of Buffalo off U.S. 16, which promises good fishing along with parking and toilets. Off U.S. 14 (roughly 27 mi. in from I-90 in the east), the **Sibley Lake Campground** offers 25 sites at 8000 ft. ($10, with electricity $13. Wheelchair accessible.) If Sibley is crowded, **Tie Flume** and **Dead Swede** (both $9) are great campgrounds off Rte. 14 about 10 mi. south of the Burgess Jct. Visitors Center. Many other campgrounds line U.S. 14 and 16; the map in *Bighorn Bits and Pieces* will guide the way. For reservations within the park, call 877-444-6777. Campgrounds rarely fill up in the Bighorns, but if they do, or if you're looking to get away from civilization altogether, free **dispersed camping** is permitted at least 100 yd. from the road. For more information call 672-0751.

US Forest Service **ranger stations** are in **Buffalo** (see p. 668), **Lovell** at 604 E. Main St. (☎548-6541; open M-F 8am-4:30pm), and **Sheridan** (see p. 667), as well as within the park. The **Burgess Junction Visitors Center**, off U.S. 14 about halfway into the area, houses loads of great info and several films on the surroundings. (Open mid-May through Sept. daily 8:30am-5pm.) The **Bighorn Canyon Visitors Center** on Rte. 14A in Lovell shows movies on the Medicine Wheel and can help out if the Lovell station is closed. (☎548-2251. Open daily 8am-6pm; off-season 8:30am-5pm.) **Area code:** 307.

DEVILS TOWER NATIONAL MONUMENT   ☎ 307

A Native American legend tells of seven sisters who were playing with their little brother when the boy turned into a bear and began to chase them. Terrified, the girls ran to a tree stump and prayed for help. The stump grew high into the sky and the girls became the stars of the Big Dipper. Others tell of a core of fiery magma that shot up without breaking the surface 60 million years ago, and of centuries of wind, rain, and snow that eroded the surrounding sandstone, leaving a stunning spire. Still others, not of this world, have used the stone obelisk as a landing strip (*Close Encounters of the Third Kind*). The massive column that figures so prominently in the myths of Native Americans, geologists, and space aliens is the centerpiece of **Devils Tower National Monument** in northeastern Wyoming. (One-week pass $8 per car, $3 per person on bike, foot, or alpaca; free map on entry.)

Devils Tower is considered one of the best technical rock climbing sites in North America, and scaling the monument's 1280 ft. is a feat indeed. Native Americans, on the other hand, consider the tower a sacred site and would rather rock climbing were banned. A semi-compromise reached in 1995 calls for a voluntary refrain from climbing in the month of June—the most sacred time because of the solstice.

Read about the rock and register to climb at the **Visitors Center**, 3 mi. from the entrance. (☎467-5283, ext. 20. Open late-May to Sept. daily 8am-8pm; Mar.-Apr. and

Oct.-Nov. usually 9am-4:45pm.) Cool **climbing demos** are given outside the Visitors Center (May, July and Aug.; call for times). For more horizontally-oriented climbers, there are several **hiking trails**. The most popular, the paved 1.3 mi. **Tower Trail**, loops the monument and provides great views. The **Red Beds Trail**, a 3 mi. loop, takes hikers up and around the bright red banks of the Belle Fourche River. Hikers can opt for a longer hike by connecting with the shorter **Valley View Trail** (0.6 mi.) for a flat walk through the prairie dog town and the **South Side Trail** (0.6 mi.), which climbs back to the bluffs of the Red Beds Trail. Ask a ranger to identify leafy spurge and poison ivy, which abound near the monument. The park maintains a **campground** near the red banks of the Belle Fourche River. (Open roughly Apr.-Oct.; call to be sure. Water, bathrooms, grills, picnic tables, and lots of noise-making prairie dogs; no showers. Sites $12.) The best camping deal around is at the **Devils Tower View Store Campground** on Rte. 24, a few miles before the monument. Though there's not much shade, there's a great view of the monument and an inexpensive restaurant next door. (Open June-Sept. Water and nice port-o-potties. $9.) To reach the monument from I-90, take U.S. 14, 25 mi. north to Rte. 24. **Area code:** 307.

CASPER   ☎307

From 1841 to 1866, some 350,000 pioneers passed through Casper on the famed Oregon, Mormon, California, and Bozeman Trails. This proliferation of travelers earned Casper the moniker "Crossroads of the West," and Casper continues this tradition today, hosting some of the hordes of tourists en route to Yellowstone, the Black Hills, and elsewhere. Stalwartly midwestern in atmosphere, Casper has managed to escape the hokey Western commercialism that overruns much of the area.

Relive the pioneer experience at **Fort Caspar,** 4100 Fort Caspar Rd., where pioneers crossed the North Platte River and cavalrymen trained for battle. The fort sponsors reenactments in June, July, and December. (☎235-8462. Open M-Sa 8am-7pm, Su noon-7pm. Free.) The **Nicolayson Art Museum,** 400 E. Collins Dr., exhibits Wyoming and world artwork and houses a children's art discovery center. (☎235-5247. Open Tu-W and F-Sa 10am-5pm, Th 10am-8pm, Su noon-4pm.) For hands-on fun, visit the **Science Adventure Center.** (Open Tu-F noon-5pm, Sa 1-5pm. Admission to both museums $3, ages 2-12 $2.) The **Central Wyoming Fair and Rodeo,** 1700 Fairgrounds Rd., gets everyone excited about livestock. (☎235-5775. July 9-13, 2002.)

Near the interstate, the **Showboat National 9 Inn,** 100 W. F St., has spacious rooms, cable TV, free local calls, and continental breakfast. (☎235-2711 or 800-524-9999. Singles $39; doubles $50.) **Fort Caspar Campground,** 4205 Ft. Caspar Rd., is a friendly RV community, but tent sites are also available. (☎234-3260. Open 8am-8pm. Free showers and laundry. Sites for 2 people $12, $60 per week; full hookup $22.50; 10% AAA discount.) Locals love **Granny's Eastside Diner,** 1705 E. 2nd St., for breakfasts ($3-6), burgers ($6), and shakes ($3). Dinner specials are a good bargain; chicken dinners range from $4-6. (☎234-4204. Open M-F 6:30am-9pm, Sa-Su 6:30am-10pm.)

Powder River Transportation Services (☎266-1904, 265-2353 or 800-433-2093), at I-25 and Center St. in the Parkway Plaza Hotel, buses to Cheyenne (4hr., 2 per day, $37) and Denver (7hr., 2 per day, $50). Office open daily 5:30am-6pm. **Casper Area Chamber of Commerce:** 500 N. Center St. (☎234-5311; open M-F 8am-5pm, Sa-Su 10am-5pm). **Post Office:** 411 N. Forest Dr. (☎266-4000; open M-F 8:30am-5pm, Sa 9am-noon). **ZIP code:** 82609. **Area code:** 307.

CHEYENNE   ☎307

The name of the Native American tribe that originally inhabited the region, "Cheyenne," was considered a prime candidate for the name of the Wyoming Territory. The moniker was struck down by vigilant Senator Sherman, who pointed out that the pronunciation of Cheyenne closely resembled that of the French word *chienne*, meaning, er, "bitch." Once one of the fastest growing frontier towns, Cheyenne has slowed down significantly. However, the historical downtown area (complete with simulated gunfights) still exhibits traditional Western charm.

PRACTICAL INFORMATION. Greyhound, 222 Deming (☎634-7744), off I-80, makes trips to Chicago (19hr., 4 per day, $128); Denver (3-5hr., 5 per day, $19-26); Laramie (1hr., 4 per day, $14); Rock Springs (5hr., 4 per day, $55); and Salt Lake City (8hr., 4 per day, $74). Station open 24hr. **Powder River Transportation** (☎634-7744), in the Greyhound terminal, honors Greyhound passes and buses daily to Rapid City (10hr., 1 per day, $65); Casper (4hr., 2 per day, $37); and Billings (11½hr., 2 per day, $70). For local jaunts, flag down one of the shuttle buses provided by the **Cheyenne Transit Program.** (☎637-6253. Buses run M-F 6:30am-6:30pm; fare $1.) **Cheyenne Area Convention and Visitors Bureau:** 309 W. Lincolnway (☎778-3133 or 800-426-5009), just west of Capitol Ave. **Domestic Violence and Sexual Assault Line;** ☎637-7233. **24hr. Internet access: Laramie County Public Library,** 2800 Central Ave. (☎634-3561. Open M-Th 10am-9pm, F-Sa 10am-6pm; mid-Sept. to mid-May also Su 1-5pm. First come, first served 30min. slots available.) **Post Office:** 4800 Converse Ave. (☎800-275-8777. Open M-F 7:30am-5:30pm, Sa 7am-1pm.) **ZIP code:** 82009. **Area code:** 307.

ACCOMMODATIONS. It's easy to land a cheap room here among the plains and pioneers, unless your visit coincides with **Frontier Days,** the last full week of July (see **Festivals and Sights,** below). Beware of doubling rates and disappearing rooms in the days approaching the annual festivities. Budget motels line Lincolnway (U.S. 30/16th St.). **Plains Hotel,** 1600 Central Ave., across from the I-180 on-ramp, one block away from downtown, offers cavernous hotel rooms with marble sinks and cable TV. (☎638-3311. Singles $35; doubles $43. Additional person $5.) The **Frontier Motel,** 1400 W. Lincolnway (☎634-7961), doubles as an espresso bar, serving $2 lattes and $3 root beer floats. The motel offers singles with a living room, large bathroom, free cable, and A/C. (Singles from $25.) The (aging) **Pioneer Hotel,** 208 W. 17th St., provides the cheapest lodgings in the downtown area. (☎634-3010. Singles with cable TV $17.) Camp at **Curt Gowdy State Park,** 1319 Hynds Lodge Rd., 24 mi. west of Cheyenne on Rte. 210/Happy Jack Rd. This year-round park is centered around two lakes with excellent fishing, horseback riding (bring your own horse), and archery. (☎632-7946. $4 per night plus $5 entrance fee.)

FOOD. Cheyenne has only a smattering of non-fast food restaurants that provide reasonably-priced cuisine. For a dirt-cheap breakfast or lunch, head to the **Driftwood Cafe,** 200 E. 18th St. at Warren St. The cafe has a mom-and-pop atmosphere that complements the homestyle cooking. The menu features cinnamon rolls ($1.35), burgers ($3.50-4.75), and $2 slices of pie. (☎634-5304. Open M-F 7am-3pm.) The walls at the popular **Sanford's Grub and Pub,** 115 E. 17th St., are littered with every type of kitschy decor imaginable. The giant menu includes burgers, sandwiches, and salads for $6-7. Sanford's has 55 beers on tap, 99 bottles of beer on the wall, and 132 different liquors. While you're waiting for your food, check out the game room downstairs. (☎634-3381. Open M-Sa 11am-12am, Su 11am-10pm.) **Lexie's Cafe,** located in a historic brick building at 216 E. 17th St., has a cheerful, cottage-style decor featuring wicker chairs and flowers. You'll find filling breakfast combos for $4-7, towering stacks of pancakes for $3, and burgers for $5. (☎638-8712. Open Tu-Th 7:30am-8pm, F-Sa 7:30am-9pm, Su 10:30am-2:30pm.)

SIGHTS AND NIGHTLIFE. During the last week in July, make every effort to attend the one-of-a-kind **Cheyenne Frontier Days,** ten days of non-stop Western hoopla. The town doubles in size when anyone who's anyone in the West comes to see the world's largest outdoor rodeo competition ($10-22) and partake of the free pancake breakfasts, parades, big-name country music concerts, and square dancing. (☎778-7222 or 800-227-6336. July 19-28, 2002.) During June and July, a "gunfight is always possible," and the entertaining **Cheyenne Gunslingers** (☎778-3133), at W. 16th and Carey, shoot each other weekdays at 6pm (Sa high noon); their soda saloon sits at 218 W. 17th St. The **Wyoming State Capitol Building,** at the base of Capitol Ave. on 24th St., has beautiful stained glass windows and a gorgeous rotunda under the gold-leaf dome. Pick up a brochure to find your way around. (☎777-7220. Open M-F 8am-4:30pm.) The **Old West Museum,** 4610 N. Carey Ave., in Frontier Park,

NAW, THAT LOOKS LIKE A... Instead of lame alphabet games or car bingo to pass the time, try a variation on the Native American vision quest. The odd formations of the Vedauwoo Rocks loom off in the distance from I-80 Exit 329 between Cheyenne and Laramie. The strange rocks look something like piles of gigantic pebbles, deliberately placed to form all kinds of shapes. Sort of like cloud watching, it's fun to try to identify different forms in the rock. The Vedauwoo rocks *(VEE-dah-voo)* take their name from the Arapaho word meaning "earthborn." Today, the Vedauwoo Recreation Area offers 57 wooded picnic sites, a campground, and hiking and biking trails. ($3 per vehicle daily fee. Water and toilets, but no hookups. Sites $10.) The Summit Rest Area on I-80 hands out info on the rocks and also displays the impressive Lincoln Monument, visible from the highway, on its grounds.

houses a large collection of Western memorabilia, including the biggest carriage collection in the world. (☎778-7290 or 800-266-2696. Open M-F 9am-5pm, Sa-Su 10am-5pm; June-Aug. M-F until 7pm. Sept.-May free, June-Aug. $4; under 12 free.)

Hang with the locals at the popular **Cowboy Restaurant and Bar**, 312 S. Greeley Hwy., and test your skill as a cowboy on the mechanical bull ($3 per ride). The live music and large dance floor always draw a crowd. (☎637-3800. Open M-Sa 11am-2am, Su noon-2am.) Shoot pool in a haze of smoke at **D.T.'s Liquor and Lounge**, 2121 E. Lincolnway (look for the pink elephant). A patio bar and sun room offer an alternative to the dark interior. (☎632-3458. Open M-Sa 7am-2am, Su 10am-10pm.)

THE SNOWY RANGE   ☎307

Local residents call the forested granite mountains to the east of the Platte Valley the Snowy Mountain Range because snow falls nearly year-round on the higher peaks. Even when the snow melts, quartz outcroppings reflect the sun, creating an illusion of a snowy peak. Enjoy 25 downhill trails, cross-country trails, and a snowboard halfpipe at **Snowy Range Ski and Recreation Area.** Take Exit 311 off I-80 to Rte. 130 W. (☎745-5750 or 800-462-7669. Open mid-Dec. to Easter. Lift ticket $31, children 6-12 $16.) The Snowy Range is part of the **Medicine Bow National Forest,** spread over much of southeastern Wyoming. Cross-country skiing is popular in the winter; campsites and hiking trails usually don't open until mid-July.

From late May to November, the **Snowy Range Scenic Byway (Rte. 130)** is cleared of snow, and cars can drive 27 mi. through seas of pine trees and around treeless mountains and picture-perfect crystal lakes to elevations nearing two vertical miles. Along the Byway, the **Libby Flats Observation Point** features a very short wildflower nature walk and an awe-inspiring view of the surrounding land. The challenging 4.5 mi. **Medicine Bow Trail** has trailheads at both **Lake Marie** and **Lewis Lake** and climbs to **Medicine Bow Peak** (12,013 ft.), the highest point in the forest. Nearby **Silver Lake** offers 17 first come, first served quiet, wooded camp sites ($10). A little west of the Centennial entrance, **Nash Fork** is another serene and untrammeled campground with 27 well-shaded sites ($10). All 16 of the park's developed campgrounds are open only in summer and have toilets and water, but no hookups or showers. Reservations for some campgrounds are available through the National Recreation Reservation Service. (☎877-444-6777; www.reserveusa.com. $10 reservation fee.) A drive up **Kennaday Peak** (10,810 ft.), at the end of Rte. 215, leads to an impressive view (take Rte. 130 to Rte. 100 and 215.)

Mountain biking is generally prohibited on high country trails because of the frail alpine plants and rocky terrain. However, biking and driving are permitted on designated trails in the high country and on trails below 10,000 ft. The 7 mi. **Corner Mountain Loop,** just west of Centennial Visitors Center (see below), is an exhilarating roller coaster ride through forest and small meadows. During the winter, mountain biking and hiking trails are used for cross-country skiing.

Brush Creek Visitors Center is located at the west entrance. (☎326-5562. Open mid-May to Oct. daily 8am-5pm.) **Centennial Visitors Center,** 1 mi. west of Centennial, guards the east entrance. (☎742-6023. Open late May to early Sept. Tu-Su 9am-4pm; in winter Sa-Su only.) Rent cross-country equipment at the **Cross Country Connection,**

222 S. 2nd St. in Laramie. (☎ 721-2851. Open M-F 10am-6pm, Sa 9am-5pm, Su noon-4pm. $10 per day, no deposit required.) Downhill ski and snowboard rentals can be found at **The Fine Edge,** 1660E N. 4th St. (☎ 745-4499. Open in winter M-Th 8am-6pm, F-Sa 7am-6:30pm, Su 7:30-5pm; in summer M-Sa 9am-6pm, Su 11am-5pm. Full-day $16, children $12. Snowboards $22/$17; boots $9. $300 credit card or check deposit required for snowboards only.) **Area code:** 307.

SARATOGA   ☎ 307

On the west side of the Snowy Range along Rte. 130, Saratoga is known for its **hot mineral springs.** Running between 104° and 120°F, the springs' soothing waters are especially popular during the early morning and evening hours. The free, 24hr. springs are located at the end of E. Walnut St., behind the public pool. A few feet away, the **North Platte River** offers excellent fishing. Fishing permits ($10) are available at the **Country Store** (☎ 326-5638) on Rte. 130. **Hack's Tackle Outfitters,** 407 N. 1st St., also sells hunting and fishing licenses. The store's knowledgeable owner offers both fishing advice and guided trips. (☎ 326-9823. Fishing tours for 2 $235 per half-day, $335 per day. Canoes $35 per day, rafts $95 per day; $100 per boat deposit required.) Stop by the **Chamber of Commerce,** 115 W. Bridge St., for additional info and for free **Internet access.** (☎ 326-8855. Open in summer M-F 9am-5:30pm, in winter M-F 9am-4pm.) The **Hotel Wolf,** 101 E. Bridge St., a renovated Victorian inn, is a howlin' good deal. (☎ 326-5525. Singles from $39; doubles from $47.) Dinner is expensive at the **Wolf Hotel Restaurant,** but the lunch menu is reasonably priced, with salads and sandwiches for $5.50-7.50. (☎ 326-5525. Lunch M-Sa 11:30am-2pm; dinner M-Th 6-9:30pm, F-Sa 6-10pm, Su 5-9pm.) For a more casual dining atmosphere, drop by the **River St. Deli,** 106 N. River St., a gourmet sandwich shop that offers the only vegetarian food in town. (☎ 326-8683. Open Tu-Th 11am-3pm, F-Sa 11am-6pm. Sandwiches $5.50-6.50.) Next door to the Wolf, the family-owned **Lolly-pops,** 107 E. Bridge St., sells ice cream (single cone $2), cafe latte ($2.75), and $2 gourmet lollipops. (☎ 326-5020. Open daily 7am-10pm.) Across from the Wolf, the **Lazy River Cantina** tempts hungry pedestrians with wafting aromas and a good selection of Mexican dishes. (☎ 326-8472. Open M-Th 11am-9:30pm, F 11am-10pm, Su 7am-9:30pm. Lunch $5-8; dinner specialties $8.) **Area code:** 307.

LARAMIE   ☎ 307

Laramie, home of the University of Wyoming (UW), the state's only four-year college, is a comfortable stop-over for those traveling across the Cowboy State. The university infused cultural diversity and urban sophistication into a town otherwise defined by a thriving ranching economy. Laramie does its darndest to bring its rough and rugged 19th-century history back to life at the **Wyoming Territorial Park,** 975 Snowy Range Rd., a reconstructed frontier town where for $5, you can have a friend or relative arrested by the town marshal. The **National US Marshals Museum** presents the history of the US marshals and their dealings with Native Americans and Western outlaws. (☎ 745-6161 or 800-845-2287. Open early June to late Aug. daily 10am-5pm. May and Sept. $10, June-Aug. $12; under 13 free.) In early July, don't miss the chance to attend a rodeo at Laramie's **Jubilee Days** festival. (☎ 745-7339 or 866-876-1012. Tickets $9-15, under 12 $4-10.)

The rooms are large and comfortable at the sprawling **Motel 8,** 501 Boswell, down the street from the Caboose on the outskirts of town. (☎ 745-4856 or 888-745-4800. Singles $45-50; doubles $51-56; cheaper in winter.) **Ranger Motel,** 453 N. 3rd St., patrols downtown, within walking distance of numerous restaurants and bars. (☎ 742-6677. HBO, fridge, microwave. Singles $37; doubles $46.) Lined with hotels and fast food, 3rd St. leads south into the heart of town, crossing Ivinson and Grand St., both of which burst with student hangouts. **Jeffrey's Restaurant,** 123 Ivinson St. at 2nd. St., doles out homemade bread and hot sandwiches for $5-9. (☎ 742-7046. Open M-Sa 11am-9pm.) **Lovejoy's Bar & Grill,** 101 Grand St., across from the railroad tracks, will put the steam back in your engine. (☎ 745-0141. Open Su-Th 11am-10pm, F-Sa 11am-2am.) Check out the local scene at the trendy **Coal Creek Coffeehouse,** 110 Grand Ave. Coffee is the speciality, but gourmet "light fare" can be had for $4-6. (☎ 745-7737. Open daily 6am-11pm.)

ROCKY MOUNTAINS

Both students and Harleys steer their way into the **Buckhorn Bar,** 114 Ivinson St., a neighborhood hangout featuring busy pool tables and live music Saturday and Sunday nights. (☎742-3554. Open M-Sa 8am-2am, Su 10am-midnight.) UW students can honestly tell their parents that they spent the weekend in the **Library,** 1622 Grand Ave. Pull up a table in their "stacks" for a salad ($4-7), steak ($11-14), or daily special ($5-6). Next door, the library's oft-frequented bar has $2-3 beers on tap. (☎742-3900. Restaurant open Su-W 11am-9pm, Th-Sa 11am-10pm. Bar open M-Sa 11am-2am, Su 11am-midnight.) Laramie's **Chamber of Commerce** is located at 800 S. 3rd. St., Exit 313 off I-80. (☎745-7339. Open M-F 8am-5pm.) **Post Office:** 152 N. 5th St. (open M-F 8am-5:15pm, Sa 9am-1pm). **ZIP code:** 82070. **Area code:** 307.

COLORADO

In the high, thin air of Colorado, golf balls fly farther, eggs take longer to cook, and visitors tend to lose their breath just getting out of bed. Oxygen deprivation lures athletes looking to loosen their lungs for a competitive edge, but most hikers, skiers, and climbers worship Colorado for its peaks and mountain enclaves. Denver—the country's highest capital—has long since shed its cow-town image and matured into the cultural center of the Rocky Mountains. Colorado's extraordinary heights are matched by its equally spectacular depths. Over millions of years, the Gunnison and Colorado Rivers have etched the natural wonders of the Black Canyon and the Colorado National Monument. Silver and gold attracted early settlers to Colorado, but it is Mother Nature that continues to enhance its appeal as a destination.

◪ PRACTICAL INFORMATION

Capital: Denver.

Visitor info: Colorado Travel and Tourism Authority, CTTA, 1127 Pennsylvania St., Denver 80203 (☎303-832-6171). For a packet of info, call 800-265-6723 or visit www.colorado.com. **US Forest Service,** Rocky Mountain Region, 740 Sims St., Golden, 80401 or P.O. Box 25127, Lakewood 80225 (☎303-275-5350). Open M-F 7:30am-4:30pm. **Ski Country USA,** 1560 Broadway, #2000, Denver 80202 provides info on all Colorado ski resorts (☎303-837-0793; ski report 825-7660; open M-F 8:30am-5:30pm). **National Park Service,** 12795 W. Alameda Pkwy., P.O. Box 25287, Lakewood 80225 (☎303-969-2000). For reservations for Rocky Mountain National Park or any national park, call 800-365-2267. **Colorado State Parks,** 1313 Sherman St., #618, Denver 80203 (☎303-866-3437). Open for calls M-F 7am-4:45pm. For reservations for any Colorado state park, call 303-470-1144 or 800-678-2267. There is a $7 reservation fee; reservations must be made at least 3 days in advance.

Postal Abbreviation: CO. **Sales Tax:** 7.4%.

DENVER ☎303

In 1858, the discovery of gold in the Rocky Mountains brought a rush of eager miners to northern Colorado. After an excruciating trek through the plains, the desperados set up camp for a breather and a stiff shot of whiskey before heading west into "them thar hills." Overnight, Denver was transformed into a flourishing frontier town. Today, Denver continues to grow at an impressive rate. The Mile High City is a bona fide melting pot of cultures and peoples, not to mention a city of surprises. Recently named the number one sports town in America, Denver is also the country's healthiest city, boasts the nation's largest city park system, brews the most beer of any metropolitan area, and has the highest number of high school and college graduates per capita. Denver has the largest performing arts complex in the world, and in 1998 the Denver Theatre Company won a Tony Award for the best regional theatre. Denver's greatest characteristic is its vibrant atmosphere; the city offers a unique combination of urban sophistication and traditional Western grit.

ROCKY MOUNTAINS

Denver

ACCOMMODATIONS
Broadway Plaza Motel, **6**
Budget Host Inn, **1**
Hostel of the Rocky Mtns. (HI-AYH) & B&Bs, **9**

FOOD
Corner Bakery, **5**
Lemon Sisters Market, **3**
The Market, **4**
Mercury Cafe, **10**
Pearl Street Grill, **7**
Swing Thai, **8**
Wynkoop Brewery, **2**

⌐ TRANSPORTATION

Airport: Denver International (DIA) (☎342-2000), 23 mi. northeast of downtown off I-70. Shuttles run from the airport to downtown and ski resorts in the area. The **RTD Sky Ride** (☎299-6000 or 800-366-7433; office hours M-F 6am-8pm, Sa-Su 8am-8pm) costs $6 (seniors and disabled $3) to DIA from downtown; buses run hourly from the Market St. station downtown from 5am-10:30pm. From the main terminal, **Supershuttle** (☎370-1300 or 800-525-3177) shuttles to downtown hotels (1hr., $17). A **taxi** to downtown costs about $45. The Supershuttle also travels to Boulder. (☎444-0808. 1-2hr. $19 from hotels, $22 from homes, businesses, and the University of CO campus.)

Trains: Amtrak, Union Station, 1701 Wynkoop St. (☎534-2812 for arrivals/departures, 825-2583 for ticket office), at 17th St. To: Salt Lake City (15hr., 1 per day, $71+); St. Louis (26½hr., 1 per day, $130+); and Chicago (19hr., 1 per day, $104+). Ticket office open daily 6am-9pm. **Río Grande Ski Train** (☎296-4754), housed in the same building, chugs 2¼hr. through the Rockies, stopping in Winter Park within walking distance of the lifts; free ground transport to town provided; lift discounts included. Dec.-Apr. same-day round-trip $45; reservations required. Runs Jan. Sa-Su, Feb. to mid-June F-Su, mid-June to mid-Aug. Sa only. Round-trip $45, under 14 $25.

Buses: Greyhound, 1055 19th St. (☎293-6555). To: Santa Fe (7½-9hr., 4 per day, $61); Salt Lake City (10-13hr., 3 per day, $46); Colorado Springs (1½hr., 7 per day, $14); and Chicago (20-22hr., 6 per day, $86). Ticket office open daily 6am-11:45pm.

Public Transit: Regional Transportation District (RTD), 1600 Blake St. (☎299-6000 or 800-366-7433). Serves Denver, as well as Longmont, Evergreen, Golden, and suburbs. Route hours vary; many lines shut down by 9pm. 75¢, seniors and disabled 25¢; peak hours $1.25. Exact change required. Major terminals are at Market and 17th St. and at Colfax and Broadway. The free 16th St. **Mall Shuttle** covers 14 blocks downtown and runs daily 5:45am-1am. **Light Rail** services the perimeter of the city and suburbs, from I-25 and Broadway north to 30th and Downing.

Taxis: Yellow Cab, ☎777-7777. **Zone Cab,** ☎444-8888.

Car Rental: Enterprise, 7720 Calawaba Ct. (☎800-720-7222), at the airport. Compact cars start at $55 per day with an extra $15 charge per day for drivers 21-25. Security deposit of $250 or a major credit card required. Open daily 7am-11pm.

▟⧮ ORIENTATION AND PRACTICAL INFORMATION

Running north-south, **Broadway** slices Denver in half. East of Broadway, **Colorado Blvd.** is also a major north-south thoroughfare. **Colfax Ave.,** running east-west, is the main north-south dividing line. Both named and numbered streets run diagonally in the downtown area. In the rest of the city, numbered avenues run east-west and count upwards as you head north. Named streets run north-south. Many of the avenues on the eastern side of the city become numbered *streets* downtown. The **16th St. Mall** is the hub of Denver's downtown and could easily be called the social, dining, and entertainment center of the city. *Avoid the west end of Colfax Ave., Federal Blvd., S. Santa Fe Blvd., the east side of town beyond the capitol (the Capitol Hill area), and the west side of the* **Barrio** *(25th-34th St.) at night.*

Visitor info: Denver Visitors Bureau, 1668 Larimer St. (☎892-1112 or 892-1505), just north of the 16th St. Mall. Open M-F 8am-5pm, Sa 9am-1pm.

Hotlines: Rape Crisis Hotline, ☎322-7273.

Bi-Gay-Lesbian Organizations: Gay and Lesbian and Bi-Sexual Community Services Center of Colorado, ☎733-7743. Open M-F 10am-6pm.

Internet access: Public Library, 10 W. 14th Ave. Open M-W 10am-9pm, Th-Sa 10am-5:30pm, Su 1-5pm.

Post Office: 951 20th St. (☎800-275-8777). Open M-F 7am-6pm, Sa 9am-1pm. General delivery open M-F 8:30am-4pm. **ZIP code:** 80202. **Area code:** 303. Ten digit dialing required.

ACCOMMODATIONS

Hostel of the Rocky Mountains (HI-AYH), 1530 Downing St. (☎861-7777). Right off E. Colfax Ave., the hostel is 10 blocks from the Capitol, next to 2 major bus routes and a trolley stop. Cheerful rooms make this Denver's best value. The hostel features TVs with built-in VCR in every room, laundry facilities, library, kitchens, a small gym, and Internet access ($1 per 20min.). Pickup from the Greyhound depot or Union Station. Bike rental ($2); tours of Denver area ($5-25). Linen $2, key deposit $5. Reception 7am-noon, 5-10pm. Reservations recommended. Dorms $14; private rooms $30-45.

Hostel of the Rocky Mountains D&Bs. The friendly staff at the hostel also operates 2 well-priced B&Bs right next door. Classier and decidedly quieter than the hostel, the rooms here are clean and spacious with shared baths. Guests can enjoy free breakfast next door at the hostel or use the kitchen facilities to fend for themselves. Prices run $32, $36, and $40, depending on the room. Call the hostel for reservations.

Broadway Plaza Motel, 1111 Broadway (☎893-0303), 3 blocks south of the Capitol building. Spacious, clean rooms within walking distance of downtown Denver. Free HBO. Singles $45-55; doubles $49-56.

Budget Host Inn, 2747 Wyandot St. (☎458-5454), has clean, comfortable rooms conveniently located near Six Flags Elitch Gardens. Great discounts on tickets to Six Flags ($19.50 per ticket, down from $33). Singles from $40; doubles from $43.

Two state parks lie in the Denver metro area. **Cherry Creek State Park,** 4201 S. Parker Rd., Aurora, is conveniently located in an urban area. A few groves of pine trees provide limited shade. The park often fills up, so arrive early. Take I-25 to Exit 200, then head north on I-225 for about 3 mi. and take the Parker Rd. exit. (Open Apr.-Oct. Sites $10; with electricity $14. Daily entrance fee $5.) The beautiful, but much less convenient **Golden Gate Canyon State Park** offers 106 rustic sites. Take I-70 west to 6th Ave., go west about 20 mi. towards Central City, and then go north about 19 mi. on Rte. 119. (Sites $10; with electricity $14; backcountry shelters $6. Daily entrance fee $4.) Contact the **State Parks Office** for info. (Reservations ☎470-1144 or 800-678-2267. Open M-F 7am-4:45pm. $7.)

FOOD

Downtown Denver offers a full range of cuisines, from Russian to traditional Southwestern. Al fresco dining and people-watching are available along the **16th St. Mall.** Gourmet eateries are located southwest of the Mall on Larimer St., in **Larimer Sq.** Sports bars and trendy restaurants occupy **LoDo,** the neighborhood extending from Wynkoop St. to Larimer Sq. between Speer Blvd. and 20th St. Outside of downtown, **Colorado Blvd.** and **6th Ave.** also have their share of posh restaurants. **E. Colfax Ave.** offers a number of reasonably priced ethnic restaurants, including Greek and Ethiopian cuisine. Colorado's distance from the ocean may make you wonder about **"Rocky Mountain oysters."** These salty-sweet delicacies (bison testicles) are sold at the **Denver Buffalo Company,** 1109 Lincoln Ave. (☎832-0880).

■ **Mercury Cafe,** 22nd and California (☎294-9281 or 294-9258 to "speak to a human"). Decorated with a new-age flair, the Merc specializes in home-baked wheat bread and a slew of reasonably priced soups ($2-3), salads ($6-8), enchiladas ($5.50-7), and vegetarian specials. Live bands provide music in the dining room and upstairs dance area. All ages admitted unless otherwise specified. Open Tu-F 5:30-11pm, Sa-Su 9am-3pm and 5:30-11pm; dancing until 2am F-Sa and 1am Tu-Th and Su.

■ **Pearl Street Grill,** 1477 S. Pearl St. (☎778-6475), in the trendy and laid-back Washington Park area. Serves gourmet food, but an evening there won't break the bank. On the dinner menu, the "PSG Favorites" range from $7-12 (the majority cost $8). Enjoy your food and the night on the patio. Open daily 11am-2am (brunch served 11am-3pm).

The Market, 1445 Larimer Sq. (☎534-5140), downtown, is popular with a young, artsy crowd, as well as suits. A variety of busy specialty counters serve cappuccino for $2.30, sandwiches for $6.50, and exotic salads for $5-9 per lb. Open M-Th 6:30am-11pm, F 6:30am-midnight, Sa-Su 7:30am-midnight.

Corner Bakery, 500 16th St. (☎572-0170), is a trendy establishment that's taken the term "bakery" to a higher level. Chicken pesto sandwiches ($6) and a variety of soups, salads, gourmet pizzas, homemade breads, and goodies are served cafeteria-style with a classy spin. Sit inside, or tempt pedestrians along the Mall with your delicious food. Open M-W 7am-7pm, Th 7am-8pm, F 7am-10pm, Sa 8am-10pm, Su 9am-5pm.

Swing Thai, 845 Colorado Blvd. (☎777-1777) is an understandably popular restaurant. With a wide assortment of high-quality food at cheap prices, Swing Thai stands out. Those sick of pizza and burgers can indulge on specialties such as the *hot* Jungle Curry ($6.50) or Pineapple Fried Rice ($5.50). A number of wok specials with gigantic portions are available for a mere $6.50. Open daily 11am-10pm.

Lemon Sisters Market, 1530 Blake St. (☎825-4133), is a hidden treasure. The tasty breakfast burritos cost just $2.50. Deli sandwiches $5. Hearty soups and a variety of specials ($3-5) are available daily. Sesame noodles, tabouli, and hummus satisfy those with more exotic cravings. Open M-Th 8am-9pm, F 8am-7pm, Sa-Su 10am-6pm.

Wynkoop Brewery, 1634 18th St. (☎297-2700), at Wynkoop across from Union Station in LoDo. Colorado's first brewpub serves beer (20 oz. $2.50), homemade root beer, lunch, and dinner (burgers from $6). Pool tables upstairs and an independent **comedy club** downstairs (☎297-2111). Happy hour M-F 3-6pm, $2 pints. Brewery open daily M-Sa 11am-2am, Su 11am-midnight. Food service M-Th until 11pm, F-Sa until midnight, Su until 10pm. Free brewery tours Sa 1-5pm.

⚙ SIGHTS

CULTURAL CONNECTION TROLLEY. One of the best tour deals around, the trolley visits over 20 of the city's main attractions. The fare is good all day on any local bus or light rail. The easiest place to begin a tour is along the 16th St. Mall, near the Mall Ride stops, but the tour can be joined at many local attractions; look for the green and red sign. (☎299-6000. Buses depart every hr. 8:30am-4:30pm. $16, under 13 $8.)

COLORADO STATE CAPITOL. Many of the best sights in Denver center around downtown, which makes touring on foot easy. The **Capitol Building** is a sensible place to start your visit to the Mile High City—the 15th step (marked by a small engraving) leading to the building's entrance sits exactly 5280 ft. (1 mi.) above sea level. Ambitious visitors can climb 93 stairs to the dome observatory for an impressive view of the city and the mountains. (☎866-2604. 40min. tours run every 30min. M-F 7am-5:30pm and Sa 9:30am-2:30pm. Visitors are welcome to climb the stairs to the dome M-F until 3:30pm and Sa-Su 2:15pm.)

DENVER ART MUSEUM. Just a few blocks west of the Capitol stands the Denver Art Museum, a unique seven-story "vertical" museum. The DAM houses a world-class collection of Native American art and pre-Colombian artifacts. Guided tours of the European and American Art Galleries run every Saturday and Sunday at 2:30pm. The gallery's impressive collection warrants several hours of exploration. (100 W. 14th Ave. Pkwy. ☎640-4433. Open Tu and Th-Sa 10am-5pm, W 10am-9pm, Su noon-5pm. Tours July-Aug. Tu-Sa 11am and 1:30pm, Su 1:30pm; Sept.-June daily at 1:30pm, Sa also at 11:30am. $4.50; seniors, students, and children $2.50; under 5 free.)

US MINT. A mere two blocks west of the Art Museum is a remnant of Colorado's silver mining days, the US Mint. The Mint issues the majority of coins in the US; just look for the small "D" embossed beneath the date to see if your pocket change was made in Denver. The lines of money-hungry tourists are often horrendously long, so arrive early or call ahead. (320 W. Colfax Ave. ☎405-4761 or 405-4765 for tour info. Open M-F 8am-3pm. In summer free 20min. tours every 15-20min. Call for reservation Oct.-Apr.)

SIX FLAGS. Next door, make a splash of your own at the Island Kingdom water park at Six Flags Elitch Gardens, at Elitch Circle and Speer Blvd., across the freeway from Mile High Stadium. The Boomerang, Mind Eraser, Sidewinder, and Tower of Doom keep thrill seekers content. (☎595-4386. Open June-Aug. daily 10am-10pm; spring and early fall Sa-Su call to confirm. $33, seniors and under 4 ft. $16.50. Look for money-saving coupons in the Elitch Gardens brochures. AAA discounts available.)

OCEAN JOURNEY. Denver's brand new aquarium guides visitors through two spectacular underwater exhibitions: the Colorado River Journey and the Indonesian River Journey. Follow the Colorado River as it descends from the Continental Divide in the Rocky Mountains to the Sea of Cortez in Mexico. The Indonesian River Journey embarks from the volcanic Barisan Mountains in Sumatra, eventually emptying into the South China Sea. The aquarium houses over 15,000 exotic marine creatures, including several species of sharks, sea otters, and the magnificent Napoleon wrasse. *(700 Water St. ☎ 561-4450. Open Sept.-May daily 10am-6pm; June-Aug. 9am-6pm. $15, ages 13-17 $13, ages 4-12 $7, seniors $13.)*

DENVER MUSEUM OF NATURE AND SCIENCE. This gigantic museum hosts a variety of interesting exhibits under its roof. You won't want to miss the Hall of Life or the Prehistoric Journey room. A super-cool **IMAX** theater with a six-story screen shows two different movies daily. *(2001 Colorado Blvd. ☎ 322-7009 or 800-925-2250. Open daily 9am-5pm. Museum $7; seniors, students, and ages 3-12 $4.50. Combination tickets to IMAX and museum $11/$7. Call for IMAX shows and times.)*

COORS BREWERY. Located in nearby Golden, this is the world's largest one-sight brewery. The brewery also holds the honor of having one of the nicest wellness centers in the corporate world—not too long ago, the workout center was deemed a necessary company addition. All 42,000 workers are allowed two free beers after every shift, and waistlines were noticeably growing. Interesting 40min. walking tours take you through the entire Coors brewing process from start to finish. Those parched and exhausted at the end of the tour can indulge themselves by sampling up to three different Coors products; free Pepsi products are available for non-drinkers. *(Take I-70 W to Exit 264; head west on 32nd Ave. for 4½ mi., then turn left on East St. and follow the signs. ☎ 303-277-2337. A shuttle bus runs from the parking lot to the brewery, but not before a very short historical tour of Golden. Tours run M-Sa 10am-4pm.)*

ROCKY MOUNTAIN ARSENAL. The best spot for bald eagles in Denver is also the town's most radioactive plot. The Rocky Mountain Arsenal, a former nuclear waste site, is a wildlife refuge. *(☎ 289-0232. Office open M-F 8am-4pm. Bald eagle viewing area open Oct.-Mar. 8:30am-dusk; refuge open Sa 12:30-8pm; in winter 8am-3pm. Call ahead.)*

🔼 OUTDOOR ACTIVITIES

Denver has more public parks per square mile than any other city, providing prime space for bicycling, walking, or lolling about. **Cheesman Park,** 8th Ave. and Humboldt St., offers picnic areas and a view of the snowcapped peaks of the Rockies. **Confluence Park,** at Cherry Creek and the South Platte River, lures bikers and hikers with paved paths along the river. Every Thursday in July, **Confluence Concerts** (☎ 455-7192) hosts live music for a broad range of musical tastes along the banks of the South Platte. **City Park** (☎ 697-4545) houses a museum, zoo, running path, and golf course. **Colorado State Parks** has the lowdown on nearby state parks. (☎ 866-3437. Open M-F 8am-5pm.) A local favorite is **Roxborough State Park,** where visitors can hike and ski among red rock formations. (Take U.S. 85 S, turn right on Titan Rd., and follow it 3½ mi. to the park. Open year-round. Day use only.)

The mammoth **Red Rocks Amphitheater and Park,** 12 mi. southwest of Denver on I-70 at the Morrison exit, is carved into red sandstone. As the sun sets over the city, performers such as R.E.M., U2, and the Denver Symphony Orchestra compete with the view behind them. The actual Red Rocks Park contains more than 600 acres and features numerous hiking trails. For concert tickets, call Ticketmaster at 830-8497. Forty miles west of Denver, the road to the top of **Mt. Evans** (14,260 ft.) is the highest paved road in North America. Take I-70 W to Rte. 103 in Idaho Springs. (☎ 303-567-2901. Open late May to early Sept.)

🎵 ENTERTAINMENT

Life in Denver is never boring for sports fans. Denver's baseball team, the **Colorado Rockies,** plays at **Coors Field,** at 20th and Blake St. (☎800-388-7625. Tickets $4-37; some $4 Rockpile tickets available day of game.) In the fall, the **Denver Broncos** move into the brand new **Invesco Field** to start the 2001-2002 season (☎433-7466). Soccer mania takes over **Mile High Stadium** during the spring and summer as the **Colorado Rapids** take the field (☎299-1570). The NBA **Nuggets** and the 2001 NHL champion **Colorado Avalanche** share the state-of-the-art **Pepsi Center,** 1000 Chopper Cir. (☎405-1100 for info on the Nuggets and the Avalanche).

Every January, Denver hosts the nation's largest livestock show and one of the biggest rodeos, the **National Western Stock Show,** 4655 Humboldt St. Here, cowboys compete for prize money while over 10,000 head of cattle compete for "Best of Breed" (Jan. 12-27, 2002). **Cinco de Mayo** (☎534-8342, ext. 106)—yes, on the 5th of May—attracts 250,000 visitors per year in celebration of Mexico's victory over the French in 1862. The **Capitol Hill People's Fair** (☎830-1651), the first full week of June, is a large outdoor celebration with food vendors and local bands at **Civic Center Park,** near the capitol. The **Renaissance Festival** takes guests back in time with jousting, music, and plenty of free spirits in medieval garb. (☎688-6010. June-July every Sa-Su.) **The Festival of Mountain and Plain: A Taste of Colorado** (☎534-6161) packs Civic Center Park Labor Day weekend for one last summer shebang. Food, crafts, free entertainment, and carnival rides are all part of the fun.

🍸 NIGHTLIFE

Downtown Denver in and around the 16th St. Mall is an attraction in itself. With ample shopping, dining, and people-watching opportunities, there's something for everyone. Many restaurants host radio stations and live bands on a regular basis, and concerts are never lacking in the Civic Center Park area. Denver's local restaurants and bars cater to a college-age and slightly older singles crowd. A copy of *Westword* gives the lowdown on LoDo.

El Chapultepec, (☎295-9126), at 20th and Market St., is a be-boppin' jazz holdover from Denver's Beat era of the 50s. No cover. 1-drink min. per set. Open daily 7am-2am.

The Church, 1160 Lincoln (☎832-3528). In a remodeled chapel, The Church offers four full bars, a cigar lounge, and a weekend sushi bar. On weekends, the congregation swells with two floors of dancing. Th 18+. Doors open Tu-Su 9pm until 1-2am.

Bluebird Theater, 3317 E. Colfax (☎322-2308). Hosts local and the occasional national act. The theater runs a free movie once a month. Due to the drinking opportunity that accompanies the films, only 21+ are allowed.

Falling Rock, 1919 Blake St. (☎293-8338). Voted the bar with the "Best Beer Selection" by the Denver Post in 1999 and 2000. With 71 beers on tap ($3.75), it is one of the best places to sample a variety of microbrews from the impressive beer menu. Open daily 11am-1:30am.

The Giggling Grizzly, 1320 20th St. (☎297-8300), is a popular late-night destination for the youthful crowd. Open M-F 4pm-1:30am, Sa 5pm-1:30am.

Bash, 1902 Blake St. (☎298-7994). A hugely popular nightclub. F ladies' night (no cover and $2.50 drinks); Sa no cover before 10pm, half-price before 11pm. Open F-Sa 9:30pm-1:40am.

Foxhole Lounge, 2936 Fox St. (☎298-7378). A popular gay-friendly bar, this is the place to be on Su nights, so get there early or expect a long wait. Th house, F lesbian night. No cover. Open Th-Sa 8am-2am, Su 2pm-2am.

Charlie's, 900 E. Colfax Ave., (☎839-8890) at Emerson, is a well-known gay bar with a big dance floor and a Western-style atmosphere. Open daily 10am-4am.

MOUNTAIN RESORTS NEAR DENVER ☎ 970

WINTER PARK

Nestled among delicious-smelling mountain pines in the upper Fraser River Valley, the popular **Winter Park Resort** is the closest ski and summer resort to Denver, only 67 miles away. **Winter Park Mary Jane Ski Area** (☎ 726-5514 or 800-453-2525) packs bowls all winter long with a 3060 ft. vertical drop and 1467 acres of glade skiing on 2886 total acres. (Single-day lift ticket $50, multiday tickets $40-45.) **Slopeside Gear and Sport,** at the base of Winter Park Resort, rents skis starting at $20 per day and snowboards from $26 per day. For snow conditions and summertime fun info, call 303-572-7669 or 800-729-5813. The **Alpine Slide** twists and turns 26 times; at 3030 ft., it is Colorado's longest. (Open June to early Sept. daily 10am-5:30pm. $8, seniors and children $7. Under 6 and over 70 free.) In the summer, mountain biking and hiking trails climb the mountains of the Continental Divide. The **Zephyr Express** chairlift blows to the summit of Winter Park Mountain, allowing mountain bikers to reach the peak, then ride down on 50 mi. of single-track trails. (Open mid-June to early Sept. daily 10am-5pm. Full-day chair pass $19. Mountain bike rentals from $9 per hr., $32 per day. A 2hr. clinic will teach you how to ride or hone your skills for $20.) Winter Park is on the vanguard of summer fun, with mountain scooters, a maze, and a zip-line. (Summer activities pass M-F $40, Sa-Su $45.) The **High Country Stampede Rodeo** bucks every Saturday at 7:30pm in July and August at the John Work Arena, west of Fraser on County Rd. 73. (☎970-726-4118, 303-422-0666, or 800-903-7275. $10, ages 6-13 $6, seniors $8.) **Mad Adventures** is a popular **whitewater rafting** company. (☎ 726-5290 or 800-451-4844. Half-day $39.50, full-day $59.50.)

The **Viking Lodge,** on Rte. 40 in Winter Park, offers tiny rooms with phones and color TVs. Lodgings include access to the hot tub and sauna, a 10% discount on rentals at the adjacent store, and winter shuttle service to the lifts. (☎ 726-8885 or 800-421-4013. Reception 8am-9pm. Singles $35-65; doubles $35-70; varies with season.) Perhaps the best family lodging deal in the Fraser Valley is the **Snow Mountain Ranch YMCA,** 12 mi. past the town of Winter Park (take I-70 W to U.S. 40 W). The ranch features a host of recreational activities, including nordic skiing. (☎887-2152, ext. 4110. Quad with private bath $67. Campsites range from $17-21 per night.) Deliciously healthy breakfasts and lunches (each $5-8) are served on the patio at **Carver's Bakery Cafe,** at the end of the Cooper Creek Mall off U.S. 40. Try the massive cinnamon rolls for $2.75 or the Almond Joy Latte for $4. (☎ 726-8202. Open daily 7am-2pm, until 3pm during peak season.) The local favorite is **The Last Waltz,** at Kings Crossing Center off Rte. 40. Hearty breakfasts such as chocolate chip pancakes ($5.25) will tide you over until lunch, when you can return for a Chicken Mango Tango sandwich for $7 or one of many vegetarian options for $6-8. (☎726-4877. Open daily 7am-2pm, Th-Su 5-9pm.)

To reach Winter Park from Denver, take I-70 W to U.S. 40. The Chamber of Commerce (see below) also serves as the **Greyhound** depot. **Home James Transportation Services** (☎970-726-5060 or 800-359-7536) runs door-to-door shuttles to and from Fraser or Winter Park and the Denver airport. (Office open daily 8am-6pm. Reservations required. $41.) From December to April, the **Río Grande Ski Train** (☎303-296-4754) leaves Denver's Union Station for Winter Park (see p. 676). **Winter Park-Fraser Valley Chamber of Commerce:** 78841 Rte. 40 (☎726-4118, 303-422-0666, or 800-903-7275; open daily 8am-5pm). **Area code:** 970.

SUMMIT COUNTY

Skiers, hikers, and mountain bikers can tap into a sportsman's paradise in the US's highest county, about 70 mi. west of Denver on I-70. The most popular ski resort in the country, **Breckenridge** (☎453-5000 or 800-789-7669; snow conditions 453-6118), has a 3398 ft. vertical drop, 139 trails, and 2043 acres of skiable terrain made accessible by 25 lifts. **Copper Mountain** (☎968-2882 or 800-458-8386; snow conditions 800-789-7609) features a 2601 ft. drop and 125 trails. **Keystone** (☎496-2316 or 800-468-5004; snow conditions 800-468-5004; reservations 888-222-9298), has a 2900 ft. drop and 116 trails, including 17 available for night skiing. All three resorts are alternatives to the more expensive resorts of Aspen and Vail. **Arapahoe Basin** (☎ 468-0718 or 888-272-7246) usually has skiing until early July, depending on snow conditions; it is the highest skiable terrain in North America.

The **Alpen Hütte,** 471 Rainbow Dr., in Silverthorne, has welcoming hosts, a familial atmosphere, clean rooms with beautiful mountain views, and year-round outdoor activities that include fly-fishing on the Blue River behind the hostel. Greyhound (from Denver) and Summit Stage stop outside the door. (☎ 468-6336. Linen and towels $1.50. Laundry, free ski storage, parking. Lockers $5 deposit. Reception daily 7-11am and 4pm-midnight. Midnight curfew. Reserve for winter 1-2 months in advance. Dorms $17; in winter $27.) There are several Forest Service campgrounds in the nearby **White River National Forest.** The **Dillon Ranger District Office,** 680 Blue River Pkwy., can provide more info. (☎ 468-5400, reservations 877-444-6777. Open M-F 8am-5pm.) Free **Summit Stage** buses connect the resorts with **Frisco, Dillon,** and **Silverthorne.** Call 668-0999 for schedule info. **Summit County Chamber of Commerce:** 11 S. Summit Blvd., in Frisco. (☎ 262-2866. Open daily 9am-5pm.) **Silverthorne-Dillon Info Center:** in the Summit Place Mall off Rte. 6 in Dillon, ¼ mi. south of I-70 on Rte. 6. (☎ 262-0817. Open M-Sa 9am-5pm.) **Area code:** 970.

BRECKENRIDGE

Fashionable Breckenridge lies west of Silverthorne on I-70, 9 mi. south of Frisco. Summer activities in this scenic town include a scenic **chairlift** ride (single ride $5, seniors and ages 7-12 $3), a superslide ($8/$7), Colorado's largest human maze ($5, children 5-12 $4), and a climbing wall ($5 per climb). The **Breckenridge Mountain Bike Park** offers a variety of biking trails on Peaks 8 and 9, accessible by chairlift ($8, children $6). More sophisticated alternatives include the **Breckenridge Music Festival,** providing a wide selection of musical performances, including the Breckenridge Music Institute Orchestra and the National Repertory Orchestra. (☎ 547-3100 for ticket information. Box office open Tu-Su 11am-5pm. Tickets $15-25, seniors $13-23, students $5.)

Despite the many expensive restaurants and stores in town, you can still find reasonably priced, smoke-free accommodations at the ◪**Fireside Inn (HI-AYH),** 114 N. French St., two blocks east of Main St. on the corner of Wellington. The indoor hot tub is great for *après-ski.* (☎ 453-6456. Office open daily 8am-9pm. Breakfast $2-4. Dorms $25-38, private rooms from $65.) Start your day at the **Cool River Coffeehouse,** 325 S. Main St., with an espresso drink and a sandwich ($5-5.25) or wrap ($4.70-6.25). Stacy's Chunky Chicken Salad sandwich ($5) is a local favorite. (☎ 453-1736. Open daily 7am-5pm, and as late as 8-9pm on weekends.) **Rasta Pasta,** 411 S. Main St., is small but jammin' with the sound of twirling forks. The Rasta Pasta namesake dish (jerk chicken, penne pasta, and a garlic tomato sauce) makes customers wail with delight. Dishes range from $4-13. (☎ 453-7467. Open daily 11:30am-9pm.) **Breckenridge Activities Center:** at Washington and Main St. (☎ 453-5579. Open daily 9am-5pm.) **Ski Conditions and Weather:** ☎ 453-6118. **Area code:** 970.

BOULDER   ☎ 303

The 60s have been slow to fade in Boulder. A liberal haven in an otherwise conservative region of the country, the city is brimming with fashionable coffeeshops, teahouses, and organic juice bars. Boulder is home to both the central branch of the University of Colorado (CU) and Naropa University, the only accredited Buddhist university in the United States. Seek spiritual enlightenment through meditation and healing workshops at Naropa, or pursue a physical awakening through local outdoor activities, including biking, hiking, and rafting along Boulder Creek.

■ ▉ **ORIENTATION AND PRACTICAL INFORMATION.** Boulder is a small, manageable city, accessible from Rocky Mountain National Park and Estes Park by Rte. 36. The most developed area lies between **Broadway (Rte. 93)** and **28th St. (Rte. 36),** two busy streets running north-south through the city. Broadway, 28th St., and **Baseline Rd.** border the **University of Colorado (CU)** campus. The area around the school is known as **the Hill.** The pedestrian-only **Pearl St. Mall,** between 9th and 15th St., is lined with cafes, restaurants, and posh shops. **Greyhound,** at 30th and Diagonal Hwy. (☎800-231-2222; open 24hr.), rolls to Denver (1hr., 2 per day, $6); Glenwood Springs (6-7hr., 2 per day, $35-37); and Vail (5-5½hr., 2 per day, $28-30). Boulder's extensive yet confusing **public transit** system is run by **RTD,** at 14th and Walnut St. in the center of town. (☎299-6000 or 800-366-7433. Station open M-F 6am-8pm, Sa-Su 8am-8pm. Call for schedules and fares.) **Taxis: Boulder Yellow Cab,** ☎442-2277. **Bike Rental: University Bicycles,** 839 Pearl St. downtown, rents mountain bikes with helmet and lock. (☎444-4196. $15 per 4hr., $20 per 4-8hr., $25 overnight; kids' bikes $12/$15/$20. Open M-F 10am-7pm, Sa 10am-6pm, Su 10am-5pm.) **Visitor info: Boulder Chamber of Commerce/Visitors Service,** 2440 Pearl St., has info and free **Internet access.** (☎442-1044; open M-Th 8:30am-5pm, F 8:30am-4pm). **University of Colorado Information,** 2nd fl. of the University Memorial Center (UMC) student union, offers free local calls. (☎492-6161. Open M-Th 7am-11pm, F-Sa 7am-midnight, Su 11am-11pm; term-time M-Th 7am-midnight, F-Sa 7am-1am, Su 11am-midnight.) **Post Office:** 1905 15th St., at Walnut St. (☎938-3704). Open M-F 7:30am-5:30pm, Sa 10am-2pm. **ZIP code:** 80302. **Area code:** 303. 10-digit dialing required.

▐ ACCOMMODATIONS AND CAMPING. As with most popular tourist destinations, budget accommodations are few and far between in Boulder. **Boulder International Hostel,** 1107 12th St. at College Ave., is the best deal in town. Youthful travelers fill the spacious downstairs lobby to watch cable TV, lounge on the comfortable couches, and surf the Internet ($2 per 30min.). The front door is locked after midnight, but guests are given a code to enter after hours. (☎442-0522. Kitchen, laundry, and TV. Linen $4. Key deposit $10. Dorm lockout 10am-5pm. Dorms $17. Private singles $39 per night, $195 per week; doubles $45/$225. Prices lower in winter.) **Lazy L Motel,** 1000 28th St., on the Frontage Rd., has standard, clean, inexpensive rooms (at least for the Boulder area) and is conveniently located near busy Rte. 36. (☎442-7525. Singles $81, in winter $63; doubles $91/$73.) **Chautauqua Association,** off Baseline Rd. at the foot of the Flatirons, has lodge rooms as well as private cottages. To get there, turn at the Chautauqua Park sign and take Kinnikinic to Morning Glory Dr., where the office is located, or take RTD bus #203. (☎442-3282. Office open M-F 8:30am-7pm, additional summer hours Sa-Su 9am-5pm. Reserve months in advance. In summer, lodge rooms $57-98, 1 bedroom suites $73-95. Cottages with 2 bedrooms $92-185, 3 bedrooms $126; 4-night min. stay.)

Camping info for **Arapahoe/Roosevelt National Forest** is available from the **Boulder Ranger District,** 2140 Yarmouth Ave. at the corner of Rte. 36. (☎444-6600 or 800-444-6777. Open M-F 8am-4:30pm, Sa 8am-2pm.) **Kelly Dahl** lies among pine trees and picnic tables 3 mi. south of Nederland on Rte. 119. (☎800-280-2267. 46 sites.) **Rainbow Lakes** is 6.5 mi. north of Nederland; turn at the Mountain Research Station (CR 119) and follow the road for 5 mi. (☎970-444-6600. 18 sites. First come, first served; no water. Open late May to mid-Sept.) The two gems of the forest are **Peaceful Valley** (18 sites) and **Camp Dick** (46 sites). Both lie north on Rte. 72 and offer cross-country skiing in the winter. (☎800-280-2267. All sites are $6, with water $12. Reservations recommended, especially on weekends.)

▐ FOOD. The streets on the **Hill** surrounding CU and along the **Pearl St. Mall** burst with good eateries, natural foods markets, and colorful bars. Boulder may have more options for vegetarians than carnivores. A Boulder classic, **The Sink,** 1165 13th St., still awaits the return of its one-time janitor, Robert Redford, who quit his job and headed to California in the late 50s. The Sink serves surprisingly upscale new cuisine and great pizzas amid wild graffiti, low ceilings, and pipes. (☎444-7465. Open M-Sa 11am-2am, Su noon-2am; food served until 10pm. Burgers $6-7.) **Johnny McGuire's,** 1220 Pennsylvania Ave., is a local favorite for its specialty deli subs and sandwiches (6 in. $5.25, 8 in. $6.25, 1 ft. $10). The walls are covered with pictures and postcards from around the globe. (☎413-9254. Open Sept.-May daily 11am-10pm, June-Aug. daily 11am-3:30pm.) **Foolish Craig's,** 1611 Pearl St., serves French crepes with an American twist ($5-7.50), such as the "Homer" crepe—"Doh!" Favorites include the Breast o'

> **FIND YOUR INNER SPIRIT...** but not by watching
> another self-motivating episode of Oprah. Instead, consult the experts at **Naropa University**, 909 14th St., the only accredited Buddhist university in the country. (☎245-4800 or 800-603-3117; www.naropa.edu/conted.) Founded in 1974, Naropa offers professional programs in such areas as Ecopsychology and Authentic Movement. However, this innovative experience is not limited to students enrolled at the university. Naropa offers a variety of summer classes, lectures, and workshops for the general public. These include a free morning meditation program (M-F 8am) and a summer writing program through the **Jack Kerouac School of Disembodied Poetics**, co-founded by Allen Ginsberg and Anne Waldman. Naropa also sponsors readings of American literature by the authors themselves. (Call 245-4715 for more info.)

Pesto chicken crepe and the classic Nutella crepe. (☎247-9383. Live bluegrass M and occasionally on weekends. Open M-Sa 8am-10pm, Su 8am-9pm.) A delightful supermarket specializing in organic foods, **Alfalfa's**, 1651 Broadway, is a good place to buy provisions. The kitchen also sells a huge selection of prepared goods, including pasta salads galore (from $4.50 per lb.) and fresh wraps ($4.50-5). A salad bar ($4.60 per lb.) and juice bar round out the organic experience. (☎442-0909. Open daily 7am-10pm.)

◉♨ **SIGHTS AND OUTDOORS.** The tiny **Boulder Museum of Contemporary Art**, 1750 13th St., focuses on regional art. (☎443-2122. Open W-F noon-8pm, Su noon-5pm; in winter Tu-Sa 11am-5pm, Su noon-5pm. $4, seniors and students $3. Kids free.) Plopped down next to the museum is the ◨**Dushanbe Teahouse**, 1770 13th St. Built by artists in Tajikstan (part of the former Soviet Union), the teahouse was piece-mailed from Boulder's sister city of Dushanbe. The building is now owned by the city and leased to restauranteur Lenny Martinelli, who lays out a scrumptious spread. (☎442-4993. Open M-Th 8am-5pm, F 8am-10pm, Sa 5-10pm, Su 5-9pm. Tea $2-4; lunch from $5.50; dinner from $7.) The intimate **Leanin' Tree Museum**, 6055 Longbow Dr., presents 200 paintings and 80 bronze sculptures depicting Western themes. (☎530-1442, ext. 299. Open M-F 8am-4:30pm, Sa-Su 10am-4pm. Free.) Minutes away, **The Celestial Seasonings Tea Company**, 4600 Sleepytime Dr., lures visitors with tea samples and free tours of the factory, including the infamous Peppermint Room. (☎581-1202. Tea shop open M-F 9am-6pm, Sa 9am-5pm, Su 11am-4pm. Tours M-Sa every hr. 10am-3pm, Su every hr. 11am-3pm.) The **Rockies Brewing Company**, 2880 Wilderness Pl., off Valmont, offers tours and free beer. (☎444-8448. Pub open M-F 11am-10pm, Sa noon-8pm; in winter M-F 11am-8pm. 25min. tours M-Sa 2pm.)

Due to its proximity to the mountains, Boulder's location supports many outdoor activities. **Boulder Creek**, at the foot of the mountains, is prime hiking and biking territory, as is **Scott Carpenter Park. Chautauqua Park** has a number of trails varying in length and difficulty that climb up and around the **Flatirons. The Enchanted Mesa/McClintock Trail** is a self-guided nature trail that is partially wheelchair accessible. Before heading out into the wilderness, learn how to protect yourself against mountain lions, and grab a trail map at the entrance of Chautauqua Park.

◧◪ **ENTERTAINMENT AND NIGHTLIFE.** An exciting street scene rocks both the Mall and the Hill; the university's kiosks have the lowdown on downtown happenings. The **University Memorial Center**, 1609 Euclid (16th St. becomes Euclid on campus), hosts many events (☎492-6161). On the 3rd fl., its Cultural Events Board (☎492-3221) has the latest word on all CU-sponsored activities. Late June through early August, the **Colorado Shakespeare Festival** is the third-largest of its kind in the US, drawing over 50,000 people annually. (☎492-0554. Tickets $16-40; previews $10-20; $2 student and senior discount.) The **Colorado Music Festival** performs July through August. (☎449-2413. Lawn seats $5; other prices vary.) The local indie music scene is on display at the popular **Fox Theater and Cafe**, 1135 13th St. (☎447-0095). From April through October, Boulder shuts down 13th St., between Canyon and Arapahoe, for a good old **Farmers Market.** (Open W 10am-2pm, Sa 8am-2pm.)

Boulder overflows with nightlife hot spots, each with its own unique spin. The **Book-end Cafe,** 1115 Pearl St., attached to the famous **Boulder Bookstore,** is an established local favorite where people go to see and be seen. Treat yourself to a muffin, cookie, or piece of pie while observing the vibrant activity along the Mall from the outdoor patio. (☎440-6699. Open M-F 6:45am-10pm, Sa-Su 8am-10pm.) For bluegrass and funk, head to **Mountain Sun Pub and Brewery,** 1535 Pearl St. (☎546-0886. Open M-Sa 11:30am-1am, Su noon-1am. Su nights feature acoustic performances from 10pm-1am.) The **West End Tavern,** 926 Pearl St., was voted "Boulder's Best" by the *Daily Camera*, a Boulder publication. Head upstairs to the Rooftop Bar and enjoy the view of downtown. (☎444-3535. Open M-Sa 11am-1:30am, Su noon-1:30am; kitchen open until 11pm. Draughts $3, bottles $2.75-3.75.) For house and trance, head over to **Soma,** 1915 Broadway. If the music doesn't get to you, the red lighted interior and dizzyingly large dance floor will make your world spin 'round. (☎402-1690. Open daily 8pm-2am.)

ROCKY MOUNTAIN NATIONAL PARK ☎970

Of all the US national parks, Rocky Mountain National Park is closest to heaven, with over 60 peaks exceeding 12,000 feet. A third of the park lies above treeline, and Longs Peak pierces the sky at 14,255 feet. Here among the clouds, a fragile alpine tundra ecosystem supports bighorn sheep, elk, dwarf wildflowers, and arctic shrubs interspersed among granite boulders and crystalline lakes.

The city of Estes Park, located immediately east of the park, hosts the vast majority of would-be mountaineers and alpinists, who crowd the shopping areas and boulevards in the summer. To the west of the park, the town of Grand Lake, located on the edges of two glacial lakes, is a more tranquil base from which to explore the park's less traversed but equally stunning western side. Trail Ridge Rd./U.S. 34 runs 48 miles through the park from Grand Lake to Estes Park.

⚒ 🛈 ORIENTATION AND PRACTICAL INFORMATION

You can reach the national park from Boulder via U.S. 36 or scenic Rte. 7, or from the northeast up the Big Thompson Canyon via U.S. 34 (but beware of flash floods).

Visitor info: Park Headquarters and Visitors Center (☎586-1206), 2½ mi. west of Estes Park on Rte. 36, at the Beaver Meadows entrance to the park. Open mid-June to late Aug. daily 8am-9pm; Sept. to mid-June 8am-5pm. Winter evening programs on park-related topics are offered Sa 7pm; in summer daily at 7:30pm; a park introduction film is shown every 30min. 8:30am-4pm. **Kawuneeche Visitors Center** (☎627-3471), just outside the park's western entrance and 1¼ mi. north of Grand Lake, offers similar info. Open mid-May to late Aug. daily 8am-6pm; Sept. 8am-5pm; Oct. to mid-May 8am-4:30pm. Evening programs Sa 7pm (during winter, on the 2nd Sa of the month). The high-altitude **Alpine Visitors Center,** at the crest of Trail Ridge Rd., has a great view of the tundra. Open mid-June to late Aug. daily 9am-5pm; late May to mid-June and late Aug. to mid-Oct. 10am-4:30pm. **Lily Lake Visitors Center,** 6 mi. south of Park Headquarters on Rte. 7, opens only in summer (daily 9am-4:30pm). Park **entrance fee** is $15 per vehicle, $5 per cyclist or pedestrian; the pass is valid for 7 days.

Park Weather and Road Conditions: ☎586-1333.

Chamber of Commerce: Estes Park, 500 Big Thompson Rd. (☎800-443-7837). Open in summer M-F 8am-8pm, Sa-Su 9am-6pm; winter hours vary. **Grand Lake** (☎627-3372 or 800-531-1019; www.grandlakechamber.com), at the corner of Rte. 34 and W. Portal Rd. Open in summer M-Sa 9am-5pm, Su 10am-4pm.

Hospital: Estes Park Medical Center, ☎586-2317. **Park Emergency:** ☎586-1399.

Internet access: Estes Park Public Library, 335 E. Elkhorn (☎586-8116). Open summer M-F 9am-9pm, F-Sa 9am-5pm, Su 1-5pm; in winter M-Th 10am-9pm, F-Sa 10am-5pm, Su 1-5pm.

Post Offices: Grand Lake, 520 Center Dr. (☎627-3340). Open M-F 8:30am-5pm. **ZIP code:** 80447. **Estes Park,** 215 W. Riverside Dr. Open M-F 8:30am-5:30pm, Sa 10am-2pm. **ZIP code:** 80517. **Area code:** 970.

ACCOMMODATIONS

ESTES PARK

Although Estes Park has an abundance of expensive lodges and motels, there are a few good deals on indoor beds near the national park, especially in winter when temperatures drop and tourists leave.

The Colorado Mountain School, 351 Moraine Ave. (☎586-5758). Tidy, dorm-style accommodations are open to travelers unless already booked by mountain-climbing students. Wood bunks with comfortable mattresses, linen, and showers. 16 beds. $25 per person. Reservations recommended 1 week in advance.

Estes Park Center YMCA, 2515 Tunnel Rd. (☎586-3341, ext. 1010), follow Rte. 36 to Rte. 66; 2 mi. from the park entrance. Extensive facilities on the 860-acre complex include mini-golf and a pool, as well as daily hikes for guests and horseback rides. A 4-person cabin with kitchen and bath from $65; 5-person cabins $120; 7-person cabins $162. A 1-day guest membership is required to stay ($3, families $5). Call ahead; reservations for summer accepted starting May 1st.

GRAND LAKE

Though inaccessible without a car in the winter, this town is the "snowmobile capital of Colorado" and offers spectacular cross-country routes. Boating and swimming are popular summertime activities.

▨ Shadowcliff Hostel (HI-AYH), 405 Summerland Park Rd. (☎627-9220); from the western entrance, veer left to Grand Lake, then take the left fork ½ mi. into town on W. Portal Rd. In downtown Grand Lake, take a left at Garfield, and turn right onto W. Portal. Hand-built pine lodge perched on a cliff overlooking Grand Lake, Shadow Mountain Lake, and the Rockies. Hiking trails, kitchen, showers and a wood burning stove. Open late May to Oct. Dorms $10, nonmembers $12, bedding rental $1. Private singles $28. Doubles $33; each additional person $5. Cabins sleeping 6-8 $80-90 per day; 6-day min. stay. Make cabin reservations as far as a year in advance.

Sunset Motel, 505 Grand Ave. (☎627-3318). Stands out against the surrounding mountains with its yellow front and baby blue trim. Friendly owners, cozy rooms, and the only heated indoor pool in Grand Lake equals a warm stay. Singles $50-60; doubles $70-100; 10% discount with *Let's Go: USA*.

Bluebird Motel, 30 River Dr. (☎627-9314), on Rte. 34 west of Grand Lake. Variety is the key word here. Some rooms have couches, many have fridges, others have complete kitchenettes. The clean and cheerful Bluebird Motel overlooks Shadow Mountain Lake and the snowcapped Continental Divide. Singles $30-50; doubles $40-55.

CAMPING

You can camp a total of seven days anywhere within the park, at which point you must look for other accommodations. In the backcountry, the maximum stay decreases to three days. All national park campgrounds are $16 (winter sites are $10). A **backcountry** camping permit ($15) is required in the summer. On the eastern slope, permits are available inside the park from the **Backcountry Permits and Trip Planning Building,** a two-minute walk from the park headquarters. (☎586-1242. Open in summer daily 7am-7pm; in winter 8am-4:30pm.) In the west, see the folks at the **Kawuneeche Visitors Center** (open daily 8am-6pm).

GRAND LAKE

The cheapest camping in the National Park is in the surrounding national forests. **Stillwater Campground,** west of Grand Lake on the shores of the hot boating spot Lake Granby, has 127 tranquil sites ($15-18). **Green Ridge Campground,** located on the south end of Shadow Mountain Lake, is also a good bet with 78 sites ($12). Both campgrounds have toilets, water, and boat ramps, and are open late May to early September. (Reservations ☎877-444-6777; www.reserveusa.com. Reserve at least 8 days in advance), or arrive early for a first come, first served spot. **Timber Creek,** 10 mi. north of Grand Lake, is the only national park campground on the western side of the park. Open year-round, it offers 100 woodsy sites on a first come, first served basis. There is no water at Timber Creek in the winter.

EAST SIDE OF THE PARK

Moraine Park, 3 mi. west of Beaver Meadows Park Headquarters on Bear Lake Rd., is open all year and has 247 sites with open, sunny spots. **Glacier Basin** (9 mi. from Estes, south of Moraine Park) is open in summer only and offers 150 secluded sites and a spectacular view of the mountains. Both Moraine Park and Glacier Basin *require* reservations in summer (☎800-365-2267; http://reservations.nps.gov). **Aspenglen,** 5 mi. west of Estes Park near the Fall River entrance, has 54 first come, first served sites late May through September. **Longs Peak Campground** (26 sites; open year-round), also first come, first served, is a prime location to begin climbing Longs Peak. There is a three-night maximum stay and no water in winter.

◨ FOOD

ESTES PARK

The Notchtop Pub, 459 E. Wonderview, #44 (☎586-0272), in the upper Stanley Village Shopping Plaza, east of downtown off Rte. 34. Locals flock to the Notchtop for homemade "natural foods and brews," including breads, pastries, and pies baked fresh every morning. A mean lunch of soups ($3), salads ($4-6), and sandwiches (starting at $5). Open M-Th 7am-10pm, F-Su 7am-11pm.

Local's Grill, 153 E. Elkhorn Ave. (☎586-6900), in the heart of downtown, is a self-proclaimed "world-famous gathering place." Customers crowd onto the front patio for gourmet sandwiches ($5-8) and pizza ($5-11). Open M-Th 11am-9pm, F-Su 11am-10pm.

GRAND LAKE

☒ Pancho and Lefty's, 1120 Grand Ave. (☎627-8773). The price is right, as are the portions; try the deliciously spicy tamales ($6.25) or crunchy *chimichangas* ($7.25), and wash it all down with a margarita ($4). Open daily 11am-9pm; in winter W-M 6am-8pm.

E.G.'s Garden Grille, 1000 Grand Ave. (☎627-8404). Patrons cool off on the shaded patio while enjoying a cool drink from the bar. Dinner is rather pricey, but lunchtime sandwiches, subs, and burgers are affordable ($7-8). Open daily 11am-9pm.

◤ OUTDOOR ACTIVITIES

SCENIC DRIVES

The star of the park is **Trail Ridge Rd.** (U.S. 34), a 48 mi. stretch that rises 12,183 ft. above sea level into frigid tundra. This main drag through the park is the highest continuously paved road in the world. Best done in the morning before the crowds, the round-trip drive takes roughly 3hr. by car; beware of slow-moving tour buses and people who stop without warning to ogle at wildlife. The road is closed October to May for weather reasons and is passable only in the afternoon well into the summer. Many sights within the park are accessible from Trail Ridge Rd. Heading west, you'll arrive at **Rainbow Curve** and then the **Forest Canyon Overlook,** both of which offer impressive views of the vast tree-carpeted landscape. The interesting 30min. **Tundra Communities Trail** provides a once-in-a-lifetime-look at the fragile alpine tundra. Signposts along the paved trail instruct on the geology and wildlife pertinent to the tundra. The **Lava Cliffs** attract large crowds, but are worth the hassle. The **Alpine Visitors Center** lies just beyond the Lava Cliffs to the west and is probably the most difficult place along Trail Ridge Rd. to find parking. Beyond the Alpine Visitors Center, the traffic and congestion become noticeably thinner.

ROCKY MOUNTAINS

A wilder alternative to Trail Ridge Rd. is **Old Fall River Rd.** Entering Rocky Mountain National Park from the east side on Rte. 34 will take you by **Sheep Lakes,** a popular crossing for Bighorn Sheep. After Sheep Lakes, veer right toward the **Alluvial Fan** and Old Fall River Rd. Most of the road is unpaved; drivers will notice the destruction caused by flooding in 1982 along the way. Starting at **Endovalley** picnic area, Old Fall River Rd. is unpaved and one-way, heading uphill. For 9 mi. the road twists around the mountain, working its way towards spectacular mountain views. The finale is worth the drive, unless you're afraid of heights. The road intersects Trail Ridge Rd. behind the Alpine Visitors Center.

Bear Lake Rd. lies south of Trail Ridge Rd. and leads to the most popular hiking trails within the park. **Moraine Park Museum,** en route to the campsites, has exhibits on the park's geology and ecosystem, as well as comfortable rocking chairs with a view of the mountains. (Open in summer 9am-5pm.) **Hollowell Park** is usually an uncrowded area with picnic tables.

SCENIC HIKES

Numerous trailheads lie in the western half of the park, including the Continental Divide and its accompanying hiking trail. Trail Ridge Rd. ends in **Grand Lake,** a small town with ample outdoor opportunities of its own. An overnight trek from Grand Lake into the scenic and remote **North** or **East Inlets** leaves the crowds behind.

Lake Nanita (11 mi., 5½hr.). Leaving from North Inlet, the trail ascends 2240 ft. through pristine wilderness to a fantastic view of the lake.

Lake Verna (7 mi., 3½hr.). Leaves from East Inlet. Gaining a total of 1800 ft. in elevation, this trail passes mountain streams before re-entering the alpine forest. The culmination of the hike is an overlook of the fjord-like lake.

Mt. Chapin (1.5 mi., 1hr.). Trailhead accessible from Old Fall River Rd. Most of the trail lies above timberline; start early to avoid unpredictable weather. You can climb Mt. Chapin or hike around it to the saddle, a great place to picnic. From here, the adventurous can continue on to **Mt. Chiquita** and **Ypsilon Mt.** (combined time 5-6hr.; 10 mi.). Watch for storms and plan accordingly—the tundra offers little protection.

Mill Creek (1.5 mi., 40min.). Beginning at Hollowell Park, a picnic area along the main road, this easy trail crosses an open meadow and then empties out into a serene field of aspen, providing a look at the significant beaver activity along the creek.

Bear Lake Hikes. The park's most popular trails can all be reached from the Bear Lake Trailhead. In the summer, the Bear Lake parking lot fills up by 9am, and the Glacier Gorge parking lot fills even earlier. If you are slow to rise, the **Bear Lake Shuttle Bus** provides convenient transportation between the Shuttle Bus parking area and Bear Lake, stopping at Glacier Gorge along the way. (Buses run every 20min. 7-9am and 5-7pm, every 8-10min. 9am-5pm.)

Flattop Mt. (4.4 mi., 3hr.). The most challenging of the Bear Lake hikes, this picturesque trail climbs 2800 ft. to a vantage point along the Continental Divide.

Nymph (0.5 mi., 15min.); **Dream** (1.1 mi., 30min.); and **Emerald Lakes** (1.8 mi., 1hr.). A series of 3 glacial pools that offer inspiring glimpses of the surrounding peaks. Although the first 2 legs of the hike are relatively easy, the Emerald Lake portion is steep and rocky at points.

Lake Haiyaha (2.3 mi., 1¼hr.), forking left from the trail, is more intimate and offers superb views of the mountains. A scramble over the rocks at the end of the trail earns you a peek at hidden (and sometimes difficult to find) Lake Haiyaha, arguably the most spectacular of the 4 lakes.

VAIL   ☎970

The largest one-mountain ski resort in all of North America, Vail also holds the ruby-encrusted crown of second most-visited ski resort in the US. (Breckenridge Mountain, p. 682, holds the diamond-encrusted crown.) The trendy town has its fair share of ritzy hotels, swank saloons, and sexy boutiques, while the mountain wows skiers with its prime snow, a vertical drop of 3330 feet, 174 ski runs, and 31 lifts. Discovered by Lord Gore in 1854, Vail and its surrounding valley were invaded by miners during the Rockies gold rush in the 1870s. According to local lore, the Ute Indians adored the area's rich supply of game, but they became so upset with the white settlers that they set fire to the forest, creating the resort's open terrain.

⁊ PRACTICAL INFORMATION. Vail Village and **Lionshead Village** form the entity known as Vail. They are pedestrian only, so visitors must park in garages off **Front- age Rd.** Parking is free during the summer. Free **Vail Transit** buses link the two vil- lages; the stops are marked by signs. Vail's two **Visitors Centers** are at either end of the village; the larger one is at the **Vail Transportation Center** on S. Frontage Rd. (☎800-525-3875. Open M-F 9am-6pm, Sa-Su 9:30am-5:30pm. Hours subject to change.) The other is in Lionshead Village, also on S. Frontage Rd. (☎800-525- 3875. Open daily 9am-7pm; in winter 8am-5pm.) **Greyhound** (☎476-5137; ticket office open daily 8am-6:30pm) buses eager skiers out of its depot, in the Trans- portation Bldg. next to the main Visitors Center, to Glenwood Springs (1½hr., 4 per day, $15.50-16.50); Denver (2hr., 5 per day, $18-19); and Grand Junction (3½hr., 4 per day, $15.50-16.50). **Avon/Beaver Creek Transit** runs bus routes between Vail and its surrounding areas, including Eagle and Edwards (each $2). Free bus service covers the area around Vail Village, Lionshead, and East and West Vail. (☎748-4120 for schedule info. Office open daily 6am-10pm.) **Weather conditions:** ☎476-5677. **Internet access: Vail Public Library,** 292 W. Meadow Dr. (☎479-2184; open M-Th 10am-8pm, F 10am-6pm, Sa-Su 11am-6pm). **Post Office:** 1300 N. Frontage Rd. W. (☎476-5217; open M-F 8:30am-5:30pm, Sa 8:30am-noon). **ZIP code:** 81657. **Area code:** 970.

⌐ ACCOMMODATIONS. The phrase "cheap lodging" is not part of Vail's vocab- ulary. Rooms in the resort town rarely dip below $175 per night in winter, and summer lodging is often equally pricey. **The Prairie Moon,** 738 Grand Ave., offers some of the cheapest lodging outside the expensive resort area. Located in Eagle, about 30 mi. west of Vail, The Prairie Moon has large, clean rooms with fridges and microwaves. (☎328-6680. Singles $55-59; doubles $57-65.) A bus shuttles visi- tors daily between Eagle and Vail (see **Practical Information,** above). The **Roost Lodge,** 1783 N. Frontage Rd., in West Vail, provides affordable lodging in a conve- nient location. The average-sized rooms are impressively clean, and come with cable TV, fridge, microwave, and phone, as well as continental breakfast and access to a jacuzzi, sauna, and pool. (☎476-5451 or 800-873-3065. Singles $55-62; in winter $134-150.) The **Holy Cross Ranger District,** right off I-70 at Exit 171 (follow signs), provides info on the six campgrounds near Vail. (☎827-5715. Open M-F 8am-5pm, Sa-Su 8am-4:30pm. Closed weekends after Labor Day.) With 25 sites, **Gore Creek** is the closest and most popular campground. Well-situated right out- side East Vail, among birch trees, wild flowers, and mountains, Gore Creek is also within hiking distance of the free East Vail Express bus route. ($12; sites have water and 10-day limit.)

⌂ FOOD. Garfinkel's, a hidden hangout accessible by foot in Vail's Lionshead Village (directly across from the gondola) offers nightly specials that include $5 burgers and $3 margaritas. Enjoy your meal on a porch that practically merges with the ski slope. DJs and the occasional live band supply Garfinkel's with tunes; Sunday nights are disco night. (☎476-3789. Restaurant open daily 11am- 10pm; bar open until 2am.) Located at the top of Bridge St., the popular **Red Lion** has been satisfying the appetites of loyal customers since 1962 with award-win- ning chili ($4-5.50) and delicious sandwiches ($8-9). The Lion also features live music from Tuesday through Saturday. (☎476-7676. Open daily 10:30am-2am; kitchen open until 10pm.)

⚡ OUTDOOR ACTIVITIES. The **Colorado Ski Museum,** in the Transportation Bldg. in Vail Village, offers a glimpse into Vail's past and houses the **Ski Hall of Fame.** (☎476-1876. Open Tu-Su 10am-5pm; closed Oct. and May. $1, under 12 free.) Before slaloming, the unequipped visit **Ski Base,** 675 W. Lionshead Circle. (☎476-5799. Open in winter daily 9am-7pm. Skis, poles, and boots start from $13 per day; snow- board and boots from $19 per day.) The store transmogrifies into the **Wheel Base Bike Shop** in the summer. (Open daily 9am-6pm. Path bikes $15 per 8hr.; mountain bikes $23 per 8hr.)

Vail caters to sun worshippers in the summer, when the ski runs turn into **hiking and biking trails.** The **Eagle Bahn Gondola** at Lionshead and the **Vista Bahn chairlift,** part of the **Vail Resort** in Vail village, whisk hikers, bikers, and sightseers to the top of the mountains for breathtaking views. (☎476-9090. Office open 8:30am-4:30pm. Eagle Bahn open in summer Su-W 10am-4pm, Th-Sa 10am-9pm; from early Sept. F-Su only. Vista Bahn open mid-July to early Sept. F-Su 10am-4pm. All-day summer pass on the Vista Bahn and Eagle Bahn $16, ages 65-69 $10, 70 and over $5, 12 and under $10; includes hauling fees.) Rental **bikes** are available atop Vail Mountain. (☎479-4380. $15 per hr., $35 per 4hr., $45 per day.) During the summer months, enjoy the **Eagle Bahn Gondola Twilight Ride** (Th and Sa 5-9pm; free). The **Gore Creek Fly Fisherman,** 183-7 Gore Creek Dr., reels in the daily catch of river info. (☎476-3296 or 800-369-3044. Open daily 7am-10pm; mid-May to June and Sept. to mid-Oct. Su-Th 8am-8pm. Rod rentals $15 per day, $25 with boots and waders.)

The **Gerald R. Ford Amphitheater** presents a number of outdoor concerts, dance festivals, and theater productions on its grounds. (☎476-2918. Box office open Tu-Sa 3-6pm. Lawn seats $5; Tu free.) The **Vilar Center for the Arts** (☎845-8497 or 888-920-2787), at Beaver Creek, hosts world renowned musicians, actors, and dancers.

ASPEN ☎970

Aspen was founded as a silver mining camp, but the silver ran out quickly and by 1940 the town was almost gone. Wealthy visionaries took one look at the location of the floundering village and transformed it into a winter playground. Today, Aspen's skiing, scenery, and festivals are matched only by the prices in the exclusive boutiques downtown. To catch Aspen on the semi-cheap, stay in Glenwood Springs (40 miles north on Rte. 82; see p. 691) and make a daytrip here or camp amid aspen groves in the nearby national forest.

◪ PRACTICAL INFORMATION. Visitors Centers: 320 Hyman Ave., in the Wheeler Opera House (open daily 10am-6pm); and 425 Rio Grand Pl. (☎925-1940 or 800-262-7736; open M-F 8am-5pm, Sa 10am-4pm). The **Aspen Ranger District,** 806 W. Hallam, provides info on hikes and camping within 15 mi. of Aspen. (☎925-3445; weather info 920-1664. Open June-Aug. M-F 8am-5pm, Sa 8am-4:30pm; Sept.-May M-F 8am-4:30pm. Topographic maps $4.) **Roads and Weather:** ☎877-315-7623. **Snow Report:** ☎925-1221 or 888-277-3676. **Post Office:** 235 Puppy Smith Rd. (☎925-7523; open M-F 8:30am-5pm, Sa 9am-noon). **ZIP code:** 81611. **Area code:** 970.

♫ ACCOMMODATIONS. If you stay in Aspen, you'll have to bite the bullet and reach deep into your pockets. The last sound deal in town, **St. Moritz Lodge,** 344 W. Hyman Ave., charms ski bums with a pool, sauna, and hot tub. (☎925-3220 or 800-817-2069. Dorm beds $26-55 depending on season. Hotel accommodations from $59.) Unless 6 ft. of snow covers the ground, **camping** is available in one of the many National Forest campgrounds that lie within 5 mi. of Aspen. Reservable and first come, first served sites scatter just west of town on Maroon Creek Rd. and southeast on Rte. 82. (☎877-444-6777. Open June to mid-Sept. 5-day max. stay throughout the district. Sites fill before noon. $9-14 per night.) A $1 search-and-rescue insurance fee can be paid at local sporting goods stores.

◳ FOOD. Main Street Bakery, 201 E. Main St., serves gourmet soups ($5), homemade granola with fruit ($6), and vegetarian sandwiches ($7). The patio is a prime people-watching spot. (☎925-6446. Open daily 7am-9:30pm.) **The Big Wrap,** 520 E. Durant Ave., rolls up gourmet wraps and fresh salads for $6 and mixes smoothies for $4. (☎544-1700. Open M-Sa 10am-6pm.) American favorites, such as burgers ($6-8) and grilled cheese ($5), take center stage at **Boogies Diner,** 534 Cooper. Boogie's is probably the only diner where you can grab a burger and then squeeze into a pair of Diesel or Versace jeans. (☎925-6610. Open M-F 11am-10pm; off-season M-F 11am-9pm, hours may vary.) The **Cooper St. Pier,** 508 E. Cooper St., is one of the best deals in town. Try the lunchtime hamburger special (burger with fries and a soda or beer) for only $6.50. (☎925-7758. Open daily 11am-10pm; bar open until 2am.)

⛷ SKIING. Skiing is the main attraction in Aspen. The hills surrounding town contain four ski areas: **Aspen Mountain, Aspen Highlands, Buttermilk Mountain,** and **Snowmass Ski Area.** Interchangeable lift tickets enable the four areas to operate as a single extended resort; for the best deal, buy multiday passes at least two weeks in advance. (☎925-1220 or 800-525-6200. Day passes vary by season, expect $60+, ages 13-27 $45, ages 7-12 $37, ages 65-69 $55, over 70 and under 7 free.) Each of the mountains offers unique skiing opportunities of varying difficulty. Buttermilk's gentle slopes are perfect for beginners interested in lessons (and snowplowing their way down the mountain). Aspen Highlands has the most diverse selection of trails and is currently expanding to include the steep cliffs of Highland Bowl. Aspen Mountain caters to expert skiers; there are no easy trails in this terrain. The granddaddy of the Aspen ski areas, Snowmass boasts 20 lifts and countless runs. All but the most timid of beginners will find something to occupy them here. Snowmass is also popular among snowboarders, with its half-pipes and terrain parks.

🏔 OTHER OUTDOOR ACTIVITIES. In summer, the **Silver Queen Gondola** heads to the 11,212 ft. summit of Aspen Mountain, providing an unparalleled panorama. (☎925-1220 or 800-525-6200. Open mid-June to early Sept. daily 10am-4pm. $15 per day, $29 per week.) At **Snowmass Mountain,** you can take a chairlift to the top and ride your mountain bike down (in summer Th-M 10am-4pm; $10). Plan on exploring the **Maroon Bells** and the unforgettable 1.8 mi. hike to **Crater Lake.** Maroon Creek Rd. is closed to traffic from 8:30am to 5pm daily in an effort to preserve the surrounding wilderness. To avoid paying $5 for a slow RFTA tour bus that departs every 30min. from **Rubey Park,** plan either an early morning or a sunset hike. In Aspen proper, the **Ute Trail** departs from Ute Ave. and weaves its way to the top of a rock ledge, a spectacular sunset-watching spot. The gentler **Hunter Trail** wanders through town and is a popular place for jogging and biking.

Entering its 53rd season, the internationally acclaimed **Aspen Music Festival** features jazz, opera, and classical music from late June through August. A variety of shows are held every night in many venues around town. A free **Music Shuttle** bus transports listeners from Rubey Park to the music tent every 30min. prior to the concert. (☎925-9042; 925-3254 for a schedule. Many concerts are free.) **Aspen Theatre in the Park** presents a variety of shows each night from late June through late August. (☎925-9313, box office 920-5770. Tickets $25-30.)

GLENWOOD SPRINGS ☎970

Picked "America's hottest place to cool off" by the Travel Channel, Glenwood Springs is much more than Aspen's little brother. The Glenwood Hot Springs are a popular year-round destination, and the spectacular Fairy Caves are considered by many to be the eighth world wonder. Glenwood Springs also allows budget travelers to stay near Aspen's famed slopes while keeping their souls out of pawn.

Glenwood Hot Springs Lodge and Pool, 401 N. River Rd., is a huge resort complex containing the world's largest outdoor hot springs pool, a waterslide, and spas at various water temperatures. (☎945-6571 or 800-537-7946. Open daily 7:30am-10pm. Day pass $9.50, after 9pm $6.25; ages 3-12 $6.25/$5.75.) Pamper yourself at **Yampah Spa and Vapor Caves,** 709 E. 6th St. Sweat the stress of travel out in these 125°F natural steam caves and then relax in the Solarium. (☎945-0667. Open daily 9am-9pm. $8.75, hostelers $4.75 with hostel pass/receipt.) While most skiers head to Aspen's fab four, relaxed family-style skiing is available at **Sunlight,** 10901 County Rd. 117, 10 mi. west of town. (☎945-7491 or 800-445-7931. $30 per day, ages 5-13 $20; hosteler discount.) Dubbed the eighth wonder of the world in 1896, the **Fairy Caves** were recently reopened to the public. **Glenwood Caverns,** 508 Pine St., offers both family-oriented and advanced tours of the caves. (☎945-4228 or 800-530-1635. Open mid-Apr. to Oct. 2hr. tours depart every hr. 9am-4pm. Family tours $12, ages 3-12 $7. Wild tours $50; 50% discount at Glenwood Springs Hostel.)

ROCKY MOUNTAINS

Within walking distance of the springs and downtown, you'll find the ■Glenwood Springs Hostel (HI-AYH), 1021 Grand Ave., which consists of a spacious Victorian house and a newer building next door. This hostel offers a wide variety of trips and tours in the area, including discounts on skiing at Aspen. Other amenities include 2 kitchens, the owner's amazing vinyl collection, a backyard patio, and a lounge with murals covering the walls. (☎945-8545 or 800-909-4776. Linen $1. Lockout 10am-4pm. Free pickup from train and bus stations. Internet access $1 for the first min., 10¢ per additional min. 4-night max. stay. Dorms $12, 4 nights $39; private singles $19; private doubles $26.) One of the least expensive motels in town is the **Frontier Lodge**, 2834 Glen Ave., providing clean, spacious rooms with cable TV, A/C, fridge, microwave, and access to a hot tub. (☎970-945-5496 or 888-606-0602. June-Aug. singles $50-80, doubles $50-100; Sept.-May $30-50/$40-60. AAA discount.)

The **Daily Bread Cafe and Bakery**, 729 Grand Ave., attracts locals with fresh, wholesome breakfasts and lunches. The $7 quiche of the day is a favorite and usually sells out by 12:30pm. (☎945-6253. Open M-F 7am-2pm, Sa 8am-2pm, Su 8am-noon.) **Doc Holliday's Saloon**, 724 Grand Ave., is the best place for burgers ($6-8) and beers. Shoot some pool while you digest. (☎945-9050. Open daily 10am-2am; food served 11am-11pm.) **Amtrak**, 413 7th St. (☎945-9563 or 800-872-7245; open daily 9:30am-4:30pm) runs to Denver (6¾hr., $49-69) and Salt Lake City (8¼hr., $55-98). **Greyhound**, at the W. Glenwood Mall (☎945-8501 or 800-231-2222; open M-F 8am-4:30pm), buses to Denver (3½hr., 5 per day, $31-33) and Grand Junction (2hr., 4 per day, $11.50-12.50). The **Roaring Fork Transit Agency (RFTA)**, at Durant and Mill St. in Aspen (☎925-8484; open M-F 9am-5pm) runs to Aspen (1½hr.; 14 per day; $6, children $5). The **White River National Forest Headquarters**, 9th and Grand Ave., has outdoor info. (☎945-2521. Open M-F 8am-5pm.) **Glenwood Springs Chamber Resort Association:** 1102 Grand Ave. (☎945-6589. Open June-Aug. M-F 8:30am-6pm, Sa-Su 10am-3pm; Aug.-June M-F 8:30am-5pm. Brochures 24hr.) **Post Office:** 113 9th St. (☎945-5611. Open M-F 8am-6pm, Sa 9am-1pm.) **ZIP code:** 81601. **Area code:** 970.

GRAND JUNCTION   ☎970

Grand Junction gets its name from its seat at the junction of the Colorado and Gunnison Rivers and the conjunction-junction of the Río Grande and Denver Railroads. Today, the name aptly describes Grand Junction's role as a transportation hub for the masses heading to southern Utah and the Colorado Rockies. While the city doesn't have the reputation of some Colorado hot spots, a unique mix of cowboys and computers makes it worth a closer look if you've got time to spare.

The lovely, historic ■Melrose Hotel, 337 Colorado Ave., between 3rd and 4th St., gives travelers the scoop on the surroundings. (☎242-9636 or 800-430-4555. Reception 9am-1pm and 4-10pm. Dorms $15; singles $30, with private bath $55; doubles $40/$65.) **Daniel's Motel**, 333 North Ave., offers clean rooms close to downtown. (☎243-1084. Check-out 10am. Singles $30-45; doubles $45-55.) Camping is available at **Fruita State Park**, 10 mi. west of downtown, off I-70 from Exit 19. (☎800-678-2267. Showers and hookups. 80 sites $10-16. Entrance fee $4 per day.)

Ying Thai, 757 U.S. 50, offers the best Thai ($6-9) for hundreds of miles in a homey setting. (☎245-4866. Open Tu-F 11am-2pm and 5-9pm, Sa 2-9pm, Su 5-9pm.) Mouthwatering breakfasts ($4-8) are the specialty at the friendly and hopping **Crystal Cafe**, 314 Main St. (☎242-8843. Open M-F 7am-1:45pm, Sa 8am-noon. Bakery open until 3pm.) **Rockslide Restaurant and Brew Pub**, 401 S. Main St., joins the avalanche of microbreweries blanketing the nation, and serves as a Grand Junction nightlife fixture. The Big Bear Stout comes in an $8.50 half-gallon growler. (☎245-2111. Half-price appetizers M-F 4-6pm. Open daily 10am-midnight.) Lying between Denver and Salt Lake City, Grand Junction's pit stop locale draws touring bands who refuse to drive 500 mi. between gigs; check local listings for concerts.

Walker Field, 2828 Walker Field Dr., is the biggest airport in Western Colorado. **Amtrak**, 339 S. 1st St. (☎241-2733), heads daily to Denver (8hr.; $49-85) and Salt Lake City (7hr.; $45-77). **Greyhound**, 230 S. 5th St. (☎242-6012), has service to Denver (5½hr.; 5 per day; $35-37); Durango (5hr.; 1 per day; $35-37); and Salt Lake City (6hr.; 1 per day; $46-49). **Grand Valley Transit** (☎256-7433) runs buses throughout the

Grand Junction area. (Runs M-F 6am-6pm. Fare $1.) For visitor info, stop by the **Grand Junction Visitors Bureau,** 740 Horizon Dr., Exit 31 off I-70, behind the Taco Bell. (☎244-1480 or 800-962-2547. Open May to mid-Oct. daily 8:30am-8pm; late Oct. to Apr. 8:30am-5pm.) **Domestic violence line,** ☎241-6704. **Community Hospital,** 2021 N. 12th St. (☎242-0920). **Post Office:** 241 N. 4th St. (☎244-3400; open M-F 7:45am-5:15pm, Sa 10am-1:30pm). **ZIP code:** 81501. **Area code:** 970.

COLORADO NATIONAL MONUMENT ☎970

Sitting on the outskirts of Grand Junction, Colorado National Monument is a 32-square-mile sculpture of steep cliff faces, canyon walls, and obelisk-like spires wrought by the forces of gravity, wind, and water. The **Rim Rock Drive** runs 23 mi. between the east and west entrances, providing views of awe-inspiring rock monoliths, the Book Cliffs, Grand Mesa, and the city of Grand Junction. **Window Rock Trail** (0.5 mi. round-trip) and **Devil's Kitchen Trail** (1.5 mi. round-trip) are easy walks to points from which you can gaze at the eerie, skeletal rock formations. The moderately strenuous 12 mi. round-trip **Monument Canyon Trail** inspires visions of grandeur, as it wanders amid the giant rocks. The strenuous 17 mi. **No Thoroughfare Trail** begins near Devils Kitchen and accesses the most remote portion of the monument as it follows the streambed that cuts No Thoroughfare Canyon. Check in at the monument's headquarters and **Visitors Center,** 4 mi. east of the western entrance, for info about ranger-led programs. (☎858-3617. Open June-Sept. daily 8am-6pm; Oct.-May 9am-5pm. Entrance fee $5 per vehicle, $3 per cyclist or hiker.) **Saddlehorn Campground,** ½ mi. north of the Visitors Center, offers 50 sites on the mesa's edge. (☎858-3617. Water and bathrooms, no showers. $10.) **Backcountry camping** is free and allowed anywhere more than ¼ mi. from roads and 100 yards from trails. A required permit is available at the Visitors Center.

COLORADO SPRINGS ☎719

Once a resort town only frequented by the elite, Colorado Springs has morphed into the second most visited city in Colorado. When early Colorado gold seekers found bizarre rock formations here, they named the region Garden of the Gods, in part because of the Ute legend that the rocks were petrified bodies of enemies hurled down by the gods above. The US Olympic Team, based in Colorado Springs, continues the quest for gold, while jets from the US Air Force Academy roar overhead.

▓▐ ORIENTATION AND PRACTICAL INFORMATION. Colorado Springs is laid out in a grid of broad thoroughfares. **Nevada Ave.** is the main north-south strip, just east of I-25. **Colorado Ave.** and **Pikes Peak Ave.** run east-west across the city. Numbered streets west of Nevada ascend as you move west. **I-25** from Denver cuts through downtown, separating Old Colorado City from the eastern sector of the town. East of Nevada Ave. remains largely residential. **Greyhound,** 120 S. Weber St. (☎635-1505; tickets sold M-Sa 4:15am-10pm, Su 5:15am-10pm), buses to Denver (1½-2hr., 7 per day, $14); Pueblo (1hr., 6 per day, $10); and Albuquerque (8hr., 4 per day, $61). **City Bus Service,** 127 E. Kiowa (☎385-7433), at Ridefinders Transport Ctr., at Kiowa and Nevada., serves Widefield, Manitou Springs, Ft. Carson, Garden of the Gods, and Peterson AFB. Pick up a schedule at the Kiowa bus terminal for exact times and locations. ($1.25, seniors and ages 5-11 60¢, under 6 free; to Ft. Carson, Widefield, Fountain, Manitou Springs, and Peterson AFB 35¢ extra; exact change required.) **Pikes Peak Tours,** 3704 Colorado Ave. (☎633-1181 or 800-345-8197; open daily 8am-5pm), offers trips to the Air Force Academy and Garden of the Gods (4hr.; $20, under 13 $12.50) and Pikes Peak (4hr., $30/$20), as well as whitewater rafting trips on the Arkansas River (7hr., includes lunch; $65/$45). **Taxis: Yellow Cab,** ☎634-5000. **Visitor info: Visitors Bureau,** 515 S. Cascade (☎635-7506 or 800-888-4748). Open daily 8:30am-5pm. **Post Office:** 201 E. Pikes Peak Ave., at Nevada Ave. (Open M-F 7:30am-5:30pm, Sa 8am-1pm.) **ZIP code:** 80903. **Area code:** 719.

⌂ ACCOMMODATIONS. Motels along **Nevada Ave.** are fairly shabby; campgrounds and lodgings along **W. Pikes Peak Ave.** and **W. Colorado Ave.** provide more favorable accommodations. The **Apache Court Motel,** 3401 W. Pikes Peak Ave., at 34th St., has pink adobe rooms with A/C, cable TV, refrigerator, and a common hot tub. (☎471-9440. Summer singles M-F $45, Sa-Su $50; in winter and on some summer weekdays $40/$55.) The simple rooms at the **Amarillo Motel,** 2801 W. Colorado Ave., at 28th and Colorado, include large kitchens equipped with fridge and microwave, as well as new TVs and access to laundry facilities. (☎635-8539 or 800-216-8539. Summer singles $40; doubles $45; in winter $28-35/$30-40.) The **Tree Haven Cottages,** 3620 W. Colorado Ave., feature tiny rooms fully equipped with cable TV, fridge, microwaves, and pool access. (☎578-1968. Singles $43; off-season $30.)

About 30min. from Colorado Springs, several **Pikes Peak National Forest** campgrounds lie in the mountains flanking Pikes Peak (generally open May-Sept.), but no local transportation serves this area. Campgrounds clutter Rte. 67, 5-10 mi. north of **Woodland Park,** which is 18 mi. northwest of the Springs on U.S. 24. Try **Colorado, Painted Rocks,** or **South Meadows** near Manitou Park. Others border U.S. 24 near the town of Lake George, 50 mi. west of the Springs (sites $11-13). You can camp on national forest property for free if you are at least 500 ft. from a road or stream. The **Pikes Peak Ranger District Office,** 601 S. Weber, has maps of the area. (☎636-1602. Open M-F 8am-5pm. $6-7.) Farther afield, visitors may camp in the **Eleven Mile State Recreation Area,** off a spur road from U.S. 24 near Lake George, on a reservoir. (☎748-3401; 800-678-2267 for reservations. Reservations 7am-4:45pm. Pay showers and laundry. Sites $10, with electricity $14; vehicle fee $4.)

◲▥ FOOD AND NIGHTLIFE. Students and the young-at-heart perch among outdoor tables in front of the cafes and restaurants lining **Tejon Ave.,** a few blocks east of downtown. **Old Colorado City** is home to a number of fine eateries. There are several **Farmers Markets** scattered throughout the city during the summer months. **Poor Richard's Restaurant,** 324½ N. Tejon Ave., is a popular local hangout, serving pizza (cheese slices $3; cheese pies $12), sandwiches, and $3-6 salads. (☎632-7721. Tu live folk music, W bluegrass, Th Celtic. Open daily 11am-10pm.) **La Baguette,** 2417 W. Colorado Ave., bakes bread and melts fondues better than you might expect in a place so far from Paris. Cheese fondue with apple slices is $6.75. (☎577-4818. Open M-Sa 7am-6pm, Su 8am-5pm.) Downtown's hottest nightspot, **Rum Bay,** 20 N. Tejon St., specializes in food, fun, and lots of rum. A 17-piece jazz band performs live every Wednesday night, and a DJ spins 90s and Top 40 hits nightly. Rum Bay also features occasional concerts by guest artists. (☎634-3522. Specialty rum drinks $6-7. Open daily 11am-2am.) **Meadow Muffins,** 2432 Colorado Ave., is a virtual museum of old movie props. The two buckboard wagons hanging from the ceiling were used to film *Gone With The Wind*, and the windmill-style fan installed above the bar was originally cast in *Casablanca*. (☎633-0583. Drafts $3. Open daily 11am-2am.)

◉ SIGHTS. Olympic hopefuls train with some of the world's most high-tech sports equipment at the **US Olympic Complex,** 750 E. Boulder St. Every 30min. to 1hr., the complex offers free 1hr. tours that include a tear-jerking film of struggle and glory. (☎578-4644, 578-4618, or 888-659-8687. Open M-Sa 9am-5pm, Su 10am-5pm.) Earlier searches for gold are recorded at the **Pioneers' Museum,** 215 S. Tejon St., which recounts the settling of Colorado Springs. (☎578-6650. Open Tu-Sa 10am-5pm; in summer only Su 1-5pm. Free.) The **United States Air Force Academy,** 12 mi. north of town off I-25, hosts over 1 million visitors annually. The cadet chapel was constructed of aluminum, steel, and other materials used in building airplanes. On weekdays during the school year, cadets gather at 11:35am near the chapel for the cadet lunch formation. (☎333-4515. Office hours 7:30am-4:30pm. Open M-Sa 9am-5pm, Su 1-5pm.) The **Barry Goldwater Visitors Center** has info. (☎333-2025 or 333-2520. Open mid-May to early Sept. daily 9am-6pm; early Sept. to mid-May 9am-5pm.)

GROUND ZERO While most Cold War era bomb shelters are buried under 5-10 ft. of dirt, the **North American Air Defense Command Headquarters (NORAD)** was constructed 1800 ft. below Cheyenne Mt. Contrary to popular myth and legend, Cheyenne Mt. is the eyes and ears of an intricate intelligence network, as opposed to a center for nuclear action. However, the center does look like something out of a James Bond movie; a three-mile tunnel leads to buildings on massive springs which house computers and detectors scanning the heavens for incoming inter-continental ballistic missiles. The center was designed to be operational even after a direct nuclear attack. Call in advance to make reservations for an informative 1½hr. slide presentation that covers the history and missions of the **Cheyenne Mountain Operation Center.** (☎474-2238 or 474-2239. Show Th 10:30am.) The **Peterson Air Force Base,** east of Academy Blvd., houses the **Edward J. Peterson Air and Space Museum,** which showcases exhibits on the history of the base as well as space and satellite operations. (☎556-4915. Museum open Tu-Sa 8:30am-4:30pm, closed on national holidays. Free.)

OUTDOOR ACTIVITIES. Between Rte. 24 (Colorado Ave.) and 30th St. in northwest Colorado Springs, the redrock towers and spires of the **Garden of the Gods** rise strikingly against a mountainous backdrop. (Open daily 5am-11pm; Nov.-Apr. 5am-9pm.) **Climbers** are regularly lured by the large red faces, and a number of exciting **mountain biking** trails cross the Garden as well. The park's hiking trails have great views of the rock formations and each can easily be completed in one day. A map is available from the park's **Visitors Center,** 1805 N. 30th at Gateway Rd. (☎634-6666. Open June-Aug. daily 8am-8pm; in winter 9am-5pm. Walking tours depart in summer at 10, 11am, 2 and 3pm; in winter 10am and 2pm.)

From any part of town, one can't help noticing the 14,110 ft. summit of Pikes Peak on the horizon. Ambitious climbers can ascend the peak along the strenuous, well-maintained **Barr Trail** (26.5 mi. round-trip). The trailhead is in Manitou Springs by the "Manitou Incline" sign on Ruxton Ave. Check the weather and with rangers before departing. Don't despair if you don't reach the top—explorer Zebulon Pike never reached it, either. There is a fee to drive up the gorgeous 19 mi. **Pikes Peak Hwy.,** a well-maintained dirt road. (☎385-7325 or 800-318-9505. Open mid-Sept. to Apr. 9am-3pm, May to mid-Sept. 7am-7pm. $35 per car or $10 per person.) Five miles west in Manitou Springs, visitors can hop on the **Pikes Peak Cog Railway,** 515 Ruxton Ave., which takes visitors to the top every 80min. From the summit, Kansas, the Sangre de Cristo Mountains, and the Continental Divide unfold before you. This lofty view inspired Kathy Lee Bates to write "America the Beautiful." (☎685-5401. Late Apr. to early Nov. daily 8am-5:20pm; call for Apr.-May and Aug.-Nov. times. Round-trip $24.50-25.50, children $13-13.50. Reservations advised.)

For adventurous hiking through subterranean passages, head for the contorted caverns of the **Cave of the Winds,** on Rte. 24, 6 mi. west of Exit 141 off I-25. A laser light show dances on the canyon walls nightly at 9pm during the summer. (☎685-5444. Guided tours daily every 15min. 9am-9pm; Sept. to late May 10am-5pm. $15, ages 6-15 $8. Light show $6, children $3.) Just above Manitou Springs on Rte. 24 lies the **Cliff Dwellings Museum,** which contains replicas of ancestral Puebloan dwelling dating from AD 1100-1300. (☎685-5242 or 800-354-9971. Open June-Aug. daily 9am-8pm; Sept.-May 9am-5pm. $8, seniors $7, ages 7-11 $6, under 7 free.) The **Seven Falls,** 10min. west of downtown on Cheyenne Blvd., are lit up at night. (☎632-0765. Before 6pm $7, ages 6-15 $4.50; after 6pm $8.50/$5.50.)

GREAT SAND DUNES NATIONAL MONUMENT ☎719

When Colorado's mountains all begin to look the same, head to the **Great Sand Dunes National Monument** at the northwest edge of the San Luis Valley. A sea of 750 ft. sand dunes, representing eons of wind-blown accumulation, laps silently at the base of the **Sangre de Cristo Range,** 37 mi. northeast of Alamosa and 127 mi. west of Pueblo on Rte. 150, off U.S. 160. The progress of the dunes through passes in the range is checked by the shallow **Medano Creek;** visitors can wade across the creek while there is still water (Apr. to mid-July). There are no designated trails through the dunes, but visitors are welcome to dive straight in and forge new paths. Hiking to the top takes about 1½hr. and loose sand makes the climb challenging (feet can sink up to 6 in. in the sand). Take at least a quart of water per person, and beware the summer's intense heat—the sand can reach 140°F (60°C). Those with high-clearance four-wheel-drive can motor over the **Medano Pass Primitive Rd.** At the southern boundary of the monument, the **Oasis** complex offers four-wheel-drive tours that huff over Medano Pass Primitive Rd. to the dunes' nether regions. (☎378-2222. 2hr. tours daily 10am and 2pm. $14, ages 5-11 $8.) Schedules of daily ranger-led hikes and talks can be found at the **Visitors Center,** ½ mi. past the entrance gate. The newsletter *Sand Dune Breezes* suggests drives and hikes. For more info, contact the **Superintendent,** Great Sand Dunes National Monument, Mosca, CO 81146. (☎378-2312. Open daily 8:30am-4:30pm; Sept.-May 9am-5pm. $3 per person, under 17 free. National Parks passes accepted.)

Pinyon Flats, the monument's primitive campground, is open year-round and includes drinking water. There are 88 individual campsites and 3 group sites available; reservations only accepted for group sites. Bring mosquito repellent in June. (☎378-2312. Arrive by early afternoon. Sites $10. No reservations.) Get free **backcountry camping** permits for the dunes from the Visitors Center. If the park's sites are full, **Oasis** (see above) will fulfill your needs with showers and two-person campsites ($12, with hookup $18.50; each additional person $2.50), cabins ($33 for 2 people), or teepees ($27.50 for 2 people). **San Luis Lakes State Park,** 8 mi. away in Mosca, has showers and 51 campsites with electricity. (☎378-2020, 800-678-2267 for camping reservations. Closed in winter. Sites $14; $4 vehicle entrance fee.) For info on nearby National Forest Campgrounds, contact the **Río Grande National Forest Service Office,** 11571 County Rd. T-5, La Jara, CO 81140. (☎274-5193. Open M-F 8am-4:30pm. Primitive sites free, with running water $12.) **Area code:** 719.

SAN JUAN MOUNTAINS

Ask Coloradans about their favorite mountain retreats, and they'll most likely name a peak, lake, stream, or town in the San Juan Range of southwestern Colorado. Four **national forests**—the **Uncompahgre** (*un-cum-PAH-gray*), the **Gunnison,** the **San Juan,** and the **Río Grande**—encircle this sprawling range. **Durango** is an ideal base camp for forays into these mountains. Northeast of Durango, the **Weminuche Wilderness** tempts the hardy backpacker with a vast expanse of rugged terrain where wide, sweeping vistas stretch for miles. Get $4 maps and hiking info from **Pine Needle Mountaineering,** 835 Main Ave., Durango 81301. (☎970-247-8726. Open in summer M-Sa 9am-9pm, Su 10am-5pm; off-season M-Sa 9am-6pm, Su 10am-5pm.)

The San Juan Mountains are easily accessible via U.S. 50, which is traveled by hundreds of thousands of tourists each summer. **Greyhound** serves the area, but very poorly; traveling by car is the best option in this region. On a happier note, the San Juans are loaded with HI-AYH hostels and campgrounds, making them one of the most economical places to visit in Colorado.

BLACK CANYON OF THE GUNNISON NATIONAL PARK   ☎970

Native American parents used to tell their children that the light-colored strands of rock streaking through the walls of the Black Canyon were the hair of a blond woman—and that if they got too close to the edge they would get tangled in it and fall. The edge of **Black Canyon of the Gunnison National Park** is a staggering place, literally—watch for those trembling knees. The Gunnison River slowly gouged out the 53-mile long canyon, crafting a steep 2500-foot gorge that is, in some places, deeper than it is wide. The Empire State Building, if placed at the bottom of the river, would reach barely halfway up the canyon walls.

The Black Canyon lies 15 mi. east of the town of **Montrose.** The **South Rim** is easily accessible via a 6 mi. drive off U.S. 50 ($7 per car, $4 walk-in or motorcycle); the wilder **North Rim** can only be reached by an 80 mi. detour around the canyon fol-

LIKE A CHICKEN WITH ITS HEAD CUT OFF

Clutching the bird in one hand, the farmer in faded dungarees picks up the wood handle of the gleaming axe. He holds the chicken firmly against the worn chopping block and with one clean, smooth motion, brings the blade slicing down across the rough, golden skin of its scrawny neck. Blood spurts across his bare forearm as he releases the mass of twitching feathers and flailing feet. In a second, the beast is on its feet and races around the farmyard—for two years! When Mike, The Headless Chicken, was beheaded in Fruita, Colorado, sometime in the middle of the last century, things didn't go exactly as planned. Rather than falling to the ground, dead as a doornail after a run-in with a farmer's axe, Mike managed to survive for more than two years. His amazed owners fed him with a medicine dropper and Mike toured the country to rave reviews. Today all that remains of Mike's legend are the tales told by Fruita old-timers and a piece of sculpture in downtown Fruita, depicting the illustrious Mike in full stride.

lowed by a gravel road from Crawford off Rte. 92. The road is closed in winter. The spectacular 8 mi. South Rim Drive traces the edge of the canyon, and boasts jaw-dropping vistas including the spectacular **Chasm View,** where you can peer 2300 ft. down the highest cliff in Colorado at the Gunnison River and the "painted" wall. Don't throw stones; you might kill a defenseless hiker in the canyon below. On the South Rim, the moderate 2 mi. round-trip **Oak Flat Loop Trail** and the North Rim's 7 mi. round-trip **North Vista Trail** both give a good sense of the terrain below. From the South Rim, you can scramble down the **Gunnison Route,** which drops 1800 ft. over a span 1 mi. Or, tackle the much more difficult **Tomichi** or **Warner Routes,** which can make good overnight hikes. Not surprising, the sheer walls of the Black Canyon make for a climbing paradise; register at the South Rim Visitors Center. Between the **Painted Wall** and **Cedar Point Overlooks,** a well-worn path leads to **Marmot Rocks,** which offer great bouldering for those not quite ready for the big walls.

At the canyon, the **South Rim Campground** has 102 well-designed sites with pit toilets, charcoal grills, water, and some with paved wheelchair access ($10). The **North Rim Campground** offers more space, rarely fills, and is popular with climbers (water and toilets; $10). Many inexpensive motels line Main St./U.S. 50 in downtown Montrose, including the **Western Motel,** 1200 E. Main St. (☎249-3481 or 800-445-7301; singles $36-40, doubles $48-57), and the **Traveler's B&B Inn,** 502 S. 1st St. (☎249-3472; singles $32, with private bath $34-36; doubles $42). **Nav-Mex Tacos,** 475 W. Main St., serves up the best Mexican cuisine around. (Open M-F 11am-9pm, Sa-Su 9am-9pm. Tacos $1.25; tostadas $3.) For tasty sandwiches ($4.50) and omelettes ($5.50), head for the **Daily Bread Bakery and Cafe,** 346 Main St. (☎249-8444. Open M-Sa 6am-3pm.)

Greyhound (☎249-6673) shuttles once a day between Montrose and the Gunnison County Airport, 711 Río Grande (☎641-0060), and will drop you off on U.S. 50, 6 mi. from the canyon ($12). **Gisdho Shuttles** conducts tours of the Black Canyon and Grand Mesa from Grand Junction. (☎800-430-4555. 10-11hr. May-Oct. W and Sa. $39.) A **Visitors Center** sits on the South Rim. (☎249-1914, ext. 23. Open daily 8am-6pm; in winter 8am-4pm.) **Post Office:** 321 S. 1st St., in Montrose. (☎249-6654. Open M-F 8am-5pm, Sa 10am-noon.) **ZIP code:** 81401. **Area code:** 970.

CRESTED BUTTE   ☎970

Crested Butte, 27 miles north of Gunnison on Rte. 135, was first settled by miners in the 1870s. The coal was exhausted in the 1950s, but a few years later, the steep powder fields on the Butte began attracting skiers. Thanks to strict zoning rules, the historic downtown district is a throwback to those early mining days. Three miles north of town, **Crested Butte Mt. Resort,** 12 Snowmass Rd., takes skiers to "the extreme limits" and offers over 800 acres of bowl skiing. Many of the other 85 runs are less spine-tingling, but the panoramic views are equally inspiring. (☎800-544-8448. Open mid-Dec. to mid-Apr. Prices vary. Day passes around $50; ages 65-69 half-price; over 70 free; children 5-16 pay the numerical value of their age.)

Come summertime, Crested Butte becomes the mountain biking capital of Colorado. During the last week of June, the town hosts the **Fat Tire Bike Festival,** four days of mountain biking, racing, and fraternizing. In 1976, a group of cyclists rode from Crested Butte to Aspen, starting the oldest mountain biking event in the world. Every September, experienced bikers repeat the trek over the 12,705 ft. pass to Aspen and back during the **Pearl Pass Tour,** organized by the **Mountain Biking Hall of Fame,** 200 Sopris St. (☎800-454-4505). Biking trail maps are available at bike shops and **The Alpineer,** 419 6th St. (☎349-5210. Open daily 9am-6pm.) Trails begin at the base of Mt. Crested Butte and extend into the exquisite Gothic area. **Trail 401** is a demanding and famous 24 mi. round-trip loop with an excellent view.

Finding budget accommodations in the winter is about as easy as striking a vein of gold, but there are a few possibilities. ☒**Crested Butte International Hostel (HI-AYH),** 615 Teocalli Ave., is a cheap place for skiers and bikers to crash. This beautifully built and situated hostel provides guests with meal plans, a large kitchen, a TV room with fireplace, and laundry. (☎349-0588 or 888-389-0588. Shower for non-guests $5, with towel $6. Reception 7:30am-10pm, lockout 10am-2pm. Dorms $20, 2 or more nights $18; in winter $30/$27. Private room $50; with private bath $60. $3 discount for HI members. $4-6 dinners in peak seasons. Packages available, such as the Mar. deal of 5 nights accommodation, 4 days skiing for $300 per person.) **Forest Queen,** 129 Elk Ave., rents out comfortable doubles at reasonable prices. (☎349-5336. Doubles $59, off-season $49; with private bath $69/$59; each additional person $10.) **Gunnison National Forest Office,** 216 N. Colorado, 30 mi. south in Gunnison, has info on area **campgrounds.** (☎641-0471. Open M-F 7:30am-4:30pm.)

Brick Oven Pizza, 3rd and Elk St., replenishes calories lost skiing and biking with authentic NY and Chicago pizza voted the best in the Butte since 1993. Tasty slices loaded with toppings are $2; large pizzas start at $11.35. (☎349-5044. Open daily 11am-9:30pm.) The **Crested Butte Brewery and Idle Spur Grille,** 226 Elk Ave., is a great place to grab a burger and a beer. Its Red Lady Ale won the 1998 Gold Medal at the Great American Beer Festival, and the Elk Burger ($9) is a local favorite. Veggie options include the $8.50 portabella mushroom burger. (☎349-5026. Open M-Th 11am-10pm, F-Su 10am-10pm.) The **Crested Butte Chamber of Commerce:** 601 Elk Ave. (☎349-6438 or 800-545-4505; open daily 9am-5pm). A free **shuttle** to the mountain leaves from the chamber. (☎349-5616. Every 40min. 7:20am-10:20am and 8pm-midnight, every 20min. 10:20am-8pm.) **Post Office:** 215 Elk Ave. (☎349-5568; open M-F 7:30am-4:30pm, Sa 10am-1pm). **ZIP code:** 81224. **Area code:** 970.

TELLURIDE   ☎970

Site of the first bank Butch Cassidy ever robbed (the San Miguel), Telluride was very much a town of the Old West. Locals believe that their city's name derives from a contraction of "to hell you ride," a likely warning given to travelers to the once hell-bent city. Things have quieted down a bit in the last few years; outlaw celebrities have been replaced with film celebrities, and six-shooter guns with cinnamon buns. Skiers, hikers, and vacationers come to Telluride to pump gold and silver *into* the mountains, and the town can also claim the most festivals per capita of any ZIP code in the US. During the summer and fall, Telluride is inundated every few weeks, a schedule that allows just enough time for the community to catch its breath before the next onslaught. Still, a small-town feeling prevails—rocking chairs sit outside brightly painted houses, and dogs lounge on storefront porches.

◪ **PRACTICAL INFORMATION.** Telluride sits on a short spur of Rte. 145, 127 mi. southeast of Grand Junction. The public **bus** line, called the **Galloping Geese,** runs the length of town on a regular basis. (☎728-5700. May-Nov. every 20min. 7:30am-6pm, Dec.-Apr. every 10min. 7am-midnight. Free.) A **gondola** runs from downtown to Mountain Village. (☎728-8888. Runs 7am-midnight. Free.) **Taxi** service from **Mountain Limo** serves the western slope. (☎728-9606 or 888-546-6894. Airport fare $8.) The **Visitors Center** is upstairs from **Rose's Grocery Store,** 666 W. Colorado Ave., near the entrance to town. (☎728-4431 or 888-288-7360. Open in summer daily 9am-7pm; ski season 8am-6pm.) Other services include: **Police,** ☎728-3818; **Rape Crisis Hotline,** ☎728-5660. **Telluride Medical Center,** 500 W. Pacific (☎728-3848); and free **Internet access** at the **Wilkinson Public Library,** 100 W. Pacific St. (☎728-4519). **Post Office:** 150 S. Willow St. (☎728-3900; open M-F 9am-5pm, Sa 10am-noon). **ZIP code:** 81435.

⌂ ACCOMMODATIONS. If you're visiting Telluride during a festival, bring a sleeping bag; the cost of a bed is outrageous. The **Oak Street Inn,** 134 N. Oak St., offers cozy rooms. (☎728-3383. Singles $42, with private bath $66; doubles $58/$66. Rates $20 higher during festivals. Showers $3 for non-guests.) **Camping** is available at the east end of Telluride in a town-operated facility with 46 sites, water, restrooms, and showers. (☎728-2173. Sites $10-12. 1-week maximum stay.) William Jennings Bryan delivered his "Cross of Gold" speech from the front balcony of the **New Sheridan Hotel,** 231 W. Colorado Ave., and if you can afford it, the luxurious rooms make it worth your while. (Rooms with shared bath from $80.) The **Telluride Town Park Campground,** east of downtown, offers particularly nice sites along the San Miguel River. (Water, full bathrooms. 7-night max. stay. Mid-May to mid-Oct. $12 per vehicle; primitive sites $10.) During festival times, you can crash anywhere; hot showers ($2) are available at the high school.

◖ FOOD. ▨**Baked in Telluride,** 127 S. Fir St., has enough rich coffee, delicious pastries, pizza, sandwiches, and 60¢ bagels to get you through a festival weekend even if you *are* baked in Telluride. The apple fritters ($2) are rightly famous, and their enormous calzones ($5-7) might be the best deal in town. (☎728-4775. Open daily 5:30am-10pm.) The subterranean locale at **Deli Downstairs,** 217 W. Colorado St., feels more like a food stand at a Grateful Dead show than a sedentary establishment, and the sandwiches ($3-8) will keep you boogying for hours. (Open daily 10am-midnight. Cash only.) The wooden benches and long tables at **Fat Alley Barbeque,** 122 S. Oak St., are reminiscent of the sawdust saloons of yore, but Telluride's miners never ate BBQ ($5-17) like this. (Open daily 11am-10pm.)

▧▨ NIGHTLIFE AND ENTERTAINMENT. Jiving with Telluride's hip and swank, **Fly Me to the Moon Saloon,** 132 E. Colorado Ave., shines with some of the area's freshest musical talent, and thrills dancers with its spring-loaded dance floor. (☎728-6666. Cover $2-5. Open daily 9pm-2:30am. Cash only.) The lively **Last Dollar Saloon,** 100 E. Colorado, is a favorite among locals. (☎728-4800. Open daily 11:30am-2am. Beer $2.75-3.75. Cash only.) The upscale **New Sheridan Bar,** 231 W. Colorado Ave., was a Butch Cassidy haunt, and a turn-of-the-century aura still lurks in the corners of the high ceilings. (☎728-3911. Open daily 3pm-2am.) The warm, welcoming **Roma Bar & Cafe,** 133 E. Colorado, is a tried-and-true joint that offers a Thursday two-for-one free-for-all and serves some of the best pizza in town. (☎728-3669. Open daily 11:30am-3pm and 5pm-2am. Dinner until 10pm.)

Given that only 1900 people live in Telluride, the sheer number of festivals in the town seems staggering. For general festival info, contact the **Telluride Visitors Center** (☎728-4431 or 888-288-7360). Gala events occur throughout the summer and fall; the most renowned is the **Bluegrass Festival.** (☎800-624-2422. 3rd weekend in June. Tickets $55 per night, 4-day pass $155.) The **Telluride International Film Festival** premiers some of the hippest independent flicks. (☎728-4401. First weekend in Sept.) Telluride also hosts a **Jazz Celebration** during the first weekend of August (☎728-7009) and a **Blues & Brews Festival** (☎728-8037) during the third weekend in September. For some festivals, volunteering to usher or perform other tasks can be exchanged for free admission. Throughout the year a number of concerts and performances go up at the **Sheridan Opera House,** 110 N. Oak St. (☎728-6363).

OUTDOOR ACTIVITIES. Biking, hiking, and backpacking opportunities are endless; ghost towns and lakes are tucked behind almost every mountain crag. The tourist office has a list of suggestions for hikes in the area. The most popular trek (about 2hr.) is up the jeep road to **Bridal Veil Falls,** the waterfall visible from almost anywhere in Telluride. The trailhead is at the end of Rte. 145. Continuing another 2.5 mi. from the top of the falls will lead to **Silver Lake,** a steep but rewarding and serene climb. For more Rocky Mountain highs, ride the free gondola to the top of the mountain. A number of hiking and biking trails run from the St. Sophia station.

In winter, even avowed atheists can be spied praying before hitting the "Spiral Stairs" and the "Plunge," two of the Rockies' most gut-wrenching ski runs. For more info, contact the **Telluride Ski Resort,** P.O. Box 11155, Telluride 81435 (☎728-3856). A free year-round gondola connects the mountain village with the rest of the town and runs from 7am-11pm. **Paragon Ski and Sport,** 213 W. Colorado Ave., rents bikes in summer and skis in winter. (☎728-4525. Open daily 9am-8pm; in ski season 8:30am-9pm. Bikes $26 per day; skis and boots $20 per day.)

SCENIC DRIVE: SAN JUAN SKYWAY

More a runway to the mountains and clouds than a terrestrial highway, the San Juan Skyway soars across the rooftop of the Rockies. Winding its way through San Juan and Uncompahgre National Forests, Old West mountain towns, and Native American ruins, the byway passes a remarkably wide range of southwestern Colorado's splendors. Reaching altitudes up to 11,000 feet, with breathtaking views of snowy peaks and verdant valleys, the San Juan Skyway is widely considered one of America's most beautiful drives. Travelers in this area inevitably drive at least parts of it as they head to destinations such as Telluride, Durango, and Mesa Verde. Many sections of the skyway skirt steep dropoffs and involve driving curvy mountain roads. The San Juan (☎970-247-4874) and Uncompahgre (☎970-874-6600) National Forests have info on road conditions on the skyway. A loop road, piggy-backing on Rte. 550, 62, 145, and 160, the skyway voyage can be started anywhere along the loop, at towns such as Durango, Ridgway, or Cortez. Beginning in Durango, the skyway heads north along Rte. 550 N (Million Dollar Hwy.), climbing into the San Juan Mountains and paralleling the Animas River.

Twenty-seven miles north of Durango, the road passes **Durango Mountain Resort** as it ascends. At Mile 64 on Rte. 550, the road peaks at Molas Point, a whopping 10,910 ft. above sea level. **Molas Lake** (☎970-749-9254 or 800-846-2172) offers visitors an oasis with tent and RV sites ($14), cabins ($25), canoe rentals ($5 per hr.), horseback riding ($20 per hr.), and picnic tables. Descending to a mere 9000 ft., the skyway arrives in the easy-going Silverton. A mining town until the early 90s, **Silverton** is a subdued mountain village that boasts some of Colorado's best ice climbing. The **Visitors Center** sits close to the entrance to town on Rte. 550. (☎970-387-5654. Open M-Sa 9am-6pm, Su 9am-5pm.) Hiking, mountain biking, and skiing at Kendall Mountain ($6 lift tickets) await those who can still catch their breath.

From Silverton, the San Juan Skyway climbs higher until it reaches 11,018 ft. at Mile 80 on Rte. 550. Known as **Red Mountain Pass,** this scenic point has some hiking and more than a few Kodak moments. Continuing north, the drive from Silverton to Ouray showcases stellar 14,000 ft. mountain peaks and defunct mines. In 1991, the Reclamation Act shut down most of the mines, leaving only remnants of the past. The skyway next arrives in **Ouray,** a yodeler's delight. With fabulous mountain views and hedonistic hot springs, this heavily Swiss-influenced town is a relaxing stop for the weary. Beyond Ouray, the skyway returns to Earth. Traversing mesas, Rte. 550 junctions with Rte. 62 in Ridgway. Rte. 62 assumes the reigns of the skyway and leads travelers to Placerville, where the skyway connects with Rte. 145.

Telluride next awaits travelers along Rte. 145. Past the Mountain Village, the dubiously named **Lizard's Pass** offers a tranquil 6 mi. hike reaching over 12,000 ft. From the pass, the skyway glides down along the Taylor Mesa through the quiet towns of Rico, Stoner, and Dolores. Rte. 145 connects with Rte. 160 just east of Cortez and west of **Mesa Verde National Park.** Moving east along Rte. 160, the skyway cuts through **Mancos** and finally returns to Durango.

DURANGO
☎970

In its heyday, Durango was one of the main railroad junctions in the Southwest. Walking down the town's main thoroughfare today, it is easy to see that Durango remains a crossroads. Dreadlocked, hemp-clad youths share the sidewalks with weathered ranchers in ten-gallon hats and stiff Wranglers, and toned, brazen mountain bikers rub shoulders in the bars with camera-toting tourists. These folks are brought together by their experiences in the great expanses of wilderness that engulf the town, be it enjoying the flora, roping dogies at the rodeo, biking the San Juans, or riding the narrow gauge railroad.

🛈 PRACTICAL INFORMATION. Durango is at the intersection of U.S. 160 and U.S. 550. Streets run perpendicular to avenues, but everyone calls Main Ave. "Main St." **Greyhound,** 275 E. 8th Ave. (☎259-2755; open M-F 7:30am-noon and 3:30-5pm, Sa 7:30am-noon, Su and holidays 7:30-10am), runs once per day to Grand Junction (5hr., $35-37); Denver (11½hr., $60-64); and Albuquerque (5hr., $42-45). The **Durango Lift** provides trolley service up and down Main Ave. every 20min. (☎259-5438. Runs daily 6am-10pm. 50¢.) Taxi: **Durango Transportation,** ☎259-4818. The **Durango Area Chamber Resort Association,** 111 S. Camino del Río, on the southeast side of town, offers info on sights and hiking. (☎247-0312 or 800-525-8855. Open M-Sa 8am-5:30pm, Su 10am-4pm.) **Road Conditions:** ☎264-5555. **Police:** 990 E. 2nd Ave. (☎385-2900). Free **Internet access** at the **Durango Public Library,** 1188 E. 2nd Ave. (☎385-2970; open M-W 9am-9pm, Th-Su 9am-5:30pm). **Post Office:** 222 W. 8th St. (☎247-3434; open M-F 8am-5:30pm, Sa 9am-1pm). **ZIP code:** 81301. **Area code:** 970.

🛏🍴 ACCOMMODATIONS AND FOOD. The **Durango Youth Hostel (HI-AYH),** 543 E. 2nd Ave., one block from downtown, maintains clean, simple bunks in a large converted house. Located near the heart of downtown, this hostel serves as a focal point for Durango's young backpacking crowd. While the men's dorm room is barracks-style, the women enjoy more comfortable accommodations. (☎247-9905. Key deposit $5. Check-in 7-10am and 5-10pm. Check-out 10am. Dorms $18, nonmembers $20.) Located right by the lift to downtown, the **Alpine Motel,** 3515 Main Ave., is one of the best places to stay in Durango for a reasonable price. (☎247-0402 or 800-818-4042. Reception 8am-10pm. June-Aug. singles $42-68; doubles $58-84; Sept.-May $28-32/$38-42.) The spacious, shag-carpeted rooms at **Budget Inn,** 3077 Main Ave., come with access to the pool, hot tub, and laundry. (☎247-5222 or 800-257-5222. June-Sept. singles $36; doubles $54; Oct.-May $27/$44.) Find great camping at **Junction Creek Campground,** Forest Rd. 171. From Main Ave., turn west on 25th St., which becomes Forest Rd. 171 after 4 mi.; the turn-off is 1 mi. past the national forest entrance. (14-night max. stay. $12 per vehicle, each additional person $6.)

Back in Durango, "dill-icious" pickles and subs abound at **Johnny McGuire's Deli,** 552 Main Ave., where you must choose between more than 25 sandwiches ($5) with names like the Free Iron Willy and the 4:20 Vegan. (☎259-8816. Open M-Sa 7am-9pm, Su 7am-6pm. Cash only.) Locals eat breakfast at **Carver's Bakery and Brewpub,** 1022 Main Ave., which has "dill-icious" (we like that word) breakfast specials ($2-7) and $8 pitchers of home-brewed beer. (☎259-2545. Open M-F 6:30am-10pm, Su 6:30am-1pm.) The best vegetarian place in town, **Skinny's Grill,** 1017 Main Ave. offers great food in a low key atmosphere. (☎382-2500. Open Su-Th 11:30am-9pm, F-Sa 11:30am-10pm.) To catch some area bands or hang with Durango hipsters, head to the **San Juan Room,** 601 E. 2nd Ave. (☎382-9880. Cover $2-5. Open M-Sa 7:30-2am.)

🎦🎭 SIGHTS AND ENTERTAINMENT. Although it's definitely more of a tourist attraction than a means of transportation, the **Durango and Silverton Narrow Gauge Train,** 479 Main St., runs along the Animas River Valley to the glistening old town of **Silverton.** Old-fashioned coal-fed locomotives wheeze through the San Juans, making a two-hour stop in Silverton before returning to Durango. In the summer, be prepared for heat and dust. It is often more comfortable and cheaper to drive the route yourself. The train also drops off and picks up at various scenic points; call for info. (☎247-2733. Office open June-Aug. daily 6am-8pm; May and mid-Aug. to Oct. 7am-7pm; Nov.-Apr. 8am-5pm. 7hr.; 2 per day; $55, ages 5-11 $30.)

The **Durango Pro Rodeo Series,** at the LaPlata County Fairgrounds at 25th and Main Ave., moseys into town every summer. Saddling up on Tuesday and Wednesday nights, the action starts at 7:30pm with a barbecue at 6pm. (☎247-1666. $13, children under 12 $5.) Some of the best Victorian-style melodramas in the US—full of high-flying vocals and tap dancing—take place at the Strater Hotel and Theater at 7th St. and Main Ave. (☎247-3400. Early June to late Sept. M-Sa. Doors open at 7:30pm, curtain at 8pm. Tickets $17.) In June and July, the annual **Shakespeare Festival** occurs. (☎247-7657. $12, students $8, under 12 $5.)

⚑ OUTDOOR ACTIVITIES. Unlike most Colorado towns that thrive on tourism, Durango's busiest season is summer, though winter is no stranger to strangers. **Durango Mountain Resort,** 27 mi. north on U.S. 550, hosts skiers of all levels. When the heat is on, travelers can trade in their skis for a sled and test out the alpine slide or take a free scenic chairlift ride. The ski slope also offers **mountain biking** in the summer. (☎800-979-9742. Open late Nov. to early Apr. daily 9am-4pm; mid-June to Aug. 10am-6pm. Lift tickets $34-48, under 12 $17-29. Slide ride $8, bike lift $5; all day $15.) Bikes are available at **Hassle Free Sports,** 2615 Main St. (☎259-3874 or 800-835-3800. Open M-Sa 8:30am-6pm, Su 10am-5pm; in winter daily 7:30am-7pm. Half-day $16; full-day $25. Ski rental packages from $12-25 per day.) **Southwest Adventures,** 1205 Camino del Río, offers mountain bikes, climbing gear, and backpacking gear. (☎259-0370. Open daily 8am-6pm.) The entire Durango area is engulfed by the **San Juan National Forest.** Call the Forest Headquarters for info on hiking and camping in the forest, especially if you're planning a trip into the massive **Weminuche Wilderness,** northeast of Durango. (☎247-4874. Open Apr. to mid-Dec. daily 8am-5pm; mid-Dec. to Mar. 8am-4:30pm.) The **Animas River** offers everything from placid Class II rapids to intense Class V battles. The largest outfitter in the area is **Mild to Wild Rafting,** 701 Main Ave. (☎247-4789 or 800-567-6745. Open daily 8am-10pm. Half-day mild $38; full-day mild $65; full-day intense $105. Reservations recommended.)

PAGOSA SPRINGS   ☎970

The Ute people—the first to discover the waters of Pagosa—believed that the springs were a gift of the Great Spirit, and the Chamber of Commerce would be hard-pressed not to think so too. Pagosa Springs, some of the hottest and largest in the world, bubble from the San Juan Mountains 60 mi. east of Durango on Rte. 160, and draw visitors from around the globe. Follow the sulfur smell to **The Springs,** 165 Hot Springs Blvd., where 15 different outdoor pools ranging from 98° to 114°F are available. (☎264-4168 or 800-225-0934. Open 24hr. $10 per person.) **Chimney Rock Archeological Area,** 17 mi. west of Pagosa Springs on U.S. 160 and Rte. 151 S, contains the ruins of a high-mesa Ancestral Puebloan village. (☎883-5359. Open mid-May to late Sept. daily 9am-4pm. 2½hr. tours leave at 9:30, 10:30am, 1, and 2pm. $5, ages 5-11 $3.) Skiing is available at **Wolf Creek,** 20 mi. east of Pagosa, which claims to have the most snow in Colorado. (☎264-5639. Call for prices and info.)

The **Mountain Express** bus line provides transportation in and around town. (☎264-2250. Daily every 1½hr. 6:30am-7:50pm. 50¢.) The **Pagosa Springs Chamber of Commerce,** 402 San Juan St., offers info on accommodations, food, and sights. (☎264-2360. Open M-F 8am-6pm, Sa-Su 9am-5pm.) **Pinewood Inn,** 157 Pagosa St., four blocks from downtown, rents cozy wood-paneled rooms with cable TVs and phones. (☎264-5715 or 800-655-7463. Singles $35-44; doubles $55-75.) **East Fork Campground,** East Fork Rd., sits 11 mi. east of town and offers shaded, rarely crowded sites. (☎264-2268. Open May-Sept. $8 per vehicle.) **Daylight Donuts & Cafe,** 2151 W. Rte. 160, is the place to start a budget day with eggs, bacon, and a massive pancake, all for $2. (☎731-4050. Open daily 6am-2pm.) **Los Amigos,** 4760 Rte. 160, a small Mexican grill 3 mi. west of downtown on Rte. 160, befriends budget travelers with $2 tacos. (☎731-2188. Open M-F 11am-8pm.) **Area code:** 970.

FOUR CORNERS **New Mexico, Arizona, Utah,** and **Colorado** meet at an unnaturally neat intersection about 40 mi. northwest of **Shiprock, NM,** on the Navajo Reservation. **Four Corners** epitomizes American ideas about land; these state borders were drawn along scientifically determined lines of longitude and latitude, disregarding natural boundaries. There's little to see; nonetheless, a large number of people veer off the highway to marvel at the geographic anomaly. At the very least, getting down on all fours to put a limb in each state is a good story for a cocktail party. (Open in summer daily 7am-8pm; in winter 8am-5pm. $2.)

MESA VERDE ☎970

Mesa Verde ("Green Table" in Spanish) rises from the deserts of southwestern Colorado, the southern-tilting slopes of its top noticeably friendlier to vegetation than the dry lands below. The landscape is not, however, the main attraction—some of the most elaborate Pueblo dwellings found today draw the largest crowds. Fourteen hundred years ago, Native American tribes began to cultivate the valleys of the area, and in the centuries that followed the Ancestral Puebloans constructed a series of cliff dwellings beneath the overhanging sandstone shelves surrounding the mesa. Around AD 1275, the Pueblo people abruptly left behind their eerie and starkly beautiful dwellings. Established in 1906, Mesa Verde National Park is the only national park set aside exclusively for archaeological remains. Mesa Verde is not for the snap-a-shot-and-go tourist; the best sites require a bit of a physical effort to reach and are too extraordinary to let the camera do all the marveling.

⚑ PRACTICAL INFORMATION. The park's sole entrance is off U.S. 160, 36 mi. from **Durango** and 8 mi. from **Mancos.** The entrance fee is $10 for vehicles, $5 for pedestrians and bikers. The **Far View Visitors Center,** is 15 mi. from the entrance on the main road. (☎529-4465. Open Apr.-Oct. daily 8am-5:30pm.) When it is closed, head to the museum (see **Sights,** below) or the **Colorado Welcome Center/Cortez Chamber of Commerce,** 928 E. Main, in Cortez. (☎565-3414. Open daily 8am-6pm.) Sights here are up to 40 mi. apart; a car is essential. **Area code:** 970.

⚐ ACCOMMODATIONS. Lodging in the park is pricey. To avoid the expensive rooms at Mesa Verde's only motel-style lodging, the **Far View Lodge** (☎592-4421), head to Mancos. Six miles west of the park entrance, the ▧**Old Mancos Inn,** 200 W. Grand Ave., lavishes guests with antique-laden private rooms for near-hostel prices. Outgoing owners and an inviting garden add to the homey feeling of the Inn. (☎533-9019. Rooms with shared bath $30, private bath $50.) The **Ute Mountain Motel,** 531 S. Broadway (☎565-8507; singles $23-30, doubles $38-45), or the **Sand Canyon Inn,** 301 W. Main St. (☎565-0125; singles $35-45, doubles $50-60), both in Cortez, are other options. Mesa Verde's **Morfield Campground** is expensive but beautiful, and its 452 sites never fills up. (☎564-1675. Sites $20; full hookup $26.)

◉ SIGHTS. A good starting point, the **Far View Visitors Center** is a long 15 mi. drive from the entrance gate along Rte. 160. At the Visitors Center, the park divides into **Chapin Mesa,** featuring the largest number of cliff dwellings, and the smaller and quieter **Wetherill Mesa.** The **Chapin Mesa Archaeological Museum,** along the first loop of the Chapin branch (before the dwellings), can give you an overview of the Ancestral Puebloan lifestyle and is a good place to start before exploring the mesa. (☎529-4465. Open daily 8am-6:30pm; Oct.-May 8am-5pm. Rangers lead tours of the cliff dwellings lasting about 1hr., departing every 30min. $2 tickets can be purchased at Far View Visitors Center.) Tours of the spectacular **Cliff Palace** (Apr.-Oct. daily 9am-6:30pm) explore the largest cliff dwelling in North America, with over 200 preserved rooms. The impressive **Balcony House** is a 40-room dwelling 600 ft. above the floor of Soda Canyon; entrance requires climbing several ladders and squeezing through a tunnel. (Open mid-May to mid-Oct. daily 9am-5:30pm.) A few self-guided tours of sites are accessible from Chapin Mesa. **Spruce Tree House** is Mesa Verde's third-largest cliff dwelling and features a reconstructed *kiva* that you can explore. This is the only dwelling open from in winter, when it is part of a tour leaving from the museum. (Trail 0.5 mi. Open daily 9am-6:30pm.) About ½ mi. north of the museum, the **Cedar Tree Tower** and **Farming Terraces Trail** give a sense of what work was like on the mesa top. (0.5 mi. Open daily 8am-sunset.) Three miles farther down the road and 2 mi. from the Visitors Center, the **Far View Sites** are comprised of five mesa-top villages. (Trail 0.8 mi. Open daily 8am-sunset.) A more low-key approach to the Chapin Mesa is the self-guided **Mesa Top Loop Rd.,** passing ruins from the 6th through the 13th century. (6 mi. Open daily 8am-sunset.)

THE SOUTHWEST

The Ancestral Puebloans (formerly Anasazi) of the 10th and 11th centuries were the first to discover that the arid lands of the Southwest could support an advanced agrarian civilization. Years later, in 1803, the United States laid claim to parts of the Southwest with the Louisiana Purchase. The idealistic hope for a Western "empire of liberty," where Americans could live the virtuous farm life, both motivated further expansion and helped create the region's individualist psychology.

Today, the vastness of the Southwestern desert, from the dramatically colored canvas of Arizona's red rock, sandstone, scrub brush, and pale sky, to the breathtaking vistas from Utah's mountains all invite contemplation, awe, and photo-ops, while the opportunity for mild and extreme outdoor activities define a side of the region that Kodak cannot capture. Be it hiking in Canyonlands, biking around Moab, river rafting on the Colorado, backpacking in the remote Gila Wilderness, or skiing the slopes of northern Utah, the rich and varied opportunities for outdoor adventure are unparalleled. At the same time, while the Southwest is best known for its dramatic landscape and recreational activities, its kaleidoscopic mix of cultures is just as intriguing. True to the eccentric spirit of the land, the Southwest can call itself home to hippies, cowboys, New Age spiritualists, Native Americans, Mexican-Americans, government scientists, conservatives, liberal outdoor junkies, and droves of tourists who have all rambled their way to the real American desert.

HIGHLIGHTS OF THE SOUTHWEST

MEXICAN FOOD. You can't get away from it, and in the tasty eateries of New Mexico's Albuquerque (p. 771) and Santa Fe (p. 764), you may not want to.

NATIONAL PARKS. Utah's "Fab Five" (p. 722) and Arizona's Grand Canyon (p. 732) reveal a stunning landscape of bizarre rock formations and brilliant colors.

SKIING. In a region famous for its blistering sun, the Wasatch Mountains (p. 716) near Salt Lake City, UT get some of the nation's choicest powder in winter.

LAS VEGAS. Attractions include casinos, casinos, and casinos (p. 707).

NEVADA

Nevada once walked the straight and narrow. Explored by Spanish missionaries and settled by Mormons, the Nevada Territory's scorched expanses seemed a perfect place for ascetics to strive for moral uplift. However, with the discovery of gold in 1850 and silver in 1859, the state was won over permanently to the worship of filthy lucre. When the precious metals ran out, gambling and marriage-licensing became big industries. The final moral cataclysms came when the state legalized prostitution on a county by county basis and spawned lounge idol Wayne Newton. But there *is* another side to Nevada. Lake Mead National Recreation Area, only 25 miles from Las Vegas, is an oasis in stunning desert surroundings, and the forested slopes of Lake Tahoe provide serene resorts for an escape from the cities.

▟ PRACTICAL INFORMATION

Capital: Carson City.

Visitor info: Nevada Commission on Tourism, Capitol Complex, Carson City 89701 (☎800-638-2328; line staffed 24hr.). **Nevada Division of State Parks,** 1300 S. Curry St., Carson City 89703-5202 (☎702-687-4384). Open M-F 8am-5pm.

Postal Abbreviation: NV. **Sales Tax:** 6.75-7%; 8% room tax in some counties.

SOUTHWEST

The Southwest

N

PACIFIC
OCEAN

0   160 miles
0   160 kilometers

LAS VEGAS
☎702

Rising out of the Nevada desert, Las Vegas is a shimmering tribute to excess. It is the actualization of a mirage, an oasis of vice and greed, and one very, very good time for those who embrace it. Nowhere else in America do so many shed their inhibitions and indulge otherwise dormant appetites. Vegas is about money and sex—but mostly money. The opulent mega-casinos that dominate Vegas are stupendously successful at snatching dollars, but the entertainment is outstanding and cheap deals are everywhere. There's a broken heart and an empty wallet for every twinkling light in the city.

▐ TRANSPORTATION

Flights: McCarran International (☎261-5211), at the southwestern end of the Strip. Main terminal on Paradise Rd. Vans to the Strip and downtown $3-5; taxi $10-12.

Buses: Greyhound, 200 S. Main St. (☎800-231-2222), downtown at Carson Ave. To Flagstaff (5-7hr., 3-4 per day, $47) and L.A. (5-7hr., 22 per day, $33).

Public Transit: Citizens Area Transit or **CAT** (☎228-7433). Bus #301 serves downtown and the Strip. Buses #108 and 109 serve the airport. All are wheelchair accessible. Buses run daily 5:30am-1:30am (24hr. on the Strip). Routes on the Strip $2, residential routes $1.25, seniors and ages 6-17 60¢. **Las Vegas Strip Trolleys** (☎382-1404) cruise the Strip every 15min. daily 9:30am-1:30am. $1.50.

Taxis: Yellow, Checker, Star (☎873-2000). Wheelchair accessible cabs available.

Car Rental: Sav-Mor Rent-A-Car, 5101 Rent-A-Car Rd. (☎736-1234 or 800-634-6779), at the airport. From $35 per day, $149 per week; 150 mi. per day included, each additional mi. 20¢. Must be 21+, under-25 surcharge $8 per day. Discounts can be found in tourist publications. Open daily 5:30am-1am.

✺⃞ ORIENTATION AND PRACTICAL INFORMATION

Driving to Vegas from L.A. is a straight, 300 mi. shot on I-15 N (5hr.). From Arizona, take I-40 W to Kingman and then U.S. 93 N Las Vegas has two major casino areas. The **downtown** area, around 2nd and Fremont St., has been converted into a pedestrian promenade. Casinos cluster together beneath a shimmering space-frame structure covering over five city blocks. The other main area is the Strip, a collection of mammoth hotel-casinos along **Las Vegas Blvd.** Parallel to the Strip and in its shadow is **Paradise Rd.,** also strewn with casinos. Always stay on well-lit pathways and don't wander too far from major casinos and hotels. *The neighborhoods just north and west of downtown are especially dangerous.*

Despite, or perhaps as a result of, its debauchery, Las Vegas has a **curfew.** Those under 18 are not allowed unaccompanied in most public places Sunday through Thursday from 10pm to 5am and Friday through Saturday from midnight to 5am. No one under 18 is allowed unaccompanied 9pm-5am on the Strip, ever.

Visitor info: Las Vegas Convention and Visitors Authority, 3150 Paradise Rd. (☎892-0711; fax 226-9011), 4 blocks from the Strip in the big pink convention center by the Hilton. Up-to-date info on headliners, conventions, shows, hotel bargains, and buffets. Open M-F 8am-5pm.

Tours: Gambler's Special bus tours leave L.A., San Francisco, and San Diego for Las Vegas early in the morning and return at night or the next day. Ask at tourist offices in the departure cities or call casinos for info. **Coach USA,** 4020 E. Lone Mountain Rd. (☎384-1234 or 800-634-6579), runs city tours (3½hr., 3 per day, $39). There are also bus tours from Las Vegas to **Hoover Dam/Lake Mead** (4hr., 2 per day, $39) and the **Grand Canyon's South Rim** (full-day, $149). Discounts with coupons in tourist publications and for ages 2-9. Reserve in advance.

Marriage: Marriage License Bureau, 200 S. 3rd St. (☎455-4415), in the courthouse. 18+ or at least 16 with parental consent. Licenses $35; cash only. No waiting period or blood test required. Open Su-Th 8am-midnight, F-Sa 24hr.

SOUTHWEST

24-Hour Crisis Lines: Gamblers Anonymous, ☎385-7732. **Rape Crisis Center Hotline,** ☎366-1640. **Suicide Prevention,** ☎731-2990.

Post Office: 301 E. Stewart Ave. (☎800-275-8777), downtown. Open M-F 8:30am-5pm. General Delivery pickup M-F 9am-2pm. **ZIP code:** 89101. **Area code:** 702.

ACCOMMODATIONS AND CAMPING

Even though Vegas has over 100,000 rooms, most hotels fill up on weekend nights. If you get stuck, call the **Room Reservations Hotline** (☎800-332-5333). The earlier you reserve, the better chance you have of snagging a special rate. Room rates at most hotels in Vegas fluctuate all the time, and many hotels have different rate ranges for weekdays and weekends. A room that costs $30 during a promotion can cost hundreds during conventions. There is a cluster of inexpensive motels north of the Strip (1200-1400 S. Las Vegas Blvd.), but these are far from the action in a sketchy part of town. *The 9% state hotel tax is not included in room rates listed below.*

Whiskey Pete's (☎800-248-8453), in Primm Valley, 45 mi. south of Vegas on I-15, just before the California border. Whiskey Pete's is cheap as fool's gold and home to the wildest roller coaster in Nevada ($6). Su-Th $19, F-Sa $50; prices vary.

Las Vegas International Hostel (AAIH/Rucksackers), 1208 S. Las Vegas Blvd. (☎385-9955). The helpful staff is an excellent source for budget advice. Tidy, spartan rooms and shared bathrooms. Key deposit $5. Reception 7am-11pm. Check-out 10am. 6-person dorms $12-14 with IHA membership or student ID; singles $26-28.

Somerset House Motel, 294 Convention Center Dr. (☎888-336-4280). A straightforward, no-frills establishment within short walking distance of the major Strip casinos. Many rooms feature kitchens; all are sizable and impeccably clean. Singles Su-Th $35, F-Sa $44; doubles $44/$55; each additional person $5; rates lower for seniors.

Circus Circus, 2880 S. Las Vegas Blvd. (☎800-444-2472). Check out the awesome Adventuredome Theme Park and clown shop. Su-Th $39-79, F-Sa and holidays $79-159; rollaway bed $12. Fills 3-4 months in advance.

Silverton, 3333 Blue Diamond Rd. (☎800-588-7711). This spooky ghost town-themed gambling den has a re-creation every Su night of a great Wild West tradition—the luau. Singles and doubles Su-Th $39-45, F-Sa $69-109.

Lake Mead National Recreation Area (☎293-8906), 25 mi. south of town on Rte. 93/95. Numerous campsites available throughout. Sites $10; hookups $14-18.

Valley of Fire State Park (☎397-2088), 60 mi. south of Vegas. A splendid campground near the ancient petroglyph site of Atlatl Rock. Sites $10. No electricity or hookups.

Circusland RV Park, 500 Circus Circus Dr. (☎734-0410). Pool, jacuzzi, convenience store, showers, and laundry. Hookups Su-Th $17.50, F-Sa $20.

FOOD

Sloshed and insatiable gamblers gorge themselves day and night at Vegas's gigantic buffets. For the bottomless gullet, there is no better value than the caloric intensity of these eateries. Beyond the buffets, Vegas has some of the best restaurants in the world, though there's little for the true budget adventurer.

Carnival World Buffet at the Río, 3700 W. Flamingo Rd. (☎252-7777). Hands down the greatest buffet in Vegas. Enjoy delicious food from any of the 11 stations. Breakfast $8 (8-10:30am), lunch $11 (11am-3:30pm), dinner $15 (3:30-11pm).

The Plaza Diner, 1 Main St. (☎386-2110), near the entrance to Jackie Gaughan's Plaza Hotel/Casino. Cheap prime rib dinner $6 (noon-midnight). $1 beers. Open 24hr.

Rincon Criollo, 1145 S. Las Vegas Blvd. (☎388-1906), across from Las Vegas International Hostel. Dine on filling Cuban food beneath a wall-sized photograph of palm trees. Hot sandwiches $3.50-4.50. Open Tu-Su 11am-9:30pm.

Battista's Hole in the Wall, 4041 Audrie Ave. (☎732-1424). Adorning the walls are 28 years' worth of celebrity photos and novelties from area brothels. Pricey at $18, but worth it. Open Su-Th 4:30-10:30pm, F-Sa 4:30-11pm.

N

TO SALT LAKE CITY, HWY. 93, & HWY. 95

TO ⬆ (10yd) DOWNTOWN (2mi)

Oakley Blvd.

St. Louis Ave.

Boston Park

Stratosphere

Sahara Ave.

Guinness World Records Museum

Sitlana

Industrial Rd.

Rancho Dr.

Highland Dr.

Circus Circus Dr.

Meade Ave.

Karen Ave.

Riviera Blvd.

Las Vegas Country Club

Desert Inn Rd.

Stardust

Stardust Rd.

Silver City

Convention Ctr. Dr.

Las Vegas Hilton

Las Vegas Convention Center

Frontier

Desert Inn Rd.

15

Spring Mtn. Rd.

Desert Inn Country Club

Treasure Island

Venetian

Sands Ave.

Paradise Rd.

Elm Ln.

Twain Ave.

Mirage

Roosevelt St.

Caesar's Palace

Flamingo Hilton

Koval Ln.

Hard Rock Casino

Bellagio

Flamingo Rd.

Industrial Rd.

Rochelle Ave.

Lana Ave.

Harmon Ave.

DESERT SPRINGS MEDICAL CENTER (1 mi)

U.N.L.V.

Harmon Ave.

The $trip

Monte Carlo

Tropicana Country Club

Naples Dr.

Burbe Ct.

Palos Verdes St.

New York-NY

Coca-Cola Store

MGM Grand

Tropicana Ave.

Leonard Fayle Res.

15

Excalibur

Luxor

Reno Ave.

TO JEAN, ⬆ (45mi).

TO BLUE DIAMOND RD. (3 mi) & ⬆

Hacienda Ave.

McCarran International Airport

Swenson St.

Wilbur St.

Maryland Pkwy.

Toni St.

Liberace Museum

Tamarus St.

Spencer St.

Gun Store

Reno Ave.

Eastern Ave.

Downtown

515

93 95

Squires Park

Cashman Field Center

Bonanza Rd.

J. Gaughan's Pl.

Fremont St. Experience

Gold Spike

93 95

Stewart Ave.

Main St.

Casino Ctr. Blvd.

3rd

Grass

Las Vegas Blvd. S.

Bonneville Ave.

Carson St.

Fremont

7th

9th

10th

11th

13th

15th

Circle Park

TO THE $TRIP

Commanche Park

Sahara Nevada Country Club

Las Vegas: The $trip

⬆ ACCOMMODATIONS

Circus Circus, 2

Las Vegas Int'l Hostel (AAIH/Rucksackers), 1

Silverton, 5

Somerset House Motel, 3

Whiskey Pete's, 4

0 — 1 mile

0 — 1 kilometer

Mediterranean Cafe, 4147 S. Maryland Pkwy. (☎ 731-6030), serves up fresh, delicious Greek and Mediterranean specialties. Try the combo plate ($9) or a falafel and hummus pita bread sandwich ($5). Open M 11am-9pm, Tu-Th 11am-1am, F-Su 11am-3am.

Saizan, 115 E. Tropicana Ave. (☎ 739-9000), in San Remo. The best sushi bar near the Strip offers only the freshest sushi and sashimi. The Yumyum roll ($8) lives up to its name. Open daily 5:30pm-midnight.

🍸 CA$INO-HOPPING AND NIGHTLIFE

Once the quintessentially Vegas themes of cheap buffets, booze, and entertainment were enough; now casinos spend millions of dollars to fool guests into thinking they are somewhere else. "Exact" images of Venice, New York, Río, Paris, Cairo (complete with the Pyramids), and Monte Carlo already thrive on the Strip. Remember: *gambling is illegal for those under 21.* If you are of age, look for casino "funbooks" which allow gamblers to buy $50 in chips for only $15. *Never bring more money than you're prepared to lose cheerfully.* Keep your wallet in your front pocket, and beware of thieves trying to nab winnings from jubilants.

Casinos, nightclubs, and some wedding chapels are open 24hr. There are far more casinos and far more attractions within them than can be listed here; use the following as a compendium of the best, but explore the Strip for yourself. Check with the Visitors Center for more casino listings.

At **Circus Circus,** 2880 S. Las Vegas Blvd. (☎ 734-0410), parents run to card tables and slot machines downstairs, while their children spend their quarters upstairs on the souped-up carnival and in the titanic video game arcade. The majestic confines of the **Mirage,** 3400 S. Las Vegas Blvd. (☎791-7111), banish all illusions from the halls of entertainment. Among its attractions are a dolphin habitat, illusionists Sieg-fried and Roy's white tigers, and an equally flaming volcano that erupts in fountains and jets of fire. A huge bronze lion guards the **MGM Grand,** 3799 S. Las Vegas Blvd. (☎891-7979), and a couple of live felines can be seen inside at the lion habitat. In addition to more than 5000 rooms, MGM also contains the Grand Adventures Amusement Park. At **Caesar's Palace,** 3570 S. Las Vegas Blvd. (☎731-7110), busts abound: some are plaster, while others are barely concealed by the low-cut cos-tumes that the cocktail waitresses have to wear; neither are real. At **New York, New York,** 3790 S. Las Vegas Blvd. (☎740-6969), towers mimic the Manhattan skyline, re-creating the glory of the Big Apple at this tacky casino. You can roll through the mean streets of New York aboard the muscular Manhattan Express Roller Coaster, a fast and acrobatic thrill.

Nightlife in Vegas gets rolling around midnight and keeps going until everyone drops. **C2K** at the **Venetian,** 2800 S. Las Vegas Blvd., is the newest resort-casino's palatial showroom transformed nightly into a mind-shattering über-club. Swim in a virtual ocean of synchronized, cyber-driven lights. (☎933-4255. Open W-Su 10:30pm-6am.) **Ra,** 3900 S. Las Vegas Blvd., is a superhot Egyptian-themed night club at the **Luxor.** Pretty people only, please. (☎262-4000. Open W-Sa 10pm-6am.)

NEAR LAS VEGAS

HOOVER DAM

Built to subdue the flood-prone Colorado River, Hoover Dam took 5000 men five years of seven-day weeks to construct. When their sweat finally dried, over 6.6 mil-lion tons of concrete had been crafted into a 726 ft. colossus that now shelters pre-cious agricultural land, pumps big voltage to Vegas and L.A., and furnishes the frazzled jet-skier with azure waters to churn. Ultimately, 96 men died during con-struction. The excellent tours and interpretive center explore the dam's history, though in a varnished and self-congratulatory way. This is a prize artifact from America's "think-big" era of ambitious landscaping and culturally transforming public works projects. The Visitors Center leads tours to the generators at the structure's bottom. (☎294-3510 or 294-3523. Open daily 8:30am-5:45pm. 30min. tours $8, seniors $7, ages 6-16 $2. More comprehensive "hardhat tours" $25.)

LAKE MEAD

The multi-tiered program of flood control, irrigation, and water storage is fulfilled by turquoise Lake Mead—a shiny blue spot in the arid wasteland between Arizona and Nevada. Dubbed "the jewel of the desert" by its residents, the lake and its envi-rons offer more than the social planning and deficit spending that created it. Lake Mead is really sustained by the multitude of Californians driving pickup trucks with jetskis in tow. Boats and other watercraft can be rented at concessionaires along the shores. **Boulder Beach** is accessible by Lakeshore Dr., off U.S. 93. (☎800-752-9669. Jetskis $50 per hr., $270 per day; fishing boats $55 per 4hr., $100 per day.)

Alongside the Park Service **campsites** ($10), concessionaires usually operate RV parks (most of which have become mobile home villages), marinas, restaurants, and occasionally motels. More remote concessionaires, including **Echo Bay Resort,** offer motel and camping options. (☎800-752-9669. Singles $80; doubles $90; hook-ups $18.) Its restaurant, **Tale of the Whale,** is decorated in nautical motifs, features a stunning view of Lake Mead, and cooks up $5 burgers. The resort rents jetskis ($50 per hr., $270 per day) and fishing boats ($12 per hr., $60 per day).

RENO   ☎775

Reno is like the mediocre younger brother of a superstar. While Las Vegas gets its name in movies, Reno gets the people who don't have the time to do Vegas. Hoping to strike it rich at the card tables, busloads of the nation's elderly flock to Reno's hedonistic splendor. A small town wrapped in urban sleaze at a Sierra scenic spot, Reno captures both the natural splendor and ultra-capitalist frenzy of the West.

⚑ PRACTICAL INFORMATION. Amtrak is at 135 E. Commercial Row. (☎800-872-7245. Open daily 8:30am-6pm.) **Greyhound,** 155 Stevenson St., a half-block from W. 2nd St., rolls to L.A. (12 per day, $52) and Salt Lake City (4 per day, $45-48). **Reno Citifare** (☎348-7433), at 4th and Center St., serves the Reno-Sparks area. Most of its buses operate daily 5am-7pm, though city center buses operate 24hr. Buses stop every two blocks. (Fare $1.25, seniors and disabled 60¢, ages 6-18 90¢.) **Reno-Sparks Convention and Visitors Center,** 300 N. Center St., sits on the first floor of the National Bowling Stadium. (☎800-367-7366. Open M-Su 9am-5pm.) **Post Office:** 50 S. Virginia St. at Mill St. (open M-F 8:30am-5pm, Sa 10am-2pm). **ZIP code:** 89501. **Area code:** 775.

⚑ ACCOMMODATIONS. While weekend prices at casinos are usually on the high side, gambler's specials, weekday rates, and winter discounts provide some great, cheap rooms. Prices fluctuate, so call ahead. **Fitzgerald's,** 225 N. Virginia St. (☎786-3663), **Atlantis,** 3800 S. Virginia St. (☎825-4700), and **Sundowner,** 340 N. Arlington Ave. (☎786-7050), have been known to offer some good deals to go along with their central locations and massive facilities. (Rates can get as low as $32, but they generally hover around $60 for a single.) Be advised—heterosexual prostitution is legal in most of Nevada (though not in Reno itself), and thus certain motels are cheap but lacking a particularly wholesome feel. Travelers of the same sex sharing a hotel room may be required to book a room with two beds. Southwestern downtown has the cheapest lodging. The prices below don't include Reno's **12% hotel tax.**

Circus Circus, 500 N. Sierra St., is deemed the family casino of Little Sin City, with over 1800 newly renovated rooms, acres of casinos, restaurants, activities, health club, a kitschy monorail-trolley, and a real live big top. Rooms are large, posh, and quiet. (☎329-0711 or 800-648-5010. M-Th from $60, F-Su from $109.) **Motel 6** has 3 clean, comfortable, and cheap locations in Reno: 866 N. Wells Ave. (☎786-9852), north on I-80 Exit 14; 1901 S. Virginia St. (☎827-0255), 1½ mi. down Virginia St. at Plumb Ln.; and 1400 Stardust St. (☎747-7390), north on I-80 Keystone Exit and west onto Stardust St. (Reserve 2 weeks in advance. Singles June-Sept. Su-Th $38, F-Sa $42; doubles $44/$48. Cheaper Oct.-May.) **El Cortez Hotel,** 239 W. 2nd St., is a 116-room downtown hotel, with A/C, cable TV, exposed pipes, and thin walls. (☎322-9161. Singles Su-Th $29, F-Sa $38; doubles $43/$49.)

⚑ FOOD. Eating in Reno is cheap. To entice gamblers and prevent them from wandering out in search of food, casinos offer a wide range of all-you-can-eat buffets and 99¢ breakfasts. However, buffet fare can be greasy and overcooked. Reno's other inexpensive eateries offer better food. The large Basque population has brought a spicy and hearty cuisine locals enthusiastically recommend. Locals swear by the tangy Basque cuisine at **Santa Fe Restaurant,** 235 Lake St., in the Santa Fe Hotel in the heart of downtown. Hearty portions of unusual food: oxtail, beef tongue, and pigs feet abound, as well as top sirloin steak and chicken. (☎323-1891. Open daily 11am-2pm and 6-9pm. Lunch $7-9. 7-course dinner $14.) **Miguel's Fine Mexican Food,** 1415 S. Virginia St., was voted best Mexican food in Nevada by *Nevada Weekly*'s readers. (☎322-2722. Open daily 11am-9pm. Entrees $5-10.)

⚑ ENTERTAINMENT. Reno is one big amusement park. Many casinos offer free gaming lessons; minimum bets vary between establishments. Drinks are either free or incredibly cheap if you're gambling, but be wary of a casino's generous gift of risk-inducing, inhibition-dropping alcohol. Don't forget that gambling is illegal if you're under 21. Almost all casinos offer live nighttime entertainment, but the shows are generally not worth the steep admission prices. **Harrah's,** 219 N. Center St. (☎786-3232), is the self-consciously "hip" complex where **Planet Hollywood** capitalizes on movie lust by magically transforming Hollywood knick-knacks into precious relics. Harrah's also features a rockumentary featuring all sorts of past dance crazes entitled **Dancin' in the Street.** At **Circus Circus,** 500 N. Sierra (☎329-0711), a small circus above the casino performs "big top" shows every 30min.

NEAR RENO: PYRAMID LAKE
Thirty miles north of Reno on Rte. 445, on the Paiute Indian Reservation, lies emerald green Pyramid Lake, one of the most heart-achingly beautiful bodies of water in

the US. The pristine tides of Pyramid Lake are set against the backdrop of a barren desert, making it a soothing and otherworldly respite from neon Reno. **Camping** is allowed anywhere on the lake shore, but only designated areas have toilet facilities. A $5 permit is required for use of the park, and the area is carefully patrolled by the Paiute tribe. Permits are available at the **Ranger Station,** 3 mi. left from Rte. 445 at Sutcliffe. (☎476-1155. Open daily 8am-7pm.) **Boat rental** (☎476-1156) is available daily at the marina near the Ranger Station; call for reservations. **Area code:** 775.

UTAH

Beginning in 1848, persecuted members of the Church of Jesus Christ of Latter-Day Saints (colloquially called Mormons) settled on the land that is now Utah, intending to establish and govern their own theocratic state. President James Buchanan struggled to quash the Mormons' efforts in 1858, as many others had tried before. The Mormons eventually gave up their dreams of theocracy and their rights to polygamy, and statehood was finally granted on January 4, 1896. Today the state's population is 70% Mormon—a religious presence that creates a haven for family values. Utah's citizens dwell primarily in the 100-mile corridor along I-15, stretching from Ogden to Provo. Outside this area, Utah's natural beauty dominates, intoxicating visitors in a way that Utah's watered-down 3.2% beer never can. Just east of Salt Lake City, the Wasatch range beckons skiers in the winter and bikers in the summer. Southern Utah is like no other place on Earth; red canyons, river gorges, and crenelated cliffs attest to the creative powers of wind and water.

⚔ PRACTICAL INFORMATION

Capital: Salt Lake City.

Visitor info: Utah Travel Council, 300 N. State St., Salt Lake City 84114 (☎801-538-1030 or 800-200-1160; www.utah.com), across from the capitol building. Distributes the *Utah Vacation Planner's* lists of motels, national parks, and campgrounds, as well as statewide biking, rafting, and skiing brochures. **Utah Parks and Recreation,** 1594 W. North Temple, Salt Lake City 84116 (☎801-538-7220). Open M-F 8am-5pm.

Controlled Substances: Mormons abstain from "strong drinks" (coffee and tea), nicotine, alcohol, and, of course, illegal drugs. While you probably won't have trouble getting a pack of cigarettes or a cup of coffee, alcohol is another matter. State liquor stores are sprinkled sparsely about the state and have inconvenient hours. Grocery and convenience stores can only sell beer. While most upscale restaurants serve wine, licensing laws can split a room, and drinkers may have to move to the bar to get a mixed drink. Law requires that waiters not offer drink menus; diners wanting a list must request one. Also, establishments that sell hard alcohol are required to be "members only"; tourists can either find a "sponsor"—i.e., an entering patron—or get a short-term membership.

Postal Abbreviation: UT. **Sales Tax:** 5.75-7.75%.

SALT LAKE CITY   ☎801

Tired from five exhausting months of travel, Brigham Young looked out across the desolate valley of the Great Salt Lake and said, "This is the place." Young knew that his band of Mormon pioneers had finally reached a haven where they could practice their religion freely, away from the persecution they had faced in the East. Today, Salt Lake City is still dominated by Mormon influence. The Church of Jesus Christ of Latter-Day Saints (LDS) welcomes visitors to Temple Sq., a city block that includes the Mormon Temple and cool, shady gardens. Despite its commitment to preserving tradition, Salt Lake is rapidly attracting high-tech firms, as well as outdoor enthusiasts drawn by world-class ski resorts, rock climbing, and mountain trails. The city has already landed perhaps the biggest prize of all, the 2002 Winter Olympics, which has Salt Lake looking temporarily war-torn from construction.

Salt Lake City

🏠 **ACCOMMODATIONS**
Avenue's Hostel, 1
Park City Int. Hostel, 8
City Creek, 10
Scenic Motel, 4
Ute Hostel, 5

🍴 **FOOD AND DRINK**
Cafe Trang, 6
Orbit Cafe, 7
The Pie, 2
Red Iguana, 9
Sage Cafe, 3

🔲 TRANSPORTATION

Airport: Salt Lake City International, 776 N. Terminal Dr. (☎575-2400), 6 mi. west of Temple Sq. UTA bus #50 runs between the terminal and downtown for $1, but don't count on it after 10pm. Taxi to Temple Sq. costs about $11.

Trains: Amtrak, 340 S. 600 W (☎531-0188). *Be aware: the station is in an unsafe area of town.* To: Denver (15hr., 1 per day, $75-112) and San Francisco (19hr., 1 per day, $77-115). Station open M-F 10am-1:30pm, Sa-Su 10pm-6am.

Buses: Greyhound, 160 W. South Temple (☎355-9579), near Temple Sq. To: Denver (7-10hr., 5 per day, $46); Las Vegas (12-13hr., 4 per day, $46); and Los Angeles (15-18hr., 4 per day, $130). Open daily 6:30am-11:30pm, ticket window until 10:30pm.

Public Transit: Utah Transit Authority (UTA) (☎743-3882). Frequent service to University of Utah campus; buses to Ogden (#70/72 express), suburbs, airport, mountain canyons, and the #11 express runs to Provo ($2). New TRAX light rail follows Main St. from downtown to Sandy. Buses every 20min.-1hr. M-Sa 6am-11pm. Fare $1-2, senior discounts, under 5 free. Maps available at libraries and the Visitors Bureau. Buses and trains traveling downtown near the major sites are free.

Taxis: Ute Cab, ☎359-7788. **Yellow Cab,** ☎521-2100.

✳️🔲 ORIENTATION AND PRACTICAL INFORMATION

Salt Lake City's grid system may seem confusing at first but makes navigation easy once you get the hang of it. Brigham Young designated **Temple Sq.** as the heart of downtown. Street names increase in increments of 100 and indicate how many blocks east, west, north, or south they lie from Temple Sq.; the "0" points are **Main St.** (north-south) and **South Temple** (east-west). State St., West Temple, and North Temple are 100 level streets. Occasionally, streets are referred to as 13th S or 17th N, which are the same as 1300 S or 1700 N. Local address listings often include two numerical cross streets, acting as a type of coordinate system (no maps needed!). A building on 13th S (1300 S) might be listed as 825 E. 1300 S, meaning the cross street is 800 E (8th E). Smaller streets and those that do not fit the grid pattern sometimes have non-numeric names.

Visitor info: Salt Palace Convention Center and Salt Lake City Visitors Bureau, 90 S. West Temple (☎534-4902). Located in Salt Palace Convention Center, 1 block south of Temple Sq. Open in summer M-F 8am-6pm, Sa-Su 9am-5pm; early Sept. to late May M-F 8am-5pm, Sa-Su 9am-5pm.

Hotlines: Rape Crisis, ☎467-7273. **Suicide Prevention,** ☎483-5444. Both 24hr.

Gay/Lesbian Information: The Little Lavender Book (☎323-0727), distributed twice yearly, presents a directory of gay-friendly Salt Lake City Services.

Internet access: Salt Lake Public Library, 209 E. 500 S (☎524-8200). Free Internet access. Open M-Th 9am-9pm, F-Sa 9am-6pm, Su 1-5pm.

Post Office: 230 W. 200 S, 1 block south and 1 block west of Visitors Bureau. Open M-F 8am-5pm, Sa 9am-2pm. **ZIP code:** 84101. **Area code:** 801.

ACCOMMODATIONS

Affordable chain motels cluster at the southern end of downtown, around 200 W and 600 S, as well as on North Temple.

Park City International Hostel, 268 Historic Main St. (☎655-7244 or 888-980-7244), 30 mi. east of Salt Lake City on I-80 and south on Rte. 224. This brand new, state-of-the-art, dazzling, and friendly hostel offers affordable beds in an exorbitant town. Free Internet, $3 continental breakfast at restaurant next door, spectacular movie/DVD theater, and a shuttle from Salt Lake City airport. Winter dorms $35, private room (sleeps up to 4) $90; summer prices significantly reduced.

Ute Hostel (AAIH/Rucksackers), 21 E. Kelsey Ave. (☎595-1645), near the intersection of 1300 S and Main. Located 2 blocks from new UTA trax line for easy downtown/ski-shuttle access. Young international crowd. Free pickups can be arranged from airport, Amtrak, Greyhound, or the Visitors Center. Free tea and coffee, parking, linen, and safe. Check-in 24hr. Dorms $15, doubles $35.

The Avenue's Hostel (HI-AYH), 107 F St. (☎359-3855), 15min. walk from Temple Sq. toward the foothills in a residential area. Guests make frequent use of TV lounge, library, and video collection. Free parking, 2 kitchens, and laundry. Blankets and linen free. Free pickup from Amtrak and Greyhound stations. Reception 7:30am-10:30pm. Dorms $17 (nonmembers), doubles $36 (nonmembers). Major credit cards accepted.

City Creek Inn, 230 W. North Temple (☎533-9149), a stone's throw from Temple Sq. Offers ranch-style rooms for reasonable downtown rates. Singles $48; doubles $58.

Scenic Motel, 1345 S. Foothill Dr., (☎582-1527). Inexpensive rooms in a safe residential area, close to the university and ski access. Singles $38; doubles $45.

The mountains rising to the east of Salt Lake City offer comfortable summer camping with warm days and cool nights. Rocky **Little Cottonwood Canyon** features two of the closest campgrounds for summer camping: **Tanners Flat** (39 sites; $12) and **Albion Basin** (26 sites; $12; higher altitude, opens later in the season). To find the campgrounds, take I-215 to Rte. 210 E. Brown recreation signs point the way to both campsites, about 30 mi. from downtown Salt Lake. On weekends, get there early to ensure a space; for summer weekends, call in advance. The **Salt Lake Ranger District** (☎943-1794) fields calls for camping reservations and more info. If you need a full hookup, **Camp VIP,** 1400 W. North Temple, has 450 RV sites and 17 tent sites. (☎328-0224. Sites $19, full hookups $26.50.)

◖ MORAL FIBER

Good, cheap restaurants are sprinkled around the city and its suburbs. Not known as an especially cosmopolitan metropolis, Salt Lake hosts a startling variety of ethnic cuisines. If you're in a hurry downtown, **ZCMI Mall** and **Crossroads Mall,** both across from Temple Sq., have standard food courts.

Red Iguana, 736 W. North Temple (☎322-1489), across the bridge from downtown in the bright orange building. Authentic pre-Hispanic Mexican food, preserving the complexity of ancient Aztec flavor. A la carte burritos, enchiladas, tacos ($5-7), and combo plates ($10). Open M-Th 11am-9pm, F 11am-10pm, Sa noon-10pm, Su noon-9pm.

Sage Cafe, 473 E. 300 S (☎322-3790). This charming organic, vegan cafe serves many variations on fresh veggies, tofu, and beans. All-you-can-eat weekday lunch buffet $6.75. Open W-Th 11am-10pm, F 11am-11pm, Sa 9am-11pm, Su 9am-10pm.

Cafe Trang, 818 S. Main (☎539-1638). Nearly 200 pan-Asian offerings, all at affordable prices ($5-9). Try the rice noodles as you gaze at the exotic fish swimming next to your table. Open M-Th 11am-10pm, F-Sa 11am-10:30pm, Su noon-10pm.

Orbit Cafe, 540 W. 200 S (☎322-3808), conveniently close to the area's nightlife, Orbit is equal parts bakery, diner, dance club, and Internet cafe. Dinner entrees ($9-12) and late-night breakfast items ($3.50-7) sate "versatile" customers. Open M-Tu 11am-midnight, W-Th 11am-3am, F 11am-4am, Sa 8am-4am, Su 8am-midnight.

The Pie, 1320 E. 200 S (☎582-0193), next to the University of Utah. This graffiti-buried college hangout serves up large pizzas (starting at $7) late into the night. Open M-Th 11am-1am, F-Sa 11am-3am, Su noon-11pm.

◉ SIGHTS

LATTER-DAY SIGHTS. Many of Salt Lake's sights are sacred to the Church of Jesus Christ of Latter-Day Saints and are all free. The seat of the highest Mormon authority and the central temple, **Temple Sq.** is the symbolic center of the Mormon religion. The square has two **Visitors Centers.** Visitors can wander around the flowery ten-acre square, but the temple itself is off-limits to non-Mormons. An automated visitor info line (☎800-537-9703) provides up-to-date hours and tour info. Forty-five-minute tours leave from the flagpole every 15min. *Legacy,* a film detailing the Mormon trek to Salt Lake City, is screened at the **Joseph Smith Memorial Building.** *(☎240-2609, show times 240-4383, tours 240-1266. Open M-Sa 9am-9pm. Free.)*

Temple Sq. is also home to the **Mormon Tabernacle** and its famed choir. Weekly rehearsals and performances are free and open to the public. *(Organ recitals M-Sa noon-12:30pm, Su 2-2:30pm; in summer also M-Sa 2-2:30pm. Choir rehearsals Th 8-9:30pm; Choir broadcasts Su 9:30am, must be seated by 9:15am.)* During summer months, there are frequent free concerts at **Assembly Hall** next door. *(☎800-537-9703 for schedules.)* The **Church of Jesus Christ of Latter-Day Saints Office Building** is the tallest skyscraper in town—check out the stunning view from the 26th floor. *(40 E. North Temple. ☎240-3789. Observation deck open M-F 9am-5pm.)* The LDS church's collection of genealogical materials is available and free. The **Family Search Center,** 15 E. South Temple St., in the Joseph Smith Memorial Building, has computers and staff to aid in your search. The actual collection is housed in the **Family History Library.** *(35 N. West Temple. ☎240-2331. Center open M-Sa 9am-9pm. Library open M 7:30am-6pm, Tu-Sa 7:30am-10pm.)*

CAPITOL HILL. At the northernmost end of State St., Utah's **capitol building** features beautiful grounds, including a garden that changes daily. *(☎538-3000. Open M-F 8am-5pm. Tours M-F 9am-4pm.)* Down State St., the **Hansen Planetarium** has free exhibits and laser shows set to music. *(15 S. State St. ☎531-4925. Open M-Th 9am-9pm, F-Sa 9:30am-midnight, Su 1-5pm. Laser show $6 star, science show $4.50.)*

MUSEUMS. At the **Children's Museum,** build houses with enormous Legos or work in the "color factory." *(840 N. 300 W. ☎322-5268. Take bus #70. Open M-Th and Sa 10am-6pm, F 10am-8pm. $3.75, under 1 year free.)* Visiting exhibits and a permanent collection of world art wows enthusiasts at the newly expanded **Utah Museum of Fine Arts,**

on the University of Utah campus. (☎581-7332. Open M-F 10am-5pm, Sa-Su noon-5pm. Free.) Also on the University campus, the **Museum of Natural History** focuses on the prehistory of the Wasatch Front. (☎581-6927. Open M-Sa 9:30am-5:30pm, Su noon-5pm. $4, ages 3-12 $2.50, under 3 free.) The **Salt Lake Art Center,** displays an impressive array of contemporary art and documentary films. (20 S. West Temple. ☎328-4201. Open Tu-Th and Sa 10am-5pm, F 10am-9pm, Su 1-5pm. Suggested donation $2.)

THE GREAT SALT LAKE. The Great Salt Lake is a remnant of primordial Lake Bonneville and is so salty that only algae and brine shrimp can survive in it. The salt content varies from 5-27%, providing unusual buoyancy; no one has ever drowned here. Decaying organic material on the lakeshore gives the lake its characteristically pungent odor. **Antelope Island State Park,** in the middle of the lake, has beaches, trails, picnic spots, and buffalo. (It is nearly impossible to get to the lake without a car; bus #37 "Magna" will take you within 4 mi. To get to the south shore, take I-80 17 mi. west of Salt Lake City to Exit 104. To get to the island, take Exit 335 from I-15 and follow signs to the causeway. ☎595-4030. Open daily 7am-10pm; in winter dawn-dusk. Vehicles $7, bicycles $3.)

⛷ SKIING

Utah sells itself to tourists with pictures of intrepid skiers on pristine powder, which many have called "the greatest snow on earth." With the Wasatch Range boasting seven ski areas within 1hr. of the city, Salt Lake is the hub of Utah's winter vacation paradise. The nearby town of **Park City** is a quintessential ski town, with expensive restaurants and accommodations and few options for budget travelers. Staying in Salt Lake is usually a more affordable option. Because they fear skiers may be scared off by the Olympic frenzy, many of the area's ski resorts are offering deals for the upcoming winter. Call individual resorts for specifics.

Alta (☎359-1078), 27 mi. southeast of the city in Little Cottonwood Canyon. The area's cheapest lift tickets provide access to magnificent skiing. Alta's slopes are strictly for skis, so ditch the snowboard. Open mid-Nov. to mid-Apr. Day pass $38; half-day $29.

Brighton (☎800-873-5512), south of Salt Lake in Big Cottonwood Canyon. A favorite for families, with its friendly terrain and no-frills approach. Open Nov. to late Apr. Day pass $37; half-day $32; night $22.

The Canyons (☎435-649-5400), in Park City. With 125 trails, 13 lifts, and 6 half-pipes, the Canyon's terrain wows skiing enthusiasts but may be intimidating to beginners. Open Nov.-Apr. Day pass $59, ages 6-12 and seniors $31, under 6 free. Free season pass in exchange for 1 day of work at the resort per week. Call ahead for more info.

Park City (☎435-649-8111). Facilities earned it the job of hosting the Olympic snowboarding events in 2002; the skiing's not bad either. The 750 acres of open bowl skiing might make you feel a bit extreme. Open mid-Nov. to mid-Apr. Lift tickets vary by season: high season full-day from $60, half-day $42; ages 65-69 $30; over 70 free.

Snowbird (☎933-2222 or 800-453-3000), in Little Cottonwood Canyon south of Salt Lake. May frighten those who don't like steeps, but the adventurous types will relish in the back bowl feeling here. A 125-passenger aerial tram ascends to an 11,000 ft. peak for spectacular views and extreme-style skiing. Open Nov.-May. Day pass with tram access $52, chairs only $42.

Snowbasin (☎399-1135), off Rte. 39 in Ogden Valley, north of the city. Host of the 2002 Olympic downhill competition. Olympic-driven construction has brought state-of-the-art lifts and comfortable lodges to the mountain. Open late Nov. to Apr. Full-day passes $39, half-day $31; child $24; seniors $27.

Solitude (☎543-1400), in Big Cottonwood Canyon south of Salt Lake. Budget prices and luxury slopes. The runs delight for skiers and snowboarders of all abilities. Open Nov.-Apr. Day pass $39, seniors 60-69 $32, over 70 free; half-day $33; multi-day $37.

🎵 🎬 ENTERTAINMENT AND NIGHTLIFE

Concerts abound in the sweltering summer months. At 7:30pm every Tuesday and Friday, the **Temple Sq. Concert Series** conducts a free outdoor concert in Brigham Young Historic Park, with music ranging from string quartet to unplugged guitar.

(☎240-2534. Call for a schedule of concerts.) The **Utah Symphony Orchestra** performs in **Abravanel Hall,** 123 W. South Temple. (☎533-6683. Office open M-F 10am-6pm. Tickets Sept. to early May $15-40. Call 1 week in advance.) On Wednesday evenings in summer, the Gallivan Center, on 200 S between State and Main, hosts **Come Alive,** a laid-back celebration of live music, beer, and food. University of Utah's **Red Butte Garden,** 300 Wakara Way (☎587-9939), offers an outdoor summer concert series with high-quality national acts.

Women's basketball's **Utah Starzz** (season June-Aug.; tickets $5-40) and the 1998 NBA Western Conference Champion **Utah Jazz** (season Oct.-Apr.; tickets $10-83) take the court at the **Delta Center,** 301 W. South Temple (☎355-3865).

Free copies of *The Event, Mountain Times, City Weekly,* or *Utah After Dark* are available at bars, clubs, and restaurants, and list events. Despite its somewhat stringent restrictions on alcohol, Salt Lake has a surprisingly active nightlife, centered on the rundown blocks just southwest of downtown. An overwhelming police presence makes the potentially dangerous neighborhood almost too safe. To meet throngs of sweaty locals pulsating to heavy beats in cramped quarters, check out either **Club Axis,** 108 S. 500 W (☎519-2947), or the **Bricks,** 200 S. 600 W. Both clubs cater to a trendy crowd and have separate 18+ and 21+ areas. The **Dead Goat Saloon,** 165 S. West Temple, showcases local jazz and blues acts in a relaxed atmosphere with pool, darts, and a grill. (☎328-4628. Open M-Sa 6pm-2am, Su 6pm-midnight.) **The Zephyr,** 301 S. West Temple, features live music and attracts national acts. (☎355-2582. Call for events schedule. Hours vary.) A diverse mix of the Salt Lake gay and lesbian crowd flocks to video-bar/dance-club **Zipperz,** 155 W. 200 S. (☎521-8200. W 80s night.) Classic movies ($4) are accompanied by microbrews ($3) at **Brewvies,** 667 S. 200 W (☎355-5500), a movie theater-*cum*-brewpub.

▓ DAYTRIP FROM SALT LAKE CITY: TIMPANOGOS CAVE

Legend has it that a set of mountain lion tracks first led Martin Hansen to the mouth of the cave that today bears his name. Hansen's cave forms but one-third of the cave system of American Fork Canyon, collectively called Timpanogos Cave. In an rich alpine environment, Timpanogos is a true gem for speleologists (cave nuts) and tourists alike. Though early miners shipped boxcar loads of stalactites and other mineral wonders back east to sell to universities and museums, enough remain to bedazzle guests for the 1 hr. walk through the caves. Today, the cave is open only to visitors via tours led by rangers.

Timpanogos Cave National Monument, administered by the National Park Service, is solely accessible via Rte. 92 (20 mi. south of Salt Lake City off I-15, Exit 287; Rte. 92 also connects with Rte. 189 northeast of Provo). The **Visitors Center** dispenses tour tickets and info on the caves. Summer tours tend to sell out by early afternoon; reservations for busy summer weekends should be made as earlier as 30 days in advance. Bring water and warm layers: the rigorous hike to the cave climbs 1065 ft. over 1.5 mi., but the temperature remains a constant 45°F inside. (☎756-5238. Open daily mid-May to mid-Oct. 7am-5:30pm. 3hr. hikes depart daily 7am-4:30pm every 15min. $6, ages 6-15 $5, Golden Age Passport and under 5 $3.)

The National Monument is dwarfed by the surrounding **Uinta National Forest,** which blankets the mountains of the Wasatch Range. The **Alpine Scenic Drive (Rte. 92)** provides excellent views of Mt. Timpanogos and other snowcapped peaks. The loopy 20 mi. trip takes almost 1hr. in one direction. The Forest Service charges $2 for recreation along the road. The **Timpooneke Trail** (16.2 mi.) leads to the sheer summit of **Mt. Timpanogos** (11,749 ft.), beginning at the Aspen Grove Trailhead (6860 ft.) and meeting the summit trail at Emerald Lake.

The Pleasant Grove Ranger District also has info on the numerous **campgrounds** in the area (☎800-280-2267; sites $11-13) and **backcountry camping** throughout the forest, which requires no permit or fee as long as you respect minimum-impact guidelines. The National Park Service forbids camping within the national monument itself. **Little Mill Campground,** on Rte. 92 past the monument, is not especially scenic, but stands closest to the national monument. Rte. 89 in nearby **Orem** and **Pleasant Grove** has gas stations, supermarkets, and fast food.

DINOSAUR NATIONAL MONUMENT AND VERNAL   ☎ 435

Dinosaur National Monument was created in 1915, seven years after paleontologist Earl Douglass happened upon an array of fossilized dinosaur bones here. The rugged landscape that today includes the beautiful Green and Yampa rivers was once home to legions of dinosaurs that left their remains for tourists to ogle. The monument's main attraction is the dinosaur quarry, but adventurous types may find more distractions in the less explored parts of the area. The town of Vernal, west of Dinosaur on U.S. 40, is a popular base for exploring the monument, Flaming Gorge, and the Uinta Mountains.

■◪ **ORIENTATION AND PRACTICAL INFORMATION.** The national monument collects an entrance fee of $10 per car, and $5 per cyclist, pedestrian, or tour-bus passenger. The national monument's western entrance lies 20 mi. east of Vernal on Rte. 149, which splits from U.S. 40 southwest of the park in Jenson, UT. Once inside the park, pay a visit to the **Dinosaur Quarry Visitors Center,** a remarkable Bauhaus building that houses exhibits, a bookstore, and an exposed river bank brimming with dinosaur bones. During summer, a **shuttle** whisks passengers ½ mi. to the Visitors Center; from September to May, cars can drive this route. (☎ 781-7700. Open June-Aug. 8am-7pm; Sept.-May 8am-4:30pm.) **Monument Headquarters** is 45 mi. along Rte. 40 from the Rte. 149 turnoff in Dinosaur, CO. (☎ 374-3000. Open June-Aug. daily 8am-6pm; Sept.-May M-F 8am-4:30pm.) **Gas** is available in Vernal, Jenson, and Dinosaur, CO.

    Greyhound runs buses to Denver (8hr.; 2 per day; $53) and Salt Lake City (4½hr.; 2 per day; $34) from Frontier Travel, 72 S. 100 W (☎ 789-0404). Jensen is a flag stop, as is Monument Headquarters, 2 mi. west of Dinosaur, CO. **The Northeast Utah Visitors Center,** 235 E. Main, provides info on regional recreational activities. The **Ashley National Forest Service Office,** 355 N. Vernal Ave., has info about hiking, biking, and camping in the Ashley and Uinta National Forests. Mail kitschy dino postcards from the **Post Office,** 67 N. 600 W. **ZIP code:** 84078. **Area code:** 435.

▟▚ **ACCOMMODATIONS AND FOOD.** For the lowdown on campgrounds, contact the park Visitors Center or the National Forest Office in Vernal. Most easily accessible, **Green River** lies along Cub Creek Rd. about 5 mi. from the entrance. (88 sites; flush toilets and water. $12.) Nearby **Split Mountain** hosts only groups during summer but is free and open to all during winter. **Echo Park,** 13 mi. along Echo Park Rd. from Harper's Corner Drive (four-wheel-drive road and impassable when wet), provides the perfect location for a crystalline evening under the stars. (9 sites. Vault toilets and water. $6.) Free **backcountry camping** permits are available from Monument Headquarters or the Quarry Visitors Center. For hookups and amenities head outside the park to **Campground Dina RV Park,** 930 N. Vernal Ave., about 1 mi. north of Main St. on U.S. 191 in Vernal. (☎ 789-2148. Heated pool, showers, laundry, convenience store. Grassy sites for 1 or 2 $17; hookups $21; $2 each additional person. Call ahead for summer weekends.)

    For those less inclined to rough it, Vernal is civilization's beacon. In high-demand summer months, prices may not always reflect quality. Directly across from the Visitors Center, the **Weston Lamplighter Hotel,** 120 E. Main, has spacious and clean rooms. (☎ 789-0312. Singles start at $46; doubles at $56; rates lower in winter.) The **Lazy K Motel,** on U.S. 40, near the outskirts of town toward the monument, has aging, minimalist rooms at dirt-cheap prices. (☎ 789-3277. Singles $25; doubles $30.)

    Imported to the Weston Inn from nearby LaPointe, **Stockman's,** 1684 W. U.S. 40, lures hordes of hungry Vernalites for an exciting menu of Southwest cuisine, steak, and seafood. Burgers ($5-7) and gargantuan, show-stopping desserts ($5-6) are highlights. (☎ 781-3030. Open Tu-Sa 10am-11pm.) Mouthwatering homemade salsa is the special at **LaLa's Fiesta,** 550 E. Main. Specialties begin with the *chile relleno* ($5 for 2), and all meals are under $9. (☎ 789-2966. Open M-Sa 11am-9pm.)

◧ **SIGHTS AND OUTDOORS.** Some 350 million tons of dinosaur remains have been carted away from this Jurassic cemetery, but over 1600 fossils remain exposed in the **Quarry Visitors Center** (see **Practical Information,** above). Scenic drives and hikes are the best way to appreciate the unique beauty and history of the area.

Stop by the Visitors Center in Vernal to pick up free guides to auto tours in the area. These pamphlets direct motorists to historical sights and beautiful vistas. **Harper's Corner,** at the confluence of the Green and Yampa Rivers, has one of the best views around. To get to the corner, take the Harper's Corner Rd. from the monument headquarters. At the end of the road, an easy 2 mi. round-trip hike leads to the view.

River trips are a popular summer diversion along the Green and Yampa Rivers. **Dan Hatch River Expeditions,** in Vernal, floats through the monument and the nearby Flaming Gorge. (☎789 4316 or 800-342-8243. Trips meet at 221 N. 400 E. One-day trip $65, age 6-12 $56; seniors 10% off.)

FLAMING GORGE NATIONAL RECREATION AREA ☎435

Seen at sunset, the contrast between the red canyons and the aquamarine water of the Green River makes the landscape glow, hence the moniker "Flaming Gorge." Apparently not everyone was satisfied with this natural beauty; legislation was passed in 1963 to dam the Green River. The resulting body of water is now home to the Flaming Gorge National Recreation Area. Boating and fishing enthusiasts descend into the gorge every summer to take advantage of this altered landscape.

The Green River below the dam teems with trout, allowing for top-notch **fishing;** in fact, the Gorge offers some of the best fly fishing in the country. To fish, obtain a **permit,** available at Flaming Gorge Lodge, Dutch John Recreation Services, and stores in Manila. For more info, call the **Utah Division of Wildlife Resources,** 1594 W. North Temple, in Salt Lake City. (☎800-538-4700. Open M-F 7:30am-6pm.) Several establishments rent the requisite gear for reservoir recreation. **Cedar Springs Marina,** 3 mi. before the dam, rents boats and accessories. (☎889-3795. Open daily 8am-6pm. 12-person pontoon boats from $120 for 3hr., from $200 per day. 6-person ski boats $130/$220; skis $15 per day.) Nearby, **Flaming Gorge Lodge** rents fishing rods. (☎889-3773. Open at 6:30am for the early catch. $10 per day.)

Hikers and bikers will delight in the area's trails, some of which snake along dangerous cliff edges. The **Canyon Rim Trail** (5 mi. one-way or a 2.7 mi. loop) has access points at Red Canyon Visitors Center and several campgrounds. Another hike (6-7hr., 10 mi.) begins at **Dowd Mountain,** off Rte. 44 west of Manila, and travels up Hideout Canyon. All trails in the area also allow bikes. The strenuous **Elk Park Loop** (20 mi.) departs Rte. 44 at Deep Creek Rd., follows it to Forest Rd. 221 and Forest Rd. 105, skirts Browne Lake, and runs single-track along **Old Carter and South Elk Park Trails.** For cars, the **Sheep Creek Geologic Loop,** an 11 mi. scenic drive off Rte. 44 south of Manila, passes towering, sculpted strata and desert wildlife.

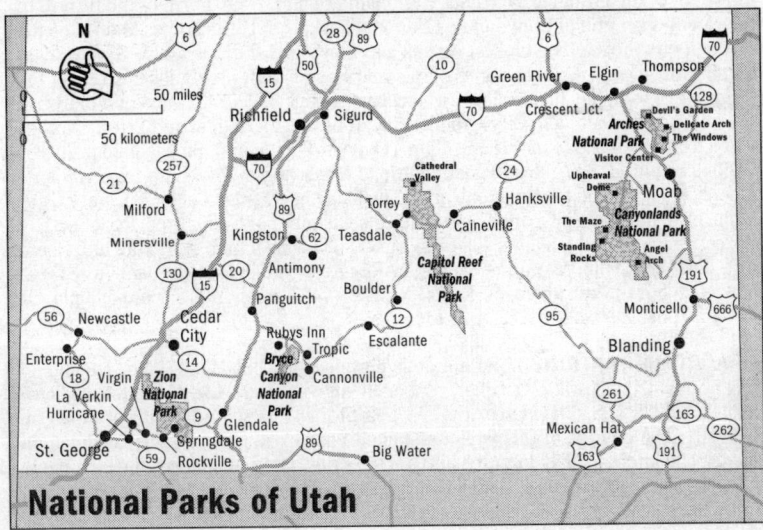

National Parks of Utah

Camping in the area is scenic and accessible. With over 30 campgrounds spread around the lake, the Visitors Centers offers sound advice for reserving sites. (☎888-444-6777; call 5 days ahead.) The 18 secluded sites at **Dripping Springs,** just past Dutch John on Rte. 191, have a prime fishing location. (Sites $13. Reservations accepted. Open year-round.) **Canyon Rim,** on the road to the Red Canyon Visitors Center, offers a feeling of high-country camping with nearby views of the red-walled gorge ($13). For a roof and four walls, the **Red Canyon Lodge,** 2 mi. south of the Visitors Center on Rte. 44, offers great location, views, and activities in line with a luxury resort but at budget prices. (☎889-3759. Private lake, restaurant. 2-person cabins $39, 4-person $49; with private bath $55/$65; $6 each additional adult, $2 per child under 12.) In **Manila,** the **Steinnaker Motel,** at Rte. 43 and 44, offers cramped but clean rooms. (☎784-3104. Check-in at the Chevron. Singles $36; doubles $44.)

From Vernal, follow U.S. 191 north to the recreation area. The reservoir extends as far north as Green River, WY, and is also accessible from I-80. A recreation pass ($2 per day, $5 per 16 days) can be obtained at the **Flaming Gorge Visitors Center,** on U.S. 191 atop the Flaming Gorge Dam, or at most stores surrounding the Gorge. The Visitors Center also offers free tours of the dam. (☎885-3135. Open daily 8am-6pm; off-season 10am-4pm.) A few miles off U.S. 191 and 3 mi. off Rte. 44 to Manila, the **Red Canyon Visitors Center** hangs 1360 ft. above the reservoir, offering staggering views into the canyon. (☎889-3713. Open June-Aug. daily 10am-5pm.) Gas and other services cluster around the dam and the towns of Manila and Dutch John. **Post Office:** 4 South Blvd., in Dutch John. (☎885-3351. Open M-F 7:30am-3:30pm, Sa 9:30am-12:30pm.) **ZIP code:** 84023. **Area code:** 435.

MOAB
☎435

Moab first flourished in the 1950s, when uranium miners rushed to the area and transformed the town from a quiet hamlet into a gritty desert outpost. Today, the mountain bike has replaced the Geiger counter, as tourists rush into the town eager to bike the red slickrock, raft whitewater rapids, and explore surrounding Arches and Canyonlands National Parks. The town itself has changed to accommodate the new visitors and athletes; microbreweries and t-shirt shops now fill the rooms of the old uranium building on Main St.

⚡🚦 ORIENTATION AND PRACTICAL INFORMATION. Moab sits 30 mi. south of I-70 on U.S. 191, just south of the junction with Rte. 128. The town center lies 5 mi. south of the entrance to Arches National Park and 38 mi. north of the turnoff to the Needles section of Canyonlands National Park. U.S. 191 becomes Main for 5 mi. through downtown. The closest **Amtrak** and **Greyhound** stations are in Green River, 52 mi. northwest of town. Some hotels and hostels will pick guests up from the train or bus for a fee. In addition, **Bighorn Express** (☎888-655-7433) makes a daily trip to and from the Salt Lake City airport, with stops in Green River and Price. Shuttles leave from the **Ramada Inn,** 182 S. Main. (Open M-F 9am-5pm, Sa 10am-2pm. Reservations required. $49.) **Roadrunner Shuttle of Moab** (☎259-9402) can take you anywhere on- or off-road in the Moab area. The **Moab Information Center,** 3 Center St. at Main, is an umbrella info organization for the Chamber of Commerce, Park Service, Forest Service, and BLM. (☎259-8825 or 800-635-6622. Open Apr.-May and Sept.-Oct. daily 8am-7pm; May-June 8am-8pm; July-Aug. 8am-9pm; Nov. 9am-7pm; Dec.-Mar. 9am-5pm.) **Post Office,** 50 E. 100 N (☎259-7427; open M-F 8:30am-5:30pm, Sa 8:30am-1pm). **ZIP code:** 84532. **Area code:** 435.

🛏 ACCOMMODATIONS. Chain motels clutter Main, but Moab is not cheap and fills up fast from April to October, especially on weekends. **Lazy Lizard International Hostel,** 1213 S. U.S. 191, is near the "A1 Self Storage" sign 1 mi. south of Moab on U.S. 191. The owners of this well-maintained hostel will give you the lowdown on Moab. The kitchen, VCR, laundry, and hot tub draw a mix of college students, backpackers, and aging hippies. (☎259-6057. Reservations recommended for spring and fall weekends. Dorms $8; singles or doubles $20; 6-person cabins $25-44; sites $6.)

A HOLE-Y PLACE Using only hand-powered drills and dynamite, Albert Christensen spent 12 years creating the bizarre **Hole 'n the Rock**, 15 mi. south of Moab on U.S. 191, a tribute to the days of Jell-O molds and chrome. This 14-room house carved out of a sandstone cliff contains 5000 sq. ft. of living space, an impressive array of equine taxidermy, and several likenesses of two of Christensen's heroes, Jesus Christ and Franklin Delano Roosevelt. Albert's wife, Gladys, kept the dream alive after his death in 1957 and opened the house to the public. She died in 1974, but this tribute to kitsch continues on. (☎686-2250. Open daily mid-Apr. to mid.-Oct. 9am-6pm; late Oct. to early Apr. 9am-5pm. Tours $4, children $3.)

Hotel Off Center, 96 E. Center St., a block off Main, the gracious owners offer eclectically lavish rooms accented by items like a miner's hat, fishing nets, and a Victrola. (☎259-4244. Open Mar.-Nov. Dorms $12; singles $39; doubles $49.) The small **Silver Sage Inn,** 840 S. Main, offers the best rates in town, with simple rooms in a somewhat institutional building. (☎259-4420. Apr.-Oct. singles $35; doubles $45; Nov.-Mar. $20/$25.)

One thousand campsites inhabit the Moab area, so finding a place to sleep out under the stars shouldn't be much of a problem. **Goose Island, Hal Canyon, Oak Grove,** and **Big Bend Campgrounds,** on Rte. 128, sit on the banks of the Colorado River three to nine miles northeast of downtown Moab. Many of the sites are shaded, and the location couldn't be better. (☎259-2100. Fire pits but no hookups or showers. Water is available at Matrimony Spring at the intersection of U.S. 191 and Rte. 128. Sites $10.) The shaded, secluded **Up the Creek Campground,** 210 E. 300 S, is just a walk away from downtown and caters solely to tent camping. (☎259-6995. 20 sites. Showers. Open Mar.-Oct. $10 per person.)

ⓒ FOOD. Retro booths at the ⬛**Moab Diner and Ice Cream Shoppe,** 189 S. Main, might take you back to the 50s, but with veggie specials and tasty green chili ($4-10), the food won't. (☎259-4006. Open Su-Th 6am-10pm, F-Sa 6am-10:30pm.) **Eddie McStiff's Microbrewery & Family Restaurant,** 57 S. Main, offers interesting beer flavors like raspberry and blueberry, great salads, and the best pizzas around ($8-14). (☎259-2337. Open M-F 5:30-10pm, Sa-Su 11:30am-10pm; bar open until 1am.) The **Peace Tree Juice Cafe,** 20 S. Main, will cool you off with a smoothie or fresh juice ($2.50-5) after a hot day in the desert. (☎259-6333. Open Su-Th 9am-5pm, F-Sa 9am-9pm.) Audrey Hepburn would be proud of **Breakfast at Tiffany's,** 90 E. Center St., which adds a little 5th Ave. flare to this Western town. Sitting on the patio you can almost imagine yourself in Paris or Rome or...Moab. (☎259-2553. Open M-F 7am-3pm, Sa-Su 7am-noon. Cash or diamonds only.) The **Río Colorado Restaurant and Bar,** 100 W. Center St, is the place to go for live music on Friday and Saturday nights, and one of few places in town that serves hard drinks. (☎259-6666. Open daily 4-9pm, bar until 1am.)

ⓝ OUTDOOR ACTIVITIES. Mountain biking and **rafting,** along with nearby national parks, are the big draws in Moab. The well-known **Slickrock Trail** (10 mi.) rolls up and down the slickrock outside of Moab. The trail has no big vertical gain, but it's technically difficult, and temperatures often reach 100°F. **Rim Cyclery,** 94 W. 1st St., rents bikes and distributes info about the slickrock trails. (☎259-5333. Open daily 9am-6pm. $31-35 per day includes helmet.)

Countless raft companies are based in Moab. ⬛**OARS/North American River Expeditions,** 543 N. Main, offers the best guides on the rivers. (☎259-5865 or 800-342-5938. Half-day $36, ages 5-17 $27; includes snacks and a natural history lesson.) **Western River Expeditions** offers good deals as well. (☎259-7019 or 800-453-7450. Half-day $34, children $27; full-day $47/$34; includes lunch.) Various outfitters also arrange horseback, motorboat, canoe, jeep, and helicopter rides. **Pack Creek Ranch** offers horseback rides to the La Sal Mountains. (☎259-5505. 1½hr. $20 per person.)

SOUTHWEST

UTAH'S NATURAL WONDERS

Arches, Canyonlands, Bryce Canyon, Zion, and Capitol Reef National Parks lie in a northeast-to-southwest-oriented line running through the southern portion of Utah, connected by a well-traveled series of scenic highways. These popular parks are geographically dwarfed by Grand Staircase-Escalante National Monument, the new kid on the block, sprawling south and east of Bryce Canyon and west of Capitol Reef. The spectacular arches, canyons, amphitheaters, plateaus, and vibrant redrock of these public lands make them one of the densest collection of geological and panoramic brilliance that the entire nation has to offer.

From Moab in the northeast, take U.S. 191 N 5 mi. to **Arches.** Continue 60 mi. north on U.S. 191 to Rte. 313 S to the Islands in the Sky area of **Canyonlands.** Or, take U.S. 191 south from Moab to Rte. 211 W to reach the Needles area of Canyonlands (87 mi.). To reach **Capitol Reef,** continue driving north on U.S. 191 and then west on I-70; leave I-70 at Exit 147, and follow Rte. 24 S to Hanksville and then west to the park (81 mi. from I-70). Rte. 24 W runs to Torrey, where scenic Rte. 12 branches south and west through the Dixie National Forest to **Bryce Canyon.** For **Zion,** continue on Rte. 12 W to U.S. 89 S through Mt. Carmel Jct., and pick up Rte. 9 W.

The two national forests in Southern Utah are divided into districts, some of which lie near the national parks and serve as excellent places to stay on a cross-country jaunt. **Manti-La Sal National Forest** has two sections near Arches and the Needles area of Canyonlands. **Dixie National Forest** stretches from Capitol Reef through Bryce all the way to the western side of Zion.

ARCHES ☎ 435

"This is the most beautiful place on earth," novelist Edward Abbey wrote of Arches National Park. Thousands of sandstone arches, spires, pinnacles, and fins tower above the desert in overwhelming grandeur. Some arches are so perfect in form that early explorers believed they were constructed by a lost civilization. Deep red sandstone, green piñon pines and juniper bushes, ominous gray thunderclouds, and a strikingly blue sky combine to etch an unforgettable palette of color best explored on foot.

■■ **ORIENTATION AND PRACTICAL INFORMATION.** The park entrance is on U.S. 191, 5 mi. north of Moab. Although no public transportation serves the park, shuttle bus companies travel to both the national park and Moab from surrounding towns and cities. While most visitors come in the summer, 100°F temperatures make hiking difficult; bring at least one gallon of water per person per day. The weather is best in the spring and fall when temperate days and nights combine to make a comfortable stay. In the winter, white snow provides a brilliant contrast to the red arches. The **Visitors Center,** to the right of the entrance station, distributes free park service maps. (☎259-8161. Open daily mid-Apr. to Sept. 7:30am-6pm; in winter 8am-4:30pm.) An **entrance pass** ($10 per carload, $5 per pedestrian or biker) covers admission for a week. Write the Superintendent, Arches National Park, P.O. Box 907, Moab 84532. **Area code:** 435.

■ **CAMPING.** The park's only campground, **Devil's Garden,** has 52 excellent campsites nestled amid piñons and giant red sandstone formations. The campsite is within walking distance of the Devil's Garden and Broken Arch trailheads; however, it is a long 18 mi. from the Visitors Center. Because Devil's Garden doesn't take reservations, sites go quickly. (No wood-gathering. Running water mid-Mar. to Oct.; 1-week max. stay. Sites $10; in winter $5.)

If the heat becomes unbearable at Arches, the aspen forests of the **Manti-La Sal National Forest** offer respite. Take Rte. 128 along the Colorado River and turn right at Castle Valley, or go south from Moab on U.S. 191 and turn to the left at the Shell Station. There are a number of campgrounds here including **Warner Lake,** where beautiful sites sit 4000 ft. above the national park and are invariably several degrees cooler. (Sites $8; Oowah Lake sites free.) **Oowah**, a three-mile hike from the Geyser Pass Rd., is a rainbow trout haven. Fishing permits are available at stores in Moab and at the Forest Service Office, 62 E. 100 N, for $5 per day. Contact the Manti-La Sal National Forest Moab/Monticello Ranger District (☎259-7155).

◪ HIKING. While the striking red slickrock around Arches may seem like attraction enough, the real points of interest here lie off the paved road. Load up on water and sunscreen and seek out on foot some of the arches that make this place famous. There are thousands of natural arches in the park, and each one is pinpointed on the free map and guide that is passed out at the fee collection booth. For more detailed maps and info on hiking, especially desert precautions, stop at the Visitors Center. Hiking in the park is unparalleled, especially in the cool days of spring and fall. Stay on trails; the land may look barren but the soil actually contains cryptobiotic life forms that are easily destroyed by footsteps. The most popular hike in the park leads to the oft-photographed **Delicate Arch.** The trail (2½hr., 3 mi.) leaves from the Wolfe Ranch parking area and climbs 480 ft; be sure to bring lots of water. To view the spectacular Delicate Arch without the 3 mi. hike, take the **Delicate Arch Viewpoint "Trail"** which begins in the Viewpoint parking area. This 300 ft. trail takes around 15min. and is wheelchair accessible. The loop through **Devils Garden** (3-5hr., 7.2 mi.) requires some scrambling over rocks, but hearty travelers will be rewarded by the eight arches visible from this trail. The trek is not recommended in wet or snowy conditions. **Tower Arch** (2-3hr., 3.4 mi.) can be accessed from the trailhead at the Klondike Bluffs parking area via Salt Valley Rd. This moderate hike explores one of the remote regions of the park, and is a good way to escape crowds. The trail ascends a steep, short rock wall before meandering through sandstone fins and sand dunes. Salt Valley Rd. is often washed out, so check at the Visitors Center before departing.

CANYONLANDS   ☎ 435

Those who make the trek to Canyonlands National Park are rewarded with a pleasant surprise: the absence of people. The sandstone spires, roughly cut canyons, and colorful rock layers of this awe-inspiring landscape are often passed up by those on a time budget. There are no amenities in the park, so those who come commit themselves to a real outdoor experience.

◪◪ ORIENTATION AND PRACTICAL INFORMATION. The Green and Colorado Rivers divide the park into three districts, and themselves comprise the fourth. Because each region is essentially self-contained, once you've entered one district, getting to another requires retracing your steps and re-entering the park, a trip that can last from several hours to a full day. To get to the **Needles**, take Rte. 211 W from U.S. 191, about 40 mi. south of Moab or 14 mi. north of Monticello. Farther north, **Island in the Sky** is the most easily accessible district from Moab—the entrance station and Visitors Center sit about 22 mi. southwest of the Rte. 313 W turn-off from U.S. 191, 10 mi. north of Moab. To reach the **Maze** district from I-70, take Rte. 24, 15 mi. west of Green River, 29 mi. to a turn-off just south of the entrance to Goblin Valley State Park. The **Rivers** district features great stretches of flat water as well as some world-class rapids.

Coyote Shuttle (☎259-8656) and **Roadrunner Shuttle of Moab** (☎259-9402) provide taxi service to the Needles and Island in the Sky districts. For general info before plunging into the different districts, visit Monticello's **Multiagency Visitors Center**, 117 S. Main (☎587-3235 or 800-574-4386; open M-F 8am-5pm, Sa-Su 10am-5pm), or the **Moab Information Center**, 3 Center St. (☎259-8825 or 800-635-6622. Open July-Aug. daily 8am-9pm; Sept.-Oct. and Apr.-May 8am-7pm; Nov. 9am-7pm; Dec.-Mar. 9am-5pm; May-June 8am-8pm.) The **Bureau of Land Management** presides over portions of the Green and Colorado upstream from the park. For more info, contact the **Grand County Travel Council** (☎800-635-6622) or the **Moab Area BLM Office** (☎259-6111). For recorded river flows, call 801-539-1311. For more info, write to Canyonlands National Park, 2282 S. W. Resource Blvd., Moab, UT 84532, or call 259-7164. **Rim Cyclery,** 94 W. 100 N (☎259-5333), and **Pagan Mountaineering,** 88 E. Center St. (☎259-1117), both in Moab, offer a full range of outdoor gear. There is no **gas** or food available in the park, and no **water** in Island in the Sky or the Maze.

☝ CAMPING. In the Needles district, **Squaw Flat's** 26 sites occupy a sandy plain surrounded by giant sandstone towers, 40 mi. west of U.S. 191 on Rte. 211. In June, insects swarm. Fuel is not abundant and water is not available October through March. (Sites $10; Oct.-Mar. free.) **Willow Flat Campground,** in the Island in the Sky district, sits high atop the mesa on Rte. 313, 41 mi. west off U.S. 191. (12 sites. Pit toilets. $5 in summer; free off-season.) You must bring your own water. Willow Flat and Squaw Flat both provide picnic tables and grills. The primitive campground at the **Maze Overlook** offers no amenities. All campgrounds operate on a first come, first served basis. Before **backcountry camping,** outdoors-types must register at the proper Visitors Center for one of a limited number of permits. ($15 for overnight permit. Backcountry voyages not recommended in summer.) Four-wheelers should also register at the Visitors Center ($30 permit).

The campsites in Canyonlands may be sweltering, but the air is almost always cooler in the **Manti-La Sal National Forest.** This forest has two campgrounds on **Blue Mountain: Buckboard,** 6½ mi. west of U.S. 191 (16 sites; 10 hookups), and **Dalton Springs,** 5 mi. west of U.S. 191 (18 sites; 10 hookups). Both campgrounds operate from late May to September and charge $8.50 per site. From Moab, go south on U.S. 191 to Monticello and then west on Rte. 1 S. More info on the Monticello District awaits at the **Multi-Agency Visitors Center** (see **Practical Information,** above).

Farther away, **Dead Horse Point State Park** perches on the rim of the Colorado Gorge. (Visitors center open daily 8am-5pm. Entrance fee $5.) The park, south of Arches and 14 mi. south of U.S. 191, accessible from Rte. 313, offers camping, with water, hookups, and picnic tables. (21 sites; half are available on a first come, first served basis. $11.) Write the Superintendent, Dead Horse Point State Park, P.O. Box 609, Moab 84532. (☎259-2614 or 800-322-3770. Open daily 6am-10pm.)

◾ HIKING. Each Visitors Center has a brochure of possible hikes. With summer temperatures regularly climbing over 100°F, bring at least 1 gallon of water per person per day. Island in the Sky offers spectacular views; a short trail makes a quick diversion. In the Maze, a guided hike into **Horseshoe Canyon** (6hr., 6 mi.) leaves the eponymous trailhead at 9am on Saturday and Sunday. If hiking in desert heat doesn't appeal to you, Jeeps and bikes are available in Moab.

In the Needles, the moderate **Chessler Park Loop** (5-6hr., 11 mi.) travels through slickrock country to the spectacular Chessler Park, 960 acres of grassy meadows surrounded by magnificently rainbowed hoodoos. Starting at the base of Elephant Hill, the hike encircles the meadow, winding through a series of deep, narrow fractures along the way, and experiences little elevation change. The **Druid Arch** (5-7hr., 11 mi.) hike follows the Chessler Park Loop for a few miles before branching off into Elephant Canyon and the arch. The moderately difficult route provides some of the most spectacular views in the Needles as it makes its way up a steep climb that requires both a ladder climb and some scrambling to the arch.

CAPITOL REEF ☎435

What do you get when you cross rock formations that strangely resemble the capitol dome of the State House in Washington with precipitous rock cliffs? A strangely inapt name for Utah's stunning, youngest national park. The hundred-mile Waterpocket Fold is a geologist's fantasy and the park's feature attraction. With its rocky peaks and pinnacles the Fold bisects Capitol Reef's 378 square miles, presenting visitors with millions of years of stratified natural history.

⚡️ ORIENTATION AND PRACTICAL INFORMATION. The middle link in the Fab Five chain, east of Zion and Bryce Canyon and west of Arches and Canyonlands, Capitol Reef is unreachable by major bus lines. The closest **Greyhound** stop is in Green River. For a fee, **Wild Hare Expeditions** (see **Sights and Outdoors,** below) will provide a shuttle service between Richfield and the park. **Entrance** to the park is free except for the scenic drive that costs $4 per vehicle. The **Visitors Center,** on Rte. 24, supplies travelers with waterproof topo maps ($8), regular maps ($4), free brochures on trails, and info on daily activities such as ranger-led jaunts. (☎425-3791. Open daily 8am-6pm; Sept.-May 8am-4:30pm.) The free park newspaper, *The Cliffline,* lists a schedule of park activities. *When hiking, keep in mind that summer temperatures average 95°F. After rain, beware of flash floods.* Contact the Superintendent, Capitol Reef National Park, HC 70 Box 15, Torrey 84775 (☎425-3791). **Post Office:** 222 E. Main St., in Fruita. (☎425-3488. Open M-F 8am-1pm, Sa 7:30-11am.) **ZIP code:** 84775. **Area code:** 435.

🍴 ACCOMMODATIONS AND FOOD. The park's campgrounds offer sites on a first come, first served basis. The main campground, **Fruita,** 1¼ mi. south of the Visitors Center off Rte. 24, contains 71 sites with water and toilets but no showers. The campground nestles between orchards, and visitors can eat all the fruit they want (sites $10). **Cedar Mesa Campground,** on the Notom-Bullfrog Rd., and **Cathedral Valley,** in the north (accessible by four-wheel-drive vehicle or on foot), have only five sites each; neither has water but they're free. Both of these sites and all backcountry camping require a free **backcountry permit,** available at the Visitors Center.

Torrey, 11 mi. west of the Visitors Center on Rte. 24, has the nearest lodging. The cheapest bed in town is at the friendly ⚑**Sandcreek Hostel,** 54 Rte. 24, featuring its own espresso bar. A single dorm room houses eight comfy beds, a minifridge, and a microwave. There are also 12 sites, 12 hookups, and two rustic cabins that can sleep up to four. (☎425-3577. Showers for non-guests $3. Linens $2. Reception 7:30am-8pm. Check-out 11am. Open Apr. to mid-Oct. Dorms $10; sites $10; hookups $14-18; cabins $28-34.) Down the road, the **Capitol Reef Inn and Cafe,** 360 W. Main, has rooms with a Southwestern theme and handmade furniture, as well as a jacuzzi and one of the best restaurants in town. (☎425-3271. Reception 7am-10pm. Check-out 11am. Open Apr.-Oct. Rooms $40, each additional person $4.)

Capitol Reef Inn and Cafe, 360 W. Main, serves up local rainbow trout (smoked or grilled) in a dining room that looks out on the russet hills. Don't miss the grilled trout sandwich ($6.75) served on a bagel with cream cheese. (☎425-3271. Open Apr.-Oct. daily 7am-11pm.) A wide range of coffees as well as an eclectic selection of books on the local area can be found at **Robber's Roost Books & Beverages,** 185 W. Main. (☎425-3265. Open Apr.-Oct. M-Tu and Th 9am-8pm, F-Sa 9am-9pm; W and Su 10am-6pm.) Greasier offerings await at **Brink's Burgers,** 163 E. Main. (☎425-3710. Open daily 11am-9pm. Take-out available. Entrees $2-5. Cash only.)

🗻 SIGHTS AND OUTDOORS. The Reef's haunting landforms can be explored from the seat of your car on the 25 mi. scenic drive, a 1½hr. round-trip jaunt next to the cliffs along paved and improved dirt roads. Along Rte. 24, you can ponder the bathroom-sized **Fruita Schoolhouse** built by Mormon settlers, 1000-year-old **petroglyphs** etched on the stone walls, and **Panorama Point. Chimney Rock** and the **Castle** are two striking sandstone formations along the route. **Wild Hare Expeditions,** 2600 E. Rte. 24, in the Best Western Capitol Reef Resort, embarks on a variety of backpacking and hiking tours. (☎425-3999 or 888-304-4273. Half day $40-50, children $35; full-day $60-75/$50. Driving tours are also available.)

For a change of scenery check out the bucolic **orchards,** which lie within the park in the Fruita region. Eat as much fruit as you like while in the orchards, but you must pay to take some home. In the northern and southern sections of the park, all hikes are considered backcountry travel. Be sure to get a **free backcountry permit** for all overnight trips. More reasonable and plebeian day hikes depart from trailheads along Rte. 24. Check at the Visitors Center for more information on hikes.

BRYCE CANYON

☎ 435

If Nature enjoys painting with a big brush in the Southwest, she discarded her usual coarse tools for finer instruments when creating Bryce Canyon. The canyon brims with slender, fantastically shaped rock spires called hoodoos. What it lacks in Grand Canyon-esque magnitude, Bryce makes up for in intricate beauty. Early in the morning or late in the evening the sun's rays bring the hoodoos to life, transforming them into color-changing stone chameleons. The first sight of the canyon can be breathtaking: as Ebenezer Bryce, a Mormon carpenter with a gift for understatement, put it, the canyon is "one hell of a place to lose a cow."

◾◼ ORIENTATION AND PRACTICAL INFORMATION. Approaching from the west, Bryce Canyon lies 1½hr. east of Cedar City; take Rte. 14 to U.S. 89. From the east, take I-70 to U.S. 89, turn east on Rte. 12 at Bryce Jct. (7 mi. south of Panguitch), and drive 14 mi. to the Rte. 63 junction; head south 4 mi. to the park entrance. There is no public transportation to Bryce Canyon. The park's entrance fee is $20 per car, $10 per pedestrian. The **Visitors Center** is just inside the park. (☎834-5322. Open June-Aug. 8am-8pm; Apr.-May and Sept.-Oct. 8am-6pm; Nov.-Mar. 8am-4:30pm.) To assuage the park's traffic problem, the Park Service has implemented a **shuttle system,** serving all destinations via three routes. Private vehicles can travel park roads, but the Park Service offers a $5 admission discount to those who park at the junction of Rte. 12 and 63 and ride the shuttle into the park. Contact the Visitors Center for details. **Post Office** is in Bryce Lodge. (☎834-5361. Open M-F 8am-noon and 1-5pm, Sa 8am-noon.) **ZIP code:** 84717. **Area code:** 435.

▐◖ ACCOMMODATIONS AND FOOD. North and **Sunset Campgrounds,** both within 3 mi. of the Visitors Center, offer toilets, picnic tables, potable water, and 210 sites on a first come, first served basis. (Sites $10; arrive early to claim the best spots.) **Backcountry camping permits** are free from the ranger at the Visitors Center. Two campgrounds lie just west of Bryce on scenic Rte. 12, in Dixie National Forest. The **King Creek Campground,** 11 mi. from Bryce on a dirt road off Rte. 12 (look for signs to Tropic Reservoir), features lakeside sites. Group sites are available with reservations. (☎800-280-2267. $8.) At 7400 ft., the **Red Canyon Campground** has 36 sites ($10) on a first come, first served basis amid the glory of the red rocks.

Sleeping inside the park requires either a tent and sleeping bag or a fat wallet. The historic **Bryce Canyon Lodge,** the only in-park hotel, offers motel-style rooms and cabins. (☎834-5361. Open Apr.-Oct. Rooms $93, cabins $103; rates quoted for two people; $5 each additional person.) Away from the park, rates drop; better deals line Rte. 12 in Tropic. Panguitch, 23 mi. west of the park on U.S. 89, has many inexpensive, independent motels. For most area accommodations, room rates fluctuate by season and quantity of tourist flow. For bright rooms with a refined country-home feel at excellent prices, head to **◪Bybee's Steppingstone Motel,** 21 S. Main, in Tropic. (☎679-8998. Singles $45; doubles $50.) The attractive garden and enchanting pastel interior of the **Marianna Inn,** 699 N. Main in Panguitch, foreshadow the quality of the rooms within. (☎676-8844. Singles and doubles $35-55.)

Inside and immediately surrounding the national park, feeding options are scarce. A quick slice of pizza or a microwave burrito await at the **Bryce Canyon General Store.** For a sit-down lunch inside the park, try the $5-6 burgers and sandwiches at **Bryce Canyon Lodge Dining Room.** With a little driving, more affordable and varied alternatives multiply. Thick, golden brown pancakes ($2) await starving passersby at the **Hungry Coyote,** on N. Main in Tropic. (☎679-8811. Open Apr.-Oct. daily 6:30-10:30am and 5-10pm.) Several miles west of the park on Rte. 12, the **Bryce Pines Restaurant** serves delicious home-cooked meals. (☎834-5441. Open in summer daily 6:30am-9:30pm. Sandwiches $4-6; dinner entrees $10-14.)

◙◪ SIGHTS AND OUTDOORS. Bryce's 18 mi. main road winds past spectacular lookouts such as **Sunrise Point, Sunset Point, Inspiration Point,** and **Rainbow Point,** but a range of hiking trails makes it a crime not to leave your car. A word to the wise: the air is thin—if you start to feel giddy or short of breath, take a rest. Also, very sturdy shoes or hiking boots are a must for hiking into the canyon. One oft-missed viewpoint is **Fairlyland Point,** at the north end of the park, 1 mi. off the main road, with some the best sights in the canyons. The **Rim Trail** (4-6hr., 11 mi.) parallels the Amphitheater and offers views over longer than a 100 mi. The part between Sunrise Point and Sunset Point is wheelchair accessible and a good way to peer onto the sea of hoodoos. The loop of the **Navajo** and **Queen's Garden Trails** (2-3hr., 3.1 mi.) leads into the canyon and by some natural bridges. More challenging options include **Peek-A-Boo Loop** (3-4hr., 3.5 mi.), winding in and out through hoodoos, and the **Trail to the Hat Shop** (4 mi.), an extremely steep trail (tough both ways). **Canyon Trail Rides** arranges guided horseback rides. (☎679-8665. $27-40 per person.)

GRAND STAIRCASE-ESCALANTE NAT'L MONUMENT   ☎435

The last virgin corner of American wilderness to be captured by a cartographer's pen, Grand Staircase-Escalante National Monument remains remote, rugged, pristine, and beautiful. The 1.9 million acre expanse of painted sandstone, high alpine plateau, treacherous canyons, and raging rivers shelters diverse areas of geological, biological, and historical interest.

Travelers just passing through the Escalante area en route to national parks east and west have a variety of options for getting a brief glimpse of the Monument's wild beauty. Scenic **Rte. 12,** tracing picturesque slickrock hills 28 mi. between Boulder and Escalante, is arguably one of the Southwest's most spectacular stretches of highway. While cresting and plunging between colored sandstone rises, Rte. 12 feels like driving through a miniature Zion. Just before descending into the farming community of Boulder, the highway threads a narrow flat between dramatic drops, the vehicular equivalent to a titillating summit-ridge hike.

A **free backcountry permit** is required for all multi-day trips into the monument. The most popular destination for backpacking trips are the **Canyons of Escalante,** in the eastern portion of the monument. Cutting through the slickrock towards Lake Powell, the Escalante and its feeder drainages create a series of canyons ripe for exploration. Many routes require technical canyoneering skills. Primary access to the canyons of Escalante comes via the **Hole-in-the-Rock Rd.,** heading south from Rte. 12 east of Escalante. One of the most challenging routes in the area, this 30 mi. trek through Death Hollow Wilderness navigates narrow slot canyons north of town and earns its ominous name with lethal flash floods. The hike involves technical climbing and long stretches of swimming with a heavy pack through pools. Two campgrounds reside in the Escalante area. The 13 shaded sites at **Calf Creek Campground,** 15 mi. east of Escalante, offer access to the Calf Creek Trail. (Toilets and water. Sites $7.) Six miles north of Boulder on Rte. 12, there are primitive sites at **Deer Creek** (7 sites; toilets, no water; $4). **Bestway Groceries,** 9 W. Main, stocks Escalante's only selection of grocery items. (☎826-4226. Open M-Sa 8am-8pm.)

Nearly two million acres is a lot of space, probably more than an entire lifetime's worth of walking could cover. Being so large, several communities serve as gateways to different portions of the monument. In the south, **Rte. 89** between Kanab and **Lake Powell** cuts into the monument and provides access to the popular **Cottonwood Canyon Rd.** At the far eastern limit of the monument, many Glen Canyon recreationalists park their boats for day hikes in the lower canyons of the Escalante drainage. Visitor information is available at the **Escalante Interagency Visitors Center,** 755 W. Main (☎826-5499), in Escalante. Helpful and friendly staff steer eager hikers to appropriate routes. The official monument headquarters is at **Kanab Field Office,** 318 N. 100 E., in Kanab. (☎644-2672. Open M-F 8am-4:30pm.)

ZION NATIONAL PARK   ☎435

Russet sandstone mountains loom over the puny cars and hikers that flock to Zion National Park in search of the promised land, and rarely does Zion disappoint. Some 13 million years ago, the ocean flowed over the cliffs and canyons of Zion. When the sea subsided, it left behind only the raging Virgin River, whose watery fingers continue to sculpt the smooth white and pink rock monuments. In the northwest corner of the park, the walls of Kolob Terrace tower thousands of feet above the river. In the 1860s, Mormon settlers came to the area and enthusiastically proclaimed that they had found Zion, the promised land. Brigham Young disagreed, however, and declared that the place was awfully nice, but "not Zion." The name "not Zion" stuck for years until a new wave of entranced explorers dropped the "not," giving the park its present name. The park might very well be the fulfillment of Biblical prophecy for outdoor recreationalists. With hiking trails nonpareil and challenging and mysterious slot canyons set against a tableau of sublime sandstone, visiting Zion is a spiritual event.

🔡 ORIENTATION AND PRACTICAL INFORMATION. The main entrance to Zion is in **Springdale**, on Rte. 9, which borders the park to the south along the Virgin River. Approaching Zion from the west, take Rte. 9 from I-15 at Hurricane. In the east, pick up Rte. 9 from U.S. 89 at Mt. Carmel Jct. **Greyhound** is in St. George (☎673-2937; 43 mi. southwest of the park on I-15), departing from a McDonald's, 1235 S. Bluff St., at St. George Blvd. The brand new, ecologically harmonious **Zion Canyon Visitors Center,** just inside the south entrance, houses an info center, bookstore, and backcountry permit station. At the west entrance to the park, the **Kolob Canyons Visitors Center** offers info on the Kolob Canyon Scenic Drive and the surrounding trail system, as well as books, and maps. (☎772-3256. Both centers open in summer daily 8am-7pm; reduced winter hours.) The park's entrance fee is $20 per car, $10 per pedestrian. **Emergency:** ☎772-3322. Zion's **Post Office** is located inside the Zion Canyon Lodge. **ZIP code:** 84767. **Area code:** 435.

👣 ACCOMMODATIONS AND CAMPING. More than 300 sites are available at the **South** and **Watchman Campgrounds,** near the brand new Visitors Center. Campgrounds fill quickly in summer; arrive before noon to ensure a spot. **Watchman Campground** takes reservations, but **South** is first come, first served. (☎800-365-2267 for Watchman reservations. Water, toilets, and sanitary disposal station. Both $14.) Avoid the crowds at the free primitive sites at **Lava Point,** a nearly one-hour drive from the Visitors Center, in close proximity to the panoramic Lava Point overlook and the Western Rim Trailhead. To find Lava Point, turn right off Rte. 9 at the sign for the Kolob Reservoir in Virgin and follow signs for the campground. **Zion Canyon Campground,** 479 Zion Park Blvd., soothes the weary, hungry, and filthy with a convenience store, pizzeria, grocery store, showers ($3 for non-guests), and laundry. (☎772-3237. Office open daily 8am-9pm. Store open daily 8am-9pm; off-season 8am-5pm. Sites for 2 $16; full hookups $20; $3.50 per additional adult, $2 each additional child under 15. Cabins $40.) **Zion Frontier Campground,** ¼ mi. from the east entrance, 1000 ft. higher and 10°F cooler than sites in the park, offers a laundromat, showers, restaurant, and gas station. (☎648-2154. Office open 24hr. 70 sites $15; 30 full hookups $25; cabins and tepees $25.) The **Zion River Resort,** on Rte. 9 in Virgin, provides new and carefully crafted sites at the area's most ritzy RV park. (☎800-838-8594. Sites from $20; full hookups $29.)

For those inclined toward indoor accommodations, Springdale's least expensive lodging, the family-owned **El Río Lodge,** 995 Zion Park Blvd., welcomes guests with clean rooms, friendly service, and dazzling views of the Watchman Face. (☎772-3205. Singles $47; doubles $52; winter rates dip to around $35.) Across the street, the **Terrace Brook Lodge,** 990 Zion Park Blvd., offers reasonably inexpensive rooms. (☎800-342-6779. Singles $49; two beds $65; $10 less in winter.)

The closest hostel is the ▨**Dixie Hostel (HI-AYH),** 73 S. Main, 20 mi. west of Zion in Hurricane. Fresh-smelling, pink-hued, and without a speck of dust, the hostel is a comfortable stay and only 2hr. from Las Vegas, Lake Powell, the North Rim, and Bryce Canyon. (☎635-8202. Linen, laundry, kitchen, continental breakfast, and 20% discount at the nearby Pah Tempe hotsprings. $15.) In the other direction, the **Canyonlands International Youth Hostel,** 143 E. 100 S, lies in the center of town, across from the police station. Though the place is a bit too primitive and earthy for some, the hostel's location makes it a good base for exploring northern Arizona and southern Utah. (☎644-5554. Dorms $10.)

OUTDOOR ACTIVITIES. Zion seems to have been made for hiking; unlike in the foreboding canyons that surround it, most of the trails won't have you praying for a stray mule to show up. However, a number of trails spiral around cliffs with narrow trails and long drop-offs. Hiking boots are recommended on trails like Angel's Landing of Hidden Canyons. The trails are serviced by a prompt shuttle bus system that delivers bright-eyed hikers to and from trailheads (runs 6:30am-11:15pm). Shuttle maps are available at the Visitors Center.

The **Riverside Walk** (1-2hr., 2 mi.), paved and wheelchair accessible with assistance, begins at the Temple of Sinawava at the north end of Zion Canyon Dr. Running alongside the Virgin River and some beautiful wildflower displays, Riverside is Zion's most popular and easiest trail. The **Emerald Pools Trail** (1-3hr., 1.2-3.1 mi.) has wheelchair access along its lower loop, but the middle and upper loops are steep and narrow. Swimming is not allowed in any of the pools. The challenging **Angel's Landing Trail** (4hr., 5 mi.) begins in the Grotto picnic area, and rises 1488 ft. above the canyon; the last terrifying stretch climbs a narrow ridge with guide chains blasted into the rock. A shorter, but equally harrowing trail is **Hidden Canyon Trail** (2-3hr., 2 mi.), rewarding hikers with impressive valley views. The difficult **Observation Point Trail** (5hr., 8 mi.) leads through **Echo Canyon**, a spectacular kaleidoscope of sandstone, where steep switchbacks explore the unusually gouged canyon. Overnight hikers can spend days on the 13 mi. course of the **West Rim Trail**.

One of the best ways to take in Zion's splendor is to ride the shuttle bus loop. Called the **Zion Canyon Scenic Loop**, this 1½ hr. narrated ride gives great views of the rocks from below. Another motorized way to take in the scenery is the 10 mi. **Zion-Mt. Carmel Highway**, connecting the east and south entrances. Spiraling around the Canyon, the highway gives excellent views of the valley, as well as a fun trip through an 80 year-old mountain tunnel.

When visiting the **Kolob Canyons**, check out **Zion Canyon**. The seven-mile dead-end road on the canyon floor rambles past the giant **Sentinel, Mountain of the Sun,** and the symbol of Zion, the **Great White Throne**. A shuttle from the Lodge runs this route every hour on the hour. (During summer daily 9am-5pm. $3.) Horseback tours by **Canyon Trail Rides** also leave from the Lodge. (☎772-3810. $15-40.)

Despite being overshadowed by the boastful Moab, the Zion area has a loyal **mountain biking** following and trails to compete with the big boy to the north. **Gooseberry Mesa**, about 15 mi. from Springdale, has some great singletrack and novice trails. **Bike Zion**, 1458 Zion Park Blvd., can hook you up with wheels and trail advice. (☎772-3929. Open daily 8am-6pm. Rigid bike full-day $23, half-day $17; front suspension $29/$22; full suspension $35/$27.)

NEAR ZION: CEDAR BREAKS NATIONAL MONUMENT ☎435

Rte. 148, diverging from scenic Rte. 14 east of Cedar City, climbs the flowered slope of the **Markagunt Plateau**, arriving at the 10,200 ft. rim as it suddenly fractures, descending 2000 ft. into an amphitheater with colorfully chiseled depths. A 30-site **campground** perched at 10,200 ft. (open June to mid-Sept.; water, flush toilets; sites $10) and the **Visitors Center** (☎586-0787; open May-Sept. daily 8am-6pm) await at **Point Supreme**. No services accommodate visitors inside the monument; the nearest gas, food, and lodging are found either in Cedar City or Brian Head. (☎586-9451. $3; under 17 free.)

Tourists travel to the Monument nearly exclusively for the view, most easily reached by parking at the Visitors Center and walking to Point Supreme, or by stopping at one of several vistas along the 5 mi. stretch of scenic Rte. 143. The Monument has two established trails that provide for a more extended visit. Originating at the **Chessman Ridge Overlook** (10,467 ft.), the popular **Alpine Pond Trail** (1-2hr., 2 mi.) follows the rim to a spring-fed alpine lake whose waters trickle into the breaks, winding toward slow evaporation in the Great Basin.

NATURAL BRIDGES NATIONAL MONUMENT ☎435

The Paiutes who inhabited this region nearly 3000 years ago called it *Ma-Vah-Talk-Tump*, or "under the horse's belly." Although Utah's first national monument now carries the more prosaic moniker of "Natural Bridges," the three rock formations are no less impressive. To appreciate the size of the monuments fully—the highest is more than 200 feet—leave the overlooks and hike down to the bridges. Once you do, it's easy to understand why the Hopi named the largest one "Sipapu," or "place of emergence"—they believed it to be the entry through which their ancestors came into the world. The park's paved **Bridge View Drive** is 9 mi. and passes the overlooks and trailheads to each of the three major bridges. It's also possible to hike various loop trails (6-8.6 mi.) connecting the bridges.

The **Visitors Center,** several miles past the entrance, offers a slide show and exhibits. (☎692-1234. Open daily Mar.-Oct. 8am-6pm; Nov.-Feb. 9:30am-5pm. Weekly park entrance $6 per vehicle, $3 per hiker or biker.) Sleep under the stars at the **campground** near the Visitors Center. Thirteen shaded sites set amid piñon pines accommodate up to nine people each and include grills and picnic tables. Sites are first come, first served (sites $10). **Water** is available at the Visitors Center. For more info, write the Superintendent, Natural Bridges, HC 60 Box 1, Lake Powell 84533. If the park campground is full, free camping is available on BLM land along a gravel road that begins at the intersection of Rte. 95 and Rte. 261, 6 mi. from the Visitors Center. The sites are flat and shaded but have no facilities.

The closest **Greyhound** and **Amtrak** stations are in Green River, several hours north. Therefore, a **car** is essential. The entrance road, **Rte. 275,** is 35 mi. northwest of Blanding and 45 mi. southeast of Hite on Lake Powell, and can be reached from almost every direction. The nearest **gas** is 25 mi. west in Fry Canyon.

ROUTE 95

This 122-mi. stretch of road between Blanding and Hanksville, known as the Bicentennial Highway because it was built in 1976, is one of the most scenic in the lower 48. From the cliff dwellings of the architecturally adept Ancestral Puebloans to the modern-day engineering feats of Lake Powell, Route 95 offers a diverse cross-section of southern Utah. The highway also mirrors part of the routes taken by Mormon settlers as they pushed into this uncharted part of the state. Traveling beside and through such natural and cultural highlights, this drive makes a good anthropology, geology, and history lesson rolled into one. Bring water, provisions, and a camera for this 2-3hr. drive.

BLANDING ☎435

The agricultural town of **Blanding** is 45 mi. northwest of Hovenweep, 47 mi. east of Natural Bridges, and 73 mi. northeast of Monument Valley. The town makes a good stop from Moab and the Four Corners, as it features the full gamut of services. The nearest **buses** run to Green River on I-70. The **San Juan County Multi-Agency Visitors Center,** 21 mi. north on U.S. 191 in Monticello, is a great resource for exploring Southeast Utah. (☎587-3235. Open Apr.-Sept. M-F 8am-5pm, Sa 10am-5pm; Oct.-Mar. M-F 8am-5pm.) **Post Office:** 90 N. Main (☎678-2627; open M-F 8am-4:30pm, Sa 8am-noon). **ZIP code:** 84511. **Area Code:** 435.

Nine miles north of town on U.S. 191, surrounded by some great views, is the **Devil's Canyon Campground** (33 primitive sites; water and pit toilets). The **Blanding Sunset Inn,** 88 W. Center St., has basic, phoneless rooms for cheap. (☎678-3323. Check-out 11am. Singles $25; doubles $35.) Unfortunately, Blanding doesn't have as many food options as it does motels. For large breakfasts ($4-6) and sandwich lunches ($5-7), try the **Homestead Steakhouse,** 121. E. Center St. (☎678-3456. Open daily 6:30am-10pm.) A better bet for meals is to head north to Monticello. The **MD Ranch Cookhouse,** 380 S. Main, serves up great dinners ($8-13) with all the fixings in a friendly atmosphere. (☎587-3299. Open daily 8am-3pm and 5-9pm.) **Mesa Java,** 516 N. Main, is the only place in the area where you can get a real cappuccino. (☎587-2601. Open daily 7am-5pm.)

SOUTHWEST

HOVENWEEP NATIONAL MONUMENT ☎435

Hovenweep, from the Ute meaning "deserted valley," was aptly named by pioneer photographer William Jackson in 1874, and today it remains one of the emptiest regions in the US. Those who have made the trip to this strip of land spanning the border between Utah and Colorado since its founding in 1923 have been treated to "national park solitude," and have gotten to explore the groups of 1000-year-old Pueblo ruins that hang precipitously from canyon-tops around the monument.

The most well-preserved and impressive remains, **Square Tower Ruins,** lie footsteps away from the Visitors Center. The **Square Tower Loop Trail** (2 mi.) loops around a small canyon, accessing **Hovenweep Castle** and the **Twin Towers.** The shorter **Tower Point Loop** (0.5 mi.), accesses the ruins of a tower perched over the canyon. For the archaeologically inclined, or those looking for a more serious hike, the outlying sites—**Cajon** in Utah and **Holly, Horseshoe & Hackberry, Cutthroat Castle,** and **Goodman Point Ruins** in Colorado—are isolated and provide a more challenging trip. All sites are accessible via dirt roads; a four-wheel-drive vehicle is recommended.

From Utah or Arizona, follow U.S. 191 to its junction with Rte. 262 E (14 mi. south of Blanding, 11 mi. north of Bluff). After about 30 mi., watch for signs to the monument. The **Visitors Center** is accessible from both the Utah and Colorado sides. (☎562-4282 or 435-692-1234. Open daily 8am-6pm; off-season 8am-5pm, except when the ranger is out on patrol. $3 per person, $6 per vehicle.) For more info, contact the Superintendent, Hovenweep National Monument, McElmo Rte., Cortez, CO 81321 (☎970-562-4282).

There is no **gas** or **food** at the monument. **Aneth,** 20 mi. south, is the closest spot for these "amenities." The **Hovenweep Campground,** a few hundred yards before the visitors center, offers 30 scenic sites ($10) with shaded picnic tables. Water and toilets are available, though campers must carry out all of their trash.

ARIZONA

Populated primarily by Native Americans until the end of the 19th century, Arizona has been hit in the past hundred years by waves of settlers—from the speculators and miners of the late 1800s, to the soldiers who trained here during World War II and returned after the war, to the more recent immigrants from Mexico. Traces of lost Native American civilization remain at Canyon de Chelly, Navajo National Monument, and Wupatki and Walnut Canyons, while deserted ghost towns are scattered throughout the state. The descendents of area tribes now occupy reservations on one-half of the state's land, making up one-seventh of the US Native American population, while urban Phoenix sprawls wider and wider. Arizona is a state always in flux, yet perhaps the majesty of the land is the one constant. No manmade structures can overshadow Arizona's natural masterpieces—the Grand Canyon, Monument Valley, and the gorgeous landscapes viewed from the state's highways.

❖ PRACTICAL INFORMATION

Capital: Phoenix.

Visitor info: Arizona Tourism, 2702 N. 3rd St. #4015, Phoenix 85004 (☎602-230-7733 or 888-520-3434; www.arizonaguide.com). Open M-F 8am-5pm. **Arizona State Parks,** 1300 W. Washington St., Phoenix 85007 (☎602-542-4174 or 800-285-3703). Open M-F 8am-5pm.

Postal Abbreviation: AZ. **Sales Tax:** variable 5%.

Time Zone: Mountain Standard Time. *With the exception of the Navajo reservation, Arizona does not observe Daylight Savings Time.*

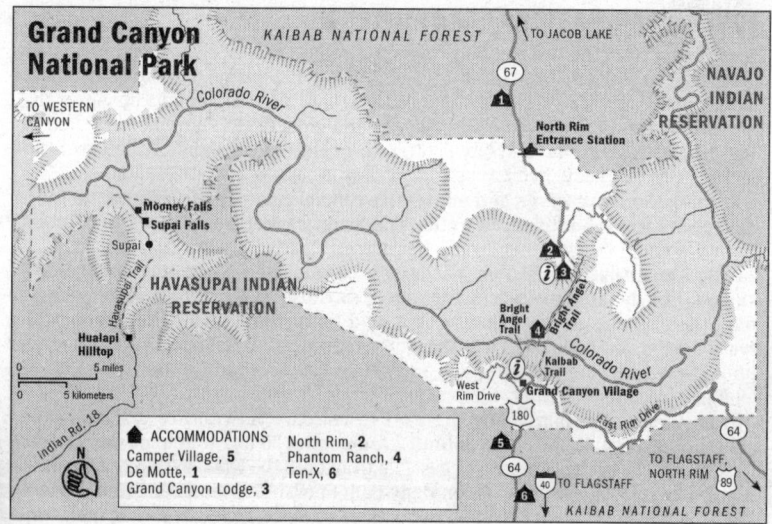

GRAND CANYON

Long before its designation as a national park in 1919, the Grand Canyon began capturing the imagination of each person who strolled to its edge and beheld its span. Every summer, millions of visitors travel from across the globe to witness this natural wonder which, in one panorama, captures the themes that make the Southwest so captivating. First, there's the space: 277 miles long and over one mile deep, the Canyon overwhelms the human capacity for perception. Then, there's the color: a panoply of hues demarcate billions of years of geologic history. Finally, there's the river: the chaotically creative force behind most of the Southwest's beautifully artful landforms is on full display. For some visitors, beholding the Canyon is a spiritual experience. For others, the Canyon demonstrates the ancient history of our earth. In all cases, the Canyon elicits reflection as deep as the Canyon itself.

The Grand Canyon extends from Lee's Ferry, AZ to Lake Mead, NV. In the north, the Glen Canyon Dam backs up the Colorado into mammoth Lake Powell. To the west, the Hoover Dam traps the remaining outflow from Glen Canyon to form Lake Mead. Grand Canyon National Park is divided into three sections: the most popular South Rim; the more serene North Rim; and the canyon gorge itself. Traveling between rims takes approximately five hours, either via a 13-mile hike or a long drive to the bridge in Lee's Ferry. Sandwiched between the national park and Lake Mead, the Hualapai and Havasupai Reservations also abut the river.

SOUTH RIM ☎928

During the summer, everything on two legs or four wheels converges on this side of the Grand Canyon. If you plan to visit during the mobfest, make reservations well in advance for lodging, campsites, or mules, and prepare to battle the crowds. That said, it's much better than Disney World. A friendly Park Service staff, well-run facilities, and beautiful scenery help ease crowd anxiety. Fewer tourists brave the Canyon's winter weather; hotels and facilities often close during the off season.

⊏ TRANSPORTATION

There are two park entrances: the main **south entrance** is about 6 mi. from the Visitors Center while the eastern **Desert View** entrance is 27 mi. away. Both are accessed via Rte. 64. From Las Vegas, the fastest route to the South Rim is U.S. 93 S to I-40 E, and then Rte. 64 N. From Flagstaff, head north on U.S. 180 to Rte. 64.

Trains: The **Grand Canyon Railway** (☎800-843-8724) runs a restored train from Williams to the Canyon (2¼hr.; leaves 10am, returns 3:30pm; $55, children $25).

Buses: Nava-Hopi Bus Lines (☎800-892-8687) departs Flagstaff depot, 114 W. Rte. 66, for the Grand Canyon daily (2hr.; leaves 7:30am, 2:30pm, returns from Flagstaff 10am, 4:30pm; $14, ages 5-15 $7). Fares don't include entrance fee. Times vary by season.

Public Transit: Free shuttle buses run the West Rim Loop (daily 1hr. before sunrise to 1hr. after sunset) and the Village Loop (daily 1hr. before sunrise to 10:30pm) every 10-30min. A free **hiker's shuttle** runs every 30min. between Grand Canyon Village and the South Kaibab Trailhead, on the East Rim near Yaki Point.

Taxis: ☎638-2822.

Auto Repairs: Grand Canyon Garage (☎638-2631), east of the Visitors Center on the main road, near Maswik Lodge. Open daily 8am-5pm. 24hr. emergency service.

❋🛈 ORIENTATION AND PRACTICAL INFORMATION

Posted maps and signs in the park make it easy to orient oneself. Lodges and services concentrate in **Grand Canyon Village**, at the end of Park Entrance Rd. The east half of the village contains the Visitors Center and the general store, while most of the lodges and the challenging **Bright Angel Trail** lie in the west section. The shorter but more difficult **South Kaibab Trail** is off East Rim Dr., east of the village. Free shuttle buses to eight rim overlooks run along **West Rim Dr.** (closed to private vehicles during the summer). Avoid walking on the drive; the rim trails are safer and more scenic. The **entrance pass** is $20 per car and $10 for travelers using other modes of transportation, including bus passengers. The pass lasts for one week. For most services in the Park, call the main switchboard number at 638-2631.

Visitor info: Canyon View Information Plaza, across from Mather Point. The Plaza houses the Visitors Center (open daily 8am-6pm), a bookstore (open daily 8am-7pm), restrooms, and helpful kiosks answering frequently asked questions. The Visitors Center stocks copies of *The Guide* (an essential), the *Backcountry Guide*, and the *Trip Planner*. The Park Service, through the Grand Canyon Association, sells a variety of informational books and packets (☎800-858-2808; www.grandcanyon.com). The **transportation info desks** in **Bright Angel Lodge** and **Maswik Lodge** (☎638-2631) handle reservations for mule rides, bus tours, plane tours, Phantom Ranch, taxis, and more. Open daily 6am-8pm.

Equipment Rental: In the General Store. Comfy hiking boots, socks included ($8 first day, $5 per additional day); sleeping bags ($7-9/$5); tents ($15-18/$9); large day packs ($6/$4), and other camping gear like stoves and backpacks. Open daily 7am-9pm.

Weather and Road Conditions: ☎638-7888.

Medical Services: Grand Canyon Clinic (☎638-2551), several mi. south of the Visitors Center on Center Rd. Open M-F 8am-8pm, Sa 9am-1pm. 24hr. emergency aid.

Post Office: 100 Mather Business Ctr. (☎638-2512), in market plaza, next to the General Store. Open M-F 9am-4:30pm, Sa 11am-3pm. **ZIP code:** 86023. **Area code:** 928.

⌂ ACCOMMODATIONS

Compared to the six million years it took the Colorado River to carve the Grand Canyon, the year it will take you to get indoor lodging near the South Rim is nothing. Summer rooms should be reserved 11 months in advance. That said, there are frequent cancellations; if you arrive unprepared, check for vacancies or call the operator (☎638-2631) and ask to be connected with the proper lodge.

Maswik Lodge (☎638-2631), Grand Canyon Village. Small, clean cabins (singles or doubles) with showers but no heat $64; motel rooms $74-118; $7-9 per extra person.

Bright Angel Lodge (☎638-2631), in Grand Canyon Village. The cheapest indoor lodging in the park. "Rustic" lodge singles and doubles with shared bath $40-50, with private bath $60. "Historic" cabins available for 1 or 2 people $74. $7 each additional person.

Phantom Ranch (☎638-2631), on the canyon floor, a day's hike down the Kaibab Trail or Bright Angel Trail. Dorms $22; seldom-available cabins for 1 or 2 people $64; $10.50 per each additional person. Reservations taken up to 23 months in advance. If you're dying to sleep on the canyon floor but don't have a reservation, show up at the Bright Angel transportation desk at 6am, and they may be able to arrange something.

🏕 CAMPGROUNDS

The campsites listed here usually fill up early in the day. In the **Kaibab National Forest**, along the south border of the park, you can pull off a dirt road and camp for free. No camping is allowed within ¼ mi. of U.S. 64. Convenient **dispersed camping** can be had along N. Long Jim Loop Rd. For quieter and more remote sites, follow signs for the Arizona Trail into the national forest between Mile 252 and 253 on U.S. 64. Sleeping in cars is *not* permitted within the park, but it is allowed in the Kaibab Forest (although Let's Go does not recommend it). For more info, contact the **Tusayan Ranger Station**, Kaibab National Forest, P.O. Box 3088, Grand Canyon, AZ 86023 (☎638-2443). Reservations for some campgrounds can be made through **SPHERICS** (☎800-365-2267).

Mather Campground (☎800-365-2267), 1 mi. south of the General Store. 320 shady, relatively isolated sites with no hookups. Check at the office even if the sign says its full. 7-night max. stay. For Mar.-Nov., reserve up to 3 months in advance; Dec.-Feb. sites first come, first served. Sept.-May $12; June-Aug. $15.

Ten-X Campground (☎638-2443), in the Kaibab National Forest, 10 mi. south of Grand Canyon Village off Rte. 64. Shady sites surrounded by pine trees. Open May-Sept. Toilets, water, no hookups, no showers. First come, first served sites $10.

Camper Village (☎638-2887), 7 mi. south of the Visitors Center in Tusayan. First come, first served tent sites; reservations required for RVs. 2-person hookups and tent sites $18-26; $2 each additional adult.

Trailer Village (☎638-2631), next to Mather Campground. Office open daily 8am-noon and 1-5pm. 84 sites designed for the RV. Showers, laundry, and groceries nearby. 2-person hookups $24; $1.75 each additional person. Reserve 6-9 months in advance.

🍴 FOOD

Fast food has yet to sink its greasy talons into the South Rim (the closest McDonald's is 7 mi. south in Tusayan), but you *can* find meals at fast-food prices. The **General Store,** near the Visitors Center, has a deli counter with the cheapest eats in the park and enough Grand Canyon apparel to clothe each member of your extended family. (☎638-2262. Open daily in summer 7am-8pm; deli open 7am-7pm. Sandwiches $2-4.) The well-stocked **Canyon Cafe,** across from the General Store, offers a wider variety of food than the deli. (Open daily 6am-10pm.) **Maswik Cafeteria,** in Maswik Lodge, serves a variety of grill food, country favorites, and Mexican specialties in a wood-paneled cafeteria atmosphere. (Open daily 6am-10pm. Hot entrees $6-7, sandwiches $3-5.) **Bright Angel Dining Room,** in Bright Angel Lodge, serves hot sandwiches for $7-9. (☎638-2631. Open daily 6:30am-10pm.) The soda fountain at **Bright Angel Lodge** chills eight flavors of ice cream and stocks a variety of snack-bar sandwiches. (Open daily 8am-8pm. 1 scoop $2.)

🥾 HIKING

Hikes into and around the Grand Canyon can be broken down into two categories: day hikes and overnight hikes. Confusing an overnight hike for a day hike can lead to disaster and a permanent residency in the canyon. Hiking to the Colorado River is reserved for overnight trips. All overnight trips require permits obtained through the Backcountry Office. In determining what is an appropriate day hike, remember that the Canyon does not have any loop hikes. Be prepared to retrace every single footstep uphill on the way back. Begin before 7am for day hikes, and consult a ranger before heading out. Park Service rangers also present a variety of free, informative talks and guided hikes; times and details are listed in *The Guide*.

The **Rim, Bright Angel, South Kaibab,** and **River** trails are the only South Rim trails regularly maintained and patrolled by the park service. There are a number of other trails and paths into and around the Canyon, such as **South Bass, Grandview,** and **Tonto.** These trails are only for the experienced hiker and may contain steep chutes and technical terrain. Consult a ranger and *The Guide* before heading out.

Rim Trail (11 mi. one-way, 4-6hr.). The Rim Trail is excellent for hikers seeking a tame way to see the Canyon. The trail follows the shuttle bus routes along Hermit Rd. past the Grand Canyon Village to Mather Point. Near the Grand Canyon Village, the Rim Trail resembles a city street crammed with people, but toward the eastern and western ends, hikers have a bit more elbow room. Hopi Point is a great place to watch the sunset with its panoramic canyon views—*The Guide* list times for sunsets and sunrises.

Bright Angel Trail (up to 18 mi. round-trip, 1-2 days). Bright Angel's frequent switchbacks and refreshing water stations make it the into-the-canyon choice of moderate hikers. The trail departs from the Rim Trail near the western edge of the Grand Canyon Village, and the first 1-2 mi. of the trail generally attract droves of day hikers. Rest houses are stationed 1.5 and 3 mi. from the rim, each with water between May and Sept. **Indian Gardens,** 4.5 mi. down, offers restrooms, picnic tables, and shade. From rim to river, the trail drops 4420 ft. Although spread over 18 mi., the round-trip is too strenuous for a day hike. With the compulsory permit, overnighters can camp at Indian Gardens or Bright Angel Campground, while day hikers are advised to go no farther than Plateau Point (12.2 mi. round-trip) or Indian Gardens (9.2 mi. round-trip). The **River Trail** (1.7 mi.) connects the Bright Angel Trail with the South Kaibab Trail.

South Kaibab Trail (7 mi. one-way to Phantom Ranch, 4-5hr. descent). Beginning at Yaki Pt. (7260 ft.), the trickier and steeper Kaibab lacks shade or water, but it rewards the intrepid with a better view of the canyon. Day hikes to Cedar Ridge (3 mi. round-trip; toilet facilities available) and **Skeleton Point** (6 mi. round-trip) are reasonable only for experienced hikers. For overnight hikes, Kaibab meets up with Bright Angel at the Colorado. Fewer switchbacks and a more rapid descent make the South Kaibab Trail 1.7 mi. shorter than the Bright Angel to this point. Guests staying at the Phantom Ranch or Bright Angel Campground use the Bright Angel or South Kaibab to reach the ranch.

◪ OTHER ACTIVITIES

Beyond using your feet, there are others ways to conquer the canyon. **Mule trips** from the South Rim are expensive and booked up to one year in advance, although cancellations do occur. (☎303-297-2757. Day trip $107, overnight including lodging and meals $308.) Mule trips from the North Rim are cheaper and more readily available (☎435-679-8665). **Whitewater rafting** trips through the canyon vary in length and book well in advance. The *Trip Planner* lists 16 commercial guides licensed to offer trips in the canyon; check the park website for info in advance of your visit.

NORTH RIM   ☎928

If you're coming from Utah or Nevada, or want to avoid the crowds at the South Rim, the park's North Rim is wilder, cooler, and more serene—all with a view almost as groovy as that from the South Rim. Unfortunately, because the North Rim is less frequented, it's hard to reach by public transportation, and by car it's a long drive. From October 15 to December 1, the North Rim is open for day use only; from December 1 to May 15, it is closed entirely. Any visit to the North Rim centers on the North Rim Lodge, an elegant structure overlooking the canyon.

> From your first glimpse of the canyon, you may feel a compelling desire to see it from the inside, an enterprise that is harder than it looks. Even the young at heart and body should remember that an easy downhill hike can become a nightmarish 50° incline on the return journey. Also keep in mind that the lower you go, the hotter it gets; when it's 85°F on the rim, it's around 100°F at Indian Gardens and around 110°F at Phantom Ranch. Heat stroke, the greatest threat to any hiker, is marked by a monstrous headache and red, sweatless skin. *For a day hike, you must take at least a gallon of water per person; drink at least a quart per hour hiking upwards under the hot sun.* Footwear with excellent tread is also necessary—the trails are steep, and every year several careless hikers take what locals morbidly call "the 12-second tour." Safety tips can be found in *The Guide,* but speak with a ranger before embarking on a hike. Parents should think twice about bringing children more than 1 mi. down any trail.

ORIENTATION AND PRACTICAL INFORMATION

To reach the North Rim from the South Rim, take Rte. 64 E. to U.S. 89 N, which runs into Alt. 89; from Alt. 89, follow Rte. 67 S to the edge. Altogether, the beautiful drive is over 200 mi. From Utah, take Alt. 89 S. from Fredonia. From Page, take U.S. 89 S to Alt. 89 to Rte. 67 S. Snow closes Rte. 67 from mid-October through mid-May, and park visitor facilities (including the lodge) close for the winter. The visitor **parking** lot lies near the end of Rte. 67, closer to both the Visitors Center and lodge.

Buses: Transcanyon, P.O. Box 348, Grand Canyon 86023 (☎638-2820). Buses run to the South Rim (4½hr.; late May to Oct. 7am, from South Rim 1:30pm; $65, round-trip $100). Reservations required.

Public Transit: A hikers' shuttle runs from the Lodge to the North Kaibab Trailhead (late May to Oct. 5:20 and 7:20am; $5, $2 each additional person).

Visitor info: North Rim Visitors Center (☎638-7864), on Rte. 67 just before the Lodge. Open daily 8am-6pm. **Kaibab Plateau Visitors Center** (☎643-7298), at Jacob Lake, next to the Inn. **Backcountry permits** are issued here. Open daily 8am-5pm.

Weather Info: ☎638-7888. Updated at 7am daily.

Camping Supplies: General store abuts North Rim Campground. Open daily 7am-9pm.

Post Office: in Grand Canyon Lodge (☎638-2611). Open M-F 8am-11am and 11:30am-4pm, Sa 8am-2pm. **ZIP code:** 86052. **Area code:** 520.

ACCOMMODATIONS AND FOOD

The North Rim has only one campground, creatively named "North Rim Campground," and it generally fills entirely by reservation during the summer. **SPHERICS** (☎800-365-2267) handles reservations. If you can't get in-park lodgings, head for the **Kaibab National Forest,** which runs from north of Jacob Lake to the park entrance. You can camp for free, as long as you're ¼ mi. from the road, water, or official campgrounds and 1 mi. from any commercial facility. Less expensive accommodations may be found in **Kanab, UT,** 80 mi. north.

Grand Canyon Lodge (☎303-297-2757 for reservations, 638-2611 for front desk). The only indoor rim lodging. Reserve well in advance. Open mid-May to Oct. Pioneer cabins shelter 4 people for $94; singles or doubles in frontier cabins $80; hotel rooms $87.

Jacob Lake Inn (☎643-7232), 32 mi. north of the North Rim entrance at Jacob Lake. Charming lodge with small store, cafe, and bakery. Reception daily 6:30am-9:30pm. Cabins for 2 $72-81, for 3 $85-94, for 4 $89-105; motel units $90-98.

Kaibab Lodge (☎638-2389), 6 mi. north of the entrance gate, is a model of rustic sophistication. 2-person basic cabin $80, 4-person modular $130.

North Rim Campground (call **SPHERICS,** ☎800-365-2267), on Rte. 67 near the rim, is the only park campground on this side of the chasm. 83 sites; no hookups. Open mid-May to mid-Oct. 7-night max. stay. Sites $15, 4 "premier sites" with canyon views $20.

DeMotte Park Campground, about 5 mi. north of the park entrance in Kaibab National Forest. 23 woodsy sites are first come, first served. $10 per vehicle per night.

Kaibab Camper Village (☎ 643-7804), 1 mi. south of Jacob Lake Inn. Open May to mid-Oct. 50 sites $12; 60 2-person hookups $22; $2 each additional person.

Feeding options on the North Rim are placed strategically at the **Grand Canyon Lodge** and tend to be pricey. (☎ 638-2612 ext. 160. Open daily 6:30-10am, 11:30am-2:30pm, and 5-9:30pm; reservations required for dinner.) The best alternative is to buy groceries at the General Store and prepare a canyon-side picnic. There is also the **Rough Rider Saloon** in the lodge, offering coffee and baked goods in the morning and beer in the afternoon and evening. (Open daily 5-9am and 11am-10pm.) North Rimers are better off eating in Kanab or stopping at the **Jacob Lake Inn** for $5-6 sandwiches and amazing $2 milkshakes. (☎ 643-7232. Open daily 6am-9pm.)

▨ OUTDOORS

Hiking in the leafy North Rim seems like a trip to the mountains. This mountain, however, is upside-down—the hike back up comes after the legs are already a little weary from hiking down. All precautions for hiking at the South Rim are even more important at the North Rim, where the elevations are higher and the air is thinner. In-depth info on trails can be found in the North Rim's version of *The Guide.* Several day hikes of variable lengths beckon the active North Rim visitor. For an indispensable resource on North Rim Trails, pick up a copy of the *Official Guide to Hiking the Grand Canyon,* available in all Visitors Centers and gift shops. Overnight hikers must get permits from the **Backcountry Office** in the ranger station (open daily 8am-noon and 1-5pm), or write to the **Backcountry Office,** P.O. Box 129, Grand Canyon, AZ 86023; it may take a few days to get a permit in person.

Bright Angel Point Trail (0.5 mi.) begins near the Visitors Center and winds around behind the Lodge, ending with a seraphic view of the Canyon. The **Uncle Jim Trail** (5 mi. round-trip) follows the **Ken Patrick Trail** along Roaring Spring Canyon and then completes a circle on a plateau that juts out between the Roaring Springs and Bright Angel Canyons, offering superior views of both. Combining Canyon views with alpine forest greenery, the 10 mi. round-trip **Widforss Trail** is perfect for a casual, if long, day's saunter. The popular and well-maintained 14.2 mi. one-way **North Kaibab Trail** descends the Roaring Spring Canyon to the Bright Angel Canyon and eventually to the Colorado. Day hikers are advised not to proceed beyond the spring, located 4.7 mi. into the hike. Some of the most scenic and least-traveled backpacking in the park is made available via the 15 mi. one-way **Thunder River Trail,** which descends steep cliffs, follows the Esplanade to Surprise Valley, and then follows Thunder River to the Colorado. The alternative **Deer Creek** route travels west from Surprise Valley through Deer Creek Valley to the Colorado.

Park Rangers also run nature walks, lectures, and evening programs at the North Rim Campground and Lodge. Check the info desk or campground bulletin boards for schedules. One-hour ($20), half-day ($45), and full-day ($95) **mule trips** through **Canyon Trail Rides** circle the rim or descend into the canyon. (☎ 435-679-8665. Open daily 7am-7pm. No credit cards.) Reservations are recommended but walk-ins can be accommodated more frequently than on the South Rim.

HAVASUPAI RESERVATION ☎ 928

To the west of the hustle and bustle of the South Rim lies the tranquility of the Havasupai Reservation. Meaning "people of the blue-green water," the Havasupai live in a protected enclave, bordered by the national park. Ringed by dramatic sandstone faces, their village, Supai, rests on the verdant shores of the Havasu River. Just beyond town, this rushing wonder of crystal-clear water cascades over a series of spectacular falls. Beneath the falls, ecstatic visitors frolic in the waters, marveling at their smallness in the face of such awesome power and cherishing their Eden-like surroundings. Such beauty attracts thousands of visitors yearly, but luckily, a grueling 10 mi. hike separates the falls from any vehicle-accessible surface and prevents the Disney-fication of the reservation. For most, blistered feet or a saddle-sore rump make bathing in the cool waters even sweeter.

SOUTHWEST

Supai and the campground can only be reached by a trail that originates on the rim at the Hualapai Hilltop. To reach the trailhead, take I-40 E until Rte. 66 at Seligman; follow Rte. 66 for 30 mi. until it meets with Indian Rd. 18, which ends at the Hilltop after 60 mi. No roads lead to Supai, although mules and helicopters can be hired to carry bags or people. For mule reservations, contact the **Havasupai Tourist Enterprise**. (☎448-2141. $75 one-way; includes 4 pieces of luggage.) The hike is not to be underestimated. The well-marked trail is a grueling, exposed 8 mi. to Supai and then an additional 2 mi. to the campground. *Do not hike down without a reservation*—you may have to turn right around and walk back to the trailhead.

Reservations for the campground, lodge, and mules can be made by calling the **Havasupai Tourist Enterprise.** Visitors must first check-in at the **Tourist Office** in Supai before heading onto the campground. In the village, there's a Post Office, a general store, and cafe. Prices are high, because everything must be brought in by mule or helicopter. Bringing your own food to the campground is advised. All trash must be packed-out. No **gas** or **water** is available past Rte. 66; stock up beforehand.

The Havasupai graciously share their natural paradise with the outside world. The tribe operates the two accommodations: the ▧**Havasupai Campground** and the Havasupai Lodge, both on the canyon floor. The friendly campground, 2 mi. beyond Supai, lies between Havasu and Mooney Falls. Many campers consider the camp sites to be heaven-on-earth, because they border the blue-green water of the Havasu River and are near to the swimmer-friendly lagoons. The Tribe charges a one-time entry fee ($20 per visitor and $10 per night) at the campground. Facilities are sparse: non-flush toilets that tend to smell up the campground, and no showers (though the falls are just a quick jaunt away). A spring provides fresh water. For those less-inclined to the great outdoors, the **Havasupai Lodge**, in Supai, offers basic accommodation ($75-95 for up to six people, plus the entrance fee).

The trail from Supai to the campground extends to **Mooney Falls** (1 mi. from campground), **Beaver Falls** (4 mi.), and the **Colorado** (7 mi.). The vertiginous hike down to Mooney Falls may turn your stomach. Extreme caution should be exercised—shoes with good tread are a must. Swimming and frolicking are both permitted and encouraged in the lush lagoons that collect at the bottom of the falls.

FLAGSTAFF

☎928

Born on the 4th of July, Flagstaff began as a rest stop along the transcontinental railroad; its mountain springs provided precious aqueous refreshment along the long haul to the Pacific. The past 100 years have echoed with the innumerable "timber!" cries of the logging industry, seen a scientist in search of canal-digging Martians, witnessed an emerging milieu of diverse cultures and ideologies, and felt the unrelenting onslaught of backpackers and fannypackers alike. One thing hasn't changed, though: Flagstaff is still a major rest stop on the way to Southwestern must-sees. Trains plow through town 72 times a day, while travelers pass through on their way to the Grand Canyon, Sedona, and the Petrified Forest—all within day-trip distance. The energetic citizens welcome travelers to their rock formations by day and their breweries by night; many have wandered into town with camera in hand and ended up settling down. Retired cowboys, earthy Volvo owners, New Agers, and serious rock climbers comprise much of the population.

⌷ TRANSPORTATION

Flagstaff sits 138 mi. north of Phoenix (take I-17), 26 mi. north of Sedona (take U.S. 89A), and 81 mi. south of the Grand Canyon's south rim (take U.S. 180).

Trains: Amtrak, 1 E. Rte. 66 (☎774-8679). 2 trains leave daily. Eastbound train leaves at 5:11am, heading to Gallup (2½hr., $33-58), and Albuquerque (5hr., $59-106). Westbound train leaves at 9:38 pm, heading to Los Angeles (12hr., $64-114). Station open daily 3:15pm-11:45am and 1:15am-8:30am.

Buses: Greyhound: 399 S. Malpais Ln. (☎774-4573). To: Albuquerque (6½hr., 4 per day, $39); Las Vegas (5-6hr., 4 per day, $49); Los Angeles (10-12hr., 9 per day, $53); Phoenix, including airport (3hr., 4 per day, $21). Terminal open 24hr. **Grayline/Nava-Hopi,** 114 W. Rte. 66 (☎774-5003 or 877-467-3329), sends shuttle buses to the Grand Canyon (2hr., 2 per day, $20 includes admission fee) and Phoenix (3hr., 3 per day, $24). **Coconino/Yavapai Shuttle Service** offers daily trips from Flagstaff to Sedona. $15 one-way, $25 return. For reservations call 775-8929 or 888-440-8929.

Public Transit: Pine Country Transit (☎779-6624). Routes cover most of town. Buses run once per hr.; route map and schedule available at Visitors Center in Amtrak station. One-way 75¢, seniors and disabled 35¢, children 60¢; book of 20 passes $13.

Taxis: Friendly Cab, ☎214-9000.

Car Rental: Enterprise Rent-A-Car (☎526-1377), on Rte. 66 near the eastern edge of town. 21+ rentals require a license and credit card. Open M-F 9am-5pm, Sa 9am-noon.

☀🕎 ORIENTATION AND PRACTICAL INFORMATION

The downtown area revolves around the intersection of **Beaver St.** and **Rte. 66** (formerly Santa Fe Ave.). **S. San Francisco St.,** two blocks east of Beaver St., marks the eastern edge of downtown. Split by Rte. 66, the northern area is slightly swanker and more upscale, while the area south of the tracks is more down to earth, housing hostels and vegetarian eateries.

Visitor info: Flagstaff Visitors Center, 1 E. Rte. 66 (☎774-9541 or 800-842-7293), in the Amtrak station. Open M-Sa 7am-6pm, Su 7am-5pm.

Equipment Rental: Peace Surplus, 14 W. Rte. 66 (☎779-4521), 1 block from Grand Canyon Hostel. Rents tents and packs for just dollars a day (with a hefty deposit), plus a good stock of other cheap outdoor gear. 3-day minimum rental on all equipment. Credit card or cash deposit required. Open M-F 8am-9pm, Sa 8am-8pm.

Internet Access: Available for free at the **Flagstaff Public Library,** 300 W. Aspen Ave. (☎774-4000). Open M-Th 10am-9pm, F 10am-7pm, Sa 10am-6pm, Su 11am-6pm.

Post Office: 2400 N. Postal Blvd. (☎714-9302). Open M-F 9am-5pm, Sa 9am-1pm. **ZIP code:** 86004. **Area code:** 928.

🏠 ACCOMMODATIONS

When swarms of summer tourists descend on Flagstaff, accommodation prices shoot up. Thankfully, the town is blessed with excellent hostels. Historic **Rte. 66** is home to many cheap motels, although the private rooms at the hostels and hotels listed below rival them both in price and in quality. *The Flagstaff Accommodations Guide*, available at the Visitors Center, lists all area accommodations.

⬛ Grand Canyon International Hostel, 19 S. San Francisco St. (☎779-9421 or 888-442-2696). Sunny, clean, and classy. Free tea and coffee, breakfast, parking, and linen. Access to kitchen, TV, Internet ($2 per 30min.), and laundry. Offers tours to the Grand Canyon ($43), and to Sedona ($25). Reception 7am-midnight. 4-bed dorms Oct.-May $14, June-Aug. $16; private rooms without bath $28/$32, with bath $31/$35.

Du Beau International Hostel, 19 W. Phoenix St. (☎774-6731 or 800-398-7112), also just behind the train station. The Du Beau lives up to its ritzy name with recently renovated dorm rooms (4-8 beds) and private bathrooms. Reception 7am-midnight. Under the same ownership as the Grand Canyon Hostel, Du Beau offers all the same services. 8-bed dorms Oct.-May $14, June-Aug. $16. Private rooms with bath $29/$32.

The Weatherford Hotel, 23 N. Leroux St. (☎779-1919), on the other side of the tracks 1 block west of San Francisco St. The oldest hotel in Flagstaff, it has spacious rooms with amazing balconies and bay windows. Reservations recommended. Rooms $50-60.

Hotel Monte Vista, 100 N. San Francisco St. (☎779-6971 or 800-545-3068), downtown. Feels like a classy hotel, with charmingly quirky decor, a bar that occasionally hosts hard-core and punk bands, and pool tables and video games downstairs. Private rooms named after movie stars who slept there start at $40.

CAMPING

Free backcountry camping is available around Flagstaff in wilderness areas. Pick up a map from the **Peaks Ranger Station,** 5075 N. 89A (☎526-0866), to find out where camping is permitted. All backcountry sites must be located at least 200 ft. from trails, waterways, and lakes. For info on campgrounds and backcountry camping, call the **Coconino Forest Service.** (☎527-3600. Open M-F 7:30am-4:30pm.)

An alternative to backcountry camping is staying at one of the numerous maintained campsites in the forest. Many of these campsites flank the lakes to the south of Flagstaff. **Lakeview Campground,** on the side of Upper Lake Marry, 11½ mi. south on Lake Mary Road (off I-17 south of Flagstaff), is surrounded by a pine forest that supports an alpine ecosystem. There are toilets and clean drinking water for a fee. (No reservations. $10 per vehicle.) **Pinegrove Campground,** 5 mi. south of Lakeview at the other end of Upper Lake Mary, is set in a similarly charming locale with identical facilities. (☎877-444-6777. Reservations available. $12 per vehicle.)

FOOD

All the arch-wielding, deep-fat frying chains are readily available outside of downtown, but near the heart of Flagstaff, the creative and offbeat rules. **Macy's,** 14 S. Beaver St., behind Motel Du Beau, is a cheery student hangout serving only vegetarian food (excellent vegan selection, too) in an earthy atmosphere. (☎774-2243. Open Su-W 6am-8pm, Th-Sa 6am-midnight. Food served until 1hr. before closing. Cash only.) **Alpine Pizza,** at 7 N. Leroux, skillfully blends the time-honored American traditions of pizza-eating and beer-drinking. Large (Alpine-sized) slices go for $2.50, while beer is comparably inexpensive. A local hang-out, Alpine has a pool table and wood-carved booths. (☎774-4109. Open Su-Th 11am-11pm, F-Sa 11am-midnight.) **The Black Bean,** 12 E. Rte. 66, is a great place for cheap on-the-go burritos. (☎779-9905. Open M-Th 11am-9pm, F-Sa 11am-10pm.) Behind demure lace curtains, **Kathy's Cafe,** 7 N. San Francisco St., prepares delicious and inexpensive breakfasts accompanied by biscuits and fresh fruit ($4-6). Lunch sandwiches include $5 veggie options. (☎774-1951. Open M-F 6:30am-3pm, Sa-Su 7am-3:30pm. Cash only.)

SIGHTS

In 1894, Percival Lowell chose Flagstaff as the site for an astronomical observatory, and then spent the rest of his life here, devoting himself to the study of heavenly bodies and culling data to support his theory that life exists on Mars. The **Lowell Observatory,** 1400 W. Mars Hill Rd., where he discovered the planet Pluto, exists as a tribute to his genius and a high-powered research center. In the day, admission includes tours of the telescopes, as well as a museum with hands-on astronomy exhibits. If you have stars in your eyes, come back at night for an excellent program about the night's sky and the constellations. (☎774-2096. Open daily 9am-5pm. Evening programs M-Sa 7:30pm; in summer 8:30pm. $3.50, ages 5-17 $1.50.)

The more down-to-earth **Museum of Northern Arizona,** off U.S. 180, a few mi. north of town, features exhibits on the native peoples of the area. Galleries house expansive collections of Native American art. There's also an intimidating dinosaur skeleton. (☎774-5213. Open daily 9am-5pm. $5, students $3, seniors $4, ages 7-17 $2.)

OUTDOOR ACTIVITIES

With the northern **San Francisco Peaks** and the surrounding **Coconino National Forest,** Flagstaff offers numerous options for the rugged outdoorsman or those simply interested in walking off last night's fun. Nature's playground provides skiing, hiking, biking, and general awe-struckedness. Due to the 7000 ft. plus altitudes, bring plenty of water, regardless of the season or activity. In late spring and summer, National and State Park Rangers may close trails if the potential for fire gets too high. The mountains occupy national forest land, so backcountry camping is free.

DEEP IMPACT Perhaps the recent American obsession with all things extraterrestrial explains the popularity of **Meteor Crater,** 35 mi. east of Flagstaff off I-40, because not much else could. Originally thought to be a volcanic cone, the crater is now believed to be the impact site of a giant nickel-iron meteorite that fell to earth 50,000 years ago. Visitors are not allowed to hike down into the crater, which measures 4100 ft. across, but must fight the hordes for an unspectacular view over the guard-railed edge. An alternative is the hour-long rim walk. (Free with admission. Every hr. 10am-2pm. Closed shoe footwear required.) Conspicuously missing in action is the meteor itself; scientists believe that most of it was vaporized at the moment of impact, since it was traveling an impressive 10 mi. per second. (☎289-5898. Open daily 6am-6pm; off-season 8am-5pm. $10, seniors $9, ages 6-17 $5.)

SKIING

The **Arizona Snow Bowl,** open from mid-December to April, operates four chairlifts and maintains 32 trails. The majestic **Humphrey's Peak,** standing a whopping 12,670 ft., is the backdrop for the Snowbowl, as well as the Hopi's sacred home of the Kachina spirits. With an average snowfall of 260 in. and 2300 ft. of vertical drop, the Snow Bowl rivals the big-boy ski resorts of the Rockies. (☎779-1951. Open daily 9am-4pm. Lift tickets $37.) To reach the Snow Bowl, take U.S. 180 about 7 mi. north to the Fairfield Snow Bowl turn-off. Cross-country skiing is available at the **Flagstaff Nordic Center** (☎779-1951), 8 mi. north of Snow Bowl Rd. on U.S. 180. The vista at the top of the **Snow Bowl's Skyride** is stunning. When the air is clear, the North Rim of the Grand Canyon, the Painted Desert, and countless square miles of Arizona and Utah can be seen from the peak. (30min. Runs daily late May to early Sept. 10am-4pm; early Sept. to mid-Oct. F-Su 10am-4pm. $9, seniors $6.50, ages 6-12 $5.)

HIKING

In the summer, these peaks attract different species: hikers and bikers. The Coconino National Forest has many trails for hikers of all abilities. Consult the **Peaks Ranger Station,** 5075 N. 89A (☎526-0866), for trail descriptions and possible closures. For the more energetic hiker, the **Elden Lookout Trail** is ideal for jaw-dropping mountain-top views. Only 6 mi. in length (round-trip), the trail climbs 2400 ft.; it is demanding, but worth the view. The trail begins at the Peaks Ranger station. The most popular trail in the area is the hike to Humphrey's Peak, Arizona's highest mountain. This 9 mi. round-trip begins in the first parking lot at the Snow Bowl ski area. For a longer hike, the moderate to strenuous 17.4 mi. round-trip Weatherford Trail offers excellent opportunities for bird- and animal-spotting. The trailhead can be found next to Schultz Tank, about 7 mi. from Flagstaff.

MOUNTAIN BIKING

Flagstaff also offers excellent mountain biking. The **Dry Lake Hills** and the **Elden Mountains** are two great areas, both north of Flagstaff, to tear it up on two wheels. Popular routes include the easy **Rocky Ridge Trail** (4.4 mi. round-trip), which begins close to the intersection of Forest Rd. 557 and 420, and can be easily combined with the **Schultz Creek Trail** and the **Oldham Trail,** as well as the **Little Bear Trail** (7 mi. round-trip), reached by a short ride up Little Elden Trail from the Little Elden Springs Horse Camp off U.S. 89. Bike rentals are available at **Absolute Bikes,** 18 N. San Francisco St. (☎779-5969), starting at $25 per day. **Sinagua Cycles,** 113 S. San Francisco St. (☎779-9969), leads free bike rides Monday to Friday at 4:30pm.

🎭🎵 NIGHTLIFE AND ENTERTAINMENT

Charly's, 23 N. Leroux St., plays live jazz and blues in one of the classiest buildings in town. (☎779-1919. Happy hour 5-7pm. Open daily 11am-10pm. Bar open daily 11am-1am.) **Joe's Place,** on the corner of San Francisco and Rte. 66, hosts indie bands weekend nights. (☎774-6281. Happy hour 4-7pm. Open 11am-1am.) **The Alley** plays to a similar crowd as Joe's and sees many out-of-towners. (☎774-7929. Happy hour M-Sa 3-7pm, Su free nacho bar. Open 11am-1pm.) If country is your thang, the **Museum Club**, 3404 E. Rte. 66, a.k.a. the **Zoo**, will rock your world. This place is the premier spot for honky-tonk action. (☎526-9434. Cover $3-5. Open daily 11am-3am.)

North of town near the museum, the **Coconino Center for the Arts** (☎779-7258 or 774-6272) houses exhibits, festivals, performers, and even a children's museum. In the middle of June, the annual **Flagstaff Rodeo** (☎800-638-4253) comes to town. Competitions and events go on all weekend at the Coconino County Fair Grounds. The town's birthday, the **4th of July,** is a foot-stomping good time with festivals and fireworks. At the end of the summer, the **Coconino Country Fair** digs its heals into Flagstaff with rides, animal competitions, and carnival games. **Theatrikos,** 11 W. Cherry Ave. (☎774-1662), stages plays year-round in their own playhouse.

⚑ DAYTRIPS FROM FLAGSTAFF

WALNUT CANYON NATIONAL MONUMENT

The remnants of more than 300 rooms in 13th-century Sinaguan dwellings make up Walnut Canyon National Monument. A glassed-in observation deck in the **Visitors Center,** 10 mi. east of Flagstaff, at Exit 204 off I-40, overlooks the whole canyon. (☎526-3367. Open daily 8am-6pm; off-season 9am-5pm. $3, under 17 free. Call ahead.) The steep, self-guided **Island Trail** snakes down from the Visitors Center past 25 cliff dwellings. The 0.75 mi. **Rim Trail** offers views of the canyon and passes rim-top sites. Every Saturday morning from 10am-1pm, rangers lead groups of five on 2 mi. hikes into Walnut Canyon to the original Ranger Cabin and more remote cliff dwellings. Reservations are required for these challenging 2½hr. hikes. There's also a trailhead for the Mexico-to-Utah portion of the Arizona trail.

SUNSET CRATER VOLCANO NATIONAL MONUMENT

The crater encompassed by Sunset Crater Volcano National Monument appeared in AD 1065. Over the next 200 years, a 1000 ft. high cinder cone took shape as a result of periodic eruptions. The self-guided **Lava Flow Nature Trail** wanders 1 mi. through the surreal landscape surrounding the cone, 1½ mi. east of the Visitors Center, where gnarled trees lie uprooted amid the rocky black terrain. Hiking up Sunset Crater itself is not permitted. The **Visitors Center,** 12 mi. north of Flagstaff on U.S. 89, supplies additional info. (☎526-0502. Open daily 8am-6pm; off-season 8am-5pm. $3, under 16 free; includes admission to Wupatki.) The **Bonito Campground,** in the Coconino National Forest at the entrance to Sunset Crater, provides tent sites.

WUPATKI NATIONAL MONUMENT

Wupatki possesses some of the Southwest's most scenic Pueblo sites, situated 18 mi. northeast of Sunset Crater, along a stunning road with views of the Painted Desert. The Sinagua moved here in the 11th century, after the Sunset Crater eruption forced them to evacuate the land to the south. Archeologists speculate that in less than 200 years, droughts, disease, and over-farming led the Sinagua to abandon these stone houses. Five empty pueblos face the 14 mi. road from U.S. 89 to the Visitors Center. Another road to the ruins begins on U.S. 89, 30 mi. north of Flagstaff. The largest and most accessible, **Wupatki,** located on a 0.5 mi. round-trip loop trail from the Visitors Center, rises three stories. The spectacular **Doney Mountain Trail** rises ½ mi. from the picnic area to the summit. Get info and trail guide brochures at the **Visitors Center.** Backcountry hiking is not permitted. *(☎679-2365. Monument and Visitors Center open daily 8am-5pm.)*

SEDONA   ☎928

Being that Sedona is a UFO sighting hot spot, one wonders if the Martians are simply mistaking its deep red-rock towers for home. The scores of tourists who descend upon the town year-round (Sedona rivals the Grand Canyon for tourist mass) certainly aren't; they come for sights that puts Newton's theories to shame. Dramatic copper-toned behemoths dotted with pines tower over Sedona, rising from the earth with such flair and crowd appeal that they feel like a manufactured tourist attraction. Some folks in town will tell you that they were manmade, perhaps by the Egyptians—Sedona is also the New Age capital of the US. Though the downtown is overrun with overpriced shops, the rocks are worth a visit.

◢◤ 🛈 ORIENTATION AND PRACTICAL INFORMATION. Sedona lies 120 mi. north of Phoenix (take I-17 north to Rte. 179) and 30 mi. south of Flagstaff (take I-17 south to Rte. 179). The **Sedona-Phoenix Shuttle** (☎282-2066) runs six trips daily ($35). The **Sedona Chamber of Commerce,** at Forest Rd. and U.S. 89A, provides info on accommodations and local attractions. (☎282-7722. Open M-Sa 8:30am-5pm, Su 9am-3pm.) **Post Office:** 190 W U.S. 89A. (☎282-3511. Open M-F 9am-5pm.) **ZIP code:** 86336. **Area code:** 928.

🛏 ACCOMMODATIONS. Lodging in town is a bit pricey, but a few deals can be had. However, it's not a bad idea to make Sedona a daytrip from Flagstaff or Cottonwood. **Hostel Sedona,** 5 Soldiers Wash Dr., off Brewer Rd., which connects with U.S. 89A uptown at the Burger King, provides basic, camp-like accommodations at a great location. (☎282-2772. Kitchen and common room. Chores required. Dorm beds $15; private room $30.) **White House Inn,** 2986 W. U.S. 89A (☎282-6680), is the second cheapest option, with singles and doubles, some with kitchenettes, for $46-58. A popular alternative to commercial lodging is renting a room in a private residence. Check the local papers or bulletin boards at New Age shops for opportunities. In addition, cheaper options can be found in Cottonwood, 15 mi. away, where a number of budget motels line U.S. 89. The **Willow Tree Inn,** off I-17 in Cottonwood, offers classy, comfortable rooms. (☎634-3678. Nov.-Apr. singles $38-42; doubles $42-48; Mar.-Oct. $42-48/$48-59.)

Most of the campsites in the area clustered around U.S. 89A as it heads north along Oak Creek Canyon on its way to Flagstaff. There are private campgrounds aplenty, but most cater to the RV crowd. The **US Forest Service campsites** along 89A provide the best, cheapest option. North of Sedona, between 9 and 20 mi. from the town, four separate campgrounds—Manzanita, Bootlegger, Cave Springs, and Pine Flat (east and west)—maintain over 150 campsites. (☎527-3600 for local info; ☎877-444-6777 national reservation service number. 7-night max. stay. Sites $12.)

🍴 FOOD. Like many things in Sedona, restaurants can be expensive. However, there are a few good deals to be had. The **Coffee Pot Restaurant,** 2050 W U.S. 89A, a local favorite, dishes up 101 varieties of omelettes ($4-7) and three varieties of tacos for $4. (☎282-6626. Open daily 6am-9pm.) Freshly made ice cream and bakery treats draw in the masses at **Black Cow Cafe,** 229 N U.S. 89A, a great spot to cool off. Baked goods ($1-3) and sandwiches ($4-6) are available. (☎203-9868. Open daily 7am-9pm.) The **Red Planet Diner,** 1665 W. 89A, beams patrons in with a flying saucer and extraterrestrial allure. Martian milkshakes ($3) and Universal noodle bowls ($6) are uncannily good. (☎282-6070. Open daily 11am-11pm.) For more down-to-earth fare, **India Palace,** 1910 W U.S. 89A, in the Basha's shopping center, has a $6 lunch buffet (served daily 11am-2:30pm), and a dinner menu with many vegetarian options, most under $10. (☎204-2300. Dinner served 5-10pm.)

◧ SIGHTS. The incredible formations at **Red Rock State Park** (☎282-6907) invite strolling or just contemplation. Located 15 mi. southwest of Sedona, the Park entrance can be found along the Red Rock Loop Road off U.S. 89A. Rangers lead daily nature hikes into the nearby rock formations and are happy to give trail recommendations. The **Chapel of the Holy Cross,** on Chapel Rd., lies just outside a 1000 ft. rock wall in the middle of red sandstone. (☎282-4069. Open daily 9am-5pm.) The view from the parking lot is a religious experience itself.

    Montezuma Castle National Monument, 10 mi. south of Sedona on I-17, is a 20-room cliff dwelling built by the Sinagua tribe in the 12th century. Unfortunately, you can't get very close to the ruins, but the view from the paved path below is excellent and wheelchair accessible. (☎567-3322. Open daily 8am-7pm; off-season 8am-5pm. $2,

CITY IN A BUBBLE The planned city of **Arcosanti,** off I-17 at Exit 262, is designed to embody Italian architect Paolo Soleri's concept of an "arcology," or "architecture and ecology working together as one integral process." When complete, the city will be entirely self-sufficient, supplying its own food, power, and all other resources. Arcosanti has been under construction since 1970 but is expected to be finished a bit later than the original goal of 2000—so far, only one building is up. The pace of the construction might have something to do with the restrictions on who is allowed to participate; rather than hiring workers, all the labor is done by students and others who take part in the community's "workshops." (☎632-7135. *Tours daily every hr. 10am-4pm; $5 donation requested. Visitors Center open daily 9am-5pm.)*

under 17 free.) A beautiful lake formed by the collapse of an underground cavern, **Montezuma Well,** off I-17 11 mi. north of the castle, once served as a source of water for the Sinagua who lived here. (Open daily 8am-7pm. Free.) Take U.S. 89A to Rte. 279 and continue through Cottonwood to reach **Tuzigoot National Monument,** 20mi. southwest of Sedona, a dramatic Sinaguan ruin overlooking the Verde Valley. (☎634-5564. Open daily 8am-7pm; in winter 8am-5pm. $2, under 17 free.)

◪ OUTDOOR ACTIVITIES. In terms of hiking, it's nearly impossible to go wrong with any of the well-maintained and well-marked trails in and around Sedona. Most trailheads are located on the forest service roads that snake from the highways into the hills and canyons around Sedona. Highlights include the 4.5 mi. **Wilson Mountain Loop,** ascending Wilson Mountain, and the 5.2 mi. round-trip **Huckaby Trail,** traversing fantastic red rocks. Biking offers similar wonders. Considered a rival to Moab, UT by those in the mountain-biking know, Sedona has some of the best tracks in the world. The **Soldier's Pass Secret Trails,** just north of town, are a playground for intense bikers. Tamer trails can be found along the **Bell Rock Pathway,** which lies south of town. Bike rentals (starting at $25 per day) and good trail information can be found at **Mountain Bike Heaven,** 1695 W U.S. 89A. They also lead occasional free bike trips (call for dates and times) and do repairs for any devilish spill. (☎282-1312. Open M-F 9am-6pm, Sa 8am-5pm, Su 9am-5pm.)

Scenic driving is nearly as plentiful as the red rocks. The Chamber of Commerce is very helpful in suggesting routes. The **Red Rock Loop** (20 mi., 1hr.) provides a little dirt road adventure and views of mind-blowing rock formations. Dry Creek and Airport Rd. are also good drives. For those hoping to see Sedona's wild off-road side, jeep tours are available from a number of companies. Generally, trips are $35-75 and 2-4hr. in length. **Sedona Adventures,** 276 N U.S. 89A (☎282-3500 or 800-888-9494), offers some of the least expensive trips in the area.

NAVAJO RESERVATION ☎520

Although anthropologists believe the Navajo descended from groups of Athabascan people who migrated to the Southwest from Northern Canada in the 14th and 15th centuries, the Navajo themselves view their existence as the culmination of a journey through three other worlds to this life, the "Glittering World." A respect for the land born out of the Navajo's beliefs still permeates the reservation.

During the second half of the 19th century, Indian reservations evolved out of the US government's *ad hoc* attempts to prevent fighting between Native Americans and Anglos while facilitating white settlement on native lands. Initially, the reservation system imposed a kind of wardship over the Native Americans, which lasted for over a century, until a series of Supreme Court decisions beginning in the 1960s reasserted the tribes' legal standing as semi-sovereign nations. Today, the **Navajo Nation** is the largest reservation in America and covers more than 27,000 sq. mi. of northeastern Arizona, southeastern Utah, and northwestern New Mexico. Home to over 250,000 Navajo, or Dineh (*dih-NEH,* "the People"), the reservation comprises one-tenth of the US Native American population. Within the Navajo borders, the smaller **Hopi Reservation** is home to around 10,000 Hopi ("Peaceable People").

For visitors to the reservation, cultural sensitivity takes on a new importance. Despite the many state and interstate roads that traverse the reservation, the land is legally and culturally distinct. Superficially, much of the Navajo Nation and other reservations resemble the rest of the US. In reality, deep rifts exist between Native American and "Anglo culture"—the term used to refer to the non-reservation US society. The Reservation has its own police force and laws. Possession and consumption of alcohol are prohibited on the reservation. General photography is allowed, unless otherwise stated, but photographing the Navajo people requires their permission (a gratuity is usually expected). Tourist photography is not permitted among the Hopi. As always, the best remedy for cultural friction is usually simple respect.

Lively reservation politics are written up in the local *Navajo-Hopi Observer* and *Navajo Times*. For a taste of the Navajo language and Native American ritual songs, tune your radio to 660AM, "The Voice of the Navajo." Remember to advance your watch 1hr. during the summer; the Navajo Nation runs on **Mountain Daylight Time**, while the rest of Arizona, including the Hopi reservation, remains on **Mountain Standard Time**. The **area code** for the Arizona portion of the reservation is 520.

Monument Valley, Canyon de Chelly, Navajo National Monument, Rainbow Bridge, Antelope Canyon, and the roads and trails that access these sights all lie on Navajo land. Driving or hiking off-road without a guide is considered trespassing. Those planning to hike through Navajo territory should head to the **Visitors Center** in Window Rock (see below) for a backcountry permit, or mail a request along with a money order or certified check to P.O. Box 9000, Window Rock, AZ 86515 ($5 per person). Fill up your gas tank before exploring the reservation; gas stations are few and far between. The "border towns" of Gallup, NM (see p. 776), Flagstaff, AZ (see p. 738), and Page, AZ (see p. 749) are good gateways to the reservations, with car rental agencies, inexpensive accommodations, and frequent Greyhound service on I-40. The only budget accommodation in the Navajo territory is the **Grey Hills Inn** (see p. 746) located in Tuba City. Budget travelers can also camp at the national monuments or Navajo campgrounds, or stay in a border town.

WINDOW ROCK ☎ 520

Unlike many historical presentations of Native Americans, **Window Rock** is a celebration of modern tribal life. The capital of the Navajo Nation and the epicenter of Reservation life, Window Rock is the seat of tribal government and home to most of the Reservation's infrastructure. For travelers, Window Rock, named after its unique geological formation, is a good starting place.

A terrific view of the eponymous rock itself can be had from **Window Rock Tribal Park,** off Rte. 12 just past the government offices. This graceful sandstone arch is sacred to the Navajo, making the surrounding area the choice for the establishment of a centralized Navajo administration in the 1930s. The **Navajo Tribal Museum,** on Rte. 264, ½ mi. east of Rte. 12, serves as a great introduction to the land and its people, with four rooms of Navajo and Navajo-related artwork and photography. (☎871-7941. Open M-Sa 8am-5pm. Free.) For those who want to observe the inner workings of the tribal government in the Navajo language, the **Navajo Nation Council Chambers** offers free tours of the governing body's meeting rooms. (☎871-6417. Open M-F 8am-noon and 1-5pm. Free.) The oldest continuously operated trading post in the US and national historic site, **Hubbell Trading Post,** 30 mi. west of Window Rock on Rte. 264 in the town of Ganado just past U.S. 191, has functioned as a store since 1876. Now part-museum, it still sells groceries and dry goods as well as Navajo arts and crafts. (☎755-3475. Open daily 8am-6pm; in winter 8am-5pm. Free.)

The limited lodging in town is expensive, but the Navajo-owned and run **Navajo Nation Inn,** 48 W Rte. 264, is an appealing option nonetheless, giving travelers a friendly welcome to the reservation. (☎871-4108 or 800-662-6189. Singles $62; doubles $67.) In the Inn, the **Navajo Nation Restaurant and Coffee Shop** serves up surprisingly affordable Navajo and American fare ($5-14) or a synthesis of the two, like the tasty Navajo burger. (☎871-4101. Open daily 6:30am-9pm.)

SOUTHWEST

The **Navajoland Tourism Department**, P.O. Box 1840, Window Rock 86515, is located about ¼ mi. east of the Rte. 264/Rte. 12 intersection, in the same building as the tribal museum. The **Visitors Center** here offers the helpful, free brochure *Discover Navajo*, which includes details on sights, accommodations, and outdoor resources in the Reservation. The center also sells a map ($3) entitled *The Visitors' Guide to the Navajo Nation*. (☎871-7941. Open M 8am-5pm, Tu-F 8am-8pm, Sa 8am-6pm.) For outdoor info, backcountry and camping permits, and guide contact info, write the **Parks and Recreation Department**, Box 9000, Window Rock 86515. (☎871-6636 or 871-6647. Open M-F 9am-5pm.) The **Post Office** is just north of the Navajo Nation Inn. (☎871-5207. Open M-F 8:30am-5:30pm, Sa 9am-12:30pm.) **ZIP Code:** 86515.

CANYON DE CHELLY NATIONAL MONUMENT   ☎520

The red hue of the cliffs of Canyon de Chelly (pronounced "*Canyon de Shay*") and the adjoining canyons in the national monument have enchanted settlers for over four millennia, giving the area a history far greater than anywhere else in the four-corners region. However, the canyon's history has been colored by repeated conflicts between Native Americans and Anglos. In 1805, in what is now called **Massacre Cave**, 115 Native American women and children were shot by Spanish men. Later in the 1860s, the famed Kit Carson starved the Navajo out of the canyon.

Although Canyon de Chelly National Monument is administered by the National Park Service, the land continues to belong to the Navajo people. To the Navajo, it is the nature of *Tsegi* (*say-he*), the spirit of their home, that brings new life to this region. So vital is the canyon to the local Native American culture that the Navajo Nation was purposely created with Canyon de Chelly at its center.

⁊ PRACTICAL INFORMATION. The most common route to the park is from **Chambers**, 75 mi. south, at the intersection of I-40 and U.S. 191; you can also come from the north via U.S. 191. Entrance to the monument is free. The **Visitors Center** sits 2 mi. east of Chinle on Navajo Rte. 7. (☎674-5500. Open daily 8am-6pm; Oct.-Apr. 8am-5pm.) One of the larger towns on the reservation, **Chinle**, adjacent to U.S. 191, has restaurants and gas stations. There is no public transportation to the park. In an **emergency**, contact the park ranger (☎674-5500, after hours 674-5524).

Camp for free in the park's **Cottonwood Campground**, 1½ mi. from the Visitors Center. This giant campground is located in a lovely cottonwood grove and enjoys gentle breezes at night. (☎674-5500. Restrooms, picnic tables, water except in winter, and dump station. 5-night max. stay. First come, first served.) The **Many Farms Inn**, 16 mi. north of Chinle and ¼ mi. north of the intersection of Navajo Rte. 59 and U.S. 191, serves as a stopover from Canyon de Chelly to Monument Valley or Navajo National Monument. Housed in the local high school, the rooms are a bit institutional with shared bathrooms, but a better deal can't be had in Navajo Nation. (☎781-6362. Open daily June-Aug.; Sept.-May weekdays only. Reception 7am-10pm. Check-out noon. Doubles $30.) **Farmington, NM**, and **Cortez, CO**, are the closest major cities with multiple cheap lodging options.

⚟ OUTDOOR ACTIVITIES. Visitors are only allowed to enter the canyon via the White House Ruin Trail. A 3 mi. round-trip hike, the trail descends into the belly of the Canyon, from a South Rim overlook. Winding its way down 600 ft., the trail passes a Navajo farm and traditional hogan and cliff dwelling ruins. To explore beyond the White House Ruin trail, a private guide must be hired. Reservations can be made through the Visitors Center, but are not required. Two hikes led by Navajo guides enter the canyon. (4 mi. round-trip, 4hr. June-Aug. daily 9am and 1pm. $10 per person.) Guides for hikes and vehicle tours of the canyon can be hired privately through Tsegi Guide Association. (3hr., $15 per hr. You provide the four-wheel-drive vehicle; free permits at Visitors Center.) Horseback tours can be arranged at Justin's Horse Rental, on South Rim Dr., at the canyon's mouth. (☎674-5678. Open daily 9am-sundown. Horses $10 per hr.; mandatory guide $15 per hr.)

You can also take one of the paved **Rim Drives** (North Rim 34 mi. round-trip, South Rim 37 mi. round-trip) skirting the edge of the 300-700 ft. cliffs; the South Rim is more dramatic. Get booklets (50¢) on the White House Ruin and Rim Drives at the Visitors Center. On the North Rim Drive, the large dwellings in **Mummy Cave Ruin** are impressive. Nearby is the somber **Massacre Cave. Spider Rock Overlook,** 16 mi. from the Visitors Center, on the South Rim Drive, is a narrow sandstone monolith towering hundreds of feet above the canyon floor. Native American lore says that the whitish rock at the top contains the bones of victims of the *kachina* spirit, or Spider Woman, who has a taste for disobedient children.

MONUMENT VALLEY   ☎ 435

The red sandstone towers of Monument Valley are one of the southwest's most otherworldly sights. Paradoxically, they're also one of the most familiar, since countless Westerns have used the butte-laden plain as their backdrop. Long before the days of John Wayne, Ancestral Puebloans managed to sustain small communities here, despite the hot, arid climate. The park's looping 17 mi. **Valley Drive** winds around 11 of the most spectacular formations, including the famous pair of **Mittens** and the slender **Totem Pole.** However, the gaping ditches, large rocks, and mudholes on this road can be jarring to both you and your car—drive at your own risk and observe the 15 mph speed limit. The drive takes at least 1½hr. Other, less-touristed parts of the valley can be reached only by four-wheel-drive vehicle, horse, or foot. *Leaving the main road without a guide is not permitted.* The Visitors Center parking lot is crowded with booths selling jeep, horseback, and hiking tours. (1½hr. jeep tour about $25 per person, full-day $100; horseback tours $30/$120.) In winter, snow laces the rocky towers. Call the Visitors Center for snow and road conditions.

The park entrance lies on U.S. 163 just across the Utah border, 24 mi. north of **Kayenta,** which is at the intersection of U.S. 163 and U.S. 160. The **Visitors Center** has info. (☎ 727-3353. Park and Visitors Center open May-Sept. $3, under 7 free.) There are few accommodations in the area. **Mitten View Campground,** ¼ mi. southwest of the Visitors Center, has showers, but no hookups. (Sites $10; in winter $5. Register at the Visitors Center.) Cheap motels are in **Mexican Hat, UT** and **Bluff, UT.**

NAVAJO NATIONAL MONUMENT   ☎ 520

Until the late 1200s, a small population of the ancestors of the modern Hopi inhabited the region, though hard times left the villages vacant by 1300. Today, the site contains three cliff dwellings. **Inscription House** has been closed to visitors since the 1960s due to its fragile condition; the other two admit a very limited number of visitors. The stunning **Keet Seel** (open late May to early Sept.) can be reached only via a challenging 17 mi. round-trip hike. Hikers can stay overnight in a free campground nearby (no facilities or drinking water). Reservations for permits to visit Keet Seel must be made up to two months in advance through the **Visitors Center.** Ranger-led tours to **Betatakin,** a 135-room complex, are limited to 25 people. (Open May to late Sept. 1 per day at 8:15am; first come, first served the morning of the tour.) If you're not up for the trek to the ruins, the paved, 1 mi. round-trip **Sandal Trail** lets you gaze down on Betatakin from the top of the canyon. The **Aspen Forest Overlook Trail,** another 1 mi. hike, overlooks canyons and aspens, but no ruins. To get to the monument, take Rte. 564 from U.S. 160, 20 mi. southwest of Kayent. The Visitors Center lies 9 mi. along this road. (☎ 672-2700. Open daily 8am-5pm.) The free **campground,** next to the Visitors Center, has 30 sites.

HOPI RESERVATION   ☎ 520

Like an island of coal-rich ore amid a sea of Navajo Nation grassland, Black Mesa and its three constitutive spurs, First Mesa, Second Mesa, and Third Mesa, have harbored the Hopi people and its traditions for over a millennium. The villages on **First Mesa** are the only places in the reservation really geared toward visitors. The **Ponsi Hall Community Center** serves as a general info center and a starting point for guided tours. (☎ 737-2262. Open June-Aug. daily 9am-6pm; Sept.-May 9:30am-5pm. Tours $5.) The villages on the **Second** and **Third Mesas** are less developed for tourism. However, on Second Mesa, the **Hopi Cultural Center,** 5 mi. west of the intersection of Rte. 264 and 87, serves as a Visitors Center and contains the reservation's only museum, displaying Hopi baskets, jewelry, pottery, and info about the tribe's history. (☎ 734-6650. Open M-F 8am-5pm, Sa-Su 9am-3pm. $3, under 14 $1.) **Free camping** is allowed at ten primitive sites next to the Cultural Center.

Visitors are welcome to attend a few Hopi **village dances** throughout the year. Often announced only a few days in advance, these religious ceremonies usually occur on weekends and last from sunrise to sundown. The dances are formal occasions; do not wear shorts, tank tops, or other casual wear. Photos, recordings, and sketches are strictly forbidden. Often several villages will hold dances on the same day, giving tourists the opportunity to village-hop. The **Harvest Dance**, in mid-September at the Second Mesa Village, is a spectacular ceremony with tribes from all over the US. Inquire at the cultural center, or the **Hopi Cultural Preservation Office** (☎ 734-2214), Box 123, Kykotsmovi 86039, for the dates and sites of all dances.

PETRIFIED FOREST NATIONAL PARK ☎ 520

Spreading over 60,000 acres, the Petrified Forest National Park looks like the aftermath of some prehistoric Grateful Dead concert—an enormous tie-dye littered with rainbow-colored trees. Some 225 million years ago, when Arizona's desert was a swampland, volcanic ash covered the logs, slowing their decay. When silica-rich water seeped through the wood, the silica crystallized into quartz, producing rainbow hues. Layers of colorful sediment were also laid down in this floodplain, creating the stunning colors that stripe its rock formations.

■■ **ORIENTATION AND PRACTICAL INFORMATION.** Roughly speaking, the park can be divided into two parts: the northern Painted Desert and the southern Petrified Forest. An entrance station and Visitors Center welcomes guests at each end and a 28 mi. road connects the two sections. With lookout points and trails strategically located along the road, driving from one end of the park to the other is a good way to take in the full spectrum of colors and landscapes.

You can enter the park either from the north or the south. (Open June-Aug. daily 7am-7pm; Sept.-May 8am-5pm. Entrance fee $10 per vehicle, $5 per pedestrian.) There is no public transportation to either part of the park. To access the southern section of the park, take U.S. 180 from St. Johns 36 mi. west or from Holbrook 19 mi. east. The **Rainbow Forest Museum** provides a look at petrified logs up close and serves as a **Visitors Center.** (☎ 524-6822. Open June-Aug. daily 8am-7pm; Sept.-May 8am-5pm. Free.) To reach the northern Painted Desert section of the park, take I-40 to Exit 311, 107 mi. east of Flagstaff and 65 mi. west of Gallup, NM. The **Painted Desert Visitors Center** is less than 1 mi. from the exit. (☎ 524-6228. Open June-Aug. daily 7am-7pm; Sept.-May 8am-5pm.) **Water** is available at both the Visitors Centers and the Painted Desert Inn. There's **gas** at the Painted Desert Visitors Center. In case of **emergency,** call the ranger dispatch (☎ 524-9726).

There are no established campgrounds in the park, but **backcountry camping** is allowed in the fantastical Painted Desert Wilderness with a free permit. Backpackers must park their cars at Kachina Point and enter the wilderness via the 1 mi. access trail. No fires are allowed. Budget accommodations and roadside diners abound on Rte. 66. To get a real taste of the road, stay at the **Wigwam Motel,** 811 W. Hopi Dr., where 19 concrete tepees await travelers. (☎ 524-3048. Reception 3-9pm. Check-out 11am. Reservations recommended. Singles $35; doubles $41.) **Gallup** and **Flagstaff** offer more lodging and eating options.

◪ **SIGHTS.** Most travelers opt to drive the 27 mi. park road from north to south. From the north, the first stop is **Tiponi Point.** From the next stop at **Tawa Point,** the **Painted Desert Rim Trail** (½ mi. one-way) skirts the mesa edge above the Lithodendron Wash and the Black Forest before ending at **Kachina Point.** The panoramas from Kachina Point are among the best in the park, and the point provides access for travel into the **Painted Desert Wilderness,** the park's designated region for backcountry hiking and camping. As the road crosses I-40, it enters the Petrified Forest portion of the park. The next stop is the 100-room

Puerco Pueblo. A short trail through the pueblo offers viewpoints of nearby petroglyphs. Many more petroglyphs may be seen at **Newspaper Rock,** but from more of a distance. The road then wanders through the eerie moonscape of **The Tepees,** before arriving at the 3 mi. **Blue Mesa** vehicle loop. The moderate **Blue Mesa Trail** (1 mi.) loops through the belly of the badlands and offers a respite from the crowds. The **Long Logs** and **Giant Logs Trails,** near the southern Visitors Center, are peppered with fragments of petrified wood. Both trails are less than 1 mi. and involve little elevation change but travel through the densest concentration of petrified wood in the world. Picking up fragments of the wood is illegal and traditionally unlucky.

LAKE POWELL AND PAGE ☎928

"Dammit!" said President Eisenhower in 1956, pressing a large red button on his desk. Many hundreds of miles away, a massive explosion shook the earth. Thus began a tremendous effort to provide water and energy to expanding desert communities. Ten years and ten million tons of concrete later, Glen Canyon Dam, the second-largest dam in the country, was completed. Stopped in its tracks in northern Arizona, the Colorado River backed-up into the once remote Glen Canyon. Today, houseboaters, fishermen, and jet-skiers have easy access to the remote slot canyons of the area. Unfortunately, the canyons now rest under hundreds of feet of water. Lake Powell, the pelagic expanse formed by the dam, has 1960 ft. of shoreline, equivalent in length to the entire Pacific coast from Washington to California. Darting around the lake on a personal watercraft or swimming in a narrow canyon, it's hard to imagine what the area looked like when John Welsey Powell led his crew down the Colorado in 1869. Page, a tourist town existing entirely to cater to visitors, lies just southeast of the dam and features a motley mix of merchants, all competing fiercely for the summertime dollar.

◪ **PRACTICAL INFORMATION. Visitor info:** The **Carl Hayden Visitors Center,** 2 mi. north of Page on U.S. 89N, offers a wealth of Lake Powell and Glen Canyon Dam info. (☎608-6404. Open May-Sept. daily 8am-7pm; Oct.-Apr. 8am-5pm.) The **Page Chamber of Commerce,** 644 N. Navajo Dr., in the Dam Plaza, carries info on local services and rentals for watersports. (☎645-2741. Open summer daily 8am-7pm; in winter M-F 9am-5pm.) **Post Office:** 44 6th Ave. (☎645-2571; open M-F 8:30am-5pm, Sa 1-4pm). **ZIP Code:** 86040. **Area code:** 928.

◪◲ **ACCOMMODATIONS AND FOOD.** Although the main drag through Page grows increasingly populated with high-end chain hotels, a few gems of an earlier, more affordable era remain. A cluster of quality budget accommodations resides on 8th Ave. between S. Navajo and Elm St. **K.C.'s Motel,** 126 8th Ave., offers spacious recently renovated, former apartment suites with cable TV for room prices. (☎645-2947; www.kcmotel.com. Online reservations accepted. Rooms start at $39.) **Bashful Bob's Motel,** 750 S. Navajo Dr., isn't embarrassed about its huge rooms with kitchens, sitting areas, cable TV, and Internet access. (☎645-3919. Singles and doubles from $39, each additional person $5; reduced winter rates.) **Red Rocks Inn,** 114 8th Ave., offers immense rooms at bargain prices. (☎845-0062. Singles and doubles $39-59; winter rates lower.) **Wahweap Campground,** 100 Lake Shore Dr., is adjacent to the exorbitant Wahweap Lodge. (☎645-1059. Sites $15; hookups $27 at campground and neighboring **Wahweap RV Park.** First come, first served.) Visitors with boats can camp nearly anywhere along the endless lakeshore, so long as they have a portable toilet. The lake's marinas rent them. Don't get caught without one—the rangers are vigilant, and besides, no one wants to swim in your sewage.

Along with the overabundance of steak and potatoes in the area come two important bonuses: hearty "cowboy appetite" portions and bargain "ranchhand" prices. The **Ranch House Grill,** 819 N. Navajo Dr., delivers gigantic portions. (☎645-1420. Open daily 5am-3pm. Breakfast served all day.) **The Sandwich Place,** 662 Elm St., in Page Plaza, offers "fast food fit for grownups" and some stellar onion rings. (☎645-5267. Open M-F 7:30am-8:30pm, Sa 10:30-4pm.) **Dos Amigos,** 608D Elm St., also in Page Plaza, prepares delectable Mexican fare. (☎645-3036. Open M-Sa 11am-10pm, Su noon-10pm. Lunch specials $5-6, a la carte tacos from $2.50.)

◨▨ **SIGHTS AND OUTDOORS.** Jaded with the thrills of cigarette boats and jet skis, many visitors to Lake Powell seek out slightly more sedate, but equally enthralling ways to spend a day. Both the **Rainbow Bridge National Monument** and **Antelope Canyon** draw countless visitors who revel in awe at the artistry of water at work on sandstone canvas. The damming of Lake Powell created easy access to Rainbow Bridge, an originally remote wonder of the natural world. Despite its current tourist-attraction status, the arch remains sacred to area native cultures. Out of respect, visitors are asked not to approach, climb on, or pass through this breathtaking lesson in erosional art. Hiking to Rainbow Bridge on Navajo land requires a **hiking permit,** obtainable by writing Navajo Nation Parks and Recreation Department, Box 9000, Window Rock 86515. Most visitors, however, come by boat. A courtesy dock floats about ½ mi. from the bridge, and is reachable after 4hr. ride from either the Wahweap, Halls Crossing, or Bullfrog Marinas. Only the park concessionaire, **ARAMARK,** has permission to offer tours. (☎800-528-6154. 7hr. full-day tours with lunch $114, children $74; 5hr. half-day tours $86\$58.)

Over the course of millions of years, raging torrents and swirling eddies have lifted particles of sand from the base and walls of Antelope Canyon. This ceaseless erosion has sculpted a canyon of exceptional variety and beauty. For ages, Native Americans have approached this canyon, called *Tse bighanilini* ("the place where water runs through rocks") in Navajo, with profound respect and spiritual reverence. Antelope Canyon is divided by Rte. 98 into two parts: upper and lower. **Upper Antelope,** the most frequently visited, is most accessible and arguably the easier to appreciate. Descending **Lower Antelope** requires climbing ladders and slipping through extremely narrow gaps. ($5 Navajo use fee; shuttle to upper canyon or guide services in lower canyon $12.50.)

For a truly low-key and highly informational afternoon, visit the **John Wesley Powell Museum,** 6 N. Lake Powell Blvd. (☎645-9496. Open in summer M-Sa 8:30am-5:30pm.) The **Carl Hayden Visitors Center,** adjacent to the dam on U.S. 89, guides visitors into the bowels of the concrete behemoth. (☎608-6404. Tours in summer every 30min. 8:30am-4:30pm; off-season every hr. Visitors Center open May-Sept. daily 8am-7pm; off-season 8am-5pm.)

Recreation opportunities abound at **Wahweep Marina,** where you can swim, rent a boat or take a boat tour. (☎528-6154, ext. 8109. Reservations recommended.) If you want to see the canyon downstream of the dam, take a day-long float trip offered by **Wilderness River Adventures.** (☎800-528-6154. Half-day $59, full-day, $79.)

PHOENIX   ☎602

The name Phoenix was chosen for a small farming community in the Sonoran desert by Anglo settlers who believed that their oasis had risen from the ashes of ancient Native American settlements like the legendary phoenix of Greek mythology. The 20th century has seen this unlikely metropolis live up to its name; the expansion of water resources, the proliferation of railroad transportation, and the introduction of air-conditioning have fueled Phoenix's ascent to its standing among America's leading cities. Shiny high-rises now crowd the business district, while a vast web of six-lane highways and strip malls surrounds the downtown area. Phoenix's rise has not been without turmoil, though: its greatest asset, the sun, is also its greatest nemesis. The scorching heat and arid landscape hinders expansion. For the traveler, the Phoenix sun can also be both friend and foe. During the balmy winter months, tourists, golfers, and business travelers flock to the resort-perfect temperatures. In the summer, the city crawls into its air-conditioned shell as temperatures climb to an average of 100°F and lodging prices plummet.

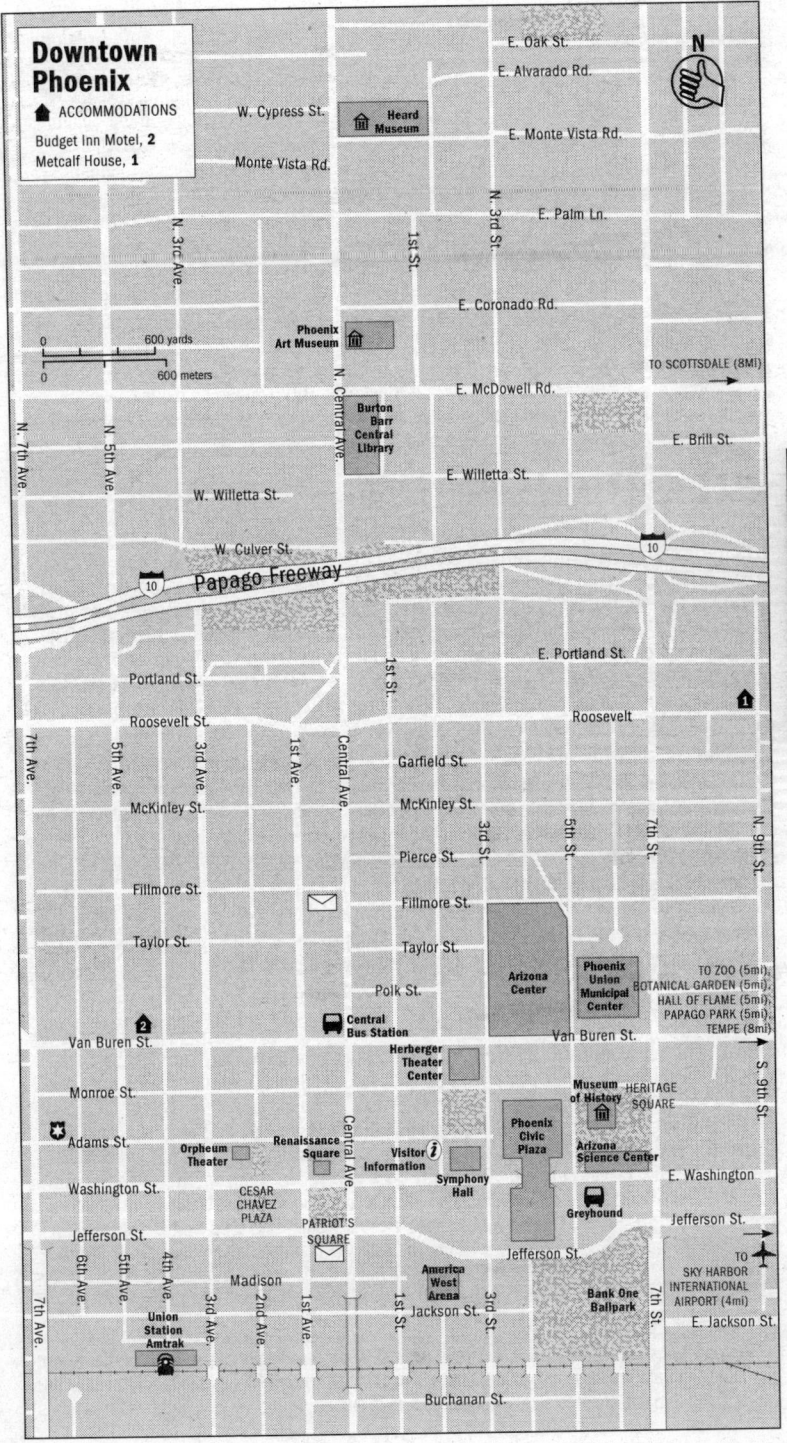

Downtown Phoenix

ACCOMMODATIONS

Budget Inn Motel, 2
Metcalf House, 1

TO SCOTTSDALE (8MI)

E. Oak St.
E. Alvarado Rd.
W. Cypress St.
Heard Museum
E. Monte Vista Rd.
Monte Vista Rd.
N. 3rd St.
E. Palm Ln.
N. 3rd Ave.
1st St.
E. Coronado Rd.
Phoenix Art Museum
N. Central Ave.
E. McDowell Rd.
Burton Barr Central Library
E. Brill St.
N. 7th Ave.
N. 5th Ave.
W. Willetta St.
E. Willetta St.
W. Culver St.
Papago Freeway
10
10

600 yards
600 meters

E. Portland St.
Portland St.
Roosevelt St.
Roosevelt
1
7th Ave.
5th Ave.
3rd Ave.
1st St.
Central Ave.
Garfield St.
McKinley St.
McKinley St.
3rd St.
5th St.
7th St.
N. 9th St.
Pierce St.
Fillmore St.
Fillmore St.
Taylor St.
Taylor St.
Polk St.
Arizona Center
Phoenix Union Municipal Center
TO ZOO (5mi), BOTANICAL GARDEN (5mi), HALL OF FLAME (5mi), PAPAGO PARK (5mi), TEMPE (8mi)
Van Buren St.
Central Bus Station
Herberger Theater Center
Van Buren St.
S. 9th St.
Monroe St.
Museum of History
HERITAGE SQUARE
Adams St.
Orpheum Theater
Renaissance Square
Visitor Information
Phoenix Civic Plaza
Arizona Science Center
E. Washington
Washington St.
CESAR CHAVEZ PLAZA
Symphony Hall
Jefferson St.
6th Ave.
5th Ave.
4th Ave.
3rd Ave.
2nd Ave.
1st Ave.
Central Ave.
PATRIOT'S SQUARE
Greyhound
Jefferson St.
Madison
America West Arena
3rd St.
Bank One Ballpark
7th St.
TO SKY HARBOR INTERNATIONAL AIRPORT (4mi)
Jackson St.
E. Jackson St.
7th Ave.
Union Station Amtrak
Buchanan St.

SOUTHWEST

⌐ TRANSPORTATION

Flights: Sky Harbor International (☎273-3300), just southeast of downtown. Take the Valley Metro Red Line bus into the city (5:45am-10pm, $1.25). The largest city in the Southwest, Phoenix is a major airline hub, and tends to be an affordable and convenient destination.

Buses: Greyhound, 2115 E. Buckeye Rd. (☎389-4200). To: El Paso (8hr., 13 per day, $35); Los Angeles (7hr., 12 per day, $33); San Diego (8hr.; 6 per day; M-Th $46, F-Su $49); Tucson (2hr., 13 per day, $14). Open 24hr. **Amtrak,** 401 W. Harrison (☎253-0121), operates connector buses to and from rail stations in Tucson and Flagstaff for those interested in train travel.

Public Transit: Valley Metro (☎253-5000). Most lines run to and from Central Station, at Central and Van Buren St. Routes tend to operate M-F 5am-8pm with reduced service on Sa. Fare $1.25; disabled, seniors, and children 60¢. All-day pass $3.60, 10-ride pass $12. Bus passes and system maps at the Terminal.

Taxis: Ace Taxi, ☎254-1999.

Car Rental: Enterprise Rent-a-car, 1402 N. Central St. (☎257-4177). Compact cars $50 per day, with lower weekly and monthly rates. No surcharge for drivers over 21. Credit card and driver's license required. N. Central St. office open M-F 7:30am-6pm, Sa 9am-midnight.

✳❼ ORIENTATION AND PRACTICAL INFORMATION

The intersection of **Central Ave.** and **Washington St.** marks the heart of downtown. Central Ave. runs north-south, Washington St. east-west. One of Phoenix's peculiarities is that numbered avenues and streets both run north-south; avenues are numbered sequentially west from Central, while streets are numbered east. Greater Phoenix includes a number of smaller municipalities. **Tempe,** east of Phoenix, is dominated by students from the Arizona State University. **Mesa,** east of Tempe, handles much of Tempe's overflow. **Scottsdale,** north of Tempe, is a swank district brimming with adobe palaces, shopping centers, and interesting sights.

Visitor info: Phoenix and Valley of the Sun Convention and Visitors Center (☎254-6500, recorded info 252-5588). Downtown: 2nd and Adams St. Open M-F 8am-5pm. Biltmore Fashion Park: 24th St. and East Camelback. Open daily 8am-5pm. Outdoors info available at the **Bureau of Land Management Office,** 222 N. Central (☎417-9200).

Hotlines: Crisis Hotline (☎254-4357). 24hr. **Gay Hotline** (☎234-2752). Daily 10am-10pm.

Internet access: Burton Barr Central Library, 1221 N. Central Ave. (☎262-4636). Open M-Th 9am-9pm, F-Sa 9am-6pm, Su 1-5pm. Sign-up required, but computers usually available.

Post Office: 1441 E. Buckeye Rd. (☎407-2051). Open M-F 7:30am-5pm. **ZIP code:** 85026. **Area codes:** 602, 623, 480. In text, 602 unless otherwise noted.

☗ ACCOMMODATIONS

Budget travelers should consider visiting Phoenix during July and August when motels slash their prices by as much as 70%. In the winter, when temperatures drop and vacancies are few, prices go up; make reservations if possible. The reservationless should cruise the rows of motels on **Van Buren St.** east of downtown, toward the airport. Parts of this area can be unsafe; *guests should examine a motel thoroughly before checking in.* Although they are more distant, the areas around Papago Fwy. and Black Canyon Hwy. are loaded with motels and may present some safer options. **Mi Casa Su Casa/Old Pueblo Homestays Bed and Breakfast,** P.O. Box 950, Tempe 85280, arranges stays in B&Bs throughout Arizona, New Mexico, southern Utah, southern Nevada, and southern California. (☎800-456-0682. Open M-F 9am-5pm, Sa 9am-noon. Singles $40-70; doubles from $60. Make winter reservations a month in advance.)

Metcalf House (HI-AYH), 1026 N. 9th St. (☎254-9803), a few blocks northeast of downtown. From Central Station, take bus #10 down 7th St. to Roosevelt St., walk 2 blocks east to 9th St., and turn left—the hostel is a half block north in a shady and quiet residential area. Last bus leaves at 7:15pm. The owner, who gushes helpful advice about the area, fosters a lively community in this decorative house. Dorm-style rooms with wooden bunks adjoin a kitchen and common room. Check-in 7-10am and 5-10pm. Chores required. $12, nonmembers $15.

Budget Inn Motel, 424 W. Van Buren St. (☎257-8331), near the junction of 4th Ave. and Van Buren. A safe and comfortable family-run motel with standard amenities. Downtown location with newly remodeled rooms. Singles May-Aug. $40, Sept.-Apr. $49; doubles $45/$59.

Phoenix Destiny RV Resorts (☎623-853-0537), 11 mi. west of Phoenix on Citrus Rd. Take I-10 to Exit 124; head ¾ mi. south to Van Buren St., then go 1 mi. west to Citrus Rd. An RV paradise with shuffleboard and a fitness center. 284 RV sites, pool, laundromat and jacuzzi. Hookups $30-36, depending on location. Sites (only 6 sites) May-Sept. $20, Oct.-Apr. $23.

◖ FOOD

While much of the Phoenix food scene seems to revolve around shopping mall food courts and expensive touristy restaurants, rest assured that hidden jewels can be found. Downtowners feed themselves mainly at small coffeehouses, most of which close on weekends. **McDowell** or **Camelback Rd.** offer a (small) variety of Asian restaurants. The **Arizona Center,** an open-air shopping gallery at 3rd St. and Van Buren, boasts food venues, fountains, and palm trees. Sports bars and grilles hover around the America West Arena and Bank One Ballpark. Tempe (along Mill Ave.) brims with college-friendly restaurants and more moderately priced menus. The *New Times* gives extensive restaurant recommendations (☎271-4000).

Los Dos Molinos, 8646 S. Central Ave. (☎243-9113). From downtown, head south on Central Ave. Go very far, and once you're sure you've gone too far, go farther. One look and you'll know why you've made the trip; Los Dos Molinos is lively, colorful, and fun. Live music at lunch and dinner, a huge menu, and lemonade in jelly jars. Locals throng here on weekends. Make sure to come early; they don't take reservations. Enchiladas $3, burritos $4-7. Open Tu-F 11am-3pm and 5-9pm, Sa 11am-9pm.

5 & Diner, 5220 N. 16th St. (☎264-5220). 24hr. service and all the sock-hop music that one can stand. Vinyl booths, smiley service, and innumerable juke boxes teach you how the fifties *might* have been. Burgers go for $6-7 and sandwiches are $5-7. You can get the best milkshakes in town for only $3. Afternoon blue plate specials (M-F 11am-4pm, $4-6) change daily, but you always get your money's worth.

Gourmet House of Hong Kong, 1438 E. McDowell Rd. (☎253-4859). For those who think that quality Chinese food vanishes between the Mississippi and the West Coast, this no-frills restaurant will surely impress. They serve so many dishes the menu comes with a table of contents. No non-smoking section. Entrees $5-7. Lunch specials $3-5. Open Su-Th 11am-9:30pm, F-Sa 11am-10:30pm.

La Tolteca, 1205 E. Van Buren St. (☎253-1511). A local favorite, this unassuming cafeteria-style restaurant/Mexican grocery serves up uncommercialized Mexican fare in *grande* portions. Big burritos $3-4, dinner plates $5-6. Open daily 6:30am-9pm.

◉ SIGHTS

DOWNTOWN. Downtown Phoenix offers a few museums and mounting evidence of America's growing consumer culture. The price of most downtown attractions hovers around $7; fortunately, the majority are worth it. The **Heard Museum** is renowned for its presentation of ancient Native American art, and also features exhibits focusing on contemporary Native Americans. *(2301 N. Central Ave., 4 blocks north of McDowell Rd. ☎252-8840; recorded info 252-8848. Open daily 9:30am-5pm. Free tours at 10am, noon, 1:30, and 3pm. $7, seniors $6, ages 4-12 $3. Natvie Americans (with status card) free.)* Three blocks south, the **Phoenix Art Museum** exhibits art of the American West, including paintings from the Taos and Santa Fe art colonies. There are also impressive collections of 19th-century European and American works. *(1625 N. Central Ave. at McDowell Rd. ☎257-1222. Open Tu-Su 10am-5pm, Th 10am-9pm; closed M. $7, students and seniors $5, ages 6-18 $2; free on Th.)* The **Arizona Science Center** offers interactive science exhibits along with an IMAX theater and a planetarium. *(600 E. Washington St. ☎716-2000. Open daily 10am-5pm. $8, seniors and ages 4-12 $6. IMAX or planetarium ticket $3 extra.)*

PAPAGO PARK AND FARTHER EAST. The **Desert Botanical Garden,** in Papago Park, 5 mi. east of downtown, grows a colorful collection of cacti and other desert plants. *(1201 N. Galvin Pkwy. ☎941-1217, recorded info 481-8134. Open daily May-Sept. 7am-8pm; Oct.-Apr. 8am-8pm. $7.50, students $4, seniors $6.50, ages 5-12 $1.50.)* Take bus #3 east to **Papago Park,** on the eastern outskirts of the city. The park has spectacular views of the desert along its hiking, biking, and driving trails. If you spot an orangutan strolling around the cacti, it's either a mirage or you're in the **Phoenix Zoo,** located within the park and boasting a formidable collection of South American, African, and Southwestern critters. *(455 N. Galvin Pkwy. ☎273-1341. Open daily mid-Sept. to May 9am-5pm; June-July 7am-noon and 6-9pm; Aug. 6-9pm. $8.50, seniors $7.50, ages 3-5 $1.50.)* The **Hall of Flame Museum of Firefighting,** just outside the southern exit of Papago Park, features antique fire engines and other fire-fighting equipment. *(6101 E. Van Buren St. ☎275-3473. Open M-Sa 9am-5pm, Su noon-4pm. $5, ages 6-17 $3, ages 3-5 $1.50.)* Still farther east of the city, in Mesa, the **Salt River** is one of the last remaining desert rivers in the US. **Salt River Recreation** arranges tubing trips, even for ice-chests. *(☎984-3305. Open daily May-Sept. 9am-4pm. Tube rental $9.)*

SCOTTSDALE SIGHTS. **Taliesin West** was originally built as the winter camp of Frank Lloyd Wright's Taliesin architectural collective; in his later years he lived there full-time. Now it serves as a campus for an architectural college run by his foundation. *(Corner of Frank Lloyd Wright Blvd. and Cactus St. ☎860-8810 or 860-2700. Open Sept.-June daily 9am-4pm; July-Aug. Th-M 9am-4pm. 1hr. or 1½hr. guided tours required. $10-14, students and seniors $8-12, ages 4-12 $3-8.)* Wright also designed the **Arizona Biltmore** hotel. *(24th St. and Missouri. ☎955-6600.)* One of the last buildings designed by Wright, the **Gammage Memorial Auditorium** wears the pink-and-beige earth tones of the surrounding environment. *(Mill Ave. and Apache Blvd., on the Arizona State University campus in Tempe. Take bus #60, or #22 on weekends. ☎965-3434. 20min. tours daily in winter.)* One of Wright's students liked Scottsdale so much he decided to stay. **Cosanti** is a working studio and bell foundry designed by the architect and sculptor Paolo Soleri. The buildings here fuse with the natural landscape even more strikingly than those at Taliesin West. *(6433 Doubletree Rd. in Scottsdale. With I-10 behind you turn right off of Scottsdale Rd.; it will be on your right in about 5 blocks. ☎480-948-6145. Open M-Sa 9am-5pm, Su 11am-5pm, $1 donation suggested.)*

🎭🎟 NIGHTLIFE AND ENTERTAINMENT

The free *New Times Weekly,* available on local magazine racks, lists club schedules for Phoenix's after-hours scene. The *Cultural Calendar of Events* covers area entertainment in three-month intervals. *The Western Front,* found in bars and clubs, covers gay and lesbian nightlife.

Char's Has the Blues, 4631 N. 7th Ave., houses local jazz acts. On Friday night, come early for the BBQ. *(☎230-0205. For shows, doors open 7pm. Cover F-Sa $7. Hours vary.)* **Phoenix Live,** 455 N. 3rd St. *(☎252-2502),* at the Arizona Center, houses three bars and a restaurant. **America's Original Sports Bar** is the largest of the three, with a DJ spinning Top-40. The dance floor at **Decades,** a retro club playing 60s-80s hits, is much larger and busier. For those who don't feel like sweating to the oldies, **Ltl Ditty's** features dueling baby grand pianos in a lounge atmosphere. *($5 weekend cover buys access to it all. Open Su-Th 4pm-midnight, F-Sa 4pm-1am.)* **The Willow House,** 149 W. McDowell Rd., is a self-proclaimed "artist's cove," combining chic coffee house, New York deli, and quirky musicians' hangout. *(☎252-0272. No alcohol. Coffee happy hour (2-for-1) M-F 4-7pm. Live music Sa starting at 8pm. Open M-Th 7am-midnight, F 7am-1am, Sa 8am-1am, Su 8am-midnight.)* A large country-western lesbian bar, **Ain't Nobody's Biz,** 3031 E. Indian School Rd. #7, has more space devoted to pool tables than to the dance floor. (☎224-9977. No regular cover, but occasionally hosts guest vocalists and charges. Open M-F 4pm-1am, Sa-Su 2pm-1am.) **Roscoe's,** 4531 N. 7th St., is a gay sports pub with pool and dart tournaments. (☎285-0833. 2-for-1 happy hour M-Sa 3-7pm, Su $1 longneck domestic beers. Open M-Sa 3pm-1am, Su 11am-1am.)

Phoenix offers many options for the sports lover. NBA basketball action rises with the **Phoenix Suns** (☎379-7867) at the **America West Arena,** while the **Arizona Cardinals** (☎379-0101) provide American football excitement. The **Arizona Diamondbacks** (☎514-8400) play at the state-of-the-art **Bank One Ballpark,** complete with a retractable roof, an outfield swimming pool, and "beer gardens." (☎462-6799. Tickets start at $6. Special $1 tickets available 2hr. before games, first come, first served. Tours of the stadium offered throughout the year; proceeds benefit local charities.)

SCENIC DRIVE: APACHE TRAIL

Steep, gray, and haunting, the **Superstition Mountains** derive their name from Pima Native American legends. Although the Native Americans were kicked out by the Anglo gold prospectors who settled the region, the curse stayed. In the 1840s, a Mexican explorer found gold in these hills, but was killed before he could reveal the location of the mine. More famous is the case of Jacob Waltz, known as "Dutchman" despite having come from Germany. During the 1880s, he brought out about $250,000 worth of high-quality gold ore from somewhere in the mountains. Upon his death in 1891, he left only a few clues to the whereabouts of the mine. Strangely, many who have come looking for it have died violent deaths—one prospector burned to death in his own campfire, while another was found decapitated in an *arroyo*. Needless to say, the mine has never been found.

Rte. 88, a.k.a. **Apache Trail,** winds from **Apache Junction,** a small mining town 40 mi. east of Phoenix, through the mountains. Although the road is only about 50 mi. long one-way, trips require at least 3hr. behind the wheel because it's only partially paved. The car-less can leave the driving to **Apache Trail Tours,** which offers on- and off-road Jeep tours. (☎480-982-7661. 2-4hr. tours $60 per person. Reserve at least a day in advance.) For more info, head to the **Apache Junction Chamber of Commerce,** 112 E. 2nd Ave. (☎480-982-3141. Open M-F 8am-5pm.)

The scenery is the Trail's greatest attraction; the dramatic views of the arid landscape make it one of the most beautiful driving routes in the nation. The deep blue waters of the manmade **Lake Canyon, Lake Apache,** and **Lake Roosevelt** contrast sharply with the red and beige-hued rock formations surrounding them. **Goldfield Ghost Town Mine Tours,** 5 mi. north of the U.S. 60 junction on Rte. 88, offers tours of the nearby mines and gold-panning in a resurrected ghost town. (☎480-983-0333. Open daily 10am-5pm. Mine tours $5, ages 6-12 $3; gold-panning $4.) "Where the hell am I?" said Jacob Waltz when he came upon **Lost Dutchman State Park,** 1 mi. farther north on Rte. 88. At the base of the Superstitions, the park offers nature trails, picnic sites, and campsites with showers but no hookups. (☎480-982-4485. Entrance $5 per vehicle; first come, first served sites $10.) Grab a saddle for a bar-stool at **Tortilla Flat,** another refurbished ghost town 18 mi. farther on Rte. 88. The town keeps its spirits up and tourists nourished with a restaurant, ice cream shop, and saloon. (☎480-984-1776. Restaurant open M-F 9am-6pm, Sa-Su 8am-7pm.) **Tonto National Monument,** 5 mi. east of Lake Roosevelt on Rte. 88, preserves 800-year-old masonry and pueblo ruins built by Ancestral Puebloans. (Open daily 8am-4pm. $4 per car.) **Tonto National Forest** offers nearby camping. (☎602-225-5200. Sites $4-11.) The trail ends at the **Theodore Roosevelt Dam** (completed in 1911), the last dam constructed by hand in the US. For those who complete the Trail, Rte. 60 is a scenic trip back to Phoenix; the increased moisture and decreased temperatures of the higher elevations give rise to lush greenery (by southern Arizona standards).

SOUTHWEST

TUCSON
☎ 520

A little bit country, a little bit rock 'n' roll, Tucson is a city that carries its own tune and a bundle of contradictions. Mexican property until the Gadsden Purchase, the city retains many of its south-of-the-border influences and shares its Mexican heritage with such disparate elements as the University of Arizona, the Davis-Monthan Airforce Base, and McDonald's. Boasting mountainous flora beside desert cacti and art museums next to the war machines of the Pima Air and Space museum, the city nearly defies categorization. In the last several years, a re-energized downtown core has attracted artists and hipsters, while families and retirees populate the sprawling suburbs. With arguably better tourist attractions and more bustle and vitality than almost any other Southwestern city, Tucson offers the conveniences of a metropolis without the nasty aftertaste.

▐ TRANSPORTATION

Flights: Tucson International Airport (☎573-8000), on Valencia Rd., south of downtown. Bus #25 runs every hr. to the Laos Transit Center; from there, bus #16 goes downtown. **Arizona Stagecoach** (☎889-1000) goes downtown for $14 for one person, $3 for each additional person. 24hr. Reservations recommended.

Trains: Amtrak, 400 E. Toole Ave. (☎623-4442), at 5th Ave. To: Las Vegas (3 per week, $124); Los Angeles (9hr., 3 per week, $72); San Francisco (12hr., 3 per week, $124). Open Sa-M 6:15am-1:45pm and 4:15-11:30pm, Tu-W 6:15am-1:45pm, Th-F 4:15-11:30pm.

Buses: Greyhound, 2 S. 4th Ave. (☎882-4386), between Congress St. and Broadway. To: Albuquerque (12-14hr., 5 per day, $85); El Paso (6hr., 12 per day, $35); Los Angeles (9-10hr., 4 per day, $38); Phoenix (2hr., 16 per day, $14). Open 24hr.

Public Transit: Sun-Tran (☎792-9222). Buses run from the Ronstadt terminal downtown at Congress and 6th St. 85¢, under 19 60¢, seniors and disabled 35¢, day pass $2. Service roughly M-F 5:30am-10pm, Sa-Su 8am-7pm.

Taxis: Yellow Cab, ☎624-6611.

Bike Rental: Fairwheels Bicycles, 1110 E. 6th St. (☎884-9018), at Freemont. $10 per day, 2-day minimum. Open M-F 9am-6pm, Sa 9am-5:30pm, Su noon-4pm.

▐▐ ORIENTATION AND PRACTICAL INFORMATION

Just east of I-10, Tucson's downtown area surrounds the intersection of **Broadway Blvd.** and **Stone Ave.,** two blocks from the train and bus terminals. The **University of Arizona** lies 1 mi. northeast of downtown at the intersection of **Park** and **Speedway Blvd.** "Avenues" run north-south, "streets" east-west; because some of each are numbered, intersections such as "6th and 6th" are possible. Speedway, Broadway, and **Grant Rd.** are the quickest east-west routes through town. To go north-south, follow **Oracle Rd.** through the heart of the city, **Campbell Ave.** east of downtown, or **Swan Rd.** farther east. The hip, young crowd swings on **4th Ave.** and on **Congress St.,** both with small shops, quirky restaurants, and a slew of bars.

Visitor info: Tucson Convention and Visitors Bureau, 130 S. Scott Ave. (☎624-1817 or 800-638-8350), near Broadway. Open M-F 8am-5pm, Sa-Su 9am-4pm.

Bi-Gay-Lesbian Organization: Gay, Lesbian, and Bisexual Community Center, 300 E. 6th St. (☎624-1779). Open M-Sa 11am-7pm.

Hotlines: Rape Crisis, ☎624-7273. **Suicide Prevention,** ☎323-9373. Both 24hr.

Post Office: 1501 S. Cherry Bell (☎388-5129). Open M-F 8:30am-8pm, Sa 9am-1pm. **ZIP code:** 85726. **Area code:** 520.

▐ ACCOMMODATIONS AND CAMPING

There's a direct correlation between the temperature in Tucson and budget accommodations: expect the best deals in summer, when rain-cooled evenings and summer bargains are strong consolation for the midday scorch.

N

TO **15** ↗

TO **5** ↗
(1mi)

Park Ave.

Tyndall Ave.

Broadway Blvd.

200 yards

200 meters

4th St.
5th St.
6th St.
7th St.
8th St.
9th St.
10th St.

Euclid Ave.

University Blvd.

1st Ave.

2nd Ave.

Bean Ave.

3rd Ave.

Huff Ave.

Catalina Park

4th Ave.

Herbert Ave.

5th Ave.

Arizona Ave.

6th Ave.

Stevens Ave.

Toole Ave.

Greyhound

Broadway Blvd.

12th St.

Armory Park

SOUTHWEST

Ferro Ave.

5th St.
6th St.
7th St.

6th Ave.

Amtrak

7th Ave.

Scott Ave.

Congress St.

Echols Ave.

8th St.

Stone Ave.

Ash Ave.

9th Ave.

Perry Ave.

Court Ave.

Council St.

Washington St.

El Presidio Park

County Courthouse

Jackson St.

Ochoa St.

Church Ave.

TO **3** ↙, **4** ↙
(10mi)

TO **1 2** ↑
(1mi)

2nd St.
3rd St.
4th St.

Queen Ave.

Meyer Ave.

Tucson Museum of Art

City Hall

Alameda St.

Brant Pl.

Tucson Convention Center

11th Ave.

Franklin St.

TO INTERNATIONAL
WILDLIFE MUSEUM (4mi),
SAGUARO
NATIONAL PARK (12mi),
ARIZONA-SONORA DESERT
MUSEUM (15mi).

Granada Ave.

Granada Ave.

10

10

Downtown Tucson

♦ ACCOMMODATIONS
Flamingo Motel, 1
Hotel Congress and Hostel, 12
Roadrunner Hostel, 14
University Inn, 2

● FOOD
India Oven, 5
La Indita, 8
Little Cafe Poca Cosa, 11
Maya Quetzal, 10
Time Market, 6

♪ NIGHTLIFE
Ain't Nobody's Biz, 15
Club Congress, 13
Gotham, 4
IBT's, 9
New West, 3
O'Malley's, 7

● SERVICES
Fairwheels Bicycles, 16

🏠 **Roadrunner Hostel,** 346 E. 12th St. (☎628-4709), wows guests with unparalleled amenities such as a giant TV, a formidable movie collection, free high-speed Internet access, free coffee and tea, and swamp cooling. Located in a pleasant house a few blocks from downtown, the hostel is exceptionally clean and friendly. Free linen, towels, lockers, and laundry soap. Dorms $16; private doubles $35.

Hotel Congress and Hostel, 311 E. Congress (☎622-8848), is conveniently located across from the bus and train stations, and offers superb lodging to night-owl hostelers. Downstairs, Club Congress booms until 1am, making it rough on early birds. Private rooms come with bath, vintage radio, and ceiling fans. Dorms $17; singles June-Aug. $29, Sept.-Nov. and May $49, Dec.-Apr. $68; doubles June-Aug. $38, Sept.-Nov. and May $53, Jan.-Apr. $82. 10% discount for students, military, and local artists.

The Flamingo Hotel, 1300 N. Stone Ave. (☎770-1901), houses not only guests, but also Arizona's largest collection of Western movie posters. Laundry facilities on-site. Singles May-Aug. $22; doubles $29; Sept.-Nov. all rooms $49; Dec.-Apr. $79.

University Inn, 950 N. Stone Ave. (☎791-7503 or 800-233-8466), strategically placed between downtown and the university, has clean rooms with A/C, cable TV, telephones, and pool access. Singles from $34; doubles $37.

In addition to the backcountry camping available in **Saguaro Park** and **Coronado Forest,** there are a variety of other camping options. **Gilbert Ray Campground** (☎883-4200), just outside Saguaro West, offers $7 campsites with toilets and drinking water. A variety of camping areas flank **Sky Island Scenic Byway** at Mt. Lemmon. All campgrounds charge a $5 road access fee in addition to the camping costs. **Spencer Canyon** (sites $12) and **Rose Canyon** ($15) have water and toilets, while **Molino Basin** and **General Hitchcock** have toilets but no potable water (both $5). Call the Santa Catalina Ranger District for more info (☎749-8700).

🍴 FOOD

As any good college town should, Tucson brims with inexpensive yet tasty eateries. Although every style of cooking is represented, south-of-the-border fare is king. Good, cheap Mexican restaurants are everywhere.

Little Cafe Poca Cosa, 20 S. Scott Ave., prides itself on fresh ingredients and an ever-changing menu. Lunch specials $5.75. Open M-F 7:30am-2:30pm. Cash only.

La Indita, 622 N. 4th Ave. (☎792-0523), on chic 4th Ave., delights customers with traditional Mexican cuisine served on tasty tortillas. Open M-Th 11am-9pm, F 11am-6pm, Sa 6-9pm, Su 9am-9pm.

India Oven, 2727 N. Campbell Ave. (☎326-8635), between Grant and Glenn, offers relief when you've had enough Mexican food. Daily $6 lunch buffet. Vegetarian dishes $6-7, tandoori meats and curries $6-9. Open daily 11am-2:45pm and 5-10pm.

Time Market, 444 E. University Blvd., has $1.75 pizza slices, enhanced by gourmet toppings like piñon nuts, shrimp, and smoked gouda. Open daily 7:30am-10pm.

Maya Quetzal, 429 N. 4th Ave. (☎622-8207), a tiny operation, serves inexpensive Guatemalan food. Open M-Th 11:30am-11:30pm, F 11:30am-9:30pm, Sa noon-9:30pm.

👁 SIGHTS

UNIVERSITY OF ARIZONA. Lined with cafes, restaurants, galleries, and vintage clothing shops, **4th Ave.** is a great place to take a stroll. Between Speedway and Broadway Blvd., the street becomes a historical shopping district. Lovely for its varied and elaborately irrigated vegetation, the **University of Arizona's** mall sits where E. 3rd St. should be, just east of 4th Ave. The **Center for Creative Photography,** on campus, houses the archives of Ansel Adams and Richard Avedon. (☎621-7968. Open M-F 9am-5pm, Sa-Su noon-5pm. Archives available to the public, but only through print-viewing appointments. Free.) The **Flandrau Science Center,** on Cherry Ave., at the campus mall, dazzles visitors with an observatory and a laser light show. (☎621-7827. Open M-Tu 9am-5pm, W-Sa 9am-5pm and 7-9pm, Su noon-5pm. $3, under 14 $2. Shows $5/$4, seniors *and students $4.50.)* The **University of Arizona Museum of Art** offers a glimpse of modern American and 18th-century Latin American art, as well as the best student art. *(1031 N. Olive. ☎ 621-7567. Open M-F 10am-3pm, Su noon-4pm. Free.)*

TUCSON MUSEUM OF ART. This major attraction presents impressive traveling exhibits in all media, in addition to its permanent collection of varied American, Mexican, and European art. *(140 N. Main Ave. ☎ 624-2333. Open M-Sa 10am-4pm, Su noon-4pm. Closed M June-Aug. $5, seniors $4, students $3, under 13 free. Everyone free on Su.)*

SIGHTS ON WEST SPEEDWAY. As Speedway Blvd. winds its way west from Tucson's city center, it passes by a variety of sights. Closest to the city, the **International Wildlife Museum** is wild but lifeless—the creatures are stuffed. *(4800 W. Gates Pass Rd. ☎ 617-1439. Open M-F 9am-5pm, Sa-Su 9am-6pm, last entrance at 4:15pm. $7, seniors and students $5.50, ages 6-12 $2.50.)* Farther west, Speedway's name changes to Gates Pass Rd. and later junctions into Kinney Rd. **Gates Pass,** west of the International Wildlife Museum on the way to Kinney Rd., is an excellent spot for watching the rising and setting sun. The left fork leads to **Old Tucson Studios,** an elaborate old-west style town constructed for the 1938 movie *Arizona. (☎ 883-0100. Open daily 10am-6pm, sometimes closed on M in winter. $15, seniors $13, ages 4-11 $9.45.)* Less than 2 mi. from the fork lies the **Arizona-Sonora Desert Museum,** a first-rate zoo and nature preserve. The living museum recreates desert habitats and features over 300 kinds of animals. A visit requires at least 2hr. *(2021 N. Kinney Rd. Follow Speedway Blvd. west as it becomes Gates Pass Rd., then Kinney Rd. ☎ 883-2702. Open Mar.-Sept. daily 7:30am-5pm; Oct.-Feb. 8:30am-5pm; June-Sept. Sa 7:30am-10pm. $10, ages 6-12 $1.75.)*

CAVES. Caves are all the rage in Tucson. The recently opened **Kartchner Caverns State Park** is enormously popular, filled with magnificent rock formations and over 1000 bats. Taking a tour is the only way to enter the cave. *(Located 8 mi. off I-10 at Exit 302. ☎ 586-4100. Open daily 7:30am-6pm. 1hr. tours run every 30min. 8:30am-4:30pm. Entrance fee $10 per vehicle, tour $14, ages 7-13 $6. Reservations strongly recommended.)* Near **Saguaro National Park East, Colossal Cave** is one of the only dormant caves in the US. In addition to 1hr. walking tours that occur throughout the day, a special ladder tour through otherwise sealed-off tunnels, crawlspaces, and corridors can be arranged. *(☎ 647-7275. Open mid-Mar. to mid-Sept. M-Sa 8am-6pm, Su 8am-7pm; mid-Sept. to mid-Mar. M-Sa 9am-5pm, Su 9am-6pm. $7, ages 6-12 $4. Ladder tour: Sa 5:30-8pm; $35, includes meal and equipment rental, reservations required.)*

PIMA AIR AND SPACE MUSEUM. This impressive museum follows aviation history from the days of the Wright brothers to its modern military incarnations. Exhibits on female and African-American aviators are interesting, but the main draw is acres of decommissioned warplanes. *(☎ 574-0462. Open M-F 7am-3pm, Sa-Su 7am-5pm; in summer daily 9am-5pm. $7.50, seniors $6.50.)* Tours of the **Davis-Monthan Air Force Base** are offered at the museum. *(5 tours per day M-F. $5, ages 6-12 $3.)*

⚑ OUTDOOR ACTIVITIES

SAGUARO NATIONAL PARK

North of the desert museum, the western half of Saguaro National Park (Tucson Mountain District) has hiking trails and an auto loop. The **Bajada Loop Drive** runs less than 9 mi., but passes through some of the most striking desert scenery the park has to offer. The paved nature walk near the **Visitors Center** passes some of the best specimens of Saguaro cactus in the Tucson area. *(☎ 733-5158. Park open 24hr.; Visitors Center daily 8:30am-5pm; auto loop 7am-sunset. Free.)*

There are a variety of hiking trails through Saguaro West; **Sendero Esperanza Trail,** beginning at the Ez-kim-in-zin picnic area, is the mildest approach to the summit of **Wasson Peak,** the highest in the Tucson Mountain Range (4687 ft.). The **Hugh Norris Trail** is a slightly longer, slightly more strenuous climb to the top of Wasson Peak.

Also known as the Rincon Mountain District, the eastern portion of the park lies east of the city on **Old Spanish Trail;** take I-10 E to Exit 279 and follow Vail Rd. to Old Spanish Trail. **Backcountry camping** is allowed; free mandatory permits may be picked up at the **Visitors Center** any time until noon on the day of camping. Mountain biking is permitted only around the **Cactus Forest Loop Drive** and **Cactus Forest Trail**, at the western end of the park near the Visitors Center. The trails in Saguaro East are much longer than those in the western segment of the park. One of the only trails that can easily be completed in a single day is the Cactus Forest.

SABINO CANYON

Northeast of downtown Tucson, the cliffs and desert pools of **Sabino Canyon** provide an ideal backdrop for picnics and day hikes. No cars are permitted in the canyon, but a shuttlebus makes trips through it. (☎749-2861. Runs July-Nov. every hr. 9am-4pm; Dec.-June every 30min. $6, ages 3-12 $2.) The national forest's **Visitors Center** lies at the canyon's entrance. (☎749-8700. Open M-F 8am-4:30pm, Sa-Su 8:30am-4:30pm.) The forest area outside the canyon is the **Pusch Ridge Wilderness**, which lies within the **Coronado National Forest**. The northern and eastern border of the wilderness is the Mt. Lemmon Hwy., and the wilderness stretches to the south and west sides of the Coronado National Forest. There is no camping allowed in Sabino Canyon, and there are seasonal and geographic restrictions on backcountry camping in the Pusch Ridge Wilderness. On the other hand, there are developed campsites as well as backcountry camping in the rest of the Coronado Forest

TUCSON MOUNTAIN COUNTY PARK

Located west of Tucson along Speedway/Gates Pass/Kinney, Tucson Mountain County Park includes Gates Pass itself as well as many of the Tucson mountains. Trailheads, picnic areas, and a campsite radiate from Kinney Road. The **McCain Loop Rd.** circle around the Arizona-Sonora Desert Museum and passes through rugged stretches of desert. Entrance is free, and mountain biking is permitted.

🎵🎭 ENTERTAINMENT AND NIGHTLIFE

The free *Tucson Weekly* is the local authority on nightlife. Throughout the year, the city of the sun presents **Music Under the Stars,** a series of sunset concerts performed by the **Tucson Symphony Orchestra** (☎792-9155). For **Downtown Saturday Nights,** on the 1st and 3rd Saturday of each month, Congress St. is blockaded for a celebration of the arts with outdoor singers, crafts, and galleries. Every Thursday, the **Thursday Night Art Walk** lets you mosey through downtown galleries and studios. For more info, call **Tucson Arts District** (☎624-9977). UA students rock 'n' roll on **Speedway Blvd.**, while others do the two-step in clubs on **N. Oracle.** Young locals hang out on **4th Ave.**, where most bars have live music and low cover charges.

Club Congress, 311 E. Congress St. (☎622-8848), has DJs during the week and live bands on weekends. Congress is the venue for most of the indie music coming through town. M is 80s night with 80¢ drinks. Cover $4. Open daily 9pm-1am.

New West, 4385 W. Ina Rd. (☎744-7744), rocks country-western music on the largest dance floor in Arizona. Alcohol not served past 1am. Two-stepping lessons W 7:15-8:15pm, F 6:15-7:15pm; Tu Hip-Hop ($5 cover); Th Latin music; Su teen night 7pm-midnight. Cover $4, 7-11pm $2. Open Tu-Th 8pm-2am, Th-Sa 7pm-2am.

Gotham shares the building with New West, and throbs to a heavy urban beat. Tu and Th-F are 18+. Alcohol not served past 1am. Cover $5, ages 18-20 $8, Tu and Th 7-11pm $2. Open Tu 7pm-2am, Th 9pm-2am, F-Sa 7pm-2am.

O'Malley's, 247 N. 4th Ave. (☎623-8600), is a good spot with decent bar food, pool tables, and pinball. As its name implies, this is a better place to nurse your pint of Guinness than it is to get your groove on. Cover Th-Sa varies. Open daily 11am-1am.

IBT's, on 4th Ave. at 6th St. (☎882-3053). The single most popular gay venue in Tucson, it pumps dance music in its classic club environment to a weekend capacity crowd. W and Su drag shows wow audiences. Open daily 9am-1am.

Ain't Nobody's Biz, 2900 E. Broadway Blvd. (☎318-4838), in a shopping plaza, is at the head of the Tucson lesbian scene. A country-western bar, it has occasional pool tournaments. No cover. Open daily 11am-1am.

⚡ DAYTRIPS FROM TUCSON

BIOSPHERE 2

Ninety-one feet high, with an area of more than three acres, Biosphere 2 is sealed off from Earth—"Biosphere 1"—by 500 tons of stainless steel. In 1991, eight research scientists locked themselves inside this giant greenhouse to cultivate their own food as they monitored the behavior of five man-made ecosystems: savanna, rainforest, marsh, ocean, and desert. After two years, they began having oxygen problems and difficulty with food production. No one lives in Biosphere 2 now, but it's still used as a research facility. The Biosphere is 30min. north of Tucson; take I-10 west to the "Miracle Mile" exit, follow the miracles to Oracle Rd., then travel north until it becomes Rte. 77 N. From Phoenix, take I-10 to Exit 185, follow Rte. 387 to Rte. 79 (Florence Hwy.), and proceed to Oracle Junction and Rte. 77. (☎896-6200 or 800-838-2462. Tours daily 9am-4:30pm, grounds open 8:30am-5:30pm, last admission at 5pm. $13, seniors and students $11.50, ages 13-17 $9, ages 6-12 $6.)

MISSION SAN XAVIER DE BAC

Built by the Franciscan brothers in the late 1700s, this is the northernmost Spanish Baroque church in the Americas, and the only such church in the US. Located on the Tohono O'odham Indian Reservation, there were few opportunities and fewer funds to restore it until the late 20th century. In the early 90s, a local group gathered money in order to preserve and protect this singular church; since then, the mortar has been restored, the frescoes have been retouched and preserved, and the statuary cleaned of centuries of candle soot and desert sand. The result is a dazzling and spectacular house of God, well-earning its nickname "white dove of the desert." (South of Tucson off of I-19 to Nogales, take the San Xavier exit and follow the signs. ☎ 294-2624. Open for viewing 8am-6pm, masses held daily. Admission is free both to the church and to small adjoining museum, although donations are accepted.)

SCENIC DRIVE: MT. LEMMON DRIVE

Climbing to 9157 ft. above sea level, the Mt. Lemmon Drive is a virtual transnational trip from the deserts of Mexico to the conifer forests of Canada. Along the ascent, drivers are witness to a breathtaking metamorphosis of terrain. *Road construction will plague the Mt. Lemmon Drive until at least the fall of 2001. Road closures and delays are frequent. Call 751-9405 for current info.*

The 50 mi. round-trip drive begins northwest of downtown Tucson along the **Catalina Hwy.**, off Tanque Verde Rd. Venturing into the **Coronado National Forest,** the road passes rolling hills of Sonoran desert scrub, Saguaro cacti, and mesquite trees. Past the Molino Canyon Vista point, a Forest Service entrance station collects fees. There is no charge to drive, but if you plan on hiking any of the numerous trails or picnic grounds that line the road, a $5 day-use permit must be purchased. As the road continues to climb beyond the entrance station, desert lowland gives way to semi-desert grassland and oak forests change into mixed pine and oak woodlands. At about 6000 ft. **Windy Point,** true to its name, provides views of Tucson, the **Patagonia Mountains,** and on clear days, the **Sierra de San Antonio** of Mexico. Just before Mile 20, the **Palisades Visitors Center** offers restrooms, brochures, and ranger advice. From there, the vegetation continues to morph into a ponderosa pine forest, as the road climbs to over 8000 ft. The final life zone is a mixed conifer forest with temperatures that are on average 20°F cooler than Tucson. At Mile 25, the drive meets the access road for the **Mt. Lemmon Ski Valley** (☎520-576-1321). The climax of the drive is the village of Summerhaven, whose surroundings look more like the Rockies than southern Arizona.

TOMBSTONE ☎520

Founded in the wake of the gold and silver rush of the 1870s, Tombstone—home to more than 100 saloons and 3000 prostitutes—was once the largest city between St. Louis and San Francisco. In recent years, tourism now keeps the old blood pumping. However, if the kitschy Old West of Ronald Reagan westerns and O.K. Corral

SOUTHWEST

shoot-em-ups isn't your cup of tea, then you should consider giving Tombstone a pass. A Cowboy Disneyland, Tombstone can give you anything you want—as long as it's a shot of rot-gut whiskey or a gunfight re-enactment.

By inviting visitors to view the barnyard where Wyatt Earp and his brothers kicked some serious butt, Tombstone has turned the **shootout at the O.K. Corral**, on Allen St. next to City Park, into a year-round tourist industry. (☎457-3456. Open daily 9am-5pm. $2.50.) The **Boothill Gunslingers**, the **Wild Bunch**, the **Vigilantes/Vigilettes,** and the **Tombstone Cowboys** perform re-enactments of famous gunfights at least seven times daily. (Times vary, but always at 11:30am, 1, and 3pm. Prices vary.) The **Hanging Chairman** can treat a friend or relative to a **public mock hanging** by one of these groups (☎457-3434). The voice of Vincent Price narrates the town's history next door to the O.K. Corral in the **Tombstone Historama**, while a plastic mountain revolves onstage and a dramatization of the gunfight is shown on a movie screen. (☎457-3456. Shows daily on the hr. 9am-4pm. $2.50.) Site of the longest poker game in Western history (8 years, 5 months, and 3 days), the **Bird Cage Theater,** at 6th and Allen, was named for the compartments suspended from the ceiling that once housed prostitutes. (☎457-3421. Open daily 8am-6pm.) John Slaughter battled outlaws at the **Tombstone Courthouse**, at 3rd and Toughnut St. (☎457-3311. Open daily 8am-5pm. $2.50, ages 7-13 $1.) The tombstones of Tombstone, largely the result of all that gunplay, stand in Boothill Cemetery on Rte. 80 just north of town. (☎457-3421 or 800-457-3423. Open daily 7:30am-6pm. Free.) For something different, the **Rose Tree Museum**, at 4th and Toughnut St., shelters the largest rose tree in the world. (☎457-3326. Open daily 9am-5pm. $2, under 14 free.)

The **Larian Motel,** on the corner of Fremont and 5th, is clean, nicely furnished, and roomy. (☎457-2272. Singles $40-45; doubles $45-59.) The rooms at the **Tombstone Motel,** across the street, are basic but clean. (☎457-3478 or 888-455-3478. Singles $39-42; doubles $55.) **Nellie Cashman's Restaurant** is little colonized by the old-west aesthetic that dominates Tombstone. Delicious ½ lb. hamburgers start at $5.50. (☎457-2212. Open daily 7:30am-9pm.) **Don Teodoro's,** 15 N. 4th St., serves Mexican plates accompanied by live guitar music. (☎457-3647. Live music W-M 6-9pm. Open Su-Th 11am-9pm, F-Sa 11am-10pm.) For a bit of moonshine and country music, smell your way to **Big Nose Kate's Saloon,** on Allen St., named for "the girl who loved Doc Holliday and everyone else too." (☎457-3107. Open daily 10am-midnight.)

To get to Tombstone, head to the Benson Exit off I-10, then go south on Rte. 80. The nearest **Greyhound** station is in **Benson,** 6080 W. 4th St. (☎586-3141). **Amtrak** is across the street. The **Douglas Shuttle** (☎364-9442) has service to Tucson ($10), Bisbee ($5), and Benson ($5). The **Tombstone Visitors Center** provides info and maps. (☎457-3929. Open M-F 9am-4pm, Sa-Su 10am-4pm.) **Internet access** is available at **Desert Gold Web Services** on Freemont. (☎457-3250. Open 7am-6pm. 15¢ per min.) The **Post Office** is at 516 E. Allen St. **ZIP code:** 85638. **Area code:** 520.

BISBEE   ☎520

One hundred miles southeast of Tucson and 20 miles south of Tombstone, mellow Bisbee, a former mining town, is known throughout the Southwest as a laid-back artists' colony. Visitors revel in the town's proximity to Mexico, picture-perfect weather, and excellent, relatively inexpensive accommodations.

Queen Mines, on the Rte. 80 interchange entering Old Bisbee, ceased mining in 1943 but continues to give educational 1¼hr. tours. (☎432-2071. Tours at 9, 10:30am, noon, 2, and 3:30pm. $10, ages 7-15 $3.50, ages 3-6 $2.) The Smithsonian-affiliated **Mining and Historical Museum,** 5 Copper Queen, highlights the discovery of Bisbee's copper surplus and the lives of the fortune-seekers who extracted it. (☎432-7071. Open daily 10am-4pm. $4, seniors $3.50, under 16 free.) For a less earthly and more heavenly experience, visit the **Chihuahua Hill Shrines.** A 25min. hike over rocky ground leads to a Buddhist, and then a Mexican Catholic shrine.

About 18 mi. west of Bisbee along Rte. 92, along the Mexican border, **Coronado National Memorial** marks the place where Francisco Coronado and his expedition first entered American territory. **Coronado Cave,** a small, relatively dry cave, is ¾ mi. from the Visitors Center along a short, steep path. A free permit is required to explore the cave, and can be picked up at the Visitors Center as long as each spe-lunker has a flashlight. (☎366-5515. Park open daily dawn to dusk. Visitors center open daily 8am-5pm.) **Ramsey Canyon Preserve,** 5 mi. farther down the road, attracts nearly as many bird-watchers as birds. In the middle of migratory routes for many North American birds, thousands of hummingbirds throng here in the late summer. (Open daily 8am-5pm. $5, under 16 free; first Sa of every month free.)

Located in the heart of downtown, the **Red Metal Miner's Hostel,** 59B Subway St., has recently changed hands, and the new owners are still in the process of expand-ing. (☎432-6671. Kitchen privileges, free Internet access, and access to laundry facilities. Dorms $18; singles $20; doubles $30.) About a 10min. walk from down-town, the **Jonquil Inn,** 317 Tombstone Canyon, offers clean and smoke-free rooms. (☎432-7371. Singles $40-45; doubles $50-60; in winter about $10 more.) On Tomb-stone Canyon Rd., the **School House Inn** houses guests in a remodeled 1918 school house. (☎432-2966 or 800-537-4333. All rooms have private bath, full breakfast included. No children under 14. Singles $55-80; 2-bed suite $90.) A number of cheap eateries line the main drags of downtown. The **Paz Cafe** is a magnet for the earthy, laid-back crowd, serving only vegetarian food. (☎432-2688. Lunch served 11am-2pm, dinner 5-8pm. Open Th and Su 10am-10pm, F-Sa 10am-1am. Meals $5-7.) A meatatarian can get a fix at **Old Tymers,** with steak ($11) and hamburger ($5) any way you like. (☎432-7364. Open Su-Th 11am-9pm, F-Sa 11am-10pm.)

The **Chamber of Commerce,** at 31 Subway St., provides maps that will help you nav-igate the labyrinthine streets of Bisbee. (☎432-5421. Open M-F 9am-5pm, Sa-Su 10am-4pm.) The **Post Office,** on Main St., is one block south of the highway exit. (☎432-2052. Open M-F 8:30am-4:30pm.) **ZIP code:** 85603. **Area code:** 520.

CHIRICAHUA NATIONAL MONUMENT ☎520

Over 25 million years ago Chiricahua was a thick heap of volcanic ash extruded from the nearby Turkey Creek Cauldera. Fortunately, since then the never-to-be-underestimated powers of erosion have sculpted the hardened rock into spectacu-lar rock formations with foreboding mountains in the background. A cross between Zion and Bryce Canyon, Chiricahua was aptly called the "Land of the Standing-Up Rocks" by Apaches and the "Wonderland of Rocks" by pioneers. And while Chir-icahua nearly equals the natural splendor of Bryce and Zion, it happily falls short of their popularity, indulging in peace and tranquility.

Chiricahua is located 40 mi. off I-10 and 70 mi. from Bisbee; take Rte. 80 E to Rte. 191 N to 181 N. The **Visitors Center** is just beyond the entrance station. (☎824-3560, ext. 104. Open daily 8am-5:30pm. Entrance fee vehicles $6, pedestrians $3.) Most of the park is federally designated wilderness; no backcountry camping, bicycles, or climbing allowed. Overnight backcountry camping is not permitted. The **Bonita Creek Campground** within the park offers 24 sites with toilets and running water, but no showers (sites $8). There is a bountiful selection of day hikes in the monument. A detailed **trail map** can be purchased for 25¢.

NEW MEXICO

Sometimes overshadowed by its more extreme neighbors, New Mexico is neverthe-less a dreamscape of varied terrains and peoples. Going back to the days when Spaniards arrived with delusions of golden riches, this expansive land of high deserts, mountain vistas, and roadrunners has always been a place where people come to fulfill their fantasies. Today, most explorers arrive in search of natural beauty, adobe architecture, and cultural treasures rather than gold. It makes sense that New Mexico is a haven for hikers, backpackers, cyclists, mountain-climbers, and skiers. Six national forests within the state provide miles and miles of beautiful and challenging opportunities for lovers of the outdoors, while the Sandía, Mogol-lon, and Sangre de Cristo mountains fulfill mountain-climbers' upward thrust. And with the mixings of Spanish, Mexican, Native American, and Anglo cultures, New Mexico is as culturally varied as it is geographically diverse.

◪ PRACTICAL INFORMATION

Capital: Santa Fe.

Visitor info: New Mexico Dept. of Tourism, 491 Old Santa Fe Trail, Santa Fe 87501 (☎800-545-2040; www.newmexico.org). Open M-F 8am-5pm. **Park and Recreation Division,** 2040 S. Pacheco, Santa Fe 87505 (☎505-827-7173). Open M-F 8am-5pm. **US Forest Service,** 517 Gold Ave. SW, Albuquerque 87102 (☎505-842-3292). Open M-F 8am-4:30pm.

Postal Abbreviation: NM. **Sales Tax:** 6.25%.

SANTA FE   ☎505

Santa Fe is like an older, wiser sibling to Albuquerque, entrenched in its old-fashioned ways but possessing a higher sophistication and elegance. Founded by the Spanish in 1608, Santa Fe is the second oldest city in the US and the only state capital to serve under the administrations of three countries. Lying at the convergence of the Santa Fe Trail, an old trading route running from Missouri, and the Camino Real ("Royal Road"), which originates in Mexico City, Santa Fe has always been a place of commerce and interaction. These days, art is the trade of choice, with Native Americans, native New Mexicans, and exiled New Yorkers all hawking their wares on the streets and in the galleries surrounding the Central Plaza. In recent years, Santa Fe's popularity has bloomed like a desert flower, allowing an influx of gated communities, ritzy restaurants, and Californian millionaires. As a result, Santa Fe can be expensive, but the fabulous art museums, traditional churches, and mountain trails are well within the price range of a budget traveler.

▐ TRANSPORTATION

Buses: Greyhound, 858 St. Michael's Dr. (☎471-0008). To: Albuquerque (1½hr., 4 per day, $12.60); Denver (8-10hr., 4 per day, $59); Taos (1½hr., 2 per day, $15.75). Open M-F 7am-5:30pm and 7:30-9:45pm; Sa-Su 7-9am, 12:30-1:30pm, 3:30-5pm, and 7:30-9:30pm.

Trains: Amtrak's nearest station is in Lamy (☎466-4511), 18 mi. south on U.S. 285. 1 train daily to: Albuquerque (1hr., $20); Flagstaff (7hr., $63-113); Kansas City (17hr., $108-192); Los Angeles (18½hr., $71-127). Call 982-8829 in advance for a shuttle to Santa Fe ($14). Open daily 9:30am-6:30pm.

Public Transit: Santa Fe Trails (☎955-2001) runs 9 downtown bus routes (M-F 6am-10pm, Sa 8am-8pm). Most bus routes start at the downtown Sheridan Transit Center, 1 block from the plaza between Marcy St. and Palace Ave. Buses #21-24 go down Cerrillos Rd., #10 goes to the museums on Camino Lejo, #5 goes to the Greyhound station. 50¢, ages 6-12 25¢; day pass $1. **Sandía Shuttle Express** (☎474-5696) runs to the Albuquerque airport (10 per day, $20) from downtown hotels. Reserve at least 1 day in advance. Open M-F 7am-6pm, Sa-Su 7am-5pm.

Taxis: Capital City Taxi, ☎438-0000.

✳ ◪ ORIENTATION AND PRACTICAL INFORMATION

Except for the museums southeast of the city center, most upscale restaurants and sights in Santa Fe cluster within a few blocks of the **downtown plaza** and inside the loop formed by the **Paseo de Peralta.** Narrow streets make driving troublesome; park your car and pound the pavement. You'll find **parking lots** behind Santa Fe Village, near Sena Plaza, and one block east of the Federal Courthouse near the plaza, while metered spaces (2hr. maximum) line the streets south of the plaza. Parking is also available along the streets near the galleries on Canyon Rd.

Visitor info: Visitors Information Center, 491 Old Santa Fe Trail (☎875-7400 or 800-545-2040). Open daily 8am-6:30pm; off-season 8am-5pm. **Santa Fe Convention and Visitors Bureau,** 201 W. Marcy St. (☎800-777-2489). Open M-F 8am-5pm.

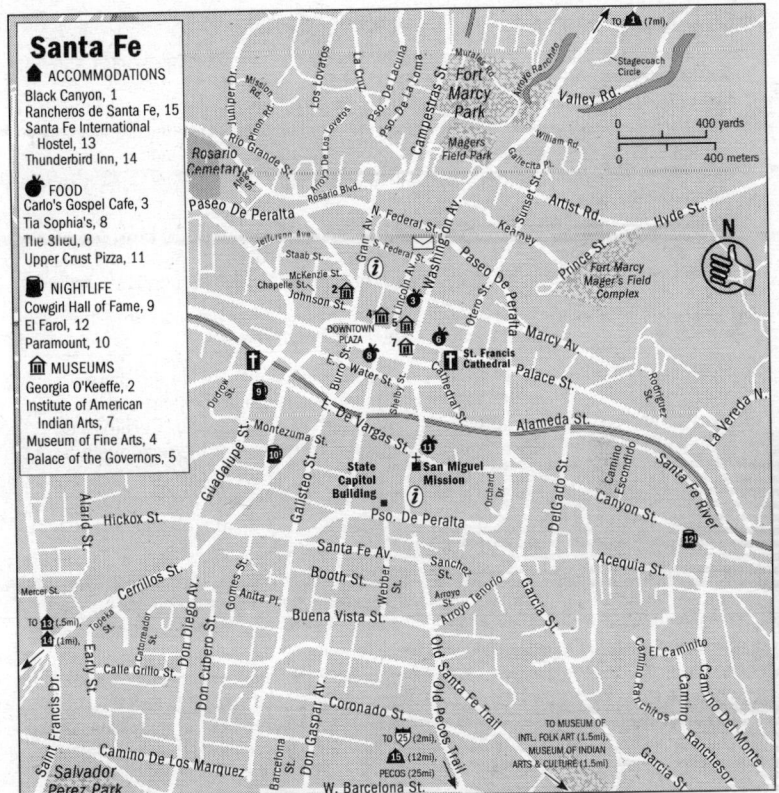

Santa Fe

ACCOMMODATIONS
Black Canyon, 1
Rancheros de Santa Fe, 15
Santa Fe International
Hostel, 13
Thunderbird Inn, 14

FOOD
Carlo's Gospel Cafe, 3
Tia Sophia's, 8
The Shed, 6
Upper Crust Pizza, 11

NIGHTLIFE
Cowgirl Hall of Fame, 9
El Farol, 12
Paramount, 10

MUSEUMS
Georgia O'Keeffe, 2
Institute of American
Indian Arts, 7
Museum of Fine Arts, 4
Palace of the Governors, 5

SOUTHWEST

Equipment Rental: Wild Mountain Outfitters, 541 W. Cordova Rd. (☎986-1152), has a large selection of outdoors gear. Open M-Sa 9am-8pm, Su 10am-5pm.

Hotlines: Rape Abuse, ☎800-721-7273 or 986-9111. On-call 24hr. **Gay and Lesbian Information Line,** ☎891-3647.

Internet access: Santa Fe Public Library, 145 Washington Ave. (☎955-6781), 2 blocks northeast of the Plaza. Open M-Th 10am-9pm, F-Sa 10am-6pm, Su 1-5pm.

Post Office: 120 S. Federal Pl., next to the courthouse. (☎988-6351. Open M-F 7:30am-5:45pm, Sa 9am-1pm.) **ZIP code:** 87501. **Area Code:** 505.

ACCOMMODATIONS

Hotels in Santa Fe tend toward the expensive side. As early as May, they become swamped with requests during the festival periods of **Indian Market** (3rd week of Aug.) and **Fiesta de Santa Fe** (2nd weekend of Sept.). Make reservations early or plan to sleep standing up. In general, the motels along Cerrillos Rd. have the best prices, but even these places run $40-60 per night. Nearby camping is pleasant even during the summer and is lighter on the wallet. Two popular sites for free primitive camping are **Big Tesuque** and **Ski Basin Campgrounds** on National Forest land. These campgrounds are both off Rte. 475 up toward the Ski Basin and offer pit toilets.

Santa Fe International Hostel and Pension (AAIH), 1412 Cerrillos Rd. (☎988-1153), 1 mi. from the bus station and 2 mi. from the plaza. Busy, but big enough to accommodate the masses. Kitchen, library, and large dorm rooms. Linen free. Office open daily 7am-11pm. Chores required. Dorms $14, nonmembers $15. Singles $25; doubles $35; with private bath $33/$43; no discount for members. No credit cards.

Thunderbird Inn, 1821 Cerrillos Rd. (☎983-4397). Slightly farther from town than the hostel, but an excellent value (for Santa Fe, anyway). Large rooms, some with fridge and microwave, all with A/C and cable TV. Reception 24hr. Summer singles $50-55; doubles $55-60; winter $39-44/$44-49.

Rancheros de Santa Fe, 736 Old Las Vegas Hwy. (☎466-3482). Take I-25 N to Exit 290, turn left and make an immediate right onto Old Las Vegas Highway. Big, friendly campground with 23 acres of land, swimming pool, laundry, groceries, and nightly movies. Tent sites in a secluded wooded area with fire pits and nearby showers. Sites $18, full hookups $25; 2-bed rustic cabins $38.

Black Canyon Campground (☎753-7331 or for reservations 877-444-6777), 7 mi. from Santa Fe on Rte. 475, is run by the Santa Fe National Forest. Sites in the pine forest have pit toilets, water, and grills. No hookups. Tent sites $9. Reservations accepted.

🍴 FOOD

Spicy Mexican food served on blue corn tortillas is a Santa Fe staple. Bistros near the plaza dish up savory chiles to tourists, businessmen, and local artists, but most run $20 an entree. Cheaper alternatives lie south of the plaza on Cerrillos and on Guadalupe St. Wandering down side streets uncovers smaller Mexican restaurants where the locals eat; grill carts in the plaza can sell you fragrant fajitas ($3) and fresh lemonade ($1). The **Santa Fe Farmers Market** (☎983-4098), at the Railyard near the intersection of Guadalupe St. and Montezuma St., has fresh fruits and vegetables (open late Apr. to early Nov. Tu and Sa 7am-noon).

🍴 **Tia Sophia's,** 210 W. San Francisco St. (☎983-9880). It looks and feels like a diner (the servers are quick and curt), but the food is exceptional. The most popular item is the Atrisco plate ($6)—chile stew, cheese enchilada, beans, *posole*, and a *sopapilla*. Arrive before noon for the fastest service. Open M-Sa 7am-2pm.

The Shed, 113½ E. Palace Ave. (☎982-9030), up the street from the plaza, feels like an open garden, even in the enclosed section. Lots of vegetarian dishes including quesadillas ($6) and excellent blue corn burritos ($8.50). Meat-eaters will enjoy the amazing chicken enchilada verde ($9). Lunch M-Sa 11am-2:30pm, dinner M-Sa 5:30-9pm.

Upper Crust Pizza, 329 Old Sante Fe Trail (☎982-0000). With a tranquil porch and live music Th-Su (winter F-Su), "crustomers" feast on Santa Fe's best pizza in a fantastic setting. Pizzas start at $6, sandwiches $5. Open Su-Th 11am-10pm, F-Sa 11am-11pm.

Carlo's Gospel Cafe, 125 Lincoln St. #117 (☎983-1841). A popular spot with locals, Carlo's is pure temptation with divinely delicious sandwiches ($5 and up) and biblically-rich pies. Open M-Sa 11am-3pm.

👁 🎵 OLD-STYLE SIGHTS AND ENTERTAINMENT

The grassy **Plaza de Santa Fe** is a good starting point for exploring the museums, sanctuaries, and galleries of the city. Since 1609, the plaza has been the site of religious ceremonies, military gatherings, markets, cockfights, and public punishments—now it holds ritzy shops and loitering tourists. Historic **walking tours** leave from the blue doors of the Palace of the Governors on Lincoln St. (May-Oct. M-Sa 10:15am. $10.) **Fiesta Tours** offers 75min. open-air van tours from the corner of Lincoln St. and Palace Ave. (☎983-1570. 3-6 per day. $7, children $4.)

MNM MUSEUMS. Sante Fe is home to six world-class and imaginative museums. Four are run by **The Museum of New Mexico.** They all hold the same hours and charge the same admission. A worthwhile four-day pass ($10) includes admission to all four museums; it can be purchased at any of them. (☎827-6463. Open Tu-Su 10am-5pm. Single visit $5, under 17 free. The 2 downtown museums—Fine Arts and Palace of the Governors—are both free on F 5-8pm.) Inhabiting a large adobe building on the northwest corner of the plaza, the **Museum of Fine Arts** dazzles visitors with the works of major Southwestern artists like Georgia O'Keeffe and Gustave Baumann, as well as exhibits of contemporary American art. (107 W. Palace Ave. ☎476-5072.) The **Palace of the Governors,** on the north side of the plaza, is the oldest public building in the US and was the seat of seven successive governments after its construction in 1610. The *haciendas* palace is now a museum with exhibits on Native American, Southwestern, and New Mexican history. Stop by the interesting display on Jewish Pioneers. *(107 W. Palace Ave. ☎ 476-5100.)* The most unique museums in town are 2½ mi. south of the Plaza on Old Santa Fe Trail. The fascinating **Museum of International Folk Art,** houses the Girard Collection, which includes over 10,000 handmade dolls, doll houses, and other toys from around the world. *(706 Camino Lejo. ☎ 476-1200.)* Next door, the **Museum of American Indian Arts and Culture** displays Native American photos and artifacts with high-tech savvy. *(710 Camino Lejo. ☎ 476-1250.)*

OTHER PLAZA MUSEUMS. While the two other Sante Fe museums have no affiliation with the Museum of New Mexico, they are just as worthwhile. The popular **Georgia O'Keeffe Museum** attracts the masses with O'Keeffe's famous flower paintings and some of her more abstract works. *(217 Johnson St. ☎ 946-1000. Open daily 10am-5pm. $5, under 17 and students with ID free; F 5-8pm free. Audio tour $5.)* The **Institute of American Indian Arts Museum,** downtown, houses an extensive collection of contemporary Indian art. *(108 Cathedral Place. ☎ 983-8900. Open M-Sa 9am-5pm, Su noon-5pm. $4, students and seniors $2, under 16 free.)* The round **New Mexico State Capitol** was built in 1966 in the form of the Zia sun symbol. The House and Senate galleries are open to the public. *(☎ 986-4589. 5 blocks south of the Plaza on Old Santa Fe Rd. Open Sept.-May M-F 7am-7pm; June-Aug. M-F 7am-7pm; Sa 8am-5pm. Free tours M-F 10am and 2pm.)*

CHURCHES. Santa Fe's Catholic roots are evident in the Romanesque **St. Francis Cathedral,** built in 1884 under the direction of the pope to bring Catholicism to the "ungodly" Westerners. *(213 Cathedral Pl. ☎ 982-5619. One block east of the Plaza on San Francisco St. Open daily 7:30am-5:30pm.)* The **Loretto Chapel** is famous for its "miraculous" spiral staircase (see "Stairway to Heaven," below), and was the first Gothic building west of the Mississippi River. *(207 Old Santa Fe Trail. ☎ 982-0092. 2 blocks south of the Cathedral. Open M-Sa 9am-5pm, Su 10:30am-5pm. $2.50, seniors and children $2.)* About five blocks southeast of the plaza lies the **San Miguel Mission,** at DeVargas St. and the Old Santa Fe Trail. Built in 1610 by the Tlaxcalan Indians, the mission is one of the oldest functioning churches in the US. Also in the church is the oldest bell in the US. *(☎ 983-3974. Open M-Sa 9am-5pm, Su 1:30-4pm; may close earlier in winter. $1.)*

GALLERIES. Santa Fe's most successful artists live and sell their work along Canyon Rd. To reach their galleries, depart the Plaza on San Francisco Dr., take a left on Alameda St., a right on Paseo de Peralta, and then a left on Canyon Rd. Extending for about 1 mi., the road is lined on both sides by galleries displaying all types of art, as well as a number of indoor/outdoor cafes. At the **Hahn Ross Gallery,** the art is hip, enjoyable, and way out of your price range. *(409 Canyon Rd. ☎ 984-8434. Open daily 10am-5pm.)* **Off the Wall** vends offbeat jewelry, pottery, clocks, and sculpture, with a cute coffee bar out back. *(616 Canyon Rd. ☎ 983-8337. Open daily 10am-5pm.)*

A BIT OF CLASS. Strange verse and distinguished acting invade the city each summer when **Shakespeare in Sante Fe** raises its curtain. The festival shows play in an open-air theater on the St. John's College campus from late June to late August. *(Shows run W 6:30pm and F-Su 7:30pm. Reserved seating tickets $15-32; lawn seating is free, though a $5 donation is requested. Tickets available at show or call 982-2910.)* The **Santa Fe Opera,** on Opera Dr. 7 mi. north of Santa Fe on Rte. 84/285, performs outdoors against a mountain backdrop. Nights are cool; bring a blanket. *(☎ 800-280-4654 or 877-999-7499. July W and F; Aug. M-Sa. Performances begin 8-9pm. Tickets $20-200, rush standing-room tickets $8-15; 50% student discount on same-day reserved seats. The box office is at the opera house; call or drop by the day of the show for specific prices and availability.)* The **Santa Fe Chamber Music Festival** celebrates the works of great Baroque, Classical, Romantic, and 20th-century composers in the **St. Francis Auditorium of the Museum of Fine Arts.** *(☎ 983-2075. Mid-July to mid-Aug. Tickets $16-40, students $10.)*

FESTIVALS. Santa Fe is home to two of the US's largest festivals. In August, the nation's largest and most impressive **Indian Market** floods the plaza (Aug. 17-18, 2002). The **Southwestern Association on Indian Affairs** *(☎ 983-5220)* has more info. Don Diego de Vargas's peaceful reconquest of New Mexico in 1692 marked the end of the 12-year Pueblo Rebellion, now celebrated in the three-day **Fiesta de Santa Fe** (☎988-7575). Held in early September, festivities begin with the burning of the *Zozobra* and include street dancing, processions, and political satires. The *New Mexican* publishes a guide and a schedule of the fiesta's events.

▲ OUTDOOR ACTIVITIES

There's a reason that *Outside Magazine* is headquartered in Santa Fe. The nearby **Sangre de Cristo Mountains** reach heights of over 12,000 ft. and offer countless opportunities for hikers, bikers, skiers, and snowboarders. Before heading into the wilderness, stop by the **Public Lands Information Center,** 1474 Rodeo Rd., near the intersection of St. Francis Rd. and I-25, for maps, guides, and friendly advice. (☎438-7542. Open M-F 8am-5pm.)

The closest **hiking** trails to downtown Santa Fe are along Rte. 475 on the way to the Santa Fe Ski Area. On this road, 10 mi. northeast of town, the **Tesuque Creek Trail** (2hr., 4 mi.) leads through the forest to a flowing stream. Near the end of Rte. 475 and the Santa Fe Ski Area, trailheads venture into the 223,000 acre **Pecos Wilderness.** A variety of extended backpacking trips can be had throughout this swath of pristine alpine forests. For a rewarding day hike 15 mi. northeast of Santa Fe on Rte. 475, the strenuous full-day climb to the top of 12,622 ft. **Santa Fe Baldy** (8-9hr., 14 mi.) affords an amazing vista of the Pecos Wilderness to the north and east.

Many **bikers** choose to ride the steep Rte. 475 that runs 17 mi. between Santa Fe and the ski area. For a backcountry ride, consider climbing Forest Rd. 150 to the top of **Tesuque Peak** (12 mi.). The uphill climb is very hard work, but the return trip is fun, fun, fun. The trailhead is 13 mi. from Santa Fe on Rte. 475.

At the end of Rte. 475, **Ski Sante Fe** heats up the winters. Located in the towering Sangre de Cristo Mountains on Rte. 475, the ski area operates six lifts, including four chairs and two surface lifts, servicing 43 trails (20% beginner; 40% intermediate; 40% advanced) on 600 acres of terrain with a 1650 ft. vertical drop. (☎982-4429. Snowboards welcome. Open late Nov. to early Apr. 9am-4pm. Lift tickets: full-day $43, teens $36, children and seniors $28. Rental packages start at $18.)

▼ NIGHTLIFE

The bars in Santa Fe attract an eclectic mixture of tourists, artists, bums, and millionaires. Nightlife in Santa Fe tends to be more mellow than in Albuquerque.

- **Cowgirl Hall of Fame,** 319 S. Guadalupe St. (☎982-2565). Nightly live music ranges from bluegrass to country. BBQ, Mexican food, and burgers served all evening, with midnight food specials. 12 microbrews on tap. Happy hour 3-6pm and midnight-1am, when Cowgirl Margaritas are only $3.50. 21+. Cover varies, but never exceeds $3. Open M-F 11am-2am, Sa 8:30am-2am, Su 8:30am-midnight.

- **Paramount,** 331 Sandoval St. (☎982-8999). The only dance club in Santa Fe. Everyone in town shows up for trash disco W. Live music Sa. 21+. Cover $5-7, Sa $5-20. Open M-Sa 9pm-2am, Su 9pm-midnight. **Bar B,** in back, has a chill, futuristic setting, with live music most nights. Cover $5-7. Open M-Sa 5pm-2am, Su 5pm-midnight.

- **El Farol,** 808 Canyon Rd. (☎983-9912). This upscale Spanish bistro has a bar with nightly live music. Flamenco shows W 9:30pm. Cover W-Th $5, F-Sa $7. Open M-F 11am-1:30am, Sa 10am-1:30am, Su 10am-11:30pm. Live music starts at 9:30pm.

▶ DAYTRIPS FROM SANTA FE

LOS ALAMOS

Known only as the mysterious P.O. Box 1663 during the heyday of the Manhattan Project, Los Alamos is no longer the nation's biggest secret. With the infamous distinction of being the birthplace of the Atomic Bomb, Los Alamos now attracts visitors with its natural beauty and outdoor activities. Overlooking the Río Grande

Valley, Los Alamos hovers above the Pueblo and Bayo Canyons on thin finger-like mesas, 35 mi. to the northeast of Sante Fe. In town, the **Bradbury Science Museum,** corner of 15th St. and Central, explains the history of the Los Alamos National Laboratory and its endeavors with excellent videos and hands-on exhibits. (☎647-4444. Open Tu-Sa 9am-5pm, Su-M 1-5pm. Free.) Not to be missed in Los Alamos is the ▓**Black Hole,** 4015 Arkansas St., which sells the junk the laboratory doesn't want anymore, including 50-year-old calculators, flow gauges, time-mark generators, optical comparators, and other technological flotsam. Leave with your very own $2 atomic bomb detonator cable. (☎662-5053. Open M-Sa 10am-5pm.) Outdoors, the town brims with great activities. The **Sante Fe National Forest** provides countless trails for hiking and biking in and along the town's many canyons. The **Valles Caldera,** an expansive and lush volcanic crater, is a wonder to see and has just recently become a National Preserve. It's 15 mi. to the east on Rte. 4 along the scenic Jemez Mountain Trail. **Los Alamos Visitors Center** is on Central Ave. just west of 15th St. (☎662-8105. Open M-F 9am-5pm, Sa 9am-4pm, Su 10am-3pm.)

BANDELIER NATIONAL MONUMENT

Bandelier, 40 mi. northwest of Santa Fe (take U.S. 285 to 502 W, then follow the signs), features some amazing pueblos and cliff dwellings, as well as 50 sq. mi. of dramatic mesas, ancient ruins, and spectacular views of surrounding canyons. The most accessible, **Frijoles Canyon,** is the site of the **Visitors Center.** (☎672-3861, ext. 517. Open June-Aug. daily 8am-6pm; Sept. to late Oct. daily 9am-5:30pm; late Oct. to late Mar. 8am-4:30pm; late Mar.-May 9am-5:30pm.) All visitors to the park should start by hiking the 1.4 mi. **Main Loop Trail** to see the **cliff dwellings** and the ruins of the Tyuonyi Pueblo. Those with more time should continue 0.5 mi. further to the **Ceremonial Cave,** a *kiva* carved into a natural alcove, high above the canyon floor. The **Frijoles Falls Trail** (3hr., 5 mi.), begins at the Visitors Center parking lot and follows the Frijoles Creek downstream 2.5 mi. to the Río Grande. Upper Frijoles Falls, dropping 80 ft., is 1.5 mi. from the trailhead. A strenuous two-day, 22 mi. hike leads from the Visitors Center to **Painted Cave,** decorated with over 50 Ancestral Puebloan pictographs. Free permits are required for backcountry hiking and camping; topographical maps ($10) are sold at the Visitors Center. Just past the main entrance, **Juniper Campground** offers the only developed camping in the park, with water and toilets (sites $10). The park entrance fee is $10 per vehicle, $5 per pedestrian; National Park passes are accepted.

TAOS   ☎505

Before 1955, Taos was a remote artist colony in the Sangre de Cristo Mountains. When the ski valley opened and the thrill-seekers trickled in, they soon realized that the area also boasted the best whitewater rafting in New Mexico, as well as some excellent hiking, mountain biking, and rock climbing. By the 1970s, Taos was a Edenic village of New-Age hippies, struggling artists, extreme athletes, and the deluge of tourists wasn't far behind. Today, Taos's once magical charm often feels eclipsed by the new hotels and traffic jams. Nonetheless, visitors who come to Taos to enjoy the natural beauty of the region will be pleasantly rewarded. To make the most of your time in Taos, get away from the town and spend a few days in the surrounding mountains. Or, head a few miles north to the village of Arroyo Seco, where locals practice yoga in the morning and kayak in the afternoon.

■▐ **ORIENTATION AND PRACTICAL INFORMATION.** Once in town, **Rte. 68** becomes Paseo del Pueblo (Sur and Norte). Drivers should park on Camino de la Placita, a block west of the plaza, or at the meters scattered on side streets. **Greyhound,** 1213A Gusdorf St. (☎758-1144), sends two buses daily to Albuquerque (3hr.; $23), Denver (7½hr.; $60), and Santa Fe (1½hr.; $17). The public local bus service, the **Chile Line,** runs buses every 15-30min. along Paseo del Pueblo from Ranchos de Taos, south of town, to and from the pueblo. In ski season, a bus runs from the center of Taos to the Ski Valley every 2½hr. (☎751-4459. Buses run daily 7am-7pm. 50¢, ski shuttle $5.) The **Chamber of Commerce,** 1139 Paseo del Pueblo Sur, offers up visitor info 2 mi. south of town at the junction of Rte. 68 and Paseo del Cañon. (☎758-

3873 or 800-732-8267. Open daily 9am-5pm.) The **Carson National Forest Office**, 208 Cruz Alta Rd., has free info on camping and hiking. (☎ 758-6200. Open M-F 8am-4:30pm.) **Post Office:** 318 Paseo Del Pueblo Norte, ¼ mi. north of the plaza (☎ 758-2081; open M-F 8am-5pm). **ZIP code:** 87571. **Area code:** 505.

▐ ACCOMMODATIONS. The **Abominable Snowmansion Hostel (HI-AYH)**, 9 mi. north of Taos in the village of Arroyo Seco, is a snowbird's delight with spacious dorm rooms and a pool table adorning the common room. A hostel by summer, ski lodge by winter, the Snowmansion is only 9 mi. west of the ski valley. Teepees and camping are available in the warmer months. (☎ 776-8298. Reception daily 8am-noon and 4-10pm. Dorms Apr. 10-Nov. 22 $14, nonmembers $16; dorm teepees $14/$16; private doubles $36/$40; tent sites $10. Dorms Nov.-Apr. $20. Reserve ahead for winter and spring break.) The **Budget Host Motel**, 1798 Paseo del Pueblo Sur, 3¼ mi. south of the Plaza, is the least expensive motel in Taos, with spacious rooms. (☎ 758-2524 or 800-323-6009. Singles $43-54; doubles $49-61. 10% AAA discount.)

Camping around Taos is easy with a car. The **Kit Carson National Forest** has three campgrounds to the east of Taos on Rte. 64. Tent sites are adjacent to a stream and are surrounded by tall pines. The closest, **Las Petacas**, is 4 mi. east of Taos and has vault toilets but no drinking water. **Capulin Campground**, 7 mi. east of Taos, and **La Sombra**, 1 mi. further, both have drinking water and vault toilets. For more info about these campgrounds, contact the Carson National Forest Office in Taos (☎ 758-6200; sites $12.50). Campgrounds on the road to Taos Ski Valley are free, but have no facilities. **Backcountry camping** doesn't require a permit. Dispersed camping is popular along Rte. 518 south of Taos and Forest Rd. 437. Park on the side of the road and pitch your tent a few hundred feet inside the forest.

▐▌ FOOD. Restaurants cluster around Taos Plaza and Bent St. Cheaper options can be found north of town along Paseo Del Pueblo. **◪Island Coffees and Hawaiian Grill**, 1032 Paseo del Pueblo Sur, just might get you lei-ed at a reasonable price, in a grass hut to boot. Popular Polynesian and southeast Asian dishes include mango coconut chicken ($6) and *lomi lomi* vegetables ($8). Many of the dishes are vegetarian. (☎ 758-7777. Open M-Sa 6:30am-9pm, Su 5-9pm.) **Casa Vaca Cafe**, 6 mi. north of Taos in Arroyo Seco, feels like it was plucked right out of New York's East Village. Have a cappuccino ($1.50) and green chile omelette ($5) for breakfast. (☎ 776-5640. Open daily 7am-6pm.) **Taos Pizza Outback**, north of town on Rte. 64, serves the town's best pizza in slices large enough to warrant their $2.75 price. (☎ 758-3112. Open June-Sept. daily 11am-10pm; Oct.-May Su-Th 11am-9pm, F-Sa 11am-10pm.)

◪ SIGHTS. Taos comes in second only to Santa Fe as a center for Southwestern art. **Galleries**, ranging from high-quality operations to glorified curio shops, can be found in Taos Plaza and on Kit Carson Rd. A well-chosen selection of early Taos paintings hangs at the **Harwood Foundation Museum**, 238 Ledoux St., off Camino de la Placita. (☎ 758-9826. Open Tu-Sa 10am-5pm, Su noon-5pm. $5, under 12 free.) The **Van Vechten-Lineberry Museum**, 501 Paseo del Pueblo Norte, features the works of the Taos Society of Artists (1915-27) with an emphasis on the art of Duane Van Vechten. (☎ 758-2690. Open Oct.-Dec. and Feb.-Apr. W-F 11am-4pm, Sa-Su 1:30-4pm; May-Sept. W-F 10am-5pm, Sa 1-5pm, Su 1-4pm. $6, students $4, children $3.) The **Taos Arts Festival** celebrates local art from mid-September to early October. In the tiny village of **Ranchos de Taos**, 4 mi. south of Taos Plaza, the **Mission of San Francisco de Asis** displays a "miraculous" painting that changes into a shadowy figure of Christ when the lights go out. (☎ 758-2754. Video shown every 30min. daily 9am-4pm. $2.) Four miles north of Taos off Rte. 522, exhibits of Native American art including Pueblo jewelry, black-on-black pottery, and Navajo rugs grace the **Millicent Rogers Museum**, 1504 Museum Rd. (☎ 758-2462. Open daily 10am-5pm, Nov.-Mar Tu-Su 10am-5pm. $6, students and seniors $5, ages 6-16 $1.) The **◪Martinez Hacienda**, 2 mi. south of downtown on Ranchos Rd., is one of the few surviving Spanish Colonial mansions in the US. Built in 1804, this 21-room fortress-like adobe structure features exhibits on the northernmost reaches of the Spanish Empire. (☎ 758-1000. Open Apr.-Oct. daily 9am-5pm; Nov.-Mar. 10am-4pm. $5, children $3.)

A SANTOS CLAUSE During the Spanish Colonial period there were few priests to serve the many Catholics in New Mexico, so people relied on representations of saints, called *santos*, to serve as intermediaries between man and God. There are two types of *santos*: *bultos* (carved figurines) and *retablos* (painted pieces of wood). *Santos* were treated as members of the family; people not only prayed to them, but also had regular conversations with them. Most families had numerous *santos*, and each saint was regarded as having a special area of expertise. For example, San Isidro was responsible for ensuring a good harvest, while San Antonio could help recover things that were missing. If a request to a *santo* was granted, family members would treat the *santo* with extra respect and honor. However, if a prayer went unanswered, the *santo* would be turned towards the wall or hidden in a drawer as punishment.

Taos Pueblo, 3 mi. northwest of the plaza, remarkable for its five-story houses, is one of the last inhabited pueblos; many buildings are off-limits to visitors. The pueblo has capitalized on its popularity—visitors must pay up. (☎758-1028. Open May-Sept. M-Sa 8am-4:30pm, Su 8:30am-4:30pm; Oct.-Apr. M-Sa 8am-4pm, Su 8:30am-4pm. $10, seniors $8, students $3, under 13 free. Camera permit $10, video cameras $20.) Feast days are celebrated with tribal dances; San Gerónimo's Feast Days (Sept. 29-30) also feature a fair and races. The Taos Pueblo Annual Powwow (2nd weekend of July) is the highlight of the summer. A free guide to Northern New Mexican Indian pueblos is available at the Taos Visitors Center.

Of the many arts-and-crafts shops in town, **Taos Drums,** on Rte. 68, 5 mi. south of the Taos Plaza, is the most unique. Local craftsmen make wooden drums in the traditional Native American style, and performers including Fleetwood Mac and Pearl Jam have used their wares. Take a free tour of the workshop and bang the largest drum in New Mexico. (☎800-424-3786. Open M-Sa 9am-5pm, Su 11am-6pm.)

⚡ OUTDOOR ACTIVITIES. Skiers flock to the Taos area when the snow falls. Hailed as one of the best ski resorts in the country, **Taos Ski Valley,** about 15 mi. northeast of town on Rte. 150, offers powder conditions in bowl sections and short but steep downhill runs that rival Colorado's. With 72 trails and 12 lifts, Ski Valley boasts over 2500 ft. of vertical drop and over 300 in. of annual snowfall. (☎776-2291, lodging info 800-992-7669, ski conditions 776-2916. Lift tickets $37-47; equipment rental from $19 per day.) Reserve a room well in advance if you plan to come during the winter holiday season. There are also two smaller, more family-oriented ski areas near Taos: **Angel Fire** (☎377-6401 or 800-633-7463; lift tickets $43) and **Red River** (☎800-494-9117; lift tickets $43). Money-saving multi-day passes are available for use at all three resorts (from $36 per day). In summer, the nearly deserted ski valley and the nearby **Wheeler Peak Wilderness** become a hiker's paradise (most trails begin off Rte. 150). Due to the town's prime location near the state's wildest stretch of the Río Grande, **river rafting** is very popular in Taos. **Far-Flung Adventures,** in Arroyo Seco, offers half-day ($40) to three-day ($375) trips. Reservations up to six weeks in advance are required for longer trips; call for details. (☎758-9072. Open daily 8am-5pm; closed in winter.) For bike rentals, visit **Gearing Up,** 129 Paseo del Pueblo Sur. (☎751-0365. Open daily 9am-6pm. Bikes $30 per day, $80 per week.)

ALBUQUERQUE   ☎505

As the crossroads of the Southwest, anyone traveling north to Denver, south to Mexico, east to Texas, or west to California passes through this commercial hub. But Albuquerque is also a place full of history and culture, with many ethnic restaurants and offbeat cafes, and raging nightclubs. Most residents still refer to Central Avenue as Route 66, and visitors can feel the energy flowing from this mythic highway. The University of New Mexico is responsible for the town's young demographic, while the Hispanic, Native American, and gay and lesbian communities chip in cultural vibrancy and diversity. From historic Old Town to modern museums, ancient petroglyphs to towering mountains, travelers will be surprised at how much there is to see and do in New Mexico's largest city.

▤ TRANSPORTATION

Airport: Albuquerque International, 2200 Sunport Blvd. SE (☎842-4366), south of downtown. Take bus #50 from 5th St. and Central Ave., or pick it up along Yale Blvd. **Airport Express** (☎765-1234) shuttles to the city ($12, 2nd person free). Their stand is open 24hr. A taxi downtown costs under $10, to Old Town $15.

Trains: Amtrak, 214 1st St. SW (☎842-9650). 1 train per day to: Flagstaff (5hr., $59-106); Kansas City (17hr., $116-207); Los Angeles (16hr., $67-120); Santa Fe (1hr. to Lamy, $16; 20min. shuttle to Santa Fe, $14). Reservations required. Open daily 10am-5:30pm.

Buses: Greyhound (☎243-4435) and **TNM&O Coaches** run from 300 2nd St. SW, 3 blocks south of Central Ave. To: Denver (10hr., 5 per day, $64); Flagstaff (6hr., 5 per day, $37); Los Angeles (18hr., 7 per day, $65); Phoenix (10hr., 5 per day, $43); Santa Fe (1½hr., 4 per day, $12.60). Station open 24hr.

Public Transit: Sun-Tran Transit, 601 Yale Blvd. SE (☎843-9200; office open M-F 8am-6pm, Sa 8am-noon). Get maps at Visitors Centers, the transit office, or the library. Most buses run M-Sa 6:30am-8:30pm and leave from Central Ave. and 5th St. #66 runs along Central Ave. 75¢, seniors and ages 5-18 25¢. Request free transfers from driver.

Taxis: Albuquerque Cab, ☎883-4888.

✳❼ ORIENTATION AND PRACTICAL INFORMATION

The city divides into four quadrants: NE, NW, SE, SW. **Central Ave.** divides the north and south, and **I-25** is a rough division between east and west. The all-adobe campus of the **University of New Mexico (UNM)** spreads along Central Ave. from University Ave. to Carlisle St. **Nob Hill,** the area of Central Ave. around Carlisle St., features coffee shops, bookstores, and art galleries. The newly revitalized **downtown** lies on Central Ave. between 10th St. and Broadway. **Old Town Plaza** lies between San Felipe, North Plaza, South Plaza, and Romero, off Central Ave.

Visitor info: Albuquerque Convention and Visitors Bureau, 401 2nd St. NW (☎842-9918 or 800-284-2282), 3 blocks north of Central Ave. in the Convention Center. Open M-F 9am-5pm. Recorded info 24hr. **Old Town Visitors Center,** 303 Romano St. NW (☎243-3215), in the shopping plaza west of the church. Open Apr.-Oct. daily 9am-5pm; Nov.-Mar. 9:30am-4:30pm. Airport **info booth** open Su-F 9:30am-8pm, Sa 9:30am-4:30pm.

Equipment Rental: Mountains and Rivers, 2320 Central Ave. SE (☎268-4876) sells camping and rock-climbing equipment and rents kayaks and canoes. Open M-F 9:30am-6:30pm, Sa 9am-5pm, Su noon-5pm.

Hotlines: Rape Crisis Center, 1025 Hermosa SE (☎266-7711). Center open M-F 8am-noon and 1-5pm, hotline 24 hr. **Gay and Lesbian Information Line,** ☎891-3647. 24hr.

Internet access: UNM Zimmerman Library (☎277-5761), at the heart of campus. Open fall and spring semesters M-Th 8am-midnight, F 8am-9pm, Sa 9am-6pm, Su 10am-midnight; in summer M-Th 8am-9pm, F 8am-5pm, Sa 10am-5pm, Su 10am-9pm.

Post Office: 1135 Broadway NE, at Mountain St. (☎346-8044). Open M-F 7:30am-6pm. **ZIP code:** 87101. **Area code:** 505

▮ ACCOMMODATIONS

Cheap motels line **Central Ave.,** even near downtown. Evaluate the motel carefully before paying; a bit more money might mean a bit more safety. During the October **balloon festival** (see **Sights,** below), rooms are scarce; call ahead for reservations.

▨ **Route 66 Youth Hostel,** 1012 Central Ave. SW (☎247-1813), at 10th St. Get your kicks at this lively and friendly hostel. Well located between downtown and Old Town, Route 66 pleases guests with a full kitchen and enthusiastic staff. Linen $1. Key deposit $5. Reception daily 7:30-10:30am and 4-11pm. Check-out 10:30am. Chores required. Dorms $14; singles with shared bath $20; doubles $25, with private bath $30.

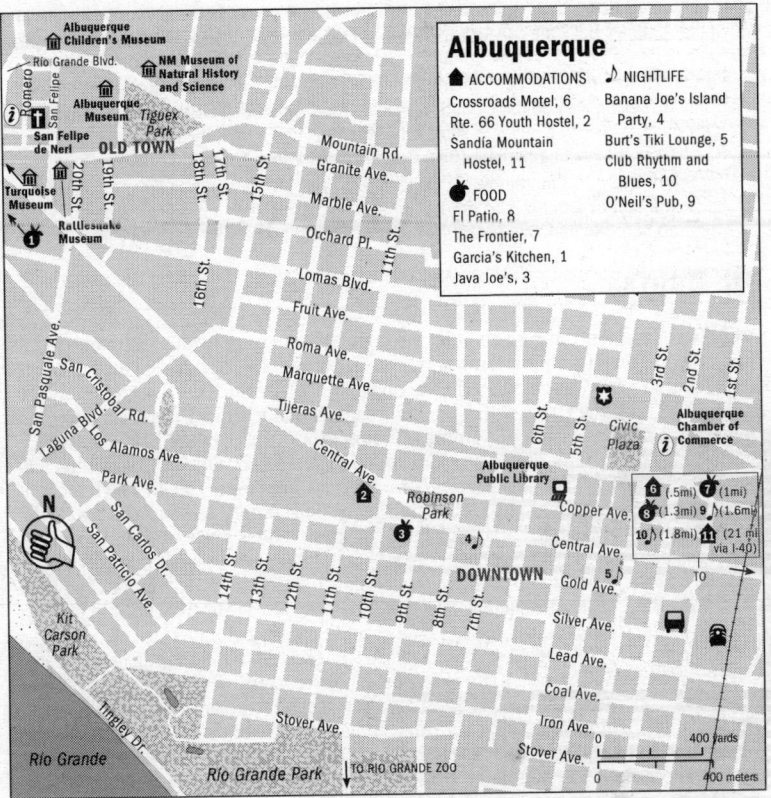

Albuquerque

🏠 ACCOMMODATIONS
Crossroads Motel, 6
Rte. 66 Youth Hostel, 2
Sandía Mountain
    Hostel, 11

🍴 FOOD
Fl Patio, 8
The Frontier, 7
Garcia's Kitchen, 1
Java Joe's, 3

♪ NIGHTLIFE
Banana Joe's Island
    Party, 4
Burt's Tiki Lounge, 5
Club Rhythm and
    Blues, 10
O'Neil's Pub, 9

Sandía Mountain Hostel, 12234 Rte. 14 N (☎281-4117), in nearby Cedar Crest. Take I-40 E to Exit 175 and go 4 mi. north on Rte. 14. Call ahead and the owners will pick you up in Albuquerque. Only 10 mi. from the Sandía Ski Area, this large wooden building boasts a comfortable living room, kitchen, and a family of resident donkeys. Hiking and mountain-biking trails across the street. Linen $1. Dorms $12; private cabins $30.

Crossroads Motel, 1001 Central Ave NE (☎242-2757), ½ mi. from the bus/train station, next to I-25. Large, bright rooms, some with fridge, all with A/C and cable. Check-out 11am. Singles $29; doubles $38. Senior and student discounts.

Coronado State Monument Campground (☎980-8256), 15 mi. north of town. Take I-25 to Exit 242 and follow the signs. A pleasant spot on the banks of the Río Grande. On-site adobe shelters offer respite from the heat. Toilets, showers, and water. Office open daily 8am-5pm; see host to check in after hours. Sites $8; full hookups $18.

🍴 FOOD

A diverse ethnic community and one big load of green chiles render Albuquerque surprisingly tasty. The area around **UNM** is the best bet for inexpensive eateries. A bit farther east, the hip neighborhood of **Nob Hill** is a haven for yuppie fare.

Java Joe's, 906 Park Ave. SW (☎765-1514), 1 block south of Central Ave., and 2 blocks from the Route 66 Hostel. This lively restaurant with a laid-back atmosphere has hearty wraps ($5), sandwiches ($5.50), salads ($4-5), and great breakfast burritos ($3). Lots of vegetarian dishes and occasional live music. Open daily 7am-4:30pm.

▓ **El Patio,** 142 Harvard St. SE (☎268-4245). Behind a blue, wooden fence, a softly strumming guitarist beckons passers-by to sit, relax, and down a few enchiladas. Mexican plates ($5-8) include veggie options. Open M-Sa 11am-9:15pm, Su noon-9:15pm.

Garcia's Kitchen, 1736 Central Ave. SW (☎842-0273). The parrots and chiles hanging from the ceiling may be fake, but the Mexican food is authentic. Breakfast (Mexican and gringo-style) is served anytime. After surveying the large menu, try the *huevos rancheros* ($4.50) or the enchilada plate ($5). Open M-Sa 6:30am-10pm, Su 6:30am-9pm.

The Frontier, 2400 Central Ave. SE (☎266-0550). If it's 3am and an insatiable appetite for some sort of ground beef product has you pressing hard on the accelerator, you'll wind up here. Remarkable breakfast burritos $3 and burgers $2-3. Open 24hr.

⊙ SIGHTS

OLD TOWN. When the railroad cut through Albuquerque in the 19th century, it missed Old Town by almost 2 mi. and thus sentenced the plaza to 90 years of being overlooked. As downtown grew around the railroad, Old Town remained untouched until the 1950s, when the city realized that it had a tourist magnet right under its nose. Just north of Central Ave. and east of Río Grande Blvd., the adobe plaza today looks remarkably as it did over 100 years ago, save for ubiquitous restaurants, gift shops, and jewelry vendors. Free walking tours of Old Town meet at the Museum of Albuquerque. *(1hr. Tu-Sa 11am.)* On the north side of the plaza, the **San Felipe de Neri Church,** dating back to 1793, has stood the test of time. *(Open daily 9am-5pm, accompanying museum open M-Sa 1-4pm; Su mass in English 7 and 10:15am, in Spanish 8:30am.)* A veritable posse of museums and attractions surrounds the plaza. To the northeast, the **Albuquerque Museum** showcases New Mexican art and history. The thorough exhibit on the Conquistadors and Spanish colonial rule is a must-see. *(2000 Mountain Rd. NW. ☎242-4600. Open Tu-Su 9am-5pm. $4, seniors and students $3, children $2. Wheelchair accessible.)* The museum also offers tours of the historic Casa San Ysidro in Corrales, NM. *(☎243-7255 for reservations.)* Across the street from the museum, two dinosaurs, Spike and Alberta, greet tourists outside the **New Mexico Museum of Natural History and Science.** The museum features a five-story dynatheater, planetarium, and simulated ride through outer space. *(1801 Mountain Rd. NW. ☎841-2802. Open daily 9am-5pm, closed M in Sept. $5, seniors $4, children $2; combination Dynamax theater ticket $9/$6/$3.)* The **Rattlesnake Museum,** just south of the plaza, has over 30 species from the deadly mojave to the tiny pygmy. *(202 San Felipe NW. ☎242-6569. Open M-Sa 10am-6pm, Su 1-5pm. $2.50, $2 seniors, under 18 $1.50.)*

UNIVERSITY MUSEUMS. The University of New Mexico has a couple of museums worth a quick stop. The **University Art Museum** rotates exhibits focusing on 20th-century New Mexican painting and photography. *(Near the corner of Central Ave. and Cornel St. ☎277-4001. Open Tu-F 9am-4pm. Free.)* The **Maxwell Museum of Anthropology** focuses on the cultural history of Native Americans in the Southwest. *(On University Blvd., just north of MLK Blvd. ☎277-5963. Open Tu-F 9am-4pm, Sa 10am-4pm. Free.)*

CULTURAL ATTRACTIONS. The **Indian Pueblo Cultural Center** provides a good introduction to the history and culture of the 19 Indian Pueblos of New Mexico. *(2401 12th St. NW. ☎843-7270. Take bus #36 from downtown. Museum open daily 9am-5pm. Art demonstrations Sa-Su 10am-3pm, Native American dances Sa-Su 11am and 2pm. $4, seniors $3, students $1.)* The brand new **Hispanic Cultural Center** has an excellent art collection and cultural exhibits. *(1701 4th St. SW, on the corner of Bridge St. Open Tu-Su 10am-5pm. $3, seniors $2, under 17 free.)*

⚠ OUTDOOR ACTIVITIES

Rising a mile above Albuquerque to the northeast, the crest of the **Sandía Mountains** is visible from just about anywhere in the city. The Spanish named Sandía (watermelon) for the pink color they turn at sunset. The mountains' proximity to Albuquerque draws hordes of outdoor adventurers. Though they don't usually provide solitude, the Sandías offer hikes for all ages and abilities. One of the most popular trails in New Mexico, **La Luz Trail** (7.5 mi. one-way) climbs the Sandía Crest, beginning at the Juan Tabo Picnic Area. From Exit 167 on I-40, drive north on Tramway Blvd. 9.8 mi. to Forest Rd. 333. Follow Trail 137 for 7 mi. and take 84 to the top. To eliminate one leg of the journey, hikers can drive or take the tram. The **North Crest Trail** (1-2 days, 12 mi. one-way) makes for a pleasant, scenic backpacking trip through the Sandía Wilderness. From town, take I-25 to Exit 242, and turn right after the ramp. Go 5 mi., turn right onto Tunnel Spring Rd. and follow 1½ mi. The Sandía Crest Trail (#130) follows the ridge to the Sandía Crest Recreation Area.

The **Sandía Peak Aerial Tramway,** on Tramway Rd. from I-25 (Exit 234) or Tramway Blvd. from I-40 (Exit 167), travels 2.7 mi. up the west face of Sandía Peak (10,378 ft.). The view from the top overlooks the city and the Río Grande Valley—a 11,000 sq. mi. panorama. The ascent is especially striking at sunset. (☎856-6419. Open June-Aug. and during the balloon festival daily 9am-10pm; Sept.-May Th-Tu 9am-8pm, W 5-8pm. During ski season Th-Tu 9am-8pm, W noon-8pm. $14, children $10.) One can also drive to the top of **Sandía Crest** (10,678 ft.). Take I-40 E to Exit 175, turn north on Rte. 14, and go 6 mi. to Rte. 536. A ranger station awaits at the top. (☎248-0190. Open June to mid-Oct. Th-Su 10am-4pm. $3 parking fee.)

Sandía Peak Ski Area, only 30min. from downtown, is a serviceable ski area for those who can't escape north to Taos or south to Ruidoso. Six lifts service 25 short trails on 200 skiable acres. The summit (10,378 ft.) tops a vertical drop of 1700 ft. (☎242-9133. Snowboards allowed. Annual snowfall 125 in. Open mid-Dec. to mid-Mar. daily 9am-4pm. Full-day $39, half-day $28, ages 13-20 $32, under 13 and seniors $28.) During the summer, the ski area, 6 mi. up Rte. 536, caters to mountain bikers. Bikes can be shuttled up on the chairlift and ridden down 35 mi. of mountain trails, covering all skill levels. (Chairlifts run June-Aug. Sa-Su 10am-4pm. Full-day lift ticket $14, single ride $8. Bike rentals at the summit $38 per day. Helmets required.)

🎭🎵 NIGHTLIFE AND ENTERTAINMENT

Within the arid expanses of the Southwest's often stale, honky-tonk bar scene, Albuquerque is an oasis. Hopping with interesting bars, jamming nightclubs, art film houses, and a large university, Albuquerque feels truly alive. Check flyers posted around the university area for live music shows or pick up a copy of *Alibi*, the free local weekly. During the first week of October, hundreds of aeronauts take flight in colorful hot-air balloons during the **balloon festival.**

Most nightlife huddles on and near Central Ave., downtown, and near the university; Nob Hill establishments tend to be the most gay-friendly. The offbeat **Guild Cinema,** 3405 Central Ave. NE, screens independent and foreign films. (☎255-1848. Open M-Th at 4:30 and 7pm, F-Su at 2, 4:30, and 7pm.)

Banana Joe's Island Party, 610 Central Ave. SW (☎244-0024), is the largest club in town. With 6 bars, a tropical outdoor patio, and 1 big dance floor, Banana Joe's delivers nightlife to the masses. Nightly live music from reggae to flamenco. DJ W-Su. Happy hour 5-8pm. 21+, except for Su teen night. Cover Th-Sa $5. Open Tu-Su 5pm-2am.

Burt's Tiki Lounge, 313 Gold Ave. (☎243-2878), at 3rd St., 1 block south of Central. Polynesian masks on the walls attract a young, lively crowd. Live music 2-3 nights a week. Live DJ Th. 21+. Open M-W and Sa 8pm-2am, Th-F 5pm-2am, Su 8pm-midnight.

Club Rhythm and Blues, 3523 Central Ave. NE (☎256-0849). Great live music M-Sa with a crowd that's not afraid to get up and dance. World beat M, open mic Tu, Latin W, jazz Th, and blues F-Sa. 21+. Cover M and W-Th $5; F-Sa $7. Open M-Sa 8pm-2am.

O'Neil's Pub, 3211 Central Ave. NE (☎256-0564), in Nob Hill. O'Neil's pours more Guinness than any pub in New Mexico. Happy hour 4-7pm and 10pm-1am. Live music Sa 10pm-1am. 21+. No cover. Open M-Sa 11:30am-2am, Su 11:30am-midnight.

SOUTHWEST

STUFF Housed within walls made of glass bottles, the Tinkertown Museum is unlike anything you've ever seen before. From a collection of wedding cake garnishes, to Otto the one-man-band, to a sailboat that has sailed around the world, to the pants of the tallest man that ever lived, this place is full of, well, doo-dads...whatchamacal-lits...you know...um, *stuff*. For full enjoyment, bring lots of quarters. Located 20min. from Albuquerque, Tinkertown sits along the Turquoise Trail on Rte. 536. Take Exit 175 off I-40 and go 6 mi. north on Rte. 14. (☎281-5233. Open Apr. 1- Nov. 1 daily 9am-6pm. $3, seniors $2.50, children $1.)

■ DAYTRIPS FROM ALBUQUERQUE

PETROGLYPH NATIONAL MONUMENT

At the western edge of Albuquerque's western suburbs, this national monument features more than 20,000 images etched into lava rocks by Pueblo Indians and Spanish settlers between 1300 and 1680. The park encompasses much of the 17 mi. West Mesa, a ridge of basalt boulders formed by volcanic activity 130,000 years ago. The most impressive petroglyphs are accessible via three short trails at **Boca Negra Canyon**, 2 mi. north of the Visitors Center. The **Rinconada Canyon Trail** (2.5 mi.), 1 mi. south of the Visitors Center, runs along the base of the West Mesa. On the west side of the park, a dirt road leads to the base of two ancient volcanoes. To reach the park, take I-40 to Unser Ave. and follow signs. By bus, take #90 from downtown to Montano and bus #27 to Unser; walk 1 mi. north to Boca Negra Canyon. (☎899-0205. Park open daily 8am-5pm. Admission to Boca Negra Canyon M-F $1, Sa-Su $2; National Parks passes accepted.)

ACOMA PUEBLO

Perched on a sheer mesa with a spectacular view, this "Sky City" is one of the longest continuously inhabited sites in the US. Today, Acoma Pueblo is a vibrant community—just as it was 900 years ago. About 30 of the Acoma people live here year-round, and on holidays hundreds drive to the mesa from the surrounding reservation for traditional celebrations and dancing. Acoma, at the end of Rte. 32, is 13 mi. south of Exit 96 off I-40, and 11 mi. south of Exit 102 off I-40. Both routes are well-marked. Visitors can only experience the pueblo through a guided tour. Video cameras are forbidden, and permits are required for still cameras. (☎800-747-0181. Open Nov.-Mar. daily 8am-4:30pm; Apr.-Oct. 8am-7pm. No tours July 10-13 and the 1st and 2nd weekends of Oct. Last tours depart 1hr. before closing. $9, seniors $8, children $6; camera permit $10.)

GALLUP ☎505

Gallup, located at the intersection of **I-40** and **U.S. 666,** falls into the unfortunate class of Western cities that seem to have been built too quickly, filling their cultural void with an empty supermarket-and-styrofoam-cups modernity. However, Gallup's proximity to the **Four Corners** (see p. 703), **Petrified Forest National Park** (see p. 747), the **Navajo Reservation** (see p. 744), **Chaco Culture National Park** (see below), and **El Morro National Monument** (see below) somewhat redeems it for travelers.

Old Rte. 66, which runs parallel to I-40 through downtown, is lined with dirt-cheap motels, often with an emphasis on dirt. The best place to stay in town, hands down, is **El Rancho Hotel and Motel**, 1000 E. 66 Ave., a step up in price from most other options, but a leap in quality. (☎863-9311. Reception 24hr. Check-in 2pm. Check-out 12pm. Singles $47; doubles $55.) One of the best spots for those watching their bottom line is the **Blue Spruce Lodge**, 119 E. Rte. 66, with clean, well-maintained rooms. (☎863-5211. Reception 8am-11pm. Check-out 11am. Singles $24; doubles $26.) You can pitch a tent in the shadow of red sandstone cliffs at **Red Rock State Park Campground**, which offers access to hiking 5 mi. east of town off Rte. 66. (☎863-1329. 142 sites with showers and hookups. Sites $10; hookups $14.) In addition to the usual fast-food suspects, diners and cafes line both sides of I-40. **Earl's**

Restaurant, 1400 E. Rte. 66, has been around since 1947, and the food and prices show why. (☎ 863-4201. Open M-Sa 6am-9:30pm, Su 7am-9pm. Entrees $4-10.) **Panz Alegra,** 1201 E. Rte. 66, is an upscale spot with deals on Mexican dishes ($7-10) and steaks. (☎ 722-7229. Open Su-Th 11am-10pm, F-Sa 11am-11pm.) **Wild Sage People's Market,** 610 E. Pershing, offers bulk organic foods and a nice respite from the rest of Gallup. (☎ 863-5383. Open Tu and F 3:30-7pm, Sa 10am-6pm.)

Greyhound, 201 E. Rte. 66 (☎ 863-3761), runs to Albuquerque (2½hr., 4 per day, $23), and Flagstaff (4hr., 4 per day, $36). **Visitors Center:** 701 Montoya Blvd., just off Rte. 66. (☎ 863-3841 or 800-242-4282; open daily 8am-5pm, June-Aug. 8am-6pm). **Post Office:** 950 W. Aztec (☎ 722-5265; open M-F 8:30am-5pm, Sa 10am-1:30pm). **ZIP code:** 87301. **Area code:** 505.

CHACO CULTURE NATIONAL HISTORICAL PARK ☎ 505

Sun-scorched Chaco Canyon served as the first great settlement of the Ancestral Puebloans. The ruins here, which date from the 9th century, are among the most well-preserved in the Southwest. Evidence of inhabitance thousands of years older than even the oldest Ancestral Pueblo dwellings enriches the landscape, though the societies that flourished during the turn of the first millennium make the site truly remarkable. The Chaco societies demonstrated superior scientific knowledge and designed their buildings in accordance to solar patterns. One such structure, **Pueblo Bonito,** is the canyon's largest pueblo; it was once four stories high and housed more than 600 rooms. Nearby **Chetro Ketl** houses one of the Southwest's largest *kivas* (prayer rooms). The largest pueblos are accessible from the main road, but **backcountry hiking trails** lead to many others; snag a free **backcountry permit** from the Visitors Center before heading off.

Chaco Canyon lies 92 mi. northeast of Gallup. From the north, take Rte. 44/550 to County Rd. 7900 (3 mi. east of **Nageezi** and 50 mi. west of **Cuba**), and follow the road for 21 mi., 16 of which are unpaved. From the south, take Rte. 9 from **Crownpoint** (home of the nearest ATM and grocery stores to the park) 36 mi. east to the marked park turn-off in Pueblo Pintado; turn north onto unpaved Rte. 46 for 10 mi.; turn left on County Rd. 7900 for 7 mi.; turn left onto unpaved County Rd. 7950 and follow it 16 mi. to the park entrance. *There is no gas in the park, and gas stations en route are few and far between.* Call the park in advance (☎ 988-6727) to inquire about the road conditions, which may deteriorate in bad weather.

The **Visitors Center,** at the east end of the park, has an excellent museum that exhibits Ancestral Puebloan art and architecture and includes an enlightening film. Star-gazing like the Chacos is offered at the center's observatory, open to visitors four nights a week (call ahead for available nights). Stock up on water here. (☎ 786-7014. Open daily 8am-6pm; in winter 8am-5pm. $8 per vehicle.) For a closer look, the **Wijiji Trail** (1½hr., 3 mi.) starts at the Wijiji parking area 1 mi. east of the Visitors Center and explores Wijiji, a great house built around AD 1100.

No food is available at the park. The **Gallo Campground,** a little more than 1 mi. from the Visitors Center, offers serene desert camping for $10 per site; register at the campground. The 48 sites have access to tables, fireplaces, and central toilets. The most accessible inexpensive lodging is in Farmington, 75 mi. north.

EL MALPAIS NATIONAL MONUMENT ☎ 505

Home to a spectacle of converging lava flows and sandstone mesas, this 15 year-old national monument and its associated BLM land feature some of the Southwest's most unique terrain—from miles of lava tubes to one of the state's largest natural arches. Despite its spectacular landscape, the monument does not receive the same crowds as its neighbors, making it a perfect spot to escape for a while.

A number of **Visitors Centers** are located throughout El Malpais. Off I-40 at Exit 85, the **Northwest New Mexico Visitors Center** sits at the northern end of the monument. (☎ 876-2783. Open May-Sept. daily 9am-6pm; Oct.-Apr. 8am-5pm.) The park service's **El Malpais Information Center** (☎ 783-4774) is 23 mi. south of I-40 on Rte. 53, while the **Bureau of Land Management's Ranger Station** is on Rte. 117, 9 mi. south of Exit 89 on I-40. (☎ 240-0300. Both open daily 8:30am-4:30pm.)

SOUTHWEST

Rte. 53 runs along the western side of the monument, while **Rte. 117** borders the eastern side. Both roads are access trailheads and are themselves excellent ways to see the diverse landscape. **Rte. 42** runs into the monument's belly, but because it is not maintained, a high-clearance vehicle is recommended. Rte. 117 runs by the most accessible wonders of the monument. The wheelchair-accessible **Sandstone Bluffs Overlook**, 10 mi. south of I-40 and 1 mi. south of the Visitors Center, offers panoramic vistas of the Malpais lava flows and environs. **La Ventana Natural Arch,** 7 mi. further south, is the largest of New Mexico's readily accessible natural arches. Less than 1 mi. further, Rte. 117 enters **The Narrows,** where lava flowed to the base of 500 ft. tall sandstone cliffs thousands of years ago. The **Narrows Rim Trail** (3-4hr., 6 mi.) begins at the southern end of the Narrows, 21 mi. from I-40, and scrambles to the top of the rim, where spectacular views of the area's wonders greet you.

There are no campgrounds at El Malpais; however, **backcountry camping** is free in designated spots in the Big Tubes and El Calderon areas. Obtaining a permit at one of the Visitors Centers is requested. For more info, contact any of the Visitors Centers or write National Park Service, P.O. Box 939, Grants, NM 87020.

EL MORRO NATIONAL MONUMENT ☎ 505

While traveling through what is now New Mexico, Native Americans, Spanish *conquistadors*, and Anglo pioneers left their inscriptions on a giant boulder. **Inscription Rock** is now part of El Morro National Monument, just west of the Continental Divide on Rte. 53, 13 mi. southeast of the Navajo town of Ramah. A half-mile loop trail winds past the boulder and neighboring spring. A longer trail continues on past two pueblos. The **Visitors Center** includes a museum and warnings against emulating the graffiti of old. A small, tranquil campground has running water and primitive toilets (9 sites; $5). Trails close 1hr. before Visitors Center. (☎ 783-4226. Open daily June-Aug. 8am-7pm; off-season 9am-5pm. $4 per vehicle, $2 per pedestrian.)

TRUTH OR CONSEQUENCES ☎ 505

In 1950, the popular radio game show, *Truth or Consequences*, celebrated its 10th anniversary by renaming a small town, formerly Hot Springs, NM, in its honor. As its maiden name suggests, T or C was a tourist attraction prior to the publicity stunt. The mineral baths infuse the town with fountain-of-youth effects and a funky down-home spirit. Maybe it's something in the water.

ORIENTATION AND PRACTICAL INFORMATION. T or C sits approximately 150 mi. south of Albuquerque on I-25. From C.W.'s Premium Water and Ice, 800 Main St., Greyhound (☎ 894-3649), runs two coaches daily from Albuquerque (3hr., $31.50) and El Paso (2hr., $26.50). **Chamber of Commerce:** 201 S. Foch St. (☎ 894-3536; open M-F 9am-5:30pm, Sa 9am-1pm). **Post Office:** 300 Main St., in the middle of town (open M-F 9am-3pm). **ZIP code:** 87901. **Area Code:** 505.

ACCOMMODATIONS. ☒**Riverbend Hot Springs Hostel (HI-AYH),** 100 Austin St. From I-25, take Exit 79, turn right, and continue 1½ mi. to a traffic light. Turn left at the light, then immediately turn right onto Cedar St. and look for the blue building at the bend in the road. On the shores of the Río Grande, this laid-back hostel offers relief to weary travelers. Use of on-site mineral baths, a meditation cove, and an outdoor barbecue grille are all free for guests. Call ahead and hostel owners will make arrangements for horseback riding, yoga, and belly dancing lessons. (☎ 894-6183. Kitchen and laundry. Reception open 8am-10pm, call ahead for late-night arrivals. Teepees or dorms $14, nonmembers $16; private rooms $30-48; tent site $10, nonmembers $12.) The **Charles Motel and Spa,** 601 Broadway, offers more plebian accommodations, but there are also mineral baths on the premises. (☎ 894-7154 or 800-317-4518. Singles $35; doubles $39; rooftop suites $45.) Campsites at the nearby **Elephant Butte Lake State Park** have access to restrooms and cold showers. (Primitive sites $8; developed sites with showers $10; with electricity $14.)

⊡ FOOD. Nearly all of T or C's restaurants are as easy on the wallet as the baths are on the body. The popular **La Cocina**, 280 N. Date St., pleases with huge portions of Mexican and New Mexican food, including free chips and salsa. A heaping combination plate goes for $7. (☎894-6499. Open daily 10:30am-10pm.) **Hot Springs Bakery Cafe**, 313 Broadway, in a stucco turquoise building, has an outdoor patio and cactus garden. Excellent pizzas go for $7-12. Open mic every Wednesday evening 6-8pm. (☎894-5555. Open Tu-Sa 8am-8pm.) **Bar-B-Que on Broadway**, 308 Broadway, serves excellent breakfast specials (starting at $2.50) and hearty lunch entrees ($5-8), as well as dishing out local gossip. (☎894-7047. Open M-Sa 7am-4pm.) **The Dam Site**, just past the **Elephant Butte Dam** on Rte. 51, is a bar and grille with an outdoor patio, offering spectacular views of the lake and surrounding mountains. (☎894-2073. Live music Sa afternoon Apr.-early Sept. Dinner entrees $7-19, drafts $2.50. Open Su-Th 11am-9pm, F-Sa 11am-10pm; bar open until midnight F-Sa.)

◒◮ SIGHTS AND OUTDOORS. T or C's **mineral baths** are the town's main attraction; locals claim that they heal everything from blisters to sunburn. The only outdoor tubs are located at the **Riverbend Hostel,** where four co-ed baths (bathing suits must be worn) abut the Río Grande. Access to the baths is $6 per hr. for the public (10am-7pm), but complementary for guests (7-10am and 7-10pm). The private indoor baths at **Charles Motel's spa** cost $4 per hr. for guests and $5 for non-guests. Rooftop jacuzzi $8 (open Su-Th). The spa offers massages and a slew of services, like reflexology and ear candling.

Five miles north of T or C, **Elephant Butte Lake State Park** holds New Mexico's largest lake. A public works project dammed the Río Grande in 1916, and the resulting lake was named after the elephantine rock formation at its southern end. The park offers sandy beaches and a marina. (Vehicles $4, bikes and pedestrians free.) The **Dam Site** rents motorized boats of all kinds. (☎894-2041. Motorboats $20 per hr., pontoon boats $30 per hr., ski boats $45 per hr.) The **Visitors Center** is at the park entrance. (☎877-664-7787. Open M-F 7:30am-4pm, Sa-Su 7:30am-10pm.)

Approximately 55 mi. north of T or C on I-25, the **Bosque del Apache Wildlife Refuge** is a favorite spot of migrating birds in winter, including cranes, eagles, and snow geese. (☎835-1828. Park open until 1hr. after sunset. Entrance fee $3.) In the summer you can see a surprising number of deer, coyote, porcupines, roadrunners, and snakes from the 15 mi. driving loop. The park also offers some short **hiking trails.** (Maps at Visitors Center. Open M-F 7:30am-4pm, Sa-Su 8am-4:30pm.)

GILA CLIFF DWELLINGS AND NATIONAL FOREST ☎505

Gila Cliff Dwellings National Monument preserves over 40 stone and timber rooms carved into the cliff's natural caves by the Mogollon tribe during the late 1200s. About a dozen families lived here for about 20 years, farming on the mesa top and along the river. During the early 1300s, the Mogollon abandoned their homes for reasons unknown, leaving the dwellings as their only trace. (Dwellings open daily 8am-6pm, off-season 9am-4pm. Entrance fee $3, under 12 free.) The **Visitors Center,** at the end of Rte. 15, shows a film and sells various maps of the **Gila National Forest.** (☎536-9461. Open daily 8am-5pm; off-season 8am-4:30pm.) The picturesque hike (1hr., 1 mi.) to the dwellings begins past Upper Scorpion Campground. A trail guide (50¢) is available at the trailhead or Visitors Center. With flush toilets and water, the free **Upper Scorpion Campground** operates on a first come, first served basis.

The **Gila National Forest** encompasses boundless hiking trails and allows **free backcountry camping.** In fact, this is the largest contiguous designated Wilderness south of Alaska. Rugged, mountainous terrain makes it ideal for extended, intense **backpacking** trips. Many trailheads lie along the road to the dwellings; rangers have hiking suggestions. To reach the monument, take Rte. 15 from Silver City, a slow, gorgeous 44 mi. drive winding through dense forests to the canyon of the Gila River. Call ahead for road conditions before attempting the drive in winter. If you're coming from Truth or Consequences, take Rte. 152 to Rte. 35, and head north on Rte. 15. This route is less steep, just as beautiful, and takes about the same time.

The nearest accommodations can be found at the comfy **Grey Feathers Lodge,** 20 mi. south at the intersection of Rte. 15 and Rte. 35. Drawing as many as 4000 hummingbirds on certain summer weekends, the lodge is a perfect place to bird-watch. (☎536-3206. Singles $45; doubles $50.) The adjoining cafe outfits travelers with sandwiches ($3-7). Otherwise, the nearest rooms and chow are in **Silver City,** south of the Gila area at the intersection of U.S. 180 and Rte. 15. The **Palace Hotel,** 106 W. Broadway, has beautiful antique-styled rooms, but only three of them are at the cheap end of the spectrum. (☎388-1811. Doubles $33-53, each additional person $5. Reservations recommended.) Chain motels flank U.S. 180 on the east side of town. For eats, the tourist favorite **Jalisco Cafe,** 100 S. Bullard St., at Spring St. in the heart of downtown, serves heaping portions of spicy Mexican food. (☎388-2060. Open M-Th 11am-8:30pm, F 11am-9pm, Sa 11am-8:30pm. Meals $5-8.)

Stopping at the Corner Cafe, 200 N. Bullard St., **Las Cruces Shuttle Service** (☎800-288-1784) offers daily trips between Silver City and Deming (3 per day, $20); Las Cruces (3 per day, $30); and El Paso (3 per day, $35). **Visitors Center:** 201 N. Hudson St. (☎538-3785 or 800-548-9373; open M-Sa 9am-5pm, in summer also Su noon-4pm). **Post Office:** 500 N. Hudson St. (☎538-2831; open M-F 8:30am-5pm, Sa 10am-noon). **ZIP code:** 88061. **Area code:** 505.

WHITE SANDS NAT'L MONUMENT ☎505

The giant sandbox of White Sands National Monument evokes nostalgia for playground days. Situated in the Tularosa Basin between the Sacramento and San Andres Mountains, the world's largest dunes formed as rainwater flushed gypsum from the nearby peaks and into Lake Lucero. As desert heat evaporated the lake, the gypsum crystals were left behind and now form the blindingly white sand dunes. These drifts of fine sand create an arctic tundra look, but don't be fooled: the midday sun assaults the shadeless with a light and heat that can be unbearable. Trekking or rolling through the dunes provides hours of mindless fun or mindful soul-searching; the sand is particularly awe-inspiring at sunset.

■■ **ORIENTATION AND PRACTICAL INFORMATION.** White Sands lies on Rte. 70, 15 mi. southwest of Alamogordo and 52 mi. northeast of Las Cruces. Rte. 70 is prone to closures due to missile testing at the nearby military base. Delays can run up to 1hr.; call 479-9199 to check the status of Rte. 70 closures. The **White Sands Visitors Center,** Box 1086, Holloman AFB 88330, is near the park entrance. (☎479-6124. Open daily 8am-7pm; mid-Aug. to late May 8am-5pm.) **Area code:** 505.

▐▞ **ACCOMMODATIONS AND CAMPING.** To use the park's **backcountry campsites,** register at the park entrance ($3 per adult plus entrance fee). **Aguirre Springs** (☎525-4300), 30 mi. to the west on Rte. 70, has free camping, but you must pay $3 to enter. For info, contact the **Forest Supervisor,** Lincoln National Forest, 1101 New York Ave., Alamogordo 88310. **Oliver Lee Memorial State Park,** 10 mi. south of Alamogordo on U.S. 54, then 5 mi. east on Dog Canyon Rd., has sites at a canyon mouth on the west slope of the Sacramento Mountains. (☎437-8284. Sites $10; hookups $14. Visitors Center open daily 9am-4pm. Park entrance fee $3 per vehicle.)

The ▨**High Desert Hostel Ranch,** the most unique accommodation in southern New Mexico, sprawls 15 mi. south of Carrizozo. The 86-year-old orange adobe ranch house offers road-weary travelers a peaceful respite. The ranch's 240 acres come complete with an orchard, plenty of land for hiking, and stunning sunsets. Guests enjoy access to all the food in the kitchen and a vast living room. The hostel is in the hamlet of Oscuro, a flag stop on the **Greyhound** route from El Paso to Albuquerque ($24 one-way from either city); call ahead for a free pickup. The hostel is 1 mi. down a dirt road from U.S. 54—follow the signs. (☎648-4007. Free laundry. Dorm beds $14; private doubles $27; triples $32. Cash or traveler's checks only.) Closer to White Sands, the town of **Alamogordo** has a large motel selection, most of which line White Sands Blvd. The **Alamo Inn,** 1450 N. White Sands Blvd., is one of the cheapest. (☎437-1000. Singles $26; doubles $35.)

⊡⚠ SIGHTS AND OUTDOORS. The 8 mi. **Dunes Drive** is a good way to begin a visit to White Sands. To really experience the uniqueness of this giant sandbox, you must get out of your car and take a walk across the dunes; off-trail hiking is permitted anywhere in the eastern section of the park. The only **wheelchair-accessible trail** in the park is the **Interdune Boardwalk** (¼ mi.), an easy walk above the sand. An interpretive brochure describes the animals and plants that live in the dune field on the **Big Dune Nature Trail** (30min., 1 mi.). The best hike in the park is the **Alkali Flat Trail** (2hr., 4.6 mi.), which loops through the heart of the dunes to the parched, salty lakebed of Lake Otero. *Do not hike the trail in strong winds.* If guided activities are your can of worms, the park does offer many ranger programs. A free guided **sunset stroll** takes place every evening at sunset (call ahead for schedule), and on **full moon nights** in the summer, the park stays open late (until 11pm, last entrance 10pm). During the **Perseid Meteor Shower** (usually the 2nd week of August), the park remains open until midnight. Park rangers lead monthly tours to **Lake Lucero,** the origin of the park's gypsum sand. (3hr. tours on last weekend of each month. Call ahead for reservations. $3, children $1.50.)

Sixty-five miles northwest of Alamogordo on the White Sands Missile Range, the **Trinity Site** was the site of the world's first atomic bomb detonation on July 16, 1945. The heat of the explosion caused the sand to melt and form a green glass called "trinitite." Part of the original trinitite has been preserved, but the area is now barren. The **Alamogordo Chamber of Commerce** organizes two tours annually to the site, on the first Saturday of April and October. (☎437-6120 or 800-826-0294. Call ahead for reservations.) **White Sands Missile Range** 34 mi. west of Alamogordo on Rte. 70, has a small museum and outdoor missile exhibit. (Open M-F 8am-4pm, Sa-Su 10am-3pm. Free. Driver's license, proof of insurance, and car registration are required.)

ROSWELL   ☎505

With giant inflatable Martians advertising used cars, streetlights donning painted-on pointy eyes, and flying saucers adorning fast-food signs, one thing is certain: aliens *have* invaded Roswell. The fascination began in July 1947, when an alien spacecraft reportedly plummeted to the earth near the dusty town. The official press release reported that the military had recovered pieces of a "flying saucer," but a retraction arrived the next day—the wreckage, the brass claimed, was actually a harmless weather balloon. Everyone admits that something crashed in the desert northwest of Roswell on that fateful night. Was the initial Army statement just a poor choice of words by some PR hack or a crack in an elaborate cover-up?

Believer or skeptic, most visitors will find the alien side of Roswell entertaining, if not enlightening. During the first week of July, the **UFO Festival** commemorates the anniversary of the alleged encounter, drawing thousands for live music, an alien costume contest, and a 5km "Alien Chase" race. With a plastic flying saucer above its storefront, the popular **International UFO Museum and Research Center,** 114 N. Main St., dedicates itself to telling the story of what happened near Roswell in 1947. Exhibits feature testimonials and newspaper clippings about the 1947 incident, as well as features on alien sightings around the world. (☎625-9495. Open Oct.-Feb. daily 10am-5pm; Mar.-Sept. 9am-5pm. Free. Audio tour $1.)

Main and 2nd St. are both lined with budget motels, with the chains on Main St. north of downtown tending to be pricier than those on 2nd St. The best deal is at the **Zuni Motel,** 1201 N. Main St. Adobe rooms have cable TV and fridges. (☎622-1930. Singles $24; doubles $28, with kitchenettes $36.) **Bottomless Lakes State Park** has lakeshore campsites, 12 mi. east on Rte. 380, then 5 mi. south on Rte. 409. (☎624-6058. Sites $10; full hookups $18.) Around the corner from the UFO Museum, the **Crash Down Diner,** 106 W. 1st St., is an out-of-this-world-themed restaurant. Try a "hungry alien" sub ($3-5), or an "unidentified" burger ($4). Even the salt and pepper shakers are shaped like other-worldly visitors. (☎627-5533. Open M-Sa 8am-6pm, Su 10am-6pm.) **Martin's Capitol Cafe,** 110 W. 4th St. delights earthling or otherwise with tasty Mexican dishes at down-to-earth prices. The gigantic burritos (starting at $3.50) scream "take me to your stomach." (☎624-2111. Open M-Sa 6am-8:30pm.)

Aside from its extraterrestrial peculiarities, Roswell is a fairly normal town. The intersection of 2nd St. (Rte. 70/380) and Main St. (Rte. 285) is the sun around which the Roswell solar system orbits. To reach Roswell from Albuquerque, head 89 mi. south on I-25 to San Antonio, then 153 mi. east on U.S. 380. **Greyhound,** 1100 N. Virginia Ave. (☎622-2510), in conjunction with TNM&O, runs buses to Albuquerque (4hr.; 2 per day Tu-Sa, 1 on Su; $35) and El Paso (4½hr.; 3 per day; $38). **Pecos Trails Transit,** 515 N. Main St., sends buses all over town. (☎624-6777. M-F 6am-10:30pm, Sa 7:10am-10pm, Su 10:30am-7pm. 75¢, students 50¢, seniors 35¢.) The cheery and helpful **Visitors Center** is at 426 N. Main St. (☎624-0889. Open M-F 8:30am-5:30pm, Sa-Su 10am-3pm.) **Post Office:** 415 N. Pennsylvania Ave. (☎623-7232; open M-F 7:30am-5:30pm, Sa 8am-noon). **ZIP code:** 88202. **Area Code:** 505.

CARLSBAD CAVERNS   ☎505

Imagine the surprise of the first European wanderers in southeastern New Mexico when 250,000 bats appeared at dusk, seemingly out of nowhere. It was the turn of the century when this swarm led to the discovery of the Carlsbad Caverns. By 1923, colonies of tourists clung to the walls of this desolate attraction. Carlsbad Caverns National Park marks one of the world's largest and oldest cave systems; even the most jaded spelunker will be struck by its unusual geological formations.

The belly of the cave can be explored by embarking on any of three tours. Plaques guide you along the self-guided **Big Room Tour** and **Natural Entrance Tour.** The Big Room Tour is relatively easy and popular, making use of the elevator on both the descent and ascent. The steep Natural Entrance tour is less trafficked as it winds its way down from the surface; the elevator is used for the ascent. (Natural Entrance open June to mid-Aug. daily 8:30am-3:30pm; mid-Aug. to May 8:30am-2pm. Big room open June to mid-Aug. daily 8:30am-5pm; mid-Aug. to May 8:30am-3:30pm. $6, age 6-15 $3. Audio tour $3.) The third option is the ranger-guided **King's Palace Tour,** which passes through four of the cave's lowest rooms and some of the most awesome anomalies. (1½hr. tours on the hr. 9-11am and 1-3pm. $8, Golden Age Passport holders and ages 6-15 $4. Advance reservations required.) Plan your visit for late afternoon to catch the magnificent **bat flight.** The ritual, during which hungry bats storm out of the cave at a rate of 6000 per min., is preceded by a ranger talk. (Daily May-Oct. just before sunset.) **Backcountry hiking** is permitted above ground, but a permit, a map, and massive quantities of water are required.

Tours of the undeveloped **Slaughter Canyon Cave** offer a more rugged caving experience. A reliable car is required to get there, however. There's no public transportation, and the parking lot is 23 mi. down a dirt road off U.S. 62/180, several mi. south of the main entrance to the park. The cave entrance is a steep, strenuous half-mile from the lot. Ranger-led tours (bring a flashlight) traverse difficult and slippery terrain; there are no paved trails or handrails. (2hr. tours; June-Aug. twice daily, Sept.-May Sa-Su only. $15, Golden Age Passport holders and ages 6-15 $7.50. Call at least 2 days ahead to reserve.) Other tours of remote caves are offered, the more adventurous of which require crawling and climbing through tight passages. (☎800-967-2283. Tours 1-4hr. $7-20. Call at least a month in advance for reservations.)

Drive 20 mi. north to **Carlsbad** to find a plethora of cheap motels. The **Park View Motel,** 401 E. Greene St., just across the Greene St. Bridge on the right, has clean, cinderblock rooms with A/C, cable, fridge, with a swimming pool outside. (☎885-3117. Singles $22; doubles $29.) The **White's City Resort RV Park,** outside the park entrance, has water, showers, and a pool. (☎785-2291 or 800-228-3767. Sites or hookups $20. Register in the Best Western lobby.) **Backcountry camping** is free; get a permit at the Visitors Center. For more camping, see **Guadalupe Mountains National Park, TX,** p. 623.

The closest town is **White's City,** a tiny tourist trap on U.S. 62/180, 20 mi. southeast of Carlsbad, 6 mi. from the park Visitors Center. Flash floods occasionally close the roads, so call ahead to the Visitors Center. **El Paso, Texas** (see p. 624), is the nearest major city, 150 mi. to the west past **Guadalupe Mountains National Park** (see p. 623).

Greyhound, in cooperation with **TNM&O Coaches** (☎887-1108), runs two buses daily between El Paso ($32) and Carlsbad ($16), making a stop at White's City. **Visitor info: Carlsbad Caverns Visitors Center** (☎785-2232. Open daily 8am-7pm, late Aug.-May 8am-5:30pm. Entrance fee $6.) White's City's **Post Office:** 23 Carlsbad Caverns Hwy., next to the Best Western. (☎785-2220. Open M-F 8am-noon and 12:30-4:30pm, Sa 8am-noon.) **ZIP code:** 88268. **Area code:** 505.

CALIFORNIA

California is a place to freak out—to redefine boundaries, identities, and attitudes. It is a land that effaces the past to experiment with the novel and unexplored, anticipating the constant changes in mass culture and channeling them into the trends of the future. Gold miners frenzied here in the 1840s, flower children went wild in the 1960s, and hungry young actors and ambitious dot-com moguls leap for the good life today. Folks dig deep for riches, imprinting California hype, commerce, industry, art, and insanity on the collective brain of the world.

Glaring movie spotlights, clanging San Francisco trolleys, and *barrio* bustle all belong to California. Vanilla-scented Jeffrey pines, alpine lakes, and ghostly, shimmering desert landscapes all belong to California. The breezy tolerance of the San Francisco Bay Area, the plastic style of L.A., and the military-fueled Republicanism of San Diego all belong to California. It is the edge of the West, the testing ground of the superlative, the drawing board for the American dream. There's so much going on you'd need a whole book (like *Let's Go: California 2002*) to describe it.

HIGHLIGHTS OF CALIFORNIA

LOS ANGELES. Follow your star to the place where media legends carouse, Ice Age fossils calcify, and boardwalk freaks commune (p. 784).

SAN FRANCISCO. Here, bluesmen resonate, iconoclasts castigate, students demonstrate, and old hippies recreate (p. 827).

SCENIC DRIVES. Along the coast, Rte. 1 and U.S. 101 breeze past earthy beach towns and along soaring cliffs, passing Santa Barbara (p. 819), Hearst Castle (p. 823), and Redwood National Park (p. 860).

NATIONAL PARKS. Hike among the granite peaks of Yosemite (p. 868), or climb a boulder and see the sunset at Joshua Tree (p. 816).

PRACTICAL INFORMATION

Capital: Sacramento.

Visitor info: California Office of Tourism, 801 K St., #1600, Sacramento 95814. Call 800-862-2543 for tourism materials 3-4 weeks in advance.

Postal Abbreviation: CA. **Sales Tax:** 7-8%, depending on county.

LOS ANGELES   ☎ 213

With a desert basin center, two mountain ranges crossing and cradling the county, and 81 miles of dazzling coastline, Los Angeles County (pop. 9.5 million; 4,061 sq. mi.) juggles multiple personalities. Myth and anti-myth stand comfortably juxtaposed in Los Angeles. Some see in its sweeping beaches and dazzling sun a demi-paradise, a land of opportunity where the most opulent dreams can be realized. Others point to its congestion, smog, and crime, and declare Los Angeles a sham—a converted wasteland where TV-numbed masses go to wither in the sun. Regardless, L.A. is a wholly American phenomenon. It's one hell of a show.

INTERCITY TRANSPORTATION

Six main arteries pump into Greater L.A. Three of them run north from the city: the **Santa Ana Freeway (I-5)**, the **Ventura Freeway (U.S. 101)**, and the **Pacific Coast Highway (Rte. 1)**, "PCH" for short. Santa Ana Fwy. also runs south, and **I-10** and **I-15** run east.

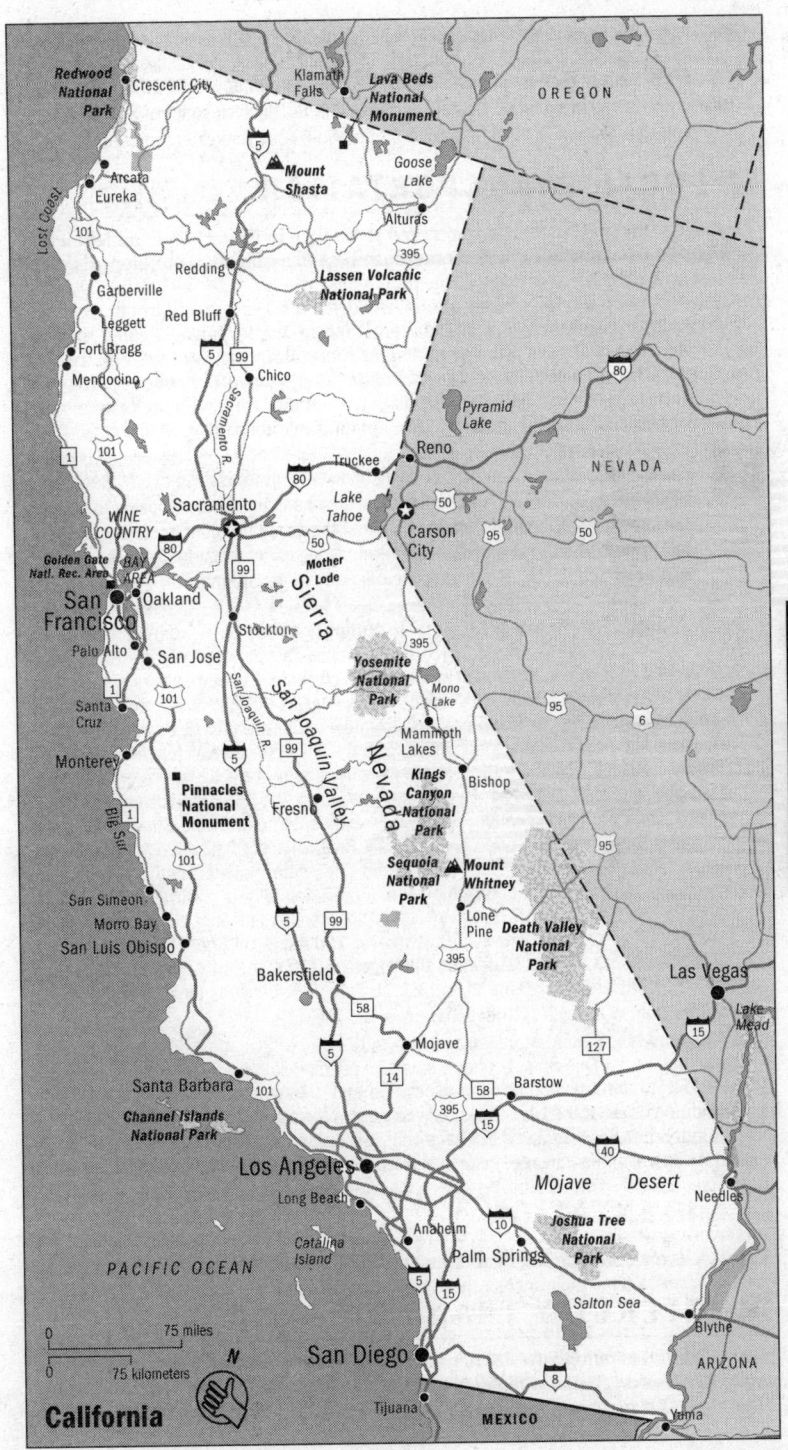

California

CALIFORNIA

Airport: Los Angeles International (LAX) (☎310-646-5252), in Westchester, 15 mi. southwest of downtown. Metro buses, car rental companies, cabs, and airport shuttles offer rides from here to requested destinations. Cab fare to downtown is $28-35.

Buses: Greyhound Information Center, 1409 N. Vine St., 1 block south of Sunset Blvd.

Trains: Union Station, 800 N. Alameda St. (☎683-6729), serves Amtrak trains.

LOCAL TRANSPORTATION

Nowhere is the god *Automobile* revered more than in L.A., often making the City of Angels a transportation hell. Sometimes it seems like all 3.5 million residents are out crowding the freeways at once, leaving little room for clean air, patience, or sanity. Hand-in-hand with cell phone use, driving takes up a major chunk of any self-respecting Angeleno's day. A little reminder: no matter how crowded the freeway is, it's almost always quicker and safer than taking city streets. For freeway info, call **CalTrans** (☎897-3693). *If you hitchhike, you will probably die.* It is uncommon and exceptionally dangerous in L.A., and anyone who picks up a hitchhiker probably has ulterior motives. Don't even think about it.

> Public transportation can be confusing, slow, and even useless in L.A. Because sights are so spread out and buses are such a headache, those looking to sightsee should get behind the wheel of a car. If this is not possible, try to base yourself in Hollywood or downtown, where many sights are clustered. While driving isn't much fun in L.A., it's usually the best way to get around.

Public Transit: The **Metropolitan Transit Authority (MTA)** does work—sort of. Some older buses may still be labeled RTD (Rapid Transit District), the MTA's former name. Bus service is dismal in the outer reaches of the city and 2hr. journeys are not unusual. Write for "sector maps," MTA, P.O. Box 194, Los Angeles 90053, or stop by a **customer service center.** There are **three centers** downtown: Gateway Transit Center, Union Station (open M-F 6am-6:30pm); Arco Plaza, 505 S. Flower St., Level C (open M-F 7:30am-3:30pm); and 5301 Wilshire Blvd. (open daily 9am-5pm). Fare $1.35, seniors and disabled 45¢; transfers 25¢/10¢. Exact change required. The **DASH shuttle** (☎808-2273) serves Chinatown, Union Station, Gateway Transit Center, and Olvera Street. DASH also operates shuttles in Hollywood (along Sunset Blvd.), Pacific Palisades, Venice, Watts, Fairfax, Midtown, Crenshaw, Van Nuys/Studio City, Warner Center, and Southeast L.A. Downtown DASH operates approximately M-F 6:30am-6:30pm, Sa 10am-5pm. Pacific Palisades shuttles do not run on Sa. Venice DASH operates June-Aug. Sa-Su every 10min. 11am-6pm. Fare 25¢; parking $2.50. With over 1000 stops in Santa Monica, L.A., and Culver City, **Santa Monica Municipal Bus Lines** (☎310-451-5444), the "Big Blue Bus" (BBBus), is faster and cheaper than the MTA. Fare 50¢; transfers for MTA buses 25¢.

Taxi: Bell Cab, ☎235-5222. **Independent,** ☎385-8294.

Car Rental: Avon, 7080 Santa Monica Blvd. (☎323-850-0826), at La Brea Ave. Open M-F 6am-7pm, Sa-Su 7am-5pm. Economy cars $29 per day with 150 mi. free, $175 per week with 750 mi. free. Insurance $9 per day. No under-25 surcharge. **Avis,** 11901 Santa Monica Blvd. (☎310-914-7700), between Barrington Ave. and Bundy St. Open M-F 7:30am-5pm, Sa 8am-5pm, Su 9am-4pm. Economy cars $34 per day or $180 per week with unlimited mileage. Insurance $9 per day. Under-25 surcharge $10 per day.

✴ ORIENTATION

A mere 419 mi. south of San Francisco and 127 mi. north of San Diego, the City of Angels spreads its wings across the flatland basin between the coast of Southern California and the San Gabriel Mountains. Greater L.A. is like a club to which the surrounding 'burbs try to belong—a vast conglomerate of over 80 cities. Before you even think about navigating L.A.'s 6500 mi. of streets and 40,000 intersections, get yourself a good **map.** Locals swear by the *Thomas Guide: Los Angeles County Street Guide and Directory* ($16 for L.A. county, $26 for L.A. and Orange County).

NEIGHBORHOODS

A legitimate **downtown** Los Angeles does exist, but it won't help orient you to the rest of the city. The predominately Latino section of L.A. known as **East L.A.** begins east of downtown's Western Ave. South of downtown are the **University of Southern California (USC), Exposition Park,** and the predominantly African-American districts of **Inglewood** and **Compton.** The area south of downtown, known as **South Central,** suffered the brunt of the fires and looting that erupted in 1992. South Central and East L.A. are considered crime-ridden and offer little to attract tourists.

Northwest of downtown is **Hollywood.** Running from downtown to the ocean, Sunset Blvd. (east-west) presents a cross-section of virtually everything L.A. has to offer: beach communities, lavish wealth, famous nightclubs, and sleazy motels. Hollywood Blvd. (east-west) runs just beneath the star-studded Hollywood Hills. West of Hollywood, the **Westside** encompasses West Hollywood, Westwood, Century City, Culver City, Bel Air, Brentwood, and (for our purposes) the independent city

L.A. Overview

CALIFORNIA

of **Beverly Hills.** The affluent Westside also is home to the University of California at Los Angeles (UCLA) and some trendy, off-beat Melrose Ave. hangouts. The area west of downtown is known as the **Wilshire District** after its main boulevard.

The Valley spreads north of the Hollywood Hills and the Santa Monica Mountains. For most people, *the* valley, is, like, the **San Fernando Valley,** where more than a million people live in the suburbs, in a basin bounded to the north and west by the Santa Susanna Mountains and the Simi Freeway (Rte. 118), to the south by the Ventura Freeway (Rte. 134), and to the east by the Golden State Freeway (I-5). The Valley also contains the suburb of **Burbank** and the city of **Pasadena.**

Eighty miles of beach line L.A.'s **Coastal Region. Zuma** is northernmost, followed by **Malibu,** which lies 15 mi. up the coast from **Santa Monica.** Just a bit farther south is the funky beach community of **Venice.** The beach towns south of Santa Monica, comprising the **South Bay,** are **Marina del Rey, Manhattan, Hermosa,** and **Redondo Beach.** South across the **Palos Verdes Peninsula** is **Long Beach.** Farthest south are the **Orange County** beach cities. Confused yet? Everyone is. Get a good map.

🔀 PRACTICAL INFORMATION

Visitor info: Los Angeles Convention and Visitors Bureau, 685 S. Figueroa St. (☎213-689-8822), between Wilshire Blvd. and 7th St. in the Financial District. Hundreds of brochures and maps. Staff speaks English, French, German, Spanish, and Tagalog. Distributes *Destination: Los Angeles*, a free booklet with tourist and lodging info. Open M-F 8am-5pm, Sa 8:30am-5pm.

Hotlines: Rape Crisis, ☎310-392-8381. 24hr.

Hospitals: Cedars-Sinai Medical Center, 8700 Beverly Blvd. (☎310-855-5000, emergency 310-423-6517). **Good Samaritan Hospital,** 616 S. Witmer St. (☎213-977-2121, emergency 213-977-2420). **UCLA Medical Center,** 10833 Le Conte Ave. (☎310-825-9111, emergency 310-825-2111).

Post Office: 71301 S. Central Ave. Open M-F 7am-7pm, Sa 7am-3pm. **ZIP code:** 90001.

> **L.A. COUNTY AREA CODES. 213** covers downtown L.A., Huntington Park, Vernon, and Montebello. **213** and **323** cover Hollywood. **310** and **424** cover Malibu, Pacific Coast Hwy., Westside, parts of West Hollywood, Santa Monica, southern and eastern L.A. County, and Catalina Island. **626** covers the San Gabriel Valley and Pasadena. **818** covers Burbank, Glendale, San Fernando Valley, Van Nuys, and La Cañada. **909** covers the eastern border of L.A. County. In text, **213** unless noted.

🔏 ACCOMMODATIONS

Cheap accommodations in Los Angeles are often unsafe; ask to see a room before you plunk down any cash. Hotels with rates below $35 are probably not the kind of place in which you would feel secure. In choosing where to stay, the first consideration should be car accessibility. If you don't have wheels, you would be wise to decide which element of L.A. appeals to you the most. Those visiting for the beaches would do well to choose lodgings in Venice or Santa Monica. Avid sightseers will probably be better off in Hollywood or the more expensive (but cleaner and nicer) Westside. Downtown has numerous public transportation connections but is unsafe after dark. *Listed prices do not include L.A.'s 14% hotel tax.*

HOLLYWOOD

Although Tinseltown has tarnished in recent years, its location, sights, and nightlife keep the tourists coming. Exercise caution if scouting out one of the many budget hotels on **Hollywood** or **Sunset Blvd.;** *especially east of the main strips, the area can be dangerous, particularly at night.* Nevertheless, the hostels here are generally excellent and a much better value than anything else in L.A.

CALIFORNIA

TO GRIFFITH PARK

Barnsdall Park

Vermont Ave.

Normandie Ave.

KOREATOWN
8th St.
Olympic Blvd.

TO DOWNTOWN

Franklin Ave.

Hollywood Fwy.

Western Ave.

N. Wilton Pl.
Van Ness Ave.

3rd St.

6th St.

Pico Blvd.

2

Sunset Blvd.
Vine St.
Cahuenga Blvd.

HOLLYWOOD

Paramount Studios

WILSHIRE DISTRICT

Crenshaw Blvd.

N

1 mile

1 kilometer

101

7

6

Highland

5

Fountain Ave.

Monica Blvd.

Warner Bros.
Studios

Melrose Ave.

La Brea Ave.

Wilshire Country Club

JEFFERSON PARK

Jefferson Blvd.

10

Franklin Ave.

Hollywood Blvd.

Fairfax Ave.

Crescent Heights Blvd.

WEST

HOLLYWOOD

Sierra Bonita Ave.
Curson Ave.
3

Spaulding Ave.
Genesee Ave.

Gardner St.

CBS Studios

Farmer's Market

Hancock Park

La Brea
Tar Pits

L.A. County
Museum of Art

Miracle Mile

San Vicente Blvd.

Washington Blvd.

Adams Blvd.

Santa

Sweetzer Ave.

Kings Rd.

Beverly Blvd.

Fairfax Ave.

Crescent Heights Blvd.

Venice Blvd.

National Blvd.

Le Parc

La Cienega Blvd.

Sunset Strip

2

Beverly Center

Robertson Blvd.

Santa Monica Blvd.

Olympic Blvd.

Pico Blvd.

WEST LOS ANGELES

Santa Monica Fwy.

Doheny Dr.
Hillcrest Rd.

Doheny Rd.

Hillcrest Rd.

Sunset Blvd.

3rd St.
Burton Way

Wilshire Blvd.

Museum of Tolerance

Castle Heights Ave.
Beverwil Dr.

10

National Pl.

Santa Monica Mtns.
Nat'l Recreation Area

Greystone Mansion
and Park

Rexford Dr.
Crescent Dr.
Canyon Dr.
Beverly Dr.
Rodeo Dr.
Camden Dr.

Elm Dr.

Golden Triangle

Beverly Dr.
Rodeo Dr.
Roxbury Dr.

Century Plaza Towers

Rancho Park

National Blvd.

Coldwater Canyon Drive

Lake Franklin

BEVERLY HILLS

Roxbury Dr.
Whittier Dr.
Walden Dr.

Moreno Dr.

Park E.

Century
Park W.

Fox Studios

Ave. of the Stars

CENTURY CITY

Federal Ave.

Benedict Canyon Rd.

Beverly Hills Hotel

Los Angeles
Country Club

Mapleton Dr.

Westwood Memorial Cemetery

Patricia Ave.

Prosser Ave.

Overland Ave.

Westwood Blvd.

Tower Rd.

Beverly Glen Blvd.

Beverly Glen Blvd.

Hilgard Ave.

WESTWOOD

Veteran Ave.
Sepulveda Blvd.

405

BEL AIR

Bel Air Rd.

Stone Canyon Rd.

Sunset Blvd.

UCLA

Gayley Ave.
Landfair Ave.
Le Conte Ave.

UCLA Hammer Museum

VETERANS
ADMIN.

Wilshire Blvd.

Barrington Ave.

405

San Diego Fwy.

BRENTWOOD

Barrington Ave.

Kentner Ave.

San Vicente Blvd.

Montana Ave.

Bundy Dr.

San Vicente Blvd.

Santa Monica Blvd.

Olympic Blvd.

2

J. Paul Getty Museum and Getty Center

TO SANTA MONICA AND VENICE

Banana Bungalow Hollywood, 2775 W. Cahuenga Blvd. (☎323-851-1129), just north of the Hollywood Bowl. This mini-compound's Hollywood Hills locale affords it space enough to cultivate a wacky and frisky summer-camp atmosphere. Pool, hoops, weight room, theater (hosts free stand-up) with big-screen TV, and "snack shack." Lockers 25¢. Continental breakfast, linen, and parking included. Meals $5. Laundry (wash $1.25, dry 75¢). Key deposit $10. On-site car rental. Check-in 24hr. Stay 7 nights and the 8th night is free. Passport and international airline ticket or college ID required. Co-ed dorms (6-10 beds) with bathroom $19-21; private doubles house up to 4 people for $67.

USA Hostels Hollywood, 1624 Schrader Blvd. (☎323-462-3777 or 800-524-6783), south of Hollywood Blvd., west of Cahuenga Blvd. Stay for more than a day at the hostel and get free pickup from airport, bus, and train stations. Kitchen, patio, free comedy nights W and Su, and themed parties ($4). To use lockers, bring your own lock or buy one for $3. All-you-can-eat make-your-own pancakes, linen, and parking included. Passport or proof of travel required. Dinner $5. Dorms (6-8 beds) with private bath $17; private rooms for 2-4 people $38-46. Prices discounted $1-2 off-season.

Hollywood International Hostel, 6820 Hollywood Blvd. (☎323-463-0797 or 800-750-6561). Front-row seats overlooking the brand new Kodak Theatre may give this hostel's property value a boost, but it doesn't change the aging interior. Enormous lounge with TV, billiards, and foosball. Free local phone calls. Toast and tea breakfast included. Lockers 25¢. Laundry ($1 wash, 50¢ dry). Reception 24hr. Reserve ahead with credit card. Ask for a discount if paying for over a week in cash up front. International passport and (sometimes) college ID required. Single-sex dorms (2-4 beds) with shared bath June-Aug. $16, Sept.-May $13; private rooms $40. Weekly dorms $105.

Orange Drive Manor, 1764 N. Orange Dr. (☎323-850-0350). This pleasant, quiet mini-mansion sitting in a low-key residential neighborhood is admittedly picky about its residents. Small TV lounge and kitchen. Spacious, clean dorms with antique furniture. Lockers 75¢. Towels $2-3. Linen included. Parking $5 per night. Reservations recommended. US citizens and non-students permitted. Max. stay 1 week, unless they really like you. Work 4-6hr. in exchange for board. Dorms (2-4 beds), some with private bath, $19-22; private rooms $39.50. Minimal discount with ISIC card. No credit cards.

SANTA MONICA, VENICE, AND MARINA DEL REY

Venice Beach hostels beckon to young budget travelers, especially foreign students, who are lured by the area's blend of beach culture and lively nightlife. Most lodgings cater to raucous party kids, but there are some quiet gems in the mix.

▧ Los Angeles/Santa Monica (HI-AYH), 1436 2nd St. (☎310-393-9913), Santa Monica. Take MTA #33 from Union Station to 2nd St. and Broadway, BBBus #3 from LAX to 4th St. and Broadway, or BBBus #10 from Union Station. This hostel welcomes travelers of all backgrounds and ages. Rooms are small but common spaces well-kept and well attended. Newly renovated kitchen, 2 nightly movies, library, central courtyard. Breakfast 7:30-10:30am. No alcohol. Quiet hours 10pm-8am. Wheelchair accessible. Safe and lockers. Laundry (wash $1, dry 75¢). 4-week max. stay in any 6-month period. 24hr. security and check-in. Dorms $23-26, nonmembers $26-29; private doubles $61-65. Prices include tax. Group packages available for 7 people or more.

Cadillac Hotel, 8 Dudley Ave. (☎310-399-8876), directly off the Ocean Front Walk, in Venice. A self-proclaimed Art Deco landmark complete with Venetian gondola and a section of the Berlin Wall, this kitschy monument draws an amiable international crowd. Sauna, sundeck, and gym. Lockers and luggage storage. Wheelchair accessible. No kitchen. 2 out of 3 of the following required: valid driver's license, credit card, or passport. Delicious ocean views for the lucky (corner doubles $110; double suite $140). 4-bed bunks with bath $25. Private doubles $102; double plus single or bunk $113.

Venice Beach Cotel, 25 Windward Ave. (☎310-399-7649), 1 block from the boardwalk above St. Mark's Restaurant, in Venice. From LAX, take BBBus #3, transfer to #2, get off at the Venice Beach Post Office, and walk 1 block toward shore. International staff and guests liven up the cramped quarters. BYOB bar area opens at 7pm nightly and offers a free cocktail at check-in. Free use of tennis rackets, table tennis, and boogie boards ($20 deposit). Linen included. Key deposit $5. Reception and security 24hr. No reservations during high season. Passport required. Dorms without ocean view $17, with bath and view $19. Doubles (some with private bath, TV, and view) $40-55; triples with bath and view $60. Oct.-May subtract $2 for dorms, $5 for private rooms.

BEVERLY HILLS, WESTWOOD, AND WILSHIRE

The relatively safe Westside has excellent public transportation to the beaches. The area's affluence, however, means less bang for your buck. Those planning to stay at least one month in summer or six months during the school year can contact the **UCLA Off-Campus Housing Office,** 350 Deneve Dr. (☎310-825-4491).

- **Orbit Hotel and Hostel,** 7950 Melrose Ave. (☎323-655-1510), west of Fairfax Ave., in West Hollywood. Opened by 2 young L.A. locals less than 2 years ago, Orbit deserves top honors for location and liveability. Spacious retro kitchen, big-screen TV lounge, small but gregarious courtyard, and party room. Parking available. Dorms accept international students with passport proof only. 6-bed ($17) or 4-bed ($20) dorms with bath. Comfortable private rooms with TV and bath $49-55.
- **Claremont Hotel,** 1044 Tiverton Ave. (☎310-208-5957 or 800-266-5957), in Westwood Village near UCLA. Pleasant and inexpensive for its locale. Clean rooms with antique dressers, ceiling fans, private baths, and phones. Microwave and free coffee offered in the lobby next to a pleasant, Victorian-style TV lounge. Daily maid service. Check-out noon. Reservations recommended, especially in June graduation season. Singles $43; doubles $51; 2 full-size beds for up to 4 people $60.
- **The Little Inn,** 10604 Little Santa Monica Blvd. (☎310-475-4422). Take one step into the courtyard and attain budget-travel nirvana. The rooms are clean and color-coordinated. A/C, cable TV, and fridges. Parking included. Check-out 11am. Let's Go readers get special rates mid-Sept. through July (excluding major holiday periods). Singles $60; doubles $65. Suite for 3 with fridge, sink, and stove $75. Stay 4 or more days and receive $5 off per day. During the high season expect prices to jump $10.
- **Bevonshire Lodge Motel,** 7575 Beverly Blvd. (☎323-936-6154), across from the Post Office at Curson Ave. Bright rooms with windows overlook both the pool courtyard and street. A/C, cable TV, daily maid service, and parking included. Singles $55-65; doubles (with kitchen) $61-71; 5-person suites $74-84. 10% ISIC discount.

🍴 FOOD

Eating in Los Angeles, the city of the health-conscious, is more than just *eating*. Thin figures and fat wallets are a powerful combination—L.A. lavishes in the most heavenly and healthy recipes. There are also restaurants where the main objective is to be seen and the food is secondary, as well as those where the food itself seems too beautiful to be eaten. Fortunately for the budget traveler, L.A. elevates fast food and chain restaurants to heights virtually unknown in the rest of the country—chains are a way of life, as all Angelenos want quality and convenience. For the supreme burger-and-fries experience, try **In 'n' Out Burger,** a beloved chain symbolized by a '57 Chevy. **Johnny Rocket's** revives the never-really-lost era of the American diner; their milkshakes are a heady experience. The current craze is lard-free, cholesterol-free "healthy Mexican"—**Baja Fresh** leads the pack. Urban yuppies crave the best Chinese chicken salad from **California Chicken Cafe,** which also serves up rotisserie chicken, a quintessential Californian food. **Quizo's** reheats its fresh baked bread with cheese for sub sandwich lovers, and surfer style meets Mexican cuisine at Hawaiian-born **Wahoo's Fish Tacos.**

HOLLYWOOD

Hollywood offers the best budget dining in L.A. **Melrose** is full of chic cafes, many with outdoor patios.

- **Roscoe's House of Chicken and Waffles,** 1514 Gower St. (☎323-466-7453). Roscoe makes the best waffles of any dive anywhere. Try "1 succulent chicken breast and 1 delicious waffle" ($5.60). The down-home feel has been known to attract celebrities. Be prepared to wait on weekends. Open Su-Th 8:30am-midnight, F-Sa 9am-4am.

■ **Duke's Coffee Shop,** 8909 Sunset Blvd. (☎310-652-3100), in West Hollywood. The legendary Duke's is the best place in L.A. to see hung-over rockers. If the seats don't testify to it, the walls will—they are plastered with autographed album covers. Communal, canteen-style tables are a regular meeting place. Try the "Spinach Special" (with mushrooms, onions, ground beef, scrambled eggs, cheese and spices) for $8.25. Entrees $5-8. Attendant parking in rear $1. Open M-F 7:30am-8:45pm, Sa-Su 8am-3:45pm.

Pink's Famous Chili Dogs, 709 N. La Brea Ave. (☎323-931-4223), at Melrose. More of an institution than a hot dog stand, Pink's has been serving up chili-slathered doggies on its outdoor patio since 1939. Mouthwatering chili dogs $2.20 and chili fries $1.85. Rumor has it that Orson Welles scarfed down 15 of Pink's chili dogs in one sitting. Open Su-Th 9:30am-2am, F-Sa 9:30am-3am. No credit cards.

Toi on Sunset, 7505½ Sunset Blvd. (☎323-874-8062). Toi, like L.A. itself, is a pastiche of unlikely elements: the walls pay homage to punk legends and rock superstars, interspersed with low-camp trimmings like leopardskin rugs; the clientele consists of edgy hipsters alongside the occasional celeb; the menu features huge portions of delectable Thai fare with a Cali twist. The net result is undeniably strange but strangely beguiling. Heaping servings of *pad kee mao* and *pad thai* $8-9. Open daily 11am-4am.

SANTA MONICA

Elevated patios along the 3rd St. Promenade and Ocean Ave. herald Santa Monica's upscale eating scene. Most menus offer organic and vegetarian choices.

■ **Fritto Misto,** 601 Colorado Ave. (☎310-458-2829), at 6th St. This "Neighborhood Italian Cafe" allows patrons to play with their own culinary inspiration with the create-your-own pasta dish option (from $6), flexible made-to-order menu ($10-14), and cheery, decision-aiding waitstaff. Numerous vegetarian entrees $8-11. Lunch specials until 5:30pm on weekdays, 4pm weekends ($6-8). Monster omelettes Su 10am-4pm ($7-8). Open M-F 11:30am-10pm, F-Sa 11:30am-10:30pm, Su 10am-9:30pm.

Big Dean's "Muscle-In" Cafe, 1615 Ocean Front Walk (☎310-393-2666). Home of the "Best Cheeseburger on the West Coast" ($4), this indoor-outdoor bar and grill is just a few steps from the Santa Monica Pier. Bratwurst $2 (with kraut $2.50), veggie burgers $6. No pretense here: it's sun, sand, sauerkraut, and *cervezas!* Happy hour ($2 beers) M-F 4-8pm. Open daily 10am-dark, or until the regulars empty out.

Britannia Pub, 318 Santa Monica Blvd. (☎310-458-5350), 2 blocks from 3rd St. Promenade. My Guinness, this is a bloody good pub—and the expats know it, too. Beer-battered mushrooms $4.25, club sandwich $6.25, and the *British Weekly* absolutely free. Beer $4. Happy hour (50¢ off everything) M-F 4-7pm. Karaoke Tu, Th, and Su; British DJ F. Open daily 11am-1:30am.

VENICE

Venetian cuisine runs the gamut from greasy to ultra-healthy, as befits its beachy-hippie crowd. The boardwalk offers cheap grub in fast food fashion.

■ **Van Go's Ear,** 796 Main St. (☎310-396-1987). This open-air cafe and art gallery gets going late night. Try the Kato Kaelin "Guest House" Salad or the Richard Simmons Fruit Salad (both $6). Entrees start at $8. Live jazz F nights. Open M-Th 7pm-3am. Open F-Sa 24hr. No credit cards.

■ **Aunt Kizzy's Back Porch,** 4325 Glencoe Ave. (☎310-578-1005), in Marina Del Rey. Done up to look like a back porch, Aunt Kizzy's is a little slice of Southern heaven. Dinner $12-13, buffet brunch $8. Save room for Aunt Kizzy's $3 sweet potato pie—"so light it can float like a feather." Rated the best soul food in the city by *L.A. Magazine,* and testified to by countless celebrities whose portraits adorn the walls. Su buffet brunch (11am-3pm) is a steal at $13. Open Su-Th 11am-10pm, F-Sa 11am-11pm.

Rose Cafe and Market, 220 Rose Ave. (☎310-399-0711), at Main St. Gigantic rose-painted walls, local art, and industrial architecture might make you think this is a museum, complete with gift shop. But the colorful cuisine is the main display. Healthy deli specials, sandwiches available starting 11:30am ($6-8), salads ($5-7). Limited menu after 3pm. Open M-F 7am-7:30pm, Sa 8am-7:30pm, Su 8am-5pm.

BEVERLY HILLS

There is budget dining in glamorous Beverly Hills; it just takes a little looking. A tip: do not eat on Rodeo Dr., and stay south of Wilshire Blvd.

▓ **The Breakfast Club,** 9671 Wilshire Blvd. (☎323-271-8903), 2 blocks west of Rodeo Dr. The diner motif dies hard in L.A., and this is Beverly Hills's designer diner. With bright vinyl booths, vintage movie posters, and Coca-Cola clocks, this was one interior decorator's labor of love. Omelettes $6, burgers $7. Open M-Sa 7am-3pm, Su 8am-3pm.

▓ **Al Gelato,** 806 S. Robertson Blvd. (☎310-659-8069), between Wilshire and Olympic St. Popular among the theater crowd for its proximity to the Beverly Hills Theater, this homemade gelato spot also does complimentary pre-buttered bread and large portions of pasta with a delicious sweet basil tomato sauce. Giant meatball ($4.50) and rigatoni ($11). Skip the tiramisu ($5.50), and just stick to the gelato ($3.75-5.75). Made-to-order cannoli ($4). Open daily 10am-midnight. No credit cards.

Nate 'n' Al Delicatessen, 414 N. Beverly Dr. (☎310-274-0101). For 55 years, this delicatessen (no mere deli) has been serving up hand-pressed potato pancakes, blintzes ($9), and Reuben sandwiches ($10). Open daily 7am-9pm.

WESTWOOD AND UCLA

With UCLA nearby, cheap food and beer can be found in abundance. If you're down to your last few bucks, head to **Subbie's Roll-Inn,** 972 Gayley Ave., for $2 subs (open daily 10am-3am), or **Jose Bernstein's,** 935 Broxton Ave., which has burritos for $4 (open Su-Th 11am-1am, F-Sa 10am-2:30am).

▓ **Gypsy Cafe,** 940 Broxton Ave. (☎310-824-2119). This cafe's fare is more Italian than French (*penne cacciatore* $7.25), and its mood is more Turkish than Italian (hookahs for rent, $10 per hr.). Don't expect fast food—the bountiful buffet is the stuff of a 5-star hotel, and the elegant dining encourages customers to linger. Kebabs $9. Organic salads, wraps, and sandwiches $6-8. The tomato soup ($5) is famous throughout Westwood. Stand-up comedy Tu and F nights. Open Su-Th 8am-midnight, F-Sa 8am-1am.

▓ **Sandbag's Gourmet Sandwiches,** 11640 San Vicente Blvd. (☎310-207 4888), in Brentwood. Other locations in Westwood (☎310-208-1133) and Beverly Hills (☎310-786 7878). The perfect place in rich man's land for a healthy, cheap lunch that comes with a complimentary chocolate cookie. Most sandwiches $5.75. Open daily 9am-4pm.

Arrosto Coffee, 923 Broxton Ave. (☎310-824-2277). In addition to the black stuff, this fun party joint serves up foot-long subs and gyro platters for $3. Arrosto packs in the students for lunch, dinner, and after-party hours. Open M-Th 6am-1am, F 6am-3am, Sa 8am-3am, Su 8am-1am.

DOWNTOWN

Financial District eateries vie for the business-person's coveted lunchtime dollar. Their formidable secret weapon is the lunch special...use it to your advantage.

▓ **Philippe, The Original,** 1001 N. Alameda St. (☎213-628-3781), 2 blocks north of Union Station. The French dip sandwich was invented here in 1918 and has been the staple of Philippe's menu ever since. Choose from pork, beef, ham, turkey ($4), or lamb ($4.50). Top it off with a large slice of pie ($2.50) or ice cream ($1) and a glass of lemonade (50¢) or a cup of coffee (9¢). Come during a Lakers game and revel in the cheapest beer in town ($1.50-2.75) with the home court fans. Open daily 6am-10pm.

The Pantry, 877 S. Figueroa St. (☎213-972-9279). Since 1924, it hasn't closed once—not for the earthquakes, not for the riots (when it served as a National Guard outpost), and not even when a taxicab drove through the front wall. There aren't even locks on the doors. Known for its large portions, free cole slaw, and fresh sourdough bread. Owned by Mayor Riordan. Giant breakfast specials ($6) are popular, especially on weekends. Lunch sandwiches $3-5. Open forever. No credit cards.

La Luz Del Día, 1 W. Olvera St. (☎213-628-7495), on the circular walking path of the El Pueblo Historic Park Plaza *kiosko*. Be serenaded by a *norteño* mariachi band while enjoying homemade soft tortillas at this *Guadalajara* Mexican restaurant whose name means "the light of day." Everything about this place is authentic—from the outpost-style building to the menu conspicuously devoid of chicken. Meal plates, which include rice and beans, run about $5-6. Open daily noon-10pm.

SAN FERNANDO VALLEY

Ventura Blvd. is lined with restaurants. Eating lunch near the studios in **Studio City** is your best stargazing opportunity. The unwritten law: stare all you like, *but don't ask for autographs.*

Miceli's, 3655 W. Cahuenga Blvd. (☎323-851-3444), in Burbank, across from Universal Studios. Would-be actors serenade dinner guests. Don't worry about losing your appetite during the Broadway and cabaret numbers—waiters must pass vocal auditions. Pasta, pizza, or lasagna $9-12. If you are looking for a romantic splurge, ask about the Valentine's table. Open Su-Th 11:30am-11pm, F 11:30am-midnight, Sa 4pm-midnight.

Dalt's Grill, 3500 W. Olive Ave. (☎818-953-7752), in Burbank. Classic, classy American grill across from Warner Studios. Frequented by the DJs and music guests from the two radio stations upstairs. Burgers and sandwiches $5-8. Chicken fajita Caesar salad $8. Open M-Th 11am-midnight, F-Sa 11am-1am (bar open until 2am), Su 9am-11pm.

◉ SIGHTS

HOLLYWOOD

Hollywood is no longer the upscale home of movie stars and production studios. In fact, all the major studios, save Paramount, have moved to the roomier San Fernando Valley. Left behind are historic theaters and museums, a crowd of souvenir shops, famous boulevards, and an American fixation. Aside from the endless string of movie premieres, the only star-studded part of Hollywood is the sidewalk, though it is lined with prostitutes, panhandlers, tattoo parlors, and porn shops.

HOLLYWOOD SIGN. The 50 ft. high, slightly erratic letters on Mt. Cahuenga north of Hollywood form a universally recognized symbol of the city. The original 1923 sign, which read HOLLYWOODLAND, was an advertisement for a new subdivision in the Hollywood Hills. You can't go frolic on the sign like Robert Downey, Jr. did in *Chaplin*—there is a $500 fine if you're caught. You can snap a great pic by driving north on Vine, turning right on Franklin, left on Beachwood, and left on Belden into the Beachwood Supermarket parking lot. To get a close-up of the sign, continue up Beachwood, turn left on Ledgewood, and drive all the way to Mulholland Hwy.

GRAUMAN'S CHINESE THEATER. Formerly Mann's, this theater is a garish rendition of a Chinese temple and the hottest spot for a Hollywood movie premiere. Pay homage to impressions made by movie stars in the cement, including Whoopi Goldberg's dreadlocks, Jimmy Durante's nose, and George Burns's cigar. *(6925 Hollywood Blvd., between Highland and La Brea Ave. ☎323-461-3331.)*

WALK OF FAME. Things get a little seedier all along Hollywood and Vine St., where the sidewalk is embedded with over 2000 bronze-inlaid stars, inscribed with the names of the famous, the infamous, and the downright obscure. The stars have no particular order so don't try to find a method to the madness. To catch a glimpse of today's (or yesterday's) stars in person, call the Chamber of Commerce for info on star-unveiling ceremonies. *(☎323-469-8311.)*

OTHER SIGHTS. Nestled in the hills, the **Hollywood Bowl** is the perfect spot to have a picnic lunch and listen to the L.A. Philharmonic strike it up at rehearsals four nights per week. The Bowl also hosts a summer jazz concert series. The Bowl's museum-within-a-bowl has several exhibits, as well as listening stations where you can swoon to Stravinsky, Aaron Copland, and the Beatles, all of whom played here in the same week during the 60s. *(2301 N. Highland Ave. ☎323-850-2058, concert line 323-850-2000. Open Tu-Sa 10am-4:30pm. Free.)* The **Capital Records Tower,** a monument to the recording industry, was designed to look like a stack of records, with fins sticking out at each floor (the "records") and a needle on top that constantly blinks H-O-L-L-Y-W-O-O-D in Morse code. *(1750 Vine St., just north of Hollywood Blvd.)* The ornate **El Capitán Theatre** hosted the 1941 Hollywood premiere of *Citizen Kane.* Current Disney movies play here with interactive post-show activities. *(6838 Hollywood Blvd. ☎467-9545 or 800-347-6396. $12, ages 3-11 and over 60 $10.)*

SANTA MONICA

Santa Monica is known more for its shoreside scene than its shore. Filled with gawkers and hawkers, the area on and around the carnival pier is the hub of local tourist activity. The fun fair spills over into the pedestrian-only **3rd St. Promenade,** where street performers and a Farmers Market (W and Sa mornings) make for cinematic "crowd" scenes. People with clipboards often sign people up for **free movie passes.** Farther inland, along Main St. and beyond, a smattering of galleries, design shops, and museums reveal the city's love affair with art and design.

The heart of the Santa Monica Beach is the famed **Santa Monica Pier,** home of the carnivalesque family funspot **Pacific Park** The centerpiece of the pier is the unrideable 1922 carousel. Look for free TV show tickets near the north entrance. *(Off PCH on the way to Venice Beach from Santa Monica Beach. Open daily 10am-11pm; ticket window closes at 10:30pm. Ticket $1.25, most rides 2-3 tickets. Parking off PCH $5 per day.)*

VENICE

Venice is a bustling beach town with rad politics and mad diversity. Its guitar-toting, Bukowski-quoting, wild-eyed, tie-dyed residents sculpt masterpieces in sand and compose them in graffiti, all before heading to the beach to slam a volleyball around. A stroll in in-line skating, bikini-flaunting, tattooed Venice is like an acid trip for the timid. *(To get to Venice from downtown L.A., take MTA #33 or 333; take 436 during rush hour. From downtown Santa Monica, take BBBus #1 or 2. Avoid hourly meter-feedings by parking in the $5-per-day lot at Pacific and Venice.)*

Venice's main beachfront drag, the **Ocean Front Walk,** is a seaside circus of fringe culture. Bodybuilders of both sexes pump iron in skimpy spandex outfits at **Muscle Beach.** *(1800 Ocean Front Walk.)* Fire-juggling cyclists, joggers, sand sculptors, groovy elders, and bards in Birkenstocks make up the balance of this playground population. Venice's anything-goes attitude attracts some of L.A.'s most innovative artists (and not just the guy who makes sand sculptures of Jesus). The **Chiat Day offices** were designed by Frank Gehry, Claes Oldenburg, and Coosje Van Brueggen to look like a pair of enormous binoculars. *(340 Main St.)* Venice's **street murals** are another free show. Don't miss the homage to Botticelli's *Birth of Venus* on the beach pavilion at the end of Windward Ave.—a woman of ostensibly divine beauty sporting short shorts, a band-aid top, and roller skates boogies out of her seashell.

WEST HOLLYWOOD

Melrose Ave. running from the southern part of West Hollywood to Hollywood, is lined with chi-chi restaurants, art galleries, and shops catering to all levels of the counter-culture spectrum. North of Beverly Center is the **Pacific Design Center,** a sea-green glass complex, nicknamed the **Blue Whale** and constructed in the shape of a wave. It hosts an awesome **Gay Pride Weekend Celebration** (see p. 801) in late June. *(8687 Melrose Ave., at San Vicente Blvd. ☎310-657-0800.)*

BEVERLY HILLS

Ready to gawk? Conspicuous consumption sometimes borders on the vulgar in this storied center of wealth and privilege. A conspicuous way to tour the city is in the trolley car replica operated by the **Beverly Hills Chamber of Commerce.** *(☎310-271-8126. June-Sept. Tu-Sa 1-5pm every hr. $5.)* If you prefer a cooler approach, go solo with a star map ($8), sold along Sunset Blvd. but not within Beverly Hills. On the palm-lined 700-900 blocks of **Beverly Dr.,** each and every manicured estate begs for attention. The heart of the city is in the **Golden Triangle,** a wedge formed by Beverly Dr., Wilshire Blvd., and Santa Monica Blvd., centering on **Rodeo Drive,** known for its flashy boutiques. Farther north, the **Beverly Hills Hotel,** 9641 Sunset Blvd., is a collection of poolside cottages. Marilyn Monroe reportedly "met" with both JFK and RFK in bungalows here. You can get a room for only $275. *(☎310-276-2251.)*

CALIFORNIA

WESTWOOD AND UCLA

Get a feel for mass academia UC-style at the **University of California at Los Angeles (UCLA),** which sprawls in the foothills of the Santa Monica Mountains. A prototypical Californian university, UCLA sports an abundance of grassy spaces, bike and walking paths, dazzling sunshine, and pristine buildings in a hodge-podge of architectural styles. *(Take the San Diego Fwy./I-405 north to the Wilshire Blvd./Westwood exit, heading east into Westwood. Take Westwood Blvd. north off Wilshire, heading straight through the center of the village and directly into the campus. By bus, take MTA route #2 along Sunset Blvd., #21 along Wilshire Blvd.; #320 from Santa Monica; #561 from the San Fernando Valley; or BBBus #1, 2, 3, 8, or 12. Parking passes $5.)*

The **Murphy Sculpture Garden,** which contains over 70 pieces scattered over five acres, lies directly in front of the Art Center. The collection includes works by Rodin, Matisse, and Miró. Opposite the sculpture garden is **MacGowen Hall,** which contains the **Tower of Masks.** Other attractions include the **Armand Hammer Museum of Art and Cultural Center** (see **Museums,** p. 798). Call the **UCLA Arts Line** for info on UCLA's many cultural offerings. *(☎ 310-825-2278.)*

BEL AIR, BRENTWOOD, AND PACIFIC PALISADES

Most of today's stars live in these three affluent communities. Next to UCLA is the well-guarded community of **Bel Air,** where **Ronald Reagan** has retired. His estate is at 668 St. Cloud, adjacent to the *Beverly Hillbillies* mansion *(750 Bel Air Rd.)* and a few blocks up from the former home of **Sonny and Cher** *(364 St. Cloud).* **Elizabeth Taylor** is literally around the corner. *(700 Nimes.)*

Farther west on Sunset Blvd. is **Brentwood,** home to many young actors and, until recently, **O.J. Simpson.** O.J.'s estate was repossessed and auctioned off for a mere $2.63 million. *(360 Rockingham.)* On Aug. 4, 1962, **Marilyn Monroe** was found dead at her home. *(12305 Fifth Helena Dr.)* Brentwood also includes the homes of Michelle Pfeiffer, Harrison Ford, Meryl Streep, and Rob Reiner.

The more secluded **Pacific Palisades** is the place to live these days. Many streets are entirely closed to anyone but residents and their guests, but if you're lucky, you might have a close encounter with **Steven Spielberg** outside 1515 Amalfi. **Arnold Schwarzenegger** and **Maria Shriver** practice family fitness at 14209 Sunset Blvd.; **Tom Hanks** lives at 321 S. Anita Ave.; and **Michael Keaton** resides at 826 Napoli Dr. Billy Crystal, Chevy Chase, and John Travolta also own homes in the area.

DOWNTOWN

The **Los Angeles Conservancy** offers Saturday tours of downtown's historic spots. *(☎ 213-623-2489. Tours $5. Reserve one week in advance.)* Those who prefer to travel solo can walk each of the respective sections but should take **DASH Shuttles** for travel between. *(References below are for M-F travel. Sa-Su the Discovery Direct "DD" route covers almost all of the sights below.)* If driving, park in a secure lot, rather than on the streets. Parking is costly; arriving before 8am enables visitors to catch early-bird specials. The guarded lots around 9th and Figueroa charge $3-4 per day. The **L.A. Visitors Center** is at 685 S. Figueroa St. *(Open M-F 8am-5pm, Sa 8:30am-5pm.)*

HISTORIC NORTH. The historic birthplace of L.A. lies in the northern section of downtown, bordered by Spring and Arcadia St. Where the city center once stood, **El Pueblo de Los Angeles Historical Monument** preserves a number of historically important buildings from the Spanish and Mexican eras. *(125 Paseo St. DASH B. ☎ 213-628-1274. Open daily 9am-9pm. Free.)* **Olvera St.,** one of L.A.'s original roads, resembles a small Mexican street market. The street is the site of the Cinco de Mayo and Día de los Muertos celebrations of L.A.'s Chicano population (see **Seasonal Events,** p. 801). **Chinatown** lies north of this area, roughly bordered by Yale, Spring, Ord, and Bernard St. Pick up maps at the **Chinatown Heritage and Visitors Center.** *(DASH B.)*

CIVIC CENTRAL. The **Civic Center** is best seen from the outside. *(Bounded by Rte. 101, Grand Ave., 1st, and San Pedro St. DASH B and D.)* One of the best-known buildings in the Southland, **City Hall** "has starred in more movies than most actors." *(200 N.*

Spring St.) The **Dorothy Chandler Pavilion** may no longer be the site of the Academy Awards (the ceremony has moved to Hollywood's new Kodak Theater), but it still houses the **Los Angeles Opera**. *(☎ 213-972-8001.)* Upscale **Little Tokyo** lies southeast of the Civic Center, on 2nd and San Pedro St. *(DASH A.)*

OTHER SIGHTS

GRIFFITH PARK AND GLENDALE. Griffith Park stretches for 4107 acres from the hills above North Hollywood to the intersection of the Ventura (Rte. 134) and Golden State Fwy. (I-5). Several of the mountain roads through the park (especially the **Vista Del Valle Dr.**) offer panoramic views of downtown L.A., Hollywood, and the Westside. Unfortunately, heavy rains have made them unsafe for cars, but foot traffic is allowed on most. The five-mile hike to the top of **Mt. Hollywood,** the highest peak in the park, is quite popular. For info, stop by the **Visitors Center and Ranger Headquarters.** *(4730 Crystal Spring Dr. ☎ 323-913-7390. Open daily 5am-10pm.)*

OBSERVATORY AND PLANETARIUM. The white stucco and copper domes of the Art Deco Observatory and Planetarium are visible from around the park. You might remember the planetarium from the denouement of the James Dean film *Rebel Without A Cause.* A telescope with a 12 in. lens is open to the public every clear night until 9:45pm. *(Drive to the top of Mt. Hollywood on Vermont Ave. or Hillhurst St. from Los Feliz Blvd., or take MTA #180 or 181 from Hollywood Blvd. ☎ 323-664-1181, recording 664-1191. Free parking, use Vermont St. entrance to Griffith Park. Planetarium: in summer M-F 3 shows per day, Sa-Su 4 per day; in winter Tu-F 2 per day, Sa-Su 4 per day; call for times. $4, seniors $3, ages 5-12 $2, under 5 free but only admitted to 1:30pm show. Observatory: ☎ 323-663-8171. Open in summer daily 12:30-10pm; in winter Tu-F 2-10pm, Sa-Su 12:30-10pm.)*

FOREST LAWN CEMETERY. A rather twisted sense of celebrity sightseeing may lead some travelers to Glendale, where they can gaze upon stars who won't run away when chased for a picture. Among the illustrious dead are Clark Gable, George Burns, Sammy Davis, Jr., and Errol Flynn. *(1712 Glendale Ave. From downtown, take MTA #90 or 91 and get off just after the bus leaves San Fernando Rd. to turn onto Glendale Ave. By car from I-5 or the Glendale Fwy., take Los Feliz Blvd. south to Glendale Ave. ☎ 800-204-3131. Open Mar.-Oct. daily 8am-6pm; Nov.-Feb. 8am-5pm.)*

SAN FERNANDO VALLEY

Movie studios have replaced the Valley Girl as the Valley's defining feature. As the Ventura Fwy. (Rte. 134) passes Burbank, you can see what are today the Valley's trademarks: the **NBC peacock,** the **Warner Bros. water tower,** and the carefully designed **Disney dwarves.** Urban legend claims that the water pipes are orchestrated such that the seven dwarves appear to urinate on daddy Disney when it rains. Most of the studios have **free TV show tapings** (see **Entertainment,** p. 800).

UNIVERSAL STUDIOS. A movie and television studio that happens to have the world's first and largest movie-themed amusement park attached, Universal Studios Hollywood is the most popular tourist spot in today's expatriate Tinseltown. Located just north of Hollywood in its own municipality, Universal City (complete with police and fire station), the park was born as a public tour of the studios in 1964. Since then, it has become a full-fledged amusement park with rides and live shows featuring Universal motion picture and television characters. The signature *Studio Tour* is a Universal Studios classic, but this attraction plays second fiddle to park's interactive adventures. *(Take Rte. 101 to Universal Center Dr. or Lankershim Blvd. exits. Or, take MTA bus #420 bus west from downtown or east from the Valley. ☎ 818-622-3801. Open July-Aug. daily 8am-10pm; Sept.-June 9am-7pm. Last tram leaves at 6:15pm; off-season 4:15pm. Tours in Spanish daily. $43, seniors $37, ages 3-11 $32. Parking $7.)*

■ SIX FLAGS THEME PARKS. At the opposite end of the Valley, 40min. north of L.A. in Valencia, lies **Magic Mountain,** not to be confused with the Thomas Mann novel of the same name. Magic Mountain has the scariest roller coasters in Southern California, if not the world. **Goliath,** the park's latest addition, drops you and a load of screaming strangers 255 ft. into a black hole. Next door, Six Flags' water-

CALIFORNIA

park **Hurricane Harbor** features the world's tallest enclosed speed slide. *(At the I-5 Magic Mountain Pkwy. exit. Magic Mountain: recorded info ☎661-255-4111, operator 661-255-413. Open June-Aug. Su-Th 10am-10pm, F-Sa 10am-midnight; Sept.-May Sa-Su 10am-6pm. $43, seniors and under 48 in. tall $21.50, under 2 free. Parking $6. Hurricane Harbor: recorded info ☎661-255-4527, operator 661-255-4806. Open in summer M-Th 10am-7pm, F-Su 10am-8pm. $22, seniors and under 48 in. tall $15, under 2 free. Combo admission to both parks $53.)*

PASADENA AND AROUND

With its world-class museums, graceful architecture, lively shopping district, and idyllic weather, Pasadena is a welcome change from its noisy downtown neighbor. **Old Town** Pasadena sequesters intriguing historic sights and an up-and-coming entertainment scene. The **Pasadena Fwy.** (Rte. 110) is one of the nation's oldest. The city provides **free shuttles** approximately every 12min. that loop between Old Town and the downtown area around Lake Ave. *(☎626-744-4055. Shuttles run downtown M-Th 11am-7pm, F 11am-10pm, Sa-Su noon-8pm; uptown M-F 7am-6pm, Sa-Su noon-5pm.)*

SAN DIMAS. San Dimas really does have a **Circle K,** 301 E. Walnut St. *(☎909-592-5085),* at Bonita St. Just try using the telephone booth in the parking lot (see *Bill and Ted's Excellent Adventure*). "San Dimas High School football rules!"

HUNTINGTON LIBRARY, ART GALLERY, AND BOTANICAL GARDENS. This massive institute was built in 1910 as the home of businessman Henry Huntington, who made his money in railroads and Southern California real estate. Its stunning botanical gardens host 150 acres of plants. The library houses one of the world's best collections of rare books, as well as British and American manuscripts, including a Gutenberg Bible, Benjamin Franklin's handwritten autobiography, a 1410 manuscript of Chaucer's *Canterbury Tales*, a number of Shakespeare's first folios, and a map from Sir Francis Drake's 1585 expedition to "West India." The art gallery is known for its 18th- and 19th-century British paintings. Tea is served in the Rose Garden Tea Room daily. *(1151 Oxford Rd., between Huntington Dr. and California Blvd. in San Marino, south of Pasadena, about 2 mi. south of the Allen Ave. exit off I-210. From downtown L.A., take MTA bus #79 out of Union Station to San Marino Ave. and walk ½ mi. ☎626-405-2100. Open June-Aug. Tu-Su 10:30am-4:30pm; in winter Tu-F noon-4:30pm, Sa-Su 10:30am-4:30pm. $10, seniors $8.50, students $7, under 12 free; 1st Th of each month free.)*

🏛 MUSEUMS

WESTSIDE

▨ **Los Angeles County Museum of Art (LACMA),** 5905 Wilshire Blvd. (info ☎323-857-6000, Docent Council 323-857-6108). A rebuttal those who say that L.A.'s only culture is in its yogurt. Opened in 1965, the LACMA is the largest museum in the West. The Steve Martin Gallery, in the Anderson Bldg., houses the famed benefactor's collection of Dada and Surrealist works, including Rene Magritte's *Treachery of Images*. (This explains how Steve was allowed to in-line skate through LACMA in *L.A. Story*.) Open M-Tu and Th noon-8pm, F noon-9pm, Sa-Su 11am-8pm. $7, seniors and students $5, under 18 $1; free 2nd Tu of each month. Free jazz F 5:30-8:30pm, chamber music Su 6-7pm. Film tickets $7, seniors $5. Parking $5, after 6pm free. Wheelchair accessible.

Petersen Automotive Museum, 6060 Wilshire Blvd. (☎323-930-2277), at Fairfax. Across the street from LACMA, this museum showcases L.A.'s most recognizable symbol—the automobile. With 300,000 sq. ft., PAM is the world's largest car museum and the nation's second largest history museum, behind the Smithsonian. Open Tu-Su 10am-6pm; Discovery Center closes at 5pm. $7, seniors and students $5, ages 5-12 $3, under 5 free. Full-day parking near LACMA $4.

La Brea Tarpits, 5801 Wilshire Blvd. (☎323-934-7243 or 857-6311). Certainly the most venerable of L.A.'s many intriguing life forms, the prehistoric critters trapped within the tarpits are worth a peek. Open July-Sept. daily 9:30am-5pm; Oct.-June Tu-Su 9:30am-5pm. Tours of grounds 1pm, museum tours Tu-Su 2:15pm. $6, seniors and students $3.50, ages 5-12 $2; 1st Tu of each month free. Parking $5.

Museum of Tolerance, 9786 W. Pico Blvd. (☎310-553-8043), at Roxbury St., just south of Beverly Hills. This hands-on, high-tech museum has interactive exhibits on the Holocaust, the Croatian genocide, the L.A. riots, and the US civil rights movement. Open M-Th 10am-4pm, F 10am-1pm, and Su 11am-5pm. Closing times are for the time of the last entry into the museum. $8.50, seniors $6.50, students $5.50, ages 3-11 $3.50. Parking free. Wheelchair accessible.

HOLLYWOOD

Hollywood Heritage Museum, 2100 N. Highland Ave. (☎323-874-2276), across from the Hollywood Bowl. Provides a provocative glimpse into early Hollywood filmmaking. Antique cameras, costumes worn by Douglas Fairbanks and Rudolph Valentino, props, and vintage film clips fill the museum. Open Sa-Su 11am-3:45pm; call ahead. $2, ages 3-12 $1, under 3 free. Ample free parking, except during Bowl events.

Hollywood Entertainment Museum, 7021 Hollywood Blvd. (☎323-465-7900). A treasure trove of authentic set designs, costumes, and props. The original sets from *Star Trek* and *Cheers* deserve the ooh-ing and aah-ing they usually receive. Open July-Aug. daily 11am-6pm; Sept.-June Th-Tu 10am-6pm. Tours every 30min. $7.50, seniors and students $4.50, ages 5-12 $4, under 5 free. Parking $2. *Cheers* cover $5.

Hollywood Wax Museum, 6767 Hollywood Blvd. (☎323-462-8860). This both fascinating and horrifying museum contains 200 figures, from Austin Powers to Jesus. Open Su-Th 10am-midnight, F-Sa 10am-1am. $10, seniors $8.50, ages 6-12 $7, under 6 free.

Frederick's of Hollywood, 6608 Hollywood Blvd. (☎323-957-5953), gives a free peep at celebrity-worn corsets and bosom-boosting brassieres in its lingerie museum. Open M-F 10am-9pm, Sa 10am-7pm, Su 11am-6pm. Free.

WESTWOOD AND BEL AIR

▨ Armand Hammer Museum of Art and Cultural Center, 10899 Wilshire Blvd. (☎310-443-7000), at UCLA. Houses a small collection of Western art from the 16th century to the present day. A who's who of European painters, Hammer's collection includes works by Rembrandt, Chagall, and Cézanne, but its real gem is Van Gogh's *Hospital at Saint-Rémy*. Open Tu-W and F-Sa 11am-7pm, Th 11am-9pm, Su 11am-5pm. $4.50, seniors and students $3, under 17 free with adult; Th free. Free tours of permanent collection Su 2pm, of traveling exhibits Th 6pm, Sa-Su 1pm. 3hr. parking $2.75.

▨ J. Paul Getty Museum and Getty Center, 1200 Getty Center Dr. (☎310-440-7330), in the Santa Monica Mountains above Bel Air. The center unites L.A.'s beloved Getty museums with its institutes on one site. The museum itself boasts the permanent Getty collection, which includes Van Gogh's *Irises,* James Ensor's *Christ's Entry into Brussels in 1889,* Impressionist paintings, Renaissance drawings, and one of the nation's best Rembrandt collections. Open Tu-W 11am-7pm, Th-F 11am-9pm, Sa-Su 10am-6pm. Free. Parking $5; reservations required.

SANTA MONICA

Santa Monica Museum of Art, 2525 Michigan Ave. (☎310-586-6467), near the intersection of Olympic and Cloverfield Blvd., exhibits the work of emerging artists. "Friday Evening Salons" are free informal public forums with up-and-coming artists. Usually open Tu-Su 11am-6pm, but call ahead. Colleagues Gallery open M noon-2pm and Th 10:30am-2pm. Suggested donation $3, seniors and students $2; galleries free.

DOWNTOWN L.A.

California Science Center (CSC), 700 State Dr. (☎323-724-3623). Located downtown in Exposition Park, the CSC is dedicated to the phenomena of California—from earthquakes to smog. The expansive, formal rose garden in front of the CSC is the last remnant of the blessed days when all of Exposition Park was an exposition of horticulture. More than 19,000 specimens of 200 varieties of roses surround walking paths, green lawns, gazebos, fountains, and a lily pond. Open daily 10am-5pm. Free. Rose garden open mid-Mar. through Dec. daily 8:30am-5:30pm. Parking $5.

PASADENA

▓ **Norton Simon Museum of Art,** 411 W. Colorado Blvd. (☎626-449-6840), at Orange Grove Blvd. The recently revamped museum features a world-class collection, chronicling Western art from Italian Gothic to 20th-century abstract, with paintings by Raphael, Botticelli, Monet, Picasso, and others. The Impressionist and Post-Impressionist hall is particularly impressive, and the collection of Southeast Asian sculpture is one of the world's best. Simon's eclectic taste gives the collection flair. Open W-Th and Sa-Su noon-6pm, F noon-9pm. $6, seniors $3, students and under 12 free.

♫ ENTERTAINMENT

A visit to the world's entertainment capital isn't complete without some exposure to the actual business of making a movie or TV show. Fortunately, most production companies oblige. **Paramount** (☎323-956-5000), **NBC** (☎818-840-3537), and **Warner Bros.** (☎818-954-1744) offer two-hour guided walking tours, but as they are made for tourists, they tend to be crowded and overpriced.

TELEVISION

The best way to get a feel for the industry is to land yourself some tickets to a TV taping. All tickets are free, but most studios tend to overbook, so holding a ticket does not always guarantee that you'll get into the taping. Show up early and you might see your favorite stars up close in the backlot of an operating studio.

NBC, 3000 W. Alameda Ave., at W. Olive Ave. in Burbank, is your best spur-of-the-moment bet. Show up at the ticket office on a weekday at 8am for passes to Jay Leno's **Tonight Show,** filmed at 5pm the same evening (2 tickets per person, must be 16+). Studio tours run on the hour. (M-F 9am-3pm; additional tours July-Aug. Sa 10am-2pm. $7, ages 5-12 $3.75.) Many of NBC's "Must-See TV" shows are taped at **Paramount Pictures,** 5555 Melrose Ave. (☎323-956-1777), in Hollywood. Sitcoms like *Dharma and Greg* and *Frasier* are taped September through May—call the studio five days in advance for tickets. NBC's most popular sitcoms, like *Friends* and *Will and Grace,* are filmed before a private audience, so unless you are a friend of a Friend, you're out of luck. As it is one of the few major studios still in Hollywood, Paramount's tours are very popular. (Every hr. M-F 9am-2pm. $15.)

A **CBS box office,** 7800 Beverly Blvd., next to the Farmers Market in West Hollywood, hands out free tickets to Bob Barker's seminal game-show masterpiece *The Price is Right* (taped M-Th) up to one week in advance. (☎323-575-2458. Open non-taping days M-Th 9am-5pm, taping days M-Th 7:30am-5pm.) Audience members must be over 18. You can request up to ten tickets on a specific date by sending a self-addressed, stamped envelope to *The Price is Right* Tickets, 7800 Beverly Blvd., L.A. 90036, about four weeks in advance.

If all else fails, **Hollywood Group Services,** 1422 Barry Ave. #8, L.A. 90025 (☎310-914-3400), and **Audiences Unlimited, Inc.,** 100 Universal City Plaza, Universal City, CA 91608 (☎818-506-0067), offer guaranteed seating, but charge $10 to no-shows. To find out what shows are available during your visit, send a self-addressed, stamped envelope to either of the services. Hollywood Group Services will fax a list of all available shows within 24hr. of a call-in request.

CINEMA

Countless theaters show films the way they were meant to be seen: in a big space, on a big screen, with top-quality sound. It would be a cinematic crime not to take advantage of the incredible experience that is movie-going in L.A. **Loews Cineplex Cinemas** (☎818-508-0588), atop the hill at Universal City Walk; **Pacific Cinerama Dome,** 6360 Sunset Blvd. (☎323-466-3401), near Vine; and **Mann's Chinese Theater,** 6925 Hollywood Blvd. (☎323-464-8111), are some of the best movie houses.

To see an **on-location movie shoot,** stop by in person at the Entertainment Industry Development Company's L.A. Film Office, 7083 Hollywood Blvd., #500, for a "shoot sheet" ($10), which lists current filming locations; the same information is available for free at www.eidc.com. Be aware that film crews may not share your enthusiasm for audience participation. (☎323-957-1000. Open M-F 8:30am-6pm.)

SO, YOU WANNA BE IN PICTURES? The quickest way to get noticed is to land yourself a job as an extra—no experience necessary. One day's work will land $40-130 in your pocket and two meals in your tummy. Step one is to stop calling yourself an extra—you're an "atmosphere actor" (it's better for both your ego and your resume). Step two is to contact a reputable casting service. **Cenex Central Casting,** 220 Flower St., Burbank 91506 (☎818-562-2755), is the biggest. You must be at least 18 and a US citizen or Green Card holder. Step three is to show up on time; you'll need the clout of DeNiro before you can waltz in after call. Don't forget to bring $20 in cash to cover the "photo fee." Step four is to dress the part: don't wear red or white, which bleed on film and render you useless. Finally, after you collect three **Screen Actors Guild (SAG)** vouchers (☎213-937-3441), you'll be eligible to pay the $1234 to join showbiz society. See you in the movies!

MUSIC

L.A.'s music venues range from small clubs to massive amphitheaters. The **Wiltern Theater** (☎213-380-5005) shows alterna-rock/folk acts. The **Hollywood Palladium** (☎323-962-7600) is of comparable size, with 3500 seats. Mid-size acts head for the **Universal Amphitheater** (☎818-777-3931) and the **Greek Theater** (☎323-665-1927). Huge indoor sports arenas, such as the **Great Western Forum** (☎310-673-1300) and the **Staples Center** (☎213-742-7100), double as concert halls for big acts. Few dare to play at the 100,000-seat **Los Angeles Memorial Coliseum and Sports Arena**—only U2, Depeche Mode, and the mighty Guns n' Roses have filled the stands. Call Ticketmaster (☎323-365-3500) to purchase tickets for any of these venues. During the week, you can catch the L.A. Philharmonic or visiting performers as they rehearse at the ▓**Hollywood Bowl,** 2301 N. Highland Ave. (☎323-850-2000).

SPORTS

Exposition Park and the often dangerous city of **Inglewood,** southwest of the park, are home to many sports teams. The **USC Trojans** football team plays at the **Los Angeles Memorial Coliseum,** 3939 S. Figueroa St. (tickets ☎740-4672), at Martin Luther King Blvd., which seats over 100,000 spectators. It is the only stadium in the world to have the honor of hosting the Olympic Games twice. Basketball's doormat, the **Los Angeles Clippers** (☎213-742-7500), and the dazzling, star-studded 2000 and 2001 NBA Champion **Los Angeles Lakers** (☎310-426-6031) play at the **Staples Center,** 1111 S. Figueroa St. (☎742-7100; box office 742-7300), along with the **Los Angeles Kings** hockey team (☎888-546-4752). The city's women's basketball team, the **Los Angeles Sparks** (☎310-330-3939), plays at the **Great Western Forum,** at the corner of Manchester and Prairie in Inglewood (☎310-673-1300). Tickets are in high demand (Lakers season runs Nov.-June; Sparks June-Aug.). Kings tickets start at $19, Lakers at $21, and Sparks at $8. For tickets, call Ticketmaster (☎480-3232).

Elysian Park, about 3 mi. northeast of downtown, curves around the northern portion of Chavez Ravine, home of **Dodger Stadium** and the popular **Los Angeles Dodgers** baseball team. Tickets ($6-17) are a hot commodity during the April to October season, especially if the Dodgers are playing well (but they rarely seem to live up to their potential). Call 323-224-1448 for info and advance tickets.

SEASONAL EVENTS

New Year's Day is always a perfect day in Southern California, or so the **Tournament of Roses Parade and Rose Bowl** (☎626-449-7673), in Pasadena, would have it. Some of the wildest New Year's Eve parties happen along **Colorado Blvd.,** the parade route. **Cinco de Mayo** (☎625-5045) explodes May 5, especially downtown at Olvera St. Huge celebrations mark the day the Mexicans drop-kicked France out of Mexico. In mid-May, **UCLA Mardi Gras** (☎310-825-8001), at the athletic field, is billed as the world's largest collegiate activity (a terrifying thought). During **Gay Pride Weekend,** Pacific Design Center, 8687 Melrose Ave., West Hollywood, L.A.'s lesbian and gay communities celebrate in full effect with art, politics, dances, and a big parade. (☎860-0701.)

Last or second-to-last weekend in June. Tickets $12.) ◪**El Día de los Muertos** is a rousing Mexican cultural celebration for the spirits of dead ancestors revisiting the world of the living. (Nov. 1, along Olvera St., downtown.)

◪ NIGHTLIFE

L.A. clubs range from tiny danceterias and ephemeral warehouse raves to exclusive lounges catering to showbiz elite. The hub of L.A. nightlife is the **Sunset Strip** along Sunset Blvd. in West Hollywood.

LATE-NIGHT RESTAURANTS

With the inconstancy of clubs and the short shelf-life of cafes, late-night restaurants have become reliable hangouts. The 24hr. **Jerry's Famous Deli** has numerous locations, including 8701 Beverly Blvd., West Hollywood (☎310-289-1811); 10923 Weyburn Ave., Westwood (☎310-208-3354); and 12655 Ventura Blvd., Studio City (☎818-980-4245).

◪ **Canter's,** 419 N. Fairfax Ave. (☎213-651-2030), in Fairfax. An L.A. institution, this deli has been the heart and soul of the historically Jewish Fairfax community since 1931. Grapefruit-sized matzoh ball in chicken broth is the best ever ($3.50). Giant sandwiches $6-8. Visit the Kibbitz Room nightly for live rock, blues, jazz, and cabaret-pop (from 9pm). Cheap beer ($2.50) served until 2am. Open 24hr.

◪ **Fred 62,** 1850 N. Vermont Ave. (☎323-667-0062), in Los Feliz. "Eat now, dine later." Headrests and toasters at every booth. Hip, edgy East L.A. crowd's jukebox selections rock the house. The waffles ($4.62) are divine. All prices end in ".62." Open 24hr.

The Rainbow Grill, 9015 Sunset Blvd. (☎310-278-4232), in West Hollywood, next to the Roxy. Dark red vinyl booths, dim lighting, and loud music set the scene. Goth girl waitresses, rock 'n' roll types, and an insane rainbow of guests play their parts. Marilyn Monroe met husband Joe DiMaggio on a blind date here. Brooklyn-quality pizza $6; calamari $7; grandma's revitalizing chicken soup $2.50 per cup, $4 per bowl. Open M-F 11am-2am, Sa-Su 5pm-2am.

Barney's Beanery, 8447 Santa Monica Blvd. (☎323-654-2287), in Hollywood. Barney's has been around since 1920—and it shows. Over 600 items on the menu, 250 bottled beers, and 200 on tap—if they don't have it, you don't need it. Janis Joplin and Jim Morrison were regulars. Pool and ping pong tables. Avoid (or target) the loud, riotous karaoke nights Su, M, and W 9:30pm-1am. Happy hour M-F 4-7pm ($2 draft, $3 appetizer). Valet parking $1.50. Open daily 10am-2am.

COFFEEHOUSES

In a city where no one eats very much for fear of rounding out that bony figure, espresso, coffee, and air are vital dining options.

◪ **Un Urban Coffeehouse,** 3301 Pico Blvd. (☎310-315-0056), in Santa Monica. 3 separate rooms of campy voodoo candles, Mexican wrestling masks, musty books, and leopard-print couches. Iced mocha blends $3.25, Italian sodas $2. Open mic comedy Th 7pm, open mic songwriters F 7:30pm, music showcase Sa 7pm. No cover. Open M-W 6am-6pm, Th-F 6am-1am, Sa 8am-1am, Su 8am-10pm.

Cow's End, 34 Washington Blvd. (☎310-574-1080), in Venice. With its asymmetrical whole-pane windows, uneven brick floor, and scantily clad beach patrons, the Cow's End is riotously popular. Sandwiches $5.50, shakes $4. Open mic Th 8pm. Live music F 8pm, Sa-Su 3pm and 8pm. Open daily 6am-midnight.

Highland Grounds, 742 N. Highland Ave. (☎323-466-1507), in Hollywood. Nightly live shows (8pm) range from folk singers to performance artists to empowerment speakers. Outdoor patio with blazing fire. Full menu. Beer and wine. Breakfast menu includes eclectic egg dishes (Bulgarian omelette $6). After 8pm, cover $2 and 1-drink min. Open M 9am-6pm, Tu-Sa 9am-midnight, Su 10am-3:30pm and 7-10pm.

BARS

While the 1996 film *Swingers* may not have transformed every bar into The 3 of Clubs, it has had a sadly homogenizing effect on L.A.'s hipsters. Grab your retro-70s shirts, sunglasses, and Cadillac convertibles, 'cause if you can't beat them, you have to swing with them, daddy-o. Unless otherwise specified, bars are 21+.

■ **Beauty Bar,** 1638 Cahuenga Blvd. (☎323-464-7676). A bar-*cum*-beauty parlor. It's like getting ready for the prom all over again, except that the drinking starts before rather than after. Manicures, "up 'dos," and henna tattoos are offered select nights of the week with a specialty drink ($10). Drinks like "Shampoo" or "Platinum Blonde" are $5-7. Smoking room with hair setting seats. DJ nightly at 10pm. Open Su-M 9pm-2am, Tu-W and Sa 8pm-2am, Th-F 6pm-2am.

■ **Miyagi's,** 8225 Sunset Blvd. (☎323-656-0100). With 3 levels, 5 sushi bars, and 7 liquor bars, this Japanese-themed restaurant, bar, and lounge is the latest Strip hot spot. "*Sake* bomb, *sake* bomb, *sake* bomb" $4. Open daily 5:30pm-2am.

The 3 of Clubs, 1123 N. Vine St. (☎323-462-6441). In a small strip mall beneath a "Bargain Clown Mart" sign, this simple, classy, spacious, hardwood bar is famous for appearing in 1996's *Swingers*. W DJ, Th live bands. Open daily 7pm-2am.

The Room, 1626 Cahuenga St. (☎213-462-7196). A speakeasy that empties into an alley, the very popular Room almost trumps The 3 of Clubs. No advertising, no sign on the door. Open daily 10pm-2am.

Daddy's, 1610 N. Vine St. (☎323-463-7777), between Hollywood and Sunset Blvd. This large, New York-style lounge sits between Cary Grant's star and Clark Gable's. Low-to-the-ground booths, candle lighting, and the cheapest jukebox in town. Sip $5 drinks and $4 beers to the mellow stylings of Al Green. Open daily 9am-2am.

CLUBS

L.A. is famous, even infamous, for its club scene. With the highest number of bands per capita in the world, most clubs book top-notch acts night after night. These clubs can be the hottest thing in L.A. one month and extinct the next, so check the *L.A. Weekly* (free everywhere) before venturing out, which prefaces its listings with "Due to the erratic lives of L.A. musicians and the capricious personalities of booking agents, all of the following are subject to change for no apparent reason."

■ **Derby,** 4500 Los Feliz Blvd. (☎323-663-8979). This joint is jumpin' with the kings of swing. Ladies, grab your snoods, because many dress the 40s part. Choice Italian fare from Louise's Trattoria next door. Full bar. Free dance lessons nightly at 8pm: Lindy Hop M, salsa Tu, swing W-Su. Happy hour daily 5-7pm; 2nd happy hour Su-Th midnight-closing ($1.50 off drinks). Cover $7-10. Open daily 5pm-2am.

Key Club, 9039 Sunset Blvd. (☎310-274-5800). Ladies, leave your snoods at home. A colossal, crowded multimedia experience complete with black lights, neon, and a frenetic dance floor. Live acts and DJ productions, depending on the night. Tequila library on the 1st floor. Cover M-Th $10, F-Sa $22. Open daily 8pm-2am.

Largo, 432 N. Fairfax Ave. (☎323-852-1073). Elegant and intimate sit-down (or, if you get there late, lean-back) club. Original rock, pop, and folk sounds. Cover $2-12. Open M-Sa 9pm-2am.

Martini Lounge, 5657 Melrose Ave. (☎323-467-4068). More people sip beer than martinis, and more people mingle than dance. Great music from R&B to indie. Cover $5-15. Shows at 8pm. Open daily until 2am.

COMEDY CLUBS

L.A.'s comedy clubs are the best in the world, unless you happen to chance upon an amateur night, which is generally a painful experience.

■ **The Improvisation,** 8162 Melrose Ave. (☎213-651-2583), in West Hollywood. L.A.'s best talent, including Robin Williams and Jerry Seinfeld, have shown their faces here; Jay Mohr and Damon Wayans sometimes join the show. Italian restaurant (entrees from $6). 18+, or 16+ with parent. Cover $10-15. 2-drink min. Shows Su-Th 8pm, F-Sa 8:30 and 10:30pm. Bar open daily until 1:30am. Reservations recommended.

CALIFORNIA

Groundling Theater, 7307 Melrose Ave. (☎323-934-9700). The best improv and comedy "forum" in town. The Groundling's alums include Pee Wee Herman and many *Saturday Night Live* regulars such as Julia Sweeney, Will Farrell, Cheri Oteri, and Chris Kattan. Don't be surprised to see *SNL* producer Lorne Michaels sitting in the back row. Lisa Kudrow (of *Friends* fame) got her start here, too. Polished skits most nights. Cover $8-18.50. Shows Tu and Th 8pm, F-Sa 8 and 10pm, Su 7:30pm.

GAY AND LESBIAN NIGHTLIFE

Many ostensibly straight clubs have gay nights. Check the *L.A. Weekly* for more listings or the free weekly magazine *fab!* Gay and lesbian nightlife centers around **Santa Monica Blvd.** in West Hollywood.

■ **Abbey Cafe,** 692 N. Robertson Blvd. (☎310-289-8410), at Santa Monica Blvd. This cafe becomes a lounge, bar, and dance club as the moon rises and the buff gay boys come out to play. Impeccable service, tasteful decor, and too many nice butts to concentrate on any of it. Open daily noon-2am.

Micky's, 8857 Santa Monica Blvd. (☎310-657-1176). Large, popular spot filled with delectable men. Music is mostly Top 40 dance. Serves lunch daily noon-4pm and hot go-go boys Tu-F and Su. "Cocktails with the stars" (many of them porn stars) Th 6-8pm. Happy hour daily 4-7pm. Cover $3-20. Open daily noon-2am.

Rage, 8911 Santa Monica Blvd. (☎310-652-7055). Its glory days have passed, but this institution rages on with nightly DJs, drag nights, and disco 'til you drop. Mostly gay men; some lesbians during the day. Half-price drinks Su 6-8pm (dance floor opens at 6pm). Full lunch and dinner menu served 2-10pm. Happy hour (half-price drinks) M-F 2-8pm. Th 18+. Open Su-Th 2pm-2am, F 2pm-3:30am, Sa 2pm-3am.

◙ BEACHES

South Bay life is beach life. **Hermosa Beach** wins both bathing suit and congeniality competitions. Its slammin' volleyball scene, gnarly waves, and killer boardwalk make this the *über*-beach. The mellower **Manhattan Beach** exudes a yuppified charm, while **Redondo Beach** is by far the most commercially suburban. Ritzy **Rancho Palos Verdes** is a coast of a different breed. From early morning to late evening, these beaches are overrun by swarms of eager skaters, bladers, volleyball players, surfers, and sunbathers. At night, the crowds move off the beach and toward Manhattan and Hermosa Ave. for an affordable nightlife scene.

South Bay harbors two of L.A.'s finest hostels. ◙**Los Angeles South Bay (HI-AYH),** 3601 S. Gaffey St., Bldg. #613, in Angels Gate Park (entrance by 36th) in San Pedro, pleases with a kitchen, laundry, TV room, volleyball courts, and free parking. (☎831-8109. Linen $2. Reception 7am-noon and 1pm-midnight; in winter 7am-11am and 4pm-midnight. 16-bed dorms $16; semi-private rooms with 2-3 beds $18.25; private rooms $40. 16-bed dorms. Nonmembers $3 extra. 7-night max. stay.) **Los Angeles Surf City Hostel,** 26 Pier Ave., half a block from the beach in Hermosa Beach, is a good-natured spot to rest, with free linen, bodyboards, and breakfast. Take the #439 bus from Union Station to 11th and Hermosa, walk two blocks north, and make a left on Pier. (☎798-2323. Key deposit $10. 4-6 bunk dorms $18; Dec.-Apr. $15.50; private rooms $47. No parking. Reservations recommended. Passport or proof of out-of-state residence required.)

Malibu's public beaches are cleaner and less crowded than any others in L.A. County, and as a whole offer better surfing. Surf's up at **Surfrider Beach,** a section of Malibu Laguna State Beach located north of the pier at 23000 PCH. You can walk onto the beach via the **Zonker Harris** access way (named after the beach-obsessed *Doonesbury* character), at 22700 PCH. **Malibu Ocean Sports,** 22935 PCH, across from the pier, rents surfboards, kayaks, boogie boards, and wetsuits, and offers surfing lessons. (☎310-456-6302. Open daily 9am-7pm. Surfboards $10 per hr., $25 per day. Kayaks: single $15 per hr., $35 per day; double $20/50. Boogie boards $12 per day. Wetsuits $10 per day. Surfing lessons $100 for 2hr. lesson and full-day gear.)

Corral State Beach, a remote windsurfing, swimming, and scuba-diving haven, lies on the 26000 block of PCH, followed by **Point Dume State Beach,** which is larger and generally uncrowded, and has better currents for scuba diving. Along the 30000 block of PCH lies **Zuma,** L.A. County's northernmost, largest, and most user-friendly county-owned sandbox. Restrooms, lifeguards, and food stands guarantee that Zuma regularly draws a diverse crowd. Sections 6-8 are popular with local kids; sections 9-11 are less populated. Swimmers should only dive near manned lifeguard stations; because of the devastating **riptide,** rescue counts are high. Free street parking is highly coveted, so expect to park in the beach lot ($6, off-peak $2). Just south of Zuma, before Point Dume, is a clothing-optional strip nicknamed Pirate's Cove. There are fewer footprints at **Westward Beach,** just southeast of Zuma, where cliffs shelter the beach from the highway.

ORANGE COUNTY ☎714

Directly south of L.A. County is Orange County. It is a microcosm of Southern California: dazzling stretches of sandy shoreline, bronzed beach bums, endless strip malls, frustrating traffic snarls, and the stronghold of the late Walt Disney's ever-expanding cultural empire. Orange County has won fame for its booming economy, which is as big as Arizona's and one of the world's 30 largest. Disneyland is the premier inland attraction, an island of singing critters with plastic smiles in the midst of the suburban sprawl. The amazing beaches run the gamut from the budget and party-friendly Huntington Beach to the opulent Newport Beach.

🔼 PRACTICAL INFORMATION

John Wayne Orange County Airport, on Campus Dr., 20min. from Anaheim, is newer, cleaner, and easier to get around than LAX. (☎949-252-5006. Domestic flights only.) **Amtrak** runs to Fullerton, 120 E. Santa Fe Ave. (☎992-0530); Anaheim, 2150 E. Katella Blvd. (☎714-385-1448); Santa Ana, 1000 E. Santa Ana Blvd. (☎547-8389); Irvine, 15215 Barranca Pkwy. (☎949-753-9713); San Juan Capistrano, Santa Fe Depot, 26701 Verdugo St. (☎949-240-2972); and San Clemente, 1850 Avenida Estacion. **Greyhound** has three stations in the area: Anaheim, 100 W. Winston St., three blocks south of Disneyland (☎999-1256; open daily 6:30am-9pm); Santa Ana, 1000 E. Santa Ana Blvd. (☎542-2215; open daily 6am-8:30pm), and San Clemente, Dad's Liquor & Deli, 2421 S. El Camino Real (☎949-366-2646; open daily 7am-8:30pm). **Orange County Transportation Authority (OCTA),** 550 S. Main St., Garden Grove, provides thorough service useful for getting from Santa Ana and Fullerton Amtrak stations to Disneyland and for coastal beach-hopping. (☎636-7433. $1, day pass $2.50.) **MTA** (☎800-266-6883) runs buses daily from L.A. to Disneyland and Knott's Berry Farm. The **Anaheim Area Visitors and Convention Bureau,** 800 W. Katella Ave., is in the Anaheim Convention Center. (☎999-8999. Open M-F 8:30am-5pm.) Anaheim's **Post Office:** 701 N. Loara (☎520-2601). **ZIP code:** 92803.

 ORANGE COUNTY AREA CODES. 714 in Anaheim, Fullerton, Fountain Valley, Santa Ana, Orange, Garden Grove; **949** in Newport, Laguna, Irvine, Mission Viejo, San Juan Capistrano, and surrounding areas; **310** in Seal Beach. In text, **714** unless noted.

🏠 ACCOMMODATIONS

The Magic Kingdom is the sun around which the Anaheim solar system revolves, so budget motels and garden-variety "clean, comfortable rooms" flank it on all sides. Keep watch for family and group rates posted on marquees and seek out establishments offering the three-for-two passport (3 days of Disney for the price of 2). O.C.'s beach communities have a few excellent hostels.

ANAHEIM

Fullerton (HI-AYH), 1700 N. Harbor Blvd. (☎738-3721, reservations 800-909-4776, ext. 25), in Fullerton, 15min. north of Disneyland. Shuttle from L.A. airport $17. OCTA bus #43 runs along Harbor Blvd. to Disneyland. In the woods and away from the thematic craziness of nearby Anaheim. Enthusiastic, resourceful staff invites questions but forbids drinking. Offers services, including ISICs. Kitchen, Internet access, relaxing living room, communal bathrooms. Linen $1. Free laundry. 5-night max. stay. Check-in 8-11am and 4-11pm. No curfew. Reservations encouraged. Single-sex and co-ed dorms $14, nonmembers $17 (including taxes); less in off-season.

Econolodge, 1126 W. Katella Ave. (☎533-4505), in Anaheim, southwest of Disneyland. Clean, newly revamped rooms with HBO, phones, and A/C. Balconies offer a good view of Disney's nightly fireworks. Small pool, many kids. Singles $79, in winter $69; doubles $99/$89. Reservations recommended; 10% discount with Internet reservations.

ORANGE COUNTY BEACH COMMUNITIES

■ **Huntington Beach Colonial Inn Youth Hostel,** 421 8th St. (☎714- 536-9206), in Huntington Beach, 4 blocks inland at Pecan Ave. Take OCTA #29 (which also goes to Knott's) or 50. This large, early 20th-century, yellow and blue house has been around the block; it was once a brothel. Things have quieted down since the neighbors moved in (quiet hours after 11pm). Common bath, large kitchen, reading/TV room, laundry, Internet access, deck, and surfboard shed. Linen and breakfast included. Key deposit $20. Check-in 7am-11pm. Americans 1 week max. stay. Reserve 2 days in advance for summer weekends. Passport required. 3-4 person dorms, $22; doubles $49.50.

HI San Clemente Beach (HI-AYH), 233 Ave. Granada (☎949-492-2848), in San Clemente, 2 blocks west of El Camino, near the shore. This airy surfer's haven is so laid-back it's almost comatose. Patio, comfy couches, and entertainment center. Lockers, laundry, kitchen, Internet access. 14-day max. stay. 20-bed male dorm, 14-bed female dorm, and private room with 3 beds ($2 surcharge per person). Reception 8-10:30am and 5-11pm. Quiet hours 11pm-7am. Open May-Oct. Dorms $14, nonmembers $17.

🔆 FOOD

Inexpensive ethnic restaurants tucked into Anaheim's strip malls allow escape from fast food. Many specialize in take-out or will deliver chow to your motel room.

■ **Rutabegorz,** 211 N. Pomona Blvd. (☎738-9339), in Fullerton. With a name derived from the unloved rutabaga and a style acquired from the worship thereof, this hippie-*cum*-hipster joint supplies a 16-page menu (printed on recycled newsprint, of course). Crepes, curries, quesadillas, and club sandwiches are all fresh and veggie-licious. Heaping salads with homemade dressings $8; Mexican casserole $6.50. Smoothies, veggie juices, and coffee drinks. Open M-Th 11am-10pm, F-Sa 11am-11pm, Su 4-9pm.

■ **Laguna Village Market and Cafe,** 577 S. Coast Hwy. (☎949-494-6344), in Laguna Beach. The restaurant is housed in an open-air gazebo, but its oceanfront terrace is the main draw. Lap up the view, along with some seafood or the chicken curry dumplings ($9.75), a house specialty. Village *huevos* $8.50; jalapeno sausage, cheese, and salsa $6.25. Open daily 8:30am-dusk.

La Cocina de Ricardo, Presidio Plaza, 401 S. Camino Real (☎949-498-7808), in San Clemente. Through a door with a sign that reads "No Lard" come troops of hungry surfers and high schoolers. The "Surfer Burrito" (beans, rice, cheese, guacamole, sour cream, lettuce, beef/chicken; $5.25) comes out "faster than McDonald's" and can be topped off at the fresh salsa stand. Open M-F 10am-9pm, Sa-Su 9am-8:30pm.

Angelo & Vinci's Cafe Ristorante, 550 N. Harbor Blvd. (☎879-4022), in Fullerton. Prepare for opera—arias, masks, even "backstage dining." Padded red chairs, iron-rod table lamps, and indoor awnings are all part of the Sicilian motif. The food is unmistakably the stuff of family recipes (*Cannelloni Vinci* $10), with more than enough to feed the family at the lunch buffet ($6). Open Su-Th 11am-9:45pm, F-Sa 11am-11:45pm.

◉ SIGHTS

DISNEYLAND. Disneyland calls itself the "Happiest Place on Earth," and there is an oh-so-smiley part of every pop culture pilgrim that agrees. Weekday and off-season visitors will undoubtedly be the happiest, but the enterprising can take advantage of the new FastPass system or wait for parades to distract the children, leaving shorter lines. *Disneyland Today!* lists parade and show times, as well as breaking news from Frontierland. (*Main entrance on Harbor Blvd. and a smaller one on Katella Ave. ☎ 781-4565; www.disneyland.com. From L.A., MTA bus #460 travels from 4th and Flower St. to the Disneyland Hotel; service to the hotel begins at 4:53am, service back to L.A. until 1:20am. Free shuttles link the hotel to Disneyland's portals, as does the Disneyland monorail. Parking in the morning is painless, but leaving in the evening is not. Open approximately Su-Th 10am-9pm, F-Sa 8am-midnight. $41, seniors $39, ages 3-12 $31, under 3 free. Parking $7.*)

K(NOT)T DISNEYLAND. Buena Park offers a cavalcade of non-Disney diversions, some of which are better than others. The first theme park in America, **Knott's Berry Farm,** is at La Palma Ave. in Buena Park just 5 mi. northeast of Disneyland. (*8039 Beach Blvd. at La Palma Ave., 5 mi. northeast of Disneyland. From downtown L.A., take MTA bus #460 from 4th and Flower St.; 1¼hr. If driving from L.A., take the I-5 S to Beach Blvd.; turn right at the end of the exit ramp and proceed south 2 mi. Recorded info ☎ 714-220-5220. Park hours vary, but are approximately Su-Th 9am-10pm, F-Sa 9am-midnight. $38, seniors $28, ages 3-11 $28, under 3 free; after 4pm all ages $17. Summer discounts. Parking $7.*) The major league **Anaheim Angels** play baseball from early April to September. (*☎ 940-2000 or 800-626-4357. General tickets $10-30.*) Happy, happy hockey takes place at the **Arrowhead Pond,** home to the NHL's **Mighty Ducks.** (*2695 E. Katella Ave, 1 block east of Rte. 57. ☎ 704-2500.*) Farther inland is the highly uncritical, privately funded monument to Tricky Dick, the **Richard Nixon Library and Birthplace.** Skeptics can investigate the Watergate Room. Museum curators portray Nixon as a victim of circumstance, plotting enemies, and his own immutable honor. (*18001 Yorba Linda Blvd. ☎ 993-5075. Open M-Sa 10am-5pm, Su 11am-5pm. $6, seniors $4, ages 8-11 $2, under 8 free.*)

ORANGE COUNTY BEACH COMMUNITIES. The various beach communities of Orange County have cleaner sand and better surf than their L.A. county counterparts. **Huntington Beach** was an epicenter of the legendary surfing craze that transformed California coast life in the early 1900s. It's still a fun hot spot for waveshredders. **Newport Beach** is the Beverly Hills of beach towns, though the beach itself displays few signs of ostentatious wealth; it is crowded with young, rowdy hedonists cloaked in neon. Nearby **Balboa Peninsula** can be reached by Rte. 1.

Laguna Beach, 4 mi. south of Newport, is between canyons. Back in the day, Laguna was a bohemian artists' colony, but no properly starving artists can afford to live here now. The surviving galleries and art supply stores nevertheless add a unique twist to the standard SoCal beach culture that thrives on Laguna's sands. **Main Beach** and the shops nearby along Ocean Ave. are the prime parading areas, though there are other, less crowded spots as well. One accessible beach is **Westry Beach,** which spreads out south of Laguna just below **Aliso Beach Park.** More tourists than swallows return every year to **Mission San Juan Capistrano,** 30min. south of Anaheim on I-5. The most beautiful of California's missions, it's still used by the Catholic Church. (*☎ 949-248-2048. Open daily 8:30am-5pm. $6, seniors $4, ages 3-12 $4.*)

BIG BEAR   ☎ 909

Hibernating in the San Bernardino Mountains, Big Bear Lake draws hordes with fluffy winter skiing and stellar summer hiking, biking, and boating. Also, the consistent winds make for some of the best sailing in the state. Prices are somewhat higher in Big Bear and increase when there is enough snow for skiing— usually mid-November to mid-April—so you'll have to just grin and bear it.

The **hiking** here is both free and priceless. Maps, trail descriptions, and the *Visitor's Guide to the San Bernardino National Forest* are available at the **Big Bear Discovery Center,** on Rte. 38. (*☎ 866-3437. Open Apr.-Sept. daily 8am-6pm; Oct.-Mar. 8am-4:30pm.*) The **Woodland Trail** or the more challenging **Pineknot Trail** offer views of the lake; high altitudes here make slow climbing necessary.

Mountain biking is a popular activity in Big Bear when the snow melts. Grab a pulpy *Ride and Trail Guide* at the Discovery Center and at **Snow Summit,** 1 mi. west of Big Bear Lake, which runs lifts in summer so that adrenaline monsters can grind serious downhill terrain. (☎866-4621. $9 per ride, day pass $19; ages 7-12 $4, $9. Helmet required.) Those without wheels of their own can rent them from **Big Bear Bikes,** 41810 Big Bear Blvd. (☎866-2224. Open daily 10am-5pm.) Many summer activities take place on the water. **Fishing licenses** are available at area sporting goods stores ($10 per day, $28 per season), and the **Big Bear Fishing Association** (☎866-6260) cheerfully dispenses info. **Holloway's Marina,** 398 Edgemor Rd., on the South Shore, rents **boats.** (☎800-448-5335. Full-day $46-130.)

When conditions are favorable, ski areas run out of lift tickets quickly. Tickets for the resorts listed below may be purchased over the phone through **Ticketmaster** (☎740-2000). The **Big Bear Hotline** (☎800-424-4232) has info on lodging, local events, and ski and road conditions. **Big Bear Resort,** 1½ mi. southeast of downtown Big Bear Lake, has 12 lifts covering 195 acres of terrain, including huge vertical drops, plus many more acres of undeveloped land for adventurous skiers. (☎585-2519. Lift tickets $32, holidays $45. Skis $23, snowboards $28.)

Big Bear has few budget accommodations, especially in the winter. The best option for daytrippers is probably to stay in Redlands or San Bernardino, although the drive down Rte. 18 can be difficult at night. **Big Bear Blvd.,** the main drag on the lake's south shore, is lined with lodging possibilities. **Mountain Lodging Unlimited** arranges lodging and lift packages. (☎800-487-3168. From about $110 per couple. Open in ski season 7am-midnight; off season 9am-midnight.) **Hillcrest Lodge,** 40241 Big Bear Blvd., is a favorite for honeymooners. Pine paneling and skylights give these cozy rooms a ritzy feel at a budget price. (☎866-7330, reservations 800-843-4449. Jacuzzi, cable, and free local calls. Small rooms $35-49, 4-person units with kitchen $64-89, deluxe doubles with hearth and kitchen $57-79; in winter $44-69/$74-125/$74-125.) **Pineknot,** south of Big Bear on Summit Blvd., has 52 isolated sites with flush toilets and water. At the base of Snow Summit, this spot is popular with mountain bikers. (☎877-444-6777. $15.) Groceries can be procured at **Stater Bros.,** 42171 Big Bear Blvd. (☎866-5211. Open daily 7am-11pm.)

To reach Big Bear Lake, take the San Bernardino Fwy. (I-10) to the junction of Rte. 30 and 330. Follow Rte. 330, also known as Mountain Rd., to Rte. 18, a *very* long and winding uphill road. About halfway up the mountain, Rte. 18 becomes Big Bear Blvd., the main route encircling the lake. **Mountain Area Regional Transit Authority (MARTA)** runs one bus per day from the Greyhound station in San Bernardino to Big Bear. (☎584-1111. $5, seniors and disabled $4.) Buses also run the length of Big Bear Blvd. (1hr.; $1, students 75¢, seniors and disabled 50¢). MARTA also operates **Dial-A-Ride** ($2, students $1.75, seniors and disabled $1).

SAN DIEGO ☎618

San Diegans are fond of referring to their garden-like town as "America's Finest City." This claim is difficult to dispute—San Diego has all the virtues of other California cities without their frequently cited drawbacks. No smog fills this city's air, and no sewage spoils its silver seashores. Its zoo is the nation's best, and its city center contains a greater concentration of museums than any spot in America save Washington, D.C. The city was founded when the seafaring Spanish prolonged an onshore foray in 1769, but it didn't become a city proper until the 1940s, when it became the headquarters of the US Pacific Fleet following the Pearl Harbor attack.

▐ TRANSPORTATION

San Diego rests in the extreme southwest corner of California, 127 mi. south of L.A. and 15 mi. north of Mexico. **I-5** runs south from L.A. and skirts the eastern edge of downtown; **I-15** runs northeast to Nevada; and **I-8** runs east-west along downtown's northern boundary, connecting the desert with Ocean Beach. The major downtown thoroughfare, **Broadway,** also runs east-west.

Downtown San Diego

⌂ ACCOMMODATIONS
J Street Inn, 4
Ocean Beach
International, 1
San Diego Metropolitan
Hostel, 3
USA Hostels San
Diego, 2

Airport: San Diego International (Lindbergh Field), at the northwest edge of downtown. Call the Travelers Aid Society (☎231-7361) for info. Open daily 8am-11pm. Bus #2 goes downtown ($1.75), as do cabs ($8).

Trains: Amtrak, 1050 Kettner Blvd. (☎239-9021 or 800-872-7245), just north of Broadway. To L.A. (11 per day 6am-8:30pm, buses at 10:15am and 3:40am; $23-28). Station has info on bus, trolley, car, and boat transportation. Ticket office open daily 5:15am-10:20pm. Additional $10 for reservations.

Buses: Greyhound, 120 W. Broadway (☎239-8082 or 800-231-2222), at 1st St. To L.A. (30 per day, 5am-11:35pm; $15). Ticket office open 24hr.

Public Transit: San Diego Metropolitan Transit System (MTS) (☎685-4900), has info on buses, trains, and trolleys. The **Transit Store,** at 1st Ave. and Broadway, has bus, trolley, and ferry tickets and timetables. Open M-F 8:30am-5:30pm, Sa-Su noon-4pm. The **Day Tripper** allows unlimited rides on buses, ferries, and trolleys for 1 day ($5), 2 days ($8), 3 days ($10), or 4 days ($12).

Car Rental: Academy Car, Jet Ski and Boat Rental, 2270 Hotel Circle N. (☎294-2227 or 888-920-2227), in the Hanalei Mission Valley Hotel. Cars from $19 per day with 150 mi. free, $139-198 per week with 700 mi. free. Ages 18-21 pay $8 per day surcharge, ages 21-25 $4. Insurance to bring the car into Mexico $6-12. Credit card required. Waverunners and boats also for rent. Open daily 8am-6pm.

Bike Info: Buses equipped with bike carriers make it possible to cart bikes almost anywhere in the city (call 233-3004 to find out which routes have carriers). Bikes are also allowed on the San Diego Trolley with a $4 permit (available at the Transit Store, see above). For more bike info, contact **CalTrans,** 4040 Taylor St., San Diego 92110 (☎231-2453), in Old Town. Biking maps and pamphlets are available. Rent bikes from

Action Sports, 4000 Coronado Bay Rd. (☎424-4466), at the Marina Dock of the Loews Coronado Bay Resort. Beach cruiser bikes $7 per hr., $20 per 4hr.; mountain bikes $9/ $25; full-suspension bikes $10/$30. Open M-F 9am-6pm, Sa-Su 8:30am-6:30pm.

✴️ 🛈 ORIENTATION AND PRACTICAL INFORMATION

In northeast downtown sits **Balboa Park,** home to many museums and to the justly heralded San Diego Zoo. The cosmopolitan **Hillcrest** and **University Heights** districts, both centers of the gay community, border the park to the northeast. South of downtown, between 4th and 6th St., is the **Gaslamp District,** full of nightclubs, chic restaurants, and coffeehouses. **Downtown** is situated between San Diego's two major bays: **San Diego Bay,** formed by **Coronado Island,** lies just to the south, while **Mission Bay,** formed by the **Mission Beach** spit, lies to the northwest. Up the coast from Mission Beach are **Ocean Beach, Pacific Beach,** and wealthy **La Jolla.**

Visitor info: International Visitor Information Center, 11 Horton Plaza (☎236-1212), downtown at 1st Ave. and F St. Helpful, multilingual staff dispenses publications, brochures, and discount coupons. 3hr. parking validation for lots with entrances on G St. and 4th Ave. Open June-Aug. M-Sa 8:30am-5pm, Su 11am-5pm; Sept.-May M-Sa 8:30am-5pm. **San Diego Convention and Visitors Bureau,** 401 B St., #1400 Dept. 700, San Diego 92101 (☎236-1212; www.sandiego.org), also provides info. **Old Town and State Park Info,** 4002 Wallace Ave. (☎220-5422), in Old Town Sq., offers free walking tours daily at noon and 2pm. Open daily 10am-5pm.

Post Office: 2535 Midway Dr. Take bus #6, 9, or 35. Open M 7am-5pm, Tu-F 8am-5pm, Sa 8am-4pm. **ZIP code:** 92186. **Area code:** 619 for most of the city; 858 in the north. In text, 619 unless noted.

🛏 ACCOMMODATIONS

San Diego offers a variety of accommodations, but rates predictably rise on weekends and during the summer season. Reservations are recommended. There is a popular cluster known as **Hotel Circle** (2-3 mi. east of **I-5** along **I-8**). Those with cars and tents can camp on the beaches outside of the city. Reservations are available through ReserveAmerica. (☎800-444-7275. Open daily 8am-5pm.)

▨ **San Diego Metropolitan Hostel (HI-AYH),** 521 Market St. (☎525-1531 or 800-909-4776, ext. 43), at 5th Ave., in the heart of the Gaslamp. Quiet, impeccable hostel near San Diego's most popular attractions and clubs. Airy common room with kitchen, pool table, and shared bath. Reception 7am-midnight. Groups welcome. Dorms (4-6 beds) members $17, nonmembers $20; doubles $40/$46.

▨ **Ocean Beach International (OBI),** 4961 Newport Ave. (☎223-7873 or 800-339-7263), in Ocean Beach. Look for international flags. Free transport to and from airport, train, and bus terminals. The OBI features cable TV and kitchen near the beach. Breakfast included. Beach gear rental. Laundry. Free barbecue and keg parties Tu and F; free pasta Tu in winter. 29 days max. stay. Proof of international travel required. Dorms (4-6 beds) $15-18; couples' rooms (some with bath) $34-40.

▨ **Banana Bungalow,** 707 Reed Ave. (☎273-3060 or 800-546-7835), just off Mission Blvd. in Mission Beach. Free pickup from airport and Greyhound terminal (call ahead), or take bus #34 to Mission Blvd. and Reed Ave. This party spot rocks with keggers and bonfires. Groovy staff ensures that you wring all the fun you can out of gorgeous Mission Beach. Internet access $1 per 10min. Breakfast included. Free linen. Bikes, skates, surfboards for rent. Check-out 11am. 2-week max. stay. Call in advance. International passport required. Dorms $20; singles with private bath June-Aug. $55, Sept.-May $45.

USA Hostels San Diego, 726 5th Ave. (☎232-3100 or 800-438-8622), between F and G St. in the Gaslamp. This Euro-style funhouse hosts keg parties every Sa and organizes Tijuana tours ($10). Breakfast included. Free linen and lockers. Coin-op laundry. Free shuttle to nearby sights. International passport required. Dorms $15-18; twin $35-40.

J Street Inn, 222 J St. (☎696-6922), near the ritzy waterfront. All 221 fabulous studio rooms have cable TV, microwave, fridge, and bath. Gym and reading room. Enclosed parking $5 per day, $20 per week. Singles and doubles $50-70. Weekly $179-249.

South Carlsbad Beach State Park (☎760-438-3143), off Pacific Coast Hwy. (Rte. 21) near Leucadia, in north San Diego County. Over 100 sites accommodate RVs. Beautiful beaches with good surfing conditions. Showers and laundry. Mar.-Nov. ocean view $22, inland $17; Dec.-Feb. $19/$14. Hookups $6 extra; extra vehicle $4; dogs $1.

San Elijo Beach State Park (☎760-753-5091), off Pacific Coast Hwy. (Rte. 21) south of Cardiff-by-the-Sea. 171 sites (23 with RV hookups) on seaside cliffs. Fresh breezes and glorious sunsets. Handicap accessible. Laundry and showers. Mar.-Nov. ocean view $22, inland $17; Dec.-Feb. $19/$14. Hookups $6 extra; extra vehicle $4; dogs $1.

🍴 FOOD

Good restaurants cluster downtown along **C St., Broadway,** and in the **Gaslamp.** The best food near Balboa Park and the Zoo is north and west in nearby **Hillcrest** and **University Heights. Old Town** is *the* place to eat Mexican cuisine.

▨ Casa de Bandini, 2754 Calhoun St. (☎297-8211). Repeatedly voted best Mexican restaurant in San Diego. Set in a Spanish-style architectural landmark (built in 1829), Bandini dishes out superb food and boisterous *mariachi* music. The colossal combo plates ($8) and heavyweight margaritas ($4-7) are the stuff of legend. Open M-Th 11am-9:30pm, F-Sa 11am-10pm, Su 10am-9:30pm.

▨ The Vegetarian Zone, 2949 5th Ave. (☎298-7302), at Quince St. The motto in this carnivore-unfriendly zone is: "the human body doesn't require any form of meat to operate wonderfully." With that in mind, savor veggie soups ($4) and protein-rich tempeh concoctions that have the taste and consistency of meat ($8-10). Open M-Th 11:30am-3pm and 5:30-9pm, F 11:30am-3pm and 5:30-10pm, Sa 9:30am-3pm and 5:30-10pm, Su 8:30am-3pm and 5:30-9pm.

Corvette Diner Bar & Grill, 3946 5th Ave. (☎542-1476). A real Corvette and booming oldies complete the pseudo-50s decor. Old-fashioned shakes $3. Serves burgers and fries because it's a diner, veggie sandwiches ($6-7) because it's Hillcrest. Open Su-Th 11am-11pm, F-Sa 11am-midnight.

El Indio Mexican Restaurant, 409 F St. (☎299-0385). Good food at good prices. Combo plates $4-6, burritos $3-4. Open M-Th 11am-8pm, F-Sa 11am-2am.

Karl Strauss' Old Columbia Brewery and Grill, 1157 Columbia St. (☎234-2739). This microbrewery is a favorite for power lunches. Barbecue ribs and pasta $8-12. Open M-Th 11:30am-midnight, F-Sa 11:30am-1am, Su 11:30am-10pm.

Rancho El Nopal (☎295-0584), in the Bazaar in Old Town. Sumptuous and bubbling concoctions of beans, rice, and cheese. Special dishes with healthy, low-fat alternatives available. Entrees $6-9. Open daily 10am-9pm.

👁 SIGHTS

DOWNTOWN

San Diego's downtown attractions are concentrated in the corridor that includes its business, Gaslamp, and waterfront districts—all testaments to San Diego's continuing renaissance. **San Diego Museum of Contemporary Art** is a steel-and-glass structure that encases 20th-century works of art from the museum's permanent collection as well as visiting works. *(1001 Kettner Blvd. ☎234-1001. Open Tu-Sa 10am-5pm, Su noon-5pm. $2; seniors, students, military, and ages 12-18 $1; under 12 free.)* The **Gaslamp Quarter** houses antique shops, Victorian buildings, and trendy restaurants. Formerly the city's Red Light District and home to the original Pappy's, Inc. adult bookstore, the area's new bars and bistros have grown popular with upscale revelers. By day, the area's charm lies in its history. The **Gaslamp Quarter Foundation** offers guided walking tours. *(410 Island Ave. ☎233-4692. Museum open M-F 10am-2pm, Sa 10am-4pm, Su noon-4pm. $5; seniors, students, and ages 12-18 $3; under 12 free.)* The **Horton Grand Hotel,** like most old buildings in San Diego, is supposedly haunted. Believers may catch a glimpse of Wyatt Earp or even Babe Ruth. *(311 Island Ave.* ☎ *544-1886. Tours W at 3pm. Free.)* The displays at the **San Diego Maritime Museum** will impress maritime history buffs. *(1306 N. Harbor Dr.* ☎ *243-9153. Open June-Aug. daily 9am-9pm; Sept.-May 9am-8pm. $6; seniors, military, and ages 13-17 $5; ages 6-12 $3; under 6 free.)*

THE SAN DIEGO ZOO AND BALBOA PARK

SAN DIEGO ZOO. With over 100 acres of exquisite fenceless habitats, this zoo well deserves its reputation as one of the finest in the world. Its unique "bioclimatic" exhibits group animals and plants together by habitat. The zoo currently showcases several **pandas** and invests over a million dollars a year on panda habitat preservation in China. Young *Homo sapiens* can watch the hatching and feeding of other species' toddlers in the **children's petting zoo.** The **Skyfari Aerial Tramway** rises 170 ft. above the park and lasts about 2min. *(*☎ *234-3153. Late June to early Sept. 7:30am-10pm; off-season 9am-dusk. $18, ages 3-11 $8, military free. Combined Zoo, Wild Animal Park, and Seaworld admission $79, ages 3-11 $56. Skyfari Aerial Tramway $1.50 one-way.)*

BALBOA PARK AND THE EL PRADO MUSEUMS. It would take several days to see all of Balboa Park's museums. Most of them reside within the resplendent Spanish colonial-style buildings that line **El Prado Street,** which runs west-to-east through the Park's central **Plaza de Panama.** The **Balboa Park Visitors Center** is in the House of Hospitality on El Prado St. at the Plaza de Panama and sells park maps ($1) and the Balboa Park passport ($25), which allows admission into 12 of the park's museums. Passports are also available at participating museums. *(*☎ *239-0512. Open daily 9am-5pm.)* Formerly a state building, the sizeable **Museum of Man** anchors the west end of the park. The museum traces human evolution with exhibits on primates and early man. *(*☎ *239-2001. Open daily 10am-4:30pm. $6, seniors $5, ages 6-17 $3, military free; free 3rd Tu of each month.)* At the east end of Balboa Park, the **Natural History Museum** displays stuffed mammals and birds. Live insects and arthropods enhance the exhibition of standard fossils. *(*☎ *232-3821. Open daily 9:30am-5pm; off-season 9:30am-4:30pm. Admission varies depending on exhibits.)* The **Aerospace Museum** displays 24 full-scale replicas and 44 original planes, as well as aviation history exhibits in the Ford Pavilion. *(2001 Pan American Plaza.* ☎ *234-8291. Open daily 10am-5:30pm; off-season 10am-5pm. $8, seniors $6, ages 6-17 $3, military and under 6 free; free 4th Tu of each month.)*

OLD TOWN

In 1769, Father Junípero Serra, supported by a brigade of Spanish infantry, established the first of 21 missions that eventually would line the California coast. Now known as Old Town, the remnants of this early settlement are one of San Diego's tourist mainstays. The **Mission Basilica San Diego de Alcalá** is still an active parish church and contains a chapel, gardens, a small museum, and a reconstruction of Serra's living quarters. *(*☎ *281-8449. Mass daily at 7am and 5:30pm; visitors welcome.)* The most popular of the area's attractions, the **Old Town State Park** contain museums, shops, and restaurants. **Seely Stable** gives visitor info and free tours of the stable's agricultural exhibits. *(*☎ *220-5422. Open daily 10am-9pm. Tours every hr. 11am-2pm.)* Take a tour of the **Whaley House,** which displays an authentic Lincoln life mask and the piano used in *Gone With the Wind.* The house stands on the site of San Diego's first gallows, which might explain why it is one of two **official haunted houses** recognized by the State of California. *(2482 San Diego Ave.* ☎ *298-2482. Open daily 10am-4:30pm. $4, seniors $3, ages 6-12 $2.)* Across the street is **Heritage Park,** a group of seven 150-year-old Victorian buildings collected from around the city. Four are open to the public. The **Serra Museum** houses exhibits documenting the settlement; outside is a really, really huge flagpole marking the former location of **Fort Stockton.** *(In Presidio Park.* ☎ *279-3258. Open Tu-Sa 10am-4:30pm, Su noon-4:30pm. $3, under 12 free.)*

CORONADO ISLAND

Lovely Coronado Island is in fact a peninsula; a slender 7 mi. strip of sand known as the "Silver Strand" tethers it to the mainland. Famous for its elegant colonial Hotel del Coronado, the island is perfect for strolling and browsing. Water babies frolic in the frothy waves that break all along the southern shore, and outdoor enthusiasts jog and bike along paved trails. Coronado has a huge military presence, and the entire northern chunk comprises the **North Island Naval Air Station,** the birthplace of American naval aviation. Among the island's many naval enterprises is the training area of the infamous SEAL (sea, air, and land) commando teams. Coronado could win "Island Least Likely to Be Invaded" in any contest. The super-helpful **Coronado Visitors Bureau** provides island info. *(1047 B Ave., just off Orange Ave. near the Hotel del Coronado. ☎437-8788 or 800-622-8300. Open M-F 9am-5pm, Sa 10am-5pm, Su 11am-4pm.)*

SEA WORLD

Take Disneyland, subtract the rides, add a whole lot of fish, and you've got Sea World. Sea World aspires to be both fun and educational. Though critics have long condemned the practice of training highly intelligent marine mammals to perform unnatural circus acts, most visitors find the playful goofballs irresistible. The A-list star here is the behemoth killer whale **Shamu,** whose signature move is a cannon-ball splash that soaks anyone in the first 20 rows (the original Shamu died long ago, but each of his ten successors has proudly borne the moniker). If it's your mind and not your water-filled pockets that needs emptying, head for the **Baywatch at Sea World** ski show, where high-speed hilarity and bursting bodices rule. The performance's plot is just as gripping as the TV show's, and part of the event is narrated by international heartthrob **David Hasselhoff.** The park's newest attraction is **Shipwreck Rapids,** Sea World's first-ever adventure ride. If you feel the need to cool off, head to the **Anheuser-Busch Hospitality Tent,** which will give each (21+) guest up to two free cups of beer. *(☎226-3901. Open M-Th 9am-11:30pm, F-Su 9am-11pm. Hours shorter in off-season. $40, ages 3-11 $30. 2-day pass $44, $34. Parking $7, RVs $9.)*

NIGHTLIFE

Nightlife in San Diego isn't centered around any one strip, but scattered in several distinct pockets of action. Upscale locals and trend-seeking tourists flock to the **Gaslamp Quarter,** where numerous restaurants and bars feature live music nightly. The **Hillcrest** area, next to Balboa Park, draws a young, largely gay crowd to its clubs and dining spots. Away from downtown, the **beach areas** are loaded with clubs, bars, and inexpensive eateries that attract college-age revelers. The city's definitive source of entertainment info is the free *San Diego Reader*, found in shops, coffeehouses, and Visitors Centers. Lesbian and gay clubs cluster in **University Heights** and **Hillcrest. Gaymart,** 550 University Ave., a clothing and video emporium, has info on the gay scene. (☎543-1221. Open daily 10am-10pm.)

Croce's Top Hat Bar and Grille and **Croce's Jazz Bar,** 802 5th Ave. (☎233-4355), at F St. Ingrid Croce, widow of singer Jim Croce, created this rock/blues bar and jazz bar side-by-side on the 1st floor of the historic Keating Bldg. Live music nightly. Cover $5-10, includes 2 shows. Open daily 7:30am-3pm and 5pm-midnight; bar open until 2am.

Pacific Beach Bar and Grill and **Club Tremors,** 860 Garnet Ave. (☎858-272-1242 and 277-7228, respectively). Live DJ packs the 2-level dance floor with a young and slinky crowd. The Bar and Grill has cheap, delicious food. Cover $5. Club open Th-Sa 9pm-1:30am. Bar open 11am-1:30am; kitchen closes at midnight.

Cafe Lu Lu, 419 F. St. (☎858-238-0114). Coffeehouse designed by local artists. See and be seen as you surreptitiously sip a raspberry-mocha espresso ($3.75). Standing room only after midnight. Open Su-Th 9am-2am, F-Sa 9am-3am.

Dick's Last Resort, 345 4th Ave. (☎858-231-9100). Buckets of Southern grub attract a wildly hedonistic bunch. Dick's stocks beers from around the globe, from Africa to Trinidad, on top of native brews. No cover for the nightly rock or blues, but you'd better be buyin'. Lunch burgers under $4, dinner entrees $10-18. Open daily 11am-1:30am.

The Crow Bar, 2812 Kettner Blvd. (☎692-1080). Live and loud, the Crow Bar hosts San Diego's up-and-coming rock 'n' roll acts. Alternative rock 6 nights per week. Happy hour ($1 drafts) daily 4-8pm. 21+. Cover W-Sa usually $5-10. Open daily 5pm-2am.

The Flame, 3780 Park Blvd. (☎295-4163), is a popular lesbian dance club with oodles of special events. Su Latin night, Tu Boys' Night Out, W drag king contests, Th karaoke. Call for cover. Open M-Th and Sa-Su 5pm-2am, F 4pm-2am.

Bourbon Street, 4612 Park Blvd. (☎291-0173), in University Heights, is a perennially popular piano bar with a gay following. Open daily 11am-1:30am.

The Brass Rail, 3796 5th Ave. (☎298-2233), in Hillcrest. San Diego's oldest gay bar. Features dancing and drag on weekends. Open daily 5pm-2am.

NORTH OF SAN DIEGO

LA JOLLA

Pronounced *la-HOY-a*, this affluent locality houses few budget accommodations or eateries, but its fabulous beaches are largely open to the public. The **La Jolla Cove** is popular with scuba divers, snorkelers, and brilliantly colored Garibaldi goldfish (the state saltwater fish). Surfers are especially fond of the waves at **Tourmaline Beach** and **Windansea Beach,** which can be too strong for novices. **La Jolla Shores,** next to Scripps/UCSD, has clean and gentle swells ideal for bodysurfers, boogie boarders, swimmers, and families. **Black's Beach** is not officially a nude beach, but let's just say there are plenty of wieners and buns at *this* lunchcart. To reach La Jolla, turn from I-5 and take a left at the Ardath exit or take buses #30 or 34 from downtown. **Area code:** 858.

ESCONDIDO

The **San Diego Wild Animal Park** is an essential part of any trip to San Diego. Visitors gawk at the beasties from the open-air **Wgasa Bush Line Railway,** a 55min. monorail safari through four simulated habitat areas. Patrons also watch butterflies and birds flutter as they walk through the Hidden Jungle greenhouses. The park has shops, restaurants, and animal shows, but for adventure, try the 1 mi. Heart of Africa hike, the open-air Photo Caravan, or the Roar and Snore overnight camping safari, available May to September. (☎738-5049 or 800-934-2267. Open daily at 9am; closing times vary. $26, ages 3-11 $19. Parking $6.) **Area code:** 760.

TIJUANA   ☎ 66

In the shadow of swollen, sulphur-spewing factories lies the most notorious specimen of a peculiar border subculture: Tijuana, Mexico. By day, swarms of tourists cross the US border to haggle with street vendors, pour gallons of tequila down their throats, and get their pictures taken with donkeys painted as zebras. By night, Revolución, the city's wide main drag, becomes a big, bad party with *mariachi* bands and exploding bottle rockets doing little to drown out the thumping dance beats blaring from the packed nightclubs. Though parts of Tijuana are dirtier than a donkey show, the city's strange charm, cheap booze, and sprawling, unapologetic hedonism continue to attract throngs of tourists.

█▐ ORIENTATION AND PRACTICAL INFORMATION. From San Diego, grab a trolley at Kettner and Broadway downtown (25min., US$20); then catch the southbound **Mexicoach** or walk across the pedestrian footbridge which continues as a walkway over the Río Tijuana and ends at the corner of Calle 1a and Revolución (10min.). The area surrounding Revolución is known as the **Zona Centro.** East-west *calles*, which are both named and numbered, cross Revolución; perpendicular to the *calles*, *avenidas* run north-south. Tijuana has two bus stations, the conveniently located **downtown station,** at Calle 1 and Madero, and the more remote **Central Camionera** (☎21 29 82). **Greyhound** (☎88 19 79) picks up passengers downtown before leaving for **Los Angeles** (3hr., every hr. 5am-midnight, US$24), and connecting to other North American cities. The **Tourist Office,** Revolución 711, at Calle 1, has friendly, English-speaking staff that doles out maps and *consejos*. (☎88 05 55. Open M-Sa 8am-5pm, Su 10am-5pm.) The **Customs Office** lies at the border on the Mexican side, after crossing the San Ysidro bridge. (☎83 13 90. Open 24hr.) Numerous countries have **consulates: Canada,** German Gedovius 10411-101, in the Zona Río. (☎84 04 61 or 800-706-2900; open M-F 9am-1pm); the **UK,** Salinas 1500, in Col. Aviación, La Mesa (☎81 73 23 or 86 53 20; open M-F 9am-3pm); and the **US,** Tapachula Sur 96, in Col. Hipódromo, adjacent to the racetrack southeast of town. (☎81

74 00 or 619-692-2154. Open M-F 8am-4:30pm.) **Red Cross:** Gamboa at Silvestre, across from Price Club (☎21 77 87, emergency 066). **Post Office:** Negrete at Calle 11 (☎84 79 50; open M-F 8am-5pm). **Postal code:** 22000. **Area code:** 66.

▚▟ **ACCOMMODATIONS AND FOOD.** There's no shortage of budget hotels in Tijuana, especially on Calle 1, between Revolución and Mutualismo. Rooms tend to be roachy—ask to see them before paying. *Exercise caution when walking in this area at night.* The strangely decorated **Hotel Perla de Occidente,** Mutualismo 758, between Calles 1 and 2, four blocks from the bedlam of Revolución, has large, soft beds, roomy bathrooms, and fans on request. (☎85 13 58. Singles 140 pesos; doubles 280 pesos.) **Hotel Colonial,** Calle 6a 1812 (☎88 16 20), between Constitución and Niños Héroes, resides in a quieter neighborhood away from Revolución. (☎88 16 20. Singles and doubles with A/C and private baths 240 pesos.) For some great food try ▨**El Pipirín Antojitos,** Constitución 878, between Calles 2 and 3. (☎688 16 02. Open daily 8:30am-9pm. Chicken burritos with rice and beans 35 pesos.) **Restaurant Ricardo's Tortas,** Madero and Calle 7, a huge, sparkling dining area, serves up the best *tortas* in town. (☎85 40 31. Open 24hr. *Super especial* with ham, *carne asada*, cheese, avocado, tomato, and mayo 36 pesos.)

◉ **SIGHTS AND SPORTS.** Photo ops abound on Revolución, where zebra-striped donkeys and gaudily costumed cowboys vie for your attention. The multi-tiered dance clubs and curio shops that share the street are often the only sights that Tijuana tourists care to see. Dedicated in 1924 to the memory of Vicente Guerrero, the shady **Parque Teniente Guerrero,** on Calle 3 and 5 de Mayo, is a favorite gathering place for families and an oasis from the circus of Revolución. The **Catedral de Nuestra Señora de Guadalupe** was built in 1902 as a modest adobe chapel; modern expansions and reinforcement have made it into a huge stone cathedral checkered in adobe orange and gray and crowned with a giant image of the Virgin of Guadalupe. The cathedral's daily mass attracts a diverse congregation of devout locals and curious passersby. The grandiose baroque **Frontón Palacio,** on Revolución at Calle 7a, hosts daily competitions of **jai alai.** (☎85 16 12. Games take place M-Sa at 8pm. Free.) If you're in town on the right Sunday, you can watch the graceful and savage battle of man versus bull in one of Tijuana's two bullrings. **El Toreo de Tijuana,** southeast of town just off of Agua Caliente, hosts the first round of fights (alternate Su, May-July). To get to El Toreo, catch a bus on Calle 2 west of Revolución.

▚ **NIGHTLIFE.** For nightlife, head to **Eclipse,** Revolución at Calle 6—a three-tiered party palace with some of the cheapest booze in town: two beers and a shot of tequila for $3. (Open daily 11am-5am.) **Animale,** Revolución at Calle 4, is the biggest, glitziest, and loudest hedonistic haven of them all. Less than a year old, Animale has already taken over the Tijuana club scene. (Open daily 10am-3am. 2 beers and a shot of tequila $4.) **Iguanas-Ranas,** Revolución at Calle 3, serves beers ($2.50) in a yellow school bus dangling above Revolución and is packed on weekends with US and Mexican twenty-somethings. (☎85 14 22. Open M-Th 10am-2am, F-Su 10am-5am.) Clubs catering to gays and lesbians cluster in the southern part of the *centro* around Calle 6 and 7 or down the hill to the north of Calle 1.

THE CALIFORNIA DESERT

Mystics and misanthropes from Native Americans to modern city slickers have long been fascinated by the austere scenery and the vast open spaces of the California desert. In winter the desert is a pleasantly warm refuge; in spring, a technicolor floral landscape; in summer, a blistering wasteland; and in fall, more of the same. A barren place of overwhelming simplicity, the desert's beauty lies in its emptiness as well as in its elusive treasures: diverse flora and fauna, staggering topographical variation, and scattered relics of the American frontier.

PALM SPRINGS ☎760

From its first known inhabitants, the Cahuilla Indians, to today's geriatric fun-lovers, the restorative oasis of Palm Springs has drawn many to its sandy bosom. With warm temperatures, celebrity residents, and more pink than a *Miami Vice* episode, this desert city provides a sunny break from everyday life.

Mt. San Jacinto State Park, Palm Springs's primary landmark, offers outdoor recreation opportunities for visitors of all fitness levels. If Mt. San Jacinto's 10,804 ft. escarpment seems too strenuous, try the **Palm Springs Aerial Tramway,** on Aerial Tramway Rd. off North Palm Canyon Dr. The observation deck has great views of the Coachella Valley. (☎325-1391. Trams run every 30min., M-F 10am-8pm, Sa-Su 8am-8pm. Round-trip $20.25, seniors $18.25, ages 3-12 $13.25, under 3 free.) The **Desert Hot Springs Spa,** 10805 Palm Dr., features six naturally heated mineral pools, as well as saunas, massage professionals, and bodywraps. Take Indian Canyon Dr. to Pierson Blvd., turn right, then turn left onto Palm Dr. (☎329-6495. Open daily 8am-10pm. M and W $5; Tu $3; Th men $3, women $5; F men $5, women $3; Sa-Su $6. After 3pm weekdays $3, weekends $4. Holidays $7.) **Oasis Water Park,** off I-10 South on Gene Autry Trail between Ramon and E. Palm Canyon Dr., has a wave pool, inner tube river, and 13 waterslides. (☎325-7873 or 327-0499. Open Mar.-Aug. daily 11am-6pm; Sept.-Oct. Sa-Su 11am-6pm. $22, seniors and under 5 ft. $15, under 3 free. Parking $5.)

Like most famous resort communities, Palm Springs caters mainly to those seeking a tax shelter, not a night's shelter. If you've gotta stay in town, there is a particular concentration of inexpensive motels at the bend in Palm Canyon Dr. where East Palm Canyon Dr. becomes South Palm Canyon Dr. **Palm Court Inn,** 1983 N. Palm Canyon Dr., between I-10 and downtown, has a melon-hued exterior that houses 107 rooms with great views, pool, and jacuzzi. (☎416-2333. Singles June-Sept. $49, Oct.-May $69; doubles $59/$79. All prices slightly higher on weekends.)

Palm Springs offers a kaleidoscope of sumptuous food, from the classic greasy spoon to ultra-trendy fusions of cuisines. However, high prices limit the scope of viable options. **Thai Smile,** 651 N. Palm Canyon Dr., offers authentic and inexpensive Thai cuisine. Don't miss the $6 lunch specials. (☎320-5503. Open daily 11:30am-10pm.) **Las Casuelas—The Original,** 368 N. Palm Canyon Dr., was the first establishment in this restaurant chain. Mexican dishes (from $6) and dingy lighting give it an outlaw, south-of-the-border feel. (☎325-3213. Open daily 10am-10pm.) **Palm Springs Regional Airport,** 3400 S. Tahquitz-Canyon Rd. (☎323-8161), offers mainly in-state service. **Greyhound,** 311 N. Indian Canyon Dr. (☎325-2053), buses to Los Angeles (9 per day; $17-19, round-trip $32-35). The local **Sun Bus** (☎343-3451) connects Coachella Valley cities. (Operates daily 5am-10pm. 75¢, transfers 25¢.) **Visitor info: Chamber of Commerce,** 190 W. Amado Rd. (☎325-1577; open M-F 8:30am-4:30pm). **Post Office:** 333 E. Amado Rd. **ZIP code:** 92262, General Delivery 92263. **Area code:** 760.

JOSHUA TREE NATIONAL PARK ☎760

When devout Mormon pioneers crossed this faith-testing desert in the 19th century, they named the enigmatic tree they encountered after the Biblical prophet Joshua. The tree's crooked limbs resembled the Hebrew general, who, with his arms upraised, seemed to beckon them to the Promised Land. Even today, Joshua Tree National Park inspires reverent awe in those who happen upon it. Piles of wind-sculpted boulders, flanked by seemingly jubilant Joshua trees, hearken to the magnificent devastation of Jericho. The park's five oases appear lushly Edenic against the desolate backdrop of the desert.

◪ PRACTICAL INFORMATION. About 160 mi. east of L.A., Joshua Tree National Park covers 558,000 acres northeast of Palm Springs. The park is ringed by three highways: **I-10** to the south, **Rte. 62 (Twentynine Palms Hwy.)** to the west and north, and **Rte. 177** to the east. The northern entrances to the park are off Rte. 62 at the towns of **Joshua Tree** and **Twentynine Palms.** The south entrance is at **Cottonwood Spring,** off I-10 at Rte. 195, south of Palm Springs near the town of Indio. The park entrance fee is $5 per person or $10 per car, valid for seven days. **Headquarters and Oasis Visitors Center:** 74485 National Park Dr., in Twentynine Palms, ¼ mi. off Rte. 62. (☎367-5500. Open daily 8am-5pm. Water available.) **Post Office:** 73839 Gorgonio Dr., in Twentynine Palms. (Open M-F 8:30am-5pm.) **ZIP code:** 92277. **Area code:** 760.

⊠ CAMPING AND ACCOMMODATIONS. Most campgrounds in the park operate on a first come, first served basis. Reservations can be made for group sites only
at Cottonwood, Sheep Pass, Indian Cove, and Black Rock Canyon through **DESTINET**
(☎800-436-7275). **Backcountry** camping is also an option. Ask at a ranger station for
details. All campsites have tables, fireplaces, and pit toilets, and are **free** unless otherwise noted. Those who plan any sort of extended stay should pack supplies,
water, and cooking utensils. Campground stays are limited to 30 days in the summer and to 14 days October through May. **▨Jumbo Rocks,** located Skull Rock Trail
on the eastern edge of Queen Valley, is the highest and coolest campground in the
park. **Hidden Valley,** in the center of the park, off Quail Springs Rd., has secluded
alcoves shaded by boulders. Its proximity to Wonderland of Rock and the Barker
Dam Trail make this a rock climber's heaven. **Indian Cove,** on the north edge of the
Wonderland of Rocks, has dramatic waterfalls and rock climbing nearby. (Sites
$10; group sites $20-35.) **Black Rock Canyon,** at the end of Joshua Ln. off Rte. 62 near
Yucca Valley, has wooded sites ($10) near flush toilets and running water. Those
who cannot stomach the thought of desert campgrounds can find indoor accommodations in **Twentynine Palms.** The **29 Palms Inn,** 73950 Inn Dr., is an attraction in
itself, with 19 distinctly different rooms that face the Mara Oasis. (☎367-3505. Doubles June-Sept. Su-Th $50-80, F-Sa $65-105; Oct.-May $10-20 extra.)

▨ OUTDOOR ACTIVITIES. Over 80% of the park is designated wilderness area,
safeguarded against development, and lacking paved roads, toilets, and campfires.
Joshua Tree offers premium backcountry hiking and camping. There's no water in
the wilderness except when a flash flood comes roaring down (beware your choice
of campsite). The park's most temperate weather is from October to December and
March to April; temperatures in other months span uncomfortable extremes.

A self-paced **driving tour** is an easy way to explore the park and linger to a later
hour. All park roads are well-marked, and "Exhibit Ahead" signs point the way to
unique floral and geological formations. One sight that should not be missed is **Key's
View,** 6 mi. off the park road just west of Ryan campground. It's a great spot for
watching the sunrise. The **Cholla Cactus Garden,** a grove of spiny succulents resembling 3D asterisks, lies in the Pinto Basin just off the road. Four-wheel-drive vehicles can use dirt roads, such as **Geology Tour Road,** climbing through fascinating rock
formations to the Li'l San Bernardino Mountains.

Hiking through the park's trails is perhaps the best way to experience Joshua
Tree. Although the **Barker Dam Trail,** next to Hidden Valley, is often packed with
tourists, its painted petroglyphs and eerie tranquility make it a worthwhile hike.
Bring plenty of water for the strenuous, unshaded climb to the summit of **Ryan
Mountain,** where the boulder formations bear an unsettling resemblance to herculean beasts of burden slouching toward a distant destination. The Visitors Center
has info on the park's many other hikes, which range from the 15min. stroll to the
Oasis of Mara to a three-day trek along the **California Riding and Hiking Trail** (35 mi.).
Joshua Tree teems with flora and fauna that you're unlikely to see anywhere else in
the world. Larger plants like Joshua trees, *cholla*, and the spidery *ocotillo* have
adapted to the severe climate in fascinating ways, and the wildflowers that dot the
desert terrain each spring attract thousands of visitors.

Energetic visitors are often drawn to Joshua Tree for its **rock climbing;** the world-
renowned boulders at **Wonderland of Rocks** and **Hidden Valley** are especially challenging and attract thousands of climbers each year. The Visitors Center provides info
on established rope routes and on wilderness areas, where the placement of new
bolts is restricted. **Joshua Tree Climbing School,** Box 29 (☎800-890-4745), in Joshua
Tree, provides instruction and equipment rental.

DEATH VALLEY NATIONAL PARK   ☎ 760

Satan owns a lot of real estate in Death Valley National Park. Not only does he grow crops (at the Devil's Cornfield) and hit the links (at the Devil's Golf Course), but the park is also home to Hell's Gate itself. Not surprisingly, the area's astonishing topographical and climactic extremes can support just about anyone's idea of the Inferno. Winter temps dip well below freezing, and summer readings rival even the hottest Hades. The second highest temperature ever recorded on Earth (134°F in the shade) was measured at the valley's Furnace Creek Ranch on July 10, 1913. Few venture to the valley floor during the summer, and it is foolish to do so; the average high in July is 116°F. A visit in winter lets visitors enjoy the splendor in comfort.

⬛ TRANSPORTATION. There is no regularly scheduled public transportation into Death Valley. **Guaranteed Tours,** with a depot at the World Trade Center on Desert Inn Rd. between Swensen and Maryland Pkwy. in Las Vegas, runs bus tours to Death Valley. (☎ 702-369-1000. Open for reservations daily 6am-10:45pm. 9½hr. tours depart Tu, Th, and Sa 8am. $120, includes continental breakfast and lunch.) The best way to get around Death Valley is by car. Of the nine **park entrances,** most visitors choose Rte. 190 from the east. The road is well-maintained, the pass is less steep, and you arrive more quickly at the Visitors Center. But the visitor with a trusty vehicle will be able to see more of the park by entering from the southeast (Rte. 178 west from Rte. 127 at Shoshone) or the north (direct to Scotty's Castle via Nevada Rte. 267 from U.S. 95). Unskilled mountain drivers should not attempt to enter via Titus Canyon or Emigrant Canyon Drive roads; neither has guard rails to prevent your car from sliding over **precipitous cliffs.** If you **hitchhike,** you walk through the Valley of the Shadow of Death. Don't.

⬛ PRACTICAL INFORMATION. Visitor info: Furnace Creek Visitors Center, on Rte. 190 in the east-central section of the valley (☎ 786-3244, info 786-2331; open daily 8am-6pm); or write the Superintendent, Death Valley National Park, Death Valley 92328. **Ranger stations** are located at **Grapevine** (☎ 786-2313), at the junction of Rte. 190 and 267 near Scotty's Castle; **Stovepipe Wells** (☎ 786-2342), on Rte. 190; and **Shoshone** (☎ 832-4308), outside the southeast border of the valley at the junction of Rte. 127 and 178. The weather report, weekly programs, and park info are posted at each station. (All open daily 8am-5pm.) The $5 per vehicle **entrance fee** is collected at the Visitors Center in the middle of the park. Get gas outside Death Valley at Olancha, Shoshone, or Beatty, NV. Radiator water (*not* for drinking) is available at a few critical points on Rte. 178 and 190 and NV Rte. 374. Those who drive along the backcountry trails should carry chains, extra tires, gas, oil, radiator and drinking water, and spare parts. **Post Office:** Furnace Creek Ranch (☎ 786-2223; open M, W, and F 8:30am-3pm; Tu and Th 8:30am-5pm). **ZIP code:** 92328. **Area code:** 760.

⬛ ACCOMMODATIONS. In Death Valley, enclosed beds and fine meals within a budget traveler's reach are as elusive as the desert bighorn sheep. During the winter months, camping out with a stock of groceries is a good way to save both money and driving time. **Furnace Creek Ranch Complex** is deluged with tour-bus refugees who challenge the adjacent 18-hole golf course and relax in the 85°F spring-fed swimming pool. (☎ 786-2345, reservations 800-236-7916. Cabins with A/C and 2 beds $94; motel-style rooms $124-149.) **Stovepipe Wells Village** is right in Death Valley. (☎ 786-2387. $58 per night for 1-2 people, each additional person $11; RV sites $15.) The National Park Service maintains nine **campgrounds,** but only Texas Springs and Furnace Creek accept reservations. Call ahead to check availability and be prepared to battle for a space if you come during peak periods. Water availability is not reliable and supplies can be unsafe at times; always pack your own. Roadside camping is not permitted, but **backcountry camping** is free and legal, provided you check in at the Visitors Center and pitch tents at least 1 mi. from main roads, 5 mi. from any established campsite, and ¼ mi. from any water source.

◪ **HIKING.** Death Valley has hiking to bemuse the gentlest wanderer and challenge the hardiest adventurer. Backpackers and day-hikers should inform the Visitors Center of their trip and take along the appropriate topographical maps. The National Park Service recommends that valley-floor hikers plan a route along roads where assistance is readily available and outfit a party of at least two people. **Artist's Drive,** 10 mi. south of the Visitors Center on Rte. 178, is a one-way loop that twists its way through rock formations of colors akin to those found in Crayola sets. About 5 mi. south is **Devil's Golf Course,** a plane of sharp salt pinnacles made of the precipitate from the evaporation of Lake Manly, the 90 mi. long lake that once filled the lower valley. **Badwater** lies 3 mi. south of Devil's Golf Course, on I-90, a briny pool four times saltier than the ocean. The surrounding salt flat dips to the lowest point in the Western Hemisphere—282 ft. below sea level. Immortalized by Antonioni's film of the same name, **Zabriskie Point** is a marvelous place from which to view Death Valley's corrugated badlands. Perhaps the most spectacular sight in the park is the vista at **Dante's View,** reached by a 13 mi. paved road from Rte. 190.

THE CENTRAL COAST

The 400-mile stretch of coastline between Los Angeles and San Francisco embodies all that is purely Californian: surf crashing onto secluded beaches, dramatic cliffs and mountains, self-actualizing New Age adherents, and always a hint of the offbeat. This is the solitary magnificence that inspired Robinson Jeffers's paeans, John Steinbeck's novels, and Jack Kerouac's musings. Among the smog-free skies, sweeping shorelines, dense forests, and plunging cliffs, there is a point where inland farmland communities and old seafaring towns join, beckoning citified residents to journey out to the quiet drama of the coast. The landmarks along the way—Hearst Castle, the Monterey Bay Aquarium, Carmel, the historic missions—are well worth visiting, but the real point of the Central Coast is the journey itself.

SANTA BARBARA ☎805

Santa Barbara epitomizes worry-free living and abandonment of responsibility—all memory seems to melt away in the endless sun. The town is an enclave of wealth and privilege, true to its soap-opera image, but in a significantly less aggressive way than its Southern Californian counterparts. Spanish Revival architecture decorates the residential hills that rise gently over a lively pedestrian district.

▐ TRANSPORTATION

Santa Barbara is 96 mi. northwest of Los Angeles and 27 mi. past Ventura on the **Ventura Freeway (U.S. 101).** Built along an east-west traverse of shoreline, the street grid is slightly skewed. The beach lies at the south end of the city, and **State St.,** the main drag, runs northwest from the waterfront. All streets are designated east and west from State St. The major east-west arteries are U.S. 101 and **Cabrillo Blvd.**

Airport: Santa Barbara Municipal Airport (☎683-4011), in Goleta. Offers state and limited national service.

Trains: Amtrak, 209 State St. (☎963-1015). *Be careful around the station after dark.* To L.A. ($16-21) and San Francisco ($46-73). Reserve in advance. Open daily 6:30am-9pm. Tickets sold until 8pm.

Buses: Greyhound, 34 W. Carrillo St. (☎962-2477), at Chapala St. To L.A. ($13) and San Francisco ($30). Open M-Sa 5:30am-8pm and 11pm-midnight, Su 7am-8pm and 11pm-midnight. **Green Tortoise** (☎415-956-7500 or 800-227-4766) picks up from Banana Bungalow Hostel. To L.A. ($15) and San Francisco ($35).

Santa Barbara Metropolitan Transit District (MTD), 1020 Chapala St. (☎683-3702), at Cabrillo Blvd., behind the Greyhound station. Bus schedules available at this transit center (open M-F 6am-7pm, Sa 8am-6pm, Su 9am-6pm). All buses wheelchair accessible. Fare $1, seniors and disabled 50¢, under 5 free; transfers free. The MTD runs a

CALIFORNIA

downtown-waterfront shuttle along State St. and Cabrillo Blvd. every 10min. Su-Th 10:15am-6pm, F-Sa 10:15am-8pm. Stops designated by circular blue signs. Fare 25¢.

Taxis: Yellow Cab Company, ☎965-5111.

✦🛈 ORIENTATION AND PRACTICAL INFORMATION

Driving in Santa Barbara can be bewildering; dead-ends and one-way streets abound. Many downtown lots and streets offer 75min. of free **parking**, including two lots at Pasco Nuevo, accessible from the 700 block of Chapala St. Parking is free on Sunday. Most streets are equipped with **bike lanes**. The **Cabrillo Bikeway** runs east-west along the beach from the Bird Refuge to the City College campus.

Visitor info: Tourist Office, 1 Garden St. (☎965-3021), at Cabrillo Blvd. near the beach. Open July-Aug. M-Sa 9am-6pm, Su 10am-6pm; Sept.-Nov. and Feb.-June M-Sa 9am-5pm, Su 10am-5pm; Dec.-Jan. M-Sa 9am-4pm, Su 10am-4pm. Outdoor computer kiosk open 24hr.

Post Office: 836 Anacapa St., 1 block east of State St. Open M-F 8am-6pm, Sa 9am-5pm. **ZIP code:** 93102. **Area code:** 805.

🏠 ACCOMMODATIONS

A ten-minute drive north or south on U.S. 101 rewards with cheaper lodgings than those found in Santa Barbara proper. All Santa Barbara accommodations are more expensive on the weekends. State campsites can be reserved through ReserveAmerica (☎800-444-7275). **Carpinteria Beach State Park,** 12 mi. southeast of Santa Barbara along U.S. 101, has 261 developed tent sites with hot showers. (☎684-2811. Sites $12, with hookup $22-28.) There are two other state beaches within 30 mi. of Santa Barbara, but neither is served by buses. North of Santa Barbara off U.S. 101, **El Capitán** (☎968-1033) has 140 well-kept sites, some with views of the Channel Islands. **Refugio** has 84 crowded, wheelchair-accessible sites just steps from the beach. (☎968-1033. Sites at both $12.) North of Santa Barbara are more than 100 sites in the **Los Padres National Forest** (☎968-6640).

Hotel State Street, 121 State St. (☎966-6586; fax 962-8459), on the main strip 1 block from the beach. Welcoming, comfortable, and run by a self-proclaimed clean freak. Pristine common bathrooms. Private rooms have sinks and cable TV; a few have skylights. Continental breakfast included. Free parking. Reservations recommended. Singles $50; doubles $70; $15-25 higher July-Aug.

Traveler's Motel, 3222 State St. (☎687-6009; fax 687-0419). Take bus #6 or 11 from downtown. Although it's a bit far from the action, this motel is clean and spacious. Cable TV, A/C, direct-dial phones, and fridges. Singles June-Sept. $55-70, Oct.-May $40; palatial rooms with kitchenettes $65/$50; each additional person (up to 4) $5.

Banana Bungalow Santa Barbara, 210 E. Ortega St. (☎963-0154), just off State St., in a busy area. Party-oriented hostel with lived-in feel and tropical motif. Young, international crowd. Kitchen, TV room, pool table, video games. Equipment rentals. Laundry and lockers. Free parking. No reservations; show up around 11am. Doors lock at 2:30am. Passport or student ID required. Co-ed and women-only dorms $24; private rooms for up to 4 with private bath $61.

🍴 FOOD

State and Milpas St. both have many places to eat; State St. is hipper, while Milpas St. is cheaper. Ice cream lovers flock to award-winning **McConnel's,** 201 W. Mission St. (☎569-2323. Open daily 10am-midnight.) There's an open-air **Farmers Market** on the 400 block of State St. (Tu 4-7:30pm), and another on Santa Barbara St. at Cota St. (Sa 8:30am-12:30pm). **Tri-County Produce,** 335 S. Milpas St., sells fresh produce and prepared foods. (☎965-4558. Open M-Sa 9am-7:30pm, Su 9am-6pm.)

Palazzio, 1026 State St. (☎564-1985). They say "people don't usually leave here hungry," and you certainly shouldn't buck the trend. The depiction of the Sistine Chapel on the ceiling is nearly as impressive as the enormous pasta dishes and the amazing garlic rolls. Tally your own intake at the serve-yourself wine bar. Lunch daily 11:30am-3pm; dinner Su-Th 5:30-11pm, F-Sa 5:30pm-midnight.

Pacific Crepes, 705 Anacapa St. (☎882-1123). Comfortable, classy French cafe is filled with the delicious smells of a full menu of crepe creations. The heavenly "Brittany" is topped with fresh strawberries and blueberries, fruit sauce, and ice cream—a perfect dessert for $5.50. Open T-Sa 8:30am-9pm, Su 8:30am-4pm.

La Super-Rica Taqueria, 622 N. Milpas St. (☎963-4940), has received rave reviews, both from culinary experts and the long lines of customers that extend out its door. Outstanding and inexpensive. Open Su-Th 11am-9:30pm, F-Sa 11am-10pm.

Napoleon, 808 State St. (☎899-1183), at De Laguerra St. This *patisserie* and *boulangerie* bakes incredible desserts (lemon tart $3.50) and serves sandwiches (*croque monsieur* $5.75). Open Su-Th 8am-10:30pm, Sa 8am-11:30pm.

◉ SIGHTS

Santa Barbara is best explored in three sections—the beach and coast, swingin' State St., and the mountains. *Santa Barbara's Red Tile Tour,* a map and walking tour guide, is free at the Visitors Center. Recently revamped, the coastal drive Cabrillo Blvd. serves as the first leg of the city's **scenic drive.** Follow the green signs as they lead you in a loop into the mountains and around the city.

SANTA BARBARA ZOO. The delightfully leafy habitat has low fences and such an open feel that the animals seem kept in captivity only through sheer lethargy. Attractions include a miniaturized African plain, or *veldt,* where giraffes stroll lazily, silhouetted against the Pacific. A miniature train provides a park tour. (*500 Niños Dr., off Cabrillo Blvd. from U.S. 101. Take bus #14 or the downtown-waterfront shuttle. ☎962-5339. Open daily 10am-5pm. $7, seniors and ages 2-12 $5, under 2 free. Train $1.50, children $1. Parking included.*)

BEACHES AND ACTIVITIES. Santa Barbara beaches are simply breathtaking. **East** and **Leadbetter Beaches** flank the wharf on either side. **Beach Rentals** will rent beachgoers a retro surrey: a covered carriage, Flintstone-esque **bicycle.** You and up to eight friends can cruise along the beach paths in this stylish buggy. They also rent in-line skates. (*22 State St. ☎966-6733. Open daily 8am-8pm. Surreys $12-32 per hr., depending on number of riders. Skates, including safety gear, $6 per hr., $9 per 2hr.,$18 per 6hr.*) For the best **sunset** view in the area, have a drink at the bar at the Four Seasons Biltmore Hotel. This five-star lodging is a little steep for the budget traveler, but the view is priceless. (*1260 Channel Dr., Montecito. ☎969-2261.*)

STATE STREET. Santa Barbara's monument to city planning, State St. runs a straight, tree-lined 2 mi. through the center of the city. Shops, restaurants, and cultural and historical landmarks are slathered in Spanish tile. The **Santa Barbara Museum of Art** owns an impressive 3000-year collection of classical Greek, Asian, and European works, mostly donated by wealthy local residents. (*1130 State St. ☎963-4364. Open Tu-Th and Sa 11am-5pm, F 11am-9pm, Su noon-5pm. Tours Tu-Su noon and 2pm. $5, seniors $3, students and ages 6-16 $2; free on Th and 1st Su of each month.*)

MISSION SANTA BARBARA. At the so-called "Queen of Missions" there are towers containing splayed Moorish windows on either side of a Greco-Roman facade, and a Moorish fountain bubbles in front. The museum contains period rooms and a sampling of items from the mission archives. (*At the end of Las Olivas St. Take bus #22. ☎682-4149. Open daily 9am-5pm. $4, under 12 free. Self-guided museum tour starts at the gift shop. Mass M-F 7:30am, Sa 4pm, Su 7:30am-noon.*)

SANTA BARBARA BOTANICAL GARDEN. Though it is quite a distance from town by car, these gardens offer enjoyable hikes through 65 acres of native Californian trees, wildflowers, and cacti. (*1212 Mission Canyon Rd. ☎682-4726. Open Mar.-Oct. M-F 9am-5pm, Sa-Su 9am-6pm; Nov.-Feb. M-F 9am-4pm, Sa-Su 9am-5pm. Tours M-W and F 2pm, Th and Sa-Su 10:30am and 2pm. $5; seniors, students, and ages 13-19 $3; ages 5-12 $1.*)

HIKING TRAILS. The trailhead for **Seven Falls Trail** is at the junction of Tunnel and Spyglass Rd. From the end of Las Canoas Rd. off Mission Canyon Rd., you can pick up the 3.5 mi. **Rattlesnake Canyon Trail,** which features many waterfalls, pools, and secluded spots. The 7.3 mi. trek from the **Cold Springs Trail** to **Montecito Peak** is considerably more strenuous. *(From U.S. 101 S, take a left at the Hot Springs Rd. exit, and another left on Mountain Dr. to the creek crossing.)*

■ NIGHTLIFE

Every night of the week, the clubs on **State St.** are packed. This town is full of locals and tourists who love to eat, drink, and be mirthful. Consult the *Independent* to see who's playing on a given night. Bars on State St. charge a fairly uniform $4 for beer, so don your sleuth gear and investigate drink specials.

The Hourglass, 213 W. Cota Street (☎963-1436), in a residential part of town. Rent a private hot tub here by the hour. Pick a sensuous indoor bath or watch the stars from a private outdoor tub. Locals report that "this is what we do in Santa Barbara." No alcohol allowed. Towels $1. 2 people $25 per hr.; each additional person $7. $2 students discount; children free with parent. Open Th-Su 5pm-midnight.

Q's Sushi A-Go-Go, 409 State St. (☎966-9177). Leopard-skin decor, a tri-level bar, and a State St. balcony. Stomach some sushi ($3.50-8.50) with your date and you'll totally score! Then again, if you still use the word "score" in regards to dating, you probably won't. M Brazilian night, W karaoke. Cover F-Sa after 9pm $5. Open daily 4pm-2am.

Madhouse, 434 State St. (☎962-5516). Decadent dive for the jet set. Sounds of Sinatra, mambo, and Afro-Cuban music mix retro and funk. W-Th live music drink and specials. Th-Sa DJ. 21+. Open W-Sa 5pm-2am, Su-Tu 7pm-2am.

SAN LUIS OBISPO ☎805

With its sprawling green hills and its proximity to the rocky coast, San Luis Obispo (SLO) is a town where things actually don't move very fast. Ranchers and oil-refinery employees make up a significant percentage of the population, but Cal Poly State University students add a young, energetic component.

⁊ PRACTICAL INFORMATION. Greyhound, 150 South St. (☎543-2121), is open daily 7:30am-9:30pm. **Visitor info: Chamber of Commerce,** 1039 Chorro St. (☎781-2777; open M-W 8am-5pm, Th-F 8am-8pm, Sa 10am-8pm). **State Parks Office,** 3220 S. Higuera St., #311 (☎549-3312; open M-F 8am-5pm). **Post Office:** 893 Marsh St. (☎543-3062; open M-F 8:30am-5:30pm, Sa 9am-5pm). **ZIP code:** 93405. **Area code:** 805.

⌐ ACCOMMODATIONS. Lodging rates in San Luis Obispo tend to "depend"—on the weather, the season, the number of travelers that day, or even on the position of the waxing and waning moon. **San Luis Obispo (HI-AYH),** 1617 Santa Rosa St., has a tight-knit atmosphere. (☎544-4678. Linen $1, towels 50¢. Reception 7:30-10:30am and 4:30-10pm. Lockout 10am-4:30pm. Parking available. No credit cards. Dorms $17.50; private rooms $40; nonmembers $3-5 extra.) The **Sunbeam Hotel,** 1656 Monterey St., looks like an apartment complex, but rooms are as sunny as the staff. (☎543-8141. Cable TV, A/C, phones, fridges.Singles $36; doubles $45-79.) **Montana de Oro State Park** (☎528-0513), on Pecho Rd., south of Los Osos, 12 mi. from SLO via Los Osos Valley Rd., offers 50 primitive sites ($12) in a gorgeous, secluded park. Outhouses and cold running water are available, but bring your own drinking water. Reserve weeks in advance during the summer.

◖⊡ FOOD AND NIGHTLIFE. Monterey St. and its cross streets are lined with restaurants and cafes. The area just south of the mission along the creek is popular with lunchtime crowds. Enticing smells will lure you into the ◼**House of Bread,** 858 Higuera St., which uses chemical-free Montana wheat in its delicious bread products. Raspberry pinwheels and huge cinnamon rolls run $2. (☎542-0255. Open M-F 7am-7pm, Sa 7am-6:30pm, Su 8am-5pm.) **Big Sky Cafe,** 1121 Broad St., was voted

"Best Restaurant in SLO" by a local magazine poll for delivering hearty, vegetarian-friendly food. (☎545-5401. Open M-Sa 7am-10pm, Su 8am-9pm.) **Tio Alberto's,** 1131 Broad St., has the best burritos between L.A. and San Francisco. (☎546-9646. Open Su-Th 9am-11pm, F-Sa 9am-3am. Burritos $3.50-5.50, combo plates $5.) One half of SLO's population is under the age of 24, so the town can't help but party. It gets particularly wild after the Thursday evening **Farmers Market** along Higuera St., more a raging block party than a market. Weekdays slow down a bit while students rescue their grades. The free weekly *New Times* lists goings-on.

◙ **SIGHTS.** San Luis Obispo grew around the **Mission San Luis Obispo de Tolosa,** and the city continues to engage in celebrations and general lunchtime socializing around its front steps. (☎543-6850. Open early Apr. to late Oct. daily 9am-5pm; late Oct. to early Apr. 9am-4pm. $2 requested donation.) The mission faces Mission Plaza, where Father Serra held the area's first mass. The Visitors Center may try to deny its existence, but **Bubble Gum Alley,** 735 Higuera St., is a crazy, squishy fact. If you'd like to add your own wad of gum to the alley, head down to the **7-11** on the corner of Broad and Marsh for a pack of Wrigley's.

South of San Luis Obispo, **Pismo Beach** is popular and congested; the lines for the public restrooms are practically social events. This raging spring break party spot is accessible by **Central Coast Area Transit** (☎541-2228) as well as **Greyhound.** Rent all kinds of beach equipment at **Beach Cycle Rentals,** 150 Hinds Ave., next to the pier. (☎773-5518. Open daily 9am-dusk.) **Shell Beach,** 1½ mi. from Pismo Beach, is the launching point for many a kayak. Gray whales, seals, otters, dolphins, and the occasional orca frequent **Montana de Oro State Park** (☎528-0513), 30min. west of SLO on Los Osos Valley Rd. The 7 mi. of shoreline remain relatively secluded. North of SLO, **Morro Bay** has dramatic coastlines formed by volcanic activity.

NEAR SAN LUIS OBISPO: HEARST CASTLE

Driving along this stretch of Rte. 1, the last thing you would expect to see is a castle that would put Disney to shame. Newspaper tycoon William Randolph Hearst built this palatial abode and invited wealthy elite to visit the most extravagant edifice this side of the Taj Mahal. Casually referred to by its founder as "the ranch," Hearst Castle, located on Rte. 1, 3 mi. north of San Simeon and 9 mi. north of Cambria, is a decadent conglomeration of castle, cottages, pools, gardens, and Mediterranean *esprit* perched high above the Pacific. It stands as a testament to Hearst's unfathomable wealth and Julia Morgan's architectural genius. **Tour One** covers the photogenic Neptune Pool, the opulent Casa del Sol guest house, fragrant gardens, and the main rooms of the house; this is the best bet for first-time visitors. **Tours Two, Three, and Four** are recommended for those already familiar with Tour One. Call weeks in advance; tours sell out. (☎927-2020, reservations 800-444-4445, international reservations 916-638-5883; wheelchair accessible reservations 805-927-2020. Tours $10, ages 6-12 $5. Evening tours feature costumed docents acting out the Castle's legendary Hollywood history; $20/$10. Each tour involves 150-370 stairs.)

BIG SUR ☎831

Host to expensive campsites and even more expensive restaurants, Big Sur holds big appeal for big crowds eager to experience the power of the redwoods, the crash of the surf, and the rhythm of the river. There are no signs to announce that you are in Big Sur, but you'll know you're there because it's the first time you'll see signs of civilization for miles in either direction. The drive from Carmel to Big Sur on **Rte. 1** is breathtaking and everyone knows it; try going early in the morning.

Big Sur's state parks and **Los Padres National Forest** beckon outdoor enthusiasts of all types. Their **hiking** trails penetrate redwood forests and cross low chaparral, offering even grander views of Big Sur than those available from Rte. 1. The northern end of Los Padres National Forest, accessible from Pfeiffer Big Sur, has been designated the **Ventana Wilderness** and contains the popular **Pine Ridge Trail,** which runs 12 mi. through primitive sites and the Sikes Hot Springs. The Forest Service ranger station supplies maps and permits for the wilderness area.

Within **Pfeiffer Big Sur State Park** are eight trails of varying lengths ($1 map available at park entrance). The **Valley View Trail** is a short, steep trail offering a view of the valley below. **Buzzard's Roost Trail** is a rugged two-hour hike up tortuous switchbacks, but at its peak are rewarding panoramic views of the Santa Lucia Mountains, the Big Sur Valley, and the Pacific Ocean.

Big Sur's most jealously guarded treasure is the splendid, USFS-operated **Pfeiffer Beach,** 1 mi. south of Pfeiffer Burns State Park and roughly 10½ mi. north of Julia Pfeiffer Burns State Park. Turn off Rte. 1 at the stop sign and the "Narrow Road Not Suitable For Trailers" sign, just past the bridge by Loma Vista. Follow the road 2 mi. to the parking area, where a path leads to the beach. An offshore rock formation protects sea caves and seagulls from the pounding ocean waves. Frequent winds can make sunbathing uncomfortable, and even if there were lifeguards, riptides make swimming and other water sports dangerous. (Parking fee $5; annual pass $15. Walk-in, bike-in, and Golden Age passport holders free.)

Camping in Big Sur is heavenly, but site prices and availability reflect high demand. Camping is free in the Ventana Wilderness at the northern end of Los Padres National Forest (permits at Big Sur Station). **Ventana Big Sur,** on Rte. 1, 30 mi. south of Carmel, has 75 shady sites in a gorgeous redwood canyon with picnic tables, fire rings, and water faucets. (☎667-2688. Sites for up to 2 people $25; day use $10; leashed dogs $5. Reservations accepted at least 2 weeks in advance.)

MONTEREY
☎831

Whaling kept Monterey alive until 1880, when sardine fishing and packaging stepped in to take its place. In the next half-century, the wharfside flourished like the fisherman's world immortalized by John Steinbeck in the 40s. Monterey has since become a sedate, tourist-oriented community. The remnants of the past and the spectacle of the present result in a restrained beauty well worth the journey.

⚠ PRACTICAL INFORMATION. Monterey-Salinas Transit (MST), 1 Ryan Ranch Rd., runs buses. (☎899-2555. Call M-F 7:45am-5:15pm, Sa 10am-2:30pm.) The free *Rider's Guide*, available on buses, at motels, and at the Visitors Center, has schedules and route info. **Monterey Peninsula Visitor and Convention Bureau:** 380 Alvarado St. (☎649-1770; open M-F 8:30am-5pm). **Post Office:** 565 Hartnell St. (☎372-5803; open M-F 8:45am-5:10pm). **ZIP code:** 93940.

⬛⬛ ACCOMMODATIONS AND FOOD. Reasonably priced hotels line **Lighthouse Ave.** in Pacific Grove (bus #2 and some #1 buses) and the 2000 block of **Fremont St.** in Monterey (bus #9 or 10). Others cluster along **Munras Ave.** between downtown and Rte. 1. The cheapest hotels in the area, however, are in the less-appealing towns of Seaside and Marina, just north of Monterey. Call the **Monterey Parks** line (☎755-4895 or 888-588-2267) for camping info and **PARKNET** (☎800-444-7275) for reservations. **Del Monte Beach Inn,** 1110 Del Monte Blvd., near downtown and across from the beach, is a Victorian-style inn with a TV room. (☎649-4410. Check-in 2-8pm. Reservations recommended. Rooms with shared bath Su-Th $55-66, F-Sa from $77.) The **Monterey Hostel (HI-AYH),** 778 Hawthorne St. is located four blocks from Cannery Row. This 45-bed hostel is spacious and pristine. (☎649-0375. Reservations essential June-Sept. Dorms $18, nonmembers $21, ages 7-17 $13.50, under 6 $9.50. Private rooms for up to 4 from $51.)

The sardines have left, but Monterey Bay teems with squid, crab, red snapper, and salmon. Seafood is bountiful, but expensive—try an early-bird special (usually 4-6:30pm). **Fisherman's Wharf** has smoked salmon sandwiches ($6) and free chowder samples. Don't despair if you loathe seafood—this is also the land of artichokes and strawberries. The Monterey **Farmers Market,** which takes over Alvarado St., has free fruit, cheese, and seafood samples. (☎655-2607. Tu 4-8pm.) The **Old Monterey Cafe,** 489 Alvarado St., has hot, hefty portions favored by locals. (☎646-1021. Open daily 7am-2:30pm. Lunch specials from $5.50.) **Thai Bistro II,** 159 Central Ave., in Pacific Grove, has good service and a patio ringed with flowers. Lunch combos ($6) come with delicious soup. (☎372-8700. Open daily 11:30am-3pm and 5-9:30pm.)

◪ SIGHTS. The extraordinary ▨**Monterey Bay Aquarium,** 886 Cannery Row, provides visitors with a window (literally) into the most curious creatures of the Pacific. Gaze through the **world's largest window** at an enormous marine habitat containing green sea turtles, giant ocean sunfish, large sharks, and impressive yellow- and blue-fin tuna. Don't miss the oozingly graceful and mesmerizing jellyfish. Arrive with a surfeit of patience; the lines for tickets, admission, viewing, and food are as unbelievable as the exhibits themselves. (☎ 648-4888. Open June to early Sept. daily 9:30am-6pm; early Sept. to late May 10am-6pm. $17; seniors, students, and ages 13-17 $14; disabled and ages 3-12 $8.)

Lying along the waterfront south of the aquarium, **Cannery Row** was once a depressed street of languishing sardine-packing plants. The ¾ mi. row has been converted into glitzy mini-malls, bars, and a pint-sized carnival complex. For a series of interpretive looks at Steinbeck's *Cannery Row,* take a peek at the **Great Cannery Row Mural;** local artists have covered 400 ft. of construction-site barrier on the 700 block with depictions of Monterey in the 30s. The lavish **Wine and Produce Visitors Center,** 700 Cannery Row, offers tastes of the county's burgeoning wine industry, with well-priced bottles, fresh produce, and free winery maps. (☎ 888-646-5446. 6 tastings $5; free with wine purchase. Open daily 11am-6pm.)

Several companies on Fisherman's Wharf offer critter-spotting boat trips around Monterey Bay. The best time to go is during gray whale migration season, November through March, but the trips are hit-or-miss at any time of year. **Chris's Fishing Trips,** 693 Del Monte Ave., has two- to three-hour daily tours at 11am and 2pm. (☎ 375-5951. $25, under 16 $20.) Sea kayaking on top of kelp forests and among prancing otters can be a heady experience. **Monterey Bay Kayaks** provides rentals, instruction, and tours. (☎ 373-5357 or 800-649-5357. Call for lesson and tour information. Open daily 9am-6pm. $25 per person, includes gear and wetsuit.)

In nearby Carmel, the extraordinary 550-acre state-run ▨**Point Lobos Reserve,** on Rte. 1, 2 mi. south of Carmel, is a wildlife sanctuary popular with skindivers and day hikers. Otters, sea lions, seals, brown pelicans, and gulls are visible from paths along the cliffs (bring binoculars). Point Lobos has tide pools and marvelous vantage points for watching the whale migration, which peaks in winter but continues throughout spring. (☎ 624-4909. Park on Rte. 1 before the tollbooth and walk or bike in for free. Accessible by MST bus #22. Open Apr.-Oct. daily 9am-7pm, Nov.-Mar. 9am-4:30pm. $5 per car (includes map), seniors $4. Day use free for state park campers. Free daily tours; call for times. Divers must call 624-8413 or email ptlobos@mbay.net for diving reservations. Dive fee $7.)

SANTA CRUZ   ☎831

One of the few places where the 60s catch phrase "do your own thing" still applies, Santa Cruz simultaneously embraces macho surfers, aging hippies, free-thinking students, and a large lesbian, gay, and bisexual community. Along the beach and boardwalk, tourism runs rampant and surf culture reigns supreme. Nearby Pacific Ave. teems with independent bookstores, cool bars, and trendy cafes, providing a safe, clean hangout for locals and tourists alike. On the inland side of Mission St., the University of California at Santa Cruz (UCSC) sprawls luxuriously across miles of rolling forests and grasslands, filled with prime biking routes and wild students.

◪▨ ORIENTATION AND PRACTICAL INFORMATION. Santa Cruz is on the northern tip of Monterey Bay, 65 mi. south of San Francisco on Rte. 1. Passing through westside Santa Cruz, Rte. 1 becomes **Mission St.** The **University of California at Santa Cruz (UCSC)** blankets the hills inland from Mission St. Southeast of Mission St. lie the waterfront and the downtown. Down by the ocean, **Beach St.** runs roughly east-west. **Greyhound,** 425 Front St. (☎ 423-1800, 423-1801, or 800-231-2222; open daily 9-11:30am and 1:30-9pm and during late bus arrivals and departures), runs to L.A. (8 per day, $40); San Francisco (4 per day, $12); and San Jose (M-Th 4 per day, $5). **Santa Cruz Metropolitan Transit District (SCMTD),** 920 Pacific Ave. (☎ 425-8600 for info M-F 6am-7pm, TDD 425-8993), at the Metro Center in the middle of the Pacific

Garden Mall, handles local transportation. The free *Headways* has route info. (Buses run daily 6am-11pm. Fare $1, seniors and disabled 40¢, under 46 in. free; day pass $3/$1.10/free.) **Yellow Cab:** ☎423-1234. **The Bicycle Rental Center,** 131 Center St., rents 21-speed mountain/road hybrids, tandems, and children's bikes. (☎426-8687. Open in summer daily 10am-6pm; off-season 10am-5pm. Bikes $7 for first hr., $2 each additional 30min.; $25 per day; $5 overnight. Helmets and locks provided.) The **Santa Cruz County Conference and Visitor Council,** 1211 Ocean St., publishes the free *Santa Cruz County Traveler's Guide.* (☎425-1234 or 800-833-3494. Open M-Sa 9am-5pm, Su 10am-4pm.) **California Parks and Recreation Dept.,** 600 Ocean St., across from the Holiday Inn, has info on camping and beaches. (☎429-2850, reservations 800-444-7275. Open M-F 8am-5pm.) **Post Office:** 850 Front St. (☎426-5200; open M-F 8:30am-5pm, Sa 9am-4pm). **ZIP code:** 95060. **Area code:** 831.

☛ ACCOMMODATIONS. Santa Cruz is packed solid during the summer, especially on weekends; rates skyrocket, availability plummets, and price fluctuation can be outrageous. Reservations are recommended and should be made early. Sleeping on the beach is strictly forbidden. **New Brighton State Beach** and **Big Basin Redwoods State Park,** the most scenic spots, are both accessible by public transportation. (Sites $12; day use $5 per car.) The **Carmelita Cottage Santa Cruz Hostel (HI-AYH),** 321 Main St., is located four blocks from the Greyhound stop and two blocks from the beach. Sporadic summer barbecues ($4) to allow hungry hostelers to feed their face. (☎429-2850. 2 kitchens, common room. Chore required. Linen $1. Strict curfew 11pm. July-Aug. 3-night max. stay; HI members preferred. Call for reservations. Reception 8-10am and 5-10pm. Lockout 10am-5pm. Dorms $15, nonmembers $18, ages 12-17 $13, ages 4-11 $9, under 3 free.) The **Harbor Inn,** 645 7th Ave., is a beautiful 19-room hotel well off the main drag. (☎479-9371. Queen-sized beds, microwaves, and fridges. Check-in 2-7pm, check-out 11am; call to arrange late check-in. Rooms Su-Th from $75, F-Sa from $100; off-season Su-Th from $65/$75.)

☐ FOOD. Santa Cruz offers an astounding number of budget eateries in various locations. Fresh local produce sells at the **Farmers Market** at Lincoln and Cedar St. in downtown (W 2:30-6:30pm). Without a doubt the best pre-picnic stop in town, **Zoccoli's,** 1534 Pacific Ave., churns out "special sandwiches" ($4-5). Daily pasta specials (about $5) come with salad, garlic bread, cheese, and a cookie. Zoccoli's uses only the freshest ingredients. (☎423-1711. Open M-Sa 10am-6pm, Su 11am-5pm.) With excellent potatoes, freshly baked bread, and enormous omelettes, **Zachary's,** 819 Pacific Ave., will fill you with reasons to laze about the beach for the rest of the day. Basic breakfast (2 eggs, oatmeal-molasses toast, and hash browns) for under $5. Beware of the crowds that congregate here on weekends. (☎427-0646. Open Tu-Su 7am-2:30pm.) The **Saturn Cafe,** 145 Laurel St. at Pacific Ave., serves excellent vegetarian meals (most under $6). Table decorations include the "body manipulations" theme and the "ruined picnic" with plastic ants. The Alien sandwich (tofu, hummus, avocado, and cheese; $6.75) is delicious. (☎429-85050. Open 24hr.) **Taquería Vallarta I,** 608 Soquel Ave., has outstanding Mexican fare, including the $4 vegetarian plate and $1 *agua fresca.* (☎457-8226. Open M-F 10am-midnight.)

▣ SIGHTS. Santa Cruz has a great beach, but the water is frigid. Without wetsuits for warmth, many casual beachgoers catch their thrills on the Boardwalk, a three-block-long strip of over 25 amusement park rides, guess-your-weight booths, shooting galleries, and caramel apple vendors. The boardwalk is a gloriously tacky throwback to 50s-era beach culture, providing a loud and lively diversion. Highly recommended is the Giant Dipper, a 1924 wooden roller coaster ($3), where Dirty Harry met his enemy in 1983's *Sudden Impact* (Harry finally impaled him on the merry-go-round's unicorn). While the Boardwalk is relatively safe, be cautious of the surrounding area at night. (Open June-Aug. daily, plus many off-season weekends and holidays. Rides $1.50-3; all-day pass $22. Mini golf $4, with all-day pass to Boardwalk $3.) The **Santa Cruz Wharf,** the longest car-accessible pier on the West Coast, juts off Beach St. Seafood restaurants and souvenir shops will try to distract you from the expansive views of the coast. Munch on candy from local favorite **Marini's** (☎423-7258) while you feed fish to the sea lions hanging out on rafters beneath the pier. (Parking $1 per hr., under 30min. free. Disabled patrons free.)

🏖️🏔️ **BEACHES AND OUTDOORS.** The **Santa Cruz Beach** (officially named Cowell Beach) is broad, reasonably clean, and packed with volleyball players. **Beach access** points line Rte. 1; railroad tracks, farmlands, and dune vegetation make several of these access points somewhat difficult, but correspondingly less crowded. To try your hand at riding the waves, contact the **Richard Schmidt Surf School**, or ask around for him at the beach. (☎423-0928. 1hr. private lesson $65, 2hr. group lesson $70. Lessons include equipment.) To learn more about the activity, stop by the well-known and ever-popular **Steamer's Lane**—the deep water off the point near the Lighthouse along West Cliff Dr.

Around the point at the end of W. Cliff Dr. is **Natural Bridges State Park.** While all but one of its natural bridges have collapsed, the park nevertheless offers a pristine beach, awe-inspiring tidepools, and tours during Monarch butterfly season from October to March. In November and December, thousands of stunning *lepidoptera* swarm along the beach. (☎423-4609. Open daily 8am-dusk. Parking $5, seniors $4.) **Parasailing** and other pricey pastimes are popular on the wharf. **Kayak Connection,** 413 Lake Ave., has ocean-going kayaks at reasonable rates. Rentals include paddle, life jacket, and a skirt or wetsuit. (☎479-1121. Open M-F 10am-6pm, Sa-Su 8:30am-6pm. Open-deck singles $27 per day, closed-deck singles $30. 4½hr. lessons $45.)

🌃 **NIGHTLIFE.** There are comprehensive weekly events listings in the free local publications *Good Times* and *Metro Santa Cruz,* and also in the *Spotlight* section of the Friday *Sentinel.* The Boardwalk bandstand offers free summertime Friday night concerts, usually by oldies bands, around 6:30 and 8:30pm. ⬛**Caffe Pergolesi,** 418A Cedar St., is a chill coffeehouse/bar perfect for reading, writing, or socializing. The cheerful color scheme and intimate tables give "Perg's" a supremely friendly atmosphere. Specialties include $2.50 pints daily 7-9pm and four varieties of hot chocolate. (☎426-1775. Open M-Th 6:30am-11:30pm, F-Sa 7:30am-midnight, Su 7:30am-11:30pm.) The **Kuumbwa Jazz Center,** 320-322 Cedar St., offers great jazz and innovative off-night programs. Tickets ($10-20) sold through **Logos Books and Music,** 1117 Pacific Ave. (☎427-5100; open daily 10am-10pm), as well as **BASS outlets** (☎998-2277). Most shows start around 8pm. (☎427-2227. Big acts M; local groups F. All ages.) A mega-popular gay-straight club, **Blue Lagoon,** 923 Pacific Ave. has won a plethora of awards, from "best bartender" to "best place you can't take your parents," from the local press. (☎423-7117. Happy hour daily 6-9pm; $2.50 drinks. Cover Su and Tu $1, M and W $3, Th-Sa $4. Open daily 4pm-2am.) **The Catalyst,** 1011 Pacific Ave., draws national, college, and local bands. (☎423-1338. Shows W-Sa. Cover and age restrictions vary widely with show; bar strictly 21+. Open M-Sa 9am-2am, Su 9am-5pm. Food served daily 9am-3pm; 9am-11pm on show days.)

SAN FRANCISCO ☎415

If California is a state of mind, then San Francisco is euphoria. Welcome to the city that will take you to new highs of all kinds, leaving your head spinning, your taste buds tingling, your calves aching, and your optic nerves reeling. Though it's smaller than most "big" cities, the City by the Bay more than compensates for its size in personality. The dazzling views, the huff-and-puff hills, the one-of-a-kind neighborhoods, and the laid-back, friendly people of SF add up to create a unique charisma. Within its mere 47 square miles, the city manages to pack an incredible amount of vitality. From its thriving art community to the bustling downtown to some of the country's most happening nightclubs, there's something for anyone who's hip.

By California standards, San Francisco is steeped in history—but it's a history of oddballs and eccentrics that resonates more today in street culture than in museums and galleries. The lineage of free spirits and troublemakers started back in the 19th century, with smugglers, pirates, and Gold Rush '49ers. In the 1950s came the brilliant, angry, young Beats, and the late 60s ushered in the most famous of SF rabble rousers—hippies and flower children, who turned on one generation and freaked out another by making love, not war. The tradition of free spirit lives on. The gay community emerged in the 1970s as one of the city's most visible and powerful groups. Anti-establishment rallies and movements continue to fill the streets and newspapers. At the same time, Mexican, Central American, and Asian immigrants have made SF one of the most racially diverse cities in the United States. Like so many chameleons, San Francisco is changing with the times, but fortunately, some things stay the same: the Bay is foggy, the hills are steep, and tourists are the only ones wearing shorts. For more coverage of the City by the Bay, see 🕮*Let's Go: San Francisco 2002.*

✈ INTERCITY TRANSPORTATION

Driving from L.A. takes 6hr. on I-5, 8hr. on U.S. 101, or 9½hr. via Rte. 1. U.S. 101 compromises between vistas and velocity, but the stunning coastal scenery along Rte. 1 makes getting there fun. From inland California, **I-5** approaches the city from the north and south via **I-580** and **I-80**, which runs across the **Bay Bridge** (westbound toll $2). From the north, U.S. 101 and Rte. 1 come over the **Golden Gate Bridge** (southbound toll $3).

Airport: San Francisco International (☎650-876-2377; www.flysfo.com), 15 mi. south of downtown via U.S. 101. Ground transportation info (☎800-736-2008). **San Mateo County Transit (SamTrans)** (within the Bay Area ☎800-660-4287, from elsewhere 650-817-1717) runs 2 buses to downtown. Express bus KX runs to the Transbay Terminal and allows 1 carry-on bag per person. Runs 35min.; 5:30am-12:50am. $3, seniors at off-peak times $1.25, under 17 $1.25. Bus #292 stops frequently along Mission St. and allows all luggage. 1hr.; 5:45am-12:30am. $2/50¢/75¢.

Trains: Amtrak (☎800-872-7245). The nearest stations are in Oakland and Emeryville. "Thruway motorcoaches" ($3.50-7) connect from both Oakland and Emeryville to downtown SF. To Los Angeles (8-12hr., 5 per day, $50). **Caltrain** (in Bay area ☎800-660-4287, from elsewhere 650-817-1717), which leaves SF from the Caltrain Depot at 4th and King St. in SoMa (M-F 5am-midnight, Sa 7am-midnight, Su 8am-10pm), is a regional commuter train that runs south to Palo Alto ($4, seniors and under 12 $2) and San Jose ($5.25, seniors and under 12 $2.50), making many stops along the way.

Buses: Golden Gate Transit (Marin County, ☎923-2000), **AC Transit** (East Bay, ☎510-891-4777), and **SamTrans** (San Mateo County) all stop at the **Transbay Terminal,** 425 Mission St. (☎495-1575), between Fremont and 1st St. downtown. **Greyhound** runs buses from the terminal to Los Angeles (8-12hr., 25 per day, $45) and Portland (14-20hr., 7 per day, $54).

▣ LOCAL TRANSPORTATION

San Francisco Municipal Railway (MUNI) (☎673-6864). System of buses, cable cars, subways, and streetcars. Fare $1, seniors and ages 5-17 35¢. Cheapest and most efficient way to get around the city. **MUNI passports** are valid on all MUNI vehicles (1-day $6, 3-day $10, 7-day $15). Weekly Pass ($9) is valid for a single work week and requires an additional $1 to ride the cable cars. The Monthly FastPass ($35) includes in-town BART trips and cable cars. Free transfers (valid for 1½hr.) if you hang onto your ticket. Coverage decreases considerably after dark. Wheelchair access varies among routes; all below-ground subway stations, but not all above-ground sites, are accessible. Runs daily 6am-1am. **Owl Service** runs limited routes daily 1am-5am.

Cable cars: Noisy, slow, and usually crammed full, but charming relics. To avoid mobs, ride in the early morning. The **Powell-Mason (PM)** line, which runs to the wharf, is the most popular. The **California (C)** line, from the Financial District up through Nob Hill, is usually the least crowded, but the **Powell-Hyde (PH)** line, with the steepest hills and the sharpest turns, may be the most fun. All lines run daily 6am-12:20am. Fare $2, seniors and disabled $1, children under 6 free, before 7am and after 9pm $1. No transfers.

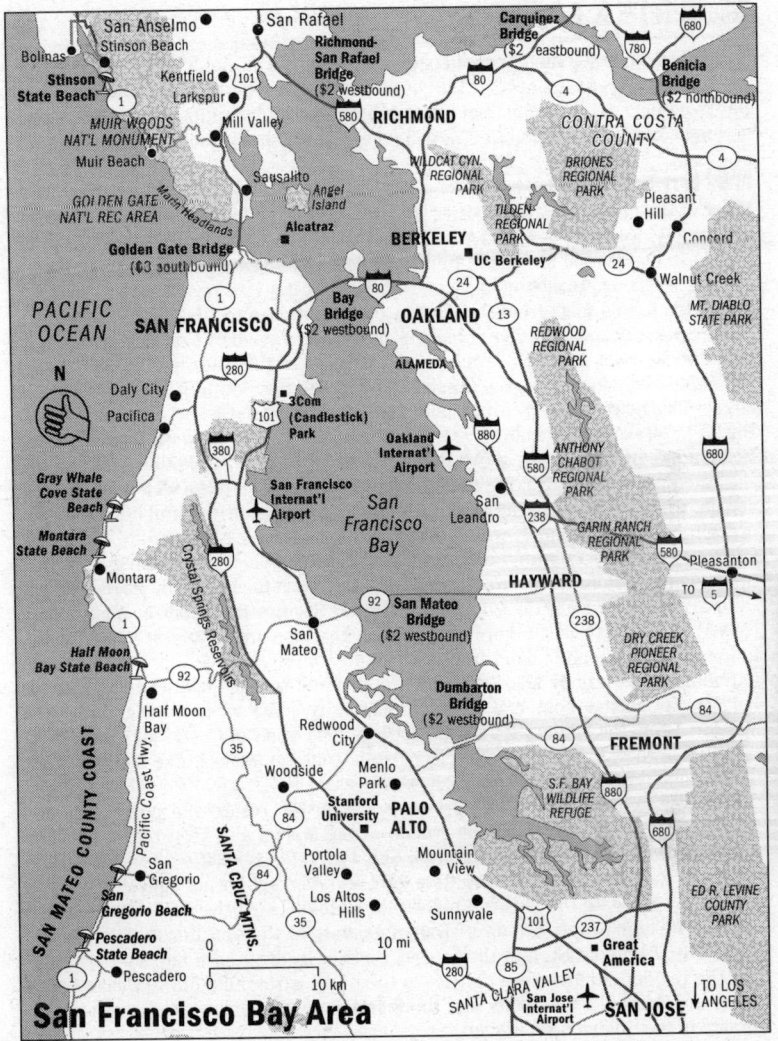

San Francisco Bay Area

Bay Area Rapid Transit (BART) (☎989-2278). BART operates carpeted trains along 4 lines connecting San Francisco with the **East Bay,** including Oakland, Berkeley, Concord, and Fremont. All stations provide maps and schedules. There are 8 BART stops in San Francisco proper, but BART is not a local transportation system. Runs M-F 4am-midnight, Sa 6am-midnight, Su 8am-midnight. Fare $1.10-6. Wheelchair accessible.

Car Rental: City, 1748 Folsom St. (☎861-1312), between Duboce St. and 14th St. Must be 21; under 25 surcharge $8 per day. Compacts from $29-35 per day, $160-170 per week. Unlimited mileage for a small fee. Weekend and advance booking specials. Open M-F 7:30am-6pm, Sa 9am-4pm. Another location at 1433 Bush St., between Van Ness Ave. and Polk St. also open Su 10am-4pm.

Taxis: San Francisco Yellow Cab, ☎626-2345. **National Cab,** ☎648-4444.

✦ ORIENTATION

San Francisco is 403 mi. north of Los Angeles and 390 mi. south of the Oregon border. The city lies at the northern tip of the peninsula separating the San Francisco Bay from the Pacific Ocean. San Francisco radiates outward from its docks, which lie on the northeast edge of the 30 mi. peninsula, just inside the lip of the Bay.

NEIGHBORHOODS

Many of the city's most visitor-friendly attractions are found within the northeastern wedge formed by **Van Ness Ave.**, which runs north-south; the **Embarcadero** along the coast; and **Market St.**, which runs northeast-southwest and interrupts the regular grid of streets. At the top of this wedge lies touristy **Fisherman's Wharf. Columbus Ave.** extends southeast from the docks to **North Beach**, a district shared by Italian-Americans, artists, and professionals. **Telegraph Hill**, topped by Coit Tower, emerges as the focal point of North Beach amid a mass of terrific eateries. To the west of Columbus Ave. are residential **Russian Hill** and **Nob Hill.** South of North Beach, the largest **Chinatown** in North America covers 24 sq. blocks. On the other side of the Bush St. Gateway to Chinatown lies the heavily developed **Financial District**, where skyscrapers fill the blocks above the northeast portion of Market St. To the west, the core downtown area centered on **Union Sq.** gives way to the well-pounded **Tenderloin**, where, despite attempts at urban renewal, drugs, crime, and homelessness prevail. In the **Civic Center**, which occupies the acute angle formed by Market St. and Van Ness Ave., cultural heavyweights like the Opera House crown a collection of municipal buildings. Just to the west, artists inhabit the newly hip **Hayes Valley.**

South of the wedge, directly below Market St., lies the **South of Market Area (SoMa).** Here, the best of San Francisco's nightclubs are scattered among warehouses. SoMa extends inland from the Bay to 10th St., at which point the largely Latino and very trendy **Mission** district begins and spreads south to quiet **Bernal Heights.** The **Castro**, center of the gay community, plays western neighbor to the Mission. From the landmark **Castro Theatre** on the corner of Castro and Market St., the neighborhood stretches to the less flamboyant **Noe Valley** in the south and the undeveloped oasis of **Twin Peaks** in the southeast.

Some interesting strips are sprinkled among the residential neighborhoods west of Van Ness Ave. The posh stucco of the **Marina** and Victorians of **Pacific Heights** run south to funkier **Fillmore St.**, which leads to the few *udon*-filled blocks of **Japantown.** Vast **Golden Gate Park** and its neighboring **Sunset** district to the south dominate the western half of the peninsula. At the park's eastern end sits the former hippie haven of **Haight-Ashbury** to the southeast. The park is bounded by Lincoln St. and the Sunset District to the south, and by Fulton St. and the residential **Richmond** district to the north, stretching out to **Ocean Beach** along the Pacific. **Lincoln Park** and the **Presidio,** at the northwestern corner, culminate in the **Golden Gate Bridge.**

⓵ PRACTICAL INFORMATION

Visitor info: Visitor Convention and Visitors Bureau, 900 Market St. (☎283-0177, TDD 392-0328; 24hr. info in English 391-2001, in Spanish 391-2122; www.sfvisitor.org), in Hallidie Plaza at Powell St. beneath street level at the BART exit. MUNI passports and maps for sale. Open M-F 9am-5pm, Sa-Su 9am-3pm.

Hotlines: Rape Crisis Center, ☎647-7273. **Drug Crisis Line,** ☎362-3400. **Suicide Prevention,** ☎781-0500. **Crisis Line for the Handicapped,** ☎800-426-4263.

Internet access: Most **public library** locations. **Chat Café,** 498 Sanchez St. (☎626-4700), at 18th St. Free with purchase ($1.25-2.50 per hr.). Open M-F 7am-8pm, Sa-Su 8am-8pm.

Post Office: Union Square Station, 170 O'Farrell St. (☎956-3570), in the basement of Macy's. Open M-Sa 10am-5:30pm, Su 11am-5pm. **Zip code:** 94108. **Area code:** 415.

TO ALCATRAZ

Pier 39

California Welcome Center

San Francisco Bay

Maritime Museum

Ghirardelli Square

FISHERMAN'S WHARF

Jefferson St.

Beach St.

Beach St.

TO FORT MASON

North Point St.

Bay St.

Bay St.

Van Ness Ave.

Francisco St.

Chestnut St.

Lombard St.

Tattoo Art Museum

Lombard St.

TELEGRAPH HILL

The Embarcadero

Coit Tower

WASHINGTON SQUARE

Filbert Steps

Filbert St.

NORTH BEACH

Union St.

Green St.

RUSSIAN HILL

Green St.

Vallejo St.

Broadway

Broadway Tunnel

Broadway

City Lights Bookstore

Pacific Ave.

Pacific Ave.

Jackson St.

Jackson St.

Justin Herman Plaza

Ferry Building

Washington St.

Cable Car Powerhouse

Transamerica Pyramid

Clay St.

Embarcadero Center

Clay St.

Grace Cathedral

NOB HILL

CHINATOWN

Sacramento St.

California St.

CALIFORNIA ST CABLE CAR LINE

Pine St.

Pine St.

EMBARCADERO

FINANCIAL DIST.

Market St.

Bush St.

101

Sutter St.

MONTGOMERY ST.

Transbay Terminal

Post St.

UNION SQUARE

Maiden Lane

Geary St.

5

O'Farrell St.

Ansel Adams Center

S. F. Museum of Modern Art

Ellis St.

TENDERLOIN

6

Yerba Buena Center for the Performing Arts

Eddy St.

Sony Metreon

POWELL

Turk St.

Moscone Center

Herbst Theatre

Golden Gate St.

Old Mint

McAllister St.

City Hall

CIVIC CENTER

Library

CIVIC CENTER

SOUTH OF MARKET

Howard St.

Opera House

Grove St.

Folsom St.

Harrison St.

TO PACIFIC BELL PARK (1 blk)

Hayes St.

Symphony Hall

Fell St.

Mission St.

Minna St.

South Park

Bryant St.

Brannan St.

10th St.

9th St.

8th St.

7th St.

6th St.

5th St.

4th St.

Townsend St.

CalTrain Depot

9th St.

7th St.

Berry St.

Mission Creek

Marina

N

280

0   250 yards

0   250 meters

San Francisco

♦ ACCOMMODATIONS

Adelaide Inn, 4
AYH Hostel at Union
    Square (HI-AYH), 5
Fort Mason Hostel, 1
Globetrotter's Inn, 6
Pacific Tradewinds Hostel, 3
San Remo Hotel, 2

⚓ ACCOMMODATIONS

Beware that some of the cheapest budget hotels may be located in areas requiring extra caution at night. Reservations are recommended at hotels.

HOSTELS

⬛ **Pacific Tradewinds Hostel,** 680 Sacramento (☎433-7970; fax 291-8801), at Kearny St. in the Financial District. While other hostels drift aimlessly in the doldrums, Pacific Tradewinds plows ahead of them, its sails filled with gusts of excellence. Clean, light, and friendly, the way a hostel should be. Linens, laundry, free DSL Internet, no curfew, no lockout. 2 week max. stay. Reception 8am-midnight. Reservations recommended. Single beds in dorm-style rooms $24; double beds $22 per person; no private rooms.

⬛ **San Francisco International Guest House,** 2976 23rd St. (☎641-1411), at Harrison St. in the Mission. Look for the blue Victorian house near the corner. Hardwood floors, wall tapestries, and house plants. Free coffee. TV area, 2 kitchens (non-smoking and smoking), and guest phones. 5-night min., 3-month max. stay. Getting in can be like escaping Alcatraz: the Guest House does not take reservations and is almost always full. All you can do is try calling. Beds in dorm-style rooms $14 ($12 if paid 25 days in advance); 1 private double $28. Passport with international stamps required.

AYH Hostel at Union Square (San Francisco Downtown; HI-AYH), 312 Mason St. (☎788-5604; fax 788-3023), between Geary and O'Farrell St., in Union Square. TV, Internet access (about $1 for 10min.), and visitor info. Free walking tours and seminar on San Francisco nightlife. Organized dinner, ballgame outings. Nightly movie. Heavily used kitchens, but no stoves. Quiet hours (midnight-7am) not always respected by Mason St. traffic. Lockers. Key deposit $5. 14 day max. stay. Reception 24hr. Wheelchair accessible. Reserve by phone or show up around 8am. July-Oct. $24, Nov.-Feb. $19, Mar.-June $20. Nonmembers $27/$21/$23. Under 13 half-price with parent.

Fort Mason Hostel (HI-AYH), Bldg. #240 (☎771-7277), in Fort Mason, behind the administrative buildings. Beautiful surroundings give this 160-bed hostel a campground feel. Not a place for partiers—strictly enforced quiet hours and other rules, such as no smoking or alcohol. Movies, walking tours, kitchen, dining room, bike storage. Huge clean kitchen; cute cafe. Usually booked weeks in advance, but a few beds are reserved for walk-ins. Minor chores expected. Lockers. Laundry (wash $1, dry $1). Parking. Reception 24hr. Check-in 2:30pm. Check-out 11am. No curfew, but lights-out at midnight. IBN reservations available. Dorms $22.50.

Easy Goin' Travel and California Dreamin' Guesthouse, 3145-47 Mission St. (☎552-8452; fax 552-8459), near Cesar Chavez St. Slightly remote location but super-friendly staff and excellent amenities. 20 dorm-style beds in 4 rooms. 10 private rooms have 2 double beds each. All rooms have TV. Kitchen, lounge with TV, laundry, Internet access, bike rental, and travel services. $20 security and key deposit. Check-in noon. Check-out 11am. Reservations recommended; 2-night min. Dorms $16, private rooms $35.

Globetrotters, 225 Ellis St. (☎/fax 346-5786), between Mason and Taylor St., in Union Square. Busy common room with TV and couches, a fully equipped kitchen, and laundry. Check-in 8am-midnight. Check-out 11am. Dorms $15, weekly $90; doubles $30.

GUEST HOUSES

⬛ **The San Remo Hotel,** 2237 Mason St. (☎776-8688), between Chestnut and Water St. in North Beach. The best value in town, with small but elegantly furnished rooms. The sparkling shared bathrooms with brass pull-chain toilets hark back to the end of the 19th century. Friendly staff will book tours, bikes, cars, and airport shuttles; they also recommend restaurants. Free modem connections; laptop rental for in-house use $5 per 15min. Check-in 2pm. Check-out 11am. Reservations required. Singles $50-75; doubles $60-85; triples $85.

⬛ **Adelaide Inn,** 5 Isadora Duncan (☎441-2261; fax 441-0161), at the end of a little alley off Taylor St. between Geary and Post St. in Union Square. Warm hosts, lovely furnishings, and reasonable prices make this quiet 18-room oasis the most charming of San

Francisco's many "European-style" hotels. Steep stairs; no elevator. All rooms have large windows, TV, and sink. Small shared hallway bathrooms. Continental breakfast included. Reception Tu-F 9am-1pm and 5-9pm, M and Sa-Su flexible. Reserve at least 10 days ahead. Singles $42-50; doubles $58-70.

The Red Victorian Bed, Breakfast, and Art, 1665 Haight St. (☎864-1978), near Belvedere St. in the Upper Haight. The "Summer of Love" lives on here. Guests come together at breakfast to meditate and chat. All 18 rooms are individually decorated by the owner, Sami Sunchild, to honor such themes as sunshine, tranquility, and butterflies. Even the hall baths have their own motifs. Free tea and coffee. Breakfast included. Reception 9am-9pm. Check-in 3-6pm or by appointment. Check-out 11am. Reservations required. Most doubles $86-126; discounts for stays of 3 or more days.

Inn On Castro, 321 Castro St. (☎861-0321), at Market St. in the Castro. Brightly refurbished Victorian exterior complements the cozy living room—the perfect place to enjoy a good book, a full breakfast, or a swig of brandy (compliments of the host). Immaculately clean, well-kept dining area and common area. Gay-owned and operated; straight-friendly. Reception 7:30am-10:30pm. Parking $15 per day. Singles $100-135; doubles $115-185; patio suite $185; neighborhood apartments $135-250 per night.

The Parker House, 520 Church St. (☎621-3222 or 888-520-7275), at 17th St. in the Castro. Serene and stylish. Voted best LGB B&B in the city. A beautiful parlor, with dark wood paneling, piano, and flowers. All rooms have cable TV and modem. Spa/steam room available. Breakfast included. Parking $15 per day. 2-night min. stay, 4-night min. stay on some holiday weekends. Check-in 3pm. Check-out noon. Reservations required. Rooms with shared bath from $119, with private bath from $149.

◘ FOOD

FISHERMAN'S WHARF AND THE MARINA

Boudin Bakery and Café, 4 locations in the Wharf area, including 156 Jefferson St. (☎928-1849) and Pier 39 (☎421-2259). Baguettes, rolls, bread bowls—you name it, they make it out of sourdough. Loaf (big enough to share) $2. Open daily 7:30am-9pm.

Soku's Teriyaki and Sushi, 2280 Chestnut St. (☎563-0162), at Scott St. in the Marina. Great service and a $4 lunch box special (2-item combo plus miso soup and rice; available 11:30am-3pm). Get take-out and wander down to the water for a view to match your meal. Open M-Sa 11:30am-10pm.

Zao, 2031 Chestnut St. (☎928-3088), between Steiner and Fillmore St. in the Marina. "The way of the noodle is long and narrow." Ponder this and other cryptic thoughts over one of the Pan-Asian noodle dishes, many vegetarian (about $7).

NORTH BEACH AND CHINATOWN

▧ L'Osteria del Forno, 519 Columbus Ave. (☎982-1124), between Green and Union St. Acclaimed Italian roasted and cold foods, plus homemade breads. Terrific thin-crust pizzas (slices $2.50-3.75, whole pizzas $10-17) and focaccia sandwiches ($5-6.50). The tiny dining room is always crowded but romantic nonetheless. Open Su-M and W-Th 11:30am-10pm, F-Sa 11:30am-10:30pm. No credit cards.

▧ Chef Jia, 925 Kearny St. (☎398-1626), at Pacific St. Serves cheap and fabulous food in a small, informal space. Yummy $4.50 lunch specials (11:30am-4pm)—try the spicy string beans with yams. Entrees $4-7. Open daily 11:30am-10pm. No credit cards.

Sam Wo, 813 Washington St. (☎982-0596), at Grant Ave. Literally translated, the name of this picturesque place means, "How is it possible to get so much tasty food for so little?" Breeze by the kitchen, climb the stairs, and find a seat by a window. Every possible soup and noodle combo $4. Open M-Sa 11am-3am, Su varies. No credit cards.

NOB HILL AND RUSSIAN HILL

▧ Zarzuela, 2000 Hyde St. (☎346-0800), at Union St. in Russian Hill. Authentic Spanish homestyle cooking. Fabulous *tapas* ($4-7) and full meals ($10-15) in a festive setting. Open Tu-Th 5:30-10pm, F-Sa 5:30-10:30pm.

CALIFORNIA

The Crêpe House, 1755 Polk St. (☎441-2421), at Washington St. in Nob Hill. Spend an extra hour after lunch traveling the information superhighway in style with a gourmet crepe ($5-7) and a cup of coffee. High-speed DSL Internet access available ($10 per hr.). Open Su-Th 7:30am-9:30pm, F-Sa 7:30am-10:30pm. No credit cards.

UNION SQUARE AND THE TENDERLOIN

☒ Café Bean, 754 Post St. (☎776-6620), and 800 Sutter St. (☎923-9539). Steaming eggs and toast ($4), brie and olive sandwich ($6.50), and Dutch pancakes ($4) made ready for tourists, businesspeople, and wayward hipsters. Free Internet access with coffee at Sutter St. location. Sutter St. location open M-Sa 6am-7pm; Su 6am-5pm; photo- and postcard-papered Post St. location open daily 6am-2pm.

☒ The California Culinary Academy, 625 Polk St. (☎292-8229), at Turk St. 600 students plus 2 restaurants equals cheap, amazing eats for you. The food is expertly prepared and served at cheaper prices than at other establishments with comparable chefs. M-W lunch ($7-11) and 3-course dinners ($22); Th French Buffet ($32.50); F Grande Buffet ($36). The **Academy Grill** offers a 3-course dinner for $13 Tu-Th. The **Tavern** has Italian fare for lunch ($7-11) and dinner ($9-16) with buffets F-Sa ($23). Under 12 half-price for all meals. Open for lunch M-F noon-1pm and dinner 6-8pm.

Lori's Diner, 336 Mason St. (☎392-8646), near Geary St. Elvis is most certainly not dead—he's working as a short-order cook at Lori's. Waitresses in period costumes careen by with stacked burger plates and huge omelettes ($6-8). Open 24hr.

CIVIC CENTER AND HAYES VALLEY

☒ It's Tops Coffee Shop (☎715-6868), on the corner of Market and Octavia. This small diner, with a soda fountain, an old-school counter, and orange booths, serves the perfect blend of nostalgia, camp, and darn good food. Breakfast $4.50-8, burgers $6-8. Open M-F 8am-3pm, M and W-F also 8pm-3am; Sa 8am-3am; Su 8am-11pm.

Ananda Fuara, 1298 Market St. (☎621-1994), at Larkin St. A vegetarian menu with vegan tendencies offers creative combos of super fresh ingredients—terrific smoothies ($3.25) and great sandwiches like the BBQ tofu burger ($5.50). The most popular dish and house specialty is the "neatloaf" (topped with mashed potatoes and gravy $10.25, in a sandwich $6.50). Open M-Tu and Th-Sa 8am-8pm, W 8am-3pm. No credit cards.

SOUTH OF MARKET AREA (SOMA)

☒ LuLu, 816 Folsom St. (☎495-5775), at 4th St. Enticing aromas, wonderful atmosphere, and delicious food. Cuisine is "nouvelle-French-Italian-Californian," but they hate labels. Unique pizzas (from $11) and huge family-style plates of fire-roasted veggies are the best budget bets on an ever-changing menu. Open Su-Th 11:30am-10:45pm, F-Sa 11:30am-11:45pm. Limited menu 3-5:30pm. Reservations essential.

☒ Buzz 9, 139 8th St. (☎255-8783), at Minna St. An homage to all things jazz and one of the coolest dinner spots around. Fantastic meals in blue-lit splendor. Check out the *Sheben* ("a shady tavern") downstairs. Offers delicious fruit smoothies like the Buzz 9 Booster ($4). Cocktails $6-8. The "Blues Man" tickles the ivories Th-F 7-8:30pm. Open daily for breakfast, lunch, and dinner M-F 11:30am-10pm, F-Sa 11:30am-11pm.

MISSION AND THE CASTRO

☒ We Be Sushi, 538 Valencia St. (☎565-0749), at 16th St. Another location at 1071 Valencia St. Serving "sushi like mom used to make," this little Japanese jewel proves that all kinds of good, cheap food abound in the Mission. Rolls $1.85-2.50. The lunch special is unreal: soup, rice, roll, and 3 pieces of *nigiri* sushi for $6. Open M-Th and Su 11:30am-10pm, F-Sa 11:30am-11pm.

Taquería El Farolito, 2279 Mission St. (☎824-7877), at 24th St. The spot for cheap and authentic Mexican *comida*—chow down as Latin beats blast through this fast-food joint. After any kind of evening activity in Mission, El Farolito is a great late-night fix. Tacos $1.75. Open Su-Th 9am-2am, F-Sa 9am-4am. No credit cards.

Welcome Home, 464 Castro St. (☎626-3600), across from the Castro Theatre. If grandma were a drag queen, this would be her kitchen: the disco lights, antique ovens,

SAN FRANCISCO ■ 835

pride flags, and fried chicken bring an all-American and decidedly queer comfort to the Castro. Dinners $7-9. Open daily 7:30am-10:30pm. No credit cards.

HAIGHT-ASHBURY

■ **Squat and Gobble,** 1428 Haight St. (☎864-8484), between Ashbury St. and Masonic Ave. This popular cafe and *crêperie* offers enormous omelettes ($5.50-6.75) and delicious crepes ($4.50-7.25). Lots of vegetarian options. Open 8am-10pm daily.

Kate's Kitchen, 471 Haight St. (☎626-3984), near Fillmore St. One of the best breakfasts in the neighborhood (served all day). It's always packed, so you'll need to sign up on a waiting list posted outside. Try the "Fruit Orgy," with fruit, yogurt, granola, and honey ($5). Open M 9am-3pm, Tu-F 8am-3pm, Sa-Su 9am-4pm. No credit cards.

RICHMOND

Taiwan Restaurant, 445 Clement St. (☎387-1789), at 6th Ave. Watch the cooks fold your dumplings in the window of this yummy, cheap, veggie-friendly spot dishing up Northern Chinese cuisine. Lines out the door on weekends and some mean dim sum. Lunch $3.50; dinner $5-8. Open M-Th 11am-10pm, F 11am-midnight, Sa 10am-midnight, Su 10am-10pm.

Schubert's Bakery, 521 Clement St. (☎752-1580), between 6th and 7th Ave. Baking up a storm since 1911. Fruit tarts, cookies, and freshly baked bread $2.50-3.50. Cookies $5 for ½ lb. Open M-F 7am-6:30pm, Sa 7am-6pm, Su 9am-5pm.

PACIFIC HEIGHTS AND JAPANTOWN

La Méditerranée, 2210 Fillmore St. (☎921-2956), between Sacramento and Clay St. Small, attractive cafe with light Mediterranean-inspired fare. Filled phyllo dough and other entrees $7.50-9. Open M-Th 11am-10pm, F-Sa 11am-11pm.

Mifune, 1737 Post St. (☎922-0337), in the Kintetsu Bldg., upper level. Excellent and much-loved noodle restaurant with minimalist wooden booths and stark red walls. Choices include *udon* (heavy flour noodles) or *soba* (slender buckwheat noodles); hot noodles from $4.50, cold noodles from $5.25. *Sake* $2.25-4.25. Open M-F and Su 11am-9:30pm, Sa 11am-10pm.

◎ SIGHTS

GOLDEN GATE BRIDGE AND THE PRESIDIO

GOLDEN GATE BRIDGE. Synonymous with San Francisco itself, the majestic Golden Gate Bridge stretches across 1¼ mi. of ocean. Its red towers loom 65 stories above the Bay, and it can sway up to 27 ft. in each direction during high winds. On sunny days, hundreds of people take the 30min. walk across the bridge; on gloomier days, the crisis counseling phones that dot the sidewalks remind walkers of the bridge's popularity among the depressed. The views from the bridge are amazing—especially those of the city from the Vista Point on the northern Marin County side. To see the bridge itself, it's best to get a bit farther away: Fort Point and Fort Baker in the Presidio, Land's End in Lincoln Park, Mt. Livermore on Angel Island, and Hawk Hill off Conzelman Rd. in the Marin Headlands all offer spectacular views of the Golden Gate on clear days. *(MUNI bus #28 or 29.)*

PRESIDIO. The Presidio, a sprawling preserve that extends from the Marina in the east to the wealthy Sea Cliff area in the west, was occupied by the US Army for nearly a century between the Mexican War and World War II. Today, the Presidio is part of the **Golden Gate National Recreation Area (GGNRA),** run by the National Park Service in conjunction with the nonprofit Presidio Trust. The Presidio Trust is raising funds to help make the park self-sufficient by 2013 and coordinating projects such as the marsh reclamation in Crissy Field and the ongoing renovation and modernization of roads, buildings, and trails in the park. *(MUNI bus #28, 29, 42, or 76 or Golden Gate Transit buses into the Presidio.)*

CALIFORNIA

OTHER SIGHTS. At the northern tip of the Presidio (and the peninsula), under the tower of the Golden Gate Bridge, **Fort Point** keeps watch over the entrance to San Francisco Bay. The site was once the nation's main coastal defense, housing a garrison of men and nearly 200 guns and cannons. The top tier of the four-story building is windy, but worth the view. Rangers give tours in Civil War garb. (☎ 561-4395. *Open Th-M 10am-5pm, though schedule may vary due to "seismic upgrading.")* **Baker Beach** offers a picturesque but chilly place to tan and swim. Wind shelter makes the northern half of the beach one of the city's most popular nude beaches.

FISHERMAN'S WHARF AND THE BAY

Piers 39 through 45 provide access to San Francisco's most famous and touristy attractions. Easily visible from boats and the waterfront is **Alcatraz Island.**

ALCATRAZ. Named in 1775 for small cormorants (*alcatraceo*) which nest on the island, this former federal prison looms over San Francisco Bay, 1½ mi. from Fisherman's Wharf. In the 30s, the federal government used it to imprison those who had wrought too much havoc in other prisons, including infamous criminals like Al Capone, "Machine Gun" Kelly, and Robert "The Birdman" Stroud. Of the 34 men who attempted to escape, 29 were recaptured or killed, and five are "presumed drowned," although their bodies have never been found. In 1964, Attorney General Robert Kennedy closed the prison, and the island remained empty until 1969-71, when 80 Native Americans occupied it as a symbolic gesture, claiming "the Rock" as theirs under terms of a broken 19th-century treaty. Alcatraz is now part of the **Golden Gate National Recreation Area.** The **Blue and Gold Fleet** runs boats to Alcatraz from **Pier 41.** Once on Alcatraz, wander alone or take the audiotape-guided tour, full of clanging chains and the ghosts of prisoners past. (*Info* ☎ 773-1188, *tickets 705-5555. Reserve at least a day and preferably a week in advance, especially in summer. If all else fails, the Blue and Gold ticket counter in the basement of the DFS Galleria in Union Square, on Geary and Stockton St., offers a number of "extra" tickets on sold out days for a $2.25 mark-up. Boats depart Pier 41 every 30min. in summer 9:15am-4:15pm; in winter 9:45am-2:45pm. Arrive 20min. before departure. Tickets $9.25, seniors $7.50, ages 5-11 $6. Entirely worthwhile audio tours $4, ages 5-11 $2. Other boating companies run shorter tours up to and around—but not onto—the island for about $10 per person.)*

GHIRARDELLI SQUARE. Ghirardelli (GEAR-ah-DEH-lee) is the most famous shopping mall in the area around Fisherman's Wharf, known for producing some of the world's best chocolate. Today, the remains of the machinery from Ghirardelli's original factory display the chocolate-making process in the rear of the **Ghirardelli Chocolate Manufactory,** an old-fashioned ice-cream parlor. If your sweet tooth outpaces your financial resources, file through the Ghirardelli store for a free sample. (*Mall: 900 North Point St.* ☎ 775-5500. *Stores open M-Sa 10am-9pm, Su 10am-6pm. Ghirardelli Store:* ☎ 771-4903. *Open Su-Th 9am-11pm, F-Sa 9am-midnight. Soda fountain: Open Su-Th 10:30am-11pm, F-Sa 10:30am-midnight.)*

OTHER SIGHTS. Pier 39 juts toward Alcatraz on pilings several hundred yards into the harbor. Toward the end of the pier is **Center Stage,** where mimes, jugglers, and magicians play the crowds. A number of the marina docks have been claimed by **sea lions** that pile onto the wharf to gawk at human tourists on sunny days. (*Pier* ☎ 981-7437. *Shops open Su-Th 10am-9pm, F-Sa 10am-10pm.)* **Pier 45** and the **Hyde St. Pier** serve as docks to old submarines and boats open for touring. **The Cannery** is a miniplaza on the wharf, with garden seating, a few cafes, and the popular Belle Roux Voodoo Lounge, a Cajun restaurant, a bar, and Cobb's Comedy Club. (*On Jefferson St., between Hyde and Leavenworth St. Belle Roux.* ☎ 771-5225; *comedy club* ☎ 938-4320.)

MARINA AND FORT MASON

▧ **PALACE OF FINE ARTS.** The Palace of Fine Arts, an imposing domed structure with curving colonnades, has been reconstructed from remnants of the 1915 Panama Pacific Exposition which commemorated the opening of the Panama Canal and signaled San Francisco's recovery from the 1906 earthquake. The grounds make one of the best picnic spots in the city, and the nighttime illumination is glorious. (*On Baker St., between Jefferson and Bay St.* ☎ 750-3600. *Open 24hr. Free.)*

FORT MASON. Fort Mason is the headquarters for the **Golden Gate National Recreation Area.** *(At Laguna and Marine St. east of Marina Green, west of Fisherman's Wharf's Municipal Pier.)* The **Magic Theatre** stages both world and American premieres. *(Bldg. D, 3rd fl. ☎ 441-8822.)* Fort Mason also boasts several excellent **museums** (see p. 843).

FINANCIAL DISTRICT

TRANSAMERICA PYRAMID. The leading lady of the area is the Transamerica Pyramid. New Age sources claim the pyramid is directly centered on the telluric currents of the Golden Dragon ley line between Easter Island and Stonehenge. An architect's joke as opted by one of the country's leading architectural firms, the building earned disdain from purists and reverence from city planners after the fact. Without a business suit and some chutzpah, one must make do with the virtual viewscapes in the lobby. A pillar of the establishment, the address was once a site of revolutionary disgruntlement, and Sun Yat-Sen scripted a dynastic overthrow in one of its offices. *(600 Montgomery St., between Clay and Washington St.)*

OTHER SIGHTS. Justin Herman Plaza and its formidable **Vaillancourt Fountain,** at the foot of Market St., invite visitors to frolic in the mist. Bands and rallyists often rent out the area during lunch. One free concert, performed by U2 in the fall of 1987, resulted in the arrest of lead singer and madcap non-conformist Bono for spraypainting "Stop the Traffic—Rock and Roll" on the fountain. The 660 ft. waterfront **Ferry Building,** at the foot of Market St., has lost a bit of grandeur over the years, as other buildings along the Embarcadero stole the spotlight.

NORTH BEACH

WASHINGTON SQUARE. Bordered by Union, Filbert, Stockton, and Powell St. is Washington Sq., a pretty lawn edged by trees and watched over by a statue of not Washington, but Benjamin Franklin. Lillie Hitchcock Coit, rescued from a fire as a girl, donated the **Volunteer Firemen Memorial,** in the middle of the square.

COIT TOWER. Lillie Hitchcock Coit also put up money to build Coit Tower, which stands a few blocks to the east of the memorial. The tower commands a spectacular view of the city and the bay from Telegraph Hill, the steep mount from which a semaphore signaled the arrival of ships in Gold Rush days. Take MUNI bus #39, or climb up the **Filbert Steps** from the Embarcadero to the tower. *(☎ 362-0808. Open daily 10am-7pm. Elevator fare $3.75, over 64 $2.50, ages 6-12 $1.50, under 6 free.)*

CITY LIGHTS BOOKSTORE. Drawn to the area by low rents and cheap bars, the Beat writers came to national attention when Lawrence Ferlinghetti's City Lights Bookstore, opened in 1953, published Allen Ginsberg's *Howl.* City Lights has expanded since its Beat days and now stocks wide selections of fiction and poetry, but it remains committed to publishing young poets and writers under its own imprint. *(261 Columbus Ave. ☎ 362-8193. Open daily 10am-midnight.)*

CHINATOWN

▨WAVERLY PLACE. Find this little alley (between Sacramento and Washington St. and between Stockton St. and Grant Ave.) and you'll want to spend all day gazing at the incredible architecture. The fire escapes are painted in pinks and greens and held together by railings made of intricate Chinese patterns. You can also visit **Tien Hou Temple,** 125 Waverly Pl., the oldest Chinese temple in the US.

GRANT AVE. The oldest street in San Francisco, Grant Ave. is a sea of Chinese banners, signs, and architecture. During the day, Grant Ave. and nearby streets fill up with a slow-moving tourist horde stopping every block to buy health balls and chirping boxes and trying to ignore the Chinese porn mags in some shop windows. Most of the picturesque pagodas punctuating the blocks were designed around 1900 or more recently. At Bush and Grant St. stands the ornate, dragon-crested **Gateway to Chinatown,** given as a gift from Taiwan in 1970. "Everything in the world is in just proportion," say the Chinese characters above the gate.

THE BONAPARTE OF THE BAY By nature California is a populist constituency, putting more questions to voter referendum than any other state—but San Franciscans have made at least one notable exception. From 1853 to 1880, locals recognized the self-proclaimed rule of **Joshua Norton the First, Emperor of the United States and Defender of Mexico.** Norton assumed the grandiose title after tough luck in rice speculation wiped out all his money—and perhaps his sanity. He donned an ostrich feather hat and faux-military attire and roamed San Francisco's streets with his dogs, Bummer and Lazarus. When he wasn't busy sending suggestions to Abraham Lincoln, Queen Victoria, and the Czar of Russia, Norton's decrees for San Francisco included starting the tradition of a Christmas tree in Union Sq. and building a bridge across the Bay. Locals didn't mind his eccentricities; good-natured merchants accepted the money he printed, and the Central Pacific Railroad allowed him to travel for free. The city even footed the bill for his new clothes. When he died, 20,000 people came to wave him on to the next world.

ROSS ALLEY. Once lined with brothels and opium dens, Ross Alley, running from Jackson to Washington St. between Grant and Stockton St., is cleaned up but still has the cramped look of old Chinatown. It has stood in for Asia in such films as *Big Trouble in Little China*, *Karate Kid II*, and *Indiana Jones and the Temple of Doom*. Watch fortune cookies being shaped by hand in the **Golden Gate Cookie Company.** *(56 Ross Alley. ☎ 781-3956. Bag of cookies $2; with "funny" or "sexy" fortunes $4.)*

CHINESE CULTURAL CENTER. A stone bridge leads from Portsmouth Square to the other side of Kearny St., where the Chinese Cultural Center operates out of the third floor of the Holiday Inn. The Center houses a gallery of Chinese-American art, displays community exhibitions, and sponsors two **walking tours** of Chinatown. *(750 Kearny St. ☎ 986-1822. Open Tu-Sa 9am-5:30pm. Gallery open Tu-Su 10am-4pm.)*

NOB HILL AND RUSSIAN HILL

THE CROOKEDEST STREET IN THE WORLD. The famous curves of **Lombard St.**—installed in the 20s so that horse-drawn carriages could negotiate the extremely steep hill—are one-of-a-kind. From the top of Lombard St., both pedestrians and passengers enjoy the view of city and harbor. The view north along Hyde St. isn't too shabby either. *(Between Hyde and Leavenworth St. at the top of Russian Hill.)*

GRACE CATHEDRAL AND HUNTINGTON PARK. The largest Gothic edifice west of the Mississippi, **Grace Cathedral** crowns Nob Hill. The castings of its portals are such exact imitations of Lorenzo Ghiberti's on the Baptistery in Florence that they were used to restore the originals. Inside, modern murals mix San Franciscan and national historical events with saintly scenes. A Keith Haring triptych graces the altar of the AIDS Interfaith Memorial Chapel. *(1100 California St. ☎ 749-6300. Open Su-F 7am-6pm, Sa 8am-6pm; Su services at 7:30, 8:30, 11am, and 3:30pm. Suggested donation $3.)* The neat, manicured spot of turf and trees in front of this behemoth of Christian modernity is **Huntington Park,** equipped with a literal playground for the rich.

OTHER SIGHTS. After the journey up Nob Hill, you will understand what inspired the development of the vehicles celebrated at the **Cable Car Powerhouse and Museum,** still the working center of the cable-car system. Displays teach about the picturesque cars, some of which date back to 1873. *(1201 Mason St. ☎ 474-1887. Open daily Apr.-Oct. 10am-6pm; Nov.-Mar. 10am-5pm. Free.)* Once the site of the enormous mansions of the four mining and railroad magnates who "settled" Nob Hill, the hilltop is now home to upscale hotels and bars.

UNION SQUARE AND THE TENDERLOIN

While Union Sq. is filled with boutiques, stores, and retail, the western blocks have cultural offerings as well, in the form of theaters and galleries. When the Barbary

Coast (now the Financial District) was down and dirty, Union Sq.'s Morton Alley was dirtier. Around 1900, murders on the alley averaged one per week, and prostitutes waved to their favorite customers from 2nd-story windows.

MAIDEN LANE. After the 1906 earthquake and fires destroyed most of the flophouses, merchants moved in and renamed the area Maiden Lane in hopes of changing the street's image. It worked. Today, the pedestrian street is as virtuous as they come. The lane's main architectural attraction is the windowless face of the **Frank Lloyd Wright Building,** the city's only Wright-designed building, which now houses the **Folk Art International Gallery.** (140 Maiden Ln. ☎392-9999. Open M-Sa 10am-6pm.)

MARTIN LAWRENCE GALLERY. The Martin Lawrence Gallery is a modest corner space that displays works by pop artists like Warhol and Haring, as well as some studies by Picasso and Chagall. Haring once distributed his work for free to New York commuters in the form of graffiti; it now commands upwards of $13,000 in print form. (366 Geary St. ☎956-0345. Open M-Th 9am-8pm, F-Sa 9am-9pm, Su 10am-6pm.)

OTHER SIGHTS. Just southwest of Union Square, the aptly named Tenderloin hosts not only more traditional ladies (and men) of the night, but also San Francisco specials: transvestite, transsexual, and transgendered streetwalkers. Unless *you* are a streetwalker, *do not walk alone here, especially at night.* Witness the scene more safely by day and check out the surprisingly vibrant cultural offerings. The **509 Cultural Center/Luggage Store** presents performing arts events and exhibitions. (1007 Market St., near 6th St. ☎255-5971.) The small **Institute of International San Francisco Art** hosts student shows in its lobby. (1172 Market St. ☎865-0198.)

CIVIC CENTER AND HAYES VALLEY

CIVIC CENTER. Most of San Francisco's theater scene dominates the beautiful, majestic Civic Center. The palatial **San Francisco City Hall,** modeled after Rome's St. Peter's Basilica, is the centerpiece of the largest US gathering of Beaux Arts architecture. (1 Dr. Carlton B Goodlett Pl., at Van Ness Ave. ☎554-4000. Open M-F 8am-8pm, Sa-Su noon-4pm.) Overlooking the Civic Center, the grandeur of the **State Building** is comparable to City Hall's in both structure and function. Home to the state Supreme Court, it also features a small but interesting art collection in the lobby at the Golden Gate Ave. entrance and an exhibition room near the McAllister St. entrance. (350 McAllister St., between Polk and Larkin St. Open M-F 7:30am-5:30pm.) The seating in the glass-and-brass **Louise M. Davies Symphony Hall** was designed to give most audience members a close-up view of performers. Visually, the building is a smashing success, as is the San Francisco Symphony. (201 Van Ness Ave. ☎552-8000, tickets 864-6000. Open M-F 10am-6pm, Sa noon-6pm.) The recently renovated **War Memorial Opera House** hosts the well-regarded **San Francisco Opera Company** and the **San Francisco Ballet.** (301 Van Ness Ave., between Grove and McAllister St.)

HAYES VALLEY. Hayes Valley is the latest San Francisco neighborhood to come into its own. Artists of all types, from architects to fashion and interior designers, have begun to open studios on and around Hayes St. For the most part, the popularity and success of the area has been due to the community's talented artists, both of the culinary and visual sort. Success has also brought higher prices—starving artists are few and far between. The area has many art galleries; one of the best is the gallery operated by **San Francisco Women Artists.** Begun in the 1880s as a women's "Sketch Club," it has developed into a non-profit organization that supports and promotes Bay Area female artists. (370 Hayes St. ☎552-7392. Open Tu-W and F-Sa 11am-6pm, Th 11am-8pm. 2nd and 3rd Su of each month 1-4:30pm. Free.)

SOUTH OF MARKET AREA (SOMA)

The area's main draw is its fantastic collection of modern and contemporary art museums (see p. 843).

MISSION

MISSION DOLORES. Established over two centuries ago and located in the old heart of San Francisco, the Mission Dolores is thought to be the city's oldest building. The mission was founded in 1776 by Father Junípero Serra. Bougainvillea, poppies, and birds-of-paradise bloom in its cemetery, which was featured in Alfred Hitchcock's 1958 film *Vertigo.* (At 16th and Dolores St. ☎ 621-8203. Open May-Oct. daily 9am-4:30pm; Nov.-Apr. 9am-4pm. $2, ages 5-12 $1. Masses in English M-F 7:30, 9am; Sa 7:30, 9am, and 5pm; Su 8 and 10am. In Spanish Su noon.)

MISSION MURALS. A walk east or north along Mission St. from the 24th St. BART stop leads to the great murals of the Mission. Continuing the long mural-painting tradition brought to fame by Diego Rivera and José Orozco, the Mission murals have long been a source of pride for Chicano artists, schoolchildren, and community members. Standouts include: the more political murals of Balmy Alley, off 24th St. between Harrison and Folsom St.; a three-building tribute to guitar god Carlos Santana at 22nd St. and Van Ness Ave. (*Inspire to Aspire;* M. Rios, C. Gonzales, J. Mayorca; 1987); the face of St. Peter's Church at 24th and Florida St. (*500 Years of Resistance,* Isaias Mata, 1993); and the urban living center on 19th St. between Valencia and Guerrero St. The library leads free weekly tours of the Mission murals in summer, meeting at Precita and Harrison St., behind Flynn Elementary School on Saturdays at 11am. The library also offers general tours of the Mission highlighting the history of the neighborhood They begin at the gold fire hydrant on the southeast corner of Church and 20th St. (380 Bartlett St., at 24th St. Mission Branch. ☎ 695-5090. Library tours ☎ 557-4266. Free.)

OTHER SIGHTS. La Galeria de la Raza celebrates local Chicano and Latino artists with exhibitions and parties. Attached to the gallery is **Studio 24,** a space where Chicano and Latino artists sell artwork, crafts, and jewelry. (2857 24th St., between Bryant and Florida St. ☎ 826-8009. Open Tu-Su noon-6pm. Free.)

CASTRO AND NEARBY

THE CASTRO. Rainbow flags raised high, out and proud lesbian, gay, bisexual, and transgendered folk find comfort and fun on the streets here. The concept, as well as the reality, of an all-queer neighborhood draws queer tourists and their friends from around the world, pushing the already absolutely fabulous Castro scene over-the-top. The people out and about are the main attraction on the picture-perfect streets, and the shops are an added novelty. **Cruisin' the Castro** is a guided tour of the area. Trevor Hailey, a resident since 1972, is consistently recognized as one of San Francisco's top tour leaders. Her four-hour walking tours cover Castro life and history from the Gold Rush to the present. (☎ 550-8110. Tours Tu-Sa 10am. $40, includes lunch. Call ahead.) Shoppers, like queens, do *not* climb hills; thus, the steeply sloped areas to the south and west of Castro Village tend to be residential. The vibrantly painted old **Victorians** here are worth wandering for—Collingwood and Noe St. both have their share. For architecture without the walk, look for the faux-baroque **Castro Theatre,** 429 Castro St.

VIEWS. West of the Castro, the peninsula swells with several large hills. From **Twin Peaks,** between Portola Dr., Clarendon Ave., and Market St., are some of the most spectacular views of the city. On rare fogless nights, the views are particularly sublime. At the hulking three-masted radio tower, known by some as the Great Satan, a pair of red warning lights blink ominously beneath a Mephistophelean crown. Significantly south of the peaks is **Mount Davidson,** the highest spot in San Francisco at 938 ft. The 103 ft. concrete cross is the resilient replacement of two earlier versions destroyed by fire. (Off Portola Dr. Accessible by MUNI bus #36.)

HAIGHT-ASHBURY

All around Haight and Ashbury St., vestiges of the 60s exist in harmony with chain stores and boutiques. Music and clothing top the list of legal merchandise. Inexpensive bars and ethnic restaurants, action-packed street life, anarchist literature, and shops selling pipes for um, tobacco, also contribute to groovy browsing possibilities. While the **Upper Haight** tends to attract a younger tourist crowd, the **Lower Haight** is the stomping ground for longtime locals, though visitors are always welcome. Can't you just feel the love?

FAMOUS HOMES. The former homes of several counterculture legends survive beautifully. Starting at the corner of Haight and Ashbury St., walk up Ashbury St. to #710, just south of Waller St., to check out the house occupied by the **Grateful Dead** when they were still the Warlocks. Look across the street for the **Hell's Angels'** house. Walk back to Haight St., go right three blocks, and make a left on Lyon St., and you can check out **Janis Joplin**'s old abode. (*122 Lyon St., between Page and Oak St.*) Cross the Panhandle, and continue three blocks to Fulton St., turn right, and wander seven blocks toward the park to see where the Manson "family" planned murder and mayhem at the **Charles Manson** mansion. (*2400 Fulton St., at Willard St.*)

WALKING TOURS. The **Flower Power Walking Tour** explains the Haight's history and visits the sights. (*☎863-1621. 2½hr., Tu and Sa 9:30am, $15.*) The **San Francisco Public Library** offers a free walking tour focused on the area's pre-hippie incarnation as a Victorian-era resort. (*☎557-4266. Tours leave Su at 11am from the Park Branch Library at 1833 Page St., near Cole St.*)

OTHER SIGHTS. Several parks dot the Haight. You may see police lurking in the bushes—the parks are rumored to be great places to buy pot. **Buena Vista Park,** which runs along Haight St. between Central and Baker St. and continues south, resembles a dense jungle. An unofficial crash pad and community center for San Francisco skaters, Buena Vista is supposedly safer than **Alamo Sq.,** which lies northeast of the Haight at Hayes and Steiner St. Across Alamo Sq.'s gentle, grassy slope, a string of beautiful and brightly colored Victorian homes known as the **Painted Ladies**—subject of a thousand postcards—glow against the metropolitan skyline.

GOLDEN GATE PARK

Take your time to enjoy this park. Intriguing museums (see p. 844) and cultural events pick up where the lush flora and fauna finally leave off, and athletic opportunities abound. In addition to cycling and skating paths, the park also has a municipal golf course, an equestrian center, sports fields, tennis courts, and a stadium. On Sundays, traffic is banned from park roads, and bicycles and in-line skates come out in full force. The **Visitors Center** is located in the remodeled Beach Chalet on the Western edge of the park on the Great Hwy. (*☎751-2766. Open daily 9am-6pm.*) **Surrey Bikes and Blades in Golden Gate Park** rents equipment. (*50 Stow Lake Dr. ☎668-6699. Open daily 10am-dusk. Bikes from $6 per hr., $21 per day; skates $7 per hr., $20 per day.*)

GARDENS. Despite its sandy past, the soil of Golden Gate Park is rich enough to support a wealth of flowers. The **Garden of Fragrance** is designed especially for the visually impaired; all labels are in Braille and the plants are chosen specifically for their textures and scents. Near the Music Concourse off South Dr., the **Shakespeare Garden** contains almost every flower and plant ever mentioned by the Bard. Plaques with the relevant quotations are hung on the back wall, and there's a map to help you find your favorite hyacinths and rue. (*Open in summer daily dawn-dusk; in winter Tu-Su dawn-dusk. Free.*) The **Rhododendron Dell**, between the Academy of Sciences and John F. Kennedy Dr., honors John McLaren with a splendid profusion of his favorite flower. The **Japanese Cherry Orchard,** at Lincoln Way and South Dr., blooms intoxicatingly the first week in April. Created for the 1894 Mid-Winter Exposition, the elegant **Japanese Tea Garden** is a serene collection of wooden buildings, small pools, graceful footbridges, carefully pruned trees, and lush plants. (*☎752-4227. Open daily 8:30am-6pm. $3.50, seniors and ages 6-12 $1.25; free daily 8:30-9:30am and 5-6pm.*)

OTHER SIGHTS. Across JFK Dr. from the Conservatory, just south of **Lily Pond,** among the fragile, flowering dogwoods and giant redwoods of **De Laveaga Dell,** rests the **National AIDS Memorial Grove.** The grove is a site for remembrance and renewal, at once somber and rejuvenating. (*☎750-8340. Tours Th 9:30am-12:30pm starting at the Main Portal of the Grove, near the corner of Middle Dr. East and Bowling Green Dr.*) In the

CALIFORNIA

extreme northwest of the park, the **Dutch Windmill** has done its last good turn. Once the muscle behind the park's irrigation system, the outdated but renovated old powerhouse (114 ft. from sail to sail) is now the purely ornamental centerpiece of the cheery **Queen Wilhelmina Tulip Garden**. Rounding out the days of yore is the **carousel** (c. 1912), accompanied by a $50,000 Gebruder band organ. *(Open daily June-Sept. 10am-5pm; Oct.-May Tu-W and F-Su 9am-4pm. $1, ages 6-12 25¢.)* Brimming **Spreckels Lake**, on John F. Kennedy Dr., is populated by crowds of turtles who pile onto a turtle-shaped rock to sun themselves—it's turtles all the way down. A dozen **bison** loll about a spacious paddock just west of Spreckels.

LINCOLN PARK AND OCEAN BEACH

CLIFF HOUSE. The precarious **Cliff House**, built in 1909, is the 3rd of that name to occupy this spot—the previous two burned down. *(At the end of Pt. Lobos Ave./ Geary Blvd. in the southwest corner of Lincoln Park.)* Along with overpriced restaurants, the Cliff House hosts a **Camera Obscura**, the **Golden Gate National Recreation Area Visitors Center**, and the **Musée Mécanique**, an arcade devoted to games of yesteryear—not Donkey Kong, but wooden and cast-iron creations dating back to the 1890s. The ingenious and addictive games are accompanied by fortune tellers, love testers, "naughty" kinescopes, player pianos, and "Laughing Sal," a roaring mechanical clown. *(Camera Obscura: ☎750-0415. Open daily 11am-sunset, weather permitting. $2. Visitors Center: ☎556-8642. Open daily 10am-5pm. Musée Mecanique: ☎386-1170. Open daily in summer 10am-8pm; in winter M-F 11am-7pm, Sa-Su 10am-8pm. Free, but most games are 25¢.)*

LINCOLN PARK. The beaches and park at the western edge of Richmond offer more views and wanderings than works of art. The grounds around Lincoln Park, which include the **Coastal Trail,** offer a romantic view of the Golden Gate Bridge. Swimming is allowed but dangerous at scenic **China Beach** at the end of Seacliff Ave. on the eastern edge of Lincoln Park. Adolph Sutro's 1896 **bathhouse** lies in ruins on the cliffs. Cooled by ocean water, the baths were capable of squashing in 25,000 occupants at a time, but after an enthusiastic opening surge, they very rarely did. *(East of Cliff House. Paths lead there from Point Lobos Ave.)*

OCEAN BEACH. Ocean Beach, the largest and most popular of San Francisco's beaches, begins south of Point Lobos and extends down the northwestern edge of the city's coastline. The strong undertow along the point is very dangerous, but diehard surfers brave the treacherous currents and the ice-cold water anyway.

JAPANTOWN AND PACIFIC HEIGHTS

PEACE PAGODA AND SOKOJI BUDDHIST TEMPLE. Stores hawk the latest Pokemon paraphernalia and karaoke bars warble J-pop along Post St. around the Japan Center. The five-tiered Peace Pagoda, a gift to the community from the Japanese government, is in a featureless paved lot. A brighter example of Japanese architecture is the Sokoji Buddhist Temple, where some meditation services are open to the public. *(1691 Laguna St., at Sutter St. ☎346-7540. Public meditation services Su 8:30am, W and F 6:30pm. Arrive 15min. early.)*

PACIFIC HEIGHTS. Near Union and Sacramento St., Pacific Heights boasts the greatest number of **Victorian buildings** in the city. The **Octagon House Museum** was built in 1861 with the belief that the odd architecture would bring good luck to its inhabitants. Its survival of San Francisco's many earthquakes and fires is proof of fortune's favor, so far. *(2645 Gough St., at Union St. ☎441-7512. Open Feb.-Dec. 2nd Su and 2nd and 4th Th of each month noon-3pm. $3 suggested donation.)* Once you've hiked up the hills of Pacific Heights, reward yourself with a breather in **Alta Plaza**, where the colorful flowers and little grassy knolls just beg for a picnic. Alta Plaza, bounded by Jackson, Scott, Steiner, and Clay St., is indeed high and has great views of the surrounding neighborhoods.

🏛 MUSEUMS

FISHERMAN'S WHARF

Ripley's Believe It Or Not Museum, 175 Jefferson St. (☎771-6188), contains bizarrely fascinating documents, models, artifacts, and folklore from Robert Ripley's 19 trips around the world. Exhibits include giant hairballs, shrunken torsos, a self-portrait of Van Gogh made entirely of toast, and a video portraying the trials and tribulations of being a 8 ft. 11 in. man. Open mid-June to early Sept. Su-Th 9am-11pm, F-Sa 9am-midnight; early Sept. to mid-June Su-Th 10am-10pm, F-Sa 10am-midnight. $10, seniors $7.50, students $8, ages 5-12 $7, under 5 free.

Maritime Museum, (☎556-3002), at Beach and Polk St. across from Ghirardelli. The museum has enormous bathrooms as well as a quiet deck with a water view. The WPA-sponsored murals, painted in the 30s, depict the mythical lost continents of Mu and Atlantis. Open daily 10am-5pm. Free.

MARINA

🏛 **Exploratorium,** 3601 Lyon St. (☎563-7337). Declared "the best science museum in the world" by *Scientific American.* Displays include interactive tornadoes, computer planet-managing, and giant power-hungry bubble-makers. Open June-Aug. M-Tu and Th-Su 10am-6pm, W 10am-9pm; Sept.-May Tu and Th-Su 10am-5pm, W 10am-9pm. $9, seniors and students $7.50, disabled and ages 6-17 $6, ages under 4 free. 1st W of each month free. Be sure to visit the **Tactile Dome,** a pitch-dark maze designed to help refine your sense of touch. (☎561-0362. $12, includes museum admission.)

FORT MASON

Museum of Craft and Folk Art, Bldg. A (☎775-0991). This museum brings together a fascinating collection of past and present creations. Exhibits showcase everything from Papua New Guinean masks, African quilts, and Japanese fashion to local metalwork sculptures. Open Tu-F and Su 11am-5pm, Sa 10am-5pm. $3, seniors and students $1, under 12 free; families $5. Free Sa 10am-noon and 1st W of each month 11am-7pm.

African-American Historical and Cultural Society Museum, Bldg. C, #165 (☎441-0640). The African-American Historical and Cultural Society Museum displays historic artifacts and artwork as well as modern works. The museum also has a permanent collection by local artists. Open W-Su noon-5pm. $2, seniors and children $1.

NORTH BEACH

Lyle Tuttle's Tattoo Art Museum, 841 Columbus Ave. (☎775-4991). While the eminently professional Tuttle, himself covered in tattoos from head to foot, continues to tattoo behind the bar, the rest of the studio displays an impressive collection of tattoo memorabilia. Tattoos start at $60, but browsing is free. Open daily noon-9pm. Free.

North Beach Museum, 1435 Stockton St. (☎391-6210), at Columbus Ave. inside Bay View Bank, depicts the North Beach of yesteryear in a series of vintage photographs. Most of the photographs long predate the Beats, but a handwritten manuscript of Ferlinghetti's *The Old Italians Dying* is on display. Open M-Th 9am-5pm, F 9am-6pm. Free.

SOMA

Yerba Buena Center for the Arts, 701 Mission St. (☎978-2787). The center runs an excellent gallery space and vibrant programs, emphasizing performance, film, viewer involvement, and local multicultural work. It is surrounded by the **Yerba Buena Rooftop Gardens,** a huge expanse of concrete, fountains, and very intentional-looking foliage next to the huge Sony Metreon. Open Tu-Su 11am-6pm, Th-F 11am-8pm. $5, seniors and students $3; 1st Th of each month free 5-8pm.

ZEUM, 221 4th St. (☎777-2800), at Howard St. Within the Yerba Buena gardens but a sight unto itself, this recently opened "art and technology center" is aimed at children and teenagers. The best draw may be the reopened carousel, created in 1906 and back in SF after a 25-year hiatus. Open in summer W-F noon-6pm, Sa-Su 11am-5pm; off-season Sa-Su 11am-5pm. $7, seniors and students $6, ages 5-18 $5, under 5 free. **Carousel:** Open Su-Th 10am-6pm, F-Sa 10am-8pm. $2 for 2 rides.

San Francisco Museum of Modern Art (SFMOMA), 151 3rd St. (☎357-4000), between Mission and Howard St. This black-and-gray marble-trimmed museum houses five spacious floors of art, with an emphasis on design. SFMOMA also has the largest selection of 20th-century American and European art this side of New York. Open M-Tu and F-Su 11am-6pm, Th 11am-9pm. $9, seniors $6, students $5, under 12 free; Th 6-9pm half-price; free first Tu of each month. 4 free gallery tours per day.

Friends of Photography Ansel Adams Center, 555 Mission St. (☎495-7000), between 3rd and 4th St. Although the center only exhibits a small number of the master's photographs, rotating shows by other photographers complete one of the largest and best collections of art photography in the country. Open daily 11am-5pm. Open 11am-8pm on first Th of each month. $5, students $3, seniors and ages 13-17 $2, under 13 free.

GOLDEN GATE PARK

▨ **California Academy of Sciences,** on the east side of the park at 9th Ave. Houses several smaller museums specializing in different fields of science. The **Steinhart Aquarium,** home to members of over 600 aquatic species, is livelier than the natural history exhibits. The **Morrison Planetarium** re-creates the heavens above with impressive sky shows. Sky shows M-F 2pm, with additional summer showings. $2.50; seniors, students, and ages 6-17 $1.25. The **Laserium** offers evening laser shows set to music. $7, seniors and students $6, ages 6-12 $4. At the **Natural History Museum,** the Earthquake Theater shakes visitors, while the Far Side of Science Gallery pays tribute to Gary Larson. Open June-Aug. daily 9am-6pm; Sept.-May 10am-5pm. $8.50; seniors, students, and ages 12-17 $5.50; ages 4-11 $2. Free first W each month (open until 8:45pm).

LINCOLN PARK

California Palace of the Legion of Honor (☎863-3330), in the middle of Lincoln Park. A copy of Rodin's *Thinker* beckons visitors into the grand courtyard. A thorough catalogue of great masters, from medieval to Matisse, hangs inside. Other draws include a pneumatically operated 4500-pipe organ, played in weekly recitals (Sa-Su 4pm) and a gilded ceiling from a 15th-century *palacio* in Toledo, Spain. Open Tu-Su 9:30am-5pm. $8, seniors $6, under 17 $5, under 12 free. $2 discount with MUNI transfer.

▣ ENTERTAINMENT

MUSIC

S.F. Weekly (www.sfweekly.com) and the *S.F. Bay Guardian* (www.sfbg.com) are the places to start looking for the latest live music listings. Hardcore audiophiles might snag a copy of *Bay Area Music (BAM)*. Many of the bars and a few of the clubs listed above feature live bands at various times.

▨ **Bottom of the Hill,** 1233 17th St. (☎621-4455, ticket info 510-601-8932), between Missouri and Texas St. in Potrero Hill. Intimate rock club with tiny stage is the last, best place to see up-and-comers before they move to bigger venues. Cover $5-10. Open M-Th and Su 3pm-2am, Sa 8pm-2am.

▨ **The Fillmore,** 1805 Geary Blvd. (☎346-6000), at Fillmore St. south of Japantown. Bands that would pack stadiums in other cities are often eager to play at the legendary Fillmore. All ages. Tickets $15-25. Wheelchair accessible. Call for hours.

Boom Boom Room, 1061 Fillmore St. (☎673-8000), at Geary St. near Japantown. Don't miss this badass blues joint, often featuring big-name acts. Live music 7 nights a week, often with popular artists. Cover Tu $1, $20 for more well-known musicians. No cover W-M. Open daily 2pm-2am.

Justice League, 628 Divisadero St. (☎440-0409, info 289-2038), at Hayes St. in Hayes Valley. Live hip hop is hard to find in SF, but the Justice League fights ever onward for a good beat. Excellent variety of artists. 21+. Cover $5-25, usually $10-14. Usually open daily 9pm-2am.

San Francisco Opera, 301 Van Ness Ave. (☎864-3330), in the **War Memorial Opera House,** near the Civic Center. Open M-Sa 10am-6pm. Tickets start at $30; box office is at 199 Grove St. Discounted standing-room-only tickets on sale at the Opera House 2hr. before performances.

THEATER

☒ **Magic Theatre,** Bldg. D, 3rd fl. (☎441-8822), in Fort Mason. Today, the theater stages both world and American premieres. F-Sa $30, W-Th $25. Senior and student rush tickets ($8) are available 30min. before the show. Shows start at 8 or 8:30pm. Previews and Su matinees start at 2 or 2:30pm ($15). Call for exact times of individual shows. Box office open Tu-Sa noon-5pm.

Theater Artaud, 450 Florida St. (☎437-2700, box office 621-7797), at Mariposa St. in the Mission. Some of the best and most diverse contemporary theater and dance in the area. Box office open Tu-Sa 1-6pm and 1hr. before shows. Ticket prices depend on the show. Seniors and students $2 discount. Volunteer to usher and see the show for free.

Geary Theater, 415 Geary St. (☎749-2228), at Mason St. in Union Square. Home to the renowned **American Conservatory Theater.** Tickets $11-61 (cheaper for weekdays and previews). Box office open Tu-Sa noon-8pm, Su-M noon-6pm. Student, teacher, and senior discounts with ID. Wheelchair accessible.

Theatre Rhinoceros, 2926 16th St. (☎861-5079; open for reservations Tu and Sa 1-6pm), at Van Ness Ave. in the Mission. The oldest queer theater in the world. Box office open 1hr. before show.

The Orpheum, 1192 Market St. (☎551-2000), at Hyde St. near the Civic Center. This famous San Francisco landmark hosts the big Broadway shows. Individual show times and ticket prices vary.

SPECTATOR SPORTS

The **San Francisco Giants** (☎467-8000 or 800-734-4268) play baseball at the newly opened **Pacific Bell Park** in SoMa, near the water off Townsend St. The Giants' season is April to October. Most games sell out before the season even starts, except for 500 seats reserved for day-of-game sale. (Tickets $10-42. Tours of the park $10.) The five-time Super Bowl champion **49ers** (☎468-2249) still play at SF's old-time field—the notoriously windy **Candlestick Park** (☎467-1994). Now officially called **3Com Park,** the stadium is 8 mi. south of the city with its own exit off U.S. 101. MUNI bus #29 will also take you right there. Football pre-season starts in early August. The main season runs from September through the last Sunday in January (Super Bowl Sunday, but these days, the 49ers probably won't be playing in it). The Bay Area is also home to baseball's **Oakland A's,** basketball's **Golden State Warriors,** hockey's **San Jose Sharks,** and soccer's **San Jose Earthquakes.**

FESTIVALS

Some of San Francisco's more popular festivals: the **Cherry Blossom Festival,** Japantown (☎563-2313; Apr. 20-21 and 27-28); the **San Francisco International Film Festival,** the oldest film festival in America (☎561-5012; Apr.-May); **Pride Day** (☎864-3733; June 30); the **San Francisco Blues Festival,** Fort Mason, the oldest blues festival in America (www.sfblues.com; 3rd weekend in Sept.); the **Folsom Street Fair,** on Folsom St., leather and chains (☎861-3247; Sept. 29); **Halloween,** the Castro (Oct. 31); **Día de los Muertos (Day of the Dead),** the Mission (☎821-1155; Nov. 2); and **Chinese New Year Celebration and Parade,** Chinatown (☎982-3000; in Feb.).

CALIFORNIA

▼ NIGHTLIFE

Nightlife in San Francisco is as varied as the city's personal ads. Everyone from the "shy first-timer" to the "bearded strap daddy" to the "pre-op transsexual top" can find places to go on a Saturday (or Tuesday) night. The spots listed below are divided into bars and clubs, but the lines get pretty blurred in SF after dark, and many cafes hop at night as well. There are tons of hot spots in the city, and you're sure to find something that fits you like a warm leather glove. Ahem. Check out the nightlife listings in the *S.F. Weekly*, *S.F. Bay Guardian*, and *Metropolitan*. **Housewares,** 1322 Haight St. (☎252-1440), is a rave clothing store and a good source of flyers for parties and events. They maintain a rave hotline (☎281-0125). An online rave bulletin is accessible at www.hyperreal.org/raves/sf. The **Be-At Line** (☎626-4087), established by the son of Mayor Willie Brown, is a rundown of the night's most happening happenings, be they well-known or obscure. It's the only resource for many professional clubbers. *Unless otherwise noted, all clubs are 21+ only.*

BARS

▨ **Tonga Room,** 950 Mason St. (☎772-5278), in the Fairmont Hotel in Nob Hill. Go down 2 floors to level "T." A local favorite, this enormous tiki (and fabulously tacky) bar features faux bamboo, muumuu-clad waitresses, and huge fruity drinks ($8-11). Simulated tropical storms roll in every 30min. Happy hour (M-F 5-7pm) features $3-7 drinks and an all-you-can-eat Polynesian buffet ($6). Open Su-Th 5-11:45pm, F-Sa 5pm-12:45am.

▨ **Hotel Utah Saloon,** 500 4th St. (☎546-6300), at Bryant St. in SoMa. Excellent and unpretentious saloon, as well as a live music venue. One of the friendliest crowds around. Build your own burger (from $7). Live music nightly and one of the best open mics in the city on M. Beer $3.75. Show cover $5-7. Open M-Sa 11:30am-3pm for lunch; 8:30pm-2am for shows.

Place Pigalle, 520 Hayes St. (☎552-2671), between Octavia and Laguna St. in Hayes Valley. Relax on the vintage velvet sofas at this big, dark, and airy *établissement*. On weekend nights the wine flows, the music blares, and crowds of boho twenty- and thirty-somethings pack the place. Occasional DJs and a rotating art exhibit liven up the back room. Happy hour daily 4-7pm (beer and house wine $2.50). Open daily 4pm-2am.

Make Out Room, 3225 22nd St. (☎647-2888), between Mission and Valencia St. in the Mission. Replete with couches and a bed for make-out ease, this loft-style bar doubles as a live music venue. Local bands play M and Su nights, while bargoers kick back and shoot some pool. Open daily 6pm-2am. No credit cards.

The Irish Bank, 10 Mark Ln. (☎788-7152), in an alley off Bush St., between Grant and Kearny St. in Union Sq. Deposit yourself on a stool and invest in a hangover at San Francisco's "most authentic" Irish pub. Tu night whiskey tasting, Th 6pm-8pm Guinness special ($2.50), Su night free live music. Video-chat for free with other drinkers around the world in an Internet-wired confessional. Open daily 11:30am-2am.

CLUBS

▨ **Backflip,** 601 Eddy St. (☎771-35470), between Larkin and Polk St. in the Tenderloin. Hipsters dive into this blue and aqua urban oasis for kitsch, cool, and infamous poolside parties. Nightly sushi. Open Tu 9pm-2am, W-F 5pm-2am, Sa 7pm-2am. *Do not walk alone in the Tenderloin at night* (see p. 839).

238, 238 Columbus Ave. (☎402-0000), between Broadway and Pacific Ave. in North Beach. Men in black leather jackets and women in tube tops break it down to house (F-Sa) and urban groove (Th) on 238's small but swanky new dance floor. Proper dress. Cover $10-20 after 10:30pm. Open Th 10pm-2am, F-Sa 10pm-4am.

Velvet Lounge, 443 Columbus Ave. (☎788-0228), between Kearny and Montgomery St. Decked-out hipsters pack this club and thump along to Top 40, hip hop, and house. F live cover bands. Proper dress. Cover usually $10. Open F-Sa 9pm-2am.

Club Deluxe, 1509-11 Haight St. (☎552-6949), near Ashbury St. in the Upper Haight. At this small but swinging retro club, *femmes fatales* banter with mysterious strangers—

and that's just the bar staff. Shiny metal and bluish lights make everyone the star of their own 1940s film noir. Smoky jazz and other live music Th-Sa. Cover varies. Open M-Sa 3pm-2am, Su 1pm-2am. No credit cards.

Nickie's Barbecue, 460 Haight St. (621-6508), at Fillmore St. in the Lower Haight. One of the chillest, friendliest small clubs in the whole city, with a low cover and even less attitude. Live DJ every night with themes ranging from world music to hip hop to funk. Great dancing, diverse crowd. Cover ranges from $4-7 based on night and attraction. Open daily 9pm-2am. No credit cards.

GAY AND LESBIAN NIGHTLIFE

Politics aside, nightlife alone is enough to make San Francisco a gay mecca. From the buff gym boys in nipple-tight Ts to tattooed dykes grinding to NIN, there's something for everybody. The boys hang in the **Castro** (around the intersection of Castro and Market St.), while the girls prefer the **Mission** (on and off Valencia St.); both genders frolic along **Polk St.** (several blocks north of Geary Blvd.), and in **SoMa.** Polk St. can be seedy and SoMa barren, so keep a watchful eye for trouble. Most clubs and bars listed above are gay-friendly. *The Sentinel* offers information on gay community events. The free *Odyssey* and *Oblivion* are excellent guides.

The Café, 2367 Market St. (☎861-3846), in the Castro. The dance floor, balcony, and patio crowds rotate in a constant game of see-and-be-seen. Repeat *Guardian* awards for best gay bar. Open M-F 2pm-2am, Sa-Su 12:30pm-2am.

The Lexington Club, 3464 19th St. (☎863-2052), at Lexington St. in the Mission. Only bar in San Francisco that is all lesbian, all the time. Jukebox plays all the favorites (k.d. lang, Sleater-Kinney, Liz Phair). Open daily 3pm-2am. Happy hour M-F 4-7pm.

The Stud, 399 9th St. (☎252-7883), at Harrison St. in SoMa. Go Tu for the wild and wacky drag and transgendered parties known as "Trannyshack," Th for Reform School boy-cruising party, F for Doll House dykes. Crowd is mostly gay male. Cover around $5. Open 5pm-3am; Sa until 4am; Su until 3am.

The EndUp, 401 6th St. (☎357-0827), at Harrison St. in SoMa. Theme nights run from mostly straight KitKat Th to Fag F to Girl Spot Sa. Cover $5-10. Open W-F 10pm-4am; Sa morning GSpot until 4pm; Sa night 9pm-4am; infamous Su Tea Dance 5:30am-2am.

Esta Noche, 3079 16th St. (☎861-5757), at Valencia St. in the Mission. SF's premier gay Latino bar hosts regular drag shows, on stage and off. *Gringos* are asked to refrain from dancing salsa without instruction. Open Su-Th 1pm-2am, F-Sa 1pm-3:30am.

THE BAY AREA

BERKELEY ☎510

Famous as an intellectual center and a haven for iconoclasts, Berkeley (pop. 99,900) lives up to its well-founded reputation. Although its political activism peaked in the 1960s and 70s—when students attended more protests than classes—**UC Berkeley** continues to cultivate consciousness and brainy brawn, even if no longer as "Berserkeley" as it once was. **Telegraph Avenue,** the Champs-Elysées of the 60s, remains Berkeley's commercial and intellectual heart, home to street-corner soothsayers, hirsute hippies, and itinerant musicians who never quite moved on.

■ ☎ **ORIENTATION AND PRACTICAL INFORMATION.** Berkeley lies across the bay northeast of San Francisco, just north of Oakland. By car, take I-80 or Rte. 24. **Bay Area Rapid Transit (BART)** has two Berkeley stops. (☎465-2278. 20-30min. to downtown SF. $2.65.) **Alameda County (AC) Transit city buses** #15, 43, and 51 run from the Berkeley BART station to downtown Oakland. ($1; seniors, disabled, and ages 5-12 65¢; under 5 free. 1hr. transfers 25¢.) **Berkeley Convention and Visitors Bureau,** 2015 Center St., has area maps. (☎800-847-4823, 24hr. hotline 549-8710. Usually open M-F 9am-5pm.) **Post Office:** 2000 Allston Way (☎649-3100; open M-F 8:30am-6pm, Sa 10am-2pm). **ZIP code:** 94704.

ACCOMMODATIONS. There are surprisingly few cheap accommodations in Berkeley, though the **Berkeley-Oakland Bed and Breakfast Network** (☎547-7726; www.bbonline.com/ca/berkeley-oakland) coordinates some great East Bay B&Bs. A good option is to stay in San Fran and make daytrips to Berkeley. **UC Berkeley Summer Visitor Housing,** puts travelers up in **Stern Hall,** 2700 Hearst Ave. (☎642-5925; www.housing.berkeley.edu. Shared baths, free Internet access, local phone calls, games, and TV room. Parking $3 per day, laundry, and meals. Make reservations online. Open June to mid-Aug. Singles $50; doubles $64.) The **Capri Motel,** 1512 University Ave., offers clean, tasteful rooms with cable TV, A/C, and fridge. (☎845-7090. Must be 18+. In summer singles $55-70, off-season $45-50; doubles $70-100/$55-70.) The **YMCA,** 2001 Allston Way, has adequate co-ed rooms. (☎848-6800. Shared bath, pool and fitness facilities, phones. No curfew. 4-night max. stay; applications available for longer stays. Reception daily 8am-9:30pm. Must be 18+. Singles $38; doubles $65; triples $75.)

FOOD. The north end of **Telegraph Ave.,** with its high concentration of pizza joints and trendy cafes, caters to student appetites and wallets. If you've maxed out on caffeine and have a car, head out to **Solano Ave.** in Albany to the north for Asian cuisine or cruise down to **San Pablo Ave.** in the west for American fare. If you want to make your own meals, the best grocery shopping in the bay awaits at ◪**Berkeley Bowl,** 2777 Shattuck Ave., a former bowling alley filled with fresh produce, seafood, and bread. (☎843-6929. Open M-Sa 9:30am-8pm, Su 10am-6pm.) A great place for wining and dining, **Cesar,** 1515 Shattuck Ave., serves savory *tapas* ($4-10), *bocadillos* (a small sandwich on french bread; $5-7), and an extensive wine selection in a bright, clean, and crisp environment. (☎883-0222. Open daily 4pm-midnight; kitchen closes Su-Th 11pm, F-Sa 11:30pm. No reservations.) **Cafe Intermezzo,** 2442 Telegraph Ave., serves up heaping salads with homemade dressing, huge sandwiches on freshly baked bread, and tasty soups, all at delicious prices. Try the salad and sandwich combo for $4.25. (☎849-4592. Open M-F 10:30am-9pm; coffee from 8:30am. No credit cards.) **Ann's Soup Kitchen,** 2498 Telegraph Ave., is a perennial student breakfast favorite. Two eggs with toast or home fries run $3; the fresh-squeezed juice tastes like a million bucks but costs only $1.35. (☎548-8885. Open M and W-F 8am-6pm, Tu 8am-3pm, Sa-Su 8am-5pm. No credit cards.)

SIGHTS. In 1868, the private College of California and the public Agricultural, Mining, and Mechanical Arts College became one as the **University of California.** Berkeley was the first of the nine University of California campuses, so by seniority it has sole rights to the nickname "Cal." Pass through **Sather Gate** into **Sproul Plaza,** both sites of celebrated student sit-ins and bloody confrontations with police, to enter the 160-acre Berkeley campus. Maps of campus are posted everywhere; the **UC Berkeley Visitors Center,** 2200 University Ave., #101, also sells campus maps and offers campus tours which leave from the center Monday through Friday at 10am. (☎642-5215. Open M-F 8:30am-4:30pm. Tours Sa 10am and Su 1pm.) Tours leave from **Sather Tower,** the tallest building on campus. You can ride to its observation level for a great view. (Open M-F 8:30am-4:30pm. $1.)

The **Lawrence Hall of Science,** on Centennial Dr., atop the eucalyptus-covered hills east of the main campus, is one of the finest science museums in the Bay Area. Take bus #8 or 65 from the Berkeley BART station (and keep your transfer for $1 off admission) or a university shuttle (☎642-5149); otherwise it's a long, steep walk. (☎642-5132. Open daily 10am-5pm. $6; seniors, students, and ages 7-18 $4; ages 3-6 $2.) You haven't really visited Berkeley until you've been on **Telegraph Ave.** which runs south from Sproul Plaza all the way to downtown Oakland. The action is near the university, where Telegraph Ave. is lined with a motley assortment of cafes, bookstores, and used clothing and record stores.

When you're ready to get out of town, Berkeley is happy to oblige. Tilden Regional Park, in the pine- and eucalyptus-forested hills east of the city, is the anchor of the extensive East Bay park system. To get there by car or bicycle, take Spruce St. to Grizzly Peak Blvd., then to Canon Ave.; AC Transit buses #7 and 8 run from the Berkeley BART station. (☎635-0135. Open daily dawn-dusk.) Hiking, biking, running, and riding trails crisscross the park and provide impressive views of the Bay Area. The **ridgeline trail** is an especially spectacular bike ride. Within the park, a 19th-century carousel delights juvenile thrill-seekers. The small, sandy beach of **Lake Anza** is a popular swimming spot during the summer, often overrun with squealing kids. (☎ 848-3385. Open 11am-6pm. $3, seniors and children $1.50.)

▉▉ ENTERTAINMENT AND NIGHTLIFE. The university offers a number of quality entertainment options. Hang out with students in or around the **Student Union** (☎ 643-0693). **The Underground** hides a ticket office, an arcade, bowling alleys, foosball tables, and pool tables, all run from a central blue desk. (☎ 642-3825. Open M-F noon-8pm, Sa 10am-6pm.) **◪Caffè Strada**, 2300 College Ave., at Bancroft Way, is a glittering jewel of the caffeine-fueled intellectual scene. (☎ 843-5282. Open daily 6:30am-midnight.) **Jupiter**, 2181 Shattuck Ave., near the BART station, houses a huge beer garden and offers terrific pizza for $6. (☎ 843-8277. Open M-Th 11:30am-1am, F 11:30am-2am, Sa noon-2am, Su noon-midnight.) **924 Gilman**, 924 Gilman St., is a legendary all-ages club and a staple of California punk. (☎ 524-8180; 24hr. info 525-9926. Cover $5 with $2 membership card, good for 1 year and sold at the door.)

SAN JOSE   ☎ 408

In 1851, San Jose was deemed too small to be California's capital, and Sacramento assumed the honors. Today, San Jose is the civic heart of the Silicon Valley and the fastest-growing city in California. The FBI named it the third safest city in the country, and taking a trip to San Jose is like taking a trip through 50s suburbia.

▉▉ ORIENTATION AND PRACTICAL INFORMATION. San Jose lies at the southern end of San Francisco Bay, about 50 mi. from San Francisco (via U.S. 101 or I-280) and 40 mi. from Oakland (via I-880). San Jose is centered around the convention-hosting malls and plazas near the intersection of east-west **San Carlos St.** and north-south **Market St. San Jose International Airport** is at 1661 Airport Blvd. (☎ 277-4759). **Amtrak**, 65 Cahill St. (☎ 287-7462), runs to San Francisco (2hr., 1 per day, $13) and Los Angeles (10½hr., 1 per day, $45). **CalTrain**, 65 Cahill St. (☎ 291-5651 or 800-660-4287), at W. San Fernando, runs to San Francisco (1½hr.; every hr. M-F 5am-10pm, Sa 6:30am-10pm, Su 7:30am-10pm) with stops at peninsula cities. **Greyhound**, 70 S. Almaden, at Santa Clara, buses to San Francisco (1hr., $7) and Los Angeles (7hr., $40). **Bay Area Rapid Transit (BART)** (☎ 510-441-2278) goes to San Francisco (1¼hr., $4.50). The **Visitor Information and Business Center**, in the San Jose McEnerny Convention Center at San Carlos and Market St., has free maps. (☎ 977-0900, events line 295-2265. Open M-F 8am-5:30pm, Sa-Su 11am-5pm.) **Post Office:** 105 N. 1st St. (open M-F 9am-5:30pm). **ZIP code:** 95113. **Area code:** 408.

▉▉ ACCOMMODATIONS AND FOOD. San Jose is surrounded by county parks with campgrounds. The hamlet of **Saratoga**, 14 mi. southwest of San Jose on Rte. 85, has a number of campsites. (Open Apr. to mid-Oct. Sites $8; with hookup $25.) and miles of horse and hiking trails in wooded **Sanborn-Skyline County Park** (☎ 867-9959, reservations 358-3751), on Sanborn Rd. From Rte. 17 S, take Rte. 9 to Big Basin Way. Along the way sits **Saratoga Springs**, a private campground with 32 sites, hot showers, and a general store. (☎ 867-9999. Sites $25; with hookup $30.) **Sanborn Park Hostel (HI-AYH)**, 15808 Sanborn Rd., in Sanborn-Skyline Park, 13 mi. west of San Jose, has dorms. (☎ 741-0166. $10, US nonmembers $12, foreign nonmembers $13, under 18 $5.) **San Jose State University**, 375 S. 9th St., is open to visitors June and July. (☎ 924-6192. $26 per person in shared room. Dorm with 2 single beds $42.)

House of Siam, 55 S. Market St., serves excellent $7-10 meat and meatless dishes. (☎ 279-5668. Open M-F 11am-3pm and 5-10pm, Sa-Su 11:30am-10pm.) **White Lotus**, 80 N. Market St., between Santa Clara and St. John, is one of the few vegetarian restaurants in the area. (☎ 977-0540. Open M-Th 11am-2:30pm and 5:30-9pm, F-Sa 11am-9:30pm, Su noon-9pm.) A wacky jukebox suits the fly clientele of **The Flying Pig Pub**, 78 S. 1st St. This mega-chill bistro serves drinks from its full bar, as well as food. (☎ 298-6710. Open M 3pm-2am, Tu-F 11am-2am, Sa 4pm-2am.)

■ **SIGHTS.** The **Tech Museum of Innovation**, 201 S. Market St., in downtown San Jose, is the closest thing to a Silicon Valley tourist attraction. Underwritten by area high-tech firms, "the Tech" features hands-on exhibits on robotics, DNA engineering, and space exploration. (☎294-8324. Open daily 10am-5pm. $9; seniors, students, and ages 3-12 $7.) Science-based toys also grace the **Children's Discovery Museum**, 180 Woz Way. (☎298-5437. Open Tu-Sa 10am-5pm, Su noon-5pm. $6, seniors $5.) The **Rosicrucian Egyptian Museum**, 1342 Naglee Ave., rises out of the suburbs like the work of a mad pharaoh. (☎947-3635. Open Tu-Su 10am-5pm. $7, seniors and students $5, ages 6-15 $3.50. Under 15 must be accompanied by adult.)

PALO ALTO
☎650

Palo Alto looks a lot like "Collegeland" in a Disney-esque theme park. Jane and Leland Stanford founded the secular, co-educational **Stanford University** in 1885, to honor a son who died of typhoid on a family trip to Italy. The Stanfords loved Spanish architecture and collaborated with Frederick Law Olmsted, designer of New York City's Central Park, to create a red-tiled campus of uncompromising beauty. Berkeley students sometimes refer to Stanford as "the World's Largest Taco Bell." The oldest part of campus is the colonnaded **Main Quadrangle**, the site of most undergraduate classes. **Memorial Church** (☎723-1762), in the Main Quad, is a non-denominational gold shrine with stained glass windows and glittering mosaic walls like those of an Eastern Orthodox church. East of the Main Quad, the observation deck in **Hoover Tower** has views of campus, the East Bay, and San Francisco. (☎723-2053. Open daily 10am-5pm. $2, seniors and under 13 $1.) The **Iris and B. Gerald Cantor Center for Visual Arts**, on Museum Way off Palm St., displays its collection for free. (☎723-4177. Open W and F-Su 11am-5pm, Th 11am-8pm.)

Hidden Villa Ranch Hostel (HI-AYH), 26870 Moody Rd., is about 10 mi. southwest of Palo Alto in Los Altos Hills. (☎949-8648. Reception 7:30-9:30am and 4:30-9pm. Open Sept.-May. 35 beds. Dorms $10.) About half of Stanford's social life happens at **The Coffee House**, in Tresidder Union, the Stanford student center, in the heart of campus. (☎723-3592. Open Su-Th 9am-2am, F-Sa 9am-midnight.) The **Mango Cafe**, 435 Hamilton Ave., boasts reggae music, wicker chairs, and Caribbean cuisine. (☎325-3229. Open M-Th 6-9:30pm, F 11:30am-2pm and 6-10pm, Sa 6-10pm.)

Palo Alto is 35 mi. southeast of San Francisco, near the southern shore of the bay. From the north, take **U.S. 101** to the University Ave. exit, or take the Embarcadero Rd. exit directly to the Stanford campus. The **Junípero Serra Hwy. (I-280)** is a slightly longer but more scenic route. Palo Alto-bound trains leave from San Francisco's **CalTrain** station, at 4th and King. (M-F 5am-midnight, Sa 7am-midnight, Su 8am-10pm. Fare $3.25; seniors, disabled and children $1.75; off-peak $2.50.) The **Palo Alto Transit Center** on University Ave., serves local and regional buses and trains. (☎323-6105. Open daily 5am-12:30am.) There is a train-only depot on California Ave., 1¼ mi. south of the Transit Center. (☎326-3392. Open daily 5:30am-12:30am.) The Transit Center connects to points south via **San Mateo County buses** and to the Stanford campus by the free **Marguerite University Shuttle. Alto Chamber of Commerce:** 325A Forest Ave. (☎324-3121; open M-F 9am-noon and 1-5pm). **Stanford University Information Booth:** across from Hoover Tower in Memorial Auditorium. Free student-led tours depart daily 11am and 3:15pm; times vary on holidays and during exam periods. (☎723-2053 or 723-2560. Open daily 8am-5pm.) **Area code:** 650.

SAN MATEO COAST
☎650

The rocky bluffs of the San Mateo County Coast quickly obscure the hectic urban pace of the city to the north. Most of the energy here is generated by the coastal winds and waves. The Pacific Coast Hwy. (Rte. 1) maneuvers its way through a rocky shoreline, colorful beach vistas, and generations-old ranches. Although it's possible to drive quickly down the coast from San Francisco to Santa Cruz, taking it slow is infinitely more rewarding—and safer.

Half Moon Bay is an old coastal community 29 mi. south of San Francisco. Recent commercialization has not infringed much on this small, easygoing beach town. The fishing and farming hamlet of **San Gregorio** rests 10 mi. south of Half Moon Bay.

San Gregorio Beach is a delightful destination; you can walk to its southern end to find little caves in the shore rocks. (Open daily 8am-dusk. Day use $2.) The **Pigeon Point Lighthouse Hostel (HI-AYH)** is on Rte. 1, 6 mi. south of Pescadero and 20 mi. south of Half Moon Bay. (☎879-0633. Call ahead. Dorms $12, nonmembers $15; private rooms $22/$25.) **Point Montara Lighthouse Hostel (HI-AYH),** is on Lighthouse Point, 25 mi. south of San Francisco and 4 mi. north of Half Moon Bay. (☎728-7177. Dorms $13, nonmembers $16; 2-person rooms $12 extra.) **The Flying Fish Grill,** at Main St. and Rte. 92, serves cheap, airborne seafood straight from the coast. (☎712-1125. Open Tu-Su 11:30am-8:30pm; off-season until 7:30pm.) *The* spot for locals is the ⬛**San Gregorio General Store,** 7615 Stage Rd., 1 mi. east of Rte. 1 on Rte. 84, 8 mi. south of Half Moon Bay. This store has served San Gregorio since 1889 with an eclectic selection of hardware, cold drinks, groceries, gourmet coffee, cast iron pots, books, candles, and more. (☎726-0565. Open M-Th 9am-6pm, F-Su 9am-7pm.)

MARIN COUNTY   ☎415

Across the Golden Gate from SF, Marin County is the jacuzzi of the bay, bubbling with money-making and mantra-spouting residents. Physically beautiful, politically liberal, and stinking rich, Marin (*muh-RIN*) epitomizes California. The county's pleasure spots are easily accessible from San Francisco, whether traveling by car, bus, ferry, or bike. A web of trails combs the string of state and national parks and watershed land, welcoming mountain bikers and hikers in search of anything from a day's adventure to a two-week trek. And if the locals seem a little smug, well, why shouldn't they? The cathedral stillness of ancient redwoods, the sweet-smelling eucalyptus, the brilliant wildflowers, and the high bluffs and crashing surf along Rte. 1 are ample justification for civic pride.

▟ TRANSPORTATION

The Marin peninsula lies at the northern end of the Bay and is connected to the city by **U.S. 101** via the **Golden Gate Bridge.** U.S. 101 extends north and inland to Santa Rosa and Sonoma County, while **Rte. 1** winds north along the coast. The **Richmond-San Rafael Bridge** connects Marin to the East Bay via **Interstate 580.**

Buses: Golden Gate Transit (☎455-2000). M-F buses #20 and 50 serve Marin City and Sausalito from San Francisco's Transbay Terminal; Sa-Su buses #10 and 25 will take you there. $2.35, seniors and disabled $1.15, under 18 $1.75, under 6 free. Buses #20, 50 and 80 go to San Rafael ($2.95, seniors and disabled $1.45, under 18 $2.25, under 6 free).

Ferries: Golden Gate Ferry (☎455-2000) runs from San Francisco to the Sausalito terminal at the end of Market St. ($5.30, seniors and disabled $2.65, under 18 $4, under 6 free), and the Larkspur terminal (M-F $3.10, seniors and disabled $1.55, under 18 $2.35, under 6 free; Sa-Su $5.30, seniors and disabled $2.65, under 18 $4). No bike fees. **Blue and Gold Fleet** (☎773-1188, tickets 705-5555) runs ferries from Pier 41 at Fisherman's Wharf to Sausalito and Tiburon ($6.75, under 5 free).

▞ PRACTICAL INFORMATION

Visitor info: Marin County Visitors Bureau, 1013 Larkspur Landing Cir. (☎499-5000), off the Sir Francis Drake Blvd. Exit from U.S. 101. Open M-F 9am-5pm. **Sausalito Visitors Center,** 780 Bridgeway Ave. (☎332-0505). Open Tu-Su 11:30am-4pm.

Park Visitor info: Marin Headlands Visitors Center, Bldg. 948, Fort Barry, (☎331-1540), at Bunker and Field Rd. One of the best information centers in the Golden Gate National Recreation Area. Open daily 9:30am-4:30pm. **Point Reyes National Seashore Headquarters** (also known as **Bear Valley Visitor Center,** ☎464-5100), on Bear Valley Rd., ½ mi. west of Olema. Open M-F 9am-5pm, Sa-Su 8am-5pm.

Post Office: 150 Harbor Dr. (☎332-4656), at Bridgeway Ave., in Sausalito. Open M-Th 8:30am-5pm, F 8:30am-5:30pm. **ZIP code:** 94965. **Area code:** 415.

CALIFORNIA

ACCOMMODATIONS

Point Reyes Hostel (☎663-8811 or 800-909-4776, ext. 61), on the Point Reyes National Seashore. Exit west from Rte. 1 at Olema onto Bear Valley Rd. Take the 2nd left at Limantour Rd. (no sign indicates the turn) and drive 6 mi. into the park. Turn left at the first crossroad. 2 cabins occupy a site near Limantour Beach, wildlife areas, and hiking trails. Kitchen, barbecue, and cozy common room. Chores expected; must be finished by check-out. Linen $1, towels $1. Reception open 7:30-9:30am and 4:30-10pm. Check-in 4:30-10pm. Check-out. Reservations recommended. Dorms $13-15. Private room available for families with children under 5. Some wheelchair access.

Marin Headlands Hostel, Bldg. 941 on Rosenstock (☎331-2777 or 800-909-4776, ext. 62), up the hill from the Visitors Center. 2 spacious Victorian houses, with 100 beds, game room, kitchens, and common rooms. Internet access 20¢ per min. Linen $1, towels 50¢. Laundry $1.50. Key deposit $10. Check-in 3:30-10:30pm. Check-out 10am. Lockout 10am-3:30pm. Reservations recommended. 15 nights max. per year Dorms $15, under 17 (with parent) $7.50; private doubles $45; family rooms $45.

The Marin Headlands (☎331-1540), offers 3 small walk-in (100 yd. to 3 mi.) campgrounds with 11 primitive campsites for individual backpackers and small groups, as well as sites for large groups. In the backpack camps, picnic tables and chemical toilets are available. Bring your own water and camp stove. 3-day max. stay. Showers and kitchen ($2 each) at Headlands Hostel. Free outdoor cold showers at Rodeo Beach. Reserve up to 90 days in advance. For all campgrounds, individual sites are free with a permit that can be obtained at the Headlands Visitors Center. Group sites $20.

FOOD

Marinites take their fruit juices, tofu, and nonfat double-shot cappuccinos very seriously; restauranteurs know this, and raise both the alfalfa sprouts and the prices.

Sartaj Indian Cafe, 43 Caledonia St. (☎332-7103), 1 block from Bridgeway in Sausalito. Generous portions of excellent Indian food. Low prices (curries $8, massive samosas $2, sandwiches $4) are even lower on W nights when Sartaj features live music. Open daily 6:30am-9:30pm.

Cafe Reyes (☎663-9493), on Rte. 1 as you enter Point Reyes Station, just before Mesa St. Decorated like something out of a Spaghetti Western, this cafe serves burgers ($7), Mexican food, quality coffee ($1.50), beer, and wine. Open daily 11am-9pm.

SIGHTS

Marin's proximity to San Francisco makes it a popular daytrip destination. Virtually everything worth seeing or doing in Marin is outdoors. An efficient visitor can hop from park to park and enjoy several short hikes along the coast and through the redwood forests in the same day, topping it off with a pleasant dinner in one of the small cities. Those without cars, however, may find it easier to use one of the two well-situated hostels as a base for explorations.

SAUSALITO. Originally a fishing center full of bars and bordellos, the city at Marin's extreme southeastern tip has long since traded its sea-dog days for retail boutiques and overpriced seafood restaurants. **Bridgeway** is the city's main thoroughfare, and practically the only one shown on Sausalito Visitors Center maps. A block away from the harbor and Bridgeway's smug shops, **Caledonia St.** offers more charming restaurants and a few more affordable stores. Perhaps the best thing to see in Sausalito is the view of San Francisco. For the best views of the city, take the ferry (see **Ferries,** p. 851) or bike across the Golden Gate Bridge. North of the town center a half-mile is the **Bay Model,** a massive working model of San Francisco Bay. Built in the 1950s to test proposals to dam the bay and other diabolical plans, the water-filled model re-creates tides and currents in great detail. *(2100 Bridgeway. ☎332-3871. Open Tu-F 9am-4pm, Sa 10am-6pm; off-season Tu-F 9am-4pm. Free.)*

MARIN HEADLANDS. Fog-shrouded hills just to the west of the Golden Gate Bridge constitute the Marin Headlands. Its windswept ridges, precipitous cliffs, and hidden sandy beaches offer superb hiking and biking within minutes of downtown San Francisco. For instant gratification, choose one of the coastal trails, which offer easy access to dark sand beaches and dramatic cliffs of basalt greenstone. One of the best short hikes is to the lighthouse at **Point Bonita,** a prime spot for seeing sunbathing California sea lions in summer and migrating gray whales in the cooler months. The **Marine Mammal Center,** at Rodeo Beach, is dedicated to saving injured, sick, or orphaned marine mammals. (☎ 289-7325. Open daily 10am-4pm. Donation requested.) Also at Rodeo Beach, the **Golden Gate Raptor Observatory** studies the annual migration of thousands of hawks across the Marin Headlands each fall. (☎ 331-0730. Ideal hawk viewing Sept.-Oct. 10am-3pm.)

MT. TAMALPAIS, MUIR WOODS, AND THE COAST. Between the upscale towns of East Marin and the rocky bluffs of West Marin rests beautiful **Mt. Tamalpais State Park** (tam-ull-PIE-us). The park has miles of hilly, challenging trails on and around 2571 ft. Mt. Tamalpais, the highest peak in the county and the original "mountain" in "mountain bike." At the center of the state park is **Muir Woods National Monument,** a 560-acre stand of coastal redwoods. Spared from logging by the steep sides of Redwood Canyon, these centuries-old redwoods are massive and stand in silence. (On Rte. 1, 5 mi. west of U.S. 101. Monument open daily 8am-dusk; Visitors Center 9am-6pm. $2.) **Rte. 1** reaches the Pacific at Muir Beach and from there twists its way up the rugged coast. It's all beautiful, especially when driving south, on the sheer-drop-to-the-ocean side of the highway. Sheltered **Muir Beach** is scenic and popular with families. (Open daily dawn-9pm.) The crowds thin out significantly after a five-minute climb on the shore rocks to the left. Six miles to the north, **Stinson Beach** attracts a younger, rowdier crowd of good-looking surfer dudes and dudettes, though cold and windy conditions often keep them landlocked. (Open daily dawn-dusk.) A near-island surrounded by nearly 100 mi. of isolated coastline, the **Point Reyes National Seashore** is a wilderness of pine forests, chaparral ridges, and grasslands. Rte. 1 enters the park from the north or south; Sir Francis Drake Blvd. comes west from U.S. 101 at San Rafael. After a day or ten exploring the seashore, the little town of **Point Reyes Station** makes a welcoming dinner destination. (On Rte. 1, 2 mi. north of Olema.)

WINE COUNTRY

NAPA VALLEY ☎ 707

Napa catapulted American wine into the big leagues in 1976, when a bottle of red from Napa's Stag's Leap Vineyard beat a bottle of critically acclaimed (and unfailingly French) Château Lafitte-Rothschild in a blind taste test in Paris. While not the oldest, and not necessarily the best, the Napa Valley is certainly the best-known of America's wine-growing regions. The big wineries here draw a mostly older, well-to-do crowd, but there are still enough bargains that the young and budget-minded can both enjoy their fill of Chardonnay and a mud bath at the end of the day.

▐ TRANSPORTATION

Rte. 29 (St. Helena Hwy.) runs through the Napa Valley from **Napa** through **Yountville** and **St. Helena** to **Calistoga.** Slow with visitors stopping at each winery, the relatively short distance takes a surprisingly long, if scenic, time. The **Silverado Trail,** parallel to Rte. 29, is a less crowded route, but watch out for cyclists. Napa is 14 mi. east of Sonoma on **Rte. 12.** From the city, take U.S. 101 over the Golden Gate, then Rte. 37 E to Rte. 121 N, which will cross Rte. 12 N (to Sonoma) and Rte. 29 (to Napa). The nearest **Greyhound** station is in Vallejo, but one bus per day passes through the valley, stopping in Napa (6:15pm, Napa State Hospital, 2100 Napa-Vallejo Hwy.), Yountville, St. Helena, and Calistoga. **Public Transit: Napa City Bus,** or **Valley Intercity**

CALIFORNIA

Neighborhood Express (VINE), 1151 Pearl St., covers the Vallejo ($1.50, students $1.10, disabled 75¢) and Calistoga ($2/$1.45/$1); transfers are free. (☎255-7631 or 800-696-6443, TDD 226-9722. Buses run M-Sa 6am-8pm, Su 8am-5:30pm.) **Car Rental: Budget**, 407 Soscol Ave., Napa. (☎224-7846. Cars $43 per day; under 26 surcharge $20. Unlimited mi. Must be 21 with credit card.)

✴❓ ORIENTATION AND PRACTICAL INFORMATION

On weekends, Napa's roads are packed with cars from San Francisco. Although harvest (early Sept.) is the most exciting time to visit, winter weekdays provide space for personal attention. **Winery tours** are offered by **Napa Valley Holidays.** (☎255-1050. $75 per person.) **Visitor info: Napa Visitors Center**, 1310 Town Center (☎226-7459; open daily 9am-5pm, phones closed Sa-Su). **St. Helena Chamber of Commerce**, 1010A Main St. (☎963-4456; open M-F 10am-4:30pm). **Calistoga Chamber of Commerce**, 1458 Lincoln Ave. (☎942-6333; open M-Tu, Th, and Sa 10am-4pm). **Post office:** 1627 Trancas St., Napa (☎255-1268; open M-F 8:30am-5pm). **ZIP code:** 94558. **Area code:** 707.

❚ ACCOMMODATIONS

Rooms in Napa are scarce and go fast despite high prices. Camping is a good alternative, although the heat can be intense in summer.

▧ Calistoga Inn and Brewery, 1250 Lincoln Ave. (☎942-4101), at the corner of Rte. 29 in Calistoga. 18 clean, simple, double- and queen-sized rooms in an old Victorian house turned microbrewery and restaurant. Shared baths. Big breakfast included. Restaurant and bar open 11:30am-11pm. Rooms $65, Sa-Su and holidays $90.

Golden Haven Hot Springs Spa and Resort, 1713 Lake St. (☎942-6793), a few blocks from the main drag in Calistoga. More of a nice motel than a resort. Large standard-issue rooms, all with TVs and phones, and many with king beds, kitchenettes, jacuzzis, and saunas. Mineral swimming pool and hot tub. Weekends 2-night min., holiday weekends 3-night min. Apr.-Oct. $75-135; Nov.-Mar. M-Th $59-125.

Tall Timbers Chalet B&B, 1012 Darms Ln. (☎252-7810), off Rte. 29 in Yountville. Eight 2- to 6-person cottages, complete with homestyle kitchens and living rooms, around a secluded garden and waterfall. Great for families and rustic romantic getaways. Check-in 3pm. Check-out noon. Reserve well in advance, especially during summer. Mar.-Oct. $150 per 2 people per cottage, each additional person $20; Nov.-Feb. $105.

Napa Valley Budget Inn, 3380 Solano Ave. (☎257-6111), in Napa, near Redwood Rd. off Rte. 29. Clean rooms and a pool. TVs, phones, and free high-speed Internet ports in each room. Continental breakfast included. Rooms with 1 or 2 double beds May-Oct. $70-145; Nov.-Apr. $62-120. Wheelchair accessible.

Bothe-Napa Valley State Park, 3801 Rte. 29 (☎942-4575, reservations 800-444-7275), north of St. Helena. 50 sites near Ritchey Creek Canyon; 3 are wheelchair accessible. Hot showers (25¢) and pool ($1, under 17 free), otherwise fairly rustic. Check-in 2pm. $12, seniors $10. Picnic area day use $2. Park open daily 8am-dusk.

❐ FOOD

Eating in Wine Country ain't cheap, but the food is usually worth it. Picnics are an inexpensive and romantic option—supplies can be bought at the numerous delis or **Safeway** supermarkets in the area. Most wineries have shaded picnic grounds, often with excellent views. The **Napa Farmers Market**, at Pearl and West St., offers a sampling of the valley's *other* produce. (☎252-7142. Open daily 7:30am-noon.)

Curb Side Café, 1245 1st St. (☎253-2307), at Randolph St., in Napa. Sublime sandwiches $6-7. This diner-like cafe's heavy breakfasts include the pancake special: 2 buttermilk pancakes, 2 eggs, and ham or sausage ($7). Open daily 9am-4pm.

Calistoga Natural Foods and Juice Bar, 1426 Lincoln St. (☎942-5822), in Calistoga. One of few natural foods stores in the area. Organic juice and sandwich bar with vegetarian specialties like the Garlic Goddess ($5). Open M-Sa 9am-6pm, Su 10am-5pm.

TASTING 101 While European wines are often known by their region of origin, California wines are generally known by the type of grape from which they are made. California **white** wines include Chardonnay, Riesling, and Sauvignon Blanc; **reds** are Pinot Noir, Merlot, Cabernet Sauvignon, and Zinfandel, which is indigenous to California. **Blush** or **rosé** wines issue from red grapes that have had their skins removed during fermentation—to leave just a kiss of pink. **Dessert** wines, such as Muscat, are made with grapes that have acquired the "noble rot" *(botrytis)* at the end of picking season, giving them an extra-sweet flavor. When tasting, be sure to follow proper procedures. Always start with a white, moving from **dry** to **sweet**. Proceed through the reds, which go from **lighter** to more **full-bodied,** depending on tannin content. You should cleanse your palate between wines with a biscuit, some *fromage,* or fruit. Tasting proceeds thus: stare, sniff, swirl, swallow (first three steps are optional). Feel free to banter about the following words during tasting sessions: dry, sweet, buttery, light, crisp, fruity, balanced, rounded, subtle, rich, woody, and complex.

Taylor's Refresher, 933 Main St. (☎963-3486), on Rte. 29 across from the Merryvale Winery, in St. Helena. A roadside stand dishing up big burgers ($5, vegetarian $6) and stellar milkshakes ($3.75) since 1949. Outdoor seating only. Open daily 11am-9pm.

⚡ WINERIES

There are more than 250 wineries in Napa County, nearly two-thirds of which line Rte. 29 and the Silverado Trail in the Napa Valley. Wine Country's heavyweights call this valley home; vineyards include national names such as Inglenook, Fetzer, and Mondavi. Some wineries have free tastings, some have free tours, and all have large selections of bottled wine available for purchase. A good way to begin your Napa Valley experience is with a tour, such as the one at **Domaine Carneros,** or a free tastings class, like the one offered on Saturday mornings at **Goosecross Cellars.**

■ Domaine Carneros, 1240 Duhig Rd. (☎257-0101), off Rte. 121 between Napa and Sonoma. Picturesque estate with an elegant terrace modeled after a French chateau. Free tour and film is a great first-stop for a day of wine-tasting. No tastings, but wines by the glass $5-9 with complimentary *hors d'oeuvres.* Open daily 10:30am-6pm.

Goosecross Cellars, 1119 State Ln. (☎944-1986), off Yountville Cross Rd. north of Yountville. Small and friendly winery is still in its natural state, nestled among the vineyards. The winemaker is always on site, and the tasting room is directly inside the production room. Free wine basics class Sa 11am. Tastings daily 10am-5pm ($3).

Robert Mondavi Winery, 7801 Rte. 29 (☎963-9611 or 800-766-3284), 8 mi. north of Napa. If you are looking to hit one massive, tourist-happy winery, this is it. Beautiful mission-style visitors complex, with 2 tasting rooms ($4-8) and a resort atmosphere. Some of the best tours in the valley cover subjects from tasting to soil conditions. Tours daily on the hour 10am-4pm; reserve 1hr. in advance; $10. Open daily 9am-5pm.

V. Sattui, 1111 White Ln. (☎963-7774 or 800-799-2337), at Rte. 29 in St. Helena. One of the best kept secrets of Napa Valley, V. Sattui is one of the few wineries in the nation that only sells at its winery. The family-owned operation has a friendly staff and a fabulous gourmet cheese and take-out shop. Picnic area. Free tastings. Open daily Mar.-Oct. 9am-6pm; Nov.-Feb. 9am-5pm.

◉ 🏔 SIGHTS AND OUTDOORS

CALISTOGA. After a hard day of wine-tasting, the rich and relaxed converge on Calistoga, the "Hot Springs of the West," to revel in mud baths, massages, and mineral showers. Standard treatment is a 30min. massage with an additional mud treatment and mineral wrap. Prices are as high as the water temperatures, hitting $80 in many spas. Massage your wallet by sticking to **Nance's Hot Springs.** (☎*942-6211. 30min. massage $25.)* **Golden Haven,** which specializes in private couple baths, is known to be one of the less pretentious. (☎ 942-6793. 30min. massages $45, 30min. facials $45; also has hot springs.) Cooler water is at **Lake Berryessa** where swimming, sailing, and sunbathing are popular along its 169 mi. shoreline. (20 mi. north of Napa, off Rte. 128. ☎ 966-2111.) If you tire of being pampered, the **Sharpsteen Museum** will educate you with exhibits detailing Calistoga's history. (1311 Washington St. ☎ 942-5911. Open daily 10am-4pm; in winter noon-4pm. Free.)

OLD FAITHFUL GEYSER OF CALIFORNIA. This steamy wonder should not be confused with its more famous namesake in Wyoming, although it performs similarly—it's one of only three faithful geysers in the world. The geyser regularly jets boiling water 60 ft. into the air; although it "erupts" about every 40min., weather conditions affect its cycle. The ticket vendor will tell you the estimated time of the next spurt. (On Tubbs Ln. off Rte. 128., 2 mi. outside Calistoga. ☎ 942-6463. Open daily 9am-6pm; in winter 9am-5pm. $6, seniors $5, disabled free, ages 6-12 $2.)

ST. HELENA. The hike up **Mt. St. Helena,** named by the Russian settlers who canvassed the area in the mid-19th century, is a moderate 3hr. climb culminating in dizzying views of the valley. There is no ranger station or facilities; bring water. (Open daily 8am-dusk.) **Robert Louis Stevenson State Park** is a nice picnic alternative for those feeling sick and penniless after a jaunt through the wineries. The beautiful park features a plaque where the Scottish writer, sick and penniless, spent a rejuvenating honeymoon in 1880. (On Rte. 29, 4 mi. north of St. Helena. ☎ 942-4575.) The **Silverado Museum** is a labor of love created by a devoted collector of Stevensoniana. Manuscript notes from *Dr. Jekyll and Mr. Hyde* number among the more memorabilia. (1490 Library Ln., off Adams St. ☎ 963-3757. Open Tu-Su noon-4pm. Free.)

BIKING. Napa's gentle terrain makes for an excellent bike tour. The area is fairly flat, although small bike lanes, speeding cars, and blistering heat can make routes more challenging, especially after several samples of wine. The 26 mi. **Silverado Trail** has a wider bike path than Rte. 29. **St. Helena Cyclery** rents bikes. (1156 Main St. ☎ 963-7736. $7 per hr., $25 per day; includes maps, helmet, lock, and picnic bag. Open M-Sa 9:30am-5:30pm, Su 10am-5pm.)

SEASONAL EVENTS. The annual **Napa Valley Wine Festival** takes place in November. Every weekend in February and March the **Mustard Festival** puts together a different musical or theatrical presentation. **Napa Valley Fairgrounds** hosts a weekend fair in August, with wine tasting, music, juggling, rides, and a rodeo. (☎ 942-5111.) In summer, there are free afternoon concerts at **Music-in-the-Park,** downtown at the riverfront. Contact **Napa Parks and Recreation Office** for more info. (☎ 257-9529.)

SONOMA VALLEY ☎ 707

Sprawling Sonoma Valley is a quieter alternative to Napa. Wineries are approachable by winding side roads rather than down a freeway strip, creating a more intimate wine-tasting experience. Charming Sonoma Plaza is surrounded by art galleries, novelty shops, clothing stores, and Italian restaurants. Distinguished by its odd mix of architecture, the town features nearly every 20th-century genre. Petaluma, west of the Sonoma Valley, has a better variety of budget lodgings than the expensive wine country.

▆ TRANSPORTATION

From San Francisco, take **U.S. 101 N** over the Golden Gate Bridge, then follow Rte. 37 East to Rte. 121 N, which crosses Rte. 12 North to Sonoma. Alternatively, follow U.S. 101 N to Petaluma, then cross over to Sonoma by Rte. 116. Allow 1 to 1½ hours from San Francisco. **Rte. 12** traverses the length of Sonoma Valley, from **Sonoma** through **Glen Ellen** to **Kenwood** in the north. The center of downtown Sonoma is **Sonoma Plaza,** which contains City Hall and the Visitors Center. **Broadway** dead-ends in front of City Hall at Napa St. Numbered streets run north-south. **Petaluma** lies to the west and is connected to Sonoma by **Rte. 116,** which becomes **Lakeville St.**

Public Transit: Sonoma County Transit (☎576-7433 or 800-345-7433) serves the entire county. Bus #30 runs from Sonoma to Santa Rosa every 30min. Runs M-F, reduced service Sa-Su. $2.30, students $1.90, seniors and disabled $1.15, under 6 free. Bus #40 goes to Petaluma M-F. $1.70, students $1.40, seniors and disabled 85¢. Within Sonoma, county buses stop when flagged down at designated bus stops. Buses run M-F 7am-6pm. 90¢, students 70¢, seniors and disabled 45¢. **Golden Gate Transit** (☎541-2000 from Sonoma County or 415-923-2000 from San Francisco, TDD 257-4554) runs buses frequently between SF and Santa Rosa. **Volunteer Wheels** (☎800-992-1006) offers door-to-door service for people with disabilities. Call for reservations. Open daily 8am-5pm.

Bike Rental: Sonoma Valley Cyclery, 20093 Broadway (☎935-3377), in Sonoma. Bikes $6 per hr., $25 per day; includes helmet. Open M-Sa 10am-6pm, Su 10am-4pm.

🛈 PRACTICAL INFORMATION

Visitor info: Sonoma Valley Visitors Bureau, 453 E. 1st St. (☎996-1090), in Sonoma Plaza. Maps $2. Open June-Oct. daily 9am-7pm; Nov.-May 9am-5pm. **Petaluma Visitors Program,** 799 Baywood Dr. (☎769-0429), at Lakeville St. Open May-Oct. M-F 9am-5:30pm, Sa-Su 10am-6pm; shorter hours off-season. The free visitor's guide has handy listings of restaurants and activities.

Post Office: 617 Broadway (☎800-275-8777), at Patten St., in Sonoma. Open M-F 8:30am-5pm. **ZIP code:** 95476. **Area code:** 707.

🏠 ACCOMMODATIONS

Pickings are pretty slim for lodging; rooms are scarce even on weekdays and generally start at $75. Cheaper motels cluster along **U.S. 101** in Santa Rosa and Petaluma.

Motel 6, 1368 N. McDowell Blvd. (☎765-0333), off U.S. 101, in Petaluma. Spacious and tastefully decorated. Cable TV. Well-maintained pool open 9am-9pm. Check-out noon. Reservations recommended weekends. Singles M-Th and Su $47, F-Sa $52; doubles $53/$58. Each additional adult $3. Under 17 free with family.

Sugarloaf Ridge State Park, 2605 Adobe Canyon Rd. (☎833-5712), off Rte. 12, north of Kenwood. 50 sites around a central meadow with flush toilets and running water, but no showers. Sites $12, seniors $10. Reserve through ReserveAmerica (☎800-444-7275; www.reserveamerica.com).

San Francisco North/Petaluma KOA, 20 Rainsville Rd. (☎763-1492 or 800-992-2267), in Petaluma off the Penngrove exit. Suburban camp with 300 sites plus a recreation hall, a petting zoo, a pool, a store, laundry, and a jacuzzi. Hot showers. Check-in 1pm. Check-out 11am. Max. tent stay 1 week. Reservations recommended. 2-person tent sites $31; each additional adult $5, child $3. RVs $36-38. Kabins $49.

🍴 FOOD

Fresh produce is seasonally available directly from area farms or at roadside stands and Farmers Markets. *Farm Trails* maps are free at the Sonoma Valley Visitors Bureau. The **Sonoma Market,** 520 W. Napa St., in the Sonoma Valley Center, is an old-fashioned grocery store with deli sandwiches ($4-6) and *very* fresh produce. (☎996-0563. Open daily 6am-9pm.)

Sonoma Cheese Factory, 2 Spain St. (☎996-1931 or 800-535-2855), in Sonoma. Forget the wine for now—take a toothpick and enjoy the free cheese samples. You can even watch the cheese-making process in the back room...ewww. Open daily 9am-6pm.

Quinley's, 310 D St. (☎778-6000), in Petaluma. This hugely popular burger counter first served slow fast food in 1946. The burgers of the best and the brightest are prepared at geriatric speed. Outdoor bar and picnic tables. Burgers $4-5; 4-scoop shake or malt $3. Open daily 11am-9pm. No credit cards.

WINERIES

Sonoma Valley's wineries, near Sonoma and Kenwood, are less touristy but just as elegant as Napa's. As an added bonus, most of the tastings in the Sonoma Valley are complimentary. Near Sonoma, white signs will help guide you through backroads. They are difficult to read but indicate the wineries' general directions. Bring a map along on the ride (they're all over the place and free), as the signs will often desert you when they're most needed.

Gundlach-Bundschu, 2000 Denmark St. (☎938-5277). Established in 1858, Gundlach-Bundschu is the second oldest winery in Sonoma and the oldest family-owned and run winery in the country. Cave and winery tours Sa-Su on the hour, the rest of the week by appointment. Free tastings. Outdoor Shakespeare performances during the summer (☎588-3400). Open daily 11am-4:30pm (and during performances).

Buena Vista, 18000 Old Winery Rd. (☎252-7117), off E. Napa St. in Sonoma. The oldest winery in the valley. Famous stone buildings are preserved just as Mr. Haraszthy built them in 1857 when he founded the California wine industry. Theater shows July-Sept. Historical presentations in summer at 2pm. Free tastings daily 10:30am-5pm.

Benziger, 1833 London Ranch Rd. (☎935-4046 or 888-490-2379). Tourists flock here for the acclaimed free tram ride. Self-guided tours lead from the parking lot through the vineyards and peacock aviary. Reserve tickets early for the tram tours, which run at 11:30am, 12:30, 1:30, 2, 3, and 3:30pm. Free tastings. Open daily 10am-5pm.

Kunde, 10155 Sonoma Hwy. (☎833-5501), near Kenwood. On hot afternoons, the cave tours at Kunde offer a cool break from the California sun. Known for its Chardonnays. Free tastings. Open daily 10:30am-4pm.

◉ SIGHTS

SONOMA STATE HISTORIC PARK. Within the park, an adobe church stands on the site of the **Mission San Francisco-Solano,** the northernmost and last of the 21 Franciscan missions. It marks the end of El Camino Real, or the "Royal Road." Built in 1826 by Padre Jose Altimira, the mission houses a fragment of the original California Republic flag, the rest of which was burned in the 1906 post-earthquake fires. (*E. Spain and 1st St., in the northeast corner of town. ☎938-9560. Open daily 10am-5pm. $1, children under 16 free; includes Vallejo's Home, the barracks, and Petaluma Adobe.*)

JACK LONDON STATE PARK. Around the turn of the 20th century, hard-drinking and hard-living Jack London, author of *The Call of the Wild* and *White Fang,* bought 1400 acres here, determined to create his dream home. London's hopes were frustrated when the estate's main building, the Wolf House, was destroyed by arsonists in 1913. London died three years after the fire and is buried in the park. The nearby House of Happy Walls, built by his widow, is now a two-story museum devoted to the writer. The park's scenic half-mile Beauty Ranch Trail passes the lake, winery ruins, and quaint cottages. (*Take Rte. 12 4 mi. north from Sonoma to Arnold Ln. and follow signs. ☎938-5216. Park open daily 9:30am-7pm; in winter 9:30am-5pm. Museum open daily 10am-5pm.*) Sonoma Cattle and Napa Valley Trail Rides also amble through the fragrant forests. (*☎996-8566. 2hr. ride $45.*)

SEASONAL EVENTS. Sonoma Plaza hosts festivals and fairs nearly every summer weekend. **Kenwood** heats up July 4, when runners gather for the Kenwood Footrace, a tough 7½ mi. course through hills and vineyards. A chili cook-off and the **World Pillow Fighting Championships** pass the rest of the day. Eager contenders straddle a metal pipe over a mud pit and beat the hell out of each other with wet pillows.

NORTHERN CALIFORNIA

MENDOCINO   ☎707

Perched on oceanside bluffs, isolated Mendocino is a stylish coastal community of art galleries, craft shops, bakeries, and B&Bs. The town's weathered wooden shingles, sloping roofs, and clustered homes seem out of place on the West Coast.

▨▨ ORIENTATION AND PRACTICAL INFORMATION. Mendocino sits on **Rte. 1**, right on the Pacific Coast, 30 mi. west of U.S. 101 and 12 mi. south of Fort Bragg. Although driving is the best way to reach Mendocino, once there the tiny town is best explored on foot (plentiful street parking available). Given Mendocino's 40-70°F weather, travelers should prepare for the chill of coastal fog.

The nearest **bus station** is 2hr. away in Ukiah. **Greyhound** runs two buses per day to Ft. Bragg. **Mendocino Stage** (☎964-0167) runs buses between Ft. Bragg and Ukiah (2 per day, $10). **Mendocino Transit Authority**, 241 Plant Rd. makes one round-trip daily between Santa Rosa, Ukiah, Willits, Fort Bragg, and Mendocino. (☎800-696-4682. $16.) **Fort Bragg Door-to-Door Taxis** has an on-call passenger van service. (☎964-8294. Operates daily 10am-2am.) For visitor info, contact the **Ford House**, 735 Main St. (☎937-5397. Open in summer daily 11am-4pm.) For **parks info,** call 937-5804, or visit **Russian Gulch Park,** on the west side of Rte. 1. (Open daily 5am-10pm.) **Catcha Canoe and Bicycles, Too!**, at Rte. 1 and Comptche Rd., rents top-quality bikes, canoes, and kayaks. (☎937-0273. Open daily 9am-5:30pm.) **Lost Coast Kayaking** gives great guided tours. (☎937-2434. $45 per person; call 24hr. in advance.) **Post Office:** 10500 Ford St. (☎937-5282; open M-F 7:30am-4:30pm). **ZIP code:** 95460. **Area code:** 707.

▨▨ ACCOMMODATIONS. It's impossible to find a hotel room in Mendocino for under $60. Fortunately, hundreds of campsites are nearby. More comfortable but less convenient, nearby Ukiah and Fort Bragg have budget motels. **Jug Handle Creek Farm,** 5 mi. north of Mendocino off Rte. 1 before the Caspar exit, is a beautiful old house sitting on 40 acres of gardens, campsites, and small rustic cabins. Guests have access to Jug Handle State Park, including beaches and trails. (☎964-4630. 30 beds. No linen. 1hr. of chores or $5 required per night. Dorms $18, students $12, children $4; sites $8. Cabins $25 per person. Reserve in advance.) **MacKerricher State Park Campground,** 3½ mi. north of Ft. Bragg, has excellent views of tide pool life, passing seals, sea lions, and migratory whales, as well as 9 mi. of beaches and a murky lake for trout fishing. (☎937-5804. Showers, bathrooms, and water. Sites $16; day use free. Reservations recommended.)

◖ FOOD. All of Mendocino's breads are freshly baked, all vegetables locally grown, all wheat unmilled, all coffee cappuccino, and almost everything expensive. Most restaurants close at 9pm. Picnicking on the Mendocino Headlands is the cheapest option and should be preceded by a trip to **Mendosa's Market,** 10501 Lansing St., the closest thing in Mendocino to a real supermarket. It's pricey (of course), but most items are fresh and delicious. (☎937-5879. Open daily 8am-9pm.) **Tote Fête,** 10450 Lansing St., has delicious tote-out food, and the crowds know it. An asiago, pesto, and artichoke heart sandwich ($4.25) hits the spot. (☎937-3383. Open M-Sa 10:30am-7pm, Su 10:30am-4pm; bakery open daily 7:30am-4pm.)

◳ SIGHTS. Mendocino's greatest attribute lies 900 ft. to the west, where the earth comes to a halt and falls off into the Pacific, forming the impressive fog-shrouded coastline of the **▨Mendocino Headlands.** Beneath wildflower-laden meadows, fingers of eroded rock claw through the pounding ocean surf and seals frolic in secluded alcoves. In **Fort Bragg,** the **Skunk Train,** at Rte. 1 and Laurel St., offers a jolly, child-friendly diversion through deserted logging towns and a recuperating forest. (☎964-6371 or 800-777-5865. 9:45am, 2:30pm; off-season 9:45am, 1:45pm.) A steam engine, diesel locomotive, and vintage motorcar take turns running between Fort Bragg and Willits via Northspur, with full- and half-day trips available. Schedule changes make it necessary to call ahead for reservations.

AVENUE OF THE GIANTS   ☎707

About 6 mi. north of Garberville off U.S. 101, the Avenue of the Giants winds its way through 31 mi. of the largest living creatures this side of sea level. Scattered throughout the area are several commercialized attractions such as the **World Famous Tree House, Confusion Hill,** and the **Drive-Thru Tree.** Travelers looking for a more authentic taste of the redwood forests may want to bypass these hokey attractions in favor of more rugged and natural tours. There are a number of great hiking trails in the area, marked on free brochures available at the **Humboldt Redwoods State Park Visitors Center,** just south of Weott on the Avenue. (☎946-2263. Open daily 9am-5pm; Nov.-Mar. Th-Su 10am-3pm.) The **Canoe Creek Loop Trail,** across the street from the Visitors Center, is an easy start. Uncrowded trails snake through the park's northern section around **Rockefeller Forest,** which contains the largest grove of old-growth redwoods (200 years and growing) in the world. The **Dyerville Giant,** in the redwood graveyard at Founder's Grove about midway through the Avenue, deserves a respectful visit. The ½ mi. loop trail includes the **Founder's Tree** and the **Fallen Giant,** whose massive trunk stretches 60 human body-lengths long and whose three-story rootball looks like a mythical ensnarlment of evil. The **Standish Hickey Recreation Area,** north of Leggett on U.S. 101, offers fishing, camping, swimming, and hiking. (☎925-6482. Camping $12, seniors $8; day use $2.)

With its sizable artist population, Garberville's art festivals are a big draw. **Jazz on the Lake** and the **Summer Arts Fair** begin in late June, followed by **Shakespeare at Benbow Lake** in late July. Early August brings **Reggae on the River,** a three-day music fest on the banks of the Eel River. **Visitor info: Chamber of Commerce,** 773 Redway (☎800-923-2613), in Garberville. **Area code:** 707.

REDWOOD NATIONAL PARK   ☎707

With ferns that grow to the height of humans and redwood trees the size of skyscrapers, Redwood National Park, as John Steinbeck said, "will leave a mark or create a vision that stays with you always." The redwoods in the park are the last remaining stretch of the old-growth forest that once blanketed two million acres of Northern California and Oregon. Wildlife runs rampant here, with black bears and mountain lions in the backwoods and Roosevelt elk grazing in the meadows.

▓ PRACTICAL INFORMATION

Redwood National Park is only one of four redwood parks between Klamath and Orick, the others being **Jedediah Smith State Park, Del Norte Coast Redwoods State Park,** and **Prairie Creek Redwoods State Park.** The name "Redwood National Park" is an umbrella term for all four parks.

Buses: Greyhound, 500 E. Harding St. (☎464-2807), in Crescent City. To San Francisco (2 per day, $55-61) and Portland (2 per day, $55-61). Open M-F 7-10am and 5-7:30pm, Sa 7-9am and 7-7:30pm. No credit cards.

Visitor info: Redwood Info Center (☎464-6101, ext. 5265), on U.S. 101, 1 mi. south of Orick. Shows free films on redwoods, gray whales, and black bears. Free maps. Info on trails and campsites from enthusiastic and helpful rangers. Open daily 9am-5pm.

Post Offices: Crescent City, 751 2nd St. (☎464-2151). Open M-F 8:30am-5pm, Sa noon-2pm. **ZIP code:** 95531. **Orick,** 121147 U.S. 101 (☎488-3611). Open M-F 8:30am-noon and 1-5pm. **ZIP code:** 95555. **Klamath,** 141 Klamath Blvd. (☎482-2381). Open M-F 8am-4:30pm. **ZIP code:** 95548. **Area code:** 707.

🏠🍴 ACCOMMODATIONS AND FOOD

Overlooking the crashing Pacific surf and housed in the historic DeMartin House, the **Redwood Youth Hostel (HI-AYH)**, 14480 U.S. 101, 7 mi. north of Klamath at Wilson Creek Rd., suggests Shaker simplicity. Chores and rules keep the house immaculate. (☎482-8265. Check-in 4:30-9:30pm. Check-out 9:30am. Dorms $14, under 17 $7.) **Nickel Creek Campground,** at the end of Enderts Beach Rd., outside Crescent City, has ocean access and toilets, but no showers or water. State Park campsites are all fully developed and easily accessible. (☎464-9533. $12.) There are more picnic table sites than restaurants in the area, so the best option for food is probably **Orick Market,** which has reasonably priced groceries. (☎488-3225. Open M-Sa 8am-7pm, Su 9am-7pm.) In Crescent City, head to the 24hr. **Safeway** in the shopping center on U.S. 101 (M St.) between 2nd and 5th. Hungry visitors can grab breakfast or lunch at the **Wild Rocket Juice Bar & Cafe,** 309 U.S. 101 in Crescent City. Delightful wraps and smoothies ($3-5) will soothe your weariness. (☎464-2543. Open M-F 6am-6pm, Sa 9am-3pm.) **Glen's Bakery and Restaurant,** 3rd and G St., serves basic diner fare such as huge pancakes ($3), sandwiches ($4-5), and burgers ($3-4), for visitors and regulars alike. (☎464-2914. Open Tu-Sa 5am-6:30pm.)

👁🎿 SIGHTS AND OUTDOORS

In the parks, you may gather berries, but all other plants and animals are protected—even feathers dropped by birds of prey are off-limits. The National Parks Service and the California Department of Parks and Recreation conduct many summer activities for all ages; call the **Redwood Information Center** (☎464-6101) for info.

ORICK AREA
The Orick Area covers the southernmost section of Redwood National and State Parks. Its **Visitors Center** lies on U.S. 101, 1 mi. south of Orick and a ½ mi. south of the Shoreline Deli (the Greyhound bus stop). A popular sight is the **Tall Trees Grove,** accessible by car to those with free permits available at the Visitors Center when the road is open. Allow at least 3-4hr. for the trip.

PRAIRIE CREEK AREA
The Prairie Creek Area, equipped with a **Ranger Station, Visitors Center,** and **State Park campgrounds,** is perfect for hikers, who can explore 75 mi. of trails in the park's 14,000 acres. Be sure to pick up a trail map ($1) at the ranger station before heading out; the loops of criss-crossing trails may be confusing without one. Starting at the Prairie Creek Visitors Center, the **James Irvine Trail** (4.5 mi.) winds through a garden of towering old-growth redwoods of humbling height. Snaking past small waterfalls that trickle down 50 ft. fern-covered walls, the trail ends at **Fern Canyon** on **Gold Bluffs Beach,** whose sands stretch for miles upon elk-scattered miles.

KLAMATH AREA
The Klamath Area to the north consists of a thin stretch of park land connecting Prairie Creek with Del Norte State Park. The town itself consists of a few stores stretched over 4 mi., so the main attraction here is the ruggedly spectacular coastline. The **Klamath Overlook,** where Requa Rd. meets the Coastal Trail, is an excellent whale-watching site with a fantastic view.

CRESCENT CITY AREA
An outstanding location from which to explore the parks, Crescent City calls itself the city "where the redwoods meet the sea." The **Battery Point Lighthouse** houses a museum open only during low tide. The curious should consult guides about the resident ghost. The lighthouse is on a causeway jutting out of Front St. Turn left onto A St. at the top of Front St. (☎464-3089. Open Apr.-Sept. W-Su 10am-4pm, tide permitting. $2, children 50¢.) From June through August, the National Park offers **tide pool walks** leaving from the Enderts Beach parking lot. (☎464-6101 for schedules. Turn-off 4 mi. south of Crescent City.)

PANNIN' FER GOALD Panning for gold is easy and fun. Find one of many public stretches of river and a 12- or 18-inch gold pan, which can be easily acquired at local stores. Dig in old mine tailings, at turns in the river, around tree roots, and at the upstream ends of gravel bars, places where heavy gold may settle. Swirl water, sand, and gravel in a tilted gold pan, slowly washing materials over the edge. Be patient, and keep at it until you are down to black sand, and—hopefully—gold. Gold has a unique color. It's shinier than brassy-looking pyrite ("fool's gold"), and it doesn't break down upon touch, like mica, a similarly glittery substance.

HIOUCHI AREA

This inland region, known for its rugged beauty, sits in the northern part of the park region along U.S. 199 and contains some excellent hiking trails, most of which are in **Jedediah Smith Redwoods State Park.** The wheelchair-accessible **Stout Grove Trail** is a ½ mi. loop through lush redwoods. The trailhead is near the eastern end of Howland Hill Rd.; the paved section is just past the trail.

GOLD COUNTRY

In 1848, California was a rural backwater of only 15,000 people. The same year, sawmill operator James Marshall wrote in his diary: "This day some kind of mettle...found in the tailrace...looks like goald." In the next four years, some 90,000 '49ers from around the world headed for California and the 120 miles of gold-rich seams called the **Mother Lode.** Despite the hype, few of the prospectors struck it rich. Miners, sustained by dreams of instant wealth, worked long and hard, yet most could barely squeeze sustenance out of their fiercely guarded claims.

Although gold remains in them thar hills, today the towns of Gold Country make their money mining the tourist traffic. Gussied up as **"Gold Rush Towns,"** they solicit tourists traveling along the appropriately numbered **Rte. 49,** which runs through the foothills along rivers, cliffs, and pastures, connecting dozens of small Gold Country settlements. Traffic from the coast connects with Rte. 49 via I-80 through Sacramento, which today serves as a tourist hub. If you tire of Gold Country lore, you're not alone; wine tasting, river rafting, and spelunking are also popular. Most of Gold Country is about two hours from Sacramento, three hours from San Francisco.

SACRAMENTO ☎916

Sacramento is a good place from which to explore the hills of Gold Country or head onward to the Sierra Nevada or Cascade mountain ranges. ◪**Sacramento Hostel (HI-AYH),** 900 H St., at 9th St., in a restored Victorian mansion, has a huge modern kitchen, three large living rooms, and a library. (☎443-1691. Chores required. Check-in 7-10am and 5-10pm. Check-out 9:30am. Doors lock at 11pm. Dorms $15, nonmembers $18. Wheelchair accessible.) At **Sacramento Econolodge,** 711 16th St., between G and H St., most rooms have refrigerators and free cable. (☎443-6631 or 800-553-2266. Singles $59; doubles $69.) ◪**The Fox and Goose,** 1001 R St., at 10th St. is a funky English pub and restaurant. (☎443-8825. Open mic nights, live bands, and wizards performing live magic. Food served M-Th 7am-midnight, F 7am-2am, Sa 8am-2am, Su 8am-1pm. Wheelchair accessible.) **Post Office:** 915 Capitol Mall, #102. **ZIP code:** 95814. **Area code:** 916.

CALAVERAS COUNTY ☎209

Unsuspecting Calaveras County turned out to be literally sitting on a gold mine—the richest, southern part of the "Mother Lode"—when the big rush hit. Over 550,000 pounds of gold were extracted from the county's earth. **Mark Twain** allegedly based "The Celebrated Jumping Frog of Calaveras County" on a tale he heard in Angels Camp Tavern. Life in this area has since imitated (or capitalized on) art; Calaveras has held **annual frog-jumping contests** since 1928. Thousands of people gather on the third weekend of May for the festivities. A drive along the scenic **Rte. 49** is a great way to glimpse Calaveras County. **San Andreas,** at the juncture of Rte. 26 and 49, is the county hub and most densely populated area, but it isn't very big.

The real attractions of Calaveras County are the natural wonders. About 20 mi. east of Angels Camp on Rte. 4 lies **Calaveras Big Trees State Park.** Here the *Sequoiadendron giganteum* (Giant Sequoia) reigns with might: the *giganteum* is the largest living thing on land. The one-mile **North Grove Trail** is wheelchair accessible, gently graded, and heavily trafficked. The less-traveled, more challenging four-mile **South Grove Trail** better captures the forest's beauty and timelessness. The park also offers swimming in **Beaver Creek** and camping. Summertime visitors should prepare for gnats and mosquitoes. Be aware that the snow comes early (sometimes in Sept.) and leaves late (mid-Apr.) at Big Trees. (☎795-2334, reservations 800-365-2267. Open 24hr. Sites $12, Day use $2, seniors $1.)

Calaveras County boasts gargantuan natural wonders below ground as well as above. **Moaning Cavern** is a vast vertical cave so large that the Statue of Liberty could live there comfortably. From Angels Camp, follow Rte. 4 east for 4 mi., turn right onto Parrot's Ferry Rd., and follow signs. Descend the 236 steps or rappel 180 ft. down into the cave. (☎736-2708. Open daily 9am-6pm; in winter M-F 10am-5pm, Sa-Su and holidays 9am-5pm. Stairs $8.75, ages 3-13 $4.50; rappelling first time $39.50, each additional time $20.) **Mercer Caverns,** 9 mi. north of Angels Camp, off Rte. 4 on Sheep Rd. in Murphys, offers one-hour walking tours of ten internal rooms. Although smaller and less dramatic than Moaning Cavern, the caves are nearly a million years old. (☎728-2101. Open M-Th 9am-6pm, F-Sa 9am-8pm. Tours every 20min. $8, ages 5-11 $4, under 5 free.) **California Caverns,** at Cave City, served as a naturally air-conditioned bar and dance floor during the Gold Rush, when a shot of whiskey could be purchased for a pinch of gold dust. The caverns sobered up on Sunday for church services when one stalagmite served as an altar. Walking tours and "wild cavern expedition trips" explore cramped tunnels, waist-high mud, and underground lakes. (☎736-2708. Tours $9, ages 3-13 $4.75. 2-3hr. expeditions $99; must be 16. Less strenuous expeditions for ages 9-16 $65.)

Calaveras County has been a producer of fine wines for nearly 150 years. Vineyards stretch along Rte. 49, and wineries abound near Plymouth. The **Stevenot Winery,** 2 mi. north of Murphy's Main St. on Sheep Ranch Rd., is the county's largest. (☎728-3436. Free tastings M-F 8am-noon and 1-5pm.) **Kautz Ironstone Vineyards,** on Six Mile Rd. 1½ mi. south of Murphy's Main St., stores wine in caverns hewn from rock. (☎728-1251. Tours daily 11:30am, 1:30, and 3:30pm. Sa additional tour 2:30pm. Tasting room open M-F 10am-6pm.) The **Calaveras County Information Center,** in downtown Angels Camp, is a great resource for info on and history of sights in the area. (☎800-225-3764. Open M-F 9am-4pm, Sa 11am-4pm, Su 11am-3pm.) **Post Office:** 1216 S. Main St. in Angels Camp. **ZIP code:** 95222. **Area code:** 209.

THE CASCADES   ☎916

The Cascade Mountains interrupt an expanse of farmland to the northeast of Gold Country. In these ranges, recent volcanic activity has left behind a surreal landscape of lava beds, mountains, lakes, waterfalls, caves, and recovering forest areas. The calm serenity and haunting beauty of these mountains draw visitors in a way that the Central Valley and Gold Country cannot.

Lassen Volcanic National Park is accessible by **Rte. 36** to the south and **Rte. 44** to the north. Both roads are about 50 mi. from **Rte. 5.** In 1914, the earth radiated destruction as tremors, streams of lava, black dust, and a series of huge eruptions ravaged the land, climaxing in 1915 when Mt. Lassen belched a seven-mile-high cloud of smoke and ashes. The destructive power of this eruption is still evident in the strange, unearthly pools of boiling water and the stretches of barren moonscape. Winter is long and snowy here. **Lassen Volcanic National Park Headquarters** are located in Mineral. (☎595-4444. Open in summer daily 8am-4:30pm; off-season closed Sa-Su.) Every summer, thousands of New Age believers, yuppie vacationers, and crunchy hikers come to ◼**Mt. Shasta** to carouse, climb, commune, and contemplate its rugged snowcapped top. **Shasta-Trinity National Forest Service,** 204 W. Alma St. (☎926-4511), charges info-crystals.

CALIFORNIA

THE SIERRA NEVADA

The Sierra Nevada is a high, steep, and physically stunning mountain range. Thrust skyward 400 million years ago by gigantic plate collisions and shaped by erosion, glaciers, and volcanoes, this enormous hunk of granite stretches 450 miles north from the Mojave Desert to Lake Almanor near Lassen Volcanic National Park. The glistening clarity of Lake Tahoe, the heart-stopping sheerness of Yosemite's rock walls, the craggy alpine scenery of Kings Canyon and Sequoia National Parks, and the abrupt drop of the Eastern Sierra into Owens Valley are sights to behold. Temperatures in the Sierra Nevada are as diverse as the terrain. Even in the summer, overnight lows can dip into the 20s. Normally, only U.S. 50 and I-80 are kept open during the snow season. Exact dates vary from year to year, so check with a ranger station for local road conditions, especially from October to June.

LAKE TAHOE   ☎ 530

In February of 1844, fearless explorer John C. Fremont led his expedition over the Sierra. Luckily for him, the sight of this beautiful alpine lake was enough to boost the morale of his 36 starved and weary companions. The lake went through several identities, from Bigler to Lake of Beer, before California officially named it Tahoe in 1945. Since settlers rolled into California in the late 18th century, Lake Tahoe has been a playground for the wealthy and a year-round outdoor haven, with miles of biking, hiking, and skiing trails, long beaches, and hair-raising whitewater.

▐ TRANSPORTATION

In the northern Sierra on the California-Nevada border, Lake Tahoe is a four-hour drive from San Francisco. The two main trans-Sierra highways, **I-80** and **U.S. 50 (Lake Tahoe Boulevard)**, run east-west through Tahoe, skimming the northern and southern shores of the lake, respectively. Lake Tahoe is 118 mi. northeast of Sacramento and 35 mi. southwest of Reno on I-80. From the Carson City and Owens Valley area, **U.S. 395** runs north along Tahoe's eastern shores.

Buses: Greyhound (☎530-543-1050), in the Thunderbird Motel on Laurel Ave., 1 block north of U.S. 50 in South Lake Tahoe. To: San Francisco (3 per day, $27) and Sacramento (3 per day, $21-23). No lockers. Station open daily 8am-7pm.

Trains: Amtrak runs a bus from its San Joaquin and Capitol train routes to Pre-Madonna Casino, off I-5 at the Pre-Madonna exit, and Whiskey Pete's Casino in Stateline, NV. These trips are long and costly. To San Francisco (11hr., $80).

Public Transit: Tahoe Casino Express (☎800-446-6128). Shuttle service between the Reno airport and South Shore Tahoe casinos. Runs daily 6:15am-12:30am. $17, up to 2 children under 12 free.) **Tahoe Area Regional Transport (TART)** (☎550-1212) connects the western and northern shores from Incline Village to Tahoe City to Tahoma (Meeks Bay in summer). Stops daily every hour 6:30am-6pm. Buses also run out to Truckee and Squaw Valley 5 times per day. Fare $1.25, exact change required; day pass $3. **South Tahoe Area Ground Express (STAGE)** (☎542-6077) operates buses around South Tahoe and every hr. to the beach; also connects Stateline and Emerald Bay Rd. $1.25; day pass $2; 10-ride pass $10. Most casinos operate free shuttle service along U.S. 50 to California ski resorts and motels. A summer bus program connects STAGE and TART at Meeks Bay for the entire lake area 6am-midnight.

☀▐ ORIENTATION AND PRACTICAL INFORMATION

The lake is roughly divided into two main regions: North Shore and South Shore. The North Shore includes King's Beach, Tahoe City, and Incline Village, while the South Shore includes Emerald Bay and South Lake Tahoe City. Rte. 28 and 89 form a 75 mi. ring of asphalt around the lake; the complete loop takes nearly 3hr.

Visitor info: ☎573-2674 (available June-Sept. daily). **South Lake Tahoe Chamber of Commerce,** 3066 Lake Tahoe Blvd. (☎541-5255). Open M-Sa 8:30am-5pm. **Lake Tahoe/Douglas Chamber of Commerce,** 195 U.S. 50, Stateline, NV (☎775-588-4591). Open M-F 9am-6pm, Sa-Su 9am-5pm.

Internet access: South Lake Tahoe Library, 1000 Rufus Allen Blvd. (☎573-3185). Open Tu-W 10am-8pm, Th-Sa 10am-5pm. **Kings Beach Library,** 301 Secline Ave. (☎546-2021), 1 block north of N. Lake Blvd. in Kings Beach. Open Tu and F 1-5pm, W 2-6pm, Th 10am-2pm, Sa 11am-3pm. Free.

Medical Services: Barton Memorial Hospital (☎541-3420), at 4th St. and South Ave., in S. Lake Tahoe. **Stateline Medical Center,** 176 U.S. 50, Stateline, NV (☎702-588-3561), at Kahle St. Open daily 8am-8pm. **Tahoe Forest Hospital** (☎587-6011), at Donner Pass Rd. and Pine Ave., Truckee.

Post Offices: Tahoe City, 950 N. Lake Blvd. #12 (☎800-275-8777), in the Lighthouse Shopping Center. Open M-F 8:30am-5pm. **ZIP code:** 96145. **South Lake Tahoe,** 1046 Tahoe Blvd. (☎544-2208). Open M-F 8:30am-5pm, Sa noon-2pm. **ZIP code:** 96151.

Area code: 530 in CA, 775 in NV; in text, 530 unless noted.

▟ ACCOMMODATIONS

The strip off U.S. 50 on the California side of the border supports the bulk of Tahoe's motels. Particularly glitzy and cheap in South Lake Tahoe, motels also line the quieter area along Park Ave. and Pioneer Trail. The North Shore offers more woodsy accommodations along Rte. 28, but rates are especially high in Tahoe City. Fall and spring are the most economical times of the year to visit.

▨ Tamarack Lodge, 2311 N. Lake Tahoe Blvd. (☎583-3350 or 888-824-6323), 3 mi. north of Tahoe City, across from Star Harbor. Clean, quiet motel in the woods. Newly refurbished exterior, outdoor BBQ and fireplace, phones, cable TV, and friendly management. Rooms with queen beds $39-54.

Cedar Glen Lodge, 6589 N. Lake Blvd. (☎546-4281 or 800-500-8246), Tahoe Vista. Family-operated motel with a private beach, pool, and indoor and outdoor hot tub and sauna. Grounds include BBQ pits, playground, hammock, lots of flowers, and spectacular rabbit hutch. Morning newspaper and continental breakfast included. Cottages with kitchens also available. Singles from $60.

Doug's Mellow Mountain Retreat, 3787 Forest St. (☎544-8065), S. Lake Tahoe. 1 mi. west of the state line, turn left onto Wildwood Rd., and after 3 blocks take a left on Forest. St. Doug's hostel is the 6th house on the left. Modern kitchen, BBQ, fireplace, Internet access. Very friendly international atmosphere. Bedding and laundry included. Dorms $15 per person, private rooms available; discounts for stays of a week or longer.

Bayview (☎544-5994) has 10 first come, first camp sites right on Emerald Bay with pit toilets but no water. 7-night max. stay. Sites $5.

D.L. Bliss State Park (☎525-7277), on Rte. 89 a few mi. north of Emerald Bay. Camp by the beach near emerald waters and granite boulders or in secluded forest sites. Popular day-use beach, but entrance restricted by the number of parking spaces. 168 sites. 14-night max. stay. Open June-Aug.; day use May-Oct. Sites $12; day parking $2.

▟ FOOD

In the south, the casinos on the Nevada side offer perpetually low-priced buffets, but there are restaurants along the lakeshore with reasonable prices, similarly large portions, and much better food. Groceries are cheaper on the California side.

Lakehouse: Pizza-Spirits-Fun, 120 Grove St. (☎583-2222), Tahoe City. On the water with a sunny lakefront deck. Standard breakfast specials $3-7, California salad $7, sandwiches, and reasonably priced pizzas. Open M-Th 8am-10pm, F-Sa 8am-11pm.

Truckee Bagel Company, 555 N. Lake Blvd. (☎582-1852), in Tahoe City. The bagels here (75¢) won't make you think you're in New York, but they're the closest thing Lake Tahoe has to the real thing. Crusty and oven-baked, these little wonders are the best in the area. Open daily 7am-3pm.

Red Hut Waffles, 2749 Lake Tahoe Blvd. (☎541-9024). Homestyle cooking. Waffle piled with fruit and whipped cream ($5.50), 4-egg monster omelettes ($5.75-7), fresh fruit bowl ($4), and bottomless coffee ($1.25). Open daily 6am-2pm. No credit cards.

Sprouts Natural Foods Cafe, 3123 Harrison Ave. (☎541-6969), at the intersection of Rte. 50 and Alameda Ave. in S. Lake Tahoe. With all-natural food and portions fit for a wrestler, this place keeps everyone satisfied. Try the pasta dinner ($6.50), the tuna burrito ($5), or the tasty smoothies ($2.50-3.25). Open daily 8am-10pm.

OUTDOOR ACTIVITIES

BEACHES

Lake Tahoe supports many beaches perfect for a day of sunning and people-watching. Parking generally costs $3-5; bargain hunters leave cars on the main road and walk. **Sand Harbor Beach,** south of Incline Village, has gorgeous granite boulders and clear waters that attract swimmers, sunners, and divers in droves. The parking lot ($6) is usually full by 11:30am. One mile away at Memorial Point, paved parking is free. **Hidden Beach,** also south of Incline Village, and **Kings Beach,** just across the California border on Rte. 28, comes complete with the latest rage (waveboards) and an alternative feel. Kings Beach has volleyball and basketball courts and a playground. **Pope Beach,** at the southernmost point of the lake off Rte. 89, is a wide, pine-shaded expanse of shoreline, less trafficked on its east side. **Nevada Beach,** 8 mi. north of South Lake Tahoe, is close to the casinos off U.S. 50, offering a quiet place to reflect on gambling losses while gazing up at the mountains. **Zephyr Cove Beach,** about 15 mi. north of South Lake Tahoe, is a favorite spot for the college crowd. **Meeks Bay,** 10 mi. south of Tahoe City, is family-oriented, with picnic tables, volleyball, motorboat and kayak rental, and a petite store. In the summer, the Tahoe City and South Tahoe Buses connect here. Five miles south of Meeks Bay, the **D.L. Bliss State Park** has a large beach on a small bay (Rubicon). Parking here ($3) is very limited, so think about parking on the road and walking in.

OTHER WATER ACTIVITIES

Rafting can be a refreshing way to appreciate the Tahoe scenery, but depending on the water levels of the American and Truckee Rivers, rafting can range from a thrilling whitewater challenge to a boring bake in the sun. If water levels are high, check out raft rental places along the Truckee River and at Tahoe City. For more info, call **Mountain Air Sports Truckee River Rafting** (☎583-7238 or 888-584-7238; open daily 8:30am-3:30pm), in Tahoe City, across from Lucky's at Fanny Bridge, or **Tahoe Truckee River Raft Co.** (☎583-0123; open daily 8:30am-3:30pm). If paddling in the north, ask around about (privately owned) **natural hot springs** on the way to the spectacular Crystal Bay. **Fishing** information and regulations can be found at Visitors Centers, and licenses are available at local sporting good stores. Because of its depth (1600 ft. in places) and strange formation, Tahoe is a notoriously difficult lake to fish; bring a good book and be prepared to walk away empty-handed.

BIKING

Lake Tahoe is a biking paradise. The excellent paved trails, logging roads, and dirt paths have not gone unnoticed; be prepared for company if you pedal around the area. The Forest Service and bike rental stores can provide advice, publications like *Bike West* magazine, maps, and trail info. No cycling is allowed in the Desolation Wilderness, or on the Pacific Crest or Tahoe Rim Trails. The expert staff at **Olympic Bike Shop,** 60 N. Lake Tahoe Blvd., Tahoe City, dispenses multitudinous maps. (☎581-2500. Open daily 9am-6pm. Bikes $5 per hr., $15 per 4hr., $21 per day.)

Known more for its ski trails, the North Shore is equipped with both flat lakeside jaunts and steeper woodsy rides. The **Tahoe Rim Trail,** from Kings Beach to Tahoe City, offers intermediate-level hilly biking. The trail can be accessed from Tahoe City or Brockway Summit (see below for more info). **Squaw Valley,** northwest of the lake on Rte. 89, opens its slope to hikers and mountain bikers during the summer. The cable car transports bikers and their wheels 2000 vertical ft. (1 ride $19, full-day pass $26). The slopes are steep, but fairly easy. The South Shore boasts a variety of scenic trails for all abilities. **Fallen Leaf Lake**, just west of South Lake Tahoe, is a dazzling destination by bike or by car, but watch out for the swerving tourists in boat- and trailer-towing vehicles. The steep mountain peaks that surround the lake are breathtaking when viewed from beside Fallen Leaf's icy blue waters. Bikers looking for a challenge can try the seven-mile ring around the lake. **U.S. 50, Rte. 89, and Rte. 28** are all bicycle-friendly, but the drivers aren't, especially in heavy traffic areas like South Lake Tahoe. Angora Ridge (4 mi.), accessible from Rte. 89, meanders past Fallen Leaf Lake to the Angora Lakes for a moderate challenge. The advanced 23 mi. **Flume Trail** begins at the Spooner Lake campground with the Marlette Lake Trail, a five-mile sandy road. The **West Shore Bike Path**, a paved ten mile stretch from Tahoe City to Sugar Pine Point, is a flat, scenic way to tour the lake.

HIKING
The Visitors Center and ranger stations provide detailed info and maps for all types of hikes. Backcountry users must obtain a wilderness permit from the Forest Service for any hike into the Desolation Wilderness. The almost completed **Tahoe Rim Trail** encircles the lake, following the ridge tops of the Lake Tahoe Basin. Hiking is moderate to difficult. On the western shore, the trail is part of the Pacific Crest Trail. Current trailheads are at Spooner Summit on U.S. 50, off Rte. 89 on Fairway Dr. in Tahoe City, Brockway on Rte. 267, and Mt. Rose on Rte. 431. (Mt. Rose is a 1.3 mi. wheelchair-accessible loop.)

ROCK CLIMBING
The **Alpenglow Sport Shop**, 415 N. Lake Blvd., Tahoe City, provides free rock and ice climbing literature and rents climbing shoes. (☎583-6917. Open M-F 10am-6pm, Sa-Su 9am-6pm.) **The Sports Exchange**, 10095 W. River St., houses Gym Works, a challenging indoor climbing gym with over 2500 sq. ft. of climbing space. (☎582-4510. Open daily 10am-6pm. $7 per day, indoor shoe rental $3 per day.) **Headwall Climbing Wall**, at Squaw Valley, offers several challenging routes in the Cable Car Building. (☎583-7673. Open daily 10am-5pm. $12 per day, indoor shoe rental $4 per day.)

DOWNHILL SKIING
With its world-class alpine slopes, knee-deep powder, and notorious California sun, Tahoe is a skier's paradise. There are approximately 20 ski resorts in the Tahoe area. The Visitors Center provides info, maps, publications like *Ski Tahoe* (free), and coupons. All the major resorts offer lessons and rent equipment. Look for multi-day discount packages. Lifts at most resorts operate daily 9am-4pm; arrive early for the shortest lines. Prices do not include rental, which generally costs $15-20 for a full day. Skiers on a budget should consider night skiing or half-day passes. Numerous smaller ski resorts offer cheaper tickets and shorter lines. **Squaw Valley**, off Rte. 89 just north of **Alpine Meadows**, was the site of the 1960 Olympic Winter Games, and its groomed bowls and tree runs make for some of the West's best skiing. The 32 ski lifts access high-elevation runs for all levels. (☎583-6955 or 800-545-4350. Day pass $52, half-day $35, seniors and under 13 $26, over 75 free.) Alpine Meadows, an excellent, accessible family vacation spot with more than 2000 skiable acres, lies 6 mi. northwest of Tahoe City on Rte. 89. (☎583-4232 or 800-441-4423. Full-day $50, ages 7-12 $10, ages 65-69 $28, over 70 or under 6 $6. Basic ski rental $26, ages 7-12 $17, under 6 $11.) **Heavenly**, on Ski Run Blvd. off U.S. 50, is the largest and most popular resort in the area, with over 4800 skiable acres, 27 lifts, and 82 trails. Reaching over 10,000 ft., it is also Tahoe's highest ski resort. (☎800-243-2826. Full-day lift ticket $46, seniors and under 13 $20; half-day $30/$15.)

CROSS-COUNTRY SKIING AND SNOWSHOEING
One of the best ways to enjoy the solitude of Tahoe's pristine snow-covered forests is to cross-country ski at a resort. Alternatively, rent skis at an independent outlet and venture onto the thick braid of trails around the lake. **Porters** (☎587-1500), at the Lucky-Longs Center, in Truckee, and 501 N. Lake Blvd., Tahoe City (☎583-2314), rents skis for $9-12. (Both open daily 8am-6pm.) **Royal Gorge** (☎426-3871), on

Old Rte. 40 below Donner Summit, is the nation's largest cross-country ski resort, with 80 trails covering 170 mi. of beginner and expert terrain. **Spooner Lake**, at the junction of U.S. 50 and Rte. 28, offers 21 trails. (☎749-5349. Trail fee $15, children $3; mid-week special $11.) **Hope Valley** (☎694-2266) has 11 free trails of varying difficulty; take Rte. 89 S from South Lake Tahoe and turn left on Rte. 88. **Snowshoes** are available at many sporting goods stores for about $15 per day. Check local ranger stations for ranger-guided winter snowshoe hikes, or trudge out on your own.

YOSEMITE NATIONAL PARK ☎209

In 1868, a Scotsman named John Muir arrived by boat in San Francisco and asked for directions to "any place that is wild." Anxious to run this crazy youngster out of town, Bay Area folk directed him to the heralded lands of Yosemite. The wonders that Muir beheld there sated his wanderlust and spawned a lifetime of conservationism. His efforts won Yosemite its national park status by 1880 and Sequoia and Kings Canyon the same reward by 1890. Yosemite remains a paradise for outdoor enthusiasts; most visitors congregate in only 6% of the park (Yosemite Valley), leaving expanses of beautiful backcountry in relative peace and quiet.

▐ TRANSPORTATION

Yosemite runs public **buses** that connect the park with Merced and Mariposa. **Yosemite VIA** runs buses from the Merced bus station at 16th and N St. to Yosemite. (☎384-1315 or 800-842-5463. 4 per day. $20, round-trip $38.) VIA also runs **Yosemite Gray Line (YGL)**, which meets trains arriving in Merced from San Francisco and takes passengers to Yosemite. Tickets can be purchased from the driver. (☎384-1315. Operates M-F 8am-5pm.) YGL also runs buses to and from Fresno/Yosemite International Airport, Fresno hotels, and Yosemite Valley ($20). **YARTS** (☎209-372-4487 or 877-989-2787) provides two daily trips to Yosemite from Merced; call ahead for fares and schedules. Amtrak runs a **bus** from Merced to Yosemite (4 per day, $10). Amtrak **trains** run to Merced from San Francisco (4 per day, $22-29) and L.A. (5 per day, $28-51). The trains connect with the waiting YGL bus. The best bargain in Yosemite is the free **shuttle bus system.** (Daily every 10min. 7am-6pm, every 20min. 6-10pm.) **Hikers' buses** run daily to Glacier Point (late June to early Sept.) and to Tuolumne Meadows/Lee Vining. (☎372-1240. $20.50 round-trip.)

Although the inner valley is often congested with traffic, the best way to achieve a rapid overview of Yosemite is by **car.** Gas-guzzlers should keep in mind that there are no gas stations in the valley; be prepared to get ripped off in a gateway town. Within the park, there are gas stations with high prices at Tuolomne Meadows and Wawona. A more relaxing (and environmentally friendly) option is to park at one of the lodging areas and ride the free shuttle to see the valley sights, using your car only to explore sights outside of the valley. Drivers intending to visit the high country in spring and fall should have snow tires (sometimes required even in summer).

▐ ▐ ORIENTATION AND PRACTICAL INFORMATION

General Park Information (☎372-0200). Info on weather, accommodations, and activities. Call the general line before calling a specific info station. All Visitors Centers have free maps and copies of *Yosemite Guide.* Listed hours valid June-Sept. unless noted.

Yosemite Valley Visitors Center (☎372-0200), in Yosemite Village. Sign language interpreter in summer. Open mid-June to Aug. daily 8am-7pm; Sept. to mid-June 9am-5pm.

Wilderness Center, P.O. Box 545, Yosemite National Park 95389 (☎372-0308). Wilderness permit reservations (☎372-0740) up to 24 weeks in advance ($5 per person per reservation, M-F 9am-4pm), or first come, first served (free). Helpful staff provides info. Open daily 7am-6pm.

Bike Rental: Yosemite Lodge (☎372-1208) and **Curry Village** (☎372-8319) for $5.25 per hr., $20 per day. Wheelchairs also available at both shops for $5 per hr., $20 per day. Both open daily 9am-5pm, weather permitting.

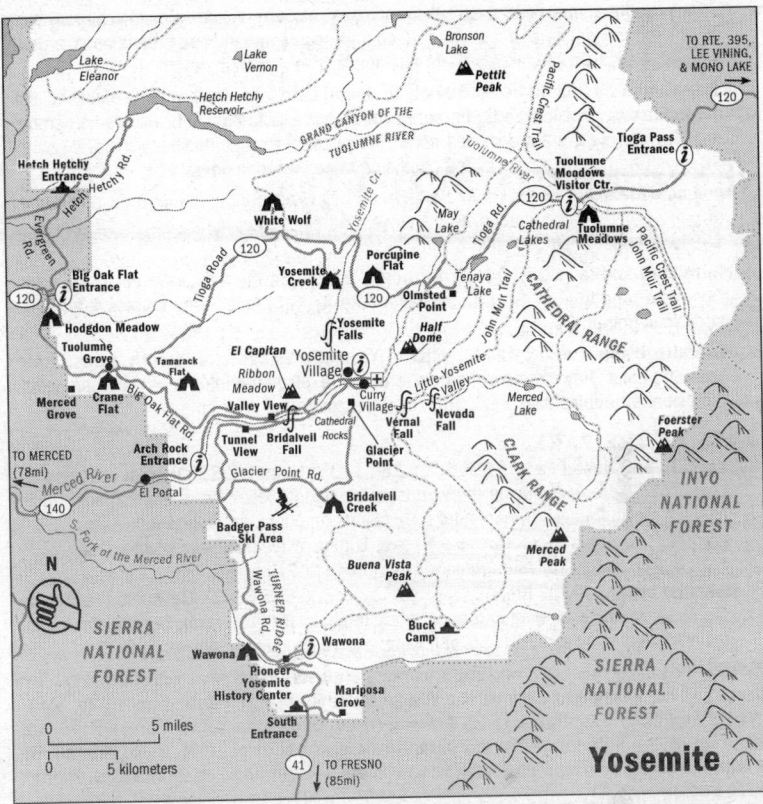

Yosemite

Equipment Rental: Yosemite Mountaineering School (☎372-8344 or 372-8436), on Rte. 120 at Tuolumne Meadows. Sleeping bags $10 per day, backpacks $8 per day; 3rd day half-price. Climbing shoes rented to YMS students only. Driver's license or credit card required for deposit. Rock climbing classes offered daily. Open daily 8:30am-5pm.

Weather and Road Conditions: ☎372-0200. 24hr.

Internet access: Yosemite Bug Hostel (☎966-6666), on Rte. 140, 30 mi. west of Yosemite in Midpines (see **Accommodations,** below). $1 per 10min.

Post Offices: Yosemite Village, next to the Visitors Center. Open M-F 8:30am-5pm, Sa 10am-noon. Lobby open 24hr. **Curry Village,** near the registration office. Open June-Aug. M-F 11:30am-3pm. **Yosemite Lodge,** open M-F 9am-1pm and 2-4:30pm. **Wawona,** open M-F 9am-5pm, Sa 9am-noon. **Tuolumne Meadows,** open M-F 9am-12:30pm and 1:30-4:30pm, Sa 9am-noon. **ZIP code:** 95389. **Area code:** 209.

🏠🏢 ACCOMMODATIONS AND FOOD

INSIDE THE PARK

Advance reservations are necessary and can be (and almost always are) made up to one year in advance by calling 252-4848. Rates fluctuate, but tend to be higher on weekends and during the summer (those given below are for summer weekends). Check-in hovers around 11am. All park lodgings provide access to dining and laundry facilities, showers, and supplies.

Housekeeping Camp (☎372-8338), ¼ mi. west of Curry Village. Canvas-capped concrete "camping shelters" accommodate up to 4 people and include 2 bunk beds, a double bed, a picnic table, a firepit with grill, lights, and electrical outlets. Cottages $43.

Curry Village (☎252-4848), southeast of Yosemite Village. Pool, nightly shows at the amphitheater, snack stands, cafeteria, and an ice rink Nov.-Feb. Ranger programs nearly every night feature stories about the history of Yosemite. Back-to-back cabins $62, with bath $82; canvas-sided cabins on raised wooden floors $44.

Tuolumne Meadows Lodge (☎372-8413), on Tioga Pass Rd., in the northeastern corner of park. Canvas-sided cabins, wood stoves, no electricity. Maid service $4. Doubles $48; additional adult $9, child $4.

White Wolf Lodge (☎372-8416), on Tioga Pass Rd. in the western area of the park. Open late June to early Sept. Cabins with bath $73.25; tent cabin doubles $44; each additional person $7.

Yosemite Lodge (☎372-1274), west of Yosemite Village and directly across from Yosemite Falls. Tiny cabins are as close to motel accommodations as the valley gets. Singles and doubles $80, each additional person $11.

OUTSIDE THE PARK

🔲 **Yosemite Bug Hostel** (☎966-6666), on Rte. 140 in Midpines, 25 mi. west of Yosemite. Look carefully for sign. Up in the woods, a low-budget resort spot. International backpacking crowd lounges in hammocks. Discounts on public transportation (45min., $10 roundtrip) to park. Internet access $1 per 10min. Wheelchair accessible. Dorm beds $16; tent sites $17; private rooms with shared bath $40-50.

Oakhurst Lodge, 40302 Rte. 41 (☎683-4417 or 800-655-6343), Oakhurst. Clean, simple motel rooms with shag carpeting, pool, large grassy back lawn. Continental breakfast included. Singles $70 ($55 with various local coupons); doubles $80-95.

Restaurants in the park are nothing special. A slim supply of pricey groceries can be found at the **Yosemite Lodge** or the **Village Store** (both open June-Sept. daily 8am-10pm; Oct.-May 8am-9pm), or at **Wawona** (open daily 8am-8pm). Consider buying all of your cooking supplies, marshmallows, and batteries in Merced, Fresno, or Oakhurst en route to the park. These towns are also home to cheaper restaurants.

▓ CAMPING

Yosemite is camping country; most of the valley's campgrounds are choked with tents, trailers, and RVs. Outside of the valley, campsite quality vastly improves. Reservations can be made up to five months in advance. (☎800-436-7275, TDD 888-530-9796, outside the U.S. 301-722-1257; www.reservations.nps.gov. Phones and web site available daily 7am-7pm, or mail NPRS, P.O. Box 1600, Cumberland, MD 21502.) **Backcountry camping** is prohibited in the valley but is encouraged outside it.

Sunnyside, at the western end of the valley past Yosemite Lodge. The only first come, first camp site in the valley. Be prepared to meet new friends; every site is filled with 6 people. Water, flush toilets, and tables. 35 sites fill up early. $5 per person.

Lower Pines, in the busy eastern end of Yosemite Valley. Commercial, crowded, and plagued by the noises of cars driving by. Next to **North Pines** campsite (81 sites; open Apr.-Sept.) and the enormous **Upper Pines** campsite (238 sites). Pets allowed. Water, toilets, tables, and showers. Open Mar.-Sept. Sites $18.

Hodgdon Meadow, on Rte. 120 near Big Oak Flat Entrance, 25 mi. from the valley. Warm enough for winter camping. 105 thickly wooded sites provide some seclusion. Water, toilets, and tables. May-Sept. sites $18; Oct.-Apr. first come, first camp $12.

Tuolumne Meadows, on Rte. 120, 55 mi. east of the Valley. 157 sites require advance reservations, 157 saved for same-day reservations. Drive into the sprawling campground or escape the RVs by ambling to the 25 sites saved for hikers without cars. Ranger programs every night and nearby trailheads. Water, toilets, and tables. Open July-Sept. Drive-in sites $18; backpacker sites $3 per person.

OUTDOOR ACTIVITIES

DRIVING

Although the view is better if you get out of the car, you can see a large portion of Yosemite from the bucket seat. The **Yosemite Road Guide** ($4 at every Visitors Center) is keyed to roadside markers and outlines a superb tour of the park—it's almost like having a ranger tied to the hood. Spectacular panoramas are omnipresent during the drive east along **Tioga Pass Road (Rte. 120).** This stretch of road is the highest highway strip in the country; as it winds down from Tioga Pass through the park's eastern exit, it plunges nearly 1 mi. to reach the lunar landscape of Mono Lake. The drive west from the pass brings you past **Tuolumne Meadows** with its open spaces and rippling creeks, to shimmering Tenaya Lake and its countless scenic views of granite slopes and canyons. No less incredible are the views afforded by the southern approach to Yosemite, **Rte. 41.** Most recognizable is the Wawona Tunnel turnout (also known as **Inspiration Point**), which most visitors will immediately recognize as the subject of many Ansel Adams photographs.

El Capitan, a gigantic granite monolith (7569 ft.), looms over awestruck crowds. If you stop and look closely (with binoculars if possible), you will see what appear to be specks of dust moving on the mountain face—they are actually world-class climbers inching toward fame. At night their flashlights shine from impromptu hammocks hung from the granite. Nearby, **Three Brothers** and misty **Bridalveil Falls** pose for hundreds of snapshots every day. A drive into the heart of the valley leads to **Yosemite Falls** (2425 ft.), **Sentinel Rock,** and mighty **Half Dome.**

Glacier Point, off Glacier Point Rd., opens up a different perspective on the valley. This gripping overlook, 3214 ft. above the valley floor, can stun even the most wilderness-weary traveler. Half Dome rests majestically across the valley, while Nevada Falls looks deceptively peaceful from such a distance.

DAY HIKING IN THE VALLEY

To have the full Yosemite experience, visitors must travel the outer trails on foot. A wealth of opportunities reward anyone willing to lace up a pair of boots, even if only for a daytrip. Day-use trails are usually as busy as the New York Stock Exchange, and are sometimes as packed as a Pearl Jam concert. Hiking just after sunrise is the best, and sometimes the only, way to beat the crowds. But even then, trails like Half Dome are already busy. A colorful trail map with difficulty ratings and average hiking times is available at the Visitors Center (50¢). The **Mirror Lake Loop** is a level three-mile walk. **Bridalveil Falls,** another Ansel Adams favorite, is an easy ¼ mi. stroll from the nearby shuttle bus stop, and its cool spray is as close to a shower as many Yosemite campers ever get. The **Lower Yosemite Falls Trail** is a favorite of all ages and starts just opposite the Yosemite Lodge. **Upper Yosemite Falls Trail,** a back-breaking 3.5 mi. trek to the windy summit, rewards the intrepid hiker with an overview of the 2425 ft. drop. Those with energy to spare can trudge on to **Yosemite Point,** where views of the valley below rival those from more-heralded Glacier Point. The trail begins with an extremely steep, unshaded ascent. Leaving the marked trail is not a wise idea—a sign warns, "If you go over the waterfall, you will die." From the Happy Isles trailhead, the less strenuous 1.5 mi. **Mist Trail** past **Vernal Falls** to the top of **Nevada Falls.** This is perhaps the most popular day hike in the park, and with good reason—views of the falls from the trails are outstanding, and the drizzle that issues from the nearby rocks is more than welcome during the hot summer months. From Nevada Falls, the trail continues to the base of **Half Dome,** Yosemite's most recognizable monument.

CLIMBING AND RAFTING

The world's best **climbers** come to Yosemite to test themselves at angles past vertical. If you've got the courage (and the cash), you can join the stellar Yosemite rock climbers by taking a lesson with the **Yosemite Mountaineering School** (see p. 869). Basic rock climbing classes (mid-Apr. to Oct.) teach simple skills on the ground such as bouldering, rappelling, and ascending an 80 ft. high cliff. Reservations are useful and require advance payment, although drop-ins are accepted if space allows. (☎372-8344. Open daily 8:30am-5pm.)

Rafting is permitted on the Merced River (10am-4pm) when the water is warm and high enough, but no motorized crafts are allowed. For organized rafting trips, **All Outdoors**, 1250 Pine St. #103, Walnut Creek 94596 (☎925-932-8993 or 800-247-2387) leads trips on the north fork of Stanislaus River (leave from Calaveras Big Trees State Park), the Merced River (Mt. View Store, Midpines), the Kaweah River (Kaweah General Store), and Goodwin Canyon (Stanislaus River Park, Sonora).

ORGANIZED ACTIVITIES

Open-air tram tours (☎372-1240) leave from Curry Village, the Ahwahnee Hotel, Yosemite Lodge, and the Village Store. Tickets are available at lodging facilities and the Village Store tour desk. The basic, two-hour **Valley Floor Tour** points out Half Dome, El Capitan, Bridalveil Falls, and Happy Isles (departs every 30min; $17.50, seniors $15.75, ages 5-12 $9.50). The four-hour **Glacier Point Tour** climbs 3200 ft. to the point for a view of the valley 7300 ft. below (June-Oct.; $20.50, ages 5-12 $11). The two-hour **Moonlight Tour,** on nights with a full (or nearly full) moon, offers unique nighttime views of the valley (2hr.; $17.50).

Park rangers lead a variety of informative hikes and other activities for visitors of all ages. Daily **junior ranger** (ages 8-10) and **senior ranger** (ages 11-12) activities allow children to hike, raft, and investigate aquatic and terrestrial life. (Free. Reservations required at least a day in advance through the **Yosemite Valley Visitors Center,** see p. 868.) Rangers also guide a number of free walks. **Discover Yosemite Family Programs** address a variety of historical and geological topics. (3hr. Daily at 9am. Most programs wheelchair accessible.) Rangers also lead strenuous, four- to eight-hour **Destination Hikes** into the high country from Tuolumne Meadows. Free **Sunrise photo walks** leave most mornings from the Yosemite Lodge tour desk.

WINTER IN YOSEMITE

Most folks never leave the valley, but a wilder, more isolated Yosemite awaits those who do. Topographical maps and hiking guides are especially helpful in navigating Yosemite's nether regions. **Cross-country skiing** is free, and several well-marked trails cut into the backcountry of the valley's South Rim at Badger Pass and Crane Flat. Both areas have markers on the trees so trails can be followed even under several feet of snow; this same snow transforms many summer hiking trails into increasingly popular **snowshoe trails.** Rangers host several snowshoe walks, but the serene winter forests are perhaps best explored sans guidance. Snowshoes and skis can be rented from the **Yosemite Mountaineering School** (see p. 869).

The state's oldest ski resort, **Badger Pass Ski Area,** on Glacier Point Rd. south of Yosemite Valley, is the only downhill ski area in the park. The resort's powder may not rival the soft stuff of Tahoe, but its family-fun atmosphere fosters learning and restraint (but no snowboards). Free shuttles connect Badger Pass with Yosemite Valley. (☎372-8430. Lifts open 9am-4:30pm. Group ski lessons $22 for 2hr., private lessons from $44. Rental packages $18 per day, under 12 $13. 1-day lift tickets M-F $22, Sa-Su $28; under 12 daily $13; some specials for those over 60 or exactly 40. Some weekday discounts available through Yosemite Lodge.)

MONO LAKE ☎760

As fresh water from streams and springs drains into this "inland sea," it evaporates, leaving behind a mineral-rich, 13 mi.-wide expanse Mark Twain once called "the Dead Sea of the West." The lake derives its lunar appearance from towers of calcium carbonate (similar to giant drip sandcastles) called tufa, which form when calcium-rich springs well up in the carbonate-filled salt water. At 1 million years old, the lake is the oldest enclosed body of water in the Western Hemisphere.

The Mono Lake Committee offers **canoe tours** of the lake. (☎647-6595. Tours $17, ages 4-12 $7. Reservations required.) The unique terrain of this geological playground makes it a great place for hikers of all levels. Easy trails include the 0.3 mi.

Old Marina Area Trail, east of U.S. 395 1 mi. north of Lee Vining, the **Lee Vining Creek Nature Trail,** which begins behind the Mono Basin Visitors Center, and the **Panum Crater Trail,** 5 mi. south on U.S. 395.

The **El Mono Motel,** on Main and 3rd St., offers a slice of modern California: faux Spanish name, white stucco exterior, espresso bar, and alternative rock in the lobby. Clean and bright rooms have cable TV but no phone. (☎647-6310. Open Apr.-Oct. Singles with shared bath $49.) None of the area's campgrounds take reservations, but sites are ubiquitous, so a pre-noon arrival time will almost always guarantee a spot. Most sites are clustered west of Lee Vining along Rte. 120. Try **Inyo National Forest Campgrounds,** which are close to town. **Lundy** and **Lee Vining Canyons** are the best locations for lakebound travelers. (No water. Open May-Oct. Sites $7.) **Ellery Lake,** on Tioga Pass Rd. at Rte. 120 across from Tioga Pass Resort, has 12 first come, first camp sites near a brook. (Running water, chemical toilets. Sites $13.)

In 1984, Congress set aside 57,000 acres of land surrounding Mono Lake and named it the **Mono Basin National Forest Scenic Area** (☎873-2408). For a $3 fee (Golden Eagle, Golden Age, and Golden Access passes accepted), investigate the **South Tufa Grove,** which harbors and awe-inspiring hoard of calcium carbonate formations. Take U.S. 395 S to Rte. 120, then go 4 mi. east and take the Mono Lake South Tufa turn-off 1 mi. south to Tufa Grove. The town of Lee Vining provides stunning access to Yosemite as well as the best access to Mono Lake and the ghost town of Bodie. Lee Vining is 70 mi. north of Bishop on U.S. 395 and 10 mi. west of the Tioga Pass entrance to Yosemite. **Mono Lake Committee and Lee Vining Chamber of Commerce** (☎647-6595) offers lodging, dining, and local services at Main and 3rd St., in the orange and blue building. **Mono Basin National Forest Scenic Area Visitors Center,** Inyo National Forest, off U.S. 395, ½ mi. north of Lee Vining, is housed in a new structure that resembles a cathedral or an *Architectural Digest* centerfold. (☎873-2408. Open M-F 9am-5:30pm.) **Post Office:** 4th St., Lee Vining, in the big brown building. (☎647-6371. Open M-F 9am-2pm and 3-5pm.) **ZIP code:** 93541. **Area code:** 760.

MAMMOTH LAKES
☎760

Home to one of the most popular ski resorts in the US, the town of Mammoth Lakes has transformed itself into a giant year-round playground. Mammoth Mountain shifts from ski park in winter to bike park in summer, with fishing, rock climbing, and hiking to boot. The weekend nightlife is lively and entirely full of athletes who come to this alpine paradise to get vertical and have mammoth fun. Mammoth Lakes is on U.S. 395 160 mi. south of Reno and 40 mi. southeast of the eastern entrance to Yosemite. Rte. 203 runs through the town as Main St. and then veers off to the right as Minaret Summit Rd. In the winter, the roads from L.A. are jammed with weekend skiers making the six-hour journey up to the slopes.

As with most ski resorts, lodging is much more expensive in the winter, but prices tend to be cheaper on weekdays. Condo rentals are a comfortable choice for groups of three or more, and start at $65 per night. **Mammoth Reservation Bureau** (☎800-462-5571) can make rental arrangements. For lone travelers, dorm-style motels are the cheapest option. Make reservations far in advance. There are nearly 20 **Inyo Forest public campgrounds** (sites $12-14) in the area, at Mammoth Lakes, Mammoth Village, Convict Lake, Red's Meadow, and June Lake. All sites have piped water, and most are near fishing and hiking. Interested parties should contact the **Mammoth Ranger District** (☎924-5500) for info. Reservations can be made for all sites, as well as at nearby Sherwin Creek. (☎877-444-6777. Reservation fee $8.65.)

One of the best views in town is from the **Davison St. Guest House,** 19 Davison Rd. (☎924-2188. Dorms $17, singles $34; in winter $18/$55.) **The Stove,** 644 Old Mammoth Rd., 4 blocks from Main St., serves big breakfasts. There's down-home cooking for dinner—the bacon avocado burger is heaven on a bun ($8). Vegetarian options are also available. (☎934-2821. Open daily 6am-2pm and 5-9pm.)

Devil's Postpile National Monument was formed when lava flows oozed through Mammoth Pass thousands of years ago, forming 40-60 ft. basalt posts. A pleasant three-mile walk from the center of Devil's Postpile Monument is Rainbow Falls, where the middle fork of the San Joaquin River drops 101 ft. into a glistening green

CALIFORNIA

pool. From U.S. 395, the trailhead is a 15 mi. drive past Minaret Summit on Rte. 203. A quick half-mile hike from the Twin Lakes turn-off culminates in spectacular views from **Panorama Dome.** Lake Mamie has a picturesque picnic area and many short hikes lead out to Lake George, where exposed granite sheets attract climbers. These trailheads and scenic spots are accessible from the **MAS shuttle.**

Mammoth Mountain High Adventure gets people high. Through adventure. And mountains. The stately climbing wall stands like a modern-day shrine to extreme sports, beckoning both the inexperienced and the professional. (☎924-5683. Open daily 10am-6pm. $6 per climb, $13 per hr., $22 per day; discount for groups of 3 or more.) The **Mammoth Mountain Gondola** reaches a view miles above the rest. (☎934-2571. Open daily 8am-4pm. Round-trip $16, children $8; day pass $25 for gondola and trail use.) Exit the gondola at the top to bike the twisted trails of **Mammoth Mountain Bike Park,** where the ride starts at 11,053 ft. and heads straight down rocky trails. (☎934-0706. Helmets required. Open 9am-6pm. 1-day pass $27, children $14.)

With 150 downhill runs, over 28 lifts, and miles of nordic skiing trails, Mammoth is one of the country's premier winter resorts. The season extends from mid-November to June (in a good year, through July). Lift tickets can be purchased at the Main Lodge on Minaret Rd. (☎934-2571. Open daily 7:30am-3pm.) A free **shuttle bus (MAS)** transports skiers between lifts, town, and the **Main Lodge.** The Forest Service provides tips on the area's cross-country trails. For info, contact the **Inyo National Forest Visitors Center and Chamber of Commerce** (☎924-5500), east off U.S. 395 north of town. **Post Office:** 3330 Main St. (open M-F 8:30am-5pm). **ZIP code:** 93546. **Area code:** 760.

CALIFORNIA

THE PACIFIC NORTHWEST

Once upon a time, approximately twelve to sixty thousand years ago, a group of nomadic hunters bravely traipsed across the (frozen) Bering Strait from Siberia into present-day Alaska and farther south into the Pacific Northwest. They spread out and developed distinct communities which found common ground in their respect for and dependence upon the land. They lived contentedly for thousands of years, until the Europeans came, exploited them, and formed a country on their land. In 1804, this country, by then called the United States, commissioned an overland exploration led by Lewis and Clark and assisted by Sacagawea (or Sakakawea), a Shoshone translator. (For more on this pivotal figure and the spelling of her name, see *Let's Go: Alaska and the Pacific Northwest 2002.*)

Several years later, the Pacific Northwest became the center of national attention again as gold rushes and the Oregon Trail ushered masses into the region, thus jump-starting the political machine that had already taken over the eastern US. In the 1840s, Senator Stephen Douglas argued, sensibly, that the Cascade Range would make the perfect natural border between Oregon and Washington. Sense has little to do with politics, and the Columbia River, running perpendicular to the Cascades, became the border between the two states. Yet even today, the range and not the river is the region's most important cultural divide: west of the rain-trapping Cascades lie the microchip, mocha, and music meccas of Portland and Seattle; to the east sprawl farmland and an arid plateau.

HIGHLIGHTS OF THE PACIFIC NORTHWEST

SEATTLE. The offbeat neighborhoods, fine museums, ample green space, and pioneering cafes of this thriving city are not to be missed (p. 876).

NATIONAL PARKS. Oregon's Crater Lake National Park (p. 913) puts the region's volcanic past on display. In Washington, Olympic National Park (p. 893) has mossy grandeur and deserted beaches; life beautifully blankets the dormant Mt. Rainier (p. 897).

SCENIC DRIVES. Rte. 20 (p. 900) winds through the emerald North Cascades, while U.S. 101 takes visitors on a spin through the Oregon Coast (p. 909).

WASHINGTON

On Washington's western shores, wet Pacific storms feed one of the world's only temperate rainforests in Olympic National Park, and low clouds linger over Seattle, hiding the Emerald City. Visitors to Puget Sound enjoy both isolation in the San Juan islands and cosmopolitan entertainment on the mainland. Over the Cascades, the state's eastern half spreads out into fertile farmlands and grassy plains, while fruit bowls runneth over near Yakima, Spokane, and Pullman.

🛈 PRACTICAL INFORMATION

Capital: Olympia.
Visitor Info: Washington State Tourism, Dept. of Community, Trade and Economic Development, P.O. Box 42500, Olympia, WA 98504 (☎800-544-1800; www.tourism.wa.gov). **Washington State Parks and Recreation Commission,** P.O. Box 42650, Olympia, WA 98504 (☎360-902-8500, info 800-233-0321; www.parks.wa.gov).
Postal Abbreviation: WA. **Sales Tax:** 7-9.1%, depending on county.

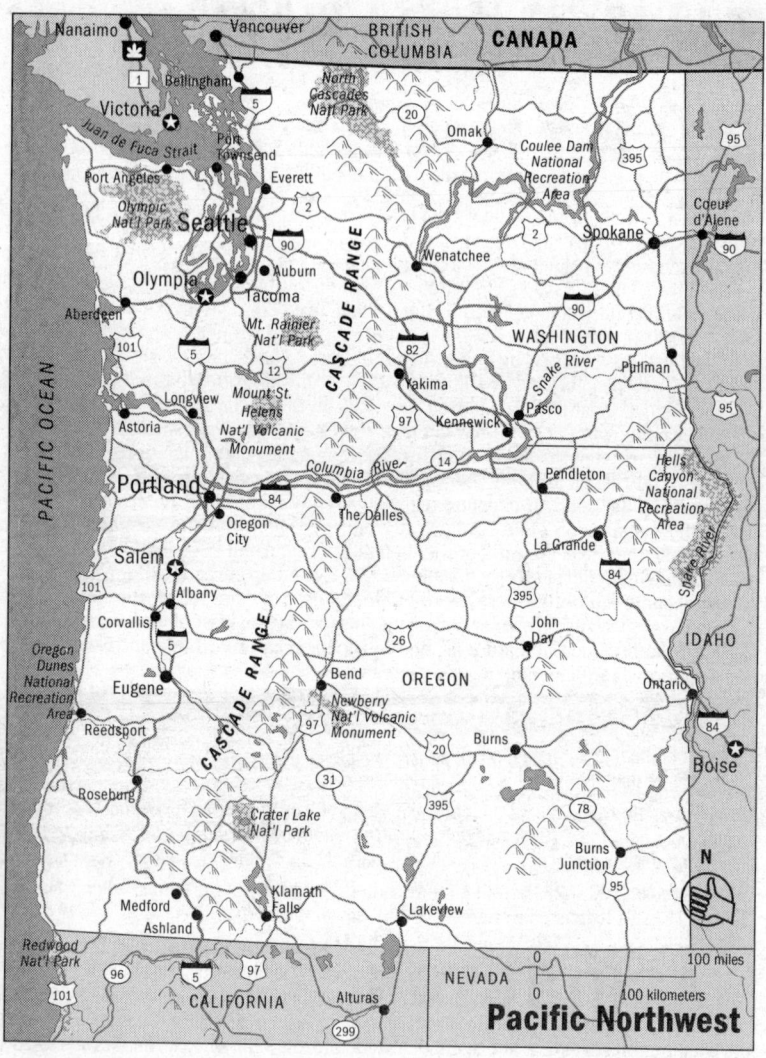

Pacific Northwest

SEATTLE

☎ **206**

Seattle's mix of mountain views, clean streets, espresso stands, and rainy weather proved to be the magic formula of the 90s, attracting transplants from across the US. Even today, newcomers arrive in droves, armed with college degrees and California license plates, hoping for computer industry jobs and a different lifestyle. Seattle duly blesses them with a magnificent setting and a thriving artistic community. The city is one of the youngest and most vibrant in the nation, and a nearly epidemic fascination with coffee has also made it one of the most caffeinated. Every hilltop in Seattle offers an impressive view of Mt. Olympus, Mt. Baker, and Mt. Rainier. The city is shrouded in cloud cover 200 days a year, but when the skies clear, Seattleites rejoice that "the mountain is out" and head for the country.

⊠ INTERCITY TRANSPORTATION

Flights: Seattle-Tacoma International (Sea-Tac) (☎431-4444), on Federal Way, 15 mi. south of Seattle, right off **I-5** (signs are clear). Bus #194 departs the underground tunnel at University St. and 3rd Ave.

Trains: Amtrak (☎800-872-7245, arrival/departure times 382-4125), King St. Station, at 3rd and Jackson St., 1 block east of Pioneer Sq. next to the stadiums. Ticket office and station open daily 6:15am-8pm. To: Portland (4 per day, $26-36); Tacoma (4 per day, $9-14); Vancouver (1 per day, $23-34).

Buses: Greyhound (☎628-5526 or 800-231-2222), at 8th Ave. and Stewart St. Try to avoid night buses, since the station can get seedy after dark. Ticket office open daily 6:30am-2:30am. To: Spokane (6 per day, $30); Vancouver (16 per day, $23); Portland (14 per day, $24); Tacoma (9 per day, $5). **Quick Shuttle** (☎604-940-4428 or 800-665-2122) makes 8 cross-border trips daily from Seattle (Travelodge hotel at 8th and Bell St.) and the Sea-Tac airport to the Vancouver airport and the Holiday Inn on Howe St. in downtown Vancouver (4-4½hr.; $31 from downtown, $39 from Sea-Tac).

Ferries: Washington State Ferries (☎464-6400 or 888-808-7977) has 2 terminals in Seattle. The main terminal is downtown, at Colman Dock, Pier 52. From here service departs to Bainbridge Island (35min.; $4.50, $8-10 with car), Bremerton on the Kitsap Peninsula (1hr., passenger-only boat 30min.; $4.50-$5.50, $8-10 with car), and Vashon Island (25min.; passengers only, $5.50). From the waterfront passenger-only ferries leave from Pier 50. The other Seattle terminal is in Fauntleroy; to reach the terminal drive south on I-5 and take Exit 163A (West Seattle) down Fauntleroy Way. Sailings from Fauntleroy to Southworth on the Kitsap Peninsula (35min.) and Vashon Island (15min.); both $2.90, $10.25-13 with car.

⊏ LOCAL TRANSPORTATION

The **Metro ride free zone** includes most of downtown Seattle (see **Public Transit**, below). The Metro buses cover King County east to North Bend and Carnation, south to Enumclaw, and north to Snohomish County, where bus #6 hooks up with **Community Transit**. This line runs to Everett, Stanwood, and into the Cascades. Bus #174 connects to Tacoma's Pierce County System at Federal Way.

Seattle is a bicycle-friendly city. All buses have free, easy-to-use bike racks (bike shops have sample racks on which to practice). Between 6am and 7pm, bikes may only be loaded or unloaded at stops outside the ride free zone. Check out Metro's *Bike & Ride*, available at the Visitors Center. For a bike map of Seattle, call **City of Seattle Bicycle Program** (☎684-7583).

Public Transit: Metro Transit, Pass Sales and Information Office, 201 S. Jackson St. (☎553-3000 or 24hr. 800-542-7876). The bus tunnel under Pine St. and 3rd Ave. is the heart of the downtown bus system. Open M-F 9am-5pm. Fares are based on a 2-zone system. **Zone 1** includes everything within the city limits (peak hours $1.50, off-peak $1.25). **Zone 2** includes everything else (peak $2, off-peak $1.25). Ages 5-18 always 50¢. Peak hours in both zones M-F 6-9am and 3-6pm. Exact fare required. Weekend day passes $2.50. Ride free daily 6am-7pm in the downtown ride free area, bordered by S. Jackson on the south, 6th and I-5 on the east, Blanchard on the north, and the waterfront on the west. Free (and often necessary) transfers can be used on any bus, including a return trip on the same bus within 2hr. The **Monorail** runs from the Space Needle to Westlake Center, on the 3rd floor. Every 15min. 9am-11pm; $1.25, seniors 50¢, ages 5-12 75¢.

Taxi: Metro Cab, ☎901-0707. **Farwest Taxi**, ☎622-1717.

Car Rental: U Save Auto Rental, 16223 Pacific Hwy. S. (☎242-9778). $33 per day for compacts, plus 22¢ per mi. over 100 mi. unlimited mileage in BC and WA. Must be 21, with a major credit card. **Enterprise**, 11342 Lake City Way NE (☎364-3127). $50 per day for compacts, plus 20¢ per mi. over 150 mi. Airport location 15667 Pacific Hwy. S. (☎242-4533) charges an additional 10% tax.

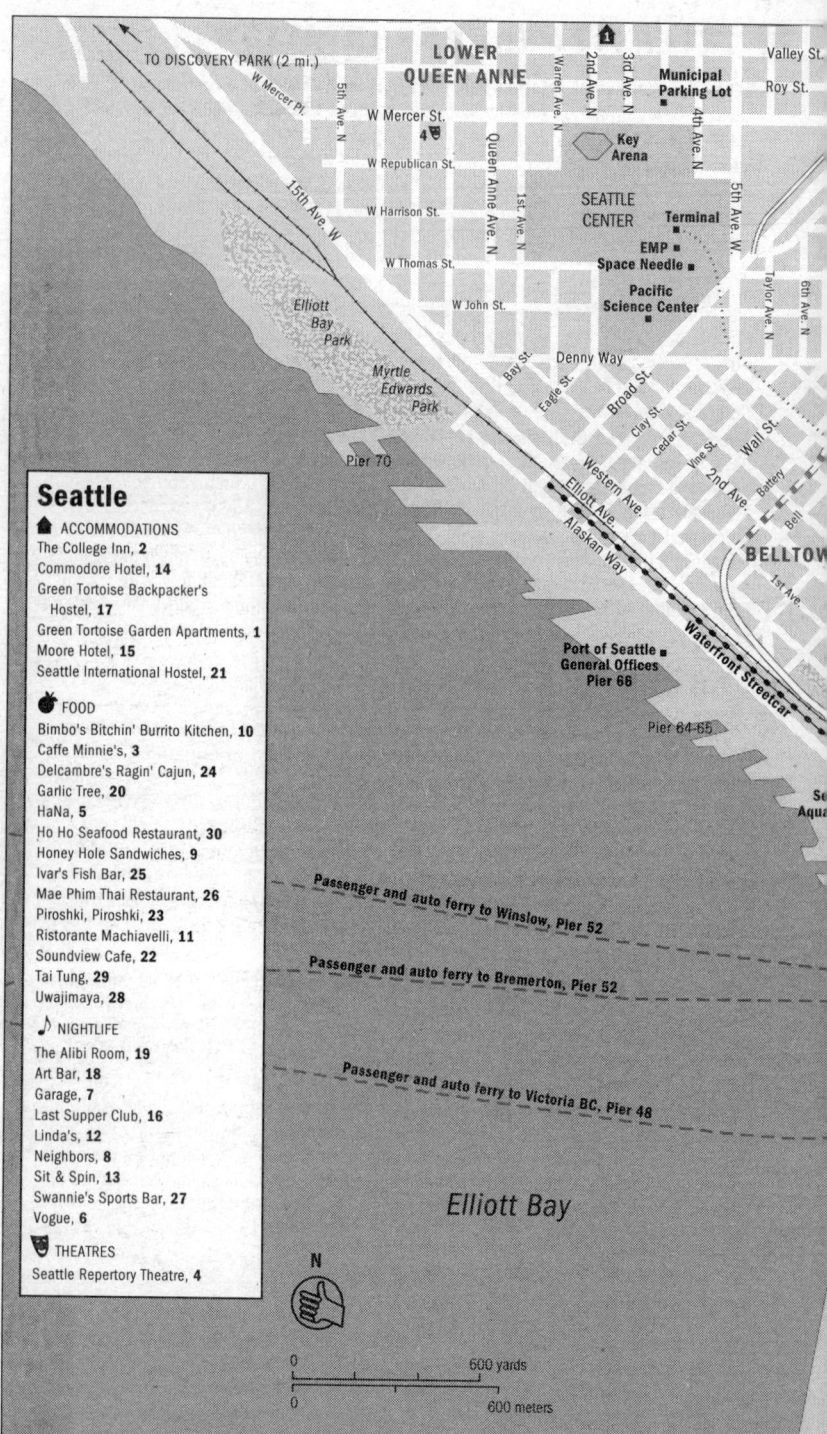

TO DISCOVERY PARK (2 mi.)

LOWER QUEEN ANNE

Valley St.
Roy St.
Municipal Parking Lot

W Mercer St.
4
Key Arena

W Republican St.

W Harrison St.

SEATTLE CENTER
Terminal
EMP
Space Needle
Pacific Science Center

W Thomas St.

W John St.

Denny Way

Elliott Bay Park

Myrtle Edwards Park

Pier 70

Western Ave.
Elliott Ave.
Alaskan Way

BELLTOW

Waterfront Streetcar

Port of Seattle General Offices
Pier 66

Pier 64-65

Se Aqua

Seattle

🏠 **ACCOMMODATIONS**
The College Inn, **2**
Commodore Hotel, **14**
Green Tortoise Backpacker's Hostel, **17**
Green Tortoise Garden Apartments, **1**
Moore Hotel, **15**
Seattle International Hostel, **21**

🍎 **FOOD**
Bimbo's Bitchin' Burrito Kitchen, **10**
Caffe Minnie's, **3**
Delcambre's Ragin' Cajun, **24**
Garlic Tree, **20**
HaNa, **5**
Ho Ho Seafood Restaurant, **30**
Honey Hole Sandwiches, **9**
Ivar's Fish Bar, **25**
Mae Phim Thai Restaurant, **26**
Piroshki, Piroshki, **23**
Ristorante Machiavelli, **11**
Soundview Cafe, **22**
Tai Tung, **29**
Uwajimaya, **28**

♪ **NIGHTLIFE**
The Alibi Room, **19**
Art Bar, **18**
Garage, **7**
Last Supper Club, **16**
Linda's, **12**
Neighbors, **8**
Sit & Spin, **13**
Swannie's Sports Bar, **27**
Vogue, **6**

🎭 **THEATRES**
Seattle Repertory Theatre, **4**

Passenger and auto ferry to Winslow, Pier 52

Passenger and auto ferry to Bremerton, Pier 52

Passenger and auto ferry to Victoria BC, Pier 48

Elliott Bay

N

0   600 yards

0   600 meters

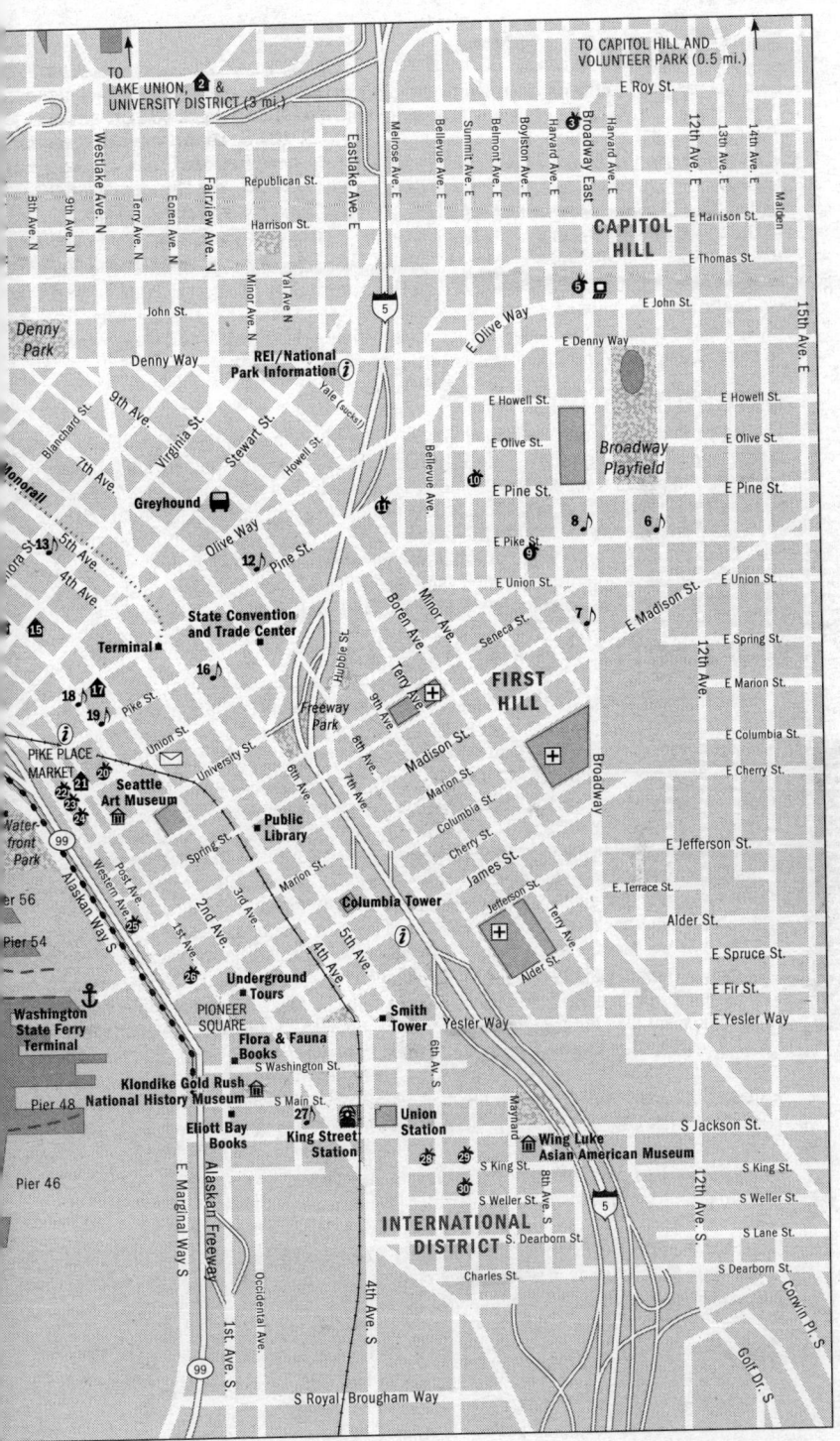

TO LAKE UNION, & UNIVERSITY DISTRICT (3 mi.)

TO CAPITOL HILL AND VOLUNTEER PARK (0.5 mi.)

E Roy St.

E Harrison St.

E Thomas St.

CAPITOL HILL

Denny Park

Republican St.

Harrison St.

John St.

Denny Way

REI/National Park Information

E Olive Way

E Denny Way

E John St.

Denny Park

Broadway Playfield

E Howell St.

E Olive St.

E Pine St.

Greyhound

State Convention and Trade Center

Terminal

Freeway Park

FIRST HILL

E Pike St.

E Union St.

E Madison St.

E Spring St.

E Marion St.

E Columbia St.

E Cherry St.

PIKE PLACE MARKET

Seattle Art Museum

Public Library

Columbia Tower

E Jefferson St.

E Terrace St.

Alder St.

E Spruce St.

E Fir St.

E Yesler Way

Water front Park

Pier 56

Pier 54

Washington State Ferry Terminal

Pier 48

Pier 46

Underground Tours

PIONEER SQUARE

Smith Tower

Flora & Fauna Books

Klondike Gold Rush National History Museum

Eliott Bay Books

King Street Station

Yesler Way

Union Station

Wing Luke Asian American Museum

INTERNATIONAL DISTRICT

S Jackson St.

S King St.

S Weller St.

S Lane St.

S Dearborn St.

Charles St.

S Royal Brougham Way

✈ ORIENTATION

Seattle is a long, skinny city, stretching from north to south on an isthmus between **Puget Sound** to the west and **Lake Washington** to the east, linked by locks and canals. The city is easily accessible by car via **I-5**, which runs north-south through the city, and by **I-90** from the east, which ends at I-5 southeast of downtown. Get to **downtown** (including **Pioneer Sq.**, **Pike Place Market,** and the **waterfront**) from I-5 by taking any of the exits from James St. to Stewart St. Take the Mercer St./Fairview Ave. exit to the **Seattle Center;** follow signs from there. The Denny Way exit leads to **Capitol Hill,** and, farther north, the 45th St. exit heads toward the **University District.** The less crowded **Rte. 99,** also called **Aurora Ave.** or the Aurora Hwy., runs parallel to I-5 and skirts the western side of downtown, with great views from the Alaskan Way Viaduct. Rte. 99 is often the better choice when driving downtown or to **Queen Anne, Fremont, Green Lake,** and the northwestern part of the city.

NEIGHBORHOODS

The finest fish, produce, and baked goods are at **Pike Place Market.** The **University District** supports inexpensive and international cuisine. The **Chinatown/International District** offers tons of rice, pounds of fresh fish, and enough veggies to keep your mother happy, all at ridiculously low prices. At night in Pioneer Square, UW students from frat row dominate the bar stools. You may prefer Capitol Hill, or up Rte. 99 at Fremont, where the atmosphere is more laid-back. For more detailed directions to these and other districts, see the individualized neighborhood listings under **Food** (p. 881), **Nightlife** (p. 888), and **Sights** (p. 884).

⑦ PRACTICAL INFORMATION

Visitor Information: Seattle-King County Visitors Bureau (☎461-5840), at 8th and Pike St., on the 1st fl. of the convention center. Helpful staff doles out maps, brochures, newspapers, and Metro and ferry schedules. Open June-Oct. M-F 8:30am-5pm, Sa-Su 10am-4pm; Nov.-May M-F 8:30am-5pm.

Outdoor Information: Seattle Parks and Recreation Department, 100 Dexter Ave. N. (☎684-4075). Open M-F 8am-5pm for info and pamphlets on city parks. **Outdoor Recreation Information Center,** 222 Yale Ave. (☎470-4060), in REI (see **Equipment Rental,** below). A joint operation between the Park and Forest services, this station is able to answer any questions that might arise as you browse REI's huge collection of maps and guides. Unfortunately, it cannot sell permits. Free brochures on trails. Open Tu-F 10:30am-7pm, Sa 9am-7pm, Su 11am-6pm; winter hours may be shortened.

Equipment Rental: REI, 222 Yale Ave. (☎223-1944), near Capitol Hill. The mothership of camping supply stores rents everything from camping gear to technical mountaineering equipment (see **Outdoor Activities,** p. 886). Open M-F 10am-9pm, Sa 10am-7pm, Su 11am-6pm. **The Bicycle Center,** 4529 Sand Point Way (☎523-8300), near the Children's Hospital. Rents bikes ($3 per hr., $15 per day; 2hr. minimum). Credit card deposit required. Open M-Th 10am-8pm, F 10am-7pm, Sa 10am-6pm, Su 10am-5pm.

Hotlines: Crisis Line, ☎461-3222. **King County Sexual Assault Center** (crisis counseling and advocacy): ☎800-825-7273.

Medical Services: International District Emergency Center, 720 8th Ave. S., Suite 100 (☎461-3235). Medics with multilingual assistance available. **Swedish Medical Center, Providence Campus,** 500 17th Ave. (☎320-2111), 24hr. for urgent care.

Internet access: The **Seattle Public Library,** 800 Pike St. (☎386-4636; TDD 386-4697), is stashed away in a temporary building near the convention center until fall 2003, when a brand new Rem Koolhaas building will open. Free 45min. access with photo ID. Open M-Th 9am-9pm, F 10:30am-6pm, Sa 9am-6pm, Su 1-5pm.

Post Office: (☎800-275-8777), at Union St. and 3rd Ave. downtown. Open M-F 8am-5:30pm, Sa 8am-noon. General delivery window open M-F 10am-noon and 1-3pm. **ZIP code:** 98101. **Area code:** 206.

ACCOMMODATIONS

Seattle's hostel scene is not amazing, but there are plenty of choices and establishments to fit all types of personalities. **Pacific Bed and Breakfast Association** arranges B&B singles in the $50-65 range. (☎800-648-2932. Open M-F 9am-5pm.)

DOWNTOWN

Green Tortoise Backpacker's Hostel, 1525 2nd Ave. (☎340-1222; fax 623-3207; www.greentortoise.net), between Pike and Pine St. on the #174 or 194 bus route. A young party hostel downtown. Often free beer Tu and F; pub crawls F. Laundry, kitchen, Internet access. $20 cash key deposit required. Blanket $1 with $9 deposit. Free breakfast 7-9:30am. Free dinner on M. Reception 24hr. No curfew. 185 beds, $18-20.

Seattle International Hostel (HI), 84 Union St. (☎622-5443 or 888-622-5443), at Western Ave., by the waterfront. Take Union St. from downtown; follow signs down the stairs under the "Pike Pub & Brewery." Great location, laundry, and Internet access. 7-night max. in summer. Reception 24hr. No curfew. Reservations recommended. 199 beds. $19, nonmembers $22. Private rooms for 2-3 $54/$60.

Moore Hotel, 1926 2nd Ave. (☎448-4851 or 800-421-5508), at Virginia, 1 block east from Pike Place Market, next to historic Moore Theater. Open lobby, cavernous halls, and attentive service. Singles $39, with bath $59; doubles $49/$67. HI discount 10%.

Commodore Hotel, 2013 2nd Ave. (☎448-8868), at Virginia. Pleasant decor, only a few blocks from the waterfront. Internet access 15¢ per min. Front desk open 24hr., no visitors past 8pm. Singles $59, with bath $79; 2 beds and bath $89.

OUTSIDE DOWNTOWN

For inexpensive motels farther from downtown, drive north on Rte. 99 (Aurora Ave.) or take bus #26 to the neighborhood of Fremont. Budget chain motels like the **Nites Inn,** 11746 Huron Ave. N., line the highway north of the Aurora bridge. (☎365-3216. Singles from $50, doubles $55.) Look for AAA approval ratings.

Green Tortoise Garden Apartments, 715 2nd Ave. N. (☎340-1222; fax 623-3207), on the south slope of Queen Anne Hill, 3 blocks east from the Space Needle and the Seattle Center. Backyard, kitchen, garden, laundry, free tea and coffee. Applications available at Green Tortoise Hostel (allow a few days for processing). Beds $300 per month and $95 each additional week (one month min.), 4 people per room. $300 deposit.

The College Inn, 4000 University Way NE (☎633-4441), at 40th St. Quiet place near UW campus and its youthful environs. Rooms are small, but turn-of-the-century bureaus and brass fixtures are so darn charming. Continental breakfast included. Singles from $49; doubles $60-70. Double with 2 beds $75-85. Credit card required.

FOOD

Although Seattleites appear to subsist solely on espresso and steamed milk, they do occasionally eat. When they do, they seek out healthy cuisine, especially seafood. The finest fish, produce, and baked goods are at **Pike Place Market** (see below). The **University District** supports inexpensive and international cuisine. **Puget Sound Consumer Coops (PCCs)** are local health food markets at 7504 Aurora Ave. N. (☎525-3586), in Green Lake, and at 6514 40th St. NE (☎526-7661), in the Ravenna District north of the university. Capitol Hill, the U District, and Fremont close main thoroughfares on summer Saturdays for **Farmers Markets.**

PIKE PLACE MARKET AND DOWNTOWN

In 1907, angry citizens demanded the elimination of the middleman and local farmers began selling produce by the waterfront. Not even the Great Depression slowed business, which thrived until an enormous fire burned the building in 1941. The early 1980s heralded a Pike Place renaissance, and today thousands of tourists mob the market daily. (Open M-Sa 9am-6pm, Su 11am-5pm. Produce and fish open earlier; restaurants and lounges close later.) In the **Main Arcade,** on the west side of

Pike St., fishmongers compete for audiences as they hurl fish from shelves to scales. Cutthroat competition will have you paying only pennies for mouth-watering cherries. The market's restaurants boast stellar views of the sound.

Even if you aren't hungry, merchants sell assorted gifts, and several stands offer stunning flower arrangements at a quarter of the cost of most florists. Be prepared to fight the masses during lunch. An **information booth** faces the bike rack by the Main Arcade, at 1st Ave. and Pike St. (☎461-5800. Open Tu-Su 10am-noon.) Restaurants south of Pike Place cater mostly to suits on lunch breaks and tourists, but there are many sandwich and pastry shops covering downtown.

Piroshki, Piroshki, 1908 Pike Pl. (☎441-6068). The Russian *piroshki* is a croissant-like dough baked around sausages, mushrooms, cheeses, salmon, or apples doused in cinnamon ($3-4). Watch the *piroshki* process in progress. Open daily 8:30am-6pm.

Delcambre's Ragin' Cajun, 1523 1st Ave. (☎624-2598), near Pike Place. A tremendous portion of spicy red beans with *andouille* (a flavorful sausage) was enjoyed by former President Clinton in 1995. Lunch $6-8. Dinner almost twice that. Open in summer daily 11am-3pm and 5-9pm. Closed for dinner earlier in the week during winter.

Soundview Cafe (☎623-5700), on the mezzanine in the Pike Place Main Arcade. Follow the neon blue sign. Self-serve breakfast. The sandwich-and-salad bar is a good place to brown-bag a moment of solace. Open M-F 7am-5pm, Sa 7am-5:30pm, Su 9am-3pm.

Garlic Tree, 94 Stewart St. (☎441-5681), one block up from Pike Place Market. The smell will drag you in. Loads of fabulous veggie, chicken, and seafood stir-fries ($7-9). Open M-Th 11am-8pm, F-Sa 11am-9pm.

THE WATERFRONT

Budget eaters, steer clear of Pioneer Square: instead, take a picnic to **Waterfall Garden,** on the corner of S. Main St. and 2nd Ave. S. The garden sports tables and chairs and a manmade waterfall that masks traffic outside. (Open daily 8am-6pm.)

Mae Phim Thai Restaurant, 94 Columbia St. (☎624-2979), a few blocks north of Pioneer Sq., between 1st Ave. and Alaskan Way. Slews of *pad thai* junkies crowd in for cheap, delicious Thai cuisine. All dishes $5. Open M-F 11am-7pm, Sa noon-7pm.

Ivar's Fish Bar (☎624-6852), Pier 54, north of the square, is named for late Seattle shipping magnate Ivar Haglund. Their fast-food window serves the definitive Seattle clam chowder ($2) and scrumptious fish and chips ($6). Open daily 11am-2am.

INTERNATIONAL DISTRICT

Along King and Jackson St., between 5th and 8th Ave. east of the Kingdome, Seattle's International District is packed with great eateries. Competition keeps prices low and quality high, and unassuming facades front fabulous food.

⊠ Uwajimaya, 600 5th Ave. S. (☎624-6248). A district veteran that just moved to bigger, better quarters. The new Uwajimaya Center is a full city block of groceries, gifts, videos, CDs, and everything else you can stick a price tag to. There is even a food court, plying goodies such as Korean BBQ and Taiwanese-style baked goods. A great place for groceries for the hostel, or just to grab a quick bite. Open M-Sa 8am-11pm, Su 9am-10pm.

Tai Tung, 655 S King St. (☎622-7372). Select authentic Chinese and Mandarin cuisine from one of the largest menus around. Grab a bite at the bar, where menus are plastered on the wall. Entrees $5-12. Open Su-Th 10am-11:30pm, F-Sa 10am-1:30am.

Ho Ho Seafood Restaurant, 653 S. Weller St. (☎382-9671). Generous portions of tank-fresh seafood. Great place for large parties to share food on round, spinning tables. Stuffed fish hanging from ceilings and large mirrors make for an interesting atmosphere. Lunch $5-7 (until 4pm), dinner $7-12. Open Su-Th 11am-1am, F-Sa 11am-3am.

CAPITOL HILL

With bronze dance-steps on the sidewalks and neon storefronts, **Broadway** is a land of espresso houses, imaginative shops, elegant clubs, and plenty of eats. Although not the cheapest place to grab a bite, it has a great variety of cuisine options. Bus #7 runs along Broadway; bus #10 runs through Capitol Hill along more sedate **15th St.** Free parking is behind the reservoir at Broadway Field, on 11th Ave.

Bimbo's Bitchin' Burrito Kitchen, 506 E. Pine (☎ 329-9978). The name explains it, and the decorations prove it (fake palm trees and lots of plastic). If the experience isn't bitchin' enough, walk right on through the door to **Cha Cha,** a similarly decorated bar. Spicy Bimbo's burrito $4. Open M-Th noon-11pm, F-Sa noon-2am, Su 2-10pm.

Caffe Minnie's, 611 Broadway Ave. E. (☎860-1360). The original Caffe Minnie (☎448-6263) is at 1st and Denny Way. Famous tomato basil soup ($4). Breakfast all day and a huge menu to chose from. Both open 24hr.

Ristorante Machiavelli, 1215 Pine St. (☎621-7941), right across the street from Bauhaus (see **Cafes,** below). A small Italian place that locals fiercely love. Not too far of a walk from downtown, either. Pasta $7-9. Open M-Th 5-10pm, F-Sa 5-11pm.

HaNa, 219 Broadway Ave. E. (☎328-1187). Packed quarters testify to the popularity of the sushi here. Sushi combo platter with rice and soup (lunch $6.25, dinner $8.75). Open M-Sa 11am-10pm, Su 4-10pm.

Honey Hole Sandwiches, 703 E. Pike (☎709-1399). The primary colors and veggie filled sandwiches make you feel happy and healthy. The hummus-loaded "Daytripper" is a treat ($5). Open daily 10am-7pm.

UNIVERSITY DISTRICT

The neighborhood around the immense University of Washington ("U-Dub"), north of downtown between Union Bay and Portage Bay, supports funky shops, international restaurants, and yes, coffeehouses. The best of each lies within a few blocks of University Way, known as "the Ave." Restaurants run rampant here. The Ave. supports everything from Denny's to bubble tea. Think student budget: this place is probably the cheapest place to eat in the city. To get there, take Exit 169 off I-5 N, or take one of buses #70-74 from downtown, or #7 or 9 from Capitol Hill.

Flowers, 4247 University Way NE (☎633-1903). This 20s landmark was once a flower shop. The mirrored ceiling tastefully reflects an all-you-can-eat vegetarian buffet ($7). Great daily drink specials: W $2 tequila shots, Sa $3 margaritas. Open W-Sa 11am-2am, Su-Tu 11am-midnight; kitchen closes for all but snacks at 10pm.

Mamma Melina, 4759 Roosevelt Way NW (☎632-2271). Right underneath the Seven Gables Cinema, this restaurant is a little slice of southern Italy transplanted onto Seattle's sodden soil. The food is fantastic, and the atmosphere great. Tu 5-9pm is when the real action happens; wine is half price, and Pappa sings his favorite Neapolitan songs. Pasta $9-12. 10% off with ticket stub from a show upstairs. Service begins 4:30pm.

Pizzeria Pagliacci, 4529 University Way NE (☎632-0421; 726-1717 for delivery), also on Capitol Hill at 426 Broadway Ave. E. (☎323-7987). Seattle's best pizza since 1986. M-F 2pm-5pm buy 2 slices, get a free drink. Open Su-Th 11am-11pm, F-Sa 11am-1am.

Tandoor Restaurant, 5024 University Way NE (☎523-7477). The lunch buffet ($6) is a great deal (11am-2:30pm), as is the Su brunch ($7). Classiness is evidenced by the higher dinner prices. Open M-Sa 11am-2:30pm and 4:30-10pm, Su 11am-3pm.

CAFES

The coffee bean is Seattle's first love. One cannot walk a single block without passing an institution of caffeination. The city's obsession with Italian-style espresso drinks has even gas stations pumping out thick, dark, soupy java.

CAPITOL HILL

Bauhaus, 305 E. Pine St. (☎625-1600). The Reading Goddess, looming above the towering bookshelves, protects patrons, and oversees service of drip coffee ($1) or Kool-Aid ($1). Open M-F 6am-1am, Sa-Su 8am-1am.

The Globe Cafe, 1531 14th Ave. (☎324-8815). Seattle's next literary renaissance is brewing here. Quotes overheard at the Globe are plastered on the tables. Fabulous all-vegan menu. Stir-fry tofu $5.50. Internet access $6 per hr. Open Tu-Su 7am-7:30pm.

B&O Cafe, 204 Belmont (☎322-5208), takes its name from the Monopoly railroad. Weekend brunches till 3pm. Delicious desserts $5.50. Open M-Th 7am-midnight, F 7am-1am, Sa 8am-1am, Su 8am-midnight.

PACIFIC NORTHWEST

UNIVERSITY DISTRICT

Espresso Roma, 4201 University Way NE (☎632-6001). Pleasant patio and quasi-former-warehouse interior result in spacious tables with an open air feel. Probably the Ave.'s cheapest coffee (mocha $1.65.) Open daily 7am-11pm.

Ugly Mug, 1309 43rd St. (☎547-3219), off University Way. Off-beat in a 10,000-Maniacs-thrift-store sort of way. Its eclectic chair collection is the perfect place to sit while enjoying the wide sandwich selection (turkey focaccia $4). Open M-F 7:30am-6pm, Sa-Su 9am-6pm.

Gingko Tea, 4343 University Way NE (☎632-7298). Gentle classical music supplies the background; tasteful wood furniture and floral cushions provide the foreground. Five types of chai $2.55; bubble tea $2.45. Open M-Th 10am-10pm, F-Su 11am-8pm.

◎ SIGHTS AND EVENTS

It takes only three frenetic days to get a decent look at most of the city's major sights, since most are within walking distance of one another or the Metro's ride free zone (see p. 877). Seattle taxpayers spend more per capita on the arts than any other Americans, and the investment pays off in unparalleled public art installations throughout the city (self-guided tours begin at the Visitors Center), and plentiful galleries. The investments of Seattle-based millionaires have brought startlingly new and bold architecture in the Experience Music Project and International Fountain. Outside cosmopolitan downtown, Seattle boasts over 300 areas of well-watered greenery (see **Outdoors,** p. 886).

DOWNTOWN

SEATTLE ART MUSEUM. Housed in a grandiose building designed by Philadelphia architect and father of Postmodernism, Robert Venturi, the SAM does a good job of balancing special exhibits, a strong collection of African, Native American, and Asian art, and an eclectic bunch of contemporary western painting and sculpture. Call for info on special musical shows, films, and lectures. Admission is also good for the **Seattle Asian Art Museum** (a branch housed in the museum's former building; see p. 885) for a week. *(100 University Way, near 1st Ave. Recording ☎654-3100, person 654-3255, or TDD 654-3137. Open Tu-W and F-Su 10am-5pm, Th 10am-9pm. Free tours 1 and 2pm, and some later. $7, seniors and students $5, under 12 free; first Th of the month free.)*

THE WATERFRONT

The **Pike Place Hillclimb** descends from the south end of Pike Place Market past chic shops and ethnic restaurants to the Alaskan Way and waterfront. (An elevator is available.) The waterfront is lined with fish and chip shops, harbor cruise companies, and t-shirt shops armed to share "authentic" Seattle with you.

■ **THE SEATTLE AQUARIUM.** The aquarium's star attraction is a huge underwater dome, but harbor seals, fur seals, otters, and plenty of fish don't disappoint either. A $1 million salmon exhibit and ladder teaches about the state's favorite fish. Don't miss the feedings that occur throughout the day. Next door, the **Omnidome** cranks out IMAX films, many of them focusing on natural events. *(Pier 59, near Union St. ☎386-4320, TDD 386-4322. Open in summer daily 10am-8pm; in winter 10am-6pm; last admission 1hr. before closing. $9, seniors $8, ages 6-18 $6.25, ages 3-5 $4.25. Omnidome ☎622-1868. Films daily 10am-10pm. $7, seniors $6.50, ages 6-18 $6. Aquarium and Omnidome combo ticket $14.50, seniors and ages 13-18 $13.50, ages 6-13 $10.75, ages 3-5 $4.25.)*

THE SEATTLE CENTER

The 1962 World's Fair demanded a Seattle Center to herald the city of the future. Now it houses everything from carnival rides to ballet, although Seattleites generally leave the center to tourists and suburbanites. The center is bordered by Denny Way, W. Mercer St., 1st Ave., and 5th Ave., and has eight gates, each with a model of the Center and a map of its facilities. It is accessible via a **monorail** which departs from the third floor of the Westlake Center. The anchor point is the Center House, which holds a food court, stage, and **Info Desk.** (*Monorail: every 15min. M-F 7:30am-11pm, Sa-Su 9am-11pm. $1.25, seniors and ages 5-12 50¢. Info Desk open daily 11am-6pm. For info about events and attractions, call 684-8582 or 684-7200.*)

EXPERIENCE MUSIC PROJECT (EMP). Undoubtedly the biggest and best attraction at the Seattle Center is the new, futuristic, abstract, and technologically brilliant Experience Music Project. The museum is the brainchild of Seattle billionaire Paul Allen, who originally wanted to create a shrine to worship his music idol Jimi Hendrix. Splash together the technological sophistication and foresight of Microsoft, dozens of ethnomusicologists and multimedia specialists, over 80,000 objects, the world-renowned architect Frank Gehry, and enough money to make the national debt appear small (okay, so it was $350 million), and you have the rock 'n' roll museum of the future. The building alone—consisting of sheet metal molded into abstract curves and then acid-dyed gold, silver, purple, blue, and red—is enough to make the average person gasp. Walk in and strap on your personal computer guide (MEG) to interact with the exhibits. Hear clips from Hendrix's famous "Star Spangled Banner" as you stare at the remnants of the guitar he smashed on a London stage. Move into the Sound Lab and test your own skills on guitars, drums, and keyboards linked to computer teaching devices. When you are ready, step up to On Stage, a karaoke gone haywire, and blast your tunes for a virtual audience. Readmission lets you go in and out several times. (*325 Fifth St., at Seattle Center. From I-5 take Exit 167 and follow signs to Seattle Center. Bus #15, 4, 3. ☎ 367-5483 or 877-367-5483. Open in summer daily 9am-11pm; in winter Su-Th 10am-6pm, F-Sa 10am-11pm. $20, seniors and ages 13-17 $16, children $15. Free live music Tu-Sa in lounge; national acts almost every F and Sa in the Sky Church.*)

SPACE NEEDLE. Until the EMP came to town, the Space Needle appeared to be something from another time—now it matches quite well with its futuristic neighbor. On a clear day, the Needle provides a great view and is an irreplaceable landmark for the disoriented. The elevator ride itself is a show—operators are hired for their unique talents. The needle houses an observation tower and a high-end 360° rotating restaurant. (*☎ 905-2100. $11, seniors $9, ages 5-12 $5.*)

THE INTERNATIONAL DISTRICT/CHINATOWN

Seattle's **International District/Chinatown** is three blocks east of Pioneer Square, up Jackson on King St.

■**SEATTLE ASIAN ART MUSEUM.** What do you do when you have too much good art to exhibit all at once? Open a second museum; which is just what SAM did, creating a wonderful stand-on-its-own attraction. The collection is particularly strong in Chinese art, but most of East Asia is admirably represented. (*In Volunteer Park, beyond the watertower. ☎ 654-3100. Open Tu-Su 10am-5pm, Th 10am-9pm. $3, under 12 free; free with SAM ticket from the previous 7 days; SAAM ticket good for $3 discount at SAM.*)

■**UNIVERSITY OF WASHINGTON ARBORETUM.** The Arboretum nurtures over 4000 trees, shrubs, and flowers, and maintains superb walking and running trails. Tours depart the **Graham Visitor Center,** at the southern end of the arboretum on Lake Washington Blvd. (*10 blocks east of Volunteer Park. Bus #11 from downtown. ☎ 543-8800. Open daily sunrise to sunset, Visitors Center 10am-4pm. Free tours Sa and Su at 1pm.*)

JAPANESE TEA GARDEN. The tranquil 3½ acre park is a retreat of sculpted gardens, fruit trees, a reflecting pool, and a traditional tea house. (*☎ 684-4725. At the south end of the UW Arboretum, entrance on Lake Washington Blvd. Open Mar.-Nov. daily 10am-dusk. $2.50; seniors, disabled, students, and ages 6-18 $1.50; under 6 free.*)

ANNUAL EVENTS

Pick up a copy of the Visitors Center's *Calendar of Events*, published every season, for event coupons and an exact listing of innumerable area happenings. The first Thursday evening of each month, the art community sponsors **First Thursday,** a free and well-attended gallery walk. Watch for street fairs in the University District

DROP THE PACK After a few months backpacking, it's no surprise that your shoulders start bruising like unrefrigerated steaks. Fortunately, there is a cure: sea kayaks. Kayaking is the perfect way to explore the nooks of Washington's labyrinthine Puget Sound, and rental boats are readily available. A truly unique resource is the Cascadia Marine Trail, a network of seaside campsites and launching spots maintained specifically for paddlers and sailors. The trail stretches from the San Juans south to Olympia, has over 40 places to pitch a tent along the way, and has been recognized as one of 16 Millennium Trails in the country. Routes in the south of the Sound tend to be shorter and more protected, perfect for beginner to intermediate boaters. Companies that rent often offer moderately priced guided trips for anywhere from half-day to multi-day excursions. Fees for camping vary from free to $10. For information and help planning a trip contact the Washington Water Trails Association, 4649 Sunnyside Ave. N., #305. (☎545-9161; www.wwta.org.)

during mid- to late May, at Pike Place Market over Memorial Day weekend, and in Fremont in mid-June. The International District holds its annual two-day bash in mid-July, featuring arts and crafts booths, East Asian and Pacific food booths, and presentations by a range of groups from the Radical Women/Freedom Socialist Party to the Girl Scouts. For more info, call **Chinatown Discovery** (☎382-1197).

Puget Sound's yachting season begins in May. **Maritime Week,** during the third week of May, and the **Shilshole Boats Afloat Show** (☎634-0911) August 14-18, 2002, gives area boaters a chance to show off their crafts. Over the 4th of July weekend, the Center for Wooden Boats sponsors the free **Wooden Boat Show** (☎382-2628) on Lake Union. Blue blazers and deck shoes are *de rigueur*. Size up the entrants (over 100 wooden boats), then watch a demonstration of boat-building skills. The year-end event is the **Quick and Daring Boatbuilding Contest,** when hopefuls go overboard trying to build and sail wooden boats of their own design, using a limited kit of tools and materials. Plenty of music, food, and alcohol make the sailing smooth.

🏔 OUTDOOR ACTIVITIES

BIKING

Over 1000 cyclists compete in the 19 mi. **Seattle to Portland Race** in mid-July. Call the bike hotline (☎522-2453) for info. On five **Bicycle Sundays** from May to September, Lake Washington Blvd. is open exclusively to cyclists from 10am to 6pm. Call the **Citywide Sports Office** (☎684-7092) for info. The **Burke-Gilman Trail** makes for a longer ride from the University District along Montlake Blvd., then along Lake Union and all the way west to Chittenden Locks and Discovery Park.

WHITEWATER RAFTING

Although the rapids are hours away by car, over 50 whitewater rafting outfitters are based in Seattle and are often willing to undercut one another with merciless and self-mutilating abandon. **Washington State Outfitters and Guides Association** (☎877-275-4964) provides advice; although their office is closed in summer, they do return phone calls and send out info. The **Northwest Outdoor Center,** 2100 Westlake Ave., on Lake Union, gives instructional programs in whitewater and sea kayaking, and leads three-day kayaking excursions through the San Juan Islands. (☎281-9694. Kayak rentals $10-15 per hr. Weekdays 3rd and 4th hours are free. Call for reservations. Open M-F 10am-8pm, Sa-Su 9am-6pm.)

LAKE UNION

Houseboats and sailboats fill Lake Union, situated between Capitol Hill and the University District. Here, the **Center for Wooden Boats,** 1010 Valley St., maintains a moored flotilla of new and restored small craft for rent. (☎382-2628. Open daily noon-6pm. Rowboats weekends $20-30, weekdays $13-19; sailboats $25-38/$16-24.)

Gasworks Park, at the north end of Lake Union, fills is a celebrated kite-flying spot.
Gasworks Kite Shop, 3333 Wallingford N., will help you fly. (☎633-4780. One block
north of the park. Open M-F 10am-6pm, Sa 10am-5pm, Su 11am-5pm.) **Urban Surf,**
2100 N. Northlake Way, rents surfboards, in-line skates, snowboards, and kite-
boards. (☎545-9463. Opposite park entrance. Boards $15 per day. Skates $5 per hr.,
$16 per day. Open M-F 10am-7pm, Sa 10am-5pm, Su 11am-5pm.)

WOODLAND PARK AND WOODLAND ZOO

Next to Green Lake are Woodland Park and the Woodland Park Zoo, 5500 Phinney
Ave. N. The park is mediocre, but the zoo has won a bevy of AZA awards (the zoo
Oscars, if you will) for best new exhibits. Both the African Savanna and the North-
ern Trail exhibits are full of zoo favorites: grizzlies, wolves, lions, giraffes, and
Sasquatch. (N. 50th St. ☎684-4800. Bus #5 from downtown. Park open daily 4:30am-
11:30pm. Zoo open May to mid-Sept. daily 9:30am-6pm; mid-March to April and mid-
Sept. to mid-Oct. until 5pm; winter until 4pm. $9, seniors $8.25, ages 6-17 $6.50.
Prices will rise slightly in 2002.)

🎭 ENTERTAINMENT

Seattle has one of the world's most notorious underground music scenes and the
third-largest theater community in the US (second to New York and Chicago), and
supports performance in all sorts of venues, from bars to bakeries. The free **Out to
Lunch** series (☎623-0340) brings everything from reggae to folk dancing to parks,
squares, and office buildings during summer.

MUSIC AND DANCE

The **Seattle Opera** performs favorites from August to May. Come January 2002 they
will move out of the Seattle Center Opera House and next door into the Mercer Arts
Arena, to make room for renovations. Buffs should reserve well in advance,
although rush tickets are sometimes available. (☎389-7676. Students and seniors
can get half-price tickets 1½hr. before the performance. From $31.) The **Pacific
Northwest Ballet** performs at the Opera House from September to June. In 2002, look
for performances of *Song and Dance*, *Tango Tonight*, and *Cinderella*. (☎441-
9411. Tickets from $15. Half-price rush tickets available to seniors and students
30min. before showtime.)

THEATER AND CINEMA

The city hosts an exciting array of first-run plays and alternative works, particularly
by many talented amateur groups. Rush tickets are often available at nearly half
price on the day of the show from **Ticket/Ticket** (☎324-2744; cash only). 🏛**The Empty
Space Theatre,** 3509 Fremont Ave. N., 1½ blocks north of the Fremont Bridge, presents comedies from October to early July. (☎547-7500. Tickets $22-30. Half-price
tickets 30min. before curtain. Box office open Tu-Su from noon.) **Seattle Repertory
Theater,** 155 Mercer St., at the wonderful Bagley Wright Theater in the Seattle Center, presents contemporary and classic winter productions. (☎443-2222. Tickets
$15-45; cheaper on weekdays, seniors $31, under 25 $10. Rush tickets 30min. before
curtain. Box office open M-F 10am-6pm, weekends noon-6pm during season.)

Seattle is a cinematic paradise. Most of the theaters that screen non-Hollywood
films are on Capitol Hill and in the University District. On summer Saturdays, outdoor cinema in Fremont begins at dusk at 670 N. 34th St., in the U-Park lot by the
bridge, behind the Red Door Alehouse. Enter as early as 7pm to catch live music
that starts at 8pm. (☎767-2593. $5.) **TCI Outdoor Cinema** shows everything from clas-
sics to cartoons for free at the Gasworks Park. (☎720-1058. Live music 7pm-dusk.)
Unless specified, the theaters below charge $5 for matinees and $8 for features. **The
Egyptian,** 801 E. Pine St. (☎323-4978), at Harvard Ave. on Capitol Hill, is an Art Deco
art house best known for hosting the **Seattle International Film Festival** in the last
week of May and first week of June. **The Harvard Exit,** 807 E. Roy St. (☎323-8986), on

Capitol Hill near the north end of the Broadway business district, has quality classic and foreign films. It is a converted women's club that has its own ghost and an enormous antique projector. **Grand Illusion Cinema,** 1403 50th St. NE, in the U District at University Way is one of the last independent theaters in Seattle and often shows old classics and hard-to-find films. (☎523-3935. $7, seniors $3.50; matinees $4.50.)

SPORTS

Seattleites cheered last summer when the home team, the **Mariners,** moved out of the Kingdome, where in 1995 sections of the roof fell into the stands. The "M's" are now playing baseball in the half-billion dollar, hangar-like **Safeco Field,** at First Ave. S. and Royal Brougham Way S., under an enormous retractable roof. (Tickets ☎622-4487. From $10.) Seattle's football team, the **Seahawks,** are stuck playing in UW's Husky Stadium until construction on their new stadium is finished. (Tickets ☎628-0888. From $10.) On the other side of town and at the other end of the aesthetic spectrum, the sleek **Key Arena** in the Seattle Center hosts Seattle's NBA basketball team, the **Supersonics.** (☎628-0888. From $9.) For college sports fans, the **University of Washington Huskies** football team has dominated the PAC-10 for years and doesn't plan to let up. Call the Athletic Ticket Office (☎543-2200) for schedules and prices.

◪ NIGHTLIFE

DOWNTOWN

▨**The Alibi Room,** 85 Pike St. (☎623-3180), across from the Market Cinema in the Post Alley in Pike Place. A local indie filmmaker hangout that is remarkably friendly in its air of culture. Bar with music open 7 nights, a downstairs dance floor opens F-Sa. Brunch Sa-Su. No cover. Open daily 11:30am-2am.

Sit and Spin, 2219 4th Ave. (☎441-9484), between Bell St. and Blanchard St. Board games keep patrons busy while they wait for their clothes to dry or for alternative bands to stop playing in the back room. F-Sa nights cover $6-8. The cafe sells everything from local microbrews on tap to bistro food. Artists cut albums in the **Bad Animal** studio down the street, where R.E.M. once recorded. Open Su-Th 9am-midnight, F-Sa 9am-2am. Kitchen opens daily at 11am.

Art Bar, 1516 2nd Ave. (☎622-4344), opposite Green Tortoise Hostel. A gallery and bar with DJs and lots of dancing. Tu funk, Th reggae, F jungle, Sa hip hop. Sa house music 4-10am. Pints $2.50 4-9pm. Cover $5-6. Open M-F 11am-2am, Sa-Su 6pm-2am.

PIONEER SQUARE

Although the local scene took a beating when several bars closed due to earthquake damage, the vibe is still intact. Most bars participate in a joint cover (F-Sa $10, Su-Th $5) that will let you wander from bar to bar to sample the bands. The larger venues are listed below. Two smaller venues, **Larry's Greenfront,** 209 1st Ave. S. (☎624-7665), and **New Orleans,** 114 1st Ave. S. (☎622-2563), feature great blues and jazz nightly. Most clubs close at 2am weekends and at midnight on weekdays.

Bohemian Cafe, 111 Yesler Way (☎447-1514), pumps reggae every night. 3 sections, a cafe, a bar, and a stage, all of them adorned with Jamaican art. Live shows 6 nights per week, often national acts on weekends. Happy hour 4-7pm. After-hours electronica F-Sa 2-8am. Part of the joint cover. Open M-Sa 4pm-2am.

Central Tavern, 207 1st Ave. S. (☎622-0209), was one of the early venues for grunge, and in a weird twist has now become a favorite for bikers. Live rock 6 nights a week, at 9:30pm. Part of the joint cover. Open daily 11:30am-2am, kitchen closes around 8pm.

Last Supper Club, 124 S. Washington St. (☎748-9975), at Occidental. 2 dance floors, DJed with everything from 70s disco F to funky house, drum and bass, and trance Sa. Su nights salsa at 8:30pm. Cover $5-10. Open W-Su 4pm-2am.

Swannie's Sports Bar, 222 S. Main St. (☎622-9353). Share drink specials with pro ballplayers who stop by post-game. Any Seattle sports junkie will swear this is the place to be. Drink specials change daily. Open M-F 11:30am-2am, Sa-Su 4pm-2am.

CAPITOL HILL

East of Broadway, Pine St. boasts cool lounge after cool lounge. Find your atmosphere and acclimatize. West off of Broadway, Pike St. has the clubs that push the limits (punk, industrial, fetish, and dance) and break the sound barrier.

■ **Linda's,** 707 Pine St. E. (☎325-1220). A very chill bar that is a major post-gig scene for Seattle rockers. Live DJ playing jazz and old rock. Expanded menu, liquor, and breakfast Sa-Su. No cover Su, Tu, and Th. Open M-F 2pm-2am, Sa-Su 10am-2am.

Vogue, 1516 11th Ave. (☎324-5778), off Pike St. If this club were a country, black leather would be the national outfit. Be prepared to dress for the night; on fetish night, only those bedecked in black can enter. Tu and Th live music, W goth night, F and Su fetish, Sa 80s/90s New Wave. Cover $2-5. Open Tu-Su 9pm-2am.

Neighbors, 1509 Broadway Ave. NE (☎324-5358). Enter from Pike Alley. A gay dance club priding itself on techno slickness. Midnight drag shows Su and Tu-Th. M, W, and F house, Tu and Th 80s, Su Latin night. Cover $1-5. Open Su-W 9pm-2am, Th 9pm-3am, F-Sa 9pm-4am.

Garage, 1130 Broadway Ave. NE (☎322-2296), between Union and Madison. This automotive warehouse turned upscale pool hall gets suave at night. Happy hour daily 3-7pm. 18 pool tables $6-14 per hr.; $4 per hr. during happy hour; $5 per hr. M; free for female sharks on Ladies' Night Su. Open daily 3pm-2am.

NEAR SEATTLE: VASHON ISLAND

Only a 25min. ferry ride from Seattle, Vashon Island has remained inexplicably invisible to most Seattleites. With its forested hills and expansive sea views, this artists' colony feels like the San Juan Islands without the tourists or an economy to cater to them, though budget travelers will feel well cared for in the island's hostel. Most of the island is covered in Douglas fir, rolling cherry orchards, wildflowers, and strawberry fields, and all roads lead to rocky beaches. **Point Robinson Park** is a gorgeous spot for a picnic, and free tours (☎217-6123) of the 1885 **Coast Guard lighthouse** are available. **Vashon Island Kayak Co.,** at Burton Acres Park, Jensen Point Boat Launch, runs guided tours (from $48) and rents sea kayaks. (☎463-9527. Open F-Su 10am-5pm. Singles $14 per hr., $35 per half-day, $50 per day; doubles $20/$50/$65.) More than 500 acres of woods in the middle of the island are interlaced with mildly difficult hiking trails. The Vashon Park District can tell you more. (☎463-9602. Open daily 9am-5pm.)

The **Vashon Island AYH Ranch Hostel (HI-AYH),** at 12119 SW Cove Rd., west of Vashon Hwy., is sometimes called the "Seattle B." Resembling an old Western town, the hostel offers bunks, open-air teepees, and covered wagons. (☎463-2592. Free pancake breakfast and 1-speed bikes. Sleeping bag $2. Open May-Oct. $11; bicyclists $10; nonmembers $14.) The hostel runs **The Lavender Duck B&B** down the road ($55).

Vashon Island stretches between Seattle and Tacoma on its east side and between Southworth and Gig Harbor on its west side. **Washington State Ferries** (☎464-6400 or 800-843-3779) runs ferries to Vashon Island from Seattle (see **Transportation,** p. 877). The local **Thriftway** (9740 SW Bank Rd.) provides maps, as does the Vashon-Maury **Chamber of Commerce,** 17633 SW Vashon Hwy. (☎463-6217).

OLYMPIA ☎360

Inside of what seems like an interminable network of otherwise bland suburbs there yet lurks a grungy, dyed core. The liberal Evergreen State College campus lies a few miles from the city center, and its highly pierced tree-hugging student body spills into the mix in a kind of chemistry experiment that gets weirder when the Olympia-as-state-capital politicians join in. The product of this grouping resists definition, but it is worth experiencing for yourself.

🔳 **PRACTICAL INFORMATION.** Olympia is at the junction of I-5 and U.S. 101. **Amtrak,** 6600 Yelm Hwy. (☎923-4602), runs to Seattle (1¾hr., 4 per day, $10-18) and Portland (2½hr., 4 per day, $13-24). Station open daily 8-11:30am, 12:45-

3:30pm, and 5:30-8:15pm. **Greyhound,** 107 E. 7th Ave. (☎357-5541), at Capitol Way, goes to Seattle (1¾hr., 6-7 per day, $8-9); Sea-Tac ($5); and Portland (2¾hr., 6-7 per day, $22-24). **Intercity Transit (IT)** provides service almost anywhere in Thurston County, even with bicycles. (☎786-1881 or 800-287-6348. Fare 75¢; day passes $1.25.) The free **Capitol Shuttle** runs from the Capitol Campus to downtown or to the east side and west side (every 15min. 6:45am-5:45pm). **Washington State Capitol Visitors Center** is on Capitol Way at 14th Ave., next to the State Capitol; follow the signs on I-5. (☎586-3460. Open M-F 8am-5pm.) The **Olympic National Forest Headquarters,** 1835 Black Lake Blvd. SW, provides info on land in and outside the park. (☎956-2400. Open M-F 8am-4:30pm.) **Post Office:** 900 Jefferson SE (☎357-2289; open M-F 7:30am-6pm, Sa 9am-4pm). **ZIP code:** 98501. **Area code:** 360.

ⁿⁱⁿ ACCOMMODATIONS AND FOOD. Motels in Olympia cater to policy-makers ($60-80), but chains in nearby Tumwater are fine. ◪**Grays Harbor Hostel,** 6 Ginny Ln., 25 mi. west of Olympia just off Rte. 8 in Elma, is the perfect place to start a trip down the coast. (☎482-3119. Hot tub, frolf course, and a shed for bike repairs. Dorms $14; private rooms $28. Bikers camp for $10.) **Millersylvania State Park,** 12245 Tilly Rd. S., is 10 mi. south of Olympia. Take Exit 95 off I-5 S or Exit 95 off I-5 N, then take Rte. 121 N, and follow signs to 6 mi. of trails and Deep Lake. (☎753-1519 or 800-452-5687. Showers 25¢ per 6min. Wheelchair accessible. 180 sites. $14; hookup $20.) Diners, veggie eateries, and Asian quickstops line bohemian 4th Ave. east of Columbia. The **Olympia Farmer's Market,** 700 N. Capital Way, proffers produce and fantastic fare. (☎352-9096. Open Apr.-Oct. Th-Su 10am-3pm, Nov.-Dec. Sa-Su 10am-3pm.) **The Spar Cafe & Bar,** 114 E. 4th Ave., is an ancient logger haunt that moonlights as a pipe and cigar shop. (☎357-6444. Restaurant open M-Th 6am-10pm, F-Sa 6am-11pm, Su 6am-9pm. Bar open Su-Th 11am-midnight, F-Sa 11am-2am.)

◪ SIGHTS. Olympia's crowning glory is **State Capitol Campus,** a complex of state government buildings, fabulous fountains, manicured gardens, and veterans' monuments. (☎586-3460. Tours depart from just inside the front steps daily on the hr. 10am-3pm. Building open M-F 8am-5:30pm, Sa-Su 10am-4pm.) The mansion-like **State Capitol Museum,** 211 W. 21st Ave., houses historical and political exhibits. (☎753-2580. Open Tu-F 10am-4pm, Sa-Su noon-4pm. $2, seniors $1.75, children $1.) Several different free tours of campus buildings leave every hr. on weekdays; call 586-8677 for info and options for the disabled. The high walls of the **Yashiro Japanese Garden,** at Plum and Union next to City Hall, contain Olympia's secret garden. (☎753-8380. Open daily 10am-dusk to picnickers and ponderers.)

◪ NIGHTLIFE. Olympia's ferocious nightlife seems to have outgrown its daylife. *The Rocket* and the daily *Olympian* list live music. At ◪**Eastside Club and Tavern,** 410 E. 4th St., old men play pool, college students slam micro pints, and local bands play often. (☎357-9985. Open M-F noon-2am, Sa-Su 3pm-2am.) The **4th Ave. Alehouse & Eatery,** 210 E. 4th St., serves "slabs" of pizza ($2.25), 26 micropints ($3), and live tunes, from blues to reggae. (☎956-3215. Music Th-Sa 9pm. Restaraunt open M-F 11:30am-8pm, F-Sa noon-8pm.) DJs spin tunes nightly at gay-friendly **Thekla,** 155 E. 5th Ave., under the neon arrow off N. Washington St., between 4th Ave. and Capitol. (☎352-1855. 21+. Cover up to $5. Open Tu-Su 5pm-2am.)

SAN JUAN ISLANDS   ☎360

The San Juan Islands are home to great horned owls, puffins, sea otters, sea lions, and more deer, raccoons, and rabbits than they can support. Pods of orcas (killer whales) patrol the waters, and pods of tourists circle the islands in all manner of watercraft. Over 1½ million visitors come ashore each year during the peak of summer. To avoid the rush but still enjoy good weather, visit in late spring or early fall.

🛈 PRACTICAL INFORMATION

Washington State Ferries (☎206-464-6400 or 800-843-3779) serves Lopez (50min.), Shaw (1¼hr.), Orcas (1½hr.), and San Juan Island (2hr.), from Anacortes; check the schedule at Visitors Centers in Puget Sound. Foot passengers travel free. To save on car fares, travel to the westernmost island on your itinerary, then return: eastbound traffic travels for free. In summer, arrive 1hr. prior to departure. ($7, vehicle $17-28, bike $3; cash only.) To reach Anacortes, take I-5 N from Seattle to Mt. Vernon, then Rte. 20 west to town and follow signs. The **Bellingham Airporter** (☎800-235-5247) shuttles between Sea-Tac and Anacortes (M-F 10 per day, Sa-Su 7 per day; $31). Short hops and good roads make the islands great for biking.

SAN JUAN ISLAND

The biggest and most popular of the islands, San Juan is the easiest island to explore, since the ferry docks right in town, roads are fairly flat, and a shuttle bus runs throughout the island. Seattle weekenders flood the island throughout the summer, bringing fleets of traffic. A drive around the 35 mi. perimeter of the island takes about 2hr., and the route is good for a day's cycle. The **West Side Rd.** traverses gorgeous scenery and provides the best chance for sighting orcas offshore. Mullis Rd. merges with Cattle Point Rd. and goes straight into **American Camp**, on the south side of the island. In the summer, every Saturday from 12:30 to 3:30pm, volunteers in period costume re-enact daily life from the time of the Pig War, a mid-19th-century squabble between the US and Britain over control of the Islands. (☎378-2902. Visitors Center open 8:30am-5pm. Camp open June-Aug. daily dawn-11pm; Sept.-May Th-Su. Guided walks Sa 11:30am.) **British Camp,** the second half of the **San Juan National Historical Park,** lies on West Valley Rd., on the sheltered **Garrison Bay.** (Buildings open late May to early Sept. daily 8am-5pm.) **Limekiln Point State Park,** along West Side Rd., is renowned as the best whale-watching spot in the area. The annual **San Juan Island Jazz Festival** (☎378-5509) swings in late July.

San Juan County Park, 380 Westside Rd., 10 mi. west of Friday Harbor on Smallpox and Andrews Bays, offers the chance to catch views of whales and a great sunset. (☎378-2992. Water and flush toilets, no showers or RV hookups. Park open daily 7am-10pm. Reservations highly recommended. Office open daily 9am-7pm. Vehicle sites $18; walk-ins $5.) **Thai Kitchen,** 42 1st St., next to the Whale Museum is a popular dinner spot with a beautiful patio for flower-sniffing or star-gazing. (☎378-1917. Open M 5-9pm, Tu-Sa 11:30am-3pm and 5-9pm. Dinners $8-12.)

San Juan Transit (☎378-8887 or 800-887-8387) circles the island every 35-55min. and will stop on request (point to point $4; day pass $10; 2-day pass $17, also good on Orcas Island). If you plan to see San Juan Island only, it may be cheaper to leave your car in Anacortes and use the shuttles. **Island Bicycles,** 380 Argyle St., up Spring St., rents for $6 per hr. and $30 per day. (☎378-4941. Open daily 9am-6pm.) The **Chamber of Commerce** (☎378-5240 or 888-468-3701) is a booth on East St. up from Cannery Landing. The **San Juan National Historic Park Information Center** is at 1st and Spring St. (☎378-2240; open M-F 8:30am-4:30pm; in winter until 4pm.)

ORCAS ISLAND

A small population of retirees, artists, and farmers dwell on Orcas Island in understated homes, surrounded by green shrubs and the red bark of madrona trees. The trail to **Obstruction Pass Beach** is the best way to clamber down to the rocky shores. **Moran State Park** is unquestionably Orcas's star outdoor attraction, with over 30 mi. of hiking trails ranging from a one-hour jaunt around **Mountain Lake** to a day-long trek up the south face of **Mt. Constitution** (2047 ft.), the highest peak on the islands. Part-way down is **Cascade Falls,** spectacular in the spring and early summer. The **Orcas Tortas** makes a slow drive on a green bus from Eastsound to the peak. (☎376-4156. $8.) **Shearwater Adventures** runs a fascinating sea kayak tour of north Puget Sound and is a great resource for experienced paddlers. (☎376-4699. 3hr. tour with 30min. of dry land training. $45.) **Crescent Beach Kayak,** on the highway 1 mi. east of Eastsound, rents. (☎376-2464. $10 per hr.; $25 per half-day. Open daily 9am-5pm.)

Doe Bay VillageResort, Star Rte. 86, off Horseshoe Hwy. on Pt. Lawrence Rd., 5 mi. out of Moran State Park, includes kitchen, health food store and cafe, a treehouse, guided kayak trips, a steam sauna and a mineral bath. (☎376-2291. Reception 8am-10pm. Sauna $4 per day, non-guests $7; bathing suits optional; coed. Reservations recommended. Beds $16; campsites $25.) To reach **Moran State Park,** Star Rte. 22 in Eastsound, follow Horseshoe Hwy. (☎376-2326 or 800-452-5687. About 12 sites and restrooms open year-round. Boats $13 per hr., $40 per day. Reservations strongly recommended May to early Sept. Sites $14.) At the ▓**Comet Cafe,** in Eastsound Sq. on N. Beach Rd., two sisters run a happy-go-lucky cafe. One bakes sweets, the other makes the savory stuff. (☎376-4220. Open Tu-Sa 9am-3pm.)

The ferry lands on the southwest tip of Orcas, and the main town of **Eastsound** is 9 mi. northeast. **Olga** and **Doe Bay** are an additional 8 and 11 mi. respectively down the eastern side of the horseshoe. **San Juan Transit** (☎376-8887) runs about every 1½hr. to most parts of the island (ferry to Eastsound $4). **Wildlife Cycle,** at A St. and North Beach Rd. in Eastsound, rents 21-speeds. (☎376-4708. Open M-Sa 10am-5:30pm, Su 11am-2pm. $7.50 per hr., $30 per day.)

LOPEZ ISLAND

Smaller than either Orcas or San Juan, "Slow-pez" lacks some of the tourist facilities of larger islands. The small **Shark Reef** and **Agate Beach County Parks,** on the southwest end of the island, have tranquil and well-maintained hiking trails, and Agate's beaches are calm and deserted. Roads on the island are ideal for biking. **Lopez Village** is 4½ mi. from the ferry dock off Fisherman Bay Rd. To rent a bike or kayak, head to **Lopez Bicycle Works,** south of the village. (☎468-2847. Open July-Aug. daily 9am-9pm. Apr.-June and Sept.-Oct. daily 10am-5pm. Bikes $5 per hr., $25 per day; kayaks from $10-15 per hr.) **Spencer Spit State Park,** on the northeast corner of the island 3½ mi. from the ferry terminal, has primitive sites on the beach and the hill. (☎468-2251 or 800-452-5687. Open Feb.-Oct. daily until 10pm. Toilets. Sites $14; hiker/biker $6. Reservations recommended; fee $6.) Ferry transport means price inflation, so it may be wise to bring a lunch. Or munch on fresh pastries at **Holly B's,** 165 Cherry Tree Ln. (☎468-2133; open M and W-Sa 7am-5pm, Su 7am-4pm).

OLYMPIC PENINSULA

Due west of Seattle and its busy Puget Sound neighbors, the Olympic Peninsula is a remarkably different world. To the west, the Pacific Ocean stretches to a distant horizon; to the north, the Strait of Juan de Fuca separates the Olympic Peninsula from Vancouver Island; and to the east, Hood Canal and the Kitsap Peninsula isolate this sparsely inhabited wilderness from the sprawl of Seattle. While getting around the peninsula is easiest by car, the determined can make the trip by bus.

PORT TOWNSEND   ☎360

Unlike the salmon industry, Port Townsend's Victorian splendor has survived the progression of time and weather. Countless cafes, galleries, and bookstores line somewhat drippy streets, cheering the urbanites who move here to escape the rat race. The **Ann Starret Mansion,** 744 Clay St., has nationally renowned Victorian architecture, frescoed ceilings, and a free-hanging, three-tiered spiral staircase. (☎385-3205 or 800-321-0644. Tours daily noon-3pm; $2.)

Two hostels crouch in old military haunts, offering bright rooms: **Olympic Hostel (HI-AYH),** in Fort Worden State Park, 1½ mi. from town, and **Fort Flagler Hostel (HI-AYH),** in Fort Flagler State Park on gorgeous Marrowstone Island, 20 mi. from Port Townsend. To get there, go south on Rte. 19, which connects to Rte. 116 E. and leads directly into the park. (Olympic: ☎385-0655. Check-in 5-10pm. Private rooms available. Dorms $14, nonmembers $17; hiker/biker $2 off. Fort Flagler: ☎385-1288. Check-in 5-10pm; lockout 10am-5pm. Book ahead. Dorms $14, nonmembers $17; hikers and bikers $2 off.) You can camp on the beach at **Fort Flagler State Park.** (☎385-1259. Book ahead. 116 sites; tents $14, RVs $20, hiker/biker $6.)

Port Townsend sits at the terminus of Rte. 20 on the northeastern corner of the Olympic Peninsula. Over land, it can be reached by U.S. 101 on the peninsula, or from the Kitsap Peninsula across the Hood Canal Bridge. **Washington State Ferries** (☎ 206-464-6400 or 800-808-7977) runs from Seattle to Winslow on Bainbridge Island, where a **Kitsap County Transit** bus runs to Poulsbo. From Poulsbo, **Jefferson County Transit** (☎ 385-4777) runs to Port Townsend. A free shuttle goes into downtown from the Park 'N' Ride lot. (Most buses do not run on Su. 50¢.) The **Chamber of Commerce** is at 2437 E. Sims Way, 10 blocks southwest of town on Rte. 20. (☎ 385-2722 or 888-365-6987. Open M-F 9am-5pm, Sa 10am-4pm, Su 11am-4pm.) **P.T. Cyclery,** 100 Tyler St., rents mountain bikes. (☎ 385-6470. Open M-Sa 9am-6pm. $7 per hr., $25 per day.) **Kayak P.T.,** 435 Water St., rents kayaks. (☎ 385-6240. Singles $25 per 4hr., doubles $40 per 4hr. Over 83 free.) **Post Office:** 1322 Washington St. (☎ 385-1600; open M-F 9am-5pm). **ZIP code:** 98368. **Area code:** 360.

OLYMPIC NATIONAL PARK ☎ 360

With glacier-encrusted peaks, dripping river valley rainforests, and jagged shores along the Pacific Coast, the landscape of ONP is wonderfully diverse. A little effort and planning may yield an afternoon shell-hunting on an isolated beach, a day salmon fishing on the Hoh River, or a week glacier-gazing from the treeline.

🛈 PRACTICAL INFORMATION

Only a few hours from Seattle, Portland, and Victoria, the wilderness of Olympic National Park is most easily and safely reached by car. U.S. 101 encircles the park in the shape of an upside-down U, with Port Angeles at the top. The park's vista-filled **eastern rim** runs up to Port Angeles, from which the much-visited **northern rim** extends westward. The tiny town of **Neah Bay** and stunning **Cape Flattery** perch at the northwest tip of the peninsula; farther south on U.S. 101, the slightly less tiny town of **Forks** is a gateway to the park's rainforested **western rim.** Separate from the rest of the park, much of the Pacific coastline comprises a gorgeous **coastal zone.**

Olympic National Park Visitors Center, 3002 Mt. Angeles Rd., is off Race St. in Port Angeles. (☎ 452-0330; TDD 452-0306. Open in summer approximately Su-F 8:30am-6:30pm, Sa 8:30am-8pm; in winter daily 9am-4pm.) Staff at the **Olympic National Park Wilderness Information Center** (☎ 565-3100), just behind the Visitors Center, helps design trips within the park. The entrance fee, good for seven days' access to the park, is $10 per car and $5 per hiker or biker, charged during the day at ranger stations and developed entrances such as Hoh, Heart o' the Hills, Sol Duc, Staircase, and Elwha. Backcountry users must pay $2 extra per night to ranger offices. $5 passes are required to park in Olympic National Forest.

🛏 ACCOMMODATIONS

The closest budget accommodations are at the **Rainforest Hostel,** 169312 U.S. 101, 20 mi. south of Forks. Follow the signs from U.S. 101 or come by bus from North Shore Brannon's Grocery in Quinault (9am, 1, and 4:35pm; 50¢). Two family rooms, a men's dorm (5 double bunks in summer), and rooms for couples require deposits. A morning chore is required. (☎ 374-2270. Curfew 11pm. Wakeup 8am. Dorms $12.)

Olympic National Park maintains six free campgrounds in the Hood Canal Ranger District, and others within its boundaries (sites $8-12); three can be reserved (☎ 800-280-2267): **Seal Rock, Falls View,** and **Klahowga.** A backcountry permit is always required. Quota limits apply to popular spots. Most drive-up camping is first come, first served. Olympic National Forest requires a trailhead pass to park at sites located off a main trail. The Washington Department of Natural Resources allows free **backcountry camping** 300 ft. off any state road on DNR land, mostly near the western shore along the Hoh and Clearwater Rivers. From July to September, most spaces are taken by 2pm. Popular sites such as those at Hoh River fill by noon.

THE GIFT THAT JUST WON'T STOP GIVING

In the early part of this century, elk were shipped from Washington to Alaska in an effort to provide more game for hunting, and mountain goats were sent from Alaska to Washington in return. The goats proliferated in Olympic National Park long after hunting was prohibited, damaging endangered native plants with their grazing, trampling, wallowing, and loitering. Park Service authorities tried many ways of removing the goats, including live capture and sterilization darts, but nothing really worked. In 1995, they resolved to liquidate the goats once and for all by shooting them from helicopters. Washington Congressman Norm Dicks got this measure postponed, and has since proposed reintroducing the native gray wolf to the park. Wolves were eliminated in the early part of this century in an effort to provide more game for hunting. To add to the mess, a 2000 study concluded that the goats neither belong in, but nor do they substantially damage, the environment. For now, the goats are left hiding peacefully deep in the interior of the park.

👁 🏔 SIGHTS AND OUTDOORS

EASTERN RIM

What ONP's western regions have in ocean and rainforest, the eastern rim matches with canals and grandiose views. Canyon walls rise treacherously, their jagged edges leading to mountaintops that offer glimpses of the entire peninsula and Puget Sound. Steep trails lead up **Mt. Ellinor,** 5 mi. past Staircase on Rte. 119. Once on the mountain, hikers can choose the 3 mi. path or an equally steep but shorter journey to the summit; look for signs to the Upper Trailhead along Forest Road #2419-04. Adventure-seekers who hit the mountain before late July should bring snow clothes to "mach" (as in Mach 1) down a ¼ mi. snow chute.

A 3¼ mi. hike ascends to **Lena Lake,** 14 mi. north of Hoodsport off U.S. 101; follow Forest Service Rd. 25 off U.S. 101 for 8 mi. to the trailhead. The Park Service charges a $3 trailhead pass. The **West Forks Dosewallip Trail,** a 10½ mi. trek to **Mt. Anderson Glacier,** is the shortest route to any glacier in the park. The road to **Mt. Walker Viewpoint,** 5 mi. south of Quilcene on U.S. 101, is steep, has sheer dropoffs, and should not be attempted in foul weather or a temperamental car. Yet another view of Hood Canal, Puget Sound, Mt. Rainier, and Seattle awaits intrepid travelers on top. Inquire about base camps and trails at **Hood Canal Ranger Station,** southeast of reserve lands on U.S. 101 in Hoodsport. (☎877-5254. Open daily 8am-4:30pm; in winter M-F 8am-4:30pm.)

NORTHERN RIM

The most developed section of Olympic National Park lies along its northern rim, near Port Angeles, where glaciers, rainforests, and sunsets over the Pacific are all only a drive away. Farthest east off U.S. 101 lies **Deer Park,** where trails tend to be uncrowded. Past Deer Park, the **Royal Basin Trail** meanders 6.3 mi. to the **Royal Basin Waterfall.** The road up **Hurricane Ridge** is an easy but curvy drive. Before July, walking on the ridge usually involves a bit of snow-stepping. Clear days provide splendid views of Mt. Olympus and Vancouver Island, set against a foreground of snow and indigo lupine. From here, the uphill **High Ridge Trail** is a short walk from Sunset Point. On weekends from late December to late March, the Park Service organizes free guided snowshoe walks atop the ridge.

Farther west on U.S. 101, 13 mi. of paved road penetrates to the popular **Sol Duc Hot Springs Resort,** where retirees de-wrinkle in the springs and eat in the lodge. (☎327-3583. Open late May-Sept. daily 9am-9pm; spring and fall Th noon-6pm, F-Su 9am-6pm. $10; ages 4-12 $7.50; last 2 hours twilight rate $6.50. Suit, locker, towel rental $3 each.) The **Sol Duc trailhead** is a starting point for those heading on up; crowds thin dramatically above **Sol Duc Falls.** The **Eagle Ranger Station** has info and permits. (☎327-3534. Open in summer daily 8am-4:30pm.)

NEAH BAY AND CAPE FLATTERY

At the westernmost point on the Juan de Fuca Strait and north of the park's western rim lies **Neah Bay,** the only town in the **Makah Reservation,** renowned as the "Pompeii of the Pacific," a remarkably preserved 500-year-old village buried in a landslide at Cape Alava. You can reach Neah Bay and Cape Flattery by a 1hr. detour from U.S. 101. From Port Angeles, Rte. 112 leads west to Neah Bay; Rte. 113 runs north from Sappho to Rte. 112. The **Makah Cultural and Research Center,** in Neah Bay on Rte. 112, just inside the reservation, beautifully presents artifacts from the archaeological site. (☎645-2711. Open June-Aug. daily 10am-5pm; Sept.-May M-F 10am-5pm. $4, seniors and students $3. Free tours W-Su 11am.) The Makah Nation, whose recorded history goes back 2000 years, still lives, fishes, and produces artwork on this land. During **Makah Days,** on the last weekend of August, Native Americans from the region come for canoe races, dances, and bone games (a form of gambling). Visitors are welcome; call the center for details. **Clallam Transit System** runs bus #14 from Oak St. in Port Angeles to Sappho, then #16 to Neah Bay. (☎452-4511. $1, seniors 50¢, ages 6-19 85¢.)

Cape Flattery, the most northwestern point in the contiguous US, is drop-dead gorgeous. Get directions at the Makah Center or just take the road through town until it turns to dirt, past the "Marine Viewing Area" sign 4 mi. to a parking area where a trailhead leads toward the cape. To the south, the reservation's **beaches** are solitary and peaceful; respectful visitors are welcome.

WESTERN RIM

In the temperate rainforests of ONP's western rim, ferns, mosses, and gigantic old growth trees blanket the earth in a sea of green. The drive along the **Hoh River Valley,** actively logged land, is alternately overgrown and barren. **Hoh Rainforest Visitors Center** sits a good 45min. drive from U.S. 101 on the park's western rim. (☎374-6925. Open mid-June to early Sept. daily 9am-6:30pm; early Sept. to mid-June 9am-4:30pm.) From there, take the quick ¾ mi. **Hall of Mosses Trail** for a whirlwind tour of the rainforest. The slightly longer **Spruce Nature Trail** leads 1¼ mi. through lush forest and along the banks of the Hoh River, with a smattering of educational panels explaining bizarre natural quirks. The **Hoh Rainforest Trail** is the most heavily traveled path in the area, beginning at the Visitors Center and paralleling the Hoh River for 18 mi. to **Blue Glacier** on the shoulder of Mt. Olympus.

Several other trailheads from U.S. 101 offer less crowded opportunities for exploration of the rainforest, amid surrounding ridges and mountains. The **Queets River Trail** hugs its namesake east for 14 mi. from the free **Queets Campground;** the road is unpaved and unsuitable for RVs or large trailers. High river waters early in the summer can thwart a trek; hiking is best in August, but there's still a risk that water will cut off trail access. A shorter 3 mi. loop passes a broad range of rainforest, lowland river ecosystems, and the park's largest Douglas fir.

The 4 mi. **Quinault Lake Loop** or the ½ mi. **Maple Glade Trail** leave from the **Quinault Ranger Station,** 353 S. Shore Rd. (☎288-2525. Open M-F 8am-4:30pm Sa-Su 9am-4pm; in winter M-F 9am-4:30pm.) Snow-seekers flock to **Three Lakes Point,** an exquisite summit covered with powder until July. **Quinault Lake** lures anglers, rowers, and canoers. The **Lake Quinault Lodge,** next to the ranger station, rents canoes and rowboats. (☎288-2900 or 800-562-6672. From $10 per hr.)

COASTAL ZONE

Pristine coastline traces the park's slim far western region for 57 mi., separated from the rest of ONP by U.S. 101 and non-park timber land. Eerie fields of driftwood, sculptured arches, and dripping caves frame flamboyant sunsets, while the waves are punctuated by rugged sea stacks. Between the Quinault and Hoh Reservations, U.S. 101 hugs the coast for 15 mi., with parking lots just a short walk from the sand. North of where the highway meets the coast, **Beach #4** has abundant tidepools, plastered with sea stars; **Beach #6,** 3 mi. north at Mile 160, is a favorite whale-watching spot. Near Mile 165, sea otters and eagles hang out amid tide pools and sea stacks at **Ruby Beach.** Beach camping is only permitted north of the Hoh Reservation between **Oil City** and **Third Beach,** and north of the Quileute Reservation between **Hole-in-the-Wall** and **Shi-Shi Beach.** Day hikers and backpackers adore the 9 mi. loop that begins at **Ozette Lake.** The trail is a triangle with two 3 mi. legs leading along boardwalks through the rainforest. One heads toward sea stacks at **Cape Alava,** the other to a sublime beach at **Sand Point.** A 3 mi. hike down the coast links the two legs, passing ancient petroglyphs. More info is available at the **Ozette Ranger Station** (☎963-2725; open intermittently). Overnighters must make permit reservations (☎565-3100) in advance; spaces fill quickly in summer.

CASCADE RANGE

Intercepting the moist Pacific air, the spectacular Cascades divide Washington into the lush, wet green of the west and the low, dry plains of the east. The Cascades are most accessible in July, August, and September. Many high mountain passes are snowed in during the rest of the year. Mounts Baker, Vernon, Glacier, Rainier, Adams, and St. Helens are accessible by four major roads. The North Cascades Hwy. (Rte. 20) is the most breathtaking and provides access to North Cascades National Park. Scenic U.S. 2 leaves Everett for Stevens Pass and descends along the Wenatchee River. Rte. 20 and U.S. 2 can be traveled in sequence as the Cascade Loop. U.S. 12 approaches Mt. Rainier through White Pass and passes north of Mt. St. Helens. I-90 sends four lanes from Seattle past the ski resorts of Snoqualmie Pass. Locals warn against hitchhiking on Rte. 20.

MOUNT ST. HELENS ☎360

In a single cataclysmic blast on May 18, 1980, the summit of Mt. St. Helens erupted, transforming what had been a perfect cone into a crater 1 mile wide and 2 miles long. The force of the ash-filled blast robbed the mountain of 1300 feet and razed entire forests, strewing trees like charred matchsticks. Ash from the crater rocketed 17 mile upward, blackening the sky for days. The explosion was 27,000 times the force of the atomic bomb dropped on Hiroshima. Mt. St. Helens National Volcanic Monument encompasses most of the blast zone, the rebounding ecosystem immediately affected by the explosion. The volcano still threatens to erupt, but is well monitored, and there's a good chance it won't blow while you're there.

🛈 PRACTICAL INFORMATION. Vigorous winter rains often spoil access roads; check at a ranger station for road closures before heading out. From the **west,** take Exit 49 off I-5 and use Rte. 504, otherwise known as the **Spirit Lake Memorial Hwy.** For most, this is the quickest and easiest daytrip to the mountain, and the main Visitors Centers line the way to the volcano. **Rte. 503** parallels the **south** side of the volcano until it connects with **Forest Service Rd. 90.** Though views from this side don't highlight recent destruction, green glens and remnants of age-old explosions make this the best side for hiking and camping. From the **north,** the towns of **Mossyrock, Morton,** and **Randle** line **U.S. 12** and offer the closest major services to the monument. From U.S. 12, both **Forest Service Rd. 25** and **Forest Service Rd. 26** head south to **Forest Service Rd. 99,** a 16 mi. dead-end road with few look-outs.

The monument charges an entrance fee at almost every Visitors Center, viewpoint, and cave. (One day, all access $6, ages 4-15 $2. Individual monument fees $3/ $1.) **Mt. St. Helens Visitors Center,** across from Seaquest State Park on Rte. 504, is most visitors' first stop, with displays and interactive exhibits. (☎274-2100 or 274-2103. Open daily 9am-5pm.) **Coldwater Ridge Visitors Center** is 38 mi. farther on Rte. 504 and emphasizes the area's recolonization by living things. (☎274-2131. Open daily 10am-6pm.) **Johnston Ridge Observatory,** at the end of Rte. 504, overlooking the crater, focuses on geological exhibits and offers the best roadside view of the steaming dome and crater. (☎274-2140. Open May-Sept. daily 10am-6pm.)

Woods Creek Information Station, 6 mi. south of Randle on Rd. 25 from U.S. 12, is a drive-through info center. (Open June-Aug. daily 9am-4pm.) **Pine Creek Information Station,** 17 mi. east of Cougar on Rd. 90, shows an interpretive film of the eruption.

(Open June-Sept. daily 9:30am-5:30pm.) **Apes Headquarters,** at Ape Cave on Rd. 8303, on the south side of the volcano, answers all of your lava tube questions. (Open June-Sept. daily 10am-5:30pm.) From mid-May through October, the Forest Service allows 100 people per day to hike to the crater rim (applications accepted from Feb. 1; $15). Procrastinators should head for **Jack's Restaurant and Country Store,** 13411 Louis River Rd., on Rte. 503, 5 mi. west of Cougar (I-5 Exit 21), where a lottery is held at 6pm each day to distribute the next day's 50 unreserved permits. (☎231-4276. Open daily 5:30am-9pm.)

✝ CAMPING. Although the monument itself contains no campgrounds, a number are scattered throughout the surrounding national forest. Free dispersed camping is allowed within the monument, but finding a site is a matter of luck. **Iron Creek Campground** is just south of the Woods Creek Information Station on Rd. 25, near its junction with Rd. 76. This is the closest campsite to Mt. St. Helens, with good hiking and striking views of the crater and the blast zone. (☎877-444-6777. Water. Sites $13-15.) Spacious **Swift Campground** is on Rd. 90, just west of the Pine Creek Info Station. (☎503-813-6666. Sites $12.) **Beaver Bay** is west of Swift Campground on the Yale Lake. (☎503-813-6666. Toilets and showers. Sites $15.)

▲ OUTDOOR ACTIVITIES. Along each approach, short interpretive trails loop into the landscape. The one-hour drive from the Mt. St. Helens Visitors Center to Johnston Ridge offers spectacular views of the crater and of the resurgence of life. Another 10 mi. east, the hike along **Johnston Ridge** approaches incredibly close to the crater where geologist David Johnston died studying the eruption. On the way west along Rd. 99, **Bear Meadow** provides the first interpretive stop, an excellent view of Mt. St. Helens, and the last restrooms before Rd. 99 ends at **Windy Ridge.** The monument begins just west of Bear Meadow, where Rd. 26 and 99 meet. Rangers lead ½ mi. walks around emerald **Meta Lake;** meet at Miner's Car at the junction of Rd. 26 and 99 (late June-Sept. daily 12:45 and 3pm). Farther west on Rd. 99, **Independence Pass Trail #227** is a difficult 3½ mi. hike, with overlooks of Spirit Lake and superb views of the crater and dome. For a serious hike, continue along this trail to its intersection with the spectacular **Norway Pass Trail,** which runs 6 mi. directly through the blast zone and ends on Rd. 26. Farther west, the two-mile **Harmony Trail #224** provides access to Spirit Lake. From spectacular **Windy Ridge** at the end of Rd. 99, a steep ash hill grants a magnificent view of the crater from 3½ mi. away. The **Truman Trail** leaves from Windy Ridge and meanders 7 mi. through the **Pumice Plain,** where hot pyroclastic flows sterilized the landscape. From the Pine Creek Information Station, 25 mi. south of the junction of Rd. 25 and 99, take Rd. 90 12 mi. west and then continue 3 mi. north on Rd. 83 to **Ape Cave,** a broken 2½ mi. lava tube formed by an ancient eruption. When exploring, wear a jacket and sturdy shoes, and take at least two flashlights or lanterns. Rangers lead ten free 30min. guided cave explorations per day. Rd. 83 continues 9 mi. farther north, ending near **Lava Canyon Trail #184** and three hikes past the **Muddy River Waterfall.**

MOUNT RAINIER NATIONAL PARK ☎360

At 14,411 ft., Mt. Rainier presides regally over the Cascade Range. The Klickitat native people called it Tahoma, "Mountain of God," but Rainier is simply "the Mountain" to most Washington residents. Perpetually snowcapped, this dormant volcano draws thousands of visitors from around the globe. Clouds mask the mountain 200 days per year, frustrating visitors who come solely to see its distinctive summit. Over 305 miles of trails weave peacefully through old-growth forests and alpine meadows, rivers, and bubbling hot springs.

⚐ PRACTICAL INFORMATION. To reach Mt. Rainier from the west, take I-5 to Tacoma, then go east on Rte. 512, south on Rte. 7, and east on Rte. 706. This road meanders through the town of **Ashford** and into the park by the **Nisqually entrance,** which leads to the Visitors Centers of **Paradise** and **Longmire.** Snow usually closes all

> ***WILLKOMMEN IN LEAVENWORTH!*** A true experiment in tourism. After the town's logging industry collapsed and the railroad switching station moved to nearby Wenatchee, Leavenworth needed a new *Weltanschauung.* Desperate officials launched "Project Alpine," a gimmick to transform the town into a German village: zoning and building codes necessitated Bavarian-style buildings, waiters learned about bratwurst, polka blasted over the loudspeakers, and German beer flowed. It worked: more than 1.5 million Americans came in 2000, with influxes peaking during the city's three annual festivals. Tasty pretzels and *schnitzel*, oddly enough, complement the nearby world-class rock climbing and camping. On the eastern slope of the Cascades, Leavenworth is near Washington's geographic center. To get there from Seattle, follow I-5 N to Everett (Exit 194), then U.S. 2 E (126 mi.; 2½hr.). From Spokane, follow U.S. 2 W (184 mi., 4hr.). The Chamber of Commerce/Visitor Information Center, 220 9th St. at Commercial St., provides a plethora of pamphlets and brochures on where to *essen* and *schlaufen.* (☎548-5807. *Open M-Th 8am-5pm, F-Sa 8am-6pm, Su 10am-4pm; winter M-Sa 8am-5pm.*)

other park roads from November to May. **Stevens Canyon Rd.** connects the southeast corner of the national park with Paradise, Longmire, and the Nisqually entrance, unfolding superb vistas of Rainier and the Tatoosh Range.

Gray Line Bus Service, 4500 S. Marginal Way, Seattle, runs from Seattle to Mt. Rainier. Buses leave from the Convention Center at 8th and Pike in Seattle at 8am and return at 6pm, allowing about 3½hr. at the mountain. (☎206-624-5208 or 800-426-7532. Runs May to mid-Sept. daily. 1-day round-trip $50, under 12 $25.) **Rainier Shuttle** (☎569-2331), runs daily between Sea-Tac Airport; Ashford (2hr., 2 per day, $40); and Paradise (3hr., 1 per day, $45). The best place to plan a backcountry trip is at the **Longmire Wilderness Center** (☎569-4453; open Su-Th 7:30am-6:30pm, F-Sa 7am-7pm), east of the Nisqually entrance; or the **White River Ranger Station** (☎663-2273; open Su-Th 8am-4:30pm, F-Sa 7am-7pm), off Rte. 410 on the park's east side. Both distribute **backcountry permits.** The entrance fee is $10 per car, $5 per hiker; permits are good for seven days, and gates are open 24hr. **Rainier Mountaineering, Inc. (RMI),** in Paradise, rents climbing gear and expert guides lead summit climbs. (☎569-2227. Open May-Oct. daily 9am-5pm. Winter office at 535 Dock St. #209, in Tacoma: ☎253-627-6242.) **Post Office:** In the National Park Inn, Longmire (open M-F 8:30am-noon and 1-5pm), and in the Paradise Inn, Paradise (open M-F 9am-noon and 12:30-5pm, Sa 8:30am-noon). **ZIP code:** Longmire 98397; Paradise 98398. **Area code:** 360.

ᖰᖯ ACCOMMODATIONS AND FOOD. Hotel Packwood, 102 Main St., in Packwood, is a charming reminder of the Old West with crisp, clean rooms and antique furniture. (☎494-5431. Shared or private bath; singles and double $32-54.) **Whittaker's Bunkhouse,** 6 mi. west of the Nisqually entrance, offers spiffy rooms with firm mattresses and sparkling clean showers, as well as a homey espresso bar, but no kitchen. Bring your own sleeping bag. (☎569-2439. Reservations strongly recommended. Bunks $25; private rooms $65-90.)

Camping in the park is first come, first served from mid-June to late September. (Off-season reservations ☎800-365-2267. Sites $10-14.) National park campgrounds all have facilities for the handicapped, but no hookups or showers (coin-operated showers are available at Jackson Memorial Visitors Center, in Paradise). **Sunshine Point** (18 sites), near the Nisqually entrance, and **Cougar Rock** (200 sites), 2¼ mi. north of Longmire, are in the southwest. The serene high canopy of **Ohanapecosh** (205 sites) is 11 mi. north of Packwood on Rte. 123, in the southeast. **White River** (112 sites) is 5 mi. west of White River on the way to Sunrise, in the northeast. **Backcountry camping** in the park requires a permit, free from ranger stations and Visitor Centers in person 24hr. beforehand, or by reservation up to two months in advance. (☎569-4453. $20 per group. Quotas limit group size.) Hikers with valid permits can use any of the free, well-established trailside camps scattered in the park. Most camps have toilet facilities and a nearby water source, and some have shelters for groups of up to 12. Glacier climbers and mountain climbers intending to scale above 10,000 ft. must register in person at ranger stations to be granted permits. Camping in national forests outside the park is free. Avoid eroded lakesides and riverbanks; flash floods are frequent. Campfires are generally prohibited.

Blanton's Market, 13040 U.S. 12, in Packwood, is the closest decent supermarket to the park and has an ATM in front. (☎494-6101. Open daily 6am-10pm.) **Ma & Pa Rucker's** on U.S. 12 in Packwood, is a pizza parlor/grill/mini-mart/ice cream store/cafe. (☎494-2651. Open M-Th 9am-9pm, F-Su 9am-10pm. Pizza $8-12.)

▨ OUTDOOR ACTIVITIES. Ranger-led interpretive hikes delve into everything from area history to local wildflowers. Each visitor center conducts hikes on its own schedule and most of the campgrounds have evening talks and campfire programs. Mt. Adams and Mt. St. Helens aren't visible from the road, but can be seen from mountain trails like **Paradise** (1.5 mi.), **Pinnacle Peak** (2.5 mi.), **Eagle Peak** (7 mi.), and **Van Trump Park** (5.5 mi.). A segment of the **Pacific Crest Trail,** which runs from Mexico to the Canadian border, dodges in and out of the park's southeast corner. The **Wonderland Trail** winds 93 mi. up, down, and around the mountain. Hikers must get permits for the arduous but stunning trek and must complete the hike in 10 to 14 days. Call the Longmire Wilderness Center (see **Practical Information,** above) for details on both hikes. A trip to the summit of Mt. Rainier requires substantial preparation and expense. The ascent involves a vertical rise of more than 9000 ft. over a distance of 9 or more mi., usually taking two days and an overnight stay at **Camp Muir** on the south side (10,000 ft.) or **Camp Schurman** on the east side (9500 ft.). Permits for summit climbs cost $15 per person. Although in opposite corners of the park, the **Ohanapecosh** and **Carbon Rivers** are in the same ranger district. One of the oldest stands of trees in Washington, the **Grove of Patriarchs** grows near the Ohanapecosh Visitors Center. An easy 1½ mi. walk leads to these 500- to 1000-year-old Douglas firs, cedars, and hemlocks. The **Summerland** and **Indian Bar Trails** are excellent for serious backpacking—this is where rangers go on their days off. **Carbon River Valley,** in the northwest corner of the park, is one of the only inland rainforests in the US and has access to the **Wonderland Trail** (see above). Winter storms keep the road beyond the Carbon River entrance in constant disrepair.

NORTH CASCADES (ROUTE 20)

A favorite stomping ground for grizzlies, deer, mountain goats, black bears, and Jack Kerouac (*The Dharma Bums*), the North Cascades are one of the most rugged expanses of land in the continental US. The dramatic peaks stretch north from Stevens Pass on U.S. 2 to the Canadian border, with the centerpiece of **North Cascades National Park** straddling the crest of the Cascades. Rte. 20 (open Apr.-Nov., weather permitting), a road designed for unadulterated driving pleasure, is the area's main thoroughfare and awards jaw-dropping views at every curve.

SEDRO WOOLLEY TO MARBLEMOUNT

The **Sedro Woolley Visitor Information Center** (☎360-855-1841; open daily 9am-4pm), in the train caboose at Rte. 20 and Ferry St., explains the **Sedro Woolley Loggerodeo** (☎855-1129), held over 4th of July weekend. Sedro Woolley houses the **North Cascades National Park and Mt. Baker-Snoqualmie National Forest Headquarters,** which will be moving down the street to 810 State Rte. 20, near the intersection with Rte. 9. If it isn't open yet, check back at 2105 Rte. 20, their old location. (☎856-5700. Open daily 8am-4:30pm.) Inquire here about camping in the forest and trail park passes and permits required. Call 206-526-6677 for snow avalanche info. Rte. 9 leads north from Sedro Woolley, providing access to **Mt. Baker** through the forks at the Nagasaki River and Rte. 542. The turn-off for **Baker Lake Hwy.** is 23 mi. east of Sedro Woolly at Mile 82, which dead-ends 25 mi. later at Baker Lake and free hot springs.

Farther east on Rte. 20, near the relatively small **Rocketry State Park** (☎853-8461; sites $14; hookup $20), Sauk Mountain Rd. (Forest Service Rd. 1030) makes a stomach-scrambling climb up **Sauk Mountain.** Trailers, RVs, and the faint of heart should not attempt it. The **Sauk Mountain Trail** near the top winds 3½ mi. to stunning views and campsites near Sauk Lake.

Three miles east of Marblemount, bunnies romp outside the **Eatery**, at Rte. 20 Mile 103.5. Dine under the American flag which the owner's grandmother made in 1890 when Washington celebrated its first 4th of July as a state (open daily 6:30am-8pm). The **Marblemount Wilderness Information Center**, 728 Ranger Station Rd., Marblemount 98267, 1 mi. north of Marblemount on a well-marked road from the west end of town, is the place to go for a backcountry permit and to plan longer hiking excursions. (☎360-873-4500, ext. 39. Open in summer Su-Th 7am-6pm, F-Sa 7am-8pm; call for winter hours.)

ROSS LAKE

Newhalem is the first town on Rte. 20 after it crosses into the **Ross Lake Recreation Area**, a buffer zone between the highway and the national park. A mystical and atonal slide show is shown at the tourist-friendly **North Cascades Visitors Center and Ranger Station**, off Rte. 20. (☎206-386-4495. Open daily 8:30am-6pm; in winter Sa-Su 9am-4:30pm.) Among the easiest hikes is the **Thunder Creek Trail**, which extends through old-growth cedar and fir forests, beginning from the Colonial Creek Campground (see below) at Rte. 20 Mile 130. The 3.3 mi. **4th of July Pass Trail** begins approximately 2 mi. into the Thunder Creek Trail and climbs 3500 ft. toward eye-popping views. The park's **Newhalem Campground**, just south of Rte. 20 in Newhalem, has 22 sites for tents and trailers, with drinking water, pit toilets, and a launch site for whitewater rafting on the Skated River. (Sites $7; water turned off after Oct., when sites are free.)

SCENIC DRIVE: ROSS LAKE TO TWISP

This is the most beautiful segment of Rte. 20. Leaving the basin of Ross Lake, the road begins to climb, exposing the jagged, snowy peaks of the North Cascades. Thirty miles of astounding views east, the **Pacific Crest Trail** crosses Rte. 20 at **Rainy Pass** on one of the most scenic and difficult legs of its 2500 miles. Canada-to-Mexico route. Near Rainy Pass, groomed scenic trails can be hiked in sneakers, provided the snow has melted (about mid-July). Just off Rte. 20, an overlook at **Washington Pass** (Mile 162) rewards a half-mile walk on a wheelchair-accessible paved trail with an astonishing view of the red rocks in **Copper Basin**. The popular 2½ mi. walk to **Blue Lake** begins just east of Washington Pass. An easier two-mile hike to **Cutthroat Lake** departs from an access road 4½ mi. east of Washington Pass. From the lake, the trail continues 4 mi. farther and almost 2000 ft. higher to **Cutthroat Pass**, treating hikers to a stellar view of towering peaks. The hair-raising 23 mi. road to **Hart's Pass** begins at **Mazama**, on Rd. 1163, 10 mi. east of Washington Pass. Awesome views await daring drivers. The road prohibits trailers and closes for snow.

Farther east is **Winthrop**, a town desperately and somewhat successfully trying to market its frontier history. **Winthrop Info Station**, 202 Riverside, is at the junction with Rte. 20. (☎509-996-2125. Open early May to mid-Oct. daily 10am-5pm.) Winthrop's summer is bounded by rodeos on Memorial and Labor Day weekends. Late July brings the top-notch **Winthrop Rhythm and Blues Festival**, where big name blues bands flock to belt their tunes, genuine radio stations, and play cowboy. (☎509-997-2541. Tickets $40 in advance; $48 at the door.) The **Methow Valley Visitors Center**, Bldg. 49, Rte. 20, hands out info on camping, hiking, and skiing. (☎509-996-4000. Open daily 9am-5pm; call for winter hours.) For more in-depth skiing and hiking trail info, call the **Methow Valley Sports Trail Association** (☎509-996-3287), which maintains 100 mi. of trails. Between Winthrop and Twisp on East Country Rd. #9129, the ⬛**North Cascades Smoke Jumper Base** is a center for airborne forest-firefighters. (☎509-997-2031. Open in summer and early fall daily 8am-6pm; tours 10am-5pm.)

Nine miles south of Winthrop on Rte. 20, the peaceful village of **Twisp** offers lower prices and far fewer tourists than its neighbor. The **Twisp Ranger Station**, 502 Glover St., employs a crunchy and helpful staff equipped with essential trail and campground guides. (☎509-997-2131. Open M-F 7:45am-4:30pm.) At **The Sportsman Motel**, 1010 E. Rte. 20, a barracks-like facade masks tastefully decorated rooms with kitchens. (☎509-997-2911. Singles $39; doubles $44.) The **Sisters Cafe**, 104 N. Glover St., serves California-style wraps. (☎509-997-1323. Open M-F 8am-5pm, Sa 9am-2pm.) Campgrounds and trails await 15-25 mi. up Twisp River Rd. off Rte. 20. Most campsites ($5). **Riverbank RV Park,** 19961 Rte. 20, is only 2 mi. west of Twisp. (☎509-997-3500 or 800-686-4498. Office open 9am-9pm. Sites $15, hookup $20.) From Twisp, Rte. 20 continues east to **Okanogan** and Rte. 153 runs south to **Lake Chelan.**

EASTERN WASHINGTON

SPOKANE   ☎509

A city built on silver mining and grown fat and prosperous after decades as a central rail link for regional agriculture, Spokane has regressed to a gateway town. Copious middle-Americana, fused with bottom-of-the-barrel prices, makes Spokane a convenient, inexpensive stopover. **Riverfront Park,** 507 N. Howard St. (☎456-4386), just north of downtown, is Spokane's civic center and greatest asset. Developed for the 1974 World's Fair, the park's 100 acres are divided down the middle by the roaring rapids that culminate in **Spokane Falls.** In the park, the **IMAX Theater** houses your basic five-story movie screen. (☎625-6686. Shows June-Sept. every hour; call for winter schedule. Open daily 11am-9pm. $7.) A 1-day pass ($15) covers the theater along with a variety of amusement rides, including the handcarved **Looff Carousel.** (Open June-Sept. Su-Th 11am-8pm, F-Sa 11am-10pm. $1.75 per whirl.) The park hosts ice-skating in the winter. South of downtown off Stevens St., at **Manito Park,** 4 W. 21st Ave., carp blow bubbles in the **Nishinomiya Japanese Garden.**

Boulevard Inn, 2905 W. Sunset Blvd., 2 mi. west of town on Rte. 2., rents rooms so clean you could eat off the floor. (☎747-1060. Singles $34; doubles $40. *Let's Go* does not recommend eating off the floor.) **Riverside State Park** is 6 mi. northwest of downtown on Rifle Club Rd., off Rte. 291 (Nine Mile Rd.); take Division St. north and turn left on Francis, then follow signs. Sites lie in a sparse Ponderosa forest next to the river. (☎800-452-5687 or 800-233-0321. Showers. Sites $14; hookup $20; hiker/biker sites $6. Wheelchair accessible.) **The Spokane Marketplace,** 1100 N. Ruby St., northwest of town at DeSmet St., sells fresh fruit, vegetables, baked goods, and crafts. (☎456-0100. Open Apr. Sa 9am-4pm; May-Dec. W and Sa 9am-4pm.) Head to the ▧**The Onion,** 302 W. Riverside Ave., at Bernard St., for an amazing burger ($6-8) or $3 huckleberry shake. (☎624-9965. Open daily 11am to about 11pm.)

Spokane lies 280 mi. east of Seattle on I-90. **Spokane International Airport** (☎624-3218) is off I-90, 8 mi. southwest of town. **Amtrak,** W. 221 1st St. (☎624-5144), at Bernard St., sends one train per day to Seattle (7hr.) and Portland (8hr.) for $34-74. **Greyhound** (☎624-5251), in the same building, runs to Seattle (6hr., 5 per day, $26) and Portland (8-10hr., 4 per day, $36). **Spokane Transit Authority** serves Spokane, including Eastern Washington University in Cheyenne. (☎328-7433. Runs until 12:00am downtown. 75¢.) **Spokane Area Convention and Visitors Bureau,** 201 W. Main St., at Exit 281 off I-90, offers free Internet access and local phone calls. (☎747-3230 or 800-248-3230. Open May-Sept. M-F 8:30am-5pm, Sa 8am-4pm, Su 9am-2pm; Oct.-Apr. M-F 8:30am-5pm.) **Post Office:** W. 904 Riverside Ave., at Lincoln (☎252-2337; open M-F 6am-5pm). **ZIP code:** 99210. **Area code:** 509.

OREGON

Over a century ago, families high-tailed it to Oregon in search of prosperity and a new way of life, liquidating their possessions and sinking their life savings into covered wagons, corn meal, and oxen. Today, Oregon remains as popular a destination as ever for backpackers, cyclists, anglers, beachcrawlers, and families. The caves and cliffs of Oregon's coastline are a siren call to tourists, and inland attractions include Crater Lake National Park and Ashland's Shakespeare Festival. Portland is idiosyncratic and casual—its name was determined by a coin toss—while the college town of Eugene embraces hippies and Deadheads. For everything from microbrews to snowcapped peaks, Oregon is worth crossing the Continental Divide.

PACIFIC NORTHWEST

⑦ PRACTICAL INFORMATION

Capital: Salem.

Visitor info: Oregon Tourism Commission, 775 Summer St. NE, Salem 97310 (☎800-547-7842; www.traveloregon.com). **Oregon State Parks and Recreation Dept.,** P.O. Box 500, Portland, OR 97207-0500 (☎800-551-6949; www.prd.state.or.us).

Postal Abbreviation: OR. **Sales Tax:** 0%.

PORTLAND   ☎503

With over 200 parks, the pristine Willamette River, and snowcapped Mt. Hood in the background, Portland is an oasis of natural beauty. Portlanders have also nursed a love of art, music, and books. Culture is constantly cultivated in the endless theaters, galleries, and bookshops around town. As the microbrewery capital of America, Portland is a flowing font of the nation's finest beer. During the rainy season, locals flood neighborhood pubs and coffeehouses for shelter and conversation. But on rare sunny days, a battalion of hikers, bikers, and runners take advantage of their sylvan surroundings.

▐ TRANSPORTATION

Portland lies in the northwest corner of Oregon, where the Willamette River flows into the Columbia River. **I-5** connects Portland with San Francisco and Seattle, while **I-84** follows the route of the Oregon Trail through the Columbia River Gorge, heading along the Oregon-Washington border toward Boise, ID. West of Portland, **U.S. 30** follows the Columbia downstream to Astoria, but **U.S. 26** is the fastest path to the coast. **I-405** runs just west of downtown to link I-5 with U.S. 30 and 26.

Airport: Portland International Airport (☎460-4234) is served by almost every major airline. The airport is connected to the city center by the **MAX** Red Line, an efficient light rail system (38min.; every 15min. daily 5am to 11:30pm; $1.55). Another option is Tri-Met bus #12 (Sandy Blvd.) outside baggage claim, which passes south through downtown on SW 5th Ave. (45min.; 6 per morning hr., 2 per evening hr.; $1.20). **Gray Line** (☎285-9845) provides **airport shuttles,** which stop at most major hotels in Portland, as well as 5th Ave. (every 45min. from 5:15am-midnight, $15).

Trains: Amtrak, 800 NW 6th Ave. (☎273-4866; reservations 800-872-7245), at Hoyt St. To Seattle (4hr., 4 per day, $23-36). Ticket counter open daily 7:45am-9pm.

Buses: Greyhound, 550 NW 6th Ave. (☎243-2310 or 800-231-2222), at NW Glisan by Union Station. Ticket counter open 5am-1am. To: Seattle (3-4½hr., 9 per day, $22); Eugene (2½-4hr., 9 per day, $14); and Spokane (about 8hr., 6 per day, $40). Student Advantage 15% discount, seniors and military 10% discount. Lockers $5 per day.

Public Transit: Tri-Met, 701 SW 6th Ave. (☎238-7433; www.tri-met.org), in Pioneer Courthouse Sq. Open M-F 9am-6pm. Several information lines available: **Call-A-Bus** info system ☎231-3199. Buses generally run 5am-midnight with reduced hours on weekends. Fare $1.20-1.50, ages 7-18 90¢, over 65 or disabled 55¢; free in the downtown. All-day pass $4; 10 fares for $10. All buses and bus stops are marked with one of seven symbols and have bike racks ($5 permit available at area bike stores). Anywhere north and east of 405, west of the river and south of Hoyt St.—the **No-Fare Zone**—all of the city's public transportation is free. **MAX** (☎228-7246), based at the Customer Service Center, is Tri-Met's light rail train running between downtown, Hillsboro in the west, and Gresham in the east. A new line, opened late in 2001, serves the airport from the main line's "Gateway" stop. Transfers from buses can be used to ride MAX. Runs M-F 4:30am-1:30am.

Taxis: Radio Cab, ☎227-1212. **Broadway Cab,** ☎227-1234.

Car Rental: Crown Rent-A-Car, 1315 NE Sandy Blvd. (☎224-8110 or 800-722-7813), across from the huge 7-Up bottle. Open M-F 8am-5pm. Transport from airport. From $25-40 per day, $140-160 per week. Must be 21 with credit card.

Downtown Portland

■ ACCOMMODATIONS
Downtown Value Inn, **14**
McMenamins Edgefield, **1**
Northwest Portland International
Hostel (HI), **3**
Portland International Hostel (HI), **13**

● FOOD
Coffee Time, **2**
Little Wing Cafe, **4**
Nicholas' Restaurant, **9**
Western Culinary Institute:
Chef's Corner Deli, **10**
Chef's Diner, **10**
Restaurant, **11**

■ THEATERS
Portland Center Stage, **12**

■ NIGHTLIFE
Boxxes, **8**
Brig, **8**
Jimmy Mak's, **6**
The Laurel Thirst Public House, **5**
The Nightclub Fez, **8**
Ohm, **7**
Red Cap Garage, **8**

⚡️❼ ORIENTATION AND PRACTICAL INFORMATION

Portland is divided into five districts by which all street signs are labeled: **N, NE, NW, SE,** and **SW. Burnside St.** divides the city into north and south, while east and west are separated by the **Willamette River.** SW Portland is known as **downtown** but also includes the southern end of Old Town and a slice of the wealthier **West Hills. Old Town,** in NW Portland, encompasses most of the city's historic sector. Some areas in the NW and SW around W. Burnside are best not walked alone at night, although on weekends district clubs and live music draw crowds. West of Old Town and Chinatown, **Pearl District** is known for art galleries and antique stores. Farther west, NW 21st and NW 23rd St. are known as **Nob Hill,** a hot spot for boutiquing and dining. **Southeast** Portland contains parks, factories, local businesses, and residential areas of all income brackets; a rich array of cafes, stores, theaters, and restaurants also lines **Hawthorne Blvd. Williams Ave.** frames "the North." **North** and **Northeast** Portland are chiefly residential, punctuated by a few small and quiet parks and the site of the **University of Portland.**

Visitor Info: Visitors Association (POVA), 701 SW Morrison St. (☎275-9750), in Pioneer Courthouse Sq. Walk through the crowds of screaming kids and between the fountains to enter. Free *Portland Book* has maps and info on local attractions. Open June-Aug. M-Sa 9am-6pm, Su 10am-4pm; Sept.-May closed Su.

Internet access: Library, 801 SW 10th Ave. (☎248-5123), between Yamhill and Taylor, has free 1hr. access. Open M-Th 9am-9pm, F-Sa 9am-6pm, Su 1-5pm.

Women's Crisis Line: ☎235-5333. 24hr.

Post Office: 715 NW Hoyt St. (☎294-2564). Open M-F 7am-6:30pm, Sa 8:30am-5pm. **ZIP code:** 97208. **Area code:** 503.

▐ ACCOMMODATIONS

Although downtown is studded with Marriott-esque hotels and the smaller motels are steadily raising prices, Portland still welcomes the budget traveler. Prices tend to drop away from the City Center, and inexpensive motels can be found on SE Powell Blvd. and the southern end of SW 4th Ave. Portland accommodations fill up, especially during the Rose Festival, so reserve early.

▩ **Portland International Hostel (HI),** 3031 SE Hawthorne Blvd. (☎236-3380), at 31st Ave. across from Artichoke Music. From downtown mall take bus #14 to SE 30th Ave. About a 20min. ride. Lively and inexpensive with much common space and a huge porch. Kitchen, laundry, and Internet access ($1 per 20min.). All-you-can-eat pancakes $1. Staff will also help arrange daytrips. Fills early in summer. Reception daily 8am-10pm. No curfew. 34 beds. Dorms $15, nonmembers $18. Private rooms $41-46.

Northwest Portland International Hostel (HI), 1818 NW Glisan St. (☎241-2783) at 18th Ave. From the downtown mall take bus #17 down Glisan to corner of 19th Ave. The snug Victorian building has a kitchen, laundry, and Sunday sundaes ($1). Tours to Mt. Hood, the Columbia River Gorge, and Mt. St. Helens ($39). Permits available for roadside parking ($5 deposit). 34 dorm beds (co-ed available). Reception 8am-11pm. No curfew. $14-16 plus tax, nonmembers $17-19. Two private doubles, $40-50.

McMenamins Edgefield, 2126 SW Halsey St. (☎669-8610 or 800-669-8610), in Troutdale. By car, take I-84 east to Exit 16, turn right at the exit, and then left at the first stoplight onto SW Halsey St. Continue down Halsey, turn right just before Edgefield's vineyards. Take MAX east to the Gateway Station, then Tri-Met bus #24 (Halsey) east to the main entrance. This beautiful 38-acre former farm is a posh escape that keeps 2 hostel rooms. Wine tasting, 3 pubs (hamburgers $5), massage service, and more. Lockers and linens included. Reception 24hr. No curfew. Call ahead in the summer. 2 single-sex dorm-style rooms with 12 beds each ($20 plus tax) are the budget option.

Downtown Value Inn, 415 SW Montgomery St. (☎226-4751), at 4th Ave. Take bus #12 through downtown to the corner of 5th Ave., or by car follow signs to the city center and Montgomery. An inexpensive option cleaner than the price would suggest. Pizza hangout downstairs. Phones, cable TV, laundry. Reception 24hr. Check-out 11am. Reservations recommended. Singles from $45; doubles from $55; rooms with jacuzzi $65.

FOOD

Portland has more restaurants per capita than any other American city, and dining is seldom dull. Downtown tends to be expensive, but restaurants and quirky cafes in the NW and SE quadrants offer great food at reasonable prices.

☒ Western Culinary Institute (☎294-9770), would totally titillate the Frugal Gourmet. WCI has 4 eateries, each catering to a different budget niche, all of them reasonable.

Chef's Diner, 1231 SW Jefferson, opens mornings to let cheerful students taste and discuss sandwiches, breakfast specials, and occasional all-you-can-eat buffets ($5). Open Tu-F 7am-noon.

Chef's Corner Deli, 1239 SW Jefferson, is good for a quick meal on the go (around $1 per dish, 3 make a nice meal). Open Tu-Th 8am-5:30pm, F 8am-6pm.

Restaurant, 1316 SW 13th Ave. Moving up the price scale, the elegant Restaurant serves a classy 5-course lunch ($10) rivaled by its superb 6-course dinner (Tu, W, and F $20). Reservations recommended. Open Tu-F 11:30am-1pm; dinner 6-8pm.

International Bistro, 3 blocks west of the Deli on Jefferson St., opened in late 2001, serving food at a price range just below the restaurant. Call for details.

☒ Nicholas' Restaurant, 318 SE Grand Ave. (☎235-5123), between Oak and Pine opposite Miller Paint. Bus #6 to the Andy and Bax stop. Lebanese and Mediterranean food at incredible prices. Sandwiches $4-8. Open M-Sa 10am-9pm, Su 11am-7pm.

Counter Culture, 3000 NE Killingsworth St. (☎249-3799). Take bus #10 to Killingsworth, or bus #6, and transfer to #72. One of the hottest restaurants in town, these rebels churn out upscale vegan cuisine that has everyone ooh-ing and ahh-ing. Seasonal menu, entrees $9-11. A dessert list finishes off the animal-free extravaganza. Open Tu-Sa 5:30-10pm, Su 5:30-9pm; brunch Sa-Su 9am-2pm.

Little Wing Cafe, 529 NW 13th Ave. (☎228-3101) off Glisan. Take bus #17. Art-hunters gather at this all-homemade cafe. Sandwiches like the Eggplant Supreme ($6). Open M-Th 11:30am-4pm and 5:30-9pm; F-Sa 11:30am-4pm and 5:30-10pm.

Coffee Time, 712 NW 21st Ave. (☎497-1090). Watch locals play chess at almost every table, as you sip on a cup of chai ($2-3). While the intelligentsia mingle on the couches, bohemians chill to music in the tapestried parlor. Open daily, 6am-3am.

 SIGHTS

PIONEER COURTHOUSE SQUARE. The fully functioning **Pioneer Courthouse,** at 5th Ave. and Morrison St., is the centerpiece of the **Square.** Since opening in 1983 it has become "Portland's Living Room." Urbanites of every ilk along with a good dose of tourists hang out in the brick quadrangle. During July and August, **High Noon Tunes** draw music lovers in droves. *(701 SW 6th Ave. Along the Vintage Trolley line and the MAX light rail. Events hotline ☎223-1613. Music W noon-1pm.)*

PARKS AND GARDENS. Portland has more park acreage than any other American city, thanks in good measure to **Forest Park,** a 5000-acre tract of wilderness in Northwest Portland. Washington Park (see below), provides easy access by car or foot to this sprawling sea of green, where a web of trails leads through lush forests, scenic overviews, and idyllic picnic areas. At the **Crystal Springs Rhododendron Garden,** over 2500 rhododendrons surround a lake and border an 18-hole public golf course. *(SE 28th Ave., at Woodstock. Take bus #63. Open Mar. to early September daily dawn-dusk; Oct.-Feb. 8am-7pm. $3, under 12 free.)* Less than 2 mi. west of downtown, in the middle of the posh neighborhoods of **West Hills,** is mammoth **Washington Park,** with miles of beautiful trails and serene gardens. From there, take the MAX to the **Rose Garden,** the pride of Portland. In summer months, a sea of blooms arrests the eye, showing visitors exactly why Portland is the City of Roses. *(400 SW Kingston. ☎823-3636.)* Across from the Rose Garden are the scenic **Japanese Gardens,** reputed to be the most authentic this side of the Pacific. *(611 SW Kingston Ave. ☎223-1321. Open Apr.-Sept. daily 10am-7pm; Oct.-Mar. 10am-4pm. Tours daily at 10:45am and 2:30pm. $6, seniors $4, students $3.50, under 6 free.)* The **Hoyt**

Arboretum, at the crest of the hill above the other gardens, features 200 acres of trees and trails. *(4000 SW Fairview Blvd. ☎ 228-8733 or 823-3655. Visitors Center open M-F 9am-4pm, Sa-Su 10am-5pm.)*

MUSEUMS. The **Portland Art Museum (PAM)** sets itself apart from the rest of Portland's burgeoning arts scene by the strength of its collections, especially in Asian and Native American art. *(1219 SW Park, at Jefferson St., on the west side of the South Block Park. Bus #6, 58, 63. ☎ 226-2811. Open Tu-Sa 10am-5pm, Su noon-5pm, and until 8pm on the first Th of the month. $7.50, seniors and students $6, under 19 $4, under 5 free; special exhibits may be more.)* Across the park from the Portland Art Museum, the **Oregon Historical Society Museum and Library** stores photographs, artifacts, and records of Oregon's past two centuries. *(1200 SW Park Ave. ☎ 222-1741. Open Tu-W and F-Sa 10am-5pm, Th 10am-8pm, Su noon-5pm. $6, students $3, ages 6-12 $1.50. Seniors free on Th.)* The **Oregon Museum of Science and Industry (OMSI)** keeps visitors mesmerized with science exhibits, including an earthquake simulator chamber and an Omnimax theater. *(1945 SE Water Ave., at SE Clay St. ☎ 797-4000 or 797-4569. Open Sept.-May daily 9:30am-7pm, Th until 8pm; in winter 9:30am-5:30pm. $6.50, ages 4-13 and seniors $4.50.)* While at OMSI, visit the **USS Blueback,** the Navy's last diesel submarine; she never failed a mission. *(☎ 797-4624. Open daily 10am-5pm. Tour $3.)*

UNIQUE ATTRACTIONS. The flagship (and only) church for "Realisticism," the **24-Hour Church of Elvis** borders somewhere between installation art and childhood nightmare. Visits to the gift store grant exit from the land of eternal grace. *(720 SW Ankeny St. ☎ 226-3671. Usually open M-Th 2-4pm, F-Sa noon-5pm and 8pm-midnight, Su noon-5pm. Call ahead.)* Downtown on the edge of the Northwest district is the gargantuan ▓**Powell's City of Books,** a cavernous establishment with almost a million new and used volumes, more than any other bookstore in the US. *(1005 W. Burnside St. ☎ 228-4651 or 800-878-7323. Open daily 9am-11pm.)*

OTHER SIGHTS. The Grotto, a 62-acre Catholic sanctuary, houses magnificent religious sculptures and gardens just minutes from downtown. *(On Sandy Blvd./U.S. 30, at NE 85th. ☎ 254-7371. Open May-Oct. daily 9am-6pm, Nov.-Jan. 9am-4pm, Feb.-Apr. 9am-6:30pm.)* The **Oregon Zoo** is renowned for its scrupulous re-creation of natural habitats and its successful elephant breeding. *(4001 SW Canyon Rd. Take #63 "zoo bus" or the MAX light rail to Washington Park stop. ☎ 226-1561. Open daily 9am-6pm. $6.50, seniors $5, ages 3-11 $4; 2nd Tu of each month is free after 1pm.)*

🎵 ENTERTAINMENT

Portland's major daily newspaper, the *Oregonian*, lists upcoming events in its Friday edition, and the city's favorite free cultural reader, the Wednesday *Willamette Week*, is a reliable guide to local music, plays, and art. **Oregon Symphony Orchestra,** 923 SW Washington St. plays classics from September to June. *(☎ 228-1353 or 800-228-7343. Box office open M-Sa 9am-5pm; off-season M-F 9am-5pm. $15-60; "Symphony Sunday" afternoon concerts $10-15. "Monday Madness" offers $5 student tickets one week before showtime.)* **High Noon Tunes** *(☎ 223-1613)*, at Pioneer Courthouse Sq., presents a potpourri of rock, jazz, folk, and world music from early July through August on Wednesday afternoons.

Portland Center Stage, in the Newmark Theater at SW Broadway and SW Main, stage classics, modern adaptations, and world premiers. *(☎ 248-6309. Late Sept.-Apr. Su and Tu-Th $21-38, F-Sa $21-44; youth matinee $10.)* The **Bagdad Theater and Pub,** 3702 SE Hawthorne Blvd., puts out second-run films and an excellent beer menu. *(☎ 225-5555. 21+. Cover $2-3.)* Basketball fans can watch the **Portland Trailblazers** at the **Rose Garden Arena,** 1 Center Ct. *(☎ 321-3211).*

Northwest Film Center, 1219 SW Park Ave., hosts the **Portland International Film Festival** in the last two weeks of February, with 100 films from 30 nations. *(☎ 221-1156. Box office opens 30min. before each show. $6.50, seniors $5.50.)* Portland's premier summer event is the **Rose Festival** *(☎ 227-2681)* during the first three weeks of June. The city decks itself in finery, coming alive with waterfront concerts, art festivals, celebrity entertainment, auto racing, parades, an air show, Navy ships, and the largest children's parade in the world. Not too long afterward, the outrageously good three-day **Waterfront Blues Festival** draws some of the world's finest blues artists. (☎282-0555 or 973-3378; in early July. Suggested donation is $3 and two cans of food to benefit the Oregon Food Bank.) The **Oregon Brewers Festival**, on the last full weekend in July, is the continent's largest gathering of independent brewers for one incredible party at Waterfront Park. (☎778-5917. Mug $3 and taste $1. Under 21 must be accompanied by parent.)

◪ NIGHTLIFE

Once an uncouth and rowdy frontier town, always an uncouth and rowdy frontier town. Portland's nightclubs cater to everyone from the clove-smoking college aesthete to the nipple-pierced neo-goth aesthete.

- **Ohm**, 31 NW 1st Ave. (☎223-9919), at Couch under the Burnside Bridge. A venue dedicated to electronic music and unclassifiable beats. W breakbeat and trance, Th spoken word; weekends often bring big-name DJs. Cover $5-15. Open M-W 8pm-2:30am, Th-F 8pm-3:30am, Sa 8pm-4am, Su 8pm-3am. After-hours for some shows and special events stretch past 6am. Kitchen service until 2am.
- **The Laurel Thirst Public House**, 2958 NE Glisan St. (☎232-1504), at 30th Ave. Bus #19. Local talent makes a name for itself in two intimate rooms of groovin', boozin', and schmoozin'. Free pool Su-Th before 7pm. Cover $3-8 after 8pm. Open Su-Th 9am-1:30am, F-Sa 9am-2am. M mornings opens at noon. Burgers and sandwiches $5-8.
- **Jimmy Mak's**, 300 NW 10th Ave. (☎295-6542), 3 blocks from Powell's Books at Flanders. Jam to Portland's renowned jazz artists. Shows 9:30pm-1am. Cover $3-6. Vegetarian-friendly Greek and Middle Eastern dinners ($8-17). Open Tu-Sa 11am-2am.
- **Brig, The Nightclub Fez, Red Cap Garage** and **Boxxes**, 341 SW 10th St. (☎221-7262), form a network of clubs along Stark St. between 10th and 11th. On weekdays the clubs are connected, but on weekends they are often sealed off. Check at the door to see what is happening where. The 23-screen video and karaoke bar is where matchmaking magic happens. Cover $2-5. Open F-Sa 9pm-4am, Su-Th noon-2:30am.
- **La Cruda**, 2500 SE Clinton (☎233-0745), serves huge veggie burritos ($5). Their name means "hangover" in Spanish. After a night of downing their killer mango margaritas ($4.50), you'll understand why. Open daily 11am-2:30am; full kitchen until midnight.

MOUNT HOOD   ☎503

The snowcapped peak of Mt. Hood, at 11,235 ft., juts above its cohorts, Adams and Bachelor—evidence of its much more recent volcanic activity. Seismicity or no seismicity, thousands of outdoor enthusiasts continue to flock here every year. From rabid downhill skiers and snowboarders to the trail-loving cross-country skiers in the winter, and the climbers, hikers, bikers, and fishers in the summer, Mt. Hood offers an unbeatable outdoor experience.

◪ **PRACTICAL INFORMATION.** Mt. Hood stands near the junction of U.S. 26 and Rte. 35, 1½hr. east of Portland and 1hr. south of the Hood River. The **Mt. Hood Information Center**, 65000 E. U.S. 26, 16 mi. west of the junction of U.S. 26 and Rte. 35 and 30 mi. east of Gresham, has topographic maps and info on both area ranger districts. (☎622-7674 or 888-622-4822. Open June-Oct. daily 8am-6pm; Nov.-May 8am-4:30pm.) **Hood River District Ranger Station**, 6780 Rte. 35, has more specialized info. (☎541-352-6002. Open late May to early Sept. daily M-F 8am-4:30pm; closed Sa-Su in winter.) The other station is **Zigzag District Ranger Station**, 7020 E. U.S. 26. (☎622-3191. Open M-F 8am-4:30pm.) **Area code:** 503.

◪ **CAMPING.** Most campgrounds in Mt. Hood National Forest cluster near the junction of U.S. 26 and Rte. 35; for reservations, call 877-444-6777. **Lost Lake Resort** offers sites with water, showers, and toilets. From Rte. 35, turn east onto Woodworth Dr., right onto Dee Hwy., then left on Lost Lake Rd. (121 sites; $15; with hookup $18.) **Trillium Lake Campground**, 2 mi. east of the Timberline turn-off on U.S.

26, has trails around the crystal-clear lake and paved sites with water and toilets. Pine trees offer some privacy. (Sites $12; premium lakeside sites $14.) Just 1 mi. west of Trillium Lake, down a dirt road off U.S. 26, **Still Creek Campgrounds** has a quieter, woodsier feel, unpaved sites, and a babbling brook. (Sites $13.) Also try **Sherwood,** 14 mi. north of U.S. 26 and just off Rte. 35, beside a rambling creek. (Potable water, pit toilets, no showers. Sites $10.)

SKIING. Three Mt. Hood ski areas are convenient to Portland. All offer night skiing and snowboard parks. **Timberline,** off U.S. 26 at Government Camp, is the largest resort in Oregon. (☎ 622-0717, snow report 222-2211. Open in winter daily 9am-4pm; in spring and fall 8:30am-2:30pm; in summer 7am-1:30pm. Lift tickets $34. Night skiing Jan.-Feb. W-F 4-9pm, Sa-Su 4-10pm. Rentals: ski package $21, ages 7-12 $13; snowboard and boots $33/$23. Cash deposit or credit card required.) Smaller **Mt. Hood Ski Bowl,** 87000 E. U.S. 26, in Government Camp, 2 mi. west of Rte. 35, has the best night skiing and a snowboard park, though the season is limited. (☎ 222-2695. Season mid-Nov. to May. Open M-Tu 3:30-10pm, W-Th 9am-10pm, F 9am-11pm, Sa 8:30am-11pm, Su 8:30am-10pm. Lift tickets $16 per day, ages 7-12 $13. $16 per night, $22-28 for both. Ski rental $18/$13. Snowboards $26.) **Mt. Hood Meadows,** 9 mi. east of Government Camp on Rte. 35, is the nicest resort in the area, offering a wide range of terrain and the most high-speed lifts. At a medium elevation (7300 ft.), it often stays open through May. Mt. Hood Meadows offers $20 lift tickets through participating hotels. (☎ 337-2222, snow report 227-7669 or 541-386-7547. Open mid-Nov. to May daily 9am-4pm. Lift tickets $41, ages 7-12 $21. Night skiing Dec.-Mar. W-Su 4-10pm; $17. Ski rental package $20, ages 7-12 $15; snowboard $28/$21. Beginner package with lift ticket, lesson, and rental $45.)

SUMMER ACTIVITIES. The most popular day hike is **Mirror Lake,** a 6 mi. loop that starts 1 mi. west of Government Camp (open June-Oct.). Mount Hood Ski Bowl opens its **Action Park,** which features Indy Kart racing ($5 per 5min.), helicopter rides ($20), bungee jumping ($25), and an alpine slide for $5. (☎ 222-2695. Open M-F 11am-6pm, Sa-Su 10am-6pm.) The Ski Bowl maintains 40 mi. of bike trails ($4 trail permit), and **Hurricane Racing** rents mountain bikes mid-June to October ($10 per hr., half-day $25, full-day $35; trail permit included). The Mt. Hood Visitors Center also lists free hiking trails on which mountain biking is allowed.

COLUMBIA RIVER GORGE   ☎ 509

Stretching 75 stunning miles east from Portland, the Columbia River Gorge carries the river to the Pacific Ocean through woodlands, waterfalls, and canyons. Heading inland along the gorge, heavily forested peaks give way to broad, bronze cliffs and golden hills covered with tall pines. Mt. Hood and Mt. Adams loom nearby, and breathtaking waterfalls plunge over steep cliffs into the river.

PRACTICAL INFORMATION. To follow the gorge, which divides Oregon and Washington, take I-84 E to Exit 22. Continue east uphill on the **Columbia River Scenic Hwy. (U.S. 30),** which follows the crest of the gorge past unforgettable views. The largest town in the gorge is **Hood River,** at the junction of I-84 and Rte. 35. **Vista House,** hanging on the edge of an outcropping, is a Visitors Center in **Crown Point State Park,** 4 mi. east of Exit 22 off I-84 E. (☎ 503-695-2230. Open mid-Apr. to mid-Oct. daily 8:30am-6pm.) **Amtrak** runs trains from Portland to the foot of Walnut St. in Bingen, WA (2hr., $8-17). Station open M-Sa 8:30am-7pm and some Su afternoons. **Greyhound** runs from 600 E. Marina Way (☎ 386-1212) to Portland (1¼hr., 4 per day, $11.50). **Hood River County Chamber of Commerce,** 405 Portway Ave., is just off City Center Exit 63. (☎ 386-2000 or 800-366-3530. Open Apr.-Oct. M-F 9am-5pm, Sa-Su 10am-5pm; Nov.-Mar. M-F 9am-5pm.) **Columbia Gorge National Scenic Area Headquarters,** 902 Wasco St., in Wyeth, offers info on hiking and a friendly earful of local lore. (☎ 386-2333. Open M-F 7:30am-5pm.) **Post Office:** 408 Cascade Ave., in Hood River (☎ 386-1584.; open M-F 8:30am-5pm). **ZIP code:** 97031. **Area codes:** In WA 509, in OR 541. In text, 509 unless noted.

⚐ ACCOMMODATIONS. The **Bingen School Inn Hostel**, a converted schoolhouse, is just across the Hood River Toll Bridge (75¢), 3½ blocks from the Amtrak stop in Bingen, WA. (☎493-3363. Sailboards $30 per day. Dorms $15; private rooms $35.) **Beacon Rock State Park,** across the Bridge of the Gods (Exit 44) and 7 mi. west on Washington's Rte. 14, has secluded sites (☎427-8265; $12). The **Lone Pine Motel**, 2429 Cascade St. Hood River, rents hostel-style rooms. (☎541-387-8882. $25-35 per night, $125 per week.)

⚐ WINDSURFING. The river widens out and the wind picks up at the town of Hood River, providing some of the world's best windsurfing. Though it was once "as fast as a waterfall turned on its side" and so full of fish that the famous comedic duo of Lewis and Clark once quipped that they could walk across without getting wet, the Columbia's waters now run slower and emptier due to damming upstream. The water near **Spring Creek Fish Hatchery** on the Washington side is the place to watch the best windsurfers in the business. Another hub is the **Event Site**, off Exit 63 behind the Visitors Center. All-day parking costs $3, although it's free if you just sit and watch. **Big Winds**, 207 Front St., at the east end of Oak St., has cheap beginner rentals. (☎386-6086. $8 per hr., $15 per half-day, $25 per day.)

⚐ OUTDOOR ACTIVITIES. Discover Bicycles, 1020 Wasco St., rents mountain bikes, suggests routes, and sells all manner of trail maps. (☎386-4820. Open M-Sa 9am-7pm, Su 9am-5pm. Bikes $6 per hr., $30 per day.) The 11 mi. round-trip **Hospital Hill Trail** provides views of Mt. Hood, the gorge, Hood River, and surrounding villages. To reach the unmarked trail, follow signs to the hospital, fork left to Rhine Village, and walk behind the power transformers through the livestock fence. At **Latourell Falls,** 2½ mi. east of Crown Point, a jaunt down a paved path leads right to the base of the falls; 5 mi. farther east, **Wahkeena Falls** is visible from the road and hosts both a short, steep scramble and a ¼ mi. trip up a paved walk. Just a half-mile farther on U.S. 30 is **Multnomah Falls,** which attracts 2 million visitors annually; I-84 Exit 31 leads to an island in the middle of the freeway from which visitors can only see the upper falls. The steep **Wyeth Trail,** near the hamlet of Wyeth (Exit 51), leads 4½ mi. to a wilderness boundary and 7¼ mi. to the road to Hood River and the incredible 13 mi. **Eagle Creek Trail** (Exit 44). Chiseled into cliffs high above Eagle Creek, this trail passes four waterfalls before joining the Pacific Crest Trail.

OREGON COAST

From Astoria in the north to Brookings down south, U.S. 101 hugs the shore along the Oregon Coast, linking a string of resorts and fishing villages that cluster around the mouths of rivers feeding into the Pacific. Breathtaking ocean views spread between these towns, while state parks and national forests allow direct access to the big surf. Seals, sea lions, and waterfowl perch on rocks just offshore, watching the human world whiz by on wheels.

ASTORIA   ☎503

Astoria's long standing dependence on maritime industries has only recently begun to yield to the tourist industry. Its Victorian homes, bustling waterfront, rolling hills, and persistent fog suggest San Francisco on a smaller scale.

The **Fort Clatsop National Memorial,** 5 mi. southwest of town, reconstructs Lewis and Clark's winter headquarters from detailed descriptions in their journals. Astoria was their last stop in 1805. Take U.S. 101 south from Astoria to Alt. U.S. 101, and follow the signs 3 mi. to the park. (☎861-2471. Open mid-June to early Sept. 8am-6pm; off-season 8am-5pm. $2, under 17 free, families $4 per car.) At the **Shallon Winery,** 1598 Duane St., owner Paul van der Velt provides tours and tastings of his vintages, including chocolate orange wine. (☎325-5978. Open afternoon; 21+ to drink.)

PACIFIC NORTHWEST

Grandview B&B, 1574 Grand Ave., offers intimate, luxurious rooms and a delicious breakfast spread. (☎325-0000, reservations 325-5555. From $45, with private bath from $71; 2nd night $36 off-season.) **Fort Stevens State Park,** over Youngs Bay Bridge on U.S. 101 S, 10 mi. west of Astoria, is the largest state park in the US, with rugged, empty beaches and bike trails. (☎861-1671, reservations 800-452-5687. Hot showers. Facilities for the disabled. $18, full hookup $21; hiker/biker $4.25 per person; yurts $29. Reservations $6.)

Pierce Pacific Stages (☎692-4437) picks up travelers at Video City, 95 W. Marine Dr., and runs to Portland (3hr., $22). **Astoria/Warrenton Area Chamber of Commerce:** 111 W. Marine Dr. (☎325-6311; open June-Sept. M-F 8am-6pm, Sa-Su 9am-6pm; Oct.-May M-F 8am-5pm, Sa-Su 11am-4pm). **Post Office:** 748 Commercial St., at 8th St. (open M-F 8:30am-5pm). **ZIP code:** 97103. **Area code:** 503.

CANNON BEACH   ☎503

Cannon Beach presents a somewhat more refined version of Astoria's commercialism, but the beach is the real draw. Ecola Point offers a view of hulking Haystack Rock, which is spotted with (and by) gulls, puffins, barnacles, anemones, and the occasional sea lion. (☎436-2844. entrance fee $3.) Ecola Point also affords views of the Bay's centerpiece, the **Tillamook Lighthouse,** which clings to a rock like a giant barnacle. A huge **Sand Castle Competition** transforms Cannon Beach into a fantastic menagerie on the 2nd Saturday of June.

Pleasant motels line Hemlock St.; none costs under $40 in summer, but family units can make a good deal. In winter, most motels offer two-nights-for-one deals. **The Sandtrap Inn,** 539 S. Hemlock St., offers picturesque, cozy rooms with fireplaces, cable TV, and kitchens. (☎436-0247 or 800-400-4106. Singles from $60; off-season $50; 2-night min. stay summer Sa-Su.) **Seaside International Hostel (HI-AYH)** is only 7 mi. north, and the stunning **Oswald West State Park** is 10 mi. south. The park provides wheelbarrows for transporting gear from the parking lot to the 36 sites which teem with surfers; arrive early. (Sites mid-May to Oct. $14; Oct.-Apr. $10.)

Sunset Transit System (☎800-776-6406) runs buses to Astoria ($2.25). **Cannon Beach Shuttle** traverses the downtown area daily 9am-6pm (75¢). **Mike's Bike Shop,** 248 N. Spruce St., rents mountain bikes. (☎436-1266 or 800-492-1266. Open daily 9am-6pm. $6-8 per hr., $20-30 per day.) **Cannon Beach Chamber of Commerce:** 207 N. Spruce St. (☎436-2623; open M-Sa 10am-6pm, Su 11am-4pm). **Post Office:** 155 N. Hemlock St. (☎436-2822; open M-F 9am-5pm). **ZIP code:** 97110. **Area code:** 503.

THE THREE CAPES LOOP

Between Tillamook and Lincoln City, the **Three Capes Loop,** a 35 mi. circle to the west of the straying U.S. 101, connects a trio of spectacular promontories. **Cape Meares State Park** and **Lighthouse,** at the tip of the promontory jutting out from Tillamook, protect one of the few remaining old-growth forests on the Oregon Coast. Another 12 mi. southwest of Cape Meares, **Cape Lookout State Park** (☎842-4981) offers picnic tables and access to the beach for drive-by dawdlers as well as some fine camping. A spectacular view of **Haystack Rock** awaits at the end of the 2½ mi. **Cape Trail. Cape Kiwanda State Park,** the southernmost promontory on the loop, reserves its magnificent shore for day use (open 8am-dusk). Home to one of the most sublime beaches on the Oregon coast, the sheltered cape draws all sorts. Massive rock outcroppings in a small bay mark the launching pad of the flat-bottomed dory fleet, one of the few fishing fleets in the world that launches beachside, directly from sand to surf. **Pacific City,** a hidden gem that most travelers on U.S. 101 never even see, is home to equally impressive **Haystack Rock.**

NEWPORT   ☎541

After the miles of malls along U.S. 101, Newport's renovated waterfront area of pleasantly kitschy restaurants and shops are a delight. Newport's claim to fame, however, is the world-class **Oregon Coast Aquarium,** 2820 Ferry Slip Rd., at the south end of the bridge. The six-acre complex features pulsating jellyfish, atten-tion-seeking sea otters, and giant African bullfrogs. (☎867-3474. Open May-June 9am-6pm; July-Sept. 9am-8pm; in winter 10am-5pm. $10.25, seniors $9.25, ages 4-13 $6.25. Wheelchair accessible.) The ◼**Mark O. Hatfield Marine Science Center,** at the south end of the bridge on Marine Science Dr., is the hub of Oregon State University's coastal research and a superior facility. (☎867-0100. Open daily 10am-5pm; in winter Th-M 10am-4pm. Admission by donation.)

City Center Motel, 538 Coast Hwy. SW, opposite the Visitors Center, is smack in the middle of town. It has spacious, oddly empty rooms with sparkling bathrooms, cable, phones, and ice. (☎265-7381 or 800-627-9099. $30; doubles $45.) **Beverly Beach State Park,** 198 123rd St. NE, 7 mi. north of town, is a year-round campground set amid gorgeous, rugged terrain. (☎265-9278 or 800-452-5687. 129 sites, $17; with electricity $20; full hookup $22; yurts $29; hiker/biker $4.25. Non-camper showers $2.) **Mo's Restaurant,** 622 Bay Blvd. SW, is a local favorite with amazing clam chow-der for $4-6. (☎265-2979. Open daily 11am-10pm.)

Greyhound, 956 10th St. SW (☎265-2253), at Bailey St. runs buses to Portland (4hr., 2 per day, $18); Seattle (9hr., 2 per day, $44); and San Francisco (17-21hr., 3-4 per day, $72-76). **Chamber of Commerce,** 555 Coast Hwy. SW (☎265-8801; open M-F 8:30am-5pm; in summer also Sa-Su 10am-4pm). **Post office:** 310 2nd St. SW (☎574-6746; open M-F 8:30am-5pm, Sa 10am-1pm). **ZIP code:** 97365. **Area code:** 541.

OREGON DUNES   ☎541

Millennia of wind and water action have formed the Oregon Dunes National Recreation Area, a 50-mile expanse between Florence and Coos Bay. Endless mounds of sand rise 500 feet above the water, shifting so quickly that the entire face of a dune can disappear and reform in the course of a day. The dunes' shifting grip on the coastline is broken at Reedsport, where the Umpqua and Smith Rivers empty into Winchester Bay, near a town of the same name. **Dunes Odyssey, Inc.,** on U.S. 101 in Winchester Bay, was the first ATV rental business on the Oregon Coast. Rent a Honda Odyssey or a Polaris Quad and explore over 10,000 acres of dunes. (☎271-3863. Open daily 8am-dusk; call for winter hours. Both $35 for the first hr., $30 for each additional hr. Odyssey: $50 deposit. Polaris Quad: $100 deposit.) Even those with little time can at least stop at the **Oregon Dunes Overlook,** off U.S. 101, about halfway between Reed-sport and Florence. Wooden ramps lead to a peek at untrammeled dunes and the ocean. (Overlook staffed daily May to Sept. 10am-3pm. Guided hikes are available. $1 parking fee.)

The **Harbor View Motel,** 540 Beach Blvd., off U.S. 101 in Winchester Bay, is so close to the marina there are boats in the parking lot. Aging rooms to charm an antique hound are comfortable and clean. (☎271-3352. Singles $34; doubles $39.) Motels with singles from $40 abound on U.S. 101, though they often fill in summer. The national recreation area is administered by **Siuslaw National Forest.** Dispersed camp-ing is allowed on public lands, 200 ft. from any road or trail. The campgrounds with dune buggy access—**Spinreel, Driftwood II, Horsfall,** and **Horsfall Beach**—are generally loud and rowdy in the summer. All have flush toilets, drinking water, and are open year-round. (Reservations ☎800-280-2267. Sites $10-13.) **Carter Lake Campground,** 12 mi. north of Reedsport on U.S. 101, is as quiet as it gets. (Open May-Sept. No ATVs. Nice bathrooms, no showers. $13.)

Oregon Dunes National Recreation Area Information Center, 855 U.S. 101 (☎271-3611), at Rte. 38 in Reedsport, south of the Umpqua River Bridge, happily answers questions on fees, regulations, hiking, and camping throughout the area. **Reedsport/Winchester Bay Chamber of Commerce** is at the same location and has dune buggy rental and motel info. (☎271-3495 or 800-247-2155. Both open June-Oct. daily 8am-4:30pm; Nov.-May M-F 8am-4:30pm, Sa 10am-4pm.) **Post Office:** 301 Fir Ave., off Rte. 38. (☎271-6790; open M-F 8:30am-5pm). **ZIP code:** 97467. **Area code:** 541.

PACIFIC NORTHWEST

INLAND OREGON

EUGENE ☎ 541

The home of the University of Oregon, and known as the track capital of the USA due to legends such as Coach Bowerman (inventor of the artificial track) and his runner Steve Prefontaine, Eugene takes due credit for its role in the running revolution of the 80s. Fitness enthusiasts sprint to this running epicenter, which is also the original hometown of Nike, Inc. (now based in Beaverton). Home to both a biking revolution and an active hippie movement, which celebrates itself each year during the Oregon Country Fair, Eugene has also earned itself a liberal reputation.

■■ **ORIENTATION AND PRACTICAL INFORMATION.** Eugene is 111 mi. south of Portland on I-5. The **University of Oregon** campus lies in the southeast corner of Eugene, bordered on the north by **Franklin Blvd.**, which runs from the city center to I-5. **First Ave.** runs alongside the winding Willamette River; numbered **streets** go north-south. **Rte. 99** is split in town: **6th Ave.** runs north and **7th Ave.** goes south. **Willamette Ave.** intersects the river, dividing the city into east and west. It is interrupted by the **pedestrian mall**, between 6th and 7th Ave. on Broadway downtown. Eugene's main student drag, **13th Ave.**, heads east to the University of Oregon. **Amtrak,** 433 Willamette St. (☎687-1383; open daily 5:15-9pm), at 4th Ave., treks to Seattle (6-8hr., 2 per day, $31-58) and Portland (2½-3hr., 2 per day, $15-27). **Greyhound,** 987 Pearl St. (☎344-6265; open daily 6:15am-9:35pm), at 10th Ave., runs to Seattle (6-9hr., 9 per day, $31) and Portland (2-4hr., 10 per day, $13). **Lane Transit District (LTD)** handles public transportation. (☎687-5555. Map and timetables at the LTD Service Center at 11th Ave. and Willamette St. Runs M-F 6am-11:40pm, Sa 7:30am-11:40pm, Su 8:30am-8:30pm. $1, seniors and ages under 18 50¢. Wheelchair accessible.) **Yellow Cab:** ☎746-1234. **Visitor info:** 115 W 8th Ave., #190, but the door is on Olive St. (☎484-5307 or 800-547-5445. Courtesy phone. Sells an indexed map for $4. Open May-Aug. M-F 8:30am-5pm, Sa-Su 10am-4pm; Sept.-Apr. M-Sa 8:30am-5pm.) **University of Oregon Switchboard**, in the Rainier Bldg. at 1244 Walnut St., is a referral service for almost anything, from rides to housing. (☎346-3111. Open M-F 7am-6pm.) **Post Office:** 520 Willamette St., at 5th Ave. (☎341-3649. Open M-F 8:30am-5:30pm, Sa 10am-2pm.) **ZIP code:** 97401. **Area code:** 541.

■■ **ACCOMMODATIONS AND FOOD.** The cheapest motels are on E. Broadway and W. 7th Ave. and tend toward seediness. Make reservations early; motels are packed on big football weekends. **Hummingbird Eugene International Hostel,** 2352 Willamette St., a graceful neighborhood home, is a wonderful escape from the city. Take bus #24 or 25 and get off at 24th Ave. and Willamette, or park in back on Portland St. (☎349-0589. Check-in 5-10pm. Lockout 11am-5pm. Dorms $16, nonmembers $18; private rooms from $37. Cash or traveler's check only.) Tenters have been known to camp by the river, especially in the wild and woolly northeastern side near Springfield. Farther east on Rte. 58 and 126, the immense **Willamette National Forest** is full of campsites ($6-16). A swamp gives the tree bark and ferns an eerie phosphorescence in the beautiful, mysterious **Pine Meadows Campground,** which lies alongside a reservoir and catches plenty of RV traffic. Take I-5 south to Exit 172, then head 3½ mi. south, then left on Cottage Grove Reservoir Rd., and go another 2½ mi. (☎877-444-6777. Sites $6-12.)

Eugene's downtown area specializes in gourmet food; the university hangout zone at 13th Ave. and Kincaid has more grab-and-go options, and natural food stores encircle the city. ◼**Keystone Cafe,** 395 W. 5th St., serves creative dinners with entirely organic ingredients. (☎342-2075. Open daily 7am-5pm. Famous pancakes $3.25.) **Park St. Cafe,** 776 W. Park, intertwined in a knot of shops, makes delicious sandwiches ($7) and offers daily lunch specials. (☎485-2089. Open M-F 9am-3pm.)

◘ SIGHTS AND EVENTS. The *Eugene Weekly* has a list of concerts and local events, as well as features on the greater Eugene community. Take time to pay homage to the ivy-covered halls that set the scene for *National Lampoon's Animal House* at Eugene's centerpiece, the **University of Oregon**. The visitor parking and info booth is just left of the main entrance on Franklin Blvd. A few blocks away, the **Museum of Natural History**, 1680 E. 15th Ave., at Agate, shows a collection of relics from indigenous cultures worldwide, including a the world's oldest pair of shoes. (☎346-3024. Open W-Su noon-5pm. Suggested donation $2.)

From June 28 to July 14, 2002, during the **Oregon Bach Festival**, Baroque authority Helmut Rilling conducts performances of Bach's concerti and his contemporaries. (☎346-5666 or 800-457-1486. Concert and lecture series $13; main events $20-45.) The vast **Oregon Country Fair** actually takes place in **Veneta**, 13 mi. west of town on Rte. 126, but its festive quakes can be felt in Eugene. From July 12-14, 2002, 50,000 people will drop everything to enjoy ten stages' worth of shows, 300 booths of art, clothing, crafts, herbal remedies, furniture, food, and free hugs. Advance tickets are available through **Fastixx** (☎800-992-8499) or at the **Hult Center**. (☎343-4298. Advance tickets F and Su $10, Sa $15. No tickets sold on site.)

▲ OUTDOOR ACTIVITIES. Canoe or kayak the **Millrace Canal**, which parallels the Willamette for 3 mi. The large and popular Cougar Lake features the Terwilliger Hot Springs, known by all as **Cougar Hot Springs**. Go 4 mi. east of Blue River on Rte. 126, turn right onto Aufderheide Dr. (Forest Service Rd. 19), and follow the road 7¼ mi. as it winds on the right side of Cougar Reservoir ($3 day fee per person).

East from Eugene, Rte. 126 runs adjacent to the beautiful McKenzie River, and on a clear day, the mighty snowcapped Three Sisters of the Cascades are visible. Just east of the town of **McKenzie Bridge**, the road splits into a scenic byway loop; Rte. 242 climbs east to the vast lava fields of McKenzie Pass, while Rte. 126 turns north over Santiam Pass and meets back with Rte. 242 in Sisters. Often blocked by snow until the end of June, Rte. 242 is an exquisite drive, tunneling its narrow, winding way between **Mt. Washington** and the **Three Sisters Wilderness** before rising to the high plateau of McKenzie Pass, where lava outcroppings served as a training site for astronauts preparing for lunar landings.

The 26 mi. **McKenzie River Trail** parallels Rte. 126 through mossy forests and leads to some of Oregon's most spectacular waterfalls, Koosah Falls and Sahalie Falls. They flank Clear Lake, a volcanic crater now filled with crystal clear waters. The trail starts about 1½ mi. west of the ranger station and ends up north at Old Santiam Rd. near the Fish Lake Old Growth Grove. The trail is now open to mountain bikers.

◙ NIGHTLIFE. According to some, Eugene nightlife is the best in Oregon. In the *Animal House* tradition, the row of hot spots by the university along 13th St. are often dominated by fraternity-style beer bashes. **Sam Bond's Garage**, 407 Blair Blvd., is a supremely laid-back gem in Whittaker neighborhood. Live entertainment goes on every night, plus an ever changing selection of local microbrews ($3 per pint). Take bus #50 or 52 or a cab at night. (☎431-6603. Open daily 3pm-1am.) **The Downtown Lounge/Diablo's**, 959 Pearl, offers a casual dance scene with pool tables upstairs and a hip party in flame-covered walls downstairs (☎343-2346. Cover $2-3. Open W-Sa 9pm-2:30am.) Across the street from 5th St. Market, **Jo Federigo's Jazz Club and Restaurant**, 259 E. 5th Ave., swings with jazz nightly. (☎343-8488. Open M-F 11:30am-2pm and 5-10pm, Sa-Su 5-10pm. Jazz club open daily 8:30pm-1am. Shows start 9:30pm.)

CRATER LAKE AND KLAMATH FALLS ☎541

The deepest lake in the US, the seventh deepest in the world, and one of the most beautiful anywhere, Crater Lake is one of Oregon's signature attractions. Formed about 7700 years ago in an eruption of the huge Mt. Mazama, it began as a deep caldera and gradually filled itself with centuries worth of melted snow. This 1936 ft. deep lake will celebrate 100 years as a national park during the 2002 summer. From the Visitors Center at the rim to the **Sinnott Memorial Overlook** it is an easy 300 ft. walk to the park's most panoramic and accessible view. **Rim Dr.,** which does not open entirely until mid-July, is a 33 mi. loop around the rim of the caldera, high above the lake. Trails to **Watchman Peak** (¾ mi. one-way, 1hr.), on the west side of the lake, are the most spectacular. The strenuous, 2½ mi. hike up **Mt. Scott,** the park's highest peak (shy of 9000 ft.), begins from near the lake's eastern edge. The steep **Cleetwood Trail** (2¼ mi. round-trip, 2hr.) leaves from the north edge of the lake and is the only route down to the water. It is also the home of **Wizard Island,** a cinder cone rising 760 ft. above the lake, and **Phantom Ship Rock,** a spooky rock formation. Picnics, fishing, and swimming are allowed, but surface temperatures reach a maximum of only 50°F. Park rangers lead free walking tours daily in the summer and periodically in the winter (on snowshoes).

Klamath Falls has several affordable hotels; it's an easy base for forays to Crater Lake. The **Townhouse Motel,** 5323 6th St., 3 mi. south of Main, on the edge of strip mall land, offers clean, comfy rooms. (☎882-0924. Cable, A/C, no phones. Double bed $30; two-bed rooms $35.) **Mazama Campground,** near the park's south entrance off Rte. 62, is swarmed by tenters and RVs from mid-June until October. (☎594-2255. Showers 75¢ per 4min. Wheelchair accessible. No reservations. 200 sites, $15; RVs $17; electric hookup $19.) **Waldo's Mongolian Grill and Tavern,** 610 Main St., will grill your choice of veggies, meats, and sauces. (☎884-6863. Open M-Th 11am-11:30pm, F-Sa 11am-1am. Medium bowl $8.50. All-you-can-eat $10.)

Rte. 62 skirts the park's southwestern edge as it arcs 130 mi. between Medford in the southwest and Klamath Falls, 56 mi. southeast of the park. From Portland, take **I-5** to Eugene, then **Rte. 58** east to **U.S. 97** south. From U.S. 97, **Rte. 138** leads west to the park's north entrance, but Crater Lake averages over 44 ft. of snow per year, and snowbound roads can keep the northern entrance closed as late as July. Before July, enter the park from the south. The **Amtrak** Spring St. depot (☎884-2822; open 6:45-10:15am and 9-10:30pm) is in Klamath Falls, on the east end of Main St.; turn right onto Spring St. and immediately left onto Oak St. One train per day runs to Portland ($36-60). **Greyhound,** 3817 U.S. 97 N (☎882-4616; open M-F 6am-2:30pm and midnight-12:45am, Sa 6-9am and midnight-12:45am), rolls one per day to Bend (3hr., $20); Eugene (10hr., $40); and Redding, CA (4hr., $30). **Visitor info: Klamath County Dept. of Tourism,** 507 Main St. (☎884-0666 or 800-445-6728; open M-Sa 9am-5pm). The **William G. Steel Center,** 1 mi. from the south entrance of the park, issues free **backcountry camping** permits. (☎594-2211, ext. 402. Open daily 9am-5pm.) **Crater Lake National Park Visitors Center:** on the lake shore at Rim Village (☎594-2211, ext. 415; open June-Sept. daily 8:30am-6pm). The park entrance fee is $10 for cars, $5 for hikers and cyclists. **Post Office:** 317 S. 7th St. in Klamath. (☎884-9828. Open M-F 7:30am-5:30pm, Sa 9am-noon.) **ZIP code:** 97604. **Area code:** 541.

ASHLAND

☎541

Set near the California border, Ashland mixes hippies and history to create an unlikely but perfect stage for the world-famous **Oregon Shakespeare Festival,** P.O. Box 158, Ashland 97520 (☎482-4331). From mid-February to October, drama devotees can choose among 11 Shakespearean and newer works performed in Ashland's three elegant theaters: the outdoor **Elizabethan Stage,** the **Angus Bowmer Theater,** and the intimate **Black Swan.** Ticket purchases are recommended six months in advance; mail-order and phone ticket sales begin in January ($22-39 in spring and fall, $29-52 in summer; $5 fee per order for phone, fax, or mail orders). At 9:30am, the **box office,** 15 S. Pioneer St., releases any unsold tickets for the day's performances and sells 20 standing room tickets for sold-out shows on the Elizabethan Stage ($11). Half-price rush tickets are sometimes available 1hr. before performances. **Backstage tours** provide a wonderful glimpse of the festival from behind the curtain (Tu-Su 10am; $10, ages 6-17 $7.50, under 6 not admitted).

In winter, Ashland is a budget paradise; in summer, hotel and B&B rates double, and the hostel bulges. Only rogues and peasant slaves arrive without reservations. ☒**Ashland Hostel,** 150 N. Main St., is well-kept and cheery, with an air of elegance. (☎482-9217. Laundry and kitchen. Check-in 5-11pm. Lockout 10am-5pm. Curfew midnight. Dorms $16; private rooms $45. Cash or traveler's checks only.) The incredible food selection on N. and E. Main St. has earned the plaza a culinary reputation independent of the festival. ◪**Pangea's,** 272 E. Main St., offers a creative menu including the $7 The Wrap of Khan. (☎552-1630. Open daily 11:30am-9pm.)

Ashland is located in the foothills of the Siskiyou and Cascade Ranges, 285 mi. south of Portland and 15 mi. north of the California border, near the junction of **I-5** and **Rte. 66. Greyhound** (☎482-8803) runs from the **BP Station,** 2073 Rte. 99 N, at the north end of town, and sends three per day to Portland (8hr., 3 per day, $43); Sacramento (7hr., 3 per day, $45); and San Francisco (11hr., 3 per day, $49). **Chamber of Commerce:** 110 E. Main St. (☎482-3486). **Ashland District Ranger Station,** 645 Washington St., off Rte. 66 by Exit 14 on I-5, provides info on hiking, biking, and the Pacific Crest Trail. (☎482-3333. Open M-F 8am-4:30pm.) **Post Office:** 120 N. 1st St., at Lithia Way. (Open M-F 9am-5pm). **ZIP code:** 97520. **Area code:** 541.

BEND
☎**541**

Defined by a dramatic landscape—volcanic features to the south, the Cascades to the west, and the Deschutes River running through its heart—Bend attracts its share of Oregon's visitors. Though young urbanites flooded the banks of U.S. 97 with malls and outlets in the 1970s, downtown has since grown into a charming crowd-pleaser, and the outdoor opportunities have only gotten better. A few miles south of Bend, the **High Desert Museum,** 59800 S. Rte. 97, is one of the premier natural and cultural history museums in the Pacific Northwest. Visitors walk through life-size dioramas of life in the Old West, while the indoor desertarium houses bats, owls, and lizards. A Native American Wing features a walk-through exhibit on post-reservation Indian life. (☎382-4754. Open daily 9am-5pm. $7.75, seniors and ages 13-18 $6.75, ages 5-12 $4.)

The **Three Sisters Wilderness Area,** north and west of the Cascade Lakes Highway, is one of Oregon's largest and most popular wilderness areas. Pick up a parking permit at a ranger station or at the Visitors Center ($5). Mountain biking is not allowed in the wilderness area, but Benders have plenty of other places to spin their wheels. Try **Deschutes River Trail** (6 mi.) for a fairly flat, basic, forested trail ending at **Deschutes River.** To reach the trailhead, go 7½ mi. west of Bend on Century Dr. (Cascade Lakes Hwy.) until Forest Service Rd. 41, then turn left and follow the signs to Lava Island Falls. A slick guide to mountain bike trails around Bend is available for $9 at most bike shops, but some of the hottest trails aren't on the maps; talk to locals.

Most of the cheapest motels line **3rd St.** just outside of town, and rates are surprisingly low. To reach **Bend Cascade Hostel,** 19 SW Century Dr., take Greenwood west from 3rd St. until the name changes to Newport. After ½ mi., take a left on 14th St.; the clean, fairly safe, and tidy hostel is ½ mi. up on the right side, just past the Circle K. (☎389-3813 or 800-299-3813. Foosball, laundry, kitchen, linen. $14, nonmembers $15.) **Deschutes National Forest** maintains a huge number of lakeside campgrounds along the **Cascade Lakes Hwy.,** west of town; all have toilets. (Free, with water $8-12. Camping in the national forest free. **Taqueria Los Jalapenos,** 601 NE Greenwood Ave. fills a simple space with locals hungry for good, cheap food, including $1.75 burritos. (☎382-1402. Open M-Sa 11am-8pm; in winter 11am-7pm.)

Bend is 160 mi. southeast of Portland either on U.S. 26 E through Warm Springs Indian Reservation to U.S. 97 S or south on I-5 to Salem, then east on Rte. 22 E to Rte. 20 E through Sisters. **U.S. 97 (3rd St.)** bisects the town. Downtown lies to the west along the **Deschutes River; Wall** and **Bond St.** are the two main arteries. **Greyhound,** 63076 U.S. 97N (☎382-2151; open M-F 8am-1:30pm and 2:30-5pm, Sa-Su 8:30am-3pm), runs to Portland (4½hr., 1 per day, $24) and Eugene (2½hr., 1 per day, $21). **Bend Chamber and Visitors Bureau,** 63085 U.S. 97 N, stocks free maps, free coffee, and Internet access. (☎382-3221. Open M-Sa 9am-5pm, Su 11am-3pm.) **Deschutes National Forest Headquarters,** 1645 U.S. 20 E, has forest and wilderness info. (☎383-5800. Open M-F 7:45am-4:30pm.) **Post Office:** 2300 NE 4th St., at Webster. (Open M-F 8:30am-5:30pm, Sa 10am-1pm.) **ZIP code:** 97701. **Area code:** 541.

PACIFIC NORTHWEST

HELLS CANYON AND WALLOWA MTS. ☎541

The northeast corner of Oregon is the state's most rugged, remote, and arresting country, with jagged granite peaks, glacier-gouged valleys, and azure lakes. East of La Grande, the Wallowa Mountains (*wa-LAH-wah*) rise abruptly, looming over the plains from elevations of more than 9000 ft. Thirty miles east, North America's deepest gorge, Hells Canyon, plunges to the Snake River. Dusty slopes and scorching heat lend credence to the canyon's name. It may take a four-wheel-drive vehicle to get off the beaten path, but those with the initiative and the horsepower will find stunning vistas and heavenly solitude in the backcountry.

◪ PRACTICAL INFORMATION. Hells Canyon National Recreation Area and the Eagle Cap Wilderness lie on either side of the Wallowa Valley, which can be reached from Baker City, La Grande, and Clarkston, WA. Three main towns offer services within the area: **Enterprise, Joseph,** and **Halfway**. The **Wallowa Valley Stage Line** (☎569-2284) makes one round-trip Monday through Saturday from Joseph to La Grande. Pickup at the Chevron on Rte. 82 in Joseph, the Amoco on Rte. 82 in Enterprise, and the Greyhound terminal in La Grande. One-way from La Grande to: Enterprise ($11); Joseph ($12); and Wallowa Lake ($17). **Wallowa County Chamber of Commerce** is at SW 1st St. and W. Greenwood Ave. in Enterprise, in the mall (☎426-4622 or 800-585-4121; open M-F 9am-5pm). **Hells Canyon Chamber of Commerce:** in the office of Halfway Motels (☎742-4222). **Wallowa Mountains Visitor Center,** 88401 Rte. 82, on the west side of Enterprise, has essential $4 maps. (☎426-5546. Open May to early Sept. M-Sa 8am-5pm; off-season M-F 8am-5pm.)

⌂ ACCOMMODATIONS. **Indian Lodge Motel,** 201 S. Main St., on Rte. 82 in Joseph, has elegant rooms with dark wood furniture and plush blue carpet. (☎432-2651 or 888-286-5484. A/C, cable, coffee-makers, fridges. Singles $37; doubles $49. In winter $32/$40.) Campgrounds here are plentiful, inexpensive, and sublime. Pick up the *Campground Information* pamphlet at the Wallowa Mountains Visitors Center for a complete listing of sites in the area. Due to 1996 budget cutbacks, most campgrounds are not fully serviced, and are therefore free—check at the Visitors Center to see whether a campground has potable water. Inexplicably, the massive **Wallowa Lake State Park campground** books solid up to a year in advance. Try your luck there if you're in the market for full-service camping. (☎432-4185 or 800-452-5687. Toilets, drinking water, and showers. Sites $16.50; full hookups $21.)

⚠ OUTDOOR ACTIVITIES. Hiking is the best way to soak in the vast emptiness of Hells Canyon, and to really get into the canyon requires a trip of at least a few days. There are over 1000 mi. of trails, only a fraction of which are regularly maintained. Bring snakebite kits, good boots, and lots of water. The dramatic 56 mi. **Snake River Trail** runs beside the river for the length of the canyon. At times, the trail is cut into the side of the rock with just enough clearance for a horse's head. Come prepared for any hazard, though outfitters and rangers patrol the river by boat at least once a day. This trail can be followed from **Dug Bar** in the north clear down to the Hells Canyon Dam or accessed by treacherously steep trails along the way. From north to south, **Hat Point, Freezeout,** and **P.O. Saddle** are possible access points. To reach Dug Bar, take Forest Rd. 4260, a steep, slippery route recommended only for four-wheel drive or high-clearance vehicles, for 27 mi. northeast from Imnaha; check conditions before heading out. The only way to get close to the canyon without taking at least a full day is to drive the **Hells Canyon National Scenic Loop Drive,** which begins and ends in Baker City, following Rte. 86, Forest Rd. 39 and 350, Rte. 82, and finally I-84. Even this paved route takes 6hr. to two days to drive; closures are routine. The most eye-popping views are from the 90 ft. fire lookout at **Hat Point Overlook;** go 24 mi. up the steep gravel Forest Rd. 4240 from Imnaha, then turn off onto Rd. 315 and follow the signs.

Without a catchy, federally approved name like "Hells Canyon," the Wallowas often take second place to the canyon in the minds of tourists, though they possess a scenic beauty equally magnificent. Over 600 mi. of hiking trails cross the **Eagle Cap Wilderness** and are usually free of snow from mid-July to October. Deep glacial valleys and high granite passes make hiking this wilderness tough going: it often takes more than a day to get into the most beautiful and remote areas. Still, several high alpine lakes are accessible to dayhikers. The 5 mi. hike to **Chimney Lake** from the Bowman trailhead on the Lostine River Rd. (Forest Rd. 8210) traverses fields of granite boulders sprinkled with a few small meadows. A little farther on lie the serene **Laverty, Hobo,** and **Wood Lakes,** where the path is less beaten. The **Two Pan trailhead** at the end of the Lostine River Rd. is the start of a forested 6 mi. hike to popular **Minam Lake,** which makes a good starting point for those heading to other backcountry spots like **Blue Lake,** 1 mi. above Minam. From the **Wallowa Lake trailhead,** behind the little powerhouse at the end of Rte. 82, a 6 mi. hike leads up the East Fork of the Wallowa River to Aneroid Lake. From there, hikes to Pete's Point and Aneroid Mountain reward with great views.

WESTERN CANADA

HIGHLIGHTS OF WESTERN CANADA

THE YUKON. Flightseeing in Kluane National Park (p. 932) and gold-panning in boom-town Dawson City (p. 929) are both unusual and memorable.

SCENIC DRIVES. The glorious Dempster Hwy. (p. 933) leads way up to Inuvik, NWT.

NATIONAL PARKS. Banff (p. 934) and Jasper (p. 937) in Alberta reign as two of the region's most beautiful. Pacific Rim National Park, BC contains the West Coast Trail (p. 927) with its isolated beaches and old growth rainforest.

BRITISH COLUMBIA

With stunning parks and vibrant cities, British Columbia (BC) is home to the third largest movie production center in the world and a huge tourism industry. This Canadian province has room for the visitors: at over 900,000 sq. km, BC is more than twice as large as California and touches four US states (Washington, Idaho, Montana, and Alaska) and three Canadian entities (Alberta, the Yukon Territory, and the Northwest Territories).

◪ PRACTICAL INFORMATION

Capital: Victoria.

Visitor Info: Tourism British Columbia, 1166 Alberni St., Ste. 600, Vancouver V6E 3Z3 (☎800-663-6000; www.hellobc.com). **British Columbia Parks Headquarters,** P.O. Box 9398, Stn. Prov. Govt., Victoria V8W 9M9 (☎250-387-5002).

Drinking Age: 19. **Postal Abbreviation:** BC. **Sales Tax:** 7% PST plus 7% GST.

> **!** All prices in this chapter are listed in Canadian dollars unless otherwise noted.

VANCOUVER ☎ 604

Like any self-respecting city on the west coast of North America, Vancouver boasts a thriving multicultural populace; the Cantonese influence is so strong that it is often referred to by its nickname, "Hongcouver." With the third largest China-town in North America and a strong influence of almost every other major culture, visitors are never hard-pressed to find exotic food or entertainment for any budget level. And while this may be the norm for big cities, Vancouver mixes its urban excitement with gorgeous surroundings and ready access to outdoor adventure.

◩ TRANSPORTATION

Flights: Vancouver International Airport (☎276-6101), on Sea Island, 23km south of the city center. A Visitors Center (☎303-3601) is on level 2. Open daily 8am-midnight. To reach downtown, take bus #100 "New Westminster Station" to the intersection of Granville and 70th Ave. Transfer there to bus #20 "Fraser." An **Airporter** (☎946-8866 or 800-668-3141) bus leaves from airport level 2 for downtown hotels and the bus station. 4 per hr.; 6:30am-midnight; $10, seniors $8, ages 5-12 $5.

Ferries: BC Ferries (☎888-223-3779; www.bcferries.bc.ca). To the Gulf Islands, Sech-elt, and Vancouver Island ($9, car $30-32, bike $2.50; fares cheapest midweek). Ferries to Victoria, Nanaimo, and the Gulf Islands leave from the **Tsawwassen Terminal,** 25km south of the city center (take Hwy. 99 to Hwy. 17). To reach downtown from Tsaw-wassen by bus, take #640 "Scott Rd. Station" or #404 "Airport" to the Ladner

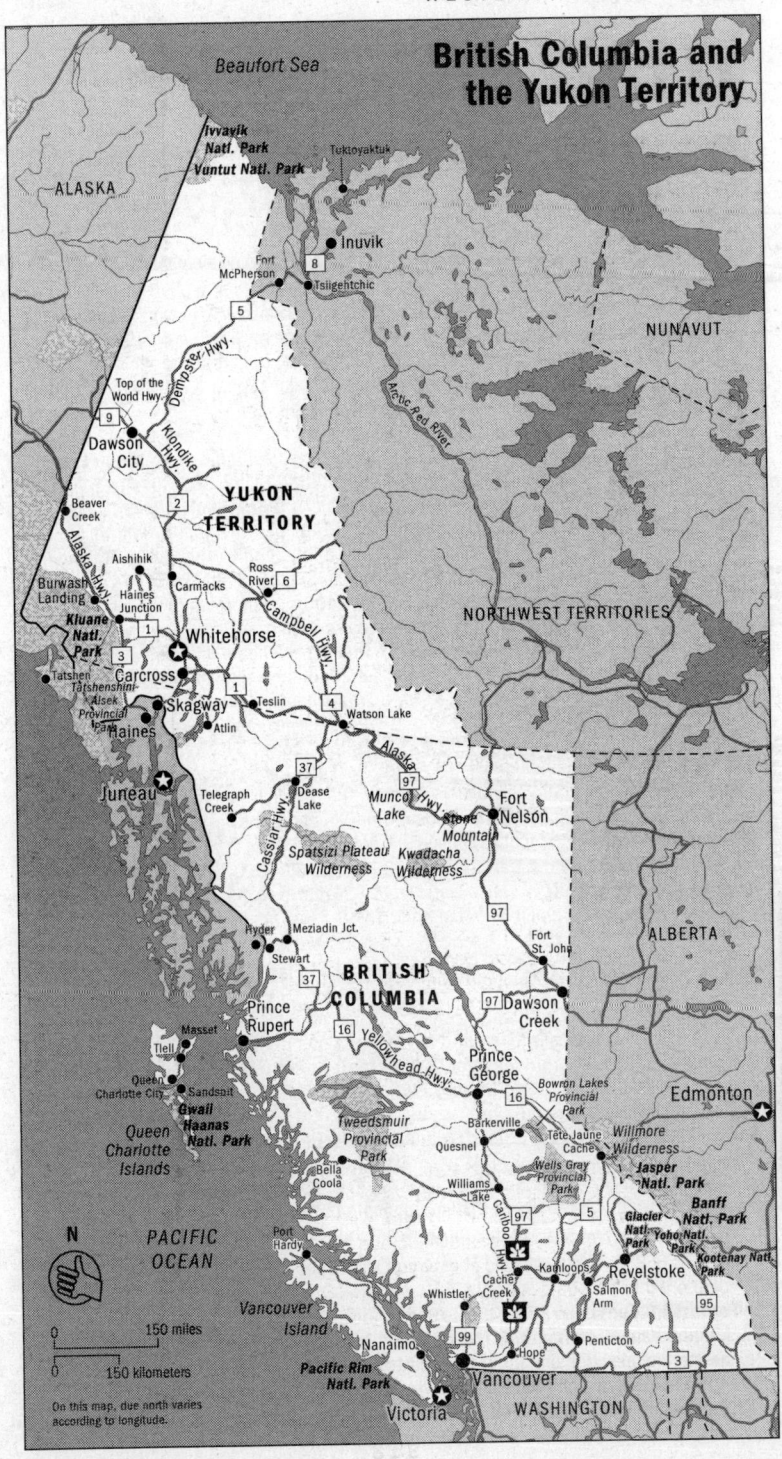

British Columbia and the Yukon Territory

Beaufort Sea

ALASKA

Ivvavik Natl. Park
Vuntut Natl. Park

Tuktoyaktuk

● Inuvik

Fort McPherson

8

Tsiigehtchic

5

NUNAVUT

Arctic Red River

Top of the World Hwy.

9

Dawson City

2

Beaver Creek

Klondike Hwy.

Dempster Hwy.

YUKON TERRITORY

Aishihik

Carmacks

Ross River

6

NORTHWEST TERRITORIES

Burwash Landing

Haines Junction

1

★ Whitehorse

Campbell Hwy.

Alaska Hwy.

3

Tatshen...

Tatshenshini-Alsek Provincial Park

Carcross

Skagway

1

Teslin

4

Watson Lake

Haines

Atlin

Alaska Hwy.

97

Fort Nelson

★ Juneau

37

Telegraph Creek

Dease Lake

Muncho Lake

Stone Mountain

Cassiar Hwy.

Spatsizi Plateau Wilderness

Kwadacha Wilderness

97

ALBERTA

Hyder

Meziadin Jct.

Stewart

37

Fort St. John

BRITISH COLUMBIA

97 Dawson Creek

Prince Rupert

16

Yellowhead Hwy.

Masset

Tlell

97

Prince George

16

Bowron Lakes Provincial Park

● Edmonton ★

Queen Charlotte City

Sandspit

Gwaii Haanas Natl. Park

Tweedsmuir Provincial Park

Barkerville

Tete Jaune Cache

Willmore Wilderness

Queen Charlotte Islands

Quesnel

Wells Gray Provincial Park

Jasper Natl. Park

Bella Coola

Williams Lake

Cariboo Hwy.

97

Glacier Natl. Park

Banff Natl. Park

Yoho Natl. Park

N

PACIFIC OCEAN

Port Hardy

5

Kootenay Natl. Park

Whistler

Kamloops

Salmon Arm

Revelstoke

95

Vancouver Island

99

Cache Creek

Hope

Penticton

3

Nanaimo

Pacific Rim Natl. Park

Vancouver

0 ___ 150 miles

0 ___ 150 kilometers

On this map, due north varies according to longitude.

★ Victoria

WASHINGTON

Exchange, then transfer to bus #601. Ferries to Nanaimo and Sechelt depart the **Horseshoe Bay Terminal** at the end of the Trans-Canada Hwy. in West Vancouver. Take "Blue Bus" #250 or 257 on Georgia St. from downtown.

Trains: VIA Rail, 1150 Station St. (☎800-561-8630, in US 800-561-9181). 3 trains per week to eastern Canada via Jasper, AB (17hr., $187). Open M, W, Th, and Sa 9:30am-6pm;

Downtown Vancouver

🏠 ACCOMMODATIONS
Cambie Int'l. Hostel, **8**
Gastown Hostel, **7**
Global Village
  Backpackers, **4**
Seymour Cambie Hostel, **6**
Vancouver Hostel
  Downtown, **1**

🍎 FOOD
Subeez Café, **5**

♪ NIGHTLIFE
The Irish Heather, **10**
Sonar, **9**
Sugar Refinery, **3**
Wett Bar, **2**

Tu, F, and Su 9am-7pm. **BC Rail,** 1311 W. 1st St. (☎984-5246), in North Vancouver at the foot of Pemberton St. Take the BC Rail Special bus on Georgia St. (June-Sept.) or the SeaBus to North Vancouver, then bus #239 west. Daily train to Whistler (2½hr., $33). Tu and F trains depart at 7pm for Williams Lake (10hr., $143); Prince George (14hr., $212); and other points north. Open daily 8am-8pm.

Buses: Greyhound Canada, 1150 Station St., in the VIA Rail station (☎482-8747 or 800-661-8747; www.greyhound.ca.) Open daily 5am-12:30am). To Calgary (15hr., 4 per day, $115). **Pacific Coach Lines,** 1150 Station St. (☎662-8074) to Victoria (3½hr., every time a ferry sails, $29 includes ferry). **Quick Shuttle** (☎940-4428 or 800-665-2122; www.quickcoach.com) makes 8 trips per day from downtown via the airport to Seattle, WA (3½hr., $34) and the Sea-Tac airport (4hr., $44). **Greyhound USA** (☎800-229-9425 or 402-330-8552) goes to Seattle (3½hr., US$20).

Public Transit: Coast Mountain Buslink (☎521-0400) covers most of the city and suburbs, with direct transport or easy connections to airport and ferry terminals. **Central zone** encompasses most of the city ($1.75). During peak hours (M-F before 6:30pm), it costs $2.50 to travel between 2 zones and $3.25 to travel through 3 zones. During off-peak hours all zones are $1.75. Ask for a **free transfer** (good for 1½hr.) when you board buses. **Day passes** ($5) are sold at 7-11, Safeway, and HI hostels. Seniors and ages 5-13 for 1 zone or off-peak travel $1.25, for 2 zones $1.75, for 3 zones $3.25. **SeaBus** and **SkyTrain** included in the normal BusFare. The SkyTrain is a light rapid transit system, running from Vancouver to Burnaby. The SeaBus shuttles passengers across the waters of Burrard Inlet from the foot of Granville St. downtown (SkyTrain: Waterfront) to **Lonsdale Quay** at the foot of Lonsdale Ave. in North Van.

Car Rental: Resort Rent-A-Car, 3231 No. 3 Rd. (☎232-3060; www.resortcars.com) in Richmond (free pickup in Vancouver). From $34 per day, $164 per week; unlimited mileage. Must be 21. Open M-F 7am-9pm, Sa-Su 7am-7pm.

✳🔢 ORIENTATION AND PRACTICAL INFORMATION

Vancouver lies in the southwestern corner of mainland British Columbia. South of the city flows the **Fraser River,** and to the west lies the **Georgia Strait,** separating the mainland from Vancouver Island. **Downtown** juts north into the Burrard Inlet from the core of the city, and **Stanley Park** goes farther north. The **Lions Gate** suspension bridge over Burrard Inlet links Stanley Park with North and West Vancouver **(West Van),** known collectively as the **North Shore;** the bridges over False Creek south of downtown link it with **Kitsilano ("Kits")** and the rest of the city. West of Burrard St. is the **West Side** or **West End.** Gastown and **Chinatown** are east of downtown. The **University of British Columbia (UBC)** lies on the west end of Kits on Point Grey, while the **airport** is on Sea Island in the Fraser River delta. The **Trans-Canada Hwy. (Hwy. 1)** enters town from the east, and **Hwy. 99** runs north-south through the city.

Visitor Information: 200 Burrard St. (☎683-2000). Open daily 8am-7pm.

Gay and Lesbian Information: The Centre, 1170 Bute St., offers counseling and info. *Xtra West* is the city's gay and lesbian biweekly, available here and around Davie St. in the West End. Open M-F 9:30am-7pm. Try www.gayvancouver.bc.ca for events.

Crisis Center, ☎872-3311. 24hr.

Downtown Vancouver

Hospital: Vancouver General Hospital, 899 W 12th Ave. (☎875-4111). **UBC Hospital,** 221 Westbrook Mall (☎822-7121), on the UBC campus.

Internet access: Library, 350 W. Georgia St. (☎331-3600). Free email terminals or pay $5 per hr. Open M-Th 10am-8pm and F-Sa 10am-5pm. Free email at 20 other branches; check white pages.

Post Office: 349 W Georgia St. (☎662-5725). Open M-F 8am-5:30pm. **Postal code:** V6B 3P7. **Area code:** 604.

⚑ ACCOMMODATIONS

Greater Vancouver B&Bs are a viable option for couples or small groups (singles from $45, doubles from $55). The Visitors Center and agencies like **Town and Country Bed and Breakfast** (☎731-5942) and **Best Canadian** (☎738-7207) list options. HI hostels are a good bet for clean rooms and quiet nights; others can be seedy or rowdy.

- **Vancouver Hostel Downtown (HI),** 1114 Burnaby St. (☎684-4565 or 888-203-4302), in the West End. Sleek and clean 225-bed facility between downtown, the beach, and Stanley Park. Four-bunk rooms, game room, library, kitchen, rooftop patio, free linen, and tours of the city. Free shuttle to Jericho Beach Hostel. Internet $6 per hr. Pub crawls twice a week; activities every day. Travel agency in the lobby. Reservations crucial in summer. Open 24hr. $20, nonmembers $24; private doubles $55/$64.
- **Global Village Backpackers,** 1018 Granville St. (☎682-8226 or 888-844-7875), on corner of Nelson, next to Ramada Inn. Shuttle from bus/train station; call for details. Airporter Bus stops at Granville St. Funky technicolor hangout in an area with great

nightlife. Internet, pool, laundry. Linen included. HI, ISIC, other hosteling members $21; doubles $57, with bath $62. Nonmembers $24/60/65.

Seymour Cambie Hostel, 515 Seymour St. (☎684-7757). The quieter of 2 downtown Cambie hostels. All rooms are twins. Pub crawls W, movie nights Su-M, soccer games Sa, free tours of Granville Island Brewery Tu (noon, 2pm, and 4pm). Laundry and Internet access. No lockers, storage available for $2 per day. No lockout. Dorms Jul.-Sept. $23, Oct.-Jun. $20; private room $40.

Cambie International Hostel, 300 Cambie St. (☎684-6466 or 877-395-5335). Atop the pub and grill of the same name, the Cambie offers easy access to—or a retreat from—the busy sights and sounds of Gastown. Common room, laundry. No kitchen, but free hot breakfast. Pool tables in the pub. Free airport pickup 9am-8pm. 24hr. reception. Dorms June-Sept. $20; Oct.-May $15. Private rooms $23.

Vancouver Hostel Jericho Beach (HI), 1515 Discovery St. (☎224-3208 or 888-203-4303), in Jericho Beach Park. Follow 4th Ave. west past Alma, bear right at the fork, or take bus #4 from Granville St. downtown. 285 beds in 14-person dorm rooms. Kitchens, TV room, laundry, cafe (breakfast $5, dinner $6-7), free linen, parking $3 per day. Bikes $20 per day. Stay-and-ski package with Grouse Mountain for $37. Reservations imperative in summer. $18, nonmembers $22; family rooms $50-60.

Gastown Hostel, 340 Cambie St. (☎684-4664). No-frills accommodations close to Water St. and the heart of downtown. Laundry available. Single or double with shared bathroom $40. Reception at the bar of the attached pub. Open daily 11am-2am.

Capilano RV Park, 295 Tomahawk Ave. (☎987-4722; fax 987-2015), at foot of Lions Gate Bridge in North Van; closest RV park to downtown. Turn onto Capilano Rd., take first right on Welch, then right on Tomahawk. Showers, pool, laundry. Reception open daily 8am-11pm. 2-person sites $25-30, extra person $4; with hookup $30-45.

🍴 FOOD

The diversity and excellence of Vancouver's international cuisine makes the rest of BC seem provincial. Vancouver's **Chinatown** and the **Punjabi Village** along Main and Fraser, around 49th St., serve cheap, authentic food. The whole world, from Chinese noodle shops to Italian cafes, seems represented along **Commercial Drive,** east of Chinatown. Produce sold along "The Drive" puts supermarkets to shame.

Restaurants downtown compete for the highest prices in the city. The **West End** caters to diners seeking a variety of ethnic cuisines, while **Gastown** lures tourists fresh off the cruise ships. Many cheap and grubby establishments along Davie and Denman St. stay open around the clock. Dollar-a-slice, all-night **pizza places** pepper downtown.

🎨 The Naam, 2724 W. 4th Ave. (☎738-7151), at MacDonald St. Bus #4 or 7 from Granville Mall. The most diverse vegetarian menu around with great prices. Crying Tiger Thai stir fry $8.50; 5 kinds of veggie burgers under $7, tofulati ice cream $3.50. Live music nightly 7-10pm. Open 24hr.

Subeez Cafe, 891 Homer (☎687-6107), at Smithe, downtown. Serves the cool kids in a cavernous and casual setting. Eclectic menu, from vegetarian gyoza ($6.50) to organic beef burgers ($9), complements a lengthy wine list and home-spun beats (DJs W and F at 10pm). Entrees $7-15. Open M-F 11:30am-1am, Sa 11am-1am, Su 11am-midnight.

Cafe Oasis, 1183 Davie St. (☎684-4760). Falafel sandwiches ($5), large tofu stew with rice ($7), breakfast wrap ($5.50), and hearty soups ($3.50) will fill a hungry stomach. Open daily 10am-1am. 10% HI discount.

Mongolian Teriyaki, 1918 Commercial Dr. (☎253-5607). Diners fill a bowl full of meats, veggies, sauces, and noodles, and the chefs will fry it up and serve it with miso soup, rice, and salad for only $5 (large bowl $6). Open daily 11am-10:30pm.

Benny's Bagels, 2505 W Broadway (☎731-9730). Every college student's dream, this eatery serves the requisite beer ($3 per glass), bagels (70¢, $2.15 with cream cheese), and sandwiches and melts ($5-7.25). Open Su-Th 7am-1am, F-Sa 24hr.

Hon's Wun-Tun House, 268 Keefer St. (☎688-0871). With 334 options and phenomenal service, this Award-winning Cantonese noodle-house is the place to go. Bowls of noodles $3.50-6. Cash only. Open daily 8:30am-10pm; in summer F-Su until 11pm.

 **SIGHTS**

DOWNTOWN AND WORLD'S FAIR GROUNDS

■ **VANCOUVER ART GALLERY.** Host to fantastic temporary exhibitions and home to a good collection of contemporary art, this gallery devotes an entire floor to the landscape paintings of British Columbian Emily Carr. An immigration officer who was murdered in 1914 is said to haunt the catacombs underneath the gallery, which is where the holding cells were in this former courthouse. (750 Hornby St. in Robson Square. ☎ 662-4700. Open F-W 10am-5:30pm, Th 10am-9pm; call for winter hours. $12.50, seniors $9, students $7, under 12 free; Th 5-9pm pay-what-you-wish; 2-for-1 HI discount.)

EXPO '86. On the city's centennial, the World Exposition brought attention, prestige, and roller coasters to Vancouver. The fairgrounds are still there, on the north shore of False Creek, and are slowly evolving into office buildings, apartment towers, and a cultural center, near False Creek and Yaletown. The big-screen star of Expo '86 was the **Omnimax Theatre,** part of **Science World,** 1455 Quebec St., at the Main St. stop of the SkyTrain. In addition to the 27m screen, Science World also features tons of hands-on exhibits and fact-crammed shows for kids. (☎ 268-6363. Open July-Aug. daily 10am-6pm; call for winter hours. $12; seniors, students, and children $8. Omnimax shows Su-F 10am-5pm, Sa 10am-9pm. $10. Combined ticket $14.75; $10.50.)

CANADA PLACE. The Canada Pavilion, or Canada Place, was built to resemble five giant sails; the masts provide a cavernous interior space free of support structures while the distinctive roof dominates the harbor. The shops and restaurants inside are outrageously expensive, but the promenades around the complex make for terrific gawking at luxury liners and their camera-toting cargo. (SkyTrain from the main Expo site or walk across the street from the Visitors Center on Burrard St.)

LOOKOUT! 555 W. Hastings St., offers fantastic 360° views of the city! Tickets are expensive! But they're good for the whole day! Come back for a more sedate nighttime skyline! (Skytrain to Waterfront Station. ☎ 689-0421. Open daily 8:30am-10:30pm; winter 10am-9pm. $9, seniors $8, students $6. 50% HI discount!)

CHINATOWN

The neighborhood bustles with restaurants, shops, bakeries, and **the world's narrowest building** at 8 W. Pender St. In 1912, the city expropriated all but a 1.8m (6 ft.) strip of Chang Toy's property in order to expand the street; he built on the land anyhow. The serene **Dr. Sun Yat-Sen Classical Chinese Garden,** 578 Carrall St., maintains imported Chinese plants, carvings, and rock formations in the first full-size authentic garden of its kind outside China. (Southeast of Gastown. Bus #22 north on Burrard St. leads to Pender and Carrall St., in the heart of Chinatown. ☎ 689-7133. Open daily 9:30am-7pm; in winter 10:30am-4:30pm. Tours every hr. 10am-6pm. $7.50, seniors $6, students $5, children free, families $18.)

UNIVERSITY OF BRITISH COLUMBIA (UBC)

The high point of a visit to UBC is the breathtaking ■ **Museum of Anthropology.** The high-ceilinged glass and concrete building houses totems and other massive carvings, highlighted by Bill Reid's depiction of Raven discovering the first human beings in a giant clam shell. Free one-hour guided walks (11am and 2pm) pick through the maze of eras and modes of expression. Behind the museum, in a courtyard designed to simulate the Pacific islands, the free re-created village displays memorial totems and a mortuary house built by Reid and Douglas Cranmer. (6393 NW Marine Dr., bus #4 or 10 from Granville St. ☎ 822-3825 or 822-5087. Open M and W-Su 10am-5pm, Tu 10am-9pm; Sept.-May closed M. $7, students $4, seniors $5, under 6 free; Tu after 5pm free.) Across the street caretakers tend to **Nitobe Memorial Garden,** the finest classical Shinto garden outside of Japan. (☎ 822-6038. $2.75, ages 65+ and students $1.75, under 6 free. Open mid-Mar. to Oct. daily 10am-6pm; Nov. to mid-Mar. M-F 10am-2:30pm.) The **Botanical Gardens** are a collegiate Eden encompassing eight gardens in the central campus, including the largest collection of rhododendrons in North

America. (6804 SW Marine Dr. ☎822-9666. $4.75, seniors and students $2.50, under 6 free. Same hours as Nitobe Garden.) In addition to its greenery, UBC has a public swimming pool. (☎822-4521. $3.75, students $2.75. Open M-F 1:30-4:30pm and 8-10pm, Sa-Su 1-10pm.) It also boasts a **Fine Arts Gallery** and free daytime and evening concerts. (Gallery ☎822-2759. $3, students free. Concert ☎822-3113. To arrange a walking tour between May and August call 822-8687.) Just east of campus in **Pacific Spirit Regional Park,** woods stretch from inland hills to the beaches of Spanish Banks. With 50km of gravel and dirt trails through dense forest make the park ideal for jogging and mountain biking. Grab free maps at the **Park Centre** on 16th Ave., near Blanca.

STANLEY PARK

Established in 1889 at the tip of the downtown peninsula, the 1000-acre **Stanley Park** (☎257-8400) is a testament to the foresight of Vancouver's urban planners. An easy escape from the nearby West End and downtown, the wooded park is laced with cycling and hiking trails and surrounded by a 10km **seawall** promenade popular with cyclists, runners, and in-line skaters. (Take #23, 35, 123, or 135 bus. A free shuttle runs between major destinations throughout the park June-Sept. daily 10am-6pm.)

■**VANCOUVER AQUARIUM.** The aquarium, on the park's eastern side not far from the entrance, features exotic aquatic animals. BC, Amazonian, and other ecosystems are skillfully replicated. Dolphin and beluga whales demonstrate their advanced training by drenching gleeful visitors in educational wetness. At the new Wild Coast exhibit, visitors get a close-up view of marine life. Outside the aquarium, an **orca fountain** by sculptor Bill Reid glistens black. (☎659-3474. Open July-Aug. daily 9:30am-7pm; Sept.-June 10am-5:30pm. Shows throughout the day from 10am-5:30pm. $14.50; seniors, students, and ages 13-18 $12; ages 4-12 $9; 3 and under free.)

FALSE CREEK AND GRANVILLE ISLAND

GRANVILLE ISLAND MARKET. Granville Island Market, southwest of downtown under the Granville Street Bridge, intersperses trendy shops, art galleries, restaurants, and countless produce stands. (☎666-5784. From downtown, bus #50 "False Creek" or 51 "Granville Island" from Granville St. Open daily 9am-6pm; Jan. closed M.)

MARITIME MUSEUM. The ferry shares the Maritime Museum dock with historic vessels. The wood-and-glass A-frame museum on shore houses the **Mounties.** The schooner **St. Roch** patrolled the Northwest Passage in the 40s; in 1950, she was the first to circumnavigate North America. (1905 Ogden Ave. ☎257-8300. $7, youths and seniors $4, families $16; Tu senior half-prices. Open late May to early Sept. daily 10am-5pm; winter Tu-Sa 10am-5pm, Su noon-5pm. Last video shown at 3:45pm.)

▲ OUTDOOR ACTIVITIES

Vancouver has kept its many beaches remarkably clean. Follow the western side of the Stanley Park seawall south to **Sunset Beach Park,** a strip of grass and beach extending all the way along **English Bay** to the Burrard Bridge. The **Aquatic Centre,** 1050 Beach Ave., at the southeast end of the beach, is a public facility with a sauna, gym, and a 50m indoor pool. (☎665-3424. Call for public swim hours, generally M-Th 9am-4:20pm and 8pm-10pm, F 9am-4:20pm and 8:20-9pm, Sa 10am-9pm, Su 1-9pm. $4, ages 13-18 $3, seniors $2.40, ages 6-12 $2.)

Kitsilano Beach ("Kits"), across Arbutus St. from Vanier Park, is another local favorite for tanning and beach volleyball. For fewer crowds, more young 'uns, and free showers, visit **Jericho Beach** (head west along 4th Ave. and follow signs). North Marine Dr. runs along the beach, and a cycling path at the side of the road leads to the westernmost end of the UBC campus. Biking and hiking trails cut through the campus and crop its edges. West of Jericho Beach is the quieter **Spanish Banks;** at low tide the ocean retreats almost a kilometer, allowing for long walks on the flats.

Most of Vancouver's 31km of beaches are patrolled by lifeguards from late May to early September between 11:30am and 9pm. Even if you don't dip a foot in the chilly waters, you can frolic in true West Coast spirit during summer weekend **vol-**

leyball tournaments, offering all levels of competition. Scare up a team at the hostel, then call 291-2007 to find out where to play. Team entry fees are around $40.

"Co-ed Naked Beach Volleyball" would make a fine t-shirt slogan, but you wouldn't wear it at **Wreck Beach.** Take entry trail #6 down the hill from SW Marine Dr. opposite the UBC campus. A steep wooden staircase leads to a totally secluded, self-contained sunshine community of nude sunbathers and guitar-playing UBC students. There are no lifeguards, but naked entrepreneurs peddle vegetarian-friendly foods, beer, and other awareness-altering goods for premium prices. Call **Wreck Beach Preservation Society** (☎273-6950) for more info.

♪ ▨ ENTERTAINMENT AND NIGHTLIFE

The **Vancouver Symphony Orchestra** (☎684-9100) plays September to May in the refurbished **Orpheum Theatre** (☎665-3050), at the corner of Smithe and Seymour. The new **Ford Center for the Performing Arts** (☎602-0616) plays Broadway musicals. The **Vancouver Playhouse** (☎873-3311), on Dunsmuir and Georgia St., and the **Arts Club Theatre** (☎687-5315), on Granville Island, stage low-key shows, often including local work. **Theatre Under the Stars** (☎687-0174), in Stanley Park's Malkin Bowl, puts on outdoor musicals. The annual **Fringe Theater Festival** features 600 shows in venues in Granville Island and Yaletown. (☎257-0350. Runs Sept. Tickets under $11.)

▨ **Sugar Refinery,** 1115 Granville St. (☎683-2004). Artsy, retro lounge where youth involved in film, art, and music go to relax. An ever-changing program of events, music, and spoken word entertains, while the tasty vegetarian meals (entrees $7.50-9, big sandwiches $5-7.50) and decadent desserts such as the popular Molestic (vanilla gelato and chocolate brownies, $5.50) please the stomach. Tap beers served in Mason jars $4.25-5.75. Open daily 5pm-3am.

Sonar, 66 Water St. (☎683-6695). A popular 2-level beat factory. Pints $3.50-4.75. W hip hop, F live DJ, Sa house. Open M-Sa 9pm-2am, Su 9pm-midnight.

The Irish Heather, 217 Carrall St. The second-highest seller of Guiness in BC, this true Irish pub and bistro serves up memories of the Emerald Isle. Draughts ($5.20), mixed beer drinks ($5.60), and a helping of bangers and mash ($14) will keep those eyes smiling. Lots of veggie dishes, too. Conservatory in the back, live music four times a week 8-11pm. Open M-F 3-11:30pm, Sa-Su 11:30am-12:30pm.

Wett Bar, 1320 Richards St. (☎662-7707). Candlelit dining booths and a weekend dress code. Wields one of the most advanced stereo and light systems in Vancouver. W house, F hip hop, Sa Top 40. Open M and W-Sa 9pm-2am, Tu 9pm-1am.

The King's Head, 1618 Yew St. (☎738-6966), at 1st St., in Kitsilano. Cheap drinks, cheap food, relaxing atmosphere, and a great location near the beach. Bands play acoustic sets on a tiny stage. Daily drink specials. $3 pints. Gullet-filling Beggar's Breakfast ($4). Open M-F 7am-1:30am, Sa 7:30am-2am, Su 7:30am midnight.

NEAR VANCOUVER: WHISTLER

Only 125km north of Vancouver on the dangerously twisty Hwy. 99, Whistler and Blackcomb mountains provides some of North America's best skiing and snowboarding and are popular mountain destinations in summer, too. The **"Village"** is commercialized and overpriced, but no amount of Disneyfication can take away from the striking beauty of the mountains or the challenge of the terrain.

Seven thousand acres of terrain, 33 lifts, and 2km of vertical drop make recently merged **Whistler/Blackcomb** the largest ski resort in North America. Parking and lift access for this behemoth is available at six points, with Whistler Creekside offering the shortest lines and easiest access to those coming from Vancouver. A lift ticket is good for both mountains. (☎932-3434 or 800-766-0449. $58; from June 12 to Aug. 7 $38. Multi-day discounts available.) Cheap tickets are often available at Super-Valu's and 7-11's in Vancouver and Squamish. While skiing is God in Whistler and lasts on the glaciers until August, the **Whistler Gondola** whisks sightseers to the top of the mountain year-round for $22 ($25 with bike), providing access in summer to the resort's extensive mountain bike park.

The gorgeous lakeside **Whistler Hostel (HI-C),** 5678 Alta Lake Rd., lies 5km south of Whistler Village on Hwy. 99. BC Rail stops at the hostel on request. (☎932-5492. $20; nonmembers $24.) The **Fireside Lodge,** 2117 Nordic Dr., 3km south of the village, offers spacious cabins with mammoth kitchens, lounge, sauna, and a game room. (☎932-4545. Check-in 3:30-8:30pm. 24 dorm beds. $20, Apr. to mid-Dec. $30.)

Greyhound (☎932-5031 or 800-661-8747) runs to Vancouver from the Village Bus Loop (2½hr., 6 per day, $20). **BC Rail's** 2½hr. Cariboo Prospector (☎984-5246) departs North Vancouver for Whistler Creek at 7am and returns at 6:20pm daily ($33). **Activity and information center:** in the heart of the Village. (☎932-2394. Open daily 9am-5pm.) **Post Office:** in the Village Marketplace. (☎932-5012. Open M-F 8:30am-5:30pm and Sa 8:30am-12:30pm.) **Postal code:** V0N 1B0. **Area code:** 604.

VICTORIA   ☎250

Clean, polite, and tourist-friendly, today's Victoria is a homier alternative to cosmopolitan Vancouver. Although many tourist operations would have you believe that Victoria fell off Great Britain in a neat little chunk, its High Tea tradition began in the 50s to draw American tourists. Double-decker buses motor past native art galleries, new-age bookstores, and countless English pubs.

⚑ PRACTICAL INFORMATION. Victoria surrounds the **Inner Harbour;** the main north-south thoroughfares downtown are **Government Street** and **Douglas Street.** To the north, Douglas St. becomes Hwy. 1, which runs north to Nanaimo. **Blanshard Street,** one block to the east, becomes Hwy. 17. The **E&N Railway,** 450 Pandora St. (☎383-4324 or 800-561-8630), near the Inner Harbour at the Johnson St. Bridge, runs daily to Nanaimo (2½hr.; $19, students with ISIC $11). **Laidlaw,** 700 Douglas St. (☎385-4411 or 800-318-0818), at Belleville St., and its affiliates, **Pacific** and **Island Coach Lines,** run buses to Nanaimo (2½hr., 6 per day, $23); Port Hardy (9hr., 1-2 per day, $93); and Vancouver (3½hr., 8-14 per day, $29). **BC Ferries** (☎656-5571 or 888-223-3779; operator 7am-10pm 386-3431) depart Swartz Bay to Vancouver's Tsawwassen ferry terminal (1½hr.; 8-16 per day; $9, bikes $2.50, car and driver $32-34), and to the Gulf Islands. **Washington State Ferries** (☎381-1551 or 656-1831; in the US 206-464-6400 or 800-843-3779) depart from Sidney to Anacortes, WA (1-2 per day; US$9, car with driver US$41). Free stopovers allowed in the San Juan Islands. **Victoria Clipper** (☎382-8100 or 800-888-2535) passenger ferries travel to Seattle (2-3hr.; 4 per day May-Sept., 1 per day Oct.-Apr.; US$79-91). **Black Public Bus #70** ($2.50) runs between downtown and the Swartz Bay and Sidney ferry terminals. **Victoria Taxi,** ☎383-7111. **Tourism Victoria:** 812 Wharf St., at Government St. (☎953-2033. Open daily 8:30am-7:30pm; in winter 9am-5pm.) **Post Office:** 621 Discovery St. (☎963-1350; open M-F 8am-6pm). **Postal code:** V8W 1L0. **Area code:** 250.

⚐ ACCOMMODATIONS. The colorful **▨Ocean Island Backpackers Inn,** 791 Pandora St., downtown, boasts a better lounge than most clubs, tastier food than most restaurants, and accommodations comparable to most hotels. Undoubtedly one of the finest urban hostels in Canada. (☎385-1788 or 888-888-4180. 140 beds in small rooms; free linen and towels, laundry, email. Dorms $20, students and HI members $17.25; doubles $40-50. Parking $5.) To reach the **The Cat's Meow,** 1316 Grant St., take bus #22 to Gernwood and Grant St. It's a mini-hostel with 12 quiet beds, 3 blocks from downtown. It offers free parking, discounts on kayaking and whale watching, and complimentary breakfast. (☎595-8878. Open 4pm-10:45am. $19; private rooms $40-45.) **Goldstream Provincial Park,** 2930 Trans-Canada Hwy., 20km northwest of Victoria, offers a forested riverside area with great hiking trails and swimming. (☎391-2300 or 800-689-9025. Flush toilets and firewood. $18.50.) The sites at **Thetis Lake Campground,** 1938 Trans-Canada Hwy., 10km north of the city center, are not large, but some are peaceful and removed. (☎478-3845. Showers 25¢ per 5min. Flush toilets, laundry. $16, full hookup $20.)

⬛📷 FOOD AND NIGHTLIFE. A diversity of food can be found in Victoria, if you know where to go; ask locals, or wander through downtown. **Chinatown** extends from Fisgard and Government St. to the northwest. Coffeeshops can be found on every corner. Cook St. Village, between McKenzie and Park Streets, offers an eclectic mix of creative restaurants. ⬛**John's Place,** 723 Pandora St., is a hopping joint serving wholesome Canadian fare with a Thai twist plus a little Mediterranean flair. (☎389-0711. Open M-F 7am-10pm, Sa 8am-4pm and 5-10pm, Su 8am-4pm and 5-9pm. Entrees $5-11.) A trip to Victoria is improper without a spot of tea; the Sunday High Tea ($10.25) at the **James Bay Tea Room & Restaurant,** 332 Menzies St., behind the Parliament Buildings, is a lower-key and significantly less expensive version of the famous High Tea at the Empress Hotel. (☎382-8282. Open M-Sa 7am-8pm, Su 8am-8pm.) The free weekly *Monday Magazine,* out on Wednesday and available downtown, lists who's playing music where. **Steamers Public House,** 570 Yates St., attracts a young, happy crowd dancing nightly to live music. (☎381-4340. Open stage M, jazz night Tu. Cover $3-5 at night. Open M 11:30am-1am, Tu-Sa 11:30am-2am, Su 11:30am-midnight.) The **Sticky Wicket,** 919 Douglas St., is a decent English-style pub, one of seven bars in the Strathacona Hotel. (☎383-7137. Open M-Sa noon-2am and Su noon-midnight.)

⬛📷 SIGHTS AND OUTDOORS. The fantastically thorough ⬛**Royal British Columbia Museum,** 675 Belleville St., presents excellent exhibits on the biological, geological, and cultural history of the province, from protozoans to the present. A new IMAX theater shows films that are larger than life. (☎387-3014. Open daily 9am-5pm. $9; students, youths, and seniors $6; under 6 free. IMAX $10, seniors $8.50, youth $6.50, child $3.50.) The public **Art Gallery of Greater Victoria,** 1040 Moss St., culls magnificent exhibits from its collection of 14,000 pieces covering contemporary Canada, traditional and contemporary Asia, North America, and Europe. (☎384-4101. Open Tu 10am-10pm, W-Sa 10am-5pm, and Su 1-5pm. $5; students and seniors $3; free M.) Across the street from the museum stands the imposing **Parliament Buildings,** 501 Belleville St., home of the provincial government. (☎387-3046. Open M-F 8:30am-5pm; Sa-Su for tours only. Free tours leave from main steps in summer daily 9am-4:30pm, 3 times per hr.) After a few days of hiking, biking, and museum-visiting, unwind with a tour of the **Vancouver Island Brewery,** 2330 Government St. The one-hour tour is educational and alcoholic. (☎361-0007. Tours F-Sa 3pm. $5 for four 4 oz. samples and souvenir pint glass. Must be 19 to have samples.)

The elaborate **Butchart Gardens** sprawl across a valley. Immaculate landscaping includes a rose garden, Japanese and Italian gardens, fountains, and wheelchair-accessible paths. (Bus #75 "Central Saanich" runs from downtown at Douglas and Pandora, $2.50, 1hr. The Gray Line (☎388-6539) runs a round-trip, direct package for $26, youth $17.25, and child $7; includes admission to gardens; 35min. each way. Recording ☎652-5256; office 652-4422. Open July-Aug. daily 9am-10:30pm. $19.25, ages 13-17 $9.50, ages 5-12 $2, under 5 free.)

Mountain bikers can tackle the **Galloping Goose,** a 100km trail beginning downtown and continuing to the west coast of the Island through towns, rainforests, and canyons. **Ocean River Sports** offers kayak rentals, tours, and lessons. (☎381-4233 or 800-909-4233. Open M-Th and Sa 9:30am-5:30pm, F 9:30am-7:30pm, and Su 11am-5pm. Full- day single kayak $42, double $50; canoe $42.) Many whale watching outfits give discounts for hostel guests. **Ocean Explorations,** 532 Broughton St., runs 3hr. tours from April to October. (☎383-6722. $70, hostelers and children $50, less in early season. Free pickup at hostels.)

PACIFIC RIM NATIONAL PARK ☎250

The Pacific Rim National Park stretches along a 150km sliver of Vancouver Island's remote Pacific coast. The region's frequent downpours create a lush landscape, rich in both marine and terrestrial life, that has beckoned explorers for over a century. Hard-core hikers trek through enormous old growth and along rugged beach trails. Long beaches on the open ocean draw beachcombers, bathers, kayakers, and surfers year-round. **West Coast Trail Express** runs daily day from Victoria to Port Renfrew via the Juan de Fuca trailhead. (☎477-8700. 2¼hr. $32. Reservations are required.) The fantastic ◧**West Coast Trail,** covering the southern third of the park between Port Renfrew and Bamfield, traces the shoreline for 75km of forests and waterfalls and scales ladders and rocky slopes; recommended hiking time is about one week. (Reservation fee $25, trail use fee $70, ferry crossing fee $25.) The **Trail Information Centre** in Port Renfrew (☎647-5434), is at the first right off Parkinson Rd. (Hwy. 14) once in "town." The trail is open May to September; reservations should be made three months in advance at **Parks Canada,** Box 280, Ucluelet V0R 3A0 (☎800-663-6000).

The park's middle section—Bamfield and the Broken Group Islands in Barkley Sound—is far more difficult to reach. Gravel roads wind toward Bamfield from **Hwy. 18** (west from Duncan) and from **Hwy. 4** (south from Port Alberni). West Coast Trail Express buses (see above) run daily from Nanaimo (3hr., $50) and Victoria (4½hr., $50). **Alberni Marine Transportation** floats April to September from Port Alberni to Bamfield. (☎723-8313 or 800-663-7192. 4½hr.; $25.)

To reach Long Beach, at the park's northern reaches, take the spectacular drive across Vancouver Island on Hwy. 4 to the **Pacific Rim Highway.** This stretch connects the towns of sleepy but expensive Ucluelet and crunchy and friendly Tofino. Hwy. 4 branches west of Hwy. 1 about 35km north of Nanaimo, leads 50km through Port Alberni, and continues 92km to the Pacific coast. **Chinook Charters** (☎725-3431) sends buses to the towns from Victoria to Tofino (7hr., $55). Alberni Marine Transportation (see above) runs daily from Port Alberni to Ucluelet (4½hr., $25). **Parks Canada Visitor Information** is 3km north of the Port Alberni junction on the Pacific Rim Hwy. (☎726-4212. Open mid-June to mid-Sept. daily 9:30am-5pm.) ◧**Whalers on the Point Guesthouse (HI),** voted as best hostel in Canada by HI, has room for 64 (4 beds per room). Relish the harborside views. Turn right on 1st St. from Campbell St. and then left on Main St. (follow to West St.). Check inside for HI discounts around town. (☎725-3443. Free sauna, billiards, linen. Check-in 7am-2pm and 4-11pm. $22, nonmembers $24; private rooms $66/$70. Camping is extremely popular in summer as well. Near Port Renfrew and adjacent to the West Coast Trail registration office, the **Pacheedaht Campground** (☎647-5521) rents sites ($10) and with hookup ($16); hikers can use the Reserve Beach for $8 per night.

The Rainforest Centre, 451 Main St., in Tofino, has assembled an excellent trail guide for Clayoquot Sound, Tofino, Ucluelet, the Pacific Rim, and Kennedy Lake (available by donation). The trails grow even more beautiful in the frequent rain and fog. (☎725-2560. Park passes available in parking lots. $8 per day; season passes $45.)

PRINCE RUPERT   ☎250

At the western end of Hwy. 16, Prince Rupert is an emerging transportation hub—a springboard for ferry travel to Alaska, the spectacular Queen Charlotte Islands, and northern Vancouver Island.

⬛ **TRANSPORTATION. Prince Rupert Airport** is on Digby Island, with a ferry and bus connection to downtown (45min., $11). **VIA Rail** (☎627-7304 or 800-561-8630), toward the water on Bill Murray Way, runs to Prince George (12hr., 3 per week, $100); **BC Rail** (☎604-984-5500 or 800-663-8238) continues the next morning from Prince George to Vancouver (14hr., $212). **Greyhound,** 6th St. and 2nd Ave. (☎624-5090), runs to Prince George (11hr., 2 per day, $92) and Vancouver (24hr., 2 per day, $183). **Alaska Marine Highway** ferries (☎627-1744 or 800-642-0066), at the end of Hwy. 16 (Park Ave.), run north from Prince Rupert along the Alaskan Panhandle to Ketchikan (6hr., US$42) and Juneau (1-2 days, US$104). Next door, **BC Ferries** (☎624-9627 or 888-223-3779) runs to Queen Charlotte Islands (6-7hr.; 6 per week; $25, car $93) and Port Hardy on northern Vancouver Island (15hr.; every other day; $106/$218). **Seashore Charter Services** (☎624-5645) runs a shuttle from the mall on

2nd Ave. to the ferry terminal by request ($3). **Prince Rupert Bus Service** (☎ 624-3343) runs downtown (Su-Th 7am-6pm; F until 10pm; $1); about every 30min., bus #52 runs from 2nd Ave. and 3rd St. to within a five-minute walk of the ferry terminal.

■◪ ORIENTATION AND PRACTICAL INFORMATION. The only major road into town is the Yellowhead Highway (Hwy. 16), leading to the ferry docks; it is known as **McBride St.** within city limits, **2nd Ave.** at the north end of downtown, and **Park Ave.** at the south end. From the docks, downtown is a 30min. walk. The **Info Centre,** at 1st Ave. and McBride St., is in a cedar building modeled after a Tsimshian bighouse. (☎ 624-5637 or 800-667-1994. Open mid-May to early Sept. M-Sa 9am-8pm and Su 9am-5pm; off season M-Sa 10am-5pm.) **Internet access: Public Library,** 101 6th Ave. W. (☎ 624-8618. Open M-Th 10am-9pm and F-Sa 10am-5pm; closed Su July-Aug. $2 per hr.) **Post office:** in the mall at 2nd Ave. and 5th St. (☎ 624-2353. Open M-F 9:30am-5pm.) **Postal code:** V8J 3P3. **Area code:** 250.

▐◪ ACCOMMODATIONS AND FOOD. Nearly all of Prince Rupert's hotels are within the six-block area defined by 1st Ave., 3rd Ave., 6th St., and 9th St. **◪Andree's Bed and Breakfast,** 315 Fourth Ave. E., in a spacious 1922 Victorian-style residence, overlooks the harbor and city. (☎ 624-3666. Breakfast included. Singles $50; doubles $65; twins $70; each additional person $15.) **Park Ave. Campground,** 1750 Park Ave., is less than 2km east of the ferry terminal via Hwy. 16. Some of the well-maintained sites in this RV metropolis are forested; others have a view of the bay. (☎ 624-5861 or 800-667-1994. Laundry facilities. Showers for non-guests $3.50. Sites $10.50; with hookup $18.50.) **◪Cow Bay Cafe,** 201 Cow Bay Rd., offers an ever-changing menu, including lunch delights ($8-9) and ten smashing dessert creations for $4-5. (☎ 627-1212. Open Tu noon-2:30pm and W-Sa noon-2:30pm and 6-9pm.)

◩◪ SIGHTS AND OUTDOORS. Prince Rupert's harbor has the highest concentration of archaeological sites in North America; **archaeological boat tours** leave from the info center daily. (2½hr. tours depart mid-June to early Sept. daily. $22, children $13, under 5 free.) The **Museum of Northern British Columbia,** in the same building as the Info Centre, documents the history of logging, fishing, and Haida culture. (☎ 624-3207. Open late May to mid-Sept. M-Sa 9am-8pm and Su 9am-5pm; mid-Sept. to late May M-Sa 9am-5pm.) Tiny **Service Park,** off Fulton St., offers panoramic views of downtown and the harbor beyond. A trail winding up the side of **Mt. Oldfield,** east of town, yields an even wider vista. The trailhead is at **Oliver Lake Park,** about 6km from downtown on Hwy. 16. (Contact the Info Centre about guided nature walks May-Oct. $5.) The best time to visit Prince Rupert may be during **Seafest** (☎ 624-9118), an annual four-day event planned for June 6-9, 2002. Surrounding towns celebrate the sea with parades, bathtub races, and beer contests.

DAWSON CREEK   ☎ 250

Mile 0 of the Alaska Highway (a.k.a. the Alcan) is Dawson Creek, BC (not to be confused with Dawson City, YT, or *Dawson's Creek*, WB), first settled in 1890 as just another pipsqueak frontier village of a few hundred souls. Its later status as a railroad terminus made it a natural place to begin building the 2600km Alaska Hwy.

Travelers cruising through Dawson Creek can't miss the **Mile 0 Cairn** and **Mile 0 Post,** both commemorating the birth of the Alaska Hwy., and both within a stone's throw of the Visitors Center. This town boomed during construction, literally. On February 13, 1943, 60 cases of exploding dynamite leveled the entire business district save the COOP building, now Bing's Furniture, opposite the Mile 0 post. In early August, the town plays host to the **Fall Fair & Stampede** (☎ 782-8911) with a carnival, fireworks, chuckwagon races, and a professional rodeo.

For a bargain price, great location, and an off-beat aura, head straight for the historic **Alaska Hotel,** above the Alaska Cafe & Pub on 10th St., one and a half blocks from the Visitors Center. (☎ 782-7998. Shared bath; no TV or phone. Singles $30; doubles $35; in winter $5 less.) The newer **Voyageur Motor Inn,** 801 111th Ave., facing

WESTERN CANADA

8th Ave., offers phones and cable in a clean, though institutional environment. (☎782-1020. Singles $45; doubles $50.) **Mile 0 Campground,** 1km west of Alaska Hwy. Mile 0 and adjacent to the Pioneer Village, is a RV city with free showers and laundry. (☎782-2590. Sites $12, hookup $17.) For excellent $5 burgers., head to the **Alaska Cafe & Pub,** "55 paces south of the Mile 0 Post" on 10th St. (☎782-7040. Open Su-Th 10am-10pm, F-Sa 11am-11pm; pub open noon-3am.) Pick up a loaf for the road at the **Organic Farms Bakery,** 1425 97th Ave. From the Visitors Center, go west along Alaska Ave. and take a right at 15th St. Breads (from $1.70) are baked with local grain. (☎782-6533. Open Tu-F 9:30am-6pm, Sa 9am-4pm.)

From Prince George, drive 402km north to Dawson Creek on the John Hart section of Hwy. 97. Greyhound, 1201 Alaska Ave. (☎782-3131; open M-F 6am-5:30pm and 8-8:30pm; Sa 6-11am, 2:30-4:30pm, and 8-8:30pm; Su 6-10:30am, 3-4:30pm, and 8-8:30pm), runs to Edmonton (8hr., 2 per day, $77); Prince George (6½hr., 2 per day, $54); and Whitehorse (20hr., June-Aug. M-Sa, $182). For road reports, stop at the Visitors Center, 900 Alaska Ave. (☎782-9595. Open mid-May to early Sept. daily. 8am-7pm; in winter Tu-Sa 9am-5pm). **Internet access:** Public Library, at 10th St. and McKellar Ave. (☎782-4661. Open Tu-Th 10am-9pm, F 10am-5:30pm, and Sa 1:30-5:30pm. Free 1hr.) **Post Office:** 104th Ave. and 10th St. (☎782-9429. Open M-F 8:30am-5pm.) **Postal code:** V1G 4E6. **Area code:** 250.

ALASKA APPROACHES

THE ALASKA HIGHWAY (HWY. 97)

Built by army troops and civilians during World War II in reaction to the Japanese bombing of Pearl Harbor and the capture of two Aleutian Islands, the Alaska Hwy. served to calm Alaskan fears of an Axis invasion. It traverses an astonishing 2451km route between Dawson Creek, BC, and Fairbanks, AK, and, in recent years, the US Army has been replaced by an annual army of over 250,000 tourists, many of them RV-borne. What the Alaska Hwy. lacks in expediency it makes up in rewarding diversions. Countless opportunities lurk off the highway for hiking, fishing, and viewing wildlife. A one-hour video shown at the Dawson Creek Visitors Center provides a praiseworthy introduction to the road and region. The free *Driving the Alaska Highway* includes a listing of emergency medical services and phone numbers throughout Alaska, the Yukon, and British Columbia, plus tips on preparation and driving; get it at Visitors Centers. **Road conditions:** ☎867-667-8215.

THE CASSIAR HIGHWAY (HWY. 37)

A growing number of travelers prefer the Cassiar Hwy. to the Alaska Hwy. since the latter has become an RV institution. The highway slices through charred forests and snowcapped peaks on its way from Hwy. 16 in BC to the Alaska Hwy. (Hwy. 97) in the Yukon. Three evenly spaced provincial parks right off the highway offer good camping, and the Cassiar's services, while sparse, are numerous enough to keep cars and drivers running. Any waiter or lodging owner along the Cassiar's 718km will readily list its advantages: less distance, consistently intriguing scenery, and fewer crowds. On the other hand, services are scarce in many portions of the highway, and the Cassiar is less maintained. Large sections past Meziadin Junction are dirt and gravel and become slippery when wet. This causes little concern for commercial trucks roaring up and down the route, but keeps the infrequent service stops busy with overambitious drivers in need of tire repair.

THE YUKON TERRITORY

The Yukon Territory lies at the end of a long drive along the Alaska Highway or the less-touristed Cassiar and Campbell Highways. Here the land rises into ranges that stretch for kilometers and sinks into lakes that snake toward the Arctic Ocean. The dry land's lonely beauty and its purple dusk are overwhelming.

ⓩ PRACTICAL INFORMATION

Capital: Whitehorse.
Visitor Info: Tourism Yukon, P.O. Box 2703, Whitehorse, YT Y1A 2C6 (☎867-667-5036; www.touryukon.com).
Police: ☎867-667-5555. For emergencies outside Whitehorse, **911 may not work.**
Drinking Age: 19. **Postal Abbreviation:** YT. **Sales Tax:** 7% national sales tax (GST).

WHITEHORSE
☎867

Whitehorse was born during the Klondike Gold Rush, when the gold-hungry used it as a layover on their journey north. Miners en route to Dawson coined the name, claiming that whitecaps on the rapids downstream resembled galloping white stallions. With 24,000 people, Whitehorse is home to 70% of the territory's population. Although as urban a setting as can be found in the Yukon, Whitehorse attracts outdoors lovers of all ages who take advantage of nearby rivers and trails.

⬛ TRANSPORTATION. The **airport** is off the Alaska Higway, just southwest of downtown. **Greyhound,** 2191 2nd Ave. (☎667-2223), on the northeast edge of town, runs to Vancouver (41hr., $314); Edmonton, AB (30hr., $246); and Dawson Creek, BC (18hr., $174). Service is reduced from September to late June. **Alaska Direct** (☎668-4833 or 800-770-6652) runs to Anchorage (15hr., 3 per week, US$165); Fairbanks (13hr., 3 per week, US$165); and Skagway (3hr., reservations only, US$50); in winter, 1 bus per week runs to the above destinations. **Whitehorse Transit**'s local buses arrive and depart downtown next to Canadian Tire on Ogilvie St. (☎668-7433. Runs M-Th 6:15am-7:30pm, F 6:15am-10:30pm, and Sa 8am-7pm. $1.50, seniors 75¢.)

⬛ⓩ ORIENTATION AND PRACTICAL INFORMATION. Whitehorse is located 1500km north of Dawson Creek, BC, along the Alaska Highway and 535km south of Dawson City, YT. **Visitors Center:** 100 Hanson St., in the Tourism and Business Centre at 2nd Ave. (☎667-3084. Open mid-May to mid-Sept. daily 8am-8pm; in winter M-F 9am-5pm.) The **Yukon Conservation Society,** 302 Hawkins St. (☎668-5678), offers maps and great ideas for area hikes. The **Kanoe People,** at Strickland and 1st Ave., rent outdoor gear. (☎668-4899. Open daily 9am-6pm. Mountain bikes $25 per day, canoes $45 per day, kayaks $35-45 per day. Credit card or deposit required.) **Internet access: Public Library,** 2071 2nd Ave. (☎667-5239. Open M-F 10am-9pm, Sa 10am-6pm and Su 1-9pm. Free.) **Post Office:** 211 Main St. (☎667-2485; open M-F 9am-6pm, Sa 11am-4pm). **General Delivery** is at 300 Range Rd. (☎667-2412). **Postal codes:** last names A-L, Y1A 3S7; M-Z, Y1A 3S8. **Area code:** 867.

⬛⬛ ACCOMMODATIONS AND FOOD. Interchangeable motels in town cost around $65. The **Hide on Jeckell Guesthouse,** 410 Jeckell (☎633-4933), lurks between 4th Ave and 5th Ave., 1 block from Robert Service Way. Stay in the continent-themed room of your choice and pick your endangered species-labeled bed and fridge bin. Services include showers, coffee, kitchen, bikes, Internet, local calls, linens, and lockers. (☎633-4933. Open year-round. 22 beds, 6 rooms. $20.) **Robert Service Campground,** 1km from town on South Access Rd. along the Yukon River, is a home-away-from-home for university students. (☎668-3721. Open late May to early Sept. Gates open 7am-midnight. Food trailer, firewood, playground, drinking water, toilets, showers. 68 sites, $12 per tent.) The 62km drive to the **Takhini Hot Springs,** the Yukon's only hot springs, offers tenting plus thermal relief. Follow the Alaska Hwy. northwest from downtown, turn right onto the North Klondike Hwy., and then left to the end of Takhini Hot Springs Rd. (☎633-2706. Restaurant, showers, and laundry. $12.50, with electricity $15.)
  ▨**Klondike Rib and Salmon Barbecue,** 2116 2nd Ave., serves charred fresh salmon or halibut with homemade bread for lunch. (☎667-7554. Open mid-May to Sept. M-F 11:30am-2pm and 4-10pm, Sa-Su 5-10pm. Lunch $8.) **The Talisman Cafe,** 2112 2nd Ave., is elegantly decorated with local art and has the best vegetarian menu in town. (☎667-2736. Open daily 9am-9pm.)

◙▲ SIGHTS AND OUTDOORS. Visitors hungry for local history can feed their heads at the **MacBride Museum,** at 1st Ave. and Wood St. The sod-roofed cabin in the courtyard was built by Sam Mcgee whose demise was famously related in verse by Robert Service. (☎667-2709. Open June-Aug. daily 10am-6pm; call for winter hours $5, students and seniors $4.50, children 5-16 $3.50, under 5 free.) The new **Yukon Beringia Interpretive Centre,** on the Alaska Hwy., 2km west of the junction with the S. Access Rd., pays homage to the forgotten continent that joined Siberia, Alaska, and the Yukon. (☎667-8855. Open mid-May to Sept. daily 8am-8pm; in winter Su 1-5pm. $6, seniors $5, children $4.)

If you think you're a weary traveler, visit the **Whitehorse Fishway** and meet the chinook salmon who swim approximately 3000km upstream before reaching the fish ladder—designed to save them from death by dam. (☎633-5965. 2.4km from town, over the bridge by the S.S. Klondike. Open June W-Su 10am-6pm. Open early July to early Sept. daily 8:30am-9pm. Admission by donation. Wheelchair accessible.) **Grey Mountain,** partly accessible by gravel road, is a somewhat rigorous day hike. Take Lewes Blvd. across the bridge by the **S.S. Klondike,** then take a left on Alsek Ave. Turn left again at the "Grey Mt. Cemetery" sign and follow the gravel road to its end. Joggers, bikers, and cross-country skiers love the **Miles Canyon trail network** that parallels the Yukon River. To get there, take Lewes Blvd. to Nisutlin Dr. and turn right; just before the fish ladder turn left onto the gravel Chadbum Lake Rd. and continue for 4km to the parking area. The **Conservation Society** leads nature walks. (Office open July-Aug. M-F 10am-2pm.) **Up North Boat and Canoe Rentals,** 86 Wickstrom Rd., lets you paddle 25km to Takhini River. (☎667-7905. 4hr. $30 including transportation. 8-day trip on the Teslin $200. Kayaks and canoes $25-30 per day.) The islands around **Sanfu Lake,** 1½hr. south of town on Atlin Rd., are snafu-free for kayaking.

Two Whitehorse festivals draw crowds from all over the world: the **Frostbite Music Festival** (☎668-4921) in February 2002, and the **Yukon International Storytelling Festival** (☎633-7550) to be held May 30-June 2, 2002. The **Commissioner's Potlatch** gathers indigenous groups and visitors in June for traditional dancing, games, artistry, and a feast. Locals, transients, and native artists perform for free at noon with **Arts in Lepage Park** on weekdays. (☎668-3136. Wood St. and 3rd Ave. From June to mid-Aug.) Call the **Yukon Arts Centre Theatre** for stage updates. (☎667-8574; www.yukonartscentre.org.) The **Yukon River** hosts the popular **Rubber Duckie Race** on Canada Day, July 1. (☎668-7979. $5 per duck. Proceeds go to charity.)

KLUANE NATIONAL PARK ☎867

The Southern Tutchone (*tuh-SHOW-nee*) people named this area Kluane (*kloo-AH-nee*), meaning "place of many fish." They might also have mentioned that Kluane National Park is a place of many Dall sheep, eagles, glaciers, and untouched mountain landscapes. It contains Canada's highest peak, Mt. Logan (5959m), as well as the world's most massive non-polar ice fields. The ice-blanketed mountains of Kluane's interior are a haven for experienced expeditioners, but render two-thirds of the park inaccessible to humbler hikers. Fortunately, the northeast part of the park (bordering the Alaska Hwy.) offers splendid, easily accessible backpacking, canoeing, rafting, biking, fishing, and dayhiking.

◪ PRACTICAL INFORMATION. Haines Junction, at the eastern park boundary, 158km west of Whitehorse, serves as park gateway and headquarters. **Alaska Direct** (☎668-4833 or 800-770-6652) runs from Haines Junction three times per week in the summer to Anchorage (13hr., US$145), Fairbanks (11hr., US$125), and Whitehorse (2hr., US$40). **Kluane National Park Visitor Reception Centre,** on Logan St. (Km 1635 on the Alaska Hwy.), provides wilderness permits ($5 per night, $50 per season); fishing permits ($5 per day, $35 per season); maps ($11); and trail and weather info. (☎634-7207. Open May-Sept. daily 9am-7pm; Oct.-Apr. M-F 10am-noon and 1-5pm.) **Sheep Mountain Info Centre,** 72km north of town at Alaska Hwy. Km 1707, registers hikers headed into the park. **24hr. road service: Triple S Garage** (☎634-2915), 1km north of Haines Jct. **Emergency: ☎**634-5555. **Ambulance/Clinic: ☎**634-4444. **Post office:** in Madley's Store on Haines Rd. (☎634-3802. Open M-F 10am-noon and 1-5pm.) **Postal code:** Y0B 1L0. **Area code:** 867.

▓▓ ACCOMMODATIONS AND FOOD. Camping by a gorgeous lakeside beats staying at a clean-but-forgettable highway motel or RV park any day. The idyllic **Kathleen Lake Campground,** off Haines Rd. 27km south of Haines Junction, is close to hiking and fishing. (Open mid-May to mid-Sept. Toilets, fire pits, and firewood. Sites $10. Wheelchair accessible.) Popular **Pine Lake,** 7km east of town, features a sandy beach. (Water, firewood, pit toilets. $8 with Yukon camping permit only.) For those who must stay in a motel, the **Stardust Motel,** 1km north of town on the Alaska Hwy., has spacious rooms with TVs and tubs, but no phones. (☎ 634-2591. Singles $49; doubles $59; shared bath.) **Village Bakery and Deli,** on Logan St. across from the Visitors Center, serves up substantial soups with bread ($3.50) and mushroom quiche ($2.50). Watch out for (or join in) live music and salmon BBQs ($13) on Monday nights. (☎ 634-2867. Open May-Sept. daily 7:30am-9pm.)

▓▓ OUTDOOR ACTIVITIES. A $1 pamphlet lists about 25 trails and routes ranging from 500m to 96km. Routes, as opposed to trails, are not maintained, do not have marked paths, are more physically demanding, and require backcountry navigation skills. Overnight visitors must register at one of the Visitors Centers ($5 per night, ages 5-16 $2.50), and use bear-resistant food canisters, which the park rents for $5 per night. The **Dezadeash River Loop** trailhead is downtown at the day-use area across from Madley's on Haines Rd. This flat, forested 5km trail will disappoint those craving vert, but it makes for a nice stroll. The more challenging 15km **Auriol Loop** has a primitive campground halfway along. The trail begins 7km south of Haines Junction on Haines Rd. and cuts through boreal forest, leading to a subalpine bench (elevation gain 400m) just in front of the Auriol Range. This is a popular overnight trip, though 4-6hr. is adequate time without heavy packs. The 5km (one-way) **King's Throne Route** is a very challenging but rewarding day hike with a 1220m elevation gain and a panoramic view. It begins at the **Kathleen Lake** day-use area at the campground (see **Accommodations,** above).

Excellent hiking awaits near **Sheep Mountain** in the park's northern section. An easy 500m jaunt up to **Soldier's Summit** starts 1km north of the Sheep Mountain Info Centre and leads to the site where the original highway was officially opened in 1942. The **Sheep Creek** trail, down a short gravel access road just north of the Visitors Center, is a satisfying dayhike up Sheep Mountain, and one of the better bets to see Dall sheep in summer (10km roundtrip, 3-6hr.; 430m elevation gain). Only experienced backpackers should attempt the trek along the **Slims River** to the magnificent **Kaskawulsh Glacier.** Two rough routes along either bank of the river are available and require three to five days to complete. One stretches 23km with an elevation gain of 910m; the other is 30km and has an elevation gain of 1340m.

The **Alsek River Valley Trail,** starting from Alcan Km 1645 and following a bumpy old mining road 14km to Sugden Creek, makes for good mountain biking. **Paddle-Wheel Adventures,** down the road from the Village Bakery in Haines Junction, arranges flightseeing over the glaciers and full-day rafting trips on the Class III and IV rapids of the **Blanchard** and **Tatshenshini Rivers.** (☎ 634-2683. $90 per person for a 30min. flight over the Kaskawulsh. Rafting $100 per person, including lunch.)

THE DEMPSTER HIGHWAY

Like no other highway in North America, the Dempster presents its drivers with naked wilderness, unmolested by logging scars or advertisements. The challenge of battling the road and taking in the divine landscape makes driving the Dempster a religious experience: those who brave it across the Arctic Circle and the Continental Divide stare into the geological beginnings of the continent—and earn the right to scratch, "I did it!" in the dust coating their car. The road is not to be taken lightly. The Dempster's dirt and gravel are notorious for eating tires and cracking windshields. Parts of it are in great condition, while other sections take on the appearance of a dry river bed. While the speed limit is posted at 90kmph, the rough road will punish you for going above 50-60kmph. The drive should be approached with careful planning. Services are limited to Klondike River Lodge (Km 0), Eagle Plains (Km 369), Fort McPherson (Km 550), and Inuvik (Km 734). Although a trip to Tombstone makes a pleasant overnight, the full drive takes at least 12hr. (two days each way to be fully and safely appreciated). The weather is erratic. Quick rainstorms or high winds can make portions of the route impassable (watch for flashing red lights that denote closed roads) and disrupt ferry service to Inuvik for as long as two weeks, leaving travelers stranded. **Northwest Territories Tourism** (☎800-661-0788) and **Road and Ferry Report** (☎867-777-2678 or 800-661-0752) provide up-to-date road info. The **Northwest Territories Visitor Centre**, in Dawson City, has a free Dempster brochure. (☎867-993-6167. Open late May to early Sept. daily 9am-8pm.) There are **government campgrounds** at Tombstone (Km 72), Engineer Creek (Km 194), Nitainlii (Km 541), and Chuk (Km 731). Hookups are only available at Nitainlii and Chuk. The **Interpretive Centre** at Tombstone loans out a detailed travel-ogue of the Dempster's natural history and wildlife.

ALBERTA

With its gaping prairie, oil-fired economy, and conservative politics, Alberta is the Texas of Canada. Petro-dollars have given birth to gleaming, modern cities on the plains, while the natural landscape swings from the mighty Canadian Rockies down to beautifully desolate badlands. For adventurous outdoor enthusiasts, Alberta is a year-round playground.

🔋 PRACTICAL INFORMATION

Capital: Edmonton.
Visitor Info: Travel Alberta, Commerce Pl., 10155 102 St., 3rd fl., Edmonton T5J 4G8 (☎780-427-4321 or 800-661-8888; www.discoveralberta.com). **Parks Canada**, 220 4th Ave. SE, #552, Calgary T2G 4X3 (☎403-292-4401 or 800-748-7275). **Alberta Environmental**, 9820 106 St., 2nd Fl., Edmonton T5K 2J6 (☎780-427-7009; www.gov.ab.ca/env/parks.html).
Drinking Age: 18. **Postal Abbreviation:** AB. **Sales Tax:** 7% GST.

THE ROCKIES

Every year, some five million visitors make it within sight of the Rockies' majestic peaks and stunning glacial lakes. Thankfully, much of this traffic is confined to highwayside gawkers, and only a tiny fraction of these visitors make it far into the forest. Of the big two national parks—Banff and Jasper—Jasper feels a little further removed from the crowds and offers great wildlife viewing from the road. Without a car, guided bus rides may be the easiest way to see some of the park's main attractions. **Brewster Tours** buses from Banff to Jasper. (☎762-6767. 9½hr.; $95.) **Bigfoot Tours** takes two days to make the trip. (☎888-244-6673 or 604-278-8224. $95.)

BANFF NATIONAL PARK   ☎403

Banff is Canada's best-loved and best-known natural park, with 6641 square kilometers of peaks, forests, glaciers, and alpine valleys. Even streets littered with gift shops, clothing shops, and chocolatiers cannot mar Banff's beauty. Itinerant twenty-somethings arrive with mountain bikes, climbing gear, and skis, but a trusty pair of hiking boots remains the park's most popular outdoor equipment.

➕🔋 PRACTICAL INFORMATION. The park hugs Alberta's border with British Columbia, 129km west of Calgary. Civilization in the park centers around the towns of **Banff** and **Lake Louise,** 58km apart on Hwy. 1. All of the following info applies to Banff Townsite, unless otherwise specified. **Greyhound,** 106 Railway Ave. (800-661-8747; depot open daily 7:30am-9pm), runs to Lake Louise (1hr., 4 per day, $12); Calgary (1½hr., 5 per day, $22); and Vancouver, BC (13hr., 4 per day, $100). **Brewster Transportation,** 100 Gopher St. (☎762-6767), runs

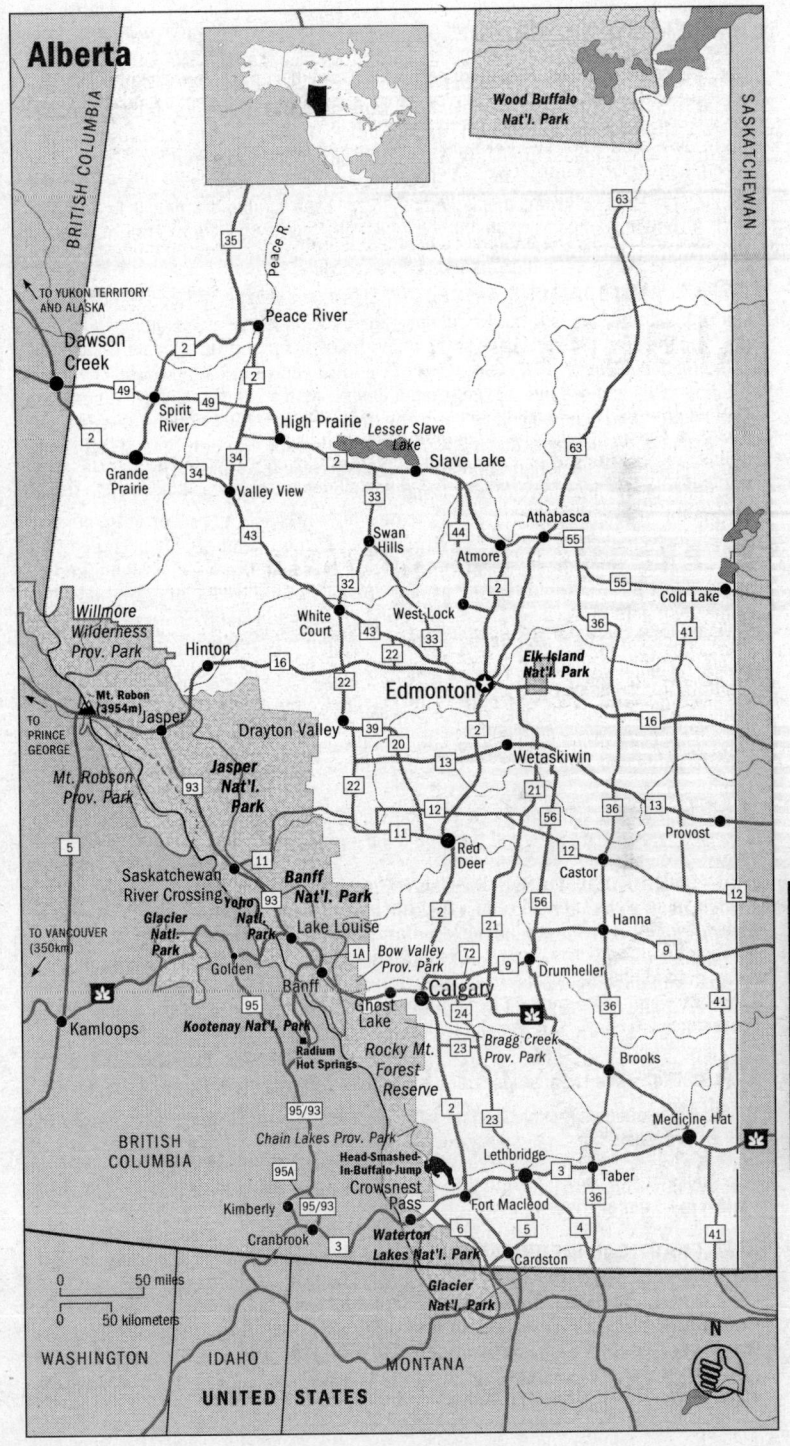

Alberta

BRITISH COLUMBIA

SASKATCHEWAN

Wood Buffalo Nat'l. Park

TO YUKON TERRITORY AND ALASKA

Peace R.

35

63

Dawson Creek

2

Peace River

49

2

Spirit River

49

49

34

High Prairie

34

Lesser Slave Lake

Slave Lake

2

Grande Prairie

Valley View

33

Swan Hills

44

Athabasca

55

Atmore

2

55

Cold Lake

32

West-Lock

36

41

Willmore Wilderness Prov. Park

White Court

43

33

22

Hinton

16

22

Edmonton

Elk Island Nat'l. Park

16

Mt. Robon (3954m)

Jasper

Drayton Valley

39

2

TO PRINCE GEORGE

20

13

Wetaskiwin

21

56

36

13

Provost

Mt. Robson Prov. Park

93

Jasper Nat'l. Park

22

12

12

Saskatchewan River Crossing

11

11

Red Deer

Castor

12

56

Hanna

12

Banff Nat'l. Park

93

Glacier Natl. Park

Yoho Natl. Park

Lake Louise

2

21

9

TO VANCOUVER (350km)

5

Golden

1A

Bow Valley Prov. Park

72

9

Drumheller

Kamloops

95

Banff

Calgary

36

41

Kootenay Nat'l. Park

Ghost Lake

24

Brooks

Radium Hot Springs

Bragg Creek Prov. Park

23

Rocky Mt. Forest Reserve

2

23

Medicine Hat

BRITISH COLUMBIA

Chain Lakes Prov. Park

Head-Smashed-In-Buffalo-Jump

Lethbridge

3

Taber

95A

95/93

Crowsnest Pass

Fort Macleod

36

4

Kimberly

95/93

6

5

Cranbrook

3

Waterton Lakes Nat'l. Park

Cardston

41

Glacier Nat'l. Park

0   50 miles

0   50 kilometers

WASHINGTON   IDAHO   MONTANA

UNITED STATES

N

WESTERN CANADA

buses to Jasper (5hr., $51); Lake Louise (1hr., $11); and Calgary (2hr., $36). The **Banff Visitor Centre,** 224 Banff Ave., includes the **Banff/Lake Louise Tourism Bureau** and the **Canadian Parks Service.** (Tourism Bureau: ☎762-8421. Parks Service: ☎762-1550. Open June-Sept. daily 8am-8pm; Oct.-May 9am-5pm.) The **Lake Louise Visitor Centre,** at Samson Mall in Lake Louise, shares a building with a museum. (☎522-3833. Open July-Aug. daily 8am-8pm; June and Sept. 8am-6pm; Oct.-May 9am-5pm.) **Emergency: Banff Police,** ☎762-2226. **Lake Louise Police,** ☎522-3811. **Banff Warden Office,** ☎762-4506. **Lake Louise Warden Office,** ☎522-1200. **Post Office:** 204 Buffalo St. (☎762-2586; open M-F 9am-5:30pm). **Postal code:** T0L 0C0. **Area code:** 403.

█▢ ACCOMMODATIONS AND FOOD. HI runs a **shuttle service** connecting all the Rocky Mountain hostels and Calgary ($8-90). Wait-list beds become available at 6pm, and the larger hostels save some stand-by beds for shuttle arrivals. ◪**Lake Louise International Hostel (HI),** 500m west of the info center in Lake Louise Townsite, on Village Rd., is more like a hotel than a hostel, with a reference library, common rooms with open, beamed ceilings, a stone fireplace, two full kitchens, a sauna, ski/bike workshops, and a cafe. (☎522-2200. Dorms $23, nonmembers $27. Private rooms available. Wheelchair accessible.) ◪**Castle Mountain Hostel (HI),** on Hwy. 1A, 1.5km east of the junction of Hwy. 1 and Hwy. 93, between Banff and Lake Louise, is a quieter alternative, with running water, hot showers, and electricity, general store, library, and fireplace. (Linen $1. Dorms $14, nonmembers $18.) Three other rustic hostels—**Hilda Creek, Rampart Creek,** and **Mosquito Creek**—can be booked by calling Banff International Hostel. At any of Banff's nine park campgrounds, sites are first come, first served ($10-24). On Hwy. 1A between Banff Townsite and Lake Louise, **Johnston Canyon** and **Castle Mountain** are close to relatively uncrowded hiking. Only Village 2 of **Tunnel Mountain Village,** 4km from Banff Townsite, on Tunnel Mountain Rd., remains open in winter.

The Banff and Lake Louise Hostels serve affordable meals ($3-8), but **Laggan's Deli** (☎522-2017), in Samson Mall in Lake Louise, is the best thing going. Thick sandwich on whole wheat cost $4-5; a fresh-baked loaf for later runs $3. **Aardvark's,** 304A Caribou St., does big business after the bars close. The place is skinny on seating but serves thick slices of pizza. (☎762-5500. Open daily 11am-4am. 10% HI discount on large pizzas. Slices $3; small pizza $6-9, large $13-21.)

▨ OUTDOOR ACTIVITIES. Near Banff Townsite, **Fenland Trail** winds 2km (1hr.) through an area shared by beaver, muskrat, and waterfowl (closed for elk calving in late spring and early summer). Follow Mt. Norquay Rd. out of town and look for signs across the tracks on the road's left side. The summit of **Tunnel Mountain** provides a dramatic view of the **Bow Valley** and **Mt. Rundle.** Follow Wolf St. east from Banff Ave., and turn right on St. Julien Rd. to reach the head of the steep 2.3km (2hr.) trail. At 2949m, **Mt. Rundle** offers a more demanding fair-weather-only day hike (5.5km one-way; 7-8hr.; 1600m elevation gain). **Johnston Canyon,** about 25km out of Banff toward Lake Louise, along the Bow Valley Pkwy. (Hwy. 1A), is a popular half-day hike, which runs past waterfalls to blue-green cold-water springs known as the **Inkpots.**

The park might not exist if not for the **Cave and Basin Hot Springs,** southwest of town on Cave Ave., once rumored to have miraculous healing properties. The **Cave and Basin National Historic Site,** a refurbished resort built circa 1914, is now a museum. (☎762-1566. Open in summer daily 9am-6pm; in winter 9:30am-5pm. Tours at 11am. $2.50, seniors $2, children $1.50.) For a dip in the hot water, follow the rotten-egg smell to the 40°C (104°F) springs.

The highest community in Canada at 1530m (5018 ft.), Lake Louise and its surrounding glaciers have often passed for Swiss scenery in movies. Once at the lake, the hardest task is escaping fellow gawkers at the posh **Château Lake Louise.** Several hiking trails begin at the water; the 3.6km **Lake Agnes Trail** and the 5.5km **Plain of Six Glaciers Trail** both end at teahouses.

Fishing is legal in most of the park's bodies of water during specific seasons, but live bait and lead weights are not. **Permits** are available at the info center. (7-days; $6.) Winter activities in the park range from world-class ice climbing to ice fishing. Those 1600km of hiking trails make for exceptional **cross-country skiing,** and three allied resorts offer a range of **skiing and snowboarding** opportunities from early November to mid-May. **Sunshine Mountain** has the largest snowfall (☎762-6500, snow report 760-7669; lift tickets $54); **Mt. Norquay** is smaller, closer to town, and less busy (☎762-4421; $47); while **Lake Louise** is the second-biggest ski area in Canada and has the most expert terrain (☎522-3555, snow report 762-4766; $54). Shuttles to all three resorts leave from most big hotels in the townsites, and most hostels have **ticket and transportation discounts** available for guests.

SCENIC DRIVE: ICEFIELDS PARKWAY

The 230km Icefields Parkway is one of the most beautiful routes in North America, heading north from Lake Louise in Banff National Park to Jasper Townsite in Jasper National Park. Free maps of the Parkway are available at info centers in Jasper and Banff, or at the **Icefield Centre,** at the boundary between the two parks, 132km north of Lake Louise and 103km south of Jasper Townsite. (☎780-852-6288. Open May to mid-Oct. daily 9am-5pm.) Although the center is closed in winter, the parkway is only closed for plowing after heavy snowfalls. An extensive campground and hostel network along the Parkway makes longer trips along the length of Jasper and Banff convenient and affordable. **Cycling** the highway is also a popular option; bikes can be rented in Banff or Jasper for a one-way trip.

However you travel the Parkway, set aside time for hikes and magnificent vistas. At **Bow Summit,** 40km north of Lake Louise, the Parkway's highest point (2135m), a 10min. walk leads to a view of fluorescent aqua **Peyto Lake,** especially vivid toward the end of June. The Icefield Centre (see above) lies in the shadow of the tongue of the **Athabasca Glacier,** a great white whale of an ice flow that flows from the 325 sq. km **Columbia Icefield,** the largest accumulation of ice and snow south of the Arctic Circle (yes, excepting Antarctica, smartass). **Columbia Icefield Snocoach Tours** carries visitors right onto the glacier in bizarre monster buses for an 80min. trip. (☎877-423-7433. Apr.-Oct. daily 9am-5pm. $27, ages 6-15 $13.50.)

JASPER NATIONAL PARK ☎780

Northward expansion of the Canadian railway system led to the exploration of the Canadian Rockies and the creation of Jasper National Park in 1907. The largest of the four National Parks in the region, Jasper encompasses herculean peaks and plummeting valleys that dwarf the battalion of motorhomes and charter buses parading through the region. In the face of this annual bloat, Jasper Townsite's permanent residents struggle to keep their sheltered home looking and feeling like a genuine small town. In the winter, the crowds melt away, a blanket of snow descends, and a ski resort welcomes visitors to a slower, more relaxed town.

▓ PRACTICAL INFORMATION. All of the addresses below are in **Jasper Townsite,** near the center of the park. **VIA Rail** (☎800-561-8630) sends 3 trains per week from the station on Connaught Dr. to Edmonton (5hr., $91) and Vancouver (16½hr., $156). **Greyhound** (☎852-3332), in the train station, runs to Edmonton (4½hr., 3 per day, $52) and Vancouver, BC (11½hr., 3 per day, $104). **Brewster Transportation Tours** (☎852-3332), in the station, runs daily to Calgary (7½hr., $71) via Banff (5½hr., $51). The **Park Information Centre,** 500 Connaught Dr., has trail maps. (☎852-6176. Open mid-June to early Sept. daily 8am-7pm; early Sept. to late Oct. and late Dec. to mid-June 9am-5pm.) **Emergency:** ☎911 or 852-4421. **Post Office:** 502 Patricia St. (☎852-3041. Open M-F 9am-5pm.) **Postal code:** T0E 1E0. **Area code:** 780.

WESTERN CANADA

Rocky Mountain Unlimited serves as a central reservation service for many local outdoor businesses. They provide prices and recommendations for rafting, fishing, horseback riding, and wildlife safaris. (☎ 852-4056. Open daily 9am-9pm; in winter 8am-6pm.) **Currie's**, in **The Sports Shop**, 406 Patricia St., rents fishing equipment and gives tips on good spots. (☎ 852-5650. Rod, reel, and line $10. 1-day boat or canoe rental $30, after 2pm $20, after 6pm $15. Pickup and dropoff service available.) **Fishing permits** are available at fishing shops and the Parks Canada info center ($6 per week, $13 per year).

⌐ **ACCOMMODATIONS.** HI runs a shuttle service connecting all the Rocky Mountain hostels and Calgary; call the Jasper Hostel for reservations. The modern **Jasper International Hostel (HI)**, 3km up Whistlers Rd. from Hwy. 93, 4km south of the townsite, also known as **Whistlers Hostel,** anchors the chain of HI hostels stretching from Jasper to Calgary. Jasper International attracts gregarious backpackers and cyclists, but a "leave-your-hiking-boots-outside" rule keeps the hardwood floors and dorm rooms clean. (☎ 852-3215 or 877-852-0781 for all HI hostels. Dorms $18. Curfew 2am.) **Maligne Canyon Hostel (HI)**, 11km east of town on Hwy. 16, has small cabins on the bank of the Maligne River. (Check-in 5-11pm. Closed W Oct.-Apr. $13, nonmembers $18.) **Mt. Edith Cavell Hostel (HI)**, 12km up Edith Cavell Rd., off Hwy. 93, offers small, cozy quarters heated by wood-burning stoves. In winter, the road is closed, but you can pick up keys at Jasper International Hostel and ski uphill from the highway. (Propane, pump water, solar shower, firepit. $13, nonmembers $18.)

Most of Jasper's campgrounds have primitive sites with few facilities ($13-22). They are first come, first served, so get there early. Call the park Info Centre (☎ 852-6176) for details. None of the surrounding campgrounds are open in winter. A 781-site behemoth, **Whistlers**, on Whistlers Rd., 3km south of the townsite, off Hwy. 93, is closest to the townsite. (Open early May to mid-Oct. $15, full hookup $24.) The highlight of the Icefields Pkwy. campgrounds is **Columbia Icefield**, 109km south of the townsite, which lies close enough to the Athabasca Glacier to intercept an icy breeze and even a rare summer night's snowfall.

⚠ **OUTDOOR ACTIVITIES.** The info center in town distributes *Day Hikes in Jasper National Park*. **Cavell Meadows Loop**, which features views of the glacier-laden peak of **Mt. Edith Cavell**, is a rewarding half-day hike. The trailhead is 30km south of the townsite; take Hwy. 93 to 93A to the end of the bumpy, twisty 15km Mt. Edith Cavell Rd. (open June-Oct.). To scale a peak in a day, climb the Sulpher **Skyline Trail**, a challenging 4-6hr. hike with views of the limestone Miette Range and Ashlar Ridge (9.6km round-trip, 700m elevation gain). The trail leaves all too conveniently from the **Miette Hot Springs**, 42km north of the townsite on Hwy. 16 and 15km along Miette Hot Springs Rd., blending chlorinated and filtered heat therapy with panoramic views. (☎ 866-3939. Open late May to late June and early Sept. to early Oct. daily 10:30am-9pm; late June to early Sept. 8:30am-10:30pm. $6; swimsuit $1.50.)

The spectacular if over-touristed **Maligne Canyon** is 11km east of the townsite on Maligne Lake Rd. From the trailhead, a 4km path follows the Maligne River as it plunges through the narrow limestone gorge, across footbridges, and eventually into Medicine Lake. Brilliant turquoise **Maligne Lake,** the longest (22km) and deepest lake in the park, sprawls at the end of Maligne Lake Rd. The **Opal Hills Trail** (8.2km loop) winds through subalpine meadows and ascends 460m to views of the lake. **Maligne Tours**, 626 Connaught Dr., rents kayaks and leads fishing, canoeing, rabbiting, horseback riding, hiking, and whitewater rafting tours (☎ 852-3370. Kayaks half-day $30, full-day $60.)

The **Jasper Tramway**, 4km up Whistlers Rd., climbs 1200m up Whistlers Mt., leading to a panoramic view of the park and, on a clear day, very far beyond. (☎ 852-3093. Open Apr.-Aug. daily 8:30am-10pm; Sept.-Oct. 9:30am-4:30pm. $19, under 14 $9.50, under 5 free.) The demanding 9km **Whistlers Trail** covers the same ground, beginning behind Jasper International's volleyball court.

CALGARY   ☎403

Mounties founded Calgary in the 1870s to control the flow of illegal whiskey, but another liquid made this city great: oil. Petroleum fuels Calgary's economy; the city holds the most corporate headquarters in Canada outside of Toronto. Calgary's dot on the map grew larger when it hosted the 1988 Winter Olympics; it is now Canada's second-fastest-growing city. The world-class Calgary Stampede, the "Greatest Outdoor Show on Earth," garbs the city in cowboy duds every July.

■☎ ORIENTATION AND PRACTICAL INFORMATION. Calgary is divided into quadrants: NE, NW, SE, and SW. **Centre St.** is the east-west divider; the **Bow River** splits the north and south sections. **Avenues** run east-west, **streets** run north-south, and numbers count up from the divides. **Calgary International Airport** is about 17km northeast of the city center. **Greyhound,** 877 Greyhound Way SW (☎265-9111 or 800-661-8747), runs to Edmonton (3½hr., 8 per day, $43); Banff (1¾hr., 4 per day, $22); and Drumheller (1¾hr., 2 per day, $24). **Brewster Tours** (☎221-8242) runs from the airport or downtown to Banff (2½hr., 4 per day, $36) and Jasper (8hr., 1 per day, $71) and offers a 15% HI discount. **Calgary Transit,** 240 7th Ave. SW, runs **C-Trains,** which are free in the downtown zone. (☎262-1000. Runs M-F 6am-11pm, Sa-Su 6am-9:30pm. Bus fare and C-Trains outside downtown $1.75, ages 6-14 $1.10; day pass $5/$3; 10 tickets $14.50/$9.) The **Visitor Service Centre,** 131 9th Ave. SW, is under the Calgary Tower. (☎750-2397. Open daily 8am-5pm.) **Post Office:** 207 9th Ave. SW (☎974-2078; open M-F 8am-5:45pm). **Postal code:** T2P 2G8. **Area code:** 403.

☎☐ ACCOMMODATIONS AND FOOD. The ▓**Calgary International Hostel (HI),** 520 7th Ave. SE, is near downtown. Go east along 7th Ave. from the 3rd St. SE C-Train station; this welcoming urban hostel is on the left just past 4th St. SE. (☎269-8239. Open 24hr. Kitchen, game room, laundry, email, and barbecue facilities. Linen $1. Wheelchair accessible. $16, nonmembers $20.) **University of Calgary,** in the NW quadrant, has rooms booked through **Kananaskis Hall,** 3330 24th Ave., a 12min. walk from the University C-Train stop. (☎220-3203. Open 24hr. Rooms available May-Aug. Shared rooms $20; singles $32, with student ID $23; doubles $39/$32. Suites with private bathrooms about $35.)

The cheapest, most satisfying food is located in Calgary's tiny Chinatown, the two square blocks at the north end of Centre St. S and 1st St. SE. Five dollars buys a feast in Vietnamese noodle-houses and Hong Kong-style cafes, many of which don't close until 3 or 4am. At ▓**Thi-Thi Submarine,** 209 1st St. SE, $2.50 will buy a 10 in. "super-sub" with pork, chicken, cilantro, carrots, cucumbers, and special sauce, served hot on a fresh baguette. The veggie sub is a ludicrous $1.50. (☎265-5452. Open daily 10am-7pm.) **Take Ten Cafe,** 304 10th St. NE, attracts clientele not for panache, but for good cuisine. All burgers under $5.75. (☎270-7010. Open Tu-Sa 9am-6pm, Su 9am-3pm.)

☐▓ SIGHTS AND NIGHTLIFE. Over a decade later, Calgary still clings to its two weeks of Olympic stardom at the **Canada Olympic Park,** 10min. west of downtown on Hwy. 1, site of the four looming ski jumps and the bobsled and luge tracks. (☎247-5452. Open daily 8am-9pm.) The **Olympic Hall of Fame,** 88 Canada Olympic Rd. SW, honors Olympic achievements with displays, films, and bobsled and ski-jumping simulators. In summer, the park opens its hills to mountain bikers. Take the lift up the hill, then cruise down—no work necessary. (☎247-5452. Open daily 9am-9pm. $7 includes chair lift and entrance to ski jump buildings, Hall of Fame, and icehouse. Guided tour, $10, $35 per family. Mountain biding open May-Oct. daily 10am-9pm. Hill pass $7 for cyclists. Bike rental $12 per hr., $31 per day.)

The **Glenbow Museum,** 130 9th Ave. SE, brings together rocks and minerals, Buddhist and Hindu art, and native Canadian history under one roof. (☎268-4100. Open Su-W 9am-5pm, Th-F 9am-9pm. $10, seniors $7.50, students and youth $6, under 6 free. 10% HI discount. Everyone $6 Th-F 5-9pm in summer; $3 F evenings in winter.) Footbridges stretch from either side of the Bow River to **Prince's Island Park,** a natural refuge blocks from the city center. Calgary's other island park, **St. George's Island**, is accessible by the river walkway to the east, and houses the **Calgary Zoo.** (☎232-9300. Parking is off Memorial Dr. on the north side of the river. Open daily 9am-5pm. $12, seniors and under 17 $6, seniors half-price Tu and Th; reduced winter rates. 20% AAA and 10% HI discounts.) On July 5-14, 2002, 1 million cowboys and tourists will converge on **Stampede Park,** just southeast of downtown, bordering the east side of Macleod Trail between 14th Ave. SE and the Elbow river. For ten days, the grounds are packed for world-class steer wrestling, bareback- and bull-riding, pig racing, wild-cow-milking, and chuckwagon races. (☎269-9822 or 800-661-1767; www.calgarystampede.com. Take C-Train to the Stampede. $10; seniors and ages 7-12 $5. Rodeo and evening cost $21-55; if not sold out, rush tickets are $10, at the grandstand 1½hr. before showtime.)

Nightclubs in Alberta only became legal in 1990, and Calgary is making up for lost time. The best areas in town for finding pubs, clubs, and live music are the Stephen Ave. Walk (8th Ave. SW), 17th Ave. SW, and 1st and 4th St. SW. ◙**The Nightgallery,** 1209B 1st St. SW, attracts clubbers with one large dance floor, one bar, and one helluva diverse program. The club breaks out the best House in town at "Sunday School" and on Thursday. Reggae-Dub draws a slightly older crowd Monday. (☎269-5924. Open daily 7:30pm-3am. Cover $5, $1.50 highballs before 11pm.) **The Vicious Circle,** 1011 St. SW, draws crowds with a solid menu and keeps them happy with a selection of 140 martinis. (☎269-3951. Open daily 11am-2am.)

ALBERTA BADLANDS

In the late Cretaceous period, these were the fertile shores of an inland sea, conditions that have created one of the richest dinosaur fossil sites in the world. Once the sea dried up, wind, water, and ice cut twisting canyons down into the sandstone and shale bedrock, creating the desolate splendor of the Alberta Badlands. The **Royal Tyrrell Museum of Paleontology** lies on the North Dinosaur Trail (Secondary Hwy. 838), 6km northwest of Drumheller. The museum has the world's largest display of dinosaur specimens. (☎403-823-7707 or 888-440-4240. Open late May to early Sept. daily 9am-9pm; mid-Sept. to mid-May Tu-Su 10am-5pm. $8.50, seniors $6.50, ages 7-17 $4.50, under 7 free; families $20.) The museum's immensely popular 12-person **Day Digs** include instruction in excavation techniques, and a chance to dig in a dinosaur quarry. The fee includes lunch and transportation, but all finds go to the museum. (July-Aug. daily 8:30am, returning at 4:30pm. $85, ages 10-15 $55. Reservations required.) **Greyhound** runs from Calgary to Drumheller (1½hr., 2 per day, $24).

ALASKA

Alaska's beauty and intrigue are born of extremes: North America's highest mountains and broadest flatlands, windswept tundra and lush rainforests, and 15 incredible national parks cover an area roughly equal to that of England and Ireland combined. The US bought Alaska for a piddling 2¢ per acre in 1867, from a Russia disillusioned with Alaska's dwindling fur trade. Critics mocked "Seward's Folly," named after the Secretary of State who negotiated the deal, but just 15 years after the purchase, huge deposits of gold were unearthed in the Panhandle's Gastineau Channel. Today, Alaskans celebrate Seward's shrewd purchase on March 27.

Many say the Klondike gold rush of 1898 was only the first in a string, from the liquid gold of the pipeline boom to the ocean gold pulled up in the form of king crab pots in the Bering Sea. Boom and bust has always been the name of the game in Alaska. The one thing that has remained constant is Alaska's overwhelming scale. From the 850-square-mile Malaspina Glacier to the 2000-mile Yukon River to the 20,320-foot Denali, Alaska is a land where everything is bigger, tougher, and more exciting. For more on Alaska and its wonders, check out *Let's Go: Alaska & the Pacific Northwest 2002*.

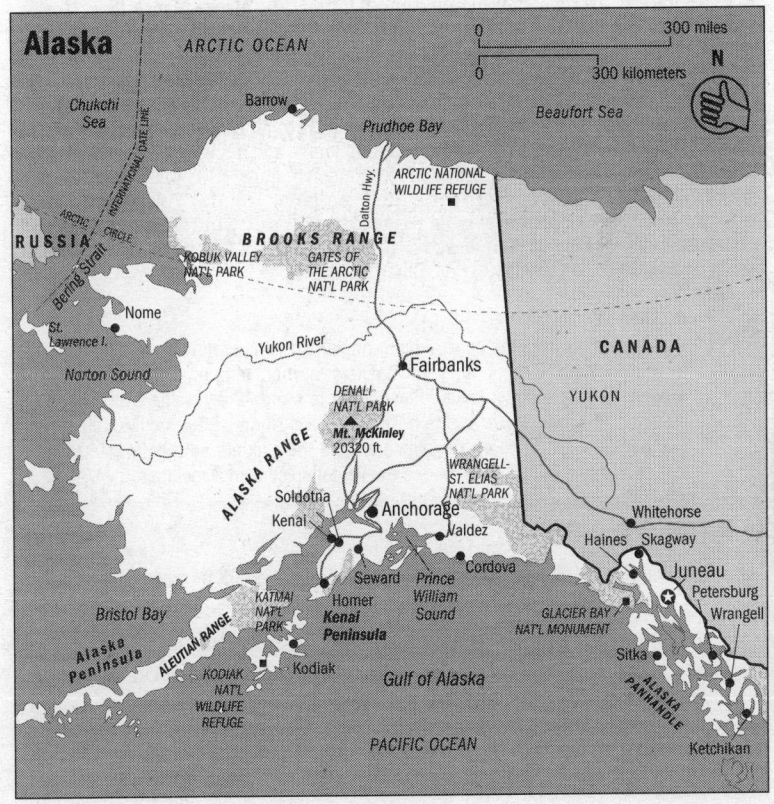

🛈 PRACTICAL INFORMATION

Capital: Juneau. **Biggest City:** Anchorage. **Biggest Party City:** Ketchikan.
Visitor Info: Alaska Division of Tourism, P.O. Box 110809, Juneau 99811 (☎907-465-2012; www.dced.state.ak.us/tourism). **Alaska Department of Fish & Game, Division of Wildlife Conservation,** P.O. Box 25526 Juneau 99802 (☎907-465-4190; www.state.ak.us/local/akpages/fish.game/wildlife/wildmain.htm).
Postal Abbreviation: AK. **Sales Tax:** 0%.

🛫 TRANSPORTATION

The **Alaska Railroad Corporation (ARRC)** (☎800-544-0552) covers 470 mi. from Seward to Fairbanks, with stops in Anchorage and Whittier. The **Alaska Marine Hwy.,** Homer Ferry Terminal, 4667 Spit Rd., #1, Homer 99603 (☎800-642-0066), remains the most practical and enjoyable way to explore much of the Panhandle, Prince William Sound, and the Kenai Peninsula. Most of the state's major **highways** are known by their name as often as their number (e.g., George Parks Hwy. is the same as Rte. 3 which is the same as The Parks). Driving to and through Alaska is not for the faint of car. Highways reward drivers with stunning views and access to true wilderness, but they barely scratch the surface of the massive state. (See p. 930 for the two major highway approaches into the state from points south.) For Alaska's most remote destinations, **air travel** is an expensive necessity. Intrastate airlines and charter services, many of them based at the busy Anchorage airport, transport passengers and cargo to virtually every village in Alaska.

CLIMATE
Weather varies from the coast inland. Anchorage temperatures range from 8°F in winter to 65°F in summer. In Alaska's interior, temperatures range from around 70°F in summer to -30°F and lower in winter. Progressing farther north, summer days and winter nights become longer. North of the Arctic Circle, the sun does not set at all on the nights around the summer solstice in late June, nor does it rise on the days around the winter solstice in December.

ANCHORAGE   ☎907

Alaska's primary metropolis, Anchorage is home to 254,000 people—two-fifths of the state's population. As far north as Helsinki and almost as far west as Honolulu, the city achieved its large size (2000 square miles) by hosting three major economic projects: the Alaska Railroad, WWII military developments, and the Trans-Alaska Pipeline. Anchorage serves as a good place to get oriented and stock up on supplies before journeying to the breathtaking wilderness just outside.

📧 **TRANSPORTATION.** Most Alaskan airstrips can be reached from **Anchorage International Airport** (☎266-2437) either directly or through a connection in Fairbanks. **Alaska Railroad,** 411 W. 1st Ave., runs to Denali (8hr., $125); Fairbanks (12hr.,

$175); and Seward (4hr., in summer only, $60). Flagstops are anywhere along the route; wave the train down with a white cloth. (☎265-2494 or 800-544-0552. Ticket window open M-F 5:30am-5pm, Sa-Su 5:30am-1pm.) **Grayline Alaska** (☎800-544-2206) sends buses daily to Valdez (10hr., $71); two times per week to Skagway ($219, overnight). **Alaska Marine Hwy.**, 605 W. 4th Ave., sells ferry tickets. (☎800-642-0066. Open daily 7:30am-4:30pm; in winter M-F.) **People Mover Bus,** in the Transit Center on 6th Ave. between G and H St., sends local buses all over the Anchorage area. (☎343-6543. Runs M-F 6am-10pm; restricted schedule Sa-Su. Fare $1, ages 5-18 50¢, over 65 25¢; tokens 90¢; day passes $2.50.) **Airport Car Rental,** 502 W. Northern Lights Blvd., charges $39 per day, with unlimited mileage. (☎277-7662. Open M-F 8am-8pm, Sa-Su 9am-6pm. Must be 21; under 25 surcharge $5 per day; credit card or cash deposit required.) **Taxi: Yellow Cab,** ☎272-2422.

◼◪ ORIENTATION AND PRACTICAL INFORMATION. Downtown Anchorage is laid out in a grid: numbered avenues run east-west, with addresses designated east or west from **C St.** North-south streets are lettered alphabetically to the west and named alphabetically to the east of **A St.** The rest of Anchorage spreads out along major highways. The **Log Cabin Visitor Information Center,** on W. 4th Ave. at F St., sells a $3.50 bike guide. (☎274-3531, events 276-3200. Open June-Aug. daily 7:30am-7pm; May and Sept. 8am-6pm; Oct.-Apr. 9am-4pm.) The **Alaska Public Lands Information Center,** Old Federal Building, 605 W. 4th Ave., between F and G St., combines the Park, Forest, State Parks, and Fish and Wildlife Services under one roof. (☎271-2737 or 271-2744. Open daily 9am-5:30pm.) **Internet access: Loussac Library,** at 36th Ave. and Denali St., is a great local library and an architectural oddity. Buses #2, 36, and 60 stop out front; bus #75 stops at C St. and 36th is within ½ block. Free for 1hr. (☎343-2975. Open M-Th 10am-8pm, F-Sa 10am-6pm; winter also Su noon-6pm.) **Post Office:** W. 4th Ave. and C St., on the lower level in the yellow mall. (Open M-F 10am-5:30pm.) **ZIP code:** 99510.

◪ ACCOMMODATIONS. Visitors can call **Alaska Private Lodgings** (☎258-1717; open M-Sa 9am-6pm) for lodgings or the **Anchorage Reservation Service** (☎272-5909) for out-of-town B&Bs (from $70). Grab a copy of *Camping in the Anchorage Bowl* (free) at the Visitors Center for crowded in-town camping, or head to nearby **Chugach State Park** (☎354-5014).

Guests take pride in the elegant kitchen and common area at the ◪**Anchorage Guesthouse,** 2001 Hillcrest Dr., and gladly earn their keep with a chore. Take bus #3, 4, 6, 36, or 60 from downtown; get off at West High School, and go west on Hillcrest. (☎274-0408. Wash, dry $1.50 each. Bikes $2.50 per hr., $20 per day. $5 key deposit. Bunks $25. Private room $65.) Originally a commune, the ◪**Spenard Hostel,** 2845 W. 42nd Pl., still retains its original character without sacrificing cleanliness. From downtown, ride bus #7 to first stop past Gweenie's. On Spenard, turn west on Turnagain Blvd., then left onto 42nd Pl. (☎248-5036. Reception 9am-1pm and 7-11pm. Chore requested; free stay for 3hr. work. $15.) Though often more packed than your pack, the **International Backpackers Hostel,** 3601 Peterkin Ave. (☎274-3870), is centrally located. The Borealis shuttle travels to and from airport (15min.; $14 for 1, $17 for 2). Only a 15min. bike ride from downtown, this popular hostel rents two-wheelers for $10 per day. (☎274-3870. Towels $1, laundry $3. $10 key deposit. Dorms $15. Sites $10, $2 for each additional person.)

◪◪ FOOD AND NIGHTLIFE. ◪**Moose's Tooth,** 3300 Old Seward, serves pizza and brews as hearty as the climbers who tackle the nearby peak. Take bus #2 or 36. (☎258-2537. Open mic M 9-11pm. Open M-Th 11am-midnight, F-Sa noon-1am, Su noon-midnight.) ◪**Sweet Basil Cafe,** 335 E. St., is run by the black labrador retriever/CEO Buba, who keeps the owner/chef turning out tasty treats. (☎274-0070. Open M-F 7:30am-4pm, Sa 9am-4pm.) **Snow City Cafe,** 1034 W. 4th St., at L St., is art-bedecked and blessed by live music F-Sa. Their other claim to fame is the best breakfast in town. (☎272-2489. Open daily 7am-4pm, W-Su also 5-9pm; reduced hours in winter. Salads and big sandwiches $4-10.)

LET'S MUSH Charlie Darwin would have liked these odds: snow, wind, and frigid cold, separating the women from the girls. The celebrated **Iditarod** dog sled race begins in Anchorage on the first weekend in March. Dogs and their drivers ("mushers") traverse a 1150 mi. trail over two mountain ranges, along the mighty Yukon River, and over the frozen Norton Sound to Nome. The Iditarod Trail began as a dog sled supply route from Seward on the southern coast to interior mining towns. The race commemorates the 1925 rescue of Nome, when drivers ferried 300,000 units of life-saving diphtheria serum from Nenana, near Fairbanks, to Nome. Today, up to 70 contestants speed each year from Anchorage to Nome, competing for a $450,000 purse but surprisingly willing to help fellow mushers in distress. The fastest time was recorded by Doug Swingley—9 days, 2hr. You can visit the **Iditarod Headquarters** at Mile 2.2 Knik Rd. in Wasilla. (☎ 376-5155 or www.iditarod.com for more info.)

The brewpub revolution has hit Anchorage, and microbrews gush from taps like oil through the pipeline. Catch a flick with brew in hand at the **Bears Tooth**, 1230 W. 27th St. (Pints $3.75. $2 cover for movie.) At **Bernie's Bungalow Lounge**, 626 D St., relax in one of many wingback chairs as you sip your lemon drop martini ($5), puff on a cigar ($3-10), and play a round of croquet in a hot spot frequented by the young and retro. (☎ 276-8808. Open daily noon-2am; in winter 3pm-2am.) **Chilkoot Charlie's**, 2435 Spenard Rd., at Fireweek, has cavernous dance floors and rock music. "Koots" is the place to dance into the night; take bus #7. (☎ 272-1010. Cover $2-5. Open Su-Th 10:30am-2:15am, F-Sa 11am-2:45am. $1 drink specials until 10pm.)

◪◩ **SIGHTS AND OUTDOORS.** Near town off Northern Lights Blvd., **Earthquake Park** recalls the 1964 Good Friday quake, the strongest ever recorded in North America, registering 9.2 on the Richter scale. ▨**Cyrano's Off Center Playhouse**, at 413 D St., between 4th and 5th, contains a cafe, a bookshop, the stage of the **Eccentric Theatre Company**, and a cinema that screens foreign and art films. (☎ 274-2599 or 263-2787. Theater at 7pm; summer F-Tu, winter Th-Su. Tickets $15; students $10.) At the ▨**Anchorage Museum of History and Art**, 121 W. 7th Ave., at A St., permanent exhibits of Native Alaskan artifacts and art mingle with national and international works. (☎ 343-4326. Open Su-Th 9am-9pm; F-Sa 9am-6pm; Sept.-May Tu-Sa 9am-6pm, Su 1-5pm. Tours daily at 10, 11am, 1, and 2pm. $6.50, seniors $6, under 18 free.) At the **Alaska Zoo**, Mile 2 on O'Malley Rd., Binky the polar bear mauled an Australian tourist in 1994 and became a local hero. (☎ 346-3242. Open daily 9am-6pm. $7, seniors $6, ages 12-18 $5, 3-11 $3.)

The 13 mi. **Tony Knowles Coastal Trail** is arguably one of the best urban bike paths in the country; in the winter, it's groomed for cross-country skiing. The serene **Chugach State Park**, cornering the city to the north, east, and south, has 25 established day hiking trails. A 15min. drive from the city center, **Flattop Mountain** (4500 ft.) is the most frequently climbed mountain in Alaska, providing an excellent view of the inlet, the Aleutian Chain, and on the rare clear day, Denali. Parking at the trailhead costs $5, or take bus #92 to Hillside Rd. and Upper Huffman Rd. From there, the trailhead is a ¾ mi. walk along Upper Huffman Rd., then right on Toilsome Hill Dr. for 2 mi.; it's a 2 mi. hike to the summit. Less frequented hikes branch from the **Powerline Trail**, which begins at the same parking lot as the Flattop Trail. The **Eklutna Lakeside Biking Trail** extends 13 mi. one-way from the Eklutna Campground, off Mile 26 of the Glenn Hwy. (Rte. 1). A relatively flat dirt road, the trail follows the blue-green Eklutna Lake for 7 mi. before entering a steep river canyon, ending at the base of the Eklutna River. **Nancy Lake State Recreation Area**, just west of the Parks Hwy. (Rte. 3) at Mile 67.3, and just south of Willow, contains the **Lynx Lake Canoe Loop**, which takes two days and weaves through 8 mi. of lakes and portages, with designated campsites along the way. The loop begins at Mile 4½ of the Nancy Lake Parkway, at the Tanaina Lake Canoe Trailhead. For canoe rental or shuttle service in the Nancy Lake Area, call **Tippecanoe**. (☎ 495-6688. Canoes $25 per day, $70 per week. Shuttle free for backpackers.)

SEWARD AND KENAI FJORDS ☎907

Seward serves as a gateway to the waterways and yawning ice fields of **Kenai Fjords National Park. Exit Glacier,** the only road-accessible glacier in the park, lies 9 mi. west on a spur from Mile 3.7 of the Seward Hwy. (Rte. 9). A **shuttle** runs here four times daily from downtown Seward; parking for the day is $5. (☎224-5770. Round-trip $20.) Beyond this glacier, boat cruises are the easiest and most popular way to see the park. **Kenai Fjords Tours** are informative and amusing. (☎224-8068 or 800-478-8068. Tours last 6-9½hr. $109-139, children $54-70.) **Major Marine Tours** brings along a ranger to explain wildlife and glacier facts. (☎224-8030 or 800-764-7300. $109; with seafood dinner $121.) **Wildlife Quest** is the only outfit with speedy catamarans. (☎888-305-2515. 5½hr. $99, children $49.) **Sunny Cove Sea Kayaking** offers a joint trip with Kenai Fjords Tours, including the wildlife cruise, a salmon bake, kayaking instruction, and a 2½hr. wilderness paddle. (☎345-5339. 8hr. $139-159.)

▓**Kate's Roadhouse,** 5½ mi. outside town on the Seward Hwy., has huge continental breakfasts with home-baking, and a heated outhouse and a flush toilet. (☎224-5888. Free shuttle service, laundry, bedding, and towels. Shared baths. Clean dorms $17; private rooms $60.) **Moby Dick Hostel,** at 3rd Ave. between Jefferson and Madison St., has single-sex rooms and a view of Mt. Marathon. (☎224-7072. Showers and kitchen. Linen $2. Office open 9-11am and 5-10pm. $17; private room $45.) Camping is available at the **Municipal Waterfront Campground,** on Ballaine Rd. between Railway Ave. and D St. (Open mid-May to Sept. Sites $6; RV sites $10, with hookup $15.)

Seward is 127 mi. south of Anchorage on the scenic **Seward Hwy. (Rte. 9).** Most services and outdoor outfits cluster in the small boat harbor on Resurrection Bay. Across from the Visitors Center at the **Alaska Railroad** depot, trains leave for Anchorage at 6:45am in summer. (4½hr.; $55, ages 2-11 half-price.) **Katchemak Bay Transit** (☎235-3795) runs daily to Anchorage (3½hr., $35). The **Alaska Marine Hwy.** (☎224-5485 or 800-642-0066) docks at 4th Ave. and Railway St., with connections all over the state. The **Seward Chamber of Commerce** is at Mile 2 on the Seward Hwy. (☎224-8051. Open M-F 8am-6pm, Sa 9am-6pm, Su 9am-4pm.) **Kenai Fjords National Park Visitors Center** is at the small-boat harbor. (☎224-3175, info 224-2132. Open daily 8am-7pm; in winter M-F 8am-5pm.) **Post Office:** at 5th Ave. and Madison St. (☎224-3001; open M-F 9:30am-4:30pm, Sa 10am-2pm). **ZIP code:** 99664.

WRANGELL-ST. ELIAS NATIONAL PARK ☎907

Wrangell-St. Elias National Park is the largest national park in the US (13.2 million acres). Beyond towering peaks and extensive glaciers, Wrangell teems with wildlife. With only two rough roads that penetrate its interior, and almost no established trails, the park's inaccessibility keeps many tourists away. **Ranger stations** lurk exclusively outside the park boundaries in Copper Center, south of Glennallen (☎822-7261; open daily 8am-6pm); Yakutat in the east (☎784-3295; open daily 8am-5pm); Chitina in the west (☎823-2205; open daily 10am-6pm); and Slana on the park's northern boundary (☎822-5238; open daily 8am-5pm). They have the lowdown on all the must-knows and go-sees of the park and sell invaluable topographical maps (entire park $9; quadrants $4). **Backcountry Connection** (☎822-5292 or 800-478-5292) runs buses daily to McCarthy from Glennallen (4hr., $70) and Chitina (3hr., $55-80). **Charter flights** from McCarthy or Nabesna start at around $60.

One of the park's access routes is the scenic **Nabesna Rd.,** extending a harsh 46 mi. from the Richardson Hwy. (Rte. 4) into the park's northern portion. The turn-off for the road is at Slana, 65 mi. southwest of Tok on the Tok Cutoff. Nabesna, at the end of the 42 mi. road, is little more than a mining ghost town, home to the **End-of-the-Road Bed & Breakfast.** (☎822-5312. Bunks $20; singles $50; doubles $65.)

The more harrowing **McCarthy Rd.** plunges 60 mi. into the park from Chitina (*CHIT-nuh*) to the western edge of the Kennicott River, where travelers must cross a footbridge and walk ½ mi. into the town of McCarthy. Free parking is available another ½ mi. back before the river. Deep in the heart of the park, McCarthy and its sister town Kennicott are quiet today, but abandoned log-hewn

WHEN WWII CAME TO ALASKA On June 3rd, 1942, the Japanese began to bomb the Aleutian Islands and occupied Attu and Kiska in an attempt to divert American forces from the southern Pacific. The US responded by constructing the Alaska Hwy. and stationing nearly 60,000 soldiers on Unalaska. The remains of their occupation still mark the landscape—the last base is only now being gradually decommissioned. With as little as 24 hours notice, the US Army evacuated Aleut residents from many of the islands, ostensibly in the interest of safety, although Caucasians were allowed to remain. In the inhumane conditions of their exile, up to 25% of the displaced Aleuts perished. Roughly 70% returned to find their property destroyed by American soldiers, and whole villages were abandoned. This little-known and shameful piece of American history, was officially silenced until the passage of the Civil Liberties Act of 1988, when the Aleuts were offered an official apology and granted financial compensation.

buildings and forgotten roads bear witness to a boom town past. **Wrangell Mountain Air** flies to McCarthy twice daily from Chitina and farther afield by arrangement. (☎554-4411 or 800-478-1160. Round-trip $140.) A **shuttle** runs the 5 mi. road between the towns from 9am to 7:30pm (round-trip $10). McCarthy's cheapest beds, six-person cabins, and a cozy common room await a ¼ mi. before the river at the **Kennicott River Lodge and Hostel.** (☎554-4441, winter 479-6822. Rooms $25; cabins $85.) Camping is free at the lot ½ mi. back along the road toward Chitina (pit toilets, no water). The food in town is expensive due to the cost of delivery to this remote location; bring groceries with you. **The Potato,** next to McCarthy Air, serves spicy breakfast, a strong cup o' joe, and good tunes from 7:30am-4pm. Try the spudniks and gravy ($5).

This is the place for flightseeing in Alaska. Even a short flight to 16,390 ft. Mt. Blackburn and the surrounding glaciers offers soul-stunning views. **Wrangell Mountain Air** makes a 35min. tour of the amazing icefalls of the Kennicott and Root Glaciers. (☎554-4411 or 800-478-1160. $60.) The best bargain is a 70min. trip up the narrow Chitistone Canyon to view the thundering Chitistone Falls and on to a slew of glaciers and peaks ($105 per person; min. 2 people). **Copper Oar** runs a daylong whitewater rafting trip down the Class III Kennicott River with a flightseeing jaunt back from Chitina. (☎554-4453 or 800-523-4453. $245.) **St. Elias Alpine Guides** (☎554-4445 in McCarthy, 888-933-5427 in Anchorage) lead a variety of guided hikes and explorations. The park maintains no trails around McCarthy; consult with a ranger station before setting out. Ranger stations need a written itinerary for independent overnight trips.

DENALI NATIONAL PARK AND PRESERVE ☎907

Six million acres of snowcapped peaks, braided streams, and glacier-carved valleys, interrupted only by a lone gravel road, Denali National Park and Preserve is not a place made for humans; nevertheless, more than a million visitors invite themselves here year after year. And why not? Such untamed, beautiful wilderness is hard to find. Visitors to the park are the guests of grizzly bears, moose, caribou, wolves, Dall sheep, and wildflowers. Denali's 20,320 ft. centerpiece, known as Mt. McKinley by the US Geological Survey but known to everyone else as Denali, is the world's tallest mountain from base to peak. (Mt. Everest reaches a higher elevation but starts from the 11,000 ft. Plateau of Tibet.) Mid- to late August is the best time to visit—fall colors peak, berries ripen, mosquito season is virtually over, and September snows have yet to arrive.

▐ TRANSPORTATION. The **George Parks Hwy. (Rte. 3)** makes for smooth and easy traveling to the park entrance north from Anchorage or south from Fairbanks. Leading east away from the park, the gravel **Denali Hwy. (Rte. 8)** starts 27 mi. south of the park entrance at Cantwell and proceeds to Paxson (closed in winter). The **Alaska Railroad** stops regularly at Denali Station, 1½ mi. from the park entrance

(☎683-2233 or 800-544-0552; open daily 10am-5pm), and runs out to Fairbanks (4½hr.; $50) and Anchorage (8hr.; $125); reserve ahead. **Parks Hwy. Express** (☎888-600-6001) runs to the park from Anchorage (5hr., $42) and Fairbanks (3½hr., $27).

Only the first 14 mi. of the park road are accessible by private vehicle; the remaining 75 mi. of dirt road can be reached only by shuttle bus, camper bus, or bicycle. **Shuttle buses** leave from the Visitors Center daily 5am to 6pm, pause at the almost inevitable sighting of any major mammal ("MOOOOOSE!"), and turn back at various points along the park road, such as Toklat, Mile 53 ($17); Eielson, Mile 66 ($23); Wonder Lake, Mile 85 ($30); and Kantishna, Mile 89 ($33). Most buses are wheelchair accessible. **Camper buses** ($18.50) transport only those visitors with campground or backcountry permits and move faster than the shuttle buses. Unlike private vehicles, bikes *are* permitted on all park roads.

⑦ PRACTICAL INFORMATION. All travelers must stop at the **Denali Visitors Center,** ½ mi. from the Parks Hwy. (Rte. 3), for orientation. Park rangers collect the **entrance fee** ($5 per person, good for 7 days). Most park privileges are first come, first served; conduct all business at the Visitors Center as early in the day as possible. (☎683-2294. Open late Apr. to late mid-May daily 10am-4pm; late May to early Sept. 7am-8pm.) **Denali Outdoor Center,** at Parks Hwy. Mile 238.9, just north of the park entrance, rents bikes. (☎683-1925. Half-day $25; full-day $40.) **Healy Clinic** is 13 mi. north of the park entrance. (☎683-2211. Open M-F 9am-5pm; Oct.-Apr. M-F 10am-3pm. On call 24hr.) **Post Office:** 1 mi. from the Visitors Center. (☎683-2291. Open May-Sept. M-F 8:30am-5pm, Sa 10am-1pm; Oct.-Apr. M-Sa 10am-1pm.) **ZIP code:** 99755.

⑦☐ ACCOMMODATIONS AND FOOD. The **⊠Denali Mountain Morning Hostel,** 13 mi. south of the park entrance, has showers, groceries, **free park shuttles** (call for schedules), and outdoor gear rental (backpacker kit $30 first day, $7 additional days). Helpful owners offer outdoor advice. (☎683-7503. Bunks $22, ages 5-13 $17. Semi-private and private rooms start at $50. Reservations recommended. Sites $15.) **Campers** must obtain a permit from the Visitors Center and may stay for up to 14 nights in the park's seven campgrounds, which line the park road. (☎272-7275 or 800-622-7275 for advance reservations. First come, first served sites are distributed rapidly at the Visitors Center.) **Riley Creek,** the only campground open year-round, has the only dump station. Most campgrounds are wheelchair accessible.

Once you board that park bus, there is no food available anywhere. At **Black Bear Coffee House,** 1 mi. north of the park entrance, the coffee is hot and strong, the muffins are fresh, and the staff is all smiles. (☎683-1656. Open May-Sept. daily 7am-10pm. Veggie sandwich with hot cup of soup $7.) **Denali Smoke Shack,** north of the park entrance at Mile 238.5, serves real Alaskan barbecue and a large vegetarian menu. (☎683-7665. Open daily 7am-3am.)

⚑ FLIGHTSEEING. Oddly, the best place for flightseeing around Denali is actually in Talkeetna, 60 mi. to the south of the mountain. If the weather cooperates, these flights are worth every penny and will leave you itching for more. Flights come in two standard flavors: a one-hour flight approaching the Mountain from the south, and a 1½hr. tour that circumnavigates the peak. Landing on a remote glacier at the base of Denali ups the cost but is an available addition for almost all flights. One-hour trips cost $100-120 per person. The 15-30min. glacier stopoff (often at a climbing base camp) costs an additional $35-45 per person. All flights are weather-dependent, with most companies offering flights over the rugged Talkeetna Mountains to the south if Denali weather is uncooperative. Many companies, such as **Doug Geeting Aviation** (☎733-2366 or 800-770-2366) provide discounts to groups of four or five. **K2 Aviation** (☎733-2291 or 800-764-2291), **McKinley Air Service** (☎733-1765 or 800-564-1765), and **Talkeetna Air Taxi** (☎733-2218 or 800-533-2219) offer standard services, plus a variety of other specialized trips. All flight services suspend glacier landings in mid-July due to unpredictable snow conditions.

ALASKA

⚠ OUTDOOR ACTIVITIES. The best way to experience Denali is to get off the bus and explore the land. Beyond Mile 14, the point which only shuttle and camper buses can cross, there are no trails. You can begin day hiking from anywhere along the park road by riding the shuttle bus to a suitable starting point and asking the driver to let you off. It's rare to wait more than 30min. to flag a ride back. **Primrose Ridge,** beginning at Mile 16 on the right side of the road, is bespangled with wildflowers and has spectacular views of the Alaska Range and its carpeted emerald valley below. A walk north from Mile 14 along the **Savage River** provides a colorful, scenic stroll through this valley. The more challenging **Mt. Healy Overlook Trail** starts from the hotel parking lot and climbs to an impressive view at 3400 ft. (5 mi. round-trip; 1700 ft. elevation gain; 3-4hr.). **Discovery hikes** are guided 3-5hr. hikes, departing on special buses from the Visitors Center. Topics vary; a ranger might lead you on a cross-country scramble or a moose trail excursion. The hikes are free but require reservations and a bus ticket. More sedate 45min. **tundra walks** leave from Eielson Visitors Center daily at 1:30pm; guided talks are also posted at the Visitors Center.

There are no trails in the backcountry. While day hiking is unlimited and requires no permit, only 2-12 backpackers can camp at one time in each of the park's 43 units. Overnight stays in the backcountry require a **free permit,** available no earlier or later than one day in advance at the backcountry desk in the Visitors Center. The quota board there reports which units are still available. Type-A hikers line up outside as early as 6:30am to grab permits for popular units. Talk to rangers and research your choices with the handy *Backcountry Description Guides* and *The Backcountry Companion,* available at the Visitors Center bookstore, which also sells essential topographic maps ($4). All but two zones in Denali require that food be carried in **bear-resistant food containers (BRFC),** available for free at the backcountry desk. These are bulky things; be sure to leave space in your backpack. With the park's cool, often drizzly weather and its many rivers, streams, and pools, your feet will get wet. **Hypothermia** can set in quickly and quietly; talk with rangers about prevention and warning signs.

FAIRBANKS

☎907

Fairbanks stands unchallenged as North American civilization's northernmost hub—witness such landmarks as the "World's Northernmost Woolworth's," "World's Northernmost Denny's," and "World's Northernmost Southern Barbecue." From here, adventuresome travelers can drive, fly, or float to the Arctic Circle and into the tundra. Most make the long and arduous trip to Fairbanks only en route to other more exciting locales, although the town is now fostering reasons to linger.

⏿ PRACTICAL INFORMATION. Most tourist destinations lie within the square formed by **Airport Way, College Rd., Cushman Blvd.,** and **University Way.** The city center lies north of the intersection of Cushman and Airport Way. Fairbanks is a bicycle-friendly city, with wide shoulders, multi-use paths, and sidewalks. The **airport** is 5 mi. from downtown on Airport Way. **Alaska Railroad,** 280 N. Cushman St. (☎456-4155 or 800-544-0552; open M-F 7am-3pm, Sa-Su 7-11am), runs one train per day to Anchorage ($175) via Denali ($50); service is reduced during the winter. **Parks Hwy. Express** (☎479-3065 or 888-600-6001) runs daily to Denali (1 per day, $27); Anchorage (1 per day, $55); Glennallen (3 per week, $45); and Valdez (3 per week, $62). **Municipal Commuter Area Service (MACS),** at 5th and Cushman St., runs through downtown and its surroundings. (☎459-1011. Fare $1.50; students, seniors, and disabled 75¢; day pass $3. Service M-F 7am-8pm; limited on Sa, no service Su.) **Fairbanks Taxi,** ☎452-3535. **Visitor Info:** 550 1st Ave., at Cushman. (☎456-5774 or 800-327-5774. Open daily 8am-8pm; in winter M-F 9am-5pm.) **Alaska Public Lands Info Center (APLIC):** 250 Cushman St., #1A, at 3rd. St. in the basement of the Federal Bldg. (☎456-0527. Open daily 9am-6pm; in winter Tu-Sa 10am-6pm.) **Post Office:** 315 Barnette St. (☎452-3203; open M-F 9am-6pm, Sa 10am-2pm). **ZIP code:** 99707.

UM, HONEY IS IT...COLD IN HERE? Those few who can brave the harsh, cold Alaskan winter come not only for the intense skiing and snowboarding opportunities but also for the marital luck. Japanese tradition has it that good fortune will follow the couple whose marriage is consummated under the northern lights. The dead of winter thus finds Fairbanks deserted except for the locals and a few blushing Japanese newlyweds.

▮▯ ACCOMMODATIONS AND FOOD. Boyle's Hostel, 310 18th Ave., has TVs in every room and provides access to 2 kitchens. (☎456-4944. Showers and laundry. No curfew or lockout. Dorms $18; private double $25; outside cabins $15 per person. Monthly rates available.) **Billie's Backpackers Hostel,** 2895 Mack Rd., is a somewhat cluttered but welcoming place to meet many international travelers. Take Westwood Way one block off College to Mack Rd. (☎479-2034. Shower and kitchen in each room. Beds $20. Sites $15.) **Chena River State Campground,** off Airport Way on University Ave., is on a quiet stretch of the Chena River. (56 sites, $15.)

An artery-blocking good time fills Airport Way and College Rd. ▨**Bun on the Run,** located in a trailer in the parking lot between Beaver Sports and the Marlin on College Rd., across from the Campus Corner Mall, whips up the best pastries in Alaska. (Open M-F 7am-6pm, Sa 9am-4pm.) ▨**Gambardella's Pasta Bella,** 706 2nd Ave., turns out the "Mother of all Lasagnas" for $15 in true Italian ambience. (Open daily M-Sa 11am-10pm.) Grab a cup o' joe in the log cabin coffeehouse **Into the Woods,** 3560 College Rd. (open M-Tu 6pm-midnight, W-Su noon-midnight).

▨▰ SIGHTS AND OUTDOORS. The ▨**University of Alaska Museum,** a ten-minute walk up Yukon Dr. from the Wood Center, features a thorough look at the Aleut/Japanese evacuation during WWII, indigenous crafts, and Blue Babe, a 36,000 year-old steppe bison recovered from the permafrost. (☎474-7505. Open June-Aug. daily 9am-7pm; May and Sept. 9am-5pm; Oct.-Apr. M-F 9am-5pm, Sa-Su noon-5pm. $5, seniors $4.50, ages 7-17 $3.) Stand upwind of the **Large Animal Research Station,** which offers a rare chance to see baby musk oxen and other arctic animals up close. Take Farmer's Loop to Ballaine Rd. and turn left on Van Kovich; the farm is 1 mi. up on the right. (☎474-7207. Tours June-Aug. Tu, Th, and Sa at 11am and 1:30pm; Sept. Sa 1:30pm. $5, seniors $4, students $2.)

Moose Mountain, 20min. northeast of town, has over 20 downhill skiing trails. (☎479-8362. Lift tickets $25; college students, seniors, military, and ages 13-17 $20; ages 7-12 $15; over 70 or under 6 free. $5 off after 1pm or if the temperature is below 0°F.) Maps for multi-use trails are available at the Wood Center, in the UAF Activities Office. Cross-country skiing trails stripe the UAF campus. The **Chena River State Recreation Area** has a variety of multi-use trails. Maps are available at the Public Lands Information Center.

▨▯ NIGHTLIFE AND ENTERTAINMENT. ▨**Howling Dog Saloon,** 11½ mi. north on the Steese Hwy. (Rte. 6) toward Fox, at the intersection of the Old and New Steese Highways, is, as the manager says "rough, tough, and good-lookin'." Volleyball, pool, and horseshoe games go on until 4am or so. (☎457-8780. Live music W-Sa. Open May-Oct. Su-Th 4pm-2am, F-Sa 4pm-4am.) In mid-July, Fairbanks citizens don old-time duds and whoop it up for **Golden Days,** a celebration of Felix Pedro's 1902 discovery that sparked the Fairbanks gold rush. Although its relation to the actual gold rush days is questionable, the **rubber duckie race** is one of the biggest events. The Fairbanks Goldpanners play their annual **Midnight Sun Baseball Game** on the solstice itself (June 21, 2002). The game begins as the sun dips at 10:30pm, features a short pause near midnight for the celebration of the midnight sun, and ends at about 2am, in full daylight. For a true sports spectacular, see the **World Eskimo-Indian Olympics,** in mid to late July. Native Alaskans from all over the state compete for three days in traditional tests of strength and survival. Witness the ear pull, for which sinew is wrapped around the ears of contestants, who then tug to see who can endure the most pain. Be warned: *ears have been pulled off in this event.* (☎452-6646. Daily pass $6, season pass $20.)

ALASKA

SOUTHEAST ALASKA

Southeast Alaska sometimes goes by "the Panhandle" or "the southeast." It spans 500 miles from the basins of Misty Fiords National Monument to Skagway at the foot of the Chilkoot Trail. The waterways weaving through the Panhandle, collectively known as the Inside Passage, make up an enormous saltwater soup spiced with islands, inlets, fjords, and the ferries that flit among them. The absence of roads in the steep coastal mountains has helped Panhandle towns maintain their small size and hospitable personalities. The **Alaska Marine Hwy.** system (see p. 942) provides the cheapest, most exciting way to explore the Inside Passage.

KETCHIKAN   ☎907

Ketchikan is the first stop in Alaska for cruise ships and would-be cannery workers. An average of nearly 12½ feet of rainfall a year can not deter visitors' delight in the fabulous proximity to Tongass National Forest (one-third of which lies in the Ketchikan area) and the Misty Fiords National Monument. A revamped "historical district" is dressed for the tourists who support the newest growth industry, but parts of Ketchikan remain economically depressed. The adjustment to a tourism-based economy has not been easy for many residents, who would prefer to turn back the clock to when fishing and logging were the only shows in town.

◪ PRACTICAL INFORMATION. Ketchikan rests on **Revillagigedo Island** (*ruh-VIL-ya-GIG-a-doe*). Upon reaching Ketchikan from Canada, roll back your watch an hour to get in step with Alaska Time. The town caters to the elite, and its attractions are extremely spread out, making bike rental a wise decision. A small **ferry** runs from the airport, across from Ketchikan on Gravina Island, to just north of the state ferry dock (every 30min.; $2.50). **Alaska Airlines** (☎800-225-2752) makes daily flights to Juneau. **Alaska Marine Hwy.** (☎225-6181 or 800-642-0066) sends wheelchair-accessible boats from the far end of town on N. Tongass Hwy. to: Wrangell ($24); Juneau ($74); and Sitka ($54). The main bus route runs a loop between the airport parking lot near the ferry terminal at one end, and Dock and Main St. downtown at the other. (Runs every 30min. M-F 5:15am-9:45pm; 1 per hr. Sa 6:45am-8:45pm, Su 8:45am-3:45pm. $1, students, seniors, and children 75¢.) Taxi: **Sourdough Cab,** ☎225-5544. **Ketchikan Visitors Bureau:** 131 Front St., on the cruise ship docks downtown. (☎225-6166 or 800-770-3300. Open daily 8am-5pm.) **Southeast Alaska Discovery Center (SEADC),** 50 Main St., provides trip-planning service, plus info on public lands around Ketchikan, including Tongass and Misty Fiords. (☎228-6220. Open May-Sept. daily 8am-5pm; Oct.-April Tu-Sa 8:30am-4:30pm.) **Post Office:** 3609 Tongass Ave., by the ferry terminal (☎225-9601; open M-F 8:30am-5pm). **ZIP code:** 99901.

◪◪ ACCOMMODATIONS AND FOOD. The **Ketchikan Reservation Service** provides info on B&Bs. (☎800-987-5337; fax 247-5337. Singles from $69.) Because of boardwalk stairs, these accommodations aren't wheelchair accessible. The **Ketchikan Youth Hostel (HI-AYH)** is at Main and Grant St. in the First Methodist Church. The social scene is skimpy since the doors close at 11pm sharp. Bring a sleeping bag for the foam mats. (☎225-3319. Common area, showers, kitchen, and free tea and popcorn every night. 4-night max. stay when full. Lockout 9am-6pm. Call ahead if arriving on a late ferry. Make reservations. Open June-Aug. $10, nonmembers $13.) **Eagle View Bed & Breakfast and Backpacker Bunks,** 2303 5th Ave., is reached via Jefferson Ave. uphill from Tongass, turn right on 5th Ave. Not as cheap as the hostel, but the B&B has free use of a kitchen, TV, sauna, BBQ, and hammocks. (☎225-5461. Laundry $3 per load. $25 per person.)

Campgrounds usually have stay limits of a week or two and are really out of the way. **Signal Creek** sits on Ward Lake Rd. Drive north on Tongass Ave. and turn right at the sign for Ward Lake, approximately 5 mi. from the ferry terminal. (Open May-Sept. Water, pit toilets. $10.) Anyone can camp for up to 30 days in **Tongass National Forest,** but may not return for six months after that time. Any clearing is free.

The freshest seafood swims in **Ketchikan Creek**; in summer, anglers frequently hook king salmon from the docks by Stedman St. ◙**Ocean View Restaurante**, 1831 Tongass Ave., serves up enchiladas and pizza with equal gusto. The fried ice cream is a winner for dessert. (☎225-7566. Open daily 11am-11pm.) **New York Cafe**, 207 Stedman St., is at the south end of Creek St. Come for the incredible soup and healthy lunch specials in this comfortable place perfect for relaxing in between seeing sights. (☎225-1800. Open M-F 6am-10pm, Sa-Su 6am-11pm.)

◙◙ SIGHTS AND NIGHTLIFE. Ketchikan's primary cultural attraction is the **Saxman Totem Park**, the largest totem park in Alaska, 2½ mi. southwest of town on Tongass Hwy. ($10 by cab, or a short ride on the Hwy. bike path). The **Totem Heritage Center**, up Park St. on the hill above downtown, houses 33 well-preserved totem poles from Tlingit, Haida, and Tsimshian villages. It is the largest collection of authentic, pre-commercial totem poles in the US, but only a few are on display. (Open May-Sept. daily 8am-5pm, Oct.-Apr. Tu-F 1-5pm. $4.) A $10 combination ticket also provides admission to the **Deer Mountain Fish Hatchery and Raptor Center**, across the creek. (☎225-6761. Open May-Sept. daily 8am-4:30pm.)

First City Saloon, ¼ mi. north of the tunnel on Water St., is the most spacious hangout in town and liberally distributes Guinness and a variety of microbrews. (☎225-1494. Live local music Tu-Su. Open daily noon-2am.) **Ketchikan Brew Pub**, 602 Dock St., has the only beer brewed in town. With true local flavor, the owner Kevin hand-picks Sitka Spruce tips grown in Ketchikan, and steeps them in Spruce Tip Beer. If you bring any bottle that seals, they'll fill it for your beer-to-go. (☎247-5221. Open M-Sa 10am-2am, Su 12:30pm-2am.) **Arctic Bar**, 509 Walter St., is a hop, skip, and stagger north of the downtown tunnel. Distinguished by their copulating bears logo, this is one of Ketchikan's most popular bars because of its deck with harbor view. (☎225-4709. Open daily until 2am.)

▨ OUTDOOR ACTIVITIES. From Ketchikan, a trail up the 3001 ft. **Deer Mountain** makes a good dayhike. Walk up the hill past the city park on Fair St.; the marked trailhead branches off to the left just behind the dump. The ascent is steep but manageable, and on a rare clear day the walk yields sparkling views of the sea and surrounding islands. While most hikers stop at the 2½ mi. point, the trail continues above the treeline to the summit along an 8 mi. route that passes Blue Lake and leads over John Mountain to Little Silvis Lake and the Beaver Falls Fish Hatchery. This portion of the trail is poorly marked, and snow and ice are common on the peaks even in the summer; only experienced and well-prepared hikers should attempt it. An A-frame cabin between Deer Mountain and John Mountain can be reserved through the Forest Service desk at SEADC (see p. 950). The trail emerges 12 mi. south of Ketchikan at the Beaver Falls power station parking lot. For swimming, a sandy beach, and picnic tables, head to **Ward Lake** at the Signal Creek Campground. A 1¼ mi. trail circles the grassy pond. Bikers can explore surrounding logging roads.

NEAR KETCHIKAN: MISTY FIORDS NATIONAL MONUMENT

The jagged peaks, plunging valleys, and dripping vegetation of **Misty Fiords National Monument**, 20 mi. east of Ketchikan, make biologists dream and outdoors enthusiasts drool. Only accessible by kayak, boat, or float plane, the 2.3 million-acre park offers superlative camping, kayaking, hiking, and wildlife-viewing. **Camping** is permitted throughout the park, and the Forest Service maintains four first come, first served shelters (free) and 14 cabins ($25). Contact the **Misty Fiords Ranger Station**, 3031 Tongass Ave., Ketchikan (☎225-2148), and ask ahead at the SEADC (see p. 950) for great advice. Kayaking neophytes might contact **Alaska Cruises**, 220 Front St.; they'll drop off at the head of Rudyard Bay. (☎225-6044. $200 per person.)

ALASKA

JUNEAU

☎907

Alaska's state capital has an air of modernity and progressiveness usually not found in the rural fishing villages of Southeast Alaska. Accessible only by water and air, Juneau is the 2nd-busiest cruise ship port in the US, after Miami. Hordes of travelers come to Juneau for the Mendenhall Glacier, numerous hiking trails, and close access to Glacier Bay. Be prepared to share the beauty.

◪ PRACTICAL INFORMATION. Franklin St. is the main drag downtown. **Glacier Hwy.** connects downtown, the airport, the residential area of the Mendenhall Valley, and the ferry terminal. The ferry and airport are both annoyingly far from the glacier and downtown. **Juneau International Airport,** 9 mi. north of Juneau on Glacier Hwy., is served by **Alaska Airlines** (☎789-0600 or 800-426-0333). **Capital Transit** runs buses from downtown to the airport and Mendenhall Glacier, with express service downtown every hr. The closest stop to the ferry is across from DeHart's General Store. (☎789-6901. Office open M-F 8:10am-5:10pm. Runs M-Sa 7am-10:30pm, Su 9am-6:30pm. Fare $1.25; exact change required.) **MGT Ferry Express** (☎789-5460) meets all ferries and runs to downtown hotels or to the airport ($5). **Alaska Marine Hwy.,** 1591 Glacier Ave. (☎465-3941 or 800-642-0066), docks at the Auke Bay terminal, 14 mi. from the city on the Glacier Hwy., and runs to Ketchikan (18-36hr., $74); Sitka (9hr., $26); and Bellingham, WA ($226). **Taku Cab** (☎586-2121) runs to the glacier ($15), the ferry ($20), and the airport ($15). **Visitors Center,** 101 Egan Dr. in Centennial Hall (☎586-2201 or 888-581-2201; www.traveljuneau.com. Open June-Sept. daily 9am-5pm; Oct.-May M-F only). **Foggy Mountain Shop** (see below) gives more genuine advice. For trail conditions, call the **trail hotline** (☎856-5330). **Alaska Dept. of Fish and Game,** 1255 W. 8th St. (☎465-4112; licensing 465-2376), close to the bridge, serves your outdoor needs. (Open M-F 8am-5pm.) **Internet access: Library,** sits over parking garage at confluence of Marine Way and S Franklin St. **Post Office:** 127 Franklin St. (Open M-F 8:30am-4:30pm, Sa-Su 9am-2pm.) **ZIP code:** 99801.

▥◫ ACCOMMODATIONS AND FOOD. The **Alaska B&B Association** can help find a room downtown (www.accommodations-alaska.com; from $65). On a steep hill, lovely ◪**Juneau International Hostel (HI-AYH),** 614 Harris St., at 6th St., enforces strict rules in a prime location. (☎586-9559. 48 beds. Wash $1.25, dry 75¢. 3-night maximum stay if they're full. Lockout 9am-5pm and midnight curfew. $7, nonmembers $10. $10 deposit mailed in advance secures a phone reservation.) **Alaskan Hotel,** 167 Franklin St., downtown, has been meticulously restored to its original 1913 decor. (☎586-1000 or 800-327-9347. Kitchenettes and TVs. Laundry for guests. Rooms $60-80; rates lower in winter.) **Mendenhall Lake Campground** is about 6 mi. from the ferry terminal on Montana Creek Rd.; take Glacier Hwy. north 10 mi. to Mendenhall Loop Rd., continue 3½ mi., and take the right fork. Bus drivers will stop within 2 mi. of camp. The 60 sites have stunning views of the glacier and convenient trails to go even closer. (Open June-Sept. Reception 7am-10:30pm. Firepits, water, flush toilets, showers, firewood. No reservations. Sites $10, with hookup $20.)

Silverbow Bagels, 120 2nd. St., is the oldest operating bakery in Alaska, and the years of experience shine through in the quality of their food. (☎586-9866. Open M-F 7am-5:30pm, Sa 8am-4:30pm, Su 9am-3:30pm. Movies Tu, Th, and Sa night. **Back Room** (in the back) restaurant open for dinner.) **Armadillo Tex-Mex Cafe,** 431 S. Franklin St., shelters locals from the cruise ship district with fast, saucy service and hot, spicy food. (☎586-1880. Open M-Sa 11am-10pm, Su noon-9pm. Huge entrees $9-14.)

◪▨ SIGHTS AND OUTDOORS. The excellent **Alaska State Museum,** 395 Whittier St., leads through the history and culture of Alaska's four major native groups: Tlingit, Athabascan, Aleut, and Inuit. (☎465-2901. Open mid-May to mid-Sept. daily 8:30am-5:30pm; mid-Sept. to mid-May Tu-Sa 10am-4pm. $3, under 18 free.) The hexagonal and onion-domed 1894 **St. Nicholas Russian Orthodox Church,** on 5th St. between N. Franklin and Gold St., holds rows of icons and a glorious altar. Services, held Sa at 6pm and Su at 10am, are conducted in English, Old Slavonic, and Tlingit. (Open in summer daily 9am-5pm. $1 donation requested.)

The **West Glacier Trail** begins off Montana Creek Rd., by the Mendenhall Lake Campground. The five- to six-hour walk yields stunning views of **Mendenhall Glacier** from the first step to the final outlook. The 3½ mi. trail parallels the glacier through the western hemlock forest and up a rocky cairn-marked scramble to the summit of 4226 ft. **Mt. McGinnis.** At the end of Basin Rd., the easy **Perseverance Trail** leads to the ruins of the Silverbowl Basin Mine and booming waterfalls. The **Granite Creek Trail** branches off the Perseverance Trail and follows its namesake to a beautiful basin, 3¾ mi. from the trailhead. The summit of Mt. Juncau lies 3 mi. farther along the ridge and, again, offers terrific views. The shorter, steeper **Mt. Juneau Trail,** which departs from Perseverance Trail about 1 mi. from the trailhead, opens up to similar vistas. Many trails are well-maintained and excellent for mountain biking. Biking off-road is sometimes prohibited.

Tracy Arm, a mini-fjord near Juneau, is known as "the poor man's Glacier Bay," for it offers the same spectacular beauty and wildlife as the national park at well under half the cost. **Auk Nu Tours,** 76 Egan Dr., is the biggest tour company. (☎800-820-2628. 8hr. $110. Lunch included.) **Juneau Outdoor Center** (☎586-8220), on Douglas Island, and **Alaska Paddle Sports,** 800 6th St. (☎463-5678), provide rental kayaks, pickups and dropoffs in Glacier Bay and elsewhere, and **guided kayak tours** in about the same price range as the tour boats. In winter, the **Eaglecrest Ski Area,** on Douglas Island, offers decent alpine skiing. (☎586-5284. $25 per day, ages 12-17 $17, under 12 $12; ski rental $20/$14/$14.) The Eaglecrest **ski bus** departs from the Baranov Hotel at 8:30am and returns from the slopes at 5pm on winter weekends and holidays. (Round-trip $6.)

GLACIER BAY NATIONAL PARK   ☎907

Glacier Bay was once referred to by explorer Jean François de Galaup de la Perouse as "perhaps the most extraordinary place in the world." Crystal monoliths, broken off from glaciers, float peacefully in fjords, while humpback whales maneuver through the maze of the icy blue depths. Glacier Bay National Park encloses nine tidewater glaciers, as well as the **Fairweather Mountains,** the highest coastal range in the world. Charter flights, tours, and cruise ships all probe Glacier Bay, providing close encounters with glaciers, rookeries, whales, and seals. The bay itself is divided into two inlets: the westward **Tarr Inlet** advances as far as the Grand Pacific and Margerie Glaciers, while the eastward **Muir Inlet** ends at the Muir and Riggs Glaciers.

Glacier Bay provides a rare opportunity to see geological and ecological processes radically compressed. A mere two centuries ago, the **Grand Pacific Glacier** covered the entire region under a sheet of ancient ice. Severe earthquakes separated the glacier from its terminal moraine (the silt and debris that insulates advancing ice from the relatively warm surrounding seawater), and the glacier retreated 45 mi. in 150 years—light speed in glacial time. As a result, the uncovered ground is virgin territory, colonized by pioneering vegetation.

Getting to Bartlett Cove, the principal access point to the bay, is relatively easy: a plane or ferry takes visitors to Gustavus, and from there a taxi or shuttle (about $12) goes to **Glacier Bay Lodge** (☎697-2225 or 800-451-5952) and the Visitors Center, both steps from the cove. The few ways to see the glaciers are expensive. Sightseers take one of a range of packages on a sightseeing cruise boat; backcountry travelers are dropped off by the same ship for their trips. Visitors should contact the **Superintendent** P.O. Box 140, Gustavus 99826 (☎907-697-2230), for assistance in planning a backcountry trip. Glacier Bay is becoming *the* destination for extended kayak trips in the region. The only food available at Bartlett Cove is at the rather expensive lodge dining room; most trippers bring provisions with them.

Wilderness camping and hiking are permitted throughout the park, though there are no trails except the two near the lodge, and hiking is very difficult in most of the park because of thick alder brush. Backcountry hiking and kayaking are possible in the Dry Bay area (the northwest corner of the park), as is rafting down the Alsek River. For info on these activities contact the **Yakutat District Office of the National Park Service,** P.O. Box 137, Yakutat 99689 (☎784-3295).

ALASKA

DISTANCES (MI.) AND TRAVEL TIMES (BY BUS)

	Atlanta	Boston	Chic.	Dallas	D.C.	Denver	L.A.	Miami	N. Orl.	NYC	Phila.	Phnx.	St. Lou.	Sa. Fran.	Seattle	Trnto.	Vanc.	Mont.
Atlanta		1108	717	783	632	1406	2366	653	474	886	778	1863	560	2492	2699	959	2825	1240
Boston	22hr.		996	1794	442	1990	3017	1533	1542	194	333	2697	1190	3111	3105	555	3242	326
Chicago	14hr.	20hr.		937	715	1023	2047	1237	928	807	767	1791	302	2145	2108	537	2245	537
Dallas	15hr.	35hr.	18hr.		1326	794	1450	1322	507	1576	1459	906	629	1740	2112	1457	2255	1763
D.C.	12hr.	8hr.	14hr.	24hr.		1700	2689	1043	1085	225	139	2350	845	2840	2788	526	3292	665
Denver	27hr.	38hr.	20hr.	15hr.	29hr.		1026	2046	1341	1785	1759	790	860	1267	1313	1508	1458	1864
L.A.	45hr.	57hr.	39hr.	28hr.	55hr.	20hr.		2780	2005	2787	2723	371	1837	384	1141	2404	1285	2888
Miami	13hr.	30hr.	24hr.	26hr.	20hr.	39hr.	53hr.		856	1346	1214	2368	1197	3086	3368	1564	3505	1676
New O.	9hr.	31hr.	18hr.	10hr.	21hr.	26hr.	38hr.	17hr.		1332	1247	1535	677	2331	2639	1320	2561	1654
NYC	18hr.	4hr.	16hr.	31hr.	5hr.	35hr.	53hr.	26hr.	27hr.		104	2592	999	2923	2912	496	3085	386
Phila.	18hr.	6hr.	16hr.	19hr.	3hr.	33hr.	50hr.	23hr.	23hr.	2hr.		2511	904	2883	2872	503	3009	465
Phoenix	40hr.	49hr.	39hr.	19hr.	43hr.	17hr.	8hr.	47hr.	30hr.	45hr.	44hr.		1503	753	1510	2069	1654	2638
St. Louis	11hr.	23hr.	6hr.	13hr.	15hr.	17hr.	35hr.	23hr.	13hr.	19hr.	16hr.	32hr.		2113	2139	810	2276	1128
San Fran.	47hr.	60hr.	41hr.	47hr.	60hr.	33hr.	7hr.	59hr.	43hr.	56hr.	54hr.	15hr.	45hr.		807	2630	951	2985
Seattle	52hr.	59hr.	40hr.	40hr.	54hr.	25hr.	22hr.	65hr.	50hr.	55hr.	54hr.	28hr.	36hr.	16hr.		2623	146	2964
Toronto	21hr.	11hr.	10hr.	26hr.	11hr.	26hr.	48hr.	29hr.	13hr.	11hr.	13hr.	48hr.	14hr.	49hr.	48hr.		4563	655
Vancvr.	54hr.	61hr.	42hr.	43hr.	60hr.	27hr.	24hr.	67hr.	54hr.	57hr.	56hr.	30hr.	38hr.	18hr.	2hr.	53hr.		4861
Montreal	23hr.	6hr.	17hr.	28hr.	12hr.	39hr.	53hr.	32hr.	31hr.	7hr.	9hr.	53hr.	23hr.	56hr.	55hr.	7hr.	55hr.	

ABOUT LET'S GO

FORTY-TWO YEARS OF WISDOM

For over four decades, travelers crisscrossing the continents have relied on *Let's Go* for inside information on the hippest backstreet cafes, the most pristine secluded beaches, and the best routes from border to border. *Let's Go: Europe*, now in its 42nd edition and translated into seven languages, reigns as the world's bestselling international travel guide. In the last 20 years, our rugged researchers have stretched the frontiers of backpacking and expanded our coverage into the Americas, Australia, Asia, and Africa (including the new *Let's Go: Egypt* and the more comprehensive, multi-country jaunt through *Let's Go: South Africa & Southern Africa*). Our new-and-improved City Guide series continues to grow with new guides to perennial European favorites Amsterdam and Barcelona. This year we are also unveiling *Let's Go: Southwest USA*, the flagship of our new outdoor Adventure Guide series, which is complete with special roadtripping tips and itineraries, more coverage of adventure activities like hiking and mountain biking, and first-person accounts of life on the road.

It all started in 1960 when a handful of well-traveled students at Harvard University handed out a 20-page mimeographed pamphlet offering a collection of their tips on budget travel to passengers on student charter flights to Europe. The following year, in response to the instant popularity of the first volume, students traveling to Europe researched the first full-fledged edition of *Let's Go: Europe*. Throughout the 60s and 70s, our guides reflected the times—in 1969, for example, we taught you how to get from Paris to Prague on "no dollars a day" by singing in the street. In the 90s we focused in on the world's most exciting urban areas to produce in-depth, fold-out map guides, now with 20 titles (from Hong Kong to Chicago) and counting. Our new guides bring the total number of titles to 57, each infused with the spirit of adventure and voice of opinion that travelers around the world have come to count on. But some things never change: our guides are still researched, written, and produced entirely by students who know first-hand how to see the world on the cheap.

HOW WE DO IT

Each guide is completely revised and thoroughly updated every year by a well-traveled set of nearly 300 students. Every spring, we recruit over 200 researchers and 90 editors to overhaul every book. After several months of training, researcher-writers hit the road for seven weeks of exploration, from Anchorage to Adelaide, Estonia to El Salvador, Iceland to Indonesia. Hired for their rare combination of budget travel sense, writing ability, stamina, and courage, these adventurous travelers know that train strikes, stolen luggage, food poisoning, and marriage proposals are all part of a day's work. Back at our offices, editors work from spring to fall, massaging copy written on Himalayan bus rides into witty, informative prose. A student staff of typesetters, cartographers, publicists, and managers keeps our lively team together. In September, the collected efforts of the summer are delivered to our printer, who turns them into books in record time, so that you have the most up-to-date information available for your vacation. Even as you read this, work on next year's editions is well underway.

WHY WE DO IT

We don't think of budget travel as the last recourse of the destitute; we believe that it's the only way to travel. Our books will ease your anxieties and answer your questions about the basics—so you can get off the beaten track and explore. Once you learn the ropes, we encourage you to put *Let's Go* down and strike out on your own. You know as well as we that the best discoveries are often those you make yourself. When you find something worth sharing, please drop us a line. We're Let's Go Publications, 67 Mount Auburn St., Cambridge, MA 02138, USA (feedback@letsgo.com). For more info, visit our website, www.letsgo.com.

INDEX

A

Acadia National Park, ME 97

Acadiana, LA 424

accommodations 48

The Adirondacks, NY 249

adventure trips 61

AIDS 46

Alabama 396–403

Birmingham 399

Huntsville 402

Mobile 402

Montgomery 397

Moundville 401

Selma 399

Tuskegee 399

Alaska 941–953

Anchorage 942

Denali National Park and Preserve 946

Fairbanks 948

Glacier Bay National Park 953

Juneau 952

Kenai Fjords National Park 945

Ketchikan 950

Misty Fiords National Monument 951

Seward 945

Tongass National Forest 950

Wrangell-St. Elias National Park 945

Albany, NY 240

Alberta 934–940

Alberta Badlands 940

Banff National Park 934

Calgary 939

Jasper National Park 937

Waterton Lakes National Park 649

Alberta Badlands, AB 940

Albuquerque, NM 771

alcohol 43

Alexandria, VA 305

alternatives to tourism 87

Amarillo, TX 622

American Express 39, 40

American University, see Washington, D.C.

Amherst, MA 144

Amtrak 75

Anaheim, CA, see Orange County, CA

Anchorage, AK 942

Ann Arbor, MI 491

Annapolis, MD 285

Apostle Islands, WI 531

Appalachian State University, see Boone, NC

Appalachian Trail 99, 102, 322, 324, 327, 350, 351

Arapahoe/Roosevelt National Forest, CO 683

Arches National Park, UT 722

architecture 24

Arco, ID 635

Arizona 731–763

Biosphere 2 761

Bisbee 762

Canyon de Chelly National Monument 746

Chiricahua National Monument 763

Coconino National Forest 740

Coronado National Forest 760

Flagstaff 738

Grand Canyon 732

Havasupai Reservation 737

Hopi Reservation 747

Kaibab National Forest 734

Lake Powell 749

Montezuma Castle National Monument 743

Monument Valley 747

Navajo National Monument 747

Navajo Reservation 744

Page 749

Painted Desert 748

Petrified Forest National Park 748

Phoenix 750

Sabino Canyon 760

Saguaro National Park 759

Sedona 742

Sunset Crater Volcano National Monument 742

Tombstone 761

Tonto National Forest 755

Tonto National Monument 755

Tucson 756

Tuzigoot National Monument 744

Walnut Canyon National Monument 742

Window Rock 745

Wupatki National Monument 742

Arkansas 427–431

Helena 359

Hot Springs 429

Hot Springs National Park 429

Little Rock 427

Ouachita National Forest 430

Ozark National Forest 431

Arlington, VA 304

art 23

Asheville, NC 365

Ashland, OR 914

Aspen, CO 690

Assateague Island, VA 288

Astoria, OR 909

Athens, GA 391

Atlanta, GA 380

Atlantic City, NJ 254

ATM cards 40

Austin, TX 602

auto racing

Daytona Beach, FL 437

Indianapolis, IN 483

auto transport companies 82

automobile clubs 80

Avenue of the Giants, CA 860

D

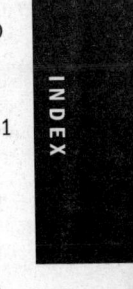

INDEX

MAPS

Will you have enough stories to tell your grandchildren?

CHOOSE YOUR DESTINATION SWEEPSTAKES

No Purchase Necessary.

**Explore the world with Let's Go® and StudentUniverse!
Enter for a chance to win a trip for two to a Let's Go destination!**
Separate Drawings! May & October 2002.

GRAND PRIZES:
Roundtrip StudentUniverse Tickets

✓ Select one destination and mail your entry to:

☐ Costa Rica
☐ London
☐ Hong Kong
☐ San Francisco
☐ New York
☐ Amsterdam
☐ Prague
☐ Sydney

* Plus Additional Prizes!!

Choose Your Destination Sweepstakes
St. Martin's Press
Suite 1600, Department MF
175 Fifth Avenue
New York, NY 10010-7848

Restrictions apply; see offical rules for
details by visiting Let'sGo.com or sending SASE
(VT residents may omit return postage) to the address above.

Name: _____

Address: _____

City/State/Zip: _____

Phone: _____

Email: _____

Grand prizes provided by:

 StudentUniverse.com   Real Travel Deals

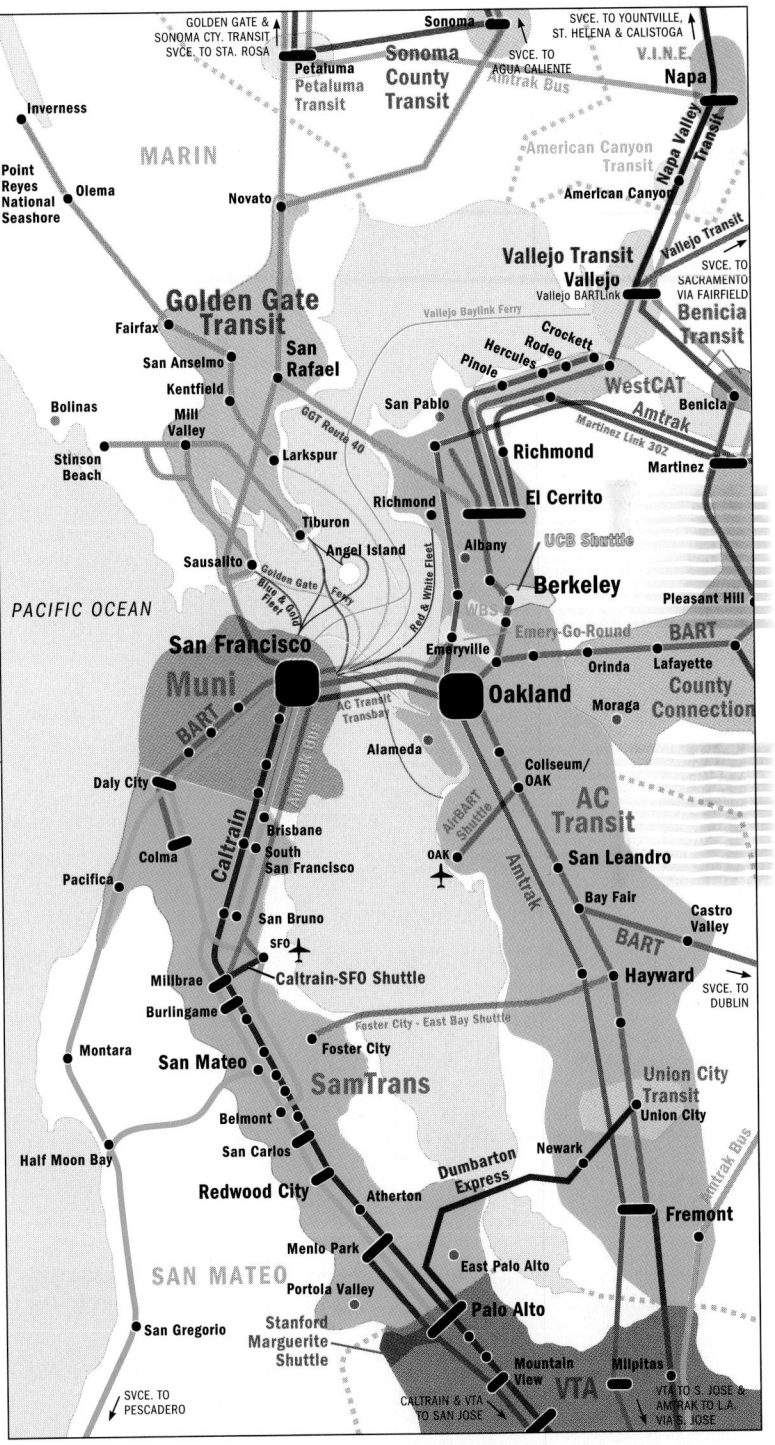

San Francisco

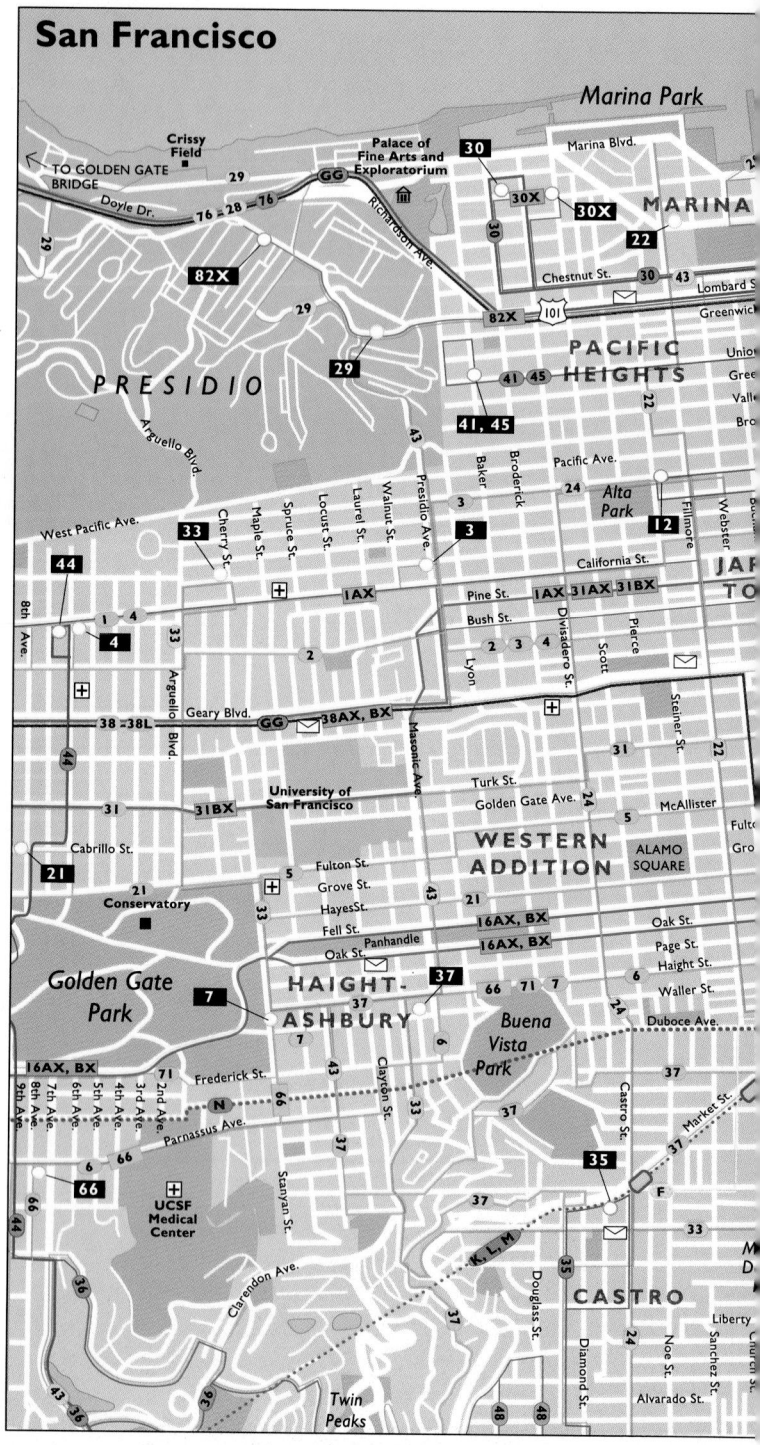

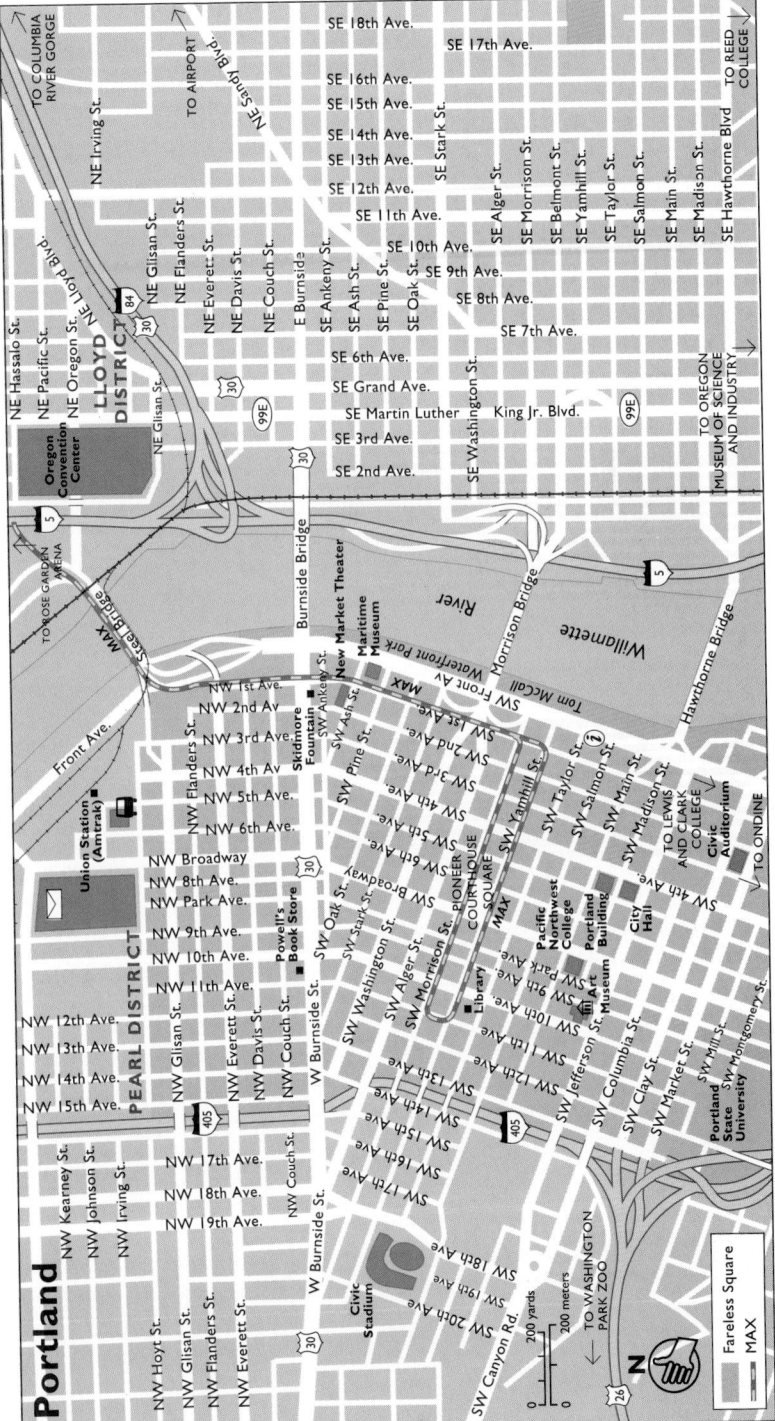

Seattle

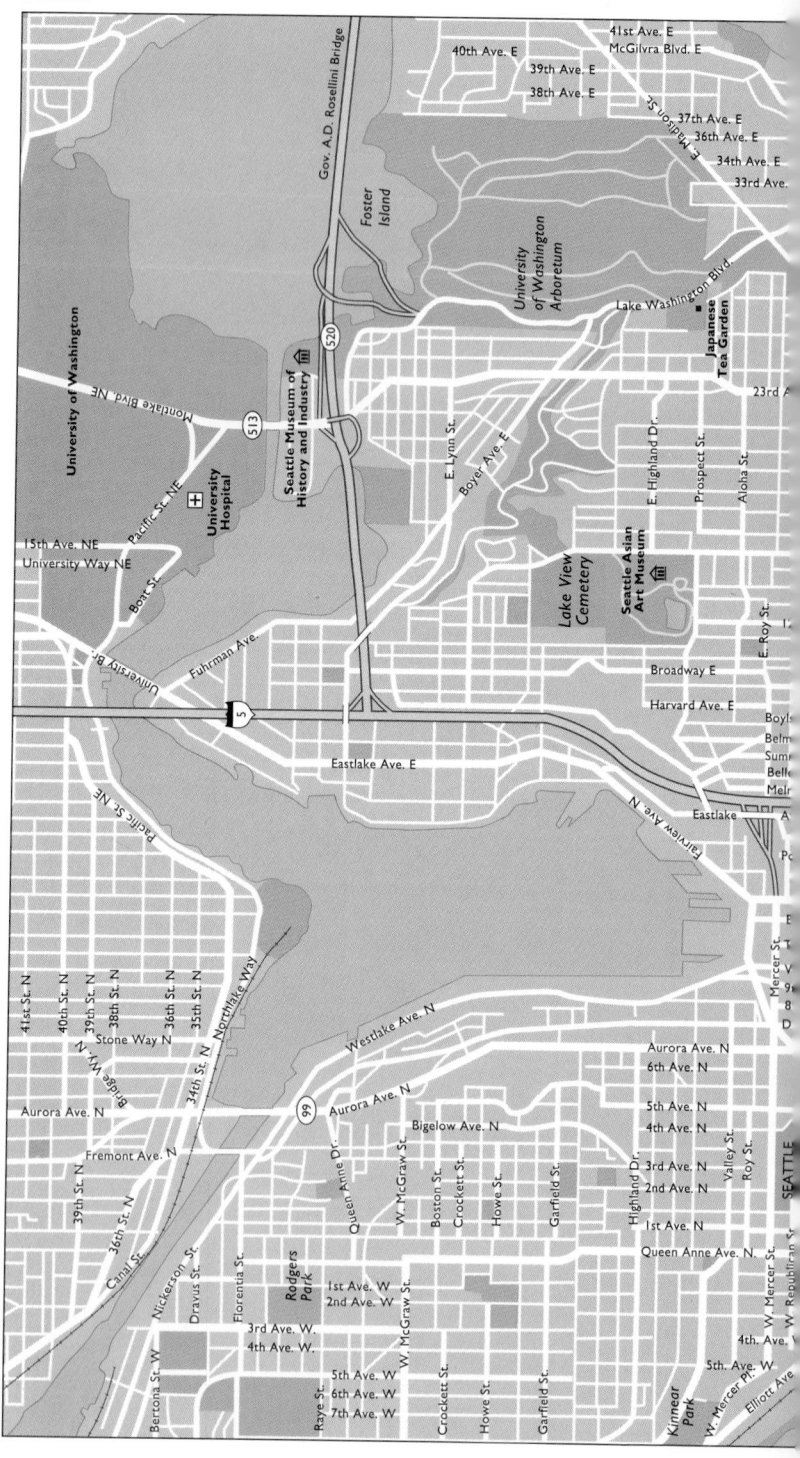

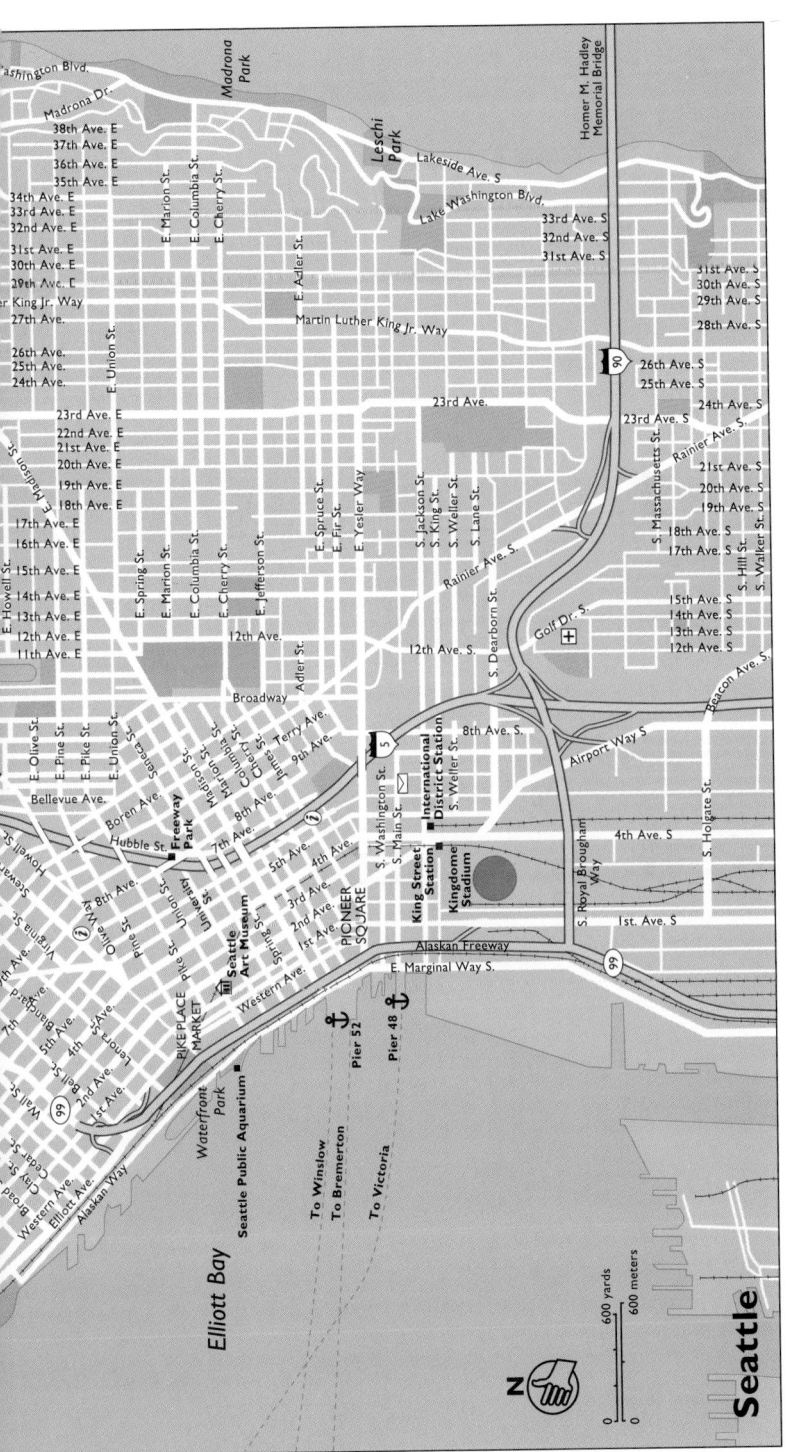

Seattle

Vancouver

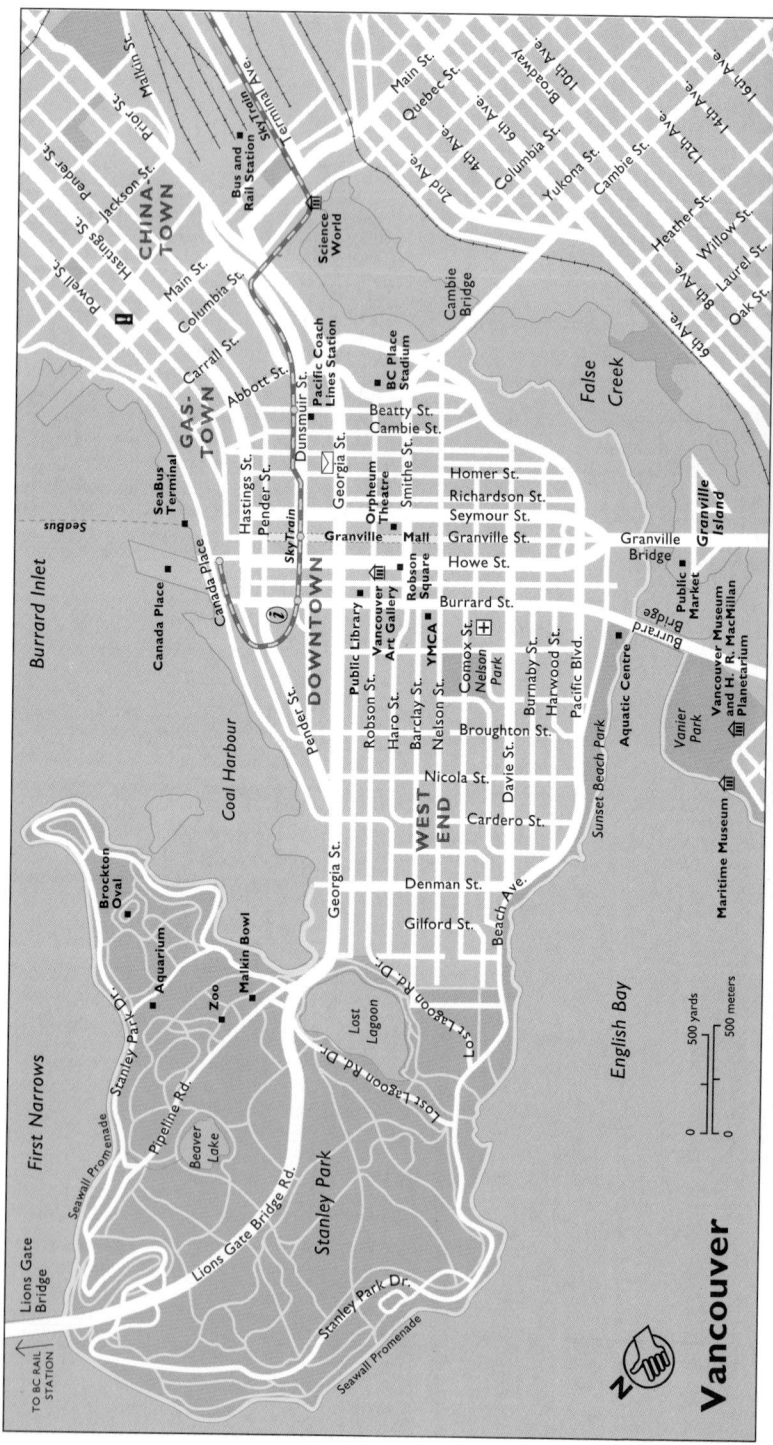

Downtown Washington, D.C.

Central Washington, D.C.

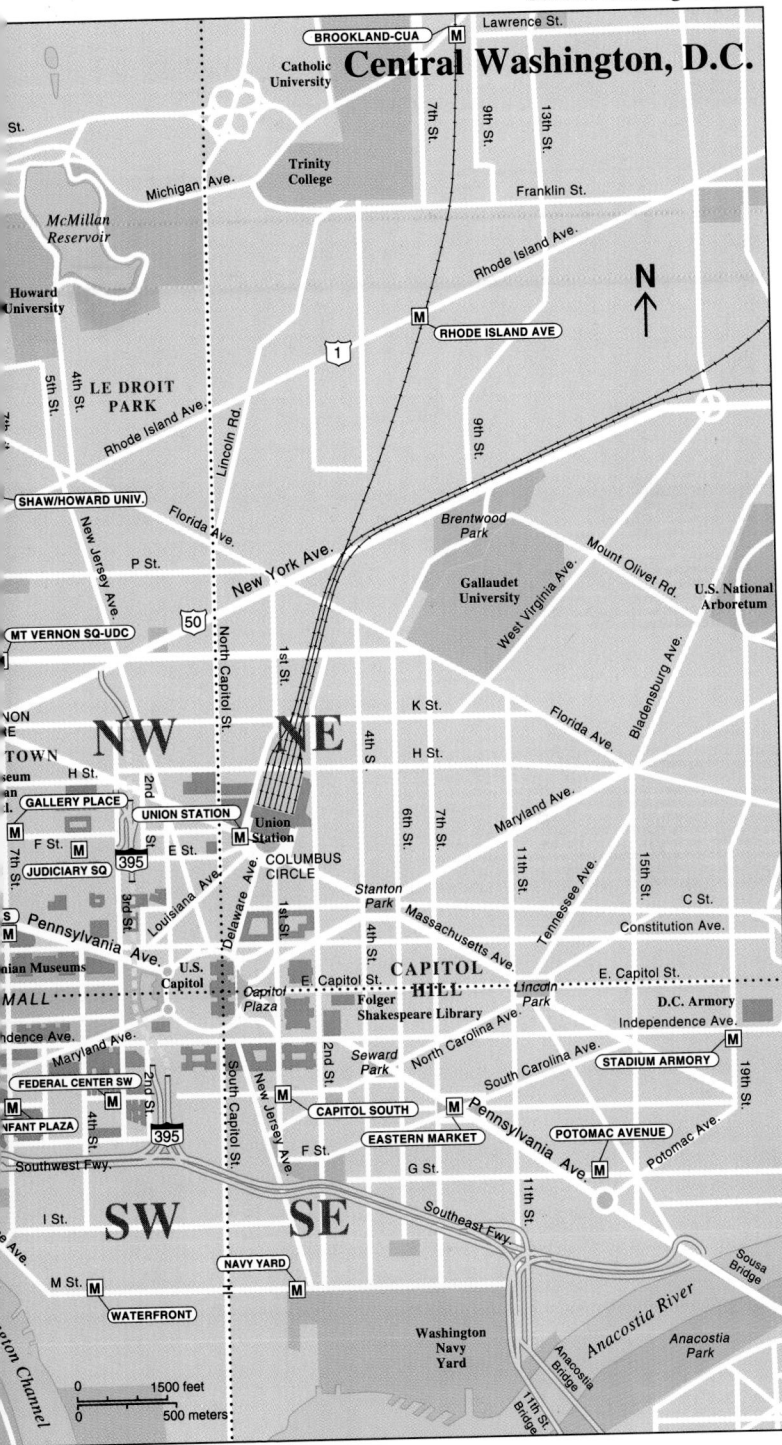

Central Washington, D.C.

The Mall Area, Washington, D.C.

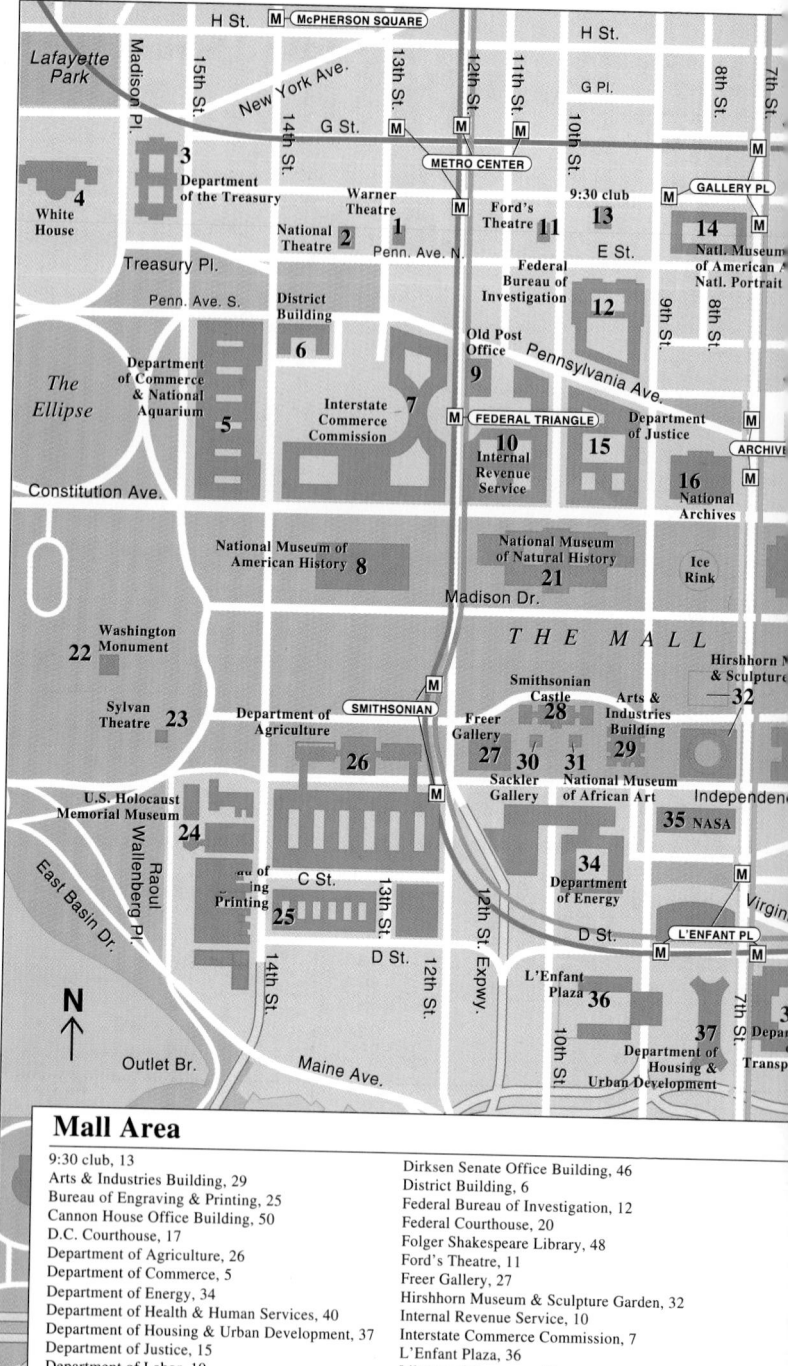

Mall Area

The Mall Area, Washington, D.C.

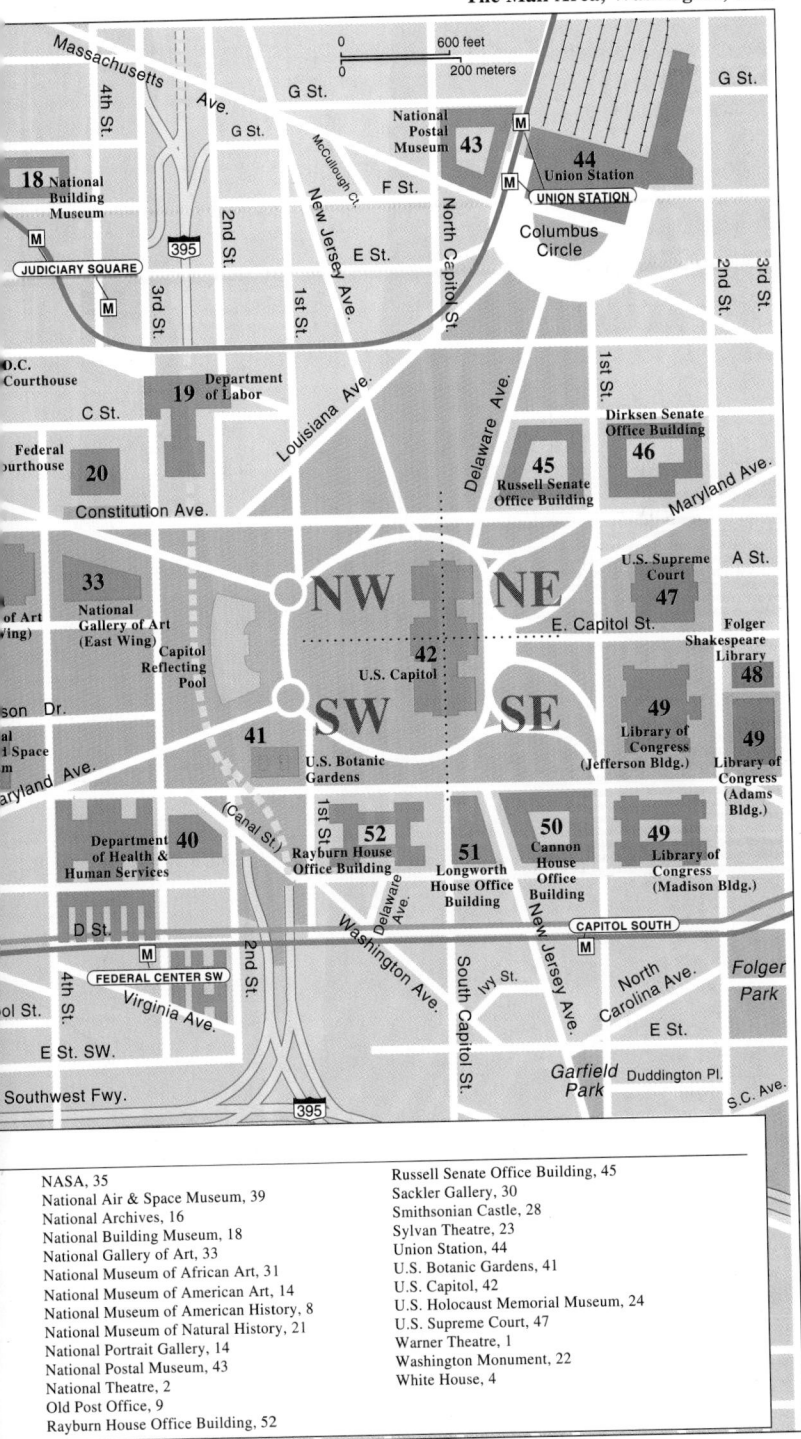

White House Area, Foggy Bottom, and Nearby Arlington

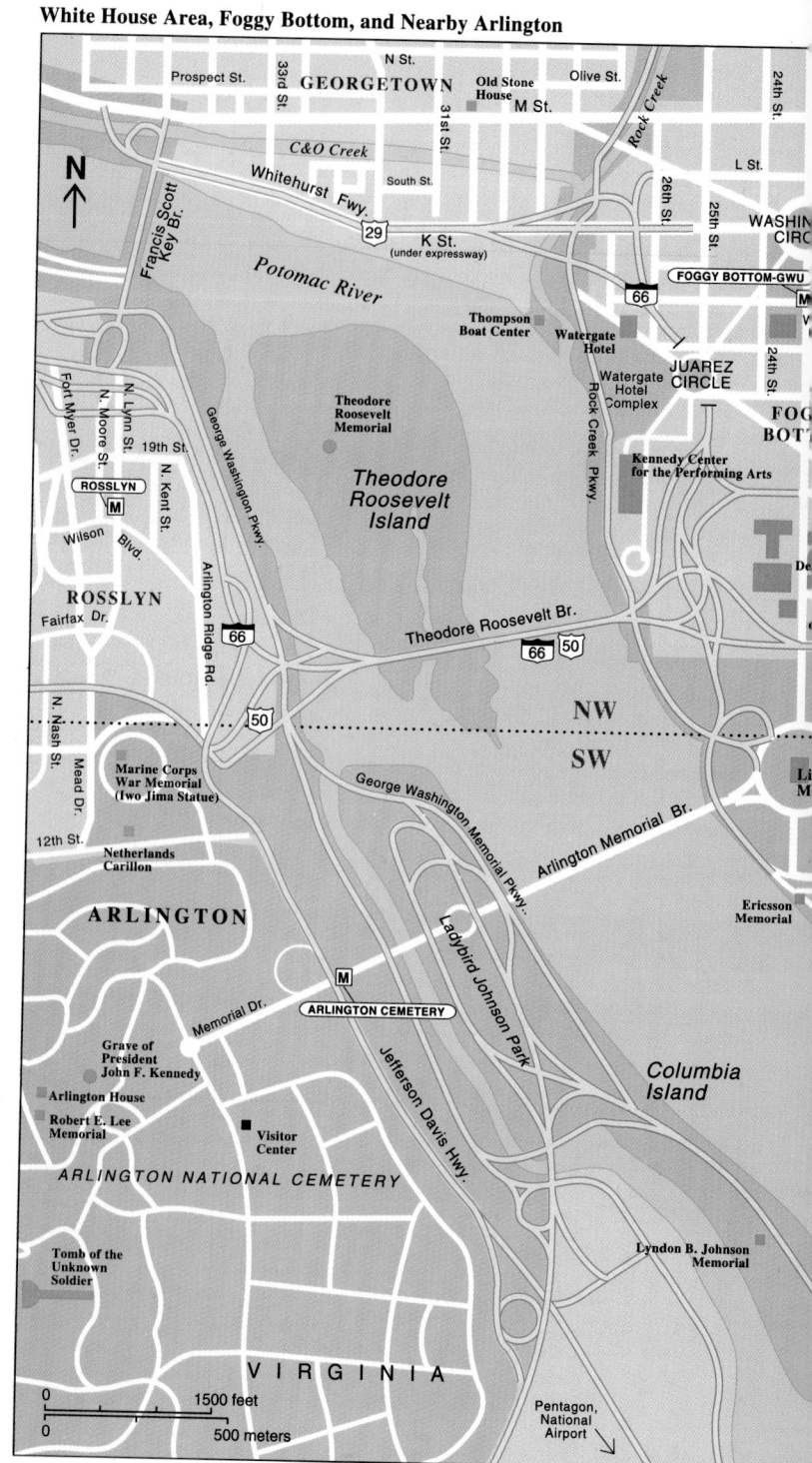

White House Area, Foggy Bottom, and Nearby Arlington

Jefferson Pl.
Connecticut Ave.
M St.
THOMAS CIRCLE
M St.
L St.
Massachusetts Ave.
MT. VERNON SQUARE
20th St.
19th St.
18th St.
DeSales St.
17th St.
National Geographic Society
15th St.
Vermont Ave.
11th St.
13th St.
12th St.
K St.
10th St.
8th St.

The Washington Post

FARRAGUT NORTH M

16th St.
McPHERSON SQUARE
Franklin Park
I St.

FARRAGUT WEST M

FARRAGUT SQUARE

U.S. Chamber of Commerce

McPHERSON SQ M

ania Ave.
H St.
St. John's Church
National Museum of Women in the Arts
New York Ave.
H St.
Convention Center

Decatur House
LAFAYETTE SQUARE
New York Ave. Presbyterian Church
Martin Luther King Jr. Library
G Pl.
G St.

World Bank
Renwick Gallery
14th St.
15th St.

St.
Blair House
Jackson Pl.
Madison Pl.
U.S. Treasury
10th St.
9:30 club

Old Executive Office Building
F St.

General Services Administration
Octagon
State Pl.
Visitor Information Center
Natl. Theatre
Warner Theatre
Ford's Theatre

St.
Corcoran Gallery
White House
Treasury Pl.
E St.
11th St.

METRO CENTER M M M M

Executive Ave.
E St.
Pennsylvania Ave.
Federal Bureau of Investigation
9th St.

St.
Interior Department
17th St.
District Building
Old Post Office
Market Pl.

C St.
D.A.R. Constitution Hall
THE ELLIPSE
Ellipse Rd.
Department of Commerce

FEDERAL TRIANGLE M
Department of Justice
National Archives

Organization of American States
D St.
S. Executive Pl.
Internal Revenue Service

stitution Ave.
Constitution Ave.

Constitution Gardens

am
rans
orial
Memorial to the Signers of the Declaration of Independence
Natl. Museum of American History
Natl. Museum of Natural History
Madison Dr.

THE MALL
Arts & Industries Building

Reflecting Pool
Washington Monument
14th St.
Freer Gallery of Art
Smithsonian Castle

st Potomac Park
Sylvan Theatre
SMITHSONIAN M

Independence Ave.

D.C. War Memorial
U.S. Holocaust Memorial Museum
Natl. Museum of African Art

endence Ave.
Kutz Br.
East Basin Dr.
Department of Agriculture
C St.
Department of Energy
9th St.

Japanese Lantern
15th St.
Bureau of Engraving & Printing
13th St.
12th St.
L'Enfant Promenade
D St.

Paddleboats
L'Enfant Plaza

Tidal Basin

West Potomac Park
W. Basin Dr.
Cherry Trees
Outlet Br.
Maine Ave.

Ohio Dr.
Jefferson Memorial
12th St. Expwy.

H St.
Maine Ave.
Water St.

Potomac River
Francis Case Memorial Br.

395

Washington Channel

George Mason Bridge
Williams Memorial Bridge
1
395

Natl. Park Service Visitors Welcome Center & Park Police Headquarters

East Potomac Park

White House Area, Foggy Bottom, and Nearby Arlington

Metrorail System, Washington, D.C.

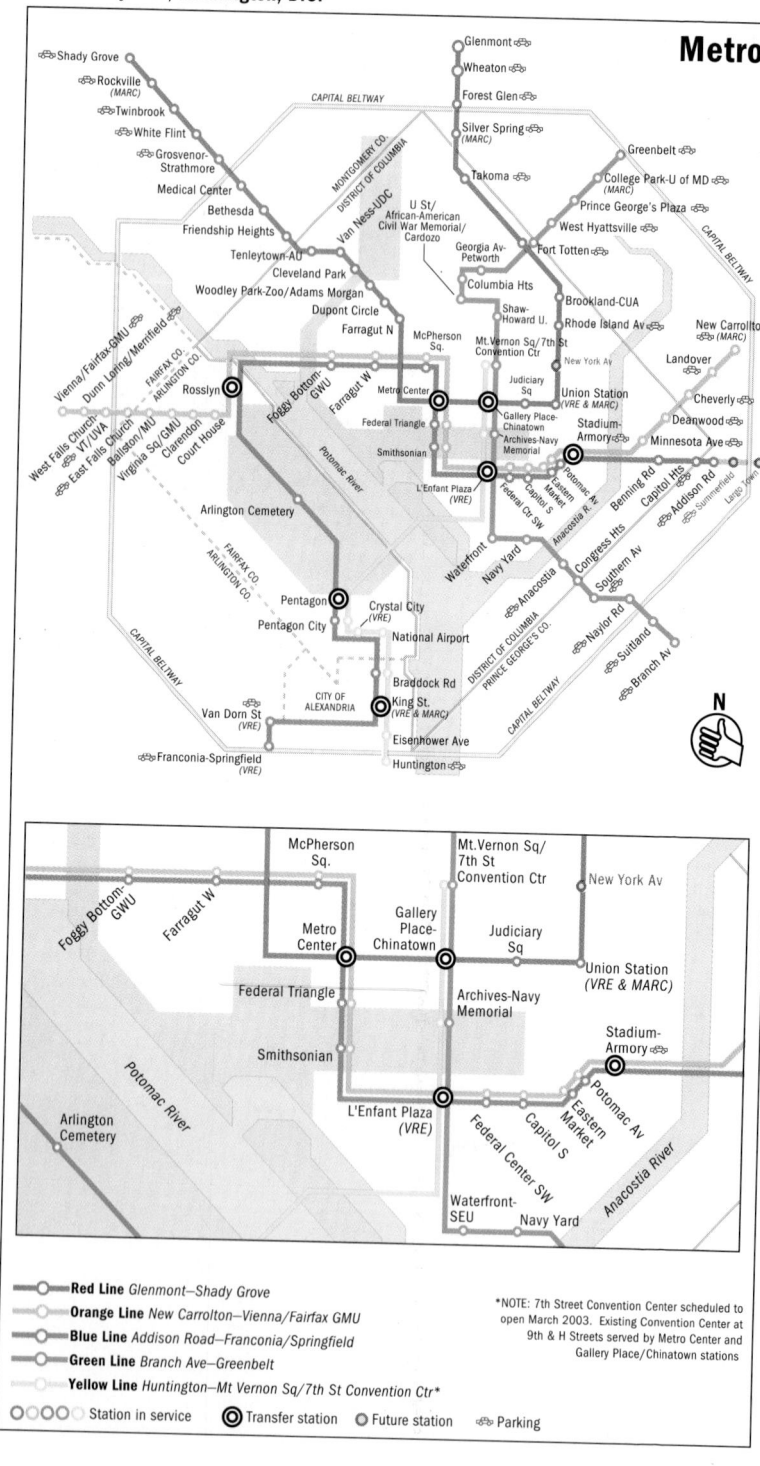

Metro

*NOTE: 7th Street Convention Center scheduled to open March 2003. Existing Convention Center at 9th & H Streets served by Metro Center and Gallery Place/Chinatown stations

- **Red Line** *Glenmont—Shady Grove*
- **Orange Line** *New Carrolton—Vienna/Fairfax GMU*
- **Blue Line** *Addison Road—Franconia/Springfield*
- **Green Line** *Branch Ave—Greenbelt*
- **Yellow Line** *Huntington—Mt Vernon Sq/7th St Convention Ctr**

○○○○○ Station in service   ◉ Transfer station   ○ Future station   🚃 Parking